# Thru the Bible
# with J. Vernon McGee

By J. Vernon McGee

# Thru the Bible
# with J. Vernon McGee

By J. Vernon McGee

## VOLUME III
### Proverbs—Malachi

Thomas Nelson Publishers
Nashville

Published in Nashville, Tennessee, by Thomas Nelson, Inc., Publishers and distributed in Canada by Lawson Falle, Ltd., Cambridge, Ontario.

From *Halfway Up the Sky* by Jane Merchant. Copyright © 1967 by Abingdon Press. Used by permission.

Reprinted from Sir Robert Anderson—*The Coming Prince*, Kregal Publications. Used by permission.

"Everyone but Thee and Me" by Ogden Nash. Copyright © 1962 by Ogden Nash and published by Little, Brown and Company. Used by permission.

Excerpt from "What is a Girl?" by Alan Beck. Reprinted with permission from the April 1951 Reader's Digest.

Unless otherwise indicated, all Scripture quotations are from the Thru the Bible Radio Special Edition of The King James Version, copyright © 1976 by Thomas Nelson Publishers.

**Library of Congress Cataloging in Publication Data**     (Revised)

McGee, J. Vernon (John Vernon), 1904-
    Thru the Bible with J. Vernon McGee.

    Based on the Thru the Bible radio program.
    Includes bibliographies.
    Contents: v. 1. Genesis—Deuteronomy—
v. 3. Proverbs—Malachi.
    1. Bible—Commentaries. I. Thru the Bible
(Radio program)    II.   Title.
BS491.2.M37        220.7'7        81-3930
ISBN 0-8407-4973-2 (Nelson) v. 1
ISBN 0-8407-4978-3 (Royal) v. 1
ISBN 0-8407-4975-9 (Nelson) v. 3
ISBN 0-8407-4980-5 (Royal) v. 3

Printed in the United States of America
    8 9 10 11 12 13 14 15 16 17 18 19 20—90 89 88

# TABLE OF CONTENTS

# PREFACE

The radio broadcasts of the Thru the Bible Radio five-year program were transcribed, edited, and published first in single-volume paperbacks to accommodate the radio audience. From the beginning there was a demand that they be published in a more permanent form and in fewer volumes. This new hardback edition is an attempt to meet that need.

There has been a minimal amount of further editing for this publication. Therefore, these messages are not the word-for-word recording of the taped messages which went out over the air. The changes were necessary to accommodate a reading audience rather than a listening audience.

These are popular messages, prepared originally for a radio audience. They should not be considered a commentary on the entire Bible in any sense of that term. These messages are devoid of any attempt to present a theological or technical commentary on the Bible. Behind these messages is a great deal of research and study in order to interpret the Bible from a popular rather than from a scholarly (and too-often boring) viewpoint.

We have definitely and deliberately attempted "to put the cookies on the bottom shelf so that the kiddies could get them."

The fact that these messages have been translated into many languages for radio broadcasting and have been received with enthusiasm reveals the need for a simple teaching of the whole Bible for the masses of the world.

I am indebted to many people and to many sources for bringing this volume into existence. I should express my especial thanks to my secretary, Gertrude Cutler, who supervised the editorial work; to Dr. Elliott R. Cole, my associate, who handled all the detailed work with the publishers; and finally, to my wife Ruth for tenaciously encouraging me from the beginning to put my notes and messages into printed form.

Solomon wrote, ". . . of making many books there is no end; and much study is a weariness of the flesh" (Eccl. 12:12). On a sea of books that flood the marketplace, we launch this series of THRU THE BIBLE with the hope that it might draw many to the one Book, *The Bible*.

J. VERNON McGEE

# The Book of
# PROVERBS
## INTRODUCTION

The Book of Proverbs is one of the books classified as the poetry of Scripture. Job, Psalms, Proverbs, Ecclesiastes, and Song of Solomon all belong in the same package because they are written as Hebrew poetry.

Solomon is the writer of three of these books of poetry: Proverbs, Ecclesiastes, and Song of Solomon. Proverbs is the book on wisdom. Ecclesiastes is the book on folly. Song of Solomon is the book on love. Love is the happy medium between wisdom and folly. Solomon was an expert on all three subjects! The Word of God says about him: "And he spake three thousand proverbs: and his songs were a thousand and five" (1 Kings 4:32). We have only one of his songs out of 1,005 that he wrote. And, actually, we have very few of his proverbs. "And he spake of trees, from the cedar tree that is in Lebanon even unto the hyssop that springeth out of the wall: he spake also of beasts, and of fowl, and of creeping things, and of fishes. And there came of all people to hear the wisdom of Solomon, from all kings of the earth, which had heard of his wisdom" (1 Kings 4:33–34).

In the Book of Proverbs we read the wisdom of Solomon. A proverb is a saying that conveys a specific truth in a pointed and pithy way. Proverbs are short sentences drawn from long experience. A proverb is a truth that is couched in a form that is easy to remember, a philosophy based on experience, and a rule for conduct. A proverb has been called a sententious sentence, a maxim, an old saying, an old saw, a bromide, an epigram.

The key verse is found in the first chapter: "The fear of the LORD is the beginning of knowledge: but fools despise wisdom and instruction" (Prov. 1:7).

The Orient and the ancient East are the homes of proverbs. Probably Solomon gathered many of them from other sources. He was the editor of them all and the author of some. This means that we have an inspired record of proverbs that are either Solomon's or from other sources, but God has put His stamp upon them, as we shall see.

Dr. Thirtle and other scholars noted that there is a change of pronoun in the book from the second person to the third person. The conclusion of these scholars was that the proverbs which used the second person were taught to Solomon by his teachers, and the proverbs using the third person were composed by Solomon himself.

There is a difference between the Book of Proverbs and proverbs in other writings. The Greeks were great at making proverbs, especially the gnostic poets. I majored in Greek in college, and I took a course that was patterned after the Oxford plan, in that I would read a great deal of Greek and then report to my professor every Monday morning. I read the entire New Testament in Greek while I was in college and then, when I got to seminary, we went over it again. The writings of the gnostic poets were among the writings that I had to read in Greek. They are very clever in the Greek language because so many of them are a play upon Greek words.

There are some characteristics and features of the Book of Proverbs that I think we should note:

1. Proverbs bears no unscientific statement or inaccurate observation. For example, "Keep thy heart with all diligence; for out of it are the issues of life" (Prov. 4:23). This is a remarkable statement, because it was about 2,700 years later that Harvey found that the blood circulates and that the heart is the pump. In contrast, in an apocryphal book called the Epistle of Barnabas, mention is made of the mythical phoenix, a bird that consumes itself by fire and rises in resurrection. Such a fable does not appear in the Book of Proverbs nor anywhere else in the Bible. It is strange that this is an ancient book containing hundreds of proverbs and not one of them is unscientific today. That in itself ought to alert any thinking person to the fact that the Book of Proverbs is God-inspired.

2. Proverbs is a book on a high moral plane. You simply will not find in its pages the immoral sayings which occur in other writings. Justin Martyr said that Socrates was a Christian before Christ—which, of course, would be an impossibility. And his admirers say that he portrays a high conception of morals. However, Socrates also gave instructions to *harlots* on how to conduct themselves! The best that can be said of him is that he was amoral.

3. The Proverbs do not contradict them-

selves, while man's proverbs are often in opposition to each other. For example: "Look before you leap" contrasted with "He who hesitates is lost." "A man gets no more than he pays for" contrasted with "The best things in life are free." "Leave well enough alone" has over against it, "Progress never stands still." "A rolling stone gathers no moss" versus "A setting hen does not get fat." The proverbs of man contradict each other, because men's ideas differ. But there is no contradiction in the Book of Proverbs because it is inspired by God.

While the Book of Proverbs seems to be a collection of sayings without any particular regard for orderly arrangement, some of us believe that it tells a story, which we will notice as we go along. It is a picture of a young man starting out in life. He gets his first lesson in Proverbs 1:7, which is the key to the book.

The advice that is given in the Book of Proverbs transcends all dispensations. Whether one lives in Old Testament or New Testament times, old Jerusalem or new Jerusalem, its truths are still true. It is a good book for anyone.

Someone may raise this objection: "There is nothing in it about the gospel." Just wait a minute, it is there. The One in this book whose wisdom it is, is none other than the Lord Jesus Christ.

The book is not a hodgepodge of unrelated statements, nor is it a discourse of cabbages and kings. It is a book that makes sense, and it does have an arrangement and an organization. Solomon has something to say about his own teaching: "And moreover, because the preacher was wise, he still taught the people knowledge; yea, he gave good heed, and sought out, and set in order many proverbs" (Eccl. 12:9).

Here is something that will make the Book of Proverbs a thrilling experience for you: There is in Proverbs a thumbnail sketch of every character in the Bible. I am going to suggest a few of them; you will enjoy finding others. Also I think you will find there is a proverb that will fit all your friends and acquaintances—but perhaps you had better not mention to them the proverb that fits some of them! There is a proverb that will fit every one of us, and we can have a good time going through this book.

Dr. A. C. Gaebelein has written this helpful analysis of the literary structure of Proverbs.

The literary form of these Proverbs is mostly in the form of couplets. The two clauses of the couplet are generally related to each other by what has been termed parallelism, according to Hebrew poetry. (Hebrew poetry does not have rhyme or meter as our poetry does. Hebrew poetry consists of a parallelism of ideas.) Three kinds of parallelism have been pointed out:

1. *Synonymous Parallelism*. Here the second clause restates what is given in the first clause. (It expresses the same thought in a different way.)

"Judgments are prepared for scorners,
And stripes for the back of fools" [Prov. 19:29].

2. *Antithetic (Contrast) Parallelism*. Here a truth, which is stated in the first clause, is made stronger in the second clause by contrast with an opposite truth.

"The light of the righteous rejoiceth,
But the lamp of the wicked shall be put out" [Prov. 13:9].

(You can see that the second statement is stating the same truth but from the opposite point of view by way of contrast.)

3. *Synthetic Parallelism*. The second clause develops the thought of the first.

"The terror of a king is as the roaring of a lion; He that provoketh him to anger sinneth against his own life" [Prov. 20:2].

# OUTLINE

I. **Wisdom and Folly Contrasted, Chapters 1–9**

II. **Proverbs of Solomon, Chapters 10–24**
   *(Written and set in order by himself)*

III. **Proverbs of Solomon, Chapters 25–29**
   *(Set in order by men of Hezekiah)*

IV. **Oracle of Agur, Unknown Sage, Chapter 30**

V. **Proverbs of a Mother to Lemuel, Chapter 31**

# CHAPTER 1

You may not consider the Book of Proverbs a very thrilling story, but it is. I hope we can get in step with the spirit of God in this book, because it has a real message for each one of us. It is particularly slanted to young men—and applies to young women also. It has a special message for youth. This is a day, as every day has been, when young people are looking for answers to the questions of life.

I want you to notice as we get into this book that it is not just a haphazard sort of thing. It has a definite message. I know a great many people who feel that we can just reach in and lift out a proverb here and there. I think it is all right to do that, but the point is that when we take it out and look at it, we should also put it back where it belongs and look at it in its context. The diamond belongs in its setting, and in this case the setting is the Book of Proverbs.

Some people are inclined to read the Book of Proverbs very much like the man who said, "I enjoy reading the dictionary, but the stories certainly are short." Maybe you feel that way about Proverbs, but I hope you will see it differently as we study the book.

**The proverbs of Solomon the son of David, king of Israel [Prov. 1:1].**

This certainly identifies the writer as King Solomon. Evidently Solomon gathered together many proverbs from other sources. He was the editor of all and the author of some. Also we are told that he wrote more proverbs than appear in this book.

The first section of the book is a contrast between wisdom and folly. This includes chapters 1–9.

## THE BOY IN THE HOME STARTING OUT IN LIFE

As the boy starts out in life, these are the instructions that God gives him.

**To know wisdom and instruction; to perceive the words of understanding;**

**To receive the instruction of wisdom, justice, and judgment, and equity;**

**To give subtilty to the simple, to the young man knowledge and discretion [Prov. 1:2–4].**

There are ten words used in this section which seem to be synonymous—and, of course, they are related—but they are not the same. I would like to take each of these words and put it under the microscope. We will find that they are not synonyms. Nor are they piled up to make an impressive beginning. Every word of God is pure, we are told, so let us look at some of these.

"To know wisdom." What is meant by wisdom? The word *wisdom* in the Scriptures means "the ability to use knowledge aright." It occurs in this book alone thirty-seven times. It is an important word in the Bible. It means the right use of knowledge. There are a great many brilliant people who have knowledge; yet they lack wisdom. They don't seem to use their knowledge aright.

Let me add something more here. *Wisdom* in the Old Testament means Jesus Christ for the believer today. "But of him are ye in Christ Jesus, who of God is made unto us wisdom, and righteousness, and sanctification, and redemption" (1 Cor. 1:30). Notice that wisdom is number one. Christ is the wisdom for the believer today. And to know wisdom is to know Jesus Christ. Paul gave as his ambition: "That I may know him . . ." (Phil. 3:10). Oh, that the same ambition to know Christ might grip your soul and my soul today! We *need* that.

Wisdom, therefore, is Christ. Wisdom is the ability to use our knowledge aright. To know Christ is not to play the fool; it is to be a wise man. I saw a bumper sticker the other day which read: "Wise men still seek Him." Friend, you may not be brilliant, but when you receive Christ and come to know Christ, then you have wisdom.

"Instruction." The word *instruction* appears twenty-six times in Proverbs. Sometimes the same Hebrew word is translated by the word *chasten*. Now that is interesting. Let me give an example of this. Proverbs 13:24 says, "He that spareth his rod hateth his son: but he that loveth him chasteneth him betimes." Here, "to chasten" actually means "to give instruction." Therefore, the word *instruction* means you teach by discipline. That is a forgotten truth today. Our contemporary society is certainly out of kilter and out of step with the Word of God. For example, we are told that lawbreakers are put in prison to discipline them and to reform them. That never was the purpose for dealing with criminals according to the Word of God. The purpose there was to judge them, punish them. No other reason was ever given. On the other hand, when you are dealing with a son, you discipline him, because that is a part of his instruction. You are to chasten him. You are to teach him by disciplining him. Your purpose is not to punish him. We often hear it said, "That child should be punished!" No, that is not the purpose of turning little Willie across your knee and paddling him. I hope you *do* paddle him. But *why* do you do it? To punish him? No, to teach him by discipline. Our purposes are all confused today—we discipline criminals and punish our children. We need to get back to God's purposes. Our schools today are practicing the "new methods" of teaching. What about the old method of teaching by discipline? That is absolutely out. I believe the board of education being applied to the seat of learning is desperately needed—both in the home and in the school.

A man asked a father, "Do you strike your children?" The father answered, "Only in self-defense." That's about what it has come to in our day—the children are bringing up the parents! They are disciplining the parents and telling them what they ought to do. I heard recently of a young man who gave his mother and father a lecture on how they should be and what they should do. Yet that young man was under a court order: he had been arrested and was out on bail! I believe the parents needed a lecture, but he wasn't the one to give it. They should have had a lesson on how to discipline their son, and it should have been given to them years earlier.

Instruction is to teach by discipline. God, our heavenly Father, is excellent at teaching in that way. I think I have learned most when He has taken me to the woodshed. Those lessons were very impressive.

"To perceive the words of understanding." Understanding means intelligence. We have another word: discernment. We need to recognize that God expects us to use our intelligence. He expects us to use a great deal of sanctified common sense.

In verse 3 is the word *justice*. Justice is righteousness, and it means "right behavior." I remember a sociology professor in college who used to teach us that right was relative. He used to ask with a smirk, "Well, what is *'right'*?" I didn't know the answer then, but now I know that right is what God says is right. It is God who separates the light from the darkness. I can't make the sun come up, and I can't make the sun go down. Only God is running His universe. He makes light; He makes darkness. God is the One who declares what is right, and God declares what is

wrong. So you may ask, "Is it right to do this or that?" If God says it is right, it is right. Or you may ask, "Is this wrong?" It is wrong if God says it is wrong. Right and wrong are not relative terms except in the minds of the contemporary average man. The prevailing feeling is that what the average man does becomes the norm; it becomes the standard. That is one of the reasons there is so much dishonesty and gross immorality today. Right and wrong have become relative terms. God says they are not. Just like light and darkness, they are absolutes.

"Judgment." Judgment means that you and I are to make judgments. It is the same as making a decision. The believer comes to crossroads in his life. He must make decisions about which way to go.

Before I came to California, I had a call to a pastorate in the East, and I had a call here to the West Coast. I honestly didn't know which way to go. I had to bring it to the Lord, and I had to test out a few things. After I had made a test, I found I was to come to California, and I thank God for it. We have to make decisions, and we should make them as the children of God.

"Equity." This refers to principle rather than conduct. The child of God is not put under rules, but we are given great principles which should guide us. For example, Romans 14:22 puts down the great principle: " . . . Happy is he that condemneth not himself in that thing which he alloweth." The believer should have enthusiasm for what he does. There is too much Christian conduct which is like walking on eggshells. People say, "I don't know whether I should do this or not." My friend, the principle is that if you cannot enter into it enthusiastically, you ought not do it at all. What we do, we ought to do with anticipation, excitement, and joy. We should be fully persuaded in our own minds that that is the right course of action. We ought not have a compunction of conscience after we have done it. Happy is the man whose conscience does not condemn him in the things which he allows. If you look back on it and say, "Oh, I wish I hadn't done that," then it was wrong for you to do. In questionable matters about which the Scriptures are silent, this is a great principle that will guide you in your conduct. If you can look back on what you did yesterday and say, "Hallelujah, it was a great day for me," then you know that what you did was *right* for you to do.

Another principle is that we ought to bear each other's infirmities, rather than simply pleasing ourselves. We should ask ourselves, *Is this thing I am doing an offense to my neighbor or to my brother in Christ?* These are great principles of conduct that should guide the believer.

"Give subtilty to the simple." Being prudent is the meaning of giving subtilty to the simple; it is to act prudently. It means to be wise in what we do. A child of God ought not to act foolishly.

I remember counseling a young couple who went to the mission field. They just shut their eyes to reality, as it were, and went to the mission field. I personally urged them not to go, because I could see they were not fitted for it. They came back as casualties. They had actually made shipwrecks of their lives by going to the mission field. They had not been prudent. They had not shown wisdom in their particular circumstances.

Remember that the Lord Jesus said, ". . . be ye therefore wise as serpents, and harmless as doves" (Matt. 10:16).

"To the young man knowledge." Knowledge is information that is useful. I remember a motto on a bulletin board in the science lab of the college which I attended. I have forgotten all the formulas I ever learned in chemistry, but I have never forgotten the motto. It was this: "Next to knowing is knowing where to find out." That is one reason it is good to have the Bible handy and to learn to read it—if you don't know, you surely can know where to find out.

"Discretion." This means thoughtfulness. This is for the young man and young people in general who are thoughtless. I am very frank to say that I was a very thoughtless young man, and I confess that I am still that way. It is always a pleasure to find a thoughtful Christian. I have several wonderful Christian friends here in Southern California. Presently I am getting ready to take a trip to the East, and at this time of year it is a little cool back there. One of these friends came by and brought me a lovely sweater. That was thoughtful. There are many wonderful Christians who are thoughtful, and it is a characteristic all of us ought to have.

The Book of Proverbs will help us see that these wonderful qualities should be incorporated into our lives.

## THE CHALLENGE

**A wise man will hear, and will increase learning; and a man of understanding shall attain unto wise counsels [Prov. 1:5].**

This has been the characteristic of all great men. They never reached the place where they felt that they had learned everything.

I listened to a young man on television the other night who had skyrocketed to fame on rock music. The thing that characterized him was his arrogance. He knew it all. I don't think anyone could tell that young man anything. Proverbs says that a wise man will hear and will increase learning.

"A man of understanding shall attain unto wise counsels." That is actually the challenge of this whole book. Solomon says that if you are smart, you will listen to what is being said in this book. The spirit of God has a lot of choice things to say in the Book of Proverbs. They are great truths, expressed in short sentences.

**To understand a proverb, and the interpretation; the words of the wise, and their dark sayings [Prov. 1:6].**

Another proverb carries this same thought: "It is the glory of God to conceal a thing: but the honour of kings is to search out a matter" (Prov. 25:2). I love that. God has given the gospel message clearly to be declared from the housetops. But there is a great deal of truth in the Word of God that is like diamonds. God has not scattered diamonds around on the ground. Jewels and that which is valuable have been hidden away for man to look for and to find. The gold and the diamonds and other precious things must be mined; oil must be drilled. That is the way that God does it. It is the glory of God to conceal a thing.

The Word of God deserves all the study that you can possibly bring to it. The Lord Jesus said, "*Search* the scriptures; for in them ye *think* ye have eternal life. . . ." He didn't say you are *not* to search the Scripture. He said *search* the scriptures. You just *think* that you have found eternal life, because you haven't really searched them. You have been reading the Bible, but you haven't found the real message that is there. The real treasure there is *Christ.* "Search the scriptures; for in them ye think ye have eternal life: and they are they which testify of me" (John 5:39). My friend, if you haven't found Christ in the Bible, you simply have not been mining for diamonds— you haven't been digging deep enough. "To understand a proverb, and the interpretation; the words of the wise, and their dark sayings." In other words, God has put these great truths here in His Book. The tragedy of the hour is the ignorance of the Word of God in both pulpit and pew. There needs to be a serious, concentrated study of the Word of God. Somehow there is an idea today that one can read over a passage once and then you have it all. I trust you will see that you cannot get the nuggets out of the Word of God without study.

When I am in Florida I always enjoy going to the home and laboratory of Thomas A. Edison at Fort Myers. There is a museum there now. The thing that has always amazed me is his search for synthetic rubber. Firestone and Henry Ford had their homes right next to Thomas A. Edison, and you can understand why they were interested in the project and were working with him. There were several hundred test tubes in his lab. Edison was taking everything that was imaginable and testing it to see if he could get synthetic rubber from it. Do you know he found some of it in dandelions, of all things. That would be the last place I would look for synthetic rubber! But that was the test he was making.

As I stood in that laboratory and looked at those hundreds of test tubes and thought of the hours that he and his helpers had spent there, testing this and that and the other thing in order to try to find it, I thought, *My, how little attention is given to the Word of God where one could do some real testing and some real study*. The challenge of the Book of Proverbs to us today is: Dig in! It is the challenge to do serious study. "Study to shew thyself approved unto God, a workman that needeth not to be ashamed, rightly dividing the word of truth" (2 Tim. 2:15).

## KEY TO THE BOOK

**The fear of the LORD is the beginning of knowledge: but fools despise wisdom and instruction [Prov. 1:7].**

There is an interesting contrast here: "The fear of the LORD is the beginning of knowledge: but fools *despise* wisdom and instruction." They do not learn from it.

I heard a little bit of nonsense to illustrate this. A man driving down the highway had a flat tire, so he pulled over to the side of the road. It happened he was parked by an insane asylum, and one of the men from the asylum was on the other side of the fence. He was watching the man as he changed the tire. He didn't say anything but just stood there and watched. As the man took off the wheel of the car, he placed all the nuts that he had taken off into the hubcap. Then he accidentally tilted the hubcap so all the nuts fell out and went down into a sewer, and he couldn't retrieve

them. He stood there scratching his head wondering what in the world he was to do. The man behind the fence who had been watching him said, "Why don't you take a nut off each of the other wheels and put them on this wheel? You could drive safely down to the filling station, and there you can buy nuts so that you can fix your wheel." The man looked at him in amazement. "Why didn't I think of that?" he asked. "You are in the institution and I am out, and yet you are the one who thought of it." The onlooker answered. "I may be crazy, but I'm not *stupid*!" Well, this Book of Proverbs is attempting to get you and me out of a position of being *stupid* in life today. I think we shall find it to be a great help to us. This book has quite a bit to say about stupidity, as we shall see.

**My son, hear the instruction of thy father, and forsake not the law of thy mother:**

**For they shall be an ornament of grace unto thy head, and chains about thy neck [Prov. 1:8–9].**

That is the important home relationship. There are many who are reading this who have come from homes in which they had a godly father and a godly mother. They were instructed by them, and they have never gotten away from the things taught them in the home. On the other hand, may God have mercy on the parents who are not instructing their little ones in the things of God!

## TEMPTATION OUTSIDE THE HOME

**My son, if sinners entice thee, consent thou not [Prov. 1:10].**

Now the movement is outside the home. When the little fellow goes away, who is the first fellow he meets? Generally that contact will be with a sinner, because most of the human race falls into that category—they have not come to Christ. All of us are sinners, but the boy will meet the unredeemed sinner who is really living in sin. So what should his attitude be? "Consent thou not."

You remember that I said you would find a proverb which would fit characters in the Bible. Probably you can also find a proverb to fit every one of your friends—although you may not want to tell them what it is! This is a proverb that fits someone in the Scriptures. Wouldn't you say it describes Joseph when he was taken as a slave down into the land of Egypt and was enticed by Potiphar's wife? He did not consent to her. This proverb is an example of his experience.

**If they say, Come with us, let us lay wait for blood, let us lurk privily for the innocent without cause:**

**Let us swallow them up alive as the grave; and whole, as those that go down into the pit:**

**We shall find all precious substance, we shall fill our houses with spoil [Prov. 1:11–13].**

The sinner has a plan and a program to get something for nothing. He lives off someone else and makes someone else suffer in order that he might prosper.

**Cast in thy lot among us; let us all have one purse [Prov. 1:14].**

This is the philosophy of the hour: Let's all live out of the same purse. Generally those who hold this philosophy are doing nothing themselves. They want the working people to share what they have worked for, but they don't have any contribution to make to it at all. That is a false philosophy, but it is one that is common among young people today. It is the thinking and the mood of the present hour. Use all kinds of methods, even crooked methods, to get something for nothing.

After my father was killed in a cotton gin accident when I was fourteen years old, my mother took my sister and me back to Nashville, which was her home. I had to go to work: I couldn't continue in school because we had no finances at all. I got a job at a wholesale hardware company. They sold practically everything, including candy. I worked in the mailing department with several other boys. I want to tell you, they were mean fellows. They had figured out a way to get into a box of candy and take out just one piece and never be detected. Since it was a wholesale place, there were about fifty boxes, and by taking one piece from each box they could fill up several boxes for themselves. I must confess that I cooperated that first day, and then my conscience bothered me that night. I thought, *This is not right. I was stealing.*

The next day I made things right, but I couldn't return the candy because I had already eaten some of it. After that, the management would let me buy a box of six candy bars wholesale. I would sell them a nickle a bar to the men and women who worked there in the office. That last candy bar was my profit because the whole box had cost me twenty-five cents wholesale. That was the way I got my candy. I had to work for it, and I felt that was the best way to do it.

It is so easy for a young man to fall in with a group that is doing shady things. And it is easy to join in with a group who "goof off" at work, as they say today. They do not return a full day's work for a full day's wages. It is so easy to cooperate in that type of thing. That is why the young man is given this advice when he leaves home.

**My son, walk not thou in the way with them; refrain thy foot from their path [Prov. 1:15].**

This is the kind of *separation* on which the Bible is very clear. "Wherefore come out from among them, and be ye separate, saith the Lord . . ." (2 Cor. 6:17) was referring to idolatry, but it certainly can be applied here. Solomon said, "Get rid of that crooked crowd that you're with."

**For their feet run to evil, and make haste to shed blood.**

**Surely in vain the net is spread in the sight of any bird.**

**And they lay wait for their own blood; they lurk privily for their own lives [Prov. 1:16–18].**

When you get into that type of thing, it will eventually lead you to your own destruction. You will be caught in your own net.

**So are the ways of every one that is greedy of gain; which taketh away the life of the owners thereof [Prov. 1:19].**

This is the condemnation of the beginning of covetousness. We live in a materialistic age today. I have an article here that is written by a Ph.D., a college professor. He takes the position that colleges must get away from the teaching of crass materialism. Therefore, they must return to religion, as he expresses it. You see, there are a few who are beginning to wake up. Covetousness is the great sin of the hour. That is what the proverb is condemning here.

## INVITATION TO THE SCHOOL OF WISDOM

**Wisdom crieth without; she uttereth her voice in the streets [Prov. 1:20].**

Wisdom is urging the young man to come to school and really learn something. Come to her college.

She crieth in the chief place of concourse, in the openings of the gates: in the city she uttereth her words, saying,

How long, ye simple ones, will ye love simplicity? and the scorners delight in their scorning, and fools hate knowledge? [Prov. 1:21–22].

Simplicity is stupidity. She asks, "How long will you be stupid?" A young man (who is in his twenties now) told me he had been on drugs for three years. He kept repeating, "Oh, how *stupid* I was, Dr. McGee." Well, here is the question: How long are you going to be stupid? When are you coming to the school of wisdom?

Turn you at my reproof: behold, I will pour out my spirit unto you, I will make known my words unto you [Prov. 1:23].

Now I will drop down to the end of the chapter:

For the turning away of the simple shall slay them, and the prosperity of fools shall destroy them [Prov. 1:32].

It is spiritual suicide to turn from Christ.

But whoso hearkeneth unto me shall dwell safely, and shall be quiet from fear of evil [Prov. 1:33].

What an expression this is! I wonder if this could speak of our nation? We are an affluent society; we measure every man by his bank account, the home he lives in, the car he drives. Are we enjoying the prosperity of fools? Are we living in a fool's paradise?

# CHAPTER 2

Let me remind you that the Book of Proverbs is not a haphazard book. It tells a story, a connected story. It is the challenge given to a young man that he be a wise young man. He is exhorted to hear, to increase his learning. He is to start learning from his father and his mother in the home; he gets his basic lesson before he enters school. Even after he gets his Ph.D., that basic lesson will still be good for him. It is this: "The fear of the LORD is the beginning of knowledge."

The way to find out about the Lord is through His Word. There are a great many people who say that a person must be very intelligent and have a high I.Q. in order to understand the Word of God. Nothing is further from the truth. God does not say that is essential. However, in this chapter where the young man starts out, it will be made clear that if he is to know the will and Word of God, he will have to *study*. He can't just dilly-dally around and pick the daisies along the highway of life; he must apply his heart unto wisdom. Therefore, he must *study* the Word of God.

## SOURCE OF TRUE WISDOM

My son, if thou wilt receive my words, and hide my commandments with thee [Prov. 2:1].

"My son"—obviously, this is advice being given to a young man. He started out as a little boy in the home. Now he has grown up enough to go out and face life, and he is given this advice by some wise person. Perhaps this is his first lesson in school— unfortunately he would not learn this in our modern schools.

"Receive my words (*sayings*)." The sayings of God are to be received. His *commandments* are to be hidden or stored up. Store them up with your valuables. I know a man who goes to his safety deposit box regularly each week. He goes to count what he has stored there. He goes to where his wealth is. He has stored up some stocks and bonds, and he just loves to go and look them over. I know a lady who owns precious jewelry. She loves to take it out often and admire it. She enjoys just looking at it. She keeps it stored up. That is the way the Word of God should be stored up, hidden, laid up. "Hide my commandments with thee."

So that thou incline thine ear unto wisdom, and apply thine heart to understanding [Prov. 2:2].

"Incline thine ear"—keep your ear open. Something is to enter the head through the ear gate, but its final destination is the heart. When the Word of God gets into the heart, it brings understanding.

He still is not through with this injunction, this urging, this challenge.

**Yea, if thou criest after knowledge, and liftest up thy voice for understanding [Prov. 2:3].**

The apostle Peter said it this way: "As new-born babes, desire the sincere milk of the word, that ye may grow thereby" (1 Pet. 2:2). Have you ever watched a little baby when his mamma is fixing the bottle? He wiggles everything he has—his hands, his mouth, and his feet—in anticipation. I tell you, he *desires* the milk in his bottle. The child of God should be that way about the milk of the Word of God. This is one of the things I have noted about the spiritual movement in our day. Where it is present, you see a renewed interest in the Word of God. I notice many young people today carrying notebooks and Bibles, and they take notes on everything. I speak around the country in many places, and I can tell if there is a real moving of the spirit of God. It is evidenced by this desire for the Word of God. "If thou criest after knowledge"—and remember that the fear of the Lord is the beginning of knowledge.

"Liftest up thy voice." If students want to have a protest movement in college, I would like to see this kind of protest movement carried on: "We want understanding!" This, you see, is advice for the young man: "Lift up thy voice for understanding."

**If thou seekest her as silver, and searchest for her as for hid treasures [Prov. 2:4].**

Out here in the desert of California there are quite a few silver mines. Stories are told about the early days when men came all the way across the country for the silver. Silver was found in the area of Death Valley, and many a man died there while trying to get to the silver. That is why it was named Death Valley. Even after the men got to the silver, they had to make all kinds of sacrifices to market it. That is the way we should go after knowledge, knowledge of the Word of God. Seek her as silver, just as if you were out mining, looking for something very valuable.

**Then shalt thou understand the fear of the Lord, and find the knowledge of God [Prov. 2:5].**

This is talking about something that is more than devotional reading. I really don't believe in devotional reading, because I know individuals and families who have been doing that kind of reading for years, and they are as ignorant of the Bible as the goat grazing on the hillside. You cannot learn the Word of God by getting in a pious frame of mind and then reading a few verses of Scripture. The way to get it is to lay it up, to incline your ear, to apply your heart, to cry after it, to lift up your voice, to seek it as silver, to search for it as if it were a hidden treasure. When you go at it like that, you will learn something. You will understand what is "the fear of the Lord, and find the knowledge of God."

I used to teach Bible when we had a Bible Institute here in Southern California, and I had several hundred students. It was always amusing to me to hear the very pious students on the morning before an exam say, "Dr. McGee, we're not prepared for the exam today. We had a prayer meeting last night." I would ask them, "What did you pray about?" They would tell how they prayed for China or Africa or some far-off place. I would answer, "You know, the most important thing in the world for you last night was not to pray." They would look at me in amazement—"We're not to pray?" I said, "Right. There is a time to *study.*" Then I would show them Proverbs 2 and tell them, "Last night was the time for you to do the digging, the searching it out. There is nothing here about a prayer meeting." They were in school to learn the Word of God. I never excused them from an exam on the pretext that they had a prayer meeting instead of a study time.

There were others who had been brought up on devotional reading. They would read a few verses and then put the Bible under their pillows. I used to tell them, "You can't learn the kings of Israel and Judah by sticking your Bible under your pillow and expecting that during the night that knowledge will come up through the duck feathers into your brain! You cannot learn the Word of God that way!"

I remember in seminary we were assigned a certain theology book. It was a boring book—certainly not like a mystery story. We had a difficult test coming up, and one of my classmates complained to the professor, "Doctor, this is the driest book I've ever read!" The professor's answer was, "Then dampen it with a little sweat from your brow."

There is no hocus-pocus way of learning the Word of God. There is no easy, pious way of learning it. There is no substitute for just digging it out. And it doesn't require a high I.Q. Notice the next verse:

**For the Lord giveth wisdom: out of his mouth cometh knowledge and understanding [Prov. 2:6].**

If you want wisdom, ask Him for it. ". . . Eye hath not seen, nor ear heard, neither have entered into the heart of man, the things which God hath prepared for them that love him." Then how are we to know them? "But God hath revealed them unto us by his Spirit: for the Spirit searcheth all things, yea, the deep things of God" (1 Cor. 2:9–10). They are revealed to us by the spirit of God. He is here today to be our Teacher. When I was a young Christian, one of the most wonderful things I learned was this truth that the spirit of God would open up the things of God to me. This is the reason that some folk who don't have a Ph.D. or a Th.D. degree have a knowledge of the Word of God which others do not have.

When I was a young preacher in Nashville, Tennessee, a 6:00 A.M. radio program was made available to the ministers in town. None of the other ministers wanted it, but I was young and single, so I didn't mind getting up at that hour. I tried to teach the Word of God, but nobody seemed to be interested in it except one person. She was a black lady who would pass my church every morning. Sometimes I would be out there changing the bulletin board as she would come by on her way to work. She would say, "Dr. McGee, I heard you this morning," and she would stand and discuss with me those things that had been on the program. She had real spiritual discernment. She told me that she only finished grade school, but I am here to tell you that that wonderful, black Christian lady knew more theology than the average Christian of any church in that city with whom I had come in contact. She knew how to discuss the Word of God. She had a Bible, and the Lord gave her wisdom. I have never seen a Bible more worn than the one she carried. She used it. She read it. And she understood it, because she was willing to let the spirit of God be her Teacher. "The LORD giveth wisdom."

Dr. Harry A. Ironside made a statement years ago: "It is to be feared that even among those who hold and value much precious truth, diligent Bible study is on the wane." I am afraid this is still true, although at the time I am writing, there is a renewed interest in Bible study. "For the LORD giveth wisdom: out of his mouth cometh knowledge and understanding." How can we hear Him speaking? As I so often say, the Bible is the *Word* of God. He speaks to us by means of this Book.

**He layeth up sound wisdom for the righteous: he is a buckler to them that walk uprightly.**

**He keepeth the paths of judgment, and preserveth the way of his saints [Prov. 2:7–8].**

Many Christians are out in the fog today; they wonder where to turn. It is obvious that the problem is that they are so far from the Word of God. This Book gives us what He is saying. The Word of God is like a foghorn. It "preserveth the way of his saints." That is what He will do, and He will not do it haphazardly. You must come to the Word of God.

**Then shalt thou understand righteousness, and judgment, and equity; yea, every good path [Prov. 2:9].**

It is sad to see so many men in public office today, guiding the destiny of nations, who are not being guided by the Lord. The Lord *wants* to guide them. Oh, if only they would go to Him for wisdom! For the man who has a deep-down desire to live in the power of the truth revealed in the Word of God, God will be a "buckler." He will be a defense for His own, keeping them safely as they tread the paths of judgment, preserving their way.

Sometimes folk write to me and say, "I see that you hold the truth." I like that, but that is not the really important thing. What is important is that the truth holds me. There is a big difference between those two. We are told that in the last days there will be vain talkers and deceivers. I don't want to be in that category. I don't want to speak with great, swelling words. I don't want to boast of a great knowledge of prophecy or dispensational teaching or ecclesiastical truth or philosophy or psychology. We have too much of that around already. What we need are people who "understand righteousness, and judgment, and equity; yea, every good path."

## THE YOUNG MAN'S ENEMIES

**When wisdom entereth into thine heart, and knowledge is pleasant unto thy soul;**

**Discretion shall preserve thee, understanding shall keep thee:**

**To deliver thee from the way of the evil man, from the man that speaketh froward things [Prov. 2:10–12].**

"When wisdom entereth into thine heart, and knowledge is pleasant unto thy soul" you won't be deceived so easily. You won't be taken in if you stay close to the Word of God.

Who leave the paths of uprightness, to walk in the ways of darkness;

Who rejoice to do evil, and delight in the frowardness of the wicked;

Whose ways are crooked, and they froward in their paths [Prov. 2:13-15].

My prayer from the very beginning of my ministry has been: "Lord, don't let me be taken in by evil men!" They are all around us, friend. We are going to learn here in the Book of Proverbs that the child of God has two enemies: the "evil man" and the "strange woman."

As the young man starts out in life he is warned of the evil man. Associating with him is always a danger for a young man. After my father died, when I was sixteen years old, I went to Detroit, Michigan, to work for Cadillac. I got into the wrong crowd in those bootleg days. We would go over into Windsor, Canada, every Saturday night, and I was introduced to a new world. It was with evil men. After a few weeks of that (and I was under conviction day and night), I got homesick and went back home. There a minister explained to me how I could have peace with God and be justified by faith. But I shall never forget the evil man. The young man should beware of him.

Then there is someone else the young man is warned about. She is the "strange woman." A better translation is the *stranger* woman.

To deliver thee from the strange woman, even from the stranger which flattereth with her words;

Which forsaketh the guide of her youth, and forgetteth the covenant of her God.

For her house inclineth unto death, and her paths unto the dead.

None that go unto her return again, neither take they hold of the paths of life.

That thou mayest walk in the way of good men, and keep the paths of the righteous.

For the upright shall dwell in the land, and the perfect shall remain in it.

But the wicked shall be cut off from the earth, and the transgressors shall be rooted out of it [Prov. 2:16-22].

Who is the strange woman? In Israel, God had made a law that no Israelite woman was to play the prostitute. I am confident that if any woman did that, she was automatically put outside the bounds of Israel, and she was classed with sinners—and later with publicans. The stranger was the Gentile who came in. She recognized that there would be a place for her to ply her trade. So the "strange woman" would be a foreigner, the stranger, who came into Israel to practice prostitution. The young man is warned about her. He is told what might happen to him. "None that go unto her return again, neither take they hold of the paths of life." They will lose their health.

An elder in a church back East told me that he almost wrecked his life with just one escapade. He said, "I went out on the town one night with the boys, and that one night I picked up a venereal disease. Back in those days it took years to get rid of the result of that. It almost wrecked my life." God warns against that.

In our contemporary culture when sex without marriage is accepted behavior, we are finding that venereal disease is reaching epidemic proportions. When I was a young fellow, I belonged to an organization whose leader was a very fine doctor. He called in a group of us fellows because he saw that we were doing a great deal of running around. He said he just wanted to have a friendly talk with us. Well, he scared the daylights out of me. People today say that we don't want to frighten our young people. Well, I thank God for what the doctor told us and for the fact that he did scare us. That is exactly what the writer here in Proverbs is doing. He warns the young man about the evil man and the strange woman.

The steps of the young man are now steps of responsibility. He has left the home and has moved out into life, out where he is coming in contact with reality. The advice that is given to him is that his steps need to be ordered according to the Word of God. Oh, how important that is! That is the reason a jeweler I know in Dallas, Texas, gave out the Book of Proverbs to thousands of young men. It contains good advice, wonderful advice.

"Wisdom" here is depicted to us as a woman. However, wisdom is for us personified in the Lord Jesus Christ. "But of him are ye in Christ Jesus, who of God is made unto us wisdom . . ." (1 Cor. 1:30). The young man actually needs Christ.

## THE BOY IS TO LISTEN TO GOD'S LAW

**My son, forget not my law; but let thine heart keep my commandments [Prov. 3:1].**

This also is directed to "My son." We are on Jewish ground here—we need to understand that. Nevertheless, it has a great importance and significance for us today.

"Let thine heart keep my commandments." Isn't that an interesting statement? This is more than simply submitting to duty. I hear so often that it is "our duty" as Christians to do this and to do that. My friend, maybe you won't like for me to say this, but it is not a duty. It is the loving devotion to the will of God. Remember what the psalmist wrote, "Thy word have I hid in mine *heart*, that I might not sin against thee" (Ps. 119:11, italics mine). Also we are told regarding a young priest named Ezra: "For Ezra had prepared his *heart* to seek the law of the LORD, and to do it, and to teach in Israel statutes and judgments" (Ezra 7:10, italics mine). There needs to be that preparation of the heart. Then, remember how the Lord Jesus talked to His own there in the Upper Room. He spoke so intimately, so personally, so wonderfully of things that had never been revealed before. He told those men, ". . . If a man love me, he will keep my words: and my Father will love him, and we will come unto him, and make our abode with him" (John 14:23). My friend, do you love Him? If you do, then He wants to talk to you. Let's not put it on the basis of duty. A man said to me the other day, "I feel that since you are on the radio, it is your *duty* to say this." Brother, just forget the duty part

of it. I *love* the Lord Jesus, and I really am trying to do what I think He wants me to do. He says for me to give out His Word. He's sowing seed today—that's the picture of Him—and I'm sowing seed under His direction. I do it because I love Him. "If a man love me, he will keep my words."

Peter certainly came to understand this. He denied the Lord, and how terrible that was. After the Resurrection, the Lord prepared a breakfast on the shore of the Sea of Galilee. When Simon Peter came into His presence, did the Lord ask him, "What do you mean by denying Me?" Is that what He said? Oh, no! He asked, ". . . Simon, son of Jonas, lovest thou me? . . . (John 21:17). If you *love* Him, my friend, it makes life so much brighter and richer and more wonderful.

**Let not mercy and truth forsake thee: bind them about thy neck; write them upon the table of thine heart [Prov. 3:3].**

"Mercy" is loving-kindness. The law was given by Moses, but grace and truth came by Jesus Christ. What is loving-kindness? It is grace; it is more than kindness. The teacher asked a little girl the difference between kindness and loving-kindness. The little girl answered, "Well, if you go in and ask your mama for a piece of bread with some butter on it, and she gives it to you, that's kindness. But if she puts a little jam on it without your asking her, that is loving-kindness." My friend, God puts a little jam on it for us—loving-kindness and truth, let not these forsake thee: "bind them about thy neck; write them upon the table of thine heart."

**So shalt thou find favour and good understanding in the sight of God and man [Prov. 3:4].**

How wonderful this is!

Now the next two verses are very familiar.

**Trust in the LORD with all thine heart; and lean not unto thine own understanding.**

**In all thy ways acknowledge him, and he shall direct thy paths [Prov. 3:5–6].**

In a service where folk are invited to give their favorite verses, these verses are invariably quoted. I'm sure I have heard them given in a thousand meetings. I sometimes wonder if those who say them realize that they come out of such a rich vein of truth. We need to remember that these verses are directed to the man who diligently studies the Word of God, to the young man who listens to God's law. It is as Paul wrote to Timothy, "Study to shew thyself approved unto God, a workman that needeth not to be ashamed, rightly dividing the word of truth" (2 Tim. 2:15). Having studied the Word of God and knowing something about the loving-kindness, the grace and truth of God—holding on to these things— "trust in Jehovah with all thine heart; and lean not on thine own understanding. In all thy ways acknowledge him, and he shall direct thy paths."

Let's pause and look at that for a moment. This is a very solemn admonition; yet it offers such wonderful assurance of guidance into a way of peace. What a contrast this is to Proverbs 28:26: "He that trusteth in his own heart is a fool. . . ." A man was telling me the other day that he was witnessing to some young folks who are in the drug culture. He told a young man, "God loves you, young man." The fellow answered, "I don't need God to love me. I love *myself*. I don't need to trust in God. I trust in *myself*." I wish the man had given him this verse: "He that trusteth in his own heart is a fool."

On the other hand, it is a wonderful thing to trust in Jehovah with all your heart, to be totally committed to Him. Total commitment to Him is sorely needed in our day.

I find myself coming back to this again and again: "Trust in the Lord with all thine heart." I may be in an airport and learn that the time of my flight has been changed or delayed by stormy weather. I just wasn't built with *wings*, and I have never cared too much for flying. (By the way, I don't expect to have wings in eternity either.) I generally go over to a corner of the airport and say, "Lord, I want to trust You with all my heart. Now just help me to sit down here and rest in You." That's when I need Him. "Trust in Jehovah with all thine heart; and lean not on thine own understanding." I go to the window and look at the sky, and I make a prognostication. But He says to me, "Don't lean on your own understanding. In all thy ways acknowledge Me, and I shall direct thy paths." *He* has led me through life.

I must confess to you that I didn't trust Him like that until I had cancer. I took every day just as it came. Shakespeare, in Act IV of *Julius Caesar*, said: "There is a tide in the affairs of men, which, taken at the flood, leads on to fortune." That was the way I took life. I

don't take it that way anymore. Every time I come to a new day, I like to go and look up at the sky and say, "Lord, thank You for bringing me to a new day." It may be a gloomy day or a bright day, whatever the day, I thank Him. "In all thy ways acknowledge him, and he shall direct thy paths." It took me a long time to learn what that meant in *life*.

Remember that the Lord Jesus, in the Sermon on the Mount, said, ". . . if therefore thine eye be single, thy whole body shall be full of light" (Matt. 6:22). That is an amazing thing. If you have committed yourself to God and you are going down a certain path, doing a certain thing, it is amazing how everything else drops into place. Then your whole body is full of light. Your whole *life* is full of light at that time.

**Be not wise in thine own eyes: fear the LORD, and depart from evil.**

**It shall be health to thy navel, and marrow to thy bones [Prov. 3:7–8].**

It could be translated this way: "It shall be healing to thy sinew and moistening to thy bones." I think that it will actually improve your health to trust in the Lord. It is wonderful to rest in Him rather than in yourself.

"Fear the LORD, and depart from evil." The apostle Paul advised young Timothy, ". . . Let every one that nameth the name of Christ depart from iniquity" (2 Tim. 2:19). It will get you away from sin, away from those things which corrode not only your spiritual life but your physical life as well.

## MATERIAL BLESSINGS HAVE A SPIRITUAL SIGNIFICANCE

**Honour the LORD with thy substance, and with the firstfruits of all thine increase:**

**So shall thy barns be filled with plenty, and thy presses shall burst out with new wine [Prov. 3:9–10].**

This represents total commitment. Remember that when God told Israel about the land He was giving to them, He said, "The land is Mine; I am giving it to you." Israel was to bring a tithe (I think they actually brought three tithes to the Lord). At the very beginning of the harvest they brought the firstfruits. That was to acknowledge that God was the owner of it all. It was an evidence of total commitment.

Don't tell me you are totally committed to

the Lord until your pocketbook is committed too. The Lord gave you everything. Some folk may say, "I have worked hard. I earned this." But who gave you the health to work? Who gave you the work to do? Who made it possible for you to make money? My friend, God did all that for you. Acknowledge Him. That is the evidence of total commitment.

Someone may complain that this sounds very mercenary. No, this is real spirituality. May I say that genuine spirituality is not the length of the prayer that you pray; it is the amount on the check that you write. That is the way one can determine spirituality.

I have learned during my years as a pastor that the person who did the most talking was the one who did the least giving. This is always true. The people who want to run the church don't do much for the treasury. You may be sure of that. However, God promises His blessing to those who honor Him with their substance.

## THE CHASTENING OF THE LORD

**My son, despise not the chastening of the Lord; neither be weary of his correction:**

**For whom the Lord loveth he correcteth; even as a father the son in whom he delighteth [Prov. 3:11–12].**

God is going to chasten you as you go along through life if you are His child. Remember that God does not whip the devil's children, but He certainly does spank His own. That is a good evidence that you belong to Him.

In the Book of Job it says, "Behold, happy is the man whom God correcteth: therefore despise not thou the chastening of the Almighty: For he maketh sore, and bindeth up: he woundeth, and his hands make whole" (Job 5:17–18). Now remember that chastening is not punishing. We have confused punishment with chastisement. The criminal is to be punished; the child is to be corrected. I believe the judges in our land have this thing all mixed up. I have seen a judge take his own little son and slap him across the face when he should have corrected him. Then he turned and let off the criminal whom he should have punished. Criminals are to be punished. Our children are to be chastened—that is, corrected and disciplined. That is what God does for His own children.

## HAPPINESS IN FINDING WISDOM

**Happy is the man that findeth wisdom, and the man that getteth understanding [Prov. 3:13].**

Happy is the man who findeth *Christ*—He is wisdom for us in our day.

**For the merchandise of it is better than the merchandise of silver, and the gain thereof than fine gold [Prov. 3:14].**

Now wisdom is portrayed as having a school. The characterization is feminine because she is in contrast to the stranger woman.

**She is more precious than rubies: and all the things thou canst desire are not to be compared unto her.**

**Length of days is in her right hand; and in her left hand riches and honour [Prov. 3:15–16].**

In the Old Testament God did promise long life for those who served Him.

**Her ways are ways of pleasantness, and all her paths are peace.**

**She is a tree of life to them that lay hold upon her: and happy is every one that retaineth her [Prov. 3:17–18].**

It requires study and effort and time to grasp the Word of God. The spirit of God does not open the Word of God to lazy minds, but to those who are alert and want to learn and know the will of God and the Word of God. One of the great problems today is that many people are not willing to make the sacrifice to study God's Word. A great deal of laziness is covered with pious jargon and pious platitudes. Many folk have developed a neat little vocabulary that sounds good and covers up a woeful ignorance of the Word of God. In these days there is no excuse for being ignorant of the Word of God. It requires work, it is true, but the ways of wisdom are the ways of pleasantness, and all her paths are peace.

**The Lord by wisdom hath founded the earth; by understanding hath he established the heavens.**

**By his knowledge the depths are broken up, and the clouds drop down the dew [Prov. 3:19–20].**

You and I live in a universe that is tremendously orderly. There are a number of folk who work in the space program who are believers. Many of them listen to our program and support it, and we rejoice in that. It is strange to me that everyone who studies the laws of nature and probes into the secrets of the universe is not brought to the realization that we live in a universe that couldn't have just happened. If it did just happen, how and when did it happen? Where is the chicken that hatched out the egg? This universe is so orderly that man can take a rocket, put men in it, send it out through space to the moon, land on the moon and come back. Man thinks he is so smart. But what he has done is to discover the laws of *God* that keep the entire universe running like a computer. My friend, if this universe just happened by chance, it would not operate so precisely. The reason the space program folk can work that little computer and send the rocket to the right place at the right time is because God has established very precise laws. God by wisdom made them. I do not mean to be irreverent when I say that our God is no dummy. We need to recognize the intelligence of God. I believe He would appreciate it if we showed more intelligence, more knowledge of Him and His ways. This we can do in His school, the Word of God. That is the only place.

**My son, let not them depart from thine eyes: keep sound wisdom and discretion [Prov. 3:21].**

"Let not them depart from thine eyes"—the word *them* refers to God's knowledge.

**So shall they be life unto thy soul, and grace to thy neck [Prov. 3:22].**

You see, life and grace come through this wisdom of studying the Word of God.

**Then shalt thou walk in thy way safely, and thy foot shall not stumble.**

**When thou liest down, thou shalt not be afraid: yea, thou shalt lie down, and thy sleep shall be sweet [Prov. 3:23–24].**

Man today has certain fears about life. These fears come to all of us. What is the solution? The Word of God is the answer to all of that. Since we spend most of our time either walking or lying down, the assurance is given that we will walk safely and our sleep shall be sweet. How wonderful it is to discover that the truth of God will hold us—it is not that you and I hold the truth, but the truth will hold us.

**Be not afraid of sudden fear, neither of the desolation of the wicked, when it cometh.**

**For the LORD shall be thy confidence, and shall keep thy foot from being taken [Prov. 3:25–26].**

These verses have meant a great deal to me because I have a fear of flying. When I sit there in a plane, I wait for the plane to fall! I think the next minute will be it. So these verses have been a great encouragement and help to me. I take them with me when I travel by plane, and I use that mode of transportation a great deal.

"Be not afraid of sudden fear"—don't be afraid of the next minute. God is taking care of me at the present moment, and He will take care of me in the next moment.

"For the LORD shall be thy confidence, and shall keep thy foot from falling." I say to the Lord, "This morning when I was in bed, before I got up, I didn't really need You as much as I do right now. Here I am, 38,000 feet in the air, and I'm just a little frightened. Now this is the test: give me the confidence, the assurance, that You are going to keep my foot from falling."

Now this is a marvelous proverb that we are coming to—in fact, there are several of them.

**Withhold not good from them to whom it is due, when it is in the power of thine hand to do it [Prov. 3:27].**

My dad didn't like the organized churches and was opposed to them because of a very bitter experience when he was young. But I always felt he had a desire to be obedient to God. Let me give you an example. When I was a boy, we were riding down a west Texas road in a buggy. A gate had come open and a man's cows had run out. My dad stopped, drove the cows back in, shut the old wire gate, and put the wire over the top to close it. He got back in the buggy and didn't say anything to anyone. He never mentioned it to the man who owned the cows.

**Say not unto thy neighbour, Go, and come again, and tomorrow I will give; when thou hast it by thee [Prov. 3:28].**

How many people today say to me, "I'm going to support your program. You can count on me—but I do have to wait until my ship comes in." Those people have a bank account and could write a check immediately. I use this as an illustration because I hear it so often. But people use this same excuse in all relations of life. They say to others, "I can't help you right now, but you come back tomorrow"—and they have the money in their pocket! We are told in Romans 13:8: "Owe no man any thing, but to *love* one another . . ." (italics mine). This kind of love reveals whether a man is a child of God or not.

Do you know that when you and I owe money to another person, that money we have is not ours? It belongs to the other man. To use it for our own purposes is actually dishonest. That is what he is saying here.

**Devise not evil against thy neighbour, seeing he dwelleth securely by thee [Prov. 3:29].**

In relationship to your neighbor, don't do things that would be to your advantage and his disadvantage. And don't try to keep up with the Joneses by undermining the Joneses.

How wonderful it is to have a neighbor say to you, "I'm going to be gone for a few days, will you sort of keep an eye on my place?" That gives you an opportunity to reveal your relationship to God in a very practical way.

**Strive not with a man without cause, if he have done thee no harm [Prov. 3:30].**

Under the Mosaic Law it was a sin to strive with another without adequate grounds. Under grace we are told, "Dearly beloved, avenge not yourselves, but rather give place unto wrath: for it is written, Vengeance is mine; I will repay, saith the Lord" (Rom. 12:19). We leave the pathway of faith and trust in God when we take matters into our own hands. If we have been treated unjustly, we should turn the matter over to God and let God deal with the situation and with the individual involved.

I have learned over a period of many years as a minister that if someone does harm you, you should go to God about it; let Him know that you have been hurt. Then turn the one who has hurt you over to God. Tell the Lord, "This is your business, You said that You would take care of it." I have watched over a

period of years, and I can say that God does deal with such people. These proverbs are wonderful and they are true. They are helpful not only for the young man but for the old man and for women and girls—they apply to the whole human race.

**Envy thou not the oppressor, and choose none of his ways [Prov. 3:31].**

"The oppressor" is the violent man.

**For the froward is abomination to the LORD: but his secret is with the righteous [Prov. 3:32].**

There are certain people who are actually an abomination to the Lord. In fact, later on in this book we will find some of the things God *hates;* He mentions them here in Proverbs. We'll be getting to that.

**The curse of the LORD is in the house of the wicked: but he blesseth the habitation of the just [Prov. 3:33].**

"The wicked" are the lawless. This proverb reminds me of King Ahab. The Lord certainly judged the house of Ahab! This proverb fits him like a glove.

**Surely he scorneth the scorners: but he giveth grace unto the lowly [Prov. 3:34].**

God seems to hate the scorner, the arrogant, and the conceited person.

**The wise shall inherit glory: but shame shall be the promotion of fools [Prov. 3:35].**

This fits quite a few people—maybe some that you know.

Through the centuries there are many folk that envy the rich. And many have discovered, as did the psalmist, that God judges the rich.

# CHAPTER 4

Although the child is now a young man who has entered the big bad and mad world, he is still counseled to remember the instruction of his father.

**Hear, ye children, the instruction of a father, and attend to know understanding [Prov. 4:1].**

"Ye children" includes the young and the old, male and female.

**For I give you good doctrine, forsake ye not my law.**

**For I was my father's son, tender and only beloved in the sight of my mother [Prov. 4:2–3].**

Solomon wrote this, and he is talking about his own father. Notice that he says, "I was my father's son, tender and only beloved in the sight of my *mother*." There are those who feel that the father's heart was wrapped up in his boy Solomon. I don't see it like that. In my opinion the historical books reveal that Solomon was not the first choice of his father. This boy, reared in the women's palace, was more or less of a sissy. I think he was a sort of playboy, and David did not have much in common with him. Solomon says, "I am my father's son, but it was my mother who really loved me and taught me." However—

**He taught me also, and said unto me, Let thine heart retain my words: keep my commandments, and live [Prov. 4:4].**

David probably gave him a great deal of advice. When Solomon was made king, David said to him, "Play the man!" I think he said that because he felt that Solomon was not manly. He said, "Let thine heart retain my words: keep my commandments, and live." David had learned by experience that you had better obey the Lord. Probably David was not as kind in teaching his son as he could have been. I have never felt that David was a success as a father. Unfortunately, that has been true of a great many famous men.

The life of David was something that Solomon could emulate. Perhaps you are saying, *Yes, but look what David did.* Well, David's great sins were committed before Solomon was born, and David had turned from that type of life altogether.

Now Solomon is giving advice to a young man, and he is really laying it on the line.

**Get wisdom, get understanding: forget it not; neither decline from the words of my mouth.**

**Forsake her not, and she shall preserve thee: love her, and she shall keep thee [Prov. 4:5–6].**

Wisdom is depicted as a lady who keeps a school and sends out her catalog. Remember that there is another woman, the stranger woman, who is also bidding for the interest of the young man. Wisdom is urging him to come to her school so that he might be wise.

Notice that he says that wisdom will "preserve" and "keep" the young man.

The great difference in contemporary educators is pinpointed in this verse. Do they *love* wisdom? In other words, do they *love* the Word of God? It was Pascal who said that human knowledge must be understood to be loved. But divine knowledge must be *loved* to be understood. So if you are going to understand the Word of God, you must bring to it love and a mind that is willing to be taught. Then the spirit of God can open up the great truths to you. How important it is to see this. He says, "*love* her, and she shall keep thee."

**Wisdom is the principal thing; therefore get wisdom: and with all thy getting get understanding [Prov. 4:7].**

Notice the way he speaks of wisdom. It is not just knowledge; it is not simply having a computer mind. It is wisdom and intelligence to use knowledge properly and to have a love for it. That is something that the souls of men need today.

The reason education is not satisfying is because of the way it is dished out. The most impressive thing here is that we are to *get wisdom.* How important it is.

**Exalt her, and she shall promote thee: she shall bring thee to honour, when thou dost embrace her.**

**She shall give to thine head an ornament of grace: a crown of glory shall she deliver to thee [Prov. 4:8–9].**

The interesting thing here is that wisdom is to be loved like a woman is loved. When we get to the New Testament, this is changed—*Christ* has been made unto us wisdom, and we are to love Him.

The real difficulty in our day is not that there are problems in the Bible. The real difficulty is that in man there is not that love and longing for God and for the things of God. When love is present in the heart, this Book will begin to open up, because the spirit of God will become the Teacher.

**Hear, O my son, and receive my sayings; and the years of thy life shall be many [Prov. 4:10].**

This sounds to me like it is Bathsheba talking to Solomon.

**I have taught thee in the way of wisdom; I have led thee in right paths.**

**When thou goest, thy steps shall not be straitened; and when thou runnest, thou shalt not stumble.**

**Take fast hold of instruction; let her not go: keep her; for she is thy life [Prov. 4:11–13].**

This is a wonderful call to the young man to seek wisdom. "Take fast hold of instruction"— it is something that should have top priority. It is like saying, "Learn all you can learn."

**Enter not into the path of the wicked, and go not in the way of evil men.**

**Avoid it, pass not by it, turn from it, and pass away [Prov. 4:14–15].**

We have noted before that the warning in this book is against the evil man and the stranger woman. That woman is a prostitute, of course. I think we shall see that this also has a spiritual application.

**For they sleep not, except they have done mischief; and their sleep is taken away, unless they cause some to fall.**

**For they eat the bread of wickedness, and drink the wine of violence [Prov. 4:16–17].**

This portrays for us how the evil man and the stranger woman live. They can't even sleep unless they have done some evil thing. You read of crimes and say, "I don't see how a man could do a thing like that; I don't see how a woman could live that kind of a life. How can they stand to live with themselves?" My friend, these folk couldn't live with themselves if they *didn't* do these wicked things. We do not know how desperate and how deep into sin the human heart can go. There is nothing which the human mind and heart cannot conceive in wickedness. We need to realize that out in this world we are rubbing

shoulders with many people who are not always nice. Of course there will be some wonderful people, but we need to be careful of the kind of people we meet.

When I was a pastor in downtown Los Angeles and rode to work on the freeways, I would pray. (When you ride these freeways in Southern California, you do well to pray for your safety, but actually, I prayed about something else.) My prayer would be something like this: "Lord, I'm going to meet new people today. Some of those people I will be able to help. Some of them would like to hurt me. Help me to be able to tell the difference. Help me to put my arm around the man who needs my help, but help me to avoid the man who would put a knife in my back." I think it is important that we recognize the kind of world in which we live.

I have learned that there are certain men who will become true friends, bosom friends, and I thank God for them. It is men like that who made my radio ministry possible. Then there have been men who have tried to destroy it—yet they profess to be Christians. It is difficult to understand their thinking. The human heart is not to be trusted. We need to be very careful; we need to have discernment as we meet mankind in our daily walk.

**But the path of the just is as the shining light, that shineth more and more unto the perfect day [Prov. 4:18].**

You will meet wonderful saints like this. Then notice the contrast:

**The way of the wicked is as darkness: they know not at what they stumble [Prov. 4:19].**

There are two ways that are set in contrast. One way is the way in which the righteous go. It is described as a "shining light, that shineth more and more unto the perfect day." There is another way, the way the lawless go. It is a way of darkness. It reminds us of the broad way that our Lord described, which I believe has been misunderstood.

I can remember when I was a boy that we would be taught about the broad way and the narrow way. Now if they had asked me which way I wanted to go, I would have said immediately, "I think you could have a lot more fun on the broad way." Unfortunately, I think that is the impression most often given. However, that is not accurate at all. The picture is altogether different.

The broad way is a wide one today. That is where the mob is. The crowd is having a "vanity fair" down that way all the time. The carnival is going on. (By the way, that word *carnival* comes from the world *carnal*, which has to do with the flesh.) Down there is the place where they indulge the flesh, and they call it the way of liberty. We hear today that we are living in a new age in which we can do as we please. That is certainly a broad way—that is, at the entrance. But notice that this broad way gets narrower and narrower and narrower. The way of the lawless is the dark way. "The way of the wicked is as darkness." There are the bright lights at the entrance, but down a little farther there are no lights. The people don't even know what they are stumbling over. That is the broad way that the Lord Jesus described. It is just like going in at the big end of a funnel and then finding that it gets narrower and narrower until finally it ends in destruction.

In contrast, the narrow way is very narrow at the entrance. The Lord Jesus said, ". . . I am *the* way . . ." (John 14:6, italics mine). It is so narrow that it is limited to one Person: Christ. No one can come to the Father but through Him. You just can't find a way any narrower than that. Peter said, "Neither is there salvation in any other: for there is none other name under heaven given among men, whereby we must be saved" (Acts 4:12). Jesus said, "I am the door: by me if any man enter in, he shall be saved, and shall go in and out, and find pasture" (John 10:9). The entrance is narrow, but after the entrance the way gets wider and wider, leading to an abundant life here and on into the light of heaven itself. My friend, we need to enter into the narrow end of the funnel, and that end is labeled, *The Lord Jesus Christ.*

That is exactly the picture we get from our verses here in Proverbs. There are two ways. There is the path of the just, and there is the way of the wicked. We will hear more of this in this book. The broad way is described in chapter 16: "There is a way that seemeth right unto a man, but the end thereof are the ways of death" (Prov. 16:25).

**My son, attend to my words; incline thine ear unto my sayings.**

**Let them not depart from thine eyes; keep them in the midst of thine heart.**

**For they are life unto those that find them, and health to all their flesh [Prov. 4:20–22].**

The psalmist said this about the Word: "Thy *word* have I hid in mine heart, that I might not sin against thee" (Ps. 119:11, italics mine). God's *words* are the words of life. It has been said of the writings of a great man of the past that if his words were cut, they would bleed. This can truly be said of the words of God. They are living words—if you cut them, they will bleed. "For they are life unto those that find them." They will bring life and light to you. They bring instruction and direction and joy. All this comes through the Word of God.

Now here is one of the great verses in the Book of Proverbs:

**Keep thy heart with all diligence; for out of it are the issues of life [Prov. 4:23].**

Another translation of this verse is: "Keep thy heart above all keeping"—with all diligence. This is the most important thing to watch over. "For out of it are the issues of life." The life of the flesh is in the blood, and it is the heart that pumps that blood. William Harvey back in the seventeenth century discovered the circulation of the blood which revolutionized medical science. Yet here in Proverbs which was written about 2,700 years earlier, there is a recognition of the importance of the heart for the maintenance of life. And the heart symbolizes the center of one's innermost being. The Lord Jesus said that it isn't what goes into a man that defiles him, but what comes out of a man. "For out of the heart proceed evil thoughts, murders, adulteries, fornications, thefts, false witness, blasphemies" (Matt. 15:19). Some of the meanest things in the world come out of the human heart. The heart is the seat of the total personality. If you want to know how important the heart is, get your concordance and look up all the references to the heart that are in the Bible. We are to keep our hearts with all diligence. What we hear is important. What we study is important. What we see is important. We should recognize that out of that heart will come all of the great issues of our lives.

Let's not miss the fact that the Book of Proverbs, written long before Harvey made the discovery of the circulation of blood, makes a statement about the heart that centuries later science demonstrated to be true. In the Book of Proverbs (and this can be said of the entire Bible) you will find no unscientific or inaccurate observation.

**Put away from thee a froward mouth, and perverse lips put far from thee [Prov. 4:24].**

The issues of life will proceed from the *heart*, but it is the *mouth* and the *lips* that will do the speaking. Someone has put it like this: "What is in the well of the heart will come up through the bucket of the mouth." How true it is that sooner or later the mouth will reveal what is in your heart.

Our mouths give us away. Mrs. McGee and I were having lunch in a little town in the Northwest and were talking to each other. We noticed that the waitress seemed very much interested and pretty soon she interrupted us. "Aren't you Dr. McGee?" I answered, "Yes, how did you know me?" She said "I've never seen you before, but I listen to you on the radio." Later my wife told me, "You had better be very careful what you say. You are recognized by people when you have no idea that you are being recognized." How true that is, but the care has to begin with the heart. What is in the well of the heart will come up through the bucket of the mouth. Our mouths will give away what is being harbored in our hearts.

**Let thine eyes look right on, and let thine eyelids look straight before thee.**

**Ponder the path of thy feet, and let all thy ways be established.**

**Turn not to the right hand nor to the left: remove thy foot from evil [Prov. 4:25–27].**

Oh, how careful a young man needs to be! A man told me the other day that he ruined his whole life by being arrested when he was a young man. He has a record against him, and that record has confronted him again and again down through the years. In this day when the use of drugs and liquor is so prevalent, especially among young folk, how careful he should be. How tragic it is to see multitudes of youngsters who are destroying themselves because they do not "ponder the path" of their feet.

# CHAPTER 5

Read this chapter carefully and you will find that the young man is counseled to live a pure life for the sake of his home. This is the kind of sex education that God gives. I like this education from God better than some of the things that I am hearing today, even in Christian services. God is saying that a pure life should be led for the sake of the home later on. A lot of the problems in the homes today don't begin there. They began way back in the premarital sex life of the individual.

## GOD'S SEX EDUCATION

**My son, attend unto my wisdom, and bow thine ear to my understanding:**

**That thou mayest regard discretion, and that thy lips may keep knowledge [Prov. 5:1–2].**

"My son." This is addressed to the young man again. This is wisdom bidding the young man to come to her school to learn of her. In the previous chapter the warning was against the evil man. In this chapter the warning is against the "strange woman," literally, the stranger woman, because the woman was a stranger, one who came from outside Israel. She was generally a Gentile, and she was a prostitute. No Israelite woman was to become a prostitute. According to the law a prostitute was to be stoned. However, as Israel got farther from God, they also sank into more and more immorality. Thus it happened that some of the Israelites did become prostitutes as is indicated in Proverbs 2:17, "Which forsaketh the guide of her youth, and forgetteth the covenant of her God." In that case the woman is still considered a stranger, a foreigner, because she is a stranger as far as her relationship to God is concerned.

**For the lips of a strange woman drop as an honeycomb, and her mouth is smoother than oil:**

**But her end is bitter as wormwood, sharp as a two-edged sword.**

**Her feet go down to death; her steps take hold on hell.**

**Lest thou shouldest ponder the path of life, her ways are moveable, that thou canst not know them [Prov. 5:3–6].**

There was an infamous gangster in the penitentiary in Atlanta. One of the officers there told me that this man had contracted syphilis, which had not been cured and went on to cause paresis and eventually insanity. That man was a blubbering idiot before he died. The officer told me this: "This man was responsible for the ruin of many a girl. But it is interesting that he didn't get by with that sort of thing. Some girl along the route got even with him." God's Word here is warning against that kind of thing.

**Hear me now therefore, O ye children, and depart not from the words of my mouth.**

**Remove thy way far from her, and come not nigh the door of her house:**

**Lest thou give thine honour unto others, and thy years unto the cruel:**

**Lest strangers be filled with thy wealth; and thy labours be in the house of a stranger;**

**And thou mourn at the last, when thy flesh and thy body are consumed [Prov. 5:7–11].**

What a warning is given here to this young man. This gives a true picture of the end result of venereal disease. At last there is mourning when the flesh and the body are consumed. Here in California venereal disease has reached epidemic proportions.

**And say, How have I hated instruction, and my heart despised reproof;**

**And have not obeyed the voice of my teachers, nor inclined mine ear to them that instructed me!**

**I was almost in all evil in the midst of the congregation and assembly [Prov. 5:12–14].**

Remember that God is not mocked. What you sow is what you shall reap. God describes here what will be the end result of such a life. I believe that our society is already reaping what it has been sowing. The gross immorality in our land stems from the lack of instruction in the Word of God.

Now God tells about the relationship that should exist between husband and wife. Here we see marriage brought to a very high plane.

## THE HOLINESS OF MARRIAGE

**Drink waters out of thine own cistern, and running waters out of thine own well.**

**Let thy fountains be dispersed abroad, and rivers of waters in the streets.**

**Let them be only thine own, and not strangers' with thee [Prov. 5:15–17].**

In other words, your offspring should be from your wife, not from a stranger.

**Let thy fountain be blessed: and rejoice with the wife of thy youth.**

**Let her be as the loving hind and pleasant roe; let her breasts satisfy thee at all times; and be thou ravished always with her love [Prov. 5:18–19].**

These verses describe love in marriage, and the Word of God makes it very clear that physical love and sexual love in marriage are to be sanctified and brought to a very high level. There was a time when speaking of these things was taboo. They were not mentioned as though they were immoral or some sort of a dirty thing even among married folk. Do you notice how God describes physical love in marriage? God lifts it to the very highest plane. Remember that marriage was designed by God Himself and was given to the human family for the welfare and good of mankind. A part of the immorality of our day is the attempt to get rid of marriage.

For the child of God the Christian home is a picture of the relationship between Christ and the church. You just cannot have a relationship higher or holier than that. That is why it is alarming to see that even Christian couples in the church are breaking up. This hasn't happened in only one or two cases but it is happening many, many times. This ought to cause the church to get down on its knees before God and find out what is wrong. It is an indication that the Word of God is not getting through to people. It is not influencing and swaying the lives of those members of the church.

"Marriage is honourable in all, and the bed undefiled: but whoremongers and adulterers God will judge" (Heb. 13:4). God calls marriage a wonderful relationship. It is high and holy and not to be treated as something that is unclean. But notice the other side of the picture: "but whoremongers and adulterers God will judge."

When I was the pastor of a certain church, a man of the congregation came to me and announced he was leaving his wife and son and was going to run off with another woman. They were all church members—whether or not they were Christians only God knows. I was a young preacher at that time, and I really laid it on the line to him. He rose in indignation and said, "Are you trying to rob me of my salvation?" I answered, "Brother, if you have salvation, I am not trying to rob you of it. But I do want to say this to you, and I want you to remember it: If you are not God's child, you are acting according to the way the devil's children act. If you happen to be a child of God, one of these days God will take you to His woodshed and He will whip you within an inch of your life. I am not sure but that He may even take your life." The fellow just sneered, and he went ahead and married the other woman. The years have gone by, and those two are the loneliest, saddest, most frustrated, most unlovely people I know. I am confident they would both say, "If only I could go back and do it over."

Peter admonishes husbands to dwell with their wives according to knowledge ". . . and as being heirs together of the grace of life; that your prayers be not hindered" (1 Pet. 3:7). This is a real test. When a husband and wife are so living before each other that they have joy and confidence and can kneel together and pray together and love together, that home represents the relationship of Christ and the church. I want to tell you, my friend, that God can and will bless such a home. Oh, how important this is!

**And why wilt thou, my son, be ravished with a strange woman, and embrace the bosom of a stranger?**

**For the ways of man are before the eyes of the LORD, and he pondereth all his goings [Prov. 5:20–21].**

This is an interesting verse. "The ways of man are before the eyes of the LORD, and he pondereth all his goings." We need to recognize that God is seeing us all the time. God is always watching us.

A man was put in a foursome for golf with three of us who were preachers. He was glad to get away from us when he found out who we were. He had ripped out an oath, and after he learned that we were preachers, he began to apologize. I said to him, "Brother, don't pay any attention to us. We are just three men like you are. But you are speaking that way before *God* all the time. I don't care whether you are on the golf course or in a bar or where you are, you are saying these things before *God*." The ways of man are before the eyes of Jehovah and God ponders—He wonders why we act and say what we do. I think that God must get really puzzled by some of the things we do and say.

**His own iniquities shall take the wicked himself, and he shall be holden with the cords of his sins.**

**He shall die without instruction; and in the greatness of his folly he shall go astray [Prov. 5:22–23].**

God says that there is a day coming, a day of accountability, a day of retribution. A payday is on the way. Man thinks he is getting by with sin. God says that no one is getting by with a thing. Man's own iniquities shall take him, and he will be held with the cords of his sins.

# CHAPTER 6

This chapter covers many different subjects. It starts with some advice that is good for the business world today, for Christians or non-Christians. These are simply some good business principles. You see, God has given a lot of good advice for all mankind, the saved as well as the unsaved.

## GOOD BUSINESS PRINCIPLES

**My son, if thou be surety for thy friend, if thou hast stricken thy hand with a stranger,**

**Thou art snared with the words of thy mouth, thou art taken with the words of thy mouth [Prov. 6:1–2].**

He mentions two things which are good advice any time. Beware of signing a friend's note. And never become a partner with a stranger. The unsaved man can follow this advice in his business, and it will be helpful to him.

The second verse would indicate that the fellow has been boasting. Apparently one of the reasons a man will co-sign a note with another man is that he wants to be the big shot. He wants to appear outstanding in the financial realm. We are to beware of that.

**Do this now, my son, and deliver thyself, when thou art come into the hand**

of thy friend; go, humble thyself, and make sure thy friend [Prov. 6:3].

Don't be afraid to go to him and get things straightened out. Be sure that you hold on to your friends, and be sure that you beware of your enemies. That is exactly what he is saying here and will repeat it in other places.

**Give not sleep to thine eyes, nor slumber to thine eyelids.**

**Deliver thyself as a roe from the hand of the hunter, and as a bird from the hand of the fowler [Prov. 6:4–5].**

Don't sleep on it; get the thing straightened out. You are just like a bird caught in a trap if you have signed a note. That is the warning.

Now he will present the positive side. Not only should one be prudent in what he does in his business and prudent in what he says in the business world, but he is also to learn something from the ants.

**Go to the ant, thou sluggard; consider her ways, and be wise:**

**Which having no guide, overseer, or ruler,**

**Provideth her meat in the summer, and gathereth her food in the harvest [Prov. 6:6–8].**

The little ant is quite a teacher. Aunt Ant can reveal great truths to us. One truth is that she is as diligent in business as anyone possibly can be. This is something that the child of God can learn from the little ant. The ant is busy doing what is the most important thing in her life—she is getting food for the winter, caring for the future, and she is *busy* about it.

I think one of the great sins among Christians today is laziness, and many of the lazy ones can be found in full-time Christian service. All of us need to ask ourselves what we do with our spare time. Do we read the Word of God? Do we study the Word of God? I think that laziness is one of the curses of the ministry today. A young man came to me and said, "I feel like I'm through as a preacher. I've been a pastor here at this place for three years, and I have run out of sermons. I feel like a dried-up well." Of course, then he became very pious, "I've spent a lot of time in prayer and meditation." Well, I asked him, "How much time do you spend in the Word of God? How much time do you spend studying it?" I couldn't get a very definite answer from him, but he inferred that he spent less than *an hour a week* in the study of the Bible! He was

a great promoter, always out doing something while the important business remained undone. I told him, "Unless you change your ways, you ought to get out of the ministry. It is a disgrace to go to the pulpit on a Sunday morning unprepared. You should have something to say from the Word of God." The ant has a lesson for that boy. "Go to the ant, thou sluggard; consider her ways, and be wise."

**How long wilt thou sleep, O sluggard? when wilt thou arise out of thy sleep?**

**Yet a little sleep, a little slumber, a little folding of the hands to sleep:**

**So shall thy poverty come as one that travelleth, and thy want as an armed man [Prov. 6:9–11].**

## THE WICKED MAN

We come now to a description of a wicked man, a son of Belial.

**A naughty person, a wicked man, walketh with a froward mouth.**

**He winketh with his eyes, he speaketh with his feet, he teacheth with his fingers [Prov. 6:12–13].**

Have you ever noticed this in a person? Everything he does and every gesture he makes is suggestive. Everything he says has a filthy connotation. There are Christians who are borderline cases in this respect.

I knew a preacher like that, and I got away from him years ago. I have known some laymen who are the same way. Everything they said had a double meaning. I know of a so-called Christian group of folk who, at their meetings, tell jokes with a double meaning. There is always that little suggestive thing in them. This is something that God is speaking against.

**Frowardness is in his heart, he deviseth mischief continually; he soweth discord.**

**Therefore shall his calamity come suddenly; suddenly shall he be broken without remedy [Prov. 6:14–15].**

"Frowardness" is perverseness. Notice that he "soweth" or casts forth discord. Here is a person who is supposed to be a child of God, and yet every movement of his body is suggestive.

In my office I have a picture of a man who has meant a great deal to me. He was not a great preacher, but he was a great man of

God. I have spent many hours with that man in the past. He always reminds me of the pureness of speech. Never have I heard him say anything that was suggestive or that had one bit of smut in it. His life was just as clear and clean as the noonday sun. That is the type of men we need today. We don't need more of the bright young fellows with the latest thing in haberdashery and the latest haircut. You see them eyeing the girls even though they are married. Their wives cannot be quite sure about them. But we say, "My, they have good personalities!"

May I say something to you, and I am going to say it very clearly. We are loaded with folk in Christian service today, and we are getting nowhere. Do you know why not? Because God is not mocked. "Be not deceived; God is not mocked: for whatsoever a man soweth, that shall he also reap. For he that soweth to his flesh shall of the flesh reap corruption; but he that soweth to the Spirit shall of the Spirit reap life everlasting" (Gal. 6:7–8). God is not fooled. Our God demands a holy life. Do you know why? Because He is holy. He is that kind of God. And that is the kind of person God is going to be interested in and bless. Oh, we need to recognize that we are dealing with a holy God! I have a wonderful preacher friend who is in what is known as the holiness movement, because the emphasis is on holiness of life. I said to him one day, "The criticism I have of you folk is that you have lost your holiness, and you are the ones who should be bearing down on that for the benefit of us who have gotten very far from God." My, what an emphasis is needed on holy living among God's people today!

## SEVEN THINGS GOD HATES

It is unbelievable to some folk that God could hate. They consider Him as only a God of love. The reason they have this kind of reaction is the result of following a deductive reasoning based on the syllogistic method of reasoning. The major premise is that God is love. That is true. The minor premise is that love is the opposite of hate, and that is also true. Then the conclusion they draw is that God cannot hate anything, but that is not true. God is love, but He hates evil.

We can see this same thing in our human relationships. You love your little child, but you hate the fever that is racking his little body. You love your child, but you hate the mad dog with the frothing mouth that comes into your yard and attempts to bite your little child. If you love your child, you will hate the

mad dog. As long as there is a world of contrasts, a world in which sin has entered, we will love the right and hate the wrong. Or, on the other hand, if you love sin, then you will hate righteousness.

The Word of God tells us to love the good and hate the evil. When we get to the Book of Ecclesiastes, we will find that it says that there is "A time to love, and a time to hate . . ." (Eccl. 3:8).

Now we find that there are seven things God hates. This is His list:

**These six things doth the LORD hate: yea, seven are an abomination unto him:**

**A proud look, a lying tongue, and hands that shed innocent blood,**

**An heart that deviseth wicked imaginations, feet that be swift in running to mischief,**

**A false witness that speaketh lies, and he that soweth discord among brethren [Prov. 6:16–19].**

God definitely says that He hates these things, and we ought to put them on our "hate list" also. This isn't the first time God has stated that He hates something. If you will turn back to Deuteronomy, you will read, "Neither shalt thou set thee up any image; which the LORD thy God hateth" (Deut. 16:22). God hates any kind of idol or anything that would take His place in our hearts. God's hate is mentioned again in Psalm 45:7, the great millennial psalm: "Thou lovest righteousness, and hatest wickedness. . . ." One follows the other as the night follows the day. God said to the early church in the Book of Revelation: "But this thou hast, that thou hatest the deeds of the Nicolaitans, which I also hate" (Rev. 2:6). You see, my friend, God loves, but also God hates. It is like the flavor of sweet and sour developed by Chinese and European chefs to a fine art. God is love but, by the same token, God is hate. And Scripture adequately states the case.

The number seven in the Bible indicates not perfection but completeness. God has a complete hatred of these things, and they are all the works of the flesh. They are things that reveal the total depravity and the utter degradation of the human species. God has gone on record that He hates them. God denies the thesis of liberal theology that He is some sentimental and senile old man who weeps but never works, that He simply shuts His eyes to the sins of mankind and is tolerant of evil, that He forgives because He hasn't the intestinal fortitude to punish sin. God says, "I *love*," but He also says, "I *hate*."

The idea that we are to be charitable to the guilty is abroad in our land because we don't have the courage to go through with a strong program of punishment. That is the thing that is corrupting and wrecking our society today. God is willing to punish the guilty. God is not afraid of public opinion. God doesn't run from any appearance of offending men. God is no coward. God says that by no means will He clear the guilty. His laws are inviolate and inexorable.

Now let's look at this ugly and hateful brood. These belong on the hate side of God's ledger:

1. "A proud look." The literal is *eyes of loftiness*. It is the attitude that overvalues self and undervalues others. This is pride. It is that thought of the heart, that little look and that turn of the face, that flash of the eye which says you are better than someone else. God says, "I *hate* it." It is number one on His list—He puts it ahead of murder and ahead of drunkenness. God hates the proud look.

It is strange that in churches today one can get by with a proud look and no one would say a thing about it. Do you know that the first overt act of sin in heaven, the original sin, was pride? It was when Satan, Lucifer, son of the morning, said in his heart, ". . . I will ascend into heaven, I will exalt my throne above the stars of God: I will sit also upon the mount of the congregation, in the sides of the north: I will ascend above the heights of the clouds; I will be like the most High" (Isa. 14:13–14). And he is the one who came to man in the Garden of Eden and said, ". . . ye shall be as gods . . ." (Gen. 3:5).

It is quite interesting that behind all psychological disturbances and psychosomatic disease there is the trunk of a tree from which the abnormality springs. Do you know what that is? It is a lack of being a complete personality. It is wanting to be somebody important, wanting certain status symbols—one of which is independence of God. It is wanting to be one's own god. It is making the little self to be God. That is the reason a salvation by works appeals to men. Little man likes to say, "I'm going to earn my own salvation. I'll do it myself, and I don't need You, God. I certainly don't need to have Your Son die for me. When I come into Your presence, I want You to move over because I am just as good as You are, and I'm going to sit down right beside

You." My friend, a work-salvation is the result of folk who are psychologically sick. God resists the proud, and He has respect unto the lowly. He says that he will bring down the high looks. God said to Job, "Look on every one that is proud, and bring him low; and tread down the wicked in their place" (Job 40:12).

In the beatitudes of the Sermon on the Mount, the Lord Jesus said, "Blessed are the *poor* in *spirit:* for theirs is the kingdom of heaven" (Matt. 5:3, italics mine). This is what the psalmist says: "Lord, my heart is not haughty, nor mine eyes lofty: neither do I exercise myself in great matters, or in things too high for me" (Ps. 131:1). We need to take the lowly place and say, "Oh God, I am weak. I can't make it. I need You."

The other day I saw a young man walk into a group of young men. He was a big, swaggering, baby boy—that is what he was. He wanted to be accepted by his peers; so he walked in, looked around, and began to curse like a sailor. I thought, *Poor little fellow! What a poor little baby he is, trying to make himself acceptable with the other fellows. Why doesn't he simply go before God and tell Him the truth?* Psychologically man adopts all this phony stuff. How much better off he would be to say to God as the psalmist said, "Lord, my heart is not haughty. I don't want to make claims that are not genuine. I don't have any righteousness." When you go to God for His salvation, that is when you become a real, full-fledged personality. Listen to what God said through Isaiah: ". . . but to this man will I look, even to him that is poor and of a contrite spirit, and trembleth at my word" (Isa. 66:2). If you are willing to come to God on that basis, God will receive you. He hates a proud look.

2. God hates a "lying tongue." Have you ever noticed that there is far more said throughout the Bible about the abuse of the tongue than is said about the abuse of alcohol? The abuse of the tongue is something that is common to all races and all languages. People talk about a tongues movement. There is a big tongues movement today. Do you know what that is? It is the lying tongue. How tragic it is!

The psalmist (probably David) said, "I said in my haste, All men are liars" (Ps. 116:11). Dr. W. I. Carroll used to tell us in class, "David said in his haste that all men are liars. I've had a long time to think it over, and I still agree with David." I'll admit that I agree with David, too. Again the psalmist said, "Deliver my soul, O Lord, from lying lips, and from a deceitful tongue" (Ps. 120:2). In David's prayer of confession, he said, "Behold, thou desirest *truth* in the inward parts: and in the hidden part thou shalt make me to know wisdom" (Ps. 51:6, italics mine). God is the God of truth. "Into thine hand I commit my spirit: thou hast redeemed me, O LORD God of *truth*" (Ps. 31:5, italics mine). How wonderful that is. How different from the lying tongue!

3. The third thing God hates is "hands that shed innocent blood." A murderer is particularly odious and objectionable both to God and to man. God says the murderer should be punished because he took that which God said is sacred—the human life. The popular idea today is completely opposite. After a man has been killed the murderer is brought to trial, then suddenly *the murderer's life* is considered to be precious. God says that human life is precious and that when a murderer kills a man, he is to forfeit his own life. That is the teaching of the Word of God.

4. The fourth thing God hates is "an heart that deviseth wicked imaginations"— thoughts of iniquity. I think all mankind has evil thoughts. The Lord Jesus said, "For out of the heart proceed evil thoughts, murders, adulteries, fornications, thefts, false witness, blasphemies" (Matt. 15:19). It is an ugly brood that comes out of the human heart. By the way, have you ever confessed to God what you have in your mind and in your heart? We all need to do that. We need to be cleansed.

God is dealing with the anatomy of evil and iniquity. It includes the eyes, the tongues, the hands, the heart, and the feet, as we shall see next.

5. "Feet that be swift in running to mischief." The heart blazes the trail that the feet will follow. Isaiah put it like this: "Their feet run to evil, and they make haste to shed innocent blood: their thoughts are thoughts of iniquity; wasting and destruction are in their paths" (Isa. 59:7). These are the things on God's hate list.

6. "A false witness that speaketh lies." It is not an uncommon thing today for people to perjure themselves. It seems to be one of the common sins of our time. It is a thing which God hates.

7. "He that soweth discord among brethren." There is a beatitude, given by our Lord, that looks at it from the positive side: "Blessed are the peacemakers: for they shall be called the children of God" (Matt. 5:9). There are multitudes of folk sowing discord, and they are not all politically motivated. They are in your neighborhood, and chances are they are in your church. You may even have one in your home, and there is a possibility that he even may be sitting where you sit. My friend, causing trouble between family members or brothers in Christ or fellow workers is something that God *hates*.

This list of seven sins is like a mirror. We look into it, and we squirm because we see ourselves. May I ask you to take a good look at yourself in this mirror of the Word of God. After you and I see ourselves as we really are, let us go to God and make a confession of these things. Let us be honest with Him and ask Him for His cleansing.

**My son, keep thy father's commandment, and forsake not the law of thy mother:**

**Bind them continually upon thine heart, and tie them about thy neck.**

**When thou goest, it shall lead thee; when thou sleepest, it shall keep thee; and when thou awakest, it shall talk with thee [Prov. 6:20–22].**

The young man has grown and has gone away to school, but he is reminded not to forget the things that were taught him by his father and his mother. The things He has learned in the home are very important. He is to keep them constantly before him.

**For the commandment is a lamp; and the law is light; and reproofs of instruction are the way of life [Prov. 6:23].**

## WARNING AGAINST SEX SINS

Now he comes back to the great sin in our contemporary society—the sex sins.

The warning again concerns the strange woman, the prostitute. It is that which can wreck the life of a young man more than anything else. The sex sins, the sins of adultery are the great sins of our day. No one can calculate the lives that have been absolutely wrecked and ruined because of them. Oh, how many marriages are broken up today because of them! Hollywood, novels, popular songs all play on the same old theme, the triangle. There is the married couple and the third party, man or woman, who is breaking up the marriage. Proverbs has much to say about them.

**To keep thee from the evil woman, from the flattery of the tongue of a strange woman.**

**Lust not after her beauty in thine heart; neither let her take thee with her eyelids [Prov. 6:24–25].**

Notice that the young man is not to lust after her beauty in his heart. We have just learned, "Keep thy heart with all diligence; for out of it are the issues of life" (Prov. 4:23). Also notice how the young man is warned against her flattery, her beauty, her fluttering eyelids. Jesus said, "Ye have heard that it was said by them of old time, Thou shalt not commit adultery: But I say unto you, That whosoever looketh on a woman to lust after her hath committed adultery with her already in his heart" (Matt. 5:27–28). The whole sinful thought begins down in the human heart.

**For by means of a whorish woman a man is brought to a piece of bread: and the adulteress will hunt for the precious life [Prov. 6:26].**

How many men have been ruined like that? I think we would all be shocked if we knew how many office "wives" there are. We have no idea of the number of people who are blackmailed today because of illicit sex. We hear of only a few. Just recently it was disclosed that a doctor in San Francisco had another wife and family in Southern California. Everyone who knew him thought that he was leading a moral, upright life. All the while he was keeping up two homes. This same kind of thing has happened in the lives of ministers! How does it all get started? The Lord says it begins in the heart—He made us and He knows us. "Lust not after her beauty in thine heart." It begins there.

Now he asks a few pointed questions:

**Can a man take fire in his bosom, and his clothes not be burned? [Prov. 6:27].**

The answer to that is obvious.

**Can one go upon hot coals, and his feet not be burned? [Prov. 6:28].**

We know of fanatics who try this, but it always burns their little tootsies to walk on hot coals.

**So he that goeth in to his neighbour's wife; whosoever toucheth her shall not be innocent [Prov. 6:29].**

If a man commit adultery, he is not innocent. He has no plea whatsoever. Now notice the illustration—

**Men do not despise a thief, if he steal to satisfy his soul when he is hungry [Prov. 6:30].**

If a man steals because he is hungry, our sympathy goes out to him. A man was arrested for stealing in my community recently, and it was found that he had some little children at home who were hungry. In a case like that you don't judge him, you want to help him. "Men do not despise a thief, if he steal to satisfy his soul when he is hungry."

**But if he be found, he shall restore sevenfold; he shall give all the substance of his house [Prov. 6:31].**

He can mortgage his house to repay it.

**But whoso committeth adultery with a woman lacketh understanding: he that doeth it destroyeth his own soul [Prov. 6:32].**

Again I draw an illustration from my own locality. A man walked into another man's room the other day, drew a gun, and shot the man dead. Why? Well, when the story came out, the man was exonerated. His home had been absolutely destroyed by the lust of the man he killed. "Whoso committeth adultery with a woman lacketh understanding: he that doeth it destroyeth his own soul."

**A wound and dishonour shall he get; and his reproach shall not be wiped away [Prov. 6:33].**

Committing adultery is something that will scar his soul for life. As a pastor (and I'm sure many other pastors know cases like this) I know a wife whose husband had an affair years ago; he repented of it, came back to her, and asked to be forgiven. She forgave him. But I happen to know the home, and I can see that it is not a happy home. Adultery is something you don't rub out. If you commit it, you lack understanding. You'll wreck your home; you will wreck your life.

**For jealousy is the rage of a man: therefore he will not spare in the day of vengeance.**

**He will not regard any ransom; neither will he rest content, though thou givest many gifts [Prov. 6:34–35].**

Oh, my friend, what tragedies result from adultery!

# CHAPTER 7

This chapter continues the subject of chapter 6. The whole thought is to beware of a woman with easy morals.

> My son, keep my words, and lay up my commandments with thee.
>
> Keep my commandments, and live; and my law as the apple of thine eye.
>
> Bind them upon thy fingers, write them upon the table of thine heart.
>
> Say unto wisdom, Thou art my sister; and call understanding thy kinswoman [Prov. 7:1–4].

Now having said that, he is going to get right down to cases.

> That they may keep thee from the strange woman, from the stranger which flattereth with her words [Prov. 7:5].

He takes an illustration out of life.

> For at the window of my house I looked through my casement.
>
> And beheld among the simple ones, I discerned among the youths, a young man void of understanding,
>
> Passing through the street near her corner; and he went the way to her house,
>
> In the twilight in the evening, in the black and dark night [Prov. 7:6–9].

This young man is taking a walk on the wrong street

> And, behold, there met him a woman with the attire of an harlot, and subtil of heart.
>
> (She is loud and stubborn; her feet abide not in her house:
>
> Now is she without, now in the streets, and lieth in wait at every corner.)
>
> So she caught him, and kissed him, and with an impudent face said unto him,
>
> I have peace offerings with me; this day have I payed my vows [Prov. 7:10–14].

Notice that she is religious! She leads him to believe that she is right with God—"I have peace offerings with me . . . I payed my vows."

> Therefore came I forth to meet thee, diligently to seek thy face, and I have found thee [Prov. 7:15].

In other words, I've been looking for you all my life, and at last I have found you!

> I have decked my bed with coverings of tapestry, with carved works, with fine linen of Egypt.
>
> I have perfumed my bed with myrrh, aloes, and cinnamon.
>
> Come, let us take our fill of love until the morning: let us solace ourselves with loves.
>
> For the goodman is not at home, he is gone a long journey:
>
> He hath taken a bag of money with him, and will come home at the day appointed [Prov. 7:16–20].

She assures him that the man of the house is out of town and won't be back until a certain day.

> With her much fair speech she caused him to yield, with the flattering of her lips she forced him.
>
> He goeth after her straightway, as an ox goeth to the slaughter, or as a fool to the correction of the stocks;
>
> Till a dart strike through his liver; as a bird hasteth to the snare, and knoweth not that it is for his life [Prov. 7:21–23].

What a picture this is!
Now he gives the warning—

> Hearken unto me now therefore, O ye children, and attend to the words of my mouth.
>
> Let not thine heart decline to her ways, go not astray in her paths.
>
> For she hath cast down many wounded: yea, many strong men have been slain by her.
>
> Her house is the way to hell, going down to the chambers of death [Prov. 7:24–27].

This warning is to be taken literally, and there is also a spiritual application for you and me today. The Scriptures have a great deal to say about spiritual adultery. God called it that when His people left Him and went after idols. They were snared by idolatry, and they were brought into subjection. They departed from the living and true God. They were to be joined to Him, but they had separated from Him. They were actually playing the harlot; they were being unfaithful and untrue to Him. That is spiritual adultery.

Today we have many cults and "isms" and all types of false religions around us. Here in Southern California we are larded with this type of thing on every hand. For example, one says, "You don't need any longer to follow Christ as you are following Him. You don't need to trust Him alone as your Savior. What you need to do is join our group and do certain things."

You would be amazed at the letters that come to me. Some time ago I was teaching Galatians, and at that time I made the statement again and again, "Faith plus nothing equals salvation." I emphasized that you must be absolutely, utterly cast upon Jesus Christ as your Savior. Oh my, did I get the letters! A great many people wrote some very ugly things. Among other things they wrote, "You said that the Mosaic Law is something that we should get rid of." I did not say anything of the kind. What I said was that the Law cannot save you. The Law was never given to save. The Law is good, but there is something wrong with *us*, and only Christ can save us. When we turn from our own efforts, from our own works and turn to Him, we can be saved.

Then there were others who wrote to tell me how wrong I was. "You should have said it is necessary to be baptized in a certain way." Others said, "You should have told them to join a certain group." Others said I should have taught that we must all keep the Mosaic Law—even if a person trusts in Christ he still must keep the Law.

May I answer this by saying that the believer is joined to Christ. Christ has said we are to keep His commandments if we love Him, and His commandments are not grievous. We are to love one another. We are to be filled with the spirit of God. We are to witness to the world. Those are His commandments today. We are joined to a living Christ; we live on a higher plane. The fruit of the Spirit should be evident in our hearts and lives.

Today there is that flattering "ism" and that flattering cult, made up like a woman of the street. She is flattering and she is calling men and women. This old gal is busy today. She knocks at your door and hands out tracts. She meets you everywhere. She is a prostitute—she wants to take you away from Christ. She wants to bring you into her system. Oh, my friend, that spiritual prostitute is out on your street today; she even comes into your home by way of radio and television, trying to lure you. We are told that to follow her is like an ox going to slaughter. It is like a fool going to the correction of the stocks. Oh, that we might not settle for anything less than the person of Jesus Christ!

In my judgment this is the finest picture we have of cults, "isms," and all false religions. Like the prostitute, they are all dressed up—attractive, alluring, offering something to man that will actually destroy him and send him down to hell, and take him away from Jesus Christ, the lover of our souls.

# CHAPTER 8

The young man has been examining the literature of the different colleges; and the school of wisdom and the school of fools are bidding for his application. In this chapter it is wisdom that sends out an invitation to him with a note of urgency. Pressure is put upon the young man now. The school bell is going to ring before long, and they want this young man enrolled.

## WISDOM CALLS TO THE YOUNG MAN

**Doth not wisdom cry? and understanding put forth her voice? [Prov. 8:1].**

As we have seen, the young man has been lured and enticed to leave the school of wisdom. Believe me, the cults and "isms" are out on the streets and ringing doorbells.

God's people should be out doing the same thing. I am very thankful for the very fine organizations that especially work with the young people today. They are out ringing doorbells. They are out doing personal witnessing. That's good. Wisdom and understanding *should* be putting forth their voice.

**She standeth in the top of high places, by the way in the places of the paths.**

**She crieth at the gates, at the entry of the city, at the coming in at the doors.**

**Unto you, O men, I call; and my voice is to the sons of man [Prov. 8:2–4].**

This is what we are trying to do by radio. We are sending out a call to come to the school of wisdom. We want you to come to wisdom in the person of Christ. It is Christ who has been made unto us wisdom.

**O ye simple, understand wisdom: and, ye fools, be ye of an understanding heart [Prov. 8:5].**

Are you willing to take that position—to admit that you are not adequate, to say you are a sinner and that you really don't have intellectual problems? Sometimes I think it is a joke to listen to folk with "intellectual" problems. A young fellow came to me and said, "I have intellectual problems about the Bible." Do you know what he really had? He had a sin problem, and he didn't want to give up his sin. I have discovered that if a person has a sin problem and will turn to Christ with that problem, it is amazing how often the intellectual problems will be solved.

**Hear; for I will speak of excellent things; and the opening of my lips shall be right things [Prov. 8:6].**

What a picture we have here!

**For my mouth shall speak truth; and wickedness is an abomination to my lips.**

**All the words of my mouth are in righteousness; there is nothing froward or perverse in them [Prov. 8:7–8].**

Many people talk about errors and problems in the Bible. There are several books written about problem Scriptures. I recognize that to an intelligent person there are problems in the Bible. I had a lot of problems with the Bible at the beginning of my study, and I still have a few. But the problem is not in the Word of God. The problem is in the mind and heart of man. God says there is nothing twisted or perverse in the words of wisdom.

**They are all plain to him that understandeth, and right to them that find knowledge [Prov. 8:9].**

You see, if it is really wisdom, it is going to be simple, and it will appeal to the simple. I'm thankful that God did not make the gospel appeal only to folk who have a high I.Q. If He had, many folk would be left out completely. This is a message to the simple. And it really is a simple message.

It is very interesting that some things which men call deep and profound are not really that at all. When I went through school, I had the viewpoint of a lot of other young fellows that I knew it all. We had a brilliant man come to lecture at our seminary. I'll be very frank with you, he was speaking right over the top of my head. I went to the man who was considered the most brilliant professor in the school and said, "I'm not getting very much out of those lectures. I must confess that they are over my head. I always had the viewpoint that I could understand anything that any man had to say, but I am not getting what he is saying." I shall never forget his answer. He said, "Mr. McGee, you know that when water is clear, you can see right to the bottom of the pool even if it is sixty feet deep, but when the water is muddy, you can't even see to the bottom of a hoofprint in the middle of the road. Some men are not deep; they are *muddy*." Well, that answered it for me. My friend, if you have an intellectual problem with something you read in the Bible—let me be very frank with you—the problem is not with the Bible; the problem is with you.

Let me refer you to a passage in the New Testament, which I think is profound, although it is very simple: "And not as Moses, which put a veil over his face, that the children of Israel could not stedfastly look to the end of that which is abolished: But their minds were blinded: for until this day remaineth the same veil untaken away in the reading of the old testament; which veil is done away in Christ" (2 Cor. 3:13–14). You may be thinking, *If they cannot understand because there is a veil over their minds, they are not responsible.* And a great many folk today are claiming that there is a veil over their minds and they are not able to understand the Bible. But notice the next verses: "But even unto this day, when Moses is read, the veil is upon their heart. Nevertheless when it shall turn to the Lord, the veil shall be taken away" (2 Cor. 3:15–16). What does it mean by "it" when it says "when *it* shall turn to the Lord"? Well, it refers back to the last principal subject, which is the "heart." It is saying that when the *heart* shall turn to the Lord, the veil shall be taken away. You see, the problem is not head trouble; it is *heart* trouble.

Let's get right down to where the rubber meets the road, right down to where we live. Don't say that there are intellectual problems which keep you from the Lord. The problem is sin in your life—there are things in your life that you do not want to change. You are not willing to bow your heart and your head and come to Jesus Christ. That is the problem. Notice that when the *heart* shall turn to the Lord an amazing thing happens—the veil shall be taken away. The problems are resolved.

A great man of the Middle Ages said, "I had many problems until I came to Christ." We may call them intellectual problems, but they are really heart problems. The Word of God is clear. The gospel message is so simple it cannot be misunderstood. But there can be deliberate, willful resistance to the gospel. That is a problem of the heart.

That is why we can actually use the Word of God as a sort of Geiger counter. A Geiger counter will tell a man where there is uranium. And the reaction to the Word of God will tell a man where there is a believing heart. There are some individuals who love the Word of God, and the arrow of the counter jumps up and down. There are others who have a pious expression and fundamental vocabulary but who register as dead. They actually resist the Word of God.

Many times people have asked me to deal with folk who resist the Word of God. I tell them that my job is simply to give out the Word. The Lord Himself will deal with them. During my years in the ministry I have seen how the Lord does deal with such people. I have seen Him move into families and deal with this one and that one. I recall a very arrogant young man who was questioning the Word of God. Then he left his wife and ran off with another woman. There was sin in his life; that was his problem. I emphasize this because God's Word is clear. There is nothing twisted or perverse in the words of God.

**Receive my instruction, and not silver; and knowledge rather than choice gold.**

**For wisdom is better than rubies; and all the things that may be desired are not to be compared to it [Prov. 8:10–11].**

When you and I come to the place, as Job did, where we get our priorities straight, when we put a proper evaluation on the things of this world and realize that wisdom is better than rubies, then we will put God first in our lives. It is as the Lord Jesus said, "But seek ye first the kingdom of God, and his righteousness; and all these things shall be added unto you" (Matt. 6:33).

## THE CHARACTERISTICS OF WISDOM

**I wisdom dwell with prudence, and find out knowledge of witty inventions [Prov. 8:12].**

The Word of God is going to make it clear that wisdom is a person, the person of the Lord Jesus Christ.

**The fear of the LORD is to hate evil: pride, and arrogancy, and the evil way, and the froward mouth, do I hate [Prov. 8:13].**

We might translate it as "the mouth of perversions do I hate." This is something that is quite real today; it is right down where we live. Wisdom is manifest. It is the character of God, and that character has been revealed in Christ. Evil, pride, arrogance, and an evil way are hateful to Him. If we belong to Him, we will hate these things also.

**Counsel is mine, and sound wisdom: I am understanding; I have strength.**

**By me kings reign, and princes decree justice.**

**By me princes rule, and nobles, even all the judges of the earth [Prov. 8:14–16].**

In the Psalms and in the prophecy of Daniel it is repeated that "the most High ruleth in the kingdom of men, and giveth it to whomsoever he will." How tremendous it is to realize that God overrules down here in the affairs of this world. Regardless of how godless a nation is, God is overruling, and His will is being accomplished. He rules in the kingdoms of men.

**I love them that love me; and those that seek me early shall find me [Prov. 8:17].**

Solomon learned this early in his life. He discovered that when he sought God, God gave him wisdom. He had sought God early—as soon as he became king. He knew it was God who had given him an unique wisdom. And God is prepared to give us wisdom if we are willing to meet the conditions: a diligent study and love of the Word of God early in our Christian life.

**Riches and honour are with me; yea, durable riches and righteousness.**

**My fruit is better than gold, yea, than fine gold; and my revenue than choice silver [Prov. 8:18–19].**

These are not stocks or bonds or real estate, but wonderful spiritual gifts He bestows.

**I lead in the way of righteousness, in the midst of the paths of judgment:**

**That I may cause those that love me to inherit substance; and I will fill their treasures [Prov. 8:20–21].**

## WISDOM PERSONIFIED IN CHRIST

From this point on, I think you will discover that the Lord Jesus Christ is speaking.

**The LORD possessed me in the beginning of his way, before his works of old [Prov. 8:22].**

This is the Lord Jesus; this is wisdom personified.

**I was set up from everlasting, from the beginning, or ever the earth was [Prov. 8:23].**

"I was set up" is I was *anointed* from everlasting. This is the One who is the subject of John's prologue: "In the beginning was the Word, and the Word was with God, and the Word was God. The same was in the beginning with God" (John 1:1–2). He was begotten, not in the sense of having a beginning of life, but as being one nature and substance with the Father. Way back yonder in eternity He was God, and He was in the beginning with God. He was in the beginning that *has* no beginning, because "in the beginning *was* the Word." He was already past tense at the time of the beginning.

He is the One and the only One who can make this clear to us. The Lord Jesus said, ". . . no man knoweth the Son, but the Father . . ." (Matt. 11:27). We could not know the Lord Jesus, had not the Father and Son sent the Holy Spirit to open our hearts. A saved person can rest in and adore the person of Christ. We are living in the midst of great unbelief in our day, but let the skeptic be skeptical. My friend, our relationship is a personal relationship with the Lord Jesus Christ, and He is the Word. ". . . the Word was with God, and the Word was God" (John 1:1). What a tremendous statement!

Wisdom is Jesus Christ.

**When there were no depths, I was brought forth; when there were no fountains abounding with water.**

**Before the mountains were settled, before the hills was I brought forth:**

**While as yet he had not made the earth, nor the fields, nor the highest part of the dust of the world.**

**When he prepared the heavens, I was there: when he set a compass upon the face of the depth [Prov. 8:24–27].**

"All things were made by him; and without him was not any thing made that was made" (John 1:3).

"When he set a compass upon the face of the depth." It is interesting that the scientists used to speak of a square universe, but God has always said it is a circle. You and I live in a world that is round, and we are going around our planetary system. And we belong to a galactic system which is a circle. All of these circles are circling around!

**When he established the clouds above: when he strengthened the fountains of the deep:**

**When he gave to the sea his decree, that the waters should not pass his commandment: when he appointed the foundations of the earth [Prov. 8:28–29].**

Have you ever stood by the seashore and wondered why the water doesn't run over? Why does it stay where it is? It says, "he gave to the sea his decree, that the waters should not pass his commandment." God has made a law that keeps the sea right where it is.

**Then I was by him, as one brought up with him: and I was daily his delight, rejoicing always before him;**

**Rejoicing in the habitable part of his earth; and my delights were with the sons of men [Prov. 8:30–31].**

Without the Lord Jesus was not anything made that was made. All things were made by Him. He is the firstborn of all creation. He is superior to all. Why? Because by Him the Father brought all things into being, for He is the uncreated God, and He was "rejoicing always before Him." These wonderful delights and joys come to us through the amazing grace of God. How wonderful all of this is!

**Now therefore hearken unto me, O ye children: for blessed are they that keep my ways.**

**Hear instruction, and be wise, and refuse it not [Prov. 8:32–33].**

Wisdom is Christ, and there must be a love for Him.

Blessed is the man that heareth me, watching daily at my gates, waiting at the posts of my doors.

For whoso findeth me findeth life, and shall obtain favour of the LORD [Prov. 8:34–35].

"Whoso findeth me findeth life." If you have Christ you have life.

But he that sinneth against me wrongeth his own soul: all they that hate me love death [Prov. 8:36].

My friend, if you hate Christ, you love death. What a picture this is! Wisdom is Christ.

# CHAPTER 9

We have come now to the place where wisdom has opened school. The young man is matriculated into the school of wisdom, and we are thankful for that. Everything is prepared, and we are able to look into this school. The school bell is about to ring.

## THE COLLEGE OF WISDOM

Wisdom hath builded her house, she hath hewn out her seven pillars:

She hath killed her beasts; she hath mingled her wine; she hath also furnished her table.

She hath sent forth her maidens: she crieth upon the highest places of the city,

Whoso is simple, let him turn in hither: as for him that wanteth understanding, she saith to him,

Come, eat of my bread, and drink of the wine which I have mingled [Prov. 9: 1–5].

Wisdom has builded a house. This is the College of Wisdom. Note there are seven pillars. Those seven pillars represent to me completeness. The school offers a complete education all the way through to the graduate course and the Ph.D. degree.

Let's not minimize the importance of a good education. There are some who like to point out the Lord Jesus chose for His disciples twelve men who were not educated men. I have had many letters, one in particular from a man who took me to task for using the title of Doctor. He pointed out that none of the twelve had a doctoral degree. May I say that an *earned* doctoral degree represents years of hard work, and I believe that the person who has earned the degree is entitled to use the title. I will freely admit that one does wonder

at some things in our educational system. I know a young man who is working on his master's degree in history. He is told to forget about dates and individuals, in order to get the *flavor* of a particular age—the life-style and the attitude of that period! Now I admit that that is a pretty slippery type of education. I believe that facts are important. And I know we still have some very fine schools which are working on that principle.

As far as the education of the apostles is concerned, anyone who spent three years with the Lord Jesus Christ was not uneducated. They learned a great deal from the greatest Teacher the world has ever seen. And, of course, the apostle Paul was well educated in the schools of his day. No one could say that he was an ignorant man. Let's remember that wisdom is the Lord Jesus Christ, and He can give you a complete education.

"She hath killed her beasts; she hath mingled her wine; she hath also furnished her table." Now it is time to come to school and start feasting on the courses that have been prepared.

"She hath sent forth her maidens: she crieth upon the highest places of the city." What a picture is given here. May I remind you that we have the same invitation in this age. A wedding feast has been prepared, and the invitations go out to all the invited guests saying that all things are ready. Many of the guests decline the invitation. Then the servants go out into the highways and byways with the invitation to the wedding feast (Matt. 22:1–14). It is interesting that wisdom must go out into the highways and byways to invite people to come in. And we are to go out on the highways and byways. Our message today is: God is reconciled to you; now you be reconciled to God. "Now then we are ambassadors for Christ, as though God did beseech you by us: we pray you in Christ's stead, be ye reconciled to God" (2 Cor. 5:20). In our day the Word is probably going out more than it ever has in the history of the world. The invitation is going out to the ends of the earth to come to the school of wisdom, that is, to come to the Lord Jesus Christ.

**Forsake the foolish, and live; and go in the way of understanding [Prov. 9:6].**

There are those who will not hear. They are the scorners. There is no use wasting your time with them. In practically every church you will find a little group that will resist the Word of God. Are we to keep on giving the Word of God to them? No. The Lord Jesus said not to cast our pearls before swine. Now notice the next three verses. Some Bible expositors think they do not belong here, that they have been inserted. But, my friend, this is exactly where they *do* belong.

**He that reproveth a scorner getteth to himself shame: and he that rebuketh a wicked man getteth himself a blot.**

**Reprove not a scorner, lest he hate thee: rebuke a wise man, and he will love thee.**

**Give instruction to a wise man, and he will be yet wiser: teach a just man, and he will increase in learning [Prov. 9: 7–9]**

If you give the Word of God to some people, they will actually hate you for it. This is a pattern that has been true down through the ages. There are people who are so shallow, empty, and ignorant that they will not receive the Word of God at all.

In our day we hear about the man who is liberal in his theology and how broad-minded he is. Did you know that it is the "broad-minded" liberal who has put religion out of our schools? They call the fundamental people bigots. I'd like to know who is the real bigot! Frankly, I don't mind evolution being taught in our schools if they will permit me to teach the Bible alongside it. But the broad-minded liberals will not allow that. Regardless of the degrees they hold, they are ignorant. They have narrow minds when they are not willing for the Word of God to be taught. The general rule is that the less a man knows, the more he thinks he knows. I have never met a liberal yet who didn't think he was a very smart cookie. He thought that he knew and understood it all; yet he doesn't understand. The more a man really knows, the more he will recognize his ignorance and his limitations. One of the truly great preachers whom I have known—and I think he had one of the best minds of any man I have ever met—often said, "The more I study the Bible the more I recognize how ignorant I am of it." My friend, you cannot study the Bible without realizing how ignorant you are of it.

However, the scorner has no interest in learning the Word of God. You waste your time by giving it to him.

**The fear of the Lord is the beginning of wisdom: and the knowledge of the holy is understanding [Prov. 9:10].**

Perhaps you are saying, *We've had this verse before.* Yes, when the little fellow was in the home, the first lesson he was given was the fear of the Lord. "The fear of the Lord is the beginning of knowledge: but fools despise wisdom and instruction" (Prov. 1:7). Now he has entered the college of life and the college of wisdom; he is in his freshman year of the university of understanding, and this is his first lesson: "The fear of the Lord is the beginning of wisdom: and the knowledge of the holy is understanding." That is where we all start. If you haven't started there, you haven't started, my friend. A man is a fool (which is what this book will say) to live without God in this world.

In our contemporary society we are so concerned with safety—safety on the highway, safety in the home, security for old age. We carry insurance for all these things, and we make sure our premiums are paid up. That is the wise thing to do. But, my brother, what about eternity? Are you making any plans; do you have insurance for that? Oh, how foolish it is to live this life without God! "The fear of the Lord is the beginning of wisdom."

**For by me thy days shall be multiplied, and the years of thy life shall be increased.**

**If thou be wise, thou shalt be wise for thyself: but if thou scornest, thou alone shalt bear it [Prov. 9:11–12].**

If you want to be smart, then make preparation for your soul for eternity. If you are going to be a scorner and ridicule all of these things, well, you are coming up for judgment. This may sound crude, but somebody ought to say it: you are on your way to hell. "If thou scornest, thou alone shalt bear it." If you are determined to go on in your own way, you will be the loser.

The town atheist in a place where I preached said to me, "You know, preacher, I don't buy this stuff about eternal life and trusting Jesus and all that sort of thing. It may be all right for some folk, but I don't care for that." I answered, "Let's suppose you are right and there is no eternal life, then you and I will come out at exactly the same place. But suppose I am right and you are wrong. Then, my friend, you are in a pretty bad spot." Another atheist said, "I would be content if it weren't for the awful fact that the Bible may be true." Yes, it may be! And if it is, it will be an awful fact for anyone who turns his back on God.

## THE SCHOOL OF THE FOOLISH WOMAN

**A foolish woman is clamorous: she is simple, and knoweth nothing [Prov. 9:13].**

You see, foolishness runs a school also. There are a lot of those around today.

**For she sitteth at the door of her house, on a seat in the high places of the city [Prov. 9:14].**

She doesn't have to go out on the highways and byways to invite folk in; they *come* to her. Thousands are going to schools like this!

**Whoso is simple, let him turn in hither: and as for him that wanteth understanding, she saith to him,**

**Stolen waters are sweet, and bread eaten in secret is pleasant.**

**But he knoweth not that the dead are there; and that her guests are in the depths of hell [Prov. 9:16–18].**

Oh, how many so-called wise men have turned in there and found a tragic end! It was Lord Byron who wrote toward the end of a life of debauchery:

My days are in the yellow leaf;
    The flowers and fruits of love are gone;
The worm, the canker, and the grief
    Are mine alone!

Byron had everything this world can offer— good looks, genius, fame, wealth, and yet he said, "the worm, the canker, and the grief are mine alone!" That is what the school of the foolish woman did for him.

A famous movie star here in California had been married to several of the beauties of the world during his life. The other day, as an old man, he committed suicide, leaving this note: "I am bored with life." How tragic.

May I say to you, foolishness still runs a college, and there is a long waiting list of those who clamor to enter. "But he knoweth not that the dead are there; and that her guests are in the depths of hell."

# CHAPTER 10

## PROVERBS OF SOLOMON, WRITTEN AND SET IN ORDER BY HIMSELF

This begins the second major division of the Book of Proverbs. Here we see that the young student is given some guidelines for his life. These are lessons that you and I also are to learn in the school of Christ.

**The proverbs of Solomon. A wise son maketh a glad father: but a foolish son is the heaviness of his mother [Prov. 10:1].**

"A wise son maketh a glad father." Have you ever noticed that when a father has a son who has gone to school and made good grades or

been outstanding as an athlete or in some other accomplishment, the old man goes around and brags about his son and tells everyone about him? "My boy has his Ph.D. and is teaching in college." "My boy is on the football team." But suppose the boy failed or didn't make the team. Then the father becomes very quiet and doesn't say anything about him at all. He just keeps his mouth shut.

"But a foolish son is the heaviness of his mother." It is the mother who grieves at a time like that. The father just keeps quiet about it and ignores it. What a picture of life this is! A boy can be a wise son or a foolish son—either one.

**Treasures of wickedness profit nothing: but righteousness delivereth from death [Prov. 10:2].**

"Treasures of wickedness profit nothing"—men who have accumulated a great fortune have had to leave it here. They couldn't take it with them, and they never really enjoyed it while they were alive.

"Righteousness delivereth from death." Christ has been made unto us not only wisdom but righteousness. And ". . . whosoever believeth in him should not perish, but have everlasting life" (John 3:16).

**The LORD will not suffer the soul of the righteous to famish: but he casteth away the substance of the wicked [Prov. 10:3].**

You will remember that I have mentioned that I think there is a proverb for everyone, and a proverb that fits certain characters in the Bible. When we remember that "The LORD will not suffer the soul of the righteous to famish," we think of Joseph. He was sold into Egypt and must have felt that he had come to the end and that God seemed far away. Yet he had faith in God. We know that God did not forsake him. God so arranged it that eventually he was brought out of prison and was made the prime minister of the land of Egypt.

**He becometh poor that dealeth with a slack hand: but the hand of the diligent maketh rich [Prov. 10:4].**

What a difference there is in people. Some wonderful Christians are so generous, and others are so stingy! It is interesting that the tight individual has that kind of life—he seems uptight all the time. By contrast, the generous man has a full life.

Don't you think this verse would fit Abraham? He was a generous man. He told his nephew Lot, "Take any part of the land you want, and I'll take what is left." It is a very generous man who will divide real estate like that! Abraham had the right to do the choosing. He certainly knew that the choice land was the well-watered plain of Jordan. Lot must have thought Abraham was very foolish not to move down there, but since Abraham had given Lot the opportunity to choose, he chose the rich land down there in the plain. With a very slack hand, very selfishly, he chose the best for himself; but, in the end, he lost everything.

"But the hand of the diligent maketh rich." There are two words that won't go together in the Bible: faith and laziness will not mingle. A lazy Christian is not a Christian with real faith in God. The one who is diligent is the one who will work, the one who will *labor*. This reminds me also of the apostle Paul. When the Lord called him, He certainly did not get a lazy individual.

**He that gathereth in summer is a wise son: but he that sleepeth in harvest is a son that causeth shame [Prov. 10:5].**

Here is another proverb of contrast. The boy who is called "wise" is the one who works in the summer. The lazy boy is the one who sleeps during the time of harvest. He is not the one who is going to get the job done.

My young Christian friend, you need to recognize that God wants to train you and school you. When I was young, I was the pastor in a little church. I wasn't satisfied; I wanted to do more for God than I was doing there. I have a wonderful wife who encouraged me to finish working on my doctor's degree and devote time to studying the Bible. I was redeeming the time; I took advantage of that period. How I thank God for it! After I became very busy pastoring a large church and carrying a radio and conference ministry, someone asked me, "You are so busy all the time, when are you able to do your preparation?" Well, back in a little town in Texas I had five years, and I spent that time studying. And the day came when God enabled me to use that preparation. I would say to any young person today who wants to be used of God: begin to prepare yourself. Remember that "he that gathereth in summer is a wise son."

These statements in the Book of Proverbs are tremendous, eternal truths. They are truths not to send you soaring into the heavenly places, but to equip you for the sidewalks of your own town. If they are not working for *you*, there is nothing wrong with them, but there is something wrong with you.

**Blessings are upon the head of the just: but violence covereth the mouth of the wicked [Prov. 10:6].**

What a picture we have here of two men in the Old Testament. "Blessings are upon the head of the just" reminds me of Samuel. "But violence covereth the mouth of the wicked (lawless)" reminds me of Saul.

**The memory of the just is blessed: but the name of the wicked shall rot [Prov. 10:7].**

I think of this in connection with certain individuals who a few years ago were famous, but today they are fading out. I am of the opinion that men of this generation will be forgotten in the next fifty years. Yet the memory of men such as Dwight L. Moody, who accomplished something for God, lives on.

### The wise in heart will receive commandments: but a prating fool shall fall [Prov. 10:8].

"Prating" is literally *word-mouthing*—he is the one who is always talking. He is wise in his own conceit. By contrast, the wise in heart will *receive* commandments. Remember there was a king by the name of Nebuchadnezzar who listened to the counsel of Daniel and prospered. There was another king by the name of Belshazzar. He was a fool. A royal banquet one night marked the end of him and his kingdom (Dan. 5).

### He that walketh uprightly walketh surely: but he that perverteth his ways shall be known [Prov. 10:9].

This is expressed in our proverb today: Honesty is the best policy.

### He that winketh with the eye causeth sorrow: but a prating fool shall fall [Prov. 10:10].

Here is something that is quite interesting. The eye and the mouth shall be in agreement. When you see a man say something and wink, it means he doesn't mean what he said. His mouth and his mind are not in agreement. When they are not in agreement, it will cause a great deal of sorrow.

Whom does this verse fit? How about Judas? The kiss of Judas certainly was a kiss of betrayal. The kiss is meant to denote affection, but it certainly didn't mean that for him.

### In the lips of him that hath understanding wisdom is found: but a rod is for the back of him that is void of understanding [Prov. 10:13].

The whole world came to hear the wisdom of Solomon, but "a rod is for the back of him that is void of understanding" characterizes his son Rehoboam. He would not listen to the advice of the wise old men; he listened to the young men who had grown up with him (1 Kings 12). As a result, he brought division and civil war to his nation.

### Wise men lay up knowledge: but the mouth of the foolish is near destruction [Prov. 10:14].

All the time the wise man is gathering up knowledge, the foolish man has one foot on the banana peel and the other one in the grave.

### The labour of the righteous tendeth to life: the fruit of the wicked to sin [Prov. 10:16].

This proverb makes me think of Cain and Abel. "The labour of the righteous tendeth to life." Abel raised sheep, and he brought a little lamb for his sacrifice. "The fruit of the wicked (the produce of the lawless) is sin." That was Cain—in rebellion he brought the fruit of the ground. The apostle Paul expressed it this way in Romans 8:6: "For to be carnally minded is death . . ."—and this is directed to the Christian. "Death" for him means separation from God in the way of fellowship. God is not going to fellowship with a carnally-minded person. When the proverb says "the labour of the righteous tendeth to life," it is fellowship with God. Abel was a saved man. "The fruit of the wicked (lawless) to sin" characterized Cain.

### He is in the way of life that keepeth instruction: but he that refuseth reproof erreth [Prov. 10:17].

This would apply to Absalom, David's son. He wouldn't accept reproof. He made a big mistake in attempting to seize the kingdom from his father.

### He that hideth hatred with lying lips, and he that uttereth a slander, is a fool [Prov. 10:18].

What a terrible thing it is to have someone pretend to be your friend and later you discover that he is really your enemy. That person is actually a fool. You catch on to him after a while. Anyone who slanders is also a fool.

God had given a specific commandment regarding this. "Thou shalt not go up and down as a talebearer among thy people . . ." (Lev. 19:16). It goes on, "Thou shalt not hate thy brother in thine heart: thou shalt in any wise rebuke thy neighbour, and not suffer sin upon him" (Lev. 19:17). Don't flatter a man when you actually hate him, but neither are you to slander the man.

This describes a man in Scripture. Remember that Joab pretended to be a friend to Abner. He lured him out of the city, and then he killed him.

The lips of the righteous feed many: but fools die for want of wisdom [Prov. 10:21].

I think again of Samuel, the great judge of Israel, in contrast to Saul, the king who played the fool.

The blessing of the LORD, it maketh rich, and he addeth no sorrow with it [Prov. 10:22].

There are those who live in pleasure and think they are living it up. But as they get closer to the end, they find life unbearable. I watched a banquet, a political affair, that was televised. All who attended the banquet were rich, and they were there for the purpose of supporting the party with a contribution. The thing I noticed was that there wasn't a happy face in the crowd. The camera panned the entire audience. I thought, *My, here they are at a banquet and jokes are being told, but I don't see a single happy face.*

"The blessing of the LORD, it maketh rich, and he addeth no sorrow with it." The contemporary Christian by his indifference to moral and doctrinal wrong, and by his laxness in his way of living, is missing a great deal that God has for him.

It is as sport to a fool to do mischief: but a man of understanding hath wisdom [Prov. 10:23].

This is good advice to the young man!

As vinegar to the teeth, and as smoke to the eyes, so is the sluggard to them that send him [Prov. 10:26].

Did you ever send a lazy boy on an errand, and then you stand first on one foot and then on the other waiting for him? That's just like "vinegar to the teeth, and as smoke to the eyes."

The fear of the LORD prolongeth days: but the years of the wicked shall be shortened [Prov. 10:27].

This certainly was true in Old Testament days. God promised long days to those who obeyed Him. Perhaps you are thinking, *Doesn't He promise that today?* No, He promises us eternal life. That will be a better quality of life as well as quantity.

The righteous shall never be removed: but the wicked shall not inhabit the earth [Prov. 10:30].

Let's look at history with that in view. All of the great world leaders, the kings and the captains, have disappeared. The pharaohs, the caesars, Alexander the Great, Napoleon— they are all gone. "The wicked shall not inhabit the earth." Neither will communism prevail and, interestingly enough, neither will democracy, because God has a form of government that is to be a monarchy. There will be no dictatorship equal to the dictatorship of Jesus Christ when He takes over the rulership of this earth. And "the righteous shall never be removed."

# CHAPTER 11

As we have seen, the young man is in college now, and wisdom—which is Christ— is the Teacher. Wisdom had to go out on the highways and byways to get her pupils, but she has a class now, and she is teaching by proverbs.

The literary form of these proverbs is mostly couplets. The two clauses of the couplet are generally related to each other by what has been termed parallelism, according to Hebrew poetry. Hebrew poetry is attained by repeating or contrasting a thought. There are three types of parallelism: synonymous parallelism that restates the thought of the first clause; antithetic parallelism which gives

contrasting truths; and synthetic parallelism in which the second clause develops the thought of the first.

This chapter will actually give the young man some good advice about business.

A false balance is abomination to the LORD: but a just weight is his delight [Prov. 11:1].

God does enter into business; you can take Him into partnership with you. However, you can't form a partnership with Him if you are crooked. If you are honest, He would like to be your partner.

The Christian businessman is to be honest

and a man of integrity. I am thankful that there are so many of these wonderful Christian businessmen. I have played golf with such a man. He lives in Chicago but had come down to Florida to attend our Bible conferences. Although we became well-acquainted, I didn't come to know much about him in his business dealings. I was so pleased when another man who knows him well told me that this man is known far and near for his honesty and integrity. And he is a successful businessman. It is wonderful to find there are still men like this.

**When pride cometh, then cometh shame: but with the lowly is wisdom [Prov. 11:2].**

The other besetting sin is pride. Immediately here in his freshman course the young man is warned about pride. This proverb contrasts pride and humility. Always with pride comes "shame." There is a great deal in Scripture, and especially in this Book of Proverbs, about pride.

**The integrity of the upright shall guide them: but the perverseness of transgressors shall destroy them [Prov. 11:3].**

This simply means that if a person wants to walk in the truth, if that is the desire of his heart, the spirit of God can be counted upon for guidance and direction. The contrast is: the "perverseness of transgressors [the treacherous] shall destroy them."

The other evening I talked with a young man who has the same problem that I had when I was going to school, which was finances. He asked me, "How do you tell the will of God; how do you know the way you should go?" My answer was this: "I had the same problem that you have. Always for me it narrowed down to only one way, and it would become very simple. The way that opened up was the way that I could go. If the door were closed, it was closed. If I didn't have the money to go to school, I simply would not go. But it seemed the Lord would always open up just one door to let me go in. That happened to me again and again, and I always interpreted it as an open door from the Lord. I believe that if you mean business with God, He will open up the door. That has been my experience."

**Riches profit not in the day of wrath: but righteousness delivereth from death [Prov. 11:4].**

Doesn't this remind you of the Lord's account of the rich man and the beggar named Lazarus? Both of them died. The riches of the rich man didn't avail him anything in the day of wrath. But righteousness delivered the beggar; it took him right to Abraham's bosom.

Those who trust riches certainly have their priorities upside down. There is nothing wrong in wealth, but we need to recognize that it has limitations. Money will buy almost anything in this world, but it can buy nothing in the next world.

**The righteousness of the perfect shall direct his way: but the wicked shall fall by his own wickedness.**

**The righteousness of the upright shall deliver them: but transgressors shall be taken in their own naughtiness [Prov. 11:5–6].**

Perhaps it will mean more to us if we translate "wicked" by the word *lawless.*

**When a wicked man dieth, his expectation shall perish: and the hope of unjust men perisheth.**

**The righteous is delivered out of trouble, and the wicked cometh in his stead [Prov. 11:7–8].**

"When a lawless man dieth, his expectation shall perish: and the hope of unjust men perisheth." Doesn't this remind you of Haman in the Book of Esther? And Mordecai was the righteous man "delivered out of trouble."

**An hypocrite with his mouth destroyeth his neighbour: but through knowledge shall the just be delivered [Prov. 11:9].**

*Hypocrite* comes from two Greek words meaning "to answer back." The hypocrite is one who answers back, and the word was used for actors in Greek plays. When one actor would give the cue to the other actor, he knew it was time for him to say his little piece. It was play-acting. To say a man is a hypocrite in religious matters means that he is a phony. He is the man who will say "Hallelujah, praise the Lord" insincerely. He is just playing a part; he is not praising the Lord in his heart.

"An hypocrite with his mouth destroyeth his neighbour." He will pretend to be your friend, but he will knife you when your back is turned in attempt to cover up the sin in his own life. Whom do you think of in the Bible in this connection? Wouldn't it be Potiphar's wife and the way she maligned Joseph? She brought false charges against Joseph to cover up her own sin. She was the guilty party, but she covered it over by accusing Joseph. Who would believe the story of a slave against the story of the wife of an official of Pharaoh? There was no need for Joseph to even open his mouth, because he didn't have a chance to defend himself.

Unfortunately, sometimes in the church we find an hypocrite who will say terrible things in order to protect himself. I have always been afraid of the man who is nice to his preacher to his face but who criticizes him behind his back. I have always felt that I needed to watch out for that kind of man. He is covering up something in his own life. Time has demonstrated to me that this was often a correct estimation of the situation. This proverb is referring to this kind of hypocrisy.

**When it goeth well with the righteous, the city rejoiceth: and when the wicked perish, there is shouting.**

**By the blessing of the upright the city is exalted: but it is overthrown by the mouth of the wicked [Prov. 11:10–11].**

I place David and Saul beside these proverbs. When David was king of Israel, Jerusalem became a great city. When King Saul died, there was not much mourning for him.

**He that is void of wisdom despiseth his neighbour: but a man of understanding holdeth his peace [Prov. 11:12].**

I believe David is an example of this proverb, too. Did you ever stop to think of the tremendous effect the life of David had upon Solomon? Even though David had committed sin with Solomon's mother, Bathsheba, David's life was a wonderful life except for that blot on it. You remember when David had to flee from the city when Absalom rebelled against him, that Shimei, of the family of Saul, cursed him. Old Joab, David's captain, wanted to go over and run a spear through him. David said, "No, he is speaking out of his heart. This is God's judgment upon me." "A man of understanding holdeth his peace."

There will be times when you will find folk are actually cursing you, maligning your character. Just keep quiet. The Lord will take care of it, as He took care of this situation with David.

These are wonderful principles in this book. They are good for young people to study. There seems to be a real spiritual movement among the young people of today. I would like to see them study the Book of Proverbs. It

would bring them to Christ, because He is the One who runs the school of wisdom and He is made unto us wisdom. Proverbs would give young people a lot of common sense. It seems to me we are short on common sense today. We seem to have a lot of high I.Q.'s and a lot of low common sense quotients.

**A talebearer revealeth secrets: but he that is of a faithful spirit concealeth the matter [Prov. 11:13].**

A talebearer is one who tells something in order to hurt someone else. Sometimes the thing he is saying is true, but he still ought not to say it to others. If he knows that a brother has sinned, he ought to go to him personally and deal with him privately about it. He should not run around and tell everyone else about it.

**Where no counsel is, the people fall: but in the multitude of counsellors there is safety [Prov. 11:14].**

Perhaps a more understandable translation is this: "Where no management is, the people fall: but in the multitude of counsellors there is safety." Regardless of how smart you are, you need good advice. You will remember that God gave Daniel to be an adviser to Nebuchadnezzar. He helped his king a great deal. Daniel was also an adviser to Cyrus, and he was a great help to him.

**He that is surety for a stranger shall smart for it: and he that hateth suretyship is sure [Prov. 11:15].**

One who goes surety for a stranger shall smart for it, and he will get smart from the experience. He will learn that he made a big mistake.

However, there was One who was surety for a stranger. Do you know who that was? Well, listen to the apostle Paul, "For ye know the grace of our Lord Jesus Christ, that, though he was rich, yet for your sakes he became poor, that ye through his poverty might be rich" (2 Cor. 8:9). He assumed your debt of sin, and mine. He had to pay the awful penalty. His experience is described prophetically in Psalm 69:4: "They that hate me without a cause are more than the hairs of mine head: they that would destroy me, being mine enemies wrongfully, are mighty: then I restored that which I took not away." And again, "He was oppressed, and he was afflicted, yet he opened not his mouth: he is brought as a lamb to the slaughter, and as a sheep before her shearers is dumb, so he openeth not his mouth" (Isa. 53:7). The penalty was exacted, and He became answerable for it. The ". . . wages of sin is death . . ." (Rom. 6:23) and Christ paid it for me. What a wonderful thing that is! Dr. H. A. Ironside in *Notes on the Book of Proverbs*, p. 121, wrote:

He bore on the tree the sentence for me;
Now both the Surety and sinner are free.

He took my place.

**A gracious woman retaineth honour: and strong men retain riches [Prov. 11:16].**

This reminds me of Ruth in the Book of Ruth. She was a widow, she was poor, and she was a woman. Yet she retained her honor. Boaz could say to her, ". . . for all the city of my people doth know that thou art a virtuous woman" (Ruth 3:11). The whole town of Bethlehem knew her. Not only did she maintain her honor in relationship with the opposite sex, but in every way she retained honor. The second part would apply to Boaz. "And strong men retain riches."

**The wicked worketh a deceitful work: but to him that soweth righteousness shall be a sure reward.**

**As righteousness tendeth to life: so he that pursueth evil pursueth it to his own death.**

**They that are of a froward heart are abomination to the LORD: but such as are upright in their way are his delight.**

**Though hand join in hand, the wicked shall not be unpunished: but the seed of the righteous shall be delivered [Prov. 11:18–21].**

Here is quite a contrast between sin and righteousness. Deceitfulness and lawlessness are going to be judged—there is no escape. And the righteousness which a believer has is the righteousness of Christ. Because we have that, we will not come into judgment but will pass ". . . from death unto life" (John 5:24).

Now here is a choice proverb—

**As a jewel of gold in a swine's snout, so is a fair woman which is without discretion [Prov. 11:22].**

Have you ever seen a pig walking around with a gold ring in its snout? Well, there are a lot of them out here in Hollywood, California. They are beautiful women with no discretion.

**The desire of the righteous is only good: but the expectation of the wicked is wrath [Prov. 11:23].**

The only way to have peace and joy is to be rightly related to Christ.

**There is that scattereth, and yet increaseth; and there is that withholdeth more than is meet, but it tendeth to poverty.**

**The liberal soul shall be made fat: and he that watereth shall be watered also himself [Prov. 11:24–25].**

This is a paradox. Dr. Ironside put it like this:

Bunyan's quaint rhyme, propounded as a riddle by Old Honest, and explained by Gaius, is in itself a suited commentary on these verses:

A man there was, though some did count
  him mad,
The more he cast away, the more he had.
He that bestows his goods upon the poor
Shall have as much again, and ten times
  more.

The Lord has said that if one sows sparingly, he shall also reap sparingly. That is a general principle. It certainly also applies to giving to the work of the Lord.

**He that withholdeth corn, the people shall curse him: but blessing shall be upon the head of him that selleth it [Prov. 11:26].**

This verse reminds me of Joseph down in Egypt. He didn't withhold the corn. He gathered it faithfully for seven years and then he was able to feed the world, including his own father and brothers and their families.

It also reminds me of Nabal—"he that withholdeth corn" certainly applies to him. He was a fool, and that is what his name means. He was married to a beautiful woman, Abigail. Why she married him, I don't know, except that he was a rich man. David, during the years he was hiding from Saul, had taken care of Nabal's sheep and had helped him on many occasions. So when David and his men were hungry, he called on Nabal for food. Nabal turned him down flat—in fact, he insulted the messengers whom David had sent. (Red-headed David would not take that lying down! He went after the man, but on his way Abigail came to meet him with an offering of peace.) This proverb fits Nabal like a glove.

Also I believe we could give this proverb a spiritual application. The corn is the Word of God. Many preachers are withholding the corn. They preach on political issues and social questions instead of teaching the Word of God. God have mercy on preachers who are withholding the corn from their people!

We *all* are to give out the corn today—this is not just for the preachers. Are you sitting on the sidelines, withholding corn from those around you? You could be a great impetus in getting a teaching of the Word of God into your area. Oh, my friend, "He that withholdeth corn, the people shall *curse* him." But what a thrill it is to have someone come and thank you for bringing them the Word of life! "Blessing shall be upon the head of him that selleth it"—or *giveth* it without money and without price.

**He that diligently seeketh good procureth favour: but he that seeketh mischief, it shall come unto him [Prov. 11:27].**

This is another evidence that ". . . whatsoever a man soweth, that shall he also reap" (Gal. 6:7).

**He that trusteth in his riches shall fall: but the righteous shall flourish as a branch [Prov. 11:28].**

When our Lord gave parables, which I believe he drew from real life, He told about a farmer who had such a bumper crop that he decided to tear down his barns to build bigger barns. He would give all his attention to that. There is nothing wrong in building bigger barns, but the Lord said that he was a fool, because he was so interested in building big barns down here that he didn't think of building anything for eternity. That is the danger of riches. No one can buy his way into heaven.

**The fruit of the righteous is a tree of life; and he that winneth souls is wise [Prov. 11:30].**

Many years ago a survey was conducted on the sons of preachers, because P.K.'s (preachers kids) come in for a lot of criticism. It was found that several United States presidents were sons of preachers, including Woodrow Wilson. Also some of our outstanding scientists were sons of preachers. Generally the children of saved folk turn out very well.

Today there seems to be a flurry of little courses on how to achieve harmony in the home. I wish we could get past that smattering of knowledge and the little surface coating that is being applied today. A little course in psychology about being sweet and nice in the home is not the answer. We need a return to the Word of God and to living a godly life in the home. A lot of our family problems would evaporate if we had righteousness in the home. "The fruit of the righteous is a tree of life."

"He that winneth souls is wise." Today a great deal of attention is being given to personal witnessing. That is good. I believe it is one of the finest things that is taking place in our day and generation. The Word of God has been saying all the time, "he that winneth souls is wise."

**Behold, the righteous shall be recompensed in the earth: much more the wicked and the sinner [Prov. 11:31].**

Judgment is coming. There can be no doubt about that.

# CHAPTER 12

In the school of wisdom, the boy is still in his freshman year, but the instruction is very important.

**Whoso loveth instruction loveth knowledge: but he that hateth reproof is brutish [Prov. 12:1].**

The man who loves instruction is a man who has a true estimate of what is top priority and what is really of superior value. That means that he will listen to instruction. However, I must say that after getting folk to listen to the Word of God, one of the great problems is getting them to obey what it says. Obedience is absolutely essential.

**A good man obtaineth favour of the LORD: but a man of wicked devices will he condemn [Prov. 12:2].**

Psalm 1:5 tells us that ". . . the ungodly shall not stand in the judgment, nor sinners in the congregation of the righteous." Regardless of fame or riches or standing high in the estimation of men, the ungodly man will come to a sorry, sad ending. God is certainly going to judge such men. "A man of wicked devices will he condemn."

**A man shall not be established by wickedness: but the root of the righteous shall not be moved [Prov. 12:3].**

Our Lord gave a parable that deals with this. In the Sermon on the Mount, He told about a man who built his house on a rock, and another who built his house on the sand (Matt. 7:24–27). The rock, of course, symbolizes Christ, the solid foundation of the Word of God.

Now here in his freshman course, the young man is given advice about choosing a wife.

**A virtuous woman is a crown to her husband: but she that maketh ashamed is as rottenness in his bones [Prov. 12:4].**

Think of the wonderful wives who are mentioned in the Old Testament. Eve must have been a wonderful person in spite of the fact that she listened to the serpent. Sarah was a model wife according to 1 Peter 3:6. The mother of Moses, Jochabed, was undoubtedly a remarkable woman.

Then there are others who were not so good and could be described as "rottenness in his bones." Job's wife was not much of a help to him. It is interesting that Satan took away from Job everything that he leaned upon except his wife, which must mean that Satan knew she wasn't very much help to Job. Then there was bloody Athalia whose mother was the wicked Jezebel. So there are many illustrations in the Scriptures of this proverb.

Ogden Nash gave advice on how to make marriage a success in a little poem that he wrote:

> To keep your marriage brimming
> With love in the loving cup,
> Whenever you're wrong, admit it;
> Whenever you're right, shut up.

That is good advice, by the way.

**The thoughts of the righteous are right: but the counsels of the wicked are deceit.**

**The words of the wicked are to lie in wait for blood: but the mouth of the upright shall deliver them.**

**The wicked are overthrown, and are not: but the house of the righteous shall stand [Prov. 12:5–7].**

Again let me change the word *wicked* to *lawless*, which is probably more accurate. You can see that God believes in law and order. He has a great deal to say about lawlessness.

**A man shall be commended according to his wisdom: but he that is of a perverse heart shall be despised [Prov. 12:8].**

"Shall be despised" is literally "shall be exposed to contempt." I think of Gideon and his son. Gideon is to be commended according to his wisdom. Abimelech, his son, was exposed to contempt.

**He that is despised, and hath a servant, is better than he that honoureth himself, and lacketh bread [Prov. 12:9].**

This proverb is rather confusing, but it seems that a contrast is being made. Another translation reads: "Better is the poor that provideth for himself." The thought appears to be that the one who is looked down upon as being lowly, but whose needs are met, is far happier and more to be envied than he who delights in appearing prosperous while feeling the pinch of poverty.

**A righteous man regardeth the life of his beast: but the tender mercies of the wicked are cruel [Prov. 12:10].**

As I have mentioned, my father was killed in an accident in a cotton gin when I was fourteen years old. I was at the age when a boy thinks his dad is a hero, and, frankly, I have never gotten over it. I remember one time we were driving on a dirt road by horse and buggy from Ardmore to Springer, Oklahoma. Ahead of us was a man in his buggy who was drunk and was beating his horse. We couldn't get around him, and my dad got out of our buggy and talked to the man about beating his animal. Of course the man, being drunk, was offended and took a swing at my dad, but he missed him. So my dad hit him and knocked him down. He took the whip away from him and told him to get back in his buggy and let his horse alone. Then we followed him as he went on ahead of us. This incident impressed me, and I am delighted to find in Scripture a proverb like this: "A righteous man regardeth the life of his beast."

A man who owns several dogs told me that he always judges a man by the reaction of his dogs to that man. Dogs seem to know character. They know whether they would be mistreated by an individual. It is interesting that the animal world seems to be able to judge human character better than some of us do.

**He that tilleth his land shall be satisfied with bread: but he that followeth vain persons is void of understanding [Prov. 12:11].**

This proverb is saying to stay on the job, keep busy, and don't do so much running around.

All the way through this chapter we have contrasts like this:

**The wicked desireth the net of evil men: but the root of the righteous yieldeth fruit [Prov. 12:12].**

There is repetition in this section for emphasis. After all, repetition is the best kind of teaching, if you can get by with it. If you keep saying a thing, your pupil will never forget it.

**The way of a fool is right in his own eyes: but he that hearkeneth unto counsel is wise [Prov. 12:15].**

You know to whom this refers, I am sure. It is Rehoboam, the son of Solomon. He refused the wise counsel of the older men in his kingdom, which resulted in his own downfall and civil war in his nation.

**He that speaketh truth sheweth forth righteousness: but a false witness deceit.**

**There is that speaketh like the piercings of a sword: but the tongue of the wise is health [Prov. 12:17–18].**

My friend, if your pastor is preaching the truth, there are times when he is going to put the sword right in your heart. And if you are not willing to accept it—well, the hypocrite always covers up with hatred and bitterness. This is the reason I am always a little afraid of a man who is highly critical of his pastor—that is, if he is nice to his face but is sticking a knife in his back.

**The lip of truth shall be established for ever: but a lying tongue is but for a moment.**

**Deceit is in the heart of them that imagine evil: but to the counsellors of peace is joy.**

**There shall no evil happen to the just: but the wicked shall be filled with mischief [Prov. 12:19–21].**

All of these verses have to do with the tongue, the lying tongue and the lips of truth. They are put in contrast. The Word of God has more to say about the tongue, more judgment on the abuse of the tongue, than it is has to say about the use and abuse of alcohol. Yet it is interesting that a lying tongue and a gossip can get by in Christian circles today, whereas a drunkard would be rejected.

**Lying lips are abomination to the LORD: but they that deal truly are his delight [Prov. 12:22].**

One of the things that should characterize a child of God is his truthfulness.

**A prudent man concealeth knowledge: but the heart of fools proclaimeth foolishness [Prov. 12:23].**

A prudent man will not say things that are going to hurt someone. But you have probably been in a crowd where there is some foolish person, a big-mouthed person, who says something that casts a reflection on another person—of course, someone who is not present in the crowd. The prudent man would not say it, but the heart of the fool will say things like that.

**The hand of the diligent shall bear rule: but the slothful shall be under tribute [Prov. 12:24].**

I believe that in our contemporary society this has been somewhat turned around. It is not always the diligent who are elected to office, and I'm not sure it is the slothful who are paying the taxes. At least I don't want to come in under the category of being lazy, and I certainly pay taxes. I have asked God for light as I have studied these proverbs, and I have come to realize that some of them should be considered in the light of eternity. I believe that the measuring stick for this proverb is eternity rather than a local situation. Aren't we told that someday we are going to rule with Christ? But Scripture does not teach that all believers will rule equally; there will be gradations. I personally would be very embarrassed if I found myself on the same plane as the apostles, sitting next to the apostle Paul. I don't belong there. However, I do think that the *diligent* are to rule with Christ.

**Heaviness in the heart of man maketh it stoop: but a good word maketh it glad [Prov. 12:25].**

Job said to his friends, "How forcible are right words! . . ." (Job 6:25). Right words can bring comfort and cheer and encouragement to those who are grieving or who have a problem or have bitterness of spirit. We certainly are not to beat down a person who is having problems. We are to give him a good word.

**The righteous is more excellent than his neighbour: but the way of the wicked seduceth them [Prov. 12:26].**

It would be clearer to translate it this way: "The righteous searcheth out his neighbor." The righteous man wants to help his neighbor, while the lawless man will try to hurt his neighbor. The righteous man will come to talk to a neighbor and face him if he finds he is wrong. That is the most helpful thing he can do.

Nathan was the best friend David had; yet it was Nathan who had the courage to point his finger at David and say, ". . . Thou art the man . . ." (2 Sam. 12:7). When there are things in our lives that need to be straightened, it is wonderful to have a good friend who will reprove us in love.

One of the best friends I ever had was a man who helped me through school. When I first started in the ministry, the Lord was gracious to me and let me be pastor of a church that had been my home church, where the people loved me and were very sympathetic with me. I was pretty much of an amateur to be pastor of such a large and prominent church in that day. They were good to me.

I went to a conference at Winona Lake and heard a man speak who I thought was great. I came back and tried to imitate him. I even tried to imitate his accent! My church members discovered that. They just sat there and smiled, very few said anything about it, and I received no harsh criticism. However, this man who had helped me through school invited me to lunch. He said just one thing that I shall never forget, and it was a good proverb. "Vernon, we would rather have a *genuine* Vernon McGee than an *imitation* anybody else." That was all he said. Friend, that is all he needed to say. From then on, I went back to being Vernon McGee—that may not have been *good*, but it was better than trying to imitate somebody else. How forcible

are right words! The righteous will search out his neighbor and help him—that is exactly what this man did for me. But the wicked (the lawless) seduceth them. He goes over and pats him on the back and then crucifies him when his back is turned. These proverbs gear right down into your neighborhood, right down into your church, right down into your place of work, don't they?

**The slothful man roasteth not that which he took in hunting: but the substance of a diligent man is precious [Prov. 12:27].**

I find this proverb quite humorous. This fellow went out and shot a deer, but he was too lazy to skin the deer and cut up the meat and cook and eat it. You must be pretty lazy to be that kind of hunter. It's like the fisherman who will fish but won't clean the fish to eat them.

"But the substance of a diligent man is precious." In other words, he takes care of what he has.

Remember when Ruth went out to glean in the field and Boaz was so generous with her that she had a surprising amount; then she beat out the grain that she had gleaned. She could have come home and thrown the gleanings down in front of Naomi and said, "Look what I have done. I worked hard all day for this. Now you can beat it out." She didn't do that. This reveals the kind of spirit that was in her.

Men, it won't hurt you to help with some of the work at home. You can even do the dishes now and then. I have learned that, since I am retired and at home more, I have become a member of the "Honey-do Club." It is, "Honey, do this," and "Honey, do that." When I was a boy I used to tell my mother, "When I grow up I'm never going to wash dishes again." Well, I must be in my second childhood, because I'm washing dishes again.

**In the way of righteousness is life; and in the pathway thereof there is no death [Prov. 12:28].**

A wonderful vista opens to the child of God! Physical death is ahead of us if the Lord tarries, but eternal life is out yonder.

# CHAPTER 13

We continue in this section where we are learning some of the great principles of life.

**A wise son heareth his father's instruction: but a scorner heareth not rebuke [Prov. 13:1].**

Although Solomon was not David's favorite son, Solomon did at least listen to him. He is an example of a wise son who heard his father's instruction. Rehoboam, the son of Solomon, is an example of the scorner who did not listen. He is an example to us of the dark side or the negative side, as we have found in many of these proverbs. But there are other examples that we could find in Scripture.

**A man shall eat good by the fruit of his mouth: but the soul of the transgressors shall eat violence.**

**He that keepeth his mouth keepeth his life: but he that openeth wide his lips shall have destruction [Prov. 13:2–3].**

There is a type of talking today which is gossip; it is foolish talking. It borders on being risqué—telling things that have a double meaning. The double entendre joke even gets into Christian circles today. And when they do, they seem to dwell on this matter of sex.

I have noticed that many of these folk take courses on sex, and then later on I hear that their home was broken up. The husband has run away with another woman and all that sort of thing. I believe much of this trouble is a result of such borderline living and borderline speaking. That is the thing we are warned about here, and the young man is told to beware of it.

**The soul of the sluggard desireth, and hath nothing: but the soul of the diligent shall be made fat [Prov. 13:4].**

You will remember that the apostle Paul put it right on the line to the Thessalonians. There were some pious souls there who said, "We're looking for the Lord to come," and they quit work. Paul wrote, ". . . if any would not work, neither should he eat" (2 Thess. 3:10). Let's not be doling out food to those who will not work. We are to work. And if you really believe that the Lord is coming, it will make you a better worker.

**A righteous man hateth lying: but a wicked man is loathsome, and cometh to shame.**

**Righteousness keepeth him that is upright in the way: but wickedness overthroweth the sinner [Prov. 13:5–6].**

This refers to truth in the inward parts. This is the background of practical righteousness. God hates that which is false; He cannot tolerate it. The child of God should recognize and deal with any sin in his life. This old nature of ours is inclined to lie. It just comes naturally to us to lie. God says He hates that, and He will have to deal with that type of thing.

**There is that maketh himself rich, yet hath nothing: there is that maketh himself poor, yet hath great riches [Prov. 13:7].**

Here is another example of the old nature that we all have. If we are poor we want to put up a front, to keep up with the Joneses. We pretend to have more than we actually have. Some people drive a Cadillac automobile simply to impress other folk, even though they really can't afford it. Some live in a neighborhood they really cannot afford.

On the other hand, there are people who are really very wealthy but are always talking about how *poor* they are. A member in one of my former churches was a very wealthy man, but he probably gave less than anyone else. He was always talking about how high prices were and how much things cost him. And he would say he'd be broke if things didn't get better.

Both sides are an abomination to God because each is hypocritical. It is putting up a front that we don't need to put up. We don't need to try to keep up with the Joneses; neither ought we to act as if we don't even know the Joneses. We are to treat them as neighbors, and then we ought to be just what we are.

**The light of the righteous rejoiceth: but the lamp of the wicked shall be put out [Prov. 13:9].**

In the study of the history of the kings of Israel, I called attention to this principle at work. One line after another became kings in the northern kingdom. Then, suddenly, they were cut off, often in a violent manner by murder. This is what God says: "The lamp of the wicked shall be put out." It happens again and again in this world. The end of Hitler was not pretty. And the end of Stalin evidently was not either.

**Only by pride cometh contention: but with the well advised is wisdom [Prov. 13:10].**

When you find contention in a group, in a neighborhood, in a church or church group, the basis of it will be found to be pride. It is *always* that. As someone has said, it takes two to make a quarrel—*always*.

**Wealth gotten by vanity shall be diminished: but he that gathereth by labour shall increase [Prov. 13:11].**

This is another proverb that should be considered in the light of eternity; that is the yardstick that you must put down alongside this. Many wealthy men apparently knew that they had very foolish offspring; so they established trust funds and put legal chains around their estates so their offspring could not get to it. Such an arrangement is made so that their offspring can live off the income, but they cannot touch the estate itself. As a result there are many rich sons in the world today, men who never made a dime in their lives, they wouldn't know how to work for a living at all; yet they are heirs to tremendous fortunes. But they have been protected so that they cannot touch the principal of their estates. If they could, they would foolishly spend it all.

Now this proverb needs to be looked at in the light of eternity. What are *true* riches? What is wealth really? Is it those stocks and bonds? Well, the individual is going to lose them someday. Death took them away from the original owner. Nobody came in and stole them; *he* stole away! He went off and left them. And that's going to happen to those who own those stocks and bonds today.

**Hope deferred maketh the heart sick: but when the desire cometh, it is a tree of life [Prov. 13:12].**

You can just keep hoping for something that doesn't come to pass—that will make the heart sick. This is the reason we ought to be in step with the will of God in our lives, because we hope for a great many things that will not be realized in our lives at all. How much better it is to accept the reality of the situation in which God has placed us!

**Whoso despiseth the word shall be destroyed: but he that feareth the commandment shall be rewarded.**

**The law of the wise is a fountain of life, to depart from the snares of death.**

**Good understanding giveth favour: but the way of transgressors is hard [Prov. 13:13–15].**

All through Proverbs there is this contrast between righteousness and wickedness. God hates pride; He hates lawlessness; He hates hypocrisy. He has no use for this type of thing that arises out of our human nature. That is the reason that God will not accept anything that we do in the old nature. It is only what He can perform through our new nature that is acceptable to Him. One thing is sure: He is not going to take Vernon McGee's old nature to heaven. I'll be glad to get rid of it. In heaven you and I will be forever parted from that old nature which produces all the sins that are inherent in each of us.

God makes what He wants very clear in Isaiah 66:2: ". . . to this man will I look, even to him that is poor and of a contrite spirit, and trembleth at my word." That is the way we must all come to God if we wish to be accepted of Him. We cannot come in pride. And we dare not despise His Word nor His commandments.

**A wicked messenger falleth into mischief: but a faithful ambassador is health [Prov. 13:17].**

We have had men in our government who have had access to government secrets, to that which is "top drawer" as far as the policy of this country is concerned, and some of these men have been homosexuals. When the enemy discovers this, it makes it possible for them to use these men. The same is true about men who have a weakness for alcohol. "A wicked messenger falleth into mischief." We need men of high integrity in our government. It is important whether a man drinks or not. I think it is tragic that so many men high up in government positions use alcohol. I think that is a part of our problem as a nation today. We need to recognize that these basic proverbs which seem so simple are *so* important to our lives as individuals and as a nation.

**He that spareth his rod hateth his son: but he that loveth him chasteneth him betimes [Prov. 13:24].**

This is real child psychology. The child of God today is told the same thing. "Children, obey your parents," but the father is told, ". . . provoke not your children to wrath . . ." (Eph. 6:1, 4). That is, don't whip them or discipline them when you are angry or talking in a loud voice. Wait until a time when you can calmly sit down with your child and talk with him and explain why he is being disciplined. That is very important. This is the reason my father's discipline was so good. He often did not deal with me until maybe a day had gone by. And I thought several times I had gotten by with it, but I hadn't. He very calmly dealt with me, and I knew he was not doing what he did because he was angry. Discipline is very important.

# CHAPTER 14

The Book of Proverbs is an important section of the Word of God. Here we find the wisdom of God distilled into small sentences. We see that they fit individuals who are mentioned in the Bible. Also they fit folk whom we know, and they fit you and me.

**Every wise woman buildeth her house: but the foolish plucketh it down with her hands [Prov. 14:1].**

"Every wise woman buildeth her house." This is not talking about the physical building of a home. I think Sarah is an example of a wife who built her house. She was the wife of a patriarch, and she built up the house of Israel. I think we can say that Jochabed, the mother of Moses, built her house. Although she was a slave in a foreign land, to save her son she hid him, watched over him, and finally became his nurse in the service of Pharaoh's daughter. She is the one who taught him about the Lord and the promise of the Lord to Israel. She was a wonderful mother, and she built her house.

"But the foolish plucketh it down with her hands." Several women in the Scriptures did that. Because of their wickedness, the house they built was destroyed. Let me point out one passage in particular. "Forty and two years old was Ahaziah when he began to reign, and he reigned one year in Jerusalem. His mother's name also was Athaliah the daughter of Omri. He also walked in the ways of the house of Ahab: for his mother was his counsellor to do wickedly" (2 Chron. 22:2–3). The counsel of his mother really brought the house of Ahab low. This is indeed a true proverb. You can take these into the laboratory of life and see them work out even today. I know of several examples of women whose personal sins have destroyed their homes.

**He that walketh in his uprightness feareth the LORD: but he that is perverse in his ways despiseth him [Prov. 14:2].**

This tells us that our walk will reveal our relationship with God. We are told by the apostle John, "He that saith he abideth in him ought himself also so to walk, even as he walked" (1 John 2:6). Our walk should be in obedience to the Father just as the walk of the Lord Jesus was.

You will remember that Samuel laid this matter before King Saul: ". . . Behold, to obey is better than sacrifice, and to hearken than the fat of rams" (1 Sam. 15:22). Obedience to the Lord is the important thing. Without that, your religion is phony and false.

**In the mouth of the foolish is a rod of pride: but the lips of the wise shall preserve them [Prov. 14:3].**

This reminds me of David and Goliath (1 Sam. 17:41–49). "In the mouth of the foolish is a rod of pride." This is a picture of Goliath. He did a lot of boasting as the champion of the Philistines. When David volunteered to fight him, Goliath reacted this way: "And the Philistine said unto David, Am I a dog, that thou comest to me with staves? And the Philistine cursed David by his gods. And the Philistine said to David, Come to me, and I will give thy flesh unto the fowls of the air, and to the beasts of the field" (1 Sam. 17:43–44).

"But the lips of the wise shall preserve them." Now notice David's answer: "Then said David to the Philistine, Thou comest to me with a sword, and with a spear, and with a shield: but I come to thee in the name of the LORD of hosts, the God of the armies of Israel, whom thou hast defied" (1 Sam. 17:45).

**Where no oxen are, the crib is clean: but much increase is by the strength of the ox [Prov. 14:4].**

This is a very interesting proverb. In several portions of Scripture the ox is used as an example to us. Also the ox was a beast of sacrifice, symbolic of Christ in sacrifice.

Now the ox was a strong animal. In fact, he was the tractor and the sedan of the families in that day. They used the ox to ride to market, and they used the ox to plow their fields.

I suppose he was rather a dirty animal in the sense that his crib needed to be cleaned out, and that was an unpleasant task because he was a big animal. Of course, the way to get rid of cleaning the crib was to get rid of the ox. That would give them a clean crib, but they would be deprived of the "strength of the ox."

This has a tremendous spiritual lesson for us. Sometimes we try to solve problems in the church and try to clean up divisions in the church by throwing out the ox. Often there is a group or clique in the church, busy as termites and with about the same result, who want to get rid of those people who insist on having Bible teaching in the church. They are going to clean the crib, they think, so they throw out the ox. I believe this has happened to church after church in our country. After a while it becomes evident that it was the oxen who pulled the plow. They were the ones who contributed financially; they were the ones who sent out the missionaries; they were the ones who paid the bills. So before one tries to do any cleaning, it is very important to find out who are the oxen in the Lord's work.

I play golf with a wonderful Christian man. He gives to our Bible-teaching program because he believes in teaching the Bible. We have wonderful fellowship together, but we disagree on a lot of things. When we are playing golf, I like to concentrate on the game. He is always talking to me about my work, saying, "Why don't you do this, and why don't you do that?" Sometimes that is a little irritating. I could get rid of him—that would be getting the crib clean—but I would be throwing out the ox! I would lose a friend who is very right in much of the advice he gives me. And he pulls the plow with me in trying to get out the Word of God. How absolutely foolish it would be to clean the crib by throwing out the ox.

**A faithful witness will not lie: but a false witness will utter lies [Prov. 14:5].**

The Lord Jesus has been called the faithful and true witness. That is the kind of witness we ought to be, too.

We hear a great deal today about being a witness for Christ. There are courses given on how to be a witness for Christ. It is wonderful to take a course that will enable you to go out and ring doorbells and tell people about the Savior. But remember, there are two kinds of witnesses: the faithful and the false. If you tell someone that Jesus saves and keeps and satisfies, are you telling the truth? You answer, "Of course, it is the truth." Yes, the facts are true, but have you proven it to be true in your own life? Or are you being a false witness?

**Fools make a mock at sin: but among the righteous there is favour [Prov. 14:9].**

Jezebel is a prime example in the Word of God of one who made "a mock at sin." We are told to turn away from people who do that and have nothing to do with them.

**The heart knoweth his own bitterness; and a stranger doth not intermeddle with his joy [Prov. 14:10].**

Every heart has some secret joy or sorrow that no one can share. No one. We may try to share it, but they do not understand. I remember some folk asked me to tell them about my operation for cancer. I told them how in the hospital I had turned to God and how at that time He had made Himself real to me. They didn't like that. I could see they turned me off. Later I said to myself, *Probably that is a secret that I can't share with anyone else.*

Have you ever had some wonderful, joyful experience, and you attempted to tell it to your loved ones? When I was a young man, some time after my dad had died, I wrote a poem. At that time I was living with an aunt, and there were several relatives there. I came in and said, "Look, I've written a poem, and I want to read it to you." I read it, and it brought great joy to me, but it didn't bring any joy to them. They turned me off when I started reading it. In fact, that experience caused me to stop writing poetry. If I were a budding poet, I was lost to the world forever, because they sure put a stop to my poetry right there! There are some things we can share with others, and there are some things we cannot share.

**There is a way which seemeth right unto a man, but the end thereof are the ways of death [Prov. 14:12].**

This is a verse which should be applied to the cults and "isms." They sound so reasonable and so nice and so attractive. Recently a friend said to me, "Why is it that this certain cult keeps growing as it does?" I said, "Because it appeals to the old nature of man. It appeals to the flesh. It tells you that if you are a nice sweet fellow and follow certain rules, you are going to make it." My friend, "there is a way which seemeth right unto a man," but notice the end of this proverb: "but the end thereof are the ways of death." The end is eternal separation from God. How important it is to be in the right way! The Lord Jesus said, ". . . I am the way, the truth, and the life: no man cometh unto the Father, but by me" (John 14:6).

**The simple believeth every word: but the prudent man looketh well to his going.**

**A wise man feareth, and departeth from evil: but the fool rageth, and is confident.**

**He that is soon angry dealeth foolishly: and a man of wicked devices is hated.**

**The simple inherit folly: but the prudent are crowned with knowledge [Prov. 14:15–18].**

The viewpoint of the world is that the Christian is a person who has a low I.Q., is very naïve, and will believe everything that is said to him. The real child of God—and the only kind of child of God is a *real* one—is not simple in that sense. He doesn't believe anything and everything.

Have you ever noticed that the disciples were constantly questioning the Lord? The man we call "doubting Thomas" was constantly raising questions. Simon Peter asked many questions: "Lord, where are You going? Why can't I follow You?" Philip, the quiet one, asked Him, "Show us the Father. That's all we need." Judas (not Iscariot) asked, "How is it You will show us these things and not show them to the world?" These fellows were always raising questions.

If you are a child of God, you will not be gullible. You're not going to swallow everything you hear. Faith is not a leap in the dark. Faith is not betting your life on something. Nor is it the little girl's definition, "Faith is believing what you know ain't so." My friend, faith rests upon a solid foundation. God says if it is not on a solid foundation, don't believe it. "The simple believeth every word." The prudent man, the wise man, tests what he hears.

The fear of the Lord causes a wise man to test what he hears. He will not be taken in. He won't believe what the preacher says just because the preacher says it. He will check what the Word of God says. I want to say to you right now that you should not believe anything I say just because I say it. I am not the oracle of Delphi; I do not speak *ex cathedra*; I am not a know-it-all. You test what I say by the Word of God. There is a lot of sweet-sounding speech going out from churches and from the media. Oh, my friend, don't believe everything you hear. Test it by the Word of God.

**The poor is hated even of his own neighbour: but the rich hath many friends [Prov. 14:20].**

That seems to be becoming more and more true. I doubt if a poor rail-splitter like Lincoln could run for the presidency in our day. A candidate has to be rich.

**He that despiseth his neighbour sinneth: but he that hath mercy on the poor, happy is he [Prov. 14:21].**

How do you feel toward those who can do nothing for you in return? Do you do something for them?

**In all labour there is profit: but the talk of the lips tendeth only to penury [Prov. 14:23].**

Some people just *talk;* they don't *do.* People can almost be classified as either talking people or doing people.

**The crown of the wise is their riches: but the foolishness of fools is folly [Prov. 14:24].**

The riches here are not necessarily material riches. There are a great many happy people who are rich, not in the things of this life, but in those things that are spiritual. That is the most important of all.

**A true witness delivereth souls: but a deceitful witness speaketh lies [Prov. 14:25].**

The Lord Jesus said it this way: ". . . if the blind lead the blind, both shall fall into the ditch" (Matt. 15:14).

**The fear of the LORD is a fountain of life, to depart from the snares of death [Prov. 14:27].**

To teach the fear of the Lord was the object of the Holy Spirit all the way through the Book of Proverbs.

**A sound heart is the life of the flesh: but envy the rottenness of the bones [Prov. 14:30].**

How true this is! Envy will not only rob you of your joy and fellowship with the Lord, but it will affect you physically.

**Righteousness exalteth a nation: but sin is a reproach to any people [Prov. 14:34].**

I wish this verse were inscribed over the United Nations instead of the verse about beating their swords into plowshares, which will not happen until Christ reigns on this earth. When Christ returns, then they will learn that righteousness *does* exalt a nation.

Today the nations do not believe that righteousness exalts them, but history bears testimony to it. The pathway of history is strewn with the wrecks, the debris, and the ruins of nations that didn't follow this principle. "Sin is a reproach to any people."

# CHAPTER 15

This chapter contrasts goodness and evil and emphasizes first the role of the tongue, then of the heart.

## THE TONGUE

**A soft answer turneth away wrath: but grievous words stir up anger [Prov. 15:1].**

I'm sure that the people who come to your mind at this proverb are Abigail and Nabal. We have seen several proverbs that are applicable to them. Abigail was the beautiful, lovely wife and woman. Nabal, her husband, was the fool but a very rich man. Someone has written a book called "Beauty and the Beast," and it is the story of Nabal and Abigail— Abigail is the beauty and Nabal is the beast. You will recall that when Abigail heard that her husband had sent an insulting answer to David, who had in kindness and consideration taken care of his flocks, she hurriedly ordered the servants to gather a great deal of food for David. Then she went to meet David and fell down on her face before him. She recognized him as the future king, and she spoke to him of the fact that his life was bound up in the bundle of life with God—a beautiful expression. She gave a soft answer, and it did turn away wrath. On the other hand, grievous words stir up anger—which certainly was true of the words of Nabal.

You will notice many illustrations of this as you go through the Word of God. We find that the Lord Jesus Himself used the strongest language in the entire Scriptures in His denunciation of the Pharisees in Matthew 23. There can be a proper time to "put it on the line," and Jesus certainly could do that. But notice how gracious He was to those who needed the grace of God. He told the poor woman in sin, ". . . Neither do I condemn

thee: go, and sin no more" (John 8:11). What a gracious thing to say to her. So we find illustrations of this again and again in the Word of God. There is a time for the very gracious, soft answer. There is also a time when the answer needs to be strong.

**The tongue of the wise useth knowledge aright: but the mouth of fools poureth out foolishness [Prov. 15:2].**

We are back again to the tongue. I'll repeat what I have said before—there is more said in the Bible about the abuse of the tongue than about the abuse of alcohol. That does not mean we commend alcohol; I think the greatest curse of this country right now is not dope or drugs but alcohol. Somehow people tend to point an accusing finger at the drug addict, but they excuse the alcoholic as being sick and needing help. He certainly does. The Word of God condemns drunkenness but even more severely condemns the abuse of the tongue. That little tongue will tell people who you really are. It will give you away. I have a little booklet entitled *Hell on Fire*. It is a scriptural title, dealing with the tongue, that dangerous little instrument.

**The eyes of the Lord are in every place, beholding the evil and the good [Prov. 15:3].**

You may look to the right hand and to the left hand and think that nobody is watching you. Even Big Brother may not be watching you, but God is watching. God sees you.

Remember that when Moses saw an Egyptian beating one of his brethren in slavery, he looked this way and he looked that way, and then he slew the Egyptian. He forgot to look up! He didn't think anyone knew. God knew. Your life and my life are an open book before God. What is secret sin down here is open scandal in heaven. "The eyes of the LORD are in every place, beholding the evil and the good."

**A wholesome tongue is a tree of life: but perverseness therein is a breach in the spirit [Prov. 15:4].**

Here is the tongue again. It can get us into a lot of trouble. It can get us out of trouble, too. It can be a blessing or a curse.

**A fool despiseth his father's instruction: but he that regardeth reproof is prudent [Prov. 15:5].**

There is so much said in the Book of Proverbs about listening to advice and instruction. It has been said that you can't tell a fool anything. That is true. You can tell him, but you can't get through to him for the very simple reason that he is not listening to instruction.

**In the house of the righteous is much treasure: but in the revenues of the wicked is trouble [Prov. 15:6].**

This contrast is not dealing with material riches. The treasure that is in the house of the righteous consists of things like joy, peace, love, sympathy, comfort—wonderful treasures. They are the great treasures of life. The contrast is with the revenues of the wicked which are trouble.

**The lips of the wise disperse knowledge: but the heart of the foolish doeth not so [Prov. 15:7].**

This changes the word from tongue to lips, but the meaning is still the same. The wise disperse knowledge.

**The sacrifice of the wicked is an abomination to the LORD: but the prayer of the upright is his delight [Prov. 15:8].**

This is a fundamental principle. The wicked cannot do good or think right. It is impossible for them to do so. Let's skip down for a moment and see another verse that states the same truth. "The thoughts of the wicked are an abomination to the LORD: but the words of the pure are pleasant words" (v. 26). The thoughts of the wicked are an abomination to the Lord and so are the sacrifices that he brings.

The reason they are an abomination is that he is wrong, wrong on the inside and wrong on the outside. He is all wrong, and whatever he does is wrong. The problem is that he has not learned to come in humility, recognizing his lost condition, coming to the Lord Jesus Christ for salvation. Someone has said, "A person who trusts so much as a single hair's breadth of his works for salvation is a lost soul." That is true. "The sacrifice of the wicked is an abomination to the LORD." A person may be religious. He may go to church and go through certain formalities, but that has no value as far as God is concerned. I do not understand why people think that if they do certain religious things, that will make them right with God. The *heart* must be changed. God does interior decorating before He can do any exterior decorating. He is not interested in *your* exterior decorating until He has done a job of interior decorating in your life.

**The way of the wicked is an abomination unto the LORD: but he loveth him that followeth after righteousness [Prov. 15:9].**

We have seen what God thinks of the *sacrifice* of the wicked and of the *thoughts* of the wicked; now we see that the *way* of the wicked is also an abomination to the Lord. But He loves the person who follows after righteousness. Remember that it is Christ who has been made unto us righteousness (see 1 Cor. 1:30).

**Correction is grievous unto him that forsaketh the way: and he that hateth reproof shall die [Prov. 15:10].**

A man hates to be told that he is wrong. There are some people who will not accept any kind of advice or admonition.

### THE HEART

**Hell and destruction are before the LORD: how much more then the hearts of the children of men? [Prov. 15:11].**

The Epistle to the Hebrews tells us, "Neither is there any creature that is not manifest in his sight: but all things are naked and opened unto the eyes of him with whom we have to do" (Heb. 4:13). God is the discerner of the thoughts and intents of the heart. "Hell" or Sheol, the unseen world which none of us has seen, and which the man of the world does not believe exists, is open before God.

Only God can make that unseen world real to a child of God, which will give him a true perspective of this life. The man who lives with the idea that this life is all there is has a different set of values and a different list of priorities from that which the child of God has. When we talk to people who are not the children of God, it is important to get their perspective of life, to see how they are thinking. But only God can reveal what is on the other side in the unseen world. You and I can't do that. Only the spirit of God can take the things of Christ and make them real to us and to them.

Jesus Christ walked on this earth in the flesh over 1,900 years ago. He stepped through the doorway of death, but He was made alive on the third day. For forty days He revealed Himself to His disciples. Then He went back to glory, and He sent His Holy Spirit to us. Only the Holy Spirit of God can make Him real to us. The Lord Jesus promised that the Holy Spirit would ". . . take of mine, and shall shew it unto you" (John 16:15). It is very important for us to be aware of this.

**A merry heart maketh a cheerful countenance: but by sorrow of the heart the spirit is broken [Prov. 15:13].**

It is known that laughter and good cheer and joy actually add to a man's health and to the length of his life. They bring to life a wonderful dimension that cannot be there if we live in sorrow and pessimism.

**The heart of him that hath understanding seeketh knowledge: but the mouth of fools feedeth on foolishness [Prov. 15:14].**

Here he is emphasizing the heart rather than the head of man. He is not talking so much about the accumulating of certain facts but about spiritual discernment or, as someone has put it, "sanctified common sense." There is a dearth, a famine, of that in the land.

**Better is little with the fear of the LORD than great treasure and trouble therewith.**

**Better is a dinner of herbs where love is, than a stalled ox and hatred therewith [Prov. 15:16–17].**

A good illustration of this is found in the life of Daniel. He was taken as a slave into Babylon when he was just a young man. He showed remarkable ability, so he was put with the wise men to be trained for government service. He was to be given a certain diet which he refused to eat because it was forbidden to the Jews by the laws of God. He asked instead for a diet of cereal. He did this because of his fear of the Lord. He wanted to serve God. My, how God honored that man! He made him prime minister to Nebuchadnezzar, the first great world ruler. When the Persians took over, God again made Daniel the prime minister to the second great world ruler, Cyrus the Great. God honored His servant.

**A wrathful man stirreth up strife: but he that is slow to anger appeaseth strife [Prov. 15:18].**

This takes us back to verse 1. A man who is crude and rough in his dealings will stir up strife.

However, it is also true that preaching the Word of God will stir up strife. Remember that the Lord Jesus was the most controversial person who has ever been on this earth. Wherever the truth is preached, strife will be the result, because there are folk who don't want to hear it. Remember that we said the Word of God works like a Geiger counter. If you run it over a congregation, you can learn who is a genuine Christian and who is not.

A young preacher having trouble in his congregation came to me about it. I told him about my experience when I was a boy. When I would go to the barn at night to feed the horse or the cow, I would light a lantern and carry it with me. When I would open the barn door and step in, two things would happen: The rats would scurry and run for cover, and the birds which were roosting on the rafters would begin to sing. Light had those two very different effects. And when the Word of God is preached you will see the rats run for cover and the birds begin to sing.

We do need to keep in mind that we are not to exaggerate the offense of the cross—just preach it.

**A wise son maketh a glad father: but a foolish man despiseth his mother [Prov. 15:20].**

The father brags about his boy when he is making good. If the boy is failing, you won't hear a word out of his dad.

**A man hath joy by the answer of his mouth: and a word spoken in due season, how good is it! [Prov. 15:23].**

It is not only *what* you say but *when* you say it. Sometimes the right word at just the right time will do the job. Many of us could testify that the right word said to us at the right time in our lives changed the whole course of our lives. That has certainly happened to me.

**The thoughts of the wicked are an abomination to the LORD: but the words**

of the pure are pleasant words [Prov. 15:26].

We have already seen that the sacrifices of the wicked, the ways of the wicked, and the thoughts of the wicked are an abomination to the Lord. The wicked must be turned from his wicked ways. He must be turned to God.

**The Lord is far from the wicked: but he heareth the prayer of the righteous [Prov. 15:29].**

Peter writes the same thing. He says that God hears the prayer—that's interesting—of the righteous; but His ears are closed to the prayer of the wicked (1 Pet. 3:12).

**The light of the eyes rejoiceth the heart: and a good report maketh the bones fat [Prov. 15:30].**

I tell you, one good way to lose weight is to hear a bad report, to get some bad news.

**The fear of the Lord is the instruction of wisdom; and before honour is humility [Prov. 15:33].**

The important lesson for man to learn is to come with humility to learn of God. We all need that lesson.

# CHAPTER 16

This is a very rich and important section— short sentences drawn from long experience, tested in the crucible of time and of suffering. They are made rich and real to us by the power of the Holy Spirit. The proverbs are for all time, although they were written specifically to the young man who was an Israelite under the Mosaic Law. However, they widen out and speak to all of our hearts in a very definite way: to rich and poor, male and female, black and white. This is a book that can reach down and touch us all.

**The preparations of the heart in man, and the answer of the tongue, is from the Lord [Prov. 16:1].**

Dr. H. A. Ironside translates this: "The purposes of the heart are of man: but from Jehovah is the answer of the tongue." Our human proverb that would go along with this is, "Man proposes, but God disposes." As the Word of God says ". . . it is not in man that walketh to direct his steps" (Jer. 10:23). You may plan, and I may plan or arrange things, but when the time comes to speak or act, God is the One who is going to have the last word. We may make a great boast, but only God can give the final answer.

**All the ways of a man are clean in his own eyes; but the Lord weigheth the spirits [Prov. 16:2].**

"All the ways of a man are clean in his own eyes." We have seen this before in Proverbs 14:12, "There is a way which seemeth right unto a man, but the end thereof are the ways of death."

If you have ever dealt with lost people and have spoken to them about their salvation, or if you have been a preacher or a teacher, you know the answer that you get most of the time: "I don't need to be saved. I'm all right. What is wrong with me? I'm willing to stand before God. I'm an honest man." It is that sort of thing on and on. A man is clean in his own eyes. I have had that thrown back at me even as a challenge.

There are even a great many Christians who think that their walk is perfect before God. The whole issue is wrapped up in this one verse of Scripture: "But if we walk in the light, as he is in the light, we have fellowship one with another, and the blood of Jesus Christ his Son cleanseth us from all sin" (1 John 1:7). We need to hold up the mirror of the Word of God to our lives, and it will reveal that things are not quite right, that we don't measure up to God's standard. You may measure up to the standard of the chamber of commerce, and it may make you Man of the Year; your club may reward you and give you a plaque; your church may pat you on the back; and your neighbors may say that you are a great guy. But, my friend, when you see yourself in the light of the Word of God, then you see that you have a need and that there are spots on your life. You will see that you have come short of the glory of God. Your way may be clean in your own eyes, but it is not clean in God's eyes. "If we say that we have fellowship with him, and walk in darkness, we lie, and do not the truth" (1 John 1:6). Now John is speaking to Christians. There are a great many folk sitting in a church pew as comfortable as you please. In fact, they tend to point their finger at other folk and say, "They're not so good, but I am. I'm really all right." I think some of the saints today have, in effect, asked God to move over. They want to sit next to Him and look down to judge their fellow Christians.

The way of a man may seem clean in his own eyes, but Jehovah weighs the spirit. God searches you. Have you ever seen a pair of scales that can weigh spirits? Well, I'll tell you one—the Word of God. It is a mirror. It is a set of scales to measure you, and it says that you come short, that you don't measure up.

Some folk have misunderstood what I said in our study of the Epistle to the Galatians. They write to me and say, "You said that the Mosaic Law is no good today, that the Law is inoperative." I didn't say that. What I said was that the law cannot *save* you. The law is *good;* Paul said it's good. It is a mirror. It reveals to you that you have come short of the glory of God. My friend, if you look at the law of God and still say that you are measuring up to it, then you haven't really seen the law yet. You don't really know what the law is saying. The law demands perfection, and you and I cannot produce it. Therefore we need a Savior. That is what the law will do: it is a schoolmaster to bring us to Christ. It will take you by the hand and bring you to the cross and say, "Little fellow, what you need is a Savior." The law is good, but it will not save you. If the ways of a man are clean in his own eyes—even with the Word of God before him—may I say, there is none blind like those who will not see. Jehovah weighs the spirits.

**Commit thy works unto the Lord, and thy thoughts shall be established [Prov. 16:3].**

The word *commit* is literally "roll." You just roll your affairs over upon the Lord, and He will take charge. That's actually the way I got saved. When I was a lad, I ran away to Detroit, got into sin, came home, and was troubled by my conscience. Then a preacher told me that God wasn't angry at me—that Jesus bore my sins and that being justified by faith I could have peace with God. At that time I just rolled my sins onto Christ. There are times, even to this day, when I can't sleep at night, that I like to just roll over in bed and say, "Lord Jesus, I am resting in You." Roll over.

Rest in Him. Commit thy works unto Jehovah.

Are you worried about tomorrow, next week, next year, or the unforeseeable future? How is it all going to work out? Why don't you just turn it over to Him? Roll it over onto Him. What a picture this is!

**The Lord hath made all things for himself: yea, even the wicked for the day of evil [Prov. 16:4].**

My friend, here is some strong medicine. This proverb is a pill that will send you on a trip, I mean a real mind-blowing trip. Jehovah hath made all things for Himself. Have you ever wondered why the ocean is salty, or why it has a tide? You may answer that it is according to certain laws of nature. But who made the laws? Why *is* the ocean salty? Because God wanted it that way! The Lord Jesus is the Creator, and He *wanted* it that way. Someone may say it is because there is salt in the land that has been filtered out by the water in the ocean. By the way, who put the salt in the land to begin with?

I don't care what you do with evolution or how far back you try to carry it, eventually you come to the place where somebody had to make something to get the whole thing *started.* You know who started it? *God* did. And not only that, He made all these things for Himself.

What is the chief end of man? I learned that in the catechism a long time ago, and the answer is good. The chief end of man is to glorify God and to enjoy Him forever. I don't care who you are or where you are, God created you for His glory. Somebody says, "What about the drunkard in the street? What about that crooked man? That lost man—what about him? You mean he's for the glory of God?" My friend, this is a strong pill—are you ready to swallow it? *All of that is for the glory of God.* "Oh," you may say, "I don't like that." I don't remember that God ever asked anyone whether or not he liked it. He has never asked me that.

Very frankly, there are certain things that I don't understand, and I think I could make some very fine suggestions to the Lord. But the Lord says, "Vernon McGee, I didn't make this universe for you. This universe exists for Me, and you exist for Me; and you are going to be for My glory whether you are good or bad, saved or lost." God is accomplishing *His* purpose today. Don't you think it is about time you got in step with God? He is the One running the thing.

So many people want to make sure that they are going with the crowd, going with the thing that is popular, going with the thing that will work out. Friend, I don't know how things are going to work out in this world, but I do know this: Ultimately it's all going to be for the glory of God. "Even the lawless for the day of evil." God is going to make the wrath of man to praise Him (Ps. 76:10). How is He going to do that? I don't know. Let's wait—He will show us someday. Are you willing to trust Him and commit your way to Him and get in step with Him?

The very wonderful thing is that God is moving this universe according to His plan and purpose. The Greeks had a proverb: "The dice of the gods are loaded." That is exactly what God is saying in this proverb. Whether you like it or don't like it, God is saying to you, "Don't gamble with Me. Don't act as if I don't exist. You can play house as if I don't exist, as if this is your universe and you are going to work it out your way. But I want you to know that if you start gambling with Me, you will lose. You see, this is My universe, and I make the dice to come up My way, not your way. My dice are loaded—I already know how they are coming up, and you don't." The thing for us to do is to get in step with God.

A man, the Scriptures say, is a fool to live without God. "The fool hath said in his heart, There is no God . . ." (Ps. 14:1). ". . . he that cometh to God must believe that he is, and that he is a rewarder of them that diligently seek him" (Heb. 11:6).

This is a pill, is it not? And it is one that is hard for men to swallow.

**When a man's ways please the Lord, he maketh even his enemies to be at peace with him [Prov. 16:7].**

I have wrestled with this proverb a great deal, and I have searched what other men have had to say on this. Do you mean to tell me that if your ways please Jehovah, you will not have an enemy? Well, if that were true, then God wouldn't have an enemy, and He *does* have an enemy.

My interpretation is that if your ways please Jehovah, then your enemy may hate you; and, by the way, he *will* hate you. But the interesting thing is that, when the chips are down, these folk will admit that God is using you. That's the important thing. One of the nicest things that has been said about me in Southern California was said by a man who very frankly says he hates me. He said, "I hate him, but he teaches the Word of God." I

say, "Thank you, Mr. Enemy, you are carrying out this proverb. You have to make that kind of acknowledgement if you're honest." I love this proverb, by the way.

**A just weight and balance are the Lord's: all the weights of the bag are his work [Prov. 16:11].**

This is a word for the butcher, the baker, and the candlestick maker.

**Pride goeth before destruction, and an haughty spirit before a fall [Prov. 16:18].**

I have that underlined in my Bible.

**Better it is to be of an humble spirit with the lowly, than to divide the spoil with the proud [Prov. 16:19].**

Here again is a thrust made against that which God hates—pride. Pride is number one on God's "hate parade" (Prov. 6:16–19). This is the thing that brought down the archangel whom we know as Satan today. He was Lucifer—son of the morning—probably the highest creature God created until sin was found in him. What was that sin? It was pride: he attempted to lift himself above God, because he was such a great creature whom God had created and given the power of free choice.

Free choice is a very dangerous weapon which God has put in the hands of some of His creatures. Now some creatures follow an instinct. For example, the ducks leave Canada in the wintertime and fly down to South America. In the summer they fly back up to Canada. Back and forth they go. They are moved by instinct, but man has a free will. Man can stay in Canada in the wintertime (I don't know why he would), and he can go south in the summertime. But where there is free choice, there is also the possibility of pride and rebellion against God.

There are so many in Scripture who illustrate this matter of pride. This is the thing that was the undoing of that man Haman in the Book of Esther. And Absalom—imagine him rebelling against his father, David! Goliath, the giant, boasted in his pride. And Ahab was filled with pride.

**Pleasant words are as an honeycomb, sweet to the soul, and health to the bones [Prov. 16:24].**

"Pleasant words." We all like to hear something good, don't we? We read the newspaper and always get the bad news. It's too bad more people don't read the Bible. It is filled with good news. That is what the gospel is— *good* news.

Also, we should learn to say it with pleasant words *now*—instead of trying to say it with flowers when it is too late.

**There is a way that seemeth right unto a man, but the end thereof are the ways of death [Prov. 16:25].**

You will recognize that we had this proverb before (Prov. 14:12). Then why is it repeated? It is because the Lord doesn't want us to miss this one. Repetition reveals its importance.

**An ungodly man diggeth up evil: and in his lips there is as a burning fire [Prov. 16:27].**

We probably all know someone who fits this proverb. I had a friend who professed to be a Christian, but almost every time I would see him he would start in, "Dr. McGee, have you heard . . . ?" Then he would go on with the latest and the juiciest gossip that was going around. Was he a godly man? I don't know. I cannot sit in judgment on him. We need to guard our own tongue and lips so that we do not do the same.

**A froward man soweth strife: and a whisperer separateth chief friends [Prov. 16:28].**

We said before that some people will believe anything if it is whispered to them. There are those people who go around and whisper things—separating friends.

**The hoary head is a crown of glory, if it be found in the way of righteousness [Prov. 16:31].**

This is a good motto for the senior citizen.

**The lot is cast into the lap; but the whole disposing thereof is of the LORD [Prov. 16:33].**

I have this verse written over the Book of Esther. In his pride Haman cast lots to determine the day of destruction of the Jewish people. But God intervened and delivered His people; and the Jewish Feast of Purim (meaning "lots") is a celebration of that providential day.

Let me say again that "the dice of the gods are loaded." Don't gamble with God. Don't take a chance with Him. Remember that it is God's universe, and it is all for His glory. It's for His purpose. Do you want to cooperate? Do you want to get in step with God or continue in rebellion? It is not your will, but God's will that shall prevail. Oh, that you and I would get in step with Him and be at peace with Him, being justified by faith!

# CHAPTER 17

**Better is a dry morsel, and quietness therewith, than an house full of sacrifices with strife [Prov. 17:1].**

This verse is very similar in thought to Proverbs 15:17: "Better is a dinner of herbs where love is, than a stalled ox and hatred therewith." The last part of the verse pictures a scene of religious activity, but activity does not always denote the working of God. A church can have a lot of meetings, a lot of organization, and a tremendous amount of activity, but all of this may cause a great deal of confusion and frustration.

I think of Elijah in the court of Ahab and Jezebel. There certainly was plenty of activity going on in Ahab's palace, including a lot of religious practices, but nothing really pertaining to God. Elijah stepped in and proclaimed

that it wasn't going to rain until God said so, and He wasn't in the mood to say so. Then Elijah walked out. Where did he go? He went far off to the Brook Cherith where he stayed a long time alone with God. God was training him out in the quietness of the desert. "Better is a dry morsel, and quietness therewith."

God took Moses out of the palace of Pharaoh (another scene of great activity and religious organization) and put him in the desert of Midian and taught him there. Both Moses and Elijah had "a dry morsel, and quietness therewith."

It is nice to get off at times and be by yourself. My wife and I are busy at many conferences, and we have had to cut down on the number of them in order to get some quietness and rest. When we get home from a series of conferences, we go nowhere but just outside on our patio. I tell my wife, "Come on out here, and let's sit down together and get acquainted with each other. I've been married to you a long time, and it's time I was getting acquainted with you." It's a good thing for us to do. God wants us to have times like that. They are very important for our spiritual refreshment.

**A wise servant shall have rule over a son that causeth shame, and shall have part of the inheritance among the brethren [Prov. 17:2].**

A servant who is faithful is better than a son who is not faithful. It is better to have a servant in whom you can have confidence than a son you cannot trust.

I think here of Abraham and his faithful servant Eliezer, and of David and his son Absalom. Abraham told the Lord that Eliezer was his only heir and that he wanted a son (Gen. 15:2). He felt it was much better to have a son, and God answered his request. But if the son is not dependable, if he is going to be like David's son Absalom, who openly rebelled against him, then certainly it is much better to have a good, faithful servant. And David had a number of faithful men who stayed right with him.

**The fining pot is for silver, and the furnace for gold: but the LORD trieth the hearts [Prov. 17:3].**

To get pure silver, the mined ore must be put into the fining pot and heated until it melts so that the dross can be removed and the pure metal remain. The same thing applies to gold; it is put in the furnace, and the dross is drawn off. And the Lord puts His servants into the fire so that He can develop something in them. He tries our hearts in order to strengthen us. He wants to produce better sons and daughters for His use.

We are more precious to God than gold or silver. Therefore, we should not be discouraged when we are tested. "Wherein ye greatly rejoice, though now for a season, if need be, ye are in heaviness through manifold temptations: That the trial of your faith, being much more precious than of gold that perisheth, though it be tried with fire, might be found unto praise and honour and glory at the appearing of Jesus Christ" (1 Pet. 1:6–7). God uses this method.

God had a purpose in allowing Job to go through the furnace of affliction. God had a purpose in giving Paul a thorn in the flesh. God had a purpose in permitting the period of martyrdom that came to the church. Persecution actually molded the church, and it has never been as rich spiritually as it was during that period.

I think one of the problems among Christians today is our affluence. This was one of the problems in Israel. Moses described it in Deuteronomy 32:15: "But Jeshurun waxed fat, and kicked: thou art waxen fat, thou art grown thick, thou art covered with fatness; then he forsook God which made him, and lightly esteemed the Rock of his salvation." I'm afraid we may have a lot of fat saints today. They have everything, and yet they become complainers, faultfinders, critics. They really are no help to the cause of Christ. So God must put the saints that He is going to use into the furnace in order that He might develop them for His use.

I received a letter from a lady who prayed that she might know the Lord Jesus better, that she might grow in grace and the knowledge of Him. What did the Lord do? He gave her cancer. Someone may say, "That's no way for God to do." But that is the way He sometimes does it, friend. You are listening to a preacher who knows all about it. I know why God gave me cancer. One mean letter sent to my wife and me said that God gave us cancer because we won't obey God and we're ignorant, and because of the kind of folk we are. Well, some of that may be true. But He didn't do it in a mean spirit, the way the letter was written. He did not do it because He hates us or because He is mean. God did it in a loving way, and you don't know how precious He has become to us because of it.

**Children's children are the crown of old men; and the glory of children are their fathers [Prov. 17:6].**

Here is a verse I am sure many of you can appreciate. "Children's children" are grandchildren. It is a verse for grandfathers. "The glory of children are their fathers." Children look to their fathers. I have always been grateful for a daughter who has loved and respected her father. We have always been able to communicate, even though she has the same kind of temper that I have—a short fuse. Every now and then we have a blowup, but then I go to her or sometimes she comes to me. We don't even let the sun go down on our disagreement. But "children's children are the crown of old men." The proverb is right. Now I am an old man with grandsons, and I could bore you to tears talking about them. Perhaps you have heard of one old man saying to another old man, "Have I ever told you about my grandson and shown you pictures of him?" The other man replied, "No, you haven't, and I want to thank you for it!" If I had known how wonderful grandchildren can be, I would have had them before I had my children! They are a pride and joy to have around, and they draw families together. The child looks to the father, but the grandfather looks back to the grandchild; that is where his affection centers.

**A reproof entereth more into a wise man than an hundred stripes into a fool [Prov. 17:10].**

Somebody says, "You know, poor Mr. So-and-So, he's a wonderful child of God, and look at the trouble he has had!" God reproves his saints, sometimes by sending trouble into their lives. God is coaching them, because they are wise men. The wise man will listen to reproof.

The fool won't listen to reproof. Even if God laid an hundred stripes on his back, it wouldn't do him any good. When you see someone prospering who is ungodly, the reason may be that he is such a fool that no matter what God would do to him, he would not change. The Lord Jesus told about the man who took down his old barns to build new barns for his crops. He was prosperous and was expanding his business. There is nothing wrong with building a new barn. The thing wrong was that the man was a fool. *I* didn't say that—*Jesus* said it. He was a fool because he did nothing about eternity. The chastening of the Lord would not have changed him. During the great tribulation the world will go through such intense suffering and judgment that people will gnaw their own tongue. But do you think they will turn to God? No. An hundred stripes will not do any good when they are applied to a fool.

This leads me to repeat that I believe we have a wrong philosophy about prisons today. A prison is not for the purpose of developing men and putting them back into society. There may be some place for that, but a prison is primarily a place of punishment, not an institution for discipline. Discipline is for a child—your own child. Punishment is for the one who has committed a crime.

**Wherefore is there a price in the hand of a fool to get wisdom, seeing he hath no heart to it? [Prov. 17:16].**

I have known a lot of boys from wealthy families who had no heart for college at all. They shouldn't have been in college. It wasn't that they were not able to pass the courses, but they didn't want to go to college in the first place. Their hearts were not in it.

I do not agree with the philosophy that every person should have a college education. I think that every person should have access to a college education, but I do not think that young folks should be forced to go to college. A lot of young people don't have a capacity for it, nor do they have the heart for it. This has nothing to do with being rich or poor. It involves the desire to learn. I believe that every poor boy who really wants to learn should have the opportunity. The door ought to be opened for him. On the other hand, there are a lot of rich boys who should not be in college at all. I was a poor boy, and I thank God for a wonderful Christian elder who took an interest in me. If it hadn't been for that man, I could never have gone to college. I thank God for opening the door to college for this poor boy.

**A friend loveth at all times, and a brother is born for adversity [Prov. 17:17].**

This verse reminds us of Jonathan who was such a wonderful friend to David. "A friend loveth at *all* times." Jonathan loved David when he was playing his music in the palace as well as when he was hiding for his life, trying to escape King Saul. Although Jonathan was the son of Saul and heir to the throne, he loved David.

It is a wonderful thing to have a friend like that. If someone doesn't love you at *all* times, that person is not your friend. It is one of the disappointments of life to have someone profess to love you and be your friend, then when the chips are down, you find that he really does not love you after all. He was a Judas Iscariot or an Absalom, who betrayed you.

**He that begetteth a fool doeth it to his sorrow: and the father of a fool hath no joy [Prov. 17:21].**

This has been repeated several times in Proverbs. The father of a son who is making good is a father full of joy. He will talk constantly about his boy. If he has a son who is not doing well, he becomes very silent, and no one hears about the boy.

**A merry heart doeth good like a medicine: but a broken spirit drieth the bones [Prov. 17:22].**

There are a lot of folk today who are actually sick with a heart sickness. It is not heart trouble. It is a heart sickness, a lack of joy. They live down in Mudville. They are the mighty Casey who struck out at bat. This description applies to many Christians.

God wants us to have a merry heart. He wants us to have a big time! Our fellowship at church should be a place of fun. We should laugh and rejoice and praise God when we go to church. We are simply too stiff and stilted in our churches.

**A wicked man taketh a gift out of the bosom to pervert the ways of judgment [Prov. 17:23].**

There are many different ways of bribing, and there is so much bribing going on in our world today.

**Even a fool, when he holdeth his peace, is counted wise: and he that shutteth his lips is esteemed a man of understanding [Prov. 17:28].**

This proverb has humor in it. It says that it pays to keep your mouth shut.

An Arkansas farmer had a son who was simple. Folks would say he was "not all there." They drove into town with a load of apples, and the father left the son to sit and hold the reins of the horses while he went off on an errand. "Now, son," said the father, "don't you say anything to anybody because if you do, they will find out you are a fool." The boy promised he wouldn't open his mouth. A man came up to the wagon and asked, "How much are your apples, son?" The boy never said a word. The man asked two or three times, but the boy just sat there and looked at him. Finally the man said, "What in the world is wrong? You act like a fool." Then he walked away. When the father returned, he asked the boy, "How did things go?" The boy answered, "I kept my mouth shut, but they found out I was a fool anyway."

# CHAPTER 18

Our young man who has entered the school of wisdom is progressing. I hope the rest of us are coming along with him and are learning the spiritual truths that are in these proverbs.

**Through desire a man, having separated himself, seeketh and intermeddleth with all wisdom [Prov. 18:1].**

Let me give a translation which I think will be helpful: "A man having separated himself for his own pleasure rageth against all sound wisdom." The important thing here is the subject of separation, and this is the wrong kind of separation.

The great division in the human family is between saved people and lost people. That is the division that God sees. He does not make divisions like we do into categories of black, white, yellow, or red. God is really "colorblind." Now the Bible does teach a separation of the saved people from the lost people: "Wherefore come out from among them, and be ye separate, saith the Lord, and touch not the unclean thing; and I will receive you" (2 Cor. 6:17). God makes it very clear that His people are to separate themselves from that which is unclean. He is referring particularly to the idolatry, the immorality, and the filthy conversation of the unsaved. There should be a separation from that. By the way, this is real segregation: segregate yourself from the evil. That is important to do. There are many saved folk who emphasize separation. They form cliques and groups and practice the wrong kind of separation. They make up their own little commandments, which are not actually in the Bible. They follow them and feel that they should separate themselves from other believers, and they feel that this makes them very special people in the sight of the Lord. They think they are superior. Generally they are not. They manifest many evidences of the flesh working in their lives. That is a wrong kind of separation.

There is another group of strong separationists, and they are among the unsaved. We find that this is what is referred to in this proverb. This is the person who has separated himself for his own pleasure. He refuses to listen to anything that is wise. Jude speaks of them as being apostates and says this: "These be they who separate themselves, sensual, having not the Spirit" (Jude 19). They withdraw themselves from any group or individual who might reprimand them and begin their own little group and become very obnoxious.

Generally they are apostates: they separate themselves from the truth. They certainly cause a great deal of sorrow in this world.

**A fool hath no delight in understanding, but that his heart may discover itself [Prov. 18:2].**

A professor sent me a collection of modern proverbs. Some of them fit the proverbs we are studying from the Bible. This is one that possibly fits here: "If I stop to think before I speak, I won't have to worry afterward about what I said before." That certainly is true.

**When the wicked cometh, then cometh also contempt, and with ignominy reproach [Prov. 18:3].**

Another modern proverb is: "Some persons cause happiness wherever they go; others, *whenever* they go." I think that is a good one and would apply to the crowd mentioned in this verse. These are some people who also bring great sorrow into the world.

**The words of a man's mouth are as deep waters, and the wellspring of wisdom as a flowing brook [Prov. 18:4].**

Every true believer in the Lord Jesus Christ is indwelt by the Holy Spirit. The Lord Jesus stood in the temple when the water was poured out at the time of the Feast of Tabernacles and said, ". . . If any man thirst, let him come unto me, and drink. He that believeth on me, as the scripture hath said, out of his belly [inmost being] shall flow rivers of living water" (John 7:37–38). Then John interprets this for us. "(But this spake he of the Spirit, which they that believe on him should receive: for the Holy Ghost was not yet given; because that Jesus was not yet glorified.)" (John 7:39). The child of God should learn to speak in the power of the Holy Spirit. This is so important in presenting the Word of God and talking about the things of God.

**It is not good to accept the person of the wicked, to overthrow the righteous in judgment [Prov. 18:5].**

Do not compromise with an evil person or a lawless person in order to overthrow a righteous person. This applies to individuals. I believe it also applies to nations. I wonder if perhaps our nation has been guilty of compromising with wicked nations. We have interfered in too many places, and we have gotten ourselves into serious difficulties. These proverbs are practical, and they can be geared right into life.

**A fool's lips enter into contention, and his mouth calleth for strokes.**

**A fool's mouth is his destruction, and his lips are the snare of his soul.**

**The words of a talebearer are as wounds, and they go down into the innermost parts of the belly [Prov. 18: 6–8].**

"The words of a talebearer" or the words of a *whisperer* are as dainty morsels that go down into the depth of the soul. We are back again to the subject of the fool. Remember that the Lord Jesus has told *us* that we are not to call anyone a fool (see Matt. 5:22). However, God calls some people fools because He knows them.

We find again that the fool is a source of trouble. He is the one who is always stirring up contention, issuing complaints, finding fault.

We can give another fitting modern proverb: "Be considerate. Most people know how to express a complaint, but few utter a gracious compliment. The bee is seldom complimented for making honey; it is just criticized for stinging." How true!

**The name of the LORD is a strong tower: the righteous runneth into it, and is safe [Prov. 18:10].**

The name of Jehovah is also the name of the Lord Jesus Christ. He is called Jesus because He saves His people from their sins. And He is called Christ because He is the Anointed One. He is the Lord of our life and our salvation. The Lord is a strong tower. You can run into it and be completely safe. This is a verse that many have used in speaking to children, and I have used it myself and found it very effective. It speaks of security and reminds us that no one can pluck us out of His hands. What a beautiful picture this is!

**The rich man's wealth is his strong city, and as an high wall in his own conceit [Prov. 18:11].**

There are basic differences between Israel and the church which we need to recognize. Material wealth was one of the promises of God to His people Israel, but He did not promise that to us. God promised them a full basket, and He made good His word. He also said He would take away their wealth as a judgment. The church is not a continuation of Israel, even though that is sometimes preached today. The church is not the next grade above Judaism. You can make a comparison, of course, and there are many likenesses. The contrasts, however, are greater. The church has not been promised material blessings. God has blessed us as believers ". . . with all *spiritual* blessings in heavenly places in Christ" (Eph. 1:3, italics mine). The child of God needs to be fortified. He needs to get into the strong tower. He needs to be in this strong city and have the high wall around him. What is it? Well, it is a knowledge of the Word of God. We need to recognize that we are living in very difficult times and we are being tested. Oh, how important is a knowledge of the Word of God! My friend, don't try to substitute these little courses that teach you how to witness and how to get along with your wife. They may have a certain value, but they are only surface stuff. There is no substitute for digging into the Word of God. My friend, learn to read the Word of God. If you don't understand it, read it again. If you don't understand it the second time, go over it once more. Then if you don't understand it the third time through, something is wrong, and you need to go to the Lord and tell Him you're not getting it. Ask Him to help you. The spirit of God is our teacher. I know I am telling you this accurately because He hasn't yet let me down in this matter of understanding His Word.

**He that answereth a matter before he heareth it, it is folly and shame unto him [Prov. 18:13].**

How often people try to pass judgment on someone else when they don't really know the person or the problem or the situation under which that person lives. How important it is to have all the facts before we express an opinion!

**The spirit of a man will sustain his infirmity; but a wounded spirit who can bear? [Prov. 18:14].**

You can break your leg and recover from that; but, if your spirit is broken, you are completely broken. Only God can encourage you at a time like that. Remember at the time of Nehemiah's governorship over the people of Israel, and even after they had rebuilt the walls, they still had not heard the Word of God. When the Word of God was read to them, they saw how far they were from God and they began to weep. Nehemiah told them not to weep because it was a time of rejoicing.

He said, ". . . the joy of the LORD is your strength" (Neh. 8:10). How important it is for us to know that the joy of the Lord is our strength. Sitting in the pastor's study of a church in Salem, Oregon, I noticed this little motto (it's a contemporary proverb) on the wall: "*Joy* is the flag that is flown in the heart when the Master is in residence." I like that. When the Lord Jesus Christ becomes first choice in your life, when He has top priority, then you will not have that broken spirit that we hear so much about today. Give God the first choice. Give of your time, your effort, your thoughts, your companionship, and your money, and see what happens. Have you tried that?

**A man's gift maketh room for him, and bringeth him before great men [Prov. 18:16].**

I hope you will nail this one down. Some critics have compared this verse with Proverbs 25:14 and have pointed it out as an apparent contradiction in the Bible; however, when we get to that chapter, we will find out that it is a contrast and not a contradiction at all.

This verse speaks of gifts, and as I have mentioned before, I believe every believer in Christ has a gift. *Gifts of the Spirit* is a message we have in print that develops this subject.

**Death and life are in the power of the tongue: and they that love it shall eat the fruit thereof [Prov. 18:21].**

"Death and life are in the power of the tongue"—think of that! Your tongue can be used to give out the gospel, and this will give life. It can also be used to say things that would drive people away from God, which makes it an instrument of death. The little tongue is the most potent weapon in this world. The Bible has much to say about the tongue, and we find a lot about it in the Book of Proverbs.

**Whoso findeth a wife findeth a good thing, and obtaineth favour of the LORD [Prov. 18:22].**

I have actually laughed at the thought that these two verses are side by side in the Word of God. The spirit of God put them together. The tongue is used when the fellow proposes to the girl. He asks her to marry him, and that is the proper way for it to be done; and death and life are in the power of the tongue. You may wish you had bitten off your tongue before you asked the fatal question. It's like the story of the old bachelor who had never met a woman whom he wanted to marry because he thought they all talked too much. He found what we used to call an old maid, one who seemed very quiet. He fell in love with her and asked her to marry him. The minute she accepted the proposal, she started talking. She talked about where they would go and how they would fix their house and on and on. Suddenly after an hour or so she realized that she was doing all the talking and that he was quiet. "Why don't you say something?" she asked. He answered, "I've said too much already!"

"Whoso findeth a wife findeth a good thing, and obtaineth favour of the LORD." I want to say that I have always thanked the Lord for my wife. It is wonderful to have a good wife—and to have someone who is able to put up with me!

**A man that hath friends must shew himself friendly: and there is a friend that sticketh closer than a brother [Prov. 18:24].**

If you want to have friends, then show yourself friendly. By the way, are you a friend to your friends?

"There is a friend that sticketh closer than a brother." Do you know who He is? He is closer to you than a brother can be. Jesus is the One, and He says, "Ye are my friends, if ye do whatsoever I command you" (John 15:14). When I hear folk singing "Jesus is a Friend of Mine," I want to go up to them and ask, "Are you obeying His commands?" Jesus says, "Ye are my friends, if ye do whatsoever I command you." If you are not obeying Him, I take it that you're not one of His friends.

Jesus is a friend who will stick closer than a brother. He is our Savior. He loved us enough to die for us. He is the one who says, ". . . lo, I am with you alway, even unto the end of the world . . ." (Matt. 28:20) and ". . . I will never leave thee, nor forsake thee" (Heb. 13:5). Also He has given us this promise: "And if I go and prepare a place for you, I will come again, and receive you unto myself; that where I am, there ye may be also" (John 14:3). There isn't anything you can do to improve such an arrangement. We have a wonderful Friend who sticks closer than any brother.

# CHAPTER 19

**Better is the poor that walketh in his integrity, than he that is perverse in his lips, and is a fool [Prov. 19:1].**

The Lord has forbidden *us* to call anyone a fool, but the spirit of God has really been using that word. Apparently there are quite a few fools in the human family.

**Also, that the soul be without knowledge, it is not good; and he that hasteth with his feet sinneth.**

**The foolishness of man perverteth his way: and his heart fretteth against the LORD [Prov. 19:2–3].**

There is an antithetic parallelism all through these proverbs. Here is a contrast between those who are the children of God and those who are not. The one is in the path of truth; the other, who is in the path of self-will and ignorance, God calls a fool.

We have a modern proverb: "Where ignorance is bliss, 'tis folly to be wise." This is a false proverb. Sometimes people—even officers of the church—pride themselves on being ignorant of the Bible. In board meetings I have heard church officers speak out saying, "Well, that is theological; that is biblical, and I don't know much about that." I had to bite my lip from saying, *Why in the world don't you know it? You are a mature man, an officer in the church, and you should not be that devoid of spiritual understanding!*

Someone sent me this proverb: "No man is uneducated who knows the Bible, and no one is truly educated who is ignorant of its teachings." Although the world does not accept this, I believe it is true. I do not think a man can be truly educated if he is ignorant of the Bible. Certainly one cannot be a mature Christian and be ignorant of the Bible. A knowledge of the Word of God should be a characteristic of the child of God.

**Wealth maketh many friends; but the poor is separated from his neighbour [Prov. 19:4].**

Wealthy people seem to have a lot of friends. Their houses are full of guests so long as the refrigerator is filled and the bar is well stocked and there is music and entertainment.

It is interesting to note that the Word of God admonishes the child of God to seek out the poor man. You will remember that James, in a practical way, speaks of a man who comes into your assembly ". . . with a gold ring, in goodly apparel, and there come in also a poor man in vile raiment; And ye have respect to him that weareth the gay clothing, and say unto him, Sit thou here in a good place; and say to the poor, Stand thou there, or sit here under my footstool" (James 2:2–3).

Unfortunately, it is true that the poor man has his problems in many of our churches. A couple was telling me about their personal experience. They are poor and not able to buy the latest in style, and what they wear looks pretty worn. They went to a church that has a reputation of being a very conservative, evangelical church. My, they were snubbed. What happened to them is terrible!

Human nature has not changed down through the centuries. The old nature is still being revealed. My mother used to ask me before she went out, "Is my petticoat showing?" Now my wife asks me the same thing. There are a lot of folk who are stepping out, going to church, and moving in the society of their particular group whose *old nature* is showing. And it shows in matters like separating the poor from their society. God lays it on the line, doesn't He? "The poor is separated from his neighbour." When they find out you are a poor boy, they don't want you around.

**A false witness shall not be unpunished, and he that speaketh lies shall not escape [Prov. 19:5].**

Drop down to verse 9 and see that it is almost the same statement. "A false witness shall not be unpunished, and he that speaketh lies shall perish". A false witness is not going to "escape." He will be found out. He will be called to account for what he has said. Not only that, he is going to "perish." God tells us that in Revelation 21:8.

We think of Ahab and Jezebel in connection with the episode of Naboth's vineyard. The record is in 1 Kings 21 and 22. Because Naboth would not give up his vineyard to the king, arrangements were made to have false witnesses bring an untrue charge against him and then stone him to death. Ahab thought he got by with this crime, but Elijah met him and

told him that where Naboth's innocent blood had been shed, the dogs would lick *his* blood. What happened was this: Ahab went into battle against Syria, with Jehoshaphat in alliance with him. He put Jehoshaphat out in front wearing his royal robes, but Ahab disguised himself as a common soldier to escape notice. But a trigger happy soldier on the enemy side "drew a bow at a venture"—he didn't even know who he was aiming at, but that old arrow had Ahab's name on it. When it went out from the bow with a *zing* it said, "Ahab, where are you? I'm looking for you." And it found him. He bled like a stuck pig, and he died. The blood ran out of the wound in the chariot, "And one washed the chariot in the pool of Samaria; and the dogs licked up his blood; and they washed his armour; according unto the word of the LORD which he spake" (1 Kings 22:38). You say that is crude and frightful. I agree. But, my friend, lying, false witnessing, and gossip in God's sight are really frightful, and God hates them. "A false witness shall not be unpunished, and he that speaketh lies shall not escape."

**Many will entreat the favour of the prince: and every man is a friend to him that giveth gifts [Prov. 19:6].**

"Many will entreat the favour of the prince"—we don't have a prince, but we write letters to our congressmen and our governor, and sometimes even to our president when we want legislation passed.

"Every man is a friend to him that giveth gifts." That is certainly true. A man will have plenty of friends as long as he is giving out gifts.

**All the brethren of the poor do hate him: how much more do his friends go far from him? he pursueth them with words, yet they are wanting to him [Prov. 19:7].**

The brethren of the poor may not hate him as we think of hateful behavior. Often they just don't have anything to do with him. They ignore him. A prosperous man may see his ne'er-do-well brother drive up in an old jalopy, so he says to his wife, "Let's get into the bedroom and lock the door and make him think that we're not home." That is what it means to hate your brother. The poor don't do very well in this world, by the way.

We hear so much from the people who campaign for office about how they are going to help us poor folk. The only thing they ever help me with is more taxes. Every time we have an election my taxes go up. Every politician promises to give us some relief. No one has yet, and I don't think anyone will. My feeling is that the problems have mounted so that no *man* can solve them. No man, I don't care who he is, is able to solve the problems of the world today.

Do you know what we need? We need politicians to call us back to God. We need someone to say, "Look, I don't have the answer to the world's problems. Let's turn to God for the answer. Let's serve Him, let's pray to Him." Since we have tried everything else to solve our problems, wouldn't it be well for us to try God for a change? It would be far better for us to listen to God than to listen to so much television. We have heard everybody else and all their opinions on the talk shows. They have strutted across the stage of human events, and it hasn't been very impressive. We need to turn to God and listen to Him.

**A foolish son is the calamity of his father: and the contentions of a wife are a continual dropping [Prov. 19:13].**

Our last proverb about this matter said that when a man finds a wife, he has found a good thing. That is, he finds the other half of him, and she is to be a helpmeet for him. She is not to be a servant. Where do people get the idea that the wife is to obey the husband? The wife is to submit herself to her husband provided he is the right kind of man. If he is not, I don't think God has asked her to submit herself. The only instructions I find about submission apply to the Christian home. A wife is to submit to a Christian husband who loves her just like Christ loves the church. When a woman has that kind of husband, she can submit herself to him.

This proverb almost makes one laugh even though it tells of a tragic situation. Think of the poor husband who has a foolish son and also has a wife who is contentious. You can imagine what kind of a home he lives in. That is why it is so wonderful to find the right kind of a wife.

**House and riches are the inheritance of fathers: and a prudent wife is from the LORD [Prov. 19:14].**

If you have a good wife, you got her from the Lord. You ought to thank the Lord for her, by the way. Have you ever done that? Thank the Lord for your good wife, because He is the One who gave her to you.

Young men, this should tell you something. Do you want a good wife? The one who gives away good wives is not the father of the daughter. Many a father is glad to get rid of his daughter. But our Heavenly Father has a lot of good wives to give away. Keep in touch with Him, and He will lead you to the right one. He wants to give you the right kind of wife. This is a very practical proverb. Don't you agree?

**Chasten thy son while there is hope, and let not thy soul spare for his crying [Prov. 19:18].**

Start with your discipline when the children are young. Don't wait until it is too late. A man who was saved later in life told me, "My wife and I were saved recently, and we are thanking God for it, but we have lost our children. We used to live like the devil, and we can see that in our children today." They had waited until too late to give their children the proper training.

Start when the children are young. Don't mind if little Willie cries when you paddle him. On the other hand, every father needs to be very careful in the way he deals with his child. No one has the right to be brutal in his dealings with his children. Dr. Ironside has translated the proverb this way: "Chasten thy son while there is hope, but set not thy soul upon slaying him." Don't be afraid to discipline, but a brutal punishment is not to be permitted. Brutality can only tear down the child and destroy his spirit. As a matter of fact, even the law of the land can, and should, step in whenever there is brutality to children.

God has given very definite commands for Christians. He tells children to obey their parents (Eph. 6:1). But then he says to the fathers, "And, ye fathers, provoke not your children to wrath . . ." (Eph. 6:4). Don't wade into them when you are angry. They know you are angry and that you are just venting your anger and frustration. At that time you will probably punish too hard—in fact, you can be brutal. The command is to bring them up in the ". . . nurture and admonition of the Lord" (Eph. 6:4), that is, the discipline and the instruction of the Lord.

**There are many devices in a man's heart; nevertheless the counsel of the LORD, that shall stand [Prov. 19:21].**

Man can come up with many explanations, many solutions, but God is the only One who can give you the right kind of advice. Many can make a computer, but only God can put sense into it.

**The desire of a man is his kindness: and a poor man is better than a liar [Prov. 19:22].**

This is a strange proverb, isn't it? "The desire [or charm] of a man is his kindness." How many folk do you know like that? They are kind, generous, lovely people. Then we are brought back to the poor man, the poor relative, who comes for dinner and stays for a couple of years to live with you. Well, it is better to have him than to have a liar.

**The fear of the LORD tendeth to life: and he that hath it shall abide satisfied; he shall not be visited with evil [Prov. 19:23].**

The fear of the Lord does not mean that you are cringing, constantly in dread, living a life of terror. This proverb makes it clear that the real fear of God means that you can rest satisfied. It means that you recognize Him, you have looked to Him, you have accepted Him, and you want to follow Him. Now you can rest satisfied.

**A slothful man hideth his hand in his bosom, and will not so much as bring it to his mouth again [Prov. 19:24].**

An alternate translation is: "A slothful man burieth his hand in the dish." Here is another proverb that is humorous. This man is so lazy that he can put his hand down into the dish to eat, but he is too lazy to bring it back up to his mouth. When you get to that place, you're lazy! Unfortunately, we often see this in the spiritual realm. The Word of God is our food. I know Christians who will hold the Bible in their hands but are too lazy to read it.

**Judgments are prepared for scorners, and stripes for the back of fools [Prov. 19:29].**

Judgment is coming—that is quite obvious. God is not soft on the guilty. The pleasures of sin are for a season, but the wages of sin last for all eternity.

# CHAPTER 20

We are still in this long section which sets before us the wisdom of Solomon. It is specifically directed to young men but actually applies to every Christian. In fact, the unbelievers can learn a great deal from these proverbs. The reading and study of the Word of God will have a definite effect upon the life of anyone. It will either bring you to God or it will drive you from Him. Your reaction to the Word of God cannot be neutral.

This is the first time there is a warning concerning alcohol or booze—I like the word *booze* because it has all the connotation of the evil that liquor has done down through the ages. I suppose that alcohol has wrecked more nations, more businesses, more homes, more individual lives than any other single factor.

**Wine is a mocker, strong drink is raging: and whosoever is deceived thereby is not wise [Prov. 20:1].**

There has always been a controversy about the "wine" in the New Testament being an intoxicant. It is my firm conviction that the Lord Jesus did not make an intoxicating drink at the wedding in Cana of Galilee (see John 2).

Anyone who attempts to make of Him a bootlegger is ridiculous and is doing absolutely an injustice. Folk like to present the argument that in the warm climate of Israel all one had to do was to put grape juice in a wine skin and in time it would ferment. Yes, but in the miracle at Cana, the Lord Jesus started out with *water*, and in the matter of a few seconds He had "wine." My friend, it didn't have a chance to ferment. And we must remember that the wedding in Cana was a religious service, and everything that had to do with leaven (which is fermentation) was forbidden. This is the reason that at the time of the Passover and the institution of the Lord's Supper the wine could not have been fermented. Fermentation is the working of leaven, and leaven was strictly forbidden in bread and in everything else. The bread and drink could not have been leavened. Intoxicants are condemned in the Word of God, and here is a verse for it: "Wine is a mocker, strong drink is raging: and whosoever is deceived thereby is not wise."

Today many folk are being trapped by this type of thing. America is becoming a nation of drunkards. I am not impressed when the news media lets us know the tremendous amount of taxes that comes from the liquor industry. What they forget to tell is the cost of the hospitals, the mental institutions and the accidents—the people who have been maimed for life—as a result of drinking drivers. That kind of cost is not reported. I understand that any derogatory news is supressed because one of the biggest advertisers is the booze industry. We hear about how bad drug abuse is today; but remember, alcohol is a drug!

A law enforcement officer told me that at the beginning of the drug craze the liquor interests helped to fight the drug traffic, because they were afraid it would hurt their business. They would much rather have a kid become a drunkard addicted to alcohol than to have him become a drug addict. That is really generous and big-hearted of the liquor industry, don't you agree? However, young people began making comparisons. I have had young folk in youth groups tell me they don't feel they should be reprimanded for smoking marijuana by a crowd that sits around drinking cocktails. And I agree with the young folk. Let the adults stop drinking liquor before they talk to our young people about the evils of marijuana. The hypocrisy of those outside the church is lots worse than the hypocrisy inside the church!

Drunkenness was the undoing of Noah, and it has been a problem from that day to the present hour. Alcohol is valuable for medicinal purposes, but the minute it is used as a beverage it becomes dangerous. The number of alcoholics is increasing every year. It is one of the greatest tax burdens we have to bear. But you don't learn of that through the news media. In fact, it is dangerous to lift your head against this hydra-headed monster. I predict that it will not be missiles but liquor that will destroy our nation.

**It is an honour for a man to cease from strife: but every fool will be meddling [Prov. 20:3].**

One of the marks of a Christian should be that he does not prolong tension and strife. Someone has said that the only persons we should try to "get even with" are the people who have helped us. In other words, repay good with good. But don't try to get even with your enemies. Do not respond with evil for evil. Instead, be yielded to God, for God has said, ". . . Vengeance is mine; I will repay, saith the Lord" (Rom. 12:19). It is on that basis that God tells us not to avenge ourselves. It is actually a departure from the pathway of faith

to attempt to take matters into our own hands. God can do it lots better than we can.

The child of God should remember what Paul said to the Philippian believers: "Let your moderation be known unto all men. The Lord is at hand" (Phil. 4:5). Matthew Arnold translated *moderation* as "sweet reasonableness." "Let your sweet reasonableness be known unto all men." That is the meaning of the proverb—"It is an honour for a man to cease from strife." How important it is!

**The sluggard will not plow by reason of the cold; therefore shall he beg in harvest, and have nothing [Prov. 20:4].**

Israel has a moderate climate, and winter is the season for preparing the soil for the spring planting. The sluggard, the lazy oaf, would say it was too cold, so he would stay by the fire. He would say he'll wait until it gets warmer. The problem would be that when it got warmer it was already too late to plow. That would be the time to be doing the planting. There is a note of humor in this verse.

It reminds me of the man whose house had a leaky roof. The reason he didn't fix it was because he didn't want to work on it when it was raining, and when it wasn't raining it didn't need fixing.

We come now to a set of proverbs that at first seem totally unrelated. However, there does appear to be a relationship based on words that speak of goodness or moral principles.

**Most men will proclaim every one his own goodness: but a faithful man who can find? [Prov. 20:6].**

The theme here is "goodness."

**The just man walketh in his integrity: his children are blessed after him [Prov. 20:7].**

The word here is "integrity."

**A king that sitteth in the throne of judgment scattereth away all evil with his eyes [Prov. 20:8].**

"Scattering away all evil" is cleaning up his kingdom.

**Who can say, I have made my heart clean, I am pure from my sin? [Prov. 20:9].**

The words here are "clean" and "pure."

**Divers weights, and divers measures, both of them are alike abomination to the Lord [Prov. 20:10].**

Falseness is contrasted to goodness.

**Even a child is known by his doings, whether his work be pure, and whether it be right [Prov. 20:11].**

The emphasis here is upon goodness even in children.

**The hearing ear, and the seeing eye, the LORD hath made even both of them [Prov. 20:12].**

The thought here is to use your head. God has given you ears, and He has given you eyes. Look and listen—that is not only good advice before you cross a railroad track, it is good when you are facing life every day.

All the way through this group of proverbs we see two great principles. First of all, "Who can say, I have made my heart clean, I am pure from my sin?" Well, can you, my friend? I am sure that neither you nor I can say that. No man by his own efforts can claim to be pure. Even the little baby in the crib cannot claim that. Those little ones reveal temper while they are still infants. At first my little grandson seemed to me to be free from sin. He was so wonderful! Then I found that he had a temper—he would get red in the face and even hold his breath! I had to realize that he was subject to the total depravity of man like the rest of us. Of course I told my wife, "I believe he's beginning to show some of the characteristics of his grandmother!" No man in his natural state can say, "I have made my heart clean, I am pure from my sin." My friend, if you would be heaven *bound*, you must first be heaven *born*. ". . . Verily, verily, I say unto thee, Except a man be born again, he cannot see the kingdom of God" (John 3:3). The Lord Jesus said that to a religious man, a good man. No man can call himself good or pure or right or clean until he has come to Christ for salvation and been clothed in the righteousness of Christ. Then he is accepted in the Beloved. But there is still that old nature that will stay with us until we enter into glory.

But notice from the proverbs that goodness does count, integrity does matter to God. Purity is worth something. A child of God should be walking in a way which commends the gospel of the grace of God.

Here is a good question which I have heard asked for many years: If you were arrested for being a Christian, would there be enough evidence to convict you? Suppose you were brought before a court on the accusation, "This fellow is a Christian." Would there be enough evidence there to convict you? Or would you be able to get off free? Would they look at your life and find you are not living like a Christian should? Would they find you do not walk in integrity? Would they find no goodness, no desire for purity?

The second thought in these proverbs is this: God has given you eyes to see and ears to hear. Use them. Stop, look, listen. Don't go blindly through life, seeing but not seeing. Use your eyes. Open your ears. God has given you a certain amount of common sense, a certain amount of "gumption." Listen to the news God has for you. You cannot make yourself pure. Only God can make you pure. God can give you a standing before Him that removes all the guilt of your sin and enables you to walk in integrity in this world.

**Love not sleep, lest thou come to poverty; open thine eyes, and thou shalt be satisfied with bread [Prov. 20:13].**

He is saying, "Go to work." You will remember this is the same thing that Paul wrote to the Thessalonians. He said that if a man doesn't want to work, neither should he eat (see 2 Thess. 3:10). Those people were so excited about the possibility of the Lord's return that they were just waiting for the Lord. It is wonderful to be looking for Him and waiting for Him. But that doesn't mean that just sitting down and gazing into space is the way to wait for Him. A true anticipation of the coming of the Lord will cause a person to put his nose to the grindstone and work harder than ever before.

**It is nought, it is nought, saith the buyer: but when he is gone his way, then he boasteth [Prov. 20:14].**

This is a humorous one, and I hope you can see the humor in it. A fellow goes in to buy an automobile, for example. He says to the man who is selling it, "I don't think this car is worth buying. The tires are almost worn out. The motor doesn't sound too good. There's a rattle back there. But I'll give you so much for it." The owner says, "All right, I'll sell it for that." The buyer says, "Well, I don't think it's really worth that, but I'll take the car." He gets in the car and drives it home and calls out his wife and the neighbors, "Look what a bargain I got!" That is human nature, isn't it?

**There is gold, and a multitude of rubies: but the lips of knowledge are a precious jewel [Prov. 20:15].**

Our sense of values is all wrong today. Man is measured by material things, rather than by the knowledge he has.

**Take his garment that is surety for a stranger: and take a pledge of him for a strange woman [Prov. 20:16].**

When you deal with certain people, you had better have them put up a little collateral. If you don't, you are sure to be taken in.

**Bread of deceit is sweet to a man; but afterwards his mouth shall be filled with gravel [Prov. 20:17].**

A person may think he is getting by with deceit, and it may seem sweet to him. No one gets by with a thing—God will see to that.

**He that goeth about as a talebearer revealeth secrets: therefore meddle not with him that flattereth with his lips [Prov. 20:19].**

The man who flatters you to your face and then goes off and gossips about you is the man you had better keep your eye on—even if he is a deacon in the church.

**Whoso curseth his father or his mother, his lamp shall be put out in obscure darkness [Prov. 20:20].**

If you have a father and a mother of whom you can boast, then boast of them. If you cannot say something good about them—and a lot of folk can't—then don't say anything. That is what this proverb is saying.

This is where Ham made his mistake. Noah, his father, got drunk, and Ham exposed his father. He should have kept silence. There are certain things that you just don't run around telling everyone.

**Man's goings are of the LORD; how can a man then understand his own way? [Prov. 20:24].**

How can a man understand his own way? We have never passed this way before—only the spirit of God can lead us. God told Moses that he needed Him to lead him. And you and I need His leading also.

**It is a snare to the man who devoureth that which is holy, and after vows to make inquiry [Prov. 20:25].**

Don't make a vow until you are sure of what you can do. Don't publicly dedicate your life to God until you have thought it through. God doesn't want that kind of a sentimental decision. I'm afraid there is too much of that today.

**The spirit of man is the candle of the LORD, searching all the inward parts of the belly [Prov. 20:27].**

"The spirit of man is the candle [or lamp] of the LORD [Jehovah]." Notice it is called the candle or lamp of Jehovah, not the *light* of Jehovah. The spirit of man is only the lamp, the vessel that holds the light. Man is just a lamp, and until we are filled by the Holy Spirit, we don't become a light. Remember the parable of the ten virgins. Five of them were wise, and five were foolish. They were just lamps. Without the oil, they could not have light.

**The glory of young men is their strength: and the beauty of old men is the grey head [Prov. 20:29].**

This proverb is saying, "Act your age." The young man is the one to be the athlete. The old man had better not try to act young. He will just make a fool of himself. He had better act his age. He should reveal a little wisdom, because that is what gray hair should indicate.

# CHAPTER 21

This is one of the great chapters in the Book of Proverbs.

**The king's heart is in the hand of the LORD, as the rivers of water: he turneth it whithersoever he will [Prov. 21:1].**

A man may be a pharaoh in Egypt, a king of Babylon, a caesar of Rome, an Alexander the Great, a Napoleon, a Joe Stalin, an Adolph Hitler, or any great ruler of the future. Regardless of how powerful a man may become politically, it can be stated as an axiom that no man can act in independence of God. Many of these rulers thought they could, and men today may still think they can. But the truth is that no man is free from God. No man can act independently. We have a Declaration of Independence in this country. Right now it is being used to declare our independence from God. We believe in liberty; so we've declared we are free from God! However, we are not free from God. We cannot act independently. "The king's heart is in the hand of the LORD," and God is going to turn him just as He turns the course of a little babbling brook that runs down a mountainside. "As the rivers of water: he turneth it whithersoever he will." No king nor ruler nor any individual can act independently of God.

I wish we had more men in public office who express a dependence upon God and *show* it in their lives. I wish they would quit telling us that *they* have the solution for all the problems of the world. They haven't. It is a misrepresentation for any man to say that. No man is independent of Almighty God, and we need to recognize our dependence upon Him. Oh, may this country be called back to a dependence upon God before it is too late. We need a new declaration, but this time it should be a declaration of *dependence* upon Almighty God. The only way such a change can come about is by the people of this nation returning to the Word of God. That is why it is so important for us to proclaim God's Word.

**Every way of a man is right in his own eyes: but the LORD pondereth the hearts [Prov. 21:2].**

Here again is this matter of man's self-righteousness. Man rationalizes, but God scrutinizes. God looks at the heart. We attempt to paint up the surface so that we have the outside looking nice. We boast, "I'm a member of a church. I teach a class and serve on a committee. I'm always busy working for the church." That may all be true, but God "pondereth the hearts." The prophet Jeremiah pointed out that "The heart is deceitful above all things, and desperately wicked: who can know it?" (Jer. 17:9). Have you gone to the Lord Jesus and spoken to Him about your desperate condition? He is the Great Physician, and He is the heart specialist. He gives you a *new* heart. He was the first One who went into this business of heart transplants. He will give you a heart that can be obedient to Him.

**To do justice and judgment is more acceptable to the LORD than sacrifice [Prov. 21:3].**

Here we have the tremendous truth stated for us again that there is no value in simply going through a religious ritual. Remember that the Old Testament sacrifices were given because they pointed to Jesus Christ. No one was more faithful about going through those rituals than the Pharisees, the religious rulers of Jesus' day. But He denounced them in withering language. He blanched them. He scorched them. He told them they looked like beautiful monuments on the outside but inside were full of dead men's bones. Why? Because sacrifices and offerings were not pleasing to the Lord when righteousness was lacking. He said He wanted mercy, not sacrifice.

Religious ritual can suggest that you are trusting in Christ when the fact is that you are not trusting in Him. A true acceptance of the sacrifice of Jesus Christ will so transform a person that he will bring forth good works. I tell you, this gets down to the marrow and to the bone of our souls. God looks at the heart. I repeat the question I asked earlier in our study: If you were arrested for being a Christian, would there be enough evidence to convict you?

**An high look, and a proud heart, and the plowing of the wicked, is sin [Prov. 21:4].**

"An high look." Maybe you walked into church on Sunday morning and saw Mrs. Jones or Mr. Smith, and you just turned your head so you wouldn't have to speak to them. I was in a group recently where there was a man who had said some unlovely things about me. He acted as if he didn't see me at all—the high look. Maybe nobody noticed the high look. Maybe the person who was given the high look was unaware of it, but God saw it. God calls it a sin. In His sight it is as much a sin as to go out and get drunk. One is just as bad as the other, although we don't measure it that way. We think the one is terrible and the other doesn't matter.

"The plowing [or tillage] of the lawless is sin." This is an interesting proverb. You might see a man out plowing his field and think, *My, he is an industrious man. He certainly should be rewarded for being so industrious.* God says that when an evil man with an evil heart is doing anything—even plowing—it will not be acceptable in His sight. That means a sinner cannot give anything to God. He cannot perform a *good* work. Not only is the high look and a proud heart sinful, but what otherwise would be meritorious is *sin* in a man who is in rebellion against God. I do not think that God will bless a gift from an unsaved person. Years ago, a brewery in Dallas, Texas, gave gifts of $50,000 each to a Christian school, a denominational college, and a hospital. The school and the college returned the money. I think they did the right thing. God wouldn't use money like that.

Notice what Paul wrote to the nation of Israel: "Brethren, my heart's desire and prayer to God for Israel is, that they might be saved. For I bear them record that they have a zeal of God, but not according to knowledge. For they being ignorant of God's righteousness, and going about to establish their own righteousness, have not submitted themselves unto the righteousness of God" (Rom. 10:1–3). When a person goes about to establish his own righteousness, God says it is *sin.* The righteousness of man is filthy rags in the sight of God.

**The thoughts of the diligent tend only to plenteousness; but of every one that is hasty only to want.**

**The getting of treasures by a lying tongue is a vanity tossed to and fro of them that seek death.**

**The robbery of the wicked shall destroy them; because they refuse to do judgment [Prov. 21:5–7].**

God can use riches that are accumulated in an honest way. There is no sin in being rich. The important thing is how the money was accumulated. If the getting of riches is by lying and robbery, God will see to it that the riches will not be enjoyed. Do you get the impression that there are certain rich men today who are not really having a good time? Their riches are not what they really need.

The story is told of an Arab who was lost out in the desert. He was about to die of thirst and starvation. The poor fellow saw a package that had dropped off a caravan. He thought it might contain food or a can of beverage. He hungrily tore open the package and eagerly looked to see what it contained. He dropped it in great disappointment, and said, "It's only pearls!" Of course they were worth a fortune, but that was not his need.

My friend, God says that you can get rich, but it won't do you a bit of good unless you make money in the right way and use it for His glory.

**The way of man is froward and strange: but as for the pure, his work is right [Prov. 21:8].**

Let me give you another translation: "The way of a guilty man is very crooked: but as for the pure, his work is right." Your life will demonstrate what kind of a person you really are. If you are right with God, that will be revealed in your life.

**It is better to dwell in a corner of the housetop, than with a brawling woman in a wide house [Prov. 21:9].**

This is the man who did not know what true happiness was until he got married—and then it was too late!

Down in Nashville the retired pastor of a church and I would repeatedly go down to the jail to get out a man who was a member of the church. He would be arrested over and over again for drunkenness. One time the retired preacher said something to me that I shall never forget: "If I were married to the woman that he is married to, I would drink also." Of course it is just as bad for a woman to be married to the wrong husband. My wife and I mentioned just the other night that we felt very sorry for a certain woman because she is married to a man like that.

We have examples of this in the Scriptures. Job didn't do so well with a wife. David was married to a daughter of Saul. I don't think there was any fellowship or any real love in that marriage. She ridiculed David when he so joyously brought the ark to Jerusalem. She told him he made a fool of himself, dancing before the ark. She called his behavior disgraceful. Believe me, if you show some enthusiasm for God, there will be a great many people who will be embarrassed. It is tragic if it is your mate who is embarrassed.

**When the scorner is punished, the simple is made wise: and when the wise is instructed, he receiveth knowledge [Prov. 21:11].**

We need to note these things so that we learn lessons from the experience of others around us.

**Whoso stoppeth his ears at the cry of the poor, he also shall cry himself, but shall not be heard [Prov. 21:13].**

This is what *God* has said. Either it is true or it is not true. I believe it is true, and I think we can find illustrations of this in public life in our day.

**A gift in secret pacifieth anger: and a reward in the bosom strong wrath [Prov. 21:14].**

Remember that when Jacob was returning home after his years in Haran, he knew he had to face Esau for the first time after he had tricked him out of his birthright and his blessing. So he sent gifts ahead in order to pacify Esau. He didn't need to do that, because God had already taken care of Esau's attitude. But men have found that a gift in secret will pacify anger.

We can easily fall into this type of thinking: "I am going to be generous because then I'll be rewarded." Or, "I am going to forgive someone because if I do that, it will make me feel better." Jane Mershon wrote a little rhyme which illustrates this type of thinking:

If I forgive an injury,
Because resenting would poison me,
I may feel noble; I may feel splendid,
But it isn't exactly what Christ intended.

No, it isn't what Christ intended. We are to forgive because God for Christ's sake has forgiven us. That is the reason we are to be kind and tenderhearted and forgiving. Our motive for forgiving is not to make us feel better.

**It is joy to the just to do judgment: but destruction shall be to the workers of iniquity.**

**The man that wandereth out of the way of understanding shall remain in the congregation of the dead [Prov. 21:15–16].**

It is my understanding that God is saying here that you cannot rehabilitate criminals. They need to be *regenerated*. These fellows need the Word of God. We need to go into crime-ridden areas and preach the Word of God. We are going about things from the wrong direction according to God.

**He that loveth pleasure shall be a poor man: he that loveth wine and oil shall not be rich [Prov. 21:17].**

In our contemporary society the entertainer has been glorified, and as a result the great moral principles of life have been turned upside down. At one time, even in the court of a king, a jester, an entertainer, was called a fool. I don't think that has been changed in God's sight. However, by our popular standards, the entertainers are the sacred cows. We hear them on talk shows glorifying themselves and each other. God still says, "He that loveth pleasure shall be a poor man: he that loveth wine and oil shall not be rich." I can think of several entertainers who have committed suicide. One man made this statement, "I am bored with life." Another said, "Life is not worth living." A comedian was dying, and his friends gathered around waiting for him to say something funny. He looked at them in stark fear and dread and said, "*This* is not funny." We have things turned upside down. Television is like the wilderness of Moab. There is really nothing to see. It becomes very boring.

**The wicked shall be a ransom for the righteous, and the transgressor for the upright [Prov. 21:18].**

Justice demands the punishment of the guilty in order that the guiltless may be delivered; but, by the grace of God, Jesus Christ, the Righteous, became a ransom for the wicked. He is the "upright," and you and I are the "transgressors."

**A wise man scaleth the city of the mighty, and casteth down the strength of the confidence thereof [Prov. 21:22].**

He is saying that wisdom is superior to brute force. A man may be able to build a seemingly impregnable fortress, but there will come along a man who is smart enough to figure out how to invade it. The ancient city of Babylon is a classic example. Belshazzar sat inside the walls of Babylon thinking he was perfectly safe. In fact, there was an inner wall around his palace. He was certain the walls of Babylon could never be penetrated, and, of course, guards were stationed all along the walls. But the general in the camp of the enemy used his wisdom and figured a way to get into Babylon. A branch of the Euphrates River went through the city, more or less like a canal. He diverted the water back into the mainstream of the river, then he was able to march his army on the riverbed under the wall where the river had flowed. The Medo-Persian army spread into the city, and the city was taken before the Babylonians knew what was happening.

Napoleon made the statement that God is always on the side of the bigger battalions. He was wrong. He should have won at Waterloo. He was a very brilliant general, but he was not quite smart enough. He had the ability to move artillery speedily, but he got bogged down in the mud. It was old General Mud that really stopped Napoleon as he went toward Warsaw. The cavalry stumbled over the artillery that was stuck in the mud. This proverb is saying that men may depend upon riches or upon brute force, but neither will be a good enough protection.

**Whoso keepeth his mouth and his tongue keepeth his soul from troubles [Prov. 21:23].**

Again he mentions using the tongue aright. He has already said that if you want friends, you must show yourself friendly. So of course you are to do some talking, but you are to watch what you say. We do need friends, and the Book of Proverbs has a great deal to say about friends and enemies. Emerson put it like this:

He who has a thousand friends has not a
    friend to spare,
And he who has one enemy will meet him
    everywhere.

How true!

**Proud and haughty scorner is his name, who dealeth in proud wrath [Prov. 21:24].**

Have you noticed that there are two subjects which seem to appear over and over again? One is the use and abuse of the tongue. The other is pride. The uncontrolled tongue, the lying tongue, the gossiping tongue, and the proud look—God says He hates them all.

**The desire of the slothful killeth him; for his hands refuse to labour [Prov. 21:25].**

"Slothful" is the lazy man. There is quite a bit said about him.

**He coveteth greedily all the day long: but the righteous giveth and spareth not [Prov. 21:26].**

The lazy man spends his time in covetousness, and he tries to use devious devices to get money without working. There are a lot of folk who are doing that. By contrast, the righteous man is not thinking so much of getting as of giving, and God will bless him. That is the thought here.

**The sacrifice of the wicked is abomination: how much more, when he bringeth it with a wicked mind? [Prov. 21:27].**

The "wicked" man is the lawless man. A lawless man is one who has not bowed himself to God and come God's way. "There is a way that seemeth right unto a man" (Prov. 16:25).— that is the lawless way. He goes *his* way and ignores God's way. In fact, he repudiates God. This doesn't mean such a man may not be religious. He may join the church, attend regularly, sing the hymns, and put on quite a front. He may even give, but he does it with a low motive. "The sacrifice of the wicked is abomination."

**A false witness shall perish: but the man that heareth speaketh constantly.**

**A wicked man hardeneth his face: but as for the upright, he directeth his way [Prov. 21:28–29].**

There were false witnesses in the trial of the Lord Jesus. Wouldn't you hate to have been one of those false witnesses? We read in Matthew's record, "Now the chief priests, and elders, and all the council, sought false witness against Jesus, to put him to death; But found none: yea, though many false witnesses came, yet found they none. At the last came two false witnesses, And said, This fellow said, I am able to destroy the temple of God, and to build it in three days" (Matt. 26: 59–61). The other false witnesses bore testimony, but it wasn't pertinent at all. These last two really lied. Jesus' response is given in the next chapter: "And Jesus stood before the governor: and the governor asked him, saying, Art thou the King of the Jews? And Jesus said unto him, Thou sayest." In other words, "You are right." "And when he was accused of the chief priests and elders, he answered nothing. Then said Pilate unto him, Hearest thou not how many things they witness against thee? And he answered him to never a word; insomuch that the governor marvelled greatly" (see Matt. 27:11–14). John's record tells us that Pilate took the Lord Jesus inside the hall of judgment and privately asked for His cooperation so he could let Him off. But he was too much of a politician to release Jesus against the wishes of the Jews. Finally, he gave in to the pressure of the mob, but all the while he knew that the witnesses against Jesus were false.

This is the trial that stands on the pages of history as being the most ignominious of all. Wouldn't you hate to have been one of those false witnesses? "A false witness shall perish."

**There is no wisdom nor understanding nor counsel against the LORD [Prov. 21:30].**

This is a remarkable verse of Scripture. It is so remarkable that I want to put beside it a New Testament verse that may have escaped your attention: "For we can do nothing against the truth, but for the truth" (2 Cor. 13:8).

Because I attended a liberal college and a liberal seminary, I used to become very alarmed by the inroads liberal theology was making. When I began my ministry, I thought it was my duty to sort of ring the fire bell every Sunday morning to defend the Word of God. Then this verse came to my attention. "There is no wisdom nor understanding nor counsel against the LORD." I began to realize that God is able to defend Himself, and He is able to defend His Word. "We can do nothing against the truth, but for the truth." Since I wanted to do something, I was to do it positively—accentuate the positive and leave the negative alone. I didn't need to defend the Bible; all He asked me to do was to proclaim it.

I had a letter from a man which I filed in the round file, known as the wastebasket. I didn't even read the whole letter, because he was trying to show me that the Bible is not the Word of God and used an asinine argument. I just thought, *Ho-hum, let's go on to something else because this man has a hangup of some sin in his life.* I have learned that if a man will turn to Christ, if he wants to get rid of his sin, if he does really desire to have a Savior, it will be amazing how the problems about the Bible that disturb him will be smoothed out.

**The horse is prepared against the day of battle: but safety is of the LORD [Prov. 21:31].**

David learned this. He wrote, "Though an host should encamp against me, my heart shall not fear: though war should rise against me, in this will I be confident" (Ps. 27:3). Asa had also learned this truth. "And Asa cried unto the LORD his God, and said, LORD, it is nothing with thee to help, whether with many, or with them that have no power: help us, O LORD our God; for we rest on thee, and in thy name we go against this multitude. O LORD, thou art our God; let not man prevail against thee" (2 Chron. 14:11). How wonderful it is to trust God.

That does not mean that we are not to be prepared. Jesus said that a strong man armed keeps his palace, and his goods are in peace. "But safety is of Jehovah." Keep your powder dry, but be sure your *faith* is in the Lord Jesus Christ and that you are resting in Him.

# CHAPTER 22

Solomon, who had all that money could buy, puts material wealth in true perspective.

**A good name is rather to be chosen than great riches, and loving favour rather than silver and gold [Prov. 22:1].**

"Good" in most Bibles is italicized, which means that it was supplied by the translators. "A *name* is rather to be chosen"—the proverb is not speaking of the name you were called by your parents when you were born, but the name you earn by the kind of person you are.

We know that David had a group of men, known as his mighty men. And they were great men. They had made a name for themselves. For example, we are told about Benaiah. "And Benaiah the son of Jehoiada, the son of a valiant man, of Kabzeel, who had done many acts, he slew two lionlike men of Moab: he went down also and slew a lion in the midst of a pit in time of snow" (2 Sam. 23:20). A lot of people won't even go to church when it snows, but this man slew a lion in the time of snow! We are told, "These things did Benaiah the son of Jehoiada, and had the name among three mighty men" (2 Sam. 23:22). He was up there in a class with the top three of the highest echelon of David's mighty men. He had a *name*. "A name is rather to be chosen than great riches."

### The rich and poor meet together: the LORD is the maker of them all [Prov. 22:2].

This means that before God all men are on the same plane. If you want to talk about a universal brotherhood of man, be very careful what you say. The Bible doesn't teach that. The Bible does teach that we are all members of the human family and that we all have a depraved nature, a nature that is alienated from God. We even need to protect ourselves from each other, because we cannot be trusted. The Bible does say that He ". . . hath made of one blood all nations of men for to dwell on all the face of the earth . . ." (Acts 17:26), and we all stand equal before Him on that basis. But we become the sons of God— not just because we are human beings—but by faith in Jesus Christ. The Lord Jesus said to the religious rulers of His day, "Ye are of your father the devil . . ." (John 8:44). So actually there are two families in the world: children of God and children of the devil. Obviously, the universal fatherhood of God does not exist.

Now notice that the proverb says: "The LORD is the maker of them all." We are all His by *creation*. God is the Creator of all but not the Father of all.

### A prudent man foreseeth the evil, and hideth himself: but the simple pass on, and are punished [Prov. 22:3].

Do you want to be a smart man? Then make arrangements for the future. There are many men today who will help you make arrangements for the future. There are all kinds of insurance companies and agencies. There are people willing to make arrangements for your old age, for the care of your children, and all that sort of thing. But I'm thinking of the next step. What about that? What about your eternal future? The Scripture calls a man a fool who has not made preparation for eternity.

When I was a young man in Nashville, Tennessee, I was very far from the Lord for awhile. I remember a fine young couple, who belonged to rich families. At a dance one night they announced their engagement, and then later they were married. Of course they made the society page of the newspaper. They had

bought a very lovely southern home with those white columns out in front. They had searched everywhere for antiques, and they furnished that home beautifully. On their wedding trip they went to the Great Smokies in East Tennessee and North Carolina. Going up into the mountains, they went around a curve and were hit and knocked off the highway down a precipice. The car caught fire, and they were both killed. The parents of the couple simply locked the door to their lovely home and left it unoccupied.

For years after I was saved, I would go by that house and reflect on all the preparation they had put into that house; yet they had not lived in it for one hour. And they went into eternity totally unprepared. Oh, how important it is for us to be making preparation for eternity!

### Train up a child in the way he should go: and when he is old, he will not depart from it [Prov. 22:6].

We are to train up a child concerning the way he should go. What he is saying is that God has a way He wants him to go, and parents are to find out that way. They are not to bring up a child in the way *they* think he should go, but in the way *God* wants him to go.

### The slothful man saith, There is a lion without, I shall be slain in the streets [Prov. 22:13].

Here we have the lazy man again. This verse has its humor in it, too. Believe me, the lazy man is full of excuses. It's too cold outside so he cannot go out to plow. Here is his new excuse: "There is a lion without, I shall be slain in the streets." I think he was lyin' about the lion!

### Foolishness is bound in the heart of a child; but the rod of correction shall drive it far from him [Prov. 22:15].

These instructions for child rearing are repeated for emphasis. Children need discipline. Proper discipline will not provoke the child to anger. Neither will it be simply the venting of our own anger. Proper discipline will help the child overcome his foolishness.

### Remove not the ancient landmark, which thy fathers have set [Prov. 22:28].

When God brought the children of Israel from Egypt, He gave them a land. Sometimes we forget that He also gave to each tribe a particular section of that land. And He gave to each family in each tribe a particular parcel of that land. Each family was to put up boundary markers for their own parcel of land. These boundary markers were generally piles of stones.

Down in front of my house in the sidewalk there is a little brass circle at one end of my lot and another little brass circle at the other end of my lot, marking where my lot begins and where it ends. This whole area used to be an avocado grove, and I have a notion that the markers were put in when it was converted into a subdivision. It was done to make sure that I stay within my own lot.

God gave Israel definite rules regarding their markers: "Thou shalt not remove thy neighbour's landmark, which they of old time have set in thine inheritance, which thou shalt inherit in the land that the LORD thy God giveth thee to possess it" (Deut. 19:14). These markers went from generation to generation and were very important. When a man got old and feeble and his eyesight began to fail him, his neighbor might want to slip over and move the marker a couple of feet to increase his own parcel of land. God said that kind of thing was forbidden. It would be totally dishonest, of course.

Now I am going to make a spiritual application of this. You may think I am a square when I say this, but I believe that today we have seen the landmarks of the Christian faith removed. They have been removed by what was first called modernism, and now is called liberalism. These folk with a liberal viewpoint say, "This old landmark, this doctrine that was taught in the days of the apostle Paul, is no longer relevant. We have learned so much that we don't need the doctrine of the plenary inspiration of the Scriptures. We can do away with that. And we can do away with the doctrine of the deity of Christ." These distinguishing doctrines of the Christian faith have been pretty well washed out by a great many of the old line denominations on the basis that

we must come up to date. Now I want to say this: Instead of moving forward and removing landmarks, we need to start moving backward to get back to many of the ancient landmarks.

Those ancient landmarks made this nation great. The landmarks of moral values, the spiritual truths, the biblical basis—all have been removed. We look around us today and hear everyone telling what he thinks the solution is, and it is always a sociological or psychological solution. I haven't heard any of our leaders suggesting a biblical solution. I say that we need to get back to the good old landmarks which our nation had at the beginning.

This chapter concludes with a word of commendation for the man who is diligent.

**Seest thou a man diligent in his business? he shall stand before kings; he shall not stand before mean men [Prov. 22:29].**

God says that He intends to reward the diligent man. You remember that the Lord Jesus said that in eternity His commendation would be: ". . . Well done, thou good and faithful servant . . ." (Matt. 25:21). His commendation will not be based on the amount of work you have done, or on the number of people to whom you have witnessed, or how hard you have worked, but on how faithful you have been to the task He has given you. He may have given you the task of being a mother to a little one in the home. Moses' mother was faithful in that way, and her name is recorded in the Word of God. The reward will be for faithfulness.

The apostle Paul put it like this in Romans 12:10–11 (and I'll give you a little more meaningful translation of my own): "As to brotherly love, have family affection one to another; for your code of honor, deferring to one another. Never flag in zeal, be aglow (fervent) with the Spirit, serving the Lord." It all adds up to being faithful to God—and that is what we should be.

# CHAPTER 23

Our young man has been attending the school of wisdom for quite some time now. I think we will have a graduation ceremony soon.

**When thou sittest to eat with a ruler, consider diligently what is before thee:**

**And put a knife to thy throat, if thou be a man given to appetite.**

**Be not desirous of his dainties: for they are deceitful meat [Prov. 23:1–3].**

I can state this in very commonplace language: Don't make a pig of yourself when you are invited out to eat—especially if you are invited to a place that serves you gourmet food, the type of food that you are not accustomed to eating. In fact, it would be better, he says, to cut your throat than make a pig of yourself! In other words, be temperate in all things. Use moderation and self-control, even when you eat.

In our day the theory is that some folk eat, not because of real hunger, but because of a psychological factor. Some people eat when they are under tension, when they are uptight. We should be relaxed and enjoy our meals but eat in moderation.

**Labour not to be rich: cease from thine own wisdom.**

**Wilt thou set thine eyes upon that which is not? for riches certainly make themselves wings; they fly away as an eagle toward heaven [Prov. 23:4–5].**

You have probably noticed that the United States dollar has an eagle on it. Believe me, that eagle will fly away if you're not careful with it. I find that the eagles on my dollars take off all the time. We cannot depend on riches.

The whole thought here is this: There is nothing wrong in being rich. There is nothing wrong in working to be rich. However, don't make that the goal in life. Wealth should not be the very object of our hearts. Some men have a lust, a thirst, a covetousness to make the almighty dollar, and the dollar becomes their god. A child of God is not to do that.

A wealthy man told me, "I do not make money for the sake of money. I make money for what it can do. At first I made money for what it could do for *me*. Now I make money for what it can do for *God*." There is nothing wrong in a man becoming wealthy. The wrong comes when there is the overweening desire of the heart for money. That is covetousness; actually it is modern idolatry.

In the United States we do not find people bowing down to worship idols. However, we do find people busily engaging their whole lives in the worship of the almighty dollar. When I pastored a church in the downtown financial district of Los Angeles, I found that men, even including some Christian men, were far more zealous in coming down early on a Monday morning to watch the stock market open than they were on Sunday morning to attend church service. I met such a man rushing to the stock market display at the brokerage on a Monday morning. He met me, greeted me cordially, and told me what he was going to do. I mentioned to him that we had been missing him at church. He said, "Well, you know, I haven't been feeling very well." That is interesting. He didn't feel well enough to come to church, but he was well enough to worship his god very early on a Monday morning. That's covetousness, and that is what the proverb is talking about. That is a false god, and that false god is an eagle that will fly away at any moment.

**Eat thou not the bread of him that hath an evil eye, neither desire thou his dainty meats:**

**For as he thinketh in his heart, so is he: Eat and drink, saith he to thee; but his heart is not with thee.**

**The morsel which thou hast eaten shalt thou vomit up, and lose thy sweet words [Prov. 23:6–8].**

Here is good advice for the young man, especially for the young preacher. On several occasions I have been warned by ministers with whom I have had Bible conferences. They have said something like this: "Now you will be invited to dinner by so-an-so, but you be very careful what you say if you go there, because they are name-droppers, as you will find out. They will ask you certain questions, and they will use your answers against you later on." Well, when I am relaxed at a meal and talking with friends, I can easily say something that can be misconstrued.

Not too long ago I had such an experience. A couple used certain things that I had said about a personal friend of mine. I was just kidding, because I love that man. He is my brother in the Lord, and we play golf together. He said to me, "What in the world are you saying about me?" I told him, and he laughed. He said, "Those people took what you said and gave it a twist." But he said that he had been over to see them and had said something about me that would be coming back to me. And it did! He kids me too, and they had twisted what he had said about me. These were the kind of folk that Solomon had in mind when he wrote, "Eat thou not the bread of him that hath an evil eye." When you are invited out to dinner, make sure that you know the people with whom you are to dine. They may not be as cordial as you think they are.

**Remove not the old landmark; and enter not into the fields of the fatherless [Prov. 23:10].**

Now we have this remark about the old landmark again. If you have lost your faith—well, you'd better not pass that on to your children, because they will really pay for it. You probably had a good background and Christian parents, but your children will have no background to protect them.

Dr. J. Gresham Machen once said, "America is coasting downhill on a godly ancestry." I agree with him, and it was my generation that had the godly ancestry; but we did not pass it on to our children. It was my generation that produced the younger generation that we are blaming for everything.

**Withhold not correction from the child: for if thou beatest him with the rod, he shall not die [Prov. 23:13].**

Now we have been over this before. Remember that Paul adds to this that the parent is not to correct the child in a fit of anger. The correction is to be for discipline, not punishment. If the discipline doesn't help to develop the character of that child, it is no good.

We should not tell our children that we are punishing them. It would be better to tell them that we are disciplining them. Paul tells the fathers not to provoke the children to wrath, but ". . . bring them up in the instruction and discipline of the Lord" (Eph. 6:4). We need to remember that it is the discipline and the instruction *of the Lord*. That is important.

**Hear thou, my son, and be wise, and guide thine heart in the way.**

**Be not among winebibbers; among riotous eaters of flesh:**

**For the drunkard and the glutton shall come to poverty: and drowsiness shall**

**clothe a man with rags [Prov. 23:19–21].**

Be very careful of the company you keep, young man. Birds of a feather flock together. Evil companions produce evil manners. This is a special warning to the young people.

**Hearken unto thy father that begat thee, and despise not thy mother when she is old [Prov. 23:22].**

The young man is almost ready to graduate from the school of wisdom. His parents may be getting old. His dad may be a square, he may even be a bit senile, but the old folks still have a lot more sense than the young man has.

You would hear an example of this if you could only talk to Absalom. He would tell you that his dad had more sense than he had. He thought he could win a rebellion against his father, King David, but old David was a warhorse. When that boy moved out to the battlefield, he made a mistake. He should never have left Jerusalem, because David knew his way around on the battlefield, and it was fatal for that boy.

**Buy the truth, and sell it not; also wisdom, and instruction, and understanding [Prov. 23:23].**

You and I do not need to buy truth with money. It is available to us without money and without price. "Ho, every one that thirsteth, come ye to the waters, and he that hath no money; come ye, buy, and eat; yea, come, buy wine and milk without money and without price" (Isa. 55:1). Christ is all of this for the child of God. He is truth and wisdom and understanding. The brilliant young Pharisee, Saul, who became the apostle Paul, tells us about it: "But of him are ye in Christ Jesus, who of God is made unto us wisdom, and righteousness, and sanctification, and redemption" (1 Cor. 1:30).

**My son, give me thine heart, and let thine eyes observe my ways [Prov. 23:26].**

Someone may say, "Dr. McGee, I thought you said that God doesn't want our old dirty, filthy hearts." That's right. He can't use them. But when He says, "My son, give me thine heart," He is not talking to the unsaved man; He is talking to His *son*. He is talking to the one to whom He has given a new heart, a new nature, who has been born again. Now He says to that one, "I want you to come to Me and I want you to yield yourself to Me. If you love Me, keep My commandments."

If you have been redeemed by the blood of Christ, you can sing:

> Take my poor heart, and let it be
> Forever closed to all but Thee.
> Take my love, my Lord; I pour
> At Thy feet its treasure-store.

**For a whore is a deep ditch; and a strange woman is a narrow pit [Prov. 23:27].**

If anyone thought I was wrong in saying the stranger was a harlot, then here is a parallelism that shows the two are synonymous. That should answer that question.

**She also lieth in wait as for a prey, and increaseth the transgressors among men [Prov. 23:28].**

The lives of two men illustrate this. There is the story of Judah in the Book of Genesis. That is a sorry chapter which tells his story when he went in to a harlot. Then there is the story of Samson. If he were here today, he would say, "I found out that a harlot is treacherous—she can betray you without a qualm."

**Who hath woe? who hath sorrow? who hath contentions? who hath babbling? who hath wounds without cause? who hath redness of eyes?**

**They that tarry long at the wine; they that go to seek mixed wine [Prov. 23:29–30].**

Here again is a warning against this matter of drunkenness. We have heard many warnings about wine and women—but there is no song. Because—

**At the last it biteth like a serpent, and stingeth like an adder.**

**Thine eyes shall behold strange women, and thine heart shall utter perverse things.**

**Yea, thou shalt be as he that lieth down in the midst of the sea, or as he that lieth upon the top of a mast.**

**They have stricken me, shalt thou say, and I was not sick; they have beaten me, and I felt it not: when shall I awake? I will seek it yet again [Prov. 23:32–35].**

What a picture of drunkenness this is!

# CHAPTER 24

This is the last chapter of the proverbs of Solomon which he wrote and arranged. After this we come to proverbs of Solomon that were arranged by the men of Hezekiah. Evidently Solomon wrote a great many proverbs. We have only a very small percentage of the total number. These are tremendous truths that have been placed in a very small compass. They can grip and direct our lives.

**Be not thou envious against evil men, neither desire to be with them.**

**For their heart studieth destruction, and their lips talk of mischief [Prov. 24:1–2].**

This has been presented to us before. We find a repetition of the things which are important. For example, a great deal has been said about the use of the tongue and about pride and about being a fool. They are things that are constantly emphasized, because they are translated into life. We find these folk, not only on the sidewalks of New York, but in your town and my town. That is the reason I said you will find a proverb to fit every person you know. We have already found a great number which fit different characters in the Bible.

Psalm 73, a psalm of Asaph, deals with the same subject as our verse here in Proverbs. Asaph writes, "For I was envious at the foolish, when I saw the prosperity of the wicked. . . . They are not in trouble as other men; neither are they plagued like other men. . . . They set their mouth against the heavens, and their tongue walketh through the earth" (Ps. 73:3–9). Asaph was disturbed about that. I am of the opinion that you have been disturbed by it also. I certainly have had these feelings. I remember as a poor boy that I couldn't understand why I had to be poor and drop out of school to work when I was only fourteen years of age. I looked about me and saw other boys who were well able to go to school but were dropping out because they hated it. I had a real question about it, because I had such a desire for an education.

Now Solomon deals with this matter: "Be not thou envious against evil men, neither desire to be with them." Why? A day of reckoning is coming. Asaph said he didn't understand why the wicked prospered—"Until I went into the sanctuary of God; then understood I their *end*" (Ps. 73:17, italics mine). God will deal with them.

As we look out upon the world, we see a great deal of injustice, and there is very little that you and I can do about it. We have been in a generation that has protested about everything. They have attempted to equalize a great many things in this world. I don't think all of the protesting has solved any problem, because the problem is in the *heart* of man. It is the *heart* of man that must be changed. God is the One who is going to level this thing off someday. We can trust Him to do that.

You and I need to recognize our place in life. It is going to make us happier people if we realize that God has put each of us in our own particular place to fulfill a purpose here on earth. I look at wicked men who are prosperous, and I don't understand it. I have told God a dozen times that I don't understand it. Don't you be afraid to tell it to God just as Asaph did. The important thing is for *you* to go on with God, trusting Him to work it all out.

We need to learn to look at things from God's point of view. The Bible is full of instances of wicked men who came to a bad end. It starts with Cain in the Book of Genesis. Even a man like Lot, although he was a saved man, chose to live in the city of Sodom and prospered there, but there came a day when he wished he had not moved to Sodom. It was a sad mistake for him to do that. So if you will go through the Word of God, you will find people who prospered for a time and then see how judgment has come time and time again. This is very important for us to understand.

**Through wisdom is an house builded; and by understanding it is established:**

**And by knowledge shall the chambers be filled with all precious and pleasant riches [Prov. 24:3–4].**

This is a wonderful picture of what we are to do. A man builds a house, and then he fills

that house with furniture, with lovely pictures and tapestries, with beautiful personal items and valuable things. It is a pleasure to see a home like that, a beautiful home that is tastefully furnished.

You and I ought to be building us a house down here, a house of wisdom, a house of knowledge. We should begin to store our minds and our hearts with all kinds of wonderful furniture, vases, pictures, and lovely things. This was the thing that Paul admonished Timothy: "Study to shew thyself approved unto God, a workman that needeth not to be ashamed, rightly dividing the word of truth" (2 Tim. 2:15). And you and I should be filling our hearts and lives with the Word of God. Oh, my friend, let's be working toward a beautiful mansion; let's not be satisfied with a hovel.

When I was down in South America visiting with a missionary, he took me to some of the homes in his area. Many of them were what we would call a "lean-to" made out of old boards. Many of them were decaying, dilapidated places. Inside there was no place to sit, not even a chair. There would be a blanket or a sheepskin in a corner where the family would sleep; there was no bed. The cooking was done on the outside. I thought how tragic it was. Frankly, it made me sick just thinking of the poverty of those people down in South America. But, my friend, up here in North America I know many Christians who should have spent their lives building a lovely home—a spiritual home—and filling it with all kinds of wonderful treasures out of the Word of God. Instead, all they have is a little hovel. And when I look inside—oh, the ignorance! There is nothing there; it is absolutely bare.

In talking to a group of preachers just the other day, they agreed with me on this: the greatest tragedy in our churches today is the ignorance of the church members. Oh, the poor little empty houses they have! "Through wisdom is an house builded; and by understanding it is established: And by knowledge shall the chambers be filled with all precious and pleasant riches."

**A wise man is strong; yea, a man of knowledge increaseth strength.**

**For by wise counsel thou shalt make thy war: and in multitude of counsellors there is safety [Prov. 24:5–6].**

There are many resources for us to use today. Not only do we have people to whom we can turn for counsel, but we also have the Word of

God. I don't believe in this method of opening the Bible to look at some verse at the time of making a decision. That is not good. The Word of God is not a roulette wheel for us to turn and hope it stops at the right place. We need to know what the whole Bible says. We need to read Moses and Joshua and Samuel and David and Micah and Zechariah and Matthew and Paul and John. They are all our counselors. We can appeal to all of them at any time of decision.

**If thou faint in the day of adversity, thy strength is small [Prov. 24:10].**

He is saying something here that is rather important: It takes a *man* to do a man's *job*. We use the old bromide, "Never send a boy to do a man's work." God uses these times of real stress and strain and testing to develop our spiritual character. That is the way He enables us to grow. It is in the hour of trial that you and I manifest the spiritual strength that we have.

It is a great comfort for us to know that many of God's men turned and ran when their test came. Elijah had been so brave on the top of Mount Carmel, but when he heard that Jezebel was after him with the intention of killing him, he took off and ran for the wilderness until he got down to Beer-sheba. He left his servant there and continued on in the desert, climbed under a juniper tree, and said, ". . . LORD, let me die" (cf. 1 Kings 19:4).

When David was hunted by King Saul, he didn't have a moment of peace. David said that he was hunted like a partridge in the mountains and that one of these days they would catch him and put him to death. He became very discouraged. But both David and Elijah learned in that hour that the Lord would and did strengthen them.

**If thou forbear to deliver them that are drawn unto death, and those that are ready to be slain;**

**If thou sayest, Behold, we knew it not; doth not he that pondereth the heart consider it? and he that keepeth thy soul, doth not he know it? and shall not he render to every man according to his works? [Prov. 24:11–12].**

Now there is somebody you could help, and you *know* you could. There is somebody to whom you could witness for Christ, and you may be the only one to whom he would listen.

Recently I talked with a man who feels that he has been responsible for the suicide of a loved one. He says that he knew he should have done something. I'm of the opinion that he should have, but he didn't do it. A man can be under great conviction because he neglected to do something at a time when he should have done it.

The Lord God is the One who ponders the heart. In such an instance when we know we have failed to do something that we should have done, there is nothing left but to turn to the Lord and say, "Lord, forgive me. I failed. I come to You now asking You to strengthen me and help me." The Lord will hear that kind of prayer. He will deliver a man from being overwhelmed by the grief and guilt of his failure.

We do well to mark the importance of this proverb and reach out to people who are in need of our help.

**For a just man falleth seven times, and riseth up again: but the wicked shall fall into mischief [Prov. 24:16].**

"A just man falleth seven times, and riseth up again." Seven is the number of completeness. It means man just keeps on falling. But the just man will get up again. Do you know a man like that? Simon Peter was one. But then notice that "the wicked shall fall into mischief." That is Judas. This proverb perfectly illustrates those two disciples of our Lord. Peter was a man who was constantly falling. We may say that he failed when he tried to walk on the water. I don't really think that he failed, because he *did* walk on the water. He walked on the water to come to Jesus, but when he took his eyes off Jesus and looked at those rolling waves, he began to go under; he began to sink. But remember that the Lord rescued him and he walked back to the boat with Jesus. But Peter certainly fell the night the Lord Jesus was arrested. He denied his Lord three times. Again and again and again Peter failed the Lord. But he always got up and went on with the Lord.

A man came to me when I was a pastor in Pasadena. He said, "I have failed so many times and I am ashamed to go back to the Lord and tell Him again that I have failed and want to start over." I told him, "You may be ashamed, but the Lord is not. He is ready to start you out again." Then he asked, "How many times do you suppose you can fail and still come back?" I told him, "I don't know, but I am working up in the hundreds myself, and I still go to Him." It is so important for us to understand that we can go back to our Heavenly Father and tell Him that we stumbled and got dirty again. He will put us right back into His service. How wonderful it is to have a Heavenly Father like that!

**Rejoice not when thine enemy falleth, and let not thine heart be glad when he stumbleth [Prov. 24:17].**

When you hear that something bad has happened to someone you haven't really liked very much, don't you say, "I'm glad that happened to him?" Now, don't tell me you have never said that, because human nature is like that. If you haven't said it, you've *thought* it. God says, "Rejoice not when thine enemy falleth." That is not the way to solve the problem. Why?

**Lest the LORD see it, and it displease him, and he turn away his wrath from him [Prov. 24:18].**

If you rejoice when your enemy falls, the Lord may turn around and start prospering that man. Then you really will be miserable. So there is a very practical reason for not rejoicing when your enemy falls.

**Fret not thyself because of evil men, neither be thou envious at the wicked [Prov. 24:19].**

You may think, *We have just read that.* Yes, it is the same thought as verse 1 of this chapter. Then why is it repeated? Again, it is to show us how important this is. The Lord wants us to learn this.

Have you noticed that some of the parables and certain of the miracles of our Lord are repeated? For example, the feeding of the five thousand is recorded in all four Gospels. Each of the Gospel writers adds details which are peculiar to his Gospel. The miracle was of such importance that it is recorded for us four times. And the teaching of this proverb needs to be repeated because of its importance.

From verse 23 to the end of the chapter there is sort of an appendix which is introduced by, "These things also belong to the wise."

**These things also belong to the wise. It is not good to have respect of persons in judgment [Prov. 24:23].**

Here is something else the young man should learn before he graduates: "It is not good to have respect of persons in judgment"—that is, it is not good to show partiality in judgment. This is an important matter in daily living and something which is needed today. Men in public office need to know this. Employers need to know this. Anyone in any position of authority needs to know this. There should not be a system of favorites, but justice should be equal to all.

**He that saith unto the wicked, Thou art righteous; him shall the people curse, nations shall abhor him [Prov. 24:24].**

There is a great deal of that today. Wicked men are *commended*. Often the wicked man is called a righteous man. That is one of the worst things that could take place.

**Say not, I will do so to him as he hath done to me: I will render to the man according to his work [Prov. 24:29].**

This repeats what we have been hearing over and over again. It is the same message which Paul wrote to the Romans: ". . . Vengeance is mine; I will repay, saith the Lord" (Rom. 12:19).

**Yet a little sleep, a little slumber, a little folding of the hands to sleep:**

**So shall thy poverty come as one that travelleth; and thy want as an armed man [Prov. 24:33–34].**

This young man is going to graduate from college. He may know a lot and he may have other good qualities, but if he is lazy, he will find *that* to be the greatest handicap he could have in life.

# CHAPTER 25

This is a new division of the Book of Proverbs. These are still proverbs of Solomon, but they were put together by the men of Hezekiah. The Septuagint calls them "the friends of Hezekiah."

**These are also proverbs of Solomon, which the men of Hezekiah king of Judah copied out.**

**It is the glory of God to conceal a thing: but the honour of kings is to search out a matter [Prov. 25:1–2].**

This is the way the proverb states what the Lord Jesus said: "Search the scriptures . . ." (John 5:39). Paul wrote the same thing: "Study to shew thyself approved unto God, a workman that needeth not to be ashamed, rightly dividing the word of truth" (2 Tim. 2:15).

We are to "search out a matter." Even then we need to recognize that there are a great many things that God has not revealed to us at all. I doubt if we would be able to understand them if He did. They are inscrutable; they are beyond the comprehension of man. As He made it very clear: "For as the heavens are higher than the earth, so are my ways higher than your ways, and my thoughts than your thoughts" (Isa. 55:9).

However, what God has revealed to us, we should study; we should consider it. It is important that we recognize our need to *search* the Word of God and to *study* it.

**The heaven for height, and the earth for depth, and the heart of kings is unsearchable [Prov. 25:3].**

Sometimes we don't understand what our rulers are doing. They probably have justification for it, because they know things that we do not know. Neither can we understand God's ways, but we are never to sit in judgment upon what God does, because whatever God does is *right*—it is the proper thing to do.

**Take away the dross from the silver, and there shall come forth a vessel for the finer.**

**Take away the wicked from before the king, and his throne shall be established in righteousness [Prov. 25:4–5].**

I think one of the worst things that can happen to any individual is to have an evil adviser, someone who leads you into difficulty

and trouble and sin. I thank God for a man in my life who led me away from that, because there was a man who had led me in the wrong direction. Think how important this is to the man in high position. A man who makes a decision in business that would affect a great many employees or a man in government whose decision would affect a great segment of the population needs to have the right kind of advisers around.

**Put not forth thyself in the presence of the king, and stand not in the place of great men:**

**For better it is that it be said unto thee, Come up hither; than that thou shouldest be put lower in the presence of the prince whom thine eyes have seen [Prov. 25:6–7].**

"Put not forth" could be translated "display not." You will remember that the Lord Jesus gave a parable to illustrate this great truth, and He did it because the religious rulers of His day were paying no attention to this proverb at all. When a great and important man invited many of his friends for dinner, he had reserved places at the table for certain ones he wanted to honor. But when the dinner bell was rung, there was a mad rush to get the best places at the table. They almost turned the thing over, I imagine, as they rushed in to get the most prominent places. The Lord Jesus was present there that day and apparently waited until everyone else had gone in. Then He said something to correct them: "When you're invited to a dinner, don't try to get the best place. You should purposely take the lowest place. Then when the one who has invited you comes in and sees you taking the lowest place—if you are his honored guest—he may say to you, 'Come on up here.' Now, if someone else has taken that place, the host would have to tap him on the shoulder and say, 'You go down and take the lowest place' " (cf. Luke 14:7–10).

There are people whom we call "pushy" today—they are pushing themselves. We have people who are pushy in Christian circles. They are ambitious. They want to get ahead in Christian things. That is a tragedy. Maybe you can't blame a man in the business world for trying to get ahead, but in Christian work it ought not to be.

**Go not forth hastily to strive, lest thou know not what to do in the end thereof, when thy neighbour hath put thee to shame [Prov. 25:8].**

Now, again, the Lord Jesus gave a parable about this. He said in essence, "When a king is ready to go forth to war, he ought to sit down and see whether he's going to be able to get the victory. And if he sees that he can't carry on the warfare, then he ought to send an ambassador to make a peace treaty with the enemy" (cf. Luke 14:31–32).

We have an example of this in the Old Testament in King Josiah. He was a good king, and he led the last great revival that Judah had. There was a great turning back to God under his leadership, but he made one grave mistake. Somehow just one flaw sometimes spoils the life of an otherwise great man. Josiah was a great man and an outstanding man of God, but he made this bad mistake. Pharaoh Nechoh, king of Egypt, came to make war, not against Josiah at all, but against an altogether different enemy. But when Josiah came out against him, Pharaoh Nechoh told Josiah, "Now look, I didn't come up to fight you. I don't want to fight you." But Josiah (he was a young man) had gone out to fight. I guess he thought it was the Lord's will. (A great many of us blame the Lord for the mistakes in our decisions.) Josiah got into real trouble and lost the battle. In fact, he was killed in the battle there at Megiddo where the war of Armageddon will be fought. Josiah made a big mistake by meddling when he should not have done that at all. That is the thing the Lord wants us to see in this proverb (cf. 2 Kings 23:28–30).

**Debate thy cause with thy neighbour himself; and discover not a secret to another:**

**Lest he that heareth it put thee to shame, and thine infamy turn not away [Prov. 25:9–10].**

You could cause a great deal of trouble by criticizing your neighbor to the man down the street. If your neighbor has faults, go and talk to him personally.

**A word fitly spoken is like apples of gold in pictures of silver [Prov. 25:11].**

Isn't that a lovely one? That is just a beautiful simile. "Apples of gold"—we do have a Golden Delicious apple today, but apparently the fruit referred to here is the orange. Oranges, as well as other citrus fruits, were common and native to Israel. Today they grow some of the finest oranges in the world. An orange is a beautiful fruit. Someone will think I am promoting oranges because I live in California,

but oranges were plentiful in Palestine at the time of Solomon.

As we go through the Word of God, we find that certain individuals said in a wonderful way just the right word at the right time. Sometimes it's a good word. Sometimes it's a word of rebuke. But the words were necessary, and they were "fitly spoken." The words fit into the picture. They were the proper thing to say.

This is something that most of us ought to pray about: what we should say and at what time. We need to recognize that many times we say the wrong thing at the right time, or sometimes we have the knack of saying the right thing but at the wrong time. And there are times when we probably ought not to open our mouths at all.

I'm sure we all know some dear Christian who has a reputation of being able to say just the right thing at the right time—"a word fitly spoken." There was a dear saint of God who lived in the country in middle Tennessee years ago. She had a reputation for always saying something very nice to the preacher at the end of every morning service. Very frankly, people would linger to hear what she had to say, because there were times they couldn't think of anything good to say about the sermon that they had heard. And one time they had a visiting preacher who was just a little worse than any they had ever had before. I tell you, people were interested that morning. What in the world could she say *nice* to that preacher about the sermon he had preached? So when she went out, she said to him, "Pastor, I want you to know that I did enjoy your sermon, because this morning you had one of the most wonderful texts in Scripture." Now that is "a word fitly spoken." It was like oranges in a picture frame of silver. The golden orange and the silver frame blend very well, as you know.

**As an earring of gold, and an ornament of fine gold, so is a wise reprover upon an obedient ear [Prov. 25:12].**

You have seen a woman's beautiful earring. In our day some men are wearing earrings, although I never saw one that I thought was attractive; but you have seen a woman beautifully wear an earring. That describes the effect of a wise reprover upon an obedient ear. There are times when a person should be reproved and rebuked. We are living in a day when if we rebuke someone, especially if it is done publicly, people will say, "My, you certainly have lost that individual. You'll never be able to win him." Friend, if he's the right kind of individual, you'll win him. And if he's the wrong kind, you wouldn't be able to win him anyway. There are times that a reproof should be made.

**As the cold of snow in the time of harvest, so is a faithful messenger to them that send him: for he refresheth the soul of his masters [Prov. 25:13].**

In that land it gets really hot at the time of harvest. And in that day they would go up to Mount Hermon and pack some of the snow and bring it down. I tell you, the snow was *good*. How wonderful it tasted! That is what a faithful messenger is. No wonder the Lord is going to say to some, ". . . Well done, thou good and faithful servant" (Matt. 25:21).

We all like to have around us *faithful* people. A man wants a faithful wife. He appreciates faithful children. An employer wants faithful employees. A pastor wants a faithful staff and a faithful congregation. And the people want a faithful pastor. Faithfulness is a wonderful quality. It is like a good, cold drink on a very hot day to have someone with us who is faithful.

**Whoso boasteth himself of a false gift is like clouds and wind without rain [Prov. 25:14].**

Some men boast of gifts they don't have. When I was a pastor, I would get letters from men who would tell me how wonderful they were. I remember one man wrote me, and he said he was an evangelist, a Bible teacher, a singer, and a pianist. He could do everything, and he wanted to hold a meeting at our church. I read the letter to the officers of the church, and they began to laugh. They said to me, "Why don't you invite him?" I said, "I'd never invite that man for two reasons. The first reason is, if he's the kind of man he says he is, after our people had heard him, they'd never want to hear me again! The second reason is I have a notion that he is a man who is boasting of a gift he does not have." What a picture this is!

And this is the picture of the apostates in the last days. Jude describes them in the most vivid language. He speaks of them as being clouds without water, fruit trees without fruit, "Raging waves of the sea, foaming out their own shame . . ." (Jude 12–13).

**Hast thou found honey? eat so much as is sufficient for thee, lest thou be filled therewith, and vomit it [Prov. 25:16].**

In the Old Testament, honey illustrates *natural* sweetness. There was no honey permitted in the bread or meal offering, because that offering speaks of Jesus Christ in His humanity. There was no natural sweetness in Him.

Have you ever met someone who was so sweet, who said so many sweet things it almost made you sick? Notice what it says here. Don't take in too much honey because it will make you sick at your tummy.

**Withdraw thy foot from thy neighbour's house; lest he be weary of thee, and so hate thee [Prov. 25:17].**

Oh, this is a good one! Don't spend too much time at the neighbor's, or else you may overhear a conversation in the kitchen where the lady of the house says, "I wish that old gossip would go home and stay home." It's better not to wear out your welcome at a place. That is what he is saying here.

**Confidence in an unfaithful man in time of trouble is like a broken tooth, and a foot out of joint [Prov. 25:19].**

For example, Judas was a bad toothache, and he was foot trouble—he was both of them. You have probably met someone like that in your life.

**If thine enemy be hungry, give him bread to eat; and if he be thirsty, give him water to drink:**

**For thou shalt heap coals of fire upon his head, and the LORD shall reward thee [Prov. 25:21–22].**

We find that the Lord Jesus repeats this principle, and Paul does, too. It is very important.

**The north wind driveth away rain: so doth an angry countenance a backbiting tongue [Prov. 25:23].**

We are living in a day of sweetness and light when we are not supposed to rebuke anyone for anything. Every now and then I get a letter from some lovely saint who rebukes me for being hard on certain groups and certain movements. May I say that I believe that is what I *should* do. "The north wind driveth away rain." An angry countenance will take care of a backbiting tongue; it will take care of those who are teaching falsely today. I think they should be dealt with, and I intend to continue to speak out when it is important to speak out.

It would be wonderful if we could have

sweetness and light all the time, but we are living in a world in which there are serpents along the pathway of life. There are pitfalls in our path: there is false doctrine and false teaching of the Word of God. And I want to speak out, but I hope I do it in a spirit of love. I have no intention of hurting any individual, but I do try to give out the truth of God. I find ample justification for that in the Word of God and here is one verse for it.

**It is better to dwell in the corner of the housetop, than with a brawling woman and in a wide house [Prov. 25:24].**

We have had this pointed out to us several times already. Solomon, who had so many wives, must have had a lot of trouble with some of them. Maybe that is why he mentioned this so often. I have wondered if he had some backseat drivers when he would go for a ride in his chariot.

A professor in seminary gave us this little poem many years ago. I'll just give you one verse and the chorus. I have part of it memorized, and I love to quote this to my wife.

'Twas at a crowded crossing; crowds hastened to the spot,
Whence came a cry of anguish and one loud pistol shot.
Inside an automobile there lay a woman dead.
Beside it stood the driver who with emotion said,

(Chorus)

"I am the lady's husband. Long years have we been wed.
I loved her very dearly and shot her through the head.
I perhaps should not have killed her; it is not right to slay
But with those backseat drivers, it is the only way."

I hope you don't mind that bit of facetious verse. Maybe Solomon had some backseat drivers in mind when he wrote this proverb.

**As cold waters to a thirsty soul, so is good news from a far country [Prov. 25:25].**

Have you heard from home lately? Or have you written home to mother? That is important. But there is something far greater in this verse than first meets the eye.

There has come good news from a far country. The Lord Jesus said, "I came forth from the Father, and am come into the world:

again, I leave the world, and go to the Father" (John 16:28). In that brief period of time, as John Wesley said, God was contracted to a span, and He wrought out your salvation and mine. That is the good news that has come to us from a far country. By the way, have you received Him? Have you accepted Him? He is the Water of Life. He is "cold waters to a thirsty soul."

**A righteous man falling down before the wicked is as a troubled fountain, and a corrupt spring [Prov. 25:26].**

When I was a little boy and went along on a hunting expedition, we never carried water with us in a container. We would come to a creek or a spring. Sometimes it would be limpid water (in that day pollution was not a big problem), but every now and then we found a spring that was green with scum. What a disappointment that would be.

This is the comparison he makes with a righteous man, a man who has stood for truth, who finally bows before the wicked. How many times that happens in business. How many times that happens in politics. A man of integrity, in order to get into office, will bow before the wicked. And it even happens in the church. A man who has stood for pure doctrine, for things that are right, will begin to compromise and cut corners. That is the heartbreak of the day. It is just like coming to a spring when you are thirsty and finding it covered with scum and pollutants. What a verse this is!

**It is not good to eat much honey: so for men to search their own glory is not glory [Prov. 25:27].**

A little honey is good, but a lot of honey makes you sick. For a man to be ambitious for self glory, especially in the ministry of God, makes you sick. We see this around us in the church—there is an inordinate ambition among some Christians today. It makes you sick at your tummy to see that type of thing.

**He that hath no rule over his own spirit is like a city that is broken down, and without walls [Prov. 25:28].**

This refers to a man or woman who cannot control his emotions, who is not self-controlled. And you know that self-control is a fruit of the Spirit. Now there is a time for a person to let go. There is a time to stand for something and to speak out with great emotion. But, my friend, we are to recognize our need to control our own spirits.

# CHAPTER 26

This first section deals with the fool. The Bible, especially Proverbs, has a great deal to say about the fool. This does not refer to the person who is mentally deficient. God is not talking to the person who is simpleminded or who has some mental aberration. The fool that God is talking to is a man who may be brilliant. In fact he may have his Ph.D. degree.

David wrote, "The fool hath said in his heart, There is no God . . ." (Ps. 14:1). A fool is a man who, though he may be brilliant, is an atheist. The Hebrew word for *fool* means "insane." The man who says there is no God is an insane man.

Intermarriage within a family can sometimes produce very brilliant offspring but can also produce mental deficiency. In the early days of a church I pastored in Tennessee one of the pastors had married into the governor's family where there had been much intermarrying. As a result, there was insanity in the family. The pastor had two daughters, and they were brilliant. They were old ladies, when I was a young pastor there, living way out in the country, up in the hills of middle Tennessee. I was holding meetings in that area, and they wanted me to come by to see them. I have never met two women who were more brilliant than those ladies. They knew all about me, about the church I was serving, about the Bible, literature, music, current events. It was amazing. But there was something odd there. The pastor who went with me had warned me not to be surprised at what I would see. When we went in, we had to shoo the chickens off the chairs so we could sit down. Then we had to be rather careful where we sat. While I was sitting there talking to them, a cow stuck her head in from the kitchen door. There was a horse in the bedroom, and there were goats all around—I didn't see them, but I sure could tell they were there. The sisters had a mental aberration, you see.

Now that is not the kind of thing the Lord means when He calls a person a fool. He means someone who has rejected Him. God calls that insanity.

**As snow in summer, and as rain in harvest, so honour is not seemly for a fool [Prov. 26:1].**

One of the marks of a fool is that he doesn't mind sacrificing his honor. Candidly, he has none.

**As the bird by wandering, as the swallow by flying, so the curse causeless shall not come [Prov. 26:2].**

Predictions that certain things will come to pass do not always happen. By the way, we have a lot of so-called prophets in our midst today. They keep telling us what is going to happen in the next few years. Some of it may come to pass, that's true, but they are not getting their information from God—because sometimes they are wrong, and God's prophet is never wrong (see Deut. 18:20–22).

**A whip for the horse, a bridle for the ass, and a rod for the fool's back [Prov. 26:3].**

That is a good one. The horse and the ass can be trained. They will respond. The only thing a fool will respond to is real discipline.

**Answer not a fool according to his folly, lest thou also be like unto him.**

**Answer a fool according to his folly, lest he be wise in his own conceit [Prov. 26:4–5].**

When I was a boy, our town atheist enjoyed pointing out contradictions in the Bible. This was one that he used. My friend, there is no contradiction here at all. These two proverbs simply set before us two possible lines of conduct in response to a fool.

I get many letters from many kinds of people. I answer some of the letters, and some of the letters I do not answer. I must make a decision about them. I conclude that some of the letters I get come from fools. If I were to answer such a letter according to its folly, I would make myself a fool. If you lay yourself wide open to a fool, you are a fool yourself.

I had this experience recently. I received a letter from a brilliant man who had some impressions about me that were entirely wrong. I thought I should try to correct him and tell him the truth, so I responded according to verse 5. I answered his letter. Then I received a letter back from him, and I have never seen such a foolish letter. It made me feel like a fool for having written to him in the first place. I do not intend to answer his second letter. I am using verse 4 for my decision. So you see, there are two lines of conduct set before us, and we need to determine whether we should respond or should not respond.

**He that sendeth a message by the hand of a fool cutteth off the feet, and drinketh damage [Prov. 26:6].**

You make a mistake if you send a message by the wrong individual!

**The legs of the lame are not equal: so is a parable in the mouth of fools [Prov. 26:7].**

I would like to extend this to the interpretation of parables. There are interpretations of parables in the Bible that are taught by some professors which tempt me to say, "So is a parable in the mouth of fools."

**As he that bindeth a stone in a sling, so is he that giveth honour to a fool [Prov. 26:8].**

Giving honor to a fool is simply giving him ammunition.

**As a thorn goeth up into the hand of a drunkard, so is a parable in the mouth of fools [Prov. 26:9].**

A thorny branch in the hand of a drunken man will probably wound him as well as others. The same is true of a fool who has the position of a teacher. He will hurt himself and those who listen.

**The great God that formed all things both rewardeth the fool, and rewardeth transgressors [Prov. 26:10].**

We can be very sure of the ultimate outcome. God will take care of things and handle all these matters.

Here is something rather frightful.

**As a dog returneth to his vomit, so a fool returneth to his folly [Prov. 26:11].**

I know of nothing as harsh as that. It is repulsive and sickening even to think of this. This is the viewpoint that Peter presents to us concerning the hypocrite: "But it is happened unto them according to the true proverb, The dog is turned to his own vomit again; and the sow that was washed to her wallowing in the mire" (2 Pet. 2:22).

Remember that when the prodigal son was in the pigpen, he knew that he was in the wrong place, and he returned to his home. Suppose when he returned home, he brought along with him one of the pigs from the pigpen. The little pig would not enjoy the father's house. Eventually he would go to the pigpen. Eventually, all the hypocrites in the church will be revealed, and there are many who only *pretend* to be sons of God—there is no question about that.

A man told me that the reason he did not join the church was that the church was filled with hypocrites. I said, "No one knows that better than I do. But that is no reason why you shouldn't be in the church. You can't hide behind a hypocrite. You should be in there revealing what is genuine."

I have talked about hypocrisy in the church before, and I receive letters from folk who don't like me to mention it. But the Bible teaches that there is a security for the believer, and also there is insecurity for the make-believer. It is to the hypocrite that the proverb refers.

**Seest thou a man wise in his own conceit? there is more hope of a fool than of him [Prov. 26:12].**

There is something worse than a fool and that is an egomaniac, one who has a high opinion of himself.

**Where no wood is, there the fire goeth out: so where there is no talebearer, the strife ceaseth [Prov. 26:20].**

Bitterness is repeatedly stirred up in certain groups because there are certain ones in there who keep putting a little wood on the fire. If no one were fueling it, the fire would go out; the strife would cease.

**As coals are to burning coals, and wood to fire; so is a contentious man to kindle strife [Prov. 26:21].**

There are certain folks who cause strife as soon as they start attending a church or join a church. You will find them in the Lord's work today. They seem to stir things up all the time. They are never really interested in the Word of God, although they may pretend to be.

**The words of a talebearer are as wounds, and they go down into the innermost parts of the belly [Prov. 26:22].**

A better translation is, "The words of a talebearer are as dainty morsels, and go down into the innermost parts of the belly." People like to hear those choice little bits of gossip. They like to hear them, but they are hard to digest and will finally make them sick. A real child of God does not wish to hear things that are ugly.

Now here we have one of the longest and strongest sections against hypocrisy, and it refers to hypocrisy among God's people.

**Burning lips and a wicked heart are like a potsherd covered with silver dross.**

**He that hateth dissembleth with his lips, and layeth up deceit within him;**

**When he speaketh fair, believe him not: for there are seven abominations in his heart.**

**Whose hatred is covered by deceit, his wickedness shall be shewed before the whole congregation.**

**Whoso diggeth a pit shall fall therein: and he that rolleth a stone, it will return upon him.**

**A lying tongue hateth those that are afflicted by it; and a flattering mouth worketh ruin [Prov. 26:23–28].**

There are folk who make a *profession* of faith in Jesus Christ, but who are not really God's children. We call them hypocrites because they are pretending to be what they are not. They are phonies. But they should not disturb those inside or outside the church for the very fact that a counterfeit necessitates a genuine and valuable original. No one counterfeits pennies or even one-dollar bills, as far as I know. They do counterfeit twenty-dollar bills. They only counterfeit that which is valuable. So we should not be surprised to see counterfeit Christians. This cluster of proverbs describes the phony and warns against him. He is the man who is two-faced. He will flatter you, yet in his heart he will hate you.

It was Tacitus who made the statement, "It is common for men to hate those whom they have injured." Dr. Ironside puts it like this: "Conscious of having wronged another, and being determined not to confess it, the dissembler will store his heart with hatred against the object of his wrongdoing. To hide his wretched feelings, such a one will flatter with his lips while all the time he is plotting the ruin of his victim."

An example of flattery and hypocrisy in the Bible is Haman. Remember how he flattered. This man plotted to destroy an entire people, including the queen upon the throne. He was an evil man. He flattered the king, and yet it was obvious that he was planning to overthrow the king.

Hypocrisy is found in Christian circles, and we need to recognize it. There is no use covering over this. There is probably no place in the world where there is so much cover-up as in the church. We try to act as if there were no wrong there. We think that if we ignore it, it will go away. We feel defeated if anyone mentions the fact that there is hypocrisy. We feel that we in ourselves are defeated if we acknowledge that even in our hearts there is this root of bitterness sometimes. Christians need to face up to these sins, and the proverbs are good at making us face up to them.

# CHAPTER 27

This chapter deals with the subject of friendship.

**Boast not thyself of to-morrow; for thou knowest not what a day may bring forth [Prov. 27:1].**

There is a philosophy of procrastination that is very familiar to all of us. It puts off until tomorrow what could be done today. South of the border, our Mexican friends have a word for it: "mañana"—tomorrow. That is the easy route. There is a Spanish proverb that says, "The road of by-and-by leads to the house of never." Usually when one says, *Mañana*, it really means, "Never." It is not that there is no intention of doing the thing in question. It is just put off. We have another proverb that puts it very bluntly, "The way to hell is paved with good intentions." The English have a proverb that says, "Procrastination is the thief of time." The Word of God puts it like this: ". . . *To-day* if ye will hear his voice, harden not your hearts" (Heb. 4:7, italics mine). And again, "(. . . behold, *now* is the accepted time; behold, *now* is the day of salvation.)" (2 Cor. 6:2, italics mine). Isaiah writes, "Come *now*, and let us reason together, saith the Lord . . ." (Isa. 1:18, italics mine). The tendency of man is to want to wait for another time. Remember that the governor Felix trembled when he heard the gospel from the apostle Paul. Paul, though a prisoner, talked to him about his soul's salvation, and Felix responded, ". . . Go thy way for this time;

when I have a convenient season, I will call for thee" (Acts 24:25). As far as we know from the Word of God, that "convenient season" never came for Felix. Also, Pharaoh in Egypt was always going to let the children of Israel go tomorrow, not today. Finally his repeated postponements cost him his oldest son and all the firstborn in the land of Egypt.

Today is always the day of salvation. You do not know what tomorrow will bring.

**Let another man praise thee, and not thine own mouth; a stranger, and not thine own lips [Prov. 27:2].**

Goliath should have listened to this proverb. He paraded in front of the army of Israel every day, flexed his muscles, told them how great he was and what a miserable bunch of cowards they were. Eventually he got into trouble with a boy named David.

**A stone is heavy, and the sand weighty; but a fool's wrath is heavier than them both [Prov. 27:3].**

If you have a fool angry with you, you are in trouble, because a fool has no discretion. He will say and do anything.

**Wrath is cruel, and anger is outrageous; but who is able to stand before envy? [Prov. 27:4].**

Envy is jealousy. ". . . jealousy is cruel as the grave: the coals thereof are coals of fire, which hath a most vehement flame" (Song 8:6).

You will remember what jealousy did in the family of Jacob. The brothers sold Joseph into slavery because of their intense jealousy.

**Open rebuke is better than secret love.**

**Faithful are the wounds of a friend; but the kisses of an enemy are deceitful [Prov. 27:5–6].**

This is a contrast of which we have many examples in the Bible. Paul rebuked Simon Peter when he withdrew from eating with the Gentiles. Peter needed that rebuke, and he accepted it from Paul. There was no ill feeling between them.

It is a wonderful thing to have a friend who will call attention to your faults in a helpful way. That's the reason a preacher needs a good wife. She can keep him humble and tell him what is wrong with him. I have come out from a service puffed up like a balloon. When we get into the car, my wife pushes a pin into the balloon. I recognize that she is the one who is right rather than the one who was flattering me.

Now the contrasting thought is, of course, exemplified in Judas who betrayed Jesus with a kiss.

**The full soul loatheth an honeycomb; but to the hungry soul every bitter thing is sweet [Prov. 27:7].**

This is the reason we have gourmet cooking in our day. We are a pampered people who have so much to eat that the food must be prepared in unusual ways or the foods must be exotic and unusual to whet our appetites. Some people need hummingbird wings or peacock tongues served to them before they can really enjoy their food. That is why cooking reached such a high degree of perfection in the European countries like France, Italy, Spain, and Germany. The ruling class had such plenty that they got tired of eating plain food. A tenderloin steak or filet mignon or strawberries and ice cream were just not good enough for them. So the chefs of that day had to concoct unusual and tasty foods for them.

Contrast this with the hungry man. Food, all food, any food tastes good to him.

One can also apply this to the Word of God. We are to eat it, chew it, ruminate on it. Actually, this is what it means to meditate on the Word of God. May God give us an appetite, a real hunger for His Word!

**As a bird that wandereth from her nest, so is a man that wandereth from his place [Prov. 27:8].**

There are many folk in churches and in other Christian works who are like round pegs in square holes or square pegs in round holes. They just don't fit in. The reason is that God has given to every believer a gift: "But the manifestation of the Spirit is given to *every* man to profit withal" (1 Cor. 12:7, italics mine). And God has a particular place for every believer to exercise the gift he has been given: "But now hath God set the members every one of them in the body, as it hath pleased him" (1 Cor. 12:18). We should get into that place and exercise our gift. In the New Testament we have examples of folk who apparently didn't exercise their gifts. For instance, Paul spoke of a young man by the name of Demas: "For Demas hath forsaken me, having loved this present world, and is departed unto Thessalonica . . ." (2 Tim. 4:10). He went back into the world. As far as we know, he never did fit into the place that God had for him.

**Ointment and perfume rejoice the heart: so doth the sweetness of a man's friend by hearty counsel.**

**Thine own friend, and thy father's friend, forsake not; neither go into thy brother's house in the day of thy calamity: for better is a neighbour that is near than a brother far off [Prov. 27: 9–10].**

I have always felt that this is a California proverb. When I first came to California, I was shocked at the few people who attended funerals. I had come from Texas, where people came from far and near to attend a funeral. The largest crowds I ever addressed were at Texas funerals. When I came to California, I conducted a funeral for a dear saint of God who lived alone. She had brought her husband out here from the East because he was sick, and she spent much of her time caring for him until he died. She didn't have many friends, although she had become active in the church to a certain extent. I thought the place would be crowded for her funeral, but there were about fifteen people there. Her family and friends were back in the East. "Better is a neighbour that is near than a brother far off." We all need friends, and it is better to make friends among our neighbors than depend on family and old friends who are great distances from us.

**A prudent man foreseeth the evil, and hideth himself; but the simple pass on, and are punished [Prov. 27:12].**

This is one of the great benefits of the study of prophecy: We know what is coming. Frankly, I would be very discouraged and pessimistic if I had to look to men to solve our problems today. I don't think man has the solution. We are moving to a crisis and a catastrophe—I don't think there is any question about that. Any man is very foolish to think that he can solve the problems of the world. The Word of God makes it clear that there is trouble ahead, and the judgment of God is coming upon this old world.

There is another thought in connection with this proverb. I will state it in rather terse language: Buy insurance. The Lord intends for you to make plans for the future. "A prudent man forseeth the evil, and hideth himself." He prepares for the difficult day that is coming. Some people have the idea that a man ought not prepare for retirement, ought not to carry insurance. The foolish reason given is that we ought to trust the Lord. Let me say that when the Lord has given us means for providing for the future, we should avail ourselves of them.

**He that blesseth his friend with a loud voice, rising early in the morning, it shall be counted a curse to him [Prov. 27:14].**

There is a great deal of irony in this statement. There are those who make such loud protestations of love and affection that you know there is some motive behind it all. Watch out for the man who is praising you more than you ought to be praised.

A scriptural illustration of this is the way in which Absalom won the hearts of the men of Israel (see 2 Sam. 15:1–6). He got up early and came to the city gate to talk to the men who came to the king with a controversy. Absalom flattered them and pretended to love them and show an interest in their cases. But his true interest was in gaining their support when he seized the throne. (Politicians have been following this same procedure from that day to this!)

I always tell this to young preachers when I am speaking in seminaries: "Young men, regardless of what church you go to, there will always be a dear saint in that church who will tell you what a wonderful preacher you are. Generally it is a sweet old lady; sometimes it is a man. The Lord puts them there to encourage young preachers. They will tell you that you are the greatest preacher they have ever heard. They will have you think you are another apostle Paul, Martin Luther, John Calvin, Billy Sunday, and Billy Graham all wrapped into one individual. It's wonderful that such a person is there to encourage you, but don't you believe what you hear. It's not true." A modern proverb goes something like this: Flattery is like perfume. The idea is to smell it, not swallow it.

**A continual dropping in a very rainy day and a contentious woman are alike.**

**Whosoever hideth her hideth the wind, and the ointment of his right hand, which bewrayeth itself [Prov. 27: 15–16].**

We are back to the subject of the contentious woman. I have already quoted the first verse of the ballad of the backseat driver. The man shot his wife because she was a backseat driver and, of course, he was brought to trial in the court. They attempted to convict him, but the last verse and chorus tell you what happened:

The judge and jury listened, then rose
and set him free.

"Your act was justified," they said, "We do agree.
We know how much you suffered, how tortured was your mind
Each time you took her driving, and this is what we find:

(Chorus)

You were the lady's husband; long years ago you wed.
You loved her very dearly and shot her through the head.
You perhaps should not have killed her; it is not right to slay,
But with these backseat drivers, it is the only way."

That's all I'll say about the contentious woman!

**Iron sharpeneth iron; so a man sharpeneth the countenance of his friend [Prov. 27:17].**

It is a wonderful thing to have a friend with whom you can sharpen your mind. You can discuss certain things with him with real profit. I used to have such a friend, and we could sit down and talk about spiritual matters. I always came away refreshed and strengthened, and I always had learned something. It is wonderful to have a friend like that.

**As in water face answereth to face, so the heart of man to man [Prov. 27:19].**

It is wonderful to have a friend to whom you can open your heart, knowing that he will not betray you. A friend is one who knows you and still loves you.

**Hell and destruction are never full; so the eyes of man are never satisfied [Prov. 27:20].**

We never see enough. We want to keep on seeing. That's the reason some of us love to travel around the world.

**As the fining pot for silver, and the furnace for gold; so is a man to his praise [Prov. 27:21].**

Be careful of praise. Make sure it has the right effect upon you. Dr. Ironside (*Notes on the Book of Proverbs*, pp. 390–391) has this comment: "There is no hotter crucible to test a man than when he is put through a fire of praise and adulation. To go on through evil report, cleaving to the Lord, and counting on Him to clear one's name is comparatively easy, though many faint in such circumstances; but to humbly pursue the even tenor of his way, undisturbed and unlifted up by applause and flattery, marks a man as being truly with God."

**For riches are not for ever: and doth the crown endure to every generation? [Prov. 27:24].**

"Riches are not for ever"—in our materialistic age we need to recognize the truth of this. You won't be taking your riches with you. There is no pocket in a shroud.

"And doth the crown endure to every generation?" Dynasties rise and fall in this world of changes. God is the only One on whom we can depend. He is the only unchangeable Friend.

This has been a great chapter on friendship.

# CHAPTER 28

**The wicked flee when no man pursueth: but the righteous are bold as a lion [Prov. 28:1].**

Sin, regardless of the viewpoint of men toward it, puts a person into a state of continual fear and self-condemnation. I was speaking to a group of young people about sin, just sin in general. A young fellow and girl in the group were living together. I had never even mentioned that as a sin, but it was interesting to hear how that young man began to defend himself—it would have been amusing if it had not been so serious. When sin was being discussed, his conscience began to prick him, and then he began defending himself. "The wicked flee when no man pursueth." No one had pointed a finger at him. I would not have known of his sin if he had kept quiet. The discussion was about sin, not his particular sin.

There is a psychological term that is used: a

guilt complex. We all have a guilt complex. A Christian psychologist, who was on the faculty of the University of Southern California, said to me, "We all have a guilt complex. It is as much a part of us as our right arm. No one can get rid of a guilt complex just by wishful thinking." Many people try to do that. He went on with an even more interesting statement: "We psychologists can shift the guilt complex from one place to another, but we cannot eliminate it."

"The righteous are bold as a lion." If a man is not guilty, he can stand up and speak out. If his own mind is free from guilt, he is not afraid of the thoughts and minds of other men.

**He that turneth away his ear from hearing the law, even his prayer shall be abomination [Prov. 28:9].**

"The Law" means the Word of God. It includes everything that had been written up to the time of Solomon: the Pentateuch, Joshua, Judges, and many of the Psalms.

The thing that God is saying here is very important. If you want God to hear you, you must hear Him first. He has made it very clear that He does not listen to the prayer of the godless man. It is just sentimental twaddle to talk about the prayers of the godless man being answered in time of trouble. Tear-jerking stories tell of a sick little daughter whose father in a very sentimental way calls upon God to raise her up. I would suggest that he call a godly friend to pray to the Lord for his little girl, because God will not hear the prayer of the ungodly man. He says he won't. "For the eyes of the Lord are over the righteous, and his ears are open unto their prayers: but the face of the Lord is against them that do evil" (1 Pet. 3:12). Here in Proverbs it says that his prayer is actually an abomination to God.

**Whoso causeth the righteous to go astray in an evil way, he shall fall himself into his own pit: but the upright shall have good things in possession [Prov. 28:10].**

This is a law of God that is operative in this world. You can find this again and again as you go through the Word of God. For example, David by his sin brought scandal into his own family and his own home.

**The rich man is wise in his own conceit; but the poor that hath understanding searcheth him out [Prov. 28:11].**

Riches will minister to pride and conceit. They seem to go along together. You hear of rich people giving testimonies at banquets, especially prominent banquets. You hear that the great men of this world give their testimony at the president's prayer breakfast. Did you ever hear of them reaching down and asking some poor little vegetable variety Christian to give his testimony? But notice what God says, "The rich man is wise in his own conceit; but the poor that hath understanding searcheth him out." The poor man, poor in this world's goods but rich in faith, can listen to the testimony of the rich and know that it is hollow, that it lacks reality. Even if it is real, it will often lack the ring of discernment and of understanding of spiritual things. I have been present at banquets where they have called upon a prominent businessman or a so-called Hollywood convert to give a testimony. I have noted the people who have real spiritual discernment bowing their heads in embarrassment at the things which were being said. This is a very practical proverb, and one that is often passed over.

**He that covereth his sins shall not prosper: but whoso confesseth and forsaketh them shall have mercy [Prov. 28:13].**

This is a great proverb. It seems a common practice today for Christians to try to cover their sins. You will find in the average church that there is a bandage Band-Aid of silence wrapped over the cancer of sin. People don't like to talk about it; in fact, they won't admit its existence. They like to think they are very good. But we are told here, "But whoso confesseth and forsaketh them shall have mercy." And we have the New Testament version of this in 1 John 1:9: "If we confess our sins, he is faithful and just to forgive us our sins, and to cleanse us from all unrighteousness." This does not refer to a public confesion of sin; confession is between you and the Lord, and sin should be *dealt* with. Trying to appear sinless before your little group of friends is a big mistake. If you confess and forsake your sin, you shall have mercy. How wonderful!

**Happy is the man that feareth alway: but he that hardeneth his heart shall fall into mischief [Prov. 28:14].**

This is what it means to walk in the fear of the Lord. Remember that "The fear of the Lord is the beginning of wisdom . . . (Prov. 9:10)." It means that our hearts are open toward God all the time. It is the opposite of "he that hardeneth his heart." The man who fears God is one who is *listening* to God. He is one who is trying to walk in a way that is *pleasing* to God. He is walking in humility before the Lord. He walks in recognition of his weakness and of his utter dependence upon God. This is the meaning of "the fear of the LORD is the beginning of wisdom."

I must pause here to say that I have received letters that read: "You have pointed out the faults of the church members, and you have given the criticism of the Christians who are in the churches today. Don't you have a word of encouragement for them?"

May I say that I attempt to teach the Word of God. We are living in days of apostasy— pastors in our churches across the land and missionaries on the foreign field are quick to acknowledge the present-day apostasy of the church. I recognize that we need encouragement, and the Bible has much to say that is encouraging to the true believer. I call attention to the local church when the Word of God makes it very clear that reference is being made to folk who are making only a profession of being Christian. I feel that to be forewarned is to be forearmed. A great many folk in and out of the church are tremendously discouraged by what they see in the lives of some Christians, and it is causing them to turn away from religion. A rebellious young man told me, "I've turned off religion." Well, knowing something of the boy's background, I almost felt like saying, *I don't blame you.* I couldn't say that to the young man, so I tried to point out to him that there are many wonderful saints in the church. Often they are in the background, and he hadn't noticed them. They are folk with whom he could have wonderful fellowship.

I felt that I should pause in our study to insert this explanation in case you may be thinking that I am too critical of the contemporary church.

Actually, the one who wrote these proverbs didn't spare any of us. Many of the proverbs fit us just like a garment!

**A man that doeth violence to the blood of any person shall flee to the pit; let no man stay him [Prov. 28:17].**

A man who is consciously guilty of having committed a horrible crime must bear a fearful load on his conscience. Often it will finally drive him to suicide. There are many cases like that today. The prime example from the Bible is Judas Iscariot who was driven to suicide because of the awful, dastardly crime which he had committed.

An FBI man told me that sometimes a crime will go unsolved for years. They will have no inkling at all of evidence nor any way to trace the guilty one. Then a man or woman pops up who has to talk, who feels impelled to make a confession. Sometimes the person is already in prison for another crime. He will confess the unsolved crime that the police are still working on. Why does he do that? Because the crime is on the mind and heart of the guilty one. There is no escape from it. God has made us that way as a means of bringing us back to Himself.

**Whoso robbeth his father or his mother, and saith, It is no transgression; the same is the companion of a destroyer [Prov. 28:24].**

A young person may think, *I'm going to inherit what my dad owns, so I'll just take a little of it now.* God says that that is a crime. The Lord Jesus rebuked the religious rulers of His day because they taught that as soon as a person had said to his father or mother, "It is Corban" or "I have dedicated to God that which would relieve your need" (see Matt. 15:5–6; Mark 7:11), he thereby consecrated all to God and was freed from using it for his parents. This, Jesus declared to be contradictory to the command of God. You see, it is so easy because of a relationship to deny support or to take something that does not belong to us. That is what our Lord condemned.

Incidentally, if you are a parent, you should not ignore acts of theft in the home.

# CHAPTER 29

**He, that being often reproved hardeneth his neck, shall suddenly be destroyed, and that without remedy [Prov. 29:1].**

God has so many ways of reproving a man; yet the man can keep going on in sin. In my own experience I have known so many folk who were warned before judgment fell upon them; they ignored the warning, and judgment fell upon them in this life.

In Dallas, Texas, one night I was walking down the street with a friend. A big crowd was gathered around out in front of a theatre. There was a wrecked automobile there and, believe me, it was really in a sad condition. When I got back to the seminary, one of the students told us the story of that car. It had been driven by a high school student and his girl friend. They had stopped to invite another girl to call her date and go out with them. She said, "No, I can't go with you tonight," but she asked them to come with her to a Bible class. They finally agreed to take her to her Bible class, but they would not go in with her. On the way over, this girl presented Christ to them. She told them that she had accepted Christ through the Bible class and that they needed Him, too. They just laughed, and let the girl out of the car. Five minutes later as they were speeding down the street, they were both killed instantly when they collided with another car.

There are many examples of this in the Bible. We think of Korah, and Dathan and Abiram, Belshazzar, Jezebel, and others. "He, that being often reproved hardeneth his neck, shall suddenly be destroyed, and that without remedy."

**When the righteous are in authority, the people rejoice: but when the wicked beareth rule, the people mourn [Prov. 29:2].**

We've seen before that when the wicked are in power, they never solve the problem, but one righteous man is able to bring blessing to a nation. That is what we need in this nation of ours above everything else. We don't need men who say they have solutions for every problem. No one has the solutions for the problems of this world, and if anyone says he does, he must say it with his tongue in his cheek. What we need today are righteous men who will stand for the right at any price. I believe just one such man is better than a whole party, regardless of what party it might be.

When the wicked rule, everyone suffers. Incidentally, for whom did you vote?

**The king by judgment establisheth the land: but he that receiveth gifts overthroweth it [Prov. 29:4].**

David was a good king. He was a righteous ruler over men, a ruler in the fear of God. Yet David made the confession that his house was not sound. Only Christ is the King who by judgment will establish the land. The coming of Christ to this earth is the only hope the world has. Thank the Lord that the church will leave before He comes to judge the earth. That is the promise that He has given.

Politicians today are influenced by the giving of gifts. That has always figured in the politics of both parties. The Lord Jesus will reign in *righteousness*.

**A man that flattereth his neighbour spreadeth a net for his feet [Prov. 29:5].**

Applause for a man who is doing a good job is certainly in order. Merit should be recognized. I think there is a time to stand up and cheer for an individual. But when flattery is used, it is like the overdose of honey that we have read about in this book. It seems there are some people who are just given to flattery. They do not really tell the thing that is upon their hearts.

When I was a pastor, there was a man who was always making requests and asking favors. I knew the minute my secretary said that he was on the phone that he wanted something. He always began the same way: "Oh Dr. McGee, I was listening to you on the radio this past week, and I want to tell you I never heard a message like that. I hope you are putting that message into print." The more flattering the things he said, the bigger the favor he was going to ask. Flattery is a dangerous thing because sometimes people believe it. It is tragic when we believe flattery.

**The bloodthirsty hate the upright: but the just seek his soul [Prov. 29:10].**

We might translate it like this: "Men of blood hate the perfect, but the just seek [or care] for his soul." The bloodthirsty man has murder and hate in his heart. The Lord Jesus said that if you hate your brother, you are guilty of murder.

Cain was a murderer, and the murder began in his heart. It shows how far and how quickly man fell. Remember that God created Adam and Eve *perfect*. When they fell, the only thing they could bring into the world was a sinner. They brought forth sons and daughters in their own likeness. Cain was one of them. He was a boy born with murder in his heart—he hated his brother.

**A fool uttereth all his mind: but a wise man keepeth it in till afterwards [Prov. 29:11].**

You talk with a fool, and he will tell you everything. A wise man will hold back. He will be very careful what he says.

**If a ruler hearken to lies, all his servants are wicked [Prov. 29:12].**

Parents need to discipline a child faithfully and set an example before him, because a child will imitate his parents. And the people will imitate their rulers and men in high position. The conduct of a ruler will be reflected in those who are under him. That is the picture we have here.

**Correct thy son, and he shall give thee rest; yea, he shall give delight unto thy soul [Prov. 29:17].**

Again we have before us the importance of discipline.

**Where there is no vision, the people perish: but he that keepeth the law, happy is he [Prov. 29:18].**

"Vision" is actually spiritual understanding. It is the work of the Holy Spirit in the life of the believer to give him understanding of the Word of God.

We read in 1 Samuel 3:1: ". . . And the word of the LORD was precious in those days; there was no open vision." The Word of the Lord was *precious*, or *rare*. There was no understanding of the Word of God, and, therefore, it was precious in those days. God had to raise up Samuel, a seer, to meet that need.

You may remember that Joshua was disturbed because some of the men prophesied in the camp. But Moses said, ". . . would God that all the LORD'S people were prophets, and that the LORD would put his spirit upon them!" (Num. 11:29).

Spiritual discernment is one of the gifts that God has given to the church—that is, an understanding of the Word of God.

This chapter concludes the collection of proverbs that were copied out by the men of Hezekiah. It concludes all the proverbs which are attributed to King Solomon. However, I believe that the final chapter of Proverbs was also written by Solomon and that he is King Lemuel.

# CHAPTER 30

In this one chapter are proverbs by an unknown sage, named Agur. The first verse tells us all we know about his parentage.

**The words of Agur the son of Jakeh, even the prophecy: the man spake unto Ithiel, even unto Ithiel and Ucal [Prov. 30:1].**

None of these named are people whom we know. Agur is an unknown seer, an unknown writer. The proper names here are like all Hebrew names in that they do mean something "*Aguar*" means gatherer and "*Jakeh*" means pious. Some versions translate the names as common nouns: "The words of a gatherer, the son of the pious."

**Who hath ascended up into heaven, or descended? who hath gathered the wind in his fists? who hath bound the waters in a garment? who hath established all the ends of the earth? what is his name, and what is his son's name, if thou canst tell? [Prov. 30:4].**

It is interesting to note that these are some of the questions God asked Job. Who is able to answer such questions? The Lord Jesus said, "And no man hath ascended up to heaven, but he that came down from heaven, even the Son of man which is in heaven" (John 3:13). This is why I constantly say that the Lord Jesus is the only authority on this matter of creation and the origin of the universe. Very candidly, I don't think any of us has the correct explanation of the origin of the universe. Scientists do not—the very fact that they come up with the evolutionary theory means that they do not have the answer to origin. The reason that we spent so much money to go to the moon was to get rocks so that we might find out about the origin of the universe!

The first verse of Genesis tells us that in the beginning God created the heaven and the earth. That is how it all began. But then the next verse: "And the earth was without form, and void; and darkness was upon the face of the deep. And the spirit of God moved upon the face of the waters" (Gen. 1:2) is considered by some to describe the act of creation. My friend, I don't think that God has told us *how* he did the creating. I believe this second verse suggests the gap theory—that God created the heaven and the earth and then there followed a space of time. Something happened to that original creation. The earth became without form and void. I recognize that this theory has been largely abandoned, but I still hold it in spite of what these sharp young men are writing today. My contention is that God has not told how He created. We just don't know—neither scientist nor theologian knows. I like the question God asked Job: "Where wast thou when I laid the foundations of the earth? . . ." (Job 38:4). That is a question which God can ask every individual. No one has the answer.

Also I like the question Agur asks. "Who hath gathered the wind in his fists?" Just think—God holds the winds just like we might hold some article in our hand. What a picture that is! Man knows very little about these things. In that same passage where the Lord Jesus said He was the One who came down from heaven, He also said, "The wind bloweth where it listeth, and thou hearest the sound thereof, but canst not tell whence it cometh, and whither it goeth . . ." (John 3:8). This is a tremendous thought.

**Every word of God is pure: he is a shield unto them that put their trust in him [Prov. 30:5].**

Nothing will clean you up like the Word of God. Every Word of God is pure. It is better than any soap; it is a miracle cleanser.

**Add thou not unto his words, lest he reprove thee, and thou be found a liar [Prov. 30:6].**

This should make us cautious in our handling of the Word of God. God doesn't mind calling a man a liar if he is one.

**Two things have I required of thee; deny me them not before I die:**

**Remove far from me vanity and lies: give me neither poverty nor riches; feed me with food convenient for me:**

**Lest I be full, and deny thee, and say, Who is the LORD? or lest I be poor, and steal, and take the name of my God in vain [Prov. 30:7–9].**

"Remove far from me vanity and lies" means I don't want to live among those who are vain and are flattering and are lying. It is like living in a rattlesnake den to live with folk like that. And then he says, "Give me neither poverty nor riches." Let me take the middle of the road. I don't want to be an extremist either way.

**There is a generation that are pure in their own eyes, and yet is not washed from their filthiness [Prov. 30:12].**

There are some church members who are like that. They are pure in their own eyes. They feel that they don't need a Savior. They are just religious.

Also there are people who are high up in business and politics who feel that they are pure—they are not guilty of wrongdoing. Even the down-and-outer may be pure in his own eyes. But none of them is washed. The only way that any of us can be clean is to be washed in the blood of Jesus Christ.

**The horseleach hath two daughters, crying, Give, give. There are three things that are never satisfied, yea, four things say not, It is enough [Prov. 30:15].**

Have you ever ridden horseback? You have two reins, and you must hold back on those reins because each one of them is constantly saying, "Give, give. Let go and let me run!" But you had better hold on to those reins or you will have a runaway horse.

This is something you and I need in life—self-control, holding back. Remember that David wrote: "Be ye not as the horse, or as the mule, which have no understanding: whose mouth must be held in with bit and bridle . . ." (Ps. 32:9). We need to commit ourselves to the Lord for His control.

Now he goes on to list the four things that are never satisfied:

**The grave; and the barren womb; the earth that is not filled with water; and the fire that saith not, It is enough [Prov. 30:16].**

First is "the grave." You and I live in a funeral procession. All of us do. It began outside the Garden of Eden with the death of Abel, and it has been coming down through the centuries. This old world on which we live is a great big cemetery. The grave is never satisfied.

"The barren womb." There are so many women who cannot have children for one reason or another. (I think they would make such wonderful mothers of adopted children.) They are never satisfied. Such a woman wants that precious little one to put his chubby arms around her neck and call her mother. And the same holds true for fathers.

"The earth that is not filled with water." We don't ever get enough rain out here in California. We need more rain.

"The fire that saith not, It is enough." We have too much fire and not enough rain. I sometimes wonder when we are going to burn off all the mountains of California. I thought we would have run out of burnable mountains long ago, but they still burn every summer.

**The eye that mocketh at his father, and despiseth to obey his mother, the ravens of the valley shall pick it out, and the young eagles shall eat it [Prov. 30:17].**

Terrible judgments are pronounced against those who turn against father and mother. God have mercy on the young people today who have turned against their parents who are believers in Christ.

**There be three things which are too wonderful for me, yea, four which I know not:**

**The way of an eagle in the air; the way of a serpent upon a rock; the way of a ship in the midst of the sea; and the way of a man with a maid [Prov. 30:18–19].**

Agur, the writer, didn't understand these things, and I don't either. Have you thought of this when you watch an eagle fly? Have you been intrigued by a serpent on a rock? Then there is the way of a ship at sea. I went across the Atlantic on the *Queen Mary* many years ago, and it was a wonder to me how that great ship of iron could float. And then the way of a man with a maid. Today we hear so much about sex; yet in spite of that, have you noticed how awkward the young boy is when he meets a girl? They are both a little embarrassed when they meet.

I well remember my first date when I was about fourteen, before I was saved. I didn't want to miss anything so I started to date early. I was walking with this girl, taking her to a movie. In those days men wore garters to hold up their socks. Well, mine came loose,

and it was dragging. Oh my! You talk about embarrassment! I never was so embarrassed in all my life. I didn't have sense enough to just stop and step aside to fix it. I just went down the street dragging that garter. After a while a crowd followed us, and that made it even worse. The girl got red in the face, and I got red in the face. I don't think we said anything to each other for a couple of hours after that happened. The way of a man with a maid. Agur says that he doesn't understand these things, and I don't understand them either.

**Such is the way of an adulterous woman; she eateth, and wipeth her mouth, and saith, I have done no wickedness [Prov. 30:20].**

We are living in a day when this has come to pass. There are those who are living in sin, and they will argue that they are not living in sin. I understand one little girl born out of wedlock was given a name that means purity. Well, in the first place the child was not pure, because *all* children are born with a sinful nature. In the second place, the name of the child could not change the fact that her mother was an adulteress. God says that adultery is sin, and God has not changed His mind. He hasn't learned anything new from this generation. God knew the sins that our generation would commit, and He has already written about them in the Book of Proverbs.

**For three things the earth is disquieted, and for four which it cannot bear:**

**For a servant when he reigneth; and a fool when he is filled with meat [Prov. 30:21–22].**

"For a servant when he reigneth"—that was Jeroboam who was a servant and became the first king of the northern kingdom of Israel.

Then "a fool when he is filled with meat" is typified by the rich fool our Lord told about who built bigger barns. With financial success like that, he was eating gourmet food, of course. He was a fool and he was "filled with meat."

The third thing is—

**For an odious woman when she is married; and an handmaid that is heir to her mistress [Prov. 30:23].**

"For an odious woman when she is married" doesn't require a comment—I think we all get the picture.

"And an handmaid that is heir to her mistress." Sometimes a very poor person, who has been walked on, suddenly becomes rich. There is no one who is more overbearing than such a person.

Now we are going to visit a zoo to look at some of the animals there. Did you know that animals have a message for us? God created them for His many purposes. One of those purposes is to give a message to us.

**There be four things which are little upon the earth, but they are exceeding wise [Prov. 30:24].**

God says we can learn from the animal world. The first group is made up of small creatures, little bitty animals. In fact, the first is an insect, the ant.

**The ants are a people not strong, yet they prepare their meat in the summer [Prov. 30:25].**

Now we are going to find two groups of animals listed here. The first group is an illustration of the way to God for the sinner. The second group is an illustration of the walk of the saints before God.

Those little creatures, the ants, are wise, and we can learn from them. We have already seen in Proverbs 6:6–8: "Go to the ant, thou sluggard; consider her ways, and be wise: Which having no guide, overseer, or ruler, Provideth her meat in the summer, and gathereth her food in the harvest." Ants do gather grain. I have seen them do it in Texas and in Palestine. A little ant will carry a grain of wheat or oats that is bigger than the ant. They store up food during those brief and bright days of harvest. The ant is an example to us of wisdom in preparing for the future with material things.

Some people think that Christians should not have insurance but that they ought to trust the Lord for their future. Friend, I think we should have everything that is available to us. If the Lord has given us means of caring for our future, we should have insurance and a savings account and a home, if it is possible. We should make a will to provide for the future of our loved ones. That is what the ant teaches us. He takes out insurance for his future by storing his food in the time of harvest.

There is a deeper message here. There are so many people who make no arrangement beyond death. They may go to the undertaker and arrange for their funeral. I saw the advertisement of an undertaker which read: "Lay away plan: pay now and go later." That is not the kind of arrangement beyond death that I mean. I am speaking of eternity. We are here for a few fleeting moments of time, and then there will be the endless ages of eternity. Isn't it foolish to care for the physical body and neglect the soul? Isn't it foolish to make no preparation for eternity?

The wicked emperor of Rome, Hadrian, said something like this when he was dying: "No more crown for this head, no more beauty for these eyes, no more music for these ears, and no more food for this stomach of mine. But my soul, oh, my soul, what is to become of you?" It is a certainty that we shall die. "And as it is appointed unto men once to die, but after this the judgment" (Heb. 9:27). It is possible to live for this life only, to eat, drink, and be merry, for tomorrow we die. A person can spend his time building bigger barns, but God tells us to be prepared to meet our God.

**The conies are but a feeble folk, yet make they their houses in the rocks [Prov. 30:26].**

Now the conies are the next animal we visit. The "conies" are not to be confused with the conies of England, which are actually rabbits. These "conies" are the *hyrax syriacus*. They have long hair, a short tail, and round ears. They are "feeble" and defenseless. They are not able to burrow in the ground, which makes them vulnerable little creatures; so they hide in the rocks to find a place of safety. They are included in the Leviticus list of unclean animals.

The coney has a message for man. Like the coney, man is poor, helpless, and unclean. We are sinners, and we need to recognize our pitiful plight. This is why David prays, ". . . Lead me to the rock that is higher than I" (Ps. 61:2). We sing this in the hymn "The Rock That is Higher Than I" by E. Johnson:

> Oh, then to the Rock let me fly,
> To the Rock that is higher than I.

That Rock is none other than the Lord Jesus Christ.

**The locusts have no king, yet go they forth all of them by bands [Prov. 30:27].**

The locust is a creature of destruction. Joel had a great deal to say about the locust plagues. We find locusts again in the Book of Revelation. They devour all the leaves and the vegetation. On one of my visits to Palestine, they were not having a real plague of them, but there were quite a few locusts, especially around the Sea of Galilee. They were doing a good job of destroying everything in their way. They are creatures of destruction.

"The locusts have no king." They have no visible head or leader, yet they go forth like soldiers in their respective regiments. They move so methodically that they seem to be acting under definite instructions and strict discipline.

To us as believers they furnish an example of subjection to one another and subjection to our unseen Head in heaven. To the world the body of believers must look like disorganized, fragmented, unrelated groups of people, with no leader and no bond of union. But, my friend, we do have a Leader. Christ is the unseen Head of the church. The apostle Paul wrote to the Corinthian believers: "For ye are yet carnal: for whereas there is among you envying, and strife, and divisions, are ye not carnal, and walk as men?" (1 Cor. 3:3). Not only is Christ the Head of all who have been redeemed by the blood of Christ, but the Holy Spirit is indwelling every believer, welding us together in one great family, ". . . every one members one of another" (Rom. 12:5). This is what the locust is teaching us.

**The spider taketh hold with her hands, and is in kings' palaces [Prov. 30:28].**

The Hebrew word for "spider" is *shemameth* and refers to a little house lizard. Delitzsch says, "The lizard thou canst catch with the hand and yet it is in kings' palaces." Somehow or other it can work its way into houses, and it has an affinity for fine tapestry and palatial mansions. It has fanlike feet which exude a sticky substance so that the lizard can actually hold onto a marble wall or a tessellated ceiling.

This teaches us about faith, the kind of faith that takes hold of the promises of God. It is the faith that enters into the very heavenly places. It lays hold of the fact that the spirit of God Himself beareth witness with our spirit, that we are the sons of God. It is the faith that says, ". . . I know whom I have believed, and am persuaded that he is able to keep that which I have committed unto him against that day" (2 Tim. 1:12). "Being confident of this very thing, that he which hath begun a good work in you will perform it until the day of Jesus Christ" (Phil. 1:6).

Now we come to the second group.

**There be three things which go well, yea, four are comely in going:**

**A lion which is strongest among beasts, and turneth not away for any [Prov. 30:29–30].**

The lion goes straight ahead and doesn't detour. He is not afraid of the pussycats in the neighborhood—they don't frighten him. A lion is known for its unflinching boldness, and this should characterize the Christian as we earnestly contend for the faith. I think of the apostle Paul who in the face of suffering and persecution said, "But none of these things move me, neither count I my life dear unto myself, so that I might finish my course with joy, and the ministry, which I have received of the Lord Jesus, to testify the gospel of the grace of God" (Acts 20:24).

I think that the curse of the church today lies in pussyfooting preachers and mealy-mouthed deacons.

It is said of Cromwell that he was a man without fear. When asked why, he said, "I have learned that when you fear God you have no man to fear."

General "Stonewall" Jackson, a Christian man, got his appellation because one day in battle the men of General Cox were ready to retreat. General Cox looked over at him and then said to his men, "Look at General Jackson; he's standing like a stone wall." He was a man of course, like a lion. That is the way the walk of the believer should be.

The next animal is a greyhound.

**A greyhound; an he goat also; and a king, against whom there is no rising up [Prov. 30:31].**

The greyhound we are speaking of here is not the Greyhound Bus! The Christian is to be like a greyhound in that he is to gird up his loins and run with patience the race that is set before him. "Wherefore seeing we also are compassed about with so great a cloud of witnesses, let us lay aside every weight, and the sin which doth so easily beset us, and let us run with patience the race that is set before us, Looking unto Jesus the author and finisher of our faith . . ." (Heb. 12:1–2).

The other animal mentioned in this verse is the goat. The mountain goat is a climber who lives way up in the top of the mountains. He finds both pleasure and safety in his high retreat.

The lesson is plain to see. The believer who walks on the high places, as did Habakkuk, will be able to rejoice in the day of trouble. "Although the fig tree shall not blossom, neither shall fruit be in the vines; the labour of the olive shall fail, and the fields shall yield no meat; the flock shall be cut off from the fold, and there shall be no herd in the stalls: Yet I will rejoice in the LORD, I will joy in the God of my salvation. The LORD God is my strength, and he will make my feet like hinds' feet, and he will make me to walk upon mine high places . . ." (Hab. 3:17–19).

# CHAPTER 31

The final chapter of Proverbs is designated as the words of King Lemuel. A popular title would be, "Advice on how to choose a wife."

**The words of king Lemuel, the prophecy that his mother taught him [Prov. 31:1].**

I believe this chapter was written by Solomon. There is no king named Lemuel. The name that God gave to Solomon is *Jedidiah*, which means "beloved of the Lord" (2 Sam. 12:25); the name *Lemuel* means "devoted to the Lord." My guess is that this was the pet name that Bathsheba had for Solomon.

I have a notion that every man reading this can remember a pet name that his mother had for him. You would almost be ashamed to say what it was, wouldn't you? Probably Solomon's mother had a pet name for him, and I think it was Lemuel. Around the palace you probably could have heard her calling, "Lemuel."

This was a mother's advice to her son. It makes a great Mother's Day sermon, by the way.

**What, my son? and what, the son of my womb? and what, the son of my vows? [Prov. 31:2].**

Bathsheba is asking, "What can I say to you?" She needed to say something, because she saw in this boy Solomon some of the characteristics of his father David. She well remembered the sin of David. I don't think it was her sin; I think it was David's sin. In the first chapter of Matthew it says, ". . . and David the king begat Solomon of her that had been the wife of Urias" (Matt. 1:6). Bathsheba's name is not even mentioned. I believe God is making it clear that it was David's sin. She sees the temptation that Solomon faces; so she gives him words of advice. "What, my son? What can I say to you, son of my womb? You're my precious boy, the son of my vows"—she had dedicated him to God.

**Give not thy strength unto women, nor thy ways to that which destroyeth kings [Prov. 31:3].**

She knew David.

**It is not for kings, O Lemuel, it is not for kings to drink wine; nor for princes strong drink:**

**Lest they drink, and forget the law, and pervert the judgment of any of the afflicted [Prov. 31:4–5].**

We are told that every day in Washington there are many cocktail parties for our government officials. Republicans and Democrats both have this in common—the party membership doesn't make any difference. It is tragic to have drinking men in high positions of government!

**Give strong drink unto him that is ready to perish, and wine unto those that be of heavy hearts.**

**Let him drink, and forget his poverty, and remember his misery no more [Prov. 31:6–7].**

She tells Solomon to use wine for medicine.

**Open thy mouth for the dumb in the cause of all such as are appointed to destruction.**

**Open thy mouth, judge righteously, and plead the cause of the poor and needy [Prov. 31:8–9].**

Oh, Solomon, be honest and just and fair!

Now she goes on to tell him how to choose a wife. This is good advice. It is God's advice.

**Who can find a virtuous woman? for her price is far above rubies [Prov. 31:10].**

"Virtuous" here means a woman of character, a woman of strength, a woman of real ability. She is not to be a shrinking violet. She is not to be like Whistler's mother, always sitting in a rocking chair. (A whimsical story is told that Whistler painted another picture of his mother, because he came in one day and found her sitting on the floor and said to her, "Mother, you're off your rocker.") I don't think you will find many mothers sitting in rocking chairs. They are busy. This is the picture of a busy mother:

**The heart of her husband doth safely trust in her, so that he shall have no need of spoil [Prov. 31:11].**

She will be faithful. "He shall have no need of spoil." She will not be a spendthrift with her husband's money. She will be a helpmate or a helpmeet for him. God never intended woman to be a servant of man. She is to be his partner, and a real partner. When God made Eve to be a helpmeet, He made the other half of Adam. Adam was only half a man until God made Eve and gave her to him.

**She will do him good and not evil all the days of her life [Prov. 31:12].**

She is a real helpmeet.

**She seeketh wool, and flax, and worketh willingly with her hands [Prov. 31:13].**

She doesn't mind working.

**She is like the merchants' ships; she bringeth her food from afar [Prov. 31:14].**

She looks for bargains to spend the money wisely.

**She riseth also while it is yet night, and giveth meat to her household, and a portion to her maidens [Prov. 31:15].**

She knows how to keep house. She runs a night shift and is a wonderful mother.

I do not recall any time when I was growing up as a boy that I got up in the morning and found my mother in bed. I just thought about that the other day. Later on when she became old, it was different, of course. But when I was a boy, by the time I got out of bed, she was up, and breakfast was usually ready and on the table.

**She considereth a field, and buyeth it: with the fruit of her hands she planteth a vineyard.**

**She girdeth her loins with strength, and strengtheneth her arms [Prov. 31:16–17].**

She is a woman of ability. She runs her household well.

**She perceiveth that her merchandise is good: her candle goeth not out by night [Prov. 31:18].**

She proves the adage, "Man's work is from sun to sun, but a woman's work is never done."

**She layeth her hands to the spindle, and her hands hold the distaff.**

**She stretcheth out her hand to the poor; yea, she reacheth forth her hands to the needy [Prov. 31:19–20].**

She is a generous person.

**She is not afraid of the snow for her household: for all her household are clothed with scarlet [Prov. 31:21].**

I was remembering that my mother kept my pants patched when I was a boy.

**She openeth her mouth with wisdom; and in her tongue is the law of kindness [Prov. 31:26].**

She is both wise and kind in her advice and admonitions.

**Favour is deceitful, and beauty is vain: but a woman that feareth the LORD, she shall be praised [Prov. 31:30].**

Young man, first you should look for a wife who is a Christian. Then I hope that you get a good-looking one in the bargain—it's nice to have both together. "A woman that feareth the LORD, she shall be praised." This is of prime importance.

**Give her of the fruit of her hands; and let her own works praise her in the gates [Prov. 31:31].**

I guess this is the reason we have Mother's Day, a day to honor our mothers. However, there are many mothers who are not worthy of the tribute given to mothers on Mother's Day.

This Book of Proverbs has been a book for young men. Also it is a wonderful book for young ladies. In fact, we all can learn from the wisdom in this remarkable book.

# BIBLIOGRAPHY

(Recommended for Further Study)

Arnot, William. *Laws from Heaven for Life on Earth*. London, England: T. Nelson and Sons, 1864.

Bridges, Charles. *An Exposition of Proverbs*. Carlisle, Pennsylvania: The Banner of Truth Trust, 1959.

Darby, J. N. *Synopsis of the Books of the Bible*. Oak Park, Illinois: Bible Truth Publishers, n.d.

Gaebelein, Arno C. *The Annotated Bible*. Neptune, New Jersey: Loizeaux Brothers, 1917.

Gray, James M. *Synthetic Bible Studies*. Old Tappan, New Jersey: Fleming H. Revell Co., 1906.

Ironside, H. A. *Notes on the Book of Proverbs*. Neptune, New Jersey: Loizeaux Brothers, 1907. (Very good.)

Jensen, Irving L. *Proverbs*. Chicago, Illinois: Moody Press, 1982.

Kelly, William. *The Proverbs*. Oak Park, Illinois: Bible Truth Publishers, n.d.

Kidner, D. *The Proverbs*. Chicago, Illinois: InterVarsity Christian Fellowship, 1964.

Mackintosh, C. H. *Miscellaneous Writings*. Neptune, New Jersey: Loizeaux Brothers, n.d.

Moorehead, W. G. *Outline Studies in the Old Testament*. Grand Rapids, Michigan: Zondervan Publishing House, 1894.

Sauer, Erich. *The Dawn of World Redemption*. Grand Rapids, Michigan: William B. Eerdmans Publishing Co., 1951. (An excellent Old Testament survey.)

Scroggie, W. Graham. *The Unfolding Drama of Redemption*. Grand Rapids, Michigan: Zondervan Publishing House, 1970. (An excellent survey and outline of the Old Testament.)

Unger, Merrill F. *Unger's Bible Handbook*. Chicago, Illinois: Moody Press, 1966.

Unger, Merrill F. *Unger's Commentary on the Old Testament*. Vol. 1. Chicago, Illinois: Moody Press, 1981. (A fine summary of each chapter.)

# The Book of
# ECCLESIASTES
## INTRODUCTION

Solomon is the writer. This fact is very well established among conservative expositors, and there is no other reasonable explanation for the book.

Solomon also wrote the Books of Proverbs and the Song of Solomon. We will find Ecclesiastes to be quite different from the Book of Proverbs. In Proverbs we saw the *wisdom* of Solomon; here we shall see the *foolishness* of Solomon. Ecclesiastes is the dramatic autobiography of his life when he was away from God.

*Ecclesiastes* indicates a preacher or philosopher. I rather like the term philosopher because it is less likely to be misunderstood.

To correctly understand any book of the Bible, it is important to know the purpose for which it was written. We need to back off and get a perspective of the book. We need to put down the telescope on the Word of God before we pick up the microscope. The necessity for this is more evident here than in many of the other books of the Bible.

This is human philosophy apart from God, which must always reach the conclusions that this book reaches. We need to understand this about Ecclesiastes, because there are many statements which contradict certain other statements of Scripture.

Actually, it almost frightens us to know that this book has been the favorite of atheists, and they have quoted from it profusely. Voltaire is an example. Today we find the cynic and the critic are apt to quote from this book. And it is quite interesting to note the number of cults that use passages from this book out of context and give them an entirely wrong meaning.

Man has tried to be happy without God; it is being tried every day by millions of people. This book shows the absurdity of the attempt. Solomon was the wisest of men, and he had a wisdom that was God-given. He tried every field of endeavor and pleasure that was known to man, and his conclusion was that all is vanity. The word *vanity* means "empty, purposeless." Satisfaction in life can never be attained in this manner.

God showed Job, a righteous man, that he was a *sinner* in God's sight. In Ecclesiastes God showed Solomon, the wisest man, that he was a *fool* in God's sight. This is a book from which a great many professors, Ph.D.s and Th.D.s, and preachers could learn a great lesson. In spite of all their wisdom, in spite of all attempts at being intellectual, unregenerate men in the sight of God are fools. That, my friend, is something that is hard to swallow for those who put an emphasis upon their I.Q. and the amount of knowledge and information that they have accumulated.

In Ecclesiastes we learn that without Christ we cannot be satisfied—even if we possess the whole world and all the things that men consider necessary to make their hearts content. The world cannot satisfy the heart, because the heart is too large for the object. In the Song of Solomon we will learn that if we turn from the world and set our affections on Christ, we cannot fathom the infinite preciousness of His love; the Object is too large for the heart.

The key word is "vanity," which occurs thirty-seven times. The key phrase is "under the sun," which occurs twenty-nine times. Another phrase which recurs is "I said in mine heart." In other words, this book contains the cogitations of man's heart. These are conclusions which men have reached through their own intelligence, their own experiments. Although Solomon's conclusions are not inspired, the Scripture that tells us about them is inspired. This is the reason for the explanatory: "I said in mine heart," "under the sun," and "vanity."

# OUTLINE

The Book of Ecclesiastes is a dramatic autobiography of King Solomon's life when he was away from God. As the Book of Proverbs reveals Solomon's wisdom, the Book of Ecclesiastes reveals his foolishness.

This is not a book without rhyme or reason—not just a bunch of verses stuck together. It begins with the problem stated: All is vanity in this world. Then we will find that experiments are made. Solomon will seek satisfaction through many different avenues, in many different fields. He will try science, the laws of nature, wisdom and philosophy, pleasure and materialism, as well as living for the "now." He will explore fatalism, egotism, religion, wealth, and morality. Then in the final verses of the book he will give us the result of his experiments.

Keep in mind that the conclusions in each experiment are human, not God's truth. This is man *under* the sun.

Do not misunderstand what is meant by "inspiration" when we say that the Bible is inspired by God. Inspiration guarantees the accuracy of the words of Scripture, not always the *thought* that is expressed. The context should be considered, and attention paid to the person who made the statement and under what circumstances the statement was made. For example, in the betrayal of Christ by Judas, the record of the event is inspired, but the act of Judas was not God-inspired; it was satanic. Also the statements that Solomon makes, while he is searching for satisfaction apart from God, are not always in accord with God's thoughts. Inspiration guarantees that what Solomon *said* has been accurately recorded in Scripture.

## PROBLEM STATED

**The words of the Preacher, the son of David, king in Jerusalem [Eccl. 1:1].**

That description doesn't fit anyone except Solomon, as far as I can tell. David did have other sons, but Solomon was the only one who was king in Jerusalem. He is the philosopher here. We know that he had been given wisdom.

I think that the wisdom God gave Solomon was a little different from what we think it was. We imagine that he was given spiritual insight, but Scripture does not tell us that he even asked for that. He had prayed: "Give therefore thy servant an understanding heart to *judge thy people*, that I may discern between good and bad: for who is able to judge this thy so great a people?" (1 Kings 3:9, italics mine). Apparently God gave him what he asked for: wisdom to rule. He was wise in political economy and probably did a marvelous job of ruling the nation. He brought in an era of peace. Other nations of the world went there to study and to behold the wisdom of Solomon. He gave a testimony for God through the temple with the altar where sacrifice was made for sinners. These were some of the things that the Queen of Sheba learned when she came from the ends of the earth. But in the area of spiritual discernment, Solomon was probably nil.

Now we find Solomon, away from God, launching out with his experiments "under the sun." The man under the sun is a great deal different from the child of God who has been blessed ". . . with all spiritual blessings in heavenly places in Christ" (Eph. 1:3).

**Vanity of vanities, saith the Preacher, vanity of vanities; all is vanity [Eccl. 1:2].**

"Vanity" here speaks of emptiness. It is to waste life without any purpose or any goal. It means to live like an animal or a bird lives. There are a great many people who live like that.

I was in a hotel in the Hawaiian Islands where the jet set come. They fly all over the world spending a few days or weeks in Hawaii, then at Acapulco in Mexico, and then the Riviera in France, then to Spain, North Africa, South Africa, and so on. They are world travelers. I watched these folk and listened to their conversation at the dinner table, out in the hotel lobby, and in the elevators. The thing that impressed me about them was how purposeless their lives really are. They talked about people they had seen in other places. They talked about plays they had seen. They would ask, "Where are you going from here?" Someone would say, "Wasn't that place where we were last year a bore!" There was no aim, no goal, no purpose in life. This is also the conclusion of Solomon. Vanity of vanities. Emptiness of emptiness. It is just like a big bag of nothing.

Solomon in the Book of Proverbs gives us gems of wisdom. In Ecclesiastes he gives us globules, not of wisdom, but of folly. Then in the Song of Solomon love is the subject. Wisdom, foolishness, and love—Solomon was an expert in all three fields. He knew how to play the fool;

he was wise in government; and his love life was quite a story. Solomon was the wisest of men, but no man ever played the fool more thoroughly than he did. He is the riddle of revelation. He is the paradox of Scripture. The wisest man was the greatest fool. The Book of Ecclesiastes will reveal this.

"Vanity of vanities; all is vanity" is life without God. It is man walking and talking "under the sun," trying to get something out of life.

There is another class of people whom I meet in motels and hotels as I travel. These are the conventioneers. This is the day of conventions. I have listened to them and watched them. They are different from the jet set, but they, too, are looking for something. They have the big cocktail party or beer bust. Then they have a huge banquet with a big show. They try it all, but there is that note of bitterness. There are dregs left in the glass of life.

Now we will find man experimenting. He is going to squeeze the juice of life out of the dry rocks of this mundane existence down here.

**What profit hath a man of all his labour which he taketh under the sun? [Eccl. 1:3].**

Let's keep in mind this is "under the sun"; it is man's viewpoint. God is not giving His viewpoint here.

## EXPERIMENT MADE

His experiments comprise the body of the book, extending from verse 4 through chapter 12, verse 12.

Now the first thing he tries is in the realm of science. He makes a study of the laws of nature. It is interesting that Solomon tried this. Men today still go into the scientific fields of study and spend years, in fact a lifetime, studying these laws of nature. This book is remarkable in giving us these laws of nature.

## SCIENCE

**One generation passeth away, and another generation cometh: but the earth abideth for ever [Eccl. 1:4].**

The earth "abideth for ever" and has a stability that man does not have because man is temporary. Contemporary man is a little different from the man of the past and probably he will be a great deal different from the man of the future, but man is temporary. The continuity of mankind is maintained through births. Most of us were not here a

hundred years ago, and we will not be here a hundred years from today. In fact, many of us won't be around much longer. However, mankind will continue through succeeding generations. Solomon has noted that: "One generation passeth away, and another generation cometh." Man is a transitory creature. Looking at life in terms of this life only, man is the most colossal failure in God's universe. He has been around only a few years. There are redwood trees in Northern California that were here when Christ was on earth, but they are newcomers compared to rocks around us which geologists tell us have been here millions, maybe billions, of years. Although no one knows how long the earth has been here, it was here before man got here, and it will be here after most of us leave. My friend, this adds a certain dimension to life that is rather discouraging and disappointing. Man is not what he thinks he is.

Now we see some very remarkable statements. Here is a revelation that Solomon made a study of the laws of nature and knew a great deal about them. It is quite interesting that these are basic in our day as far as science is concerned.

**The sun also ariseth, and the sun goeth down, and hasteth to his place where he arose.**

**The wind goeth toward the south, and turneth about unto the north; it whirleth about continually, and the wind returneth again according to his circuits.**

**All the rivers run into the sea; yet the sea is not full; unto the place from whence the rivers come, thither they return again [Eccl. 1:5–7].**

It is very interesting that these accurate observations come from the days of Solomon. Dr. Arthur T. Pierson comments on this fact:

There is a danger in pressing the words in the Bible into a positive announcement of scientific fact, so marvellous are some of these correspondencies. But it is certainly a curious fact that Solomon should use language entirely consistent with discoveries such as evaporation and storm currents (vv. 6–7). Some have boldly said that Redfield's theory of storms is here explicitly stated. Without taking such ground, we ask, who taught Solomon to use terms that readily accommodate facts that the movement of the winds which seem to be so lawless and uncertain, are ruled by laws as positive as those which rule the growth of the plant; and that by evaporation, the waters that fall on the earth are continually rising again, so that the sea never overflows. Ecclesiastes 12:6 is a poetic description of death. How the "silver cord" describes the spinal marrow, the "golden bowl" the basin which holds the brain, the "pitcher" the lungs, and the "wheel" the heart. Without claiming that Solomon was inspired to foretell the circulation of the blood, twenty-six centuries before Harvey announced it, is it not remarkable that the language he uses exactly suits the facts— a wheel pumping up through one pipe to discharge through another?

There are three very interesting statements in verses 5–7.

1. "The sun also ariseth, and the sun goeth down." There is a monotony in nature, but also that which you can depend upon. You can count on the sun coming up and you can depend on it going down—we still use that terminology although we know that the coming up and going down of the sun really is caused by the rotation of the earth. We are standing on a pretty solid piece of earth, and it looks to us as if the sun comes up and the sun goes down. The terminology has accommodated man in all ages. The amazing thing is the precise, regular way that the sun appears and disappears; it is obeying certain laws.

2. "The wind goeth toward the south, and turneth about unto the north." Today we know that the wind follows certain patterns. Even with our modern gadgets we are not able to predict it well enough to forecast the weather as we would like to. Here in Southern California where we have a monotony of good weather, the weatherman misses the exact prediction about half the time. I have watched this very carefully over the years. The Lord Jesus said, "The wind bloweth where it listeth"—that is, where it wants to blow. It is blowing according to laws. "And thou hearest the sound thereof, but canst not tell whence it cometh, and whither it goeth . . ." (John 3:8)—we can't tell where it is coming from and where it is going. As I am making this study of Ecclesiastes, we have had quite a bit of disturbance across the country. Here in Southern California we never get rain in June or July or August—but we've been having showers! I couldn't believe it when I got in my car the other night and had to use the windshield wipers. The weatherman tells us that there is a low pressure here and a high pressure there. There is movement; winds are blowing. "The wind bloweth where it listeth." Or, as Solomon put it, "The wind goeth toward the south, and turneth about unto the north." At one place the wind is moving south, and in another place it is moving north. In Arizona they even had flooding in desert communities, all because of the wind. It is obeying certain laws as it is blowing. How did Solomon know that? He didn't have the gadgets which we have nor the background on which to base his conclusions.

3. "All the rivers run into the sea; yet the sea is not full." Solomon is tacitly speaking of the law of evaporation, of the elevation of moisture into the air. Then the wind comes along, blows that moisture over the land, and it pours out on the earth. The whole process follows certain definite, specific laws. There is nothing haphazard happening, although we may think so. Including verse 4, we have four remarkable statements concerning the laws of nature that make sense and fit right into what men know today. Compare this with other writings that come from one thousand years before Christ. You will find a great deal of false conclusions and superstitions in contrast to the accuracy you find in the Word of God.

Here is another remarkable observation—

**All things are full of labour; man cannot utter it: the eye is not satisfied with seeing, nor the ear filled with hearing [Eccl. 1:8].**

This may not have seemed true before, but since the advent of television it is obvious. Many people watch television for hours day after day. Why? Because the eye is never satisfied with seeing; the ear is never filled with hearing. Most of us love to go to new places and see new scenes. This is one of the enjoyments of life. It is one of the things we can enjoy in this big, wonderful country. I get kidded because I come from Texas, but I must say in all honesty that I have never been in a state that I didn't like. They are all wonderful. We live in a wonderful country and in a wonderful universe.

Man cannot exhaust the exploration of the universe. The more he learns, the more he sees that he should learn. The more he learns, the more he sees how much more there is to learn. This is frustrating. The physical universe is too big for little man. Yet man alone of all God's creatures—as far as we know—is able to comprehend the universe. When a dog bays at the moon, I don't think he knows the distance to the moon, and I don't think he cares. I don't think he recognizes that he lives in a vast universe. I believe that the world of a dog is a very small world. It is no bigger than a bone most of the time. But the eyes and ears of man are never satisfied; he wants to explore.

**The thing that hath been, it is that which shall be; and that which is done is that which shall be done: and there is no new thing under the sun.**

**Is there any thing whereof it may be said, See, this is new? it hath been already of old time, which was before us [Eccl. 1:9–10].**

People think we have come up with something new when we have manufactured a new gadget. I remember what a novelty the telephone was. In West Texas we were on a party line, and when the telephone would ring, you could hear a dozen receivers being taken off the hook. That was the best way to make a public announcement in those days! You say, "Well, television is new, how can it be said that there is nothing new under the sun?" Let me illustrate this.

My grandfather courted my grandmother on an old horsehair sofa in a very staid living room in Mississippi. He proposed to her there. She accepted, and they were married. My dad courted my mother on a train—he met her in a day coach. They traveled by horse and buggy to Tyler, Texas, where they were married. I proposed to my wife down in Texas, as we were sitting in a car. My little grandson may propose to his wife in an airplane or maybe even in a space capsule. You may ask, "Isn't that new?" No, not really. The feeling that my granddad had when his proposal was accepted is the same feeling that I had, and I don't think my little grandson will feel any differently. There is really nothing new under the sun. The environment may change, and there may be new gadgets around, but there really is nothing new under the sun. Man stays the same. Only the stage setting may vary a bit from age to age.

It is said that the atom bomb is new, but the atom has been around for a long time. Actually, the atom is older than man, although man did not know it existed during all that time. All man has accomplished is to make the little atom a very difficult neighbor. The nosy human should have let sleeping dogs lie, but we probe around. Perhaps you are asking, "Well, isn't the computer new?" Not really. God created us with computer brains and electric nervous systems. A mechanical computer brings to man no deep and abiding satisfaction. Man has learned that none of these gadgets contributes anything really new to him.

There is one exception. There is one thing that is new—the New Birth. This is something that comes when you receive Jesus Christ as your Savior. This, my friend, is about the only thing *new* that will come your way.

**There is no remembrance of former things; neither shall there be any remembrance of things that are to come with those that shall come after [Eccl. 1:11].**

Solomon had tried to find satisfaction in the study of science, but he had to come to this conclusion. Man tries to be important. He tries everything in the world to keep himself before the public, but it isn't long until he passes off the stage. "There is no remembrance of former things."

Do you remember who were the popular entertainers of fifty years ago? Do you remember the popular athletes of fifty years ago? Could you name the president of the United States of fifty years ago? Our memories aren't very long. The Scripture says that we spend our time down here as a tale that is told and we can't go back over it again.

You see, this man Solomon is making tremendous experiments, and he is making them in the laboratory of life. He is trying everything that is available to man. In his day and position he was able to go into any field that he chose. Not many men even today would be able to do what Solomon did. He first gave himself to the study of the laws of nature, as we have seen, but he found nothing he could learn in nature, in science, which was new in the sense that it would bring new life to him.

Solomon's next experimentation will be in the area of wisdom and philosophy.

## WISDOM AND PHILOSOPHY

**I the Preacher was king over Israel in Jerusalem.**

**And I gave my heart to seek and search out by wisdom concerning all things that are done under heaven: this sore travail hath God given to the sons of man to be exercised therewith [Eccl. 1:12–13].**

Solomon spent a lot of time studying the philosophy of the world. He lived nearly a thousand years before Christ, and since we live two thousand years on this side, three thousand years have elapsed. Man has come up with a great deal of gadgetry in that time, but actually man doesn't know any more about philosophy and wisdom than he knew three thousand years ago. There has been no improvement in philosophy and wisdom, neither do they satisfy the heart.

**I have seen all the works that are done under the sun; and, behold, all is vanity and vexation of spirit [Eccl. 1:14].**

All systems of philosophy lead up a blind alley. You can make the same experiment yourself. You can spend your time in studying this subject, and you will find it is actually a waste of time.

We are living in a day when educators are declaring that all the past methods of education were just a waste of time. I wonder how good our present method is. I think that it is also a waste of time. Man can never learn the really important thing—he cannot know God by wisdom and philosophy. His knowledge of God comes *only* through revelation. Philosophy generally leads a person to a pessimistic viewpoint of life.

You cannot take natural man—man who is a lost sinner alienated from God—and give him an education, expecting that education to solve the problems of his life. It will not do that. Philosophy and psychology cannot change human nature, nor can they correct the old nature of man.

**That which is crooked cannot be made straight: and that which is wanting cannot be numbered [Eccl. 1:15].**

"That which is crooked cannot be made straight"—as the twig is bent, the tree inclines. The tree grows crooked because the twig was bent. You and I start out in life with an old nature. We can educate it and do many things to improve it, but, as the Lord Jesus said, "That which is born of the flesh is flesh." It will always be flesh, my friend. That is the reason we must have a new nature—". . . that which is born of the Spirit is spirit" (John 3:6).

For a time we thought that education would solve the problems of life. Now higher education, in fact all education, is coming under the scrutiny of a great many thoughtful people. A committee to study higher education has come up with a novel explanation of our present conditions. They say the rebellion and the general immorality in our schools is taking place because the young people today are more inquiring and more interested in politics and what is happening in their world. I agree that people are more aware of the many terrible things that are happening. The media gather news from the four corners of the earth and broadcast it the same evening. This makes us more aware of what takes place in the world than ever before. There was a time when it took six weeks to complete all the information after an election; so it took that long to find out who had been elected president. Today they can tell you who is going to be elected before they have the election! So I agree with the fact that young people are more aware today. But I heartily disagree with the implication that the things happening on our campuses are actually an *improvement* because the young people are so well informed. There is a deterioration on our campuses. We have come to the day when evil is called good, and good evil. Only an educated man could come up with the conclusion that the deterioration on campuses is not deterioration but actually improvement! If you believe fairy stories, you may want to believe that, but we need to face reality. Education cannot solve the problems of life. Neither can psychology provide the answer. In our day there are clever men and women who have come up with little psychological clichés to explain and solve the problems of life. They coat them with a little Bible, like a bitter pill that is covered with a sugar coating, to make them appear as the biblical solutions. My friend, the Word of God in its entirety contains for the Christian the answers to the problems of life. There are no easy solutions. Studying the Word of God requires a great deal of time and effort and mental "perspiration." Oh, how that is needed among Christians!

Solomon discovered that wisdom and philosophy did not provide the answers to the problems of life.

**I communed with mine own heart, saying, Lo, I am come to great estate, and have gotten more wisdom than all they that have been before me in Jerusalem: yea, my heart had great experience of wisdom and knowledge [Eccl. 1:16].**

I believe that Solomon was led to a certain amount of arrogance, a certain amount of conceit, since he was wiser than the others. Paul writes that "Knowledge puffeth up . . ." (1 Cor. 8:1). It can inflate an individual like a balloon if he feels that he is a little smarter or better educated than those around him.

Remember that education is based on experience, and experience cannot be trusted. Experience must be tested by the Word of God. Unfortunately, many folk today are testing the Word of God by their experience. My friend, if your experience is contrary to the Bible, then it is your experience, not the Word of God, which is wrong.

**And I gave my heart to know wisdom, and to know madness and folly: I perceived that this also is vexation of spirit [Eccl. 1:17].**

"To know madness and folly"—it is interesting that wisdom and playing the fool are not very far apart. Many smart men in the history of the world have played the fool. Solomon is the notable example of that. King James of England, the one for whom our King James Version of the Bible is named, certainly was not capable of translating. He was called James the fool, because that's what he was, although he thought he was a very smart individual.

Our nation has produced a generation that thinks it is very intelligent and very smart. Yet we cannot even solve the problems that are about us, much less the problems of the world. Solomon gave his heart to know wisdom and also to know madness and folly. He did both.

"I perceived that this also is vexation of spirit." In other words, it was not worth the effort.

**For in much wisdom is much grief: and he that increaseth knowledge increaseth sorrow [Eccl. 1:18].**

Joy and satisfaction do not increase in ratio to the increase of knowledge. Someone has said that when ignorance is bliss, 'tis folly to be wise. There is a certain amount of truth in that. In much wisdom there is much grief. The more we know, the more we increase our problems. Life has become more tedious, has produced more tensions, and all of our scientific gadgets about us are making life almost unbearable. A Christian friend said to me the other day, "I think I will lose my mind if I don't get away from these computers that are controlling life today. The machines that we think are so wonderful and practically worship are drowning us in pollution and driving us to madness." How accurate Solomon was in saying "in much wisdom is much grief," and Solomon did not live in the machine age. He did not see the Industrial Revolution, but he knew what he was talking about.

# CHAPTER 2

In this chapter we will find Solomon following another course to find satisfaction in life. This is a popular route for modern man who seeks satisfaction in pleasure.

## PLEASURE

**I said in mine heart, Go to now, I will prove thee with mirth, therefore enjoy pleasure: and, behold, this also is vanity [Eccl. 2:1].**

Solomon probably tried everything known in the way of pleasure. We are a sex-mad people. And what do we have to show for it? Well, we certainly have low morals, and we have venereal disease in epidemic proportions. Today the church has entered the field also. I suppose most pastors have a sermon on sex; some of them have a whole series. There are many who feel that the church should have a course to teach our young people about sex. I think that is a tragic mistake.

This generation is getting sex right up to their ears—all they need and more. Now Solomon was an expert in the area of sex. He had one thousand wives and concubines, and they were all available to him. A man who had a thousand women around him is some sort of an expert. Solomon tried that way to seek satisfaction. Also he went in for drinking and for entertainment. I suppose he could have put on a performance that would make Las Vegas look like it was penny ante or just a sideshow in a small circus. Solomon went all out for pleasure. "I said in mine heart, Go to now, I will prove thee with mirth, therefore enjoy pleasure." But notice his conclusion: "Behold, this also is vanity"—empty.

**I said of laughter, It is mad: and of mirth, What doeth it? [Eccl. 2:2].**

He probably had a comedian or court jester to entertain him and tell him the latest jokes—

probably many of them questionable. He said, "I found this to be a great waste of time."

**I sought in mine heart to give myself unto wine, yet acquainting mine heart with wisdom; and to lay hold on folly, till I might see what was that good for the sons of men, which they should do under the heaven all the days of their life [Eccl. 2:3].**

"Under the heaven"—remember that Solomon is a man probing and making experiments apart from God.

**I made me great works; I builded me houses; I planted me vineyards [Eccl. 2:4].**

These were hobbies with Solomon. Even today the ruins of the stables of Solomon can be seen right in Jerusalem and in several other places. At Megiddo a tourist guide will show you ruins of the troughs where the horses ate. Solomon had stables all over that land, although the Mosaic Law had expressly forbidden a king to multiply horses.

**I made me gardens and orchards, and I planted trees in them of all kind of fruits:**

**I made me pools of water, to water therewith the wood that bringeth forth trees [Eccl. 2:5–6].**

He had irrigation.

**I got me servants and maidens, and had servants born in my house; also I had great possessions of great and small cattle above all that were in Jerusalem before me [Eccl. 2:7].**

He had a ranch out at the edge of town where he raised cattle. You may be wondering how he could afford all this. Well, Solomon had cornered the gold in his day. He had plenty of spending money, and he built in all the comforts of life.

It is now known that snow was brought down from Mount Hermon so that he could have cold drinks in the summertime. I think Solomon tried everything that a man could try for pleasure. I doubt that modern man could have anything that Solomon did not have.

**I gathered me also silver and gold, and the peculiar treasure of kings and of the provinces: I gat me men singers and women singers, and the delights of the sons of men, as musical instruments, and that of all sorts [Eccl. 2:8].**

He brought in the best nightclub acts from Las Vegas. He had all kinds of music—from symphony to rock, but it didn't satisfy his heart.

**So I was great, and increased more than all that were before me in Jerusalem: also my wisdom remained with me.**

**And whatsoever mine eyes desired I kept not from them, I withheld not my heart from any joy; for my heart rejoiced in all my labour: and this was my portion of all my labour [Eccl. 2:9–10].**

Mrs. McGee and I are out in conferences a great deal of the time. In the evenings after a service we need to get away from everyone for a while, and one of the things we like to do is just go walking through a shopping area. I have said to her, "Would you like sometime to be able to buy everything that you see and want?" She answered that she wondered how it would feel to be able to do that. Well, Solomon did just that. Anything his little heart desired, he bought. As he looked out upon this world, there was nothing that it withheld from him.

You would think that all men in that position would be happy. Well, I don't know why, but they are not. I am told that we have more suicides here in Southern California than the average for the country. One would think it would be the bums on skid row, the down-and-outers, who would be the ones to commit suicide. Life certainly wouldn't seem to be worth much to them. Actually, those are not the ones with the high suicide rate. It is the rich, the famous, the Hollywood movie and television stars, the folk who seem to have made it. They are the ones who commit suicide. Why? They have come to the same conclusion that Solomon did. He had tried everything in the way of pleasure and concluded:

**Then I looked on all the works that my hands had wrought, and on the labour that I had laboured to do: and, behold, all was vanity and vexation of spirit, and there was no profit under the sun [Eccl. 2:11].**

What a statement from a man who had everything! A great many people will not take Solomon's word for it; they have to make the same experiments—although not to the extent that Solomon did. Eventually they arrive at the same conclusion. They say, "Life is empty."

Solomon said, "All was vanity and vexation of spirit, and there was no profit under the sun."

Throughout the remainder of this chapter Solomon moves into another area. I wish I had a better word for it, but I simply call it materialism.

## MATERIALISM

This is living for the *now*, and this should be understood by people today because we say we are the "now generation." It is a materialistic concept. It is a living for the here and now, living for self, selfishness. Each of these words describes a facet of this type of living.

**And I turned myself to behold wisdom, and madness, and folly: for what can the man do that cometh after the king? even that which hath been already done [Eccl. 2:12].**

In other words, no one could live it up more than Solomon did. He said they would have to repeat what he had done and would find it very monotonous.

**Then I saw that wisdom excelleth folly, as far as light excelleth darkness [Eccl. 2:13].**

It is better to be a wise man than to be a fool. It is better to be an educated man than to be an ignorant man.

**The wise man's eyes are in his head; but the fool walketh in darkness: and I myself perceived also that one event happeneth to them all [Eccl. 2:14].**

"The wise man's eyes are in his head"—I've heard my parents and my school teachers say to me, "Use your mind. Use your head. Use your eyes." That is what Solomon is saying. A wise man uses his head and his eyes, but "the fool walketh in darkness."

"I myself perceived also that one event happeneth to them all." Regardless of how smart you are, you don't really get too far away from the fool, because you both are going to be carried out feet forward and laid to rest somewhere. You both will end up in the same way.

**Then said I in my heart, As it happeneth to the fool, so it happeneth even to me; and why was I then more wise? Then I said in my heart, that this also is vanity [Eccl. 2:15].**

You would think that a smart fellow would find another way out. "Then I said in my heart, that this also is vanity." It is interesting that modern man with all his tremendous inventions and scientific advances has not been able to extend human life very long. Oh, I know that the average life span has been extended by ten years or more. But put that ten years down by a thousand years, or put it down beside eternity, and what do you have? You don't even have a second on the clock of eternity, my friend. Man really hasn't done very much for himself here on this earth.

**For there is no remembrance of the wise more than of the fool for ever; seeing that which now is in the days to come shall all be forgotten. And how dieth the wise men? as the fool [Eccl. 2:16].**

They die just the same way.

You may be innately intelligent. You may have a high I.Q. You may have been educated, even have several doctoral degrees, but none of this will help you when it is your time to die. Neither will any of that stop you from dying. When it is your time to go out the door, you will go, and there is nothing in this world that can keep you from it.

**Therefore I hated life; because the work that is wrought under the sun is grievous unto me: for all is vanity and vexation of spirit [Eccl. 2:17].**

Let me repeat: "Vanity" means that which is empty, meaningless, purposeless. With "all the work that is wrought under the sun" what has been done?

Thomas A. Edison is an example. He worked in a laboratory and developed many things such as the electric light bulb and the Victrola. All of our recording instruments really go back to the work of Edison. He was a genius, but he died just like everyone else. What good did it do him after all?

His laboratory is preserved in Fort Myers, Florida. If you are ever down there, it is worth the time to visit the Edison home and laboratory. He worked in that laboratory day and night. He had insomnia of the worst kind, so he had a little bed in his lab where he would lie down for little naps. He worked day and night, trying out many, many things that never worked out at all. I don't get the impression that life was a thrill for him. I think that Thomas A. Edison found life very boring.

**Yea, I hated all my labour which I had taken under the sun: because I should leave it unto the man that shall be after me [Eccl. 2:18].**

I have to go off and leave all of this someday. Have you ever stopped to think about that? What good is it going to do *you*? Oh, how many folk have worked all their lives to accumulate a little of this world's goods, then they leave it to some godless relative. Some folk intend to leave it to a Christian organization so that their money can propagate the gospel after they are gone, but have you ever stopped to think how many Christian organizations have become apostate and have departed from teaching the Word of God?

For example, Mr. John Harvard, who founded Harvard University, was a fundamental believer, and he left his money to propagate the fundamental Christian faith. Today you wouldn't find fundamental faith within ten yards of Harvard. They have departed from the faith. The money which Mr. Harvard left has come to be used for the very opposite of what he intended.

People today leave money to so-called Christian organizations, but they have no assurance that the organizations will remain true to the faith.

We know that Solomon faced this same kind of problem, and 1 Kings 12 tells us what happened. He left the kingdom to his son, and it was his son's foolish arrogance that divided the kingdom. What a tragedy that was.

**And who knoweth whether he shall be a wise man or a fool? yet shall he have rule over all my labour wherein I have laboured, and wherein I have shewed myself wise under the sun. This is also vanity [Eccl. 2:19].**

Solomon saw that it was a waste of time to work for something and then to turn it all over to a fool.

**Therefore I went about to cause my heart to despair of all the labour which I took under the sun [Eccl. 2:20].**

Notice again that this is "under the sun." It is the view of the man apart from God. This is not the man in Christ seated in the heavenly places of Ephesians 2:6. This view under the sun always leads to pessimism.

**For all his days are sorrows, and his travail grief; yea, his heart taketh not rest in the night. This is also vanity [Eccl. 2:23].**

Solomon found out that it didn't do any good to worry about it, because there was nothing he could do about it.

**There is nothing better for a man, than that he should eat and drink, and that he should make his soul enjoy good in his labour. This also I saw, that it was from the hand of God.**

**For who can eat, or who else can hasten hereunto, more than I?**

**For God giveth to a man that is good in his sight wisdom, and knowledge, and joy: but to the sinner he giveth travail, to gather and to heap up, that he may give to him that is good before God. This also is vanity and vexation of spirit [Eccl. 2:24–26].**

If you are living just for self—whether you are God's man or an unregenerate sinner—it will come to naught. It will lead to bitterness in your heart, and you will be holding nothing but dead leaves in your hands at the end.

# CHAPTER 3

In this chapter we see that Solomon adopts a certain philosophy of life known as fatalism. This was common among pagans; Buddhism is a fatalistic system; Platonism is fatalism. In our day certain cults give the impression of having a glorious faith in God, but actually the "faith" is fatalism.

The philosophy of fatalism is very popular in modern America. It is my custom to conclude my Bible conferences on Thursday evenings and fly back home on Fridays. On Friday afternoons I board a plane in some distant city and find myself with almost 100 percent male passengers. Who are they? Well, they are married men for the most part who are salesmen or representatives of certain companies. Their families live here in Southern California, and every Friday they get on a plane to come home. Most of them are tired. Their faces show the effect of a week's work.

Many of them who are carrying attaché cases will open them up and begin to work out a final report to hand in at the office if they get back in time. Or they will probably put it in the mail when they get home so it will be there for the president of the company to see on Monday. They take their drinks, and after they have their cocktails, they begin to laugh. I can sense that it is the liquor that is laughing. Every now and then, if I sit by one of them and there is an exchange of viewpoints, I find out that they have a fatalistic viewpoint of life.

On one occasion I came home on a plane that passed through some very rough weather. The man next to me looked unconcerned. I said to him, "You didn't seem to be frightened when we went through that bad weather." His response was, "No, there's no use being frightened. What is going to be *will* be. You can't change it. If it's time for your number to come up, it will come up—there's nothing you can do about it." There he sat, gritting his teeth with a philosophy of life that is very popular. It is called many things, but basically it is fatalism. A great many folk are facing life with that viewpoint.

## FATALISM

Now we find Solomon seeking satisfaction in fatalism.

**To every thing there is a season, and a time to every purpose under the heaven:**

**A time to be born, and a time to die; a time to plant, and a time to pluck up that which is planted;**

**A time to kill, and a time to heal; a time to break down, and a time to build up;**

**A time to weep, and a time to laugh; a time to mourn, and a time to dance;**

**A time to cast away stones, and a time to gather stones together; a time to embrace, and a time to refrain from embracing;**

**A time to get, and a time to lose; a time to keep, and a time to cast away;**

**A time to rend, and a time to sew; a time to keep silence, and a time to speak;**

**A time to love, and a time to hate; a time of war, and a time of peace [Eccl. 3:1–8].**

This is Solomon's viewpoint as he expresses it. In our day we hear the expression, "Take life as it comes."

There is "a time to get, and a time to lose." You played the stock market, and you lost your money. Well, that's the way it was to be.

You were a traveling man away from home, and a certain woman was easy to get, and you invited her up to your room. Your philosophy was that there is "a time to embrace, and a time to refrain from embracing." Taking life as it comes is a philosophy of fatalism.

**What profit hath he that worketh in that wherein he laboureth? [Eccl. 3:9].**

What's the use? Why fight it? If you can't fight them, join them. That is the kind of cliché that is bandied about among men today. This is the way men operate, especially godless men in the business world. Money is made on this kind of basis.

I think that you will find that men who live like this are not filled with joy. They are difficult to live with. I imagine their wives have real problems. They have a cocktail in the evening, and then they become sociable for several hours. After that it is better to stay out of their way.

**I have seen the travail, which God hath given to the sons of men to be exercised in it [Eccl. 3:10].**

Solomon has looked around—"I see people in trouble everywhere; so if I've escaped a little of it, I just consider myself lucky—that's all."

**He hath made every thing beautiful in his time: also he hath set the world in their heart, so that no man can find out the work that God maketh from the beginning to the end [Eccl. 3:11].**

God has allowed men to "set the world in their heart" so they will see that the world does not satisfy—their hearts are still empty. Many men start out with the philosophy that they are going to get all they can out of life. They say, "Life is like an orange, and I'm going to squeeze it for all it's worth." Solomon did that, but it didn't satisfy him at all.

**I know that there is no good in them, but for a man to rejoice, and to do good in his life [Eccl. 3:12].**

There is another group in this crowd: the do-gooders. A man on a plane said to me, "Well, I think a man ought to do good as much as he can. That's what I try to do." Let me tell you that he wasn't doing much *good*, but that was his philosophy of life.

And also that every man should eat and drink, and enjoy the good of all his labour, it is the gift of God [Eccl. 3:13].

This fellow said, "I see nothing wrong in drinking." And from his point of view, there wasn't anything wrong. This is the fatalism of modern man.

I know that, whatsoever God doeth, it shall be for ever: nothing can be put to it, nor any thing taken from it: and God doeth it, that men should fear before him [Eccl. 3:14].

They talk about God's will as primary, but with this viewpoint a man will say, "If it's not God's will for me to be saved, I won't be saved." You see, fatalism leaves no place for the mercy and grace of God. Fatalism says that God does not hear and answer prayer. My friend, it is God's grace and mercy and love that make life exciting and bring joy into life and give peace to the human heart.

We come to another philosophy at this point, which we call egotism or egoism. It is excessive love of self; an individual's self-interest is the *summum bonum* of life.

## EGOTISM

And moreover I saw under the sun the place of judgment, that wickedness was there; and the place of righteousness, that iniquity was there [Eccl. 3:16].

He is saying that all men are wicked. You can't trust anybody. This is a cynical, although I must confess a rather accurate, viewpoint of the human race.

I was speaking at a conference at which the director said, "Now we want to treat all of you folk who are here as Christian ladies and gentlemen." That was the last thing he should have done, because they didn't act like ladies and gentlemen, I assure you.

A friend of mine says that when some men do business, they trust the other individual until he proves himself untrustworthy. He says that he has learned to treat people as crooks until they prove that they are not. Now that is a cynical attitude. Unfortunately, it is reasonably accurate, and I must say that my friend is a successful businessman. He faces the reality as God has said it: ". . . All have sinned . . ." (Rom. 3:23).

Solomon goes on in this vein of thought—

I said in mine heart, God shall judge the righteous and the wicked: for there is a time there for every purpose and for every work.

I said in mine heart concerning the estate of the sons of men, that God might manifest them, and that they might see that they themselves are beasts [Eccl. 3:17–18].

That's not very encouraging!

For that which befalleth the sons of men befalleth beasts; even one thing befalleth them: as the one dieth, so dieth the other; yea, they have all one breath; so that a man hath no pre-eminence above a beast: for all is vanity.

All go unto one place; all are of the dust, and all turn to dust again [Eccl. 3:19–20].

You recognize, I am sure, that there are several cults which build on this statement. However, we must remember that this is the viewpoint of man *under* the sun, living for self-interest.

Living for self, enjoying life for self, is the reason men get involved in some projects which are good. For example, many men get interested in athletics and give themselves to it. Others give themselves to art, others to literature, others to music, and many different things. These things are not wrong, but they are selfish; they gratify man's selfish desires.

This viewpoint does not accept the optimist's conclusion. You see, evolution says that man *was* a beast but that he now has become a man. Egoism or egotism or self-interest says that man *is* a beast, which causes the individual to despise others. This philosophy produced the caste system in India and the class system in other parts of the world. It leads to vanity and the feeling of being better than the other man. It has a pessimistic viewpoint of death: man dies as an animal dies. I heard a man say, "Man dies just like a dog dies. When you're dead, you're dead—and that's all there is to it." Since he expects to die like an animal dies, he is going to live for himself in this life and get all he can out of it. This type of teaching is in the contemporary schoolroom. Evolution is a form of it, although it says man *was* a beast, and this says man *is* a beast. It is only a difference of time periods. Both agree that you are going to die like an animal, that you have no soul nor spirit; so you might as well live like an animal.

It is interesting to observe animal behavior with this in mind. I watched a family of little kittens the other day. Believe me, they had no regard for each other. They played together all right, but when food was given to them, they didn't mind pushing one little fellow out. The owner of the cats had to personally feed that little kitten—his brothers and sisters would have been perfectly willing to let him starve to death. Don't they have any compassion? No. Their egoism is their philosophy of life. You see little birds in a nest acting the same way. Each little fellow is taking care of himself. That is the viewpoint of the animal world. The reason man is beginning to react like an animal is because he is being taught in our schools that he *is* an animal.

**Who knoweth the spirit of man that goeth upward, and the spirit of the beast that goeth downward to the earth? [Eccl. 3:21].**

Solomon recognizes that man is different from the beast, for the spirit of man goes upward while the spirit of the beast goes downward—because he is only an animal.

**Wherefore I perceive that there is nothing better, than that a man should rejoice in his own works; for that is his portion: for who shall bring him to see what shall be after him? [Eccl. 3:22].**

In other words, this life is all we are going to get. Again, this is a modern teaching—call it whatever you wish—that the only thing worthwhile is to identify oneself with his environment and live like an animal lives. By the way, this is the ancient version of the "hippie" philosophy which came out of our schools a few years ago.

# CHAPTER 4

This chapter continues the record of Solomon's search for satisfaction through the philosophy of egotism.

**So I returned, and considered all the oppressions that are done under the sun: and behold the tears of such as were oppressed, and they had no comforter; and on the side of their oppressors there was power; but they had no comforter [Eccl. 4:1].**

Does this sound to you like any political philosophy in modern America? The egoist rebels against the establishment. He is opposed to it. However, whatever system exists, whoever is ruling, the poor are oppressed. Frankly, the poor always get the bad deal—there is no question about that. They are the ones who are oppressed. So the protest movements begin at this particular juncture.

**Wherefore I praised the dead which are already dead more than the living which are yet alive [Eccl. 4:2].**

You have heard the expression: "I wish I were dead." Then, "I'd rather be red than dead" is just reversing it, but both are rebellion against the establishment. Death appears to hold no terror for him whatsoever.

**Yea, better is he than both they, which hath not yet been, who hath not seen**

**the evil work that is done under the sun [Eccl. 4:3].**

Here is the other side of the coin: It would be better for future generations if they were never born. "I wish I had never been born" is the way we hear it.

**Again, I considered all travail, and every right work, that for this a man is envied of his neighbour. This is also vanity and vexation of spirit [Eccl. 4:4].**

It is interesting that the egoist rebels against the establishment, against the oppressor, against that which is wrong, but what about the man who is doing right? What about the man who is trying to do something about it? Well, he says that is no good either. It is a waste of time. This is really a pessimistic view of life!

**The fool foldeth his hands together, and eateth his own flesh [Eccl. 4:5].**

Does this mean a foolish man is a cannibal? No, it means that he is not willing to do anything to protect himself. He will not work for himself. We have developed quite a society like that today; people want everything given to them.

**Better is an handful with quietness, than both the hands full with travail and vexation of spirit [Eccl. 4:6].**

Candidly, this is a very good point. Of course this man wants to do "his own thing," but I would say it is better to have it that way than to have the hands full with travail and vexation of spirit.

**Then I returned, and I saw vanity under the sun [Eccl. 4:7].**

Anyway you go, it is wrong. There is no way out. This is the worst kind of pessimism. No wonder that campuses which major in an egoistic philosophy have the highest incidence of suicide. It is the old sore that has broken out in corruption. Behind all of it is the same pessimism of a philosophy of egoism which teaches that all comes to naught.

**There is one alone, and there is not a second; yea, he hath neither child nor brother: yet is there no end of all his labour; neither is his eye satisfied with riches; neither saith he, For whom do I labour, and bereave my soul of good? This is also vanity, yea, it is a sore travail [Eccl. 4:8].**

What a picture this is! Even if you work for somebody else and help them, you are just wasting your time.

**Two are better than one; because they have a good reward for their labour [Eccl. 4:9].**

Now he is going to give some reasons for teaming up with someone else, but it will be a selfish reason—you may be sure of that. He says that two are better than one "because they have a good reward for their labour." You'll be able to acquire more by teaming up with someone than by trying to do it alone.

**For if they fall, the one will lift up his fellow: but woe to him that is alone when he falleth; for he hath not another to help him up [Eccl. 4:10].**

Solomon made the discovery that attempting to live just for yourself doesn't mean you can go it alone. You need someone to help you and stand with you. "Woe to him that is alone when he falleth." That is the reason they tell us to team up if we go on a hike rather than going alone. In case of an accident it is well to have someone else around. This is a problem of the many retired folk who live alone. They may fall and break a hip and be unable to get to the telephone. Sometimes it is a day or two before a neighbor looks in on them. So it is better that two be together. If one falls, the other can render help.

**Again, if two lie together, then they have heat: but how can one be warm alone? [Eccl. 4:11].**

And then one member of a team can give warmth to the other member of the team. I remember as a little boy, I always liked to sleep with my dad in the wintertime because he would warm me up. It was cold. Ours was not a warm house, and we slept in rooms that were unheated. It made quite a difference to sleep with my dad.

**And if one prevail against him, two shall withstand him; and a threefold cord is not quickly broken [Eccl. 4:12].**

If two is company, then three is a crowd, and sometimes it is well to have a crowd, especially if someone is coming against you.

We have problems with crime on our streets today. Often it is the person who is alone who is the victim of crime. I am told that in Washington, D.C., a woman is not permitted to go alone to a public restroom. There must always be another to go along with her. It is tragic that we live in such a day. In spite of what the liberals say, we are in need of law and order in our day. The Bible teaches clearly that unregenerate man has a *sinful* nature. It should be obvious that "civilized" man has not lost his sinful nature and needs restraint rather than liberty. The liberty being exercised in our day is the liberty to hold people up on the street, liberty to mug them, liberty to make obscene calls, liberty to blare out music that only one or two people want to hear, liberty to express oneself in any way. My friend, liberty is not license. You have liberty to swing your fist, but where my nose begins is where your liberty ends. We need to change many of our concepts today.

The self-centered man will not find satisfaction in this life. To be alone in your work may satisfy for a while, but finally you get tired of it. I don't like to travel alone. I go to many conferences in my work, and I take my wife with me everywhere I go. Most of us find that we don't like to go alone.

**Better is a poor and a wise child than an old and foolish king, who will no more be admonished [Eccl. 4:13].**

Solomon was both—a wise child and a very foolish king.

**For out of prison he cometh to reign; whereas also he that is born in his kingdom becometh poor [Eccl. 4:14].**

We should be interested in what happens in federal and state governments because it is going to affect our living. A great many people become poor because the politicians become rich and influential. Certainly folk have a right to protest against that. The corruption that has arisen in our country is wrecking business, making many people poor, and retired folk suffer from it.

**I considered all the living which walk under the sun, with the second child that shall stand up in his stead.**

**There is no end of all the people, even of all that have been before them: they also that come after shall not rejoice in him. Surely this also is vanity and vexation of spirit [Eccl. 4:15–16].**

"The second child that shall stand up in his stead." It is interesting to notice that Solomon was a second child. He was the second child of Bathsheba. He was not the child whom David would have chosen to be the next king. Solomon apparently had noted that since Isaac was not the first child and Jacob was not the first child, God has a way of choosing seconds. If you feel that you are second-class today, remember that you are first-class with God.

The second thing to notice is that later on things seem different from what they were at the time. "They also that come after shall not rejoice in him." Someone, such as a president, may be very popular during his day. Then, as time begins to recede from him, when the glamor boys and publicity men are no longer heard, and the news media are no longer building him up, we can see that his time in office was not a blessing to the nation but actually a time of deterioration. "There is no end of all the people, even of all that have been before them: they also that come after shall not rejoice in him."

# CHAPTER 5

Now Solomon tries something else, and this is something that may interest you a great deal. He tries to find satisfaction in religion, and he does *not* find it. I am going to say several things which may be startling to you, but don't reject them until you think about them just a little.

Did you know that religion has damned more people in this world than anything else has? Take a look at what the pagan religions have done for people in the past and in the present. Look at the condition of India. These people do not have a lower mentality than other peoples of the world. It is their religion that keeps them down. Consider China. As I write, China is in the grip of a terrible dictatorship, but it has made China a nation to be reckoned with. Their pagan religions did not do even that much for them. The Moslem world is fractured and is in sad condition. South America is as rich in natural resources as North America; yet most of the people remain in a miserable condition, and its religion tries to keep it that way. Look at what liberal Protestantism and liberal Romanism have done to this country. When this country began to give up its belief in God and its respect for the Bible, when liberalism came into the pulpits of our nation, then deterioration began in our land.

My friend, if you have a religion, I suggest you get rid of it and exchange it for Christ. I personally do not think one can call Christianity a religion. There is no ritual whatsoever given with Christianity. Have you ever stopped to think of that? This is the reason we can have all kinds of churches with different forms of worship—for instance you can sing the doxology if you want to, but you don't have to. Christianity was never given a form to follow. Why? Because Christianity is a Person. To be a Christian means that you trust Christ. Religion has never been very helpful to man.

## SEEKING SATISFACTION IN RELIGION

Listen to what Solomon is saying now—this is terrific!

**Keep thy foot when thou goest to the house of God, and be more ready to hear, than to give the sacrifice of fools: for they consider not that they do evil [Eccl. 5:1].**

Going to some churches is not only a waste of time; it is *wrong*. It is wrong to give your approval to a liberal pulpit. It is wrong when you do not give your support to a fundamental pastor who is giving out the Word of God. Solomon tried being religious. He went up to the temple, but he warns, "Have as little to do with it as possible; keep your mouth shut. Go and sit, but for goodness' sake don't commit yourself to anything."

**Be not rash with thy mouth, and let not thine heart be hasty to utter any thing before God: for God is in heaven, and thou upon earth: therefore let thy words be few [Eccl. 5:2].**

He is warning, "Do not make any decision under the stress of emotion." Cry at the movies, but don't do it in church. Don't sign a pledge. If you are going to rent an apartment or a house, it's all right to sign for that, but don't commit yourself to God in writing. In other words, make it a religion; go through the form but avoid reality.

My friend, Solomon is not the only one who tried that. There are a lot of unhappy people in our churches today. They never get involved; they just go through a nice sweet little ritual. There is nothing as deadening as that!

**For a dream cometh through the multitude of business; and a fool's voice is known by multitude of words [Eccl. 5:3].**

There are a lot of things being said in church that should not be said.

**When thou vowest a vow unto God, defer not to pay it; for he hath no pleasure in fools: pay that which thou hast vowed [Eccl. 5:4].**

Don't go forward at an invitation unless you are really doing business with God. I recall conducting a service after which I was severely criticized because I would not let young people come forward. It was obvious to me that it would have been merely a display. I felt it was better to let them make a decision for Christ right where they were sitting. Oh, how many folk have come forward in a meeting when it has meant nothing to them at all! "When thou vowest a vow unto God, defer not to pay it." Don't break your vow—not to God. You can't promise God things, fail to make good on them, and then expect to maintain a vital relationship with Him.

There is a lot of pious talking and pious promising that is absolutely meaningless because it is never carried out.

Do you know that God actually gave a law concerning vows? Read Leviticus 27. I deal with this chapter in the second volume of my book, *Learning Through Leviticus*. My friend, when you make a vow to God, you had better mean what you say, because God is going to hold you to it. There is many a person who is no longer a missionary, many a preacher who is out of the pulpit, many a Christian who has been put on the shelf because they promised God that which they didn't mean at all. It is not a religious ceremony when you are dealing with God. You are dealing with a Person who hears you and expects you to keep your promise.

**Better is it that thou shouldest not vow, than that thou shouldest vow and not pay.**

**Suffer not thy mouth to cause thy flesh to sin; neither say thou before the angel, that it was an error: wherefore should God be angry at thy voice, and destroy the work of thine hands? [Eccl. 5:5–6].**

After making a vow to God, we are not to say, "It was an error—I should never have said it; I didn't really mean it." We are dealing with a living God. It seems there are many people who don't know that. As a result, they stand way out on the fringe of the things of God. God is a reality, and we need to be very careful in our dealings with Him.

**For in the multitude of dreams and many words there are also divers vanities: but fear thou God [Eccl. 5:7].**

In "dreams and many words there are also divers vanities"—that is, all kinds of emptiness. They are no substitute for a personal relationship with God. So many people say, "I have had a dream," or, "I have had an experience." And they are putting their trust in that. There are many people today who use an experience to test the Word of God. It *must* be the other way around: All experience must be tested by the Word of God. We are instructed to *try* the spirits to see whether they are of God or not (see 1 John 4:1). Too many people go out on a tangent of experience and live by that. That is merely religion. That is an appeal to the emotion, an appeal to the aesthetic sense.

My friend, does your faith in Christ rest upon experience, or does it rest upon the naked Word of God? Do you have religion, or do you have Christ?

**If thou seest the oppression of the poor, and violent perverting of judgment and justice in a province, marvel not at the matter: for he that is higher than the highest regardeth; and there be higher than they [Eccl. 5:8].**

In our country we have heard much about corruption in the poverty program. There are so many today who are attempting to get rich at the expense of the poor. God will judge that. "For he that is higher than the highest regardeth." God sees what is going on. I think that any Christian who is in a program in which he sees corruption should get out of the program. If *you* see corruption in a program, believe me, *God* sees the corruption in the program, and God will deal with it in judgment.

The history of this world bears that out. God watches what governments do to the poor. Governments that have exploited the poor have fallen. An example is the French Revolution. It wasn't a nice, pretty thing by any means. It was an awful thing. I think it was the judgment of God upon the corruption of a nation in which a few were living at the expense of the many poor.

God has much to say about the relief of the poor. When the Lord Jesus comes to reign during the kingdom age which we call the Millennium, then they will find that there is One reigning who really means business when He says that He is going to do something for the poor. There will be justice and righteousness for them. I don't think that He will put them on any kind of dole system. But each person will make his contribution and will receive justice at His hands.

This brings us to a new section in Solomon's experiments to find satisfaction in life. As we have seen, he tried science, the study of natural laws. He tried wisdom and philosophy, pleasure, and materialism. He tried living for the "now." He tried fatalism. He tried egoism, living for self. Then, of all things, he tried religion.

Now we will see Solomon engage in another experiment. Solomon was in a position to pursue and enjoy wealth better than anyone else. He was probably the richest man who has ever been on this earth. He gave himself over to the accumulation of gold, and he could buy anything that he wanted. The riches of Solomon was the factor that finally brought the downfall of the nation. The greed of the surrounding nations was aroused. They wanted to move in to get some of that wealth. God had put up a wall of protection around Israel, but that wall crumbled, and God allowed the nations to come into Israel and help themselves.

## SEEKING SATISFACTION IN PURSUIT AND ENJOYMENT OF WEALTH

**He that loveth silver shall not be satisfied with silver; nor he that loveth abundance with increase: this is also vanity [Eccl. 5:10].**

The president of a great corporation comes to the end of the year and sees a tremendous profit, but that actually does not satisfy him. A man may have a big bank account, which offers him some measure of security, but it will not really satisfy him. Wealth will not bring satisfaction in life.

Wealth is not wrong in itself. The Scripture never condemns wealth. It condemns the *love* of money. Not the money itself, but the *love* of money is a root of all evil (see 1 Tim. 6:10). To accumulate wealth for wealth's sake is wrong. The miser thinks dollars are flat so they can be stacked; the spendthrift thinks they are round so they can be rolled. Both are entirely wrong.

Man's attitude toward money is the issue. There is nothing wrong with our profit system itself. The wrong is in the people who are in it. It is the love of money which is wrong. The love of money makes people try to get rich for riches' sake.

We see men who are held together, bound together in an arrangement just to make money for money's sake. I was interested in hearing a comedian tell about a play he had a part in producing. He was thanking all those who had participated and was telling how they had all cooperated. It was a very lovely speech with no trace of humor in it. When he got to the end, he said, "And we have all been held together in this endeavor by one thing"— he paused a moment—"*greed!*" Yes, greed was the ingredient that held them together to make the production. That is the ingredient that holds big business together. It holds the Mafia together. It holds a great many organizations together.

I must confess that I believe it is wrong for one man or one organization to accumulate so much money when others are in poverty and need. This may sound radical, but I do believe that eventually something must be done about that. Look at India for an example. The maharaja has become immensely wealthy while the masses are poverty-stricken. God condemns that kind of thing. He condemns it because of the love of money and the use which is made of it. In our own country greed is the thing that is wrong with godless capitalism and godless labor. Greed—the love of money. It would be so wonderful if man would *make* money for the glory of God. It would be wonderful if man *labored* for money for the glory of God. It would be so wonderful if money were put to its proper use. The only cure for greed, of course, is to have Christ in the heart!

**When goods increase, they are increased that eat them: and what good is there to the owners thereof, saving the beholding of them with their eyes? [Eccl. 5:11].**

Growth just for the sake of growth is no good at all. This is true of a business or even of a Christian organization or church. I have learned it by personal experience.

For years I was the pastor of a large church. Just to grow for the sake of growing so one can have a big church is nothing in the world but a big headache. There is no fun in it. There is no joy in it. The Lord taught me that to grow for the glory of God is to be my one purpose in life. I keep this goal before me: Vernon McGee, you do this *one* thing, get out the Word of God.

**The sleep of a labouring man is sweet, whether he eat little or much: but the abundance of the rich will not suffer him to sleep [Eccl. 5:12].**

The laboring man may not have too much to eat. That keeps him from being a glutton, and he probably sleeps a lot better by not overeating. The rich man has an abundance. In fact, he has gourmet food all the time, and he gets pretty tired of it. He loses his appetite for it. Besides that, he has to worry about his riches, which keeps him awake at night. When we were in Hawaii with one of our tours, we were permitted to stay in a lovely hotel because of the size of our tour. I noticed how unhappy the people in the hotel seemed to be. They were people who had come to Hawaii to have a good time, but they were always worrying about their things. One woman spent thirty minutes getting her jewels in a safe-deposit box. When I got to the desk, the girl said, "She's been here before and she'll be back a dozen times to check on them or take out a piece to wear and bring it back again." You know, I was glad my wife didn't have that kind of problem. That rich woman had a real problem—probably one hundred thousand dollars worth of jewels to worry about. Riches multiply anxieties. Maybe that is one reason the Lord didn't let me become rich!

**There is a sore evil which I have seen under the sun, namely, riches kept for the owners thereof to their hurt [Eccl. 5:13].**

Riches actually hurt rather than help a great many people. Sometimes the poor man is happier than the rich man. However, the apostle Paul said that he knew both how to abound and how to be abased (see Phil. 4:12). Frankly, I'd like to try both.

**But those riches perish by evil travail: and he begetteth a son, and there is nothing in his hand [Eccl. 5:14].**

He is saying that a man can accumulate a fortune and leave it to a son, and the boy will run through it—he will spend it all. Today men have become pretty wise about that. A man doesn't leave the money to his son directly, but in a trusteeship so that someone else doles out the money to the boy in small amounts to preserve the family fortune.

There are a lot of prominent men today who never made a dime in their lives. The reason they are rich is because they inherited it. They lack discernment in the use of the money; yet they are in positions of influence. This is one of our problems today.

I think that eventually there will be a division in our nation which will not be between races, but will narrow down to the rich and the poor. That has always been the line of demarcation. I believe many rich people sense this, which explains why so many of the wealthy are politically liberal in their thinking. They already have their money, and no one can touch it; so they are willing to bring in liberal programs which will be supported by the taxes that you and I pay. The wealthy do not pay for those programs. That is a real problem. Solomon understood and spoke into that kind of situation. Solomon learned that wealth does not satisfy, nor is it the solution to the problems of life.

# CHAPTER 6

This chapter concludes Solomon's pursuit and enjoyment of wealth in his search for satisfaction.

**There is an evil which I have seen under the sun, and it is common among men:**

**A man to whom God hath given riches, wealth, and honour, so that he wanteth nothing for his soul of all that he desireth, yet God giveth him not power to eat thereof, but a stranger eateth it: this is vanity, and it is an evil disease [Eccl. 6:1–2].**

A friend told me that when he was in a hotel in Florida, he saw John D. Rockefeller, Sr., sitting and eating his meal. He had just a few little crumbs, some health food, that had been set before him. Over at a side table my friend saw one of the men who worked as a waiter in the hotel sitting with a big juicy steak in front of him. The man who could afford the steak couldn't eat one; the man who could not afford the steak had one to eat because he worked for the hotel. It is better to have a good appetite than a big bank account!

**If a man beget an hundred children, and live many years, so that the days of his years be many, and his soul be not filled with good, and also that he have no burial; I say, that an untimely birth is better than he (Eccl. 6:3].**

The rich man can eat only three meals a day, he can sleep on only one bed at a time, and he cannot live longer than the poor man—no matter how many doctors he may have—and he takes nothing with him when he leaves. There is no pocket in a shroud. Job was a rich man, and he said that he had come here with nothing and he was going out the same way. It is rather empty to give one's life to the pursuit of that which does not bring happiness here and has no value hereafter. Some people spend their lives in this kind of an emptiness.

# CHAPTER 7

This is the last experiment that Solomon tries. He has made experiments in everything under the sun to see if any of it would bring satisfaction and enjoyment to him. He tried science, the study of the natural laws of the universe, which made some contribution but did not satisfy him. Then he went into the study of philosophy and psychology. They didn't satisfy. He went the limit on pleasure and materialism. He tried fatalism, which is such a popular philosophy of life today. He tried egoism, living for self. Then he tried religion—no religion can satisfy, because only Christ can satisfy the heart. Wealth was another thing which Solomon tried. He was the wealthiest man in the world, but he found that wealth did not bring satisfaction in and of itself.

Now we will see him try the last experiment: morality. Today we would call him a "do-gooder." I would say that this is the place to which the majority of the people in America are moving. (I think the majority would still be classified as do-gooders.) They are going down the middle of the road on the freeway of life. This group can be described as the Babbitts, doing business in the Big City, under a neon sign, living out in suburbia, in a sedate, secluded, exclusive neighborhood, and taking it easy. Their children go to the best schools. They move with the best crowds. They go to the best church, the richest church in the neighborhood, the one with the tallest steeple, the loudest chimes, and the most educated preacher, who knows everything that man can possibly know, except the Bible (of course, if he did know and preach the Bible, he would lose his job). This is the kind of do-good society Solomon now tries.

## SEEKING SATISFACTION IN MORALITY THE GOOD LIFE

**A good name is better than precious ointment; and the day of death than the day of one's birth [Eccl. 7:1].**

That is true, by the way. There is nothing wrong with that statement. A good name *is* better than precious ointment. It is gratifying to a man to have people say he is a wonderful neighbor and that they have never had an argument with him, that he won't discuss religion or politics, or won't get involved in any kind of bad situation. He just smiles and goes right down the middle of the road, never veering to the right or to the left. He is a respectable person, recognized in the community. He joins different organizations of the town and does business with all kinds of people. Some day at his funeral the preacher will say all kinds of good things about him to try to push him into heaven. Solomon says a good reputation and a long eulogy at your funeral are what we should strive for down here. But will that satisfy the heart?

**It is better to go to the house of mourning, than to go to the house of feasting: for that is the end of all men; and the living will lay it to his heart [Eccl. 7:2].**

All of this life of morality and do-goodism is done in a dignified manner. People go to a club meeting and listen to a man come and talk about pollution. They don't *do* anything about it, but they sit and talk about it in a very dignified way. The next week someone talks to them on civic problems. They sit and listen to that, and again nothing will be done. Then they all go to the funeral of one of the men in their fraternal lodge and hear nice things said about him. Nobody is particularly moved; no one will miss him too much. This is just how life is in our hometown.

That kind of life cannot satisfy the needs of man. To me, that life would be *blah*. I am glad I have never lived like that, and I don't live like that today. It is not really *living*. I think this is the worst situation of them all. Frankly, I cannot blame a lot of young people who are rebelling against that kind of society.

**Sorrow is better than laughter: for by the sadness of the countenance the heart is made better [Eccl. 7:3].**

People today do anything to avoid sorrow. We have it arranged now so that you can laugh all the way to the cemetery. Reality is so covered over with flowers and soft music and a preacher saying a lot of easy things, nice things, that everyone goes home and says, "My, that was a nice funeral"—and forgets the grim reality of death as soon as possible.

**The heart of the wise is in the house of mourning; but the heart of fools is in the house of mirth [Eccl. 7:4].**

They don't get more than fifty yards from the cemetery until someone tells a joke and they all have a good laugh. This is living in the presence of death. Somehow it doesn't occur to these folk, as they see their friends slipping out of this life, that they, too, are moving along to death. Doesn't it occur to them that it might be well for them to check to see where they are going? Are they saved? Are they lost? Are they rightly related to God? They don't consider that important. They give to the Community Chest and are active in Red Cross. They are involved citizens in the community. They wouldn't dare confess Christ and take a public stand for Him.

**It is better to hear the rebuke of the wise, than for a man to hear the song of fools.**

**For as the crackling of thorns under a pot, so is the laughter of the fool: this also is vanity [Eccl. 7:5–6].**

Solomon's point is this: Why not try both groups? Listen to the rebuke of a wise person, then go down and listen to a rock band and enjoy that also. One may be better than the other, but it is easier to go with both groups. This is the picture through the remainder of this chapter.

**Be not hasty in thy spirit to be angry: for anger resteth in the bosom of fools [Eccl. 7:9].**

Don't get angry at anything. Be a nice fellow, stay friends with everyone because that will help business. Go the easy way, walk softly. Don't be an extremist, be willing to compromise. Go with one crowd to be popular with them, and the next night go with a different crowd to be popular with them. You see, the do-gooder in this chapter is the man who lives like hell on Saturday night and then goes to church and passes for a Christian on Sunday. A man who had been stone drunk on Saturday night saw me on Sunday morning and said, "I want you to know that I am a Christian. What do you think I am, a pagan?" And that's what he was, a pagan.

**Wisdom is good with an inheritance: and by it there is profit to them that see the sun [Eccl. 7:11].**

In the Book of Proverbs we see that "wisdom" is another name for Christ. Christ has been made unto us wisdom. Oh, how this do-gooder needs to have Christ!

**For wisdom is a defence, and money is a defence: but the excellency of knowledge is, that wisdom giveth life to them that have it [Eccl. 7:12].**

"Money is a defence"—this man wants plenty of money, but he doesn't want Christ.

"Wisdom giveth life to them that have it." And you can't buy life with money. Medical science may be able to extend your life for a few years, but it doesn't give eternal life here and out yonder in eternity. Only wisdom, which is Christ, can do that.

**Also take no heed unto all words that are spoken; lest thou hear thy servant curse thee [Eccl. 7:21].**

Don't be disturbed by reports that somebody who knows you well says you are a crook. If you take the middle of the road, in the long run the community will applaud you.

My friend, seeking satisfaction in life by just trying to be a do-gooder is living like a vegetable, not a man! Yet this is the lifestyle of the majority in modern America. They will go to the burlesque show on Saturday night and to church on Sunday morning! What hypocrisy! We have seen our youth rebelling against this type of living. There are two thousand of them over on the island of Hawaii. I had the privilege of ministering to some of them, and quite a few turned to Christ. They have tried everything else. But why didn't they find Christ in their homes in which their parents were church members? They saw that there was something radically missing in their homes and in their churches. They have seen the hypocrisy, the emptiness of the life of the moralist, the do-gooder.

I believe it is easier to reach a godless atheist than a hypocritical churchgoer. The godless atheist may respond when he hears the gospel for the first time, but the hypocritical churchgoer has heard the gospel again and again and has become hardened to it. That is the real tragedy.

# CHAPTER 8

**T**his chapter continues with the man who is lukewarm. He blows neither hot nor cold. The moralists and the do-gooders say that they are living by the Golden Rule, but they don't seem to have any idea of what the Golden Rule is and what it requires. Solomon observes that there doesn't seem to be much difference between the wicked and the righteous.

**Who is as the wise man? and who knoweth the interpretation of a thing? a man's wisdom maketh his face to shine, and the boldness of his face shall be changed [Eccl. 8:1].**

Only Christ who is real wisdom can change a man's life. He can come into a life and bring excitement, joy, and peace. He can give us all the things that are needed today to deliver us from living a mediocre existence.

**I counsel thee to keep the king's commandment, and that in regard of the oath of God.**

**Be not hasty to go out of his sight: stand not in an evil thing; for he doeth whatsoever pleaseth him [Eccl. 8:2–3].**

He is saying, "Be careful what you do. Don't get into trouble."

**Where the word of a king is, there is power: and who may say unto him, What doest thou? [Eccl. 8:4].**

Now the king can take a stand for what he believes because he has the liberty to do so. My friend, why don't you live like a king and take a stand for Christ?

I talked to a young vagrant who had adopted what was then called the hippie lifestyle. I asked him, "Why in the world do you take up this life-style? Why are you dressed like you are?" He said, "Man, I want liberty; I want freedom. I want to live as I please." I said, "Let me ask you this one question: If you changed your garb and went back to your crowd, would they accept you?" He thought a moment and then said, "I guess they wouldn't." So I asked, "Then you don't have much liberty, do you?"

Young people feel that they *must* have the approval of the crowd, of the pack, so they really don't know what liberty is. A great many of them take drugs for no other reason than to be accepted by the crowd. I asked the young man, "Do you think that I don't have freedom because I dress as I dress?" He answered, "Yes, I would say that." Then I told him that I have a freedom which he didn't have. I told him that I don't dress like this all the time. I can dress any way that I please—and I do. I don't conform to a pattern. I have liberty. I said, "You and I are living in a world where there is rebellion against God—that is the direction mankind is moving. But I can bow my knee to the Lord Jesus Christ. I can call Him my Lord and my Savior. That is *real* freedom. I am not going in the direction of the crowd. I have made my choice. Young man, if you want real freedom, come to Christ. Jesus said, 'If the Son therefore shall make you free, ye shall be free indeed' " (John 8:36). That is freedom.

It is hard for people to understand that the do-gooder is just as much in rebellion against God as the criminal in the jail and that he is bound as securely by the rules of his group and the patterns they set. He is bound to a life-style that goes down the middle of the road.

**There is no man that hath power over the spirit to retain the spirit; neither hath he power in the day of death: and there is no discharge in that war; neither shall wickedness deliver those that are given to it [Eccl. 8:8].**

If he continues taking that cocktail to conform to the group he associates with, one of these days he is going to be an alcoholic. (Oh, there are millions of them in our country, and they are all do-gooders!) And finally death will come to him—"neither hath he power in the day of death."

**Because sentence against an evil work is not executed speedily, therefore the heart of the sons of men is fully set in them to do evil [Eccl. 8:11].**

What a picture of that which is happening in our contemporary society! When judgment is not executed, men do more and more evil work, because evil is in the hearts of men. Even men who call themselves Christian continue in sin, saying, "Look, I've been in sin for five years, and God has done nothing about it!" Well, that already reveals His judgment upon you. He has done nothing about it because He is way down the road waiting for you. In fact, He can wait until eternity—*you* can't. ". . . Behold, now is the accepted time; behold, now is the day of salvation" (2 Cor. 6:2). God grants you *today* so that you can turn to Him.

**There is a vanity which is done upon the earth; that there be just men, unto whom it happeneth according to the work of the wicked; again, there be wicked men, to whom it happeneth according to the work of the righteous: I said that this also is vanity [Eccl. 8:14].**

Solomon observes that when you look at the surface of things, there does not seem to be too much difference between the wicked and the righteous. It seems that it really doesn't make any difference whether one is wicked or righteous because both come to the same end.

**Then I commended mirth, because a man hath no better thing under the sun, than to eat, and to drink, and to be merry: for that shall abide with him of his labour the days of his life, which God giveth him under the sun [Eccl. 8:15].**

"Eat, . . . drink, and . . . be merry"—he concludes that the best thing to do is to enjoy life and to enjoy the labor "which God giveth him under the sun." That is the most empty philosophy of life that anyone can have.

# CHAPTER 9

We have labeled the moralist as the do-gooder. This is where we see him in action. We have seen that this is the man who says, "I believe that if you pay your honest debts and live a good life, God will accept you." He is like the average American who travels down the middle of the road on the freeway of life. He is Babbitt on Main Street in Big City, doing business under a neon sign, but living in the sedate, secluded, and exclusive neighborhood in the suburbs. He is the one who feels that he is going to heaven on his own propulsion. "I am working out my own salvation, and I'm really a pretty good fellow after all." He has a hard philosophy of life and very little real joy. Oh, he has his "happy hour" each evening when he has his cocktail, but he comes to some very doleful and pessimistic conclusions.

We have seen that many of the teachings of

the Book of Ecclesiastes are quite radical. They present the philosophy of man *under the sun*. They do not present the Christian viewpoint, nor do they represent God's viewpoint. They tell us the inevitable conclusions that are reached by the man under the sun. I find it a doleful book, and I find this chapter especially so. This book of the Bible is like a black sheep in a flock of sheep. One can take many passages out of this book which seem to contradict the other portions of Scripture. They express ideas that are contrary to some of the great teachings of Scripture, which explains why this book has been a favorite among atheists. Volney and Voltaire quoted from it frequently. It fosters a pessimistic philosophy of life like Schopenhauer had. Some of the modern cults predicate the main thesis of their systems on this book.

How did this book get into the canon of Scripture? Well, it is obvious that one must go back to the purpose of the author. What is his thesis? What is he demonstrating? Is he trying to set forth Christian principles? We must always remember that Solomon is speaking of life apart from God. He has tried to make an experiment to see how to be happy without God. These are the conclusions that he has come to "under the sun." This is the way the man of the world looks at life. So then it is no surprise that unbelievers would quote from this book.

Let me give you an illustration to help you to understand this book. Halfway between high tide and low tide is what they call the *mean* tide, which is sea level. There is a realm of life below sea level; there is a realm of life above sea level. Actually, they are like two different worlds. In the world below sea level there are certain chemical elements in a world that is aqueous. Above the sea level there are different combinations of chemical elements in a world that is gaseous. Below sea level are the fish with fins. Above are the birds with wings. There are two ways of life. The mockingbird does not tell the tuna fish that he is all wrong because he doesn't have feathers. The monkey and the barracuda could actually have a big debate on which direction is sea level. The monkey would say that sea level is down; the barracuda would argue that sea level is up.

Now Ecclesiastes is "under the sun." The Christian life is in the heavenly places where God is. Man under the sun will have a different view of life from the view of God who is above the sun. We are looking at two different worlds, two different ways of life. Life *under*

the sun is a mundane existence apart from God. It views a future and an eternity without God. The Christian life is a contrast to this in every way, because man has been saved by the grace of God and is a display of His grace.

So there are two different spheres, and the laws and principles of one will not apply to the other. They are as far apart as that which is below sea level and that which is above sea level. Because this is true, it is a waste of time to tell the non-Christian, "If ye then be risen with Christ, seek those things which are above, where Christ sitteth on the right hand of God" (Col. 3:1). That man is not even in Christ; he is not risen with Christ. Therefore he *cannot* seek those things which are above. He first needs to be born again, to become a new creature. You see, it is no use talking to a non-Christian as if he were a man in Christ, because he isn't. It would be like trying to teach a mud turtle to fly. The mud turtle likes the mud; he is not even interested in flying.

As we have seen, Ecclesiastes is the record of experiments that Solomon made with life. He tried everything "under the sun" to see if he could find satisfaction for his soul. Everything must be interpreted in that light.

Solomon tried the pursuit of knowledge and came to the conclusion, ". . . of making many books there is no end " (Eccl. 12:12). He tried pleasure and the outcome was, "I hated life." He tried riches and came to the conclusion, "He that loveth silver shall not be satisfied with silver" (Eccl. 5:10). Then he tried religion and concluded that it will make one become a lunatic or a racketeer, a crank or a crook, a nut or a bum. Then he tried fame and a good name; he tried morality. All he could say was that it was all vanity and vexation of spirit.

Thackeray wrote a wonderful novel called *Vanity Fair*. It is the story of a girl named Becky, and it is set in the time of the wars of Napoleon. It tells of the littleness and of the sin in the lives of the characters as they lived their lives apart from God (Thackeray was a Christian). He concluded the book by saying, "The play is over. We put the puppets back in the box. All is vanity and vexation of spirit."

By the way, you could do the same thing with the entertainment and pleasure capitals of our country. They are places of fame and riches and also places that have a monopoly on sleeping pills and narcotics. Life is empty without God and without Christ.

Augustine gave us that often-quoted expression, "Thou hast made us for Thyself, and the heart of man is restless until it finds its rest in Thee" (Confessions, Bk. 1, Sec. 1). The human heart is so constructed that you could put the whole world in it and still it would not be filled.

Quotations from Ecclesiastes have been used to support socialism. There is only one answer for statism or regimentation. Christ is the answer, the only answer. All other routes lead to emptiness and frustration. With Him there is life abundant.

**For all this I considered in my heart even to declare all this, that the righteous, and the wise, and their works, are in the hand of God: no man knoweth either love or hatred by all that is before them [Eccl. 9:1].**

He is not worried about the future. Eternity is a realm he doesn't even think about because he knows nothing about it.

**All things come alike to all: there is one event to the righteous, and to the wicked; to the good and to the clean, and to the unclean; to him that sacrificeth, and to him that sacrificeth not: as is the good, so is the sinner; and he that sweareth, as he that feareth an oath [Eccl. 9:2].**

It looks to him as if it doesn't make any difference which direction you go. They all come out the same way anyhow. Remember, this is not God's answer. This is the way it looks to man under the sun as he observes the lives of people around him.

**This is an evil among all things that are done under the sun, that there is one event unto all: yea, also the heart of the sons of men is full of evil, and madness is in their heart while they live, and after that they go to the dead [Eccl. 9:3].**

Why should anyone work at all? Life is just a big lottery, and you are the victim of your circumstances. The fellow who was lucky enough to get his share of it, ought to share it with you. The philosophies of our day are not saying anything new. Karl Marx didn't say anything new—Solomon was way ahead of him.

**For to him that is joined to all the living there is hope: for a living dog is better than a dead lion [Eccl. 9:4].**

If you follow along this basic premise, it is eat, drink, and be merry for tomorrow you die. Then, whether you are a fool or a wise man doesn't make much difference. It's still better to be alive than dead, even if you are a fool while you are alive—"for a living dog is better than a dead lion."

**For the living know that they shall die: but the dead know not any thing, neither have they any more a reward; for the memory of them is forgotten [Eccl. 9:5].**

This is where the idea of a "soul sleep" arises (see also v. 10). All of this is the observation of the man under the sun. This is the way it looks if death is the end and there is nothing after death. That is why he says it would be better to be a living dog than a dead lion.

God has told us what happens after death. The body is put into the grave, and it is the *body* that sleeps in the grave. Scripture makes it very clear that the soul of the child of God goes to be with the Lord: "Therefore we are always confident, knowing that, whilst we are at home in the body, we are absent from the Lord: (For we walk by faith, not by sight:) We are confident, I say, and willing rather to be absent from the body, and to be present with the Lord" (2 Cor. 5:6–8). The soul, the real person, goes to be with the Lord—absent from the body, present with the Lord. The bodies you and I are living in are only our earthly tabernacles or tents, and we'll move out of them someday. So you see, soul sleep is not even a Christian viewpoint.

**Also their love, and their hatred, and their envy, is now perished; neither have they any more a portion for ever in any thing that is done under the sun [Eccl. 9:6].**

I told you that this is a doleful chapter. It looks as if life is futile, purposeless and without meaning. If death is the end of everything, then man is just like an animal. The evolutionist says that man once was an animal, and this man under the sun says man is like an animal now. The end result of both is the same. Man dies like an animal.

How different it is for us who know that we have come from the creative hand of God and that we are going back to God.

**Go thy way, eat thy bread with joy, and drink thy wine with a merry heart; for God now accepteth thy works [Eccl. 9:7].**

The do-gooder who thinks that death is the end of it all finds his joy in the "happy hour." "Drink thy wine with a merry heart." This is about the most monotonous life in the world.

**Let thy garments be always white; and let thy head lack no ointment [Eccl. 9:8].**

He dresses up and keeps up a good front.

**Live joyfully with the wife whom thou lovest all the days of the life of thy vanity, which he hath given thee under the sun, all the days of thy vanity: for that is thy portion in this life, and in thy labour which thou takest under the sun [Eccl. 9:9].**

Enjoy your marriage, he advises. There are many non-Christian couples who are enjoying their lives together—I have met several of them. Oh, they have their problems and their dark days, but their attitude is, "Let's make the best of it."

Now here is another verse on which the theory of soul sleep is based.

**Whatsoever thy hand findeth to do, do it with thy might; for there is no work, nor device, nor knowledge, nor wisdom, in the grave, whither thou goest [Eccl. 9:10].**

It is certainly true that the body in the grave can no longer hold a hammer in its hand. The brain is no longer able to study or perform any mental chores. Solomon is speaking only of the body. "Whatsoever thy *hand* findeth to do, do it with thy might." He is talking about the hand, not the soul. It is the hand that will be put into the grave. If you are a child of God, you will go into the presence of the Lord. If you are not a child of God, you will go to the place of the dead until you are raised to be judged at the Great White Throne. This life does not end it all. This book does not teach soul sleep.

Now he will deal with social injustice and the minority groups.

**I returned, and saw under the sun, that the race is not to the swift, nor the battle to the strong, neither yet bread to the wise, nor yet riches to men of understanding, nor yet favour to men of skill; but time and chance happeneth to them all [Eccl. 9:11].**

The observation of the man under the sun leads him to believe that life is a matter of time and chance. It is nothing but a big lottery. If you happen to be born black, you will have your problems. If you are born white, you will have your problems. If you are born yellow, you will have your problems. It's all

chance, and there is nothing you can do about it. That is the thought here.

**For man also knoweth not his time: as the fishes that are taken in an evil net, and as the birds that are caught in the snare; so are the sons of men snared in an evil time, when it falleth suddenly upon them [Eccl. 9:12].**

If time and chance are the regulators of life, then you are just as helpless as the fish caught in a net. This is an awful viewpoint, the worst kind of fatalism. This is the philosophy of the men I mentioned who fly home at the end of the week, coming back to Southern California from Dallas, Kansas City, Chicago, and Seattle. They sit in the airplane and grit their teeth in the midst of the turbulence of a storm and say, "If the plane is going to go down, it will go down. If my number comes up, there is nothing I can do about it." A man is just like a fish caught in a net. For the do-gooder, there is no other explanation. He is forced to come to this fatalistic philosophy.

Now Solomon gives a little parable:

**There was a little city, and few men within it; and there came a great king against it, and besieged it, and built great bulwarks against it [Eccl. 9:14].**

Come a little closer, Mr. Marxist, and listen to this parable. Do you want to lift up the burden of the downtrodden? Do you want to defend a minority group and the cause of the underdog? Is that the thing you're interested in? Well, may I say to you, there will arise a dictator. "A great king" will come against a people that let down their defenses and spend all their time with social problems which unsaved men *cannot* solve. (They've had probably six thousand years or longer, and they have not yet solved the problems of life. How much longer do you think God ought to give man to work these out?) "A great king" will take over such a city when socialistic methods are adopted.

**Now there was found in it a poor wise man, and he by his wisdom delivered the city; yet no man remembered that same poor man [Eccl. 9:15].**

Who was that man who came and brought deliverance? His name was Wisdom, and *Wisdom* is another name for Christ. He came to this earth in poverty. Jesus could actually say, ". . . The foxes have holes, and the birds of the air have nests; but the Son of man hath not where to lay his head" (Matt. 8:20). He was a poor man.

**Then said I, Wisdom is better than strength: nevertheless the poor man's wisdom is despised, and his words are not heard.**

**The words of wise men are heard in quiet more than the cry of him that ruleth among fools [Eccl. 9:16–17].**

Eventually the voice of the Lord Jesus will prevail. When He comes, His voice will be like the shout of the archangel and like the sound of a trumpet. There is a babble of voices in this world today, but there is coming a time when His voice will prevail in this world.

**Wisdom is better than weapons of war: but one sinner destroyeth much good [Eccl. 9:18].**

Here is his conclusion of all he has said in this chapter. "Wisdom is better than weapons of war." And Christ is better than atomic energy.

"Wisdom is better than weapons of war." Years ago I crossed the ocean in the H.M.S. *Queen Mary*, and I shall never forget the morning when we came into Southampton. I got up early to watch it. It was a tremendous feat to bring that great ship into port. The pilot had brought her across the trackless ocean. How had he done it? He had done it by the principles that were set down by a little-known Greek philosopher years ago working in geometry. That's the way it was done. "Wisdom is better than weapons of war."

"But one sinner destroyeth much good." There is a tremendous influence exerted by the life of one individual. And the influence is more potent when it is in the wrong direction. History will bear this out.

Adam sinned and his sin has affected the entire race of mankind. Achan sinned, and because of him an entire nation went down in defeat. They had to deal with the sin of Achan before they could achieve a victory. Rehoboam's sin split the kingdom of Israel. The sin of Ananias and Sapphira brought the first defect into the early church, and from that day on the church has not been as potent as it was in the beginning.

You and I have an influence, either for good or for bad. No matter who you are, you occupy a place of influence. "For none of us liveth to himself, and no man dieth to himself" (Rom. 14:7). Every person is a preacher. No one can keep himself from being a preacher.

I made that same statement to a man, an alcoholic, who lived with his mother in a house down the street from the church. His mother was brokenhearted over her boy, and she asked me to talk to him about Christ. One day I got him into my study. He had been drinking, but he was not what you would call drunk. I told him he was breaking his mother's heart, and I told him how low down and good for nothing his life was. He was not moved; he just sat there and took it. Then I asked him, "Do you know that you are a preacher?" At that he stood up and drew back his fist—he was going to hit me. "You can't call me a preacher!" He would allow me to call him any kind of name but not a preacher! My friend, all of us are preachers. *You* are preaching to those around you by the life that you live.

I personally believe that the do-gooder, the man who boasts of his moral life apart from God, is the greatest detriment. He actually stands in the way; he blocks the way to God, because his message is, "Live like I do. I live without God. I just do good." There is nothing quite as deadening as that.

You are a preacher, whoever you are. It may be in a very small circle, but you are affecting someone. You are a preacher in your own home. This reminds me of a father who kept a jug of whiskey hidden in the corn crib. It was his habit to go out there every morning and get himself a drink. On a snowy morning he went out to the barn as was his habit, but this time he heard someone behind him. He turned around and found that it was his little son following him, stepping in the footsteps in the snow where his father had walked. The father asked, "What are you doing, son?" The boy answered, "I'm following in your footsteps." He sent the boy back into the house, and then he went out to the corn crib and smashed that jug of whiskey. He realized that he didn't want his boy to be following in his footsteps. Someone in *your* home is following in your footsteps. Where are you leading him?

You may be influencing a wide circle of human society. You may have influence in the business world. You have influence in your neighborhood and in your community. You have influence in your Sunday school. Somebody is looking at you and watching to see whether or not you mean business with God. Does your going to church mean anything more to you than going to a drive-in to pick up a hamburger? Does your life suggest that there is a heaven to gain and a hell to shun? You have influence.

You remember that Peter preached a mighty sermon on the Day of Pentecost. Andrew just sat on the sidelines and could say, "That is my brother. I brought him to Christ." That was Andrew's influence. You, today, are pointing men to heaven or to hell. Now, if you want to go to hell, that's your business, but you have no right to lead a little boy there. You have no right to lead your family and those who surround you there. Even if you want to go, it's awful to lead others. Influence—"One sinner destroyeth much good." Think about it.

# CHAPTER 10

We see here that the injustice of life suggests the adoption of a moderate course.

**Dead flies cause the ointment of the apothecary to send forth a stinking savour: so doth a little folly him that is in reputation for wisdom and honour [Eccl. 10:1].**

Life is full of illustrations of this truth. One night on the town can mean a lifetime in the darkness of disease or even death. An officer in a church I served years ago told me, "I was brought up in a Christian home, and I really never did run around, but when I went away from home and got a job, I went out with the fellows one night. That is the only night in my life that I went out, and that is the night I got a venereal disease. I had to postpone marriage for several years, and I had to break off an engagement with a sweet, lovely girl." Just one dead fly will ruin the ointment of the apothecary. How tragic!

A mother spends twenty-one years teaching a son to be wise, and some girl will come along and make a fool out of him in five minutes. What a picture! A little folly, a little foolishness—that is all it takes. It can be the thing that can ruin a life and spoil the lives of others.

**A wise man's heart is at his right hand; but a fool's heart at his left [Eccl. 10:2].**

The right hand is the hand of strength. A wise man's heart is at his right hand. Whatever he does, he does it with all his heart. He doesn't do it reluctantly. The fool's heart is at his left hand. He just does things in a half-hearted way.

My friend, whatever you do, do it with heart. If you are going to serve God, do it with joy and excitement. Don't make the Christian life a drudge. Make it something worthwhile. Whatever you do, do it with excitement.

**Yea also, when he that is a fool walketh by the way, his wisdom faileth him, and he saith to every one that he is a fool [Eccl. 10:3].**

A fool does not have to carry a placard on himself that says, "I am a fool." The fact of the matter is that all he has to do is open his mouth. Sometimes he doesn't even have to open his mouth to prove that he is a fool.

Sometimes at community meetings people will get up to express a viewpoint. A man will make a thoughtful suggestion, and I will think, *My, I didn't know my neighbor was so intelligent.* Then a fellow gets up to speak, and the minute he opens his mouth, I look at my friend sitting next to me and arch my eyebrows. The Bible calls him a fool, and he tells everyone what he is.

**If the spirit of the ruler rise up against thee, leave not thy place; for yielding pacifieth great offences [Eccl. 10:4].**

The man under the sun is going to take the position of yielding in order to pacify. In other words, "If you can't fight city hall, join them."

**There is an evil which I have seen under the sun, as an error which proceedeth from the ruler:**

**Folly is set in great dignity, and the rich sit in low place [Eccl. 10:5–6].**

This is one of the things that has happened in our day and age: a dignity has been given to sin. There was a time when sin was down on the sidestreet. It was considered dirty and filthy, and it savored of that which was low and foul. But today sin has moved up on the boulevard. Sin is committed with great dignity, and it has been given a prominent place. It is given a prominent place on TV shows.

I noticed the other day that they interviewed a stripper on a TV show, that is, a girl who takes off her clothes in a nightclub. When I was a young fellow in my teens, living a life away from God, we would sneak off on Saturday night to go to such shows. It was dirty; it was filthy. Today they call it an art form! Today sin is handled in such a dignified way. "Folly is set in great *dignity*, and the rich sit in low place."

Have you heard interviews with the ordinary citizen or with the ordinary Christian? These are the people who are making the finest contribution to their community and to their society. Are they the ones who are interviewed? No, they occupy a low place. You never hear of them. The attention is focused on the ones who are the sinners and oddballs.

**I have seen servants upon horses, and princes walking as servants upon the earth [Eccl. 10:7].**

To work hard, save your money, and study late do not always mean that you will become a success. The fool next door may inherit a million dollars. Sometimes it is the fool who rides the horse, while the prince walks as the servant.

I know many wonderful Christians—across this land I have had the privilege of meeting some of the most wonderful people who are humble folk. Many of them live in humble homes; some of them are financially well-to-do. But they are ignored. They are "princes walking as servants upon the earth" today. What a picture!

**He that diggeth a pit shall fall into it; and whoso breaketh an hedge, a serpent shall bite him [Eccl. 10:8].**

If you think that you can get by with sin, especially if you are a child of God, you are very foolish. God may not act immediately, but all you need to do is wait; God will eventually judge you for it. I have watched that over the years. Christians do things that are wrong and seem to get by with it, but somewhere down the line God begins to move in on them, and He takes them to His woodshed.

**Whoso removeth stones shall be hurt therewith; and he that cleaveth wood shall be endangered thereby [Eccl. 10:9].**

Removing stones in that day was removing the markers of property lines. This is saying again that one cannot get by with sin. Whatsoever a man sows, that shall he also reap. If you try to cheat someone out of his property, or anything else, God will see to it that you will get hurt. This is the reason the Lord tells us that we are not to avenge ourselves. The Lord says, ". . . Vengeance is mine; I will repay . . ." (Rom. 12:19). The Lord is the One who will settle the accounts.

**If the iron be blunt, and he do not whet the edge, then must he put to more strength: but wisdom is profitable to direct [Eccl. 10:10].**

If the hoe gets dull, you will sharpen it, if you have any sense at all. A dull hoe makes digging that much harder. Unfortunately, many people are not willing to do the thing that will sharpen the hoe.

A young man told me the other day that God had called him to preach, and he wanted to take a short course to prepare himself. I said, "Young man, don't do that. Sharpen your hoe. Sharpen your sword. Don't go out untrained. Take the time for sharpening." It is foolish to take out a dull hoe and expect to cut down many weeds. Sharpen the hoe and then move in on the weed patch. This Book of Ecclesiastes has some great lessons for us to learn. It is an unusual book.

**Surely the serpent will bite without enchantment; and a babbler is no better [Eccl. 10:11].**

We need to understand the practices of the East if we are going to understand this verse. It is very similar to Psalm 58:4–5: "Their poison is like the poison of a serpent: they are like the deaf adder that stoppeth her ear; Which will not hearken to the voice of charmers, charming never so wisely." The same idea is found in Jeremiah. "For, behold, I will send serpents, cockatrices, among you, which will be charmed, and they shall bite you, saith the LORD" (Jer. 8:17).

The adder is a very deadly reptile. We have all seen pictures of the Indian fakirs (and I believe it would be just as correct to spell it fakers) who play a doleful sort of tune on a horn to charm the cobra. The cobra does a sort of dance; I suppose one could call it the cobra hula dance. The cobra will not strike as long as the tune is being played on that horn. Now I don't know about you, but if I had one of those horns, and a cobra came along, I'd be a long-winded person—I'd play as long as I possibly could. But there will come a time when the cobra or the adder will not listen, and finally he will strike. When he does strike, it means death.

The "serpent" in the passages we have quoted probably is not referring to literal snakes. I think it is referring to that person, "babbler," who will deceive you, who will betray you, a Judas Iscariot. After all, that's what Antichrist will be to the nation of Israel in the Great Tribulation Period.

Even among people in the church you will find those who will say things that are not true. "Surely the serpent will bite without enchantment; and a blabber is no better." He may pose as your friend, but he is going to bite you like a serpent no matter how nice you are to him.

This was the kind of sorrow that David felt when his friend Ahithophel turned against him. Ahithophel had been his counselor and his personal friend, but he left David and went with Absalom when Absalom rebelled. That broke David's heart. I think David was a broken man after the rebellion of Absalom. Up to that time, I doubt that there had ever been a ruler like King David in his prime. After that time of rebellion David became an old man. He pours out his heart in Psalm 55, and this is the picture we get.

Solomon is saying that in view of the possibility of this happening, one should be very careful. I would say that that is the philosophy of life of the average person today. He is the do-gooder who walks in the middle of the road. He has been told to be careful with So-and-So, who can repeat what he says and twist it. So when Mr. Do-gooder faces these people, he adopts a very sweet attitude toward them, but he is very careful what he says.

Sometimes it seems that we actually should confront the kind of person who takes facts and twists them and point out to them exactly what they are doing. However, I know from experience that if you point them out, you will be attacked in a most vicious manner.

**The words of a wise man's mouth are gracious; but the lips of a fool will swallow up himself [Eccl. 10:12].**

"The lips of the fool will swallow up himself" and those who are around him as well. That is why one should be careful in making friends and choosing the right kind of friends. When I taught school, I always advised the freshman class, "You are going to make friends here that will be friends with you for life. You may even meet your mate here (and of course some

of them did), so be careful about the friends you make."

When my daughter went away to college, I gave her that same advice. I told her she would have the greatest opportunity of all her life to make some wonderful friendships. But I advised her to be careful in choosing her friends. There are some people who will try to destroy you.

There are people who are like the adder or the serpent. If you are nice to them and can keep them charmed, things will go well. But be very careful how you act in their presence. This is good advice, my friend, but it is a middle-of-the-road course, as you can see.

**The beginning of the words of his mouth is foolishness: and the end of his talk is mischievous madness.**

**A fool also is full of words: a man cannot tell what shall be; and what shall be after him, who can tell him? [Eccl. 10:13-14].**

How true this is. Have you ever noticed that if you have a group and you throw out a topic for an open discussion, there will generally be some loquacious person in that group. (I believe that now they call such sessions "rap" sessions. When I was young, we called them "bull" sessions.) Usually some person who likes to talk will take over the discussion, and often he will say foolish, absurd things. The group begins to wish that one person would keep his mouth shut.

This is one reason why I am not very fond of open discussions. When I have a question and answer period, I always encourage people to write out their questions. If you don't do that, you will almost invariably find one babbler in the group, one talker who comes under this category of being a troublemaker. Someone has described such a person as one whose brain starts his mouth working, and then the brain goes off and leaves it.

**The labour of the foolish wearieth every one of them, because he knoweth not how to go to the city [Eccl. 10:15].**

Today we would say the fool doesn't know enough to come in out of the rain.

**Woe to thee, O land, when thy king is a child, and thy princes eat in the morning! [Eccl. 10:16].**

They give themselves over to pleasure instead of ruling the people properly and being a blessing to the land.

**Blessed art thou, O land, when thy king is the son of nobles, and thy princes eat in due season, for strength, and not for drunkenness! [Eccl. 10:17].**

The big problem in our country is not drugs but liquor. The number of alcoholics in this country is now in the millions. Probably we cannot get an accurate figure on the number of alcoholics because of the liquor interests, but it is a real cause for alarm. There are too many cocktail parties in Washington where the political decisions are being made. "Blessed art thou, O land, when . . . thy princes eat in due season, for strength, and not for drunkenness!"

**By much slothfulness the building decayeth; and through idleness of the hands the house droppeth through [Eccl. 10:18].**

This is an indictment of laziness, of the refusal to work. I'm afraid that is becoming a way of life in our country today. A common greeting is, "Take it easy" and "Have a good day." In other words, do as little as possible and have as much fun as you can.

**A feast is made for laughter, and wine maketh merry: but money answereth all things [Eccl. 10:19].**

Many of the rich have moved to the middle of the road. They want to be liberal and yet they want to be conservative.

**Curse not the king, no not in thy thought; and curse not the rich in thy bedchamber: for a bird of the air shall carry the voice, and that which hath wings shall tell the matter [Eccl. 10:20].**

"Curse not the king." Regardless of our president's political party or his views, I do not feel that he should be caricatured or made an object of ridicule. In the New Testament Peter says, ". . . Honour the king" (1 Pet. 2:17).

# CHAPTER 11

This chapter gives the best course to follow for the do-gooder, for the moral man, the man who wants to live the good life and wants to go down the middle, neither hot nor cold, neither right nor left.

**Cast thy bread upon the waters: for thou shalt find it after many days [Eccl. 11:1].**

Don't be afraid of doing good, although the reward may be late in arriving.

**Give a portion to seven, and also to eight; for thou knowest not what evil shall be upon the earth [Eccl. 11:2].**

When you are doing good, be sure to help more than one person. Help quite a few people, because you may get into trouble yourself at some later time, and there will be many people who will be willing to help you.

The Lord Jesus told a parable along this line, and it is recorded in Luke 16. There was an "unjust" steward who was really a crook. He made friends for himself by reducing their debts to his master, so that when he lost his job he could go to them for help.

**If the clouds be full of rain, they empty themselves upon the earth: and if the tree fall toward the south, or toward the north, in the place where the tree falleth, there it shall be [Eccl. 11:3].**

If rain is predicted, you had better carry an umbrella. After a big redwood tree falls, it is hard to move it. What is he saying here? It is best to have a clear understanding of a situation at the very beginning before you launch a venture because, after it begins, it is very difficult to make any change.

**He that observeth the wind shall not sow; and he that regardeth the clouds shall not reap [Eccl. 11:4].**

That is, act wisely in what you do. If a man wants to sow seed, he had better wait until there is no wind. If a man wants to reap a harvest, he will not begin if rain is threatening.

**As thou knowest not what is the way of the spirit, nor how the bones do grow in the womb of her that is with child: even**

so thou knowest not the works of God who maketh all [Eccl. 11:5].

The formation of the fetus and the physical birth of a baby are still great mysteries today. Spiritual rebirth is an even greater mystery. You do not know how the Spirit will move. The Lord Jesus said that. "The wind bloweth where it listeth, and thou hearest the sound thereof, but canst not tell whence it cometh, and whither it goeth: so is every one that is born of the Spirit" (John 3:8). There is a great deal that we do not know.

I believe his point is simply this: Don't let what you don't know disturb what you do know. Let me give an example. Any person knows enough to sit in a chair. There is an empty chair in my study right now. I don't mind getting up and going over there to sit down. Now there are a lot of things I don't know about that chair. I don't know anything about its construction—who made it or how it was made—but I do know that I can sit in that chair and it will hold me up. That is really all I need to know about the chair. So don't let what you don't know disturb what you do know.

**Truly the light is sweet, and a pleasant thing it is for the eyes to behold the sun:**

**But if a man live many years, and rejoice in them all; yet let him remember the days of darkness; for they shall be many. All that cometh is vanity [Eccl. 11:7–8].**

Some day you will get old, my friend. Life for the senior citizen is not always as pleasant as the advertising folders say it is going to be.

**Rejoice, O young man, in thy youth; and let thy heart cheer thee in the days of thy youth, and walk in the ways of thine heart, and in the sight of thine eyes: but know thou, that for all these things God will bring thee into judgment.**

**Therefore remove sorrow from thy heart, and put away evil from thy flesh: for childhood and youth are vanity [Eccl. 11:9–10].**

Remember, young man, now is the time to make your decisions in every category of life. It is very important that you make the right choices now. How many men have lived wasted lives and are living them today, because they made the wrong choices in their youth.

Your youthful days are empty if they are not lived right. Life is a gift that is given to us by God, given one day at a time, in fact, one second at a time. It is a precious gift, and it is to be used for the glory of God. What is the chief end of man? The chief end of man is to glorify God and to enjoy Him forever.

# CHAPTER 12

We have seen the experiments that Solomon made in life. He is probably the only man who ever lived who was able to experiment in all of these different areas, attempting to find a solution and satisfaction apart from God. Throughout Ecclesiastes the key expression has been "under the sun." He tried nature and natural science as his first experiment.

A great many people today feel that they will solve their problems by getting back to nature. There is a great exodus out of the cities and into the suburbs and beyond the suburbs to a little cabin by a lake or by a river or up in the mountains. "Let's get away from it all. Let's get back to nature." Well, this didn't solve Solomon's problems, and it will not solve our problems. So Solomon tried wisdom and philosophy; he tried pleasure and materialism; he experimented with fatalism; he tried living life for self. He turned to religion and found ritual but no reality. Then he tried to find the answer in wealth. Finally Solomon tried the good life, the life of the moralist, which he found to be an insipid sort of existence. I think that is why the young people today rebel against it.

Solomon now comes to his final conclusion in this chapter.

## POETIC PICTURE OF OLD AGE

This chapter is going to have something for the young person and for the senior citizen. Both ends of the spectrum of life meet here.

**Remember now thy Creator in the days of thy youth, while the evil days come not, nor the years draw nigh, when thou shalt say, I have no pleasure in them [Eccl. 12:1].**

In view of the fact that nothing under the sun can satisfy the human heart, Solomon says, "Get back to God." While you are young, make your decision for God. It is going to be obvious why this should be done.

Solomon will paint a picture of old age, and it is not a pretty picture. Nevertheless, it is your picture and my picture in old age. When I first preached on this chapter of Ecclesiastes, I was a very young preacher, and I wondered if it would really be like this. Now I am here to testify that the description of old age in Ecclesiastes is accurate.

One often hears the liberal and the skeptic say, "I believe in a religion of the here and now. I'm not interested in a religion of the hereafter." Well, here is a religion for the "here," which means to get rightly related to God and live for Him. Why? Well, let's look at this picture he paints of old age—a tremendous picture.

**While the sun, or the light, or the moon, or the stars, be not darkened, nor the clouds return after the rain [Eccl. 12:2].**

Does he mean that the sun, the moon, the stars, the lights are all going out? No, he means that you don't see them as you used to.

Mrs. McGee and I took a walk when we were in the Hawaiian Islands, under a full moon, and it was beautiful. I said to her, "My, isn't that a beautiful moon? But you know, it doesn't seem as romantic as it once did. How do you feel?" She replied, "No, I don't think it is as romantic as it once was. I used to think Hawaii was the most romantic place in the world." Well, my friend, when you get old, the luster dims.

Time flies, and one sad experience follows another—"the clouds return after the rain." When you get old, you can go out and have a great day but, believe me, you must take three or four days to rest up afterward. I have learned that.

I used to have a heavy schedule of conferences and just kept on going and enjoying every minute of it. Now Mrs. McGee and I find that we need to change our whole life-style. Conferences are becoming wearing on us. "The clouds return after the rain."

**In the day when the keepers of the house shall tremble, and the strong men shall bow themselves, and the grinders cease because they are few, and those that look out of the windows be darkened [Eccl. 12:3].**

This is the description of the body, the physical body, in old age. "The keepers of the house shall tremble." Those are the legs. The old person begins to totter.

My staff and my close friends try to kid me by saying, "Oh, you're looking so strong and so well." Yet I notice when I get in and out of a car, they are at my elbow to help me. Do you know why? Because my legs don't move quite as fast as they once did.

When I get up in the morning and come down the steps, I groan. My wife gets after me and asks, "Why do you groan?" I tell her it is scriptural to groan. Paul tells us, "For we that are in this tabernacle do groan, being burdened . . ." (2 Cor. 5:4). So I tell her that I want to be scriptural. But honestly I groan because my knees hurt when I come down the steps. "The keepers of the house shall tremble."

I find that I stumble more than I used to, and I must be more careful when I climb a ladder. An old person gets himself a walking stick, and I've been thinking about that, too.

"And the strong men shall bow themselves." Those are the shoulders. They are no longer erect. My wife told me the other day, "You'd look lots better if you would stand erect like you used to stand. When you were young, you had broad shoulders, and now you are all stooped over." Well, friend, the "strong men" are bowing themselves. They don't stay back like they once did. The shoulders begin to round off, and I can assure you it is more comfortable that way.

"The grinders cease because they are few." The grinders are the teeth. You are going to lose your teeth as you get older. You will need to have some bridges put in or full dentures. I haven't had to resort to false teeth yet—I'm thankful I still have my own—but they have all been capped now for years.

"Those that look out of the windows be darkened" refers to failing eyesight. The other night in a restaurant a man came up to me, we shook hands, and I talked with that man for two minutes before I even recognized who he was. I just couldn't place him. I met another friend at a meeting. We talked a while and after he left, I asked my wife who he was. She told me his name. It was a man whom I had known for years. I said, "To tell you the truth, I didn't know him. He surely has changed." She said, "Yes, I think he has, but you have, too." So you see that the windows get darkened. Even with my trifocals, I don't see as well as I did. Things don't look quite as bright as they once did.

**And the doors shall be shut in the streets, when the sound of the grinding is low, and he shall rise up at the voice of the bird, and all the daughters of music shall be brought low [Eccl. 12:4].**

"The doors shall be shut in the streets" means that the hearing is failing. My wife tells friends, "You'll have to speak a little louder. He's getting hard of hearing." I'm not really, by the way. She says that I often don't hear what she says. Maybe sometimes it is that I don't want to hear. Several years ago I had a neighbor who wore a hearing device. His wife would get after him when he got out to trim trees or prune his fruit trees. He would be up on the ladder working, and she would come out and rebuke him for it. All he did was take out his hearing aid. She would talk to him for fifteen minutes, and he wouldn't hear a word she said. Finally she would say, "I don't think you are wearing your hearing aid," and he wasn't. He would just keep on doing what he wanted to do.

Well, noise, even out on the street, is not as loud as it once was. "The doors shall be shut in the streets." And "when the sound of grinding is low." The grinding is literally the grinding women. They don't seem to make as much noise as they used to.

"He shall rise up at the voice of the bird." I can remember when I was a boy that even a loud alarm clock wouldn't wake me up in the morning. When my wife and I were young, we didn't mind the noise of children. We didn't mind the noise of music coming from the neighbors. We could sleep in motels and hotels, and none of the noises bothered us. Now even the little chirp of a bird disturbs us! Now when we travel and we come to a motel or hotel I always ask, "Can you give us a quiet room?" We are getting old, and we rise up at the voice of the bird. Any little noise disturbs our sleep.

"And all the daughters of music shall be brought low." You don't find too many older people singing in the choir anymore. The voice gets thin, and it gets harder to carry a tune. I remember dear brother Homer Rodeheaver.

What a marvelous music director and song leader he was! I remember him as a young man when he traveled with Billy Sunday. How he thrilled me when I heard him as a boy. He played the trombone, sang, and led the singing. What a voice he had! Then I invited him to come to the church I pastored in downtown Los Angeles. He was in his seventies by then. I would help him up, and he would go tottering up to the platform. He was still a marvelous song leader; I don't think anyone could ever excel him. But every now and then he would sing a stanza, and my feeling was that he would have done better to *read* the stanza. It was no longer the glorious voice that we had heard years before.

Even the people who once had beautiful singing voices lose the quality of their voices as they get older. Those of us who never could sing very well should realize that we had better praise the Lord in our *hearts*. That is the reason I never open my mouth in a song service. I don't dare. I couldn't sing when I was young, and now it is positively frightful. "The daughters of music shall be brought low."

Now he continues on as he speaks of old age. And now, to me, it gets to the place where it's tragic, because we're looking at the psychological effects.

**Also when they shall be afraid of that which is high, and fears shall be in the way, and the almond tree shall flourish, and the grasshopper shall be a burden, and desire shall fail: because man goeth to his long home, and the mourners go about the streets [Eccl. 12:5].**

"They shall be afraid of that which is high." I never did enjoy flying, but I was getting over my fear and began to enjoy it. Then old age slipped up on me, and I find today I have the same old fear of flying that I had at the very beginning. Little things disturb me, little things that didn't disturb me at all when I was younger.

"And fears shall be in the way." We just don't enjoy things as much as we once did. We have always enjoyed traveling and have conducted many tours to the Bible lands and to the Hawaiian Islands. I have noticed that as we and our friends get older, we find traveling much more difficult. We worry and wonder about things we never even thought of before.

When we were young, my wife and I would start out in an old jalopy to go across the country. We never made any reservations. It didn't worry us if we stopped at motels and found that they were all filled. It didn't bother us if we had to sleep on the side of the road. But today there is always a nagging fear. When we get ready to make a trip, I have all the reservations made well in advance, and I go over the road map again and again and again. "Fears shall be in the way."

"The almond tree shall flourish." A blossoming almond tree is white. And the senior citizen is going to turn white on top, or else there won't be anything left on the top—it is one or the other.

"The grasshopper shall be a burden." How can a little grasshopper be a burden? Well, when old age comes little things that never used to bother now become a burden. We love our grandchildren dearly and enjoy having them with us, but after a while, we are glad to see them go home again. Strength fails, endurance fails, patience fails. Many *little* things become a burden.

"Desire shall fail." Romance is gone. You can try to act as if you are just as young as you were, but you don't fool anyone. I remember listening to an evangelist who had married a young girl. He hopped on the platform, jumped in the air, and said, "I'm just as young as I ever was." He wasn't fooling anybody but himself, and he died shortly after that.

"Because man goeth to his long home, and the mourners go about the streets." That "long home" is eternity. Death is getting near.

**Or ever the silver cord be loosed, or the golden bowl be broken, or the pitcher be broken at the fountain, or the wheel broken at the cistern [Eccl. 12:6].**

Here is a list of the organs of the body. At the end, they no longer function. The "silver cord" is the spinal cord. The "golden bowl" is the head, the bowl for the brain. The functioning of the brain decreases in its efficiency as one gets older, and at death it ceases to function at all. The pitcher is the lungs. "The pitcher is broken at the fountain." The wheel is the heart—"the wheel broken at the cistern." It is no longer pumping blood through the body. All of this is a picture of the deterioration of old age leading to death. Life cannot be sustained without the functioning of these organs.

**Then shall the dust return to the earth as it was: and the spirit shall return unto God who gave it [Eccl. 12:7].**

There is no soul sleep. I wish the people who try to use verses from this Book of Ecclesiastes to support their idea of soul sleep would just read on until they get to this verse.

The body sleeps, but the spirit, or the soul, returns unto God who gave it.

Let me repeat that the New Testament assures us that to be absent from the body means to be present with the Lord (see 2 Cor. 5:8). The soul immediately returns to God. This body is just a tabernacle, or a tent, that we live in. It is just the outer covering. The soul goes to be with God.

When President Adams became an old man, someone asked him how he was getting along. His reply was something like this: "Oh, I'm doing fine, but this house I live in is growing very feeble, and I think I'll be moving out of it before long." That was true. He did move out of his old house shortly after that.

**Vanity of vanities, saith the preacher; all is vanity [Eccl. 12:8].**

Young man, life is empty if you are just living for the here and now. One day you will find that all you have in your hand is a fistful of ashes, and you will have eternity ahead of you.

When as a child, I laughed and wept,
   Time crept;
When as a youth, I dreamed and talked,
   Time walked;
When I became a full grown man,
   Time ran;
When older still I daily grew,
   Time flew;
Soon I shall find in traveling on,
   Time gone.
            —Author unknown

The psalmist writes: "So teach us to number our days, that we may apply our hearts unto wisdom" (Ps. 90:12), and Wisdom is the Lord Jesus Christ.

Thinking of old age, someone has written this bit of whimsey:

Thou knowest, Lord, I'm growing older.
My fire of youth begins to smolder;

I somehow tend to reminisce
And speak of good old days I miss.

I am more moody, bossy, and
Think folk should jump at my command.

Help me, Lord, to conceal my aches
And realize my own mistakes.

Keep me sweet, silent, sane, serene,
Instead of crusty, sour, and mean.

            —Author unknown

May the Lord, give us the grace to grow old gracefully!

> And moreover, because the preacher was wise, he still taught the people knowledge; yea, he gave good heed, and sought out, and set in order many proverbs.
>
> The preacher sought to find out acceptable words: and that which was written was upright, even words of truth.
>
> The words of the wise are as goads, and as nails fastened by the masters of assemblies, which are given from one shepherd [Eccl. 12:9–11].

We should not by any means despise the wisdom of the past, nor should we refuse to be taught.

> And further, by these, my son, be admonished: of making many books there is no end; and much study is a weariness of the flesh [Eccl. 12:12].

Education will not solve the problems of life.

## THE RESULT OF THE EXPERIMENT

> Let us hear the conclusion of the whole matter: Fear God, and keep his commandments: for this is the whole duty of man [Eccl. 12:13].

"Fear God." This is the message of the Book of Proverbs as well as the message here. In view of the experiment made "under the sun," the wise thing is to fear God, which means to reverence, worship, and obey Him.

"And keep his commandments" would mean to meet God's conditions for salvation—in any age—grounded on faith in God. For Cain it meant bringing a lamb. For Abraham it meant believing the promises of God. For the people of Israel it meant approaching God through sacrifice in the tabernacle and in the temple. For us it is to ". . . Believe on the Lord Jesus Christ, and thou shalt be saved . . ." (Acts 16:31).

> For God shall bring every work into judgment, with every secret thing, whether it be good, or whether it be evil [Eccl. 12:14].

"For God shall bring every work into judgment." God will judge every man, for every man is a sinner who is guilty before God. Christ bore our judgment; He died a judgment death. Our sins are either on Christ by faith in Him, or else we must come before the Great White Throne for judgment.

"Remember now thy Creator in the days of thy youth." Why? Well, for a very definite reason: because in the matter of salvation your chances of being saved are greater; and in the subject of service you'll have something to offer to God. Statistics show that more come to Christ when they are young.

This does not mean that old people cannot accept Christ and be saved. On one of our radio programs we gave an invitation for those who wanted to accept Christ to put up their hands. A lady walked into the room where her ninety-year-old father was listening to the program, and she saw that he sat there in the rocking chair listening to us with his hand in the air. When she questioned him, she found that he had accepted Christ Jesus as his Savior. How wonderful! It is never too late.

The second reason why Solomon makes a special appeal to young people is that they have a lifetime to offer to God in service to Him. The men who have had real service, who have had something to *give* to God, have been young men: Joseph, Moses, Gideon, David, Jeremiah, Saul of Tarsus, Timothy—and oh, the host of young missionaries in the past few centuries, such as Robert Moffat, who was "wee Bobby Moffat" when he came to Christ as a child and became a great missionary to South Africa.

My friend, there is no answer to the problems of life "under the sun." Jesus Christ is the *only* solution for the problems of life. The Lord Jesus has given His promise to people of any and all ages: ". . . him that cometh to me I will in no wise cast out" (John 6:37).

# BIBLIOGRAPHY

(Recommended for Further Study)

Darby, J. N. *Synopsis of the Books of the Bible*. Addison, Illinois: Bible Truth Publishers.

Gaebelein, Arno C. *The Annotated Bible*. 1917. Reprint. Neptune, New Jersey: Loizeaux Brothers, 1971.

Glickman, S. Craig. *A Song for Lovers*. Downers Grove, Illinois: InterVarsity Press, 1976. (A fine treatment of Song of Solomon.)

Gray, James M. *Commentary on the Whole Bible*. Old Tappan, New Jersey: Fleming H. Revell Co., 1906.

Hadley, E. C. *The Song of Solomon*. Sunbury, Pennsylvania: Believer's Bookshelf, n.d.

Ironside, H. A. *Addresses on the Song of Solomon*. Neptune, New Jersey: Loizeaux Brothers, 1933. (An excellent treatment.)

Jensen, Irving L. *Ecclesiastes and the Song of Solomon*. Chicago, Illinois: Moody Press, 1974. (A self-study guide.)

Kelly, William. *Lectures on the Song of Solomon*. Addison, Illinois: Bible Truth Publishers, n.d.

Miller, Andrew. *The Song of Solomon*. Addison, Illinois: Bible Truth Publishers, n.d.

Unger, Merrill F. *Unger's Bible Handbook*. Chicago, Illinois: Moody Press, 1966.

Unger, Merrill F. *Unger's Commentary on the Old Testament*. Vol. I. Chicago, Illinois: Moody Press, 1981.

# The
# SONG OF SOLOMON

## INTRODUCTION

The first verse of this little book identifies Solomon as its writer: "The song of songs, which is Solomon's." Solomon also wrote the Books of Proverbs and Ecclesiastes.

This book is actually not a story at all; it is a song. We read in 1 Kings 4:32: "And he [Solomon] spake three thousand proverbs: and his songs were a thousand and five." Solomon wrote three thousand proverbs, but it is quite interesting that if you count the proverbs in the Book of Proverbs, and even include the Book of Ecclesiastes, you come up with quite a few less than three thousand. So we have very few of all that Solomon wrote. However, we can say two things about those that we do have: first, we have the best that he wrote—surely we would have that; second, we have those that the Spirit of God wanted us to have.

This verse also tells us that "his songs were a thousand and five." Think of that—more than a thousand songs! That makes him quite a song writer. He would have fit in on Tin Pan Alley any day. It is interesting to note that the Word of God is very specific when it says that he wrote one thousand *and five* songs. It doesn't simply give us a round number. Probably those which have been preserved for us are those five. Most of Solomon's songs, of course, we do not have. In fact, we generally say that we have only one song. But the Song of Solomon is also called the Book of Canticles. A canticle is a little song, and that means that in this book we have several canticles, several little songs. There is a difference of opinion as to how many songs there are. The old position is that there are five, and I agree with that. I notice that *The New Scofield Reference Bible* states that there are thirteen. That is an excellent Bible, but I will continue to accept the old division of the book into five songs.

"Beloved" is the name for Him; "love" is the name for her.

"I am my beloved's, and my beloved is mine: he feedeth among the lilies" (Song 6:3).

"Many waters cannot quench love, neither can the floods drown it: if a man would give all the substance of his house for love, it would utterly be contemned" (Song 8:7).

The Song of Solomon is a parabolic poem. The *interpretation*, not the inspiration, causes the difficulty. There are some who actually feel it should not be in the Bible; however, it is in the canon of Scripture. The Song of Solomon is the great neglected book of the Bible. The reader who is going through the Word of God for the first time is puzzled when he comes to it. The carnal Christian will misunderstand and misinterpret it. Actually this little book has been greatly abused by people who have not understood it. When Peter was puzzled by some of Paul's epistles, he wrote, "As also in all his epistles, speaking in them of these things; in which are some things hard to be understood, which they that are unlearned and unstable wrest, as they do also the other scriptures, unto their own destruction" (2 Pet. 3:16). I think this is also true of the Song of Solomon.

Origen and Jerome tell us that the Jews would not permit their young men to read this book until they were thirty years old. The reason was that they felt there was the danger of reading into it the salacious and the suggestive, the vulgar and the voluptuous, the sensuous and the sexual. On the contrary, this is a wonderful picture of physical, human, wedded love. It gives the answer to two erroneous groups of people: those who hold to asceticism and think it is wrong to get married, and those who hold to hedonism and think that the satisfying of their lusts is of primary importance. This book makes it very clear that both are wrong. It upholds wedded love as a very wonderful thing, a glorious experience.

Sometimes young preachers are counseled not to use the Song of Solomon until they become old men. A retired minister advised me not to preach on it until I was sixty years old. Do you know what I did? I turned right around and preached on it immediately—that's what a young preacher would do. Now that I am past sixty years, I think I am qualified, at least as far as the chronology is concerned, to be able to speak on it. This book means more to me today than it did forty years ago. The elaborate, vivid, striking, and bold language in this book is a wonderful, glorious picture of our relationship with the Lord Jesus Christ. I know of no book that will draw you closer to Him or be more personal than the Song of Solomon.

If you were to compare the Song of Solomon with other Oriental poetry of its period—such as some of the Persian poetry—you would find the Song of Solomon to be mild and restrained. Reading the Persian poetry, on the other hand, would be like reading some of the modern, dirty stuff that is being written today.

By contrast, the Jews called the Song of Solomon the Holy of Holies of Scripture. Therefore, not everyone was permitted inside its sacred enclosure. Here is where you are dwelling in the secret place of the Most High. That is one reason I hesitate to discuss this book. It will be abused by unbelievers and carnal Christians. But if you are one who is walking with the Lord, if the Lord Jesus means a great deal to you and you love Him, then this little book will mean a great deal to you also.

The Song of Solomon is poetic and practical. Here God is speaking to His people in poetic songs which unfold a story. We need to take our spiritual shoes from off our feet as we approach this book. We are on holy ground. The Song of Solomon is like a fragile flower that requires delicate handling.

There have been four different and important meanings found in this book:

1. The Song of Solomon sets forth *the glory of wedded love*. Here is declared the sacredness of the marital relationship and that marriage is a God-given institution. This little book shows us what real love is. The Jews taught that it reveals the heart of a satisfied husband and that of a devoted wife.

Today we see a great movement toward "sexual freedom," which many people seem to think is good. One young man who had lived and believed in "free love" told me that he had come to realize that such a life is the life of an animal. He said, "For several years I lived like an animal. If you want to know the truth, I don't think sex meant any more to my group of friends than it means to an animal." The younger generation today is geared to sex; their life-style is one of sexual expression. But I am of the opinion that they actually know very little about it. All they know about sex is

what an animal knows. A dog out on the street knows as much as they do. Something is missing—there is a terrible void in their lives.

This generation may have a great deal of experience with sex but knows little about love. They know the Hollywood version of love; yet they think they know it all. The story is told of the father who wanted to talk to his young boy about sex. He beat around the bush and finally blurted out, "Son, I'd like to talk to you about some of the facts of life." The boy said, "Sure, Dad, what would you like to know?" The boy knew the raw facts about sex, so he thought he knew more than his dad knew. There was a veteran movie queen who had had five husbands. She knew about sex, but she didn't know anything about real love; so she committed suicide. Reading our modern novels and plays is like taking a trip through the sewers of Paris! There is a stark contrast between the ideas of our generation and the glory of wedded love as it is portrayed in the Song of Solomon.

2. This little book sets forth *the love of Jehovah for Israel*. That is not a new thought which is found in this book alone. The prophets spoke of Israel as the wife of Jehovah. Hosea dwells on that theme. Idolatry in Israel is likened to a breach in wedded love and is the greatest sin in all the world, according to Hosea.

The scribes and the rabbis of Israel have always given these two interpretations to this book, and they have been accepted by the church. However, there are two other interpretations set forth by the church.

3. The Song of Solomon is *a picture of Christ and the church*. The church is the bride of Christ. This is a familiar figure in the New Testament (see Eph. 5; Rev. 21). However, in this book God uses a picture of human affection to convey to our dull minds, our dead hearts, our distorted affections, and our diseased wills, His so great love. He uses the very best of human love to arouse us to realize the wonderful love that He has for us. This book can lead you into a marvelous, wonderful relationship with the Lord Jesus which you probably have never known before. My friend, what we need today is a knowledge of the Word of God and a personal relationship with Jesus Christ. I am afraid that very few of us are experiencing this today.

4. This book depicts *the communion of Christ and the individual believer*. It portrays the love of Christ for the individual and the soul's communion with Christ. Many great saints of God down through the years have

experienced this. Paul could say, ". . . the Son of God, who loved me, and gave himself for me" (Gal. 2:20). Samuel Rutherford could spend a whole night in prayer. His wife would miss him during the night and would get up and go looking for him. Even on cold nights she would find him on his knees praying, and she would take his big overcoat and throw it around him. Men like Dwight L. Moody and Robert McCheyne came into a real, personal relationship with the Lord Jesus Christ. This is not some kind of second experience, as some people try to describe it. It is more than an experience. It is *a personal relationship* with Jesus Christ—seeing how wonderful He is, how glorious He is. We need to come to the place where it can truly be said of us that we love Him because He first loved us. To open up this little book will be like the breaking of Mary's alabaster box of ointment, and I trust that the fragrance of it will fill our lives and spread out to others.

People are being deluded today. They feel that living the Christian life is like following the instructions for putting together a toy. The instructions for a little truck or house will say to take piece "A" and put it down by piece "D" and then take piece "C" and fit it between them. I want to tell you, some of those instructions are really complicated! I know, because I buy them for my little grandsons. It almost takes a college degree to be able to put some of those gadgets together. Some people think that the Christian life is like that. They have the impression that if you get together a little mixture of psychology, a smattering of common sense, a good dash of salesmanship, and a few verses from the Bible as a sugarcoating over the whole thing, that makes a successful formula for living the Christian life.

My friend, may I say that what we need is a personal relationship with Jesus Christ. We need a hot passion for Him. The Lord is not pleased with this cool, lukewarm condition which exists today in the churches among so-called dedicated Christians. Too many who are called dedicated Christians are actually as cold as a cucumber. Some are even unfriendly and arrogant in their attitudes. What we all need is a real, living, burning passion for the person of the Lord Jesus Christ.

This little book is going to be personal. It is not for the ear of the unsaved man. It is for the blood-tipped ear of the man who has a personal relationship with the Lord Jesus Christ.

Since the Song of Solomon is a series of scenes in a drama which is not told in chronological sequence, I will make no attempt to outline the book. What we find in this little book is the use of antiphony; that is, one character speaks and another responds. We have many characters: the young bride (she is a Shulamite), the daughters of Jerusalem, the bridegroom, and the Shulamite's family. In the family there is the father (who is dead), the mother, two daughters, and two or more sons.

One interpretation of the story given in the Song of Solomon came out of the German rationalistic schools of the nineteenth century. (It was from these schools that liberalism first crept into the church. Actually, liberalism was and is simply unbelief.) These people tried to interpret the story so that the Shulamite girl was kidnapped by Solomon; at first she did not want to go with him, and then finally she did.

To a child of God who sees in this book the wonderful relationship between Christ and the church, such an interpretation is repugnant. Men like Rutherford, McCheyne, and Moody—this was their favorite book—could not accept this kidnapping interpretation. Neither could the late Dr. Harry Ironside. So he got down on his knees and asked God for an interpretation. Much of what I am going to pass on to you is based on Dr. Ironside's interpretation.

The setting of the drama is the palace in Jerusalem, and some of the scenes are flashbacks to a previous time. There is a reminder here of the Greek drama in which a chorus talks back and forth to the protagonists of the play. The daughters of Jerusalem carry along the tempo of the story. These dialogues are evidently to be sung. Several lovely scenes are introduced at Jerusalem which find a counterpart in the church.

The Shulamite girl says, "Look not upon me, because I am black, because the sun hath looked upon me: my mother's children were angry with me; they made me the keeper of the vineyards; but mine own vineyard have I not kept" (Song 1:6). The elder daughter of this poor Shulamite family is a sort of a Cinderella, and she has been forced to keep the vineyard. She is darkened with sunburn from working out in the vineyard. Apparently this family lived in the hill country of Ephraim, and they were tenant farmers. We would call them croppers or hillbillies. We get this picture from a verse in the last chapter: "Solomon had a vineyard at Baal-hamon; he let out the vineyard unto keepers; every one for the fruit thereof was to bring a thousand pieces of silver" (Song 8:11).

I think that is the setting where the first scene takes place. The girl is sunburned and she feels disgraced. In that day a sunburn meant you were a hardworking girl. The women in the court wanted to keep their skin as fair as they possibly could. It was exactly the opposite of our situation here in California. Here the young girls go down to the beach and lie out in the sun all day in order to get a suntan. Today, it's not a disgrace to have a suntan; in fact, it is a disgrace if you don't have one!

Not only was this girl sunburned from working out in the vineyard, but she says that she was unable to keep her own vineyard. That means she hadn't been to the beauty parlor. Apparently she was a naturally beautiful girl, but she hadn't been able to enhance her beauty or groom herself.

She was an outdoor girl, a hardworking girl. Apparently her brothers also made her watch the sheep. "If thou know not, O thou fairest among women, go thy way forth by the footsteps of the flock, and feed thy kids beside the shepherds' tents" (Song 1:8). So she worked in the vineyards and also had to herd the sheep.

The place where she worked was along a caravan route there in the hill country. Perhaps some of you have traveled in that land, and you know how rugged it is. A tour bus goes up through there today, and the tourists take a trip into that part of the country. I have been through that rugged territory twice, and I have pictures of some Arab girls working in the fields. I think that is exactly the way it was with the Shulamite girl.

When she would look up from her work, she would see the caravans that passed by going between Jerusalem and Damascus. We see her reaction: "Who is this that cometh out of the wilderness like pillars of smoke, perfumed with myrrh and frankincense, with all powders of the merchant?" (Song 3:6). She would see the caravans of merchants and also the caravans that carried beautiful ladies of the court. They were the ones who didn't have a sunburn. They had a canopy over them as they traveled on camels or on elephants. The girl would see the beautiful jewels and the satins. She never had anything like that, and she would dream about it, you know.

She also would smell the frankincense and the myrrh as the caravans passed by. We shall see how this is a wonderful picture of the Lord Jesus both in His birth and in His death. They brought Him myrrh as a gift when He was born; when He was dead, they brought myrrh to put on His body. There are wonderful spiritual pictures here, truths that will draw us to the person of Christ.

One day while the girl was tending her sheep, a handsome shepherd appeared. He fell in love with her. I must run ahead enough to tell you it is a picture of Christ and the church. This is what he said to her, "As the lily among thorns, so is my love among the daughters" (Song 2:2). Again, he says, "Behold, thou art fair, my love; behold, thou art fair; thou hast doves' eyes within thy locks: thy hair is as a flock of goats, that appear from mount Gilead" (Song 4:1). This is beautiful poetic language. It is a picture of the love of Christ for the church. Christ loved the church and gave Himself for it.

Finally she gave her heart to the shepherd: "As the apple tree among the trees of the wood, so is my beloved among the sons. I sat down under his shadow with great delight, and his fruit was sweet to my taste" (Song 2:3).

Remember that the word *love* is used when it is speaking of the bride, and *beloved* is the word that refers to the bridegroom.

The Lord Jesus has given us an invitation: "Come unto me, all ye that labour and are heavy laden, and I will [rest you]" (Matt. 11:28). Do you know what it is to rest in Jesus Christ? Is He a reality to you? Do you *rest* in Him? How wonderful this relationship can become to you! I am not talking about religion or about an organization. I am talking about a personal relationship, a love relationship with Jesus Christ.

After she gave her heart to him, they were madly in love. There is nothing quite like marital love such as they experienced. "My beloved is mine, and I am his: he feedeth among the liles" (Song 2:16). How wonderful! They had that wonderful, personal relationship.

Apparently he took her to dinner one time as he traveled through the country. (All she knew of him was that he was a shepherd, but evidently a very prominent one.) "He brought me to the banqueting house, and his banner over me was love" (Song 2:4).

He was a most peculiar shepherd. He didn't have any sheep that she could see. She asked him about his sheep: "Tell me, O thou whom my soul loveth, where thou feedest, where thou makest thy flock to rest at noon . . . ?" (Song 1:7). Where are his sheep? He is an unusual shepherd.

Then one day he announced that he was going away but that he would return. This is an obvious parallel to the words of the Lord Jesus: "Let not your heart be troubled: ye believe in God, believe also in me. In my Father's house are many mansions: if it were not so, I would have told you. I go to prepare a place for you. And if I go and prepare a place for you, I will come again, and receive you unto myself; that where I am, there ye may be also" (John 14:1–3).

The days passed and she waited. Finally, her family and friends began to ridicule her. They said, "You are just a simple, country girl taken in by him." This is exactly what Peter said would happen in our time: "Knowing this first, that there shall come in the last days scoffers, walking after their own lusts, And saying, Where is the promise of his coming? for since the fathers fell asleep, all things continue as they were from the beginning of the creation" (2 Pet. 3:3–4).

Yet she trusted him. She loved him. She *dreamed* of him: "By night on my bed I sought him whom my soul loveth: I sought him, but I found him not" (Song 3:1). Now let me ask you a very personal question. Do you really miss Christ? Do you long for Him?

One night she lay restlessly upon her couch when she noticed a fragrance in the room. In that day it was a custom that a lover would put some myrrh or frankincense in the opening to the door handle. She smelled the perfume and went to the door. "I rose up to open to my beloved; and my hands dropped with myrrh, and my fingers with sweet smelling myrrh, upon the handles of the lock" (Song 5:5). She knew that he had been there. She knew that he really hadn't forgotten.

Are there evidences of the fragrance and the perfume of Christ in your life today? Oh, my friend, don't ever be satisfied with religious gimmicks. Why not get right down to where the rubber meets the road? What does Christ mean to you right now? Is the fragrance of Christ in your life today?

Now she knew that her lover was near. The Lord Jesus said, ". . . Lo, I am with you alway, even unto the end of the world" (Matt. 28:20). Paul could say while he was in prison that the Lord stood by him. The Lord Jesus has promised, ". . . I will never leave thee, nor forsake thee" (Heb. 13:5).

One day she is in the vineyard, working with the vines. "Take us the foxes, the little foxes, that spoil the vines: for our vines have tender grapes" (Song 2:15). She is lifting up the vines so that the little foxes cannot get to the grapes. In that land, they raise the grapes right down on the ground. They do not string them up as we do in this country. So she is lifting up the vines and putting a rock under them so that the little foxes will not get to the grapes.

While she is doing this, down the road there comes a pillar of smoke. "Who is this that cometh out of the wilderness like pillars of smoke, perfumed with myrrh and frankincense, with all powders of the merchant?" (Song 3:6). The cry is passed along, "Behold, King Solomon is coming!" But she is busy, and she doesn't know King Solomon. Then someone comes to her excitedly and says to her, "Oh, King Solomon is asking for *you*!" And she says, "Asking for *me*? I don't know King Solomon. I've never met him, why would he ask for *me*?"

"The voice of my beloved! behold, he cometh leaping upon the mountains, skipping upon the hills. My beloved is like a roe or a young hart: behold, he standeth behind our wall, he looketh forth at the windows, shewing himself through the lattice. My beloved spake, and said unto me, Rise up, my love, my fair one, and come away" (Song 2:8–10). And so she is brought into the presence of King Solomon. Do you know who King Solomon is? Why, he is her shepherd, and he has come for her.

This is the promise of the Lord Jesus: "My sheep hear my voice, and I know them, and they follow me: And I give unto them eternal life; and they shall never perish, neither shall any man pluck them out of my hand" (John 10:27–28). Paul writes, "For the Lord himself shall descend from heaven with a shout, with the voice of the archangel, and with the trump of God: and the dead in Christ shall rise first: Then we which are alive and remain shall be caught up together with them in the clouds, to meet the Lord in the air: and so shall we ever be with the Lord" (1 Thess. 4:16–17). The Lord Jesus has promised that He is coming again for us. "For, lo, the winter is past, the rain is over and gone; The flowers appear on the earth; the time of the singing of birds is come, and the voice of the turtle is heard in our land; The fig tree putteth forth her green figs, and the vines with the tender grape give a good smell. Arise, my love, my fair one, and come away" (Song 2:11–13). One of these days He is going to call us out of this world.

By the way, how much are you involved in the world? Would it break your heart if He were to come right now and take us all out of the world? I have a feeling there are some people who are so satisfied down here, who are doing so well in this affluent society, that if He should come for them, they would go crying all the way to heaven because they have so much here in this life. He says to her, "Arise, my love, my fair one, and come away. O my dove, that art in the clefts of the rock." That is where the Lord puts us—in the cleft of the rock until the storm passes. "In the secret places of the stairs, let me see thy countenance, let me hear thy voice; for sweet is thy voice, and thy countenance is comely" (Song 2:13–14). What a glorious thing!

"He brought me to the banqueting house, and his banner over me was love" (Song 2:4). Salvation is a love affair—we love Him because He first loved us. That is the story that this little book is telling.

# CHAPTER 1

It is important for you to read the beautiful story of this book before you come to the text. I have given this in some detail in the introduction.

There are five canticles or brief songs in the book. They depict the experience and the story of a country girl, a Shulamite, up in the hill country. A shepherd came one day, and she fell in love with him, and he fell in love with her. He left her but promised to return. He didn't return as soon as she had expected. One day it was announced that King Solomon had arrived and wanted to see her. She couldn't believe it. When she was brought into his presence, she recognized that he was her shepherd-lover.

Some interpreters feel that this is a connected story told in sequence. I personally do not hold that view. I think the scene shifts, and there are flashbacks to earlier times. However, the primary concern for us in our study is the application of this book to you and me as believers. It is a picture of the beautiful love relationship between the believer and the Lord Jesus Christ.

**The song of songs, which is Solomon's [Song 1:1].**

I suppose one could liken this book to a piece of folk music, or more likely to an opera. These canticles are put together to give us a glorious, wonderful story. This is one of the methods God used in speaking to His people. It rebukes asceticism, but it also condemns lust and unfaithfulness to the marriage vow. This is no soap opera. It is not a cheap play in which the hero is a neurotic, the heroine is erotic, and the plot is tommyrotic. Rather, it is a beautiful song of marital love.

## HIS KISS

In this first song, we find the bride and the bridegroom together in a wonderful relationship.

**Let him kiss me with the kisses of his mouth: for thy love is better than wine [Song 1:2].**

The kiss in that day was the pledge of peace, a token of peace. Solomon's very name means peace. He was a prince of peace and he ruled in Jerusalem, the city of peace. The Shulamite girl is the daughter of peace.

The kiss indicates the existence of a very personal, close relationship, such as the Lord Jesus has with His own. He is able to communicate His message personally to you and me through the Word of God. That is why there needs to be a return to a study of the Word of God—more than just learning the mechanics of the Bible, or even memorizing the Word, but a personal relationship with Him so that He can speak through His Word to our hearts. "Let him kiss me with the kisses of his mouth." He has spoken peace to us, you see. He alone can speak peace to the human heart.

In the Old Testament we have seen types of Christ. A. Moody Stuart has written: "Moses and the prophets have come, Aaron and the priests have come, and last of all, David and the kings have come; but let Him now come himself, the true prophet, priest, and king, of all his people." And Bernard, one who had drawn very close to Christ, commented: "I hear not Moses for he is slow of speech, the lips of Isaiah are unclean, Jeremiah cannot speak because he is a child, and all the prophets are dumb; Himself, himself of whom they speak, let him speak" (*The Song of Songs: An Exposition of the Song of Solomon*, p. 95).

The one who has ears to hear and has heard Him speak peace—peace through the blood of His cross by forgiveness of sin—can take the next step. If you have been reconciled to God by redemption in Christ, He entreats the kiss of the solemn, nuptial contract. It is the kiss which seals the marriage vow between Christ and the believer.

We find this same custom in our marriage ceremonies today. When I perform a marriage ceremony and both couples have said "I will" and "I do," I say, "Lift the bride's veil and give the marriage kiss." The kiss is a solemn thing; it seals the marriage covenant.

In redemption, the Lord Jesus not only gives us deliverance, but He also gives us freedom. "If the Son therefore shall make you free, ye shall be free indeed" (John 8:36). What kind of freedom is that? It is the freedom now to come to Him and to say, "I present my body as a living sacrifice to You" (see Rom. 12:1). It is the freedom of dedication, which brings us into a personal relationship with Jesus Christ, our Savior.

Are you such a child of God? Are you a trembling soul who is afraid to lay hold of His grace? He *wants* you to appropriate it for yourself. In Ephesians we are told that He is rich in mercy and He is rich in grace, and He wants to share with us the riches of His glory. I don't know how you feel about this, but I know that I need His mercy, and I need His grace. His invitation is, "Come unto me, all ye that labour and are heavy laden, and I will give you rest" (Matt. 11:28). This is a real rest. It is not rest for just one day on the Sabbath. This is a rest for the seven days of the week. It is resting in His finished redemption. Then He says, "Take my yoke upon you, and learn of me; for I am meek and lowly in heart: and ye shall find rest unto your souls. For my yoke is easy, and my burden is light" (Matt. 11:29–30). Being yoked up with Him is a wonderful, glorious relationship. And He is the One who carries the load for you.

Erskine expressed it poetically:

His mouth the joy of heaven reveals;
    His kisses from above,
Are pardons, promises, and seals
    Of everlasting love.

## HIS LOVE

"**F**or thy love is better than wine." In that day wine typified the highest of the luxuries this earth offered. It was the champagne dinner, which included everything from soup to nuts. It speaks of that which brings the highest joy to the heart. Paul wrote, "And be not drunk with wine, wherein is excess; but be filled with the Spirit" (Eph. 5:18). Oh, to be filled with the Holy Spirit so that we might experience that excitement, that exhilaration, that ecstasy of belonging to Christ and of having fellowship with Him!

Friend, I am talking about something that neither you nor I know very much about, do we? We play at church. We talk about being dedicated Christians simply because we are as busy as termites, and often have the same effect. We need to come to that attitude of which Peter wrote: "Whom having not seen, ye love; in whom, though now ye see him not, yet believing, ye rejoice with joy unspeakable and full of glory" (1 Pet. 1:8).

Habakkuk stated it like this: "Although the fig tree shall not blossom, neither shall fruit be in the vines; the labour of the olive shall fail, and the fields shall yield no meat; the flock shall be cut off from the fold, and there shall be no herd in the stalls: Yet I will rejoice in the LORD, I will joy in the God of my salvation" (Hab. 3:17–18). Have you arrived at that place? No wonder it says, "Thy love is better than wine."

I do not mean to be irreverent, but do you get a kick out of life? Well, this is the way to get it. Wine is excess and may lead you to alcoholism. Wine will give a temporary lift, I grant you, but it will let you down. My friend, allow the Spirit of God to come into your life. He will shed abroad in your heart the love of God. That is one reason we need the Holy Spirit.

**Because of the savour of thy good ointments thy name is as ointment poured forth, therefore do the virgins love thee [Song 1:3].**

The "ointment" is the perfume. When He began His life on earth, myrrh was brought to Him as a gift. When He died, myrrh was brought to be put on His body. There was a fragrance in His entire life on earth from His birth to His death. Oh, the fragrance of His love for us when He died upon the cross!

## HIS DRAWING POWER

**Draw me, we will run after thee: the king hath brought me into his chambers: we will be glad and rejoice in thee, we will remember thy love more than wine: the upright love thee [Song 1:4].**

**T**his is a wonderful passage of Scripture. It is the expression of one who is in love with Him, who desires a close fellowship with Him. But then comes the awareness that we can't reach that state; we cannot attain to it because it is too high for us. That is the position from which we say, "Draw me."

Bonar expressed his love in these lines:

I love the name of Jesus,
    Immanuel, Christ the Lord,
Like fragrance on the breezes,
    His name abroad is poured.

What does the name of Jesus mean to you? If you know that you have never experienced that wonderful relationship, then listen to the bride, and give her response, "Draw me." If you are a child of God, then say, "Draw me." Let Him lift you up and bring you to this place which you cannot reach yourself. Recognize that in yourself you cannot rise to that level. Francis Quarles has expressed this thought beautifully:

But like a block beneath whose burden lies
That undiscovered worm that never dies,
I have no will to rouse, I have no power to rise.
For can the water-buried axe implore
A hand to raise it, or itself restore,
And from her sandy deeps approach the dry-foot shore?

So hard's the task for sinful flesh and
  blood,
To lend the smallest help to what is good;
My God, I cannot move the least degree.
Ah! if but only those who active be,
None should thy glory see, thy glory none
  should see.
Lord, as I am, I have no power at all
To hear thy voice, or echo to thy call.

Give me the power to will, the will to do;
O raise me up, and I will strive to go:
Draw me, O draw me with thy treble-
  twist;
That have no power, but merely to resist;
O lend me strength to do, and then com-
  mand thy list.

God tells us that His power is available to us. He says that His strength is made perfect in our weakness. He will answer the heart cry, "Draw me," Lord. There is an excitement and an ecstasy of being brought into the presence of Christ by the Spirit of God. He can make Christ real to us.

"No man can come to me, except the Father which hath sent me draw him . . ." (John 6:44). The Lord Jesus said to His own, "Ye have not chosen me, but I have chosen you . . ." (John 15:16)—"I am the One who went after *you*." We did not seek after God; God sought after us. He is still seeking us today. We can only rouse ourselves to say, Lord, "draw me." We need the Spirit of God to give to us the Water of Life. If we will drink of that Water of Life, we will have rivers of living water gushing up within us and flowing out from us.

"We will run after thee." The idea here is not that we ask to be drawn because we are lazy and indifferent, but we are helpless. We have the desire—the spirit is willing, but the flesh is weak. We want to run after Him, but He will have to give us the legs to do it. He must give us that enablement, that divine enablement. He must draw us. "Wherefore . . . let us run with patience the race that is set before us, Looking unto Jesus the author and finisher of our faith . . ." (Heb. 12:1–2). "But they that wait upon the LORD shall renew their strength; they shall mount up with wings as eagles; they shall run, and not be weary; and they shall walk, and not faint" (Isa. 40:31).

## HIS CHAMBERS

So when we cry, "Draw me, we will run after thee," He responds—"the king hath brought me into his chambers." The chamber is the secret of His presence, His pavilion, like the Holy of Holies within the sanctuary. It is the secret place away from the noise and the crowd. It is the place in the cleft of the rock which He has made for us, where He can cover us with His hand and commune with us. It is like Christ's invitation: "Behold, I stand at the door, and knock: if any man hear my voice, and open the door, I will come in to him, and will sup with him, and he with me" (Rev. 3:20). Oh, what a privilege to fellowship with Him!

Yet we withdraw and cry out with Isaiah, ". . . Woe is me! for I am undone; because I am a man of unclean lips, and I dwell in the midst of a people of unclean lips: for mine eyes have seen the King, the LORD of hosts" (Isa. 6:5). But "the king hath brought me into his chambers"—He is the One who has provided a redemption. He is the One who took the coals from the altar and touched our lips. He is the One who made the supreme sacrifice.

"We will be glad and rejoice in thee." We need more joy in our churches, and we need more joy in our lives. Jesus said, ". . . I am come that they might have life, and that they might have it more *abundantly*" (John 10:10, italics mine). And John wrote, ". . . These things write we unto you, that your *joy* may be full" (1 John 1:4, italics mine). The Lord means for us to live life to the hilt.

Oh, let's quit playing church, and let's quit saying, "I belong to a certain group, and I have had an *experience*." The point is, is Christ close to you *today*? "The king hath brought me into his chambers: we will be glad and rejoice in thee, we will remember thy love more than wine: the upright love thee."

At this moment there are probably millions of people across the country who are crawling up onto a bar stool. Well, if I were in their situation, I'd crawl up there too. They need something to face life. Many a man feels he needs that drink in order to face his business. Many a person needs that drink in order to face a lonely evening. Life is too much for them. It is too complicated. May I say to you, if you are a child of God, you can always know that God loves you. The love of God is shed abroad in our hearts by the Holy Spirit who has been given to us. He wants to make His love real to us. He wants to manifest His love to us. That is a lot better than crawling up onto a bar stool. ". . . Be not drunk with wine, wherein is excess; but be filled with the Spirit" (Eph. 5:18).

If we would read on in Ephesians 5, we

would find the next verse going on to say, "Speaking to yourselves in psalms and hymns and spiritual songs, singing and making melody in your heart to the Lord" (Eph. 5:19). I have always been glad that Paul didn't write, "*Singing* to yourselves," because I can't sing. But I can speak it. I can say it. It wouldn't hurt for you to say it either. In fact, it would be good to hear a "Praise the Lord" from all of us believers. Oh, we need to praise the Lord in this day. "We will be glad and rejoice in thee, we will remember thy love more than wine."

"The upright love thee." Who are the upright? They are those who belong to Him. They are those who have said to Him, "Draw me." He has placed them on their feet, and they are to run the race of life, looking unto Jesus, the author and finisher of their faith.

The Christian life is a love affair. We love Him because He first loved us. He loved us enough to give Himself for us. Now He says to us, "I want your love." That seals it. If you don't love Him, then don't go on pretending. Be honest and chuck the whole thing. It is all meaningless if you do not love Him.

Now listen to the believer's loving response, as we find it in Psalm 63: "O God, thou art my God; early will I seek thee: my soul thirsteth for thee, my flesh longeth for thee in a dry and thirsty land, where no water is" (Ps. 63:1). My friend, are you thirsty for God? The Lord Jesus said, ". . . If any man thirst, let him come unto me, and drink" (John 7:37).

"To see thy power and thy glory, so as I have seen thee in the sanctuary" (Ps. 63:2)— this is the bride's secret place of communion.

"Because thy lovingkindness is better than life, my lips shall praise thee. Thus will I bless thee while I live: I will lift up my hands in thy name. My soul shall be satisfied as with marrow and fatness; and my mouth shall praise thee with joyful lips" (Ps. 63:3–5). Oh, friend, let's get our lips busy praising Him!

"Because thou hast been my help, therefore in the shadow of thy wings will I rejoice" (Ps. 63:7). You remember that the Lord Jesus said that He wanted to gather the people of Jerusalem under His wings like a hen gathers her chicks (see Matt. 23:37). This gives to us a picture of His love and the great desire to protect the helpless ones from harm.

"My soul followeth hard after thee: thy right hand upholdeth me. But those that seek my soul, to destroy it, shall go into the lower parts of the earth. They shall fall by the sword: they shall be a portion for foxes. But the king shall rejoice in God; every one that sweareth by him shall glory: but the mouth of them that speak lies shall be stopped" (Ps. 63:8–11). What a glorious picture of a believer's devotion to Christ!

## THE SUNBURNED SLAVE GIRL

**I am black, but comely, O ye daughters of Jerusalem, as the tents of Kedar, as the curtains of Solomon.**

**Look not upon me, because I am black, because the sun hath looked upon me: my mother's children were angry with me; they made me the keeper of the vineyards; but mine own vineyard have I not kept [Song 1:5–6].**

"The tents of Kedar" were made of the skin of the black sheep and the black goats. In that land even today one can see many of these nomad people who have black tents.

When the bride says here that she is black, she is not referring to her race. She was a Jewish girl from the area of Shunem. She explains the blackness herself. Her family were tenant farmers on one of the vineyards owned by Solomon, and they made her work out in the vineyard. She is sunburned—"I am black, because the sun hath looked upon me." She is black, but she is beautiful. Black is beautiful, we hear today. It certainly can be. Black is beautiful when the heart is right with the Lord. The pigment of the skin is of no importance whatever. The condition of the heart is the important matter.

It is interesting that most of the rays of the sun do not bother our skin. It is the ultraviolet segment of the sun's rays that burns our skin. Those rays can come through clouds, so that we can get sunburned on cloudy days, even when we are unaware of it. Since I have had cancer, my doctor warns me about sunlight. He tells me to keep my head covered, even on the cloudy days. He warns me against going out into the sunlight. The ultraviolet rays can burn, and they can cause cancer.

A great many people think they can come into the light of the holy presence of God without a covering. I tell you, no one can come into the holy presence of God without the covering of the righteousness of Christ. That is our protection—which is another meaning of being covered with His wings. You and I need to be clothed in the righteousness of Christ to come into the presence of God.

Let's get back to our girl who is blackened with sunburn. She has been working outside because her mother's children were angry with her, and they made her keep the vineyards. Then she says, "But mine own vineyard have I not kept." This is the bride's portrait of herself. She has some natural beauty, but she has nothing to commend her because she hasn't been able to take care of herself. She has had no time to go to the beauty parlor. She hasn't been able to have her hair styled. She hasn't been able to get a facial. She hasn't been able to get whatever it would take to enhance her beauty. That has been neglected because she has been made to work so hard.

Mankind is not beautiful in the presence of God. Sometimes we tend to think that the reason God is interested in us is because we are such nice, sweet little children. Actually we are ugly; we are sunburned. We are not attractive to Him as we are, but He says that He is going to make us His beautiful bride. That is the wonderful picture given to us in Ephesians 5. The example given to husbands is the love of Christ for the church. "Husbands, love your wives, even as Christ also loved the church, and gave himself for it; That he might sanctify and cleanse it with the washing of water by the word, That he might present it to himself a glorious church, not having spot, or wrinkle, or any such thing; but that it should be holy and without blemish" (Eph. 5:25–27). You see, Christ is taking us to the beauty parlor. He will fashion us into His bride, without spot or wrinkle, holy and without blemish!

## THE PASTURE

Now the story moves on. The Shulamite speaks to the shepherd whom she has just met.

**Tell me, O thou whom my soul loveth, where thou feedest, where thou makest thy flock to rest at noon: for why should I be as one that turneth aside by the flocks of thy companions? [Song 1:7].**

He seemed to be an unusual shepherd in that he didn't have any sheep that she could see. So she raised a question concerning his sheep. The shepherd seemed to be evasive. Now let's look beneath the surface and see something very precious.

The Lord Jesus said, "I am the good shepherd, and know my sheep, and am known of mine. . . . And other sheep I have, which are not of this fold: them also I must bring, and they shall hear my voice; and there shall

be one fold, and one shepherd" (John 10:14, 16). We all tend to raise questions, as the Shulamite girl asked the shepherd, about "the other sheep," the heathen. Are they lost? We want to know about the doctrine of election. We want to know about this one or that one—is he saved, or isn't he saved? We tend to pass judgment on those who are around us. Instead of questioning another's position in Christ, we need to make sure that *we* are His sheep. That is our direct concern.

The shepherd answers her.

**If thou know not, O thou fairest among women, go thy way forth by the footsteps of the flock, and feed thy kids beside the shepherds' tents [Song 1:8].**

And this would be the answer of the Lord Jesus to us.

"Feed thy kids"—the little lambs need to be fed, and all of us, my friend, come under that classification. Peter put it this way, "As newborn babes, desire the sincere milk of the word, that ye may grow thereby" (1 Pet. 2:2).

"Feed thy kids beside the shepherds' tents." Believers need to feed themselves beside the shepherds' tents, because that is the place where the grass would be unusually green. Of course it is the Word of God on which we are to feed. We cannot feed others and tell them about the joy of the Word of God unless it is a joy to us. Herbert puts it this way:

My soul's a shepherd too, a flock it feeds
   Of thoughts and words and deeds;
The pasture is thy word, the streams thy
     grace,
   Enriching all the place.

We need to feed upon the Word of God, then we need to get the Word out to others, you see. The Bride of Christ, who is to be presented to Him in the future, is to get the Word of God out today. As the body of believers, we are failing to do this.

"If thou *know not*, O thou fairest among women"—there are many things for which we do not have the answer. When I was a young preacher, I tried to get the answer to everything. I was given some good advice: "Don't let what you don't know disturb what you do know!" Do you know that Christ died for your sins? Do you know that you are trusting in Him? Are you resting upon Him? You can say, ". . . I know that my redeemer liveth . . ." (Job 19:25). You can say, ". . . I know whom I have believed . . ." (2 Tim. 1:12)—Paul could say that, but I don't find Paul saying that he knew all about the doctrine of election. So let's not permit what we don't know to disturb what we do know. That is what the shepherd is saying to this girl. Don't worry about what you don't know. Just be sure to feed *your* sheep. That is your responsibility.

There is a bedridden lady in Ohio who hears our radio broadcasts. She contacts about one thousand people each month, and she asks them to listen to the Bible being taught by radio. She is a real missionary! Now I am sure that she is puzzled by many things and has questions to ask about things she doesn't know, but so far I have never received a letter from her with a question in it. She isn't spending her time asking questions. She is spending her time getting out the Word of God. That is exactly what the shepherd tells the girl. He says, "You don't need to know about all these other sheep. You just feed your sheep." Be sure *you* get the Word of God to them.

## THE BRIDE'S ADORNING

The shepherd uses a comparison as he goes on to say:

**I have compared thee, O my love, to a company of horses in Pharaoh's chariots [Song 1:9].**

As I have mentioned before, when the word *love* is used, it is the bridegroom speaking to the bride. When the person is addressed as *beloved*, it is the bride who is speaking to the bridegroom.

"I have compared thee, O my love, to a company of horses in Pharaoh's chariots." When Moses and the children of Israel came to the Red Sea in their flight from Egypt, they found that any retreat was blocked by Pharaoh's chariots which were rapidly approaching. It was a fearsome army with horses and chariots and banners flying above the chariots. It was an overwhelming sight. The bridegroom is saying that he is overwhelmed by the beauty of this country, hillbilly girl. She has none of the graces of the court. She has never been to a beauty parlor. She really has never taken care of herself. But she has a striking natural beauty.

He goes on to describe the things that he notices.

**Thy cheeks are comely with rows of jewels, thy neck with chains of gold.**

**We will make thee borders of gold with studs of silver [Song 1:10–11].**

"Thy cheeks are comely." Her neck is beautiful. How lovely this is and how intimate. He says that he intends to cover her with jewelry. He sees her cheeks comely with jewels, her neck with chains of gold. He speaks of the parts of the body that appeal in a love affair. I am sure there are many of you ladies who noticed the eyelashes of your husband—of all things! You noticed his physique. You husbands noticed the cheeks and the eyes of your wife, and even the little ears, like shells—and all that sort of thing. He is speaking of this girl who will be his bride.

Now in the spiritual sense, the bride is the church, and the bridegroom is the Lord Jesus Christ. Does He find any beauty in the church? Friend, He found all of us lost sinners. The Shulamite girl had a natural beauty even though it had been neglected, but we don't even have that. There is nothing about us that could be appealing to Christ. We bring nothing to Him; He provides everything for us.

The same picture can be applied to Israel. When He came down to deliver the children of Israel, He didn't say, "I'm going to free you because you're such a superior people, superior to the Egyptians." They weren't. Actually, they were small and inferior. Neither did He say, "You have been so faithful to Me." They had been unfaithful—completely faithless, living in idolatry. They had deserted God. They had turned their backs upon God and were engaged in gross immorality. Then what was it that appealed to God? Why did He waste His time with them? The answer is given by God to Moses: ". . . I have heard their groaning" (Acts 7:34). *That* appealed to God. The answer lies totally in His love and grace. It was the lost condition that caused Him to provide a salvation for Israel. And He said that He remembered His covenant with Abraham, Isaac, and Jacob. God is faithful to His Word. When He says He will do a thing, He intends to make that promise good.

And it was our wretched, lost condition that caused Him to provide a salvation for us, for the church. God tells us that we will be saved if we will do nothing more than put our trust in Christ!

"We will make thee borders of gold with studs of silver"—this is a picture of what our heavenly Bridegroom will do for believers. The passage in Ephesians 5 makes this so very clear. Christ loved the church and gave Himself for the church. He did it so that He might sanctify and cleanse the church with the washing of water by the Word. That is a real miracle soap, by the way. He did this so that

He might present the church to Himself, a glorious church without a spot or wrinkle but holy—set apart for Him—and without blemish. What has happened to the church? He has redeemed us. He has paid the price for us. He has subtracted our sins and has added His righteousness. We are covered with the righteousness of Christ, we stand complete in Him, accepted in the Beloved.

## FEASTING AT THE ROUND TABLE

**While the king sitteth at his table, my spikenard sendeth forth the smell thereof [Song 1:12].**

Some have translated this, "While the king is on his circuit." They interpret it to mean while he is out going through the kingdom. Others have translated this, "While the king is at his banquet," which I think is probably the best translation that could be given. Very literally it is, "While the king sitteth at his round table"—that is the circuit. It is actually a round table where he either sits or reclines with his guests around the banquet table.

The translation is important because this verse carries with it a deeper spiritual meaning. The bridegroom brings in all of His invited guests to the banquet table. We can go down through history and mark those who have accepted the invitation to the banquet of the Bridegroom. When He was born, the shepherds came down from the hilltops to see Him in the stable. Then wise men came out of the East to present Him with gifts of gold and frankincense and myrrh. John Milton expressed it like this:

See how from far upon the Eastern road,
The star-led wizards haste with odours sweet;
O run, prevent them with thy humble ode,
And lay it lowly at his blessed feet;
Have thou the honor first thy Lord to greet.

David had the round table in mind when he wrote, "Thou preparest a table before me in the presence of mine enemies: thou anointest my head with oil; my cup runneth over" (Ps. 23:5).

A towheaded boy in southern Oklahoma heard the invitation and, thank God, accepted it. I have been sitting at His table for a long, long time. Are you sitting at that round table? You have an invitation to come. Jesus says to you, "Behold, I stand at the door, and knock: if any man hear my voice, and open the door, I will come in to him, and will sup with him, and he with me" (Rev. 3:20). Say, why don't you come and sit at the round table? Sir Lancelot may have had the privilege of sitting at King Arthur's round table, but that was nothing compared to Christ's round table!

"While the king sitteth at his table, my spikenard sendeth forth the smell thereof." The spikenard is the fragrance of Christ's life —how wonderful it is! This same fragrance should be in our lives by association with Him. Sitting at His table will do this for us. The ordinance of the Lord's Supper is a very important service if it is a time of real communion with Him. If it is merely a form and ritual to you, forget it—it is of no value.

I received a letter from a lady in Miami who wrote, "I had never heard anyone say that we should tell the Lord Jesus we love Him. I had never said it, but I have loved Him. Ever since I heard you say that we should tell Him, at morning, noon, and night (I have been making up for lost time), I tell Him that I love Him." Then she added, "The Word of God has taken on a new color—a new meaning." How wonderful! We need the fragrance of Christ in our lives.

## THE BUNDLE OF MYRRH IN THE BOSOM

Now the bride makes a statement which is quite intimate—but don't be afraid of it and run from it.

**A bundle of myrrh is my wellbeloved unto me; he shall lie all night betwixt my breasts [Song 1:13].**

The original permits us to translate this several different ways: "*It* shall lie all night betwixt my breasts." What is "it"? Well, it is the bundle of myrrh.

For the believer, the bundle of myrrh represents Christ. You recall that one of the gifts the wise men brought to Him was myrrh. When Christ died, Joseph and Nicodemus brought myrrh to put on His body. The myrrh speaks of His entire life from birth to death. My friend, Christ should lie heavy upon your breast and upon your heart at night. When you wake up during the night, what do you think about? Do you begin to worry about the next day? I must confess that I do a lot of that. But it is wonderful to be able to turn that off and to turn to *Him* at night when I'm anxious or worried. We need to follow the admonition in Philippians 4:8: "Finally, brethren [when you get to the end of your rope], whatsoever things are true [that is Christ], whatsoever things are honest [that is also Christ], whatsoever things are just [that is the Lord Jesus], whatsoever things are pure [He is pure], whatsoever things are lovely, whatsoever things are of good report; if there be any virtue, and if there be any praise, *think* on these things" (italics mine). In other words, meditate upon the Lord Jesus Christ.

> A bundle of mellifluous myrrhe,
> Is my Beloved best
> To me, which I will bind between
> My breasts, while I do rest
> In silent slumbers.
>
> —*Troth-plight Spouse*

A friend of mine said it this way: "When I go to bed at night, the last thing I do is pull up the covers, look up and say, 'Lord Jesus, I love you.' " Isaac Watts wrote it like this:

> As myrrh new bleeding from the tree,
> Such is a dying Christ to me;
> And while He makes my soul his guest,
> My bosom, Lord, shall be thy rest.

Oh, friend, let's think upon the Lord Jesus Christ. How wonderful He is!
Erskine wrote it this way:

> From this enfolded bundle flies
> His savor all abroad:
> Such complicated sweetness lies
> In my Incarnate God.

My Christian friend, you miss so much when you are satisfied with some little course on how to live the Christian life or on going through some little ritual. Oh, to have *Him* as the very object of your life, the One who brings in the excitement, the ecstasy, the fellowship, and the joy. His grace and His love and His mercy are all yours—just open the door. Jesus is knocking right now.

## THE CLUSTER OF CAMPHIRE

The bride continues to speak of her delight in her bridegroom.

**My beloved is unto me as a cluster of camphire in the vineyards of En-gedi [Song 1:14].**

The "camphire" mentioned here is the cypress. In some versions it is translated "henna flowers," and the flowers of the cypress are that color. Scholars have done a great deal of

study of different plants mentioned in this book. The cypress is a tree that grows in profusion in Palestine and in Turkey. As I traveled in that area, I was most impressed by the great rows of cypress trees. Here is a statement about the cypress from Kitto, which I would like to pass on to you. The camphire "is now generally agreed to be the Henna of the Arabians. The deep color of the bark, the light green of the foliage, and the softened mixture of white-yellow in the blossoms, present a combination as agreeable to the eye as the odour is to the scent. The flowers grow in dense clusters, the grateful fragrance of which is as much appreciated now as in the time of Solomon. The women take great pleasure in these clusters, hold them in their hand, carry them in their bosom, and keep them in their apartments to perfume the air."

Now notice the comparison of camphor or cypress to the bridegroom—what a lovely thing it is: "My beloved is unto me as a cluster of camphire in the vineyards of En-gedi."

En-gedi, another place that I have visited, is down by the Dead Sea. It is one of those wonderful oases in the desert, because there are springs there. You may recall that the area around En-gedi is a wilderness where David hid from Saul. It is a good hiding place—I don't see how anyone could be found in those barren hills. But at En-gedi many kinds of lovely spices are grown. It is a very interesting spot in the midst of that desolate desert, and the bridegroom is like a cluster of camphor in the vineyards of En-gedi. He is like a row of those stately trees with that lovely fragrance.

Christ as our Beloved is represented here as being full of attractive beauty and an aromatic fragrance. I emphasize the deity of Christ very often, but I wonder sometimes if I give a lopsided view of Him. Have you ever stopped to think how lovely He was in His person? He came and took upon Himself our humanity, and He was in all points tempted as we are, yet without sin. There was no sin in Him. How wonderful He was! There was nothing lopsided about His personality. You may recall that in the Old Testament the meal offering typified the even quality of Christ's personality. It was well-beaten flour—never coarse or lumpy.

Frankly, most of us are lumpy—I don't mean physically, but psychologically. All of us are a little "off" in one way or another. We all have our peculiarities. One man talking to another made the statement, "You know we all have our peculiarities." The man replied, "I don't believe that. I don't think I have any peculiarities." The first man said, "All right. Let me ask you a question. Do you stir your coffee with your right hand or your left hand?" He answered, "I stir it with my right hand." "There," he said triumphantly, "that's your peculiarity. Most people use a spoon!" So, you see, we may not stir our coffee with our hand, but we all have peculiarities. We are lumpy; He was not.

He is the perfect human in His incarnation. He is lovely. He is the bundle of camphor. He is the One of whom John could say with enthusiasm and deep expression, ". . . Behold the Lamb of God, which taketh away the sin of the world" (John 1:29). If you will hear Him, your soul shall live. Or, as the psalmist says, "O taste and see that the LORD is good . . ." (Ps. 34:8). The Lord Jesus was a sacrifice—He ". . . hath given himself for us an offering and a sacrifice to God for a sweet-smelling savour" (Eph. 5:2). He typified the burnt offering that ascended up to heaven. It all speaks of the fact that God is completely satisfied with what Jesus did for you and for me. He is satisfied with Jesus. He said, ". . . This is My beloved Son, in whom I am well pleased" (Matt. 3:17). He has never said that about Vernon McGee, and probably He has never said it about you. But He has declared that He is satisfied with Jesus.

Friend, are you satisfied with Jesus? I don't think many people are. If they were, they wouldn't be running here and there over the face of the earth, trying to find satisfaction in something else. People run to hear this thing and that thing, always searching for something that is new. We can even become so engrossed in the mechanics and the details of Bible study that we lose sight of the person of Jesus Christ. How wonderful He is! "My beloved is unto me as a cluster of camphire in the vineyards of En-gedi."

There is another interesting symbol in the "bundle" of camphire. There is a great emphasis in the Scriptures on the oneness of the Lord Jesus Christ. He is the *only* begotten Son of the Father. He is the *one* good Shepherd. He is the *one* true Vine. He is the *one* Light of the world. He is the *one* Servant of the Father. He is the *one* Sacrifice for sin. He is the *one* Way, the *one* Truth, the *one* Life. Yet in His perfect unity there is a fullness that is absolutely inexhaustible. He is also a cluster of fragrant flowers. There is a oneness in Him; but, oh, in Him there is *everything*. Innumerable graces crowd harmoniously together in the Lamb of God. In Him we

can find the faith of Abraham, the persuasiveness of Jacob, the meekness of Moses, the zeal of Elijah, the holiness of Job, the love of John. They are all full and perfect in Him. In Him are found truth, righteousness, wisdom, love, pity, friendship, majesty, might, sovereignty, lowliness, patience, faith, zeal, courage, holiness, and all the graces. If I have left out any of His qualities, they ought to be included in this list because He is everything. He is all in all. And He is ours. That is the wonder of it all.

## BEHOLD, THOU ART FAIR

Now after the bride has expressed her adoration of the bridegroom, he says this to her:

**Behold, thou art fair, my love; behold, thou art fair; thou hast doves' eyes [Song 1:15].**

And her instant response is in the following verse: "Behold, thou art fair, my beloved."

She is the one who said, "Look not upon me, because I am black, because the sun hath looked upon me." But he says to her, "Behold, thou art fair, my love; behold, thou art fair."

My friend, we as the bride of Christ have sinned. We can confess with Daniel, "We have sinned, and have committed iniquity, and have done wickedly, and have rebelled, even by departing from thy precepts and from thy judgments" (Dan. 9:5). This is the confession of every person if he is a child of God. But our Lord Jesus intercedes for us: ". . . thine they were, and thou gavest them me; and they have kept thy word" (John 17:6). That is our High Priest pleading for you and me. Because we are in Christ, the Father sees no iniquity in us, as God would not see the iniquity of Jacob or perverseness in Israel and would not permit Balaam to curse them. God went down and dealt with His own people; He wouldn't let them get by with sin. But God would not let a heathen prophet curse Israel. He saw Israel in Christ. That is the way He sees us today. "Behold, thou art fair."

The secret of this beauty is in this: "Thou hast doves' eyes." Doves are common emblems of chastity and constancy. Her eyes are fixed upon the bridegroom, and all her beauty is the reflected beauty of the bridegroom. Jesus said, "The light of the body is the eye: if therefore thine eye be single, thy whole body shall be full of light" (Matt. 6:22)—and also full of beauty. "But if thine eye be evil [or double], thy whole body shall be full of darkness . . ." (Matt. 6:23). A believer who has an eye for anything equally with Christ has no beauty in His sight. Jesus laid it on the line: "He that loveth father or mother more than me is not worthy of me: and he that loveth son or daughter more than me is not worthy of me" (Matt. 10:37). It is important for you to answer this question: Do you have your eye fixed upon the Lord Jesus today?

I hear a great deal about "dedication" as I attend many conferences around the country. Folk are always talking about how dedicated they are and how they want to manifest Christ, but these very people are actually lazy. Their service is slipshod. You see, dedication is not something to *talk* about; dedication to Christ is something you *reveal*. It will be manifested in your life. If your eye is upon Him, then His beauty will be reflected in you.

The bridegroom has told the bride how wonderful she is. Now she turns right around and says the very same thing to him.

**Behold, thou art fair, my beloved, yea, pleasant: also our bed is green.**

**The beams of our house are cedar, and our rafters of fir [Song 1:16–17].**

The Bridegroom is beautiful to those of us who believe. He is altogether lovely. Augustine wrote: "He is fair in heaven, fair in the earth; fair in the virgin's womb [He was that holy thing], fair in the arms of His parents, fair in the miracles, fair in His stripes . . . fair in laying down His life, fair in receiving it again; fair on the cross, fair in the sepulchre." This was the way Augustine, that great saint of God of the past, described the Lord Jesus.

"Yea, pleasant"—the word is the Hebrew *naim*, and it is used to describe the wonderful melodies of the sanctuary: ". . . sing praises unto his name; for it is pleasant" (Ps. 135:3). Christ is pleasant; He is lovely. Why would anyone want to run away from the Lord Jesus! He is so wonderful. The word is also used to describe a chosen earthly friend. David said of his loyal friend, Jonathan, "I am distressed for thee, my brother Jonathan: very pleasant hast thou been unto me . . ." (2 Sam. 1:26).

What can we say of the One who is greater than Jonathan? Can you say that Jesus is pleasant to you? It is sweet to be with Him. He is the One who can bring rest to us. Are you satisfied with Him? God the Father is satisfied with Him. "Behold, thou art fair, my beloved, yea, pleasant."

"Also our bed is green." The "bed" is the English translation for lack of a better word. It is actually the reclining couch where they sat around the banquet. Especially at the time of a marriage feast the banquet couch would be strewn with flowers and green leaves. I think this would be the meaning of the green "bed" if the setting is in Jerusalem.

However, it may be that this is referring back to the time when they first met and is speaking of the green grass where the sheep were. Maybe they just sat on the grass while the sheep were grazing, and that is where they first got acquainted with each other. It would signify the place of communication.

This reminds us of David's psalm: "He maketh me to lie down in green pastures . . ." (Ps. 23:2). When the sheep lies down in green pastures, he is satisfied. He has eaten enough and is full. It is the answer to Christ's invitation to come to Him and rest. He invites all those who are weary and heavy laden to come to Him. The green pastures are there for us. Christian friend, if you are tired and weary, you can rest in Him.

It has been expressed this way by A. Moody Stuart: " 'Heavy laden' and hopeless thou art, seeking peace afar off and passing Him who is near, like Hagar in the desert, with the last drop drained from the now shriveled water-skin, thou art ready to lie down and die. But open thine ears and thou wilt hear one say, 'Come unto Me and I will give you rest'; open thine eyes and thou wilt see the well and the green sward around it; and with a full heart thou wilt answer him, 'Behold Thou art pleasant, also our couch is green.' " What a beautiful picture this is!

Do you remember where He reclined? When He first came to this earth, they put Him in a manger. The last place they laid Him was in the tomb of Joseph. He went to that place so that you and I might sit with Him in green pastures.

# CHAPTER 2

## THE ROSE OF SHARON

**I am the rose of Sharon, and the lily of the valleys [Song 2:1].**

In my printed notes on this verse I have said that here the bride speaks of herself, that she is not boasting, but comparing herself to the lowly and humble flowers of that land. Some of the newer translations indicate that she is the one who is speaking here. Well, I want to say that I no longer believe that this is her voice, but that it is the voice of the bridegroom. If she is the one who is speaking, this is actually a picture of the Lord Jesus Christ and His reflected beauty. "I am the rose of Sharon, and the lily of the valleys" is a statement that none of the sons of men could be making. I believe these are the words of the Lord Jesus, not the words of the bride. Many of the older translators have tried to make it clear that it is the king speaking. In the old English Bibles this is said to be the voice of Christ, the bridegroom. In the French and Italian and Portuguese Bibles this is designated as the voice of Christ. Many of the church fathers applied these words to the Lord Jesus.

These words describe the Lord Jesus. He says, ". . . for I am meek and lowly in heart" (Matt. 11:29). If you put a statement like that on my lips, or your lips, or the lips of the angel Gabriel, it wouldn't be humility at all; it would actually be pride. It is true humility from the lips of the Lord Jesus because He stooped in order that He might become meek and lowly. He came down from heaven's glory, and anything beneath heaven is humility on His part.

So here He says, "I am the rose of Sharon, and the lily of the valleys." These are two very interesting flowers. I suppose that among all the flowers the rose has always been—especially in the East—the one that tops the list. And the rose of Sharon is an unusually beautiful flower. The valley of Sharon is that coast valley that goes all the way from Joppa up to Haifa. I have traveled the length and breadth of it several times. It is beautiful at any season of the year. It is a valley where you can see a great many flowers. I took pictures of them, especially the poppy fields. You have probably heard that the finest citrus fruit in the world is grown in Israel. Sharon is the valley where most of it is grown. The rose grows in profusion in that valley. It is the very beautiful flower that speaks of Him.

I do not think roses originally had thorns. I don't think they were intended to be thorny. But as we know them today, they still have thorns. Even the very beautiful rose reminds us that the earth is under a curse and brings forth thorns and thistles (see Gen. 3:18).

An ancient author wrote: "If the king were set over flowers, it would be the rose that should reign over them, being the ornament of the earth, the splendor of plants, the eye of flowers, the beauty of the field."

Now here is something quite interesting. When Jesus said, ". . . I am the bread of life . . ." (John 6:35), He was saying that He is something that is necessary. Bread is the staff of life. We need it to keep us going. It is a necessity of life. He is that food to the perishing sinner. Thousands have reached up a dying hand, a feeble hand, in faith, and have taken the bread. And they have eaten, and they have lived. Jesus also said, "I am the true vine . . ." (John 15:1). As the true vine, He gives the glorious, wonderful joy of the Lord. The Scripture says, "Give strong drink unto him that is ready to perish, and wine unto those that be of heavy hearts" (Prov. 31:6). Christ gives joy—not the alcoholic beverage, but the real joy of the Lord. However, when He says that He is "the rose of Sharon," He is presenting Himself not as a necessity but as an object of pure admiration and delight to the children of men. What a wonderful human being He was! We need to behold Him and let Him occupy our thoughts. He is the One of truth and honesty and purity and beauty upon whom we are to think.

As He walked along with His disciples through the fields, He said, ". . . Consider the lilies of the field, how they grow; they toil not, neither do they spin" (Matt. 6:28). I think He would say to you and me today, "Consider the Rose of Sharon!" In other words, consider *Him.* We find this same invitation in Hebrews: "Wherefore, holy brethren, partakers of the heavenly calling, *consider* the Apostle and High Priest of our profession, Christ Jesus" (Heb. 3:1). Consider Jesus Christ.

## THE LILY OF THE VALLEYS

"I am . . . the lily of the valleys." This may be a reference to the valley of Esdraelon. This valley has beautiful flowers in it, too. Actually, there is a profusion of flowers in all the valleys—along the coast south of Joppa, in the Jordan valley, around the Sea of Galilee. What is the lily of the valleys? There have been questions as to which flower is meant. Apparently it was the iris. The iris grows wild over there, and one can still see a great many of them. I am of the opinion that it does refer to that humble plant, the iris. He is the beautiful, stately rose and the humble iris. "I am the rose of Sharon, and the lily of the valleys."

**As the lily among the thorns, so is my love among the daughters [Song 2:2].**

Bonar expressed it in this way: "Close by these lilies there grew several of the thorny shrubs of the desert; but above them rose the lily, spreading out its fresh green leaf as a contrast to the dingy verdure of these prickly shrubs—'like the lily among thorns, so is my love among the daughters.' " In other words, among "daughters" (meaning here, the daughters of Jerusalem) the bride stands out as a lily among thorns.

Christ is the lily of the valleys—He is pure, He is lovely, He is beautiful, therefore His bride is a lily also, because she bears the image of His loveliness and reflects it to men. This is what the church is to do today. We are to reveal to a world that is filled with thorns, briars, and thistles, the beauty of Christ.

## THE APPLE TREE IN THE WOOD

Now the bride speaks of her beloved using the "trees of the wood" in her comparison—

**As the apple tree among the trees of the wood, so is my beloved among the sons. I sat down under his shadow with great delight, and his fruit was sweet to my taste [Song 2:3].**

"The apple tree among the trees of the wood" is a picture of Christ.

Now you may wonder what kind of tree she is talking about. Actually, apples are not grown in that land. I suppose they could be grown, but they would not be very good. The climate is much as it is here in Southern California. We can grow apples, but they are not very good apples, because apples require a colder climate. The "apple" referred to here is actually a *citron* fruit, probably an orange tree. I have three orange trees in my yard here in Pasadena, and they make very good shade trees. They are a tree of beauty, and when they blossom, I sit on my patio and enjoy the fragrance of the orange blossoms in spring. No wonder they are used for weddings! And the luscious fruit which the tree bears is both beautiful and healthful.

There are citrus groves in the valley of Sharon, which are said to produce the finest citrus fruit in the world. It has always grown there. The citrus was transplanted to California years ago; it didn't grow here naturally. But it is native to Palestine. There the green of the citrus groves is beautiful to see.

Notice that she says, "I sat down under his shadow with great delight, and his fruit was sweet to my taste." The orange tree affords thick shade like the " . . . shadow of a great rock in a weary land" (Isa. 32:2) and refreshing fruit. Christ is like this wonderful fruit tree in contrast to the fruitless trees of the woods.

## THE BANQUETING HOUSE

**He brought me to the banqueting house, and his banner over me was love [Song 2:4].**

In this is the story of the Shulamite girl whose heart was won by a shepherd who later came as King Solomon to claim her and who takes her back to the palace in Jerusalem. Now he takes her to the banqueting house.

In this there is a beautiful picture of the church which will be the bride of Christ. It also reveals the personal relationship which is possible between the Lord Jesus Christ and each individual believer.

"He brought me to the banqueting house." This probably looks forward to that day of the final banquet which is called the "marriage supper of the Lamb." You and I as believers will be there by the grace of God. That is when full satisfaction will be made. But already He has brought me to the table of salvation, and He has brought me to the table of fellowship with Him. He prepares the table before me, the table of the Word of God, and He tells me to eat and be full. He brings me to a table of good things. How good and gracious He is!

We can go back to the birth of the Lord Jesus and see that already He has brought joy unspeakable to a group of people. There were old Simeon and Anna back in the temple who were waiting for Him. They had great hope that He would come during their lifetime. One day Joseph and Mary brought the little boy Jesus into the temple. My, that day the temple became a banqueting house for those two old people who had looked for the salvation of the Lord.

Even before that, God had brought Joseph and Mary to the banqueting house. When the angel announced to Mary that she should be the mother of the Savior, she realized that she who was in the line of David would be the one who would bear this child. Notice what she says in her Magnificat: "He hath filled the hungry with good things . . ." (Luke 1:53), using exactly the same picture as we have in the Song of Solomon: "He brought me to the banqueting house." What a picture we have here!

You recall in chapter 1, verse 4, the girl's prayer was, "Draw me, we will run after thee." We cannot know the ecstasy of this experience unless the Spirit of God gives us discernment and opens our eyes to behold Christ in His beauty and glory. Oh, my friend, let's not be satisfied with eating scraps or, like the prodigal son, getting down to eat with the pigs when God has prepared such a banquet for us!

## THE BANNER OF LOVE

"**H**e brought me to the banqueting house, and his banner over me was love." That banner is still floating over us today. The banner in that day had many meanings. Armies would carry banners with them when they went to war. I think all the various meanings of banners are included when she says, "His banner over me was love."

The banner of an army, as, for example, the banners of the Roman legions, was an emblem of conquest. The Son of God still goes forth to war. There is a battle today for the souls of men. I remember how I resisted Him. I shall never forget the excuses I made for not going to a young people's conference. I thought they were a bunch of sissies who were going there, and I didn't want to go with that crowd. I wasn't interested. But, you know, He opened up the way, and the first thing I knew I was there. Before I knew it, I had made a decision in my heart for Him. His banner over me was a banner of conquest.

The banner is also an emblem of protection. When the Lord Jesus came into this world, the Father testified, ". . . This is my beloved Son, in whom I am well pleased" (Matt. 3:17), and the enemies of Jesus could not touch Him until His hour had come. He was protected. When the time had come, they took Him and crucified Him. We will never understand how terrible that was. He cried out in that hour, ". . . My God, my God, why hast thou forsaken me?" (Matt. 27:46). His enemies thought that since God had forsaken Him they could do as they pleased with Him. They mocked saying, "He trusted in God; let him deliver him now, if he will have him: for he

said, I am the Son of God" (Matt. 27:43). But God *was* still pleased with His Son; He delighted in Him, and He raised Him from the dead. He delivered Him from death. And now that banner of salvation and protection is over all those who are His. "And the peace of God, which passeth all understanding, shall keep [that is, be on guard duty over] your hearts and minds through Christ Jesus" (Phil. 4:7). He will protect you.

The banner is also an emblem of enlistment. You can enlist as a soldier. By the way, His army is entirely a volunteer army. "I beseech you therefore, brethren, by the mercies of God, that ye present your bodies a living sacrifice, holy, acceptable unto God, which is your reasonable service" (Rom. 12:1). "If ye love me, keep my commandments" (John 14:15). What if you don't love Him? Then forget it! This is a banner for enlistment on a voluntary basis. "His banner over me was love."

## LOVESICK

**Stay me with flagons, comfort me with apples: for I am sick of love [Song 2:5].**

**T**he Holy Spirit of God has brought the saved soul into a personal relationship with Christ that is satisfying. I repeat: God is satisfied with Jesus and what He did for you. Are you satisfied? Do you find joy and satisfaction and delight in the person of Christ? Spend time in this Song of Solomon. Great men of God down through the ages have spent time in this book, men like Moody and McCheyne. Personally, I have spent too little time in this book, but it has become very meaningful to me.

When I went to Nashville, Tennessee, to pastor a church, I succeeded a great man of God. I always loved to go out to visit him. I never talked to that man without learning something new from the Word of God. One day he told me, "Vernon, the other night I was lying in bed, and I thought how wonderful Christ is. It just seemed to me that there was glory all around my bed. Don't misunderstand—I was not seeing things. It was just so wonderful to contemplate the person of Christ. Finally my body was so worked up that I couldn't go to sleep, and I had to cry out to God, 'Oh Lord, turn off the glory. This old body of mine can't stand any more of it.' " Imagine the experience of Paul when he was caught up to the third heaven! You see, most of us haven't even gotten our foot in the door yet. We know so little about what it is to have this kind of fellowship with Him. Of course it will have its final fulfillment when we come to "the marriage supper of the Lamb."

Erskine, who has written many wonderful things, expressed it like this:

The love, the love that I bespeak,
    Works wonders in the soul;
For when I'm whole it makes me sick,
    When sick, it makes me whole.

I'm overcome, I faint, I fail,
    Till love shall love relieve;
More love divine the wound can heal,
    Which love divine did give.

More of the joy that makes me faint,
    Would give me present ease;
If more should kill me, I'm content
    To die of that disease.

This wonderful love of God is a paradox. We long for it, and yet the glory of it all is more than we can bear.

**His left hand is under my head, and his right hand doth embrace me [Song 2:6].**

"His left hand is under my head"—He is able to save us to the uttermost. "His right hand doth embrace me"—He is able to keep us from temptation and protect you and me down here.

**I charge you, O ye daughters of Jerusalem, by the roes, and by the hinds of the field, that ye stir not up, nor awake my love, till he please [Song 2:7].**

What is it that will wake Him up? What is it that would disturb Him in His fellowship with you? It is the sin and waywardness in your life. Not only are we to be satisfied with Him, but, oh, that He might be satisfied with us!

We have come now to the second song. Apparently, Solomon has been away on a trip. The bride has been looking forward in great anticipation to his coming home. What a wonderful thing it is to see the excitement of the bride as she looks forward to the coming of the bridegroom. We will find its final fulfillment, I believe, in the anticipation of the church for the return of Christ to take the church out of the world.

### THE VOICE OF THE BELOVED

**The voice of my beloved! behold, he cometh leaping upon the mountains, skipping upon the hills [Song 2:8].**

"**T**he voice of my beloved!" The Lord Jesus had this to say concerning His voice: "My sheep hear my voice, and I know them, and they follow me: And I give unto them eternal life; and they shall never perish, neither shall any man pluck them out of my hand" (John 10:27–28). "The voice of my beloved! behold, he cometh. . . ." Have you ever considered that at the Rapture of the church it is the voice of the Son of God that is to be heard? The church is made up of those people who have heard about Him. We have heard of His death and burial and resurrection. We have trusted Him. We listen to Him today, so when He comes we are going to know His voice. Jesus said, "My sheep hear My voice." The sheep know who He is.

When the Lord Jesus comes to take His church out of this world, ". . . the Lord himself [He will come personally] shall descend from heaven with a shout, with the voice of the archangel, and with the trump of God . . ." (1 Thess. 4:16). The "shout," the "voice," and the "trump" are all *His* voice. "The voice of my beloved! behold, he cometh." What a picture of the Rapture!

Contrast this to the coming of the Lord Jesus to rule and to reign on this earth. Then it will not be the sound of a voice but a tremendous sight of glory. The appeal is not to the ear as it is in the Rapture; the appeal is to the eye when He comes to the earth. "And then shall appear the sign of the Son of man in heaven: and then shall all the tribes of the earth mourn, and they shall see the Son of man coming in the clouds of heaven with power and great glory" (Matt. 24:30). But at the Rapture it will be the "voice of my beloved!"

"Behold, he cometh leaping upon the mountains, skipping upon the hills." This is poetic language, of course. This is a song, and God is trying to speak to us through it.

There is a great deal said about the feet of Jesus. In fact, I developed a series of messages several years ago about the members of the body of the Lord Jesus Christ. I spoke of the eyes of Jesus that were stained with tears. I spoke of the lips of Jesus, and I spoke of His hands. I spoke of the feet of Jesus.

"He maketh my feet like hinds' feet, and setteth me upon my high places" (Ps. 18:33). *Aijeleth Shahar*, which means the "hind of the morning," is the title to Psalm 22. It reveals the Lord Jesus Christ in the day of His sorrow, in His suffering and death upon the cross. It is a picture of the hind of the morning. All night long the dogs had been following the hind. They had torn at his flesh. They had attempted to destroy him. "For dogs have compassed me: the assembly of the wicked have enclosed me: they pierced my hands and my feet" (Ps. 22:16). But when the sun comes up, what do we find? He is the hind of the morning, standing on the mountain peak. He has been delivered out of death. He is coming back, my friend. He is skipping upon the hills; He is leaping upon the mountains. I can't think of a more wonderful, more poetic picture of the Lord Jesus Christ in His return to earth.

I like the way Erskine expresses it:

> When manifold obstructions met,
> My willing Saviour made
> A stepping-stone of every let,
> That in his way was laid.

He took stumbling blocks and made them into stepping stones. He made a way for us, and He *is* the way for us. We have the picture of Him coming again, this One who is the hind, or the roe, or the young hart who is leaping upon the mountains and skipping upon the hills.

Now He is drawing closer—

> The voice of my Beloved sounds,
> Over the rocks and rising grounds;
> O'er hills of guilt, and seas of grief,
> He leaps, he flies to my relief.

## BEHIND OUR WALL

**My beloved is like a roe or a young hart: behold, he standeth behind our wall, he looketh forth at the windows, shewing himself through the lattice [Song 2:9].**

Today He stands behind the wall. He has gone to be at God's right hand, and we are way down here. It is like the time He went to the mountain to pray after He had fed the five thousand, and His disciples were down on the Sea of Galilee in a storm. That is the way it is today. I am down here in a storm; He is up yonder at God's right hand.

He is on the other side of the wall, and everything under the sun is trying to keep us from Him: the world, the flesh, and the devil. But He still says to us the same thing that He said to Zacchaeus: ". . . Make haste, and come down; for to-day I must abide at thy house" (Luke 19:5). He still tells us that he wants to come in and sup with us, as He went into the home of that old publican and had fellowship with him. He will come to you if you will invite Him in. This is the One of whom John the

Baptist said, ". . . there standeth one among you, whom ye know not" (John 1:26). And today the world does not know Him. He is behind a wall—a wall of indifference, a wall of rebellion against God, a wall of sin. What a picture!

## THE SONG OF HIS RETURN

**My beloved spake, and said unto me, Rise up, my love, my fair one, and come away.**

**For, lo, the winter is past, the rain is over and gone;**

**The flowers appear on the earth; the time of the singing of birds is come, and the voice of the turtle is heard in our land;**

**The fig tree putteth forth her green figs, and the vines with the tender grape give a good smell. Arise, my love, my fair one, and come away [Song 2:10–13].**

"Rise up, my love, my fair one, and come away." Christ loved the church and gave Himself for it. He did it because He is going to come to take the church out of this world. He is going to present it to Himself as a church that is purified—all of us believers *need* that purifying. He sanctifies and cleanses us with the washing of water by the Word. That is the reason we have Bible study. He wants to present to Himself a glorious church, without a spot or wrinkle. He wants it to be holy and without blemish. That is why He calls, "Arise, my love, my fair one, and come away."

"For, lo, the winter is past"—it is cold down here in this world.

"The rain is over and gone"—the storms of life will then have abated. Are you having a hard time today, Christian friend? Christ said you would: ". . . In the world ye shall have tribulation . . ." (John 16:33). Don't be upset if you are having trouble. It is one of the marks that you belong to Him, that you are a child of God. But when He comes, all the trouble will be over. He will wipe away all tears from your eyes. Every broken heart will be healed. Every sorrow will have vanished away when we are in His presence. "The winter is past, the rain is over and gone."

"The flowers appear on the earth." When the Lord Jesus comes for His own and takes them out of this world to the beautiful home which He has prepared, I believe it will be to a beautiful garden of flowers. I like to think that in the New Jerusalem there will be a profusion of flowers.

"The time of the singing of birds is come, and the voice of the turtle [turtledove] is heard in our land." "The time of the singing of birds" is another very lovely expression. There is going to be a great deal of singing when we come into His presence.

Have you ever noticed that there is a great deal of singing that opens the story of the Gospels? Dr. Luke is the writer who starts farther back in the account of the birth of Christ than any of the other gospel writers, and he recorded the songs. There is the song of Zacharias, the song of Elisabeth, the song of Mary, the song of Anna, and the song of Simeon. There were a lot of songs connected with His birth. The church began singing, and the joy of these people is what called attention to them in the Roman world. Some day when we come into His presence we will sing a new song to the Lord, for He has done wondrous things! I can't sing it now because God didn't create me with a voice that could sing, but when I have a new body, I'm going to sing that new song. Until then I can lift my heart in the praise that is due Him. The very singing of the birds of the air and the bursting buds of the flowers of the earth should remind us of the debt of joyful gratitude we owe for His great salvation. Kingwellmersh expressed it poetically:

O sing unto this glittering glorious king,
O praise his name let every living thing;
Let heart and voice, like belles of silver,
    ring
The comfort that this day did bring.

It is interesting to note that in our older Bibles "the time of singing" is rendered "the time of pruning." The season of the singing of birds is also the season of the pruning of the vines. The branch that is pruned for fruit and the song that is pruned for beauty are expressed in the same way by the Hebrew writers, which makes it difficult to determine whether "singing" or "pruning" is intended. Pruning the vines is exactly what the Lord Jesus said he was going to do. He said, "I am the true [genuine] vine, and my Father is the husbandman. Every branch in me that beareth not fruit he taketh away: and every branch that beareth fruit, he purgeth [or *prunes*] it, that it may bring forth more fruit" (John 15:1–2). My friend, you and I are living

in the time of pruning, but the time of singing is ahead of us. What a picture this is!

"The voice of the turtle [turtledove] is heard in our land." The turtledove is the wild dove which is common today. I saw them in Israel. They looked very similar to the doves in California, only I think they were somewhat smaller. The dove has always been the emblem of peace. The reason for that is that the dove went out and brought back an olive leaf to Noah after the waters of the Flood had receded. That spoke of peace, because the judgment was over.

Also the turtledove speaks to us of our salvation which is complete because the judgment is past. It is past because Christ bore the judgment for us. He has endured it in our behalf. I am saved, not because of who I am, but because of what *Christ* did. My friend, your sins are either on you or they are on Christ. If your sins are on you, you are yet to come up for judgment. If you have trusted Christ, your sins are on Him. He bore them for you, and the judgment is past. By faith you appropriate the salvation. The turtledove speaks of the peace that He has made for us.

This is the reason that not just a *few* of the saints will go to meet Christ at the Rapture. There are some folk who believe that only the super-duper saints will go. However, the hope of *every* believer is to be taken with Christ when He comes for His church. We will go to be with Him, not because we have been super-duper saints, but because He has made peace by the blood of His cross. The turtledove is symbolic of this.

The "turtle" is the turtledove of the morning. Where I live, the turtledove is the first bird to get up in the morning. It heralds a new day that is coming. I love the way Isaac Watts has expressed it—evidently he spent a great deal of time studying the Song of Solomon:

The legal wintery state is gone,
The mists are fled, the spring comes on;
The sacred turtle-dove we hear
Proclaim the new, the joyful year.
And when we hear Christ Jesus say,
Rise up my Love, and come away,
Our hearts would fain outfly the wind,
And leave all earthly joys behind.

"The fig tree putteth forth her green figs, and the vines with the tender grape give a good smell"—these are signs of springtime. "Arise, my love, my fair one, and come away." First Thessalonians 4:16 tells us that ". . . the dead in Christ shall rise first." The Lord Jesus said,

". . . I go to prepare a place for you. And if I go and prepare a place for you, I will come again, and receive you unto myself; that where I am, there ye may be also" (John 14:2–3). "Rise up, my love, my fair one, and come away."

## THE DOVE IN THE CLEFTS OF THE ROCK

**O my dove, that art in the clefts of the rock, in the secret places of the stairs, let me see thy countenance, let me hear thy voice; for sweet is thy voice, and thy countenance is comely [Song 2:14].**

The psalmist made this plea: "O deliver not the soul of thy turtledove unto the multitude of the wicked . . ." (Ps. 74:19). Will the Lord deliver us? We are told He will hide us in the clefts of the rock, and that Rock symbolizes Christ. He is the Rock upon whom the church is built. He bore our judgment, and we can rest in Him. That should bring us not only satisfaction but also security. If you are on the Rock today, you are safe. Even if you do not recognize the assurance of this, you are still safe. A little Scottish lady was speaking with great assurance about her salvation. Someone said, "You act as if you were safe and secure on the rock." She answered, "I am. Sometimes I do tremble on the Rock, but the Rock never trembles under me."

The dove is also an emblem for the Holy Spirit. He descended like a dove on the Lord Jesus. And everyone who is in Christ has that dove-like Spirit dwelling in him. ". . . if any man have not the Spirit of Christ, he is none of his" (Rom. 8:9). And true believers are like doves in their simplicity and their gentleness. Our Lord admonished us to be ". . . wise as serpents, and harmless as doves" (Matt. 10:16). Now, I suspect that a dove is a rather stupid bird. The other day as I was driving along, I accidentally hit a dove. The crazy dove stood there on the highway without making a move until the car was about to hit him. I regretted doing that, but I said, "You stupid little bird for staying there like you did!" You see, you and I need not only to be as harmless as doves, but we had better be as wise as serpents in our world today—or we'll get run over also.

The dove is a timid bird. The Lord says, "They shall tremble as a bird out of Egypt, and as a dove out of the land of Assyria: and I will place them in their houses, saith the LORD" (Hos. 11:11). The dove needs a hiding place in the clefts of the rock. Christ is a beautiful picture of the Rock who was wounded for us. As someone has said, "I got into the heart of Christ through a spear wound." Augustus M. Toplady's wonderful hymn is based on this thought.

Rock of Ages, cleft for me,
Let me hide myself in Thee;
Let the water and the blood,
From Thy wounded side which flowed,
Be of sin the double cure,
Cleanse me from its guilt and power. . . .

Nothing in my hand I bring,
Simply to Thy cross I cling;
Naked, come to Thee for dress,
Helpless, look to Thee for grace;
Foul, I to the fountain fly;
Wash me, Saviour, or I die.

While I draw this fleeting breath,
When my eyelids close in death,
When I soar to worlds unknown,
See Thee on Thy judgment throne,
Rock of Ages, cleft for me,
Let me hide myself in Thee.

## THE LITTLE FOXES

**Take us the foxes, the little foxes, that spoil the vines: for our vines have tender grapes [Song 2:15].**

They could put up a fence or a wall that would keep out the big foxes, but they had trouble with the little foxes. Those little fellows could sneak through. They were the ones that would sneak in and destroy the grapes and tear up the young vines. This has a message for us. "Foxes" are both subtle sins and fox-like men who corrupt others. Both were resolutely dragged into the light of day by John the Baptist. Regarding the subtle sins, he said, ". . . He that hath two coats, let him impart to him that hath none; and he that hath meat, let him do likewise. . . . Exact no more than that which is appointed you. . . . Do violence to no man, neither accuse any falsely; and be content with your wages" (Luke 3:11, 13–14). Then John the Baptist pointed his finger at Herod whom our Lord called "that old fox" (see Luke 13:32) and told him that he had no right to be married to another man's wife. I tell you, a preacher doesn't make himself popular when he says that kind of thing! Old Herod had John the Baptist killed by chopping off his head.

However, it is the young foxes that get into the contemporary church and cause trouble. The little sins spoil the fellowship among be-

lievers and spoil a Christian's life. For example there are the little sins of omission. "Therefore to him that knoweth to do good, and doeth it not, to him it is sin" (James 4:17). Here is one of those little foxes. This is the sin of omission. How often we see something that we should do for God, but we don't do it. How often have we sinned in this way? We are told that the Lord Jesus went about doing good.

> I read
> In a book
> Where a man called
> Christ
> Went about doing good.
> It is very disconcerting
> To me
> That I am so easily
> Satisfied
> With just
> Going about.
> —Author unknown

How often we have intended to write a letter, but we didn't write it. How often we have intended to do something for missions, but we neglected to do it. How many times we should have been praying for someone, but we neglected to pray. We think of the words of the prophet Samuel: ". . . God forbid that I should sin against the LORD in ceasing to pray for you . . ." (1 Sam. 12:23). These are little sins of omission. They are the little foxes that spoil the vineyard.

Here is another of those little foxes. ". . . Whatsoever is not of faith is sin" (Rom. 14:23). How often do we take a step on our own, but we try to call it a step of faith. We know it is not really faith; we know we just want to have our way. That is a sin. It is a little fox. It gets in and spoils the work of God. We have a tendency to lean on that very lame and broken reed and try to hold ourselves up with it and maintain a pious attitude. We say, "I am doing this because God is leading me," when we know it is not true. We say it so lightly. Romans tells us that whatever we do that is not of faith is sin.

Showing partiality is another little fox that is seen among God's people. James lowers the boom on that: "But if ye have respect [show partiality] to persons, ye commit sin, and are convinced of the law as transgressors" (James 2:9). I have had this happen to me just as James described it. I went to a certain church just to visit, not wanting to be recognized. I wanted to hear the preacher. When I went in, the usher was absolutely insulting to me. He said, "You wait right here." Then he came back and said, "Well, I don't have a seat for you. You'll have to stand here in the back." He looked at me for a moment, then said, "Oh, you're Dr. McGee! I'll get a chair and let you sit right here!" How tragic it is to see in some churches a well-known or a wealthy man acknowledged in the service and some poor man, who probably is more godly, absolutely ignored. That is a little fox that really wrecks God's work in our day.

Then there is the little fox of not giving freely to God. It is not the amount of the giving that is the only thing that is wrong about it. It is the attitude of giving, the hypocrisy of it all. We sing songs such as, "Were the whole realm of nature mine, that were a present far too small"—then we put a quarter into the collection plate! We actually sing lies. We pretend we have given ourselves and all that we have to the Lord. Oh, my friend, it is the little foxes that are destroying a lot of the grapes today.

## THE NIGHT BEFORE DAYBREAK

The next wonderful statement follows closely after the song of the bridegroom's return, which is symbolic of the Rapture, that is, Christ's coming again for the church.

**My beloved is mine, and I am his: he feedeth among the liles [Song 2:16].**

This Song of Solomon expresses the highest spiritual state of the relationship between the Lord Jesus Christ and the believer. There is no other book of the Bible which portrays this relationship any better than this little book, and there is no higher plane than this right here: "My beloved is mine, and I am his." This is one of the deepest, most profound of all theological truths which our Lord Jesus put into seven simple words: ". . . ye in me, and I in you" (John 14:20). The bride says, "My beloved is mine, and I am his."

The Lord Jesus said in effect, "Down here I took your place when I died on the cross. I am in you. Now you are to show forth My life down here in this world." (Of course we can only do that in the power of the Holy Spirit.) But we are *in Him* up there—seated in the heavenly places, accepted in the Beloved, joined to Him, risen with Christ. "If ye then be risen with Christ, seek those things which are above, where Christ sitteth on the right hand of God" (Col. 3:1). How wonderful! Oh, my friend, if you are a child of God, why don't you tell Him that you *love* Him?

You and I live in a day when we may not have very much of this world's goods; yet we

are *rich*. We don't glory in men; we glory in Christ. "Therefore let no man glory in men. For all things are yours; Whether Paul, or Apollos, or Cephas, or the world, or life, or death, or things to come; all are yours; And ye are Christ's; and Christ is God's" (1 Cor. 3:21–23). We belong to Christ. He is ours. He belongs to us. He is our Savior. He is our Shepherd. We ought to draw very close to Him and appropriate these wonderful spiritual blessings that are ours. It is a high level of spiritual life when you and I can say, "My beloved is mine, and I am his."

"He feedeth among the lilies." This again refers to the flower-strewn couch upon which He reclines at the banqueting table. It speaks of satisfaction, of fellowship, of joy, of everything that is wonderful. This world is seeking these things. This world is looking for a good time. This world wants to "live it up." Well, let's have a good time and live it up by sitting at Christ's table and rejoicing in Him. This is a high spiritual level. I'm afraid that many of us do not ". . . attain unto it" (Ps. 139:6). Therefore we have to cry out as the bride did, "Draw me, we will run after thee." We can't run, we cannot run the race that is set before

us until we not only see Jesus but *appropriate* His power in our lives. "My beloved is mine, and I am his."

**Until the day break, and the shadows flee away, turn, my beloved, and be thou like a roe or a young hart upon the mountains of Bether [Song 2:17].**

We come back to that picture of Christ as the hind of the morning. Remember that we saw Him on that bright morning (v. 8) standing on the mountain peak in triumph. All during the night the hunters had been after His life, and the fierce dogs had been leaping at Him. How terrible it was! He went down through the doorway of death, but He came up through the doorway of resurrection. Now, in light of that, although you and I are presently living in a dark world, we can look forward to the daybreak. My friend, let the redemption that you have in Christ, and all that He has done for you, be meaningful to you. Rest upon that. Let that be your comfort; let that be the pillow for your head during the dark hours of this life—"until the day break, and the shadows flee away."

# CHAPTER 3

As we begin chapter 3 we are still in the second song, but I would say that we have come to the second stanza of it. However, this does begin a new section, which is set in an altogether different scene.

At the beginning of this book we were up in the hill country of Ephraim where we saw a girl and her family who were tenant farmers. Now Solomon has won her heart and has brought her back with him to Jerusalem.

## THE MIDNIGHT SEARCH

**By night on my bed I sought him whom my soul loveth: I sought him, but I found him not.**

**I will rise now, and go about the city in the streets, and in the broad ways I will seek him whom my soul loveth: I sought him, but I found him not [Song 3:1–2].**

Now the scene has shifted to the palace in Jerusalem to which the king has taken

her. She has been left alone—the king, perhaps, being away on business. What is recorded here is a dream that reflects the anguish of their separation in which she finally goes out to look for him in the streets of the city.

"By night on my bed I sought him." This has a marvelous spiritual application to our relationship with Christ. When we have a big day ahead of us, we think we must have a good night's sleep. If sleep is preferred to Christ, we may get in our eight hours, but we have lost Him who is far better than rest. A. Moody Stuart has put it like this: "But if Christ is first and best and most necessary, if he is more to us than food or sleep, he is often, though not always, quickly found, without actual loss either of the time or of the sleep which we were willing to sacrifice for his sake. Our sleep is then sweet unto us and refreshing, for the Lord himself is dwelling in us, and resting with us."

"I will rise now, and go about the city in the

streets." The getting out of bed and going about the city in her search indicates a determination to seek the Lord.

"I sought him, but I found him not." This is her honest confession. A great many folk never find Christ because they never seek Him. Oh, how many Christians sit in a church pew every Sunday and never face honestly the fact: "I found Him not." However, He has promised that He will be found of those who seek Him with their whole heart. Or, as James put it, "Draw nigh to God, and he will draw nigh to you . . ." (James 4:8).

**The watchmen that go about the city found me: to whom I said, Saw ye him whom my soul loveth? [Song 3:3].**

The watchmen seem to have been helpful in directing her to the Beloved. At least, it was only a short distance from them that she found Him.

**It was but a little that I passed from them, but I found him whom my soul loveth: I held him, and would not let him go, until I had brought him into my mother's house, and into the chamber of her that conceived me [Song 3:4].**

Oh, my friend, what a tremendous reward for her search—"I found him whom my soul loveth!" Again I quote A. Moody Stuart (p. 231): "I found him—I, a man, found the Lord of Glory; I, a slave to sin, found the great Deliverer; I, the child of darkness, found the Light of life; I, the uttermost of the lost, found my Saviour, and my God; I, widowed and desolate, found my Friend, my Beloved, my Husband! Go and do likewise, sons and daughters of Zion, and He will be found of you, 'for then shall ye find, when ye search with all your heart.' "

"I held him, and would not let him go." Maintaining unbroken fellowship with Christ requires effort on our part. It is easy to let other interests crowd into our lives so that we lose the sense of His presence. Stuart has well said, "Unheld, the King will go away; He is willing to be held, yet not willing to remain without being held." (This, of course, has no reference to a believer losing his salvation, but of losing his fellowship with Christ.)

"I . . . brought him into my mother's house, and into the chamber of her that conceived me." When she found Him, she went right back to the place where she had been born, where she had met Him. Many of us need to get back to that first love. Do you remember when you came to Christ? Do you remember how much He meant to you then?

**I charge you, O ye daughters of Jerusalem, by the roes, and by the hinds of the field, that ye stir not up, nor awake my love, till he please [Song 3:5].**

Now that wonderful fellowship with Him is restored.

## THE ENTRANCE OF SOLOMON WITH HIS BRIDE

This last part of the chapter is a little gem in itself. It depicts the return of the king for his bride. This little Shulamite girl had waited a long time for the return of the shepherd to whom she had given her heart. One day she is out in the vineyard working. Down the road there comes a pillar of smoke, and the cry is passed along from one group of peasants to another, "Behold, King Solomon is coming!"—but she has work to do. Then someone comes to her excitedly, saying, "Oh, King Solomon is asking for *you!*" Mystified, she says, "Asking for *me*? I don't know King Solomon!" But when she is brought into his presence, she recognizes that he is her shepherd-lover who has come for her.

He places her at his side in the royal chariot and the procession sweeps on, leaving the amazed country folk speechless at the sudden change in the position of her who had been just one of them.

How beautifully this pictures the glorious reality of the return of Christ, our Beloved, when He comes for His own. "For the Lord himself shall descend from heaven with a shout, with the voice of the archangel, and with the trump of God: and the dead in Christ shall rise first: Then we which are alive and remain shall be caught up together with them in the clouds, to meet the Lord in the air: and so shall we ever be with the Lord" (1 Thess. 4:16-17).

**Who is this that cometh out of the wilderness like pillars of smoke, perfumed with myrrh and frankincense, with all powders of the merchant? [Song 3:6].**

This is a description of Solomon as he rides into Jerusalem with his bride. The glory that was Solomon's is beyond description. We will get a glimpse of it in the next few verses.

We as believers are to go through this world as witnesses of the Lord Jesus Christ. As witnesses we are made new in Christ. Each of us is like the bride who is brought before the Bridegroom and the fragrance of Christ should be upon us as we witness to the

world—"perfumed with myrrh and frankincense." How wonderful the Lord Jesus is! The myrrh speaks of His death and the frankincense of His life. Both were sweet; both were glorious.

**Behold his bed, which is Solomon's; threescore valiant men are about it, of the valiant of Israel [Song 3:7].**

His "bed" is the traveling couch in which the King is carried by bearers.

"Threescore valiant men are about it, of the valiant of Israel." They are living in days of danger. These are the guards, and they are there for his protection. They are the Secret Service men who have charge of his person to watch over him.

May I say that I think that we need to guard the person of the Lord Jesus. In other words we need to declare our belief in the deity of Jesus Christ, that He was God manifest in the flesh. We must reject the teaching of liberalism. We must reject anything that makes Him just a human Jesus. He was God manifest in the flesh.

**They all hold swords, being expert in war: every man hath his sword upon his thigh because of fear in the night [Song 3:8].**

Notice that the guards all have swords. The Scriptures tell us that our sword is the Word of God. They are "expert in war." And we need to know how to use the Word of God. The Word of God is the sword of the Spirit, and that is the weapon of a good soldier of Jesus Christ.

**King Solomon made himself a chariot of the wood of Lebanon.**

**He made the pillars thereof of silver, the bottom thereof of gold, the covering of it of purple, the midst thereof being paved with love, for the daughters of Jerusalem [Song 3:9–10].**

He has a chariot made out of the cedars of Lebanon. "The bottom thereof of gold"—imagine, the floor made of gold!

"The midst thereof being paved with love, for [or from] the daughters of Jerusalem." Solomon's chariot is adorned by the needlework of the women of Jerusalem. What beauty there is. But, also, what tremendous emotion and love is displayed there.

**Go forth, O ye daughters of Zion, and behold king Solomon with the crown wherewith his mother crowned him in the day of his espousals, and in the day of the gladness of his heart [Song 3:11].**

It says, "his mother crowned him." If you go back to the story in 1 Kings 1, you will find that David didn't really want to crown him. Another son of David, Adonijah, was carrying on a bit of strategy and was trying to get to the throne himself. David was an old man, and he didn't do anything at all about the situation. His favorite son, Absalom, had been killed, and David just didn't seem to have much heart for Solomon. So Nathan the prophet went to Bathsheba, the mother of Solomon, and said, "We'd better get busy or Adonijah may become the new king." So Bathsheba and Nathan went to King David, and King David said, "Well, bring him in. We'll make him the king." That is the way Solomon was made the king of Israel. I like the way it is stated here: "his *mother* crowned him." It was his mother who was interested in him. I really think that David was not much interested in making Solomon the new king, even though he was David's son.

"Behold king Solomon." This is a picture of Christ. Behold Him. Behold Him in His birth. Behold Him in His life. Behold Him in His death. Behold Him in His resurrection. Behold Him in His glory today. And behold Him as the One who is coming again for His bride.

This entire chapter except the last verse is the song of the bridegroom. It expresses Solomon's love for this girl whom he had met up in the hill country and had brought to town, as it were. I suppose that she wore shoes for the first time. Now she is wearing lovely dresses, and she sits at the table of Solomon. What a privilege she had, and she was rejoicing in it.

As we read this chapter, we should see that the Spirit of God is trying to show us Christ's love for us. It is expressed through this very wonderful and personal relationship. It shows to us the love of Christ for the church and His love for the individual believer. This is the love song of the Bridegroom, or the love song of the Lord Jesus Christ.

It is obvious that He speaks of the church when He says, "Thou art all fair, my love; there is no spot in thee" (v. 7). This is Christ speaking of the church, of each believer; He is speaking to you and me. Does that mean then that we are going to have to become perfect? Oh, no. In Ephesians Paul says, ". . . as Christ also loved the church, and gave himself for it; That he might sanctify and cleanse it with the washing of water by the word" (Eph. 5:25–26). He's already cleansed us by the blood; through His sacrifice we have the forgiveness of sin, so that there is no charge brought against us. But He is also going to sanctify us and cleanse us by the Word of God. "That he might present it to himself a glorious church, not having spot, or wrinkle, or any such thing; but that it should be holy and without blemish" (Eph. 5:27). *He* will be the One who will make the church without spot or wrinkle—we will be seen *in Christ*. Now He can look at the church and say, "Thou art all fair, my love; there is no spot in thee" because He removed the spot from the church and from each believer.

**Behold, thou art fair, my love; behold, thou art fair; thou hast doves' eyes within thy locks: thy hair is as a flock of goats, that appear from mount Gilead [Song 4:1].**

We find here a very minute description of this girl. It describes the parts of her body, if you please. Now there are two extreme viewpoints of marriage. One is that the emphasis is put upon sex. The other is that there is no emphasis put on sex, that marriage is such a high, holy state that sex doesn't enter into it at all. But when the emphasis is placed com-

pletely on sex, then the relationship becomes more like that between two animals. True marriage lies between these two extreme viewpoints. When the bridegroom holds the bride in his arms, their love, their physical love, is consummated.

**Thy teeth are like a flock of sheep that are even shorn, which came up from the washing; whereof every one bear twins, and none is barren among them.**

**Thy lips are like a thread of scarlet, and thy speech is comely: thy temples are like a piece of a pomegranate within thy locks [Song 4:2–3].**

This is how the bridegroom sees the bride. I'm sure every young fellow has looked into the eyes of some girl and told her what beautiful eyes she has. I met my wife when she was a young school teacher. She had black hair, black as a raven's wing, and dark brown eyes. Today there is some gray in that hair. I tell you, when I met her, I thought her hair was beautiful, and I told her so. I told her she had beautiful eyes. Now I never told her she had beautiful big toes, because I really don't think her big toes are beautiful. But I do think she is beautiful.

This reveals to us that the Lord Jesus not only loves us but the Lord Jesus *knows* us. We need to quit kidding ourselves, because we are not kidding Him at all. This means that we can go to Him and tell Him everything. There is no use in trying to cover up, no use in trying to use subterfuge, no use in trying to beat around the bush. We can tell Him everything that we have on our hearts. We can tell Him all about our weaknesses, about our sin, about all the things that are in our hearts and lives. That is the way to deal with them.

Do you have an inferiority complex? Then tell the Lord Jesus about it. He is the only One who has an answer for that. An eminent Christian psychologist here in Southern California years ago told me, "You can't get rid of an inferiority complex. All that the psychologist can do is to shift an inferiority complex from one place in the personality to another. The only place where anyone finds a solution to it is at the cross of Christ." I believe that is where people should go with their complexes. Augustine said that our hearts are restless until we come to the Lord. Paul wrote, "I can do all things through Christ which strengtheneth me" (Phil. 4:13). Maybe you don't even

need to get rid of your inferiority complex. It may help you to find your strength in Him. It may keep you from being a proud, arrogant Christian. It may help you to give all the glory to Him.

Do you have a bad habit which you would like to change? Then go to Him and confess it. He is rich in mercy. I think that for years I must have gone to Him two or three hundred times to tell Him about something. He was *rich* in mercy to me, which means He has a whole lot of it. Although I failed again and again, I kept going back in repentance. It was wonderful to go to Him. Do you know what happened? When the time came, He gave me the victory in *His* way. Our Lord moves in a mysterious way His wonders to perform. He doesn't follow my rules or your rules. He doesn't do it through some gimmick which men have worked out. He helps in His own time and His own way.

May I say to you, He knows us intimately. He knows every tiny detail of our lives. We should never be afraid to go to Him and tell Him everything.

**Until the day break, and the shadows flee away, I will get me to the mountain of myrrh, and to the hill of frankincense [Song 4:6].**

This is the place where we need to go for the solution to our problems. "The mountain of myrrh" is symbolic of the cross of Christ, because myrrh speaks of His death. That is where you will find comfort and salvation and help and hope.

"The hill of frankincense" refers to His life, but not simply His earthly life. Paul writes, "Wherefore henceforth know we no man after the flesh: yea, though we have known Christ after the flesh, yet now henceforth know we him no more" (2 Cor. 5:16)—now we know Him as the glorified Christ.

The solution to your problem is in knowing Christ. "Let this mind be in you, which was also in Christ Jesus" (Phil. 2:5). That, my friend, is the reason that I keep saying the answer is in the Word of God. It is ignorance of His Word that causes people to search elsewhere for answers. It makes a person vulnerable to false teachers who trade on and take advantage of those who are ignorant of the Word of God. But it is through the Word of God that we get acquainted with Jesus Christ and learn to sit at that round table in the banqueting hall which we have seen here in the Song of Solomon. There we can feast with Him, and find satisfaction and joy in Him.

You and I do not realize how much He really loves us. Listen to Him:

**Thou hast ravished my heart, my sister, my spouse; thou hast ravished my heart with one of thine eyes, with one chain of thy neck.**

**How fair is thy love, my sister, my spouse! how much better is thy love than wine! and the smell of thine ointments than all spices! [Song 4:9–10].**

The bridegroom speaking of the bride typifies the Lord Jesus speaking of believers, those who are His own. This is how much He loves us today. Oh, it would break your heart and my heart if we knew how much He loves us. Only the Spirit of God can make this love real to us. Some folks write out a little motto and stick it on their car bumper and then drive around with it. It says, "Jesus loves you." I wonder, how do you know He loves you? Have you experienced that love yourself? Are you conscious of His love right now? Oh, my friend, He loves you! Fall in love with Him.

Now the bride speaks:

**Awake, O north wind; and come, thou south; blow upon my garden, that the spices thereof may flow out. Let my beloved come into his garden, and eat his pleasant fruits [Song 4:16].**

Remember how the Lord Jesus taught His disciples in the Upper Room in that wonderful discourse that is found in John 13–17. In the midst of it, in John 14, we find that the Lord Jesus is interrupted again and again by the disciples asking Him questions. The last one to interrupt Him was Judas. Have you ever noticed the question which he asked the Lord? "Judas saith unto him, not Iscariot, Lord, how is it that thou wilt manifest thyself unto us, and not unto the world?" (John 14:22). He is saying in effect, "Lord, it is wonderful to be here. You are revealing these wonderful truths about Yourself to us, but what about the world outside?"

Now the bride is getting the message. "O north wind"—that north wind is cold, and it may cause the bride to get very cold. But, "*Awake*, O north wind." Why? That this spice, this wonderful fragrance might be blown out to others and they might enjoy it. Dr. Ironside adds: "It indicates her yearning desire to be all that he would have her to be." The north wind, he continues, is "that cold, bitter, biting,

wintry blast. Naturally she would shrink from that as we all would, and yet the cold of winter is as necessary as the warmth of summer if there is going to be perfection in fruitbearing. It takes the cold to bring out the flavor of apples. And it is so with our lives. We need the north winds of adversity and trial as well as the zephyrs of the south so agreeable to our natures. The very things we shrink from are the experiences that will work in us to produce the peaceable fruits of righteousness. If everything were easy and soft and beautiful in our lives, they would be insipid; there would be so little in them for God that could delight

His heart; and so there must be the north wind as well as the south."

It is this kind of life that the Lord Jesus uses to reach the world. He has not forgotten the world.

The bride says to her beloved, "Let my beloved come into his garden, and eat his pleasant fruits." This is an invitation he will accept. And in that Upper Room the Lord Jesus said to His questioning disciples, ". . . If a man love me, he will keep my words: and my Father will love him, and we will come unto him, and make our abode with him" (John 14:23).

# CHAPTER 5

In this chapter there seems to be a certain amount of conflict in the mind of the bride about whether they should spend time in fellowship and communion or in going out to discharge their responsibilities. Both are essential. We need to be doing both. We need to sit at the feet of Jesus, but we also need to follow those feet as they go out on the hillsides looking for the lost sheep. We need to follow those feet out into the world, which is a field in which to plant the seed of the Word of God.

**I am come into my garden, my sister, my spouse: I have gathered my myrrh with my spice; I have eaten my honeycomb with my honey; I have drunk my wine with my milk: eat, O friends; drink, yea, drink abundantly, O beloved [Song 5:1].**

He is inviting her to join with him in fellowship. Our Lord says, "Behold, I stand at the door, and knock: if any man hear my voice, and open the door, I will come in to him, and will sup with him, and he with me" (Rev. 3:20). That is the fellowship we need. And in connection with fellowship, John writes, ". . . These things write we unto you, that your joy may be full" (1 John 1:4). Not only does He want us to have fellowship, but He wants us to have a good time. Are you having a good time as a Christian?

Wonderful letters come to me in response to our radio broadcasts. There are people in hospitals and in rest homes who tell about their sufferings and the diseases with which they are afflicted. But they also write about the

wonderful fellowship they have with the Lord Jesus. The tears came to my eyes when I read a letter from one dear lady, who wrote, "At night when the nurse tucks me in I cannot sleep but lie awake for another hour or two. During that time I pray for you until I go to sleep. Then I wake up about 4:30 in the morning and I pray for you again." Then she continues in her letter to tell how wonderful it is to have fellowship with the Lord Jesus. That is beautiful!

## THE WAKING SLEEP

Now we come to the fourth canticle, or the fourth song. These are like folk songs. Now it is the bride who speaks.

**I sleep, but my heart waketh: it is the voice of my beloved that knocketh, saying, Open to me, my sister, my love, my dove, my undefiled: for my head is filled with dew, and my locks with the drops of the night [Song 5:2].**

She says her heart is awake. She is on the alert, watching for him.

"The voice of my beloved"—he has been busy out in the night while the bride crawled into bed.

The church needs to hear this message today. All believers need to hear this message. Let's get out of bed and get busy. If the Lord has given us health, let us start moving out for Him.

**I have put off my coat; how shall I put it on? I have washed my feet; how shall I defile them? [Song 5:3].**

Now she starts to rationalize. She is already in bed. She has washed her feet to go to bed, and she doesn't want to get out of bed and get her feet dirty.

**My beloved put in his hand by the hole of the door, and my bowels were moved for him [Song 5:4].**

Her "bowels," that is, her emotions, were moved for him.

**I rose up to open to my beloved; and my hands dropped with myrrh, and my fingers with sweet smelling myrrh, upon the handles of the lock [Song 5:5].**

The background for this was a lovely custom that they had in that day. When a man was in love with a girl and wanted to express his love, he would go to her home and instead of leaving a calling card, he would leave a fragrance. The door was so constructed as to leave an opening so that one could reach through to the inside and remove the bar unless it was locked as well as barred—which was the case on this occasion. When there was no response from the sleeping bride, the bridegroom placed myrrh on the inside handle of the door to let her know that he had been there. When she finally came to open the door, the wonderful fragrance was transferred to her fingers. He had left the sweetness of his presence.

The bride is a picture of the church today. The church doesn't go very far from home. Very few get out from under the shadow of the church steeple. Most folks don't even get off the church steps. As a result, they have lost fellowship with the Lord Jesus. Actually, that is one of those little foxes which destroy the grapes. We lose our fellowship when we step out of the will of God. That is what it means to quench the Spirit (see 1 Thess. 5:19). It is quenching the Spirit to refuse to go where He wants us to go or to do what He wants us to do.

I think that if we today would get up off our beds, begin to move out and start doing something for God, we would find the sweetness of His presence on the handle of our own bed chamber. We would experience the sweetness of His fellowship.

This is the briefest of the songs, but what a little gem it is!

## THE SORROWING SEARCH FOR THE BELOVED

Now we come to the fifth song. In this love story King Solomon has brought this humble Shulamite girl from the hill country of Ephraim to the palace in Jerusalem. In these songs the bride reveals how impressed she is by everything there—the palace, the throne, and the banquet table of the king. Her song includes her worship and adoration of the king.

But when he came to rouse her to come with him as he was out doing his work as a shepherd, looking for the sheep that were lost, she didn't want to get out of bed. When she finally did go to the door, he was gone. She opened the door and called to him, then she went out to look for him.

**I opened to my beloved; but my beloved had withdrawn himself, and was gone: my soul failed when he spake: I sought him, but I could not find him; I called him, but he gave me no answer [Song 5:6].**

You see, the fellowship had been broken.

I personally believe that there are a great many Christians who have done one of two things: they have grieved the Spirit by sin in their lives, or they have quenched the Spirit by not being obedient to Him. That breaks fellowship with Him and causes us to lose our joy. It does not mean that we lose our salvation, but we will surely lose the *joy* of our salvation. It does not mean that we have lost the Holy Spirit. He still indwells the believer. We can grieve Him, but we cannot grieve Him away. However, we certainly can lose fellowship with Him, and many Christians are in that position.

Sometime ago a man said to me, "You speak of the reality of Christ in your life. I don't have it." That was a dead giveaway that he was quenching the Spirit of God. He was out of the will of God. I know the man quite well, and I believe the problem was that he was doing what *he* wanted to do instead of doing what he knew was the will of God. A person can try to mask the truth and say that he is doing the will of God. If he does not have the joy of the Lord, it is a giveaway that he is actually doing his own will.

The bride here has lost her fellowship. I tell you, if you are not doing something for the Lord, you haven't lost your salvation, but you surely are missing sweet fellowship with Him.

**The watchmen that went about the city found me, they smote me, they wounded me; the keepers of the walls took away my veil from me [Song 5:7].**

Do you realize how impotent and powerless we are if we attempt to go out on our own? We

may go out with a great deal of enthusiasm, but enthusiasm will never replace fellowship with Him. Today there is a lot of enthusiasm for knocking on doors and witnessing to people. There are certain people who ought to be doing that; there are others who had better not. I have a friend in another state who, when I am there, asks me to play golf with him. I enjoy playing with him, but I have discovered that he is a man who lacks tact even though he has a zeal to witness for the Lord. I have seen him make waitresses angry. I have seen him make strangers that we meet angry. He says to me, "You know, there is surely a lot of opposition to the gospel today, isn't there?" Well, I couldn't help but say to him, "I don't think there is as much opposition as you think there is. It might have something to do with the way we present the gospel."

Then I called his attention to the way the Lord Jesus witnessed to the woman at the well. One of the most hostile persons that the Lord Jesus ever approached was that Samaritan woman who came down to the well. She was defiant. Have you ever noticed how He approached her? He didn't approach her as if He had something to cram down her throat. He asked her for a drink of water. He took the lowly place by asking her for something. Then He very courteously said, "Oh, I could have given you living water if you had asked for it." Finally she did ask for it, but He didn't offer it until she asked for it.

Before we attempt to cram the gospel down the throats of people, we need to give them a little appetite for it. They should see something in our lives that will make them *want* to know about the Lord Jesus.

However, it is true that there is an opposition to the Word of God, and we find it coming sometimes from unexpected quarters.

"The watchmen that went about the city found me, they smote me." This girl is having a difficult time. She is being hurt by those who should have been protecting her.

This same situation occurs in Christian circles. Many a preacher in our society finds himself deserted by a board that has turned against him because his preaching bothers their consciences. Many times opposition to the gospel comes from those who should be protecting it.

Now this girl, the bride, meets the daughters of Jerusalem. Here we find antiphonal singing. The bride sings one part, and the daughters of Jerusalem sing an answering part. This sounds very much like an opera.

The bride says:

**I charge you, O daughters of Jerusalem, if ye find my beloved, that ye tell him, that I am sick of love [Song 5:8].**

"If you find him, tell him how much I miss him. Tell him how much I love him, and let him know that I am looking for him." Her heart is sick and her whole being is yearning after him. The garden has lost its fragrance; the myrrh and frankincense don't mean much to her now; and the beauty of the flowers has withered.

Now in this antiphony the daughters of Jerusalem answer:

**What is thy beloved more than another beloved, O thou fairest among women? what is thy beloved more than another beloved, that thou dost so charge us? [Song 5:9].**

Their answer sounds rather skeptical. In effect they are saying, "This one that you say means so much to you, why is he more to you than you might expect another to be to us?" "What is thy beloved more than another beloved?" Who is this Jesus anyway? What makes you think Jesus is different from anyone else? There have been other great religious leaders. Why do you think that Jesus is different from them? Why do you think that He is who He claims to be? Jesus was only a man. That is the kind of skepticism we hear.

May I say to you, there has been a lot of discussion about Jesus. There has been more controversy about Him than any person who has ever lived. He is the most controversial figure in history. Let me ask you a question. If someone today tried to show that Julius Caesar was a real rascal, would you get all excited about it and rise to his defense? If someone tried to show that Julius Caesar was a saint, would you be all excited about that and try to argue about it? It wouldn't excite me. I'd let anyone think whatever he wanted to think about Julius Caesar. I wouldn't argue with him. But the minute you mention Jesus Christ, the whole human family chooses sides. It is interesting that God forces us to make a decision about His Son. He wouldn't let Pilate off without making a decision. Pilate tried to evade any involvement. He called for a basin of water and washed his hands, saying, ". . . I am innocent of the blood of this just person . . ." (Matt. 27:24). How wrong he was! The oldest creed of the church, which has been recited for over nineteen hundred years by multitudes of people, includes these words: "Crucified under Pontius Pilate." Pontius Pi-

late, you didn't wash your hands; you made a decision. God forced you to make a decision. Pilate thought that he was the judge and that Jesus was the prisoner. He didn't realize that Christ was the judge and he was the prisoner. And still in our contemporary society every man must make a decision.

"What is thy beloved more than another beloved?" In anthologies of religion, great religious leaders are listed who are called founders of religions: Moses, Jesus, Mohammed, Ghandi, Buddha, and all the rest. According to Tertullian, the early church father, the Christians in the early church would rather have died than have Jesus put down on a place with the heathen deities of the Roman Empire. They refused to even take a pinch of incense and place it before the image of Caesar. They just wouldn't do it, because their Beloved was different; He was God.

## THE BEAUTY OF THE BELOVED

Now the bride is going to answer. She is going to respond to their skepticism. You would think that they had her cooled off and that she would tone down what she says about the bridegroom. But it didn't work that way. Actually, she now waxes eloquent concerning him.

**My beloved is white and ruddy, the chiefest among ten thousand.**

**His head is as the most fine gold, his locks are bushy, and black as a raven.**

**His eyes are as the eyes of doves by the rivers of waters, washed with milk, and fitly set.**

**His cheeks are as a bed of spices, as sweet flowers: his lips like lilies, dropping sweet smelling myrrh.**

**His hands are as gold rings set with the beryl: his belly is as bright ivory overlaid with sapphires.**

**His legs are as pillars of marble, set upon sockets of fine gold: his countenance is as Lebanon, excellent as the cedars.**

**His mouth is most sweet: yea, he is altogether lovely. This is my beloved, and this is my friend, O daughters of Jerusalem [Song 5:10–16].**

There is something here that is very obvious, and that is that she describes him in minute detail. Do you know what that means? It means that she knew him. She knew him intimately.

My friend, if you are going to defend the Lord Jesus Christ today, if you are going to witness for Him, you must know Him. Not only do you need to know who He is, but you need to know Him enough to be able to wax eloquent on His behalf. When I say be eloquent, I don't necessarily mean eloquent in language. I mean full of enthusiasm, excitement, love, and zeal for His person. You and I need not only to know Him, but we must *love* Him. That is the challenge that we find here. The bride knew Him. She knew Him and she loved Him. She says that He is the chiefest among ten thousand.

Many people have written about the person of Christ because He is altogether lovely even in His humanity. Dr. C. I. Scofield, the man who wrote the first notes for *The Scofield Reference Bible*, wrote about the Lord Jesus in a tract he entitled, "The Loveliness of Jesus." Let me share part of it with you:

All other greatness has been marred by littleness, all other wisdom has been flawed by folly, all other goodness has been tainted by imperfection; Jesus Christ remains the only Being of whom, without gross flattery, it could be asserted, "He is altogether lovely."

My theme, then, is: The Loveliness of Christ.

First of all, as it seems to me, this loveliness of Christ consists in His perfect humanity. Am I understood? I do not now mean that He was a perfect human, but that He was perfectly human.

In everything but our sins, and our evil natures, He is one with us. He grew in stature and in grace. He labored, and wept, and prayed, and loved. He was tempted in all points as we are—sin apart. With Thomas, we confess Him Lord and God; we adore and revere Him, but beloved, there is no other who establishes with us such intimacy, who comes so close to these human hearts of ours; no one in the universe of whom we are so little afraid. He enters as simply and naturally into our twentieth century lives as if He had been reared in the same street. He is not one of the ancients. How wholesomely and genuinely human He is! Martha scolds Him; John, who has seen Him raise the dead, still the tempest and

talk with Moses and Elijah on the mount, does not hesitate to make a pillow of His breast at supper. Peter will not let Him wash his feet, but afterwards wants his head and hands included in the ablution. They ask Him foolish questions, and rebuke Him, and venerate and adore Him all in a breath; and He calls them by their first names, and tells them to fear not, and assures them of His love. And in all this He seems to me altogether lovely.

He is altogether lovely. Now the important question is this: Is He altogether lovely to you? Are you able to speak of Him with the enthusiasm the bride had for her bridegroom? We must know Christ intimately if we are to witness of Him. And we must love Him. When one comes to Christ it is not a business transaction. He is wonderful, and I do not think that we laud Him, glorify Him, lift Him up, worship Him, and bow before Him with thanksgiving enough. He is wonderful any way that you look at Him.

Let me quote again from Dr. Scofield's essay:

The saintliness of Jesus is so warm and human that it attracts and inspires. We find in it nothing austere and inaccessible, like a statue in a niche. The beauty of His holiness reminds one rather of a rose, or a bank of violets.

Jesus receives sinners and eats with them—all kinds of sinners. Nicodemus, the moral, religious sinner, and Mary of Magdala, "out of whom went seven devils"—the shocking kind of sinner. He comes into sinful lives as a bright, clear stream enters a stagnant pool. The stream is not afraid of contamination but its sweet energy cleanses the pool.

I remark again, and as connected with this that His sympathy is altogether lovely.

He is always being "touched with compassion." The multitude without a shepherd, the sorrowing widow of Nain, the little dead child of the ruler, the demoniac of Gadara, the hungry five thousand—what ever suffers touches Jesus. His very wrath against the scribes and Pharisees is but the excess of His sympathy for those who suffer under their hard self-righteousness.

Did you ever find Jesus looking for "deserving poor"? He "healed all their sick." And what grace in His sympathy! Why did He touch that poor leper? He could have healed him with a word as He did the nobleman's son. Why, for years the wretch had been an outcast, cut off from kin, dehumanized. He lost the sense of being a man. It was defilement to approach him. Well, the touch of Jesus made him human again.

A Christian woman, laboring among the moral lepers of London, found a poor street girl desperately ill in a bare, cold room. With her own hands she ministered to her, changing her bed linen, procuring medicines, nourishing food, a fire, and making the poor place as bright and cheery as possible, and then she said, "May I pray with you?"

"No," said the girl, "you don't care for me; you are doing this to get to heaven."

Many days passed with the Christian woman unwearily kind, the sinful girl hard and bitter. At last the Christian said:

"My dear, you are nearly well now, and I shall not come again, but as it is my last visit, I want you to let me kiss you," and the pure lips that had known only prayers and holy words met the lips defiled by oaths and by unholy caresses—and then, my friends, the hard heart broke. That was Christ's way.

As I read this essay from Dr. Scofield, my thoughts turn back to the very beginning of the Song of Solomon in chapter 1, verse 2: "Let him kiss me with the kisses of his mouth: for thy love is better than wine." He wants to bestow His love, His affection, His care, His grace, His mercy upon us today, and we are as hard as that poor sinning girl.

Again, I quote from Dr. Scofield:

Can you fancy Him calling a convention of the Pharisees to discuss methods of reaching the "masses"? That leads me to remark that His humility was altogether lovely, and He, the only one who ever had the choice of how and where He should be born, entered this life as one of the "masses."

What meekness, what lowliness! "I am among you as one that serveth." He "be-

gan to wash His disciples' feet." "When He was reviled He reviled not again." "As a sheep before her shearers is dumb, so He openeth not His mouth." Can you think of Jesus posing and demanding His rights?

But it is in His way with sinners that the supreme loveliness of Christ is most sweetly shown. How gentle He is, yet how faithful; how considerate, how respectful. Nicodemus, candid and sincere, but proud of his position as a master in Israel, and timid lest he should imperil it, "comes to Jesus by night." Before he departs "the Master," Nicodemus has learned his utter ignorance of the first step toward the kingdom, and goes away to think over the personal application of "they loved darkness rather than light, because their deeds were evil." But he has not heard one harsh word, one utterance that can wound his self-respect.

When He speaks to that silent despairing woman, after her accusers have gone out, one by one, He uses for "woman" the same word as He used when addressing His mother from the cross.

Follow Him to Jacob's well at high noon and hear His conversation with the woman of Samaria. How patiently He unfolds the deepest truths, how gently, yet faithfully He presses the great ulcer of sin which is eating away her soul. But He could not be more respectful to Mary of Bethany.

Even in the agonies of death He could hear the cry of despairing faith. When conquerors return from far wars in strange lands they bring their chiefest captive as a trophy. It was enough for Christ to take back to heaven the soul of a thief.

Yea, He is altogether lovely. And now I have left myself no room to speak of His dignity, of His virile manliness, of His perfect courage. There is in Jesus a perfect equipoise of various perfections. All the elements of perfect character are in lovely balance. His gentleness is never weak. His courage is never brutal. My friends, you may study these things for yourself. Follow Him through all the scenes of outrage and insult on the night and morning of His arrest and trial. Behold Him before the high priest, before Pilate, before Herod. See Him browbeaten, bullied, scourged, smitten upon the face, spit upon, mocked. How His inherent greatness comes out. Not once does He lose His self-poise, His high dignity.

Let me ask some unsaved sinner here to follow Him still further. Go with the jeering crowd without the gates; see Him stretched upon the great rough cross and hear the dreadful sound of the sledge as the spikes are forced through His hands and feet. See, as the yelling mob falls back, the cross, bearing this gentlest, sweetest, bravest, loveliest man, upreared until it falls into the socket in the rock. "And sitting down, they watched Him there." You watch, too. Hear Him ask the Father to forgive His murderers, hear all the cries from the cross. Is He not altogether lovely? What does it all mean?

"He bore our sins in His own body on the tree."

"By Him all that believe are justified from all things."

"Verily, verily, I say unto you, he that believeth on Me hath everlasting life."

I close with a word of personal testimony. This is my beloved, and this is my friend. Will you not accept Him as your Saviour, and beloved and friend?

That is the end of the quotation, and I want to add my own "Amen" to it. That means I agree with every word of it. My Beloved is the chiefest among ten thousand. He is the One who is altogether lovely.

Was it merely the son of Joseph and Mary who crossed the world's horizon more than nineteen hundred years ago? Was it merely human blood that was spilled on Calvary's hill for the redemption of sinners? What thinking man can keep from exclaiming, "My Lord and my God"?

"This is my beloved, and this is my friend, O daughters of Jerusalem" (v. 16). She knew Him. She loved Him. She makes Him known.

# CHAPTER 6

## FROM SKEPTICS TO BELIEVERS

**Whither is thy beloved gone, O thou fairest among women? whither is thy beloved turned aside? that we may seek him with thee [Song 6:1].**

The daughters of Jerusalem are not so skeptical and cynical now. They are willing to go with the bride to help her find him. They want to see this one whom the bride has told them about. They conclude that he must be wonderful, and they want to see him for themselves.

The Bible tells us that whoever seeks will find. The Lord Jesus has said that if anyone would come to Him, He would in nowise cast him out.

**My beloved is gone down into his garden, to the beds of spices, to feed in the gardens, and to gather lilies.**

**I am my beloved's, and my beloved is mine: he feedeth among the lilies [Song 6:2–3].**

She has located the bridegroom. What assurance, what satisfaction, what joy she has!

God is satisfied with Jesus. He has said, ". . . This is my beloved Son: hear him" (Luke 9:35). He is satisfied with the work which Christ accomplished for us on the cross. He says that if we will come to His Son, we will not perish but have everlasting life. What an invitation has gone out!

## THE KING'S DELIGHT IN THE BRIDE

**Thou art beautiful, O my love, as Tirzah, comely as Jerusalem, terrible as an army with banners.**

**Turn away thine eyes from me, for they have overcome me: thy hair is as a flock of goats that appear from Gilead.**

**Thy teeth are as a flock of sheep which go up from the washing, whereof every one beareth twins, and there is not one barren among them.**

**As a piece of a pomegranate are thy temples within thy locks.**

**There are threescore queens, and fourscore concubines, and virgins without number.**

**My dove, my undefiled is but one; she is the only one of her mother, she is the**

choice one of her that bare her. The daughters saw her, and blessed her; yea, the queens and the concubines, and they praised her [Song 6:4–9].

"Thou art beautiful, O my love, as Tirzah"—the beautiful expressions throughout this section are the bridegroom's response to the long, intense, sorrowful, and patient search for his presence. A. Moody Stuart gives us this helpful background: "Tirzah was the royal city of one of the ancient kings of Canaan, and afterwards for a time of the kings of Israel. The word signifies pleasant, and the situation of the city, as well as the town itself, was probably remarkable for beauty. . . . 'Beautiful as Tirzah'—how gracious the address to the slothful, sorrowing, smitten Bride! but 'whom he loveth he loveth unto the end,' though we change, He is 'the same yesterday, to-day, and for ever.' "

**Who is she that looketh forth as the morning, fair as the moon, clear as the sun, and terrible as an army with banners? [Song 6:10].**

This shows us how the Lord views the Rapture of the church. It is natural that we look at the Rapture from the viewpoint of our expectations: "For the Lord himself shall descend from heaven with a shout, with the voice of the archangel, and with the trump of God: and the dead in Christ shall rise first" (1 Thess. 4:16). But the Lord looks at it from His side. He will be calling His own. When the church comes into His presence, the angelic hosts will see one of the greatest sights that will be beheld in all of eternity. This will be the most thrilling event for us and for Him, too. Then they will say about the church, "Who is she that looketh forth as the morning, fair as the moon, clear as the sun, and terrible as an army with banners?" This same union of Christ and the church is pictured for us in the lives of Isaac and Rebekah. Isaac was walking in the field when he looked up and saw the caravan of camels coming. Rebekah was on one of the camels in that caravan. She got off the camel and came to meet her bridegroom. What a glorious picture of the time when you and I will go into the presence of the Lord Jesus.

## THE RESPONSE OF THE BRIDE

**I went down into the garden of nuts to see the fruits of the valley, and to see**

whether the vine flourished, and the pomegranates budded.

**Or ever I was aware, my soul made me like the chariots of Amminadib [Song 6:11–12].**

I just can't resist intruding here with a little anecdote. A friend of mine who is a preacher went to speak to a group of unbelievers. They were a group that included college professors. Many of their theories were way out in left field. They really understood very little about the real issues of life. I asked my friend, "What do you think you accomplished by going to that group?" He answered, "I don't know that I accomplished very much, but I was certainly scriptural. I went down into the garden of nuts." There's no question about that!

Seriously, the bride had something very different in mind. It is interesting that this is the third garden we see in the Song of Solomon. A. Moody Stuart calls our attention to this: "The first garden is in spring, full of flowers and tender grapes with nothing mature; the second garden is in autumn, full of spices and ripe fruits with nothing imperfect; and this third garden is in the end of winter, but with the immediate prospect of a new spring. . . . It is still winter, but the winter is on the very point of bursting in a new spring, and the Bride descends into the garden of nuts to watch the first sproutings of the valley, the earliest blossoming of the vine, and the budding of the pomegranate."

Stuart compares this to the experience of the disciples of our Lord after His ascension as they wait in Jerusalem for the promise of the Father. In a sense they go into the garden to watch for a fresh outbreak of a new spring. The entire Old Testament is a new treasure to them since Jesus had ". . . expounded unto them in all the scriptures the things concerning himself" (Luke 24:27). While gathering and breaking open those old treasures of the past, the Spirit came in an unexpected manner and with unexpected power, which could not be described more exactly than in the words of the Song, "or ever I was aware, my soul made me like the chariots of Amminadib."

My friend, the Word of God is a garden, a whole garden of unopened nuts. There are innumerable kernels in the Word of God waiting to be opened and enjoyed by the bride of Christ.

**Return, return, O Shulamite; return, return, that we may look upon thee. What will ye see in the Shulamite? As it were the company of two armies [Song 6:13].**

The statement is made that the bride of Christ will be for the demonstration of God's grace throughout the ages: "That in the ages to come he might shew the exceeding riches of his grace in his kindness toward us through Christ Jesus" (Eph. 2:7). All of the created universe is going to see us. None of us is worthy to be there, but we are going to be there because we are in Christ. It is because He loved us and gave Himself for us. We will be there for His glory and for our good. I can't think of anything better than that!

# CHAPTERS 7–8

## PORTRAIT OF THE BRIDE

In the first nine verses of chapter 7 the bridegroom tells of his delight in his bride, using one beautiful figure after another. Harry A. Ironside makes this comment: "It is a wonderful thing to know that the Lord has far more delight in His people than we ourselves have ever had in Him. Some day we shall enjoy Him to the fullest; some day He will be everything to us; but as long as we are here, we never appreciate Him as much as He appreciates us. But as she listens to his expression of love, her heart is assured; she has the sense of restoration and fellowship."

## SATISFACTION OF THE BRIDE

She says all she needs to say about her beloved in one verse:

**I am my beloved's, and his desire is toward me [Song 7:10].**

Twice before we have heard the bride say, "My beloved is mine, and I am his," but A.

Moody Stuart draws our attention to the fact that this is an expression of far greater fullness. Although it implies the outgoing of desire from the heart of Christ, it expressly declares what is much more precious: that the *believer* knows the strength of Christ's desire toward him. Stuart puts it this way: 'I know', saith the Lord, 'the thoughts that I think towards you, thoughts of good and not of evil'; the Lord who thinks them knows them, but he toward whom they are thought is often ignorant, or doubtful, or unbelieving regarding them; and most blessed are the souls that can respond, 'We have known and believed the love that God hath to us.' " *We* are objects of *His* desire—what wondrous grace!

## THE VERY BROTHER

**O that thou wert as my brother, that sucked the breasts of my mother! when I should find thee without, I would kiss thee; yea, I should not be despised [Song 8:1].**

"**M**y brother, that sucked the breasts of my mother" refers, of course, to a brother born of the same mother, implying the nearest possible relationship. It is this kind of a brother the Lord Jesus has become to us—"For verily he took not on him the nature of angels; but he took on him the seed of Abraham" (Heb. 2:16), becoming flesh of our flesh and bone of our bone.

"I would kiss thee; yea, I should not be despised." A great many true believers are afraid or ashamed to openly confess that they love Christ. Oh, my friend, don't *say* you love Him if you don't, but if your life reveals that you do love Him, folk will not despise you for speaking of it.

**I would lead thee, and bring thee into my mother's house, who would instruct me: I would cause thee to drink of spiced wine of the juice of my pomegranate [Song 8:2].**

"I would cause thee to drink of spiced wine of the juice of my pomegranate." Stuart has well said, "It is our part to give Christ the best entertainment in our power, to spare nothing on him, to gather all for him and present all to him, that is choicest and best. But the full reference of these words is to the final 'marriage of the Lamb when his wife shall have made herself ready,' and when Christ 'shall drink the fruit of the vine new with her in his Father's kingdom.' "

## THE RELYING WEAKNESS OF LOVE

**Who is this that cometh up from the wilderness, leaning upon her beloved? I raised thee up under the apple tree: there thy mother brought thee forth: there she brought thee forth that bare thee [Song 8:5].**

"**L**eaning upon her beloved." The final stage of the true believer's life is characterized by weakness, by dependence, and by love. In youth we ". . . mount[ed] up with wings as eagles . . ." (Isa. 40:31) when His banner over us was love. In manhood we ran without being wearied—even when (as Stuart says) we sought Him sorrowing through the streets of Jerusalem—but in our declining years we are more apt to lean heavily upon Him in childlike trust. And when we finally recognize our utter dependence upon Christ and the truth of His statement that without Him we can do *nothing*, then He can use our service.

**Set me as a seal upon thine heart, as a seal upon thine arm: for love is strong as death; jealousy is cruel as the grave: the coals thereof are coals of fire, which hath a most vehement flame [Song 8:6].**

"For love is strong as death." Death, with all its terrors, was the price of the love of the Lord Jesus Christ to lost men, but it did not deter Him—He loved us and gave Himself for us, enduring the cross and despising the shame. Also death has been ten thousand times before the bride of the slain Lamb, and she ". . . loved not [her life] . . . unto the death" (Rev. 12:11); for, ". . . neither death, nor life . . . shall be able to separate us from the love of God, which is in Christ Jesus our Lord" (Rom. 8:38–39).

"Jealousy is cruel as the grave"—the all-devouring grave knows no pity. Stuart reminds us that it was jealousy cruel as the grave that moved Elijah, who was very jealous for the Lord God of hosts, to slay the prophets of Baal at the brook Kishon and let not one escape. And "it was jealousy that stirred Paul to utter the righteous and holy, yet tremendous curse—'if any man love not the Lord Jesus Christ, let him be Anathema Maranatha.' This jealousy, with its grave-like cruelty, our protesting and suffering forefathers knew better than we; and it produced a remarkable but noble mingling of ardent love to Jesus with tenderness of conscience and manly boldness, which made little account

either of their lives or those of others, when placed in competition with the honour of the Lord Jesus Christ."

"The coals thereof are coals of fire." This reminds us of the love that burned in the heart of the Lord Jesus Christ when He said, ". . . The zeal of thine house hath eaten me up" (John 2:17). Stuart adds: "Ascending to the right hand of the Father, he kindled within the hearts of his disciples the same divine fire that burned within himself; sending down the Holy Ghost to rest upon them as flames or tongues of fire: and the fire of love burned more mightily within them, than the visible flames that encircled their heads."

**Many waters cannot quench love, neither can the floods drown it: if a man would give all the substance of his house for love, it would utterly be contemned [Song 8:7].**

"Many waters cannot quench love." Oh, how many times we have failed Him; yet our repeated failures have not quenched His love, nor has it been drowned by the floods of our sins.

"If a man would give all the substance of his house for love, it would utterly be contemned." The word *contemned* means to be loathed, despised. God is not asking for our money or our service; He is asking for our *love*. If we don't love Him, He *despises* the so-called Christian work we try to do and the money we put in the offering plate.

## THE LITTLE SISTER

**We have a little sister, and she hath no breasts: what shall we do for our sister in the day when she shall be spoken for? [Song 8:8].**

The "little sister" is, many Bible teachers feel, symbolic of the church of the Gentiles. "What shall we do for our sister" was the thorny question in the early church. Acts 15 records the Council at Jerusalem which was convened to resolve the conflict between the Gentile converts and the Hebrew converts who had no intention of giving up the Mosaic system.

"In the day when she shall be spoken for." Well, who would speak for her? Nobody would want her. Gentiles were outcasts. But the day came when this sister was spoken for by the great Bridegroom of the church who called her to Himself. My friend, He did not choose us because we were attractive, but because He saw our lost condition and loved us.

Now that the "little sister" is accepted by Christ, what kind of reception will she get from the elder sister?

**If she be a wall, we will build upon her a palace of silver: and if she be a door, we will enclose her with boards of cedar [Song 8:9].**

"If she be a wall, we will build upon her a palace of silver." Since the Gentiles were being accepted by God, they were being ". . . builded together [with the Hebrew Christians] for an habitation of God through the Spirit" (Eph. 2:22). The Jewish church faced the question: what should be built on it? Circumcision, ceremonies, different rites and ordinances—yokes which neither the Hebrew fathers nor children were able to bear? James expressed the feeling of the elder sister: ". . . my sentence is, that we trouble not them, which from among the Gentiles are turned to God" (Acts 15:19). The council agreed not to force Gentile believers into the Mosaic system, but to accept them as they were and do everything possible to build them up in the faith.

**I am a wall, and my breasts like towers: then was I in his eyes as one that found favour [Song 8:10].**

This is the rejoicing of the "little sister." When the gentile church received the good news of the council's decision, ". . . they rejoiced for the consolation" (Acts 15:31). Recognized now as a wall in God's temple, they greatly rejoiced in the privilege. "Now therefore ye are no more strangers and foreigners, but fellow-citizens with the saints, and of the household of God; And are built upon the foundation of the apostles and prophets, Jesus Christ himself being the chief corner stone; In whom all the building fitly framed together groweth unto an holy temple in the Lord: In whom ye also are builded together for an habitation of God through the Spirit" (Eph. 2:19–22).

"My breasts like towers"—the little sister, symbolic of the gentile church, soon nourished many sons and daughters with the sincere milk of the Word. The Gentile church grew with amazing rapidity so that the little sister now has become both more beautiful and more honored than the elder.

There is a missionary message in this parable of the little sister. You and I need to recognize that the little sister includes all nations in our day. In many parts of the world there are folk who have never responded to

the call of the Bridegroom simply because they have not heard His voice. And ". . . how shall they hear without a preacher?" (Rom. 10:14).

## THE TRANSFER OF THE VINEYARD

**Solomon had a vineyard at Baal-hamon; he let out the vineyard unto keepers; every one for the fruit thereof was to bring a thousand pieces of silver [Song 8:11].**

**"S**olomon had a vineyard." Solomon is symbolic of Christ. The bride, which is the united church of Jews and Gentiles, tells the story of the vineyard. First it was under the charge of its original keepers, the nation of Israel, and next it was committed to her own care. It is the same parable that Jesus told in Matthew 21:33–46 about a certain householder who planted a vineyard, put a wall around it, dug a winepress in it, and built a tower, then rented it out to vinegrowers while he went on a long journey. At harvest time he sent his servants to receive the produce, and they were beaten or killed. Finally he sent his own son. "But when the husbandmen saw the son, they said among themselves, This is the heir; come, let us kill him, and let us seize on his inheritance. And they caught him, and cast him out of the vineyard, and slew him. When the lord therefore of the vineyard cometh, what will he do unto those husbandmen?" (Matt. 21:38-40). The answer is that he will come and destroy the husbandmen and will give the vineyard to others.

**My vineyard, which is mine, is before me: thou, O Solomon, must have a thousand, and those that keep the fruit thereof two hundred [Song 8:12].**

"Those that keep the fruit thereof two hundred"—they are to be paid for their work. "Even so hath the Lord ordained that they which preach the gospel should live of the gospel" (1 Cor. 9:14).

"Thou, O Solomon, must have a thousand," promising, unlike her predecessor, that full revenue shall be the Lord's; yet she tends it with her whole heart as if it were her own— "my vineyard, which is mine, is before me."

Historically the early church kept the vine-

yard just that way. But, unfortunately, the church in our day presents a different picture. Oh that you and I, as members of the bride of Christ, will be faithful in the portion of the vineyard God has allotted to our care!

**Make haste, my beloved, and be thou like to a roe or to a young hart upon the mountains of spices [Song 8:14].**

The bride is saying to the Lord of the vineyard, "Return!" Over in the Book of Revelation the last thing she says is, ". . . Even so, come, Lord Jesus" (Rev. 22:20).

My friend, I don't believe you can honestly say that unless you *know* Him, unless you *love* Him, and unless you *make Him known*. Can you look up and say, "Come, Lord Jesus, I want you to come"? Paul said that God will give a crown to those who *love* His appearing. And to love His appearing means to love Him—even as a bride eagerly anticipates and prepares for the coming of the bridegroom, her beloved.

Let us conclude this marvelous Song of Solomon with the lines of Herbert:

Come, Lord, my head doth burn, my
   heart is sick,
  While thou dost ever, ever stay:
Thy long deferrings wound me to the
   quick,
  My spirit gaspeth night and day.
    O show thyself to me,
    Or take me up to thee!

Yet if thou stayest still, why must I stay?
  My God, what is this world to me?
This world of woe? hence all ye clouds,
   away!
  Away! I must get up and see.
    O show thyself to me,
    Or take me up to thee!

We talk of harvests; there are no such
   things,
  But when we leave our corn and hay.
There is no fruitful year, but that which
   brings
  The last and loved, though dreadful,
   day.
    O show thyself to me,
    Or take me up to thee!

# BIBLIOGRAPHY

(Recommended for Further Study)

Darby, J. N. *Synopsis of the Books of the Bible*. Addison, Illinois: Bible Truth Publishers.

DeHaan, Richard W. *The Art of Staying Off Dead-End Streets*. Grand Rapids, Michigan: Radio Bible Class, 1974. (A study in Ecclesiastes.)

Gaebelein, Arno C. *The Annotated Bible*. 1917. Reprint. Neptune, New Jersey: Loizeaux Brothers, 1971.

Goldberg, Louis. *Ecclesiastes*. Grand Rapids, Michigan: Zondervan Publishing House, 1983.

Gray, James M. *Commentary on the Whole Bible*. Old Tappan, New Jersey: Fleming H. Revell Co., 1906.

Jennings, F. C. *Meditations on Ecclesiastes*. Sunbury, Pennsylvania: Believer's Bookshelf, 1920.

Jensen, Irving L. *Ecclesiastes and the Song of Solomon*. Chicago, Illinois: Moody Press, 1974. (A self-study guide.)

Kaiser, Walter C. Jr. *Ecclesiastes: Total Life*. Chicago, Illinois: Moody Press, 1979.

Unger, Merrill F. *Unger's Bible Handbook*. Chicago, Illinois: Moody Press, 1966.

Unger, Merrill F. *Unger's Commentary on the Old Testament*. Vol. I. Chicago, Illinois: Moody Press, 1981.

# The Book of
# ISAIAH
## INTRODUCTION

Beginning with Isaiah and continuing through the Old Testament, there is a section of Scripture which is called the prophetic portion of the Bible. That does not mean that prophecy begins with Isaiah, because there are prophecies as far back as the Pentateuch, which was written by Moses. Although the predictive element bulks large in this section, the prophets were more than foretellers. They were men raised up by God in a decadent day when neither priest nor king was a worthy channel through which the expressions of God might flow.

These books of prophecy also contain history, poetry, and law, but their primary message is prophecy. Each writer, from Isaiah to Malachi, is a prophet of God. Today we make an artificial division of the prophets by designating them as the *major prophets* and the *minor prophets*. All of the prophets are in the major league as far as I am concerned—I don't think you can put any of them back in the minors. This artificial division was determined by the length of the book, not by content. Some of the minor prophets are like atom bombs—they may be small, but their content is potent indeed.

These prophets not only spoke of events in the distant future, but they also spoke of local events in the immediate future. They had to speak in this manner in order to qualify for the prophetic office under God according to the Mosaic code. Codes for the priest, the king, and the prophet are given in the Book of Deuteronomy. Note the code for the prophet: "But the prophet, which shall presume to speak a word in my name, which I have not commanded him to speak, or that shall speak in the name of other gods, even that prophet shall die. And if thou say in thine heart, How shall we know the word which the LORD hath not spoken? When a prophet speaketh in the name of the LORD, if the thing follow not, nor come to pass, that is the thing which the LORD hath not spoken, but the prophet hath spoken it presumptuously: thou shalt not be afraid of him" (Deut. 18:20–22). If the local event did not transpire *exactly* as the prophet predicted, he was labeled a false prophet and was so treated. You may be sure that the message of the false prophet is not in the library of inspired Scripture. The prophetic books are filled with events that are local and fulfilled.

If you had lived in Isaiah's day, how would you have known that he was a true prophet? You would have judged him on his local prophecies. He not only spoke of events far in the future, like the first and second comings of Christ, but he also spoke of local things that would happen in the near future. If his local predictions had not come to pass exactly the way they were given, he would have been recognized as a false prophet and stoned.

The prophetic books are filled with local prophecies already fulfilled. All of the prophets gave local prophecies to prove that they were genuine. Remember that a sharp distinction needs to be drawn between fulfilled and unfulfilled prophecy. When any prophecy was first given, it was of course unfulfilled. Since the time the prophecies were given, a great many of them have been fulfilled. One of the greatest evidences that these men were speaking the words of God is that hundreds of their prophecies have been fulfilled—fulfilled literally.

Man cannot guess the future. Even the weatherman has difficulty in prognosticating the weather for twenty-four hours in advance, although he has the advantage of all sorts of scientific and mechanical devices to assist him. The fact of the matter is that no weatherman that you and I listen to so intently would survive as a prophet in Israel!

The law of compound probability forbids man from consistently foretelling the future. Each uncertain element which he adds decreases his chance of accuracy 50 percent. The example of hundreds of prophecies which have had literal fulfillment has a genuine appeal to the honest mind and sincere seeker after the truth. Fulfilled prophecy is one of the infallible proofs of plenary verbal inspiration of Scripture.

Let me illustrate: Suppose I make a prophecy that it is going to rain tomorrow. I would have a fifty-fifty chance of being right. It is either going to rain or it is not going to rain—that is for sure. Now I will add another element to my prophecy by predicting that it will begin raining at eleven o'clock in the morning. That reduces my chance of being right another 50 percent, but I still have a 25 percent chance of being correct. But I don't stop there. I not

only say that it will start raining at eleven o'clock, but I also say that it will stop raining at three o'clock. I have reduced my chances again and have only a 12½ percent chance of being right. If I keep adding uncertain elements until I have three hundred prophecies, you know they would never be literally fulfilled. No man can guess like that. Only the Holy Spirit of God could give such information. A man would not have a ghost of a chance of being right that many times, and yet God's Word has over three hundred prophecies concerning the first coming of Christ, which have been literally fulfilled.

Why did God give so many prophecies concerning the first coming of Christ to earth? There is a logical and obvious answer. The coming of the Lord Jesus Christ to earth was an important event. God did not want the children of Israel to miss Him. God marked Him out so clearly that Israel had no excuse for not recognizing Him when He was here on this earth.

Let me use a homey illustration: Suppose I am invited to your hometown. You ask me, "When you arrive at the airport, how will I know you?" I would write back and say, "I am arriving at the airport at a certain time on a certain flight. I will be wearing a pair of green-checked trousers and a blue-striped coat. I will have on a big yellow polka dot necktie and a pink shirt with a large purple flower on it. I will be wearing one brown shoe and one black shoe and white socks. On my head you will see a derby hat, and I will be holding a parrot in a cage in one hand, and with the other hand I will be leading a jaguar on a chain." When you arrive at the airport, do you think you would be able to pick me out of the crowd?

When Jesus came to earth more than nineteen hundred years ago, those who had the Old Testament and knew what it said should have been waiting at the inn in Bethlehem or waiting for the news of His birth, because they had all the information they needed. When the wise men appeared, looking for the Lord Jesus, the Israelites at least should have been interested enough to hitch a ride on the back of the camels to take a look themselves. Oh, how tremendously important His coming was, and how clearly God had predicted it!

The prophets were extremely nationalistic. They rebuked sin in high places as well as low places. They warned the nation. They pleaded with a proud people to humble themselves and return to God. Fire and tears were mingled in their message, which was not one of doom and gloom alone, for they saw the Day of the Lord and the glory to follow. All of them looked through the darkness to the dawn of a new day. In the night of sin they saw the light of a coming Savior and Sovereign; they saw the millennial kingdom coming in all its fullness. Their message must be interpreted before an appreciation of the kingdom in the New Testament can be attained; the correct perspective of the kingdom must be gained through the eyes of the Old Testament prophets.

The prophets were not supermen. They were men of passions as we are, but having spoken for God, their message is still the infallible and inspired Word of God. This is substantiated by writers of the New Testament. Peter tells us: "Of which salvation the prophets have inquired and searched diligently, who prophesied of the grace that should come unto you: Searching what, or what manner of time the Spirit of Christ which was in them did signify, when it testified beforehand the sufferings of Christ, and the glory that should follow" (1 Pet. 1:10–11).

"Moreover I will endeavour that ye may be able after my decease to have these things always in remembrance. For we have not followed cunningly devised fables, when we made known unto you the power and coming of our Lord Jesus Christ, but were eyewitnesses of his majesty. For he received from God the Father honour and glory, when there came such a voice to him from the excellent glory, This is my beloved Son, in whom I am well pleased. And this voice which came from heaven we heard, when we were with him in the holy mount. We have also a more sure word of prophecy; whereunto ye do well that ye take heed, as unto a light that shineth in a dark place, until the day dawn, and the day star arise in your hearts: Knowing this first, that no prophecy of the scripture is of any private interpretation. For the prophecy came not in old time by the will of man: but holy men of God spake as they were moved by the Holy Ghost" (2 Pet. 1:15–21).

It was William Cowper who said, "Sweet is the harp of prophecy; too sweet not to be wronged by a mere mortal touch."

Most of the prophets moved in an orbit of obscurity and anonymity. They did not project their personalities into the prophecy they proclaimed. Jeremiah and Hosea are the exceptions to this, which we will see when we study their books. Isaiah gives us very little history concerning himself. There are a few scant references to his life and ministry. In Isaiah 1:1 he gives the times in which his life

was cast: during the reigns of Uzziah, Jothan, Ahaz, and Hezekiah, all kings of Judah. In Isaiah 6 he records his personal call and commission.

The days in which Isaiah prophesied were not the darkest days in Judah internally. Uzziah and Hezekiah were enlightened rulers who sought to serve God, but the days were extremely dark because of the menace of the formidable kingdom of Assyria in the north. The northern kingdom of Israel had already been carried away into captivity.

Isaiah 36–39 records the historical section of the ministry of Isaiah during the crisis when the Assyrian host encompassed Jerusalem. Beyond these few personal sections, Isaiah stands in the shadow as he points to Another who is coming, the One who is the Light of the world.

There are those who believe that Isaiah belonged to the royal family of David. This is supposition and certainly cannot be proven. Likewise it has been stated that he is referred to in Hebrews 11:37 as the one "sawn asunder."

Whether or not this is true, the liberal critic has sawn him asunder as the writer of the book. They have fabricated the ghastly theory that there are several Isaiahs. According to this theory the book was produced by ghost writers whom they have labeled "Deutero-Isaiah" and "Trito-Isaiah." The book will not yield to being torn apart in this manner, for the New Testament quotes from all sections of the book and gives credit to one Isaiah. The critics have cut up Isaiah like a railroad restaurant pie, but history presents only one Isaiah, not two or three.

A friend of mine, who has made quite a study of the Dead Sea Scrolls, tells me that Isaiah is the scroll the scholars work with the most. There is a great section of Isaiah intact, and only one Isaiah is presented. It is quite interesting that the Lord let a little shepherd boy reach down into a clay pot, in Qumran by the Dead Sea, and pick out a scroll that confounds the critics. The Lord will take care of the critics.

Let me illustrate how ridiculous the double or triple Isaiah hypothesis really is. Suppose a thousand years from today some archaeologists are digging in different parts of the world. One group digs in Kansas, another in Washington, D.C., and another group digs in Europe. They come up with the conclusion that there must have been three Dwight Eisenhowers. There was a General Eisenhower, the military leader of the victorious Allied forces of World War II in the European theater. There was another Eisenhower who was elected president of the United States in 1952 and 1956. There was still another Eisenhower, an invalid and victim of a heart attack and of a serious operation for ileitis. This illustration may seem ridiculous to some people, but that is exactly how I feel when I hear the critics talk about three Isaiahs. Of course there was only one man by the name of Dwight Eisenhower who fulfilled all the requirements without any absurdity. The same is true of Isaiah.

The prophecy of Isaiah is strikingly similar to the organization of the entire Bible. This similarity can be seen in the following comparison:

| BIBLE | ISAIAH |
|---|---|
| 66 Books | 66 Chapters |
| 39 Books—Old Testament | 39 Chapters—Law, Government of God |
| 27 Books—New Testament | 27 Chapters—Grace, Salvation of God |

There are sixty-six direct quotations from Isaiah in the New Testament. (Some have found eighty-five quotations and allusions to Isaiah in the New Testament.) Twenty of the twenty-seven books of the New Testament have direct quotations. Isaiah is woven into the New Testament as a brightly colored thread is woven into a beautiful pattern. Isaiah is discernible and conspicuous in the New Testament. Isaiah is chiseled into the rock of the New Testament with the power tool of the Holy Spirit. Isaiah is often used to enforce and enlarge upon the New Testament passages that speak of Christ.

The historic interlude (chs. 36–39) leaves the high plateau of prophecy and drops down to the record of history. Even the form of language is different. It is couched in the form of prose rather than poetry.

The third and last major division (chs. 40–66) returns to the poetic form but is in contrast to the first major section. In the first we had judgment and the righteous government of God; in the last we have the grace of God, the suffering, and the glory to follow. Here all is grace and glory. The opening "Comfort ye" sets the mood and tempo.

It is this section that has caused the liberal critics to postulate the Deutero-Isaiah hypothesis. A change of subject matter does not necessitate a change of authorship. It is interesting that for nineteen hundred years

there was not a word about a second Isaiah. John refers to this section as authored by Isaiah (see John 1:23). Our Lord likewise referred to this section as written by Isaiah (see Luke 4:17–21). Philip used a chapter from this section to win an Ethiopian to Christ (see Acts 8). There are numerous other references which confirm the authorship of Isaiah.

Isaiah prophesied many local events. When Jerusalem was surrounded by the Assyrian army, Isaiah made a very daring prophecy: "Therefore thus saith the LORD concerning the king of Assyria, He shall not come into this city, nor shoot an arrow there, nor come before it with shields, nor cast a bank against it" (Isa. 37:33). Also see Isaiah's prophecy concerning the sickness of Hezekiah in Isaiah 38.

There are other prophecies which were not fulfilled in his lifetime, but today they stand fulfilled. See, for instance, his prophecies concerning the city of Babylon: "And Babylon, the glory of kingdoms, the beauty of the Chaldees' excellency, shall be as when God overthrew Sodom and Gomorrah. It shall never be inhabited, neither shall it be dwelt in from generation to generation: neither shall the Arabian pitch tent there; neither shall the shepherds make their fold there. But wild beasts of the desert shall lie there; and their houses shall be full of doleful creatures; and owls shall dwell there, and satyrs shall dance there. And the wild beasts of the islands shall cry in their desolate houses, and dragons in their pleasant palaces: and her time is near to come, and her days shall not be prolonged" (Isa. 13:19–22).

Further fulfillments relative to Babylon are recorded in Isaiah 47. Excavations at Babylon have revealed the accuracy of these prophecies. More than fifty miles of the walls of Babylon have been excavated. The culture of this great civilization is still impressive but lies in dust and debris today according to the written word of Isaiah. This is one of many examples that could be given. Others will come before us in this study as we proceed through the book.

The New Testament presents the Lord Jesus Christ as its theme, and by the same token Isaiah presents the Lord Jesus Christ as his theme. Isaiah has been called the fifth evangelist, and the Book of Isaiah has been called the fifth gospel. Christ's virgin birth, His character, His life, His death, His resurrection, and His second coming are all presented in Isaiah clearly and definitively.

# OUTLINE

I. **Judgment (Poetry), Chapters 1–35**
   *Revelation of the sovereign on the throne*
   A. Solemn Call to the Universe to Come into the Court Room to Hear God's Charge against the Nation Israel, Chapter 1
   B. Preview of the Future of Judah and Jerusalem, Chapter 2
   C. Present View of Judah and Jerusalem, Chapter 3
   D. Another Preview of the Future, Chapter 4
   E. Parable of the Vineyard and Woes Predicated for Israel, Chapter 5
   F. Isaiah's Personal Call and Commission as Prophet, Chapter 6
   G. Prediction of Local and Far Events, Chapters 7–10
      *(Hope of future in coming child)*
   H. Millennial Kingdom, Chapters 11–12
   I. Burdens of Surrounding Nations (Largely Fulfilled), Chapters 13–23
      1. Burden of Babylon, Chapters 13–14
      2. Burden of Moab, Chapters 15–16
      3. Burden of Damascus, Chapter 17
      4. Burden of the Land beyond the Rivers of Ethiopia, Chapter 18
      5. Burden of Egypt, Chapters 19–20
      6. Burden of Babylon, Edom, Arabia, Chapter 21
      7. Burden of the Valley of Vision, Chapter 22
      8. Burden of Tyre, Chapter 23

   J. Kingdom, Process, and Program by Which the Throne is Established on Earth, Chapters 24–34
   K. Kingdom, Mundane Blessings of the Milliennium, Chapter 35

II. **Historic Interlude (Prose), Chapters 36–39**
   *(This section is probably a prophetic picture of how God will deliver His people in the Great Tribulation, see 2 Kings 18–19; 2 Chron. 29–30.)*
   A. King Hezekiah and the Invasion of Sennacherib, King of Assyria, Chapter 36
   B. King Hezekiah's Prayer and the Destruction of the Assyrian Hosts, Chapter 37
   C. King Hezekiah's Sickness, Prayer, and Healing, Chapter 38
   D. King Hezekiah Plays the Fool, Chapter 39

III. **Salvation (Poetry), Chapters 40–66**
   *Revelation of the Savior in the Place of Suffering (There is a threefold division marked by the concluding thought in each division, "There is no peace to the wicked.")*
   A. Comfort of Jehovah Which Comes through the Servant, Chapters 40–48
      *(Polemic against idolatry—Help and hope come only through the Servant)*
   B. Salvation of Jehovah Which Comes through the Suffering Servant, Chapters 49–57
      1. Redeemer of the Whole World, Who Is God's Servant, Chapters 49–52:12
      2. Redemption Wrought by the Suffering Servant, Who Is God's Sheep (Lamb), Chapters 52:13–53
      3. Results of the Redemption Wrought by the Redeemer, Who Is God's Only Savior, Chapters 54–57

   C. Glory of Jehovah Which Comes through the Suffering Servant, Chapters 58–66
      1. Sin Hinders the Manifestation of the Glory of God, Chapters 58–59
      2. Redeemer Is Coming to Zion, Chapters 60–66
         *(Nothing can hinder God's progress—He will judge sin)*

# CHAPTER 1

***THEME:*** *God's charge against the nation Israel*

Chapter 1 is God's solemn call to the universe to come into the courtroom to hear God's charge against the nation Israel.

Isaiah lived in a time of tension. In many respects it was a time of crisis in the history of the world. World-shaking events were transpiring. Catastrophic and cataclysmic judgments were taking place. There was upheaval in the social order.

A new nation had arisen in the north; it was moving toward world domination. Assyria, the most brutal nation ever to put an army on the battlefield, was marching to world conquest. Already the northern kingdom of Israel had been taken into Assyrian captivity. The southern kingdom of Judah was in a precarious position, and an Assyrian army, 185,000 strong, was just outside the walls of Jerusalem.

In this dire, desperate, and difficult day Hezekiah entered the temple and turned to God in prayer. God sent His prophet with an encouraging word. He asserted that Assyria would never take Judah, the army of Assyria would never set foot in the streets of Jerusalem, and they would never cross the threshold of any gate of the city of the great King. But God was preparing another nation, Babylon, the head of gold down by the banks of the River Euphrates; this nation would eventually take Judah into captivity unless she turned to God.

God was giving Judah another chance. In order to establish the justice of His cause, God called her into court; He held her before His bar of justice. He gave her opportunity to answer the charge, to hear His verdict, and to throw herself on the mercy of His court. God invites us into the court to see if He is just. It is well for this day and generation to go into the courtroom and see God on the throne of judgment in this sensational scene.

In the thinking of the world, God has been removed from the throne of judgment. He has been divested of His authority, robbed of His regal prerogative, shorn of His locks as the moral ruler of His universe; He has been towed to the edge of the world and pushed over as excess baggage. This is a blasphemous picture of God! He is still the moral ruler of His universe. He is still upon the throne of justice; He has not abdicated. He punishes sin.

Isaiah records the principles upon which God judges the nations. God raises up nations, and He puts them down. The kingdoms of this world today are Satan's, but God overrules them. God has permitted great nations to rise, and He has permitted Satan to use them; but when it is time in God's program for certain nations to move off the stage, He moves them off—Satan notwithstanding. Even God's own people, the Jews, are a testimony of the fact that He rules in the affairs of the nations of this world.

There is an expression that keeps recurring in my thinking from the Song of Moses which the children of Israel sang as they crossed the Red Sea. The expression is, "Jehovah is a man of war." Yes, He is! And He will not compromise with sin. He will not accept the white flag of surrender. He is moving forward in undeviating, unhesitating, and uncompromising fury against it. There would be hope today for man if he could say with Isaiah, "I saw also the Lord sitting upon a throne" (Isa. 6:1).

**The vision of Isaiah the son of Amoz, which he saw concerning Judah and Jerusalem in the days of Uzziah, Jotham, Ahaz, and Hezekiah, kings of Judah [Isa. 1:1].**

First of all, note that this is a vision "concerning Judah and Jerusalem." I am sure that we will not make the mistake of locating either one anywhere in the Western Hemisphere. There is, however, a marvelous application for America today—one that we need to hear and heed.

"In the days of Uzziah, Jotham, Ahaz, and Hezekiah." Uzziah, the tenth king of Judah, became a leper because he intruded into the holy place, which even a king was not permitted to do. However, Uzziah is classed as a good king. Jotham, his son who followed him, was also a good king. But Ahaz, the grandson of Uzziah, was a bad king. Finally, Hezekiah, the last king mentioned, was a good king. He was the king who asked that his life be prolonged, and God granted his desire. Asking this was probably a mistake on Hezekiah's part, because many bad things took place during his last years that actually were the undoing of the kingdom.

**Hear, O heavens, and give ear, O earth: for the LORD hath spoken, I have nourished and brought up children, and they have rebelled against me [Isa. 1:2].**

God begins this prophecy in a majestic manner. This is God's general judgment against Judah. He is calling the world, if you please, to come into the courtroom and listen to the proceedings as He tries His people. God does not do anything in a corner or in the dark. This language is strangely similar to the way Deuteronomy 32 begins: "Give ear, O ye heavens, and I will speak; and hear, O earth, the words of my mouth." When God put the nation Israel in the land, having taken them out of the land of Egypt, He put down the conditions on which He was "homesteading" them in the Promised Land. He called the created intelligences of heaven and earth to witness these conditions.

Now, after five hundred years, God says, "I have nourished and brought up children, and they have rebelled against me." He is ready to take them out of the land and send them into Babylonian captivity. He calls the created intelligences of heaven and earth to witness that He is just and right in His dealings. His charge against them is rebellion. The condition upon which they were allowed to dwell in the land was obedience. They were disobedient; and, according to the Mosaic Law, when a man had a rebellious son, that son was to be stoned to death. God's charge against them is a serious one. As His children, they had rebelled against the Mosaic Law in this connection. In the Book of Deuteronomy note the law concerning an incorrigible son: "If a man have a stubborn and rebellious son, which will not obey the voice of his father, or the voice of his mother, and that, when they have chastened him, will not hearken unto them: Then shall his father and his mother lay hold on him, and bring him out unto the elders of his city, and unto the gate of his place; And they shall say unto the elders of his city, This our son is stubborn and rebellious, he will not obey our voice; he is a glutton, and a drunkard. And all the men of his city shall stone him with stones, that he die: so shalt thou put evil away from among you; and all Israel shall hear, and fear" (Deut. 21:18–21).

This was what the Law did with a prodigal son. The crowd that heard Christ tell of the Prodigal Son was dumbfounded when He said that the father told the servant to kill the fatted calf instead of killing the son! When the Prodigal Son got home, he asked his father for forgiveness, and even before he finished his confession, his father had thrown his arms around the boy, kissed him, and forgiven him. Instead of stripes, the son was given a wonderful feast. God is not only just, but merciful; but the rebellion of a son is a serious thing. Scripture has a great deal to say about it.

In order to emphasize His charge and break the tension of the courtroom, God indulges in a bit of humor. I trust that you recognize humor in the Bible—it will make you enjoy it a great deal more. I think that when we get into eternity, and get past the time of sin on earth and are finished with the program God is working out at this present time, we are going to have a good time. I think we are going to have many laughs and enjoy many hilarious situations. It does not hurt Christians to have the right kind of humor. God has put a lot of humor in the Bible. A lady, who was a member of a church I pastored, was upset every time I found humor in the Bible. She would make a trip down the aisle and tell me that I was being irreverent. She has been home with the Lord for a long time, and I do hope she has had a couple of good laughs, because she certainly never had them down here. The fact of the matter is, she acted like she had been weaned on a dill pickle. Unfortunately, she never found humor in this life, and she didn't seem to enjoy the Christian life as God has intended us to enjoy it.

**The ox knoweth his owner, and the ass his master's crib: but Israel doth not know, my people doth not consider [Isa. 1:3].**

This verse is a splendid piece of satire. The two animals that are used for illustrations do not have a reputation for being very intelligent. Neither the ox nor the long-eared donkey has a very high I.Q. The expression "dumb as an ox" is still often used. The donkey does not wear a Phi Beta Kappa key. I should qualify that statement: I admit that I have met a few who do! However, even these animals have intelligence enough to know who feeds them.

When I was a pastor in Texas, there was a grassy vacant lot across the street from the church to which a very poor man with many patches on his overalls would bring his little donkey. While the donkey was grazing, many of the little boys and girls in the neighborhood would ride him, and even the preacher rode him once in a while. When I would get on his back, he wouldn't pay any attention to me—or to anyone else. Late in the afternoon the donkey's owner would come for him. When he came tottering along, the donkey would prick up his long ears. He *knew* his owner. He knew who was going to feed him that night.

On the contrary, a number of folk today do

not have intelligence enough to know that God provides for all their needs. They don't know that God feeds them. They do not even recognize that He exists. What a commentary on this sophisticated generation that no longer needs God. The story is told of a little boy, reared in a Christian home, who was having his first visit away from home. Although he was only going next door for the evening meal, he was eagerly anticipating the experience, and at five o'clock he was dressed and ready to go. When it came time for all of them to sit down at the table, the little fellow, who was accustomed to hearing the giving of thanks at the table, bowed his head and shut his eyes. But the home to which he had been invited was not a Christian home, and they immediately began to pass the food. Because he didn't want to miss anything, he opened his eyes and looked around. The little fellow was just a bit embarrassed, but not having any inhibitions, he raised the question: "Don't you folks thank God for your food?" Then the host was a bit embarrassed but confessed that they did not. The young lad was thoughtful for a moment and then blurted out, "You're exactly like my dog: you just start in." There are many people like that today. Multitudes of people live just like animals.

God said, "The ox knows his owner, and the donkey his master's crib, but my people do not know." We hear today that man has descended from animals. Who says he has? Man acts like animals act; in fact, it could be said that some animals are smarter than some men. Instead of man descending from animals, maybe animals descended from men; maybe they have evolved into something better than man. Man has dropped pretty low. I think what the Lord said, when He opened up court, reveals that.

He continues His charge in verse 4:

**Ah sinful nation, a people laden with iniquity, a seed of evildoers, children that are corrupters: they have forsaken the Lord, they have provoked the Holy One of Israel unto anger, they are gone away backward [Isa. 1:4].**

We see God as the Judge of all the earth and of His own people Israel. It seems a strange thing to think of God as a judge, because in the thinking of the world today God has been removed from the throne of judgment. He has been divested of His authority. He has been robbed of His regal prerogatives and shorn of His locks as moral ruler of the universe. He has been driven to the edge of the world and has been driven to the edge of the world and

pushed over as excess baggage. Don't think I am being irreverent when I say that modern teaching has given us a warped conception of God. He is characterized as a toothless old man with long whiskers, sitting on the edge of a fleecy cloud with a rainbow around His shoulders. He is simple, senile, and sentimental. He is overwhelmed with mushy love that slops over on every side, dripping honey and tears. He does not have enough courage or backbone to swat a fly or crush a grape. His proper place is in the corner by the fireplace, where He can either crochet or knit. This is the world's conception of God, but that is not how the Bible describes Him. God is going to judge this universe just as He judged His own people. That ought to be a warning not only to nations but also to individuals.

Israel is described as "a people laden with iniquity." This phrase throws a world of light upon the personal invitation that the Lord Jesus gave in the New Testament. He said, "Come unto me, all ye that labour and are heavy laden, and I will give you rest" (Matt. 11:28). Now we know what He meant—"laden with iniquity." The people of Israel were laden with sin. Today His invitation goes out to those who are laden with sin to bring that burden and load to Him and find rest, the rest of redemption.

In this verse God spells out Israel's condition. They are backslidden, they have turned away from God, and they are a people laden with iniquity. Now He is going to spell out in detail the charge that He has made against them.

This brings to mind the philosophy of human government upon which God operates. This system is presented to us in the Book of Judges, and you see this cycle of the history of human government working itself out in the nation. In the Book of Judges we saw Israel serving God, being blessed of God, and prospering. They began, in their prosperity, to turn away from God, and they finally turned to idolatry. They were in rebellion against God; in fact, they forgot Him. Then God delivered them into the hands of the enemy. In a short time they began to cry out to God for deliverance. When they turned to God, He delivered them from their enemies and put them back in the place of blessing. This picture follows all the way through Scripture, and history corroborates the fact that there are three steps in the downfall of any nation. There is religious apostasy, then moral awfulness, and finally political anarchy. Many people don't pay any attention to the cycle until

the stage of political anarchy is reached, and then they cry out that the government should be changed and a new system adopted. Well, the problem is not in the government. The problem in Jerusalem was not in the palace, but the problem was within the temple. The trouble begins when there is spiritual apostasy.

**Why should ye be stricken any more? ye will revolt more and more: the whole head is sick, and the whole heart faint.**

**From the sole of the foot even unto the head there is no soundness in it; but wounds, and bruises, and putrifying sores: they have not been closed, neither bound up, neither mollified with ointment.**

**Your country is desolate, your cities are burned with fire: your land, strangers devour it in your presence, and it is desolate, as overthrown by strangers [Isa. 1:5–7].**

What God says in these verses is absolutely true. There is moral awfulness and political anarchy, but God is holding back. This still is not the charge that He is bringing against them.

**And the daughter of Zion is left as a cottage in a vineyard, as a lodge in a garden of cucumbers, as a besieged city.**

**Except the LORD of hosts had left unto us a very small remnant, we should have been as Sodom, and we should have been like unto Gomorrah [Isa. 1:8–9].**

In other words, if there had not been a faithful remnant, God would have destroyed Israel as He did Sodom and Gomorrah. But there has always been a remnant of God's people. There is a remnant today: there are Christians scattered throughout the world.

**Hear the word of the LORD, ye rulers of Sodom; give ear unto the law of our God, ye people of Gomorrah [Isa. 1:10].**

Now God is spelling it out. The whole problem is spiritual apostasy.

**To what purpose is the multitude of your sacrifices unto me? saith the LORD: I am full of the burnt offerings of rams, and the fat of fed beasts; and I delight not in the blood of bullocks, or of lambs, or of he goats [Isa. 1:11].**

God specifies His charges against His people. He has put His hand upon a definite thing, and He is going to prove that particular point in which they are wrong. He puts His finger on the *best* thing in Judah, not the worst. He shows them what is exceedingly wrong. Israel has a God-given religion and a God-appointed ritual in a God-constructed temple, but they are wrong in that which represented the best. They are bringing sacrifices and going through the ritual according to the letter of the Law, but their hearts are in rebellion against God. Their religion is not affecting their conduct. Frankly, that is a problem among believers today. A great many of us have reached the place where we have a form of godliness, but we deny the power thereof.

**When ye come to appear before me, who hath required this at your hand, to tread my courts?**

**Bring no more vain oblations; incense is an abomination unto me; the new moons and sabbaths, the calling of assemblies, I cannot away with; it is iniquity, even the solemn meeting [Isa. 1:12–13].**

Even doing that which God has commanded becomes wrong when the heart is not in it and when it does not affect the believer's conduct.

If the Lord Jesus were to come into your church next Sunday, would He commend you? Would He compliment you for your faithfulness to Him? Would He tell you how much He appreciates your attendance at the services and your giving to Him? I think not! The One who has "feet as burnished brass," whose "eyes are as a flame of fire," and from whose mouth there goes " a sharp two-edged sword," would not commend us (cf. Prov. 5:4; Dan. 10:6; Rev. 1:14–16). I think He would tell most of us that all of our outward form, all of our lovely testimonies and loud professions, are making Him sick. Would He not tell us that we need to repent and come in humility to Him? Surely this is a warning to the churches of America. Fundamentally, our difficulty today is spiritual; and, until the professing church repents and has genuine revival, there is no hope for America.

**And when ye spread forth your hands, I will hide mine eyes from you: yea, when ye make many prayers, I will not hear: your hands are full of blood.**

**Wash you, make you clean; put away the evil of your doings from before mine eyes; cease to do evil;**

**Learn to do well; seek judgment, relieve the oppressed, judge the fatherless, plead for the widow [Isa. 1:15–17].**

God says, "You are nothing in the world but a bunch of phonies. You come into My presence as if you are really genuine. You go through the sacrifices, but they have become absolutely meaningless to you." God has spelled out His charge against them. They are guilty of spiritual apostasy. It has led to moral awfulness and to political anarchy in the nation. God has called Israel into court and has proved His charge against them. Israel is like a prisoner standing at the bar waiting for the sentence of judgment. God can now move in to judge them.

But even at this late date God is willing to settle the case out of court. He says to Israel, "Don't go into court with Me, because you are going to lose." The Judge has something else to say, and we stand amazed and aghast at what He says next:

**Come now, and let us reason together, saith the LORD: though your sins be as scarlet, they shall be as white as snow; though they be red like crimson, they shall be as wool [Isa. 1:18].**

God is saying to Judah, "Do not force Me to render sentence. Settle your case out of court." In Matthew 5:25 the Lord Jesus said, "Agree with thine adversary quickly, whiles thou art in the way with him . . ."—don't wait until he takes you to court. God says that He has a secret formula, a divine alchemy, a potent prescription, a powerful potion, a heavenly elixir that will take out sin. It is not a secret formula like the newest bomb, but it is more potent. You will find it in Isaiah 53 as the One who was more marred, who suffered more, who died differently, who was wounded for our transgressions. Because He paid the penalty, the Judge is able now to extend mercy to us. The blood of Jesus Christ, God's Son, keeps on cleansing from all sin.

This is God's charge against His people, and this is the basis on which they may turn to Him. If they will turn to Him, He will preserve the nation—He will give them almost one hundred years—then if they don't turn to Him and change their ways, He will send them into captivity.

We see an application of this to our own country. In my beloved country I see political anarchy. It is obvious to most of us that men cannot solve the problems of this nation, and certainly not of the world.

The historical Gibbon gives five reasons for the decline of the Roman Empire in his book, *The Decline and Fall of the Roman Empire*. As the first step towards decline, he lists the undermining of the dignity and the sanctity of the home, which is the basis of human society. The second step includes higher and higher taxes, and the spending of public money for free bread and circuses for the populace. The third was the mad craze for pleasure and sports becoming every year more exciting, more brutal, and more immoral. The fourth step was the building of great armaments when the real enemy was within: the decay of individual responsibility. The fifth was the decay of religion, fading into mere form, losing touch with life, and losing power to guide the people.

You see, a nation's decline begins with spiritual apostasy, which is followed by moral awfulness, and results in political anarchy.

Is there spiritual apostasy in this land of ours? Every informed Christian is aware that modernism has taken over most of the great denominations of America today; and, in this dire day, modernism, by its own confession, has failed. Dr. Reinhold Niebuhr, one of the mouthpieces of liberalism, is quoted as saying that liberal Protestantism has been inclined to sacrifice every characteristic Christian insight if only it could thereby prove itself intellectually respectable, but that liberalism finds itself unable to cope with the tragic experiences of our day.

I find in my file an interesting article clipped from the *Wall Street Journal* several years ago: "What America needs more than railway extension, western irrigation, a low tariff, a bigger cotton crop, and a larger wheat crop is a revival of religion. The kind that father and mother used to have. A religion that counted it good business to take time for family worship each morning right in the middle of wheat harvest. A religion that prompted them to quit work a half hour earlier on Wednesday so that the whole family could get ready to go to prayer meeting." America's problem is the same today; it is a spiritual problem.

Dr. Albert Hyma, when he was professor of history at the University of Michigan in Ann Arbor, said, "The United States of America in the past fifty years has been dominated to a large extent by persons who do not understand the spiritual heritage bequeathed by their own ancestors." Dr. J. Gresham Machen said, "America is coasting downhill on a godly ancestry, and God pity America when

we hit the bottom of the hill." Friend, we have hit the bottom of the hill, but God is saying to us, "Come, let us reason together, though your sins be as scarlet, they shall be as white as snow." There is a way out for America, but, if we go the same direction as other nations, our time is limited.

Aaron Burr was a grandson of the great Jonathan Edwards, who, upon an occasion, conducted meetings at Princeton, where Aaron Burr was a student. There was a great spiritual movement in the school. One night Jonathan Edwards preached on the subject, "The Mastery of Jesus." Aaron Burr was deeply stirred, and he went to the room of one of his professors to talk to him about making a decision for Jesus. The professor urged him not to make a decision under any sort of an emotional appeal, but to wait until after the meetings were over. Aaron Burr postponed making a decision and went on to murder a great American and to betray his country. When he was an old man, a young man came to him and said, "Mr. Burr, I want you to meet a Friend of mine." Aaron Burr said, "Who is he?" The young man replied, "He is Jesus Christ, the Savior of my soul." A cold sweat broke out on the forehead of Aaron Burr, and he replied, "Sixty years ago I told God if He would let me alone, I would let Him alone, and He has kept His word!"

There is a way out for America, and there is a way out for you and for me. Someone has stated it this way:

Philosophy says: Think your way out.
Indulgence says: Drink your way out.
Politics says: Spend your way out.
Science says: Invent your way out.
Industry says: Work your way out.
Communism says: Strike your way out.
Fascism says: Bluff your way out.
Militarism says: Fight your way out.
The Bible says: Pray your way out, but
Jesus Christ says: "I am the way (out). . . ."

After the Lord brings His charges against Judah and offers them salvation and a way out of their trouble, He continues gently with a warning.

**If ye be willing and obedient, ye shall eat the good of the land:**

**But if ye refuse and rebel, ye shall be devoured with the sword: for the mouth of the LORD hath spoken it [Isa. 1:19–20].**

The government of God and the grace of God are two aspects emphasized in the Book of Isaiah. During the remainder of chapter 1 God is attempting to move Judah back to Himself. He is giving the people a warning.

**Therefore saith the Lord, the LORD of hosts, the mighty One of Israel, Ah, I will ease me of mine adversaries, and avenge me of mine enemies:**

**And I will turn my hand upon thee, and purely purge away thy dross, and take away all thy tin:**

**And I will restore thy judges as at the first, and thy counsellors as at the beginning: afterward thou shalt be called, The city of righteousness, the faithful city [Isa. 1:24–26].**

Judah's destiny depends upon the people's response to God's offer of forgiving grace. If they are willing to turn from their sin and obey God, He will bestow His favor upon them materially and spiritually and protect them from their enemies.

**Zion shall be redeemed with judgment, and her converts with righteousness.**

**And the destruction of the transgressors and of the sinners shall be together, and they that forsake the LORD shall be consumed.**

**For they shall be ashamed of the oaks which ye have desired and ye shall be confounded for the gardens that ye have chosen [Isa. 1:27–29].**

This has to do with idolatry because the idols were placed under the oak trees, and a garden was planted around them.

**For ye shall be as an oak whose leaf fadeth, and as a garden that hath no water.**

**And the strong shall be as tow, and the maker of it as a spark, and they shall both burn together, and none shall quench them [Isa. 1:30–31].**

God has been misrepresented in the sense that He has been pictured as losing His temper and breaking forth in judgment. That is never a true picture of God. The fact is that our sin is like a wick, and when we play with the spark of sin, the fire will follow. "Be not deceived; God is not mocked: for whatsoever a man soweth, that shall he also reap" (Gal. 6:7).

# CHAPTER 2

**THEME:** *Prophecy concerning the last days: the kingdom and the Great Tribulation*

Isaiah chapters 2 through 5 constitute one complete prophecy. These chapters look beyond the present time to the last days concerning Israel (the total nation of twelve tribes). As we move through these chapters, God makes it clear that He is speaking of all the tribes of Israel which will be brought back together. God always thinks of Israel as one nation.

The last days of Israel need to be distinguished from the last days of the church. God is not talking about the church in these chapters. There is no way of making what He says applicable to the church. We can be sure of this fact, because in the New Testament Paul says that the church was a mystery which was not revealed in the Old Testament at all. In writing to the Romans, Paul makes this very clear: "Now to him that is of power to stablish you according to my gospel, and the preaching of Jesus Christ, according to the revelation of the mystery, which was kept secret since the world began" (Rom. 16:25). Now if Isaiah had known about the church, it would not have been a new revelation in Paul's day. From Paul's day to the present time the church has been God's agency through which He is giving His message to the world.

However, the church will be removed from the world at the time of the Rapture. Isaiah's message looks beyond the time of the church to the day when God will begin to move in a new way. We call it the Great Tribulation Period, at the close of which He will set up His kingdom.

## PREVIEW OF THE FUTURE FOR JUDAH AND JERUSALEM

**The word that Isaiah the son of Amoz saw concerning Judah and Jerusalem [Isa. 2:1].**

When Isaiah speaks of Israel, Judah, and Jerusalem, he means exactly these people and places. Judah means Judah, Israel means Israel, and Jerusalem means Jerusalem. If Isaiah uses figures of speech, he will make it perfectly clear that they are figures of speech. The prophet will let you know when he is making a different application. Beware of the fallacy of spiritualizing prophecy in con-formity to some outmoded theological cliché which fits into some church's program.

**And it shall come to pass in the last days, that the mountain of the LORD'S house shall be established in the top of the mountains, and shall be exalted above the hills; and all nations shall flow unto it [Isa. 2:2].**

"It shall come to pass in the last days, that the mountain of the LORD'S house shall be established in the top of the mountains." Again let me say that this is *not* speaking of the last days of the church. The last days of the church pertain to the time of spiritual apostasy. Paul makes this clear in his pastoral epistles of 1 and 2 Timothy: "Now the Spirit speaketh expressly, that in the latter times some shall depart from the faith . . ." (1 Tim. 4:1). You can see that the "latter times" of the *church* and the "last days" of *Israel* are not identical, nor are they contemporary, although there is some overlapping. Certainly they do not refer to the same period of time. It is important to note this. The "last days" in this verse refer to the Great Tribulation Period. The Lord Jesus Christ made it clear, when His disciples asked Him, "When shall these things be?" (Luke 21:7 refers to the destruction of Jerusalem) that by the "last days" He meant the Great Tribulation Period. The Great Tribulation ends with the coming of Christ to earth and the setting up of His kingdom. The first section of Isaiah, chapters 2–5, deals with the Great Tribulation Period and the kingdom that shall be set up on this earth.

"The mountain of the LORD'S house shall be established in the top of the mountains." This pertains to the nation of Israel after the church has been removed. The word *mountain* in Scripture means "a kingdom, an authority, or a rule." Daniel makes this clear in his prophecy. "The LORD'S house shall be established in the top of the mountains"—that is above all the kingdoms of this earth. The kingdoms of this world shall become the kingdom of the Lord Jesus Christ, and He will be King of Kings and Lord of Lords. One of the reasons that today Israel is such a hot spot and such a sensitive piece of real estate is because it is the very spot that God has chosen to be the political and religious center of the world during the kingdom age. Speaking of those days

Daniel says, "Then was the iron, the clay, the brass, the silver, and the gold, broken to pieces together, and became like the chaff of the summer threshingfloors; and the wind carried them away, that no place was found for them: and the stone that smote the image became a great mountain, and filled the whole earth" (Dan. 2:35). God's kingdom will be exalted above the kingdoms of this world.

**And many people shall go and say, Come ye, and let us go up to the mountain [the kingdom] of the LORD, to the house of the God of Jacob; and he will teach us of his ways, and we will walk in his paths: for out of Zion shall go forth the law, and the word of the LORD from Jerusalem [Isa. 2:3].**

Both government and religion will center in Jerusalem. The Lord Jesus Christ will sit upon the throne of David. One of the primary concerns of those who inhabit the earth will be to discover and do the will of God. They will seek to learn His ways and walk in His paths.

**And he shall judge among the nations, and shall rebuke many people: and they shall beat their swords into plowshares, and their spears into pruninghooks: nation shall not lift up sword against nation, neither shall they learn war any more [Isa. 2:4].**

"He shall judge among the nations, and shall rebuke many people." The period of the reign of Christ on the earth during the Millennium is another trial period for mankind. And there will be a great many judged during that period; and, of course, multitudes will be saved during that time also.

"They shall beat their swords into plowshares, and their spears into pruninghooks"—the rule of the Lord upon earth at this time will be righteous, and He will compel the nations to practice justice and fairness with each other. For the first time all countries will dwell together in peace. Only during the kingdom age will the people be able to beat their swords into plowshares. Joel 3:10 tells us that during the Tribulation just the opposite will be true: the people will beat their plowshares into swords. In fact, we are living in times like that right now. The idea of disarming nations and disarming individuals is, in my judgment, contrary to the Word of God. In the New Testament the Lord Jesus said, "When a strong man armed keepeth his palace . . ." (Luke 11:21). If you are going to have peace and safety, you must have law and order. The

prophecy of beating swords into plowshares will be fulfilled during the Millennium, when the Lord Jesus is reigning. Then you will be able to take the locks off of your doors, and you will be able to walk the streets at night in safety. You will not be drafted, because there will be no more war. There will be no more need for weapons for defense. The kingdom that the Lord is going to establish upon earth will be one of peace. He is the Prince of Peace.

It is futile, nonsensical, and asinine for any man or nation to promise to bring peace upon the earth today. The United Nations, which was founded to help bring peace on earth, is one of the greatest places to carry on battles. It has proven how impotent it is. It cannot bring peace on earth. It has only increased dictatorship on the earth. We do not have peace in the world. If you are a child of God with your thinking cap on and begin to think God's thoughts after Him, you will find that you are living in a big bad, evil world. If you expect to see a brotherhood of all men, you are doomed to disappointment, because man is not capable of bringing peace to this earth. There will be no peace as long as there is sin in the hearts of men and an overweening ambition to rule over other people.

**O house of Jacob, come ye, and let us walk in the light of the LORD [Isa. 2:5].**

In view of the future that is coming, certainly we should walk in the light of the Lord. This is the only way of peace. When you leave God out, you will never have peace.

**Therefore thou hast forsaken thy people the house of Jacob, because they be replenished from the east, and are soothsayers like the Philistines, and they please themselves in the children of strangers.**

**Their land also is full of silver and gold, neither is there any end of their treasures; their land is also full of horses, neither is there any end of their chariots:**

**Their land also is full of idols; they worship the work of their own hands, that which their own fingers have made:**

**And the mean man boweth down, and the great man humbleth himself: therefore forgive them not [Isa. 2:6–9].**

Judah adopted new ideas from the heathen and incorporated them into their own religion. They embraced all kinds of ways from Assyria

and Babylon. Before long they had joined the rest of the nations in worshiping the creature more than the Creator.

> Enter into the rock, and hide thee in the dust, for fear of the LORD, and for the glory of his majesty.

> The lofty looks of man shall be humbled, and the haughtiness of men shall be bowed down, and the LORD alone shall be exalted in that day.

> For the day of the LORD of hosts shall be upon every one that is proud and lofty, and upon every one that is lifted up; and he shall be brought low [Isa. 2:10–12].

God intends to break down the proud man—the man who thinks he can rule himself and the man who thinks he can rule the world without God.

> And upon all the cedars of Lebanon, that are high and lifted up, and upon all the oaks of Bashan [Isa. 2:13].

The cedars of Lebanon and the oaks of Bashan represent, I believe, the pride of man.

> And upon all the high mountains, and upon all the hills that are lifted up [Isa. 2:14].

This has reference to government and society.

> And upon every high tower, and upon every fenced wall [Isa. 2:15].

This is a reference to the military, which will be judged.

> And upon all the ships of Tarshish, and upon all pleasant pictures [Isa. 2:16].

Commerce and art are going to be judged.

> And the loftiness of man shall be bowed down, and the haughtiness of men shall be made low: and the LORD alone shall be exalted in that day [Isa. 2:17].

God is going to put down all of the pride and pomp of men.

> And the idols he shall utterly abolish [Isa. 2:18].

God is going to get rid of all false religion.

> And they shall go into the holes of the rocks, and into the caves of the earth, for fear of the LORD, and for the glory of his majesty, when he ariseth to shake terribly the earth [Isa. 2:19].

The Book of Revelation repeats what man will do in that day of judgment: "And the kings of the earth, and the great men, and the rich men, and the chief captains, and the mighty men, and every bondman, and every free man, hid themselves in the dens and in the rocks of the mountains; And said to the mountains and rocks, Fall on us, and hide us from the face of him that sitteth on the throne, and from the wrath of the Lamb" (Rev. 6:15–16).

All you see on television today has to do with the political economy, government, commerce, art, the pomp and pride of man—and the religion of man. The day is coming when all of man's pride is going to be brought low, and the Lord Jesus Christ will be *exalted* on earth. Today He is not being given His proper place in government, in society, in business, in art, or in the pomp and ceremony of the world—or even in the religion of the world. He is left out today. When He comes again, men are going to run for the caves of the earth. I don't know whether men were ever cavemen or not, but a day is coming in the future when men are going back to the caves.

> In that day a man shall cast his idols of silver, and his idols of gold, which they made each one for himself to worship, to the moles and to the bats;

> To go into the clefts of the rocks, and into the tops of the ragged rocks, for fear of the LORD, and for the glory of his majesty, when he ariseth to shake terribly the earth [Isa. 2:20–21].

"When he ariseth to shake terribly the earth" is the time of the Great Tribulation.

> Cease ye from man, whose breath is in his nostrils: for wherein is he to be accounted of? [Isa. 2:22].

Don't put your confidence in man. You and I exhale, but we don't know whether we are going to inhale the next breath. That is the frailty of man—if he misses one breath he is out of the picture. Multitudes today going about their daily business will have fatal heart attacks and disappear from the earth's scene. Don't put your confidence in man. Put your confidence in the Lord Jesus Christ today.

# CHAPTER 3

*THEME: The cause of Israel's undoing: weak government; loose and low morals*

This is a continuation of the prophecy begun in chapter 2 (chs. 2–5 constitute a complete prophecy). In this section on judgment, chapter 3 reveals God's judgment leveled particularly against the nation of Israel. Although it has application to other nations, the interpretation is definitely to Israel. Further along in this judgment section we will see God's judgment of surrounding nations, which are among the most remarkable prophecies in the Word of God, and many of them have been literally fulfilled. However, we find that God's judgment against Israel is more severe and intense than against any other nation. Why? Well, Israel was the nation God had chosen in a peculiar way, and it enjoyed a particularly close relationship to God. Privilege creates responsibility.

Because privilege always creates responsibility, I believe God will judge the United States more severely than He will judge any of our contemporary nations—like China, for example. The United States has been privileged to know the Word of God as no other nation has—except Israel.

Israel as a nation had more light than any of its neighbors, and light rejected brings severe punishment, as will be illustrated in this book.

The subject of God's judgment may be offensive to you, but please don't hide your head in the sand like the proverbial ostrich. Let's face reality whether we like it or not. God does judge sin. Not only will He judge sin in the future, He has judged it in the past. And He makes no apology for it.

The prophecy before us is a picture of Isaiah's day, and it has been fulfilled. However, its fulfillment does not exhaust its meaning, because the conditions described will prevail again at the end times and will bring down the wrath of God in judgment—not only upon Israel but upon the nations of the world.

The first fifteen verses deal with the subject of weak government and women's dress. These seem to be totally unrelated subjects, but we shall see that they are not as far removed as they appear to be. Weak government is caused by a lack of leadership, as evidenced by women rulers—and we will see what he means by this.

## WEAK GOVERNMENT

**For, behold, the Lord, the LORD of hosts, doth take away from Jerusalem and from Judah the stay and the staff, the whole stay of bread, and the whole stay of water [Isa. 3:1].**

This verse confines us to Jerusalem and Judah.

Although man does not live by bread alone, he surely needs it. This famine is a judgment of God. There are thirteen famines mentioned in the Word of God, and every one of them is a judgment from Him upon the nation of Israel.

**The mighty man, and the man of war, the judge, and the prophet, and the prudent, and the ancient,**

**The captain of fifty, and the honourable man, and the counsellor, and the cunning artificer, and the eloquent orator [Isa. 3:2–3].**

God is going to remove not only bread and water but all the men of leadership. Qualified men for high positions are lacking, and this is a judgment from God.

This can be brought up to date. Have you been impressed by the fact that there are no great men on the contemporary scene? There are quite a few men who are passing themselves off as great, but they would have been pygmies in the days of Washington, Lincoln, Jackson, Teddy Roosevelt, or the men who wrote the Declaration of Independence. I am not taking sides with any political party when I say this, but today there are many ambitious men, young and old alike, who have practically no qualifications as statesmen. One hundred years ago they would have been called cheap politicians, but today they are called statesmen!

We have men of war, but we have no great generals. Our army would not be in the situation it is in today if it had strong leadership. There is lack of leadership in our judicial system. We have an alarming crime wave because we have pygmies sitting in the seats of judgment. Where is the prophet, the prudent, and the ancient? We have no statesmen at all today. What we have is a group of clever politicians who know how to compromise. I am not talking about a certain political party. I am simply saying that it is always the mark of a decadent age and the judgment of God when a nation is not producing great men.

Moving into the field of the arts—what

greatness do you see on the television screen? I get rather bored with the television talk programs. Generally the master of ceremonies comes out and says, "I am going to introduce you to a great artist, a genius." And some little peanut comes out on stage, strums a guitar—doesn't play any music at all—just yells at the top of his voice. And he is hailed as a genius! Another man comes along who is introduced as a great literary light, and all that he has written is a dirty book. My friend, we lack greatness in this day, but we are not willing to admit it because we have become a proud nation.

Where is greatness in the field of education? We used to believe that the educators had the solution to the problems of the world. Today it is obvious that educators cannot control even their own campuses.

It is said that we used to have wooden ships and iron men, but now we have iron ships and wooden men. I would go further than that and call them paper doll men. Our leadership is just a string of paper dolls!

**And I will give children to be their princes, and babes shall rule over them [Isa. 3:4].**

As far as ability is concerned, men in high positions today should be wearing diapers. Juvenile adults are our rulers, and they are totally incompetent. That is exactly what brought Israel down to ruin in that day. Their leaders had the mental level of children, and God sent them into captivity. He judged them.

**And the people shall be oppressed, every one by another, and every one by his neighbour: the child shall behave himself proudly against the ancient, and the base against the honourable [Isa. 3:5].**

My friend, it sounds as if Isaiah were talking about our day, but the same was true in his day. The child, the little college student, is saying, "Listen to me. I have something to say." I have been listening to them for years, and I haven't heard them say anything yet. One class is set against another class. "The people shall be oppressed, every one by another." We have groups of minorities who want to inflict their ways on others. Christians are a minority also, but certainly we are not being heard.

**For Jerusalem is ruined, and Judah is fallen: because their tongue and their doings are against the Lord, to provoke the eyes of his glory [Isa. 3:8].**

"Jerusalem is ruined, and Judah is fallen"—that's what the prophet says. We don't have many of God's men in our day standing up, pointing at our nation, and saying, "*Our* cities are ruined," although it is as true as it was in Isaiah's time.

"Because their tongue and their doings are against the Lord, to provoke the eyes of his glory." This is the key to the chapter, and it is the key to the ruin of Israel and of any other nation. God judges nations by their relationship to Him.

The problem with the United States of America is that God has been run out of Washington, D.C. God has been ruled out in every area of our lives. A few little men think they can rule the world. How we need to be humbled, and I think we have been humbled. Russia has humbled us. China has humbled us. And little Vietnam humbled us. We are being humbled all over the world; yet we don't wake up. We continue merrily on our way, coasting downhill on our godly ancestry.

**The shew of their countenance doth witness against them; and they declare their sin as Sodom, they hide it not. Woe unto their soul! for they have rewarded evil unto themselves [Isa. 3:9].**

Sin is out in the open. What used to be done in the backyard has been moved to the front yard. What was done under cover, is now done in the open. The boast is that we are more honest now. No, we're not more honest; we are the same hypocrites that our fathers were. They were hypocrites because they hid their sin, and we are hypocrites because we are sinning out in the open and trying to say that the sin is *good!* This is exactly what Israel was saying.

**Say ye to the righteous, that it shall be well with him: for they shall eat the fruit of their doings [Isa. 3:10].**

God promises to deliver His own people.

**Woe unto the wicked! it shall be ill with him: for the reward of his hands shall be given him [Isa. 3:11].**

This is another way of saying, "Whatsoever a man sows, that shall he also reap."

**As for my people, children are their oppressors, and women rule over them. O my people, they which lead thee cause**

thee to err, and destroy the way of thy paths [Isa. 3:12].

"Children are their oppressors." The greatest problem in our day is juvenile delinquency. The greatest increase in crime is among young people, and the age drops every year.

"Women rule over them." Oh, "women's lib" will not like Isaiah, and they won't like me any better. "O my people, they which lead thee cause thee to err, and destroy the way of thy paths." Whether women rulers are meant here or effeminate men is not clear. I think it is a little of both. The women's liberation movement is another sign of a decadent age. When women act like men, they are not coming up to a high level but are descending to the male level. The woman has been given a greater amount of tenderness, but when she becomes as blasé and brutal as a man, she actually becomes worse than he is. And that is the downfall of the nation. That was true in Israel's case, and it will be true in our own nation. Go to Italy and see the ruins of Pompeii, and then consider what removed the Romans from the earthly scene. The nation that once ruled the world collapsed—not because they were attacked by someone on the outside, but they fell from within.

Listen to Him now as He pleads with His people:

**The LORD standeth up to plead, and standeth to judge the people.**

**The LORD will enter into judgment with the ancients of his people, and the princes thereof: for ye have eaten up the vineyard; the spoil of the poor is in your houses [Isa. 3:13–14].**

"The ancients" and "the princes" are the leaders of the nation. God lays the blame on the adult leadership. The juvenile problem did not originate with young people.

In Isaiah's time there were a few who were trying to get rich and rule over everyone else. "The spoil of the poor is in your houses." Godless capitalism and godless labor are big problems in our nation, and one is as bad as the other. The whole difficulty is that we are away from God. God is standing up ready to plead *or* ready to judge, and He will let the nation determine which it will be. We can have it either way. He will do one or the other.

## WOMEN'S DRESS

**Moreover the LORD saith, Because the daughters of Zion are haughty, and**

**walk with stretched forth necks and wanton eyes, walking and mincing as they go, and making a tinkling with their feet [Isa. 3:16].**

What a picture of womanhood! The problem, of course, is in the heart. In 1 Peter 3:1–4 we read, "Likewise, ye wives, be in subjection to your own husbands; that, if any obey not the word, they also may without the word be won by the conversation of the wives; While they behold your chaste conversation [or, conduct] coupled with fear. [This doesn't mean that she is to take abuse from him, but she is to live a godly life before him.] Whose adorning let it not be that outward adorning of plaiting the hair, and of wearing of gold, or of putting on of apparel; [if you are trying to hold your husband with sex, you'll lose him]. But let it be the hidden man of the heart, in that which is not corruptible, even the ornament of a meek and quiet spirit, which is in the sight of God of great price."

When I counsel with young couples I always tell them that there are three cords that hold marriage together, and a threefold cord is not easily broken. There is the physical cord, and that is important. Also there is the psychological cord—the same interests. Third, there is the spiritual cord—the same love for God and His work. If a wife is trying to hold her husband with only her physical attraction, the time will come when he is no longer interested. This is what Peter is saying. A wife's attraction should be more than the way she dresses and styles her hair. Her beauty should be in the way she lives her life with a gentle and quiet spirit.

Isaiah pictures the women of his day as haughty and sexy, "mincing as they go, and making a tinkling with their feet."

**Therefore the Lord will smite with a scab the crown of the head of the daughters of Zion, and the LORD will discover their secret parts [Isa. 3:17].**

He is talking about a disease. Do you know that there is an epidemic of venereal disease in our nation right now? So many of our young girls look appealing, but they are like serpents along the way, as many a man is finding out to his sorrow.

**In that day the Lord will take away the bravery of their tinkling ornaments about their feet, and their cauls, and their round tires like the moon.**

**The chains, and the bracelets, and the mufflers,**

The bonnets, and the ornaments of the legs, and the headbands, and the tablets, and the earrings,

The rings, and nose jewels,

The changeable suits of apparel, and the mantles, and the wimples, and the crisping pins,

The glasses, and the fine linen, and the hoods, and the veils.

And it shall come to pass, that instead of sweet smell there shall be stink; and instead of a girdle a rent; and instead of well set hair baldness; and instead of a stomacher a girding of sackcloth; and burning instead of beauty [Isa. 3:18–24].

Women's dress is the barometer of any civilization. When women's dress is modest it tells something about the nation as a whole.

In these last few verses twenty articles of women's wear are mentioned by name. There certainly is nothing wrong with a woman dressing in style—if the style is not immodest. I feel that all of us should look the best we can with what we have, even though some of us don't have too much to work with. God is not condemning the women of Israel for dressing in the style of their day. He is talking about the inner life. They were haughty and brazen. Real adornment is beneath the skin, not from the skin outward. Women's dress is the key to a nation's morals.

Thy men shall fall by the sword, and thy mighty in the war.

And her gates shall lament and mourn; and she being desolate shall sit upon the ground [Isa. 3:25-26].

There was a Roman medal which showed a woman weeping; the insignia beneath her read, *Judea capta*. It represented the captives of Israel. Because Israel did not heed the warnings God gave them, they went into captivity.

As I write this, the terrible loss of our young men in Vietnam is still fresh in our minds. But now we are a nation at peace, and we feel very comfortable. But, my friend, the bombs are yet to fall on our nation, which I believe will be God's judgment upon us.

# CHAPTER 4

**THEME:** *Conditions that did prevail during the Babylonian captivity and will prevail at the establishment of the kingdom*

This chapter is a continuation of one complete prophecy which began in chapter 2 and will conclude in chapter 5. In these chapters we actually have a synopsis of the entire Book of Isaiah, because he touches all the bases here that he will touch upon in the rest of the book.

Chapter 4 is the briefest chapter in the book; it is only six verses long. We have set before us a description of the conditions which prevailed at the time of the Babylonian captivity and also of the conditions which will exist during the Great Tribulation Period right before the setting up of the messianic kingdom.

The structure of the chapter is very simple. The first verse is the only one that depicts conditions during the time of the Great Tribulation, or the last days. The remainder of the chapter sets before the reader the preparation that will be necessary for entering the kingdom. This section, of course, is entirely anticipatory.

And in that day seven women shall take hold of one man, saying, We will eat our own bread, and wear our own apparel: only let us be called by thy name, to take away our reproach [Isa. 4:1].

These conditions will prevail because of the frightening casualties of war. That has been true of all wars, and these conditions will exist in the time of the Great Tribulation. In other words, because the manpower population will be so decimated by war, there will be a surplus of women, so much so that seven women will be willing to share one man in that day! And all of them will be willing to hold down a job. I suppose a man will do nothing in the world but keep books for the women and make

sure that they turn in their proper share. It is an awful condition that will prevail. After World War II we experienced, to an extent, a manpower shortage in this country and also following our involvement in the Vietnam war. At that time, when I heard that there was something like a surplus of 80,000 women, I kidded my wife that she had better take good care of me as there just weren't enough men to go around!

**In that day shall the branch of the LORD be beautiful and glorious, and the fruit of the earth shall be excellent and comely for them that are escaped of Israel [Isa. 4:2].**

"In that day" refers to the Day of the Lord. This phrase will occur again and again in Isaiah (and in all the prophets), and it will be mentioned in the New Testament. Joel particularly will have something to say about it. It begins as every Hebrew day always begins—at sundown. It begins with darkness and moves to the dawn. It begins with the Great Tribulation and goes on into the millennial kingdom.

There is also a reference in this verse to the Lord Jesus Christ for He is "the branch." There are eighteen Hebrew words translated by the one English word *branch*. All of them refer to the Lord Jesus. In this verse the word *branch* means "sprout." Later, we are going to be told that He is a branch out of a dry ground. He is something green that has sprung up in the desert.

**And it shall come to pass, that he that is left in Zion, and he that remaineth in Jerusalem, shall be called holy, even every one that is written among the living in Jerusalem [Isa. 4:3].**

There will be those of God's people, both of Israel and the Gentiles, during the Great Tribulation, who will survive that period. (Those who are martyred will, of course, be resurrected at the end of that time.) In Matthew the Lord Jesus expressed it in a way that may seem strange, but He is looking at the end of the Tribulation when He says, ". . . he that shall endure unto the end, the same shall be saved" (Matt. 24:13). Well, they were *sealed* at the beginning to make sure they got through it. The Shepherd is able to keep His own sheep, and therefore they are going to endure unto the end. We have the same thought in Revelation 7 which speaks of that great company, both Jew and Gentile, who were sealed at the beginning of the Great Tribulation and came through that period.

**When the Lord shall have washed away the filth of the daughters of Zion, and shall have purged the blood of Jerusalem from the midst thereof by the spirit of judgment, and by the spirit of burning [Isa. 4:4].**

Zechariah 13:1 tells us, "In that day there shall be a fountain opened to the house of David and to the inhabitants of Jerusalem for sin and for uncleanness."

God's people must be *prepared* to enter the kingdom. This brings up a very pertinent question. Each year as we stand on the threshold of a new year, we say we are going to do better. We have been saying the same thing for years. My question is, "Are you fit today for heaven?" Suppose God took you to heaven as you are right now. Would you be fit for heaven? I cannot answer this question for you, but God is going to have to do a great deal of repair work on Vernon McGee to make him ready for heaven. That is what life is all about: it is a school to prepare us for eternity. Many people make a sad mistake to think that this life is all there is. Preparation is made on earth for *eternity*. Suppose God took you to heaven as you are. Would you be a square peg in a round hole? I am afraid I would be. Beloved, it does not yet appear what we shall be. He is going to have to make some changes.

**And the LORD will create upon every dwelling place of mount Zion, and upon her assemblies, a cloud and smoke by day, and the shining of a flaming fire by night: for upon all the glory shall be a defence [Isa. 4:5].**

The glory of God will be upon every house in the kingdom, not just upon the temple. What a glorious thing that will be!

**And there shall be a tabernacle for a shadow in the daytime from the heat, and for a place of refuge, and for a covert from storm and from rain [Isa. 4:6].**

Security will come to the nation Israel in that day—at last. Today Israel does not have peace. Therefore this prophecy is not being fulfilled. The Jews are not back in the land with every man dwelling under his vine and fig tree in peace.

Note that peace always follows grace, mercy, and cleansing. The problem has never

been with a political party. The real problem has never been with a foreign country. The problem is in the human heart. We war because it is in our hearts. Man is a warlike creature because he is a sinner and he refuses to deal with that question. There will be one war right after the other until the heart of man is changed.

# CHAPTER 5

**THEME:** *The song of the vineyard; the six woes that follow*

This chapter brings us to the end of the section which was begun in chapter 2. The first seven verses are the song of the vineyard which tells of the sins of the nation Israel and the coming captivity. The balance of the chapter gives the six woes or the six specific sins which bring down the judgment of God upon the nation. The penalty for each sin is listed.

## THE SONG OF THE VINEYARD

Those who can read the song of the vineyard in Hebrew tell me that it is without doubt one of the most beautiful songs that has ever been written. There is nothing quite like it; there is nothing to rival it. It is a musical symphony, and it is absolutely impossible to reproduce in English. It is truly a song and comparable to any of the psalms.

The vineyard is the house of Israel (v. 7). Thus, the vineyard becomes one of the two figures in Scripture that are taken from the botanical world to represent the whole nation of Israel. The fig tree is the other figure that is used.

Before His death our Lord gave a parable of the vineyard which obviously referred to the whole house of Israel (see Matt. 21:33–46). In Isaiah the prophet announces the imminent captivity of the northern kingdom into Assyria and of the southern kingdom into Babylon. In Matthew the Lord Jesus Christ showed that God had given Israel a second chance in their return from the seventy-year Babylonian captivity, but the nation's rejection of the Son of God would usher in a more extensive and serious dispersion.

Now listen to the song of the vineyard:

**Now will I sing to my wellbeloved a song of my beloved touching his vineyard. My wellbeloved hath a vineyard in a very fruitful hill [Isa. 5:1].**

"My beloved" is the Lord Jesus Christ. He is the Messiah of Israel and the Savior of the world.

"A very fruitful hill"—there is nothing wrong with the soil. The problem is with the vineyard itself, that is, with the vine. Verse 7 makes it quite clear that the vineyard is the house of Israel; it is Judah. It is not the church or something else. This is clear; we do not have to guess at these things.

God is again inviting us into court to consider His charges against Israel. And, my friend, the minute you listen to Him and to His charge against Israel, you will find yourself condemned.

**And he fenced it, and gathered out the stones thereof, and planted it with the choicest vine, and built a tower in the midst of it, and also made a winepress therein: and he looked that it should bring forth grapes, and it brought forth wild grapes [Isa. 5:2].**

God took the nation Israel out of Egypt and placed them in the Promised Land. He expected them to produce the fruits of righteousness and required them to glorify His name. They failed ignominiously.

**And now, O inhabitants of Jerusalem, and men of Judah, judge, I pray you, betwixt me and my vineyard [Isa. 5:3].**

God asks these people to judge, to equate the difference between God and Israel. Very candidly, friend, when you look at your own life, are you ready to complain against God? I know how I whined and howled when I got cancer. I thought the Lord was being unfair. Then I had the opportunity of lying alone on that hospital bed and looking at my life. My friend, God wasn't wrong—*I* was wrong and I needed to face up to it. We need to get rid of the idea that somehow we are something special. God is not going to do anything to us that is unjust. He is not going to do anything that is wrong. You and I are wrong; God isn't wrong.

**What could have been done more to my vineyard, that I have not done in it? wherefore, when I looked that it should bring forth grapes, brought it forth wild grapes? [Isa. 5:4].**

God states that He made every provision on His part for them to produce the fruits of righteousness. Their failure under these circumstances becomes serious indeed.

**And now go to; I will tell you what I will do to my vineyard: I will take away the hedge thereof, and it shall be eaten up; and break down the wall thereof, and it shall be trodden down:**

**And I will lay it waste: it shall not be pruned, nor digged; but there shall come up briers and thorns: I will also command the clouds that they rain no rain upon it [Isa. 5:5–6].**

This is a clear prediction of the forthcoming captivities of both the kingdoms. For over five hundred years God had kept the great nations of the world off the land bridge of three continents—Palestine. He put a wall around the children of Israel. God would not let anybody touch them, though many times He could have judged them. But God says, "You are my vineyard. I have hedged you in, but now I am breaking down the wall." First Syria, then Assyria, then Babylon—they all poured into Israel's land and laid it waste. And in spite of everything that has been done in that land today, it is still a pretty desolate looking place. God has judged it.

"I will also command the clouds that they rain no rain upon it." For over a thousand years, the former (fall) and the latter (spring) rains did not fall. That is why that land is so desolate today. The former rains, I understand, have begun, but not the latter.

**For the vineyard of the LORD of hosts is the house of Israel, and the men of Judah his pleasant plant: and he looked for judgment, but behold oppression; for righteousness, but behold a cry [Isa. 5:7].**

You don't have to guess whom the prophet is talking about. The vineyard refers to the whole house of Israel, and this verse makes that crystal clear. And in that vineyard God "looked for judgment, but behold oppression; for righteousness, but behold a cry."

## THE SIX WOES

Once again God is going to spell it all out. Six woes are mentioned here, and each

one tells of a certain sin for which God is judging Israel. If you want to apply these to your life or to the life of our nation, you can do it. But the interpretation is for Israel; it has already been fulfilled for them. We can certainly make application to our own hearts and lives, however.

**Woe unto them that join house to house, that lay field to field, till there be no place, that they may be placed alone in the midst of the earth! [Isa. 5:8].**

This is the first sin of Israel. What is it? This sin is the lust of the eye; more specifically, it is covetousness. Colossians 3:5 tells us: "Mortify therefore your members which are upon the earth; fornication, uncleanness, inordinate affection, evil concupiscence, and covetousness, which is idolatry." Covetousness is idolatry. It is a big business expanding at the expense of the little man. That is what happened in Israel—the little man was squeezed out. It was done so that great fortunes might be accumulated. The only excuse for such expansion is the insatiable greed for more property and possessions. God will judge the people for that.

It is a sad story that we have here. The picture is one of a great complex of farms. In Isaiah's day the people were agricultural people. They built big corporations, big complexes. This was not done for the good of the little man, the small operator. It was done to accumulate wealth. Anything to which you give yourself completely becomes your religion. Many people today are worshiping at the altar of covetousness.

Covetousness is a mean-looking god. It has the face of a silver dollar or a dollar bill. It is one thing that brought down Israel and for which God judged them. Instead of following God's instructions, they were beginning to take all of the richness from the soil. We are doing the same thing today. We are living in a world which is actually depleted of its energy. We are frantically searching for oil, for any kind of energy that can be used. Why? Because men are covetous, and that covetousness is depleting the earth of its riches. That is a judgment of God.

**In mine ears said the LORD of hosts, Of a truth many houses shall be desolate, even great and fair, without inhabitant.**

**Yea, ten acres of vineyard shall yield one bath, and the seed of an homer shall yield an ephah [Isa. 5:9–10].**

God is simply saying that even though they expand their lands, the yield will not be great because there will be a famine which will decimate the crop. Extended holdings will not produce a bumper crop at all.

The earth you and I are living on is running short of energy. We are running out of oil. We are running out of arable lands. This subject of ecology is an important matter. Pollution is destroying much of the earth. One of these days we are going to be on a desolate planet. We are quickly running out of energy. If you are planning on taking a trip, you had better go now, because there is going to be a shortage of fuel. It may not happen in our lifetime, but there are those who believe that it will be in our lifetime. This is the judgment that God made on the nation Israel in that day.

**Woe unto them that rise up early in the morning, that they may follow strong drink; that continue until night, till wine inflame them!**

**And the harp, and the viol, the tabret, and pipe, and wine, are in their feasts: but they regard not the work of the LORD, neither consider the operation of his hands [Isa. 5:11–12].**

This is the second woe, the second sin. Drunkenness and pleasure on a national scale are the sins mentioned here, and they lead to the deadening of all spiritual perception.

I notice that the news media do not release today, as they did a number of years ago, the number of alcoholics that we have in this country. The last report I got, which was several years ago, was that there were ten million alcoholics in the United States. They *do* put in the paper what is done with the tax money the liquor industry pays. It goes to take care of the alcoholics and to maintain police forces who take care of the accidents caused by drunk drivers! Of course, no one can pay for the lives of the innocent victims taken in such useless accidents. No one knows how many decisions are made in our government by people who have just come from a cocktail party. These are the things that lower the morals of a nation. They destroy a nation and eat at its vitals like a cancer. Such a nation is on the verge of falling prey to an enemy without.

**Therefore my people are gone into captivity, because they have no knowledge: and their honorable men are famished, and their multitude dried up with thirst [Isa. 5:13].**

The majority of the people in this country think it is rather sophisticated to drink, that it is the thing to do. I was very much interested in an article in which the man being interviewed was the director of a therapeutic community for drug addicts in New York. One of the questions he was asked was, "Is there anything parents can do to prevent children from turning to drugs?" This man, whose answers indicated that he probably was not a Christian, said that of paramount importance is an attitude in the home of not using drugs, pills, or alcohol as a means of solving life's problems. He went on to say that he didn't mean that taking an occasional social drink was taboo (of course, he would not go so far as to say that!), but that the old rule, "Monkey see, monkey do," is just as valid on this issue as it is on any other. He said that youngsters who grow up in an atmosphere of drug abuse will be among the first to try marijuana or pills when confronted with their own problems.

Father, mother, if you continue to drink cocktails—and I see it in many restaurants as I travel across the country—don't be surprised if your Willie or Mary gets on dope. They will probably move in that direction. After all, why do *you* drink? The problem of young people on drugs started in the home where parents drink in order to face life. That is what destroys the home and the nation. Drunkenness is one of the things that brought down Israel. What about our nation?

**Therefore hell hath enlarged herself, and opened her mouth without measure: and their glory, and their multitude, and their pomp, and he that rejoiceth, shall descend into it [Isa. 5:14].**

The word translated "hell" in this verse is actually "the grave." It is not a reference to the lake of fire as we think of hell today. It is the Hebrew word *sheol*. It means that "the grave demands." You find this same word in Proverbs 30:16 which says, "The grave; and the barren womb; the earth that is not filled with water; and the fire that saith not, It is enough." Death, or the grave, (both satisfactory translations of *sheol*) is never satisfied. This is the question to ask when you stand at the grave of someone: Where is he? Job asked this question, "But man dieth, and wasteth away: yea, man giveth up the ghost, and where is he?" (Job 14:10). That is the question everybody is going to have to ask.

*Hell* at first did not have the idea of a local-

ity, but in time it was thought that since God was in heaven or above, hell or the grave must be below or down. In the New Testament the word *hades* is the same as the Old Testament *sheol*. The Lord Jesus used this word when He said, "And thou, Capernaum, which art exalted unto heaven, shalt be brought down to hell [hades] . . ." (Matt. 11:23). The Lord was not talking about a literal descent into the heart of the earth. He simply meant that Capernaum was going to be brought down, and all you have to do is look at the ruins of that place today to know that what He said was true. We always attach strong moral connotations to the terms of direction, *up* and *down:* up towards God and down towards hell. Here Isaiah is saying that the nation of Israel will be brought down. They are going to be taken into captivity, they are going to be brought down to the grave, and the glory of the nation will be turned into dust because of her drunkenness and pleasure.

Rudyard Kipling was a prophet as well as a poet when he wrote in his "Recessional":

> "Lo, all our pomp of yesterday
> Is one with Nineveh and Tyre."

**Woe unto them that draw iniquity with cords of vanity, and sin as it were with a cart rope [Isa. 5:18].**

This can be translated: "Woe to those whose wickedness is helped by words of lying, who in their pride and unbelief the wrath of God define." You can make a poem out of it, you see. This is the third woe, or the third sin. This is the picture of a nation giving itself in abandon to sin without shame or conscience.

**That say, Let him make speed, and hasten his work, that we may see it: and let the counsel of the Holy One of Israel draw nigh and come, that we may know it! [Isa. 5:19].**

In other words, they challenge God to do anything about their sin. It is interesting to note that no penalty is mentioned. The very silence here is frightening: the penalty is too awful to mention. The history of the deportation of the nation to Babylon tells something of the frightful judgment of God upon a people who sin with impunity against Him and defy Him. God will judge them.

Do you remember Psalm 137? In that psalm Israel prayed against Babylon. They prayed that there would be an eye for an eye and a tooth for a tooth. They said, "Happy shall he

be, that taketh and dasheth thy little ones against the stones" (Ps. 137:9). That is horrible beyond words, but that is the judgment that came to Israel. My friend, God is a God of love, but when you reach the place where you defy Him and turn your back on Him, there is no hope for you. Judgment comes. There are just too many instances in history to deny this fact, unless you want to shut your eyes to them.

**Woe unto them that call evil good, and good evil; that put darkness for light, and light for darkness; that put bitter for sweet, and sweet for bitter! [Isa. 5:20].**

This is the fourth sin against which the fourth woe is leveled. It is an attempt to destroy God's standards of right and wrong by substituting man's values which contradict His moral standards. This is the confusion that comes upon a nation when they abandon God after He has blessed them in the past for their acknowledgment of Him. England is a present-day example of this, and America is fast deteriorating in the same direction.

We have this confusion in our standards of marriage today. I listened to a very beautiful little girl tell her story on a television interview program. She was living with a man to whom she was not married, and the reason she gave was that she was being honest—she did not believe in being a hypocrite. I have news for her: she is not only a hypocrite and dishonest, she knows that what she is doing is wrong and that she should be married. God says she is living in adultery. God calls him an adulterer and her an adulteress. I don't care, my friend, what you might think about it—that's what God says.

**Woe unto them that are wise in their own eyes, and prudent in their own sight! [Isa. 5:21].**

This is the fifth woe, the sin of pride. God hates this above all else. Proverbs 6:16–17 tell us, "These six things doth the LORD hate: yea, seven are an abomination unto him: A proud look, a lying tongue, and hands that shed innocent blood." Pride was the sin of Satan according to 1 Timothy 3:6, "Not a novice, lest being lifted up with pride he fall into the condemnation of the devil." Pride is number one on God's hate parade.

**Woe unto them that are mighty to drink wine, and men of strength to mingle strong drink:**

**Which justify the wicked for reward, and take away the righteousness of the righteous from him!** [Isa. 5:22–23].

This is the sixth and last woe. Here a people have become so sodden with drunkenness that they have lost their sense of justice. Injustice and crookedness prevail, and the righteous man is falsely accused. No nation can long survive which drops so low in morals that it loses its sense of values.

Ours is a day when people are saying that wrong is right and right is wrong. In my younger days I was in a little theater group, and I remember memorizing a line from *The Great Divide:* "Wrong is wrong from the moment it happens 'til the crack of doom, and all the angels in heaven working overtime cannot make it different or less by a hair." My friend, wrong is still wrong.

**Therefore as the fire devoureth the stubble, and the flame consumeth the chaff, so their root shall be as rottenness, and their blossom shall go up as dust: because they have cast away the law of the LORD of hosts, and despised the word of the Holy One of Israel** [Isa. 5:24].

"As the fire devoureth the stubble." Though the process of deterioration and rottenness is slow and unobserved, the penalty comes like a fire in the stubble. It is fast and furious and cannot be deterred. It is the anger of the Lord bursting forth in judgment. It moves the frightful judgment of God in the last days.

In Matthew 12:20 the Lord Jesus Christ said, "A bruised reed shall he not break, and smoking flax shall he not quench, till he send forth judgment unto victory." He was quoting from Isaiah 42:3. There are certain sins that bring their own judgment; drunkenness is one, and drug abuse is another. I could give many instances of men I have seen engaged in these sins, and the sin worked in their own lives, in the lives of their families, and in their bodies until it destroyed them. God didn't have to do a thing. The smoking flax *will* break into flame, and that bruised reed *will* die. The very sin that we commit is the sin that will destroy us.

When I was a young man in Nashville, Tennessee, I went to a dentist who was also a good friend. One day he told me something which had happened in that town several years before. He told me that one of the most reputable doctors in the city had headed up a dope ring. It was difficult for the law to reach

him because of his position. One day the doctor tightened up on the dope in order to get a higher price. For a brief period of time he cut off the supply of dope. This, of course, pushed the price up higher. During that time both his son and daughter were exposed as addicts. He knew nothing about their problem until he cut off the dope supply. That man had the shock of his life, and it apparently led to his death, which occurred shortly afterward. God doesn't have to put His hand in and judge every time. In many instances He just lets sin take its course.

The sin of drinking is all around us today. God doesn't do anything about it. He doesn't have to. Drunkenness will bring its own judgment. Judgment will come to the individual, and it will come to the nation. Those of us who have been in the ministry for a long time have seen drinking increase through the years, and I have seen some heavy drinkers be converted and turn to the Lord. But some of them would leave a bottle in the icebox, just in case. That is what leads many back into the awful sin of drinking. That is what Paul is talking about in Romans 8:12 when he says, "Therefore, brethren, we are debtors, not to the flesh, to live after the flesh." In other words, make no arrangements with the flesh to do what it wants to do. Don't leave a bottle in the refrigerator. Take the bottle out and break it. Many of us kid ourselves about our sins, but some of these sins touch all of us, I am sure.

**Therefore is the anger of the LORD kindled against his people, and he hath stretched forth his hand against them, and hath smitten them: and the hills did tremble, and their carcases were torn in the midst of the streets. For all this his anger is not turned away, but his hand is stretched out still** [Isa. 5:25].

"Therefore is the anger of the LORD kindled against his people." This is a strange verse for many who want to talk about just the love of God. The love of God is real, and you cannot keep Him from loving you; but God hates sin, my friend. If you are going to love sin, still He will love you, but you can expect His judgment. The anger of the Lord is kindled against *His* people—not against the neighbors.

"But his hand is stretched out still." If Israel had gone to the Lord and trusted Him, He would have delivered them. The judgment of God is in the Book of Isaiah but so is His grace. The government of God and the grace of God—they are not in conflict. If you are

going to continue in sin, if you refuse the grace of God, then you *will* know what the government of God is.

In the rest of this chapter we see an accumulation of the judgment of God.

**And in that day they shall roar against them like the roaring of the sea: and if one look unto the land, behold darkness and sorrow, and the light is darkened in the heavens thereof [Isa. 5:30].**

Take a good look at the land of Israel today. Many people who have traveled to Israel come back and say, "It certainly is wonderful. We are seeing the fulfillment of prophecy. The land is being reclaimed." They go on and on about how prophecy is being fulfilled. I don't see it that way at all. I see a people still in darkness. I see a people far from God. I see a people who are not living in peace and who need God. They are living in fear and are in great danger in that land today. My heart goes out to them. This is the judgment of God.

Consider the following poem:

## OUR PRAYERLESS SIN

We have not wept for thy grief,
  Israel, scattered, driven,
Shut up to darkened unbelief
  While we have heaven.

We have not prayed for thy peace,
  Jerusalem forsaken;
Thy root's increase, by God's great
  grace,
  We age-long have partaken.

How trod thy street our Saviour's feet;
  How fell His tears for thee;
How, loving Him, can we forget,
  Nor long thy joys to see.

Zion, thy God remembers thee
  Though we so hard have been;
Zion, thy God remembers thee,
  With blood-bought right to cleanse,
    may He
Remove our prayerless sin.

　　　　　　　—Selected and revised

God is punishing His own people.

# CHAPTER 6

***THEME:*** *The call and commission of Isaiah to the prophetic office*

Chronologically, as well as logically, the Book of Isaiah begins with this chapter, which constitutes the crisis in the life of Isaiah and brings him into the prophetic office. Prior to this, we have no record of his life or relationship to God. His ministry began at the death of King Uzziah.

## THE VISION OF THE LORD
## SEEN BY ISAIAH

In verses 1–4 are the time, place, person, glory, and holiness of the Lord in the vision seen by Isaiah. Now notice the time, the place, and the Person:

**In the year that king Uzziah died I saw also the Lord sitting upon a throne, high and lifted up, and his train filled the temple [Isa. 6:1].**

Isaiah opens this chapter on a very doleful note taking us to the funeral of Uzziah. Uzziah

has been a good king. Now he is dead. It is the belief of many that he was the last great king of the southern kingdom of Judah and that after his death the glory of the Lord was no longer to be seen. I am not sure but what that is true. Uzziah brought the Philistines, the Arabians, and the Ammonites into subjection. He had ruled for fifty-two years, and the nation had been blessed materially during that period according to God's promise. As F. Delitzsch says, "The national glory of Israel died out too with King Uzziah and has never been recovered to this day." I heartily concur with that statement.

In the year that King Uzziah died, Isaiah is thinking, *Good King Uzziah is dead, and things are going to the bowwows now. Israel will be taken captive. Prosperity will cease. A depression will come, and famine will follow.* In that frame of mind Isaiah does what every person ought to do—he goes into the temple.

He goes to the proper place, the place where he could meet with God. Psalm 29:9 says, ". . . in his temple doth everyone speak of his glory." In God's temple Isaiah makes the discovery that the true King of the nation is not dead.

"I saw also the Lord sitting upon a throne, high and lifted up, and his train filled the temple"—*God* is on the throne.

Isaiah has already told us not to put confidence in man, whose breath is in his nostrils. When man exhales, he doesn't know for sure that he ever will be able to inhale again. A man can have a heart attack and die, just like that. Don't put your confidence in man. Old King Uzziah is dead. Yes, it is true, and the throne looks pretty bleak right now but behind the earthly throne is the heavenly throne. Isaiah sees the Lord sitting upon a throne.

That is a vision that some of God's people need in this day. I see no reason for being pessimistic. This is the greatest day in the history of the world. I would rather live right now than in any other period of time. Somebody says, "Oh, look at the terrible condition of the world. Look at our nation and the deteriorating condition in our cities." Well, the Lord said it was going to be that way. He said that tares were going to be sown in among the wheat. And He was going to let them both grow together. My business today is sowing the seed of the Word of God. I know that it is going to bring forth a harvest. And it is heading up today—there is no question about that. We don't need to be disturbed. God will take care of the harvest. Our business is to sow the seed, that is, to get the Word of God out to needy hearts.

This is a great day in which to live. Do you know that the Word of God is going out to more people than it ever has before? Even my radio broadcast is reaching more people in a half hour than I was able to reach in all my years of preaching behind a pulpit. And the message is going around the world! I realize the world conditions are alarming. The tares are really growing, but we have a good stand of wheat also. The wheat is growing right along. It is thrilling to be sowing the Word of God in this day!

When Isaiah goes into the temple, he finds that the Lord is still on the throne. And some of us need to be reminded that God is still on the throne in our day. He still hears and answers prayers. He is still doing wonderful things. Isaiah also makes another discovery when he goes into the temple. He finds out that God is high and lifted up and that His train fills the temple. That is the second thing we need to discover about God. God is high and lifted up, and He will not compromise with sin.

**Above it stood the seraphims: each one had six wings; with twain he covered his face, and with twain he covered his feet, and with twain he did fly [Isa. 6:2].**

Seraphim are around the throne of God. This is one of the few mentions of these created intelligences in Scripture. Practically nothing is known concerning them. *Seraph* means "to burn." It is the word used in connection with the sin offerings and judgment. Apparently the seraphim are in contrast to the cherubim. The seraphim search out sin, and the cherubim protect the holiness of God. Never is the word *seraph* connected with the sweet incense or sweet savor offerings, those offerings which speak of the person of Christ. The seraph is active, and the cherub is passive. We will find both of them in the Books of Ezekiel and Revelation as the "living creatures." The seraphim in Isaiah's vision are protecting the holiness of God. He is "high and lifted up."

God will not compromise with evil. I thank Him for that. He will not compromise with evil in your life, nor in my life, because evil and sin have brought all of the sorrows in this world. Sin is that which puts gray in the hair, creates the tottering step and the stooped shoulder. It is the thing that breaks up homes and lives, and fills the grave. I am glad that God does not compromise with it. God says that He hates sin and He intends to destroy it and remove it from this universe. Today our God is moving forth uncompromisingly, unhesitatingly, and undeviatingly against sin. He does not intend to accept the white flag of surrender from it. He intends to drive sin from His universe. That is what God says. He is high and lifted up. My friend, you and I are going to have to bow before Him. When Isaiah saw God on the throne, it brought him down upon his face. Oh, how desperately the church needs another vision of God, not just of His love, but of His holiness and righteousness! Because God is holy, He moves in judgment against sin—and He has never asked me to apologize for Him. So I won't. God is angry against sin, and He will punish those who engage in it. He *says* He will.

He also says that He is your Friend and will save you. But you have to come His way. You

have to put your faith and trust in His Son, the Lord Jesus Christ. In John 14:6 Jesus said, ". . . I am the way, the truth, and the life: no man cometh unto the Father, but by me."

**And one cried unto another, and said, Holy, holy, holy, is the LORD of hosts: the whole earth is full of his glory [Isa. 6:3].**

This pictures the holiness and glory of our God. He is high and lifted up; and, if we would see Him today in that position, we would be delivered from low living. It would also deliver some folk from this easy familiarity that they seem to have with Jesus. They talk about Him as if He were a buddy and as if they could speak to Him in any way they please. My friend, you cannot rush into the presence of God. He doesn't permit it. You come to the Father through Christ. This is the only way He can be approached. You can never come into the presence of the Father because of who you are. You come into His presence because you are *in Christ.* The Lord Jesus made that very clear when He said, "No man cometh unto the Father, but by me." If you are His child, you can come with boldness to the throne of grace, but you cannot come to Him on any other basis.

**And the posts of the door moved at the voice of him that cried, and the house was filled with smoke [Isa 6:4].**

"The voice of him that cried" is the voice of the seraphim as they proclaim God's holiness.
What effect is this going to have on Isaiah?

**Then said I, Woe is me! for I am undone; because I am a man of unclean lips, and I dwell in the midst of a people of unclean lips: for mine eyes have seen the King, the LORD of hosts [Isa. 6:5].**

Isaiah was God's man before he had this experience, but it still had a tremendous effect on him. The reaction of Isaiah to such a vision is revolutionary. He sees himself as he really is in the presence of God—undone. It reveals to him his condition. When he had seen God, he could see himself. The problem with many of us today is that we don't walk in the light of the Word of God. If we did, we would see ourselves. That is what John is talking about in the first chapter of his first epistle: "But if we walk in the light, as he is in the light, we have fellowship one with another, and the blood of Jesus Christ his Son cleanseth [keeps on cleansing] us from all sin" (1 John 1:7). If

we walk in the light of His Word, we are going to see exactly what Isaiah saw—that we are undone and men of unclean lips. You have never really seen the Lord, my friend, if you feel that you are worthy, or merit something, or have some claim upon God.

Job had an experience similar to Isaiah's, and his reaction was "I abhor myself." Job was a self-righteous man. He could maintain his integrity in the presence of his friends who were attempting to tear him to bits. They told him that he was a rotten sinner, but he looked them straight in the eye and said, "As far as I know, I am a righteous man." From his viewpoint he was right, and he won the match against them. But he was not perfect. When Job came into the presence of God, he no longer wanted to talk about maintaining his righteousness. When Job really saw who he was, he said, "I have heard of thee by the hearing of the ear: but now mine eye seeth thee. Wherefore I abhor myself, and repent in dust and ashes" (Job 42:5–6). If you walk in the light of the Word of God, you will see yourself, and you will know that even as a child of God you need the blood of Jesus Christ to cleanse you from all sin.

You will find that other men had the same reaction when they came into the presence of God. John, on the Isle of Patmos, wrote, "And when I saw him, I fell at his feet as dead . . ." (Rev. 1:17). When Daniel saw the Lord, he said, "Therefore I was left alone, and saw this great vision, and there remained no strength in me: for my comeliness was turned in me into corruption, and I retained no strength" (Dan. 10:8). That was also the experience of Saul of Tarsus, who became Paul the apostle. After Paul met the Lord, he no longer saw himself as a self-righteous Pharisee, but as a lost sinner in need of salvation. He then could say, "But what things were gain to me, those I counted loss for Christ" (Phil. 3:7). He saw his need of Jesus Christ.

**Then flew one of the seraphims unto me, having a live coal in his hand, which he had taken with the tongs from off the altar [Isa. 6:6].**

This "live coal" has come from the burnt altar where sin had been dealt with. In the next chapter we will see the prediction of the birth of Christ, but it is not the incarnation of Christ that saves us, it is His death upon the cross. For this reason, Isaiah needs the live coal from off the burnt altar, which is symbolic of Christ's death. This living coal represents

the cleansing blood of Christ that keeps on cleansing us from all sin.

**And he laid it upon my mouth, and said, Lo, this hath touched thy lips; and thine iniquity is taken away, and thy sin purged [Isa. 6:7].**

Isaiah is a man of unclean lips, and the condition for cleansing is confession: "If we confess our sins, he is faithful and just to forgive us our sins, and to cleanse us from all unrighteousness" (1 John 1:9). I believe it would be more accurate to say that this glowing coal is symbolic of none other than the Lord Jesus Christ. He was the One high and lifted up on the throne, and He was the One lifted up on the cross. It is absolutely essential that He be lifted up, because He came down to this earth and became one of us that He might become ". . . the Lamb of God which taketh away the sin of the world" (John 1:29).

And so the lips of this man Isaiah are cleansed. I take it that this act of putting the coal on his lips was just an external manifestation of what happened in the inner man. It is what proceeds out of the heart of a man that goes through the lips; and, when the lips are cleansed, it means that the heart is cleansed also.

There was a man in the New Testament who also was "undone." His name was Paul, and he cried out, "O wretched man that I am! who shall deliver me from the body of this death?" (Rom. 7:24). When Paul said this, he was not a lost sinner but a saint of God, learning the lesson from God that he needed to walk in the Spirit because he could not live for God by himself. Living for God can only be accomplished by divine grace. Man's responsibility is to confess his sinfulness and his inability to please God. Therefore, we need to have the redemption of Christ applied to our lives again, and again, and again.

After Isaiah's lips are cleansed, something happens:

**Also I heard the voice of the Lord, saying, Whom shall I send, and who will go for us? Then said I, Here am I; send me [Isa. 6:8].**

It is interesting that up to this time Isaiah had never heard the call of God.

I think many Christians have never felt like they were called to do anything for God because they have never been cleansed. They have not seen this great need as Christians. God is not going to use a dirty vessel, I can assure you of that. It is true that God does bless His Word even when it is given out by those who are playing around with sin, but in time God judges them severely. I don't dare mention any names, but I have known certain ministers who for awhile enjoyed the blessing of God. Then they got into sin, and it wasn't long until the judgment of God fell upon them.

Isaiah heard God's call: "Whom shall I send, and who will go for us?" I don't need to call attention to the fact that you have both the singular and the plural in this verse, and I believe it sets forth the Trinity. Isaiah's response was, "Here am I; send me." Isaiah heard God's call for the first time and responded to it, as a cleansed individual will do. There are too many people today who are asked to do something in the church who first of all ought to get cleansed and straightened out with the Lord. They need to have their lips touched with a living coal. They need to confess the sins in their lives, because their service will be sterile and frustrating until that takes place.

Now notice the commission to Isaiah:

**And he said, Go, and tell this people, Hear ye indeed, but understand not; and see ye indeed, but perceive not [Isa. 6:9].**

The message Isaiah is told to give is very, very strange. "This people" means, of course, the nation of Israel.

**Make the heart of this people fat, and make their ears heavy, and shut their eyes; lest they see with their eyes, and hear with their ears, and understand with their heart, and convert, and be healed [Isa. 6:10].**

At first glance it looks as if the prophet is being sent to those who are blind, deaf, and hardened people, but I think I can safely say that God never hardens hearts that would otherwise be soft. God simply brings the hardness to the surface; He does not make the heart hard. He does not make blind the eyes of those who want to see, but apart from His intervention they would never see. Nothing but the foolish blasphemy of men would say that God hardens or blinds.

Isaiah's job was to take a message of light to the people. Light merely reveals the blindness of the people. In darkness they do not know if they are blind or not. Matthew 13:14–15 records the words of our Lord: "And in them is fulfilled the prophecy of Esaias, which saith, By hearing ye shall hear, and shall not

understand; and seeing ye shall see, and shall not perceive: For this people's heart is waxed gross, and their ears are dull of hearing, and their eyes they have closed; lest at any time they should see with their eyes, and hear with their ears, and should understand with their heart, and should be converted, and I should heal them."

Let me illustrate this. When I was a boy in Oklahoma, I used to have to milk a stubborn old cow. When it grew dark early in the evenings, I would have to take a lantern out to the barn with me. When I reached the corn-crib two things would happen. The rats ran for cover—I could hear them taking off—and the little birds that were roosting up in the rafters would begin to twitter around and sing. The presence of light caused one to flee and the other to sing. Now, did the light make a rat a rat? No. He was a rat before the light got there. The light only revealed that he was a rat. When the Lord Jesus came into the world, He was the Light of the world. In His presence two things happened: He caused the birds to sing and the rats to run.

Let me illustrate this same thought with another story. Years ago there was a big explosion in a mine in West Virginia, and many men were blocked off in the mine because of the cave-ins. After several days a rescue party dug through to the trapped men. And one of the first things they managed to get through to them was a light. After the light came on, a fine young miner said, "Why doesn't someone turn on a light?" The other miners looked at him startled, suddenly realizing that he had been blinded by the explosion. But it took a light to reveal that he was blind.

God blinds nobody. He hardens no heart. When the light shines in, it reveals what an individual is, and that is what Isaiah means. That is exactly why the Lord Jesus Christ quoted this passage.

Paul wrote, "Now thanks be unto God, which always causeth us to triumph in Christ, and maketh manifest the savour of his knowledge by us in every place. For we are unto God a sweet savour of Christ, in them that are saved, and in them that perish: To the one we are the savour of death unto death; and to the other the savour of life unto life. And who is sufficient for these things?" (2 Cor. 2:14–16). I have often said, as I have given an invitation to receive Christ, "If you have rejected Christ—if you come into this church as a lost person and are leaving a lost person—I am no longer your friend, because you cannot now go into the presence of God and say that you never heard the gospel."

You see, the light of the gospel revealed that they were blind, and they rejected Jesus Christ. He didn't make them blind, but He only revealed their blindness.

"Now thanks be unto God, which always causeth us to triumph in Christ"—we always triumph. There are those who like to boast of the number who are being saved, but I would much rather boast of the fact that thousands and even several millions of people are hearing the Word of God. My business is sowing the seed, the Word of God. It is the business of the Spirit of God to touch the hearts of those who hear.

# CHAPTER 7

**THEME:** *Prediction of the virgin birth of Immanuel and of Assyria's invasion of Judah*

Verses 1 and 2 of this chapter speak of the civil war between Judah and Israel with Syria allied to Israel, resulting in a state of fear in Judah. Verses 3–9 tell us about the conduit of the upper pool where Isaiah and his son Shear-jashub meet Ahaz, king of Judah, with an encouraging word from the Lord. Verses 10–16 speak of the confirmation by the sign of the virgin birth to the house of David when Ahaz refuses to ask for a sign. Verses 17–25 tell of the coming invasion of the land of Judah by Assyria, which is predicted as a judgment.

**And it came to pass in the days of Ahaz the son of Jotham, the son of Uzziah, king of Judah, that Rezin the king of Syria, and Pekah the son of Remaliah, king of Israel went up toward Jerusalem to war against it, but could not prevail against it [Isa 7:1].**

In 2 Kings 16:2 we read, "Twenty years old was Ahaz when he began to reign, and reigned sixteen years in Jerusalem, and did not that which was right in the sight of the LORD his God, like David his father." The prophecy of chapter 7 follows the call and commission of Isaiah in chapter 6, which took place at the death of Uzziah. Jotham, his son, succeeded him to the throne; and he reigned sixteen years. In 2 Kings 15:32–34 we are told, "In the second year of Pekah the son of Remaliah king of Israel began Jotham the son of Uzziah king of Judah to reign. Five and twenty years old was he when he began to reign, and he reigned sixteen years in Jerusalem. And his mother's name was Jerusha, the daughter of Zadok. And he did that which was right in the sight of the LORD: he did according to all that his father Uzziah had done." Jotham was a good king, as was his father Uzziah. Ahaz, Jotham's son, succeeds him, and he does that which was evil.

Ahaz will reign for sixteen years, and he will be a very bad king indeed. There will be a time of civil war during his reign. It will be a time of great distress in Israel. If you want to know just how bad things were, the record is in 2 Kings 16:3–4: "But he [Ahaz] walked in the way of the kings of Israel, yea, and made his son to pass through the fire, according to the abominations of the heathen, whom the LORD cast out from before the children of Israel. And he sacrificed and burnt incense in the high places, and on the hills, and under every green tree." Ahaz is a bad egg, I can assure you of that, and he is frightened because Israel in the north teamed up with Syria, and they are coming against him. Although they do not prevail at first, Ahaz has every reason to believe that they finally will prevail.

**And it was told the house of David, saying, Syria is confederate with Ephraim. And his heart was moved, and the heart of his people, as the trees of the wood are moved with the wind [Isa. 7:2].**

Ahaz cannot expect the blessing of God upon him or the nation. As a result, the alliance of Rezin, king of Syria, with Pekah, king of Israel, terrifies him and his people. Previously both Syria and Israel had attempted to take Judah. Alone they could not prevail, but together Ahaz is confident that they will be able to take Jerusalem. In spite of the fact that Ahaz is a godless king, God is not yet ready to let the people of Judah go into captivity. As we already know from history, Judah is not going to go into captivity in the north, but many years later they will be taken captive to Babylon.

**Then said the LORD unto Isaiah, Go forth now to meet Ahaz, thou, and Shear-jashub thy son, at the end of the conduit of the upper pool in the highway of the fuller's field [Isa. 7:3].**

Because God is not ready to deliver the kingdom of Judah into captivity, He wants to encourage the king so he will not make an unwise and frantic alliance with Egypt. So God tells Isaiah to meet with Ahaz.

There are several things we need to look at in this verse. First of all, Isaiah is to meet Ahaz "at the end of the conduit of the upper pool." The place where he is to meet the king is suggestive. It is from this conduit that the life-giving waters pour for thirsty Jerusalem. It is here that the people can quench their thirst. You can't get much satisfaction from a pipe filled with water—you must have a spigot on it somewhere. You must go to the place where the water comes out of the pipe.

Now this is symbolic of the fact that you are not going to get any blessing out of that house of David, but way down at the end of his line One is coming as the "water of life." That One was the Lord Jesus Christ. He came in the line of David to bring the water of life.

Isaiah is to meet the king at the upper "pool." The word for "pool" is *berekah* from the root word meaning "blessing." I can assure you that in that land a pool of water is a blessing. This same word is used in Psalm 84:6, ". . . the rain also filleth the pools [*berakah*]," everywhere else is rendered "blessing." This is a very interesting thing.

Notice also that it is "the *upper* pool." *Upper* is the word used over thirty times for the Most High. You may recall that it was said of the one who came out to minister to Abraham that he was the priest of the Most High God (see Gen. 14:18). Now the blessing of the Most High God was given "at the end of the conduit" when Jesus came into the world.

"In the highway of the fuller's field." The highway is a path which is elevated above the surrounding land to keep the traveler's feet clean. The spiritual application of the word *highway* is made clear in Proverbs 16:17: "The highway of the upright is to depart from evil. . . ." This highway is the way of holiness. Isaiah will use this same figure in Isaiah 35:8: "And an highway shall be there, and a way, and it shall be called The way of holiness." This very interesting symbolism refers to the

One who is the way, the truth, and the life. The psalmist wrote in Psalms 84:5: "Blessed is the man whose strength is in thee; in whose heart are the ways of them." That is, blessed is the one who has the One who is the way, the truth, and the life.

Notice also that the meeting was to take place in the "fuller's field." The fuller's field was the place where folk went to wash their clothes. It was the laundry of that day. Applying this to our own lives, if we want to get our lives cleansed, we must come to the Lord Jesus Christ. He said, ". . . ye are clean through the word which I have spoken unto you" (John 15:3).

So you see, it is no accident that Isaiah is sent to this very interesting place for his meeting with Ahaz. It has a wonderful spiritual meaning for us.

Isaiah is told to take his son Shear-jashub with him. That is quite a name for a boy, but it is nothing compared to the second son whom we shall meet in chapter 8. *Shear-jashub* means "a remnant shall return." The interesting thing is that God has always had a remnant that was true to Him.

**And say unto him, Take heed, and be quiet; fear not, neither be fainthearted for the two tails of these smoking firebrands, for the fierce anger of Rezin with Syria, and of the son of Remaliah.**

**Because Syria, Ephraim, and the son of Remaliah, have taken evil counsel against thee, saying,**

**Let us go up against Judah, and vex it, and let us make a breach therein for us, and set a king in the midst of it, even the son of Tabeal:**

**Thus saith the Lord GOD, It shall not stand, neither shall it come to pass.**

**For the head of Syria is Damascus, and the head of Damascus is Rezin; and within threescore and five years shall Ephraim be broken, that it be not a people.**

**And the head of Ephraim is Samaria, and the head of Samaria is Remaliah's son. If ye will not believe, surely ye shall not be established. [Isa. 7:4–9].**

The tenor of the message is to let Ahaz know that he need not fear the alliance of his two enemies in the north. God has determined that their venture will be a failure. The problem is, how will Ahaz know it? To begin with,

he is a skeptic, a doubter, and an unbeliever. How will he be convinced that what Isaiah is saying is true?

God has never asked anyone to believe anything that does not rest upon a foundation. Faith does not mean to move blindly into some area and say, "Oh, I am trusting God." That is very foolish. God never asks us to do that. For example, in our salvation we do not bring a little lamb to offer as a sacrifice; our faith rests upon the historical facts of the death, the burial and the resurrection of the Son of God. God never asks us to take a leap in the dark. He asks us to believe and trust something which rests upon a firm foundation, and it is the *only* foundation, "For other foundation can no man lay than that is laid, which is Jesus Christ" (1 Cor. 3:11). If any person is an honest unbeliever and sincerely wants to know God, he will come to a saving faith. Folk with whom I have dealt who say that they cannot believe are not being honest. For example, a young fellow in San Francisco told me, "Oh, I want to believe; I am searching for the truth." There he was, living with a girl in an adulterous relationship and saying that he was searching for the truth! The fact of the matter is that no man's eyes are blindfolded unless he himself chooses to be blindfolded. If a person really wants to know God and will give up his sin and turn to Christ, God will make Himself real to him. In our day the problem is that a great many folk do not really mean business with God.

That is the problem with King Ahaz—he doesn't mean business with God. Listen to him—

**Moreover the LORD spake again unto Ahaz, saying,**

**Ask thee a sign of the LORD thy God; ask it either in the depth, or in the height above [Isa. 7:10–11].**

God knows that Ahaz does not have faith, and He is willing to give the king faith; but Ahaz is nothing but a pious fraud—and there are a lot of those around today. Listen to his false piety:

**But Ahaz said, I will not ask, neither will I tempt the LORD [Isa. 7:12].**

Isn't that sweet of him? He sounds so nice, but he is one of the biggest hypocrites you will find in Scripture. This sort of thing is sickening, and I believe God feels that way about it.

**And he said, Hear ye now, O house of David; Is it a small thing for you to**

**weary men, but will ye weary my God also? [Isa. 7:13].**

I hope you won't mind my telling a little story. One day, in a Sunday school class for junior boys and girls, the teacher was telling the story about the Good Samaritan. As she related the parable, she was painting a vivid picture. She told how the man fell among thieves, how he was beaten up, and blood was gushing out from the wounds in his body. She told about the priest, and the Pharisee, and finally she came to the Good Samaritan. She wanted to clinch her presentation by making an application to the lives of the children. She first asked a little girl, "What would you have done?" She said, "Oh, I would have stayed and nursed him for a few days." The next little boy didn't want to be outdone, so he said, "And I would have brought him a box of candy." The teacher went around the class with her question, and finally came to a little girl who had a very distressed look on her face. The teacher said to her, "What would you have done?" She said, "I think I would have *thrown up!*" Believe me, the teacher had painted a gory picture, and that little girl was being honest.

I think God feels that way about our piosity. My friend, don't think you are being pious when you say, "Oh, I won't test God." God says, "Test Me. Try Me, and see if I am not good." I actually feel fatigued when I talk to some folk who say that they are just going to step out on "faith." Oh, my friend, wait until God puts a rock underneath you. Wait until God gives you definite leading before you make a fool of yourself and bring criticism upon the cause of Christ.

God says to this unbelieving king, "I'm not asking you to believe My message just because Isaiah said it. I want to put a foundation under it. I want to give you a supernatural sign so you will know that the message is from Me." But Ahaz refuses to ask for a sign. So God is going to give a sign—not to Ahaz—but to the whole house of David.

**Therefore the Lord himself shall give you a sign; Behold, a virgin shall conceive, and bear a son, and shall call his name Immanuel [Isa. 7:14].**

God puts a foundation under His prophecy; and, if you want to know whether or not the virgin birth is true, you can find out if you read the four Gospels. For example, in Matthew we read, "Now the birth of Jesus Christ was on this wise: When as his mother Mary was espoused to Joseph, before they came together, she was found with child of the Holy Ghost. Then Joseph her husband, being a just man, and not willing to make her a public example, was minded to put her away privily. But while he thought on these things, behold, the angel of the Lord appeared unto him in a dream, saying, Joseph, thou son of David, fear not to take unto thee Mary thy wife: for that which is conceived in her is of the Holy Ghost. And she shall bring forth a son, and thou shalt call his name JESUS: for he shall save his people from their sins. Now all this was done, that it might be fulfilled which was spoken of the Lord by the prophet, saying, Behold, a virgin shall be with child, and shall bring forth a son, and they shall call his name Emmanuel, which being interpreted is, God with us" (Matt. 1:18–23).

Isaiah 7:14 has become one of the most controversial verses in Scripture because of the prophecy concerning the virgin birth. Unbelievers have quite naturally discounted it and have sought desperately, but in vain, for a loophole to reject the virgin birth. The battle has been waged about the meaning of the Hebrew word *almah*, which is translated "virgin."

The fact that the angel quotes this prophecy in Isaiah 7:14 to Joseph as an explanation for Mary's being with child before her marriage to him is satisfactory evidence that the prophecy referred to an unmarried woman who had a son without physical contact with any man. The word used by Matthew (see Matt. 1:23) is the Greek word *parthenos*, which definitely means "virgin." The same Greek word was used for the Parthenon, the Greek temple to the goddess Athena, which the Greeks characterized as being a virgin.

When the Revised Standard Version of the Bible was first published, the Hebrew word *almah* was translated "young woman," with "virgin" in the footnotes—of course, it should have been reversed. Their argument was that *almah* meant only a young woman. While it is true that there are places in the Scriptures where it is translated "young woman," it is evident that it means "virgin."

For example, when Abraham's servant went to Haran in search of a bride for Isaac and he prayed that God would direct him to the right girl, this is how Rebekah was described: "And the damsel was very fair to look upon, a virgin, neither had any man known her . . ." (Gen. 24:16). The word *damsel* is the Hebrew word *naarah*, meaning "young woman," but that she was a virgin was made clear also. Then when the servant was

rehearsing this experience of praying for God's guidance, he said, "Behold, I stand by the well of water; and it shall come to pass, that when the virgin cometh forth to draw water . . ." (Gen. 24:43), the Hebrew word *almah* is translated "virgin." I don't think that anyone could misunderstand what is being said here. When the word *almah* was used, it referred to a virgin young woman, that is, one who had had no sexual relationship with a man.

When the liberal theologian says that the Bible does not teach the virgin birth of Jesus, I feel like asking him if his papa had talked to him when he was a boy about the birds and the bees. He can deny that he believes in the virgin birth of Jesus, but he cannot deny that Isaiah and Matthew are talking about the virgin birth of Jesus.

Notice again Isaiah's prophecy: "Behold, a virgin shall conceive, and bear a son, and shall call his name Immanuel." Isaiah said that His name would be Immanuel, but you cannot find any place in the Gospels where He is called by that name. *Immanuel* means "God with us." They called Him "Jesus" because He would save His people from their sins. But, friend, He cannot save the people from their sins unless He is Immanuel, "God with us." Everytime you call Him Jesus, you are saying, "God with us." He is God. He is God with us and God for us. He is our Savior, born of a virgin. Have you put your trust in Him?

When Isaiah gave this prophecy in 7:14, someone probably came to him and said, "When will this take place?" I have a notion that Isaiah looked down through the centuries and said, "It will be a long time." Then how would the people of his generation know the prediction was true? The virgin birth of Christ would come to pass, just as Isaiah said it would, because God had spoken through Isaiah on many other things that were fulfilled during the days in which he spoke them. One

of them was his prophecy about Hezekiah and the Assyrians, which we shall see in the historic section of Isaiah. The Assyrians once gathered outside the walls of Jerusalem, and they were 150,000 strong. Things looked bad for Jerusalem. It looked as if the city would fall. So Hezekiah went into the temple, got down on his knees, and fell on his face before God. He cried out for deliverance, and God sent Isaiah to him with a message. Isaiah told Hezekiah that he didn't have to worry. The Assyrians would not come into the city, nor would they take it. In fact, Isaiah told the king that not even one arrow would be shot into Jerusalem. There were 150,000 soldiers outside the walls of Jerusalem and each soldier had a quiver full of arrows on his back and a bow in his hand. You would think that out of that many soldiers there would be one that was trigger-happy, one who would shoot an arrow over the wall just to see if anyone would yell. If just *one* soldier had shot one arrow over the wall into the city, Isaiah would have rightly been declared a false prophet. But no arrows were shot; the city was spared. What Isaiah had told Hezekiah came true. And the New Testament bears witness to the fact that the virgin birth of the Lord Jesus Christ came to pass exactly as Isaiah had predicted.

**Butter and honey shall he eat, that he may know to refuse the evil, and choose the good [Isa. 7:15].**

Jesus was reared as a poor peasant in Palestine. This food was the simple diet of the poor.

**For before the child shall know to refuse the evil, and choose the good, the land that thou abhorrest shall be forsaken of both her kings [Isa. 7:16].**

This verse would be fulfilled by the time the Messiah came. This seemed unlikely in Ahaz' day.

*THEME: The birth of the prophet's second son as a sign; prediction of Assyria's invasion of Immanuel's land*

Chapters 7–12 constitute a series of prophecies given during the reign of Ahaz. Some have attempted to identify the virgin's Son of chapter 7 with the prophet's son in chapter 8. The names preclude that possibility, and the additional information in chapter 9 makes it an impossibility for the two to be identical. The prophet's son is a sign (see v. 18).

This chapter is rather significant as it contains the prediction of the invasion of Immanuel's land by the king of Assyria. God had kept the flood tide of foreign invasions walled off from His people for over five hundred years. Now He opens the floodgates and permits an enemy to cover the land like a flood. The people are looking to a confederacy rather than looking to God for help.

This chapter concludes with a warning against spiritualism as the last resort of people who have rejected God's counsel and turned in desperation to the satanic world. The end will be trouble, darkness, and anguish.

## THE BIRTH OF THE PROPHET'S SECOND SON AS A SIGN

**Moreover the LORD said unto me, Take thee a great roll, and write in it with a man's pen concerning Maher-shalal-hash-baz [Isa. 8:1].**

If you thought Shear-jashub was a strange name for a boy, try this one on for size! Maher-shalal-hash-baz is a remarkable name for a boy in any language. How would you like to carry this cognomen through life? That's what Isaiah's son had to do. I don't know what his nickname was. They may have shortened his name to Maher, or Hash, or even Baz. There is a reason, however, why God wants Isaiah to give his sons these unusual names. The reason is found in verse 18 which says, "Behold, I and the children whom the LORD hath given me are for signs and for wonders in Israel from the LORD of hosts, which dwelleth in mount Zion." Both sons are signs, and their names carry a message.

*Maher-shalal-baz* means "hasten booty, speed prey." This simply means that God is against those who are against His people. Paul puts it like this: ". . . If God be for us, who can be against us?" (Rom. 8:31).

This boy's name is also a message for Ahaz, the man on the throne. He is a godless man, and God is trying to reach him. He tells Isaiah to get a great tablet and write on it with a "man's pen"—or, the stylus of a frail, mortal man. He is then to hang it up in a prominent place like a billboard so that everyone can read it. God wants this boy's name written down so that the most humble person in the kingdom will see it, read it, and understand it. God is trying to reach Ahaz, first through Isaiah's first son, Shear-jashub ("a remnant shall return"), and then through Maher-shalal-hash-baz ("hasten booty, speed prey"). This second son's name is to assure Ahaz that God will take care of the enemies of His people.

**And I took unto me faithful witnesses to record, Uriah the priest, and Zechariah the son of Jeberechiah [Isa. 8:2].**

*Uriah* means "Jehovah is my light." *Zechariah* means "Jehovah remembers." *Jeberechiah* means "Jehovah will bless." This is an interesting combination, is it not? Thus, the one witness says by his name, "Jehovah is my light," and the other says, "Jehovah's purpose is to bless." The offspring of these is the grace of God—that is, He will never forget His people.

In all of Isaiah's actions there is a message for the people. He is acting out and writing out his message so that the people will understand it. The Book of Isaiah is a picture parable. Our Lord used this method also. The reason is that people will look at a picture. It is somewhat like television. It is amazing how many of us will sit in front of the television screen and watch things from that idiot box which under different circumstances we wouldn't waste our time on. Because God knows the inclination of mankind, He tries to get a message across to these people by using a picture.

**And I went unto the prophetess; and she conceived, and bare a son. Then said the LORD to me, Call his name Maher-shalal-hash-baz [Isa. 8:3].**

"The prophetess" in this verse is Isaiah's wife, Mrs. Isaiah. She conceives and bears a son, and the child's name is given to him before he is born.

For before the child shall have knowledge to cry, My father, and my mother, the riches of Damascus and the spoil of Samaria shall be taken away before the king of Assyria [Isa. 8:4].

Before this child is able to say "Mommy" and "Daddy," the Assyrians will invade Syria and Samaria. The enemy in the north that is planning to come against Judah is going to be taken away into captivity. It will not be due to the brilliant military ability of Ahaz to work out a strategy that will bring victory. The victory will be due to the sovereign grace of God—God is making this perfectly clear.

The LORD spake also unto me again, saying,

Forasmuch as this people refuseth the waters of Shiloah that go softly, and rejoice in Rezin and Remaliah's son;

Now therefore, behold, the Lord bringeth up upon them the waters of the river, strong and many, even the king of Assyria, and all his glory: and he shall come up over all his channels, and go over all his banks [Isa. 8:5–7].

This is another remarkable passage of Scripture. The people "refuseth the waters of Shiloah," which means "sent." They refuse the peace God offered them, a peace here typified by this gentle, rippling brook. In contrast, we see in verse 7 "the waters of the river, strong and many." This is evidently the Euphrates River where Assyria was located. These waters came down like a flood. In other words, the flood waters of the Euphrates represent the judgment of God and are contrasted with the gentle waters of Shiloah. God is giving a message to His people through these two rivers. As Shakespeare put it in his play *As You Like It*, there are "tongues in trees, books in the running brooks, sermons in stones, and good in everything."

Shiloah is a softly flowing little spring. It doesn't amount to much today, but it did in Isaiah's day. It flows between Mount Zion and Mount Moriah. There is a message in that little stream, a message that you will hear if you have a blood-tipped ear. It is a message sweeter than the rippling music of the stream itself. It is the story of grace, of Mount Zion, which stands in contrast to Mount Sinai, which is symbolic of the Mosaic Law. Moriah is where Abraham offered his son, where David bought the threshingfloor of Araunah, and where Solomon put up the temple. And

down at the end of that great shaft of rocks is Golgotha, where Christ was crucified. This speaks of grace. Moriah is where God provided Himself a Lamb. He spared Abraham's son, but He did not spare His own Son.

So here God is speaking grace to this man, Ahaz. He is saying to him, "I'll spare you, if only you will turn to Me."

And he shall pass through Judah; he shall overflow and go over, he shall reach even to the neck; and the stretching out of his wings shall fill the breadth of thy land, O Immanuel [Isa. 8:8].

God will permit Assyrians to overflow the land of Judah, but He will never permit them to take Jerusalem.

## PRONOUNCEMENT AGAINST A CONFEDERACY AS A SUBSTITUTE FOR GOD

Associate yourselves, O ye people, and ye shall be broken in pieces; and give ear, all ye of far countries: gird yourselves, and ye shall be broken in pieces; gird yourselves, and ye shall be broken in pieces [Isa. 8:9].

This is a warning against nations who form an alliance against God's land. Beginning with Isaiah 13, we are going to have a series of messages to the nations that were contiguous to Israel, or at least had dealings with them in that day, and we will find that the judgment of God will come upon them. That section which goes all the way from Isaiah 13 to Isaiah 35 is a most remarkable section in God's Word. Most of it is fulfilled prophecy. God says that the nations will never deter His purpose here on earth. It is interesting that the nations of the world no longer seek wisdom or counsel from God. God does have a purpose, and His purpose *will* prevail. If a nation goes in the other direction, judgment will come upon it.

Take counsel together, and it shall come to nought; speak the word, and it shall not stand: for God is with us.

For the LORD spake thus to me with a strong hand, and instructed me that I should not walk in the way of this people, saying,

Say ye not, A confederacy, to all them to whom this people shall say, A confederacy; neither fear ye their fear, nor be afraid [Isa. 8:10–12].

Judah is not to be alarmed by the confederacy of Syria and Samaria. Fear had caused those in the north to unite, and God urges His people, "neither fear ye their fear." In other words, they are not to turn to an ally among the nations, which probably would have been Egypt. Later on they will ally themselves with Egypt, which brings great tragedy to the land.

**Sanctify the LORD of hosts himself; and let him be your fear, and let him be your dread.**

**And he shall be for a sanctuary; but for a stone of stumbling and for a rock of offence to both the houses of Israel, for a gin and and for a snare to the inhabitants of Jerusalem [Isa. 8:13–14].**

They are to fear God above and look to Him. He will be either their salvation or a stone of stumbling. Cromwell was once asked why he was such a brave man. He had the reputation of being one of the bravest men who ever lived. He said, "I have learned that when you fear God, you have no man to fear." Paul said in 1 Cor. 1:23, "But we preach Christ crucified, unto the Jews a stumblingblock, and unto the Greeks foolishness." The Lord Jesus said that either you will fall on this stone—and He is that stone—fall on Him for salvation, rest upon Him who is the only foundation, and you will be saved; or He, the stone, will fall on you, judge you, and it will grind you to powder (see Matt. 21:44). You have two options: you can either accept Him or reject Him.

"Sanctify the LORD of hosts himself" is a strange injunction. Peter used this: "But sanctify the Lord God in your hearts: and be ready always to give an answer to every man that asketh you a reason of the hope that is in you with meekness and fear" (1 Pet. 3:15). This is what God's people need to do. Today there is this light thinking about God, a lack of reverence for Him and for His Word. There are those who sometimes ridicule things that are sacred, making light of things that should not be made light of. You and I need to sanctify the Lord God in our hearts, because there are multitudes of people today who are not convinced that ". . . the LORD is in his holy temple: let all the earth keep silence before him" (Hab. 2:20). If they believed, my friend, that He is in your church on Sunday morning, they would not be at the beach, at some picnic area, or out mowing the back lawn. They would be with you in church. You and I haven't convinced them, have we?

## PRONOUNCEMENT AGAINST SPIRITUALISM AS A SUBSTITUTE FOR THE WORD OF GOD

**And when they shall say unto you, Seek unto them that have familiar spirits, and unto wizards that peep, and that mutter: should not a people seek unto their God? for the living to the dead? [Isa. 8:19].**

We are seeing a resurgence of spiritualism today. More than fifteen years ago I wrote, "God forbids His people to dabble in this satanic system. When a people turn from God, they generally go after the occult and abnormal" (see Lev. 20:27; Deut. 18:9–12).

There is a great turning today to the occult, to the spirit world, and to demonology. There are churches of Satan in Southern California and in the San Francisco Bay area. The members worship the Devil; many are worshiping Satan today. Even Christians are dabbling in the occult. Many of them talk about casting out demons. My friend, I am not in that business. I preach the gospel of the grace of God and the Word of God. That will take care of all the demons. I say that we need to let the occult alone because it is dangerous, and it is growing by leaps and bounds. Some people don't believe there is any reality in it, but it is real, just as Satan is real. God warns us against it. Let us heed that warning.

**And they shall pass through it, hardly bestead and hungry: and it shall come to pass, that when they shall be hungry, they shall fret themselves, and curse their king and their God, and look upward.**

**And they shall look unto the earth; and behold trouble and darkness, dimness of anguish; and they shall be driven to darkness [Isa. 8:21–22].**

These final verses reveal the final issue of pursuing a life of disobedience which will lead you into spiritualism. The result is dimness, darkness, and despair. Disobedience will take you there every time.

# CHAPTER 9

This chapter is one with which Christians are generally familiar because of the prophecy concerning the coming Child, who is Christ. Handel's use of this chapter in *The Messiah* has added to the familiarity of the church with this particular passage. I am always thrilled when I listen to a presentation of Handel's work, especially when they sing, "And his name shall be called Wonderful, Counsellor, The mighty God, The everlasting Father, The Prince of Peace."

The material presented in Isaiah 7–12 contains prophecies that Isaiah made during the reign of Ahaz. Ahaz was the one bad king that reigned during the period in which Isaiah prophesied. Isaiah began to prophesy at the death of Uzziah, who reigned for fifty-two years and was a good king. The next king was Jotham, Uzziah's son, who was also a good king. The next king was Ahaz, the grandson of Uzziah and the son of Jotham, who was a bad king and a phony besides. It was during the reign of Ahaz that Isaiah made these prophecies concerning the Messiah. It was a dark period in the history of the nation.

## THE HOPE OF ISRAEL

In verses 1–7 we find that the hope of Israel is in the Divine Child in both His first and second comings.

**Nevertheless the dimness shall not be such as was in her vexation, when at the first he lightly afflicted the land of Zebulun and the land of Naphtali, and afterward did more grievously afflict her by the way of the sea, beyond Jordan, in Galilee of the nations [Isa. 9:1].**

The translation of this verse is not established. Actually, contrary meanings are suggested. This poses no problem to the reverent mind but reveals a divine purpose in permitting both to be possible.

"And afterward did more grievously afflict her by the way of the sea, beyond Jordan, in Galilee of the nations." Others have translated it: "But in the latter time hath he made it glorious, by the way of the sea, beyond the Jordan, Galilee of the nations." It is difficult to see how both translations, "more grievously afflict" and "made it glorious," can be sustained, but I believe it is enigmatic for a rea-

son. The first translation would refer to the near fulfillment when God did afflict the northeastern portion of the land comparatively lightly in the invasions of the Syrians and later brought heavier suffering upon them in the carrying away of the people into captivity by the Assyrians (see 2 Kings 15:29).

But the other translation, "hath he made it glorious," refers to the far fulfillment in the first coming of Christ. He *did* "make glorious" that area. Galilee was the despised area because it was a place where Gentiles had congregated. The Lord Jesus passed by Jerusalem, the snobbish religious center of the day. Jesus was neither born nor reared in Jerusalem. Nazareth was His hometown; and, when Nazareth rejected Him, He went down to Capernaum, which is on the Sea of Galilee in the despised periphery of the kingdom. Zebulun and Naphtali were located in the north, with Naphtali along the west bank of the Sea of Galilee and Zebulun adjoining Naphtali on the west. Nazareth was in Zebulun, and Capernaum (Jesus' headquarters) was in Naphtali. As far as I can tell, the Lord Jesus never changed His headquarters from Capernaum. In fact, that explains why He pronounced such a severe judgment upon Capernaum—it had access to light as no other place had.

Matthew 4:12–16 tells us, "Now when Jesus had heard that John was cast into prison, he departed into Galilee; And leaving Nazareth, he came and dwelt in Capernaum, which is upon the sea coast, in the borders of Zabulon and Nephthalim: That it might be fulfilled which was spoken by Esaias the prophet, saying, The land of Zabulon, and the land of Nephthalim, by the way of the sea, beyond Jordan, Galilee of the Gentiles; The people which sat in darkness saw great light; and to them which sat in the region and shadow of death light is sprung up." You will note that Matthew omitted the questionable clause. Otherwise, we would have the Holy Spirit's own interpretation of the passage. I believe that the double meaning is intended by the Holy Spirit. Both are surely true.

**The people that walked in darkness have seen a great light: they that dwell**

**in the land of the shadow of death, upon them hath the light shined [Isa. 9:2].**

Regardless of the way verse 1 is translated or interpreted, it is obvious that the people in despised Galilee were in the darkness of paganism and religious tradition. That is one place where the Old Testament and paganism from the outside mingled and mixed. When the Lord Jesus began His ministry in that area, the people did see a great light. They saw the Lord Jesus Christ, the Light of the world. "Then spake Jesus again unto them, saying, I am the light of the world: he that followeth me shall not walk in darkness, but shall have the light of life" (John 8:12). This was fulfilled at the first coming of Christ. I think it is safe to say that the first two verses refer to our Lord's first coming.

But to what period do the following verses refer? It is the belief of certain outstanding Bible expositors, among whom are Dr. F. C. Jennings and Dr. H. A. Ironside, that there is a hiatus, an interval, between verses 2 and 3, so that while the first two verses refer to Christ's first coming, verse 3 refers to His second coming, as we shall see.

**Thou hast multiplied the nation, and not increased the joy: they joy before thee according to the joy in harvest, and as men rejoice when they divide the spoil [Isa. 9:3].**

The nation had been greatly multiplied and the people were more religious, but the joy was gone. They had a lot of religion, but they never had Christ. It was a period of great manifestation but no real joy.

The hiatus between verses 2 and 3 has already been two thousand years long. Why didn't Isaiah give any prophecy about this period? Because during this interval God is calling out the church which was unknown to Isaiah. In Romans 16:25–26 Paul says, "Now to him that is of power to stablish you according to my gospel, and the preaching of Jesus Christ, according to the revelation of the mystery, which was kept secret since the world began, But now is made manifest, and by the scriptures of the prophets, according to the commandment of the everlasting God, made known to all nations for the obedience of faith." Paul makes it very clear that the prophets passed over that which they did not see, as Isaiah does in the chapter before us. In Isaiah 63 we will come to a place where with

just a comma Isaiah passes over a period of time that is already two thousand years long. The people in Isaiah's day had no revelation concerning the church, but today the church has been revealed and the interval is filled in. This makes it clear that the rest of this chapter refers to the nation Israel, and the nation that was "multiplied" was the nation over which Ahaz was king. Notice that Paul says it was "made known to *all* nations for the obedience of faith." So, you see, the revelation of the church was for a different congregation. Isaiah was speaking only to one nation, his own nation of Israel.

**For thou hast broken the yoke of his burden, and the staff of his shoulder, the rod of his oppressor, as in the day of Midian [Isa. 9:4].**

When will the burden be broken? It will be broken when Christ comes again. Why is it that Israel today cannot enjoy peace? Why are they plagued along every border? They are having all this trouble because they rejected the only One who can bring peace, their own Messiah, the Lord Jesus Christ. The power of the oppressor will not be broken until the Lord comes the second time.

**For every battle of the warrior is with confused noise, and garments rolled in blood; but this shall be with burning and fuel of fire [Isa. 9:5].**

What a sad thing it was when those fine young Jewish athletes were killed during the Olympic Games in Munich a few years ago. They were murdered by terrorists; and, when their bodies were sent back to Israel, their loved ones and the whole nation mourned. What is in back of all this? Israel has a Messiah whom they have rejected. He is the Prince of Peace, and He is the only One who can bring peace to this troubled and persecuted people.

While these verses complete the thought of verse 3, they also look beyond the immediate time to the Great Tribulation Period which is coming in the future.

Now we see the prediction of their Messiah's coming:

**For unto us a child is born, unto us a son is given: and the government shall be upon his shoulder: and his name shall be called Wonderful, Counsellor, The mighty God, The everlasting Father, The Prince of Peace.**

Of the increase of his government and peace there shall be no end, upon the throne of David, and upon his kingdom, to order it, and to establish it with judgment and with justice from henceforth even for ever. The zeal of the Lord of hosts will perform this [Isa. 9:6–7].

How will this come about? "The zeal of the Lord of hosts will perform this." Is this a reference to the first coming of Christ? Most Christians seem to think it is, because they quote it at Christmas time. However, I feel sure that it refers to the second coming of Christ when He will be "born" to the nation of Israel. This is a complete prophecy of the Lord Jesus Christ at His second coming, as Isaiah 53 is of His first coming. These verses continue the thought which we picked up in verse 3, and they look forward to the second coming of Christ.

The question arises of how "a child is born" at His second coming. First of all, let me clearly state that He was not born "unto us," the nation Israel, at His first coming. They didn't receive Him. "He came unto his own, and his own received him not" (John 1:11). Although He was born at Bethlehem the first time, He was not received by the nation—only a few shepherds welcomed Him. The wise men who came to worship Him were Gentiles from a foreign land. If you read verse 6 carefully, you will see that it was not fulfilled at His first coming, neither were verses 3, 5, and 7.

To say that Christ will be born to the nation Israel might be better stated. Actually, Israel will be born as a nation "at once," which is made perfectly clear in the final chapter of Isaiah: "Before she travailed, she brought forth; before her pain came, she was delivered of a man child. Who hath heard such a thing? who hath seen such things? Shall the earth be made to bring forth in one day? or shall a nation be born at once? for as soon as Zion travailed [that is the Great Tribulation], she brought forth her children" (Isa. 66:7–8).

Israel is to be "delivered of a man child" in the future, not by His birth, but by Israel's birth. This will be the new birth of the nation Israel when Christ comes again. Israel will be born at the second coming of Christ.

I see no objection to calling attention to the fact that the child is born—that is, His humanity. The son is given, which will be true at His second coming. In other words, it will be the same Jesus who was here nearly two thousand years ago.

"The government shall be upon his shoulder." The shoulder speaks of strength. The government of this world will be placed on His strong shoulders at His second coming; it was not at His first coming.

Notice the names that are given to our Lord:

"Wonderful"—this is not an adjective; this is His name. In Judges 13:18 we see the preincarnate Christ appearing as the Captain of the hosts of the Lord: "And the angel of the Lord said unto him, Why askest thou thus after my name, seeing it is secret?" "Secret" in this verse is the same word as is translated "Wonderful." In Matthew 11:27 the Lord Jesus said, ". . . no man knoweth the Son, but the Father. . . ." The people did not know it, but He was Wonderful, and people still don't know it today. There are Christians who have trusted Him as Savior but really don't know how wonderful He is.

He is going to put down rebellion when He comes to earth the second time, and He is going to reign on earth. His name is "Wonderful!"

"Counsellor"—He never sought the counsel of man, and He never asked for the advice of man. "For who hath known the mind of the Lord? or who hath been his counsellor?" (Rom. 11:34). God has no counsellor. The Lord Jesus Christ never called His disciples together and said, "Now, fellows, what do you think I ought to do?" You don't read anything like that in Scripture. The Lord called them together and said, "This is what I am going to do, because this is My Father's will." And Christ has been made unto us wisdom (see 1 Cor. 1:30). Most of us are not very smart. We must go to Him for help.

"The mighty God"—The Hebrew word for this name is El Gibbor. He is the one to whom "all power is given." He is the omnipotent God. That little baby lying helpless on Mary's bosom held the universe together. He said, "All power is given unto me in heaven and in earth." He is the Mighty God!

"The everlasting Father"—Avi-ad, Father of eternity. This simply means that He is the Creator of all things, even time, the ages, and the far-off purpose of all things. As John said, "All things were made by him; and without him was not any thing made that was made" (John 1:3). In Colossians 1:16 Paul said, "For by him were all things created, that are in heaven, and that are in earth, visible and invisible, whether they be thrones, or dominions, or principalities, or powers: all things were created by him, and for him." Then in

Hebrews 1–2 we read, "God. . . . Hath in these last days spoken unto us by his Son, whom he hath appointed heir of all things, by whom also he made the worlds [ages]." The translation of the Greek word *aiōn* should be "ages" instead of "worlds," and that is the thought in this title of His—Father of eternity.

"The Prince of Peace"—*Sar-Shalohim*. There can be no peace on this earth until He is reigning. His government is not static; there is increase and growth. No two days are going to be alike when Jesus is reigning. He is going to occupy the throne of David. This is a literal throne which He will occupy at His second coming. Justice will be dominant in His rule. God's zeal, not man's zany plans, will accomplish this.

## THE HELP OF ISRAEL

The remainder of the chapter, verses 8–21, covers the local situation in Isaiah's day and will be partially fulfilled in the immediate future, but it also looks forward to the time of the Great Tribulation for a full and final fulfillment. God will continue to punish this nation and all nations that have turned their backs on Him, until He comes again. Modern men don't like to hear this—they would rather listen to something comforting. Check your history books and see what happened to Israel and other nations who left God out. They have had a sad, sordid story, and I am afraid that you and I live in a nation that is getting ripe for judgment. If we escape, we will be the only nation in the history of the world that has escaped.

# CHAPTER 10

**THEME:** *Judgment of Assyria after she executes God's judgment on Israel; the Great Tribulation and Battle of Armageddon*

Once again I would like to remind you that this is a series of prophecies which began with chapter 7 and goes through chapter 12. They are prophecies which were given during the reign of Ahaz, a wicked king. On a black background Isaiah gives his predictions, speaking into a local situation, but also he looks down through the ages of time to that day when God is going to set up His kingdom here on earth.

This is another remarkable chapter in God's Word. Great principles and gigantic programs in God's dealings with men and nations are set forth. The chapter opens with a brief discussion on the courts of that day. The injustices of the courts of the nation are reflected in the culture of the people and the chastisement of God.

God will use the Assyrians as we shall see, to judge His people. And Assyria is a symbol of the future "king of the north" who shall come up against Immanuel's land in the last days. This prophecy reaches beyond the immediate future of Isaiah's day and extends down to the last days of the nation Israel. Isaiah identifies the period by the designation, "in that day." The chapter concludes with the awesome picture of the approach of the enemy from the north to the Battle of Armageddon.

## UNJUST JUDGES WILL BE JUDGED OF GOD

**Woe unto them that decree unrighteous decrees, and that write grievousness which they have prescribed [Isa. 10:1].**

"Woe unto them that decree unrighteous decrees"—that is, hand down unrighteous decisions. They should represent justice, but they do not give justice. These first few verses may appear at first to be a discourse of Plato or one of the moralists. The one notable exception is that behind human justice is the justice of God. The judge and throne down here on earth are to reveal His justice and are answerable to Him.

**To turn aside the needy from judgment, and to take away the right from the poor of my people, that widows may be their prey, and that they may rob the fatherless! [Isa. 10:2].**

This verse is very much up-to-date. I think we are seeing the working out of this in our contemporary culture, because the courts are to

hand down justice and mirror the justice of God, and they don't. Lawlessness abounds. People sink into degradation. The idea of freedom has been distorted. Every criminal who is arrested ought to be given a fair trial but in order that my family and your family can walk the streets in peace, criminals will have to be punished. Many who are guilty of crimes are set free by a softhearted, softheaded judge. That judge is not giving justice to me and my family or to you and your family.

We hear a lot about justice today, and that is what I want. I want the criminal punished so that I can walk the streets in safety, and so that I can live in my home in safety. In our land it is no longer safe for women to walk on the streets at night. It is not even safe for men in many places. What is the problem? The problem is in our *courts*—that is where God puts His finger down. The courts are not administering justice.

Now God mentions the poor and the widows and the fatherless; they are the ones who need justice. One of the leading political analysts in this country recently stated on a telecast that every program that has been devised to *help* the poor has *hurt* the poor. What is wrong? The only One who will give justice to the poor is God. Judges are supposed to represent God on earth. Today many *godless* men are judges. They are in no position to judge at all until they recognize that they are representing God.

One of the wonderful things about the founders of our country was the way they believed. Although Thomas Jefferson, for example, was a free thinker, he had great respect for the Bible. He was not what we would call a Christian, but he held God's Word in high esteem and respected the statements made in it. We have gotten so far away from God and His Word that our courts and government don't even recognize Him. It is a farce to have a man put his hand on the Bible and take an oath in a court of law today, because most judges do not believe it is the Word of God. The lawyers, the jury, and the men who are taking the oath probably do not believe it is God's Word. When you don't believe it, you might as well take an oath on a Sears and Roebuck catalog. Some of them may have more respect for that than they do for the Bible.

God is dealing with principles; and, until a judge represents God, he cannot represent the people. We have gotten so far from this concept that I am sure I sound like a square! And that's what I am.

**And what will ye do in the day of visitation, and in the desolation which shall come from far? to whom will ye flee for help? and where will ye leave your glory? [Isa. 10:3].**

God is saying to the judges, "You are to represent Me, and the day is coming when I am going to judge *you.*" I feel that every judge ought to recognize the fact that he is one day going to stand before God and give an account of how he has handled his responsibility here on earth. Judges in our day seem to have bleeding hearts; they want to show mercy to the poor criminal. Well, they should be meting out justice to both rich and poor. In the day of reckoning, the unjust judges will stand before the Just Judge.

**Without me they shall bow down under the prisoners, and they shall fall under the slain. For all this his anger is not turned away, but his hand is stretched out still [Isa. 10:4].**

This distortion of justice works itself out in all strata of society. It affects all men and brings about deterioration and degradation. Today we are at a new low as far as morals are concerned.

## JUDGEMENT OF ASSYRIA AFTER SHE EXECUTES GOD'S JUDGMENT ON ISRAEL

Now we come to the key to the entire passage. Here God makes one of the strangest statements in the Bible, and it is too much for a great many folk. My friend, if you don't like it, take your objections to God, because He is the one who said it.

**O Assyrian, the rod of mine anger, and the staff in their hand is mine indignation [Isa. 10:5].**

This is the key verse of the entire passage, and it sheds light on the whole purpose of God, for this verse says He will use Assyria as a rod to chasten His people Israel. This is an amazing thing. Just as you take up a switch to paddle a little fellow who has done wrong, so God is using Assyria as a switch. He is using Assyria to discipline His people. The destruction which Assyria will wreak is what the hand of the Lord God will wreak. This is difficult for modern man to swallow.

**I will send him against an hypocritical nation, and against the people of my wrath will I give him a charge, to take the spoil, and to take the prey, and to**

tread them down like the mire of the streets [Isa. 10:6].

God goes so far as to say that He is responsible for sending Sennacherib, the Assyrian, against Israel and for sending the northern kingdom of Israel into captivity.

Assyria is a symbol of another kingdom in the north whom God will use in the last days. Many Bible expositors believe this verse has reference to the "beast" which will come out of the sea, mentioned in Revelation 13, who would be the ruler in the Roman Empire. I prefer to be specific and think it is a reference to Russia. Have you noticed that ever since World War II the Russians have won every diplomatic battle? They have won, and they have our country on the ropes today. I wonder if God may not be using them. You might say, "You don't mean that God would use godless Russia?" Well, He used godless Assyria to spank His people in Isaiah's day. God may be using Russia to humiliate us today, and she may have already done that. When we fought in Vietnam, we were not fighting the North Vietnamese; we were fighting Russia. It was a very nice, polite war, and it was embarrassing. It was tragic and horrible. Was God permitting our humiliation in an attempt to bring us to our senses? It didn't seem to work—we have not turned to God.

**Howbeit he meaneth not so, neither doth his heart think so, but it is in his heart to destroy and cut off nations not a few.**

**For he saith, Are not my princes altogether kings? [Isa. 10:7–8].**

If you had asked the Assyrian if he was being used as a rod to chasten Israel, he would have laughed at you. If you had asked Russia's dictators if they knew they were rods in the Lord's hands, they would have given you a great ha-ha! They would think such talk was ridiculous. Neither did the Assyrian have any notion that he was prompted of God, nor would he admit it. The Assyrians were having great victories on every hand, and their pride blinded them to their true status. Because they were resting on their own strength and supremacy and were victorious everywhere they turned, they were like Little Jack Horner who sat in a corner, put his thumb in the pie, pulled out a plum, and said, "What a smart boy am I." There are some rulers of nations who are like Little Jack Horner today, but God overrules, though He may be using them to accomplish His purpose.

**Wherefore it shall come to pass, that when the Lord hath performed his whole work upon mount Zion and on Jerusalem, I will punish the fruit of the stout heart of the king of Assyria, and the glory of his high looks [Isa. 10:12].**

When God gets through using Assyria to punish His people, God will deal with the Assyrians and judge them. They do not escape, either; history is a testimony to the fact. God judged them. Isaiah shows that God controls and judges all the nations of the earth.

Now He asks a very pointed question:

**Shall the axe boast itself against him that heweth therewith? or shall the saw magnify itself against him that shaketh it? as if the rod should shake itself against them that lift it up, or as if the staff should lift up itself, as if it were no wood [Isa. 10:15].**

Imagine an axe out in the woods. You are walking through the woods and hear something patting itself on the back and saying, "Look at this big tree I cut down." You walk over to the axe and find nothing but the axe. You say to the axe, "What do you mean, *you* cut down the tree?" The axe replies, "The tree is down, and I did it." You say that is silly. Somebody had to be using the axe, and that is exactly how it was with Assyria and other nations of the world. God *uses* nations. That is the reason it is so important today for men in our nation to recognize God, men who look to God for leading and guidance. But we have a divided nation today. In fact, we are lots more divided than we will admit. We have this minority group, that minority group, and the other minority group. However, the real minority is God. Although He is in the minority, Martin Luther said, "One with God is a majority," and if you are with God, you are with the majority. We need to be sure that we are on God's side today, because He is running the universe. As a nation we are a Johnny-come-lately. A two hundred-year-old nation is a baby compared to many of the other nations in history, and we have just about had it. The Assyrians are only instruments in the hand of God.

## THE GREAT TRIBULATION AND PRESERVATION OF THE REMNANT

Now we have a vision of the Jewish remnant during the Great Tribulation:

**And it shall come to pass in that day, that the remnant of Israel, and such as**

are escaped of the house of Jacob, shall no more again stay upon him that smote them; but shall stay upon the LORD, the Holy One of Israel, in truth [Isa. 10:20].

In this verse Isaiah begins to look beyond the immediate circumstances which concern the Assyrian to "that day." As we have seen, "that day" is the day of the Lord, which begins with the Great Tribulation Period.

**Therefore thus saith the Lord GOD of hosts, O my people that dwellest in Zion, be not afraid of the Assyrian: he shall smite thee with a rod, and shall lift up his staff against thee, after the manner of Egypt [Isa. 10:24].**

This is a word of comfort to Judah that she shall be spared from captivity by the Assyrians.

**And it shall come to pass in that day, that his burden shall be taken away from off thy shoulder, and his yoke from off thy neck, and the yoke shall be destroyed because of the anointing [Isa. 10:27].**

## THE BATTLE OF ARMAGEDDON

Again Isaiah moves beyond, "in that day."

**He is come to Aiath, he is passed to Migron; at Michmash he hath laid up his carriages:**

**They are gone over the passage: they have taken up their lodging at Geba; Ramah is afraid; Gibeah of Saul is fled.**

**Lift up thy voice, O daughter of Gallim: cause it to be heard unto Laish, O poor Anathoth.**

**Madmenah is removed; the inhabitants of Gebim gather themselves to flee.**

**As yet shall he remain at Nob that day: he shall shake his hand against the mount of the daughter of Zion, the hill of Jerusalem [Isa. 10:28–32].**

This is a remarkable section of prophecy. It gives certain geographical locations, all of them north of Jerusalem, and it shows the route taken by Assyria and of the future invader from the north, who I think will be Russia. The invader comes from the land of Magog (see Ezek. 38–39).

Now notice the places mentioned: "Aiath" is about fifteen miles north of Jerusalem. "Migron" is south of Aiath and is the pass where Jonathan got a victory over the Philistines (see 1 Sam. 14). I understand that General Allenby secured a victory over Turkey in the same place. "Geba" and "Ramah" are about six miles north of Jerusalem. "Anathoth" was about three miles north of Jerusalem. This is the home of the prophet Jeremiah. "Laish" is in the extreme north of Palestine, in the tribe of Dan. "Madmenah" (dunghill) is a garbage dump north of Jerusalem. "Gebim" is probably north of Jerusalem. The exact site is not known. "Nob" is the last place mentioned, and it is north of the city and in sight of Jerusalem.

This passage clearly charts the march of the enemy from the north, which brings a state of paralysis and defeat to Jerusalem.

**Behold, the Lord, the LORD of hosts, shall lop the bough with terror: and the high ones of stature shall be hewn down, and the haughty shall be humbled [Isa. 10:33].**

God intervenes and delivers His people. I believe this is a reference to the second coming of Christ to establish His kingdom.

**And he shall cut down the thickets of the forest with iron, and Lebanon shall fall by a mighty one [Isa. 10:34].**

I believe the "mighty one" is Christ when He comes to the earth.

# CHAPTER 11

**THEME:** *The Person and power of the King; the purpose and program of the kingdom*

Chapter 11 is a continuation of the prophecy begun in chapter 7 which will conclude with chapter 12. There is progress and development through this section of prophecies which were all given during the reign of Ahaz. In the preceding chapters we have seen a time of judgment, a time that the Lord Jesus called the Great Tribulation Period. Chapter 11 is one of the great messianic prophecies of Scripture. It speaks of the coming of Christ to establish His kingdom and the type of program He will have. In chapter 12 we will have the culmination of this section where we will see the worship of the Lord in the kingdom.

## THE PERSON AND POWER OF THE KING

**And there shall come forth a rod out of the stem of Jesse, and a Branch shall grow out of his roots [Isa. 11:1].**

It is interesting that it says "a rod of the stem of Jesse." David is not mentioned; the one who is mentioned is David's father. Of course that means He is in the line of David, but why does Isaiah go back to Jesse? Well, the royal line did begin with David. Jesse was a farmer, a sheepherder who lived in a little out-of-the-way place called Bethlehem. But by the time of Jesus, the line of David had sunk back to the level of a peasant. It no longer belonged to a prince raised in a palace, but it belonged to One raised in a carpenter shop. Isaiah, therefore, very carefully says that the rod comes "out of the stem of Jesse."

*Branch* means "a live sprout." This is the second time we have had a reference to the "Branch." The first time it was mentioned was in Isaiah 4:2. There are eighteen words in the Hebrew language translated by our English word *branch*. This is one of the titles given to the Lord Jesus Christ. In Isaiah 53 He is "a root out of a dry ground." Delitzsch, the great Hebrew scholar, wrote, "In the historical fulfillment even the ring of the words of the prophecy is noted: the *nehtzer* (Branch) at first so humble, was a poor *Nazarene*" (see Matt. 2:23). Christ had a humble beginning, born yonder in Bethlehem, a city of David, but a city of Jesse also.

**And the spirit of the LORD shall rest upon him, the spirit of wisdom and understanding, the spirit of counsel and might, the spirit of knowledge and of the fear of the LORD [Isa. 11:2].**

This is the sevenfold spirit which rested upon the Lord Jesus Christ. The plentitude of power is the sevenfold spirit: (1) of the LORD; (2) of wisdom; (3) of understanding; (4) of counsel; (5) of might; (6) of knowledge; and (7) of the fear of the LORD. The number seven in Scripture does not necessarily mean perfection. The primary thought is fullness, completeness. John 3:34 tells us, ". . . for God giveth not the Spirit by measure unto him." In Ephesians 5:18 we are admonished, ". . . be filled with the Spirit." Some of us just have a few drops at the bottom, others are one-fourth filled, and some are half filled. Very few Christians you meet are really *filled* with the Spirit. A little girl once prayed, "Lord, fill me with the Spirit. I can't hold very much, but I can run over a whole lot." Very few Christians are just brimming full, running over on all sides. The Lord Jesus was the exception to that.

1. "The spirit of the LORD shall rest upon him." The Lord Jesus Christ in His humanity went forth in the power of the Spirit. When He comes again, He is going to rule in the power of the Spirit.

2. "The spirit of wisdom." He has been made unto us wisdom (1 Cor. 1:30). He is the only One who can lead and guide you and me through this life. We are no match for the world today. The Lord Jesus Christ could say, ". . . for the prince of this world cometh, and hath nothing in me" (John 14:30). Satan cannot find anything in Christ, but he can always find something in us. We need the Spirit of wisdom, and the Lord Jesus Christ is that Spirit of wisdom.

3. "And understanding," which means spiritual discernment. It is distressing to find that so few Christians have any discernment at all. I am amazed the way some people will follow a certain man purely on a human basis. They like his looks, or the sound of his voice, and they never really comprehend what he is saying, or if what he is saying is true to the Word of God. Christians need the Spirit of understanding. That is one thing for which I have always prayed, and I seem to need it more today than ever before. We need to be aware of who is for the Lord and who isn't.

Not long ago, while driving a car in another

city, I was listening to the radio. A man who was preaching blessed my heart, but he went on to say that if he did not get support he would no longer be able to broadcast. I said to myself, "You would think the people in this city would have enough spiritual discernment to support him." He is so much better than many who are being supported. I spoke to a pastor in that city about the man whom I had heard on the radio. He told me that he was a wonderful man, very humble, and a great Bible teacher, but he simply was not getting the support he needed. The Christians in that city need the spirit of understanding. My friend, have you ever prayed for the spirit of understanding? Ask God to give you the understanding that you lack.

4. "The spirit of counsel." All of us need counsel. Did you ever notice that the Lord Jesus Christ never asked anyone for advice? He never asked for counsel; He *gave* it.

5. "Might"—that is, power. Oh, how we need power. Paul says, "That I may know him, and the *power* of his resurrection . . ." (Phil. 3:10, italics mine). We need that today.

6–7. "The spirit of knowledge" and "of the fear of the LORD." I think these come through a study of the Word of God.

## THE PURPOSE OF THE KINGDOM

**And shall make him of quick understanding in the fear of the LORD: and he shall not judge after the sight of his eyes, neither reprove after the hearing of his ears:**

**But with righteousness shall he judge the poor, and reprove with equity for the meek of the earth: and he shall smite the earth with the rod of his mouth, and with the breath of his lips shall he slay the wicked [Isa. 11:3–4].**

**"T**he wicked" should be "the wicked one." Satan will have his heyday on earth during the Great Tribulation. There will be no deliverance for the world at that time, humanly speaking. Even Israel will cry out, but help will not come from the north, the south, the east, or the west. Help will come from above. At that time the Messiah will come and establish His kingdom. The reason for the Lord Jesus coming to earth is quite evident: this earth needs a ruler. The world has not voted for Him, and it would not vote for Him, but *God* has voted for Him. And since this is God's universe, God will establish Him on earth and He is going to judge—not after the sight of His eyes. There won't be a lengthy court case, where, in the end, the criminal is turned loose. The whole thing is rather terrifying: there will be two judgments, one for believers and one for unbelievers. At the beginning of the Tribulation believers will appear before the judgment seat of Christ. Then 1,007 years later there will be the Great White Throne judgment for the lost.

One day I am going to stand before the Lord Jesus Christ. Everything that is phony in my life will be brought out in the open, and so I have been trying to get rid of that which is phony. I want things to be crystal clear, because someday the Lord is going to turn a light on my life and everything will be exposed. What a light that is going to be. It is rather terrifying.

**And righteousness shall be the girdle of his loins, and faithfulness the girdle of his reins [Isa. 11:5].**

The thing that will gird the Lord's reign will be righteousness and faithfulness. The purpose of the reign of Christ on this earth is to bring in a reign of righteousness and justice as well as to restore the dominion lost by Adam.

## THE PARTICULARS OF THE KINGDOM

**The wolf also shall dwell with the lamb, and the leopard shall lie down with the kid; and the calf and the young lion and the fatling together; and a little child shall lead them.**

**And the cow and the bear shall feed; their young ones shall lie down together: and the lion shall eat straw like the ox [Isa. 11:6–7].**

**D**uring the time when the Lord reigns on earth the calf and the young lion will lie down together. The only way they can lie down together today is if the calf is *inside* the lion!

"The lion shall eat straw like the ox." That seems ridiculous to us. Anybody knows that a lion does not eat straw. But a Bible teacher, who has a very sharp mind, once said, "I will tell you what I'll do. If you can make a lion, I will make him eat straw." The One who made the lion will be able to make him eat straw when the time comes.

**They shall not hurt nor destroy in all my holy mountain: for the earth shall be full of the knowledge of the LORD, as the waters cover the sea [Isa. 11:9].**

This kingdom shall extend over the entire earth.

## THE PROGRAM OF THE KINGDOM

**And in that day there shall be a root of Jesse, which shall stand for an ensign of the people; to it shall the Gentiles seek: and his rest shall be glorious [Isa. 11:10].**

The key to this verse is the phrase "in that day." "That day" begins with the Tribulation Period and extends on into the kingdom. The Gentiles shall have a part in the millennial kingdom.

**And it shall come to pass in that day, that the Lord shall set his hand again the second time to recover the remnant of his people, which shall be left, from Assyria, and from Egypt, and from Pathros, and from Cush, and from Elam, and from Shinar, and from Hamath, and from the islands of the sea [Isa. 11:11].**

God shall restore the nation Israel to the land. They were established the *first* time in the land when Moses led them out of Egypt, and Joshua brought them into the land.

**And he shall set up an ensign for the nations, and shall assemble the outcasts of Israel, and gather together the dispersed of Judah from the four corners of the earth [Isa. 11:12].**

What is the "ensign"? That ensign is none other than the Lord Jesus Christ. It will not be some banner that will be lifted up, but *He* will be the rallying center for the meek of the earth in that day. That will be the day when the meek will inherit the earth. That is God's plan. That is His program, and He will bring it to pass.

**And there shall be an highway for the remnant of his people, which shall be left, from Assyria; like as it was to Israel in the day that he came up out of the land of Egypt [Isa. 11:16].**

A great super highway will extend from Assyria to Egypt over the great land bridge of Palestine. Apparently the nations of the world shall come over this to Jerusalem to worship (see Zech. 14:16–18).

# CHAPTER 12

***THEME:** The worship of the Lord in the Millennium; the kingdom age*

We have been following a series of prophecies beginning with chapter 7 and concluding with chapter 12. The series began with the judgment of God upon His people. In Isaiah 11 we saw that the kingdom would be established on earth and that the Lord Jesus would reign personally.

Here in chapter 12 we reach a high note. The Tribulation is past, and the storms of life are all over. Now Israel has entered the kingdom, and we find them worshiping and singing praises to God. And we find Israel at the temple, not at the wailing wall. Israel is at the wailing wall today, which is one of the proofs that Israel's return to the land at the present time does not fulfill prophecy.

This brief chapter reads like a psalm—for that is what it is. It is a jewel of beauty. Here is set before us the praise of a people under the direct and personal reign of Christ. It is pure praise from redeemed hearts to God because of His salvation and creation. The curse has been removed from the earth, which is an occasion for praise to God for His display of goodness in creation. You and I have not seen anything like this in nature because of the curse that rests upon it. Today nature has a sharp fang and a bloody claw. During the kingdom age that will change entirely.

## PRAISE OF JEHOVAH
## FOR HIS SALVATION

**And in that day thou shalt say, O Lord, I will praise thee: though thou wast angry with me, thine anger is turned away, and thou comfortedst me [Isa. 12:1].**

Once again we have the expression "in that day," which marks the beginning of the Great Tribulation Period and goes through the coming of the kingdom that Christ is going to establish upon the earth.

This verse expresses the thought that the night of sin is over and the day of salvation is come. Israel has gone through the terrible night of the Tribulation, and now the light has come. The Tribulation is over, and they enter the peace and joy of the kingdom. This is an occasion for praise! The thing that will characterize the kingdom age is pure joy.

**Behold, God is my salvation; I will trust, and not be afraid: for the LORD JEHOVAH is my strength and my song; he also is become my salvation [Isa. 12:2].**

Note that they will not say that God *provided* salvation but that He *is* salvation. Salvation is a Person, not a program, or a system, or a ritual, or a liturgy. Salvation is a Person, and that Person is the Lord Jehovah, the Lord Jesus Christ. They are praising Him for His salvation.

**Therefore with joy shall ye draw water out of the wells of salvation [Isa. 12:3].**

The "wells" speak of abundance. His salvation gives satisfaction and joy to the heart. During the kingdom period there will be a time of great joy, which is what the Lord wants for His own. He wants us to be happy now. Our salvation should cause us to rejoice and sing praises to the Lord. I do not think we are ever witnesses to Him until we have that joy.

## PRAISE OF JEHOVAH
## FOR HIS CREATION

**And in that day shall ye say, Praise the LORD, call upon his name, declare his doings among the people, make mention that his name is exalted [Isa. 12:4].**

**“I**n that day," of course, refers to the Millennium, the light part of the day. The "day of the Lord" opened with the night of sin. Our day begins with sunrise, but the day in the Old Testament began with sun-

down. "Weeping may endure for a night, but joy cometh in the morning" (Ps. 30:5). The time of the Millennium is the morning of joy and the time of thanksgiving to God for salvation—but not only that it is to thank Him for the fact that He is the Creator. His mighty and expansive "doings" are to be declared among the people, and His name exalted. The "doings" of God include not only His work in creation, but everything He does.

"In that day shall ye say, Praise the LORD"—*hallelujah* is the word.

**Sing unto the LORD; for he hath done excellent things: this is known in all the earth [Isa. 12:5].**

God has done great things. When the six days of renovation and creation came to an end, God looked upon His work and said that it was good. When God says it is good, it *is* good! I think it would be well for us to thank Him for a perfect salvation and thank Him for creation, even though sin has marred it. In my backyard I notice that the gophers have been burrowing under the fence, and ants get into the house, but in spite of these annoyances there is the singing of the birds and the beauty of the flowers and trees. Even though the earth has been cursed with sin, it is still beautiful. Just think how beautiful it will be when the curse is removed. We will have an occasion to sing praises to God in that day as well as today.

**Cry out and shout, thou inhabitant of Zion: for great is the Holy One of Israel in the midst of thee [Isa. 12:6].**

This is one great throbbing and pulsating outburst of a redeemed soul who is giving to God all that a poor creature can—his hallelujah! We talk of our dedication to God, but we don't even know what dedication means. In that glorious day Israel will know its meaning, and we will too.

# CHAPTER 13

**THEME:** *Destruction in the Day of the Lord and in the immediate future*

Chapter 13 brings us to an altogether different section. The tone changes immediately. Chapters 13–23 contain "burdens" imposed on nine surrounding nations. A burden is something that you bear, and these burdens are judgments of God upon these nine nations. You could substitute the word *judgment* for "burden" and it would be just as accurate. This is a remarkable passage of Scripture, because most of the prophetic judgments have already been fulfilled. They are now facts of history. Each of these nations had some contact with Israel, and most of them were contiguous to her borders or not very far away. Israel suffered at the hands of some of them—and is suffering today—and will suffer again in the future.

You will find some names in this chapter that are strangely familiar. Egypt is one of them. While some of these judgments will take place in the future, the chief characteristic of this section is that much has been fulfilled and stands today as an evidence of fulfilled prophecy. All of this adds singular interest and importance to these eleven chapters. In this section the Assyrian is no longer the oppressor; another set of nations headed by Babylon takes his place.

It was not pleasant to the prophet to deliver this type of message. This was not the way to win friends and influence people. But God's prophets were not in a popularity contest.

Babylon is the subject of the first burden. It is suggestive of many things to the reverent student of Scripture. First of all, the literal city of Babylon is the primary consideration. This is indeed remarkable, as Babylon in Isaiah's day was an insignificant place. It was not until a century later that Babylon became a world power. God pronounced judgment upon Babylon before it became a nation!

This section does not end with the "burdens" on nine surrounding nations but extends through six woes in chapters 28–33 and concludes with the calm and blessing after the storm in chapters 34 and 35. These last two chapters again give us a millennial picture.

In chapter 13 we will see the punishment of Babylon in the Day of the Lord. I believe this looks forward to the Great Tribulation Period for its final fulfillment.

## PUNISHMENT OF BABYLON IN THE DAY OF THE LORD

### The burden of Babylon, which Isaiah the son of Amoz did see [Isa. 13:1].

The literal city of Babylon in history is in view in this chapter and also in chapter 14. It became one of the great cities of the ancient world. In fact, it became the first great world power and is so recognized in Daniel's prophecy. Nebuchadnezzar was the "head of gold" of Babylon. He was the king of the first great world power.

The city of Babylon will be rebuilt in the future. Babylon is the symbol of united rebellion against God, which began at the Tower of Babel and will end in Revelation 17 and 18 where we will see religious Babylon and political Babylon ruling the world. During the Great Tribulation Period Babylon will go down by a great judgment from God. This possibly is the first mention of it in Scripture.

### I have commanded my sanctified ones, I have also called my mighty ones for mine anger, even them that rejoice in my highness [Isa. 13:3].

In this verse the word *sanctified* means "set apart for a specific use by some agency." God says, "I have also called my mighty ones for mine anger." God has "sanctified" or raised up Babylon for a specific purpose. He did the same thing with Assyria. In Isaiah 10:5 God said through the prophet Isaiah, "O Assyrian, the rod of mine anger, and the staff in their hand is mine indignation." God used Assyria to punish His people, and then He judged Assyria. This is what He is going to do with Babylon. Anything can be sanctified if it is set apart for God. Assyria and Babylon were set aside to punish Israel. They were instruments in His hands for a specific purpose.

### The noise of a multitude in the mountains, like as of a great people; a tumultuous noise of the kingdoms of nations gathered together: the LORD of hosts mustereth the host of the battle [Isa. 13:4].

This verse explains what we mean by "sanctified ones." Babylon will come against the

southern kingdom of Judah (as Assyria did against the ten northern tribes of Israel) and take it into captivity.

> They come from a far country, from the end of heaven, even the LORD, and the weapons of his indignation, to destroy the whole land [Isa. 13:5].

The Babylonians will be the "weapons of his indignation."

> Howl ye; for the day of the LORD is at hand; it shall come as a destruction from the Almighty [Isa. 13:6].

This prophecy looks beyond anything that now is in history and projects into the Great Tribulation.

> Therefore shall all hands be faint, and every man's heart shall melt.
>
> And they shall be afraid: pangs and sorrows shall take hold of them; they shall be in pain as a woman that travaileth: they shall be amazed one at another; their faces shall be as flames.
>
> Behold, the day of the LORD cometh, cruel both with wrath and fierce anger, to lay the land desolate: and he shall destroy the sinners thereof out of it [Isa. 13:7–9].

During the Great Tribulation God will again use the power (called Babylon here) to judge these people, just as He did in the past. The Tribulation is spoken of as a time of travail, with men in travail. The Day of the Lord opens with this time of travail.

Now this identifies it as the Great Tribulation:

> For the stars of heaven and the constellations thereof shall not give their light: the sun shall be darkened in his going forth, and the moon shall not cause her light to shine [Isa. 13:10].

This is prophesied again by the Lord Jesus in Matthew 24:29: "Immediately after the tribulation of those days shall the sun be darkened, and the moon shall not give her light, and the stars shall fall from heaven, and the powers of the heavens shall be shaken." Revelation 8:12 tells us, "And the fourth angel sounded, and the third part of the sun was smitten, and the third part of the moon, and the third part of the stars; so as the third part of them was darkened, and the day shone not for a third part of it, and the night likewise."

> And I will punish the world for their evil, and the wicked for their iniquity; and I will cause the arrogancy of the proud to cease, and will lay low the haughtiness of the terrible [Isa. 13:11].

"I will punish the world for their evil"—We are living in a world today that is moving toward judgment.

> I will make a man more precious than fine gold; even a man than the golden wedge of Ophir [Isa. 13:12].

When Christ died for you and me on the cross, that added value to us.

Verses 13–16 go on to tell us that the Tribulation will be a time of worldwide destruction when no "flesh would survive" except for the fact that God will preserve a remnant for Himself.

## DESTRUCTION OF BABYLON IN THE DAY OF MAN

> Behold, I will stir up the Medes against them, which shall not regard silver; and as for gold, they shall not delight in it [Isa. 13:17].

Who are the Medes? Media and Persia became a dual nation and a mighty empire that conquered Babylon. Isaiah is speaking of that which was going to take place in the immediate future. He identifies those who will destroy Babylon: "the Medes."

> And Babylon, the glory of kingdoms, the beauty of the Chaldees' excellency, shall be as when God overthrew Sodom and Gomorrah [Isa. 13:19].

This prophecy has been fulfilled. Babylon was the greatest kingdom that has ever existed upon this earth. The Macedonian empire was great; the Egyptian Empire was great, as was the Roman Empire. At one time Great Britain could have been named a great nation, but I don't think anything can compare to the glory of Babylon. God's Word calls it "the beauty of the Chaldees' excellency," and that excellency God overthrew as He did Sodom and Gomorrah. All you have to do is to look at the ruins of ancient Babylon to recognize that that has happened.

It was a great city that was never rebuilt. Other great cities have been rebuilt. This is especially true of Jerusalem. Rome was destroyed and rebuilt. Cities in Germany were bombed out—absolutely obliterated—and were rebuilt. Frankfurt, Germany, was lev-

eled, and it arose out of the ashes a great city. But Babylon did not arise. God said that it would never again be inhabited. It is true that Babylon will be rebuilt in the future, but not on the ancient site of Babylon. It will be built in a different place.

Babylon represents confusion, and the future Babylon will be a great commercial center, a great religious center, a great political center, a power center, and the educational center of the world again.

**It shall never be inhabited, neither shall it be dwelt in from generation to generation: neither shall the Arabian pitch tent there; neither shall the shepherds make their fold there [Isa. 13:20].**

How can Babylon be destroyed and yet appear in the last days as a literal city again? Already the ancient site of the ancient Babylon is seven to nine miles from the Euphrates River. The river ran in a canal right through the ancient city of Babylon. The ancient site will never be rebuilt, but Babylon will be rebuilt on another site. The ruins of ancient Babylon stand as a monument to the accuracy of fulfilled prophecy.

Several archaeologists of the past who have excavated Babylon say that they were never able to get the Arabians to stay in the camp beside the ruins. The Arabians would always go outside the area and stay. They were superstitious. It is interesting that God said they would not pitch their tents in Babylon.

**But wild beasts of the desert shall lie there; and their houses shall be full of doleful creatures; and owls shall dwell there, and satyrs shall dance there.**

**And the wild beasts of the islands shall cry in their desolate houses, and dragons in their pleasant palaces: and her time is near to come, and her days shall not be prolonged [Isa. 13:21–22].**

"Wild beasts of the desert shall lie there." Lions have been found making their homes amid the ruins.

"Satyrs shall dance there." Satyrs are demons. Satyrs shall dance in Babylon. If you want to go to the dance of the demons, Babylon is the place to go. I hear of folk here in Southern California who worship Satan. One young fellow who claims to belong to a church that worships Satan came to me after a meeting and attacked me in a very vitriolic manner. He insisted that demons are real, and he worshiped them. I agreed that demons are real, but I cautioned him about worshiping them. Then I asked him if He had ever danced with the demons. He looked at me with amazement and said, "No!" So I told him where their dance hall is. I told him that demons dance in the ruins of Babylon. I said to him facetiously, "Why don't you go over there? Brother, if you are going to go halfway, go all the way." Babylon was the headquarters for idolatry in the ancient world. Apparently demons have this spot as a rallying place.

The future Babylon will become a great center on earth. The Man of Sin, the willful king, called the Antichrist, will reign in that place. It will be destroyed just as the ancient Babylon was destroyed. Babylon is a memorial to the fact of the accuracy of fulfilled prophecy and a testimony to the fact that God will also judge the future Babylon.

# CHAPTER 14

*THEME:* *The millennial kingdom established after the final destruction of Babylon; the origin of evil and its judgment; and the burden of Palestine*

This chapter is a continuation of the burden of Babylon begun in chapter 13. The burden of Babylon is actually a judgment on Babylon. Babylon was the first of several nations upon which the judgment of God was to fall. All of the nations to be judged had something to do with Israel—either by physical proximity or political involvement. Great issues are at stake in chapter 14. The origin of evil and its judgment and final removal from this earth is the theme of this section.

Local situations and nations are the expression of these worldwide themes and eternal issues. This chapter looks at nations and the problems of life through the telescope rather than placing them under the microscope for inspection.

This chapter opens on a joyful note because of the final judgment of Babylon. The millennial kingdom is established with all fears and dangers removed. No enemy of God is abroad. The judgment here and elsewhere in this Book of Isaiah is explained. We will see here God's plan and purpose for the earth.

This chapter is a mixture of light and darkness. The chapter changes from the ecstasy of the kingdom to the punishment of hell. Satan and the problem of evil are brought before us. There is an extended section on the final destruction of Babylon. This chapter of great subjects and strong contrasts closes with the insertion of the burden of Palestine, which was probably brought about by the sudden demise of King Ahaz (see 2 Kings 16:19–20).

## THE FUTURE RESTORATION OF ISRAEL
## AND THE PEACE OF
## THE KINGDOM

**For the LORD will have mercy on Jacob, and will yet choose Israel, and set them in their own land: and the strangers shall be joined with them, and they shall cleave to the house of Jacob [Isa. 14:1].**

This verse reaches down to the end times. God has said again and again that the nation Israel will be restored to her land. Now I do not think you see the fulfillment of the prophecies there today. When God restores them to the land, Israel will not have any problems with other nations. They won't need to turn to Russia, or the United States, or to the United Nations for help. The Lord Jesus will reign there.

There are many people who say they believe in the verbal, plenary inspiration of the Scriptures, but they will turn right around and say that this passage is not literal. When you deny its reality and the fact that it is literal, you deny the inspiration of Scripture. "For the LORD will have mercy on Jacob, and will yet choose Israel"—He has said that too many times for anyone to say, "I didn't quite get it." Or, "It means something else."

**And the people shall take them, and bring them to their place: and the house of Israel shall possess them in the land of the LORD for servants and handmaids: and they shall take them captives, whose captives they were; and they shall rule over their oppressors [Isa. 14:2].**

My friend, this has not yet been fulfilled. "The people" in this verse are Gentiles. The Gentiles are going to return them to Palestine. But the Gentiles up to this point have actually hindered them. Even Great Britain, when they had a mandate in the land, would not let the Jews return after World War II. But the Jews went in anyway, because they had to go somewhere. How the multitudes went to that land is a real saga of suffering. As I write, Russia is hindering the Jews from returning to Palestine. Other nations are not concerned for them either. Now the Jews throughout the world *are* interested in helping their brethren return to the land, but Gentiles are not helping them. I take it, therefore, that we are not seeing the fulfillment of Scripture.

**And it shall come to pass in the day that the LORD shall give thee rest from thy sorrow, and from thy fear, and from the hard bondage wherein thou wast made to serve [Isa. 14:3].**

The Jews have sorrow in that land today, and they are in fear. I walked through the streets of Jerusalem and through the streets of some other cities in Palestine some time ago, and there were soldiers everywhere. Why? The nation is fearful. Even if things were settled,

they would still be in fear. There is no rest from sorrow for them.

**That thou shalt take up this proverb against the king of Babylon, and say, How hath the oppressor ceased! the golden city ceased! [Isa. 14:4].**

I think "Babylon," in this passage, represents the great enemy in the last days who will be headquartered in Babylon. It represents all the enemies of Israel. Babylon was an inveterate hater of this nation.

**The LORD hath broken the staff of the wicked, and the sceptre of the rulers.**

**He who smote the people in wrath with a continual stroke, he that ruled the nations in anger, is persecuted, and none hindereth [Isa. 14:5–6].**

These verses speak of the final judgment at the end of the Great Tribulation Period. Judgment has to take place. This earth *must* be judged. There is too much injustice here. Someone is going to have to handle the judgment, and I thank the Lord that it won't be me. I am thankful that we don't have to look to men in these matters. The Lord Jesus will do the judging.

**The whole earth is at rest, and is quiet: they break forth into singing.**

**Yea, the fir trees rejoice at thee, and the cedars of Lebanon, saying, Since thou art laid down, no feller is come up against us [Isa. 14:7–8].**

What is described in this passage has not yet taken place. After the war of Armageddon and the coming of Christ, rest and peace come to the earth. Instead of sorrow there is singing. Weeping is only for the night. The morn of joy has come.

## THE FINAL RULER OF THE WORLD CAST INTO SHEOL

**Hell from beneath is moved for thee to meet thee at thy coming: it stirreth up the dead for thee, even all the chief ones of the earth; it hath raised up from their thrones all the kings of the nations [Isa. 14:9].**

"Hell," in this verse, is *Sheol*. It can mean the grave or the place of torment. Evidently the latter meaning is in view here.

**All they shall speak and say unto thee, Art thou also become weak as we? art thou become like unto us?**

**Thy pomp is brought down to the grave, and the noise of thy viols: the worm is spread under thee, and the worms cover thee [Isa. 14:10–11].**

All the pomp and glory of man is removed.

## THE ORIGIN OF SATAN AND EVIL

**How art thou fallen from heaven, O Lucifer, son of the morning! how art thou cut down to the ground, which didst weaken the nations! [Isa. 14:12].**

"Lucifer" is none other than Satan. Lucifer, according to Ezekiel 28, is the highest creature that God ever created. But he was a Judas Iscariot—he turned on God. He set his will over God's will. In Luke 10:18 the Lord Jesus says, ". . . I beheld Satan as lightning fall from heaven." In 1 John 3:8 we are told, "He that committeth sin is of the devil; for the devil sinneth from the beginning. For this purpose the Son of God was manifested, that he might destroy the works of the devil." Then in Revelation 12:7–9 we are told, "And there was war in heaven: Michael and his angels fought against the dragon; and the dragon fought and his angels, And prevailed not; neither was their place found any more in heaven. And the great dragon was cast out, that old serpent, called the Devil, and Satan, which deceiveth the whole world: he was cast out into the earth, and his angels were cast out with him." This is a picture of this creature Lucifer at the very beginning.

What was the sin of this creature created higher than any other? Well, what is sin in its final analysis? I'm not speaking philosophically, but theologically—what is sin?

**For thou hast said in thine heart, I will ascend into heaven, I will exalt my throne above the stars of God: I will sit also upon the mount of the congregation, in the sides of the north:**

**I will ascend above the heights of the clouds; I will be like the most High [Isa. 14:13–14].**

These are the five "I wills" of Lucifer. He was setting his will over against the will of God. This is sin in embryo. This is the evolution of evil. There is no evolution of man, but there is an evolution of sin. It began by a creature setting his will against the will of God. As a free moral agent, the creature must be allowed to do this. It is nonsense to talk about

a creature who has a free moral will, who can do anything he wants to, but is restricted in his movements in a certain area. Lucifer had a free will.

This is man's original sin: "All we like sheep have gone astray; we have turned every one to *his own way;* and the LORD hath laid on him the iniquity of us all" (Isa. 53:6). Murder is sin, not just because God says it is, but because it is contrary to the will and character of God. Anything that is contrary to the character and will of God is sin, regardless of what it is. I think that some people can even displease God by going to church.

Imagine little bitty puffed-up creature man, who says to God, "I won't do what You want me to do. I am going to do it my way." That is exactly what man is saying today. Well, friend, you are *not* going to do things your way, because God's will is going to prevail in the final analysis. Therefore, the prayer of all God's people should be, ". . . Thy will be done in earth, as it is in heaven" (Matt. 6:10). Anything contrary to His will is sin, regardless of what it is.

The sin of Satan was overweening pride. He did not go out and get drunk, and he didn't steal anything. He went against God's will. He was created as an angel of light; he was the "son of the morning," a perfect being. He was given a free moral will—he could choose what he wanted. But he was lifted up—so lifted up by pride that he set his will against the will of God. It wasn't the purpose of Satan to be different from God; he wanted to be like God. In other words, he wanted *to be God.* He put his will above the will of God, and any creature who does that puts himself in the place of God.

There are many men like Lucifer today. They put their wills above the will of God and take His place. That is what sin is all about in the human family. There are only two ways: God's way and man's way. That is what the Lord Jesus Christ meant when He said, ". . . I am the way, the truth, and the life: no man cometh unto the Father, but by me" (John 14:6). My friend, you live in God's universe today. You breathe His air and enjoy His sunshine. He never sends you a bill for either one or for the life He furnishes. You are His creature. You owe Him a great deal. You are to obey Him.

In his natural state, man is unable to obey God; that is why we have to come to Him through the Lord Jesus Christ as lost sinners. Then we are given a new nature. That is what it means to be born again.

**Yet thou shalt be brought down to hell, to the sides of the pit.**

**They that see thee shall narrowly look upon thee, and consider thee, saying, Is this the man that made the earth to tremble, that did shake kingdoms;**

**That made the world as a wilderness, and destroyed the cities thereof; that opened not the house of his prisoners? [Isa. 14:15–17].**

God is yet going to judge Satan, and that judgment will be severe. Satan is finally going to be cast into the lake of fire which was prepared for him.

God is working out a great plan and purpose that is far beyond the thinking of anyone here on this earth. It is not for you and me to question it. Rather, we need to trust Him, because He is prepared to extend to us mercy, grace, and love.

## THE FUTURE REBELLION OF BABYLON

**All the kings of the nations, even all of them, lie in glory, every one in his own house [Isa. 14:18].**

Babylon was controlled by Satan. You remember that Satan offered to the Lord Jesus the kingdoms of this world (see Luke 4:5–7). Babylon belonged to him. Back of Babylon and all the kingdoms of this world is Satan. In the future, Babylon will evidently become the rallying point for all the nations which are against God.

**For I will rise up against them, saith the LORD of hosts and cut off from Babylon the name, and remnant, and son, and nephew, saith the LORD.**

**I will also make it a possession for the bittern, and pools of water: and I will sweep it with the besom of destruction, saith the LORD of hosts [Isa. 14:22–23].**

If you have ever seen pictures of the ruins of Babylon, you realize how literally these verses have been fulfilled. In the future, Babylon will be rebuilt (though at a different site). It will once again be a place of world rulership, and it will be a Tower of Babel lifted against God. And again God will come down to judge, and that will be the final judgment. The reason that these great truths have been given to us is so that we will know what is coming in the future.

**The LORD of hosts hath sworn, saying, Surely as I have thought, so shall it come to pass; and as I have purposed, so shall it stand:**

**That I will break the Assyrian in my land, and upon my mountains tread him under foot: then shall his yoke depart from off them, and his burden depart from off their shoulders [Isa. 14:24–25].**

"The Assyrian" represents the king that is coming from the north.

Verses 19–27 give a detailed account of the coming judgment of Babylon and all that it represents. It has been only partially fulfilled in the past, but it has been fulfilled quite literally.

## THE FIERCE REPUDIATION OF PALESTINE

**In the year that king Ahaz died was this burden [Isa. 14:28].**

There is inserted at this point the burden of Palestine which was precipitated by the death of Ahaz. Ahaz had reigned for sixteen years and had been an evil king. The people felt he would be followed by an evil king, but they were delighted to be rid of him. There was a bare possibility that a good king might follow him—and they did get one, by the way.

**Rejoice not thou, whole Palestina, because the rod of him that smote thee is broken: for out of the serpent's root shall come forth a cockatrice, and his fruit shall be a fiery flying serpent [Isa. 14:29].**

Two more good kings ruled after Ahaz, but the worst kings are yet to come. The people are to understand that just the rule of man will not bring about an improvement in the world. In this country we seem to feel that if we change presidents or parties there is going to be an improvement. We have done that, and there has been no improvement. God tells Palestine not to rejoice just because Ahaz is dead. Things are not going to get any better at all.

Before the kingdom blessings prevail, there will be a severe judgment of God upon that land. It will be more severe than that of the surrounding nations, because this nation had light, and light creates responsibility. Isaiah is looking into the future when there will be the Great Tribulation Period and the Antichrist's rule.

There are those who do not feel that the burden mentioned here is much of a burden, but it is called a burden, and it is about Palestina. The name *Palestina* is quite interesting. It refers to those who gave that name to the land, the Philistines. They had come up the coast out of Egypt, and they slipped into the land. They were there when Israel arrived. Apparently the Philistines had not been in the land during the days of Abraham, because the Canaanites were then in the land. But when the children of Israel returned four hundred years later, the Philistines had come into the land. In the Books of Zephaniah and Zechariah are specific prophecies against Ashdod and Ashkelon, two Philistine cities. They were to be destroyed, and it was literally fulfilled. Verses 30–32 describe the judgment in detail, and it is fierce!

# CHAPTERS 15–16

*THEME:* The burden of Moab

This brief chapter records the third burden, the burden of Moab. Chapters 15 and 16 deal with Moab. This seems strange in light of the fact that there were only two chapters that dealt with Babylon, and Babylon was the first great world power. Compared to Babylon, Moab may seem to us like it was very small potatoes. But in Isaiah's day—in fact, as early as the time of David—this land was very important, and it was a great kingdom.

Moab was the nation which came from Lot through the incestuous relationship with his elder daughter. Moab, the illegitimate son of this sordid affair, was the father of the Moabites. These people became the inveterate and persistent enemies of the nation of Israel. Balak, their king, hired Balaam, the prophet, to curse Israel, for he feared them when they passed through the land of Moab.

The lovely story told in the Book of Ruth concerns a maid of Moab. This maiden of Moab was a very wonderful person. I am in love with Ruth and have been for a long time—not only the Book of Ruth, but also with my wife

whose name is Ruth. David was part Moabite, for his father Jesse was a descendant of Obed, the son of Boaz and Ruth. David had relatives in Moab, and he took his father and mother there when Saul was pursuing him.

Today the nation of Moab has disappeared, but who are the modern Moabites? I feel that Moab is representative of those who make a profession of being children of God but actually have no vital relationship with Him (see Heb. 12:8). Like Felix and Festus, the Moabites were "almost persuaded." They were not very far from the kingdom, but they never quite made it. They were neighbors of God's people but never became followers of God.

The modern "Moabite" is easily discovered. He is in our churches today. He parades as a Christian. He is the one Paul describes in 2 Timothy 3:5: "Having a form of godliness, but denying the power thereof: from such turn away." Jude 16 also describes him: "These are murmurers, complainers, walking after their own lusts; and their mouth speaketh great swelling words, having men's persons in admiration because of advantage." The modern Moabites are ungodly. They pretend to be godly, but they are not. They flatter you with great swelling words when they think they can get something from you, but drop you the minute they find that they cannot get anything from you.

Moab was a dangerous friend to have. It was never a trusted ally of Israel.

## THE SUDDEN DESTRUCTION OF MOAB

**The burden of Moab. Because in the night Ar of Moab is laid waste, and brought to silence; because in the night Kir of Moab is laid waste, and brought to silence [Isa. 15:1].**

"In the night"—the burden of Moab came suddenly. This expression is repeated twice to emphasize the suddenness of the storm which struck the nation. The storm came at night, and their night of weeping never ended. Assyria destroyed this nation in a way that is unbelievable and almost unspeakable. They seemed to wipe Moab off the face of the earth.

"Kir" is Kerak on a mountain peak about ten miles from the southeast corner of the Dead Sea.

**He is gone up to Bajith, and to Dibon, the high places, to weep: Moab shall howl over Nebo, and over Medeba: on**

**all their heads shall be baldness, and every beard cut off [Isa. 15:2].**

There are several places mentioned in this verse with which I do not think we are acquainted. "Bajith" means house and apparently refers to the temple of Chemosh which was in that land. "Dibon" was a town on the east side of Jordan where the Moabite stone was found. "Nebo" is the mountain from which Moses saw the Promised Land. "Medeba" was a city that belonged to Reuben (see Josh. 13:16).

All of these cities and places belonged to Moab during Isaiah's day. They were going to be destroyed because, although the Moabites professed to know God, they spent their time in heathen temples dedicated to pagan gods, saying that they were worshiping the living and true God.

**In their streets they shall gird themselves with sackcloth: on the tops of their houses, and in their streets, every one shall howl, weeping abundantly [Isa. 15:3].**

When I was in Amman, Jordan, I had a very funny feeling. It is a weird sort of place. It is a very poor land now, but in Isaiah's day it was a rich country. I felt as if the judgment of God was still on that place.

## THE SYMPATHY OF THE PROPHET FOR ZOAR

The judgment upon Moab was so serious that even Isaiah was moved:

**My heart shall cry out for Moab; his fugitives shall flee unto Zoar, an heifer of three years old: for by the mounting up of Luhith with weeping shall they go it up; for in the way of Horonaim they shall raise up a cry of destruction [Isa. 15:5].**

Although Moab was the enemy of Israel, Isaiah's heart goes out to them in sympathy because of the terror that has come upon them. This reveals the heart of God. In spite of people's sin today, God still loves them and will extend His mercy to them if they will but turn to Him.

The rest of the chapter gives a detailed description of the further ravaging of the land of Moab. It has been literally fulfilled.

## THE FINAL OVERTURE OF MERCY OFFERED TO MOAB

Chapter 16 opens with a last call to Moab to avail herself of the mercy of God which He has provided for her.

**Send ye the lamb to the ruler of the land from Sela to the wilderness, unto the mount of the daughter of Zion [Isa. 16:1].**

A lamb was to be sent from Moab to Israel for an offering on the altar there. The lamb was the animal of sacrifice which best depicts Christ, ". . . the Lamb of God, which taketh away the sin of the world" (John 1:29). If they sent a lamb, Moab would signify that they recognized the God of Israel. They did not send a lamb. The Moabites wanted to be religious without acknowledging the fact that they were subject to a higher will and were sinners in the sight of God. This was their great sin.

**For it shall be, that, as a wandering bird cast out of the nest, so the daughters of Moab shall be at the fords of Arnon [Isa. 16:2].**

I crossed that little river of Arnon. It is not much of a river, and it certainly could not separate the Moabites from the Assyrians. They were taken there.

**And in mercy shall the throne be established: and he shall sit upon it in truth in the tabernacle of David, judging, and seeking judgment, and hasting righteousness [Isa. 16:5].**

In Acts 15:16 James mentions that the "tabernacle of David" is "fallen down," but that after God has called out the Gentiles to form the church, He will turn again and rebuild the tabernacle of David. This is what Isaiah is talking about here.

## THE FIERCE PRIDE OF MOAB

**We have heard of the pride of Moab; he is very proud: even of his haughtiness, and his pride, and his wrath: but his lies shall not be so [Isa. 16:6].**

The reason that God had to reject and judge Moab was that their pride had led them to reject God's proffered offer of mercy. God would have delivered them, but instead they trusted in their own righteousness.

## THE FULFILLMENT OF JUDGMENT WITHIN THREE YEARS

**This is the word that the LORD hath spoken concerning Moab since that time.**

**But now the LORD hath spoken, saying, Within three years, as the years of an hireling, and the glory of Moab shall be contemned, with all that great multitude; and the remnant shall be very small and feeble [Isa. 16:13–14].**

When God deals with the nations that have to do with Israel, He uses a calendar. He *never* uses a calendar with the church. Within three years the Moabites were to be destroyed, and within three years God used Assyria to destroy this nation. It was the judgment of God upon them because of their pride.

Lucifer, the son of the morning, was also lifted up with pride. He wanted to lift his throne above the throne of God. He wanted to establish his own self-contained kingdom and be independent of God. Basically, this is the position of all liberal theology. Pride is the thing that causes people to reject God's Word and His revelation. Most people want a do-it-yourself religion. They want to *do something* to be saved, because it ministers to their pride. Many accuse church members of being hypocritical, selfish, and some actually anti-God. All this rests basically on the pride of the human heart: "we have turned every one to his own way" (Isa. 53:6).

Judgment came upon Moab. This out-of-the-way nation, entirely forgotten today, has had a message for us.

**THEME:** *The burden of Damascus and Ephraim; the burden of the land beyond the rivers of Ethiopia*

## THE BURDEN OF DAMASCUS AND EPHRAIM

Damascus was the leading city of Syria, and it still is that today. Many have called it the oldest living city in the world. There are, of course, several places that make the same claim. In Greece, the city of Mycenae claims to be the oldest, but there is not much there today except a very good Greek restaurant! By the Jordan there is a sign giving the kilometers to "Jericho, The World's Oldest City." I guess about every country in the world claims to have the oldest city. I have been waiting for my native state of Texas to make the same claim—I am sure they will dig it up some day. However, Damascus does have a good claim to it. It was Vitringa who wrote, "Damascus has been destroyed oftener than any other town . . . it rises again from ashes." But "Damascus" in this chapter refers to the entire nation of Syria.

*Ephraim* is the name of a tribe of Israel, it is the name of a city, it is the name of a mountain, and it is the name of a man. *Ephraim* is often used in Scripture to refer to the ten northern tribes of Israel. The prophets used it in that way: "For Israel slideth back as a backsliding heifer. . . . Ephraim is joined to idols . . ." (Hos. 4:16–17).

Therefore, we have here in chapter 17 the burden of Damascus and Ephraim, or in other words, the burden of the nations of Syria and Israel. Because of the confederacy between Syria and Israel (often for the purpose of coming against Judah), Israel is linked with the judgments pronounced on Syria. Partners in crime means partners in judgment.

**The burden of Damascus. Behold, Damascus is taken away from being a city, and it shall be a ruinous heap [Isa. 17:1].**

"It shall be a ruinous heap"—there will be those quick to point out that this has not been fulfilled, inasmuch as the present-day city of Damascus claims to be the same as the original city. As I have said before, there is a far-off fulfillment of all these prophecies and a local or contemporary fulfillment also. There are two possible explanations for the problem presented by this prophecy:

1. Historians are not always accurate in their identification of such things as the locations of ancient cities. One man wrote a profound history not long ago and then made the statement that the biggest liars in the world have been historians. In the area of present-day Damascus there happen to be many ruins of a city, and any one of these ruins could be the original Damascus. Damascus is like a great many of the ancient cities in that when it was destroyed in one place, they did not always rebuild on the same site, but shifted it somewhat to another location. (Other cities, such as the sacred city of Jerusalem, were rebuilt on exactly the same site because of the significance of the location to the people.) We will just leave this problem to the archaeologist who hasn't come up with the answer yet as to which of the ruins is old Damascus.

2. Damascus has withstood the ravages of war throughout history and has never ceased being a city, although it has shifted locations. It probably is the oldest city in the world. It thus far has survived every catastrophe that has come upon the earth, particularly in a land that has seen army after army march through it. But it *will not* survive during the Great Tribulation Period. It will be destroyed; and, as Isaiah says here, it will cease being a city. It will become a ruinous heap.

Both of these explanations show the accuracy of the prophecy that Isaiah gives here.

**The cities of Aroer are forsaken: they shall be for flocks, which shall lie down, and none shall make them afraid [Isa. 17:2].**

"The cities of Aroer" is a suburban area near Damascus. This entire area would be destroyed. This probably has happened in the past, and it will happen again.

**The fortress also shall cease from Ephraim, and the kingdom from Damascus, and the remnant of Syria: they shall be as the glory of the children of Israel, saith the Lord of hosts [Isa. 17:3].**

The northern kingdom of Israel must bear her share of the burden or judgment of Damascus because of the alliance they have. Both were

besieged by Tiglath-pileser, as recorded in 2 Kings 15:29, and were finally deported by the Assyrian, Shalmaneser, as recorded in 2 Kings 17:6. This certainly was a partial fulfillment of Isaiah's prophecy; and, as far as many are concerned, it is the total fulfillment. But I feel that all of this is looking even to a future day. Certainly this has been fulfilled partially at least, but oftentimes in the Word of God we find that God is letting us know by giving an earlier partial fulfillment, that a prophecy will be completely fulfilled.

In the remainder of this chapter we find that the judgment is going to be carried out. I will not go into much detail here.

**Because thou hast forgotten the God of thy salvation, and hast not been mindful of the rock of thy strength, therefore shalt thou plant pleasant plants, and shalt set it with strange slips [Isa. 17:10].**

Isaiah is talking to the northern kingdom of Israel, and what he says has been literally fulfilled. It has its spiritual application also, as all of this does. The land of Israel in our day has been planted with pleasant plants and slips. I had the privilege personally of setting out five trees in Israel. The forests of the cedars of Lebanon have almost been removed, but there are many trees in that land. The Mount of Olives was covered with trees, but while the Turks controlled Palestine, practically all the land was denuded of its greenery. After World War I England began a movement to plant trees in that land, and the present government of Israel has continued this policy, so that literally millions of trees have been set out.

## THE BURDEN OF THE LAND BEYOND THE RIVERS OF ETHIOPIA

Chapter 18 deals with the fifth burden, that of the land "beyond the rivers of Ethiopia." The exact nation that Isaiah had in mind has not been clearly established, so there have been many interpretations. Some have thought that he is talking about Egypt, but the description does not fit that country. Also, Egypt is the subject of the next chapter, where we see that God is not through with that kingdom. Prophecy literally has been fulfilled concerning her. Those who say that chapter 18 is referring to England and the United States weary me with that interpretation. I feel like yawning, as that is certainly not sound interpretation of the Word of God!

I believe that Ethiopia best suits the text and tenor of Scripture. But which Ethiopia is intended? There are two mentioned in Scripture. The word for Ethiopia is Cush. There is one in Asia (see Gen. 2:13), and there is one in Africa. I believe we are talking about the Ethiopia that is in Africa. It is the land "beyond the rivers," and the rivers of Ethiopia are the Nile River.

Now God calls the world's attention to Ethiopia:

**Woe to the land shadowing with wings, which is beyond the rivers of Ethiopia [Isa. 18:1].**

"Woe" is an unfortunate translation. Actually, it is the same word that is translated as "ah" in Isaiah 1:4, where it is a sigh, or as "ho" in Isaiah 55, where it is a form of address that demands attention. Here God is saying, "Ho, to the land—Hear Me, listen to this!"

"Shadowing with wings" might better be translated "rustling with wings." This is quite interesting. A missionary to the land for quite some years told me that Ethiopia is noted for its birds. It is called "the land of wings." This helps to confirm that the land in question here is Ethiopia.

**That sendeth ambassadors by the sea, even in vessels of bulrushes upon the waters, saying, Go, ye swift messengers, to a nation scattered and peeled, to a people terrible from their beginning hitherto; a nation meted out and trodden down, whose land the rivers have spoiled! [Isa. 18:2].**

Some have held this sea power to be England or the United States, but "vessels of bulrushes" would not characterize the boats of any modern nation! Dr. F. C. Jennings, in his profound work on Isaiah, makes a good case for the steamboat, but since modern ships use oil, this seems to have no place in our day.

"A nation scattered and peeled" is Israel. This is patently evident, and most of the sound students of the Word of God concur in this.

**All ye inhabitants of the world, and dwellers on the earth, see ye, when he lifteth up an ensign on the mountains; and when he bloweth a trumpet, hear ye [Isa. 18:3].**

Many students of the Word consider the "ensign" mentioned here to be the ark of the tabernacle, which was later transferred to the temple. It disappeared at the time of the

Babylonian captivity, and there is a tradition which says it was carried to Ethiopia. I have been told that there is a church in that land that claims to have the ark. I don't know if that is true or not, but an ensign will come out of that land.

**In that time shall the present be brought unto the LORD of hosts of a people scattered and peeled, and from a people terrible from their beginning hitherto; a nation meted out and trodden under foot, whose land the rivers have spoiled, to the place of the name of the LORD of hosts, the mount Zion [Isa. 18:7].**

This is evidently a reference to the time when the kingdom of Christ will be established on this earth and the Ethiopians will come again to Jerusalem to worship. There is no judgment spoken against them. In Psalm 87:4, evidently in reply to what he is doing in Jerusalem, the Ethiopian answers that he was born there. God has wonderful things to say about Ethiopia!

# CHAPTERS 19–20

*THEME: The burden of Egypt—through gloom to glory*

Chapters 13–23 present eleven judgments against nations that surrounded the nation Israel. The burden of Egypt is the sixth burden. Egypt is certainly one nation we would expect to find on this list. This is one of the greatest passages that illustrate the accuracy of the Word of God. Certainly fulfilled prophecy is proof that the Bible is the Word of God. No nation figures more prominently on the pages of Scripture than Egypt in its relationship to Israel. Egypt has a longer history than any nation mentioned in Scripture, including Israel. In fact, it was down in the land of Egypt that the nation Israel was born. Seventy souls from the family of Jacob journeyed there, and four hundred years later they left Egypt with at least a million and a half people. Egypt was an old nation at that time. It has had a continuous history right down to the present day. It is in existence today and plays a prominent part in world events. And it has a glorious future predicted in this chapter. This chapter contains all the elements which enter into the history of the nation—its past, present, and future.

Egypt came into prominence early in Scripture when Abraham ran away to Egypt and got into difficulties. Later Joseph was sold into Egypt, and during a famine Jacob and his sons went down into Egypt with their families. There Israel became a great nation as slaves in the brickyards. Later on, after the children of Israel returned to the Promised Land, two of their kings, Ahaz and Hezekiah, made an alliance with Egypt and found her an unreliable ally.

During the intertestamental period, between Malachi and Matthew, Israel suffered grievously at the hand of Egypt. When the Lord Jesus Christ was born, He was taken down into Egypt. The gospel made many converts in Egypt during the first three centuries of the Christian era. Out of that section of North Africa came three great saints of the church—Athanasius, Origen, and Augustine—and others also. In our day, Egypt has been a thorn in the side of the new nation of Israel.

## FULFILLED PROPHECY CONCERNING EGYPT

**The burden of Egypt. Behold, the LORD rideth upon a swift cloud, and shall come into Egypt: and the idols of Egypt shall be moved at his presence, and the heart of Egypt shall melt in the midst of it [Isa. 19:1].**

The idolatry of Egypt is the chief target of God's condemnation. We will pick up this theme again when we get to the Book of Ezekiel where God says that every idol would disappear from Egypt. Perhaps no people were ever given over to idolatry more than the Egyptians, with the possible exception of Babylonia, which was the fountainhead of idolatry. What Paul said in Romans 1:21–23 fits Egypt like a glove: "Because that, when they knew God, they glorified him not as God,

neither were thankful; but became vain in their imaginations, and their foolish heart was darkened. Professing themselves to be wise, they became fools, And changed the glory of the uncorruptible God into an image made like to corruptible man, and to birds, and four-footed beasts, and creeping things."

History bears testimony to the fact that Egypt was originally monotheistic, that is, they worshiped one God; but they gradually lapsed into the basest sort of idolatry where every creature under heaven was worshiped, including the bull, the frog, the scarab (a bug), the fish, and all sorts of birds. When Moses was ready to deliver the children of Israel from Egypt, God had to carry on warfare, which I call the battle of the gods, in which God through Moses brought down plagues upon Egypt. Jehovah struck at all forms of idolatry in Egypt—from the sun in the heavens and the River Nile to frogs and lice in the land. Each plague was directed against one of the gods or idols of Egypt.

Now God comes down again in a cloud like a chariot to destroy the idols of Egypt. It is interesting to know that idolatry has long since disappeared from the land, though the people dwell in the ignorance and superstition of the Moslem religion. I have visited Egypt twice, and there is no darkness like the darkness in the land of Egypt. Isaiah's prophecy has been fulfilled.

**And I will set the Egyptians against the Egyptians: and they shall fight every one against his brother, and every one against his neighbour; city against city, and kingdom against kingdom [Isa. 19:2].**

At about the time of Isaiah several pharaohs arose who could no longer control this great kingdom, and the army no longer obeyed them. The people no longer respected the government. This caused the setting up of weak city-states that were self-governing for a period of time. For this reason there were great cities such as Thebes and Karnak in Upper Egypt, and in Lower Egypt there was another cluster of great cities. There was a break-up of cities also at Memphis, known in Scripture as Noph.

**And the spirit of Egypt shall fail in the midst thereof; and I will destroy the counsel thereof: and they shall seek to the idols, and to the charmers, and to them that have familiar spirits and to the wizards [Isa. 19:3].**

The proud nation of Egypt had advanced its civilization much further than other nations. There is not a nation under the sun today that does not owe a great deal to the civilization of Egypt. There came a time when Egypt turned to idols and finally in desperation resorted to spiritism. You find that at the time of Moses, for instance, the magicians who were called in could actually duplicate some of the miracles that Moses did. The time came when they could no longer duplicate what Moses did, but what they did at first reveals the fact that they were not fakers; they actually had satanic powers.

"The spirit of Egypt shall fail." The time came when the nation was brought down to a low level.

**And the Egyptians will I give over into the hand of a cruel lord; and a fierce king shall rule over them, saith the Lord, the LORD of hosts [Isa. 19:4].**

This "cruel lord" cannot be positively identified from history, as Egypt was attacked and subdued by a series of invaders who eventually reduced the nation to poverty.

**And the waters shall fail from the sea, and the river shall be wasted and dried up [Isa. 19:5].**

The "sea" in this verse refers to the River Nile which was the main artery of the nation and a large body of water. "The rivers" are the canals that were built especially at the mouth of the river. That delta area had to be kept open in that day because so much soil was being brought down by the River Nile.

**And they shall turn the rivers far away; and the brooks of defence shall be emptied and dried up: the reeds and flags shall wither [Isa. 19:6].**

It is quite interesting that even today those "brooks," those outlets to the sea there at the delta, are filled up. It had been a wonderful place like the Garden of Eden, but it is not that now by any means. Those who have traveled to the land of Egypt are amazed to see that there is no great growth of vegetation along the banks of the Nile. There is no forest or heavy foliage such as is common along other great rivers.

Now notice what God says specifically:

**The paper reeds by the brooks, by the mouth of the brooks, and every thing sown by the brooks, shall wither, be driven away, and be no more [Isa. 19:7].**

The "paper reeds" are the papyri which were used in that day as paper is used today. It was one of the main industries of Egypt, and it added a great deal to the wealth of Egypt. After clay tablets, papyrus became the writing material of man. The Phoenicians introduced papyrus all over the civilized world of their day, and the main source of this writing material was raised along the Nile River. You won't find it there today. It no longer grows along the banks where it was indigenous. If you go there today, you will find papyri in front of the museum beside the pool that is there, and you see it growing at some of the wealthy homes, especially in the British colony at Cairo. It is a luxury plant; it is no longer the common plant which grew plentifully along the River Nile. God said it would cease. You can try to find a natural explanation for its dying out, but I believe that God had something to do with it.

**The fishers also shall mourn, and all they that cast angle into the brooks shall lament, and they that spread nets upon the waters shall languish [Isa. 19:8].**

Fishing was another great industry in Egypt, as the Nile River abounded in fish. When the children of Israel came out of Egypt, they missed the fish they had eaten in Egypt. Of course, there were no fish in the desert. God gave them flesh to eat when He sent them quail; but, very frankly, they didn't care too much for quail on toast. They much preferred the fish in Egypt. The fish have disappeared, and to this day fishing is not one of the industries along the Nile. This prophecy was literally fulfilled. When I was in Egypt, I particularly watched for people fishing in the Nile. I don't think I saw over two or three people fishing! In Florida you see hundreds of people fishing along the canals, but you don't see fishing like that in Egypt. God said that the fishermen would mourn and lament—because they wouldn't catch anything.

**Moreover they that work in fine flax, and they that weave networks, shall be confounded [Isa. 19:9].**

Egypt raised flax, and they wove it into remarkable linen. It even excelled the linen made in Ireland in our day. I have been told that while the Irish linen mills get about 180,000 feet of strands per pound, the Egyptian mills got 300,000—almost twice the amount. It was very much like silk. It is said that a fisherman could take a net made of that fine twined byssus linen and pull it through the ring on his hand! It was this Egyptian linen that was used in Israel's wilderness tabernacle. The people had brought that wonderful linen with them.

Now God said that that industry would disappear, and it certainly has disappeared. This prophecy has been literally fulfilled.

**And they shall be broken in the purposes thereof, all that make sluices and ponds for fish [Isa. 19:10].**

The entire fishing industry was to disappear. This has been fulfilled literally. Dr. F. C. Jennings writes, "Egypt's wealth, as already said, practically consists in her river, because of its volume here called a sea." All of that has disappeared.

**Surely the princes of Zoan are fools, the counsel of the wise counsellors of Pharaoh is become brutish: how say ye unto Pharaoh, I am the son of the wise, the son of ancient kings? [Isa. 19:11].**

The royal line of the pharaohs intermarried so much—actually brother married sister—that it produced offspring who were morons. God said:

**The princes of Zoan are become fools, the princes of Noph are deceived; they have also seduced Egypt, even they that are the stay of the tribes thereof [Isa. 19:13].**

"Noph" is Memphis as we know it.

"They have also seduced Egypt." We all know the sordid story of Cleopatra (a Greek) who became queen of Egypt.

**The LORD hath mingled a perverse spirit in the midst thereof: and they have caused Egypt to err in every work thereof, as a drunken man staggereth in his vomit [Isa. 19:14].**

This is a vivid picture of the reduction of Egypt to a base kingdom.

**Neither shall there be any work for Egypt, which the head or tail, branch or rush, may do [Isa. 19:15].**

According to this verse there would be the failure of industry and commerce. They would die, and poverty and wretchedness would overtake the nation. Isaiah has predicted that there will be failure of false religion, failure of material resources, and failure of spiritual power. When these disappeared, the prophecy that Egypt would become a base kingdom

was fulfilled. All you have to do is to go to Cairo today to have this confirmed.

## UNFULFILLED PROPHECY

**In that day shall Egypt be like unto women: and it shall be afraid and fear because of the shaking of the hand of the Lord of hosts, which he shaketh over it [Isa. 19:16].**

The phrase, "In that day," places this section in the future. "In that day" Egypt will be afraid like women; that will be their condition when they go into the Great Tribulation Period.

**And the land of Judah shall be a terror unto Egypt, every one that maketh mention thereof shall be afraid in himself, because of the counsel of the Lord of hosts, which he hath determined against it [Isa. 19:17].**

You may be thinking that this verse is being fulfilled in our day when we see buildings in Egypt, like the museum in Cairo, sandbagged and protected against a bomb attack.

**In that day five cities in the land of Egypt speak the language of Canaan, and swear to the Lord of hosts; one shall be called, The city of destruction [Isa. 19:18].**

This entire section looks toward the Day of the Lord for a complete fulfillment.

**In that day shall there be an altar to the Lord in the midst of the land of Egypt, and a pillar at the border thereof to the Lord.**

**And it shall be for a sign and for a witness unto the Lord of hosts in the land of Egypt: for they shall cry unto the Lord because of the oppressors, and he shall send them a saviour, and a great one, and he shall deliver them [Isa. 19:19–20].**

"An altar to the Lord" has been interpreted by some of the cults as the pyramid. The pyramid is neither an altar nor a pillar, but a monstrous mausoleum for the burying of kings and queens. What will be "a sign"? What will be an ensign? The cross will yet be the place to which Egypt will look instead of to a crescent.

**And the Lord shall be known to Egypt, and the Egyptians shall know the Lord in that day, and shall do sacrifice and oblation; yea, they shall vow a vow unto the Lord, and perform it.**

**And the Lord shall smite Egypt: he shall smite and heal it: and they shall return even to the Lord, and he shall be entreated of them, and shall heal them [Isa. 19:21–22].**

Egypt has a glorious future. The nation will enter and enjoy the kingdom with Israel. It may not look like this could be possible in the present hour. Only God can do this.

**In that day shall there be a highway out of Egypt to Assyria, and the Assyrian shall come into Egypt, and the Egyptian into Assyria, and the Egyptians shall serve with the Assyrians [Isa. 19:23].**

This freeway will not be for soldiers and armies but for those going to Jerusalem to serve Christ the King.

**In that day shall Israel be the third with Egypt and with Assyria, even a blessing in the midst of the land [Isa. 19:24].**

Note the exalted position of Egypt in the Kingdom.

**Whom the Lord of hosts shall bless, saying, Blessed be Egypt my people, and Assyria the work of my hands, and Israel mine inheritance [Isa. 19:25].**

A blessing is yet to come to Egypt, a despised and debased nation.

The one great thought in chapter 20 is that in three years Israel would be invaded. Chapter 19 closed on the high note of future blessing for Egypt in the millennial kingdom, and this chapter predicts coming events in the *near* future, which will prove the reliability of Isaiah as a prophet of God.

**In the year that Tartan came unto Ashdod (when Sargon the king of Assyria sent him,) and fought against Ashdod, and took it [Isa. 20:1].**

Tartan was a general in the Assyrian army, mentioned in 2 Kings 18:17. Ashdod was a city in the northern kingdom of ten tribes. Sargon succeeded Shalmaneser (see 2 Kings 17:3).

This is the only place the name of Sargon is mentioned in the Bible. As recent as one hundred years ago historians maintained that Sargon never lived, because they could find no reference to him in secular history. However, archaeologists discovered that the Assyrian

form of his name is Sharrukin. Abundant historical materials concerning his reign have come down to us.

**At the same time spake the LORD by Isaiah the son of Amoz, saying, Go and loose the sackcloth from off thy loins, and put off thy shoe from thy foot. And he did so, walking naked and barefoot [Isa. 20:2].**

Isaiah was to become a walking parable to Israel as a warning not to become confederate with Egypt. Probably Isaiah was not asked to go in the nude. Clothing was and is so essential to the customs of the East and nudity is so revolting that it is obvious that this was not intended. Isaiah was to lay aside his outward tunic of mourning. This would attract immediate and startling attention to the prophet. It would enable Isaiah to make his point publicly. It is well to note the words of F. Delitzsch at this point, "What Isaiah was therefore directed to do was simply opposed to common custom and not to moral decency."

**And the LORD said, Like as my servant Isaiah hath walked naked and barefoot three years for a sign and wonder upon Egypt and upon Ethiopia [Isa. 20:3].**

Isaiah was to walk through Israel to let them know what would happen to Egypt. As he walked, we are told, he would be for a sign and wonder for the people.

**So shall the king of Assyria lead away the Egyptians prisoners, and the Ethiopians captives, young and old, naked and barefoot, even with their buttocks uncovered, to the shame of Egypt [Isa. 20:4].**

Since Egypt could not protect herself (nor could Ethiopia), she would not be a reliable ally for Israel. Both Egypt and Ethiopia were invaded by Sargon of Assyria, and this shame which Isaiah had predicted came upon Egypt.

# CHAPTER 21

**THEME:** *Three burdens: Babylon "desert of the sea," Edom "Dumah," and Arabia*

Isaiah is enumerating eleven "burdens," or judgments. In this chapter we are going to consider burdens seven, eight, and nine, which are against Babylon, Edom, and Arabia. These burdens are set forth by expressive symbols, and in the day they were given I am sure they were as clear to the people as the noonday sun. In fact, they were as clear to the people in Isaiah's day as the expressions "stars and stripes" and "Old Glory" are to every American. The insignia in this chapter are not quite so clear to us today, and as a result there has been some disagreement among Bible expositors about their meaning. They can be identified as Babylon, Edom, and Arabia, and each one will be considered separately as we go through this chapter. All were enemies or potential enemies of Israel. Each brought a particular misery upon God's people. Each has been judged in time.

This chapter is a neglected part of the Word of God. To prove this, let me ask you a question. When was the last time you heard a sermon or Bible study on this chapter of the Bible? I have a notion that you have *never* heard a study on Isaiah 21. This is another section of Scripture which confirms my position of a premillennial, pretribulation, dispensational interpretation of the Word of God. It is the only interpretation which would satisfy a passage like this, which is the reason all other systems stay clear of this chapter and other portions of God's Word with like teaching.

The remarkable thing in this chapter is that symbols are used. Now I believe in a *literal* interpretation of Scripture, but when symbolism is used, it always pictures *reality*. That is an important thing to remember. Many expositors call a teaching of Scripture symbolism in an attempt to make it disappear. Like a magician says, "hocus-pocus," and it's gone—so don't worry about it. My friend, let's not try to evaporate this section of Scripture, but let's study it to see what God is saying.

**The burden of the desert of the sea. As whirlwinds in the south pass through;**

**so it cometh from the dessert, from a terrible land [Isa. 21:1].**

"The desert of the sea" is a strange expression. It is like saying "the dryness of the water," or "how dry the water is." This may not be too peculiar to us since we have "dry ice" and "cold heat." Dr. F. C. Jennings translates this verse, "As sweep the whirlwinds through the south, so comes it from the desert, from the land that strikes with terror." This is a good interpretation of the verse, but it does not identify the nation. But if you keep reading, the nation is identified in verse 9: "Babylon is fallen, is fallen." So we know "the desert of the sea" is Babylon. Before Babylon became a world power, her doom was again predicted. We have already seen that. The first burden in chapters 13–14 was against Babylon. Babylon became so awe-inspiring and frightful, and represented so much in Scripture, that we have this further word concerning its doom. It was the first place of united rebellion against God at the tower of Babel, and it represents the last stronghold of rebellion against God. We find this in Revelation 17 and 18. Religious Babylon is presented in Revelation 17, and commercial Babylon is set forth in Revelation 18.

The expression, "desert of the sea," is a paradoxical phrase. Babylon was geographically located on a great desert plain beside the Euphrates River. It was irrigated by canals from the river. Jeremiah gives this description of Babylon, "O thou that dwellest upon many waters, abundant in treasures, thine end is come, and the measure of thy covetousness" (Jer. 51:13). The desert and the sea form a weird amalgamation here. This same fusion of desert and sea is made by John in Revelation. "So he carried me away in the spirit into the wilderness: and I saw a woman sit upon a scarlet coloured beast, full of names of blasphemy, having seven heads and ten horns" (Rev. 17:3). This is the desert where John beheld the mystery Babylon: ". . . Come hither; I will shew unto thee the judgment of the great whore that sitteth upon many waters" (Rev. 17:1). It was in the desert that John saw the "many waters." These two verses are symbolic, but they carry through the same pattern. We will find it again in Jeremiah.

Babylon, with its glitter and glamour and as the fountainhead of idolatry and false religion, was a mirage upon the desert. Isn't this tremendous!—"desert of the sea"—what a picture! Babylon was not a wonderful place. It was a mirage in the desert. It wasn't a spring or an oasis at all, but a place filled with idols and false religion. There was no life-giving water there for the souls of men. This is something that every pastor, every radio preacher, every church, and every church member ought to turn over in his mind. Is my church or am I a life-giving fountain, or am I just a mirage upon the desert of life?

**A grievous vision is declared unto me; the treacherous dealer dealeth treacherously, and the spoiler spoileth. Go up, O Elam; besiege, O Media; all the sighing thereof have I made to cease [Isa. 21:2].**

God commands the two-fold nation of Media-Persia to destroy and spoil the city. "Go up, O Elam [Persia]: besiege, O Media." That is exactly what happened. This is a prophecy that was given before the invasion took place.

**Therefore are my loins filled with pain: pangs have taken hold upon me, as the pangs of a woman that travaileth: I was bowed down at the hearing of it; I was dismayed at the seeing of it.**

**My heart panted, fearfulness affrighted me: the night of my pleasure hath he turned into fear unto me [Isa. 21:3–4].**

Once again Isaiah is moved with great feeling and emotion when he learns of the coming devastation. This is the heart of God revealed, desiring to show mercy and loath to judge even so frightful a foe. God's love is as evident here as in the tears of Jeremiah. No one can rejoice in the judgment of God. God says that His judgment is His "strange" work. He does not want to judge you; He wants to save you, but the choice is yours. He doesn't want to judge nations either, and that choice is up to them.

**Prepare the table, watch in the watchtower, eat, drink: arise, ye princes, and anoint the shield [Isa. 21:5].**

This verse reads as if it were an eyewitness account of the destruction of Babylon as recorded by Daniel (see Dan. 5). Remember, this was recorded about two hundred years before it transpired. In the midst of the banquet of Belshazzar, the Median general, Gobryas, detoured the river that flowed through the city and marched his army on the dry river bed underneath the walls of the city. He took the city by surprise and shock. This is something that God said would take place.

**And he cried, A lion: My Lord, I stand continually upon the watchtower in the**

daytime, and I am set in my ward whole nights:

**And, behold, here cometh a chariot of men, with a couple of horsemen. And he answered and said, Babylon is fallen, is fallen; and all the graven images of her gods he hath broken unto the ground [Isa. 21:8–9].**

The watchman on the walls of the city tells the people inside what he sees. He says, "As I look out on the desert, here comes a chariot of men, with a couple of horses." They are messengers, and their message is "Babylon is fallen, is fallen." The watchman brings word to the king of Babylon that it has fallen (see Jer. 51:31–33). All of Babylon's graven images of her gods are broken unto the ground. This is a sigh of sorrow as well as relief. Babylon was the source of all idolatry.

**O my threshing, and the corn of my floor: that which I have heard of the LORD of hosts, the God of Israel, have I declared unto you [Isa. 21:10].**

Harvest is the time of judgment. In John 4:35 our Lord said, "Say not ye, There are yet four months, and then cometh harvest? behold, I say unto you, Lift up your eyes, and look on the fields; for they are white already to harvest." Our Lord said this at the end of the age of law, when judgment was coming against Israel who had had the Law for almost fifteen hundred years. Harvest is the time of judgment.

There is a book I would like to recommend to you at this point, because we are going to study some more about Babylon in the Books of Jeremiah, Ezekiel, and Daniel. Hislop's book, *The Two Babylons*, would be a valuable addition to your library.

## BURDEN OF EDOM

**The burden of Dumah. He calleth to me out of Seir, Watchman, what of the night? Watchman, what of the night? [Isa. 21:11].**

Who is "Dumah"? Dumah is a symbolic word. Isaiah played upon words to bring out a deeper meaning. We have already seen that. He used words to carry a message to the people. "Dumah" is Edom with the *E* removed. You take the *E* off Edom, and you have *Dumah* which means "silence." Our word *dumb* is closer to the intent and purpose of Isaiah. Edom is still a land of deathlike silence.

*Seir* means "rough or hairy." Esau was the first Seir man (see Gen. 25:25). He was hairy, and he dwelt in Mount Seir (see Gen. 36:8). *Seir* also means "storms." It was a land swept with storms. "Silence and Storm." What a play on words, and what a message!

Edom is obviously the country involved. Out of the land of silence and storm comes this inquiry, which is twice repeated: "Watchman, what of the night?" In other words, "How much of the night is gone?" How long will it be before God's glory will be revealed when the ". . . Sun of righteousness [shall] arise with healing in his wings . . ." (Mal. 4:2)?

**The watchman said, The morning cometh, and also the night: if ye will inquire, inquire ye: return, come [Isa. 21:12].**

You see, both morning and night are coming. What will be glory for some will be doom for others. What will be light for God's people will be night for Edomites, the men of the flesh who have rejected God.

## BURDEN OF ARABIA

**The burden upon Arabia. In the forest in Arabia shall ye lodge, O ye travelling companies of Dedanim [Isa. 21:13].**

"Arabia" seems clear enough, but again this is a word with a double meaning. It can be made to mean *evening* by changing the vowel points. The Hebrew language is a language of consonants with no vowels. Instead it had vowel points, which are little marks above the consonants. Scholars have added vowels to the Hebrew words to make them more readable. In this verse the meaning is quite obvious: it was evening in the history of Arabia. It was later than they thought. Arabia was the land of the Ishmaelites, the Bedouin tribes of the desert— the modern Arabs. It is interesting that God speaks of them. Abraham's sons, Ishmael and Isaac, never did get along. Their descendants don't get along today either. The Arabs and the Jews are still at each other's throats. If Abraham could see what is going on now, I wonder if he would think the sin he committed was a small sin. My friend, sin never ceases working itself out in the human story.

**The inhabitants of the land of Tema brought water to him that was thirsty, they prevented with their bread him that fled.**

For they fled from the swords, from the drawn sword, and from the bent bow, and from the grievousness of war.

For thus hath the Lord said unto me, Within a year, according to the years of an hireling, and all the glory of Kedar shall fail [Isa. 21:14–16].

There was a coming judgment upon this land and its people. This chapter of poetic beauty and heart sorrow should not end on this note. It may be "evening" here, but God's day is reckoned "the evening and the morning"— ". . . the evening and the morning were the first day" (Gen. 1:5).

The morning is coming; the night of weeping will soon be over, and the new day will dawn. Man's evening of failure, sin, and darkness will end, and God's morning will be ushered in by the coming of the Sun of Righteousness.

# CHAPTER 22

***THEME:*** *The burden of the valley of vision (Jerusalem); the history of Shebna and Eliakim*

This burden evidently refers to Jerusalem, as we shall point out under the comments on the verses. The burdens began way off at a distance in Babylon, and they have continued to come nearer to Jerusalem. Now the storm breaks in all of its fury upon the Holy City.

## BURDEN OF JERUSALEM

The burden of the valley of vision. What aileth thee now, that thou art wholly gone up to the housetops? [Isa. 22:1].

The "valley of vision" refers to Jerusalem, as verses 4, 8, 9, and 10 imply. The expression, "valley of vision," is another of Isaiah's paradoxical statements. *Mountain* of vision would be understood, because the mountain is the place of the far view. Moses stood on Mount Nebo to view the land of promise. Our Lord looked over Jerusalem from the Mount of Olives. But in Scripture a valley symbolizes a place of sorrow, humbleness, and death. Because the vision here is one of sorrow and coming battle, the valley is the proper place for this vision.

Curiosity and fear send people to the housetop to inquire about the approaching danger. See the Assyrian siege of Jerusalem in Isaiah 36 and 37. In the last siege our Lord warns these people to leave the housetops and flee (see Matt. 24:16–17).

Therefore said I, Look away from me: I will weep bitterly, labour not to comfort me, because of the spoiling of the daughter of my people [Isa. 22:4].

"My people" are, of course, the people of Israel.

Ye have seen also the breaches of the city of David, that they are many: and ye gathered together the waters of the lower pool.

And ye have numbered the houses of Jerusalem, and the houses have ye broken down to fortify the wall [Isa. 22:9–10].

Hezekiah actually took these precautions in defending Jerusalem (see 2 Chron. 32). One of the things he did was to put a wall around the fountain so that the city would not run out of water. You can still see it in the land today.

This section refers to the future. As Dr. F. C. Jennings puts it, "The history eventuated in the deliverance of Jerusalem, the prophecy in its capture; therefore the history does not fulfill it."

Just what siege and enemy is in the mind of the prophet? Persia is mentioned by name, but Jerusalem was in ruins while Persia was in power. Apparently all the enemies who have come up against Jerusalem are before us here, from the Assyrians who only laid a siege but did not enter the city, to the last enemy from the north who will threaten the city but will not enter. The interval between these two has seen this city captured more than any other. This is the burden of Jerusalem.

## BRIEF FROM THE CASE OF SHEBNA AND ELIAKIM

The unusual insertion at this point of an historical document out of the archives of

Jerusalem during the reign of Hezekiah is worth noting.

Many have seen a picture of the Antichrist in Shebna, while Eliakim sets before us none other than the Lord Jesus Christ who will supplant the Antichrist in this world.

**Thus saith the Lord GOD of hosts, Go, get thee unto this treasurer, even unto Shebna, which is over the house, and say [Isa. 22:15].**

Shebna was secretary of the treasury, a cheap politician under Hezekiah. Apparently he was misappropriating funds (see 2 Kings 18:18; 19:2; Isa. 36:3; 37:2).

**What hast thou here? and whom hast thou here, that thou hast hewed thee out a sepulchre here, as he that heweth him out a sepulchre on high, and that graveth an habitation for himself in a rock? [Isa. 22:16].**

Shebna was building a tomb to perpetuate his name. It was ironical, as he was to die and be buried in a foreign land (vv. 17–18).

**And I will drive thee from thy station, and from thy state shall he pull thee down [Isa. 22:19].**

Shebna, I think, is just an adumbration of Antichrist.

**And it shall come to pass in that day, that I will call my servant Eliakim the son of Hilkiah:**

**And I will clothe him with thy robe, and strengthen him with thy girdle, and I will commit thy government into his hand: and he shall be a father to the inhabitants of Jerusalem, and to the house of Judah [Isa. 22:20–21].**

Eliakim was the statesman who succeeded Shebna. Eliakim was an unselfish man. He and Shebna are in contrast here. Isaiah has brought together these men who are more than paradoxes—they are opposites. Shebna pictures the Antichrist, and Eliakim pictures Christ. The language is typical.

**And the key of the house of David will I lay upon his shoulder; so he shall open, and none shall shut; and he shall shut, and none shall open [Isa. 22:22].**

This verse reminds us of the words of Christ in the New Testament: "And to the angel of the church in Philadelphia write; These things saith he that is holy, he that is true, he that hath the key of David, he that openeth, and no man shutteth; and shutteth, and no man openeth" (Rev. 3:7). How wonderful it is, my friend, to place our lives in the hands of Him who is able to close or open any door!

**And I will fasten him as a nail in a sure place; and he shall be for a glorious throne to his father's house.**

**And they shall hang upon him all the glory of his father's house, the offspring and the issue, all vessels of small quantity, from the vessels of cups, even to all the vessels of flagons [Isa. 22:23–24].**

Our salvation likewise hangs on Him.

**In that day, saith the LORD of hosts, shall the nail that is fastened in the sure place be removed, and be cut down, and fall; and the burden that was upon it shall be cut off: for the LORD hath spoken it [Isa. 22:25].**

"In that day" refers to the Great Tribulation Period, as we have seen, and this verse refers to Shebna as he pictures the Antichrist. A great many people will put their trust in the Antichrist who is to come. They will look to him for help. They will think he is Christ, but he will be just a nail that will fall.

My friend, have you ever had that experience? You drive a good nail into the wall, hang a heavy coat on it, and it comes down. The Lord Jesus Christ is the nail in a sure place. Shebna was a nail that came down, and so will all others who are like him. Are you hanging everything you've got on the nail that is in a sure place? Many people are not. They are hanging everything they have on something that is not sure. For instance, they make investments. A man told me, "I trusted a lawyer, and he made a mistake." He wasn't a nail in a sure place. Some folk have even trusted a preacher and have found that he was not a nail in a sure place. Only Christ is a nail in a sure place. I hope you are hanging your life and everything you have on Him.

# CHAPTER 23

**THEME:** *The burden of Tyre*

In this chapter we come to the eleventh and last burden against the nations. A burden, as we have seen, is a judgment, and these judgments were leveled against the nations around Israel. Each one of these great nations represents or sets before us some principle, philosophy, or system which God must judge. Let me give a recapitulation of these eleven nations and what they represent.

1. *Babylon* represents false religions and idolatry. Idolatry in our land is covetousness, which is the overwhelming desire to have more and to give ourselves to the accumulation of the material things of the world.

2. *Palestine* represents true religion which has become apostate. Today you find that the same thing has happened in many churches. They go through rituals, they even repeat the Apostles' Creed and the Lord's Prayer. From all outward appearances they seem to be resting upon the Bible, but in reality they deny everything that is in it. They are apostate, which means they are standing away from what they once believed.

3. *Moab* represents formal religion; that is, having a form of godliness, but denying the power thereof.

Many of us today could be identified with one of these three. Some of us are giving our lives to the accumulation of material things, and our eyes are filled with the things we want. We are covetous.

Some of us have been brought up in Bible-believing churches but have turned away from their teachings. Others of us go to church and follow forms, ceremonies, and rituals, which are beautiful but dead as a dodo bird.

4. *Damascus* represents compromise. That is the position that most churches (even fundamental churches) are in today. Thank God for those churches that are standing true!

5. *Ethiopia* represents missions. How we need to be involved in getting out the Word of God!

6. *Egypt* represents the world. Israel was told to stay out of Egypt—that is where Abraham got into trouble. And we are admonished, "Love not the world." Many of us are having trouble with the world.

7. *Persia* (Babylon) represents luxury. My, how most of us love luxury in our affluent society.

8. *Edom* represents the flesh. Many people serve the flesh today.

9. *Arabia* represents war. There are two groups of people in our contemporary society: the hawks and the doves. Both are of the world, and the only difference I see in them is that the peace group tells us they are for peace, but they are willing to *fight* for it!

10. *Valley of vision*, which is Jerusalem, represents not religion but politics. Some think that in politics will be found the solutions to the problems of the world.

11. *Tyre* represents commercialism (big business). I would say that the great sin of America today is commercialism, believing that the almighty dollar can solve all our problems. When a problem comes up, Congress votes for a little more money, and people for whom it is intended never get it, of course. Every poverty program has hurt rather than helped the poor. Why? Because godless men just don't have the right solutions. The poor haven't learned that yet, because they are also far from God. It is only the Lord Jesus Christ who has any love for the poor and really knows how to help them.

Now let us look at the burden of Tyre. Tyre and Sidon were the two great cities of the Phoenicians. Sidon was the mother city, and she was soon surpassed by her proud and rich daughter, Tyre.

The ships of the Phoenicians entered all ports of the Mediterranean Sea and even penetrated the uncharted ocean beyond the Pillars of Hercules. The vessels of Phoenicia brought tin from Great Britian—in fact, the meaning of *Brittania* is "the land of tin." The Phoenicians were aggressive and progressive people. Carthage, in North Africa, was settled by them. Carthage, the great enemy of Rome, was a Phoenician city, and Cyprus owed its prosperity to trading with Tyre. There were also other centers that the Phoenicians founded—Tarshish for instance. You remember that when Jonah tried to flee from the Lord, he bought a ticket for Tarshish. Tarshish was on the southern coast of Spain. Who founded it? The Phoenicians did. It is also of interest that the Phoenicians invented the alphabet.

Hiram, king of Tyre, was one of the great friends of King David. When we get to Ezekiel 26, we are going to see a remarkable prophecy concerning Tyre, which had an exact fulfillment. God said that Tyre would be destroyed by Babylon and would be taken into

captivity for seventy years just as Judah went into captivity for seventy years. The people of Tyre returned to their land, as did Israel, after the captivity and rebuilt their city on an island in the Mediterranean Sea about half a mile from the old city. God said that the ruins of the old city would be *scraped* (see Ezek. 26:4), and, later, Alexander the Great scraped the ancient site of Tyre to make a causeway to the island city. He was wise enough not to attempt a battle by sea, because the Phoenicians were experts with ships; so he built a causeway from the old city on the mainland to the new city on the island. I've walked down that causeway and it is filled with broken pieces of pottery. I could have filled tubs with pieces of pottery, but, of course, no one is allowed to do that. I put one little piece in my pocket, because it looked as if there was plenty to spare. Where did all the pottery and pillars and rubble come from? It came from the ruins of ancient Tyre. Alexander the Great literally scraped the surface of the old city to build his causeway, and you cannot tell where the site of the old Tyre used to be—it's all out there in the causeway. When Alexander took the city, the prophecy of Ezekiel was fulfilled exactly as God said it would be: "And I will make thee like the top of a rock: thou shalt be a place to spread nets upon; thou shalt be built no more: for I the LORD have spoken it, saith the Lord GOD" (Ezek. 26:14). My friend, today there is a little Turkish town near there, but the site of ancient Tyre is still in ruins.

If an atheist wants to disprove the Word of God, I suggest that he do more than stand on a street corner and blab about the fact that he doesn't believe in God. I challenge him to go over to the ancient site of Tyre and rebuild the city. However, I warn him that others have tried to do it and have failed.

In fact, there is a ready-made city, the rock-hewn city of Petra, that is all ready to be moved into. The only problem is that God said it would not be inhabited. Anyone can try to start a colony there, but he won't succeed. A German unbeliever took a group of people to Petra and tried to start a colony, but it didn't last long. You won't succeed either, friend. *God* said that Tyre won't be rebuilt and that Petra won't be inhabited.

## DIVINE RESPONSIBILITY FOR TYRE'S DESTRUCTION

**The burden of Tyre. Howl, ye ships of Tarshish; for it is laid waste, so that there is no house, no entering in: from the land of Chittim it is revealed to them [Isa. 23:1].**

The picture here is that of ships coming home to Tyre from Tarshish where there is a colony of the Phoenicians. Word is brought to them that Tyre has been destroyed. As they sail near, they see the smoke of the city. Then they see that the city has been leveled and the harbor blocked. It will no longer be a great commercial center.

**Be still, ye inhabitants of the isle; thou whom the merchants of Zidon, that pass over the sea, have replenished [Isa. 23:2].**

"Zidon," or Sidon, was about thirty miles up the coast from Tyre. Tyre and Sidon go together like pork and beans go together. They were the two leading cities of the Phoenicians. The prominent sea merchants of Sidon had made Tyre the great city it was. It is interesting that the prophecy concerning the destruction of Tyre was literally fulfilled. But destruction was not predicted for Sidon, and Sidon continues as a city today. Currently Sidon is the place to which oil is brought to be loaded on shipboard and taken to other parts of the world.

**And by great waters the seed of Sihor, the harvest of the river, is her revenue; and she is a mart of nations [Isa. 23:3].**

*Sihor* means "black" and refers to the Upper Nile, the silt of which flooded Egypt and made it fertile. The wealth of Egypt had flowed through the port of Tyre, and now that is ended, and there is going to be a depression— a real one!

**Be thou ashamed, O Zidon: for the sea hath spoken, even the strength of the sea, saying, I travail not, nor bring forth children, neither do I nourish up young men, nor bring up virgins [Isa. 23:4].**

There is a suggestion here that Tyre is the daughter of Sidon. Historically this is accurate.

**As at the report concerning Egypt, so shall they be sorely pained at the report of Tyre [Isa. 23:5].**

The destruction of Tyre ruined the commerce of Egypt in that day.

**Pass ye over to Tarshish; howl, ye inhabitants of the isle [Isa. 23:6].**

The fall of Tyre caused universal mourning, even to a colony that was way over on the southern coast of Spain. Some of the inhabitants of Tyre escaped in ships to Tarshish, when Nebuchadnezzar destroyed the city.

**Is this your joyous city, whose antiquity is of ancient days? her own feet shall carry her afar off to sojourn [Isa. 23:7].**

Any great commercial center is a city which is also a fun center because there will be many things in that city that are pleasing to the flesh. Now the Tyrians are urged to flee as far as possible because this city which was formerly a "joyous city" has come to an end.

**Who hath taken this counsel against Tyre, the crowning city, whose merchants are princes, whose traffickers are the honourable of the earth? [Isa. 23:8].**

"The crowning city" means the *giver of crowns.* You see, Tyre established crown colonies. Great Britain has done the same thing in more recent times. A crown colony is under the legislation and administration of the crown rather than having its own constitution and representative government.

**The LORD of hosts hath purposed it, to stain the pride of all glory, and to bring into contempt all the honourable of the earth [Isa. 23:9].**

It was the Lord of hosts who had determined the destruction of Tyre. He offers no apologies for making the arrangement.

## HUMAN RESPONSIBILITY FOR TYRE'S DESTRUCTION

**Pass through thy land as a river, O daughter of Tarshish: there is no more strength [Isa. 23:10].**

The "river" is the Nile. As the Nile has overflowed her banks, the colony of Tarshish is now free to do as she pleases since Tyre has fallen and is no longer able to control her.

"There is no more strength" means that there is no girdle that holds her up or binds her.

**He stretched out his hand over the sea, he shook the kingdoms: the LORD hath given a commandment against the merchant city, to destroy the strong holds thereof [Isa. 23:11].**

Have you noticed this threefold description of Tyre? In verse 7 Tyre is called a "joyous city." In verse 8 Tyre is called a "crowning city." In verse 11 Tyre is called a "merchant city." All three of these are apt descriptions of Tyre.

**And he said, Thou shalt no more rejoice, O thou oppressed virgin, daughter of Zidon: arise pass over to Chittim; there also shalt thou have no rest [Isa. 23:12].**

What is suggested in verse 4 is plainly declared here. Tyre is the daughter of Sidon. Sidon was the older city, and rich merchants from there had founded Tyre and given her prestige. The joy of prosperity was to disappear. Both Tyre and Sidon would suffer.

"Pass over to Chittim"—probably some thought that by fleeing to Cyprus they might make a fresh beginning. In this, too, they were to be disappointed. God was responsible for what happened to them, although He used human instruments.

**Behold the land of the Chaldeans; this people was not, till the Assyrian founded it for them that dwell in the wilderness: they set up the towers thereof, they raised up the palaces thereof; and he brought it to ruin [Isa. 23:13].**

When Assyria was a great nation, Chaldea (Babylon) was just a hick town. Now Babylon is the ruler of the world.

**Howl, ye ships of Tarshish: for your strength is laid waste [Isa. 23:14].**

## RECOVERY OF TYRE— PARTIAL AND COMPLETE

**And it shall come to pass in that day, that Tyre shall be forgotten seventy years, according to the days of one king: after the end of seventy years shall Tyre sing as an harlot [Isa. 23:15].**

Tyre was to go into captivity for seventy years.

**And it shall come to pass after the end of seventy years, that the LORD will visit Tyre, and she shall turn to her hire, and shall commit fornication with all the kingdoms of the world upon the face of the earth [Isa. 23:17].**

At the end of seventy years Tyre was to return and begin once again her world commerce. Once more she would become a great commercial center, and she would commit fornication with all the kingdoms of the world upon the face of the earth. The prophet compares Tyre to a harlot plying her unholy trade. That is the way God speaks of these great commercial centers.

Now we move down the ages to the last days, the time of the Great Tribulation. Here we find that Tyre will again be a great nation and will enter the Millennium.

**And her merchandise and her hire shall be holiness to the LORD: it shall not be treasured nor laid up; for her merchandise shall be for them that dwell before the LORD, to eat sufficiently, and for durable clothing [Isa. 23:18].**

"Her merchandise shall be for them that dwell before the LORD." Now it is all dedicated to the Lord. "And the daughter of Tyre shall be there with a gift; even the rich among the people shall entreat thy favour" (Ps. 45:12).

# CHAPTER 24

*THEME: Coming—the Great Tribulation*

This brings us to a new section, although the theme is still judgment. Chapter 23 concluded the judgment against the nations. We have seen God's judgment snowballing from nation to nation, and now it comes down to the final judgment that is coming upon the earth, which our Lord Jesus Christ labeled the Great Tribulation Period. Both F. Delitzsch and F. C. Jennings consider this section thoroughly eschatological; that is, it refers to the final judgment from God which will come upon the whole world. In contrast to the judgments upon the nations in chapters 13–23 which have largely been fulfilled, this final judgment is entirely future.

## WORLDWIDE JUDGMENT FROM GOD

**Behold the LORD maketh the earth empty, and maketh it waste, and turneth it upside down, and scattereth abroad the inhabitants thereof [Isa. 24:1].**

"**E**arth" in this verse is the Hebrew word *erets* and could mean either the land of Israel or the whole world. The whole world conforms better to the context in this chapter. Actually, the judgment could be said to be twofold, referring not only to the land of Israel, but to the entire world.

**Therefore hath the curse devoured the earth, and they that dwell therein are desolate: therefore the inhabitants of the earth are burned, and few men left [Isa. 24:6].**

God promised Noah that He would never destroy the earth again with a flood. Note here that the judgment is fire— "burned." Second Peter 3:6–7 says, "Whereby the world that then was, being overflowed with water, perished: But the heavens and the earth, which are now, by the same word are kept in store, reserved unto fire against the day of judgment and perdition of ungodly men."

## PRESERVATION OF THE SAINTS

In verses 13–15 we see that the saints are preserved through the Great Tribulation Period.

**When thus it shall be in the midst of the land among the people, there shall be as the shaking of an olive tree, and as the gleaning grapes when the vintage is done.**

**They shall lift up their voice, they shall sing for the majesty of the LORD, they shall cry aloud from the sea.**

**Wherefore glorify ye the LORD in the fires, even the name of the LORD God of Israel in the isles of the sea [Isa. 24:13–15].**

The remnant will be small, and they will lift up their voices to glorify God. Now in the time of testing, during the Tribulation, they will be able to glorify the Lord, "even the name of the LORD God of Israel." So there is to be a remnant at that time, which will be of Israel, and also out to the very "isles of the sea," which will include the whole earth, of course.

## UNIVERSAL AND UNPARALLELED SUFFERING

**From the uttermost part of the earth have we heard songs, even glory to the righteous. But I said, My leanness, my leanness, woe unto me! the treacherous dealers have dealt treacherously; yea, the treacherous dealers have dealt very treacherously [Isa. 24:16].**

"My leanness, my leanness"—when the prophet sees the awful character of the destruction of the Great Tribulation, he cries out, as Dr. Jennings translates it, "My misery, my misery." It is going to be a terrible time.

Our Lord described this period of time in just as striking language when He said, "For then shall be great tribulation such as was not since the beginning of the world to this time, no, nor ever shall be. And except those days should be shortened, there should no flesh be saved: but for the elect's sake those days shall be shortened" (Matt. 24:21–22).

**Fear, and the pit, and the snare, are upon thee, O inhabitant of the earth [Isa. 24:17].**

This verse states that there are three dangers that will be upon the inhabitants of the earth in that day.

1. "Fear"—there is no freedom from fear here. From the time of the Atlantic Truce, drawn up by Winston Churchill and Franklin Roosevelt, politicans have talked about bringing freedom from fear to the world. How about it? Is the world free from fear today? Mobs are marching. Dissatisfaction and fear are everywhere. And fear will be multiplied during the Tribulation.

2. "Pit"—is danger of death. Hanging over the world today is the threat of the atom bomb, and it spells frightful death to the population of the world. God says He won't let the population be destroyed. The Lord Jesus said, "Except those days be shortened, no flesh would be able to survive," but He is going to shorten those days.

3. "Snare"—is deception. What the Lord Jesus Christ said as He began the Olivet discourse fits right into the Great Tribulation Period. In Matthew 24:4 the Lord said, ". . . Take heed that no man deceive you." It will be a time when people will believe that they are entering into the Millennium. We get the impression today that some of the great world leaders think they are going to bring in the Millennium. Well, they are going to bring

in nothing but the Great Tribulation Period, and the Antichrist will take over. The world will think they are entering the Millennium, when in fact they are entering the Tribulation. One of the things that will characterize the Antichrist is deception. He will be a deceiver. After all, that is what his papa, the Devil is.

How many people there are who are being deceived today! They are deceived about life. How many people are even thinking about eternity? Not many. Most people think only of the here and now. Science is now rejecting the creation account—they don't want it. This is a great day of deception. You can be deceived by science; you can be deceived by politicians; you can be deceived by the news media; you can be deceived by the military; and you can be deceived by all of the malcontents who are protesting today. The only help available is the Lord Jesus Christ. Turn to Him. He has been made unto us wisdom, and He is the only hope. During the Tribulation people will be deceived; the Antichrist will be able to look at the world and privately say, "Suckers!" And that's what they will be. The Devil has said that about the human race for a long time, and that is what we *are* unless we turn to Christ.

**And it shall come to pass, that he who fleeth from the noise of the fear shall fall into the pit; and he that cometh up out of the midst of the pit shall be taken in the snare: for the windows from on high are open, and the foundations of the earth do shake [Isa. 24:18].**

Those who don't go down into the pit of death will be snared. The Book of Revelation says that one fourth of the population is going to be taken out at one time in a great judgment, and at another time one third of the population will die.

## TRIBULATION SAINTS ARE RAISED FROM THE DEAD

This is a marvelous passage of Scripture that speaks of resurrection.

**And they shall be gathered together, as prisoners are gathered in the pit, and shall be shut up in the prison, and after many days shall they be visited [Isa. 24:22].**

They shall go down into death; then they will be raised from the dead. I believe the meaning of this is that the Tribulation saints will have

part in the first resurrection. They will be raised from the dead (see Rev. 20:4).

The Great Tribulation will end with the coming of the King (see Rev. 19:11–16).

**Then the moon shall be confounded, and the sun ashamed, when the LORD of hosts shall reign in mount Zion, and in Jerusalem, and before his ancients gloriously [Isa. 24:23].**

"The moon shall be confounded, and the sun ashamed"—even nature is going to respond to the King when He comes to rule. Christ Jesus is the only One who can end this period known as the Great Tribulation.

# CHAPTERS 25–27

### *THEME:* Coming—the kingdom

After the Lord Jesus comes and ends the Tribulation, He establishes the kingdom. Chapters 25 and 26 bring us into the kingdom age. The King is coming, and there will be the kingdom of heaven upon this earth. This has been predicted throughout the Old Testament. And when John the Baptist began his ministry, his message was, ". . . Repent ye: for the kingdom of heaven is at hand" (Matt 3:2). Then the Lord Jesus took up the theme, ". . . the kingdom of heaven is at hand" (Matt. 4:17).

But He was rejected as King. You can't have a kingdom without a king. When He was rejected as King, He could then say to individuals, "Come unto me, all ye that labour and are heavy laden, and I will give you rest" (Matt. 11:28). This is still His invitation today. It is a message to be sent out to individuals in our day asking them to exercise their free wills. Whether you know it or not, you are making a decision today. You are either accepting Him or rejecting Him. There is no neutral ground. Our Lord said, "He that is not with me is against me . . ." (Matt. 12:30).

This wonderful twenty-fifth chapter is a song, a song of three stanzas. This chapter, like chapter 12, is a paean of praise, a song of undiluted joy.

## PRAISE TO GO FOR DELIVERANCE FROM ALL ENEMIES

**O LORD, thou art my God; I will exalt thee, I will praise thy name; for thou hast done wonderful things; thy counsels of old are faithfulness and truth [Isa. 25:1].**

This is praise to God for deliverance. This is a song of sheer delight, wonder, and worship. This comes from a heart full to overflow-

ing, for the worshiper has come into a new knowledge of who God is and what He has done.

This is not the average song service that you have in church on Wednesday night. Some of the saints sit there and wonder why they came in the first place. Those who are singing this song are those who are eager to worship God because of His faithfulness and because He is true. These are the attributes of Deity, and they are foreign to humanity. The psalmist says, "It is better to trust in the LORD than to put confidence in man" (Ps. 118:8). Faithfulness is the fruit of the Spirit, not the work of the flesh. Truth is the very opposite of man. In Psalm 116:11 David said, "I said in my *haste*, All men are liars" (italics mine). I remember Dr. W. I. Carroll commenting, "I have had a lot of time to think it over, and I still agree with David."

**For thou hast made of a city an heap; of a defenced city a ruin: a palace of strangers to be no city; it shall never be built [Isa. 25:2].**

All of the past is gone now. They are delivered from the enemies of the past. They no longer need a wall around a city to protect them.

**Therefore shall the strong people glorify thee, the city of the terrible nations shall fear thee [Isa. 25:3].**

Does this mean worldwide conversion? I believe it does, for this is the Millennium. Man will turn to God in that day. The greatest turning to God is in the future when the night of sin and Great Tribulation will be past. Weeping shall endure for a night, but joy cometh in the morning. That is what we have here. There will be boundless joy during the kingdom age.

**Thou shalt bring down the noise of strangers, as the heat in a dry place; even the heat with the shadow of a cloud: the branch of the terrible ones shall be brought low [Isa. 25:5].**

They recall the awful blasphemy of the last days personified in one of whom it is written: "Who opposeth and exalteth himself above all that is called God, or that is worshipped; so that he as God sitteth in the temple of God, shewing himself that he is God" (2 Thess. 2:4). The Antichrist will be put down as are all the enemies of God.

## PRAISE TO GOD FOR PROVISION OF PRESENT NEEDS

**And in this mountain shall the LORD of hosts make unto all people a feast of fat things, a feast of wines on the lees, of fat things full of marrow, of wines on the lees well refined [Isa. 25:6].**

"Fat things" have to do with physical provision certainly. The redeemed earth will produce bountifully. (Eating fat things in that day will not be a problem—you won't have to worry about putting on weight!) However, the "fat things" are likewise the wonderful spiritual feast in that day. I think there will be Bible classes held during the Millennium. I don't know, but maybe the Lord will let me teach one of them.

**He will swallow up death in victory; and the Lord GOD will wipe away tears from off all faces; and the rebuke of his people shall he take away from off all the earth: for the LORD hath spoken it [Isa. 25:8].**

This verse is quoted by Paul in 1 Corinthians 15:54, which says, "So when this corruptible shall have put on incorruption, and this mortal shall have put on immortality, then shall be brought to pass the saying that is written, Death is swallowed up in victory."

## PRAISE TO GOD IN ANTICIPATION OF FUTURE JOYS

**And it shall be said in that day, Lo, this is our God; we have waited for him, and he will save us: this is the LORD; we have waited for him, we will be glad and rejoice in his salvation [Isa. 25:9].**

As we come to the final stanza, attention is drawn to the person of God. It is with Him that men have to do. The world will be deceived by Antichrist, but the real Christ, the real Messiah, the real Ruler of this earth will come. His salvation is going to be vital to man in that day. Man "will be glad and rejoice in his salvation."

Now this is a strange verse:

**For in this mountain shall the hand of the LORD rest, and Moab shall be trodden down under him, even as straw is trodden down for the dunghill [Isa. 25:10].**

Why is Moab introduced here? I will be very frank with you; it is difficult to say. When Moab is up, God is down. When God is up, Moab is down. In the kingdom Moab is down, and God will be on top. As you may remember, Moab represents a form of godliness but denies the power thereof.

**And the fortress of the high fort of thy walls shall he bring down, lay low, and bring to the ground, even to the dust [Isa. 25:12].**

All the pride of man will be brought down. This is the period when the meek shall inherit the earth (Matt. 5:5). The meek are not doing too well in our day!

Chapter 26 continues the kingdom theme.

## THE KINGDOM

**In that day shall this song be sung in the land of Judah; We have a strong city; salvation will God appoint for walls and bulwarks [Isa. 26:1].**

This is their prospect. In that day this song will be sung in Judah. They don't have this song today, friend. It is obvious that the present return to Israel is not a fulfillment of prophecy.

**With my soul have I desired thee in the night; yea, with my spirit within me will I seek thee early: for when thy judgments are in the earth, the inhabitants of the world will learn righteousness [Isa. 26:9].**

"With my soul have I *desired* thee in the night." I wonder if you and I recognize the great need for communion with Christ. In the little book of the Song of Solomon, the bride said, "Let him kiss me with the kisses of his mouth . . ." (Song 1:2). That was the kiss of pardon and of peace and of passion. Then the bride, recognizing that she can't rise to the heights she desires, says, "Draw me, we will run after thee . . ." (Song 1:4). Isaiah is expressing the same thought here. "With my

soul have I *desired* thee in the night." My friend, do we have that passion for God? I hear a lot of pseudo-love today, and a smattering of spirituality. I see people pretending to be pious and hear them quoting platitudes. I get tired of hearing, "Oh, I love the Lord, and I want to serve Him." My friend, when you lie on your bed at night, do you have a *desire* for God? Do you really want Him? Do you have a real passion for Him? Are you able to say, "Draw me, and I will run after thee."

In the time of the Millennium they will be saying, "With my soul have I desired thee in the night; yea; with my spirit within me will I seek thee early."

I confess that many times I find myself running from Him. I find myself running ahead of Him, out of His will, and then the tensions come. I am frustrated, and I say, "O, I've left Him. I've gotten away from Him. I am not close to Him." I don't see many people crying out for God today. I don't mean to be critical, but I don't see much of it today, and when I do detect it, what a blessing it is to my own heart.

> **LORD, in trouble have they visited thee, they poured out a prayer when thy chastening was upon them [Isa. 26:16].**

In the past the remnant turned in prayer to God. Now they go back in retrospect to those difficult days:

> **Like as a woman with child, that draweth near the time of her delivery, is in pain, and crieth out in her pangs; so have we been in thy sight, O LORD [Isa. 26:17].**

In the Great Tribulation the nation Israel was like a woman in childbirth, so great was their suffering. The prophet is now looking back over that period (which is yet future). He saw it from the other side of the river of time.

> **We have been with child, we have been in pain, we have as it were brought forth wind; we have not wrought any deliverance in the earth; neither have the inhabitants of the world fallen [Isa. 26:18].**

"We have as it were brought forth wind"— that is, the suffering produced no fruitful results. This period did not change the heart of the wicked. They continued to blaspheme the God of heaven.

Today the suffering that comes to you, like a birth pang, will either bring forth something worthwhile, or it can just be wind. I am afraid many of us have suffered for *nothing*, simply because we do not see that all things work together for the glory of God. Remember that Isaiah is talking about the coming Millennium, and we could be living in a state similar to the Millennium if we would only seek Him early.

> **Thy dead men shall live, together with my dead body shall they arise. Awake and sing, ye that dwell in dust: for thy dew is as the dew of herbs, and the earth shall cast out the dead [Isa. 26:19].**

Chapter 27 concludes the threefold song of the coming of the kingdom which we have in chapters 25–27.

## SONG OF THE VINEYARD

> **In that day the LORD with his sore and great and strong sword shall punish leviathan the piercing serpent, even leviathan that crooked serpent; and he shall slay the dragon that is in the sea [Isa. 27:1].**

"**I**n that day"—projects us immediately into the future. As we have said, this is a technical expression that refers to the Day of the Lord. It is a day that begins, as the Hebrew day did, with the evening, the time of the Great Tribulation, and it goes on into the millennial kingdom. I personally feel that it goes on into eternity, as that will be a sunrise that will never end.

"The LORD with his sore and great and strong sword." The Lord's sword is the Word of God. In describing the coming of the Lord Jesus, Revelation 1:16 says, "And he had in his right hand seven stars: and out of his mouth went a sharp two-edged sword: and his countenance was as the sun shineth in his strength." With that sword He will smite the nations. An amillennialist will say, "You say you take the Bible literally. Is this a literal sword?" Well, I've discovered that the tongue is really a sharp thing. And Hebrews 4:12 tells us, "For the word of God is quick, and powerful, and sharper than any two-edged sword. . . ." I take it that the Word of God is meant here. It is by His Word—that's all He needs. By His Word He created all things, and by His Word shall He judge.

Whom is He going to judge? "Leviathan the piercing serpent, even leviathan that crooked serpent." In that day, at the beginning of the kingdom, the Lord Jesus will bring judgment upon the serpent, leviathan, who is Satan. In Revelation 20:1–3 we are told that Satan will

be shut up in the bottomless pit for one thousand years. In Revelation 12:9 we read, "And the great dragon was cast out, that old serpent, called the Devil, and Satan, which deceiveth the whole world: he was cast out into the earth, and his angels were cast out with him." Job 41:15 says of him, "His scales are his pride. . . ." The scales are for his protection, and Satan thinks he is invulnerable, that he cannot be touched. This is his pride. He doesn't realize, even today, as I understand it, that he can be judged. He probably thinks he is beyond the judgment of Almighty God.

There are a great many people today who think that there is no judgment coming. They laugh at the idea. That is the thinking of Satan, my friend.

F. Delitzsch has suggested that "the piercing serpent," or literally "swift-fleeing serpent," represents the Tigris River and thereby the nation of Assyria. The "crooked serpent" represents the winding Euphrates and thereby the nation of Babylon. "The dragon that is in the sea" represents the Nile River and thereby the nation of Egypt. This would not militate against "levithan," meaning Satan, but would enforce that interpretation, since Satan was the power behind these kingdoms.

**In that day sing ye unto her, A vineyard of red wine [Isa. 27:2].**

Actually, I believe that chapter 27 begins with verse 2 and that verse 1 belongs with the previous chapter. However, that is a technical point with which I will not get involved. There is a change of subject at this point.

"In that day sing ye unto her." This is the Millennium, and we all can sing now—even I will be able to sing.

"A vineyard of red wine" speaks of abundance, fruitfulness, bounty, and joy. What a contrast this is to Isaiah 5! In Isaiah 5 we had the song of the vineyard, but it was a dirge. That vineyard was Israel, and God was going to bring judgment because she hadn't brought forth fruit. Here we are in the Millennium, and there is an abundance of fruit. Why?

**I the LORD do keep it; I will water it every moment: lest any hurt it, I will keep it night and day [Isa. 27:3].**

The Lord is the husbandman here, and never again will He ever let the vineyard out to others. He is the husbandman who keeps an eye continually upon it. He watches it night and day so that no enemy may enter. This

ought to say something to those who believe that God is through with Israel. Scripture makes it clear that He is *not* through with Israel.

**Or let him take hold of my strength, that he may make peace with me; and he shall make peace with me [Isa. 27:5].**

The enemy can make peace with God even in the kingdom, for God never ceases to be merciful. Thank God for that! He is rich in mercy, which means that He has plenty of it. I need a lot of it myself. He is rich in grace. We will find out that ten million years from today His grace will still be available to us. I think we will need it even in heaven.

"That he may make peace with me." This is the only place in Scripture where it is even suggested that man can make peace with God. Of course here it has to do with obedience to the King and not the acceptance of Christ as Savior. Man cannot make peace with God about the sin question. God has already done that. Romans 5:1 says, "Therefore being justified by faith, *we have peace* with God through our Lord Jesus Christ" (italics mine). When you are ready to agree with God and trust Him for what He has done through Christ on the cross, then you will have peace. You won't have it until then. This verse is not talking about our day but about the time of the Millennium.

## SMITING OF ISRAEL AND HER ENEMIES

**Hath he smitten him, as he smote those that smote him? or is he slain according to the slaughter of them that are slain by him? [Isa. 27:7].**

This verse poses a question that has been partially answered already in the Book of Isaiah: Why does God judge Israel more than other nations? Light creates responsibility. In view of the fact that Israel had more light, her sin was blacker and her punishment was greater. She received more stripes than the nations who smote her. In Amos 3:2 we read, "You only have I known of all the families of the earth: therefore I will punish you for all your iniquities." Her punishment was severe, but God did not destroy Israel as He did some other nations. Psalm 118:18 tells us, "The LORD hath chastened me sore: but he hath not given me over unto death." God will *not* allow Israel to be destroyed.

**By this therefore shall the iniquity of Jacob be purged; and this is all the fruit**

to take away his sin; when he maketh all the stones of the altar as chalkstones that are beaten in sunder, the groves and images shall not stand up [Isa. 27:9].

It was not the suffering for sin that atoned for Israel's sin. The sin of Jacob was purged by a blood offering, and the sin of the nation will be expiated by the blood of Christ. Just as you were saved as a sinner, that is the way it will take place in that day. Those who say that God is through with Israel simply have not read passages of Scripture like this:

Yet the defenced city shall be desolate, and the habitation forsaken, and left like a wilderness: there shall the calf feed, and there shall he lie down, and consume the branches thereof.

When the boughs thereof are withered, they shall be broken off: the women come, and set them on fire: for it is a people of no understanding: therefore he that made them will not have mercy on them, and he that formed them will shew them no favour [Isa. 27:10–11].

However, the cities that Israel built are to be destroyed like any city that man builds apart from God. The great ruins in the world are the result of the judgment of Almighty God. Why? Because they rejected light. They not only rejected light, they rejected the person of the Son of God.

And it shall come to pass in that day, that the LORD shall beat off from the channel of the river unto the stream of Egypt, and ye shall be gathered one by one, O ye children of Israel.

And it shall come to pass in that day, that the great trumpet shall be blown, and they shall come which were ready to perish in the land of Assyria, and the outcasts in the land of Egypt, and shall worship the LORD in the holy mount at Jerusalem [Isa. 27:12–13].

This section reveals that God definitely intends to restore the nation Israel to the Promised Land, and I have no argument with those who deny it. I just want to say this: It is not a question of whether Israel is going to be restored to the land. It is a question of whether or not you believe the Word of God. If you believe God's Word, what are you going to do with a passage like this? You cannot spiritualize it, because the prophet talks about Assyria, Egypt, Israel, and Jerusalem. These are *literal* places. Israel is going to be literally restored. If you have a high view of the inspiration of Scripture, then believe what God says.

This prophecy has never been fulfilled in the past. Its fulfillment is yet future. My friend, when God moves the Jews into the land, God will *move* them. When they come, they will worship Him. Just as He called you and me, He will call them. We are not seeing the fulfillment of this today.

# CHAPTER 28

*THEME: The immediate invasion of Ephraim by Assyria is a picture of the future and a warning to Jerusalem*

This chapter brings us to an entirely new section. The prophecies which were totally future are included in chapters 24–27 inclusively. From chapters 28–35 we have prophecies which have a local and past fulfillment, and also there are those that reach into the future and cover the same period as in the previous section. This new section is identified by six woes, and it culminates in the great war of Armageddon in chapter 34, followed by the millennial benefits brought to the earth in chapter 35.

Now the chapter before us is a fine illustration of the combination of the near and far view, the past and future events, the local and immediate, and the general and far distant prophecies. We will see that which has been fulfilled and that which is yet to be fulfilled.

The northern kingdom of Israel, designated here by the term *Ephraim*, was soon to go

into Assyrian captivity. This was a preview of the coming future day, but it was to be a warning to the southern kingdom of Judah. The first part was fulfilled when Shalmaneser, king of Assyria, invaded Ephraim in 721 B.C., overthrew the northern kingdom, and took the people into captivity.

## THE IMMEDIATE CAPTIVITY OF EPHRAIM

The first woe is against the northern kingdom.

**Woe to the crown of pride, to the drunkards of Ephraim, whose glorious beauty is a fading flower, which are on the head of the fat valleys of them that are overcome with wine! [Isa. 28:1].**

Ephraim and Israel are synonymous terms for the ten northern tribes, also called Samaria. The picture here of drunkards is both literal and spiritual. They were in a stupor as far as spiritual understanding was concerned. To be spiritually drunk is to be filled with pride.

**Behold, the Lord hath a mighty and strong one, which as a tempest of hail and a destroying storm, as a flood of mighty waters overflowing, shall cast down to the earth with the hand [Isa. 28:2].**

The Assyrian is designated here as a strong one, a destroying storm, and a flood of mighty waters.

**The crown of pride, the drunkards of Ephraim, shall be trodden under feet [Isa. 28:3].**

Maybe you don't like this, but God does not apologize for it; He simply tells us that this is what He did. The prophet picks up the future of the drunkard here. A high level of civilization had been developed in the northern kingdom with its comforts and outward beauty expressed in homes and gardens and trees. All you have to do to confirm this is go to the hill of Samaria and see the palace built by Omri and Ahab. This is the place where Ahab and Jezebel lived. It seems that the Lord always gives the wicked and the rich the best places to live, and I think it is poetic justice. It is not going to be so good for the wicked and rich in the next world; so they have it pretty good here. The hill of Samaria is one of the most beautiful spots in the land. When I stood there I could see the Mediterranean Sea, the Jordan valley, Mount Hermon in the north covered with snow, and the walls of Jerusalem

in the south. My friend, you could not ask for a more beautiful place to live. If a real estate man develops that hill and sells lots, I hope I can buy one and build a little house there. It's a great place, but God judged these people in the northern kingdom, and He brought down their high civilization.

## THE FAR DISTANT JUDGMENT

Now the prophet begins to move into the future. The expression "in that day" refers to the Day of the Lord, which begins with the Great Tribulation and extends on through the Millennium.

**In that day shall the LORD of hosts be for a crown of glory, and for a diadem of beauty, unto the residue of his people [Isa. 28:5].**

This looks into the future to the millennial kingdom which is coming. The thing that caused the downfall of Ephraim, the northern kingdom, was their pride—they wore a crown of pride. But in that future day when God brings them back to the land, it will be a crown of glory.

**And for a spirit of judgment to him that sitteth in judgment, and for strength to them that turn the battle to the gate.**

**But they also have erred through wine, and through strong drink are out of the way; the priest and the prophet have erred through strong drink, they are swallowed up of wine, they are out of the way through strong drink; they err in vision, they stumble in judgment [Isa. 28:6–7].**

A businessman recently told me some of the things that go on in big business. I don't suppose there is a day that goes by that he doesn't make deals with men who make big investments for large profits. He told me about one of these men who was beginning to indulge in sin. He was not faithful to his wife, and he was drinking heavily. He has recently made certain judgments about investments that have caused this businessman to withhold loaning money to him. He told me that when a man begins to drink and indulge in sin he loses his sharpness in business. He said, "Because I am a Christian I may be biased, but I have found over the long haul, over a period of years, that this is factual. I have learned it through bitter experiences."

Now God is making this same observation regarding the northern kingdom: "they are

out of the way through strong drink; they err in vision, they stumble in judgment."

**But the word of the LORD was unto them precept upon precept, precept upon precept; line upon line, line upon line; here a little, and there a little; that they might go, and fall backward, and be broken, and snared, and taken [Isa. 28:13].**

Sections like this have caused some expositors of the past to call Isaiah "the prophet of the commonplace." Teaching is a slow, patient, and continuous work. This is the way that even spiritual truth is imparted. God does not impart it in a flash to a lazy and lethargic soul. As the people lapse into apostasy in any age, it becomes increasingly difficult to impart spiritual truth.

There are many Christians today who are not satisfied with their Christian lives. To be brutally frank, they are ignorant of the Word of God. Then they hear about a wonderful two-week course that will give them the answers to all their problems. They will learn how to handle their marital problems, how to get along with their mother-in-law, how to guide their children aright, and how to become model employees. My friend, let me say this to you very candidly. Neither a little course nor some great emotional experience will solve your problems. There is no shortcut to success in the Christian life. There is only one way to grow as a Christian, and it is so commonplace and ordinary that I hesitate to say it. The Word of the Lord was given unto Israel precept upon precept, line upon line, here a little, and there a little. It was the daily grind of getting into God's Word. What happened? Israel did not follow through. They fell backward; that is, they were in a backslidden state. There are many Christians in the same condition today. It is not that they are weaker than anybody else; it is simply that they do not spend enough time in the Word of God. I realize that this method is not very exciting, but line upon line and precept upon precept is the only way you are going to grow in the Christian life.

## THE WARNING TO JUDAH

**Wherefore hear the word of the LORD, ye scornful men, that rule this people which is in Jerusalem [Isa. 28:14].**

The judgment coming to Israel in the north should be a warning to Judah in the south. Ephraim speaks to Jerusalem, Jerusalem

speaks to us today, and the Word of God speaks to all of us. It looks as if God wrote this Book, not yesterday, but tomorrow. In fact, it is way ahead of tomorrow's newspaper.

**Because ye have said, We have made a covenant with death, and with hell are we at agreement; when the overflowing scourge shall pass through, it shall not come unto us: for we have made lies our refuge, and under falsehood have we hid ourselves [Isa. 28:15].**

What is this covenant with death and Sheol? Daniel tells us about a future covenant which Israel will make with the Antichrist, the prince who is coming, the Man of Sin, the godless man, the willful king, the beast out of the sea and the beast out of the land, the one who is controlled by Satan (see Dan. 9:27).

**Therefore thus saith the Lord GOD, Behold, I lay in Zion for a foundation a stone, a tried stone, a precious corner stone, a sure foundation: he that believeth shall not make haste [Isa. 28:16].**

What is the answer today to the falsehood in the lives of people and the deception that is abroad which will continue to snowball right on down into the Great Tribulation Period? Well, God has already put that answer down. It is a foundation; it is a tried stone, a precious cornerstone, a sure foundation. One who believes in it doesn't need to be in a hurry. He can rest in Him. First Peter 2:6–8 speaks of Him: "Wherefore also it is contained in the scripture, Behold, I lay in Sion a chief corner stone, elect, precious: and he that believeth on him shall not be confounded. Unto you therefore which believe he is precious: but unto them which be disobedient, the stone which the builders disallowed, the same is made the head of the corner, And a stone of stumbling, and a rock of offence, even to them which stumble at the word, being disobedient: whereunto also they were appointed." Simon Peter makes it very clear that this stone is Christ.

**Judgment also will I lay to the line, and righteousness to the plummet: and the hail shall sweep away the refuge of lies, and the waters shall overflow the hiding place [Isa. 28:17].**

Judgment for these people is going to come gradually. I think it comes that way today. Sometimes it comes suddenly. But gradual judgment is worse than sudden judgment, for

usually the process is so slow that you don't detect it.

> For the bed is shorter than that a man can stretch himself on it: and the covering narrower than that he can wrap himself in it [Isa. 28:20].

Have you ever gone to a hotel or a motel and found that the covers on the bed were not quite long enough? They don't come up to your neck, and if you pull them up, then your feet stick out. Have you ever slept in a short bed, where your feet hang over the edge, or you have to prop your head up, or you have to sleep at an angle? That's not so good, is it? God says to these people, "I am giving you a short bed. The cover won't be quite long enough." From then on the judgment of God will come. It didn't come to Judah for about one hundred years, but it finally came.

## THE FINAL JUDGMENT OF GOD UPON HIS PEOPLE

The remainder of this chapter is almost the parable of the wheat and the tares. He talks about the different kinds of grain, the hard grains and the soft grains, and the different methods of threshing it.

> When he hath made plain the face thereof, doth he not cast abroad the fitches, and scatter the cummin, and cast in the principal wheat and the appointed barley and the rie in their place? [Isa. 28:25].

The grains are "fitches" (sometimes translated *fennel* or *dill*), "cummin, wheat, barley, and rie."

> For the fitches are not threshed with a threshing instrument, neither is a cart wheel turned about upon the cummin; but the fitches are beaten out with a staff, and the cummin with a rod.

> Bread corn is bruised; because he will not ever be threshing it, nor break it with the wheel of his cart, nor bruise it with his horsemen [Isa. 28:27–28].

A farmer has to be careful about the way he harvests soft grains. Each grain is different.

Now he says that this is the way God judges. Judgement is spoken of as the harvest. The individual or nation actually determines the character of the judgment which is to fall upon them. In other words, if you are hard and resist God, you are a hard grain. You are a hard nut to crack, and the judgment is going to be severe for you. A man came to me and told me that he had lost his wife and two children before he came to himself. He said, "God had to knock me down *three* times because I was such a hardened sinner." God will thresh you; and, if you are hard, the judgment will be hard.

The Lord Jesus put it like this in Matthew 13:30, "Let both grow together until the harvest: and in the time of harvest I will say to the reapers, Gather ye together first the tares, and bind them in bundles to burn them: but gather the wheat into my barn." In Matthew 13:41 the Lord goes on to say, "The Son of man shall send forth his angels, and they shall gather out of his kingdom all things that offend, and them which do iniquity." How tremendous this is! We ourselves determine our own judgment. If we only will listen to Him, He will put us over where the wheat is and spare us the severity of His judgment.

# CHAPTER 29

**THEME:** *Jerusalem—prophecies of immediate future and reaching on into the kingdom*

The prophecies in this chapter are confined to Jerusalem but extend from the invasion of Sennacherib through the time when Jerusalem will be trodden down of the Gentiles until the last invader (see Zech. 14:1–7) shall have destroyed Jerusalem and, finally, to the establishment of the kingdom when the Messiah shall come and His feet shall touch the Mount of Olives.

It will prove profitable to compare this chapter with our Lord's discourse on Jerusalem in Matthew 23:37–24:2 and with Luke 13:34–35; 21:20–24.

## JERUSALEM—HISTORY AND PROPHECY

**Woe to Ariel, to Ariel, the city where David dwelt! add ye year to year; let them kill sacrifices [Isa. 29:1].**

It is necessary to establish the fact that Jerusalem is the city designated under the title of Ariel. *Ariel* means "lionlike." The word occurs in 2 Samuel 23:20 which says, "And Benaiah the son of Jehoiada, the son of a valiant man, of Kabzeel, who had done many acts, he slew two lionlike men of Moab. . . ." A lionlike man is an "Ariel" man. The word also carries the meaning of "the lion of God." In Ezekiel 43:16 the same word is translated "altar" and, under certain circumstances, could mean "the altar of God." Both designations are a fitting title for the city of Jerusalem. It is further identified here as "the city where David dwelt." The lion is the insignia of that family. Our Lord is called the ". . . Lion of the tribe of Juda" (Rev. 5:5). Likewise Jerusalem was the place where the temple of God was, and the altar, of course, was there.

This is a remarkable prophecy concerning Jerusalem. The prophecy began to be fulfilled in Isaiah's day and has continued right down to today. If you walk down the streets of Jerusalem, you will see this prophecy being fulfilled, and it will continue to be fulfilled.

**Yet I will distress Ariel, and there shall be heaviness and sorrow: and it shall be unto me as Ariel [Isa. 29:2].**

This is judgment upon Jerusalem.

**And I will camp against thee round about, and will lay siege against thee with a mount, and I will raise forts against thee.**

**And thou shalt be brought down, and shalt speak out of the ground, and thy speech shall be low out of the dust, and thy voice shall be, as of one that hath a familiar spirit, out of the ground, and thy speech shall whisper out of the dust.**

**Moreover the multitude of thy strangers shall be like small dust, and the multitude of the terrible ones shall be as chaff that passeth away: yea, it shall be at an instant suddenly [Isa. 29:3–5].**

This prophecy was given before Nebuchadnezzar came up to the city of Jerusalem and destroyed it, which marked the beginning of the ". . . times of the Gentiles . . ." (Luke 21:24). Our Lord said that Jerusalem would be trodden down of the Gentiles until the Time of the Gentiles be fulfilled. The Gentiles have marched through her streets and still do today.

Jerusalem has been besieged and captured more often than any other city. I have in my files a list of twenty-seven sieges that have been leveled against this city throughout history. Almost every time it was taken, it was destroyed. That is why it is not quite accurate for people to say, "Go to Jerusalem and walk where Jesus walked." You are not going to walk where He walked, because Jerusalem is much higher today than it was in His day. For example, the pool of Bethesda was about fifty feet down from the level of the ground today. The Lord Jesus walked down there. It is quite evident that Solomon's temple was probably more than one hundred feet beneath where the Mosque of Omar stands today. The city has been destroyed many times, and each time it was leveled off and rebuilt on the wreckage. That is what Nehemiah did—out of the debris and wreckage he rebuilt the walls of Jerusalem. Rocks did not have to be hauled in for repair work because there are more rocks over there than they could ever use. I heard a few years ago that stones were being shipped from Indiana to Jerusalem to rebuild the temple. That report was proven false, but how foolish it would have been. There is no place on the topside of this earth that is as

rocky as Jerusalem and the surrounding area. It is a rugged terrain. That is one reason Jerusalem was so difficult for the enemy to take.

> Thou shalt be visited of the LORD of hosts with thunder, and with earthquake, and great noise, with storm and tempest, and the flame of devouring fire.

> And the multitude of all the nations that fight against Ariel, even all that fight against her and her munition, and that distress her, shall be as a dream of a night vision.

> It shall even be as when an hungry man dreameth, and, behold, he eateth; but he awaketh, and his soul is empty: or as when a thirsty man dreameth, and, behold, he drinketh; but he awaketh, and, behold, he is faint, and his soul hath appetite: so shall the multitude of all the nations be, that fight against mount Zion [Isa. 29:6–8].

The final siege of Jerusalem will be the worst of all (see Zech. 14), but God will intervene at the last moment and deliver His people from extermination. All the dreams of the enemies of God to bring in their own kingdom will be frustrated, and God will put them down. He will build His own kingdom and establish it Himself, just as He said He would do.

### JERUSALEM—MEANING AND MESSAGE

> Stay yourselves, and wonder; cry ye out, and cry: they are drunken, but not with wine; they stagger, but not with strong drink.

> For the LORD hath poured out upon you the spirit of deep sleep, and hath closed your eyes: the prophets and your rulers, the seers hath he covered [Isa. 29:9–10].

I have said that Isaiah is the prophet of the commonplace, and what he says fits into our contemporary culture. Did God actually make them sleepy? How did He do it? He kept giving Israel light; and, as He gave them light, they kept rejecting it. They would not accept the truth that He gave them. They could not see it, which revealed that they were blind. That is the way God puts people to sleep and the way He reveals that they are blind. Even the prophets and princes did not anticipate this deliverance from God. They were as blinded to the future as the enemies of God. They were as men who were dead drunk.

> And the vision of all is become unto you as the words of a book that is sealed, which men deliver to one that is learned, saying, Read this, I pray thee: and he saith, I cannot; for it is sealed:

> And the book is delivered to him that is not learned, saying, Read this, I pray thee: and he saith, I am not learned [Isa. 29:11–12].

The attitude of the people, including God's people, before their final deliverance by God was that prophecy was too obscure to be understood, that it was a sealed subject about which they could know nothing. This is the present-day attitude of many church leaders and preachers. I have heard seminary professors and ministers say, "Well, you know, the Book of Revelation is a sealed book. Nobody can understand it." Those who insist that Revelation is a sealed book and that we are not supposed to understand it are saying exactly what the people in Isaiah's day were saying about prophecy. Or, people today will say that they are too busy, that they don't have time to study the Word of God. All kinds of excuses are offered by Christians for their own ignorance of the Scriptures.

The word *revelation* is from the Greek word *apocalypse*, which means "unveiled." God took the seal from the Book of Revelation so that it *can* be understood. In one sense Revelation is the simplest book in the Bible, but you must have an understanding of the sixty-five books that precede it. It is the last book of the Bible, and certainly it is not the place you should *begin* reading. No book is so organized, and I found it to be the easiest book in the Bible to outline. It is nonsense to say that it is symbolic, a sealed book that we are not supposed to understand. That is what they were saying in Isaiah's day. God will judge you for that kind of thinking because when He gives light and you will not open your eyes, you become blind to the light. Listen to what God says of Revelation in Revelation 1:3, "Blessed is he that readeth, and they that hear the words of this prophecy, and keep those things which are written therein: for the time is at hand." Revelation 22:10 says, "And he saith unto me, Seal not the sayings of the prophecy of this book: for time is at hand." It is *not* a sealed book.

> Wherefore the Lord said, Forasmuch as this people draw near me with their

mouth, and with their lips do honour me, but have removed their heart far from me, and their fear toward me is taught by the precept of men [Isa. 29:13].

If you had lived in Isaiah's day, you would have wondered what Isaiah really meant because the people were going to the temple. It was crowded—anytime a sacrifice was offered you would find people there. There was a place for the men, a court for the women, and a court for the Gentiles. Why was God finding fault with these people? They were all coming to church, but they went through all of the ritual with their mouths. It was as if they could say the Lord's Prayer and the Apostles' Creed, but it did not mean anything to them. They did not believe what they were saying; they did not accept God's Word. God said that their hearts were far from Him. That is the reason He judged them, and that is the reason He is going to judge us today.

The curse of the world today is religion. God would like you to get rid of religion and come to Christ. Religion is the greatest barrier for many people today. I made that statement to a man not long ago. Immediately he countered by saying, "I want you to know, Dr. McGee, that I am a religious man. I am religious by nature." He had a fallen nature, but he had a religious nature. I think I shocked him when I told him that he ought to get rid of his religion and that I was not a religious man. He said, "I cannot believe that there is a preacher who is not religious. If you are not religious, what are you then?" I told him that I am a sinner who came to Christ and that I have a personal relationship with Him today. It is not a religion but a relationship. Do you have Christ, or don't you? That is the important thing.

Woe unto them that seek deep to hide their counsel from the Lord, and their works are in the dark, and they say, Who seeth us? and who knoweth us? [Isa. 29:15].

Things are so serious for His people that He puts in another "Woe" here. This chapter contains two woes because (1) the people act as if God does not see or know, and (2) they act as if they are getting by with it.

## JERUSALEM—HONOR AND GLORY

Is it not yet a very little while, and Lebanon shall be turned into a fruitful field, and the fruitful field shall be esteemed as a forest? [Isa. 29:17].

Now we see into the future. The time will come when there will be honor and glory in Jerusalem and in the land. God is not through with that city. Today it looks like a layer cake with one city built on top of the other. God has judged them, and He will judge them again. But Jerusalem will be rebuilt once again, and *then* it will be the city of God.

And in that day shall the deaf hear the words of the book, and the eyes of the blind shall see out of obscurity, and out of darkness [Isa. 29:18].

The deaf are going to hear, and the blind are going to see.

The meek also shall increase their joy in the Lord, and the poor among men shall rejoice in the Holy One of Israel [Isa. 29:19].

You have heard the old bromide, "No one is so blind as those who will not see." Today, as in Isaiah's day, there is a willful blindness. In that day, in the Millennium, they are going to see.

Therefore thus saith the Lord, who redeemed Abraham, concerning the house of Jacob, Jacob shall not now be ashamed, neither shall his face now wax pale.

But when he seeth his children, the work of mine hands, in the midst of him, they shall sanctify my name, and sanctify the Holy One of Jacob, and shall fear the God of Israel.

They also that erred in spirit shall come to understanding, and they that murmured shall learn doctrine [Isa. 29: 22–24].

What are they going to do with the name of God? They are going to make it holy—they are going to set it apart as something wonderful. Today, God's people, by their lives, should sanctify the name of God. It is a holy name—but do we treat it that way?

*THEME: Judah admonished not to turn to Egypt for help against Assyria; exhorted to turn to the Lord*

These two chapters present largely a local situation, although a larger prophecy of a future time grows out of it. The local prophecy has been literally fulfilled. The southern kingdom of Judah heard and heeded the prophet's warning and did not join with Egypt in order to be delivered from the Assyrian. The northern kingdom of Israel made the mistake of ignoring the prophet's warning, and they went into Assyrian captivity (see 2 Kings 17:4). This is one time when the southern kingdom profited by the experience of the northern kingdom.

## ADMONITION NOT TO SEEK ALLIANCE WITH EGYPT

**Woe to the rebellious children, saith the LORD, that take counsel, but not of me; and that cover with a covering, but not of my spirit, that they may add sin to sin [Isa. 30:1].**

This is the fourth woe. It is a woe because it is a warning. God says in effect, "Don't go to Egypt for help, because it won't be a good thing for you to do. Help down there is a mirage on the desert."

**For the Egyptians shall help in vain, and to no purpose: therefore have I cried concerning this, Their strength is to sit still [Isa. 30:7].**

## EXHORTATION TO TURN TO JEHOVAH FOR DELIVERANCE

God says, "Turn to Me, and I will deliver you" (see v. 15). This is a marvelous verse, one of the gems of Scripture:

**And therefore will the LORD wait, that he may be gracious unto you, and therefore will he be exalted, that he may have mercy upon you: for the LORD is a God of judgment: blessed are all they that wait for him [Isa. 30:18].**

Don't be in a hurry. Don't say, "We are at the end of the age, and the Lord is going to come this year or next—or at least before the year two thousand." God says, "Let *Me* work this out. I have not given you any dates." Learn to wait upon the Lord. This matter of looking for the Lord Jesus to come to take His own out of the world is a matter of *waiting*. And we are

told that they who wait on the Lord will renew their strength. You cannot rush God. He is in no hurry. Maybe things are not working out the way you think they should; maybe you and I would like to rearrange them, but let God work things out. He has eternity ahead of Him; and, when you and I get in step with Him, life will be much easier for us down here.

## DECLARATION THAT GOD WILL DEAL WITH THE FINAL ASSYRIAN

**For through the voice of the LORD shall the Assyrian be beaten down, which smote with a rod.**

**And in every place where the grounded staff shall pass, which the LORD shall lay upon him, it shall be with tabrets and harps: and in battles of shaking will he fight with it.**

**For Tophet is ordained of old; yea, for the king it is prepared; he hath made it deep and large: the pile thereof is fire and much wood; the breath of the LORD, like a stream of brimstone, doth kindle it [Isa. 30:31–33].**

The Assyrian here is the final enemy of God in the Great Tribulation. "Tophet" was a place in the valley of the son of Hinnom where the most abominable idolatries were practiced. Little children were offered as sacrifices! It speaks in this passage of the worst spot in the lake of fire.

"The king" mentioned represents the beast and the false prophet: "And the devil that deceived them was cast into the lake of fire and brimstone, where the beast and the false prophet are, and shall be tormented day and night for ever and ever" (Rev. 20:10).

In chapter 31 the prophet warns God's people again not to look to Egypt for help but to trust the Lord to defend Jerusalem. So pressing is the danger, and so evident is the likelihood of the Israelites turning to Egypt, that Isaiah continues to warn Judah of the futility of such a measure. In the future Israel will turn to the wrong ally. They will accept the Antichrist, and God is warning them about it here. God will judge those who turn to outside help instead of to Him.

**Woe to them that go down to Egypt for help; and stay on horses, and trust in**

chariots, because they are many; and in horsemen, because they are very strong; but they look not unto the Holy One of Israel, neither seek the LORD! [Isa. 31:1].

This is the fifth woe. It is pronounced on those who go down to Egypt for help.

This has a message for you and me. Woe to you and woe to me when we turn away from God and turn to some materialistic or human help. Don't misunderstand me—He doesn't intend that you launch out into space and hang there. God expects you to be reasonable. But in the final analysis God wants top priority as far as giving help is concerned. My friend, where do you go for help? To your banker? To your preacher? Every now and then I receive a letter from someone who asks me what he should do in a given situation. Well, I don't know what to do with many problems that arise in my own life! Although it is nice to ask others for advice, in the final analysis we must go to God for help. The psalmist wrote: "Some trust in chariots, and some in horses: but we will remember the name of the LORD our God (Ps. 20:7).

Materialistic philosophy says that it is smart to trust in the stock market or your investments, that it is smart to look to "Egypt." Most of us have some "Egypt" upon which we depend for help. The real source of Israel's difficulty was that they did not look to God, nor did they seek Him. Since they did not trust Him, they turned frantically to some outside, physical display of power.

As birds flying, so will the LORD of hosts defend Jerusalem; defending also he will deliver it; and passing over he will preserve it [Isa. 31:5].

The Lord will defend and preserve Jerusalem in the days of Hezekiah, as we shall see. God assures them that it is a sure thing that the Assyrians will not take the city of Jerusalem.

Then shall the Assyrian fall with the sword, not of a mighty man; and the sword, not of a mean man, shall devour him: but he shall flee from the sword, and his young men shall be discomfited [Isa. 31:8].

"Not of a mighty man"—God says it is not because you are going to be strong enough to drive them away. You won't. *God* will deal with the Assyrians. Jerusalem's confidence should be in the Lord.

This is a great chapter to read for our own help and strength.

# CHAPTER 32

**THEME:** *The coming King, the coming Tribulation, and the coming Spirit*

This chapter is a bright note between the fifth and sixth woes; it is a ray of light to God's people in a dark place in that day.

It has been some time since the person of the King has been before us, but we find Him introduced again at this point, for there can be no Millennium or blessing to this earth without Him.

## THE KING WHO IS TO REIGN

Behold, a king shall reign in righteousness, and princes shall rule in judgment [Isa. 32:1].

This verse projects into the kingdom age. The King is none other than the Lord Jesus Christ. The character of His reign is righteousness. The world has never had a kingdom like this so far.

And a man shall be as an hiding place from the wind, and a covert from the tempest; as rivers of water in a dry place, as the shadow of a great rock in a weary land [Isa. 32:2].

The Lord is not only King, He is also a Savior-King. He bore the winds and tempest of the judgment of sin for us. He is a Rock for our protection. He was set before us in Isaiah 26:4 as the Rock of ages. This is another aspect of His ministry under the figure of the rock. He is a place of hiding for believers in our day also.

And the eyes of them that see shall not be dim, and the ears of them that hear shall hearken [Isa. 32:3].

In other words, there will be spiritual understanding given to all of God's people. "For now we see through a glass, darkly; but then face to face . . ." (1 Cor. 13:12). True spiritual values will then be ascertained and made obvious. And that which should have top priority *will* have top priority. In our day moral values are gone. One of the great problems in this country is that we have lost the sense of moral values. For many years now our schools have been teaching the evolutionary theory which makes man an animal. Moral values are not taught. If you advocate law and order and a high state of morality, you are considered a square, a back number, and somehow not as smart as are the sophisticated and clever crooks. Therefore, the feeling is, "Let's not listen to that old stuff." Well, the "old stuff" is going to be the future stuff also, because the earth will have a King reigning in righteousness. Then the moral values will come back into place.

**The vile person shall be no more called liberal, nor the churl said to be bountiful [Isa. 32:5].**

I love this—it is about as up to date as we can get. We have today what is known as the limousine liberals. The rich, for the most part, are liberal. Why? They already have their wealth which is not being taxed, but the middle man is being taxed unmercifully to pay for new projects that the rich are promoting. You can be sure of one thing: the rich man could afford to be liberal. Lazarus sat on the floor and caught the crumbs that fell from the rich man's table. That rich man was liberal—he was very liberal with his crumbs—but that was all.

In our day a "vile person" is "called liberal." In that day a vile person will no longer be called liberal, because he will be seen for what he really is. He is a villain, and his heart will work iniquity. The human heart is desperately wicked. Everything in that future day will be seen in its true colors. There will be no false values. Every man will be seen for what he is. There will be no "putting on a front" or assuming what they are not. The mask of hypocrisy will be removed. This, of course, applies to everyone—not only to Christians. The biggest hypocrites are actually not in the church. They are all those who pretend to be something they are not.

All of this will take place when the King comes who will reign in righteousness.

## THE PRECEDING TIME OF TROUBLE

Before Christ, the King, comes to reign, there will be a time of trouble, which will be the Great Tribulation.

**Rise up, ye women that are at ease; hear my voice, ye careless daughters; give ear unto my speech [Isa. 32:9].**

Why does he say this? Because naturally women are more sensitive than men, and they sense danger before a man does. My friend, every man before he goes into a business partnership or any kind of partnership should let his wife meet the person who is to be his partner. She is apt to give him a true evaluation of his nature and character. In my home I try to maintain my place as the head of the house, but I have discovered over a period of years that I am no judge of human character. Time after time my wife has said to me, "Well, you misjudged that person." Either I put confidence in someone when I should not have, or I failed to recognize that certain people are really wonderful folk. So I have learned that the best thing to do is to listen to her, especially in the evaluation of character. Now God says that in the days prior to the Tribulation Period women will become so insensible that they will not recognize the danger that is coming. It is quite interesting that there will be women living in pleasure in that day to such extent that they will have no sense of coming judgment.

## THE PROMISE OF THE SPIRIT

Now we come to the third division: the promise of the Spirit to be poured out in the last days.

**Until the spirit be poured upon us from on high, and the wilderness be a fruitful field, and the fruitful field be counted for a forest [Isa. 32:15].**

Here is a case where you need to pay attention to the development of prophecy in the Word of God. When will the Spirit be poured out? The Spirit will be poured out during the Millennium when Christ reigns. That is going to be the greatest time of spiritual blessing and turning to Christ, for at that time He will be reigning in person. That doesn't mean that every knee is going to bow to Him at that time. Every knee will bow to Him eventually, but the kingdom will be a time of testing. Joel mentions it: "And it shall come to pass afterward, that I will pour out my spirit upon all flesh; and your sons and your daughters shall

prophesy, your old men shall dream dreams, your young men shall see visions: And also upon the servants and upon the handmaids in those days will I pour out my spirit" (Joel 2:28-29). This looks forward to the coming kingdom. This prophecy was not fulfilled at Pentecost nor any time since then.

In Acts 2:15–21 Peter quotes from Joel 2:28–29 and explains the passage. Peter did not say that Pentecost was a fulfillment of the prophecy in Joel, but that Pentecost was similar to what Joel described. The people who were filled with the Holy Spirit in Peter's day were ridiculed as being drunk early in the morning. Now that could happen in Los Angeles today, but people did not get drunk in the morning in Peter's day. Peter was saying that what was happening at Pentecost was similar to what would take place during the millennial kingdom.

What Joel and Peter described will take place during the kingdom age when the Lord pours out His Spirit upon all flesh. On the Day of Pentecost it was poured out on only a few

people, but it was similar to that which will occur during the Millennium.

Joel's prediction was of tremendous phenomena: "And I will shew wonders in the heavens and in the earth, blood, and fire, and pillars of smoke. The sun shall be turned into darkness, and the moon into blood, before the great and the terrible day of the LORD come" (Joel 2:30–31). My friend, these tremendous signs have never yet taken place.

Notice also that Joel predicted, ". . . and your sons and your daughters shall prophesy, your old men shall dream dreams . . ." (Joel 2:28). Today our young people are not fulfilling this prophecy, and our old men are in a retirement place playing golf. These things did not happen on the Day of Pentecost, neither are they happening today. This prophecy looks forward to the coming kingdom. There is always a danger of pulling out a few verses of Scripture and trying to build on them a system of prophecy. We are just to let the Word of God speak to us—line upon line and precept upon precept—as He wants to do it. This is the way God gives it to us.

# CHAPTER 33

**THEME:** *The final woe is pronounced on all who spoil God's people and land*

This chapter, in particular, pronounces a judgment upon those who seek to destroy God's people and lay waste His land. It refers to the Assyrians in the immediate purview but extends to the final enemy of the last days. The chapter is geocentric. The land is the thing of primary importance.

## PRAYER OF THE REMNANT FOR DELIVERANCE

**Woe to thee that spoilest, and thou wast not spoiled; and dealest treacherously, and they dealt not treacherously with thee! when thou shalt cease to spoil, thou shalt be spoiled; and when thou shalt make an end to deal treacherously, they shall deal treacherously with thee [Isa. 33:1].**

This is Isaiah's way of expressing the great spiritual principles, which God put down from the time man sinned. It is stated well in Galatians 6:7: "Be not deceived; God is not mocked: for whatsoever a man soweth, that shall he also reap."

The "spoiler" here is Sennacherib who came against Jerusalem during the reign of Hezekiah (Isa. 36–37). I believe this is the unanimous conclusion of all sound scholars. However, it does not limit this chapter to the Assyrians. God says in effect, "You spoil My people, and I'll spoil you." God promises to take vengeance on behalf of His people. For this reason we as believers should always let God handle all of our revenge. God says that we are not to avenge ourselves, but *He* will repay. Turn it over to God. He can do a better job than we can do.

Now this is also a picture of that final day of consummation after God has brought together again the restored Roman Empire, and Antichrist will destroy the land of Israel again. God will take care of him at the second coming of Christ.

Now in view of that, we hear this prayer:

**O LORD, be gracious unto us; we have waited for thee: be thou their arm every morning, our salvation also in the time of trouble [Isa. 33:2].**

This is the prayer of the godly remnant then and in the future.

## PLAINTIVE CRY OF AMBASSADORS WHO FAILED

**Behold, their valiant ones shall cry without: the ambassadors of peace shall weep bitterly.**

**The highways lie waste, the wayfaring man ceaseth: he hath broken the covenant, he hath despised the cities, he regardeth no man [Isa. 33:7–8].**

You would think that we would have learned a lesson today, but we have not. A great peace conference was held at the Hague; and, while it was going on, Germany began World War I and broke all of the treaties. At the end of that war the League of Nations was formed; and, when President Woodrow Wilson went to be our representative, the idea was to make the world safe for democracy. What they forgot, however, was to make democracy safe for the world. Peace didn't come. It led to World War II. Now the United Nations is making the world ready for World War III. We talk about peace, but we are not doing it God's way.

## PETITION FOR ALL TO CONSIDER GOD'S DEALINGS

**Hear, ye that are far off, what I have done; and, ye that are near, acknowledge my might [Isa. 33:13].**

Two groups of people are addressed here: "Ye that are far off" are the Gentiles, and "ye that are near" are the people of Israel. The call is to recognize God.

**The sinners in Zion are afraid; fearfulness hath surprised the hypocrites. Who among us shall dwell with the devouring fire? who among us shall dwell with everlasting burnings? [Isa. 33:14].**

"Sinners in Zion" are those of Israel who are not Israel. There are godless Israelites just as there are godless Gentiles.

"The devouring fire" does not refer to the lake of fire mentioned in the Book of Revelation, but rather to the fact that "our God is a consuming fire." He is a holy God, and He intends to judge in that day.

Today there is a tremendous godless movement abroad. It is growing by leaps and bounds. That is the reason we are giving out the Word of God. We don't know how much longer we can do it, but we are going to continue as long as the Lord allows. God is going to bring judgment, and God's people need to be concerned about getting His Word out. Judgment is not a pretty subject. It is not one that will make friends, but these are the words of Isaiah, and Isaiah's message is God's message, and He would like the human family to hear it.

**He that walketh righteously, and speaketh uprightly; he that despiseth the gain of oppressions, that shaketh his hands from holding of bribes, that stoppeth his ears from hearing of blood, and shutteth his eyes from seeing evil [Isa. 33:15].**

The one who has been declared righteous by his faith in Christ is called to walk in righteousness. In that awful day we find that where sin abounds, grace will much more abound.

## PRAISE TO GOD FOR FINAL DELIVERANCE

Now we come to the fourth division, where there is praise to God for final deliverance.

**Look upon Zion, the city of our solemnities: thine eyes shall see Jerusalem a quiet habitation, a tabernacle that shall not be taken down; not one of the stakes thereof shall ever be removed, neither shall any of the cords thereof be broken.**

**But there the glorious LORD will be unto us a place of broad rivers and streams; wherein shall go no galley with oars, neither shall gallant ship pass thereby [Isa. 33:20–21].**

Babylon could boast of the Euphrates River, Assyria could boast of the Tigris and upper Zab, and Egypt could boast of the Nile, but Jerusalem was a landlocked city with neither river nor harbor. However, Zechariah gave an amazing prophecy which leads us to believe that God will provide a harbor for Israel during the Millennium (see Zech. 14:4–8). It is my understanding that the earthquake he describes will open up a deep valley to the Mediterranean Sea, and Jerusalem will be a seaport town during the Millennium.

The literal fulfillment of the prophecy also has a spiritual application. "The glorious LORD

will be unto us a place of broad rivers and streams." The Lord Himself is the source of Israel's defense and blessing.

**And the inhabitant shall not say, I am sick: the people that dwell therein shall be forgiven their iniquity [Isa. 33:24].**

This is a glorious prospect which is held out for Jerusalem. The eye of faith looks beyond the immediate hard circumstances to the glorious prospect of the future. This is the day when the *King* will be in Jerusalem. The Prince of peace will then bring peace to the earth.

# CHAPTER 34

*THEME: The final world clash—the Battle of Armageddon*

This chapter brings to an end the section which in my outline I call the "Kingdom, Process, and Program by which the Throne is Established on Earth." Judgment has been the theme all the way through this section. We have looked at six woes and followed a progression in this matter of prophecy. We saw a local situation into which Isaiah spoke and then watched him move into that broader area, as he looked down through the centuries to the time of judgment that was coming in the future, which the Lord Jesus called the Great Tribulation. Beyond that we saw the coming of the King.

However, in our day we are not looking for the King, we are looking for our Savior. We are "Looking for that blessed hope, and the glorious appearing of the great God and our Saviour Jesus Christ" (Titus 2:13). After He takes the church out of the world, those who remain will go through the frightful Tribulation Period, which will end with the war or the campaign of Armageddon.

This chapter is in contradiction to the philosophy of the world. You see, man expects to so improve the world by his own efforts that he will build a Utopia. He plans to bring in a millennium, although he may call it something else. Man thinks he is capable of lifting himself by his own bootstraps. The basic philosophy of evolution (and evolution is a philosophy rather than a science) is that there is improvement as we go along. It is onward and upward forever! Or, as the slogan has it, "Every day in every way I am getting better and better." Man has woven this philosophy into the fabric of life; he thinks we are moving into something which is great and good.

The Word of God also looks forward to a wonderful future for this earth, but it is not the consummation of man's efforts. Everything that man has built apart from God is coming under a frightful judgment. All of man's work is contrary to God and must come into a final conflict. That conflict is set before us here as the Battle of Armageddon. The sin of man will finally be headed up in the Man of Sin, who will attempt to bring in a kingdom for himself, and that kingdom is the Great Tribulation period. It can only be ended with the coming of Christ to the earth to establish His kingdom.

This chapter looks entirely to the future. The Assyrians have disappeared, F. Delitzsch has made this statement, which I think is quite accurate: "We feel that we are carried away from the stage of history , and are transported into the midst of the last things," and these chapters are the "last steps whereby our prophet rises to the height at which he soars in chapters 40 to the end. After the fall of Assyria, and when darkness began to gather on the horizon again, Isaiah broke away from his own time—'the end of all things' became more and more his home. . . . It was the revelation of the mystery of the incarnation of God, for which all this was to prepare the way."

**Come near, ye nations, to hear; and hearken, ye people: let the earth hear, and all that is therein; the world, and all things that come forth of it [Isa. 34:1].**

In Isaiah 1:2 God called heaven and earth to witness His judgment upon His people Israel. In this chapter God calls only the nations of the earth to witness His final judgment upon the nations.

**For the indignation of the LORD is upon all nations, and his fury upon all their armies: he hath utterly destroyed them, he hath delivered them to the slaughter [Isa. 34:2].**

Observe carefully the words chosen to depict this judgment: *indignation, fury, utterly destroyed,* and *delivered to the slaughter.* They are the strongest possible expressions that could be used. The judgment is universal, and it is severe. It is not only the ". . . time of Jacob's trouble" (Jer. 30:7), but it is the time of the earth's travail. Our Lord spoke of this as a time of suffering that will be unparalleled in the history of the world. The seals, trumpets, and vials in the Book of Revelation all intensify and confirm this. Whether you believe it or not, the earth is moving toward the judgment of God. Instead of a wonderful day coming for sinful man, a time of judgment is coming. As we look around us at our contemporary civilization, everything we see is going to come under the judgment of our Almighty God.

**Their slain also shall be cast out, and their stink shall come up out of their carcases, and the mountains shall be melted with their blood [Isa. 34:3].**

This description is to me the most terrible and repulsive in the Bible. I can't think of anything worse than this. It confirms what the Lord Jesus said when He was here and what the Book of Revelation teaches about a coming judgment upon this earth.

I realize that a great many people doubt this, which reminds me of an incident when a tropical hurricane broke on the Gulf coast several years ago. I traveled along that area several years later, drove for miles and saw entire sections of cities that the storm had taken out. Even after several years, nothing is there. I also saw places where jungle in the area was absolutely removed. I was told about an apartment house in the area where a group of people were living fast and loose. When they heard the warnings about the storm, they decided that they would not leave. They didn't believe the storm was going to be severe; so they had a big beer bust. Instead of evacuating, they all got drunk. They ridiculed the storm forecast, and they were all killed. You can do the same thing concerning the judgment that is coming on this earth. God says that judgment is coming, and it is coming.

**And all the host of heaven shall be dissolved, and the heavens shall be rolled together as a scroll: and all their hosts shall fall down, as the leaf falleth off from the vine, and as a falling fig from the fig tree [Isa. 34:4].**

When you see a little leaf fall from a tree, you can attempt to glue it back on the branch, but it won't stay and it won't live. Just as surely, judgment is coming, and you can't keep it from coming. There is only one thing you can do: make sure that you have a shelter. Listen to God and remember that the Lord Jesus is the shelter in the time of storm which is coming upon the earth.

## IDUMEA, REPRESENTING ALL GOD'S ENEMIES

**For my sword shall be bathed in heaven: behold, it shall come down upon Idumea, and upon the people of my curse, to judgment [Isa. 34:5].**

God bathes that sword in heaven—that is important to see. When you and I take the sword down here, it is for vengeance or some ulterior motive. When God takes the sword, it is for justice and righteousness upon the earth. His sword is bathed in heaven, and it is going to fall in judgment.

Idumea is Edom, and Edom is Esau, and Esau represents the flesh. Esau represents all in Adam who are rebellious against God and His people. God said, ". . . Jacob have I loved, but Esau have I hated" (Rom. 9:13). God will judge Edom because they are against God, against His people, against His Word, against everything that is right and good.

## INTENTION OF THE LORD

**For it is the day of the LORD'S vengeance, and the year of recompences for the controversy of Zion [Isa. 34:8].**

This is the day of the Lord's vengeance. We will see this again in Isaiah 63:1–6. You can't do anything to stop it, just like there is nothing you can do to stop Niagara Falls from flowing. God says that things have to be made right upon this earth. To make them right He has to put down the evil and rebellious man upon this earth. Many people will not bow to God; but, since this is God's universe, where will they go? He has only one place for them, which is called hell. You may have your own concept of it, but it undoubtedly is lots worse than a place of literal fire. God's Word is in-

violable and the Lord Jesus said, "Till heaven and earth pass, one jot or one tittle shall in no wise pass from the law, till all be fulfilled" (Matt. 5:18). My friend, it is wise to read the weather report and when a storm is forecast to make arrangements to escape it.

# CHAPTER 35

**THEME:** *The blessings of the Millennium, a picture of the kingdom*

As we come to this chapter, we can thank God that the war of Armageddon is not the end of all things. Chapter 35 is a poetic gem. There is a high sense of poetic justice in this chapter which concludes the section on judgment. The fires of judgment have now burned out, and the sword of justice is sheathed. The evening of earth-trouble is ended, and the morning of millennial delights has come. This section closes on the high plane of peace, having been through suffering to peace, through the night to the dawn, through judgment to salvation, through tears to joy in the morning.

The calm of this chapter is in contrast to the storms of judgments of the previous chapter and even those that preceded it. We can say with the writer of the Song of Solomon, the winter is past, and the flowers appear on the earth.

## MATERIAL EARTH WILL BE RESTORED

First we see that the material earth will be restored and the curse of sin lifted. This is the *body* of the earth.

**The wilderness and the solitary place shall be glad for them; and the desert shall rejoice, and blossom as the rose [Isa. 35:1].**

We are informed today that the deserts of the world are being enlarged each year; they are not being reduced in size. Drought and soil erosion are hastening this process. Today pollution is filling the earth. All of this will be reversed for the Millennium. The smog will be lifted, and the curse of sin will be removed. The familiar and beautiful statement, "the desert shall . . . blossom as the rose" is an apt and happy picture of the earth's future. If you are familiar with the great desert area of the southwestern section of our country, you will be impressed with this statement. This out-line was written while we were crossing the southeast section of Colorado where the drought has been so severe and where the vast grasslands have been eroded by sandstorms. During the Millennium all of this will be reversed.

**It shall blossom abundantly, and rejoice even with joy and singing: the glory of Lebanon shall be given unto it, the excellency of Carmel and Sharon, they shall see the glory of the LORD, and the excellency of our God [Isa. 35:2].**

Paul tells us that creation is groaning and travailing in pain (see Rom. 8:22), while in the Millennium all creation will rejoice.

## MEN WILL BE RENEWED

The bodies of men will be renewed, as will the psychological part of man.

**Strengthen ye the weak hands, and confirm the feeble knees [Isa. 35:3].**

Creation is waiting for us to get our new bodies.

**Say to them that are of a fearful heart, Be strong, fear not: behold, your God will come with vengeance, even God with a recompence; he will come and save you [Isa. 35:4].**

In the midst of the storm of judgment, God's people can rejoice because they will know that God will come and save them. The church has the added hope and joy of never experiencing the Great Tribulation Period.

**Then the eyes of the blind shall be opened, and the ears of the deaf shall be unstopped.**

**Then shall the lame man leap as an hart, and the tongue of the dumb sing: for in the wilderness shall waters break**

out, and streams in the desert [Isa. 35: 5-6].

Sickness and disease and all affliction are the result of man's sin. These will be lifted in the kingdom.

**And the parched ground shall become a pool, and the thirsty land springs of water: in the habitation of dragons, where each lay, shall be grass with reeds and rushes.**

**And an highway shall be there, and a way, and it shall be called The way of holiness; the unclean shall not pass over it; but it shall be for those: the wayfaring men, though fools, shall not err therein.**

**No lion shall be there, nor any ravenous beast shall go up thereon, it shall not be found there; but the redeemed shall walk there [Isa. 35:7-9].**

What a beautiful picture we have here of the earth during the kingdom age.

## MEMBERS OF GOD'S FAMILY WILL RETURN TO ZION

Here we see the *spirit* of earth; that is, man will be renewed spiritually.

**And the ransomed of the LORD shall return, and come to Zion with songs and everlasting joy upon their heads: they shall obtain joy and gladness, and sorrow and sighing shall flee away [Isa. 35:10].**

Can you think of anything nicer than this? This not only includes Israel, but it will include the redeemed who enter the Millennium upon the earth. In Zechariah 14:16-17 we read, "And it shall come to pass, that every one that is left of all the nations which came against Jerusalem shall even go up from year to year to worship the King, the LORD of hosts, and to keep the feast of tabernacles. And it shall be, that whoso will not come up of all the families of the earth unto Jerusalem to worship the King, the LORD of hosts, even upon them shall be no rain."

We can say with that old Puritan, Richard Baxter, "Hasten, O Saviour, the time of Thy return. Delay not, lest the living give up their hope. Delay not, lest earth shall grow like hell, and Thy Church shall be crumbled to dust. O hasten, that great resurrection day, when the graves that received but rottenness, and retain but dust, shall return Thee glorious stars and suns. Thy desolate Bride saith, Come. The whole creation saith, Come, even so come, Lord Jesus. The whole creation groaneth and travaileth in pain, waiting for the revealing of the sons of God."

Thus ends the first major division of the Book of Isaiah with all the blessing of the Millennium.

# HISTORIC INTERLUDE

We have come to the second major division of the Book of Isaiah. This section is unlike that which precedes it and that which follows it. This section leaves the high plateau of prophecy and drops down to the record of history. Even the form of language changes from poetry to prose. The first section dealt with the government of God and the method by which God judges. In the last section we will see the grace of God—salvation instead of judgment. Between these two sections is this historic interlude of four brief chapters. Why are they wedged in between the two major sections of this book? This is a reasonable question which requires investigation and rewards the honest inquirer. There are several significant factors which are worthy of mention.

1. Sacred and secular history are not the same. F. C. Jennings, in his fine work, *Studies in Isaiah*, says, "Divine history is never merely history, never simply a true account of past events." This means that there are great *spiritual* truths couched in sacred history that are seen only by the eye of faith. The Holy Spirit must teach us the divine purpose in recording spiritual history. I want to note several suggested reasons for this:

a. These incidents might seem trite to the average historian who records great world movements, but events that concerned *God's people* were important according to the standards of heaven.

b. These chapters note the transfer of power from Assyria to Babylon. Babylon was the first great world empire and was the real

menace to God's people. Babylon was to begin the period designated by our Lord as ". . . the times of the Gentiles . . ." (Luke 21:24).

c. This section is a record of a son of David who was beset by enemies and who went down to the verge of death, but was delivered and continued to reign. In this he foreshadows the great Son of David who was also beset by enemies, was delivered to death, but was raised from the dead, and who is coming again to reign. Hezekiah was only a man who walked in the ways of David, another weak man. Hezekiah lived to play the fool. Our Lord was greater than David, and as the crucified and risen Son of God, He is made unto us ". . . wisdom, and righteousness, and sanctification, and redemption" (1 Cor. 1:30). There are other great spiritual truths which are noted in the chapter outlines.

2. The second significant factor in this historic section is that these particular events are recorded *three* times in Scripture—2 Kings 18–19, 2 Chronicles 29–30, and here in Isaiah. The fact that the Holy Spirit saw fit to record them three times is in itself a matter of great importance. The records are not identical but are similar. Some scholars think that Isaiah is the author of all three, or at least also of the one in the Book of Kings. Surely the Spirit of God has some special truth for us here which should cause us not to hurry over these events as if they were of no great moment.

3. Three significant and stupendous miracles are recorded in this brief section:

a. The death angel slays 185,000 Assyrians (Isa. 37:36–38).

b. The sun retreats ten degrees on the sundial of Ahaz (Isa. 38:7–8).

c. God heals Hezekiah and extends his life fifteen years (Isa. 38:1–5).

4. This section opens with Assyria and closes with Babylon. There are two important letters which Hezekiah received:

a. The first was from Assyria, which Hezekiah took directly to God in prayer. God answered his prayer and delivered His people (Isa. 37:14–20).

b. The second letter was from the king of Babylon, which flattered Hezekiah and which he did not take to the Lord in prayer. As a result, it led to the undoing of Judah (Isa. 39:1–8).

Chapter 36 tells about King Hezekiah and the invasion of Sennacherib, king of Assyria. Chapter 37 tells about King Hezekiah's prayer and the destruction of the Assyrian hosts. Chapter 38 records King Hezekiah's sickness, prayer, and healing. Chapter 39 finds King Hezekiah playing the fool.

# CHAPTERS 36–37

**THEME:** *Hezekiah and Assyria*

Sennacherib, king of Assyria, had come down like a flood from the north, taking everything in his wake. He had captured every nation and city that stood in his path, or they had capitulated to him. Flushed with victory, he appears with the Assyrian hosts before the walls of Jerusalem. He is surprised and puzzled that Hezekiah would attempt to resist him. He seeks for some explanation, as Hezekiah must have some secret weapon. Rab-shakeh, his representative, ridicules all known possibilities of aid. Arrogantly he demands unconditional surrender. The chapter closes with the terms and threats reported to Hezekiah.

## ASSYRIA THREATENS TO INVADE JERUSALEM

**Now it came to pass in the fourteenth year of king Hezekiah, that Sennacherib king of Assyria came up against all the defenced cities of Judah, and took them [Isa. 36:1].**

You will recall that Isaiah began his prophetic ministry when King Uzziah died, and he continued it through the reigns of Jotham, Ahaz, and now Hezekiah. Hezekiah was one of the five great kings of Judah. During the reigns of these five kings (Asa, Jehoshaphat, Joash, Hezekiah, and Josiah) revival came to the land of Judah. Hezekiah was actually a great king. Second Chronicles 29: 1–2 tells us, "Hezekiah began to reign when he was five and twenty years old, and he reigned nine and twenty years in Jerusalem. And his mother's name was Abijah, the daughter of Zechariah. And he did that which was right in the sight of the LORD, according to all that David his father had done."

Although Hezekiah was a good king, he exhibited weakness when he attempted to stave off the invasion of Jerusalem by bribing Sennacherib (see 2 Kings 18:13–16). He stripped the gold and silver from the temple to meet the exorbitant demands of the king of Assyria. It was to no avail, however, as the army of Assyria was outside the gates of Jerusalem. Payment did not help at all. This policy was not something new then, and it is still with us. Our nation, since World War II, has followed a very weak policy. We have used the almighty dollar to try to buy friends throughout the world, and we don't have many friends today. You cannot get friends by buying them. Our problem is that we haven't learned who our real Friend is. He is the One to whom Hezekiah finally had to turn, the Lord God.

**And the king of Assyria sent Rab-shakeh from Lachish to Jerusalem unto king Hezekiah with a great army. And he stood by the conduit of the upper pool in the highway of the fuller's field [Isa. 36:2].**

Sennacherib did not condescend to come personally, but instead he sent an army under Rab-shakeh. They are parked now outside the gates of Jerusalem, and General Rab-shakeh is attempting to put fear into the hearts of Hezekiah and the people of Jerusalem so that they will surrender.

Hezekiah sent out a delegation to meet with him.

**Then came forth unto him Eliakim, Hilkiah's son, which was over the house, and Shebna the scribe, and Joah, Asaph's son, the recorder [Isa. 36:3].**

Hezekiah sent forth this embassage of three to receive the terms offered by Sennacherib.

## ASSYRIA DEMANDS SURRENDER OF JERUSALEM

**And Rab-shakeh said unto them, Say ye now to Hezekiah, Thus saith the great king, the king of Assyria, What confidence is this wherein thou trustest? [Isa. 36:4].**

**R**ab-shakeh arrogantly expresses surprise that Hezekiah would even dare resist, and he wants to know about the secret weapon in which Hezekiah trusts. He suggests first of all that it might be Egypt.

**Lo, thou trustest in the staff of this broken reed, on Egypt; whereon if a man lean, it will go into his hand, and pierce it: so is Pharaoh king of Egypt to all that trust in him [Isa. 36:6].**

The Assyrian host was then on the way to Egypt to capture that kingdom and was incensed that Jerusalem blocked the way. The facts were that Hezekiah had hoped for help from Egypt as had Ahaz his father before him. But Hezekiah wouldn't get any help from Egypt—Rab-shakeh was right about that.

Then he suggests another possibility:

**But if thou say to me, We trust in the LORD our God: is it not he, whose high places and whose altars Hezekiah hath taken away, and said to Judah and Jerusalem, Ye shall worship before this altar? [Isa. 36:7].**

Next Rab-shakeh asks, "Is it true that you are depending upon your God?" Here is where his lack of spiritual discernment gave him a wrong cue. He says, "Don't you know that Hezekiah had all the high places destroyed?" He thought the worship at the heathen altars out yonder on those hilltops was the same as the worship of the living God in Jerusalem. He thought Hezekiah had destroyed the worship of the people so that they had no gods to turn to.

Many people today have no spiritual discernment. Every now and then someone will write to me or say, "All churches are the same. They are all striving to get to the same place." These people are like old Rab-shakeh. They don't seem to know the difference. When they say that it does not make any difference what you believe as long as you are sincere, they contradict the words of our Lord. "Jesus saith unto him, I am the way, the truth, and the life: no man cometh unto the Father, but by me" (John 14:6).

Now the third possibility suggested by Rab-shakeh reveals the haughty attitude of the Assyrian:

**Now therefore give pledges, I pray thee, to my master the king of Assyria, and I will give thee two thousand horses, if thou be able on thy part to set riders upon them.**

**How then wilt thou turn away the face of one captain of the least of my master's servants, and put thy trust on Egypt for chariots and for horsemen? [Isa. 36:8–9].**

There was the bare possibility that Hezekiah was depending on his own resources and man-

power to defend Jerusalem; so Rab-shakeh offers to make things just about equal by giving Hezekiah two thousand horses! He, of course, is ridiculing them.

The fourth possibility suggested by Rab-shakeh is the most subtle of all:

**And am I now come up without the LORD against this land to destroy it? the LORD said unto me, Go up against this land, and destroy it [Isa. 36:10].**

He suggests that Jehovah of Israel has *sent* the Assyrian against Jerusalem and that He is therefore on the side of the Assyrian.

It is interesting to note that in World War I the Germans thought God was with them, and we thought God was on our side. I doubt seriously that God was on either side. In this particular case the true God used the Assyrian to destroy His people, but He is not going to let the enemy take Jerusalem.

**Then said Eliakim and Shebna and Joah unto Rabshakeh, Speak, I pray thee, unto thy servants in the Syrian language; for we understand it: and speak not to us in the Jews' language, in the ears of the people that are on the wall [Isa. 36:11].**

Now Eliakim, Shebna, and Joah ask Rab-shakeh to speak in the Syrian language. All this time he has been speaking so loudly in the Hebrew language that the soldiers on the walls of Jerusalem could hear. He was great at giving out propaganda; enemies always do that. He was yelling out his ideas at the top of his voice so that the soldiers on the wall would get the word to the people in Jerusalem; he wanted to get it past these emissaries. Of course, their protest only caused Rab-shakeh to talk a little louder.

**Beware lest Hezekiah persuade you, saying, The LORD will deliver us. Hath any of the gods of the nations delivered his land out of the hand of the king of Assyria?**

**Where are the gods of Hamath and Arphad? where are the gods of Sepharvaim? and have they delivered Samaria out of my hand?**

**Who are they among all the gods of these lands, that have delivered their land out of my hand, that the LORD should deliver Jerusalem out of my hand? [Isa. 36:18–20].**

Arrogantly Rab-shakeh boasts that none of the gods of other people have delivered them. Why should the Israelites expect Jehovah to deliver Jerusalem? He placed Jehovah on a par with heathen idols.

## REPRESENTATIVES REPORT ASSYRIA'S BITTER TERMS

Finally the emissaries bring the word to Hezekiah, the king:

**Then came Eliakim, the son of Hilkiah, that was over the household, and Shebna the scribe, and Joah, the son of Asaph, the recorder, to Hezekiah with their clothes rent, and told him the words of Rabshakeh [Isa. 36:22].**

The messengers return to report these doleful words to Hezekiah.

"Clothes" speak of the dignity and glory of man. The saying is that clothes make the man. Well, "clothes rent" indicates humiliation and shame. This is a dejected and discouraged delegation that brings to Hezekiah the message from the king of Assyria.

## REACTION OF HEZEKIAH TO THE REPORT

Now notice what Hezekiah does when this report reaches him.

**And it came to pass, when king Hezekiah heard it, that he rent his clothes, and covered himself with sackcloth, and went into the house of the LORD [Isa. 37:1].**

His reaction to the report of his messengers reveals a man of faith. In his extremity he turns to God and goes to the house of the Lord.

**And he sent Eliakim, who was over the household, and Shebna the scribe, and the elders of the priests covered with sackcloth, unto Isaiah the prophet the son of Amoz. [Isa. 37:2].**

Hezekiah now sends his messengers to Isaiah the prophet. This is another act of faith. He wants a word from God.

**And they said unto him, Thus saith Hezekiah, This day is a day of trouble, and of rebuke, and of blasphemy: for the children are come to the birth, and there is not strength to bring forth [Isa. 37:3].**

The message to Isaiah is ominous, black, and pessimistic. It is a day of trouble, rebuke, and blasphemy.

> It may be the LORD thy God will hear the words of Rabshakeh, whom the king of Assyria his master hath sent to reproach the living God, and will reprove the words which the LORD thy God hath heard: wherefore lift up thy prayer for the remnant that is left [Isa. 37:4].

He speaks of the Lord as "thy God," not as "our God." Why didn't he say "our God" to begin with? However, he will correct this in his prayer in verse 20.

## ENCOURAGEMENT FROM THE LORD THROUGH ISAIAH

> So the servants of king Hezekiah came to Isaiah.

> And Isaiah said unto them, Thus shall ye say unto your master, Thus saith the LORD, Be not afraid of the words that thou hast heard, wherewith the servants of the king of Assyria have blasphemed me [Isa. 37:5–6].

God gives assurance to Hezekiah that the blasphemy of the Assyrian has not escaped His attention. Likewise, God cannot, nor will not, ignore it.

> Behold, I will send a blast upon him, and he shall hear a rumour, and return to his own land; and I will cause him to fall by the sword in his own land [Isa. 37:7].

He would not be killed near Jerusalem but in his own land. This had literal fulfillment, as we shall see. God declares the destruction of Assyria.

## THREATENING LETTER TO HEZEKIAH

When Rab-shakeh got back to his army, he learned that the king of Assyria had left Lachish and was going to war against Libnah. A rumor came that the main force of the Assyrian army was being attacked by the Egyptian army. Rab-shakeh withdrew from Jerusalem temporarily to assist the main force of the Assyrian army, but to "save face" he dispatched a letter from Sennacherib to Hezekiah saying, "I'll be back!"

The message of the letter was another attempt to shake Hezekiah's faith in God's deliverance.

> Thus shall ye speak to Hezekiah king of Judah, saying, Let not thy God, in whom thou trustest, deceive thee, saying, Jerusalem shall not be given into the hand of the king of Assyria [Isa. 37:10].

He repeats the same words of Rab-shakeh.

> Behold, thou hast heard what the kings of Assyria have done to all lands by destroying them utterly; and shalt thou be delivered?

> Have the gods of the nations delivered them which my fathers have destroyed, as Gozan, and Haran, and Rezeph, and the children of Eden which were in Telassar? [Isa. 37:11–12].

Here he goes beyond the former word and boasts that no gods of any nation had delivered their people out of the hand of the Assyrian.

> Where is the king of Hamath, and the king of Arphad, and the king of the city of Sepharvaim, Hena, and Ivah? [Isa. 37:13].

He quotes historical facts that were difficult to answer.

## HEZEKIAH'S PRAYER

Now notice the action of Hezekiah—I love this!

> And Hezekiah received the letter from the hand of the messengers, and read it: and Hezekiah went up unto the house of the LORD, and spread it before the LORD [Isa. 37:14].

When Hezekiah received the letter, he went to God directly and spread the letter before Him. Then follows one of the truly great prayers of Scripture.

> And Hezekiah prayed unto the LORD, saying,

> O LORD of hosts, God of Israel, that dwellest between the cherubims, thou art the God, even thou alone, of all the kingdoms of the earth: thou hast made heaven and earth [Isa. 37:15–16].

No instructed Israelites believed that God was a *local* deity who dwelt in the temple—just a little box in Jerusalem! King Solomon had prayed: "But will God indeed dwell on the earth? behold, the heaven and heaven of heavens cannot contain thee; how much less

this house that I have builded" (1 Kings 8:27). Every Israelite recognized that He was the God of heaven, the Creator of heaven and earth.

Hezekiah pleads with Him to hear and deliver His people from the threatening Assyrian:

Incline thine ear, O LORD, and hear; open thine eyes, O LORD, and see: and hear all the words of Sennacherib, which hath sent to reproach the living God [Isa. 37:17].

Hezekiah shows God the letter and calls attention to the fact that it is directly against God.

Of a truth, LORD, the kings of Assyria have laid waste all the nations, and their countries,

And have cast their gods into the fire: for they were no gods, but the work of men's hands, wood and stone: therefore they have destroyed them [Isa. 37:18–19].

Hezekiah acknowledges the truth of the letter. There was no need to deny or ignore it. When we deal with God, it is wise to tell Him the truth, especially about ourselves, and not try to conceal anything.

Now therefore, O LORD our God, save us from his hand, that all the kingdoms of the earth may know that thou art the LORD, even thou only [Isa. 37:20].

## GOD'S ANSWER THROUGH ISAIAH

God says that He has heard the blasphemy of the Assyrian. Notice how He will deal with him:

Because thy rage against me, and thy tumult, is come up into mine ears, therefore will I put my hook in thy nose, and my bridle in thy lips, and I will turn thee back by the way by which thou camest [Isa. 37:29].

Now God gives this word of comfort and assurance to His people:

And this shall be a sign unto thee, Ye shall eat this year such as groweth of itself; and the second year that which springeth of the same: and in the third year sow ye, and reap, and plant vineyards, and eat the fruit thereof [Isa. 37:30].

The primary thought is that the children of Judah would continue on in the land a little longer.

Note the boldness of this prophecy:

Therefore thus saith the LORD concerning the king of Assyria, He shall not come into this city, nor shoot an arrow there, nor come before it with shields, nor cast a bank against it [Isa. 37:33].

If one of the 185,000 Assyrians had accidentally shot an arrow over the walls of Jerusalem, God's Word would have been inaccurate! How wonderful are the promises of God!

By the way that he came, by the same shall he return, and shall not come into this city, saith the LORD [Isa. 37:34].

This is specific and was also literally fulfilled.

## GOD DESTROYS THE ASSYRIAN ARMY

Then the angel of the LORD went forth, and smote in the camp of the Assyrians a hundred and fourscore and five thousand: and when they arose early in the morning, behold, they were all dead corpses [Isa. 37:36].

In the morning the men who were stationed on the walls of Jerusalem saw an amazing sight! The enemies they so feared were now lifeless corpses.

So Sennacherib king of Assyria departed, and went and returned, and dwelt at Nineveh [Isa. 37:37].

Now let's see what happened to the king of Assyria.

And it came to pass, as he was worshipping in the house of Nisroch his god, that Adrammelech and Sharezer his sons smote him with the sword; and they escaped into the land of Armenia: and Esarhaddon his son reigned in his stead [Isa. 37:38].

Secular history confirms the fact that Sennacherib was murdered by his sons. It was about this time that the great kingdom of Assyria began to disintegrate and eventually was taken over by Babylon. God has already let Isaiah know that He was preparing a kingdom down on the banks of the Euphrates River, which would be the one to take the southern kingdom into captivity. God knew that though He delivered His people by this tremendous miracle in the days of Hezekiah, soon the day would return when He again would say, "Ah sinful nation, a people laden with iniquity, a seed of evildoers, children

that are corrupters: they have forsaken the LORD, they have provoked the Holy One of Israel unto anger, they are gone away backward" (Isa. 1:4).

# CHAPTER 38

**THEME:** *Prayer of Hezekiah when told he is to die; promise of healing—miracle of the sundial; Hezekiah's poem of praise*

This chapter deals with King Hezekiah's illness, prayer, and healing. It is well to keep in mind that while Hezekiah was beset by the danger of the Assyrian host, he was plagued by a "boil." His deliverance from death must have been prior to the destruction of the Assyrian host. It was while the siege was going on, and the answer to prayer must have encouraged his heart relative to Isaiah's prediction of the coming deliverance of Jerusalem. Hezekiah reigned twenty-nine years. He reigned fifteen years after this event; so his sickness was in the fourteenth year of his reign, and we are told that Sennacherib came up against Jerusalem in the fourteenth year of Hezekiah's reign (see Isa. 36:1). All of this happened in the same year—the sickness of Hezekiah and the siege of Jerusalem by the Assyrians.

## PRAYER OF HEZEKIAH WHEN TOLD HE IS TO DIE

**In those days was Hezekiah sick unto death. And Isaiah the prophet the son of Amoz came unto him, and said unto him, Thus saith the LORD, Set thine house in order: for thou shalt die, and not live [Isa. 38:1].**

It is interesting the way this chapter opens. We have seen that "in that day" is a technical expression that speaks of the Tribulation and millennial days. This verse does not open by saying, "In that day," but by saying, "In those days." What "days" is Isaiah talking about? He is talking about those days in which he and Hezekiah lived. Hezekiah was sick unto death. He was having trouble with a "boil" that was just about to kill him. On top of that he was having trouble with the Assyrians. There are those who believe that Hezekiah's "boil" was either cancer or leprosy, or something similar. Whatever it was, it was a terminal disease, and his time to die had come.

The sentence of death was delivered to Hezekiah by Isaiah. It is true that this sentence of death rests upon each one of us, although we do not know the day nor the hour. But we do know this: ". . . it is appointed unto men once to die, but after this the judgment" (Heb. 9:27). This is a divine date. If each one of us knew the exact time, our life-style would change.

Some years ago I received a letter from a fine young minister who had been told by his doctor that he had cancer and that his days were limited. He sent out a letter to some of his friends, and I was privileged to be included in that list. Here is a brief quotation from his letter so that you might know the thinking of a man under the shadow of death: "One thing I have discovered in the last few days. When a Christian is suddenly confronted with a sentence of death, he surely begins to give a proper evaluation of material things. My fishing gear and books and orchard are not nearly so valuable as they were a week ago." I conducted this young preacher's funeral. And many years later I had the experience of having cancer myself. My doctor told me he thought I had only about three months to live. I can bear witness to the accuracy of the young preacher's statement. It was amazing how certain things suddenly became very unimportant. One of those things was my home. I thought I would not be living in it but a few more weeks, and it certainly became unimportant to me; but where I was *going* became very important. Well, God had other plans for me, for which I am indeed grateful. I thank and praise Him for each new day He gives to me.

When Hezekiah was confronted with death, what did he do?

**Then Hezekiah turned his face toward the wall, and prayed unto the LORD [Isa. 38:2].**

We have seen Hezekiah in prayer before when he spread Sennacherib's letter before the Lord.

And said, Remember now, O LORD, I beseech thee, how I have walked before thee in truth and with a perfect heart, and have done that which is good in thy sight. And Hezekiah wept sore [Isa. 38:3].

This is a time when a man can weep. I wept when I was told I was going to die. I am sure the young preacher wept when he heard the news from his doctor. You are bound to weep at a time like that. But Hezekiah also prayed on the basis of his life. This man had a good reputation before God, and under the Mosaic Law this was the accurate thing to do. Second Kings 18:5 says concerning Hezekiah: "He trusted in the LORD God of Israel; so that after him was none like him among all the kings of Judah, nor any that were before him." Hezekiah was an outstanding man. He was not boasting when he made that claim.

## PROMISE OF HEALING—
## MIRACLE OF THE SUNDIAL

Then came the word of the LORD to Isaiah, saying,

Go, and say to Hezekiah, Thus saith the LORD, the God of David thy father, I have heard thy prayer, I have seen thy tears: behold, I will add unto thy days fifteen years [Isa. 38:4-5].

God did hear and answer his prayer and extended his life by fifteen years. He did it, not for Hezekiah's sake, but for David's sake.

That is not the basis upon which our prayers are heard today. Our prayers are heard for the sake of David's greater Son, the Lord Jesus Christ. In John 16:23–24 the Lord says, "And in that day ye shall ask me nothing. Verily, verily, I say unto you, Whatsoever ye shall ask the Father in *my* name, he will give it you. Hitherto have ye asked nothing in my name: ask, and ye shall receive, that your joy may be full" (italics mine). You and I can go to our Heavenly Father with our requests in the name of Christ. To pray in the *name* of Christ means that you are *in* Christ, and you are praying for *His* will to be done. It means that it is to please Him. Sometimes He will heal and sometimes He won't. He is the One to decide.

And I will deliver thee and this city out of the hand of the king of Assyria: and I will defend this city [Isa. 38:6].

God ties in His deliverance of Jerusalem from the Assyrian with the deliverance of Hezekiah from death. God's answer to one request will encourage the believer's heart that He will answer the other requests. To be honest with you, I have been greatly strengthened in my own faith since God heard and answered the prayers of a host of radio listeners concerning my health.

And this shall be a sign unto thee from the LORD, that the LORD will do this thing that he hath spoken;

Behold, I will bring again the shadow of the degrees, which is gone down in the sun dial of Ahaz, ten degrees backward. So the sun returned ten degrees, by which degrees it was gone down [Isa. 38:7-8].

God gave him a sign, which was an assurance that He would answer his prayer.

F. C. Jennings (*Studies in Isaiah*, p. 438) translates the verse like this: "Behold, I will cause the shadow of the steps to return, which is gone down on the steps of Ahaz with the sun, backward ten steps. And the sun returned ten steps by the steps which it had gone down." You see, the translation of "degrees" can also be "steps." Dr. Jennings comments: "We can now transport ourselves in spirit to Hezekiah's palace, and into his chamber. There lies the king, still prone on his couch, but with his face no longer turned to the wall, but joy and hope brightening his eye as he looks out of the window to the gardens, in the midst of which, and in full view, stands an obelisk, or column, with a series of steps leading up to it, and at least ten of these are lying in the column's shadow; for the sun has gone so far down as to throw the shadow over that number of steps. But look again, the once darkened steps are now in clearest sunlight— 'tis the sign for which the king had asked!"

## HEZEKIAH'S POEM OF PRAISE

The writing of Hezekiah king of Judah, when he had been sick, and was recovered of his sickness [Isa. 38:9].

The verses following are a fine thesis on death by one who was very near to it. Many believe that Hezekiah composed Psalm 116 at this time.

Now the question arises: Was Hezekiah right in asking God to extend his life?

The LORD was ready to save me: therefore we will sing my songs to the

**stringed instruments all the days of our life in the house of the LORD [Isa. 38:20].**

At this time there was a great welling up of praise in the heart of Hezekiah. His song of praise to God was evidently set to music and sung.

However, after this experience Hezekiah became rather proud and arrogant. In the Book of Chronicles, which is God's viewpoint of history, we are told: "But Hezekiah rendered not again according to the benefit done unto him; for his heart was lifted up: therefore there was wrath upon him, and upon Judah and Jerusalem" (2 Chron. 32:25). Here is evidence to the fact that maybe he should not have asked for an extension of life because it led to pride in his life—*he* was raised up!

When I became ill, I remembered the story of Hezekiah. I went to the Lord and said, "If you will let me live, I will promise to do your will, and I will continue to get out your Word." That is the reason I have over-extended myself in conferences and meetings. I didn't want to let the Lord down. But He has made it pretty clear to me that I should not kill myself by overdoing, since He has extended my life. Now I am trying to be reasonable in what I do.

After experiencing a miracle like Hezekiah did, there is a danger of withdrawing from the Lord. You would think that it would draw one closer to Him, but instead there is a grave danger of getting away from Him.

Was he right in asking God to extend his life? Should he not have died when the time came? There is another consideration which leads me to believe that he should have died when he was so ill. Manasseh, his son, was twelve years old when he began to reign, which means that he was born after Hezekiah's sickness. Manasseh was the worst king who reigned in either kingdom. I consider Manasseh worse than Ahab and Jezebel put together. I think that it was during his reign that the Shekinah glory departed. If it didn't depart during his reign, I can't think of any reason it would depart afterward. Manasseh was very much like Antichrist, the Man of Sin who is yet to come.

In the next chapter we will see that Hezekiah played the fool after his experience in healing.

Now *how* did God perform the healing of Hezekiah? Did he have Isaiah pray over him? Or did Isaiah lay his hand on him so hard that he fell backward? No. Notice what Isaiah did—

**For Isaiah had said, Let them take a lump of figs, and lay it for a plaster upon the boil, and he shall recover [Isa. 38:21].**

In other words, he did the two things that James recommends: "Is any sick among you? let him call for the elders of the church; and let them pray over him, anointing him with oil in the name of the Lord" (James 5:14). This anointing is not religious nor ceremonial. The oil is for healing; it is medicinal. And the elders are to pray for the one who is sick. What God said through Isaiah and through James is the same. When you get sick, pray and call for the doctor. God expects us to be sensible.

# CHAPTER 39

### *THEME: Hezekiah and Babylon*

The transfer of the enemy of Judah from Assyria to Babylon is one of the outstanding features of this section. At this time Babylon was a struggling city on the banks of the Euphrates, unable to overcome Assyria. However, Babylon was to become the great head of gold in the times of the Gentiles, and that makes this chapter significant.

This chapter reveals the great blunder of Hezekiah's life and also his human frailty and weakness. It is after the hour of great spiritual triumph that our worst defeats come.

## HEZEKIAH RECEIVES THE BABYLONIAN EMBASSAGE

**At that time Merodach-baladan, the son of Baladan, king of Babylon, sent letters and a present to Hezekiah: for he had heard that he had been sick, and was recovered [Isa. 39:1].**

Merodach-baladan is a meaningless king to us, but his name is full of meaning. F. C. Jennings calls our attention to the fact that *Merodach* means "a rebel" and *baladan* means "not the Lord." Behind this king, of course, is Nimrod, the founder of Babylon, and Satan, who is the archrebel against God and is the "god of this world."

These ambassadors brought a letter which flattered Hezekiah. They said, "The king of Babylon has been concerned about you. He heard that you were sick and have recovered; so he sends a gift to rejoice with you."

**And Hezekiah was glad of them, and shewed them the house of his precious things, the silver, and the gold, and the spices, and the precious ointment, and all the house of his armour, and all that was found in his treasures: there was nothing in his house, nor in all his dominion, that Hezekiah shewed them not [Isa. 39:2].**

At this time Hezekiah had not lost very many of the riches that David and Solomon had gathered. He made the mistake of showing his silver and gold, for he was immensely wealthy. We are told in 2 Chronicles 32:27-28, "And Hezekiah had exceeding much riches and honour: and he made himself treasuries for silver, and for gold, and for precious stones, and for spices, and for shields, and for all manner of pleasant jewels; Storehouses also for the increase of corn, and wine, and oil; and stalls for all manner of beasts, and cotes for flocks."

It is interesting how Hezekiah received the embassage from Babylon. They gave him a gift and a get-well card from the king. Instead of taking the letter and opening it before the Lord like he did the letter from the Assyrians, he just put it aside. They had flattered him, and so he gave the visitors the VIP treatment. He took them on a tour of the grounds of Jerusalem. Solomon had cornered the world's gold market, and also he had cornered the market on quite a few other things. All of it was stored away in Jerusalem. Hezekiah foolishly showed this great wealth to his visitors, who went back to their king and told him that when he was strong enough, they knew where he could get all of the gold, silver, and jewels that he would need to carry on warfare.

Hezekiah made a big mistake, and Isaiah heard about what he had done.

**Then came Isaiah the prophet unto king Hezekiah, and said unto him, What said these men? and from whence came they unto thee? And Hezekiah said, They are come from a far country unto me, even from Babylon [Isa. 39:3].**

Hezekiah thought it was wonderful, but Isaiah recognized the danger.

**Then said he, What have they seen in thine house? And Hezekiah answered, All that is in mine house have they seen: there is nothing among my treasures that I have not shewed them [Isa. 39:4].**

It was a very foolish thing that Hezekiah had done.

**Then said Isaiah to Hezekiah, Hear the word of the LORD of hosts:**

**Behold, the days come, that all that is in thine house, and that which thy fathers have laid up in store until this day, shall be carried to Babylon: nothing shall be left, saith the LORD.**

**And of thy sons that shall issue from thee, which thou shalt beget, shall they take away; and they shall be eunuchs in the palace of the king of Babylon [Isa. 39:5-7].**

Hezekiah played the fool. He should never have shown his treasures to strangers. Isaiah's prophecy was literally fulfilled (see 2 Kings 24-25; Dan. 1).

**Then said Hezekiah to Isaiah, Good is the word of the LORD which thou hast spoken. He said moreover, For there shall be peace and truth in my days [Isa. 39:8].**

Hezekiah's reply to Isaiah is very strange. He said in effect, "I am glad this prophecy won't take place in my day." He was grateful that these things would not come to pass in his days, but what about his children and grandchildren and great grandchildren? It did take place in their day.

Hezekiah's life was extended for fifteen years. Was it good? It was not good. He lived to play the fool. Three terrible things took place during those years.

This chapter concludes the historic section.

# CHAPTER 40

*THEME: Comfort, a message from God; creation, a revelation of God; consideration, a call from God*

Chapter 40 brings us to the final major division of the Book of Isaiah. There is a sharp contrast between the first and last sections of this book. The first section was a revelation of the *Sovereign* upon the throne, while this final section is a revelation of the *Savior* in the place of suffering. In chapter 6 we saw the *crown*; in chapter 53 we shall see the *cross*. The theme in the first section was the *government* of God; in this section it is the *grace* of God.

The opening words, "Comfort ye," set the mood and tempo for this final section. The message from God is comfort rather than judgment which we saw in the first section.

The change of subject matter has led the liberal critic to postulate the Deutero-Isaiah hypothesis. Because the subjects are entirely different, they suppose that they were written by different writers—two Isaiahs. Well, a change of message certainly does not necessitate a change of authorship. The message has changed but not the messenger. Many authors write on subjects that are entirely different. For example, I have a booklet on Psalm 2, which is God's judgment, and one on Psalm 22, which is God's salvation—two entirely different subjects, but written by the same individual.

In this section of Isaiah the thunders and lightnings of Sinai are subdued, smothered by the wonderful message of grace which comes from God.

## COMFORT, A MESSAGE FROM GOD

**Comfort ye, comfort ye my people, saith your God [Isa. 40:1].**

All of the "woes" and the "burdens" of the first section have been lifted because there is now a burden-bearer, One who later on will fulfill everything that Isaiah said about Him. He will be the One to give the invitation, "Come unto me, all ye that labour and are heavy laden, and I will give you rest." (Matt. 11:28). The Lord Jesus Christ lifts burdens.

"Comfort ye, comfort ye" is a sign of yearning from the pulsating heart of God. Our God is the God of "all comfort." That is the way Paul speaks of Him in 2 Corinthians 1:3–4: "Blessed be God, even the Father of our Lord Jesus Christ, the Father of mercies, and the God of all comfort; Who comforteth us in all

our tribulation, that we may be able to comfort them which are in any trouble, by the comfort wherewith we ourselves are comforted of God." The Holy Spirit is called "the Comforter." The Lord Jesus said, "And I will pray the Father, and he shall give you another Comforter, that he may abide with you for ever" (John 14:16). He is today *our* Comforter.

**Speak ye comfortably to Jerusalem, and cry unto her, that her warfare is accomplished, that her iniquity is pardoned: for she hath received of the LORD'S hand double for all her sins [Isa. 40:2].**

It has been suggested that when there was an indebtedness or mortgage on a house in Israel, the fact was written on a paper, a legal document, and put on the doorpost so that all their neighbors and friends would know that they had a mortgage on their place. Another copy was kept by the one who held the mortgage. When the debt was paid, the second copy, the carbon copy, was nailed over the other doorpost so that all might see that the debt was paid. This is the meaning of "she hath received of the LORD'S hand double for all her sins." The sins of Jerusalem were paid for by the One who suffered outside her gates. This is the difference between the dealings of God with His people in the Old Testament and with us in our day. It actually separates Christianity from all pagan religions and from the Mosaic Law. The difference is all wrapped up in that little word *propitiation*. In the heathen religions the people bring an offering to their gods to appease them, and that is what *propitiation* means. Many people think that that is what it means in the Bible, that they have to "do" something—because God is angry—to win Him over. The people in heathen religions are always doing that because their gods are always angry and difficult to get along with. Their feelings are easily hurt, and they are not very friendly. The fact is that sin, man's sin, has alienated him from God, but it is *God* who did something. And today God is propitious. You don't have to do anything to win Him over. *Propitiation* is toward God, and *reconciliation* is toward us. God has done everything that needs to be done. Today *we* are asked to be reconciled to God, not to do

something to win Him over. God is already won over; that is what Jesus Christ did for us on the cross. We need only accept what Christ has done. This is the word of comfort for a lost world today.

**The voice of him that crieth in the wilderness, Prepare ye the way of the LORD, make straight in the desert a highway for our God [Isa. 40:3].**

All four writers of the gospel records—Matthew, Mark, Luke, and John—quote this verse as applying to John the Baptist. Since it appears four times in the New Testament, I'm not going to argue about it. I say that it refers to John the Baptist.

**Every valley shall be exalted, and every mountain and hill shall be made low: and the crooked shall be made straight, and the rough places plain:**

**And the glory of the LORD shall be revealed, and all flesh shall see it together: for the mouth of the LORD hath spoken it.**

**The voice said, Cry. And he said, What shall I cry? All flesh is grass, and all the goodliness thereof is as the flower of the field [Isa. 40:4–6].**

Luke quotes this as applying to John the Baptist.

**The grass withereth, the flower fadeth: because the spirit of the LORD bloweth upon it: surely the people is grass.**

**The grass withereth, the flower fadeth: but the word of our God shall stand for ever [Isa. 40:7–8].**

Man is compared to the grass of the field. The question is, How can there be comfort in being reminded that we are like grass? Hence in California grass is beautiful after the spring rain; but not many weeks later, after the sun has beat upon it for a few days, it begins to wither and die. Man is just like that.

You say, "Well there is no comfort in that!" Yes, there is. Man is faint, frail, and feeble, but the Word of God is strong, sure, and secure. God's Word is our hiding place, a foundation upon which we can rest; it is our sword and buckler, high tower, protection, security, and salvation. In 1 Peter 1:23–25 we read, "Being born again, not of corruptible seed, but of incorruptible, by the word of God, which liveth and abideth for ever. For all flesh is as grass, and all the glory of man as the

flower of grass. The grass withereth, and the flower thereof falleth away: But the word of the Lord endureth for ever. And this is the word which by the gospel is preached unto you." It is only the gospel that gives eternal life to man who naturally is just a transitory creature on this earth.

Now note the wonderful message—

**O Zion, that bringest good tidings, get thee up into the high mountain; O Jerusalem, that bringest good tidings, lift up thy voice with strength; lift it up, be not afraid; say unto the cities of Judah, Behold your God! [Isa. 40:9].**

"Good tidings" is the gospel, and the "good tidings" of John the Baptist was "Behold your God!" Until you have seen Jesus Christ as God manifest in the flesh, you haven't really seen Him. You must come to Him as He is—not just as a Man, but as God, Immanuel, God with us. If He is just a human, He cannot be my Savior; but He is *Immanuel*, and He is my Savior. How wonderful this is!

**Behold the Lord GOD will come with strong hand, and his arm shall rule for him: behold, his reward is with him, and his work before him [Isa. 40:10].**

Now Isaiah, as he generally does, draws together the first and second comings of Christ. This verse looks forward to His second coming. Actually, the gospel includes both the first and second comings of Christ. We are apt to get sidetracked and put all the emphasis on Jesus' first coming or on His second coming. Well, let's put our emphasis on both Comings, which is the totality of the gospel.

**He shall feed his flock like a shepherd: he shall gather the lambs with his arm, and carry them in his bosom, and shall gently lead those that are with young [Isa. 40:11].**

The Lord Jesus took the title of Shepherd when He came the first time. "I am the good shepherd: the good shepherd giveth his life for the sheep" (John 10:11). He also said, ". . . I lay down my life for the sheep" (John 10:15).

## CREATION, A REVELATION OF GOD

The next verse introduces the section that speaks of the greatness of God as Creator.

**Who hath measured the waters in the hollow of his hand, and meted out heaven with the span, and comprehended the dust of the earth in a**

measure, and weighed the mountains in scales, and the hills in a balance? [Isa. 40:12].

Who has done that? To begin with, when you get out into space, you don't weigh anything; so who is doing the weighing today, and where is it going to be weighed? This verse makes me feel like singing "How Great Thou Art"!

**Who hath directed the spirit of the LORD, or being his counsellor hath taught him?**

**With whom took he counsel, and who instructed him, and taught him in the path of judgment, and taught him knowledge, and shewed to him the way of understanding? [Isa. 40:13–14].**

God knows no equal nor is there anyone to whom He can go for advice. Someone has asked the rather facetious question, "What is it that you have seen that God has never seen?" The answer is very simple. God has never seen His equal. I see mine every day.

**To whom then will ye liken God? or what likeness will ye compare unto him? [Isa. 40:18].**

You and I know very little. All we know is what He has revealed in the Word of God, and I don't think He has told us everything. To begin with, we can't even comprehend what He *has* told us.

Isaiah is contrasting God to idols. "To whom then will ye liken God? or what likeness will ye compare unto him?" Look around you at the pictures of Him. Personally, I don't care for any picture of Jesus because they are *not* pictures of Jesus. I don't become very popular when I say this. Stores that sell such pictures and people who are rather sentimental think I am terrible. But, my friend, we don't need pictures of Him. I agree with the old Scottish philosopher who said years ago, "Men never thought of painting a picture of Jesus until they had lost His presence in their hearts."

Now here is the first rather ironical attack that Isaiah will make against idolatry—

**The workman melteth a graven image, and the goldsmith spreadeth it over with gold, and casteth silver chains [Isa. 40:19].**

The rich make a very ornate idol. They have a rich god.

**He that is so impoverished that he hath no oblation chooseth a tree that will not rot; he seeketh unto him a cunning workman to prepare a graven image, that shall not be moved [Isa. 40:20].**

The poor can have only a crude idol; he whittles out a god from a piece of wood. How preposterous idolatry is!

**Have ye not known? have ye not heard? hath it not been told you from the beginning? have ye not understood from the foundations of the earth? [Isa. 40:21].**

It is utterly ridiculous to compare God to some dumb idol.

**It is he that sitteth upon the circle of the earth, and the inhabitants thereof are as grasshoppers; that stretcheth out the heavens as a curtain, and spreadeth them out as a tent to dwell in [Isa. 40:22].**

The Old Testament does not teach that the earth is flat; but scientists in the days of Columbus taught this theory. Those so-called scientists did not pay attention to the Word of God in that day, and they missed something. And I think scientists are missing something today. It is clearly stated in this verse that the earth is a sphere, a circle positioned in an even greater universe, and that God's throne is far beyond the penetration of the most powerful telescopes as they search out the limitless vault of space.

## CONSIDERATION, A CALL FROM GOD

In the light of all of this, God calls us to consider.

**Why sayest thou, O Jacob, and speakest, O Israel, My way is hid from the LORD, and my judgment is passed over from my God? [Isa. 40:27].**

God *knows* about the difficulties and problems of His people. If you belong to Him, He is able to quiet the storms of life, but sometimes there are lessons for His own to learn in the storm. When you find yourself in the midst of a storm, instead of sitting and weeping and criticizing God, why don't you look around and find out what lesson He wants you to learn? God will not let you go through trials unless He has something for you to learn.

The lesson may be this:

**Hast thou not known? hast thou not heard, that the everlasting God, the LORD, the Creator of the ends of the**

earth, **fainteth not, neither is weary?
there is no searching of his understanding** [Isa. 40:28].

We have a great God. He never gets tired. He
is not like man.

**Even the youths shall faint and be
weary, and the young men shall utterly
fall:**

**But they that wait upon the LORD shall
renew their strength; they shall mount
up with wings as eagles; they shall run,
and not be weary; and they shall walk,
and not faint** [Isa. 40:30–31].

There are three degrees of power here, and
several expositors have likened them to the
three stages of Christian growth that you
have in 1 John 2:12–14. These three stages of
growth are: (1) the young Christian shall
mount up as an eagle; (2) the adult Christian

shall run; and (3) the mature Christian shall
walk.

This reminds me of the black preacher down
in my southland who preached a very wonderful sermon, in which he said, "Brethren, this
church, it needs to walk." And one of the
deacons said, "Amen." He continued, "Brethren, this church needs to run." And the
deacon said, "Hallelujah." Then he said,
"Brethren, this church needs to fly." And this
deacon said, "Amen and hallelujah." Then the
minister said, "Well, it's going to cost money
to make this church fly." To this the deacon
replied, "Let her walk, brother, let her walk."

My friend, regardless of who you are, if you
are going to move with God through this
earth, it will cost you something. But God will
furnish you strength whatever your condition.
If you need strength to walk, He will give it to
you. If you need strength to fly, He has that
for you also. This is a wonderful chapter
revealing the comfort of God as our Creator,
as our Savior, and as our Sustainer.

# CHAPTER 41

**THEME:** *God overrules individuals; God overtures Israel to
trust Him; God overturns idols*

This chapter continues the thought of chapter 40 in setting forth the greatness of
God. The emphasis here is not upon God as
Creator so much as upon His *dealings* with
man. The greatness of God is revealed in both
creation and human history.

There are also some things in this chapter
that are rather enigmatic. It seems that there
is a bare profile of prophecy in the background, but the theme is that God will protect
and lead His children through the world which
is fraught with pitfalls and dangers. Therefore, comfort is here for the child of God.

## GOD OVERRULES INDIVIDUALS

**Keep silence before me, O islands; and
let the people renew their strength: let
them come near; then let them speak:
let us come near together to judgment**
[Isa. 41:1].

The whole world of individuals is moving
toward judgment.
The showdown is coming between light and

darkness, between God and mammon, between faith and unbelief. God is now calling
upon individuals to turn to Him and accept the
salvation He has to offer. God is propitious.
He is not demanding anything of you. He is
simply asking you to accept the grace and
salvation that He has to offer.

**Who raised up the righteous man from
the east, called him to his foot, gave the
nations before him, and made him rule
over kings? he gave them as the dust to
his sword, and as driven stubble to his
bow** [Isa. 41:2].

"Righteous man from the east" is a strong
expression. There are those who feel that this
is a veiled suggestion of Cyrus. Cyrus will be
mentioned by name shortly, but this is not the
place. I believe that the word actually refers
to a quality—*righteousness*—rather than to a
person. It could be a reference to the rule of
righteousness which Christ will establish at
His return to earth. We find this thought developed in this section.

They helped every one his neighbour; and every one said to his brother, Be of good courage [Isa. 41:6].

Since God is coming to right the wrongs and relieve injustices, individuals who are right with God can be of good courage. There is hope for the little man who trusts God. He doesn't have to worry about the future.

## GOD OVERTURES ISRAEL TO TRUST HIM

Here again we have a reference to idolatry.

So the carpenter encouraged the goldsmith, and he that smootheth with the hammer him that smote the anvil, saying, It is ready for the soldering: and he fastened it with nails, that it should not be moved [Isa. 41:7].

In an emergency some folk hammered themselves out a god, that is, a temporary idol. But now God says:

But thou, Israel, art my servant, Jacob whom I have chosen, the seed of Abraham my friend [Isa. 41:8].

God now turns to Israel to comfort them in their distress. God says, "Instead of hammering out an idol, why not turn to Me?" After all, He knows they are sinners. He still calls them Jacob, and Jacob was the crooked one. It is *God* who made him Israel, a prince with God. And God wants to do that for the *sons* of Jacob.

Abraham is called the "friend" of God, and God wants to bring these people into a right relationship with Himself.

Fear thou not; for I am with thee: be not dismayed; for I am thy God: I will strengthen thee; yea, I will help thee; yea, I will uphold thee with the right hand of my righteousness [Isa. 41:10].

This verse has been a real pillar of strength and a source of comfort to God's children of every age.

As he moves on, he says that if they oppose God it will be the very height of folly, because they are moving toward the day when all these adjustments will have to be made.

Now note this remarkable verse:

For I the LORD thy God will hold thy right hand, saying unto thee, Fear not; I will help thee [Isa. 41:13].

Here is God's gracious overture to trust Him—what comfort! God wants to take us into His confidence. He wants to enable us to walk with Him, have fellowship with Him, and know Him. My, what mankind is missing today! Some people can even get so involved in *church* work that they miss all this.

Fear not, thou worm Jacob, and ye men of Israel; I will help thee, saith the LORD, and thy redeemer, the Holy One of Israel [Isa. 41:14].

You may think you are something, but you are a "worm"—a nobody. It is only God who can make any of us important. Only God can make man a somebody. Little man frets and struts across the stage of life, as Shakespeare put it. He huffs and puffs like the old wolf around the little pigs' houses. Where is man going, and exactly what is he getting out of what he is doing? Some people see the futility of it all and take their own lives. Where else can they turn? The only place man can turn is to God. Oh, what man is missing! God's fellowship, His salvation, His goodness, His grace—all of these are yours if you but turn to Him.

Then He talks to them about the material blessings of the Millennium—they will be there. And God would like to talk to you and me about the spiritual blessings which are available to us now and those we will have in eternity.

## GOD OVERTURNS IDOLS

Produce your cause, saith the LORD; bring forth your strong reasons, saith the King of Jacob [Isa. 41:21].

This is a challenge to idolatry. Now who is an idolater? Have you ever considered the possibility that *you* may be? Anything you put between your soul and God is your idol—regardless of what it is. It is anything to which you are giving your time and your energy; it could actually be your religion. Anything that you allow to take the place of a personal relationship with God is your idol.

What can idols do? Can they explain the origin of the universe? Are you satisfied today with the explanations that evolution has given? Of course there have been several explanations, but God says, "Bring them all out."

Let them bring them forth, and shew us what shall happen: let them shew the former things, what they be, that we may consider them, and know the latter

**end of them; or declare us things for to come [Isa. 41:22].**

Man doesn't know his beginning or the origin of the universe. He simply doesn't *know*—I don't care what theory he is following. I predict that the evolutionist will be embarrassed in the next fifty years or so, because evolution will be just one of the many theories which will be left along the highway of time with the other wreckage. There have been many explanations of the origin of the universe which were called scientific at one time but are exploded today. Evolution will be exploded in time. Then man will turn to another theory. Man doesn't know his origin, and he doesn't know the future. Man is a very ignorant creature. Have you ever stopped to think how little you know?

There are many Ph.D.'s who don't know very much either. I heard of a man working on his Ph.D. degree who was studying the eye of the mosquito. Now there is an unusual subject! One day as he was doing his research, it suddenly occurred to him that he did not want to spend the rest of his life looking a mosquito in the eye. And I can understand that—I wouldn't mind taking one or two looks, but after that I think it would become monotonous! This man came to the conclusion that he should do something else. He found the Lord Jesus Christ as his Savior, was granted his degree, and he decided to dedicate his life to something worthwhile. Today he is a minister of the gospel.

It is quite interesting that man can be very well-educated, even have his doctor's degree, and still know very little. He knows nothing about his origin or where he is going, and no idol can give him that information. So it is well to turn to the One who does have the answers. This doesn't mean He will *give* you all the answers, but it is nice to know *Him* who knows the answers. I have never learned much about science, but I did learn a motto that was posted in the science building of the college I attended, which read: "Next to knowing is knowing where to find out." Now there are many things I don't know, but I know the One who knows everything. If there is something I *need* to know, God will tell me.

**Behold, ye are of nothing, and your work of nought: an abomination is he that chooseth you [Isa. 41:24].**

Man cannot explain his past, and he does not know his future apart from God. That makes all of man's effort apart from God a very vain thing, an empty thing. During my first pastorate a man came to me and said, "If you can't give me a good reason for living, I am going to solve all of my problems by taking my life." What do you do with a man like that? He had an old rusty .45; it was a big old gun. I said to him, "Now look, if you can show me you can solve your problems by taking your life, I will get you a better gun than the one you have so you can do it right. Candidly, if you are not going to turn to Christ—if you are not going to bring Him into your life—you might as well use your gun. I see no reason why you shouldn't." Well, he was really taken aback. He expected me to give him arguments on reasons for living. That fellow put down his gun and left. Although he didn't turn to Christ at that time, he did later on. And he found that Christ had the answer to his problems.

**Behold, they are all vanity; their works are nothing: their molten images are wind and confusion [Isa. 41:29].**

"Confusion" is the end result of idolatry or any philosophy which is anti-God or atheistic. It does not have the answers to the problems of life. These man-made systems cannot satisfy the human heart. The answer is found in the One who brings good tidings of great joy.

# CHAPTER 42

**THEME:** *The Servant of Jehovah—Jesus; the scourge of idola-*
*try—images; the servant of Jehovah—the nation*

In each chapter Isaiah is gradually working up to his condemnation of idolatry.

We find in this chapter that the nation Israel is called the servant of Jehovah. Also, the Lord Jesus Christ is the Servant of Jehovah and is so called in the Gospel of Mark. He made it very clear: "For even the Son of man came not to be ministered unto, but to minister, and to give his life a ransom for many" (Mark 10:45). And in Matthew 12:17–21 there is an application of this prophecy to the Lord Jesus.

## THE SERVANT OF JEHOVAH, JESUS

**Behold my servant, whom I uphold; mine elect, in whom my soul delighteth; I have put my spirit upon him: he shall bring forth judgment to the Gentiles [Isa. 42:1].**

"**B**ehold" is a word that is a bugle call to consider the Lord Jesus Christ.

**A bruised reed shall he not break, and the smoking flax shall he not quench: he shall bring forth judgment unto truth [Isa. 42:3].**

This verse characterizes the life and ministry of the Lord Jesus when He was here. "A bruised reed shall he not break." The Lord didn't move in with a club against sin. He simply let sin bring its own judgment. "The smoking flax shall he not quench"—the man who keeps on in sin will find that it will break out in flames finally. The wages of sin is death; it always is that. You can't change it.

This is a marvelous section as it presents the Lord Jesus as God's Servant.

**I the LORD have called thee in righteousness, and will hold thine hand, and will keep thee, and give thee for a covenant of the people, for a light of the Gentiles;**

**To open the blind eyes, to bring out the prisoners from the prison, and them that sit in darkness out of the prison house [Isa. 42:6–7].**

Christ performed these miracles as credentials of His Kingship when He was here the first time. He came as the Light of the world. As old Simeon prophesied, "A light to lighten the Gentiles, and the glory of thy people Israel" (Luke 2:32).

## THE SCOURGE OF IDOLATRY—IMAGES

Now Isaiah begins God's polemic against idolatry.

**I am the LORD: that is my name: and my glory will I not give to another, neither my praise to graven images [Isa. 42:8].**

God will not share His glory with another.

Now he talks about the scourge of idolatry, and the judgment of God which it will bring.

**I will make waste mountains and hills, and dry up all their herbs; and I will make the rivers islands, and I will dry up the pools [Isa. 42:15].**

The physical earth will be affected by His judgment.

**And I will bring the blind by a way that they knew not; I will lead them in paths that they have not known: I will make darkness light before them, and crooked things straight. These things will I do unto them, and not forsake them [Isa. 42:16].**

This is the way God leads His own. You and I are blind to the future, but He is not, and He will lead all who put their trust in Him.

**They shall be turned back, they shall be greatly ashamed, that trust in graven images, that say to the molten images, Ye are our gods [Isa. 42:17].**

The idolaters, you see, are warned that judgment is coming.

## THE SERVANT OF JEHOVAH, THE NATION

**Who is blind, but my servant? or deaf, as my messenger that I sent? who is blind as he that is perfect, and blind as the LORD'S servant? [Isa. 42:19].**

He identifies the blind servant here as His own people Israel.

This is God's condemnation of His own people—

**But this is a people robbed and spoiled; they are all of them snared in holes,**

and they are hid in prison houses: they are for a prey, and none delivereth; for a spoil, and none saith, Restore [Isa. 42:22].

The nation Israel is the subject in this verse. They are "a people robbed and spoiled." Why? Because they turned away from God, and they have turned to idols.

Who gave Jacob for a spoil, and Israel to the robbers? did not the LORD, he against whom we have sinned? for they would not walk in his ways, neither were they obedient unto his law [Isa. 42:24].

The people and nation are identified as Israel. God scattered them—but He will also regather them.

Therefore he hath poured upon him the fury of his anger, and the strength of battle: and it hath set him on fire round about, yet he knew not; and it burned him, yet he laid it not to heart [Isa. 42:25].

The chastening of the Lord did not cause the nation to repent and return to Him. Did this thwart the purposes of God? The answer, of course is *no*, as we will see in the following chapter.

# CHAPTER 43–44

**THEME:** *Retrospect—creation, redemption, preservation of Israel; Prospect—future judgment, deliverance, redemption of Israel; promise of the Spirit; polemic against idolatry; prophecy concerning Cyrus*

This section of Scripture, and particularly this chapter, reveals that God is not through with the nation Israel. It is tantamount to unbelief to deny that God has a future purpose for the nation of Israel. In the New Testament Paul asks the question, ". . . Hath God cast away His people?" And the answer is, "God forbid . . ." (Rom. 11:1). That is a very dogmatic answer. God is not through with these folk, as He makes clear in the chapter before us.

## RETROSPECT—CREATION, REDEMPTION, PRESERVATION OF ISRAEL

But now thus saith the LORD that created thee, O Jacob, and he that formed thee, O Israel, Fear not: for I have redeemed thee, I have called thee by thy name; thou art mine [Isa. 43:1].

This statement is as clear-cut as could be made. God addresses the nation *Israel* in this entire section, and I do not think you could misunderstand Him unless you deliberately wanted to misunderstand.

He speaks of their origin: "the LORD that *created* thee." God took a sad specimen like old Jacob, whose name means "crooked"—he was a supplanter—and made a nation out of him.

God took the dust of the ground, breathed into it the spirit of life, and it became a living human being. And that human being rebelled, but now God makes sons of God out of those who will trust Christ. That is *my* beginning, and it was a very bad beginning. I don't accept the evolutionary theory that I evolved from a monkey; I came from something worse than a monkey! I came from a rebellious sinner who on the physical side had been taken from the ground. That first man passed on to me a fallen nature which will never be reformed or repaired. But God has given me a new nature.

Beginning with Jacob, God created a nation. Then He *redeemed* them by blood and power from Egypt, and they became Israel, a prince with God. They belong to God because of creation and because of redemption.

When thou passest through the waters, I will be with thee; and through the rivers, they shall not overflow thee: when thou walkest through the fire, thou shalt not be burned; neither shall the flame kindle upon thee [Isa. 43:2].

This is a promise which specifically applies to Israel and the manner in which God delivered them in the past, for example, when they crossed the Red Sea and the Jordan River.

It also has a marvelous spiritual application for all of God's children in all times. "When

thou passest through the waters, I will be with thee." Sometimes in my experience I get into what I could call "deep water" when I can't touch bottom. But I have the assurance that God is going through the experience with me. I think I'm going to drown, but He has promised, "they shall not overflow thee," and He intervenes and delivers me.

**For I am the LORD thy God, the Holy One of Israel, thy Saviour: I gave Egypt for thy ransom, Ethiopia and Seba for thee [Isa. 43:3].**

He does not lower His high standard in salvation. How could God give Egypt and Ethiopia a ransom for Israel? The answer is simple. God says in effect, "I used these nations to discipline you. I *gave* them, that is, I *permitted* them to treat you as they did, and now I will judge them."

In Proverbs 21:18 we read, "The wicked shall be a ransom for the righteous, and the transgressor for the upright." Have you ever wondered why God permitted the enemy to cross your path and cause you all the trouble he did? He did it in order to bring you into line and in order to develop you spiritually. God gave him for your deliverance. Proverbs 11:8 says, "The righteous is delivered out of trouble, and the wicked cometh in his stead." God has let several people really mistreat me, and I talked to Him about it. I thought God was treating me wrong, but I noticed that the Lord paddled these individuals, and I must confess that I was rather satisfied about it. The Lord used these people to straighten things out in my life, and then He straightened them out.

**Since thou wast precious in my sight, thou hast been honourable, and I have loved thee: therefore will I give men for thee, and people for thy life [Isa. 43:4].**

We cannot imagine how much God loves Israel. We cannot imagine how precious we are to God.

**Fear not: for I am with thee: I will bring thy seed from the east, and gather thee from the west;**

**I will say to the north, Give up; and to the south, Keep not back: bring my sons from far, and my daughters from the ends of the earth [Isa. 43:5–6].**

God states in clear-cut language that He will regather the nation Israel. In Jeremiah 31:10 He reaffirms this: "Hear the word of the LORD, O ye nations, and declare it in the isles afar off, and say, He that scattered Israel will gather him, and keep him, as a shepherd doth his flock." God says, "Hear the word of the LORD, O ye nations." What He means is this: "Hear the word of the Lord, ye liberals. Hear the word of the Lord, ye amillennialists, and ye postmillennialists, and ye premillennialists—some of you haven't been quite sure whether or not I am through with Israel." We are to listen to *Him*. Regardless of what the world situation might be, God says He intends to regather Israel. We have His word for it.

**Ye are my witnesses, saith the LORD, and my servant whom I have chosen: that ye may know and believe me, and understand that I am he: before me there was no God formed, neither shall there be after me [Isa. 43:10].**

God has no competitor or equal. He alone is God. He alone holds this unique position.

**I, even I, am the LORD; and beside me there is no saviour [Isa. 43:11].**

It is interesting that of all the religions of the world only Christianity guarantees salvation. Others put down quite a program, but they certainly do not guarantee salvation. God says, "Beside me there is no saviour."

God now opens up the subject of idolatry.

**I have declared, and have saved, and I have shewed, when there was no strange god among you: therefore ye are my witnesses, saith the LORD, that I am God [Isa. 43:12].**

God is saying, "As long as you will not go into idolatry or turn to that which will lead you away from Me, I will bless you."

## PROSPECT—FUTURE JUDGMENT, DELIVERANCE, REDEMPTION OF ISRAEL

**Yea, before the day was I am he; and there is none that can deliver out of my hand: I will work, and who shall let it? [Isa. 43:13].**

The word *let* in this verse means to hinder. No creature can slip out of the hand of God or escape out of His reach.

**Thus saith the LORD, your redeemer, the Holy One of Israel; For your sake I have sent to Babylon, and have brought down all their nobles, and the Chal-**

deans, whose cry is in the ships [Isa. 43:14].

The ultimate destruction of Babylon is foretold.

**I am the LORD, your Holy One, the creator of Israel, your King [Isa. 43:15].**

Surely it is inescapable that the nation Israel is the subject. *God* takes responsibility for bringing them into existence. Let every anti-Semite take note of this. He is their *King.* This is another affirmation of the deity of Christ, for He is their King. When the Lord Jesus came to earth and made His claim to Kingship, Israel knew that He was claiming to be Immanuel, ". . . God with us" (Matt. 1:23). The instructed Israelite understood that.

We have seen that God claims Israel because He created them. Now He speaks of the fact that even the beasts of the field honor Him.

**The beast of the field shall honour me, the dragons and the owls: because I give waters in the wilderness, and rivers in the desert, to give drink to my people, my chosen [Isa. 43:20].**

I have a notion that even the animal world is a little more conscious of God than His creature man, who has fallen into sin.

**I, even I, am he that blotteth out thy transgressions for mine own sake, and will not remember thy sins [Isa. 43:25].**

God is saying that He intends to forgive them on the same basis that He has forgiven us.

**Thy first father hath sinned, and thy teachers have transgressed against me [Isa. 43:27].**

This evidently is a reference to Abraham. Surely Scripture records his failures and sins. We have only to mention the matter of his lying to Pharaoh about Sarah, his wife.

*Thy teachers* means "interpreters." Those who interpreted God to the people had faults and sins. Remember Samson, Samuel, and David.

**Therefore I have profaned the princes of the sanctuary, and have given Jacob to the curse, and Israel to reproaches [Isa. 43:28].**

This is the present condition of Israel. They have no peace today because they have departed from the living and true God. This is not, however, their final state.

Chapter 44 continues the theme of chapter 43. However, the last chapter closes with the dark mention of coming judgment. This chapter moves into the light of the coming kingdom and the promise of the Holy Spirit.

There is in this chapter a brilliant and bitterly devastating satire against idolatry. This is the recurring theme of this particular section. The human heart has a way of turning from God to some idol. Today, we do not go after graven images, but anything to which a person gives himself instead of the true God is an idol. It can be a career, the making of money, seeking for fame, pleasure, sex, alcohol, self-adoration, or business. These are our idols, O America! The high point of the prophet's polemic against idolatry will come in chapter 46. There we shall have occasion to consider this subject further and to examine the real distinction between God and an idol.

## PROMISE OF THE SPIRIT

God calls to Israel as His chosen one and assures her of His help. Then there is this remarkable prophecy of the Holy Spirit:

**For I will pour water upon him that is thirsty, and floods upon the dry ground: I will pour my spirit upon thy seed, and my blessing upon thine offspring [Isa. 44:3].**

This, I believe, is a reference to the pouring out of the Spirit, which corresponds to Joel 2:28–32. If you read Joel's prophecy very carefully, you will find that it was not fulfilled on the Day of Pentecost. When Peter quoted from it, he did two things: First, he said, "this is that"—he did not say it was a fulfillment (see Acts 2:16). The crowd there in Jerusalem was ridiculing the disciples because they were speaking in different languages of the ". . . wonderful works of God" (Acts 2:11). The people were accusing them of being ". . . full of new wine" (Acts 2:13), instead of the Holy Spirit. So Peter says in substance, "This should not amaze you, because this is similar to what will take place in the last days." Now how do we know it wasn't fulfilled on the Day of Pentecost? There are several reasons: (1) Joel said, "And I will shew wonders in the heavens and in the earth, blood, and fire, and pillars of smoke. The sun shall be turned into darkness, and the moon into blood . . ." (Joel 2:30–31). This did not take place on the Day of Pentecost. (2) The record in Acts tells us that the Spirit was not poured out on all people, but Joel said: ". . . I will

pour out my spirit upon all flesh . . ." (Joel 2:28). In Acts there were first 120 disciples, then 3,000 believers—not ever "all," and after nineteen hundred years it still is not *all*. There were probably a half million to a million people in Jerusalem at that time, but by no stretch of the imagination can anyone say that Joel's prophecy was fulfilled at that time. But the fulfillment of Joel's prophecy is coming in the future. This is the reason I continually say that the greatest days for God are in the future.

## POLEMIC AGAINST IDOLATRY

In verses 9–20 we have a brilliant polemic against idolatry. The way the prophet deals with the subject is devastating. Those who make images are witnesses to the senseless character of their gods. An image does not even have the five senses of a human being. An idol can't hear, see, talk, smell, or feel. Paul called them "nothings," and that is what they are. They cannot help anyone.

**Who hath formed a god, or molten a graven image that is profitable for nothing? [Isa. 44:10].**

The prophet asks the question, "Why do you spend all of your time making a god? You ought to be ashamed. You have everything mixed up. *You* don't make a god; *God* made you!"

Now he goes on to describe idol making—

**The smith with the tongs both worketh in the coals, and fashioneth it with hammers, and worketh it with the strength of his arms: yea, he is hungry, and his strength faileth: he drinketh no water, and is faint [Isa. 44:12].**

The artificer of metals works hard in forging a god from some metal, but this labor weakens him and reveals that he is but a man. After all of his labor, talent, time, and money that he puts into making a god, what does he get? Nothing! He gets a beautiful little "nothing."

The origin of a man-made god begins in a forest; yet it is God who made the tree to begin with! Only God can make a tree.

**Then shall it be for a man to burn: for he will take thereof, and warm himself; yea, he kindleth it, and baketh bread; yea, he maketh a god, and worshippeth it; he maketh it a graven image, and falleth down thereto [Isa. 44:15].**

The chips and scraps from the production of a god are used to kindle a fire for the man to warm himself and to bake bread. This is the only practical and helpful contribution that comes from the making of a god. In fact, the scraps are helpful, but that idol is no good to you at all. It cannot warm you; it cannot cook your food; it cannot help you; it cannot save you. An idol cannot do anything for you. God is calling Israel's attention to how absurd idolatry really is.

My friend, many of us give ourselves to those things that take us away from God. They don't help us, they don't lift us up, they don't bring us joy, and it is a fact that they can never save us.

## PROPHECY CONCERNING CYRUS

**That saith of Cyrus, He is my shepherd, and shall perform all my pleasure: even saying to Jerusalem, Thou shalt be built; and to the temple, Thy foundation shall be laid [Isa. 44:28].**

Keep in mind that this verse really belongs in the next chapter. This is a remarkable prophecy concerning Cyrus. He is named here about two centuries before his birth. He is designated as "my shepherd." This is the only instance where a pagan potentate is given such a title. We shall develop this in the next chapter.

# CHAPTER 45

*THEME: Calling of Cyrus before he was born; creation of the universe; continuance of Israel*

This chapter continues the theme of the preceding chapter. This chapter begins with Cyrus as the last chapter closed with him. It is rather unfortunate that the final verse of chapter 44 is not the first verse of this chapter, but I am sure you understand that chapter and verse divisions were made of men. It is said that a monk of the Middle Ages, marked off the chapters while riding a donkey through the Alps. Each time the donkey came to a halt, he came forward with his pen, and that marked the end of a chapter. Of course, this is a fable, but it looks as if certain places were certainly divided that way. In fact, there are times when I get the impression that perhaps the donkey did some dividing on his own!

Let me repeat the final verse of chapter 44, since it properly belongs here:

**That saith of Cyrus, He is my shepherd, and shall perform all my pleasure: even saying to Jerusalem, Thou shalt be built; and to the temple, Thy foundation shall be laid [Isa. 44:28].**

Cyrus was named and identified almost two hundred years before he was born. This unusual prophecy has caused the liberal critic to construct out of the web of his imagination the figment of "the great unknown" writer of this section of the Book of Isaiah. The fact that Isaiah could name a man two centuries before he appears is too strong a tonic for the weak faith of an unbeliever.

The question is, Why was Cyrus marked out like this two centuries before he was born? I believe there are three reasons. Primarily it was for identification. When Cyrus did appear on the scene, there would be no misunderstanding about whom Isaiah had talked. Also, Cyrus would be the man responsible for a decree that would return the nation Israel to her land.

Another reason why Isaiah called Cyrus by name through the revelation of God was so that his accuracy could be demonstrated. If in two hundred years Isaiah would be accurate about Cyrus, he also would be accurate in his prophecy concerning the One born of a virgin, Immanuel, God with us, who was to come seven hundred years later. The instructed Israelite should have been prepared for Christ's coming.

Notice that God calls Cyrus "my shepherd," and says that he "shall perform all my pleasure" and shall rebuild Jerusalem.

Remember that God used Assyria to take the northern kingdom of Israel into captivity. Then He used Babylon to destroy Jerusalem and take the southern kingdom into captivity. The men God used to do this were wicked, and God judged them for what they had done. But Cyrus is different. God calls him "my shepherd" who shall "perform all my pleasure."

When we get to heaven I believe there will be two things that will be a surprise to all of us; (1) the folk who will be there whom we didn't expect to make it—and I think Cyrus is going to be one of them, and (2) the folk whom we expected to be there who won't be there. And, my friend, the reason any of us will be there is because Christ is our Savior.

It is interesting to note that God says that Cyrus "shall perform all my *pleasure*"—not only God's *will*, but also His *pleasure*. After all, both Sennacherib and Nebuchadnezzar performed God's *will* in taking Israel and Judah into captivity, but Cyrus will perform God's *pleasure*, and that is a little different.

## CALLING OF CYRUS BEFORE HE WAS BORN

**Thus saith the LORD to his anointed, to Cyrus, whose right hand I have holden, to subdue nations before him; and I will loose the loins of kings, to open before him the two leaved gates; and the gates shall not be shut [Isa. 45:1].**

This is a remarkable prophecy. Cyrus did not appear in the pages of history until two hundred years after Isaiah spoke of him. Cyrus came out of the East, from Persia. The ruins of his tomb have been found in Pasargadae, Iran, and you cannot read the inscription without recognizing that he was a humble man who trusted God. Most of the great rulers of the past were braggarts and most of them were liars. Everything they said you have to take with a grain of salt. The records they left magnified their greatness (sort of like the ones left by modern politicans) and cannot be trusted. But Cyrus was different. He made no great claims; he did not boast, and yet, he conquered the world!

Also note that God calls Cyrus "his anointed," a title that applies only to the Lord Jesus. Why did God give such a title to Cyrus? Because he carried out the will of God and delivered the Israelites from captivity and permitted them to return to the land of promise. Also he encouraged the Israelites who did not return to send rich gifts of gold, silver, and precious things with those who did go back. In that respect Cyrus was a gentile messiah of Israel and a vague foreshadowing of the One who was to come.

"The two leaved gates" is evidently, a reference to the numerous gates of Babylon which shut Israel out from returning to Palestine. Cyrus opened those gates and said that the Israelites could walk out. They were free to return to their homeland.

Now God says this of Cyrus:

**And I will give thee the treasures of darkness, and hidden riches of secret places, that thou mayest know that I, the LORD, which call thee by thy name, am the God of Israel [Isa. 45:3].**

The rich treasures of Babylon, which the kings of Babylon had taken as spoils of war from all nations, especially from Jerusalem, fell to Cyrus.

**For Jacob my servant's sake, and Israel mine elect, I have even called thee by thy name: I have surnamed thee, though thou hast not known me.**

**I am the LORD, and there is none else, there is no God beside me: I girded thee, though thou hast not known me [Isa. 45:4–5].**

God chose Cyrus before he knew the Lord. It is reasonable to conclude that Cyrus came to know the living and true God. "Thus saith Cyrus king of Persia, The LORD God of heaven hath given me all the kingdoms of the earth; and he hath charged me to build him an house at Jerusalem, which is in Judah" (Ezra 1:2).

## CREATION OF THE UNIVERSE

Here is a remarkable statement relative to the creation of the universe before all time.

God says:

**I form the light, and create darkness: I make peace, and create evil. I the LORD do all these things [Isa. 45:7].**

Zoroastrianism began in Persia. It teaches that Mazda is the god of light. God says He creates light, and that it is no god. The Persians were getting very close to the truth. Many have wondered why they worshiped one god in the midst of idolatry. Well, you must remember that they came in contact with the nation Israel, and Israel was a witness to the world. In Zoroastrianism darkness was Ahriman, the god of evil. God takes responsibility for creating the darkness also.

"And create evil"—the word *evil* does not mean wickedness in this instance, but rather "sorrow, difficulties, or tragedies"—those things which are the fruit of evil, the fruit of sin. This is the Old Testament way of saying, "The wages of sin is death . . ." (Rom. 6:23). If you indulge in sin, there will be a payday for it!

By the way, let me introduce something else at this point, since we are living in a day when it is said that good and evil are relative terms, that whatever you *think* is good, *is* good. The argument is put forth: The Bible says "Thou shalt not kill" and "Thou shalt not steal" (Exod 20:13, 15), But what is the Bible? Who should obey it? Or why should we listen to the God of the Bible?

The Lord has another very cogent argument. God says that if you indulge in sin, you will find that sin has its payday. It pays a full wage, by the way. This is what God is saying through Isaiah. God has so created the universe that when you break over the bounds that He has set, you don't need a judge, a hangman's noose, or an electric chair; God will take care of it.

He says, therefore, that He is the One who creates light and darkness. He is answering Zoroastrianism which worshiped the god of light. God says, "I want you to know that light is no god; *I* created it."

**Woe unto him that striveth with his Maker! Let the potsherd strive with the potsherds of the earth. Shall the clay say to him that fashioneth it, What makest thou? or thy work, He hath no hands? [Isa. 45:9].**

Why fight against God? You are going to lose anyway. The Greeks had a proverb that went something like this: The dice of the gods are loaded. That is exactly what God says in His Word. He says, "Don't gamble with Me. Don't strive with Me. Don't think that you can fight Me. Settle your case out of court." "Come now, and let us reason together, saith the LORD: though your sins be as scarlet, they shall be as white as snow; though they be red like crimson, they shall be as wool" (Isa. 1:18).

My friend, don't gamble with God, because when He rolls the dice He knows exactly how they are coming up—you don't. This is tremendous!

Now the Lord makes some other claims.

**I have made the earth, and created man upon it: I, even my hands, have stretched out the heavens, and all their host have I commanded [Isa. 45:12].**

It is interesting that God says He "stretched out the heavens." This is no accident. It was Sir James Jeans, a Christian astronomer in Great Britain, who advanced a theory that today most astronomers follow. I notice here in Pasadena that some of the men connected with Cal Tech, who work in the field of astronomy, take the position that you and I live in a universe which Sir James Jeans called an expanding universe. It gets bigger every minute. The planets and worlds and galactic systems are all moving out away from each other. God says, "I stretched out the heavens." That is the way He did it, although He hasn't told us exactly *how* He did it—or how He could take nothing and make something out of it. Regardless of what theory you adopt, you have to move back to the place where there is *nothing* and then there is *something*. If you can tell me how nothing becomes something, then I will listen to you. Until you can answer that you can talk about tadpoles and monkeys all you want and I'll just sit and smile at you. I'm a skeptic; I don't believe you. Only God has a reasonable answer. God says, "I created it." By His fiat word He brought the universe into existence. Do you have a more intelligent answer than what God has given to us in His Word?

## CONTINUANCE OF ISRAEL

This brings us to the third division: the continuance of Israel for all time and eternity. God won't let us forget this subject.

**But Israel shall be saved in the LORD with an everlasting salvation: ye shall not be ashamed nor confounded world without end [Isa. 45:17].**

Those who believe that God is through with Israel should take a long look at this passage. Israel's salvation is everlasting. God says, "Yes, you are going to be judged, Israel. You are going to Babylon, but you are going to return to the land. Rebellion is still in your heart, but ultimately I am going to save you."

Again He gives them an invitation—it was wide open then and it is wide open today.

**Look unto me, and be ye saved, all the ends of the earth: for I am God, and there is none else [Isa. 45:22].**

This is the verse that an ignorant man used which was responsible for the conversion of Charles Spurgeon. Spurgeon was on his way to church one Sunday morning when a snowstorm hit London. Because he couldn't make it to his church, he stopped at a little church along the way. The storm was so severe that the preacher did not make it to this little church, so a man got up and said a few words. Spurgeon never knew the man's name; he only knew that he was an uneducated man. He chose Isaiah 45:22 as his text, and what he lacked in lightning, he made up for in thunder. He said, "This verse says, 'Look unto me, and be ye saved.'" He began to talk about the verse. "God says you should *look* to Him and be *saved*." By that time he ran out of ammunition. He had said all he could say about the verse, so he went into the thunder department and began to roar and pound the pulpit, "Look to God, all the ends of the earth, and be saved." He looked way back in the congregation and saw the young fellow Spurgeon sitting there with a very miserable look on his face. The man said to Spurgeon, "You look to Jesus, and you will be saved." Spurgeon was a very brilliant man, but he did what this ignorant man suggested—he looked to Jesus and was saved.

# CHAPTER 46

*THEME: Pronouncement of judgment against idols*

This chapter contains one of the finest satires against idolatry that is found in the Word of God. It opens with the announcement of defeat against the idols of Babylon in particular. This seems strange since Babylon had not yet come to the front as a world power and was not the enemy of Israel. Nevertheless, Babylon was the source of all idolatry, and it is fitting that after announcing the defeat of the idols of Babylon the prophet proceeds to denounce all idolatry with an injunction to Israel not to forsake the true God.

## PRONOUNCEMENT OF JUDGMENT AGAINST IDOLS

**Bel boweth down, Nebo stoopeth, their idols were upon the beasts, and upon the cattle: your carriages were heavy loaden; they are a burden to the weary beast [Isa. 46:1].**

Bel and Nebo are gods of Babylon. *Bel* is the shortened form of Baal and is found in the first part of Beelzebub—which is one of Satan's names. *Nebo* means "speaker or prophet." When Paul and Barnabas went to Lystra, the people thought Barnabas was Bel or Jupiter and Paul was Nebo or Mercury because he did the talking.

Behind the idols of that day was satanic worship, which is becoming rather popular in our contemporary society. The Word of God repeatedly warns us that our warfare is *spiritual* warfare.

God contrasts the helplessness of the idol, which is a burden to carry, to His own love and strength.

**Hearken unto me, O house of Jacob, and all the remnant of the house of Israel, which are borne by me from the belly, which are carried from the womb [Isa. 46:3].**

God, says, "I have been carrying you, Israel, as a woman carries a child in her womb."

**And even to your old age I am he; and even to hoar hairs will I carry you: I have made, and I will bear; even I will carry, and will deliver you [Isa. 46:4].**

This is the real distinction between that which is true and that which is false. God had not only been carrying the nation Israel, but He had carried each individual from the cradle to the grave. Let me ask you the question, "Is your religion carrying you, or are you carrying your religion?" God carries our sins. "He hath borne our griefs, and carried our sorrows" (Isa. 53:4). He also carries our cares, our burdens: "Casting all your care upon him; for he careth for you" (1 Pet. 5:7). And God carries us today: "The eternal God is thy refuge, and underneath are the everlasting arms: and he shall thrust out the enemy from before thee; and shall say, Destroy them" (Deut. 33:27).

Now notice how He speaks of idolatry:

**To whom will ye liken me, and make me equal, and compare me, that we may be like? [Isa. 46:5].**

The reason that it is so difficult to explain God is because He is infinite and we are finite and live in a finite universe. There is nothing with which to compare Him. He cannot be reduced to our terminology without losing all meaning. He cannot be translated into human language. This explains one of the reasons why God became a man. The only way we can know God is through Jesus. He revealed God.

This is a brilliant satire on idolatry—

**They lavish gold out of the bag, and weigh silver in the balance, and hire a goldsmith; and he maketh it a god: they fall down, yea, they worship [Isa. 46:6].**

This is a metallic image that excels the wooden image in beauty and value. The wealth of man is expended in making an idol. If a man doesn't have much money, he has a cheap god. If he is rich, he has a rich god. It actually amounts to men worshiping their own workmanship, which is self-worship. It is a form of humanism.

Now here is the real test:

**They bear him upon the shoulder, they carry him, and set him in his place, and he standeth; from his place shall he not remove: yea, one shall cry unto him, yet can he not answer, nor save him out of his trouble [Isa. 46:7].**

They lug their god around on their shoulders and put him in the corner when they get home! Listen to what God says to them—

**Remember the former things of old: for I am God, and there is none else; I am**

God, and there is none like me [Isa. 46:9].

There is a lot of modern idolatry about. Face up to it. Do you receive anything when you go to church? For many folk church-going is a real burden to them. It is like a useless god they have to carry around.

Oh, my friend, God wants to communicate to *you*. He has something for *you*. He doesn't want you to carry Him; He wants to carry *you*.

# CHAPTER 47

*THEME: The decline and fall of Babylon*

This is the third time in this book (chs. 13–14; 21) that we have considered the prediction of the doom of Babylon. There was also a suggestion of the fall of Babylon in chapter 46, which opened with God's judgment upon the idols. The time given to this subject is remarkable in view of the fact that Babylon at this time was a very small and insignificant kingdom. It was almost a century before it would become a world power. It had been in existence since the days of the Tower of Babel and had influenced the world religiously. Babylon was the fountainhead and the mother of all idolatry. Again I recommend for your study Alexander Hislop's book, *The Two Babylons*. All through the Old Testament books of prophecy a great deal is said about drunkenness and idolatry. These are the two things that will bring the downfall of any nation.

There is a spiritual meaning for us of the present who have nothing to do with Babylon of the past or of the future. The Babylon of the past lies under the rubble and ruins of judgment. Its glory is diminished by the accumulated dust of the centuries. We can see this Babylonian tendency today in the political realm as represented in the United Nations. Babel is the place where all the political power of the world comes together, which will finally be under the willful king, the Antichrist. We see the commercial combine coming to pass in the breaking down of economic barriers among the nations of Europe. We see the religious combine in both Romanism and the World Council of Churches. We will see all of this prefigured in ancient Babylon.

## DECLINE OF BABYLON

Come down, and sit in the dust, O virgin daughter of Babylon, sit on the ground: there is no throne, O daughter of the Chaldeans: for thou shalt no more be called tender and delicate [Isa. 47:1].

"Come down" is the command of God to Babylon, the same as a dog is called to obedience. It is like saying, "Down Rover, down Fido." That is the way God is going to talk to the great world power Babylon when the time comes for it to be brought low. God will say, "Down Fido, down Babylon." That is the way the Lord Jesus dealt with the storm on the little sea of Galilee. When the Lord spoke to the waves and the wind, He literally said, "Be muzzled," like you would muzzle a dog. The same thought is here in Isaiah.

Babylon is called a virgin because she had not yet been captured by an enemy. Babylon was just now coming to power, although it had a very ancient history, going back to Nimrod (see Gen. 10) and to Babel where the Tower of Babel (see Gen. 11) was located. All the ziggurats in that valley were patterned after the Tower of Babel.

He predicts the tremendous humiliation of Babylon—

Take the millstones, and grind meal: uncover thy locks, make bare the leg, uncover the thigh, pass over the rivers [Isa. 47:2].

This depicts the indescribable humiliation to which Babylon was finally subjected. She had mistreated the people of Israel, and the day came when she was brought low.

Nudity is becoming rather popular today. Men play with the subject like a child playing with a new toy, but it degrades humanity. It was no accident that God clothed mankind. A person who wants to go without clothes has a hangup—a real hangup. For Babylon nudity was part of her humiliation.

Thy nakedness shall be uncovered, yea, thy shame shall be seen: I will take vengeance, and I will not meet thee as a man [Isa. 47:3].

## DELIVERANCE OF ISRAEL TO BABYLON

Here we see that God delivered Israel into the hands of Babylon—

I was wroth with my people, I have polluted mine inheritance, and given them into thine hand: thou didst shew them no mercy; upon the ancient hast thou very heavily laid thy yoke [Isa. 47:6].

God is making it clear to them that the reason Babylon was able to take His people was because He permitted it and not because Babylon was so superior. They had a great sense of power, and they gave themselves credit for overthrowing Israel. They were wrong. God delivered His people into the hands of Babylon because they had sinned against Him. He was judging His own people. This is the message of the little prophecy of Habakkuk.

And thou saidst, I shall be a lady for ever: so that thou didst not lay these things to thy heart, neither didst remember the latter end of it [Isa. 47:7].

God's judgment of His people deceived Babylon. They thought it was by their might and power that they had taken God's people.

Therefore hear now this, thou that art given to pleasures, that dwellest carelessly, that sayest in thine heart, I am, and none else beside me; I shall not sit as a widow, neither shall I know the loss of children [Isa. 47:8].

Babylon was arrogant, lifted up, and careless, not believing that a frightful fall was coming. Nebuchadnezzar, the Babylonian king, looked over the beautiful and glorious city of Babylon, and said, "This is great Babylon that I have built," giving no credit to God. God sent him out to the field like an ox to eat grass, having a form of amnesia—probably the psychiatrist would call it hysteria today. For a long time he did not know who he was, and he lived like an animal. It was God's judgment upon him.

## DETAILS FOR THE DESTRUCTION OF BABYLON

For thou hast trusted in thy wickedness: thou hast said, None seeth me.

Thy wisdom and thy knowledge, it hath perverted thee; and thou hast said in thine heart, I am, and none else beside me [Isa. 47:10].

There is always a grave danger of a nation or a man being lifted up by pride and feeling that he is able to make it on his own. We are living in a country today where men can become rich, not by doing some great service or by making a contribution to mankind, but by being in an industry that brings men down—degrades them instead of building them up. Think of the millions of dollars that are being made through entertainment and the multitudes who are getting rich through the sale of liquor. We are in many questionable businesses as a nation, and our methods of business are not always honorable. We attempt to cover up these things, but God sees, and He will judge as He judged Babylon.

## DILEMMA OF BABYLON

Stand now with thine enchantments, and with the multitude of thy sorceries, wherein thou hast laboured from thy youth; if so be thou shalt be able to profit, if so be thou mayest prevail [Isa. 47:12].

God satirically urges Babylon to turn to the witchcraft in which she has trusted and which has gotten her into trouble. In substance God asks, "You thought it was so great, why don't you trust it to get you out of trouble?"

Thou art wearied in the multitude of thy counsels. Let now the astrologers, the stargazers, the monthly prognosticators, stand up, and save thee from these things that shall come upon thee [Isa. 47:13].

Confusion characterizes Babylon at this time. The city lives up to its name—Babylon means "confusion," and confusion besets them. That great city depended upon its economic strength and its total gross product. But something happened to that nation, and it was dying within. We are living in a country today that depends upon its economic strength, but something is also wrong with us, and we won't face up to it. Our problem is moral. As a nation we have departed from the living and true God. The ancient city of Babylon, which at first glance seems so unrelated to us, has a message for us. The stones of the debris of Babylon are crying out a warning to us.

# CHAPTER 48

**THEME:** *Last call to the house of Jacob; longing call of God to the remnant*

All three of these last sections conclude with the phrase, "no peace . . . to the wicked" (Isa. 57:21). The Messiah brings peace, but those who reject Him will never know peace. Turning to idols is turning from the Messiah. As we have seen, this section has majored in a denunciation of idolatry. Idolatry is a road that leads to Babylon. God, in this book, is traveling the lonely road to Calvary.

## LAST CALL TO THE HOUSE OF JACOB

**Hear ye this, O house of Jacob, which are called by the name of Israel, and are come forth out of the waters of Judah, which swear by the name of the LORD, and make mention of the God of Israel, but not in truth, nor in righteousness [Isa. 48:1].**

There are those who say that Judah and Israel are different. God contradicts that thinking in this verse. Don't try to change the name God has given them. The whole house of Israel is addressed here, and they belong to the chosen line through Abraham, Isaac, and Jacob. The apostate nation back then and in our day should listen to this final injunction to turn back to God. They speak of the God of Israel as if they knew Him. Actually, they neither know Him nor serve Him. They have a religion without any strength whatsoever. They will not find the solution to their problems by turning to the United States, or to Russia, or to the Arab nations. Help will come when they turn to God. That is their solution and our solution.

**For they call themselves of the holy city, and stay themselves upon the God of Israel; The LORD of hosts is his name [Isa. 48:2].**

They boast of being citizens of Jerusalem and of being children of God, but they only have a name; they are actually strangers to God.

**Because I knew that thou art obstinate, and thy neck is an iron sinew, and thy brow brass [Isa. 48:4].**

From the very beginning, when God took Israel out of Egypt, He knew they were stiff-necked people. My friend, God did not choose them because they were superior, nor did He choose us because we are superior. God chose them and us because of His grace and because He saw our great need.

## LONGING CALL OF GOD TO THE REMNANT

He is pleading with His people to listen to Him.

**Hearken unto me, O Jacob and Israel, my called; I am he; I am the first, I also am the last [Isa. 48:12].**

It would seem that God is no longer addressing the nation as a whole but confines His word to the remnant labeled, "my called."

**I, even I, have spoken; yea, I have called him: I have brought him, and he shall make his way prosperous [Isa. 48:15].**

This is the heartcry of God.

**Come ye near unto me, hear ye this; I have not spoken in secret from the beginning; from the time that it was, there am I: and now the Lord GOD, and his spirit, hath sent me [Isa. 48:16].**

It is Isaiah who becomes God's messenger. He is pleading with them, and as He pleads you can hear the Lord Jesus Christ. F. Delitzsch (p. 253) appropriately says, "Since the prophet has not spoken in his own person before; whereas, on the other hand, these words are followed in the next chapter by an address concerning Himself from that servant of Jehovah who announces Himself as the restorer of Israel and light of the Gentiles, and who cannot be therefore either Israel, as a nation," or Isaiah, it can be none other than the Lord Jesus Christ Himself.

God has never been able to bless the nation Israel to the fullness of His promise, and you and I have never been blessed as much as God would like to bless us. Whose fault is it? Is it God's fault? No! It is Israel's fault and the fault of you and me.

**Thy seed also had been as the sand, and the offspring of thy bowels like the gravel thereof; his name should not have been cut off nor destroyed from before me [Isa. 48:19].**

Then he concludes this section, as the three sections of this last major division of Isaiah conclude:

**There is no peace, saith the LORD, unto the wicked [Isa. 48:22].**

This is the solemn benediction of this section where God's Servant is set over against all the idols of the heathen. He alone gives peace. If a person is away from God, living in sin, he cannot find peace in the world today. We have several thousand years of recorded history which tell us that anyone away from God hasn't had peace.

# CHAPTER 49

*THEME: Discourse of Christ to the world; discussion of Jehovah with Israel; digression—judgment of Israel's oppressors*

In this third and final division of the Book of Isaiah there is a threefold division which is marked off with the words, "There is no peace, saith the LORD, unto the wicked." We have seen in the first division the *comfort* of Jehovah which comes through the servant. Now chapter 49 begins the second division, which I call *salvation* of Jehovah which comes through the suffering Servant.

We are now beginning to move toward a definite revelation of the Lord Jesus Christ as the suffering Servant of God. We have been moving toward that revelation from the very beginning, but at first we saw Him more as a silhouette in the background as the Servant who brings comfort to God's people. The closer we get to chapter 53, where we have that wonderful revelation of the cross of Christ, the more clear He will become to us.

Israel was the servant of Jehovah, but as such Israel had failed. Now God speaks of another Servant, and that Servant is the Lord Jesus Christ. The prophetic Scriptures spoke primarily of *Israel* as God's servant; yet the final meaning is found in the Person of Christ. A classic illustration is in Hosea 11:1, where it is recorded: "When Israel was a child, then I loved him, and called my son out of Egypt." This was fulfilled in Christ (see Matt. 2:15). The nation failed, but the One who came out of the nation will succeed.

## DISCOURSE OF CHRIST TO THE WORLD

As we open this chapter, we are listening in on a discourse by Christ as truly as the twelve apostles listened to Him in Galilee. In this chapter we see Christ moving out to become the Savior of the world. In this movement Israel is not forsaken, for her assured restoration to the land is reaffirmed.

There is nothing to correspond to this remarkable discourse of our Lord Jesus Christ in the religions of this world. Here is One who is looking at a *world*, and He is looking at it as the Servant of God, who has come as the Savior of the world. Every religion is confined to an ethnic group or to several ethnic groups. Generally they do not move beyond the borders of a tribe, a people, or a nation so that most deities are *local* deities. However, the Deity in the Word of God is the living God, the Creator of the universe and the Redeemer of mankind. This fact makes the discourse before us remarkable indeed.

**Listen, O isles, unto me; and hearken, ye people, from far; The LORD hath called me from the womb; from the bowels of my mother hath he made mention of my name [Isa. 49:1].**

Christ is calling upon the nations of the world to hear. He was given the name of Jesus before He was born, and this name is to be proclaimed throughout the world because it is the name of the *Savior*, and the world needs a Savior.

**And he hath made my mouth like a sharp sword; in the shadow of his hand hath he hid me, and made me a polished shaft; in his quiver hath he hid me [Isa. 49:2].**

The sharp sword that went out of His mouth is the Word of God, and the explanation of His enemies when He walked on this earth was, ". . . Never man spake like this man" (John 7:46). And the *revelation* of this One concludes with these words: "And out of his mouth goeth a sharp sword, that with it he should smite the nations . . ." (Rev. 19:15). It is the judgment of the nations by the Word of God.

Notice the identification:

And said unto me, Thou art my servant, O Israel, in whom I will be glorified [Isa. 49:3].

This will be true of the nation Israel, and it is true of Christ.

Now this is a remarkable statement:

Then I said, I have laboured in vain, I have spent my strength for nought, and in vain: yet surely my judgment is with the LORD; and my work with my God [Isa. 49:4].

Though the Lord was rejected, and it may look as if He labored in vain, His confidence is in God. Even the *death* of the Lord Jesus Christ was a victory; in fact, it is the greatest victory the world has seen up to the present time. The emphasis in this section, therefore, is on the suffering Servant.

At His first coming He did not gather Israel, as they rejected Him. At His first coming He did something far more wonderful—He wrought salvation for the world. Therefore, God's purposes were not thwarted by man's little machinations.

And now, saith the LORD that formed me from the womb to be his servant, to bring Jacob again to him, Though Israel be not gathered, yet shall I be glorious in the eyes of the LORD, and my God shall be my strength [Isa. 49:5].

I submit this to you as being one of the most remarkable passages in the Word of God.

Thus saith the LORD, the Redeemer of Israel, and his Holy One, to him whom man despiseth, to him whom the nation abhorreth, to a servant of rulers, Kings shall see and arise, princes also shall worship, because of the LORD that is faithful, and the Holy One of Israel, and he shall choose thee [Isa. 49:7].

Paul said it like this: "Now if the fall of them be the riches of the world, and the diminishing of them the riches of the Gentiles; how much more their fulness?" (Rom. 11:12). The rejection of Christ by Israel meant that the gospel went to the ends of the earth. Just think how great it will be some day in the future when God regathers Israel!

## DISCUSSION OF JEHOVAH WITH ISRAEL

From this section, the discussion of Jehovah with Israel regarding their restoration, I shall lift out only a few verses:

Thus saith the LORD, In an acceptable time have I heard thee, and in a day of salvation have I helped thee: and I will preserve thee, and give thee for a covenant of the people, to establish the earth, to cause to inherit the desolate heritages [Isa. 49:8].

God heard the prayer of Christ, and He whom the nation crucified will be the One before whom kings will bow, and every knee must bow and acknowledge His Lordship.

Sing, O heavens; and be joyful, O earth; and break forth into singing, O mountains: for the LORD hath comforted his people, and will have mercy upon his afflicted [Isa. 49:13].

God's purposes in the *earth* center in the nation Israel. When they are back in the land, then both the heavens and the earth can rejoice. Today, however, everything is more or less out of place as far as the world is concerned. Israel should be in their land, in the place of blessing, serving God. They are not. The church should be in heaven with Christ, but the church is still in the world. The Devil should be in hell, but he is walking around the earth seeking whom he may devour. The Lord Jesus Christ should be sitting upon the throne of the earth, ruling the earth, but He is at the right hand of God. There are many things that have to be shifted around and put in the right socket. Then the lines of Robert Browning as written in "Pippa Passes" will be true: "God's in His heaven: All's right with the world," which at the moment just do not fit the world in which you and I live.

Even the people of Israel think they are forsaken of God—

But Zion said, The LORD hath forsaken me, and my Lord hath forgotten me.

Can a woman forget her sucking child, that she should not have compassion on the son of her womb? yea, they may forget, yet will I not forget thee.

Behold, I have graven thee upon the palms of my hands; thy walls are continually before me [Isa. 49:14–16].

What beautiful assurance God gives them that they are not forsaken of Him! Israel may forsake Him—as they are doing yet today—but God will never forsake them.

My friend, if you still have doubts that God will restore Israel, I submit this section to you for your careful study.

## DIGRESSION—JUDGMENT OF ISRAEL'S OPPRESSORS

**Thus saith the Lord God, Behold I will lift up mine hand to the Gentiles, and set up my standard to the people: and they shall bring thy sons in their arms, and thy daughters shall be carried upon their shoulders [Isa. 49:22].**

God assures Israel that the Gentiles will assist Him in the final restoration of the nation to the land. Heretofore, the Gentiles have *scattered* them, which makes this a rather remarkable prophecy even for today. Great Britain did open the land for the Jews; yet Great Britain was the country that issued the mandate which forbade them to enter the land—so they came by ship *without* permission, and they have been hindered in one way or another since that time. It has taken persecution to push them out of other countries, and at the time I am writing this they are being blocked from leaving Russia, which probably has the third largest Jewish population in the world. Russia doesn't want to get rid of them; yet it subjects them to a great deal of anti-Semitic oppression. However, in *that* day, that is, in the end times, God will bring them back into their land, and He will use Gentiles to move them back!

# CHAPTER 50

**THEME:** *The reason for the rejection of Israel: Israel's rejection of Christ*

Israel's rejection of Christ is the real hurdle that they must get over before there can be blessing for them. He came as their Messiah; He actually was one of them. "He came unto his own, and his own received him not" (John 1:11). He came to His own people, and His own people did not receive Him.

## GOD THE FATHER STATES THE REASON

**Thus saith the Lord, Where is the bill of your mother's divorcement, whom I have put away? or which of my creditors is it to whom I have sold you? Behold, for your iniquities have ye sold yourselves, and for your transgressions is your mother put away [Isa. 50:1].**

Under the Mosaic Law (see Deut. 24:1) a man could put away his wife on the slightest pretext. A cruel and hardhearted man would take advantage of this to get rid of his wife. God asks Israel if they know on what grounds He set them aside. Certainly God is not cruel or brutal. Israel is spoken of as the wife of Jehovah—this is the theme of Hosea. It was not a whim of God that caused Israel to be set aside, but God makes it very clear that their sin brought about their rejection.

**Wherefore, when I came, was there no man? when I called, was there none to answer? Is my hand shortened at all, that it cannot redeem? or have I no power to deliver? behold, at my rebuke I dry up the sea, I make the rivers a wilderness: their fish stinketh, because there is no water, and dieth for thirst [Isa. 50:2].**

"When I came"—when did Jehovah come directly to His people, not through His prophets but *Himself*, to Israel and expect such a welcome? It was not when He descended on Mount Sinai to give them the Mosaic Law. He looked for no welcome then but insisted that they keep their distance. But He came again as a man, a humble man, and there was no reception of Him at all. Israel did not welcome Him at His birth; they didn't receive Him when He began His ministry. They rejected and killed their Messiah. Simon Peter on the Day of Pentecost put it like this: "Ye men of Israel, hear these words; Jesus of Nazareth, a man approved of God among you by miracles and wonders and signs, which God did by him in the midst of you, as ye yourselves also know: Him, being delivered by the determinate counsel and foreknowledge of God, ye have taken, and by wicked hands have crucified and slain: Whom God hath raised up, having loosed the pains of death: because it was not possible that he should be holden of it" (Acts 2:22–24). God makes it very clear that because they rejected their Messiah, they have been set aside.

## GOD THE SON SPEAKS
## OF HIS HUMILIATION

**The Lord God hath given me the tongue of the learned, that I should know how to speak a word in season to him that is weary: he wakeneth morning by morning, he wakeneth mine ear to hear as the learned [Isa. 50:4].**

The title by which Christ, the perfect Servant, addresses God is revealing. It is "Jehovah Adonai." The Lord Jesus Christ made Himself known to His people as "Jehovah Adonai." He came meek and lowly to do the Father's will.

"He wakeneth mine ear to *hear* as the learned" means the Lord Jesus was studying the Word of God. The question is asked, What did the Lord Jesus do the first thirty years of His life? Generally the answer is that He worked as a carpenter. But that is only half the truth. The other half is that He studied the Word of God. How tremendous! If *He* needed to study the Word of God, what about you? What about me? I think we need to get with it!

It is nonsense to say, "Oh, I believe the Bible from cover to cover; I will defend it with my life," when you don't study it! If God has spoken between the pages of Genesis 1:1 and Revelation 22:21, then somewhere between God has a word for you and for me. If God is speaking to us, we ought to listen.

**The Lord God hath opened mine ear, and I was not rebellious, neither turned away back [Isa. 50:5].**

This speaks of the Lord's true submission in His crucifixion. In Exodus 21:1–6 we are told that when a servant wanted to become a permanent servant, his master would bore or pierce a hole in his ear. "Then his master shall bring him unto the judges; he shall also bring him to the door, or unto the door post; and his master shall bore his ear through with an awl; and he shall serve him for ever" (Exod. 21:6). He could wear an earring after that, and I am convinced that he did. It indicated that he was a slave for life to his master.

Now the reason he would become a slave forever is twofold. First, he loved his master; and second, he had married a slave girl and he refused to go without her.

Do you see how this was applied to the Lord Jesus? The psalmist, referring to this custom, wrote, ". . . mine ears hast thou opened . . ." (Ps. 40:6). Now notice how this is quoted in Hebrews 10:5: "Wherefore when he cometh into the world, he saith, Sacrifice and offering thou wouldest not, but a body hast thou prepared me." In the psalm it says, "mine ears hast thou opened," and in Hebrews it says, "a body hast thou prepared me." When the Lord Jesus came down to this earth and went to the cross, His ear wasn't "opened" or "digged"; He was given a body, and that body was *nailed* to a cross. He has taken a glorified body bearing nail prints back to heaven. He did more than have his ear bored through with an awl; He gave His *body* to be *crucified* because He loved us and would not return to heaven without us!

**I gave my back to the smiters, and my cheeks to them that plucked off the hair; I hid not my face from shame and spitting [Isa. 50:6].**

This was literally fulfilled when Jesus was arrested. Matthew, Mark, and John all record the fact that He was spit upon, scourged, buffeted, and smitten. This is something we don't like to think about and would like to pass over, but it was literally fulfilled.

## GOD THE HOLY SPIRIT SUGGESTS
## MEN TRUST THE SON

**Who is among you that feareth the Lord, that obeyeth the voice of his servant, that walketh in darkness, and hath no light? let him trust in the name of the Lord, and stay upon his God [Isa. 50:10].**

This is the wooing word. The Holy Spirit speaks a soothing and imploring word to trust and rest in God's Servant.

He turns from this and gives a warning word:

**Behold, all ye that kindle a fire, that compass yourselves about with sparks: walk in the light of your fire, and in the sparks that ye have kindled. This shall ye have of mine hand; ye shall lie down in sorrow [Isa. 50:11].**

First it is the wooing word as He implores them; then He gives a warning word to those who walk in the light of their own fire, rejecting the One who is the light of the world.

Some time ago a man said to me, "McGee, I heard you on the radio, and I disagree with you about salvation. Let me tell you what *I* think about it." Well, he was ready to build a fire, and he wanted both of us to sit there and warm ourselves by his fire. I knew it was a

phony fire, which would give off no heat or light. So I frankly said to him, "I don't mean to be ugly or rude, but I don't want to hear what *you think*, because what you think and what I think are quite meaningless. It is what *God says* that we need to know." And we need to walk in the light of the Lord Jesus. He is the Light of the World. If we reject Him who is the Light of the World, then we generally walk in the light of our own little fire down here. The Holy Spirit gives this warning: You will lie down by that little fire of yours in sorrow, which means you will be eternally lost.

# CHAPTER 51

**THEME:** *Israel's origin from past history; Israel's outlook for the future; outline of Israel's present conditions*

It is impossible to read this chapter without realizing that God has a future purpose for the nation Israel—just as He has a future purpose for the church and for you and me.

Let me remind you that the final verse of chapter 50 concluded with a warning, which might lead you to an amillennialist interpretation. And God doesn't want us to hold the view that Israel as a nation has been set aside permanently and that when He speaks of Israel, He means the church. My friend, when God says *Israel*, He means *Israel*. If He had meant the church instead of Israel, somewhere along the line He would have said, "I hope you understand that when I say Israel I mean the church." No, He makes it very clear that He means Israel. Just as Israel has had a past rooted in a very small beginning, just so today they are small and set aside. But this does not mean God has forsaken them.

To illustrate this I use the figure of a train. God is running through the world a twofold program: One of them is expressed in the words, "Yet have I set my king upon my holy hill of Zion (Ps. 2:6)—that train will be coming through later, but now it is on the side-track. On the main track He is ". . . bringing many sons unto glory" (Heb. 2:10), which refers to believers (or the church). When this train has come into the Union Station on time, God will put back on the main track the program of Israel and the gentile nations which are then upon the earth. And He is going to bring that train through on time also.

God's time piece is not B-U-L-O-V-A or G-R-U-E-N, but I-S-R-A-E-L. In this chapter God turns on the alarm to awaken those who are asleep that they might know that the eternal morning is coming soon. In Romans 13:11–12 we read, "And that, knowing the time, that now it is high time to awake out of sleep: for now is our salvation nearer than when we believed. The night is far spent, the day is at hand: let us therefore cast off the works of darkness, and let us put on the armour of light."

## ISRAEL'S ORIGIN FROM PAST HISTORY

**Hearken to me, ye that follow after righteousness, ye that seek the LORD: look unto the rock whence ye are hewn, and to the hole of the pit whence ye are digged [Isa. 51:1].**

"Hearken unto me," is God turning on the alarm. This is a call to every sincere heart in Israel that longs to be righteous and desires to know God. He says, "Wake up! Hear Me! I have a plan."

**Look unto Abraham your father, and unto Sarah that bare you: for I called him alone, and blessed him, and increased him [Isa. 51:2].**

God is saying, "I called Abraham when he was over in Chaldea in idolatry, and look what I've done through him! Now I want to move in your heart and life."

## ISRAEL'S OUTLOOK FOR THE FUTURE

**Hearken unto me, my people; and give ear unto me, O my nation: for a law shall proceed from me, and I will make my judgment to rest for a light of the people [Isa. 51:4].**

"O my nation" is Israel. This is a word of glorious anticipation for them.

My righteousness is near; my salvation is gone forth, and mine arms shall judge the people; the isles shall wait upon me, and on mine arm shall they trust [Isa. 51:5].

"My righteousness is near"—righteousness is Christ. He is made unto us "righteousness."

"The isles" are all the continents which are inhabited by the human family. God says, "I have a salvation which I will send out to them."

"On mine arm shall they trust—the arm of God, as we shall see in Isaiah 53, is His salvation. The question is asked, "to whom is the [bared] arm of the LORD revealed?" (Isa. 53:1). God wants that bared arm of redemption in Christ to be revealed to the lost world. Therefore He is sending out this message that this bared arm will deliver Israel in the future.

Therefore the redeemed of the LORD shall return, and come with singing, unto Zion; and everlasting joy shall be upon their head: they shall obtain gladness and joy; and sorrow and mourning shall flee away [Isa. 51:11].

"Zion" is a geographical location (in Jerusalem) on *earth*. We need to understand that God means what He says here.

The captive exile hasteneth that he may be loosed, and that he should not die in the pit, nor that his bread should fail.

But I am the LORD thy God, that divided the sea, whose waves roared: The LORD of hosts is his name [Isa. 51:14–15].

Just as God brought their father Abraham from the ends of the earth, God intends to bring Israel back to the land. This is what the prophet Jeremiah is saying: "But, The LORD liveth, which brought up and which led the seed of the house of Israel out of the north country, and from all countries whither I had driven them; and they shall dwell in their own land" (Jer. 23:8). The day will come when Israel will no longer remember the deliverance out of Egypt, so great will be their deliverance in the future. My friend, this is tremendous! You can't just set it aside and ignore it. God is saying, "Wake up! This is what I'm going to do."

## OUTLINE OF ISRAEL'S PRESENT CONDITIONS

The present conditions of Israel ought to tell us something. God is still telling us to wake up.

Awake, awake, stand up, O Jerusalem, which hast drunk at the hand of the LORD the cup of his fury; thou hast drunken the dregs of the cup of trembling, and wrung them out [Isa. 51:17].

All you have to do is look at Jerusalem today. It is a city in turmoil. I have no desire right now to stay there permanently, although it was a favorite spot of David, and it is also God's favorite spot on earth. But God has *yet* to make it beautiful. He has *yet* to bring His people there. God is saying, "Wake up, O Jerusalem. I am going to make you a great city."

Thus saith thy Lord the LORD, and thy God that pleadeth the cause of his people, Behold, I have taken out of thine hand the cup of trembling, even the dregs of the cup of my fury; thou shalt no more drink it again [Isa. 51:22].

God has been pressing the cup of fury to their lips because of their rejection of Christ, but the day is coming when He will remove the cup. The day will come when God will take away judgment and bless them. How can you say that God is through with the nation Israel? Even poetic justice demands that after all these years of judgment upon the land and upon the people, God should bless them. God will get the victory, and that is what He is telling us here.

But I will put it into the hand of them that afflict thee; which have said to thy soul, Bow down, that we may go over; and thou hast laid thy body as the ground, and as the street, to them that went over [Isa. 51:23].

The enemies of Israel will not escape the judgment of God. Every nation that has majored in anti-Semitism has fallen: Egypt, Persia, Rome, Spain, Belgium, and Germany. This chapter should alert the believers today that God will yet choose Israel, and that the events in the Near East indicate that we are fast approaching the end times, although no specific prophecy is being fulfilled in this hour.

# CHAPTER 52

*THEME: Invitation to the redeemed remnant of Israel; institution of the kingdom to Israel; introduction of the suffering servant*

As we have been moving through Isaiah, we have seen in the shadows or in the background the Servant of Jehovah. Now as we approach chapter 53 we will see very clearly that the Servant of Jehovah is none other than our Lord Jesus Christ.

In the preceding chapter, the "alarm clock" chapter, the alarm was going off—"Awake, awake!" Now again in the chapter before us we have the alarm sounding.

## INVITATION TO THE REDEEMED REMNANT OF ISRAEL

**Awake, awake; put on thy strength, O Zion; put on thy beautiful garments, O Jerusalem, the holy city: for henceforth there shall no more come into thee the uncircumcised and the unclean [Isa. 52:1].**

When God says, "O Zion," He doesn't mean Los Angeles, or Pocatello, Idaho, or Muleshoe, Texas. He means *Zion*, which is a geographical place in the land of Israel. It is actually the high point in the city of Jerusalem. It was David's favorite spot. Blessing is going to come upon Jerusalem, and it will no longer be an unattractive place. I was not impressed when I saw Jerusalem for the first time. I came up from Jericho and made that turn around the Mount of Olives by Bethany; then I was within sight of the temple area, the wall, and the east gate—that was a thrill. It was late in the afternoon and a shadow was over the city. I could hardly wait until the next morning to enter the city and visit around. Well, the next day was a great disappointment to me. That city is not beautiful in my opinion. Yet the Word of God says it is beautiful for situation; so that's God's viewpoint. I will agree with Him that the situation of it is beautiful, but not the city. However, He makes it clear here that it will be beautiful some day—because of our Lord's work of redemption. You see, Christ will redeem this physical universe, which now is groaning and travailing together in pain. All the world will become a beautiful spot because of redemption in Christ. He will redeem our bodies; we will get new bodies, and when this takes place, all creation will be redeemed. Redemption is not only of the person but of the property. This is the type of redemption that God permitted in the Mosaic Law, which serves as an illustration of it.

**Shake thyself from the dust; arise, and sit down, O Jerusalem: loose thyself from the bands of thy neck, O captive daughter of Zion [Isa. 52:2].**

Today the Arab is there. All the sacred spots are covered with churches—Russian Orthodox, Greek Orthodox, Roman Catholic, Lutheran, and the Church of All Nations—they are all over the place! Jerusalem needs to be released from religion. It needs to be turned loose from the sin and the low degree of civilization that is there right now. Release is coming some day, and it will come during the Millennium. For twenty-five hundred years that city has been captive and trodden down of the Gentiles, but the day is coming when the shackles of slavery will be removed.

**For thus saith the LORD, Ye have sold yourselves for nought; and ye shall be redeemed without money [Isa. 52:3].**

Since God received nothing from those who took His holy city captive, He will give nothing in return. He will take it from them and restore it again.

**For thus saith the Lord GOD, My people went down aforetime into Egypt to sojourn there; and the Assyrian oppressed them without cause [Isa. 52:4].**

Jacob went down to Egypt by invitation, but his children were made slaves. The Assyrians, and others likewise, have oppressed them. That will end when the Millennium begins.

**Now therefore, what have I here, saith the LORD, that my people is taken away for nought? they that rule over them make them to howl, saith the LORD; and my name continually every day is blasphemed [Isa. 52:5].**

God received no gain from the years of His people's rejection. Therefore He says:

**Therefore my people shall know my name: therefore they shall know in that day that I am he that doth speak: behold, it is I [Isa. 52:6].**

This is a lovely thought! When the Lord was here over nineteen hundred years ago, they did not know Him. If they had only known the day of His visitation! Well, they *will* know Him when He comes again, and He will say, "Behold, it is I." This expression is rendered freely by Lowth: "Here I am." The world has rejected Christ; it doesn't know Him. One day He will say to the Christ-rejecting world, "Here I am,"; and it will be too late then for multitudes who have rejected Him to turn to Him.

## INSTITUTION OF THE KINGDOM TO ISRAEL

**Break forth into joy, sing together, ye waste places of Jerusalem: for the Lord hath comforted his people, he hath redeemed Jerusalem [Isa. 52:9].**

O ne of the things you will note about the present-day Jerusalem is the lack of a joyful song. It is even true of the churches there. I listened for it but never heard a joyful song. Around the Mosque of Omar (which stands on the temple site) everything is in a minor key. If you go to the wailing wall, wailing is what you will hear and the Jews are knocking their heads against it. But in the Millennium everybody is going to have fun— they will "Break forth into joy" and they will "sing together." It will be a joyous time!

Even today I don't think God likes to see us saints walking around with long faces, complaining and criticizing. He wants us to have joy. The apostle John wrote, "And these things write we unto you, that your joy may be *full*" (1 John 1:4, italics mine)—not just a little fun, but fun all the time!

The Millennium is the time when God answers the prayer which our Lord taught His disciples: "Thy kingdom come . . ." (Matt. 6:10). The tears and the sorrow will be gone; no longer will there be weeping on the earth. Instead there will be joy, and they will know that the millennial kingdom has come.

## INTRODUCTION OF THE SUFFERING SERVANT

M y friend, somebody will have to travail if you are going to rejoice at a birth, a new birth and a new world. Therefore we have here the suffering of the Servant.

**Behold, my servant shall deal prudently, he shall be exalted and extolled, and be very high [Isa. 52:13].**

Several of the administrations in Washington over the past few years have used the word *prudent* to excess. They speak of being prudent in their conduct. There is some question about whether they were prudent or not. If you think the Democrats have been prudent, ask the Republicans. If you think the Republicans have been prudent, ask the Democrats. You will find out that nobody has been prudent. Man today has not dealt prudently; but, when the Lord Jesus Christ comes, He will deal prudently. That is the picture we have here.

"He shall be exalted and extolled, and be very high." Paul writing to the Philippian believers says, "Wherefore God also hath highly exalted him, and given him a name which is above every name: That at the name of Jesus every knee should bow, of things in heaven, and things in earth, and things under the earth; And that every tongue should confess that Jesus Christ is Lord, to the glory of God the Father" (Phil. 2:9–11).

Now we see the suffering Servant—

**As many were astonied at thee; his visage was so marred more than any man, and his form more than the sons of men [Isa. 52:14].**

This is a picture of the crucifixion of Christ, and this statement prepares the way for chapter 53. I want to be careful, because it is not always a sign of orthodoxy to dwell upon the sufferings of Christ upon the cross; sometimes it is only being crude.

During that time of darkness when men could no longer do anything, the Son of God was working on the cross. It was during those three hours in blackness that the cross became an altar and the Son of Man, the Lamb of God, paid for the sins of the world. After the three hours of darkness, the crowd must have been startled when the light broke upon the cross. He did not even look human—just a bloody piece of quivering human flesh. It was unspeakable. We will see in the next chapter that there was "no beauty that we should desire him" (Isa. 53:2). That is the reason God put the mantle of darkness down on the cross. There was nothing there to satisfy the morbid curiosity of man.

"His visage was so marred more than any man." When I was a pastor in Nashville, Tennessee, there was a wonderful elder on the church board who was a captain in the fire department. He always talked about the importance of having a first aid kit, and he taught classes in first aid. He asked me a

dozen times if I had a first aid kit in my car, and because of his urging I finally got one. Early one morning there was a fire alarm and the firemen responded to the call. On the way to the fire, the hook and ladder truck on which he was riding was hit by a milk truck and flipped over. The men riding on it were dragged along on the asphalt. I received a call about five o'clock in the morning and was told that he was in the hospital. He was still alive when I arrived, and his father was sitting beside his bed. When I looked at him I saw that his face was so marred that I didn't even recognize him. All I could see was a mouth and I could tell that he was breathing—that was all. He didn't last very long. In an hour's time he was gone.

Many times since then I have thought of the fact that the Lord Jesus was marred more than any man, which means He had to be marred more than the captain of the fire company. He was just a piece of quivering human flesh. That is what my Lord went through on the cross!

I don't feel that we should move into the realm of being crude in describing Him, because the next verse says:

**So shall he sprinkle many nations; the kings shall shut their mouths at him: for that which had not been told them shall they see; and that which they had not heard shall they consider [Isa. 52:15].**

"So shall he sprinkle many nations" could be translated, "So shall He make with astonishment many nations." This carries the thought that His death will *startle* people when they properly understand it. The death of Christ should never become commonplace to anyone. His death was different. We have not explained it properly unless it *startles* people.

This prepares us for the profound mystery of the next marvelous chapter.

# CHAPTER 53

**THEME:** *The suffering of the Savior; the satisfaction of the Savior*

Those who are acquainted with God's Word realize that Isaiah 53 and Psalm 22 give us a more vivid account of the crucifixion of Christ than is found elsewhere in the Bible. This may be a shock to many who are accustomed to think that the four Gospels alone describe the sad episode of the horrible death of the Son of God. If you will examine the Gospel accounts carefully, you will make the discovery that only a few unrelated events connected with the Crucifixion are given and that the actual Crucifixion is passed over with reverent restraint. The Holy Spirit has drawn the veil of silence over that cross, and none of the lurid details are set forth for the curious mob to gaze at and leer upon. It is said of the brutal crowd who murdered Him that they sat down and watched Him. You and I are not permitted to join that crowd. Even they did not see all, for God placed over His Son's agony the mantle of darkness. Some sensational speakers gather to themselves a bit of notoriety by painting, with picturesque speech, the minutest details of what they *think* took place at the crucifixion of Christ.

Art has given us the account of His death in ghastly reality. You and I probably will never know, even in eternity, the extent of His suffering.

> But none of the ransomed ever knew
> How deep were the waters crossed,
> Nor how dark was the night that the
> Lord passed thro'
> Ere He found His sheep that was lost.
> —Elizabeth C. Clephane,
> "The Ninety and Nine"

Very likely God did not want us to become familiar with that which we need not know. He did not wish us to treat as commonplace that which is so sacred. We should remind ourselves constantly of the danger of becoming familiar with holy things. "Be ye clean, that bear the vessels of the LORD" (Isa. 52:11).

Isaiah, seven hundred years before Christ was born, lets us see something of His suffering that we will not find anywhere else. Before going any further, we should pause a

moment to answer the question that someone, even now, is doubtless asking: "How do you know that Isaiah is referring to the death of Christ? Isaiah wrote seven hundred years before Christ was born." Well, that is just the question that the Ethiopian eunuch raised when Philip hitchhiked a ride from him in the desert. The Ethiopian was going from Jerusalem back to his own country, and he was reading the fifty-third chapter of Isaiah. We are even told the very place in the chapter where he was reading (see Acts 8:32).

When I was a little boy in Sunday school, I was given a picture of the Ethiopian eunuch sitting in his chariot, holding in one hand the reins and in the other hand the book he was reading. Well, with a little thought we would realize that it couldn't have happened that way.

This man was an official of the government of Ethiopia. He was going across the desert in style. I am sure that he was under some sort of a shade as he sat there reading. He had a chauffeur who was doing the driving for him.

As the Ethiopian was reading Isaiah 53:7–8 his question to Philip was, ". . . I pray thee, of whom speaketh the prophet this? of himself, or of some other man?" (Acts 8:34). How can we be sure that Isaiah was referring to the Lord Jesus Christ in the fifty-third chapter? Listen to Philip. He will answer the Ethiopian's question and our question as well. "Then Philip opened his mouth, and began at the same scripture, and preached unto him Jesus" (Acts 8:35).

Also Christ Himself in John 12:38 quoted from Isaiah 53 and made application to Himself. And the apostle Paul in Romans 10:16 quotes from this same chapter in connection with the gospel of Christ. My friend, Scripture leaves no doubt that Isaiah 53 refers to Christ. Even more than that, it is a photograph of the cross of Christ as He was dying there.

The first nine verses will tell us of the suffering of the Savior. The remainder of the chapter tells the satisfaction of the Savior.

You will find that these two themes belong together—suffering and satisfaction. Suffering always precedes satisfaction. Too many folk are trying to take a shortcut to happiness by attempting to avoid all the trying experiences of life. I want to tell you that there is no short route to satisfaction. This is the reason I condemn short-term courses that claim they have the answers to all of life's problems and will equip you with the whole armor of God. Well, that's the way God does it. There is no

short route. Even God did not go the short route. He could have avoided the cross and accepted the crown. That was Satan's suggestion. But suffering always comes before satisfaction. Phraseology bears various expressions: through trial to triumph; sunshine comes after the clouds; light follows darkness; and flowers come after the rain clouds. That seems to be God's way of doing things. Since it is His method, then it is the very best way. Perhaps you are sitting in the shadows of life today. Trials confront you, and problems overwhelm you, and the fiery furnace is your present lot, and you have tasted the bitter without the sweet. If that is your case right now, then let me encourage your heart and fortify your faith by saying that you are on the same pathway that God followed, and that it leads at last to light if you walk with Him. ". . . weeping may endure for a night, but joy cometh in the morning" (Ps. 30:5).

Now with this in mind, let's look at the suffering Savior.

## THE SUFFERING OF THE SAVIOR

This chapter opens with the enigmatic inquiry:

**Who hath believed our report? and to whom is the arm of the LORD revealed? [Isa. 53:1].**

The prophet seems to be registering a complaint because his message is not believed. This which was revealed to him is not received by men, and this is always the sad office of the prophet. When God called this man Isaiah, back in chapter 6, He told him, "You are going to get a message that the people won't hear. When you tell them My words, they won't believe you." That certainly was Isaiah's experience.

God's messengers have not been welcomed with open arms by the world. The prophets have been stoned, and the message unheeded. That is still true today. After World War I, when everyone was talking about peace and safety, it was very, very unpopular even to suggest that there might be another war. Public opinion then demanded that we sink all the battleships and disarm ourselves, because our leaders told us that the world was safe for democracy. There were a few prophets of God in that period, standing in the pulpits of the land. They were not pacifists, but they did not care for war either. They declared in unmistakable terms that God's Word said there would be wars and rumors of war so long as there was sin, unrighteousness, and evil in the

world. They stated that war was not a skin disease, but a heart disease, and they were proven correct when we entered World War II. When others declared that Christ was a pacifist, they called attention to the fact that He had said that a strong man armed keepeth his palace. I can recall that the church I attended as a boy had just such a minister. He was a faithful servant of Christ, and he sought to please God rather than men. But his message was largely rejected, and he was not popular with the crowd—they preferred the liberal preacher in the town. But time has now proven that he was right, and current events demonstrate that he was a friend of this nation, not an enemy. He was a prophet of God and could say with Isaiah, "Who has believed our report?" There are a few prophetic voices lifted up right now in America. They are trying to call this nation back to God before it is too late, but the crowd is rushing headlong after another delusion.

Personally I am overwhelmed by the marvelous response to our Bible teaching program on radio. But every now and then we are reminded that we are in a Christ-rejecting world. Our program has been put off the air by several radio stations because they did not like our message. One radio manager called in to say that he did not like the kind of "religion" I was preaching. He wanted to know if it weren't possible to give something a little bit more cheerful, because mankind was on the up-and-up and getting better and better. They weren't sinners, and things were not as bad as I seemed to think they were. This man's call, and others like it, simply serve to remind us that we are in a Christ-rejecting world, and we must accept it as such and keep on going. We rejoice today that we have as large an outlet as we do. I believe that there are many prophetic voices in our nation today trying to call us back to God before it is too late. In spite of that, the majority of the people are following any Pied Piper of liberalism who has a tune they can jig by and who makes them feel like everything is going to be all right.

Paul said the preaching of the cross is to them that perish foolishness. From ideas publicly expressed we are given to know that there are many to whom the preaching of the cross is foolishness. I admit there is a lot of foolish preaching, and I offer no apology for it. But God said they would identify the preaching of the cross with foolishness. This message is a challenge to those folk, for there is a reason for their thinking as they do. God says,

"But the natural man receiveth not the things of the Spirit of God: for they are foolishness unto him: neither can he know them, because they are spiritually discerned" (1 Cor. 2:14). Would that they would give God a chance to talk with them!

It must be remembered that God does not use man's methods and ways to accomplish things. God chooses the weak things of the world to confound the mighty and the foolish things to confound the wise. If we were to call in a specialist in a time of illness, we certainly would not expect him to use the same home remedies normally used by us. His procedure might appear foolish to us, but we would follow it faithfully. Then should we not accord to God the same dealing of fairness as we do to the specialist?

But we still have to say with Isaiah, "Who hath believed our report? and to whom is the arm of the LORD revealed?"

There is a very definite reason why men do not believe in God's gospel. Men like to think of God as sitting somewhere in heaven upon some lofty throne. The ancients spoke of the gods whose dwelling was not with mankind. The Greeks placed their deities upon Mount Olympus, and the Romans had Jupiter hurling thunderbolts from the battlements of the clouds. It is foreign to the field of religion that God has come down to this earth among men and that He suffered upon the shameful cross. That is too much to comprehend. The modern mind calls that defeatism—they do not care for it. A suffering deity is contrary to man's thinking.

However, there is a peculiar fascination about this fifty-third chapter of Isaiah. There we see One suffering as no one else ever suffered. There we behold One in pain as a woman in travail. We are strangely drawn to Him and His cross. He said, "And I, if I be lifted up from the earth, will draw all men unto me" (John 12:32). Suffering has a singular attraction. Pain draws us all together. When you and I see some poor creature groaning in misery and covered with blood, our hearts instinctively go out in sympathy to the unfortunate victim. Somehow we want to help. That is the reason the Red Cross makes such an appeal to our hearts. Our sympathy is keen toward those who are war's victims, or the victims of twentieth century civilized barbarism. Pain places all of us on the same plane. It is a common bond uniting all the frail children of suffering humanity. Therefore look with me upon the strange sufferings of the Son of God. Let Him draw our cold hearts into

the warmth of His sacrifice and the radiance of His love.

Isaiah enlarges upon his first question by asking further, "To whom is the [bared] arm of the LORD revealed?" "Bared arm" means that God has rolled up His sleeve, symbolic of a tremendous undertaking. When God created the heavens and the earth, it is suggested that it is merely His *fingerwork*. For instance, Psalm 19:1—"The heavens declare the glory of God; and the firmament sheweth his handiwork." That word *handiwork* is literally "fingerwork." Dr. T. DeWitt Talmage used to say that God created the physical universe without half trying. When God created the heavens and the earth, it was without effort. He merely *spoke* them into existence. When He rested on the seventh day, He wasn't tired; He had just finished everything; it was completed. But when God redeemed man, it required His "bared arm," for salvation was His greatest undertaking. One of the objections offered to God's salvation is that it is *free*. If by that is meant that for man it is free, then this is correct. Man can pay nothing, nor does he have anything to offer for salvation. The reason that it is free for man is because it cost God everything. He had to bare His arm. He gave His Son to die upon the cross. Redemption is an infinite task that only God could perform. Salvation is free, but it certainly is not cheap.

Now we have brought before us the person of Christ. We are told something of His origin on the human side.

**For he shall grow up before him as a tender plant, and as a root out of a dry ground: he hath no form nor comeliness; and when we shall see him, there is no beauty that we should desire him [Isa. 53:2].**

Christ was a root out of a dry ground. This means that at the time of the birth of Christ the family of David had been cut off from the kingship. They were no longer princes; they were peasants. The nation Israel was under the iron heel of Rome. They were not free. The Roman Empire produced no great civilization. They merely were good imitators of great civilizations. There was mediocre achievement and pseudoculture. The moral foundation was gone. A virile manhood and a virtuous womanhood were supplanted by a debauched and pleasure-loving citizenry. The religion of Israel had gone to seed. They merely performed an empty ritual, and their hearts remained cold and indifferent. Into such a situation Christ came. He came from a noble family that was cut off, from a nation that had become a vassal to Rome, in a day and age that was decadent. The loveliest flower of humanity came from the driest spot and period of the world's history. It was humanly impossible for His day and generation to produce Him, but He came nevertheless, for He came forth from God.

Let me use a ridiculous illustration. Christ coming where He did and when He did would be like our walking out in the desert in Arizona, without a green sprig anywhere, and suddenly coming upon a great big head of iceberg lettuce growing right out of that dry, dusty soil. We would be amazed. We would say, "How in the world can this head of lettuce grow out here?" It would be a miracle. The coming of Christ was just like that. His day could never have produced Him. Evolution has always tried to get rid of the Lord Jesus, because it cannot produce a Jesus. If it can, why doesn't it? The interesting thing is that He is different. Therefore He is the root out of a dry ground.

Now the prophet focuses our attention immediately upon His suffering and death upon the cross.

"He hath no form nor comeliness [majesty]; and when we shall see him, there is no beauty that we should desire him." Some have drawn the inference from this statement that Christ was unattractive and misshapen in some way. Some even dare to suggest that He was repulsive in His personal appearance. That cannot be true because He was the *perfect* man. The Gospel records do not lend support to any such viewpoint. It was on the *cross* that this declaration of Him became true in a very real way. His suffering was so intense that He became drawn and misshapen. The cross was not a pretty thing; it was absolutely repulsive to view. Men have fashioned crosses that look very attractive, but they do not represent *His* cross. His cross was not good to look upon; His suffering was unspeakable; His death was horrible. He endured what no other man endured. He did not even look human after the ordeal of the cross, as we saw in the previous chapter. He was a mass of unsightly flesh.

Naturally, we are eager to learn why His death was different and horrible. What is the meaning of the depths of His suffering?

**Surely he hath borne our griefs, and carried our sorrows: yet we did esteem him stricken, smitten of God, and afflicted [Isa. 53:4].**

He was "smitten of God, and afflicted." The prophet was so afraid that you and I would miss this that he mentioned it three times: "The LORD hath laid on him the iniquity of us all." "Yet it pleased the LORD to bruise Him." "He hath put him to grief." Consternation fills our souls when we recognize that it was *God the Father* who treated the perfect Man in such terrible fashion.

Candidly, we do not understand it, and we are led to inquire why God should treat Him in this manner. What had He done to merit such treatment? Look for a moment at that cross. Christ was on the cross six hours, hanging between heaven and earth from nine o'clock in the morning until three o'clock in the afternoon. In the first three hours man did his worst. He heaped ridicule and insult upon Him, spit upon Him, nailed Him without mercy to the cruel cross, and then sat down to watch Him die. At twelve o'clock noon, after He had hung there for three hours in agony, God drew a veil over the sun, and darkness covered that scene, shutting out from human eye the transaction between the Father and the Son. Christ became the sacrifice for the sin of the world. God made His soul an offering for sin. Christ Jesus was treated as *sin*, for we are told that He was made sin for us who knew no sin. If you want to know if *God* hates sin, look at the cross. If you want to know if God will punish sin, look at the Darling of His heart enduring the tortures of its penalty. By what vain conceit can you and I hope to escape if we neglect so great a salvation? That cross became an altar where we behold the Lamb of God taking away the sin of the world. He was dying for somebody else— He was dying for you and me.

Listen to the prophet:

**But he was wounded for our transgressions, he was bruised for our iniquities: the chastisement of our peace was upon him; and with his stripes we are healed.**

**All we like sheep have gone astray; we have turned every one to his own way; and the LORD hath laid on him the iniquity of us all [Isa. 53:5–6].**

The phrase "with His stripes we are healed" may cause questions in your mind. Of what are we healed? Are we healed of physical diseases? Is that the primary meaning of it? I am going to let Simon Peter interpret this by the inspiration of the Spirit of God. First Peter 2:24 says, "Who his own self bare our sins in his own body on the tree, that we, being dead to sins, should live unto righteousness: by whose stripes ye were healed." Healed of what? Peter makes it quite clear that we are healed of our trespasses and sins. Now notice that marvelous sixth verse. It begins with "all" and ends with "all." "All we like sheep have gone astray"—not some of us, but all of us. What is really the problem with mankind? What is your basic and my basic problem? It is stated in this clause: "We have turned every one to his own way." That is our problem. Man has gone *his* way, neglecting *God's* way. And the Scripture further says: "There is a way which seemeth right unto a man, but the end thereof are the ways of death" (Prov. 14:12). Another proverb admonishes: "In all thy ways acknowledge him, and he shall direct thy paths" (Prov. 3:6). Although our Lord Jesus said, ". . . I am the way, the truth and the life: no man cometh unto the Father, but by me" (John 14:6), we have turned every one to his own way.

"And the LORD hath laid on him the iniquity of us all." Isaiah is making it clear that when Christ died on the cross He was merely taking your place and mine. He had done nothing amiss. He was holy, harmless, undefiled, separate from sinners. He was the Substitute whom the love of God provided for the salvation of you and me.

Surely our hearts go out in sympathy to Him as He expired there upon the tree. Certainly we are not unmoved at such pain and suffering. We would be cold-blooded, indeed, if our own hearts were not responsive. It is said that when Clovis, the leader of the Franks, was told about the crucifixion of Christ, he was so moved that he leaped to his feet, drew his sword, and exclaimed, "If I had only been there with my Franks!" Yet, my friend, Christ does not want your sympathy. He did not die to win that. He didn't die to enlist us in His defense. Remember that when He was on the way to the cross and the women of Jerusalem were weeping for Him, He said, ". . . weep not for me, but weep for yourselves, and for your children. . . . For if they do these things in a green tree, what shall be done in the dry?" (Luke 23:28, 31). He did not want their sympathy and He does not want ours.

Someone may be thinking that He died a martyr's death. He did not die a martyr's death, for He did not espouse a lost cause! He did not die as martyrs who in their death sang praises of joy and confessed that Christ was standing by them. Compare His death to that of Stephen's. Stephen in triumph said,

". . . behold, I see the heavens opened, and the Son of man standing on the right hand of God" (Acts 7:56). Our Lord didn't die like that. He was *forsaken* of God. He said, ". . . My God, my God, why hast thou forsaken me?" (Matt. 27:46). His death was different. He died alone—alone with the sins of the world upon Him.

Someone else may feel like saying what a wonderful influence the death of Christ should exercise upon our lives. As we contemplate His life and death, most assuredly we ought to be persuaded to turn from sin. However, that has not been the experience of men. By the way, how did it work in your life? That view will not satisfy as an explanation of this verse: "All we like sheep have gone astray; we have turned everyone to his own way; and the LORD hath laid on him the iniquity of us all." None of these will suffice to explain His death, for He is the Lamb of God that taketh away the sin of the world. He took our place.

## THE SATISFACTION OF THE SAVIOR

At this point let me quote verse 3 which speaks of Christ's grief.

**He is despised and rejected of men; a man of sorrows, and acquainted with grief: and we hid as it were our faces from him; he was despised, and we esteemed him not [Isa. 53:3].**

Christ is identified as "a man of sorrows, and acquainted with grief," and the inference is that Christ was a very unhappy Man while He was here upon this earth. To fortify this position a few isolated incidents are quoted which speak of His weeping. Now I want to correct this impression if I can. In verse 4 it says that "he hath borne our griefs, and carried our sorrows." Notice that it was *our* sorrows and *our* griefs that He bore. He had no grief or sorrow of His own. He was supremely happy in His mission here upon earth. In the Epistle to the Hebrews it is said of Him ". . . for the *joy* that was set before him he endured the cross" (Heb 12:2, italics mine). These pictures that show Him looking long-faced and very solemn misrepresent Him. Even on the cross He joyfully took our place. He made that cross an altar upon which He offered a satisfactory payment for the penalty of your sins and mine. *Willingly* He died there, for in verse 7 we read "as a sheep before her shearers is dumb, so he openeth not his mouth."

Perhaps you are saying to yourself, "Preacher, that does not make sense to me. I do not believe that, nor do I care for that sort of religion. I do not want God to make a sacrifice for me. I did not ask Him to do it." Well, it is true that you did not ask Him to do it, but let me ask you a very plain and fair question. I am sure that you will agree that man has gotten this world into a very sad predicament today. The wisdom of man has failed to settle the issues of this life. Had you ever thought that man may be wrong about the next life when he dismisses God's remedy with a snap of the fingers? Vain philosophy and false science have not solved the problems of daily living. Since they are wrong in so many other areas, they may also be wrong about the Bible.

Suppose for a moment that God *did* give His Son to die for you and that He *did* make a tremendous sacrifice. Grant that the cross is God's remedy for the sin of the world and that it is the very best that even God can do. Suppose also that you go on rejecting this gracious offer of salvation. Do you think that you can reasonably expect God to do anything for you in eternity? If God exhausted His love, His wisdom, and His power in giving Christ to die and patiently has waited for you to turn to Him, what else can He do to save you? What else do you suppose God can do for you, or for anyone, who rejects His Son? He would come again at this moment and die again if that would be the means to save you! It is no light thing to turn down God's love gift to you.

This does not end the gospel story. We do not worship a dead Christ; we worship a *living* One. He not only died, He rose again from the grave in victory. He ascended back into heaven. At this moment He is sitting at God's right hand, and the prophet says:

**He shall see of the travail of his soul, and shall be satisfied: by his knowledge shall my righteous servant justify many; for he shall bear their iniquities [Isa. 53:11].**

We have a living and rejoicing Savior, for His suffering led to *satisfaction*. He took our hell that we might have His heaven. He is happy, for down through the ages multitudes, yes, millions, have come to Him and found sweet release from guilt, pardon for wrongdoing, and healing from the leprosy of sin. Christ said there is *joy* in heaven over one sinner that repenteth, and that number can be multiplied by millions. Think of the joy and satisfaction of Christ today! We have a happy Christ, a joyful Christ, and it is going to be fun to be in His presence.

You can bring added joy to His heart by

accepting the gift of eternal life that He longs to give to you. He is not asking anything of you—He wants to *give* you something. It is for ". . . him that worketh not, but believeth on him that justifieth the ungodly, his faith is counted for righteousness" (Rom. 4:5). All you have to do is accept Him right where you are. He invites you to the foot of the cross where you will find forgiveness for your sins. May this be your prayer and mine:

> Beneath the cross of Jesus
> I fain would take my stand—
> The shadow of a mighty Rock
> Within a weary land;
> A home within the wilderness,
> A rest upon the way,
> From the burning of the noontide heat,
> And the burden of the day.
>
> Upon the cross of Jesus
> Mine eye at times can see

> The very dying form of One
> Who suffered there for me:
> And from my stricken heart with tears
> Two wonders I confess—
> The wonders of redeeming love
> And my unworthiness.
> —Elizabeth C. Clephane,
>       "Beneath the Cross of Jesus"

What a marvelous prayer this is for a sinner to pray! It makes it very clear that all men will not be saved, that all men must accept the Substitute or they will be lost. It also makes clear that the total depravity of man is taught in the Bible, that we are in no condition to save ourselves. All without exception are involved in guilt, and all without exception are involved in sin, and all without exception are guilty of straying, and all without exception have turned away from God, and all without exception have chosen their own way.

# CHAPTER 54

**THEME:** *The regathered and restored wife of Jehovah; the rejoicing and righteous restored wife of Jehovah*

This is the logical chapter to follow Isaiah 53, because it is the song that accompanies salvation and the future glories of Israel. You see, the Redeemer is coming to Zion, and some day they will behold Him.

## THE REGATHERED AND RESTORED WIFE OF JEHOVAH

He is speaking directly to Israel saying they should sing.

**Sing, O barren, thou that didst not bear; break forth into singing, and cry aloud, thou that didst not travail with child: for more are the children of the desolate than the children of the married wife, saith the LORD [Isa. 54:1].**

I can't sing. If you can, that's wonderful. But some day I am going to be able to sing. Redemption brings a song into the world. The world produces the blues; the redeemed sing of blessings. The world has its rock; the redeemed sing of redemption. The world plays jazz; the redeemed have the reality of joy. Only the redeemed have a song of joy. The redeemed will sing the song of redemption

whether on earth or in heaven. "And they sung a new song, saying, Thou art worthy to take the book, and to open the seals thereof: for thou wast slain, and hast redeemed us to God by thy blood out of every kindred, and tongue, and people, and nation; And hast made us unto our God kings and priests: and we shall reign on the earth" (Rev. 5:9–10). What a picture we have here! You see, it is the church mentioned in Revelation, but in Isaiah 54 it is the nation Israel. The church is called a chaste virgin while Israel is characterized as the restored wife.

"Sing, O barren." In the past Israel has been as a barren wife. Sarah's life was this in miniature. She was barren, childless, an old women eighty years old with no children. God caused the barren to bring forth a son, and just think of the millions that have come from her!

So the first word after the crucifixion in chapter 53 is "Sing." It is a call to Israel to sing. But the Jews are not singing over in their land today. In the past Israel has been as a barren wife, but in the future her travailing will be over. Her travailing so far has pro-

duced only wind—like the mountain that travailed and brought forth a mouse! But her future is glorious because she will have many children in the future.

**Enlarge the place of thy tent, and let them stretch forth the curtains of thine habitations: spare not, lengthen thy cords, and strengthen thy stakes [Isa. 54:2].**

The nation Israel has never occupied the entire land given to them by the Lord. The land God marked out for them in Joshua 1:4 is about 300,000 square miles. Even in Israel's heyday, when they reached their zenith under David and Solomon, they only occupied 30,000 square miles—that is quite a difference. Now God says they are going to lengthen their cords and strengthen their stakes. And they are going to be safe in the land. They won't need to be afraid of the Arab in that day. During the Millennium, Israel will occupy the total borders of the land. Also, the city of Jerusalem will push out into the suburban areas, and there will be no traffic jams.

**For thou shalt break forth on the right hand and on the left; and thy seed shall inherit the Gentiles, and make the desolate cities to be inhabited [Isa. 54:3].**

The Gentiles have occupied most of the Land of Promise—they have it today. But they will have to withdraw to their own borders. The problem in the world today is not only that individuals are trying to step over into somebody else's territory, but nations are trying to expand their borders. This causes problems. People just keep wanting more and more and more, which is what produces wars.

**For thy Maker is thine husband; the LORD of hosts is his name; and thy Redeemer the Holy One of Israel; The God of the whole earth shall he be called [Isa. 54:5].**

God will own them then as His redeemed in that day.

**For the LORD hath called thee as a woman forsaken and grieved in spirit, and a wife of youth, when thou wast refused, saith thy God [Isa. 54:6].**

Israel is today like a wife that has been divorced for adultery. That is the figure of speech that is used.

**For a small moment have I forsaken thee; but with great mercies will I gather thee [Isa. 54:7].**

In that day not only Israel, but all of us are going to look back at what we thought was terrible down here in this life, and it will seem as Paul described it "a light affliction, which is but for a moment." And it will work for us an "exceeding and eternal weight of glory." We need to get our eyes focused on things which are not seen rather than things that are seen (see 2 Cor. 4:17–18).

**For the mountains shall depart, and the hills be removed; but my kindness shall not depart from thee, neither shall the covenant of my peace be removed, saith the LORD that hath mercy on thee [Isa. 54:10].**

If you feel that God is going to break His covenant which He made with Abraham, Isaiah would have you know that you are wrong. God will not break His covenant; He will never break it.

## THE REJOICING AND RIGHTEOUS RESTORED WIFE OF JEHOVAH

**O thou afflicted, tossed with tempest, and not comforted, behold, I will lay thy stones with fair colours, and lay thy foundations with sapphires [Isa. 54:11].**

Now God begins to comfort Israel that she might rejoice.

**And all thy children shall be taught of the LORD; and great shall be the peace of thy children [Isa. 54:13].**

This is the day when the knowledge of the Lord shall cover the earth. This brings peace.

**In righteousness shalt thou be established: thou shalt be far from oppression; for thou shalt not fear: and from terror; for it shall not come near thee [Isa. 54:14].**

Following righteousness is freedom from fear. Now notice this marvelous verse of Scripture.

**No weapon that is formed against thee shall prosper; and every tongue that shall rise against thee in judgment thou shalt condemn. This is the heritage of the servants of the LORD, and their righteousness is of me, saith the LORD [Isa. 54:17].**

Even in the past and in the present, God has been opposed to anti-Semitism. No enemy of God's chosen nation has ever prospered. The

witnesses to this truth are Pharaoh, Haman, Herod, and Hitler. There are a lot of anti-Semites in this country who ought to read this verse. This verse is a *promise* of God.

# CHAPTER 55

*THEME: Invitation to the world; the ways of God; institution of the Word of God*

The work of the suffering Servant in chapter 53 makes possible the offer of salvation in this chapter. In chapter 54 the invitation was confined to Israel. In this chapter the invitation is extended to the entire world. The gospel went first to Israel and then to the Gentiles. I think this is what Paul meant when he said, "For I am not ashamed of the gospel of Christ: for it is the power of God unto salvation to every one that believeth; to the Jew first, and also to the Greek" (Rom. 1:16). This does not mean that the Jew has top priority today, but he shouldn't have bottom priority either; he is on the same par as everyone else. The Jew did receive the gospel first. Peter on the Day of Pentecost preached to an all-Jewish congregation—there wasn't a Gentile in the lot. Now this invitation goes out to the *world*. This is remarkable because there have been very few religious leaders who have had a global view. The work of the suffering Servant in chapter 53 makes possible now the offer of salvation to a lost world.

God's invitation has yet to find its complete fulfillment in Israel. Today it is worldwide, with only one condition, as we shall see. This is not a mechanical offer locked in the airtight compartment of God's election, but it rests upon the free-flowing will of each hearer. He is urged—in fact, he is commanded—to seek the Lord.

## INVITATION TO THE WORLD

**Ho, every one that thirsteth, come ye to the waters, and he that hath no money; come ye, buy, and eat; yea, come, buy wine and milk without money and without price [Isa. 55:1].**

The chapter opens with the heart cry of God to *every one* to pause and consider His salvation.

"Ho" is like a startled cry for help in the night. He wants every weak soul to behold His mighty bared arm of salvation.

The invitation is ecumenical. I don't believe in the ecumenical movement that men talk about today, but I do believe in God's ecumenical movement, which is that the invitation of the gospel is to go out to the world. However, it is limited to one class: "Ho, every one that thirsteth." This invitation is to every man, woman, and child on the topside of the earth. It means every man of every station in life, in all strata of society, from every race, tribe, tongue, condition, and color. All are included. The invitiation is "Ho, every one."

But notice that it is limited to only certain ones—"every one that *thirsteth*." It is for those whose thirst has not been slaked by the man-made cisterns and bars of this earth. The invitation is to drink deep and long of the eternal springs. Dr. F. C. Jennings has written: "Let us listen then, as if we had never heard the melody of this tender and gracious invitation before. Who are the guests here invited? *All who thirst!* All that is needed to be welcome then, is—not to *need* (for that is true of all)—but to *want* what is offered. Am I utterly dissatisfied with myself? I thirst! Am I dissatisfied with all the world can offer me, and of which I have tasted? I thirst! Is my spirit altogether dissatisfied with all the formalism of religion? Then do I thirst! Blessed thirst! It is the only prerequisite to enjoyment!" (*Studies in Isaiah*, p. 645).

This is the invitation: "Ho, everyone that thirsteth." If you say, "I am not interested. I am not thirsty. I am satisfied with the things of this life," then it is not for you, my friend. It is not for you until you are thirsty. Here in California you will be riding along in the desert and all of a sudden you will see on a billboard the picture of a bottle pushed down into some cracked ice. My, it looks good! There is only one word printed on the sign—"THIRSTY?" The company that put up the sign hopes you are thirsty. They want you to stop at the next service station and buy a coke or whatever they are selling. If you have your thermos bottles filled with iced tea, or orange juice, you say, "I am not thirsty," and drive

on. But if you are thirsty, you will pull off at the next service station and get your drink.

At the crossroads of life God has put up a sign: "THIRSTY?" Ho, every one that is thirsty. Are you tired of this world? Have you found that it does not satisfy? Do you long for something better? God says, "I have something for you." Then He mentions a variety of things and says that you can buy these things without money. A bottled drink used to cost a nickel, now you have to pay forty cents and by the time you read this, the price may have gone even higher. But God's offer is without money. Why? Because back in Isaiah 53 the Lord Jesus paid the price for it on the cross. This is God's invitation to you, "Come ye, buy, and eat." Not only drink, but He offers the bread of life, too.

Notice that there are three types of drink offered:

1. "Waters"—the plural form is used. In the Hebrew the plural expresses a superlative degree. This water is too wonderful to be expressed by the singular form. "Waters" also speaks of abundance, of quantity as well as quality. This is water for the *soul*. This is the kind of water that the Lord Jesus offered—and He used the same symbolism—when He stood in the temple area that day and cried, ". . . If any man thirst, let him come unto me, and drink" (John 7:37). Now we know where the fountain is—that fountain is Christ, who is the Water of Life and our Savior.

2. "Wine" is the second type of drink offered, which symbolizes joy. In Proverbs 31:6 we read, "Give strong drink unto him that is ready to perish, and wine unto those that be of heavy hearts." And 1 Thessalonians 1:6 says, "And ye became followers of us, and of the Lord, having received the word in much affliction, with *joy* of the Holy Ghost" (italics mine). Joy is what you have when Christ is not only your Savior but when He becomes the Master of your life. When you come to *know* Him, you have joy. In 1 John 1:4 John says, "And these things write we unto you, that your *joy* may be full" (italics mine). I saw this motto in a preacher's study in Salem, Oregon: "Joy is the flag that is flown in the heart when the Master is in residence." That is a marvelous drink that will put genuine joy in your heart!

3. "Milk" is the third type of drink offered. Milk is essential for growth and development, especially for babies. The dairy industry has been trying to tell people: "Everybody needs milk." Well, the milk of the Word of God is essential for spiritual growth. Now, since I am a teacher of the Word of God, that makes me a milkman. I give out the milk of the Word. Peter said it like this, "As newborn babes, desire the sincere milk of the word, that ye may grow thereby" (1 Pet. 2:2). Have you ever seen a little baby while his mama gets his bottle ready? That hungry little fellow, lying in his crib, is wiggling his feet, his hands; in fact, he is wiggling all over. With his mouth he is making all kinds of commotion and a great deal of noise! Why? Because he desires milk. And a child of God ought to want the milk of the Word of God with equal longing! My friend, if you are a believer, there is something wrong with you if you don't like to study the Word of God. The greatest problem in our churches today is that we are entertaining, we are giving nice little courses in this and that and the other thing, we are giving banquets and dinners, and we are putting folk on committees. We are doing everything but giving them the Word of God. Many church members are stillborn—they have no spiritual life. My friend, if you are a believer, you ought to want the sincere milk of the Word of God.

**Wherefore do ye spend money for that which is not bread? and your labour for that which satisfieth not? hearken diligently unto me, and eat ye that which is good, and let your soul delight itself in fatness [Isa. 55:2].**

Many folk, even Christians today, are spending money for so-called Christian enterprises that don't feed anybody. I hear some groups today calling money *bread*—I rather like that expression. The Word of God is "bread" also. A lot of Christians put their money into that which is not bread, although they think it is. It would be well to investigate where you give your money. It may be that you are buying a load of sawdust, which won't satisfy your heart and life.

The question is asked, "Wherefore do ye spend money for that which is not bread?" The pleasures of this world are expensive. You have to pay for them. Not only are they expensive, but they never satisfy. They are counterfeit. They are sawdust and cannot satisfy the soul. Then where is happiness? You won't find it in money. Jay Gould, an American millionaire, had plenty of that. When he was dying, he said: "I suppose I am the most miserable devil on earth." You won't find happiness in pleasure either. Lord Byron had fame, genius, money, and lived a life of pleasure; yet he wrote in his poem "On My

Thirty-sixth Year": "The worm, the canker, and the grief are mine alone."

Why don't you come to the table where you can get some water, wine, milk, and bread that satisfies? That's where we all need to be today.

> **Incline your ear, and come unto me: hear, and your soul shall live; and I will make an everlasting covenant with you, even the sure mercies of David [Isa. 55:3].**

God was merciful to David, and He will be merciful to you and me today. I heard a man speaking in Pershing Square in Los Angeles one day, deriding and ridiculing the Bible. One Sunday evening I saw him in church when I was a pastor in downtown Los Angeles. After the service he came to talk to me, feigning a humble approach, and said, "Pastor, I have a question to ask you. Why did God choose a man like David?" Then he leered at me, and I knew exactly what the old rascal was thinking. I said, "I'll tell you why God chose a man like David. It was so that you and I would have the courage to come to Him. If God would take David, He might take *you*, and He might take *me!*" The sure mercies of David—how wonderful they are!

> **Behold, I have given him for a witness to the people, a leader and commander to the people [Isa. 55:4].**

Jesus is called the true witness for us in our day.

> **Behold, thou shalt call a nation that thou knowest not, and nations that knew not thee shall run unto thee because of the LORD thy God, and for the Holy One of Israel; for he hath glorified thee [Isa. 55:5].**

"Behold, thou shalt call a nation that thou knowest not"—at that time Isaiah didn't know about the United States of America, but we are included in his prophecy.

## THE WAYS OF GOD

> **Seek ye the LORD while he may be found, call ye upon him while he is near [Isa. 55:6].**

The way of God and the way of man are put in contrast and conflict. The objection is often made that this is not a legitimate gospel call for today since man is not asked to seek God, but rather God is seeking man. This certainly is accurate, but nonetheless this call is for today, as the human aspect is in view here. Human responsibility is not defeated by the sovereign purposes and election of God. Therefore the Lord Jesus could say, "All that the Father giveth me shall come to me; and him that cometh to me I will in no wise cast out" (John 6:37). You can sit on the sidelines and argue that you are not one of the elect; but the minute you come, you are elect. And the coming is up to you.

> **Let the wicked forsake his way, and the unrighteous man his thoughts: and let him return unto the LORD, and he will have mercy upon him; and to our God, for he will abundantly pardon [Isa. 55:7].**

The problem people have today is not mental. You may say, "I have great intellectual hurdles to surmount before I can come to Christ." No, you don't. You have only one—that is sin in your life that you don't want to give up. That is the one thing that keeps men from God. "Let the wicked forsake his way," and when you do, then you will be ready to turn to Him. That is when you really get thirsty.

Now God says—

> **For my thoughts are not your thoughts, neither are your ways my ways, saith the LORD [Isa. 55:8].**

God's way is different from man's way. The gospel is God's way. It is not man-made. No man could ever have devised it. "But I certify you, brethren, that the gospel which was preached of me is not after man. For I neither received it of man, neither was I taught it, but by the revelation of Jesus Christ" (Gal. 1:11–12). The gospel came down from heaven. It is God's gospel.

> **For as the heavens are higher than the earth, so are my ways higher than your ways, and my thoughts than your thoughts [Isa. 55:9].**

The gospel could come only by revelation, since man's reason never follows the redemption route.

## INSTITUTION OF THE WORD OF GOD

When the gospel is given out, the emphasis is placed on the accuracy and the reliability and the importance of the Word of God.

> **For as the rain cometh down, and the snow from heaven, and returneth not thither, but watereth the earth, and**

maketh it bring forth and bud, that it may give seed to the sower, and bread to the eater.

So shall my word be that goeth forth out of my mouth: it shall not return unto me void, but it shall accomplish that which I please, and it shall prosper in the thing whereto I sent it [Isa. 55:10–11].

In this closing section there is a prominence given to the Word of God. The only place where the gospel is found is in the Word of God. Salvation is a revelation of God, and the Word of God is likened to the rain that comes down from heaven. You see, the gospel is not asking *you* to do something. Neither is the gospel something that man has thought up. Man does not work his way up to God by some Tower of Babel effort, but he receives God's revelation which comes down from heaven like rain. The rain causes the earth to become fruitful. The seeds germinate and fructify and bring forth abundantly. The Word of God is also the seed; and, when the rain and seed get together in the human heart, there will be fruit.

For ye shall go out with joy, and be led forth with peace: the mountains and the hills shall break forth before you into singing, and all the trees of the field shall clap their hands [Isa. 55:12].

The rain causes the earth to respond with a green blanket of praise to God. During the Millennium the earth will respond with a note of praise to the Creator and Redeemer. "For we know that the whole creation groaneth and travaileth in pain together until now" (Rom. 8:22).

Instead of the thorn shall come up the fir tree, and instead of the brier shall come up the myrtle tree: and it shall be to the LORD for a name, for an everlasting sign that shall not be cut off [Isa. 55:13].

This verse looks forward to the Millennium when the earth will be redeemed from the curse of sin. The curse of sin is expressed by the thorn and brier. When Christ died, He not only redeemed sinners, He also redeemed a sin-cursed earth.

# CHAPTER 56

**THEME:** *Grand particulars of the future kingdom; predicament of the present kingdom*

The chapter before us follows a pattern that goes back to that marvelous fifty-third chapter, which tells of the salvation of the Lord provided for lost mankind by the sacrifice of His Son upon the cross.

Now Isaiah the prophet returns to the nation of Israel and is speaking to his own people. What we have in this chapter is not a retreat to Mount Sinai (as some seem to think) but rather a victory march through the arch of triumph into the Millennium. It is a forward movement which is the logical outworking of what has preceded. It pertains particularly to Israel and radiates out into a widening circle of global benefits. This all rests on the New Covenant which God has made with Israel. It will be the blessing for the earth in the future. At that time the Mosaic Law, which the Lord Jesus lifted to the nth degree in His Sermon on the Mount, will be enforced on the earth because Christ will be reigning. It will be His will and it will be His law.

The emphasis in this chapter is on ethics, not on events. The emphasis is on practice, not prophecy. All of this should influence our living today. The study of prophecy is not to entertain the curious or to intrigue the intellect but to encourage holy living. Remember that the apostle John wrote: "And every man that hath this hope in him purifieth himself, even as he is pure" (1 John 3:3). The study of prophecy gives us a purifying hope.

Isaiah now is looking forward into the kingdom age, the Millennium. The Lord Jesus is reigning. As we said, our Lord lifted the Mosaic Law to the nth degree in His Sermon on the Mount, which makes it absolutely impossible for anybody to be saved by keeping the Law. For instance, He said, ". . . whosoever is angry with his brother without a cause shall be in danger of the judgment: and whosoever shall say to his brother, Raca [a word of contempt], shall be in danger of the council: but whosoever shall say, Thou fool,

shall be in danger of hell fire" (Matt. 5:22). On that kind of basis, very few of us would escape. How, then, are we going to be saved? Well, we have a Savior who saves us. But when He is reigning on earth, there will be no hijacking of planes, no kidnapping, no murdering, no mugging. We will be able to walk in safety down Glory Boulevard and Hallelujah Avenue in Jerusalem; the earth will be a safe place in that day. Every man will dwell in peace under his own vine and fig tree, which means he is going to be a capitalist. Everyone will own property and will not be taxed for it. That's going to be great, isn't it!

## GRAND PARTICULARS
## OF THE FUTURE KINGDOM

**Thus saith the LORD, Keep ye judgment, and do justice: for my salvation is near to come, and my righteousness to be revealed [Isa. 56:1].**

**"My** salvation is near to come"—apparently the prophets expected the establishment of the kingdom immediately. Although they made allowance for the possibility of an interval, they speak of it in the immediate future. "Salvation" is the *national* salvation of Israel. This is what was in the mind of the apostle Paul in Romans 11:26 when he said, "And so all Israel shall be saved: as it is written, There shall come out of Sion the Deliverer, and shall turn away ungodliness from Jacob." Anticipation of the coming salvation was to be an incentive to do justice—just as our hope of the coming of the Lord Jesus Christ is an incentive today to lead a holy life.

**Blessed is the man that doeth this, and the son of man that layeth hold on it; that keepeth the sabbath from polluting it, and keepeth his hand from doing any evil [Isa. 56:2].**

This, you see, is for a people who are back under the Sabbath. The Sabbath will be restored to this earth during the Millennium. During this present day of grace we are definitely told: "Let no man therefore judge you in meat, or in drink, or in respect of an holyday, or of the new moon, or of the sabbath days" (Col. 2:16). Therefore, you and I are not under the Sabbath—which ought to be evident to everyone. But God intends to restore it to the earth when Christ reigns, for the law will go forth from Jerusalem.

**Neither let the son of the stranger, that hath joined himself to the LORD, speak, saying, The LORD hath utterly separated me from his people: neither let the eunuch say, Behold, I am a dry tree [Isa. 56:3].**

The Gentile in that day is not to feel that he is an outsider because of God's peculiar arrangement with Israel. On the contrary, he is invited to step up and share the blessings. A eunuch could not serve as a priest under the Mosaic economy. In other words, a physical handicap will shut no one out in that future day.

**For thus saith the LORD unto the eunuchs that keep my sabbaths, and choose the things that please me, and take hold of my covenant;**

**Even unto them will I give in mine house and within my walls a place and a name better than of sons and of daughters: I will give them an everlasting name, that shall not be cut off [Isa. 56:4–5].**

The handicapped, the strangers, and all outcasts are invited to accept God's gracious overture of a position that is better than a son or daughter and a security that is everlasting. This the Law did not give. He is talking about the Millennium, of course.

**Also the sons of the stranger, that join themselves to the LORD, to serve him, and to love the name of the LORD, to be his servants, every one that keepeth the sabbath from polluting it, and taketh hold of my covenant [Isa. 56:6].**

The stranger will be given a new heart that he might love the Lord in that day.

**Even them will I bring to my holy mountain, and make them joyful in my house of prayer: their burnt offerings and their sacrifices shall be accepted upon mine altar; for mine house shall be called an house of prayer for all people [Isa. 56:7].**

This is the verse from which the Lord quoted when He cleansed the temple the second time. It was God's original intention that the temple was to be for *all* peoples irrespective of their race, tongue, class, or condition. It had long ceased to function as such in Christ's day.

Also the present-day church is as far removed from its primary objective as the temple. The church has become like a suburban country club. It has moved from the downtown area and into the suburban area where it

is serving good meals and has good volleyball and basketball teams. But there are few personal workers bringing the lost to the Lord.

**The Lord GOD which gathereth the outcasts of Israel saith, Yet will I gather others to him, beside those that are gathered unto him [Isa. 56:8].**

The kingdom is to be worldwide in its extent and will include members of every family of the human race. God says in that day they are going to go out after folk. I believe that the greatest time of turning to Christ will take place during the Millennium.

## PREDICAMENT OF THE PRESENT KINGDOM

Now that we have seen the marvelous view of the future kingdom, Isaiah returns to the predicament of the kingdom in his day. And we see the same things as we look around us today.

**All ye beasts of the field, come to devour, yea, all ye beasts in the forest [Isa. 56:9].**

Our vision is now shifted from the lofty contemplation of the glorious future kingdom to the sorry condition of the then existing kingdom. God was permitting the nations of the world to come in like wild and ferocious beasts, and they were robbing and pillaging His people. Assyria had already broken in, and Babylon was soon to break in; later others would come to plunder and destroy. If you have ever seen pictures of the walls of Jerusalem and the wailing wall, you can see that they are built of stones from different periods of civilizations. It is quite evident that the city has been destroyed repeatedly. History tells us that Jerusalem has been destroyed at least twenty-seven times, and today it is built upon debris. To go down to the place where Christ walked this earth you would have to dig thirty to fifty feet below the present surface. God permitted nations to come against Israel. Why? Because Israel failed Him so.

Note this remarkable verse—

**His watchmen are blind: they are all ignorant, they are all dumb dogs, they cannot bark; sleeping, lying down, loving to slumber [Isa. 56:10].**

This is a picture of the prophets and priests who spoke for God in that day. God permitted the enemy to take Jerusalem because of the weak and inadequate leadership of the people. They were blind. They were ignorant. They

were dumb dogs. In the New Testament Paul warned the people to beware of dogs (see Phil. 3:2). What did he mean? Well, he's not talking about being wary of a stranger's dog that barks at you. He is referring to false teachers and preachers who are not declaring the full counsel of God. In Isaiah's day every shepherd had a dog to help him watch the sheep. The dog would lie down at night and keep one eye open. The minute a dangerous animal or a human being came to harm or to steal a sheep, the dog would bark. Watchmen—the prophets and the priests who should have been warning God's people and giving out the Word of God—were ignorant of it. They were like dumb dogs who did not bark when there was danger. It was easier for them to keep quiet.

Liberalism, in my judgment, came into being because of the cowardly position that many ministers took. When you preach the Word of God, you step on toes. I know this—I have been doing it for years. I try to be as nice as I can about preaching the Word, but it is strong and this verse is very strong. The man who stands in the pulpit and won't give out God's Word is a *dumb dog!* I didn't say that, but Isaiah did say it, and Isaiah wrote at the direction of the Holy Spirit of God. A dumb dog is a man who won't give out the Word of God. He lies down and sleeps. He cannot bark. He loves to slumber. It is much more comfortable for the pastor to try to please his people.

Over the years I have received many letters from pulpit committees asking me to recommend a pastor. Then they list the qualifications they want him to have. The top priority qualification is personality. They want a friendly pastor who knows how to communicate to all age groups—a man that the senior citizens will love and the young people will love. Some of the letters don't even ask for a man with the ability to teach the Word of God! As a result, there are a lot of dumb dogs in pulpits. I am sorry to say this, but it is true, and Isaiah said it before I did.

**Yea, they are greedy dogs which can never have enough, and they are shepherds that cannot understand: they all look to their own way, every one for his gain, from his quarter [Isa. 56:11].**

"They are greedy dogs." They are concerned with their own personal interests rather than the welfare of their people.

One day I had lunch with a preacher friend of mine who is retired. He said to me, "McGee, you are making your message on the

radio a little strong, aren't you? Suppose people turn against you and won't support your program?" I replied, "Then I'll go off the air and just tell the Lord about it. If He intends for me to stay on the air, He intends for me to give out His Word. Very frankly, I think that this is *His* problem, not mine. I'll just give out His Word."

**Come ye, say they, I will fetch wine, and we will fill ourselves with strong drink; and to-morrow shall be as this day, and much more abundant [Isa. 56:12].**

These people drowned their sad plight and condition in drink, and they faced the future as drunkards and blind optimists. There are many people today who are facing life like that. They drown their troubles in drink. In our nation today, my friend, we have an alcohol problem among adults and young people—and even children! I am seeing more drunkards today than I have ever seen before in my long life. When I was on a plane the other day, I was seated near a dear old grandmother. She was the sweetest looking little thing, and I just wished she were my grandmother. I was thinking, *Well, she is one person on this plane who won't be ordering a cocktail.* And, do you know, she ordered a Bloody Mary! Oh, boy, she tossed them down! Obviously she was accustomed to that sort of thing. The morality of our nation is gone, my friend. And a great many Christians don't want to hear about it; they would rather listen to soft, sweet music.

Well, you don't get into trouble when you play soft music, but you do when you give out the Word of God. But Isaiah told it like it was, and that's what I intend to do also.

# CHAPTER 57

**THEME:** *Contrast between the righteous and wicked; comfort for the righteous; condemnation of the wicked*

Now I grant you that today the wicked have it easy—they are the ones in *comfort.* They are the ones with the money, and they seem to be on top. But when we get to the end of the age, it will be comfort for the righteous and condemnation for the wicked.

This chapter marks the end of the second section of the final division of Isaiah, which I have labeled, "The salvation of Jehovah which comes through the suffering Servant." Those who come in humility and accept it are made righteous. Those who reject it, proceed on their wicked way to judgment. This chapter brings us to the crossroads where the way that leads to life goes one way and the broad way to destruction goes another way. The destination and division are right here.

## CONTRAST BETWEEN THE RIGHTEOUS AND WICKED

**The righteous perisheth, and no man layeth it to heart: and merciful men are taken away, none considering that the righteous is taken away from the evil to come [Isa. 57:1].**

"The righteous perisheth." Many of God's wonderful saints are being taken away today through the doorway of death. God is removing them from a lot of trouble that is going to come in the future. When I started my ministry, I worried about myself. Then I had a child and I worried about her. Now I have two grandsons, and I worry about them. I no longer worry about myself or my daughter, but I do worry about those two little fellows because their lot in the future is going to be rough.

**He shall enter into peace: they shall rest in their beds, each one walking in his uprightness [Isa. 57:2].**

"He shall enter into peace"—he shall have peace in his heart. "They shall rest in their beds, each one walking in his uprightness." If death comes to him while he is in bed, he will be removed from the Great Tribulation and will be taken into the presence of Christ. They will have peace regardless of what may come to them.

**But draw near hither, ye sons of the sorceress, the seed of the adulterer and the whore [Isa. 57:3].**

Now God addresses the wicked. Even their ancestry is bad—note the label given their mothers!

**Against whom do ye sport yourselves? against whom make ye a wide mouth, and draw out the tongue? are ye not children of transgression, a seed of falsehood [Isa. 57:4].**

They have been the persecutors of the righteous. Up to this point God has not intervened. Look around you today. Attacks are being made upon the righteous. They are not having an easy time. The attacks are coming hard and fierce, and the wicked seem to get by with it.

**Enflaming yourselves with idols under every green tree, slaying the children in the valleys under the clifts of the rocks? [Isa. 57:5].**

The wicked in the last days are the idolaters who have turned their backs on God. They are guilty of gross immorality and murder. Adultery and murder are two of the terrible sins of *our* day also—coupled with covetousness, which is idolatry. This is the condition of the wicked at the present time.

**Among the smooth stones of the stream is thy portion; they, they are thy lot: even to them hast thou poured a drink offering, thou hast offered a meat offering. Should I receive comfort in these? [Isa. 57:6].**

They will even worship the smooth stones in the brook that once slew a giant. They worship everything except the living and true God.

**Upon a lofty and high mountain hast thou set thy bed: even thither wentest thou up to offer sacrifice [Isa. 57:7].**

Now idolatry, associated with the groves on the mountain tops, gives place to scenes of the vilest immorality. It is a picture of the last days.

**Behind the doors also and the posts hast thou set up thy remembrance: for thou hast discovered thyself to another than me, and art gone up; thou hast enlarged thy bed, and made thee a covenant with them; thou lovedst their bed where thou sawest it [Isa. 57:8].**

In the past, sin was committed in secret, but at the present time sin has become brazen and flaunts itself. Somebody asked me, "Don't you think there was as much immorality in the past as there is now?" I agreed that there may have been as much, but it was kept secret. Men were ashamed of their sin, but today

they are not. The other day I listened to a pretty little girl on television talk about the man she lives with who is not her husband. She was commended by others on the program for not being a hypocrite. She may not be a hypocrite, but she is a sinner in God's sight. What would not even have been whispered about a few years ago is done in the open today. Sin has become a way of life. There are no longer high standards. The wheat and the tares are growing together exactly as the Lord said they would.

We see the contrast between the righteous and the wicked all through this section.

## COMFORT FOR THE RIGHTEOUS

In the second division Isaiah speaks of comfort for the righteous.

**For thus saith the high and lofty One that inhabiteth eternity, whose name is Holy; I dwell in the high and holy place, with him also that is of a contrite and humble spirit, to revive the spirit of the humble, and to revive the heart of the contrite ones [Isa. 57:15].**

God in the last days comforts His own because of who He is—"the high and lofty One." He is the God of eternity. How feeble man is with his threescore years and ten down here. Man doesn't last very long on earth. The eternal God promises to take those who do not trust in themselves, but trust in Him, and He covers them as a mother hen covers her brood. What peace and security there is for those who belong to God! This verse looks beyond our day to the time of the Great Tribulation; we are coming here to the end of the age.

**For I will not contend for ever, neither will I be always wroth: for the spirit should fail before me, and the souls which I have made [Isa. 57:16].**

He is the eternal God, but He will not always be angry with sin, because sin is to be removed.

**For the iniquity of his covetousness was I wroth, and smote him: I hid me, and was wroth, and he went on frowardly in the way of his heart [Isa. 57:17].**

God explains why He punishes the wicked. The wicked are covetous, and they go on in rebellion against God. I am sure that any intelligent person knows that a holy God will one day stop rebellion. God will have to punish those with rebellious and proud hearts.

**I have seen his ways, and will heal him: I will lead him also, and restore comforts unto him and to his mourners [Isa. 57:18].**

For those who will forsake the wickedness of their ways, He will heal and save them. He is a gracious God toward the righteous.

**I create the fruit of the lips; Peace, peace to him that is far off, and to him that is near, saith the LORD; and I will heal him [Isa. 57:19].**

God alone can speak peace to the heart of the sinner.

## CONDEMNATION OF THE WICKED

Each one of these last three divisions can be marked off at the place where God says, as He did in Isaiah 48:22, "There is no peace, saith the LORD, unto the wicked." I think this is something that is quite evident. Man's history is one of warfare and constant conflict. It is not only true among nations, but also between individuals—although they call it competition. You will find it in the business world, the social world, and in the religious world. You will find conflict in practically every town, every hamlet, and in many homes in our country. God says that there is no peace for the wicked. You cannot make peace in the human heart apart from God. So far *no* one has been able to do it.

**But the wicked are like the troubled sea, when it cannot rest, whose waters cast up mire and dirt [Isa. 57:20].**

This is probably one of the most picturesque descriptions of the wicked in Scripture. Like the troubled and restless sea, the wicked person can find no rest or peace in his wicked ways. He continues on like a hunted criminal looking for deliverance and safety.

Several years ago an eighty-year-old man walked into the police station in Jackson, Mississippi, and said, "For fifty years I have been carrying on my conscience a murder. Another man has already paid the penalty for it, but I'm the one who is guilty. I *have* to make the confession of it." They found that, according to law, when another man had already paid the penalty, they couldn't execute the actual criminal or even hold him because another man had served the sentence. Probably the worst punishment this man had was fifty years of misery with a guilty conscience. He had had no peace of heart and mind at all.

**There is no peace, saith my God, to the wicked [Isa. 57:21].**

If the world can have peace today without God, then it is a contradiction of the Word of God. You cannot contradict God's Word. The wicked cannot have peace in the world, and they *don't* have it today. God says that the wicked will have no peace. That is an axiom of God, and it is like the law of gravity—it works.

# CHAPTER 58

**THEME:** *Exposure of Israel's wicked ways; explanation from God for rejecting religious acts; God's concern for their welfare*

This chapter brings us to the final division of the prophecy of Isaiah—"The Glory of Jehovah which comes through the suffering Servant." We move on in this section to the glory of the kingdom. Inward wicked ways and outward religious forms delay the grace and glory of God and hurt the cause of Christ as much as anything. Men who are religious and are church members and yet curse like pagans, men who are dishonest in business, immoral in their social lives, yet talk about being good enough to meet God's standards, actually block the grace and glory of God.

The explanation is given here as to why the glory was withheld. The people were supercilious and cynical about their relationship to God. They were observing forms and dared to question the actions of God toward them. They sat in judgment upon God and His methods. A lot of people still do this today. In spite of their outward observance of religion they indulge in their own wicked ways.

This same spirit was manifested after the Babylonian captivity, which reveals that the captivity did not cure them. In Malachi 3:13–14 we read, "Your words have been stout against me, saith the LORD.. Yet ye say, What have we spoken so much against thee? Ye

have said, It is vain to serve God: and what profit is it that we have kept his ordinance, and that we have walked mournfully before the LORD of hosts?" They were criticizing God for not blessing them—yet look how religious they were! They went to the temple and they made sacrifices. It was brazen effrontery and audacity to question God! This is the spirit of the natural man with his outward show of religion. His heart is far from God, and his way is wicked. The veneer of godliness is nauseating to the Lord Jesus Christ. The Lord said to the Laodicean church, "So then because thou art lukewarm, and neither cold nor hot, I will spue thee out of my mouth" (Rev. 3:16). This is the attitude of the Lord Jesus to a lot of churchianity in our day.

## EXPOSURE OF ISRAEL'S WICKED WAYS

**Cry aloud, spare not, lift up thy voice like a trumpet, and shew my people their transgression, and the house of Jacob their sins [Isa. 58:1].**

The prophet is commanded to cry aloud a message that is always unpopular, which is to point out the transgressions and sins of a people who think they are very religious. This will bring down the bitter displeasure and caustic invective upon one's head. Only a very brave man will do it. I would say that the basic weakness of liberalism in the pulpit is its aim to please the natural man without telling him the real truth about his fatal disease. The medical profession today would be guilty of gross negligence if they followed the same procedure with the physical part of man that religion plays with the spiritual part of man. When the doctor told me I had cancer, I tried my best to get him to say that it was something else. He said, "I am going to tell you exactly what is wrong with you. I will tell it exactly like it is. If I don't, you won't have any confidence in me." God is telling it exactly like it is. And He wants His servants to tell mankind that they are suffering from the fatal disease of sin, which is going to eventuate in *eternal death*, eternal separation from almighty God.

**Yet they seek me daily, and delight to know my ways, as a nation that did righteousness, and forsook not the ordinance of their God: they ask of me the ordinances of justice; they take delight in approaching to God [Isa. 58:2].**

I think there is an element of God's biting satire in this statement. These people were attending the temple worship regularly. They were going through the ordinances punctiliously. They were meticulous in following the forms of worship. They actually *enjoyed* going to church; yet their lives bore no resemblance to those of Christians. What was true in that day is also true today.

**Wherefore have we fasted, say they, and thou seest not? wherefore have we afflicted our soul, and thou takest no knowledge? Behold, in the day of your fast ye find pleasure, and exact all your labours [Isa. 58:3].**

These people are petulantly complaining. They ask the reason for fasting and self-infliction if God doesn't take note of it and pat them on the back for the ritual. Yet their hearts are far from God. They evidently had made fasting an important part of their religion. God never gave them fast days; He gave them feast days. It is true that they were to afflict their souls in connection with the great Day of Atonement, and in times of sin they were to fast. Fasting was the outward expression of the soul, but they had made it a form which ministered to their ego and pride. They *boasted* of the fact that they fasted. Fasting was to be a private matter between the soul and God—not a public show. Our Lord condemned them for abusing the fast. When He was here He said, "Moreover when ye fast, be not, as the hypocrites, of a sad countenance: for they disfigure their faces, that they may appear unto men to fast. Verily I say unto you, They have their reward [which was to be seen of men]" (Matt. 6:16). They needn't expect anything from God, for they didn't do it because of the relationship with Him. The Lord Jesus said to those who are His own: "But thou, when thou fastest, anoint thine head, and wash thy face; That thou appear not unto men to fast, but unto thy Father which is in secret: and thy Father, which seeth in secret, shall reward thee openly" (Matt. 6:17–18). Real religion is a personal relationship with Christ, and it is as secret and private as anything can possibly be. Do you go around and tell others about your intimate relationship with your wife or your husband? Of course you don't. My friend, if you have a personal relationship with Jesus Christ, it is a precious secret between the two of you. You witness for Him, but you don't reveal your intimate moments with Him. My friend, are you boasting about your religion, or about going

through a certain ceremony or ritual? Shame on you! They are nothing in the sight of God—unless they reveal what is within your heart. Oh, how we need reality rather than ritual!

I am of the opinion that many folk in that day questioned Isaiah's message. They probably said, "Isaiah, what in the world are you talking about? You criticize these people who are very religious, who go regularly to the temple and make their sacrifices!" But, you see, God knows the heart. Their religion was only superficial. They had no real relationship with God.

## EXPLANATION FROM GOD FOR REJECTING RELIGIOUS ACTS

In this next section God explains His reason for rejecting their show of religion.

**Behold, ye fast for strife and debate, and to smite with the fist of wickedness: ye shall not fast as ye do this day, to make your voice to be heard on high [Isa. 58:4].**

God explains why He cannot accept their fasting. They thought it gave them special acceptance with Him.

**Is it such a fast that I have chosen? a day for a man to afflict his soul? is it to bow down his head as a bulrush, and to spread sackcloth and ashes under him? wilt thou call this a fast, and an acceptable day to the LORD? [Isa. 58:5].**

God had not commanded their fasting, and their acts of worship were entirely outward and did not reveal the condition of the heart.

This is largely the condition of the contemporary church. I don't say it is the condition of *your* church—there are many wonderful churches. But, by and large, the organized church has only a form of godliness.

**Is not this the fast that I have chosen? to loose the bands of wickedness, to undo the heavy burdens, and to let the oppressed go free, and that ye break every yoke? [Isa. 58:6].**

This is tremendous—it gets right down to the nitty-gritty, right down where the rubber meets the road. God says in effect, "If you really want to fast, let Me tell you what to do: Instead of fasting and going around with a pious look, stop your sinning. Stop your gossiping. Stop the things that reveal the wickedness and the evil in your hearts. Demonstrate your faith in Me by your con-

duct. Start being honest in your dealings. Be truthful in what you say. Instead of seeing you in sackcloth and covered with ashes, I'd like to see you clean on the inside."

My friend, I am of the opinion that the Lord could stop many church services today and say, "Listen, let's cut this out. Why are you going through this form? You are not getting close to me. You are not pleasing Me. When you leave this service, you gossip, you have bitterness in your heart, you are not moral in your conduct, and you are living loose lives. You think you are pleasing Me by your religious form. I want you to know that you are not pleasing Me. That is the reason I am rejecting you."

**Is it not to deal thy bread to the hungry, and that thou bring the poor that are cast out to thy house? when thou seest the naked, that thou cover him; and that thou hide not thyself from thine own flesh? [Isa. 58:7].**

They were turning their backs on the poor and needy. They even refused to show kindness and love to their own flesh and blood. Their religion was as cold as the north side of a tombstone in January! They didn't have a heart for God. When you have a heart for God, my friend, you will also have a heart for other folk. You will want to be helpful to them and be a blessing to them. You cannot be hateful and fundamental in your theology at the same time. All of the criticism and unloveliness today is harmful to the cause of Christ. Isaiah has a tremendous message for us!

God told His people that He didn't want their so-called worship—they were just going through a form. They were just "playing church." He told them that they might think they were having fun, but it was going to become a burden to them because they would become weary trying to keep up a front before the world. God said to them, "Come clean. Demonstrate in your lives that you have reality."

Do you see why Isaiah is not popular? You will never find liberalism dealing with this part of the Bible. They like to turn to the Sermon on the Mount and pick out a few verses, such as: "Blessed are the merciful: for they shall obtain mercy" (Matt. 5:7). That is great, but the important thing is to confess your sin to God and allow Christ to live His life through you. Religion is a great cover-up today. Oh, how we need a personal relationship with Christ!

## GOD'S CONCERN FOR THEIR WELFARE

God wants His people to turn to Him in a real way.

**Then shall thy light break forth as the morning, and thine health shall spring forth speedily: and thy righteousness shall go before thee; the glory of the Lord shall be thy rereward [Isa. 58:8].**

God could not manifest His blessing and glory to a people who practiced their religion so badly. This is one of the reasons the world today is not convinced that God is in His holy temple. The world is passing by the church. Why? They don't believe God is there. And I suspect they might be right. God says here, "I can't manifest myself because of your lives." How many of us are blocking the way! The story is told that when Alexander the Great returned from one of his campaigns, he rushed to find his old teacher, Aristotle, the great Greek philosopher. It so happened that Aristotle was taking a bath when his visitor arrived. Alexander told him about his campaign and then said, "Now what can I do for you?" The old philosopher was not at all impressed with this young upstart and continued his bathing. Alexander repeated the question, "Now what can I do for you?" Finally old Aristotle replied, "Well, you can get out of my light!" Perhaps we are saying to God, "What can I do for You?" I think God would answer, "You can get out of my light!" Let's allow His light to shine through us. That's the important thing.

**Then shalt thou call, and the Lord shall answer; thou shalt cry, and he shall say, Here I am. If thou take away from the midst of thee the yoke, the putting forth of the finger, and speaking vanity [Isa. 58:9].**

God *wanted* to hear their prayers and He *wanted* to bless. He wanted to open the windows of heaven and pour out a blessing upon them, but their hearts weren't open to receive it. We say, "Our prayers are not answered." Why? Is it because God does not want to answer them? No! The problem is that our hearts are not open to receive the blessing God really wants to give us. God says, "The minute you cry to Me, here I am."

When I was a boy, I had typhoid fever and double pneumonia at the same time. I lived in a little country town, and one night the country doctor thought I was going to die. My mother sat by my bed all night. I was delirious most of the time, but I can still remember coming out of it and calling her name, "Mama?" She would say, "Here I am." What a comfort that was for a little boy. And today what a comfort to know that when we go to God in prayer, He is there. He says, "Here I am." In effect, God says, "It's up to you from now on. If you come in the name of My Son, make a request that is in My will, and your heart is right, I'm going to move right along with you." When we have prayers which are not being answered, the problem is with *us*.

**And if thou draw out thy soul to the hungry, and satisfy the afflicted soul; then shall thy light rise in obscurity, and thy darkness be as the noon day [Isa. 58:10].**

God asked them to practice one specific thing that He might bless them. He only picked out one thing. He could have picked out a dozen things, but He chose only one. God *promised* to bless them if they would show reality in their religion.

**And the Lord shall guide thee continually, and satisfy thy soul in drought, and make fat thy bones: and thou shalt be like a watered garden, and like a spring of water, whose waters fail not [Isa. 58:11].**

God wanted to bless them, you see.

**If thou turn away thy foot from the sabbath, from doing thy pleasure on my holy day; and call the sabbath a delight, the holy of the Lord, honourable; and shalt honour him, not doing thine own ways, nor finding thine own pleasure, nor speaking thine own words [Isa. 58:13].**

God gave the sabbath to the nation Israel. God said, "It is a sign between me and the children of Israel for ever . . ." (Exod. 31:17). For something interesting, read the entire passage of Exodus 31:12–18. Now God turns to this specific thing that He commanded them as a people.

For us today it is a little different. We are told: "Let us therefore fear, lest, a promise being left us of entering into his rest, any of you should seem to come short of it" (Heb. 4:1). The word for "rest" is *sabbath*—we should not come short of entering into His rest. "For he that is entered into his rest [that is, the sabbath], he also hath ceased from his own works, as God did from his" (Heb. 4:10). Now have you entered into His sabbath,

which is the rest of redemption? Have you come to the place where you completely, fully trust Christ—that He has done everything necessary for your salvation and you are resting in His finished work? Or do you feel compelled to *do* something in order to earn or not lose your salvation? My friend, He wants us to fully trust Christ. To enter into His rest will mean not only great blessing for us, but it will open up an avenue of service for us. The thing that brought the apostle Paul to a life of missionary activity was to enter into the rest of redemption.

**Then shalt thou delight thyself in the LORD; and I will cause thee to ride upon the high places of the earth, and feed thee with the heritage of Jacob thy father: for the mouth of the LORD hath spoken it [Isa. 58:14].**

The horizon here is extended, and the vista of the future opens before us. They may delay the approaching glory, but they cannot destroy God's plan for the coming manifestation of His glory.

# CHAPTER 59

***THEME:*** *Condemnation of Israel; confession of Israel; coming of the Redeemer to Israel*

This remarkable chapter continues God's charges against Israel, and He spells them out. Their sins had brought about their sad state. Religion had become a cover-up for their sins. God refused to hear because of their iniquities, not because He was hard of hearing. Many people today think God has a hearing problem. God hears us all right. The problem lies with us.

Their sins are referred to thirty-two times. Many words are used to describe their sins: iniquities, sins, defiled with blood, lies, perverseness, vanity, mischief, adder's eggs, spider's web, viper, works, violence, evil, wasting, destruction, crooked paths, darkness, transgressions, departing, oppression, revolt, conceiving, and uttering falsehood. There are twenty-three separate charges brought against them. What a picture this is! For Israel there will be a time of national confession of sin. In that day there shall be a great mourning in Jerusalem. We are told about it in Zechariah 12:11–14: "In that day shall there be a great mourning in Jerusalem, as the mourning of Hadadrimmon in the valley of Megiddon. And the land shall mourn, every family apart; the family of the house of David apart, and their wives apart; the family of the house of Nathan apart, and their wives apart; The family of the house of Levi apart, and their wives apart; the family of Shimei apart, and their wives apart; All the families that remain, every family apart, and their wives apart."

## CONDEMNATION OF ISRAEL

**Behold, the LORD'S hand is not shortened, that it cannot save; neither his ear heavy, that it cannot hear [Isa. 59:1].**

The reason that Israel was not saved in Isaiah's day was not due to any weakness in the "mighty bared arm of Jehovah" which we saw in Isaiah 53. The Lord's hand was not shortened. Neither was it due to any faulty connection in His communication with man. Likewise in our day it is not the mental hurdles that man has to surmount nor any of his many problems, but his *sin* separates him from God.

**But your iniquities have separated between you and your God, and your sins have hid his face from you, that he will not hear [Isa. 59:2].**

Let me quote the comment of Alexander Maclaren in *The Books of Isaiah and Jeremiah:* "It is not because God is great and I am small, it is not because He lives for ever, and my life is but a hand-breadth, it is not because of the difference between His omniscience and my ignorance, His strength and my weakness, that I am parted from Him: 'Your sins have separated between you and your God.' And no man, build he Babels ever so high, can reach thither. There is one means by which the separation is at an end, and by which all objective hindrances to union, and all subjective hindr-

ances, are alike swept away. Christ has come, and in Him the heavens have bended down to touch, and touching to bless this low earth, and man and God are at one once more."

Now throughout this first section God spells out their sins. It is rather a discouraging picture of the human family—and of you and me. Then we have a confession of Israel, which is coming in the future when the Redeemer comes to Zion.

## CONFESSION OF ISRAEL

**Therefore is judgment far from us, neither doth justice overtake us: we wait for light, but behold obscurity; for brightness, but we walk in darkness [Isa. 59:9].**

The change of pronoun here indicates that there is another speaker. Instead of "your" and "their," it is "we" and "our" and "us" now. This is Israel's confession. They confess they are in darkness. They confess that their religious rituals have all been a pretense.

Many folk need to do this in our day. I played golf with a dentist and a broker some time ago in Tulsa, Oklahoma. Both of these men told me how they came to know the Lord. Both of them had been members in rich liberal churches. They were both wealthy men. One of the men told me that one day he simply got tired of being a hypocrite, so he went to the Lord and confessed that he was a hypocrite and wanted reality. He accepted Jesus Christ as his Savior. Oh, how this is needed today! It could actually bring revival to our churches.

Now notice Israel's confession:

**We grope for the wall like the blind, and we grope as if we had no eyes: we stumble at noon day as in the night; we are in desolate places as dead men [Isa. 59:10].**

You see, they are in darkness. What a picture of the man who does not have a personal relationship with God!

But when Israel will make this confession—

and they *will* make it in the future—to these specific charges, they also will repudiate their sins. My friend, our confessions to God should be specific and then the sins repudiated. Each sin should be confessed privately to God.

I have no heart to go through this list of Israel's sins—I have problems enough with my own.

## COMING OF THE REDEEMER TO ISRAEL

Notice that the pronoun changes again. The Redeemer will come to Zion.

**And the Redeemer shall come to Zion, and unto them that turn from transgression in Jacob, saith the LORD [Isa. 59:20].**

Many people ask, "Will the whole nation be saved?" No, "For they are not all Israel, which are of Israel" (Rom. 9:6). Those saved will only be a remnant. And there appears to be only a remnant in the church who are actually saved.

But the Redeemer is coming some day to Zion, and at that time there will be a great confession of sin. Zechariah 12:10 tells us about it: "And I will pour upon the house of David, and upon the inhabitants of Jerusalem, the spirit of grace and of supplications: and they shall look upon me whom they have pierced, and they shall mourn for him, as one mourneth for his only son, and shall be in bitterness for him, as one that is in bitterness for his firstborn."

**As for me, this is my covenant with them, saith the LORD; My spirit that is upon thee, and my words which I have put in thy mouth, shall not depart out of thy mouth, nor out of the mouth of thy seed, nor out of the mouth of thy seed's seed, saith the LORD, from henceforth and for ever [Isa. 59:21].**

God has made a covenant that the Redeemer is coming to Zion. There will never be a time when this promise will be entirely forsaken, for this is God's purpose. It *will* be fulfilled in His good time.

# CHAPTER 60

***THEME:*** *The Redeemer and Gentiles come to Jerusalem; the return of Israel to Jerusalem; Jerusalem's realization of all God's promises*

The last part of Isaiah, I have a notion, is virgin territory to a great many folks because no school of prophecy dwells on this particular section of Scripture. In this chapter we see the Sun of Righteousness rising upon Israel; it is that which Malachi said would come to pass in the last days. When He comes, it will be like the sun rising into midnight darkness. In that day the nation Israel will reflect the glory light here upon the entire earth. The church, in the meantime, has gone to be with Christ. To attempt to make the nation Israel and the church synonymous is an interpretation that bogs down when you get into an area like this. It is an unsatisfactory interpretation which does not meet the dimensions of these prophecies. I emphasize this because it has caused so much confusion. Certain schools of Bible interpretation place little importance on prophecy because they neglect sections like this great chapter in the Word of God.

This third and final division of the Book of Isaiah presents the Redeemer on the cross (ch. 53). Following that there has been a definite progress and development which speaks not of the *government* of God (as the first part of Isaiah did), but rather of the *grace* of God. In the first section the emphasis was upon *law*; here it is upon *grace*. We find here—as we found also in the first section—that there is *love* in law. Also in this section we find that there is *law* in love.

The chapter before us brings us to the full manifestation of the Millennium. Chapter 59 closed by saying that the Redeemer will come to Zion. Now as we move along in chapter 60, He has come. In the Hebrew language there is what is known as the prophetic tense—when the prophet goes beyond the event and looks back at it as if it were history. Isaiah speaks of many future things as having already taken place. For example he begins by saying, "Arise; shine, for thy light *is* come, and the glory of the Lord *is* risen upon thee." And you can understand that for God to say a thing is going to happen, He is already on the other side of it—for Him it is just the same as having taken place. In other words, prophecy is the mold into which history is poured.

## THE REDEEMER AND GENTILES COME TO JERUSALEM

**Arise, shine; for thy light is come, and the glory of the Lord is risen upon thee [Isa. 60:1].**

The Light now has come of which Malachi has spoken: "But unto you that fear my name shall the Sun of righteousness arise with healing in his wings . . ." (Mal. 4:2).

**For, behold, the darkness shall cover the earth, and gross darkness the people: but the Lord shall arise upon thee, and his glory shall be seen upon thee [Isa. 60:2].**

The Lord Jesus Christ is the Light of the world—that was one of His claims when He was here. When He comes to the earth the second time, He is that Light.

"For, behold, the darkness shall cover the earth." The coming of the Light is necessitated by the night of spiritual darkness that has covered the earth—and covers the earth today. In spite of the preaching of the Gospel for nineteen hundred years, there is a wider circle of darkness today than ever before. Light *must* precede the future blessings. The Sun of Righteousness *must* rise to bring the millennial day. The preaching of the gospel was never God's intention to bring in the Millennium, because it takes the Light to bring in the Millennium. And who is the Light? The Lord Jesus. We need the presence of the Redeemer in Zion, and He is going to bring the Gentiles from afar.

**And the Gentiles shall come to thy light, and kings to the brightness of thy rising [Isa. 60:3].**

I believe that the greatest revival—that is, the greatest turning to God is yet in the future. In Romans 11:15 Paul says, "For if the casting away of them [Israel] be the reconciling of the world, what shall the receiving of them be, but life from the dead?" It will be the resurrection of the nation Israel and the resurrection of the world. You and I live on a little clod of earth in space that is just a glorified cemetery!

**Lift up thine eyes round about, and see: all they gather themselves together,**

they come to thee: thy sons shall come from far, and thy daughters shall be nursed at thy side [Isa. 60:4].

Rebellious and scattered, they are going to come back to the Land of Promise—but in obedience to God. The women who are weaker than men are carried, like women in the East often carry their children, on their hips.

**Then thou shalt see, and flow together, and thine heart shall fear, and be enlarged; because the abundance of the sea shall be converted unto thee, the forces of the Gentiles shall come unto thee [Isa. 60:5].**

Here you see the tremendous movement of all peoples toward Jerusalem—by land, by sea, and by air—which will be an occasion of astonishment.

**The multitude of camels shall cover thee, the dromedaries of Midian and Ephah, all they from Sheba shall come: they shall bring gold and incense; and they shall shew forth the praises of the LORD [Isa. 60:6].**

Again wise men, not only from the East but from all over the world, will come with gifts of gold and incense for the Redeemer. Notice that they are not bringing myrrh. Why? Because myrrh spoke of Christ's death at His first coming. At His second coming they bring no myrrh. This is a remarkable verse!

**All the flocks of Kedar shall be gathered together unto thee, the rams of Nebaioth shall minister unto thee: they shall come up with acceptance on mine altar, and I will glorify the house of my glory [Isa. 60:7].**

Flocks are brought to Jerusalem for sacrifice. The sacrifices will be reinstituted in the millennial temple. This may be difficult for some to accept, but the Old Testament is very definite at this point. Read, for example, Ezekiel 40–44. These sacrifices, I believe, will point *back* to the death of Christ as in the Old Testament they pointed forward to His death. They will have the same meaning.

## THE RETURN OF ISRAEL TO JERUSALEM

**Who are these that fly as a cloud, and as the doves to their windows? [Isa. 60:8].**

If there is any prophecy in Scripture that suggests the airplane, this is it, but I think the direct reference is to ships of the sea. It does not refer to what is happening today, although I understand that Jews who have come from farther East than Israel thought this prophecy was being fulfilled as they were brought by American airplanes to the land of Israel; but it does not quite meet the dimensions of the prophecy.

**Surely the isles shall wait for me, and the ships of Tarshish first, to bring thy sons from far, their silver and their gold with them, unto the name of the LORD thy God, and to the Holy One of Israel, because he hath glorified thee [Isa. 60:9].**

"Tarshish," as used here, evidently refers to all seagoing nations whose ships will be used to return Israel to the Land of Promise. The nations who once destroyed Israel will assist in her recovery. At that time Russia will send the Jews back to their land. Instead of demanding payment, they will send the Jews off with gifts as the Egyptians did. After all, Israel only collected their back pay from the Egyptians, and they had a great deal coming, because they had been in slavery for four hundred years.

**Therefore thy gates shall be open continually; they shall not be shut day nor night; that men may bring unto thee the forces of the Gentiles, and that their kings may be brought [Isa. 60:11].**

The nations of the world that are saved are going to come to Jerusalem in the Millennium.

**For the nation and kingdom that will not serve thee shall perish; yea, those nations shall be utterly wasted [Isa. 60:12].**

The Lord Jesus made it clear that His judgment upon the nations would be based on their treatment of the Jews (see Matt. 25:31–46).

In the Millennium every knee shall bow and every tongue shall confess that Jesus Christ is Lord (see Phil. 2:10–11). In the Millennium all mankind will be forced to bow to Jesus. The force, of course, will be the force of public opinion in that day. In their hearts there will be those who won't want to bow, but they will go through the motions. Then when Satan is released at the end of the Millennium, those with rebellious hearts will naturally gravitate toward him, which will be the last rebellion. Then the eternal aspect of the kingdom will be introduced. I believe at that time certain radical changes will take place. It won't be a

patched-up earth, but a new earth and new heavens will come into existence. God is going to make all things new, and He is going to let me start over again. I am looking forward to that! I haven't done so well since I began my life in Texas many years ago. I would like to start over. God is going to make all things new. He is not going to retool the old nature; He is going to give me a new nature, and He is going to give a new nature to everyone who has trusted in Him. What a glorious, wonderful day that will be!

## JERUSALEM'S REALIZATION OF ALL GOD'S PROMISES

**Whereas thou hast been forsaken and hated, so that no man went through thee, I will make thee an eternal excellency, a joy of many generations [Isa. 60:15].**

As Isaiah said in chapter 2, Jerusalem will become the center of the earth. A great deal of blessing will come in that day.

**Thou shalt also suck the milk of the Gentiles, and shalt suck the breast of kings: and thou shalt know that I the LORD am thy Saviour and thy Redeemer, the mighty One of Jacob [Isa. 60:16].**

The riches of Jerusalem, which were taken away by the nations, will be restored with interest.

**For brass I will bring gold, and for iron I will bring silver, and for wood brass, and for stones iron: I will also make thy officers peace, and thine exactors righteousness [Isa. 60:17].**

It is interesting that we see so many objects of brass in that land today. The markets of Egypt and Lebanon sell many brass objects, but in that future day they will be replaced by silver and gold objects for sale. In other words, precious metals will become commonplace again. Now notice some other wonderful things which will take place:

**The sun shall be no more thy light by day; neither for brightness shall the moon give light unto thee: but the LORD shall be unto thee an everlasting light, and thy God thy glory.**

**Thy sun shall no more go down; neither shall thy moon withdraw itself: for the LORD shall be thine everlasting light, and the days of thy mourning shall be ended [Isa. 60:19–20].**

Jesus, the Light of the world, will be there. He is also the Light of the New Jerusalem. The universe no longer will need street lights on the corners. After all, the suns and stars are street lights out in space. God did not light up the universe very well because sin had come in, but in that day He is really going to light things up!

**A little one shall become a thousand, and a small one a strong nation: I the LORD will hasten it in his time [Isa. 60:22].**

Human strength will be increased in that day without resorting to vitamins! The Lord Jesus called attention to the fact that the spirit is willing but the flesh is weak. In my own experience I find that my flesh just doesn't keep up with me! I would like to go much faster, but my body holds me back. However, in that future day all of this will be corrected—corrected here on earth as it will be corrected for the heavenly people.

# CHAPTER 61

*THEME: Distinction between the first and second coming of Christ; delights of the Millennium*

This chapter is of peculiar interest in view of the fact that the Lord Jesus opened His public ministry in Nazareth by quoting from it. This chapter continues the full blessings of the Millennium with Israel as the center of all earthly benefits. The last section projects us into the total benefits of the Millennium.

## DISTINCTION BETWEEN THE FIRST AND SECOND COMINGS OF CHRIST

Here in the first three verses we have one of the most remarkable passages of Scripture, and it helps us to correctly interpret the Bible.

The spirit of the Lord GOD is upon me; because the LORD hath anointed me to preach good tidings unto the meek; he hath sent me to bind up the brokenhearted, to proclaim liberty to the captives, and the opening of the prison to them that are bound;

To proclaim the acceptable year of the LORD, and the day of vengeance of our GOD; to comfort all that mourn [Isa. 61:1–2].

Now here we are given a system of biblical interpretation. If I were to read this without knowing the New Testament, I would not be sure about whom he is talking. Who is it who says, "The spirit of the Lord GOD is upon me"? If He is the Lord Jesus, does it refer to His first or second coming? Well, in the New Testament we have God's interpretation. When the Lord Jesus went into the synagogue in His hometown of Nazareth, He read this section: "And he came to Nazareth, where he had been brought up: and, as his custom was, he went into the synagogue on the sabbath day, and stood up for to read. And there was delivered unto him the book of the prophet Esaias. And when he had opened the book, he found the place where it was written, The Spirit of the Lord is upon me, because he hath anointed me to preach the gospel to the poor; he hath sent me to heal the brokenhearted, to preach deliverance to the captives, and recovering of sight to the blind, to set at liberty them that are bruised, To preach the acceptable year of the Lord" (Luke 4:16–19). Now, my friend, if you will look again at Isaiah 61:1–2, you will see that He is not even through with the sentence. Why didn't He keep

reading? The rest of the sentence is "and the day of vengeance of our God"—why didn't He preach that? Notice this: He *closed* the book. That was a deliberate action. "And he closed the book, and he gave it again to the minister, and sat down. And the eyes of all them that were in the synagogue were fastened on him. And he began to say unto them, This day is this scripture fulfilled in your ears" (Luke 4:20–21). Isaiah's prophecy up to that point was fulfilled by Christ's first coming. Isaiah had not made the distinction between the first and second comings of Christ, but the Lord Jesus made the distinction. In Isaiah's prophecy a little "and" separates the first and second comings of Christ. You might say that this little *and* is more than nineteen hundred years long! The prophets wrote of the first and second comings of Christ; they saw these two great events, but they did not know the length of time that lay between them. The apostle Peter confirms this: "Of which salvation the prophets have inquired and searched diligently, who prophesied of the grace that should come unto you: Searching what, or what manner of time the Spirit of Christ which was in them did signify, when it testified beforehand the sufferings of Christ, and the glory that should follow" (1 Pet. 1:10–11). Peter says that the prophets spoke of the sufferings of Christ and the glory of Christ—we see this in both the first and second sections of Isaiah.

Let me illustrate the problem the prophets had as they looked into the future. Behind my home in Pasadena, California—several miles from the foothills—looms Mount Wilson upon which Mount Wilson Observatory and the antennas of several radio stations are situated. Behind Mount Wilson I can see another mountain, Mount Waterman. It looks as if the two mountains are right there together, but I've been up in those mountains and I know there are at least twenty-five miles between them. It is impossible to see that distance between them unless you are there.

Now the prophet was way down in the valley looking into the future. He saw the first and second comings of Christ. Perhaps Isaiah was a little confused. In one breath how could he say that the Lord was going to bind up the brokenhearted, and open the prisons, and at the same time announce the day of the

vengeance of our God? How can both be true? If the prophet had stood where we stand today, he would have understood. We are in the valley between the first and second comings of Christ. We can look back to the first coming when He came to fulfill Luke 4:20–21 and to die on the cross as our Redeemer, as we saw in Isaiah 53. Somewhere beyond that mountain peak is the next one, the second coming of Christ. Before He comes again, however, the church will be removed from the earthly scene. In John 14:3 Jesus said, "And if I go and prepare a place for you, I will come again, and receive you unto myself; that where I am, there ye may be also."

"To proclaim the acceptable year of the LORD, and the day of vengeance of our God." When He comes to earth the second time to establish His kingdom, it will be with vengeance. We will see that in chapter 63 where He is treading the winepress of the wrath of God. It is not a pretty scene—God didn't say it would be pretty. But Christ is going to put down the rebellion that is here on this earth. You see, this little earth is still under His control. Emerson was wrong when he said that *things* are in the saddle and ride mankind. The *Lord Jesus Christ* is in the saddle, and He is in control. He is the King, and He is coming some day to put down all rebellion; that will be "the day of vengeance of our God."

"To comfort all that mourn." Immediately after announcing the day of vengeance, He says He is going to comfort all that mourn—those who mourn over their sin, who long in their hearts for a better day, and who want to be obedient unto Him.

Not only will He comfort *all* who mourn but all that mourn in *Zion*—

**To appoint unto them that mourn in Zion, to give unto them beauty for ashes, the oil of joy for mourning, the garment of praise for the spirit of heaviness; that they might be called trees of righteousness, the planting of the LORD, that he might be glorified [Isa. 61:3].**

I believe that Isaiah knew his geography, and when he said "Zion," he meant Zion—not Los Angeles, Salt Lake City, Florida, or South America. Zion, the highest spot in Jerusalem, was well known to Isaiah.

Now, speaking specifically of the Jews, he says, "to give unto them beauty for ashes, the oil of joy for mourning, the garment of praise

for the spirit of heaviness; that they might be called trees of righteousness, the planting of the LORD, that he might be glorified." You can see that beyond the "day of vengeance," which will be amplified in chapter 63, is the peace and the prosperity of the Millennium.

Isaiah makes a play upon words with "beauty" and "ashes"—it is like saying in English that God will exchange joy for judgment or a song for a sigh. After the sighing and the judgment there will be joy and singing.

**And they shall build the old wastes, they shall raise up the former desolations, and they shall repair the waste cities, the desolations of many generations [Isa. 61:4].**

The land of Israel is yet to receive a face-lifting, which will restore its Edenic beauty. What is happening in our day in Israel is wonderful. It has caused Dr. W. F. Albright, a great Hebrew scholar, to take the position that he now believes in prophecy—since a nation that has been out of their land for twenty-five hundred years is back in their land. It apparently has made a believer out of him. But let us be very careful not to call it the fulfillment of *this* prophecy. The "face-lifting" that this verse is talking about will take place at the beginning of the Millennium, and we are not at that place in time right now.

**And strangers shall stand and feed your flocks, and the sons of the alien shall be your plowmen and your vinedressers [Isa. 61:5].**

This is a real picture of prosperity.

**But ye shall be named the Priests of the LORD: men shall call you the Ministers of our God: ye shall eat the riches of the Gentiles, and in their glory shall ye boast yourselves [Isa. 61:6].**

"Men shall call you the Ministers of our God." Israel is going to be a priesthood of believers during the Millennium. It was God's original intention that the entire nation would be priests. In Exodus 19:6 God said of Israel, "And ye shall be unto me a kingdom of priests, and an holy nation. These are the words which thou shalt speak unto the children of Israel." Because of their sin this was never attained, but it will be attained in the Millennium.

**For your shame ye shall have double; and for confusion they shall rejoice in**

their portion: therefore in their land they shall possess the double: everlasting joy shall be unto them [Isa. 61:7].

In other words, everlasting joy shall be Israel's portion. It will be fullness of joy! What a great day that will be.

For I the LORD love judgment, I hate robbery for burnt offering; and I will direct their work in truth, and I will make an everlasting covenant with them [Isa. 61:8].

Their lives then will *adorn* their religious ritual. We have looked at several passages which spoke of the fact that Israel went through all of the rituals, but God condemned her for it because her heart was not in it. Things will be changed in that future day.

And their seed shall be known among the Gentiles, and their offspring among the people: all that see them shall acknowledge them, that they are the seed which the LORD hath blessed [Isa. 61:9].

Anti-Semitism will end, and pro-Semitism will begin because they are genuine witnesses for God. In our day neither Israel nor the church is fulfilling what God intended—although I believe we are following God's program, and it is working out as He said it would. He warned us that the day would come when we would have a form of godliness but deny the power thereof.

## DELIGHTS OF THE MILLENNIUM

I will greatly rejoice in the LORD, my soul shall be joyful in my God; for he hath clothed me with the garments of salvation, he hath covered me with the robe of righteousness, as a bridegroom decketh himself with ornaments, and as a bride adorneth herself with her jewels [Isa. 61:10].

"**I** will greatly rejoice in the LORD, my soul shall be joyful in my God"—my, they're going to have fun then! I wish that in our day more Christians had fun going to church. I wish they enjoyed it more. I wish the study of the Bible was a thrilling and exciting experience for all of us. It ought to be, and God intended that it should be.

"For he hath clothed me with the garments of salvation, he hath covered me with the robe of righteousness, as a bridegroom decketh himself with ornaments, and as a bride adorneth herself with her jewels." The Messiah continues to speak here, and as He does, all who are His can join in the psalm of praise. They will greatly rejoice in the Lord. The problem in our day is that a great many Christians can't rejoice in the Lord because they are out of fellowship. They have sin in their lives, they are way out of the will of God, and they are going on in their self-will.

For as the earth bringeth forth her bud, and as the garden causeth the things that are sown in it to spring forth; so the Lord GOD will cause righteousness and praise to spring forth before all the nations [Isa. 61:11].

Not only will there be material benefits and physical improvements, but the true blessings will be *spiritual* in that day.

# CHAPTER 62

**THEME:** *The ambition of the Messiah for Israel; the anticipation for the Millennium; announcement for that future day*

**T**he yearning of the Messiah for these anticipated joys is before us in this chapter, and there ought to be a yearning in the hearts of believers for these joys. There is a danger today of believers looking for the coming of Christ to take us out of the world so we can get away from our problems; we use it as an escape mechanism. People get into real difficulty, and then they want the Lord to come and get them out of it. When I was attending seminary, one of my fellow students was a Canadian. He was a great fellow, but he did not have much of a sense of humor, and other students, myself included, enjoyed kidding him. On certain nights after dinner he would go outside, look up into the sky, and say, "Oh, if only the Lord would come!" He would say this on the nights just before he had Hebrew class the following day. Hebrew was a difficult class, and when he said he wished the Lord would come, what he was really saying was that he wished the Lord would come

because he didn't want to study Hebrew. However, at graduation time, he received his degree one day and the next day he was married to a beautiful girl who had come down from Canada. The night before graduation this fellow went outside, looked up into the sky, and said, "I hope the Lord *doesn't* come for a few more days." Yes, that is the way it is with many of us. When things are bad, we want the Lord to come right away because we are on a hot seat and we want to get off it.

## THE AMBITION OF MESSIAH FOR ISRAEL

**For Zion's sake will I not hold my peace, and for Jerusalem's sake I will not rest, until the righteousness thereof go forth as brightness, and the salvation thereof as a lamp that burneth [Isa. 62:1].**

The reason Jerusalem can't have peace today is because her Messiah is not there. He is seated at God's right hand *longing* to rule that city in righteousness. You can call it the holy city if you want to, but it is anything but holy as it is now. However, it will be holy some day and the zeal of Jehovah of Hosts will perform it. Man won't make the kingdom, and the United Nations won't do it—that is obvious now. I don't think that anyone can bring peace into the world but this One. Only the zeal of the Lord of Hosts will accomplish it. The heart of the prophet Isaiah, as well as the heart of every godly soul on earth, enters into this longing. All of creation and all believers are groaning in their present state as they contemplate the future. Christian pilgrim, are you weary of the earthly journey, and do you desire the fellowship of the Father's house? That is a question each believer should consider.

**And the Gentiles shall see thy righteousness, and all kings thy glory: and thou shalt be called by a new name, which the mouth of the LORD shall name [Isa. 62:2].**

A new heart, a new situation, a new earth, a new righteousness demand a new name. I don't know what the new Vernon McGee will be like, but I'll be glad that the old Vernon McGee is gone. We will be new, and we are to be in the New Jerusalem. What a wonderful picture is given here of the future.

Redemption involves not only the church, but the nation Israel and this earth. Now we are all groaning and travailing, waiting for that grand day of deliverance.

**Thou shalt also be a crown of glory in the hand of the LORD, and a royal diadem in the hand of thy God [Isa. 62:3].**

Israel is also going to have a new position.

**Thou shalt no more be termed Forsaken; neither shall thy land any more be termed Desolate: but thou shalt be called Hephzibah, and thy land Beulah: for the LORD delighteth in thee, and thy land shall be married [Isa. 62:4].**

I have heard people sing that song about "Beulah land, sweet Beulah land," and I knew they did not have the foggiest notion what "Beulah land" meant or where it was. Let's see what this verse is talking about.

Israel has been "Forsaken"—this is the picture and name of Israel since the crucifixion of Christ. When you look at that land today, the word that comes to your mind is *forsaken*—desolate. That is the description of the land right now, but in the coming kingdom Israel shall be called *Hephzibah*, which means "delightful." It is going to be a delightful spot. I have made the statement before that I don't like Jerusalem as it is today, but it will be delightful in that future day.

"And thy land Beulah"—*Beulah* means "married." In other words, the King is present to protect it, and His presence means joy.

**For as a young man marrieth a virgin, so shall thy sons marry thee: and as the bridegroom rejoiceth over the bride, so shall thy God rejoice over thee [Isa. 62:5].**

God will delight over Israel as a bridegroom delights over a bride.

## THE ANTICIPATION FOR THE MILLENNIUM

**I have set watchmen upon thy walls, O Jerusalem, which shall never hold their peace day nor night: ye that make mention of the LORD, keep not silence [Isa. 62:6].**

This longing is contagious. The thirsty soul longs to drink. Every right-thinking person can pray for the peace of Jerusalem and long for that day when there will be peace.

**And give him no rest, till he establish, and till he make Jerusalem a praise in the earth [Isa. 62:7].**

God says that He ". . . will overturn, overturn, overturn . . . until he comes whose right it is . . ." to rule (Ezek. 21:27).

## ANNOUNCEMENT FOR THAT FUTURE DAY

Now let's drop down to the announcement of the Lord for that future day—

**Behold the Lord hath proclaimed unto the end of the world, Say ye to the daughter of Zion, Behold, thy salvation cometh; behold, his reward is with him, and his work before him [Isa. 62:11].**

This announcement is pertinent for the present hour, as this verse indicates. The salvation of Israel is part of God's overall plan of salvation. We ought to present the gospel to every Israelite. The Messiah is their Savior

today. And the second coming of Christ means the second coming of Christ to establish His kingdom on earth for these people.

**And they shall call them, The holy people, The redeemed of the Lord: and thou shalt be called, Sought out, A city not forsaken [Isa. 62:12].**

Israel cannot be called a holy people today. They are not redeemed today. Jerusalem is a forsaken city right now, but the day will come when things will be different. The experience of God's salvation will work a transformation in the nation Israel and also in the physical earth. The people will be called an holy people, and the land will be greatly desired. The contrary is true today. What a glorious future we have!

# CHAPTER 63

*THEME: The winepress of judgment; in wrath the Savior remembers mercy*

The content of the first six verses of this chapter is certainly in contrast to the preceding section. It really seems out of keeping with the tenor of this entire section of Isaiah, but judgment precedes the kingdom, and this has always been the divine order.

When Isaiah 53:1 described Christ at His first coming "there was no beauty that we should desire Him," but here there is majesty and beauty, which identifies it with His second coming. Also, the day of vengeance has been identified already with Christ's second coming rather than His first coming, as the Lord Himself clearly stated. Compare Isaiah 61:2 with Luke 4:18–20.

I find no delight in the first part of this chapter, because we see the wrath of Christ likened to a winepress in His coming judgment. Then the second part of the chapter reveals the loving-kindness which Christ manifests toward His own.

## THE WINEPRESS OF JUDGMENT

**Who is this that cometh from Edom, with dyed garments from Bozrah? this that is glorious in his apparel, traveling in the greatness of his strength? I that speak in righteousness, mighty to save [Isa. 63:1].**

The form used here is an antiphony. Those who ask the question concerning the One coming from Edom are overwhelmed by His majesty and beauty. He comes from Edom and the east, and we are told elsewhere that His feet will touch the Mount of Olives on the east. "Edom" and "Bozrah" are geographical places, and are to be considered as such, but this does not exhaust the mind of the Spirit. Edom is symbolic of the flesh and the entire Adamic race, and here we see the judgment of man.

**Wherefore art thou red in thine apparel, and thy garments like him that treadeth in the winevat? [Isa. 63:2].**

In that day men would get into the winepress barefooted to tread out the grapes. The red juice would spurt out of the ripe grapes and stain their garments. That is the picture you have in this verse, and that is why this question is asked. The spectators see that there is blood on His beautiful garments just as if He had trodden the winepress.

Now listen to His answer—

**I have trodden the winepress alone; and of the people there was none with me: for I will tread them in mine anger, and trample them in my fury; and their**

**blood shall be sprinkled upon my garments, and I will stain all my raiment [Isa. 63:3].**

Notice that it is *their* blood, not His.

The early church fathers associated these first six verses with the first coming of Christ. They mistook the winepress as the suffering of Christ on the cross. Such an interpretation is untenable, as the blood upon His garments is not His blood but that of others. It is the day of vengeance. It is identified already with the second coming of Christ rather than with His first coming. The Lord Jesus made that clear in Luke 4:18–20 when He read Isaiah 61:2. The Lord Jesus shed His own blood at His first coming, but that is not the picture which is presented here. He was trodden on at His first coming, but here He does the treading. This is a frightful picture of judgment.

Now we are told the reason for His judgment—

**For the day of vengeance is in mine heart, and the year of my redeemed is come [Isa. 63:4].**

He has come to save forever His redeemed ones from their vicious oppressors. This is His judgment upon the earth, and it is defined as the day of vengeance.

**And I looked, and there was none to help; and I wondered that there was none to uphold: therefore mine own arm brought salvation unto me; and my fury, it upheld me [Isa. 63:5].**

The Lord Jesus Christ wrought salvation alone when He was on the cross, and judgment is His solo work also.

**And I will tread down the people in mine anger, and make them drunk in my fury, and I will bring down their strength to the earth [Isa. 63:6].**

This is the end of man's little day upon the earth. The King is coming to the earth in judgment. There are those who will say, "This is frightful. I don't like it." Then, like the proverbial ostrich, they will put their heads in the sand and read John 14 or some other comforting passage of Scripture. However, we have to face up to this verse. The next time the Lord comes it will be in judgment. Can you think of any other way He can come and set up His kingdom? Suppose the Lord Jesus came the second time the way He came the first time, as the Man of Galilee, the Carpenter of Nazareth who walked the countryside

telling people that He had come from heaven. Suppose He knocked on the door of the Kremlin. Do you think those people are ready for Him? I don't think they are. I think they would put Him before a firing squad before the sun came up. No nation and no church today is prepared to turn their affairs over to Jesus. If they *are* prepared, why don't they do it? He was rejected when He came nearly two thousand years ago, and He has been rejected ever since. I can't think of any other way for Him to come the second time but in judgment.

Now others may say, "This verse is in the *Old* Testament. You have a God of wrath in the Old Testament, but when you get to the New Testament, He is a God of love." One of the reasons that the Book of Revelation has never been popular with the liberal is because it is filled with judgment. The Book of Revelation is in the *New* Testament, and the language is the strongest in the Bible (except what came from the lips of the Lord Jesus who spoke more of hell than anyone else). The Book of Revelation speaks of Christ's coming to put down the unrighteousness and rebellion and godlessness that is on the earth. Consider this one segment of the Book of Revelation: "And I heard a great voice out of the temple saying to the seven angels, Go your ways, and pour out the vials of the wrath of God upon the earth. And the first went, and poured out his vial upon the earth; and there fell a noisome and grievous sore upon the men which had the mark of the beast, and upon them which worshipped his image. And the second angel poured out his vial upon the sea; and it became as the blood of a dead man; and every living soul died in the sea. And the third angel poured out his vial upon the rivers and fountains of waters; and they became blood. And I heard the angel of the waters say, Thou art righteous, O Lord, which art, and wast, and shalt be, because thou hast judged thus" (Rev. 16:1–5). You see, immediately the critic will say, "God is not fair; He is not righteous to do this." God lets us know that when He judges like this, He is indeed being righteous. "For they have shed the blood of saints and prophets, and thou hast given them blood to drink; for they are worthy. And I heard another out of the altar say, Even so, Lord God Almighty, true and righteous are thy judgments" (Rev. 16:6–7). God is *right* in what He does—whether we think so or not. After all, to compare you and me with this tremendous universe would make it obvious that we don't amount to very much. Your opinion and my opinion, even when they are put together,

aren't worth very much. It is what *God* says that is important. When God says He is righteous, but we don't think He is, that means that we are wrong. God *is* righteous in what He does. "And the fourth angel poured out his vial upon the sun; and power was given unto him to scorch men with fire. And men were scorched with great heat, and blasphemed the name of God, which hath power over these plagues: and they repented not to give him glory" (Rev. 16:8–9). You would think that all of this would cause them to turn to God, but they didn't react that way. Instead it just brought out what they really were—just as the plagues of Egypt did in Pharaoh's day. "And the fifth angel poured out his vial upon the seat of the beast; and his kingdom was full of darkness; and they gnawed their tongues for pain" (Rev. 16:10). I have quoted this extensive passage from the New Testament to show the agreement between the Old and New Testaments. Don't let anyone tell you that we have a God of wrath in the Old Testament and a God of love in the New Testament! The God of love is the One making these statements in both the Old and New Testaments, because there is love in law—in fact, there is law in love.

Judgment is frightful, but He is coming in judgment when He returns to this earth, and He has not asked me to apologize for Him.

### IN WRATH THE SAVIOR REMEMBERS MERCY

In this section we see that in wrath the Lord Jesus remembers mercy to those who are His.

**I will mention the lovingkindnesses of the LORD, and the praises of the LORD, according to all that the LORD hath bestowed on us, and the great goodness toward the house of Israel, which he hath bestowed on them according to his mercies, and according to the multitude of his lovingkindnesses [Isa. 63:7].**

The entire content and intent changes abruptly at this point. It is like coming out of darkness into the sunlight of noonday. It is like turning from black to white. Our God is glorious in holiness, fearful in praises, doing wonders, and this is only one aspect of His many attributes. He is good, and He exhibits loving-kindness. He is also a God of mercy. If these attributes were not in evidence, we would all be consumed today—you may be sure of that! He has to come in judgment to take over this earth. It seems to me that He

has given men an extra long time to turn to Him.

**For he said, Surely they are my people, children that will not lie: so he was their Saviour [Isa. 63:8].**

His "people" here are believing Israelites and also a great company of Gentiles who will turn to Christ during the Great Tribulation. (Of course here the church has already gone to be with Him and has been in His presence for some time.)

"Children that will not lie." It sounds as if He had high hopes of them, but they disappointed Him. Certainly He expects you and me to live lives well-pleasing to Him, and He specifically admonished us, "Lie not one to another."

**In all their affliction he was afflicted, and the angel of his presence saved them: in his love and in his pity he redeemed them; and he bare them, and carried them all the days of old [Isa. 63:9].**

How tender are these words. I believe that the angel of the Lord is none other than the pre-incarnate Christ. We are told that in His love and pity He redeemed and carried them. He entered into the sufferings of His people.

Now there has been some question about whether "in all their affliction he was afflicted" should be positive or negative. We have good manuscript evidence for the translation given to us here. But we also have good manuscript evidence for the negative: "in all their affliction he was *not* afflicted." Which is true? Well, both are true, but I personally like the negative much better. Let me give you my reason. When the Lord went through the wilderness with the children of Israel, He wasn't afflicted when they were afflicted. For example, when they were bitten by the fiery serpents, He wasn't bitten. In all their affliction He was not afflicted. He was like a mother or a father who just stood by and waited for them. He didn't go on without them. The pillar of cloud and the pillar of fire were there. God was waiting for them. For forty years through that wilderness experience He was patient with them, patient like a mother.

When I was a pastor in Pasadena, my study was right by a street that led to a market. I used to watch a mother who had two children. One child she carried, and the other little fellow often walked along by himself. Sometimes the little fellow would stop, and his mother

always waited for him. Sometimes when he would fall down, or stray a little, doing something he shouldn't do, she would wait patiently for him. I often thought to myself, *That is the way God has been doing with me all of these years.* I fall down, or I get in trouble, and God waits for me. That is the way He does with His people.

**But they rebelled, and vexed his holy spirit: therefore he was turned to be their enemy, and he fought against them [Isa. 63:10].**

I think the Holy Spirit gets rather tired of you and me! But He is patient with us. Thank God for that!

**Then he remembered the days of old, Moses, and his people, saying, Where is he that brought them up out of the sea with the shepherd of his flock? where is he that put his holy spirit within him? [Isa. 63:11].**

I think this is a direct reference to Israel, but at the same time it is a picture of the entire human family. Some expositors do not feel that the reference here is to the Holy Spirit, the third Person of the Godhead, because the Old Testament does not contain a clear-cut distinction of the Holy Spirit. However, I believe that the Holy Spirit mentioned here is the Holy Spirit that today dwells in believers. Although in the Old Testament we do not have a clear-cut distinction of the work of the Holy Spirit, I believe this is definitely a mention of it.

The Holy Spirit is the One—

**That led them by the right hand of Moses with his glorious arm, dividing the water before them, to make himself an everlasting name?**

**That led them through the deep, as an horse in the wilderness, that they should not stumble? [Isa. 63:12–13].**

Once again God refers to the history of their deliverance out of Egypt. Then He continues their history of how He has led them.

Here the prophet and the people plead with God to look upon their great need and desire.

**Look down from heaven, and behold from the habitation of thy holiness and of thy glory: where is thy zeal and thy strength, the sounding of thy bowels and of thy mercies toward me? are they restrained?**

**Doubtless thou art our father, though Abraham be ignorant of us, and Israel acknowledge us not: thou, O LORD, art our father, our redeemer; thy name is from everlasting [Isa. 63:15–16].**

God was the *Father* of the nation Israel, but there is no thought in the Old Testament that He was the Father of the individual Israelite. It is a corporate term rather than a personal one in the Old Testament. In the New Testament it becomes personal, not corporate. As Abraham was the father of the nation and not of each individual Israelite, so God, too, was the Father of the nation.

**O LORD, why hast thou made us to err from thy ways, and hardened our heart from thy fear? Return for thy servants' sake, the tribes of thine inheritance [Isa. 63:17].**

This is a pleading prayer, asking God to intervene for them.

**We are thine: thou never barest rule over them; they were not called by thy name [Isa. 63:19].**

Now they surrender completely to God. This should be the attitude of the Christian today—complete yielding to God. Most of us are afraid to yield to God because we are afraid He will be hard on us. God wants to be gentle with us if we will give Him a chance. But remember that He also is the God of judgment. He is the One who is coming to earth some day to tread the winepress of the fierceness of His wrath.

God is not trying to frighten you; He is just telling you the truth.

# CHAPTER 64

**THEME:** *God's control of the universe recognized; man's condition in the universe confessed*

This chapter continues the pleading of the hungry hearts for the presence of God in life's affairs. No child of God today can be immune to such ardent petitions. The Christian can cry with the same passionate desire, "Even so, come, Lord Jesus!" (See Rev. 22:20).

This, too, is a neglected section of the Word of God. We have attempted to emphasize this section so that you can see why we hold the premillennial viewpoint and why we believe Christ is coming before the Great Tribulation Period. The church will be taken out of the world before the Tribulation. The Lord will come at the end of the Tribulation to establish His kingdom. This is not just a theory. This is what we find in the Book of Isaiah. We have looked at Isaiah almost verse by verse, and the prophet has presented a very definite program. The Word of God simply does not give isolated verses to prove some particular theory of interpretation, but whatever your or my theory is, it has to fit in place. Some of the theories I hear today remind me of the lady who went into the shoestore to get a pair of shoes. The salesman asked, "What size do you wear?" The lady replied that she could wear a size four, but a size five felt so much better that she always bought a size six or sometimes a seven. There are some theories, as far as the Word of God is concerned, that require a size change because they simply don't fit.

## GOD'S CONTROL
## OF THE UNIVERSE RECOGNIZED

**Oh that thou wouldest rend the heavens, that thou wouldest come down, that the mountains might flow down at thy presence [Isa. 64:1].**

The prophet is a representative of the believing remnant of Israel in that future day. Again he is using the past tense, which is called a prophetic tense. That is, God sees it as having already taken place, and He gives the prophecy to Isaiah from the other side, looking back at the event.

The prophet is pleading with God just as the remnant of Israel will do in that day of the Great Tribulation. This Scripture is not written to us—the church is not in view here. It is addressed to the remnant of Israel, but as

believers we can identify with them. Our prayer today should be for the return of the Lord. "Even so, come, Lord Jesus." But it is clear in this section that Isaiah is predicting Israel's prayer during the Great Tribulation Period.

**As when the melting fire burneth, the fire causeth the waters to boil, to make thy name known to thine adversaries, that the nations may tremble at thy presence! [Isa. 64:2].**

Just as fire makes water boil, so the presence of God would make the nations tremble. Today the nations are not conscious of the existence of God. There are people who wonder how we can sit down with godless nations like Russia or China. The reason is that we are just about as godless as they are. In our day the nations of the world are not turning to God, nor do they recognize Him. However, as the end of the age approaches, I believe there will be a very real consciousness that God is getting ready to break through. There was that consciousness throughout the world at the time of the birth of Christ, and several Roman historians have called attention to that fact.

**When thou didst terrible things which we looked not for, thou camest down, the mountains flowed down at thy presence [Isa. 64:3].**

The very mountains melt—that is, become molten—at His presence. The enemies then will cry for the mountains to hide them from ". . . the wrath of the Lamb" (Rev. 6:16).

**For since the beginning of the world men have not heard, nor perceived by the ear, neither hath the eye seen, O God, beside thee, what he hath prepared for him that waiteth for him [Isa. 64:4].**

Paul expresses this same thought in 1 Corinthians 2:9 when he says, "But as it is written, Eye hath not seen, nor ear heard, neither have entered into the heart of man, the things which God hath prepared for them that love him." Paul goes on to say, "But God hath revealed them unto us by his Spirit: for the Spirit searcheth all things, yea, the deep things of God" (1 Cor. 2:10). First Corinthians

2:9 is obviously a quote from Isaiah, but verse 10 tells us that in our day the Holy Spirit will reveal these things unto us. In that day of the Great Tribulation they will have to wait until Christ comes. And even for us it can be said, "For now we see through a glass, darkly; but then face to face: now I know in part; but then shall I know even as also I am known" (1 Cor. 13:12).

All through this section we can identify with these people, for we have a hope also. We are looking for Him to take us *out* of the world, and they will be looking for Him to come and establish a kingdom here *on* the earth.

My friend, it seems to me that the only folk who miss this distinction are the theologians. Failure to recognize that Christ is going to take the church *up* to meet Him in the air and that He is coming *down* to the earth to establish His kingdom gives us some upside down theology.

**Thou meetest him that rejoiceth and worketh righteousness, those that remember thee in thy ways: behold, thou art wroth; for we have sinned: in those is continuance, and we shall be saved [Isa. 64:5].**

Here begins the acknowledgment of sins and, at the same time, an expression of confidence in the redemption of the Savior.

## MAN'S CONDITION
## IN THE UNIVERSE CONFESSED

**But we are all as an unclean thing, and all our righteousnesses are as filthy rags; and we all do fade as a leaf; and our iniquities, like the wind, have taken us away [Isa. 64:6].**

This verse is familiar because it is used very frequently to establish the fact that man has no righteousness *per se;* that is, man has no righteousness in himself whatsoever. This is not only true of Israel but it is also true of the entire human family. Both Jew and Gentile alike have sinned and come short of the glory of God. "We are all as an unclean thing, and all our righteousnesses are as filthy rags." It does not matter what we might consider to be good works. It may sound pretty good to give a million dollars to feed the poor and hungry or to care for little orphans and widows, but in God's sight anything that the flesh produces is as filthy rags. You cannot bring a clean thing out of an unclean thing. A lost sinner is unable to do anything that is

acceptable to God—he must first come to God *His* way. This is very difficult for man to accept—especially the unsaved man who is depending upon his good works to save him.

**But now, O Lord, thou art our father; we are the clay, and thou our potter; and we all are the work of thy hand [Isa. 64:8].**

God is our Father by creation, but man lost that image. You and I can become sons of God in only one way, and that is through Christ. The New Testament revelation of the sons of God is not by creation at all, but on an entirely different basis. In John 1:12–13 we read, "But as many as received him, to them gave he power to become the sons of God, even to them that believe on his name: Which were born, not of blood, nor of the will of the flesh, nor of the will of man, but of God."

"We all are the work of thy hand" is a recognition that God is our Creator. He is the Potter, the One who creates. Now, a man that makes a vessel or a pretty vase is, in a sense, the father of it. In this same way we speak of George Washington as being the father of our country.

Paul makes this distinction in his speech in Athens: "For in him we live, and move, and have our being; as certain also of your own poets have said, For we are also his offspring. Forasmuch then as we are the offspring of God, we ought not to think that the Godhead is like unto gold, or silver, or stone, graven by art and man's device" (Acts 17:28–29). Man is the *offspring* of God in that he was created by Him, but not all men are the born again *sons* of God. Paul is saying that, since God has created us, we ought not to make an image and say that it is a likeness of God. In doing so we would be attempting to create God, and God has forbidden that.

**Thy holy cities are a wilderness, Zion is a wilderness, Jerusalem a desolation [Isa. 64:10].**

The description given in this verse was not true in Isaiah's day, but it came to pass shortly afterwards when Babylon came against Jerusalem. Second Kings 25:9–10 tell us, "And he burnt the house of the Lord, and the king's house, and all the houses of Jerusalem, and every great man's house burnt he with fire. And all the army of the Chaldees, that were with the captain of the guard, brake down the walls of Jerusalem round about." Isaiah's prophecy was literally fulfilled.

Our holy and our beautiful house,
where our fathers praised thee, is
burned up with fire: and all our
pleasant things are laid waste [Isa.
64:11].

Isaiah writes as if this has already taken
place, but it didn't happen until about one
hundred years after Isaiah. The temple was
destroyed at the same time Jerusalem was
destroyed.

Wilt thou refrain thyself for these
things, O Lord? wilt thou hold thy

peace, and afflict us very sore? [Isa.
64:12].

The prophet closes this chapter with a question: Will God refuse to act? The remainder of
Isaiah's prophecy is God's answer to this question. God rejected Israel only after they rejected Him, but it did not thwart His plan and
purpose for them and for the earth. God has
carried through with His program which is
yet to be finalized.

# CHAPTER 65

**THEME:** *Redeemer's reason for rejecting the nation; reservation of a remnant; revelation of the new heavens and the new
earth*

In chapter 64 we noted the fervent prayer of
the prophet and the people pleading with
the King to break through all barriers and
come to earth. Chapters 65 and 66 contain
God's answer to that plea. God makes it very
clear that their sins and unfaithfulness are
responsible for His judgment upon them, but
that their sins have not frustrated His promises and purposes concerning the coming kingdom. God has preserved a remnant through
which He will fulfill all of His prophecies.
Again He gives a vision of the kingdom and a
prospectus of the eternal position of Israel in
the new heavens and new earth. This will take
us to the end of the Book of Isaiah which goes
down in a blaze of glory.

## REDEEMER'S REASON FOR
## REJECTING THE NATION

I am sought of them that asked not for
me; I am found of them that sought me
not: I said, Behold me, behold me, unto
a nation that was not called by my
name [Isa. 65:1].

He is speaking here of the Gentiles to
whom the gospel has now come. When
Paul came to Philippi he had had the vision of
the man in Macedonia. However, when he got
over there, he found, not a *man* looking for
him wanting to hear the gospel, but a *woman*
by the name of Lydia who was holding a
prayer meeting down by the river. Although
she may not have recognized her need, Paul
brought the gospel to her.

Paul quotes this verse in Romans 10:20:
"But Esaias is very bold, and saith, I was
found of them that sought me not; I was made
manifest unto them that asked not after me."
That is the way it happened to us, my friend.
Our ancestors were heathen barbarians. They
were not down on the shore with their hands
held out, saying, "Oh please, send us missionaries!" They didn't want them; they even
killed some of those who did come. Today the
heathen are not begging for the gospel—
nobody's begging for the gospel. God has responded to people who didn't even call upon
Him. I never asked to be saved—He just
saved me. I was like the black boy down South
who said, "I ran from Him as fast as my sinful
legs would carry me and as far as my
rebellious heart would take me, and He took
out after me and ran me down." That is the
way it happened for all of us who have been
saved.

I have spread out my hands all the day
unto a rebellious people, which walketh
in a way that was not good, after their
own thoughts [Isa. 65:2].

Now He is talking to the Jew, to the nation
Israel. God first gave the gospel to him; it was
given "to the Jew first." Again, in Romans
10:21, Paul says, "But to Israel he saith, All
day long have I stretched forth my hands unto
a disobedient and gainsaying people." God rejected them only after they rejected Him. In
Acts 13:46 we read: "Then Paul and Barnabas
waxed bold, and said, It was necessary that

the word of God should first have been spoken to you: but seeing ye put it from you, and judge yourselves unworthy of everlasting life, lo, we turn to the Gentiles." That is the way it all came about. In other words, if Jerusalem refuses the gospel, Ephesus will receive it. If Los Angeles rejects the gospel, then maybe Bombay, India, or some out-of-the-way place is going to hear. The flood tide of God's grace *will* spill over somewhere in this world. Thank God for that.

> **A people that provoketh me to anger continually to my face; that sacrificeth in gardens, and burneth incense upon altars of brick [Isa. 65:3].**

This is the reason that blessings were withheld from Israel: they were continually going into idolatry and rebelling against God.

> **Which remain among the graves, and lodge in the monuments, which eat swine's flesh, and broth of abominable things is in their vessels;**
>
> **Which say, Stand by thyself, come not near to me; for I am holier than thou. These are a smoke in my nose, a fire that burneth all the day [Isa. 65:4–5].**

This is just a partial list of the reasons for Israel's rejection. They were breaking the commandments God gave to them.

> **Behold, it is written before me: I will not keep silence, but will recompense, even recompense into their bosom.**
>
> **Your iniquities, and the iniquities of your fathers together, saith the LORD, which have burned incense upon the mountains, and blasphemed me upon the hills: therefore will I measure their former work into their bosom [Isa. 65:6–7].**

Israel walked in pride. They practiced the externalities of a God-given religion, but their hearts were far from God. They practiced iniquity as easily as they practiced the rituals of religion. In so doing, they blasphemed God.

## RESERVATION OF A REMNANT

A remnant is reserved through which all of God's promises are to be fulfilled. God always has had a remnant.

> **Thus saith the LORD, As the new wine is found in the cluster, and one saith, Destroy it not; for a blessing is in it; so will I do for my servants' sakes, that I may not destroy them all [Isa. 65:8].**

In spite of their sins, God would not totally exterminate them because of the believing remnant. The remnant is compared to a cluster of wonderful grapes that has been passed over in the vineyard.

> **And I will bring forth a seed out of Jacob, and out of Judah an inheritor of my mountains: and mine elect shall inherit it, and my servants shall dwell there [Isa. 65:9].**

"A seed out of Jacob" could refer to the Lord Jesus Christ, and in one sense I think it does, but more particularly it refers to the remnant out of Israel that is to be saved. For the sake of the remnant God will make good His promises.

> **And Sharon shall be a fold of flocks, and the valley of Achor a place for the herds to lie down in, for my people that have sought me [Isa. 65:10].**

You see, there was to be a place, a place of safety for the little flock, for the remnant.

> **But ye are they that forsake the LORD, that forget my holy mountain, that prepare a table for that troop, and that furnish the drink offering unto that number.**
>
> **Therefore will I number you to the sword, and ye shall all bow down to the slaughter: because when I called, ye did not answer; when I spake, ye did not hear; but did evil before mine eyes, and did choose that wherein I delighted not [Isa. 65:11–12].**

But for the remainder of the nation that went headlong without heeding the Word of God there remains nothing but punishment. I do not understand how intelligent people who believe in the existence of God can fail to realize that there must finally come a judgment and a straightening out of things. If they continue on in sin they will be judged, as surely as God judged the bulk of the nation Israel.

> **Behold, my servants shall sing for joy of heart, but ye shall cry for sorrow of heart, and shall howl for vexation of spirit [Isa. 65:14].**

Just as God made a distinction between the nation as a whole and the remnant, He makes the same distinction in the contemporary church. The church is a vast organization with a tremendously bloated membership. The question is asked as to whether the church

will go through the Great Tribulation Period. Well, there is a church that will go through the Great Tribulation. It is called an old harlot in Revelation 17. It is just an organization and does not belong to Christ. It is not His bride at all. The true believers in the body of Christ will be taken out before the Great Tribulation Period. We need to recognize that there is a distinction to be made between that which is merely outward and that which is genuine.

## REVELATION OF THE NEW HEAVENS AND THE NEW EARTH

**For, behold, I create new heavens and a new earth: and the former shall not be remembered, nor come into mind [Isa. 65:17]**

Here the creation of the new heavens and the new earth seems to precede chronologically the setting up of the kingdom. But I think when we examine it closely we find that the remnant has already entered the kingdom. The others have been judged and do not enter the kingdom. The Lord Jesus made this clear in Matthew 25:34 when He said, ". . . Come, ye blessed of my Father, inherit the kingdom prepared for you from the foundation of the world." The others were to be cast into outer darkness and would not enter the kingdom.

Now at the end of the millennial kingdom— that is, at the end of the thousand-year reign of Christ, after that final rebellion—the creation of the new heavens and new earth takes place. You see, after the Rapture and during the Millennium tremendous changes in the earth will be made. The desert is going to blossom as the rose. But when you get to the new heavens and the new earth, there will not be any sea and there actually will not be any desert. It will be a *new* earth. We will have traded in the old model and gotten a new one.

I deal with this subject further in a little book I have called *Three Worlds in One*. The message comes from 2 Peter 3 where we find that there are three worlds. There is the world that was—that which was destroyed by the waters of the Noahic flood. Then there is the present world, which is going to be destroyed by fire. And finally there will come into existence the new heavens and the new earth.

**But be ye glad and rejoice for ever in that which I create: for, behold, I create Jerusalem a rejoicing, and her people a joy [Isa. 65:18].**

Here Isaiah is definitely speaking of the millennial blessings as well as the eternal blessings. The millennial kingdom is a phase of the eternal kingdom, but it is also a time of judgment. I do not think you can bring in a new heaven and a new earth until God's program of judgment is completed. When judgment is over, then we are ready for all things to be made new. I believe that after the Millennium there is something even more wonderful in store for the child of God. Man's potential will be greatly increased. Jerusalem will be a city of joy. It is not that today. It has a Wailing Wall and very few smiling people. But the day will come when God will make it a city of joy.

**And I will rejoice in Jerusalem, and joy in my people: and the voice of weeping shall be no more heard in her, nor the voice of crying [Isa. 65:19].**

What a change there is going to be for Jerusalem!

**There shall be no more thence an infant of days, nor an old man that hath not filled his days: for the child shall die an hundred years old; but the sinner being an hundred years old shall be accursed [Isa. 65:20].**

The longevity of life that predated the patriarchs will be one of the features of the kingdom. People will live a long time. There won't be any need for senior citizen homes because there won't be any senior citizens. All of us will be young!

**And they shall build houses, and inhabit them; and they shall plant vineyards, and eat the fruit of them [Isa. 65:21].**

Prosperity is another feature of the kingdom. It will be a time of real blessing.

**They shall not build, and another inhabit; they shall not plant, and another eat: for as the days of a tree are the days of my people, and mine elect shall long enjoy the work of their hands [Isa. 65:22].**

There will be permanence and stability.

**The wolf and the lamb shall feed together, and the lion shall eat straw like the bullock: and dust shall be the serpent's meat. They shall not hurt nor destroy in all my holy mountain, saith the LORD [Isa. 65:25].**

This is not what happens today, my friend. If

the wolf and the lamb lie down together, it is the wolf feeding on the lamb. A wolf likes lamb chops. But in that day they will be together, and the lion will eat straw. I like to tell the story of the young upstart who publicly questioned Dr. George Gill in a meeting, saying, "Who ever heard of a lion eating straw? Anyone knows that a lion never eats straw!" Dr. Gill, in his characteristically easygoing manner, said, "Young man, if you can make a lion, then I will make him eat straw. The One who created the lion will equip him to eat straw when He wants him to do it." In other words, in that day the sharp fang and the bloody claw will no longer rule animal life. The law of the jungle will be changed to conform to the rule of the King. There will be nothing to hurt or harm or make afraid in the whole world. It will be a *new* world then, will it not?

# CHAPTER 66

**THEME:** *The Creator, Ruler, Redeemer, Judge, Regenerator, and Rewarder; the Lord decides the destiny of both the saved and the lost*

Today our prayer is, "Thy kingdom come . . ." (Matt. 6:10). In Isaiah 66 the kingdom has come.

## THE CREATOR, RULER, REDEEMER, JUDGE, REGENERATOR, AND REWARDER

**Thus saith the LORD, The heaven is my throne, and the earth is my footstool: where is the house that ye build unto me? and where is the place of my rest? [Isa. 66:1].**

"The earth is my footstool"—this little earth on which you and I live is not very important. It is only a footstool for God!

"Where is the house that ye build unto me? and where is the place of my rest?" Any temple down here on this earth could not contain Him. Solomon recognized that. In his prayer of dedication for the first temple, he said, "But will God indeed dwell on the earth? behold, the heaven and heaven of heavens cannot contain thee; how much less this house that I have builded?" (1 Kings 8:27). Therefore, the eternal character of the kingdom seems to me to be the very presence of God. You won't need a temple there. I think that the New Jerusalem (Rev. 21) will be a place to which the people on earth will come to worship and visit.

Listen to the God of creation, the God who is high and holy and lifted up:

**For all those things hath mine hand made, and all those things have been, saith the LORD: but to this man will I look, even to him that is poor and of a contrite spirit, and trembleth at my word [Isa. 66:2].**

The God who created this vast universe, who is above it and beyond it, condescends to dwell with the humble and contrite of heart. Oh, what condescension on the part of God! In that day the meek shall inherit the earth; in fact, they will inherit all things.

**He that killeth an ox is as if he slew a man; he that sacrificeth a lamb, as if he cut off a dog's neck; he that offereth an oblation, as if he offered swine's blood; he that burneth incense, as if he blessed an idol. Yea, they have chosen their own ways, and their soul delighteth in their abominations [Isa. 66:3].**

Apparently the sacrificial system will be dispensed with after the Millennium. To offer an ox without spiritual comprehension is the same as murder. Everything in eternity must point to Christ—or that which was once commanded becomes sin.

**Hear the word of the LORD, ye that tremble at his word; Your brethren that hated you, that cast you out for my name's sake, said, Let the LORD be glorified: but he shall appear to your joy, and they shall be ashamed [Isa. 66:5].**

God will make the distinction between the true and the false—that which is real and that which is not. Christ said to let the wheat and tares grow together, that He would separate them. Now that time has come. The Pharisee who was meticulous in his religious practice is to be cast out. The publican who stood afar off and repented will be received.

**A voice of noise from the city, a voice from the temple, a voice of the LORD that rendereth recompence to his enemies [Isa. 66:6].**

God will finally deal with the enemies of Israel—they are *His* enemies also.

**Before she travailed, she brought forth; before her pain came, she was delivered of a man child [Isa. 66:7].**

The Great Tribulation was a time of travail. Israel went through the Great Tribulation *after* Christ was born in Bethlehem—"before her pain came, she was delivered of a man child" who is Christ Jesus. This is a remarkable verse.

**Shall I bring to the birth, and not cause to bring forth? saith the LORD: shall I cause to bring forth, and shut the womb? saith thy God [Isa. 66:9].**

God will make sure that all He has promised is accomplished. The 144,000 Jews who were sealed at the beginning of the Great Tribulation will come through it—not just 143,999, but everyone of them will be there. How wonderful!

Now he can say:

**Rejoice ye with Jerusalem, and be glad with her, all ye that love her: rejoice for joy with her, all ye that mourn for her [Isa. 66:10].**

What a time of blessing it will be.

## THE LORD DECIDES THE DESTINY OF BOTH THE SAVED AND THE LOST

**For I know their works and their thoughts: it shall come, that I will gather all nations and tongues; and they shall come, and see my glory [Isa. 66:18].**

All nations must appear before Him. The Lord Jesus mentioned this in Matthew 25:31–32. "When the Son of man shall come in his glory, and all the holy angels with him, then shall he sit upon the throne of his glory: And before him shall be gathered all nations: and he shall separate them one from another, as a shepherd divideth his sheep from the goats." At that time a great company of Gentiles are going to be saved as well as many from Israel. The nations are going to come and worship in Jerusalem.

**For as the new heavens and the new earth, which I will make, shall remain before me, saith the LORD, so shall your seed and your name remain [Isa. 66:22].**

God's purposes and promises for Israel are as eternal as the new heavens and the new earth.

**And it shall come to pass, that from one new moon to another, and from one sabbath to another, shall all flesh come to worship before me, saith the LORD [Isa. 66:23].**

The redeemed of all ages will worship God throughout eternity. That will be the most engaging and important business of eternity.

**And they shall go forth, and look upon the carcases of the men that have transgressed against me: for their worm shall not die, neither shall their fire be quenched; and they shall be an abhorring unto all flesh [Isa. 66:24].**

In other words, "There is no peace, saith my God, to the wicked" (Isa. 57:21). That is going to be their condition throughout eternity—no peace, no rest, no contentment, no God. The Book of Isaiah closes with this third warning that there is no peace for the wicked. "He that hath ears to hear, let him hear" (Matt. 11:15).

# BIBLIOGRAPHY

(Recommended for Further Study)

Criswell, W. A. *Isaiah*. Grand Rapids, Michigan: Zondervan Publishing House, 1977.

Gaebelein, Arno C. *The Annotated Bible*. Neptune, New Jersey: Loizeaux Brothers, 1917.

Ironside, H. A. *Expository Notes on Isaiah*. Neptune, New Jersey: Loizeaux Brothers, 1952.

Jennings, F. C. *Studies in Isaiah*. Neptune, New Jersey: Loizeaux Brothers, n.d.

Jensen, Irving L. *Isaiah and Jeremiah*. Chicago, Illinois: Moody Press. (A self-study guide.)

Kelly, William. *An Exposition of Isaiah*. Addison, Illinois: Bible Truth Publishers, 1896.

Martin, Alfred. *Isaiah: The Salvation of Jehovah*. Chicago, Illinois: Moody Press, 1956. (A fine, inexpensive survey.)

Martin, Alfred and John A. *Isaiah*. Chicago, Illinois: Moody Press, 1983.

McGee, J. Vernon. *Initiation Into Isaiah*. 2 vols. Pasadena, California: Thru the Bible Books, 1957.

Unger, Merrill F. *Unger's Bible Handbook*. Chicago, Illinois: Moody Press, 1966.

Unger, Merrill F. *Unger's Commentary on the Old Testament*. Chicago, Illinois: Moody Press, 1982. (Highly recommended.)

Vine, W. E. *Isaiah*. Grand Rapids, Michigan: Zondervan Publishing House, 1946.

# The Book of
# JEREMIAH
## INTRODUCTION

Jeremiah, the prophet of the broken heart, is the writer of this book. It is one of the most remarkable books in the Bible. Every book in the Bible is remarkable, but this book is remarkable in a very unusual way. Most of the prophets hide themselves and maintain a character of anonymity. They do not project themselves on the pages of their prophecy. But Jeremiah is a prophet whose prophecy is largely autobiographical. He gives to us much of his own personal history. Let me run through this list of facts about him so that you will know this man whom we will meet in this book.

1. He was born a priest in Anathoth, just north of Jerusalem (Jer. 1:1).

2. He was chosen to be a prophet before he was born (Jer. 1:5).

3. He was called to the prophetic office while he was very young (Jer. 1:6).

4. He was commissioned of God to be a prophet (Jer. 1:9–10).

5. He began his ministry during the reign of King Josiah and was a mourner at his funeral (2 Chron. 35:25).

6. He was forbidden to marry because of the terrible times in which he lived (Jer. 16:1–4).

7. He never made a convert. He was rejected by his people (Jer. 11:18–21; 12:6; 18:18), hated, beaten, put in stocks (Jer. 20:1–3), imprisoned, and charged with being a traitor (Jer. 37:11–16).

8. His message broke his own heart (Jer. 9:1).

9. He wanted to resign, but God wouldn't let him (Jer. 20:9).

10. He saw the destruction of Jerusalem and the Babylonian captivity. He was permitted to remain in the land by the captain of the Babylonian forces. When the remnant wanted to flee to Egypt, Jeremiah prophesied against it (Jer. 42:15–43:3); he was forced to go with the remnant to Egypt (Jer. 43:6–7); and he died there. Tradition says that he was stoned by the remnant.

Jeremiah was a remarkable man. I call him God's crybaby, but not in a derogatory sense. He was a man in tears most of the time. God chose this man who had a mother's heart, a trembling voice, and tear-filled eyes to deliver a harsh message of judgment. The message that he gave broke his own heart. Jeremiah was a great man of God. Candidly, I don't think that you and I would have chosen this kind of man to give a harsh message. Instead we would have selected some hard-boiled person to give a hard-boiled message, would we not? God didn't choose that kind of man; He chose a man with a tender, compassionate heart.

Lord Macaulay said this concerning Jeremiah: "It is difficult to conceive any situation more painful than that of a great man, condemned to watch the lingering agony of an exhausted country, to tend it during the alternate fits of stupefaction and raving which precede its dissolution, and to see the symptoms of vitality disappear one by one, till nothing is left but coldness, darkness, and corruption" (*Studies in the Prophecy of Jeremiah*, W. G. Moorehead, p. 9). This was the position and the call of Jeremiah. He stood by and saw his people go into captivity.

Dr. Moorehead has given us this very graphic picture of him: "It was Jeremiah's lot to prophesy at a time when all things in Judah were rushing down to the final and mournful catastrophe; when political excitement was at its height; when the worst passions swayed the various parties, and the most fatal counsels prevailed. It was his to stand in the way over which his nation was rushing headlong to destruction; to make an heroic effort to arrest it, and to turn it back; and to fail, and be compelled to step to one side and see his own people, whom he loved with the tenderness of a woman, plunge over the precipice into the wide, weltering ruin" (pages 9, 10).

You and I are living at a time which is probably like the time of Jeremiah. Ours is a great nation today, and we have accomplished many things. We have gone to the moon, and we have produced atom bombs. Although we are a strong nation, within is the same corruption which will actually carry us down to dismemberment and disaster. It is coming, my friend. Revolution may be just around the corner. I know that what I am saying is not popular today. We don't hear anything like this through the media. Instead, we have panels of experts who discuss how we are going to

improve society and how we can work out our problems. Today God is left out of the picture totally—absolutely left out. If the Bible is mentioned, it is mentioned with a curled lip by some unbeliever. The ones who are believers and have a message from God are pushed aside. I *know* that. That is why I say to you that I think we are in very much the same position that Jeremiah was in. For that reason I know this book is going to have a message for us today.

Another author has written, "He was not a man mighty as Elijah, eloquent as Isaiah, or seraphic as Ezekiel, but one who was timid and shrinking, conscious of his helplessness, yearning for a sympathy and love he was never to know—such was the chosen organ through which the Word of the Lord came to that corrupt and degenerate age."

"When Jesus came into the coasts of Caesarea Philippi, he asked his disciples, saying, Whom do men say that I the Son of man am? And they said, Some say that thou art John the Baptist: some, Elias; and others, Jeremias, or one of the prophets" (Matt. 16:13–14). There was a difference of opinion, and none of them seemed to really know who He was. Folk had some good reasons for thinking He was Elijah and also good reasons for thinking He was John the Baptist. Now there were those who thought He was Jeremiah, and they had a very good reason for believing it, because Jeremiah was a man of sorrows and acquainted with grief. The difference between him and the Lord Jesus was that the Lord Jesus was bearing *our* sorrows and *our* grief, while Jeremiah was carrying his *own* burden, and it was breaking his heart. He went to the Lord one time and said, "I can't keep on. This thing is tearing me to pieces. I'm about to have a nervous breakdown. You had better get somebody else." The Lord said "All right, but I'll just hold your resignation here on My desk because I think you'll be back." Jeremiah did come back, and he said, "The Word of God was like fire in my bones; I had to give it out." He did that even though it broke his heart. God wanted that kind of man, because he was the right kind of man to give a harsh message. God wanted the children of Israel to know that, although He was sending them into captivity and He was judging them, it was breaking *His* heart. As Isaiah says, judgment is God's *strange* work (see Isa. 28:21).

Jeremiah began his ministry about a century after Isaiah. He began his work during the reign of King Josiah, and he continued right on through the Babylonian captivity. He is the one who predicted the seventy years' captivity in Babylon. He also saw beyond the darkness of the captivity to the light. No other prophet spoke so glowingly of the future. We will have occasion to see that as we study his marvelous prophecy.

The message of Jeremiah was the most unwelcome message ever delivered to a people, and it was rejected. He was called a traitor to his country because he said that they were to yield to Babylon. Isaiah, almost a century before him, had said to resist. Why this change? In Jeremiah's day there was only one thing left to do: surrender. In the economy of God, the nation was through. The times of the Gentiles had already begun with Babylon as the head of gold (see Dan. 2).

Characterizing Jeremiah's message is the word *backsliding*, which occurs thirteen times. It is a word that is used only four other times in the Old Testament, once in Proverbs and three times in Hosea—Hosea's message is also that of the backsliding nation.

The name that predominates is *Babylon*, which occurs 164 times in the book, more than in the rest of Scripture combined. Babylon became the enemy.

# OUTLINE

# CHAPTER 1

*THEME: Call of prophet during reign of Josiah*

It will help our understanding of the prophets to weave them into 1 Samuel through 2 Chronicles, the historical books which cover the same period of time. The prophets prophesied during the time period covered by those historical books—with the exception of Haggai, Zechariah, and Malachi, who prophesied after the Exile (and fit into the time period of the historical Books of Ezra and Nehemiah).

**The words of Jeremiah the son of Hilkiah, of the priests that were in Anathoth in the land of Benjamin [Jer. 1:1].**

Here is a reference to "Hilkiah" who is the father of Jeremiah. He was the high priest who found the Book of the Law during the time of Josiah. It was the finding of the Law of the Lord as given to Moses that sparked the revival during the reign of Josiah. Revivals are not caused by men; they are caused by the Word of God. Never a man, but the Book. The Word of God is responsible for every revival that has taken place in the church. It is true that God has used men, but it is the Word of God that brings revival. The record of this revival and its effect is found in the historical books in 2 Kings 22 and in 2 Chronicles 34.

"Anathoth" was the hometown of Jeremiah. It is a few miles directly north of Jerusalem.

**To whom the word of the LORD came in the days of Josiah the son of Amon king of Judah, in the thirteenth year of his reign [Jer. 1:2].**

Josiah was eight years old when he came to the throne, and he reigned for thirty-one years. Jeremiah began his ministry when Josiah was twenty-two years old. Apparently Jeremiah was about twenty years old himself; so both of them were young men and were probably friends. Jeremiah prophesied during eighteen years of Josiah's reign, and he was a mourner at his funeral (see 1 Chron. 35:25).

Josiah had done a very foolish thing—even men of God sometimes do foolish things. He went over to fight against the pharaoh of Egypt at Carchemish although the pharaoh had not come up against Judah at all. For some reason Josiah went out to fight against him in the valley of Esdraelon or Armageddon at Megiddo, and there Josiah was slain. Jeremiah mourned over his death because Josiah had been a good king. The last revival that

came to these people came under the reign of Josiah, and it was a great revival. After the death of Josiah, Jeremiah could see that the nation would lapse into a night out of which it would not emerge until after the Babylonian captivity.

**It came also in the days of Jehoiakim the son of Josiah king of Judah, unto the end of the eleventh year of Zedekiah the son of Josiah king of Judah, unto the carrying away of Jerusalem captive in the fifth month [Jer. 1:3].**

This and the preceding verse give to us the exact time of the ministry of Jeremiah—from the thirteenth year of the reign of Josiah and continuing through the carrying away of Jerusalem into captivity.

We know that when Judah went into captivity, Nebuchadnezzar allowed Jeremiah to stay in the land: "Now Nebuchadnezzar king of Babylon gave charge concerning Jeremiah to Nebuzar-adan the captain of the guard, saying, Take him, and look well to him, and do him no harm; but do unto him even as he shall say unto thee" (Jer. 39:11–12). Of course Jeremiah didn't want to go to Babylon with the others—they had rejected his message and were being led away captives as he had predicted. Since Nebuchadnezzar gave him his choice, he chose to stay in the land with the few who remained. However, those fugitives took off and went down to Egypt, doing it against the advice of Jeremiah and taking him with them. In Egypt Jeremiah continued faithfully giving them God's Word.

Second Chronicles 36 fills in the history which is omitted. Jehoahaz, a son of Josiah, is not mentioned in Jeremiah's record. He reigned for three months—he didn't even get the throne warm before they eliminated him. Then the king of Egypt placed his brother Eliakim on the throne and changed his name to Jehoiakim. He reigned for eleven years. Jeremiah warned him not to rebel against Nebuchadnezzar, king of Babylon. However, Jehoiakim did not listen to the advice from Jeremiah and was taken captive to Babylon. After the removal of Eliakim, the king of Babylon put Jehoiachin on the throne in Jerusalem. He reigned three months and ten days. He is not mentioned here either because he, too, barely got the throne warm and then was eliminated. Nebuchadnezzar took him captive

to Babylon. After that it was Zedekiah, the brother of the father of Jehoiachin, who was placed on the throne at Jerusalem. He reigned eleven years. When Zedekiah rebelled, Nebuchadnezzar came and destroyed Jerusalem, slew the sons of Zedekiah, put out Zedekiah's eyes, and took him captive to Babylon.

All of this sounds very brutal, and it was brutal. But we must remember that Nebuchadnezzar had been very patient with the city of Jerusalem. Also the people there refused to listen to God's warning through Jeremiah.

Jeremiah continued his ministry to the remnant that was left at Jerusalem. After they forced him to go to Egypt with them, he still continued his ministry in Egypt until the time of his death. We can say that two things characterized the life of Jeremiah: weeping and loneliness. They are the marks of his ministry.

**Then the word of the LORD came unto me, saying [Jer. 1:4].**

The "word of the LORD" came to Jeremiah. I can't emphasize that too much. If you are not prepared to go along with that, you might just as well put the book down. It will have no message for you. This is the Word of God. I don't propose to tell you how God got it through to Jeremiah, but He did get it to him, and it is recorded for us as the Word of God.

**Before I formed thee in the belly, I knew thee; and before thou camest forth out of the womb I sanctified thee, and I ordained thee a prophet unto the nations [Jer. 1:5].**

I am glad that Jeremiah's mother did not practice abortion—he would never have been born. Many people today are asking, "When is a child a child?" May I say to you, a child is a child at the very moment he is conceived. Read Psalm 139. David says, "My substance was not hid from thee, when I was made in secret, and curiously wrought in the lowest parts of the earth" (Ps. 139:15). That is, he was formed in the womb of his mother; and, at that moment, life began. I am told by a gynecologist that there is tremendous development in the fetus at the very beginning. Abortion is murder, unless it is done to *save* a life. That is the way the Word of God looks at it. God said to Jeremiah, "Before you were born, I knew you and I called you."

Now why did God say these things to Jeremiah? My friend, God is going to ask Jeremiah to give a message to the people of Judah that will be rejected. Jeremiah is going to be imprisoned because of his stand for God. His message will break his own heart because he loved his people, and he hated to tell them what was going to come to them.

But God wanted a man like this, a tender man, to bring His message. To the court of old Ahab and Jezebel, God had sent a hard-boiled prophet by the name of Elijah. But before the kingdom of Judah goes into captivity, God wants His people to know that He loves them and that He wants to save them and deliver them. For this reason He chose this man Jeremiah.

Therefore God is saying these things to Jeremiah to encourage him. He said, "I want you to know, Jeremiah, that the important thing is that I am the One who has called you, I have ordained you, and I have sanctified you."

*Sanctification* simply means "to set aside for the use of God." Those old vessels that were used in the tabernacle and temple—old beaten-up pots and pans which were used in God's service—were called *holy* vessels, *sanctified* vessels. When they looked as if they should be traded in for a new set, why were they called holy? Because they were for the use of God. Anything that is set aside for the use of God is sanctified.

God says, "Before you were born, Jeremiah, I set you aside for My use. So don't worry about the effect of your message. You just give the message."

Frankly, God expects the same of me. I feel very comfortable as I prepare these messages. I'm not pulling any punches; I'm giving the Word of God just as it is. That is my responsibility. I say this kindly, I am not responsible to you; I am responsible to God, and I turn my report in to Him. It is just too bad if what I say does not please you. I'm sorry; I wish it did. When I was still in the active pastorate, people would often say, "My, how people love you!" But you know, in every church there was a little group of dissidents—cantankerous troublemakers who were not always honest. However, if you are giving out the Word of God, you are responsible to God and set aside for that ministry.

God goes on to say, "I ordained thee a prophet unto the nations." This gave authority to Jeremiah. It offered him encouragement that would help him through many a dark day.

Now here is Jeremiah's response:

**Then said I, Ah, Lord GOD! behold, I cannot speak: for I am a child [Jer. 1:6].**

Jeremiah was probably about twenty years old at the time, but this verse would not lead you to think so. Actually, he was not a child as we think of a child. "Child" here is the same word that is translated "young man" in Zechariah 2:4: "And said unto him, Run, speak to this young man. . . ." Jeremiah was actually a young man. What he is saying in effect is, "I'm a young, inexperienced fellow. I am not capable of doing such a job. I am not prepared for this."

Have you ever noticed that the man whom God uses is the man who doesn't think he can do it? If you think you can do it today, then I say to you that I don't think God can use you.

A young preacher came in to see me who was absolutely green with jealousy of another man in the same town. He said to me, "I'm a better preacher than he is. I'm a better pastor than he is. I'm a better speaker than he is. I want to know *why* God is using that man and He is not using me! My ministry is falling flat." So I told him, "You *think* you can do it. I happen to know the other man, and he really doesn't believe that he can do it. God always uses that kind of a man. God chooses the weak things of this world."

Jeremiah felt inadequate, unfit, unequipped. Listen to God's answer to him:

**But the Lord said unto me, Say not, I am a child: for thou shalt go to all that I shall send thee, and whatsoever I command thee thou shalt speak [Jer. 1:7].**

"Whatsoever I command thee thou shalt speak." While there are more liberal pulpits in our country, it is the fundamental churches which are really growing in the size of their congregations. It is in the Bible-believing churches where things are really moving today. The problem in the liberal churches is that the man in the pulpit doesn't believe what he is saying. He is giving out *theories* and *ideas*. He holds panel discussions where he tells what *he thinks*. God says, "You give what I command you to give, and give it with that authority." May I say to you, when you are giving out God's Word, it's very comfortable, it's very wonderful. I love Jeremiah, and I would love to have comforted him. He surely has comforted me.

**Be not afraid of their faces: for I am with thee to deliver thee, saith the Lord [Jer. 1:8].**

"Be not afraid of their faces." One of the comfortable things about my ministry of teaching the Bible on the radio is that my listeners cannot get to me when I say something that displeases them. I heard from a man in Oakland, California, who is now a wonderful Christian. He wrote that he had belonged to a certain cult which believed in certain rituals and gyrations that he had to go through in order to be saved. He would hear our broadcast when he was driving to his work as a contractor. He said, "You made me so mad. You kept telling me I was a sinner. If I could have gotten to you, I would have punched you in the nose." He is a big fellow; so I think he could have done it. That is one reason it is comfortable to be on radio, because when I stay true to the Word of God, I will say things that people don't like to hear. The interesting thing is that this man kept listening morning after morning, and one day he turned to the Lord Jesus and said, "I *am* a sinner, save me." He accepted Christ as his personal Savior. That is the joy of giving out the Word of God. That is why God says to go ahead and give out His Word with courage and with conviction—it will never return void; it will accomplish God's purpose.

Our pulpits today desperately need men to speak with authority what God has written down in His Word. That is all He asks us to do. It is a simple task in one way, and in another it is a most difficult task.

God says to Jeremiah, "Be not afraid . . . for I am with thee to deliver thee." He is saying, "Look, I am on your side." Martin Luther said, "One with God is a majority." That is always true. As Christians we may feel that we are in the minority, but we really are in the majority.

**Then the Lord put forth his hand, and touched my mouth. And the Lord said unto me, Behold, I have put my words in thy mouth [Jer. 1:9].**

"I have put my words in thy mouth." This is very important. God has inspired the *words* of Scripture—not just the thoughts and ideas of Scripture. For example, the Devil was not inspired by God to tell a lie, but the record in Scripture that the Devil told a lie are inspired words.

This idea is too often misunderstood in our day, which is the reason I cannot commend certain so-called translations of the Bible. They may be good interpretations, but they are very poor translations—because the very words of Scripture are inspired.

Let me illustrate the importance of accurate translation. There was a girl who aspired to

be a singer, and the time for her recital had come. After her recital performance she went back to the dressing room where she was met by friends. She eagerly asked, "What did my teacher say?" A very diplomatic friend replied, "He said that you sang *heavenly*." She said, "Did he really say that? Did he say that in so many words?" "Well, that was not exactly the word he used, but that's what he meant," the friend responded. "But I want to know exactly the words he used. Did he say that I sang *heavenly*?" she persisted. "Well," the friend answered, "he meant that, but what he really said was that it was an *unearthly* noise."

You see, it is very important to realize that the words of Scripture are inspired by God. God said to Jeremiah, "I'm going to put *My words* in your mouth."

**See, I have this day set thee over the nations and over the kingdoms, to root out, and to pull down, and to destroy, and to throw down, to build, and to plant [Jer. 1:10].**

Jeremiah prophesied during the reigns of Josiah, Jehoiakim, Jehoahaz, Jehoiachin, and Zedekiah. All these kings had various bureaus and government projects. They were all going to improve Jerusalem. They were going to deal with the ecology and get rid of the slums. They each had a poverty program. But none of them paid much attention to Jeremiah—they ignored him. Now almost three thousand years have passed by. Could you mention any of those government projects today? Can you tell me anything worthwhile that was done by Zedekiah? Can you mention anything that Jehoiachin or Jehoiakim did? Not a good thing is mentioned. Yet in their day everybody thought they were doing the right thing, the popular thing. Jeremiah was ignored. But whom do we read today? We read Jeremiah.

The Book of Jeremiah is the Word of God, my friend. It has survived and is going to survive through our day. America is a nation that no longer hears God. They don't listen to Him in Washington, D.C. They are not hearing Him in the classrooms of our universities today. And they are not hearing God in the military. The scientists do not listen to Him. But God is speaking and His Word will survive.

God is telling Jeremiah that He is going to put him in charge of giving His Word to the nation of Judah. And poor little Jeremiah wants to retire before he even gets the job! God now gives Jeremiah two tremendous pictures concerning his call to the prophetic office.

**Moreover the word of the LORD came unto me, saying, Jeremiah, what seest thou? And I said, I see a rod of an almond tree [Jer. 1:11].**

The almond tree was known as the "waker" or the "watcher." It was actually the first tree to come out of the long night of winter and bloom in the spring. Like the almond tree, Jeremiah was to be an alarm clock—an awaker. He was going to try to wake people up, but they didn't want to be awakened. No one who is asleep likes to be wakened. An alarm clock is one of the most unpopular things in the world. In my college dormitory every alarm clock was battered up; I threw mine against the wall many a morning. Jeremiah is going to be a "waker" to the nation of Judah.

**Then said the LORD unto me, Thou hast well seen: for I will hasten my word to perform it [Jer. 1:12].**

God said, "That's right. I will give you a word that will wake them up. It will shake them out of sleep."

**And the word of the LORD came unto me the second time, saying, What seest thou? And I said, I see a seething pot; and the face thereof is toward the north [Jer. 1:13].**

What was the "seething pot"? In Jeremiah's time Egypt and Assyria were no longer a danger to the southern kingdom of Judah, but around the Fertile Crescent in the north was a boiling pot: the rising power of Babylon, which was to eventually destroy Judah. It was to be Jeremiah's job to constantly warn his people what was going to happen to their nation.

**Then the LORD said unto me, Out of the north an evil shall break forth upon all the inhabitants of the land.**

**For, lo, I will call all the families of the kingdoms of the north, saith the LORD; and they shall come, and they shall set every one his throne at the entering of the gates of Jerusalem, and against all the walls thereof round about, and against all the cities of Judah [Jer. 1:14, 15].**

A century earlier God had delivered Jerusalem, and now all the false prophets were

running around saying that He was going to do it again.

All of God's prophets of the past—Hosea, Joel, Amos, Micah and Nahum, all those who had been contemporaries of Isaiah—had now passed off the scene. I think Zephaniah and Habakkuk were still living. Ezekiel and Obadiah were also contemporary with Jeremiah, but they are not going to prophesy until the captives are actually in Babylon. Daniel, too, will be prophesying later on. But at this time, Jeremiah stands alone, and he is to utter these judgments that are to come upon the nation.

What will be the reaction to his message?—

**And they shall fight against thee; but they shall not prevail against thee; for I am with thee, saith the Lord, to deliver thee [Jer. 1:19].**

The Lord says, "Go ahead, Jeremiah, they're going to resist you, they won't listen to the message, but you *give* the message." Jeremiah feels incapable and unworthy of the office of prophet, and he has offered that as an excuse. But God says, "I'm going to put My words in your mouth, and you will be giving My words."

I do not believe that any man ought to stand in the pulpit and give a message until he is sure that he is giving the Word of God. If he has any doubts or if he feels that he should give his own ideas and preach a liberal, social gospel—he ought to stay out of the pulpit. Regardless of how much homiletics, or hermeneutics, or theology, or sophisticated training he has had, unless he is confident that he is giving the Word of God, he ought to stay out of the pulpit. That is very important. Jeremiah could be confident that he was giving out the very words of God.

# CHAPTER 2

### *THEME: Twofold condemnation of Judah*

In the first chapter we saw the impressive call and commission of Jeremiah. God called him when he was a young man, probably about twenty years of age. We know also that the king Josiah was twenty-one or twenty-two years old when God called Jeremiah. So here we have two young men in the land of Israel, the young king and the young prophet.

Jeremiah made it very clear that he felt incapable and unworthy of such a calling. He felt that he could not measure up to the office of a prophet, and he offered that as an excuse. God answered him that He would put His words into Jeremiah's mouth. He would be giving God's words, not his own.

Chapters 2 through 6 were given during the first five years of Jeremiah's ministry. And since he began to prophesy in the thirteenth year of the reign of Josiah, these messages were given in those five years before the finding of the Book of the Law in the temple. The messages in chapters 7 through 9 have to do with the cleansing of the temple and the discovery of the Book of the Law, which took place in the eighteenth year of the reign of Josiah. Then in chapters 10 through 12 are the messages which came in the period of reform and revival *after* the finding of the Book of the

Law. We will discover that the revival was a surface sort of thing because there was not proper emphasis placed upon the Word of God.

Friend, we need to remember that there will never be a real revival until there is a real emphasis placed upon the Word of God.

In order to orient ourselves for this period of history, we need to study the historical books along with the prophetic books. Therefore we will turn back to the thirty-fourth chapter of 2 Chronicles to fit the messages of Jeremiah into this particular place in history: "Josiah was eight years old when he began to reign, and he reigned in Jerusalem one and thirty years. And he did that which was right in the sight of the Lord, and walked in the ways of David his father, and declined neither to the right hand, nor to the left" (2 Chron. 34:1–2). Here is an outstanding king who reigned during the twilight of the kingdom of Judah.

"For in the eighth year of his reign, while he was yet young, he began to seek after the God of David his father: and in the twelfth year he began to purge Judah and Jerusalem from the high places, and the groves, and the carved images, and the molten images

(2 Chron. 34:3). Jeremiah's first five years of prophesying were during this period.

"And they brake down the altars of Baalim in his presence; and the images, that were on high above them, he cut down; and the groves, and the carved images, and the molten images, he brake in pieces, and made dust of them, and strowed it upon the graves of them that had sacrificed unto them. And he burnt the bones of the priests upon their altars, and cleansed Judah and Jerusalem. And so did he in the cities of Manasseh, and Ephraim, and Simeon, even unto Naphtali, with their mattocks round about. And when he had broken down the altars and the groves, and had beaten the graven images into powder, and cut down all the idols throughout all the land of Israel, he returned to Jerusalem. Now in the eighteenth year of his reign, when he had purged the land, and the house, he sent Shaphan the son of Azaliah, and Maaseiah the governor of the city, and Joah the son of Joahaz the recorder, to repair the house of the LORD his God" (2 Chron. 34:4–8). It was during this time of cleaning out and repairing the house of the Lord that Hilkiah the priest found a Book of the Law as it had been given to Moses. In those days probably there were only two copies—one was for the king and one was for the high priest. You see, before Josiah had come to the throne, Judah had sunk to a new low under the wicked and godless reins of his grandfather, Manasseh, and his father, Amon. They had no regard for God or His Word, and the one or two copies in existence were finally lost in the rubbish which collected in the neglected temple.

Jeremiah's first message (2:1–3:5) is to this people who had forsaken the living God. It would be difficult to find any portion of Scripture that would surpass it in genuine pathos and tenderness. It is the eloquent and earnest pleading of a God who has been forgotten and insulted. His grace and compassion toward the guilty nation are blended with solemn warnings of dreadful days to come if hearts are not turned back to Him. This is one of the great discourses in the Word of God. The young king Josiah was truly seeking the Lord, but he didn't have the Word of God! He did know, however, that idolatry must be put down. Now he has a young man, a young prophet, who will encourage him in his resolve.

## THEY REJECTED JEHOVAH

**Moreover the word of the LORD came to me, saying,**

**Go and cry in the ears of Jerusalem, saying, Thus saith the LORD; I remember thee, the kindness of thy youth, the love of thine espousals, when thou wentest after me in the wilderness, in a land that was not sown.**

**Israel was holiness unto the LORD, and the firstfruits of his increase: all that devour him shall offend; evil shall come upon them, saith the LORD [Jer. 2:1–3].**

God is doing something quite wonderful. He is asking Israel to remember the springtime of their relationship to Him when He called them out of the land of Egypt—how they followed the pillar of fire at night and the pillar of cloud by day. Out in that frightful and terrible wilderness they sought the Lord. God now reminds them of that. After God had blessed them and given them a good land, they turned from Him. As Hosea had said of the northern kingdom, "Ephraim waxed fat and wicked." In their comfortable and sophisticated society, they turned away from the living God to serve idols.

One cannot help but note that there is an analogy between Judah and our own nation. God is left out today. Our nation was founded by men and women who believed that the Book was the Word of God, and everything they did was based on that Book. As one of our outstanding historians has observed, our nation is controlled by men who do not know its spiritual heritage. We have turned away from God. We are going after the idol of the almighty dollar. The best news out of New York is a vigorous stock market. The best news out of Washington is that which will put more money in our pockets. Money is the god of the present hour. The Ephesians chanted, ". . . Great is Diana of the Ephesians" (Acts 19:28). The cry of America is, "Great is the almighty American dollar," and God is left out.

"I remember thee." God says, "I remember *you*." They had forgotten Him, but God had not forgotten them. Oh, how gracious God is!

Listen to His longing: "Israel was holiness unto the LORD. Don't you remember back there how you were? You belonged to Me. You followed Me and you were led by Me."

**Hear ye the word of the LORD, O house of Jacob, and all the families of the house of Israel [Jer. 2:4].**

Although the ten tribes had been conquered by the Assyrians, they were still around. They hadn't wandered over to Great Britain

or America. He addresses the house of Jacob and *all* the families of Israel. (And they are the same people today, by the way.) God's message was to them in that day although they were in the Assyrian captivity.

**Thus saith the LORD, What iniquity have your fathers found in me, that they are gone far from me, and have walked after vanity, and are become vain? [Jer. 2:5].**

Without doubt this is one of the great passages of Scripture. Notice the wonderful way in which God approaches them: "What did I do wrong that you have turned from Me?"

In our day, my friend, what is wrong with God that we are not more interested in Him? Why are we not serving Him? Is there unrighteousness with God? Is God doing something wrong today? He asks, "What iniquity have your fathers found in me?"

**Neither said they, Where is the LORD that brought us up out of the land of Egypt, that led us through the wilderness, through a land of deserts and of pits, through a land of drought, and of the shadow of death, through a land that no man passed through, and where no man dwelt? [Jer. 2:6].**

People just didn't go through that country, and there are not many who go through that country today. I have been at the edge of it, and that is as far as I have wanted to go. Yet God kept His people in that frightful wilderness for forty years, and He took care of them.

**And I brought you into a plentiful country, to eat the fruit thereof and the goodness thereof; but when ye entered, ye defiled my land, and made mine heritage an abomination [Jer. 2:7].**

Today we hear a great deal about ecology and the fact that we need to clean up the land. That is good—it needs cleaning up. But let's recognize that there is a lot of moral filth around and a lot of degradation and deterioration in character. This is the thing that the Lord God is talking about here. They had polluted God's land. God intended that they be a witness to Him; instead, they are as bad as the people before them.

**The priests said not, Where is the LORD? and they that handle the law knew me not: the pastors also transgressed against me, and the prophets proph-**
esied by Baal, and walked after things that do not profit [Jer. 2:8].**

God puts the responsibility on the spiritual leaders. And I believe that the problems in my country began in the church. No nation falls until it falls first spiritually. There is first of all a spiritual apostasy, then a moral awfulness, and finally a political anarchy. That is the way every nation makes its exit as a great nation.

"The priests said not, Where is the LORD?" There are too many folk today who are supposed to be Bible teachers and preachers and witnesses for Him, even among the laymen, who do not know the Word of God. I am sorry to say that, but it happens to be true. As a result of not knowing the Word of God, they don't really know *God*. It is necessary to know the Word of God in order to know Him.

**Wherefore I will yet plead with you, saith the LORD, and with your children's children will I plead [Jer. 2:9].**

God says, "I have not given you up. I am still going to plead with you." How wonderful that is.

**For my people have committed two evils; they have forsaken me the fountain of living waters, and hewed them out cisterns, broken cisterns, that can hold no water [Jer. 2:13].**

Israel had committed two evils. First of all, they rejected Jehovah, the fountain of living waters. Second, they hewed out cisterns for themselves, broken cisterns that couldn't hold water.

Oh, how many people today have hewn out a little cistern for themselves, and they drink from their own cistern! Of course they are not finding satisfaction. For example, every man who has made a million dollars thirsts for more—he wants to make the second million. The same is true of fame. There is never enough to satisfy.

God goes on to deal with these people, mentioning their backsliding for the first time.

**Thine own wickedness shall correct thee, and thy backslidings shall reprove thee: know therefore and see that it is an evil thing and bitter, that thou hast forsaken the LORD thy God, and that my fear is not in thee, saith the Lord GOD of hosts [Jer. 2:19].**

In chapter 3 we will find that backsliding is mentioned in one chapter as many times as it

is mentioned in the rest of the Bible; so it must be rather important to God.

## THEY REARED THEIR OWN GODS

The remainder of chapter 2 is a polemic against idolatry, which continues in chapter 3. Rather than quote this section, I want to recommend that you read it in your Bible, read it all the way through. As you become familiar with the prophecy of Jeremiah, you will be surprised how wonderful it will become to you.

It is interesting to see that when man rejects God, he always will make an idol. When people make their own god, they make it as *they* want it. They make a god whose demands they can meet. In other words, it is actually a projection of the old nature of man.

# CHAPTER 3

### *THEME: Josiah begins reforms in the nation*

In Jeremiah's first message, begun in chapter 2, God has condemned Judah on two scores: they have rejected Jehovah, and they have reared their own gods. The first five verses of chapter 3 will continue on this theme. The messages found in chapters 2 through 6 were given during the first five years of Jeremiah's ministry before the Book of the Law was found. During this time, however, Josiah, a young man like Jeremiah, was seeking the Lord and instituting certain reforms in the nation. Primarily, he was trying to clean up the idolatry in Judah. The nation had forsaken the living God and had gone over into idolatry. You can see that the combined efforts of this young king and the young prophet Jeremiah had a tremendous effect upon the nation.

Judah had gone over to idolatry because it was the easy way and the popular way, but it was a pathway that led to the lowering of their standards and brought them down to a low moral level.

**They say, If a man put away his wife, and she go from him, and become another man's, shall he return unto her again? shall not that land be greatly polluted? but thou hast played the harlot with many lovers; yet return again to me, saith the Lord [Jer. 3:1].**

Judah had sunk to a very low level—there was gross immorality in the land. She had played the harlot; yet God asks her to return to Him.

**Lift up thine eyes unto the high places, and see where thou hast not been lien with. In the ways hast thou sat for them, as the Arabian in the wilderness; and thou hast polluted the land with thy whoredoms and with thy wickedness [Jer. 3:2].**

Idolatry is not simply making a little idol to worship. Anything that a man gives himself to wholeheartedly is idolatry. The Bible teaches that covetousness is idolatry, because when a man covets something, he gives his time, his energy to that—he is dedicated to it. Especially in these last days we see a great many people who are dedicated to sin, and the energy they put into sin is tremendous. But, you see, the minute a man turns away from the living God, he will turn to something else. It will be something he has made, and it becomes his god, his idol.

Dr. G. Campbell Morgan has made this very fine statement about the nature of idolatry and the worship of the true God:

... When a man makes a god according to the pattern of his own being, he makes a god like himself, an enlargement of his own imperfection. Moreover, the god which a man makes for himself will demand from him that which is according to his own nature. It is clearly evident in Mohammedanism. Great and wonderful and outstanding in his personality as Mohammed was, yet the blighting sensuality of the man curses the whole of Islam today. Men will be faithful to those gods who make no demands upon them which are out of harmony with the desires of their own hearts.

When God calls men, it is the call of the God of holiness, the God of purity, the God of love; and He demands that they rise to His height. He cannot accommodate Himself to the depravity of their nature. He will not consent to the things of desire within them that are of impurity and evil. He calls men up, and even higher, until they reach the height of perfect

conformity to His holiness. God's call to humanity is always first pure, and then peaceable; first holy, and then happy; first righteous, and then rejoicing (*Studies in the Prophecy of Jeremiah*, p. 36).

God said that Jeremiah's generation in Judah had gone wholeheartedly into idolatry, and as a result there was gross immorality in the land. When He says, "Lift up thine eyes unto the high places," you must understand how grossly immoral those high places were. A high place was a grove of trees where an idolatrous altar had been built. All kinds of sex orgies and drunken revelries were carried on there. Judah had sunk to a very low level.

The comparison to our own nation today is obvious, is it not? America has forsaken the living and true God, which is evident in the moral condition of this country. What lawlessness, dishonesty, and corrupt speech we find everywhere! We have even taught our children the use of very foul language.

**Therefore the showers have been withholden, and there hath been no latter rain; and thou hadst a whore's forehead, thou refusedst to be ashamed [Jer. 3:3].**

God tells them that He has already begun to judge them by withholding rain. Even today that land is dry. Their greatest need is water—even more than oil. They didn't find oil in the Negeb, but they found water, and that is much more precious to them. I believe that when the Jews return to Israel under the blessing of God, they are going to have all the water they need. God has said that He will supply it.

I think that we can see God's judgment upon our own nation in the many national calamities which we have suffered over the past several years. Unfortunately, it doesn't seem to wake us up and bring us back to Him.

## CHARGE OF BACKSLIDING DURING THE REIGN OF JOSIAH

We come now to the second message of Jeremiah. It begins in verse 6 of chapter 3 and extends all the way through chapter 6. In this message God charges the people with backsliding. The word *backsliding* is used seven times in this chapter, and that is more than half the number of times in the entire book. In Jeremiah we find this word more often than in the rest of the Bible put together. He and Hosea are the ones who use it.

*Backsliding* does not simply mean "to slide backwards" as we usually think of it. God gives us a vivid picture of what He means by backsliding when He tells us, "For Israel slideth back as a backsliding heifer . . ." (Hos. 4:16). Do you have any idea what it is like to try to load calves into a truck or wagon? When I was a boy, we lived next door to a southern Oklahoma rancher. He had two sons who were my friends. (They were mean boys, and I ran with them—but, of course, I was a good boy!) Sometimes we would go out to the ranch and help load the heifers. Do you know what they do when you try to get them up the ramp? They set their front feet and make themselves as stiff as they can. They brace themselves so that you cannot move them at all. When we would try to move them, they would start slipping backwards. That is God's picture of what it means to backslide.

Backsliding is a refusal to go God's way, a refusal to listen to Him. And when we do as the heifers do, when we set our wills against God's will, we wind up going backwards every time. If we rebel against the Lord and His will, we only get farther and farther away from Him.

**The LORD said also unto me in the days of Josiah, the king, Hast thou seen that which backsliding Israel hath done? she is gone up upon every high mountain and under every green tree, and there hath played the harlot [Jer. 3:6].**

God tells Judah to take a lesson from Israel which had already gone into captivity. He tells them to take notice of the fact that Israel had done exactly what they are doing. "Israel slideth back as a backsliding heifer." But God had tried to get Israel to return to Him, and they would not return. As a result they were taken off into captivity. What happened to Israel should serve as a lesson and should be a warning to Judah.

In verse 1 of this chapter God said, "Yet return again to me, saith the LORD." He says, "Though you have played the harlot, you belong to Me. If you come back to Me, I'll receive you." That is the reason any prodigal son or any prodigal daughter or any prodigal family or any prodigal church or any prodigal nation can always come back to God. God will receive you. The prodigal son didn't get any kicks when he came home. He had gotten those in the far country! He received kisses instead. He had nearly starved in the far country, but his father prepared a banquet for him when he came home.

But Israel had not returned to God. They

went into idolatry, and God sent them into captivity. Now He says to Judah, "Let this be a lesson to you."

**And I said after she had done all these things, Turn thou unto me. But she returned not. And her treacherous sister Judah saw it [Jer. 3:7].**

God says, "I gave Israel an opportunity to turn to me. I would have taken her back, but she wouldn't come. And her treacherous sister Judah saw it." The sin of Judah is compounded. I think her captivity was much worse than that of the ten northern tribes, and the reason is self-evident: Judah had Israel's captivity as an example and refused to profit by it.

The tragedy in this country is that we have a Bible, but very few are reading it. I get a little weary of hearing people say, "We live in a land where we have an open Bible, and we can read the Bible." Well, thank God for that, but who is *reading* it? How many people are really reading it? Judah did not turn to God even though they had an example. You and I have the Word of God today, and therefore I believe God will judge this country more harshly than He will judge nations such as the Soviet Union. They don't have Bibles over there, but you and I do. I believe God will judge us according to the opportunities He gives us.

**And it came to pass through the lightness of her whoredom, that she defiled the land, and committed adultery with stones and with stocks [Jer. 3:9].**

They made idols of sticks and stones.

**And yet for all this her treacherous sister Judah hath not turned unto me with her whole heart, but feignedly, saith the LORD [Jer. 3:10].**

The revival under King Josiah was a revival—there is no question about it. Many people turned to God. But it was so popular that for many it was nothing but a surface return to God. By and large, as far as the nation is concerned, it was a superficial experience with God.

I believe that there is a renewed interest in the Word of God today, and I think more people are being saved than at any time during the years of my ministry. But let's be very careful—it is not a revival. A great deal of it is quite surface. Don't be deceived by the large crowds in places or by the number who are reported to have accepted Christ. Just divide that number by two, and you'll probably get the number of those who have been *genuinely* converted. We see a great surface movement as well as that which is genuine.

**And the LORD said unto me, The backsliding Israel hath justified herself more than treacherous Judah [Jer. 3:11].**

God is making it clear that the sin of Judah is worse than the sin of Israel. The northern tribes didn't have the same opportunity as the southern tribes. They did not have the temple nor did they have a copy of the Word of God. Therefore the judgment on Judah was greater. I believe the judgment on us will be greater also.

**Go and proclaim these words toward the north, and say, Return, thou backsliding Israel, saith the LORD; and I will not cause mine anger to fall upon you: for I am merciful, saith the LORD, and I will not keep anger for ever [Jer. 3:12].**

God tells Israel that He will bring them back into the land if they will turn to Him. How gracious God is! How wonderful He is!

**Only acknowledge thine iniquity, that thou hast transgressed against the LORD thy God, and hast scattered thy ways to the strangers under every green tree, and ye have not obeyed my voice, saith the LORD [Jer. 3:13].**

Today the big problem is a lack of confession of sin. I find that repentance is lacking in much of the so-called spiritual movement of today. An example is a book I read recently which disturbed me. The author constantly used the first person pronoun, and the Lord received none of the glory. He told what God had done for him, how He had made him a millionaire, a big success. But I didn't find anywhere a statement that God had saved him from sin. We need to confess our iniquity.

My friend, do you say that you are a Christian? What do you mean by that? Perhaps you say that you have trusted Christ. Trusted Him for *what?* You may say that you trust Him as your Savior. Fine! I'm glad to hear that. Did He save you from *sin?* Remember that He died on the cross to save you from *sin,* not to give you a new personality or to make you a millionaire. He died to save us all from our sins. He was delivered for our offenses—we were all very offensive to God. The word of God through Jeremiah is "acknowledge

thine iniquity," and it is directed to us as well as to Judah.

**Turn, O backsliding children, saith the Lord; for I am married unto you: and I will take you one of a city, and two of a family, and I will bring you to Zion [Jer. 3:14].**

Oh how gracious God was!

**And I will give you pastors according to mine heart, which shall feed you with knowledge and understanding [Jer. 3:15].**

My friend, if you have a Bible-teaching pastor, you ought to run over and put your arm around him. You ought to protect him, because he is valuable. Such men are few and far between.

**And it shall come to pass, when ye be multiplied and increased in the land, in those days, saith the Lord, they shall say no more, The ark of the covenant of the Lord: neither shall it come to mind: neither shall they remember it; neither shall they visit it; neither shall that be done any more [Jer. 3:16].**

"In those days" is a reference to the millennial kingdom. All the way through the Book of Jeremiah we will find these rays of light. Have you ever been out on a cloudy day when all of a sudden the sun breaks through and you see a rainbow? This is how it will be throughout Jeremiah—we will have these glorious prophecies of the future.

**At that time they shall call Jerusalem the throne of the Lord; and all the nations shall be gathered unto it, to the name of the Lord, to Jerusalem: neither shall they walk any more after the imagination of their evil heart.**

**In those days the house of Judah shall walk with the house of Israel, and they shall come together out of the land of the north to the land that I have given for an inheritance unto your fathers [Jer. 3:17–18].**

This is a glorious prophecy. It is like a little gem.

**But I said, How shall I put thee among the children, and give thee a pleasant land, a goodly heritage of the hosts of nations? and I said, Thou shalt call me, My father; and shalt not turn away from me [Jer. 3:19].**

"Thou shalt call me, My father." No individual Israelite ever called God his Father. He was a Father to the *nation* of Israel, and He said ". . . Israel is my son . . ." (Exod. 4:22). But, he never called David His son; He said, ". . . David my servant" (Ps. 89:3). He never called Moses His son; He called him, "Moses my servant . . ." (Josh. 1:2). It is only in this day of grace that we are called the sons of God. How privileged we are today! "But as many as received him, to them gave he power [the right] to become *the sons of God*, even to them that believe on his name" (John 1:12). Those who do no more and no less than simply trust in His name become the sons of God. Is He your Savior from sin? If He is, you are not only a saved sinner, you are a *son* of God. How wonderful that is!

**Return, ye backsliding children, and I will heal your backslidings. Behold, we come unto thee; for thou art the Lord our God [Jer. 3:22].**

The Lord says that He will heal. I can tell you that you have a little sore in a very prominent place if you do a lot of backsliding my friend. God says, "I will heal you if you will come to Me."

**Truly in vain is salvation hoped for from the hills, and from the multitude of mountains: truly in the Lord our God is the salvation of Israel [Jer. 3:23].**

In Psalm 121 David says, "I will lift up mine eyes unto the hills, from whence cometh my help. My help cometh from the Lord, which made heaven and earth" (Ps. 121:1–2). Help does not come from those high places on the hills. Salvation comes from the Lord.

**We lie down in our shame, and our confusion covereth us: for we have sinned against the Lord our God, we and our fathers, from our youth even unto this day, and have not obeyed the voice of the Lord our God [Jer. 3:25].**

Judah did not confess their sins. Jeremiah confessed their sins for them and for himself, also.

You know, it wouldn't hurt for us to have a little confession of sin today. We hear so much about special gifts and about God's blessing in special ways. That is wonderful. We should thank God because He has blessed us. But have you ever heard a confession that we come short of the glory of God? Have you gone to Him yourself and told Him how far you fall short of His glory? We need to be humble before Him.

Judah was not humble before God, and God had to send them into captivity. I often wonder whether the Lord is getting ready to chastise us. We need to be humble before Him.

# CHAPTERS 4–6

**THEME:** *Jeremiah deals with backsliding of the people*

We are in that period of time when Josiah the king was carrying on a reformation, but it was before the Word of God had been found in the temple. Therefore it was reformation and *not* revival. That which was taking place was very shallow. Josiah was sincere, and he was certainly moved toward God. He listened to Jeremiah. But the people were not turning back to God in any genuine sort of way, even though Jeremiah had struck home in some of the prophecies he had given.

We are in the second message which Jeremiah gave (it began in ch. 3 and continues through ch. 6). He deals with the backsliding of the people. "And yet for all this her treacherous sister Judah hath not turned unto me with her whole heart, but feignedly, saith the LORD" (Jer. 3:10). They were turning to God in a merely outward manner. They were going to the temple and were going through the rituals, but their heart was not in it at all. It was something Josiah was trying to produce. This reveals that there can be reformation without revival. Reformation without revival is never a genuine change.

I am not quite sure that what we are seeing around us as I write this book is true revival. This renewed interest in the Word of God could become revival, but it may be merely an experience jag that a great many people are on at the present. It remains to be seen whether they are genuinely converted or not.

Although in Jeremiah's time there was reformation rather than a real turning to God, it was enough to prompt Jeremiah to give a tremendous prophecy in Jeremiah 3:16–18. He says that "in those days" all the nations will gather to the house of God in Jerusalem. Even that fact should have alerted Judah not to make their temple worship ritualistic, but they did not respond. Yet the Lord continues to plead with them. "Return, ye backsliding children, and I will heal your backslidings." (Jer. 3:22).

At the beginning of chapter 4 we find an expression of the Lord's response to any movement on the part of the people toward Him.

> **If thou wilt return, O Israel, saith the LORD, return unto me: and if thou wilt put away thine abominations out of my sight, then shalt thou not remove [Jer. 4:1].**

He is vitally interested in them, and He wants to bring them back into a right relationship to Himself. He tells them that He will not remove them from the land if they will but turn to Him.

> **And thou shalt swear, The LORD liveth, in truth, in judgment, and in righteousness; and the nations shall bless themselves in him, and in him shall they glory.**

> **For thus saith the LORD to the men of Judah and Jerusalem, Break up your fallow ground, and sow not among thorns [Jer. 4:2–3].**

In other words, reformation is no good. You can sow the seed on the ground, but the ground must first be prepared for it. There is no use sowing seed on thorny ground. Our Lord expressed it another way, ". . . neither cast ye your pearls before swine . . ." (Matt. 7:6). I believe there are certain times and certain places where there is no point in giving out the Word of God. There are times when men attempt evangelism because it is spectacular and sensational. God says, "Break up your fallow ground." As Dr. H. A. Ironside has put it, "The plowshare of conviction must overturn the hardened soil of the heart."

In the remainder of this section, there will first be an impeachment of the people. God will pronounce a judgment upon them and will call to them to return to Jehovah. Finally, there will be a clear foretelling of judgment. Believe me, Jeremiah will not mince words about that.

My feeling is that there ought to be more of the message of the prophets rather than the message of comfort in our own day. The fallow ground needs to be broken up. We are a nation in danger. We say we are one of the greatest nations in the world, but we could fall

overnight. Babylon the great fell in one night; Alexander the Great died in a night, and his entire empire crumbled; the Roman Empire fell from within, and we can go down just like that. Our greatness does not depend upon our atom bombs or the almighty dollar. We are decaying from within. There is deterioration, moral deterioration. Somebody needs to be saying something about it, but very little is being said. It seems to me that we are sowing seed on ground that is thorny. The Lord warns us against doing that.

God continues to offer to Judah an opportunity to come back to Him.

> **Circumcise yourselves to the LORD, and take away the foreskins of your heart, ye men of Judah and inhabitants of Jerusalem: lest my fury come forth like fire, and burn that none can quench it, because of the evil of your doings [Jer. 4:4].**

They were going through the outward form of circumcision. Circumcision was a badge that showed they belonged to the nation Israel, but God hadn't given it just as a form or a ceremony. Circumcision has been shown to have a very definite therapeutic value, but the important thing was its spiritual value. Their *hearts* needed to be turned to God.

Now Jeremiah lets them know that there will come a power out of the north—that will be Babylon—which will eventually destroy them.

> **Set up the standard toward Zion: retire, stay not: for I will bring evil from the north, and a great destruction.**

> **The lion is come up from his thicket, and the destroyer of the Gentiles is on his way; he is gone forth from his place to make thy land desolate; and thy cities shall be laid waste, without an inhabitant.**

> **For this gird you with sackcloth, lament and howl: for the fierce anger of the LORD is not turned back from us [Jer. 4:6–8].**

Judah had seen the ten tribes of the north go into captivity. Now Jeremiah is asking them to take warning from that. God is raising up a power, a new power in the north, and that power will come down and will finally destroy them.

The natural man cannot produce any righteousness at all. That is why Jeremiah calls the people to a circumcision of their hearts. But we see here that the people refused to turn to God; and, when a nation or a church or an individual rejects God, God rejects them. Remember that the Lord Jesus came and offered Himself as the King to Israel. When they rejected Him, He in turn rejected them. He said to them, "Behold, your house is left unto you desolate" (Matt. 23:38). Read that whole chapter of Matthew 23—if that doesn't make you blanch with fear, nothing will. Don't talk about the gentle Jesus! They rejected Him as their King, and then He rejected them.

Friend, you are free to reject God—that is your free will. But remember, if you reject God, God will reject you. He is gracious; He is good; He is patient and longsuffering; He gives you ample opportunity to turn to Him. But it is sobering to see what happens to any privileged people who refuse God, be it Israel or be it the church. God finally refuses them, and then all other men count them as reprobate, refuse, and worthless.

We have too many people today who give a pretense of being a follower of the living and true God. Many of them are members in the churches today. We often hear the expression that we are a Christian nation in America. I say we are not a Christian nation. There is no emphasis on the Word of God, and we are not following the living and true God.

The *Reader's Digest* published an article quite some time ago entitled, "The Book Almost Nobody Reads." Of course, they were referring to the Bible. I agree with that title. But notice what was said: "In short, one way to describe the Bible, written by many different hands over a period of 3,000 years and more, would be to say it is a disorderly collection of 60-odd books which are often tedious, barbaric, obscure and teeming with contradictions and inconsistencies. It is a swarming compost of a book, an Irish stew of poetry and propaganda, law and legalism, myth and murk, history and hysteria." Now that is a *lie*, my friend! The man who wrote the article knows nothing about the content of the Word of God.

I say to you that we are in the same kind of position today as were those people in the days of Jeremiah. The nation at that time had rejected God, but the people were still making a pretense of following Him. Such a people will find themselves rejected by God and by the world. America is following that same path. We are not loved by the world today. After World War II we were the pious people who were going to bring democracy to the

world. What have we done? We have brought lawlessness into our own land. Do you think we should bring lawlessness into the trails of the jungle as we have into the streets of our cities? Is that the kind of civilization we are going to bring to people?

We find ourselves despised by other nations. God said it would be that way. No people can pretend to be God-fearing, be hypocritical about it, and still expect the world to look up to them. God has ordered it that way. I know it is not popular to say this—Jeremiah wasn't very popular in his day, either. I am not expecting to win any popularity contest. The chamber of commerce will never elect me to be the man of the year. They would rather give me the boot, I am sure. But I must tell you honestly the message of this Book: A people who turn away from God will find that God turns away from them.

Now let me lift out some high points as we go through this message.

**For my people is foolish, they have not known me; they are sottish children, and they have none understanding: they are wise to do evil, but to do good they have no knowledge [Jer. 4:22].**

It is interesting to note that our government uses the help of those they call the intellectuals. Perhaps it was Franklin Roosevelt who started this with his "brain trust"—this idea of going to Harvard or some other prestigious university and getting the advice of some of the boys with high IQs. Oh, we are wise in doing evil! We think we have been real clever cookies in our dealings around the world. We think we are big business. We are big in everything but righteousness, my friend. We are not very big on knowing God. God says that those who pretend to know Him and don't really know Him are foolish.

The man who wrote the article that I just quoted was no more competent to write about the Word of God than I am to write about the *Congressional Record* or the Smithsonian Institution! I know nothing about those things. These famous intellectuals who are not real believers are not capable of writing about the Word of God. They do not know God, and you must know *Him* in order to know His Book. It is interesting that you can read a human book and understand it without knowing the author of the book. A human book by a human author can be understood by another human being. But if you want to know the Bible, you need to know the Author and have Him as your

Teacher. Only the spirit of God can make the Word of God real to you.

## JEREMIAH SPELLS OUT SPECIFIC SINS

**Run ye to and fro through the streets of Jerusalem, and see now, and know, and seek in the broad places thereof, if ye can find a man, if there be any that executeth judgment, that seeketh the truth; and I will pardon it [Jer. 5:1].**

You remember the story of old Diogenes, the Greek philosopher, who went through the streets of Athens with a lantern. They asked him what he was looking for, and his answer was, "I am looking for an honest man." He never did find one. I think you would have the same trouble in Los Angeles and maybe also in your town.

"If ye can find a man . . . I will pardon it." Why didn't Abraham keep on pleading with God for Sodom and Gomorrah? He stopped praying after he had asked God to spare the city for ten righteous men. God would have saved the city for *one* righteous man. He had to get that one man, Lot, out of the city before He could destroy it.

Look at how God speaks of His people—

**They were as fed horses in the morning: every one neighed after his neighbour's wife [Jer. 5:8].**

What is the big sin in our nation today? It is sexual sin, only we don't call it that. We call it "the new morality." But *God* still calls adultery sin. In fact He uses sarcasm of the first water: He says, "Every man is neighing like a horse for his neighbor's wife." What a picture of our contemporary culture!

**As a cage is full of birds, so are their houses full of deceit: therefore they are become great, and waxen rich [Jer. 5:27].**

In our generation we have seen a great many kids walk away from their homes because of the conditions which exist in them. I have talked to many of these young people, and I believe this verse gives a valid evaluation of what has happened.

## JUDAH REFUSES TO LISTEN

Now Jeremiah concludes his message in chapter 6.

**For from the least of them even unto the greatest of them every one is given**

to covetousness; and from the prophet even unto the priest every one dealeth falsely [Jer. 6:13].

The entire nation was obsessed with covetousness. And covetousness is the great sin in America. There is the coveting of gold and silver, riches, fame, and the neighbor's wife. Those are the things men covet.

They have healed also the hurt of the daughter of my people slightly, saying, Peace, peace; when there is no peace [Jer. 6:14].

There was a reformation on the surface. There was a little healing, but it was like pouring talcum powder on a cancer and then saying it is healed. People were saying "Peace," when there was no peace. And we hear a great deal about peace today, but I think that in reality we are getting ready for the final conflict.

Hear, O earth: behold, I will bring evil upon this people, even the fruit of their thoughts, because they have not hear-

kened unto my words, nor to my law, but rejected it [Jer. 6:19].

In rejecting the Word of God, they have rejected God. And when men reject God there is always something that follows—

Reprobate silver shall men call them, because the Lord hath rejected them [Jer. 6:30].

*Reprobate* is actually the same word as *reject*. Therefore, it could read, "Rejected silver shall men call them, because the Lord hath rejected them."

God says to the people of Judah, "You have rejected My law, and I will reject you and when I reject you, the men of the world are going to reject you also." Interesting, isn't it? It worked out that way in Jeremiah's day, and it is working that way in our day. We have spent billions of dollars to buy friends throughout the world; yet we are not loved by this big, bad world because we have rejected God and God will reject us. This is a very solemn message, and we ought not to treat it lightly.

# CHAPTERS 7–10

***THEME:*** *Warning delivered in the gate of the Lord's house*

We have seen in chapters 2–6 the prophecies which Jeremiah delivered during the first five years of his ministry. As a young man around twenty years of age, he delivered those severe predictions, condemning his people and pronouncing judgment upon them.

Now the prophecies in chapters 7–10 were given after the Law of the Lord had been discovered in the temple during the time of cleansing ordered by the young king Josiah. Josiah was greatly concerned about his people, which revealed that he had a personal relationship with God as a young man. He and Jeremiah, being approximately the same age and both zealous for God, were probably good friends. Hilkiah the priest, who was evidently the father of Jeremiah, is the one who found the law of the Lord. The temple was cleaned out and repaired and back in use, which was, of course, a very wonderful thing. Now Jeremiah stands in the gate of the Lord's house and gives a prophecy to his people. This is the way chapter 7 opens—

The word that came to Jeremiah from the Lord, saying,

Stand in the gate of the Lord's house, and proclaim there this word, and say, Hear the word of the Lord, all ye of Judah, that enter in at these gates to worship the Lord [Jer. 7:1–2].

"Stand in the gate of the Lord's house." There are some who think this is very similar to the prophecy that is found in chapter 26 of Jeremiah. The prophecy is similar, but you will notice that it was delivered in the *court* of the house of the Lord—he was no longer standing by the gate but had gone into the court—and it was given during the reign of another king. However, the message is very much the same; Jeremiah had not changed his viewpoint.

Now that the temple has been repaired and the Book of the Law has been found, the people are returning to the temple in droves. Coming back to the temple is the popular thing to do, and they are talking about return-

ing to God. Young Jeremiah hears the conversation of the people, and he gives the following message—

## PLEA TO AMEND THEIR WAYS

**Thus saith the LORD of hosts, the God of Israel, Amend your ways and your doings, and I will cause you to dwell in this place [Jer. 7:3].**

It is evident that, although they are going to the temple and are returning back to temple worship, there is no real change in their lives. They are still living as they did when they were worshiping idols. It is only an outward revival at this time. The time would come when it was more real, but at this point it is only a surface movement.

Now we see the attitude of the people, which was the thing that concerns Jeremiah.

**Trust ye not in lying words, saying, The temple of the LORD, The temple of the LORD, The temple of the LORD, are these [Jer. 7:4].**

You can imagine how the people felt about all of this. They were exclaiming, "My, look at the temple! Isn't it beautiful? Didn't they do a good job of repairing it? Isn't it nice to get back to the temple; it's just like old times!" You see, there was enthusiasm about the temple, but there was no genuine turning to God. This is the thing that Jeremiah noticed. So he said, "Don't trust these lying words that you're saying. You act as if it is the greatest thing in the world just to return to the temple."

If you will turn back to 2 Chronicles and read chapters 34 and 35, it will be very helpful for you to understand what is going on at this time in history. What happened was truly wonderful. Hilkiah gave the Book of the Law to Shaphan, who read it before the king. The king gathered together all the elders of Judah and Jerusalem, and they had the Law read to all the people. Then they made a covenant with God to walk before Him. They celebrated a passover in Jerusalem: "And there was no passover like to that kept in Israel from the days of Samuel the prophet; neither did all the kings of Israel keep such a passover as Josiah kept, and the priests, and the Levites, and all Judah and Israel that were present, and the inhabitants of Jerusalem. In the eighteenth year of the reign of Josiah was this passover kept" (2 Chron. 35:18–19). They reinstituted the services in the temple with all the sacrifices and feasts. That was good and wonder-

ful. Then what was the problem? The problem was that they were not changing their ways. They lived just as they had lived before. He refers back, not to the Ten Commandments, but to that which the Lord gave them after the Ten Commandments, instructions in Exodus 21–23, which dealt with everyday life in Israel and their relationships to one another.

**Will ye steal, murder and commit adultery, and swear falsely, and burn incense unto Baal, and walk after other gods whom ye know not;**

**And come and stand before me in this house, which is called by my name, and say, We are delivered to do all these abominations? [Jer. 7:9–10].**

Although the people were talking about how wonderful the temple was, they were still worshiping Baal. Their philosophy was that, since the temple was repaired and they were at least tipping their hat to God on the Sabbath day, He would protect them. Now it is true that when people genuinely turn to God, He will protect them, but they were resting on a fact that did not apply to them. They had taken up quite an offering for the rebuilding of the temple, and people who had given generously felt this was all that was necessary for God's blessing.

I know of no book that fits into the present hour with a message for us better than this Book of Jeremiah. After World War II there was a little wave of revival. There were several evangelists out at that time, and the crowds came. During that time I began my Bible studies which were said to have the largest attendance of any midweek service in America. During that time we would hear pastors say that church attendance had doubled and tripled. They were putting chairs in the aisles and building new buildings. Churches were moving out to the suburbs. One pastor I know built a very wonderful church out in suburbia, and he was packing them in—two thousand people in a service. He said, "The trouble was that when I got a new church, I didn't get new people. The same people should have been made new, but they were not." It was the same old people in a new church. They mistook growth in numbers for spiritual growth and development. This is the point that Jeremiah is making.

Now Jeremiah says something further. In fact, our Lord quoted him in His day—

**Is this house, which is called by my name, become a den of robbers in your**

eyes? Behold, even I have seen it, saith the LORD [Jer. 7:11].

This is the same charge that the Lord Jesus used when He cleansed the temple centuries later. In the days of Jeremiah he called it a den of robbers because the people were spending the week robbing their brethren and then would piously come to the temple. There was no change in their business habits or in their relationship with one another.

People today still think there is something valuable in great religious splurges and conventions. This type of thing doesn't appeal to me, because I am not an organization man, nor am I a joiner. I have never enjoyed organizations and conventions. Some people love them. The problem is that some people mistake enthusiasm for a moving of the spirit of God. Now I will probably be as unpopular as Jeremiah when I say that kind of thing is not revival. Nothing is true revival unless it transforms lives.

The Wesleyan movement in England changed lives. It just about put the liquor industry out of business in England. It changed conditions in factories and resulted in the enactment of child labor laws. It was a spiritual movement that reached into the lives of the people. I want to see a spiritual movement today that will reach into the ghetto. When the government reaches into the ghetto with so-called social reform as we have it today, there is crookedness and misappropriation of funds, and nothing is made right. What we need is true revival, which is the only thing that will really change the ghetto.

That was the message of Jeremiah in his day. You can see how popular that young man would have been as he stood there in the gates of the temple and delivered God's message. I can picture him there—a lonely fellow, heartbroken at the message he is giving to his people. But he is giving it faithfully, and it does bring partial revival.

## JUDGMENT FOR IDOLATRY

Therefore pray not thou for this people, neither lift up cry nor prayer for them, neither make intercession to me: for I will not hear thee [Jer. 7:16].

God says, "Jeremiah, you don't need to pray for these people until they turn to Me." This is an awesome verse. God says that it is no longer useful to pray for the people. The nation has gone too far away from God. Unless they will turn to God, there is no hope for them.

I believe there are times when we do not need to pray for folk to be blessed. I visited a member of my church in the hospital and prayed for him, then a man in the other bed asked me to pray for him. I asked him whether he was a Christian, and he said he believed in God. I told him that didn't make him a Christian, and then I explained the gospel to him and asked him to put his trust in the Lord Jesus Christ. He said he could not accept that, but he wanted me to pray for him. I told him, "Brother, I will pray for you, but not the way you want me to pray for you. You want me to pray that you will get well and that God will bless you. I am going to pray that you will be *saved*—that is the only prayer I can pray for you." I believe we do too much praying for people to be blessed of God when we ought to be praying that those people will be saved.

This is what God is saying to Jeremiah. "Don't stand there in the temple and pray that these people will not go into captivity. Pray that they will turn back to Me. You are giving them My message, and that is the important thing to do." This gets right down to the nitty-gritty, doesn't it? God is not as interested in your ritual on Sunday as He is in your behavior on Monday. The place to judge whether a Christian is genuine or not is not to watch him in church on Sunday but to see him at work on Monday.

But this thing commanded I them, saying, Obey my voice, and I will be your God, and ye shall be my people: and walk ye in all the ways that I have commanded you, that it may be well unto you [Jer. 7:23].

God clearly states for them again that what He wants is their obedience. Coming to the temple is wonderful, but it is no substitute for obedience.

It has been said that some people go to church to eye the clothes and others go to close their eyes. That may be true in a great number of cases. Their purpose is not really to worship God. Their lives have not been changed. They still gossip, still crucify other Christians behind their backs, still live their lives out in the world—just as Jeremiah's people were still going to the altar of Baal—living without a testimony for the Lord. There is a certain testimony given by going to church, but it is the testimony you give out in the world that counts. This is very real and very personal, isn't it?

Yet they hearkened not unto me, nor inclined their ear, but hardened their

neck: they did worse than their fathers.

Therefore thou shalt speak all these words unto them; but they will not hearken to thee: thou shalt also call unto them; but they will not answer thee [Jer. 7:26–27].

Jeremiah did not have people come forward and declare themselves for God. His message went unheeded; yet it was his responsibility to deliver the message. God told him to do the job, to give out His Word, even if there was no response to it. It is not important for us to be able to count noses and see a response to our message. The important thing is the report we must give to God, to be faithful in giving out His Word and backing it up with our lives.

Cut off thine hair, O Jerusalem, and cast it away, and take up a lamentation on high places; for the LORD hath rejected and forsaken the generation of his wrath [Jer. 7:29].

God calls them "the generation of his wrath." Judgment will come to Jerusalem.

And they have built the high places of Tophet, which is in the valley of the son of Hinnom, to burn their sons and their daughters in the fire; which I commanded them not, neither came it into my heart [Jer. 7:31].

"Tophet" was the high place of the valley of Hinnom, where the children were sacrificed upon the heated brass arms of Moloch.

## NO ONE REPENTED
## OF HIS WICKEDNESS

Chapter 8 continues Jeremiah's message as he stands in the gate of the Lord's house.

The wise men are ashamed, they are dismayed and taken: lo, they have rejected the word of the LORD; and what wisdom is in them? [Jer. 8:9].

Their crowning sin is that they are rejecting the Word of the Lord.

This is the crowning sin of America also. The prevailing feeling is that if our economy is all right, we are all right. However, many folk are beginning to realize that the economy can be all right and we can be all wrong.

After World War II we hastened to get the atom bomb into our arsenal of weapons. Of course we need to protect ourselves, but we forgot that any nation, any church, or any individual disintegrates from the *inside*. It is

not what happens on the outside, but what happens on the inside that is the crucial issue.

Jeremiah enters deeply into the feelings of his people, sharing with them this wail—

The harvest is past, the summer is ended, and we are not saved.

For the hurt of the daughter of my people am I hurt; I am black; astonishment hath taken hold on me.

Is there no balm in Gilead; is there no physician there? why then is not the health of the daughter of my people recovered? [Jer. 8:20–22].

Although God had made adequate provision for their restoration, they refuse the remedy.

## JEREMIAH SHARES
## GOD'S HEARTBREAK

Chapter 9 begins with an expression of Jeremiah's personal heartbreak as he sees his people spurn the tender solicitude of God.

Oh that my head were waters, and mine eyes a fountain of tears, that I might weep day and night for the slain of the daughter of my people! [Jer. 9:1].

This is the effect it had on Jeremiah. How did he give his message? Was he a hard-boiled kind of man who liked to criticize others and rule them out? No, he stood there and gave his message with tears streaming down his face. The message that he gave broke his heart. Centuries later, people of Israel saw Jesus weeping over the city of Jerusalem when He had a harsh message to deliver to that city and were reminded of Jeremiah, the weeping prophet, and some of them even thought Jesus was Jeremiah who had returned to them.

Oh that I had in the wilderness a lodging place of wayfaring men; that I might leave my people, and go from them! for they be all adulterers, an assembly of treacherous men [Jer. 9:2].

He longed to get away into a wilderness place where he would not have to see the sin of his people which was bringing his nation to ruin.

Thus saith the LORD, Let not the wise man glory in his wisdom, neither let the mighty man glory in his might, let not the rich man glory in his riches:

But let him that glorieth glory in this, that he understandeth and knoweth

me, that I am the LORD which exercise lovingkindness, judgment, and righteousness, in the earth: for in these things I delight, saith the LORD [Jer. 9:23–24].

These are two wonderful verses of Scripture. They can stand alone and are often quoted alone. However, we need to remember that they were spoken to a people who had rejected the Word of God.

As a nation, what are the things we glory in? Obviously, we trust in human wisdom, in riches, and in power. We need to be reminded that our strength is not in the brain trust in Washington. Our strength is not in Wall Street, the stock market, and the economy. Our strength does not lie in the cleverness of politicians. Our strength is not found in the fact that we have nuclear weapons. Any strength that we have must lie in our spiritual values, our moral values, our character, and our purpose. And these things are not even taught in our schools and colleges today. We have brought forth a generation that is rude, a generation that has no sense of moral purpose. In fact, we have lost our way—as Jeremiah said to his people—on the dark mountains. In our day America is just coasting along; and, when you start coasting, you are going downhill.

I know it is not popular to say these things. I am afraid I am not making friends and influencing people—but neither did Jeremiah. I am going to stand with him, because I believe there is still hope for revival in our land.

"Let him that glorieth glory in this, that he understandeth and knoweth me." What we need desperately is a group of leaders who know something other than the present godless philosophy. We need people who know God, who know His Word and are obeying it. The great need in this country today is a return to God. We need to set aside our hypocrisy and our sophistication and our illusion that we are such a smart people. We brag about our achievements when our great need is to walk in a way that will glorify God.

Chapter 10 concludes Jeremiah's message in the gate of the Lord's house, and it begins a section (chs. 10–12) of reform and revival after finding the Book of the Law.

The finding of the Book of the Law had a tremendous effect on King Josiah. He realized how far the people had fallen from God's intention for them. It moved that man, and he was tremendously changed. He brought his people into a covenant with God that they would serve Him.

## THE FOOLISHNESS OF IDOLATRY

In this chapter we see that the people were substituting something for God. People have always had substitutes for God. Anyone who is not worshiping the true and living God has some substitute for Him. It may be that the person himself becomes his god—there are a great number of people who actually worship themselves. Others worship money and are willing to be dishonest to become rich. Others worship fame and will sell their honor in order to obtain some unworthy goal. There are many substitutes for God, and Jeremiah talks about this:

Hear ye the word which the LORD speaketh unto you, O house of Israel:

Thus saith the LORD, Learn not the way of the heathen, and be not dismayed at the signs of heaven; for the heathen are dismayed at them [Jer. 10:1–2].

People today are still doing what they did in the time of Jeremiah, trying to regulate their lives by the zodiac. They want to know what sign they were born under and all that nonsense. It is given out through our news media as though it were genuine!

God warns, "Learn not the way of the heathen." My friend, the astrology that is being promoted today is something which has been picked up from the pagan world.

For the customs of the people are vain: for one cutteth a tree out of the forest, the work of the hands of the workman, with the axe.

They deck it with silver and with gold; they fasten it with nails and with hammers, that it move not [Jer. 10:3–4].

There are some folk who interpret Jeremiah's denunciation of idolatry to be a condemnation of the modern Christmas tree. That is utterly preposterous and ridiculous. Jeremiah is not talking about Christmas trees—nobody in his day had a Christmas tree! He is talking to his people about worshiping idols.

"The customs of the people are vain"—they are empty. Obviously Jeremiah is talking about idolatry. He is ridiculing with bitter irony the idolatry of his day. He reminds them that they go out to the woods, cut down a tree, shape it into an image, deck it with silver and gold, fasten it with nails—and that's their god! It is like worshiping a scarecrow! Now,

my friend, if at Christmas time you fall on your knees before your Christmas tree and worship it, Jeremiah's warning could have reference to you. But I don't know of even an unsaved pagan in the country who *worships* a Christmas tree. They use it as a decoration, then throw it out with the trash when Christmas is over. Rather than worshiping a Christmas tree, the danger I see is the worship of self at Christmastime—*getting* everything possible for self.

**Forasmuch as there is none like unto thee, O LORD; thou art great, and thy name is great in might [Jer. 10:6].**

The Lord cannot be compared to anything. How ridiculous it is to turn from the true and living God to worship the things around you and get your leading from the zodiac!

**Thus shall ye say unto them, The gods that have not made the heavens and the earth, even they shall perish from the earth, and from under these heavens [Jer. 10:11].**

The gods of the heathen did not create the universe. Our God, the living God, created it.

**He hath made the earth by his power, he hath established the world by his wisdom, and hath stretched out the heavens by his discretion [Jer. 10:12].**

The stars are up there in their places because *God* put them there. He placed them where *He* wanted them. He didn't ask you or me how we wanted them arranged. This is *His* universe, and He is the only One who is worthy of our worship. We may smile at the people of previous centuries who cut down a tree to make a god. We call ourselves intelligent and civilized; yet our people spend millions of dollars to try to discern their future by the zodiac, going to fortune tellers and palm readers and all that sort of thing. If people today are so intelligent, why don't they worship the living and true God and get into reality?

**O LORD, I know that the way of man is not in himself: it is not in man that walketh to direct his steps [Jer. 10:23].**

No man can walk aright apart from the revelation of God in His Word. The minute a man turns from the Word of God, he is on a detour. That is our natural course. In fact, we begin that way. I used to take my little grandson for a walk around the block when he was learning to walk. He was a wonderful little fellow, but he wore me out because he wanted to walk up the sidewalk of every house we passed; and when we came to a driveway, he would want to run out in the street, and when we would get to a corner he would want to go the wrong way. I have never seen a little fellow who wanted to go in as many wrong ways as he did. One day when we finally got home, I said to him, "Kim, you're just like your grandfather. When he gets away from the Word of God, he always goes down a detour." My friend, "it is not in man . . . to direct his steps." We are dependent upon the omniscient God for direction in every area of our lives.

# CHAPTERS 11–13

*THEME: Israel disobeyed God's covenant made in the wilderness*

In chapters 11 and 12 Jeremiah delivers this tremendous message after the Law has been read to the people. I must remind you that following the giving of the Ten Commandments in Exodus 20, God went on to pronounce certain judgments if the Law were disobeyed. These are the things that Jeremiah emphasizes, the aspects of the Law which condition the way we live our lives—the way you treat your neighbor, the way you conduct your business, and the kind of social life you are living. Are you one of these church members who is actually worshiping sex? I know men who have left their wives to marry some little girl who didn't have anything upstairs but had a whole lot downstairs, and they think they can still serve the Lord! Jeremiah makes it clear that if you have done that, you've gone down a detour and are far away from God.

Many people talk about being fundamental and correct in their doctrine (I hope you understand that I insist upon that), but what is

equally important is the kind of life that you are living. How *honest* are you? How *clean* are you in your living? That is what Jeremiah is insisting upon here. Most of us, if we were honest, would get down before God and confess our need to walk with Him, to be close to Him. But the people didn't do it in Jeremiah's day, and there won't be many who do it in our day either.

> **The word that came to Jeremiah from the Lord, saying,**

> **Hear ye the words of this covenant, and speak unto the men of Judah, and to the inhabitants of Jerusalem [Jer. 11:1–2].**

"This covenant"—When the Law was found and read to the people, King Josiah called in the leaders and they made an oath that they were going to follow the Word of God.

> **And say thou unto them, Thus saith the Lord God of Israel; Cursed be the man that obeyeth not the words of this covenant [Jer. 11:3].**

Before they found the Book of the Law, the people did not know the Law. Now they know it and their responsibility is great: God says, "*Cursed* be the man that obeyeth not the words of this covenant."

I have said many times that I would rather be a heathen in some dark corner of the earth bowing down before an idol, than to be a member of a church where the pastor faithfully preaches the Word of God and to have done nothing in response to it. May I say, I have more respect for that heathen man, and God may yet bring the gospel to him. But that church member who has heard the gospel and rejected it—God will certainly judge him.

Now this chapter closes with the fact that Jeremiah is actually rejected by his hometown, Anathoth.

> **But I was like a lamb or an ox that is brought to the slaughter; and I knew not that they had devised devices against me, saying, Let us destroy the tree with the fruit thereof, and let us cut him off from the land of the living, that his name may be no more remembered.**

> **But, O Lord of hosts, that judgest righteously, that triest the reins and the heart, let me see thy vengeance on them: for unto thee have I revealed my cause.**

> **Therefore thus saith the Lord of the men of Anathoth, that seek thy life, saying, Prophesy not in the name of the Lord, that thou die not by our hand [Jer. 11:19–21].**

God tells Jeremiah, "There is no use speaking to Anathoth anymore. They have rejected Me, and they want to kill you. Don't bother to prophesy to them any longer."

There are churches today who no longer stand for the things of God or teach the Word of God as they once did. And some people think it is terrible that their memberships are dwindling and that the churches are being deserted. What *is* terrible is that the Word of God is not being taught in their pulpits. Jeremiah stopped giving the Word of God in Anathoth. He went somewhere else, because the people were going to kill him; they had rejected the Word of God.

What a picture we have here! It *cost* this man Jeremiah something to stand for God. It broke his own heart and alienated his hometown from him. In John 4:44 we read, ". . . Jesus himself testified, that a prophet hath no honour in his own country." Our Lord had to leave his hometown of Nazareth and move his headquarters to Capernaum. That is what young Jeremiah had to do also.

Jeremiah is delivering a message to these people unlike any we hear today. Today we say, "Come to Jesus, and He will give you a new personality, and He may even make you rich. You're going to get along real well." That's not what we learn from Jeremiah and his life. Jeremiah says that it will cost you something to turn to God—but it will be worth everything you have to pay.

In spite of the fact that Judah made a covenant to serve God, the revival in the land proved to be a largely surface movement. There is no question that the words of Jeremiah had their effect and that there were some who in genuineness turned to the Lord. Jeremiah had preached, "Then the Lord said unto me, Proclaim all these words in the cities of Judah, and in the streets of Jerusalem, saying, Hear ye the words of this covenant, and do them" (v. 6).

However, things in the nation were deteriorating. After the revival, interest in spiritual things began to wear off, and the people returned to their old ways. Even King Josiah made a grave blunder. He went out to battle against the king of Egypt, Pharaoh-nechoh, and they fought at Megiddo. Josiah was fatally wounded, and Jeremiah mourned for

him: "And Jeremiah lamented for Josiah: and all the singing men and the singing women spake of Josiah in their lamentations to this day, and made them an ordinance in Israel: and, behold, they are written in the lamentations" (2 Chron. 35:25).

Jeremiah wept because he knew that the people not only would return to idolatry but they would sink even farther into immorality. And, of course, they did. Jeremiah had to give the people a message that they didn't want to hear. They rejected his message and were plotting to kill him, so that he had to leave his hometown of Anathoth. Had Josiah still been alive, he would have protected Jeremiah, but Josiah was gone now.

Jehoahaz came to the throne but reigned for only three months. Pharaoh-nechoh then raised Jehoiakim to the throne of Judah. Jehoiakim had to pay a tax to Egypt, so he taxed the land heavily. It wasn't very long until Nebuchadnezzar defeated the Egyptian king and Jehoiakim became a vassal of Babylon. This lasted for three years, and then Jehoiakim rebelled against the king of Babylon, ignoring Jeremiah's warning not to do so. Jeremiah had also warned earlier against the alliance with Egypt as a source of false confidence, but the kings of Judah paid no attention to him and continually became more corrupt.

## JEREMIAH'S QUESTION

As we come to chapter 12 we have entered a very evil period in the life of the nation, and the only light remaining is this man Jeremiah. Josiah has been slain, Jeremiah has been forced to leave his hometown, and evil men have come to the throne. Conditions seem only to get worse. At this point Jeremiah—and I believe every honest Christian—has doubts come into his heart. Dark thoughts come into his mind, and he wonders why God permits certain things. Every pastor who has ever stood for the things of God at times wonders why God does not move. He looks around and sees that it is his very best people who are suffering; the most spiritual folk seem to be having more trouble than anyone else. We all wonder why God permits this. Even David questioned God when he saw ". . . the wicked in great power, and spreading himself like a green bay tree" (Ps. 37:35). Listen now to Jeremiah as he talks to the Lord:

**Righteous art thou, O Lord, when I plead with thee: yet let me talk with thee of thy judgments: Wherefore doth the way of the wicked prosper? wherefore are all they happy that deal very treacherously?**

**Thou hast planted them, yea, they have taken root: they grow, yea, they bring forth fruit: thou art near in their mouth, and far from their reins [Jer. 12:1–2].**

"Oh, they talk about You, Lord, but they're far from You, and they prosper. Why do You permit that?" That was Jeremiah's question. That's my question too. I'd like to ask God that today: "Lord, why do You permit it?" I don't have the answer, and I don't think Jeremiah or David ever had the answer either. God allows the wicked to prosper, and we see them spreading themselves like a green bay tree. Why doesn't God prosper those who are really interested in supporting fine Christian missionaries? I've asked Him that, and I don't have the answer.

**But thou, O Lord knowest me: thou hast seen me, and tried mine heart toward thee: pull them out like sheep for the slaughter, and prepare them for the day of slaughter [Jer. 12:3].**

Jeremiah says, "Why don't You judge them? They are the ones who should be judged."

**How long shall the land mourn, and the herbs of every field wither, for the wickedness of them that dwell therein? the beasts are consumed, and the birds; because they said, He shall not see our last end [Jer. 12:4].**

"How long shall the land mourn"—in other words, "Lord, why don't You move?" God's answer to Jeremiah and to you and me today is one that we must accept—it's the best we have. God says, "I know what I'm doing. You *trust Me*, rest in Me." Remember Jeremiah began this passage, "*Righteous* art thou, O Lord." My friend, what God is doing today—however peculiar it may seem to us—is *right*, and we will be able to see and understand that someday. That is where faith must enter in. We walk by faith and not by sight.

Jeremiah alone stands for God. Jehoiakim, a corrupt ruler, is on the throne. Things are getting worse, and he wonders what is going to happen. God has already assured Jeremiah that He will take care of the situation. In chapter 11 verse 16 "The Lord called thy name, A green olive tree, fair, and of goodly fruit: with the noise of a great tumult he hath kindled fire upon it, and the branches of it are

broken." Paul refers to this in Romans 11 saying that the good olive tree has been cut off and set aside. That is exactly what God did to these people. And today, out of that same root, He's bringing forth a wild olive tree. That is you and me: the church has been grafted into that root which is Christ. He is the ". . . root out of a dry ground . . ." (Isa. 53:2), and He brings life. God says to Jeremiah, "I'll take care of this. I'll be the One who will deal with this." God has a plan which extends far beyond the circumstances that Jeremiah could see.

> **If thou hast run with the footmen, and they have wearied thee, then how canst thou contend with horses? and if in the land of peace, wherein thou trustedst, they wearied thee, then how wilt thou do in the swelling of Jordan? [Jer. 12:5].**

You'll forgive me, I'm not trying to be irreverent, but this is actually what God is saying to Jeremiah: "If you are troubled now by what things are going to happen, well, you ain't seen nothing yet! Things are to get lots worse, Jeremiah. And if you're troubled now, what are you going to do when it really gets bad?"

Friend, things may look bad to us today, but they are going to get worse. I hope the knowledge of that will help draw you closer to God. He does not explain all the details to us as we might wish He would, but He does tell us that we can trust Him to always do the right thing.

> **Mine heritage is unto me as a speckled bird, the birds round about are against her; come ye, assemble all the beasts of the field, come to devour [Jer. 12:9].**

Don't tell me God doesn't have a sense of humor. He says here, "Jeremiah, you're a speckled bird!" You see, every crow thinks his little offspring is blacker than any other crow, but when an egg hatches and it's speckled, that tells you something. And Jeremiah was a speckled bird. The people said to him, "We thought you were for us, that you were one of us. But you're not, you're speckled." Well, my friend, I'm a speckled bird too, and I have a notion you might be one. If you're standing for God, you *are* a speckled bird! God says, "Jeremiah, you might as well accept it: you're a speckled bird, if you stand with Me."

> **And it shall come to pass, after that I have plucked them out I will return, and have compassion on them, and will bring them again, every man to his heritage, and every man to his land [Jer. 12:15].**

Why is it that the rich are prospering? God says, "Jeremiah, I'll take care of that. And I'll tell you what is going to happen: They are going into captivity. But I have remembered the land, and I'm going to bring them back into the land."

## PARABLE IN ACTION— THE LINEN GIRDLE

Chapter 13 is another great chapter. I think it is interesting because, even when conditions are so terribly serious, you just can't help but smile. God is giving a parable to Judah, and it is the parable of the *girdle*!

> **Thus saith the LORD unto me, Go and get thee a linen girdle, and put it upon thy loins, and put it not in water [Jer. 13:1].**

I just can't help but smile at this. I don't think that Jeremiah was putting on weight. In fact, I would think he had been losing weight. God told him to get a girdle and wear it. But it wasn't because he was getting fat—a girdle wasn't worn for that purpose in that day. You see, today a girdle is used to try to achieve an hourglass figure when it is more like a barrel! In that day a girdle was something worn to bind up the flowing garments to ready oneself for service.

The girdle is a sign of service. The Lord Jesus spoke of His servants having their ". . . loins . . . girded about . . ." (Luke 12:35). That is, they are to be ready for service. You remember that He girded Himself with a linen cloth and began to wash the disciples' feet. This had a twofold meaning: *He*, the great Servant, was preparing *them* for service by washing their feet so they could have fellowship with Him. For if you don't have fellowship with Him, you can't serve. Service is fellowship with Christ. It is not teaching a Sunday school class, singing a solo, or preaching a sermon. Service is fellowship with Christ. It is being cleansed and used for what He wants to do. God doesn't use dirty cups or dirty vessels.

Now Jeremiah is told to do something very interesting with this girdle:

> **And the word of the LORD came unto me the second time, saying,**

> **Take the girdle that thou hast got, which is upon thy loins, and arise, go to**

Euphrates, and hide it there in a hole of the rock.

So I went, and hid it by Euphrates, as the LORD commanded me [Jer. 13:3–5].

There has always been a lot of debate as to whether Jeremiah actually went down to the Euphrates and hid the girdle. I think he did. There was traffic in the day going to and fro between nations, and I think Jeremiah actually made this trip. He did this very strange thing, and when he came back, people probably said, "Where have you been, Jeremiah?" He would reply, "I've been down to Babylon." "What have you been doing down there? Did you go as a representative of the king, or did you go down there on a business trip?" Jeremiah would have to answer, "No, I went down there to hide a girdle!" Now, my friend, I think the crowd laughed at that.

And it came to pass after many days, that the LORD said unto me, Arise, go to Euphrates, and take the girdle from thence, which I commanded thee to hide there.

Then I went to Euphrates, and digged, and took the girdle from the place where I had hid it: and, behold, the girdle was marred, it was profitable for nothing [Jer. 13:6–7].

Jeremiah was to wear the girdle and not wash it but let it get dirtier and dirtier. I think it finally got so dirty that he couldn't bear to wear it anymore. Then God told him to bury it in Babylon as an object lesson. When he returned and dug it up, he found "it was profitable for nothing." What does this strange action mean?

Then the word of the LORD came unto me, saying,

Thus saith the LORD, After this manner will I mar the pride of Judah, and the great pride of Jerusalem [Jer. 13:8–9].

God is saying that because the people of Judah are continually sinking into iniquity they will reach the place where there is no hope for them. He is going to send them into Babylonian captivity. The object lesson was impressive. God uses some very funny things to teach His people.

Give glory to the LORD your God, before he cause darkness, and before your feet stumble upon the dark mountains, and, while ye look for light, he turn it into the shadow of death, and make it gross darkness [Jer. 13:16].

God says to His people, "It's getting nighttime now. It's going to be dark, and you won't know where to go because you are lost in the mountains." Yet He still asks them to turn to Him.

The cities of the south shall be shut up, and none shall open them: Judah shall be carried away captive all of it, it shall be wholly carried away captive [Jer. 13:19].

God tells them exactly what is going to happen. He makes it very clear what He will do.

Can the Ethiopian change his skin, or the leopard his spots? then may ye also do good, that are accustomed to do evil [Jer. 13:23].

It is impossible for an unsaved person to do good. All of the do-gooders are not really pleasing God. Until a man does his work in the name of the Lord Jesus Christ and for His glory and honor, he is simply doing the work for himself for selfish reasons. No genuine goodness can come out of an evil heart.

*THEME: Backsliding nation judged by drought and famine*

Up to this point Jeremiah has been prophesying during the reign of Josiah. Now we find him delivering a prophecy during the reign of Jehoiakim. King Josiah during the last part of his reign did a very foolish thing. He fought against Nechoh, a pharaoh of Egypt, and there at Megiddo Josiah was killed. Jeremiah mourned for him; he had been his friend. After the death of Josiah, the nation began to drop back into idolatry; in fact, its plunge downward was swift and terrible, as we shall see in this section.

## DROUGHT

God's first warning to the nation was drought.

**The word of the LORD that came to Jeremiah concerning the dearth.**

**Judah mourneth, and the gates thereof languish; they are black unto the ground; and the cry of Jerusalem is gone up [Jer. 14:1–2].**

The drought was apparently a very severe one. There had been a drought during the reign of Ahab, and at that time Elijah was the messenger from God. Now there is a drought, and Jeremiah is the messenger to the southern kingdom of Judah.

**Because the ground is chapt, for there was no rain in the earth, the plowmen were ashamed, they covered their heads [Jer. 14:4].**

The ground is barren and cracked for want of rainfall.

**Yea, the hind also calved in the field, and forsook it, because there was no grass [Jer. 14:5].**

Even the cattle would leave their offspring because there was no water to drink and no grazing land. It would mean death to the calf and to the mother also. All of this revealed the fact that God was judging them. This is one of the thirteen famines mentioned in Scripture, and all of them were judgments of God upon the land. Just as the land was barren and unfruitful, so were the lives of the people because they had rejected the water of life. God was showing them that what was happening to the physical earth was also happening in a spiritual sense to their hearts.

Jeremiah goes to God to confess the sins of the people.

**O LORD, though our iniquities testify against us, do thou it for thy name's sake: for our backslidings are many; we have sinned against thee [Jer. 14:7].**

Notice that Jeremiah takes his place with his people as being one of the sinners. There is no boasting here. He does not show any signs of a critical attitude toward the people. He says, "*We* have backslidden, and *we* have sinned." It is so easy for God's people to be critical of others. They pray almost like the Pharisee whom our Lord Jesus told us about in Luke 18:11–12. "I thank You, Lord, that I am so good. I am a separated Christian and I do this and I don't do that. I am a nice, sweet Sunday school Christian. Now Mr. So-and-So over there is a dirty old man, and Mrs. So-and-So never does anything for You, and Miss So-and-So is a real gossip." That is not identifying oneself with the people of God! You will notice that Jeremiah didn't pray that kind of a prayer. He identified himself with God's sinning people and said, "We have backslidden, and we have sinned." My friend, if you can take your place before God, confessing your own sins as well as the sins of your people, then you can speak to them about the judgment of God. But until you can do that, you shouldn't try to speak on God's behalf.

As we move on through this chapter, we see that the darkness has gathered, and the people are stumbling on the dark mountains.

**Then said I, Ah, Lord GOD! behold, the prophets say unto them, Ye shall not see the sword, neither shall ye have famine; but I will give you assured peace in this place [Jer. 14:13].**

The false prophets were predicting peace and prosperity—everything was going to be wonderful.

**Then the LORD said unto me, The prophets prophesy lies in my name: I sent them not, neither have I commanded them, neither spake unto them: they prophesy unto you a false vision and divination, and a thing of nought, and the deceit of their heart [Jer. 14:14].**

You see, Jeremiah is very much alone now that King Josiah is dead. And he is wondering—*Am I giving the correct message, or are the other prophets right?* He is not quite sure; so he goes to God about it. God reassures him, "I want you to know that the false prophets are lying. I didn't send them. You are the one giving My message." You can see that this will put Jeremiah right back on the firing line.

**Therefore thou shalt say this word unto them; Let mine eyes run down with tears night and day, and let them not cease: for the virgin daughter of my people is broken with a great breach, with a very grievous blow [Jer. 14:17].**

The message was breaking the heart of Jeremiah. He was weeping as he gave the message to his people. God wanted the people to know that *His* heart was breaking. Jeremiah was not only giving the message from God, but he was expressing the feelings of God as well.

We all need to realize that we are witnesses for God. If you are a child of God, you are a witness for God, and you are saying something by your life. We need to be very careful when we speak the Word of God that our lives conform to it. We are not to be giving out the Word in a coldhearted manner. There must be feeling in it. If there is not, then there is something radically wrong with us.

## INEVITABLE JUDGMENT

In chapter 15 we see that Jeremiah is a brokenhearted man who wants to go to God to pray for his people. That was very right and fine. However, God has something interesting to say to him:

**Then said the LORD unto me, Though Moses and Samuel stood before me, yet my mind could not be toward this people: cast them out of my sight, and let them go forth [Jer. 15:1].**

The people have gone too far, and judgment must come upon them. They have gone over the borderline where there is absolutely no possibility for reprieve. They will not escape captivity. The Lord tells Jeremiah that he shouldn't think that God is not hearing his prayers. There was nothing wrong in Jeremiah's prayers. God says that even if *Moses* stood before Him, He would not listen. You will remember in Exodus 32 that Moses was a marvelous intercessor for the people. When God threatened to destroy the people, Moses had stood before Him as their intercessor.

God answered his prayer and spared the people. But now, even if Moses were acting as the intercessor for the people, it wouldn't do any good. Samuel was another who had prayed for the people. Judgment had been averted again and again because of Samuel. But God says that even if *Samuel* were to pray now, there could be no averting of the judgment. The people had stepped across the borderline, and judgment was inevitable.

Now we can understand why Jeremiah is giving a message of nothing but judgment.

**For who shall have pity upon thee, O Jerusalem? or who shall bemoan thee? or who shall go aside to ask how thou doest?**

**Thou hast forsaken me, saith the LORD, thou art gone backward: therefore will I stretch out my hand against thee, and destroy thee; I am weary with repenting [Jer. 15:5–6].**

"Thou art gone backward"—that's backsliding.

"I am weary with repenting." They have come to Him over and over with their weeping and their promises to do better, but they continually go right back into the same old sin. God is tired of it all, and He says the time has now come when He intends to judge them.

## JEREMIAH'S PERSONAL DISTRESS

You can see that this message would not increase the popularity of poor Jeremiah. King Josiah was his friend, but not King Jehoiakim. Jehoiakim was an evil man. Jeremiah was the fly in the ointment for Jehoiakim. He considered Jeremiah nothing but a troublemaker.

In spite of the fact that Jeremiah is a weeping prophet who must deliver this very difficult message, he really had a sense of humor. He went to the Lord and cried out:

**Woe is me, my mother, that thou hast borne me a man of strife and a man of contention to the whole earth! I have neither lent on usury, nor men have lent to me on usury; yet every one of them doth curse me [Jer. 15:10].**

Jeremiah says, "Nobody likes me, I don't lend money on interest and I don't borrow money on interest, yet everyone curses me." We still have an adage today that says if we want to lose a friend, lend him money.

I have seen what the lending of money can do to Christian friends. I remember a man

who lent money to his friend who had some project in mind and thought he could double the money in a hurry. Actually, he lost all the money and couldn't pay back his friend. That broke up a good friendship and wrecked their relationship. So if you want to start losing your friends, lend them money! Jeremiah says, "You'd think I had been lending money around here—nobody wants to have anything to do with me."

During this difficult time, Jeremiah turns to the Word of God—remember that the law of the Lord had been found in the Temple and was available to him.

**Thy words were found, and I did eat them; and thy word was unto me the joy and rejoicing of mine heart: for I am called by thy name, O LORD God of hosts [Jer. 15:16].**

He found his consolation in it. He ate it and he digested it and it became a part of him. Oh, how we need to get into the Word of God today. We don't need just a little surface learning of a few rules, or just a little guideline of a few steps to take. We need to digest it so that it becomes part of our being. It will bring joy and rejoicing to the heart just as it did for Jeremiah. Only the Word of God can do this.

I received a letter from a man who heard our broadcast when I was in Galatians. He heard one word: *Father.* That arrested his attention. May I say to you that God is still using His Word today. Oh, how important the Word of God is!

Jeremiah is in real difficulty. Remember that his hometown rejected him and got rid of him. His own family rejected him. His life is actually in danger.

**And I will make thee unto this people a fenced brasen wall: and they shall fight against thee, but they shall not prevail against thee: for I am with thee to save thee and to deliver thee, saith the LORD.**

**And I will deliver thee out of the hand of the wicked, and I will redeem thee out of the hand of the terrible [Jer. 15:20–21].**

God says, "You just stay on the firing line, and I will take care of you."

# CHAPTERS 16–17

***THEME:** God forbids Jeremiah to marry*

The days are becoming increasingly difficult. The nation of Judah is coming to the end of its rope. As nearly as I can judge, it is within ten years of the destruction of Jerusalem at this particular time.

**The word of the LORD came also unto me, saying,**

**Thou shalt not take thee a wife, neither shalt thou have sons or daughters in this place.**

**For thus saith the LORD concerning the sons and concerning the daughters that are born in this place, and concerning their mothers that bare them, and concerning their fathers that begat them in this land;**

**They shall die of grievous deaths; they shall not be lamented; neither shall they be buried; but they shall be as dung upon the face of the earth: and they shall be consumed by the sword, and by famine; and their carcases shall be meat for the fowls of heaven, and for the beasts of the earth [Jer. 16:1–4].**

God reveals to Jeremiah the horror that is to come. He tells Jeremiah not to get married, and I think the reason is quite obvious. If you will turn to Psalm 137, which was written after the Babylonian captivity, you will see the fate children suffered. In the last two verses it says that Babylon will be destroyed and they will do to her just *as she had done to Judah*: "O daughter of Babylon, who art to be destroyed; happy shall he be, that rewardeth thee as thou hast served us. Happy shall he be, that taketh and dasheth thy little ones against the stones" (Ps. 137:8–9). When Nebuchadnezzar took the city of Jerusalem, the conquerors seized little children and dashed their heads against the stones! God

asked Jeremiah not to get married because He wanted to spare Jeremiah this anguish.

Under certain circumstances it is best not to bring children into this world. I sometimes wonder about the times in which we live. My heart goes out to the little ones today. I look at my own grandchildren and, actually, tears come into my eyes. They may live out their lives through some terrible times, so I pray for them and ask the Lord to protect them. A great deal could be said about this. There is a time when it would be better not to have children.

Here is a bright note—

**Therefore, behold, the days come, saith the LORD, that it shall no more be said, The LORD liveth, that brought up the children of Israel out of the land of Egypt;**

**But, the LORD liveth, that brought up the children of Israel from the land of the north, and from all the lands whither he had driven them: and I will bring them again into their land that I gave unto their fathers [Jer. 16:14–15].**

In this dark moment in Judah's history, God let Jeremiah see a brilliant future. It is as if he looks down the dark tunnel of the future and sees the light at the other end. It is interesting that this theme recurs throughout the writings of the prophets. It never got so dark but what the prophets didn't see the light that was coming, and the darker the night was, the brighter the light appeared to be. God says the day is coming when He will bring them back from captivity, back home to their own land.

**Therefore, behold, I will this once cause them to know, I will cause them to know mine hand and my might; and they shall know that my name is The LORD [Jer. 16:21].**

It is my personal opinion that God is going to have to teach my country that He is the Lord. I get the impression that America doesn't know God is out there. When He does make Himself known, I am afraid it will be very impressive.

## MESSAGE OF THE UNMARRIED PROPHET

**The sin of Judah is written with a pen of iron, and with the point of a diamond: it is graven upon the table of their heart, and upon the horns of your altars;**

**Whilst their children remember their altars and their groves by the green trees upon the high hills [Jer. 17:1–2].**

There was evil in everything they did. It even permeated their religion.

**Thus saith the LORD; Cursed be the man that trusteth in man, and maketh flesh his arm, and whose heart departeth from the LORD [Jer. 17:5].**

It might be well for us to put that up as a motto today. Sometimes we think we can depend on certain men or on certain political parties to work out the problems of the world. You and I are cursed people if we put our trust in men and what men can do. This is the day to trust *God*.

**Blessed is the man that trusteth in the LORD, and whose hope the LORD is [Jer. 17:7].**

We shall be blessed if we trust Him.

**For he shall be as a tree planted by the waters, and that spreadeth out her roots by the river, and shall not see when heat cometh, but her leaf shall be green; and shall not be careful in the year of drought, neither shall cease from yielding fruit [Jer. 17:8].**

This is the same thought that we find in the first psalm: Blessed is the man whose ". . . delight is in the law of the LORD; and in his law doth he meditate day and night. And he shall be like a tree planted by the rivers of water, that bringeth forth his fruit in his season; his leaf also shall not wither; and whatsoever he doeth shall prosper" (Ps. 1:2–3).

**The heart is deceitful above all things, and desperately wicked: who can know it? [Jer. 17:9].**

This is true of your heart and my heart. Unfortunately, we all have heart trouble.

**I the LORD search the heart, I try the reins, even to give every man according to his ways, and according to the fruit of his doings [Jer. 17:10].**

Only God can make a heart transplant. Man is now doing that sort of thing in the physical sense, but God has been doing it in the spiritual sense for a long time. When we come to Him, He gives us new life—we are born anew and given a new nature. Sometimes we who

are ministers use the expression, "Give your heart to the Lord." Well, what would God want with that old, dirty, filthy heart of yours or mine? He doesn't want it. The heart is deceitful. He wants to give you a new heart. He is a heart specialist; He is the Great Physician.

Now we will conclude this chapter with a great verse:

**A glorious high throne from the beginning is the place of our sanctuary [Jer. 17:12].**

This is the hope of man. All men have hearts which are deceitful, dirty, filthy, and wicked. But there is a sanctuary. "A glorious high throne from the beginning is the place of our sanctuary." A sanctuary is not only a place of worship; it is a place of safety, a place of peace. God gave to His people certain cities which were to be cities of refuge, sanctuaries where they would be protected.

My friend, these are difficult days. It is dangerous to walk the streets of our cities. Even in our homes we are not safe from a bomb that may come from the other side of the world. Where can we go to be safe? There is a sanctuary, and it is the high throne of our God. That is the place where you and I can go. And He *asks* us to come. "Having therefore, brethren, boldness to enter into the holiest by the blood of Jesus, By a new and living way, which he hath consecrated for us, through the veil, that is to say, his flesh; And having an high priest over the house of God; Let us draw near with a true heart in full assurance of faith . . ." (Heb. 10:19–22).

# CHAPTERS 18–19

## *THEME:* Sign at potter's house

Now we go with Jeremiah down to the potter's house. For folk who are sophisticated and hardened in sin it is difficult to get them to listen to the *Word* of God; so God has a sign for the nation of Judah, and He has an object lesson for you and me.

**The word which came to Jeremiah from the Lord, saying,**

**Arise, and go down to the potter's house, and there I will cause thee to hear my words.**

**Then I went down to the potter's house, and, behold, he wrought a work on the wheels.**

**And the vessel that he made of clay was marred in the hand of the potter: so he made it again another vessel, as seemed good to the potter to make it.**

**Then the word of the Lord came to me, saying,**

**O house of Israel, cannot I do with you as this potter? saith the Lord. Behold, as the clay is in the potter's hand, so are ye in mine hand, O house of Israel [Jer. 18:1–6].**

One Sunday evening a potter, who also was one of our radio listeners, came to put on a demonstration for the congregation at an evening service. He brought in a potter's wheel which was operated by a foot pedal, and on that wheel he put clay. While I was giving the message, he molded the clay into a vessel. It was a very simple experiment, but I never repeated it—the congregation that evening was so intent on watching the potter that I don't think anyone heard my message!

Many years before this, when I was a seminary student, traveling from my home in Tennessee to the seminary at Dallas, Texas, I had to cross the state of Arkansas, and always passed by a large pottery plant near Arkadelphia. One day we took time out (several other fellows were traveling with me) to stop and see the pottery being made.

There were two very impressive and striking sights there that I have not forgotten. Behind this plant was as ugly a patch of mud as I've ever seen. It was shapeless and gooey. It looked hopeless to me. Out in front of the plant they had a display room, and in that room were some of the most exquisite vessels I have ever seen.

Then we went inside the plant, and there we saw many potters at work. There they

stood, bent over many wheels which were power-driven. They didn't even have to use foot pedals; so they could give their full attention to working with that helpless, hopeless, ugly, mushy, messy clay. They were intent on transforming it and translating it into objects of art. The difference between that mass of mud out back and those lovely vessels in the display room were these men, the potters, working over their wheels.

Now it was to such a place that God sent this man Jeremiah. He sent him down to see a sermon. Actually it is a very simple sermon. It is easy to make identification in this very wonderful living parable that Jeremiah gives us. We have no difficulty in identifying the potter, and we have no difficulty in identifying the clay. In fact, God does it for us. God is the Potter, and Israel is the clay in particular here. Also it is very easy to make application to mankind in general and to each individual personally. Each individual is the clay. If I may be personal, *you* are clay on the Potter's wheel. Regardless of what else may be said about you, you are clay today on the Potter's wheel—as is every man who has ever lived on this earth.

The figure of the potter and clay is carried over in the New Testament. We find Paul in his epistle to the Romans using the same simile: "Hath not the potter power over the clay, of the same lump to make one vessel unto honour, and another unto dishonour?" (Rom. 9:21). Then Paul used the other side of this very wonderful figure of speech when he wrote to Timothy: "If a man therefore purge himself from these, he shall be a vessel unto honour, sanctified, and meet for the master's use, and prepared unto every good work" (2 Tim. 2:21). So we see that this figure is carried all the way through the Word of God.

Now notice what the potter did. He was fashioning a vessel, and it became marred in his hands. It wouldn't yield. The clay has to be just the right texture. Maybe it was too hard or too soft. So he pitched it aside. Then later he picked it up and made it into another kind of vessel.

There are two things we want to see in this section: the power of the potter and the personality of the clay.

## POWER OF THE POTTER

Like a giant Potter, God took clay and formed man, the physical part of man. "And the LORD God formed man of the dust of the ground, and breathed into his nostrils the breath of life; and man became a living soul" (Gen. 2:7). God was the Potter.

Now let's go down to the potter's house and stand with Jeremiah as we watch the potter at work. The potter has a wheel, an old-fashioned one. He works the pedal with his foot to make the wheel turn. As he pedals, his hands are deftly, artistically working with the clay, and attempting to form out of it a work of art.

Note, now, the first principle: God is sovereign.

The potter is absolute. That is, he has power over the clay and that power is unlimited. No clay can stop the potter, nor can it question his right. No clay can resist his will, nor "say him nay," nor alter his plans. The clay cannot speak back to him. You remember in the delightful little story we heard in the nursery about the gingerbread boy that talked back. But the clay can't talk back.

I recall a very whimsical story of a little boy who was playing in the mud down by a brook. He was attempting to make a man. He worked on him and had gotten pretty well along when his mother called him. They were going downtown and he must come along. He wanted to stay, but she insisted that he come. By this time he had finished his mud man except for one arm. But he had to leave. While he was in town with his mother and father, he saw a one-armed man. He eyed him for awhile. Finally he went up to him and said, "Why did you leave before I finished you?"

The clay on the potter's wheel can't get up when it wants to. The clay on the potter's wheel can't talk back. The clay on the potter's wheel is not able to do anything. It can only yield to the potter's hand.

Nowhere, I repeat, *nowhere* will you find such a graphic picture of the sovereignty of God than in this. Man, the clay upon the potter's wheel, and God, the Potter. You won't find anything quite like this.

And our contemporary generation resists it because this is the day of the rights of man. We are hearing a great deal today about freedom, and every group is insisting upon its freedom—freedom to protest, freedom to do what it chooses. We seem to have forgotten about the rights of God. Today men will permit a racketeering gangster to plead the fifth amendment because we must protect his rights. God has incontestable authority. His will is inexorable, it is inflexible, and it will prevail. He has irresistible ability to form and fashion this universe to suit Himself. He can form this little earth on which we live to suit

Himself. And, my friend, you, an individual, and I, an individual, can be nothing but clay in His hands. He has power to carry through His will and He answers to no one. He has no board of directors. He has no voters to whom He must respond. He has absolute authority. He is *God*. You and I live in a universe that is running to please God. And the rebellion of little man down here on this speck of dust that we live on is a "tempest in a teapot!" Our little earth, as we see in the pictures taken from the moon, is just a speck in the infinity of space. And, my friend, God rides triumphantly in His own chariot.

You will find that the Word of God has some very definite things to say concerning Him: "Thou wilt say then unto me, Why doth he yet find fault? For who hath resisted his will? Nay but, O man, who are thou that repliest against God? Shall the thing formed say to him that formed it, Why hast thou made me thus? Hath not the potter power over the clay, of the same lump to make one vessel unto honour, and another unto dishonour?" (Rom. 9:19–21).

It was Bengel who wrote this: "The Jews thought that in no case could they be abandoned by God, and in no case could the Gentiles be received by God." And Dr. Lange, the great German expositor, said: "When man goes the length of making to himself a god whom he affects to bind by his own rights, God then puts on His majesty, and appears in all His reality as a free God, before whom man is a mere nothing, like the clay in the hand of the potter. Such was Paul's attitude when acting as God's advocate, in his suit with Jewish Pharisaism."

God is absolute!

## PERSONALITY OF THE CLAY

Now for a moment let's look at the personality of the clay. I realize someone will be saying, "Believe me, you have a mixed metaphor here! You mean to tell me that *clay* has personality?" Clay is formless, it's shapeless, it's lifeless, it's inept, it's inert, it's incapable, it's a muddy mess. The psalmist wrote, ". . . he remembereth that we are dust" (Ps. 103:14). Dr. George Gill used to say in class, "God remembers that we are dust, but man sometimes forgets it, and he gets stuck on himself. And when dust gets stuck on itself, it's mud." We do sometimes forget this, but God remembers we are dust. I look at the clay on that wheel down at the potter's house. That clay has no wish; it has no rights; it has

no inherent ability. It is helpless, and it is hopeless.

The Scriptures confirm this. Listen to Paul in Ephesians 2:1. Although he is writing to the Ephesians, it can apply to you and me as well: ". . . you . . . who were *dead* in trespasses and sins" (italics mine). That's man. Then he amplifies this later on in the same chapter: ". . . having no hope, and without God in the world" (Eph. 2:12). That clay on the potter's wheel is no different. Then Paul said to the Romans, "For when we were yet without strength, in due time Christ died for the ungodly" (Rom. 5:6).

You and I need to recognize that our God is a sovereign God and that we are the clay. We were dead in trespasses and sin, without strength. God is the Potter with the power. "So then it is not of him that willeth, nor of him that runneth, but of God that sheweth mercy" (Rom. 9:16). God is the One who is in charge. None of us has any claim on God. "For he saith to Moses, I will have mercy on whom I will have mercy, and I will have compassion on whom I will have compassion" (Rom. 9:15).

When Moses pleaded with God, God said to him, "Moses, I'm going to hear you, but I'm not going to hear you because you are Moses; I am going to hear you because I extend mercy." That is the reason God heard him. God is not obligated to save any man. God is free to act as He wishes. He is righteous, and He is holy. This is a lost world, and it could remain like that, and no one would have the right to raise a question.

Now look at the other side of the coin. Let's talk now about the power of the clay and the personality of the potter. This is the other side. "And the vessel that he made of clay was marred in the hand of the potter: so he made it again another vessel, as seemed good to the potter to make it." There is not only a principle here which is that God is sovereign, but also there is a purpose here.

## POWER OF THE CLAY

Look now at the power of the clay. That clay on the potter's wheel is like Browning's "dance of plastic circumstance." This wheel is the wheel of circumstance. That's what it is!

I do not believe that life's big decisions are made in a church sanctuary. I believe they are made out in the work-a-day world—in the office, in the school, in the workshop, at the crossroads of life—there is where the Potter is working with the clay. There is the place He is working with you, my friend.

You and I live in a world that seems to have no purpose or meaning at all. Multitudes of people see no purpose in life whatever and find confusion on every hand. Someone has expressed it in a little jingle:

In a day of illusions
And utter confusions,
Upon our delusions
We base our conclusions

—Author unknown

How true that is of life today!

Look away, for a moment, from the potter's wheel. Behind him we see shelf upon shelf of works of art. Those objects of beauty were one time on the potter's wheel as clay—clay that yielded to the potter's hand. Once they all were a shapeless mass of mud. What happened? That lifeless clay was under the hand of the potter, and as the wheel of circumstance turned, he molded and made them into the vessels that now stand on display.

I outlined the Book of Jeremiah for our Thru the Bible Radio program while my wife and I were down at Fort Myers in Florida. We had an apartment there for a few days. Every morning we would eat breakfast in the apartment, and I would work for a few hours on Jeremiah; then we would go over to one of the islands to hunt for shells. I discovered something. There are literally thousands of varieties of shells. I didn't dream there were so many. Anything God does He does in profusion. My wife bought a book on shells, and we identified many of them.

In my hand I am holding a little shell that I picked up on Sanibel Island. It is a beautiful little shell. I had been working on the eighteenth chapter of Jeremiah that morning, and when I found this, it occurred to me that the Lord was trying to say something to us. God started with just some little animal, a tiny mollusk, and around it He formed this shell. I thought, *Well, since the great Architect has spent all that time with a little shell in the bottom of the ocean, what about man today?*

Look again at those works of art which the potter has lining the shelves behind him. Don't speak disparagingly of the clay! I'm sorry for what I said about it. It has marvelous capacity and resilience. This, my friend, and I am saying it reverently, this is what the Potter wants—*clay*. He doesn't want steel. He doesn't want oil. He doesn't want rock. He wants clay. He wants something that He can put in His hand to mold and fashion. This is the stuff He is after—clay. God wants to work with human beings.

Someone may say, "Yes, but here is where the analogy breaks down. The distance between God and man is greater than between the potter and the clay." I disagree with that. Actually God is nearer man than the potter is to the clay.

This is what I mean: the clay on the wheel down at the potter's house to which Jeremiah takes us has no will. I *do!* That clay cannot cooperate with the potter. I *can!* I quoted the Genesis account of the creation of man for a purpose—God created man in His own likeness. He took man physically out of the dust of the ground; He made man. Then He breathed into his breathing-places the spirit of life, and man became a living soul. Man today has a free will, and he can exercise it. That clay has no will. But you and I do have a will; we can cooperate with the Potter.

Now I want to ask the Potter a question. What's Your purpose in putting me on the potter's wheel? Why do You bear down on me? Why do You keep working with me? Why, Potter, do You do this? I'm not being irreverent, but I am like the little gingerbread boy, I talk back. Why, O Potter, do you do this? What are You after?

Well, I go back to the potter's house. Follow me now very carefully. I do not discover the purpose, but I learn something more important than the purpose for my life. I learn that the *potter* has a purpose, which is more important to know. I watch the potter there. He is serious. He means business. He's not playing with the clay. This is his work. He is giving his time, his talents, his ability to working with the clay.

Notice again in verses 3–4: "Then I went down to the potter's house, and, behold, he wrought a work on the wheels. And the vessel that he made of clay was marred in the hand of the potter: so he made it again another vessel, as seemed good to the potter to make it." My friend, this is not a cat-and-mouse operation. This is not the potter's avocation. It is his vocation. This is not his hobby. This is not something with which he is amusing himself. He knows what he is doing. This tells me that God is not playing with me today. He is not experimenting with us. He has purpose. And, friend, that comforts me. This is the second great principle we see here: the Potter has a purpose.

As a sightseer, I stand with Jeremiah, and I say, "What's he going to make?" Jeremiah says, "I don't know. Let's watch him." The sightseer cannot tell as he watches, but the potter knows. He has a plan. He knows what

he is doing. The clay does not know his purpose.

But, friend, someday we will know. When He puts us on the plastic wheel of circumstance, He means to accomplish something. He has a purpose. The psalmist says, ". . . I shall be satisfied, when I awake, with thy likeness" (Ps. 17:15). Someday *I'll* be like Him! ". . . it doth not yet appear what we shall be: but we know that, when he shall appear, we shall be like him; for we shall see him as he is" (1 John 3:2). That's going to be a fair morning. That's going to be a new day. And God will be vindicated—He was not being cruel when He caused us to suffer. Some day, some glorious someday, we'll see that the Potter had a purpose in your life and in mine. Notice how Paul writes to the Ephesians. He began the second chapter with the doleful words which I have already quoted: "And you hath he quickened [made alive], who were dead in trespasses and sins" (Eph. 2:1). And if that is all, then I'm through too. But, my friend, there is more: "That in the ages to come he might shew the exceeding riches of his grace in his kindness toward us through Christ Jesus" (Eph. 2:7). In the ages to come we'll be a demonstration, and we'll be yonder on display. We will reveal what the Potter can do with lifeless clay. He gets the glory. It will be wonderful to be a vessel in the Master's hand.

## PERSONALITY OF THE POTTER

In conclusion let us consider the personality of the potter. This is the most important and wonderful thing of all. To do this we must take one final look in the potter's house.

I say to Jeremiah, "The potter is a kindly looking man." Jeremiah answers, "He is. He doesn't want to hurt the clay. He wants the clay to yield because he wants to make something out of it." I gaze into the face of the potter. Oh, how intent he is. How interested he is in the clay.

Oh, what a Potter God is! If I could only see my Potter! But Scripture says I cannot see God. Philip asked the question, which I certainly would have asked, when he said to Jesus, ". . . Lord shew us the Father, and it sufficeth us" (John 14:8). The Lord Jesus said to him, ". . . he that hath seen me hath seen the Father . . ." (John 14:9).

My friend, let us look at the Potter very carefully now. See the Potter's feet as He is working them on the pedals, turning, turning that wheel of circumstance. See the hands of the Potter as He deftly, artistically, oh, so intently and delicately, kindly and lovingly works with the clay. I look at Him. Those feet have spike wounds in them. And there are nail prints in those hands.

That's not all.

I turn over to Matthew's gospel and read: "Then Judas, which had betrayed him, when he saw that he was condemned, repented himself, and brought again the thirty pieces of silver to the chief priests and elders, Saying, I have sinned in that I have betrayed the innocent blood. And they said, What is that to us? see thou to that. And he cast down the pieces of silver in the temple, and departed, and went and hanged himself. And the chief priests took the silver pieces, and said, It is not lawful for to put them into the treasury, because it is the price of blood. And they took counsel, and bought with them the potter's field, to bury strangers in. Wherefore that field was called, The field of blood, unto this day. Then was fulfilled that which was spoken by Jeremy the prophet, saying, And they took the thirty pieces of silver, the price of him that was valued, whom they of the children of Israel did value; And gave them for the potter's field, as the Lord appointed me" (Matt. 27:3–10).

Two verses startle me: "And they took counsel, and bought with them the potter's field, to bury strangers in. Wherefore that field was called, The field of blood, unto this day." They probably did not know what they were doing when they called it the field of blood, but I hope you don't miss it. This Potter is more wonderful than any other potter. He shed His blood that He might go into that field and take those broken pieces and put them again on His potter's wheel to make them again another vessel.

Just this past week I talked with a woman who has a broken home and a broken life. Is God through with her? Is He through with us when we make a failure of our lives? Oh, no. He's not through with us—that is, if the clay will yield to Him. All that is necessary is the clay yielding to the Potter. He paid the price for the field, it's a field of blood. You may look back on your life and say, "Oh, what failure! I don't think God could use me." My friend, He is working with those broken pieces today, and He'll work with you if you'll let Him. He has already paid the price for your redemption. You can't make anything out of yourself for Him, and I can't either, but He can take us and put us on the wheel of circumstance and shape us into a vessel of honor.

We are the clay; He is the Potter.

## THE SIGN OF THE BROKEN VESSEL

In the first verse of chapter 19 God sends Jeremiah to get a potter's earthen bottle and tells him to take elders of the people and of the priests with him as witnesses.

**And go forth unto the valley of the son of Hinnom, which is by the entry of the east gate, and proclaim there the words that I shall tell thee [Jer. 19:2].**

"The valley of the son of Hinnom" was at this time the place where the horrible worship of Moloch was conducted. God spells it out for them—

**Because they have forsaken me, and have estranged this place, and have burned incense in it unto other gods, whom neither they nor their fathers have known, nor the kings of Judah, and have filled this place with the blood of innocents;**

**They have built also the high places of Baal, to burn their sons with fire for burnt offerings unto Baal, which I commanded not, nor spake it, neither came it into my mind [Jer. 19:4–5].**

Because of these things, God says that the valley of the son of Hinnom would soon be known as the valley of slaughter, because as they had killed their children as offerings to Baal and Moloch, God would allow their enemies to kill them there (see vv. 6–9).

After pronouncing this frightful judgment upon the people of Jerusalem, God directed Jeremiah to break the clay bottle in the sight of the witnesses—

**And shalt say unto them, Thus saith the LORD of hosts; Even so will I break this people and this city, as one breaketh a potter's vessel, that cannot be made whole again: and they shall bury them in Tophet, till there be no place to bury [Jer. 19:11].**

Returning from Tophet, or the valley of Hinnom, Jeremiah went to the court of the Lord's house and gave this final word:

**Thus saith the LORD of hosts, the God of Israel; Behold, I will bring upon this city and upon all her towns all the evil that I have pronounced against it, because they have hardened their necks, that they might not hear my words [Jer. 19:15].**

He had warned, pleaded, and entreated, but their hearts were unrelenting. The clay had resisted the hand of the Potter too long. Very soon the enemy would come and shatter the nation in pieces.

# CHAPTERS 20–22

*THEME: Jeremiah's persecution and prophecies during Zedekiah's reign*

When Jeremiah went down to Tophet and broke the bottle as the Lord had told him to do, the message he gave to the people of Judah was that they were going into captivity. Josiah, the great and good king, is dead, and he has been followed by Jehoahaz and Jehoiakim. Zedekiah, the last king of Judah, is now on the throne. He is the worst and the weakest of all the kings who ever ruled Judah. It is during his reign that the Babylonian captivity prophesied by Jeremiah will take place.

We will now see a change take place in the life and ministry of Jeremiah. When he gives out the Word of God, he's adamant, he's strong, and he's hard-nosed, but personally, as a man, he has a very tender heart. When his beloved friend Josiah died, Chronicles records that Jeremiah wept for him. The three evil kings who followed Josiah reject the ministry of Jeremiah in a very definite way. He is given a cold shoulder, and his message is absolutely ignored, but he has not been persecuted personally. As we come to chapter 20, we will find Jeremiah being personally and physically persecuted for the first time.

**Now Pashur the son of Immer the priest, who was also chief governor in the house of the LORD, heard that Jeremiah prophesied these things.**

**Then Pashur smote Jeremiah the prophet, and put him in the stocks that were in the high gate of Benjamin,**

which was by the house of the LORD [Jer. 20:1–2].

Notice with whom the persecution originates: it began in organized religion. Today the Word of God is being hurt and hindered the most by the organized, liberal church which has rejected the Word of God. They will align themselves with some very shady characters boasting of their brotherhood, their love for everyone, and their broad-mindedness. But when it comes to accepting a fundamentalist, someone who stands for the Word of God, I have found that their broad-mindedness and love disappears. There is more opposition to the furtherance of the gospel originating in the organized church than there is in the liquor industry or in any political group that I know of today. This physical persecution of Jeremiah began in the organized religion of his day.

**And it came to pass on the morrow, that Pashur brought forth Jeremiah out of the stocks. Then said Jeremiah unto him, The LORD hath not called thy name Pashur, but Magor-missabib [Jer. 20:3].**

"Magor-missabib"—that's quite a name, and it means "terror on every side." Jeremiah is telling Pashur that there is terror in store for him and for everyone connected with him.

**For thus saith the LORD, Behold, I will make thee a terror to thyself, and to all thy friends: and they shall fall by the sword of their enemies, and thine eyes shall behold it: and I will give all Judah into the hand of the king of Babylon, and he shall carry them captive into Babylon, and shall slay them with the sword [Jer. 20:4].**

This is now the prophecy that Jeremiah will emphasize again and again: the southern kingdom is going into captivity, and nothing can stop it. God has said that it would not help if even Moses or Samuel were alive. It is too late. The people have gone too far in their rejection of God as has been revealed by the actions of the present king and the two who have been on the throne ahead of him.

We need to consider what has happened to Jeremiah. He has been ignored and rejected, but up to this point he has not been persecuted physically. But now he is, and because of all this—remember that his message is breaking his own heart—he decides he will turn in his resignation to God. Your heart

cannot help but go out to this man. He is not indifferent to what is happening. He feels all this very deeply, and it is sapping his strength. I think he may even have been on the verge of a nervous breakdown.

**Then I said, I will not make mention of him, nor speak any more in his name. But his word was in mine heart as a burning fire shut up in my bones, and I was weary with forbearing, and I could not stay [Jer. 20:9].**

What Jeremiah is saying is this: "The message is breaking my heart, and all it has earned for me is the persecution of the religious rulers and the rejection of the people; therefore I'm resigning." But when he attempted to resign he found that the Word of God was in his bones like a fire. He says, "I had to speak out. I couldn't forbear."

Such urgency to speak should be the mark of any man who is giving out the Word of God. How do *you* really feel about it? Is your ministry just a job you have, or is your heart really in it? If you love the Word of God and you really want to give it out, then you would feel pretty bad if you didn't have that privilege and opportunity. Unless it really means something to you, I don't believe you should be attempting to give out the Word of God.

You can understand the conflict that is going on in the heart of Jeremiah, and he indulges in something that seems to have been a habit with God's men in the Old Testament. He does something that Jonah did, that Job did, and Elijah did. He begins to sing an old song that won't do him any good. It's the blues, the religious blues: "Why was I born?" A lot of folk sing that song. Listen to Jeremiah:

**Cursed be the day wherein I was born: let not the day wherein my mother bare me be the blessed.**

**Cursed be the man who brought tidings to my father, saying, A man child is born unto thee; making him very glad [Jer. 20:14–15].**

Oh boy, does Jeremiah hate himself and wish he had never been born!

**Wherefore came I forth out of the womb to see labour and sorrow, that my days should be consumed with shame? [Jer. 20:18].**

Behold, it's the old story: Why was I born? Elijah crawled up under a juniper tree and

said, "Let me die!" (see 1 Kings 19:4). Job wanted to die and cursed the day he was born. Old Jonah got pretty downhearted about everything, and he also wanted to die. Well, to wish that you had not been born is about as foolish as anything you could wish. My friend, you have already been born, and there is nothing you can do about it. You can sing the blues that you want to die, but you will never die by wishing it—no one ever has. Jeremiah is way down, is he not? You wish that you could put your arm around him, pat him on the back, and encourage him somehow. He is so discouraged; yet he wants to give out the Word of God.

Chapters 21 through 29 contain the prophecies delivered during the reign of Zedekiah, the last king of Judah. This will bring us right down to the time of the destruction of Jerusalem and the captivity. There is not a harsher message than the one Jeremiah gives here in chapters 21 and 22.

## ANSWER TO ZEDEKIAH REGARDING NEBUCHADNEZZAR

**The word which came unto Jeremiah from the LORD, when king Zedekiah sent unto him Pashur the son of Melchiah, and Zephaniah the son of Maaseiah the priest, saying.**

**Inquire, I pray thee, of the LORD for us; for Nebuchadrezzar king of Babylon maketh war against us; if so be that the LORD will deal with us according to all his wondrous works, that he may go up from us [Jer. 21:1–2].**

It is interesting that when Zedekiah got into real trouble he went to the man he knew was giving the Word of God. He went right past Pashur and his crowd—he didn't seek help from organized religion. I find that a great many people today belong to a liberal church, but they listen to a Bible broadcast on the radio. For some strange reason they feel they can reconcile those two things. My friend, when you are in trouble nothing is going to satisfy you but the Word of God.

Zedekiah comes to Jeremiah but he doesn't get any comfort from him at all. Jeremiah tells him that Nebuchadnezzar is coming and he will destroy the city unless there is a turning to God. Jeremiah really lays it on the line to him.

**And unto this people thou shalt say, Thus saith the LORD; Behold, I set be-**

fore you the way of life, and the way of death [Jer. 21:8].**

That is exactly what God says to you today about His salvation provided in the Lord Jesus Christ. God says that He gave His Son to die for you, to pay the penalty of your sin. He arose so that you might have righteousness. If you are to be saved, you must be *in* Him. You get into Him by the baptism of the Holy Spirit when you put your trust in Jesus Christ as your Savior. When you do that, you become a child of God. God says, "This is My way that I offer to you. You can take it or leave it. I set before you life and death." That is the way God has put it. God also pleads with tears in His eyes.

Now the choice before the people of Judah was to stay in the city and die or to surrender to the king of Babylon and live.

**He that abideth in this city shall die by the sword, and by the famine, and by the pestilence: but he that goeth out, and falleth to the Chaldeans that besiege you, he shall live, and his life shall be unto him for a prey.**

**For I have set my face against this city for evil, and not for good, saith the LORD: it shall be given into the hand of the king of Babylon, and he shall burn it with fire [Jer. 21:9–10].**

King Zedekiah didn't follow through. He was a weakling and the worst of the kings. He does not turn to God at all. He evidently thought something like this: *Well, look, God didn't let Nebuchadnezzar destroy this city when Jehoiachin was on the throne and he was about as bad as I am. Why should it happen now?*

## JUDGMENT OF JEHOIAKIM

Chapter 22, therefore, contains what I feel is the harshest judgment that is pronounced in the Word of God. It is harsher than the judgment pronounced by God upon Cain or by the Lord Jesus upon Judas. It is frightful, and at the same time one of the most remarkable prophecies in the Word of God.

Before we consider the judgment against Coniah, or Jehoiachin, there is first the judgment against his father, Jehoiakim. He was an evil ruler also, but during his reign there was prosperity. The rich were getting richer, and the poor were being ground underfoot. It is very interesting that the Word of God has so much to say about the poor. God pays so much

attention to them, both in the Old and New Testaments, that we cannot ignore it.

This begins God's message concerning Jehoiakim:

**Woe unto him that buildeth his house by unrighteousness, and his chambers by wrong; that useth his neighbour's service without wages, and giveth him not for his work [Jer. 22:13].**

Men were getting rich through wrong methods. The poor were being underpaid.

**That saith, I will build me a wide house and large chambers, and cutteth him out windows; and it is ceiled with cedar, and painted with vermilion.**

**Shalt thou reign, because thou closest thyself in cedar? did not thy father eat and drink, and do judgment and justice, and then it was well with him? [Jer. 22:14–15].**

"Thy father"—Jeremiah is referring back to Josiah, the good king, and this is what he says about him:

**He judged the cause of the poor and needy; then it was well with him: was not this to know me? saith the LORD.**

**But thine eyes and thine heart are not but for thy covetousness, and for to shed innocent blood, and for oppression, and for violence, to do it [Jer. 22:16–17].**

Josiah had "judged the cause of the poor and needy"; but in Jehoiakim's day the rich were getting richer by wrong methods, and the poor were getting poorer.

God has a great deal to say on this subject. Jeremiah called attention to the fact that the rich men were heaping up wealth by the labor of others and treading down the poor. In their pride and in their arrogance they built themselves palaces and lived as though God had forgotten their iniquitous means for the acquisition of their wealth. In the New Testament we read: "Go to now, ye rich men, weep and howl for your miseries that shall come upon you. Your riches are corrupted, and your garments are motheaten. Your gold and silver is cankered; and the rust of them shall be a witness against you . . ." (James 5:1–3). There are two things for which God condemns the rich: the way they get their money, and the way they spend their money or the way they use it.

Have you noticed that everything is slanted for the rich man? I find that I am paying more taxes than some men who are worth a million dollars. You would think I am a millionaire judging from the taxes I must pay! The tax laws are geared to protect the rich. The politicians gear everything in favor of the rich, those who have given to their political campaigns. That is what the rich people support. Most of them don't give to the work of the Lord; they don't give in order to get out the Word of God. God notices that. He notices when the rich get rich at the expense of the poor, and He notices when they spend their wealth on themselves, building palaces to live in.

Very frankly, it is sinful to live in a mansion when there are so many people in such poverty. I do not believe a Christian should do that. There are a lot of poor Christians who need help from the wealthier Christians. And I am not sure that Christian organizations should have plush and luxurious accommodations either.

May I say also that there is too much of a tendency for religion to cater to the rich. I often hear preachers boast that they have a millionaire or two in their congregation. I'd like to know what they are doing to get the Word of God out.

I played golf with a man who is reported to be worth twenty million dollars. I was told he might be interested in supporting our radio broadcast. After he asked me about it, I told him all about the broadcast and the needs of the program. He was interested, and he assured me he listens to the broadcast. Do you know how much support he has given the program? Not one dime. I give this isolated case as an example, but I would hate to be a Christian who left a million dollars when I died and have to face the Lord to account for what I had done with my money. I do not think this means we are not to enjoy what the Lord gives us—the comforts that He has made possible—but if He has given you wealth, He is going to hold you responsible for using it for His glory.

"He judged the cause of the poor and needy . . . was not this to know me? saith the LORD." God says, "Josiah knew Me, and he knew that he could not be My follower and not have a concern for the poor and needy." God says that *He* has a concern for these people.

Do you know who are the two groups of people that are the hardest to reach with the gospel? They are the very rich and the very poor. God wants to equalize that because He wants them to hear the gospel and be saved.

He wants the rich way up at the top to help those way down at the bottom. And He is concerned that both be reached with the Word of God.

The fundamental social problem in America today is not a racial or a class struggle. It is a question of the rich and the poor. Communism would never have risen in the world if it were not for the struggle between the filthy rich and the very poor. And it is this inequality that God says He judges.

## JUDGMENT OF CONIAH

Now we come to the very frightful and harsh judgment against the man Coniah.

**As I live, saith the Lord, though Coniah the son of Jehoiakim king of Judah were the signet upon my right hand, yet would I pluck thee thence;**

**And I will give thee into the hand of them that seek thy life, and into the hand of them whose face thou fearest, even into the hand of Nebuchadrezzar king of Babylon, and into the hand of the Chaldeans [Jer. 22:24–25].**

"Coniah" is Jehoiachin who was also called Jeconiah. Why does God call him Coniah? It is because the "Je" in Jeconiah stands for Jehovah. God is saying, "Don't identify Me with that man!" He goes on to say, "Why, if he were the ring on My finger, I would throw him away!"

**Is this man Coniah a despised broken idol? is he a vessel wherein is no pleasure? wherefore are they cast out, he and his seed, and are cast into a land which they know not?**

**O earth, earth, earth, hear the word of the Lord.**

**Thus saith the Lord, Write ye this man childless, a man that shall not prosper in his days: for no man of his seed shall prosper, sitting upon the throne of David, and ruling any more in Judah [Jer. 22:28–30].**

God cries to the whole earth to be His witness: No descendant of Coniah will sit on the throne of David or rule anymore in Judah. This is one reason that Joseph could not have been the father of Jesus. Joseph was in the line of Jeconiah, and God says no child of that line will sit on the throne of David.

Does that mean the throne of David would be vacant from then on? Listen to another prophecy: "For thus saith the Lord; David shall never want a man to sit upon the throne of the house of Israel" (Jer. 33:17). There *will* be Someone on the throne of David, but He will not be a descendant in the line of Jeconiah. In Jeremiah 36:30 we read: "Therefore thus saith the Lord of Jehoiakim king of Judah; He shall have none to sit upon the throne of David: and his dead body shall be cast out in the day to the heat, and in the night to the frost." I remind you that Jehoiakim was the father of Jeconiah. God cut off that line.

Now the remarkable thing is that there are two recorded genealogies of Jesus Christ, and there is a reason for that. The one recorded in Matthew chapter 1 leads to Joseph. It comes from David, through Solomon and *Jeconiah*, to Joseph. Joseph's line gave to Jesus the *legal* title to the throne. But Joseph was not the father of Jesus. Jesus is not a descendant of that line. The second genealogy is in Luke 3:23–38. This is the genealogy of Mary, and it does not come through Solomon but comes through another son of David, Nathan. There is no curse and no judgment on that line. The Lord Jesus Christ was virgin born, and He came through Mary's line. That is where He got the *blood* title to the throne of David. I find this to be one of the most remarkable things that has occurred in this world!

That is why God calls the earth to listen: "O earth, earth, earth, hear the word of the Lord." He wants the earth to see that this is the way He has worked it out. God's purposes will not be thwarted. He is able to bring judgment upon whomever He wills; yet He was able to fulfill His promise that the coming Messiah would be a descendant of King David.

*THEME: Bright light in a dark day and parable of two baskets of figs*

Every cloud has a silver lining, so the song says, and the dark clouds of the previous chapter also have a silver lining. It never got so dark that the prophets could not see light at the end of the tunnel. After chapter 22, which has the harshest judgment in the Bible against Coniah, the sun breaks through. However, we'll have two more verses before we see the sun—

**Woe be unto the pastors that destroy and scatter the sheep of my pasture! saith the LORD [Jer. 23:1].**

The "pastors" here are not preachers. He will speak about the religious rulers later on. Here the pastors refer to the kings, the politicians, the people who are ruling, the ones who are responsible for the laws of the land. God says, "Woe be unto them."

**Therefore thus saith the LORD God of Israel against the pastors that feed my people; Ye have scattered my flock, and driven them away, and have not visited them: behold, I will visit upon you the evil of your doings, saith the LORD [Jer. 23:2].**

God said He was going to judge them, and He did.

Now the sun breaks through:

**And I will gather the remnant of my flock out of all countries whither I have driven them, and will bring them again to their folds; and they shall be fruitful and increase.**

**And I will set up shepherds over them which shall feed them: and they shall fear no more, nor be dismayed, neither shall they be lacking, saith the LORD [Jer. 23:3–4].**

God says, "The day is coming when I intend to take over, and when I do, the poor will be taken care of." This refers specifically to the return of the Jews to their land after the present dispensation has closed and the church has been raptured. At that time the King whom they once rejected will tenderly set over them faithful shepherds. It will be an altogether different type of government from what we have in the world now.

**Behold, the days come, saith the LORD, that I will raise unto David a righteous Branch, and a King shall reign and prosper, and shall execute judgment and justice in the earth [Jer. 23:5].**

There is a King coming in David's line. The king Coniah and all of his line, although they are in David's line, shall be rejected and cut off. However, no one can destroy God's purpose, although they may think they can. God knows what He will do. We know from the New Testament that through another line, the line of Nathan, another son of David, came a peasant by the name of Mary, a girl up in Nazareth, who bore Jesus, the Messiah, the King. When Jesus presented Himself to the world, He said, ". . . Repent: for the kingdom of heaven is at hand" (Matt. 4:17). Since you can't have a kingdom without the king, in effect He was saying to the people, "Your King is here!" The people rejected the King, but He had the last word. He said that some-day the King would come back and set up that kingdom.

**In his days Judah shall be saved, and Israel shall dwell safely: and this is his name whereby he shall be called, THE LORD OUR RIGHTEOUSNESS [Jer. 23:6].**

Have you ever heard of this as a plank in a political platform? I have never heard a candidate claim that he is righteous and that he will follow God's plan and program for government. I've heard politicians make almost every other claim under the sun but that one! They wouldn't dare make it. But *righteousness* will characterize the kingdom when the Lord Jesus Christ reigns.

**Therefore, behold, the days come, saith the LORD, that they shall no more say, The LORD liveth, which brought up the children of Israel out of the land of Egypt;**

**But, the LORD liveth, which brought up and which led the seed of the house of Israel out of the north country, and from all countries whither I had driven them; and they shall dwell in their own land [Jer. 23:7–8].**

This is one of the most remarkable prophecies in the Word of God. The oldest religious holiday celebrated today is the Jewish Passover. Regardless of whether the Jew is reformed or orthodox, he remembers the Passover, because it is the celebration of the miraculous deliverance of the Jews out of Egypt. Now God is saying, "The day is coming when I will bring them back into their land that they will *forget* the deliverance out of Egypt and they will *remember* this new deliverance which I intend to accomplish." It will be that tremendous! Obviously God is not through with the nation Israel, my friend.

**Thus saith the Lord of hosts, Hearken not unto the words of the prophets that prophesy unto you: they make you vain: they speak a vision of their own heart, and not out of the mouth of the Lord.**

**They say still unto them that despise me, The Lord hath said, Ye shall have peace; and they say unto every one that walketh after the imagination of his own heart, No evil shall come upon you [Jer. 23:16–17].**

The false prophets persisted in prophesying peace. God repudiates them. Today there are dreamers who are talking about how *they* are going to bring in world peace, and all of them are talking along that same line. God says, "You won't do it—you can't do it." God said through Isaiah, "There is no peace . . . unto the wicked" (Isa. 48:22). The problem is not that the people don't want peace; the trouble is that the heart of man is desperately wicked. We don't realize how bad we really are. Wicked men in power today cannot bring peace on this earth. If they could, it would be a contradiction of the Word of God.

God turns now to the religious rulers.

**I have not sent these prophets, yet they ran: I have not spoken to them, yet they prophesied [Jer. 23:21].**

He has already said you can't trust the political rulers. They cannot bring in peace. They ignore the poor. Now God says that He did not send the bunch of prophets that were filling the land in that day. God denies that their message comes from Him. God rejected both the political rulers and the religious rulers.

Today I believe that God would say the same thing to the world. Who is seeking God in our day? The religious rulers of the world are out for religion. They are religious up to their eyebrows and are so pious, but how many of them are seeking out the living and true God?

**Therefore, behold, I am against the prophets, saith the Lord, that steal my words every one from his neighbour [Jer. 23:30].**

The contemporary liberal theologians are casting reflections upon the Word of God, saying it is not truly the Word of God, thereby stealing it out of the hearts of the people. I would cringe if I were one of the godless college professors or godless preachers who is wrecking the faith of believers. God says that He is going to do something about it someday. God is in no hurry—don't be deceived because God's judgment against an evil work is not executed speedily. That day of judgment is coming. It is in the hearts of the sons of man to do evil. They think they are getting by with it. God says, "I have eternity ahead of Me, and I am still running this show. The time will come when I will judge the religious rulers."

Chapter 24 is a sort of appendix, relating a vision given after Jeconiah had been carried away into captivity. Therefore it was during the early part of Zedekiah's reign. In a vision Jeremiah was shown two baskets of figs (the fig tree is a well-known symbol of Judah). One basket contained good figs and the other very bad figs. They symbolized two classes of people in Judah.

**Thus saith the Lord, the God of Israel; Like these good figs, so will I acknowledge them that are carried away captive of Judah, whom I have sent out of this place into the land of the Chaldeans for their good.**

**For I will set mine eyes upon them for good, and I will bring them again to this land: and I will build them, and not pull them down; and I will plant them, and not pluck them up [Jer. 24:5–6].**

Notice that God had sent them away into captivity "for their good." He promises to watch over them and eventually restore them (a remnant) to their land. That their restoration to the land does not refer to the return under Ezra and Nehemiah is clear from the final words "and not pluck them up." Obviously they have been plucked up again. The reference is to their restoration during the Millennium when "they shall return unto me with their whole heart" (v. 7).

The bad figs represented Zedekiah and

those who remained in Jerusalem and finally went down to Egypt in defiance of God's Word.

**And I will deliver them to be removed into all the kingdoms of the earth for their hurt, to be a reproach and a pro-** **verb, a taunt and a curse, in all places whither I shall drive them [Jer. 24:9].**

Secular history gives us the accurate fulfillment of this prophecy which Jeremiah faithfully delivered to his people.

# CHAPTER 25

*THEME: God spells out seventy-year captivity*

This chapter deals with a prophecy which was given about seventeen or eighteen years before that of the previous chapter. (Keep in mind that the Book of Jeremiah is not arranged in a chronological order.) The son of Josiah, Jehoiakim, was on the throne. He was very different from his godly father, as 2 Kings 24:4 records: ". . . he filled Jerusalem with innocent blood; which the LORD would not pardon."

Jeremiah makes this pointed charge:

**And the LORD hath sent unto you all his servants the prophets, rising early and sending them; but ye have not hearkened, nor inclined your ear to hear [Jer. 25:4].**

Because they will not hear God's Word, the land will be invaded by Babylon.

**Behold, I will send and take all the families of the north, saith the LORD, and Nebuchadrezzar the king of Babylon, my servant, and will bring them against this land, and against the inhabitants thereof, and against all these nations round about, and will utterly destroy them, and make them an astonishment, and an hissing, and perpetual desolations [Jer. 25:9].**

"Nebuchadrezzar the king of Babylon, my servant"—God calls Nebuchadrezzar His servant! (The variant spelling Nebuchadrezzar is probably more nearly correct than the common Nebuchadnezzar.) He was God's instrument of judgment.

A great many people wonder why the land of Israel is not a land flowing with milk and honey today. There is a desperate need for water in that land. God said He would make it a perpetual desolation, and He intends to let the world know that He not only judged the people but He also judged the land. There is a judgment of God upon that land specifically just as the curse of sin is on the entire earth—the earth does not produce what it is capable of producing because of the curse of sin upon it.

**Moreover I will take from them the voice of mirth, and the voice of gladness, the voice of the bridegroom, and the voice of the bride, the sound of the millstones, and the light of the candle [Jer. 25:10].**

God will take away from them all the fun they have been having. Neither will there be any more marrying and giving in marriage. "The sound of the millstones" will cease, which means that business and commerce will end. "The light of the candle"—they won't enjoy evenings at home anymore.

**And this whole land shall be a desolation, and an astonishment; and these nations shall serve the king of Babylon seventy years [Jer. 25:11].**

When God is dealing with the nation of Israel, He deals with the calendar. He spells out *time* in relation to their history. When God deals with the church, He does not give any times. Therefore you and I are not able to say when the Lord Jesus is coming. We have no right to say even that He is coming soon—we have not been told the *time* of His coming.

The seventy-year period of time is very significant. When the people of Israel were about to enter the land, the Lord told them that every seventh year was to be a Sabbath in which the ground was to lie fallow (see Lev. 25). Not only did God promise blessing if His Word was obeyed, but He warned of judgment if it was not. If they walked contrary to Him, He would walk contrary to them. Notice that God foresaw their disobedience: "Then shall the land enjoy her sabbaths, as long as it lieth desolate, and ye be in your enemies' land; even then shall the land rest, and enjoy her

sabbaths. As long as it lieth desolate it shall rest; because it did not rest in your sabbaths, when ye dwelt upon it" (Lev. 26:34–35). For approximately 490 years the sabbatic year was not kept—seventy Sabbaths had been neglected. God says through Jeremiah that for seventy years they will live in a strange country while their land has its rest. Then after the lost sabbatic years have been made up, Israel will be permitted to return to the land. Listen to Jeremiah:

**And it shall come to pass, when seventy years are accomplished, that I will punish the king of Babylon, and that nation, saith the Lord, for their iniquity, and the land of the Chaldeans, and will make it perpetual desolations [Jer. 25:12].**

At the time of Jeremiah this was a prophecy. It is now history. God has done that. There is no argument here.

### THE WINE CUP OF FURY

At the time this prophecy was given, Nebuchadnezzar had already deported to Babylon Jehoiachin with all his nobles, soldiers, and artificers. Those who remained under Zedekiah were all paying tribute (taxes) to Babylon. All the kings after Josiah were evil. Jeremiah had pronounced final judgment—Nebuchadnezzar would come and destroy Jerusalem and take all but a small remnant into captivity. He has told them that the captivity will definitely last for seventy years. But that does not conclude his prophecy.

He gives them now a picture using the figure of the wine cup of the wrath of God. This is a figure of speech that several of the prophets used. They spoke of the sin of man as he continues in rebellion against God.

**For thus saith the Lord God of Israel unto me; Take the wine cup of this fury at my hand, and cause all the nations, to whom I send thee, to drink it.**

**And they shall drink, and be moved, and be mad, because of the sword that I will send among them.**

**Then took I the cup at the Lord's hand, and made all the nations to drink, unto whom the Lord had sent me [Jer. 25: 15–17].**

Now he lists the nations.

**To wit, Jerusalem, and the cities of Judah, and the kings thereof, and the**

**princes thereof, to make them a desolation, an astonishment, an hissing, and a curse; as it is this day [Jer. 25:18].**

First, of course, Jerusalem and the cities of Judah, the kings and the princes are mentioned. Although this especially relates to the sin of Israel, it is not confined to God's own people. All the nations of the world are guilty. Like a wine cup gets full, there is a filling up of the wrath of God.

After Israel, he mentions Egypt:

**Pharaoh king of Egypt, and his servants, and his princes, and all his people [Jer. 25:19].**

Then He mentions Uz and the land of the Philistines and Ashkelon and Azzah and Ekron and Ashdod and Edom and Moab and Ammon and Tyre and Zidon and "the kings of the isles which are beyond the sea" (v. 22). They all are to take the wine cup of the wrath of God. Man's sin and continuous rebellion against God is like a wine cup which is filling up with God's anger. When it is full, the judgment of God will break upon the earth.

**Therefore thou shalt say unto them, Thus saith the Lord of hosts, the God of Israel; Drink ye, and be drunken, and spue, and fall, and rise no more, because of the sword which I will send among you [Jer. 25:27].**

He makes them drink that cup, which is, of course, the judgment of God. All of the nations in the area of Israel and beyond it were to be judged of God because they had gotten so far away from Him. This reveals the fact that all the nations of the world are responsible to God.

**Therefore prophesy thou against them all these words, and say unto them, The Lord shall roar from on high, and utter his voice from his holy habitation; he shall mightily roar upon his habitation; he shall give a shout, as they that tread the grapes, against all the inhabitants of the earth [Jer. 25:30].**

The judgment would not be confined to Israel. Babylon, you see, will be God's instrument of judgment, and we know from history that Babylon did become the first great world power which dominated all the nations of the civilized world at that time.

**Thus saith the Lord of hosts, Behold, evil shall go forth from nation to nation, and a great whirlwind shall be**

raised up from the coasts of the earth [Jer. 25:32].

This is descriptive of the tremendous movement of Nebuchadnezzar, king of Babylon, as he moved out over the civilized world of his

day and brought even Egypt and Tyre and Sidon—these great powers—under his sovereignty. The verses that conclude this chapter give a graphic description of the day of the Lord's anger with the nations and their "shepherds," or kings.

# CHAPTERS 26–28

**THEME:** *Message in temple court during reign of Jehoiakim and parable of yokes*

You may recall that in chapter 7 Jeremiah was told to stand at the *gate* of the Lord's house and speak to the people. Here he is told to stand in the *court*.

**Thus saith the Lord; stand in the court of the Lord's house, and speak unto all the cities of Judah, which come to worship in the Lord's house, all the words that I command thee to speak unto them; diminish not a word [Jer. 26:2].**

This is a message that he had already given in the time of Jehoiakim. Now it is repeated at the time of Zedekiah. Chapters 26–30 record the message which delivered the final words of God to these people before the captivity.

I am of the opinion that the people were still coming to the temple as usual. There was this outward show of worship, and there was prosperity in the land at that time; nobody seemed to be complaining. It looked as if God were being petulant to make such prophecies, but in actuality the people were far from God, and there was awful sin in the land. Jeremiah was to continue to cry out against this.

**If so be they will hearken, and turn every man from his evil way, that I may repent me of the evil, which I purpose to do unto them because of the evil of their doings [Jer. 26:3].**

"That I may repent me of the evil." When God repents, it does not mean that He has changed His mind. He means that the people have changed. If the people will change, God will not judge; He will bless. It looks as if God had changed His mind, but the fact is that God will always punish sin and will always pardon the sinner who will come to Him. That never changes. When a sinner, who has been under the judgment of God, turns to God and is blessed and saved, it looks as if God has

changed His mind. However, in fact, it is the sinner who has changed his mind. God tells them that if they will change, then He will not destroy them; He will not judge them.

**And thou shalt say unto them, Thus saith the Lord; If ye will not hearken to me, to walk in my law, which I have set before you,**

**To hearken to the words of my servants the prophets, whom I sent unto you, both rising up early, and sending them, but ye have not hearkened;**

**Then will I make this house like Shiloh, and will make this city a curse to all the nations of the earth [Jer. 26:4–6].**

"Then will I make this house like Shiloh"— meaning that it would be destroyed.

"And will make this city a curse to all the nations of the earth"—Jerusalem has been a burden to this world, and it is at the present moment. At the time I am writing this commentary, Jerusalem does not even belong to the nation Israel; it is like a pawn on the chessboard of the earth controlled by Russia and America. God said that He would make it a burden to all nations, and He certainly has done that.

## JEREMIAH THREATENED WITH DEATH

**Now it came to pass, when Jeremiah had made an end of speaking all that the Lord had commanded him to speak unto all the people, that the priests and the prophets and all the people took him, saying, Thou shalt surely die [Jer. 26:8].**

Things are getting bad. They have resisted the message of God through Jeremiah,

and now they want to *kill* Jeremiah. Now this gets rather complicated because there are three groups in this section: the princes, the priests and the prophets, and the people.

**Then spake the priests and the prophets unto the princes and to all the people, saying, This man is worthy to die; for he hath prophesied against this city, as ye have heard with your ears [Jer. 26:11].**

The priests and the prophets were of one mind; they had determined his death. They never changed their minds about that at all. However, the princes decided they had better hear Jeremiah, and the people who had been of the same mind as the priests and prophets came over on the side of the princes.

**Then spake Jeremiah unto all the princes and to all the people, saying, The LORD sent me to prophesy against this house and against this city all the words that ye have heard.**

**Therefore now amend your ways and your doings, and obey the voice of the LORD your God; and the LORD will repent him of the evil that he hath pronounced against you [Jer. 26:12–13].**

He makes it clear why God is threatening to judge them.

Let's keep in mind that it was considered blasphemy when Jeremiah prophesied that the city and the temple would be destroyed. This branded him as a heretic. The false prophets were saying that God would never let the temple fall. It was His temple, and Jerusalem was His city. God would not let that happen. Jeremiah said, "You are entirely wrong. You are disassociating religion from morality."

This is a problem with a number of people who are very fundamental in their belief. They make the Word of God almost a fetish. I don't believe there is anyone more fundamental in his doctrine than I am. People say that I lean backwards, I am so fundamental. But I do want to say that it is entirely wrong to divorce *morality* from your faith, be it ever so fundamental. One can make religion and the Word of God a sort of good-luck charm.

It reminds me of the story of a soldier who carried a New Testament in his pocket. The bullet hit the book in his shirt pocket, and that saved his life. Well, the book didn't stop the bullet because it was a New Testament—it could have been any kind of a book. How foolish to make the Word of God a sort of fetish.

Oh, my friend, we can't divorce our manner of life from the teachings of the Word of God and still expect His blessing. This is what the false prophets were doing. And in our day many folk are saying, "Because I am fundamental in my doctrine, no harm can come to me." Well, it *can* come to you. When you and I get away from God, He will judge us.

I point out again how interesting it is that the priests and the false prophets did not change their minds about putting Jeremiah to death. The princes did, and that is the thing that saved the life of Jeremiah. The princes were willing to hear him. It has been my experience that when a spiritual authority becomes corrupt and debased it is far more evil than when the politicians become corrupt and debased. When the civil authority is corrupt, that is bad; but when the religious authority becomes corrupt, that is a lot worse. Let me remind you that it was the *priests* who put the Lord Jesus to death on the cross. It was the religious rulers who insisted that He must die; they were the ones who persuaded the people to shout, "Crucify Him!" And the *religious* leaders in Jeremiah's time were determined to kill him.

This reveals another fallacy: We hear the expression, *Vox populi, vox Dei*, that is, "the voice of the people is the voice of God." There are a lot of people in America who believe that. They consider public opinion as the authority. However, the mass of people is a fickle crowd that will follow one TV personality after another. It will elect a man to office if he has charisma even though he may be the biggest fool in the world and utterly corrupt in his life. The voice of the people is the very worst basis for authority. I thank God that He is not going to let the world vote the Lord Jesus into office! If God were to put it up to a public vote, Jesus Christ would never enter into His kingdom. I rejoice that God will send the Lord Jesus to this earth to put down rebellion.

During those last troubled days of the kingdom of Judah, God is saying that the people are wrong, the princes are wrong, the priests are wrong, and the prophets are wrong. Jeremiah isn't even sure of himself; he is only sure that he is giving out the Word of God.

The Word of God is the only and final authority. People today are turning to the signs of the zodiac and the horoscope—we have mentioned the utter foolishness of that. But we find some Christians, often ministers and

leaders, who feel that they are a final authority. I appreciate this Book of Jeremiah. It helps me, because I confess that the more I study the Word of God the more aware I am of my own ignorance of it. It disturbs me that so many men think they know it all and are the final authority.

It is said that Socrates made the statement that he was the wisest man in Athens. When asked on what grounds he made such a claim he replied that he was the wisest man because he realized that his wisdom was worthless!

The only claim I can make today is that I know I am ignorant of the Word of God. A Persian proverb puts it this way:

He who knows not and knows not that he
    knows not is a fool. Shun him.
He who knows not and knows that he
    knows not is a child. Teach him.
He who knows and knows not that he
    knows is asleep. Wake him.
He who knows and knows that he knows
    is wise. Follow him.
               —Author unknown

I will accept the first three statements, but not the last one, because I don't think we do know. This is also Jeremiah's position—all he knows is the Word of God. Although the false prophets insist that nothing is going to happen, Jeremiah believes God, and he *knows* something is going to happen.

In chapter 27 the message is to go out again to all the nations that they are to yield to the king of Babylon. This time his message is illustrated—

**Thus saith the Lord to me; Make thee bonds and yokes, and put them upon thy neck,**

**And send them to the king of Edom, and to the king of Moab, and to the king of the Ammonites, and to the king of Tyrus, and to the king of Zidon, by the hand of the messengers which come to Jerusalem unto Zedekiah king of Judah [Jer. 27:2–3].**

God reminds these nations that He is the Creator and He gives power to whomever He chooses—

**And now have I given all these lands into the hand of Nebuchadnezzar the king of Babylon, my servant; and the beasts of the field have I given him also to serve him [Jer. 27:6].**

Although God clearly told these nations to yield to the king of Babylon, they did not obey. Had they done as He said, they would have saved literally thousands of human lives—

**And it shall come to pass, that the nation and kingdom which will not serve the same Nebuchadnezzar the king of Babylon, and that will not put their neck under the yoke of the king of Babylon, that nation will I punish, saith the Lord, with the sword, and with the famine, and with the pestilence, until I have consumed them by his hand [Jer. 27:8].**

## HANANIAH, THE FALSE PROPHET

Chapter 28 continues the prophecy of the yokes. One of the false prophets, Hananiah, refutes the prophecy of Jeremiah and claims to give the true Word of the Lord:

**Thus speaketh the Lord of hosts, the God of Israel, saying, I have broken the yoke of the king of Babylon.**

**Within two full years will I bring again into this place all the vessels of the Lord's house, that Nebuchadnezzar king of Babylon took away from this place, and carried them to Babylon:**

**And I will bring again to this place Jeconiah the son of Jehoiakim king of Judah, with all the captives of Judah, that went into Babylon, saith the Lord: for I will break the yoke of the king of Babylon [Jer. 28:2–4].**

Well, Jeremiah made it clear that Hananiah was not a prophet of God and that he was giving the people a lie. Hananiah actually took the wooden yoke from off Jeremiah's neck and broke it, saying, "Thus saith the Lord; Even so will I break the yoke of Nebuchadnezzar king of Babylon from the neck of all nations within the space of two full years (v. 11)."

As a judgment upon him, God said to tell him that he would die within the year. Notice what happened:

**Then said the prophet Jeremiah unto Hananiah the prophet, Hear now, Hananiah; The Lord hath not sent thee; but thou makest this people to trust in a lie.**

**Therefore thus saith the Lord; Behold, I will cast thee from off the face of the**

earth: this year thou shalt die, because thou hast taught rebellion against the LORD.

So Hananiah the prophet died the same year in the seventh month [Jer. 28:15–17].

He died, just as God said he would.

You would think this would alert the people and they would say, "Look, Jeremiah is the one who is calling the shots. Jeremiah is the one who is giving us God's Word." However, they were not convinced, but went on in their rebellion against the Word of God.

Judah listened to the wrong voices, and we have done the same thing in our own recent history. Since the time of World War II we have not had any true leaders in this country. Someone once asked Gladstone, the great English jurist, what was the mark of a great statesman. He gave this answer: "A great statesman is a man who knows the direction God is going for the next fifty years." My friend, we certainly have not had leaders like that. As a result, we have missed a great opportunity as a nation for leadership in the world, and the great middle class of our nation has been corrupted. We are headed down, just as England went down, and just as Judah went down. We have refused to listen to the Word of God.

# CHAPTER 29

**THEME:** *Message of hope to first delegation of captives*

## JEREMIAH'S LETTER OF ENCOURAGEMENT

**Now these are the words of the letter that Jeremiah the prophet sent from Jerusalem unto the residue of the elders which were carried away captives, and to the priests, and to the prophets, and to all the people whom Nebuchadnezzar had carried away captive from Jerusalem to Babylon [Jer. 29:1].**

Chapter 29 records Jeremiah's letter to the people who had been taken into captivity when Jehoiachin was king (see 2 Kings 24:10–16). The complete captivity of Judah came eleven years later (2 Kings 25:1–7).

This is God's instruction to them:

**Thus saith the LORD of hosts, the God of Israel, unto all that are carried away captives, whom I have caused to be carried away from Jerusalem unto Babylon;**

**Build ye houses, and dwell in them; and plant gardens, and eat the fruit of them;**

**Take ye wives, and beget sons and daughters; and take wives for your sons, and give your daughters to husbands, that they may bear sons and daughters; that ye may be increased there, and not diminished [Jer. 29:4–6].**

That is, settle down in Babylon. Don't think you will be released any moment. Go ahead and plan for your future—get married and establish homes, because you are going to be there a long time.

**And seek the peace of the city whither I have caused you to be carried away captives, and pray unto the LORD for it: for in the peace thereof shall ye have peace [Jer. 29:7].**

"Seek the peace of the city" in which you are living, and pray for it. They were not to rebel or instigate revolt. They were to settle down and be law-abiding citizens.

**For thus saith the LORD, That after seventy years be accomplished at Babylon I will visit you, and perform my good word toward you, in causing you to return to this place [Jer. 29:10].**

God tells them the exact number of years they will be in captivity, then assures them that He has not forsaken them but will restore them to their homeland.

## LIES OF THE FALSE PROPHETS

There were false prophets in Babylon who refused to accept Jeremiah's letter as a message from God. They wrote letters to Jerusalem claiming that God had appointed a new priest and that Jeremiah was to be silenced.

**Then came the word of the LORD unto Jeremiah, saying,**

**Send to all them of the captivity, saying, Thus saith the LORD concerning Shemaiah the Nehelamite; Because that Shemaiah hath prophesied unto you, and I sent him not, and he caused you to trust in a lie:**

**Therefore thus saith the LORD; Behold, I will punish Shemaiah the Nehelamite, and his seed: he shall not have a man to dwell among this people; neither shall he behold the good that I will do for my people, saith the LORD; because he hath taught rebellion against the LORD [Jer. 29:30–32].**

Of course, God pronounces a judgment against these false prophets.

God speaks very impressively in history. He has told Judah that what is happening to them is happening because of their sin. He will always judge sin. God has not changed. Many people would like to think that the God of the New Testament is different from the God of the Old Testament. He is the same Person; He hasn't changed one bit. He hasn't grown old. He hasn't even learned anything new. He is the same God.

Not only has God spoken in history, but He has spoken in His Word. Listen to Simon Peter: "Knowing this first, that no prophecy of the scripture is of any private interpretation" (2 Pet. 1:20). "Knowing this first"—this is primary stuff, something we should learn in the first grade. There are two ways this verse has been understood which are incorrect. One is that when you study prophecy, you need to consider the whole of prophecy; you cannot take one prophecy by itself and study it to the exclusion of others. That is a true statement, but it is not what this passage is teaching. Then there are those who say you have no right to interpret prophecy on your own.

Well, that not only takes away the freedom of the first amendment from me, but it also removes the free will that God gave to me. This is not what Peter is saying. He is not speaking at all about the end result of God's revelation; what he is talking about is the *origin* of it. No writing of Scripture was of private interpretation at its origin. The prophets who wrote and spoke in olden times are not giving you the result of their observations. They are speaking what *God* told them to speak.

When you and I approach the Word of God, we must come to the place where we are ready to lie in the dust. I do not mean to simply acknowledge that we are nothing, that we are sinners; but we must be willing to lay into the dust our opinions, our self-will, and our own viewpoints—to put it all down and listen to what *God* has to say. This was the problem with the priests and prophets and princes in Jeremiah's day. It is our problem today. Every man has his own little viewpoint, is doing his own little thing, carrying his own little placard of protest—and he's doing it out of limited knowledge.

God has all knowledge—He has all the facts, knows all the background. It is unbelievable that some people presume to sit in judgment of Him. Little man stands up and says, "Lord, if You're up there—and I'm not sure You are; I'm pretty hard to convince because I have a giant intellect, and my intellect says You may not even be up there—but if You're up there, I just want to say that You are *wrong*." Oh, my friend, what arrogance! If a little, old ant were to crawl into my house and onto my chair and look at me and say, "Look, I don't like the way you built this house; I don't like the way you plant flowers and trees around here; and I don't like what you eat," do you know what I would do to that ant? I would flick him off my chair and *step* on him. That would be the end of that little ant! But God is so gracious to man. He doesn't step on us. He has given us a second chance.

# CHAPTER 30

**THEME:** *The coming Great Tribulation*

Chapters 30–39 form the fourth major section of the Book of Jeremiah, and they contain prophecies concerning the future of the twelve tribes of Israel and the near captivity of Judah. The prophecies in this section are not in chronological order.

The message in these chapters comes from Jeremiah to Judah in the darkest days she has ever had. It never got so dark that he didn't have a wonderful message of encouragement, however.

This is the situation: the army of Nebuchadnezzar is outside the walls of the city of Jerusalem, and they mean business. This time Nebuchadnezzar will destroy the city and burn the temple. Jeremiah has been arrested and shut up in the courtyard. Literally, he is in jail. It has been seven years since he had his conflict with the false prophets. Events have moved along rather quietly, but every day reveals the accuracy of Jeremiah's message. The false prophet Hananiah had said that the power of Babylon would be broken within two years. Seven years have gone by, and Nebuchadnezzar is outside the city wall. His power is not going to be broken; instead *he* is about to break Jerusalem. The vessels of the Lord's house are not going to be restored to the temple. Jeconiah will not be returned to the city. Things have gone from bad to worse. They are out of the frying pan into the fire. The life of the nation of Judah has gone down. With Jerusalem already under the shadow of Babylon, God's prophet is held captive by the rebellious spirit of a sinning nation which refuses to hear the Word of the Lord.

Can any hour be darker? Can any circumstances be more calculated to fill the heart with despair? Yet it is at this time that the prophetic note of Jeremiah's message goes all the way from the basement to the top floor of the Empire State Building. He is no longer singing low bass; now he's going to sing high tenor, if you please. He is going to reach the heights. He has come all the way through darkness into the light. The night cometh, but also the morning is coming.

**The word that came to Jeremiah from the LORD, saying,**

**Thus speaketh the LORD God of Israel, saying, Write thee all the words that I have spoken unto thee in a book [Jer. 30:1–2].**

He is *writing* his prophecy now. After all, he's in jail; he won't be in the pulpit on Sunday morning.

**For, lo, the days come, saith the LORD, that I will bring again the captivity of my people Israel and Judah, saith the LORD: and I will cause them to return to the land that I gave to their fathers, and they shall possess it.**

**And these are the words that the LORD spake concerning Israel and concerning Judah.**

**For thus saith the LORD; We have heard a voice of trembling, of fear, and not of peace [Jer. 30:3–5].**

Believe me, the people had gotten the message from Jeremiah that there would be no peace. The false prophets had said, "Peace, peace," and there was none.

**Ask ye now, and see whether a man doth travail with child? wherefore do I see every man with his hands on his loins, as a woman in travail, and all faces are turned into paleness?**

**Alas! for that day is great, so that none is like it: it is even the time of Jacob's trouble; but he shall be saved out of it [Jer. 30:6–7].**

Jeremiah sees the great Day of the Lord coming of which the other prophets, including Isaiah, also spoke. They said it is to be a day of darkness and not of light, that the people will go through the night of the Great Tribulation Period before they will see the brightness of day. In effect God is saying, "You haven't seen anything yet. The Great Tribulation Period will be far worse than what you are going through now."

## THE COMING KINGDOM

**For it shall come to pass in that day, saith the LORD of hosts, that I will break his yoke from off thy neck, and will burst thy bonds, and strangers shall no more serve themselves of him:**

**But they shall serve the LORD their God, and David their king, whom I will raise up unto them [Jer. 30:8–9].**

Out of that awful time of trouble, the people of Israel will return to the land. David

will be raised from the dead and will rule over them as they enter the kingdom age.

> Thus saith the LORD; Behold, I will bring again the captivity of Jacob's tents, and have mercy on his dwelling-places; and the city shall be builded upon her own heap, and the palace shall remain after the manner thereof [Jer. 30:18].

This is the sure promise of the Lord. When will these things take place?—

> The fierce anger of the LORD shall not return, until he have done it, and until he have performed the intents of his heart: in the latter days ye shall consider it [Jer. 30:24].

"In the latter days"—this is a prophecy which is to be fulfilled in the future. It refers to the kingdom age which is, of course, still future in our day.

# CHAPTER 31

### THEME: The "I Will" chapter

Chapters 30 through 33 constitute one very bright and encouraging song. Up to this point Jeremiah's emphasis has been upon judgment, but his message now is in sharp contrast to that. E. W. Hengstenburg calls these chapters "the triumphal hymn of Israel's salvation." They were written at the darkest moment in the history of Judah.

As the last king of Judah, Zedekiah corresponds to Hoshea who was the final ruler of the northern kingdom of Israel. But, of course, the northern kingdom of Israel has long since departed and gone into captivity. At this moment Nebuchadnezzar's army is outside the wall of Jerusalem, ready to destroy the city and burn the temple. The promises of the false prophets have been proven false. Seven years earlier Hananiah had said that Babylon would be broken within two years. But Nebuchadnezzar is not broken; he is alive—too much alive for the people of Judah.

Jeremiah's message is a message of encouragement. In chapter 30 he spoke of the Day of the Lord opening with the Great Tribulation Period. In verse 7 of that chapter he called it "the time of Jacob's trouble." But beyond the Great Tribulation is coming the restoration of the land and the return of the people to it.

I have labeled chapter 31 "the 'I will' chapter," because "I will" occurs fifteen times, and the One who says it is none other than God. When God says "I will" fifteen times, He is telling us what *He* is going to do.

> At the same time, saith the LORD, will I be the God of all the families of Israel, and they shall be my people [Jer. 31:1].

This prophecy has not yet been fulfilled; that time has not come. The present return of Israel to the land cannot be interpreted as being the fulfillment of this prophecy—because they have not returned to God. I am told there is real persecution of Christians in that land today. They talk about religious freedom, but it does not really exist. The people have returned to the land, but they have not returned to the Lord.

> Thus saith the LORD, The people which were left of the sword found grace in the wilderness; even Israel, when I went to cause him to rest.

> The LORD hath appeared of old unto me, saying, Yea, I have loved thee with an everlasting love: therefore with loving-kindness have I drawn thee [Jer. 31:2–3].

We have here the reason God is going to restore the people to the land. I believe with all my heart that God intends to restore the nation Israel to that land in His own time and in His own plan and in His own purpose. The basis for that is given right here: "I have loved thee with an everlasting love." This verse ranks high among the many favorite statements in the Word of God.

There are those who will ask, "*How* can God love these people?" That is a good question, but let's widen it out just a little and ask, "How can God love *us* today?" He has said, ". . . God so loved the world . . ." (John 3:16). Not only does God love Israel, He loves the world—He loves you and me. It is easy to point a finger at the Jews and be critical of them, but God says, "I have loved thee

[Israel] with an everlasting love." There is nothing you can do with that—God has said it. Instead of pointing the finger at others, we need to turn it around and point at ourselves. In God's sight we are as great sinners as anyone who is still unbelieving. It took the death of Christ to provide a redemption for you and me. Don't limit it to a few and say, "How can God love *them?*" My friend, how can God love *me?* How can God love *you?* We should be amazed that He loved any of us.

Frederick W. Faber has expressed this very well in a song:

How Thou canst think so well of us
Yet be the God Thou art,
Is darkness to my intellect
But sunshine to my heart.

"I have loved thee with an everlasting love." "Everlasting"—I must confess that I know very little about the meaning of that word. I once asked a little boy, "How long is *everlasting* and how long is *never?*" He simply answered, "I reckon it's a pretty long time."

"Love"—what is love, by the way? The only explanation I have for why God loves us is that it is not because of anything He sees in us but it is *because of who He is.* He finds the explanation in Himself. John wrote "Herein is love, not that we loved God, but that he loved us . . ." (1 John 4:10). Now that is love. Cramer commented on what John said: "The love of God toward us comes from love, and has no other cause above or beside itself, but is in God, and remains in God, so that Christ Who is in God is its Centre" (in *Studies in the Prophecy of Jeremiah,* G. Campbell Morgan, p. 167). God loves you and me, my friend, and I really cannot tell you why.

Again, let me quote Faber:

Yet Thou dost think so well of us,
Because of what Thou art;
Thy love illumines our intellect,
Yet fills with fear our heart.

I am overwhelmed by the love of God. If He were to change His mind tomorrow, I would be eternally lost and so would you. But He says His love is everlasting, and that's a pretty long time.

I have a great many amillennial friends who believe that God is through with the nation Israel. May I say to you, if He's through with Israel, then He's through with you and He's through with me. But He says, "I have loved you with an everlasting love." It doesn't make

any difference what you and I think—God is not through with Israel.

**Behold, I will bring them from the north country, and gather them from the coasts of the earth, and with them the blind and the lame, the woman with child and her that travaileth with child together: a great company shall return thither [Jer. 31:8].**

It is going to be such a big undertaking to bring the people back to the land you might think that He would leave the blind and the lame behind and just bring the best physical specimens. God says, "Nothing of the kind. I am going to bring them all back."

**They shall come with weeping, and with supplications will I lead them: I will cause them to walk by the rivers of waters in a straight way, wherein they shall not stumble: for I am a father to Israel, and Ephraim is my firstborn [Jer. 31:9].**

"I am a father to Israel, and Ephraim is my firstborn." God never said that He was Father to any individual Israelite. He said, "Moses, My *servant*" (see Josh. 1:2), and "David, My *servant*" (see Ps. 89:3). But when He speaks of the whole nation as a corporate body, God says, "I am a *father* to Israel" (see Exod. 4:22).

**Hear the word of the LORD, O ye nations, and declare it in the isles afar off, and say, He that scattered Israel will gather him, and keep him, as a shepherd doth his flock [Jer. 31:10].**

I am grateful that the Lord has given to me a radio ministry that reaches around the world each day. I am delighted that I can say what God also says, that I want the isles of the earth to hear the message. I want all mankind to hear that He scattered Israel. It was a judgment upon them, but He loves them with an everlasting love, and He is going to bring them back to the land.

He loved Israel and He judged them. This is a bittersweet message. All through Jeremiah you have a note of joy, but you also have a note of sorrow. It is like the Chinese dishes that are called "sweet and sour." God judged Israel, but He also said, "He that scattered Israel will gather him, and keep him, as a shepherd doth his flock." And a shepherd really watches over his flock.

God is not through saying what He *will* do:

Then shall the virgin rejoice in the dance, both young men and old together: for I will turn their mourning into joy, and will comfort them, and make them rejoice from their sorrow.

And I will satiate the soul of the priests with fatness, and my people shall be satisfied with my goodness, saith the LORD [Jer. 31:13–14].

I don't know about you, but this makes me feel like saying, "Hallelujah!" and throwing my hat in the air. This is what *God* says He is going to do for *Israel*; let's allow Him to say it, for it's what He wants to do.

Yet Israel's immediate condition was tragic. They had rebelled against God, and they were backslidden.

How long wilt thou go about, O thou backsliding daughter? for the LORD hath created a new thing in the earth, A woman shall compass a man [Jer. 31:22].

There are those who believe that this verse refers to the virgin birth of Jesus Christ, and I see no reason to rule that out.

Beginning at verse 31 we have the new covenant that God intends to make with Israel—all twelve tribes. And if you think that ten of the tribes are lost, God does not. He is going to make this covenant with all twelve tribes.

Behold, the days come, saith the LORD, that I will make a new covenant with the house of Israel, and with the house of Judah:

Not according to the covenant that I made with their fathers in the day that I took them by the hand to bring them out of the land of Egypt; which my covenant they brake, although I was an husband unto them, saith the LORD:

But this shall be the covenant that I will make with the house of Israel; Af-

ter those days, saith the LORD, I will put my law in their inward parts, and write it in their hearts; and will be their God, and they shall be my people [Jer. 31:31–33].

This new covenant is going to be different from the one given to Moses at Mount Sinai. The grand distinction is that it will be engraved upon the hearts of the people and not upon cold tables of stone.

And they shall teach no more every man his neighbour, and every man his brother, saying, Know the LORD: for they shall all know me, from the least of them unto the greatest of them, saith the LORD: for I will forgive their iniquity, and I will remember their sin no more [Jer. 31:34].

Their sins will be forgiven.

Notice how God confirms this covenant to Israel:

Thus saith the LORD, which giveth the sun for a light by day, and the ordinances of the moon and of the stars for a light by night, which divideth the sea when the waves thereof roar; The LORD of hosts is his name:

If those ordinances depart from before me, saith the LORD, then the seed of Israel also shall cease from being a nation before me for ever [Jer. 31:35–36].

This covenant will never be changed or abrogated. Just as we cannot change the course of the moon or pull it out of the sky, so His covenant with Israel cannot be changed. On a trip to the moon we brought back two hundred pounds of rock. If we kept doing that for a few million years, maybe we would eventually move the whole thing to earth—but I don't think we're going to do that! God says this is an everlasting covenant that He will make with them.

# CHAPTERS 32–33

**THEME:** *Imprisoned Jeremiah buys real estate; coming kingdom as promised to David*

In chapter 32 Jeremiah is in prison, and Jerusalem is under siege by Nebuchadnezzar; yet Jeremiah buys a piece of real estate in Anathoth!

> **The word that came to Jeremiah from the LORD in the tenth year of Zedekiah king of Judah, which was the eighteenth year of Nebuchadrezzar.**
>
> **For then the king of Babylon's army besieged Jerusalem: and Jeremiah the prophet was shut up in the court of the prison, which was in the king of Judah's house [Jer. 32:1–2].**

Notice how Jeremiah pinpoints the time: it was "the tenth year of Zedekiah," the year Nebuchadnezzar breached the walls of Jerusalem and destroyed it. It was a dark day indeed.

> **Behold, Hanameel the son of Shallum thine uncle shall come unto thee, saying, Buy thee my field that is in Anathoth: for the right of redemption is thine to buy it [Jer. 32:7].**

The Lord told Jeremiah that he would have the opportunity to buy a piece of land from his relative, Hanameel.

> **And I bought the field of Hanameel my uncle's son, that was in Anathoth, and weighed him the money, even seventeen shekels of silver [Jer. 32:9].**

At the darkest hour in Judah's history, Jeremiah buys real estate—this was the time to be *selling* real estate! I imagine that the real estate men in Jerusalem and the surrounding country were dumping all the real estate they possibly could. Why did Jeremiah buy this piece of land at this time? It was to show the people he believed God when He said that they were going to return to the land. This is very remarkable.

But Jeremiah had a question which was too hard for him to answer, and in the following verses he brings this question to the Lord in prayer.

> **Now when I had delivered the evidence of the purchase unto Baruch the son of Neriah, I prayed unto the LORD, saying,**
>
> **Ah Lord GOD! behold, thou hast made the heaven and the earth by thy great power and stretched out arm, and there is nothing too hard for thee [Jer. 32:16–17].**

Jeremiah's question is too hard for him to answer, but it is not too hard for God.

In verses 18 through 23, Jeremiah recounts the way the Lord has protected and provided for Israel down through her history, but now the situation is very grave.

> **Behold the mounts, they are come unto the city to take it; and the city is given into the hand of the Chaldeans, that fight against it, because of the sword, and of the famine, and of the pestilence: and what thou hast spoken is come to pass; and, behold, thou seest it.**
>
> **And thou hast said unto me, O Lord GOD, Buy thee the field for money, and take witnesses; for the city is given into the hand of the Chaldeans [Jer. 32:24–25].**

Jeremiah is no hypocrite. He trusts the God who made heaven and earth, the God who had so wonderfully cared for Israel. But now the Chaldeans are right outside the city and are going to take it; yet God told Jeremiah to buy a field. He obeyed, but it didn't make good sense to him. So he brings his question to the Lord.

My friend, there is nothing wrong with asking why. If you have a doubt or a question, talk to the Lord about it. That is what He wants us to do. Just don't put up this pious hypocritical front that we sometimes see. While he says he trusts the Lord, he is crying and complaining and asking why. Let's be honest like Jeremiah. He obeyed the Lord, but he admitted his doubts, taking them to the Lord in prayer.

God answers Jeremiah's prayer in verses 26 through 44.

> **Then came the word of the LORD unto Jeremiah, saying,**
>
> **Behold, I am the LORD, the God of all flesh: is there any thing too hard for me? [Jer. 32:26–27].**

The Lord begins by putting down the axiom that nothing is too hard for Him.

And now therefore thus saith the LORD, the God of Israel, concerning this city, whereof ye say, It shall be delivered into the hand of the king of Babylon by the sword, and by the famine, and by the pestilence;

Behold, I will gather them out of all countries, whither I have driven them in mine anger, and in my fury, and in great wrath; and I will bring them again unto this place, and I will cause them to dwell safely:

And they shall be my people, and I will be their God:

And I will give them one heart, and one way, that they may fear me for ever, for the good of them, and of their children after them:

And I will make an everlasting covenant with them, that I will not turn away from them, to do them good; but I will put my fear in their hearts, that they shall not depart from me [Jer. 32:36–40].

God is delivering the city over to the Chaldeans, and in His own time He will deliver the city *from* the Chaldeans.

Yea, I will rejoice over them to do them good, and I will plant them in this land assuredly with my whole heart and with my whole soul.

For thus saith the LORD; Like as I have brought all this great evil upon this people, so will I bring upon them all the good that I have promised them [Jer. 32:41–42].

Now Jehovah is delivering Judah unto judgment. In a future day, He will deliver them in mercy—this is His promise.

When we go to God and let Him know how we feel, He will encourage our hearts as He did for Jeremiah. Oh, my friend, He wants you to come to Him.

The day is very dark for Judah, but God allows Jeremiah to look down through the tunnel to where light can be seen at the other end. In chapter 33 God confirms and reaffirms the covenant that He made with David. There is a day coming when He will restore the people to the land of Israel and to fellowship with Himself.

Moreover the word of the LORD came unto Jeremiah the second time, while he was yet shut up in the court of the prison, saying [Jer. 33:1].

Jeremiah is still in jail, you see.

Thus saith the LORD the maker thereof, the LORD that formed it, to establish it; the LORD is his name;

Call unto me, and I will answer thee, and shew thee great and mighty things, which thou knowest not [Jer. 33:2–3].

This last verse I have heard quoted frequently at testimony meetings. It is a very wonderful verse, but I think it is more meaningful if it is remembered in the context of this chapter. Despite the fact that he is in prison, this man was told by God to buy a piece of real estate. Jeremiah acted by faith and bought the real estate, but he has a great many questions in his mind. Why was God permitting Judah to go into captivity? Frankly, I think it is an example of great faith when a believer has these moments of doubt. Someone will ask how that can be. My friend, if you are walking with God and are in fellowship with Him, He is so wonderful and He does such wonderful things that there will be times when you do not understand what He is doing. Our question is bound to be, "Why are You doing this?" Don't you have questions like that?

I have had questions like that. I remember one evening going to the hospital to see my wife and our firstborn baby. The nurse said to me, "The doctor wants to speak to you," and she looked very serious. The doctor said to me, "The little baby died." He hadn't told my wife, so he and I went in and told her and we wept together. I walked out (I never shall forget) to an open-air porch there at the hospital. It was summertime, and I looked up at the heavens and the stars. I had a question. Do you know what that question was? Why? Why? I still look up and ask that same question. Over the years I have learned to put my hand in His and just keep walking in the dark. Many times I talk this over with Him, and I tell Him about my doubts, but I also tell Him that I trust Him. I'm glad that Jeremiah was that kind of a man. And there are other men in Scripture who also had questions they asked God. In the Book of Habakkuk, we find that Habakkuk had a lot of questions. In fact, his book is just a great big "WHY?". Jonah also had some questions to ask the Lord. My friend, such questions are not a revelation of a lack of faith, but it is hypocrisy to pretend that we have accepted God's ways and are walking in complete submission to Him when actually we

are having questions deep inside. I believe that God wants us to be completely honest with Him above everything else. And this is His promise to us: "Call unto me, and I will answer thee, and shew thee great and mighty things, which thou knowest not."

Now God is going to reaffirm the covenant He made with David in 2 Samuel 7. He made a covenant with David that there would be one to sit on his throne forever. This covenant became the theme song of every prophet, so much so that they all sound like a stuck record. They all refer back to this covenant and rest upon it. Listen to Jeremiah:

**Behold, the days come, saith the Lord, that I will perform that good thing which I have promised unto the house of Israel and to the house of Judah.**

**In those days, and at that time, will I cause the Branch of righteousness to grow up unto David; and he shall execute judgment and righteousness in the land [Jer. 33:14–15].**

"In those days" refers to the day which is coming, the Day of the Lord.

"The Branch of righteousness to grow up unto David." There hasn't been a righteous branch so far except One, the One who was born in Bethlehem.

"He shall execute judgment and righteousness in the land." We haven't had any ruler like that yet.

**In those days shall Judah be saved, and Jerusalem shall dwell safely: and this is the name wherewith she shall be called, The Lord our righteousness [Jer. 33:16].**

"The Lord our righteousness" in the Hebrew is *Jehovah-tsidkenu*. If you and I have any righteousness it is in Jesus Christ. *He* is our righteousness.

**For thus saith the Lord; David shall never want a man to sit upon the throne of the house of Israel [Jer. 33:17].**

Where do you think this man is today? There is not an Israelite on topside of the earth who can make the claim to David's throne. The One who has that claim is sitting at God's right hand as the psalmist explained: "The Lord said unto my Lord, Sit thou at my right hand, until I make thine enemies thy footstool" (Ps. 110:1). God is busy calling out a people to His name, getting things ready to put His Son on the throne of this universe.

**And the word of the Lord came unto Jeremiah, saying,**

**Thus saith the Lord; If ye can break my covenant of the day, and my covenant of the night, and that there should not be day and night in their season;**

**Then may also my covenant be broken with David my servant, that he should not have a son to reign upon his throne; and with the Levites the priests, my ministers.**

**As the host of heaven cannot be numbered, neither the sand of the sea measured: so will I multiply the seed of David my servant, and the Levites that minister unto me [Jer. 33:19–22].**

At the time this prophecy was given, Zedekiah was on the throne of Judah. He was as corrupt as any man ever was. Nebuchadnezzar will put out his eyes and carry him into captivity. You would think that this would put an end to the line of David. It would end the line of any other nation, I can assure you. There is no one around to claim the throne of the king of Babylon. There is no one to take Alexander the Great's place. There is no Pharaoh in Egypt today. But there is One in David's line who can claim his throne. God says that He intends to put Him on the throne of this universe someday. This is a great prophecy and one which is very difficult to ignore or to spiritualize. I think God means exactly what He says.

**THEME:** *Zedekiah's captivity foretold; Rechabites obey God and Jehoiakim destroys Word of God*

The word which came unto Jeremiah from the Lord, when Nebuchadnezzar king of Babylon, and all his army, and all the kingdoms of the earth of his dominion, and all the people, fought against Jerusalem, and against all the cities thereof, saying,

Thus saith the Lord, the God of Israel; Go and speak to Zedekiah king of Judah, and tell him, Thus saith the Lord; Behold, I will give this city into the hand of the king of Babylon, and he shall burn it with fire:

And thou shalt not escape out of his hand, but shalt surely be taken, and delivered into his hand; and thine eyes shall behold the eyes of the king of Babylon, and he shall speak with thee mouth to mouth, and thou shalt go to Babylon.

Yet hear the word of the Lord, O Zedekiah king of Judah; Thus saith the Lord of thee, Thou shalt not die by the sword:

But thou shalt die in peace: and with the burnings of thy fathers, the former kings which were before thee, so shall they burn odours for thee; and they will lament thee, saying, Ah lord! for I have pronounced the word, saith the Lord [Jer. 34:1–5].

Jeremiah is to prophesy that the city of Jerusalem is to be burned with fire by the king of Babylon and that Zedekiah himself will be taken captive.

This is the word that came unto Jeremiah from the Lord, after that the king Zedekiah had made a covenant with all the people which were at Jerusalem, to proclaim liberty unto them;

That every man should let his manservant, and every man his maidservant, being an Hebrew or an Hebrewess, go free; that none should serve himself of them, to wit, of a Jew his brother [Jer. 34:8–9].

Zedekiah made an agreement with the people that all the Hebrew servants should be set free.

And ye were now turned, and had done right in my sight, in proclaiming liberty every man to his neighbour; and ye had made a covenant before me in the house which is called by my name:

But ye turned and polluted my name, and caused every man his servant, and every man his handmaid, whom ye had set at liberty at their pleasure, to return, and brought them into subjection, to be unto you for servants and for handmaids [Jer. 34:15–16].

The Lord said that the covenant was "right in my sight" (see Exod. 21:2).

But Zedekiah did not make good on his covenant, and the Lord said of him, "ye turned and polluted my name." In other words, Zedekiah profaned the name of God. By truly granting liberty to the people, Zedekiah, as king of Judah, could have demonstrated to the world that he was different, that he served the living and true God. But it was just a pretense; he didn't make good on his promise. He not only brought himself into disrepute, but he profaned the name of God.

It is the *life* of the child of God that the world will always look at. God's name and the furtherance of His Word is hurt more by those who profess to know Him than by all the godless professors in our colleges today. The lives of those who name the name of Christ can hurt His cause more than those who are unbelieving. God says, "You have polluted My name; you have profaned My name."

The princes of Judah, and the princes of Jerusalem, the eunuchs, and the priests, and all the people of the land, which passed between the parts of the calf;

I will even give them into the hand of their enemies, and into the hand of them that seek their life: and their dead bodies shall be for meat unto the fowls of the heaven, and to the beasts of the earth.

And Zedekiah king of Judah and his princes will I give into the hand of their enemies, and into the hand of them that seek their life, and into the hand of the king of Babylon's army, which are gone up from you [Jer. 34:19–21].

"Which passed between the parts of the calf." This is the way men made a covenant or a contract in that day. They took a sacrifice and cut it in half, putting half of the animal on one side and half on the other. The men then went between and joined hands. This is also the way God made His covenant with Abraham. It is like going to the notary public in our day. Zedekiah, the princes, the priests, and the people had all violated God's covenant in not granting liberty to the servants, and therefore God pronounces this judgment upon them.

In chapter 35 we find the Rechabites who are part of the believing remnant, and they are in sharp contrast to the nation as a whole. God has given us this account to remind us that there has always been a remnant—He will never leave the world without a witness to Himself. Even in the darkest time in history the world will ever know—the Great Tribulation Period which is yet future, when the 144,000 will have been forced underground—there will still be two witnesses who are going to stand for God. That is just the way God is going to have it. Even at the time when Satan is being allowed to run the whole show, God says, "I will keep two witnesses around, and they will be inviolate—you won't be able to touch them—until their mission has been accomplished."

**The word which came unto Jeremiah from the Lord in the days of Jehoiakim the son of Josiah king of Judah, saying,**

**Go unto the house of the Rechabites, and speak unto them, and bring them into the house of the Lord, into one of the chambers, and give them wine to drink [Jer. 35:1–2].**

The Lord tells Jeremiah to bring the Rechabites to the house of the Lord and give them wine to drink.

**And I set before the sons of the house of the Rechabites pots full of wine, and cups, and I said unto them, Drink ye wine.**

**But they said, We will drink no wine: for Jonadab the son of Rechab our father commanded us, saying, Ye shall drink no wine, neither ye, nor your sons for ever [Jer. 35:5–6].**

On the basis of a command that had been given to their family many years before, the Rechabites refuse the wine that Jeremiah gives to them.

**Thus saith the Lord of hosts, the God of Israel; Go and tell the men of Judah and the inhabitants of Jerusalem, Will ye not receive instruction to hearken to my words? saith the Lord.**

**The words of Jonadab the son of Rechab, that he commanded his sons not to drink wine, are performed; for unto this day they drink none, but obey their father's commandment: notwithstanding I have spoken unto you, rising early and speaking; but ye hearkened not unto me.**

**I have sent also unto you all my servants the prophets, rising up early and sending them, saying, Return ye now every man from his evil way, and amend your doings, and go not after other gods to serve them, and ye shall dwell in the land which I have given to you and to your fathers: but ye have not inclined your ear, nor hearkened unto me [Jer. 35:13–15].**

God draws this sharp contrast between the Rechabites who faithfully obey the commands of their earthly father and the children of Judah who have failed to hearken to the commands of their loving heavenly Father. In the remainder of the chapter He goes on to pronounce judgment on the people of Judah and blessing upon the Rechabites.

Chapter 36 reveals the attitude which Jehoiakim had toward the Word of God and the messages God sent to him through His prophet, Jeremiah.

**And it came to pass in the fourth year of Jehoiakim the son of Josiah king of Judah, that this word came unto Jeremiah from the Lord, saying,**

**Take thee a roll of a book, and write therein all the words that I have spoken unto thee against Israel, and against Judah, and against all the nations, from the day I spake unto thee, from the days of Josiah, even unto this day [Jer. 36:1–2].**

God told Jeremiah to record all His words in a book; so Jeremiah dictated all of God's words to Baruch who wrote them down for him. Then Jeremiah commanded Baruch to take the roll into the house of the Lord and read it in the hearing of all the people. When the princes heard what had taken place, they sent for Baruch and had him read the roll in their presence.

Then said the princes unto Baruch, Go, hide thee, thou and Jeremiah; and let no man know where ye be.

And they went in to the king into the court, but they laid up the roll in the chamber of Elishama the scribe, and told all the words in the ears of the king.

So the king sent Jehudi to fetch the roll: and he took it out of Elishama the scribe's chamber. And Jehudi read it in the ears of the king, and in the ears of all the princes which stood beside the king.

Now the king sat in the winterhouse in the ninth month: and there was a fire on the hearth burning before him.

And it came to pass, that when Jehudi had read three or four leaves, he cut it with the penknife, and cast it into the fire that was on the hearth, until all the roll was consumed in the fire that was on the hearth [Jer. 36:19–23].

That shows you what Jehoiakim thought of the Word of God: he took it and just flung it into the fire! He didn't care for it. He didn't accept it. He didn't believe it.

I am not impressed that the Bible is still the best seller of all books. Who is actually *reading* the Bible today? Ignoring the Bible is really no different from throwing it into the fire as Jehoiakim did. Here is a sad little jingle that someone sent to me that illustrates the condition in our country today:

"Maw, I found an old, dusty thing high upon the shelf. Just look!"

"Why, that's a Bible, Tommy dear, be careful. That's God's Book."

"God's Book?" the young one said, "Then, Maw, before we lose it

We'd better send it back to God, 'cause you know we never use it."

Yet they were not afraid, nor rent their garments, neither the king, nor any of his servants that heard all these words [Jer. 36:24].

There was no fear or remorse because of what they had done.

If you think God is going to stop here because Jehoiakim has destroyed His Word, you are wrong.

Take thee again another roll, and write in it all the former words that were in the first roll, which Jehoiakim the king of Judah hath burned [Jer. 36:28].

God tells Jeremiah to write it all over again and to send a message to Jehoiakim:

Therefore thus saith the LORD of Jehoiakim king of Judah; He shall have none to sit upon the throne of David: and his dead body shall be cast out in the day to the heat, and in the night to the frost [Jer. 36:30].

This is exactly what happened to Jehoiakim. He has no one to sit upon the throne of David today. The Lord Jesus who does have claim to that throne did not come in his line. Mary was born in the line of Nathan, another son of David, and it is through her that the Lord Jesus has blood title to the throne of David. No one in the line of Jehoiakim will ever sit on that throne.

# CHAPTERS 37–39

**THEME:** *Word of God destroyed; Jeremiah imprisoned but then released; Judah begins captivity*

We move now into a new section of the book which places the emphasis on the historical events. Jeremiah could be saying, "I told you so," but he is too much involved. He is crushed and broken by the message which he has had to give to the people and now by its fulfillment as the city that he loves is destroyed and the nation he loves goes into captivity. Jeremiah has been faithful in revealing God and acting as His witness. If you want to know how God feels about all that is taking place, look into the face of Jeremiah with the tears streaming down his cheeks.

Over thirty years of ministry have gone by for Jeremiah. We saw him start as a young man of about twenty years of age, a young priest who was called to be a prophet of God. Now he is in prison, and the army of the king of Babylon is outside the walls of Jerusalem. They have been there for a long siege of eigh-

teen months duration. Jeremiah gives some of this history in chapter 52, and more is recorded in 2 Kings and in 2 Chronicles.

This is now the third and final time that Nebuchadnezzar has come down against Jerusalem. The other two times he had taken a certain number of the people captive and had placed Zedekiah on the throne as his vassal. Zedekiah wanted to get out from under the king of Babylon, so he made an overture to Pharaoh of Egypt. Pharaoh decided to come up to try to relieve Zedekiah. Of course, what he planned to do was to put Judah under the rule of Egypt. When Pharaoh came up to Jerusalem, the commanders of Nebuchadnezzar turned aside, and instead of besieging the city they withdrew. At this point it looked as if the prophecies of Jeremiah might be wrong. So God gave to Jeremiah this very strong word:

Thus saith the Lord, the God of Israel; Thus shall ye say to the king of Judah, that sent you unto me to inquire of me; Behold, Pharaoh's army, which is come forth to help you, shall return to Egypt into their own land.

And the Chaldeans shall come again, and fight against this city, and take it, and burn it with fire.

Thus saith the Lord; Deceive not yourselves, saying, The Chaldeans shall surely depart from us: for they shall not depart.

For though ye had smitten the whole army of the Chaldeans that fight against you, and there remained but wounded men among them, yet should they rise up every man in his tent, and burn this city with fire [Jer. 37:7–10].

The destruction of Jerusalem was determined by God. Even though it looked as if Babylon's armies had been frightened away, they would be back.

There are five recorded imprisonments of the prophet. The imprisonment described in this chapter was due to the fact that Jeremiah had said to the king that he was not to make an alliance with Pharaoh but was to surrender to Babylon.

And it came to pass, that when the army of the Chaldeans was broken up from Jerusalem for fear of Pharaoh's army,

Then Jeremiah went forth out of Jerusalem to go into the land of Benjamin,

to separate himself thence in the midst of the people [Jer. 37:11–12].

While the city is being relieved, Jeremiah comes out of Jerusalem to go up to his hometown of Anathoth. Now notice what happens—

And when he was in the gate of Benjamin, a captain of the ward was there, whose name was Irijah, the son of Shelemiah, the son of Hananiah; and he took Jeremiah the prophet, saying, Thou fallest away to the Chaldeans [Jer. 37:13].

He made the accusation against Jeremiah that he was going over to the enemy.

Then said Jeremiah, It is false; I fall not away to the Chaldeans. But he hearkened not to him: so Irijah took Jeremiah, and brought him to the princes.

Wherefore the princes were wroth with Jeremiah, and smote him, and put him in prison in the house of Jonathan the scribe: for they had made that the prison [Jer. 37:14–15].

Poor Jeremiah was not only put in prison, but he was put in the dungeon—for how long, we are not told. The next verse says only that it was for "many days." This was a time of great suffering for Jeremiah, but God had not forgotten. He moved the king to call for him.

Then Zedekiah the king sent, and took him out: and the king asked him secretly in his house, and said, Is there any word from the Lord? And Jeremiah said, There is: for, said he, thou shalt be delivered into the hand of the king of Babylon [Jer. 37:17].

Then Jeremiah takes this occasion to plead for his life:

Therefore hear now, I pray thee, O my lord the king: let my supplication, I pray thee, be accepted before thee; that thou cause me not to return to the house of Jonathan the scribe, lest I die there [Jer. 37:20].

The king didn't release him, but at least he saved his life.

Then Zedekiah the king commanded that they should commit Jeremiah into the court of the prison, and that they should give him daily a piece of bread

out of the bakers' street, until all the bread in the city were spent. Thus Jeremiah remained in the court of the prison [Jer. 37:21].

Jeremiah will remain in prison now until the armies of Babylon take the city of Jerusalem.

## JEREMIAH NARROWLY ESCAPES DEATH

When we come to chapter 38, Jeremiah is still confined to the court of the prison, and he faithfully relays God's Word to his people even though his personal safety is endangered.

The princes of Judah consider him a traitor to his country and a demoralizing influence among the people; so they get permission from the king to silence Jeremiah by putting him in the dungeon.

Then took they Jeremiah, and cast him into the dungeon of Malchiah the son of Hammelech, that was in the court of the prison: and they let down Jeremiah with cords. And in the dungeon there was no water, but mire: so Jeremiah sunk in the mire [Jer. 38:6].

Again God sent someone to his rescue (vv. 7–13). This is a thrilling rescue—I hope you will read the text carefully. After this, Zedekiah the king secretly asked Jeremiah to tell him what the Lord was saying to him now. And he promised to save Jeremiah from those who were seeking his life.

Then said Jeremiah unto Zedekiah, Thus saith the Lord, the God of hosts, the God of Israel; If thou wilt assuredly go forth unto the king of Babylon's princes, then thy soul shall live, and this city shall not be burned with fire; and thou shalt live, and thine house [Jer. 38:17].

Again he said, "Surrender! You can't resist this man."

But if thou wilt not go forth to the king of Babylon's princes, then shall this city be given into the hand of the Chaldeans, and they shall burn it with fire, and thou shalt not escape out of their hand.

And Zedekiah the king said unto Jeremiah, I am afraid of the Jews that are fallen to the Chaldeans, lest they deliver me into their hand, and they mock me.

But Jeremiah said, They shall not deliver thee. Obey, I beseech thee, the voice of the Lord, which I speak unto thee: so it shall be well unto thee, and thy soul shall live [Jer. 38:18–20].

Jeremiah is pleading with Zedekiah to surrender to save his own life and the life of his people. His refusal to follow the course of action which Jeremiah presents will doom his nation.

Zedekiah is a coward at heart. He tries to make peace with everybody and to please everybody. He is a typical politician. As a result, he pleases nobody.

But if thou refuse to go forth, this is the word that the Lord hath shewed me:

And, behold, all the women that are left in the king of Judah's house shall be brought forth to the king of Babylon's princes, and those women shall say, Thy friends have set thee on, and have prevailed against thee: thy feet are sunk in the mire, and they are turned away back [Jer. 38:21–22].

A study of this period of Judah's history reveals that womanhood was pretty much corrupt. When womanhood becomes corrupt in any nation, there is very little hope for it on the moral plane. This is the picture here.

The foolish king will not heed the warning of God through Jeremiah. Instead he will continue to listen to the optimistic forecast of the false prophets.

In chapter 39 the awful carnage that Jeremiah had been predicting takes place.

In the ninth year of Zedekiah king of Judah, in the tenth month, came Nebuchadrezzar king of Babylon and all his army against Jerusalem, and they besieged it.

And in the eleventh year of Zedekiah, in the fourth month, the ninth day of the month, the city was broken up [Jer. 39:1–2].

In the following verses we see the fall of Jerusalem. King Zedekiah and the army attempt to escape from the city by night, but the army of Babylon overtakes them and delivers them to Nebuchadnezzar their king.

Then the king of Babylon slew the sons of Zedekiah in Riblah before his eyes: also the king of Babylon slew all the nobles of Judah.

**Moreover he put out Zedekiah's eyes, and bound him with chains, to carry him to Babylon [Jer. 39:6–7].**

The last chapter of the Book of Jeremiah gives a view of this horrible time in retrospect. It mentions the things that evidently were impressed upon the mind of Jeremiah. There he mentions again the fact that the king of Babylon killed the sons of Zedekiah before his eyes, then blinded Zedekiah.

## JEREMIAH RELEASED BY THE ENEMY

It is interesting to note that Nebuchadnezzar instructed his men to release Jeremiah from prison and to treat him well.

**Take him, and look well to him, and do him no harm; but do unto him even as he shall say unto thee [Jer. 39:12].**

God was still taking care of His faithful prophet.

**Even they sent, and took Jeremiah out of the court of the prison, and committed him unto Gedaliah the son of Ahikam the son of Shaphan, that he should carry him home: so he dwelt among the people [Jer. 39:14].**

This begins that period which our Lord called "the times of the Gentiles." He said, ". . . and Jerusalem shall be trodden down of the Gentiles, until the times of the Gentiles be fulfilled" (Luke 21:24). I insist that Gentiles are still trodding down Jerusalem. The Gentiles are still actually in control, and Israel doesn't really control the holy places in that land—except the Wailing Wall where they can go and weep. The words of the Lord Jesus are still true.

It is difficult for our contemporary generation to accept the fact of the judgment of God—that the judgment of God can come upon a nation, upon a family, upon an individual. Jeremiah had proclaimed the Word of Jehovah for forty years. He had denounced the sins of the people and had called these people to repentance. God had been very patient with them, and His very patience had deceived them. It enabled the false prophets to say, "See, the words of Jeremiah have not come to pass." But now his words have come to pass, and it is too late. God is patient with people and will let them go on and on until there comes a time when there is no remedy.

Judah is an outstanding example of this. God pleaded with them through Jeremiah right up to the last moment. They spurned God, and the day finally came when Nebuchadnezzar leveled the city.

Humanity—all of mankind—does not like to hear that God is going to judge. It is hard for people to believe that God ever gets angry. Some folks try to say that it is the God of the Old Testament who is a God of wrath, that the New Testament gives a different picture of God. May I say to you there is more said about divine wrath and anger in the New Testament than there is in the Old. Read Matthew 23 and listen to the frightful things said by the gentle Jesus: "Woe unto you, scribes and Pharisees, hypocrites. . . . Ye serpents, ye generation of vipers, how can ye escape the damnation of hell?" (Matt. 23:29,33). Then read the Book of Revelation where the bowls of the wrath of God are poured out. There is nothing to equal that in the Old Testament. Don't try to say that the God of the Old Testament is a God of wrath and the God of the New Testament is a God of love. I tell you that He is always in every age both the God of love and the God of wrath. God punishes sin. You will always find divine judgment and divine mercy side by side. The throne of God is a throne of grace, a place to find mercy and help, but that very same throne will judge this earth some day. Man today finds this very difficult to understand.

God's laws are inexorable, and judgment is the penalty for disobedience of those laws. It seems so difficult for men to understand this in the moral and spiritual sphere when it is perfectly obvious in the natural sphere. If you don't believe that is true, I suggest you go to Yosemite Valley where there is a sheer surface of a rock several thousand feet high called El Capitan. If you step off El Capitan, you know what will happen. In nature there are certain laws that are inexorable. If you obey them, you may live; if you disobey them, you will die.

We think it is such a wonderful feat for men to walk on the moon, and it is. But do you realize that it was possible only because those men were *obeying* all the natural laws of God? They didn't *dare* break them. When they started for the moon, they didn't aim for the moon; they aimed for the position the moon would be in when they would arrive there. They knew exactly where it would be at the time of their arrival because the movements of this universe are governed by laws. If those

fellows had ignored those laws of space and movement, they would have been lost out there in space and would be dead.

Human history should teach us the same lesson. All we need to do is walk down through the corridor of time and look at the debris and the ashes and the wreckage of the great civilizations of this world. They testify that God is a God of vengeance, a God of punishment, a God of judgment. When nations turned from high ideals and lofty moral planes to base ideals, they went down and passed off the stage of human history. It is about time for the intellectuals in this country to begin to read history correctly and to see that God moves in human history.

Now I admit that I feel like a square for saying this, but I don't feel bad about it because Jeremiah was also a square in his day. From our perspective in the twentieth century we can see that the king, old Zedekiah, was *pigheaded*! And the intellectuals, the sophisticates, the ones who had ruled God out, were *stupid*! So I don't mind being called an intellectual obscurantist, because I find that I am in very good company. I am going to be like Jeremiah was—just a man who believes God.

# CHAPTERS 40–42

**THEME:** *Jeremiah prophesies to remnant left in land*

In these three chapters we find Jeremiah speaking to those who were left in the land of Judah after the destruction of Jerusalem. They were the very poor, the blind, the crippled, the lame, and another group which would be called the criminal element, a hard group of people. Jeremiah chose to stay with the people in the land. He had a message for them.

### JEREMIAH RELEASED

**The word that came to Jeremiah from the LORD, after that Nebuzaradan the captain of the guard had let him go from Ramah, when he had taken him being bound in chains among all that were carried away captive of Jerusalem and Judah, which were carried away captive unto Babylon.**

**And the captain of the guard took Jeremiah, and said unto him, The LORD thy God hath pronounced this evil upon this place.**

**Now the LORD hath brought it, and done according as he hath said: because ye have sinned against the LORD, and have not obeyed his voice, therefore this thing is come upon you.**

**And now, behold, I loose thee this day from the chains which were upon thine hand. If it seem good unto thee to come with me into Babylon, come; and I will look well unto thee: but if it seem ill unto thee to come with me into Babylon, forbear: behold, all the land is before thee: whither it seemeth good and convenient for thee to go, thither go [Jer. 40:1–4].**

Nebuchadnezzar permitted Jeremiah to do what he wished to do. He could have gone with the captives to Babylon, but, interestingly enough, Jeremiah did not want to do that. I think he would have been given special privileges if he had gone, but Jeremiah couldn't bear to see his brethren suffer as they did there by the canals of Babylon where they sat down and hung up their harps and wept when they remembered Zion. Jeremiah did not want to go with them. They had rejected his message, and they had rejected him. In Babylon God would raise up another prophet, Ezekiel, who would speak to them. Jeremiah chose to remain in Judah with the poor remnant which were left there.

Who really loved that land? Jeremiah. Who was the real patriot? Jeremiah. Who really had the best interests of the people at heart? It was Jeremiah. This is quite obvious now.

You will remember that Jeremiah had urged them to surrender to Nebuchadnezzar. I believe that if they had obeyed God and gone willingly, they would not have gone into captivity. They probably would have received the kind of treatment that Jeremiah received from Nebuchadnezzar, and they probably would have been permitted to stay in the land.

Now in verse 8 we are introduced to Ishmael who plots to murder Gedaliah whom

Nebuchadnezzar had made governor over the cities of Judah.

## GEDALIAH MURDERED

In chapter 41 we have the bloody record of the slaying of Gedaliah with the Chaldeans and Jews who were with him. Then Ishmael captures the people of the city (Mizpah), intending to take them to the land of the Ammonites. They are overtaken by Johanan. Then Johanan, fearing the reprisal of the king of Babylon because his governor Gedaliah had been killed, plans to escape with the whole remnant of the people to Egypt.

## JEREMIAH CONSULTED

In chapter 42 we see that before leaving for Egypt Johanan and all the captains come to Jeremiah. It is interesting that the people turned to Jeremiah under these strange circumstances. They needed to know what to do. Should they stay in the land or leave the land? Where should they go?

**Then all the captains of the forces, and Johanan the son of Kareah, and Jezaniah the son of Hoshaiah, and all the people from the least even unto the greatest, came near,**

**And said unto Jeremiah the prophet, Let, we beseech thee, our supplication be accepted before thee, and pray for us unto the Lord thy God, even for all this remnant; (for we are left but a few of many, as thine eyes do behold us:)**

**That the Lord thy God may shew us the way wherein we may walk, and the thing that we may do [Jer. 42:1–3].**

This sounds very nice, doesn't it? You would think that these people would actually walk with God now. They promised to obey the voice of the Lord.

**Then Jeremiah the prophet said unto them, I have heard you; behold, I will pray unto the Lord your God according to your words; and it shall come to pass, that whatsoever thing the Lord shall answer you, I will declare it unto you; I will keep nothing back from you [Jer. 42:4].**

They came to Jeremiah, and they knew that they could depend upon Jeremiah to speak the truth.

Any person who is attempting to speak for God, no matter whether his medium be the pulpit, radio, or even a soapbox, should lay aside all attempts at being clever and subtle. He should give forth the Word of God with no attempt at being sophisticated and saying smooth words to please the people. When the pulpit majors in positive thinking and ignores the negatives, it becomes weak and is only a sounding board just to say back to the people what they want to hear. Paul wrote to Timothy, "For the time will come when they will not endure sound doctrine; but after their own lusts shall they heap to themselves teachers, having itching ears; And they shall turn away their ears from the truth, and shall be turned unto fables" (2 Tim. 4:3–4). Unfortunately, I think that is much of what the modern pulpit is today. That is the reason it has become extremely weak and has no message for this hour in which we live. When the pulpit can give out God's Word as Jeremiah did, with nothing being held back, letting it say what God means for it to say, then the Word of God will become effective again in our day.

Now Jeremiah is going to tell the remnant exactly what God says they are to do—

**And said unto them, Thus saith the Lord, the God of Israel, unto whom ye sent me to present your supplication before him;**

**If ye will still abide in this land, then will I build you, and not pull you down, and I will plant you, and not pluck you up: for I repent me of the evil that I have done unto you [Jer. 42: 9–10].**

God assures them that He will not continue to judge them if they will obey Him. After all, God wants to bless; judgment is His *strange* work.

**Be not afraid of the king of Babylon, of whom ye are afraid; be not afraid of him, saith the Lord: for I am with you to save you, and to deliver you from his hand.**

**And I will shew mercies unto you, that he may have mercy upon you, and cause you to return to your own land [Jer. 42:11–12].**

Jeremiah delivers the Word as the Lord gave it to him. It was a good word, an encouraging word. You would think by now they would know that Jeremiah spoke God's Word, because it had been proven true. You would think they would believe God, but God knows they won't. He adds this warning—

For thus saith the LORD of hosts, the God of Israel; As mine anger and my fury hath been poured forth upon the inhabitants of Jerusalem; so shall my fury be poured forth upon you, when ye shall enter into Egypt: and ye shall be an execration, and an astonishment, and a curse, and a reproach; and ye shall see this place no more.

The LORD hath said concerning you, O ye remnant of Judah; Go ye not into Egypt: know certainly that I have admonished you this day.

For ye dissembled in your hearts, when ye sent me unto the LORD your God, saying, Pray for us unto the LORD our God; and according unto all that the LORD our God shall say, so declare unto us, and we will do it [Jer. 42:18–20].

Experience has taught them nothing. They still will not obey God. They will not hear the message from Jeremiah. God has told them not to go down into Egypt. So where will they go? They go to Egypt.

# CHAPTERS 43–44

### THEME: *Prophecies to remnant in Egypt*

We have come now to the sixth and last section of prophecy of the book. This contains prophecies during Jeremiah's last days in Egypt and extends from chapters 43 to 51. Chapters 43 and 44 contain his words to the remnant in Egypt.

## JEREMIAH'S MESSAGE REJECTED

And it came to pass, that when Jeremiah had made an end of speaking unto all the people all the words of the LORD their God, for which the LORD their God had sent him to them, even all these words,

Then spake Azariah the son of Hoshaiah, and Johanan the son of Kareah, and all the proud men, saying unto Jeremiah, Thou speakest falsely: the LORD our God hath not sent thee to say, Go not into Egypt to sojourn there:

But Baruch the son of Neriah setteth thee on against us, for to deliver us into the hand of the Chaldeans, that they might put us to death, and carry us away captives into Babylon [Jer. 43:1–3].

These people go through the same routine again. They say that God hadn't really told Jeremiah to say that. The problem is that he is not saying what they want him to say. They had hoped he would tell them to go to Egypt. Instead, God tells them not to go into Egypt.

But Johanan the son of Kareah, and all the captains of the forces, took all the remnant of Judah, that were returned from all nations, whither they had been driven, to dwell in the land of Judah;

Even men, and women, and children, and the king's daughters, and every person that Nebuzaradan the captain of the guard had left with Gedaliah the son of Ahikam the son of Shaphan, and Jeremiah the prophet, and Baruch the son of Neriah.

So they came into the land of Egypt: for they obeyed not the voice of the LORD: thus came they even to Tahpanhes [Jer. 43:5–7].

Johanan and the captains forced the remnant into Egypt, including the prophet Jeremiah. So they return to Tahpanhes, a place near where they had begun as a nation in the land of Goshen in Egypt. They forced Jeremiah to go with them against his will, but he still is speaking to them.

## JEREMIAH'S WARNING TO THE REMNANT IN EGYPT

Then came the word of the LORD unto Jeremiah in Tahpanhes, saying,

Take great stones in thine hand, and hide them in the clay in the brickkiln, which is at the entry of Pharaoh's house in Tahpanhes, in the sight of the men of Judah [Jer. 43:8–9].

They are back down in the brickyards of Egypt. We can see that disobedience to God does not help them to advance—they are right back where they started.

And say unto them, Thus saith the LORD of hosts, the God of Israel; Behold, I will send and take Nebuchadrezzar, the king of Babylon, my servant, and will set his throne upon these stones that I have hid; and he shall spread his royal pavilion over them.

And when he cometh, he shall smite the land of Egypt, and deliver such as are for death to death; and such as are for captivity to captivity; and such as are for the sword to the sword [Jer. 43:10–11].

They ran off to the land of Egypt to escape from Nebuchadnezzar, but God is going to permit Nebuchadnezzar to take the land of Egypt. They are worse off than if they had obeyed God and stayed in the land. They will be right back under Nebuchadnezzar; but now they are out of the land, and Nebuchadnezzar will put them into slavery.

## THE REMNANT IN EGYPT REJECTS GOD

Chapter 44 records the absolute refusal of the remnant in Egypt to obey God.

Again God patiently explains that He is the One responsible for the invasion and desolation of Judah.

Thus saith the LORD of hosts, the God of Israel; Ye have seen all the evil that I have brought upon Jerusalem, and upon all the cities of Judah; and, behold, this day they are a desolation, and no man dwelleth therein,

Because of their wickedness which they have committed to provoke me to anger, in that they went to burn incense, and to serve other gods, whom they

knew not, neither they, ye, nor your fathers [Jer. 44:2–3].

Again God gives the reason for His punishment.

Therefore now thus saith the LORD, the God of hosts, the God of Israel; Wherefore commit ye this great evil against your souls, to cut off from you man and woman, child and suckling, out of Judah, to leave you none to remain;

In that ye provoke me unto wrath with the works of your hands, burning incense unto other gods in the land of Egypt, whither ye be gone to dwell, that ye might cut yourselves off, and that ye might be a curse and a reproach among all the nations of the earth? [Jer. 44:7–8].

What a revelation of God's love! He still pleads with them to return to Him.

Their insolent reply is an example of the utter depravity of the human heart.

As for the word that thou hast spoken unto us in the name of the LORD, we will not hearken unto thee.

But we will certainly do whatsoever thing goeth forth out of our own mouth, to burn incense unto the queen of heaven, and to pour out drink offerings unto her, as we have done, we, and our fathers, our kings, and our princes, in the cities of Judah, and in the streets of Jerusalem: for then had we plenty of victuals, and were well, and saw no evil [Jer. 44:16–17].

There is nothing left for them now but judgment.

# CHAPTER 45

**THEME:** *Prophecy to Baruch*

**B**aruch was a friend who acted as sort of an assistant to Jeremiah. He was the one who wrote the words of Jeremiah on the scroll which was sent to King Jehoiakim, and the king cut the scroll with a knife and pitched it into the fire (ch. 36). When Jeremiah was in prison and bought the property in Anathoth, Baruch carried out the transaction for him. He had the papers signed and carried through with all the necessary work for the purchase of the land (ch. 32). Finally, Baruch was taken down into Egypt with Jeremiah according to chapter 43:6.

The prophecy to Baruch which we have here in chapter 45 was actually given during the reign of Jehoiakim. That is the reason we said at the beginning of the book that although there is a certain semblance of chronological order in the Book of Jeremiah, it is not arranged chronologically. Although the prophecy was given back during the reign of Jehoiakim, it is recorded here, and I think there is a reason for that. I believe it is recorded here as an encouragement to Baruch. The Lord had already revealed to him what would happen to him if he identified himself with Jeremiah the prophet. This should be an encouragement to him when he was forced to go to Egypt with the remnant of Judah.

**Thus saith the Lord, the God of Israel, unto thee, O Baruch;**

**Thou didst say, Woe is me now! for the Lord hath added grief to my sorrow; I fainted in my sighing, and I find no rest [Jer. 45:2–3].**

Things were pretty bad during the reign of Jehoiakim, but that was nothing compared with what was going to follow. The really bad time would occur after the era of Jehoiakim.

**Thus shalt thou say unto him, The Lord saith thus; Behold, that which I have built will I break down, and that which I have planted I will pluck up, even this whole land [Jer. 45:4].**

Even though things were going to get very much worse, God wanted Baruch to know that He was the One who was responsible for it. God assumed responsibility for what would happen to the land of Judah; therefore, Baruch could go along with the program.

**And seekest thou great things for thyself? seek them not: for, behold, I will bring evil upon all flesh, saith the Lord: but thy life will I give unto thee for a prey in all places whither thou goest [Jer. 45:5].**

This prophecy was given to Baruch when he was still a young man. God told him that he couldn't expect to arrive at some high goal for himself at this tragic time in the history of the nation. He would live through very troubled times, but he would come through it with his life because God would preserve him. Now Jeremiah and Baruch, his friend and associate, are old men in Egypt. They have seen how God did preserve them through the troubled times in which they lived.

# CHAPTERS 46–48

**THEME:** *Prophecy to Egypt, Philistia, and Moab*

**J**eremiah is in Egypt, having been taken there against his will by the remnant who disobeyed God and went to Egypt. Now Jeremiah gives prophecies to the different nations round about.

God tells them what will happen to Egypt. The remnant which left from Judah went down to Egypt because they thought they would have peace and plenty there. God says, "I have news for you: the war is going to move down to Egypt, and Nebuchadnezzar will take Egypt, too"—which he did.

**They did cry there, Pharaoh king of Egypt is but a noise; he hath passed the time appointed [Jer. 46:17].**

In other words, they can't depend on Pharaoh any longer. Egypt will go down in defeat.

**O thou daughter dwelling in Egypt, furnish thyself to go into captivity: for**

**Noph shall be waste and desolate without an inhabitant [Jer. 46:19].**

The survivors of Judah made a big mistake to put their trust in Pharaoh and in Egypt. They should have put their trust in God. They should have believed and obeyed the Lord. Yet, in spite of all that, Jeremiah includes a wonderful prophecy of comfort to them.

**But fear not thou, O my servant Jacob, and be not dismayed, O Israel: for, behold, I will save thee from afar off, and thy seed from the land of their captivity; and Jacob shall return, and be in rest and at ease, and none shall make him afraid.**

**Fear thou not, O Jacob my servant, saith the LORD: for I am with thee; for I will make a full end of all the nations whither I have driven thee: but I will not make a full end of thee, but correct thee in measure; yet will I not leave thee wholly unpunished [Jer. 46:27–28].**

My friend, after you read these two verses, if you believe the Word of God to be true, you must believe that God is not through with the nation Israel. God tells them He must punish them but that He will not make a full end of them. Here is one of the many answers to the question ". . . Hath God cast away his people? . . ." (Rom. 11:1). If we believe the Word of God, we must let this Word stand and accept it at face value.

Chapter 47 gives the prophecy of Jeremiah against the Philistine country.

This little remnant from Judah began to look from one nation to another. Where should they go? On which nation might they depend? Some of these nations were their enemies. Should they go to them for refuge? The answer is no because the land of the Philistines will be conquered also.

In chapter 48 we see a prophecy against Moab. Moab ceased from being a nation.

**And Moab shall be destroyed from being a people, because he hath magnified himself against the LORD [Jer. 48:42].**

The present-day Hashemite Kingdom of Jordan on the east bank of the Jordan River occupies the same land that the country of Moab and the people of Moab once occupied. Yet God is not through with the people of Moab. I don't know where they are today; I doubt whether anyone could locate them. But God is able to locate them—

**Yet will I bring again the captivity of Moab in the latter days, saith the LORD. Thus far is the judgment of Moab [Jer. 48:47].**

God will bring again the captivity of Moab in the latter days. Evidently Moab will enter the Millennium. However, at the time of Jeremiah, there was no use for the people to flee to Moab. They wouldn't be safe there either.

# CHAPTER 49

*THEME: Prophecies to nations surrounding Israel*

We have seen that the people who had been left in Judah made the mistake of going down into Egypt. They went there in disobedience to God, and they went out of the frying pan into the fire. The war was over in the land of Israel. No enemy would want to come in to take that land now. The cities had been absolutely run over, burned, left with nothing but debris. Only the ashes of a former civilization were left there. The remnant should have stayed. They could have built up their land, but instead they ran off to Egypt. God knew that Egypt would be the area of the next big campaign of Nebuchadnezzar. When he took Egypt, he would take these people for

the second time. They would be captured again and would suffer again. They thought they were running away from war. They thought they were going to a land where they would have plenty to eat. They thought only of safety and full stomachs.

My friend, when our attitudes and actions and goals are not based on a desire to live for God, when God's truth is no longer our guide, we have sunk to a low level which won't bring peace or plenty. This has been the experience down through the annals of history. History has great lessons to teach us if we will but listen.

This chapter continues God's prophecies

through Jeremiah concerning the judgment which was coming to the nations surrounding Israel.

## PROPHECY TO AMMON

The remnant of Judah need not look to Ammon for shelter, because it will be destroyed. There is no nation of Ammon in our day, but notice what God says—

> **And afterward I will bring again the captivity of the children of Ammon, saith the LORD [Jer. 49:6].**

Ammon is to be restored.

These are remarkable prophecies, remarkable verses of Scripture.

## PROPHECY TO EDOM

There is more space given to the prophecy directed to Edom—probably because Edom was related to Israel. Esau and Jacob were brothers, and the two nations Edom and Israel have come from these two men. Edom and Israel have not been friendly down through the years. Edom had become a great nation, for God had said that He would make a great nation out of Esau.

> **Concerning Edom, thus saith the LORD of hosts; Is wisdom no more in Teman? is counsel perished from the prudent? is their wisdom vanished?**

> **Flee ye, turn back, dwell deep, O inhabitants of Dedan; for I will bring the calamity of Esau upon him, the time that I will visit him [Jer. 49:7–8].**

Edom was in the territory that is south and more to the east of the Dead Sea, an area between the Dead Sea and the Gulf of 'Aqaba. Edom was in for a judgment from God. They had become a great nation and had furnished advisors to other nations. The rock-hewn city of Petra was such a secure place that it acted as a depository for the great nations. Both Babylon and Egypt carried a bank account there. This was a place where they could store their treasures and feel safe about them. The city was hewn out of solid rock on both sides, and there was only one little entrance into this rock-hewn city. It was a tremendous place in its day, but God took away all the greatness which it once enjoyed. Their greatness depended largely on the nations round about them that looked to them because they felt Petra was so secure.

> **For I have sworn by myself, saith the LORD, that Bozrah shall become a desolation, a reproach, a waste, and a curse; and all the cities thereof shall be perpetual wastes [Jer. 49:13].**

Bozrah is Petra and Edom. That rock-hewn city is still there today, completely deserted. It is a ready-made city, and if you are looking for an apartment, I can tell you where you can get one that is rent free. Those rock-hewn apartments are lovely, and you could move into one tomorrow if you wished to do so. It's all there today, and you can have it. No one will come around to collect the rent. No one will try to sell you any of the property. I caution you, however, that you won't stay there very long. People who tried to live there just didn't stay. Some years ago the Germans tried to colonize Petra. The colony that was sent into Petra didn't make a go of it, and before long the people scattered.

> **Thy terribleness hath deceived thee, and the pride of thine heart, O thou that dwellest in the clefts of the rock, that holdest the height of the hill: though thou shouldest make thy nest as high as the eagle, I will bring thee down from thence, saith the LORD [Jer. 49:16].**

The great sin of the Edomites was pride, and for this they were judged. They were in a place that was remarkably protected. The entrance to Petra was through a deep and narrow defile, called the Sik, which was about a mile in length. It was just sort of a cleft in the rock in the valley known as the Wadi Musa. The nation had a history of about one thousand years. Then the Nabataean Arabs took it. The Greeks made two fruitless expeditions against it but found it to be an impregnable city. It was inaccessible for modern men until the airplane. We have had the experience of going into the city of Petra with some of our tours and have found it a remarkable place.

The city was influenced by Babylon, Egypt, Greece, and Rome. One can see it in the architecture and the remnants of their civilization. God judged Edom and brought her down.

Now God says this concerning it, and Ezekiel has a more complete prophecy—

> **Also Edom shall be a desolation: every one that goeth by it shall be astonished, and shall hiss at all the plagues thereof.**

> **As in the overthrow of Sodom and Gomorrah and the neighbour cities thereof, saith the LORD, no man shall**

abide there, neither shall a son of man dwell in it [Jer. 49:17–18].

This is a prophecy which has been literally fulfilled. The city is still there. It cannot be destroyed since it is hewn right into the rocks. God said it would not be inhabited, and it isn't. Every now and then an Arab pitches his tent there for the night, but he's on his way the next day. The Arabs have very superstitious feelings about the city. Although the Germans didn't have superstitious feelings, they couldn't colonize it either. The Word of God says that "neither shall a son of man dwell in it." It is a ready-made city; yet it will not become an abiding place for men.

This is even more remarkable when you place this prophecy beside the prophecy against Tyre. God had said that Tyre would be scraped so that there would be absolutely nothing left of it, but that it would be inhabited after that. Tyre is an inhabited city today. In contrast, Petra is a city that has never been destroyed yet is without an inhabitant.

> Therefore hear the counsel of the LORD, that he hath taken against Edom; and his purposes, that he hath purposed against the inhabitants of Teman: Surely the least of the flock shall draw them out: surely he shall make their habitations desolate with them [Jer. 49:20].

The city has become desolate, and the nation of Edom has disappeared.

## PROPHECY TO DAMASCUS

> Concerning Damascus. Hamath is confounded, and Arpad: for they have heard evil tidings: they are faint-hearted; there is sorrow on the sea; it cannot be quiet.

> Damascus is waxed feeble, and turneth herself to flee, and fear hath seized on her: anguish and sorrows have taken her, as a woman in travail [Jer. 49:23–24].

Damascus is said to be the oldest inhabited city. There are many other cities that make the same claim, but Damascus probably has some right to it. Here is a prophecy against Damascus stating that the city would be destroyed. It has been destroyed, and it has shifted its position several times. However, the name Damascus continues on with the city, and today it is the capital of Syria.

## PROPHECY TO KEDAR, HAZOR, ELAM

Then there is a prophecy against two very prosperous places, Kedar and Hazor. We know very little about them. They were told that Nebuchadnezzar would smite them, and he did. Then there is also a prophecy against Elam.

> Thus saith the LORD of hosts; Behold, I will break the bow of Elam, the chief of their might [Jer. 49:35].

Elam is to be destroyed but will be restored in "the latter days" (v. 39).

All of these nations are to suffer the same fate as Israel, so that there is no place for the remnant of Judah to flee for safety. They could turn to no one for help. They looked every place but *up*. Their only help was in the Lord, but they did not turn to Him. He had given them direction, but they would not receive it.

They, of course, decided to go to Egypt—to their ultimate destruction.

**THEME:** *Prophecy to Babylon*

Here is the prophecy against the nation which at that time was the top nation of the world. It was the first great world power but would also be destroyed. Judgment would come to Babylon.

> The word that the LORD spake against Babylon and against the land of the Chaldeans by Jeremiah the prophet.

> Declare ye among the nations, and publish, and set up a standard; publish, and conceal not: say, Babylon is taken, Bel is confounded, Merodach is broken in pieces; her idols are confounded, her images are broken in pieces [Jer. 50:1–2].

When this was written, it looked as if Israel would disappear from the face of the earth and that Babylon would continue as a world power. Yet God says that Babylon would be destroyed.

> In those days, and in that time, saith the LORD, the children of Israel shall come, they and the children of Judah together, going and weeping: they shall go, and seek the LORD their God [Jer. 50:4].

Israel will survive. This prophecy looks forward to the last days when Israel will turn to God.

God says he will judge Babylon; she shall be conquered by the Medo-Persians—

> For, lo, I will raise and cause to come up against Babylon an assembly of great nations from the north country: and they shall set themselves in array against her; from thence she shall be taken: their arrows shall be as of a mighty expert man; none shall return in vain [Jer. 50:9].

It was by a clever maneuver that Gobryas was able to invade Babylon.

> Because of the wrath of the LORD it shall not be inhabited, but it shall be wholly desolate: every one that goeth by Babylon shall be astonished, and hiss at all her plagues [Jer. 50:13].

That this verse has been literally fulfilled is obvious to every tourist who visits the ruins of ancient Babylon.

> Israel is a scattered sheep; the lions have driven him away: first the king of Assyria hath devoured him; and last this Nebuchadrezzar king of Babylon hath broken his bones.

> Therefore thus saith the LORD of hosts, the God of Israel; Behold, I will punish the king of Babylon and his land, as I have punished the king of Assyria [Jer. 50:17–18].

The destruction of Babylon will come suddenly and take her unaware.

> I have laid a snare for thee, and thou art also taken, O Babylon, and thou wast not aware: thou art found, and also caught, because thou hast striven against the LORD [Jer. 50:24].

You can read the account of this in Daniel 5.

> Come against her from the utmost border, open her storehouses: cast her up as heaps, and destroy her utterly: let nothing of her be left [Jer. 50:26].

You can look at Babylon today; it is a heap of ruins. It was utterly destroyed.

> The voice of them that flee and escape out of the land of Babylon, to declare in Zion the vengeance of the LORD our God, the vengeance of his temple [Jer. 50:28].

The report of the destruction of Babylon is to be announced in Zion.

> A drought is upon her waters; and they shall be dried up: for it is the land of graven images, and they are mad upon their idols.

> Therefore the wild beasts of the desert with the wild beasts of the islands shall dwell there, and the owls shall dwell therein: and it shall be no more inhabited for ever; neither shall it be dwelt in from generation to generation.

> As God overthrew Sodom and Gomorrah and the neighbour cities thereof, saith the LORD; so shall no man abide there, neither shall any son of man dwell therein [Jer. 50:38–40].

The destruction of Babylon is compared to the destruction of Sodom and Gomorrah.

They shall hold the bow and the lance: they are cruel, and will not shew mercy: their voice shall roar like the sea, and they shall ride upon horses, every one put in array, like a man to the battle, against thee, O daughter of Babylon [Jer. 50:42].

This is exactly what happened when Gobryas, the Median, entered the city.

Chapter 51 continues the prediction of God's judgment on Babylon.

Flee out of the midst of Babylon, and deliver every man his soul: be not cut off in her iniquity; for this is the time of the LORD'S vengeance; he will render unto her a recompence.

Babylon hath been a golden cup in the LORD'S hand, that made all the earth drunken: the nations have drunken of her wine; therefore the nations are mad.

Babylon is suddenly fallen and destroyed: howl for her; take balm for her pain, if so she may be healed [Jer. 51:6–8].

Babylon was to be destroyed suddenly—that, of course, was literally fulfilled.

Behold, I am against thee, O destroying mountain, saith the LORD, which destroyeth all the earth: and I will stretch out mine hand upon thee, and roll thee down from the rocks, and will make thee a burnt mountain.

And they shall not take of thee a stone for a corner, nor a stone for foundations; but thou shalt be desolate for ever, saith the LORD [Jer. 51:25–26].

And it certainly is desolate today.

Therefore thus saith the LORD; Behold, I will plead thy cause, and take vengeance for thee; and I will dry up her sea, and make her springs dry.

And Babylon shall become heaps, a dwellingplace for dragons, an astonishment, and an hissing, without an inhabitant [Jer. 51:36–37].

Note that this utter desolation is to follow, not some future overthrow, but the sack of the city resulting from the turning aside of the waters of the river. The Euphrates River, which flowed directly through Babylon, was diverted from its course, which left an entryway at each end for the warriors of the enemy to enter under the walls in the dry riverbed. By this maneuver they were able to appear suddenly in the streets and take the city by surprise.

## CHAPTER 52

*THEME: Fulfillment of the prophesied destruction of Jerusalem*

We have already briefly looked at this chapter because it is a review in retrospect of the destruction of Jerusalem and the captivity of Judah. What Jeremiah had first given as prophecy he now writes as history. He recounts again the capture of King Zedekiah and tells how his sons were slain and his eyes put out by the king of Babylon.

Jeremiah also tells us what happened to Jehoiachin after he had been captured and taken to Babylon:

And it came to pass in the seven and thirtieth year of the captivity of Jehoiachin king of Judah, in the twelfth month, in the five and twentieth day of the month, that Evil-merodach king of Babylon in the first year of his reign lifted up the head of Jehoiachin king of Judah, and brought him forth out of prison,

And spake kindly unto him, and set his throne above the throne of the kings that were with him in Babylon,

And changed his prison garments: and he did continually eat bread before him all the days of his life.

And for his diet, there was a continual diet given him of the king of Babylon, every day a portion until the day of his death, all the days of his life [Jer. 52:31–34].

Jehoiachin died in Babylon. Jeremiah had prophesied that no king from this line would again sit on the throne of David; this ends the

line of David through his son Solomon. The Son of David who will sit on that throne through all eternity was born through another line, the line of Nathan. Mary was born in that line, and it is in that line that Jesus Christ has claim to the throne of David. This is why the Book of Jeremiah ends with these important details about the royal line.

# BIBLIOGRAPHY

(Recommended for Further Study)

Feinberg, Charles L. *Jeremiah*. Grand Rapids, Michigan: Zondervan Publishing House, 1982. (Excellent, comprehensive treatment.)

Gaebelein, Arno C. *The Annotated Bible*. Neptune, New Jersey: Loizeaux Brothers, 1917.

Gray, James M. *Synthetic Bible Studies*. Old Tappan, New Jersey: Fleming H. Revell Co., 1906.

Ironside, H. A. *Notes on Jeremiah*. Neptune, New Jersey: Loizeaux Brothers, 1946.

Jensen, Irving L. *Jeremiah: Prophet of Judgment*. Chicago, Illinois: Moody Press, 1966.

Jensen, Irving L. *Isaiah and Jeremiah*. Chicago, Illinois: Moody Press. (A self-study guide.)

Meyer, F. B. *Jeremiah: Priest and Prophet*. Fort Washington, Pennsylvania: Christian Literature Crusade, 1894. (A rich devotional study.)

Sauer, Erich. *The Dawn of World Redemption*. Grand Rapids, Michigan: Wm. B. Eerdmans Publishing Co., 1951. (An excellent Old Testament survey.)

Scroggie, W. Graham. *The Unfolding Drama of Redemption*. Grand Rapids, Michigan: Zondervan Publishing House, 1970. (An excellent survey and outline of the Old Testament.)

Unger, Merrill F. *Unger's Commentary on the Old Testament*. Chicago, Illinois: Moody Press, 1982. (Highly recommended.)

# HELPFUL BOOKS ON BIBLE PROPHECY

Hoyt, Hermann A. *The End Times*. Chicago, Illinois: Moody Press, 1969.

Pentecost, J. Dwight. *Things to Come*. Grand Rapids, Michigan: Zondervan Publishing House, 1958.

Ryrie, Charles C. *The Basis of the Premillennial Faith*. Neptune, New Jersey: Loizeaux Brothers, 1953.

Ryrie, Charles C. *What You Should Know About the Rapture*. Chicago, Illinois: Moody Press, 1981.

Sauer, Erich. *From Eternity to Eternity*. Grand Rapids, Michigan: Wm. B. Eerdmans Publishing Co., 1954.

Unger, Merrill F. *Beyond the Crystal Ball*. Chicago, Illinois: Moody Press, 1973.

Walvoord, John F. *Armageddon, Oil; and the Middle East Crisis*. Grand Rapids, Michigan: Zondervan Publishing House, 1974.

Walvoord, John F. *The Millennial Kingdom*. Grand Rapids, Michigan: Zondervan Publishing House, 1959.

Walvoord, John F. *The Rapture Question*. Grand Rapids, Michigan: Zondervan Publishing House, 1957.

Wood, Leon J. *The Bible and Future Events*. Grand Rapids, Michigan: Zondervan Publishing House, 1973.

# The Book of
# LAMENTATIONS
## INTRODUCTION

The Book of Lamentations normally and naturally follows the prophecy of Jeremiah. In this little book the soul of the prophet is laid bare before us. These are the lamentations of Jeremiah.

Dr. Alexander Whyte, one of the great expositors of the Word of God of days gone by, has said: "There is nothing like the Lamentations of Jeremiah in the whole world. There has been plenty of sorrow in every age, and in every land, but such another preacher and author, with such a heart for sorrow, has never again been born. Dante comes next to Jeremiah, and we know that Jeremiah was the great exile's favorite prophet."

Jeremiah began his ministry during the reign of Josiah. Both he and Josiah were young men, and they were evidently friends. It was Josiah who led the last revival in Judah. It was a revival in which a great many hearts were touched, but on the whole it proved to be largely a surface movement. Josiah met his untimely death in the battle at Megiddo against Pharaoh-nechoh, a battle that Josiah never should have been in. Jeremiah, however, continued his prophetic ministry during the reigns of the four wretched kings who followed Josiah: Jehoahaz, Jehoiakim, Jehoiachin, and Zedekiah, the last king of Judah. His was a harsh message as he attempted to call his people and his nation back to God, but he was never able to deter the downward course of Judah. He witnessed the destruction of Jerusalem; and as he saw it burn, he sat down in the warm ashes, hot tears coursing down his cheeks.

The Book of Lamentations is composed of five chapters, and each chapter is an elegy, almost a funeral dirge. These elegies are sad beyond description. In them we see Jeremiah as he stood over Jerusalem weeping. This book is filled with tears and sorrow. It is a paean of pain, a poem of pity, a proverb of pathos. It is a hymn of heartbreak, a psalm of sadness, a symphony of sorrow, and a story of sifting. Lamentations is the wailing wall of the Bible.

Lamentations moves us into the very heart of Jeremiah. He gave a message from God that actually broke his heart. How tragic and wretched he was. If you were to pour his tears into a test tube to analyze them from a scientific viewpoint and determine how much sodium chloride, or salt, they contained, you still would not know the sorrow and the heartbreak of this man. He has been called the prophet of the broken heart. His was a life filled with pathos and pity. His sobbing was a solo. Ella Wheeler Wilcox has written a piece of doggerel that goes like this:

Laugh, and the world laughs with you;
Weep, and you weep alone:
For this sad old earth must borrow its mirth,
But it has trouble enough of its own.

Tears are generally conceded to be a sign of weakness, crying is effeminate, and bawling is for babies. Years ago when I was pastor of a church here in Pasadena where I still live, the playground for our summer Bible school was right outside my study window. One little boy brought his even younger sister, and it was interesting to watch how he hovered over her and watched after her. Neither one of them was very big. But one day she fell on the asphalt and scratched up her knee. She began to cry, as a little child would. He tried to give her a sales talk in order to quiet her down. Oh, she shouldn't cry, he said, only women cry. Well, I don't know what he thought she was, but nevertheless it worked, and she stopped crying.

This man Jeremiah had a woman's heart. He was sensitive. He was sincere. He was sympathetic. He was as tender as a mother. Yet he gave the strongest and harshest message in the Bible: he announced the destruction of Jerusalem, and he pronounced judgment, counseling the people to surrender to Nebuchadnezzar. His message did nothing but get him into all kinds of trouble.

Now what kind of a man would you have chosen to deliver such a rough, brutal, tough message as that? Would you have wanted Attila the Hun or a Hitler or a Mussolini? Of one thing I am sure: none of us would send Casper Milquetoast to give the message! But God did choose such a man, a man with a tender heart.

Dr. G. Campbell Morgan tells the story

about Dr. Dale of Birmingham who used to say that Dwight L. Moody was the only man who seemed to him to have the right to preach about hell. When someone asked Dr. Dale why he said that, he replied, "Because he always preaches it with tears in his voice." That is the type of man God wants today. We have too many who are not moved by the message they give.

David Garrick, one of the great Shakespearean actors of the past, told about the day he was walking down the street in London and found a man standing on the corner just yearning over the people. Garrick said, "I stood on the outside of the crowd, but I found myself imperceptibly working myself in, until I stood right under that man, and there came down from his breast hot tears." He went on to say that there was a woman there, pointing her shaking, withered finger at the man who spoke, and she said, "Sir, I have followed you since you preached this morning at seven o'clock and I have heard you preach five times in the streets of this city, and five times I have been wet with your tears. Why do you weep?" That preacher was George Whitefield, a cross-eyed man who was burlesqued on the English stage and denounced from almost every pulpit in the country. David Garrick went on to say, "I listened to George Whitefield, and as I listened to him I saw his passion and his earnestness. I knew that he meant that without Christ men would die. As I listened to him, he came to the place where he could say nothing more. He reached up those mighty arms, his voice seemed almost like a thunderstorm as he said one final word: 'Oh!' " Why, he could break an audience with that word! When George Whitefield said "Oh!" men bowed before the Holy Spirit like corn bows under the wind. Garrick went on, "I would give my hand full of golden sovereigns if I could say 'Oh!' like George Whitefield. I would be the greatest actor that the world has ever known." The only difference was that George Whitefield was sincere—he was not acting. Jeremiah was that kind of a preacher also.

I am afraid that we have developed a generation in our day that has no feeling, no compassion for this lost world. There is little concern for getting out the Word of God. There is little attention given to moral fiber or a high sense of duty.

Several years ago in a *Reader's Digest* arti-

cle, young people were counseled that their highest chances of success in life would be found "by engaging in work you most enjoy doing, and which gives fullest expression to your abilities and personality." If Jeremiah had read that article and heeded its advice, he probably would have gone into some other kind of business. But Jeremiah could say that it was the Word of God that he rejoiced in: "Thy words were found, and I did eat them; and thy word was unto me the joy and rejoicing of mine heart: for I am called by thy name, O LORD God of hosts" (Jer. 15:16). How wonderful this man was!

The young people today who have been trained—even many in Christian work—are simply looking for a job where they can punch a clock, go home to watch TV, and forget all about it. They hold their feelings and emotions in reserve and are unwilling to become really involved in getting out the Word of God.

I don't always understand Jeremiah, but I admire him and look up to him. Mrs. Elizabeth Cook wrote this about him:

A woman's heart—tender and quick and
  warm;
But man's in iron will and courage strong.
His harp was set to weird, pathetic song,
Yet when time called for deeds, no wrath-
  ful storm
From throne or altar could his soul dis-
  arm—
His disheartening battle fierce and long.

This is Jeremiah, the man who had a sorrow.

Jeremiah reminds us of Another who sat weeping over Jerusalem. The only difference is that Jerusalem was in ruins and the temple already burned as Jeremiah gazed upon the debris. Jesus wept over the same city about six centuries later because of what was going to happen to her. To Jeremiah the destruction of Jerusalem was a matter of history. To Jesus the destruction of Jerusalem was a matter of prophecy.

The key verse in the Book of Lamentations explains the reason Jerusalem lay in ruin: "The LORD is righteous; for I have rebelled against his commandment: hear, I pray you, all people, and behold my sorrow: my virgins and my young men are gone into captivity" (Lam. 1:18).

# CHAPTER 1

## THEME: Elegy 1

The first elegy in Lamentations opens on a doleful note. Jeremiah is singing in a minor key.

> How doth the city sit solitary, that was full of people! how is she become as a widow! she that was great among the nations, and princess among the provinces, how is she become tributary! [Lam. 1:1].

The great city of Jerusalem has fallen. What is the explanation? Jeremiah makes two tremendous statements that will help us understand.

> Jerusalem hath grievously sinned; therefore she is removed: all that honoured her despise her, because they have seen her nakedness: yea, she sigheth, and turneth backward [Lam. 1:8].

"Jerusalem hath grievously sinned"—this is the first explanation for the fall of the city. Her nakednesss was revealed—what a picture!

> Is it nothing to you, all ye that pass by? behold, and see if there be any sorrow like unto my sorrow, which is done unto me, wherewith the LORD hath afflicted me in the day of his fierce anger [Lam. 1:12].

People don't like to hear about the fierce anger of God today. That aspect is often left out of the gospel message, and I have observed this particularly in the religious programs that are shown on TV, even by so-called gospel churches. In one Christmas program I saw, they did say that Christ was born of a virgin and that He was God manifest in the flesh—I rejoiced in that. But the program was a travesty of the gospel because it said that Christ came to give you a new personality, to bring peace and love—and oh, how insipid it was! It was a message for comfort and for compromise. The excuse that is often given for such an approach with the gospel is that it is trying to reach the man of the world. Jeremiah, too, was trying to reach a lost world, and he wasn't very successful; but at least he gave God's message as God had given it to him. God judged Judah because of her sin, and He still will judge sin today.

> The LORD is righteous; for I have rebelled against his commandment: hear,

> I pray you, all people, and behold my sorrow: my virgins and my young men are gone into captivity [Lam. 1:18].

Jeremiah mourned the destruction of Jerusalem alone. He stood among the ashes weeping. Why had the city been destroyed? The city had sinned. The second explanation is "The LORD is righteous." God did it, and God was right in what He did.

This is difficult to understand, and I must say I feel totally inadequate to deal with this. I merely stand at the fringe of the sorrow of this man and find I cannot enter in. I can merely look over the wall into his garden; I am not able to walk up and down in it. He has revealed two things to us, the bitter and the sweet: Jerusalem has sinned, yet God loves Jerusalem. "Jerusalem hath grievously sinned," and "the LORD is righteous." God loved them, He said, "with an everlasting love." He brought this upon them because He is righteous.

A statement from G. Campbell Morgan may help us to understand this. Of the revelation of God's anger, he said: "This is a supreme necessity in the interest of the universe. Prisons are in the interest of the free. Hell is the safeguard of heaven. A State that cannot punish crime is doomed; and a God Who tolerates evil is not good. Deny me my Biblical revelation of the anger of God, and I am insecure in the universe. But reveal to me this Throne established, occupied by One Whose heart is full of tenderness, Whose bowels yearn with love; then I am assured that He will not tolerate that which blights and blasts and damns; but will destroy it, and all its instruments, in the interest of that which is high and noble and pure" (*Studies in the Prophecy of Jeremiah*, p. 248).

You and I are living in a universe where there is a God, a living God, a God whose heart goes out in love and yearning over you. But I want to say this to you: if you turn your back on Him, He will judge you even though He still loves you. He is the righteous God of this universe. I am not sure I understand all that, but I know it is what He says in His Word. Someday He will make it clear to us that hell is actually there because He is a God of love and a God of righteousness and a God of holiness. The whole universe, including Satan himself, will admit that God is righteous

and just in all He does. My friend, God is so great and wonderful and good we dare not trifle wih Him.

Jesus could say to the scribes and Pharisees, the religious leaders of His day, "Woe unto you, scribes and Pharisees, hypocrites!" Why did He call them hypocrites? Because ". . . ye devour widows' houses . . ." (Matt. 23:14)—that was one of the reasons. My friend, if your Christianity does not affect your heart, your life in your home and in your business, and your social life, then you are a hypocrite. I didn't say it; He said it, my beloved. And He is the One who wept over these men. My eyes are dry, but His eyes are filled with tears for you and for me today. Oh, my friend, don't turn your back on the God who loves you like this! It will be tragic indeed if you do.

God does what He does because He is a righteous God. He cannot shut his eyes to evil. When His own children disobey Him, God must discipline them, even though it breaks His heart. Jeremiah reveals to us the heart of God: when Jeremiah weeps, God is weeping; when he sorrows, God is sorrowing. When we don't understand what is happening, the important thing is to trust in knowing that God is righteous in what He does. Although it broke His heart, He was right in letting Jerusalem be destroyed and in letting the people go into captivity.

G. Smith wrote a poem about Jerusalem that gives us some insight into this man Jeremiah:

I am the man sore smitten with the wrath
    Of Him who fashion'd me; my heart is
        faint,
    And crieth out, "Spare, spare, O God!
        Thy saint";
But yet with darkness doth He hedge my
    path.

My eyes with streams of fiery tears run
    down
    To see the daughter of my people slain,
    And in Jerusalem the godless reign;
Trouble on trouble are upon me thrown.

Mine adversaries clap their sinful hands
    The while they hiss and wag their
        heads, and say,
    "Where is the temple but of yester-
        day—
The noblest city of a hundred lands?"
We do confess our guilt; then, Lord,
    arise,
Avenge, avenge us of our enemies!

Jeremiah cries out—he wants to know why, and God assures him that He is righteous, right, in what He is doing to Jerusalem.

Another anguished question that Jeremiah has is this: "Is it nothing to you, all ye that pass by?" (v. 12). In other words, How much are the people involved? Do they really care?

Man does not want to accept the fact that God is angry with sin. Instead, the fact that God is love is played for all its worth. I agree that God is love, and the church certainly needs to learn to take the love of God into the marketplace of life. We have often failed to do that, but I feel that it has led to an overemphasis on the love of God in this generation. God is righteous, and God is holy, and God is just in what He does.

The question remains: How do you feel about your sin and God's anger toward it? Is it nothing to you? Jeremiah sat *weeping* over the city. There were not many others weeping with him. Oh, we are told in Psalm 137 that the captives who had been taken to Babylon sat down and wept when they remembered Zion. They cried out for vengeance, and I feel they had a perfect right to do that, but was there any genuine repentance? Or was it the repentance of a thief who is merely sorry he has been caught but does not repent of his thievery? The people who were carried into captivity wept. But Jeremiah, who did not go into captivity, wept also over the debris, the wreckage, the ashes, and ruins of the city. He was a free man, but he was moved, he was involved, and he was concerned.

Again, may I refer to the religious programs we have on television in our day. They are often finished, polished, and professional in their presentation. I think it is a credit to the church to do something in a professional way—that is good and right—but I am concerned that there was one word I did not hear: the word *sin*. Their message did not emphasize at all that God is righteous and He must punish our sin.

The Virgin Birth, the deity of Christ, His death and resurrection are all important, but the question is: *Why* did He die? That is the question raised in Psalm 22:1, "My God, my God, why hast thou forsaken me? . . ." Our Lord said that while He was hanging on the cross. We find the answer to that question in the same psalm: "But thou art *holy*, O thou that inhabitest the praises of Israel" (Ps. 22:3, italics mine). He is holy. He is righteous. Christ died on that cross because you and I are sinners, hell-doomed sinners.

Look at the cross today—"Is it nothing to

you, all ye that pass by?" (v. 12). He didn't have to die. He suffered as no man has had to suffer. God forsook Him, but God will never forsake you as long as you live. He forsook Christ so that He would not have to forsake you. May I ask you, is it nothing to you?

McCheyne was a wonderful man of God in the past who had a real experience with the Lord. He wrote a poem about *Jehovah-Tsidkenu*, which means "the Lord our Righteousness" (see Jer. 23:6; 33:16), and Dr. H. A. Ironside quoted it in *Notes on the Prophecy and Lamentations of Jeremiah* (pp. 315, 316).

> I oft read with pleasure, to soothe or engage,
> Isaiah's wild measure, or John's simple page:
> But e'en when they pictured the blood--sprinkled tree,
> Jehovah Tsidkenu was nothing to me.
>
> Like tears from the daughters of Zion that roll,
> I wept when the waters went over His soul;
> Yet thought not that *my sins* had nailed to the tree
> Jehovah Tsidkenu: 'twas nothing to me.
>
> When free grace awoke me by light from on high,
> Then legal fears shook me—I trembled to die.
> No refuge, no safety in self could I see;
> Jehovah Tsidkenu my Saviour must be.
>
> My terrors all vanished before that sweet name;
> My guilty fears banished, with boldness I came,
> To drink at the fountain, life-giving and free;
> Jehovah Tsidkenu *is all things to me*.

My friend, "Is it nothing to you, all ye that pass by?" Have you come to Jesus just to get a new personality? To bring a little peace into your soul, or to create a little love on your altar? Is *that* the reason He died on the cross? Will you hear me, my friend? He died on the cross to save you from *hell*.

The Holy Spirit has come into the world to reveal Christ as Savior, and He has come to convict the world of sin. What kind of sin? Murder? Thievery? Yes, but something is worse than that: they sinned ". . . *because they believe not on me*" (John 16:9, italics mine). God has a remedy for the thief. The thief on the cross was saved. I think Paul was guilty of murder, that he was responsible for the death of Stephen, but he got saved. Moses also was a murderer. God has a remedy for the murderer, the thief, and the liar, but God does not have a remedy for the man who rejects Jesus Christ. That is the greatest sin you can commit.

Rejection of Christ is a state rather than an act. You can never commit the act of rejecting Christ, but you can gradually come to the place where Christ and what He has done for you is absolutely meaningless. Jerusalem reached the place where God told Jeremiah, "Don't be disturbed that they are not listening to you. If Moses or Elijah or Samuel were here to pray for them, I would not answer their prayers either. It is too late; they have crossed over." There are many living in our sophisticated day who have crossed over to that place.

Now we cannot judge when a man has reached the point of having totally rejected Christ. I have seen the conversion of many folk whom I'm sure I would have considered to be hopeless cases. One man I know of who lived in the San Francisco Bay area was on drugs and was guilty of several crimes, but he was marvelously and wonderfully converted. So neither you nor I are the ones to say that someone has stepped over that line, but it does happen.

Jerusalem had rejected God. An individual can reject God. What does Jesus Christ mean to you? What does His death mean to you? "Is it nothing to you, all ye that pass by?" (v. 12).

# CHAPTER 2

## THEME: *Elegy 2*

The Lord was as an enemy: he hath swallowed up Israel, he hath swallowed up all her palaces: he hath destroyed his strong holds, and hath increased in the daughter of Judah mourning and lamentation [Lam. 2:5].

God took full responsibility for what Nebuchadnezzar did. God allowed him to destroy the city of Jerusalem. God used him as a rod, just as He had used the Assyrians against Israel for their punishment.

Have you ever stopped to think in your own personal life why God permits certain people to cross your path? Do you wish that you had never met certain people? Are there people whom you would call your enemies? Someone may have caused you sorrow, but it is all for His purpose. God has permitted all that for a definite purpose. Learn to recognize the hand of God in your life.

The Lord hath cast off his altar, he hath abhorred his sanctuary, he hath given up into the hand of the enemy the walls of her palaces; they have made a noise in the house of the LORD, as in the day of a solemn feast [Lam. 2:7].

The very temple which God had blessed—He had given the instructions for building it, His very presence had been there at one time—now He says, "The day came that I abhorred that temple."

Churchgoing folk need to investigate their own lives. If you go to church, is that something that God takes delight in? Or is it actually something that hurts His cause? Is your frame of mind right when you go, or are you critical? Can the spirit of God use you? I think that it can even be sinful to go to church. Do you know where the most dangerous place was the night Jesus was arrested? Was it down with that bunch of rascals who were plotting His death? No, my friend, the most dangerous place that night was in the Upper Room where Jesus was! Do you know why? *Satan* was there. He put it into the heart of Judas Iscariot to betray Him, and he also got into the heart of Simon Peter to deny Him. Just because you are going to church doesn't mean you are pleasing God.

The elders of the daughter of Zion sit upon the ground, and keep silence: they have cast up dust upon their heads; they have girded themselves with sackcloth: the virgins of Jerusalem hang down their heads to the ground [Lam. 2:10].

All the people went through the outward gyrations of grief, but notice how Jeremiah was affected:

Mine eyes do fail with tears, my bowels are troubled, my liver is poured upon the earth, for the destruction of the daughter of my people; because the children and the sucklings swoon in the streets of the city [Lam. 2:11].

"Mine eyes do fail with tears"—he cried so much he couldn't even see. "My bowels are troubled"—this thing tore him to pieces, it wrecked his health. He was involved; it broke his heart.

How many of us are willing to be really involved in God's work? Are we willing to endanger our health? Are we willing to give ourselves over to God?

All that pass by clap their hands at thee; they hiss and wag their head at the daughter of Jerusalem, saying, Is this the city that men call The perfection of beauty, The joy of the whole earth? [Lam. 2:15].

The enemy without is elated at the misery of Jerusalem.

I am sometimes severe in my comments about the condition of the church in our day. I am retired from the active pastorate—although I am not retired from the work of God—and I need to ask myself how involved I am with my brethren who are in the ministry? When I see the problems in the church today, is it nothing to me? Do I just sit on the sidelines as a critic, or does it bring sorrow to my heart? I can say that I have been moved, and I want to be an encouragement to the many wonderful Bible-teaching pastors in our country. It is too easy to be harsh in our criticism when it means nothing to us at all.

# CHAPTER 3

## THEME: Elegy 3

Each one of the chapters in this little Book of Lamentations forms an acrostic. That is, there are twenty-two letters in the Hebrew alphabet, and each of the twenty-two verses in each chapter begins with the succeeding letter. However, in this chapter there are sixty-six verses, which means that there are three verses that begin with each letter of the alphabet.

> **I am the man that hath seen affliction by the rod of his wrath.**
>
> **He hath led me, and brought me into darkness, but not into light.**
>
> **Surely against me is he turned; he turneth his hand against me all the day.**
>
> **My flesh and my skin hath he made old: he hath broken my bones [Lam. 3:1–4].**

This man Jeremiah has seen and gone through great trouble. His health is wrecked because of his concern for Jerusalem. Jeremiah was not unmoved by the destruction he had seen come to the nation. He did not run around saying, "I told you so!" Actually, he was heartbroken. His response also shows us how *God* feels. God is not removed; He goes with those who are His own. The Lord Jesus said, ". . . I will never leave thee, nor forsake thee" (Heb. 13:5). Whatever you are going through, you can be sure He is there.

> **This I recall to my mind, therefore have I hope.**
>
> **It is of the LORD'S mercies that we are not consumed, because his compassions fail not.**
>
> **They are new every morning: great is thy faithfulness.**

> **The LORD is my portion, saith my soul; therefore will I hope in him [Lam. 3:21–24].**

If I were to give a title to these last three chapters of Lamentations, it would be, "When Tomorrows Become Yesterdays." Jeremiah is now looking back upon the past. He had predicted the judgment that came upon Jerusalem, and Jeremiah sits in the rubble and ruin of Jerusalem weeping as he writes this lamentation.

These verses are the only bright spot in all of the five lamentations. "It is of the LORD'S mercies that we are not consumed, because his compassions fail not. They are new every morning: great is thy faithfulness." In spite of the severe judgment of God—and many thought it was too severe—Jeremiah can see the hand of God's mercy. They would have been utterly consumed had it not been for the *mercy* of God. If they had received their just deserts, they would have been utterly destroyed—they would have disappeared from the earth.

Was Judah's deliverance from such a fate due to something in them? No, it was all due to the *faithfulness* of God. He had promised Abraham that He would make a nation come from him—and *this* was the nation. He had promised Moses that He would put them into the land. He had promised Joshua that He would establish them there. He promised David that there would come One in his line to reign on the throne forever. The prophets all said that God would not utterly destroy this people but that He would judge them for their sin. God is faithful. He has judged them, but He will not utterly destroy them. A faithful remnant has always remained, and ultimately they will become a great nation again.

Will God judge America? A great many people think not, but I think He will.

# CHAPTER 4

This fourth lamentation is a meditation. Sitting amidst the debris and ashes of Jerusalem, Jeremiah describes the horror of the destruction of his city and the carrying into captivity of the people by Nebuchadnezzar. It is so terrifying that I might be tempted to shun giving such a doomsday message. But we need to face up to the fact that God is a righteous God as well as a God of love. God judges sin, and He is righteous in doing so. Judah did not receive full judgment because of the mercies of God. Habbakuk said, ". . . in wrath remember mercy" (Hab. 3:2). God never forgets to be merciful. There is always a way out for God's people if they will come God's way.

**How is the gold become dim! how is the most fine gold changed! the stones of the sanctuary are poured out in the top of every street.**

**The precious sons of Zion, comparable to fine gold, how are they esteemed as earthen pitchers, the work of the hands of the potter! [Lam. 4:1–2].**

Jeremiah is comparing gold to the young men of Zion. The fine young men of Judah who were like gold vessels are now like earthen vessels of clay. They have been broken. That is the terrifying thing about warfare: it eliminates the finest young men of a nation.

We are a proud people in this country. Even Christians are told that they need to think well of themselves. I heard of a Christian psychologist who teaches that you should get up every morning, look in the mirror, and say, "I love you!" Well, a lot of the saints don't need to be told that—they already love themselves! The apostle Paul says that we are not to think more highly of ourselves than we ought. If we don't think of ourselves more highly than we ought, we will find that we are merely clay vessels. In 2 Timothy Paul likens the believer to a clay vessel. However, the issue is not of what material the vessels are made, but how they are being used. Are we vessels for the Master's use or for our own use?

At the wedding in Cana of Galilee the Lord Jesus had the servants bring out those old beaten water pots, which had apparently been stuck back in a corner until after the wedding. He used those old pots to supply the crowd with drink. He could use those pots, but He had to fill them with water. The water is the Word of God. When we, as old water pots, get filled with the Word of God, God can use us.

The young men of Judah had not been serving God, and they were now just broken pieces of pottery. What a tragic picture this is!

**The tongue of the sucking child cleaveth to the roof of his mouth for thirst: the young children ask bread, and no man breaketh it unto them [Lam. 4:4].**

The siege of Jerusalem by Nebuchadnezzar was a horrible thing. The people suffered inside the city. Instead of surrendering, they held out and saw their little babies die. Shakespeare has Lady Macbeth say: "I have given suck and know How tender 'tis to love the babe that milks me: I would, while it was smiling in my face, Have pluck'd my nipple from his boneless gums, And dash'd the brains out, had I so sworn as you" (*Macbeth*, Act 1, scene 7). That is a bitter awful thing! But don't point your finger back to the terrible things these people did, for today, my friend, abortion is the *murder* of little children.

**They that did feed delicately are desolate in the streets: they that were brought up in scarlet embrace dunghills [Lam. 4:5].**

They had lived in luxury, they had had big supermarkets, but now the shelves of the supermarkets are bare. They no longer can enjoy the conveniences they once had—in fact, they don't have any at all.

Have you ever stopped to think what could happen to the place where you live? Suppose those supermarket shelves which now groan with food were all empty next week when you do your shopping. Suppose you flipped the switch in your home and the lights did not come on. Suppose there was no heat, no air conditioning, no gas for the automobile. A howl of despair would go up in this nation. We would be a helpless people. That's what happened to Jerusalem. God judged them.

**For the punishment of the iniquity of the daughter of my people is greater than the punishment of the sin of Sodom, that was overthrown as in a moment, and no hands stayed on her [Lam. 4:6].**

God judged Sodom and Gomorrah, but God judged Jerusalem more severely. Why was that? Because the sin of Jerusalem was worse than that of Sodom and Gomorrah. Sodom and Gomorrah were destroyed by homosexuality. That is an awful sin, but there is something worse than that. It is worse for a man to sit in the church pew and hear the gospel and do nothing about it. That might be true of someone reading this book. Jesus Christ died for you. God is merciful to you today, and you have turned your back on Him. When God judges, your judgment will be more severe than for the heathen in Africa or in the islands of the sea. Don't worry about the heathen out there; worry about yourself. How have you responded to God's offer of grace in Jesus Christ?

**Her Nazarites were purer than snow, they were whiter than milk, they were more ruddy in body than rubies, their polishing was of sapphire [Lam. 4:7].**

Boy, they looked good, didn't they? Religion today looks good. We have new churches today—new sanctuaries and nice Christian education buildings where we have a place to play volleyball and basketball. We've got a baseball team. We have a nice room for banquets. It all looks good on the outside. Now Jeremiah is saying that a Nazarite was one who took a voluntary oath, and many did it. They were complimented; they looked good, you know. But it was all on the outside; their hearts were not changed. While it is wonderful to have beautiful churches—I'm not opposed to them; I'm excited about them—it is tragic when the people on the inside are not new creatures in Christ Jesus. They are still doing the same old sins. That is the picture Jeremiah gives us of the people of Judah.

**They that be slain with the sword are better than they that be slain with hunger: for these pine away, stricken through for want of the fruits of the field [Lam. 4:9].**

Even though Jeremiah has witnessed the awful destruction of Jerusalem and those who had died, he says he would rather be dead than alive, for the condition of those who remained was so terrible.

**The hands of the pitiful women have sodden their own children: they were their meat in the destruction of the daughter of my people [Lam. 4:10].**

The same thing took place when Titus destroyed Jerusalem in A.D. 70. The people got so hungry that mothers had to give their own babies to be eaten! We look back and think how horrible this was but today many mothers are having abortions, actually murdering their babies. If we don't want a baby, we must take responsibility for our actions before a baby becomes a reality. God has made us capable of having babies and when one has been conceived, it is His intention for that child to come into the world. The moment the child is conceived, he is a *person* and to abort a pregnancy is murder of a human being.

**For the sins of her prophets, and the iniquities of her priests, that have shed the blood of the just in the midst of her [Lam. 4:13].**

Because the false prophets and the priests did not tell the people the truth, they are guilty of murder—that is God's estimate of it. A preacher who won't preach the Word of God and tell the people how they might be saved is put in this classification. *I* didn't say that— *God* said it. God says if you don't give out the Word of God, you are guilty.

**The anger of the LORD hath divided them; he will no more regard them: they respected not the persons of the priests, they favoured not the elders [Lam. 4:16].**

The people paid no attention to the priests who *were* giving out the Word of God. Jeremiah was a prophet of God, and they paid no attention to him at all. God judged the people for that.

**As for us, our eyes as yet failed for our vain help: in our watching we have watched for a nation that could not save us [Lam. 4:17].**

This is something the modern nation of Israel needs to learn. *God* did not put them back in the land in 1948; the *United Nations* made them a nation, and since that time they have never known one minute of peace. There have been war and threats of war continually. They have not turned to God, and God did not put them back into the land.

Don't misunderstand me, I think the return of the Jews to Israel was a tremendous thing. Dr. W. F. Albright has made this statement: "It is without parallel in the annals of human history that a nation carried into captivity for seventy years should return to resume its national life, and that after nearly six hundred

years, this same nation should again be scattered worldwide for nearly two thousand years and retain its identity." To see how God has dealt with this nation has caused many to turn to Him.

The Lord says that the problem was that Judah was looking to Egypt for help, and Egypt was *not* a help; they were an enemy. The United States should recognize that it is not the war machines we need to give to Israel. We need to give them the Word of God, the Word which they gave to us so many years ago.

**The breath of our nostrils, the anointed of the LORD, was taken in their pits, of whom we said, Under his shadow we shall live among the heathen [Lam. 4:20].**

What a picture of that people as they are today! They are scattered among the heathen.

**The punishment of thine iniquity is accomplished, O daughter of Zion; he will no more carry thee away into captivity: he will visit thine iniquity, O daughter of Edom; he will discover thy sins [Lam. 4:22].**

After the judgment, God has promised that He will permanently place them in the land.

# CHAPTER 5

### *THEME: Elegy 5*

This fifth and final lamentation is a prayer of Jeremiah.

**Remember, O LORD, what is come upon us: consider, and behold our reproach [Lam. 5:1].**

Judah had lost the honor and respect which she had had among the nations.

**They ravished the women in Zion, and the maids in the cities of Judah.**

**Princes are hanged up by their hand: the faces of elders were not honoured.**

**They took the young men to grind, and the children fell under the wood [Lam. 5:11–13].**

Their women were ravished, and their princes hanged; they had lost everything. The young men who survived were put into slavery to work for Nebuchadnezzar.

**The joy of our heart is ceased; our dance is turned into mourning [Lam. 5:15].**

The joy of their hearts had ceased.

**Thou, O LORD, remainest for ever; thy throne from generation to generation.**

**Wherefore dost thou forget us for ever, and forsake us so long time?**

**Turn thou us unto thee, O LORD, and we shall be turned; renew our days as of old [Lam. 5:19–21].**

This is the prayer of Jeremiah for his people. We could learn a lesson from this: before it is too late, we had better turn to the Lord.

Daniel Webster made this statement many years ago, and it sounds like a prophecy: "If religious books are not circulated among the masses and the people do not turn to God, I do not know what is to become of us as a nation. If truth be not diffused, error will be. If God and His Word are not received, the devil and his works will gain the ascendency. If the evangelical volume does not reach every hamlet, the pages of a corrupt and licentious literature will. If the power of the Gospel is not felt through the length and the breadth of the land, anarchy, misrule, degradation, misery, corruption, and darkness will reign without mitigation or end." What a picture! Today we live in a day when you cannot read the Bible in the schools, but pornography is permitted because we must be free to do what we want to do! Well, can't some of us have the Bible in our schools, especially when it is desired by the majority?

When our great nation was founded during the period from 1775 to 1787, the following statement by Benjamin Franklin was still widely accepted: "The longer I live the more convincing proofs I see of the truth that God governs in the affairs of men." Unless a marked change takes place in the United States of America, it's doomed just as sure as was ancient Babylon.

Dr. Machen said, "America is coasting

downhill on a godly ancestry." Now we have reached the bottom of the hill. What a message Lamentations would have for us today, but it will not be selected as the Book of the Month or the Book of the Year. It is unfortunate that we will not listen.

(For Bibliography to Lamentations, see Bibliography at the end of Jeremiah.)

# The Book of
# EZEKIEL
## INTRODUCTION

Ezekiel was a priest (Ezek. 1:3), but he never served in that office because he was taken captive to Babylon during the reign of Jehoiachin (2 Kings 24:10–16), who was the king of Judah who followed Jehoiakim. It was during the eleven-year reign of Jehoiakim that the first deportation took place when Daniel was taken captive. Jehoiachin then came to the throne and reigned only three months. In 597 B.C. the second deportation took place, and Ezekiel was taken captive.

Ezekiel was a contemporary of Jeremiah and Daniel. Jeremiah was an old man at this time. He had begun his ministry as a young man during the reign of young King Josiah. He had remained with the remnant in the land and then was taken by them down into Egypt. Therefore his ministry at this time was confined to the remnant in Egypt. Daniel had been taken into the court of the king of Babylon and had become his prime minister. Ezekiel, then, was with the captives who had been brought down to the rivers of Babylon. The captives had been placed by the great canal that came off the River Euphrates, which was several miles from Babylon itself. Ezekiel's ministry was among those people.

Psalm 137 is the psalm of the remnant in Babylon: "By the rivers of Babylon, there we sat down, yea, we wept, when we remembered Zion. We hanged our harps upon the willows in the midst thereof" (Ps. 137:1–2). But at the same time Ezekiel writes: "The heavens were opened, and I saw visions of God" (Ezek. 1:1). What a contrast! While these people had already put their harps on a willow tree and sat down to weep, this man Ezekiel was seeing visions of God!

Jeremiah, Ezekiel, and Daniel were all prophets, but each had a particular and peculiar ministry to a certain group of people, and apparently they never came into contact with each other. From the record in the Book of Daniel you would not gather that Daniel ever visited his people in Babylon where Ezekiel was; yet he had a great concern for them and he actually defended them. But did Daniel and Jeremiah know each other? Well, we know from his book that Daniel was acquainted with the prophecies of Jeremiah. I have a notion that as a young man in his teens he listened to

Jeremiah in Jerusalem. Ezekiel also was a young man when he was taken captive, and he too had probably heard Jeremiah, but had no personal acquaintance with Daniel.

The message of Ezekiel is the most spiritual of all the prophets because he dealt particularly with the Person of God. Someone has said, "Ezekiel is the prophet of the Spirit, as Isaiah is the prophet of the Son, and Jeremiah the prophet of the Father."

During the first years of the captivity the false prophets were still saying that the people were going to return to Jerusalem and that the city would not be destroyed. The city was not destroyed even at the time of the second deportation. It was not until about 586 B.C., when Nebuchadnezzar came against the city the third time, that he burned and destroyed Jerusalem. Therefore for a period of about ten years, these false prophets were saying that the people would return and the city would not be destroyed. Jeremiah had sent a message to Babylon saying the city would be destroyed, and Ezekiel confirmed his message. He warned the people that they must turn to God before they could return to Jerusalem. When the time came, a very small remnant did turn to God, and they returned to Jerusalem very discouraged.

Ezekiel began his ministry five years after he was taken captive at about the age of thirty. In many ways, he spoke in the darkest days of the nation. He stood at the bottom of a valley in the darkest corner. He had to meet the false hope given by the false prophets and the indifference and despondency begotten in the days of sin and disaster. The people would not listen to his message. Therefore, he resorted to a new method. Instead of speaking in parables, as the Lord Jesus did, he acted out the parables. He actually did some very interesting stunts. We read in Ezekiel 24:24, "Thus Ezekiel is unto you a sign: according to all that he hath done shall ye do: and when this cometh, ye shall know that I am the Lord GOD." The people would not listen to his words, so he would act them out, and he attracted a great deal of attention that way.

We have folk who use this very same method today. We have placard carriers, flagpole sitters, and walkathons. People do these

things to attract attention and gain publicity. This, too, was Ezekiel's method. One time he walked into a house, locked himself in, and then started digging himself out. When he came out, he came out in the middle of the street! Here in Pasadena, California, it is nothing new to be digging in the middle of the street, for the city workers keep digging up the streets all the time. But in Ezekiel's time, when a man came up out of the middle of the street one day, people naturally gathered around and said, "What's the big idea?" Ezekiel had a message for them, and he gave it to them (see Ezek. 12:8–16).

Ezekiel is the prophet of the glory of the Lord. There were three prophets of Israel who spoke when they were out of the land. They are Ezekiel, Daniel, and John (who wrote from the island of Patmos). All three of these men wrote what is called an apocalypse. They all used highly symbolic language; yet they saw the brightest light and held the highest hope of all the prophets. Ezekiel saw the Shekinah glory of the Lord leave Solomon's temple, but he also saw the return of the glory of the Lord which was projected into the future and will come to pass during the kingdom age, or the Millennium.

The meaning of Ezekiel is seen in this coming of the glory during the kingdom age. Ezekiel looked beyond the sufferings of Christ to the glory that should follow. As Peter said of the prophets, they saw the sufferings and they saw the glory that would follow (1 Pet. 1:11). I think Ezekiel saw it better than any of the other prophets.

# OUTLINE

I. **Glory of the Lord; Commission of the Prophets, Chapters 1–7**
   A. Display of the Glory, Chapter 1
   B. Prophet's Call and Endowment with Power for the Office, Chapter 2
   C. Prophet's Preparation; Office as Watchman, Chapter 3
   D. Judgment of Jerusalem, Chapter 4
   E. Sign of Prophet Shaving Hair, Chapter 5
   F. Sword to Fall Upon Jerusalem; Remnant to be Saved, Chapter 6
   G. Prophecy of Final Destruction of Jerusalem, Chapter 7

II. **Glory of the Lord; Complete Captivity of Jerusalem and Israel; Departure of the Glory, Chapters 8–24**
   A. Vision of the Glory; Temple Defilement by Idolatry Explains its Destruction, Chapter 8
   B. Shekinah Glory Prepares to Leave Temple, Chapter 9
   C. Shekinah Glory Fills Holy Place; Leaves the Temple, Chapter 10
   D. Prophecy Against Rulers of Jerusalem, Chapter 11
   E. Ezekiel Enacts Destruction of Jerusalem, Chapter 12
   F. Prophecy Against Pseudo Prophets and Prophetesses, Chapter 13
   G. Prophecy Against Idolatry of Elders; Certain Destruction of Jerusalem, Chapter 14
   H. Vision of the Vine, Chapter 15
   I. Jerusalem Likened to Abandoned Baby Adopted by God, Chapter 16
   J. Riddle of Two Eagles, Chapter 17
   K. Wages of Sin is Death, Chapter 18
   L. Elegy of Jehovah over Princes of Israel, Chapter 19
   M. Review of Sins of Nation; Future Judgment and Restoration, Chapter 20
   N. King of Babylon to Remove Last King of Davidic Line Until Messiah Comes, Chapter 21
   O. Review of Abominations of Jerusalem, Chapter 22
   P. Parable of Two Sisters (Samaria and Jerusalem), Chapter 23
   Q. Parable of Boiling Pot, Chapter 24

III. **Glory of the Lord; Judgment of Nations, Chapters 25–32**
   A. Against Ammon, Moab, Edom, and Philistia, Chapter 25
   B. Against Tyre, Chapters 26–28
   C. Against Egypt, Chapters 29–32

IV. **Glory of the Lord and the Coming Kingdom, Chapters 33–48**
   A. Recommission of the Prophet, Chapters 33–34
   B. Restoration of Israel, Chapters 35–36
   C. Resurrection of Israel, Chapter 37
   D. Repudiation of Gog and Magog, Chapters 38–39
   E. Rebuilt Temple, Chapters 40–42
   F. Return of the Glory of the Lord, Chapters 43–48

# CHAPTER 1

***THEME:*** *Display of the Lord's glory*

Ezekiel's vision of the glory of the Lord may very well be a key to all of the visions in the entire Word of God; it certainly is the key to the rest of the Book of Ezekiel. Many people think of the Book of the Revelation as resting upon the prophecy of Daniel and the Olivet Discourse of our Lord. That is true, but I believe it rests primarily upon the apocalypse of Ezekiel; you will find a striking similarity between the vision in Ezekiel 1 and chapters 4 and 5 of Revelation.

This vision is a very difficult one to deal with. John Calvin said, "If anyone asks whether the vision is lucid, I confess its obscurity, and that I can scarcely understand it." I am certainly a Calvinist in the sense that I must concur with his statement—neither do I understand Ezekiel's vision clearly.

However, there is one thing that I am confident this vision is not: it is *not* a vision of the present mechanical age. Ezekiel's vision of the wheels within wheels is not a prophecy of the airplane! When the old propeller planes were first developed, several prophetic teachers were saying that this vision was a prophecy of the airplane. Today we have jet planes and they have no wheels within wheels, and we must set aside that interpretation. Such interpretations are juvenile. Silly and senile chatter like that is what has brought prophecy into disrepute.

What we do have in this first chapter of Ezekiel, I believe, is a vision of the glory of the Lord. In the Book of Isaiah we have the *principles* of the throne of God; in Jeremiah we have the *practice* of that throne; but in Ezekiel we have the *Person* who is on the throne. I want to hasten to add that we do not have God Himself exposed in this vision—you do not have a window display of Him. When I began my ministry I considered this to be a vision of God, but it is not that. It is instead a vision of the *glory* of God, a vision of the *presence* of God.

We see here a vision of the chariot of God as He rides triumphantly and irresistibly through time. There is one feature of this vision which shocked me when I discovered it: the chariot is vacant. I had taken for granted that God was there. There are four living creatures, the cherubim, connected with the chariot; yet they are distinct from it. Above all, there is a throne, and on the throne there is a Man. This is the highest vision of God that

we are given, and it is most difficult to understand. We will note just a few of its impressive aspects:

**Now it came to pass in the thirtieth year, in the fourth month, in the fifth day of the month, as I was among the captives by the river of Chebar, that the heavens were opened, and I saw visions of God [Ezek. 1:1].**

"Now it came to pass in the thirtieth year" would seem to indicate that Ezekiel was thirty years of age. However, it is the belief of many scholars that this is geared to a little different calendar. I will not go into any detail on this as, frankly, it gets a little intricate, and I do not feel that it is essential.

"I saw visions of God." While the captives in Babylon had sat down and wept by the rivers of Babylon (see Ps. 137:1), Ezekiel was seeing visions of God. What a contrast—seeing visions and weeping!

**In the fifth day of the month, which was the fifth year of king Jehoiachin's captivity [Ezek. 1:2].**

We have not quite come to the time of the destruction of Jerusalem which took place during the reign of Zedekiah.

**The word of the Lord came expressly unto Ezekiel the priest, the son of Buzi, in the land of the Chaldeans by the river Chebar; and the hand of the Lord was there upon him [Ezek. 1:3].**

"The word of the Lord came expressly unto Ezekiel the priest." Ezekiel belonged to the tribe of Levi, apparently the priestly branch, and probably to the sons of Kohath. We are told that he was "the son of Buzi."

"Chebar" was the main canal that came off the Euphrates River, which watered that area. Evidently, the Jewish captives were put there to till the land. This area was removed by quite a few miles from Babylon, and that may be the reason that Daniel and Ezekiel did not have the opportunity to meet together for a meal. Daniel may have visited the area, but I doubt that Ezekiel would have been permitted to visit Daniel.

**And I looked, and, behold, a whirlwind came out of the north, a great cloud, and a fire infolding itself, and a bright-**

ness was about it, and out of the midst thereof as the colour of amber, out of the midst of the fire [Ezek. 1:4].

"Behold, a whirlwind came out of the north." I know that many people have made a great deal of this idea that there is a great vacant space up yonder in the north and that this is the direction that leads to the presence of God. Our modern radio electronic telescopes with their big dishes have shown that there are stars out there—it is not vacant. However, "the north" is used in Scripture to point to the throne of God. In Isaiah 14:13 we read (speaking of the fall of Satan): "For thou hast said in thine heart, I will ascend into heaven, I will exalt my throne above the stars of God: I will sit also upon the mount of the congregation, in the sides of the north." I believe the idea is that, instead of pointing to the north pole, we are to look up—God's throne is out yonder, not relative to any direction at all. After all, its location is not something you and I can understand. We are told, ". . . look up . . . for your redemption draweth nigh" (Luke 21:28). That is the direction in which our attention should be focused today.

Also in Psalm 75:5–7 we read: "Lift not up your horn on high: speak not with a stiff neck. For promotion cometh neither from the east, nor from the west, nor from the south. But God is the judge: he putteth down one, and setteth up another." The only direction that is not mentioned is *north*, and I would say the thought is that it is *up*—God's throne is out yonder, even beyond space.

This whirlwind out of the north, then, indicates a tremendous movement from the throne of God—it is a judgment from God.

"And a fire infolding itself, and a brightness was about it, and out of the midst thereof as the colour of amber, out of the midst of the fire." This is the first thing we observe—a light flashing forth, revealing and also concealing. Obscuring and yet bringing out where it can be seen, it is a light brighter than the sun. Perhaps it could be compared to the inside of an atomic blast. It was incandescent, like lightning.

The Word of God says that " . . . our God is a consuming fire" (Heb. 12:29), and that ". . . God is light . . ." (1 John 1:5). Paul said that at the time of his conversion he saw ". . . a light from heaven, above the brightness of the sun . . ." (Acts 26:13). All of this speaks of the unapproachable presence of God (see also vv. 13–14).

Also out of the midst thereof came the likeness of four living creatures. And this was their appearance; they had the likeness of a man [Ezek. 1:5].

This verse and also verse 26 ("the appearance of a man") speak of the incarnation of Christ, the fact that God became a man. "And the Word was made flesh, and dwelt [pitched His tent] among us . . ." (John 1:14). Isaiah 52:7 tells us, "How beautiful upon the mountains are the feet of him that bringeth good tidings, that publisheth peace; that bringeth good tidings of good, that publisheth salvation; that saith unto Zion, Thy God reigneth!" God came to earth a Man, walked the dusty trails of Palestine, and finally spikes were driven into His feet.

As for the likeness of their faces, they four had the face of a man, and the face of a lion, on the right side: and they four had the face of an ox on the left side; they four also had the face of an eagle [Ezek. 1:10].

These four faces (compare this with Rev. 4:6–8) remind us of the four Gospels in which Christ is revealed in four aspects: His kingship (Matthew) symbolized here by the lion; His servanthood (Mark) symbolized by the ox; His perfect humanity (Luke) symbolized by the face of a man; and His deity (John) symbolized by the flying eagle.

These four living creatures resemble the description we have of the cherubim who were in the Garden of Eden to guard the way of the Tree of Life. They were not shutting man out from God; they were keeping the way open. What did Adam and Eve see when they looked back as they left the garden? They saw a slain animal whose skins they were wearing. And they saw the cherubim overshadowing, keeping open the way to God. It is the blood that makes an atonement for the sin of man. When Moses made the mercy seat, there were cherubim above which looked down upon the blood of the sacrifices—the same thing Adam and Eve had seen. Through the blood is the only way man can approach God. The Lord Jesus said, ". . . no man cometh unto the Father, but by me" (John 14:6).

And they went every one straight forward: whither the spirit was to go, they went; and they turned not when they went [Ezek. 1:12].

God is moving forward undeviatingly, unhesitatingly toward the accomplishment of

His purpose in this world today. Nothing will deter Him—nothing can sidetrack Him at all.

**As for the likeness of the living creatures, their appearance was like burning coals of fire, and like the appearance of lamps: it went up and down among the living creatures; and the fire was bright, and out of the fire went forth lightning.**

**And the living creatures ran and returned as the appearance of a flash of lightning [Ezek. 1:13–14].**

The Scripture tells us ". . . God is light . . ." (1 John 1:5). This is a tremendous vision of the glory of God, a vision out of the person of God. The Lord Jesus said, ". . . I am the light of the world . . ." (John 8:12). What does this reveal to us? It reveals the righteousness and holiness of God. "But if we walk in the light, as he is in the light, we have fellowship one with another, and the blood of Jesus Christ his Son cleanseth us from all sin" (1 John 1:7). We would be scorched by the holiness of God if we had not been redeemed by the blood of Christ and covered with His righteousness.

God is not exposed in this vision—He is portrayed. It is still true that no man has seen God at any time. Moses said, ". . . Shew me thy glory," and God hid him in the cleft of the rock so that Moses saw only the glory of God, not the person of God. The Lord told him, ". . . Thou canst not see my face: for there shall no man see me, and live" (Exod. 33:18–23). Man has been forbidden to make a likeness of God (see Exod. 20:4). We do not know what He looks like. We do not even know how the Lord Jesus who became a man looked. But there is in the human heart a longing to see God; I think every idol witnesses to that desire. Although idols are perverted and profane representations, they reveal that men want to *see* God. Yet God has not chosen to reveal His Person to man.

**Now as I beheld the living creatures, behold one wheel upon the earth by the living creatures, with his four faces.**

**The appearance of the wheels and their work was like unto the colour of a beryl: and they four had one likeness: and their appearance and their work was as it were a wheel in the middle of a wheel [Ezek. 1:15–16].**

Again may I emphasize that this is not a prophecy of the present mechanical age or even of the invention of the wheel. I am sure that in the beginning man felled a tree, cut off part of the trunk, and found that he had a wheelbarrow. When he put two wheels on it, he had a cart. Then when he put four wheels on it, he had a Ford automobile! If that is what you want to see in this vision, may I say to you, that is silly and senile, that is garbage and rubbish. We need to read further to gain an understanding of these wheels within wheels.

**As for their rings, they were so high that they were dreadful; and their rings were full of eyes round about them four [Ezek. 1:18].**

God is a God of intelligent purpose. You and I are not living in a universe that is moving into the future aimlessly and without purpose. God has a purpose for every atom which he has created, and he has a purpose for you, my friend, in His plan and program. The very fact that you and I are alive today reveals that we are to accomplish a purpose for God. God is intelligently carrying out His purpose in the world.

**And when the living creatures went, the wheels went by them: and when the living creatures were lifted up from the earth, the wheels were lifted up.**

**Whithersoever the spirit was to go, they went, thither was their spirit to go; and the wheels were lifted up over against them: for the spirit of the living creature was in the wheels [Ezek. 1:19–20].**

Now we can see more clearly that these wheels speak of the ceaseless activity and energy of God. Our God is omnipotent. The Lord Jesus said, ". . . All power is given unto me in heaven and in earth" (Matt. 28:18). God is moving forward, and He *will* accomplish His purposes.

In Revelation 4 we again read of these four living creatures of Ezekiel's vision. They are set to guard the throne of God, and in guarding the throne they do two things: (1) they protect the throne in the sense that they do not allow man in his sin to come into the presence of God; and (2) they indicate the way that man is to come. "I must needs go home by the way of the cross, there's no other way but this" ("The Way of the Cross Leads Home" by Jessie Brown Pounds). The cherubim show the way.

However, I think that Ezekiel saw something infinitely greater. He saw the cherubim over the world, extending mercy to this little

piece of dirt that is flying through space. Someone has said that man "is nothing in the world but a rash on the epidermis of a second-rate planet." But God made the whole world a mercy seat when Christ died down here, and God is hovering over this world today, ready to receive any sinner who will come through Christ to Him.

**And above the firmament that was over their heads was the likeness of a throne, as the appearance of a sapphire stone: and upon the likeness of the throne was the likeness as the appearance of a man above upon it.**

**And I saw as the colour of amber, as the appearance of fire round about within it, from the appearance of his loins even upward, and from the appearance of his loins even downward, I saw as it were the appearance of fire, and it had brightness round about [Ezek. 1:26–27].**

I see here an amber throne in the azure blue—a sapphire-studded throne flashing like a diamond and colored like a rainbow. The light blinds and obscures. The throne is filled with energy, like a missile on launching. It is moving like a chariot. It is not leaving the earth; it is coming to the earth. I see the cherubim over the world. I see a cross, a Lamb, and the blood. I see a mercy seat: there is mercy with the Lord. In the hymn "Only Trust Him" by J.H. Stockton we sing:

> Come, ev'ry soul by sin oppressed,
> There's mercy with the Lord.

In Romans 9:15 Paul wrote, "For he saith to Moses, I will have mercy on whom I will have mercy, and I will have compassion on whom I will have compassion." We are also told, "The soul that sinneth, it shall die" (Ezek. 18:20). God is saying to us—not only to the house of Israel, but to the whole word—"You *can* come to Me."

**As the appearance of the bow that is in the cloud in the day of rain, so was the appearance of the brightness round about. This was the appearance of the likeness of the glory of the LORD. And when I saw it, I fell upon my face, and I heard a voice of one that spake [Ezek. 1:28].**

"This was the appearance of the likeness of the glory of the LORD." Ezekiel saw more than Moses saw, more than David, Isaiah, or Daniel saw. He saw a vision of the glory of God—not His Person, but His glory. The presence of God was there. When the Lord Jesus came to this earth and took upon Himself our humanity, His glory was not seen. Ezekiel saw the glory of the Lord.

"And when I saw it, I fell upon my face." This vision had a tremendous effect upon Ezekiel, and it should have this effect upon us: "Oh, God, I am undone. I'm lost and I need You. I turn to You and accept You."

We find throughout the Old Testament that when men came into the presence of God, they went down on their faces. This was true of Isaiah who said: ". . . Woe is me! for I am undone; because I am a man of unclean lips, and I dwell in the midst of a people of unclean lips: for mine eyes have seen the King, the LORD of hosts" (Isa. 6:5). In the presence of the Lord, this man found himself horizontal with the ground. That was the position Daniel took also. It was the position John took on the isle of Patmos: "And when I saw him, I fell at his feet as dead . . ." (Rev. 1:17).

What a picture of our holy God we have here! I must say that I stand merely on the fringe, thankful that I'm hidden in the cleft of the rock. Someday I am going to look upon the face of my Savior. I do not know what He looks like, but I am looking forward to that day.

## EZEKIEL'S CALL

**And he said unto me, Son of man, stand upon thy feet, and I will speak unto thee [Ezek. 2:1].**

Apparently after the vision Ezekiel had seen, he was not standing up, but was down on his face. He will now receive a call and commission and an endowment with power for the office to which God has called him.

"Son of man"—God addresses him as "son of man." This title is found exactly one hundred times in the Book of Ezekiel. Daniel, also, is called the son of man. Only these two men in the Old Testament were called by this title. This is also the title that the Lord Jesus appropriated to Himself; eighty-six times in the New Testament He used this title for Himself. It speaks of Him in His rejection, His humiliation, and His exaltation; He is the Son of Man.

Ezekiel did pass through a great deal of suffering. If someone were to ask me whose position I would rather not have—Daniel's, Jeremiah's or Ezekiel's—I would say I would rather not have Ezekiel's. Certainly Daniel was in danger in the court of Babylon—just ask the lions down there in the den where Daniel spent a night with them! If God had not intervened, Daniel would have been lion food. But I would prefer his job to Ezekiel's because he at least had luxurious quarters there in the palace of the king of Babylon. Also, Jeremiah at this time was pretty much retired, although he had been in grave danger during his active ministry until the deportation of the people into captivity. However, this man Ezekiel was sent to do a hard job, a very difficult job. He had the job of speaking to an apostate people. He was sent to people who thought they were God's people, but actually they were in rebellion against God.

The Spirit of God now comes upon Ezekiel and prepares him for this office:

**And the spirit entered into me when he spake unto me, and set me upon my feet, that I heard him that spake unto me [Ezek. 2:2].**

The Spirit of God gave Ezekiel the power to do the job He had given him to do. I believe that when God calls you to do a job He will give you the power to do that job. In fact, God's work can *only* be done with the power of God. If God has called you to do a certain thing, He'll give you the power to do it. The best position you can come to is to recognize that you are not able to do the job the Lord has given to you. Moses finally came to the realization—after forty years in the wilderness—that he could not deliver the people. God said to him, "I can do it through you." God called him to deliver the people, and he was able to do it—not because there was anything in Moses, but because there was a great deal in God.

This is so practical for us today: it works in the ministry, in the pew, and on the mission field. A young couple once came to me saying they had been called to the mission field. I questioned them carefully because I frankly did not feel they were called, although I could not be sure and certainly did not want to stand in their way. They went to the mission field but came back a casualty. As I talked to them, I found they were bitter and felt that God had let them down. They had been willing to go, willing to be martyrs; yet God had not used them. I asked them, "Did it ever occur to you that if you had been called to the mission field, He would have given you the power to do the job?" They had never looked at it from that viewpoint. My friend, we need to recognize that, if we are called of God, He is going to give us the power to do the job. The important thing then is to make sure that we are truly called of God to do a certain thing.

Ezekiel was called to do a harder job than any man I can think of. God is going to tell him about his job. I think that if God had told me something like this when I entered the ministry I would have said, "Now wait a minute, Lord, I'm handing in my resignation right now. I think I'll continue in my job as a bank clerk and see if I can work myself up in the banking world." I'm glad He didn't tell me what He told Ezekiel, because I must confess I am a coward and I come from a long line of cowards. I admire this man Ezekiel. Notice what God tells him about his job:

**And he said unto me, Son of man, I send thee to the children of Israel, to a rebellious nation that hath rebelled against me: they and their fathers have**

transgressed against me, even unto this very day.

**For they are impudent children and stiffhearted. I do send thee unto them; and thou shalt say unto them, Thus saith the Lord God [Ezek. 2:3-4].**

This is a tremendous statement that God makes: "I am going to send you to these people—they are 'a rebellious nation.' " The word *rebellious* occurs again and again in the Book of Ezekiel. They are a people in rebellion against God.

The word that is translated "nation" is not the word that God generally used for His chosen people. The word in the Hebrew is *goi*, and it is the word that Israel used to speak of the Gentiles, the pagans, the heathen. What has happened is that Israel has sunk to the level of the heathen people who lived round about them. God says that they are "a rebellious nation"—they've rebelled against Him—and they are "impudent children."

My friend, the hardest people to reach with the gospel today are church members—those who are in church and who have rejected the gospel and rejected the Word of God. Although they are in church, they are actually against God. They think that being a Christian means to be nice little boys and girls. They play at church—it's a nice game for them. They seek to be sweet and to keep their noses clean. They want to live a life on the surface which is very sedate and comfortable. They don't want anyone coming in and telling them they are lost sinners who need to be saved and to become obedient to God. They are hard people to reach, and my heart goes out to my brethren who are in the ministry today—they are sitting on a hot seat. And I would counsel any young man who is considering the ministry to be sure about his call. If he is not sure of his call, maybe he should sell insurance or something else rather than go into the ministry. To be in the ministry today is not easy *if* you are going to stand for the Word of God.

**And they, whether they will hear, or whether they will forbear, (for they are a rebellious house,) yet shall know that there hath been a prophet among them [Ezek. 2:5].**

God says to Ezekiel, "I am calling you to go to these people, and whether they hear you or whether they don't, they are going to know that there was a prophet of God among them—I'll make sure of that." After Ezekiel was gone, the people would say that he was certainly a prophet of God, although they disagreed with him.

I'll be frank with you, all I want after I'm gone is for people to say that I preached the Word of God the best I knew how. That is what is important.

**And thou, son of man, be not afraid of them, neither be afraid of their words, though briers and thorns be with thee, and thou dost dwell among scorpions: be not afraid of their words, nor be dismayed at their looks, though they be a rebellious house [Ezek. 2:6].**

Apparently Ezekiel was going to be in danger, but God says, "Be not afraid of them, neither be afraid of their words." The Lord really lays it on the line to Ezekiel just what his job was going to be like.

## PREPARATION OF THE PROPHET

In chapter 3 we have the preparation of the prophet for a hard job, a difficult assignment. Jeremiah was a different type of individual from Ezekiel. Jeremiah was the prophet of the broken heart, tears often streaming from his eyes. At that crucial moment in history God needed Jeremiah to let His people know that it was breaking His heart to send them into captivity. Now the people have gone into captivity, and they are bitter and rebellious. However, at this time the temple had not yet been burned or the city of Jerusalem destroyed. It would not be until seven years after this delegation of captives arrived in Babylon that that destruction would occur. Therefore, the false prophets were still telling the people that they were God's people and they would go back home. They said to this man Ezekiel, "Who do you think you are to tell us these things? We are God's people, and we are going back to our land. We will not be in captivity a long time." But God had told Ezekiel, "You tell them they are *not* going back. They are going to be in captivity for seventy years just as Jeremiah said. They are going to be in Babylon seventy years, and they are going to work hard there along the canals, working in the fields and building buildings. It is going to be a hard lot for them."

**Moreover he said unto me, Son of man, eat that thou findest; eat this roll, and go speak unto the house of Israel [Ezek. 3:1].**

"Son of man"—again, this is the title the Lord gives Ezekiel in this hard job, in the suffering he would experience.

"Eat that thou findest; eat this roll, and go speak unto the house of Israel." This is quite a diet—he is to eat the Word of God. The Word of God should become part of us, my friend. No man ought to preach the Word whose heart is not in it and who doesn't believe every word he says. Otherwise, he should get out of the ministry. The pulpit is no place for flowery speech and high-flown excess verbiage. The pulpit is the place to declare the Word of God.

**So I opened my mouth, and he caused me to eat that roll.**

**And he said unto me, Son of man, cause thy belly to eat, and fill thy bowels with this roll that I give thee. Then did I eat it; and it was in my mouth as honey for sweetness [Ezek. 3:2–3].**

For a good diet study the Word of God. May I ask you, do you love the person of Christ? Maybe I ought to first ask, do you love the Word of God? You will never love Him unless you love the Word of God.

A seminary professor asked me one time, "What *theory* of inspiration do you hold?" I said to him, "The theory I hold is no theory at all—*love the Book.*" You have to love the Word of God before it will ever become meaningful to you. The Word of God reveals a Person to you and then you fall in love with Him. Ezekiel said, "It was in my mouth as honey for sweetness"—he loved the Word of God.

**And he said unto me, Son of man, go, get thee unto the house of Israel, and speak with my words unto them.**

**For thou art not sent to a people of a strange speech and of an hard language, but to the house of Israel [Ezek. 3:4–5].**

Ezekiel was not sent to speak to foreigners but to his own people. He would not go as a missionary who has to learn a foreign tongue and a hard language—God sent him "to the house of Israel."

**Not to many people of a strange speech and of an hard language, whose words thou canst not understand. Surely, had I sent thee to them, they would have hearkened unto thee.**

**But the house of Israel will not hearken unto thee; for they will not hearken unto me: for all the house of Israel are impudent and hardhearted [Ezek. 3:6–7].**

"Ezekiel, I am sending you to a congregation that is impudent and in rebellion against Me. They won't hear Me, and they are not going to hear you, either."

**Behold, I have made thy face strong against their faces, and thy forehead strong against their foreheads.**

**As an adamant harder than flint have I made thy forehead: fear them not, neither be dismayed at their looks, though they be a rebellious house [Ezek. 3:8–9].**

The Lord tells Ezekiel, "You are to go ahead and give them My Word, and I am going to make your head hard." Now God didn't make Jeremiah's head hard. Jeremiah had a soft heart, and he couldn't stand up against all the trouble he faced. At one time he even went to the Lord and resigned. Ezekiel is not about to resign. God says, "The children of Israel are hardheaded, and I am going to make your head harder than theirs."

A man came to me one time and said, "You know, our preacher really talked hard to the board the other night, and I don't think a preacher ought to talk that way to the board." "Well," I said, "what kind of a board is it?" He replied, "They've caused the pastor a lot of trouble." I told him, "That's the kind of problem Ezekiel had, but God made his head harder than Israel's. I just hope your preacher's head is harder than anyone's on the board."

## HIS OFFICE AS WATCHMAN

Now God tells Ezekiel what he is to do and how he is to warn Israel.

**Then I came to them of the captivity at Tel-abib, that dwelt by the river of Chebar, and I sat where they sat, and remained there astonished among them seven days.**

**And it came to pass at the end of seven days, that the word of the LORD came unto me, saying,**

**Son of man, I have made thee a watchman unto the house of Israel: therefore hear the word at my mouth, and give them warning from me.**

**When I say unto the wicked, Thou shalt surely die; and thou givest him not**

**warning, nor speakest to warn the wicked from his wicked way, to save his life; the same wicked man shall die in his iniquity; but his blood will I require at thine hand.**

**Yet if thou warn the wicked, and he turn not from his wickedness, nor from his wicked way, he shall die in his iniquity; but thou hast delivered thy soul [Ezek. 3:15–19].**

God gives to Ezekiel the job of being a watchman to warn His people. They may not want it, but he is to warn them. God says to him, "If you do not warn them that they are going to die in their sins I am going to hold you responsible. However, if you warn them and they continue in their disobedience and die in their sins, you will not be responsible."

My friend, I would hate to be in the place of a minister who does not give out the Word of God. I'd hate to be in his position and stand before the Lord Jesus someday in judgment. A man who has the Word of God should have the intestinal fortitude to declare the Word of God. This was Ezekiel's responsibility, and God chose the right man for the job— he was as hard as a hickory nut.

The watchman held a very important position in the ancient world, in that day of walled cities. The cities were walled for protection, and the gates were closed at nightfall. A watchman then ascended the wall to begin the vigil of the long, dark night. With a trained eye he peered into the impenetrable darkness which surrounded the city. With a trained ear alert to every noise, he listened for the approach of danger, for the approach of an enemy.

The Word of God has quite a bit to say about the watchman. In Isaiah 62:6 we read: "I have set watchmen upon thy walls, O Jerusalem, which shall never hold their peace day nor night. . . ." And then in Psalm 127:1 it says, "Except the LORD build the house, they labour in vain that build it: except the LORD keep the city, the watchman waketh but in vain."

In the Hebrew culture, the watchmen functioned in three watches of the night; that is, they had three shifts: from dark until about midnight; from midnight until cockcrow, which was probably about two or three o'clock; and from then until dawn. The watchman in the morning watch was the one who announced the dawn. The Romans had the night divided into four watches.

We might think that the practice of having watchmen belongs to a backward age and a day that is past, that at the dawn of civilization it was satisfactory but it's not needed today. However, we are finding out again that we need watchmen. The police who patrol all during the night in our cities are watchmen. I personally feel they should have more support from the citizens and from the legal profession. We should stand behind them. I know that some of them individually are not what they should be, but we should respect their office and respect the fact that they do protect us during the night. But if we continue on the lawless path on which we are now, I am afraid that the day will come when they will not be able to help us at all.

The Book of Isaiah teaches us that the watchman had not only a responsibility, but also a visibility. He was to be able to distinguish the enemy out there in the darkness. Today, the minister is to be the watchman for his community. He should be able to give a warning of danger—he is *responsible* to give that type of message.

**Again, When a righteous man doth turn from his righteousness, and commit iniquity, and I lay a stumblingblock before him, he shall die: because thou hast not given him warning, he shall die in his sin, and his righteousness which he hath done shall not be remembered; but his blood will I require at thine hand [Ezek. 3:20].**

This verse has been used to argue that a believer can fall from grace, a teaching which is not found in the Word of God. Galatians 5:4 is the only place where you will find the expression ". . . fallen from grace." There it is not speaking of salvation but of those who have been saved by grace but have fallen down to a legal level and are attempting to live by the law instead of living by grace. The great teaching of Galatians is that we are saved by grace and are to live by grace.

Here in Ezekiel we have a man who is living under the time of law. His life was determined by righteous acts. Under normal circumstances the righteous acts he might perform might look very good. But under time of stress and strain he might turn from God, and he would be judged for it. We are not to construe that he was once saved. He will be tested at the end of his life as to whether he is a child of God or not.

Today you and I are living under grace, and righteousness is determined in a little different way. We are constituted righteous by

447 EZEKIEL 2-3

faith in Jesus Christ. We are saved by grace through faith. In Romans 4:5 we are told "But to him that worketh not, but believeth on him that justifieth the ungodly, his faith is counted [reckoned] for righteousness." The true believer today may fall into sin, but he will not deliberately practice and live in sin: "Whosoever is born of God doth not commit [practice] sin . . ." (1 John 3:9). If a believer falls into sin, a gracious provision is made—we have an Advocate with the Father, and we can come to Him in confession of our sins.

The emphasis in Ezekiel is not so much upon this man living under law but upon the responsibility of the watchman. The watchman is to warn the man who has turned from good works to living in a way that conforms to the standard of the enemy.

**And the hand of the LORD was there upon me; and he said unto me, Arise, go forth into the plain, and I will there talk with thee [Ezek. 3:22].**

Having been told he is to be a watchman, God now tells Ezekiel to leave these people. For seven days he has sat among them overwhelmed by how far they have apostatized and turned from God. God calls him to leave them.

**Then I arose, and went forth into the plain: and, behold, the glory of the LORD stood there, as the glory which I saw by the river of Chebar: and I fell on my face [Ezek. 3:23].**

The subject of the glory of God will appear again and again in the Book of Ezekiel. What is *glory*, by the way? Some will say that glory is something you cannot see, that it is intangible. I feel that is entirely wrong. Glory is something that produces a sensation on all five of our senses. Glory has size. How big is it? Is it long or square or round? May I say, glory has the size of the infinity of space. The Word of God tells us, "The heavens declare the glory of God; and the firmament sheweth his handiwork" (Ps. 19:1). The glory of God is seen in this tremendous universe that you and I live in. Glory also has a beauty to it: ". . . whose glorious beauty is a fading flower . . ." (Isa. 28:1). Glory is beautiful. My, heaven is going to be a beautiful place. How lovely it's going to be! Glory has to do with adornment. We read in Scripture that He was

". . . glorious in his apparel . . ." (Isa. 63:1). He is really dressed up and lovely in the garb that he wears. There is a majesty about glory. Psalm 8:1 declares, "O LORD our Lord, how excellent is thy name in all the earth! who hast set thy glory above the heavens." This is the majesty of God; it is bright and light, precious and pure. Finally, glory also sets forth honor and dignity. Daniel said, "O thou king, the most high God gave Nebuchadnezzar thy father a kingdom, and majesty, and glory, and honour" (Dan. 5:18). The very name of God suggests His dignity, His glory. Ezekiel saw the glory of the Lord.

**Then the spirit entered into me, and set me upon my feet, and spake with me, and said unto me, Go, shut thyself within thine house.**

**But thou, O son of man, behold, they shall put bands upon thee, and shall bind thee with them, and thou shalt not go out among them [Ezek. 3:24-25].**

The usual interpretation of this verse is that the enemy binds Ezekiel so that they can take him out of the house. However, Ezekiel wanted to stay in that house and he would not go although they had bound him.

Instead of speaking a great deal, Ezekiel is going to act out the parables which God gives to him. This is one of them: he goes into his house and locks himself in. Why? To show that God has rejected this rebellious people.

**And I will make thy tongue cleave to the roof of thy mouth, that thou shalt be dumb, and shalt not be to them a reprover: for they are a rebellious house.**

**But when I speak with thee, I will open thy mouth, and thou shalt say unto them, Thus saith the Lord GOD; He that heareth, let him hear; and he that forbeareth, let him forbear: for they are a rebellious house [Ezek. 3:26-27].**

Ezekiel's job is to say, "Thus saith the Lord GOD." Back in chapter 2, verse 7 we read, "And thou shalt speak my words unto them." This man is to give God's Word to these people, and that is the only time he's to speak to them. He is to be dumb at other times. He had only the Word of God to give them.

# CHAPTERS 4–5

**THEME:** *Judgment of Jerusalem; sign of the prophet shaving his hair*

In chapters 4 and 5 Ezekiel is going to use certain signs and act out certain parables before the people. At this time Jerusalem was not yet destroyed, and the false prophets were telling the people of Israel that they were going to have peace. They were saying that the Jews already in Babylonian captivity would return to their land shortly, but Ezekiel is going to confirm the word of Jeremiah, who had told them they would not be going back and that Jerusalem would be destroyed.

G. K. Chesterton writing in the early twentieth century said, "This is the age of pacifism, but it is not the age of peace." Throughout history man has engaged in fifteen thousand wars and he has signed some eight thousand peace treaties; yet during five or six thousand years of history he has never enjoyed more than two to three hundred years of true peace. Man is a warlike creature, whether he likes to think so or not. Paul wrote in 1 Thessalonians 5:3, "For when they shall say, Peace and safety; then sudden destruction cometh upon them, as travail upon a woman with child; and they shall not escape." May I say to you, there is only one Prince of Peace, the Lord Jesus Christ.

## JUDGMENT OF JERUSALEM

Ezekiel is going to show these people that there is not going to be any peace and that Jerusalem is going to be destroyed.

> Thou also, son of man, take thee a tile, and lay it before thee, and portray upon it the city, even Jerusalem [Ezek. 4:1].

"A tile" in that day meant a brick. This was their writing material; the Babylonians used clay bricks on which they kept their records. Many, many of these bricks have been found, and they have writing upon them. They are almost square, about fourteen by twelve inches in size.

What Ezekiel was to do was to draw the city of Jerusalem on the brick (I do not know just how he did it), and then he was to break the brick to show that the city was going to be destroyed.

> Moreover take thou unto thee an iron pan, and set it for a wall of iron between thee and the city: and set thy face against it, and it shall be besieged, and thou shalt lay siege against it. This shall be a sign to the house of Israel [Ezek. 4:3].

Now Ezekiel was to take an iron pan and put it between himself and this picture of Jerusalem which he had made to show that God had put a wall between Himself and the city of Jerusalem. The destruction of the city was inevitable; it could not be stopped. What a tremendous way in which to bring God's message to these people!

The sign of the tile portrayed the siege of Jerusalem. The second sign of the pan showed the hardships of divine judgment, that the people were to go through terrible suffering. A third sign describes additional punishments to come upon Jerusalem. It is the sign of the defiled bread:

> Take thou also unto thee wheat, and barley, and beans, and lentils, and millet, and fitches, and put them in one vessel, and make thee bread thereof, according to the number of the days that thou shalt lie upon thy side, three hundred and ninety days shalt thou eat thereof.
>
> And thy meat which thou shalt eat shall be by weight, twenty shekels a day: from time to time shalt thou eat it.
>
> Thou shalt drink also water by measure, the sixth part of an hin: from time to time shalt thou drink.
>
> And thou shalt eat it as barley cakes, and thou shalt bake it with dung that cometh out of man, in their sight.
>
> And the LORD said, Even thus shall the children of Israel eat their defiled bread among the Gentiles, whither I will drive them [Ezek. 4:9–13].

These instructions would be overwhelming to most of us, but they were especially difficult for Ezekiel to follow because he was a priest and had never eaten anything unclean:

> Then said I, Ah Lord GOD! behold, my soul hath not been polluted: for from my youth up even till now have I not eaten of that which dieth of itself, or is torn in pieces; neither came there

abominable flesh into my mouth [Ezek. 4:14].

However, this was to be a sign from the Lord of the famine the people would experience at the time of the destruction of the city of Jerusalem. Despite the continued promises of the false prophets, the city and the people were going to be lost. These various signs described the horrors that were to come.

## SIGN OF THE PROPHET SHAVING HIS HAIR

Chapter 5 opens with Ezekiel acting out yet another sign to the people:

And thou, son of man, take thee a sharp knife, take thee a barber's razor, and cause it to pass upon thine head and upon thy beard: then take thee balances to weigh, and divide the hair.

Thou shalt burn with fire a third part in the midst of the city, when the days of the siege are fulfilled: and thou shalt take a third part, and smite about it with a knife: and a third part thou shalt scatter in the wind; and I will draw out a sword after them.

Thou shalt also take thereof a few in number, and bind them in thy skirts [Ezek. 5:1–3].

This must have looked something like one of our modern commercials for an electric razor—only they didn't have electric razors in those days! Just what was the meaning of this? Ezekiel was to shave his head and his beard, which was unusual for a priest to do. I imagine the people gathered all around to watch as Ezekiel shaved himself out there in the open.

After he shaved, Ezekiel carefully divided the hair into three parts. One third of the hair he took and burned inside the city. This represented the people who were going to be besieged and burned with fire inside the city at the time of its destruction—this is exactly what happened to them. The second third of the hair he took and smote—he really worked it over. This depicted what was to happen to those people who lived through the siege—they fell by the sword. The last third of the people were scattered out; this group included those who went down to Egypt taking Jeremiah with them. The small remnant of God's people who eventually returned to the city is pictured by the few hairs that were bound up in Ezekiel's skirts.

A third part of thee shall die with the pestilence, and with famine shall they be consumed in the midst of thee: and a third part shall fall by the sword round about thee; and I will scatter a third part into all the winds, and I will draw out a sword after them [Ezek. 5:12].

This is the message that Ezekiel brought, and he made its meaning very clear.

So will I send upon you famine and evil beasts, and they shall bereave thee; and pestilence and blood shall pass through thee; and I will bring the sword upon thee. I the LORD have spoken it [Ezek. 5:17].

Ezekiel's warning to the people went unheeded. The destruction of Jerusalem and the suffering endured by the people should be a warning to us of the reality of divine judgment. But we are so far removed from it, and very few people are really acquainted with the Word of God today. (The greatest sin among Christians is ignorance of the Word of God.) God gave this warning to the people of Jerusalem, but it has a message for us also, as does all Scripture. My friend, when the judgment of God begins, it is going to be too late to make your decision. Today, if you will hear His voice, He says, "(. . . behold, now is the accepted time; behold, now is the day of salvation.)" (2 Cor. 6:2, italics mine). The real "Now Generation" are those who have not postponed their decision but have already accepted God's salvation.

# CHAPTER 6

**THEME:** *Sword to fall upon Jerusalem; remnant to be saved*

The book of Ezekiel is a very orderly book, and up to this point we have had prophecies which largely concerned Jerusalem. However, the prophet will now turn his attention to the whole land of Israel: judgment is going to come upon the whole land.

Ezekiel is with the second delegation of people who were taken captive by Nebuchadnezzar. They were slaves of the government of Babylon working in the agricultural area by the river Chebar, the great canal running off the Euphrates River. Most of the people, however, were still back in the land, and Jerusalem had not yet been devastated. The false prophets continued to assure the people that everything was going to be all right and that the captives would be able to return shortly. Meanwhile, Jeremiah was saying that the captivity would last seventy years, but they paid no attention to him. They listened to the false prophets because their message sounded better and was very optimistic.

I have found the same attitude among people throughout the years of my ministry. After I preached a series of messages on the judgments of God found in the books of the prophets, one very prominent man in my church at that time withdrew from the church. He said, "I go to church to be comforted, and I am not being comforted." He did not want to hear the Word of God. I discovered later that in his business dealings he did not need to be comforted; the judgment messages were good for him—they were digging in right where he was! Another lady stopped coming to my church, saying, There were times when Dr. McGee made me feel very bad. Now I go to church, and the preacher makes me feel very good." Frankly, her church was a cult, and its message concerned how to make friends and influence people. It emphasized the power of positive thinking: just feel good about it, and it will be good. May I say to you, that is *not* the message of the Word of God.

In chapters 6 and 7 we have two messages of judgment. Ezekiel now is going to speak on that which concerns all of the land, and his message is that the idolaters are to die and the land is to be desolated.

## SWORD TO FALL UPON JERUSALEM

**And the word of the LORD came unto me, saying [Ezek. 6:1].**

This verse opens the first of the two messages; the second message in chapter 7 begins the same way: "Moreover the word of the LORD came unto me, saying" (Ezek. 7:1). The people would not accept what Ezekiel said, but Ezekiel told them, "I'm not telling you what I *think*, and I'm not telling you what I *hope* or what I'd *like* to see come to pass. I'm telling you what *God* says."

It is also interesting to note that both of these messages conclude with "and they shall know that I am the LORD." God sent this judgment upon them so that they would know He was the Lord; one of the purposes of judgment is that men might know that God is a holy God.

This world needs to know that God is a holy God. We have had a great deal of emphasis upon the fact that God is love. While it is true that God is love, it is only half the story. We need to look on the other side of the coin: God is holy, and God *will* punish sin. If you turn in disobedience from Him, if you deny Him and do not accept His salvation, there is only one alternative left—judgment. Men today try to excuse themselves; they do not want to recognize that they are sinners. They attempt to write God off and bow Him out of His universe by saying He does not even exist.

A brilliant young Hebrew, who was a chaplain at the University of Pittsburgh a number of years ago, attempted to show that God did not exist. His argument was based on the premise that the God of the Hebrew Bible is depicted as the faithful protector of His chosen people, but at least six million Jews had died at the hands of the Nazis. He wrote, "To believe in the God of the covenant today you must affirm that their Creator [that is, of the nation Israel] used Adolph Hitler as the rod of His wrath to send His people to the death camps, and I find myself utterly incapable of believing this. Even the existentialist's leap of faith cannot resurrect this dead God after Auschwitz." This young rabbi speaks of the death of God as a cultural event. Wistfully and sadly he comes to the conclusion that there is no God because the God of the covenant is a God who would protect Israel and would never let anything happen to them. May I point out that he never takes into consideration, as Ezekiel did, that there might be something wrong with the people upon whom the judgment came. They had turned their backs

upon God and had denied Him. They had been given a special privilege, and that privilege created a responsibility which they did not measure up to.

Ezekiel is telling the people that it is God who is sending this judgment that He might confirm to them that He is a *holy* God. His judgment is an awful thing. Paul wrote, "Knowing therefore the terror of the Lord, we persuade men . . ." (2 Cor. 5:11). Because Ezekiel was made aware of God's holiness at the beginning of his ministry, he devoted his life to the ministry of "persuading men."

**Son of man, set thy face toward the mountains of Israel, and prophesy against them [Ezek. 6:2].**

The judgment is to come upon the entire land.

**And say, Ye mountains of Israel, hear the word of the Lord GOD; Thus saith the Lord GOD to the mountains, and to the hills, to the rivers, and to the valleys; Behold, I, even I, will bring a sword upon you, and I will destroy your high places [Ezek. 6:3].**

"Mountain" in Scripture, if used figuratively, speaks of government, but you need to determine if it is being used literally or figuratively. I believe Ezekiel is speaking of that land, the good old terra firma—right down where there's plenty of dirt.

"I will destroy your high places." In that land under every kind of tree there was a heathen altar around which the grossest immorality took place. This is what the heathen, the Gentiles did, but now this nation, God's chosen people, had given themselves over to the same idolatry. God says to them, "Judgment is coming upon you."

**And your altars shall be desolate, and your images shall be broken: and I will cast down your slain men before your idols.**

**And I will lay the dead carcases of the children of Israel before their idols; and I will scatter your bones round about your altars [Ezek. 6:4–5].**

It is too bad that the Jews in Germany did not read the Book of Ezekiel rather than turning to a man like Hitler, which the entire nation did at the beginning. Israel should have turned to the living and true God and been acquainted with His method of dealing with men. You cannot trifle with God, my friend. Judgment does come.

America struggles to bring peace to the world; but, instead of solving our problems, they continue to mount up. Why? Because God judges. Do you think God is a senile old man with long whiskers, sitting on a cloud and weeping crocodile tears? My friend, God is a *holy* God. In chapter 1 Ezekiel saw a vision of a holy God: those wheels within wheels depicting the energy of God as He moves forward to accomplish His purposes, and the fire and whirlwind showing that God does move in judgment upon this earth in which we live. To understand God in this way may be a bitter pill, but when we take the bitter pills the doctor gives us, they do help us. We need to swallow this bitter pill: we are dealing with a holy God, and He is not wrong; we are the ones who are wrong. Are you willing to admit that?

God is saying, "I am going to judge Israel, and it is not going to be easy." I am afraid Israel was not at all willing to admit their wrong.

## REMNANT TO BE SAVED

**Yet will I leave a remnant, that ye may have some that shall escape the sword among the nations, when ye shall be scattered through the countries [Ezek. 6:8].**

There were some among these people who remained faithful to God. The nation as a whole went away from God, but there was a believing remnant. This is true of the church today. Liberalism has taken over the bulk of the organized church, but there are many of God's people left. God takes note of the faithful ones.

**And they that escape of you shall remember me among the nations whither they shall be carried captives, because I am broken with their whorish heart, which hath departed from me, and with their eyes, which go a-whoring after their idols: and they shall loathe themselves for the evils which they have committed in all their abominations [Ezek. 6:9].**

"And they that escape of you shall remember me among the nations whither they shall be carried captives." What is this remnant going to do? They are going to be a witness for God.

"Because I am broken with their whorish heart, which hath departed from me" would be better translated "when I shall have broken their whorish heart which has de-

parted from me." They are people who belong to Him, but they have played the harlot, they have committed spiritual adultery. The organized church which will remain after Christ takes His true church out of the world is also called a harlot in Revelation 17. That is the most frightful chapter in the Word of God—it presents a terrible picture.

"They shall loathe themselves for the evils which they have committed in all their abominations." This was one of the results of judgment, but we do not see this result in our world today. This means simply that there will be more judgment, and that judgment is coming during the Great Tribulation Period. The people at that time will gnaw their tongues because of the judgment of God. You would think there would be a great wave of repentance, but there will not be among that crowd.

In Ezekiel's day there were those who loathed themselves—they repented because they were still close to God. That will be true of God's people always. If you do not hate yourself whenever you serve the Devil, then you must not be one of God's people.

**And they shall know that I am the Lord, and that I have not said in vain that I would do this evil unto them [Ezek. 6:10].**

"And they shall know that I am the Lord"— this is said three times in this chapter, and it is another result of judgment. Again, we do not see this result happening in our own day. Instead of recognizing the hand of God, people are saying that He is not even there. They argue that if He did exist, He would always help them. Oh, my friend, where do we get that idea? God is judging sin. People rebel against this; they do not want a God who judges. You can make a God after your own likeness if you want to, but the holy God is still out there. You might wish He would go away, but He is not going to go away. He will continue to judge.

**Then shall ye know that I am the Lord, when their slain men shall be among their idols round about their altars, upon every high hill, in all the tops of the mountains, and under every green tree, and under every thick oak, the place where they did offer sweet savour to all their idols [Ezek. 6:13].**

I happen to know that the persecution under Hitler drove many wonderful Jews to God. There is a great company of believers today in Europe as a result of that. We forget about them, and very little is said about them. I received a letter once from a wonderful girl whose parents died in those gas chambers, and she testified to the fact that the horrible experience had been the means of her salvation. We need to recognize the hand of God— He is a holy God. If He did not spare His own Son, but let Him die when He became sin for us, why in the world do sinners think they will escape His judgment?

"Their altars, upon every high hill"—God spells out the reason He judged them in the land. My friend, the judgment of God is still upon that land. Many folk like to speak of it as "the land of milk and honey." Don't kid yourself—it is not the land of milk and honey today. The people are not turning to Him, and His judgment is still on that land.

**So will I stretch out my hand upon them, and make the land desolate, yea, more desolate than the wilderness toward Diblath, in all their habitations: and they shall know that I am the Lord [Ezek. 6:14].**

I do not know about "the wilderness toward Diblath," but I do know what it is like between Jerusalem and Jericho right now, and I am not interested in buying real estate there. If it were not for their need of protection, I think Israel would be willing to turn it back to the Arabs and let them have it!

"They shall know that I am the Lord"— again, this is one of His tremendous purposes in judgment.

# CHAPTER 7

**THEME:** *Prophecy of the final destruction of Jerusalem*

Chapter 7 contains the second of two messages of judgment against the entire land of Israel. Through chapter 5 Ezekiel's messages had concerned Jerusalem, but now the whole land is in view. Jerusalem had not yet been destroyed and, although most of the inhabitants had been removed from the land, many people still remained there. However, the events which had already taken place did not cause them to turn to God.

**Moreover the word of the LORD came unto me, saying [Ezek. 7:1].**

Ezekiel is passing on to the people of Israel what *God* has to say. The first message, given in chapter 6, opened with the same words.

**Also, thou son of man, thus saith the Lord GOD unto the land of Israel; An end, the end is come upon the four corners of the land [Ezek. 7:2].**

Judgment was to come upon that land, and of course it would include the people of the land. The land of Israel and the nation Israel are always considered together in the Word of God.

A new element is added to Ezekiel's prophecy in this message—this is now the prophecy of the *final* destruction of the land and of Jerusalem. The final deportation will take place, and the city will be destroyed.

**Now is the end come upon thee, and I send mine anger upon thee, and will judge thee according to thy ways, and will recompense upon thee all thine abominations [Ezek. 7:3].**

This message is in the form of marvelous Hebrew poetry, and throughout this chapter I would like to quote to you a translation by the late Dr. A. C. Gaebelein (*The Prophet Ezekiel*, p. 48). He has translated this quite literally in poetic form. This then is his translation of verses 1–3.

And the Word of Jehovah came unto me, saying, And thou Son of Man, thus saith Jehovah unto the land of Israel:

An end cometh! The end
Upon the four corners of the land.
Now cometh the end upon thee
And I will send mine anger upon thee,
And I will judge thee according to thy ways,

And I will bring upon thee all thine abominations.

God says to Israel, "I am going to judge you according to your ways." The judgment or the punishment will fit the crime.

We need to ask ourselves: How serious is it to be a professed witness for God and yet really be a phony? How serious is it to be a church member and not be saved? That brings the issue right down to where the rubber meets the road for us in this day. I have said many times that I would rather be a Hottentot in the darkest corner of Africa, bowing down to an idol, than to be a church member sitting in the pew, professing to be a Christian, yet not knowing the Lord Jesus Christ as my Savior! I will not argue with you about what God will do with the Hottentot—the Lord has His plan for him. I will talk about church members who are not truly saved. That is the issue in our day which corresponds to what Ezekiel is talking about. Ezekiel says that such a man's responsibility is great, because he has heard the Word of God, and he has turned his back upon it. The more he hears, the greater his responsibility grows, I can assure you of that.

**And mine eye shall not spare thee, neither will I have pity: but I will recompense thy ways upon thee, and thine abominations shall be in the midst of thee: and ye shall know that I am the LORD.**

**Thus saith the Lord GOD; An evil, an only evil, behold, is come.**

**An end is come, the end is come: it watcheth for thee; behold, it is come.**

**The morning is come unto thee, O thou that dwellest in the land: the time is come, the day of trouble is near, and not the sounding again of the mountains.**

**Now will I shortly pour out my fury upon thee, and accomplish mine anger upon thee: and I will judge thee according to thy ways, and will recompense thee for all thine abominations.**

**And mine eye shall not spare, neither will I have pity: I will recompense thee according to thy ways, and thine abominations that are in the midst of thee;**

**and ye shall know that I am the Lord that smiteth [Ezek. 7:4–9].**

Again, let me give you Dr. Gaebelein's translation (*The Prophet Ezekiel*, p. 48) of these verses:

And mine eyes shall not spare thee,
Neither will I have pity:
Because I will bring thy ways upon thee
And thine abominations shall be in the
    midst of thee:
And ye shall know that I am Jehovah.

Thus saith the Lord Jehovah!
An evil—an only evil!—behold it com-
    eth.
An end is come—the end is come!
It awaketh against thee. Behold it com-
    eth!
O inhabitant of the land, thy doom is
    come unto thee
The set time is come, the day is near,
The day of tumult.
And not the joyous shouting upon the
    mountains;
Now will I soon pour out my fury upon
    thee
And accomplish mine anger against thee.
I will judge thee according to thy ways,
And I will bring upon thee all thine
    abominations.
Mine eye shall not spare, neither will I
    have pity.
According to thy ways will I render unto
    thee,
And thine abominations shall be in the
    midst of thee,
And ye shall know that I am Jehovah,
    who smiteth.

This is a tremendous passage of Scripture which, I dare say, few deal with today—it is totally unknown to multitudes of church members. Someone will argue, "Well, it belongs way back in the Old Testament, and that makes it different." My friend, Ezekiel's language is tame compared to the Book of Revelation and to the words of the Lord Jesus in Matthew 25. Ezekiel's words here are those of a sissy compared to many passages in the New Testament. The God of the New Testament is the same Person as the God of the Old Testament, and He will punish sin in any age.

I mentioned in the previous chapter a young Jewish rabbi who wants to dismiss God altogether because he cannot reconcile what happened to the six million Jews in Hitler's Germany. All I want to say is that that ought

to be a warning to the church of God today. Will God judge? Yes, He will! It is no wonder that Paul said, "Knowing therefore the terror of the Lord, we persuade men . . ." (2 Cor. 5:11).

Many are playing church today, making it a cheap sort of thing. They speak of their "allegiance," their "dedication," but do not have a full commitment to Jesus Christ. That is the tragedy of this moment. Our problem is not that we do not have enough church members—the problem is we have too many who are not genuine Christians. There was a great preacher in New York City many years ago who made this statement: "One cold church member hurts the cause of Christ more than twenty blatant, blaspheming atheists." Ezekiel's message was not popular in his day, nor is it today.

**Behold the day, behold, it is come: the morning is gone forth; the rod hath blossomed, pride hath budded.**

**Violence is risen up into a rod of wickedness: none of them shall remain, nor of their multitude, nor of any of theirs: neither shall there be wailing for them.**

**The time is come, the day draweth near: let not the buyer rejoice, nor the seller mourn: for wrath is upon all the multitude thereof.**

**For the seller shall not return to that which is sold, although they were yet alive: for the vision is touching the whole multitude thereof, which shall not return; neither shall any strengthen himself in the iniquity of his life.**

**They have blown the trumpet, even to make all ready; but none goeth to the battle: for my wrath is upon all the multitude thereof [Ezek. 7:10–14].**

Here is Dr. Gaebelein's rendering (*The Prophet Ezekiel*, pp. 49-50) of this passage:

Behold the Day! Behold it cometh!
Thy doom advanceth:
The rod hath blossomed, pride hath
    budded.
Violence has risen up into a rod of wick-
    edness;
None of them shall remain; yea none of
    their multitude
Nor their wealth; neither shall there be
    eminency among them.
The time is come, the day draweth near;

Let not the buyer rejoice, nor the seller
  mourn,
For wrath is upon all the multitude
  thereof.
For the seller shall not return to that
  which is sold,
Even though he were yet amongst the
  living.
In the vision touching the whole multi-
  tude thereof
It shall not be revoked;
And none shall through his iniquity
  assure his life.
They have blown the trumpet and made
  all ready,
But none goeth to the battle;
For my wrath is upon all the multitude
  thereof.

The thing that characterized these people was
that they were a bunch of protesters—they
were pacifists and wouldn't go to war. They
refused to stand for that which was right, my
friend. The judgment came, and when the
enemy came in, he didn't have any silly notions about pacifism. I mentioned before
G. K. Chesterson's comment, "This is the age
of pacifism, but it is not the age of peace." It is
true that men today are weary of war, but as
long as there is iniquity in the human heart
God has said, "There is no peace . . . to the
wicked" (Isa. 57:21). Isaiah repeated that
truth three times in his prophecy.

**They shall cast their silver in the
streets, and their gold shall be removed:
their silver and their gold shall not be
able to deliver them in the day of the
wrath of the LORD: they shall not satisfy their souls, neither fill their
bowels: because it is the stumblingblock of their iniquity [Ezek. 7:19].**

Dr. Gaebelein's translation (*The Prophet Ezekiel*, p. 51) is:

They shall cast their silver in the streets,
And their gold shall be as an unclean
  thing;
Their silver and their gold shall not be
  able to deliver them
In the day of Jehovah's wrath;
They cannot satisfy their souls, neither
  fill their bowls,
Because it was the stumbling block of
  their iniquity.

Too often in America we have felt that the
almighty dollar could solve every problem of
life. We have spent billions of dollars throughout the world in pursuit of peace. We haven't
done a very good job, but we sure have spent
a lot of money. It is very comfortable to have a
few dollars on hand, but they will not solve
life's problems. This is what God is saying
here to the people of Israel who felt that their
accumulated wealth would protect them—it
did not.

**As for the beauty of his ornament, he
set it in majesty: but they made the
images of their abominations and of
their detestable things therein: therefore have I set it far from them.**

**And I will give it into the hands of the
strangers for a prey, and to the wicked
of the earth for a spoil; and they shall
pollute it.**

**My face will I turn also from them, and
they shall pollute my secret place: for
the robbers shall enter into it, and defile it [Ezek. 7:20–22].**

Dr. Gaebelein continues on page 51:

And the beauty of their ornaments, they
  turned it to pride,
And the images of their abominations,
  their detestable things made they of it.
And I shall give it to the hands of strang-
  ers for a prey,
And to the wicked of the earth for a spoil;
  and they shall profane it.
For I will turn my face from them,
And they shall defile my secret place,
And robbers shall enter into it and pro-
  fane it.

This is an awesome description of the judgment of God, but if you want to read something even more awesome and which still lies
ahead for the world, read Revelation 18 and
19, which describe the destruction of commercial Babylon. It speaks of a day in which
men trust in big business and the stock market and depend on the success of Fifth Avenue. It is a day in which the boys in grey
flannel suits make business successful, and
the government assures that everything in
life will go all right. But it wasn't all right, and
it didn't save them. When they needed deliverance, it could not deliver them.

**Make a chain: for the land is full of
bloody crimes, and the city is full of
violence.**

**Wherefore I will bring the worst of the heathen, and they shall possess their houses: I will also make the pomp of the strong to cease; and their holy places shall be defiled [Ezek. 7:23–24].**

These verses are translated on page 51 by Dr. Gaebelein for us:

Form a chain,
For the land is full of bloody crimes,
And the city full of violence.
Therefore will I bring the worst of the
  nations,
And they shall possess their houses;
And I will make the pride of the mighty
  to cease,
And their sanctuaries shall be defiled.

"The land is full of bloody crimes, and the city is full of violence"—what an accurate picture of our own day!

"Wherefore I will bring the worst of the heathen, and they shall possess their houses." There are many today who want to believe that God will never permit Russia to destroy America. Where do we get that idea? God permitted Babylon, a pagan nation, to destroy His own people. Can America come down? People will say, "Oh, no. We are sending missionaries. We are such nice, lovely people." My friend, it is not safe to walk the streets of America. There's violence; there's crime. Until a nation will become a law-abiding people, God cannot bless them.

You see, people do not like to read Ezekiel's message; they would rather read John 14. Don't misunderstand me—I love John 14, too. But we must remember that Ezekiel 7 is in the Bible also. I do not know where we got the idea that one chapter was a little bit more important than another to read. We need to at least give Ezekiel 7 equal time and let him present his case.

# CHAPTER 8

*THEME: Vision of the glory; temple destroyed because of defilement*

We now come to the second major section of the prophecy of Ezekiel. In this division of the book the complete captivity of Jerusalem and Israel will become a reality, and the glory of the Lord will depart from the temple in Jerusalem.

## VISION OF THE GLORY

In chapter 8 Ezekiel has another vision of the glory of the Lord. The vision transports Ezekiel to Jerusalem, and God's glory appears in the temple at Jerusalem. The question always arises: Was Ezekiel *actually* transported to Jerusalem? I will give you my viewpoint, but this is an issue on which no one can be dogmatic and on which few agree. One answer to the question is that Ezekiel simply saw a vision and he saw it there by the river Chebar. A second explanation is given that Ezekiel literally went to Jerusalem and walked around and saw all that he records here. I do not accept either of these interpretations.

I believe that Ezekiel's experience was very similar to the experiences that the apostles

Paul and John had. Paul said that he had been caught up to the third heaven (2 Cor. 12:1–3). It is my feeling that that occurred at the time he was stoned in Lystra in the Galatian country and was left for dead. I believe he actually was dead and that God raised him from the dead, and that at that time he was caught up to the third heaven. John also, as recorded in Revelation 4, was caught up into heaven. In this I feel John is a picture of the rapture of the church, in which all true believers will be caught up to be with the Lord. Chapters 2 and 3 of Revelation frequently mention "the church," but after John's experience in chapter 4, the church (the "called-out body") is no longer mentioned. She is now the "bride" of Christ, the church which is no longer on the earth but is with her Lord. Therefore, I see John's being caught up into heaven as a picture of the Rapture.

Ezekiel was actually caught up as Paul and John were, but I do not think that the people at Jerusalem and of the surrounding area were aware that he was there. We are not dealing with the natural, and I cannot offer you a

natural explanation. God caught him up, and what happened was supernatural.

> **And it came to pass in the sixth year, in the sixth month, in the fifth day of the month, as I sat in mine house, and the elders of Judah sat before me, that the hand of the Lord GOD fell there upon me [Ezek. 8:1].**

Ezekiel was sitting among the elders. I imagine it was a pretty doleful crowd there.

> **Then I beheld, and lo a likeness as the appearance of fire: from the appearance of his loins even downward, fire; and from his loins even upward, as the appearance of brightness, as the colour of amber [Ezek. 8:2].**

This is very similar to a part of Ezekiel's vision recorded in chapter 1. That tremendous vision of the glory of God is the basis of every vision in the Book of Ezekiel, and I personally think it is the basis of the Book of Revelation.

> **And he put forth the form of an hand, and took me by a lock of mine head; and the spirit lifted me up between the earth and the heaven, and brought me in the visions of God to Jerusalem, to the door of the inner gate that looketh toward the north; where was the seat of the image of jealousy, which provoketh to jealousy.**

> **And behold, the glory of the God of Israel was there, according to the vision that I saw in the plain [Ezek. 8:3-4].**

"And he put forth the form of an hand." God is a Spirit; He doesn't have a hand like I have. But when the Scripture tells me that the *fingerwork* of God is in the heavens then I am able to understand, because I could not understand how God could make the world without a hand. Scripture uses our own finite terms to aid our understanding of the infinite.

"And he took me by a lock of mine head." You will remember that Ezekiel had shaved himself—his face and his head—but that had been about a year before this, and his hair has had time to grow out. God took him by the hair of his head.

"And the spirit lifted me up between the earth and the heaven, and brought me in the visions of God to Jerusalem." Ezekiel was actually caught up and removed by the Spirit of God to Jerusalem. Whether or not his body went along with him is a point I will not argue

about, but I rather think it did. Ezekiel's withdrawal to Jerusalem is not something new in Scripture. Elijah also was caught up (2 Kings 2), and in the New Testament we read of Philip: "And when they were come up out of the water, the Spirit of the Lord caught away Philip, that the eunuch saw him no more: and he went on his way rejoicing" (Acts 8:39). Philip was removed bodily, and that is exactly what happened to Elijah and possibly to this man Ezekiel.

"To Jerusalem, to the door of the inner gate that looketh toward the north; where was the seat of the image of jealousy, which provoketh to jealousy." I believe this "image of jealousy" may be a reference to the idol which Manasseh put in the temple (see 2 Kings 21; 2 Chron. 33) which was an abomination and a blasphemy. Perhaps that old idol had been pushed into a corner and forgotten for awhile, but now in Ezekiel's day it has been pulled out, and the people who should have turned to God in repentance are again worshiping that idol.

In chapters 8–10 of Ezekiel we are going to see the gradual withdrawal of the glory of the Lord from the temple and from Israel. I feel that the glory actually departed back during the reign of Manasseh and that Ezekiel is given a vision of that here. I know that most expositors of Scripture feel that the glory left at the time of the Captivity, but I do not feel that is accurate. If the glory did not leave during the exceedingly evil reign of Manasseh, I cannot see any other period in Israel's history which would cause the glory, the presence of God, to leave.

In this chapter we do not have the complete vision of the departure of the glory. Here we see the glory, and then, because the people did not turn back to God, the glory lifted up from the temple and went out over the city to the east and waited there. It will not be until chapter 10 that we will see the final departure of the glory.

I do not think there is any evidence after the reign of Manasseh that the glory of the Lord was in the temple. This vision was given to Ezekiel to show that God is merciful. He was loath to leave and was ready to save the people of Israel if they would turn to Him. God is merciful, and God is love. But He is also a righteous and just God who cannot permit evil in His universe. He cannot permit that which is contrary to Himself.

Today, God cannot save us by our righteousness or our perfection—we have none to present to Him. He cannot accept anything less than righteousness. He therefore had to

provide a redemption for man, and we must come His way through faith in the Lord Jesus Christ. If we do not, we have an old nature that is in rebellion against God, and God is not going to permit that in His universe, anymore than a policeman should harbor a criminal in his home.

## TEMPLE DESTROYED BECAUSE OF DEFILEMENT

**Then said he unto me, Son of man, lift up thine eyes now the way toward the north. So I lifted up mine eyes the way toward the north, and behold northward at the gate of the altar this image of jealousy in the entry [Ezek. 8:5].**

The temple is defiled. The people are no longer worshipping the living and true God but are breaking the first two commandments.

**And he brought me to the door of the court; and when I looked, behold a hole in the wall.**

**Then said he unto me, Son of man, dig now in the wall: and when I had digged in the wall, behold a door.**

**And he said unto me, Go in, and behold the wicked abominations that they do here [Ezek. 8:7–9].**

If Ezekiel is over there just in his spirit, how in the world could he crawl through a hole? How does a spirit dig a hole? If he were a spirit, he wouldn't *need* to dig a hole. I believe he was there bodily, and he dug a hole and was apparently brought down into a basement or a cave. What does he find down there?

**So I went in and saw; and behold every form of creeping things, and abominable beasts, and all the idols of the house of Israel, portrayed upon the wall round about [Ezek. 8:10].**

These people are worshiping the creature rather than the Creator—this is as low as they could go. Man will turn to this type of thing when he has absolutely repudiated the living and true God. This is what they were doing in Egypt at the time of the Exodus; they were worshiping every kind of beast. That is the reason the plagues upon Egypt were aimed at the different gods of Egypt. In Romans 1 we read: "Because that, when they knew God, they glorified him not as God . . . . Who changed the truth of God into a lie, and worshipped and served the creature more than

the Creator, who is blessed for ever . . ." (Rom. 1:21, 25). This means that Israel has sunk down to the level of the nations round about her, and she is no longer a witness for the living and true God. For this reason, He will destroy the temple.

**And there stood before them seventy men of the ancients of the house of Israel, and in the midst of them stood Jaazaniah the son of Shaphan, with every man his censer in his hand; and a thick cloud of incense went up.**

**Then said he unto me, Son of man, hast thou seen what the ancients of the house of Israel do in the dark, every man in the chambers of his imagery? for they say, The LORD seeth us not; the LORD hath forsaken the earth [Ezek. 8:11–12].**

You see, they have dismissed God. They said He was not watching them. And those today who say that God is dead are really trying to say that God is not looking at us, that we are not responsible to Him, we owe Him nothing and may do as we please. That is what Israel was doing. They were apparently worshiping this idol, and they were doing it in secret. Talk about a secret lodge—they sure had one in the temple there.

My friend, in this day the believer's *body* is God's temple on earth. Is He pleased by what He sees going on in our minds and hearts?

**He said also unto me, Turn thee yet again, and thou shalt see greater abominations that they do.**

**Then he brought me to the door of the gate of the LORD'S house which was toward the north; and, behold, there sat women weeping for Tammuz.**

**Then said he unto me, Hast thou seen this, O son of man? turn thee yet again, and thou shalt see greater abominations than these [Ezek. 8:13–15].**

"There sat women weeping for Tammuz." This was an awful thing that was going on. Tammuz was the Babylonian Dumuzi, the god of spring vegetation. He died in the fall and winter and went down to the netherworld to be revived again each returning summer. The worship of this god was practiced in Phoenicia and spread to Greece, where Adonis was Tammuz' counterpart. These weeping women were celebrating the death of this god; his worship was actually the worship of nature

and connected with it were some vile and immoral ceremonies.

**And he brought me into the inner court of the Lord's house, and, behold, at the door of the temple of the Lord, between the porch and the altar, were about five and twenty men, with their backs toward the temple of the Lord, and their faces toward the east; and they worshipped the sun toward the east [Ezek. 8:16].**

The greatest of all the abominations was the worship of the sun. This was happening right in the temple between the porch and the altar. They can sink no lower than this.

**Then he said unto me, Hast thou seen this, O son of man? Is it a light thing to the house of Judah that they commit the abominations which they commit here? for they have filled the land with violence, and have returned to provoke me to anger: and, lo, they put the branch to their nose [Ezek. 8:17].**

"And, lo, they put the branch to their nose." There are many ways of interpreting this; Jewish commentators of the past have said that it speaks of shocking, low, and degrading religious rites. Perhaps it could be compared with a man "thumbing his nose" today. This is what they were doing to God!

God now expresses His anger—

**Therefore will I also deal in fury: mine eye shall not spare, neither will I have pity: and though they cry in mine ears with a loud voice, yet will I not hear them [Ezek. 8:18].**

Israel has stepped over the line—they can go no lower than this. God will now judge them.

My friend, God loves you and will save you if you will come to Him by faith and trust Christ as your Savior. God also judges, and He is a holy and righteous God, and He makes no apology for it. We can say with Paul, ". . . Is there unrighteousness with God? God forbid" (Rom. 9:14). God is right in everything He does; if He judges, He is right to do so. It will be quite a revelation to this generation when it is shown that it is wrong and God is right. God will judge sin.

# CHAPTERS 9–10

**THEME:** *Shekinah glory prepares to leave temple; Shekinah glory fills the holy place; Shekinah glory departs*

### SHEKINAH GLORY PREPARES TO LEAVE THE TEMPLE

In chapter 9 the Shekinah glory prepares to leave the temple at Jerusalem. I believe that from the days of Manasseh there was the coming and going of the Shekinah glory. God is merciful; He doesn't, in a petulant mood, give up on people. God is longsuffering and not willing that any should perish.

**And, behold, six men came from the way of the higher gate, which lieth toward the north, and every man a slaughter weapon in his hand; and one man among them was clothed with linen, with a writer's inkhorn by his side: and they went in, and stood beside the brasen altar.**

**And the glory of the God of Israel was gone up from the cherub, whereupon he was, to the threshold of the house. And he called to the man clothed with linen, which had the writer's inkhorn by his side [Ezek. 9:2–3].**

"Six men came from the way of the higher gate." These six men are angels—I see no other explanation for them. Angels are used by God in the judgment of this world. They are associated with the nation Israel and have nothing to do with the church. On the Day of Pentecost the Holy Spirit came—*not* angels—and when the Lord Jesus Christ comes to take the church out of the world, there will be no angels with Him. However, when He comes to the earth to establish His kingdom, He will send forth His angels. We read in Matthew 13:41, "The Son of man shall send forth his angels, and they shall gather out of his kingdom all things that offend, and them which do iniquity." Then in Matthew 16:27: "For the

Son of man shall come in the glory of his Father with his angels; and then he shall reward every man according to his works." Finally, Paul wrote: "And to you who are troubled rest with us, when the Lord Jesus shall be revealed from heaven with his mighty angels, In flaming fire taking vengeance on them that know not God, and that obey not the gospel of our Lord Jesus Christ" (2 Thess. 1:7–8). After the third chapter in Revelation, there is no mention of the church which had been previously mentioned frequently. Why? The church is gone from the earth, and *angels* have taken over the judgment upon the earth.

"And the glory of the God of Israel was gone up from the cherub." That is, it had gone up from the Holy Place. The "cherub" were above the mercy seat. This is where the glory had been, but now it lifts up. The glory was a token of the presence of God, and it is now departing.

**And the LORD said unto him, Go through the midst of the city, through the midst of Jerusalem, and set a mark upon the foreheads of the men that sigh and that cry for all the abominations that be done in the midst thereof [Ezek. 9:4].**

God has said, "Mark out the men who want these abominations and are seeking after them. I am going to judge them." But this man with the inkhorn marks out those "that sigh and that cry for all the abominations." These are the remnant which God will save in that city.

**Then said he unto me, The iniquity of the house of Israel and Judah is exceeding great, and the land is full of blood, and the city full of perverseness: for they say, The LORD hath forsaken the earth, and the LORD seeth not [Ezek. 9:9].**

It was as if the people were saying, "God is blind, and He can't make it to the earth." That is the same as those who say today that God is dead. It may be easy to say that God is not out there and He doesn't know what is going on in the earth, but when you really think about it, it is absurd. My friend, just because you haven't seen God and have seen no evidence of Him is no proof that He does not exist. I have never been to Tokyo, Japan, but I believe there is a great city by the name of Tokyo in Japan. I have never been there, and I can act as if it's not there, but the fact remains that it does exist. Just because a man has had no

intimate relationship with God does not mean that God does not exist. The people of Israel were trying to say that God had forsaken the earth. Why? Because *they* had forsaken God.

**And as for me also, mine eye shall not spare, neither will I have pity, but I will recompense their way upon their head [Ezek. 9:10].**

The destruction of Jerusalem at the hands of Nebuchadnezzar and the burning of the temple were frightful things. Why did God do it? He has said, "I will recompense their way upon their head." God is running things, my friend; and, if you are out of step with Him, it might be well to get in step with Him. If I saw a lion coming down the street toward me, I wouldn't meet him head on. I would turn and be going the same direction as he was going and as far ahead of him as I could go! You can defy God if you want to, but may I say to you, the chariot of the Lord is riding triumphantly, and God have mercy on you if you get in His way.

**And, behold, the man clothed with linen, which had the inkhorn by his side, reported the matter, saying, I have done as thou hast commanded me [Ezek. 9:11].**

There were those who were picked out for judgment, and there was the remnant which was to be saved. Our God is merciful when men will turn to Him; that fact makes His judgment actually more frightful.

## SHEKINAH GLORY FILLS THE HOLY PLACE

In chapter 10 we continue Ezekiel's vision of the departing glory of the Lord. God has supernaturally transported Ezekiel to Jerusalem to let him see these things and then return to report to the major portion of the people of Israel who were already in captivity in Babylon. They were being told there by the false prophets that everything was fine in Jerusalem and they would return there shortly. Ezekiel will be able to go back and tell them why God is going to destroy the city and permit judgment to come upon them. We saw in chapter 8 that there was sufficient proof of the sin in the life of the people in Jerusalem—God made that evident to Ezekiel.

We need to see the fact that God judges; it is one of the evidences we have of the living God. We do not get by with our sin, and the very fact that we don't get by with it is proof that God exists. The "wheels within wheels"

which Ezekiel saw speak of the energy of God as He moves in the affairs of men.

The glory of the Lord was above the cherubim—between the cherubim in the Holy of Holies in the temple. The nation of Israel had what no other nation had and, indeed, that which the church does not have today: the visible presence of God. In the ninth chapter of Romans, Paul lists about eight different points of identification which were unique to the nation of Israel, and one of them was "the glory." These people had the Shekinah glory, the visible presence of God, that which Ezekiel saw in his vision in the first chapter.

The glory began its departure in the previous chapter, and will now continue to depart. It moved out from the temple and hovered over it. Now we read:

**Then I looked, and, behold, in the firmament that was above the head of the cherubims there appeared over them as it were a sapphire stone, as the appearance of the likeness of a throne.**

**And he spake unto the man clothed with linen, and said, Go in between the wheels, even under the cherub, and fill thine hand with coals of fire from between the cherubims, and scatter them over the city. And he went in in my sight [Ezek. 10:1–2].**

The man clothed with linen is to scatter these coals from off the altar. The blood of the sacrifice was taken from the altar and put on the mercy seat. These coals speak of judgment. The people had refused the grace and mercy and redemption of God; now they must bear the judgment.

It is just as simple as this: God sent His Son because He loves you. Because He is holy, He had to pay the penalty for your sin and mine; He had to die on the cross. Christ is the propitiation, He is the mercy seat for our sins—not for ours only, but for the sins of the whole world. There is a mercy seat which you can come to, but, if you reject it, the judgment of God must come upon you. Christ bore your judgment, and that is the only way God forgives you. It is not because you are a sweet little boy or a nice little Pollyanna glad-girl. You are a sinner and in rebellion against Him. The best that Christians can say today is that we are *saved* sinners; we are not superior people at all.

Judgment is now going to come to Jerusalem, the city that is the center of the earth. It is the very navel of the earth—that is what God calls it. It will be the center of the millennial kingdom, and it will be the eternal center of the earth. It is today the most sensitive piece of real estate on topside of the earth. Someone has put it like this: "Palestine became the nerve-center of the earth in the days of Abraham. Later on, the country became the truth-center because of Moses and the prophets. Ultimately, it became the salvation-center by the manifestation of Christ. His rejection led to its becoming the storm-center, as it has continued to be throughout many centuries. The Scriptures predict that it is to be the peace-center under the messianic kingdom, and it will be the glory-center in a new universe yet to be experienced." We are seeing through the vision of Ezekiel the departure of the glory from that city, but God has an eternal purpose in this city.

**Then the glory of the LORD went up from the cherub, and stood over the threshold of the house; and the house was filled with the cloud, and the court was full of the brightness of the LORD'S glory [Ezek. 10:4].**

The Shekinah glory had been confined to the Holy Place, the place which denoted the approach of these people to God. However, now the glory leaves the Holy Place there between the cherubim and hovers over the temple to see if the people will return to God.

**And the sound of the cherubim's wings was heard even to the outer court, as the voice of the Almighty God when he speaketh.**

**And it came to pass, that when he had commanded the man clothed with linen, saying, Take fire from between the wheels, from between the cherubims; then he went in, and stood beside the wheels.**

**And one cherub stretched forth his hand from between the cherubims unto the fire that was between the cherubims, and took thereof, and put it into the hands of him that was clothed with linen: who took it, and went out.**

**And there appeared in the cherubims the form of a man's hand under their wings [Ezek. 10:5–8].**

Again, this "hand" denotes the activity of God in performing certain things. "The heavens declare the glory of God; and the firmament

sheweth his handiwork [actually, *fingerwork*]" (Ps. 19:1). The universe is the fingerwork of God, but God's work in His redemption of man was greater than that in creation. Isaiah said, "Who hath believed our report? and to whom is the *arm* of the LORD revealed?" (Isa. 53:1, italics mine). He used His *bared* arm. The only way that I can understand the work of God is to use terms with which I am acquainted. I use my *fingers* to do certain things, my *hands* to do other tasks, and my *arms* to do even heavier tasks. The greatest thing God has done is to perform the wonderful redemptive love act at the cross of Christ—that was His bared arm; but when God created the universe He just used His fingers, or, as John Wesley put it: "God created the universe and didn't even half try." Ezekiel says here that the *hand* of God is moving in judgment.

**And when I looked, behold the four wheels by the cherubims, one wheel by one cherub, and another wheel by another cherub: and the appearance of the wheels was as the colour of a beryl stone [Ezek. 10:9].**

Have you ever watched a wheel when it is going around? There's that flashing light, you know, like that of a precious stone. These wheels are in ceaseless activity and speak of the fact that God is busy. The Lord Jesus said, ". . . My Father worketh hitherto, and I work" (John 5:17). The Lord Jesus has been very busy on our behalf ever since He ascended back to heaven.

**And as for their appearances, they four had one likeness, as if a wheel had been in the midst of a wheel.**

**When they went, they went upon their four sides; they turned not as they went, but to the place whither the head looked they followed it; they turned not as they went [Ezek. 10:10–11].**

God has never had to come back to pick up something He has forgotten. He doesn't need to deviate from one side to the other; He never detours. He goes straight forward today toward the accomplishment of His purpose in the world.

**And their whole body, and their backs, and their hands, and their wings, and the wheels, were full of eyes round about, even the wheels that they four had.**

**As for the wheels, it was cried unto them in my hearing, O wheel.**

**And every one had four faces: the first face was the face of a cherub, and the second face was the face of a man, and the third the face of a lion, and the fourth the face of an eagle [Ezek. 10:12–14].**

This, of course, is highly figurative, and I do not want to press this point, but I believe we have the messages of the four gospels set before us. In the face of the eagle is pictured the *deity* of Christ—that's John's gospel. In the face of the lion is pictured the *kingship* of Christ, the lion of the tribe of Judah—that's Matthew's gospel. In the face of the man is pictured the *humanity* of Christ—that's Luke's gospel. Finally, the face of the cherub (sometimes it is the ox) pictures the *servanthood* of Christ—that's Mark's gospel. He shed His blood that you and I might have eternal life—He made a mercy seat. In the temple the cherubim looked down upon the blood of the sacrifice.

**And the cherubims were lifted up. This is the living creature that I saw by the river of Chebar [Ezek. 10:15].**

Ezekiel refers to his first vision recorded in chapter 1.

### THE GLORY LEAVES THE TEMPLE

**Then the glory of the LORD departed from off the threshold of the house, and stood over the cherubims [Ezek. 10:18].**

The glory of the Lord lifts up from the temple.

**And the cherubims lifted up their wings, and mounted up from the earth in my sight: when they went out, the wheels also were beside them, and every one stood at the door of the east gate of the LORD's house; and the glory of the God of Israel was over them above [Ezek. 10:19].**

The cherubim mounted up, and the glory moved out and stood at the east gate.

**This is the living creature that I saw under the God of Israel by the river of Chebar; and I knew that they were the cherubims.**

**Every one had four faces apiece, and every one four wings; and the likeness**

of the hands of a man was under their wings.

And the likeness of their faces was the same faces which I saw by the river of Chebar, their appearances and them-selves: they went every one straight forward [Ezek. 10:20–22].

I believe this vision pictures the fact that God would become incarnate, or, as John put it, "And the Word was made flesh . . ." (John 1:14).

# CHAPTERS 11–13

*THEME: Prophecy against Jerusalem's rulers; Ezekiel's enacting Jerusalem's destruction; prophecy against pseudoprophets, prophetesses*

In chapter 11 there is a prophecy against the rulers who were still in Jerusalem. Although most of the people had been carried into captivity, Jerusalem had not yet been destroyed. Zedekiah was still on the throne. Not only were the rulers in rebellion against God, they were in rebellion against the king of Babylon, Nebuchadnezzar.

Moreover the spirit lifted me up, and brought me unto the east gate of the LORD'S house, which looketh eastward: and behold at the door of the gate five and twenty men; among whom I saw Jaazaniah the son of Azur, and Pelatiah the son of Benaiah, princes of the people [Ezek. 11:1].

Specific individuals are named who were princes of the people.

Then said he unto me, Son of man, these are the men that devise mischief, and give wicked counsel in this city:

Which say, It is not near; let us build houses: this city is the caldron, and we be the flesh [Ezek. 11:2–3].

In other words, these rulers were saying, "This city is our cup of tea—it's ours now. Most everybody has left, and we are going to continue. We're going to have peace and plenty and prosperity." Theirs was materialism of the worst sort.

Therefore prophesy against them, prophesy, O son of man.

And the spirit of the LORD fell upon me, and said unto me, Speak; Thus saith the LORD; Thus have ye said, O house of Israel: for I know the things that come into your mind, every one of them [Ezek. 11:4–5].

God knows even what we are thinking. He knows our thoughts afar off.

Ye have multiplied your slain in this city, and ye have filled the streets thereof with the slain [Ezek. 11:6].

Apparently the rulers have slain those who stood for God.

Ye shall fall by the sword; I will judge you in the border of Israel; and ye shall know that I am the LORD [Ezek. 11:10].

God's purpose in judgment is that the people might know Him.

This city shall not be your caldron, neither shall ye be the flesh in the midst thereof; but I will judge you in the border of Israel [Ezek. 11:11].

God says that He *is* going to judge them.

Again the word of the LORD came unto me, saying,

Son of man, thy brethren, even thy brethren, the men of thy kindred, and all the house of Israel wholly, are they unto whom the inhabitants of Jerusalem have said, Get you far from the LORD: unto us is this land given in possession.

Therefore say, Thus saith the Lord GOD; Although I have cast them far off among the heathen, and although I have scattered them among the countries, yet will I be to them as a little sanctuary in the countries where they shall come [Ezek. 11:14–16].

God says, "There will be a remnant who will see Me. When they do, I'm going to be a little temple, a little sanctuary, and they will be able to approach Me." This was God's arrangement during the time the temple was destroyed. Daniel and many others were among those who sought the LORD during this period.

> Therefore say, Thus saith the Lord GOD; I will even gather you from the people, and assemble you out of the countries where ye have been scattered, and I will give you the land of Israel.
>
> And they shall come thither, and they shall take away all the detestable things thereof and all the abominations thereof from thence.
>
> And I will give them one heart, and I will put a new spirit within you; and I will take the stony heart out of their flesh, and will give them an heart of flesh:
>
> That they may walk in my statutes, and keep mine ordinances, and do them: and they shall be my people, and I will be their God [Ezek. 11:17–20].

God would return the people to the land. Who was it that came back? Those who were seeking God. There were less than 60,000 in the remnant which returned at the end of the seventy-year captivity.

> But as for them whose heart walketh after the heart of their detestable things and their abominations, I will recompense their way upon their own heads, saith the Lord GOD [Ezek. 11:21].

The judgment of God is coming. It is a great tragedy today that the ministry ignores the fact that judgment is coming upon this earth. God's judgment is one of the sure proofs of His existence.

> Then did the cherubims lift up their wings, and the wheels beside them; and the glory of the God of Israel was over them above.
>
> And the glory of the LORD went up from the midst of the city, and stood upon the mountain which is on the east side of the city [Ezek. 11:22–23].

The glory of the Lord moves from Jerusalem out to the Mount of Olives east of the city.

> Afterwards the spirit took me up, and brought me in a vision by the spirit of God into Chaldea, to them of the captivity. So the vision that I had seen went up from me [Ezek. 11:24].

Ezekiel is brought back to Babylon where he began.

> Then I spake unto them of the captivity all the things that the LORD had shewed me [Ezek. 11:25].

He returns to tell the people that the false prophets have lied to them. He has seen the vision—Jerusalem will be destroyed, and full captivity is near at hand. He will be able to tell them why God will judge them. The people are not going to listen to Ezekiel, but he is to continue to be a sign unto them.

## EZEKIEL'S ENACTING JERUSALEM'S DESTRUCTION

Chapter 12 opens a section in which Ezekiel continues to proclaim that judgment is imminent, but the people will not believe. The important thing here is the proclamation of the Word of God; Ezekiel is to make sure that he gives the Word of God—

> The word of the LORD also came unto me, saying [Ezek. 12:1].

Five times in this chapter (vv. 1, 8, 17, 21, and 26), Ezekiel says, "The word of the LORD came unto me, saying." Do you get the impression that Ezekiel is trying to tell these people that he is giving them the Word of the Lord? He is giving them nothing short of that.

> Son of man, thou dwellest in the midst of a rebellious house, which have eyes to see, and see not; they have ears to hear, and hear not: for they are a rebellious house [Ezek. 12:2].

Of course, God had warned Ezekiel before about these people, but He is reminding him because Ezekiel may get discouraged. God said way back at the beginning of Israel's history, "Yet the LORD hath not given you an heart to perceive, and eyes to see, and ears to hear, unto this day" (Deut. 29:4). These people had their eyes closed and their ears stopped. Ezekiel was not the only prophet who confirmed this truth about these people—Isaiah (Isa. 6:9–10) and Jeremiah (Jer. 5:21) did also. In addition, the Book of Acts closes with this statement: "Saying, Go unto this people, and say, Hearing ye shall hear, and shall not understand; and seeing ye shall see,

and not perceive: For the heart of this people is waxed gross, and their ears are dull of hearing, and their eyes have they closed; lest they should see with their eyes, and hear with their ears, and understand with their heart, and should be converted, and I should heal them" (Acts 28:26–27). These people had closed eyes and ears.

Today, when people say they cannot believe, it is not a mental problem, it is a matter of the will of the heart—they do not *want* to believe. Some say they have certain "mental reservations," mental hurdles which they cannot get over. My friend, your mind is not big enough to take even one little hurdle. The problem is never in the mind but in the will. There is sin in the life and a man does not want to turn to God; he does not want to believe Him.

Israel is just a miniature of the world; that is, the condition of Israel described here is the condition of the world today. In her spirit of unbelief she was a little microcosm of the entire world. That is why we need to look carefully at what the Book of Ezekiel has to say.

I remember talking to a college professor who told me that he appreciated my ministry and what I had to say about the Bible, but that he had certain mental reservations. I had to bite my tongue—I do not believe he was so far ahead of me intellectually that he could see so much more than I! You know what his real problem was? He was having an affair with a former student from one of his classes. *She* was his "intellectual problem"—he did not want to forsake the sin in his life. Blindness in part had happened in Israel, and this is true of our world today.

Because of Israel's unbelief, Ezekiel is not only going to give the people a parable, he is actually going to act it out. Ezekiel was a very brilliant man, but I think he also had a real sense of humor. I would love to have seen his face when he went through some of these mechanics! I think he might have been somewhat of a ham actor and been greatly amused as he did these things.

**Therefore, thou son of man, prepare thee stuff for removing, and remove by day in their sight; and thou shalt remove from thy place to another place in their sight: it may be they will consider, though they be a rebellious house.**

**Then shalt thou bring forth thy stuff by day in their sight, as stuff for removing: and thou shalt go forth at even in**
their sight, as they that go forth into captivity.

**Dig thou through the wall in their sight, and carry out thereby.**

**In their sight shalt thou bear it upon thy shoulders, and carry it forth in the twilight: thou shalt cover thy face, that thou see not the ground: for I have set thee for a sign unto the house of Israel [Ezek. 12:3–6].**

I tell you, this is a good one! Here's what Ezekiel does: He goes into his house (the houses then were right on the street, by the way); he packs his baggage like he's going on a trip, digs through the wall, and comes up out in the street. You can imagine the effect that would have—a man coming out through the wall bringing his suitcases with him! People would *have* to stop and look.

Here in Pasadena, California, where I live, digging up the street is not anything new. Actually, the city here plays a game with all of us. They dig up one street, and so you decide to get smart and use another street. So the next day they find out what new street you're using, and then they go dig up that street too! It gets to be quite a puzzle, like a maze, finding your way around dug-up streets. But I have a notion that when this man Ezekiel came up in the middle of the street with his suitcase, it was something new, and people stopped to ask, "Where are you going? What's the big idea?" Ezekiel had an answer for them:

**And in the morning came the word of the LORD unto me, saying,**

**Son of man, hath not the house of Israel, the rebellious house, said unto thee, What doest thou?**

**Say thou unto them, Thus saith the Lord GOD; This burden concerneth the prince in Jerusalem, and all the house of Israel that are among them.**

**Say, I am your sign: like as I have done, so shall it be done unto them: they shall remove and go into captivity.**

**And the prince that is among them shall bear upon his shoulder in the twilight, and shall go forth: they shall dig through the wall to carry out thereby: he shall cover his face, that he see not the ground with his eyes [Ezek. 12:8–12].**

Zedekiah was on the throne in Jerusalem, and the false prophets were saying to the captives, "Look, Nebuchadnezzar has made two sieges of Jerusalem, and he's carried away captives, but he did not destroy the city, he did not burn the temple, and he did not execute the king. You are going to be able to return soon. There's nothing to worry about." But Ezekiel says, "I have news for you: What I have just done is a picture of what is happening back in Jerusalem. The king over there, the prince (that's Zedekiah), thinks he's very clever. He thinks he will be able to slip out of the city during the siege, but he won't. When he leaves the city, he won't even see the ground."

Do you know why Zedekiah didn't see the ground? Read the historical record in 2 Kings 25:1–7; Nebuchadnezzar put out his eyes. Zedekiah was a deceptive, wicked fellow, and he had broken his treaty with Nebuchadnezzar. Nebuchadnezzar, the pagan king, was more honorable than the man on Israel's throne. There is nothing that hurts the church more today than a dishonest Christian, particularly when it is a layman who is active in the Lord's work but in the business world has a poor reputation. Zedekiah was like that, and Ezekiel's message was a bitter pill for those captives to swallow when the false prophets had said, "It's so wonderful back in Jerusalem."

**Moreover the word of the LORD came to me, saying,**

**Son of man, eat thy bread with quaking, and drink thy water with trembling and with carefulness;**

**And say unto the people of the land, Thus saith the Lord GOD of the inhabitants of Jerusalem, and of the land of Israel; They shall eat their bread with carefulness, and drink their water with astonishment, that her land may be desolate from all that is therein, because of the violence of all them that dwell therein [Ezek. 12:17–19].**

This is quite a stunt Ezekiel is going to pull. He is to bring his table out into the street and sit there, trembling as he eats. Then the people will come and say, "What's the matter with you? Have you got a chill, or is it something you ate?" Ezekiel will give them God's message: "I want you to know what's happening over yonder in Jerusalem. There's a famine over there. There's fear over there.

God is destroying the city." What an awesome message he has to bring.

**Son of man, what is that proverb that ye have in the land of Israel, saying, The days are prolonged, and every vision faileth?**

**Tell them therefore, Thus saith the Lord GOD; I will make this proverb to cease, and they shall no more use it as a proverb in Israel; but say unto them, The days are at hand, and the effect of every vision [Ezek. 12:22–23].**

Ezekiel is saying, "God has been patient, but it's all up now. The captivity is coming, and God is not going to wait any longer."

**Therefore say unto them, Thus saith the Lord GOD; There shall none of my words be prolonged any more, but the word which I have spoken shall be done, saith the Lord GOD [Ezek. 12:28].**

Everybody wants to believe that the future out yonder is beautiful. My friend, the only beautiful thing that lies ahead is the fact that someday the Lord Jesus will take His church out of the world—that is the *only* hope we have. This world is not going to get better, and we are not going to have peace. In all of recorded history there have only been two to three hundred years of what could actually be called peace—man is not building the new world he thinks he is.

### PROPHECY AGAINST PSEUDO PROPHETS AND PROPHETESSES

In chapter 13 we have the prophecy against the false prophets, the pseudoprophets and prophetesses. Notice that the women were also getting involved in this. Have you ever noticed how many cults and isms have been founded by women or how women play a very prominent part in them? It may not be popular to say that, but it was true in Ezekiel's day and it is true in ours.

Ezekiel continues to give the Word of the Lord:

**And the word of the LORD came unto me, saying,**

**Son of man, prophesy against the prophets of Israel that prophesy, and say thou unto them that prophesy out of their own hearts, Hear ye the word of the LORD;**

**Thus saith the Lord GOD; Woe unto the foolish prophets, that follow their own spirit, and have seen nothing! [Ezek. 13:1–3].**

What was the problem? These prophets prophesied "out of their own hearts." God have mercy on the man who stands in the pulpit and gives his own viewpoints and does not give the Word of God. Now it is possible to make a mistake in interpretation, and I have sometimes made mistakes. However, let me make it clear that I am attempting to interpret the *Word of God*. These men were merely giving what they thought: how to make friends, influence people, think positively, be self-reliant, and think of yourself as a wonderful individual, not as a sinner. This was their message: "Everything is all right in Jerusalem."

**Likewise, thou son of man, set thy face against the daughters of thy people, which prophesy out of their own heart; and prophesy thou against them,**

**And say, Thus saith the Lord GOD; Woe to the women that sew pillows to all armholes, and make kerchiefs upon the head of every stature to hunt souls! Will ye hunt the souls of my people, and will ye save the souls alive that come unto you? [Ezek. 13:17–18].**

Ezekiel is to resist the false prophetesses— "Set thy face against the daughters of thy

people . . . and prophesy thou against them."

In Genesis 10:8–9, Nimrod is called a mighty hunter before the Lord. Actually, he was a hunter of the souls of men. That is also what these false cults do—they hunt out the souls of men.

The women were involved in this also. In 2 Peter 2:1 Peter said, "But there were false prophets also among the people [that is, Israel], even as there shall be false teachers among you, who privily shall bring in damnable heresies, even denying the Lord that bought them, and bring upon themselves swift destruction." Today we have many women who are involved in spiritualism with its mediums and fortune-tellers and necromancers and witches. There are quite a few in Southern California—I always thought we had them, but now they openly claim they are witches.

"Woe to the women that sew pillows to all armholes." What these women were doing was giving out amulets, a little something to put on your arm, to keep you from getting sick or to protect you from harm. "And make kerchiefs upon the head of every stature to hunt souls!" They give you a handkerchief which they have prayed over, and it will help you get well (as if there were merit in that rather than in the Lord)! My friend, what you see about you today is *not* new. It is as old as the human race. When Ezekiel clearly denounced it in his day, it was "the word of the LORD," not his own word.

# CHAPTERS 14–16

**THEME:** *Prophecy against the elders' idolatry; vision of the vine; Jerusalem likened to an abandoned baby adopted by God*

Chapter 14 is divided into two major sections: the prophecy against the idolatry of the elders and the certainty of the destruction of Jerusalem. Both sections open with, "The word of the LORD came unto me" (vv. 2, 12). The Lord continues in this chapter to outline why He judged the city of Jerusalem as He did. The principles that are put down here are operative today also. God still judges nations.

## PROPHECY AGAINST THE ELDERS' IDOLATRY

In these verses Ezekiel will call the elders of Israel to repent. I have noticed throughout

both the Old and New Testaments *repentance* is God's message to His own people, those who profess to belong to Him. "Repent and turn to God"—that will be Ezekiel's message here.

**Then came certain of the elders of Israel unto me, and sat before me [Ezek. 14:1].**

The elders come to Ezekiel, and oh, how pious these fellows are! They pretend they want to listen to the prophet. It is like coming to church with a big Bible under your arm, pretending you want to serve the Lord.

And the word of the LORD came unto me, saying,

Son of man, these men have set up their idols in their heart, and put the stumblingblock of their iniquity before their face: should I be inquired of at all by them? [Ezek. 14:2–3].

In effect the elders say, "Oh, brother Ezekiel, we don't worship idols!" It was true they had not made idols, but the Lord said, "These men have set up their idols in their heart."

Samson was also a man who pretended to be God's man, and the Spirit of God *did* come upon him at times. The Holy Spirit—never his hair—was the secret of his power. But there came a day when he went out and ". . . he wist it not . . ." (Lev. 5:17)—he knew not that the Spirit of God had departed from him. He had kept toying and playing with sin and at the same time wanting to be God's man. How many people today in the church keep toying and playing with sin and think they are getting by with it? My friend, they are *not* getting by with it. Judgment is inevitable. They may go through the form and ritual of religion, keeping up a false front, but they actually have idols in their hearts.

Ezekiel is told by the Lord that these men are phonies. They pretend they want to hear his message, but they do not hear it at all. When he turns around, they will put a knife in his back.

Therefore speak unto them, and say unto them, Thus saith the Lord GOD; Every man of the house of Israel that setteth up his idols in his heart, and putteth the stumblingblock of his iniquity before his face, and cometh to the prophet; I the LORD will answer him that cometh according to the multitude of his idols [Ezek. 14:4].

God says He will judge these men. The Lord Jesus called the religious rulers of His day *hypocrites.* He used that frightful, awful word more than anyone. Ezekiel is speaking to the spiritual leaders of the people. How tragic this is! God is going to judge them. God will always judge phony religion. I believe that whenever a church or an individual departs from the truth, God will judge.

Therefore say unto the house of Israel, Thus saith the Lord GOD; Repent, and turn yourselves from your idols; and turn away your faces from all your abominations [Ezek. 14:6].

God has laid it on the line that these men are phonies, not genuine, having idols in their hearts, sin in their hearts. Again, someone might say about Samson, "My, isn't that terrible about Samson!" I'd hate to live like that man did and have that judgment come upon *me.*" However, I am afraid that there are folk who sit in the church pew and yet would like to live in sin, to taste the fruits of sin. The very thing they condemn outwardly is the thing in their heart they would like to do. This old nature we have is bad, but God says, "Repent. Come to Me." He is gracious to Israel. He is giving them an opportunity to become genuine, but they will not.

## CERTAIN DESTRUCTION OF JERUSALEM

The false prophets were still running around saying, "God will spare Jerusalem. It is His city—He loves it. He says His eye is there." They could quote an abundance of Scripture about it. It is possible to quote an isolated Scripture or two to support false doctrine today. However, you cannot take a verse here and there; you must look at the whole picture presented in Scripture. When you do, you will not be able to support false theories. These prophets were wrong, and God is saying very explicitly that Jerusalem is to be judged.

The word of the LORD came again to me, saying,

Son of man, when the land sinneth against me by trespassing grievously, then will I stretch out mine hand upon it, and will break the staff of the bread thereof, and will send famine upon it, and will cut off man and beast from it [Ezek. 14:12–13].

God says to Ezekiel, "The city is a rebellious city which has continuously rebelled against Me. I have given them opportunity to return to Me, and they will not."

God is very definite, and He means what He says. Judgment is unavoidable. Listen to just how serious He is:

Though these three men, Noah, Daniel, and Job, were in it, they should deliver but their own souls by their righteousness, saith the Lord GOD [Ezek. 14:14].

If Noah were in the city of Jerusalem, the Lord says, they would not listen to him. Just imagine what a warning Noah would have been to those people! But the people in Noah's

day did not listen to him, and the people of Jerusalem would not have listened to him had he been there.

I get rather amused over the excitement about the search for Noah's ark. I think they may find it, but let me ask you: How many believers do you think its discovery will make? If Noah himself were here today, who would believe him? They would call him a square and an old fogey! (One thing nice about being a square is that you don't go around in circles as do a lot of other people. Some of those going around in circles really think they are big wheels, too!)

They wouldn't have listened to Noah, and they wouldn't have listened to Daniel. Nebuchadnezzar listened to Daniel, however. What a tribute that is to Daniel! Yonder in the palace of the world's first great ruler, Nebuchadnezzar, is Daniel. The Babylonians knew Daniel, and they knew he was God's man. The Lord says that the Israelites would not have listened to Noah *or* Daniel *or* Job!

**Or if I bring a sword upon that land, and say, Sword, go through the land; so that I cut off man and beast from it [Ezek. 14:17].**

God says that He intends to bring a sword upon the land. He is going to allow Nebuchadnezzar into the land, and he will destroy it.

**Though Noah, Daniel, and Job, were in it, as I live, saith the Lord GOD, they shall deliver neither son nor daughter; they shall but deliver their own souls by their righteousness [Ezek. 14:20].**

Noah would not have been able to save his own family in that city—"they shall but deliver their own souls by their righteousness." Daniel saved a couple of empires, but if he had been in that city he could not have helped them at all. That is the reason that God got Daniel out of Jerusalem. God's people wouldn't hear him, but an old pagan king in Babylon listened to Daniel and made him prime minister.

How many churches are there today where the people will really listen to the Word of God? I do not think there are many. That is one reason that this hour God is permitting His Word to go to the world via radio and why He is allowing the Word to reach groups of people that many Christians had given up on. My friend, if the folk in churches are not going to listen to the Word of God, He is going to go out yonder where people *will* receive it. Daniel would not have done any good in Jeru-

salem, but he was made top man in Babylon and there a pagan king listened to him. My friend, God is going to let people hear the gospel who are willing to listen to Him.

## VISION OF THE VINE

Chapter 15 is the parable of the vine that would not bear fruit. The vine is one of the figures of the nation Israel. In Isaiah 5 the vine set before us is the nation Israel. We do not need to speculate about that because Isaiah said, "For the vineyard of the LORD of hosts is the house of Israel . . ." (Isa. 5:7).

**Son of man, What is the vine tree more than any tree, or than a branch which is among the trees of the forest?**

**Shall wood be taken thereof to do any work? or will men take a pin of it to hang any vessel thereon?**

**Behold, it is cast into the fire for fuel; the fire devoureth both the ends of it, and the midst of it is burned. Is it meet for any work? [Ezek. 15:2–4].**

God makes a very interesting application here. Just what is the purpose of a vine? The Lord Jesus also used the vine as a picture of believers today in John 15. He said, by the way, that Israel was no longer a vine, but "I am the true [genuine] vine . . ." (John 15:1). The Lord Jesus was not talking about salvation in that chapter. Again, I ask you: What is the purpose of a vine? It is to do one thing—bear fruit—nothing else. What God is saying here in Ezekiel is that you do not go to the furniture store and ask for a Louis XIV bedroom set made of grapevine wood! The salesman would look at you in amazement and say, "We do not have anything made of grapevine wood. It's not good for anything like that. It's just good for bearing fruit." Furthermore, God says, if a vine will not bear fruit, the only thing it is good for is burning. In John, the Lord Jesus said that if a believer does not bear fruit, you do not lose your salvation, but you are removed from the place of fruit bearing. God sets men aside in many, many ways if they do not bear fruit. The Lord Jesus said, "Herein, is my Father glorified, that ye bear much fruit . . ." (John 15:8).

The people of Israel were not bearing fruit, and God said, "There is nothing left for me to do but to burn Jerusalem." That is the reason He did it—the people were supposed to represent God, and they had failed to do it.

If you have been given great privilege as a Christian today, then you have a great

responsibility. Have you ever thought of that poor fellow in Africa or China or Russia who has not had the privilege of hearing the Word of God? We who have heard His Word have a great responsibility. God wants us to be bearing fruit today.

## JERUSALEM LIKENED TO AN ABANDONED BABY ADOPTED BY GOD

Chapter 16 contains yet another parable—the parable of an abandoned little orphan, a dirty and filthy little child, for whom it would seem there is nothing that can be done.

**Again the word of the LORD came unto me, saying [Ezek. 16:1].**

Ezekiel is not going to let us forget that he is giving us the Word of the Lord. We may not accept it, but it is still His Word.

**Son of man, cause Jerusalem to know her abominations [Ezek. 16:2].**

Who is the little orphan? Who is the little dirty, filthy child who has been thrown out? Who is this illegitimate child? It is the city of Jerusalem.

**And say, Thus saith the Lord GOD unto Jerusalem; Thy birth and thy nativity is of the land of Canaan; thy father was an Amorite, and thy mother an Hittite [Ezek. 16:3].**

This does not speak of the origin of the *nation* Israel; it is not speaking of Abraham and Sarah. The origin of the *city* of Jerusalem is in view here. The history of Jerusalem is that it was an Amorite city. We read in Genesis 15:16, "But in the fourth generation they [that is, the children of Israel] shall come hither again: for the iniquity of the Amorites is not yet full." Jerusalem was a Hittite city also. The Hittites were a great nation, and they controlled that land at one time. This is the background of Jerusalem, and it is nothing to brag about at all.

**And as for thy nativity, in the day thou wast born thy navel was not cut, neither wast thou washed in water to supple thee; thou wast not salted at all, nor swaddled at all.**

**None eye pitied thee, to do any of these unto thee, to have compassion upon thee; but thou wast cast out in the open field, to the loathing of thy person, in the day that thou wast born [Ezek. 16:4–5].**

She was an illegitimate orphan child who was just thrown out—abandoned and not cared for.

**And when I passed by thee, and saw thee polluted in thine own blood, I said unto thee when thou wast in thy blood, Live; yea, I said unto thee when thou wast in thy blood, Live.**

**I have caused thee to multiply as the bud of the field, and thou hast increased and waxen great, and thou art come to excellent ornaments: thy breasts are fashioned, and thine hair is grown, whereas thou wast naked and bare.**

**Now when I passed by thee, and looked upon thee, behold, thy time was the time of love; and I spread my skirt over thee, and covered thy nakedness: yea, I sware unto thee, and entered into a covenant with thee, saith the Lord GOD, and thou becamest mine [Ezek. 16:6–8].**

God says to Jerusalem, "I adopted you and made you My child."

**Then washed I thee with water; yea, I throughly washed away thy blood from thee, and I anointed thee with oil.**

**I clothed thee also with broidered work, and shod thee with badgers' skin, and I girded thee about with fine linen, and I covered thee with silk.**

**I decked thee also with ornaments, and I put bracelets upon thy hands, and a chain on thy neck [Ezek. 16:9–11].**

He says, "This is what I did for Jerusalem."

I think the application to our lives is quite obvious: you and I have a pretty bad background. Adam and Eve became sinners, and you and I were born in iniquity. David said, ". . . in sin did my mother conceive me" (Ps. 51:5), and David is no different from you and me. What do you have to boast about? Even if your ancestors *did* come over on the Mayflower, they were just a bunch of sinners saved by the grace of God. That is our origin, our background—we were dead in trespasses and sin.

What did God do for Jerusalem? God said to her, "Live" (v. 6). To us He has said, ". . . Ye must be born again" (John 3:7). He has made a covenant that if you will trust Christ, He will save you. "For God so loved the world, that he gave his only begotten Son, that whosoever believeth in him should not perish, but have

everlasting life" (John 3:16). The Lord took that little illegitimate child, dirty and filthy in its own blood, and He said, "Then washed I thee with water." Likewise, we can know the washing of regeneration and the renewing of the Holy Spirit. "I throughly washed away the blood from thee"—the Lord Jesus bore my guilt on the cross; there is no blood guilt on a child of God today. "And I anointed thee with oil"—He anoints the child of God today with the oil of the Holy Spirit. "I girded thee about with fine linen"—we can be covered with the righteousness of Christ in order that we might stand in the presence of God.

What happened to this city? God says that when she became grown, a beautiful young lady, she played the harlot. She went over into idolatry and turned her back on Him. God have mercy on the Christian who will sell himself to the world for a bowl of pottage. Yes, Esau *did* sell out cheap, but many Christians also sell out cheap to the world today. The Devil could buy a lot of us, my friend. We so easily find ourselves going off again and again away from God and away from fellowship with Him. Oh, to be true to God in this hour in which we live!

**When I shall bring again their captivity, the captivity of Sodom and her daughters, and the captivity of Samaria and her daughters, then will I bring again the captivity of thy captives in the midst of them:**

**That thou mayest bear thine own shame, and mayest be confounded in all that thou hast done, in that thou art a comfort unto them.**

**When thy sisters, Sodom and her daughters, shall return to their former estate, and Samaria and her daughters shall return to their former estate, then thou and thy daughters shall return to your former estate [Ezek. 16:53–55].**

Verses 53 and 55 (as well as ch. 37) have been used by several cults to teach the doctrine of restitutionalism; that is, that everybody ultimately will be saved. Again, this is a case of resting doctrine on a few isolated verses of Scripture which will result in weird and unscriptural doctrine. In these verses and in Ezekiel 37:12, where God says, "I will open your graves, and cause you to come up out of your graves," God is *not* talking about the resurrection of the wicked to eternal life. In both instances He is talking about the restoration of a city or a nation, and it has no reference to the people who lived there years ago. Here in Ezekiel 16 He is saying that the city of Sodom is to be rebuilt. Now, personally, I don't see anything there to attract anybody, but there is tremendous development today along the coast of the Dead Sea in that area. And in chapter 37 the Lord is speaking of the restoration of a nation, the nation of Israel.

Actually, in the Old Testament we do not have the divine revelation concerning the future state that we have in the New Testament. God had no plan to bring back from the dead the saints of the Old Testament and to take them out yonder to a place prepared for them. He has told us that that is His plan for us, but nowhere did He tell the Old Testament saints that. He told them there was to be a heaven down here on this earth, and that is the resurrection Abraham looked for. There is to be a restoration of the nation. You cannot read what is New Testament development of this doctrine into this Old Testament passage. However, every Old Testament passage will conform also to New Testament teaching. The New Testament makes it very clear that there will be a twofold resurrection: the resurrection of the saved, and the resurrection of the lost who are *lost* when they are raised from the dead. Therefore, these verses deal only with the restoration of a nation. We must read them in their context and not draw any more from them than is there.

This chapter concludes in a most glorious way: God is going to make good His covenants with the nation Israel. The sin of these people, their rebellion, their constant departure from Him, their backsliding, will not annul, abrogate, or destroy God's covenant with them.

**Nevertheless I will remember my covenant with thee in the days of thy youth, and I will establish unto thee an everlasting covenant.**

**Then thou shalt remember thy ways, and be ashamed, when thou shalt receive thy sisters, thine elder and thy younger: and I will give them unto thee for daughters, but not by thy covenant.**

**And I will establish my covenant with thee; and thou shalt know that I am the LORD:**

**That thou mayest remember, and be confounded, and never open thy mouth any more because of thy shame, when I am pacified toward thee for all that**

thou hast done, saith the Lord God
[Ezek. 16:60–63].

God says that not only will He make good on
the past covenants but He is also going to
make a new covenant with them. Unfortunately, these passages of Scripture are not
studied very much at all. When they are, they
make it very clear that God still has a future
purpose with the nation Israel.

# CHAPTER 17

*THEME: Riddle of the two eagles*

## RIDDLE OF THE TWO EAGLES

And the word of the LORD came unto
me, saying,

Son of man, put forth a riddle, and
speak a parable unto the house of Israel
[Ezek. 17:1–2].

66 **P**ut forth a riddle, and speak a parable
unto the house of Israel"—because
they would not listen to him, Ezekiel had to
come to these people in a strange and unusual
way.

And say, Thus saith the Lord God; A
great eagle with great wings, long-
winged, full of feathers, which had divers colours, came unto Lebanon, and
took the highest branch of the cedar:

He cropped off the top of his young
twigs, and carried it into a land of traffic; he set it in a city of merchants.

He took also of the seed of the land, and
planted it in a fruitful field; he placed it
by great waters, and set it as a willow
tree [Ezek. 17:3–5].

This great eagle is none other than Babylon
and Nebuchadnezzar, the present king of
Babylon. The eagle is a figure that is used of
Babylon elsewhere in Scripture. Jeremiah
used it in Jeremiah 48:40 as he wrote of
Nebuchadnezzar: "For thus saith the LORD;
Behold, he shall fly as an eagle, and shall
spread his wings over Moab." Then in Jeremiah 49:22 he wrote, "Behold, he shall come
up and fly as the eagle, and spread his wings
over Bozrah: and at that day shall the heart of
the mighty men of Edom be as the heart of a
woman in her pangs." Daniel saw the Babylonian empire rising up out of the sea, and it was
in the form of a lion with eagle's wings (Dan.
7:4). Therefore, what we have here is a picture of Nebuchadnezzar, king of Babylon, who
is going to come and crop the top of the tree.

Who is the tree? It is the nation Israel and,
specifically, the royal house of David. Nebuchadnezzar is going to clip it off and bring it to
naught. That is exactly what he did with
Zedekiah.

There was also another great eagle with
great wings and many feathers: and,
behold, this vine did bend her roots
toward him, and shot forth her
branches toward him, that he might
water it by the furrows of her planta-
tion [Ezek. 17:7].

The other eagle is Egypt which was still a
great power at this time. Zedekiah had been
put on the throne by Nebuchadnezzar, and
they made a covenant together. However,
Zedekiah broke that covenant and turned to
Egypt. That is pictured here by the branches
which lean toward Egypt. The vine is planted
in the soil of Egypt, seeking to draw strength
from her, but there will not be any strength
because Egypt will go down. Nebuchadnezzar
took Egypt and destroyed it and made it subject to himself.

Now this is the message which grows out of
Ezekiel's parable:

Say now to the rebellious house, Know
ye not what these things mean? tell
them, Behold, the king of Babylon is
come to Jerusalem, and hath taken the
king thereof, and the princes thereof,
and led them with him to Babylon.

And hath taken of the king's seed, and
made a covenant with him, and hath
taken an oath of him: he hath also
taken the mighty of the land:

That the kingdom might be base, that it
might not lift itself up, but that by
keeping of his covenant it might stand.

But he rebelled against him in sending his ambassadors into Egypt, that they might give him horses and much people. Shall he prosper? shall he escape that doeth such things? or shall he break the covenant, and be delivered? [Ezek. 17:12–15].

The interesting thing is that Nebuchadnezzar kept his side of the covenant. God's people broke the covenant, but the pagan nation kept their side of it. What a picture! In some churches you will find people still carrying their Bibles, but their hearts are far from God and you cannot believe what they say. On the other hand, there are businessmen who, although they are unsaved, are men of integrity.

Nebuchadnezzar is going to come and destroy Zedekiah:

Seeing he despised the oath by breaking the covenant, when, lo, he had given his hand, and hath done all these things, he shall not escape [Ezek. 17:18].

God says, "I intend that Zedekiah be judged for this." My friend, I sure would hate to be some Christians who are someday going to be taken to the woodshed for the lives they have lived down here. God will certainly judge.

And all the trees of the field shall know that I the LORD have brought down the high tree, have exalted the low tree, have dried up the green tree, and have made the dry tree to flourish: I the LORD have spoken and have done it [Ezek. 17:24].

Sometimes God allows a godless nation to harass and actually destroy a people who claim to be God's people but have departed from Him. There has been a great breakdown in morals in America, and apostasy is in earnest. We have not had much peace in this world, either internally or externally. There is trouble everywhere. God says that we will not get by with our sin—there will be a judgment.

# CHAPTERS 18–19

THEME: *Jerusalem an example of "the wages of sin is death"; elegy of Jehovah over the princes of Israel*

In chapter 18 God will show that in His judgment He deals specifically and individually with each person.

The word of the LORD came unto me again, saying [Ezek. 18:1].

Again, it is clear that Ezekiel is not giving his own opinion. This is God's Word.

What mean ye, that ye use this proverb concerning the land of Israel, saying, The fathers have eaten sour grapes, and the children's teeth are set on edge? [Ezek. 18:2].

The children of Israel had a proverb they used, and it is mentioned twice by Jeremiah. In Jeremiah 31:29 we read, "In those days they shall say no more, The fathers have eaten a sour grape, and the children's teeth are set on edge." And then in Lamentations 5:7 we find, "Our fathers have sinned, and are not; and we have borne their iniquities." I believe the people had built this proverb upon

a passage back in Exodus: "Thou shalt not bow down thyself to them, nor serve them: for I the LORD thy God am a jealous God, visiting the iniquity of the fathers upon the children unto the third and fourth generation of them that hate me" (Exod. 20:5). The problem is that the proverb they drew from this verse is incorrect. That is the danger in lifting out one verse of Scripture without considering its context. This is a false proverb: The fathers ate the grapes, and the children paid the penalty. That is true to a certain extent, but God judges the individual, father or son, according to his conduct. This is not a judgment for eternal life, but a judgment in *this* life according as a man obeys or disobeys Him.

As I live, saith the Lord GOD, ye shall not have occasion any more to use this proverb in Israel [Ezek. 18:3].

The word *live* or some form of it occurs thirteen times in this chapter, and the word *die* occurs fourteen times. We have life and death

presented here, but it is not eternal life or eternal death that God is talking about. God is speaking of the way in which He judges individuals in this life. We need to look at this entire chapter from that viewpoint.

**Behold, all souls are mine; as the soul of the father, so also the soul of the son is mine: the soul that sinneth, it shall die [Ezek. 18:4].**

God says here that all souls belong to Him. If the sins of the fathers come upon the children, it is because the children have followed the wickedness of their fathers. Every man shall be put to death for his own sin. We read in Deuteronomy 24:16, "The fathers shall not be put to death for the children, neither shall the children be put to death for the fathers: every man shall be put to death for his own sin."

"The soul that sinneth, it shall die"—God will judge each individual.

**But if a man be just, and do that which is lawful and right,**

**And hath not eaten upon the mountains, neither hath lifted up his eyes to the idols of the house of Israel, neither hath defiled his neighbour's wife, neither hath come near to a menstruous woman,**

**And hath not oppressed any, but hath restored to the debtor his pledge, hath spoiled none by violence, hath given his bread to the hungry, and hath covered the naked with a garment;**

**He that hath not given forth upon usury, neither hath taken any increase, that hath withdrawn his hand from iniquity, hath executed true judgment between man and man,**

**Hath walked in my statutes, and hath kept my judgments, to deal truly; he is just, he shall surely live, saith the Lord God [Ezek. 18:5–9].**

"Hath not eaten upon the mountains"—he has not engaged in idolatry. This man is a just man who has walked in God's statutes and kept His ordinances. "He shall surely live, saith the Lord God." He is talking about this life, not eternal life. God will bless him in this life—this is the blessing of the Old Testament.

**If he beget a son that is a robber, a shedder of blood, and that doeth the like to any one of these things [Ezek. 18:10].**

However, the just man may have an ungodly son.

**Hath given forth upon usury, and hath taken increase: shall he then live? he shall not live: he hath done all these abominations; he shall surely die; his blood shall be upon him [Ezek. 18:13].**

God will judge that son—not the father.

**Now, lo, if he beget a son, that seeth all his father's sins which he hath done, and considereth, and doeth not such like [Ezek. 18:14].**

On the other hand, a son may decide not to follow in the footsteps of his wicked father. There were several instances of this in the history of Israel. Old Ahaz was a wicked king, but his son Hezekiah led in a revival. Josiah was a wonderful man, and he had a very wicked father.

**That hath taken off his hand from the poor, that hath not received usury nor increase, hath executed my judgments, hath walked in my statutes; he shall not die for the iniquity of his father, he shall surely live.**

**As for his father, because he cruelly oppressed, spoiled his brother by violence, and did that which is not good among his people, lo, even he shall die in his iniquity [Ezek. 18:17–18]**

God is saying that each man is judged in this life for the way he lives his life. Remember that He is not speaking of eternal life but about judgment here and now. He wants Israel to know this is the basis on which he intends to judge them.

**The soul that sinneth, it shall die. The son shall not bear the iniquity of the father, neither shall the father bear the iniquity of the son: the righteousness of the righteous shall be upon him, and the wickedness of the wicked shall be upon him [Ezek. 18:20].**

"The soul that sinneth, it shall die." We have this twice in this chapter—here and in verse 4.

**Cast away from you all your transgressions, whereby ye have transgressed; and make you a new heart and a new spirit: for why will ye die, O house of Israel? [Ezek. 18:31].**

The teaching of this chapter answers the new psychology we have today. Psychology argues that the reason a person is a brat or an oddball is because his mother didn't treat him right but neglected him and didn't love him. My friend, you stand alone. You are a sinner because you are a sinner yourself. There's an old bromide that is rather crude, but it certainly expresses it well: Every tub must sit on its own bottom. Every individual will stand before God, and he won't be able to blame his papa and mama at that time. Ezekiel makes it very clear that the Israelite will be judged in this life on the basis of the life he lived, whether he was a believer or not.

**For I have no pleasure in the death of him that dieth, saith the Lord GOD: wherefore turn yourselves, and live ye [Ezek. 18:32].**

Again, this refers to physical death. God does not take any delight today in seeing anyone die. That is something that is foreign to Him; He didn't intend death for mankind. Remember that the Lord Jesus *wept* at the tomb of Lazarus, even though He was going to bring him back into this life. By man came death, not through the working of God, but because of man's sin.

## ELEGY OF JEHOVAH OVER THE PRINCES OF ISRAEL

In chapter 19 we have two lamentations: the lamentations over the princes of Israel (vv. 1–9), and the lamentation over the land of Judah, the southern kingdom of Israel (vv. 10–14).

**Moreover take thou up a lamentation for the princes of Israel,**

**And say, What is thy mother? A lioness: she lay down among lions, she nourished her whelps among young lions.**

**And she brought up one of her whelps: it became a young lion, and it learned to catch the prey; it devoured men [Ezek. 19:1–3].**

This is not the lamentation of Ezekiel, as some Bible commentators have attempted to say. This is the lamentation of the Lord, actually the lamentation of the same One who later wept over Jerusalem (Matt. 23:37–39). He is the One who is here weeping over the princes of Judah. The princes were a group of people in that land who had very few who were concerned about them. But God was concerned. Who shed tears over them? God did.

By the way, who is concerned about you today? I suspect there are very few. Are the people where you work really concerned about you? Are the people in your church really concerned about you? Is your family concerned? A successful businessman once told me, "I honestly wonder who really cares about me today. Everybody, including my family, is only interested in what they can get out of me." How sad that is! But God is concerned about you, and He is concerned about me. That's quite comforting in this tremendous universe in which I live. I could get lost in it, I am so small. But He has His eye out and has a concern for each one of us.

The princes of Judah were people for whom not too many in that day wanted to shed tears. They were Jehoahaz and Jehoiachin, two kings who were about as sorry as they come. God alone is concerned over them.

When He begins to speak of the "lion," He is speaking of the lion of Judah. "Judah is a lion's whelp . . ."—that is the way Judah was marked out by Jacob in Genesis 49:9 as he gave his prophecies concerning each of his twelve sons. In Numbers 23:24 we read, "Behold, the people shall rise up as a great lion, and lift up himself as a young lion. . . ." The Lord Jesus is called the Lion of the tribe of Juda in Revelation 5:5: "And one of the elders saith unto me, Weep not: behold, the Lion of the tribe of Juda, the Root of David, hath prevailed to open the book, and to loose the seven seals thereof."

**Thy mother is like a vine in thy blood, planted by the waters: she was fruitful and full of branches by reason of many waters.**

**And she had strong rods for the sceptres of them that bare rule, and her stature was exalted among the thick branches, and she appeared in her height with the multitude of her branches.**

**But she was plucked up in fury, she was cast down to the ground, and the east wind dried up her fruit: her strong rods were broken and withered; the fire consumed them [Ezek. 19:10–12].**

This now is the lamentation over the land of Judah. These people came into that land, and God blessed them. They were like a vine planted in the land. Now He has plucked up the vine, and they are carried away into captivity. This is a sad song depicting the sordid history of the nation.

# CHAPTER 20

**THEME:** *Review of Israel's long history of sins; future judgment and restoration*

Chapters 20–24 contain the final predictions concerning the judgment of Jerusalem. There are two things to which I would like to call your attention in this section. First, notice how long and drawn out is God's message to these people. Right down to the very day that Nebuchadnezzar besieged the city, God was willing to spare them. God would have removed Nebuchadnezzar from the city as He had done previously to the Assyrians and would not have permitted him to destroy it. However, the people did not turn to God, and the judgment came. Right down to the last moment there was mercy extended to them. Second, the very day that the siege of Jerusalem began, the wife of Ezekiel died, and God told him not to mourn or weep for her at all. I consider this man Ezekiel a sharp contrast to the prophet Jeremiah. Jeremiah had a woman's heart, and he wept; the message he gave broke his own heart. Because He wept, the Lord Jesus was compared to Jeremiah. I'll be honest with you though; Ezekiel is almost like an actor playing a part. He goes through his part, but he is not moved by it. He seems to be pretty hardboiled all the way through. Ezekiel was simply a mouthpiece for God.

## REVIEW OF ISRAEL'S LONG HISTORY OF SINS; FUTURE JUDGMENT AND RESTORATION

In chapter 20 we have a retrospect of the nation's sins. Again, it is Ezekiel giving not his word, but God's Word. He was very much like a Western Union boy who brings you a message. It may be a message of joy, it may be a message of sorrow, but the Western Union boy just delivers the message—you are the one who is moved by it.

**And it came to pass in the seventh year, in the fifth month, the tenth day of the month, that certain of the elders of Israel came to inquire of the LORD, and sat before me [Ezek. 20:1].**

More and more they are beginning to turn to this man Ezekiel—they come now to get a word. This occurred in approximately 590 B.C. The destruction of Jerusalem took place shortly after, somewhere around 588–586 B.C.

I do not think we can be dogmatic about these dates.

**Then came the word of the LORD unto me, saying [Ezek. 20:2].**

He is not giving his word; he is giving God's Word.

**Son of man, speak unto the elders of Israel, and say unto them, Thus saith the Lord GOD; Are ye come to inquire of me? As I live, saith the Lord GOD, I will not be inquired of by you.**

**Wilt thou judge them, son of man, wilt thou judge them? cause them to know the abominations of their fathers [Ezek. 20:3–4].**

These people are coming to complain and to criticize God. They say He is unfair to judge them and unfair to destroy Jerusalem. It is beginning to penetrate their thinking that it is really going to happen.

Ezekiel is going to go over this ground again with them, because God does not mind stating His charge or reviewing His reasons for the judgment He is to bring.

**And say unto them, Thus saith the Lord GOD; In the day when I chose Israel, and lifted up mine hand unto the seed of the house of Jacob, and made myself known unto them in the land of Egypt, when I lifted up mine hand unto them, saying, I am the LORD your God [Ezek. 20:5].**

God goes back to the very beginning when He called these people out of the land of Egypt, delivered them out of their slavery there, and brought them into the wilderness.

**But the house of Israel rebelled against me in the wilderness: they walked not in my statutes, and they despised my judgments, which if a man do, he shall even live in them; and my sabbaths they greatly polluted: then I said, I would pour out my fury upon them in the wilderness, to consume them [Ezek. 20:13].**

The generation that went into the wilderness rebelled against God, and He let them die in the wilderness.

Notwithstanding the children rebelled against me: they walked not in my statutes, neither kept my judgments to do them, which if a man do, he shall even live in them; they polluted my sabbaths: then I said, I would pour out my fury upon them, to accomplish my anger against them in the wilderness.

Nevertheless I withdrew mine hand, and wrought for my name's sake, that it should not be polluted in the sight of the heathen, in whose sight I brought them forth [Ezek. 20:21–22].

The next generation was rebellious also.

Wherefore I gave them also statutes that were not good, and judgments whereby they should not live;

And I polluted them in their own gifts, in that they caused to pass through the fire all that openeth the womb, that I might make them desolate, to the end that they might know that I am the LORD [Ezek. 20:25–26].

This is a strange passage of Scripture, and there is a difference of opinion among commentators as to what it means. I feel that the thought here is the same thought Paul had in 2 Corinthians 2:15–16—"For we are unto God as a sweet savour of Christ, in them that are saved, and in them that perish: To the one we are the savour of death unto death; and to the other the savour of life unto life. . . ." When God gave these people His Word and they rejected it, He gave them over to their own way. The very law that was good became bad, because it condemned them and judged them. The same thing is true of the gospel today. If you listen to the gospel and reject it, it would actually be better if you had never heard it. If you reject it, the gospel becomes a savor of death unto you. You can never go before God and say that you had not heard it.

Considering this tremendous condemnation, you would think God was through with these people. But tucked in here and there throughout the Book of Ezekiel we find marvelous, wonderful passages of promise. At

the darkest time in their history, the light of prophecy shone the brightest.

As I live, saith the Lord GOD, surely with a mighty hand, and with a stretched out arm, and with fury poured out, will I rule over you:

And I will bring you out from the people, and will gather you out of the countries wherein ye are scattered, with a mighty hand, and with a stretched out arm, and with fury poured out [Ezek. 20:33–34].

God tells them that He intends to bring them back into the land. God's purpose with Israel will yet be fulfilled. He will someday be declared right by those who had said He was not right.

Moreover the word of the LORD came unto me, saying,

Son of man, set thy face toward the south, and drop thy word toward the south, and prophesy against the forest of the south field;

And say to the forest of the south, Hear the word of the LORD; Thus saith the Lord GOD; Behold, I will kindle a fire in thee, and it shall devour every green tree in thee, and every dry tree: the flaming flame shall not be quenched, and all faces from the south to the north shall be burned therein [Ezek. 20:45–47].

"Prophesy against the forest of the south field"—some commentators feel this refers to Judah, and others think it means the Negeb. At least, it is south. If you were to see the Negeb, you would wonder what happened to the forest. Well, my friend, God judged it; He said He would remove it. That land was once the land of milk and honey, but you cannot come to that conclusion when you look at it today. Not only is it not the land of milk and honey, they do not even have enough water there.

This is a remarkable prophecy. God is not through with these people or with that land.

# CHAPTER 21

*THEME: Babylon removes last Davidic king until Messiah comes*

It is important to study the Book of Ezekiel because it is so often neglected and its message is very pertinent for this hour in which we are living today. Although the words of Ezekiel were spoken many years ago, it was the Word of God as he has almost monotonously repeated: "The word of the LORD came unto me, saying." Since it is the Word of God, it has an application for us in this day and in this nation. The liberal argues that, like the Book of Revelation, the Book of Ezekiel cannot be understood and does not have a message for us. Ezekiel's visions are tremendous, and I do not propose to have the final word on their interpretation. I just stand in awe and wonder. But in this section of the book we are down to the nitty-gritty where the rubber meets the road, and I am sincere when I say that Ezekiel is not difficult to understand and he is very practical for us.

Chapter 21 is one of the most important chapters in the Book of Ezekiel as it makes it very clear that the king of Babylon is going to remove the last king of the Davidic line until Messiah comes.

**And the word of the LORD came unto me, saying [Ezek. 21:1].**

Ezekiel will repeat this three times in this chapter. There is only one alternative for you: either you agree that the Lord said this, or you take the position that Ezekiel is lying. I believe that the Lord said this to him and that Ezekiel is not giving his viewpoint. I do not think that Ezekiel's feelings entered into his message very much. Jeremiah was overwhelmed by his feelings; they entered into every word he spoke. I do not think that is true of Ezekiel. In the beginning of his ministry when God gave Ezekiel his commission, He told him that he was going to speak to a rebellious and hardheaded people. God also said at that time He would make Ezekiel's head harder than theirs. I think maybe a little of that hardness got down to his heart, and so he could really lay it on the line to these people. You actually love the man for this, for, if his feelings had entered into it, this man would have been crushed by the message that he had to give.

**Son of man, set thy face toward Jerusalem, and drop thy word toward the holy places, and prophesy against the land of Israel,**

**And say to the land of Israel, Thus saith the LORD; Behold, I am against thee, and will draw forth my sword out of his sheath, and will cut off from thee the righteous and the wicked [Ezek. 21:2–3].**

Judgment is impending and apparently now is inevitable. Up to this point, the mercy of God has been extended, but now judgment is coming and there is no alternative.

"Thus saith the LORD; Behold, I am against thee." This is the first time He has said this about His city of Jerusalem.

"And will cut off from thee the righteous and the wicked." This sounds strange, does it not? Who are the righteous? The ones who say they are righteous? In our day they are the ones who are church members but are not saved at all, the ones who go through the ritual, who are religious. A great many people have the band-aid of religion over the sore of sin. They need to pull that old band-aid off and get that sore lanced, before it destroys them. It's a cancerous sore, and you simply do not cure cancer by putting a band-aid over it. Neither do you cure sin by becoming religious. God said, "I'm cutting it off now; I'm moving in with the sword, and I intend to destroy the city."

**Seeing then that I will cut off from thee the righteous and the wicked, therefore shall my sword go forth out of his sheath against all flesh from the south to the north [Ezek. 21:4].**

He is going to draw out the sword from its sheath—all the way from the south to the north.

**That all flesh may know that I the LORD have drawn forth my sword out of his sheath: it shall not return any more [Ezek. 21:5].**

"It shall not return any more"—the time for judgment has come.

**Sigh therefore, thou son of man, with the breaking of thy loins; and with bitterness sigh before their eyes.**

**And it shall be, when they say unto thee, Wherefore sighest thou? that thou**

shalt answer, For the tidings; because it cometh: and every heart shall melt, and all hands shall be feeble, and every spirit shall faint, and all knees shall be weak as water: behold, it cometh, and shall be brought to pass, saith the Lord GOD [Ezek. 21:6–7].

God asks Ezekiel to do something here, and I am not prepared to say whether Ezekiel's feelings are in it or not. He didn't do it naturally—God told him to do it—so I would say that he is acting the part. However, in doing so, he is revealing the heart of God.

The people have complained about Ezekiel's giving parables to them. In Ezekiel 20:49 we read, "Then said I, Ah, Lord GOD! they say of me, Doth he not speak parables?" In effect, they were saying, "We don't get his message." They didn't *want* to get it; they didn't like to be told that things were wrong. We sometimes think that the parables of the Lord Jesus are obtuse and difficult to understand. They are not, if you *want* to understand them. The religious rulers in His day understood what He was saying—that is the reason they hated Him. They understood He was speaking judgment against them.

**Again the word of the LORD came unto me, saying [Ezek. 21:8].**

Just in case you didn't get the message, Ezekiel repeats it again.

**Son of man, prophesy, and say, Thus saith the LORD; Say, A sword, a sword is sharpened, and also furbished:**

**It is sharpened to make a sore slaughter; it is furbished that it may glitter: should we then make mirth? it contemneth the rod of my son, as every tree [Ezek. 21:9–10].**

God is going to judge the city. This is a frightful and fearful word which comes from the lips of God, the One who had yearned over Jerusalem. The Lord Jesus, too, *wept* over Jerusalem because He loved the city: "O Jerusalem, Jerusalem, thou that killest the prophets, and stonest them which are sent unto thee, how often would I have gathered thy children together, even as a hen gathereth her chickens under her wings, and ye would not! Behold, your house is left unto you desolate" (Matt. 23:37–38). If you want to know how terrible that judgment was, read what happened when Titus the Roman came in A.D. 70 and leveled that city—just as Nebuchadnezzar is about to do in Ezekiel's time.

God makes it clear what He is going to do, and the message is not a brand new one by any means. In the Book of Isaiah we find: "For by fire and by his sword will the LORD plead with all flesh: and the slain of the LORD shall be many (Isa. 66:16). And again we read, "Fear, and the pit, and the snare, are upon thee, O inhabitant of the earth" (Isa. 24:17). Ezekiel is to sigh because of the judgment that is coming. The Lord Jesus said of the day that is still coming, "Men's hearts failing them for fear, and for looking after those things which are coming on the earth: for the powers of heaven shall be shaken" (Luke 21:26). Ezekiel is to sigh and weep because God has now drawn the sword of judgment. Judgment lies ahead in our day, my friend. That is not a popular message, just as it was not in Ezekiel's day.

**The word of the LORD came unto me again, saying [Ezek. 21:18].**

Believe me, he will not let us forget this!

**Also, thou son of man, appoint thee two ways, that the sword of the king of Babylon may come: both twain shall come forth out of one land: and choose thou a place, choose it at the head of the way to the city [Ezek. 21:19].**

In other words, Nebuchadnezzar wanted to decide which way he was going to come to Jerusalem. Now, do you think he's going to turn to the Lord? No, he is pagan. He is going to use divination and necromancy:

**For the king of Babylon stood at the parting of the way, at the head of the two ways, to use divination: he made his arrows bright, he consulted with images, he looked in the liver [Ezek. 21:21].**

These are methods which were used in that day and are actually used today also.

"He made his arrows bright" would be better translated as, "he shook his arrows to and fro." This was sort of like rolling dice or looking at tea leaves. He dropped his arrows down to see which direction they pointed to determine which direction he should take to Jerusalem. Nebuchadnezzar was entirely a pagan and heathen king. God, however, will overrule his actions—that is important to remember.

**And thou, profane wicked prince of Israel, whose day is come, when iniquity shall have an end [Ezek. 21:25].**

"Thou, profane wicked prince of Israel"—he is speaking of Zedekiah. "Whose day is come, when iniquity shall have an end"—the time for judgment has come; this is the end time.

Scripture has a great deal to say about the end of this age. The correct translation of Ezekiel's phrase would be, "in the time of the iniquity of the end." Daniel also used this expression, ". . . the time of the end . . ." (Dan. 11:35). The disciples asked the Lord Jesus, ". . . Tell us, when shall these things be? and what shall be the sign of thy coming, and of the end of the world?" (Matt. 24:3), and the Lord answered that question for them. Paul also spoke of it a great deal in 2 Thessalonians. This man, Zedekiah, then is a picture of that future wicked prince, the false messiah, the Antichrist, who is coming at the time of the end.

**Thus saith the Lord GOD; Remove the diadem, and take off the crown: this shall not be the same: exalt him that is low, and abase him that is high [Ezek. 21:26].**

Zedekiah is to be brought low, and there will not be another king to sit upon the throne of David "until Shiloh come," until the Messiah comes.

**I will overturn, overturn, overturn, it: and it shall be no more, until he come whose right it is; and I will give it him [Ezek. 21:27].**

This is a remarkable prophecy. "Until he come whose right it is; and I will give it him," that is, the Lord Jesus. From Zedekiah down to the Lord Jesus there has been no one in the line of David who ever sat on that throne. Ezekiel is saying that no one would ever be able to do so. The Lord Jesus is the only One who will. Right now He is sitting at God's right hand, waiting until His enemies are made His footstool when He comes to this earth to rule.

This remarkable prophecy began back in Genesis 49:10, when Jacob was giving the prophecies concerning his twelve sons who became the twelve tribes of Israel. He said there: "The sceptre shall not depart from Judah, nor a lawgiver from between his feet, until Shiloh come; and unto him shall the gathering of the people be." "The sceptre" means the king. The Hebrew word for "until He come" is very similar to the word, *Shiloh*. It speaks of the Lord Jesus—this is the way He was introduced in Scripture. This is the reason that John the Baptist said, ". . . Repent ye: for the kingdom of heaven is at hand" (Matt. 3:2). Why? Because it was "at hand" in the Person of the One who had come, the One of whom all the prophets had spoken.

**Whiles they see vanity unto thee, whiles they divine a lie unto thee, to bring thee upon the necks of them that are slain, of the wicked, whose day is come, when their iniquity shall have an end [Ezek. 21:29].**

Ezekiel is speaking of the judgment of the Ammonites, but we also have again the expression, "when their iniquity shall have an end," suggesting the end of this age. In 2 Thessalonians 2:8 Paul writes: "And then shall that Wicked be revealed, whom the Lord shall consume with the spirit of his mouth, and shall destroy with the brightness of his coming." The Lord Jesus Christ will put down this enemy in the last days.

**And I will pour out mine indignation upon thee, I will blow against thee in the fire of my wrath, and deliver thee into the hand of brutish men, and skilful to destroy.**

**Thou shalt be for fuel to the fire; thy blood shall be in the midst of the land; thou shalt be no more remembered: for I the LORD have spoken it [Ezek. 21: 31–32].**

Ezekiel's generation was going to go into captivity—that would be the end as far as they were concerned. It would be their children who would return back to the land of Israel.

# CHAPTERS 22–24

*THEME: Review of Jerusalem's abominations; the parable of two sisters; the parable of the boiling pot*

We continue in this section which contains the last prophecies concerning the judgment that was coming upon the nation Israel (chs. 20–24). In the beginning, Ezekiel's messages were directed to the first two delegations which had gone into captivity. They were holding on to the belief that God would never destroy the temple; it was His sanctuary, and His glory had been there.

They believed that God would not allow Nebuchadnezzar to touch it. The false prophets encouraged the captives in their unbelief, making them think it was not necessary for them to come back to God, or to give up their idolatry and other evil ways.

There is something very subtle that happens often in our day which I think we need to be very careful about. A great many men are eulogized today even before they die, but particularly at their funerals; though they were godless blasphemers, some preacher tries to push them right into heaven with his words of praise. Unless we have God's mind on the matter, we need to be very careful what we say about folk. Otherwise, an unbeliever may measure his goodness by the life of someone who is praised (he knows how great a sinner that man was!), and may be led to believe that he does not need the Savior. It is tragic today that gospel messages are frequently given to a crowd of saints, but not given at a time and place the worldly and unsaved man is present. Too often, the preacher trims his message to please the crowd—that is what the false prophets of Ezekiel's day did.

Ezekiel has really been laying it on the line in these final prophecies. In chapter 20 he gave a prophecy concerning the Negeb, the southern part of Israel around Beersheba. In that prophecy God said, "I'll kindle a fire in thee." I have been through that area, and it is as baldheaded as a doorknob; there is no vegetation of any size whatsoever. I never saw a tree any larger than my arm in the entire place. There used to be a forest there, but God judged it, and He did a pretty good job of it. Then in chapter 21, there was the remarkable prophecy that there would be no one to sit on David's throne until the Lord Jesus came. That is what the angel was talking about when he said to Mary, "I am going to give to Him the throne of His father David." You see, even at Christmastime it's nice to have Ezekiel around to add to our understanding. The background the prophets give us is so needful today.

## REVIEW OF THE ABOMINATIONS OF JERUSALEM

Chapter 22 lists the abominations of the city of Jerusalem.

**Moreover the word of the LORD came unto me, saying,**

**Now, thou son of man, wilt thou judge, wilt thou judge the bloody city? yea, thou shalt shew her all her abominations [Ezek. 22:1–2].**

"The bloody city"—this is what Ezekiel calls Jerusalem. Isaiah said the same thing in Isaiah 1:21, "How is the faithful city become an harlot! it was full of judgment; righteousness lodged in it; but now murderers." The Lord Jesus wept over the city and said, "O Jerusalem, Jerusalem, which killest the prophets, and stonest them that are sent unto thee . . ." (Luke 13:34). After all, didn't they slay Him also? They turned Him over to the Romans who did the killing job. It was Stephen who said to the Jews, "Which of the prophets have not your fathers persecuted? and they have slain them which shewed before of the coming of the Just One; of whom ye have been now the betrayers and murderers" (Acts 7:52). At the death of Christ, the crowd cried out to Pilate, ". . . His blood be on us, and on our children" (Matt. 27:25).

The leaders of Israel were involved in apostasy and gross sins:

**There is a conspiracy of her prophets in the midst thereof, like a roaring lion ravening the prey; they have devoured souls; they have taken the treasure and precious things; they have made her many widows in the midst thereof [Ezek. 22:25].**

1. Her false *prophets* were saying, "Everything is fine. We're getting along nicely."

**Her priests have violated my law, and have profaned mine holy things: they have put no difference between the holy and profane, neither have they shewed difference between the unclean and the clean, and have hid their eyes from my**

sabbaths, and I am profaned among them [Ezek. 22:26].

2. Her *priests* blatantly violated the law of God.

**Her princes in the midst thereof are like wolves ravening the prey, to shed blood, and to destroy souls, to get dishonest gain [Ezek. 22:27].**

3. Her *princes* were "like wolves ravening the prey." Paul has warned the church about wolves in sheep's clothing (see Acts 20:29), and we do have them in the church today.

Why was Jerusalem called a bloody city? Because of the prophets, the priests, and the princes.

**And I sought for a man among them, that should make up the hedge, and stand in the gap before me for the land, that I should not destroy it: but I found none.**

**Therefore have I poured out mine indignation upon them; I have consumed them with the fire of my wrath: their own way have I recompensed upon their heads, saith the Lord God [Ezek. 22:30–31].**

There was not a man to be found in the land who could stand in the gap. I thank God He did find a Man to stand between my sin and a holy God. That Man is the Lord Jesus Christ, and God sees those who belong to Him in Christ. I am thankful for the Man who stands in the gap today!

## PARABLE OF TWO SISTERS

Once again, in chapter 23, Ezekiel goes way out on a limb, he goes way out into left field, and he tells the people another strange parable. It is the parable of two sisters: one was named Aholah, and the other was Aholibah. I think that when he began to give this parable, the people actually smiled and said, "Where in the world is this fellow going with a story like that?"

**The word of the Lord came again unto me, saying [Ezek. 23:1].**

Ezekiel didn't make this story up—God gave him this message.

**Son of man, there were two women, the daughters of one mother:**

**And they committed whoredoms in Egypt; they committed whoredoms in their youth: there were their breasts**

pressed, and there they bruised the teats of their virginity [Ezek. 23:2–3].

The two sisters were no longer virgins but had become harlots. What in the world is Ezekiel talking about?

**And the names of them were Aholah the elder, and Aholibah her sister: and they were mine, and they bare sons and daughters. Thus were their names; Samaria is Aholah, and Jerusalem Aholibah [Ezek. 23:4].**

"Samaria is Aholah"—that is, the northern kingdom of Israel is Aholah. "And Jerusalem Aholibah"—Jerusalem and Judah in the south is Aholibah.

The meaning of *Aholibah* (Jerusalem and Judah) is, "My tent is inner." Who is saying this? God is saying, "My tent is inner." In other words, in the southern kingdom, in Jerusalem, was the wonderful temple of Solomon. It was patterned after the tabernacle in the wilderness, and it was the place where the people approached God. That was wonderful.

*Aholah* means "her own tent." The northern kingdom rebelled and separated from the southern part of Israel. Old King Jeroboam put up two golden calves, one in Beth-el and one in Samaria, and tried to keep his people from going south to worship in Jerusalem.

It was very easy for the prophets and the people of the southern kingdom to say that God will judge those golden calves in the north—and He surely did. However, He is going to judge the southern kingdom also, because they were going through the ritual of a dead religion; they thought they were right with God, but they actually were living in sin.

One of the things that is cutting the nerve of the spiritual life even of fundamental Christians and fundamental churches today is the lives of some church members. Of course you are saved by grace—that is the only way you and I can ever be saved. If God is not going to save by grace, then I couldn't possibly be saved, but that does not mean that I am not to live for Him. That doesn't mean that He will not judge you and me. That does not mean that our lives cannot kill the spiritual life in a church.

Ezekiel attracted a little attention with his story about these two girls, Aholah and Aholibah. This incident reminds me of the whimsical story which comes out of my southland about a poor tenant farmer who had a little donkey. He hitched the donkey up to a wagon in which one line was leather and the other

was a cotton rope. One day he was going to give a friend a ride into town. The friend got into the wagon, but the farmer went and got a two-by-four out of the wagon, took it up to the front and hit his donkey on the head! The friend was thunderstruck; he couldn't believe what he saw. "Why in the world did you do that?" he asked. "Well," the farmer said, "I always have to get his attention before I start." Ezekiel was dealing with a lot of hard-headed people, and he tells this parable to get their attention. Sometimes preachers are criticized for using sensational subjects for their messages, but I have great sympathy for them. How else are you going to get people to listen today? Ezekiel used some unusual methods.

**She doted upon the Assyrians her neighbours, captains and rulers clothed most gorgeously, horsemen riding upon horses, all of them desirable young men [Ezek. 23:12].**

This refers to an historical event which took place when Old King Ahaz was on the throne in the southern kingdom. He went up to Damascus to meet Tiglath-pileser, king of Assyria, and he saw there an altar he thought was the prettiest altar he'd ever seen. So he sent Urijah the priest to get the pattern of it in order to make one just like it (2 Kings 16:10–18). He wanted to "improve the worship," you know—he went in for that type of thing. Well, God took note of that, and He judged the northern kingdom for it.

Now the Babylonian invasion of the southern kingdom is about to take place—there's no alternative to it. God is judging both the northern and the southern kingdoms because they have turned away from the living and true God; one went brazenly into idolatry, and the other *pretended* to worship the Lord.

My friend, it might be well for all of God's people to heed Paul's warning: "Examine yourselves, whether ye be in the faith . . ." (2 Cor. 13:5). Someone may ask, "Don't you believe in the security of the believer?" Yes, I do, but I also believe in the insecurity of make-believers. We need to examine ourselves. When you go to church do you really worship God? Do you draw close to the person of Christ? Do you really love Him? He doesn't want your service unless you do. In John 21 He asked Peter, "Lovest thou me?" When Peter could say that he did, then the Lord said, "Feed my sheep." Only then could the Lord use him.

## PARABLE OF THE BOILING POT

In chapter 24 we have the parable of the boiling pot and the death of Ezekiel's wife. God will use both of these to speak to the people.

**Again in the ninth year, in the tenth month, in the tenth day of the month, the word of the Lord came unto me, saying,**

**Son of man, write thee the name of the day, even of this same day: the king of Babylon set himself against Jerusalem this same day [Ezek. 24:1–2].**

This is the first time that Ezekiel has dated his message. At this very moment Nebuchadnezzar was breaking through the wall of Jerusalem. There was no television in that day to let Ezekiel know what was happening. There was no satellite to convey this message from Jerusalem to Babylon. The only way he could get this message was by God revealing it to him. The liberal theologians have always had a problem with this verse; one of them has said: "This verse forces on us in the clearest fashion the dilemma either Ezekiel was a deliberate deceiver, or he was possessed of some kind of second sight." He certainly was possessed of second sight—God's sight, by the way. The liberal doesn't recognize it as that, of course.

**Wherefore thus saith the Lord God; Woe to the bloody city, to the pot whose scum is therein, and whose scum is not gone out of it! bring it out piece by piece; let no lot fall upon it [Ezek. 24:6].**

Again, Jerusalem is called "the bloody city." There is a pot, and there is scum in the pot. The pot is the city of Jerusalem; the citizens are in that pot. Their sin is the scum that's in the pot.

Sometimes we hear somebody say concerning another group of people, "They are the scum of the earth." Do you want to know what God says? He says your sin and my sin is the scum of the earth. Listen carefully: We are *all* in the same pot. The pot of Jerusalem is the pot of the world for you and me today. I get a little weary of all this talk about different "ethnic groups." We're all in the same pot, and we are the scum of the earth—that is, our sin is the scum of the earth. I don't know how you could say it more strongly than that.

**Also the word of the Lord came unto me, saying,**

**Son of man, behold, I take away from thee the desire of thine eyes with a stroke: yet neither shalt thou mourn nor weep, neither shall thy tears run down [Ezek. 24:15–16].**

Apparently, the prophet had married a lovely, young Israelite girl, and they loved each other. But down there in captivity, she became sick and died. I imagine it was a heartbreak to Ezekiel, but again he must act a part:

**Forbear to cry, make no mourning for the dead, bind the tire of thine head upon thee, and put on thy shoes upon thy feet, and cover not thy lips, and eat not the bread of men [Ezek. 24:17].**

God told him, "Don't act like you're mourning at all." And the people didn't understand it. The people came to Ezekiel and said, "What in the world does this mean? Your wife has died, and you are not mourning at all! What kind of man are you?"

All of this Ezekiel is doing to get a message through to the people. Verse 24 is the key to this entire Book of Ezekiel:

**Thus Ezekiel is unto you a sign: according to all that he hath done shall ye do: and when this cometh, ye shall know that I am the Lord God [Ezek. 24:24].**

At that very moment, Jerusalem was being destroyed, and later on word came to the captives about its destruction: "And it came to pass in the twelfth year of our captivity, in the tenth month, in the fifth day of the month, that one that had escaped out of Jerusalem came unto me, saying, The city is smitten" (Ezek. 33:21). Into the camp came these stragglers; they must have looked terrible. They said, "We've escaped from the city. The false prophets were wrong. The city is burned. The temple has been leveled, and the city is debris and ashes."

Ezekiel was right in not mourning. The reason they were not to mourn is found in verse 27:

**In that day shall thy mouth be opened to him which is escaped, and thou shalt speak, and be no more dumb: and thou shalt be a sign unto them; and they shall know that I am the Lord [Ezek. 24:27].**

"They shall know that I am the Lord." Jerusalem was *God's* city, and the temple was *His* house. They were God's witness to the world. And when the people of Israel failed, God said, "I will destroy even My own witness on the earth. I want you to know the city is destroyed. The rest of your people are being brought into captivity. But there's no use weeping, there's no use howling to Me now. I have done this—I am responsible for it."

To each of the seven churches in the Book of Revelation, the Lord Jesus said, "You had better be careful of your witness to the world, or I will come and remove your lampstand." The lampstand of all seven of those churches has been removed, my friend. Not one of those churches remains today. This ought to be a message to us: If you are a Christian and are not going to stand for God today, He will remove your lampstand—there will be no light.

This is a strong message; it is not the lovey-dovey, sloppy stuff we hear so often. This is Ezekiel, and he is speaking for God. He has said again and again, "The word of the Lord, came unto me, saying." If you want to argue with his message, take it to the Lord, but remember He's right and we are the ones who are wrong.

# CHAPTER 25

*THEME: Prophecies against the nations: the Ammonites, Moab, Edom, the Philistines*

This brings us to a new section (chs. 25–32) which deals with the prophecies concerning the nations around Israel. All of these nations, as far as we are concerned today, have long since disappeared from the face of the earth, and the prophecies about them have been literally fulfilled.

Up to this point, Ezekiel has been giving out prophecies concerning Jerusalem and the land of Israel because the *final* deportation of the children of Israel has not yet arrived. To the very last, the people held on to the faint hope, at the urging and encouragement of the false prophets, that God would not destroy Jerusalem, and the land of Israel would remain. After all, wasn't it God's method of communication to the world? When the destruction of Jerusalem occurred, the people were startled; they were dumbfounded. I imagine the word came when the headline in the *Babylonian Bugle* read: JERUSALEM DESTROYED! And the opening line read something like this: "On this day Nebuchadnezzar with his armies entered the city of Jerusalem, having breached the wall."

Ezekiel was proved accurate in his prophecies, and from here on he will not be giving any prophecies concerning the destruction of Jerusalem, because he is not writing *history;* he is writing *prophecy.* So now he turns to the surrounding nations. What will be their fate?

There is a tremendous message for us in this chapter. There lies God's city in ruins. I see standing over that city a man by the name of Jeremiah. Tears are coursing down his cheeks; he is a man with a broken heart. He is the one who mirrors the One who will be coming to earth in five hundred or so years. He, too, will sit over Jerusalem on the Mount of Olives and will weep over the city knowing that destruction is coming again because its people will have turned their backs on the living and true God.

I see another prophet. He is not weeping, and I will tell you why. At this same time his lovely wife died, and the Scriptures make it clear that he loved her. This prophet is Ezekiel, and he is told not to mourn. On the surface he is hard-boiled.

God said that He would be that way. Jeremiah and Ezekiel reveal the two sides of God in this matter. This is something we need to see today. God is tenderheated. Like Jeremiah, the Lord Jesus Christ is merciful and kind. He was not willing that any should perish, so He died on the cross for us. But listen to Him speaking to the cities that rejected Him: "Woe unto thee, Chorazin! woe unto thee Bethsaida! for if the mighty works had been done in Tyre and Sidon, which have been done in you, they had a great while ago repented, sitting in sackcloth and ashes. But it shall be more tolerable for Tyre and Sidon at the judgment, than for you. And thou, Capernaum, which art exalted to heaven, shalt be thrust down to hell" (Luke 10:13–15). That is strong language coming from the gentle Jesus! He also said, "Woe unto you, scribes and Pharisees, hypocrites! for ye are as graves which appear not, and the men that walk over them are not aware of them" (Luke 11:44). The Lord denounced them in such a way that it makes your hair curl! There are two sides to God, and He is the same today. We get a warped view of Him when all we hear is, "God is love, God is love." It is true that God is love, but don't lose sight of the fact that God is also holy. He is righteous and He will judge. You are not rushing into heaven on the little love boat today. You will go to heaven only if you put your faith and trust in Jesus Christ, who shed His blood and gave His life on the cross. Then you will have eternal life and will be covered with the righteousness of Christ, standing complete and acceptable in Him. If you reject His salvation, there will be nothing left but judgment.

We have a warped view of God today. In this connection I always think of a judge who lived in west Texas many years ago. He had a reputation for making quick decisions. Other judges just didn't move as fast as he did. A friend asked him one day, "What is the secret of your making quick decisions?" "Well," he replied, "I'll tell you what I do. I just listen to the defense, and then I hand in a decision." The friend was startled. He asked the judge, "Don't you ever listen to the prosecution?" The judge said, "I used to, but that always confused me." And there are a lot of confused folks running around talking about the love of God, but we must never forget that He is also a God of judgment. Maybe that is the reason Ezekiel is a closed book, a sealed book to so many people. Liberal ministers encourage this by saying, "Nobody can understand the

Book of Ezekiel." Well, you cannot understand it until you study it, that is for sure. We have had a remarkable principle laid down for us so far, and I hope we don't miss its message for us.

Now we come to the judging of the nations around Israel. I am not going to spend much time with them because they have long since passed off the stage, but they are important because they are to return. Only God can bring them back, and he says He will do that.

## PROPHECY AGAINST THE AMMONITES

The Ammonites had a very bad beginning. They were a nomadic race descended from an incestuous relationship between Lot and his younger daughter (see Gen. 19:33–38). Their country lay along the Dead Sea. God said they would be made subject to Nebuchadnezzar, and they were.

Now God gives the reason for His judgment against them:

> And say unto the Ammonites, Hear the word of the Lord GOD; Thus saith the Lord GOD; Because thou saidst, Aha, against my sanctuary, when it was profaned; and against the land of Israel, when it was desolate; and against the house of Judah, when they went into captivity [Ezek. 25:3].

The Ammonites applauded the enemy that destroyed Israel. They were allies. But the same enemy destroyed Ammon. In Jeremiah 49:6 we read concerning them, "And afterward I will bring again the captivity of the children of Ammon, saith the LORD." God judged them so that they might know that He is the Lord.

> Behold, therefore I will stretch out mine hand upon thee, and will deliver thee for a spoil to the heathen; and I will cut thee off from the people, and I will cause thee to perish out of the countries: I will destroy thee; and thou shalt know that I am the LORD [Ezek. 25:7].

## PROPHECY AGAINST MOAB

The Moabites were more civilized than the Ammonites, but they too were descended from an incestuous relationship—between Lot and his older daughter (Gen. 19:33–38). Moab was situated on the east of Israel but along the northern part of the Dead Sea. This is the land that Ruth the Moabitess came from. She was an ancestor of King David, which makes her also an ancestor of the Lord Jesus Christ—her name appears in His genealogy (Matt. 1:5).

Notice the reason God will judge Moab:

> Thus saith the Lord GOD; Because that Moab and Seir do say, Behold, the house of Judah is like unto all the heathen;

> Therefore, behold, I will open the side of Moab from the cities, from his cities which are on his frontiers, the glory of the country, Beth-jeshimoth, Baal-meon, and Kiriathaim [Ezek. 25:8–9].

## PROPHECY AGAINST EDOM

Edom is the nation that came from Esau, whose beginning is found in Genesis 25. The little Book of Obadiah details the judgment against Edom and the rock-hewn city of Petra. God gives His reason for judging Edom:

> Thus saith the Lord GOD; Because that Edom hath dealt against the house of Judah by taking vengeance, and hath greatly offended, and revenged himself upon them;

> Therefore thus saith the Lord GOD: I will also stretch out mine hand upon Edom, and will cut off man and beast from it; and I will make it desolate from Teman; and they of Dedan shall fall by the sword [Ezek. 25:12–13].

Edom's treatment of His chosen people is the cause of God's judgment.

## PROPHECY AGAINST THE PHILISTINES

> Thus saith the Lord GOD; Because the Philistines have dealt by revenge, and have taken vengeance with a despiteful heart, to destroy it for the old hatred;

> Therefore thus saith the Lord GOD; Behold, I will stretch out mine hand upon the Philistines, and I will cut off the Cherethims, and destroy the remnant of the sea coast.

> And I will execute great vengeance upon them with furious rebukes; and they shall know that I am the LORD, when I shall lay my vengeance upon them [Ezek. 25:15–17].

The Philistines have disappeared; they are no longer in that land. This judgment against them has been so literally fulfilled that

the unbelieving critic wants to place Ezekiel's prophecy at a much later date so it can be considered history!

My friend, we will do well to take note of the fact that God judged the nations who had sinned against Him and His people.

# CHAPTER 26

*THEME: Judgment against Tyre*

## JUDGMENT AGAINST TYRE

Chapters 26–28 give us prophecies against Tyre and Sidon. Tyre and Sidon belong together like pork and beans, or ham and eggs. You never think of one without the other. These chapters are a marvelous example of the exactness of the literal fulfillment of prophecy.

Tyre was the capital of the great Phoenician nation which was famous for its seagoing traders. They plied the Mediterranean and even went beyond that. We know today that they went around the Pillars of Hercules and the Rock of Gibraltar, and into Great Britain, where they obtained tin. They established a colony in North Africa. Tarshish in Spain was founded by these people. They were great colonizers and went a lot farther than we used to think they did in their explorations.

Tyre was a great and proud city. Hiram, king of Tyre, had been a good friend of David and supplied him with building materials. Solomon and Hiram did not get along as well as David and Hiram had. Apparently Hiram was a great king. But also the center of Baal worship was there in Tyre and Sidon. Jezebel, the daughter of a king and former priest, married Ahab, king of Israel, and introduced Baal worship into the northern kingdom.

Now let's look at the tremendous prophecy God gives concerning Tyre and Sidon.

**And it came to pass in the eleventh year, in the first day of the month, that the word of the LORD came unto me, saying,**

**Son of man, because that Tyrus hath said against Jerusalem, Aha, she is broken that was the gates of the people: she is turned unto me: I shall be replenished, now she is laid waste [Ezek. 26:1–2].**

Tyre was destroyed at the same time Jerusalem was destroyed. Nebuchadnezzar took Tyre.

**Therefore thus saith the Lord GOD; Behold, I am against thee, O Tyrus, and will cause many nations to come up against thee, as the sea causeth his waves to come up [Ezek. 26:3].**

When God says, "Behold, I am against thee," you can be sure He is against that place. Just as the waves break on the shore, God says, nations will come against Tyre, that great commercial center that had been invincible.

**And they shall destroy the walls of Tyrus, and break down her towers: I will also scrape her dust from her, and make her like the top of a rock [Ezek. 26:4].**

Nebuchadnezzar came against the city and destroyed it, but he didn't scrape it.

**It shall be a place for the spreading of nets in the midst of the sea: for I have spoken it, saith the Lord GOD; and it shall become a spoil to the nations [Ezek. 26:5].**

God said it would be a fishing village—not the proud commercial capital—and that is what it is today.

**And her daughters which are in the field shall be slain by the sword; and they shall know that I am the LORD [Ezek. 26:6].**

"Her daughters" are, I believe, the colonies that she established. She had established one on the island of Cyprus, by the way. *Cyprus* means "copper", and she obtained copper from there. The Phoenicians were the traders who brought these metals into the ancient civilized world.

**For thus saith the Lord GOD; Behold, I will bring upon Tyrus Nebuchadrezzar king of Babylon, a king of kings, from the north, with horses, and with chariots, and with horsemen, and companies, and much people.**

He shall slay with the sword thy daughters in the field: and he shall make a fort against thee, and cast a mount against thee, and lift up the buckler against thee.

And he shall set engines of war against thy walls, and with his axes he shall break down thy towers.

By reason of the abundance of his horses their dust shall cover thee: thy walls shall shake at the noise of the horsemen, and of the wheels, and of the chariots, when he shall enter into thy gates, as men enter into a city wherein is made a breach [Ezek. 26:7–10].

Nebuchadnezzar breached the walls of ancient Tyre, just as he had at Jerusalem, and this prophecy was literally fulfilled.

With the hoofs of his horses shall he tread down all thy streets: he shall slay thy people by the sword, and thy strong garrisons shall go down to the ground [Ezek. 26:11].

It is very interesting to note that verses 7–11 clearly predict that Nebuchadnezzar will take the city, and the pronoun *he* is all through that section. But now, beginning with the next verse the pronoun changes to *they*. God had said that the nations were coming and here is that prediction:

And they shall make a spoil of thy riches, and make a prey of thy merchandise: and they shall break down thy walls, and destroy thy pleasant houses: and they shall lay thy stones and thy timber and thy dust in the midst of the water.

And I will cause the noise of thy songs to cease; and the sound of thy harps shall be no more heard.

And I will make thee like the top of a rock: thou shalt be a place to spread nets upon; thou shalt be built no more: for I the LORD have spoken it, saith the Lord GOD [Ezek. 26:12–14].

Now this prophecy waited centuries for fulfillment. For three hundred years the ruins of Tyre lay there, and they were very impressive. Although Nebuchadnezzar had destroyed the city, this second prophecy had not been fulfilled. Who was going to take up the stones and even scrape the dust into the ocean?

Well, out of the west there comes Alexander the Great, symbolized as the he goat in Daniel's prophecy. You see, after the return of the Tyrians from Babylonian captivity, they decided to rebuild their city on an island and forget all about the mainland. Since they were a seafaring power, they could better protect themselves on an island. Well, when Alexander got there, he saw the ruins of the city, but the inhabited new city was out yonder on the island out of his reach. He had plenty of time and he had plenty of soldiers, so he decided to build a causeway to the city. Where did he get the material to construct it clear out there in the ocean? He took the building material of old Tyre, the stones, the pillars, and even the dust of the city, and built a causeway over which his army marched right into the new city of Tyre. He destroyed the city, and from that day to this it has never been rebuilt.

My friend, this is a remarkable prophecy! As I mentioned, the critics try to explain away the prophecy regarding Nebuchadnezzar's destruction of the city by saying that Ezekiel wrote it after it had happened, but it is impossible for them to claim that Ezekiel wrote after Alexander the Great! Only God can prophesy with such accuracy.

I have walked out on the isthmus that Alexander made from the mainland to the island and have seen the ruins. The ruins are being excavated and there were all kinds of broken pieces of pottery and artifacts around. Ezekiel's prophecy was literally fulfilled. You cannot look at the ruins of Tyre and say that the Word of God is guesswork.

Sidon stands today as it always has, but Tyre is gone. Nobody has tried to rebuild it. Lebanon hasn't tried. God's Word says that Tyre will never be rebuilt. If you can rebuild Tyre, you can contradict God's Word, but I advise you to invest your money somewhere else.

# CHAPTER 27

*THEME: Lamentation for Tyre*

## LAMENTATION FOR TYRE

The preceding chapter gave us the prophecy concerning the destruction of Tyre, and we saw that the prophecy was literally fulfilled. The ruins of Tyre stand today as a witness to the accuracy of the Word of God. This was an impressive city in Ezekiel's day. Even though he may never have been there, he gives a lamentation for Tyre in this chapter. He laments the fact that this great city will fall. It was a *great* city—I don't want to minimize its beauty and magnificence. This is a sad and beautiful chapter in which Ezekiel likens Tyre, the capital of the Phoenician Empire, to a great ship that is wrecked. I cannot think of a better picture for a seagoing people.

What was it that brought Tyre down?

**The word of the LORD came again unto me, saying,**

**Now, thou son of man, take up a lamentation for Tyrus;**

**And say unto Tyrus, O thou that art situate at the entry of the sea, which art a merchant of the people for many isles, Thus saith the Lord GOD; O Tyrus, thou hast said, I am of perfect beauty [Ezek. 27:1–3].**

What brought Tyre down? The same thing that brought down the rock-hewn city of Petra also brought down the great city of Tyre: "The pride of thine heart hath deceived thee . . ." (Obad. 3). Pride in the glory, pomp, and prosperity is the thing that has brought down many great nations of the world and reduced them to ruins. This chapter speaks of how extensive the kingdom of Phoenicia was. It begins with Chittim (Cyprus), meaning copper, which was one of their colonies, and extends all the way to Tarshish, which means smelting plant or refinery. Tarshish was sort of a jumping-off place for the Phoenicians. Jonah bought a ticket to that city, but he never saw it—instead he saw the interior of a big fish!

**The ships of Tarshish did sing of thee in thy market: and thou wast replenished, and made very glorious in the midst of the seas [Ezek. 27:25].**

Tyre was a great commercial center. Merchants came from all over the world to buy and sell. You could find just about anything you wanted in Tyre. In verse 17 it says that Israel traded in her markets. "Minnith" was perhaps olives or figs made into some kind of preserves. You could buy anything and everything in the markets of Tyre.

If you want a picture of Tyre as the great commercial center, you will see it depicted in a prophecy of Babylon in the future when it will become the commercial, religious and political center of the world. It will be the capital of the Antichrist. "The merchandise of gold, and silver, and precious stones, and of pearls, and fine linen, and purple, and silk, and scarlet, and all thyine wood, and all manner vessels of ivory, and all manner vessels of most precious wood, and of brass, and iron, and marble, And cinnamon, and odours, and ointments, and frankincense, and wine, and oil, and fine flour, and wheat, and beasts, and sheep, and horses, and chariots, and slaves, and souls of men. And the fruits that thy soul lusted after . . ." (Rev. 18:12–14).

This also is a picture of London, Paris, Rome, New York City, and Los Angeles. You can buy anything you want in these cities. If you have the money, you can buy it. Today is the age of materialism, just as it was in the days of Tyre.

Tyre was like a great ship. Everything the people needed was on board, and the music was playing. There was laughter, and the wine and champagne flowed. It was all there. Then it all disappeared. God judged it. Now here is the lamentation and the weeping over that great city. That is exactly what is going to happen in the last days. In those last days the stock market will fail, and everything you have in your safe deposit boxes won't be worth a dime, and everything you thought was valuable will suddenly become dust and ashes in your hands. What a tragic day it was when Tyre fell; what a tragic day it will be when the same thing happens in the future!

Be careful. Don't put all of your eggs in one basket. I think people ought to enjoy the affluent society we have today. I see nothing wrong in it, provided it does not become an obsession or an idol. Unfortunately, it has become that to many folk. Even in many of our good churches there is really very little Bible teaching. We play games. We pat each other on the back, and we have "fellowship"—we

love to talk about that. And we quote a Bible verse now and then to make sure we are religious and pious, and we go through the little ceremonies of the church. They did that in Tyre; they did it in Jerusalem, and God destroyed them. He destroyed them because they had an opportunity, a privilege, and a responsibility that they shrugged off.

**And in their wailing they shall take up a lamentation for thee, and lament over thee, saying, What city is like Tyrus, like the destroyed in the midst of the sea? [Ezek. 27:32].**

Tyre was like a great ship that had gone down at sea.

**In the time when thou shalt be broken by the seas in the depths of the waters thy merchandise and all thy company in the midst of thee shall fall [Ezek. 27:34].**

All will be swallowed up by the sea.

**The merchants among the people shall hiss at thee; thou shalt be a terror, and never shalt be any more [Ezek. 27:36].**

As I walked through the ruins of Tyre I heard no music nor laughter. I could not see the buildings or the gold and silver. All I saw were broken pieces of pottery and the wreck and ruin of what had once been a great city. And the God of heaven says, "I judged you." There must be a message in this picture of Tyre for our day and generation.

# CHAPTER 28

**THEME:** *Judgment against the prince of Tyre; judgment against the king*

## JUDGMENT AGAINST THE PRINCE OF TYRE

In this chapter we find the judgment of the prince and king of Tyre and Sidon. The prophecy looks beyond the local ruler to the one who is behind the kingdoms of the world—Satan.

**The word of the Lord came again unto me, saying,**

**Son of man, say unto the prince of Tyrus, Thus saith the Lord God; Because thine heart is lifted up, and thou hast said, I am a God, I sit in the seat of God, in the midst of the seas; yet thou art a man, and not God, though thou set thine heart as the heart of God [Ezek. 28:1–2].**

Again the word of the Lord comes to Ezekiel, and this time there are two messages: one for the prince of Tyre and one for the king of Tyre. In back of the great kingdom, the great commercial center, the great political center, and the great stronghold of Tyre, we are going to find the one who apparently also controls all the kingdoms of this world. He is Satan. He offered the kingdoms of the world

to the Lord Jesus during his temptation in the wilderness: "And the devil, taking him up into a high mountain, shewed unto him all the kingdoms of the world in a moment of time. And the devil said unto him, All this power will I give thee, and the glory of them: for that is delivered unto me; and to whomsoever I will I give it. If thou therefore wilt worship me, all shall be thine" (Luke 4:5–7). The Lord rejected Satan's offer, but not because He didn't recognize his ownership—Christ knew that Satan did have the kingdoms. Ultimately Christ will rule over the kingdoms of the world—but not as the vice-regent of Satan! Today, however, the Devil is still the prince of the power of the air. He is the one who is in back of the kingdoms of our world, whether we like it or not.

Here is, I believe, a type of Antichrist. Actually, it takes two persons to fulfill all that Scripture says about *the* Antichrist (and John says there are many). One will deny the Person of Christ—be His enemy; the other will imitate Him. There will be a religious ruler and a political ruler. Now here in Ezekiel we have, I believe, the combination set before us.

This is the vicegerent of Satan: "Because thine heart is lifted up, and thou hast said, I

am a God"—this is exactly what the Antichrist is going to say. The apostle Paul says this of him: "Who opposeth and exalteth himself above all that is called God, or that is worshipped; so that he as God sitteth in the temple of God, shewing himself that he is God" (2 Thess. 2:4). And this prince of Tyre says, "I sit in the seat of God, in the midst of the seas."

But God says, "Yet thou art a man, and not God, though thou set thine heart as the heart of God."

**Behold, thou art wiser than Daniel; there is no secret that they can hide from thee [Ezek. 28:3].**

Here is another reference to Daniel. Ezekiel and Daniel, you remember, were contemporaries. This young man Ezekiel had great respect for Daniel, who was prime minister in Babylon, and who really stood for the Lord. I personally think that Ezekiel had the hardest job. He lived with and preached to the captives. As I said earlier, I would have much preferred to live in the palace and spend one night in the lions' den than to work with the captives, but Ezekiel had no choice in the matter.

Ezekiel refers to Daniel's wisdom. Ezekiel says that this prince of Tyre was a smart boy. If you don't think there were wise men in that day, you are wrong. I think the wise men in that day would make the so-called intellectual crowd that centers in Harvard today look like beginners in kindergarten. These great men in Ezekiel's day were really *wise* men.

Now I believe that this prince of Tyre represents the religious ruler aspect of the Antichrist. And I think he comes out of Israel. You see, the Antichrist, the political ruler, comes out of the sea of the nations of the world. I think he will be a Gentile. His advisor, the religious ruler, will come out of the land. The religious ruler will be like a prime minister to the political ruler, like Daniel was in Babylon, or like Joseph in Egypt, or Disraeli in England. Perhaps I should not make that kind of comparison, but I think it serves to illustrate the two positions.

## JUDGMENT AGAINST THE KING

**Moreover the word of the LORD came unto me, saying [Ezek. 28:11].**

Ezekiel is not going to let anyone forget that he is not giving his own opinion, but he is telling forth God's message.

We have had a lamentation of the city of Tyre. We have talked about the prince of Tyre, and now we come to a lamentation of the king of Tyre. Immediately we pass beyond the local king of Tyre—there were many of them. It wasn't safe to be a king in those days. Uneasy lies the head that wears the crown. The glory did not last long. It was like the bromide *sic transit gloria mundi*, which is Latin for "thus passeth the glory of the world."

In back of the kingdom and the king is Satan. Ezekiel 28 is one of the few passages in the Word of God that gives us the origin of the Devil and of evil. I don't want to press this too much, but read carefully these words—

**Son of man, take up a lamentation upon the king of Tyrus, and say unto him, Thus saith the Lord GOD; Thou sealest up the sum, full of wisdom, and perfect in beauty [Ezek. 28:12].**

Satan was the wisest creature God ever created. Keep in mind that Satan is a created being. He was created perfect in beauty. If you think of Satan as a creature with horns, a forked tail, and cloven feet, you are wrong. You have been reading the literature of the Middle Ages which has its origin in Greek mythology that goes back into Asia Minor. There was a great temple of Apollo in Pergamum; also there was one in Corinth, and in Ephesus, just to name a few. This is a description of the god Pan, or Bacchus, the god of pleasure. He has horns, he runs through the grape vineyard, he is the god of the grape, the god of wine. From his waist down he is represented as a goat. The creature with horns, a forked tail, and cloven feet is right out of Greek mythology.

The Word of God does not present Satan in that manner. The Bible presents him as perfect in beauty. If you could see him, you would find that he is the most beautiful creature you have ever seen. I have heard many people say how good looking the men of certain cults are. When I was a boy, I heard such a man. He was in one of the cults. He had silver gray hair and was a fine looking man—in fact, he was very handsome. Some women would almost swoon at his presence. People treated him as if he were a god, a claim that he almost made. Do you know what he was? He was a minister of Satan; I don't mind saying it. When I was a boy, with no instruction in the things of God, he almost led me astray. Oh, how terrible the ministers of Satan are!

Paul has something to say about the ministers of Satan. "For such are false apostles, deceitful workers, transforming themselves

into the apostles of Christ. And no marvel; for Satan himself is transformed into an angel of light. Therefore it is no great thing if his ministers also be transformed as the ministers of righteousness . . ." (2 Cor. 11:13–15).

Ezekiel says of this one: "Thou sealest up the sum, full of wisdom, and perfect in beauty." What was it that brought him down? We will see that when we come to verse 15.

**Thou hast been in Eden the garden of God; every precious stone was thy covering, the sardius, topaz, and the diamond, the beryl, the onyx, and the jasper, the sapphire, the emerald, and the carbuncle, and gold: the workmanship of thy tabrets and of thy pipes was prepared in thee in the day that thou wast created [Ezek. 28:13].**

"Thou hast been in Eden the garden of God"— no king of Tyre has been in the Garden of Eden!

"Every precious stone was thy covering"— can you imagine what a beautiful creature he was!

"The workmanship of thy tabrets and of thy pipes was prepared in thee." Not only could he sing, he was a band; he was music itself. Do you know the origin of music on this earth? Go back to Genesis 4:21, and you will see that it originated with the progeny of Cain. And when I hear some of the music of my contemporaries, I am confident that it came out of the pit—it couldn't come from any place else! Satan was a musician.

**Thou art the anointed cherub that covereth; and I have set thee so: thou wast upon the holy mountain of God; thou hast walked up and down in the midst of the stones of fire [Ezek. 28:14].**

Satan was the "anointed cherub that covereth"—that is, he protected the throne of God. This is not the Eden which was on earth, but apparently is a picture of heaven itself. Satan had access to heaven, of course.

**Thou wast perfect in thy ways from the day that thou wast created, till iniquity was found in thee [Ezek. 28:15].**

Satan protected God's throne. He had the highest position a created being could have. What was it that brought him down? Ezekiel doesn't tell us, but Isaiah 14:12-15 has already told us: "How art thou fallen from heaven, O Lucifer, son of the morning! how art thou cut down to the ground, which didst weaken the nations! For thou hast said in thine heart, I will ascend into heaven, I will exalt my throne above the stars of God: I will sit also upon the mount of the congregation, in the sides of the north: I will ascend above the heights of the clouds; I will be like the most High. Yet thou shalt be brought down to hell, to the sides of the pit." The thing that brought him down was *pride!* Satan wanted to lift up his throne. He wanted to divorce himself from God and be God. He was in rebellion against God.

Now, let me say this: If you are one of the saints today who thinks you have arrived, that you are perfect, and you have set yourself up as a standard, remember that Satan was the angel of light; he was perfect—but he fell. Since *he* fell, what about you? What about me? We are only frail human beings.

God cannot tolerate rebellion, so what is He going to do?

**By the multitude of thy merchandise they have filled the midst of thee with violence, and thou hast sinned: therefore I will cast thee as profane out of the mountain of God: and I will destroy thee, O covering cherub, from the midst of the stones of fire [Ezek. 28:16].**

Satan will be judged for his sin. He is only a creature. I don't know about you, but this is comforting to me. I frankly would not be able to overcome him. I am no match for him. I am thankful, therefore, that God is going to deal with him.

**Thine heart was lifted up because of thy beauty, thou hast corrupted thy wisdom by reason of thy brightness: I will cast thee to the ground, I will lay thee before kings, that they may behold thee [Ezek. 28:17].**

"Thine heart was lifted up because of thy beauty"—pride.

"Thou hast corrupted thy wisdom by reason of thy brightness." You see, Solomon, the wisest man, played the fool. And here we see that the greatest creature whom God ever created, perfect (filled with all that could be learned), played the fool. Oh, my friend, God's children can do the same today!

"I will cast thee to the ground, I will lay thee before kings, that they may behold thee." God is going to make a spectacle of Satan someday.

**All they that know thee among the people shall be astonished at thee: thou shalt be a terror, and never shalt thou be any more [Ezek. 28:19].**

At some time in the future God is going to get rid of Satan in His universe, and we pray for that day to come.

In verses 20–24 judgment is pronounced on Sidon, but not complete destruction. He says that there will be blood in the streets, and that is exactly what happened. It is a matter of history. It is interesting to note that Tyre, the prominent city and capital city, was destroyed, scraped like a rock, never to be rebuilt; yet Sidon, about fifteen miles from Tyre, was also judged, but not destroyed. That city exists today; it is the place where oil is brought in from the Near East. It comes by pipeline and is loaded onto ships. Sidon is a thriving port, whereas down the coast is Tyre lying in ruins, with only a little fishing village there. God says that Tyre will never be rebuilt. God knew what He was talking about. In this chapter He has made the prophecies clear-cut: Tyre would be destroyed and never be rebuilt; Sidon would be judged but not destroyed. Today after approximately twenty-five hundred years, Tyre is gone and Sidon lives on.

**Thus saith the Lord GOD; When I shall have gathered the house of Israel from the people among whom they are scat-tered, and shall be sanctified in them in the sight of the heathen, then shall they dwell in their land that I have given to my servant Jacob.**

**And they shall dwell safely therein, and shall build houses, and plant vineyards; yea, they shall dwell with confidence, when I have executed judgments upon all those that despise them round about them; and they shall know that I am the LORD their God [Ezek. 28:25–26].**

God says, "I intend to regather Israel." Satan cannot disturb His plan and program with the children of Israel. Neither can any theologian today dismiss God's plan to restore Israel to the land in peace. One reason that so many theologians are believed when they say that God is through with the nation Israel is because God's people are not acquainted with Isaiah, Jeremiah, Ezekiel, Daniel, and the minor prophets. The theme song of these prophets is that God is *not* through with Israel as a nation. For this reason they should be studied. They throw new light on the Word of God so that it is no longer a jigsaw puzzle, but everything falls into place.

# CHAPTERS 29–30

**THEME:** *Prophecy against Egypt, lamentation for Egypt*

## PROPHECY AGAINST EGYPT

Many conservative commentators take the position that the prophecies concerning Egypt are of more interest than the one concerning Tyre. I must confess that I do not concur in that—the prophecies concerning Tyre are remarkable. Also the ones concerning Egypt are interesting, and we will find a remarkable prophecy in this chapter. Egypt was a great nation, and it had not been destroyed. It had maintained its integrity down through the centuries. It was one of the most ancient nations. It did not need to put up a wall of defense. After all, the desert was a pretty good defense. There was only one entrance, and that was through the Nile River valley. All Egypt had to do for protection was put up a good defense there. You will find that the cities of Egypt were not walled—walls were not necessary.

Now God says that the Egyptians will go into captivity for forty years.

**In the tenth year, in the tenth month, in the twelfth day of the month, the word of the LORD came unto me, saying,**

**Son of man, set thy face against Pharaoh king of Egypt, and prophesy against him, and against all Egypt [Ezek. 29:1–2].**

God takes a very definite position against the land of Egypt. It was this nation that had reduced His people to slavery in the brickyards and had introduced them to idolatry. Egypt had been a thorn in the flesh of Israel

for years; yet Israel was constantly running to Egypt for help. For some reason the children of Israel seemed to lean upon Egypt. Now God says He is against Egypt and it will be destroyed.

**Speak, and say, Thus saith the Lord GOD; Behold, I am against thee, Pharaoh king of Egypt, the great dragon that lieth in the midst of his rivers, which hath said, My river is mine own, and I have made it for myself [Ezek. 29:3].**

The crocodile, apparently, is the "great dragon" or sea monster here. Pharaoh is likened unto the crocodile that says, "This is my river." It is interesting to note that Egypt worshiped all manner of birds, beasts, and bugs. You will notice that the plagues against Egypt (Exod. 7–11) were leveled against the gods which Egypt worshiped. I think that in spite of how terrible the plagues were, they also reveal that God has a sense of humor. Imagine worshiping Heka, the frog-headed goddess, and then waking up one morning and finding frogs all over your bedroom. What are you going to do? Start killing off your goddess? I think the Lord must have smiled at that.

The Pharaoh mentioned here is Pharaoh Hophra, also called Apries in the Greek. He was the grandson of Pharaoh Nechoh, who defeated King Josiah of Judah at Megiddo; in fact, Josiah was slain in that battle. Kings Jehoiakim, Jehoiachin, and Zedekiah all turned to Pharaoh Hophra when Jerusalem was besieged. The Egyptian army came up, went through Phoenicia, and forced the Chaldeans to raise the siege of Jerusalem. The prophet Jeremiah announced the doom of Pharaoh Hophra: "The LORD of hosts, the God of Israel, saith; Behold, I will punish the multitude of No, and Pharaoh, and Egypt, with their gods, and their kings; even Pharaoh, and all them that trust in him: And I will deliver them into the hand of those that seek their lives, and into the hand of Nebuchadrezzar king of Babylon, and into the hand of his servants: and afterward it shall be inhabited, as in the days of old, saith the LORD" (Jer. 46:25–26).

You may find it interesting to note that the critic has made an issue of the fact that the prophecy of the destruction of Egypt was not fulfilled at this time. It was fulfilled seventeen years later. However, if you read the prophecy carefully, you will see that, although the prophecy was given through Ezekiel at this time, nothing is said about immediate fulfillment. Egypt was destroyed seventeen years later as God said it would be.

Now notice what God says will happen to Egypt:

**Yet thus saith the Lord GOD; At the end of forty years will I gather the Egyptians from the people whither they were scattered [Ezek. 29:13].**

Seventeen years later, to be exact, the king of Babylon, Nebuchadnezzar, came and took the Egyptians into captivity. They were in captivity for forty years, not seventy years like Israel.

**And I will bring again the captivity of Egypt, and will cause them to return into the land of Pathros, into the land of their habitation; and they shall be there a base kingdom [Ezek. 29:14].**

Now notice carefully this next verse—

**It shall be the basest of the kingdoms; neither shall it exalt itself any more above the nations: for I will diminish them, that they shall no more rule over the nations [Ezek. 29:15].**

Egypt had been the great power of the ancient world. They came out of the dawn of history as a great nation. Their monuments and tombs reveal the fact that they had a civilization that was second to none. It is believed today by many historians that the Greeks got a great deal of their information from the Egyptians. Egypt was a great nation, but God said, "I am going to let Nebuchadnezzar take you. Not only that, you are going to be in captivity for forty years, and at the end of that time you are going to return to your land, but you are going to be a base kingdom—in fact, the basest of the kingdoms." My friend, on our tours we visit many lands in the Near East, and we can see how accurate God's prediction was. No one can go to Cairo without his heart being sick when he sees the poverty and the low levels to which the people have sunk.

**Therefore thus saith the Lord GOD; Behold, I will give the land of Egypt unto Nebuchadrezzar king of Babylon; and he shall take her multitude, and take her spoil, and take her prey; and it shall be the wages for his army.**

**I have given him the land of Egypt for his labour wherewith he served against**

it, because they wrought for me, saith the Lord GOD [Ezek. 29:19–20].

Babylon, you see, was to conquer all these nations—including Tyre, Egypt, and, of course, Israel. Babylon was the first great empire.

## LAMENTATION FOR EGYPT

This brings us to chapter 30, which is considered a lamentation. Ezekiel speaks of the desolation of Egypt, and it is indeed a desolate nation.

**The word of the LORD came again unto me, saying [Ezek. 30:1].**

Here we go again. This phrase has been repeated I don't know how many times. Ezekiel doesn't want there to be a doubt in any mind whose word this is.

**Son of man, prophesy and say, Thus saith the Lord GOD; Howl ye, Woe worth the day! [Ezek. 30:2].**

This is a time of wailing and mourning, a lamentation.

**For the day is near, even the day of the LORD is near, a cloudy day; it shall be the time of the heathen [Ezek. 30:3].**

A cloudy day was unusual. They don't have many clouds in the land of Egypt because they have less than an inch of rain in that section. They depend upon the river Nile for the water they need. By the way, they worshiped the crocodile of the Nile, as well as everything else in the animal world.

"The time of the heathen" is better translated the time of the *nations*, and we are certainly living in that day when the nations are really stirring throughout the world.

**And the sword shall come upon Egypt, and great pain shall be in Ethiopia, when the slain shall fall in Egypt, and they shall take away her multitude, and her foundations shall be broken down [Ezek. 30:4].**

At times there was an alliance between Egypt and Ethiopia, although a great deal of the time there was enmity and warfare between the two nations. It is believed by many conservative scholars that Moses, when he was Pharaoh's daughter's son, would have been the next Pharaoh, and that he actually led an expedition against Ethiopia.

**Ethiopia, and Libya, and Lydia, and all the mingled people, and Chub, and the men of the land that is in league, shall fall with them by the sword [Ezek. 30:5].**

At this time there was an alliance among these nations, but they would all become subject to Nebuchadnezzar, who was actually a world ruler. In fact, he is the head of gold in Daniel's prophecy (ch. 2) of the four great world kingdoms.

**Thus saith the LORD; They also that uphold Egypt shall fall; and the pride of her power shall come down: from the tower of Syene shall they fall in it by the sword, saith the Lord GOD [Ezek. 30:6].**

Not only Israel, but all of these other nations had looked to Egypt for help, and they will all be judged together.

**And I will make the rivers dry, and sell the land into the hand of the wicked: and I will make the land waste, and all that is therein, by the hand of strangers: I the LORD have spoken it [Ezek. 30:12].**

These rivers, as we have seen before, are actually the different branches down in the delta of the Nile, and there were many of them. There were also canals in that very rich fertile area. Near there was the land of Goshen, where the Israelites settled when they first came to Egypt.

"I will make the rivers dry, and sell the land into the hand of the wicked." Egypt fell later on to Alexander the Great, and when he died his generals took over the nations he had conquered. Cleopatra, who was not an Egyptian but a Greek, ruled over Egypt.

"I will make the land waste, and all that is therein, by the hand of strangers." "Strangers" are foreigners. Egypt came under the control of foreign nations, and the canals were allowed to fill up. Although I have never gotten into that delta section, a friend of mine whom I met in Cairo had just come from there, and he told me that it is really a swamp in that section. God had said that He would make the land waste, and that is what it is today.

Now here is another remarkable prophecy—

**Thus saith the Lord GOD; I will also destroy the idols, and I will cause their images to cease out of Noph; and there shall be no more a prince of the land of Egypt: and I will put a fear in the land of Egypt [Ezek. 30:13].**

"I will cause their images to cease out of Noph." Noph is Memphis, and in Ezekiel's time it was the great city of Egypt. It was a very wealthy city, and it had idols in profusion—up and down both sides of the streets were idol after idol. They were the city's decoration! No other place has ever had idols like Memphis had them. Here God says that He would make the idols to cease out of Memphis.

I have walked over what is supposed to be the ruins of Memphis, and all that is left of the idols is one great big statue of Raamses. It lies on its back, and a building has been erected around it to house the statue. That is the only thing left in Memphis. God did exactly what He said He was going to do. He made the idols to cease.

"There shall be no more a prince of the land of Egypt." There is no royal line in Egypt any more. Neither can any of the rulers be called great men. They all have had to look to other nations for aid and support.

**And I will pour my fury upon Sin, the strength of Egypt; and I will cut off the multitude of No [Ezek. 30:15].**

"I will pour out my fury upon Sin"—which is Pelusium, now completely buried in the sand. "I will cut off the multitude of No"—this is Thebes, which was a great city in the upper Nile. The ruins are there, but its greatness is all gone.

In the next verses God continues to speak of these great cities of Egypt which have now disappeared altogether.

**Son of man, I have broken the arm of Pharaoh king of Egypt; and, lo, it shall not be bound up to be healed, to put a roller to bind it, to make it strong to hold the sword.**

**Therefore thus saith the Lord God; Behold, I am against Pharaoh king of Egypt, and will break his arms, the strong, and that which was broken; and I will cause the sword to fall out of his hand [Ezek. 30:21–22].**

God states once again that Egypt will fall. The pictures of Egyptian rulers always show them holding the scepter in their hands. The scepter was a token of their power. God says, "I have broken the arm of Pharaoh." It is hard to hold a scepter with a broken arm! And God goes on to say, "It shall not be bound up to be healed." Babylon was going to conquer Egypt, and Pharaoh would be powerless to stop it. All of this was literally fulfilled.

# CHAPTERS 31–32

**THEME:** *Judgment against Pharaoh; Pharaoh's greatness and glory; Pharaoh's fall; lamentation over the fall*

## JUDGMENT AGAINST PHARAOH

These two chapters conclude the section regarding the judgment of Egypt (chs. 29–32). It is interesting that Ezekiel devotes four chapters to Egypt and also Isaiah and Jeremiah and the minor prophets deal with Egypt. Egypt looms large in the history of the nation Israel. It is rather ironic that Egypt is such a thorn in the flesh to Israel at the present time. Egypt, in fact, is a dog in the manger. Israel didn't want the Baby in the manger; so it got the dog in the manger!

In chapter 31 we see the fall of Pharaoh. It is described in a parabolic form and represents both Pharaoh and his subjects. Verses 1–9 give the greatness and glory of Pharaoh in Egypt; verses 10–14 give the fall of Egypt in the parable of the tree; and verses 15–18 give the lamentation over the fall of the tree and the crisis which came to the nations of the world because of it. It had the same effect in that day as it would at the present time if the United States were destroyed overnight. That would certainly change the situation in the world, I am sure.

I trust you have seen how important the Book of Ezekiel is. It is a book that reveals the glory of the Lord and the fact that our God is a holy God who will judge sin. Now God is merciful, and He is kind. He loves mankind; He wants to save the human family, and He is not willing that any should perish, but He also judges sin. He intends to judge, and He will not spare you if you reject His gracious offer.

That is what happened to Israel, and that is what happened to Egypt. Egypt was judged on the basis of the light she had, and she had been given a great deal of light.

## THE GREATNESS AND GLORY OF PHARAOH

**Son of man, speak unto Pharaoh king of Egypt, and to his multitude; Whom art thou like in thy greatness? [Ezek. 31:2].**

God recognized the greatness of Egypt—probably over a couple of millenniums this vast kingdom had dominated the world. It was the breadbasket for the world because it did not have to depend on the rainfall. The Nile River overflowed each year to water their crops. It was a nation of tremendous power.

**Behold, the Assyrian was a cedar in Lebanon with fair branches, and with a shadowing shroud, and of an high stature; and his top was among the thick boughs [Ezek. 31:3].**

God says, "I liken Assyria, that great nation in the north, to a great cedar tree." Now there is more than one tree in a forest, because one tree won't make a forest. Assyria stood way above the other trees and dominated. But God brought Assyria down. This message should have gotten through to Pharaoh and his people. Pharaoh, too, is a great tree. He has dominated everything. The people of Egypt are great, but now they are going to be brought low. As we saw in chapter 29, Egypt is going to become a base kingdom. Well, for a period of over two thousand years now it has been a base kingdom. It will never be a world empire again.

## THE FALL OF PHARAOH

**Therefore thus saith the Lord GOD; Because thou hast lifted up thyself in height, and he hath shot up his top among the thick boughs, and his heart is lifted up in his height [Ezek. 31:10].**

The phrase, "Therefore thus saith the Lord GOD," indicates the divisions in this chapter. In this division we see that Pharaoh is lifted up in pride. Pride is in the human heart, and his greatness blinded him to the danger that he was in.

**I have therefore delivered him into the hand of the mighty one of the heathen; he shall surely deal with him: I have driven him out for his wickedness [Ezek. 31:11].**

At this point in history who is the mighty one of the nations? It is Nebuchadnezzar, king of Babylon. I don't think Ezekiel is speaking about Satan because Satan has had Egypt for years, so this wasn't something new. If you want to confirm the fact that this "mighty one" was Nebuchadnezzar, read the Book of Daniel. Daniel said to king Nebuchadnezzar, "You are the head of gold"—the greatness of this man has not been exceeded.

"I have therefore delivered him," he is talking about Pharaoh of Egypt. God is going to deal with him; He is going to drive him out because of his wickedness.

**And strangers, the terrible of the nations, have cut him off, and have left him: upon the mountains and in all the valleys his branches are fallen, and his boughs are broken by all the rivers of the land; and all the people of the earth are gone down from his shadow, and have left him [Ezek. 31:12].**

Egypt would be taken, and it would be a shock to the world.

## LAMENTATION OVER THE FALL OF PHARAOH

This is a very remarkable section of the Word of God. If you are a student of the Word, I recommend that you spend a great deal of time here.

**Thus saith the Lord GOD; In the day when he went down to the grave I caused a mourning: I covered the deep for him, and I restrained the floods thereof, and the great waters were stayed: and I caused Lebanon to mourn for him, and all the trees of the field fainted for him [Ezek. 31:15].**

The word "grave" in this verse is *sheol*. This verse speaks of Pharaoh who is going to go down in defeat and be killed. Sheol, although at times does mean the grave, means here the unseen world, the unknown region, or the abode of the dead—not just the grave where the physical body is placed after death. It is the place where the spirit goes. You remember that Solomon spoke about the fact that the body returns to the earth, and the spirit goes to God: "Then shall the dust return to the earth as it was: and the spirit shall return unto God who gave it" (Eccl. 12:7). The human

body is nothing in the world but dust. Speaking of man the psalmist says, "For he [God] knoweth our frame; he remembereth that we are dust" (Ps. 103:14). Sometimes we forget we are only dust, and when dust gets stuck on itself, it becomes mud! We need to remember that as far as our bodies are concerned, they are dust. When we put our bodies in the ground, they will go back to dust. The Lord Jesus spoke of the fact that when a believer dies his body sleeps. And Paul speaks of the physical body as sleeping in 1 Thessalonians 4:13.

Where do the spirits of the lost go? They, too, go to sheol, the unseen world. We know from a parable—which is also a true-life story which Jesus told (Luke 16:19–31) about two men who died—that sheol is divided into two compartments. One is called the place of torment, and that is where the rich man went. The other is called Abraham's Bosom, which is the place where the beggar went when he died. The place of torment is not to be confused with hell or the lake of fire of the New Testament. Apparently sheol was a temporary "abode of the dead," as the Lord Jesus emptied the section called paradise or Abraham's Bosom when he ascended (Eph. 4:8–10). The section called the place of torment will not be emptied until all who are there will stand before the great white throne for their final judgment (Rev. 20:11–15).

With this background in mind, notice that Ezekiel gives a picture of Pharaoh going down into sheol. Remember that God is not speaking of Pharaoh's body here. The grave receives the bodies, but the immaterial part of man, that which has endless being, goes to sheol.

"I covered the deep for him, and I restrained the floods thereof, and the great waters were stayed: and I caused Lebanon to mourn for him." When he died, the entire world mourned. Up there in Lebanon, which was in the great nation of Phoenicia, there was great mourning. The nations of the world mourned when Egypt went down. All were dependent upon it—their economy rested upon it, and its allies were protected by it. What a picture this is!

**I made the nations to shake at the sound of his fall, when I cast him down to hell with them that descend into the pit: and all the trees of Eden, the choice and best of Lebanon, all that drink water, shall be comforted in the nether parts of the earth [Ezek. 31:16].**

"When I cast him down to hell [sheol] with them that descend into the pit [the grave]." Now the tree, representing Pharaoh, is cut down. And where does Pharaoh go? To sheol. Now notice what he discovers:

**To whom art thou thus like in glory and in greatness among the trees of Eden? yet shalt thou be brought down with the trees of Eden unto the nether [lower] parts of the earth: thou shalt lie in the midst of the uncircumcised with them that be slain by the sword. This is Pharaoh and all his multitude, saith the Lord God [Ezek. 31:18].**

When Pharaoh got to sheol, he found other rulers that had been slain were there too.

He discovered something else: there is democracy in death. We talk a great deal today about integration. There is nothing that will integrate the rich and the poor, the black and the white, the male and the female, those at the top of the social ladder and those at the bottom of it, like *death!* Death will bring them all to the same level, not only the placing of their bodies in the grave, but also their spirits.

Probably one of the startling things to some people will be the realization that they haven't died as an animal dies. An atheist said to me, "When a man dies it is just like a dog that dies. He simply ceases to exist. There is no life after death." Well, he is going to be surprised when he moves into sheol and finds out who all is there. It will be quite a company of people who did not believe that there was an afterlife or a judgment to come. They will all be on the same par. This is total integration! The spirits of all those who have rejected the Lord Jesus will be there—not because they are sinners but because they have rejected Christ as their Savior. It is the sin of *rejecting Christ* that will take them to sheol and finally to the Great White Throne of judgment and the lake of fire. The Lord Jesus made this clear when He said, "Of sin, because they believe not on me" (John 16:9). How terrible it is not to trust Christ as your Savior.

This passage of Scripture opens up a new area altogether. Someone has called this the "Dante's Inferno of the Bible." And it is like that. The lost do go to a definite *place.* The Lord Jesus called it a place of torment and a place where the lost wait for judgment. Some people say, "Oh, I am going to appear before God all right, but I will get things straightened out there because I have been a pretty good fellow." But when they stand in the pres-

ence of the One who was crucified for them, they are going to find out that their puny works did not amount to much. They will discover that they have a fallen nature with no capacity for God, and no interest in Him at all. Where else could God put them? Do you think He could take anyone to heaven with Him who is in rebellion against Him? My friend, this is a very important passage of Scripture.

In chapter 32 the lamentation continues—

**Son of man, take up a lamentation for Pharaoh king of Egypt, and say unto him, Thou art like a young lion of the nations, and thou art as a whale in the seas: and thou camest forth with thy rivers, and troubledst the waters with thy feet, and fouledst their rivers [Ezek. 32:2].**

"Thou art as a whale in the seas" is better translated "thou art like a monster, the crocodile." The Egyptians worshiped both the lion and the crocodile.

"Thou camest forth with thy rivers, and troubledst the waters with thy feet, and fouledst their rivers." You see, back there they had an ecology problem. Old Pharaoh was muddying the water.

**Thus saith the Lord GOD; I will therefore spread out my net over thee with a company of many people; and they shall bring thee up in my net [Ezek. 32:3].**

"Thus saith the Lord GOD; I will therefore spread out my net over thee"—"just as you put nets in the Nile River to get fish, that's the way I am going to catch you, you monster of the Nile River, you crocodile!" It is as if God is saying, "I am going to pull you out and move you to a place where you won't live in a palace. You will find yourself on the same plane with your subjects." Death surely does level out humanity, does it not?

**For thus saith the Lord GOD; The sword of the king of Babylon shall come upon thee [Ezek. 32:11].**

The king of Babylon will take Egypt.

**Son of man, wail for the multitude of Egypt, and cast them down, even her, and the daughters of the famous nations, unto the nether parts of the earth, with them that go down into the pit.**

**Whom dost thou pass in beauty? go down, and be thou laid with the uncircumcised [Ezek. 32:18–19].**

Now Pharaoh will find that the other rulers are down there in sheol—

**Asshur is there and all her company: his graves are about him: all of them slain, fallen by the sword [Ezek. 32:22].**

"Asshur" is Assyria. And he finds somebody else is there—

**There is Elam and all her multitude round about her grave, all of them slain, fallen by the sword, which are gone down uncircumcised into the nether parts of the earth, which caused their terror in the land of the living; yet have they borne their shame with them that go down to the pit [Ezek. 32:24].**

"There is Elam and all her multitude round about her grave." You see, the body was put in the grave, but *they* have gone to another place, to sheol, the unseen world. Our Lord Jesus called it the place of torment for those who are lost. The saved are in the section which He called Abraham's Bosom; then later to the repentant thief on the cross He called it paradise: "Today thou shalt be with me in paradise."

Here are others Pharaoh finds in sheol—

**There is Meshech, Tubal, and all her multitude: her graves are round about him: all of them uncircumcised, slain by the sword, though they caused their terror in the land of the living [Ezek. 32:26].**

And Edom is there also—

**There is Edom, her kings, and all her princes, which with their might are laid by them that were slain by the sword: they shall lie with the uncircumcised, and with them that go down to the pit [Ezek. 32:29].**

Now listen to this—

**For I have caused my terror in the land of the living: and he shall be laid in the midst of the uncircumcised with them that are slain with the sword, even Pharaoh and all his multitude, saith the Lord GOD [Ezek. 32:32].**

Ezekiel only gives us a glimpse of that unseen world called sheol. Remember, we see only a fleeting view of this place. Don't try to build a skyscraper, or a merchandise center, or a mall, or a shopping area, on a place that only has a foundation big enough for a tool shed! In

other words, you can't build a theology on this, because all we have had is a little peek into the unseen world. And it is all God intended for us to see.

# CHAPTER 33

*THEME:* Recommission of Ezekiel

Chapter 33 brings us to the last major division of this book. From chapters 33–48 we will see the glory of the Lord and the coming millennial kingdom. Chapter 32 concluded the predictions concerning the nations that were round about Israel. Some of these nations were contiguous to the land of Israel. They were very closely related to them, of course—actually related by blood. These prophecies were given before the destruction of Jerusalem. Now we come to the second part of this prophetic book, which contains Ezekiel's prophecies *after* the fall of Jerusalem.

Ezekiel again is speaking of Jerusalem, and the land of Israel will be his subject, but his message is different. Up to chapter 25 everything pointed to the destruction of Jerusalem. Then Jerusalem was destroyed exactly as he had predicted. Now he will look forward to the future of the coming millennial kingdom when the glory of the Lord will be seen again on this earth. That makes this a very interesting section.

Not only is Ezekiel's commission renewed, he will also be commended for the fact that he has done a good job up to this point. From now on he is going to be speaking to those in captivity, telling them that they are to live in the expectancy of the future. Before, these captives had no hope because of their sins. But in the future, Ezekiel sees hope for the children of Israel.

Today believers also have a hope. It is not anchored in anything that men do here on earth, or in any of the gyrations of psychoanalysis. Our hope today is not a philosophy. It rests upon the Word of God and what He has said will take place in the future. This is the lodestar of the child of God in our day. It is not the same as Israel moving into the Millennium. We are moving actually into the New Jerusalem. This is what is immediately ahead of us as believers.

## RECOMMISSION OF THE PROPHET

**Again the word of the Lord came unto me, saying [Ezek. 33:1].**

This phrase is a stuck record as far as Ezekiel is concerned. He wants us to remember constantly that he is not giving us his theories or ideas, but he is giving out the Word of the Lord.

**Son of man, speak to the children of thy people, and say unto them, When I bring the sword upon a land, if the people of the land take a man of their coasts, and set him for their watchman:**

**If when he seeth the sword come upon the land, he blow the trumpet, and warn the people [Ezek. 33:2–3].**

God reverts to the commission that he gave to Ezekiel at the beginning of his ministry. He likens him to the watchman of a city. In that day most of the cities of importance were protected by walls. Those in authority appointed a watchman to watch for invaders from the top of the wall all during the hours of darkness. I imagine that during the night he would call off the watches with a shout of "All's well" when there was no moving of an approaching enemy out there in the darkness. The interesting thing is that the false prophets were saying "All's well" when the enemy was coming. They were too blind to see him. Ezekiel had been a faithful watchman and had given the people warning that the enemy, which was Babylon, was coming.

**But if the watchman see the sword come, and blow not the trumpet, and the people be not warned; if the sword come, and take any person from among them, he is taken away in his iniquity; but his blood will I require at the watchman's hand [Ezek. 33:6].**

Now the people are going to be judged for their sin, but the watchman will be held responsible if he doesn't warn them. Ezekiel had warned them; the false prophets had not. Ezekiel had done a good job.

**So thou, O son of man, I have set thee a watchman unto the house of Israel;**

therefore thou shalt hear the word at my mouth, and warn them from me [Ezek. 33:7].

Ezekiel has fulfilled that commission.

When I say unto the wicked, O wicked man, thou shalt surely die; if thou dost not speak to warn the wicked from his way, that wicked man shall die in his iniquity; but his blood will I require at thine hand [Ezek. 33:8].

The responsibility of the watchman is to warn the wicked that they are going to be judged. Ezekiel was faithful in giving the warning, although the people would not listen to him. To sound the warning was the only way the watchman could clear himself.

Today the man who is teaching the Word of God is not required to get results. Many people say, "Let's get an evangelist who can get *results*." To get people to come forward in a meeting is not of primary importance. The preacher giving the people the Word of God is the important thing. I don't look at the folks who have come forward; I look at the people who walk out after the benediction. Have they been warned? That should be our concern. We have been looking at the wrong crowd. We say, "Oh, So-and-so gave such a sweet gospel invitation, and a lot of sweet people came forward. No decisions were actually made, but we had a movement going on." Oh, my friend, let's make sure that the fellow who hears has been properly warned. If he is not warned, the speaker is held responsible. He will have to answer to God for neglecting his duty.

Say unto them, As I live, saith the Lord GOD, I have no pleasure in the death of the wicked; but that the wicked turn from his way and live: turn ye, turn ye from your evil ways; for why will ye die, O house of Israel? [Ezek. 33:11].

It is quite obvious from this verse that God does not want to judge. Isaiah said that judgment was His *strange* work. God wants to save them, and He is urging them to turn to Him and accept life.

Yet the children of thy people say, The way of the Lord is not equal: but as for them, their way is not equal [Ezek. 33:17].

The children of Israel had another complaint. They said that God was not fair in His judgment. He judged everybody alike; yet there were some "good people" among the captives.

When the righteous turneth from his righteousness, and committeth iniquity, he shall even die thereby [Ezek. 33:18].

This verse is not speaking about somebody losing salvation. God is saying that when one of His children gets into sin, He will judge him. That is exactly what Paul said in 1 Corinthians 11:31: "For if we would judge ourselves, we should not be judged." And God says through John that there is a sin unto death (1 John 5:16). He is speaking about a child of God. What kind of death is he talking about? He is talking about physical death. Some Christians are judged for their sins by physical death. I am amazed that more folks don't catch on to God's discipline after a time. There are others who are in the Lord's work, but what they are doing is not prospering, and they are getting deeper and deeper into debt. You would think that the message would come through loud and clear that perhaps God is moving in judgment, that what they are doing is not pleasing to Him.

But if the wicked turn from his wickedness, and do that which is lawful and right, he shall live thereby [Ezek. 33:19].

God is righteous in what He does. If a wicked man will turn to God, God will save him.

Yet ye say, The way of the Lord is not equal. O ye house of Israel, I will judge you every one after his ways [Ezek. 33:20].

Godly men, too, were carried away into captivity. Those who had trusted God were carried off just like the most wicked people, and these godly people are complaining. It looks like God is being unfair.

You and I experience this same principle in many ways. For example, we have to pay excessive insurance premiums today because there are a lot of alcoholics. I don't drink, but I have to pay for the ones who do. I have to pay high taxes because we have a lot of folks in Washington today who spend money foolishly. We are identified with our nation.

And the good people in Israel were suffering because they were identified with the nation. But there is more to it than that. Notice what God says—

"O ye house of Israel, I will judge you every one after his ways." In other words, I am going to judge every one of you. And, my friend, whoever you are, you will have to stand before God for judgment some day. If

you are a child of God, He will judge you for the sins you have committed, but you will not lose your salvation. However, if you are a lost person, you have no claim on God whatsoever. He has made that clear in the New Testament. In 1 Peter 3:12 we read, "For the eyes of the Lord are over the righteous, and his ears are open unto their prayers: but the face of the Lord is against them that do evil." God doesn't say that He won't hear the prayer of the wicked; He just says that He hears the prayers of the righteous, which implies that He feels no obligation to hear the prayer of the unsaved person. Of course, if he would cry out for salvation, God would hear and answer, but the point is that the unsaved person has no claim on God whatsoever. When you hear an unsaved person ask, "Why does God let this happen to me?" you know that he has no claim whatever on God's mercy. God is *righteous* when He is judging a lost world, and sometimes we forget that this happens to be *His* world.

## THE CITY IS SMITTEN!

**And it came to pass in the twelfth year of our captivity, in the tenth month, in the fifth day of the month, that one that had escaped out of Jerusalem came unto me, saying, The city is smitten [Ezek. 33:21].**

Ezekiel had already said that Jerusalem was destroyed because God had told him, but as yet he had been given no information about it. When the news of the destruction of the city was brought to these people, it absolutely dumbfounded them. They were overwhelmed by the news. They never believed that anything like this could possibly take place. On the very day that this news was brought, Ezekiel's wife died, and God said to him in effect, "Don't grieve for your wife. I want these people to know that I have repudiated their city. They think that I have to have Jerusalem. They think that I won't destroy it. They don't believe I will judge sin, but I will. Therefore, don't weep for your wife. Let the people know that at this time the city is being destroyed because of its sin. The city is smitten."

**Now the hand of the LORD was upon me in the evening, afore he that was escaped came; and had opened my mouth, until he came to me in the morning; and my mouth was opened, and I was no more dumb [Ezek. 33:22].**

You see, at the end of chapter 24 God announced to Ezekiel the destruction of Jerusalem, the bloody city. From that point on (chs. 25–33) He had given him no prophecy for Jerusalem; instead He had given him messages for the surrounding nations. Now when we come here to chapter 33, we find that God no longer makes Ezekiel dumb about Jerusalem. He says to him, "I have some messages for you about Jerusalem now."

**Then the word of the LORD came unto me, saying,**

**Son of man, they that inhabit those wastes of the land of Israel speak, saying, Abraham was one, and he inherited the land: but we are many; the land is given us for inheritance [Ezek. 33:23–24].**

The people of Israel are remembering how God took care of Abraham; yet there was only one of him, and there are a whole lot of them. They expect Him to take care of them in the same way. They are ignoring the fact that there was a great deal of difference between Abraham and themselves. Abraham believed God, and it was counted to him for righteousness. These people do not believe God.

**Wherefore say unto them, Thus saith the Lord GOD; Ye eat with the blood, and lift up your eyes toward your idols, and shed blood: and shall ye possess the land? [Ezek. 33:25].**

God says to them, "I won't let you have the land. I put the heathen and the pagan out of this land because of their sin, and you are doing the same things they did."

**For I will lay the land most desolate, and the pomp of her strength shall cease; and the mountains of Israel shall be desolate, that none shall pass through [Ezek. 33:28].**

I cannot get as elated about the land of Israel as some of my very good minister friends do. When they get into that land, they go into ecstasy. The way some of them act you would think they were on drugs! They exclaim, "Isn't it wonderful to see this land!" I want to tell you that the land is just about as desolate as any place you could possibly find today. That land is desolate because the judgment of God is upon it. There is a water shortage—put a little water on that land and it blossoms like a rose—but they can't get enough water. That is the great problem. God's judgment is not only upon a people; it is also upon a land.

Also, thou son of man, the children of thy people still are talking against thee by the walls and in the doors of the houses, and speak one to another, every one to his brother, saying, Come, I pray you, and hear what is the word that cometh forth from the LORD [Ezek. 33:30].

The people are shaken, and they want to listen to Ezekiel now, but they won't follow through.

And they come unto thee as the people cometh, and they sit before thee as my people, and they hear thy words, but they will not do them: for with their mouth they shew much love, but their heart goeth after their covetousness [Ezek. 33:31].

On the surface they appeared to be turning to the Lord. They wanted to hear what the Lord had to say but had no intention of obeying Him. They were like folk who go to church in our day to hear an interesting and well-delivered sermon, but what they hear does not change their lives. The epistle of James gets down where the rubber meets the road when he says, "But be ye doers of the word, and not hearers only, deceiving your own selves" (James 1:22). This is what God says to Ezekiel about these folk in captivity, "They hear thy words, but they do them not."

And, lo, thou art unto them as a very lovely song of one that hath a pleasant voice, and can play well on an instrument: for they hear thy words, but they do them not.

And when this cometh to pass, (lo, it will come,) then shall they know that a prophet hath been among them [Ezek. 33:32–33].

Now that Jerusalem has fallen, as Ezekiel had prophesied, the people know he is a true prophet of God. Although they know he is giving them God's Word, they still will not obey it. My friend, unbelief is *willful;* it is not because mankind has a great mentality that cannot accept what God says. The real problem is that people do not want to give up their sin. That was the problem with the people to whom Ezekiel ministered. They were willing to come and listen to what Ezekiel had to say, but it had no effect upon them whatsoever. You would think that the people would now turn to God, but that was not the case. God said to Ezekiel, "Don't let the crowds deceive you. It is true that they are coming and listening, but they are not heeding what you say. They are not doers of the Word at all. They like it when they hear you talk about love, and the future, and prophecy, but it has not affected their lives one whit. They are still living the same way—far from Me."

Ezekiel was the *only* man who said that Jerusalem would be destroyed. All of the false prophets said that it would not be destroyed. The word of confirmation has come. Jerusalem is destroyed. Ezekiel is declared a true prophet.

# CHAPTER 34

*THEME: Israel's false shepherds; God's true shepherd*

### ISRAEL'S FALSE SHEPHERDS

The false prophets of Israel have now been shown to be liars because the destruction of Jerusalem as prophesied by Ezekiel has become a reality. God has a word to say about these false prophets:

And the word of the LORD came unto me, saying,

Son of man, prophesy against the shepherds of Israel, prophesy, and say unto them, Thus saith the Lord GOD unto the shepherds; Woe be to the shepherds of Israel that do feed themselves! should not the shepherds feed the flocks? [Ezek. 34:1–2].

Ezekiel did not say these things about the false prophets—God said them.

Very candidly, I have always been opposed to promotion—that is, furthering the growth or development of a Christian work. This does not mean that there aren't many very wonder-

ful and fine works which deserve our financial support. My point is that they should not be just a promotion agency; they should be feeding the people—they should be giving out the Word of God. I feel that an organization has no right to fleece people for an offering when it has not given the people something first. We should be able to support ministries where we ourselves have received a blessing. The business of the ministry is not to beg for money all the time, but to give out the Word of God and to be feeding the sheep.

This was God's criticism of the false prophets—they had not given the people the Word of God. I feel this should still be the standard by which we judge a ministry today.

**The diseased have ye not strengthened, neither have ye healed that which was sick, neither have ye bound up that which was broken, neither have ye brought again that which was driven away, neither have ye sought that which was lost; but with force and with cruelty have ye ruled them [Ezek. 34:4].**

All of us are needy people, and the only thing which can minister to our deep needs is the Word of God. If a minister is not giving the Word of God, he is not ministering to the people. The Word *must* be given out. These little sermonettes delivered to Christianettes by preacherettes are not quite doing the job today.

**And they were scattered, because there is no shepherd: and they became meat to all the beasts of the field, when they were scattered [Ezek. 34:5].**

"Meat" could also be translated "food." In other words, when people are not being fed in a church, they will scatter. They'll go find some place where they can be fed. There is no point in criticizing them, because sheep want to be fed. That is also the nature of the child of God: he wants to hear the Word of God.

**Therefore, ye shepherds, hear the word of the LORD;**

**As I live, saith the Lord GOD, surely because my flock became a prey, and my flock became meat to every beast of the field, because there was no shepherd, neither did my shepherds search for my flock, but the shepherds fed themselves, and fed not my flock;**

**Therefore, O ye shepherds, hear the word of the LORD;**

**Thus saith the Lord GOD; Behold, I am against the shepherds; and I will require my flock at their hand, and cause them to cease from feeding the flock; neither shall the shepherds feed themselves any more; for I will deliver my flock from their mouth, that they may not be meat for them [Ezek. 34:7–10].**

God holds these false shepherds responsible. He says, "I am against them, and I am as much opposed to them as I am to any sinner or any sin. I'm going to hold them responsible."

## GOD'S TRUE SHEPHERD

**For thus saith the Lord GOD; Behold, I, even I, will both search my sheep, and seek them out [Ezek. 34:11].**

Here you have God's Shepherd—Jesus, who said "I am the Good Shepherd." Ezekiel said that Christ would come, and, my friend, He is coming again because He has not yet fulfilled all the prophecies concerning His shepherding of this earth.

Now we begin to look into the future. These are God's words of comfort to the children of Israel in their captivity—they should listen to Him. He's the Shepherd, the Good Shepherd, the Great Shepherd, and the Chief Shepherd of the sheep. He says, "I will search out my sheep." David said, "The LORD is my shepherd; I shall not want" (Ps. 23:1).

The thing that impresses us in the rest of this chapter is the repetition of a wonderful statement by God, "I will," which occurs eighteen times in verses 11 through 29. I get a little weary listening to men speak of what they have done. This is a new note here—God says, "I will." This is grace when God says this. The Good Shepherd one day said, "Come unto me, all ye that labour and are heavy laden, and *I will* give you rest [rest you]" (Matt. 11:28, italics mine). The Shepherd also said, "*I [will]* give unto them eternal life; and they shall never perish . . ." (John 10:28). That is what my wonderful Shepherd said.

**As a shepherd seeketh out his flock in the day that he is among his sheep that are scattered; so will I seek out my sheep, and will deliver them out of all places where they have been scattered in the cloudy and dark day [Ezek. 34:12].**

The Good Shepherd came more than nineteen hundred years ago, and He still says, "My sheep hear my voice . . ." (John 10:27). Do you know why they hear His voice? There are

two reasons: He is *calling* them, and His sheep *know* Him. They hear His voice, and they know Him. What a wonderful Shepherd we have!

**And I will bring them out from the people, and gather them from the countries, and will bring them to their own land, and feed them upon the mountains of Israel by the rivers, and in all the inhabited places of the country [Ezek. 34:13].**

The Shepherd is talking about the nation of Israel, what He is going to do for them in the future. They are in captivity now because of their sin and because they listened to the false prophets. But He says, "I am not through with them. I have not thrown them overboard. You amillennialists ought to read the Book of Ezekiel; then you would find out that I am not through with My sheep—I intend to bring them back to their land."

**I will feed them in a good pasture, and upon the high mountains of Israel shall their fold be: there shall they lie in a good fold, and in a fat pasture shall they feed upon the mountains of Israel.**

**I will feed my flock, and I will cause them to lie down, saith the Lord GOD [Ezek. 34:14–15].**

He will feed them in a good pasture, and when they lie down they will be safe. Obviously this is for a future time. The land of Israel does not lie in safety at all today.

**I will seek that which was lost, and bring again that which was driven away, and will bind up that which was broken, and will strengthen that which was sick: but I will destroy the fat and the strong; I will feed them with judgment [Ezek. 34:16].**

When He has one lost sheep, this Shepherd goes out to find it. He will do that for the nation Israel, and He will do that for the church today. When our Lord told the parable of the lost sheep, that shepherd had one hundred sheep, and one sheep got lost. What did the shepherd do? Did he just forget about that sheep? Did he say, "Well, if one little one wants to run off, that's all right; after all, ninety-nine sheep is a pretty good number to come through with"? No, this shepherd said, "I started out with one hundred and I am going to come through with one hundred." My friend, Vernon McGee is going to be in

heaven—not because he's a smart sheep; all sheep are stupid—I am going to be there because I've got a wonderful Shepherd, and He says, "I will, I will," again and again.

**Therefore thus saith the Lord GOD unto them; Behold, I, even I, will judge between the fat cattle and between the lean cattle [Ezek. 34:20].**

God is going to do the separating. In Matthew 13, the Lord Jesus gave the parable of the tares among the wheat. He told of a man who sowed good seed in his field, but an enemy came in and sowed tares among the good seed. The man's servant said, "Let's go pull up the tares," but the man said, "You let them alone; let the wheat and the tares grow together. I'll do the separating." I am glad that the separating is the Lord's job. That is His business. When someone comes to me and says, "Do you think So-and-so is a believer?" I have to say that I don't know. That's not my business; that's the Lord's business. He knows the ones who are His.

**Because ye have thrust with side and with shoulder, and pushed all the diseased with your horns, till ye have scattered them abroad;**

**Therefore will I save my flock, and they shall no more be a prey; and I will judge between cattle and cattle.**

**And I will set up one shepherd over them, and he shall feed them, even my servant David; he shall feed them, and he shall be their shepherd.**

**And I the LORD will be their God, and my servant David a prince among them; I the LORD have spoken it [Ezek. 34:21–24].**

It is my firm conviction that the earth will be the eternal home of Israel and that David will rule here on this earth throughout eternity. He will be vice-regent of the Lord Jesus. I believe the church will be in the New Jerusalem with the Lord—the Lord Jesus said that He was coming again to take the church, ". . . that where I am, there ye may be also" (John 14:3). And throughout eternity when He comes to earth, we will come also, but just for a visit. Therefore, don't buy too much real estate down here—you won't be needing it—but be sure you are sending up plenty of material to build a good home in heaven!

"I the LORD have spoken it." My friend, He says He is *not* through with the nation Israel.

And I will make with them a covenant of peace, and will cause the evil beasts to cease out of the land: and they shall dwell safely in the wilderness, and sleep in the woods [Ezek. 34:25].

It is quite interesting that the land and the people of Israel go together in Scripture. When they are in the land and being blessed, that means that the people are in a right relationship to God.

And they shall no more be a prey to the heathen, neither shall the beast of the land devour them; but they shall dwell safely, and none shall make them afraid [Ezek. 34:28].

The day will come when Israel will "no more be a prey to the heathen [the nations]." They are still that today, but God says, "I will," and when He says that, He *is* going to do it, my friend.

# CHAPTERS 35–36

*THEME: Edom judged; prediction of Israel's sins judged and forgiven*

Chapters 35 and 36 deal with the future restoration of Israel. There are two things which must happen before the people can be restored to the land in peace: Edom must be judged, and Israel's past sins must be judged and forgiven. The judgment predicted here was fulfilled upon Edom, but it also is prophetic of the judgment which is in store for the enemies of Israel which is still future in our day.

## EDOM JUDGED

Chapter 35 deals with the judgment and removal of Mount Seir (or Edom) which must take place before Israel can be restored to the land.

Moreover the word of the LORD came unto me, saying,

Son of man, set thy face against mount Seir, and prophesy against it,

And say unto it, Thus saith the Lord GOD; Behold, O mount Seir, I am against thee, and I will stretch out mine hand against thee, and I will make thee most desolate.

I will lay thy cities waste, and thou shalt be desolate, and thou shalt know that I am the LORD [Ezek. 35:1–4].

These verses refer to Edom, and in Edom there was the rock-hewn city known as Petra. The city is still there, but there is no more desolate area anywhere than that place.

Because thou hast had a perpetual hatred, and hast shed the blood of the children of Israel by the force of the sword in the time of their calamity, in the time that their iniquity had an end [Ezek. 35:5].

God gives the reason for the judgment of Edom. Edom is the people descended from Esau, Jacob's brother. Esau was Jacob's bitterest enemy, and the people of Edom probably hurt the people of Israel more than any other enemy they had. Edom represents the enemy of God in this world today, that enemy who is going to rise against God in the last days under the Antichrist.

I will make thee perpetual desolations, and thy cities shall not return: and ye shall know that I am the LORD [Ezek. 35:9].

Ezekiel has previously mentioned Edom's judgment in Ezekiel 25:12–14. Why does he mention it here again? I believe that it is to show that God has a program for the nation Israel. They are to be restored to the land, a place of blessing. They will be put back in the land in peace. However, the enemy is still about, and so God will judge the enemy. The people will be back in the land worshiping God, and living in peace and blessing. What a glorious future is ahead for them!

## ISRAEL'S PAST SINS JUDGED AND FORGIVEN

In chapter 36 we find that Israel's past sins must be judged and forgiven before she can be restored to the land.

**Therefore thus saith the Lord GOD; Surely in the fire of my jealousy have I spoken against the residue of the heathen, and against all Idumea, which have appointed my land into their possession with the joy of all their heart, with despiteful minds, to cast it out for a prey [Ezek. 36:5].**

God is determined that the wicked will not inherit the earth. He has made it clear: ". . . the meek . . . shall inherit the earth" (Matt. 5:5). The meek are not inheriting it today. The wicked are the ones who have it, and they are the ones who are prospering.

This chapter contains the prophecy concerning the fact that the land of Israel is to be restored. All you have to do is drive through that land, and you will know this prophecy is not yet fulfilled. A great many people like to think they see prophecy being fulfilled on every hand, but when *God* brings them back to the land, the land is to be *blessed.* It is not blessed today, my friend.

**Prophesy therefore concerning the land of Israel, and say unto the mountains, and to the hills, to the rivers, and to the valleys, Thus saith the Lord GOD; Behold, I have spoken in my jealousy and in my fury, because ye have borne the shame of the heathen:**

**Therefore thus saith the Lord GOD; I have lifted up mine hand, Surely the heathen that are about you, they shall bear their shame.**

**But ye, O mountains of Israel, ye shall shoot forth your branches, and yield your fruit to my people of Israel; for they are at hand to come [Ezek. 36:6–8].**

"For they are at hand to come" could be translated "For they are *soon* to come." "Soon" to God is different from what it is to us; after all, a day is as a thousand years with Him.

**Moreover the word of the LORD came unto me, saying,**

**Son of man, when the house of Israel dwelt in their own land, they defiled it by their own way and by their doings: their way was before me as the uncleanness of a removed woman.**

**Wherefore I poured my fury upon them for the blood that they had shed upon the land, and for their idols wherewith they had polluted it [Ezek. 36:16–18].**

Again may I emphasize that the land and the people belong together. The Mosaic Law was not only given to a people, it was given for a land.

**And I scattered them among the heathen, and they were dispersed through the countries: according to their way and according to their doings I judged them [Ezek. 36:19].**

God says, "I scattered them among the heathen [the nations]," but listen to Him:

**But I had pity for mine holy name, which the house of Israel had profaned among the heathen, whither they went.**

**Therefore say unto the house of Israel, Thus saith the Lord GOD; I do not this for your sakes, O house of Israel, but for mine holy name's sake, which ye have profaned among the heathen, whither ye went.**

**And I will sanctify my great name, which was profaned among the heathen, which ye have profaned in the midst of them; and the heathen shall know that I am the LORD, saith the Lord GOD, when I shall be sanctified in you before their eyes [Ezek. 36:21–23].**

You see, God has yet to defend His name in this earth. There are a great many people who ridicule the church today and the people who are in it. They blaspheme God because of it. God is going to justify Himself in this earth, and he is going to sanctify His name down here. Many take His name in vain today, but God says, "That's going to stop, and you are going to honor Me." This is *His* world, you see.

**A new heart also will I give you, and a new spirit will I put within you: and I will take away the stony heart out of your flesh, and I will give you an heart of flesh [Ezek. 36:26].**

God says what He is going to do. A change is going to take place. "A new heart also will I give you"—they are going to be born again.

**And I will put my spirit within you, and cause you to walk in my statutes, and ye shall keep my judgments, and do them [Ezek. 36:27].**

This is what Joel meant in his prophecy—there is a day coming when God will pour out His Spirit on all flesh, not just *some.* The Spirit was poured out upon very few on the

Day of Pentecost. All Peter said on that day was, "Don't ridicule us and say we are drunk. This is *like* what Joel said is going to happen in the last days." The Spirit has come upon a few, and today God is calling out a people for His name. The minute you turn to Christ, you are regenerated by the Holy Spirit; you are indwelt and baptized by the Holy Spirit; you are put in the body of believers. "In that day," God says, "I'll put My Spirit within you."

**And ye shall dwell in the land that I gave to your fathers; and ye shall be my people, and I will be your God.**

**I will also save you from all your un-cleannesses: and I will call for the corn, and will increase it, and lay no famine upon you [Ezek. 36:28–29].**

They will dwell in the land, and there will be prosperity in the land. God has promised to them *physical* blessings, just as He has promised to us *spiritual* blessings.

This chapter concludes with a great prophecy:

**And they shall say, This land that was desolate is become like the garden of Eden; and the waste and desolate and ruined cities are become fenced, and are inhabited.**

**Then the heathen that are left round about you shall know that I the Lord build the ruined places, and plant that that was desolate: I the Lord have spoken it, and I will do it.**

**Thus saith the Lord God; I will yet for this be inquired of by the house of Israel, to do it for them; I will increase them with men like a flock.**

**As the holy flock, as the flock of Jerusalem in her solemn feasts; so shall the waste cities be filled with flocks of men: and they shall know that I am the Lord [Ezek. 36:35–38].**

"And they shall say, This land that was desolate is become like the garden of Eden." You can say that if you want to, but it wouldn't be true today.

"And they shall know that I am the Lord." They don't know that in Israel, they don't know it in the United States, and they don't know it in the world today. But the day is coming, my friend, when Israel will know that He is the Lord.

# CHAPTER 37

**THEME:** *Vision of the valley of dead bones, picturing the Resurrection of Israel*

## THE VISION OF THE VALLEY OF DEAD BONES

In this chapter we have the vision of the valley of dead bones which served as the basis for a Negro spiritual written some years ago, entitled, "Dem Bones." The interpretation of this chapter concerns the future restoration of Israel. That restoration has to do both with the *national* entity of Israel as well as the *spiritual* revival or restoration which the Lord announced in the preceding chapter.

We have here a remarkable vision, and I would like to make it very clear that this vision does *not* have to do with the resurrection of the dead saints of the church. That is the giant leap in interpretation made by the many who spiritualize the prophetic section of the Old Testament. My friend, when we take prophecy *literally*, it will make sense. We are talking here about the nation Israel, and we are not talking about a spiritual or physical resurrection of individuals. In my notes I have labeled this chapter, "The Resurrection of Israel," and I think that is a good title, but it is sometimes misunderstood. Some think that I am referring to the raising of the dead from Abraham on. It has no reference to that, but it definitely refers to the *nation* of Israel.

God gives to Ezekiel a real living parable and to do so He takes him to the valley of dead bones:

**The hand of the Lord was upon me, and carried me out in the spirit of the Lord, and set me down in the midst of the**

**valley which was full of bones [Ezek. 37:1].**

Before Jerusalem was destroyed by Nebuchadnezzar, Ezekiel was transported to Jerusalem (see ch. 8), and I do not believe God had any difficulty doing that. If man today can make a jet plane which can carry him halfway around the world in half a day, I see no reason why God cannot do something which is commensurate with who He is. So I don't think that God had any difficulty getting Ezekiel up and taking him to Jerusalem.

Here again, I believe God literally moves Ezekiel. When Ezekiel says that He "carried me out in the spirit of the LORD," he is saying that the Spirit of the Lord carried him out to the valley which was full of bones.

**And caused me to pass by them round about: and, behold, there were very many in the open valley; and, lo, they were very dry [Ezek. 37:2].**

Back in 1849, Lewis Manly and his partner by the name of John Rogers crossed Death Valley in California to bring back supplies to the stranded Bennett-Arcane party. The Bennett-Arcane group had mistakenly wandered into Death Valley and would have perished if these two men had not crossed the valley to rescue them. They were actually the first white men to cross this valley and gaze upon its grand scene of death and desolation. Few men have seen such sights, but what Ezekiel saw some twenty-five hundred years earlier must have been even more bleak. He saw a vision of another "death valley," more desolate, more fearsome, and more awesome than Death Valley, California.

The valley which Ezekiel saw was filled with dead bones, and the thing which characterized them is that they were very dry and they were scattered.

**And he said unto me, Son of man, can these bones live? And I answered, O Lord GOD, thou knowest [Ezek. 37:3].**

These bones scattered all over the place are human bones, and the question that is put to Ezekiel is, "Can these bones live?" Ezekiel answers, "O Lord GOD, thou knowest." In other words, he said, "I don't see how they could. It's beyond me—You alone know whether these dead bones can live or not!"

**Again he said unto me, Prophesy upon these bones, and say unto them, O ye dry bones, hear the word of the LORD [Ezek. 37:4].**

This is something rather ironical and even humorous. I have always insisted that God has a sense of humor, and here is an illustration of that. If you can't see where it's funny, that's all right—just pass it by. But imagine Ezekiel now as God says to him, "Prophesy on these bones. Start out by saying, 'O ye dry bones, hear the word of the LORD.'" I have a notion Ezekiel said, "Now, Lord, you really don't mean for me to start *talking* to these dry bones here! The man with the white coat and the net will be out looking for me if I do that!" Really, that isn't a very good sermon introduction is it? No preacher would begin by saying to his Sunday morning congregation, "Oh, you dry bones!" A friend of mine (who also has a good sense of humor) said to me, "You know, I have a congregation with which I'd like to begin as Ezekiel did—the bones I speak to are as dry as Ezekiel's—but I don't dare do that."

Ezekiel is looking out on this valley filled with dry bones, and he's to speak to them. Every congregation that a preacher speaks to includes those who are saved and those who are unsaved. Those who are saved may have ears to hear, but not hear. And the ones who are not saved are dead in trespasses and sins—they haven't been redeemed yet. The preacher is just as helpless as Ezekiel, for any preacher who understands the real state and condition of those who are lost recognizes his own helplessness in speaking to them. Ezekiel is to say to these bones, "I want you to hear what God has to say."

**Thus saith the Lord GOD unto these bones, Behold I will cause breath to enter into you, and ye shall live.**

**And I will lay sinews upon you, and will bring up flesh upon you, and cover you with skin, and put breath in you, and ye shall live; and ye shall know that I am the LORD [Ezek. 37:5–6].**

God says, "I want you to speak to them and tell them I'll be the One who will give them life." That is our condition today—if God doesn't move, no one has spiritual life. I receive letters from people who say, "You saved me." My friend, I save no one. I just speak to dry bones, giving them the Word of God—that's all I do. The Spirit of God is the One who has to bring life. That is the only way life can come. This is the *application* of these verses; we are going to see that they also have a tremendous *interpretation*.

**So I prophesied as I was commanded: and as I prophesied, there was a noise, and behold a shaking, and the bones came together, bone to his bone [Ezek. 37:7].**

"So I prophesied as I was commanded"—this man Ezekiel obeys God.

"There was a noise, and behold a shaking, and the bones came together, bone to his bone." This is the point where that Negro spiritual, "Dem Bones," is really accurate—when the bones start coming together. I'm of the opinion Ezekiel had a rather funny feeling when in his vision he saw all these bones come together!

**And when I beheld, lo, the sinews and the flesh came up upon them, and the skin covered them above: but there was no breath in them [Ezek. 37:8].**

We have here a method which I want you to notice. The first state of the bones is that they are scattered, dry, and dead. Then gradually they come together, and the sinews and flesh come upon them. This is a process—it is not instantaneous at all. At this point in the vision all you have is a bunch of bodies, actually corpses; it is just an undertaking establishment down in that valley. They are no longer bones, but bodies with flesh upon them. They are human beings even, but they do not have any life in them.

**Then said he unto me, Prophesy unto the wind, prophesy, son of man, and say to the wind, Thus saith the Lord God; Come from the four winds, O breath, and breathe upon these slain, that they may live.**

**So I prophesied as he commanded me, and the breath came into them, and they lived, and stood up upon their feet, an exceeding great army [Ezek. 37:9–10].**

Ezekiel spoke, and life came into those bodies. What happened here resembles the creation of man at the very beginning. God took man of the dust of the earth; Ezekiel started with bones, but God didn't. God started with just the dirt of the earth, and then He breathed life into man.

Now what has happened to these bones has occurred in three stages: (1) they were scattered bones, just as dead as they could be; (2) then they came together, and flesh and skin came upon them—they were bodies, but *dead* bodies; and finally (3) they were made alive.

We will find in these three stages a real key to understanding Bible prophecy concerning the nation Israel.

Now this verse explains the meaning of the vision:

**Then he said unto me, Son of man, these bones are the whole house of Israel: behold, they say, Our bones are dried, and our hope is lost: we are cut off for our parts [Ezek. 37:11].**

"Son of man, these bones are the whole house of Israel." We are not talking here about the church; we are talking about *the house of Israel*.

"Behold, they say, Our bones are dried, and our hope is lost: we are cut off for our parts." You see, the people in captivity had gone from one extreme to another. As long as Jerusalem had stood and the false prophets continued to say they would return, they maintained a false hope. Now that Jerusalem has been destroyed, they go to the other extreme—they have what psychologists call manic depressive psychosis. They are in a bad state: they were high up one day, but now they have hit the very depths. They say, "We have no hope." This vision is being given to them to let them know they do have a hope, and it is for the whole house of Israel.

**Therefore prophesy and say unto them, Thus saith the Lord God; Behold, O my people, I will open your graves, and cause you to come up out of your graves, and bring you into the land of Israel [Ezek. 37:12].**

After reading this verse, someone is apt to say, "Wait a minute. You said this vision was not concerning physical resurrection." I still insist upon that. Let's drop down to verse 21:

**And say unto them, Thus saith the Lord God; Behold, I will take the children of Israel from among the heathen, whither they be gone, and will gather them on every side, and bring them into their own land [Ezek. 37:21].**

This is what God meant in verse 12 when He said, "I will cause you to come up out of your graves." Israel is buried in the nations of the world, and they are to be brought back and become a nation again.

I want to say something very carefully now concerning the three stages of the bones Ezekiel saw. I have said they are the key to understanding the future of the nation Israel, and I now want to add that if there is any

place we have fulfilled prophecy it is in these three stages. I don't go much for finding prophecy being fulfilled on every hand, but I do see it here. Follow me carefully: The nation Israel was buried and scattered in the nations of the world, and was dead to God, dead to the things of God—that's the first stage of the bones that we saw. Now since 1948 they have come back as a nation, but it is really a corpse over there today. They have a flag, they have a constitution, they have a prime minister, and they have a parliament. They have a police force and an army. They have a nation, and they even have Jerusalem. They have everything except spiritual life. If you walk from the old Arab section of Jerusalem where Islam dominates and come over into the Israeli section, there is no spiritual life. I want to say this kindly, but, as far as I am concerned, there is as much spiritual deadness on the one side as the other. There is a great deal more of that which is materialistic, which is intellectual, and which denotes civilization on the Israeli side, but there is no spiritual life whatsoever. This is symbolized by the second stage of the bones—bodies, but without life. That is where Israel stands today.

In verses 15–28 Ezekiel mentions two sticks. I will not go into any detail here other than to say that they typify the northern (Israel) and southern (Judah) kingdoms which will again become one nation. This means, my friend, that there must not be any "ten lost tribes of Israel"—at least, if there are, God knows where they are, and I am confident that it is not Great Britain which will be joined to them in that land!

**And I will make them one nation in the land upon the mountains of Israel; and one king shall be king to them all: and they shall be no more two nations, neither shall they be divided into two kingdoms any more at all [Ezek. 37:22].**

God will make them one nation.

**And David my servant shall be king over them; and they all shall have one shepherd: they shall also walk in my judgments, and observe my statutes, and do them [Ezek. 37:24].**

That one Shepherd is none other than the Lord Jesus Christ. When He came, He was born in the line of David. Read Matthew 1; Luke 1–2—both very carefully record that He came in the line of David. The One that came in that line is the Shepherd, and He will rule over them. I personally believe that God will raise up David to reign over Israel, either in the Millennium or in the eternal kingdom which will be ushered in immediately following the Millennium. Some commentators say he will reign in the Millennium; others say it will be the eternal kingdom. I believe he will reign during both, that he will serve as the vice-regent of the Lord Jesus Christ down here on this earth.

**And the heathen shall know that I the Lord do sanctify Israel, when my sanctuary shall be in the midst of them for evermore [Ezek. 37:28].**

This is going to come to pass—it has not yet come to pass.

"When my sanctuary shall be in the midst of them for evermore." There will be a millennial temple and an eternal temple down here on the earth. In Revelation where it speaks of there not being a temple, it is referring to the New Jerusalem, which is where the church will be and which is not to be upon this earth. The eternal home of the children of Israel will be upon this earth, and God's temple will be in their midst. Although there is no doubt that Israel is the subject of Ezekiel, and especially of chapters 37–39, we can certainly make an application of it for our personal lives. The world that you and I live in today is a death valley, full of dead bones, dead people, if you please. Oh, people talk about being alive and say they are where the action is, but they are really dead in trespasses and sins. They have no spiritual life. That is the reason they have to have a drink or two, or take some sort of drugs, or do something to liven up the old corpse.

God has made it very clear that "He that hath the Son hath life; and he that hath not the Son of God hath not life" (1 John 5:12). If you have the Son of God, you have life. If you do not have the Son, you are dead. There are two kinds of people: live people and dead people. "He that believeth on the Son hath everlasting life: and he that believeth not the Son shall not see life; but the wrath of God abideth on him" (John 3:36). That means that the person without the Son is dead.

God is saying to you today that you are dead if you are not a Christian. Ye dry bones, hear the Word of the Lord. You can come to life. Accept Jesus Christ as your Savior. This is the application we can draw from this portion of Scripture, but the subject of the prophecy is the nation Israel.

# CHAPTERS 38–39

*THEME: Russia's (Gog's) invasion of Israel*

If there is any section in the prophecy of Ezekiel that is familiar, it is chapters 38 and 39. These two chapters tell of the repudiation of Gog and Magog. I am going to attempt to handle these chapters just a little differently than I generally do because I am anxious to lift out certain great truths for our consideration. Unfortunately, these chapters have been interpreted by men who apparently have no knowledge of the prophecy of Ezekiel and what goes with it. As a result they have come up with some very odd interpretations. They remind me of the advertisement that was put in the *Mines Magazine* in El Paso, Texas, by some fellows who were mining experts and engineers. They put an ad in that magazine in a deadpan way, as though it was serious. "Wanted: Man to work on nuclear fissionable isotopes, molecular reactive counters and three-phased cyclotronic uranium photosynthesizers. No experience necessary." Well, it is equally as humorous to try to interpret Ezekiel without knowing what the entire book is about.

We saw in chapter 37 that God has a definite purpose for Israel in the future, and these two chapters deal with that subject. They tell about the final enemy that will come against Israel in the last days.

In chapters 38 and 39 I believe that the enemy mentioned is Russia. When I entered the ministry, I did not believe that it referred to Russia. I refused to accept that interpretation because I had attended my denominational seminary which taught amillennialism. They did not believe that Russia was being referred to in this portion of Scripture. Even after I had worked for my doctoral degree, even at the time of my graduation, I still had not accepted it. Finally I came to the conclusion that I had better study the subject on my own, and I am convinced that the enemy of chapters 38 and 39 is Russia. Three points of contact make me know this in my own heart and mind: You have here what is known as the linguistic phenomenon, the geographic phenomenon, and the philosophical or ideological phenomenon.

## LINGUISTIC PHENOMENON

**And the word of the LORD came unto me, saying,**

**Son of man, set thy face against Gog, the land of Magog, the chief prince of Meshech and Tubal, and prophesy against him [Ezek. 38:1–2].**

Gog is a word for ruler, meaning roof, which actually means "the man on top." I can't think of a better name for a dictator than Gog. If he is not on top, he is not a dictator, and if he is on top, he is a dictator.

*Magog* means "head"; it is the Hebrew word *Rosh*, which means head. Dean Stanley, in his exhaustive *History of the Eastern Church*, published half a century ago, has a note founded on Gesenius, the great Hebrew scholar, to the effect that the word *Rosh* should be *Russia*. Then Dean Stanley adds that this is the only reference to a modern nation in the entire Old Testament. This is indeed remarkable.

Bishop Lowther made the statement that *Rosh* taken as a proper name in Ezekiel signified the inhabitants of Scythia from whom the modern Russians derive their name. You see, Russia was first called Muscovy, derived from Meshech. Ivan the Fourth, a czar of Russia, who was called Ivan the Terrible, came to the Muscovite throne in 1533. He assumed the title of Czar, which was the first time the title was used. I am sure you detect that the names Meshech and Tubal certainly sound like Moscow, and Tobolsk, which is way over in Siberia. The linguistic phenomenon certainly leads us to believe that Ezekiel is talking about Russia in this passage.

## GEOGRAPHIC PHENOMENON

Now the second proof that identifies Russia is the geographic position. Here we have mentioned the nations which will be with Russia in the last days: "Gomer, and all his bands: the house of Togarmah of the north quarters, and all his bands: and many people with thee" (v. 6). "Gomer" is Germany, and "the house of Togarmah" is Turkey. "Of the north quarters" gives us the geographic location. Again in verse 15 we read: "And thou shalt come from thy place out of the north parts," and in chapter 39 verse 2 the same location is given: "and will cause thee to come up from the north parts." Whenever I give an illustrated message on this passage in Scripture, I always show a map of Israel and Russia. The literal meaning here is the "uttermost parts of the north." If you look at a map, you will find that Russia is directly north and

northeast. In fact, it covers Israel just like that picture you have seen of the fellow under a great big sombrero. That hat covers him just like Russia covers the nation Israel. When you start going north of Israel, you end up in Russia, and when you get through Russia you will be among the icebergs. You and the polar bears are going to be the only ones there.

Directions in the Bible are in relation to the land of Israel. North in the Bible does not mean north of California or north of where you live. In the Bible north is north of the land of Israel. South is south of the land of Israel. West is west of the land of Israel, and east is east of the land of Israel. In other words, Israel is the geographical center of the earth as far as the Word of God is concerned.

## PHILOSOPHICAL PHENOMENON

Finally we come to the philosophical or ideological phenomenon, which helps us identify Gog and Magog with Russia.

**And say, Thus saith the Lord God; Behold, I am against thee, O Gog, the chief prince of Meshech and Tubal [Ezek. 38:3].**

This is strange language. Here in the Book of Ezekiel God has said several times that He is against certain nations. He said it about Babylon; He said it about Egypt; and He said it about the nations which were against His people and against His person. Now here is a nation that is to arise in the last days, a nation which is against God. The reason we know it is against God is because God says, "I'm against you." This makes it different from any other nation, because God has said this about nations already in existence that have exhibited enmity and rejection of Him, but this nation hadn't even come into existence when Ezekiel gave this prophecy. Yet God says he is against it.

My friend, you and I have seen something that no generation in the past has seen. We have seen a nation arise whose basic philosophy is atheism. The political economy of Russia rests upon the premise that there is no God. It is atheistic. No other nation has assumed the dominant position of atheism.

Someone may be thinking, "What about the heathen, pagan nations of the past? Weren't they atheistic?" No, they were not. They were polytheistic. They believed in many gods. In the beginning men went off the track, but they did not become atheists. The reason they did not become atheists is, I think, easy to

understand. They were too close to the mooring mast of revelation. After all, in Noah's day you did not have atheists. That was not the problem with that crowd at all. The problem with them was that they had gone off into sin, and they worshiped many gods. Man at that point was polytheistic. All the great nations of the past were polytheistic, and the judgments God has pronounced in this book are against polytheistic nations. He said of Memphis that all of the idols would disappear, and they have disappeared. There were probably no people so given over to idolatry—with the possible exception of the Babylonians. Polytheism characterized the ancient world. But Russia is a nation whose basic philosophy is atheistic, a nation that is against God.

Do you realize that God did not give a commandment against atheism at the beginning? He did, however, give the first two commandments against polytheism: "Thou shalt have no other gods before me" (Exod. 20:3); and "Thou shalt not make unto thee any graven image, or any likeness of any thing that is in heaven above, or that is in the earth beneath, or that is in the water under the earth" Exod. (20:4). So, you see, there are commandments against polytheism, but none against atheism.

When you reach the time of David, atheism is beginning to appear. In Psalm 14:1 we read, "The fool hath said in his heart, There is no God." How ridiculous atheism is! It is almost an untenable position for little man, and here is a *nation* that says there is no God! Concerning Russia, men in high places have warned, "You cannot negotiate with them." Mr. Churchill said of Russia, "A riddle wrapped in a mystery inside an enigma." Rube Goldberg, who drew one of those crazy cartoons years ago, called Joe Stalin, "The Great Upsidedown Philosopher." Underneath the cartoon was written: "Top is bottom, black is white, far is near, and day is night. Big is little, high is low, cold is hot, and yes is no." Unreasonable? Insane? But that has been the basic philosophy of Russia, and it is a nation that has risen in our day.

Mr. Stalin once said, "We have deposed the czars of the earth, and we shall now dethrone the Lord of heaven." When Russia put a rocket past the moon, called the *Sputnik*, and when it was nearing the sun, the following was heard on the radio in Russia: "Our rocket has bypassed the moon. It is nearing the sun. We have not discovered God. We have turned out lights in heaven that no man will be able to put on again. We are breaking the yoke of the

gospel, the opiate of the masses. Let us go forth and Christ shall be relegated to mythology." I have often wondered what they had in mind when they said that. Did they think that God was playing peekaboo on the other side of the moon? Because they got a glimpse of the other side of the moon and did not see God, did that prove He did not exist? That is the reasoning of the upside-down philosopher. God, however, has beaten them to the draw. Before Russia even came into existence, God said, "I am against thee."

You can see how Gog and Magog may be identified with Russia by this threefold reason: (1) the linguistic phenomenon; (2) the geographic phenomenon; and (3) the philosophical or ideological phenomenon. These are the three points of identification, and when we get to chapter 39 of Ezekiel, God repeats once again that He is against Russia.

This chapter will tell us that this nation in the north with other nations with him will come down against Israel.

## WHY RUSSIA WILL INVADE ISRAEL

Now the question is: Why will they come against the land of Israel?

**And I will turn thee back, and put hooks into thy jaws, and I will bring thee forth, and all thine army, horses and horsemen, all of them clothed with all sorts of armour, even a great company with bucklers and shields, all of them handling swords [Ezek. 38:4].**

God says, "I will . . . put hooks into thy jaws, and I will bring thee forth." This has been interpreted to mean that God was going to put hooks in their jaws to get them *out* of Israel after they had invaded it. But that is not what He says. He makes it clear that He is going to judge them *in* the land of Israel, and that they will not come out alive. In chapter 39, verse 11, He says, "And it shall come to pass in that day, that I will give unto Gog a place there of *graves in Israel.*" As we read this section, it becomes obvious that God is not going to lead out the invading nations, but there will be a slaughter the like of which probably has not been seen in the history of the world.

Then what does God mean by saying that He will put hooks in their jaws? Well, it seems obvious to me that He is saying, "I am going to put hooks in your jaws and bring you down into the land of Israel." When this time comes, Israel will be back in their own land. For centuries that land was not occupied by them. After the destruction by Titus the Roman in

A.D. 70, the Jewish people were sold into slavery throughout the world, and they were scattered throughout the world.

The land was no longer a land of milk and honey. We have seen in the Book of Ezekiel that even the Negev was at one time covered with forest. God said that He was going to burn that out, and He did. That is the place where Elijah went when Jezebel threatened to kill him. He kept going until he was so tired he stopped and crawled under a juniper tree. If Elijah were here today, he would have trouble finding a juniper tree to crawl under; he would have to find something else. The forests are gone.

Mark Twain said concerning the land of Israel, "Palestine sits in sackcloth and ashes, desolate and unlovely. It is a hopeless, dreary, heartbroken land. And why should it be otherwise? Can the curse of the Deity beautify a land? Palestine is no more of this work-day world. It is sacred to poetry and tradition. It is dreamland."

Dr. Theodor Herzl, the playwright from Austria who began the tremendous Zionist movement back to the land of Palestine, made this statement: "There is a land without a people. There is a people without a land. Give the land without a people to the people without a land."

Dr. Chaim Weizmann, the first president of Israel, speaking before the Anglo-American Commission of Inquiry, said, "The Jewish nation is a ghost nation. Only the God of Israel has kept the Jewish people alive."

David Ben-Gurion, the first prime minister and minister of defense in Israel, made this statement: "Ezekiel 37 has been fulfilled, and the nation Israel is hearing the footsteps of the Messiah."

Today Israel has turned from this thinking. I have a picture, taken on Israel's twenty-first anniversary, of a motto in the auditorium at Tel Aviv, written in Hebrew and English. It said, "Science will bring peace to this land." The Old Testament says that Messiah will bring peace to that land, so apparently they are chasing a new messiah today.

Russia will invade the land of Israel. Lord Beverly made the statement that Russia would not move into western Europe but would move into Asia and the Near East. General Douglas MacArthur concurred with him in that viewpoint. At the time Lord Beverly made that statement almost everyone thought that Russia would move into western Europe after World War II, but they did not move into that area at all. In fact, up

to this day they have not moved into that area.

God says, "I will put hooks into thy jaws, and I will bring thee forth." Today I believe that we can already see three of the hooks that God could use to bring them down into that land:

1. Russia needs a warm-water entrance into the waterways of the world. Israel offers that, and Russia is moving in this direction. A few years ago I sat in the dining room on the top floor of the Hilton Hotel in Istanbul and watched Russian ships coming out of the Black Sea, moving through the Bosporus, and heading for the Mediterranean Sea. This took place after the Six-Day War, and Russian naval strength had increased tremendously. What are the Russians looking for? They are looking for a warm-water port. Admiral Sergei Gorshkov made this statement, "The flag of the Soviet navy now proudly flies over the oceans of the world. Sooner or later the United States will have to understand that it no longer has mastery of the seas." Russia is looking for a warm-water port. Where are they going? All I know is that they are headed for the Mediterranean Sea. What nation along the east side of the Mediterranean would be suitable as a port? Israel certainly would be. Russia is interested in moving southward today. God has put a hook in their jaw.

2. God has a second hook—oil. The oil deposits of the Near East are essential for the survival of modern nations. Russia needs oil. Today we are being constantly reminded that the world is running short of energy. Oil is one of the resources in short supply. As a result, the world is turning to the places where they can get oil. There is oil in the Near East. Whether or not the oil is actually in the land of Israel is not the important thing. The important consideration is that, in spite of the strained relations between the Arabs and the Jews, a great deal of that oil is going through the land of Israel. When ships were not able to go through the Suez Canal, they put the oil off at a port which had been taken by Israel, and then the oil was taken across the land of Israel to the Mediterranean ports. As far back as 1955 I delivered a message stating that Russia was hungering for the Arabian oil. An editor of a paper in downtown Los Angeles heard my message and disagreed with it. Sometime later he made a trip over to the Near East area. When he returned, he wrote an article (and I have a copy of it) in which he said, "Russia hungers for Arabian oil." He changed his viewpoint after he had been to the Near

East and had seen things with his own eyes. It is a pretty good hook God has in Russia's jaws, because any modern nation must have oil.

3. The third hook concerns the Dead Sea. The mineral deposits in the Dead Sea are so great that they cannot be evaluated on today's market. Chemicals saturated in the water represent untold wealth. It is estimated that the Dead Sea contains two billion tons of potassium chloride, which is potash—needed to sweeten and enrich the soil that is readily being depleted around the world, including our own area. The Dead Sea also contains twenty-two billion tons of magnesium chloride, twelve billion tons of sodium chloride, and six billion tons of calcium chloride. The Dead Sea, in addition to all of this, contains cerium, cobalt, manganese, and even gold. Believe me, friend, there is much effort being made today to extract this wealth from the Dead Sea.

If you had been around a few million years ago and had seen the Lord forming this earth, particularly the Dead Sea, you would probably have asked Him, "Why are you damming up that sea? You are going to have a pretty salty place." He would have replied, "I am baiting a hook." Then you would have said, "Baiting a hook for what?" Then the Lord would have said, "In a few million years there will be a nation in the north that I am going to bring into the land of Israel. I am just baiting one of the hooks a little ahead of time." And that is what God has been doing—baiting a hook.

## WHEN RUSSIA WILL INVADE ISRAEL

The question is: When will Russia come down? This is where many expositors disagree. There are those who believe that Russia will invade the land of Palestine at the end of this age, before the church is raptured. Others believe that Russia will come against Israel at the beginning of the Tribulation Period, and others believe it will be at the end of the Tribulation. There are some who believe this will take place at the beginning of the Millennium. I am not going to discuss these different viewpoints in detail. My particular viewpoint is this: Russia will come in the "latter days" (v. 16); these "latter days" (as we have seen in the other prophets) is a technical term that specifically refers to the Tribulation Period. These will be the days when the Antichrist comes to power, and he is going to come to power on a peace platform. As a result there will be a false peace for the first part of

the Tribulation Period; then in the midst of the seven years, Russia will come down from the north into the land of Israel. Russia will trigger the *Great* Tribulation by breaking the false peace made by the Antichrist and invading Israel.

> **After many days thou shalt be visited: in the latter years thou shalt come into the land that is brought back from the sword, and is gathered out of many people, against the mountains of Israel, which have been always waste: but it is brought forth out of the nations, and they shall dwell safely all of them [Ezek. 38:8].**

When Israel is back in the land, they will be under the domination of the Antichrist, who will make them believe that peace has come to the earth, that all of the problems of the earth are settled and they are entering the Millennium. But this is not true, and they will find in the midst of the Tribulation Period that out of the north will come their enemy, Russia.

> **And thou shalt come up against my people of Israel, as a cloud to cover the land; it shall be in the latter days, and I will bring thee against my land, that the heathen may know me, when I shall be sanctified in thee. O Gog, before their eyes [Ezek. 38:16].**

Since Israel is dwelling in peace, and Antichrist has deceived everyone, God is Israel's only source of help. He Himself will deal with Russia. War will break out. The *Great* Tribulation will begin (which is the final three and one-half years of the Tribulation Period) in all of its frenzied fury. The whole earth will be a holocaust. Judgments, one right after the other, will come upon the earth. War will reign. Christ said concerning this brief period, ". . . except those days should be shortened, there should no flesh be saved. . ." (Matt. 24:22).

I recommend that you read in your Bible the remainder of this chapter. This is God's judgment upon the invading armies of Russia.

## RESULTS OF THE INVASION

Chapter 39 continues the prophecy against Gog and furnishes added details about the destruction of this formidable enemy.

> **And I will turn thee back, and leave but the sixth part of thee, and will cause thee to come up from the north parts, and will bring thee upon the mountains of Israel [Ezek. 39:2].**

"Leave but the sixth part of thee" is literally "I will six thee," or better still, "I will afflict thee with six plagues." These plagues are listed in chapter 38 verse 22 as pestilence, blood, overflowing rain, great hailstones, fire, and brimstone. This is the way God destroyed Sodom and Gomorrah. According to the record, "Then the LORD rained upon Sodom and Gomorrah brimstone and fire from the LORD out of heaven" (Gen. 19:24). And this is exactly the way God intends to destroy this army which will come out of the north against His people to destroy them. You must remember that Russia has always been anti-Semitic. At the present writing the largest population of Jews—outside the land of Israel and the United States—is over there in Russia. We are hearing a great deal of criticism of Russia for not permitting the Jews to leave. Well, in these last days God will deal with Russia for its treatment of His people.

There is a message for us here. When God was ready to destroy Sodom and Gomorrah, Abraham thought He was being unjust. He asked God, "Will you destroy the righteous with the wicked? Will you spare the city if there are fifty righteous—forty-five—forty—thirty—twenty—ten?" God said no, He would not destroy the city if ten righteous were found there. But there were not ten, and God sent His angels to get Lot out of the city, saying that they could not destroy the city until Lot was out of it. My friend, this is one reason I believe that God will not let the Tribulation come until He takes His church—that is, all born-again believers—out of the world. Let me illustrate this with the following diagram:

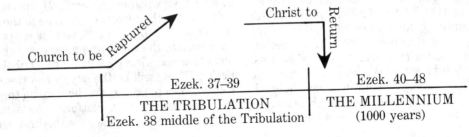

To put it very bluntly, all hell will break loose on the earth during the Tribulation Period. It will be a frightful, terrible time. I don't understand the folk who insist that God's redeemed ones, which we designate as the church, will go through the Tribulation. The Bible makes it clear that those who will be witnessing on the earth during this time will be the 144,000 Jews.

God, having dealt in judgment with the enemy that invaded Israel from the north, allows Antichrist to be the world ruler for the remainder of the Tribulation Period. Then the Lord Jesus Christ will come to the earth to establish His kingdom; we have that pictured in chapter 19 of Revelation. In chapter 20 of the Book of Revelation the kingdom, the Millennium, begins.

With these tremendous events in mind, it would be well to pause a moment and consider the material we have studied. After a careful examination of three of the four major prophets: Isaiah, Jeremiah, and Ezekiel, certain great principles emerge, which the fourth prophet, Daniel, will confirm. These principles have an ageless application for nations of the world and for believers (when I say "believers," I am speaking about those who have trusted the Lord Jesus Christ as Savior and believe that the Bible is the Word of God). In Ezekiel we have seen God dealing with Israel. My friend, when God says "Israel" He means Israel; He does not mean the church. How some can believe that God means the church when He says Israel is a flip on the flying trapeze of theology that is beyond me. Let's allow God to mean what He says and realize that He has been dealing in these prophecies with the literal people of Israel. That is the correct interpretation. However, there is an application we can make since God's dealing with Israel is a microcosm of His dealings with the world in which we live. The principles God has used in dealing with His own people Israel are *eternal*, for they are linked to the character and attributes of God. I have stated some of them in the Books of Isaiah and Jeremiah, and now I am prepared to draw certain conclusions from Ezekiel.

No prophet emphasizes the glory and the holiness of God more than Ezekiel. He *saw* the glory of God—that was the great vision he had at the beginning of his book. He never forgot it. And we should not forget it either. His emphasis, therefore, is upon God's judgment. God is longsuffering, not willing that any should perish, and He warned his people again and again that, if they did not turn to Him, He

would judge Jerusalem. Then Jerusalem was destroyed, and Ezekiel offered the people encouragement as they looked into the future. "But," he said, "another enemy is coming." When the Lord Jesus Christ was on earth, He wept over the city of Jerusalem because He knew that Titus the Roman would be around in a few years to destroy the city, just as Nebuchadnezzar had done in the past.

Things were wrong in Jerusalem; and, if that city was to enjoy the blessings of God, those things had to be made right. The liars should cease lying; the thieves should cease stealing; the lawless should become law-abiding; and righteousness should prevail in the city. Only when God was acknowledged and respected in the land could blessing rest upon Jerusalem. Righteousness must prevail before any nation or individual can experience the love, mercy, and goodness of God. Jerusalem was *wrong*—the people were thinking wrong; they were acting wrong. They were in sin, and God was *right* in judging them. God never blesses that which is wrong.

This is made evident when we contrast Ezekiel with Jeremiah. I want you to notice this again because I consider it rather important. Jeremiah reveals the heart of God. God does not want to judge. As He said in Isaiah, judgment is *strange* work. He would rather save—that is His business. He is not willing that any should perish. He is very much involved with the human race. The great statement in John's gospel is that He became *flesh* and came down here among us. This reveals His love and concern for us. It broke His heart that Jerusalem would be destroyed. Jesus wept over it just as Jeremiah had wept over it centuries before.

In Ezekiel we have something altogether different. At the very time Jerusalem was being destroyed Ezekiel's wife died, and God forbad him to mourn or sorrow for her. He was to act like nothing happened. God wept over Jerusalem, but He did not *mourn*. He did not repent for what He had done, because He was right in doing it. God, with tears in His eyes, punished Jerusalem and destroyed the city, but He was doing that which was in keeping with His character. He did what was right because what God does is right. Paul asks, ". . . Is there unrighteousness with God? God forbid" (Rom. 9:14). Of course there is no unrighteousness with God. Whatever God does is right. His *glory* is manifested in *judgment*. His *grace* is manifested in *redemption*. If God had not provided redemption for

us, there would be no salvation for man whatsoever.

In chapters 38 and 39 of Ezekiel we saw that the kingdom in the north which is going to invade Israel (which I believe is Russia) will be destroyed in the future. The question is: *Why* will God destroy Russia? Let's read this verse again: "And thou shalt come up against my people of Israel, as a cloud to cover the land; it shall be in the latter days, and I will bring thee against my land, that the heathen may know me, when I shall be sanctified in thee, O Gog, before their eyes" (Ezek. 38: 16). What is God going to do? He is going to *destroy* them. I can hear someone exclaim, "Do you mean God will actually do such a thing?" Certainly He will. The liberal theologian has a problem with the Creator destroying what He chooses, such as the Lord Jesus cursing a fig tree and also destroying a few pigs. I was in a conference one time when a man who was a liberal in his theology almost wept because Jesus destroyed those pigs (Matt. 8:30–32)! Yet every morning *he* ate bacon for breakfast! He was like the Walrus and the Carpenter who wept, but were busy eating oysters as fast as they could. I am not impressed with these people who get upset with God because He judges. I have a notion that God gets a little upset with them.

Now let me cite two other verses:

**And I will send a fire on Magog, and among them that dwell carelessly in the isles: and they shall know that I am the LORD.**

**So will I make my holy name known in the midst of my people Israel; and I will not let them pollute my holy name any more: and the heathen shall know that I am the LORD, the Holy One in Israel [Ezek. 39:6–7].**

Is God going to destroy Russia? He says that He will send fire on Magog and among those that dwell securely in the coastlands. The question is: Where is God today? Why doesn't He move in defense of His people in our day? I shall never forget watching a newscast on television several years ago when a group of Christians appeared at the American Embassy in Moscow and appealed, actually weeping, for permission to leave Russia because of being persecuted. Our country did nothing. And the Russian soldiers came and took these people away. I waited for a long time to hear what had happened to them, but there was never a further word in the media. The Soviet authorities were never dealt with. And Russia has been guilty of more anti-Semitism than any other nation over a period of years. Oh, the injustice in the world! I see very little fear of God throughout the world. The feeling is that He is a jolly old Man who shuts His eyes to the injustice in the world. Why doesn't God move against injustice? Well, He *will* move when it is time. He will vindicate His glory, but He will not do it in a vindictive, revengeful, and petulant manner. He will judge, and when He does, there will be a respect and reverence for God in this world, and little man will bow before Him.

Romans 2:3 tells us, "And thinkest thou this, O man, that judgest them which do such things, and doest the same, that thou shalt escape the judgment of God?" Man is not going to escape judgment. He thinks he will get away with his sin, but he will not. In Hebrews 2:3 we read, "How shall we escape, if we neglect so great salvation; which at the first began to be spoken by the Lord, and was confirmed unto us by them that heard him." My friend, do you realize that this is a question which even God cannot answer? How *shall* we escape, if we neglect so great salvation? Well, we can't escape. There is no answer to that question.

Now let me use an old-fashioned expression that gags the liberal preachers (and also some evangelicals who are attempting to make the world a better place for people to go to hell in). Here it is: Hell, my friend, is an awful *reality*. You can interpret it any way you want to, but it is a place where a holy God puts those who are in rebellion against Him, those who sin with impunity, those who blaspheme God and His holy name at will, those who live like animals in the name of freedom but who are indulging in gross immorality. My friend, God's holy name is going to be vindicated.

How will God's holy name be vindicated? In love? He is demonstrating His love today in giving His Son. Those of us who name His name need to learn a lesson. We need to learn that we cannot trifle with Him. We cannot get familiar with Him. We cannot live as we please and then get buddy-buddy with Him. Our God is holy. Neither can we presume upon Him. We cannot sin and get by with it. If that were possible, then God would be no better than we are. Man is only a creature. The will of God will prevail, and our proper position is to bow before Him. Our only liberty today is in the will of God. He remembers that we are dust, but I can say with Paul, ". . . I

obtained mercy . . ." (1 Tim.1:13). My friend, if you deny Him, He will trample you under His feet. He has loved you enough to give His Son, but if you reject His mercy and grace He will reject you. This is His universe, this is His earth, and He is running it according to His perfect plan. My friend, we need to get in step with Him.

# CHAPTERS 40–48

*THEME: Description of the millennial temple, worship in the millennial temple; return of the glory of the Lord*

In this concluding section of the Book of Ezekiel we find a description of the millennial temple, the worship of the millennial temple, and a vision concerning the land.

## THE MILLENNIAL TEMPLE

Chapters 40–42 contain a description of the millennial temple. Now since this is the millennial temple, I expect to see it and maybe go into it, but I don't intend to worship there. The temple will be here on this earth, but I am going to be in the place which is described in Revelation 21—the New Jerusalem. That will be the address of the believer for eternity. If you want to give someone your address as a believer for eternity, I don't know what street you will be on (I hope I'm on Glory Blvd.), but I do know the city—it will be the New Jerusalem. One thing that John tells us about this city is, "And I saw no temple therein: for the Lord God Almighty and the Lamb are the temple of it" (Rev. 21:22). Therefore the church is going to be in a place where there won't be a temple; we won't need one, but the earth will have one for the duration of the Millennium at least. I rather like the fact that we won't have a temple because, very candidly, I have never gone in much for ritual. I'm going to be delighted to be up there with the Lord God and the Lamb as the temple of the New Jerusalem. We will be with them, and I cannot even conceive how wonderful that is going to be.

We have seen a certain progress and development in the Book of Ezekiel: after the enemy is put down, Israel enters the Millennium, and there will be a temple here on this earth. We are talking about the earth, and that means we are talking about Israel and the gentile nations which will be saved. The church of Christ is up yonder with Him in the New Jerusalem at this time.

**In the five and twentieth year of our captivity, in the beginning of the year, in the tenth day of the month, in the fourteenth year after that the city was smitten, in the selfsame day the hand of the LORD was upon me, and brought me thither [Ezek. 40:1].**

Jerusalem has been destroyed and the temple is burned, but Ezekiel is to be shown now the temple that will be in that city during the millennial kingdom.

**In the visions of God brought he me into the land of Israel, and set me upon a very high mountain, by which was as the frame of a city on the south.**

**And he brought me thither, and, behold, there was a man, whose appearance was like the appearance of brass, with a line of flax in his hand, and a measuring reed; and he stood in the gate [Ezek. 40:2–3].**

Every time in Scripture that we find a man with a measuring rod—it generally is an angel, and it is an angel here—it means that God is getting ready to move again in dealing with His earthly people. We find this again in the minor prophets and in the Book of Revelation.

**And the man said unto me, Son of man, behold with thine eyes, and hear with thine ears, and set thine heart upon all that I shall shew thee; for to the intent that I might shew them unto thee art thou brought hither: declare all that thou seest to the house of Israel [Ezek. 40:4].**

It is my personal feeling that Ezekiel was brought literally to Jerusalem and shown there a vision of the millennial temple of the future.

And behold a wall on the outside of the house round about, and in the man's hand a measuring reed of six cubits long by the cubit and an hand breadth: so he measured the breadth of the building, one reed; and the height, one reed [Ezek. 40:5].

Beginning with verse 5 and continuing through these chapters we are given a great deal of detailed information concerning the temple which I will not go into. Its environs are given to us, and it will obviously be a thing of great beauty.

And in the porch of the gate were two tables on this side, and two tables on that side, to slay thereon the burnt offering and the sin offering and the trespass offering [Ezek. 40:39].

In verses 39–42 we find that the Mosaic system will be restored with the reinstating of the levitical liturgy and the burnt offering, the sin offering, and the trespass offering.

Four tables were on this side, and four tables on that side, by the side of the gate; eight tables, whereupon they slew their sacrifices [Ezek. 40:41].

There will be sacrifices offered in the millennial temple. I will discuss this further in chapter 45.

And without the inner gate were the chambers of the singers in the inner court, which was at the side of the north gate; and their prospect was toward the south: one at the side of the east gate having the prospect toward the north [Ezek. 40:44].

There will also be music and singers in the temple.

So he measured the court, an hundred cubits long, and an hundred cubits broad, foursquare; and the altar that was before the house [Ezek. 40:47].

Our attention is again called to the fact that there will be an altar for sacrifices. In the Holy Land Hotel in Jerusalem there is a miniature replica of the city as it was in the days of Herod and the Lord Jesus. Actually it is quite a large model, and as far as I could tell when examining it closely, there is no altar for sacrifice in the temple model—it has been left out. The orthodox Jews are a little embarrassed by an altar, and the liberal Jews want to get rid of it altogether. However, in the millennial temple there will be an altar.

## WORSHIP IN THE MILLENNIAL TEMPLE

Chapters 43–46 describe the worship of the millennial temple. As we consider the millennial temple, we need to remember that in the last days of the temple of Solomon, the *shekinah* glory, the presence of God, was absent. However, here in chapter 43 the glory returns to the temple, and, as we see the worship in the millennial temple, the One Israel worships is now in the temple. He is none other than the Lord Jesus Christ.

Afterward he brought me to the gate, even the gate that looketh toward the east:

And, behold, the glory of the God of Israel came from the way of the east: and his voice was like a noise of many waters: and the earth shined with his glory [Ezek. 43:1–2].

The glory of God comes from the east and fills the temple. This is the return of Christ to the earth, and He brings the *shekinah* glory with Him. When he came to Bethlehem more than nineteen hundred years ago, the glory was not with Him.

And the glory of the LORD came into the house by the way of the gate whose prospect is toward the east [Ezek. 43:4].

Apparently the Lord will come from the east. We will look at this again in chapter 44.

And thou shalt give to the priests the Levites that be of the seed of Zadok, which approach unto me, to minister unto me, saith the Lord GOD, a young bullock for a sin offering [Ezek. 43:19].

In this section we are dealing with the worship in the temple. The sacrifices offered will be memorial in character. They will look back to the work of Christ on the cross, as the offerings of the Old Testament anticipated His sacrifice. In chapter 45 we will go into more detail about this.

In chapter 44 Ezekiel is told that a prince will enter the city through the eastern gate:

Then he brought me back the way of the gate of the outward sanctuary which looketh toward the east; and it was shut.

Then said the LORD unto me; This gate shall be shut, it shall not be opened, and no man shall enter in by it; because

the LORD, the God of Israel, hath entered in by it, therefore it shall be shut.

It is for the prince; the prince, he shall sit in it to eat bread before the LORD; he shall enter by the way of the porch of that gate, and shall go out by the way of the same [Ezek. 44:1–3].

The eastern gate of present-day Jerusalem is shut—it is completely walled up. Some of my premillennial brethren feel that this is a fulfillment of these verses in Ezekiel and that the gate will not be opened again until the Messiah comes. I have two objections to this viewpoint that I would like to mention.

My first point is that the prince mentioned here who is coming is *not* the Lord Jesus Christ. Ezekiel tells us that this prince offers a sacrifice and worships God (chs. 45–46); therefore he cannot be the Lord Jesus. The Lord Jesus *is* God, and He never has and never will offer a sacrifice. It is not necessary for Him to do so, for He is still able to say, "Which of you convinceth [convicteth] me of sin? . . ." (John 8:46). This prince is not the Lord Jesus Christ. I personally feel that the prince is David. There are many fine men who do not agree that it is David, but they do agree that it is not the Lord Jesus. Many of them feel that the prince is simply another man in the line of David.

My second objection is that the gate in question is obviously not the gate of the city—it is the gate of the temple. It is true that the temple is not there yet, and the temple must be built before any of this can take place. The walled-up gate to the city has nothing to do with it. He probably will come through that eastern gate of the city, but it could be the present gate, or the wall could be torn down and an entirely new wall and gate be built before then. We must remember that the wall that is there now is neither the wall that Christ knew nor that Ezekiel knew—both of those walls have long since been destroyed.

Chapter 45 tells us that the Feast of the Passover will be kept:

Thus saith the Lord GOD; In the first month, in the first day of the month, thou shalt take a young bullock without blemish, and cleanse the sanctuary:

And the priest shall take of the blood of the sin offering, and put it upon the posts of the house, and upon the four corners of the settle of the altar, and upon the posts of the gate of the inner court.

And so thou shalt do the seventh day of the month for every one that erreth, and for him that is simple: so shall ye reconcile the house.

In the first month, in the fourteenth day of the month, ye shall have the passover, a feast of seven days; unleavened bread shall be eaten.

And upon that day shall the prince prepare for himself and for all the people of the land a bullock for a sin offering [Ezek. 45:18–22].

The Passover definitely refers to Christ: we are told in 1 Corinthians 5:7, ". . . For even Christ our passover is sacrificed for us."

At this point we must answer a major question: Since all the sacrifices of the Old Testament were fulfilled in Christ, why are they restored again during the Millennium? This is a major argument that amillennialists have against the premillennial position. I personally find no conflict here. I feel that the sacrifices offered during the Millennium are going to look back to the coming of Christ and His death upon the cross in the same way that in our day the Lord's Supper looks back to them. Someone will ask why the *literal* offering of sacrifices will be necessary. My friend, the human family has a great deal of difficulty learning a lesson. For the same reason, I believe that the literal blood of Christ is going to be in heaven. It will be there to reveal to us the horrible pit out of which we were digged. Our salvation from sin and hell unto heaven was a pretty big job, one that only God could undertake. The blood of Christ will be in heaven to remind the church of this, and the sacrifices will also be restored here on earth to reveal to the people of Israel how they were redeemed.

## A VISION CONCERNING THE LAND

In chapters 47–48 Ezekiel is given a picture of the land during the millennial kingdom.

Afterward he brought me again unto the door of the house; and, behold, waters issued out from under the threshold of the house eastward: for the forefront of the house stood toward the east, and the waters came down from under from the right side of the house, at the south side of the altar.

Then brought he me out of the way of the gate northward, and led me about the way without unto the utter gate by

the way that looketh eastward; and, behold, there ran out waters on the right side [Ezek. 47:1–2].

"Behold, waters issued out from under the threshold of the house eastward"—that is, they came from the altar. That is where all blessings originate—at the altar. Everything that comes to us by way of blessings comes through the death of Christ for you and me upon the cross.

The water here is a type of the Holy Spirit, and many spiritual lessons may be drawn from this passage:

And when the man that had the line in his hand went forth eastward, he measured a thousand cubits, and he brought me through the waters; the waters were to the ankles [Ezek. 47:3].

"The waters were to the ankles." This speaks of the walk of the believer in the Spirit.

Again he measured a thousand, and brought me through the waters; the waters were to the knees. Again he measured a thousand, and brought me through; the waters were to the loins [Ezek. 47:4].

"The waters were to the knees"—this speaks of prayer.

"The waters were to the loins." We are to gird up our loins for service. The walk and service of a believer rest upon the redemption we have in Christ.

Afterward he measured a thousand; and it was a river that I could not pass over: for the waters were risen, waters to swim in, a river that could not be passed over [Ezek. 47:5].

"Waters to swim in" indicates the fullness of the Spirit. This looks forward to the day when God will pour out His Spirit upon these people; He is not doing that today.

Now when I had returned, behold, at the bank of the river were very many

trees on the one side and on the other [Ezek. 47:7].

"Many trees"—this is the fruit that will be in our lives.

I have given you an *application* of this passage which we can make to our own lives. However, its *interpretation* for the people of Israel is that there will be an eternal spring of water coming out of that altar in that day which will bring blessing to that land. And, my friend, they *need* water in that land today.

Chapter 48 gives us the division of the land among the twelve tribes. Of particular interest to us is the tribe of Dan:

Now these are the names of the tribes. From the north end to the coast of the way of Hethlon, as one goeth to Hamath, Hazarenan, the border of Damascus northward, to the coast of Hamath; for these are his sides east and west; a portion for Dan.

And by the border of Dan, from the east side unto the west side, a portion for Asher [Ezek. 48:1–2].

The tribe of Dan is present in the Millennium although it is absent from those sealed in the Great Tribulation Period (see Rev. 7:4–8). Danites do not serve in the Great Tribulation, but the grace of God brings them into the Millenium. We, too, are saved by grace but rewarded for service.

The Book of Ezekiel has closed with a picture of the city, the millennial temple, and the land during the Millennium—all the curse is removed. What a picture we have here!

It was round about eighteen thousand measures: and the name of the city from that day shall be, The LORD is there [Ezek. 48:35].

The prophet Ezekiel closes on a high note: "The LORD is there."

# BIBLIOGRAPHY

(Recommended for Further Study)

Alexander, Ralph. *Ezekiel*. Chicago, Illinois: Moody Press, 1976. (Fine, inexpensive survey.)

Feinberg, Charles L. *The Prophecy of Ezekiel*. Chicago, Illinois: Moody Press, 1969. (Excellent.)

Gaebelein, Arno C. *The Prophet Ezekiel*. 1918. Reprint. Neptune, New Jersey: Loizeaux Brothers, 1972. (Excellent.)

Grant, F. W. *The Numerical Bible, Ezekiel*. 6 vols. Neptune, New Jersey: Loizeaux Brothers, n.d.

Gray, James M. *Synthetic Bible Studies*. Old Tappan, New Jersey: Fleming H. Revell, Co., 1906.

Ironside, H. A. *Expository Notes on Ezekiel*. Neptune, New Jersey: Loizeaux Brothers, 1959.

Jensen, Irving L. *Ezekiel and Daniel*. Chicago, Illinois: Moody Press. (Self study guide.)

Kelly, William. *Notes on Ezekiel*. 1876. Reprint. Addison, Illinois: Bible Truth Publishers.

Sauer, Erich. *The Dawn of World Redemption*. Grand Rapids, Michigan: William B. Eerdmans Publishing Co., 1951. (An excellent Old Testament survey.)

Scroggie, W. Graham. *The Unfolding Drama of Redemption*. Grand Rapids, Michigan, Zondervan Publishing House, 1970. (An excellent survey and outline of the Old Testament.)

Unger, Merrill F. *Unger's Bible Handbook*. Chicago, Illinois: Moody Press, 1966.

Unger, Merrill F. *Unger's Commentary on the Old Testament*, Vol. 2. Chicago, Illinois: Moody Press, 1982. (Highly recommended.)

# The Book of

# DANIEL

## INTRODUCTION

The Book of Daniel is one of the most thrilling books in the Bible, and it is, of course, a book on prophecy. Because prophecy bulks large in the Bible, I would like to say a word about it before we look at the Book of Daniel specifically. One fourth of the books in the Bible are of prophetic nature; the subject and statement of the books are eschatological, that is, they deal with prophecy. One fifth of the content of Scripture was predictive at the time of its writing; a large segment of that has been fulfilled. Therefore, the prophecy in Scripture can be divided into fulfilled and unfulfilled prophecy. We will find a great deal of fulfilled prophecy in Daniel.

There are certain great subjects of prophecy. They are like planes flying into an airport from all sections of the world, and you can go to the Book of Revelation and see all these great subjects brought to a final fruition. The main subject of prophecy is the Lord Jesus Christ. Other topics include Israel, the gentile nations, evil, Satan, the Man of Sin, the Great Tribulation Period, and how this age will end. The church is also a subject of prophecy; however, the church is never mentioned in the Old Testament, and therefore there will be no reference to it in the Book of Daniel. Then, of course, there are the subjects of the kingdom, the Millennium, and eternity future. These are the great subjects of prophecy.

I do not believe that one can have a full-orbed view of the Bible or be a well-rounded student of Scripture without a knowledge of eschatology, or prophecy. The neglect of the study of prophecy has produced certain harmful results which I think are quite evident today. Many of the cults have gone off the track in prophetic areas. This is largely because the teaching of prophecy has been neglected by the great denominations. For example, Dr. Charles Hodge, a great theologian at Princeton in the past, made this statement: "The subject [prophecy] cannot be adequately discussed without taking a survey of all the prophetic teachings of Scripture both of the Old Testament and of the New. This task cannot be satisfactorily accomplished by anyone who has not made a study of the prophecies a specialty. The author [that is, Dr. Hodge], knowing that he has not such qualifications for the work, purposes to confine himself in a great measure to an historical survey of the different schemes of interpreting the Scriptures prophetically." That certainly was a startling and sad admission on the part of Dr. Hodge. As a result, we find men in a great many of our denominations today who are ill-equipped to speak on prophecy. They dismiss it with a wave of the hand as being unimportant. And those who do go into the study of prophecy often come up with that which is sensational and fanatical. The Book of Daniel, particularly, is the subject of many such sensational writers on prophecy.

The Book of Daniel is a very important one, and it has therefore been the object of special attack by Satan in the same way that the Book of Isaiah has been. Isaiah has been called the prince of the prophets, and I would like to say that Daniel, then, is the king of the prophets. Both of these prophecies are very important in Scripture and have been especially attacked by unbelievers.

The Book of Daniel has been a battlefield between conservative and liberal scholars for years, and much of the controversy has had to do with the dating of the writing of the book. Porphyry, a heretic in the third century A.D., declared that the Book of Daniel was a forgery written during the time of Antiochus Epiphanes and the Maccabees. That would place its writing around 170 B.C., almost four hundred years *after* Daniel lived. The German critics seized upon this hypothesis and, along with Dr. S. R. Driver, developed this type of criticism of the book. These critics, as well as present-day unbelievers, assume the premise that the supernatural does not exist. Since foreknowledge is supernatural, there can, therefore, be no foretelling, no prophesying.

However, the very interesting thing is that the Septuagint, the Greek version of the Old Testament, was translated before the time of Antiochus Epiphanes, and it contains the Book of Daniel! The liberal scholars have ignored similar very clear testimony from the Dead Sea Scrolls. Those scrolls confirm the fact that there was only one author of the Book of Isaiah. The liberal has wanted to argue that there was a duet or even a trio of "Isaiahs" who wrote that book. The Dead Sea

Scrolls are very much alive, and they refute the liberal critic on that point.

It is interesting how these questions which are raised concerning the Bible are always answered in time. The heretic, the critic, and the cultist always move in an area of the Bible where we do not have full knowledge at the time. Everyone can speculate, and you can speculate any way you want to—generally the speculation goes the wrong way. However, in time, the Word of God is proven accurate.

Flavius Josephus *(Antiquities of the Jews,* Vol. 1, p. 388) also records an incident during the time of Alexander the Great which supports the early authorship of Daniel. When Alexander's invasion reached the Near East, Jaddua, the high priest, went out to meet him and showed him a copy of the Book of Daniel in which Alexander was clearly mentioned. Alexander was so impressed by this that, instead of destroying Jerusalem, he entered the city peaceably and worshiped at the temple.

These arguments clearly contradict the liberal critics; yet there are those who blindly ignore them. It is not in the purview of these brief comments to enter into useless argument and fight again about that which has already been settled. I simply want to say that I accept the findings of conservative scholarship that the man Daniel was not a deceiver and that his book was not a forgery. I feel the statement of Pusey is apropos here: "The rest which has been said is mostly mere insolent assumptions against Scripture, grounded on unbelief." Sir Isaac Newton declared, "To reject Daniel is to reject the Christian religion."

Furthermore, our Lord Jesus called the Pharisees "hypocrites," but He called Daniel "the prophet" (see Matt. 24:15; Mark 13:14). Very frankly, I go along with the Lord Jesus who, by the way, never reversed His statement. The endorsement of the Lord Jesus Christ is valid and sufficient for every believer, whether or not he has examined the arguments of the critics, and it satisfies the sincere saint without his having to study the answers of conservative scholarship.

We know more about Daniel the man than we do of any other prophet. He gives us a personal account of his life from the time he was carried captive to Babylon in the third year of the reign of Jehoiakim (about 606 B.C.) until the first year of King Cyrus (about 536 B.C.). Daniel's life and ministry bridge the entire seventy years of captivity. At the beginning of the book he is a boy in his teens. At the end he is an old man of fourscore and more years.

Here is God's estimate of the man Daniel: "O Daniel, a man greatly beloved" (Dan. 10:11). I would not want to be one of those critics who have called the Book of Daniel a forgery. Someday I am going to face Daniel in heaven and find that he has a pretty good reputation—"a man greatly beloved."

There are three words which characterize Daniel's life: purpose, prayer, and prophecy.

1. Daniel was a man of *purpose* (Dan. 1:8; 6:10). When the king made a decree that everyone had to eat the same thing, Daniel and his friends decided they would abide by the law of Moses—and they did. Daniel was a man of purpose, and we can see this all the way through his book. Here was a man who stood on his own two feet and had the intestinal fortitude to speak God's Word.

God have pity today on men who claim to be His messengers to the world but haven't got the courage to declare the Word of God. I also thank God that there are many who are declaring the whole Word of God, including prophecy, in our day. You see, the proper study of prophecy will not lead us to sensationalism and fanaticism, but it will lead us to a life of holiness and fear of God. John said in 1 John 3:3, "And every man that hath this hope in him purifieth himself, even as he is pure." The study of prophecy will purify our lives, my friend.

2. Daniel was a man of *prayer* (Dan. 2:17–23; 6:10; 9:3–19; 10). There are several incidents recorded in this book about Daniel's prayer life. By the way, prayer got Daniel into the lion's den. How about that for answered prayer? Well, God also miraculously saved him from the lions. Daniel was a man of prayer.

3. Daniel was a man of *prophecy.* The Book of Daniel divides itself equally: the first half is history, and the last half is prophecy. Daniel gives us the skeleton of prophecy on which all prophecy is placed. The image in Nebuchadnezzar's dream (Dan. 2) and the beasts (Dan. 7) are the backbone of prophecy; the Seventy Weeks (Dan. 9) are the ribs which fit into their proper place.

The key verse to the Book of Daniel is Daniel 2:44: "And in the days of these kings shall the God of heaven set up a kingdom, which shall never be destroyed: and the kingdom shall not be left to other people, but it shall break in pieces and consume all these kingdoms, and it shall stand for ever."

Dr. G. Campbell Morgan gave this theme

for the Book of Daniel: "Persistent Government of God in the Government of the World." This is the book of the universal sovereignty of God. Prophecy is here interwoven with history to show that God is overruling the idolatry, blasphemy, self-will, and intolerance of the Gentiles.

More specially, Daniel 12:4 brings together ". . . the times of the Gentiles . . ." (Luke 21:24) and "the time of the end" (see also Dan. 8:17; 11:35, 40) for the nation Israel in the Great Tribulation Period. This coming crisis eventuates in Christ's setting up the millennial kingdom. "But thou, O Daniel, shut up the words, and seal the book, even to the time of the end: many shall run to and fro, and knowledge shall be increased" (Dan. 12:4).

The Book of Daniel deals with political issues apart from ecclesiastical matters, giving the final outcome of events and issues which are at work in the world today. He answers the question—Who will rule the world?—not, How will the world be converted?

The Book of Daniel is the key to understanding other Scriptures. Our Lord, in the Olivet Discourse, quoted only from the Book of Daniel. The Book of Revelation is largely an enigma without the Book of Daniel. Paul's revelation concerning the ". . . man of sin . . ." (2 Thess. 2:3) needs Daniel's account for amplification and clarification.

# OUTLINE

I. **The Historic Night with Prophetic Light, Chapters 1–6**
   A. Decline of Judah; Fall of Jerusalem; Daniel Taken Captive to Babylon; His Decision to be True to God, Chapter 1
   B. Dream of Nebuchadnezzar about a Multimetallic Image; Interpretation by Daniel Concerning the Four Kingdoms of "The Times of the Gentiles," Chapter 2
   C. Decree of Nebuchadnezzar to Enforce Universal Idolatry; Three Hebrews Cast into the Furnace for Refusal to Bow to Image of Gold, Chapter 3
   D. Dream of Nebuchadnezzar about a Great Tree Hewn Down to a Stump; Fulfilled in Subsequent Period of Madness of the King, Chapter 4
   E. Downfall of Babylon Foretold by Daniel as He Read the Handwriting on the Wall at the Feast of Belshazzar, Chapter 5
   F. Decree of Darius, the Median, to Enforce Worship of Himself; Daniel Cast into Den of Lions for Praying to the God of Heaven, Chapter 6

II. **The Prophetic Light in the Historic Night, Chapters 7–12**
   A. Daniel's Vision of Four Beasts Concerning Four Kingdoms of "The Times of the Gentiles," Chapter 7
   B. Daniel's Vision of Ram and He Goat and Another Little Horn, Chapter 8
   C. Daniel's Vision of Seventy Weeks Concerning the Nation of Israel, Chapter 9
   D. Daniel's Vision Relating to Israel in Immediate Future and Latter Days; Historical Little Horn and Little Horn of the Latter Days, Chapters 10–12
      1. Preparation for Vision by Prayer of Daniel; Appearance of a Heavenly Messenger, Chapter 10
      2. Prophecy Concerning Persia and Grecia, Historical "Little Horn"; Eschatological "Little Horn," Chapter 11
      3. Preview of Israel in Latter Days; Great Tribulation; Resurrections; Rewards; Final Word about The End Times, Chapter 12

# CHAPTER 1

*THEME: Decline of Judah and Fall of Jerusalem; Daniel decides to be true to God; Delight of Nebuchadnezzar in the development of Daniel and his three friends*

## DECLINE OF JUDAH AND FALL OF JERUSALEM

**In the third year of the reign of Jehoiakim king of Judah came Nebuchadnezzar king of Babylon unto Jerusalem, and besieged it [Dan. 1:1].**

Jehoiakim was placed on the throne of Judah by Pharaoh Nechoh to succeed his brother, Jehoahaz. Both of these evil men were sons of Josiah, the godly king who led in the last revival in Judah (see 2 Kings 23:31–37). Jehoiakim's name was actually Eliakim. During his reign Nebuchadnezzar first came against Jerusalem. The year was about 606 B.C.; he took the city in about 604 B.C. The city was not destroyed, but the first group of captives was taken to Babylon. Among these were Daniel, his three friends, and literally thousands of others.

When Jehoiakim died, his son Jehoiachin came to the throne. He rebelled against Nebuchadnezzar who, in 598 BC., again besieged Jerusalem. Once more Jerusalem was not destroyed, but the king, his mother, and all the vessels of the house of the Lord were taken away to Babylon, along with an even larger group of captives. Evidently among this latter group was Ezekiel (see 2 Kings 24:6–16).

Zedekiah, the uncle of Jehoiachin, was subsequently made king and also rebelled against Nebuchadnezzar. This time Nebuchadnezzar came against the city, destroyed the temple, and burned Jerusalem. The sons of Zedekiah were slain in his presence, and then his own eyes were put out. He, along with the final deportation, went into captivity about 588 or 587 B.C. All this, by the way, was in fulfillment of Jeremiah's prophecy in Jeremiah 25:8–13. Both Jeremiah and Ezekiel had told the people that the false prophets were wrong and that Jerusalem would be destroyed. These two men just happened to have been right.

**And the Lord gave Jehoiakim king of Judah into his hand, with part of the vessels of the house of God: which he carried into the land of Shinar to the house of his god; and he brought the vessels into the treasure house of his god [Dan. 1:2].**

Only some of the vessels were taken to Babylon at this time; the remainder were removed when Jehoiachin surrendered (see 2 Kings 24:13). Nebuchadnezzar took these vessels and carried them into the land of Shinar to the house of his god. We want to keep this in mind, because later on King Belshazzar (probably a grandson of Nebuchadnezzar) will bring them out for his banquet.

**And the king spake unto Ashpenaz the master of his eunuchs, that he should bring certain of the children of Israel, and of the king's seed, and of the princes [Dan. 1:3].**

Nebuchadnezzar always took for himself the cream of the crop of the captives from any nation. I think they were given tests to determine their IQ's, and those selected were trained to be wise men to advise the king of Babylon. We will find that Daniel was included in this group and that the king did consult them.

"And the king spake unto Ashpenaz the master of his *eunuchs*." Verse 9 of this chapter also says: "Now God had brought Daniel into favour and tender love with the prince of the *eunuchs*." Daniel and his three friends were made eunuchs in fulfillment of Isaiah 39:7, "And of thy sons that shall issue from thee, which thou shalt beget, shall they take away; and they shall be eunuchs in the palace of the king of Babylon."

Most conservative scholars agree that Daniel was taken captive when he was about seventeen years old. He was made a eunuch, and so you can understand why Daniel never married or had any children. Some people wonder what kind of an oddball Daniel was. Actually, he was no oddball—this was something the king did, and it did not destroy the mental development of these young men. It served the purpose of making them more docile toward the king, and it also enabled them to give all their time to the studies which were given to them. I am sure that it is true today as it was when I was in college: I spent half of my time taking a "course" that was known as dating. I had a lot of good times—I did a great deal of studying, but I could have done lots more! But, you see, the king wanted

these boys to spend their time studying, and his way of doing that was to make them eunuchs. Daniel was in this group.

**Children in whom was no blemish, but well favoured, and skilful in all wisdom, and cunning in knowledge, and understanding science, and such as had ability in them to stand in the king's palace, and whom they might teach the learning and the tongue of the Chaldeans [Dan. 1:4].**

I want to submit to you that the Bible was not written by a bunch of ninnies—it wasn't written by men who were ignorant. Moses was learned in all the wisdom of Egypt. The Egyptians were quite advanced; they knew the distance to the sun, and they knew that the earth was round. It was a few Greeks who came along later and flattened out the earth. They were the "scientists" in that day, you see. Science taught that the earth was flat. The Bible never did teach that; in fact, it said it was a circle (see Isa. 40:22). Daniel, too, as a young man was outstanding. He must have rated high on the list of these young men who were given tests in the court of Nebuchadnezzar. The apostle Paul, who wrote much of the New Testament, was up in that bracket intellectually also. All these were brilliant young men who were exposed to the learning of their day. I get weary of these so-called eggheads who act as if the Bible was written by a group of ignoramuses. If you feel that way about it, you are mistaken. Daniel was nobody's fool. He was a brilliant young man, and he was taught as few men have been taught. Don't despise the learning of that day. There were many men who were well advanced in knowledge, in science, and in many other areas. Daniel is going to be exposed to all that.

**And the king appointed them a daily provision of the king's meat, and of the wine which he drank: so nourishing them three years, that at the end thereof they might stand before the king [Dan. 1:5].**

"Meat" could be translated "food." This, of course, was the diet of pagans, and it would include unclean animals. Remember that Daniel was a Jew and was under the Mosaic Law. They had been told not to eat certain meats, certain fowl, and certain fish.

## DANIEL DECIDES TO BE TRUE TO GOD

**Now among these were of the children of Judah, Daniel, Hananiah, Mishael, and Azariah:**

**Unto whom the prince of the eunuchs gave names: for he gave unto Daniel the name of Belteshazzar; and to Hananiah, of Shadrach; and to Mishael, of Meshach; and to Azariah, of Abed-nego [Dan. 1:6-7].**

The prince of the eunuchs actually changes their Hebrew names and gives them pagan names. He gave Daniel the name of *Belteshazzar* which means "worshiper of Baal," a heathen god. He named Hananiah Shadrach, and Mishael Meshach, and Azariah Abed-nego. Notice that the names with which we are acquainted are the heathen names. I think maybe these four boys registered the highest IQ's of the whole group. You see, Babylon wanted the best brains as well as good physical specimens.

These four young men from Judah are singled out and identified to us, and the reason is that they are going to take a stand for God. If all these boys were the same age as Daniel, I would say they were around seventeen years of age. Dr. Arno C. Gaebelein, who was a very able expositor of the Old Testament and especially of the prophetic books, felt that Daniel was about fourteen years old. Sir Robert Anderson gave him the age of around twenty. Therefore, seventeen would be a good conservative estimate of the age of these four.

**But Daniel purposed in his heart that he would not defile himself with the portion of the king's meat, nor with the wine which he drank: therefore he requested of the prince of the eunuchs that he might not defile himself [Dan. 1:8].**

This boy takes a real stand for God, and he does it in a heathen court. Under normal circumstances, this would have been fatal. Obviously, Daniel was not trying to win a popularity contest. He wasn't attempting to please Nebuchadnezzar. His decision did not reflect the modern softness of compromise which we find all around us today; nor was it dictated by the false philosophies of "How to Win Friends and Influence People" and "The Power of Positive Thinking." Daniel knew nothing of the opportunist's policy of "When in

Babylon, do as the Babylonians do." Daniel was not conformed to this world, but he was transformed by the renewing of his mind, and the will of God was the all-absorbing purpose of his life.

Daniel and his friends represented in their day that Jewish remnant which God has had in all ages. This is the remnant of which Paul spoke in Romans 11:5—"Even so then at this present time also there is a remnant according to the election of grace."

Now these boys don't want to eat the king's food; they are going to rebel against a Babylonian diet. Actually, an attempt will be made to brainwash these young men, to make them Babylonians inwardly and outwardly. They were supposed to eat like Babylonians, dress like Babylonians, and think like Babylonians.

However, Daniel and his friends were under the Mosaic system, and God made what they were to eat very clear to His people in the Old Testament. We read in Leviticus 11:44–47: "For I am the LORD your God: ye shall therefore sanctify yourselves, and ye shall be holy; for I am holy: neither shall ye defile yourselves with any manner of creeping thing that creepeth upon the earth. For I am the LORD that bringeth you up out of the land of Egypt, to be your God: ye shall therefore be holy, for I am holy. This is the law of the beasts, and of the fowl, and of every living creature that moveth in the waters, and of every creature that creepeth upon the earth: To make a difference between the unclean and the clean, and between the beast that may be eaten and the beast that may not be eaten." Certain meats were specifically forbidden, and they are listed in the Book of Leviticus; also, meats offered to heathen idols were repulsive to godly Israelites.

Perhaps Daniel and these other Hebrew children were Nazarites to whom even wine was forbidden: "He shall separate himself from wine and strong drink, and shall drink no vinegar of wine, or vinegar of strong drink, neither shall he drink any liquor of grapes, nor eat moist grapes, or dried" (Num. 6:3).

These young men were following the injunction of Isaiah: "Depart ye, depart ye, go ye out from thence, touch no unclean thing; go ye out of the midst of her; be ye clean, that bear the vessels of the LORD" (Isa. 52:11).

However, believers today have not been given a diet chart or menu. Paul tells us in 1 Corinthians 10:25–27: "Whatsoever is sold in the shambles [that is, out yonder in the meat market], that eat, asking no question for conscience sake: For the earth is the Lord's, and the fulness thereof. If any of them that believe not bid you to a feast, and ye be disposed to go; whatsoever is set before you, eat, asking no question for conscience sake." Then again, in 1 Corinthians 8:8, he says, "But meat commendeth us not to God: for neither, if we eat, are we the better; neither, if we eat not, are we the worse."

These Hebrew young men were taking a stand under the Mosaic Law, and they were taking a stand for God.

**Now God had brought Daniel into favour and tender love with the prince of the eunuchs [Dan. 1:9].**

Now, you see, Daniel is already a favorite, and that is no accident. God was working on Daniel's behalf, even as He worked in the life of Joseph down in the land of Egypt.

**And the prince of the eunuchs said unto Daniel, I fear my lord the king, who hath appointed your meat and your drink: for why should he see your faces worse liking than the children which are of your sort? then shall ye make me endanger my head to the king [Dan. 1:10].**

The prince of the eunuchs did not want to force the diet upon them, but he was really on a hot seat. He was caught between a rock and a hard place. He liked Daniel, but what was he to do?

**Then said Daniel to Melzar whom the prince of the eunuchs had set over Daniel, Hananiah, Mishael, and Azariah,**

**Prove thy servants, I beseech thee, ten days; and let them give us pulse to eat, and water to drink [Dan. 1:11–12].**

"Pulse"—some translators have felt that this means vegetables, but I don't think that is exactly it. Actually, it was a grain they wanted to eat. To tell the truth, what Daniel was saying was, "Let us have our pulse, and in a few days we'll show you that we are all right, that we are in just as good physical condition as the others are."

**Then let our countenances be looked upon before thee, and the countenance of the children that eat of the portion of the king's meat: and as thou seest, deal with thy servants [Dan. 1:13].**

In other words: "Test us out, and put us on this diet for a few days to see if we are not in

as good condition as the other fellows are." Well, God had brought favor from this man Melzar to Daniel, and so Melzar is going to make the test.

The Bible tells us that Daniel's decision to refuse the Babylonian diet was something he "purposed in his heart." I want to comment for a moment on this issue of making Christian living and separation from the world a matter of a few little rules that have to do with eating and with conduct. There is always a tendency in this area to be dogmatic and forbid certain questionable things, things which are actually debatable.

I received a letter once from a lady who joined a small group shortly after she had become a Christian, and they told her there were certain things she couldn't do and certain things she could do. In the letter which she wrote to me she said, "I have followed all these rules, and yet I am still miserable."

In the history of the church we can see times when people set up a system of doing things and not doing things—systems that actually were *good* at first. For example, the monasteries which began in the Roman Empire were actually a protest against the licentiousness of their day. But before long it was worse on the inside of the monastery than on the outside.

Remember that Christ said to the Pharisees, ". . . Now do ye Pharisees make clean the outside of the cup and the platter; but your inward part is full of ravening and wickedness" (Luke 11:39). In other words, "You make the outside of the cup clean, but inside it's dirty. It is just like whitewashing a tomb." Today it is "Not by works of righteousness which we have done, but according to his mercy he saved us, by the washing of regeneration, and renewing of the Holy Ghost" (Titus 3:5). In order to live a life of holiness, we must first receive new life from God—we must be born from above.

"Daniel purposed in his heart" (v. 8)—it all began in the heart of Daniel. He was not a papier-mâché; he had a heart, and his convictions came from his heart. That should be our experience also. We are captives in this world in which we live; gravitation holds all of us by the seat of our pants, and we cannot jump off this earth. The Lord Jesus said that we are in the world, but not of the world. And He said, ". . . Ye cannot serve God and mammon" (Matt. 6:24). However, we cannot serve God by following a set of rules; we must have a purpose in our hearts. Jesus said that it was out of the heart that the issues of life proceed;

the things which we put into our bodies are not the most important. Daniel purposed in his heart that he would obey God's law given to God's people Israel—this was to be his testimony.

**So he consented to them in this matter, and proved them ten days [Dan. 1:14].**

The prince of the eunuchs was rather reluctant to go along with Daniel's suggestion because he had been brought up in Babylonian culture and believed that this diet was the thing which produced geniuses. However, he liked Daniel and gave them ten days to test it out.

## DELIGHT OF NEBUCHADNEZZAR IN THE DEVELOPMENT OF DANIEL AND HIS THREE FRIENDS

**And at the end of ten days their countenances appeared fairer and fatter in flesh than all the children which did eat the portion of the king's meat [Dan. 1:15].**

Daniel's diet worked in their behalf. This ought to tell us something. God wanted His people Israel to be different from the surrounding nations, but He did not give them a special diet just to make them different—there was also a health factor involved. I firmly believe that if we followed the diet outlined in Leviticus, we would be healthier than our neighbor who eats just anything. But we *can* eat anything we want; we are not under the law. I have found, though, that it is a matter of health. I have had a number of physical problems and have discovered, among other things, that pork just isn't the best thing for us. Israel's God-given diet was very meaningful healthwise, and it had more than just a ceremonial basis for it.

**Thus Melzar took away the portion of their meat, and the wine that they should drink; and gave them pulse.**

**As for these four children, God gave them knowledge and skill in all learning and wisdom: and Daniel had understanding in all visions and dreams [Dan. 1:16–17].**

Just as God blessed Solomon, God is blessing these Hebrew children who were in a foreign court. Daniel will eventually become prime minister to two great world empires.

"Daniel had understanding in all visions and dreams." Daniel was still in the time of revela-

tion, the time in which God used dreams and visions. Now don't *you* say that God has spoken to you in a dream, because I must contradict you. I do not think that God is speaking to us that way—He speaks to us today in His Word.

For a great many people it is easier to *dream* about the Word than it is to *study* it. I used to have students in a Bible institute who would very piously pray the night before an exam. They didn't study much, but they were very pious about it all. One student told me that he stuck his Bible under his pillow the night before an examination! I asked him, "Do you really think the names of the kings of Israel and Judah will come up through the duck feathers and get into your brain?" The Holy Spirit is not a help and a crutch for a lazy person. You are going to have to *study* the Word of God. God speaks to us through His written Word today.

However, God is speaking audibly to Daniel, for he is now writing one of the books of the Bible. In spite of what the critics say, Daniel wrote it—it was not written three or four hundred years later.

**Now at the end of the days that the king had said he should bring them in, then the prince of the eunuchs brought them in before Nebuchadnezzar [Dan. 1:18].**

Nebuchadnezzar is going to look at the training which was given to them to see if it has been the proper training. I honestly believe the Communists have been very stupid in their methods of brainwashing. They attempt to break a man down. You can break down any human being; he will finally give in, of course. A man can only take so much. But this man Nebuchadnezzar really knew how to do it. He gave them a lot of food, he tested them, and finally he placed them in a fine position. He did all this in a friendly way. This was his philosophy, his way of making friends and influencing people.

**And the king communed with them; and among them all was found none like Daniel, Hananiah, Mishael, and Azariah: therefore stood they before the king [Dan. 1:19].**

Nebuchadnezzar talked with those four boys and found they were geniuses, and so he gave them good positions in his kingdom.

**And in all matters of wisdom and understanding, that the king inquired of them, he found them ten times better than all the magicians and astrologers that were in all his realm [Dan. 1:20].**

Daniel is moved to the head of the class.

**And Daniel continued even unto the first year of king Cyrus [Dan. 1:21].**

With verse 1 and this verse we can learn Daniel's life span. Coming to Babylon at about the age of seventeen, he died when he was about ninety years of age. He bridged the entire seventy years of captivity. He did not return to Israel but apparently died before the people left Babylon. We actually have no record about that.

# CHAPTER 2

*THEME: The dream of Nebuchadnezzar about a multimetallic image, and the interpretation of Daniel concerning the four kingdoms of "the times of the Gentiles"*

We are in one of the great sections of the Word of God as far as prophecy is concerned. The multimetallic image (ch. 2), the four beasts (ch. 7), and the seventy weeks of Daniel (ch. 9) form the backbone and ribs of biblical prophecy. You could never have a skeleton of prophecy without these passages of Scripture in the Old Testament.

Everything the Lord Jesus said in the Olivet Discourse was based on the Book of Daniel. The disciples asked Him, ". . . Tell us, when shall these things be? and what shall be the sign of thy coming, and of the end of the world?" He replied, "When ye therefore shall see the abomination of desolation, spoken of by Daniel the prophet . . ." (Matt. 24:3, 15). This chapter, then, is a very important chapter in the Word of God.

Men everywhere are asking, "What is this world coming to? How are things going to be

worked out today? There are crises everywhere." My friend, the times of the Gentiles are going to run out. The Gentiles have not done a very good job of running the world. We can see the beginning of that way back in the Book of Daniel, and we may come close to seeing the end of it. However, the church of Jesus Christ will leave this earth before the fullness of the Gentiles comes in; and, when the church leaves, Christ will come back to the earth to rule.

This prophetic chapter is basic to the understanding of all prophecy. That is why I keep insisting that to know just a few little verses of Scripture and to be able to interpret them can be a dangerous thing. This is the way the cults begin: they use only certain verses of Scripture. The men who start these cults understand history and human nature; they know man's need for a doctrine which satisfies the natural mind. Liberalism and the social gospel appeal to the natural mind.

A young preacher in the East told me of a minister in a neighboring town who was building a great empire of his church. Yet that man drinks and curses and goes out with the boys, probably doing everything else the boys do. The young preacher asked me, "How is that man drawing people to his church? They come to hear him and to join his church—not mine. But I am attempting to preach the Word of God!" I told that young man that we need to realize that if we are going to represent God in the ministry, we are going to be in the minority. The other minister was appealing to the natural mind. He may have baptized many—he may have got them under the water and got a lot of water on them—but he had not led people to a saving knowledge of Christ.

Saint Augustine, who became a great man of God, was asked why he had succumbed earlier to the Manichean heresy of his day. He replied that it was "so complete and reasonable." The philosophical approach used by so many preachers today is probably the most dangerous approach to the Word of God that is imaginable. They never think to go to the Word of God as the foundation and the authority. Rather, they want to give you the interpretation of some man of the past, such as Plato. When I was preparing to enter the ministry, that is the direction I wanted to take because it appeals to people and it shows how smart you are. Thank God that I got under the assistance and influence of two men who put me on the track of simply teaching the Bible, letting the chips fall where they may. It is so important to study the *entire* Word of God, and therefore this section is important to us.

## THE DREAM OF NEBUCHADNEZZAR AND HIS DEMANDS UPON THE WISE MEN OF BABYLON

**And in the second year of the reign of Nebuchadnezzar, Nebuchadnezzar dreamed dreams, wherewith his spirit was troubled, and his sleep brake from him [Dan. 2:1].**

I am confident that Nebuchadnezzar, who had now been lifted and exalted to a very high position, wondered about this great empire that had come into existence under his leadership. Actually, Babylon was the first great world empire. Nebuchadnezzar had done something that the Egyptians had not been able to do because Egypt was self-contained. The biggest mistake any pharaoh ever made was to leave the Nile River. If he just stayed there, he was well protected—he had a wall of desert around him which nobody could breach. All he needed to do was guard the Nile River which was the only entrance into Egypt. The Egyptians began to reach out, but they never did become what you would call a world empire, although they did influence the world as few nations have.

However, this man Nebuchadnezzar began as a petty chieftain and united several tribes. Then he took over the Assyrian empire, then the Syrian, and he was on the march. And he overcame the Egyptians. The Greeks would have been unable to offer resistance, but he made no effort to move in their direction. He didn't need to, as he was actually ruling the then-known world. Nebuchadnezzar had to think this thing over, and when he did, he found he had a world empire on his hands. It was sort of like the old bromide about getting a lion by the tail—you can't hold on and you can't turn him loose. That is the position Nebuchadnezzar was in, and God spoke to him at that time.

This man was troubled in his sleep, wondering about the future of this great empire he had founded: Where was it all going to end? Do you know that after about 2500 years of human history since Nebuchadnezzar we are still wondering about that. We have the answer here in this chapter, by the way.

**Then the king commanded to call the magicians, and the astrologers, and the sorcerers, and the Chaldeans, for to shew the king his dreams. So they came and stood before the king [Dan. 2:2].**

Nebuchadnezzar called in all his wise men. These were the men who had been trained even as Daniel and his friends had been trained. They were the old boys who were called in for this conference. In other words, the king summoned his cabinet.

These wise men were men of great intellect and learning. It is true that they held many superstitions and concepts of a heathen religion, but, my friend, I don't know how much farther we've come today. I know some Ph.D.'s who reject the Bible—I think they are heathen and a little superstitious, by the way. Isn't it interesting that the Bible has been ruled out of our schools; yet they are teaching astrology and all kinds of superstitions which have been rejected by civilized people in the past. Don't look down on the wise men of Babylon—they are just as smart as some of our Ph.D.'s and Th.D.'s today.

These men comprised the brain trust of Babylon, and they were brought before the king to hear his unique command:

**And the king said unto them, I have dreamed a dream, and my spirit was troubled to know the dream [Dan. 2:3].**

The king explains that he has had an unusual dream which he believes to have some far-reaching significance. You see, God made it clear to him that He had something to say, but this man in his darkness knew only that it was something important.

**Then spake the Chaldeans to the king in Syriac, O king, live for ever: tell thy servants the dream, and we will shew the interpretation [Dan. 2:4].**

"Then spake the Chaldeans to the king in Syriac, O king, live for ever." To me that seems to be about the silliest thing they could ever say, but that was the way they flattered the king—"O king, live for ever." I am sure that many a king who sat there on the throne had a heart condition and might well have said, "Well, boys, you are wrong. I'm not going to live forever. I'm going to have a heart attack one of these days, and I won't be around." However, they seem to have avoided that issue.

It is important to note that at this juncture in the Book of Daniel there is a change from the Hebrew to the Aramaic or Syriac language, as it is called here in verse 4. From verse 4 of this chapter through verse 28 of chapter 7, the book is written in Aramaic or Syriac. Aramaic was the court language, the diplomatic language of that day. It was the language of the Gentiles, the language of the world. It would correspond to what French was a few years ago; today I think English is the language that has supplanted French in that position.

The significance of this change is quite remarkable: God is now speaking to *the world*, not just to His nation. Israel has gone into Babylonian captivity. God has taken the scepter out of the line of David, and He has put it in gentile hands. It will stay there until the day He takes the scepter back. When He does, nail-pierced hands will take the scepter, because it is God's intention for Jesus to reign.

The subject here is a worldwide kingdom. The idea that the Word of God is confined to some local deity and that the Bible has quite a limited view is entirely wrong. If we examine it carefully, we find that God has in mind a worldwide kingdom. In Psalm 89:27 He says of the covenant He made with David: "Also I will make him my firstborn, higher than the kings of the earth." Then in verses 34–37 of the same psalm He says: "My covenant will I not break, nor alter the thing that is gone out of my lips. Once have I sworn by my holiness that I will not lie unto David. His seed shall endure for ever, and his throne as the sun before me. It shall be established for ever as the moon, and as a faithful witness in heaven." In other words, God is saying, "If you can go out and see that the sun has disappeared from the heaven and the moon is not out at night, then you will know that I have changed My mind; but as long as you see the sun and moon, you will know that I am going to put *My* king over this earth."

We are talking now about that which is global and not some local situation. This concerns the first great world ruler, and the language used is the language of the world of that day.

**The king answered and said to the Chaldeans, The thing is gone from me: if ye will not make known unto me the dream, with the interpretation thereof, ye shall be cut in pieces, and your houses shall be made a dunghill [Dan. 2:5].**

This would be a rather extreme judgment, but you can see what the king wants. Frankly, a faulty translation of this verse gives the impression that the king had forgotten his dream. He hadn't forgotten his dream. He knows the dream, senses its importance, and refuses to divulge it to the wise men. Why? He wants to get a correct interpretation of it.

In the margin, the American Standard Version of 1901 translates "The *thing* is gone from me" as, "The *word* is gone forth from me." In other words, Nebuchadnezzar is saying to these men, "I will not change my mind about this judgment I am pronouncing. Don't beg me to tell you the dream—I'm not going to do it. You are going to come up with the dream if I am to listen to your interpretation of it." The Berkeley Version has a helpful translation at this point also: "The king answered the Chaldeans, 'This word I speak, I mean! If you do not tell me the dream and what it means, you shall be torn limb from limb and your houses will be destroyed.'" That translation really tones it down, but nevertheless the penalty is still excessive and extreme. Nebuchadnezzar is putting fear in these men. They have to come up with the interpretation of the dream, but they first of all have to give what the dream is.

**But if ye shew the dream, and the interpretation thereof, ye shall receive of me gifts and rewards and great honour: therefore shew me the dream, and the interpretation thereof [Dan. 2:6].**

Conversely, Nebuchadnezzar could be generous and charitable. This man was greatly governed by his emotions, as we are going to see. He tells them, "I am going to amply reward you if you give me the correct interpretation."

**They answered again and said, Let the king tell his servants the dream, and we will shew the interpretation of it [Dan. 2:7].**

The wise men realized their dangerous predicament, and they again cautiously suggest to the king that he supply the dream and they will supply the interpretation.

**The king answered and said, I know of certainty that ye would gain the time, because ye see the thing is gone from me [Dan. 2:8].**

The king says, "You see that I mean business and so you are stalling. You want a little more time." The Berkeley Version clarifies this verse: "The king replied, 'I see plainly that you are trying to gain time; because you see how capital punishment awaits you.'" That is taking a little liberty with the translation, but that actually is the meaning of it.

**But if ye will not make known unto me the dream, there is but one decree for you: for ye have prepared lying and cor-**rupt words to speak before me, till the time be changed: therefore tell me the dream, and I shall know that ye can shew me the interpretation thereof [Dan. 2:9].**

The king really reveals here his lack of confidence in the wise men of Babylon. I think they probably had failed him on previous assignments, just as the prophets of Baal failed old Ahab (but since Ahab died in battle, he didn't have a chance to retaliate). Nebuchadnezzar feels these men have been feeding him a great deal of malarkey, and he is now putting them to a real test. His reasoning at this point is very logical: If they can tell him his dream, then it is reasonable to conclude that their interpretation is genuine. If they cannot tell him his dream, any interpretation would be under suspicion.

## DECREE TO DESTROY THE WISE MEN FOR THEIR FAILURE

**The Chaldeans answered before the king, and said, There is not a man upon the earth that can shew the king's matter: therefore there is no king, lord, nor ruler, that asked such things at any magician, or astrologer, or Chaldean [Dan. 2:10].**

This is the first true statement the wise men have made—no man on earth could give the dream, only God could. In desperation they are pleading for their lives, trying to show the unreasonableness of the king's demand. If you leave out the supernatural, of course his demands are unreasonable. However, they have made claim to be superior, and he is asking them to demonstrate that.

**And it is a rare thing that the king requireth, and there is none other that can shew it before the king, except the gods, whose dwelling is not with flesh [Dan. 2:11].**

What they are saying is that they have no communication with heaven. They even confessed that their gods were not giving them very much information. They conclude their argument by saying that no human being could meet the king's demands. This paves the way for Daniel to come onto the scene.

**For this cause the king was angry and very furious, and commanded to destroy all the wise men of Babylon [Dan. 2:12].**

The king exhibits here a violent temper for which he was noted. It is another symptom of the psychosis he is suffering and which we will see later on. The king orders the wise men to be destroyed summarily.

**And the decree went forth that the wise men should be slain; and they sought Daniel and his fellows to be slain [Dan. 2:13].**

The king's decree includes Daniel and his brethren. Although they are just being trained, they are being taught by the same crowd in which the king has now lost confidence. The rash order to destroy the wise men of Babylon is going to take in a great many men who were really innocent and who could not be held responsible. The dictatorship of Nebuchadnezzar could be carried to the *nth* degree—he could do what he wanted to.

## DANIEL'S DESIRE TO TELL THE DREAM

**Then Daniel answered with counsel and wisdom to Arioch the captain of the king's guard, which was gone forth to slay the wise men of Babylon:**

**He answered and said to Arioch the king's captain, Why is the decree so hasty from the king? Then Arioch made the thing known to Daniel [Dan. 2:14–15].**

Daniel is really puzzled at the hasty and unjust decree of the king, but he uses tact as he approaches Arioch. Arioch is the captain of the king's guard—he is in charge of the Secret Service of that day—and, naturally, is often in the presence of the king. It would be interesting to know all that Arioch communicated to Daniel. I wonder if he suggested to Daniel that the king was off his rocker or that the king didn't have all his marbles. It is not recorded here if he did, but I think he touched his head and said, "You know how the king is!"

**Then Daniel went in, and desired of the king that he would give him time, and that he would shew the king the interpretation [Dan. 2:16].**

Daniel got an audience with the king—he is already in favor—and he requested the king to give him time to tell him the dream. This seems presumptuous; in fact, it seems to be the act of a very brash young man. However, succeeding events will reveal that it was the confidence of a man with faith in God.

**Then Daniel went to his house, and made the thing known to Hananiah, Mishael, and Azariah, his companions:**

**That they would desire mercies of the God of heaven concerning this secret; that Daniel and his fellows should not perish with the rest of the wise men of Babylon [Dan. 2:17–18].**

"That they would desire mercies of *the God of heaven.*" This is an expression which you will find only in the books of the captivity, including Ezra, Nehemiah, and Daniel. You see, after the departure of the glory of God from Jerusalem, from the Holy of Holies in the temple, He is now addressed as "the God of heaven." These Hebrew young men knew that God did not dwell in some little temple in Jerusalem. He is "the God of heaven."

"That they would desire *mercies*" reveals the basis of their prayers. God does not answer prayer because of the worth or the effort or the character or the works of the one who is praying. All prayer must rest upon His mercy. To pray today in Jesus' name simply means that we come to God, not on our merit, but on His merit, looking to Him for mercy.

## DANIEL DESCRIBES THE DREAM AS A MULTIMETALLIC IMAGE

**Then was the secret revealed unto Daniel in a night vision. Then Daniel blessed the God of heaven [Dan. 2:19].**

I would think that the way God revealed this to Daniel was to give him the same dream He gave to Nebuchadnezzar. This would seem to be the reasonable explanation.

**Daniel answered and said, Blessed be the name of God for ever and ever: for wisdom and might are his:**

**And he changeth the times and the seasons: he removeth kings, and setteth up kings: he giveth wisdom unto the wise, and knowledge to them that know understanding:**

**He revealeth the deep and secret things: he knoweth what is in the darkness, and the light dwelleth with him.**

**I thank thee, and praise thee, O thou God of my fathers, who hast given me wisdom and might, and hast made known unto me now what we desired of thee: for thou hast now made known unto us the king's matter [Dan. 2:20–23].**

This is one of the several recorded prayers of Daniel. Daniel was a man of purpose, a man of prayer, and a man of prophecy. God alone has revealed this secret to Daniel, and this is his tremendous prayer of thanksgiving. Now Daniel is ready to go in and ask again for an audience with the king.

**Therefore Daniel went in unto Arioch, whom the king had ordained to destroy the wise men of Babylon: he went and said thus unto him, Destroy not the wise men of Babylon: bring me in before the king, and I will shew unto the king the interpretation [Dan. 2:24].**

Daniel wants to stop the bloody slaughter that would have taken place, and apparently Arioch has no heart for the matter either—he doesn't want to slay all the wise men.

**Then Arioch brought in Daniel before the king in haste, and said thus unto him, I have found a man of the captives of Judah, that will make known unto the king the interpretation [Dan. 2:25].**

Arioch rushes Daniel into the presence of the king with the good news that the dream will be divulged.

**The king answered and said to Daniel, whose name was Belteshazzar, Art thou able to make known unto me the dream which I have seen, and the interpretation thereof? [Dan. 2:26].**

Quite obviously and, I think, logically, the king was rather skeptical. All of these wise men had not been able to come up with the dream and its interpretation, but here comes this young fellow Daniel who says *he* will be able to. The king asks him, "Do you mean to tell me that all the other wise men had no answer, but you think you can answer me? Maybe this is just another attempt of the wise men to stall for time!" His question sounds rather cynical, but Daniel has a marvelous answer for him:

**Daniel answered in the presence of the king, and said, The secret which the king hath demanded cannot the wise men, the astrologers, the magicians, the soothsayers, shew unto the king;**

**But there is a God in heaven that revealeth secrets, and maketh known to the king Nebuchadnezzar what shall be in the latter days. Thy dream, and the visions of thy head upon thy bed, are these [Dan. 2:27–28].**

Daniel immediately makes a distinction between the wisdom of Babylon and the wisdom of God. The apostle Paul wrote, ". . . hath not God made foolish the wisdom of this world?" and also, ". . . the foolishness of God is wiser than men; and the weakness of God is stronger than men" (1 Cor. 1:20, 25).

Daniel now has the unique privilege of introducing to the darkened mind of this pagan king the living and true God. He says, "There is a God in heaven that revealeth secrets, and maketh known to the king Nebuchadnezzar *what shall be in the latter days*." This is very important because it is going to be the emphasis in the Book of Daniel; this dream refers to the end of the times of the Gentiles.

The end of "the times of the Gentiles" runs concurrently with "the latter days" of the nation Israel: both come to their fulfillment during the Great Tribulation Period. The day in which you and I live is "man's day." Paul said in 1 Corinthians 4:3, "But with me it is a very small thing that I should be judged of you, or of man's judgment [day]: yea, I judge not mine own self." We are living in the day of man.

It is also well to note that the term, "the times of the Gentiles," is not synonymous with the term, "the fulness of the Gentiles." Romans 11:25 says, "For I would not, brethren, that ye should be ignorant of this mystery, lest ye should be wise in your own conceits; that blindness in part is happened to Israel, until the fulness of the Gentiles be come in." The fulness of the Gentiles ends with the Rapture of the church. The terms, "the latter days" and "the times of the Gentiles," are not synonymous with "the last days" of the church which come to a fulfillment at the Rapture and *precede* the Great Tribulation. "The times of the Gentiles" will continue right on into the Great Tribulation, and at that time God will again turn His attention back to the nation Israel.

**As for thee, O king, thy thoughts came into thy mind upon thy bed, what should come to pass hereafter: and he that revealeth secrets maketh known to thee what shall come to pass [Dan. 2:29].**

Nebuchadnezzar was bothered as he lay in bed at night, wondering what the future held. Although he started out as a petty king, he now finds himself a world ruler.

**But as for me, this secret is not revealed to me for any wisdom that I have**

**more than any living, but for their sakes that shall make known the interpretation to the king, and that thou mightest know the thoughts of thy heart [Dan. 2:30].**

The dream had to do with the future of Nebuchadnezzar's kingdom and the outcome of his great world empire. Nebuchadnezzar was troubled about the future of this empire of which he suddenly found himself the possessor and dictator. The dream was God's answer to his problem.

Daniel makes it clear that he himself deserves no credit, that God in heaven has revealed the dream, that God was prompted to reveal the dream to spare the lives of the wise men as well as to satisfy the curiosity of this man Nebuchadnezzar.

God is going to speak to Nebuchadnezzar in a language that he will understand, the language of the outward splendor and glory of his kingdom. In the dream God showed him the outward splendor of his kingdom. This dream was also the dream of a Gentile, and in it God spoke to him by using an image. The image in Nebuchadnezzar's dream was not an image to be worshiped; but, because Nebuchadnezzar did fall down before images in the city of Babylon, God used an image in his dream. In this land of idolatry, such a vision was the only language Nebuchadnezzar could truly understand. Babylon was known as the fountainhead of pagan religion, the womb of heathen idols.

We will see in this section the history of the rule of this world by the Gentiles. Because of the failure of the house of David, God is now taking the scepter of this universe out from the hands of the line of David, and He is putting it in the hands of the Gentiles. It will be there until Jesus Christ comes again to this earth. Then Christ will take the scepter and rule on this earth as King of Kings and Lord of Lords. From the day of Nebuchadnezzar right on down through our day until the Lord comes to reign is "the times of the Gentiles."

**Thou, O king, sawest, and behold a great image. This great image, whose brightness was excellent, stood before thee; and the form thereof was terrible [Dan. 2:31].**

That is, the image excited terror—it was awe-inspiring. It was very glamorous, terrific, and stupendous. As Daniel began to describe the dream, I wish that I could have been there to see the expression on Nebuchadnezzar's face

change from cynicism to unconcealed amazement. When Daniel began to say, "You saw a great image, the brightness of which was terrific and stupendous," I think the eyes of Nebuchadnezzar lighted up. He shifted to the edge of his throne and said, "Boy, that's it! You are starting out right!"

**This image's head was of fine gold, his breast and his arms of silver, his belly and his thighs of brass,**

**His legs of iron, his feet part of iron and part of clay [Dan. 2:32–33].**

—gold—BABYLON

—silver—MEDIA-PERSIA

—brass—GRAECO-MACEDONIA

—iron—ROME

—clay inserted—LAST FORM OF ROMAN RULE

When Daniel said this, I think the king again said, "Boy, you are exactly right!" Now Nebuchadnezzar is prepared to listen to the interpretation. Tregelles has said of this dream: "Here all is presented as set before the king according to his ability of apprehension— the external and visible things being shown as man might regard them." As we have said, God is speaking to him in a language that he can understand.

This tremendous image that is before him just stands there. There is no movement at all. It is simply awe-inspiring, glamorous, terrific, and stupendous. The head was of gold, the breast and arms of silver, the belly and thighs of brass, the legs of iron, and the feet were iron and clay mixed together. The image

therefore consisted of a very strange assortment of metals. It was not an alloy of metals, but a multimetallic image of four metals plus a silicon (that is, sand or clay).

**Thou sawest till that a stone was cut out without hands, which smote the image upon his feet that were of iron and clay, and brake them to pieces.**

**Then was the iron, the clay, the brass, the silver, and the gold, broken to pieces together, and became like the chaff of the summer threshingfloors; and the wind carried them away, that no place was found for them: and the stone that smote the image became a great mountain, and filled the whole earth [Dan. 2:34-35].**

We will get the interpretation of this later on. We will let Daniel give the interpretation—we do not need to guess about it at all. The thing to note here is that, as Nebuchadnezzar beheld the image in awe and wonder, the stone, coming from beyond the environs of the image and without human origin or motivation, smote the image on the feet of iron and clay with such force that all the metals were pulverized. Then a wind blew the dust of the image away, so that it entirely disappeared. Then the stone began to grow as a living stone, and it filled the whole world, taking the place of this image.

## DEFINITION OF FOUR WORLD EMPIRES AND THEIR DESTINIES

**This is the dream; and we will tell the interpretation thereof before the king.**

**Thou, O king, art a king of kings: for the God of heaven hath given thee a kingdom, power, and strength, and glory.**

**And wheresoever the children of men dwell, the beasts of the field and the fowls of the heaven hath he given into thine hand, and hath made thee ruler over them all. Thou art this head of gold [Dan. 2:36-38].**

Nebuchadnezzar was the first great world ruler. I think that this was God's ideal for Adam—he was given dominion, but he lost it. The world has known four great world rulers; there have been four great nations who have attempted to rule the world. They all just butchered the job—none of them made a real success of it—but the first one, Nebuchadnezzar, did the best job.

Daniel immediately began to interpret the dream. The different metals represent world empires. Nebuchadnezzar is identified as the head of gold. He exercised rulership over the then-known world. No one questioned his authority. His was an absolute monarchy, and there have been very few since then, by the way. More is said about this Babylonian empire in other sections of the Bible, including Daniel 5:18-19 and Jeremiah 27:5-11. Through Jeremiah God said: "I have made the earth, the man and the beast that are upon the ground, by my great power and by my outstretched arm, and have given it unto whom it seemed meet unto me. And now have I given all these lands into the hand of Nebuchadnezzar the king of Babylon, my servant; and the beasts of the field have I given him also to serve him. And all nations shall serve him, and his son, and his son's son, until the very time of his land come . . ." (Jer. 27:5-7). God made Nebuchadnezzar the one at the top; He made him the first great world ruler, and there has been none like him since then.

**And after thee shall arise another kingdom inferior to thee, and another third kingdom of brass, which shall bear rule over all the earth [Dan. 2:39].**

The kingdom which will come after Nebuchadnezzar will be inferior to his. The third one will be inferior to the second, and the fourth will be inferior to the third. That means the fourth one is the worst form of all. That is where we are today.

There are two kingdoms mentioned in this verse. The arms of silver represent Media and Persia. In Daniel 5:28 we are told the future of the Babylonian kingdom: "Thy kingdom is divided, and given to the Medes and Persians." We don't need to speculate as to who the second kingdom is—it is made clear. Remember that Daniel lived in both the kingdom of Nebuchadnezzar and the kingdom of Media-Persia. We read in Daniel 6:8, "Now, O king, establish the decree, and sign the writing, that it be not changed, according to the law of the Medes and Persians, which altereth not."

The third kingdom would be a kingdom of brass and would "bear rule over all the earth." This is the Graeco-Macedonian empire of Alexander the Great.

This brings us to the fourth kingdom. It is important to note that there are only four—there is no fifth kingdom. The period of the fourth kingdom is where we are today.

**And the fourth kingdom shall be strong as iron: forasmuch as iron breaketh in**

**pieces and subdueth all things: and as iron that breaketh all these, shall it break in pieces and bruise.**

**And whereas thou sawest the feet and toes, part of potters' clay, and part of iron, the kingdom shall be divided; but there shall be in it of the strength of the iron, forasmuch as thou sawest the iron mixed with miry clay.**

**And as the toes of the feet were part of iron, and part of clay, so the kingdom shall be partly strong, and partly broken.**

**And whereas thou sawest iron mixed with miry clay, they shall mingle themselves with the seed of men: but they shall not cleave one to another, even as iron is not mixed with clay [Dan. 2:40–43].**

This is a remarkable passage of Scripture. More attention is directed to this fourth kingdom than to the other three kingdoms put together. Four verses are used here by Daniel to describe it and interpret it. Only one verse, verse 39, is used to describe the second and third kingdoms, the Media-Persian and the Graeco-Macedonian empires.

The fourth kingdom is the kingdom of the latter days. Remember that Daniel had told Nebuchadnezzar that that was the reason for the image. God is speaking to Nebuchadnezzar, an idol worshiper, through this image, and He is telling Nebuchadnezzar what shall be in the latter days. He is a world ruler, and he is concerned about where it is all going to end. My friend, we are living in the period of the latter days, and that is still the question today: What is this world coming to?

We need to stand back and look at this image again for a moment. It is awe-inspiring and of tremendous size. I think it towered over the entire plain of Babylon as Nebuchadnezzar saw it in his vision. It is a multimetallic image. It has a head of gold, and that speaks of Babylon. The breast and arms are of silver—Media-Persia. The brass is Graeco-Macedonia. The legs are of iron, and that is Rome. In the feet, clay is inserted into the iron, which is the last form of the Roman Empire.

The image represents four empires, and there are several observations to be made about them. There is a definite deterioration from one kingdom to another, and this is made clear in several very specific ways. This deterioration is contrary to modern philosophy and opinion. Our viewpoint today is that we are all getting better and better every day: evolution is at work, and it is onward and upward forever. We feel that we have the best form of government and that we are superior people—neither of which is true. The human race has always liked to pat itself on the back as Little Jack Horner did:

Little Jack Horner
Sat in the corner,
Eating of Christmas pie:
He put in his thumb,
And pulled out a plum,
And said, "What a good boy am I!"

However, what we have here is the *deterioration* from one kingdom to the other—each is inferior to its predecessor. This is revealed through the image in several ways:

1. The *quality* of the metals: gold is finer than silver, and silver is finer than brass. Brass is finer than iron, and iron is better than clay. There is definite deterioration.

2. The *specific gravity* of the metals: each metal shows deterioration; Tregelles (as quoted by Culver) is the scholar who called attention to this factor.

3. The *position* of each metal: the head has more honor than do the feet.

4. The specific *statement of Scripture:* "And after thee shall arise another kingdom inferior to thee" (v. 39). Scripture is clear that each kingdom is to be inferior to the one before it.

5. The *division of sovereignty:* the definite division of sovereignty denotes weakness. Nebuchadnezzar is the head of gold, but there are two arms of the Media-Persian empire. The Babylonian Empire was strong because there was not that division. The Graeco-Macedonian Empire begins with one, but soon is divided into four. Rome has two legs of iron, but it eventuates into ten toes which are composed of both iron and clay.

In the United States today we like to believe we have the very best form of government, and people eagerly say they "believe in democracy." Actually, our form of government is not a democracy, but a representative form of government. No one asks me to come to Washington, D.C., to make any decisions. There are many who do go to Washington to tell them how to do it, and I think somebody needs to tell them. The problem is that it is the wrong people who are doing the telling. I am of the opinion that a democracy is really not the best form of government.

God's form of government is going to be just exactly like that head of gold, only the ruler will be that Rock that is "cut out without hands"—none other than the Lord Jesus Christ. He is going to reign over this earth, and He is not going to ask anybody for advice about it. He will not have a Congress, and He will not have a Cabinet, and He will not be calling upon you to vote for Him. In fact, if you don't make a decision for Him in this life, my friend, you just won't be there at all. Don't rebel against that fact, because this happens to be His world—He created it. You and I are just little pygmies running around down here. God has as much right to remove you and me from this little world as I have to remove those ants that get into my house and yard. I set out poison for those fellows—I want to get rid of them. Why? Because they don't fit into my program. There are a lot of us who don't fit into God's program. This is His world, and He is going to make it to suit Himself.

God's form of government is going to be one of the most strict forms of government that the world has ever seen. I do not think a rooster is going to crow in that day without His permission to do so. The Lord Jesus Christ is going to be a dictator, and if you are not willing to bow to Him, I don't think you would even want to be in His kingdom when He establishes it here upon the earth. Maybe it is good that He has another place for folk like that, because it will not be pleasant for them to be here—they wouldn't enjoy it at all. God's form of government is the absolute rule of a king, the sovereignty of one ruler. It is going to be autocratic, dictatorial, and His will is going to prevail. That is the reason it is well for you and me to practice bowing to Him and acknowledging Him. He is going to take over one of these days.

Before we move on, we need to notice one more thing: No great world power follows Rome. The Roman Empire is the last, and it will be in existence in the latter days. Actually, it exists today. All of these other empires were destroyed by an enemy from the outside, but no enemy destroyed Rome. Attila the Hun came in and sacked the city, but he was so awestruck by what he saw that he realized he could not handle it. He took his barbarians and left town. The Roman Empire fell apart from within—no enemy destroyed it. Rome is living in the great nations of Europe today: Italy, France, Great Britain, Germany, and Spain are all part of the old Roman Empire. The laws of Rome live on, and her language also. No one speaks Latin today, but it is basic to understanding French, Spanish, and other languages. Her warlike spirit lives on also: Europe has been at war ever since the empire broke up into these kingdoms.

What is happening in Europe today? There is a new psychological viewpoint developing. The young people there do not want to be called Italians or Germans; they like to be called Europeans. Such thinking is creating a basis for the man who is coming someday to put the Roman Empire back together again. He is known in Scripture as the Man of Sin, or the Antichrist. They have a Common Market in Europe today, and they may be well along in restoring the Roman Empire. But not until God takes down the roadblock will that man appear and all this come to fruition. Because he is Satan's man, God will not let him appear until He has called out His people to His name. When He has done that, He will remove His church from the earth. God *is* carrying out His program whether it looks like that or not.

Therefore, there is one coming who will put the Roman Empire together again. I never speak of the *resurrection* of the Roman Empire; that implies that it died. Let me again quote a nursery rhyme:

Humpty-Dumpty sat on a wall,
Humpty-Dumpty had a great fall;
All the King's horses, and all the King's men
Could not put Humpty-Dumpty together again.

You see, the Roman Empire fell apart like Humpty-Dumpty. There have been a lot of men who tried to put it together again, but they have not succeeded. That was one of the missions of the Roman Catholic church at the beginning. Also, Charlemagne attempted to put it back together. Napoleon tried to do so, and also several emperors of Germany. Hitler and Mussolini attempted it, but so far the man has not yet appeared who will accomplish it. God is not quite ready for him to appear.

## DESTRUCTION OF GENTILE WORLD POWERS—ESTABLISHMENT OF THE KINGDOM OF HEAVEN UPON EARTH

What will be the final end of this last kingdom, the kingdom of iron mixed with clay? The clay, I believe, represents the masses, the different nations of the ten toes. The iron speaks of the fact that Rome lives on in this final form of the old empire. How is it all

going to end? We are given the answer in this concluding section of chapter 2.

**And in the days of these kings shall the God of heaven set up a kingdom, which shall never be destroyed: and the kingdom shall not be left to other people, but it shall break in pieces and consume all these kingdoms, and it shall stand for ever.**

**Forasmuch as thou sawest that the stone was cut out of the mountain without hands, and that it brake in pieces the iron, the brass, the clay, the silver, and the gold; the great God hath made known to the king what shall come to pass hereafter: and the dream is certain, and the interpretation thereof sure [Dan. 2:44–45].**

The Antichrist, or the Man of Sin (he has about thirty-five aliases in Scripture), is the one who will bring back the Roman Empire. He will be a world dictator—he will rule the world just as Nebuchadnezzar did at the beginning (see Rev. 13). That is an ideal form of government, but if the wrong man is at the top, it is horrible. This was true of Nebuchadnezzar, as we will see, and it will certainly be true of the Antichrist.

When the Lord Jesus comes, He is going to rule as an autocratic ruler, and He is going to put down all rebellion against Him: "Thou shalt break them with a rod of iron; thou shalt dash them in pieces like a potter's vessel" (Ps. 2:9). I don't think He wants me to apologize for Him today. If you don't like it, I suggest you get on the next trip to the moon or Mars and get off this earth. He is going to take over this earth, and I think He may take over the place you choose, also. This is His universe—it belongs to Him.

"The stone [which] was cut out of the mountain without hands" represents none other than the Lord Jesus Christ. This is not a man; this is God's Anointed. The Lord Jesus Himself made it clear that He is that Stone. In His day there were probably more people who understood what He was saying than there are today. In Matthew 21:44 He said, "And whosoever shall fall on this stone shall be broken: but on whomsoever it shall fall, it will grind him to powder." He is the Stone, the living Stone, the foundation—"For other foundation can no man lay than that is laid, which is Jesus Christ" (1 Cor. 3:11). If you fall on that Stone—that is, rest in Him by faith, come just as you are without one plea but that

His blood was shed for you—you are broken, you come as a sinner, with nothing to offer. But He is a wonderful Stone to rest upon.

The Stone is one of many figures of speech in Scripture which speak of Christ in His office as both Savior and Judge. He is the Rock of salvation (see Deut. 32:15), and He is the Rock of judgment (see Deut. 32:4).

These verses in Daniel speak of the time when He is coming to the earth as Judge to put down earth's rebellion against God. The reference here is to the second coming of Christ to the earth, which is depicted for us in detail in Revelation 19:11–21. His coming is going to be climactic, catastrophic, and cataclysmic. It is mentioned again and again in Scripture (see Zech. 14:1–3; Joel 3:2, 9–16; Isa. 34:1–8; Ps. 2).

Man's boast of ruling this earth and establishing a utopia will end in the dismal destruction of this so-called civilization. It is hard for us to get this fact in our thinking: We live in a world that is *judged*. This world is not on trial. I hear people say, "I'll take my chances." My unsaved friend, you do not have a chance. You are lost. You are without God. You have no capacity for God. All you have in your heart is perhaps a little desire to be religious. You'd like to win a few more ribbons for going to Sunday school—you don't intend to miss a Sunday. But, my friend, you need to trust Christ as Savior, and that is not easy to do, is it? It is not easy to bow to Him and to acknowledge Him. However, either you are going to come to that Stone, or that Stone is coming to you. I'd rather come to the Stone.

God is going to end man's little day down here. God's kingdom will prevail, and for one thousand years the earth will be tested under the personal reign of Christ. Apart from a brief moment in which Satan and sin will be permitted to make their last assault on the righteous reign of God, the kingdom will continue on into eternity (see Rev. 20).

**Then the king Nebuchadnezzar fell upon his face, and worshipped Daniel, and commanded that they should offer an oblation and sweet odours unto him.**

**The king answered unto Daniel, and said, Of a truth it is, that your God is a God of gods, and a Lord of kings, and a revealer of secrets, seeing thou couldest reveal this secret [Dan. 2:46–47].**

The effect of Daniel's interpretation upon Nebuchadnezzar is so profound that he actually worships Daniel and commands others

to do likewise. He doesn't know any better; he only knows the worship of physical objects, and he intends thus to worship the living and true God. This was his introduction to the God of heaven. In this book we can watch the growth of faith in the heart of this idolatrous king. It will break through the darkness of paganism, and he is going to come into the marvelous light of the knowledge of God.

**Then the king made Daniel a great man, and gave him many great gifts, and made him ruler over the whole province of Babylon, and chief of the governors over all the wise men of Babylon.**

**Then Daniel requested of the king, and he set Shadrach, Meshach, and Abednego, over the affairs of the province of Babylon: but Daniel sat in the gate of the king [Dan. 2:48–49].**

Sitting in the gate of the king is a practice that is mentioned elsewhere in Scripture. In Genesis, Lot sat in the gate of Sodom; that meant that he was a judge. And in the Book of Esther, Mordecai was also given that office—he sat in the gate as a judge.

Daniel now is rewarded and elevated by Nebuchadnezzar, but he does not forget his three Hebrew friends. They likewise receive high positions in the government of Babylon. This young boy Daniel is moved into a position of sitting in the gate. He was a judge, a Supreme Court Justice, but he also acted in the capacity of prime minister. Throughout this book we will find that he is the one with whom Nebuchadnezzar confers. He judges the people, and he is also prime minister of the kingdom of Babylon.

# CHAPTER 3

**THEME:** *The decree of Nebuchadnezzar to enforce universal idolatry; the three Hebrew children cast into the furnace when they refuse to bow to the image of gold*

In the first chapter of Daniel heathen customs were judged; in the second chapter heathen philosophy was judged; and in the third chapter heathen pride is judged.

## CONSTRUCTION OF THE IMAGE OF GOLD

**Nebuchadnezzar the king made an image of gold, whose height was threescore cubits, and the breadth thereof six cubits: he set it up in the plain of Dura, in the province of Babylon.**

**Then Nebuchadnezzar the king sent to gather together the princes, the governors, and the captains, the judges, the treasurers, the counsellors, the sheriffs, and all the rulers of the provinces, to come to the dedication of the image which Nebuchadnezzar the king had set up [Dan. 3:1–2].**

"An image of gold"—this reveals the lavish display of wealth and workmanship which went into the construction of this impressive image.

Some scholars think that Nebuchadnezzar constructed this image in memory of his father, Nabopolassar. Others are equally convinced that he made it to Bel, the pagan god of Babylon. It is more likely that he made it of himself. Daniel had declared that Nebuchadnezzar was the head of gold in the image of his dream. Instead of humbling himself before God, the dream caused Nebuchadnezzar to be filled with excessive pride, and he made an entire image of gold to represent the kingdom he had built.

The image was sixty cubits high and six cubits in breadth—that was a pretty good-sized image. A cubit is approximately eighteen inches, which would make the image ninety feet high. Babylon was situated on a plain, surrounded by flat country. Although it was a city of skyscrapers for its day, the sheer height of the image made it visible for a great distance. The plain of Dura was like an airport—flat and expansive—allowing a great multitude to assemble for the worship of the image, actually the worship of the king.

All the leaders and government officials

were present for the dedication of the image. Only the big brass were invited, and they were to sell this project to the people. This was the first step in the brainwashing program. These bureaucrats comprised a great company.

What did Nebuchadnezzar really have in mind in making this image? We can observe here three things: (1) The making of this image shows the rebellion of Nebuchadnezzar against the God of heaven who had given him world dominion. Instead of gratitude, this is a definite act of rebellion. (2) This also shows his vaunted pride in making an image which evidently was self-deification. The Roman emperors also attempted this later on. (3) Obviously, Nebuchadnezzar was seeking a unifying principle to weld together the tribes and tongues and peoples of his kingdom into one great totalitarian government. In other words, he was attempting to institute a world religion. This was nothing in the world but a repetition of the tower of Babel—a forming of one religion for the world.

There are many who are working toward a world religion today, including the denominations which make up the World Council of Churches. They are moving toward a world religion, and, my friend, they are going to leave Jesus out altogether. All of these attempts are not toward the worship of the living and true God; they actually oppose Him. It is a movement which is going to lead to the Great Tribulation Period, to the Man of Sin, and the False Prophet. This, of course, is after the true church is removed from the earth (the true church is all those who make up the body of believers). Every believer in Christ—whoever he is, whatever his color of skin, whatever his denomination, if he is trusting Christ—will all go out together.

## DEDICATION OF THE IMAGE OF GOLD

**Then the princes, the governors, and captains, the judges, the treasurers, the counsellors, the sheriffs, and all the rulers of the provinces, were gathered together unto the dedication of the image that Nebuchadnezzar the king had set up; and they stood before the image that Nebuchadnezzar had set up [Dan. 3:3].**

The day of dedication had arrived. All were present, except Daniel. We believe he had a good and legitimate reason for his absence. He probably was away on state business. He was in a unique position of being the chief advisor to the king of Babylon who was now the ruler of the world.

The sight of the image of gold on the plain of Dura was very impressive—as impressive as an Atlas missile set up on the launching pad at Cape Canaveral, Florida. It must have made a tremendous appeal to the eye.

**Then an herald cried aloud, To you it is commanded, O people, nations, and languages,**

**That at what time ye hear the sound of the cornet, flute, harp, sackbut, psaltery, dulcimer, and all kinds of music, ye fall down and worship the golden image that Nebuchadnezzar the king hath set up:**

**And whoso falleth not down and worshippeth shall the same hour be cast into the midst of a burning fiery furnace [Dan. 3:4-6].**

They knew nothing of the freedom of worship at this dedication service. When the orchestra began to play, they were to fall down and worship this image. There was no room here for spontaneous, personal religion—this is all prearranged.

Notice the different instruments in this orchestra: the cornet—that's a wind instrument; the flute—a wind instrument; the harp—a stringed instrument; the sackbut—a trombone, or perhaps a high-stringed instrument; the psaltery—a stringed instrument like the harp; and the dulcimer—a drum with strings above which was played with a stick. Then, it says, "and all kinds of music," which means there were instruments and types of music that are not listed.

I would like to give this orchestra a name: the Babylonian Beboppers; or maybe it should be the Babylonian Beatles, or the Royal Rock Quartet Plus Two (or however many instruments there were), or the Chaldean Philharmonic Orchestra.

The point is this: this was more than a dedication—people were forced to worship. However, true worship is an expression of the heart; it cannot be forced. So it is more accurate to say that at least these people went through the outward form of worship.

The music was used to appeal to the flesh. Music that is spiritual is a wonderful aid to worship, but in some of our churches today it is very difficult to tell the difference between spiritual music and worldly music.

Paul had a great deal to say about the im-

portance of music for the believer in worship. He says in Ephesians 5:19, "Speaking to yourselves in psalms and hymns and spiritual songs, singing and making melody in your heart to the Lord." And then in Colossians 3:16 we read: "Let the word of Christ dwell in you richly in all wisdom; teaching and admonishing one another in psalms and hymns and spiritual songs, singing with grace in your hearts to the Lord."

However, at the very beginning, music got off to a bad start. It was mentioned in the godless line of Cain, back in Genesis 4:21— "And his brother's name was Jubal: he was the father of all such as handle the harp and organ."

Whenever music or ritual appeals to the flesh, it degrades man rather than elevates him, and it is not an aid to true worship. It cancels worship out; it deadens everything. However, music can also lift a worship service; it can help the spiritual ministry and be a great blessing.

I recall one particular incident when I was speaking in special meetings held in a fine church in the East. Before my first message, a young lady was called on to sing, and she was quite a showman. Rather than selecting a song which contributed to the worship, she sang a number that simply gave opportunity to show off her voice. When I realized it had deadened the meeting spiritually, I had the congregation sing another hymn before I went on with my message. When I spoke to the pastor about it afterwards, he told me that she was the daughter of one of his leading officers and she always sang at the opening of any special series of meetings!

May I say, music can be helpful to a service or it cannot. Worldly music has a tremendous influence upon people, and it has gotten into many of our churches today. I thank God that many ministers are taking a stand against it.

Nebuchadnezzar had established a terrible penalty for those who refused to worship this image. The music helped prepare for this worldly worship, and you can be sure that everyone in that crowd went down on their faces before the image—with the exception of three young men.

**Therefore at that time, when all the people heard the sound of the cornet, flute, harp, sackbut, psaltery, and all kinds of music, all the people, the nations, and the languages, fell down and worshipped the golden image that**

**Nebuchadnezzar the king had set up [Dan. 3:7].**

This movement of dedication was an outward act of worship, and practically unanimous. There may have been many who were not convinced in their hearts, but they gave no visible evidence that they were contrary. I am sure they were inwardly attempting to justify their position by some form of rationalization.

We rationalize our own compromises today, also. One man told me that the reason he continued in the liberal church of which he was a member was that his father had been a leader in the church, an outstanding layman, and when he died, the church had dedicated a stained glass window to him. That was the reason he felt he couldn't leave the church! My friend, it would have been better for him to buy a replacement for that window and take the one dedicated to his father with him, than to have continued in that church upon such an unfortunate excuse.

## THE THREE HEBREW CHILDREN FAIL TO WORSHIP THE IMAGE

**Wherefore at that time certain Chaldeans came near, and accused the Jews [Dan. 3:8].**

The king had apparently appointed observers to note any irregularities in the service. "Certain Chaldeans" may indicate that they had been watching these three Jews particularly, perhaps because they were jealous or had some personal animosity toward them. The only Jews who were involved, of course, were the three Hebrew children who were among the officers of Nebuchadnezzar. The other Jews in captivity who had no position of leadership were not present at this meeting.

**They spake and said to the king Nebuchadnezzar, O king, live for ever.**

**Thou, O king, hast made a decree, that every man that shall hear the sound of the cornet, flute, harp, sackbut, psaltery, and dulcimer, and all kinds of music, shall fall down and worship the golden image:**

**And whoso falleth not down and worshippeth, that he should be cast into the midst of a burning fiery furnace.**

**There are certain Jews whom thou hast set over the affairs of the province of Babylon, Shadrach, Meshach, and Abed-nego; these men, O king, have not regarded thee: they serve not thy gods,**

nor worship the golden image which thou hast set up [Dan. 3:9–12].

This must have been a very famous orchestra in that day—this is the third time we have been given a list of its instruments.

The Chaldeans' accusation before the king was very formal and according to protocol. They made a direct charge against the three Hebrew children by name. There is no misunderstanding as to whom they referred. Although their insinuation—"These men, O king, have not regarded thee"—was absolutely false. The Hebrews' refusal to worship the image was not an act of disloyalty toward the king personally. It was their recognition of a higher power—they were obedient to their God, which will be revealed by their own answer to this charge.

## THE THREE HEBREW CHILDREN DECLARE THE POWER OF GOD

Then Nebuchadnezzar in his rage and fury commanded to bring Shadrach, Meshach, and Abed-nego. Then they brought these men before the king [Dan. 3:13].

"Nebuchadnezzar in his rage and fury"—this man had a real psychological problem, and such actions characterize his form of insanity. He suffered from hysteria, and a sort of manic-depressive psychosis: one moment he was hot with anger and the next he was laughing his head off.

Nebuchadnezzar spake and said unto them, Is it true, O Shadrach, Meshach, and Abed-nego, do not ye serve my gods, nor worship the golden image which I have set up? [Dan. 3:14].

Nebuchadnezzar asked them if the charge were true. Had they refused to worship his gods and the image which he had set up?

Now if ye be ready that at what time ye hear the sound of the cornet, flute, harp, sackbut, psaltery, and dulcimer, and all kinds of music, ye fall down and worship the image which I have made; well: but if ye worship not, ye shall be cast the same hour into the midst of a burning fiery furnace; and who is that God that shall deliver you out of my hands? [Dan. 3:15].

The king gives them another opportunity to change their minds and fall down before the image. Their submission now would be a worse reproach than it would have been at the outset. Nebuchadnezzar again recites the penalty for refusal and shows the fallacy of it. The king has heard of their God before, and he assures them that He is unable to deliver them.

Shadrach, Meshach, and Abed-nego, answered and said to the king, O Nebuchadnezzar, we are not careful to answer thee in this matter [Dan. 3:16].

They address Nebuchadnezzar, but they do not say, "O king, live forever."

"We are not careful to answer thee in this matter" means that they have carefully weighed the consequences of refusing to obey the king. They have counted the cost and are not being "careful" in giving an answer; in other words, they are not being concerned for their own well-being in the answer they give to the king.

The wise men in Babylon would have advised the Hebrews to fall down and worship, but God had said: "Thou shalt have no other gods before me. Thou shalt not make unto thee any graven image, or any likeness of any thing that is in heaven above, or that is in the earth beneath, or that is in the water under the earth: Thou shalt not bow down thyself to them, nor serve them: for I the LORD thy God am a jealous God, visiting the iniquity of the fathers upon the children unto the third and fourth generation of them that hate me; And shewing mercy unto thousands of them that love me, and keep my commandments" (Exod. 20:3–6). These Hebrew children were being true to God, and it took a great deal of courage for them to take this position.

If it be so, our God whom we serve is able to deliver us from the burning fiery furnace, and he will deliver us out of thine hand, O king.

But if not, be it known unto thee, O king, that we will not serve thy gods, nor worship the golden image which thou hast set up [Dan. 3:17–18].

They make it very clear: "If it is God's will, He will deliver us out of your hand." Regardless of the outcome, these three had purposed to serve God and not the idol of Nebuchadnezzar.

## THE THREE HEBREWS ARE PRESERVED IN THE FIERY FURNACE

Then was Nebuchadnezzar full of fury, and the form of his visage was changed

against Shadrach, Meshach, and Abednego: therefore he spake, and commanded that they should heat the furnace one seven times more than it was wont to be heated.

And he commanded the most mighty men that were in his army to bind Shadrach, Meshach, and Abed-nego, and to cast them into the burning fiery furnace [Dan. 3:19–20].

"Full of fury"—Nebuchadnezzar had an uncontrollable temper. In an extreme outrage of emotionalism, Nebuchadnezzar vented his anger against these men whom he had previously favored. The fire in the furnace was to be built up *seven times* larger and hotter than usual! This was not necessary, but it reveals what was in this man's heart.

Then these men were bound in their coats, their hosen, and their hats, and their other garments, and were cast into the midst of the burning fiery furnace [Dan. 3:21].

"Their hosen" means their stockings. In other words, they were in full dress for this trip to the fiery furnace.

Therefore because the king's commandment was urgent, and the furnace exceeding hot, the flame of the fire slew those men that took up Shadrach, Meshach, and Abed-nego.

And these three men, Shadrach, Meshach, and Abed-nego, fell down bound into the midst of the burning fiery furnace [Dan. 3:22–23].

The haste and high temperature caused those who threw in the captives to perish in the flames.

Then Nebuchadnezzar the king was astonied, and rose up in haste, and spake, and said unto his counsellors, Did not we cast three men bound into the midst of the fire? They answered and said unto the king, True, O king.

He answered and said, Lo, I see four men loose, walking in the midst of the fire, and they have no hurt; and the form of the fourth is like the Son of God [Dan. 3:24–25].

This furnace apparently was an open furnace, and Nebuchadnezzar, who expected these men to expire at once, was amazed to see them alive and walking about in the fire.

Another amazing fact was to see a fourth Man whom Nebuchadnezzar described as being in the form "like the Son of God." That should be translated "like a son of gods." Nebuchadnezzar had no knowledge of the living and true God at this time, although Daniel had spoken of Him. Having no spiritual perception, Nebuchadnezzar could only testify to His unusual appearance—He looked like one of the sons of the gods. However, I do believe that the fourth Man was the Son of God, the preincarnate Christ.

The preservation of these faithful few in the fiery furnace was miraculous. There is no other explanation—you either accept that or reject it. Either the Book of Daniel is misrepresenting things, or it is telling the truth. We have a group today, often identified as neo-orthodox, who rob the language of Scripture of its true meaning. They castrate the meaning of the language, saying it doesn't mean what it says, but that it means something "spiritual." That type of rationalism is not only hypocritical, it is deceptive.

Several years ago a retired pastor told me of his visit to an outstanding church in Southern California where the son of a friend of his was the pastor. He told me that in his sermon the young man used language that he was accustomed to hearing in the pulpit, and he went up afterwards and congratulated him, "Why, you used in your message the same language John Wesley used!" The young man responded to this retired preacher, "I used the same language John Wesley used, but I do not mean what John Wesley meant by it." That was positively deceptive—taking language and trying to explain away its real meaning.

My point is that there are many miracles in Scripture that such men have attempted to explain away. For instance, Jesus didn't walk on the water—He walked on the shore, and the disciples *thought* He was walking on the water. The widow's son was not really dead—they only *thought* he was—and Jesus just woke him up. That type of double-talk is deceptive and hypocritical. You either believe this miracle or you don't. No three men can be thrown into a fiery furnace without being absolutely destroyed, unless a miracle takes place. I believe a miracle took place, and that the fourth Man present was none other than the Lord Jesus Christ.

The events recorded here in this chapter are an historical incident, but we should also note that it is an adumbration, a prophetic

picture, of the Great Tribulation Period. The fiery furnace represents the suffering that will occur during the Great Tribulation. This man Nebuchadnezzar represents the beast out of the sea, the Antichrist, the last great world ruler. This image of gold represents the abomination of desolation of which the Lord Jesus spoke. These three Hebrew children represent the remnant which will be miraculously preserved during the Great Tribulation Period. And then, quite interestingly, Daniel is not mentioned in this chapter at all. He wasn't around. Apparently he acted not only as a Supreme Court Justice, but also as prime minister of the kingdom. He was out on kingdom business, out on the king's highway somewhere. He is, therefore, a picture of the redeemed ones who are to be removed before the Great Tribulation. What a very wonderful picture is presented here!

In the fourth Man present in the furnace, we see that the Lord Jesus was there with them. He will be with them also in the day of the Great Tribulation, with those who are His as they go through the trials of that period. My friend, He is with you and me today as we go through our trials. He said, "These things I have spoken unto you, that in me ye might have peace. In the world ye shall have tribulation: but be of good cheer; I have overcome the world" (John 16:33). He also said, ". . . lo, I am with you alway, even unto the end of the world" (Matt. 28:20). He promises never to leave or forsake His own.

**Then Nebuchadnezzar came near to the mouth of the burning fiery furnace, and spake, and said, Shadrach, Meshach, and Abed-nego, ye servants of the most high God, come forth, and come hither. Then Shadrach, Meshach, and Abed-nego, came forth of the midst of the fire.**

**And the princes, governors, and captains, and the king's counsellors, being gathered together, saw these men, upon whose bodies the fire had no power, nor was an hair of their head singed, neither were their coats changed, nor the smell of fire had passed on them [Dan. 3:26–27].**

Nebuchadnezzar acknowledges that these three are "servants of the most high God." I think he is getting a little closer to a knowledge of God. These men came forth with not a hair singed, nor the smell of smoke on their garments! This is a clear-cut miracle.

## NEBUCHADNEZZAR'S DECREE CONCERNING THE GOD OF THE HEBREW CHILDREN

**Then Nebuchadnezzar spake, and said, Blessed be the God of Shadrach, Meshach, and Abed-nego, who hath sent his angel, and delivered his servants that trusted in him, and have changed the king's word, and yielded their bodies, that they might not serve nor worship any god, except their own God.**

**Therefore I make a decree, That every people, nation, and language, which speak any thing amiss against the God of Shadrach, Meshach, and Abed-nego, shall be cut in pieces, and their houses shall be made a dunghill: because there is no other God that can deliver after this sort.**

**Then the king promoted Shadrach, Meshach, and Abed-nego, in the province of Babylon [Dan. 3:28–30].**

There is nothing personal in this expression of Nebuchadnezzar; yet he recognizes the omnipotence of the living God and His power in delivering these three men. He grants that their God is superior to his. This is Nebuchadnezzar's conviction; in the next chapter, we will read his personal testimony of conversion. I believe he came to the knowledge of the living and true God. It took this man a long time to move out of the paganism and heathenism in which he was saturated.

Now these three Hebrew children are back in Nebuchadnezzar's favor. Twice they had the sentence of death upon them, twice they have been miraculously delivered, and twice they have been promoted.

In the same way the Lord Jesus is able to keep His own in the world today. That ought to be a comforting thought to many of us. He said in John 10:27–28: "My sheep hear my voice, and I know them, and they follow me: And I give unto them eternal life; and they shall never perish, neither shall any man pluck them out of my hand." And again in John 17:11—"And now I am no more in the world, but these are in the world, and I come to thee. Holy Father, keep through thine own name those whom thou hast given me, that they may be one, as we are." He continued, "I pray not that thou shouldest take them out of the world, but that thou shouldest keep them from the evil [one]" (John 17:15). In Hebrews 7:25 we read: "Wherefore he is able also to save them to the uttermost that come unto

God by him, seeing he ever liveth to make intercession for them." And finally, Paul wrote, "For the which cause I also suffer these things: nevertheless I am not ashamed: for I know whom I have believed, and am persuaded that he is able to keep that which I have committed unto him against that day" (2 Tim. 1:12).

My friend, you and I are living in a world today in which we *are* going to have trouble. Some of God's children do get into a fiery furnace, but He is able to keep them even there, and He is able to bring them out of it. We simply do not trust the Lord like we should—we do not have the faith of these three Hebrew children.

# CHAPTER 4

*THEME: Testimony of Nebuchadnezzar; tree dream of Nebuchadnezzar; tree dream interpreted by Daniel; the mental malady of Nebuchadnezzar; dream fulfilled and Nebuchadnezzar's reason restored*

This chapter is going to give us a great deal more information about this man Nebuchadnezzar than we have had before. Actually, there was a skeleton in the family closet—something I am sure they didn't boast of: Nebuchadnezzar suffered from a form of insanity. This chapter is a leaf of history taken from the archives of Babylon. Nebuchadnezzar's form of insanity is pretty well identified and known today, and it is something which a number of world rulers have suffered from.

We are living in a day when a great deal of attention is given to mental illness and various forms of abnormal behavior. I wonder sometimes just who *is* normal in this mad world in which we live! A psychologist will tell you that the bulk of mankind is normal, a few are abnormal, and a few are above normal or geniuses. Who is to say who is sane and who is not sane? The standard, of course, is the way most of us act—the behavior of the majority is called normal. When just a few react, that is abnormal, which, of course, is an arbitrary distinction. Who in the world is going to say that what the majority is doing today is normal? That could be quite a subject of debate, and I think it would be very difficult to sustain a thesis that the majority of us are normal. In Shakespeare's play *Hamlet*, Hamlet was sent from Denmark over to England (they thought he was a little touched in the head) because, they said, in England everyone was abnormal!

There is the story of the man who had trouble sleeping at night because he had the feeling that there was someone under his bed. He was losing sleep because he had to get up many times during the night to look under the bed and satisfy himself that no one was there. He finally went to the psychiatrist with his problem. The psychiatrist told him, "Well, you really do have a problem, and it is going to be difficult to bring you back to normal, but I think we can do it. It will take ten sessions, and it will cost you twenty-five dollars for each session." The man left, saying he would think it over and let him know. However, he never returned. Several weeks later the psychiatrist met the man on the street and asked him why he had never come back. The man replied that he had been cured with the help of a carpenter friend of his. He had told his friend his problem, and the carpenter said he could fix it for him. He came over to the man's house with his saw and simply sawed off the legs of the bed. "Now that fellow *can't* get under my bed!" the man told the psychiatrist. I guess a lot of us suffer some kind of abnormality, but this man Nebuchadnezzar had a real problem.

## TESTIMONY OF NEBUCHADNEZZAR

**Nebuchadnezzar the king, unto all people, nations, and languages, that dwell in all the earth; Peace be multiplied unto you.**

**I thought it good to shew the signs and wonders that the high God hath wrought toward me.**

**How great are his signs! and how mighty are his wonders! his kingdom is an everlasting kingdom, and his dominion is from generation to generation [Dan. 4:1–3].**

This is Nebuchadnezzar's marvelous testimony, and it shows development in the faith of this man. Back in Daniel 3:29 he issued a decree and expressed a conviction. Here he gives a personal testimony. There it was a decree; here it is a decision. There it was a conviction, and here it is conversion. Chronologically, this testimony should come at the end of the chapter because it grew out of his experience recorded here.

Nebuchadnezzar sends a message of peace to "all peoples, nations, and languages" of his kingdom. He is not speaking of peace among nations—he already has such peace, attained by his military might and enforced by his superior power. Rather, he speaks here of the peace of heart which comes to a sinner when he knows he has been accepted of God and is at peace with God. This man's own tranquility was restored to him, as we shall see in this chapter.

He speaks also of what "the high God hath wrought toward *me.*" His testimony is very personal. God is no longer the God of only the three Hebrew children. He also testifies to God's signs, His wonders, and His dominion. He recognizes and acknowledges that God's rule, God's kingdom, is above his.

The peace of which Nebuchadnezzar speaks can only come to the human heart when it knows God. "Therefore being justified by faith, we have peace with God through our Lord Jesus Christ" (Rom. 5:1)—that is the peace which He made by the blood of the cross. It is the peace which can come to a sinner's heart that all is right now because of the penalty which Christ paid—God is for him now and God is on his side. Back of all the trouble and travail that is in the world today, back of all the troubled hearts, is the question of sin. Things are not right. One young fellow expressed it this way to me: "I'm not at peace with myself. I'm not at peace with my parents. I'm not at peace with my teachers. I'm not at peace with anybody." Fundamentally, man must make peace with God. When there is peace in the human heart, then there can be peace made with those round about us; but, until then, man does not know peace.

I am sure that much of what is called abnormality and insanity today could be cured by bringing the gospel and the knowledge of God to the people who are so afflicted. I thought it was absurd that hospitals were set up to receive the Vietnam War POW's as they arrived in the Philippine Islands. They were to be examined and given psychological tests there. However, the men came bounding off the planes, ready to make phone calls to a wife, a mother, or some other loved one. Many of them testified that God had been with them. They had learned to pray, and Christ had been with them. They didn't need a lot of psychological treatment.

Everything in the world is being taught in our schools and colleges except the Word of God. It is the Word of God which can bring peace to the human heart. This is the problem Nebuchadnezzar had, but he made his peace with God, and God made peace with him. Today, God has already made peace with you—He is waiting for you to make peace with Him. When you have settled that, you won't need to spend much time on the psychiatrist's couch. Instead, you will be a radiant Christian.

## TREE DREAM OF NEBUCHADNEZZAR

We find the first symptom of Nebuchadnezzar's form of insanity in verse 4—

**I Nebuchadnezzar was at rest in mine house, and flourishing in my palace [Dan. 4:4].**

The personal pronouns—*my, I,* and *mine*—are already used three times in just this one verse. You will find them about three times in every verse from verse 4 through verse 10. Nebuchadnezzar had a bad case of what I call "perpendicular I-itis." Job had that problem also.

**I saw a dream which made me afraid, and the thoughts upon my bed and the visions of my head troubled me [Dan. 4:5].**

It is all about me and mine.

**Therefore made I a decree to bring in all the wise men of Babylon before me, that they might make known unto me the interpretation of the dream.**

**Then came in the magicians, the astrologers, the Chaldeans, and the soothsayers: and I told the dream before them; but they did not make known unto me the interpretation thereof.**

**But at the last Daniel came in before me, whose name was Belteshazzar, according to the name of my god, and in whom is the spirit of the holy gods: and before him I told the dream, saying,**

**O Belteshazzar, master of the magicians, because I know that the spirit of**

**the holy gods is in thee, and no secret troubleth thee, tell me the visions of my dream that I have seen, and the interpretation thereof [Dan. 4:6–9].**

Again the wise men were called in and were unable to give an interpretation of the dream. It was God who gave both of his dreams, and only God can give the interpretation. Finally, Daniel was called in. Nebuchadnezzar had learned that Daniel was a Spirit-filled man and that interpretations were given him by God.

Nebuchadnezzar is introducing the vision that he has had, and he gives us a surplus of the personal pronoun *I*.

I think that the family had kept this man's insanity quiet. They didn't talk much about it, but those closest to him did recognize it. I believe the psychiatrists today would label it hysteria. Hysteria is a highly emotional mental disease. It is psychotic, rather than a structural form of insanity (in other words, Nebuchadnezzar was not insane because he had been dropped on his head as a baby). It manifests itself in somnambulism (sleepwalking) and amnesia (loss of memory), and it is thought to be hereditary. An historian tells us that a number of other world rulers have suffered from some form of mental instability: Antiochus Epiphanes, Charles VI of France, Christian VII of Denmark, George III of England, Otho of Bavaria, Alexander the Great, Julius Caesar and Napoleon. It has also been in the Spanish royal line, the Russian line (among the czars), and also in the English line. Henry VI of England was a real madhatter, and suffered from something similar to hysteria. Hitler also had that problem. And here, the head of gold, Nebuchadnezzar, was a lunatic. He had bats in his belfry. He was not ruling with a full deck in his hands. He was just a little off, if you please. All of this was revealed in his extreme emotionalism—he would move in any direction and to an extreme.

The whole key to this chapter is found in verse 17, and it is important to note it at this point: "This matter is by the decree of the watchers, and the demand by the word of the holy ones: to the intent that the living may know that the most High ruleth in the kingdom of men, and giveth it to whomsoever he will, and setteth up over it the basest of men." God says that He puts on the thrones of this world the basest of men. In other words, God gives us the kind of rulers we deserve and the kind we want. There have been many rulers who had bats in their belfries and who were off their rockers. God says He sets over the kingdoms the basest of men: twenty-five hundred years of history since Nebuchadnezzar have demonstrated the truth of this statement.

**Thus were the visions of mine head in my bed; I saw, and behold, a tree in the midst of the earth, and the height thereof was great.**

**The tree grew, and was strong, and the height thereof reached unto heaven, and the sight thereof to the end of all the earth:**

**The leaves thereof were fair, and the fruit thereof much, and in it was meat for all: the beasts of the field had shadow under it, and the fowls of the heaven dwelt in the boughs thereof, and all flesh was fed of it.**

**I saw in the visions of my head upon my bed, and, behold, a watcher and an holy one came down from heaven;**

**He cried aloud, and said thus, Hew down the tree, and cut off his branches, shake off his leaves, and scatter his fruit: let the beasts get away from under it, and the fowls from his branches:**

**Nevertheless leave the stump of his roots in the earth, even with a band of iron and brass, in the tender grass of the field; and let it be wet with the dew of heaven, and let his portion be with the beasts in the grass of the earth:**

**Let his heart be changed from man's, and let a beast's heart be given unto him; and let seven times pass over him [Dan. 4:10–16].**

These verses contain the substance of Nebuchadnezzar's dream which centers around a tree that grew tall to heaven, wide enough to fill the earth. The tree was evidently an evergreen, for its leaves were fair. It was a fruit tree, and its fruit was eaten by all. Beasts stood in its shadow, and birds rested in its branches.

In Scripture, a tree can represent a number of things. A tree can represent a man: "And he shall be like a tree planted by the rivers of water, that bringeth forth his fruit in his season; his leaf also shall not wither; and whatsoever he doeth shall prosper" (Ps. 1:3; see also Jer. 17:8; Isa. 56:3). Also a tree can repre-

sent a nation (see Ezek. 31:3–14; Matt. 24:32–33). The mustard tree in Matthew 13:31 and 32 represents Christendom today. The olive tree represents both Israel and the Gentiles (see Rom. 11:16–24). The tree here represents Nebuchadnezzar primarily and also his kingdom of Babylon—the king and kingdom are inseparable.

The "watcher" and "holy one" are of an order of God's created intelligences. The watchers are the holy ones who administer the affairs of this world. The Book of Daniel makes it very clear that God has created intelligences who administer His universe and this world in which you and I live. God has His administrators under which are many created intelligences. Over against that, Satan also has his minions who have charge over certain areas of certain nations. We will see more of this in the Book of Daniel.

These watchers see all, hear all, and tell all. Many believers today think they can live in secret, that they are not under the eye of God. We talk about wanting to enjoy our privacy, but if you want to know the truth, you and I haven't any privacy. Psalm 139:7–12 tells us that we cannot get away from God, no matter where we go. Secret sin on earth is open scandal up yonder in heaven. His created intelligences know all about you, and if you are a Christian, you had better go to God with that "secret" sin in your life and get it straightened out.

Now the tree was hewn down, and a band of iron and brass was put around its stump to indicate that it would grow and flourish again in seven years. And the heart of the ruler (that is, of the "tree") was to be changed into that of a beast—the vegetable was to become an animal.

**This matter is by the decree of the watchers, and the demand by the word of the holy ones: to the intent that the living may know that the most High ruleth in the kingdom of men, and giveth it to whomsoever he will, and setteth up over it the basest of men [Dan. 4:17].**

There are three things that we are to learn from Nebuchadnezzar's dream:

1. "The most High ruleth in the kingdom of men." If you think that God has abdicated today and has withdrawn from this universe, you are wrong. The universe has not gotten loose from Him. Emerson was wrong when he said, "Things are in the saddle, and they ride

mankind." There happens to be Somebody else in the saddle, and He is in control on this earth. "He that sitteth in the heavens shall laugh: the Lord shall have them in derision. Then shall he speak unto them in his wrath, and vex them in his sore displeasure. Yet have I set my king upon my holy hill of Zion" (Ps. 2:4–6). God says He is going on with His purpose in the world. He is permitting Satan to carry out a nefarious plot for a very definite reason: God is demonstrating something to His created intelligences today. There are a lot of silly things being said about Satan which are entirely unscriptural.

Nations rise and fall to teach men that God rules and overrules the kingdoms of this world. If you think our nation happens to be His special little pet, you are entirely wrong. I believe we have already been put on the auction block: we are already judged. The downward course which this nation is traveling is going to take us right to the judgment of God. He rules in the kingdom of men.

2. He "giveth it to whomsoever he will." You probably thought that the Democrats and the Republicans put men in power. They *think* they do, but God disposes of these kingdoms according to His will. That thought may cause someone's chest to puff up, and he will say, "Well, I am occupying this office by the will of God." A lot of kings in the past had the foolish notion that they were ruling in God's place. Don't believe a word of it—God puts them in power. Notice that Paul says in Romans 13:1, ". . . the powers that be are ordained of God." Why in the world does God permit certain powers to rule on this earth?

3. He "setteth up over it the basest of men." This third statement should be humbling to both the Democrats and the Republicans—and to all of mankind. If you think we pick the best men, we don't—all you need to do is to read human history to see this. My study of English history shows that our ancestors in the British Isles were some pretty bloody ancestors. They were terrible, and they had some rulers who were unspeakable! May I say to you, God "setteth up over it the basest of men," and we get the kind of ruler that we deserve. People complain about our government, our Congress, and all that sort of thing. My friend, we put them in their offices; we voted for them. God lets the basest of men come to power. That ought to be humbling to all of us—from Washington, D.C., on down. You will never hear of someone who is trying to curry the favor of our leaders speaking on this verse at a Presidential breakfast or upon

any occasion in Washington! This verse is quite upsetting, is it not?

History will substantiate the truth of this statement. The head of gold, Nebuchadnezzar, was insane; yet he was a brilliant ruler who formed the first world kingdom. He had times when he was as mad as a mad-hatter and didn't even know who he was. As we have mentioned before, many of the great world rulers have suffered problems similar to his. And the reason our forefathers did not establish the United States of America as a kingdom is because they believed that no man could be trusted to rule. God has been demonstrating this now over quite a length of time: He "setteth up over it the basest of men."

**This dream I king Nebuchadnezzar have seen. Now thou, O Belteshazzar, declare the interpretation thereof, forasmuch as all the wise men of my kingdom are not able to make known unto me the interpretation: but thou art able; for the spirit of the holy gods is in thee [Dan. 4:18].**

Now Daniel will interpret Nebuchadnezzar's dream.

## TREE DREAM INTERPRETED BY DANIEL

**Then Daniel, whose name was Belteshazzar, was astonied for one hour, and his thoughts troubled him. The king spake, and said, Belteshazzar, let not the dream, or the interpretation thereof, trouble thee. Belteshazzar answered and said, My lord, the dream be to them that hate thee, and the interpretation thereof to thine enemies [Dan. 4:19].**

The dream is a great shock and a blow to Daniel. Nebuchadnezzar has become his friend, and Daniel is his prime minister. The first dream Nebuchadnezzar had had dignified him, but this dream debases him. It is so bad that Daniel is reluctant to reveal it to the king.

Daniel resists whatever temptation there may have been to withhold from Nebuchadnezzar the full story. He is going to give the entire interpretation to the king. The question is often raised as to whether a doctor should tell his patient that he is suffering from a fatal disease. I personally feel that if a man is getting ready to take the biggest step of his life, he ought to know it—that is, if there is someone else who knows it. I have always appreciated the fact that my doctor, who is a Christian and a cancer specialist, said to me when he had discovered that I had cancer: "Dr. McGee, I'm going to tell you exactly what the situation is, because if I didn't, you would never trust me." I appreciated that. Many people simply want their doctor to butter them up and assure them they are well.

Daniel is going to lay it on the line to Nebuchadnezzar, and he uses a great deal of tact in approaching the problem. First, he tells Nebuchadnezzar that the good in the dream is for the enemies of the king.

**The tree that thou sawest, which grew, and was strong, whose height reached unto the heaven, and the sight thereof to all the earth;**

**Whose leaves were fair, and the fruit thereof much, and in it was meat for all; under which the beasts of the field dwelt, and upon whose branches the fowls of the heaven had their habitation:**

**It is thou, O king, that art grown and become strong: for thy greatness is grown, and reacheth unto heaven, and thy dominion to the end of the earth [Dan. 4:20–22].**

The tree represents Nebuchadnezzar. He has grown strong and become great. He is a world ruler and has filled the then-civilized world. The picture here is of Nebuchadnezzar personally and of his dominion.

**And whereas the king saw a watcher and an holy one coming down from heaven, and saying, Hew the tree down, and destroy it; yet leave the stump of the roots thereof in the earth, even with a band of iron and brass, in the tender grass of the field; and let it be wet with the dew of heaven, and let his portion be with the beasts of the field, till seven times pass over him;**

**This is the interpretation, O king, and this is the decree of the most High, which is come upon my lord the king [Dan. 4:23–24].**

The tree (Nebuchadnezzar) is to be cut off but not totally rejected. For seven years, Nebuchadnezzar is to live with and like the beasts of the field. He won't even recognize who he is.

**That they shall drive thee from men, and thy dwelling shall be with the**

beasts of the field, and they shall make thee to eat grass as oxen, and they shall wet thee with the dew of heaven, and seven times shall pass over thee, till thou know that the most High ruleth in the kingdom of men, and giveth it to whomsoever he will.

And whereas they commanded to leave the stump of the tree roots; thy kingdom shall be sure unto thee, after that thou shalt have known that the heavens do rule [Dan. 4:25–26].

Daniel makes it clear why this dream was given to Nebuchadnezzar and why he is going to have this experience. Nebuchadnezzar is lifted up with pride which was evidenced when he made that tremendous image and forced all mankind to fall down and worship him. This man is certainly filled with pride, and now God is going to humble him. He is to be driven out of his palace, out to the pasture where he will take his abode with the oxen and forget what manner of man he was. However, God is also going to bring Nebuchadnezzar out of his insanity.

Evidently Nebuchadnezzar suffered from hysteria; some of the symptoms which are evident in his life are characteristic of this form of abnormality. One of the symptoms is excessive emotionalism, actually a sort of manic-depressive psychosis. One moment the patient is joyful and friendly, and the next he is morose and antagonistic. Someone has expressed it as "Easy gloom, easy glow"—it is an up and down state. Many people suffer from it to some extent. We all know people who are moody at times and then very joyful at others. But this was a very real problem for Nebuchadnezzar. It was a functional problem and not a structural one; it was not the result of some injury to his brain.

Nebuchadnezzar's hysteria also manifested itself in amnesia. Those afflicted with this malady don't know who they are for a period of time. There are those in mental institutions, for example, who think they are Napoleon or some such person. Nebuchadnezzar thought he was an animal.

Another thing that identifies hysteria is extreme egotism and pride. This became an obsession with Nebuchadnezzar (see Dan. 4:30). We saw how in verses 4 through 10, he talked about I, I, I—he had a bad case of perpendicular I-itis.

Pride is one of the things God hates, and it is something that characterizes man. Old Caesar Augustus said of a city which he captured, "I found it brick, I left it straw." He had utterly destroyed it. Another caesar made the statement "I found Rome wood, and I left it marble." You see, pride is the besetting sin of the human family. But what does man have to be proud of? Jeremiah 9:23–24 says, "Thus saith the Lord, Let not the wise man glory in his wisdom, neither let the mighty man glory in his might, let not the rich man glory in his riches: But let him that glorieth glory in this, that he understandeth and knoweth me, that I am the Lord which exercise lovingkindness, judgment, and righteousness, in the earth: for in these things I delight, saith the Lord."

God's salvation rules out pride—that is one thing you cannot have when you come to Christ for salvation. Paul said, "For I determined not to know any thing among you, save Jesus Christ, and him crucified" (1 Cor. 2:2). We have nothing in which we can glory. Again, the apostle wrote, "For who maketh thee to differ from another? and what hast thou that thou didst not receive? now if thou didst receive it, why dost thou glory, as if thou hadst not received it?" (1 Cor. 4:7). And finally, in 2 Corinthians 10:17, we read: "But he that glorieth, let him glory in the Lord." Pride is number one on God's "hate parade"— He hates pride (see Prov. 6:16–19). Our Lord Jesus gave us the ultimate example of humility: "And being found in fashion as a man, he humbled himself, and became obedient unto death, even the death of the cross" (Phil. 2:8).

Finally, it is characteristic of hysteria that it runs in cycles. In Nebuchadnezzar's case, it was a cycle of seven years.

Wherefore, O king, let my counsel be acceptable unto thee, and break off thy sins by righteousness, and thine iniquities by shewing mercy to the poor; if it may be a lengthening of thy tranquillity [Dan. 4:27].

This man Nebuchadnezzar is disturbed within his own heart—he has no peace. He has brought peace to the world—there is no one to challenge his authority at this time—but he is living in sin. Daniel tells Nebuchadnezzar that he needs to repent of and turn from his sins. He needs to turn to God and to a life of righteousness. Daniel advises him to repent in order to reverse the coming judgment. There is still hope for deliverance—Nebuchadnezzar could know the peace and tranquillity of God. I think this is God's final warning to Nebuchadnezzar.

A great deal of the mental and emotional

abnormalities that we see today are actually the result of spiritual problems. Now I do not say that they all are, as I know that there is sometimes a structural basis for such a problem. However, much of the disturbed condition we see in the lives of men is rooted in the spiritual condition of men. There is peace for them, if they would only come to Christ.

## THE MENTAL MALADY OF NEBUCHADNEZZAR

**All this came upon the king Nebuchadnezzar.**

**At the end of twelve months he walked in the palace of the kingdom of Babylon.**

**The king spake, and said, Is not this great Babylon, that I have built for the house of the kingdom by the might of my power, and for the honour of my majesty? [Dan. 4:28–30].**

Nebuchadnezzar did not heed the warning of Daniel. One year of grace went by before judgment fell. How patient God is! But His graciousness and longsuffering are not understood by the wicked (see Eccl. 8:11).

The king was on the verge of a break. He looked about his great kingdom, the kingdom which God had already told him that *He* had given to him. Despite that, Nebuchadnezzar now says, "Is not this great Babylon, that I have built?"

There have been a multitude of men and women throughout history who have tried to build little empires, and they have looked upon them with pride. I sometimes have opportunity to advise young preachers, and I tell them, "Look fellows, don't try to build a little empire of your church. I started out with that viewpoint, and I'll be honest with you, I have never been more disturbed or unhappy as I was then." This passage of Scripture in Daniel really spoke to me one day, and I realized I was trying to be an empire builder—and that wasn't what God intended for me to be. My ministry is building the lives of people, not trying to build a great empire. So I tell young preachers, "Start building in the lives of people, and I think the Lord will let you have what He wants you to have."

**While the word was in the king's mouth, there fell a voice from heaven, saying, O king Nebuchadnezzar, to thee it is spoken; The kingdom is departed from thee.**

**And they shall drive thee from men, and thy dwelling shall be with the beasts of the field: they shall make thee to eat grass as oxen, and seven times shall pass over thee, until thou know that the most High ruleth in the kingdom of men, and giveth it to whomsoever he will.**

**The same hour was the thing fulfilled upon Nebuchadnezzar: and he was driven from men, and did eat grass as oxen, and his body was wet with the dew of heaven, till his hairs were grown like eagles' feathers, and his nails like birds' claws [Dan. 4:31–33].**

Nebuchadnezzar moves out of the palace, out yonder to live with nature. God deals with this man personally. As he departs from the plane of normality and rationality, his kingdom slips from him. The insane of that day were driven out rather than being placed in an institution for treatment. Under ordinary circumstances Nebuchadnezzar would never have been able to return to the throne; yet God promised that he would do so after he had learned his lesson.

History corroborates this event in the life of Nebuchadnezzar. Dr. Philip R. Newell has this note from Albert Barnes, "Josephus attributes to the Babylonian historian, Berosus, a definite reference concerning a strange malady suffered by Nebuchadnezzar before his death" (*Daniel, the Man Greatly Beloved, and His Prophecies, p. 54*).

## DREAM FULFILLED AND NEBUCHADNEZZAR'S REASON RESTORED

**And at the end of the days I Nebuchadnezzar lifted up mine eyes unto heaven, and mine understanding returned unto me, and I blessed the most High, and I praised and honoured him that liveth for ever, whose dominion is an everlasting dominion, and his kingdom is from generation to generation [Dan. 4:34].**

His understanding comes back to him, and he adds these brief words to the testimony which he gave at the opening of this chapter.

**And all the inhabitants of the earth are reputed as nothing: and he doeth according to his will in the army of heaven, and among the inhabitants of the earth: and none can stay his hand,**

or say unto him, What doest thou? [Dan. 4:35].

Nebuchadnezzar has learned now that God is running things, that He is in control of this universe. Nebuchadnezzar accepted this thing that had come to him as the will of God for him, yielding his proud mind to the will of God. That is what a great many believers need to do today.

**At the same time my reason returned unto me; and for the glory of my kingdom, mine honour and brightness returned unto me; and my counsellors and my lords sought unto me; and I was established in my kingdom, and excellent majesty was added unto me.**

**Now I Nebuchadnezzar praise and extol and honour the King of heaven, all whose works are truth, and his ways judgment: and those that walk in pride he is able to abase [Dan. 4:36–37].**

Nebuchadnezzar's reason returned to him. His position as king of Babylon was restored to him, and his officials once again surrounded him. The kingdom was not jeopardized during his long period of absence, and added majesty came to him because he had now come to the knowledge of the living and true God.

# CHAPTER 5

*THEME: Feast of Belshazzar; fingers of God write upon the wall; failure of the wise men to read the handwriting; Daniel spurns the king's gifts; Daniel interprets the handwriting on the wall; fall of Babylon—fulfillment that very night*

The events recorded in chapter 5 took place a great deal later than those in the previous chapters. Again, this is just a page lifted from the historical records of Babylon, and much has taken place since the events of chapter 4.

## FEAST OF BELSHAZZAR

**Belshazzar the king made a great feast to a thousand of his lords, and drank wine before the thousand [Dan. 5:1].**

Now who was Belshazzar and how did he get to the throne? In the previous chapter the king was Nebuchadnezzar. Belshazzar has been a controversial figure in history, so we do need to take a moment to look at him. Even Dean Farrar said, "There was no such king as Belshazzar." John Walvoord in his book *Daniel, the Key to Prophetic Revelation*, p. 114, states: "Until the discovery of the Nabonidus Cylinder, no mention of Belshazzar, whom Daniel declares to be king of Babylon, had been found in extrabiblical literature. Critics of the authenticity and historicity of Daniel accordingly were free to question whether any such person as Belshazzar existed. Since the publication of Raymond Dougherty's scholarly research on Nabonidus and Belshazzar, based on the Nabonidus Cylinder and other sources, there is no ground for questioning the general historicity of Belshazzar. . . ." The name of Bel-shar-usur (Belshazzar) has been found on cylinders in which he is called the son of Nabonidus. It is now generally accepted that Belshazzar acted as a regent under his father, Nabonidus.

A resumé of the events which succeeded Nebuchadnezzar's reign would be helpful at this point. At the death of Nebuchadnezzar his only son, Evil-merodach, succeeded him, at about 561 B.C. (see 2 Kings 25:27). Evil-merodach was murdered by Nergal-sharezer who had married one of Nebuchadnezzar's daughters and now replaced him on the throne at about 559 B.C. Nergal-sharezer was succeeded by his young son who reigned only a few months before he was murdered by Nabonidus (the husband of another of Nebuchadnezzar's daughters). Nabonidus, the last ruler of the Babylonian empire, spent much of his time away from the kingdom on foreign expeditions, and Belshazzar his son remained at Babylon as his co-regent. All this reveals the accuracy of what Jeremiah the prophet had said: "And now have I given all these lands into the hand of Nebuchadnezzar the king of Babylon, my servant; and the beasts of the field have I given him also to serve him. And all nations shall serve him, and his son, and his

son's son, until the very time of his land come: and then many nations and great kings shall serve themselves of him" (Jer. 27:6–7). In other words, the Babylonian kingdom would last through the reign of a son and grandson of Nebuchadnezzar, and then the reign of the Babylonian kingdom as the head of gold would end.

We have further evidence of Belshazzar from a prayer of Nabonidus to the moon god for his son which was discovered on a clay cylinder: "My son, the offspring of my heart, might honor his godhead and not give himself to sin." Herodotus, the Greek historian, also mentions this and confirms it.

During the time of the events recorded in chapter 5, Nabonidus was on the field of battle while Belshazzar his son remained in Babylon. We will notice that when Belshazzar offers Daniel a position in the kingdom, it is to be the *third* ruler in the kingdom. Why not *second* to Belshazzar? Well, Belshazzar himself was number two—his father was really the king.

During the feast of Belshazzar introduced here in verse 1, Gobryas, the Median general, was besieging the city of Babylon from without. Xenophon, the Greek historian, describes how they took the city by detouring a canal of the Euphrates River back into its main channel and then letting the army flow under the walls of the city.

Therefore the events of this chapter, which for many years had been discounted by the critics, have today been confirmed by secular history. I would rather say that secular history has been confirmed by the Word of God. We know that historians are sometimes liars, and we cannot always depend upon their writings. However, here the historical research does agree with the account of Scripture.

"Belshazzar the king made a great feast to a thousand of his lords, and drank wine before the thousand." Note the arrogance of this young upstart Belshazzar who puts on this lavish affair while the armies of Gobryas were in full view of the city. Perhaps Belshazzar thought the city was impregnable. Nebuchadnezzar had built it to withstand any siege. The city wall was actually fifteen miles square and was constructed of brick. It was three hundred feet high and wide enough for four chariots to travel abreast around the city walls. In other words, they could have put a freeway around the top of the city. He had supplies of grain and water to last for years—in fact, there was a canal channeled off the Euphrates River which went right through the city.

Belshazzar's feast may have been in de-fiance of the enemy on the outside, or perhaps he wanted to build up the morale of those within. We are told here that it began with a big cocktail party.

Liquor today is a temporary prop for weak men and women, and alcohol is still the number one drug problem in the United States. I thought it rather ironical when a group of well-meaning citizens in Los Angeles—leaders from the schools, the churches, and politics—met together to discuss the drug problem among young people. You know how they opened their meeting? With a cocktail party! How hypocritical can you be? My friend, there are far more alcoholics in this country than drug addicts. Do you know that more than half of those killed in traffic accidents each year have alcohol in their blood at the time of the accident? Many billions of dollars are spent annually by Americans for alcoholic beverages. Alcohol is doing great damage—in automobile accidents and in homes being absolutely wrecked. The liquor problem is an alarming problem, and it is a problem common to all of mankind. Many nations have gone down because of liquor—and not because of marijuana. Don't misunderstand me—I am not supporting the use of marijuana. I just cannot get enthusiastic about these reformers who want to solve the drug problem but will not give up their alcohol. I don't care for that hypocrisy.

Old Belshazzar started off with a big cocktail party to get his guests high so they would enjoy the banquet that he was also going to put on for them.

**Belshazzar, whiles he tasted the wine, commanded to bring the golden and silver vessels which his father Nebuchadnezzar had taken out of the temple which was in Jerusalem; that the king, and his princes, his wives, and his concubines, might drink therein.**

**Then they brought the golden vessels that were taken out of the temple of the house of God which was at Jerusalem; and the king, and his princes, his wives, and his concubines, drank in them [Dan. 5:2–3].**

This man is not only defying the enemy outside, but now under the influence of alcohol he does an audacious thing which his grandfather would never have done. When Nebuchadnezzar took Jerusalem, he was an old, pagan, heathen king, and he took the vessels from the temple in Jerusalem. But when he came to the

knowledge of the living and true God, he had them stored away. To Belshazzar as a boy growing up in the palace, I guess they were a no-no—he had to leave those vessels alone. Now he drags them out and is going to serve his guests with them.

The vessels were no longer holy vessels. *Holy* means "that which is set aside for the use of God." However, Belshazzar *is* defying God by this act. And men today are defying God by their actions. We are prompted to speak out and to wonder why God doesn't deal with such people. My friend, God has plenty of time. He will take care of the situation, just as He is going to take care of Belshazzar.

Belshazzar knew that his grandfather had come to the knowledge of God and had praised and honored Him (see v. 22); yet he deliberately defied and profaned God. Proverbs 29:1 says, "He, that being often reproved hardeneth his neck, shall suddenly be destroyed, and that without remedy."

Everyone at the banquet was now beastly drunk. It was a scene of real debauchery and licentiousness. Ever since I was a boy, I have heard preachers preach on this banquet of Belshazzar—it must have been a real banquet according to some of them! One of the preachers talked about the dancing girls and the drinking and the laughter and all that sort of thing. If the truth were told, the sermon was like a vicarious trip to a nightclub, and we all enjoyed it. However, Scripture gives us no such details.

**They drank wine, and praised the gods of gold, and of silver, of brass, of iron, of wood, and of stone [Dan. 5:4].**

They toasted the gods, and it would have taken more than one night to toast all they had in Babylon. They cloaked their sin as an act of worship and veiled their blasphemy in the name of religion.

## FINGERS OF GOD WRITE UPON THE WALL

**In the same hour came forth fingers of a man's hand, and wrote over against the candlestick upon the plaster of the wall of the king's palace: and the king saw the part of the hand that wrote [Dan. 5:5].**

God now directly intervenes. He does not speak by dream or vision because this is a man whom He doesn't intend to reach. God would not endure this impious insult to heaven, so He writes on the wall of the banqueting hall. Is it done in anger? Very frankly, I think it is, and I believe the One who wrote this is the same One who wrote in the sand when they brought a sinful woman before Him (John 8:1–11). At that time it was a message of forgiveness; here, for Belshazzar, it is a message of doom. He has ignored the God of heaven, as Daniel will soon make clear to him.

**Then the king's countenance was changed, and his thoughts troubled him, so that the joints of his loins were loosed, and his knees smote one against another [Dan. 5:6].**

Belshazzar couldn't stand up. A few moments ago he had been too drunk to stand up. Although he's suddenly sober he still cannot stand up. What he has seen on the wall has scared him nearly to death; he is overwhelmed with fear.

**The king cried aloud to bring in the astrologers, the Chaldeans, and the soothsayers. And the king spake, and said to the wise men of Babylon, Whosoever shall read this writing, and shew me the interpretation thereof, shall be clothed with scarlet, and have a chain of gold about his neck, and shall be the third ruler in the kingdom [Dan. 5:7].**

Notice that the reward was to be "the *third* ruler in the kingdom." How accurate Daniel is! The man who wrote this book had to have been there and understood the circumstances: Nabonidus was the real king, and Belshazzar was only second in the kingdom.

## FAILURE OF THE WISE MEN TO READ THE HANDWRITING

**Then came in all the king's wise men: but they could not read the writing, nor make known to the king the interpretation thereof [Dan. 5:8].**

When Belshazzar finally got his senses back he had the wise men trotted in, and he asked them to give the interpretation of the writing on the wall. Although he offered them a handsome reward, they could only stand there looking at him. They didn't know the answer, and they didn't know what to do. This is the third time the wise men of Babylon have failed. On the third strike, you're out, you know—I think maybe this incident put them out of business.

**Then was king Belshazzar greatly troubled, and his countenance was changed**

in him, and his lords were astonied [Dan. 5:9].

You can imagine the change which took place in that banquet room. A few moments before they all had been laughing and drunk. Now they are sober and perplexed and troubled.

**Now the queen, by reason of the words of the king and his lords, came into the banquet house: and the queen spake and said, O king, live for ever: let not thy thoughts trouble thee, nor let thy countenance be changed [Dan. 5:10].**

The "queen" here is the queen mother, the wife of Nebuchadnezzar. She heard what had happened at the banquet, and she came in to speak to the king.

**There is a man in thy kingdom, in whom is the spirit of the holy gods; and in the days of thy father light and understanding and wisdom, like the wisdom of the gods, was found in him; whom the king Nebuchadnezzar thy father, the king, I say, thy father, made master of the magicians, astrologers, Chaldeans, and soothsayers [Dan. 5:11].**

"Nebuchadnezzar thy father"—relationships were indicated with one word; therefore "father" could refer to a father, a grandfather, a great-grandfather, or a great-great-grandfather.

**Forasmuch as an excellent spirit, and knowledge, and understanding, interpreting of dreams, and shewing of hard sentences, and dissolving of doubts, were found in the same Daniel, whom the king named Belteshazzar: now let Daniel be called, and he will shew the interpretation [Dan. 5:12].**

The queen mother has come to help her grandson out of his predicament. She tells him there is a man in his kingdom by the name of Daniel, a Spirit-filled man, who can decipher the writing.

## DANIEL SPURNS THE KING'S GIFTS

**Then was Daniel brought in before the king. And the king spake and said unto Daniel, Art thou that Daniel, which art of the children of the captivity of Judah, whom the king my father brought out of Jewry?**

**I have even heard of thee, that the spirit of the gods is in thee, and that light and**

understanding and excellent wisdom is found in thee [Dan. 5:13–14].

Daniel is now brought in. He evidently had been set aside and pushed out of office after the death of Nebuchadnezzar.

**And now the wise men, the astrologers, have been brought in before me, that they should read this writing, and make known unto me the interpretation thereof: but they could not shew the interpretation of the thing:**

**And I have heard of thee, that thou canst make interpretations, and dissolve doubts: now if thou canst read the writing, and make known to me the interpretation thereof, thou shalt be clothed with scarlet, and have a chain of gold about thy neck, and shalt be the third ruler in the kingdom [Dan. 5:15–16].**

Belshazzar butters him up and tells him that if he can give the interpretation which the wise men have failed to give, then he will be made the third ruler in the kingdom. Thus Daniel is offered the same reward which had been offered to the wise men.

**Then Daniel answered and said before the king, Let thy gifts be to thyself, and give thy rewards to another; yet I will read the writing unto the king, and make known to him the interpretation [Dan. 5:17].**

Daniel spurned these gifts. He was absolutely contemptuous of Belshazzar. I am sure that if the king had not been so filled with fear, he would not have ignored Daniel's insult. After all, why did Daniel need this reward? He would not have had it but for a few hours.

Before Daniel interprets the handwriting on the wall, he gives to this young king who is reigning under his father the best sermon he probably ever could receive. Daniel is not the young man who went into the presence of old King Nebuchadnezzar; he is now an old man going into the presence of a young king. There had been no generation gap with Nebuchadnezzar, and there is not one now. Listen to what Daniel tells Belshazzar:

**O thou king, the most high God gave Nebuchadnezzar thy father a kingdom, and majesty, and glory, and honour:**

**And for the majesty that he gave him, all people, nations, and languages, trembled and feared before him: whom**

he would he slew; and whom he would he kept alive; and whom he would he set up; and whom he would he put down [Dan. 5:18-19].

Nebuchadnezzar had been an absolute ruler on this earth. I believe there has not been another ruler like him and there will not be another until Antichrist rules. Daniel recites for Belshazzar how God had dealt with his grandfather: God had put him on the throne and had given him a world kingdom. Then he tells Belshazzar of the experience Nebuchadnezzar had had:

But when his heart was lifted up, and his mind hardened in pride, he was deposed from his kingly throne, and they took his glory from him:

And he was driven from the sons of men; and his heart was made like the beasts, and his dwelling was with the wild asses: they fed him with grass like oxen, and his body was wet with the dew of heaven; till he knew that the most high God ruled in the kingdom of men, and that he appointeth over it whomsoever he will.

And thou his son, O Belshazzar, hast not humbled thine heart, though thou knewest all this;

But hast lifted up thyself against the Lord of heaven; and they have brought the vessels of his house before thee, and thou, and thy lords, thy wives, and thy concubines, have drunk wine in them; and thou hast praised the gods of silver, and gold, of brass, iron, wood, and stone, which see not, nor hear, nor know: and the God in whose hand thy breath is, and whose are all thy ways, hast thou not glorified:

Then was the part of the hand sent from him; and this writing was written [Dan. 5:20-24].

Daniel preaches a very pointed and powerful sermon to Belshazzar. God had given the kingdom to Nebuchadnezzar, and he had been an absolute sovereign whom no man could question or hinder and whose wishes and whims were the law of the realm. However, when Nebuchadnezzar became filled with pride, God humbled him to a tragic episode. When Daniel reminds Belshazzar of Nebuchadnezzar's humiliating experience, you wonder if Daniel is rubbing it in. Perhaps he

is. He is reminding this young proud king that if he is lifted up by pride, it is either because of his drinking or because he is insane.

Belshazzar was a proud and vain man. Although he knew of his grandfather's insanity and of his descent to the level of a beast, he had not profited by this experience. Instead, he had committed sacrilege in using the vessels taken from God's temple in Jerusalem. He had defied the living and true God; and, by the profane use of that which had been holy, he had mocked God and insulted Him. Knowing the truth, he yet rejected it.

God destroys only those who have known the truth and have refused it. During the Great Tribulation Period those who will be deluded are those who have rejected the light. Paul writes in 2 Thessalonians 2:9-12, "Even him, whose coming is after the working of Satan with all power and signs and lying wonders, And with all deceivableness of unrighteousness in them that perish; because they received not the love of the truth, that they might be saved. And for this cause God shall send them strong delusion, that they should believe a lie: That they all might be damned who believed not the truth, but had pleasure in unrighteousness." Daniel is telling Belshazzar the principle by which God operates and which Paul has also since confirmed. The Lord Jesus also made this very clear when He said: "I am come in my Father's name, and ye receive me not: if another shall come in his own name, him ye will receive" (John 5:43).

The people in Germany who accepted Hitler were the same people that had rejected the Word of God in Christ. When you turn your back on the truth, you are wide open for any cult or ism which comes along. Why is it that cults and isms are growing today? Why is it that we hear so much about demonism and the worship of Satan? These things are being manifested in our nation because it is a nation that has had the Word of God and has rejected it.

We desperately need the *teaching* of the Word of God. We have enough preaching—we have enough people telling us what they think. What does *God* say? What difference does it make what you or I think? What God thinks—that is what is important.

Daniel concludes his sermon by stating that the handwriting was from God whom Belshazzar had spurned and ridiculed and blasphemed. Some people wonder if he had committed an unpardonable sin. I'll let you answer that. I just know that he had an oppor-

tunity here to receive the truth, and he turned it down.

## DANIEL INTERPRETS
## THE HANDWRITING ON THE WALL

**And this is the writing that was written, MENE, MENE, TEKEL, UPHARSIN [Dan. 5:25].**

I can't resist telling you the story of a man who was a foreigner in this country and was finally persuaded by his daughter to go to church, although he had great difficulty understanding English. However, he agreed to go with his daughter, Minnie, on the Sunday the preacher had unfortunately chosen for his text the account of this writing on the wall: MENE, MENE, TEKEL, UPHARSIN. As soon as the preacher mentioned this, the man grabbed Minnie his daughter by the hand and took her out of the church. "Father, what in the world is the matter?" she asked. With a very heavy accent, he replied, "Did you hear what that preacher said? He said, "Minnie, Minnie, come tickle the parson'!" Well, that is *not* the interpretation of this writing upon Belshazzar's wall. Daniel gives the interpretation:

**This is the interpretation of the thing: MENE; God hath numbered thy kingdom, and finished it [Dan. 5:26].**

*MENE* is translated "number", and it is repeated—Number, Number. It meant that God had numbered the kingdom of Babylon. We have a common colloquialism today, "His number is up." That is an accurate expression of the idea here. Also, in Psalm 90:12, we read, "So teach us to number our days, that we may apply our hearts unto wisdom." Only God knows when "our number is up"—when our earthly journey is over.

There was a young man who had never flown on a plane before, and his friends were encouraging him to take a trip to California. Well, he didn't want to go because he was afraid the plane might go down. His friends assured him, "It doesn't matter where you are—if your number's up, it's up—whether you're on a plane or not." But the boy said, "I'm not worried about *my* number being up. I just worry whether it's time for the *pilot's* number to be up. If it is, I'd rather not be on that plane!"

"MENE, MENE" means that God had numbered the Babylonian kingdom. He keeps track of every moment of every day. He determines beforehand the length of our days, and we cannot change that.

**TEKEL; Thou art weighed in the balances, and art found wanting [Dan. 5:27].**

*TEKEL* simply means "weight." Babylon had been put on the divine scales and had been found wanting. The people of Babylon didn't weigh enough—they were lightweight. God had raised up Babylon, and now He is going to put it down. Why? Because Babylon had not measured up to God's standards.

We read in the second and third chapters of the Book of Revelation about the seven churches of Asia Minor. There we see the Lord Jesus in the midst of the lampstands which represent the churches. He trims the wicks, pours in the oil, and snuffs out those which fail to light. He also judges the church today. Now we may weigh out at sixteen ounces to the pound on the Toledo scales we have down here, but Christ weighs us on the divine scale, and he had to say to every one of the churches, "Repent. You haven't measured up." He says the same thing to you and me today. Our righteousness is not only insufficient, it is filthy rags. Only His righteousness is going to stand the test and weigh out at sixteen ounces to the pound. Romans 3:21–23 says, "But now the righteousness of God without the law is manifested, being witnessed by the law and the prophets; Even the righteousness of God which is by faith of Jesus Christ unto all and upon all them that believe: for there is no difference: For all have sinned, and come short of the glory of God." You see, God weighs the actions of mankind.

**PERES; Thy kingdom is divided, and given to the Medes and Persians [Dan. 5:28].**

*PERES* is the singular form of *UPHARSIN* (as it was given in verse 25), and it means "divisions." The kingdom of Babylon is now to be divided and given to the Medes and Persians. In other words, the head of gold is to be removed; it is now time for the arms of silver to come into place. God is in supreme command of the kingdoms of the earth. Ezekiel wrote, "I will overturn, overturn, overturn, it: and it shall be no more, until he come whose right it is; and I will give it him" (Ezek. 21:27). God will continue to turn over kingdoms until Christ comes. I think He is doing a pretty good job. I remember a few years ago when Mussolini and Hitler and Stalin were real terrors to the world—all that crowd is gone now.

God is still in charge, and Christ is that "stone . . . cut out without hands" (Dan. 2:34) who is going to establish His kingdom down here someday.

**Then commanded Belshazzar, and they clothed Daniel with scarlet, and put a chain of gold about his neck, and made a proclamation concerning him, that he should be the third ruler in the kingdom [Dan. 5:29].**

Again, note that it is "the third ruler in the kingdom." How accurate the Book of Daniel is. Nabonidus was really the king, and Belshazzar, the grandson of Nebuchadnezzar, was second in command.

### FALL OF BABYLON—
### FULFILLMENT THAT VERY NIGHT

**In that night was Belshazzar the king of the Chaldeans slain.**

**And Darius the Median took the kingdom, being about threescore and two years old [Dan. 5:30–31].**

At the very time this banquet was being held, the Medes were marching underneath the walls of Babylon where the waters of the canal had flowed. As I mentioned earlier, underneath the wall of that city had been a canal which had brought water through the city, and now the waters had been cut off and channeled back into the main stream of the Euphrates River. This man Gobryas was marching his army into the inner city where the palace was located. History records that he and his men were on the inside of the inner city before the guards had even detected that anything was wrong. It is Xenophon, the Greek historian, who recorded for secular history the way in which the Persians took the city.

Belshazzar was slain—he had been weighed and found wanting. God does that, and He uses His scale and His standards. He says to you and me, ". . . all have sinned, and come short of the glory of God" (Rom. 3:23). You and I are not 100 percent wool, a yard wide and warranted not to wrinkle or unravel. We just do not measure up to God's standard. We are not on trial today; we are lost, and God is offering us salvation. Belshazzar had rejected God, and he was slain.

Darius the Median became the ruler of the kingdom of silver. He came with a sudden attack and destroyed Babylon. Isaiah had prophesied the fall of Babylon in Isaiah 21. In a future day another Babylon will fall by the hands of God (see Rev. 18)—thus will end man's vaunted civilization.

## CHAPTER 6

**THEME:** *Position of Daniel under Darius the Mede; plot to destroy Daniel; prayer of Daniel; Daniel in the den of lions; Daniel's deliverance, prosperity of Daniel and the decree of Darius*

Chapter 6 of the Book of Daniel is perhaps one of the most familiar in the Bible and certainly is the most well-known of this book. It is the account of Daniel in the den of lions. Have you ever stopped to think that Daniel spent only one night in the den of lions, but he spent a lifetime—from a boy of seventeen until he was about ninety—in the palace of pagan kings? It was more dangerous to live in that palace than it was to spend a night in the den of lions. The lions could not touch him, but yonder in the palace of Nebuchadnezzar, Nabonidus, Belshazzar, Darius the Median, and Cyrus who were pagan men, Daniel was in constant danger. However, he had the privilege of leading some of these men to a knowledge of the living and true God.

Daniel spent only one night in the den of lions, but we are going to look at it because it has a message for us today. This chapter concludes the strictly historical section of the Book of Daniel, and each historical event has been recorded for us for a purpose. This particular episode in Daniel's life is another illustration of the keeping power of God, and it is another adumbration of the way in which God will protect the remnant during the Great Tribulation Period. This chapter is a counterpart of chapter 3 where God preserved Daniel's three friends in the fiery furnace. As

there was a question as to the whereabouts of Daniel in chapter 3, there is also a question as to the whereabouts of the three Hebrew children here in chapter 6. Surely they would have followed Daniel in his obedience to God. Perhaps, since there has been a lapse of time, they are no longer living.

Chapters 3 and 6, therefore, give two aspects of the preservation of the remnant—both of Israel and of the Gentiles—during the Great Tribulation Period. In chapter 3 the emphasis is upon the pressures which are brought to bear by human hatred and persecution. In this chapter the emphasis is rather upon satanic hatred and persecution. The message for us today is, "Be sober, be vigilant; because your adversary the devil, as a roaring lion, walketh about, seeking whom he may devour" (1 Pet. 5:8). You and I live in a lions' cage. That cage is the world, and there is a big roaring lion prowling up and down the cage. Peter calls him our adversary, the Devil.

## POSITION OF DANIEL UNDER DARIUS THE MEDE

**It pleased Darius to set over the kingdom an hundred and twenty princes, which should be over the whole kingdom;**

**And over these three presidents; of whom Daniel was first: that the princes might give accounts unto them, and the king should have no damage [Dan. 6:1–2].**

With the opening of this chapter, we have again moved ahead historically. The kingdom of Babylon, the head of gold, has now disappeared; it has been removed from the number one spot of world power. Instead of Babylon, we have the Media-Persian empire which was represented by the arms of silver in the dream of Nebuchadnezzar. "Darius" is the Darius Cyaxares II of secular history, and he ruled for only two years. Cyrus, who followed him, was the son of Darius' sister Mundane and of Cambyses the Persian. This was what brought the empire together into the Media-Persian empire which now ruled the world.

Although we have moved into another empire, we still find Daniel in the position of prime minister under Darius the Mede. When we were considering the multimetallic image of gold, silver, brass, iron, and clay (ch. 2), we suggested that it pictured deterioration in a number of ways. There was deterioration in position, in the type of metal, etc. Here we can see that the inferiority of this kingdom to Nebuchadnezzar's is quite evident. Nebuchadnezzar's reign was autocratic and absolute—he did not share authority with anyone. Darius had "an hundred and twenty princes" who shared the responsibility and leadership with him. Over this group Darius placed "three presidents" who served as liaison officers between the princes and the king. There was therefore a distribution of responsibility and rulership. We are told that these three presidents (Daniel was one of them) held their position so that "the king should have no damage." This suggests that the presidents were to prevent the princes from stealing from or undermining the king in any way. Daniel was number one of the three presidents, and I take it that he was a man of about eighty years of age at this time.

**Then this Daniel was preferred above the presidents and princes, because an excellent spirit was in him; and the king thought to set him over the whole realm [Dan. 6:3].**

Daniel not only had seniority in this group, he had superiority. That he possessed "an excellent spirit" means Daniel was a Spirit-filled man. The king had such confidence in him that he placed Daniel next to himself in position and power.

## PLOT TO DESTROY DANIEL

**Then the presidents and princes sought to find occasion against Daniel concerning the kingdom; but they could find none occasion nor fault; forasmuch as he was faithful, neither was there any error or fault found in him [Dan. 6:4].**

One thing is for sure: When you find yourself the number one man in any position—whether it be in church, in politics, in school, or even in the home—you are the one who will be watched by those who have a jealous spirit. If there is a flaw in your life, if you have an Achilles' heel, they are going to discover that weak spot and may use it against you.

Now Daniel had a remarkable life behind him. These men could not find anything in this man's character or in his past life which they could seize upon and make something of. There has been many a politician who wished he had lived and acted a little differently—

actually, that could be said of mankind generally.

Today a child of God ought to live so that the charges which inevitably will be leveled against him will be a lie. You cannot keep people from talking about you, but you can so live as to make them liars when they do talk about you. The apostle Paul enjoins all believers: "That ye may be blameless and harmless, the sons of God, without rebuke, in the midst of a crooked and perverse nation, among whom ye shine as lights in the world" (Phil. 2:15). This was Paul's personal testimony—"And herein do I exercise myself, to have always a conscience void of offence toward God, and toward men" (Acts 24:16). In other words, Paul could lie down at night and go to sleep, and he did not have a bad conscience troubling him. That ought to be true of every believer. Someone has said that a conscience is something that only a good man can enjoy.

**Then said these men, We shall not find any occasion against this Daniel, except we find it against him concerning the law of his God [Dan. 6:5].**

Daniel was different—God had made His people different. When he was first brought to the court of Nebuchadnezzar as a boy slave, he had asked for a different diet. From then on, the life of Daniel was different, and these men were aware of that. They said, "If we are going to find anything wrong with him, we are going to have to find it in his religion." When they said "wrong," they meant something which they could accuse him of before the king. The only vulnerable spot in Daniel, as these politicians saw it, was his religion. This was certainly a case of Daniel's good being "evil-spoken of." They knew that Daniel was faithful to God and was dependent upon Him. His prayer life was something that was well-known. Therefore, they are going to have to draw a conflict between the king and Daniel's religion.

**Then these presidents and princes assembled together to the king, and said thus unto him, King Darius, live for ever.**

**All the presidents of the kingdom, the governors, and the princes, the counsellors, and the captains, have consulted together to establish a royal statute, and to make a firm decree, that whosoever shall ask a petition of any God or man for thirty days, save of thee, O king, he shall be cast into the den of lions [Dan. 6:6–7].**

The plot of these princes and presidents and petty politicians was very subtle. King Darius was a good man. That is obvious from secular history, and I think it is certainly the implication of the Book of Daniel. But Darius had a vulnerable spot (many of us have it), and that was his vanity—he yielded to flattery.

One of the tragedies of our day is that there are many Christians, especially of financial means, who give only to organizations where the leader of the organization flatters them and butters them up. It is my conviction that we do not need to stoop to flattering people to get them to contribute financially to a ministry; God will speak to people's hearts, if He wants them to support a ministry.

A long time ago I discovered that I am not as bad as my enemies say and I am not nearly as good as my friends say that I am. There is always a danger of being carried away by flattery. I used to tell my students in seminary, "Fellows, it does not matter how poor a preacher you are or what church you are in, the Lord will always have some dear lady who will tell you how wonderful you are. She will come up to you after you have preached the lousiest sermon in the world, and she will tell you, 'My, I think you are another Dwight L. Moody on the scene!' It is nice to have such dear ladies who want to encourage you like that, but just don't believe them. There is a danger if you do."

These men flattered Darius, and he yielded to it. He thought, *My, this is great!* So he drafted a bill, and it was made a statute. He thus elevated himself to the position of deity, and prayer was to be offered only to him.

**Now, O king, establish the decree, and sign the writing, that it be not changed, according to the law of the Medes and Persians, which altereth not.**

**Wherefore king Darius signed the writing and the decree [Dan. 6:8–9].**

Darius yielded to his weakness, and now this decree which has gone out, signed by the king, cannot be changed. Even the king of the Medes and Persians himself cannot change it after it has been passed. All this puts Daniel in a bad spot.

## PRAYER OF DANIEL

**Now when Daniel knew that the writing was signed, he went into his house; and his windows being open in his chamber toward Jerusalem, he kneeled upon his knees three times a day, and**

prayed, and gave thanks before his God, as he did aforetime [Dan. 6:10].

Notice the reaction of Daniel to this new law. He did not do anything audacious or foolhardy when he opened those windows—he had been doing that for years. He simply did not back down. He did not act in a cowardly and compromising manner by closing the windows but went about his usual prayer life.

I would like to note that he *kneeled* to pray. The proper posture of prayer is often a question. I really doubt that the posture of prayer is the important thing. Victor Hugo said that the soul is on its knees many times regardless of the position of the body. The posture of the *spirit* of the man is what is important. However, if you want to select a posture for prayer, it is kneeling, and that is set before us here.

Notice also that Daniel prayed toward Jerusalem. That was the direction of Daniel's life, and he didn't intend to change because of Darius' decree. When away from the temple in Jerusalem, God's people of that day were to pray facing in that direction. Today, no earthly place is preferred above another; the Lord Jesus said, ". . . ye shall neither in this mountain, nor yet at Jerusalem, worship the Father. . . . God is a Spirit: and they that worship him must worship him in spirit and in truth" (John 4:21, 24).

**Then these men assembled, and found Daniel praying and making supplication before his God [Dan. 6:11].**

These men were waiting for Daniel, and that was really a compliment. This man had a reputation, and they had a feeling that he would not back down from his convictions.

**Then they came near, and spake before the king concerning the king's decree; Hast thou not signed a decree, that every man that shall ask a petition of any God or man within thirty days, save of thee, O king, shall be cast into the den of lions? The king answered and said, The thing is true, according to the law of the Medes and Persians, which altereth not.**

**Then answered they and said before the king, That Daniel, which is of the children of the captivity of Judah, regardeth not thee, O king, nor the decree that thou hast signed, but maketh his petition three times a day.**

Then the king, when he heard these words, was sore displeased with himself, and set his heart on Daniel to deliver him: and he laboured till the going down of the sun to deliver him [Dan. 6:12–14].

These men called attention to the fact that Daniel was disobeying: he was at an open window praying toward Jerusalem. Believe me, this was something which distressed the king. Darius could not change his own law; Nebuchadnezzar would have been able to. This is evidence of the deterioration from one kingdom to the next.

**Then these men assembled unto the king, and said unto the king, Know, O king, that the law of the Medes and Persians is, That no decree nor statute which the king establisheth may be changed [Dan. 6:15].**

Daniel is to be put in the den of lions, and there is nothing the king can do about it.

### DANIEL IN THE DEN OF LIONS

**Then the king commanded and they brought Daniel, and cast him into the den of lions. Now the king spake and said unto Daniel, Thy God whom thou servest continually, he will deliver thee [Dan. 6:16].**

I am of the opinion that the king did not believe what he said. It was like one of the halfhearted things some of us saints say today. We tell someone else, "Oh, the Lord will take care of you," but if we were in that predicament, we wouldn't quite trust Him like that. King Darius, though, had come a long way. He recognized that the God of Daniel was omnipotent and sovereign and could deliver him. He also saw that Daniel was faithful to God. Daniel's testimony in the dissolute court of two world powers was nothing short of miraculous. His unaffected and unassuming life was a powerful witness to the saving grace of God in that day.

**And a stone was brought, and laid upon the mouth of the den; and the king sealed it with his own signet, and with the signet of his lords; that the purpose might not be changed concerning Daniel [Dan. 6:17].**

They put a stone against the mouth of the den of lions, and Daniel spent the night down there. These lions were fierce and wild beasts—they were not toothless old lions.

There is the story about the man who got a job at a zoo, and he was asked to go into the lions' cage to feed the lions. When he refused, the keeper said, "Look, those lions are toothless!" The man replied, "Yes, I noticed that, but they could *gum* me to death."

Daniel's lions had teeth, and they were fierce, but the safest place that night just happened to be the den of lions. I think Daniel got a pretty good night's sleep down there. The interesting thing is that the king was more disturbed than Daniel and was probably in more danger.

## DANIEL'S DELIVERANCE

**Then the king went to his palace, and passed the night fasting: neither were instruments of music brought before him: and his sleep went from him [Dan. 6:18].**

The king didn't sleep, but Daniel did! Darius passed a sleepless night due to his concern for Daniel.

**Then the king arose very early in the morning, and went in haste unto the den of lions.**

**And when he came to the den, he cried with a lamentable voice unto Daniel: and the king spake and said to Daniel, O Daniel, servant of the living God, is thy God, whom thou servest continually, able to deliver thee from the lions? [Dan. 6:19–20].**

I don't know if the king expected Daniel to answer, but Daniel answered:

**Then said Daniel unto the king, O king, live for ever.**

**My god hath sent his angel, and hath shut the lions' mouths, that they have not hurt me: forasmuch as before him innocency was found in me; and also before thee, O king, have I done no hurt [Dan. 6:21–22].**

"O king, live for ever" was Daniel's polite and respectful greeting. It was as if Daniel said, "Did you have a good night?" And of course, the king hadn't had a good night, but Daniel had.

Daniel evidently had been given the same assurance as had his three friends in the fiery furnace that God could and would deliver him. "His angel" was evidently the same One Nebuchadnezzar had seen in the fiery furnace—the pre-incarnate Christ Himself.

**Then was the king exceeding glad for him, and commanded that they should take Daniel up out of the den. So Daniel was taken up out of the den, and no manner of hurt was found upon him, because he believed in his God [Dan. 6:23].**

The king loved Daniel and was sincerely delighted at his preservation. Daniel was saved by faith: "Who through faith subdued kingdoms, wrought righteousness, obtained promises, *stopped the mouths of lions*" (Heb. 11:33, italics mine).

**And the king commanded, and they brought those men which had accused Daniel, and they cast them into the den of lions, them, their children, and their wives; and the lions had the mastery of them, and brake all their bones in pieces or ever they came at the bottom of the den [Dan. 6:24].**

The dastardly plot of those who were enemies of Daniel was uncovered. Together with their families, they were cast into the den of lions. The viciousness of the lions is now demonstrated in all its hideousness.

## PROSPERITY OF DANIEL AND THE DECREE OF DARIUS

**Then king Darius wrote unto all people, nations, and languages, that dwell in all the earth; Peace be multiplied unto you [Dan. 6:25].**

Darius sent out a worldwide decree which was his personal testimony. He had found the same peace that had come to Nebuchadnezzar (see Dan. 4:1). This testimony of peace comes from the same man who could not sleep the night before.

**I make a decree, That in every dominion of my kingdom men tremble and fear before the God of Daniel: for he is the living God, and stedfast for ever, and his kingdom that which shall not be destroyed, and his dominion shall be even unto the end.**

**He delivereth and rescueth, and he worketh signs and wonders in heaven and in earth, who hath delivered Daniel from the power of the lions [Dan. 6: 26–27].**

Darius commands men to fear the God of Daniel and testifies that He is the living God (in contrast to idols) and that He is sovereign.

Darius was brought to God through the miracle of the den of lions.

**So this Daniel prospered in the reign of Darius, and in the reign of Cyrus the Persian [Dan. 6:28].**

Daniel's position was secure, and he maintained it to the end of his life which came during the reign of Cyrus. It was Cyrus who made the decree permitting the Jews to return to Palestine (see 2 Chron. 36:22–23; Ezra 1:11).

This concludes the strictly historical section of the Book of Daniel. From this point on the book will be mainly concerned with the visions and prophecies which were given to Daniel over the long period of his life spent in a foreign land.

# CHAPTER 7

*THEME: Daniel's vision of the four beasts; the visions of the Son of Man coming in clouds of heaven; the definition of the four beasts; the explanation of the fourth beast*

Chapter 7 opens a new and different section of the Book of Daniel. The first six chapters contained the historic night with prophetic light; the last six chapters are prophetic light in the historic night. Whereas in the first section of the book the emphasis was upon the historical, the emphasis will now be on the prophetic, yet still with an historical background.

God gives to Daniel several visions of four beasts which are quite remarkable. Daniel had these visions at different periods. The vision of chapter 7 was in the first year of King Belshazzar. In chapter 8 the vision was seen in the third year of the reign of Belshazzar. In chapter 9 it was in the first year of Darius; in chapter 10 it was the third year of Cyrus; and in chapters 11 and 12 the vision was seen in the first year of Darius. Daniel did not record these visions in the historical section but gathered these prophetic visions together in this second section of his book.

## DANIEL'S VISION OF THE FOUR BEASTS

Nebuchadnezzar of Babylon was a very brilliant man who found himself suddenly elevated to the position of the first great world ruler. He had territory on three continents. He had taken Egypt in North Africa, and he also had territory in Europe. He had a tremendous empire, greater than any the world had ever known. But Nebuchadnezzar wondered about the future: What would happen to him and to his empire? He dreamed a dream about a multimetallic image, and through Daniel God gave the interpretation of the dream (see Dan. 2).

There were *four* different kinds of metals in Nebuchadnezzar's image—not five, but four metals. Now Daniel's vision of the beasts is of *four* beasts—the lion, the bear, the panther (or leopard), and a composite beast which has been called a nondescript beast. The last was a wild-looking animal which has never been seen on land or sea or in the air—it simply does not exist as a real beast. Well, after he had had visions and dreams like that, I don't think Daniel slept much that night. He probably got a better night's sleep in the den of lions than he did the night he had this dream!

I imagine that, after God gave him Nebuchadnezzar's image dream and its interpretation, Daniel was quite puzzled. As a good student and follower of the Old Testament, Daniel knew of the covenant which God had made with David—that One was coming in his line who would be a world ruler. Now with the four world kingdoms of Nebuchadnezzar's dream before him, he wondered how God's plan and program of raising up a world ruler from David would fit into all this. The rest of the Book of Daniel is going to answer that question. It will give us world history prewritten, history that has been followed right down to the minutest detail for twenty-five hundred years since the time it was written.

God speaks to Daniel through his vision of the four beasts to satisfy his heart and to give him the explanation he needed. In Daniel's vision of the multimetallic image the outward

splendor and glory of the kingdoms was demonstrated—that was what God knew would attract Nebuchadnezzar's attention. But in the vision He gives to Daniel, God lets him in on the inward character and the true nature of these kingdoms. What are these kingdoms? These are like wild beasts, carnivorous in nature, and destructive killers every one of them.

The four beasts of Daniel's vision of course correspond to the four metals in the image of Nebuchadnezzar's vision. *In the Decline and Fall of the Roman Empire*, the historian Edward Gibbon, who was not a Christian, said, "The four empires are clearly delineated; and the invincible armies of the Romans are described with as much clearness in the prophecies of Daniel, as in the histories of Justin and Diodorus." The following chart summarizes the correspondence between the two visions and the four kingdoms they represent:

| MULTI-METALLIC IMAGE (Chapter 2) | FOUR BEASTS (Chapter 7) | NATIONS DESIGNATED |
|---|---|---|
| Head of Gold | Lion | Babylon |
| Arms of Silver | Bear | Media-Persia |
| Sides of Brass | Panther (leopard) | Graeco-Macedonia |
| Legs of Iron; | Composite beast | Rome |
| Feet of Iron and Clay | | |

**In the first year of Belshazzar king of Babylon Daniel had a dream and visions of his head upon his bed: then he wrote the dream, and told the sum of the matters [Dan. 7:1].**

The time of this vision is pinpointed historically for us in the first year of Belshazzar; that is, toward the end of the time that the head of gold, or Babylon, was ruling in the world. Belshazzar was reigning in Babylon the night Gobryas came with his army under the city wall where the canal had once flowed and took the city.

"Visions" suggests that the first three beasts are given in the first vision, the second vision concerned the fourth beast only, and the third vision is a scene in heaven. Therefore, there are actually three visions which are recorded here.

"He wrote the dream." Daniel was in obscurity in Babylon at this time, and I think he had more opportunity to give attention to the Word of God and to writing. Perhaps it was in this period that he recorded the first part of the Book of Daniel.

**Daniel spake and said, I saw in my vision by night, and, behold, the four winds of the heaven strove upon the great sea [Dan. 7:2].**

The four winds broke violently "upon the *great sea*," that is, upon the Mediterranean Sea, for that is the word given to it. The "winds" speak of agitation, propaganda, public opinion, and disturbance. The "sea" suggests the masses, the mob, and the peoples of the Gentiles (see Matt. 13:47; Rev. 13:1; Isa. 57:20). In Revelation we read: "And there came one of the seven angels which had the seven vials, and talked with me, saying unto me, Come hither; I will shew unto thee the judgment of the great whore that sitteth upon many waters. . . . And he saith unto me, The waters which thou sawest, where the whore sitteth, are peoples, and multitudes, and nations, and tongues" (Rev. 17:1, 15). The sea, therefore, is this conglomerate population of Gentiles throughout the world.

Customarily the wind blows from only one direction at a time, but here it is a tornado of great violence with the wind coming from all directions. It refers not only to the disturbed conditions out of which these four nations arose, but particularly to the last stage of the fourth kingdom (vv. 11, 12, 17) in which certain ideologies shall strive to capture the thinking of the disturbed masses of all nations and tribes. We are in that last stage of the fourth kingdom today. We are very close, apparently, to the time when the Roman Empire will be brought back together again. It still exists—it lives in Italy, France, Germany, Spain, and all the nations in Europe which were in the Roman Empire. All it needs is someone who will put it back together. We apparently are near that time—how near I do not think we even ought to speculate.

All these nations are to be brought back together with their different ideologies, forms of government, and viewpoints. At this point we should call attention to the deadly parallel between the circumstances herein described and our own modern world situation. This is the reason I say we are evidently drawing toward the end of the age. Entire continents are awakening today, and all are demanding a place in the sun. People who have had a primitive civilization for centuries have suddenly been catapulted into the jet age. Radios and missiles have changed the thinking of the

masses. New ideologies have captured their minds, and our disturbed world is desperately trying to avoid World War III.

I wonder if you have noticed as you listen to radio and look at television today that we are being brainwashed? All kinds of propaganda are being given to us. The disturbed masses are being fed propaganda. I do not mind confessing that I am interested in giving out propaganda also—the propaganda of the Word of God. I wish that I could brainwash everyone who reads this book and make him a believer in the Lord Jesus Christ.

It is the "little horn" of this chapter who will succeed in capturing the minds of the masses. He is described as having "a mouth speaking great things" (v. 8). He is going to sell himself to the world when he appears. He will be Satan's man. The Lord Jesus said, "I am come in my Father's name, and ye receive me not: if another shall come in his own name, him ye will receive" (John 5:43).

Humanism today is glorifying mankind everywhere. They are glorifying public officials, and they are glorifying stage and screen actors (who also glorify one another). These are the people who are in control of the various media today. They have made the theater respectable, whereas it was clearly the theater which corrupted the morals of the Greeks and which is corrupting our morals today.

I hear young people talking about their "freedom," but they use the same line of talk and wear the same clothes that can be found everywhere across the country. They really have no freedom at all. People are being brainwashed today. We would all be better off if we would get brainwashed with the Word of God.

This is a frightful picture and a disturbed scene that Daniel is presenting to us. Don't misunderstand me—I am not saying that what we see today is a fulfillment of prophecy. I am simply saying that the winds are beginning to blow; it may be a pretty long storm.

**And four great beasts came up from the sea, diverse one from another [Dan. 7:3].**

The four beasts are different kinds of beasts: the lion, the bear, the panther, and the beast with ten horns. I have never seen a beast with ten horns except in this book. These beasts represent kingdoms formed out of many peoples, tongues, tribes, and nations.

**The first was like a lion, and had eagle's wings: I beheld till the wings thereof were plucked, and it was lifted up from the earth, and made stand upon the feet as a man, and a man's heart was given to it [Dan. 7:4].**

The lion with eagle's wings represents Babylon in particular. King Nebuchadnezzar is intended also, as verse 17 declares that the four beasts represent four kings.

This lion had eagle's wings, and that makes it an unusual lion. These eagle's wings denote the ability that Babylon had of moving an army speedily, which has been the secret of any great world power down through history. It was a Tennessean named Gen. Nathan Bedford Forrest who, when he was asked how to win battles, said, The one that gets there "the first with the most" is the one that is going to win. Nebuchadnezzar had the ability to move an army speedily, and that was the thing which brought him to world power. Such was the secret of Alexander the Great, the Roman caesars, and of course Napoleon. The coming in of the airplane was significant in World War I, and then World War II was won largely by air power. The one who can move the quickest with the greatest power will be the world ruler. This was true of Babylon in the past, and it will probably be the determining factor in the future.

"The wings thereof were plucked" evidently refers to the humbling of Nebuchadnezzar in his mental lapse and loss of identity.

"And made stand upon the feet as a man"—denotes Nebuchadnezzar's restoration. He became like a beast and acted like one, but his mind was restored, and he was brought back to sanity.

"A man's heart was given to it." I believe this refers to Nebuchadnezzar's conversion. I think he came to know the living and true God.

The lion corresponds to the head of gold, Babylon. Today she is a heap of ruins; but, as predicted by Jeremiah, those very ruins bear eloquent testimony to the outward glory that was hers. Among those ruins one can see a proud lion standing on a pedestal; it was the thing which represented that great empire. Excavation of the city of Babylon reveals the glory that was once there. The hanging gardens of Babylon were one of the seven wonders of the ancient world. Nebuchadnezzar had married a girl from the hill country, but since Babylon was built down on a plain—just like west Texas—he built the hanging gardens for her so that she wouldn't be homesick. It was a thing of great beauty. There was also a

great ziggurat evidently patterned after the Tower of Babel. It was made of brick, and around it like a corkscrew ran a runway that went to the top. There at the top were altars on which were offered human sacrifices. The Babylonians had a postal system second to none. They had interior bathtubs with brass plumbing. They were a literate people with a tremendous library there in the city. Around the city was a three hundred foot high wall, wide enough that four chariots could ride abreast upon it, and which well protected the entire city.

While the head of gold on the multimetallic image represents the outward glory of this advanced civilization, the cruel nature of the lion describes the brutal paganism of this kingdom which is clearly illustrated in chapters 2 and 3 of the Book of Daniel.

**And behold another beast, a second, like to a bear, and it raised up itself on one side, and it had three ribs in the mouth of it between the teeth of it: and they said thus unto it, Arise, devour much flesh [Dan. 7:5].**

The bear, representing the kingdom of Media-Persia, corresponds to the arms of silver of Nebuchadnezzar's image. As the bear raised itself up on one side, the image was ambidextrous. First he struck with the strong left hand of Medes, conquering Babylon; then he followed through with the right uppercut of the Persians who took over Egypt and the rest of the world which had been ruled by Babylon.

"Three ribs in the mouth" are the three kingdoms that constituted this empire: Babylon, Lydia, and Egypt.

There are no wings on this bear, but it was told, "Arise, devour much flesh." The army of the Media-Persians moved like a great, lumbering, and rumbling bear—they even took their families along with them. It was Xerxes who led about 300,000 men and three hundred ships against Greece at Thermopylae and was defeated. His fleet was destroyed by a storm because God did not intend the East to control the West at that particular time.

**After this I beheld, and lo another, like a leopard, which had upon the back of it four wings of a fowl; the beast had also four heads; and dominion was given to it [Dan. 7:6].**

"Leopard" would perhaps be better translated "panther." A panther, which leaps with suddenness upon its helpless prey, represents the Graeco-Macedonian empire of Alexander the Great.

"Four wings" further accentuates the ability of Alexander to move his army with rapidity and to strike suddenly. In comparison it would have made Nebuchadnezzar's army look like it was on a slow train through Arkansas. Strong nations which have gained world dominion have developed the ability to move and strike with great speed. Today, in the cold war, we are witnessing a missiles race as a further refinement of the process of adding more "wings" to a nation.

The "four heads" depict the division of Alexander's empire at the time of his death in his early thirties. Babylon went down on a drunken orgy and so did Alexander—they both went the same way. Our nation is going down the same path today. We are living in a day when the social drink is accepted. Our people don't want their young people on drugs, but they don't mind if they go out drinking. Following the death of Alexander, four of his generals divided the world empire which he had carved out, because each of them knew they could not control the whole. Cassander took Macedonia; Lysimachus took Asia Minor; Seleucus took Syria, out of which came the "little horn" of Daniel 8, Antiochus Epiphanes, who wrought such havoc with the temple in Jerusalem; and finally, Ptolemy took Egypt, and of course, Cleopatra came along later in that line.

Scripture does not give us an historical record of the Graeco-Macedonian kingdom. It falls chronologically between the Old and New Testaments—the period known as the intertestament period. It was, however, the time when the remnant in Palestine endured the greatest suffering at the hands of Egypt and Syria.

**After this I saw in the night visions, and behold a fourth beast, dreadful and terrible, and strong exceedingly; and it had great iron teeth: it devoured and brake in pieces, and stamped the residue with the feet of it: and it was diverse from all the beasts that were before it; and it had ten horns [Dan. 7:7].**

This nondescript beast with ten horns represents the Roman Empire, just as the legs of iron of Nebuchadnezzar's image did. We will find this interpreted in detail in verses 19–28. We want to get the explanation that the Spirit of God has given to us, and that will deliver us from any speculation.

More attention is given to the fourth beast than to all of the other three put together. This section is very important to us because we are living in the time of the fourth beast—the time when the ten toes and horns are beginning to manifest themselves.

The fourth beast is altogether different from the others, and he is given in a separate vision. All the other beasts have counterparts in the jungles and zoos today. We all have seen a lion, or a bear, or a panther, but we have never seen a beast like this on land or sea or in the air. This is really an unusual beast. After you have had a night of dreaming about beasts like this, I don't think an aspirin tablet or a sleeping pill would do you any good at all! I think you would be awake the rest of the night.

The beast is described as "dreadful and terrible, and strong exceedingly." This beast which represents the Roman Empire is characterized by strength. It incited dread and terror, and it bore no resemblance to any beast that preceded it.

"It had great iron teeth," and this identifies it with the legs of iron of the image vision—which is the Roman Empire. The iron heel of Rome was on the neck of this world for one millennium. A great deal has been said about the Roman Empire, and even to this day it amazes historians. Gibbon has said of it: "The empire of the Romans filled the world, and when the empire fell into the hands of a single person, the world became a safe and dreary prison for his enemies. To resist was fatal and it was impossible to fly."

Another writer, Dr. Robert D. Culver, who has a very fine book on Daniel entitled *Daniel: Decoder of Dreams*, has made this statement: "Two millennia ago, Rome gave the world the ecumenical unity which the League of Nations and the United Nations organizations have sought to give in our time. The modern attempts are not original at all (as many of our contemporaries suppose), but are revivals of the ancient Roman ideal which never since the time of Augustus Caesar has been wholly lost."

The Roman Empire simply fell apart; it lives on in many nations of Europe, in those nations which border the Mediterranean and in North Africa—all those which were a part of the Roman Empire. No one overcame Rome, but it fell apart into these different nations.

This unusual beast had ten horns which obviously correspond to the feet of the image with ten toes. The emphasis here is not upon the *origin* of this empire, but rather upon the *end time*—the period of the ten horns.

The vision of this fourth beast is made further important to us because it is yet unfulfilled. Apparently we are living in some period toward the end time. The visions of the three beasts have been fulfilled, which means that three-fourths of this prophecy has already been literally fulfilled; there remains for the future only the time of the "horns." The fourth kingdom of Rome has already appeared. Although it fell apart, it will come back together in ten kingdoms. It will be put together by the one whom the Word of God has labeled the Antichrist.

**I considered the horns, and, behold, there came up among them another little horn, before whom there were three of the first horns plucked up by the roots: and, behold, in this horn were eyes like the eyes of man, and a mouth speaking great things [Dan. 7:8].**

Our attention is now directed to the ten horns. Notice that they do not represent a fifth kingdom: they grow out of the head of the fourth beast and are the last development of the fourth beast. In the toes of the first vision, the vision of the image, they are iron and clay. Iron is still there—Rome is still there, but the clay, the weakness, is there also. I think the iron represents the autocratic rule of one man, and the clay represents the crowd, a democracy.

Very candidly, we see that type of weakness in democracy today. We are proud of the freedom we have—I thank God we have it—but it is almost a joke to talk about how important John Q. Public is. You and I are not very important, to tell the truth. Oh, every now and then when it's time for elections, the politicians tell us how important and wonderful and educated we are. However, we have very little to do with the control of our government or with the choice of our president. The lobbyists and the politicians are making the choices. I thank God for the liberty we have, but we have been brainwashed to think as they think.

God's ideal government is not a democracy—it is a real dictatorship. When Jesus Christ rules on this earth, He is not going to ask anyone what he wants done. He is going to make the choices, and this earth is going to be run the way He wants to run it. That is the reason it would be best if you and I would become conformed to His image; otherwise we will be very uncomfortable under His dic-

tatorship. Actually, He will put out of His kingdom anything that offends, anyone who is in rebellion against Him. We are to bow to Him and to His absolute rule.

Rome fell apart because of internal corruption and rottenness and drunkenness. All four of these empires went down with drunkenness. In our own country we say drugs are a problem, but liquor is legal. Who are we kidding? My friend, there are millions of alcoholics trying to hold down jobs today. That is only part of the problem, because that does not include the number of housewives and even children who are alcoholics but are not represented in the statistics. No one knows about them until they commit suicide or need to be put into a mental institution. That is the picture of America in the dark hour in which we live.

Rome is going to be put together again, and it is interesting that men are looking for someone who will be able to do it. The German historian Hoffman has said this: "When Germans and Slavs advanced partly into Roman ground, anyhow into the historical position of the Roman Empire, their princes intermarried with Roman families. Charlemagne was descended from a Roman house; almost at the same time the German Emperor Otho II and the Russian Grand-Prince Vladimir intermarried with daughters of the East-Roman Emperor. This was characteristic for the relation of the immigrating nations to Rome; *they did not found a new kingdom, but continued the Roman.* And so it continues to the end of all earthly power, until its final ramification into ten kingdoms. To attempt now to mark out these would be as misplaced as to fix the Coming of Christ (with which they stand connected) tomorrow or the next day."

"Another little horn" becomes the key to the entire situation. He uproots three of the ten horns and establishes himself over all. I do not know who the ten kingdoms are, but they come from the disintegration of the Roman Empire.

"In this horn were eyes," denoting human intelligence and genius.

"A mouth speaking great things" denotes the blasphemy of this man.

## THE VISIONS OF THE SON OF MAN COMING IN CLOUDS OF HEAVEN

**I beheld till the thrones were cast down, and the Ancient of days did sit, whose garment was white as snow, and the hair of his head like the pure wool:**

**his throne was like the fiery flame, and his wheels as burning fire [Dan. 7:9].**

The scene shifts to heaven, and the throne of God is revealed. This is the same scene described in chapters 4 and 5 of the Book of Revelation. It is the preparation for the judgment of the Great Tribulation and the second coming of Christ to the earth.

"I beheld till the thrones were cast down [placed]" corresponds to Revelation 4:4. While in Revelation John gives the number of the elders and other details, Daniel is not concerned with such since his subject does not include the church and its future.

"The Ancient of days" is the eternal God.

"Whose garment was white as snow" refers to His attributes of holiness and righteousness.

"The hair of his head like the pure wool" speaks of His infinite wisdom.

"His throne was like the fiery flame" speaks of judgment (see Rev. 4:5).

"His wheels as burning fire" speaks of the resistless energy and restless power of God (cf. Ezek. 1:13–21).

**A fiery stream issued and came forth from before him: thousand thousands ministered unto him, and ten thousand times ten thousand stood before him: the judgment was set, and the books were opened [Dan. 7:10].**

This is not the Great White Throne judgment which occurs after the Millennium, but is the setting for the judgment of the Great Tribulation and the return of Christ to establish His millennial kingdom here upon earth (see Rev. 5:11–14).

**I beheld then because of the voice of the great words which the horn spake: I beheld even till the beast was slain, and his body destroyed, and given to the burning flame [Dan. 7:11].**

While God is setting the judgment scene in heaven to determine who will enter the kingdom, on earth "the little horn" is blaspheming and boasting the loudest (see Rev. 13:5–6). However, his judgment is fixed and his kingdom is doomed.

The emphasis with this kingdom, represented by the last beast, is not on its beginning but on its end. The appearance of "the little horn" is shortly before Christ comes to judge living nations and individuals. This period equates the Great Tribulation Period.

As concerning the rest of the beasts, they had their dominion taken away: yet their lives were prolonged for a season and time [Dan. 7:12].

Although the first three beasts were destroyed, the ideology and philosophy of the kingdoms they represent apparently live on and will be manifested in the Great Tribulation Period.

I saw in the night visions, and, behold, one like the Son of man came with the clouds of heaven, and came to the Ancient of days, and they brought him near before him [Dan. 7:13].

The Son of God in heaven is here invested with the authority to take the kingdoms of this world from the Gentiles and establish His kingdom. Jesus referred to this passage when He was put on oath at His trial before the Sanhedrin: ". . . Again the high priest asked him, and said unto him, Art thou the Christ, the Son of the Blessed? And Jesus said, I am: and ye shall see the Son of man sitting on the right hand of power, and coming in the clouds of heaven" (Mark 14:61–62). The angel prophesied at the time of His birth: "He shall be great, and shall be called the Son of the Highest: and the Lord God shall give unto him the throne of his father David" (Luke 1:32).

Therefore what we have here is a very clear-cut statement that the Lord Jesus is that "stone cut out without hands" which smites the image—He will establish His kingdom here upon earth. In the second Psalm we read: "I will declare the decree: the LORD hath said unto me, Thou art my Son; this day have I begotten thee" (Ps. 2:7). He was begotten from the dead—this refers to His resurrection, not to His birth in Bethlehem. The apostle Paul gives us this interpretation in Acts 13:33. The psalmist goes on to say: "Ask of me, and I shall give thee the heathen for thine inheritance, and the uttermost parts of the earth for thy possession" (Ps. 2:8). Jesus Christ is going to take over the kingdom. How will He do it?—"Thou shalt break them with a rod of iron; thou shalt dash them in pieces like a potter's vessel" (Ps. 2:9). When He comes to the earth, the Millennium will not be there waiting for Him. *He* will put out all rebellion, and those who are obedient will enter into the kingdom.

And there was given him dominion, and glory, and a kingdom, that all people, nations, and languages, should serve him: his dominion is an everlasting dominion, which shall not pass away, and his kingdom that which shall not be destroyed [Dan. 7:14].

This prepares the way for the coming of Christ and the smashing of the image by the "stone cut out without hands" (see Rev. 19:11–16).

"An everlasting dominion" seems to contradict the idea of a millennial kingdom of one thousand years. However, at the end of the thousand years, which is a test period with Christ ruling, there will be a brief moment of rebellion against Him when Satan is released for a brief season, and then the kingdom will go right on into eternity.

Revelation 20:6 says, "Blessed and holy is he that hath part in the first resurrection: on such the second death hath no power, but they shall be priests of God and of Christ, and shall reign with him a thousand years." The thousand-year kingdom is but a phase of the everlasting kingdom. The steps are outlined clearly in Revelation 20: Christ reigns a thousand years on the earth under heavenly conditions. After this period, Satan is released. The unregenerate human heart, still in rebellion against God, rallies to Satan's leadership, and he assembles them to make war against Christ. Satan and the rebellious betrayers are cast into the lake of fire. The lost dead are raised for judgment before the Great White Throne. After this, the eternal aspect of the kingdom comes into purview (see v. 27).

The Word of God makes it very clear that the location of this kingdom is on the earth. In Micah 4:2 we read: "And many nations shall come, and say, Come, and let us go up to the mountain of the LORD, and to the house of the God of Jacob; and he will teach us of his ways, and we will walk in his paths: for the law shall go forth of Zion, and the word of the LORD from Jerusalem."

## THE DEFINITION OF THE FOUR BEASTS

I Daniel was grieved in my spirit in the midst of my body, and the visions of my head troubled me.

I came near unto one of them that stood by, and asked him the truth of all this. So he told me, and made me know the interpretation of the things [Dan. 7:15–16].

As the dream of the image troubled Nebuchadnezzar, this vision disturbs

Daniel. He approaches one of the heavenly creatures for an explanation.

> **These great beasts, which are four, are four kings, which shall arise out of the earth [Dan. 7:17].**

These four beasts are not only kingdoms but kings. Nebuchadnezzar, together with his kingdom of Babylon, was represented by the head of gold and the two-winged lion. Alexander the Great, synonymous with the Graeco-Macedonian empire, is depicted by both the sides of brass and a panther. These wild beasts of prey, with their carnivorous and voracious natures, are representative of the character of both the king and the kingdom.

> **But the saints of the most High shall take the kingdom, and possess the kingdom for ever, even for ever and ever [Dan. 7:18].**

The identity of "the saints" is the important factor of this statement. There are five verses in this chapter which mention them (see also vv. 21–22, 25, 27). Reference to them occurs again in Daniel 8:24. Immediately one school of prophetic interpretation assumes they are New Testament saints. A great many people think even narrower than that; they feel that their denomination or their little group are the only saints there are. My friend, God has a pretty big family. In the Old Testament He had Old Testament saints. The nation Israel were called saints; the Gentiles who came in as proselytes were called saints of God. That's a different company from New Testament saints today who are in the church. Don't get the idea that your little group is the only group that will be saved or even the idea that believers in this dispensation of grace are the only ones to be saved. God saved people before the Day of Pentecost, and He is going to be saving people after the Rapture. God is in the saving business; maybe the church is failing to reach people with the gospel as it should be, but God is not failing at all.

Daniel 8:24 says, "His power shall be mighty, but not by force of arms; in astonishing ways he shall bring ruin. He shall succeed in what he undertakes. He shall destroy mighty opponents; also the holy people." The "holy people" are the saints. Exodus 19:6 identifies Israel as the holy nation or saints: "And ye shall be unto me a kingdom of priests, and an holy nation . . . ."

The Greek word for "saints" is *hagios*, and it occurs two hundred times in the New Testament. Ninety-two times *hagios* is translated "holy" in combination with "spirit," for the Holy Spirit. It is also used to speak of believers in the church who are called "saints" or "holy ones." In the New Testament, "saints" are the sinners who have been declared righteous because of their faith in Christ (see Rom. 1:7). *Hagios* is used likewise for Old Testament believers (see Matt. 27:52–53) and for tribulation saints (see Rev. 13:7). In the Book of Daniel, therefore, "the saints" refer to people of Israel—not to all Israel but to the believing remnant only. That the church saints are not in view here is evident since Daniel does not refer to the church in any sense.

## THE EXPLANATION OF THE FOURTH BEAST

The emphasis is placed on the fourth beast. Here is where Daniel put the emphasis and where God put the emphasis. We ought to also, as our period in history fits somewhere in the time of the fourth beast.

> **Then I would know the truth of the fourth beast, which was diverse from all the others, exceeding dreadful, whose teeth were of iron, and his nails of brass; which devoured, brake in pieces, and stamped the residue with his feet;**
>
> **And of the ten horns that were in his head, and of the other which came up, and before whom three fell; even of that horn that had eyes, and a mouth that spake very great things, whose look was more stout than his fellows [Dan. 7:19–20].**

Everything here speaks of power and fierceness. The ferocity of the beast, with its iron teeth and brass nails, is noted again. Rome was hated by her captive nations. Hannibal vowed vengeance against her cruel power and lived to execute it; yet he was finally subdued by Rome. Rome rejected the Son of God, the Savior, through her puppet Pilate, who asked the cynical and contemptuous question of Jesus, "What is truth?" Rome crucified Jesus and persecuted the church.

The ten horns grow out of the beast, denoting a later development, not a separate kingdom. Note that the horns do not grow out of a dead beast. Rome *lives* in the fragmentation of the empire in the many existing nations of Europe and North Africa, including perhaps some of Asia. However, I do not think we can specifically identify the nations.

At the time of the end, three of the horns will fall before "the little horn" who is dominant in personality, ability, propaganda, and public appeal. "The little horn" is Antichrist, the Man of Sin (2 Thess. 2:3–4), and the first Beast (Rev. 13:3–6).

**I beheld, and the same horn made war with the saints, and prevailed against them [Dan. 7:21].**

It should be noted that Rome will again be a world power under Antichrist. We are told in Revelation 13:7—"And it was given unto him to make war with the saints, and to overcome them: and power was given him over all kindreds, and tongues, and nations." This will be a brief period in the last part of the Great Tribulation (see Rev. 11:3; 12:6; 13:5). The church will be removed before the Tribulation begins.

The Romans have been a warlike people. Our ancestors in Europe have been warlike people for fifteen hundred years, and we still are. You cannot go into any city or small town in this country today without seeing a monument to our war dead. G.K. Chesterton said, "One of the paradoxes of this age is that it is the age of pacifism, but not the age of peace." Oh, people carry placards about peace, but we are not a peaceful people. The Bible says, "For when they shall say, Peace and safety; then sudden destruction cometh upon them, as travail upon a woman with child; and they shall not escape" (1 Thess. 5:3). War is in our hearts. In recorded history man has engaged in fifteen thousand wars and has signed some eight thousand peace treaties; yet in all that time, he has enjoyed only two to three hundred years of true peace. Man is a warlike creature.

The Roman Empire is to be put together again, and the Antichrist will be the one to do it. He will march to world power and will become the world ruler. We are told he will blaspheme the God of heaven: "And he opened his mouth in blasphemy against God, to blaspheme his name, and his tabernacle, and them that dwell in heaven" (Rev. 13:6).

What is the picture in Europe today? Early in the 1950s a University of Oklahoma professor traveled through Europe, and although it was less than a decade since the close of World War II with all of its death and destruction, he reported that there was ample evidence the people were looking for a strong man, a leader like Hitler or Napoleon, who would restore their nations to the grandeur and glory and prosperity they once knew.

Even a man like Bishop Fulton J. Sheen made this statement: "The Antichrist will come disguised as the great humanitarian. He will talk peace, prosperity, and plenty, not as a means to lead us to God but as ends in themselves. He will explain guilt away psychologically and make men shrink in shame if their fellowmen say they are not broadminded and liberal. He will spread the lie that men will never be better until they make society better."

My friend, the world is moving toward the time when Europe will come together. I don't know how long away it is. The Common Market is evidence that Europe is moving in that direction; yet it does not mean that we have come to the end.

Another thing has happened in Europe that provides the psychological basis for its coming together. The young people of Italy, France, and Germany, for instance, do not want to be called Italians, French, and Germans. They like to be called *Europeans*. What a preparation for the coming of Antichrist! Europe today is like ripe fruit hanging on a tree—all the Antichrist needs to do is come and pick it. However, he is not going to come until the Lord removes the church from the world as we read in 1 and 2 Thessalonians.

**Until the Ancient of days came, and judgment was given to the saints of the most High; and the time came that the saints possessed the kingdom [Dan. 7:22].**

"The Ancient of days" is Christ; He is the only One Who is going to be able to put down Antichrist.

"The saints." Again, we are not talking about New Testament saints—this is the Old Testament. Let the Bible say what it wants to say and don't try to make it fit *your* little jigsaw puzzle of doctrine.

**Thus he said, The fourth beast shall be the fourth kingdom upon earth, which shall be diverse from all kingdoms, and shall devour the whole earth, and shall tread it down, and break it in pieces [Dan. 7:23].**

The fourth beast is identified here as a *kingdom* and in verse 17 as a *king*. It is impossible to separate the king from his kingdom; both belong together like two sides of a door.

**And the ten horns out of this kingdom are ten kings that shall arise: and another shall rise after them; and he shall**

be diverse from the first, and he shall subdue three kings [Dan. 7:24].

There are ten horns that come out of this fourth beast, and they denote the final form of the fourth kingdom. Each of these kings represents a kingdom. An eleventh king, "the little horn," will arise. He is going to be diverse from the others and will move to world power by subduing three of the kings. He will actually become the dictator of the entire world. This is the picture that is given to us in Revelation 13:7—"And it was given unto him to make war with the saints, and to overcome them: and power was given him over all kindreds, and tongues, and nations." He is the Man of Sin, the Antichrist, and he is going to rule the world during the Great Tribulation Period, which is a period of seven years.

And he shall speak great words against the most High, and shall wear out the saints of the most High, and think to change times and laws: and they shall be given into his hand until a time and times and the dividing of time [Dan. 7:25].

The little horn is a blasphemer. "And there was given unto him a mouth speaking great things and blasphemies; and power was given unto him to continue forty and two months. And he opened his mouth in blasphemy against God, to blaspheme his name, and his tabernacle, and them that dwell in heaven" (Rev. 13:5–6).

One of the characteristics of Antichrist is that he is against God and *against Christ*. That is one of the meanings of "antichrist"; the other meaning is to *imitate Christ*. I believe that the two beasts of Revelation 13 represent these two aspects of Antichrist: (1) that he is against Christ and a blasphemer; and (2) that he is a false prophet and attempts to imitate Christ; although he acts like a lamb, he really is a wolf in sheep's clothing.

We are also told that he "shall wear out the saints of the most High." That doesn't mean like some of us preachers wear out the saints on Sunday mornings! It means literally to afflict and persecute the saints (see Rev. 12:13–17).

"And think to change times and laws"—the little horn will change customs and laws.

The period of the little horn's reign is of short duration: "they shall be given into his hand until a time and times and the dividing of time."

| "Time" | 1 | year |
|---|---|---|
| "Times" | 2 | years |
| "Dividing of time" | ½ | years |
| | 3½ | years |

It is during the last three and one-half years of the Great Tribulation that he will reign over the earth (see Rev. 11:2–3; 12:6; 13:5).

But the judgment shall sit, and they shall take away his dominion, to consume and to destroy it unto the end [Dan. 7:26].

"The judgment shall sit" reminds us of the scene in heaven in Revelation 4 and 5 where thrones are depicted. It is determined by the One on the central throne and by the Lamb who is the executor of the judgment, and it is the agreement of all God's created and redeemed intelligences of heaven that the beast must be put down. His dominion must be ended and he himself judged. "The judgment shall sit"—this cannot be changed. This judgment continues through the Great Tribulation and is consummated by the return of Christ to the earth to establish His kingdom (see Rev. 19:11–21). Thus will end "the times of the Gentiles" which began with Nebuchadnezzar and will continue until the return of Christ.

And the kingdom and dominion, and the greatness of the kingdom under the whole heaven, shall be given to the people of the saints of the most High, whose kingdom is an everlasting kingdom, and all dominions shall serve and obey him [Dan. 7:27].

This is a reference to the eternal kingdom which appears first in its millennial aspect (see Rev. 20) and then opens up into eternity. Those who find fault with the premillennial position say that the Millennium is not an accurate interpretation but that the kingdom is an *eternal* kingdom. However, the Millennium is simply a thousand-year period of testing such as we are in today, and it leads and eventuates into the eternal kingdom.

This is the statement of Irenaeus, one of the early church fathers: "But when this Antichrist shall have devastated all things in this world, he will reign for three years and six months, and sit in the temple at Jerusalem; and then the Lord will come from heaven in the clouds, in the glory of the Father, sending this man and those who follow him into the lake of fire; but bringing in for the righteous the times of the kingdom, that is, the rest, the hallowed seventh day; and restoring to Abra-

ham the promised inheritance in which king-dom the Lord declared that 'Many coming from the east and from the west should sit down with Abraham, Isaac, and Jacob. . . .' " It is wearisome to hear men try to dissipate and dissolve the Millennium and God's dis-pensational program for this world by saying that the early church fathers were not pre-millennial.

Note also this statement by the historian, Philip Schaff: "The most striking point in the eschatology of the ante-Nicene age is the prominent chiliasm, or millenarianism, that is the belief of a visible reign of Christ in glory on earth with the risen saints for a thousand years, before the general resurrection and judgment. It was indeed not the doctrine of the church embodied in any creed or form of devotion, but a widely current opinion of dis-tinguished teachers." May I say to you, you are in good company today if you believe we are going to have a Millennium here on earth.

**Hitherto is the end of the matter. As for me Daniel, my cogitations much trou-bled me, and my countenance changed in me: but I kept the matter in my heart [Dan. 7:28].**

Daniel did not divulge to his contemporaries the visions and their contents since they be-longed to the end time. They were disturbing to Daniel, however, and made such an impres-sion upon him as to alter his entire outlook. This was something brand new to him.

The study of prophecy in this day is not for the selfish gratification of idle curiosity or vain knowledge. Rather, the careful, prayer-ful study of prophetic Scripture has a trans-forming effect upon the life of a believer.

# CHAPTER 8

**THEME:** *The vision of the ram and he goat; the meaning of the vision*

The vision recorded by Daniel in this chap-ter was prophetic when it was given, but it has since been fulfilled. Because it has been so clearly and literally fulfilled, this chapter is the basis for the liberal critic giving a late date for the writing of the Book of Daniel. His argument rests on the fact that prophecy con-cerning the future is supernatural and he does not believe in the supernatural; therefore, this prophecy could not have been written at the time of Daniel but must have been written afterward as history. That is a very weak argument, and I won't say anymore than that the Book of Daniel was written by the prophet Daniel. You know, there is a debate among some scholars as to whether Shakespeare wrote Shakespeare. Mark Twain's amusing reply to that question was that if Shakespeare didn't write Shakespeare, it must have been written by another man of the same name! Well, if Daniel did not write the Book of Daniel at about 600 B.C., then it must have been written by another man of the same name at the same date.

Daniel's prophetic vision of the ram with two unmatched horns and the he goat with one horn places a microscope down on the conflict between the second and third world empires and the struggle between the East and the West, between the Orient and Occi-dent, between Asia and Europe. This was the struggle between the Media-Persian and the Graeco-Macedonian empires. The vision in-cludes another "little horn," who has already been fulfilled in Antiochus Epiphanes, the great persecutor of the Jews called "the Nero of Jewish history."

We should also note that the preceding sec-tion (see Dan. 2:4–7:28) was written in Arama-ic, the original language of Syria and the world language of these four great empires. With the beginning of chapter 8, the book returns to the use of the Hebrew language.

## THE VISION OF THE RAM AND HE GOAT

**In the third year of the reign of king Belshazzar a vision appeared unto me, even unto me Daniel, after that which appeared unto me at the first [Dan. 8:1].**

This is the third year of the reign of Bel-shazzar, the last king of Babylon. The

vision given in chapter 7 was in the first year of his reign; therefore, both of these visions took place toward the end of the Babylonian empire.

**And I saw in a vision; and it came to pass, when I saw, that I was at Shushan in the palace, which is in the province of Elam; and I saw in a vision, and I was by the river of Ulai [Dan. 8:2].**

In the vision Daniel finds himself at Shushan, which is Susa, the capital of Media-Persia, the second world empire.

"In the palace" is more accurately, "near the fortress."

"Ulai" is the Kerkhah River which flowed by Susa.

The reason for the setting of the vision being at Susa rather than at Babylon is that this vision concerns the second and third world empires. The events foretold in this vision were all fulfilled within two hundred years. Such fulfillment is so remarkable that the liberal critic insists upon a late dating of the Book of Daniel. That is, he maintains that Daniel was written *after* these events had transpired and so is merely an historical record. This is an attempt to get rid of the miraculous, which is embarrassing to his system of interpretation.

**Then I lifted up mine eyes, and saw, and, behold, there stood before the river a ram which had two horns: and the two horns were high; but one was higher than the other, and the higher came up last [Dan. 8:3].**

"A ram which had two horns" will be identified later as Media-Persia (see v. 20).

"The higher came up last." In other words, the horn representing Media came up first when Gobryas the Median general destroyed Babylon. Then later the Persian monarchs gained the ascendency over the Medes and took the great empire to its highest peak. This ram, then, with its two horns and one horn more prominent than the other, is the Media-Persian empire with the Persians being in the ascendancy.

**I saw the ram pushing westward, and northward, and southward; so that no beasts might stand before him, neither was there any that could deliver out of his hand; but he did according to his will, and became great [Dan. 8:4].**

"I saw the ram pushing westward, and northward, and southward." Why doesn't it say he was pushing eastward? Persia was in the east and made no further advance into the Far East. If they had gone farther in that direction, they would have stepped into the Orient, into India and China. However, they were projecting their empire in all other directions. This is the empire which was represented by the bear in chapter 7; they were motivated by the spirit of conquest.

**And as I was considering, behold, an he goat came from the west on the face of the whole earth, and touched not the ground: and the goat had a notable horn between his eyes [Dan. 8:5].**

As Daniel was marveling at the power and ability of the ram, yonder from the west came a goat with great movement and a dominant horn. The goat represents Greece (see v. 21), and the horn typifies Alexander the Great.

Under Xerxes, Persia intended to move west, but from the west came this goat which was moving so fast it "touched not the ground"—that corresponds to the four wings of the panther and denotes the speed with which Alexander moved his army.

**And he came to the ram that had two horns, which I had seen standing before the river, and ran unto him in the fury of his power.**

**And I saw him come close unto the ram, and he was moved with choler against him, and smote the ram, and brake his two horns: and there was no power in the ram to stand before him, but he cast him down to the ground, and stamped upon him: and there was none that could deliver the ram out of his hand [Dan. 8:6–7].**

"He was moved with choler" means that he was moved with anger and great hatred. He ran into him in order to destroy him.

Xerxes was the last great ruler of Persia, and he made a foray against Europe, against Greece. He moved with an army of 300,000 men and their families. The Greeks were smart—they didn't go out to meet him. Instead, they waited until he got to Thermopylae, which was a narrow pass into which he could not fit a big army. Since one Greek soldier was equal to at least ten of the Media-Persians who were not a trained and disciplined army as the Greeks were, the Greeks gained the victory at Thermopylae. They decimated that tremendous Persian army as it attempted to advance through the pass a few

soldiers at a time. And then at Salamis, Xerxes' fleet of three hundred vessels was destroyed by a storm. When word was brought to him that his fleet had been destroyed, he went down to the sea, took off his belt, and beat the waves with it—they had destroyed his fleet! I would say that that was not the action of an outstanding and intelligent man, by any means.

This marked the last effort of the East to move toward the West; no great advance was ever made again. It is true that the great hordes of Mohammed, the Moors, came up through Spain, but Charles Martel stopped them at the battle of Tours. It is also true that the Turks attempted to come through the East, through the Balkans, but they failed.

Now there rises in the West this tremendous general, a young man, Alexander the Great. He was only thirty-two years old when he died. He was a military genius, one of the greatest. He could move a striking force by land quicker than any man ever had.

**Therefore the he goat waxed very great: and when he was strong, the great horn was broken; and for it came up four notable ones toward the four winds of heaven [Dan. 8:8].**

"When he was strong, the great horn was broken." What was it that broke this horn? There was no human power that could break it. We are told that when he came to power, the whole world was under the heel of Alexander the Great. Tradition says that he sat down and wept because there were no more worlds to conquer—he had conquered the then-known world. However, in the midst of his vast projects, he was seized by a fever after a nightlong drinking bout, and he died in Babylon in the year 323 B.C. at the age of thirty-two. "When he was strong, the great horn was broken."

All three of these empires—the Babylonian, the Media-Persian, and the Graeco-Macedonian—went down in a drunken orgy. Let me say that I do not think our nation will be destroyed by marijuana or heroin, but alcohol will destroy it. Don't misunderstand me—I am not for legalizing marijuana, and I believe the drug traffic is a grave danger, but we have lost sight of the fact that alcohol destroys nations.

According to the latest 1981 statistics I have seen, about 26,000 Americans are killed and another million suffer crippling and other serious injuries every year in drunk-driving incidents. We have had protest movements over the deaths caused by war, but do we see anyone carrying a whiskey bottle, saying, "This is the real danger to America today"? The drinking-driver problem creates an estimated economic cost of more than five billion dollars annually. There are no statistics on the unemployed who are alcoholics. Billions of dollars are spent each year for liquor. The facts are alarming.

The great empire of Alexander the Great went down because he was an alcoholic. He conquered the world, but he could not conquer Alexander the Great. There is a grave danger in Washington, D.C., today, which is that many decisions of our government are made during cocktail parties. Why do we think we are something special? Why are there people who think that the United States happens to be God's little pet nation? We think we are so superior intellectually, the ultimate product of the evolutionary process, and there is no chance that we will go down as a nation. My friend, it is time someone blew the whistle and announced that we are on the way out. If I read prophecy correctly, we *are* on the way out.

"And for it came up four notable ones." When Alexander died, his empire was divided among four men (which correspond to the four heads of the panther in ch. 7). These were the four generals who divided the empire: Cassander, who was married to Alexander's sister and took the European section (Macedonia and Greece); Lysimachus who took the great part of Asia Minor, which is modern Turkey; Seleucus who took Asia, all the eastern part of the empire, except Egypt; and Ptolemy who took Egypt and North Africa.

**And out of one of them came forth a little horn, which waxed exceeding great, toward the south, and toward the east, and toward the pleasant land [Dan. 8:9].**

"The pleasant land" is Israel.

The "little horn" of this chapter is not the same as described in the previous chapter. There the little horn arises out of the fourth kingdom; here the little horn comes out of the third kingdom. This little horn is historical, while the little horn of chapter 7 is to be revealed in the future. The little horn being presently considered came out of Syria from the Seleucid dynasty. He was Antiochus IV, or Epiphanes, the son of Antiochus the Great. He is sometimes called Epimanes, "the madman"—he was another demented ruler.

Antiochus came to the throne in 175 B.C.

and he made an attack on Jerusalem. It was against him that the Maccabees were raised up in Judah. Anti-Semitic to the core, he tried to exterminate the Jews. He placed an image of Jupiter in the Holy Place in the temple in Jerusalem. This was the first "abomination of desolation." He also poured swine broth over all the holy vessels.

**And it waxed great, even to the host of heaven; and it cast down some of the host and of the stars to the ground, and stamped upon them [Dan. 8:10].**

This statement is admittedly difficult to interpret. I think that the natural interpretation is that Antiochus challenged God and was permitted to capture Jerusalem and the temple. This warfare included the spiritual realm where angels and demons were involved. Some of the feats attributed to Antiochus are astounding; if they are true, demonic power was exhibited.

**Yea, he magnified himself even to the prince of the host, and by him the daily sacrifice was taken away, and the place of his sanctuary was cast down [Dan. 8:11].**

Antiochus was a devotee of Jupiter of whom he may have thought himself an incarnation. He chose for himself the title *Theos Epiphanes*, meaning "God manifest."

**And an host was given him against the daily sacrifice by reason of transgression, and it cast down the truth to the ground; and it practised, and prospered [Dan. 8:12].**

It was by the *permissive* will of God that this little horn practiced and prospered during this period.

**Then I heard one saint speaking, and another saint said unto that certain saint which spake, How long shall be the vision concerning the daily sacrifice, and the transgression of desolation, to give both the sanctuary and the host to be trodden under foot? [Dan. 8:13].**

*Saint* is an "holy one" and refers to one of God's created intelligences other than man—what we would call a supernatural creature. (I often wonder what angels call us, by the way.)

This profaning of the temple is called here a "transgression of desolation."

**And he said unto me, Unto two thousand and three hundred days; then**

**shall the sanctuary be cleansed [Dan. 8:14].**

There has always been a great deal of disagreement as to the interpretation of these twenty-three hundred days. Seventh-Day Adventism grew out of the "great second advent awakening" in which this verse was given the day-year interpretation and the date for Christ's second coming was set for the year 1843. William Miller and his followers, among whom was Ellen G. White, understood "the sanctuary" to be the earth which would be cleansed at His coming. Miller was a sincere but badly mistaken Baptist preacher. The day-year interpretation was a fragile and insecure foundation for any theory of prophecy, and history has demonstrated it to be false.

However, if the twenty-three hundred days are taken as being literal twenty-four-hour days, the period would be between six and seven years, which approximates the time of Antiochus who began to perpetrate his atrocities in about 170 B.C. Finally the Jewish priest, Judas Maccabeus ("the hammer"), drove out the Syrian army, at which time the temple was cleansed and rededicated after its pollution. This cleansing is celebrated in the Feast of Lights. In John 10:22 we read: "And it was at Jerusalem the feast of the dedication [rededication or Lights], and it was winter." This was one of the holy days celebrated at the time of Christ and which is still remembered by the Jews. It is a feast not mentioned in the Old Testament at all, because it was established in the intertestamental period between the Old and New Testaments.

## THE MEANING OF THE VISION

**And it came to pass, when I, even I Daniel, had seen the vision, and sought for the meaning, then, behold, there stood before me as the appearance of a man.**

**And I heard a man's voice between the banks of Ulai, which called, and said, Gabriel, make this man to understand the vision [Dan. 8:15-16].**

Daniel was puzzled by the vision, and he desired to learn the meaning of it. There appeared to him the angel Gabriel. This is the first time Gabriel is introduced to us in the Bible.

**So he came near where I stood: and when he came, I was afraid, and fell upon my face: but he said unto me, Un-**

derstand, O son of man: for at the time of the end shall be the vision [Dan. 8:17].

Gabriel, in the explanation that follows, will make it clear that Antiochus Epiphanes is but a picture in miniature of the coming Antichrist.

"For at the time of the end shall be the vision." Notice that it is for "the time of the end," not the end of time. Nowhere in the Bible are we told about the end of time. "The time of the end" locates the complete fulfillment of this prophecy in the period which our Lord Jesus called the Great Tribulation. The man referred to is the Antichrist, also called the Man of Sin and the little horn of chapter 7. This prophecy goes beyond the immediate future and is projected into the distant future—even in our day it is still future. Antiochus is merely an adumbration of the other "little horn" who will come at the end of the "times of the Gentiles," which is made abundantly clear by the use of these eschatological terms.

Now as he was speaking with me, I was in a deep sleep on my face toward the ground: but he touched me, and set me upright [Dan. 8:18].

Notice the physical effect of this vision upon Daniel.

And he said, Behold, I will make thee know what shall be in the last end of the indignation: for at the time appointed the end shall be [Dan. 8:19].

Again Gabriel moves from the local fulfillment in Antiochus to the end of the Times of the Gentiles.

The ram which thou sawest having two horns are the kings of Media and Persia [Dan. 8:20].

They are clearly identified for us; we do not have to speculate. The ram definitely represents the kings of Media and Persia.

And the rough goat is the king of Grecia: and the great horn that is between his eyes is the first king [Dan. 8:21].

So the "rough goat" is likewise labeled the king of Greece, and the "great horn" is the first king, Alexander the Great.

Now that being broken, whereas four stood up for it, four kingdoms shall stand up out of the nation, but not in his power [Dan. 8:22].

In other words, none of these kings would have the power that Alexander the Great had.

And in the latter time of their kingdom, when the transgressors are come to the full, a king of fierce countenance, and understanding dark sentences, shall stand up [Dan. 8:23].

The "little horn" is Antiochus Epiphanes of the line of the Seleucidae that took Syria. The only adequate explanation of this verse and of the facts of history is that this man was demon possessed. In this respect he is also a picture of the coming Antichrist. The Lord Jesus made reference to him when He said, "For there shall arise false Christs, and false prophets, and shall shew great signs and wonders; insomuch that, if it were possible, they shall deceive the very elect" (Matt. 24:24).

And his power shall be mighty, but not by his own power: and he shall destroy wonderfully, and shall prosper, and practise, and shall destroy the mighty and the holy people [Dan. 8:24].

"The holy people" refers to Israel. The slaughter of these people by Antiochus Epiphanes seems almost unbelievable. He was as bad as Hitler. However, he is merely an adumbration of the Antichrist who is coming, of whom it is said: "And it was given unto him to make war with the saints, and to overcome them: and power was given him over all kindreds, and tongues, and nations" (Rev. 13:7).

And through his policy also he shall cause craft to prosper in his hand; and he shall magnify himself in his heart, and by peace shall destroy many: he shall also stand up against the Prince of princes; but he shall be broken without hand [Dan. 8:25].

Antiochus was but a faint type of this king who is coming. And he will do four things which Antiochus did in pygmy style:

1. "He shall cause craft to prosper in his hand." We are told in Revelation 13:17 that no man will be able to buy or sell save the one who has the mark of the beast. He will control the economy with a vengeance.

2. "He shall magnify himself in his heart." Revelation 13:5 says that he is given a mouth speaking great things and blasphemies. He will be given power to continue forty-two months. Humility is not a characteristic of the Antichrist! He is like Satan who was filled with pride.

3. "By peace shall destroy many." He

comes in as a lamb, but he goes out as a lion. In Revelation 6 he is the rider on the white horse. Notice that right after him comes the red horse of *war*—he has brought in a false peace.

4. "He shall stand up against the Prince of princes." You see, he will oppose and fight against Christ. One of the marks of Antichrist and of that first beast in Revelation 13 is that he is against Christ.

**And the vision of the evening and the morning which was told is true: wherefore shut thou up the vision; for it shall be for many days [Dan. 8:26].**

Daniel was told that the vision would be for the distant future—"for it shall be for many days" to come.

**And I Daniel fainted, and was sick certain days; afterward I rose up, and did the king's business; and I was astonished at the vision, but none understood it [Dan. 8:27].**

The physical and psychological effect of this vision upon Daniel was devastating. At this point God was beginning to mesh the "times of the Gentiles" into the history of the nation Israel. That was the thing that puzzled Daniel at the first, and it still puzzles a great many people. How can God mesh His program with Israel into His program for the Gentiles in the world? And today to further complicate it, there is His program with the church. The answer is quite simple, of course. In our day God is calling out a people to His name—we label this called-out group "the church." When that is concluded, and the church is removed from the earth at the Rapture, then He will again turn to His purpose with Israel and the gentile nations.

# CHAPTER 9

**THEME:** *The prayer of Daniel; prophecy of the Seventy Weeks*

This is another one of those remarkable chapters in Scripture. Dr. Philip Newell evaluates it, "The greatest chapter in the book and one of the greatest chapters of the entire Bible." The double theme is prayer and prophecy. If one were to choose the ten greatest chapters of the Bible on the subject of prayer, this chapter would be included on any list. If the ten most important chapters on prophecy were chosen, this chapter would again be included on any list. The first 21 verses give us the prayer of Daniel, and the final 6 verses give us the very important prophecy of the Seventy Weeks.

## THE PRAYER OF DANIEL

This prayer of Daniel is actually a culmination of a life of prayer. Daniel asked for a prayer meeting to learn the dream of Nebuchadnezzar at the beginning of the book, and he has been a man of prayer all the way through. The prayer in this chapter gives the pattern of his prayer life and acquaints us with the conditions of prayer. Here are some of the basic elements in the prescription of prayer:

*Purposeful Planning.* Prayer was no haphazard matter with Daniel. He wrote, "And I set my face unto the Lord God, to seek by prayer and supplications, with fasting, and sackcloth, and ashes" (v. 3). Prayer was not just a repetition of idle words or the putting together of pretty phrases with flowery grammar. The Lord Jesus said, "But when ye pray, use not vain repetitions, as the heathen do: for they think that they shall be heard for their much speaking" (Matt. 6:7). Such is not real prayer.

*Painful Performance.* Daniel prayed with fasting and sackcloth and ashes. This was not done for outward show but to reveal the sincerity of his heart. One doesn't see many prayer meetings like that today.

*Perfect Plainness.* Daniel was candid and straightforward in his confession. He got right down to business with God.

There is the story of a preacher in a Scottish prayer meeting who got up and started one of his long-winded prayers. Finally a dear old lady pulled his coattail and said, "Parson, call Him 'Father' and ask Him for something." We need more plainness in prayer.

*Powerful Petition.* Daniel received an answer while he was speaking and praying. The angel Gabriel appeared to him to give him some explanation. This man got *answers* to

his prayers. "And this is the confidence that we have in him, that, if we ask any thing according to his will, he heareth us" (1 John 5:14).

*Personal and Private.* Daniel did not call a public prayer meeting; he prayed privately. This prayer of his is of three minutes' duration. Our Lord often prayed privately. His prayer which is recorded in John 17 is also three minutes long. There are many of us who want to call a public prayer meeting when we ought to spend more time in *private* prayer.

*Plenary (full) Penetration.* Prayer is the only force that has penetrated outer space to the throne of God. Sir Isaac Newton said that he could take up a telescope and look at the nearest star, but he could put down the telescope, get down on his knees and penetrate the outer heavens to the very throne of God.

Prayer for Daniel was a real exercise of soul in spiritual travail. Such prayer is arduous work. It requires effort and endurance and suffering.

**In the first year of Darius the son of Ahasuerus, of the seed of the Medes, which was made king over the realm of the Chaldeans [Dan. 9:1].**

"First year of Darius . . . of the seed of the Medes." The two significant questions are: Who was Darius and what was the date? Darius the Mede *may* be identified as Cyaxares II of secular history (Dan. 5:31). "Darius" is more an official title, such as king, czar, or emperor, than an actual name. There has been some disagreement as to the exact date. Newell thinks it is 538 B.C.; Culber places it at 536 B.C. I think either date would fit into the background. This man conquered Babylon in 538 B.C.

**In the first year of his reign I Daniel understood by books the number of the years, whereof the word of the LORD came to Jeremiah the prophet, that he would accomplish seventy years in the desolations of Jerusalem [Dan. 9:2].**

This is in the first year of the reign of Darius. Daniel has now seen a new great world empire come into position, and he is wondering about the future and especially the future of his own people. So Daniel turns to a study of the Word of God. He reads the book of the prophet Jeremiah who said that Israel would be in captivity for seventy years. The date is about 537 B.C. in this chapter. Daniel is between eighty-five and ninety years of age. He had been captured back in 606 B.C. when he was

about seventeen. That means that the seventy-year period is coming to a close. It is about the time that these people will be given the opportunity to return to their own land.

Daniel was concerned about his people. I think he was shaken by that little horn in chapter 8, Antiochus Epiphanes, the Syrian king of the Seleucid dynasty. He would abuse Daniel's people, and he would desecrate the temple. All of this caused Daniel great concern.

We should notice that the determining factor which brought Daniel to this prayer was his study of the Word of God. The Word reveals the will of God. A study of God's Word, followed by prayer, is the formula for determining God's will. These are the promises which Daniel read: "And this whole land shall be a desolation, and an astonishment; and these nations shall serve the king of Babylon seventy years" (Jer. 25:11). "For thus saith the LORD, That after seventy years be accomplished at Babylon I will visit you, and perform my good word toward you, in causing you to return to this place" (Jer. 29:10).

Keep in mind that Daniel had been studying Jeremiah's prophecy about these seventy years. When Gabriel used the expression, "seventy weeks" (v. 24), he was extending the time of the seventy years. The Seventy Weeks will cover the entire time of the nation Israel in this time of testing before the kingdom is established on earth.

Just reading Daniel's prayer reveals how different prayer was in his day from what it is now. Notice first the conditions—

**And I set my face unto the Lord God, to seek by prayer and supplications, with fasting, and sackcloth, and ashes:**

**And I prayed unto the LORD my God, and made my confession, and said, O Lord, the great and dreadful God, keeping the covenant and mercy to them that love him, and to them that keep his commandments [Dan. 9:3–4].**

"To seek by prayer and supplications, with fasting." We are told that the Lord Jesus fasted, but fasting was never given to the people of God as a service. It was something that one could do over and above what was required. It is mentioned that in the early church there were many who fasted. Paul wrote to the Christians at Corinth: "In weariness and painfulness, in watchings often, in hunger and thirst, in fastings often, in cold and nakedness" (2 Cor. 11:27).

Daniel demonstrated a purposeful persistence in prayer. Even Jacob in his prayer cried, ". . . I will not let thee go, except thou bless me" (Gen. 32:26).

This prayer of Daniel is very personal. It concerns him and his people, which is evident by the repeated use of the first person pronouns, *I*, *we*, and *our*. They appear forty-one times in this prayer. You may remember that we pointed out how Nebuchadnezzar used the personal pronoun in chapter 4. What is the difference? For Nebuchadnezzar it was a mark of pride, a mark of being lifted up. The contrast of Daniel's use of the personal pronoun is striking. It denotes humility, confession, and "confusion of faces" in contrast to Nebuchadnezzar's pride and self-adulation.

Daniel is down on his face before God. He recognizes the attributes of God. First we see that he rests upon his personal relationship to God. He calls Him, *"My God,"* appealing to God in a very personal way. Before he makes his confession, he dwells on the greatness of God. "Dreadful God" actually means worthy of reverence. One cannot trifle with God.

Daniel acknowledges that God keeps the covenant and mercy to them that love Him. He not only makes promises, but He keeps them. He is immutable and, therefore, He is faithful. He is also a God of mercy. It was by His mercy that the nation Israel had been preserved. It is by His mercy that you and I have been brought to this present moment. It is by His mercy that He saves us. "It is of the LORD's mercies that we are not consumed, because his compassions fail not" (Lam. 3:22). God is gracious, but God also expects us to mean business, and God expects to be obeyed.

Now notice Daniel's confession of sin—

**We have sinned, and have committed iniquity, and have done wickedly, and have rebelled, even by departing from thy precepts and from thy judgments:**

**Neither have we hearkened unto thy servants the prophets, which spake in thy name to our kings, our princes, and our fathers, and to all the people of the land [Dan. 9:5–6].**

"We have sinned." Daniel identifies himself with his people back there in the land of Israel when they rebelled against God, which resulted in their captivity. He is specific in his confession. He labels each sin: iniquity, wickedness, rebellion, disobedience, and refusal to hear God's prophets. He writes them all down. He doesn't leave any out.

My friend, I believe that our confession of sin requires exactly that. It isn't enough to go to God and say, "I have sinned." It means to tell God exactly what we have done. When my wife sends me to the grocery store, she doesn't say, "Get some groceries." She always gives me a list of items. I am to get this, get that, and get the other thing—and four or five more things. I have to go through that list. And I feel that confession of sins should be that specific. Spell it out to Him. Maybe we don't like to do that because it is an ugly thing. But spell it out to Him; He already knows how ugly it is. We need to come to Him in frank, open confession.

**O Lord, righteousness belongeth unto thee, but unto us confusion of faces, as at this day; to the men of Judah, and to the inhabitants of Jerusalem, and unto all Israel, that are near, and that are far off, through all the countries whither thou hast driven them, because of their trespass that they have trespassed against thee [Dan. 9:7].**

"All Israel, that are near, and that are far off." The people of Israel were scattered, but there were no lost tribes—it is a misnomer to call them that. Some of the tribes were near Daniel there in Babylon and others were far off, but he knew where they were. He didn't say they were lost. But they were scattered "through all the countries whither thou hast driven them, because of their trespass that they have trespassed against thee."

**O Lord, to us belongeth confusion of face, to our kings, to our princes, and to our fathers, because we have sinned against thee.**

**To the Lord our God belong mercies and forgivenesses, though we have rebelled against him;**

**Neither have we obeyed the voice of the LORD our God, to walk in his laws, which he set before us by his servants the prophets.**

**Yea, all Israel have transgressed thy law, even by departing, that they might not obey thy voice; therefore the curse is poured upon us, and the oath that is written in the law of Moses the servant of God, because we have sinned against him.**

**And he hath confirmed his words, which he spake against us, and against**

our judges that judged us, by bringing upon us a great evil: for under the whole heaven hath not been done as hath been done upon Jerusalem.

As it is written in the law of Moses, all this evil is come upon us: yet made we not our prayer before the LORD our God, that we might turn from our iniquities, and understand thy truth.

Therefore hath the LORD watched upon the evil, and brought it upon us: for the LORD our God is righteous in all his works which he doeth: for we obeyed not his voice [Dan. 9:8–14].

Up to this point have you noticed how Daniel contrasted God's goodness with Israel's sin? He contrasted His righteousness with their "confusion of face" which was their shame. They were scattered because of their trespass against God. They *deserved* the punishment they had received. God was righteous in sending them into captivity. God was right; they were wrong.

Oh, my friend, if you go to God and make excuses for your sin, if you say to Him, "Lord, you know that I am weak and I was in this and that circumstance," you are blaming your sin upon God. You are saying that God made a mistake—He should have taken those things into consideration. He has been too hard on you! My friend, you and I are getting exactly what we deserve. And we need to go to God in confession of our sin. In our day I hear folk implying that God may be wrong in what He is doing. God is *not* wrong; we are the ones who are wrong.

Daniel's attitude is the proper attitude that each of us should take as we approach our God in prayer. God will not utterly forsake us, but He certainly is not going to move on our behalf until you and I get to the place where we can claim the *mercy* of God and stop making excuses for ourselves.

And now, O Lord our God, that hast brought thy people forth out of the land of Egypt with a mighty hand, and hast gotten thee renown, as at this day; we have sinned, we have done wickedly.

O Lord, according to all thy righteousness, I beseech thee, let thine anger and thy fury be turned away from thy city Jerusalem, thy holy mountain: because for our sins, and for the iniquities of our fathers, Jerusalem and thy people

are become a reproach to all that are about us.

Now therefore, O our God, hear the prayer of thy servant, and his supplications, and cause thy face to shine upon thy sanctuary that is desolate, for the Lord's sake.

O my God, incline thine ear, and hear; open thine eyes, and behold our desolations, and the city which is called by thy name: for we do not present our supplications before thee for our righteousnesses but for thy great mercies [Dan. 9:15–18].

This is Daniel's petition and plea. He recalls how God led Israel out of Egypt. God did it because of *His* righteousness, not because of theirs. He found the explanation for their deliverance in Himself, not in the people. "And God heard their groaning, and God remembered his covenant with Abraham, with Isaac, and with Jacob. And God looked upon the children of Israel, and God had respect unto them" (Exod. 2:24–25). The only thing that made an appeal to God from the people was their groaning. In other words, God saw their misery, and He remembered His mercy.

Now Daniel asks God to repeat Himself by delivering them again because of His righteousness. God is righteous when He extends His mercy to us, because Jesus Christ has fully paid all the penalty for our sin. "To declare, I say, at this time his righteousness: that he might be just, and the justifier of him which believeth in Jesus" (Rom. 3:26).

Now notice Daniel's impassioned plea—

O Lord, hear; O Lord, forgive; O Lord, hearken and do; defer not, for thine own sake, O my God: for thy city and thy people are called by thy name [Dan. 9:19].

This is the climactic plea of Daniel. He asks God to hear and answer because of who He is and what He has promised. No good thing rests upon Israel. Daniel doesn't plead because he is Daniel. Rather, he associates himself with his people and says, "*We* have sinned," including himself, you see. God's name is at stake, and Daniel is deeply concerned about the name of God and the glory of God. This is the basis for his plea.

Now we shall see that while Daniel was praying, an answer was on its way.

And whiles I was speaking, and praying, and confessing my sin and the sin

of my people Israel, and presenting my supplication before the LORD my God for the holy mountain of my God [Dan. 9:20].

"Whiles I was speaking, and praying, and confessing my sin." Notice Daniel says, "*my* sin." Daniel confessed that *he* was a sinner. It is interesting that there is no place in the Bible which mentions any sin that Daniel committed. In fact, when his enemies were trying to find some wrongdoing in his life, they could find *nothing*—and we may be sure that they left no stone unturned.

Now I have often made the statement that no one has ever been saved by keeping the Ten Commandments. And I have suggested that if anybody knew one in the Old Testament who was saved by keeping the Ten Commandments to let me know about it. Well, one night after a service in which I had said that no one in the Old Testament was ever saved by keeping the Ten Commandments, a UCLA student came up to me and said, "I found a man in the Old Testament who didn't sin. It's Daniel." I told him very frankly that he was right. One cannot find a recorded sin which Daniel committed. Then I showed him this verse where Daniel says, "I was speaking, and praying, and confessing my sin." If Daniel had never sinned but *said* that he was confessing his sin, then he would be lying to say he was confessing his sin if, in fact, he had never sinned! So Daniel is a sinner, any way you take it. I think the UCLA student was convinced that the Bible is correct when it says, "For *all* have sinned, and come short of the glory of God" (Rom. 3:23, italics mine).

Now if you are wondering what sin Daniel committed, let me say that it is none of your business, and it is none of my business. God did not record it in His Word.

So Daniel was a sinner, and I can still say that no one was ever saved by keeping the Ten Commandments. Daniel was casting himself and his people upon the mercy of God.

"Presenting my supplication before the LORD my God for the holy mountain of my God"—which would be Jerusalem and the kingdom of God that will be there (see Isa. 2:1–2).

Yea, whiles I was speaking in prayer, even the man Gabriel, whom I had seen in the vision at the beginning, being caused to fly swiftly, touched me about the time of the evening oblation [Dan. 9:21].

"The man Gabriel"—Gabriel was an angel and apparently appeared in human form. The time of his appearance was at the hour of the evening sacrifice at Jerusalem, which would be approximately three o'clock in the afternoon.

## PROPHECY OF THE SEVENTY WEEKS

Now here is the prophecy delivered by Gabriel which makes this chapter of such great importance in the study of eschatology.

And he informed me, and talked with me, and said, O Daniel, I am now come forth to give thee skill and understanding.

At the beginning of thy supplications the commandment came forth, and I am come to shew thee; for thou art greatly beloved: therefore understand the matter, and consider the vision [Dan. 9:22–23].

Notice that Daniel gets an immediate answer to his prayer. I heard Dr. Gaebelein say that it took him three minutes to read Daniel's prayer in Hebrew. By the time Daniel finished his prayer, the angel Gabriel was there. So Dr. Gaebelein reasoned and explained with a twinkle in his eye, "It took Gabriel three minutes to get from heaven to earth." Of course, if Daniel had his eyes closed while he was praying, it may be that Gabriel was standing on one foot and then on the other for two minutes, waiting for Daniel to get finished. The Lord God has promised, "And it shall come to pass, that before they call, I will answer; and while they are yet speaking, I will hear" (Isa. 65:24).

Note that Daniel was "greatly beloved" in heaven. That is wonderful. The believer in Jesus Christ is seen by God as being in Christ. According to Ephesians 1:6 we are accepted in the Beloved—so the believer is loved in heaven because he is in Christ.

Seventy weeks are determined upon thy people and upon thy holy city, to finish the transgression, and to make an end of sins, and to make reconciliation for iniquity, and to bring in everlasting righteousness, and to seal up the vision and prophecy, and to anoint the most Holy [Dan. 9:24].

"Seventy weeks" does not mean weeks of seven days any more than it means weeks of seven years or seven other periods of time. The Hebrew word for "seven" is *shabua*, meaning "a unit of measure." It would be com-

parable to our word *dozen*. When it stands alone, it could be a dozen of anything—a dozen eggs, a dozen bananas. So here, Seventy Weeks means seventy sevens. It could be seventy sevens of anything. It could be units of days or months or years. In the context of this verse it is plain that Daniel has been reading in Jeremiah about *years*, seventy years. Jeremiah had been preaching and writing that the captivity would be for seventy years. The seventy years of captivity were the specific penalty for violating seventy sabbatic years. That would be seventy sevens, a total of 490 years. In those 490 years, Israel had violated exactly seventy sabbatic years; so they would go into captivity for seventy years. "To fulfil the word of the LORD by the mouth of Jeremiah, until the land had enjoyed her sabbaths: for as long as she lay desolate she kept sabbath, to fulfil threescore and ten years" (2 Chron. 36:21).

1 week = 7 years
70 weeks = 490 years
70 weeks divided into 3 periods:
7 weeks—62 weeks—1 week

Now Daniel was puzzled as to how the end of the seventy years of captivity would fit into the long period of Gentile world dominion which the visions in chapters 7 and 8 had so clearly indicated. He obviously thought that at the end of the seventy years his people would be returned to the land, the promised Messiah would come, and the kingdom which had been promised to David would be established. How could both be true? It appeared to him, I am sure, to be an irreconcilable situation created by these seemingly contradictory prophecies.

The Seventy Weeks, or the seventy sevens, answer two questions. Israel's kingdom will not come immediately. The seventy sevens must run their course. These seventy sevens fit into the Times of the Gentiles and run concurrently with them. They are broken up to fit into gentile times. The word for *determined* literally means "cutting off." These seventy sevens are to be cut off, as the following verses will indicate. The seventy sevens for Israel and the Times of the Gentiles will both come to an end at the same time, that is, at the second coming of Christ. This is important to know in the correct understanding of the prophecy.

The Seventy Weeks concern "thy people," meaning the people of Daniel. That would be Israel. And they concern "thy holy city," which can be none other than Jerusalem. Six things are to be accomplished in those Seventy Weeks or 490 years. We will see as we progress in our study that sixty-nine of those "weeks" have already passed, and one "week" is yet to be fulfilled.

Here are the six things to be accomplished:

1. "To finish the transgression." This refers to the transgression of Israel. The cross provided the redemption for sin—for the sin of the nation, but not all accepted it. Today the word has gone out to the ends of the earth that there is a redemption for mankind. But in that last "week" we are told that God says, "And I will pour upon the house of David, and upon the inhabitants of Jerusalem, the spirit of grace and of supplications . . ." (Zech. 12:10). And in Zechariah 13:1: "In that day there shall be a fountain opened to the house of David and to the inhabitants of Jerusalem for sin and for uncleanness." That has not been opened yet. All you have to do is to look at the land of Israel and you will know this has not been fulfilled.

2. "To make an end of sins." The national sins of Israel will come to an end at the second coming of Christ. They are just like any other people or any other nation. They are sinners as individuals and as a nation. They have made many mistakes as a nation (so have we), but God will make an end to that.

3. "To make reconciliation for iniquity." During this period of Seventy Weeks, God has provided a redemption through the death and resurrection of Christ. This, of course, is for Jew and Gentile alike.

4. "And to bring in everlasting righteousness" refers to the return of Christ at the end of the 490 years to establish the kingdom.

5. "To seal up the vision and prophecy" means that all will be fulfilled, which will vindicate this prophecy as well as all other prophecies in Scripture.

6. "To anoint the most Holy" has reference to the anointment of the holy of holies in the millennial temple about which Ezekiel spoke (Ezek. 41–46).

**Know therefore and understand, that from the going forth of the commandment to restore and to build Jerusalem unto the Messiah the Prince shall be seven weeks, and threescore and two weeks: the street shall be built again, and the wall, even in troublous times.**

**And after threescore and two weeks shall Messiah be cut off, but not for himself: and the people of the prince**

# The 70 WEEKS of DANIEL 9

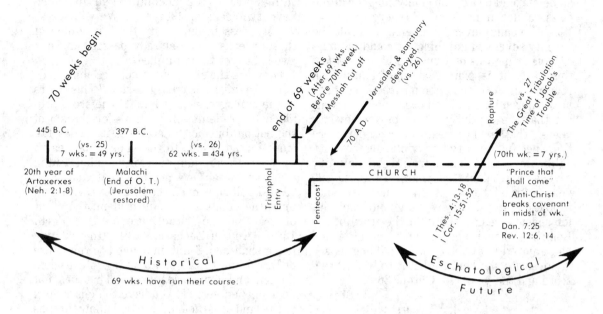

(See Sir Robert Anderson's *The Coming Prince*)

that shall come shall destroy the city and the sanctuary; and the end thereof shall be with a flood, and unto the end of the war desolations are determined.

And he shall confirm the covenant with many for one week: and in the midst of the week he shall cause the sacrifice and the oblation to cease, and for the overspreading of abominations he shall make it desolate, even until the consummation, and that determined shall be poured upon the desolate [Dan. 9:25–27].

The starting point for this period of 490 years is essential to the correct understanding of the prophecy. Since this period is projected into the Times of the Gentiles, it must fit into secular history and originate from some date connected with the Times of the Gentiles. Of course there have been many suggestions for a starting point: the decree of Cyrus (see Ezra 1:1–4); the decree of Darius (see Ezra 6:1–12); the decree of Artaxerxes (at the seventh year of his reign—Ezra 7:11–26); but I feel that the decree of Artaxerxes in the twentieth year of his reign (Neh. 2:1–8) meets the requirements of verse 25. The commandment to rebuild the city of Jerusalem was issued in the month Nisan 445 B.C. That, then, will be our starting point.

The first seven weeks of forty-nine years

bring us to 397 B.C. and to Malachi and the end of the Old Testament. These were "troublous times," as witnessed to by both Nehemiah and Malachi.

Sixty-two weeks, or 434 years, bring us to the Messiah. Sir Robert Anderson in his book, *The Coming Prince*, has worked out the time schedule. From the first of the month Nisan to the tenth of Nisan (April 6) A.D. 32, are 173,880 days. Dividing them according to the Jewish year of 360 days, he arrives at 483 years (69 sevens). On this day Jesus rode into Jerusalem, offering Himself for the first time, publicly and officially, as the Messiah.

After the 69 weeks, or 483 years, there is a time break. Between the sixty-ninth and Seventieth Week two events of utmost importance are to take place:

1. Messiah will be cut off. This was the crucifixion of Christ, the great mystery and truth of the gospel: "From that time forth began Jesus to shew unto his disciples, how that he must go unto Jerusalem, and suffer many things of the elders and chief priests and scribes, and be killed, and be raised again the third day" (Matt. 16:21). "That whosoever believeth in him should not perish, but have eternal life" (John 3:15).

2. Destruction of Jerusalem, which took place in A.D. 70, when Titus the Roman was the instrument.

The final "week" (the seventieth), a period

of seven years, is projected into the future and does not follow chronologically the other sixty-nine. The time gap between the sixty-ninth and seventieth weeks is the age of grace—unknown to the prophets (Eph.3:1–12; 1 Pet. 1:10–12). The Seventieth Week is eschatological; it is the final period and is yet unfulfilled.

"The prince" is a Roman; he is the "little horn" of Daniel 7; he is "the beast" of Revelation 13. After the church is removed from the earth, he will make a covenant with Israel.

Israel will accept him as her Messiah, but in the midst of the "week" he will break his covenant by placing an image in the temple (Rev. 13). This is the abomination of desolation. What Israel thought to be the Millennium will turn out to be the Great Tribulation (Matt. 24:15–26). Only the coming of Christ can end this frightful period (Matt. 24:27–31).

My friend, you and I are living in the age of grace, and the Seventieth Week of Daniel, the Great Tribulation, as the Lord Jesus called it, is yet to take place.

# CHAPTER 10

**THEME:** *Time, place, and preparation of Daniel for the vision; the vision of Christ glorified; transforming effect on Daniel; message of an unidentified heavenly messenger; Daniel assured and strengthened*

These last three chapters should be treated as one vision. It relates to the nation Israel in the immediate future and also in the latter days. For example, there is the historical "little horn" and also the "little horn" of the latter days.

Some expositors consider this last vision to be the greatest of all the visions of Daniel. Although it may not have such stature, it is indeed the most unique section. There are features here which are different from all other chapters. In this last vision even the method of revelation was changed.

Another outstanding feature is that it fills in much detail of the preceding visions. While all was prophetic when it was given, at the present time much has been fulfilled and belongs to history. There is also a great deal that is yet prophetic—to be fulfilled in the last days. The line of demarcation between what has been fulfilled and what is yet to be fulfilled is not always clear. We have already seen the principle of double reference, which refers to predictions that have a near and local fulfillment and also have a distant fulfillment. Of course, the fulfillment in the *immediate* future gives us the key for the far future fulfillment. For example, the historical fulfillment in Antiochus Epiphanes gives us a picture of the future fulfillment which will be in Antichrist.

The key to understanding these last three chapters is found in the explanation the angel gives to Daniel: "Now I am come to make thee understand what shall befall thy people in the latter days: for yet the vision is for many days" (v. 14). In other words, it will be a long time before this will be fulfilled, and it concerns Daniel's people, the people of Israel. (Let me caution you against trying to put the church in this section, because Daniel is making it very clear that he is talking about his people.)

We are moving into a very eerie section. Maybe you would call it weird or strange. The veil of the spiritual world is partially and momentarily pulled aside, and we get a look into the unseen world. There is nothing here to satisfy the morbid curiosity of an idle spectator. However, there is enough to produce a beneficial and sobering effect upon the humble believer similar to the effect that it produced upon Daniel.

This intrusion into the spiritual realm introduces the believer to the order of angels—both good and bad angels, fallen and unfallen. We will see something about the kingdom of Satan, which is about us today. There has been a great deal said and written about that recently. Many people take a little fact and then add a whole lot of fiction to it. We are going to stick to the facts that the Bible gives us here.

Apparently angels exercise a free will since

some of them by their own volition followed Satan in his rebellion against God. Some of these belong to the order of demons to which frequent reference is made in the gospels. The angels are in different orders, ranks, positions and have various powers and abilities. "For by him were all things created, that are in heaven, and that are in earth, visible and invisible, whether they be thrones, or dominions, or principalities, or powers: all things were created by him, and for him" (Col. 1:16). This makes a separation in God's creation, not only of that which is in heaven and that which is in earth, but that which is visible and that which is invisible. There is a great realm today that is invisible. We are discovering that there are a great many things in this world of energy that we know very little about.

We are told that He created *thrones*, which would be the archangels like Michael and Gabriel and other special envoys. There are *dominions*, which would be the cherubim and seraphim. There are *principalities*, which would be the generals, "the brass" of the angel hosts. And *powers* would be the privates such as serve as guardian angels (Heb. 1:4).

Some angels in the rank of principalities, that is, the generals, fell away to join with Satan. Notice what is said about "principalities": "For we wrestle not against flesh and blood, but against *principalities*, against powers, against the rulers of the darkness of this world, against spiritual wickedness in high places" (Eph. 6:12, italics mine).

Satan also has his angels organized according to rank. Just as one army is set over against another army, there are generals on both sides. Satan's "principalities," or generals, seem to have the oversight of nations. His "powers" are the privates of his army who are demons who seek to possess human beings. The "rulers of the darkness of this world" are demons who have charge of Satan's worldly business, and I think he has a lot of monkey-business going on down here. Then there is "spiritual wickedness" in the heavenlies, which are the demons who have charge of religion. You may not realize it, but Satan's department of religion is the largest department of all. He is in the business of religion. Many folk think Satan is against religion. No indeed, he is promoting religion—not Christ, but religion.

These two groups move in the arena of this universe in which we live. They are engaged in ceaseless warfare to capture the souls of men. We will see more of this as we go through this section.

## TIME, PLACE, AND PREPARATION OF DANIEL FOR THE VISION

**In the third year of Cyrus king of Persia a thing was revealed unto Daniel, whose name was called Belteshazzar; and the thing was true, but the time appointed was long: and he understood the thing, and had understanding of the vision [Dan. 10:1].**

The "third year of Cyrus" was 534 B.C., which was about four years after the vision of the Seventy Weeks. Daniel was an old man by this time and probably retired from public office.

"A thing [word] was revealed unto Daniel" suggests a new mode of communication.

"The thing [word] was true, but the time appointed was long" indicates that the final fulfillment was in the distant future, not the immediate future.

"He understood the thing [word], and had understanding of the vision" means that this vision was made crystal clear to Daniel.

**In those days I Daniel was mourning three full weeks.**

**I ate no pleasant bread, neither came flesh nor wine in my mouth, neither did I anoint myself at all, till three whole weeks were fulfilled [Dan. 10:2–3].**

Daniel didn't take a bath for three weeks!

The cause of Daniel's mourning is not told us, but we can speculate. Remember that it was the third year of Cyrus' reign, and in his first year he had made the decree which permitted Israel to return to her land (see Ezra 1:1–4). Two full years had passed and only a paltry few had returned to the land of Israel under Zerubbabel. This is before the group under Ezra and the group under Nehemiah had returned. This was a rigorous time for Daniel. It brought grief to the heart of this aged prophet of God, now past ninety, to see that his people did not want to return to their homeland. Probably retired now from active participation in office, evidently having served through the first year of Cyrus, he gave himself entirely to the service of God. He fasted for three weeks because he did not get an immediate answer to his prayer.

**And in the four and twentieth day of the first month, as I was by the side of the great river, which is Hiddekel [Dan. 10:4].**

Now he gives us the exact place and date when he received his vision and revelation.

He was by the great river Hiddekel, which is the Tigris River. The time was the twenty-fourth of Nisan, April 24. Daniel is dealing with exact dates. This makes it difficult for the critics to wrestle with, because the one who wrote this was dealing with specific dates and he was not giving a *late* date for the Book of Daniel!

## THE VISION OF CHRIST GLORIFIED

I think that Daniel saw the transfiguration of Christ before either Moses or Elijah saw it. You see, there have always been three representatives: Moses represented the law, Elijah represented the prophets, but Daniel represented a very particular group of those who had been in exile, and now he is given this vision of the glorified Christ ahead of time for his encouragement.

**Then I lifted up mine eyes, and looked, and behold a certain man clothed in linen, whose loins were girded with fine gold of Uphaz:**

**His body also was like the beryl, and his face as the appearance of lightning, and his eyes as lamps of fire, and his arms and his feet like in colour to polished brass, and the voice of his words like the voice of a multitude [Dan. 10:5–6].**

This is a new method of revelation. No longer does Daniel see an image or visions of beasts or weeks. He sees a certain man. Who is that certain man? Some very excellent expositors hesitate to identify him, and they dodge the dilemma by saying he was a heavenly visitor. Well, that is really generalizing, and you can't be very wrong if you call him a heavenly visitor. But that is not an exegesis of the passage. I believe this Person is Christ.

When the Lord Jesus was on earth, He gave many parables, and some of them concerned the activity of "a certain man." That "certain man" was either God the Father or God the Son. In the verse before us the "certain man" is identified even further by His person and His dress. What a striking similarity there is to the vision of Christ after His ascension into glory as it was seen by John in the Revelation! "And I turned to see the voice that spake with me. And being turned, I saw seven golden candlesticks; And in the midst of the seven candlesticks one like unto the Son of man, clothed with a garment down to the foot, and girt about the paps with a golden girdle. His head and his hairs were white like wool, as white as snow; and his eyes were as a flame of fire; And his feet like unto fine brass, as if they burned in a furnace; and his voice as the sound of many waters. And he had in his right hand seven stars: and out of his mouth went a sharp two-edged sword: and his countenance was as the sun shineth in his strength" (Rev. 1:12–16). Now that is a vision of Christ, and I believe Daniel saw Christ—not in His preincarnation, but he saw Him as the postincarnate Christ, in His office as priestly Intercessor and Judge and the great Shepherd of the sheep. After all, both Israel and the church are called His sheep. It is interesting to recall that Moses and Elijah were present at the transfiguration of Jesus as recorded in the gospel records, but Daniel was not present. Why? Well, I think it may be because he had already witnessed the transfiguration of Jesus, and this is the record of it.

## TRANSFORMING EFFECT ON DANIEL

**And I Daniel alone saw the vision: for the men that were with me saw not the vision; but a great quaking fell upon them, so that they fled to hide themselves [Dan. 10:7].**

I do not think that any ordinary angel or even an archangel would have this effect upon these men.

Although others were with Daniel, he alone saw the vision. It is evident from many recorded incidents that only the Holy Spirit can identify Christ for men, and that is what He is doing for Daniel. The Lord Jesus said, "He shall glorify me: for he shall receive of mine, and shall shew it unto you" (John 16:14). The apostle Paul had a similar experience on the road to Damascus. "And the men which journeyed with him stood speechless, hearing a voice, but seeing no man. And Saul arose from the earth; and when his eyes were opened, he saw no man: but they led him by the hand, and brought him into Damascus" (Acts 9:7–8). Paul was blinded—he had seen the glorified Christ.

**Therefore I was left alone, and saw this great vision, and there remained no strength in me: for my comeliness was turned in me into corruption, and I retained no strength [Dan. 10:8].**

Daniel was left alone. That is the marvelous, wonderful experience of that man of God, and many have shared eagerly and joyfully a like experience. Abraham left Ur, and finally his kindred, and he was alone with God. Moses

was sent to the backside of the desert of Midian, and at the burning bush he was alone with God. Elijah was disciplined by the Brook Cherith, and God was with him. Jeremiah walked a lonely path, but God was with him. John the Baptist was in the desert alone, but God was there. Paul had two years of solitary confinement on that same desert—that was God's opportunity to train him. The apostle John was exiled on the lonely isle of Patmos, but God was with him.

There are so many people who want to get together to have a great prayer meeting or other great gatherings. Friend, have you ever tried being alone? That is where God will meet with you. Take the Word of God and go off alone with Him. It will do you a lot of good.

I love speaking on my radio program. I have been asked, "Dr. McGee, are you speaking to an audience when you make those tapes?" The answer is, "No. I am all alone." I am in the studio with all the doors shut. I am alone, alone with God. It is wonderful. I think this is when God speaks to me. It is at this time that God has been able to use this weak bit of clay to get out the Word of God. He makes that Word go out, and He gives it its effectiveness.

In contrast, the ungodly and the unbeliever are gregarious. They want to go to the nightclubs to have a drink with somebody. They run in packs, and they like to have people around them. They don't like to be alone. You remember that Jacob tried to avoid being alone, but God pushed him into a corner so that one night God wrestled with him and finally crippled him in order to get him.

Now in this Scripture before us Daniel is alone with God, and he has this vision of the Lord Jesus Christ. He says, "there remained no strength in me"—it had a tremendous effect upon him.

**Yet heard I the voice of his words: and when I heard the voice of his words, then was I in a deep sleep on my face, and my face toward the ground [Dan. 10:9].**

Daniel apparently lapsed into unconsciousness. I don't know how long he was there. The Lord Jesus left him, and when Daniel regained consciousness, he found that an angel had come and ministered to him.

## MESSAGE OF AN UNIDENTIFIED HEAVENLY MESSENGER

Daniel apparently is just sprawled down, prone on the earth. Then a hand touches him.

**And, behold, an hand touched me, which set me upon my knees and upon the palms of my hands [Dan. 10:10].**

This heavenly messenger was sent by the postincarnate Christ to answer Daniel's petition. Who could he have been? Well, I suggest that he was Gabriel, since Gabriel was sent to Daniel on other occasions; yet he could have been any other angel.

**And he said unto me, O Daniel, a man greatly beloved, understand the words that I speak unto thee, and stand upright: for unto thee am I now sent. And when he had spoken this word unto me, I stood trembling [Dan. 10:11].**

You see, at first Daniel was horizontal with the ground. Then he was brought up on all fours, and now he is told to stand up.

"A man greatly beloved"—again Daniel is reminded of the fact that he is greatly beloved of God. That is a nice reputation to have in heaven, by the way!

**Then said he unto me, Fear not, Daniel: for from the first day that thou didst set thine heart to understand, and to chasten thyself before thy God, thy words were heard, and I am come for thy words.**

**But the prince of the kingdom of Persia withstood me one and twenty days: but, lo, Michael, one of the chief princes, came to help me; and I remained there with the kings of Persia [Dan. 10:12–13].**

Here a veil is lifted momentarily, and it reveals a heavenly warfare going on. It reveals that there is a great deal more about this universe in which we live than meets the eye. There is a great deal more to it than we know. Very little is revealed to us, and we should not try to know more than is revealed about the unseen world.

This reveals that in the world which is unseen by us there is a conflict going on, a conflict of the ages between good and evil, light and darkness, God and Satan. It reveals that there are satanic forces and heavenly forces.

"From the first day . . . thy words were heard, and I am come for thy words." The angel is saying that Daniel's prayer was heard immediately and he was sent as a messenger with an answer. But on the way his pathway was blocked; he couldn't get through to Daniel. This is an amazing statement! This throws some light on what Paul said to the

Ephesian believers: "Put on the whole armour of God, that ye may be able to stand against the wiles of the devil. For we wrestle not against flesh and blood, but against principalities, against powers, against the rulers of the darkness of this world, against spiritual wickedness in high places" (Eph. 6:11–12).

Again, here are the gradations of rank in the forces of Satan. Their power may explain the reason your prayer and my prayer have not yet been answered. Actually, prayer is fighting a spiritual battle always. Paul made it clear that prayer was a spiritual battle for him. "Now I beseech you, brethren, for the Lord Jesus Christ's sake, and for the love of the Spirit, that ye strive together with me in your prayers to God for me" (Rom. 15:30). "Strive together" is the Greek word *sunagōnizom*—from this root we get our English word *agonize*. You and I are to agonize in prayer.

Prayer has been made a light sort of thing today. Most of the prayers I hear are either very flowery or very theological, and I think we could do without both kinds. Real prayer is agonizing. It is getting through the barriers to release spiritual power. It is not done by trying to entertain the Lord with flowery language or by trying to be very profound and theological. My friend, we are fighting a spiritual *battle!*

Again, the angel said to Daniel, "When you began to pray, God sent me to answer your prayer, but I couldn't get through to you because on the way the prince of the kingdom of Persia withstood me for twenty-one days." Who is he? No earthly or human prince could do such a thing. This evidently was an envoy of Satan, one of the demons. We know that God has his angels organized, and apparently Satan also has his demons organized like an army. There are the generals and the colonels, the lieutenants and second lieutenants, sergeants and corporals, and so on. Apparently this angel was outranked by the satanic angel who was the prince of the kingdom of Persia, and so he couldn't get through and had to send back for reinforcements. In fact, Michael, the archangel, had to come to open up the way for him.

Why would the way be blocked? Daniel is going to be given information about the kingdom of Persia and about the kingdom of Greece—we will see that when we get to the next chapter. Satan didn't want that kind of information to get out. It was secret information that he didn't want released to the human family. But God wanted the information to be gotten through to Daniel.

"Michael, one of the chief princes, came to help me; and I remained there with the kings of Persia." Apparently there was a conflict going on involving the kings of Persia (remember that Daniel was in Persia), and there needed to be some heavenly forces to help. This was about the time that Daniel had the experience of being put into the den of lions. You see, the Lord was active on Daniel's behalf without his knowing anything about it.

Oh, my friend, we need to recognize as believers that we are in a spiritual warfare. It is amazing how many times the Devil short-circuits our prayer life.

One of the reasons that public prayer and prayer meetings are so dead is because those who go there say some pretty little prayers without realizing that there is a battle going on. There is a *war* that must be fought and won. Paul mentions this again in 2 Corinthians 10:3–5: "For though we walk in the flesh, we do not war after the flesh: (For the weapons of our warfare are not carnal, but mighty through God to the pulling down of strong holds;) Casting down imaginations, and every high thing that exalteth itself against the knowledge of God, and bringing into captivity every thought to the obedience of Christ."

Friend, the Christian life is a bigger undertaking than any of us ever dreamed it to be. You and I need to recognize how much we need the power of the Holy Spirit in our lives and how much we need the presence of Christ. We need to be more conscious of the fact that we are engaged in a spiritual warfare.

**Now I am come to make thee understand what shall befall thy people in the latter days: for yet the vision is for many days [Dan. 10:14].**

This is the key which opens the door to the understanding of the remainder of the Book of Daniel. There are three features which characterize this closing vision.

1. The vision concerns "thy people." I think we can dogmatically and categorically identify the prophecy as having Israel as its subject. If anyone tries to interpret this in any other way, then semantics and syntax are meaningless. "Thy people" means Israel.

2. It will be accomplished "in the latter days." This places the final fulfillment in the period of the Seventieth Week, which is the time of the Great Tribulation Period. The "latter days" places it at the end of that period.

3. "Yet the vision is for many days." This emphasizes the fact that a long period of time

is involved—not only in fulfillment—but before the vision will be finalized.

We will come now to the two parts of the vision: the historical (it was prophetic when it was given, but now has been fulfilled) and the prophecy yet to be fulfilled.

### DANIEL ASSURED AND STRENGTHENED

**And when he had spoken such words unto me, I set my face toward the ground, and I became dumb.**

**And, behold, one like the similitude of the sons of men touched my lips: then I opened my mouth, and spake, and said unto him that stood before me, O my lord, by the vision my sorrows are turned upon me, and I have retained no strength [Dan. 10:15–16].**

This was having a tremendous effect upon Daniel physically, as you can see.

**For how can the servant of this my lord talk with this my lord? for as for me, straightway there remained no strength in me, neither is there breath left in me.**

**Then there came again and touched me one like the appearance of a man, and he strengthened me [Dan. 10:17–18].**

When I hear people today tell me that they have had a vision of an angel but it doesn't seem to have affected them very much, I know they didn't really see an angel. The experience of seeing an angel certainly had a tremendous effect upon Daniel.

**And said, O man greatly beloved, fear not: peace be unto thee, be strong, yea, be strong. And when he had spoken unto me, I was strengthened, and said, Let my lord speak; for thou hast strengthened me.**

**Then said he, Knowest thou wherefore I come unto thee? and now will I return to fight with the prince of Persia: and when I am gone forth, lo, the prince of Grecia shall come [Dan. 10:19–20].**

Another angel that represents Greece will come—another satanic principality. The angel who was speaking to Daniel had to get back to the battle that was going on.

**But I will shew thee that which is noted in the scripture of truth: and there is none that holdeth with me in these things, but Michael your prince [Dan. 10:21].**

"That which is noted in the scripture of truth"—the angel turns Daniel to the Word of God. *Noted* means "recorded or registered." In other words, Daniel will not hear or see anything that is contradictory to the Word of God.

My friend, the Word of God is the only weapon available to the child of God for effective use in our spiritual warfare. It is called the sword of the Spirit, and some of us don't know how to use our swords.

# CHAPTER 11

**THEME:** *Vision continued; Antiochus Epiphanes identified; vicious and vocal volition of the Man of Sin; victory of the willful king is temporary*

Chapters 10–12 all deal with the same vision, and therefore chapter 11 is a continuation of the previous chapter. It is a very important chapter because it fills in some of the details of the Seventy Weeks of chapter 9, which specifically concern Daniel's people, Israel. It also fills in some of the details of the last three of the four nations symbolized in the multimetallic image of chapter 2 and in the beasts of chapter 7. The very importance of this chapter caused Satan to hinder the angel in coming to give Daniel the answer to his prayer, because this prophecy does concern two of the nations which were all-important in relation to Daniel's people. The two nations were Persia and Greece.

A further notable contribution of this chapter is that it bridges prophetically part of the gap between the Old and New Testaments. We speak of the intertestamental period be-

tween the Old and New Testaments as being a period of silence, which is not exactly accurate. The intertestamental period was the time of Israel's greatest travail. They suffered at the hands of both Syria and Egypt. As these two nations warred against each other, Palestine was caught in the middle as the armies of these two nations seesawed back and forth, up and down, across the land of Israel.

During the intertestamental period came the rise of Antiochus Epiphanes (who is a type of the Antichrist of the future). He was a member of the Seleucid family, and we will identify him when we come to him in this chapter. He was a persecutor of the Jews, far exceeding any Pharaoh or Haman or Hitler or modern Russia. He has been called the Nero of Jewish history. He has also been called the Great Profaner.

There is a remarkable division in the chapter which separates history and prophecy— the historical from the eschatological section. Remember, it was all future when it was originally written, but part of it has been fulfilled.

This prophecy is rather complicated and goes into prophecy a little deeper than the average person likes to go into it. Most people seem to like the exciting, sensational part of prophecy, but they do not want to dig down into the Word of God to see what it really says. However, if you are one who enjoys a deep and detailed study of prophecy, you will be thrilled by this section of the remarkable Word of God.

## VISION CONTINUED

This prophecy bridges the gap from Media-Persia over to Greece, from Asia to Europe. It tells of the transition of world powers from one continent to another, from the East to the West. Remember that the prophecy concerns the people of Daniel. It was especially important to Israel because they would be caught in a vise between these different powers. It would be a period of great suffering for these people.

**Also I in the first year of Darius the Mede, even I, stood to confirm and to strengthen him [Dan. 11:1].**

The speaker here is the angel, and this is a continuation from chapter 10. The angel may have been Gabriel; we are not told his name. Remember that it occurred during the reign of Darius when Daniel was thrown into the den of lions. Darius tried in vain to deliver Daniel, but he was trapped by his own decree. Yet he said to Daniel, "Thy God whom thou servest continually, he will deliver thee" (Dan. 6:16).

"I stood to confirm and strengthen him." The angel confirmed and strengthened Darius in his faith. He also comforted and assisted Daniel. And Daniel said, you recall, "My God hath sent his angel, and hath shut the lions' mouths" (Dan. 6:22).

So historically this is where the vision fits in, and it bridges the gap between the Old and New Testaments, the intertestamental period.

**And now will I shew thee the truth. Behold, there shall stand up yet three kings in Persia; and the fourth shall be far richer than they all: and by his strength through his riches he shall stir up all against the realm of Grecia [Dan. 11:2].**

From here through verse 34 is one of the most remarkable examples of prewritten history. This section has caused the destructive critic to demand a late date for the composition of the Book of Daniel. Here are clear-cut statements of prophecy which have been literally fulfilled.

The prophecy of this chapter is so detailed and so accurate that the liberal critic will not accept the fact that it was written before it happened. He insists that Daniel's prophecy was written after it had become history. Personally, I do not like the liberals to be called liberal. To me they are the most narrow-minded people I know anything about. Yet they like to speak of their broad-mindedness and that they don't have a narrow conception of Scripture. Let me give you an example. One of them right here in Southern California said to me, "McGee, I listen to you on the radio sometimes." (He said that in a condescending manner as though I should have been honored.) Then he said, "I notice that you accept prophecy as being reliable," and he cited this Book of Daniel. So I asked him, "What authority do you have for rejecting the early dating of Daniel and accepting a late date of Daniel?" His reply was this, "Well, it's very simple. We know that miracles are impossible, that they do not happen. Therefore if this were written beforehand, it would be a miracle; so it must have been written afterward." Now, my friend, I ask you, is that being narrow-minded, prejudiced, and biased? Obviously, this chapter before us is one of the most remarkable passages of prewritten history in the Word of God, and conservative scholarship can sustain the early

date of Daniel. This means that you have a miracle on your hands.

When the angel gave this information to Daniel, he knew that Daniel would not live to see it fulfilled. Obviously, it was recorded for the comfort and encouragement of the people of God who would live through the difficult days it describes. Also it was written for all generations as a testimony of the fact that God knows the end from the beginning.

The angel told him that there would be four notable kings of Persia to follow Cyrus. We think we can identify them today: (1) Cambyses, 529 B.C.; (2) Pseudo-Smerdis, 522 B.C.; (3) Darius Hystaspis, 521 B.C.; and (4) Xerxes who invaded Greece in 480 B.C. He was defeated and never again did Media-Persia make a bid for world dominion. Incidentally, I believe that Xerxes is the Ahasuerus of the Book of Esther. He was very rich, as the prophecy here said he would be.

**And a mighty king shall stand up, that shall rule with great dominion, and do according to his will [Dan. 11:3].**

"A mighty king" is Alexander the Great who came to power in 335 B.C. over the Graeco-Macedonian Empire. He put down Persia and assumed world dominion.

**And when he shall stand up, his kingdom shall be broken, and shall be divided toward the four winds of heaven; and not to his posterity, nor according to his dominion which he ruled: for his kingdom shall be plucked up, even for others beside those [Dan. 11:4].**

Alexander the Great was a world ruler and probably the greatest military strategist the world has ever seen, but he died an alcoholic in 323 B.C. His own posterity did not inherit his vast kingdom. Four of his generals divided the empire into four geographical areas, each ruled by one general. The division was roughly this: Cassander took Macedonia; Lysimachus took Asia Minor (modern Turkey); Seleucus Nicator took Syria and the remainder of the Middle East; and Ptolemy took Egypt. All four families warred among themselves. Eventually they all lost their kingdoms when the Romans marched east.

**And the king of the south shall be strong, and one of his princes; and he shall be strong above him, and have dominion; his dominion shall be a great dominion [Dan. 11:5].**

"The king of the south." South of what? Directions in the Bible are reckoned from Palestine as the center of the earth. The king of the south is not from south of Los Angeles or Chicago or New York. It is the king from the south of Israel, so this would be the king from Egypt. This king of the south would be one of the Ptolemies.

**And in the end of years they shall join themselves together; for the king's daughter of the south shall come to the king of the north to make an agreement: but she shall not retain the power of the arm; neither shall he stand, nor his arm: but she shall be given up, and they that brought her, and he that begat her, and he that strengthened her in these times [Dan. 11:6].**

"The king of the north" refers to the line of the Seleucidae. This verse brings us to about 250 B.C. Although historians differ on some of the minor details, they have recorded some of the manipulations that went on in the courts of that day, which fulfill this prophecy very accurately. To form an alliance between these two warring families, Ptolemy Philadelphus of Egypt gave his daughter Berenice in marriage to Antiochus Theos of Syria. Antiochus was already married to Laodice, whom he divorced. After two years Ptolemy Philadelphus died; so Antiochus Theos put away Berenice with her son and took back his first wife, Laodice. She, in turn, poisoned Antiochus Theos and ordered the death of Berenice and her son. Then Laodice put her own son, Seleucus Callinicus, on the throne. That was some juggling act, and it is interesting how this is covered in the prophecy given to Daniel.

**But out of a branch of her roots shall one stand up in his estate, which shall come with an army, and shall enter into the fortress of the king of the north, and shall deal against them, and shall prevail [Dan. 11:7].**

This was Ptolemy Euergetes, brother of Berenice, who came with an army and captured Syria, and he seized the fort which was the port of Antioch in that day.

**And shall also carry captives into Egypt their gods, with their princes, and with their precious vessels of silver and of gold; and he shall continue more years than the king of the north.**

So the king of the south shall come into his kingdom, and shall return into his own land [Dan. 11:8–9].

It is recorded that Ptolemy Euergetes took into Egypt as booty four thousand talents of gold, forty thousand talents of silver, and twenty-five hundred idols. Do you see how this Scripture was literally fulfilled?

But his sons shall be stirred up, and shall assemble a multitude of great forces: and one shall certainly come, and overflow, and pass through: then shall he return, and be stirred up, even to his fortress.

And the king of the south shall be moved with choler, and shall come forth and fight with him, even with the king of the north: and he shall set forth a great multitude; but the multitude shall be given into his hand.

And when he hath taken away the multitude, his heart shall be lifted up; and he shall cast down many ten thousands: but he shall not be strengthened by it.

For the king of the north shall return, and shall set forth a multitude greater than the former, and shall certainly come after certain years with a great army and with much riches [Dan. 11:10–13].

There was continual warfare between Egypt and Syria. Without going into detail, let me say that during this period Israel seemed repeatedly to make the wrong choice and found herself being made captive first by one, then by the other.

And in those times there shall many stand up against the king of the south: also the robbers of thy people shall exalt themselves to establish the vision; but they shall fall [Dan. 11:14].

Many in the nation of Israel were slain at this time. They incurred untold sufferings from both the king of the north and the king of the south.

So the king of the north shall come, and cast up a mount, and take the most fenced cities: and the arms of the south shall not withstand, neither his chosen people, neither shall there be any strength to withstand.

But he that cometh against him shall do according to his own will, and none shall stand before him: and he shall stand in the glorious land, which by his hand shall be consumed [Dan. 11:15–16].

"He shall stand in the glorious land." Now we know why this has been recorded and given to Daniel—it concerns the "glorious land," which is Israel, the land that God had vouchsafed to Abraham and to those coming after him.

These two verses predict what history now records as the victory of Antiochus the Great over Egypt. It was a decisive victory, and it caused Israel to suffer immeasurably. I am going to pass over some of the secular history of this period. If you care to go into detail, I suggest that you consult one of the larger Bible encyclopedias, such as *Hastings'* or the *International Standard Bible Encyclopedia*, and read in detail the secular history covered in this section. You will find that Daniel's prophecy was fulfilled in a remarkable way. There is a period of 125 years that was fulfilled in detail.

He shall also set his face to enter with the strength of his whole kingdom, and upright ones with him; thus shall he do: and he shall give him the daughter of women, corrupting her: but she shall not stand on his side, neither be for him [Dan. 11:17].

This brings us to about 198 or 195 B.C. when Antiochus the Great made a treaty with Egypt and gave his daughter Cleopatra to Ptolemy Epiphanes in marriage.

After this shall he turn his face unto the isles, and shall take many: but a prince for his own behalf shall cause the reproach offered by him to cease; without his own reproach he shall cause it to turn upon him.

Then he shall turn his face toward the fort of his own land: but he shall stumble and fall, and not be found.

Then shall stand up in his estate a raiser of taxes in the glory of the kingdom: but within few days he shall be destroyed, neither in anger, nor in battle [Dan. 11:18–20].

"He shall turn his face unto the isles" refers to Greece and all the Greek islands. This is where Antiochus the Great was beginning to move at this time—not only against Ptolemy in the south, but against Lysimachus in the west.

"A prince for his own behalf" would refer to another line, that is, Rome which was beginning to arise in the west and move toward the east. Rome, you see, exacted taxes from the Syrians. The Romans were probably the best tax assessors and tax gatherers in the world until modern America perfected the system. Our system of collecting taxes would put even Rome to shame! As Rome began to rise, she was building a tremendous empire by taxing the people she was capturing. As the Syrians began to fall before Rome, there were many historical details that could be filled in. For further reading I would suggest to you *The Prophet Daniel* by A. C. Gaebelein and *The Coming Prince* by Sir Robert Anderson, a former chief of Scotland Yard.

## ANTIOCHUS EPIPHANES IDENTIFIED

Introduced to us now is the vile person, Antiochus Epiphanes, who was king in Syria and is easily identified in history.

This is the "little horn" that has already been fulfilled, as we studied back in chapter 8.

**And in his estate shall stand up a vile person, to whom they shall not give the honour of the kingdom: but he shall come in peaceably, and obtain the kingdom by flatteries [Dan. 11:21].**

This prophecy is concerned with one king in the line of the Seleucidae, Antiochus Epiphanes. Most fundamental interpreters of Scripture consider this section to be a direct reference to this man. The prophecy fits the history of Antiochus Epiphanes like a glove. (He is at the same time a type of the Antichrist, thus illustrative and figurative of the Man of Sin who is yet to come. The careers of both are strikingly similar.)

Antiochus Epiphanes came to the throne in 175 B.C. He is called vile because of his blasphemies. He came to the throne with a program of peace. (The Antichrist will come to power in the same way. He will introduce the Great Tribulation with three and one half years of peace, and the people of the world will think they are entering the Millennium when they are really entering the Great Tribulation Period.) Antiochus was a deceiver and a flatterer. My friend, beware of that type of person. You can find them even in the ministry. They have hurt the church more than anything. We do not need men who will deceive and butter up folk for their own advantage; we need honest forthright men who will stand in the pulpit and tell it like it is. Unfortunately, they are getting few and far between, but, thank God, there are still many of them about.

**And with the arms of a flood shall they be overflown from before him, and shall be broken; yea, also the prince of the covenant.**

**And after the league made with him he shall work deceitfully: for he shall come up, and shall become strong with a small people.**

**He shall enter peaceably even upon the fattest places of the province; and he shall do that which his fathers have not done, nor his fathers' fathers; he shall scatter among them the prey, and spoil, and riches: yea, and he shall forecast his devices against the strong holds, even for a time [Dan. 11:22–24].**

"The prince of the covenant" was probably the high priest, Onias III, who was deposed and murdered at this time by the deceitful devices of Antiochus when he came to power.

**And he shall stir up his power and his courage against the king of the south with a great army; and the king of the south shall be stirred up to battle with a very great and mighty army; but he shall not stand: for they shall forecast devices against him.**

**Yea, they that feed of the portion of his meat shall destroy him, and his army shall overflow: and many shall fall down slain.**

**And both these kings' hearts shall be to do mischief, and they shall speak lies at one table; but it shall not prosper: for yet the end shall be at the time appointed.**

**Then shall he return into his land with great riches; and his heart shall be against the holy covenant; and he shall do exploits, and return to his own land [Dan. 11:25–28].**

These verses describe the campaign of Antiochus and his victory over the king of Egypt which brought him much riches and prestige.

"They shall speak lies at one table" refers to the fact that he was an unreliable liar. It also reveals that the conference tables of that day were very much like the conference tables of our own day where nations meet and make treaties which become meaningless scraps of paper.

At the time appointed he shall return, and come toward the south; but it shall not be as the former, or as the latter.

For the ships of Chittim shall come against him: therefore he shall be grieved, and return, and have indignation against the holy covenant: so shall he do; he shall even return, and have intelligence with them that forsake the holy covenant [Dan. 11:29–30].

Antiochus made a second campaign against Egypt but was not successful due to the navy of Rome, "the ships of Chittim." He broke his covenant with Israel, but notice that some of the Jews betrayed their own people—"he shall even return, and have intelligence with them that forsake the holy covenant."

And arms shall stand on his part, and they shall pollute the sanctuary of strength, and shall take away the daily sacrifice, and they shall place the abomination that maketh desolate [Dan. 11:31].

Antiochus came against Jerusalem in 170 B.C., at which time over one hundred thousand Jews were slain! He took away the daily sacrifice from the temple, offered the blood and broth of a swine upon the altar, and set up an image of Jupiter to be worshiped in the holy place of the temple of God. This was an "abomination that maketh desolate," but it was not the abomination to which our Lord Jesus refers which was future when He was on earth and is still future in our day. It is the abomination which Antichrist will set up. Antiochus set up an image of Jupiter in the holy place, and the Antichrist will probably set up an image of himself in the holy place.

And such as do wickedly against the covenant shall he corrupt by flatteries: but the people that do know their God shall be strong, and do exploits [Dan. 11:32].

There were a few in the nation Israel who played the role of a Judas, but there were many who knew God and were strong and did exploits. It was during this time that God raised up the family of the Maccabees. In 166 B.C. Mattathias the priest raised a revolt against the awful blasphemy. The family was called the Maccabees, that is, the hammer. Although they are not recorded in Scripture, I am convinced that they were God's men for that particular hour.

And they that understand among the people shall instruct many: yet they shall fall by the sword, and by flame, by captivity, and by spoil, many days.

Now when they shall fall, they shall be holpen with a little help: but many shall cleave to them with flatteries [Dan. 11:33–34].

This period lies between the Testaments and is a saga of suffering. There were many in this time who served God as faithfully and courageously as had Gideon or David or Elijah or Jeremiah or Daniel. If you are not familiar with this period of history, you should look into the apocryphal books of *1 and 2 Maccabees* as well as the writings of Josephus.

And some of them of understanding shall fall, to try them, and to purge, and to make them white, even to the time of the end: because it is yet for a time appointed [Dan. 11:35].

"The time of the end" leaps forward in prophecy from Antiochus Epiphanes to the Antichrist. We move now from the history of that day into that which is yet in the future. All of this prophecy was in the future when Daniel gave it—some is now history and some is yet future.

## VICIOUS AND VOCAL VOLITION OF THE MAN OF SIN

And the king shall do according to his will; and he shall exalt himself, and magnify himself above every god, and shall speak marvellous things against the God of gods, and shall prosper till the indignation be accomplished: for that that is determined shall be done [Dan. 11:36].

At this point history ends and prophecy begins. The text passes from a vile person to a vicious character, moving over a bridge of unmeasured time. Antiochus Epiphanes was certainly a contemptible person, but he could not measure up to the king described in verses 36–39. Antiochus was an adumbration of Antichrist, and I believe that this passage of Scripture thus indicates that Antichrist will rise out of the geographical bounds of the ancient Grecian empire.

There will be a political Antichrist, the one who is mentioned here, a Gentile raised out of the Roman Empire. There will also be a religious Antichrist who will pretend to be Christ and who will arise out of the land of

Israel—he will be like a wolf in sheep's clothing.

Antichrist is given many names in Scripture. J. Dwight Pentecost, in his book *Things to Come* (p. 334), gives a list of names compiled by Arthur W. Pink (*The Antichrist*, pp. 59–75) which are applicable to Antichrist: "The Bloody and Deceitful Man (Ps. 5:6), the Wicked One (Ps. 10:2–4), the Man of the Earth (Ps. 10:18), the Mighty Man (Ps. 52:1), the Enemy (Ps. 55:3), the Adversary (Ps. 74:8–10), the Head of Many Countries (Ps. 111:6 [sic]), the Violent Man (Psalm 140:1), the Assyrian (Isa. 10:5–12), the King of Babylon (Isa. 14:2), the Sun [sic] of the Morning (Isa. 14:12), the Spoiler (Isa. 16:4–5; Jer. 6:26), the Nail (Isa. 22:25), the Branch of the Terrible Ones (Isa. 25:5), the Profane Wicked Prince of Israel (Ezek. 21:25–27), the Little Horn (Dan. 7:8), the Prince that shall come (Dan. 9:26), the Vile Person (Dan. 11:21), the Wilful King (Dan. 11:36), the Idol Shepherd (Zech. 11:16–17), the Man of Sin (2 Thess. 2:3), the Son of Perdition (2 Thess. 2:3), the Lawless one (2 Thess. 2:8), the Antichrist (1 John 2:22), the Angels [sic] of the Bottomless Pit (Rev. 9:11), the Beast (Rev. 11:7; 13:1). To these could be added: the One Coming in His Own Name (John 5:43), the King of Fierce Countenance (Dan. 8:23), the Abomination of Desolation (Matt. 24:15), the Desolator (Dan. 9:27)."

"The king shall do according to his will." Antichrist is self-willed. How contrary this is to the Lord Jesus Christ who said, "I can of mine own self do nothing: as I hear, I judge: and my judgment is just; because I seek not mine own will, but the will of the Father which hath sent me" (John 5:30).

"He shall exalt himself." The little horn (the name given to Antichrist in ch. 7) tries to be a big horn. Again, how unlike the Lord Jesus this is! Paul wrote of Him: "Let this mind be in you, which was also in Christ Jesus: Who, being in the form of God, thought it not robbery to be equal with God: But made himself of no reputation, and took upon him the form of a servant, and was made in the likeness of men: And being found in fashion as a man, he humbled himself, and became obedient unto death, even the death of the cross" (Phil. 2:5–8).

"And magnify himself above every god." In 2 Thessalonians 2:4 Paul wrote of the Antichrist: "Who opposeth and exalteth himself above all that is called God, or that is worshipped; so that he as God sitteth in the temple of God, shewing himself that he is God."

And in Revelation 13:8 we are also told: "And all that dwell upon the earth shall worship him, whose names are not written in the book of life of the Lamb slain from the foundation of the world."

It is blasphemous rebellion against God which marks the willful king as the final and logical expression of humanism. He is the typical representative of that which is against God and that which is *our* old nature: "Because the carnal mind is enmity against God: for it is not subject to the law of God, neither indeed can be. So then they that are in the flesh cannot please God" (Rom. 8:7–8). The carnal mind of men will turn to the Antichrist. When men choose their own rulers and leaders, what kind of man do they choose? Generally it is one who is like they are, and that is the reason we are getting such sorry leaders in the world today. The leadership of the world is frightful—they are the kind of folk we picked out. God has said right here in the Book of Daniel that He would set over the kingdoms of this world the basest of rulers.

"And shall prosper till the indignation be accomplished." The willful king will be successful at first and for a brief time. God will permit this to come to pass during the last half of Daniel's Seventieth Week.

**Neither shall he regard the God of his fathers, nor the desire of women, nor regard any god: for he shall magnify himself above all [Dan. 11:37].**

"Neither shall he regard the God of his fathers." It has been assumed from this statement that Antichrist would have to be an Israelite. However, this statement could refer to a Protestant, a Roman Catholic, or a heathen. Wherever he comes from, he will not regard the God of his fathers. We have examples of this in history. Smith, the head of the now defunct organization, the American Association for the Advancement of Atheism, was the son of a Methodist minister, and Stalin at one time studied in a theological seminary.

As I have stated previously, I believe that it takes two men to fulfill this office, and they are both presented in chapter 13 of Revelation. This first one is a political ruler who comes out of the Roman Empire and probably the Greek section of the Roman Empire. He is the one who doesn't have to be an Israelite at all. The second beast that arises is a religious leader, and he imitates Christ—I assume he will be an Israelite.

"Nor the desire of women." This refers evidently to the desire of Hebrew women to

be the mother of the Messiah. Not only will the Lord Jesus Christ be absolutely rejected, He will become the enemy. Antichrist leads a rebellion against God and Christ. As Psalm 2 puts it: "The kings of the earth set themselves, and the rulers take counsel together, against the LORD, and against his anointed, saying, Let us break their bands asunder, and cast away their cords from us" (Ps. 2:2–3).

"Nor regard any god." That means very plainly that he will oppose all religions and worship, except worship of himself. He is not only a believer in the ecumenical movement, he promotes it; in fact, he is *it*. One religion for one world will be his motto, and *he* is that religion.

"He shall magnify himself above all" is the final fruition of the self-will of this willful king. His total ambition is self-adulation.

This is the frightful prospect of the final days of the Great Tribulation Period: "And he had power to give life unto the image of the beast, that the image of the beast should both speak, and cause that as many as would not worship the image of the beast should be killed. And he causeth all, both small and great, rich and poor, free and bond, to receive a mark in their right hand, or in their foreheads: And that no man might buy or sell, save he that had the mark, or the name of the beast, or the number of his name" (Rev. 13:15–17). You will not be able to go to a restaurant to eat or buy a ticket on a plane or train without the mark of the beast. I tell you, that is going to be dictatorship with a vengeance!

**But in his estate shall he honour the God of forces: and a god whom his fathers knew not shall he honour with gold, and silver, and with precious stones, and pleasant things [Dan. 11:38].**

"The God of forces" should be more accurately translated "the God of fortresses." It is true that we are living in a day, as someone has written, in which man is increasingly making gods out of forces, but that is not what Daniel is saying here. I am quoting Dr. Newell: "We know from pagan mythology that both Cybele and Diana are variously represented as crowned with multi-tiered crowns, plainly setting forth the idea of fortification with turrets, battlements, and so forth" (*Daniel, The Man Greatly Beloved, and His Prophecies*, p. 178). I am sure you have seen pictures of these heathen idols with their multi-tiered crowns with all kinds of fortresses on them which represent the kingdoms of this world. Antichrist will honor the god of fortresses who has the kingdoms of the world. Who is that? Well, it was Satan who offered to Christ the kingdoms of this world, and our Lord rejected his offer. Apparently, Satan had a right to make that offer. Antichrist will accept the offer and become the world's dictator. We are told in 2 Thessalonians 2:4 and Revelation 13:4 that Antichrist will accept worship and will have the world worshiping Satan in that day. All the kingdoms of the world will be under his rulership, the first truly worldwide dictatorship.

**Thus shall he do in the most strong holds with a strange god, whom he shall acknowledge and increase with glory: and he shall cause them to rule over many, and shall divide the land for gain [Dan. 11:39].**

This is going to be Satan's hour. He will make the most of it, as he knows his time is short. "Therefore rejoice, ye heavens, and ye that dwell in them. Woe to the inhabiters of the earth and of the sea! for the devil is come down unto you, having great wrath, because he knoweth that he hath but a short time" (Rev. 12:12). Antichrist will be the pliant tool to completely do the will of Satan in that day. He will rule over many people and dispose of property as he pleases. He is the willful king and the final world dictator.

## VICTORY OF THE WILLFUL KING IS TEMPORARY

**And at the time of the end shall the king of the south push at him: and the king of the north shall come against him like a whirlwind, with chariots, and with horsemen, and with many ships; and he shall enter into the countries, and shall overflow and pass over [Dan. 11:40].**

It is "the time of the end," not the end of time. It is the end which Daniel has had in mind all through this section, the last days of the nation Israel which the Lord Jesus labeled the Great Tribulation.

"The king of the south" is evidently a ruler of Egypt, but it is impossible for us to identify him. Actually, Egypt has not had a native ruler for years. God has done a pretty good job of putting over that nation the basest of rulers. However, this one who is going to arise at the time of the end will probably unite

all of Africa as no leader of Egypt has ever been able to do, and he will come against Antichrist.

"The king of the north" is more easily identified. He takes the place of the Seleucidae dynasty, and I believe he is the one who comes out of the north mentioned in Ezekiel 38 and 39. The king of the north is Russia. Russia will open the campaign of Armageddon which will not be just a battle, but an entire war. At the very beginning, the king of the north will be eliminated as God moves in judgment upon that nation.

**He shall enter also into the glorious land, and many countries shall be overthrown: but these shall escape out of his hand, even Edom, and Moab, and the chief of the children of Ammon [Dan. 11:41].**

The entrance of Russia into Palestine precipitates the great crisis and conflict of the Great Tribulation Period.

When Antichrist enters Palestine, that is, "the glorious land," he will find that he is going to have trouble with Edom, Moab, and Ammon. That is the territory where the sons of Ishmael, the Arabs, are today. He is going to have trouble with them, for a while at least.

**He shall stretch forth his hand also upon the countries: and the land of Egypt shall not escape [Dan. 11:42].**

Egypt and the king of the south will yield to the Antichrist.

**But he shall have power over the treasures of gold and of silver, and over all the precious things of Egypt: and the Libyans and the Ethiopians shall be at his steps [Dan. 11:43].**

He will have control of the wealth of this world. He will control the entire money markets of the world at that time. Libya and Ethiopia will surrender to him—he will have control of Africa.

**But tidings out of the east and out of the north shall trouble him: therefore he shall go forth with great fury to destroy, and utterly to make away many [Dan. 11:44].**

"Tidings out of the east"—that means the Orient with its teeming millions. A great army will come from there to the Battle of Armageddon, and this world ruler will be troubled. At that time, there will be no hope for the world, and certainly there will be no hope for God's people, except in God Himself.

**And he shall plant the tabernacles of his palace between the seas in the glorious holy mountain; yet he shall come to his end, and none shall help him [Dan. 11:45].**

"The seas" refer to the Mediterranean Sea, and "the glorious holy mountain" is Jerusalem. In other words, at that time Antichrist will establish his headquarters for world conquest between the Mediterranean Sea and Jerusalem. However, instead of ruling from there, he will be destroyed by the personal return of the Lord Jesus Christ (Rev. 19:17–20). Evil will have taken over, and only in the personal coming of Christ to establish His kingdom will any on this earth be delivered and saved.

# CHAPTER 12

**THEME:** *The Great Tribulation; the resurrections of Old Testament saints and sinners; sealing of prophecy till the time of the end; the abomination of desolation*

Chapter 12 now concludes the vision which began back in chapter 10. This is all one vision, and everything about it must fit together like a jigsaw puzzle. The problem is that some people dip into this prophecy here and there, making applications as they see fit. We need to remember that this is all one vision, and we were told concerning it: "Now I am come to make thee understand what shall befall thy people in the latter days: for yet the vision is for many days" (Dan. 10:14). There are three important things that we note from this verse:

1. "Thy people" means that it concerns the nation Israel after the church is removed from the earth.

2. It is "in the latter days." The latter days of the Old Testament are identified with the last days of the New Testament which the Lord Jesus called the Great Tribulation Period and which correspond to the Seventieth Week of Daniel.

3. "Yet the vision is for many days," that is, there will be a long time before all of this is worked out and before you come to the latter days. It has been a long time since Daniel had these visions; in fact, at least twenty-five hundred years have gone by. Whether we are moving into the orbit of these days, I do not know. The church will have to be removed first—that is the next happening in the program of God. We have no date for that—we have no sign for it. Anyone who tries to set a date for the Rapture is dealing with something that is not found in the Word of God.

## THE GREAT TRIBULATION

**And at that time shall Michael stand up, the great prince which standeth for the children of thy people: and there shall be a time of trouble, such as never was since there was a nation even to that same time: and at that time thy people shall be delivered, every one that shall be found written in the book [Dan. 12:1].**

By what authority do we call this period the Great Tribulation Period? By the authority of the Lord Jesus, because He used the same language in speaking of the Great Tribulation that Daniel uses here. He said that this would be a brief period, a time of trouble, and that there would never be a time like it before or afterward. This is the time the Lord Jesus called the Great Tribulation Period. He knew what He was talking about, and we will accept what He said (see Matt. 24:15–26).

"At that time" identifies the time frame as the time of the end (Dan. 11:35, 40; 12:4) and the latter days (Dan. 10:14). This is now the end of the vision given to Daniel, and it ends with the Great Tribulation Period. Dr. Robert Culver wrote in *Daniel and the Latter Days*, p. 166: "Another expression, 'at the time of the end' (11:40), seems to indicate eschatological times. I do not feel that this evidence, taken by itself, can be pressed too far, for obviously the end of whatever series of events is in the mind of the author is designated by the expression, 'time of the end.' This is not necessarily a series reaching on to the consummation of the ages. However, it is quite clear from 10:14, which fixes the scope of the prophecy to include 'the latter days,' that the 'time of the end' in this prophecy is with reference to the period consummated by the establishment of the Messianic kingdom."

"Michael" is identified for us here. He is the only angel given the title of archangel (see Jude 9). His name means "who is like unto God?" He is the one who is going to cast Satan out of heaven (see Rev. 12:7–9). He is the one who protects the nation Israel and stands in her behalf, as Daniel makes clear here. His strategy is outlined by John in Revelation 12:14–16.

"For the children of thy people." This is positively the nation Israel. Otherwise the language has no meaning whatsoever.

"And there shall be a time of trouble." This is the Great Tribulation Period as our Lord so labeled it in Matthew 24:21.

The believing remnant of Israel will be preserved (see Matt. 24:22; Rom. 11:26; Rev. 7:4). "And I heard the number of them which were sealed: and there were sealed an hundred and forty and four thousand of all the tribes of the children of Israel" (Rev. 7:4).

## THE RESURRECTIONS
## OF OLD TESTAMENT SAINTS
## AND SINNERS

**And many of them that sleep in the dust of the earth shall awake, some to everlasting life, and some to shame and everlasting contempt [Dan. 12:2].**

"**A**nd many of them that sleep in the dust of the earth shall awake, some to everlasting life." The remnant of Israel living in the Great Tribulation Period will be preserved, and that great company of Gentiles who are to be saved during that time also will be preserved. Those of the Old Testament who died belonging to the remnant and the Gentiles saved during the Old Testament will be raised to everlasting life at the end of the Great Tribulation.

The Old Testament saints are not raised at the Rapture of the church. Scripture clearly states that at the Rapture those ". . . which sleep *in Jesus* will God bring with him" (1 Thess. 4:14, italics mine). Only, ". . . the dead *in Christ* shall rise first" (1 Thess. 4:16, italics mine). We are *in Christ* by the baptism of the Holy Spirit which began on the Day of Pentecost and will end at the Rapture. This particular body of believers is called the church. We are told in 1 Corinthians 12:12–13, "For as the body is one, and hath many members, and all the members of that one body, being many, are one body: so also is Christ. For by one Spirit are we all baptized into one body, whether we be Jews or Gentiles, whether we be bond or free; and have been all made to drink into one Spirit." Christ told His disciples who were members of the nation Israel that they would be baptized by the Holy Spirit and put into the body of believers, the church—"For John truly baptized with water; but ye shall be baptized with the Holy Ghost not many days hence" (Acts 1:5).

When the church is raptured out of the world, the Old Testament saints will not yet be raised. Why? Because the time to enter the kingdom is at the end of the Great Tribulation Period when Christ comes to establish His kingdom on the earth. Then the Old Testament saints will be raised. Abraham, Isaac, and Jacob will all be raised to enter the kingdom on this earth at that time. However, if they were raised at the time of the Rapture of the church, they would just have to stand around with their harps for seven years! I think that would get a little monotonous. However, Scripture makes it clear that they will be raised at the *end* of the Great Tribulation.

"Some to shame and everlasting contempt" refers to the lost of the Old Testament who are raised for the Great White Throne judgment at the end of the Millennium (see Rev. 20:11–15).

**And they that be wise shall shine as the brightness of the firmament; and they that turn many to righteousness as the stars for ever and ever [Dan. 12:3].**

God's servants in the dark days of the Great Tribulation will shine as lights. Believers are to do the same thing today, by the way. "That ye may be blameless and harmless, the sons of God, without rebuke, in the midst of a crooked and perverse nation, among whom ye shine as lights in the world" (Phil. 2:15). The remnant in that day will be God's witness in the world, and they are going to "turn many to righteousness." That righteousness is Christ, the only righteousness which is acceptable to God. Our righteousness is as filthy rags (see Isa. 64:6) in His sight—not in *our* sight; we think we are pretty good. We pat each other on the back and tell each other how wonderful we are, while all we produce is a bunch of dirty laundry, my friend. God is not accepting our works; He is accepting the righteousness of Christ, and that is provided only by faith.

## SEALING OF PROPHECY TILL THE
## TIME OF THE END

**But thou, O Daniel, shut up the words, and seal the book, even to the time of the end: many shall run to and fro, and knowledge shall be increased [Dan. 12:4].**

**T**hese prophecies were to be sealed until "the time of the end." This does not mean the end of time but refers to that definite period of time which in the Book of Daniel is the Seventieth Week. In view of the fact that we are in the interval immediately preceding this period, it is difficult to know just how much we understand. Since so many good men differ today on the interpretation of prophecy, it would seem to indicate that there is much that we do not understand. All of this will be opened up when we reach this particular period. This is the reason we need to keep our eyes upon one thing—"Looking for that blessed hope, and the glorious appearing of the great God and our Saviour Jesus Christ" (Titus 2:13).

"Many shall run to and fro." I personally

believe that this refers to running up and down the Bible in the study of prophecy—many shall search it through and through. There is a serious study of prophecy being made by many scholars today which has not been done in the past. Different great doctrines of the church have been studied and developed during different periods of the history of the church. At the very beginning, the doctrine of the inspiration of the Scriptures was pretty well established—also the doctrine of the deity of Christ and of redemption. Other doctrines were developed down through history. Today I think we are seeing more study of prophecy than ever before.

"Knowledge shall be increased." I believe this means knowledge of prophecy. It is true that knowledge has increased in every field today, but this refers primarily to the study of prophecy.

**Then I Daniel looked, and, behold, there stood other two, the one on this side of the bank of the river, and the other on that side of the bank of the river.**

**And one said to the man clothed in linen, which was upon the waters of the river, How long shall it be to the end of these wonders?**

**And I heard the man clothed in linen, which was upon the waters of the river, when he held up his right hand and his left hand unto heaven, and sware by him that liveth for ever that it shall be for a time, times, and an half; and when he shall have accomplished to scatter the power of the holy people, all these things shall be finished [Dan. 12:5-7].**

These verses return us to the vision which Daniel had seen at the beginning of chapter 10.

"The man clothed in linen" has been previously identified as the postincarnate Christ. Two others join Him here—one stands on one bank of the Tigris River and the other on the opposite bank. One asks how long these events will take, and the postincarnate Christ swears that it will be three and one half years, which is the last half of Daniel's Seventieth Week.

"To scatter the power of the holy people" is a strange phrase. It may mean that the rebellion of Israel will have finally been broken by the end of the Great Tribulation Period and that there will have been a great turning to God at that time.

**And I heard, but I understood not: then said I, O my Lord, what shall be the end of these things? [Dan. 12:8].**

Though Daniel was a witness to this scene, he did not understand what he saw and heard. Daniel was puzzled and wanted to know how all of these things he had just witnessed would work out.

**And he said, Go thy way, Daniel: for the words are closed up and sealed till the time of the end [Dan. 12:9].**

Daniel is reminded again that these things would take place in the time of the end and are temporarily sealed (see v. 4).

## THE ABOMINATION OF DESOLATION

**Many shall be purified, and made white, and tried; but the wicked shall do wickedly: and none of the wicked shall understand; but the wise shall understand [Dan. 12:10].**

These great principles of God prevail from Daniel's day to the time of the end, irrespective of dispensations:

1. "Many shall be purified" refers to those who have come to Christ, "Not by works of righteousness which we have done, but according to his mercy . . ." (Titus 3:5).

2. "None of the wicked shall understand" refers to the natural man. "But the natural man receiveth not the things of the Spirit of God: for they are foolishness unto him: neither can he know them, because they are spiritually discerned" (1 Cor. 2:14).

3. "But the wise shall understand." "Howbeit when he, the Spirit of truth, is come, he will guide you into all truth: for he shall not speak of himself; but whatsoever he shall hear, that shall he speak: and he will shew you things to come" (John 16:13).

**And from the time that the daily sacrifice shall be taken away, and the abomination that maketh desolate set up, there shall be a thousand two hundred and ninety days [Dan. 12:11].**

The importance of this verse cannot be overemphasized as the Lord Jesus referred to it in Matthew 24:15—"When ye therefore shall see the abomination of desolation, spoken of by Daniel the prophet, stand in the holy place, (whoso readeth, let him understand)." This is the signal to the remnant that the Great Tribulation has begun.

For 1290 days the idol of the Beast remains in the temple. Actually, this is thirty days

beyond the three and one half years. The last half of the Great Tribulation is 1260 days, and for some unexplained reason the image of Antichrist will be permitted to remain 30 days after Antichrist himself has been cast into the lake of fire.

**Blessed is he that waiteth, and cometh to the thousand three hundred and five and thirty days [Dan. 12:12].**

Another series of days is given to us here with no other explanation than "blessed is he that waiteth, and cometh" to them. No one has the interpretation of this—it is sealed until the time of the end. I think sometimes we try to know more than is actually given to us.

**But go thou thy way till the end be: for thou shalt rest, and stand in thy lot at the end of the days [Dan. 12:13].**

Daniel is told (as the Lord Jesus told Simon Peter) that he would die. He would not live to see the return of Christ, but he would be raised from the dead to enter the Millennium.

"In thy lot" means that Daniel will be raised with the Old Testament saints at the beginning of the Millennium.

"At the end of the days" brings us to the abundant entrance into Christ's kingdom. My friend, that is the future that is before us right now, a future that says Jesus is coming to this earth to establish His kingdom. This is the hope we should keep before us in these days.

# BIBLIOGRAPHY

(Recommended for Further Study)

Campbell, Donald K. *Daniel: Decoder of Dreams*. Wheaton, Illinois: Victor Books, 1977.

Criswell, W. A. *Expository Sermons on the Book of Daniel*. Grand Rapids, Michigan: Zondervan Publishing House, 1968.

DeHaan, M. R. *Daniel the Prophet*. Grand Rapids, Michigan: Zondervan Publishing House, 1947.

Gaebelein, Arno C. *The Prophet Daniel*. Neptune, New Jersey: Loizeaux Brothers, 1911.

Ironside, H. A. *Lectures on Daniel the Prophet*. Neptune, New Jersey: Loizeaux Brothers, 1911. (Especially good for young Christians.)

Kelly, William. *Lectures on the Book of Daniel*. Addison, Illinois: Bible Truth Publishers, 1881.

Larkin, Clarence. *The Book of Daniel*. Philadelphia: The Larkin Estate, 1929. (Very helpful charts.)

Luck, G. Coleman. *Daniel*. Chicago, Illinois: Moody Press, 1958. (Fine, inexpensive survey.)

McClain, Alva J. *Daniel's Prophecy of the Seventy Weeks*. Winona Lake, Indiana: Brethren Missionary Herald Co., 1940.

McGee, J. Vernon. *Delving Through Daniel*. Pasadena, California: Thru the Bible Books, 1960.

Strauss, Lehman. *The Prophecies of Daniel*. Neptune, New Jersey: Loizeaux Brothers, 1969. (Very practical.)

Walvoord, John F. *Daniel, The Key to Prophetic Revelation*. Chicago, Illinois: Moody Press, 1971. (Excellent, comprehensive interpretation.)

Wood, Leon J. *Daniel: A Study Guide Commentary*. Grand Rapids, Michigan: Zondervan Publishing House, 1975. (Excellent for individual and group study.)

# HELPFUL BOOKS ON BIBLE PROPHECY

Hoyt, Hermann A. *The End Times*. Chicago, Illinois: Moody Press, 1969.

Pentecost, J. Dwight. *Things to Come*. Grand Rapids, Michigan: Zondervan Publishing House, 1958.

Ryrie, Charles C. *The Basis of the Premillennial Faith*. Neptune, New Jersey: Loizeaux Brothers, 1953.

Ryrie, Charles C. *What You Should Know About the Rapture*. Chicago, Illinois: Moody Press, 1981.

Sauer, Erich. *From Eternity to Eternity*. Grand Rapids, Michigan: Wm. B. Eerdmans Publishing Co., 1954.

Tatford, Frederick A. *The Minor Prophets*. Minneapolis, Minnesota: Klock & Klock, n.d.

Walvoord, John F. *Armageddon, Oil, and the Middle East Crisis*. Grand Rapids, Michigan: Zondervan Publishing House, 1974.

Walvoord, John F. *The Millennial Kingdom*. Grand Rapids, Michigan: Zondervan Publishing House, 1959.

Walvoord, John F. *The Rapture Question*. Grand Rapids, Michigan: Zondervan Publishing House, 1957.

Wood, Leon J. *The Bible and Future Events*. Grand Rapids, Michigan: Zondervan Publishing House, 1973.

# The Book of
# HOSEA
## INTRODUCTION

**B**eginning with Hosea and concluding with Malachi, there are twelve short prophecies designated as the Minor Prophets, while Isaiah, Jeremiah, Ezekiel, and Daniel are called the Major Prophets. The Minor Prophets are so called because of the size of the books, not because of their content. However, even that criterion for division is not completely accurate since Hosea is a longer book than Daniel. Actually, the so-called Minor Prophets are not minor. Each of them batted in the major league and was a star in the message that he brought.

The Minor Prophets were exceedingly nationalistic, but they were not isolationists. They dealt with the fact that God's people had broken the law of God, the Ten Commandments. This necessarily puts an emphasis on works, good works. For this reason the liberals and the promoters of the social gospel have used the Minor Prophets a great deal. Unfortunately, they have missed the main message of these prophets. We will see some of that when we get into the prophecy of Hosea. The Minor Prophets warned against godless alliances with other nations. They were extremely patriotic and denounced political and moral corruption. They warned Israel against an isolationism from God.

Hosea lived during the time of the divided kingdom. He was a prophet to the northern kingdom which is called the kingdom of Israel, distinguished from the southern kingdom known as the kingdom of Judah. "The word of the LORD that came unto Hosea, the son of Beeri, in the days of Uzziah, Jotham, Ahaz, and Hezekiah, kings of Judah, and in the days of Jeroboam the son of Joash, king of Israel" (Hos. 1:1).

Hosea mentions the four kings of Judah first, and then he mentions the king of Israel, the northern kingdom. Because they were all contemporary with Hosea, he mentions them all. He was a prophet to the northern kingdom of Israel, as the content of the book reveals.

Hosea was a contemporary of Amos, another prophet to Israel. He was also a contemporary of Micah and Isaiah, prophets to Judah. His ministry extended over half a century, and he lived to see the fulfillment of his prophecy in the captivity of Israel.

He can be compared to Jeremiah in the southern kingdom. Jeremiah warned his people of the southern kingdom that they would go into captivity, and he lived to see it. Hosea warned the northern kingdom that they would be going into Assyrian captivity, and he lived to see it. Jeremiah and Hosea have a great many things in common.

The theme of this book is a plea to return unto the Lord. I have a message entitled, "The Greatest Sin in All the World," which emphasizes the great theme of this book. I shall let it serve as the introduction to this marvelous prophecy of Hosea.

The accusation is often made that the present-day pulpit is weak and uncertain. Furthermore, it is charged that instead of being a ". . . voice . . . in the wilderness . . ." (John 1:23), the modern pulpit has settled down comfortably to become a sounding board for the whims and wishes of an indifferent people with itching ears. If the charge is true (and in many cases it is), it is because the pulpit is reluctant to grapple with the great issues of life. This hesitancy is born of a desire to escape criticism and a dread of becoming offensive to the finer sensibilities. More often it is due to a cowardly fear of facing the raw realities of life and wrestling with the leviathan of living issues. The pulpit quotes poetry and sprinkles rose water. It lives in a land of make-believe instead of saying, "Believe on the Lord Jesus Christ, and thou shalt be saved . . ." (Acts 16:31).

The theater, the monthly magazine, and other agencies of communication deal with life stripped of its niceties. These instruments for reaching and teaching the masses take the gloves off and grapple with the problems that we face daily.

Not so the pulpit. The pulpit has avoided these issues. As we come to this prophecy of Hosea, we cannot avoid dealing with the problems and issues of life, for that is the story that is behind the headlines in the prophecy of Hosea. It is not a pretty story, but we must understand it if we are to understand the message of Hosea.

The story behind the prophecy of Hosea is the tragedy of a broken home. The personal experience of Hosea is the background of his

message. He walks out of a broken home to speak to the nation from a heart that is breaking. He knew exactly how *God* felt, because *he* felt the same way.

The home is the rock foundation of society and has been that for all peoples. God has given the home to mankind. He gave it to man at the very beginning. It is the most important unit in the social structure. It is to society what the atom is to the physical universe. The little atom has been called the building block of the universe. Well, the home is the building block of society. The character and color of a building is determined by the individual bricks that go into it. No nation is any stronger than the homes that populate it, for the home determines the color and complexion of society. The home is the chain of a nation that holds it together, and every individual link is important.

Home is where we live and move and have our being. It is in the home where we are ourselves. We dress up physically and psychologically when we go out. We put up quite a front when we go through our front door and move out upon the street. But it is within the walls of the home that we take off our masks and are really ourselves.

Because of the strategic position of the home, God has thrown about it certain safeguards to protect it. He has surrounded it with certain bulwarks because of its importance. One of these is marriage. God has given more attention to the institution of marriage than He has to any other institution in this world. Society did not *make* marriage; society *found* marriage. It is God who made marriage, and He gave it to mankind. Marriage rests upon His direct Word, ". . . What therefore God hath joined together, let not man put asunder" (Matt. 19:6). God performed the first marriage ceremony. He gave the first bride away. He blessed the first couple. Marriage is more than a legal contract, more than an economic arrangement, more than a union of those with mutual love; it is an act of God. It rests upon His fiat command. Many folk think that all they need in order to get married is a license and a preacher. My friend, if you are going to have a successful marriage, you have to have God. If God does not make the marriage, it will go on the rocks.

God has given a drive to the race to reproduce within the framework of marriage. That is what makes the home. The ". . . twain shall be one flesh . . ." (Mark 10:8). Before man walked out of the Garden of Eden, God gave him this institution. Besides the skins that Adam and Eve wore, the only thing they had was a marriage certificate from God. That is all. That is the only institution that came out of the Garden of Eden.

Marriage is a sacred relationship; it is a holy union. The New Testament sums up the mind of God on this when it says, "Marriage is honourable in all . . ." (Heb. 13:4). Therefore, my beloved, marriage cannot be broken by a little legal act. It cannot be broken by a fit of temper. It cannot be broken by self-will. I personally believe there are only two acts that break a marriage—I mean a *real* marriage.

The first act is death, of course, which automatically severs the relationship.

The second act is unfaithfulness—unfaithfulness on the part of either the husband or the wife. That rips a relationship in two. In the Old Testament, the one guilty of adultery was to be dealt with in the harshest manner imaginable. For example, notice the importance God attached to the act: "And the man that committeth adultery with another man's wife, even he that committeth adultery with his neighbour's wife, the adulterer and the adulteress shall surely be put to death" (Lev. 20:10). For an unmarried girl accused of adultery the Law said, "But if this thing be true, and the tokens of virginity be not found for the damsel: Then they shall bring out the damsel to the door of her father's house, and the men of her city shall stone her with stones that she die: because she hath wrought folly in Israel, to play the whore in her father's house: so shalt thou put evil away from among you" (Deut. 22:20–21).

There are a few words I think we should say here by way of explanation. There are some zealous Christians who use Romans 7:2–3 as the basis for the extreme viewpoint that a divorced person who has a living mate can never remarry. Verse 2 says, "For the woman which hath an husband is bound by the law to her husband so long as he liveth; but if the husband be dead, she is loosed from the law of her husband." They forget that under the Law the married person who was guilty of fornication was stoned to death and the innocent party under the Law did not have a living partner. The guilty person was pushing up daisies through the rock pile. If that were enforced in Southern California today, we wouldn't have freeways because we wouldn't be able to get around all the rock piles.

I am not sure but what Paul includes desertion under the heading of unfaithfulness in 1 Corinthians 7:15: "But if the unbelieving depart, let him depart. A brother or a sister is

not under bondage in such cases: but God hath called us to peace."

Another item concerning the Law which needs amplification is the reference in Deuteronomy which seems to preclude the man from any charge of guilt. You may wonder why the woman is picked on—isn't the man guilty? Yes, but there are two things you need to bear in mind: one is that the word used is always the generic term, *anthropōs*, meaning "mankind." We have the same distinction in legal terminology. I notice that some contracts read, "The party of the first part, if he . . ." when the person is really a she. The term is used for either one. Also we must remember that marriage is a picture of Christ and the church, and He is never guilty, but the church is guilty. The Scriptures do not teach a double standard, but I do think they teach a different standard.

Personally, I think that God has made woman finer than man. For this reason, when she goes bad, she goes farther down than a man goes. It is not that sin in one is worse than in another, but the results are far more detrimental. In my limited ministry, I have seen children overcome the handicap of a ne'er-do-well father, but I have never seen children turn out right when the mother has been bad. A sorry father is a serious handicap for a child, but a good mother more than compensates. Mother is the center of the home. Some time ago I heard of a woman who was asked to accept an office in a church organization. She refused the office and gave as her reason, "I am a missionary to the nursery. There are three pairs of eyes watching me, and I want to direct them to God." God has placed a mother in a home and made her all-important in that place.

Every woman was once a little girl very much like the description composed by Alan Beck, and which he has entitled "What is a Girl?"

Little girls are the nicest things that happen to people. They are born with a little bit of angel-shine about them and though it wears thin sometimes, there is always enough left to lasso your heart—even when they are sitting in the mud, or crying temperamental tears, or parading up the street in mother's best clothes.

A little girl can be sweeter (and badder) oftener than anyone else in the world. She can jitter around, and stomp, and make funny noises and frazzle your nerves, yet just when you open your mouth, she stands there demure with that special look in her eyes. A girl is Innocence playing in the mud, Beauty standing on its head, and Motherhood dragging a doll by the foot.

God borrows from many creatures to make a little girl. He uses the song of a bird, the squeal of a pig, the stubbornness of a mule, the antics of a monkey, the spryness of a grasshopper, the curiosity of a cat, the slyness of a fox, the softness of a kitten. And to top it off, He adds the mysterious mind of a woman.

A little girl likes new shoes, party dresses, small animals, dolls, make-believe, ice cream, make-up, going visiting, tea parties, and one boy. She doesn't care so much for visitors, boys in general, large dogs, hand-me-downs, straight chairs, vegetables, snow suits, or staying in the front yard. She is loudest when you are thinking, prettiest when she has provoked you, busiest at bedtime, quietest when you want to show her off, and most flirtatious when she absolutely must not get the best of you again.

She can muss up your home, your hair, and your dignity—spend your money, your time, and your temper—then just when your patience is ready to crack, her sunshine peeks through and you've lost again.

Yes, she is a nerve-racking nuisance, just a noisy bundle of mischief. But when your dreams tumble down and the world is a mess, when it seems you are pretty much of a fool after all, she can make you a king when she climbs on your knee and whispers, "I love you best of all!"

God shapes that little-girl charm into a fine and delicate instrument, a woman. But when a woman goes wrong, the tragedy is immeasurable.

The background of the prophecy of Hosea is the story of a fallen woman and a broken home. It is a story of that which must be contrasted to God's ideal of marriage and of womanhood. God uses this to tell His own story.

In the hill country of Ephraim, in one of the many little towns not on the maps of the world, lived two young people. One was a boy by the name of Hosea, the other was a girl by the name of Gomer. They fell in love—it is the same story which has been repeated millions

of times but never grows old. I don't think it is stretching the imagination to say that they fell madly in love with each other. Then for some unaccountable reason, Gomer went bad. She resorted to the oldest profession known to mankind. Hosea was brokenhearted, and shame filled his soul. He must have thought about his recourse to the Mosaic Law. He could have brought her before the elders of the town and demanded the law be enforced. In that case she would have been stoned, for she had betrayed him. He would have been justified.

Does this remind you of another story that took place some seven hundred years later in that same hill country when a man by the name of Joseph was engaged to a girl by the name of Mary? The principal difference is that Joseph's information was wrong, and an angel came from heaven to correct it; but Hosea's information was right, for Gomer was guilty.

At this particular juncture the Book of Hosea opens. "The beginning of the word of the LORD by Hosea. And the LORD said to Hosea, Go, take unto thee a wife of whoredoms and children of whoredoms: for the land hath committed great whoredom, departing from the LORD" (Hos. 1:2). There are expositors who take the position that this is nothing but an allegory, that it did not really happen. Such trifling with the Word of God waters it down to a harmless solution which is more sickening than stimulating. Let's face it—God commanded Hosea to break the Mosaic Law. The Law said to stone her, but God said to marry her. The thing God commanded Hosea to do must have caused him to revolt in every fiber of his being, but Hosea did not demur—he obeyed explicitly. He took Gomer in holy wedlock, and he gave her his name. She came into his home as his wife. Listen to the apostle Paul as he speaks of such a relationship: "What? know ye not that he which is joined to an harlot is one body? for two, saith he, shall be one flesh" (1 Cor. 6:16).

My friend, you may be sure that the tempo of gossip really picked up in that little town. Hosea's home became a desert island in a sea of criticism. It was the isolation ward in local society. A case of leprosy in the home would not have broken off contact with the outside world more effectively. Poor Hosea!

Children were born in this home. There were three—two boys and one girl. Their names, in their meanings, tell the awful story. And there is the larger meaning and message for the nation Israel.

Jezreel was the oldest. His name means "God will scatter, and God will avenge." The reference, God told Hosea, was directly to the house of Jehu. Although Jehu had carried out God's instructions to destroy the house of Ahab, he had done it with hatred and great personal vengeance. For this, God says, "I'll judge. I'll scatter Israel, but there will be mercy in My judgment."

The second child was Lo-ruhamah, which means that she never knew a father's pity. It was not that she was an orphan, but she did not know who her father was. What a scandal in the home of Hosea! God is saying through this circumstance to the people of the northern kingdom who had gone into idolatry, "You will not know My pity, for I am not your Father."

The third child was Lo-ammi—which means "not my people." If you put this in the singular, it would mean "not my child." What a message that was to Hosea's day! And what a message it is to our own day when liberal theology claims that everyone is a child of God. God says they are wrong. He has no illegitimate children. God says, "I know who My children are. Do you think that My children are the offspring of a man-made union? Absolutely not! A person becomes My child only through faith in Jesus Christ." And the Lord Jesus said to the men in His day who claimed to be the sons of Abraham, "Ye are of your father the *devil* . . ." (John 8:44, italics mine). They could make no claim of being God's children.

My friend, are you Lo-ammi? Are you God's child, or are you an illegitimate child? Let me assure you that you can become a child of God—"But as many as received him, to them gave he power [the right, the authority] to become the sons of God, even to them that believe on his name" (John 1:12).

The story of Hosea's home is a sad one, and the story continues. Gomer left home. She returned to her former profession and became a common prostitute. Certainly God is going to say to this man, "Hosea, you have done all that you can. You tried to reform the woman, but it didn't do any good. Let her go." But no, God says, "Go get her and bring her back to your home." Hosea went after her. She refused to come back. He sent the children to plead with their mother. Still she would not return. Then, as women of this sort did in those days, she sold herself into slavery. Hosea went to her and *bought* her and brought her back to the home.

Oh, my friend, what a picture this is of our Savior. He created us and we belong to Him.

Then we were guilty of going from Him and giving our love, our affection, our time, to the things of the world. And while we were yet sinners, He came down to this earth and *bought* us in our ugly condition that He might make us His legitimate children. What love!

After this experience, did Gomer become a faithful wife? The record does not tell us. But we see Hosea, stepping out of a home scarred by shame and going before a nation with a heart that is breaking. His sorrow is intolerable; with scalding tears coursing down his cheeks, he denounces the nation Israel, saying, "You have been faithless to God! I know how God feels, because I feel the same way. You have broken the heart of God." What a picture!

Hosea denounced the nation. He declared a verdict of guilty for the crime of all crimes. He said simply but specifically that their sin was as black as it could be and they could expect God's punishment. This people who had known God, whom He had redeemed out of Egypt, to whom He had said, "Ye have seen what I did unto the Egyptians, and how I bare you on eagles' wings, and brought you unto myself" (Exod. 19:4), turned their backs on God and made a golden calf! And still in Hosea's day they had not learned their lesson, for at that moment in the northern kingdom there stood two golden calves. The people had turned from the living and true God back to calf worship! Israel was playing the harlot. Their sin was the greatest sin in the world.

You may be saying, "I thought unbelief was the greatest sin." In one sense unbelief is the greatest sin, but it is not an act, it is a state. We all are born in rebellion against God. But, thank God, Christ's death paid the penalty for our sin, and if you and I exercise faith in Jesus Christ, He will save us. It is true that unbelief is a terrible sin for which there is but one remedy—the remedy is to trust Christ. When you continue in unbelief, you reject the remedy.

There is another sin which you may consider the greatest in the world: it is sin against light. To have the light of the gospel of Jesus Christ and reject it is sinning against light. Frankly, I would rather stand before God's throne of judgment as an idolater from the darkest jungle of Africa, than as a church member who has repeatedly heard the gospel and rejected it. But this is not the greatest sin.

The greatest sin in all the world is sin against love. This is worse than all others, and this is the message of Hosea. Gomer was not only guilty of breaking the marriage vow, which was bad enough, but she sinned against the one who loved her. That is sin at its worst. My friend, to sin against God and the Savior who loves you is worse than the animism and animalism of the heathen world. The sin of paganism is nothing compared to the sin of those who reject God's love. It is deeper and darker than the immorality of the underworld and the demonism of the overworld.

Hosea knew what sin was, and he knew what love was. Sin against love makes the sin more heinous.

Israel knew the love of God as no other nation knew it. She knew His deliverance, His redemption, His protection, His forgiveness, His revelation, and His love. Yet Israel turned to dumb idols and gave herself to them. This is sin at its worst.

However, God would not give her up. Love will triumph. Let me lift out just three verses from Hosea's prophecy which will tell God's story:

First, here is the charge: "Ephraim is joined to idols: let him alone" (Hos. 4:17). The name *Ephraim* is synonymous with the name *Israel*, and He charges Israel with spiritual adultery.

Then notice the great pulsating passion of the infinite God: "How shall I give thee up, Ephraim? how shall I deliver thee, Israel? how shall I make thee as Admah? how shall I set thee as Zeboim? mine heart is turned within me, my repentings are kindled together" (Hos. 11:8). God is saying that He can't give Israel up; He loves her too much. This is His reason for sending Hosea back to get Gomer a second and a third time. He wanted Hosea to know how He felt about Israel.

Finally, here is the victory: "Ephraim shall say, What have I to do any more with idols? I have heard him, and observed him: I am like a green fir tree. From me is thy fruit found" (Hos. 14:8). There is a day coming when Israel will turn back to God. This leads us to believe that Gomer finally did change and become a good wife and mother. We cannot be sure of this, but we can be sure that Israel will one day return to God with her whole heart.

Is there an application for you and me here? Does this shocking description of spiritual adultery fit the believer in our day? Yes, the church is described as the bride of Christ— ". . . I have espoused you . . . that I may present you as a chaste virgin to Christ" (2 Cor. 11:2). And to the church at Ephesus the Lord Jesus said, "I know thy works, and

thy labour, and thy patience, and how thou canst not bear them which are evil. . . . Nevertheless I have somewhat against thee, because thou hast left thy first love" (Rev. 2:2, 4).

My friend, it is not enough to be correct in your doctrine and be active in your service for Christ. These are important and have their place, but the essential thing is love. Have you left your first love? Do you *love* Him today?

The name *Hosea* means "salvation"; it is another form of *Joshua*, which is the Hebrew name of the Greek form *Jesus*. The church is the bride of the New Testament Hosea, but our Hosea is joined to a spiritual harlot!

In Revelation, chapter 17, is the most frightful picture in the Bible. It personifies the church and calls her the great harlot, Mystery Babylon. This is the trend which the organized church is following in our day. Oh, how many believers are covering up their frustration and their lack of reality in their spiritual experience by just being busy. It is nothing in the world but nervous agitation. Down underneath they cannot honestly say, "I love Him. I am true to Him." With hot tears our Lord accuses the church of being lukewarm. God pity the man who is married to a lukewarm woman. God pity our Savior who is joined to a church that is only lukewarm. He says, "Oh, how I wish that you were either hot or cold!"

Let me be very personal and ask about *your* relationship with Christ. Has any cloud come between your soul and your Savior? An incident is told of Spurgeon who suddenly stopped in the middle of the street he was crossing and prayed. When he reached the other side, his companion asked him, "Why did you stop to pray in the middle of the street?" Spurgeon's reply was something like this, "A cloud came between my soul and Christ, and I could not let it remain there even long enough to reach the other side of the street." Before the Lord Jesus put Simon Peter in harness, He asked the heart-searching question, ". . . Lovest thou me? . . ." (John 21:17). This is just as poignant and pertinent now as it was that early dawn by the Sea of Galilee.

My friend, when you turn your back on the one who so loved the world that He gave His only begotten Son, you are not only doing something bad, you are not merely turning away in unbelief, you are committing the greatest sin of all. You are turning away from a God who loves you and died for you. There is no other sin equal to that.

# OUTLINE

I. **Personal—The Prophet and His Faithless Wife, Gomer, Chapters 1–3**
   A. Marriage of Hosea and Gomer, the Harlot, Chapter 1
   B. Gomer Proves Faithless; Israel Proves Faithless; God Proves Faithful, Chapter 2
   C. Hosea Commanded to Take Gomer Again, Chapter 3

II. **Prophetic—The Lord and the Faithless Nation Israel, Chapters 4–14**
   A. Israel Plays the Harlot, Chapters 4-5
      1. Israel Guilty of Lawlessness, Immorality, Ignorance of God's Word, and Idolatry, Chapter 4
      2. Israel Turns from God; God Turns from Israel; Deterioration within Follows, Chapter 5
   B. Israel *(Ephraim)* Will Return in the Last Days; Presently to Be Judged for Current Sins, Chapter 6
   C. Israel *(Ephraim)* Could Escape Judgment by Turning to God Who Loves Her *(Key: 11:8)*, Chapters 7–12
      1. Israel *(Silly Dove)* Turns to Egypt and Assyria, Chapter 7
      2. Israel Turns to Golden Calves and Altars of Sin, Chapter 8
      3. Israel *(Backsliding Heifer)* Turns to Land Productivity; Will Be Driven from Land, Chapters 9–10
      4. Israel Turns from God—Must Be Judged; God Will Not Give up on Her, Chapters 11–12
   D. Israel *(Ephraim)* Will Turn from Idols to God in Last Days, Chapters 13–14
      1. Israel Will Be Judged in the Present, Chapter 13
      2. Israel Will Be Saved in the Future, Chapter 14

# CHAPTER 1

**THEME:** *The marriage of Hosea and Gomer, the harlot*

When we come to the prophecy of Hosea, we are coming to one of the great books of the Bible and to a man who was a remarkable prophet. I personally do not like the classification of the prophets as Major and Minor. Every one of these men, whether they wrote a long prophecy or not, was an outstanding man. You wouldn't call Elijah a minor prophet simply because he never wrote a prophecy, would you? And John the Baptist, the last of the prophets, never wrote anything; yet he was a prophet of God and announced the coming of the Savior.

The prophets were not grouped as Major and Minor in the Hebrew Bible. They were arranged as we have them by the church around the third century. If I could have had my way in the arrangement of the books of the Bible, I would have placed each prophet with the historical book to which it corresponds. You will notice that the messages of nearly all the writing prophets belong to the period of the divided kingdom. When the kings failed, God then raised up prophets to speak to the nation.

Chronologically, therefore, the prophecy of Hosea belongs before Jeremiah. Hosea was contemporary with Isaiah, Micah, and his compatriot, Amos, in the northern kingdom. Hosea and Amos were prophets in the northern kingdom, Isaiah and Micah in the southern kingdom.

Hosea compares in many respects to Jeremiah. Jeremiah was the last prophet before the southern kingdom went into captivity; but more than a hundred years before that, Hosea was a prophet in the northern kingdom. He, like Jeremiah, warned the nation of its impending captivity. Both men spoke out of a heartbreaking personal experience, although Jeremiah's was more public. Hosea's experience was in the home while Jeremiah's was in the nation. Jeremiah loved his nation, and it broke his heart to give them such a harsh message, but God chose a very tenderhearted man for the job. Perhaps Hosea was not as tenderhearted as Jeremiah, but we will see that he came from the experience of a broken home with a broken heart. His wife was unfaithful to him and became a harlot. He loved her so much that he went back and took her again. And again she played the harlot. Coming from this experience, this man walked out before the nation Israel, with hot tears streaming down his cheeks, and said, "I want to tell you how God feels about you, because I feel the same way. I have had a personal experience in my own home." Because this man's heart had been broken, he could speak God's message to his nation.

In the first three chapters of Hosea we have that which is *personal*, the story of the prophet and his faithless wife, Gomer. We have here the scandal of his home and the gossip of the town.

## THE MARRIAGE OF HOSEA AND GOMER, THE HARLOT

**The word of the LORD that came unto Hosea, the son of Beeri, in the days of Uzziah, Jotham, Ahaz, and Hezekiah, kings of Judah, and in the days of Jeroboam the son of Joash, king of Israel [Hos. 1:1].**

"Uzziah, Jotham, Ahaz, and Hezekiah, kings of Judah"—these were the kings in the south at this particular time.

"Jeroboam the son of Joash, king of Israel"—there couldn't have been a worse king than this king of the northern kingdom.

**The beginning of the word of the LORD by Hosea. And the LORD said to Hosea, Go, take unto thee a wife of whoredoms and children of whoredoms: for the land hath committed great whoredom, departing from the LORD [Hos. 1:2].**

What the Lord says to the prophet is a rather startling thing, and many interpreters do not take Him literally. I highly recommend *The Scofield Reference Bible*, and I use the older edition a great deal. Some folk feel that those of us who recommend this Bible believe its notes are inspired. I do not believe they are inspired, and the first note given for this verse in *The New Scofield Reference Bible* is one that I totally disagree with. It reads: "God did not command Hosea to take an immoral wife but permitted him to carry out his desire to marry Gomer, warning him that she would be unfaithful, and using the prophet's sad experience as a basis for the presentation of lessons about God's relation to Israel." I consider this a very nice way to get God off the hook, but you do not have to get Him off the hook—He takes full responsibility for this. The way that I understand this verse is that

God said to Hosea, "Go." When my parents said that to me as a boy—"*Go* to the store," or "*Go* to school"—I always interpreted that as a command. When God said to Hosea, "Go," He was not just granting him permission to marry Gomer; it was a *command* to do so. Hosea probably was a young man, probably living in the Ephraim country of the northern kingdom. He met this beautiful girl and fell madly in love with her, and then she played the harlot. Naturally he wanted to put her aside. He might have wanted to marry her, but he wouldn't dare do that in a little town— and the Mosaic Law said to stone her. What is he going to do? God said, "Go and marry her." God is actually asking him to break the Mosaic Law. Someone will say, "That's terrible." Not when God tells you to do it, my friend. God said to him, "Hosea, you were in love with her, and now you want to put her aside. I don't want you to put her aside; I want you to marry her. She is a wife of harlotry and child of harlotry." Apparently there was a record of unfaithfulness in her family.

Here at the very beginning, the Lord makes clear to Hosea how He is going to use this experience in the prophet's life. He said, "For the land hath committed great whoredom, departing from the LORD." He is comparing that which is physical harlotry or adultery to that which is spiritual harlotry or adultery.

This is applicable to the believer today. You can play fast and loose with God, and you are nothing in the world but a harlot, a spiritual harlot, in His sight. That is exactly the language He uses here, and God uses pretty plain language. I wish the pulpit today were a little stronger than it is. We all are trying to be very nice and, as a result, we sometimes do not speak as strongly as the Word of God does.

**So he went and took Gomer the daughter of Diblaim; which conceived, and bare him a son.**

**And the LORD said unto him, Call his name Jezreel; for yet a little while, and I will avenge the blood of Jezreel upon the house of Jehu, and will cause to cease the kingdom of the house of Israel.**

**And it shall come to pass at that day, that I will break the bow of Israel in the valley of Jezreel [Hos. 1:3–5].**

Not only the marriage but also the children are going to present a real spiritual lesson for the nation Israel. (Remember that Isaiah's children also had a spiritual message for the nation.) *Jezreel* is the name of the son; it means "God will scatter." God says, "I will avenge the blood of Jezreel." Jezreel is the name of a city and also of a famous plain, the plain of Armageddon, or the Valley of Esdraelon. It has a long, bloody history and will have a similar future as the place where the last war will end. God is saying here that He is going to scatter the northern kingdom.

**And she conceived again, and bare a daughter. And God said unto him, Call her name Lo-ruhamah: for I will no more have mercy upon the house of Israel; but I will utterly take them away [Hos. 1:6].**

God named her *Lo-ruhamah*, which means that she "never knew a father's pity." As I indicated previously, it was not that she was an orphan, but she did not know who her father was. This reveals the scandal in the home of Hosea! God is saying through this circumstance to the people of the northern kingdom who had gone into idolatry, "You will not know My pity, for I am not your Father."

There has always been the question as to the possibility of a person stepping over a line—that is, sinking so low in sin that the grace of God cannot reach him. While I do not believe that you could ever get to a place where God by His grace *could* not save you, I do believe that if you persist in rejecting God's grace and mercy, the day will come when you will step over that line. This does not mean the grace of God cannot reach you, but it does mean that there will be nothing in you that the grace of God can lay hold of.

Let me illustrate this with the story of a man I met when I first came to Pasadena, California, as a pastor in 1940. His wife wanted me to visit him in his home because he was sick and dying. She asked me to present the gospel to him, and I did. He was a very polite man, and he listened to me. Then he said, "I would say, 'Yes, I will accept Christ as my Savior'—in fact, I am going to do it. But I want to tell you this: I have played and trifled with God all my life. I have been down to an altar twenty-five times. I have made promises to Him and then turned from Him, and I have never been sincere. Honestly, I cannot tell you right now whether I am sincere or not." All I could do at his funeral as I looked down at him was to say under my breath, "Oh, God, I hope he was sincere. I

hope he really meant it. I hope Your grace reached down and touched him."

You *can* trifle with God too long. The nation Israel did, and the day came when God said, "I will no longer have mercy on you."

**But I will have mercy upon the house of Judah, and will save them by the Lord their God, and will not save them by bow, nor by sword, nor by battle, by horses, nor by horsemen [Hos. 1:7].**

"However," God said, "I am not ready yet to judge the house of *Judah*." Why will He spare Judah and not Israel? For the sake of David. God had said that for the sake of David He would not divide the kingdom under the rule of Solomon. Again and again He said that for the sake of David He would save the southern kingdom. Someone may want to criticize this and say that it is not fair. I don't know whether it is fair or not, but I thank God that He showed mercy to me, that He was patient and continued to show mercy. And He continues to do so even today.

"And will save them by the Lord their God, and will not save them by bow, nor by sword, nor by battle, by horses, nor by horsemen." In effect, God says, "I am not going to save them by the fact that they have phantom jets and atom bombs. I am not going to save them by the means of arms." If you read 2 Kings 19 and Isaiah 37, you will learn how God miraculously delivered the people of the southern kingdom at this time. But He did not deliver the northern kingdom.

**Now when she had weaned Lo-ruhamah, she conceived, and bare a son [Hos. 1:8].**

In that country they take about two to three years to wean a child. When Lo-ruhamah was weaned, Gomer had another son.

**Then said God, Call his name Lo-ammi: for ye are not my people, and I will not be your God [Hos. 1:9].**

The third child was *Lo-ammi*, which means "not my people." If you put this in the singular, it would mean "not my child." There was a question about the second child; there is no question about this one. And God is saying to the nation Israel, "Ye are not my people, and I will not be your God." If this were the only verse in the Bible, I would have to agree with the amillennialists who say that God is

through dealing with the nation Israel. All of us—including many of my premillennial brethren—need to be very careful not to reach into the Bible and pull out a verse here or there and say that it is being fulfilled. If the entire prophecy of Hosea is read, no one can convincingly argue that God is through with the nation Israel. The next verse makes this very clear—

**Yet the number of the children of Israel shall be as the sand of the sea, which cannot be measured nor numbered; and it shall come to pass, that in the place where it was said unto them, Ye are not my people, there it shall be said unto them, Ye are the sons of the living God [Hos. 1:10].**

"Yet the number of the children of Israel shall be as the sand of the sea, which cannot be measured nor numbered." The Hebrew people have been decimated again and again by persecution—think of what Hitler did! Yet here is a marvelous prophecy that God is going to increase their number.

"And it shall come to pass, that in the place where it was said unto them, Ye are not my people, there it shall be said unto them, Ye are the sons of the living God." In that day there will be a great turning to God. God is not through with Israel—that is clear when you read the entire Word of God.

**Then shall the children of Judah and the children of Israel be gathered together, and appoint themselves one head, and they shall come up out of the land: for great shall be the day of Jezreel [Hos. 1:11].**

"Then shall the children of Judah and the children of Israel be gathered together." The nation shall come together. There are no "ten lost tribes of Israel," by the way.

"And appoint themselves one head." They don't have that today—they are not all in agreement with their leadership. The "one head" referred to in Hosea's prophecy is the Messiah, of course.

"And they shall come up out of the land: for great shall be the day of Jezreel"—what a wonderful prophecy this is. However, I disagree with the viewpoint that the present return to Israel is a fulfillment of Old Testament prophecy. We shall deal with that in greater detail as we go through the Book of Hosea.

# CHAPTER 2

**THEME:** *Gomer proves faithless; Israel proves faithless; God proves faithful*

**T**his chapter opens with the fifth very remarkable prophecy concerning the nation Israel. In the last two verses of the preceding chapter we saw that (1) Israel will experience a great increase in population; (2) in the nation there will be a great turning to God; (3) the northern and southern kingdoms will reunite so that the twelve tribes will again form a single nation; (4) they will appoint themselves one head, who will be the Messiah; and (5)—

**Say ye unto your brethren, Ammi; and to your sisters, Ruhamah [Hos. 2:1].**

*Ammi* means "my people," and *Ruhamah* means "pitied." God is saying to the nation that the day is coming when He is going to say, "You *are* My people." My friend, God is not through with the nation Israel, as we will see in chapter 3. This is very important to understand. Those who teach that God is through with Israel either spiritualize or discount a great deal of the Old Testament. If you can strip the Old Testament of its literal meaning, that gives you the liberty to do the same to the New Testament. Do you want to rob the Epistle of Romans and even John 3:16 of their literal meaning? You cannot do that with the New Testament, and I don't believe you can do it with the Old Testament either.

**Plead with your mother, plead: for she is not my wife, neither am I her husband: let her therefore put away her whoredoms out of her sight, and her adulteries from between her breasts [Hos. 2:2].**

"Plead" carries the thought of a great contention, because Israel like Gomer was unfaithful and went back to practicing prostitution. God is applying Gomer's sin to the nation. Hosea married a girl who had become a harlot, and, even after they had been married for some time and had three children, she went back to prostitution again. And all the while this man Hosea *loved* her! The greatest sin in all the world is not murder or theft or lying or possibly, under certain circumstances, adultery. But judging from what Scripture teaches, the worst sin one can commit is to become unfaithful to one who loves you.

Applying this to our own lives, what is the greatest sin a Christian can commit? Many people feel that it is murder or lying or even coveting, but the greatest sin is unfaithfulness to God who has redeemed you and who loves you. There is no sin greater than that, my friend.

God says, "Go to your mother and contend with her. Tell her to come back to Me. Tell her to turn away from her idolatries."

**Lest I strip her naked, and set her as in the day that she was born, and make her as a wilderness, and set her like a dry land, and slay her with thirst [Hos. 2:3].**

If she does not repent, God will judge her. Regarding Hosea, the implication is that he was not quite as tenderhearted as the prophet Jeremiah was. I imagine he said, "I intend to have her stoned if she continues this kind of life—I have no alternative."

**And I will not have mercy upon her children; for they be the children of whoredoms [Hos. 2:4].**

"And I will not have mercy upon her children." God is applying the sin of the nation to the individuals who compose the nation. They are illegitimate children, and God will judge them. At this time in Israel's history apparently the entire nation had turned to idolatry. God says that He will not have mercy on the children of Israel, for they are the children of harlotry.

**For their mother hath played the harlot: she that conceived them hath done shamefully: for she said, I will go after my lovers, that give me my bread and my water, my wool and my flax, mine oil and my drink [Hos. 2:5].**

She is doing it for money! There is money in prostitution—it is one of the big rackets in our day also. This may imply that Hosea was not a wealthy man and was not able to provide the luxuries which Gomer wanted; so she practiced harlotry on the side.

Israel's sin was the same: she had turned to idols, which was spiritual adultery. The people of Israel were giving the idols credit for providing for them. "I will go after my lovers, that give me my bread and my water" —those are the necessities; "my wool and my flax, mine oil and my drink"—those are the

luxuries. And all the while it was her loving God who was providing all these things for her.

Oh, the ingratitude of the human race—and especially professing Christians—for all that God has provided! I hear a great deal of complaining about rising prices today. If you are one of those who are complaining, let me ask you something: You had at least one good meal today, didn't you? You have clothing in your closet, haven't you? Perhaps you even have some luxuries. Who do you think provided these? "Well," you may say, "I am an intelligent, hard-working person; I provided them for myself." I have news for you: God has provided all of those material things for you. He is the one who gave you intelligence. He is the one who gave you a measure of health and strength, and He is the one who provided the job for you. In fact, He is the one who created this earth with a well-stocked pantry and with clean air and clean water and sunshine. And yet you are ungrateful. You can't sin much worse than that, my friend. It is true that we live in a day when terrible crimes are being committed—stealing, lying, murdering—but the worst sins are being committed by the children of God who are ungrateful. I realize this is not a popular thing to say, but here in the Book of Hosea, this is His charge against Israel.

**Therefore, behold, I will hedge up thy way with thorns, and make a wall, that she shall not find her paths [Hos. 2:6].**

And it is my opinion that it was God who sent the depression to my country, then the "dust bowl." I think He was speaking to us in judgment. If we had repented and had heard God at that time, we would never have had to fight World War II. We would not have been involved in warfare in Korea and then in Vietnam. If we had been sending our boys over there as missionaries to give those people the gospel, we would not have had to send our boys over there to die or to suffer in the prison camps. Back of all our problems is the big problem that we are not recognizing God.

**And she shall follow after her lovers, but she shall not overtake them; and she shall seek them, but shall not find them: then shall she say, I will go and return to my first husband; for then was it better with me than now [Hos. 2:7].**

There comes a day when that girl who has become a harlot is no longer beautiful and her lovers lose interest in her. She finds herself being put out. This was exactly what was happening to the nation Israel. The people were saying, "Now we will go back to God."

**For she did not know that I gave her corn, and wine, and oil, and multiplied her silver and gold, which they prepared for Baal.**

**Therefore will I return, and take away my corn in the time thereof, and my wine in the season thereof, and will recover my wool and my flax given to cover her nakedness [Hos. 2:8–9].**

God says that He will judge Israel. I think we can apply the same thing to our own nation. We entered into difficult times beginning in World War I because we thought we were such a sophisticated nation. We have become so sophisticated that we think homosexuality should be considered normal in our society. We don't like to punish murderers anymore; we would rather accept them into our society. God calls murder and homosexuality *sin*, and He says that, when these things become prevalent in a nation, it is a sign that the nation is going down the tube. We have too many judges who know a great deal about the law but know nothing about how God overrules even the laws of a nation, especially when the laws are wrong and the wrong men sit on the benches of our judicial system.

**And now will I discover her lewdness in the sight of her lovers, and none shall deliver her out of mine hand.**

**I will also cause all her mirth to cease, her feast days, her new moons, and her sabbaths, and all her solemn feasts.**

**And I will destroy her vines and her fig trees, whereof she hath said, These are my rewards that my lovers have given me: and I will make them a forest, and the beasts of the field shall eat them.**

**And I will visit upon her the days of Baalim, wherein she burned incense to them, and she decked herself with her earrings and her jewels, and she went after her lovers, and forgat me, saith the Lord [Hos. 2:10–13].**

The greatest sin in all the world is to forget God.

**Therefore, behold, I will allure her, and bring her into the wilderness, and speak comfortably unto her.**

**And I will give her her vineyards from thence, and the valley of Achor for a door of hope: and she shall sing there, as in the days of her youth, and as in the day when she came up out of the land of Egypt [Hos. 2:14–15].**

The *valley of Achor* literally means "the valley of trouble." It refers to the incident recorded in Joshua 7. You will recall that when the children of Israel entered the Promised Land, they faced three major enemies in the center of that land who had to be conquered first so that Joshua could divide the enemy and then concentrate on taking one section at a time. The first enemy was Jericho; Jericho represents the world, and God got the victory for them at Jericho. Next they made an attack upon Ai, and they thought it would be an easy victory because Ai was a small city. Ai represents the flesh, and a great many people think they can live the Christian life in their own strength; that is, by means of the flesh—which always means defeat. Joshua was defeated at Ai, but a great lesson was learned there. God had instructed the men not to take any of the unclean things at the destruction of Jericho, but one man disobeyed. As a result, the army suffered a great defeat at Ai.

Joshua went down upon his face and cried out to God. He was as pious as I have been at times, complaining to the Lord. The Lord said to him, "Get up off your face. Israel has *sinned*. You must deal with the sin before you can have a victory." So they had to ferret out the one who had sinned and finally found him to be Achan. Achan and his property were taken to the Valley of Achor where they were destroyed and buried. From then on it was victory for Israel under General Joshua. And, friend, when you and I deal with the sins of the flesh, we will have victory in the Christian life.

"And the valley of Achor for a door of hope." In effect, God is saying, "I'll judge your sin, and after I have judged your sin, there will be a glorious, wonderful hope for you in the future."

"And she shall sing there, as in the days of her youth, and as in the day when she came up out of the land of Egypt." My friend, even today in the land of Israel, you don't find it quite like this. Although Israel is back in her land, this particular area is up near Shechem—near the place where Joseph is buried—an area characterized by Arab/Israeli conflict and not by singing. The fulfillment of this promise is still future. The day is going to come when God will bless them there.

**And it shall be at that day, saith the Lord, that thou shalt call me Ishi; and shalt call me no more Baali [Hos. 2:16].**

This is interesting, and the meaning of it is quite lovely. *Ishi* means "my husband," and *Baali* is connected with Baal and means "my lord or my master." You see, the people of Israel were placing the true God on the level of Baal and were trying to worship both. Of course, it is impossible to do that, and God says to them that the day is coming when Israel will call Him, "my husband."

Now let's think about this for a moment. The husband relationship implies that which is intimate and personal and is based on love. It is the highest relationship in the human family. The loveliest expression of it is found in the Song of Solomon where the bride says, "I am my beloved's, and my beloved is mine . . ." (Song 6:3).

When you have that relationship in a marriage, you have a happy home. You won't have to attend seminars that instruct you on how to live as man and wife. The secret is love; when you don't have that, you don't have anything. But if you have love, you have everything. You can work out your financial problems; you can adjust your personality conflicts; you can work together in dealing with your children if you love each other. However, if you don't love each other, you can't work out anything.

My friend, it is wonderful to have that kind of relationship with God. We can go to the Lord Jesus and say, "I *love* You. I belong to You." When that kind of relationship exists, Paul says, ". . . For all things are yours; Whether Paul, or Apollos, or Cephas, or the world, or life, or death, or things present, or things to come; all are yours; And ye are Christ's; and Christ is God's" (1 Cor. 3:21–23). Can you call Christ yours? Do you belong to Him, and does He belong to you? If He does, then you have something good going. There is no relationship equal to that. And one day Israel will say to God, "You are *my* husband."

"And shalt call me no more Baali." As we have seen, *Baali* is connected with the hideous idol Baal, and means "my lord"—that is all it means. Remember that the Lord Jesus said, "Not every one that saith unto me, Lord, Lord, shall enter into the kingdom of heaven; but he that doeth the will of my Father which is in heaven. Many will say to me in that day, Lord, Lord, have we not prophesied in thy name? and in thy name have cast out devils? and in thy name done many wonderful works?

And then will I profess unto them, I never knew you: depart from me, ye that work iniquity" (Matt. 7:21–23). Oh, my friend, the all-important thing is a personal relationship with the Lord Jesus Christ—it is not to mouth platitudes about His being your Lord and claim to be doing great things for Him. It narrows down to the thing He said to Simon Peter by the Sea of Galilee, "Lovest thou me?" Do you *love* Him?

**For I will take away the names of Baalim out of her mouth, and they shall no more be remembered by their name [Hos. 2:17].**

Even the name of Baal will be forgotten. They will turn from idolatry.

**And in that day will I make a covenant for them with the beasts of the field, and with the fowls of heaven, and with the creeping things of the ground: and I will break the bow and the sword and the battle out of the earth, and will make them to lie down safely [Hos. 2:18].**

In that land, as in our own land, there is a danger of many species of animals becoming extinct—some already have. God created the animals and placed them here. They have a right to this world, and in that future day He will make a covenant with them. In that day, which we designate as the Millennium, the lion and the lamb will lie down together. In our day when they lie down together, the lamb is always inside the lion, but in the Millennium they will lie down together in peace. As I am writing, there is a new interest in ecology and in the preservation of animal life. Have you ever noticed that all through the Bible God has considered the animals? Also He has considered the land itself and speaks of blessing the land. It is man who is the polluter. Man is a sinner on the inside, and he is also a sinner on the outside. He contaminates everything he touches. I recall a drive home from the Mojave Desert when the rays of the setting sun were hitting the road at an angle, and lining both sides of the road were beams and flashes of light. I have never seen anything like it. Do you know what it was? It was the broken beer bottles and whiskey bottles and perhaps a few soft drink bottles reflecting those rays of the sun! Man is a polluter everywhere he goes. Well, God says that He is going to take care of this earth. I thank God for that, because I don't think man will be able to do it.

**And I will betroth thee unto me for ever; yea, I will betroth thee unto me in righteousness, and in judgment, and in lovingkindness, and in mercies.**

**I will even betroth thee unto me in faithfulness: and thou shalt know the Lord [Hos. 2:19–20].**

We are seeing something very wonderful here. The word *betrothed* means literally to "woo a virgin"; it means to court a girl. If you are a married man, you can remember when your wife was a girl, and how pretty she was and how you courted her. You said a lot of sweet things then. One evening some time ago my wife and I were sitting out on the patio. I was recuperating from surgery, and we were just talking about the fact that we are getting old. I took a look at her, and I would have to say that she is getting old like I am, but I can remember that girl I first saw down in Texas with her hair as black as a raven's wing and those flashing brown eyes. She had a sultry look, let me tell you, because her complexion is dark. As we remembered those wonderful days, we got just a little sentimental. We talked about the times when we used to drive up to Fort Worth to eat in a restaurant there. We ordered steaks and do you know what we paid for a steak in that day? It was fifty cents apiece! She was a school teacher, and I was a poor preacher; so I made her pay for her own—even at fifty cents! I've tried to make up for that through the years since then, I can assure you. To woo a virgin is a wonderful experience. That is what God said He would do to Israel. What a beautiful, lovely picture this is. God says, "I intend to win you for Myself."

How is God going to do this? He says, "I will betroth thee unto me in righteousness, and in judgment, and in lovingkindness, and in mercies." You see, there was mercy under the Mosaic system, too. You will find that there was love in law just as there is law in love. You cannot completely segregate one from the other.

This is another reason why I do not think the present return of Israel to their land is a fulfillment of prophecy. It certainly does not fulfill this one. God says that when He woos Israel and brings her back into the land it will be in righteousness and in justice and in lovingkindness and in mercies. Today Israel is just like any other nation. Some think they are unnecessarily brutal, but they are on the defensive and their survival depends on a

strong defense system. They are not back in the land of Israel in fulfillment of prophecy. Although they have returned to the land, they have not returned to the Lord. When they do return to the Lord, there will be blessing.

"I will even betroth thee unto me in faithfulness." They never were faithful in the past. In fact, they are very much like the apostate church in our day.

"And thou shalt know the LORD." They certainly do not know Him today.

**And it shall come to pass in that day, I will hear, saith the LORD, I will hear the heavens, and they shall hear the earth [Hos. 2:21].**

"In that day" is a technical expression which refers to the last days as they pertain to the nation Israel, the Great Tribulation Period, and the coming of Christ to set up His kingdom on earth.

"I will hear the heavens, and they shall hear the earth"—heaven and earth will be in tune.

**And the earth shall hear the corn, and the wine, and the oil; and they shall hear Jezreel [Hos. 2:22].**

"Jezreel" means that God will scatter or sow them, but in that future day God will regather them.

**And I will sow her unto me in the earth; and I will have mercy upon her that had not obtained mercy; and I will say to them which were not my people, Thou art my people; and they shall say, Thou art my God [Hos. 2:23].**

These final two verses are a play upon the names of Gomer's children. Not only will God regather them, but they will no longer be Lo-ruhamah, like the unpitied daughter of harlotry. God will have mercy upon them. In our day Israel is Lo-ammi—"not my people," but in that future day God will say, "You are My people," and they will say, "You are my God." My friend, they are not saying that today; they are not turning to God. This is a prophecy for the Millennium.

# CHAPTER 3

*THEME: Hosea commanded to take Gomer again*

Although Hosea finds out that his wife has proved unfaithful, he is commanded to go and take Gomer again.

**Then said the LORD unto me, Go yet, love a woman beloved of her friend, yet an adulteress, according to the love of the LORD toward the children of Israel, who look to other gods, and love flagons of wine [Hos. 3:1].**

"Go yet, love a woman"—that is, love your wife; she is your woman. "Beloved of her friend"—Hosea loved her although she had been unfaithful.

"Yet an adulteress, according to the love of the LORD toward the children of Israel who look to other gods, and love flagons of wine." "Flagons of wine" should actually be translated as "cakes of raisins." This is a reference to the cakes of raisins which were used in the sacrificial feasts of the Canaanites. They were a part of the heathen worship of idols, which the children of Israel had adopted. You see that God is making an application here. In

effect He says to Hosea, "Now you know how I feel. I want you to go and take Gomer again. She's been unfaithful to you, but you are to love her and take her back. That is what I am going to do with My people. Israel has been unfaithful to Me, and I am going to punish her, but some day I will bring her back to Myself."

**So I bought her to me for fifteen pieces of silver, and for an homer of barley, and an half homer of barley [Hos. 3:2].**

Perhaps Gomer had sold herself to some group of racketeers who were running brothels in that land. Hosea had to go buy her back. "So I bought her to me."

Do you know that you and I have been redeemed? The picture here is not very pretty—that is the reason it is not being preached more today. We hear a great deal in conservative circles about dedication, about commitment, and about turning your life over to the Lord. But, my friend, the first thing you need to do is to come as a *sinner* to God—

He has to redeem you. Just as Hosea bought this harlot, that is the way God redeemed us. Until you and I see that, we can know nothing of real commitment to God.

"So I bought her to me for fifteen pieces of silver, and for an homer of barley, and an half homer of barley." Gomer wasn't worth it, and we are not worth the redemption price which was paid for us. "Forasmuch as ye know that ye were not redeemed with corruptible things, as silver and gold . . . But with the precious blood of Christ . . ." (1 Pet. 1:18–19). He had to shed His blood; He had to suffer and die that you and I might be redeemed. Why? Because we were lost sinners, sold under sin.

I have a friend who is a great preacher, but he has gotten to the place where he no longer mentions the gospel. He does not mention the fact that a man must come to God as a sinner. Oh, he tells people, "You ought to love Jesus. You ought to serve God and obey Him," and all that sort of thing. But, my friend, that is not where you begin. You might as well go out to a graveyard and say, "Listen, fellas and girls, let's all start doing better. Let's all start committing our lives to the Lord." Why, everybody out there is dead! They can't do anything. And until we have come to God for salvation, you and I are *dead* in trespasses and sins. We have no life to commit to Him. Until the sin issue is settled—until we are born again and have received a new nature—we can do *nothing* that is pleasing to God.

**And I said unto her, Thou shalt abide for me many days; thou shalt not play the harlot, and thou shalt not be for another man: so will I also be for thee [Hos. 3:3].**

A man told me the sad story not long ago of how he had found out that his wife was unfaithful to him. He had actually had her followed by a detective to establish the facts. Imagine the feeling of that man! Oh, what a heartbreak it was to find out that she was unfaithful to him. I cannot think of anything worse than that. And God says to His people, "That is what you have been doing. You've been playing the harlot. Oh, you call Me, 'Lord,' but you have gone after other gods, you have turned from Me and no longer serve Me."

The Lord Jesus also said in Matthew 7: 22–23, "Many will say to me in that day, Lord, Lord, have we not prophesied in thy name? and in thy name have cast out devils? and in thy name done many wonderful works? And then will I profess unto them, I never knew

you . . . ." Now I am going to say perhaps the strongest thing you have ever heard: If a so-called church has a man in the pulpit who denies the Word of God, denies the deity of Christ, and denies that He died for sinners, it is not a church. It is a brothel—a spiritual *brothel!* I didn't say that; God says that right here. This is the strongest language you can imagine, and you can understand why Hosea was not elected "Man of the Year" in Israel at that particular time. He didn't win any popularity contest in his hometown, you can be sure. He is telling his people, "You have become a *brothel* as a nation. You've turned to idolatry and have turned from the living and true God."

Verses 4–5 of this chapter are probably two of the most important prophetic verses which supply an answer to those students of prophecy who have begun to set dates for the coming of the Lord. Although this is a brief chapter, having only five verses, it is one of the great prophetic passages in the Word of God. Dr. Charles Feinberg, a Jewish believer and an outstanding Hebrew scholar, says of this chapter, "It rightfully takes its place among the greatest prophetic pronouncements in the whole revelation of God."

In connection with this passage, you ought to read chapters 9–11 of the Epistle to the Romans. I consider those chapters to be the dispensational section of the epistle which concerns the nation Israel. In chapter 9 you have the past dealings of God with Israel, in chapter 10 His present dealings with Israel, and in chapter 11 His future dealings with them.

Now concerning Israel, Hosea writes—

**For the children of Israel shall abide many days without a king, and without a prince, and without a sacrifice, and without an image, and without an ephod, and without teraphim [Hos. 3:4].**

"For the children of Israel shall abide *many days* without a king." You will notice that He does not give a specific number of days. This is unusual because the children of Israel were told three times that they were to be put out of their land and they would be returned three times. Each time God put them out of that land, He told them how long they would be out—except the last time. The first time, God told Abraham, "I am going to give you this land—it's yours, but I am going to put your children out of this land for 430 years. They will be down in the land of Egypt, and after

430 years, I will bring them back." They did come back—that prophecy was literally fulfilled. A second time, God said through Jeremiah, "Because of your sins, you are going to be sent into captivity in Babylon. You are going to be down there for seventy years." Again, that was fulfilled literally. Now, here Hosea is speaking to the northern kingdom (which never actually returned to the land), and he says, "Israel shall abide many days without a king."

How long is "many days"? Right now we have some folk who are saying that the Lord Jesus is going to come again by A.D. 2000. I do not know where they find that in Scripture! They sound as if they have a private line into heaven! And at least one other to whom I have listened says that the generation living today is the one that is going to see the coming of Christ. May I say, that sounds good to a lot of untaught Christians, but you cannot find such teaching in the Word of God. Nowhere does Scripture tell us how long the time will be until His return. We have a lot of sensational prophecy-mongers about today.

Why did the Lord say "many days" and not give us the specific number? It is because in the interval between the time Israel left the land in A.D. 70 and the time at which they will return, He has been calling out a people to His name from among the Gentiles and has been building His church. I want to say first of all that I believe we are living in the last days. Someone will say, "Do you mean then that the Lord will be coming soon?" Well, I do not know how soon because we have been in the "last days" for more than nineteen hundred years. The Lord Jesus said, "Behold, I come quickly . . ." (Rev. 3:11; 22:7), and that was nineteen hundred years ago. Therefore I am not prepared to say He will come tomorrow or next week or next year or even in this century. I just don't happen to know that. But I do believe we are seeing the setting of the stage, and the action will begin when the church is removed from this earth.

The reason the date is not given here in Hosea is that in Scripture the church is nameless and dateless. We who belong to the true church are a heavenly people, having no name. I suppose some of you folk thought the name of the church was Baptist or Presbyterian or Methodist or Christian or even Independent. I have news for you: the church has no name; Scripture has never given it a name. The Greek word *ecclesia* simply means "a called-out body." He is calling out a body today which is going to be His bride. I could

make a suggestion today for a name for the church. In the parable of the pearl of great price (see Matt. 13:45–46), the pearl represents the church which the merchantman, Jesus, came and bought. He paid a big price for the church, you know. The word for pearl is *margarites*. If the church is to have any name at all, I think it should be Margaret. Have you ever heard of the Margaret Church? One time I told a fellow that I went to the Margaret Church; he thought I was kidding, but I really was serious about it.

The church is nameless, and it is also dateless. If you had met Simon Peter an hour before the Holy Spirit came on the Day of Pentecost and you had asked him, "Do you know what's going to happen here in a little while?" he would have said, "No. What's going to happen?" He didn't know, because the birth of the church had been announced, but no date had been given. And we are not given the date of the Rapture, the time when the church will be removed from this earth. For that reason we are told "the children of Israel shall abide *many days* without a king"—no specific time period is given to us.

Israel is going to abide many days "without a king." There are those in that land today who claim that they can tell you the tribe to which they belong. I have serious doubts about that, but they make that claim. However, there is no Israelite living today who can say, "I am in the line of David, and I have a right to the throne of David." The only One who can claim that is this moment sitting at God's right hand. He is the Lord Jesus, King of Kings and Lord of Lords. Israel has rejected their King.

"Without a prince"—they have no one to succeed to the throne. If the Lord Jesus Christ is not their Messiah, they have none and have no prospect for one.

"Without a sacrifice." Luke 21:24 tells us that ". . . Jerusalem shall be trodden down of the Gentiles, until the times of the Gentiles be fulfilled." Therefore, many people argue that we must be to the end of the "times of the Gentiles" because Israel now has Jerusalem. Do they really have Jerusalem today? All of the holy places in old Jerusalem are in the hands of either the Moslems, the Russian Catholics, the Greek Catholics, the Armenian Church, or the Roman Catholics. And all of them have built cathedrals or churches over these spots. Israel does not possess these sacred spots, and they dare not touch them. I said once to a Jewish guide with whom I had become acquainted, "You have Jerusalem

now. Why don't you go and tear down that Mosque of Omar and put up your own temple?" He said, "What do you want us to do—start World War III?" That would surely start it, my friend—you can be sure of that. Israel does not possess that temple area, and they do not have a sacrifice today. The only holy place they have is the Wailing Wall—they are still at the Wailing Wall. They have no sacrifice except the one which you and I have—Jesus. He died nineteen hundred years ago outside the city, was raised from the dead, and is today at God's right hand.

"Without an image." God did not give Israel any images. He had said to them, "Thou shalt not make unto thee any graven image, or any likeness of any thing . . ." (Exod. 20:4). But He had given them many things; for instance, "an ephod" and "a teraphim." The ephod was the sacred garment worn by the high priest. Teraphim were small objects which they carried around like good luck charms and which they began to worship. God says here that they are going to get away from idolatry, that they will not have any images. That is one thing that you can say about Israel today—they are not in idolatry. Although they have not turned to God, they certainly have turned away from idolatry.

**Afterward shall the children of Israel return, and seek the Lord their God, and David their king; and shall fear the Lord and his goodness in the latter days [Hos. 3:5].**

"Afterward shall the children of Israel return." *Afterward* does not mean in the year A.D. 2000. I do not know when it will be, but they are going to return to the land according to God's timetable.

When they do return, this is the way they will return: they shall "seek the Lord their God, and David their king; and shall fear the Lord and his goodness in the latter days." I am going to say something that may be very startling to you. They have returned to that land, and it is remarkable what has happened over there, but it is not the fulfillment of this prophecy. The prophecy says that when they return, they will return to God, and there is no real turning to God in that land. It is the belief of at least two outstanding prophetic students whom I know, that Israel may be put out of that land again before we have the real fulfillment of this prophecy. When they return to the land, they will also return to God.

There is much evidence that Israel has not turned to the Lord. When they celebrated their twentieth anniversary as a nation some years ago, they displayed a large motto which read, "Science will bring peace to this land." The Scriptures say it is the Messiah who is going to bring peace. They are not turning to the Messiah but to science. They are looking to prosperity and depending upon economics. Sometime ago they had a large economic conference which was attended by one of the Rockefellers and one of the Fords. There were a hundred outstanding men there who each put up a million dollars to invest in that land. They are building over there like I have never seen anywhere else.

A very reputable missionary in Israel was specifically asked this question: "How many true Christians are there in this land today?" This missionary is an intelligent man who speaks several languages. He was a professor who became a Christian and is doing missionary work there. He gave this reply: "Today in Israel there are fewer than three hundred Israelites who are real believers in Christ." I know that that statement may cause a great deal of discussion and disagreement because there are those who are saying that hundreds are turning to Christ in that land. That just does not happen to be true. There are actually more Arab Christians in Israel than Jewish Christians. Missionary work in Israel is really a tough job, and there are very few missionaries in that land. Israel has not returned to God.

I know when I insist that this present return to the land is not the fulfillment of the Word of God, it is contrary to what you hear so often today. However, this prophecy is evidence of that fact; and, when we consider the whole of the Word of God and not just a verse here and there, we must face up to the fact that this return is not a fulfillment of prophecy.

Many ridiculous things result when people take a verse here or there and say that what is happening in Israel is a fulfillment of prophecy. We heard some time ago that they were shipping Indiana stone over to Israel to build the temple. If you have been to Jerusalem, you know that one thing they do *not* need is stone! Jerusalem is located on a rocky place and every hill around it, including the Mount of Olives, is loaded with rocks. Now, if Indiana wants to buy some stone, I could tell them where to get it: Israel would be glad to export some of her stone.

Another example of so-called fulfilled prophecy is the argument that the growing of

oranges in Israel is a fulfillment of the "strange slips" which Isaiah said would grow in that land (see Isa. 17:10). However, in the Song of Solomon where it speaks of the apples and the apple tree, that is actually the orange tree. Oranges grow in that land, and it is the belief of some that oranges were taken from there to Spain and then to Florida and California. Israel is the land that grows oranges, and they are not a "strange slip." How ridiculous these things can become! We need to stay close to the Word of God and not become one of these prophetic fanatics who are abroad today.

"And shall fear the Lord and his goodness in the latter days." "The latter days" are yet in the future. They refer to the nation Israel and to the time beginning with the Great Tribulation and going through the second coming of Christ and on into the Millennium.

# CHAPTER 4

**THEME:** *Israel guilty before God*

From this point on in the Book of Hosea we will not be seeing much about the private and personal life of the prophet. Beginning actually with the two closing verses of the previous chapter, the private life of Hosea fades into the background, and the emphasis is now upon the Lord and the faithless nation of Israel which has been playing the harlot. We have left that section of the book which is personal, and in chapters 4–14 we will be dealing with that which is *prophetic*.

## ISRAEL GUILTY BEFORE GOD

Out of the heartbreaking experience in his own home, Hosea now comes to speak to the nation—and he knows how God feels about them. Everything that has been said up to this point has been in the way of generalization. God has said, "They have sinned. They have played the harlot and been unfaithful to Me." Now God is going to bring them into court, spell out certain charges against thcm, and prove those charges. The message of chapter 4 is that Israel is guilty of lawlessness, immorality, ignorance of God's Word, and idolatry. We can compare this chapter with the first chapter of Isaiah in which Isaiah speaks to the southern kingdom, spelling out God's charge against that nation.

I believe that you could interchange these same sins of Israel with the sins of our own nation. It is true that the nation Israel was God's chosen people, and He gave the Mosaic Law to them. However, we need to understand this: the law is His pattern for any nation which wants to be blessed. Therefore, I think that our nation is guilty of the same sins that Israel was guilty of when God judged them and sent them into captivity. Someone will disagree with me and say, "Well, we're not idolaters." My friend, covetousness is idolatry, and I do not know of a nation that is more greedy and worships the almighty dollar more than this nation of ours today. We might read the Book of Hosea and point our finger at Israel and say, "It is a shame how they turned from God," but we need to look around and see if the same thing is not true of us.

In the first verse of this chapter, the Lord confronts Israel with the fact that they have no knowledge of Him—

**Hear the word of the Lord, ye children of Israel: for the Lord hath a controversy with the inhabitants of the land, because there is no truth, nor mercy, nor knowledge of God in the land [Hos. 4:1].**

He says three things here: there is no mercy; there is no truth; and there is no knowledge of God in the land. These people had become brainwashed through their idolatry. Although God had instructed them to be merciful, they were no longer showing mercy. The Lord had told them in Leviticus 19:10, "And thou shalt not glean thy vineyard, neither shalt thou gather every grape of thy vineyard; thou shalt leave them for the poor and stranger: I am the Lord your God." In other words, He said, "This is the way I take care of the poor, and you are to do this also." Why? "Because I am the Lord your God, and I am a holy God." The people had forgotten this—there was no knowledge of God in the land—and they were no longer being merciful. Oh, there was a

great deal of religion, but no real knowledge of God.

Notice that they were breaking the Ten Commandments:

**By swearing, and lying, and killing, and stealing, and committing adultery, they break out, and blood toucheth blood [Hos. 4:2].**

In each of these sins they were breaking the Ten Commandments. Read them in the twentieth chapter of Exodus: "Thou shalt not kill. Thou shalt not commit adultery. Thou shalt not steal. Thou shalt not bear false witness . . ." (Exod. 20:13–16). And all of this that they were doing was happening even among relatives—"blood toucheth blood."

I want to say something very carefully, and I want you to follow me very carefully. God gave the Ten Commandments, which were only a part of the Mosaic system, to the nation Israel, but in them God expressed His will.

The church today is not under the Ten Commandments as the way of salvation or the way to live the Christian life, but that does not mean that we can *break* the commandments; it simply means that He has called us to a higher plane of living and has enabled us so to live by the power of the Holy Spirit.

However, since through the Ten Commandments God expresses His will, they are a pattern for the laws of every nation. The nation Israel, which He chose and dealt with, furnishes a pattern to the other nations of the world. We have a so-called Christian civilization in Europe today. It has never really been Christian but has had the semblance of Christianity because its laws were patterned after the Ten Commandments. These laws are the laws for all nations.

God has said, "Thou shalt not kill. Thou shalt not commit adultery," and there are other things which He has condemned in Scripture. God has condemned drunkenness, and He has condemned homosexuality. He uses the strongest language in speaking of homosexuality. God says that when a people or an individual indulges in that, He will give them up. God gave Israel up to captivity because they were guilty of indulging in these sins.

We in the United States today are guilty of the same thing: there is no knowledge of God in this land. Oh, I know that there seems to be a church on every corner and on Sunday mornings you can hear church bells everywhere, but a very small percentage of the population actually attends church, and very few are really being reached with the Word of God. There is a Gideon Bible in every hotel or motel room in which I stay, but I do not know how much they are being read. The Gideons report that they receive many letters telling of conversions—and I thank God for that—but I am afraid that many of the Bibles are never opened. My point is that, although we have the Bible freely available, we are actually a nation of Bible ignoramuses. We do not know the Word of God today in this land. For example, a political leader some time ago made the statement on television that the four Gospels contradict one another; he not only misquoted Scripture, he also misinterpreted it. I would have liked to demand equal time to answer him that there is *no* contradiction in the four Gospels. When a man makes a statement like that, he reveals a woeful ignorance of the Word of God.

The consumption of alcohol is another area in which our land is in the same condition as Israel was in that day. We were told a few years ago that there were 128 cocktail parties every day in Washington, D.C. With the trend as it is, I am sure that number has increased greatly. Whatever the actual statistics, we know that there is a great deal of drinking going on in our nation's capital. Like Israel, we too are being brainwashed by liberal propaganda. A local newspaper in one large city in Southern California dared to publish an article a number of years ago with the following headline: "Alcoholics Cost Area Businesses Ten Million Dollars." People cry out about the high cost of living, the high cost of war, and the high cost of government—all of which is true—but who is crying out against liquor today? We are told that millions of American workers are alcoholics. What do you suppose that has to do with the cost of what we buy at the store today? Someone may say, "Preacher, this is none of your business." My friend, the pulpit has become extremely silent on these issues, but I must insist that our government and our nation are engaged in gross immorality and are breaking the Ten Commandments. And we will not get by with it as a nation. An alarming percentage of the deaths on U.S. highways and streets is the result of alcohol drinking. We have had much protest about the killing in war, but I have found no one leading a protest in front of a brewery or a cocktail lounge.

It is argued in our day that alcoholism is a disease and not a sin. That has been answered by a medical doctor, who writes:

Alcoholism, a disease? If so:

It is the only disease contracted by an act of will.

It is the only disease that is habit forming.

It is the only disease that comes in a bottle.

It is the only disease causing hundreds of thousands of family disruptions.

It is the only disease promoting crime and brutality.

It is the only disease contributing to hundreds of thousands of automobile accidents.

It is the only disease playing a major part in over 50 percent of the more than 50,000 annual highway deaths.

It is the only disease which is sold by license.

It is the only disease that is bought in grocery stores, drug stores, and well-marked retail outlets.

It is the only disease that is taxed by the government. . . .

Our eyes have been shut to all these facts because the liquor interests have tremendous control in our country, and we have been brainwashed by them. As a result, our nation sinks lower and lower.

We have what we call the "new morality" today, but it isn't new at all. Israel was practicing it way back yonder in 700 B.C. They were breaking all the commandments, and God condemned them for it. It wasn't even the "new" morality in their day, for homosexuality was practiced as far back as the day of Sodom and Gomorrah, cities which were judged by God and destroyed because of it. Today we have legislatures which are filled with men who are ignorant of the Word of God and ignorant of the commandments which have been basic for this nation, and they are passing legislation which condones the life style of sexual perverts.

The liberal church argues that homosexuals are not sinners, but may I say to you, Jesus Christ says to homosexuals, "You must be born again" (see John 3:7). He can deliver you from it. When homosexuality is treated for what it really is—sin—then God can deal with it.

We as a nation are doomed as much as Israel was condemned and sent into captivity. After all, they were God's chosen people and we are not—by no stretch of the imagination can we make that claim. However, we have here in Hosea the basis on which God judges

nations, and the United States stands condemned as did Israel. The pulpits in this country are strangely silent in this connection, and one reason for that is that they seldom if ever study the Book of Hosea; he is one of the forgotten prophets.

**Therefore shall the land mourn, and every one that dwelleth therein shall languish, with the beasts of the field, and with the fowls of heaven; yea, the fishes of the sea also shall be taken away [Hos. 4:3].**

"Therefore shall the land mourn." Suddenly we have found in this country that we are polluting everything around us. But when I was a boy in southern Oklahoma, we used to go swimming in old Phillips Creek, and the water was so clear you could see twenty-five feet to the bottom of that creek. Today it smells to high heaven. We've polluted the land, and the land is mourning today.

Another interesting thing is that a few years ago there was plenty of everything—the granaries were filled with grain—but today we often hear about the scarcity of this or that. You see, when God judges a nation, the land itself is involved and even the beasts and fowls suffer because of the sin of man.

**Yet let no man strive, nor reprove another: for thy people are as they that strive with the priest [Hos. 4:4].**

The priest in that day was not doing his duty; he was not warning the people. Therefore, God raised up the prophets.

**Therefore shalt thou fall in the day, and the prophet also shall fall with thee in the night, and I will destroy thy mother [Hos. 4:5].**

"And I will destroy thy mother"—that is, God will destroy the nation. There were false prophets in Israel—even as we have false prophets today—telling the people, "Everything is going to be all right. We live in a new age. The Bible is an outmoded book, and the Ten Commandments belong to our grandfathers and grandmothers. We have learned to be broad-minded and tolerant." My friend, the truth is that we are a dirty lot, and we have sunk very low as a nation and as a people.

Verse 6 is perhaps the most familiar verse in the Book of Hosea—

**My people are destroyed for lack of knowledge: because thou hast rejected knowledge, I will also reject thee, that**

thou shalt be no priest to me: seeing thou hast forgotten the law of thy God, I will also forget thy children [Hos. 4:6].

"My people are destroyed for lack of knowledge." The background of their sin was a lack of knowledge of the Word of God. My friend, if you are a Christian, the minute you get away from the Word of God, you are doomed to failure in the Christian life. Regardless of the number of conferences or seminars you attend that tell you how to be a success in your home, in your business, and in your social life, you will be a failure. This book makes it crystal-clear that we do not live the Christian life by these little gimmicks and methods, but by a personal knowledge of the Word of God. This is the reason I am concerned with teaching the Word of God—and the reason I teach even the Book of Hosea. People are destroyed for lack of knowledge.

"Because thou hast rejected knowledge, I will also reject thee, that thou shalt be no priest to me." God intended that the whole nation of Israel be priests unto Him; in the Millennium they will be that. But at this time, God says, "You are not even going to *have* priests."

"Seeing thou hast forgotten the law of thy God, I will also forget thy children." God says to the people of this nation, "I will forget you, because you have forgotten Me." Because they have gone through a long, sordid history of departing from the Lord, they have now come to the time of judgment. God has proved His case against these people; in the beginning of the chapter He enumerated their sins—they have broken the Ten Commandments. Therefore He hands down His decision that He is going to judge them.

**As they were increased, so they sinned against me: therefore will I change their glory into shame [Hos. 4:7].**

God had promised Abraham to bless the nation by multiplying them, and the nation did increase, but all that it did was bring more sinners into the world. After all, that is what happened when I was born—another sinner came into the world. But, thank God, the grace of God reached down, and someone gave me the Word of God, and I was able to trust Christ as my Savior. However, these people were ignorant and had no knowledge of the Word of God.

"Therefore will I change their glory into shame." Now the "glory" of Israel was the temple with the Shekinah glory upon it—His visible presence with the nation and His definite leading of them, and their witness of monotheism to the world of polytheism of their day as they worshiped the living and true God. That was their glory, and it brought the Queen of Sheba from the ends of the earth.

God is saying through Hosea, "I will remove My glory from you. I'll remove My blessing from you, and I will judge you by letting the enemy come upon you and take you into captivity."

Of course the enemy is going to be able to say, "Look, they said they were God's chosen people, but look what is happening to them! Apparently their God is not a very strong God." My friend, we are seeing today in this land of ours something very similar to that. God is judging many churches, and He is closing many doors. We are inclined to say, "Isn't it a shame to see a decline in a certain church." Well, maybe *God* is closing the door. We need to recognize that God can afford to judge His own people, and this is what He is doing.

**They eat up the sin of my people, and they set their heart on their iniquity [Hos. 4:8].**

The people not only sinned, but they liked to brag about it. As a young fellow I ran with a pretty fast crowd from the bank where I worked. Especially on Monday mornings we liked to brag about what we had done on our weekend, and the blacker the sin was, the more we enjoyed bragging about it. That is what these people were doing—"they set their heart on their iniquity."

**And there shall be, like people, like priest: and I will punish them for their ways, and reward them their doings [Hos. 4:9].**

The unfortunate thing was that the priesthood in Israel had sunk down to the level of the congregation. When I started out in the ministry, I wore a Prince Albert coat and a wing collar (a friend of mine told me that I looked like a mule looking over a whitewashed fence!), but I soon gave that up and began to dress just like the man sitting out there in the pew. Although I'm no different from the man in the pew, I do want to give out the Word of God in the pulpit and not sink to the level of the man of the world when I'm out of the pulpit. There are many ministers who seek to be "good guys." One man boasting of his pastor said, "You know, my preacher comes out

to our golf club and plays golf with us." That much sounds good. I think it is great to mix with folk like that. Then he added, "And after the game he goes into the barroom and has a drink with us. He is just one of the fellows. I sure do like him." Well, I wonder what God thinks of him—"Like people, like priest: and I will punish them for their ways, and reward them their doings."

**For they shall eat, and not have enough: they shall commit whoredom, and shall not increase: because they have left off to take heed to the LORD [Hos. 4:10].**

"For they shall eat, and not have enough"—in other words, famine is coming to the land. Who would have believed that we would ever hear anything about scarcities in this country—that there would ever be times when we could not buy meat or bread in the market—yet we have learned in recent years that such circumstances are a real possibility. Again may I say that I believe God judged this nation in the years of the depression and the "dust bowl," but no one listened to Him. Then we had to fight World War II, and still we didn't come back to God. We have had very little peace and a whole lot of troubles since then.

"They shall commit whoredom, and shall not increase." I know what I am saying when I tell you that you can never, never enjoy the sexual relationship in the way in which God really wants you to enjoy it unless it is within the bonds of marriage. When you can put your arms around a woman whom you have been loving and can say to her, "I love you above everything else in the world," then it is wonderful and there will be an increase. Otherwise, there is really no satisfaction in it; it is just a temporary sort of release, and you hate yourself afterward. I know that some of you know that, and God knows that—He is spelling that out for us here.

**Whoredom and wine and new wine take away the heart [Hos. 4:11].**

Part of our problems in Washington, D.C., today are caused by these two sins—harlotry or adultery and liquor. They are responsible for men lying and doing any number of crooked things. This is not confined to just one political party or group; the whole crowd is guilty. One writer said that in Washington you do not know whom to trust—what a sad commentary on our nation! Do not tell me that the "new" morality is working today. It didn't

work for Israel either when they got away from the Word of God and decided to try something new. In the northern kingdom they had sin galore. They put up two golden calves to replace God and practiced Baal worship which involved the grossest form of immorality.

**My people ask counsel at their stocks, and their staff declareth unto them: for the spirit of whoredoms hath caused them to err, and they have gone a-whoring from under their God [Hos. 4:12].**

He is speaking here of the harlotry, the spiritual adultery, which is turning from God—they went to inquire of idols. Today we find people running after the gurus of India. One of the gurus who came to this country said very candidly that he had come for the money and that it was nothing in the world but a religious racket as far as he was concerned—yet people went after him! People are going off into all types of things today, including the worship of Satan. I have a newspaper clipping which reports that a group of Satan cultists tortured and beat a seventeen-year-old youth to death, believing he was an undercover narcotics agent. The worship of Satan today is certainly not helping the morality of our country. And in Israel, idolatry simply led them into gross immorality and finally to God's judgment.

**They sacrifice upon the tops of the mountains, and burn incense upon the hills, under oaks and poplars and elms, because the shadow thereof is good: therefore your daughters shall commit whoredom, and your spouses shall commit adultery [Hos. 4:13].**

They put their idols on top of a hill under a grove of trees. The center of this idolatrous worship was in these groves; it was cool there and a nice place to go.

"Therefore your daughters shall commit whoredom, and your spouses shall commit adultery." Our idolatry in this country today is covetousness and greed, and it has caused many a family to try to get on in the world. They want to move to a better neighborhood, to have a swimming pool, and to have a boat. They say they are doing it for the children—but all of a sudden the children leave the home. There are thousands and thousands of young people wandering up and down this country and all over the world. I have seen them in the Hawaiian Islands, and I talked to

three of them in Constitution Square in Athens some time ago. There were two young men and a young lady, and I am sure they were not beyond their teens—one of them could have been twenty. I tried to talk with them as they sat there under the influence of drugs. They told me, "We're nobody. We don't count. We've dropped out." What has happened to them? The problem is back there in the home. Their parents are idolatrous, worshiping the almighty dollar. We have forgotten God. We've turned away from the living and true God, and we no longer worship Him. We need to turn to the Savior who can redeem us and help us.

**I will not punish your daughters when they commit whoredom, nor your spouses when they commit adultery: for themselves are separated with whores, and they sacrifice with harlots: therefore the people that doth not understand shall fall [Hos. 4:14].**

God says that ignorance of the law excuses no one. He is saying, "Although these people have gone off into sin, I am not going to judge them for the sin they are committing right now. I am going to judge them because they have turned from the living and true God and from His way." I made this point to a man on the golf course who joined with my two preacher friends and myself to make a foursome. He said he guessed he was a sinner going to hell because of the various sins he had committed. I said to him, "You know, you're not going to hell because you commit those sins." He said, "What do you mean I'm not going to hell? I thought that's what you preachers say." I told him, "This preacher never said that. You're going to hell because you have rejected Jesus Christ." Israel was not judged because they had become harlots, but because they had turned from the living and true God.

**Though thou, Israel, play the harlot, yet let not Judah offend; and come not ye unto Gilgal, neither go ye up to Beth-aven, nor swear, The LORD liveth [Hos. 4:15].**

God is saying, "I am going to hold Judah back. I will not judge Judah yet. And Judah, don't you come up and worship these calves which Israel has put up here."

**For Israel slideth back as a backsliding heifer: now the LORD will feed them as a lamb in a large place [Hos. 4:16].**

I want to look at what backsliding really is. A great many people think that backsliding is when you have become a Christian, have joined the church, and then drop back into sin. That is not backsliding in the way it is used here—God illustrates it so that you cannot miss its meaning: "For Israel slideth back as a backsliding heifer." In the little town in which I lived in southern Oklahoma as a boy, there lived next door to us a rancher who had a big cattle ranch and two boys who were about my age. We three played together. We enjoyed riding heifers out in the lot. We would tie a rope around them—as we said in that day, a bellyband—and we would hold on to that until the heifer bucked us off. Every now and then that rancher would need to load up some of those heifers into his wagon to take them to market. He had a runway constructed out of boards which he would put at the back end of the wagon, and then he would try to run the heifers up that. He put a rope around the heifer to lead her up and then would have someone push her from the rear. The heifer would go up part of the way, and then she would stiffen those front feet of hers. You know what would happen? You couldn't push her, and you couldn't pull her. She would simply start sliding backwards. My friend, that's what backsliding is—"a backsliding heifer." Israel was stiffening her front feet, and instead of being led of God, she was slipping backward all the time. My friend, you are backsliding when you turn your back on God, stiffen that little neck of yours and that little mind of yours, and you say, "I don't have to obey God's Word." When you refuse to go the way God wants to lead you, then you are backsliding. God called Israel a backsliding heifer.

The word *backsliding* is used three times in this book. It is used in Scripture only by Jeremiah and Hosea, both of whom spoke to a nation ready to go into captivity. Israel and Judah were guilty of backsliding, guilty of refusing to be led of God and refusing to come to God.

**Ephraim is joined to idols: let him alone [Hos. 4:17].**

"Ephraim" occurs thirty-six times in this book. God has picked out the name of one of the ten tribes in the north and applied it to all ten of the tribes. I used to wonder just how God used this term: was it a term of endearment or a term of ridicule? I have come to the conclusion that it was a term of endearment, actually His pet name for the northern king-

dom. These ten tribes had revolted, and Israel in the north actually had no name as a nation; it was Judah in the south who was really the nation. I think God gave this to them as a pet name—Ephraim. It is used throughout this Book of Hosea.

"Ephraim is joined to idols: let him alone." God says this in a longing sort of way but with a note of finality. If a man continues in a backslidden condition, refusing to listen to God, there will come a day when God can no longer speak to that man.

**Their drink is sour: they have committed whoredom continually: her rulers with shame do love, Give ye [Hos. 4:18].**

"Their drink is sour"—You will become an alcoholic if you keep drinking, my friend. And it is not a disease; it is sin.

"They have committed whoredom continually: her rulers with shame do love." The sad thing is that men high in our government, instead of using language that is clean and chaste, love to curse and to drink. They love shame more than glory.

**The wind hath bound her up in her wings, and they shall be ashamed because of their sacrifices [Hos. 4:19].**

People are carried away by every wind of doctrine, and God says that they are going to be made ashamed before it is over.

# CHAPTER 5

*THEME: Israel turns from God and God turns from Israel*

This chapter continues to deal with the sin of the northern kingdom and the fact that judgment is coming upon them; therefore it is not a very happy or pleasant section of the Word of God.

We must keep in mind the personal background of the prophet Hosea. As a young man he fell in love with a very lovely, beautiful young lady who became a prostitute. I imagine that she was attracted to prostitution by the money, by the fact that she would be able to get the luxuries that she otherwise could not have had. God sent Hosea to marry her in spite of this. He loved her and married her. After she had borne three children, again she played the harlot. And again Hosea went after her—he bought her and brought her back to himself. Hosea had a broken heart and a broken home. With that background, he said to the northern kingdom of Israel, "God says that you are playing the harlot, that you have been unfaithful to Him. I know exactly how He feels. He loves you and will never let you go, but He is going to judge you because of your sin."

## ISRAEL TURNS FROM GOD AND GOD TURNS FROM ISRAEL

God begins by condemning the leadership in the nation—the priests and the king.

**Hear ye this, O priests; and hearken, ye house of Israel; and give ye ear, O house of the king; for judgment is toward you, because ye have been a snare on Mizpah, and a net spread upon Tabor [Hos. 5:1].**

"Mizpah" was in the southwest section of the kingdom, and "Tabor" is Mount Tabor which was way up in the northeast section of the kingdom. In other words, the people were worshiping idols under every green tree they could find—there were idols all over the land.

He speaks to the priests and to the king as representing the leadership of the nation. We saw in chapter 4 that God said, "Like people, like priest." The priests who should have been setting an example were unable to rise above the level of the lowest man in society; that was true of the king also.

Unfortunately, we are living in a day in which our spiritual and political leadership is certainly not worthy of emulation. Liberalism is predominant in theology; liberalism is predominant in politics; and our news media are altogether liberal. Spiritual deterioration and decline in a nation will eventually bring it to destruction. That is what happened to Israel, and that nation furnishes a pattern for what can happen to us today.

**And the revolters are profound to make slaughter, though I have been a rebuker of them all [Hos. 5:2].**

God rebuked Israel for their brutality—there was murder, there was violence, and there was warfare. It is my conviction that the United States is today feeling the effects of God's judgment upon us. In Vietnam we fought perhaps the most disgraceful war that was ever fought, and we did so against the warnings of generals who said that we should never fight a land war in Asia. We made a terrible blunder by getting involved in that, and what has happened in that land is tragic. Did we help them? I think not, and the judgment of God is upon us and, actually, upon the white man. This has been called "the white man's day," and it certainly has been that. Earlier in history it was the sons of Ham who headed up the great pagan civilizations of Egypt, Babylon, and Assyria. However, it is the sons of Japheth, the white man, who has made the greatest blunder of all, and that is this: We have had the Word of God, the Bible, and we have not sent missionaries as we should have done. We did too little in getting the Word of God out to China, and God closed the door—I say *God*, not communism, closed the door. We did not send Bibles to Vietnam; we sent bullets and bombs over there. Because we did not send men to give out the Word of God, we had to send boys to die on the battlefield. We ought to wake up today to the fact that we cannot take God to the end of His universe and dismiss Him and tell Him we do not need Him anymore. We are feeling the effects of His judgment upon us, just as Israel did.

**I know Ephraim, and Israel is not hid from me: for now, O Ephraim, thou committest whoredom, and Israel is defiled.**

**They will not frame their doings to turn unto their God: for the spirit of whoredoms is in the midst of them, and they have not known the LORD [Hos. 5:3–4].**

I have said previously that I think "Ephraim" is a pet name that God chose for the nation Israel. Although it was the name of just one of the tribes, He used it to represent all ten of the northern tribes. But I think there is a second reason that God chose Ephraim to represent all of the northern kingdom: Ephraim was the very center of idolatry in Israel. The first golden calf was set up by Jeroboam in Beth-el; later on, a second one was set up in

Samaria. Both of these places were in the tribe of Ephraim—Beth-el was probably in the tribe of Benjamin, but that area revolted with Ephraim and the rest of the northern kingdom. Ephraim was the very heart of idolatry, and idolatry was the great sin of the nation Israel.

"I know Ephraim, and Israel is not hid from me: for now, O Ephraim, thou committest whoredom, and Israel is defiled." God knows what He is talking about. Although the calf worship, or the worship of Baal, had been set up in the tribe of Ephraim, it had defiled all ten of the tribes and even had had its effect upon the southern kingdom. Their sin was the sin of a people who had the Word of God and who knew God but had turned from Him and no longer knew Him or worshiped Him. As a result, gross immorality and deterioration set in throughout every part of the nation, affecting even the ecology of the nation. God said that even the land and the animals were affected, and I think the curse of God is still upon that land today. What little irrigation has been done has not yet made the ". . . desert . . . blossom as the rose" (Isa. 35:1).

**And the pride of Israel doth testify to his face: therefore shall Israel and Ephraim fall in their iniquity; Judah also shall fall with them [Hos. 5:5].**

God is saying that all ten tribes will be conquered, and "Judah also shall fall with them," but He does not say, "at the same time." However, Judah was finally brought down, and both of these kingdoms were carried away into captivity. The northern kingdom was carried into captivity by Assyria; about a century later, the southern kingdom was taken to Babylon. From that captivity there has never actually been the return to the land which the Word of God speaks about. This Book of Hosea makes it abundantly clear that when God brings them back, the *world* will know it, and there will be peace in the land.

**They shall go with their flocks and with their herds to seek the LORD; but they shall not find him; he hath withdrawn himself from them [Hos. 5:6].**

In other words, the people have deserted God, but when trouble comes upon them and after they have tried every other resource, they will turn to God. God is their last resource, but they will not find Him because He has withdrawn Himself from them.

For many people, turning to God is the last resort. There is told the story of a ship which

was crossing the Atlantic years ago, and the ship hit an iceberg. The captain sent out the order all over the ship, "To prayers, to prayers!" One woman on board the ship came rushing up to the captain and said, "Captain, has it come to this?" She was implying that if they were going to pray, they had come to the last resort. That is the way many people treat God. To them He is like a spare tire which they have on hand but are always hoping they won't have to use. Or He is like a life insurance policy or a fire extinguisher—you hope you never have to use them but they are there just in case the emergency arises.

**They have dealt treacherously against the LORD: for they have begotten strange children: now shall a month devour them with their portions [Hos. 5:7].**

"For they have begotten strange children"— that is, they are strange to God. The people did not bring up their children in the nurture and admonition of the Lord, in the discipline and instruction of the Lord. Back in the Book of Deuteronomy God told His people that they were to be continually teaching His Word to their children. They were to put it on the doorposts and teach it as they sat in their homes and as they walked together and even when they were going to bed at night. But now He says, "You have begotten *strange* children—they don't even know Me."

**Blow ye the cornet in Gibeah, and the trumpet in Ramah: cry aloud at Bethaven, after thee, O Benjamin [Hos. 5:8].**

"Beth-aven" is Beth-el. That part of the tribe of Benjamin had apparently revolted with the northern kingdom. God is saying here that the word of warning is to go out over all the land and to all the people.

**Ephraim shall be desolate in the day of rebuke: among the tribes of Israel have I made known that which shall surely be [Hos. 5:9].**

In other words, God had not failed to warn the people. He had warned them, He had rebuked them, and they still would not hear.

**The princes of Judah were like them that remove the bound: therefore I will pour out my wrath upon them like water [Hos. 5:10].**

The southern kingdom had apparently attempted to move its boundaries as far north as it possibly could, and there evidently was a real division caused by the fact that the two nations could not agree on the boundary. God had a message through Hosea for the southern kingdom as well, although he primarily was a prophet to the northern kingdom.

**Ephraim is oppressed and broken in judgment, because he willingly walked after the commandment [Hos. 5:11].**

Ephraim willingly followed the idols and the worship of idols—he went with the crowd.

**Therefore will I be unto Ephraim as a moth, and to the house of Judah as rottenness [Hos. 5:12].**

The prophets use figures of speech which are quite interesting. There is great profit in studying the prophets, if I may make a play on words, because they reach out into nature and use certain figures of speech which are helpful to us in understanding the Word of God. "Therefore will I be unto Ephraim as a moth." What does a moth do? A moth can get into your closet, and if you do not have mothballs in there, it can ruin a suit of clothes. The story is told about the man who had bought some mothballs at a drugstore but brought them back, saying they didn't work. When the druggist asked him what he meant, the man said, "I stayed up half the night throwing these balls at the moths, but I never hit one of them!" My friend, moths are something you do not want in your closet, because in just one night they can ruin a very valuable wool garment. God says, "I am going to be to Ephraim like a moth; I will judge him in a hurry."

"And to the house of Judah as rottenness." It takes a wooden board or a wooden foundation of a house a long time to become rotten. God has said to Ephraim, the northern kingdom, "I'm going to judge you *now*. However, in the southern kingdom rottenness is also setting in, and, finally, it will collapse—but it will take longer for that to take place."

Our foundations are being removed in every way imaginable in our nation today, and rottenness has already begun in that which is left. It may take a while, my friend, but we cannot continue in sin like we are and expect to escape God's judgment. The situation is enough to make us weep today.

**When Ephraim saw his sickness, and Judah saw his wound, then went Ephraim to the Assyrian, and sent to king Jareb: yet could he not heal you, nor cure you of your wound [Hos. 5:13].**

"When Ephraim saw his sickness"—Ephraim was sick, sick nigh unto death. "And Judah saw his wound"—Judah was hurt at this time also, because Assyria had come against them but did not take them into captivity.

"Then went Ephraim to the Assyrian, and sent to king Jareb: yet could he not heal you, nor cure you of your wound." Ephraim went to a quack doctor. They thought that the king of Assyria would help them, but he is the one who took them into captivity—they appealed for help to the wrong one.

**For I will be unto Ephraim as a lion, and as a young lion to the house of Judah: I, even I, will tear and go away; I will take away, and none shall rescue him [Hos. 5:14].**

Here is another marvelous figure of speech. God says, "To Ephraim I am going to be as a lion, but to the southern kingdom I am going to be a young lion, a lion cub." The other evening I was watching on television a nature picture about lions. It showed how the mother lion protects her cubs. One of those little fellows looked just like a great big roly-poly cat—I wished I could have one as a pet. But that mother lion was vicious, especially when another animal would come near her cubs. She would really go after that animal, and the little cubs would just keep on playing. God said to the northern kingdom that He was

going to be a lion—He intended to destroy them. To the southern kingdom He was going to be just a lion cub. But what happens to a lion cub? He grows up and some day is just as vicious as his mama. This was a warning to the southern kingdom that some day judgment was coming to them also.

"I, even I, will tear and go away; I will take away, and none shall rescue him." God was going to let Ephraim go into captivity, and they could whine and cry all they wanted to, but He would not rescue them. God judged their sin.

God judges sin even today—no one is really getting by with it. We have failed our young people today. Venereal disease is in epidemic stages, and we say, "What in the world is happening?" I'll tell you what is happening: God says you do not get by with *sin*—He is judging sin, and He will continue to judge sin, my friend.

**I will go and return to my place, till they acknowledge their offence, and seek my face: in their affliction they will seek me early [Hos. 5:15].**

Although this has been a doleful chapter entirely about judgment, it closes here with a note of hope. The time will come when Israel will again seek God, but He will not deliver them until they turn to Him.

# CHAPTER 6

**THEME:** *Israel will return in the last days; Israel presently to be judged for current sins*

## ISRAEL WILL RETURN IN THE LAST DAYS

**Come, and let us return unto the LORD: for he hath torn, and he will heal us; he hath smitten, and he will bind us up [Hos. 6:1].**

This is God's last call to the northern kingdom in that day, but it also looks to the future of that nation when God will heal them; although He has torn them, He intends to bind them up. This should be a warning that God will judge the sin of any nation that makes a profession of being a Christian nation

and which has had the benefit of the Word of God.

**After two days will he revive us: in the third day he will raise us up, and we shall live in his sight [Hos. 6:2].**

"In the third day he will raise us up"—this is very interesting in light of the fact that the resurrection of Christ was on the third day. He was raised for the justification of both Jew and Gentile. This will also be applicable in that future day when God will bring Israel back into that land and bring them to Himself. In Ezekiel 37 God speaks of that day as a

resurrection, and that resurrection will be based on the One who was raised on the third day; for in Christ's resurrection there is provided, for any man who will accept it, a redemption and a justification which will bring him into a right relationship with Almighty God.

The apostle Paul develops the subject of the future of Israel in Romans 11. In our day, God's purpose in building His church is to draw to Himself both Jew and Gentile, people out of every tongue and tribe and nation, who are going to come before Him to worship. When God completes His purpose in the church and takes it out of the world, He will again turn to the nation Israel and will raise her up. Every prophet who wrote in Scripture—and even some who didn't write—spoke of God's future purpose for the nation Israel. Even before the children of Israel could get into the land, Moses began to talk about the coming day when God would restore them back to the land for the third time. The third time—on the third day, so to speak—the restoration to the land would be a permanent restoration. There is a correlation between this restoration and Christ's being raised from the dead on the third day.

**Then shall we know, if we follow on to know the LORD: his going forth is prepared as the morning; and he shall come unto us as the rain, as the latter and former rain unto the earth [Hos. 6:3].**

"And he shall come unto us as the rain, as the latter and former rain unto the earth." The former rains were the heavy rains which fell toward the end of October, and the latter rains were the heavy showers of March and April which came right before the harvest. There are folk who say that the latter rain has returned to that land, but I do not think you can say that either the former or latter rain has returned. The rainfall in Israel is much less than we have in Southern California, and here it is not the rain which makes this area a so-called Garden of Eden (despite its smog and traffic); it is irrigation that makes the land productive. But in Israel there is not enough water to irrigate all the land, and we are not seeing the fulfillment of the promised return of the rains to that land. When these people again turn to God, however, the blessing will come not only to the people, but also to the land and the animal world.

"Then shall we know, if we follow on to know the LORD." That is the very secret of the solution to the problems of life—to know the Lord. The apostle Paul, even when he had come to the end of his life, had this ambition: "That I may know him [that is, the Lord Jesus Christ], and the power of his resurrection, and the fellowship of his sufferings, being made conformable unto his death" (Phil. 3:10). There is no way for improvement in this life apart from a knowledge of God. The Word of God is very emphatic about that, and either it is right or it is wrong. Over thousands of years the Word of God has been proven right, and I do not think the present generation is upsetting it by any means.

## ISRAEL PRESENTLY TO BE JUDGED FOR CURRENT SINS

**O Ephraim, what shall I do unto thee? O Judah, what shall I do unto thee? for your goodness is as a morning cloud, and as the early dew it goeth away [Hos. 6:4].**

God sounds as if He is just a little bit frustrated here. In effect, He is saying, "What am I going to do with you? I love you, but you continue on in sin and I am going to have to judge you!" This puts God on the horns of a dilemma. Judgment is the strange work of God—He wants to *save*, not judge. But when people keep turning away from God, then the day comes when He has to judge them.

The people of Israel were religious, but they had no knowledge of God and were far from Him. We today have a lot of religion, and I am opposed to it. Let me illustrate my point with a letter which a man wrote to the editor of a newspaper:

In today's society, religion has outlasted its usefulness. Man at long last has outgrown the necessity for this opiate. No longer does he have to explain the unknown with folktales and the worship of a superior being. In a complex society such as ours, religion can only mute and cloud the mind. Religion blurs and distorts important details and information, interferes with important decisions, and promotes bigotry and prejudice. Now is the time for humanity to discard this mental blindfold.

This may startle you, but I agree with what that man wrote; I wish that we could get rid of

religion. Someone answered this letter, and his reply was also published. He expressed it so much better than I could:

> In response to the April 26 letter entitled "Religion Termed Mental Blindfold," I agree with Mr. _____ about the effects of religion, for religion is man's attempt to reach God through his own efforts. I have never been a religious man, but about four years ago, something happened that has really changed my life. I invited Jesus Christ to take control of my life and accepted the fact that I cannot reach God by myself, but that He has made a relationship with Him possible through His Son Jesus Christ. Since that commitment, I have grown increasingly aware of my social responsibility and have grown to love and accept myself and other people regardless of age, race, creed, or color.

Today many are saying, "Out with religion," and I say, fine, let's sweep it out the back door, and let's invite Jesus Christ, the Light of the world, to come in.

The Israelites were religious, but their goodness was like "a morning cloud"—just form and ritual and ceremony. "As the early dew it goeth away"—that is all their religion amounted to. Many people wear religion like you would wear a loose-fitting garment; it is something they can put on or off at any time. God condemned these people because they were religious, but they did not know Him, and they had never had a transforming, life-changing, experience with Him.

**Therefore have I hewed them by the prophets; I have slain them by the words of my mouth: and thy judgments are as the light that goeth forth [Hos. 6:5].**

In other words, God says, "I skinned them alive by the prophets." I appreciate the many letters I receive that commend us for giving out the Word of God as it is, for hewing to the line and letting the chips fall where they may. I have always tried to do that throughout the years of my ministry, and I have found that the folk who sincerely want to hear the Word of God will appreciate it. Others will oppose it, and I expect to hear their criticism also. God says to His people here, "I've skinned you alive by the prophets—they have been faithful in telling it like it is—but you have not listened to them." And in our day, although there is a great interest in and turning to the Word of God, we wonder how much of it has really transformed the hearts and lives of those who hear.

"I have slain them by the words of my mouth: and thy judgments are as the light that goeth forth." They were not sinning because of *ignorance*—there was no lack of information. God had sent the prophets to them, but they had turned their backs on God and His Word.

**For I desired mercy, and not sacrifice; and the knowledge of God more than burnt offerings [Hos. 6:6].**

The people were merely going through a form. My friend, you can go to church on Sunday and be as fundamental as you can be. You may criticize the preacher, criticize the choir, criticize everybody—maybe they deserve it, I don't know—but God's desire is that you put His Word into shoe leather, that you allow it to get down where the rubber meets the road, and that there be an evidence of *mercy* in your own heart and life. Don't think that going to a church banquet is somehow a substitute for truly eating the Bread of Life or of enjoying a big porterhouse steak from the Word of God. No church function is a substitute for really studying the Word of God.

**But they like men have transgressed the covenant: there have they dealt treacherously against me [Hos. 6:7].**

"The covenant"—that is, the covenant which God had made with this nation.

**Gilead is a city of them that work iniquity, and is polluted with blood [Hos. 6:8].**

The city of Gilead is best known to us for the ". . . *balm* in Gilead . . ." (Jer. 8:22, italics mine), which was an aromatic gum or resin used for medical purposes. However, in Hosea's day only iniquity came out of Gilead.

**And as troops of robbers wait for a man, so the company of priests murder in the way by consent: for they commit lewdness [Hos. 6:9].**

In other words, the priests in refusing to give the people the Water of Life and the Bread of

Life were actually committing murder. To be honest with you, I think that a minister who stands in the pulpit and does not give out the Word of God is guilty just as it is stated right here. I did not think that up—it is the Word of God which says that.

**I have seen an horrible thing in the house of Israel: there is the whoredom of Ephraim, Israel is defiled.**

**Also, O Judah, he hath set an harvest for thee, when I returned the captivity of my people [Hos. 6:10–11].**

This is a warning to Judah that their day of judgment is also coming. "When I returned the captivity of my people"—there is a future day when God will bring the people back to the land, but at that time He had to judge them for their sin.

# CHAPTER 7

*THEME: Israel turns to Egypt and Assyria*

Chapters 7–12 deal with the fact that Israel could escape judgment by turning to God who loves her. God is dealing with Israel in a harsh way; yet in tenderness He is attempting to call the people back to Himself before judgment comes.

Israel turns to Egypt and Assyria instead of turning to God.

## ISRAEL TURNS TO EGYPT AND ASSYRIA

**When I would have healed Israel, then the iniquity of Ephraim was discovered, and the wickedness of Samaria: for they commit falsehood; and the thief cometh in, and the troop of robbers spoileth without [Hos. 7:1].**

Samaria was the capital of the northern kingdom—that is, Omri made it the capital, and then Ahab and Jezebel built a palace there.

On our recent trips to Israel I insisted that Samaria be included in the tour. I wanted the folk to go to that hill of Samaria and see the fulfillment of prophecy. The judgment of God is on what is probably one of the most beautiful spots in the world. It would be a lovely spot for a palace, or for that matter, for a home. From the top of the hill there is a view of the entire area. To the west is the Mediterranean Sea, to the east the Jordan Valley, to the north Mount Hermon and Megiddo, to the south the city of Jerusalem. It is a choice spot with nothing to obstruct the view in any direction. But today it is a desolate waste. Indeed the judgment of God is upon it.

What was happening in Israel during Hosea's day was that the sin which had been covered was being uncovered. That which they had been doing secretly they were now doing openly. There was no shame, no conviction, no conscience relative to their sin. The Lord would forgive their iniquity if they would repent and turn to Him. Instead, they persisted in their wickedness and went farther and farther into it.

It is one thing to sin in secret—that is bad enough—but it is even worse to bring your sin out in the open and flaunt it before the world. To do that is to sink to the very bottom. This is the reason that I believe Hosea has a message for my own nation as well as all other nations. Since the people of Israel were God's chosen people, and yet God sent them into captivity when they persisted in sinning against Him, does it seem likely that any other nation could get by with the same type of sin?

For example, when I was growing up in Nashville, Tennessee, the few homosexuals who lived there kept their homosexuality under cover. They operated rather secretly and concealed their sin. However, now across the country they are very open about their perversion and are demanding acceptance and protection of their activity. The fact is being uncovered that there are not only call girls but call boys and that homosexuals are numbered in the thousands. What was formerly done in secret is now brought out into the open, and this is characteristic of other sins as well.

Someone said to me just recently, "Dr. McGee, in our day people sinned just as they do today."

"Yes, they did," I agreed. "Before I was saved, I was with that crowd, and I know."

"Well, then, what's the difference?"

"I'll tell you the difference. In my day we kept it under cover. There was still some shame connected with sin. Today sin is brought out in the open and is flaunted before the world." It is called a new morality, and actually a sort of halo is put around sin today. The sinner is commended for doing something new and daring and courageous. The other day I heard a girl *complimented* as being honest and courageous because she was living with a man to whom she was not married and had an illegitimate child. Well, I am a square, I know (as someone said, being a square keeps me from going around in circles), but we must face the fact that God's Word has not changed. The openness of sin is not a mark of advancement, but it indicates that we are losing the civilization which formerly carried some semblance of Christian culture.

**And they consider not in their hearts that I remember all their wickedness: now their own doings have beset them about; they are before my face [Hos. 7:2].**

God is saying, "I knew about their sins before, but now they have taken a further step away from Me and are doing their sinning out in the open." In other words, they have now reached the lowest depths of immorality.

**They make the king glad with their wickedness, and the princes with their lies [Hos. 7:3].**

The king and the princes applauded this sort of behavior. In our day it is tragic when the leadership in any field—education, science, politics, or the church—give themselves over to foul and blasphemous language, as they are now doing. That is something else that is out in the open. A foulmouthed leader is applauded as being a he-man. Well, it also indicates that he has a very poor vocabulary and is not able to express himself. Unfortunately, this verse is applicable to our nation, and history tells us that it has been applicable to great nations in the past that have now passed off the stage of human events and lie in rubble, covered by the dust of the centuries.

**They are all adulterers, as an oven heated by the baker, who ceaseth from raising after he hath kneaded the dough, until it be leavened [Hos. 7:4].**

This figure of speech is tremendous. The baker had his oven ready but didn't bring up the heat until the dough was kneaded and ready to bake. Here God is not talking about spiritual adultery but about gross immorality. They had formerly kept their sin under cover, but now they are like an open oven, hot with passion. In our day I get the impression that men are trying to prove that they are virile and women are trying to prove that they are sexually alert. In modern America there is a tremendous open obsession with sex.

**In the day of our king the princes have made him sick with bottles of wine; he stretched out his hand with scorners [Hos. 7:5].**

The king has become an alcoholic, and he is making a fool of himself. We have mentioned this before, but it is so important that we will keep repeating it. What was it that brought down the northern kingdom? It was idolatry, a turning away from God. That will always manifest itself in gross immorality. Wine and women, the bottle and the brothel, sauce and sex are the things that occupied the attention of the northern kingdom.

Now if you think I am a square or unfair or a bigot, will you let me ask you a fair question? As you look about you today, what is the chief occupation of men and women in all walks of life? Isn't it an occupation with liquor and with sex? Haven't these two become the prominent things in this civilization of ours? Isn't it true that it is being brought out in the open today as never before in our country? When these sins were brought out in the open in Israel, God said that He would have to move and judge them.

**For they have made ready their heart like an oven, whiles they lie in wait: their baker sleepeth all the night; in the morning it burneth as a flaming fire [Hos. 7:6].**

Everything is done to stir up the passions of men and women. In our day we hear this so-called sophisticated argument about pornography: "We are adults and should have the right to choose what we want to see and what we want to hear." Well, there isn't much freedom to choose what we want to see and what we want to hear when we are bombarded with filth everywhere we turn. I don't have the liberty to choose what is presented on television or the radio or the advertising media. I think there are a great many people who would like to see better things and hear better things than are presented to us today, but that freedom is denied us in order that the

other crowd can have their freedom to give themselves over to sin.

**They are all hot as an oven, and have devoured their judges; all their kings are fallen: there is none among them that calleth unto me [Hos. 7:7].**

"All their kings are fallen." The northern kingdom did not have one good king. If you were to look back in the historical books and go through the list of the kings of Israel and Judah, you would note that Judah had a few good kings—in fact, five kings of Judah led in revivals—but the northern kingdom didn't have a good king in the lot. Every king was as wicked as he could be. Ahab and Jezebel reached the bottom of the list, but some of the others would run them a close second.

Many of the kings in the northern kingdom were assassinated. They made nine different changes of dynasty in their short history. The kings in the northern kingdom started off with Jeroboam, but you don't get very far into the story until someone gets in and murders his line. Another line of kings starts out, and it doesn't go very far until someone else is murdered. Several of the kings had a short reign, and their sons didn't even make it to the throne. That was a judgment of God upon them. You see, God had chosen and promised to bless the line of David; He made no such promise to the kings of the divided kingdom in the north.

**Ephraim, he hath mixed himself among the people; Ephraim is a cake not turned [Hos. 7:8].**

"Ephraim, he hath mixed himself among the people." God never goes in for mixtures. Have you noted that? He seems to want His children to stay in their own crowd.

"Ephraim is a cake not turned." Here we go again with another good, homely illustration, and Hosea has many of them. What does he mean? In that day they cooked on the top of a stove and made little cakes like our pancakes. They still make those kind of cakes there today. Now you know that a pancake that is not turned can be burned on the one side and raw on the other side. That is the picture of Ephraim. The nation was hot on one side but raw on the other side.

They blew hot and cold toward God. There is a whimsical little story told of a man who had been wandering through the woods and came up to a cottage. The man who lived in the cottage invited him into his home. As the man came in out of the cold, he began to blow on his hands. "Why do you blow on your hands?" asked the host. "To make them warm," answered the wanderer. Then the host offered the visitor a bowl of hot soup. The man began to blow on the soup. "Why do you blow on the soup?" asked the host. "To make it cool," answered the guest. So the host jumped up and ran out of his own house, saying, "I don't like anybody who can blow hot and cold!" Well, my friend, that is the way a great many people are as far as Christianity is concerned. With one crowd they blow hot and with another crowd they blow cold. They are like Ephraim—a cake (a pancake) not turned.

**Strangers have devoured his strength, and he knoweth it not: yea, gray hairs are here and there upon him, yet he knoweth not.**

**And the pride of Israel testifieth to his face: and they do not return to the LORD their God, nor seek him for all this.**

**Ephraim also is like a silly dove without heart: they call to Egypt, they go to Assyria [Hos. 7:9–11].**

This is another interesting illustration. If you have ever been dove hunting, you know that if a dove has a nest with eggs or little ones in it she will act as if she has a broken wing and actually let you get very close to her. She tries to lure you away from her nest. Actually, that is not a very smart move on the part of the dove for two reasons. When a dove lets you get that close to her, you know there is a nest nearby. Secondly, she endangers her own life.

Now here was Ephraim. She refused to run to God for help. So first she ran down to Egypt for help. When Egypt wouldn't give her the help she wanted, she went up to Assyria and asked for help. She went back and forth like a silly dove. What a picture!

**When they shall go, I will spread my net upon them; I will bring them down as the fowls of the heaven; I will chastise them, as their congregation hath heard [Hos. 7:12].**

I can remember as a boy that we would get a big box, prop up one end, and put corn under it. We would have the corn lead right under the box. We would hide in the barn, and the doves would come to eat the corn. They would follow the corn right under the box. Then we would pull a string, and the box would come down on them. Silly doves. That is what God says here. He will spread His net upon them. They will be caught.

Woe unto them! for they have fled from
me: destruction unto them! because
they have transgressed against me:
though I have redeemed them, yet they
have spoken lies against me [Hos. 7:13].

God had a redemption for them, and yet these
people were continuing to turn from the living
and true God.

And they have not cried unto me with
their heart, when they howled upon
their beds: they assemble themselves
for corn and wine, and they rebel
against me [Hos. 7:14].

They didn't realize that the famine they were
having was a judgment of God upon them.
They were crying about having no food.

Though I have bound and strengthened
their arms, yet do they imagine mischief against me.

They return, but not to the most High:
they are like a deceitful bow: their
princes shall fall by the sword for the
rage of their tongue: this shall be their
derision in the land of Egypt [Hos.
7:15–16].

"They are like a deceitful bow." You put an
arrow in it to shoot at something and the
string breaks. It is a deceitful bow—you can't
depend upon it.

"This shall be their derision in the land of
Egypt." He is saying that Egypt will begin to
mock them and ridicule them for the way they
are acting.

You can see that this is a very severe section of the Word of God. Hosea was not the
most popular prophet in his day. He wouldn't
be a popular prophet today, either. However,
he still has a message for us, and we do well to
listen.

# CHAPTER 8

**THEME:** *Israel turns to golden calves and altars of sin*

All of the prophets had not only a local
message but also one that reaches into
the future even beyond us today. However,
their message does have an application for us.
There are no prophecies more applicable to us
than those of Hosea and Jeremiah. Each of
these prophets prophesied right at the time of
the downfall of this nation. Their messages
ought to alarm us as a nation today, but I do
not have the faith that they will. I am afraid
that we may have stepped over the line and
that judgment is inevitable, just as it was for
Israel.

## ISRAEL TURNS TO GOLDEN CALVES
## AND ALTARS OF SIN

As Israel turned from God, they looked to
their king and their wealth to deliver
them—

Set the trumpet to thy mouth. He shall
come as an eagle against the house of
the LORD, because they have transgressed my covenant, and trespassed
against my law.

Israel shall cry unto me, My God, we
know thee.

Israel hath cast off the thing that is
good: the enemy shall pursue him.

They have set up kings, but not by me:
they have made princes, and I knew it
not: of their silver and their gold have
they made them idols, that they may be
cut off [Hos. 8:1–4].

"Because they have transgressed my covenant, and trespassed against my law"—God is
explaining why He is going to send them into
captivity. Previously He spelled out their sins
and showed that they had broken His commandments, but their sins had also resulted in
their breaking the covenant which God had
made with them. God had made a covenant
with Abraham which was applicable to them,
and He had made a covenant with Moses
which was applicable to them, especially as it
pertained to that land and how He would bless
them in the land; but if they did not serve Him
He would put them out of the land. And then
God also made a covenant with David. Now
the people had broken these covenants, but
God will never break them. The covenant
which God made with Abraham and the covenant which He made with David were both

unconditional (the Mosaic covenant was conditional). The people could transgress the covenant, and when they did they were judged. They were put out of the land, but that has never altered the fact that God will give them that land for an eternal possession. It simply means that that generation was put out of the land, but another generation will be brought back. That is what happened when they came out of Egypt. Since the people would not enter the land because of their unbelief, God said they would never enter the land but that their children would inhabit it.

"They have set up kings, but not by me." God had said that the line of David was to rule over Israel. Jeroboam led a rebellion, and the line of kings which he set up did not include men who turned to the living God. These kings never attempted in any way to bring the people into the worship of God. Instead, they all went into idolatry. Jeroboam, at the very beginning, put up those two golden calves—one in Samaria and one in Beth-el—and he did that to keep the people from returning to Jerusalem in the south to worship in the temple. God judged them because they had set up kings of whom He did not approve.

**Thy calf, O Samaria, hath cast thee off; mine anger is kindled against them: how long will it be ere they attain to innocency? [Hos. 8:5].**

"How long will it be ere they attain to innocency?" They were guilty, they were sinful, they were not innocent at all.

"Thy calf, O Samaria." Samaria had become the capital of Israel under Omri, the father of Ahab. Ahab married Jezebel whose father was a priest in Sidon among the Phoenicians, worshipers of Baal. Jezebel had transported to Israel several hundred prophets of Baal, and many Israelites became worshipers of Baal.

"Mine anger is kindled against them"—God intended to judge them. Samaria is a desolate place even today. I insisted on taking our tour group to see it. Though it is a beautiful spot, the desolation there is appalling; you cannot help but be overwhelmed by it. But there were once palaces of ivory in Samaria. The archaeologists say that they have found very lovely ivory perfume bottles and all kinds of beautiful ivory bric-a-brac in the ruins there. I noticed that the people on our tour were depressed after viewing the ruins, and rightly so. God has judged Samaria. It was a beautiful spot with lovely buildings, but God's judgment came upon it because the people had turned from Him and were worshiping the calf there.

**For from Israel was it also: the workman made it; therefore it is not God: but the calf of Samaria shall be broken in pieces [Hos. 8:6].**

I do not know where you would find that golden calf today. The archaeologists certainly have not found any piece of it there. It was probably taken somewhere and broken to pieces, maybe even melted down. God says to these people, "You have turned from Me to worship this, but it is not God and it is not able to help you."

**For they have sown the wind, and they shall reap the whirlwind: it hath no stalk: the bud shall yield no meal: if so be it yield, the strangers shall swallow it up [Hos. 8:7].**

This verse speaks of the judgment both of famine and of the enemy who was to come into that land.

**Israel is swallowed up: now shall they be among the Gentiles as a vessel wherein is no pleasure [Hos. 8:8].**

"Israel is swallowed up." Do you know where the ten tribes are today? So many people have the idea that the United States is the tribe of Ephraim—I cannot think of anything more absurd. If you think that is true, read these chapters here about God's judgment on Ephraim; nothing but judgment is mentioned of Ephraim.

"Now shall they be among the Gentiles as a vessel wherein is no pleasure." We are not able to locate or identify the tribes of Israel today. I am confident that the people of Israel mixed with the tribe of Judah when they returned to the land after their captivity, and there has been no way to separate them since that time. They are scattered throughout the world today. Actually, there are more Jews in New York City than there are in the whole nation of Israel; there are at least four times as many outside of the land than are in Israel today.

**For they are gone up to Assyria, a wild ass alone by himself: Ephraim hath hired lovers [Hos. 8:9].**

Here is another specific action which brought God's judgment upon Israel. What a condemnation this is! They are like one of these long-eared donkeys. Israel went up to Assyria

for help and tried to buy off Assyria—
"Ephraim hath hired lovers."

However, they found they could not buy off
Assyria. Instead God would use Assyria to
judge them—

**Yea, though they have hired among the
nations, now will I gather them, and
they shall sorrow a little for the burden
of the king of princes.**

**Because Ephraim hath made many
altars to sin, altars shall be unto him to
sin [Hos. 8:10–11].**

An altar is a place of worship, and God had
given Israel an altar. We see in the Book of
Hebrews that the church has a heavenly altar;
the throne of God is today a throne of grace to
us, and the Lord Jesus is our Great High
Priest at that altar making intercession for us.
An altar is to be a place of worship, but here
God says, "Because Ephraim hath made many
altars to sin, altars shall be unto him to sin."
Israel had turned to religion, to the worship of
idols. It did not help them and only brought
judgment upon them.

My friend, religion has been the most damn-
ing thing this world has ever experienced.
Religion has damned the world. Look at India
today where they cannot eat steak because
the cows are sacred; there are multitudes
starving to death, and yet they will not use
cattle for food. Look at the condition of China
today or at our ancestors yonder in the wilder-
nesses of England. Throughout history religion has not helped us but has crippled and
damned the human race. Only the Lord Jesus
can deliver us.

**I have written to him the great things
of my law, but they were counted as a
strange thing [Hos. 8:12].**

"But they were counted as a strange thing"—
that is, the people did not know anything
about God's law. I say this often because there
are so few who are saying it at all. God is
saying here, "I have given them my written
Word, and to them it is a strange thing—they
are *ignorant* of it." That was the condemnation of Israel and, my friend, that is the condemnation of our nation today. We try to pass
as a civilized, Christian nation, and we are
anything but that. The ignorance of the Word
of God is to me one of the most amazing things
in this land. That is the reason we are committed to teaching the Bible. The most important business the church has is to get out the
Word of God. I do not think your pastor is to

be a business administrator. I do not think he
is called to be a social lion who mixes and
mingles with people. The important thing is
whether he gives out the Word of God when
he stands in that pulpit. If he does, then you
should stand behind him. But I do not ask you
to support a man who is playing around and
riding the fence in liberalism. Across this land
there are many men who are teaching the
Word of God, and they are the ones who are
getting a hearing today. However, their
ministries and the ministry of a Bible teaching
radio program like ours are just a drop in the
bucket—this nation is ignorant of the Word of
God.

**They sacrifice flesh for the sacrifices of
mine offerings, and eat it; but the LORD
accepteth them not; now will he
remember their iniquity, and visit their
sins: they shall return to Egypt [Hos.
8:13].**

They go through the ceremony, they've got
the ritual, and they know the vocabulary, but
that is all it is. The Lord knows them and He
doesn't accept them. I discovered as a pastor
that you have a few people who learn the
vocabulary of fundamentalism; they know
when to say, "Praise the Lord" and "the Lord
bless you." Those are wonderful expressions,
but in the mouths of some people they are
meaningless. "The LORD accepteth them not."

"Now will he remember their iniquity, and
visit their sins: they shall return to Egypt." It
is evident that when Babylon destroyed
Assyria, many from the ten tribes joined with
the ones who were taken into Babylonian
captivity from Judah and returned to the land.
Also, we know from the Book of Jeremiah that
at the time of the Babylonian captivity many
of the people went into Egypt. I believe that
that is what Hosea is speaking of here, but
there are many fine Bible expositors who
would not agree with me.

**For Israel hath forgotten his Maker,
and buildeth temples; and Judah hath
multiplied fenced cities: but I will send
a fire upon his cities, and it shall devour the palaces thereof [Hos. 8:14].**

"For Israel hath forgotten his Maker, and
buildeth temples." They had tried to build
substitutes for the temple in Jerusalem. It
was in that temple and in that temple *only*
that God had said sacrifices were to be made
to Him. "And Judah hath multiplied fenced
cities"—Judah had sinned also, and God will
judge them later. The thing that is going to

happen first is that these temples in Israel are to be destroyed. It is interesting that the northern section of Israel seems to be more desolate than any other section of that land. Way down in the Negeb where they don't get any rain, you expect it to be that way, but up in the northern section—especially in the valley of Esdraelon, which is one of the richest valleys in the world—you do not expect the desolation which is there. Yet all around, even to this day, you see evidences of the judgment of God which came upon that land.

# CHAPTER 9

**THEME:** *Israel turns to land productivity*

At this time Israel was beginning to look to prosperity as the indication that everything was all right in the nation. In other words, they were trying to increase the value of their money, and they were attempting to increase the production of the land. But God said that they were nothing but a backsliding heifer. He had blessed them with prosperity, and that had blinded them to the reality of their spiritual condition. In fact, they are right on the verge of captivity, which was the judgment of God.

**Rejoice not, O Israel, for joy, as other people: for thou hast gone a-whoring from thy God, thou hast loved a reward upon every cornfloor [Hos. 9:1].**

"Rejoice not, O Israel, for joy, as other people"—they were sinning more and enjoying it less.

"For thou hast gone a-whoring from thy God." God says, "You have played the harlot."

"Thou hast loved a reward upon every cornfloor." In other words, Israel was trying to increase their production, but instead it became a judgment upon them. The stock market was up, and there was abundance. The shelves of the supermarket were groaning with food; there was plenty of liquor to be bought, plenty of wine, all of which deceived Israel.

Our nation today has also been deceived by prosperity. We are finding out that these great big combines, these large corporations, are probably not the blessing that we thought at one time they would be. Even farming is often done by large corporations. However, the important thing today is the stock market. Certainly the stock market is more important to our nation than are the Scriptures. That was what was happening in Israel—there was a false prosperity in the land, and they were far from dependent upon God.

I believe that one of the methods God has used to judge the United States is that He has judged us with prosperity. After World War II, I predicted that we were going to have to suffer as the other nations had suffered during the war. We did not have any bombing as did England, France, Germany, and Japan. We escaped all that, but I felt at the time that God would judge us somehow. After the war we became the most prosperous nation in the world, and it seemed a contradiction of the statements I was making. It took me about ten years to see what God was doing. God judged us with prosperity, and that is what He did to Israel. He said, "I have provided everything for you, and you're giving credit to your own ingenuity and your own ability. You're a proud people, and you're not looking to Me nor giving Me credit at all." That is the picture of Israel and, my friend, that just happens to be a picture of my nation since World War II.

**The floor and the winepress shall not feed them, and the new wine shall fail in her [Hos. 9:2].**

In other words, there is going to be scarcity rather than abundance.

**They shall not dwell in the LORD'S land; but Ephraim shall return to Egypt, and they shall eat unclean things in Assyria [Hos. 9:3].**

"They shall not dwell in the LORD'S land." God makes it clear that He is going to put them out of the land. Although He said He would never forget His covenants with Abraham, Moses, and David, Israel's tenure in the land always depended on their obedience to God. Now He is going to put them out of the land.

"And they shall eat unclean things in Assyria." The people had been turning from God and breaking His law. Now God says, "I'm really going to give you a diet of unclean things." They are not going to have any more fun—they were sinning more, but enjoying it less. I am of the opinion that that is true of a great many people today. I talked once with a man in some meetings in the East, who said to me, "The reason I came tonight, Dr. McGee, is that I've tried everything in this world, and I am *so* sick of sin, just sick of it." He was sinning more, but enjoying it less, and that was what finally brought that man to Christ.

**They shall not offer wine offerings to the Lord, neither shall they be pleasing unto him: their sacrifices shall be unto them as the bread of mourners; all that eat thereof shall be polluted: for their bread for their soul shall not come into the house of the Lord.**

**What will ye do in the solemn day, and in the day of the feast of the Lord?**

**For, lo, they are gone because of destruction: Egypt shall gather them up, Memphis shall bury them: the pleasant places for their silver, nettles shall possess them: thorns shall be in their tabernacles [Hos. 9:4–6].**

Many of them went down into the land of Egypt following the captivity. Out of the land, they could not worship God as He intended them to.

**The days of visitation are come, the days of recompence are come; Israel shall know it: the prophet is a fool, the spiritual man is mad, for the multitude of thine iniquity, and the great hatred [Hos. 9:7].**

Israel had lost its way spiritually. Why? Because of the leadership.

When I started out to study for the ministry, the big debate in the church in this country was between what was then known as fundamentalism and modernism. Modernism espoused the social gospel. They were the do-gooders, and they claimed they had a high ethical standard. Frankly, I was inclined to agree with them because I found that many fundamentalists didn't operate on high ethics. It disturbed me a great deal to think that the liberals had one strike on us in that connection. But I watched them carefully and found that they didn't really have a high ethical standard. Hosea said it, and you can blame it on him; he said, "The prophet is a fool."

For example, there was a young man who attended Yale and had there an outstanding

liberal preacher who taught ethics. This preacher taught young men to burn their draft cards—and that's against the law. In certain protest meetings he taught and espoused that there is a higher law than the law of the land. The young man heard these things and thought, *Well, if that's ethics, then I will follow that.* He was led into very serious trouble because of such teaching.

May I say to you, liberalism has lost even its moral standard today. I was in Portland, Oregon, at the time it was discovered through the testimony of a policewoman that the place where the young people were getting narcotics was run by the liberal churches. Hosea said, "The prophet is a fool"—he has led the nation astray.

Liberalism is also responsible for the policy this nation followed after World War II, and the trouble we are in today is a trouble that has been produced by liberalism. I will say this, fundamentalism may act fanatically at times, but the fact of the matter is that fundamentalism did not lead this country into the trouble we are in today. Before I even entered seminary I listened to men like Dr. Harry Ironside, Dr. Harry Rimmer, and Dr. Arthur Brown, and I heard my liberal professors and preachers call them fanatics. But what those men said and preached is true today, and the things I was taught by those liberal professors are not true at all—it just didn't work out the way they said.

Israel had turned their backs on God, and judgment was coming because of it. They had no spiritual discernment. It is the ignorance of the Word of God that disturbs me about our nation today. We receive many letters from people who are coming out of various cults and "isms"—and we rejoice in that—but how did they get trapped in all of these groups? There is only one explanation: ignorance of the Word of God and lack of spiritual discernment. God said that He intended to judge Israel, and that should be an illustration to any nation which makes a pretense of being a Christian nation.

**The watchman of Ephraim was with my God: but the prophet is a snare of a fowler in all his ways, and hatred in the house of his God [Hos. 9:8].**

"The watchman of Ephraim was with my God"—evidently there were a few fanatical fundamentalists around in that day warning the people of the coming judgment.

"But the prophet is a snare of a fowler." That is harsh language, and I would never use that kind of language to speak of the liberal today. However, I do believe that liberalism is in control in my day, especially over the news media. They have sacred cows known as freedom of the press and freedom of speech, but they allow the fundamentalists very little freedom, I can assure you of that. Liberalism—whether it is in politics, the news media, or in the pulpit—is a snare; it is like a trap, and it brainwashes people. As a result, this nation has been in trouble ever since World War II. It is time someone made the diagnosis and gave the prognosis of the case: the problem is that we have turned from God as a nation. *God* has become a big swear word in Washington, D.C. His name is often used in the form of blasphemy but seldom in the form of prayer or in worship of Him.

**They have deeply corrupted themselves, as in the days of Gibeah: therefore he will remember their iniquity, he will visit their sins [Hos. 9:9].**

There are no ifs, ands, or buts about it—God intends to judge sin. Maybe you don't like it, but that is what He says: He intends to judge sin.

**I found Israel like grapes in the wilderness; I saw your fathers as the first-ripe in the fig tree at her first time: but they went to Baal-peor, and separated themselves unto that shame; and their abominations were according as they loved [Hos. 9:10].**

The vine and the fig tree are symbols of the nation Israel which are used throughout the Word of God.

Israel not only established calf worship in both Samaria and Beth-el, but, under Ahab and Jezebel, they also brought in the prophets of Baal.

**As for Ephraim, their glory shall fly away like a bird, from the birth, and from the womb, and from the conception [Hos. 9:11].**

Have you ever been duck hunting and spent the cold hours of the morning in a duck trap or in a boat out on the lake? Then right before the sun comes up and you can finally start shooting, someone else out there fires a gun, and every duck on the lake and anywhere nearby takes off! You just sit there and watch them fly away. That is the picture of the glory of Ephraim—it was departing. This nation had made a tremendous impact upon the ancient world, but its glory was flying away like a bird.

**Though they bring up their children, yet will I bereave them, that there shall not be a man left: yea, woe also to them when I depart from them! [Hos. 9:12].**

This is another judgment which God was going to bring upon them. God had promised Abraham not only to give him the land but also to multiply his seed. God had said that Abraham's seed would be like the sand on the seashore and like the stars in the heavens. God made good that promise, but now the people have sinned and He says, "You're going to have a real decline in your birthrate as part of My judgment upon you."

"Not be a man left" is not a declaration that God would completely wipe out the population, but that there would be no man left who would stand for God.

**Ephraim, as I saw Tyrus, is planted in a pleasant place: but Ephraim shall bring forth his children to the murderer [Hos. 9:13].**

"Tyrus" is Tyre. God had not yet judged Tyre, and it was at that time a great commercial center. Its prosperity was like a fever, and it had caught on in the northern kingdom which also became a commercial center. There was a false prosperity in the land, and the people were deceived by it.

**Give them, O LORD: what wilt thou give? give them a miscarrying womb and dry breasts [Hos. 9:14].**

Their women were barren. It was the judgment of God upon them.

**All their wickedness is in Gilgal: for there I hated them: for the wickedness of their doings I will drive them out of mine house, I will love them no more: all their princes are revolters [Hos. 9:15].**

In other words, God says to them, "Their sin in Gilgal brought My judgment upon them, although I loved them. This should be a warning to you. I will judge you again, and you will come to the conclusion that I do not love you anymore."

**Ephraim is smitten, their root is dried up, they shall bear no fruit: yea, though they bring forth, yet will I slay even the beloved fruit of their womb [Hos. 9:16].**

God's judgment was to come not only upon the fruit of the ground, but also on the birth of children.

**My God will cast them away, because they did not hearken unto him: and they shall be wanderers among the nations [Hos. 9:17].**

God says that He intends to cast them out and that they would be "wanderers among the nations." The ten tribes as such did not return after the captivity. It is true that they came back with Judah as a mixture, and they spread throughout the land. In fact, we find Joseph and Mary who were members of the tribe of Judah living way up in Galilee. There was a tremendous scattering even in the land when they returned after the Babylonian captivity, so that today most Jews could not tell you to which tribe they belong.

# CHAPTER 10

*THEME: Israel will become an empty vine*

We are in a section in which God pronounces His judgment upon Israel. In this chapter we discover something else that Israel was doing which would bring God's judgment upon her.

## ISRAEL WILL BECOME AN EMPTY VINE

**Israel is an empty vine, he bringeth forth fruit unto himself: according to the multitude of his fruit he hath increased the altars; according to the goodness of his land they have made goodly images [Hos. 10:1].**

He was not saying that Israel was a vine which was not producing fruit, because during this period Israel was very prosperous. God was still being good to them, although He was warning them of coming judgment. "He bringeth forth fruit unto himself" means that he was a vine that was emptying itself of its fruit—just pouring out fruit upon the people. You see, although God had made Israel prosperous, He was not given credit for it. Their urban areas were growing, they were putting up apartments and condominiums, and as a result, they thought everything was all right. Their prosperity was blinding them to their true condition.

It is my belief that this same thing has happened to my own country. As a nation, God blinded us with prosperity and with power at the end of World War II, while other nations suffered. We became the big brother to the world. Well, we have been eager to send bombs, but we have not sent what we should have sent: *Bibles.* I am weary of protestations decrying the fact that we used our bombs on other nations but never telling us what we should have sent instead of bombs. My friend, it is the Bible which has made our nation great, and we are pitifully ignorant of it today. The logical, rational conclusion, judging from history, is that God will judge our nation. There is many a great nation lying in rubble and ruin, which reveals God's judgment upon them.

"According to the multitude of his fruit he hath increased the altars." As the population increased, the images increased. In other words, their *sin* increased as the population increased.

This figure of the vine reminds us of what the Lord Jesus said in John 15 to His Jewish disciples. He said, "I am the true [*genuine*] vine . . ." (John 15:1, italics mine). He was saying that until then they had felt that their identification with the *nation* gave them access to God and a relationship to Him. Now this was no longer true. The Lord Jesus was beginning to call out a people to His name. He would be the Head, and the church which He would be forming would be His body. When He said, "I am the genuine vine," He meant that no longer would His people worship through the temple, but they would come through *Him* to the living God.

**Their heart is divided; now shall they be found faulty: he shall break down their altars, he shall spoil their images [Hos. 10:2].**

"Their heart is divided." Actually they did worship God—we can't say that they didn't. Many of them went down to Jerusalem for the feast days as they had done in former years and joined in the worship of God. However, they would come right back up to the golden calves that had been set up, and they would also worship Baal. Their hearts were divided—one day they would worship God; the next day they would worship Baal.

This is the condition which James mentions in his epistle. "A double-minded man is unstable in all his ways" (James 1:8). I believe this is the reason we find so much inconsistency in the lives of men in public office today. They talk out of one side of their mouths saying one thing; then they talk out of the other side of their mouths saying the opposite thing. I understand that the language of some of our leaders is absolutely the foulest speech one can imagine. Then some of those same people can appear on television and quote a Bible verse so that you would think they were sprouting wings under their coats! That is having a divided heart.

My friend, you cannot go to church on Sunday and sing, "Praise God from whom all blessings flow," then walk out, and on Monday morning go to your work and take His name in vain—lose your temper and use His precious name to damn everything that irritates you. That kind of divided living is exactly the same kind of divided heart that brought judgment upon Israel.

**For now they shall say, We have no king, because we feared not the LORD; what then should a king do to us? [Hos. 10:3].**

They were saying, "Go down and look at the southern kingdom, and you will see that their king is not helping them very much." Their basic problem was not that they had godless kings (they never had one good king in the northern kingdom), but their own hearts were not right with God. My friend, it is easy for you and for me to blame our government for our problems today when the basic problem is in our own hearts—yours and mine.

**They have spoken words, swearing falsely in making a covenant: thus judgment springeth up as hemlock in the furrows of the field [Hos. 10:4].**

The last days of the northern kingdom must have been parallel to our times. "They have spoken words." They were very loquacious, great talkers. I believe that in our day radio and television and the printed page have made our generation the most talkative people on earth. Man is a pretty talkative "animal"—there is no monkey in a tree that does more chattering than man does. Talk, talk, talk, talk, reams and reams of printed material, and about 99.44 percent of all of it is not worth

listening to. It would be better if most of it had never been said. Yet people are being paid fortunes for what they say and for what they write. Out of it all you hear practically nothing said about bringing people back to God, about a return to God and to the Word of God, about looking to Christ as the Savior.

"They have spoken words, swearing falsely in making a covenant." They just talk, talk, talk, and you can believe almost nothing they say. I hear some Christian people say today that it is terrible that we don't ask people to put their hand on the Bible anymore when they swear to tell the truth in a courtroom. Frankly, I'm glad the Bible is being left out of it. If they are going to lie anyway, all an oath on the Bible would do is blaspheme the Book. If the Bible means nothing to people, why in the world should it be used? I *resent* seeing someone put his hand on the Bible and swear to tell the truth and then hear him lie!

How many Christian people have spoken words to make a false covenant? How many people have marched down to an altar to dedicate their lives to God, have done it repeatedly, and still nothing changed? How often do we say words but not really mean business with God?

"Thus judgment springeth up as hemlock in the furrows of the field." Or, getting it down to the level of most of us, judgment will spring up like weeds in our planted gardens.

**The inhabitants of Samaria shall fear because of the calves of Beth-aven: for the people thereof shall mourn over it, and the priests thereof that rejoiced on it, for the glory thereof, because it is departed from it [Hos. 10:5].**

"Beth-aven" is a term of ridicule for Beth-el. Since one golden calf was located at Beth-el and the other at Samaria, the inhabitants of these two cities were jealous of one another over who had the biggest calf or the most gold in it.

"For the people thereof shall mourn over it." The actions of people mourning over these calves is really more the idea of trying to outdo one another over it. It would be in our day like "keeping up with the Joneses." They bought a Cadillac, so we must buy a Continental. They built a house with three bedrooms and three baths, so we must build one with six bedrooms and six baths. They were trying to outdo each other in their calf worship!

"The priests thereof that rejoiced on it, for the glory thereof, because it is departed from it." God is saying, "All the glory of your religion that your priests have boasted in will one day disappear." The word *Ichabod*, meaning "the glory is departed," will be written over the door.

What will happen to it?

**It shall be also carried unto Assyria for a present to king Jareb: Ephraim shall receive shame, and Israel shall be ashamed of his own counsel [Hos. 10:6].**

Those golden calves are going to be carried into Assyria for a present to the king. They would make a gift fit for a king—after all, there was a lot of gold in those calves.

"Ephraim shall receive shame, and Israel shall be ashamed of his own counsel." Their counsel will come to naught.

**As for Samaria, her king is cut off as the foam upon the water [Hos. 10:7].**

God makes it very plain that He is going to cut off the king of the northern kingdom. He'll be "cut off as the foam upon the water"—that royal line, as well as the royal line from the southern kingdom, will spend their time singing, "I'm Forever Blowing Bubbles." In other words, they will be reduced to nothing.

**The high places also of Aven, the sin of Israel, shall be destroyed: the thorn and the thistle shall come up on their altars; and they shall say to the mountains, Cover us; and to the hills, Fall on us [Hos. 10:8].**

"The high places also of Aven . . . shall be destroyed." As we have seen before, they worshiped their idols in groves of trees on the mountains.

"They shall say to the mountains, Cover us; and to the hills, Fall on us." They want to be hidden from the judgment that is coming upon them. This will also be said in the Great Tribulation (see Rev. 6:15–17).

**O Israel, thou hast sinned from the days of Gibeah: there they stood: the battle in Gibeah against the children of iniquity did not overtake them [Hos. 10:9].**

This probably refers to the terrible events recorded in Judges 19–20. Even after the civil war, and the men of Gibeah were wiped out, the sin remained, and Gibeah was emblematic of gross and cruel sensuality. Along with the idolatrous practices of Israel were also gross sensual sins.

**It is in my desire that I should chastise them; and the people shall be gathered against them, when they shall bind themselves in their two furrows.**

**And Ephraim is as an heifer that is taught, and loveth to tread out the corn; but I passed over upon her fair neck: I will make Ephraim to ride; Judah shall plow, and Jacob shall break his clods [Hos. 10:10–11].**

"Ephraim is as an heifer that is taught, and loveth to tread out the corn." Ephraim is like an heifer that loves to tread out the corn. They enjoyed the wonderful, bountiful harvest that they got, but they sure didn't like the idea of going out and plowing the ground to break up the clods. God is saying that He will force Ephraim to go back to doing the thing he does not want to do.

**Sow to yourselves in righteousness, reap in mercy; break up your fallow ground: for it is time to seek the Lord, till he come and rain righteousness upon you [Hos. 10:12].**

This is a principle that runs throughout the Bible. It is exactly what Paul wrote to the believers in Galatia: "Be not deceived; God is not mocked: for whatsoever a man soweth, that shall he also reap. For he that soweth to his flesh shall of the flesh reap corruption; but he that soweth to the Spirit shall of the Spirit reap life everlasting" (Gal. 6:7–8). Hosea is saying that if they would sow in righteousness, they would reap in mercy. It is always true that we cannot live by the Devil's standards and then expect to reap a reward from God!

**Ye have plowed wickedness, ye have reaped iniquity; ye have eaten the fruit of lies: because thou didst trust in thy way, in the multitude of thy mighty men [Hos. 10:13].**

Israel hadn't learned her lesson. She plowed wickedness, so she would reap iniquity. They have eaten the fruit of lies. They trusted in mighty men, in their leaders who lied to them. They believed these men rather than God. So they got exactly what was coming to them—the *fruit* of lies.

In Daniel we read that God set over the nation the ". . . basest of men" (Dan. 4:17). My friend, in our day, regardless of what political party you are talking about, a sinful, godless people cannot elect a righteous leader. If the people are liars, they will get a liar as a leader. If they are adulterers, they will get an adulterer. If they are thieves, that's the kind of ruler they will have. My friend, you cannot beat God at this. As the Greek proverb puts it, "The dice of the gods are loaded." You can't gamble with God without losing. If you think that you can be a liar, an adulterer, a thief, and get by with it, I have news for you. When you roll the dice of life, you think they are going to come up in such a way that you will be the winner. Well, God already knows how they will come up, because He has loaded them. When you sow sin, you will reap sin. That is inescapable. If you think that you can escape the results of sin, you are making God out a liar and the Bible a falsehood. It is true that some have thought that they have gotten by with sin, but no one ever has. If we could bring Ahab and Jezebel or Judas back to testify, they would tell you that they did not get by with sin. And if we could bring back to life some Americans who have died, they would testify to the same thing.

**Therefore shall a tumult arise among thy people, and all thy fortresses shall be spoiled, as Shalman spoiled Beth-arbel in the day of battle: the mother was dashed in pieces upon her children [Hos. 10:14].**

"Shalman" is an abbreviated form of Shalmaneser, the King of Assyria. "Beth-arbel" apparently refers to a place the Greeks call Arbela. It is in the northern part of the country in the region of Galilee. It seems there was a battle here, although it is difficult to identify in secular history just which incident is being referred to in this verse.

"The mother was dashed in pieces upon her children." This was a method used not only by the Assyrians, but also used later on by the Babylonians. This was mentioned by the children of Israel as they wept in Babylon. "O daughter of Babylon, who art to be destroyed; happy shall he be, that rewardeth thee as thou hast served us. Happy shall he be, that taketh and dasheth thy little ones against the stones" (Ps. 137:8–9).

Those people used an awful, brutal, uncivilized method of destruction in war. Was it so uncivilized? Are we any better today? Have you read of things that are done by those in the drug culture, by homosexuals, by demon worshipers, by the new morality of our day? Was dashing the heads of little babies against the stones any worse than the sins that are committed today?

A brokenhearted man in Atlanta, Georgia, said to me one day, "The day I sent my boy to college it would have been better for him if I had taken him to the cemetery and buried him instead." In other words, it would have been better for him to have been brutally killed as a baby by a ruthless pagan. But the ruthless pagans of the present hour are not condemned by our society. Instead they are accepted and even approved.

**So shall Beth-el do unto you because of your great wickedness: in a morning shall the king of Israel utterly be cut off [Hos. 10:15].**

The Assyrians came, and overnight Israel was being transported to Assyria and a life of slavery.

# CHAPTERS 11–12

***THEME:** Israel must be judged, but God will not give her up*

Chapter 11 opens on a new note. Up to this point the emphasis has been on the disobedience of God's people, but now there is a new note sounded. That new note is the love of God—how wonderful it is!

**When Israel was a child, then I loved him, and called my son out of Egypt [Hos. 11:1].**

This verse speaks primarily of the nation Israel—there is no question about that. It reveals the close relationship between God and the nation. In effect God is saying, "Israel as a nation was my son, and I took him out of Egypt. I did not take them out of Egypt because they were wonderful people who were serving Me. They were not serving Me but were in idolatry even then. It was not because of their ability, their superiority; they had nothing like that. I took them out of Egypt because I loved them." My friend, that is the reason He saved you and me. Love is not the basis of salvation, but it is the motive of salvation. Back of the redemption we have in

Christ, the fact that He would die, is ". . . God so *loved* the world . . ." (John 3:16, italics mine). "When Israel was a child, then I loved him," God says. "I took him out of Egypt not because he was worthy, not because he performed good works, but because I loved him."

Matthew in his gospel applied this verse to the Lord Jesus (see Matt. 2:15). This is an example of how statements in the Old Testament can also have application to the future. That baby boy who was born yonder in Bethlehem is identified with these people— He is an Israelite. The woman of Samaria knew this when He came there to the well. She said to him, ". . . How is it that thou, being a Jew, askest drink of me, which am a woman of Samaria? for the Jews have no dealings with the Samaritans" (John 4:9). God sent Him down to this world to die, and the Lord Jesus came and identified Himself with His people. As a baby He was taken down to the safety of Egypt, but the time came when God called Him out of the place of safety back to the place of danger within the land. He moved into the arena of life where He was to demonstrate the love of God by dying upon the cross—to furnish a redemption that man might have a righteous basis on which his sins could be forgiven. He identified with His people; He identified with humanity; He identified with you and me. "For God so loved the world, that he gave his only begotten Son, that whosoever believeth in him should not perish, but have everlasting life" (John 3:16).

**As they called them, so they went from them: they sacrificed unto Baalim, and burned incense to graven images [Hos. 11:2].**

God had put the Canaanites and the other pagans out of the land because they worshiped Baalim. However, when the Hebrews got into the land they also turned to the worship of Baalim and to carved images.

**I taught Ephraim also to go, taking them by their arms; but they knew not that I healed them [Hos. 11:3].**

God blessed Israel in many different ways, and His blessing was the gentle way in which He led them.

**I drew them with cords of a man, with bands of love: and I was to them as they that take off the yoke on their jaws, and I laid meat unto them [Hos. 11:4].**

God says, "I did not force them to serve Me." God will not force Himself upon you either,

my friend. Many people say, "Why doesn't God break through today? Why doesn't He do this or that?" I don't know why God doesn't do a lot of things—He just hasn't told me. He is God, and I happen to be a little creature down here and I lack a great deal of information. Although I'm not able to answer that, I do know this: God will not force you. The only band He will put on you is the band of love. He says, "I won't bridle you, I won't push you, the only appeal I make to you is that I love you." My friend, that is the appeal that God makes to you and to me today. He moved heaven and hell to get to the door of your heart, but He stopped there and politely knocks on the door and says, "Behold, I stand at the door, and knock . . ." (Rev. 3:20). That is where He is—He has never crashed the door; He is not going to push Himself in. You will have to respond to His love.

It is interesting that love has always been the strongest appeal. It is said that Napoleon made the statement, "Charlemagne, Alexander the Great, and other generals have built up empires, and they built them on force, but Jesus Christ today has millions of people who would die for Him, and He built an empire on love." That is His only appeal to you—don't think He will use any other method. He will judge you, but He will not draw you to Himself except by love. That is the strongest appeal that can possibly be made. The band is a band of love.

**He shall not return into the land of Egypt, but the Assyrian shall be his king, because they refused to return [Hos. 11:5].**

Israel ran down to Egypt to get help but then found out that Egypt was his enemy. Then he ran up to Assyria to get help there. God said, "I'm going to make Assyria his king"— Assyria is where He sent Israel into captivity.

**And the sword shall abide on his cities, and shall consume his branches, and devour them, because of their own counsels.**

**And my people are bent to backsliding from me: though they called them to the most High, none at all would exalt him [Hos. 11:6–7].**

This is the second time in Hosea that the word *backsliding* occurs. Again, it is the figure of the backsliding heifer, that little calf who, when you try to push her up the runway into the old wagon, simply puts down her front feet and begins to slide backwards—and you just have to start all over again. That is a picture of what backsliding is—it is to refuse to listen to God, to refuse to come to Him.

> **How shall I give thee up, Ephraim? how shall I deliver thee, Israel? how shall I make thee as Admah? how shall I set thee as Zeboim? mine heart is turned within me, my repentings are kindled together.**
>
> **I will not execute the fierceness of mine anger, I will not return to destroy Ephraim: for I am God, and not man; the Holy One in the midst of thee: and I will not enter into the city [Hos. 11: 8–9].**

This is a plaintive note. It seems as if God is on the horns of a dilemma here, as if He is frustrated. Listen to Him: "How shall I give thee up, Ephraim?" He doesn't want to give them up. God loves them, but because of their sin God must judge them.

"How shall I deliver thee, Israel?" My friend, God has no other way to save you except by the death of Christ. You may think you have two or three different ways yourself, but God has but one way. Since He says, "There is no saviour beside me" (Hos. 13:4), you had better listen to Him. You and I are not in the saving business, but He is.

"How shall I make thee as Admah? how shall I set thee as Zeboim?" Admah and Zeboim were cities down on the plain which God judged along with Sodom and Gomorrah. God is saying to Israel, "I hate to judge you like that." However, God had to judge them, and today it is just as desolate in Samaria as it is there along the Dead Sea where these cities were once located.

"Mine heart is turned within me, my repentings are kindled together. I will not execute the fierceness of mine anger." In other words, Israel did not receive half of what they deserved. Why? Because God says, "I will not return to destroy Ephraim"—He intends to redeem them and to put these people back in that land some day. Their present return to the land is not a fulfillment of this at all; do not blame God for what is happening in that land today.

However, God *will* put them back in the land. Why will He do it? For one reason: "For I am God, and not man; the Holy One in the midst of thee: and I will not enter into the city." This is something else we need to learn today. We feel like we live in a democracy and that our government exists for us and exists to carry out the decisions we make, but God says, "I am the sovereign God. I'm not accountable to anyone. I do not have a board of directors, and nobody elected Me to office. I do what I please." My friend, if you do not like what God is doing today, it's too bad for you, because God is going to do it—He is not accountable to you. There are a lot of things which God does that I don't understand, but He is God, and He is surely not accountable to Vernon McGee. He does not come down and hand in a report to me. The folk who work for me at "Thru the Bible" headquarters hand in reports to me, but God doesn't give me a report. Why? Because He is *God*, and He doesn't have to report to me.

> **They shall walk after the LORD: he shall roar like a lion: when he shall roar, then the children shall tremble from the west [Hos. 11:10].**

God intends to judge, my friend—a judgment upon the nations in the west. And the United States happens to be *west* from the land of Israel.

> **They shall tremble as a bird out of Egypt, and as a dove out of the land of Assyria: and I will place them in their houses, saith the LORD.**
>
> **Ephraim compasseth me about with lies, and the house of Israel with deceit: but Judah yet ruleth with God, and is faithful with the saints [Hos. 11:11–12].**

Judah still had a few good kings in the southern kingdom, but there were none in the northern kingdom. Some of the kings made a profession, but they were using lies and deceit. My friend, I believe we live in a day when you can fool everyone. Abraham Lincoln made the statement (everybody believes it because good old Abe said it), "You can fool some of the people all of the time, and all of the people some of the time, but you cannot fool all of the people all of the time." Lincoln did not live in this day of television and brainwashing. You can fool all the people all the time. There has never been such a day of brainwashing as today. But nobody is fooling God. He knows, and someday He will judge according to truth.

Chapter 12 continues God's statement of judgment against Israel.

> **Ephraim feedeth on wind, and followeth after the east wind: he daily increaseth lies and desolation; and they**

do make a covenant with the Assyrians, and oil is carried into Egypt [Hos. 12:1].

"Ephraim feedeth on wind, and followeth after the east wind." This is a reference to the east wind which comes over the burning Arabian desert and blows through that land. God is saying, "I intend to let the Assyrians come through the land just like the east wind."

**The LORD hath also a controversy with Judah, and will punish Jacob according to his ways; according to his doings will he recompense him.**

**He took his brother by the heel in the womb, and by his strength he had power with God:**

**Yea, he had power over the angel, and prevailed: he wept, and made supplication unto him: he found him in Beth-el, and there he spake with us [Hos. 12: 2–4].**

Many people have questioned why God put it in His Word that Jacob took hold of his brother Esau's heel. It is interesting to note that today medicine and psychology have said that probably the most important period of a man's life is when he is in the womb, because even in the womb character is being formed as well as the human body. This little fellow Jacob began to reveal something in the womb—he revealed that he wanted to be the firstborn. Although Esau beat him out, Jacob wanted to be the firstborn. I do not know how to explain it other than to say that it was in his heart from the very beginning. He wrestled at his birth, and God had to wrestle with him later on in his life at Peniel to bring him to submission so that He would be able to bless him. "Yea, he had power over the angel, and prevailed." How did he prevail? Was he a better wrestler? Would he appear on television today as an outstanding wrestler? No, Jacob wasn't much of a wrestler. He had his ears pinned back and his shoulders pinned to the mat. God had him down, but he won. How did he win? By surrendering. My friend, you can fight God all you want to, but you'll never win until you surrender to Him.

**Even the LORD God of hosts; the LORD is his memorial [Hos. 12:5].**

The name *Jehovah*, or "the LORD," is a name God gave to Israel as a memorial. He said, "You will always know Me by My name. I am Jehovah, the self-existing one, the living God." We do not need images to remind us of God. His very name expresses His nature.

**Therefore turn thou to thy God: keep mercy and judgment, and wait on thy God continually [Hos. 12:6].**

These people needed to practice what they preached. In our day, the worship of Satan and the giving over to homosexuality is leading to the basest of crimes. Only by coming to the living God and waiting upon Him continually will we have mercy and justice; they go together—you will not have one without the other.

**He is a merchant, the balances of deceit are in his hand: he loveth to oppress [Hos. 12:7].**

This speaks of dishonesty in business, something of which God does not approve.

**And Ephraim said, Yet I am become rich, I have found me out substance: in all my labours they shall find none iniquity in me that were sin [Hos. 12:8].**

In other words, Ephraim felt he was able to buy his way with money. He had made his money dishonestly, but he thought he was being blessed of God.

**And I that am the LORD thy God from the land of Egypt will yet make thee to dwell in tabernacles, as in the days of the solemn feast [Hos. 12:9].**

God is saying to Israel, "I am not through with you—I'll not give you up."

**Is there iniquity in Gilead? surely they are vanity: they sacrifice bullocks in Gilgal; yea, their altars are as heaps in the furrows of the fields [Hos. 12:11].**

"Is there iniquity in Gilead?" Gilead is the place where there should be a balm to heal the wound, but Gilead was then a place of sin.

**Ephraim provoked him to anger most bitterly: therefore shall he leave his blood upon him, and his reproach shall his Lord return unto him [Hos. 12:14].**

"Therefore shall he leave his blood upon him." His blood shall rest upon his own head, for he is guilty and deserves death. Blood had been shed profusely, and the guilt of his sin remained upon him.

Israel had turned from God, and therefore He must judge them.

*THEME: Israel will be judged in the present; Israel will be saved in the future*

## ISRAEL WILL BE JUDGED IN THE PRESENT

In chapter 13 we see that God's judgment of Israel is inevitable.

**When Ephraim spake trembling, he exalted himself in Israel; but when he offended in Baal, he died [Hos. 13:1].**

In other words, when Ephraim served the living God, God exalted him; but when he began the worship of Baal, he died. My friend, not only did Ephraim die and was put out of the land, but the land also died, and I do not think that it has come back today. The ruins of Samaria and the other cities in that area are the most desolate that you will find anywhere on the earth.

**And now they sin more and more, and have made them molten images of their silver, and idols according to their own understanding, all of it the work of the craftsmen: they say of them, Let the men that sacrifice kiss the calves [Hos. 13:2].**

This was a form of worship. The people were actually going up and kissing those golden calves!

There are many people today who think that to kiss a certain image or to kiss a certain area of ground is to worship God. On one of our tours to Israel there was a lady who got down on her hands and knees at the Garden Tomb and started kissing the place. I immediately took her by the arm and reminded her that we had been told not even to drink the water in that land and that she must get up out of the dirt. "Oh," she said, "that doesn't make any difference. This is a holy place; this is where my Lord was buried." Then I said to her, "He's not here today. He is the living Christ at God's right hand. You cannot kiss Him today, but you can worship Him and praise Him." It is nonsense to go around kissing something as an act of worship of the living and true God. You worship Him, my friend, by the life that you live. You worship Him in the way you conduct your business, carry on your social life, the way you run your home, and the way you act out on the street— not only in the way you act in the sanctuary. We are the ones who have made a distinction between the sanctuary and the street, but in God's sight there is no difference at all.

**Therefore they shall be as the morning cloud, and as the early dew that passeth away, as the chaff that is driven with the whirlwind out of the floor, and as the smoke out of the chimney.**

**Yet I am the LORD thy God from the land of Egypt, and thou shalt know no god but me: for there is no saviour beside me [Hos. 13:3–4].**

Listen to Him, my friend. You may work out a plan of salvation, but *He* is the only Savior, and since He is, you had better come His way. The Lord Jesus said, ". . . I am the way, the truth, and the life: no man cometh unto the Father, but by me" (John 14:6). Now either that's true or it's not true. Millions of people have come that way, and they have found it to be true. You may think you have your way of salvation, but God is the only Savior, and He is the only one who can offer you a plan of salvation.

**I did know thee in the wilderness, in the land of great drought.**

**According to their pasture, so were they filled; they were filled, and their heart was exalted; therefore have they forgotten me [Hos. 13:5–6].**

God says, "I have been your God, the one who brought you out of Egypt. I am not about to give you up, but I am going to judge you."

**Therefore I will be unto them as a lion: as a leopard by the way will I observe them:**

**I will meet them as a bear that is bereaved of her whelps, and will rend the caul of their heart, and there will I devour them like a lion: the wild beast shall tear them [Hos. 13:7–8].**

There is a prophetic sidelight here that is very interesting. In Daniel's vision (ch. 7) Babylon is pictured as a lion, Greece (under Alexander the Great) is pictured as a leopard, and the empire of Media-Persia is pictured as the bear. Now here in Hosea's prophecy God is saying that in the future He will come against them like a lion and a leopard, but in the *immediate* future He will come like a bear—represented by Media-Persia, which at that early date was dominated by Assyria. God says, "I will meet them as a bear that is bereaved of her whelps." There is nothing more ferocious than a mother bear that has been robbed of her cubs, and she is an apt illustration of the brutal Assyrian army.

**O Israel, thou hast destroyed thyself; but in me is thine help [Hos. 13:9].**

We often blame God for what happens to us. When you feel like that, this is a good verse to turn to. *You* have destroyed *yourself*, and you are responsible for your condition. But you can get help from God; *He* will furnish help to you.

**I will be thy king: where is any other that may save thee in all thy cities? and thy judges of whom thou saidst, Give me a king and princes?**

**I gave thee a king in mine anger, and took him away in my wrath [Hos. 13: 10–11].**

"I gave thee a king in mine anger." When Israel asked for a king, God gave Saul to them. "And took him away in my wrath." He took the last king, Hoshea, away from the northern kingdom, He took Zedekiah away from the southern kingdom, and He did it in His wrath. Judgment! It was His judgment in the beginning, and His judgment at the end.

**Samaria shall become desolate; for she hath rebelled against her God: they shall fall by the sword: their infants shall be dashed in pieces, and their women with child shall be ripped up [Hos. 13:16].**

"Samaria shall become desolate." I have been to Samaria, and I agree with God. It is a desolate place today.

## ISRAEL WILL BE SAVED IN THE FUTURE

Chapter 14 is a wonderful chapter, for it speaks of the future salvation of Israel.

**O Israel, return unto the LORD thy God; for thou hast fallen by thine iniquity [Hos. 14:1].**

The Lord tells the people that it is because of their sin that they will go into captivity.

**Asshur shall not save us; we will not ride upon horses: neither will we say any more to the work of our hands, Ye are our gods: for in thee the fatherless findeth mercy [Hos. 14:3].**

Imagine making something with your hands and then falling down and worshiping it! Many men today worship their own ability. They worship their brain, their intellect. They worship what they are doing and what they are able to do. You are nothing but a pagan and a heathen when you do that, my friend.

**I will heal their backsliding, I will love them freely: for mine anger is turned away from him.**

**I will be as the dew unto Israel: he shall grow as the lily, and cast forth his roots as Lebanon.**

**His branches shall spread, and his beauty shall be as the olive tree, and his smell as Lebanon.**

**They that dwell under his shadow shall return; they shall revive as the corn, and grow as the vine: the scent thereof shall be as the wine of Lebanon [Hos. 14:4–7].**

"I will heal their backsliding." God says, "The people have been backsliding, slipping away from Me, but I am going to heal them. I will love them freely, for Mine anger is turned away from them."

**Ephraim shall say, What have I to do any more with idols? I have heard him, and observed him: I am like a green fir tree. From me is thy fruit found.**

**Who is wise, and he shall understand these things? prudent, and he shall know them? for the ways of the LORD are right, and the just shall walk in them: but the transgressors shall fall therein [Hos. 14:8–9].**

Verse 8 is one of the most wonderful verses in the Bible. This is a victory song. "Ephraim *shall* say"—this is future. God is finally going to win. Love is going to win the victory here. God has said to Ephraim, "Oh, Ephraim, how shall I give you up?" And He said, "Ephraim—let him alone because he has turned to idols." Now God says, "But there is a day coming when Ephraim will see that he's made a great blunder and mistake, and he will turn back to Me. He is going to say, 'I don't have anything more to do with idols.' "

I cannot help but believe in the midst of this tragedy of sin, this drama of human life which is being enacted down here in this world today, that God is going to come out the victor. I believe that there are going to be more people saved than there will be lost. That was Spurgeon's belief also; he said that many times. You and I have our noses pressed against the present hour. We look around at the world today, and all we see is the little flock the Lord Jesus talked about—that is, the church, the people whom He is calling out of this world. But there are many whom He has saved in the past. For example, at one time He saved the entire population of Nineveh (although a hundred years later they reverted to sin, and He judged them). There have been other great revival movements in the past also, but the greatest turning to God is to take place in the future. That will occur, of all times, during the Great Tribulation Period. The Millennium is also going to be a period of salvation, by the way. God is going to win, my friend. Love will triumph. Our God today is riding victoriously in His own chariot—He is the sovereign God. God pity the man who gets under those chariot wheels! I don't know about you, but I want to go along with God— I'm hitchhiking a ride with Him today. That is the reason it is so urgent that we know His Word—to find out how to stay in His will in this difficult day in which we are living.

# BIBLIOGRAPHY

(Recommended for Further Study)

Feinberg, Charles L. *The Minor Prophets*. Chicago, Illinois: Moody Press, 1976.

Gaebelein, Arno C. *The Annotated Bible*. 1917. Reprint. Neptune, New Jersey: Loizeaux Brothers, 1971.

Ironside, H. A. *The Minor Prophets*. Neptune, New Jersey: Loizeaux Brothers, n.d.

Jensen, Irving L. *Minor Prophets of Israel*. Chicago, Illinois: Moody Press, 1975.

Unger, Merrill F. *Unger's Commentary on the Old Testament*, Vol. 2. Chicago, Illinois: Moody Press, 1982.

# The Book of
# JOEL
## INTRODUCTION

The prophecy of Joel may seem unimportant as it contains only three brief chapters. However, this little book is like an atom bomb—it is not very big, but it sure is potent and powerful.

We know very little about the prophet Joel. All we are told concerning him is in Joel 1:1, "The word of the LORD that came to Joel the son of Pethuel." *Joel* means "Jehovah is God," and it was a very common name. There have been some people who have jumped to the conclusion that the prophet Joel was a son of Samuel because 1 Samuel 8:1–2 says, "And it came to pass, when Samuel was old, that he made his sons judges over Israel. Now the name of his firstborn was Joel. . . ." But if we read further the next verse tells us, "And his sons walked not in his ways, but turned aside after lucre, and took bribes, and perverted judgment" (1 Sam. 8:3). Samuel's son could not have been the same as the prophet Joel.

We can be sure that Joel prophesied in Jerusalem and the Jerusalem area. Throughout his prophecy he refers again and again to "the house of the LORD." For instance, in Joel 1:9 we read, "The meat offering and the drink offering is cut off from the house of the LORD; the priests, the LORD's ministers, mourn." He also mentions Jerusalem in Joel 3:20, "But Judah shall dwell for ever, and Jerusalem from generation to generation." And then again, in Joel 3:17, we read, "So shall ye know that I am the LORD your God dwelling in Zion, my holy mountain: then shall Jerusalem be holy, and there shall no strangers pass through her any more." Therefore we know that this man was a prophet in the southern kingdom of Judah.

Joel prophesied as one of the early prophets. Actually there were quite a few prophets—at least fifty—and it is generally conceded by conservative scholars that Joel prophesied about the time of the reign of Joash, king of Judah. That would mean that he was contemporary with and probably knew Elijah and Elisha.

Joel's theme is "the day of the LORD." He makes specific reference to it five times: Joel 1:15; 2:1–2; 2:10–11; 2:30–31; and 3:14–16. Isaiah, Jeremiah, Ezekiel, and Daniel all refer to the Day of the Lord. Sometimes they call it "that day." Zechariah particularly emphasizes "that day." What is "that day"? It is the Day of the Lord, or the Day of Jehovah. Joel is the one who introduces the Day of the Lord in prophecy. Yonder from the mountaintop of the beginning of written prophecy, this man looked down through the centuries, seeing further than any other prophet saw—he saw the Day of the Lord.

The Day of the Lord is a technical expression in Scripture which is fraught with meaning. It includes the millennial kingdom which will come at the second coming of Christ, but Joel is going to make it very clear to us that it begins with the Great Tribulation Period, the time of great trouble. If you want to set a boundary or parenthesis at the end of the Day of the Lord, it would be the end of the Millennium when the Lord Jesus puts down all unrighteousness and establishes His eternal kingdom here upon the earth.

The Day of the Lord is also an expression that is peculiar to the prophets of the Old Testament. It does not include the period when the church is in the world, because none of the prophets spoke about a group of people who would be called out from among the Gentiles, the nation Israel, and all the tribes of the earth, to be brought into one great body called the church which would be raptured out of this world. The prophets neither spoke nor wrote about the church.

James, at the great council of Jerusalem, more or less outlined the relationship between the church age and this period known as the Day of the Lord. He said, "Simeon hath declared how God at the first did visit the Gentiles, to take out of them a people for his name. And to this agree the words of the prophets; as it is written, After this I will return, and will build again the tabernacle of David, which is fallen down; and I will build again the ruins thereof, and I will set it up" (Acts 15:14–16). James says, "After this"— after what? *After* He calls out the church from this world, God will again turn to His program with Israel, and it is to this time that the Day of the Lord refers. James went on to say, "That the residue of men might seek after the Lord, and all the Gentiles, upon whom my name is called, saith the Lord, who doeth all these things" (Acts 15:17). Today God is calling *out* of the Gentiles a people; in that day, *all* the Gentiles who will be entering the kingdom will seek the Lord. I think there will be a tremendous turning to God at that time unlike any the church has ever witnessed.

Someone may question, "Why is God following this program?" James said, "Known unto God are all his works from the beginning of the world" (Acts 15:18). Don't ask me why God is following this program—ask Him, because I do not know and nobody else knows. He is following this program because it is *His* program and it is *His* universe. He is not responsible to you or to me. God doesn't turn in a report at the end of the week to tell us what He's been doing and to receive our approval. My friend, all I can say is that it is just too bad if you and I don't like it because, after all, we are just creatures down here in this world.

There are several special features about the prophecy of Joel which I would like to point out. Joel was the first of the writing prophets, and as he looked down through the centuries, he saw the coming of the Day of the Lord. However, I do not think he saw the church at all—none of the prophets did. When the Lord Jesus went to the top of the Mount of Olives, men who were schooled in the Old Testament came and asked Him, "What is the sign of the end of the age?" Our Lord didn't mention His cross to them at that time. He didn't tell them then about the coming of the Holy Spirit. He didn't tell them about the church period or mention the Rapture to them. Instead, the Lord went way down to the beginning of the Day of the Lord. He dated it, but it's not on your calendar or mine; the events He predicted will identify it for the people who will be there when the Day of the Lord begins: "When ye therefore shall see the abomination of desolation, spoken of by Daniel the prophet, stand in the holy place, (whoso readeth, let him understand:)" (Matt. 24:15). That is how we are to know the beginning of the Day of the Lord. Joel will make it clear to us that it begins with night—that is, it begins as a time of trouble. After all, the Hebrew day always began at sunset. Genesis tells us, "And the evening and the morning were the first day" (Gen. 1:5). We begin at sunup, but God begins at sundown. The Day of the Lord, therefore, begins with night.

It is remarkable to note that, unlike Hosea, Joel says practically nothing about himself. In Hosea we find out about the scandal that went on in his home, about his unfaithful wife. We do not know whether Joel had an unfaithful wife or not; we don't even know if he were married. The very first verse of the prophecy gives us all that we are to know: "The word of the LORD that came to Joel the son of Pethuel" (Joel 1:1).

Unlike many of the other prophets, Joel does not condemn Israel for idolatry. Earlier in their history, at the time Joel was prophesying, idolatry was not the great sin in Israel. Joel will only mention one sin, the sin of drunkenness.

Joel opens his prophecy with a unique description of a literal plague of locusts. Then he uses that plague of locusts to compare with the future judgments which will come upon this earth. The first chapter is a dramatic and literary gem. It is a remarkable passage of Scripture, unlike anything you will find elsewhere in literature.

Finally, Joel's prophecy contains the very controversial passage in which he mentions the outpouring of the Holy Spirit which was referred to by the apostle Peter on the Day of Pentecost (see Joel 2:28–29). There is a difference of interpretation concerning the pouring out of the Holy Spirit, and we will look at that in detail when we come to it.

# OUTLINE

# CHAPTER 1

*THEME: Literal and local plague of locusts; looking to the Day
of the Lord (prelude)*

The prophecy of Joel contains only three very brief chapters, but it holds an important position in Scripture. As the first of the writing prophets, it is Joel who introduces and defines the term, "the day of the LORD."

## LITERAL AND LOCAL PLAGUE OF LOCUSTS

**The word of the LORD that came to Joel the son of Pethuel [Joel 1:1].**

There are those who have thought that Joel was a son of Samuel (see 1 Sam. 8:1–2), but Samuel's sons were very wicked and this Joel certainly is not. This boy's father was Pethuel. Joel was a common name, and it means "Jehovah is God."

**Hear this, ye old men, and give ear, all ye inhabitants of the land. Hath this been in your days, or even in the days of your fathers? [Joel 1:2].**

Apparently Israel was in the midst of a great locust plague at this time. Locust plagues were rather commonplace in that land, but Joel calls to the old men and says, "Did anything like this ever happen in your day? Did it happen in the day of your fathers? Have you ever heard anything like *this* locust plague?" Of course, they had to say, "No, this is the worst we've ever had." The trouble with most of us as we begin to get older is that we have grandiose ideas about the past. If some young person comes and says to us, "Say, we just had a wonderful meeting at our church," we like to say, "That's wonderful, that was a great meeting, but we had a meeting that was twice as good back in my hometown when I was young." Joel said, "You old men have never heard of anything like this"—and the old men had to agree that they had not.

**Tell ye your children of it, and let your children tell their children, and their children another generation [Joel 1:3].**

Joel goes on to say, "You can pass this on down. Tell your children about this and have them tell their children, because there's not going to be a plague of locusts like this ever again." Does this remind you of another passage of Scripture? In the Olivet Discourse in Matthew 24, when the Lord Jesus identified the period which He Himself labeled the

Great Tribulation Period, He said the same thing about it. He said that there has never been anything like it before, and there is not going to be anything like it afterward. Now that more or less puts parentheses around that period and slips it into a unique slot in history. During the Great Tribulation no one will be able to say, "This reminds me of when I was a young fellow—we had a real time of trouble back then." We have never had a period like the Great Tribulation. For all periods of recorded history in the past, there have always been previous times in history that could match it. However, the Lord Jesus made it very clear concerning the Great Tribulation: "For then shall be great tribulation, such as was not since the beginning of the world to this time, no, nor ever shall be" (Matt. 24:21). When people are in the midst of the Great Tribulation, there will be none of this questioning that we hear today: "Do you think that the Great Depression was the Great Tribulation?" Or, "Do you think that all this turmoil today is the Great Tribulation?" The answer is very easy to come by when we turn to the words of the Lord Jesus. He said there is nothing like it in the past. We've had times like this before, my friend—they can all be duplicated in the past. And since things are not getting better but getting worse, neither can we say there will be nothing like this in the future.

In a very dramatic way, Joel is saying, "Look, this locust plague is unique—there has never been anything like it, but there is coming another unique period called the Day of the Lord." The Day of the Lord will open with the Great Tribulation after the church has left this world. It will be a frightful time on this earth, horrible beyond description, and then Christ will come and establish His kingdom. I wish the people who deny that the Bible teaches these things would study the total Word of God and not just lift out a few verses here and there. We need to study the *entire* Word of God to know what it says.

This plague of locusts stands alone as being different from any other plague that has taken place. The plague of locusts in the land of Egypt at the time of Moses was a miraculous plague—it was a judgment of God. However, this plague was what we would call a natural event.

There are several things that we need to understand about the locust as many of us are not familiar with them at all. As a boy I always enjoyed lying on my bed before an open window on a summer evening and listening to the locusts in the trees. However, they were never a plague, and they probably were not the same kind of locusts which were in Israel in Bible times or even today. If you have ever seen pictures of fields after a plague of locusts, you know that locusts seem to have a scorched earth policy of their own—it looks just as if a fire had burned over the field and destroyed everything.

The Word of God speaks of locusts, and one passage I will draw your attention to is Proverbs 30:27, "The locusts have no king, yet go they forth all of them by bands." Locusts march as an army, and they are divided into different bands as they go. That will help us understand Joel's description of this locust plague as we come to verse 4—

**That which the palmerworm hath left hath the locust eaten; and that which the locust hath left hath the cankerworm eaten; and that which the cankerworm hath left hath the caterpillar eaten [Joel 1:4].**

It is true that four different words are used here—the palmerworm, the locust, the cankerworm, and the caterpillar. There are those who believe that this refers to four different types of insects, but there really is no basis for that. The *palmerworm* means "to gnaw off." The word for *locust* in Hebrew is *arbeh* and it suggests that there are many of them and they are migratory—they move as a great swarm. The *cankerworm* means "to lick off," and the *caterpillar* means "to devour or to consume." These four words describe the locust and what he does. The locusts move in bands just like an army. First of all, there are the planes which come over and drop the bombs. Then after the bombs have been dropped by the air corps, the artillery comes through and destroys every section, leaving great areas devastated, but a great deal remains. Then the infantry comes along—that's the third group—and they get what has been left. The mop-up crew follows after that, and they will get what little may still be there. What we have here, therefore, are four words which describe the different bands of locusts. They have no general, they have no king, they have no lieutenants or sergeants, but they move just like an army.

Locusts were often sent by God as a judg-ment, but we would put this plague in the category of a natural plague. I believe that it was not necessarily a judgment, but a warning to the people, a warning to the nation. Joel was the first writing prophet, and he prophesied at the same time as Elijah. As Elijah was warning the northern kingdom, this man Joel, in a most dramatic manner, was warning the southern kingdom of a judgment that was coming. He will move from the local judgment—it was the method of all the prophets to move from the local situation into the future—to the judgment that is coming at the Day of the Lord.

The Day of the Lord is one of the most misunderstood terms and yet one of the most important in Scripture. Joel was the first to use it, and he makes very clear what the Day of the Lord is. After him, all the other prophets had to do was to speak of "that day," and it was understood as to what they were referring.

Now I am getting a little bit ahead of this chapter, but I want to say that Joel will move from this literal and local plague of locusts to speak of the Day of the Lord which begins with the Great Tribulation Period. How does the Great Tribulation Period open? It opens with the four horsemen of the Apocalypse: there is a false peace, then war breaks out, followed by a famine, and then finally the pale horse of death. I see a tremendous parallel between these four bands of locusts and the four horsemen of the Apocalypse. During the Great Tribulation Period it will not be literal locusts, but it will be something far worse that is going to ride, not just through that land, but through the entire world. The world will be totally devastated when the Lord Jesus Christ returns to the earth to set up His kingdom.

**Awake, ye drunkards, and weep; and howl, all ye drinkers of wine, because of the new wine, for it is cut off from your mouth [Joel 1:5].**

The locusts have gotten to the grapes first. They have stripped all the vineyards, and there will be no more wine for the drunkards. The man who was an alcoholic in that day found himself taking the cure before he intended to, because there was no more wine to drink.

This reveals that, even at the beginning of the downfall of the nation Israel, the great sin was drunkenness. We are frequently reminded that most of the accidents which take place on our highways are caused by some individual who is exercising his freedom and right to drink. Entire families have been killed on the highway while out on a holiday because some drunk driver has hit them head-on. I may be criticized for moving into the realm of politics but, my friend, I am studying the Word of God, and when it talks about drunkenness, I am going to talk about drunkenness. And when God's Word speaks about the king being a drunkard, then I will talk about drunkenness in my nation's capital. When we are told that there are dozens of cocktail parties every day in Washington, D.C., it is no wonder that some of the decisions which are being handed down look as if they were coming from men who are not in their right minds.

"Awake, ye drunkards, and weep; and howl, all ye drinkers of wine." At the very beginning, drunkenness was beginning to chip away the foundation of the nation Israel. This is the only sin Joel will mention. He will not mention idolatry at all, the great sin of turning from God, which eventually brought the nation down. At this time the people still made a profession of worshiping God.

**For a nation is come up upon my land, strong, and without number, whose teeth are the teeth of a lion, and he hath the cheek teeth of a great lion [Joel 1:6].**

Here the locusts are compared to an invading army and its destructiveness. These little bitty insects, the locusts, can tear a tree down. They can move through a field of grain and absolutely leave nothing but bare ground. They came along in these four bands with no leader, no king. They came, in most cases, as a judgment from God, but this plague was a warning from God. Later Joel will move ahead to that which is still future, the Day of the Lord which will be just like a locust plague upon the earth. The four horsemen of the Apocalypse are yet to ride.

**He hath laid my vine waste, and barked my fig tree: he hath made it clean bare, and cast it away; the branches thereof are made white [Joel 1:7].**

The locusts actually can kill a fig tree. They absolutely stripped a fig tree of its bark, leaving nothing but the naked wood exposed.

Joel is sending out a message to the people, and he is going to tell them what they are to do at a time like this. He will tell them ten things they are to do—

**Lament like a virgin girded with sackcloth for the husband of her youth [Joel 1:8].**

He says something now that is unusual: (1) They are to *lament*. Like a young bride who has lost her husband, perhaps killed in battle, that is the way this nation should weep.

**The meat offering and the drink offering is cut off from the house of the LORD; the priests, the LORD's ministers, mourn [Joel 1:9].**

"The meat offering and the drink offering is cut off from the house of the LORD." In other words, they are not able to make an offering at all. (2) "The priests, the LORD's ministers, *mourn.*" All through this passage the same thing is said. The drunkards mourned and the priests mourned—the entire economy was affected by this plague.

This verse and other verses lead us to believe that the prophet Joel was in Jerusalem. He speaks here to the priests who minister in the house of the Lord.

**The field is wasted, the land mourneth; for the corn is wasted: the new wine is dried up, the oil languisheth [Joel 1:10].**

There was no olive oil and no grapes and no grain. The three staple crops which they had were now destroyed. Even the land is to mourn. You see, the land and the people were very closely intertwined. The Mosaic Law was not only given to a people, it was given to a land.

Joel has spoken to the drunkards, he has spoken to the priests, and now he will speak to the farmers:

**Be ye ashamed, O ye husbandmen; howl, O ye vinedressers, for the wheat and for the barley; because the harvest of the field is perished.**

**The vine is dried up, and the fig tree languisheth; the pomegranate tree, the palm tree also, and the apple tree, even all the trees of the field, are withered: because joy is withered away from the sons of men [Joel 1:11–12].**

(3) "*Be ye ashamed,* O ye husbandmen." (4) "*Howl,* O ye vinedressers." The vinedressers are vineyard owners. "The apple tree" is actually the orange tree which is indigenous to that land.

**Gird yourselves, and lament, ye priests: howl, ye ministers of the altar: come,**

**lie all night in sackcloth, ye ministers of my God: for the meat offering and the drink offering is withholden from the house of your God [Joel 1:13].**

(5) *"Gird yourselves,"* (6) *"and lament,* ye priests: howl, ye ministers of the altar." The priests could not perform their function because there was nothing for them to use for the offerings. They were to lie all night girded with sackcloth and ashes because there was no meat offering and no drink offering. The economy of the land was wrecked, and there was not even enough to make an offering to God. However, God makes it clear that it was not the ritual that was important but the hearts of the people.

In these verses God is asking the people to do something that He had not asked before. When God gave the Mosaic Law, He gave seven feast days to these people, and He made it clear that He did not want them to come before Him with a long face. He wanted them to come to His house rejoicing and with joy in their hearts.

Have you noticed today that when Christians meet together in church it is generally not a very joyful occasion? I am even rebuked for telling funny stories. Sometimes I see a lot of saints who just sit there and do not even crack a smile. I wish they would—I think it would do them good. There is no joy today, and there was no joy in Joel's day.

Why is God for the first time telling His people, "I want you to lament. I want you in sackcloth and ashes. I want you to mourn"? Before He had told them, "I want you to come before Me with joy." The reason is because of sin in the nation. That is the same reason there is such a lack of joy today. The world is surely working hard today. The music has to be loud and fast, and the jokes have to be dirty to even get a laugh. Even in our churches it is considered almost sinful to laugh out loud. Oh, my friend, where is our joy today? It is gone because of sin. God won't let us have joy. He said to these people, "Come before Me now with your mourning. I do not like it, but you are sinful and I want to see your repentance."

**Sanctify ye a fast, call a solemn assembly, gather the elders and all the inhabitants of the land into the house of the LORD your God, and cry unto the LORD [Joel 1:14].**

(7) *"Sanctify ye a fast."* God had never asked them to do that before. God had given them feast days—He never gave them a fast day until they plunged into sin. The one sin Joel mentions which was destroying the nation was drunkenness. It was robbing people of their normal thinking; they were not able to make right judgments.

(8) *"Call a solemn assembly."* In other words, they were to come together. God had wanted them to come together and rejoice in His presence, but now He says this is to be a solemn assembly.

(9) *"Gather the elders* and all the inhabitants of the land into the house of the LORD your God." This was a time to go to church. During World War II there were two rather godless men who were good friends and belonged to all different kinds of clubs (drinking clubs, most of them), but they met one Sunday at church. One of them said, "Well, I didn't know you went to church!" The other replied, "I don't usually go to church—this is my first time. But I've got a son over there fighting in this war, and I thought it was about time I got to church." My friend, times of great trouble drive people to God. The people of the land were to come together for a fast day.

(10) *"Cry unto the LORD."* Why? Because God is merciful. God is gracious. God wants to forgive. Our God is a wonderful God. They were to come to Him in this time of difficulty, and He would hear and answer their prayer.

Joel has given a warning to these people, and he has given them these injunctions. These are the things they are to do if they want the blessing of God upon them.

## LOOKING TO THE DAY OF THE LORD (PRELUDE)

In a masterly way, Joel now moves from the local situation, this plague of locusts, down to the end of the age and the Day of the Lord.

**Alas for the day! for the day of the LORD is at hand, and as a destruction from the Almighty shall it come [Joel 1:15].**

"Alas for the day!" What day are you talking about, Joel? "For the day of the LORD is at hand, and as a destruction from the Almighty shall it come." Like a little model, a little adumbration of that which is coming in the future, this local plague of locusts was a warning, a picture of the coming Day of the Lord. It should have alerted the people.

Joel is now going to tell them about something in the future. That which was coming in the future, the thing which had been promised to David, was a kingdom. David would be raised up to rule over that kingdom. War would cease, and there would be peace on the earth. All the prophets spoke about that, but they also spoke about what Joel is saying here—the coming of the Day of the Lord.

The Day of the Lord must be understood in contrast to the other days which are mentioned in Scripture. You and I are living today in what Scripture calls *man's day*. It began with Nebuchadnezzar, and the Lord Jesus labeled it "the times of the Gentiles." He said, ". . . Jerusalem shall be trodden down of the Gentiles, until the times of the Gentiles be fulfilled" (Luke 21:24). We are living in a man's day. Man is the one who makes the judgments today. We appeal to the Supreme Court, but we do not appeal to God. We have forgotten Him altogether. His name is just a word to swear by and to blaspheme.

Dr. Lewis Sperry Chafer makes this comment concerning man's day: "This theme, obscured at times by translators, is referred to but once in the New Testament, namely, 1 Corinthians 4:3, which reads, 'But with me it is a very small thing that I should be judged of you, or of man's judgment: yea, I judge not mine own self.' Now in this passage the phrase, 'man's judgment' is really a reference to human opinion current in this age, which might properly and literally be translated, 'man's day.' "

We are living in the day of man. Believe me, humanism abounds today. Man believes he can solve the problems of the world, but what has man really done? He has gotten the world into an awful mess right now. Every new politician who comes along thinks he has the answer. My friend, they do not have the answers; man cannot solve the problems of this world. I understand there have been some admissions in the cloakrooms of our own government and the chancelleries of the great nations of the world that man is incapable of solving the problems of the world today.

Scripture speaks of another day that is coming—the *Day of the Lord Jesus Christ*. Paul wrote in 1 Corinthians 1:7–8: "So that ye come behind in no gift; waiting for the coming of our Lord Jesus Christ: Who shall also confirm you unto the end, that ye may be blameless in the day of our Lord Jesus Christ." What is the Day of the Lord Jesus Christ? It is the day when He will come to take His church out of this world, and then the church will come before the judgment seat of Christ. My life verse is Philippians 1:6 which reads, "Being confident of this very thing, that he which hath begun a good work in you will perform it until the *day of Jesus Christ*" (italics mine). He is

going to keep us until that day when He takes us out of the world and we appear before Him to see whether we receive a reward or not.

Both the Old and the New Testament speak of the *Day of the Lord*. Second Thessalonians 2:2 tells us, "That ye be not soon shaken in mind, or be troubled, neither by spirit, nor by word, nor by letter as from us, as that the day of Christ is at hand." The Thessalonian believers were afraid that they would miss the Rapture. Our translation of this verse is an unfortunate one—the word *Christ* should have been translated as "Lord"—in other words, "as the day of the Lord is at hand." Paul is assuring the believers that they will not go through the Day of the Lord.

Joel will make very clear what the Day of the Lord is. He will say that the Day of the Lord is a dark, gloomy, and difficult day. The Hebrew viewpoint was that they would enter immediately into the kingdom—that life would be a breeze with no problems at all. But Joel says that the Day of the Lord begins with night, with darkness. That darkness is the Great Tribulation Period. It will be like this locust plague that has come with its four bands of locusts like the four horsemen of the Apocalypse who will ride in the Great Tribulation Period. Then the Day of the Lord will include the coming of Christ to the earth to establish His kingdom. Then His people will enter into the sunshine of His presence. That was the Old Testament hope; that was the thing the Old Testament taught.

My friend, you can see how important it is to study all of the Bible. One man wrote to me to explain what he thought the day of the Lord was. He wrote several pages, giving Scripture after Scripture, but he never gave one verse from Joel. He didn't understand that Joel is the very key. Joel was the first of the writing prophets. You cannot say the Day of the Lord is something other than what Joel says it is; it must fit into the program which he describes. All the prophets who came after him used this term many times. "The Day of the Lord" occurs about seventy-five times in the entire Bible; "the day of the LORD" occurs five times and "that day" one time in the Book of Joel. All of the prophets have a great deal to say about the Day of the Lord, and we need to recognize that it is a technical term which is defined and used consistently in Scripture.

To summarize, there is (1) man's day, the day in which we are living now; (2) the Day of the Lord Jesus Christ, when He will take the church out of this world; then (3) the Day of the Lord beginning with the Great Tribulation

Period. After all, we label the different days of the week: Monday, Tuesday, Wednesday, and so on. God has labeled these different periods of time also. This is not something men thought of, but it is what the Word of God teaches.

I should say that the Day of the Lord is not the same as the Lord's Day that is mentioned in Revelation 1:10. The Lord's Day is the first day of the week, which the New Testament makes very clear. Many people say the Day of the Lord and the Lord's Day are the same just because they use the same two words. That is ridiculous—as ridiculous as saying there is no difference between a chestnut horse and a horse chestnut. If you take two words and turn them around, you get something altogether different. In the one you've got a nut, and in the other you've got a horse! The Day of the Lord and the Lord's Day are two different things.

**Is not the meat cut off before our eyes, yea, joy and gladness from the house of our God? [Joel 1:16].**

Joel continues talking about this plague of locusts. There was no more joy and gladness in the house of God. I have had the privilege in the past few years of my ministry of speaking in the great pulpits of this country and at many of the great Bible conferences. I have noted that there is a sadness in congregations as they come together today. In many places I have found that at the first service there is an air of expectancy. You can feel it, the air is charged with it, but there is no note of gladness. At some meetings in Florida, a man with the FBI said to me, "I've been watching your method. I've noted that you get up before a congregation, and you slide very quietly and slowly into a funny story to get the people into a good humor." I said, "You've noticed that?"

And he said, "Yes, and I think I know why you do it. I think you're doing it because there is a low level of joy among the people today." I told the man that he was right. The joy was gone in Israel, and today, even when we have everything, there is no joy in our services.

**The seed is rotten under their clods, the garners are laid desolate, the barns are broken down; for the corn is withered [Joel 1:17].**

"The seed is rotten under their clods." The grain couldn't even come up, because the locusts had just gnawed off the shoots even with the ground. "The garners are laid desolate"—they could not fill up the granary.

**How do the beasts groan! the herds of cattle are perplexed, because they have no pasture; yea, the flocks of sheep are made desolate.**

**O LORD, to thee will I cry: for the fire hath devoured the pastures of the wilderness, and the flame hath burned all the trees of the field [Joel 1:18–19].**

The locusts have their own scorched earth policy. It was just as if the ground had been entirely burned off.

**The beasts of the field cry also unto thee: for the rivers of waters are dried up, and the fire hath devoured the pastures of the wilderness [Joel 1:20].**

This was a very terrible, treacherous time. Even the animal world—both the animals in the barnyard and the wild animals out yonder in the forest—were being affected by this plague. It was a judgment that touched all life in that land in that day, and it becomes a picture of the Day of the Lord that is coming.

# CHAPTER 2

*THEME: Looking to the Day of the Lord; God's plea; promise of deliverance; promise of the Holy Spirit*

This chapter continues the prelude which was begun in 1:15, and, of course, continues the theme.

## LOOKING TO THE DAY OF THE LORD

You recall that God had promised David a kingdom, and that wonderful future kingdom became the theme song of all the prophets after David. The great message is that the millennial kingdom is coming upon this earth. As we read the prophets, it sounds like a stuck record as one after another looks forward to it.

Now Joel, the first of the writing prophets, makes it clear that the Day of the Lord—which includes the millennial kingdom—will not be all peaches and cream. Before the millennial kingdom (when the Lord Jesus will be ruling on this earth), there will be a time which the Lord Jesus defined as the Great Tribulation Period. Chapter 2 will make this clear to us.

> **Blow ye the trumpet in Zion, and sound an alarm in my holy mountain: let all the inhabitants of the land tremble: for the day of the LORD cometh, for it is nigh at hand [Joel 2:1].**

"The day of the LORD cometh." Let me remind you that Joel is the first of the writing prophets, and he looks way down through the centuries and sees the Day of the Lord. It begins with darkness, that is, with judgment. Then Christ comes to the earth and establishes His kingdom. Malachi speaks of Him as the ". . . Sun of righteousness [who will] arise with healing in his wings . . ." (Mal. 4:2).

"Blow ye the trumpet in Zion, and sound an alarm in my holy mountain." "Zion" and "my holy mountain" refer to Jerusalem. He says they should blow the trumpet and sound an alarm. It is important for us to understand the significance of the trumpet. One needs to have a full-orbed view of the Bible so that on any given subject we are able to put our thinking down on all four corners and make an induction. Understanding the background will enable us to appreciate what the writer is saying.

What is the significance of the blowing of the trumpet? Back in the Book of Numbers we learn that when the children of Israel started through the wilderness, God commanded them to make two silver trumpets. He gave the instructions to Moses: "And the LORD spake unto Moses, saying, Make thee two trumpets of silver; of a whole piece shalt thou make them: that thou mayest use them for the calling of the assembly, and for the journeying of the camps" (Num. 10:1–2). When Israel was in the wilderness, God used the trumpets to move them on the wilderness march. The first blowing of the trumpet was a signal that everybody should get ready to march. When the pillar of cloud would lift and move out, they would take down the tabernacle. Then immediately the trumpet would sound again, and Moses and Aaron would move up front ahead of the tribe of Judah, and the ark would go out ahead with them. You will remember that Israel was encamped around the tabernacle on all four sides, three tribes on each side. Now each section would move out in turn, signaled by the blowing of the trumpets. Actually, to get the whole camp on the march, the trumpets were blown seven different times.

Now when we come to Revelation, the final book of the Bible, we find the blowing of the trumpets again. Although some expositors feel that this is in relation to the church, there is no blowing of the trumpet for the church. The sound of the trumpet at the time of the Rapture (1 Thess. 4:16) will be the shout of Christ Himself: "For the Lord himself shall descend from heaven with a shout, with the voice of the archangel, and with the trump of God . . ."—His voice will be like a trumpet.

The seven trumpets in Revelation have nothing to do with the church. The church will have been completed and will have been taken out of the world. The seven trumpets are identified with the nation Israel, just as there were the seven trumpet calls in the wilderness march.

If we turn back to the Book of Numbers, we will see that the different trumpet calls meant certain definite things. They were a way of giving instructions to Israel: "And when they shall blow with them, all the assembly shall assemble themselves to thee at the door of the tabernacle of the congregation. And if they blow but with one trumpet, then the princes, which are heads of the thousands of Israel, shall gather themselves unto thee. When ye blow an alarm, then the camps that lie on the east parts shall go forward. When ye blow an alarm the second time, then the camps that lie on the south side shall take their journey: they shall blow an alarm for their journeys. But when the congregation is to be gathered together, ye shall blow, but ye shall not sound an alarm" (Num. 10:3–7). Then he gives instructions for the time they will be in the Promised Land: "And if ye go to war in your land against the enemy that oppresseth you, then ye shall blow an alarm with the trumpets; and ye shall be remembered before the LORD your God, and ye shall be saved from your enemies" (Num. 10:9). During the time of war the trumpet would call the men of war to defend their country when an enemy was coming.

Now here in Joel's prophecy he says, "Blow ye the trumpet in Zion, and sound an *alarm* in my holy mountain." Why? "Let all the inhabitants of the land tremble: for the *day of the LORD cometh*, for it is nigh [near] at hand." You see, after the Lord has called His church out of the world, He will turn again to the nation of Israel, which becomes the object of worldwide anti-Semitism. This is the beginning of the Day of the Lord.

Now in this second chapter, Joel is going to give a blending of the plague of locusts together with the threat of the Assyrian army and then look down the avenue of time into the future and the Day of the Lord. Of course the liberal theologian would say this refers simply to the locust plague and the local situation. He would like to dismiss a great deal of meaning from the Word of God. The other extreme view is to say this refers only to the Great Tribulation Period.

I think we need to see that in Joel there is a marvelous blending. He moves right out of the locust plague to the Day of the Lord which is way out yonder in the future. You recall that was the practice of the prophets to speak into a local situation and then move out into the future Day of the Lord—which includes the Tribulation Period and the Millennium.

The local situation was the plague of locusts, and in the near future the Assyrian army was coming down: "But I will remove far off from you the *northern army*" (v. 20). I think it would be rather ridiculous to call a plague of locusts the northern army, but the plague of locusts was a picture of the Assyrian army that would be coming out of the north, and the Assyrian army becomes the picture of the enemy which will be coming out of the north in the last days. As we see in chapters 38 and 39 of Ezekiel, the northern army refers to present-day Russia which will invade Israel. In fact, Russia's coming will usher in the last half of the Great Tribulation Period.

Let me remind you that the Day of the Lord is not a twenty-four hour day, but a period of time. The apostle Paul used it in that sense when he said, ". . . now is the accepted time; behold, now is the *day* of salvation" (2 Cor. 6:2, italics mine), speaking of the age of grace.

Let me repeat that the Day of the Lord is different from the Lord's Day, which refers to the first day of the week. Although the two words are the same, their arrangement makes all the difference. The difference is as great as between a chestnut horse and a horse chestnut!

Now Joel will put down God's definition that will condition and limit the prophets who will speak in the future. After this, all of them will speak into this period. It is interesting to find that none of them contradict each other, even though some of the prophets didn't know what the others were prophesying.

**A day of darkness and of gloominess, a day of clouds and of thick darkness, as the morning spread upon the mountains: a great people and a strong; there hath not been ever the like, neither shall be any more after it, even to the years of many generations [Joel 2:2].**

This is the same period about which the Lord Jesus said, "For then shall be great tribulation, such as was not since the beginning of the world to this time, no, nor ever shall be" (Matt. 24:21). The Great Tribulation opens the Day of the Lord, because that is the way the Hebrew day opens; it begins in the evening at the time of darkness. I have a notion that when the plague of locusts came over the land, they would actually darken the sky because there would be so many of them. And the Day of the Lord will begin with darkness.

**A fire devoureth before them; and behind them a flame burneth: the land is as the garden of Eden before them, and behind them a desolate wilderness; yea, and nothing shall escape them [Joel 2:3].**

Before the plague of locusts came, the earth looked like the Garden of Eden. Everything was green with rich, luxurious foliage. The land was beautiful. After the locusts left, there was not a bit of green to be seen. It looked as if a fire had swept over the land.

The Day of the Lord will be the same in that it will be a time of destruction. When the four horsemen of the Apocalypse ride through this world, there will be war and famine and death. In one fell swoop, one fourth of the population will be wiped out, and at another time, one third of the population will be destroyed.

**The appearance of them is as the appearance of horses; and as horsemen, so shall they run [Joel 2:4].**

As I indicated before, the head of the locust resembles a horse's head, and the Italian word for locust means "little horse"; the German word means "hay horse." As the horse eats hay, the locusts would eat up everything green. Joel is describing the locust plague and is beginning to make application of it to the Day of the Lord.

**Like the noise of chariots on the tops of mountains shall they leap, like the noise of a flame of fire that devoureth the stubble, as a strong people set in battle array.**

**Before their face the people shall be much pained: all faces shall gather blackness [Joel 2:5–6].**

"All faces shall gather blackness"—that is, they will be scorched.

**They shall run like mighty men; they shall climb the wall like men of war; and they shall march every one on his ways, and they shall not break their ranks [Joel 2:7].**

In the Book of Proverbs it says this: "The locusts have no king, yet go they forth all of them by bands" (Prov. 30:27). They don't need a king or a leader—each one knows his place. They come in bands. When Joel describes four different groups of locusts here, I believe he is describing the movement of a great army—an army of locusts. In the last days, there will come against that land another enemy, and it will come like a locust plague. This is a preparation for the Book of Revelation in which the apostle John writes of a locust plague that will take place on the earth during the first woe which follows the blowing of the fifth trumpet: "And the fifth angel sounded, and I saw a star fall from heaven unto the earth: and to him was given the key of the bottomless pit. And he opened the bottomless pit; and there arose a smoke out of the pit, as the smoke of a great furnace; and the sun and the air were darkened by reason of the smoke of the pit. And there came out of the smoke locusts upon the earth: and unto them was given power, as the scorpions of the earth have power. And it was commanded them that they should not hurt the grass of the earth, neither any green thing, neither any tree; but only those men which have not the seal of God in their foreheads" (Rev. 9:1–4).

This is an unusual locust that will not attack anything green—that is all the normal locust would attack. They did not attack human beings. But these locusts will attack "only those men which have not the seal of God in their foreheads."

It will be such a terrifying time that men will seek death and will not be able to find it; that is, they will not be able to commit suicide: "And to them it was given that they should not kill them, but that they should be tormented five months: and their torment was as the torment of a scorpion, when he striketh a man. And in those days shall men seek death, and shall not find it; and shall desire to die, and death shall flee from them" (Rev. 9:5–6).

Now notice this description of the locusts: "And the shapes of the locusts were like unto horses prepared unto battle; and on their heads were as it were crowns like gold, and their faces were as the faces of men. And they had hair as the hair of women, and their teeth were as the teeth of lions" (Rev. 9:7–8). My friend, that is an unusual type of locust! This plague will take place during the Great Tribulation.

You can see that Joel, way back here at the beginning of the writing prophets, prepares the ground for the apostle John to come later and give the detailed description of the locusts as they will appear in the Day of the Lord.

May I just say that this is the reason I think it is tragic today to find so many people who have just been converted who think they are qualified to start a Bible class. What books do they like to start to teach? Usually you will find they choose either the Gospel of John or the Book of Revelation. In my judgment, that is not the place to begin with new believers. I believe Matthew is the key book to the Bible. Until you understand Matthew, I don't think you will quite get the message of the Gospel of John and I *know* you will miss the message of the Book of Revelation. And this little prophet Joel, who has been by and large ignored, sheds a great deal of light on the last days which he calls the Day of the Lord.

When Joel writes: "They shall run like mighty men; they shall climb the wall like men of war," he is beginning to move from the local locust plague into the future which he has labeled the Day of the Lord.

In the next verse we will see that he *is* talking about the Day of the Lord.

**Neither shall one thrust another; they shall walk every one in his path: and when they fall upon the sword, they shall not be wounded.**

**They shall run to and fro in the city; they shall run upon the wall, they shall climb up upon the houses; they shall enter in at the windows like a thief.**

**The earth shall quake before them; the heavens shall tremble: the sun and the moon shall be dark, and the stars shall withdraw their shining [Joel 2:8–10].**

Obviously this is more than a local locust plague or else Joel is exaggerating; the prophets spoke God's Word as He gave it to them—they didn't exaggerate. This is the same picture that John gives us in the Book of Revelation.

**And the Lord shall utter his voice before his army: for his camp is very great: for he is strong that executeth his word: for the day of the Lord is great and very terrible; and who can abide it? [Joel 2:11].**

This is the third time Joel has mentioned the Day of the Lord.

"Who can abide it?" This is very much the same as Jesus said, "Except those days should be shortened, there should no flesh be saved" (Matt. 24:22). And Joel asks, "Who can abide it?" Well, John gives the answer in Revelation. In chapter 7 he says that God will shut down the forces of nature, withholding the winds from blowing (which are judgments of God upon the earth) until the two great companies of the redeemed are sealed and made secure. If God's people are going to make it through the terrible time of tribulation, they will have to be sealed. When Joel asks, "Who can abide it?" the "it" is the Day of the Lord, which begins in darkness, the night of the Great Tribulation.

## GOD'S PLEA

Now the question is: What can a sinner do in a period like this? Well, Joel gives the answer for that:

**Therefore also now, saith the Lord, turn ye even to me with all your heart, and with fasting, and with weeping, and with mourning [Joel 2:12].**

"Turn ye even to me with all your heart." The word *turn* means "repent." God says to His people whose hearts are turned from Him, "Repent." Repent means primarily to change your mind. You indicate a change of mind by turning around. It is true there may be some shedding of tears along with the repentance, but that is only a by-product of repentance. Repentance really means to change your mind.

When I first entered the ministry, I went to my home church in Nashville as a pastor. I had some of the most wonderful people in that church—they had to be wonderful to put up with me! It was my first pastorate, and I was as green as grass. I could be very serious but also rather frivolous. I was not married yet; so I would take off to go to Atlanta, Georgia, or to Memphis, Tennessee, because I knew some girls in both places.

The man who was humanly responsible for my entering the ministry was in that church. He had arranged a loan for me, because I was a poor boy with no money. Also he had helped me get a job. He was like a father to me, and I loved him as a father.

One day I went to the bank to tell him something that I had in mind. He let me know immediately that my idea was not a very good idea, as many of mine have not been. He let me know in no uncertain terms. That angered me, so I turned and started out the door. When I got to the street, I thought, "This is not right. I owe this man a great deal." So I turned around and went back. Do you know why I turned around? Because it came into my mind and into my heart that I ought to do it. When I got back to his office I saw tears coming from his eyes. By the way, when my wife and I were in Nashville on our honeymoon, he said to her, "I don't know much about you, whether or not you get angry quickly, but Vernon has a very high temper, and don't both of you get angry at the same time!" Well, one of the things that made my wife so attractive to me was her mild, even temper, and she has put up with a whole lot from this poor preacher! But the day I returned to his office I repented of the thing I had done, and I manifested it in turning and going back to him.

Now when God says, "Turn ye even to me with all your heart," He means to repent, and the by-product of it will be fasting, weeping, and mourning. Unfortunately, a great many people think that if they go down to an altar and shed enough tears, they are converted. Well, I went through that process as a boy and found it to be absolutely meaningless.

**And rend your heart, and not your garments, and turn unto the Lord your God: for he is gracious and merciful, slow to anger, and of great kindness, and repenteth him of the evil [Joel 2:13].**

You see, this was to be a heart experience, not some outward gesture. Actually, the Mosaic Law forbade the priest from tearing his garments. Repentance was not to be shown by being a fanatic. The tear was to be in the heart.

"And turn unto the Lord your God" is repentance.

Now he gives the reason for turning to the Lord: "For he is gracious and merciful, slow to anger, and of great kindness, and repenteth him of the evil." In the Books of Exodus and Jonah, I deal more thoroughly with the question of what it means when God repents. When Israel was in Egypt it looked as if God changed His mind. He sent plague after plague to Egypt to give Pharaoh the opportunity to repent and turn to Him, but he didn't. Also in Jonah's day, God sent Jonah to preach to the Ninevites that He would destroy the city. However, Nineveh repented and turned to God; so God did not destroy the city. It looked as if God had changed His mind after He said that He would destroy the city, but He did not change His mind. God is immutable. He is always gracious; He is always merciful, and He is always slow to anger.

My friend, you can always depend upon God. He never changes, He is immutable; but when a *sinner* repents and turns to Him, God says in effect, "You were under My judgment, and I was going to judge you, but now that you have turned to Me, I will not judge you." God is always gracious and ready to forgive.

**Who knoweth if he will return and repent, and leave a blessing behind him; even a meat offering and a drink offering unto the Lord your God? [Joel 2:14].**

In other words, "The Lord will bless you again in the field and in the vineyard, and you will have a drink offering and you'll have a meat offering to bring to Him."

Incidentally, the drink offering is mentioned here; yet there is no instruction in Leviticus for a drink offering. The drink offering was poured on the other offerings and became a part of them. When it was poured on the sacrifice, it went up in steam on the hot coals. The apostle Paul, you recall, said that he wanted his life to be like that—just a drink offering on the sacrifice of Christ.

**Blow the trumpet in Zion, sanctify a fast, call a solemn assembly [Joel 2:15].**

At the beginning of this chapter we saw that the blowing of the trumpet was used to call an assembly and also to sound an alarm. In verse 1 it was to sound an alarm. Now here at verse 15 it is to call an assembly. The people were to be brought together to hear God's message so that they might have the opportunity to turn to God. He is gracious and good, and He is willing to accept them.

"Sanctify a fast, call a solemn assembly." As we have seen, in the Mosaic system God gave His people only feast days. They were to come before Him with rejoicing. But now that they are in sin and rebellion against Him and have turned from Him, they are to fast and come before Him in a solemn assembly.

My friend, the only way we can come to Him is to come as sinners wanting to turn from our sins. If you have been turning *from* God and now will turn *to* God, all you have to do is call upon Him and He will save you. ". . . Believe on the Lord Jesus Christ, and thou shalt be saved . . ." (Acts 16:31). You don't need to do anything but that. You don't need to join a church, go through a ceremony, or promise Him something. You simply turn as a sinner to Christ for His mercy.

It is interesting that the word for preaching or evangelizing or heralding the gospel is a word that means trumpet. The trumpet call of the New Testament is the gospel message that we are to get out to the world. "Blow the trumpet in Zion." This is to call a solemn assembly. When people respond to an altar call and come down to the front of the church, it is a solemn moment. They are testifying that they are turning to God from sin. That is serious business and should not be done lightly. However, I emphasize again that it is not merely going to the altar of a church that constitutes real repentance.

A lovely young couple in Memphis responded to an altar call and came down to the front of the church after a message I had given. I went down to talk to them and asked them, "Is this the first time you have responded to a call?"

"No, we come down every Sunday."

"Then why do you come down to the altar?"

"Because we want all that God has for us."

"Do you think you will get that by just coming down here."

"We hope so."

"Let me ask you another question. Do you think you have it now?"

"No, we don't."

"Then I would get a little discouraged if I were you. Maybe this isn't the way it is to be done. Maybe you are trying man's way, and God has another way. God wants to be good and gracious to you, and He wants to save you, but you must come to Him His way. No man comes to the Father but by the Lord Jesus Christ. He is the only door to heaven." Jesus Himself said, "I am the door: by me if any man enter in, he shall be saved, and shall go in and out, and find pasture" (John 10:9).

**Gather the people, sanctify the congregation, assemble the elders, gather the children, and those that suck the breasts: let the bridegroom go forth of his chamber, and the bride out of her closet [Joel 2:16].**

"Gather the children, and those that suck the breasts" sounds as if the little children were to be taken care of in the nursery so their mothers could give this assembly their full attention. Notice that even the bridegroom is to go to the assembly. When a man was married in Israel, he was excused from going to war for one year. In fact, he was excused from a lot of duties so he could get acquainted with his bride. I guess that was an advantage of getting married! However, God is saying here that everybody is to be gathered together—even the bridegroom and the bride if they are on their honeymoon.

**Let the priests, the ministers of the Lord, weep between the porch and the altar, and let them say, Spare thy people, O Lord, and give not thine heritage to reproach, that the heathen should rule over them: wherefore should they say among the people, Where is their God? [Joel 2:17].**

The priests and the ministers of the Lord are to weep. Joel is in Jerusalem, you see; he is a prophet of the southern kingdom.

They were to pray, "Spare thy people, O Lord, and give not thine heritage to reproach, that the heathen [nations] should rule over them." Israel has been scattered throughout the world to this day. Although they have a nation and a government and a flag, they are still pretty well subject to the nations of the world. As I write this, they are caught in the oil slick which is causing them a great deal of trouble, and it will continue to cause trouble because they are not back in the land today in fulfillment of prophecy. When God puts them back into the land, there will be no problem relative to the oil situation.

Golda Meir made a statement which inferred that Moses had made a mistake. She said something like this: "Imagine! Moses led all of our people around through the wilderness for forty years and brought them to the only place in this area that has no oil!" Well, if she believed the Old Testament, she would know that they were led by a pillar of fire by night and a pillar of cloud by day, and that God had a definite purpose for keeping them from settling on land that was rich with oil. They would never have gotten their land back—that's for sure! Actually what Israel needs is not oil but water. They don't have enough water because the judgment of God is upon them. Moses made no mistake because he was following the orders of God, and certainly God makes no mistakes.

"Wherefore should they say among the people, Where is their God?" They were wondering what was happening to them. And today that is still their question. In Israel I talked with a sharp young Jewish fellow at the King David Hotel. He said, "If it is as you say that we are God's chosen people, why doesn't He intervene for us today?" I told him very candidly, "Because right now, you are not with God. Until you come back in repentance to Him, He is not dealing with you as His chosen people. Today God is doing a new thing: He is calling out from among your people and my people—Jews and Gentiles—a people to His name. You are just not up to date with God. You are going way back to the Mosaic system which is outmoded. The latest thing, the newest model, is the church of the Lord Jesus Christ." You see, God is inviting "whosoever will" to trust Christ and become a part of the new organism which He calls the church.

## PROMISE OF DELIVERANCE

Now he is definitely moving into the future. Notice the time-word "Then." It will appear several times in this chapter.

**Then will the Lord be jealous for his land, and pity his people [Joel 2:18].**

In the Olivet Discourse (see Matt. 24–25), the Lord Jesus used the word *then* to advance in time the happenings that will take place in the

Great Tribulation Period. At the end of the Great Tribulation Period, just before the Lord returns to this earth, *then* will He be jealous for His land and pity His people.

**Yea, the LORD will answer and say unto his people, Behold, I will send you corn, and wine, and oil, and ye shall be satisfied therewith: and I will no more make you a reproach among the heathen [Joel 2:19].**

At that time the Lord will give them corn and wine and oil; they will be satisfied, and no longer will they be a reproach among the heathen. Even the most radical radical today would not say that this is being fulfilled now. The largest population of Israel is not in the land. There are more Jews in New York City than there are in Israel. And there is a great company of them even in Russia. This is not being fulfilled at this time. This still looks forward to the future. It is definitely the period known as the Day of the Lord, which will begin with darkness and move on into the dawn of the Millennium, past man's rebellion that breaks out on the earth, and on to the beginning of the eternal kingdom. From here on we are bottled into that particular period.

**But I will remove far off from you the northern army, and will drive him into a land barren and desolate, with his face toward the east sea, and his hinder part toward the utmost sea, and his stink shall come up, and his ill savour shall come up, because he hath done great things [Joel 2:20].**

"I will remove far off from you the northern army" certainly is not talking about locusts but an army coming down from the north. This was partially fulfilled when Assyria came down and took the northern kingdom, but God miraculously delivered the southern kingdom from them. It was another hundred years before the southern kingdom went into captivity—and then it was to the Babylonians, not the Assyrians.

However, there is still a future fulfillment of the removal of the northern army. This is given in more detail in Ezekiel 38–39. In the Great Tribulation Period Russia will come down from the north, but God will deliver Israel. The description given here fits the description of the Battle of Armageddon. "And will drive him into a land barren and desolate, with his face toward the east sea, and his hinder part toward the utmost sea, and his stink shall come up, and his ill savour shall

come up, because he hath done great things." The Sea of Galilee is on one side and the Mediterranean Sea is on the other side of the Valley of Esdraelon where Armageddon will take place. God will intervene as we have seen in Ezekiel. He will destroy this enemy that comes from the north, and He does it to glorify His name.

God is glorified when He judges sin just as much as He is when He saves a sinner. That is hard for us to believe; it is a bitter pill for man to swallow. God is holy, and a holy, righteous God is going to judge. Every one of the prophets says that. The Word of God has a lot to say about the judgment of God. But He doesn't like to judge. We have already seen that He is gracious and merciful and slow to anger. Judgment is a strange work for God. That is why He holds out His hands all the day long and asks us to come to Him. When people refuse to turn to Him, He must judge them in His righteousness and in His holiness.

This is true even for the children of God. When we do wrong, if we do not judge ourselves, God must judge us. He chastens us to bring us back to Himself. To be honest with you, I have had some chastening from the Lord. I want to stick very close to my Heavenly Father because, I can tell you, I don't enjoy the chastening of the Lord.

**Fear not, O land; be glad and rejoice: for the LORD will do great things [Joel 2:21].**

The Tribulation Period will lead to the coming of Christ to earth to establish His kingdom. Today that land is still under a curse. They need water. The land is far from being a Garden of Eden. Anyone who has driven from Jerusalem to Jericho will have to admit it is just as desolate as the desert in Arizona and California.

You will notice that the church is not in this picture. Neither do we find the church in the Olivet Discourse nor in the Book of Revelation after chapter 4. The believers have been raptured, and there is no longer a church on earth. And when the church gets to heaven it will no longer be called the church (*ekklesia*, meaning "called out"), but the figure changes and the believers will be called the *bride* of Christ.

**Be not afraid, ye beasts of the field: for the pastures of the wilderness do spring, for the tree beareth her fruit, the fig tree and the vine do yield their strength [Joel 2:22].**

This day has not come yet.

**Be glad then, ye children of Zion, and rejoice in the LORD your God: for he hath given you the former rain moderately, and he will cause to come down for you the rain, the former rain, and the latter rain in the first month [Joel 2:23].**

Who are the "children of Zion"? Of course they are the people of the southern kingdom—that is where Zion is located. You and I may sing lustily, "We're marching to Zion," but we are not marching to the Zion here upon this earth.

When he speaks of the "rain," he is talking about literal rain. In verse 28 Joel will make application of it in the pouring out of the Holy Spirit, but he is referring to literal rain in this verse. The former rain came in October, and the latter rain came in April. There are other passages in the Bible that speak of the former and the latter rains which were quite literal rains in the land of Israel (see Lev. 26:3–4; Deut. 11:14–17; 1 Kings 8:35–36; Jer. 3:3; Hos. 6:3).

Before I went over to Israel, I heard that the latter rain was returning to that land. Well, I have been over there in April, and it rained a little. But, gracious, I don't think people would call that the kind of rain which the Lord is talking about. In former days they really had rain. All those rugged hills of that land were covered with trees. The enemies came in and denuded the land, and today they are trying to set out trees, but they are having trouble making those trees grow because there is not enough of the latter rain. Joel is talking about these literal rains—H$_2$O—which God has promised in the future.

**And the floors shall be full of wheat, and the vats shall overflow with wine and oil.**

**And I will restore to you the years that the locust hath eaten, the cankerworm, and the caterpillar, and the palmerworm, my great army which I sent among you [Joel 2:24–25].**

"I will restore to you the years that the locust hath eaten." There have been a great many sermons preached on this, spiritualizing this passage. And it certainly can be used as an application, since it states a great principle. We find the same thought in the Book of Revelation where God says, ". . . Behold, I make all things new . . ." (Rev. 21:5). He is speaking of the New Jerusalem in this chapter. Those of the church, the sinners who have trusted Christ, are going to be there. He tells us how wonderful it will be and about the fact that He will wipe away all tears from our eyes. What a change that will be! There are a lot of tears in this old world. I rejoice that He will make all things new.

I don't know about you, but I can say that I am not satisfied with my life down here. I have never preached the sermon I have wanted to preach—I wish I could do it. I have had it in my heart and in my mind, but somehow I have never been able to preach as well as I have wanted to. I have never been the husband that I have really wanted to be. I wish that I could have been a much better husband to my wife. When I was sick, she and I went back over the days when we met and how we courted, and all that sort of thing. As I told her, I wish I could change many things which would make it lots more wonderful than it was. Neither have I been the father that I wanted to be. I have never really been the man that I have wanted to be. That is why I love Revelation 21:5: ". . . Behold, I make all things new. . . ." My Lord will say, "Vernon McGee, you didn't quite make it down there on the earth. You never really accomplished your goals. You were frustrated. You were limited. You were down there with that old sinful nature. Now I am going to make all things new. I'm going to give you a new scratch pad and a new pencil without an eraser. You can write it all out now. You can accomplish what you wanted to accomplish."

My friend, that will really make heaven *heaven* for a lot of us. We will be able to do the things and be the person that we have wanted to be down here. Oh, to be free from the hindrances of circumstances, of sin, of the environment, and even of heredity. What a glorious experience to be free of all this and to be in the presence of Christ! He will make all things new. He will restore the years that the locusts have eaten.

**And ye shall eat in plenty, and be satisfied, and praise the name of the LORD your God, that hath dealt wondrously with you: and my people shall never be ashamed.**

**And ye shall know that I am in the midst of Israel, and that I am the LORD your God, and none else: and my people shall never be ashamed [Joel 2:26–27].**

This will take place when he is "in the midst of Israel"; that is, when Christ has come to the earth and has established His kingdom. At that time there will be a fulfillment of all the physical blessings which God has promised to the nation Israel. And the blessings in the Old Testament were largely physical blessings. God promised to bless the land so that they would have bumper crops and their cattle would thrive and multiply. Actually the spiritual blessings seem almost secondary. In contrast to this, the blessings God has promised the church are spiritual blessings—*only*. We have all spiritual blessings in Christ Jesus.

Even though the primary blessings to Israel were physical blessings, we come now to a passage which speaks of spiritual blessing to Israel. This is a very controversial passage of Scripture.

## PROMISE OF THE HOLY SPIRIT

As we come to this section, it is important to keep in mind that we are in the prophecy of Joel that began with the record of a frightful locust plague which he compared to that which is coming in the future, which he calls the Day of the Lord. We have seen that the Day of the Lord will begin with the Tribulation Period, after which Christ will come and establish His kingdom on the earth. In verse 27 we have just read that the Lord at this time will be in the midst of them. Now let's see what He is going to do.

**And it shall come to pass afterward, that I will pour out my spirit upon all flesh; and your sons and your daughters shall prophesy, your old men shall dream dreams, your young men shall see visions:**

**And also upon the servants and upon the handmaids in those days will I pour out my spirit.**

**And I will shew wonders in the heavens and in the earth, blood, and fire, and pillars of smoke.**

**The sun shall be turned into darkness, and the moon into blood, before the great and the terrible day of the LORD come.**

**And it shall come to pass, that whosoever shall call on the name of the LORD shall be delivered: for in mount Zion and in Jerusalem shall be deliverance, as the LORD hath said, and in the remnant whom the LORD shall call [Joel 2:28–32].**

There are many wonderful things that we could say about this passage of Scripture. Dr. Charles L. Feinberg, a Jewish Christian, and an outstanding Hebrew scholar, has written a fine series of books on the Minor Prophets which have been very helpful to me. In *Joel, Amos, and Obadiah*, pp. 26–27, he calls attention to something that I had not known before: "Verses 28 through 32 form chapter 3 in the Hebrew text; and chapter 3 in the English translations is chapter 4 in the original. No one will be inclined to doubt that the disclosure of truth in 2:28–32 is of sufficient importance to warrant its appearing in a separate chapter." I certainly agree that these five verses are important enough to make them a separate chapter.

In understanding this prophecy, it is of utmost importance to note the time of fulfillment indicated in this passage: "And it shall come to pass *(afterward)*." Joel has been telling us about the coming Day of the Lord. As the first of the writing prophets, he introduced it, and he tells what is going to take place during that period. He has emphasized the fact that it will begin with the darkness of the Great Tribulation Period (our Lord Jesus gave it that name). We noted the importance of the time sequence in Hosea. In chapter 3, verse 5 of that prophecy it is written: "Afterward shall the children of Israel return, and seek the LORD their God, and David their king; and shall fear the LORD and his goodness in the latter days." We identified the "latter days" as that time of the Great Tribulation Period which ushers in the kingdom by the coming of Christ to the earth, which is the beginning of the Millennium. This leads us to conclude that Joel is now speaking of a very definite period of time, that this prophecy is to be fulfilled during the Day of the Lord, after the night of the Great Tribulation Period. Then God will pour out His Spirit upon all flesh.

Although Joel is the first of the writing prophets, he is not the only one to mention the pouring out of the Spirit. In Isaiah we read: "Until the spirit be poured upon us from on high, and the wilderness be a fruitful field, and the fruitful field be counted for a forest" (Isa. 32:15). He is speaking of the kingdom which is coming on the earth, and the pouring out of the Spirit has reference to the Millennium. Of course none of the prophets spoke of the church age; all of them spoke of the last days in reference to the nation Israel.

Ezekiel 36:27 says this: "And I will put my spirit within you, and cause you to walk in my statutes, and ye shall keep my judgments, and do them." Then he continues, "And ye shall dwell in the land that I gave to your fathers; and ye shall be my people, and I will be your God" (Ezek. 36:28). Now he is talking to a particular people and a particular land—Israel. It is also a particular period of time when God will pour out His Spirit. Also Ezekiel says: "And shall put my spirit in you, and ye shall live, and I shall place you in your own land: then shall ye know that I the LORD have spoken it, and performed it, saith the LORD" (Ezek. 37:14). That's not all: "Neither will I hide my face any more from them: for I have poured out my spirit upon the house of Israel, saith the Lord GOD" (Ezek. 39:29).

Zechariah is one of the last of the writing prophets. He says, "And I will pour upon the house of David, and upon the inhabitants of Jerusalem, the spirit of grace and of supplications: and they shall look upon me whom they have pierced, and they shall mourn for him, as one mourneth for his only son, and shall be in bitterness for him, as one that is in bitterness for his firstborn" (Zech. 12:10).

Joel also makes it clear in the passage we are discussing—"And it shall come to pass, that whosoever shall call on the name of the LORD shall be delivered: for in *mount Zion* and in *Jerusalem* shall be deliverance"—that he refers to a certain spot on the map.

The question arises: What did Peter mean when he referred to this passage of Scripture on the Day of Pentecost? Did he mean that the prophecy of Joel was fulfilled? No, he didn't say that. He never claimed that this prophecy was fulfilled.

On the Day of Pentecost, when the Holy Spirit came upon the disciples they began to speak to Jews who had come to Jerusalem from all over the Roman Empire. Every man heard the message in his own tongue. These were not *unknown* tongues in which the disciples were speaking the message. Each tongue was the native tongue of one or more of the men who were gathered there from all over the Roman Empire and even beyond the empire.

Well, many believed, but others began to mock and say that the disciples were drunk—filled with new wine. So Simon Peter is the one who gets up to answer them. He acted as the spokesman for the group, and he gave an answer to the accusation that they were drunk. ". . . Ye men of Judaea, and all ye that dwell at Jerusalem, be this known unto you, and hearken to my words: For these are not drunken, as ye suppose, seeing it is but the third hour of the day" (Acts 2:14–15). Peter says you wouldn't find people drunk in the morning. (It's a little different in modern America—some people start drinking pretty early in the day.)

Peter continues, "But this is that which was spoken by the prophet Joel" (Acts 2:16). You will notice that Peter does not say that this is in *fulfillment* of what the prophet Joel said. All the Gospel writers and the apostle Paul are very clear when they say that something is the fulfillment of a prophecy. I couldn't begin to mention all of the passages. For examples, turn to Matthew 2:17–18: "Then was *fulfilled* that which was spoken by Jeremy the prophet, saying, In Rama was there a voice heard, lamentation, and weeping, and great mourning, Rachel weeping for her children, and would not be comforted, because they are *not*" (italics mine). That was a fulfillment of prophecy that had to do with incidents associated with the birth of Christ. Drop down to verse 23: "And he came and dwelt in a city called Nazareth: that it might be *fulfilled* which was spoken by the prophets, He shall be called a Nazarene" (italics mine). Or turn to Acts 13 to the sermon of Paul at Antioch in Pisidia. He speaks of the resurrection of Jesus Christ and says, "And we declare unto you glad tidings, how that the promise which was made unto the fathers, God hath *fulfilled* the same unto us their children, in that he hath raised up Jesus again; as it is also written in the second psalm, Thou art my Son, this day have I begotten thee" (Acts 13:32–33, italics mine). The Bible is very definite about fulfillment of prophecy.

What does Peter say in Acts 2:16? ". . . this is *that* which was spoken by the prophet Joel" (italics mine). He does not say it was a fulfillment of what Joel had predicted. Rather, he said, "This is *that*"—this is like that or similar to that. If you will go back in your mind to the Day of Pentecost, you will realize that Peter was not talking to Gentiles; he was speaking to Jews who were schooled in the Old Testament. They *knew* the Old Testament. They were Jews from all over the empire who had come to Jerusalem for the feast; they had traveled long distances because they were keeping what was required of them according to the Mosaic Law. Peter says to them in effect, "Don't mock, don't ridicule this thing which you see happening. This is like that which is going to take place in the Day of the Lord as it is told to us by the prophet Joel."

He quotes Joel's prophecy. "And it shall come to pass in the last days, saith God, I will pour out of my Spirit upon *all* flesh . . ." (Acts 2:17, italics mine). This is to occur in the last days. Then the Spirit of God will be poured out upon all flesh. Was that fulfilled on the Day of Pentecost? Hardly. It was experienced by those enumerated in the previous chapter. And three thousand were saved. Even if it had been three hundred thousand who were saved, it still would not have been a pouring out of the Spirit upon all flesh. It would still not have been a fulfillment of Joel's prophecy.

In effect, Peter is saying to them, "Don't mock at what you see happening. You ought to recognize from your own Word of God that Joel says the day is coming when God will pour out His Spirit on all flesh. If it is poured out on a few people today, you ought not to be surprised at that."

Then Peter went on to quote the rest of Joel's prophecy regarding what would take place: "I will shew wonders in the heavens and in the earth, blood, and fire, and pillars of smoke. The sun shall be turned into darkness, and the moon into blood, before the great and terrible day of the LORD come" (vv. 30–31). Was that fulfilled on the Day of Pentecost? Of course not. There were no earthquakes, no changes in the sun and moon. These will occur on "that great and notable day of the Lord." Joel calls it "the great and the terrible day of the LORD." The Day of Pentecost was a great day, but it was not a terrible day. It was a wonderful day!

My friend, if we understand the Book of Joel, we will never come to the conclusion that Peter was saying that the prophecy of Joel was being fulfilled on the Day of Pentecost. Simon Peter was merely using Joel's prophecy as an introduction to answer those who were mocking.

Now the question arises: What was the *sub-ject* of Simon Peter's message? On the Day of Pentecost the subject of Simon Peter's sermon was the resurrection of the Lord Jesus Christ. Now when he comes to his text, he uses Psalm 16:8–10, which prophesied the resurrection of Christ. Notice how he applies it to Christ: "This Jesus hath God raised up, whereof we all are witnesses. Therefore being by the right hand of God exalted, and having received of the Father the promise of the Holy Ghost, he hath shed forth this, which ye now see and hear (Acts 2:32–33).

The conclusion both in Joel and in Peter's address is, "And it shall come to pass, that whosoever shall call on the name of the LORD shall be delivered [Peter says, Shall be saved]." This is one of the many passages that causes me to make the statement that I think the greatest time of salvation is yet in the future. I believe God will save more of the human race than will be lost. I agree with Spurgeon who said that he believed God would win more to Himself than would be lost. When Christ comes to the earth to establish His kingdom, there is going to be the greatest time of individuals turning to God that the world has ever seen. Also during the Tribulation Period there will be a great turning to the Lord—much greater than there has been during the church age. The resurrection of Jesus Christ whom God has made both Lord and Christ is the whole point of Peter's sermon. He is not emphasizing the phenomenon they had witnessed. The important issue is coming to know Jesus Christ. Oh, my friend, don't be so occupied with having an experience that you miss coming to *know* Christ. What place does He occupy in your thinking, in your life, in your ministry?

This section of Joel's prophecy is all-important, but it is yet to be fulfilled.

# CHAPTER 3

**THEME:** *Looking at the Day of the Lord (postlude)*

**For, behold, in those days, and in that time, when I shall bring again the captivity of Judah and Jerusalem [Joel 3:1].**

"For, behold, in those days." What day? The Day of Pentecost? No, for He says, "when I shall bring again the captivity of Judah and Jerusalem." He did not bring them back at Pentecost; in fact, the Lord Jesus reversed the order when He said, ". . . ye shall be witnesses unto me both in Jerusalem, and in all Judaea, and in Samaria, and unto the uttermost part of the earth" (Acts 1:8). Instead of bringing the captivity back to Jerusalem, Christ, as head of the church, said to those who now have been born again and are in the body of believers, "Go to the ends of the earth. Take the message out that I am raised from the dead. Tell them that God is gracious and longsuffering and merciful, and that whosoever will call upon the name of the Lord will be saved."

The gospel seems so simple that a lot of smart people miss it today. How wonderful it is! All you do is believe. I want to say that I do not believe in a works salvation—that is obvious—but I do believe in a salvation that works. That is important to see. If you have been saved, you'll want to get the gospel out. If you don't want to, my friend, I'd question your faith—not your works, but your faith—because faith *works*.

**I will also gather all nations, and will bring them down into the valley of Jehoshaphat, and will plead with them there for my people and for my heritage Israel, whom they have scattered among the nations, and parted my land [Joel 3:2].**

"I will also gather all nations, and will bring them down into the valley of Jehoshaphat"—that is there at Jerusalem.

"And will plead with them there for my people and for my heritage Israel, whom they have scattered among the nations, and parted my land." Before the Lord Jesus comes again to the earth, believers will already have appeared before His judgment seat to see whether or not they are to receive a reward. When He comes to the earth, then He will judge to see who will enter the kingdom. We have this marvelous prophecy here, but it is not found only in the Book of Joel. Joel is the first of the writing prophets, but all of the prophets mentioned it. One of the last prophets, Zechariah, said the same thing, "Sing and rejoice, O daughter of Zion: for, lo, I come, and I will dwell in the midst of thee, saith the Lord. And many nations shall be joined to the Lord in that day, and shall be my people: and I will dwell in the midst of thee, and thou shalt know that the Lord of hosts hath sent me unto thee" (Zech. 2:10–11). This is the same thing Joel told the people at the beginning. This was their great hope, their bright hope, that the Lord will come to establish His kingdom on the earth and the Spirit will be poured out on all flesh.

**And they have cast lots for my people; and have given a boy for an harlot; and sold a girl for wine, that they might drink [Joel 3:3].**

This is an awful thing that Joel describes here. I get a little provoked sometimes with the Society for the Prevention of Cruelty to Animals which has come up with some unusual demands as to how we should treat animals. They are opposed to the foxhunt, although the fox generally gets away and they don't really need to worry about him at all; they also are opposed to all types of hunting and shooting of game. However, they haven't been down to the stockyards yet to stop the slaughter of cattle, because most of them like their porterhouse and sirloin steaks as well as their prime rib roast. But that is really not my point, because I agree that animals should not be mistreated and that they often suffer because of man's sin. The greatest cruelty today, however, is cruelty toward children. It is one of the most appalling things that is happening in our day. I read sometime ago of a mother who had co-habited with some no good, ne'erdo-well man who beat her little boy. A precious little boy—what a beautiful child he was at the beginning. But they also showed a picture of him near the end; he'd been beaten and mistreated and finally killed by that man! Actually, there was not much protest over that. The mistreatment of a dog has caused more furor in our communities than did the mistreatment of that child. Such cruelty toward children is one of the signs of the end of an age.

Why are so many children running away from home in this day? I think any parent who has a runaway child needs to get down on his knees before God and ask Him what he has done wrong. Someone will say, "Well, the child got in with the wrong crowd. We need the help of a psychologist." My friend, we don't need that—we need to read the Word of God. God says the evil day will come when "they have cast lots for my people; and have given a boy for an harlot." How many fathers today are setting the right example for their sons? "And sold a girl for wine, that they might drink." How many girls are being plunged into immorality because of liquor in their homes? One young girl, who had become a harlot and was arrested, was asked where she took her first drink. She said that it had been with her mother. God have mercy on a mother who would do a thing like that! Someone needs to speak out today in this so-called suave and sophisticated age that wants to think we are advancing in civilization. My friend, we are going down the tubes so fast it's making us dizzy.

**Yea, and what have ye to do with me, O Tyre, and Zidon, and all the coasts of Palestine? will ye render me a recompence? and if ye recompense me, swiftly and speedily will I return your recompence upon your own head [Joel 3:4].**

God says that they have gone past the time and are unable to turn to Him sincerely.

**Because ye have taken my silver and my gold, and have carried into your temples my goodly pleasant things:**

**The children also of Judah and the children of Jerusalem have ye sold unto the Grecians, that ye might remove them far from their border [Joel 3:5–6].**

Even at this time the children of Israel were being sold into slavery, yet this was before Rome had come to power.

**Behold, I will raise them out of the place whither ye have sold them, and will return your recompence upon your own head:**

**And I will sell your sons and your daughters into the hand of the children of Judah, and they shall sell them to the Sabeans, to a people far off: for the LORD hath spoken it [Joel 3:7–8].**

God's judgment of Tyre and Sidon, prophesied also by Ezekiel, Jeremiah, and Isaiah, has all been literally fulfilled.

**Proclaim ye this among the Gentiles; Prepare war, wake up the mighty men, let all the men of war draw near; let them come up:**

**Beat your plowshares into swords, and your pruninghooks into spears: let the weak say, I am strong [Joel 3:9–10].**

"Beat your plowshares into swords, and your pruninghooks into spears." Someone will say, "I thought the Bible said to beat your swords into plowshares." It does say that, but the time to do that is when the kingdom is established on the earth (see Isa. 2:4; Mic. 4:3). When Christ is ruling you can get rid of your sword, but until then you'd better keep your ammunition dry and you'd better be prepared. I do not agree that we should get rid of guns today. I think we need to protect our homes, our loved ones, and our nation. You and I are living in a big, bad world in which there are a lot of wild animals loose—they are human beings and they are two-legged, but they're mean and ferocious and they will destroy you. Also there are nations which are like that. In fact, that is the way God describes nations; He calls one a lion, another a bear, another a panther, and another a nondescript beast. Believe me, my friend, the nations of the world are like wild beasts, and we need to keep a few atomic bombs in our arsenal. Paul said, "For when they shall say, Peace and safety; then sudden destruction cometh upon them . . ." (1 Thess. 5:3). I am afraid we are going to have our teeth jarred out one of these days by the falling of a bomb, and we won't be able to retaliate because we have had too many soft-hearted and soft-headed leaders. The United Nations has as its motto the verse in Isaiah which says to beat your swords into plowshares; I think they ought to have *this* verse from Joel: "Beat your plowshares into swords." We need to be prepared today—we live in a bad, bad world.

**Assemble yourselves, and come, all ye heathen, and gather yourselves together round about: thither cause thy mighty ones to come down, O LORD.**

**Let the heathen be wakened, and come up to the valley of Jehoshaphat: for there will I sit to judge all the heathen round about [Joel 3:11–12].**

In the Olivet Discourse the Lord Jesus said that He will judge the nations and that He will judge them according to the way they have treated His people. Someone will ask, "Are they peculiar? Are they better?" No. Why, then, will He judge in this way? Because the 144,000 Jewish witnesses are going to be the only witnesses upon this earth after the church is removed. The Lord said that if anyone gave a cup of cold water in His name to one of these witnesses He would reward him. Many people think that that excuses them for giving only a dime or a quarter in the offering plate. However, may I say to you, in that day it would cost you your life to give a cup of cold water to one of the 144,000 who will be witnessing for Christ throughout the world.

**Put ye in the sickle, for the harvest is ripe: come, get you down; for the press is full, the vats overflow; for their wickedness is great [Joel 3:13].**

When he speaks of a "harvest," he is speaking of the end of the age.

**Multitudes, multitudes in the valley of decision: for the day of the LORD is near in the valley of decision [Joel 3:14].**

Joel identifies this period as "the day of the LORD." All that Joel says falls within the parentheses of the Day of the Lord which begins after the Rapture of the church with the Great Tribulation and continues through the second coming of Christ to establish His kingdom and the judgment as to who will enter the kingdom. Then Christ will reign for one thousand years; there will be a brief period of rebellion when Satan is let loose, then the final judgment at the Great White Throne, and eternity will begin. All of that is included in the Day of the Lord.

Again Joel speaks of the disturbance in the heavenly bodies—

**The sun and the moon shall be darkened, and the stars shall withdraw their shining.**

**The LORD also shall roar out of Zion, and utter his voice from Jerusalem; and the heavens and the earth shall shake: but the LORD will be the hope of his people, and the strength of the children of Israel.**

**So shall ye know that I am the LORD your God dwelling in Zion, my holy mountain: then shall Jerusalem be holy, and there shall no strangers pass through her any more [Joel 3:15–17].**

Jerualem is still being trodden down by Gentiles. The Garden Tomb was so crowded with tourists the last time we were there that we could not get into it. It was not Jews who were there, but it was Gentiles from all over the world—tourists coming and going all the time. The day is coming when the Garden Tomb will not be the tourist attraction in Jerusalem. Someday the Lord Himself will be there!

Now we move into the time of the kingdom—

**And it shall come to pass in that day, that the mountains shall drop down new wine, and the hills shall flow with milk, and all the rivers of Judah shall flow with waters, and a fountain shall come forth of the house of the LORD, and shall water the valley of Shittim [Joel 3:18].**

"And it shall come to pass in that day"—that is, the Day of the Lord. "The mountains shall drop down new wine"—this is in the time of the kingdom. "And the hills shall flow with milk, and all the rivers of Judah shall flow with waters." Israel is short of water today, but they will not be short in that day.

"And a fountain shall come forth of the house of the LORD, and shall water the valley of Shittim." This is interesting because the valley of Shittim is on the other side of the Jordan River. How could these waters flow from Jerusalem across the Jordan? Zechariah tells us that the mountain will be split in that day. Instead of the great rift running from north of Byblos in Lebanon, down through the Sea of Galilee, through the Jordan valley, through the Dead Sea and into Africa, it is going to run the opposite direction—it is going to run east and west.

**Egypt shall be a desolation, and Edom shall be a desolate wilderness, for the violence against the children of Judah, because they have shed innocent blood in their land [Joel 3:19].**

God will judge Egypt and Edom even into the millennial kingdom. They have always been enemies of the nation Israel.

**But Judah shall dwell for ever, and Jerusalem from generation to generation.**

**For I will cleanse their blood that I have not cleansed: for the LORD dwelleth in Zion [Joel 3:20–21].**

"For I will cleanse their blood that I have not cleansed"—the Lord has not yet moved in their behalf. "For the LORD dwelleth in Zion"—He doesn't dwell there today. Jerusalem is as pagan and heathen as any city on topside of the earth, but the day is coming when the Lord will dwell there. Then we will see all these things fulfilled. We would need to see Christ Himself there to say that these things are being fulfilled today. But that is not where we see Him, for at this very moment He is at God's right hand. It is my prayer that we might be continually conscious of Him and have the reality of His presence in our lives.

# BIBLIOGRAPHY

## (Recommended for Further Study)

Feinberg, Charles L. *The Minor Prophets.* Chicago, Illinois: Moody Press, 1976.

Gaebelein, Arno C. *The Annotated Bible.* 1917. Reprint. Neptune, New Jersey: Loizeaux Brothers, 1971.

Ironside, H. A. *The Minor Prophets.* Neptune, New Jersey: Loizeaux Brothers, n.d.

Jensen, Irving L. *Minor Prophets of Israel.* Chicago, Illinois: Moody Press, 1975.

Unger, Merrill F. *Unger's Commentary on the Old Testament,* Vol. 2. Chicago, Illinois: Moody Press, 1982.

# The Book of
# AMOS
## INTRODUCTION

Amos' prophetic ministry took place during the reigns of Jeroboam II, king of Israel, and Uzziah, king of Judah. He was contemporary with Jonah and Hosea who were prophets in the northern kingdom of Israel and with Isaiah and Micah who were prophets in the southern kingdom of Judah.

Amos presents God as the ruler of this world and declares that all nations are responsible to Him. The measure of a nation's responsibility is the light which a nation has. The final test for any nation (or individual) is found in Amos 3:3, "Can two walk together, except they be agreed?" In a day of prosperity, Amos pronounced punishment. The judgment of God awaited nations which were living in luxury and lolling in immorality.

Amos is, in my words, "The Country Preacher Who Came to Town." I want us to get acquainted with him personally, because to get acquainted with Amos is to love him and to understand his prophecy better. We will find that he was born in Judah, the southern kingdom, but he was a prophet to the northern kingdom. His message was delivered in Beth-el at the king's chapel. It was most unusual for a man to have come from such a country, out-of-the-way place with a message of judgment against all of the surrounding nations. Amos had a global view of life and of God's program for the entire world—not only for the present but also for the future. All this makes this man a most remarkable prophet.

In Amos 1:1 we read, "The words of Amos, who was among the herdmen of Tekoa, which he saw concerning Israel in the days of Uzziah king of Judah, and in the days of Jeroboam the son of Joash king of Israel, two years before the earthquake." Tekoa was Amos' birthplace and his hometown. Six miles south of Jerusalem there is the familiar little place of Bethlehem of which the prophet Micah said, "But thou, Beth-lehem Ephratah, though thou be little among the thousands of Judah, yet out of thee shall he come forth unto me that is to be ruler in Israel; whose goings forth have been from old, from everlasting" (Mic. 5:2). Bethlehem has become famous, but there was another little place that was another six miles southeast of Bethlehem called Tekoa which is not so well known. In fact, Amos himself is

not even mentioned anywhere else in the Old Testament. There is an Amos in Mary's genealogy given in the Gospel of Luke, but he is no relation to the prophet Amos. And the little town of Tekoa from which he came is practically an unknown place. It is the place where a prophetess came and gave David a message (see 2 Sam. 14); David was familiar with this area because it was the area to which he fled to hide from King Saul.

Tekoa is located on a hilly ridge which overlooks a frightful desert wilderness that continues down to the very edge of the Dead Sea. Wild animals howl by night, and by day the only thing you can see are spots here and there which indicate the remains of the camps of the Bedouins. There is nothing but the blackened ground left by these nomads and vagabonds of the desert who moved through that area. Dr. Adam Smith said, "The men of Tekoa looked out upon a desolate and haggard world."

Today the nation Israel has constructed a modern highway along the Dead Sea that leads to Masada. The highway comes back through Arad and up through Hebron and Bethlehem, but it never gets near Tekoa because Tekoa is over in that wilderness. I'm sure most of you have never heard of it for, even in its heyday, Tekoa was never more than a wide place in the road. It was a whistle-stop, a jumping-off place. The name *Tekoa* means "a camping ground." It was really only a country crossroads out on the frontier. Years ago I heard a man say that, to reach the place where he was born, you go as far as possible by buggy and then you get off and walk two miles! Tekoa was that sort of place, and it was the birthplace of Amos—that is its only claim to greatness.

We need to turn to chapter 7 to get a little personal insight into this man and his ministry in Samaria, the northern kingdom of Israel. There we read: "Then Amaziah the priest of Beth-el sent to Jeroboam king of Israel, saying, Amos hath conspired against thee in the midst of the house of Israel: the land is not able to bear all his words. For thus Amos saith, Jeroboam shall die by the sword, and Israel shall surely be led away captive out of their own land. Also Amaziah said unto Amos, O thou seer, go, flee thee away into the land of

Judah, and there eat bread, and prophesy there: But prophesy not again any more at Beth-el: for it is the king's chapel, and it is the king's court. Then answered Amos, and said to Amaziah, I was no prophet, neither was I a prophet's son; but I was an herdman, and a gatherer of sycomore fruit: And the LORD took me as I followed the flock, and the LORD said unto me, Go, prophesy unto my people Israel" (Amos 7:10–15).

Amos tells us he was a "herdman." An unusual word is used here which means that he was the herdsman of a peculiar breed of desert sheep. They were a scrub stock, but they grew long wool because of the cold in the wintertime. He also says that he was a "gatherer of sycomore fruit"; the literal is a "pincher of sycamores." This was a fruit like a small fig which grew on scrub trees down in the desert. These trees grew at a lower level than the sycamore that we know today.

We can see, then, that Amos had to travel to his job. He was a migrant worker, if you please. His sheep and his sycamores pushed Amos far out into that desert. He was truly a farmer. He was a country rube. He was a rustic. He was a yokel and a hayseed. He was a country preacher. He was a clumsy bumpkin who was "all thumbs" among the ecumenical preachers up yonder in Beth-el.

But before you laugh at Amos, may I say this? He was one of God's greatest men, and he was a remarkable individual. Listen to what Amos says: "And the LORD took me as I followed the flock, and the LORD said unto me, Go, prophesy unto my people Israel" (Amos 7:15). God sent Amos all the way from down there in the desert and the wilderness up to Beth-el, one of the capital cities of the northern kingdom where he found city folk living. God called him to preach, God gave him a message, and God sent him to Beth-el.

Beth-el was, at first, the capital of the northern kingdom, and it was the place where Jeroboam I had erected one of his golden calves. It was the center of culture and also of cults. The people worshiped that golden calf and had turned their backs upon almighty God. Beth-el was where the sophisticated and the suave folk moved; the jet set lived there. It was a place that was blasé and brazen. It was also the intellectual center. They had a School of Prophets there. The seminaries taught liberalism. They would have taught the Graf-Wellhausen hypothesis which denies the inspiration of the Pentateuch and gone in for all the latest theories of a theologian like Rudolf Bultmann.

What was done in Beth-el was the thing to do. When filter-tipped cigarettes were introduced, Beth-el was the first place they were advertised and used, and from there they spread everywhere. It was the place where you could see the styles which would be popular the next year. Are we going to wear the wider lapel next year? Will there be two or three buttons on the suit coat? Should you leave the last button unbuttoned to be in style? Well, you would go to Beth-el to find out all that.

Then here comes to town this country preacher, this prophet of God with a message—a most unusual message, different from any other prophet. Amos' suit of clothes was not cut to the style of Beth-el and neither was his message. He did not give the type of messages they were used to hearing. In the king's chapel there was always a mild-mannered preacher, very sophisticated and well educated, but a rank unbeliever who stood in the pulpit giving comforting little words to the people. He gave them pabulum; saccharine sweetness was in his message. But now here's a different kind of man. When Amos first arrived, people stared at him. But they were very indulgent, of course (they were broad-minded, you know), so they smiled at him. I think he had on high-buttoned yellow shoes which were not in style that year, and his suit probably didn't fit him and was buttoned improperly. He had on his first necktie, and it looked like it had been tied by a whirlwind. Everyone was embarrassed except Amos. Amos was not embarrassed at all. He must have created quite a stir. He had left the backwoods and had arrived on the boulevard. He had left the desert; now he entered the drawing room. He had been with the long-haired sheep out on the desert all of his life; now he was with the well-groomed "goats" up yonder in Beth-el. He had left the place of agriculture and had come to the place of culture.

I think almost everyone came to hear him at first. They said, "We don't believe he can preach." They came out of curiosity, saying, "We don't think this man has any message." They came in amusement, but they left in anger. He was a sensational preacher, for his sermons weren't cut to the style of Beth-el. However, today we do not have any record of the liberal sermons of that day, but we certainly have the sermons and the prophecy of Amos.

Amos preached the Word of God. Many people were moved, and some turned to God;

but he disturbed the liberal element. Organized religion in Beth-el, the worship of Baal and of the golden calf, got together. They had the ecumenical movement going there, so they had the same program. If you don't believe anything, my friend, there is nothing to keep you apart. If *I* don't believe anything and *you* don't believe anything, we can get together. That is the ecumenical movement, and it was going great guns even in that day.

Amos was in the midst of all this organized religion which was plotting against him to silence him and to run him out of town. Some of the leading ecumenical leaders called a meeting. They wanted to remove Amos; they wanted to withdraw support from him; they told him he'd lose his pension if he didn't change his message. There were also some fundamental leaders called evangelicals in Beth-el who began to criticize him because he was drawing the crowds. They tried to undermine his ministry. But God blessed him, and Amos would not compromise but continued to preach the Word of God.

They had a mass meeting of all the religions in Beth-el—it was really the first meeting of the World Council of Churches—and the motto of this first meeting was, "Away with Amos, away with Amos." And the inevitable happened at this meeting: they appointed a committee chairman, Amaziah, to go and confront Amos. Amaziah was a priest who had gone into idolatry. (Does all of this sound modern to you? It's the same old story; we think it's modern, but this sort of thing has been happening ever since man got out of the Garden of Eden.) Amaziah was the hired hand of religion. He was polished, he was educated, he was proud, he was scholarly, he was pious, and he was a classic example of a pseudosaint.

Cleverly and subtly, Amaziah worked a master stroke. He went to Jeroboam II and poisoned his mind against Amos. Amaziah got the king to support him because he believed that the church and state, religion and politics, should be combined. This is what happened: "Then Amaziah the priest of Beth-el sent to Jeroboam king of Israel, saying, Amos hath conspired against thee in the midst of the house of Israel: the land is not able to bear all his words. For thus Amos saith, Jeroboam shall die by the sword, and Israel shall surely be led away captive out of their own land" (Amos 7:10–11). Let me ask you, friend, is that what Amos said? No, he had not said that. His actual words were that God had said, "I will rise against the house of Jeroboam with the sword" (Amos 7:9). If you fol-

low the record, you will find that Amos' pronouncement was accurate. It is too bad that Jeroboam II did not believe Amos because his grandson was later slain with the sword, thus ending his kingly line. It was true that Amos had said something about the sword and about Jeroboam, but he had not said that Jeroboam personally would die by the sword. Amaziah was an ecclesiastical politican who was twisting the truth, and that is the worst kind of lying.

I think Amaziah had two other men on his committee when he went to see Amos. There was Dr. Sounding Brass, president of the School of Prophets—*false* prophets, by the way. Proud and pompous, he was a politician par excellence. There was also Rev. Tinkling Cymbal. He was the pastor of the wealthiest and most influential church in town. He was the yes-man to the rich. He couldn't preach, but he was a great little mixer. It is amazing the things he could mix, by the way. He didn't pound the pulpit because he didn't want to wake up his congregation, but he could sure slap their backs during the week. This is the committee which waited upon Amos.

Amaziah, with biting sarcasm, with a rapier of ridicule, and with a condescending manner, said to Amos, "O thou seer." In other words, he's calling him, "Parson." "Also Amaziah said unto Amos, O thou seer, go, flee thee away into the land of Judah, and there eat bread, and prophesy there" (Amos 7:12). In effect, Amaziah said to Amos, "Who told you that you were a preacher? Where is your degree? What school did you go to? Who ordained you? Where did you preach before you came here? Go, flee away." In other words, he's saying to him, "Get out of town. Get lost." Then Amaziah adds, "And there eat bread." He is insinuating to Amos, "You're just in it for the money, and therefore we don't want you here."

Verse 13 is the crowning insult of all: "But prophesy not again any more at Beth-el: for it is the king's chapel, and it is the king's court" (Amos 7:13). That is the height of Amaziah's insolence and his arrogance. He uses here a satire that is not only biting but also poisonous. He says in effect, "Remember, you've been speaking in the leading church here in Beth-el, the king's chapel. You have been in the king's sanctuary, and he's dissatisfied with you. Your message disturbs him. In fact, there are a lot of people who do not like you. You don't use a very diplomatic method. You don't pat them on the back and tell them how wonderful they are. You do not patronize the rich and the affluent. And you're not very reverent. You tell funny stories every now and then. You're not dignified. You pound the pulpit, and you lack graceful gestures. You do not use a basso profundo voice as if you were thundering out of heaven. What you need is a course in homiletics. And you don't seem to have read the latest books. By the way, *have* you read the latest, *Baal Goes to Yale?*" And, of course, poor Amos hadn't read the latest book.

I want you to listen to the answer that this great prophet of God gave, this man who preached the righteousness of God and the judgment of God. There are those who like to call him a hell-fire prophet, but will you listen to his answer and notice how gracious it really is: "Then answered Amos, and said to Amaziah, I was no prophet, neither was I a prophet's son; but I was an herdman, and a gatherer of sycomore fruit: And the LORD took me as I followed the flock, and the LORD said unto me, Go, prophesy unto my people Israel" (Amos 7:14–15). And then Amos continued with his message in which he has some pretty harsh words to say to this man Amaziah.

Now I ask you a fair question: Does his answer sound like that of a fanatic? Frankly, I have one criticism of Amos. He is too naive. He's rather artless; he's rather simple. Down in the desert of Tekoa, he knew his way around. He could avoid the dangers in that howling wilderness which was filled with wild beasts, but, in the asphalt jungle of Beth-el, he was rather helpless.

By the way, there is a jungle today in this world. You will find that in church circles—in liberal churches and even in fundamental churches—it's a little dangerous. You're not really safe because there is often someone who will want to tear you to pieces. There will be the roar of some big lion, such as Mr. Gotrocks who is on the board of deacons. I tell you, you had better pat him on the back, you had better play up to him, or else he may give you real trouble. There is also the hiss of a serpent in the asphalt jungle today, Mrs. Joe Doaks who has a poison tongue. James, in his epistle, talked about those who have poison under their lips (see James 3:8). It is worse than a rattlesnake bite to have some of these folk criticize you.

This man Amos is very naive. He says,

"You say that I'm no preacher. I know it—I'm no preacher. And you say I'm not a prophet. You're right, I'm no prophet. I'm not even a prophet's son. I'm a country boy, *but God called me.*" Listen to him: "And *the* LORD took me as I followed the flock, and *the* LORD said unto me, Go, prophesy unto my people Israel" (Amos 7:15, italics mine). Amos says, "You want my credentials? Here they are: God called me."

May I say to you, if you give out the Word of God today, you are going to be challenged. I recently received a letter from a man in Salt Lake City, Utah, which presents a very devious argument. He concludes by saying, "I am interested in knowing how you got your authority." I can answer that very easily. When I was in my teens, *God called me,* and I knew He called me. Maybe you think that was because I had great faith. No, as a poor boy, I didn't even have enough faith to believe that the Lord would get me through school. I'll be very frank with you, I had no faith at all. I just had a tremendous and overweening desire to continue. Now since I'm toward the end of the journey, I have no doubt that I was called of God—and *that* is my authority. Amos was naive, but he was called of God, and the Lord was leading him all the way.

Amos was God's man giving God's message. Simply because Israel was being religious on the surface did not guarantee that God would not judge their sin. Because of their rejection of His law—their deceit and robbery and violence and oppression of the poor—God said, "I hate, I despise your feast days. . . . Though ye offer me burnt offerings and your meat offerings, I will not accept them. . . . Take thou away from me the noise of thy songs. . . . But let judgment run down as waters, and righteousness as a mighty stream" (Amos 5:21–24).

It was a day of false peace. In the north was Assyria hanging like the sword of Damocles ready to fall, and in the next half century it would destroy this little kingdom. Israel was trying to ignore it, and they kept talking about peace. But Amos said, "Behold, the eyes of the Lord GOD are upon the sinful kingdom, and I will destroy it from off the face of the earth" (Amos 9:8). His message was not a popular message. He warned that it was God's intention to punish sin.

# OUTLINE

**I. Judgment on Surrounding Nations, Chapters 1:1–2:3**
- A. Introduction, Chapter 1:1–2
- B. Judgment against Syria for Cruelty, Chapter 1:3–5
- C. Judgment against Philistia for Making Slaves, Chapter 1:6–8
- D. Judgment against Phoenicia for Breaking Treaty, Chapter 1:9–10
- E. Judgment against Edom for Revengeful Spirit, Chapter 1:11–12
- F. Judgment against Ammon for Violent Crimes, Chapter 1:13–15
- G. Judgment against Moab for Injustice, Chapter 2:1–3

**II. Judgment on Judah and Israel, Chapters 2:4–6:14**
- A. Judgment against Judah for Despising the Law, Chapter 2:4–5
- B. Judgment against Israel for Immorality and Blasphemy, Chapter 2:6–16
- C. God's Charge against the Whole House of Israel (Twelve Tribes), Chapter 3 *(Privilege creates responsibility; the higher the blessing, the greater the punishment.)*
- D. Israel Punished in the Past for Iniquity, Chapter 4
- E. Israel Will Be Punished in the Future for Iniquity, Chapter 5
- F. Israel Admonished in the Present to Depart from Iniquity, Chapter 6

**III. Visions of Future, Chapters 7–9**
- A. Visions of Grasshoppers, Chapter 7:1–3
- B. Vision of Fire, Chapter 7:4–6
- C. Vision of Plumbline, Chapter 7:7–9
- D. Historic Interlude, Chapter 7:10–17 *(Personal Experience of the Prophet)*
- E. Vision of Basket of Summer Fruit, Chapter 8
- F. Vision of Worldwide Dispersion, Chapter 9:1–10
- G. Vision of Worldwide Regathering and Restoration of Kingdom, Chapter 9:11–15

Amos was a fearless man with a message from God. Not only was Amos an unknown when he arrived in Beth-el of the northern kingdom of Israel, but he is still rather unknown today. In our country, Amos is a name that is associated with Andy because of the popular radio program of the past generation, "Amos and Andy." Actually, we should associate the Amos of Bible times with Hosea. They were contemporary prophets, and I am sure they knew each other. Hosea's message emphasized the love of God, but a God of love who also intends to judge. Amos spoke of the lofty justice and the inflexible righteousness of God which leads Him to judge.

It is startling to see that Amos had a world view, a global conception. He spoke first to the nations which were contiguous to and surrounding the nation Israel. He spoke to the great world powers of that day—that in itself isn't something unique. The later prophets—Isaiah, Jeremiah, Ezekiel, and Daniel—did it also. But the method of these other prophets was first to speak of God's judgment of the nation Israel and then to take up the judgment of the other nations. Amos reverses that method. He spoke first of God's judgment of the nations round about and then of Israel's judgment.

When Amos first spoke in Beth-el, saying that God was going to judge Syria, Philistia, Phoenicia, Edom, Ammon, and Moab, everybody filled the king's chapel. He really was drawing a crowd. They were very glad for him to preach on the sins of the Moabites, you see, but not on *their* sins. There are people even today who like the preacher to preach on the sins of the Moabites which were committed four thousand or more years ago, but any preacher who mentions the people's own sins is in real trouble. Amos exercised a great deal of diplomacy, it seems to me, in speaking of the other nations first. He was an eloquent man. Although he was a country preacher from out yonder in the desert, he used the language of a Shakespeare. He was, in my judgment, a great preacher.

**The words of Amos, who was among the herdmen of Tekoa, which he saw concerning Israel in the days of Uzziah king of Judah, and in the days of Jeroboam the son of Joash king of Israel, two years before the earthquake [Amos 1:1].**

"In the days of Jeroboam the son of Joash king of Israel"—this is Jeroboam II, by the way.

"Two years before the earthquake." This earthquake is also mentioned by Zechariah nearly two hundred years later. According to the historian Josephus, it took place during the reign of Uzziah. The important thing is that this does help us to see that Amos was contemporary with Hosea, he was one of the first of the prophets, and he was a prophet to the northern kingdom of Israel.

**And he said, The LORD will roar from Zion, and utter his voice from Jerusalem; and the habitations of the shepherds shall mourn, and the top of Carmel shall wither [Amos 1:2].**

"And he said, The LORD will roar from Zion." This is very figurative and eloquent language in many ways. You may recall that Joel also used this expression. It suggests the roar of a lion as it pounces upon its prey. Believe me, this is an arresting way for Amos to begin his message! It speaks of the coming judgment of God upon the nations which were round about.

"And the habitations of the shepherds shall mourn, and the top of Carmel shall wither." Apparently, a drought and a famine would come upon that land, a famine that would extend throughout the entire land.

When I was in Israel some time ago, I came over Carmel where Haifa is located, and I noticed how beautiful it is there. There are wonderful shrubbery and lovely flowers there today. It must have been that way in the day of Amos also, but now he says that there is coming a drought so severe that beautiful Carmel "shall wither."

## JUDGMENT AGAINST SYRIA FOR CRUELTY

We begin now a section of this prophecy which deals with the judgments of God upon the nations which were contiguous to the nation Israel, that is, those that surrounded that nation. This man Amos gives us a world view. The Word of God, even the Old Testament, shows that God is not only the God of the nation Israel but He is also the God of the Gentiles. In the New Testament, Paul is the one who makes that abundantly clear. And God *judges* the nations. Although in this day of grace God has one great purpose, that of calling out a people to His name, that does not mean that He has taken His hands off the affairs of this world—He has not. He still moves in judgment upon the nations of the world, and this Book of Amos has a tremendous message along that line.

The first nation that is considered is Syria of which Damascus was the capital—

**Thus saith the LORD; For three transgressions of Damascus, and for four, I will not turn away the punishment thereof; because they have threshed Gilead with threshing instruments of iron [Amos 1:3].**

"For three transgressions of Damascus, and for four." Amos is not attempting to give us a list of their transgressions. He could have said, "Not for three, not for four, or five, or six, but for many transgressions." In other words, the cup of iniquity was filled up, and nothing could now hold back the judgment of God that was coming upon Syria.

"Because they have threshed Gilead with threshing instruments of iron." This is the atrocity which Syria had committed and for which they were to be judged. Those threshing instruments were sharp and were to be used to beat out the grain. It is believed that with them they had torn and mangled the bodies of the people of Gilead. In 2 Kings 10:32–33, we read: "In those days the LORD began to cut Israel short: and Hazael smote them in all the coasts of Israel; From Jordan eastward, all the land of Gilead, the Gadites, and the Reubenites, and the Manassites, from Aroer, which is by the river Arnon, even Gilead and Bashan." Syria came down against these tribes first and actually destroyed them.

What does Amos mean by "Gilead"? Gilead was on the east bank of the Jordan River. It was the land which came up as far as the Sea of Galilee where the tribes of Reuben and Gad and the half tribe of Manasseh remained on the wrong side of the Jordan. Syria is located right to the north and came down against them. Even as I am writing this there is constantly a dogfight going on in the air between Syria and Israel around the Golan Heights which would correspond to the ancient land of Gilead. In that day, Syria had come down against God's people and simply threshed them, and He says He is going to judge them for their cruelty and for their brutality.

**But I will send a fire into the house of Hazael, which shall devour the palaces of Ben-hadad.**

**I will break also the bar of Damascus, and cut off the inhabitant from the plain of Aven, and him that holdeth the sceptre from the house of Eden: and the people of Syria shall go into captivity unto Kir, saith the LORD [Amos 1:4–5].**

A fire is to come upon Hazael, the king, and upon the palaces of Ben-hadad. If you have ever been to Damascus, you know that you do not see there the original city or its original location. It claims to be the oldest city in the world, but it has actually shifted around in the area to several different locations. It has burned to the very ground a number of times, and this is one of the occasions when that took place.

"And cut off the inhabitant from the plain of Aven." If you travel from Beirut to Damascus, you go by a place known as Baalbek, and Baalbek is in the plain of Aven. The ruins there are spectacular. The Romans attempted to colonize it because it was such a lovely area. The temple ruins there testify to that. But Baalbek has been destroyed, and the great population is no longer in that area.

"And the people of Syria shall go into captivity unto Kir" means that they were to be taken captive by the Assyrians. Kir was a province in the Assyrian empire. It is good to have a knowledge of the geography of this area as it makes all of this more understandable. You must remember that when you are reading the Bible, you are not reading about the never-never land and you are not reading about some place in outer space. It deals with reality; even when the Bible talks about heaven, it is talking about that which is real.

### JUDGMENT AGAINST PHILISTIA FOR MAKING SLAVES

**Thus saith the LORD; For three transgressions of Gaza, and for four, I will not turn away the punishment thereof; because they carried away captive the whole captivity, to deliver them up to Edom:**

**But I will send a fire on the wall of Gaza, which shall devour the palaces thereof:**

**And I will cut off the inhabitant from Ashdod, and him that holdeth the sceptre from Ashkelon, and I will turn mine**

hand against Ekron: and the remnant of the Philistines shall perish, saith the Lord God [Amos 1:6–8].

"**F**or three transgressions of Gaza, and for four." As we said before, this is an idiomatic expression which means that there could be listed here quite a few transgressions. The cup of iniquity had been filled up.

"Gaza" was in Philistia, or the Philistine empire.

The judgment against the Philistines was for making slaves. They took a certain number of Israelites, and they sold them into slavery to Edom and also to Phoenicia. The Phoenicians were great traders, and they in turn sold them as prisoners of war into slavery. They would send them all over the Mediterranean world. Because of this, God says that He intends to judge Philistia.

It is quite interesting that as I am writing this the territory we know as the Gaza Strip is still an unknown quantity; that is, it is an Arab area which is now under the control of Israel. Israel is having a real problem with that territory, as you know. However, "Ashdod" and "Ashkelon" are still in Israel. Today you will find that in Ashdod there is a great refinery, and a new harbor has been constructed there. It will probably become a more important shipping place than even Haifa has become. I think it is probably better located than Haifa. Ashkelon is directly south of Ashdod. There you can still see the remains of the temple of Dagon where Samson was (see Jud. 16). All of these are very real places.

The judgment of God came upon these places exactly as God said it would. He said, "I will send a fire on the wall of Gaza, which shall devour the palaces thereof." In the historical record of the reign of Hezekiah, we read: "He [Hezekiah] smote the Philistines, even unto Gaza, and the borders thereof, from the tower of the watchmen to the fenced city" (2 Kings 18:8). The record goes on to say how Hezekiah destroyed all that particular area. Amos' prophecy, you see, was *literally* fulfilled. This example of fulfilled prophecy makes this section particularly interesting. It also puts down a pattern for the way in which God will fulfill prophecy in the future.

## JUDGMENT AGAINST PHOENICIA FOR BREAKING TREATY

**W**e come now to the judgment against Phoenicia. The judgment against them is not only for selling slaves—the Philistines sold slaves to Phoenicia, and Phoenicia in turn sold them out in the world—but the judgment is for breaking their treaty with Israel. Hiram, king of Tyre, had been a personal friend of David, and they had enjoyed many years of friendship. No king of Israel or Judah had ever made war upon Phoenicia. Now Phoenicia had broken the treaty.

**Thus saith the LORD; For three transgressions of Tyrus, and for four, I will not turn away the punishment thereof; because they delivered up the whole captivity to Edom, and remembered not the brotherly covenant [Amos 1:9].**

"Thus saith the LORD; For three transgressions of Tyrus, and for four." He is not just giving them *ad seriatim*. He says, "I will not give one, two, three, four, five, six, seven, eight, nine, ten reasons." He could have listed probably a hundred, but he will mention the main ones.

"I will not turn away the punishment thereof; because they delivered up the whole captivity to Edom, and remembered not the brotherly covenant." In other words, they had broken a covenant that they had with Israel.

**But I will send a fire on the wall of Tyrus, which shall devour the palaces thereof [Amos 1:10].**

First the Assyrian came against Tyre, and he was not able to take the city. Then there has been some question whether the Chaldeans under Nebuchadnezzar took the city or not. However, it is conceded that Nebuchadnezzar forced the Tyrians (Tyre was the great city of the Phoenicians) to retire to an island that was out to sea about one-half mile. The Tyrians built their city there, and Nebuchadnezzar destroyed the old city that was on the mainland. About 250 years later, Alexander the Great came along. He saw that very prosperous, very wealthy city out on the island, and he built a causeway out to it. In doing so, he fulfilled Ezekiel's prophecy in which God said that they would absolutely scrape the ground of old Tyre and throw it into the ocean (see Ezek. 26). Alexander made a causeway out to the island; he took it and destroyed it, bringing Tyre to an end. Amos' prophecy concerning Tyre was literally fulfilled.

## JUDGMENT AGAINST EDOM FOR REVENGEFUL SPIRIT

**T**he judgment against Edom is because of their revengeful spirit. Back of revenge one ordinarily finds jealousy. The Edomites were jealous of their brothers. You see, Edom came from Esau, and Israel from Jacob; Jacob and Esau were twin brothers, the sons of Isaac.

> Thus saith the LORD; For three transgressions of Edom, and for four, I will not turn away the punishment thereof; because he did pursue his brother with the sword, and did cast off all pity, and his anger did tear perpetually, and he kept his wrath for ever:

> But I will send a fire upon Teman, which shall devour the palaces of Bozrah [Amos 1:11–12].

In the rock-hewn city of Petra, the capital of Edom, which is located in Teman, everything was destroyed that would burn. The palaces of Bozrah have been destroyed and have disappeared. This prophecy against Edom has been literally fulfilled. Judgment came upon them because of their revengeful spirit, because they were jealous of their brother, Israel.

## JUDGMENT AGAINST AMMON FOR VIOLENT CRIMES

We come now to Ammon, the nation of the Ammonites. If you will notice, geographically, we are moving around almost in a circle. We began with Syria, came over to Phoenicia, down to Philistia, then over to Edom on the south, and now to Ammon.

What was the cause of God's judgment against the Ammonites? Theirs was a violent crime—

> Thus saith the LORD; For three transgressions of the children of Ammon, and for four, I will not turn away the punishment thereof; because they have ripped up the women with child of Gilead, that they might enlarge their border [Amos 1:13].

The Ammonites were located over on the east bank of the Jordan, and they joined with the Syrians in fighting against the two and one-half tribes of Israel which were in the land of Gilead. They did it "that they might enlarge their border."

> But I will kindle a fire in the wall of Rabbah, and it shall devour the palaces thereof, with shouting in the day of battle, with a tempest in the day of the whirlwind:

> And their king shall go into captivity, he and his princes together, saith the LORD [Amos 1:14–15].

"But I will kindle a fire in the wall of Rabbah, and it shall devour the palaces thereof." This is God's judgment against the Ammonites. Rabbah was a great city and the capital city of the Ammonites. Later on it was called Philadelphia by the Greeks. It was named after Ptolemy Philadelphus of Egypt. We know it today as Amman, the capital of the nation of Jordan. You can see ruins there of the great civilization of the past which was totally destroyed. Modern Jordan has been built upon the ruins of the nation of the Ammonites.

We can turn to 2 Kings 8 to see the sin that had prompted God's judgment against them. "And Hazael said [to Elisha], Why weepeth my lord? And he answered, Because I know the evil that thou wilt do unto the children of Israel: their strong holds wilt thou set on fire, and their young men wilt thou slay with the sword, and wilt dash their children, and rip up their women with child. And Hazael said, But what, is thy servant a dog, that he should do this great thing? And Elisha answered, The LORD hath shewed me that thou shalt be king over Syria" (2 Kings 8:12–13). In other words, Elisha said to Hazael, "You say that only a dog would do such a thing, but you are going to do it." Whether Hazael was a dog or not, he did the very thing he said only a dog would do. We read in these verses of the violent things he would do to the children of Israel. He was going to dash their children and rip up their women with child. It was a horrible, awful thing, and it was for this crime that God would judge the Ammonites.

**Thus saith the LORD; For three transgressions of Moab, and for four, I will not turn away the punishment thereof; because he burned the bones of the king of Edom into lime [Amos 2:1].**

I consider this man Amos to be a great preacher. The mold was broken after he was made—there is only one of him. He uses unusual expressions. "For three transgressions of Moab, and for four"—that is his way of saying that there were many transgressions; but, as usual, he will mention only one specifically.

## JUDGMENT AGAINST MOAB FOR INJUSTICE

"I will not turn away the punishment thereof; because he burned the bones of the king of Edom into lime." The judgment against Moab is for an awful spirit of revenge. The Moabites had gained a victory in battle over their enemies, the Edomites, and had killed their king. You would think that that would be enough, but they even burned the bones of the king of Edom into lime. The Moabites carried their revengeful spirit to the nth degree, and God says here that He will judge them for that.

**But I will send a fire upon Moab, and it shall devour the palaces of Kirioth: and Moab shall die with tumult, with shouting, and with the sound of the trumpet:**

**And I will cut off the judge from the midst thereof, and will slay all the princes thereof with him, saith the LORD [Amos 2:2–3].**

"Moab shall die with tumult"—that is, they will go out with a real bang, and the nation will be ended. This proud nation was brought to extinction later on at the hands of Nebuchadnezzar, and you haven't seen a Moabite since then.

But isn't it interesting that, many years before, out of this heathen country had come that gentle, lovely, and beautiful girl by the name of Ruth who became the wife of Boaz? Her story is recorded in one of the loveliest books in the Bible. Ruth is in the genealogical line which leads to Jesus Christ. And she had come from Moab, of all places. They were really a heathen, pagan people with a sad and sorry beginning and just as sad and tragic an end as a nation. But Ruth's story reveals what the grace of God *can* do in the life of a believer if the believer will let Him do it.

## JUDGMENT AGAINST JUDAH FOR DESPISING THE LAW

Now Amos turns to the nation Israel in a reverse of the method which the other prophets used later on. They would always mention God's judgment of Israel and then the judgment of the other nations which surrounded them. However, Amos has taken up these other nations first before he turns to Israel against whom the judgment of God will be greater. The reason for their greater judgment is quite obvious: Privilege *always* creates responsibility. The more light that you have, the more responsible you are to God. I believe that you and I are more responsible to God than people who are denied Bibles and who are not hearing the Word of God at all. We are more responsible than they are. We often like to sit in judgment of these other nations round about us, but have you ever stopped to think of the tremendous responsibility that you and I have because of the privilege of having the Word of God? We boast of the fact that we have the Bible, but the important thing is our own personal obedience to the Word of God and whether or not we are doing anything to help get it out to others.

As Amos turns from the surrounding nations, he takes up the sins of God's people. He begins with Judah, the southern kingdom, from which he himself had come.

**Thus saith the LORD; For three transgressions of Judah, and for four, I will not turn away the punishment thereof; because they have despised the law of the LORD, and have not kept his commandments, and their lies caused them to err, after the which their fathers have walked [Amos 2:4].**

"Thus saith the LORD; For three transgressions of Judah, and for four, I will not turn away the punishment thereof." God could enumerate many transgressions of which they were guilty, but here is the key one.

"Because they have despised the law of the LORD, and have not kept his commandments, and their lies caused them to err, after the which their fathers have walked." This is saying in a very brief way what the prophets Isaiah and Jeremiah and Ezekiel took quite a few pages to say; that is, that God would judge the southern kingdom. For what would He judge them? They did not keep the commandments of God; they despised God's law. Judah had the law of God and despised it. They even had the temple which was in Jerusalem. Therefore, God now judged them according to the Law.

Have you noticed that God did not judge any of these other nations on that basis whatsoever? He judged them for certain specific sins which are common to the natural man. Because these other nations did not have God's law, they were not judged according to God's law.

> **But I will send a fire upon Judah, and it shall devour the palaces of Jerusalem [Amos 2:5].**

Again and again, Amos mentions, as do the other prophets, that there is to be a judgment by fire. When Nebuchadnezzar came against the city, he absolutely burned Jerusalem to the ground. There was nothing left but the stones—of which there is an abundance in that particular area.

## JUDGMENT AGAINST ISRAEL FOR IMMORALITY AND BLASPHEMY

Remember that Amos is delivering these messages in Beth-el of the northern kingdom. He is speaking in the king's chapel. I think that every time he got up to speak, he would take as his subject one of these nations, and he would pronounce God's judgment upon it. Now he has even talked about Judah, and that's getting pretty close to home. It may be that a few people squirmed in their pews when he mentioned Judah. However, the ten northern tribes and the two southern tribes were at war with one another a great deal of the time. There were several occasions when they made alliances, but that was only because of fear and of the necessity to stand together against a common enemy. Most of the time they were enemies. Therefore, when Amos gave his message of judgment against the southern kingdom, everyone was present and "amened" him. They agreed that God should judge Jerusalem and Judah. But what about the northern kingdom? Beginning with verse 6, he will speak to the northern kingdom. Beth-el is the city where the king worshiped, and this man was speaking in the king's chapel. Amos is getting closer to home. He's going to start meddling.

The story is told of the preacher who one Sunday morning was preaching against various sins. He preached about the sin of drunkenness, and a woman sitting in the congregation loudly "amened" him. He preached against the sin of smoking, and she "amened" him for that. Then when he started preaching against the sin of chewing tobacco, she shifted her wad to the other cheek and grumbled, "Now he's quit preachin' and has gone to meddlin'!"

Amos is starting to meddle now. He is going to talk about the sin of the congregation which was before him. No longer will his message be about the sins of the "Moabites" but the sins of the northern kingdom. They, too, had God's law, and they were schooled in the commandments of God. Listen to Amos as he speaks—

> **Thus saith the LORD; For three transgressions of Israel, and for four, I will not turn away the punishment thereof; because they sold the righteous for silver, and the poor for a pair of shoes [Amos 2:6].**

"Thus saith the LORD." May I say to you, I personally have never felt that I have any right to stand in the pulpit and speak unless I can speak on the basis of "Thus saith the LORD." What the Word of God has to say should be the basis of all pulpit ministry.

"For three transgressions of Israel, and for four, I will not turn away the punishment thereof." There are more transgressions than that, and Amos will mention more than that. He is going to deal with the Mosaic Law. He will not deal with the Ten Commandments as he did with Judah, but with the Mosaic Law which had to do with man's everyday life.

"Because they sold the righteous for silver, and the poor for a pair of shoes." The ten tribes in the north had the Mosaic Law, but they were committing the same sins as the nations that were round about them. The fact of the matter is that the very people whom God had put out of that land were guilty of the same sins that Israel was now committing.

First of all, we have here the mistreatment of the poor. You will find that Amos has a great deal to say about the poor. In Amos 4:1 we read, "Hear this word, ye kine of Bashan, that are in the mountain of Samaria, which oppress the poor, which crush the needy, which say to their masters, Bring, and let us drink." Listen again to Amos: "Forasmuch therefore as your treading is upon the poor . . ." (Amos 5:11).

In studying the prophets, I see again and again that the poor are not going to get justice, nor will they be treated fairly upon this earth until Jesus Christ reigns. The only hope of the poor is in the Lord Jesus Christ. We are told today that certain political parties will take care of the poor. Well, they've been taking care of us all right! Every time another politician wants my vote, he tells me how much he's going to help me. I vote for him and then my taxes go up, and they keep going up and up and up. I will be very frank with you, I find that most of these politicians are rich men. They are millionaires, and they don't know my problem. They do not understand the poor. I am thankful there is one, the Lord Jesus Christ, who is someday going to bring justice to the poor.

God will judge a nation for its mistreatment of the poor. He gave a number of laws regarding this, but I will mention just one: "Thou shalt not wrest judgment; thou shalt not respect persons, neither take a gift: for a gift doth blind the eyes of the wise, and pervert the words of the righteous" (Deut. 16:19). God put down this law to protect the poor. In that day a man might be absolutely innocent, but his adversary could slip a bribe under the table to the judge and thus receive a favorable verdict for himself. By the way, that practice doesn't seem to be out of style today. Other styles change, but this one has not. It is difficult for the poor to receive justice today when money seems to be the determining factor. Amos was speaking to a very pertinent problem of his day when even a pair of shoes would pervert judgment and cause the poor to suffer.

**That pant after the dust of the earth on the head of the poor, and turn aside the way of the meek: and a man and his father will go in unto the same maid, to profane my holy name [Amos 2:7].**

"That pant after the dust of the earth on the head of the poor." This could mean several things, but I personally think it means that these selfish, greedy, rich judges even resented that the poor had enough dust left to throw upon their heads in mourning. Believe me, that is the covetousness, the modern idolatry, of our day. God judges nations for that.

"And turn aside the way of the meek." Justice was being turned aside in disfavor to the meek. Why? Because the meek did not speak out. The old saying is true: "It's the squeaky wheel that gets the grease." The meek are not inheriting the earth today. It is inherited by those who are forward and are grabbing for all they can get. The poor and the meek were not receiving justice in Israel, nor are they receiving justice anywhere in the world today.

"And a man and his father will go in unto the same maid, to profane my holy name." Apparently, Amos is talking about a maid who is a prostitute. Both the father and the son went in to her. God says that adultery profanes His holy name. May I say to you, what we call "the new morality" isn't new at all. Israel was practicing the new morality, but God said He hated it. They were breaking the laws which He had put down concerning these things.

You can see that Amos is not going to be popular. He took the side of the poor, and he condemned unrighteousness. He condemned injustice. He condemned the fact that the poor were getting a bad deal, and he condemned immorality.

**And they lay themselves down upon clothes laid to pledge by every altar, and they drink the wine of the condemned in the house of their god [Amos 2:8].**

"And they lay themselves down upon clothes laid to pledge by every altar." God had a very lovely law concerning this: "And if the man be poor, thou shalt not sleep with his pledge: In any case thou shalt deliver him the pledge again when the sun goeth down, that he may sleep in his own raiment, and bless thee: and it shall be righteousness unto thee before the LORD thy God" (Deut. 24:12–13). A very poor man would have nothing to put up as collateral for a small loan except his outer garment, and that is what he needed to keep himself warm. God said, "You can take it as a pledge, but when the sun goes down, let him have it back in order that he might not be cold in sleeping that night." Now God points out that Israel had broken this law and was not obeying Him at this point either.

We talk about how just our own laws are today, but how sad it is that we will permit an entire family to be moved from their home when they cannot pay the rent because of poverty. My friend, the Word of God has a great deal to say in behalf of the poor.

"By every altar." God had given Israel only one altar, and that was in the temple in Jerusalem. This reveals that they had gone into idolatry and had a multitude of altars.

"And they drink the wine of the condemned in the house of their god." He condemns their drunkenness.

**Yet destroyed I the Amorite before them, whose height was like the height of the cedars, and he was strong as the oaks; yet I destroyed his fruit from above, and his roots from beneath [Amos 2:9].**

Notice the expressive and figurative language of this country preacher who had come up from Tekoa in the desert in Judah. Through Amos, God says of the Amorite, "He was tall like the cedar. He was strong like the oaks, but I destroyed him. I destroyed the fruit above, and I destroyed the roots from beneath." God got rid of the Amorites. We read in Joshua 24:8, "And I brought you into the land of the Amorites, which dwelt on the other side Jordan; and they fought with you: and I gave them into your hand, that ye might possess their land; and I destroyed them from before you." We have already said that there are no Moabites around today, and I wonder when the last time was that you saw an Amorite.

God had said to Abraham way back yonder, "I cannot put you in the land right now because the Amorite is in the land, and his iniquity is not yet full. I am going to give him an opportunity to turn to Me, to turn from these gross sins that he is committing." You may want to say to me, "Dr. McGee, after all, these heathen nations didn't have the Mosaic Law, and they didn't know any better." Paul makes a very interesting statement in his Epistle to the Romans: "For as many as have sinned without law shall also perish without law: and as many as have sinned in the law shall be judged by the law; (For not the hearers of the law are just before God, but the doers of the law shall be justified. For when the Gentiles, which have not the law, do by nature the things contained in the law, these, having not the law, are a law unto themselves" (Rom. 2:12–14). Why would Gentiles who do not have the Mosaic Law refrain from murder? Why would they refrain from lying? Why would they refrain from stealing? Paul continues, "Which shew the work of the law written in their hearts, their conscience also bearing witness, and their thoughts the mean while accusing or else excusing one another;)" (Rom. 2:15). You and I have a conscience, and even if we had never heard of the Ten Commandments, our consciences would either accuse us or excuse us. We would either say, "I'm guilty," or we would be free of any sense of guilt. Man has been given a sense of that which is right and that which is wrong.

It was on that basis that God judged the Amorite—he continued in sin. God said to Abraham, "I am going to put your offspring down in Egypt for 420 years until the iniquity of the Amorite is full." I do not think that even the most rabid liberal would want to ask God to give the Amorites more than 420 years of opportunity to repent. I personally will go along with the Lord that when you give a nation 420 years to decide what to do, they have had long enough.

The fact of the matter is that the Amorites did not turn to God. When Joshua crossed over the Jordan River, he came into the land of the Amorites. Jericho was an Amorite city, and the harlot Rahab was an Amorite. She and her family were the only ones who were not destroyed. The Moabites disappeared, but Ruth the Moabitess is in the genealogy of Jesus Christ. The Amorites, too, have long since disappeared, but Rahab the harlot is also in the line that led to the Messiah.

God is saying to Israel, "I judged the Amorites for the same sins which you are now committing. I have given you My law, and you have broken it."

**Also I brought you up from the land of Egypt, and led you forty years through the wilderness, to possess the land of the Amorite.**

**And I raised up of your sons for prophets, and of your young men for Nazarites. Is it not even thus, O ye children of Israel? saith the LORD [Amos 2:10–11].**

In effect God is saying, "I wanted you to serve Me in the land. I wanted you to bring up your young men to serve Me, to be prophets, and to be Nazarites." But what had happened?—

**But ye gave the Nazarites wine to drink; and commanded the prophets, saying, Prophesy not [Amos 2:12].**

A Nazarite was an Israelite who took a vow voluntarily to dedicate himself to God. There were three things that a Nazarite did not do. First, he did not cut his hair. Why? Because for a man to have long hair, Paul says, is a shame to him (see 1 Cor. 11:14). When I look around me today and see some fellows, I agree with Paul that it is sort of a shame for a man to have long hair. But I will simply say that the Nazarites let their hair grow because they were willing to bear shame.

The second thing was that a Nazarite was

not permitted to drink wine or touch any fruit of the vine. They were not to eat grapes or even raisins. The Israelites were causing a Nazarite to break his vow when they gave him wine.

The Nazarite also was not to touch a dead body or come near to one. When a loved one died, he did not even attend the funeral. This was done as an evidence of the fact that he had put God first in his life.

"And commanded the prophets, saying, Prophesy not." The people said to the prophets, "We don't want to hear you. We don't want to have any messages from you at all." They refused to listen to God's prophets.

Let me again make an analogy to our own nation today. We are following the same pattern that Rome followed when she went down. Rome was not destroyed from the outside, and I do not believe that there will come a missile over the North Pole which will destroy America. I think the missile which will destroy us is the propaganda that is abroad today. Through it we have become convinced that we are a sophisticated, very progressive nation and that nothing can happen to us. The truth is that we are probably going down as fast as any nation in history. A leading statesman has said, "This nation has gone down faster in the past ten years than it did in its entire history from its inception." How true that is!

There are two things which are bringing us down as a nation. One of them is drunkenness. There are a shocking number of alcoholics in this country. A majority of the fatal accidents that take place on our highways involve drunk drivers. Yet we are criticized if we speak out about this. We make laws concerning the use and abuse of drugs, and I agree with those laws; but what about liquor, my friend? Liquor is one of the things that is destroying us as a nation.

The other thing that characterizes us today is that we are not hearing the Word of God. The liberal preacher is the popular preacher. If we are going to hear the opinion of a minister on television, it will be the liberal preacher. The other day there was a panel discussion on television about abortion. They included a minister on the panel. You guessed it—he was a liberal. Recently I also viewed a discussion about women's rights. Again, the minister who spoke was a liberal. They do not ask a Bible-teaching preacher to tell what God has said on the subject. And yet we talk about religious liberty! My friend, the voice of God is not being heard in this land except for a few

of us weak fellows who are trying to declare the Word of God.

The same thing was happening in Israel. Amos said, "You are giving the Nazarite wine, causing him to break his vow and turning him from God. And you say to the prophets, 'Prophesy not.' You say to me, 'Don't talk like that. We want to hear something that will butter us up and make us feel good.' "

**Behold, I am pressed under you, as a cart is pressed that is full of sheaves [Amos 2:13].**

There are different ways of interpreting this verse, even different ways of translating it. It is the belief of some that it is rather degrading to think of God as being pressed down like a cart. I do not feel that way about it. God is saying here, "You have put Me in a difficult situation. You are My people. I put you in the land, and I put the Amorite out. Now here you are committing the same sins they commit! Do you expect Me to shut My eyes to your sin because you are My people? I'm being pressed down 'as a cart is pressed that is full of sheaves.' "

**Therefore the flight shall perish from the swift, and the strong shall not strengthen his force, neither shall the mighty deliver himself:**

**Neither shall he stand that handleth the bow; and he that is swift of foot shall not deliver himself: neither shall he that rideth the horse deliver himself.**

**And he that is courageous among the mighty shall flee away naked in that day, saith the Lord [Amos 2:14–16].**

There are some expositors who believe this refers to the earthquake mentioned in the first verse of Amos' prophecy. I do not think there is any reference here to an earthquake at all. The point is this: Israel was a strong nation. God had kept the enemy out, and no one had ever advanced into their land. Now everything is breaking down, even the walls of the city. The enemy has come in, and the strong are no longer strong.

We as a nation today ought to do a little thinking about what has happened in our land. In two world wars we were able to cross the sea and to bring an end to the conflict. In that we became a great nation, and we were very proud. We felt we didn't need God at all—we had the atom bomb. Then a little country called North Vietnam came along, and we thought that we would subdue them overnight. I am not attempting to fix blame on anyone, but I do say that America should have learned a lesson from that. We did not win a victory. We were never able to subdue the little enemy and we were divided at home. It is true that we did not want to bring the full force of our military power to bear, but this reveals the fact that we are becoming weak as a nation. We ought to wake up instead of shutting our eyes to the condition of our land.

We ought to begin to call attention to the fact that God is already beginning to bring us down as He brought His own people down.

God said to Israel, "You are becoming weak, and you do not seem to realize that I have already begun to judge you." That was Amos' message, and it is no wonder that the people wanted to run him out of town. It is no wonder they didn't want to hear the message he had for them. And he is not through yet!

# CHAPTER 3

**THEME:** *God's charge against the whole house of Israel*

**Hear this word that the LORD hath spoken against you, O children of Israel, against the whole family which I brought up from the land of Egypt, saying [Amos 3:1].**

Now God is ignoring the fact that the nation is split. He says that He is speaking to the whole family of Israel which He brought out of Egypt. In His eyes there were not two nations but one. The twelve tribes are one family before Him.

**You only have I known of all the families of the earth: therefore I will punish you for all your iniquities [Amos 3:2].**

This is getting right down to where the rubber meets the road, which shows the kind of prophet Amos was. He didn't beat around the bush. He didn't mince words. He comes right out and says that God will punish Israel for her iniquities. It's too bad the politicians and the priests wouldn't listen to him. If they had, it could have been a different story for Israel.

"You only have I known of all the families of the earth." After the disaster of the Flood, man was still in such sin that at the Tower of Babel all mankind had departed from God. It was total apostasy. Then God reached down to Ur of the Chaldees and called a man, told him to get away from his home of idolatry and to go to a place which He would show him. God said that from this one man, Abraham, He would make a nation and give them a land. This is what God means when He says, "You only have I known of all the families of the earth."

In order to get a message through to the world, God had to use this method. At the Tower of Babel, man was not building an escape in case there should be another flood—that was never the point. It was an altar that was built, apparently, to the sun. It was a place of worship. After the Flood men had the false idea that the god of darkness and the god of the storm had brought the Flood. So now they are going to worship the sun. It was sun worship that prevailed in the Tigris-Euphrates valley and continues until this very day. In the religion of Zoroaster there is the worship of light even down to the present.

God chose Abraham from among the nations, out of Abraham He brought forth the nation Israel, and to the nation He gave His Word. His purpose was that this nation would give His Word to the world. And this is God's purpose for us, my friend. For this reason I am attempting to get out His whole Word—all sixty-six books—by all means available to me.

"Therefore I will punish you for all your iniquities." God is saying, "I intend to judge you." The nation Israel occupied a unique relationship to God. God had given to them His commandments. And the reason He would judge Israel so severely is because they had broken so many of His commandments. You see, light creates responsibility. An enlightened nation has a greater responsibility than a nation which is in darkness.

This is a great principle that God puts down here. He intends to judge in a harsher manner those who have received light than those who are in darkness. The Lord Jesus also mentioned the fact that some would receive fewer stripes and others would receive more stripes. Many times I have made the statement that I would rather be a heathen Hottentot in the darkest corner of this earth, bowing down before an ugly, hideous idol of stone, than to be the so-called civilized man in this country, sitting in church on Sunday morning while he hears the gospel preached and does nothing about it. The man who hears the Word of God has a greater responsibility than the man who doesn't. Therefore, there are different degrees of punishment.

God makes it clear that He intends to punish them for their iniquities. Now a great many people today like to hear of the *love* of God. The love of God is indeed wonderful, and I don't think any teacher has emphasized it more than I have. It is something we need to rest upon and rejoice in. The love of God is manifested in the cross of Christ—"For God so loved the world, that he gave his only begotten Son . . ." (John 3:16). The cross is where God revealed His love, and when that love is rejected, there is nothing left but punishment. A great many folk feel that God should not punish; but, since they are not running the universe, I am of the opinion that their viewpoint will not be followed. God has already said that He is holy, righteous, just and that He intends to punish. Judgment upon sin is the logical consequence.

In fact, there will be a set of questions asked and answered, which reveal what a logical matter-of-fact prophet Amos really was. He deals with certain basic truths. He was a man from the edge of the wilderness down in Tekoa, and he draws from his long experience down there. He takes his lessons from the world of nature. He learned some things that folk still need to learn today.

I shall never forget the day my daughter went to a dairy on a school excursion. She had grown up in Pasadena, so she was a city girl. She came home from the excursion that day with the most exciting news you have ever heard. She told us that milk came from a *cow!* She had thought that milk came from the market and had originated there.

Well, this man Amos is a country man, and he has observed many wonderful things in nature.

Notice his first question:

**Can two walk together, except they be agreed? [Amos 3:3].**

Can two walk together? Yes, but they cannot go together unless they are in agreement. I watched a young couple the other day who hadn't been married long. They were walking down the street arm in arm. All of a sudden she turned around, stamped her little foot, and started walking back toward their home—but he kept on going. They weren't walking together any more because there had been some disagreement. Can two walk together, except they be agreed?

Here is a cause and an effect. The cause: there must be agreement if you are to walk together with God. The effect: you will walk with Him when you are in agreement. This doesn't mean that God will come over and agree with you. You and I will have to go over to His side and agree with Him. As someone has said, God rides triumphantly in His own chariot. And if you don't want to get under the wheels of that chariot, you had better get aboard and ride. After all, God is carrying through *His* purpose in the world.

It was very interesting to me to visit England and see Windsor Castle and Hampton Court. I think of Henry VI, Henry VIII, and Richard II, who were some of the boys who made the Tower of London famous because they sent many there who lost their heads. They had their way for a while—especially Henry VIII, but no one today is paying much attention to what Henry VIII thought or to what he did. My friend, God is running His universe *His* way and is not asking advice from little man. If you and I are going to walk with God, we will have to go His way. Amos has stated a great principle in his first question: "Can two walk together, except they be agreed?"

Now here is Amos' second question:

**Will a lion roar in the forest, when he hath no prey? will a young lion cry out of his den, if he have taken nothing? [Amos 3:4].**

"Will a lion roar in the forest, when he hath no prey?" Of course not. A lion moves about stealthily, quietly, silently on his padded feet. He is noiseless until he pounces on his prey. When he has captured his prey, then you can hear him roar.

"Will a young lion cry out of his den, if he have taken nothing?" No. The little lion doesn't make a sound because his mamma told him to keep quiet while she was away getting something for him to eat. But when she comes back with his supper, then he lets out a cry—but not until then.

You see, there is always a cause and a result. And the judgment of God *will* follow man's iniquity.

Amos has another question:

**Can a bird fall in a snare upon the earth, where no gin is for him? shall one take up a snare from the earth, and have taken nothing at all? [Amos 3:5].**

A "gin" is a trap. Of course a bird is not going to get caught in a snare unless a trap is laid for him. When I was a boy, they used to tell me that I could catch a bird if I put salt on its tail. So I ran all over the neighborhood trying to get salt on a bird's tail—and found it didn't work! I found that I couldn't catch a bird without a trap. In nature there is always the principle of cause and effect. If you are going to catch a bird, you will have to have a trap.

Now here is another question: "Shall one take up a snare from the earth, and have taken nothing at all?" A man is not going to keep setting a trap if he doesn't catch anything in it. I used to have six traps when I was a boy. In the fall of the year, I would ride down on my bicycle every morning before school to see if I had caught anything. In one of those six traps I would usually have a possum or a rabbit, sometimes I would have a skunk. (I always gave the skunk to a friend of mine. Although I could get more for the fur, I didn't care for the scent.) After I had left a trap in a place day after day and caught nothing, it would be foolish for me to continue to leave the trap there; so I would move it to some other place. If you are going to put out a trap, you expect to catch something in the trap.

**Shall a trumpet be blown in the city, and the people not be afraid? shall there be evil in a city, and the LORD hath not done it? [Amos 3:6].**

"Shall a trumpet be blown in the city, and the people not be afraid?" God has said that He is going to judge the people, and judgment *is* coming. It is rather *foolish* to fail to respond. It should have had an effect on their lives, but they are not listening to the prophet—any more than our nation is listening to the Word of God today.

"Shall there be evil in a city, and the LORD hath not done it?" First of all, let's understand that the word "*evil*" does not mean something which is sinful or wrong. It means calamity or judgment. Amos is saying, "Shall there be a calamity in the city, and the Lord has not done it?" This means, my friend, that there is no such thing as an accident in the life of a child of God. There *must* be a cause for the effect. God is not moving this universe in a foolish, idle manner. Therefore, when calamity strikes, there is a lesson to be learned from it. I believe that if America had learned the lesson of the "dust bowl" and of the drought period and of the depression, we would never have had to fight World War II. But we did not learn. Neither did we listen to God's warning in World War II, so we fought a tragic war in Vietnam, and still we are not listening to God. My friend, God will not let any nation dwell in peace and prosperity when it is in sin. Oh, it may have a period of peace and prosperity, but judgment *will* come.

Amos asks seven questions which illustrate that for every effect there is a cause and that the judgment of God which is coming is not accidental but is a result caused by the sin of the people.

**Surely the Lord GOD will do nothing, but he revealeth his secret unto his servants the prophets [Amos 3:7].**

Amos is saying that God will not move in judgment until He gives His message to the prophets. He will let them know what He intends to do.

**The lion hath roared, who will not fear? the Lord GOD hath spoken, who can but prophesy? [Amos 3:8].**

The prophets were giving God's message to Israel.

The problem in our day is not that people do not have a Word from God; the problem is that they will not hear that Word from God. His warnings are given in His Word. I feel that the Bible is more up to date than tomorrow morning's newspaper. After all, tomorrow morning's paper will be out of date by noon when the afternoon edition comes off the press. But the Word of God will be just as good the next day and on to the end of time.

It has always been God's method to reveal information to those who are His own concerning future judgment. You will recall that during Noah's day, God told him of a coming flood judgment and gave Noah 120 years to warn his generation. But the world did not heed his message. Also, remember that God let Abraham know ahead of time regarding the destruction of Sodom and Gomorrah. It is a good thing He did that, because if He had not, it would have given Abraham a wrong viewpoint of the almighty God. It has always been God's method to reveal such things to His own. When He was here in the flesh, He told His disciples, "Henceforth I call you not servants; for the servant knoweth not what his lord doeth: but I have called you friends; for all things that I have heard of my Father I have made known unto you" (John 15:15). There are many examples of this throughout the Bible. He gave a forewarning to Joseph in Egypt of the seven years of famine that were to come upon the earth. Also, Elijah was forewarned of the drought that would come upon Israel. He walked into the courts of Ahab and Jezebel to announce to them that they were in for a drought—". . . As the Lord God of Israel liveth, before whom I stand, there shall not be dew nor rain these years, but according to my word—[and I'm not saying anything!]" (1 Kings 17:1). Then he walked out of the court and dropped out of sight for over three years. Since it is God's method to warn of impending judgment, our Lord told His apostles, when He was gathered with them on the Mount of Olives, that Jerusalem would be destroyed—not one stone would be left upon another.

It is God's method always to give a warning of impending judgment, and that is all that Amos is doing here although his contemporaries are very critical of him. Folk just don't want to hear about judgment. They would much rather hide their head in the sand like the proverbial ostrich. Some people will not even go to a doctor because they do not want to know that something is wrong with them. The human family does not want to hear the bad news of judgment which is coming. If you preach and teach the truth, they will say you are a pessimist, a killjoy, a gloom-caster. However, God follows the principle that for every effect there is a cause, and God sends judgment only upon a sinning people.

God also makes it clear that the prophet is *obligated* to give His message—regardless of what it is. In fact, he ought to be in fear if he fails to relay God's message to the people. Frankly, I feel sorry today for the liberal who is refusing to declare God's message. He ought to be in fear. "The lion hath roared, who will not fear?" God has spoken. Now let's speak what God has to say. Let's get off this social gospel—which is almost like being on dope and taking a trip of sweetness and light, rose water and sunshine, expecting everything to work out beautifully. Well, I have been told all my life by politicians and preachers that there is a pot of gold at the end of the rainbow and we are going to arrive there shortly. But I've been on this trip for most of this century, and we haven't arrived yet—in fact, conditions get worse and worse. They refuse to face up to the fact that the real problem is sin in the heart of man.

**Publish in the palaces at Ashdod, and in the palaces in the land of Egypt, and say, Assemble yourselves upon the mountains of Samaria, and behold the great tumults in the midst thereof, and the oppressed in the midst thereof [Amos 3:9].**

"Publish in the palaces at Ashdod." Ashdod is in the country of the Philistines. At the time I am writing this, Israel has Ashdod. They have built a great many apartment buildings, a man-made harbor, and have erected a big oil refinery there so that oil is brought into Ashdod today.

A friend of mine who teaches prophecy attempts to find fulfilled prophecy in modern Palestine. When the oil pipeline came into Haifa in the northern part of Israel and an oil refinery was in operation and oil tankers were loading there, my friend said, "See, here is the fulfillment of the prophecy that Asher will dip his foot in oil!" However, that pipeline was cut, and the only oil brought into Haifa was by tankers. Now there is a pipeline across the Negeb from the Red Sea to Ashdod. Oil is piped from the tankers across to the refinery in Ashdod. It looks like it would be the tribe of Dan that gets its foot in oil today! My friend doesn't mention the fulfillment of this particular prophecy anymore because he can see it doesn't apply. I personally do not think that prophecy is being fulfilled in that land at all. However, I *do* see the setting of the stage that will later on bring the fulfillment of prophecy. It is foolish to pick out these little specific prophecies and insist that they are currently being fulfilled.

However, when Amos was giving his prophecy, Ashdod was a prominent city of the Philistines and stands here in this particular verse as representative for all of Philistia. "And in the palaces in the land of Egypt." God was instructing His prophets to spread this word upon the palaces of Ashdod and Egypt. Now notice what the invitation was—

"Assemble yourselves upon the mountains of Samaria, and behold the great tumults in the midst thereof, and the oppressed in the midst thereof." Samaria was the capital of the northern kingdom of Israel, and the palace of Ahab and Jezebel was there. Samaria was built on one mountain, but there were other mountains surrounding the city. From these surrounding mountains, people could see what was going on in the city. Sin was going great guns. "The great tumults" were riots caused by the oppression of the poor. If the pagan nations of Philistia and Egypt condemned Israel, wouldn't a holy God condemn them?

**For they know not to do right, saith the Lord, who store up violence and robbery in their palaces [Amos 3:10].**

Samaria was storing up in their palaces that which they had been stealing.

**Therefore thus saith the Lord God; An adversary there shall be even round about the land; and he shall bring down thy strength from thee, and thy palaces shall be spoiled [Amos 3:11].**

My friend, today the palaces of Samaria lie in ruins—I have seen them on several occasions.

**Thus saith the Lord; As the shepherd taketh out of the mouth of the lion two legs, or a piece of an ear; so shall the children of Israel be taken out that dwell in Samaria in the corner of a bed, and in Damascus in a couch [Amos 3:12].**

After God's judgment has fallen on Samaria, the remaining remnant is likened to a piece of an ear and two legs which are all that are left of a lamb after a lion has devoured it. You see, God's judgment was severe because Samaria had light from heaven which made their responsibility great.

**Hear ye, and testify in the house of Jacob, saith the Lord God, the God of hosts,**

**That in the day that I shall visit the transgressions of Israel upon him I will also visit the altars of Beth-el: and the horns of the altar shall be cut off, and fall to the ground [Amos 3:13–14].**

"The altars of Beth-el" refer to the worship of the golden calf. "The horns of the altar shall

be cut off." God is saying that He intends to remove this gross idolatry from His land.

**And I will smite the winter house with the summer house; and the houses of ivory shall perish, and the great houses shall have an end, saith the Lord [Amos 3:15].**

"The houses of ivory shall perish." Ahab and Jezebel had built on the top of the hill in Samaria. Their tremendous palace was in a most beautiful location. I particularly noticed that on my last trip there. That palace covers the very brow of the hill, the tip-top of the hill. From their palace they could look in every direction. To the west they could see the Mediterranean Sea on a clear day. To the east they could see the Jordan valley. To the north they could see the Valley of Esdraelon with Mount Hermon in the distance. To the south they could see Jerusalem. What a view!

There they built a palace of *ivory*. Of course, the enemy in days gone by has carted away that beautiful ivory, but excavations have been going on there recently. In fact, Israel is excavating there now. Our guide told us that they have found several very delicate vessels of ivory. Apparently one of them was for perfume. The other vessels were probably for wine. Ivory was the color scheme of the palace, if you please. Everything was done in ivory. Apparently, Ahab and Jezebel had the best interior decorator of the period come up and decorate for them. It was a palace of luxury.

God said He would destroy it and bring it to an end. I do not know of a more desolate spot today than the ruins of Samaria on top of that hill. I have many pictures that I took of it. God has certainly fulfilled that prophecy. Although we do not see prophecy which is *being* fulfilled in that land today, we can see that many prophecies *have been* fulfilled in the past. However, I repeat, that certainly the stage currently is being set for the fulfillment of *future* prophecies in the land of Palestine.

# CHAPTER 4

***THEME:*** *Israel punished in past for iniquity*

Beginning with this chapter, we have a series of three chapters which deal specifically with Israel, the ten tribes of the northern kingdom. In chapter 4 we will be reminded that God in the past punished Israel for iniquity. Then in chapter 5 we will see that in the future Israel will be punished for her iniquity. Finally, in chapter 6 we will see Amos admonishing his generation in the present to depart from iniquity. You see that this section has a very practical application to us as well as to Israel in the days of Amos.

As Amos is attempting to call the people back to God, he uses sarcasm that is really cutting.

**Hear this word, ye kine of Bashan, that are in the mountain of Samaria, which oppress the poor, which crush the needy, which say to their masters, Bring, and let us drink [Amos 4:1].**

"Ye kine of Bashan"—kine are cows. Bashan is a territory on the east of the Jordan River between the mountains of Gilead in the south and Mount Hermon on the north. It was settled by the three tribes that stayed on the wrong side of Jordan, and it was part of the northern kingdom of Israel. It was a very fertile area and noted for its fine breed of cattle. The cows of Bashan were strong and sleek in appearance because of the lush grazing lands.

Now whom is Amos addressing? Who are the "cows of Bashan"? Because the word *cows* is feminine, some expositors believe he is speaking to the women who were living in luxury, well fed, well dressed, well groomed. To enable them to enjoy this wealth, the poor were oppressed. In fact, Amos says, "which oppress the poor, which crush the needy." Generally, a nation reveals its moral position and its economic standard by the way women dress. When women are well dressed and bejeweled, it denotes a time of affluence in the nation. So Amos could be referring to the women of Bashan.

However, I believe that Amos is speaking to the rulers. Why, then, does he use the feminine gender? Well, that crowd was homosexual. If you will read the first chapter of the Epistle to the Romans, you will see that homosexuality is a thing which God judges. We know from history that when a nation starts to go down, homosexuality comes to the forefront. It was that which began the downfall of Rome. Nero was a homosexual. Nero was known as a mad king. He was mad, yes, in a very unnatural way. In his great palace, he had one separate room which was reserved for the basest kind of sexual deviation imaginable. It was given over to the satisfying of his homosexual cravings. This certainly can be brought up to date. What is taking place in our own country is alarming, and it can spell our national doom. We need an Amos to speak out against the growing acceptance and even encouragement of homosexuality today.

**The Lord GOD hath sworn by his holiness, that, lo, the days shall come upon you, that he will take you away with hooks, and your posterity with fishhooks [Amos 4:2].**

God uses the picture of having a hook in the jaw of the northern kingdom to drag them off into captivity. We sometimes speak of people being "hooked" on drugs. A person can be "hooked" by any besetting sin. God says these people are "hooked" for judgment. They are going to be dragged out of the land. We know from history that their conquerors did lead off their captives by a hook through the nose.

**And ye shall go out at the breaches, every cow at that which is before her; and ye shall cast them into the palace, saith the LORD [Amos 4:3].**

In effect, God is saying, "If you think because you are rich or because you are a ruler living in a palace that you will be spared, you are wrong." And we read in the historical record that when Assyria finally came and took them into captivity, the king was taken also. This was true also of the southern kingdom when it went into Babylonian captivity.

Now we come to an arresting expression:

**Come to Beth-el, and transgress; at Gilgal multiply transgression; and bring your sacrifices every morning, and your tithes after three years:**

**And offer a sacrifice of thanksgiving with leaven, and proclaim and publish the free offerings: for this liketh you, O ye children of Israel, saith the Lord GOD [Amos 4:4–5].**

I am sure you recognize that Amos is using bitter sarcasm as he invites them to come up to Beth-el (the place where they went to worship the golden calf.) "Come to Beth-el, and transgress; at Gilgal multiply transgression." The word *Gilgal* means "circle, or to roll along." It was the first place to which Israel came after they had crossed the Jordan River under Joshua's leadership, and it became a sacred place to them. Later it became a center of idolatry, and here again it is associated with idolatry. So Amos invites them to "multiply transgression" at Gilgal. That would be saying today, "Come to church to sin." Obviously, one goes to church for the very opposite. Amos is using pungent satire and taunting rebuke. He makes such an ironical and ridiculous statement to alert the people as to what they are actually *doing.*

Do you know that sometimes it can actually be dangerous to go to church? The Devil goes to church, you know. I think that he gets up bright and early on a Sunday morning, and wherever there is the preaching and teaching of the Word of God, he is there trying to wreck their work in any way he can. That is the reason we ought to pray for Bible-preaching and Bible-teaching pastors. The Devil doesn't need to be busy in cults or in liberal churches which deny the Word of God. Those places are already in his domain. He must concentrate his efforts in those places where there is spiritual life and the Word of God is being given out.

When Jesus Christ was about to die and His enemies were plotting the details of His execution, He spent time in the Upper Room with His twelve disciples. You would think that was the most sacred spot in all the world at that moment. You might expect that the Devil was busy with those who were plotting the death of Jesus. But do you know where the Devil was that evening? He was in the Upper Room! He hadn't been invited, but he was there. Satan had entered into the heart of Judas Iscariot to betray Him, and he walked into the Upper Room on the legs of Judas. That's how he got there. And, my friend, sometimes he walks into our so-called conservative, fundamental churches on the legs of a deacon or a Sunday school teacher or another church member. It is tragic today to fail to recognize our enemy and to be ignorant of his devices.

In the days of Amos, the people of Israel were coming to the place of worship in a very pious manner. Amos indicates that they were offering a sacrifice of thanksgiving with leaven. If you are familiar with the Book of Leviticus, you may think it was strange that they used leaven in their offerings since in the Scriptures leaven represents evil—evil or wrong doctrine and evil living. In the Levitical system, at the Feast of Passover, the Feast of Unleavened Bread and the Feast of Firstfruits, the use of leaven was forbidden. However, at the Feast of Pentecost, there was to be a meal offering to the Lord, which was to be presented in two loaves of fine flour baked *with leaven* (see Lev. 23). Pentecost was to depict the beginning and origin of the church. There has never yet been a church in which there wasn't at least a little leaven— that is, a little error or a little sin. For this reason leaven is included in the offering at Pentecost.

Also, leaven was used in the thanksgiving offerings. Leviticus 7 gives the law of the sacrifice of the peace offerings: "If he offer it for a thanksgiving, then he shall offer with the sacrifice of thanksgiving unleavened cakes mingled with oil, and unleavened wafers anointed with oil, and cakes mingled with oil, of fine flour, fried" (Lev. 7:12). This is the Godward side of the offering. You see, the Lord Jesus Christ has made peace with God for us. Because it represents Christ, there is no leaven in this first offering. In the New Testament this is made clear: "Therefore being justified by faith [not by works—we could never be justified by anything but faith], we have peace with God through our Lord Jesus Christ" (Rom. 5:1). Now, although the first offering represents Christ and contains no leaven, the second represents the manward side; the one who is bringing the sacrifice of thanksgiving offers *himself* to God: "Besides the cakes, he shall offer for his offering leavened bread with the sacrifice of thanksgiving of his peace offerings (Lev. 7:13).

We can make an application of this to our own lives. You and I can dedicate our lives to the Lord. Sometimes this is done in a ritual which is called a "consecration" service. Since the literal meaning of consecration is to set something apart as being holy, that is really a misnomer for that kind of ritual. We can never present ourselves holy or perfect before God. We will always contain some "leaven." So present yourself as a living sacrifice to God, as we are admonished in Romans 12:1. But don't ever think that you can present yourself *perfect* to God. If you are waiting for that before you feel you can present yourself to God, you will be waiting your whole lifetime.

Now, when Amos sarcastically invites the people of Israel to come to Beth-el and Gilgal to transgress, it is very significant that he tells them to "offer a sacrifice of thanksgiving with leaven." He doesn't even mention the first unleavened part of the offering. Why? Because the people are totally removed from the living and true God. Therefore, the only thing they can do is offer evil to God. Of course, God will not accept that at all. This prophet Amos, just a country preacher, has a lot on the ball! He is an outstanding minister of the Word of God. This is tremendous.

My friend, I hope you understand the satire and sarcasm of Amos when he invites people to Gilgal to transgress. He is not asking them to sin, but in biting sarcasm he is saying, "That's what you do when you come to Beth-el and to Gilgal. You come to *sin*, not to worship God!"

Next Sunday morning when you put on your Sunday-go-to-meeting clothes, it might be well to first get down on your knees and ask God about the condition of your heart. Will you be taking a clean heart to church? Will you be taking lips that will not speak anything to hurt the cause of Christ? The message of Amos is very pertinent even in our day. If Amos were still around and if I were still a pastor, I would invite him to my church to preach. I think the modern church needs ministers like him. There are many ministers who give only nice little messages on comfort and how to solve personal problems. Somebody needs to say something very strong about *sin* in people's hearts in our day. Sin is rampant in and out of the church, and it is rampant in your heart and in my heart this very day. The biggest problem you and I have is to overcome the sin which is in our lives. There is no use trying to cover it up by church attendance or by going to some little course or seminar. The essential thing is to have a confrontation with the Lord Jesus Christ and to get your relationship with Him straightened out.

Amos now reminds the people of Israel of the judgments God had sent upon them—

**And I also have given you cleanness of teeth in all your cities, and want of bread in all your places: yet have ye not returned unto me, saith the Lord [Amos 4:6].**

They didn't have "cleanness of teeth" because God had given them a new toothpaste or new mouthwash! The reason they had clean teeth was that they had nothing to eat. God had judged them with famine, but it had not awakened them to their spiritual condition.

"Yet have ye not returned unto me, saith the Lord." It made no impression on them.

**And also I have withholden the rain from you, when there were yet three months to the harvest: and I caused it to rain upon one city, and caused it not to rain upon another city: one piece was rained upon, and the piece whereupon it rained not withered.**

**So two or three cities wandered unto one city, to drink water; but they were not satisfied: yet have ye not returned unto me, saith the Lord [Amos 4:7–8].**

Then God sent a drought. God is the one who controls the rainfall—some think the weatherman does it! God withheld the rain three months before it was time to harvest, which was disastrous. And note that God caused it to rain on one city and not on another. God did this to show them that the rainfall was not by chance but by His sovereign will. The drought was so serious that people from one city would go to another city where there was water, and they would carry a little water home in a jug or wineskin. This should have turned them to God. "Yet have ye not returned unto me, saith the Lord."

Those of us from Texas can appreciate this. It was a three-year drought in West Texas that caused my Dad to leave there when I was a small boy. People in Dallas, Texas, can remember the drought that dried up the water supply for that city. They had to draw water from the Red River into which oil had been poured. I want to tell you, I have never tasted any other drinking water that was as bad as that! People who had friends or relatives in the little towns around Dallas would go there to fill up a jug of water to take it home for drinking. This wasn't new; it was the same thing the people were doing in the days of Amos. It was a warning from God, but they paid no attention to it.

**I have smitten you with blasting and mildew: when your gardens and your vineyards and your fig trees and your olive trees increased, the palmerworm devoured them: yet have ye not returned unto me, saith the Lord [Amos 4:9].**

"Blasting and mildew." The crops were blasted by the scorching east wind from the desert, and the mildew was from excessive drought, not moisture. "The palmerworm devoured them" refers to a locust plague which devoured what was left. "Yet have ye not returned unto me, saith the LORD."

**I have sent among you the pestilence after the manner of Egypt: your young men have I slain with the sword, and have taken away your horses; and I have made the stink of your camps to come up unto your nostrils: yet have ye not returned unto me, saith the LORD [Amos 4:10].**

"The stink of your camps" was the stench of the dead bodies from the pestilence and from the warfare. Yet with all of this, they did not return to the Lord!

**I have overthrown some of you, as God overthrew Sodom and Gomorrah, and ye were as a firebrand plucked out of the burning: yet have ye not returned unto me, saith the LORD [Amos 4:11].**

Some Bible expositors feel that this is sort of a summation of the previous plagues. I rather doubt that, because we know from the Book of Jonah that at this time the Assyrians were making forays down into the northern kingdom. Assyria would strike here and there and sometimes would take an entire community into captivity. God was permitting the Assyrian, just like a bird, to peck here and there in the kingdom. This should have been a warning to all the people that the whole kingdom might fall some day. They didn't accept the warning from God but continued on in their evil ways. "Yet have ye not returned unto me, saith the LORD."

**Therefore thus will I do unto thee, O Israel: and because I will do this unto thee, prepare to meet thy God, O Israel [Amos 4:12].**

God does not tell them here what He is going to do. He simply says, "*Thus* I will do unto thee" and "because I will do *this* unto thee." It is going to be a surprise. We know now that it was the Assyrians who came down upon them suddenly and took them into captivity. In other words, the people of Israel simply did not believe God and did not turn to Him.

God goes even beyond the judgment of the Assyrian captivity. He says, "Prepare to meet thy God, O Israel." When Assyria came down, they didn't take all the people into captivity. Many of them were slain. This means that they were to meet God in death, which is something that every individual must do. We all must meet God in death. "Prepare to meet

thy God, O Israel." This is a message to every individual even today.

God has dealt very definitely with a friend of mine because of the sin that was in his life. He told me the story of how God had dealt with him. The judgment that had come upon him was rather severe, although it was something that a man could bear. As I was sympathizing with him about it, he said to me, "McGee, the judgment that has come upon me is not the thing that disturbs me. I have *yet* to stand before God, and I tremble."

I answered him, "You know that Vernon McGee is also going to stand before God. If I stood before Him as I am, I would be frightened to death. But I am not going to stand before Him as Vernon McGee. I am in Christ, and God is going to see Christ. I have been made acceptable in the Beloved." My friend answered, "Yes, that is the only comfort that I have for the life that I have lived."

Well, my friend, that message is for *you* also. Prepare to meet thy God. Suppose at this very moment you went into the presence of God—perhaps both you and I will be going there shortly. Suppose this life is past. The things that were so important to you down here will have no importance any more, I assure you. Life on earth is over, you're through, you're out of it, and you are in God's presence. How are you going to stand before Him? Perhaps you have lived to please people and have tried to keep up with the Joneses. Don't you know that you cannot stand in your own strength, your own life, your own character? You and I have nothing to offer to God—we are bankrupt, friend. We were *dead* in trespasses and sins. The only way you and I can stand there is in Christ. He "was delivered for our offences, and was raised again for our justification" (Rom. 4:25), that you and I might stand before Him justified. We stand before God in the righteousness of Christ.

Now our country preacher will tell us who this God is whom we are to meet. This is one of the most majestic awe-inspiring statements in the Word of God—

**For, lo, he that formeth the mountains, and createth the wind, and declareth unto man what is his thought, that maketh the morning darkness, and treadeth upon the high places of the earth, The LORD, The God of hosts, is his name [Amos 4:13].**

Amos presents Him as the omnipotent, omniscient, and omnipresent God. He is the omnipotent Creator. He has all power. It was He who formed the mountains and created the wind. He is omniscient, knowing your thoughts afar off. And He is omnipresent—He "treadeth upon the high places of the earth." No matter where you go, even to the moon, you won't get away from Him, friend. Perhaps you have been able to keep up a pretty good front so that your friends and neighbors (and maybe even your mate) think you are a fine person. But in heaven, the psalmist says, "Thou hast set our iniquities before thee, our secret sins in the light of thy countenance"

(Ps. 90:8). God *knows* you. There is no use trying to keep up a front. You might as well go to Him and turn yourself in. The FBI or the police may not be after you, but God knows your transgressions. As Dr. Louis Sperry Chafer used to say to us in class, secret sin on earth is open scandal in heaven. God not only knows *us* through and through, but He also knew personally the people to whom Amos was speaking. With intensity of feeling Amos urged them, "Prepare to meet thy God, O Israel."

# CHAPTER 5

*THEME: Israel will be punished in the future for iniquity*

The previous chapter closed with a bang, with a note of finality. It would seem as if God had closed the door, that judgment was inevitable, and that there was no hope for Israel at all. Although chapter 5 reaches into the future and makes it very clear that God will punish them for their iniquity, in the first fifteen verses God pleads with Israel to seek Him so that judgment can be averted. As long as He did not bring that final stroke of judgment, their captivity, there was hope for them.

**Hear ye this word which I take up against you, even a lamentation, O house of Israel [Amos 5:1].**

He is taking up a dirge. He is singing a funeral song, a very sad one. He speaks of them now with tenderness—

**The virgin of Israel is fallen; she shall no more rise: she is forsaken upon her land; there is none to raise her up [Amos 5:2].**

When Hosea began his prophecy, he spoke of the experience he had had in his home. He had married a harlot, and God sent him out to speak to the northern kingdom, saying, "You're a harlot, but God still loves you." Here Amos says, "You were a virgin, God espoused you to Himself." That is the picture of every believer today. Paul said even to the Corinthians, "I espoused you as a chaste virgin to Christ" (see 2 Cor. 11:2). When we come to Him, our sins are forgiven, and we start new with Him. But how about it, friend?

How has it been going the past few years? Have you done what Israel did? Have you played the harlot? Have you turned away from the One who loves you? Have you been led astray into the world and into the things of the flesh? Is the Devil leading you around like a pig with a ring in its snout? A great many Christians are in that condition today. This is a sad funeral dirge: "The virgin of Israel is fallen; she shall no more rise: she is forsaken upon her land; there is none to raise her up."

**For thus saith the Lord GOD; The city that went out by a thousand shall leave an hundred, and that which went forth by an hundred shall leave ten, to the house of Israel [Amos 5:3].**

"The city that went out by a thousand shall leave an hundred." Amos is saying, "Prepare to meet your God. Look at the number that are going to be slain." "That which went forth by an hundred shall leave ten, to the house of Israel." These are the ones who will be left back in the land, but a great company of them will be slain.

Listen to Amos. This is, as it were, a last call to the nation—

**For thus saith the LORD unto the house of Israel, Seek ye me, and ye shall live [Amos 5:4].**

The invitation is still open. The Word has gone out. God is calling upon them to turn to Him; if they do even now, they will live.

**But seek not Beth-el, nor enter into Gilgal, and pass not to Beer-sheba: for**

**Gilgal shall surely go into captivity, and Beth-el shall come to nought [Amos 5:5].**

"But seek not Beth-el." Beth-el is where one of the golden calves was erected. By the way, you cannot find Beth-el today. I have had two different spots pointed out to me by guides, so we cannot be sure just where it is. The general location is pretty well known, but to be able to pinpoint it seems to be a problem.

"Nor enter into Gilgal." Gilgal is the place where Israel camped when they crossed the Jordan River when they first came into the land under the leadership of Joshua. There they set up the tabernacle, and there was the staging area for their march upon Jericho. It became a very sacred place. In fact, God had told them to tell their children that that was the place where He had delivered them. Instead, these people had gone into idolatry, and these places that had been sacred for God became places to set up an idol.

"And pass not to Beer-sheba." Beer-sheba was way down in the southern kingdom of Judah in the Negeb. It is another very famous place. It was at Beer-sheba that Abraham and Abimelech made a covenant, and then Abraham called on the name of the Lord (see Gen. 21). The expression, ". . . from Dan to Beer-sheba . . ." (e.g., see Jud. 20:1), is used in Scripture to designate the whole land of Israel from north to south. In the days of Amos, the people in the northern kingdom were making pilgrimages to Beer-sheba for the worship of idols.

"For Gilgal shall surely go into captivity, and Beth-el shall come to nought." Why doesn't Amos mention Beer-sheba at this point? Because Beer-sheba is not in the northern kingdom but in the southern. It will be more than another hundred years before Beer-sheba goes into captivity with the southern kingdom. However, these two in the northern kingdom, both Beth-el and Gilgal, are about to go into captivity. How accurate Amos is in his statement here!

But he goes on to say that there is still hope for them—

**Seek the Lord, and ye shall live; lest he break out like fire in the house of Joseph, and devour it, and there be none to quench it in Beth-el [Amos 5:6].**

"Seek the Lord, and ye shall live"—what a wonderful invitation this is! "Lest he break out like fire in the house of Joseph." God says,

"If you do not turn to Me, I will have to judge you."

**Ye who turn judgment to wormwood, and leave off righteousness in the earth [Amos 5:7].**

The man who was liberal in his theology used to make a great deal of this section of Scripture. He presented a "works salvation," finding justification for it in this passage. Unfortunately, he did not consider Amos' entire message. The condition of the people of Israel was that they were going through the *form* of worship that God had prescribed. They were offering sacrifices, they were going through a ritual that God had given to them, but their lives did not commend their profession. In other words, their practice did not equal the profession which they made.

Years ago Dr. G. Campbell Morgan said that he was more afraid of the blasphemy of the secular than he was of the blasphemy of the sanctuary. Many people think that if you participate in all the forms and rituals of the church, you are very pious, but if you do something in the sanctuary which is not according to the ritual of the church, it is blasphemous. My friend, I do not feel that the real danger is in that sort of thing. The real danger is in the man who goes to church and sings the doxology, "Praise God from whom all blessings flow," but outside the church is living a life in which he is not honest and a life in which there is neither justice nor righteousness. That is the blasphemy of the secular or the blasphemy of the street. *That* is the thing that God is condemning in the lives of the people of Israel.

I am not saying that a living faith in Christ is not essential. It is absolutely essential to trust in Christ for your salvation. But, my friend, if you make a profession of trusting in Christ and your life outside the church does not commend the gospel at all, then, may I say to you, there is not but one word to describe that. It is a harsh word, but the Lord Jesus is the one who used this word more than anyone else. He called the religious rulers of His day, "Ye *hypocrites*." That is His word for it—I did not think of it. It is brazen hypocrisy today, either in the pulpit or in the pew, when a profession is given and a protestation is made of our wonderful love for and trust in Christ, and then we go out and live a life which condemns the very gospel we are supposed to be professing. This is the thing that hurts the cause of the gospel today. A great many Christians do not want this mentioned because they are very active in Christian work but not very active in living for the Lord in their business and social lives.

I knew a man who was married and very active in the church; I do not think there was an organization within the church in which he was not active. But he got involved with a lady in the choir. He dropped out for a time, and without making any amends, without any apparent change of life whatsoever, he wanted to come back into active service in the church. As pastor, I absolutely condemned that sort of thing, and I was made out to be the unreasonable party because of it.

Amos condemns this idea of making a profession and then not living up to it—this was basic in his message. You see, God had to bring Amos from way down south in the southern kingdom in order to get a man who would give this kind of message. The paid preachers up there in Beth-el and Samaria were saying only what the people wanted them to say.

A leading Bible expositor made the statement several years ago that the modern pulpit had become a sounding board for the thinking of the congregation. Paul wrote to Timothy, "For the time will come when they will not endure sound doctrine; but after their own lusts shall they heap to themselves teachers, having itching ears; And they shall turn away their ears from the truth, and shall be turned unto fables" (2 Tim. 4:3–4). The people's ears itch to hear something nice and sweet, and then they go up and pat the preacher on the back, telling him how sweet *he* is. It becomes like the old Egyptian game: "You scratch my back, I'll scratch your back, and we both will have a good time." A great deal of that type of thing is going on in our churches today; liberalism has done it for years, and we find it in many conservative churches today.

The people of Israel were insulted that this man Amos would even suggest that they were not very religious or very pious, but that was his message to them.

**Seek him that maketh the seven stars and Orion, and turneth the shadow of death into the morning, and maketh the day dark with night: that calleth for the waters of the sea, and poureth them out upon the face of the earth: The LORD is his name [Amos 5:8].**

Again, this is God's gracious call. God is long suffering. God is much more patient than I would be. I have found out that I need to learn to be patient with the patience of God. How long suffering and patient He is!

"Seek him that maketh the seven stars and Orion." Orion is one of the many constellations in the heavens, and it was the one, of course, familiar to these people in that day.

"And maketh the day dark with night: that calleth for the waters of the sea, and poureth them out upon the face of the earth." That is, it is God who makes the rain fall. It is true that rainfall is controlled by the law of hydrodynamics, but who made the law of hydrodynamics? Who is the one who pulls the water up out of the ocean, puts it on the train (they call it a cloud), moves those clouds with the wind until they get to just the right place, then turns loose the rain? *God* is the one doing that, my friend. Amos says, "The LORD is his name." In effect, he is saying to the people of Israel, "You have turned to idols, and your life does not commend your profession of a faith in the living God, the living God who is the Creator."

**That strengtheneth the spoiled against the strong, so that the spoiled shall come against the fortress.**

**They hate him that rebuketh in the gate, and they abhor him that speaketh uprightly [Amos 5:9–10].**

"They hate him that rebuketh in the gate." The one who rebuketh in the gate would be a judge. The courthouse of that day was the gate of the walled city. You will find all the way through Scripture that the judges sat in the gate. Boaz brought the nearer kinsman to the gate of Bethlehem to settle the inheritance of Naomi and Ruth. When Lot went down to Sodom, he became involved in politics down there, and we are told that he sat in the gate. What was he doing there? He was a judge. Amos says that the judge who rebuked that which was wrong was the one who was hated; therefore, most of the judges chose to cooperate with the evil doers.

"And they abhor him that speaketh uprightly." When a judge insisted upon justice and upon that which was right, he became very unpopular. I am not sure that human nature has changed very much since Amos' day.

**Forasmuch therefore as your treading is upon the poor, and ye take from him burdens of wheat: ye have built houses of hewn stone, but ye shall not dwell in them; ye have planted pleasant vine-**

**yards, but ye shall not drink wine of them [Amos 5:11].**

"Forasmuch therefore as your treading is upon the poor, and ye take from him burdens of wheat." The poor are the ones who do not get justice. I know that, for I have been on that side of the line for a long time.

"Ye have built houses of hewn stone, but ye shall not dwell in them; ye have planted pleasant vineyards, but ye shall not drink wine of them." The beautiful palaces that were built at Samaria are in ruins today. They were destroyed shortly after this message was given and have been in ruins now for nearly three thousand years.

**For I know your manifold transgressions, and your mighty sins: they afflict the just, they take a bribe, and they turn aside the poor in the gate from their right [Amos 5:12].**

The poor could not get justice in the court of that day. Has it changed today?

One of the reasons offered for repealing the death penalty has been that the rich man can always escape the gas chamber or the electric chair. I do not think that that is a legitimate reason, although it is true that the rich man can do that. The poor man, when he is found guilty, does not stand a chance of escaping the penalty. The rich man can keep appealing the case, and it takes him a long time to find his way to jail; in fact, in many cases, he never even gets there.

God takes notice when there is no justice in a nation. God has turned over to human government the responsibility of running this earth. The nations of the earth are God's arrangement, and He holds them accountable. When they fail, He removes them, as Rome was removed from the scene.

**Therefore the prudent shall keep silence in that time; for it is an evil time [Amos 5:13].**

In other words, a man in that day knew he could not get justice, and many good people were keeping quiet. It was the prudent thing to do because, if he had attempted to protest, it wouldn't have done him a bit of good. The tragedy of the hour in which we live is that we talk about the freedom of the press, the freedom of religion, and the freedom of speech, but there is not much of it left. The news media have definitely become a brainwashing agency. It is true that only he who has money can get a public hearing today. As a result, we do have a silent majority in this country, be-cause they know that their voices would not amount to anything at all. We are in a tragic day, very much like the day to which Israel had come.

**Seek good, and not evil, that ye may live: and so the LORD, the God of hosts, shall be with you, as ye have spoken [Amos 5:14].**

Again, the Lord calls upon Israel to turn to Him.

**Hate the evil, and love the good, and establish judgment in the gate: it may be that the LORD God of hosts will be gracious unto the remnant of Joseph [Amos 5:15].**

In our day, a man who is liberal and supported by some rich organization can betray our government and escape any penalty (in fact, he is even made a hero), while some poor fellow who is espousing an honest cause does not stand a chance of gaining a hearing. God says, "Hate the evil, and love the good, and establish judgment in the gate."

"It may be that the LORD God of hosts will be gracious unto the remnant of Joseph." In other words, Amos says, "It's a slim chance, but there is hope for you."

Now Amos moves into another area, the warning of an approaching judgment, the Day of the Lord.

**Therefore the LORD, the God of hosts, the Lord, saith thus; Wailing shall be in all streets; and they shall say in all the highways, Alas! alas! and they shall call the husbandman to mourning, and such as are skilful of lamentation to wailing.**

**And in all vineyards shall be wailing: for I will pass through thee, saith the LORD [Amos 5:16–17].**

Because God knew that they would not repent, He now clearly states the judgment which is to come. Death will touch everyone; all will mourn.

**Woe unto you that desire the day of the LORD! to what end is it for you? the day of the LORD is darkness, and not light [Amos 5:18].**

A great many people were very piously saying that they desired the Day of the Lord. Amos expresses it here as a "Woe"—"Woe unto you that desire the day of the LORD!" But for them it is nothing in the world but pious sentiment.

That day is not going to be as pleasant for them as they think it is going to be.

Amos uses here the expression, "the day of the LORD." Joel is the one who introduced this subject in prophecy, and every one of the prophets after him has something to say about it. Many people have thought that the Day of the Lord refers to the Millennium; in fact, at the beginning of my theological training that is what I was taught. Joel was very careful (and Amos will be also) to say that the Day of the Lord is not light but it is darkness. The Day of the Lord begins with judgment and moves on to the coming of Christ to establish His kingdom here upon this earth.

There are a number of commentators who feel that the people of Israel were becoming rather cynical and were ridiculing the Day of the Lord. I do not see that here at all; I do not see how that interpretation could possibly be true. Rather, I see that the people were becoming very pious. They were going through the Mosaic rituals, but they were also worshiping idols. It was just religion to them, just as churchgoing is to many people today. There is nothing vital, nothing real in going through a ritual. The reason many church services are so dead is that they are nothing more than ritual. It may be beautiful, it may appeal to your eyes and your ears, but does it change your life? Is it transforming? Is it something you can live by in the marketplace? There are many people today who are premillennial and pretribulational in their theology and who very piously say, "Oh, if only the Lord would come!" If you are one of them, let me ask you this: Do you really want Him to come? Or are you using the Rapture of the church as a sort of an escape mechanism to get you out of your troubles down here?

In seminary a fellow student and I were studying Hebrew. After dinner in the evening, when we had a difficult Hebrew assignment to prepare for the next day, he would look up to the heavens and say, "Oh, if the Lord would only come tonight!" What was he after? He didn't want to study Hebrew! But I never shall forget the night before graduation (he was to be married and go on his honeymoon the day after graduation) when he came out of the cafeteria, looked up to the sky, and said, "I sure hope the Lord doesn't come now for several days!" My friend, many of us look forward to the Rapture, not because we love Christ's appearing, but because we want to escape an unpleasant situation.

Amos says to these people, "You pious folk are just going through the religious rituals, you don't really know God—you are worshiping idols also! The Day of the Lord is not something which you are to desire. It is not light, but it is a day of darkness. You will first go through a great period of tribulation when the Day of the Lord comes. What you expect to do is to jump right into the Millennium, but that is not the way it is going to happen.

Those of us who believe that the church will not go through the Tribulation should be aware that we will not escape all judgment. My friend, some of us may think we have gotten into the Tribulation after we get to heaven! Do you know why? Listen to what Paul has to say in 2 Corinthians 5:9–10: "Wherefore we labour, that, whether present or absent, we may be accepted of him. For we must all appear before the judgment seat of Christ; that every one may receive the things done in his body, according to that he hath done, whether it be good or bad." The judgment seat of Christ is the *bema;* it is not the Great White Throne judgment at all. It is to the *bema* that all Christians come "that every one may receive the things done in his body, according to that he hath done, whether it be good or bad." Is this a judgment for salvation? No, Paul says, "For other foundation can no man lay than that is laid, which is Jesus Christ" (1 Cor. 3:11). There is no other foundation any man can lay, but you can build on that foundation. You can build with wood, hay, and stubble; or you can build with gold, silver, and precious stones. But every man's *work*—not his salvation, not his person—will be tested by fire. If any man's work survives the fire, he will receive a reward. But suppose his work does not survive the fire? Paul says, "He himself shall be saved; yet so as by fire" (see 1 Cor. 3:12–15). This is the reason I often make the statement that, although many people are saved, they are going to smell like they were bought at a fire sale when they get to heaven. Everything they did here on earth they did in the flesh, they did it for some earthly reason, for some present satisfaction.

I want to be very frank with you: as I am now getting toward the sunset of life, I'm wondering how Vernon McGee is going to fare at the judgment seat of Christ. You may say that I will get a great reward because of my Bible-teaching ministry through the years. But you don't know me like I know myself; if you did, you might not want to listen to me. But wait a minute, don't put the book down, because if I knew you like you know yourself, I wouldn't want to talk to you.

My friend, the lives which we live down

here are to be *tested*, and it is pious nonsense to pretend to be so interested in the coming of Christ when the truth is that some of us will get to heaven and think that we didn't miss the Great Tribulation after all. Notice what Paul went on to say after speaking of our judgment at the *bema* of Christ: "Knowing therefore the terror of the Lord, we persuade men . . ." (2 Cor. 5:11). If you think that when you appear in His presence He is going to give you a nice little Sunday school medal because you didn't miss Sunday school for fifteen years, I think you are wrong. I do not think that that is even going to be an issue. I think that the life you live in your home, your witness in your business and social life, your conduct with the opposite sex are the things which are going to come before the judgment seat of Christ—it will be the things that were done in the body down here.

Do you want to go to heaven now? Do you have everything straightened out? Paul writes, "For if we would judge ourselves, we should not be judged" (1 Cor. 11:31). This is the reason I try to keep everything confessed to the Lord. I want to run short accounts with Him every day. If I don't, He is going to straighten it out up there someday. You lost your temper and gave a poor witness today. Or you gossiped about another believer. Do you think that when you come into the presence of Christ He will pat you on the back and say what a nice little fellow you were? He is going to judge those things, my friend. Things must be made right in heaven, and that is the purpose of the judgment seat of Christ.

Amos is really putting it on the line to these people. He says, "Cut out this nonsense that you desire the Day of the Lord. It is not a day of light but of darkness. There will be a Great Tribulation that you will go through." If you are a believer and therefore do not go through that, there will still be the judgment seat of Christ for you. I do not think that it is going to be as pleasant as some folk think it is going to be.

**As if a man did flee from a lion, and a bear met him; or went into the house, and leaned his hand on the wall, and a serpent bit him [Amos 5:19].**

Amos is one of the most dramatic preachers that you will find in Scripture. He uses such figurative language. He uses the idiom of the earth and draws his illustrations from nature. Here he describes a man who is out in the woods, and suddenly there is a lion on the trail in back of him. As he runs away from the lion,

he sees a bear coming toward him. In other words, if you say you want the Lord to come so that you can get out of your troubles down here, it may be like jumping out of the frying pan into the fire (to use an adage of our day). Seeing the bear coming toward him, the man takes off over the hill and reaches his home. He puts his hand upon the wall to rest and get his breath, only to have a serpent come out of the wall and bite him. It might have been better if the lion or the bear had gotten him than to have the poison of a serpent in him!

Amos is saying that we had better be very careful about the life we are living for God down here. As believers, our *salvation* is not in jeopardy—Christ has paid the penalty for our sins, but if our sins as believers are not dealt with and made right, *He* will make them right. My friend, He *must* do that—He is holy and righteous and just, and heaven is a place where things are right. Therefore, you and I will have to be right when we get there. This is something that a great many people do not realize today.

**Shall not the day of the LORD be darkness, and not light? even very dark, and no brightness in it? [Amos 5:20].**

"The day of the LORD" begins with a period of judgment that is yet to come upon the nation of Israel. There is more than a period of judgment that is included in the Day of the Lord, however. The Day of the Lord also includes the second coming of Christ to the earth and the time of the millennial kingdom here upon earth.

**I hate, I despise your feast days, and I will not smell in your solemn assemblies.**

**Though ye offer me burnt offerings and your meat offerings, I will not accept them: neither will I regard the peace offerings of your fat beasts.**

**Take thou away from me the noise of thy songs; for I will not hear the melody of thy viols [Amos 5:21–23].**

Behind their going through the rituals were lives that were dishonest. God's people need to recognize that their faith must be real. Faith is not fake or fable; it is reality. Faith must lay hold of a person. Believing is not deceiving. Many people say, "If you believe, it is because you are blind. You have a blind faith." My friend, if it is a blind faith, forget it, because God does not accept that. Faith must have an effect upon the life; James says,

".  .  . faith without works is dead?" (James 2:20). Paul said that we have been saved in order that we might produce good works. All of this is important.

The people of Israel were living lives of sin. They were engaged in idolatry; yet they were going through all the Mosaic ritual. God says here, "I despise it. I have no use for it." In some of our song services which we consider to be so enthusiastic, if the hearts of the people are not in it, if there is nothing but a big mouth in it, do you really think God accepts that? If He came to your church or my church, what do you think His viewpoint would be?

**But let judgment run down as waters, and righteousness as a mighty stream.**

**Have ye offered unto me sacrifices and offerings in the wilderness forty years, O house of Israel?**

**But ye have borne the tabernacle of your Moloch and Chiun your images, the star of your god, which ye made to yourselves [Amos 5:24–26].**

Apparently, the people of Israel offered sacrifices in the wilderness, but when they met a heathen people, they wanted to take on the worship of their gods also. The worship of Moloch was that in which small children were put into the arms of a red-hot idol and made human sacrifices. The screams of those children were terrible. God is saying to us, "You come to church on Sunday and go through the motions of worshiping Me, but during the week you worship Moloch, you worship the idol of covetousness as you go after the almighty dollar."

Cardinal Wolsey was banished from Hampton Court by Henry VIII who would also have had him executed if Wolsey had not died a natural death before the execution could take place. On his deathbed, the cardinal said, "If I had only served my God like I served my king!" Many a Christian will have to say on his deathbed, "I have served the god of Moloch down here; I have served the idol of covetousness. I've worshiped the things of the flesh and have not served my God." My friend, it does not matter how sweet the music will be, nor what nice words the preacher will say at the funeral, you and I are going to stand at the judgment seat of Christ. I will be frank with you, that disturbs me somewhat. Therefore, I want to keep things straightened out with Him down here.

**Therefore will I cause you to go into captivity beyond Damascus, saith the LORD, whose name is The God of hosts [Amos 5:27].**

Israel is to be punished in the future. They will go into captivity "beyond Damascus" (that is, beyond Syria), and beyond Damascus was Nineveh. God is telling Israel that the Assyrian would take them into captivity.

# CHAPTER 6

**THEME:** *Israel admonished in the present to depart from iniquity*

Amos begins this chapter with a "Woe." He is not a prophet who majors in woes, but you will find them in several other of the prophets and in the Book of Revelation. "Woe" also means "Whoa!"—it means to stop, look, and listen, because this is something that is important. The word *woe* is one that ought to draw our special attention to that which follows.

**Woe to them that are at ease in Zion, and trust in the mountain of Samaria, which are named chief of the nations, to whom the house of Israel came! [Amos 6:1].**

Zion was, of course, in the southern kingdom of Judah; so both parts of the nation, Judah and Israel, are addressed here. Zion was the center of religion—God's temple was there, and Samaria was the metropolis of a powerful kingdom.

"Woe to them that are at ease in Zion." The common expression at departure a few years ago was, "Well, take it easy!" Today we often say, "Have a good day!" which I take to mean practically the same thing. That is what Israel was doing: they were taking it easy. "Woe to them that are at ease in Zion." They were sitting in the lap of luxury in a day of affluence. We have been doing that as a nation since the depression and World War II—we have been sitting in the lap of luxury in a day of affluence.

"And trust in the mountain of Samaria." It was as if Samaria was the place where they stored their atom bombs. It was the capital of the northern kingdom, Ahab and Jezebel had lived there, and lovely palaces of ivory were built there. The mountains of Samaria provided such excellent natural fortifications that the city was able to stand the Assyrian siege for three years before it fell. Samaria was such an important city that, after the Assyrians had destroyed it, Herod later rebuilt it. Herod was quite a builder, and he built all over Palestine. He built Caesarea right from the ground up, but Samaria he rebuilt because it was such a marvelous location. With all this luxury and excellent fortifications, Israel felt secure and well protected.

"Which are named chief of the nations, to whom the house of Israel came!" "Chief of the nations" probably refers to Israel's princes who were men of rank and authority. To these godless and careless heads of the nation the people of Israel came for justice and for help. But the princes were interested only in their own ease and self-indulgence. The term *chief of the nations* may also refer to Israel herself, as she was recognized among the nations in that day. In other words, she belonged to the United Nations and had a great deal of influence.

**Pass ye unto Calneh, and see; and from thence go ye to Hamath the great: then go down to Gath of the Philistines: be they better than these kingdoms? or their border greater than your border? [Amos 6:2].**

"Pass ye unto Calneh, and see." Calneh is one of the cities that was in the intersection of the Tigris River and the upper Zab River. Nineveh was there, Calneh was there, and that area constituted a great center.

"And from thence go ye to Hamath the great." Hamath is the chief city in Syria. We are going south now.

"Then go down to Gath of the Philistines." Gath is way south in Philistia and was the leading city of the Philistines.

"Be they better than these kingdoms? or their border greater than your border?" In other words, "Go look at these other nations. Why do you think that you are superior to these nations? You're not superior. You are engaged in the same sins that they are, and your responsibility is greater. They have no

revelation from God, but you do have a revelation from God."

Now Amos will mention the three national sins of Israel. These are the three sins which brought the northern kingdom down. They also brought the southern kingdom down; they brought Babylon down; they brought Egypt down; they brought Greece down; and they brought Rome down. They have brought down many great nations. They are the reason that France and Great Britain have become second-rate nations today. At one time we said, "The sun never sets on the British Empire," but today it looks as if the British Empire itself is setting. These three sins are national sins, and they are sins for which God will judge the nations.

**Ye that put far away the evil day, and cause the seat of violence to come near [Amos 6:3].**

Israel was saying, "Yes, a day of judgment is coming, but it is not near. We do not need to worry about it." That was the thing that Hezekiah said to Isaiah when Isaiah told him that judgment was coming on the southern kingdom and that they were to be carried into captivity. Hezekiah said, "Will it be in my day?" Isaiah said, "No, it won't be in your day." And even Hezekiah, who was a great king, said, "Well, then, that's all right."

Our present generation is passing on to our grandchildren a nation that is in debt and in great trouble. I used to worry about my daughter and the day in which she would live. Now I worry about my two little grandsons and the world that they are moving into and in which they will live. The evil day is coming.

What are the three sins which destroy a nation? The first sin is given in verse 4—

**That lie upon beds of ivory, and stretch themselves upon their couches, and eat the lambs out of the flock, and the calves out of the midst of the stall [Amos 6:4].**

Illicit sex and gluttony are the two sins that are mentioned here, and they are sins of the flesh.

"That lie upon beds of ivory." Ahab and Jezebel had built an ivory palace in Samaria. It has been thoroughly excavated now, and the workmen have found there many very fine, delicate vessels that were in the rubble and ruin of that great palace. That palace represented the life of the upper class of that day. "They lie upon beds of ivory"—they all had king-sized beds. They were taking it easy.

"And stretch themselves upon their couches" suggests their preoccupation with sex. That was the thing that they were engaged in, and it is that which characterizes our own day. Someone tried to answer the current women's liberation movement by saying that the woman's place is in the kitchen and in the bedroom. May I say to you, that is an awful thing to say. I totally disagree with that comment, but it does show the color and complexion of our nation today. Much has been reported in the press regarding the social life in our nation's capital. We are told that when they get together, they are heavily involved in drinking and that the main topic of conversation is who is dating whose wife. Such activity is not limited to those of any particular political party. Thank God there are individuals who are exceptions to this type of thing, but I am afraid that more attention is paid to sex in Washington, D.C., than to any of the problems which face this nation. When our lawmakers appear on television, they become very serious, but their social life—this is not true of all of them, of course—seems to be very corrupt.

No nation has been able to survive such involvement in sin. Rome was probably the greatest of all nations; then why did it fall apart? No outside enemy destroyed Rome. It was like "Humpty-Dumpty"—

Humpty-Dumpty sat on a wall,
Humpty-Dumpty had a great fall;
All the King's horses, and all the King's men
Could not put Humpty-Dumpty together again.

Why did Rome fall? Gibbon, in his *Decline and Fall of the Roman Empire*, mentions that the destruction of the family was one of the important reasons Rome fell. When immorality came in, then the nation began to go down.

The second national sin is given in verse 5—

**That chant to the sound of the viol, and invent to themselves instruments of music, like David [Amos 6:5].**

They came up with a lot of new tunes in that day. You may think that jazz, rock and roll, and hard rock music are something new, but Israel had it back in that day. The character of music can destroy a nation, and as far as I'm concerned, we have arrived at that point in our nation. I know that I sound like a square and a real backward fellow, and that I am. Someone will say, "You just don't know any-

thing about music." While it is true that I do not know much about music, I do know what I like and what I don't like; a lot of it I don't like today, and I simply do not listen to it.

"They chant to the sound of the viol, and invent to themselves instruments of music, like David." But the music was no longer used as it was in David's day. David was a genius whose music was to praise and glorify God. Israel also had geniuses in Amos' day, but they were not writing music to the praise and glory of God. Instead, it was that which took people away from God and from the worship of God.

Now we come to the third national sin—

**That drink wine in bowls, and anoint themselves with the chief ointments: but they are not grieved for the affliction of Joseph [Amos 6:6].**

"That drink wine in bowls"—not just in little glasses but in bowls; they were really alcoholics.

"And anoint themselves with the chief ointments: but they are not grieved for the affliction of Joseph." In that day there was a great deal of attention given to the matter of getting the right kind of ointment for the underarms. I don't mind mentioning this because it is mentioned on television all the time. It was pretty important in Israel that you use the right kind of deodorant, but it was *drunkenness* that was destroying the nation.

Drunkenness is the thing that is destroying our nation today along with these other sins—and we are not getting by with it, my friend. There is an alarming number of alcoholics in this country and many, many more people whose lives are directly affected by the alcoholic. A majority of the fatal automobile accidents are caused by alcohol. More people are being killed in automobile accidents in this country than were ever killed in Vietnam, but no one is protesting about that.

I was amazed a few years ago when one of the distilleries ran an advertisement about young people drinking, saying they were concerned about the problem. In their ad, they said: "Teenagers, especially in a group, are often tempted to do things they might not do on their own, like taking a drink when they know they shouldn't. We are sure you are concerned about this problem." Imagine the liquor makers telling you and me that they think we are concerned because they are concerned! Well, why don't they quit making the stuff? Their ad continued: "You don't have to worry much about it, if you've shown your youngster over the years that your ideas about drinking are healthy and mature." What are "healthy and mature" ideas about drinking? Drinking is drinking, isn't it? They certainly were not running an advertisement for prohibition!

I would like to share with you this poem, "It's Nobody's Business"—

It's nobody's business what I drink.
   I care not what my neighbors think,
Or how many laws they choose to pass.
   I'll tell the world I'll have my glass.
Here's one man's freedom cannot be
   curbed.
   My right to drink is undisturbed.
So he drank in spite of law or man,
   Then got into his old tin can,
Stepped on the gas and let it go,
   Down the highway to and fro.
He took the curves at fifty miles,
   With bleary eyes and a drunken smile.
Not long 'til a car he tried to pass,
   Then a crash, a scream, and breaking
   glass.
The other car was upside down,
   About two miles from the nearest
   town.
The man was clear, but his wife was
   caught,
   And he needed the help of that drunken
   sot,
Who sat in a maudlin, drunken daze
   And heard the scream and saw the
   blaze,
But too far gone to save a life.
   By helping the car from off the wife.
The car was burned and a mother died,
   While a husband wept and a baby
   cried.
And a drunk sat by, and still some think
   It's nobody's business what they drink.
                —Unknown

The sins of the flesh (illicit sex and gluttony), heathen music, and drunkenness are the three great sins which have brought great nations down. I simply cannot believe that our nation will be the exception to the rule. It is enough to break any person's heart to see what is happening in this great nation of ours. Yet we try to explain it away by saying that now we are civilized, now we have a new morality, now we have grown up and gotten rid of the old Puritan notions. By the way, the Puritans and the Pilgrims founded a great nation. Are we, the sophisticated and suave folk, going to keep that great nation, or are we losing it?

This message from Amos was fulfilled in his day. The northern kingdom was destroyed and went into captivity. These are the sins that brought it down. In verse 4 it was gluttony and illicit sex; in verse 5 it was heathen music; and in verse 6 it was drunkenness. It is the same old story: wine, women, and song. That is what a great many people think life is all about. Actually, that is not what life is all about but what death is all about. It is the philosophy which says, "Eat, drink, and be merry, for tomorrow we die." Or the philosophy which says, "Pick the daisies while you can"—the day is coming when you won't be able to pick them. In other words, satisfy self. But if a man (or a nation) goes down that line, he will find out that it does not lead to a pot of gold; it is a dead-end street with the emphasis upon *dead*. It has led to the death of individuals and of nations.

All of this reveals something quite interesting about the human heart. You can put the whole world into the heart and it still will not be satisfied. That is remarkable, is it not? Only God can fill the vacuum of the human heart. The iniquity of Israel is going to lead to the destruction of the nation—

**Therefore now shall they go captive with the first that go captive, and the banquet of them that stretched themselves shall be removed [Amos 6:7].**

"Therefore." One preacher has said that when you come to *therefore* in the Bible, you'd better investigate what it's there for. Here it leads to this great statement that, because of these three great sins, the northern kingdom will go into captivity first. That is the direction in which they were moving, and they were moving rapidly. They were much closer to it than they could really believe.

**The Lord GOD hath sworn by himself, saith the LORD the God of hosts, I abhor the excellency of Jacob, and hate his palaces: therefore will I deliver up the city with all that is therein [Amos 6:8].**

Their palaces were places of corruption and storehouses of plunder from the poor. God hated all this. If you want to know God's attitude toward the present-day philosophy of the new morality, of illicit sex, gluttony, degrading music, and drunkenness, He makes it very clear here. God says He *hates* them. As a result of these sins, Israel had become a godless nation. These are the things which will take you away from God or prevent your coming to Him in the first place.

**And it shall come to pass, if there remain ten men in one house, that they shall die [Amos 6:9].**

Some expositors believe that this refers to the coming of a devastating plague, such as often follows warfare.

**And a man's uncle shall take him up, and he that burneth him, to bring out the bones out of the house, and shall say unto him that is by the sides of the house, Is there yet any with thee? and he shall say, No. Then shall he say, Hold thy tongue: for we may not make mention of the name of the LORD [Amos 6:10].**

This is a strange statement. I shall give you Dr. Charles L. Feinberg's explanation (from his book *Joel, Amos and Obadiah* pp. 89–90), which is probably accurate:

How widespread the plague will be is noted for us in verse 10. When one's next of kin, to whom the duty of burial belonged, would come to carry the corpse out of the house to burn it, he would find but one remaining out of the ten who lived there formerly. And that last surviving one hidden away in the innermost recesses of the houses fearfully awaiting the hour when the plague would carry him away also. In ancient Israel in accordance with the words of Genesis 3:19 burial was the accepted method of disposal of the dead. In this the New Testament doctrine of the body concurs. Hence cremation was considered wrong and not countenanced (see Amos 2:1). But when God's judgment falls upon His people, there will be so many dead that they will not bury but burn them. The cases here and 1 Samuel 31:12 are exceptional cases. Here cremation is resorted to in order to prevent contagion; in 1 Samuel it was done to obviate further dishonor of the bodies of Saul and his sons by the Philistines. When asked if there are others alive, the remaining occupant of the house will say there is none. Immediately he will be told to hold his peace for fear he would mention the name of the Lord in announcing the death of the others in the household, or in praising God for his own deliverance. Punishment will so work fear and despair in them all that they will refrain from even the mention of the

name of the Lord (which should be their sole refuge in such an hour) lest further wrath come upon them.

**For, behold, the LORD commandeth, and he will smite the great house with breaches, and the little house with clefts [Amos 6:11].**

High and low, great and small were going into Assyrian captivity.

**Shall horses run upon the rock? will one plow there with oxen? for ye have turned judgment into gall, and the fruit of righteousness into hemlock [Amos 6:12].**

"Shall horses run upon the rock?" If you have ever ridden horseback in mountain country where there is a great deal of rock, you know that a horse can slip and fall there. As a young fellow I belonged to the cavalry division of the National Guard. We were out on patrol duty, and I was riding a big, tall red horse. The section I patrolled was a very rocky one up in middle Tennessee. My horse slipped and fell on one of my feet. As a result, I got out of patrol duty and was sent home because they did not want me hanging around. That got me out of a lot of hard work, and very frankly, I have always appreciated that old red horse. "Shall horses run upon the rock?" Well, they'd better not because they will slip and fall.

"Will one plow there with oxen?" You *cannot* run a plow over a rock.

"For ye have turned judgment into gall, and the fruit of righteousness into hemlock." Israel had done that which was contrary to reason, that which was contrary to righteousness. Amos is saying to them, "You've acted foolishly"—as foolish as I was in riding that old red horse over rocky terrain.

**Ye which rejoice in a thing of nought, which say, Have we not taken to us horns by our own strength? [Amos 6:13].**

"Have we not taken to us horns by our own strength?" Since in the Scriptures "horns" are symbolic of power, this is probably a reference to the military strength of Jeroboam II in which Israel was trusting.

**But, behold, I will raise up against you a nation, O house of Israel, saith the LORD the God of hosts; and they shall afflict you from the entering in of**

Hemath unto the river of the wilderness [Amos 6:14].

"They shall afflict you from the entering in of Hemath;" that is, from all the way up in Syria, for Hemath was the chief city of Syria.

"Unto the river of the wilderness" should be translated "unto the river of Arabah." Arabah is the river on the other side of the Jordan River which flowed into the Dead Sea.

God is saying, "Through the whole extent of your land this enemy will come down from the north." That enemy was not Ben-hadad of Syria, but it was the king of Assyria who would take these people into captivity.

# CHAPTER 7

*THEME: Visions of future*

Chapter 7 opens the third and last major division of the Book of Amos. These final three chapters contain visions of the future. Although this fellow Amos might be called a clodhopper and a country preacher, he could soar to the heights. Some of the visions the Lord gave to him are quite remarkable.

## VISION OF GRASSHOPPERS

**Thus hath the Lord GOD shewed unto me; and, behold, he formed grasshoppers in the beginning of the shooting up of the latter growth; and, lo, it was the latter growth after the king's mowings [Amos 7:1].**

"Thus hath the Lord GOD shewed unto me; and, behold, he formed grasshoppers in the beginning of the shooting up of the latter growth." These are called grasshoppers in our translation, but they were, of course, locusts.

"And, lo, it was the latter growth after the king's mowings." There were two crops that could be harvested from the land in that day, and the first crop went to the king as taxes. Actually, the people paid more than one-tenth as a tithe. It is estimated that they paid out about three-tenths of what they took from the land, and here we can see an example of that. However, this time, after the king had gotten his due, a plague of grasshoppers or locusts came in and took *their* share so that there was nothing left for the people who had really done the work. This was a judgment that should have shaken the people and should have awakened them.

**And it came to pass, that when they had made an end of eating the grass of the land, then I said, O Lord GOD, forgive, I beseech thee: by whom shall Jacob arise? for he is small [Amos 7:2].**

Amos says to the Lord, "We have been cut down to size. This has so weakened us that we'll not be able to stand." He calls out to God to forgive and help them. And notice, the Lord is still patient with Israel—

**The LORD repented for this: It shall not be, saith the LORD [Amos 7:3].**

The Lord said, "I will not do it—I will not weaken you in this way." He got rid of the grasshoppers, and He gave them a good crop. You would think that because of His tender mercy the people would return to God, but they did not.

## VISION OF FIRE

**Thus hath the Lord GOD shewed unto me: and, behold, the Lord GOD called to contend by fire, and it devoured the great deep, and did eat up a part [Amos 7:4].**

Many commentators believe the fire here was actually a drought. I am perfectly willing to say that a drought has to go along with the fire. When we have dry weather here in Southern California, we often have fires in the mountains. We have a great many fires here due, in my judgment, to the carelessness of the public. Many of them have been started by cigarettes. Nevertheless, the high fire danger is usually brought on by a drought. But the thing which did the destroying, I believe, was a literal fire, and I think Amos makes that very clear.

**Then said I, O Lord GOD, cease, I beseech thee: by whom shall Jacob arise? for he is small.**

**The LORD repented for this: This also shall not be, saith the Lord GOD [Amos 7:5–6].**

Apparently, God sent rain, and the fires were put out. Again, God heard them. When it says that God "repented," it is because of the prayers of the people. God was tenderhearted and would not go through with it. The awful thing, my friend, in rejecting Christ and thus being lost eternally, is the fact that you have to do it against a God who is tenderhearted and who is gracious and loving. God *loves* you, and to sin against that love is an awful, dreadful, and terrible thing.

## VISION OF PLUMBLINE

**Thus he shewed me: and, behold, the Lord stood upon a wall made by a plumbline, with a plumbline in his hand.**

**And the LORD said unto me, Amos, what seest thou? And I said, A plumbline. Then said the Lord, Behold, I will set a plumbline in the midst of my people Israel: I will not again pass by them any more [Amos 7:7–8].**

We find the plumbline used many places in the Word of God. In Jeremiah 31:38–39 we read, "Behold, the days come, saith the LORD, that the city shall be built to the LORD from the tower of Hananeel unto the gate of the corner. And the measuring line shall yet go forth over against it upon the hill Gareb, and shall compass about to Goath." The "measuring line" is the plumbline, if you please. Every time that you have a vision of the plumbline in Scripture (see Isa. 28:17; Zech. 2:1–2), it means that God is getting ready to judge. In the Book of Daniel, the prophet of God said to King Belshazzar, ". . . Thou art weighed in the balances, and art found wanting" (Dan. 5:27). When God begins to measure either in length or in weight, you can be sure that the people have not measured up to God's requirements, and judgment is the thing which He has in mind. Amos does not intercede for the people again, realizing that God's judgment is just.

**And the high places of Isaac shall be desolate, and the sanctuaries of Israel shall be laid waste; and I will rise against the house of Jeroboam with the sword [Amos 7:9].**

In other words, God says that Jeroboam will not have peace. God's principle is, "There is

no peace, saith the LORD, unto the wicked" (Isa. 48:22). And Jeroboam will not have peace.

## PERSONAL EXPERIENCE OF THE PROPHET

We have wedged in here, between these visions, a little historic interlude, a very personal experience of the prophet Amos. I have considered this section at length in the Introduction, and it also fits very well into the story here.

**Then Amaziah the priest of Beth-el sent to Jeroboam king of Israel, saying, Amos hath conspired against thee in the midst of the house of Israel: the land is not able to bear all his words.**

**For thus Amos saith, Jeroboam shall die by the sword, and Israel shall surely be led away captive out of their own land [Amos 7:10–11].**

If you go back and read verse 9 carefully, you will find that Amaziah is lying here. This is one of the tragic things that goes on in the church today. When I teach I try to speak as simply and as plainly as I possibly can, and yet I discover that people will misquote me. They represent me as having said something that I have not said at all. Sometimes this is done through simply not understanding or failing to comprehend what was said; other times it is done deliberately.

Amaziah was the priest of the golden calf, and you can imagine the type of individual he was. He was a hired preacher—he said what the king wanted him to say. And I suppose that he was very cultured and used very flowery language. I'm sure he was a good backslapper; he wasn't a pulpit-pounder but a backslapper. And he could, of course, entertain. He had charisma, and he was very attractive in many ways.

Amaziah went in and deliberately lied to the king about Amos. Amos had not said that Jeroboam would perish with the sword, and Jeroboam did not. Amos had said, "And I [God] will rise against the house of Jeroboam with the sword," which meant that warfare would come, and it *did* come. Israel was finally taken into captivity to Assyria.

**Also Amaziah said unto Amos, O thou seer, go, flee thee away into the land of Judah, and there eat bread, and prophesy there:**

**But prophesy not again any more at Beth-el: for it is the king's chapel, and it is the king's court [Amos 7:12–13].**

Amaziah came to Amos, insulted him, and, in effect, called him an ignoramus. I'd like to know where the books are that Amaziah wrote. We have had one book preserved now for over twenty-five hundred years that was written by Amos but none that were written by Amaziah. Amaziah called Amos a country rube and insinuated that he was not fit to speak in the king's chapel. He said, "We want soft words spoken here. We don't want anyone to be offended."

"O thou seer, go, flee thee away into the land of Judah." In other words, "Get out of town and get lost. We don't want you here anymore. You've been speaking in the king's chapel and, after all, you are just not up to it. You're not the caliber of preacher that should be in the pulpit there." Now although Amos was a country man without seminary training, he was no slouch by any means. I hope we agree that he was thoroughly capable of filling the pulpit; in fact, he was a great preacher of God. The people knew when they listened to him that they were getting the Word of God. It is always a comfort to people to have a pastor who is giving the Word of God—that is something very important in these days.

**Then answered Amos, and said to Amaziah, I was no prophet, neither was I a prophet's son; but I was an herdman, and a gatherer of sycomore fruit:**

**And the LORD took me as I followed the flock, and the LORD said unto me, Go, prophesy unto my people Israel [Amos 7:14–15].**

Amos answered in such a proper manner that it was evident that he was a moderate man. He wasn't giving out the wild utterances of a prophecy monger. He was no fanatic at all. He said, "Why, I know I'm no prophet. I never claimed to be a prophet. I never went to your seminaries. I'm not even a prophet's son. I was just a herdsman, a gatherer of sycamore fruits, and the Lord took me, and the Lord told me to prophesy. I'm here because *the Lord* put me here." When a man has that kind of confidence, he's really got confidence, my friend.

A man should be very sure that he has a call from God if he is going to be in the ministry. If there is any doubt in his mind, he ought not to do it. Some say that if you can do anything else, then don't go into the ministry. I don't quite agree with that, because a great many of us could have done something else and might have preferred doing it, by the way. The important thing is: Did God call you? If God has called you, my friend, you ought not to let anything stand in the way.

Now Amos has a personal prophecy for Amaziah, and this is strong medicine for him. Many folk say to me, "Dr. McGee, you are very harsh at times with certain people or certain groups or certain churches." In answer to that, I can truly say that I carry no bias or hatred in my heart against any of those that I mention. What I am trying to do is to say what the Word of God says. The argument given to me is that, as a Christian, I ought to be sweet and nice and I ought not to speak harshly. Love is to be the theme today: Love, love, love! My friend, listen to Amos as he talks to "brother Amaziah"—

**Now therefore hear thou the word of the LORD: Thou sayest, Prophesy not against Israel, and drop not thy word against the house of Isaac.**

**Therefore thus saith the LORD; Thy wife shall be an harlot in the city, and thy sons and thy daughters shall fall by the sword, and thy land shall be divided by line; and thou shalt die in a polluted land: and Israel shall surely go into captivity forth of his land [Amos 7: 16–17].**

"Therefore thus saith the LORD"—Amos says that he has a word from God to this man Amaziah. This is a very disturbing prophecy, and it's a very strong prophecy, but the thing is that it was a *true* prophecy. When Assyria came down, they did make the women harlots. The sons and daughters were destroyed, and those who were not destroyed were taken into captivity. And this old priest of the golden calf, Amaziah, was taken into Assyrian captivity. I am sure that Amaziah's word on his deathbed would have been like that of old Cardinal Wolsey (whom I mentioned earlier) who wished that he had served his God as he had served his king. Cardinal Wolsey had tried to play politics with Henry VIII and did not really tell him what the Word of God had to say.

If we as ministers fail to give out the Word of God, there is no reason for us to point our fingers at the politicians in Washington and accuse them of failing our country and jeopardizing our nation. My friend in the ministry, if you are not giving out the Word of God, there is no other traitor in this land today as guilty as you are. If you are called to be a minister, you are called to be a minister of *the Word of God.* If you are not giving that Word out, you are a traitor to the cause of Christ today. Those are strong words, I know, just as Amos' words were strong.

# CHAPTER 8

*THEME: Vision of basket of summer fruit*

This is the fourth vision, and it takes in the entire eighth chapter of this book. It is important to get the meaning of this vision, because that will help us in the interpretation of passages that come later on. Especially it will clarify some of the things that our Lord Jesus said.

**Thus hath the Lord GOD shewed unto me: and behold a basket of summer fruit [Amos 8:1].**

A great deal can be said about a basket of summer fruit. I love fruit. To me all fruits are delicious. I enjoy the citrus fruits of California or Florida, the fruits of northern California and Oregon and Washington. Wherever I am, I enjoy the fruit produced in that locality. There is nothing more attractive than a basket of summer fruit, and that basket of summer fruit has a message.

First of all, a basket of summer fruit represents a harvest. It tells us that the tree is no longer producing. My apricot tree had some lovely apricots on it this past summer, but there is no need for me to go out now to see if there is fruit on the tree. The limbs are bare; there is no fruit. The harvest is past. There will be no fruit until next year. So we see that, although a basket of summer fruit is delightful and delicious, it also speaks of the end of the harvest.

A basket of summer fruit also tells us of rapid spoilage and quick deterioration. Back in the time of World War II, a missionary from South America wrote to us from the East that she was coming to the West Coast. Since she was a personal friend and would be staying with us during her time in California, she told us the day of her arrival. You may remember that in those days trains were crowded and the military had priority over all else. When our friend reached Chicago, she learned that her reservation had been cancelled. She had to wait a week before she could come out to California. We had prepared the guest room for her for the day we had expected her to arrive. I had gone out and picked some lovely apricots off my tree and had put a basket of apricots in her room. When we got the telegram from her telling us of her delay, we just closed the door to her room. We forgot all about the basket of apricots. Then when the time came for her to arrive, we opened the door to her room, and I want to tell you the odor was not very pleasant! In fact, it took us weeks to get the odor out of that room. There is a message in a basket of summer fruit. God gives us a dramatic and a figurative illustration.

**And he said, Amos, what seest thou? And I said, A basket of summer fruit. Then said the LORD unto me, The end is come upon my people of Israel; I will not again pass by them any more [Amos 8:2].**

We have seen in chapter 7 in the previous visitations of God's judgments that Amos prayed for the survival of Israel and that God changed His mind and withheld His hand. But now the basket of summer fruit indicates that the harvest is past. The jig is up. The northern kingdom of Israel has come to the end of the line. Judgment will come, and harvest is symbolic of that.

Since harvest speaks of a time of judgment and falls at the end of an age, I think that some things our Lord said are misunderstood if one does not understand what is meant by the harvest. Jesus said to His disciples, ". . . The harvest truly is plenteous, but the labourers are few; Pray ye therefore the Lord of the harvest, that he will send forth labourers into his harvest" (Matt. 9:37–38). Our Lord was speaking at the end of an age when the dispensation of the law was coming to an end. Christ was going to go to the cross. He said that He needed harvesters to go out into Israel.

After His death on the cross, it is a different picture. For this age of grace He gives His parable of the sower. A sower went forth to sow seed. ". . . Go ye into all the world, and preach the gospel . . ." (Mark 16:15), is the message for our age. Go out into the world and sow the seed. This is the time for sowing the Word of God. My business and your business is just sowing the seed. It is the Lord's business to do the converting. We believe that the Spirit of God will take the Word of God and make a son of God. We are just seed-sowers. We are not harvesters. Harvest speaks of judgment, and it speaks of the end of an age. Our business today is to be out sowing the seed. I wish so much that I could get this message across to people. I wish I could motivate all believers to do what God has called us to do. Our business is to sow the seed of the Word of God.

**And the songs of the temple shall be howlings in that day, saith the Lord God: there shall be many dead bodies in every place; they shall cast them forth with silence [Amos 8:3].**

The place for praising God will be changed into a place of wailing. The place of rejoicing before God will be changed into a place of weeping. The slain bodies will be everywhere. This is a terrifying prophecy.

**Hear this, O ye that swallow up the needy, even to make the poor of the land to fail [Amos 8:4].**

Again God is speaking of the exploitation of the poor. Although I have commented on this before, I feel it is important for us to realize how God feels about the poor of this world. I have experienced being poor. My dad was a workman. I remember him wearing his overalls and drawing his paycheck on Saturday. After he would pay the grocery bill and the doctor bill and the rent, he always gave my sister and me a nickel each, but I remember one Saturday night when he had only one nickel left. He told me to go to the store and buy a sack of candy. I got gumdrops, because I could get a big sack of them for a nickel in those days, and my sister and I divided the gumdrops.

My dad died when I was fourteen, and it was up to me to support my mother and sister. At fourteen I had to secure a special permit to get a job. Then, after I was converted and felt called to the ministry, some folk took an interest in me and helped me get through school. Believe me, I am for the poverty pro-

gram—but not the one we have had in our society that puts money in the pockets of those who already have it. I want to see a poverty program that will really help the poor get on their feet and enable them to work.

In the days of Amos, God accuses them of even making "the poor of the land to fail." That is, the poor were brought down to such a low poverty level that they never could escape from it. The poor always suffer more acutely in a godless nation—I don't think that statement can be successfully contradicted.

**Saying, When will the new moon be gone, that we may sell corn? and the sabbath, that we may set forth wheat, making the ephah small, and the shekel great, and falsifying the balances by deceit? [Amos 8:5].**

If you had been among the people in that day—especially down in Jerusalem at the temple—you would have wondered what the Lord was talking about. You would have seen them going through the rituals which God had prescribed. But, you see, God knew what was in their hearts. "The new moon" and "the sabbath" were holy days on which business was not transacted. God is saying that even when the rich went to the temple to praise God, they were so greedy and covetous that they were thinking about business the next day and how they could make more money by cheating their customers. They not only practiced their sin during the week, but they carried it into the temple. What a picture this gives us of Israel in that day—and of modern man as well.

**That we may buy the poor for silver, and the needy for a pair of shoes; yea, and sell the refuse of the wheat? [Amos 8:6].**

"That we may buy the poor for silver." The poor even had to sell themselves into slavery. That was permitted in that land under the Mosaic system. They would buy the needy for a pair of shoes—that's how cheap they were! And they would sell the poor the refuse of the wheat. That means they got the "seconds," the leftovers which an honest dealer throws away.

I have never felt right about giving old clothes to help the poor in the church. I have never felt they should be given the leftovers of anything. When I was just starting my ministry, a dairyman in Georgia told me he generally had a quart of skim milk left over and he would leave it for me since I preached in a little church there. I didn't accept the milk even though I could have used it. I felt it would not be fair to the man to give him the feeling he was doing a great service to the Lord by giving his leftovers. Remember how David said, ". . . neither will I offer burnt offerings unto the LORD my God of that which doth cost me nothing . . ." (2 Sam. 24:24).

It is no accident that the Lord Jesus, when He was here on earth, sat and watched how the people gave in the temple. Was that His business? Yes. And He is interested in how much *we* give to Him and how much we keep for ourselves.

I guess you can tell that I can identify with Amos. Maybe the reason I love this man Amos so much is that he talks my language. He was a poor man himself, and he says the thing that I understand.

You see, Amos is explaining why Israel was like a basket of summer fruit. The goodness of Israel was just as perishable and just as soon deteriorated as summer fruit. One evidence of this was the way they treated the poor.

**The LORD hath sworn by the excellency of Jacob, Surely I will never forget any of their works [Amos 8:7].**

"The LORD hath sworn by the excellency of Jacob." The excellency of Jacob is the Lord Jesus Christ. The Lord has sworn by the Messiah who is coming. No oath could be taken that is higher than that.

Now notice what it is that He has sworn: "Surely I will never forget any of their works." As we have seen previously in this book, God does not forget the works of any of us—believer or unbeliever. Those of us who are believers will one day ". . . appear before the judgment seat of Christ; that every one may receive the things done in his body, according to that he hath done, whether it be good or bad" (2 Cor. 5:10). In the days of Amos, they had heaped up sins unto the day of God's wrath, and He remembered every one of them.

**Shall not the land tremble for this, and every one mourn that dwelleth therein? and it shall rise up wholly as a flood; and it shall be cast out and drowned, as by the flood of Egypt [Amos 8:8].**

Some commentators think this refers to an earthquake. That is possible, and I certainly wouldn't want to rule that out. However, I think it is the fact that God is coming down hard upon them in judgment that makes the land tremble. Even today one cannot go through places like Samaria and the rugged hill country around Gilgal and Beth-el without being impressed by the frightful state of the land. It once was a very fruitful area with a great deal of vegetation, including a great many trees, but today the land has been pretty much denuded. It shows the evidence of judgment upon it. God came down heavily upon the land. We will see in the next chapter that the promise for the future includes a promise for the land.

When we study prophecy, we need to remember that, whether God promised judgment or blessing, the land was involved as well as the people. That is one reason why I cannot accept the idea that the prophecies of the Scripture are being fulfilled in the present return of Jews to that land. Although they have returned physically to the land, they have not returned spiritually to the Lord. It is obvious today that God's blessing is not upon that land. It hasn't changed. It is true that a great deal of hard work has gone into it, areas have been recovered from swamps, and irrigation has reached the desert in many places (which has made it blossom like a rose), but those places are few and far between even in that small land. Therefore, it cannot be said that these great prophecies are being fulfilled. Israel's last return to the land has not yet taken place. Let's remember that there are more Jews in New York City than there are in the entire nation of Israel—that ought to tell us something.

**And it shall come to pass in that day, saith the Lord GOD, that I will cause the sun to go down at noon, and I will darken the earth in the clear day [Amos 8:9].**

Now here is Amos speaking of "that day," which we have already seen is a technical expression that refers to the Day of the Lord. And generally it refers to the Great Tribulation because that comes first—the day begins at night as far as Israel was concerned.

Amos gives a mingling of prophecy of the near future and the far distant future. The Day of the Lord has not yet arrived. The sun has not gone down at noon, nor has the earth been darkened in the clear day. When Amos wrote this, this was still in the far distant future.

Now he turns to the more immediate future for Israel—

**And I will turn your feasts into mourning, and all your songs into lamenta-**

**tion; and I will bring up sackcloth upon all loins, and baldness upon every head; and I will make it as the mourning of an only son, and the end thereof as a bitter day [Amos 8:10].**

"And I will turn your feasts into mourning." God gave to the nation Israel seven feasts. The males of Israel were required to come before Him for three of those great feasts. They were to come with rejoicing. It was to be a time of praise and thanksgiving and glorifying God. Now God says that, since they have been celebrating the feasts but not giving praise to Him, He will turn their feasts into mourning. They will become the very opposite of what He intended them to be. "And all your songs into lamentation." When God's judgment falls upon them, there will be no more singing—no more joy—only lamentation.

Although I am certainly no music critic, I have been interested to observe the trend of modern music. When I was a young fellow, the popular music was the blues. That was followed by jazz and then rock and roll. Today it is hard rock. Do you detect any joy in that music? Oh, the songs have a beat to them so that you hop up and down like a yo-yo, but it is almost a mindless kind of motion which requires no thinking. That kind of music stimulates the flesh but certainly gives no real joy. This is the type of music that the world produces. It is mournful and it is tragic. When I had the privilege of being in Vienna, I attended an opera there. It was the first opera I had ever heard, and I have to confess that I enjoyed it. However, it was a tragedy. The boy didn't get the girl. It was a tragic story, and the songs were lamentations and wailings. Now that is the type of music which the world produces. I am struck with the fact that God has said, "I will turn . . . all your songs into lamentation."

"And I will make it as the mourning of an only son, and the end thereof as a bitter day." Sackcloth on all loins and baldness on every head are indications of deepest mourning. This was literally fulfilled in the judgment that was to come unto them presently.

**Behold, the days come, saith the Lord God, that I will send a famine in the land, not a famine of bread, nor a thirst for water, but of hearing the words of the Lord [Amos 8:11].**

Here is a most unusual famine. God had given them His Word, and they had rejected it. They had despised it and turned aside from it.

Now God tells them that the day is coming when they will no longer have the privilege of hearing His Word.

God tells any church or any nation that, if they will not hear His Word after He has given it to them, He will withdraw it from them. I think we can see this happening in America. There has been a rejection of the Word of God. The churches have turned to liberalism, and the Word of God is no longer preached. There has come a famine of the Word of God. So many of the formerly great churches of this country, the great downtown churches, have turned from the Word of God. As a consequence, many of them have had to close shop. Others are just barely operating, and many of them are operating in the red. Even those which have stayed open have lost their influence and have lost their drawing power.

Actually, very little of the Word of God is getting out in this land today. There is a Gideon Bible in every room in every hotel and motel in this country. Nearly everyone *owns* a Bible. But who is studying it? Who is reading it? Who is believing it? I think we are beginning to see the famine of the Word of God in this country.

**And they shall wander from sea to sea, and from the north even to the east, they shall run to and fro to seek the word of the Lord, and shall not find it [Amos 8:12].**

The distraught people will wander from sea to sea seeking the Word of God but will not find it. God in His great love for His chosen people had sent His Word by prophet after prophet, but they had rejected His Word, persecuted and even slain His prophets. Now one of God's judgments will be His silence.

We see something of this same situation in our own land. I receive numerous letters from folk all over the country who tell me that they have no Bible teaching in their town or community and haven't had any for many years. The famine has already set in for this land of ours. My friend, the most important thing in the world that we can do is to give out God's Word by every means at our disposal.

**In that day shall the fair virgins and young men faint for thirst [Amos 8:13].**

Even the young people, the most hopeful and vigorous members of society, will faint for thirst after the Word of God.

**They that swear by the sin of Samaria, and say, Thy god, O Dan, liveth; and, The manner of Beer-sheba liveth; even they shall fall, and never rise up again [Amos 8:14].**

It was their custom to swear in the name of their gods. "The sin of Samaria" refers to the golden calf which was located at Beth-el. The second golden calf was located at Dan, and there was an idolatrous sanctuary at Beer-sheba, as we have seen. God's judgment upon them from such idolatry concludes this chapter: "they shall fall, and never rise up again." This indicates the dissolution and permanent downfall of the northern kingdom. The ten tribes are going into captivity, and they will never return as the northern kingdom of Israel. When they come back to their land, they will come as part of the twelve tribes.

# CHAPTER 9

*THEME: Vision of worldwide dispersion, regathering and restoration*

This chapter concludes the message of judgment which Amos has been delivering to Israel. Then Amos looks into the far future and gives the glorious prospect of the restored kingdom of Israel.

**I saw the Lord standing upon the altar: and he said, Smite the lintel of the door, that the posts may shake: and cut them in the head, all of them; and I will slay the last of them with the sword: he that fleeth of them shall not flee away, and he that escapeth of them shall not be delivered [Amos 9:1].**

This describes the coming of the Assyrians. We need to understand that "the altar" is not the altar of Solomon's temple in Jerusalem but is probably the altar of the temple to Baal in Samaria. I have seen the ruins of this temple in Samaria.

"Smite the lintel of the door, that the posts may shake: and cut them in the head, all of them." At the time of the siege, the people would seek refuge in the temples, but the temples would be brought down so suddenly that many of the people would be trapped when the pillars crumbled.

"He that fleeth of them shall not flee away, and he that escapeth of them shall not be delivered." Those who would escape alive from the city would be carried into captivity.

Now notice this frightful statement—

**Though they dig into hell, thence shall mine hand take them; though they climb up to heaven, thence will I bring them down [Amos 9:2].**

"Though they dig into hell." The word translated "hell" is the Hebrew word *sheol*, meaning "the grave or the place of the dead."

There are two things which cause the terror of the wicked. In our day, folk have been so brainwashed by our society that many of them try to blot it out of their minds; but if they give any thought to it at all, the two things which bring terror to the heart of the wicked person are the omnipresence and the immutability of God. God is omnipresent; that is, He is everywhere. Even death cannot separate you from Him. And the immutability of God means that God never changes. Jesus Christ is the same yesterday, today, and forever. These two truths are a great comfort to God's children, but they are frightening to the wicked.

To the child of God the omnipresence of God assures him that God will never leave him. The Lord Jesus said, ". . . I will never leave thee, nor forsake thee" (Heb. 13:5). How wonderful that is! Also He said, ". . . him that cometh to me I will in no wise cast out" (John 6:37). When He receives you, He receives you for eternity. No one can take you out of His hand; and, if you are in His hand, you are very close to Him, you see. The Lord Jesus also likened our relationship to Him to that of a vine and its branches. What can be closer to a vine than its branch? The omnipresence of God is a great comfort to the believer.

However, for the unbeliever, the omnipresence of God is a terror. Many people commit suicide because they want to get away from it all. A prominent man here in Southern California left a suicide note which read, "I want to end it all and get rid of this life." Well, he got rid of his problems and a great many things which were annoying him here—he was in deep trouble—but he didn't get rid of God. Death didn't separate him from God. David understood this when he wrote, "Whither shall I go from thy spirit? or whither shall I flee from thy presence? If I ascend up into heaven, thou art there: if I make my bed in hell, behold, thou art there" (Ps. 139:7–8). And the poet Francis Thompson was not being irreverent when he characterized God as "the hound of heaven" because, regardless of who you are, God is right on your track. You cannot get rid of Him.

Then there is the immutability of God. God didn't learn anything new by reading the morning newspaper. The president or the Senate or the college professors or the scientists cannot teach God anything that is new to Him. He doesn't change His mind. He never changes. "Jesus Christ the same yesterday, and to-day, and for ever" (Heb. 13:8). That is wonderful for the child of God to know. The same One who walked by the Sea of Galilee, who was so gracious and merciful to people, is still the same One who walks with the believer today.

**And though they hide themselves in the top of Carmel, I will search and take them out thence; and though they be hid from my sight in the bottom of the sea, thence will I command the serpent, and he shall bite them [Amos 9:3].**

"And though they hide themselves in the top of Carmel, I will search and take them out thence." The city of Haifa is located on Carmel today. Mount Carmel is wooded and rises to a height of about eighteen hundred feet. I have been there several times and have noted the caves which are along the sides of that mountain. It is said that there are over a thousand caves there, especially on the side toward the sea. But even there God said He would search them out. And although they should try to hide in the bottom of the sea, they would find God there. They could not escape Him.

**And though they go into captivity before their enemies, thence will I command the sword, and it shall slay them: and I will set mine eyes upon them for evil, and not for good [Amos 9:4].**

"And though they go into captivity before their enemies"—that is, going voluntarily in order to spare their lives, they still will not escape God's judgment.

My friend, the wicked do well to fear God and to fear the future. There is no escape for them. The man who commits suicide, thinking that he will get rid of his troubles, will move into real trouble when he faces God. It is like jumping from the frying pan into the fire— and *that* almost literally.

**And the Lord God of hosts is he that toucheth the land, and it shall melt, and all that dwell therein shall mourn: and it shall rise up wholly like a flood; and shall be drowned, as by the flood of Egypt [Amos 9:5].**

You cannot go through that land today without being conscious of the fact that it certainly is no longer a land of milk and honey. Even with all the irrigation and cultivation, it is far from that. Judgment has come upon it.

When I was in a hotel there, I met a lovely Jewish couple in the elevator. We began to talk about the land. They had come out to buy an apartment. They thought they might retire permanently to Israel or at least spend part of the year there. He told me very candidly, "Although we bought the apartment because we want to help our people in this land, we really don't ever expect to use it. I don't think this is the land that the Bible says it is." Obviously, he had not read the prophecy of Amos and did not realize that God's judgment had come upon the land.

**It is he that buildeth his stories in the heaven, and hath founded his troop in the earth; he that calleth for the waters of the sea, and poureth them out upon the face of the earth: The Lord is his name [Amos 9:6].**

In this beautiful way Amos is reminding his people of the omnipotence of God. Not only is He omnipresent, but He is also omnipotent. It is He who does all of this. Out yonder in the heavens, the sun, the moon, the planets, the tremendous galaxies, the quasars, the whole universe obeys God. He has made certain laws by which they are to move, and they obey those laws. But little man—little man is in rebellion against the omnipotent God. In effect, Amos is asking Israel, "Do you think we can escape such a God?"

Now here is one of the strangest statements in the Bible, and it is quite wonderful—

**Are ye not as children of the Ethiopians unto me, O children of Israel? saith the Lord. Have not I brought up Israel out of the land of Egypt? and the Philis-**

tines from Caphtor, and the Syrians from Kir? [Amos 9:7].

When God wanted them to know how much He loved them, He said, "I love you as I love the Ethiopians!" At the time that the Italians under Mussolini invaded Ethiopia in 1935, I made a study of the biblical prophecies concerning Ethiopia. It was amazing to me to discover the place which Ethiopia has in the program of God for the future. It is a nation which may seem very unimportant to us, but it is very important to God.

**Behold, the eyes of the Lord GOD are upon the sinful kingdom, and I will destroy it from off the face of the earth; saving that I will not utterly destroy the house of Jacob, saith the LORD [Amos 9:8].**

"The sinful kingdom" is Israel, of course. "I will destroy it from off the face of the earth" means that He will destroy it as a separate kingdom. When God returns the people of Israel to their land, they will not be a divided kingdom but will be one nation under the sovereignty of the One sitting on the throne of David.

**For, lo, I will command, and I will sift the house of Israel among all nations, like as corn is sifted in a sieve, yet shall not the least grain fall upon the earth [Amos 9:9].**

"I will sift the house of Israel among all nations." If you want to know where the so-called "lost tribes of Israel" are, look in your phone book for the Cohens, the Goldbergs, etc. They are scattered throughout the world, but they are not "lost" as far as God is concerned. "Yet shall not the least grain fall upon the earth." God will not lose one of them.

**All the sinners of my people shall die by the sword, which say, The evil shall not overtake nor prevent us [Amos 9:10].**

How about the sinners? They are going to die. He will judge the individuals who won't turn to Him. We have the same analogy in the contemporary church. Not all church members are saved. Believe me, if you have been a pastor as long as I have, you would *know* that not all church members are genuine believers—but they *are* church members. And the apostle Paul says, ". . . For they are not all Israel, which are of Israel" (Rom. 9:6). There are two kinds of Israelites, the natural and the spiritual Israel. Although "not the

least grain" will fall to the ground, all sinners of the nation will perish, especially the defiant ones whom Amos has been addressing.

This brings us to the final vision of Amos, that of the worldwide regathering and restoration of the kingdom of the Lord. Amos saw beyond the terrible days of judgment and scattering of His people, even beyond the Great Tribulation (which is still future in our day).

**In that day will I raise up the tabernacle of David that is fallen, and close up the breaches thereof; and I will raise up his ruins, and I will build it as in the days of old [Amos 9:11].**

The phrase "in that day" refers to the last days of Israel. "In that day will I raise up the tabernacle of David that is fallen." To follow through on this, listen to James in Acts 15 where he quotes this prophecy of Amos: "And after they had held their peace, James answered, saying, Men and brethren, hearken unto me: Simeon hath declared how God at the first did visit the Gentiles, to take out of them a people for his name. And to this agree the words of the prophets; as it is written, After this I will return, and will build again the tabernacle of David, which is fallen down; and I will build again the ruins thereof, and I will set it up: That the residue of men might seek after the Lord, and all the Gentiles, upon whom my name is called, saith the Lord, who doeth all these things. Known unto God are all his works from the beginning of the world" (Acts 15:13–18).

Today God is calling out a people for His name among the Gentiles. After this He will raise up the tabernacle of David. In other words, he is speaking of the kingdom age, the Millennium, the greatest day which is yet in the future.

**That they may possess the remnant of Edom, and of all the heathen, which are called by my name, saith the LORD that doeth this [Amos 9:12].**

There will be many nations which will enter the Millennium.

**Behold, the days come, saith the LORD, that the plowman shall overtake the reaper, and the treader of grapes him that soweth seed; and the mountains shall drop sweet wine, and all the hills shall melt [Amos 9:13].**

This is the proof of what I have mentioned previously, that when the people of Israel are being blessed, the land of Israel is being blessed. The people and the land belong together. God makes it clear that when *He* returns the people of Israel to their land, it will again be the land of milk and honey. The land is not that now; so I take it that the present return is not the one which is predicted. Although Jews are returning to their land, they are not returning to their God.

**And I will bring again the captivity of my people of Israel, and they shall build the waste cities, and inhabit them; and they shall plant vineyards, and drink the wine thereof; they shall also make gardens, and eat the fruit of them [Amos 9:14].**

God is going to restore Israel to the land. Never again will it be the southern kingdom of Judah and the northern kingdom of Israel. It will all be Israel, an undivided kingdom, as it was in the beginning of its history. It will be all twelve tribes. They are scattered over the whole world today. They are sifted among all nations. Any idea that "the lost tribes" are the people of Great Britain and of the United States is unscriptural. The prophecy clearly states that they will be sifted among all nations. Just look around you. Has God done that, or hasn't He done it? But it will not be that way forever. God will return them to the land. "I will bring again the captivity of my

people of Israel, and they shall build the waste cities, and inhabit them."

**And I will plant them upon their land, and they shall no more be pulled up out of their land which I have given them, saith the LORD thy God [Amos 9:15].**

When God puts them in the land, they will be there permanently.

These are the things God has said He will do for His people: (1) He is going to restore the Davidic dynasty. Who do you think will be the king? It will be a son of David by the name of Jesus, born in Bethlehem of the house and lineage of David. He will be the ruler. (2) Israel will take her place among the nations of the world. She will no longer go to the United Nations with her hat in her hand (nor will she be shutting out Arabs). She will be a nation that is going to be blessed of God and will occupy a place among the nations of the world. (3) In addition to this, there will be a conversion of the nations of the world! This will occur after the church leaves this earth. The greatest conversion to Christ is still in the future. What a day that will be! When God returns Israel to her land, (4) they will build the waste cities and inhabit them. (5) They will eat the fruit of their gardens and drink the wine of their vineyards. The curse on the land will be lifted, and it will produce bountifully. (6) And the people of Israel "shall no more be pulled up out of their land which I have given them, saith the LORD thy God."

# BIBLIOGRAPHY

(Recommended for Further Study)

Cohen, Gary G. and Vandervey, H. Ronald. *Hosea and Amos*. Chicago, Illinois: Moody Press, 1981.

Feinberg, Charles L. *The Minor Prophets*. Chicago, Illinois: Moody Press, 1976.

Gaebelein, Arno C. *The Annotated Bible*. 1917. Reprint. Neptune, New Jersey: Loizeaux Brothers, 1971.

Ironside, H. A. *The Minor Prophets*. Nep-

tune, New Jersey: Loizeaux Brothers, n.d.

Jensen, Irving L. *Minor Prophets of Israel*. Chicago, Illinois: Moody Press, 1975.

Tatford, Frederick A. *The Minor Prophets*. Minneapolis, Minnesota: Klock & Klock, n.d.

Unger, Merrill F. *Unger's Commentary on the Old Testament*, Vol. 2. Chicago, Illinois: Moody Press, 1982.

# The Book of
# OBADIAH
## INTRODUCTION

The name *Obadiah* means "servant of Jehovah." He is one of four prophets about whom we know absolutely nothing except that he wrote prophecy. The other three prophets are Habakkuk, Haggai, and Malachi. These four prophets are cloaked in anonymity. Obadiah is like a ghost writer in that he is there, but we do not know him. He lived up to his name, for he was a servant of Jehovah. A servant boasts of no genealogy neither exploits nor experiences. He doesn't push himself forward. He has to demonstrate by what he *does* that he can even claim the place of a servant. So Obadiah is just a prophet who wrote one of the great prophecies of the Scripture. Dr. Pusey said, "God has willed that his name alone and this brief prophecy should be known to the world." Obadiah is a little book, but it is an example of an atomic bomb in the Bible. It is a small thing, but it has a potent message.

The chief difficulty with the prophecy of Obadiah is where to fit it into the history of the nation Israel. There are some who give the date of 887 B.C., which fixes the time during the reign of Jehoram and the bloody Athaliah (see 2 Kings 8:16–26). Dr. Pusey placed it during the reign of Jehoshaphat (see 2 Chron. 17:7). Although the name *Obadiah* does occur in this passage, it was a common name in that day and probably was not the same Obadiah who wrote this prophecy. Canon Farrar gave the date as 587 B.C., and Dr. Moorehead concurred in this, suggesting that Obadiah was probably a contemporary of Jeremiah's. The whole question seems to hinge on verse 11: "In the day that thou stoodest on the other side, in the day that the strangers carried away captive his forces, and foreigners entered into his gates, and cast lots upon Jerusalem, even thou wast as one of them." Either this was written as prophecy before it happened or it is an historical record of what did happen. The natural interpretation, of course, is to accept it as history rather than prophecy, which places the date of Obadiah's prophecy around 587 B.C., after the Babylonian captivity and during the ministry of the prophet Jeremiah.

The little kingdom of Edom is the subject of this brief prophecy. Verse 6 is the key verse: "How are the things of Esau searched out! how are his hidden things sought up!"

## OUTLINE

I. **Edom—Destruction, vv. 1–16**
   A. Charge against Edom, vv. 1–9
   B. Crime of Edom, vv. 10–14
   C. Catastrophe to Edom, vv. 15–16
   (Poetic justice [*lex talionis*]—law of retaliation)

II. **Israel—Restoration, vv. 17–21**
   A. Condition of Israel, v. 17
   B. Conflagration of the House of Esau, v. 18
   C. Consummation of All Things, vv. 19–21
   (*"And the kingdom shall be the Lord's"*)

# OBADIAH

*THEME: Edom—destruction; and Israel—restoration*

Obadiah is the shortest book in the Old Testament—only twenty-one verses. There are many folk who feel that this book is not worth reading and that if it were omitted from the Bible, it would not be missed. However, the brevity of the message does not render it less important or less significant. Like the other Minor Prophets, the message is primary, it is pertinent, it is practical, and it is poignant. It is a message that can be geared into this day in which we are living.

None of these so-called Minor Prophets are extinct volcanoes; rather, they are distinct action. There is no cold ash in any of them; they are spewing hot lava. Obadiah's prophecy is of devastating judgment against the little kingdom of Edom.

## CHARGE AGAINST EDOM

**The vision of Obadiah. Thus saith the Lord GOD concerning Edom; We have heard a rumour from the LORD, and an ambassador is sent among the heathen, Arise ye, and let us rise up against her in battle [Obad. 1].**

Obadiah tells us immediately, bluntly, and to the point that this is a vision given to him by God Himself.

Who is Obadiah? As I mentioned in the Introduction, he is one of the Minor Prophets about whom we know absolutely nothing. His name was a very common one in Israel, and it means "servant of Jehovah."

"Thus saith the Lord GOD concerning Edom." Edom is the key to this little book, and so we shall have to go back to Genesis to determine the identity of Edom. In Genesis, where we have the record of the generations of Esau, notice this comment: "Now these are the generations of Esau, who is Edom" (Gen. 36:1). Also this: "Thus dwelt Esau in mount Seir: Esau is Edom. And these are the generations of Esau the father of the Edomites in mount Seir" (Gen. 36:8–9).

That is the record that is given to us here, and it is repeated three times. Although I am sure Moses did not know, the Spirit of God knew that this would need to be emphasized—Esau is Edom and Edom is Esau. The Edomites were those who were descended from Esau, just as the Israelites are those who are descended from Jacob.

The story of Esau is that of twin brothers,

sons of Isaac and Rebekah. The boys were not identical twins; actually, they were opposites. The record given back in Genesis 25 begins as Rebekah is about to give birth to these twins: "And the children struggled together within her; and she said, If it be so, why am I thus? And she went to inquire of the LORD. And the LORD said unto her, Two nations are in thy womb, and two manner of people shall be separated from thy bowels; and the one people shall be stronger than the other people; and the elder shall serve the younger" (Gen. 25:22–23). From the very beginning these two brothers were struggling against each other. Esau was an outdoor fellow who loved to hunt. Jacob would rather stay in the house and learn to cook. He was tied to his mama's apron strings. However, Jacob had a spiritual discernment that Esau did not have. Esau was a man of the flesh and did not care for spiritual things. In fact, he so discounted his birthright that he traded it to Jacob for a bowl of soup! "And Esau said to Jacob, Feed me, I pray thee, with that same red pottage; for I am faint: therefore was his name called Edom. And Jacob said, Sell me this day thy birthright. And Esau said, Behold, I am at the point to die: and what profit shall this birthright do to me? And Jacob said, Swear to me this day; and he sware unto him: and he sold his birthright unto Jacob. Then Jacob gave Esau bread and pottage of lentiles; and he did eat and drink, and rose up, and went his way: thus Esau despised his birthright" (Gen. 25:30–34).

He didn't sell his birthright because he was so hungry that he was about to perish, nor because there wasn't anything else to eat in the home of Isaac, but because his was a desire of the flesh and he was willing to trade all of his spiritual heritage for a whim of the moment. The man who had the birthright was in contact with God, and he was the priest of his family. He was the man who had a covenant from God. He was the man who had a relationship with God. In effect Esau said, "I would rather have a bowl of soup than have a relationship with God."

This is an illustration of a great truth for believers today. It is a picture of Christians. A believer has two natures within him, and they are struggling with each other and against each other. In Galatians 5:17 Paul says, "For the flesh lusteth [wars] against the

Spirit, and the Spirit against the flesh: and these are contrary the one to the other: so that ye cannot do the things that ye would." These are the two natures of the believer, the new nature and the old nature. They are opposed to each other. Esau pictures the flesh, the old nature, and Jacob pictures the spirit, the new nature.

The name *Edom* means "red or sunburned." A sunburn occurs when the skin is able to absorb all the rays of light except the rays that make it red. The sunburned man in Scripture is the man who could not absorb the light of heaven, and it burned him. My friend, the light of heaven will either save you or burn you. You will either absorb it, or you will be burned by it. This is always true. Esau represents the flesh. He became Edom. Jacob, who became Israel, a prince with God, represents the spirit.

Having seen Esau in the first book of the Old Testament, look now at the last book of the Old Testament and read this strange language: "I have loved you, saith the Lord. Yet ye say, Wherein hast thou loved us? Was not Esau Jacob's brother? saith the Lord: yet I loved Jacob, And I hated Esau . . ." (Mal. 1:2–3). This is a strange thing for God to say— "I loved Jacob, and I hated Esau." It immediately presents a problem.

A student once approached Dr. Griffith Thomas with this question, "Dr. Thomas, I am having a problem with this statement in Malachi. I cannot understand why God says He hated Esau." Dr. Thomas replied, "Young man, I am having a problem with that verse also, but my problem is different from yours. I can understand why He hated Esau, but I cannot understand why He loved Jacob."

Well, the thing that lends importance to the little Book of Obadiah is that it is the only place in the Word of God where we find the explanation of why God hated Esau.

Ginsburg, the great Hebrew scholar, translated Obadiah 6 like this: "How are the things of Esau stripped bare!" In other words, they are laid out in the open for you to look at for the first time. Obadiah puts the microscope down on Esau, and when you look through the eyepiece you see *Edom*. Not only did Obadiah focus the microscope on him, but Obadiah *is* God's microscope! Come here and look through the microscope. Look! One Esau— oh, he is magnified!—one Esau is now 250,000 little Esaus, and that is Edom. The photographer takes a miniature and makes a great enlarged picture. He says, "I blew up the picture." Obadiah is the "blown up" picture of

Esau. You inflate a tire tube to find a tiny leak in it. You could not find that leak until you inflated it. Just so, Obadiah presents Esau inflated so that you can see where the flaw is in his life, and you can see why God said He hated him. What at the beginning was a little pimple under the skin is now a raging and angry cancer. What was small in Esau is now magnified 100,000 times in the nation. God did not say at the beginning that He hated Esau; He had to wait until he became a nation and revealed the thing that caused God to hate him.

God never said that He hated Esau or loved Jacob until He came to the last book in the Old Testament. Both men have become nations, Edom and Israel. Israel has been mightily used of God through the centuries. Israel produced men like Moses, Joshua, Samuel, David, Hezekiah, Nehemiah, Ezra, and on down the line. But the nation that came from Esau became a godless nation. Edom turned its back upon God, but what was it that caused God to hate Esau and to hate the nation?

**Behold, I have made thee small among the heathen: thou art greatly despised [Obad. 2].**

This great people—they *were* a great people, as we are going to see in this book—are now going to be brought down. Obadiah gives this as a prophecy which looks to the future, but from where we stand today, we see that it has been fulfilled.

What was the great sin of Edom which brought about God's judgment upon her?

**The pride of thine heart hath deceived thee, thou that dwellest in the clefts of the rock, whose habitation is high; that saith in his heart, Who shall bring me down to the ground? [Obad. 3].**

"The pride of thine heart hath deceived thee." What was it for which God hated Edom? It was *pride.* I am confident that, the minute I say this, the wind is taken out of the sails of many of my readers. They are going to say, "Is that *all?* Pride is bad, but it's not that bad, is it?"

Let me illustrate to you how we today have things all out of proportion concerning sin. Suppose that I knew of a certain Christian who was drinking very heavily and that I came to ask your advice as to what his church should do with him. I am sure that you would say that he ought to be put out of the membership of the church, and I would agree with you. Now suppose that I told you of an officer in a church who was caught by the police the other night in a supermarket as he was breaking into the safe. I'm sure that you would say he ought to be put out of the church and that he ought to be disciplined. I'd agree with you on that. Suppose, though, that I told you that I knew of a certain church member who was filled with pride, who was one of the proudest persons I had ever met. I dare say that you would not suggest that he be put out of the church. Many who have a very tender heart would say, "I think the pastor should talk to him and tell him that it's wrong to have pride. But it's not such a bad sin after all. At least, it's one that doesn't show. It's not like getting drunk; it's not like stealing; it's not like lying." Would I surprise you if I told you that, in the sight of God, pride is a much worse sin than getting drunk? Now the Bible does have a great deal to say about the sin of drunkenness. God condemns drunkenness. It contributed to the downfall of Israel, Babylon, the kingdom of Alexander the Great, and Rome. It has brought down all the great nations, and it will bring down our nation. But, may I say to you, in God's sight, pride is worse than drunkenness. This is something which gets right down to where we live today. This is right where the bat hits the ball. This is where the plane of your life and my life touches down on the runway of the life of God. We are given here a proper perspective concerning pride. Pride is the sin of sins. It is one of the worst sins of all. It is something that Scripture condemns above everything. God has said that He hates pride, and if that is the thing that Edom is eaten up with, God can say, "Esau have I hated because of his pride."

Notice what the writer of the Proverbs says: "These six things doth the LORD hate: yea, seven are an abomination unto him." And then he gives us the list: (1) "A proud look"; (2) "a lying tongue"; (3) "hands that shed innocent blood"; (4) "an heart that deviseth wicked imaginations"; (5) "feet that be swift in running to mischief"; (6) "a false witness that speaketh lies"; and (7) "and he that soweth discord among brethren" (Prov. 6:16–19). Do you see what is number one on God's hate parade? A proud look. When a man or woman walks into church and looks at some poor saint who is known to have committed a sin, and that man lifts his head and puts his nose in the air, or the woman draws her skirts about her, that in the sight of God is worse than getting drunk. This is not to condone drunkenness; it is saying that drunkenness is bad, but pride is much worse.

This is not all that God has to say about pride. God says that He resists the proud, but He is always on the side of the humble. "The fear of the LORD is to hate evil: pride, and arrogancy, and the evil way, and the froward mouth, do I hate" (Prov. 8:13). John tells us, ". . . the pride of life, is not of the Father . . ." (1 John 2:16). Where does the pride of life come from? If there is anything that comes from the Devil, that is it.

A great many saints today have pride of race, pride of face, and pride of grace—they are even proud they have been saved by grace! My friend, your salvation ought not to make you proud; it is not even something to brag about. It is something about which to glorify God, and it is something that should humble you. Aren't you ashamed of yourself that you have to be saved by grace because you are such a miserable sinner? I wish I had something to offer God for salvation, but I have nothing. Therefore, I must be saved by grace, and I cannot even boast of that. There are too many folk boasting of the fact that they have been sinners. God gives grace to the *humble*. Paul writes, "Let this mind be in you, which was also in Christ Jesus" (Phil. 2:5). What kind of mind did He have? Lowliness of mind. He said, "Take my yoke upon you, and learn of me; for I am meek and lowly in heart . . ." (Matt. 11:29). Pride is that which is destroying the testimony of many Christians and has made them very ineffective for God. They go in for show, but the thing they are building is a big haystack. They are not building on the foundation of Christ with gold and silver and precious stones. Pride has a great many saints down for the count of ten; it has pinned the shoulders of many to the mat today.

Pride, after all, was the sin of Satan. He said, "I will exalt my throne above the stars of God . . . . I will be like the most High" (see Isa. 14:13–14). Pride was also actually the root of Nebuchadnezzar's insanity. He strutted like a peacock in the palace of his kingdom of Babylon. "The king spake, and said, Is not this great Babylon, that I have built for the house of the kingdom by the might of my power, and for the honour of my majesty?" (Dan. 4:30). And what happened to Nebuchadnezzar? "While the word was in the king's mouth, there fell a voice from heaven saying, O king Nebuchadnezzar, to thee it is spoken; The kingdom is departed from thee. And they shall drive thee from men, and thy dwelling shall be with the beasts of the field . . ." (Dan. 4:31–32). That was no accident, my friend.

The psychologists today would call Nebuchadnezzar's condition hysteria which leads to a form of amnesia. This man did not know who he was, and he went out and acted like an animal of the field. Why? Because, when a man is lifted up with pride, he's not lifted *up* but has come *down* to the level of beasts. God debased Nebuchadnezzar and brought him down to the level of the beasts of the field.

What is pride? Let me give you a definition of it: Pride of heart is the attitude of a life that declares its ability to live without God. We find here in the Book of Obadiah that pride of heart had lifted up this nation of Edom just like Esau who had despised his birthright. Even in the home of Isaac, where there was plenty to eat, he liked that bowl of soup, and he liked it more than he liked his birthright. He didn't care for God at all. In despising that birthright, he despised God. And now Esau had become a great nation that had declared its ability to live without God.

"Thou that dwellest in the clefts of the rock, whose habitation is high; that saith in his heart, Who shall bring me down to the ground?" He lived in a very unique place. He lived in the rocky mountain fastness of the rock-hewn city of Petra. It is still in existence today and can be viewed. Many who see it are overwhelmed by the size of the city. It is a ready-made city hewn out of the rock. It is protected by the entrance way which is very narrow in places. A horse and rider can get through but with just a bit of twisting and turning. It was, therefore, a city which could easily be defended. Everything was secure. It was like the First National Bank in that many of the nations of the world deposited vast sums of gold and silver there because they felt that the city could never be taken.

They dwelt "in the clefts of the rock." They were living in great buildings which were hewn out of solid rock inside this great canyon and up and down the sides of it. They were perfectly secure—at least they thought they were. The Edomites had signed a declaration of independence. They had a false sense of security and had severed all relationship with God. They had seceded from the government of God. They had revolted and rebelled against Him.

Now what is God going to do in a case like this?

**Though thou exalt thyself as the eagle, and though thou set thy nest among the stars, thence will I bring thee down, saith the LORD [Obad. 4].**

"Though thou exalt thyself as the eagle." The eagle is used in Scripture as a symbol of deity. The Edomites were going to overthrow God, as Satan had attempted to do, and they were going to become deity. They were going to handle the business that God was supposed to handle. "And though thou set thy nest among the stars"—this was the sin of Satan, for he sought to exalt his throne above the stars. God says, "Thence will I bring thee down."

How many people today are attempting to run their lives as if they were God? They feel that they don't need God, and they live without Him. The interesting thing is that when God made us He did not put a steering wheel on any of us. Why? Because *He* wants to guide our lives. He wants us to come to Him for salvation first, and then He wants to take charge of our lives. When you and I run our lives, we are in the place of God. We are in the driver's seat. We are the ones who are the captains of our own little ships or our own little planes, and we are going through the water or the air just to suit ourselves. That is pride, and anyone who reaches that position, if he continues in it, is committing a sin which is fatal because it means he will go into a lost eternity.

Will you come now and look down into the microscope again? Edom is the incarnation of Esau. There stands Esau. What do you see? You see a human animal; you see animalism in the raw. Oh, the terrifying ugliness of it all! At this point you may say to me, "I thought we descended from animals, but here you are saying that men act like animals." That is exactly what I am saying, my friend. We didn't descend up, we descended down. There has been no ascension, there has been a descension.

The teaching of evolution as a fact of science is the greatest delusion of the twentieth century. When we do come out of the fog, the unbeliever will move to another explanation for the origin of things. Actually, evolution does not give the origin of things at all. It has been accepted by the average man as gospel truth because he has been brainwashed through radio, television, our schools, and our publications to believe that evolution is a proven fact—and it absolutely is not. The strong and intelligent objections that have been given by reliable scientists are entirely ignored today. I am not going to discuss the pros and cons of evolution—that is not my point—but it is something that I became interested in even before I was sixteen years of age. I had a great desire to read and study, and I appealed to the wrong man, a minister who was a liberal, and he urged me to read Darwin. I read *The Origin of Species, The Descent of Man*, and other miscellaneous papers. I studied it, of course, later in college and again in a denominational seminary. At the seminary they taught theistic evolution, which is probably the most absurd of all interpretations of the origin of things. I want to say to you that I totally reject the godless propaganda of evolution—this idea that it is from mud to man, from protoplasm to personality, from amoeba to animation! I would like to dismiss the argument with a quotation from Dr. Edwin Conklin, the biologist, who said: "The probability of life originating from accident is comparable to the probability of the unabridged dictionary resulting from an explosion in a printing shop." That is good enough for me.

The chief difficulty with the theory of evolution is its end results. Evolution leads to an awful, fatal pessimism. It leads man to believe that he has arrived, that he is something, that he is actually up at the top; and that belief has led to a fatal pessimism today. That pessimism is seen in our colleges and in the alarming rate of suicide among young people. I attribute it to the teaching of evolution. It was Dr. Albert Einstein who made this statement: "The man who regards his own life and that of his fellow creatures as meaningless is not merely unfortunate but almost disqualified for life." That is a good statement.

If you want to see how this teaching has affected men, listen to the poetry of the late Wystan Hugh Auden:

Were all the stars to disappear or die,
I should learn to look at an empty sky
And feel its total dark sublime,
Though this might take me a little time.

How pessimistic! And then he added this:

Looking up at the stars, I know quite well
That, for all they care, I can go to hell.

May I say to you, that is pessimism, and that is the thinking to which evolution has led.

But wait just a minute! The startling and amazing thing is that the little Book of Obadiah is God's trenchant answer to evolution, and this is the reason He said what He did about Edom.

On Wilshire Boulevard in Los Angeles there are what are known as the La Brea Tar Pits, where they have also now built a great museum. The tar pits and this museum are a tourist attraction in Southern California. When I first came to California as a tourist, I went there when it was just a small museum. The museum showed, according to the scientists, how man lived one hundred thousand to two hundred thousand years ago in California. They showed that he lived like an animal and that he looked like an animal, according to the picture that they displayed. By the way, they didn't have a photograph of him. The fellow must have turned around before they could get the picture! Of course, they didn't have a photograph but composed an imaginary picture of him.

God has something to say to us, my friend. Will you hear me carefully? Why go back one hundred thousand years? Right this moment, if you were to ride down that same Wilshire Boulevard, you would see men and women who are living like animals. They don't look like animals—some of them are called "the beautiful people"—but they are living like animals. The fact is that they have come down from the high plane where God had created them to the plane where they do not depend on God. Not only do they live like animals, they live lower than animals. No animal gets drunk or beats his wife or shoots his children or murders or practices homosexuality. Only mankind does that. Man lives in our day lower than animals, and they were living like that yonder in Edom in Obadiah's day.

You may have heard the story of the pig in Kentucky that got out of its pen, wandered out in the woods, and found a still. Mash had leaked out of this still, and the pig began to eat it and also to drink the liquid leaking out with it. The pig got drunk, and I mean drunk. He couldn't walk, and he sprawled right down in the mud. He stayed there for twenty-four hours until he sobered up. Then as he started off grunting, he was heard to say, "I'll never play the man again."

Or, as someone else has expressed it:

How well do I remember,
'Twas in the bleak December
As I was strolling down the street in manly pride,
When my heart began to flutter
And I fell into a gutter,
And a pig came up and lay down by my side.

As I lay there in the gutter,
My heart still all a-flutter,

A man passing by did chance to say,
"You can tell a man that boozes
By the company he chooses,"
And the pig got up and slowly walked
    away.

—Unknown

No, my friend, man has not evolved from the animal world. Tremendous though his achievements are, man can sink lower than an animal when he determines that he is going to live without God.

Remember that God said to the Edomites: "Though thou exalt thyself as the eagle, and though thou set thy nest among the stars, thence will I bring thee down."

Obadiah continues to set forth the complete destruction of Edom—

**If thieves came to thee, if robbers by night, (how art thou cut off!) would they not have stolen till they had enough? if the grapegatherers came to thee, would they not leave some grapes? [Obad. 5].**

Obadiah is saying that if a thief came to rob them, he would take only what he wanted—he wouldn't take everything. That would also be true of a grape gatherer—he would leave some grapes. But God said to Edom, "When I judge you, the destruction will be complete."

**How are the things of Esau searched out! how are his hidden things sought up! [Obad. 6].**

This is the key verse to the Book of Obadiah. "How are the things of Esau searched out!" Let me repeat that Ginsburg, the Hebrew scholar, translates this, "How are the things of Esau stripped bare!" Or, as we have put it, God has put Esau under a microscope, and God says, "Come, look. Look through the Word of God, and look at this man. I hate him. Why do I hate him? It is because of his pride of life. He has turned his back on Me and has declared his ability to live without Me." That is the pride of life, my friend.

"How are his hidden things sought up!" Frankly, when I read the story of Esau back in the Book of Genesis, I don't quite understand it, but although I missed it in Genesis, I sure don't miss it here. I can now take the microscope and go back and look at Esau and see why he wanted to trade in his birthright for a bowl of soup. It was for the very simple reason that the birthright meant that he would be the priest in the family and it meant a relationship to God. Frankly, Esau would rather have had a bowl of soup than to have had a relationship with God. When you reach that place, my friend, you have sunk to the level of the pig that got down in the gutter.

**All the men of thy confederacy have brought thee even to the border: the men that were at peace with thee have deceived thee, and prevailed against thee; they that eat thy bread have laid a wound under thee: there is none understanding in him [Obad. 7].**

Edom was a nation which all the enemies of that day just passed by. They just couldn't be bothered with him because he was safely holed up in the rock-hewn city of Petra. However, Nebuchadnezzar was able to get spies inside the city, and through them he was able to take the city. Just as God used Nebuchadnezzar to destroy Jerusalem, the city of Jacob's sons who had turned from God, He used Nebuchadnezzar also to reach in and take Edom, the nation of Esau's sons.

**Shall I not in that day, saith the Lord, even destroy the wise men out of Edom, and understanding out of the mount of Esau? [Obad. 8].**

Not only was Edom noted for the fact that they were well protected in their rocky mountain fastness, in the beautiful city of Petra, but they also had developed a wisdom and learning and superstition. Petra was a pagan center where there were many "pillar cults." Expeditions have excavated the great high place on top of the mountains round about Petra where bloody human sacrifices had been offered. Also Edom was famous for its wisdom. Job's friend Eliphaz was a Temanite (see Job 4:1). People traveled from afar to hear the wisdom of its wise men (see Jer. 49:7). God says that He will destroy the wise men out of Edom and understanding out of the mount of Esau.

**And thy mighty men, O Teman, shall be dismayed, to the end that every one of the mount of Esau may be cut off by slaughter [Obad. 9].**

"Teman" takes it name from a grandson of Esau and is located in the southern portion of Edom. The Temanites were noted for their courage.

## CRIME OF EDOM

In verses 10 through 14, Obadiah is going to give a list or a catalog of the reasons that

God is going to destroy Edom. The pride of life, we have said, was their great sin, but it led also to the committing of other sins. Pride is an attitude, but it is an attitude that you cannot conceal very long. It is going to break out like a running cancer because it is such a tremendous driving force in man. Your philosophy of life is going to gradually work its way down into your fingers, your feet, your eyes, and all your senses. You are going to express that philosophy in some way. If you are godless, you are going to lead a godless life. If you are godly, you are going to lead a godly life—that naturally follows. Therefore, Obadiah is now going to spell out the terrible sins that came from Edom's pride of life.

You must remember at this point that Esau and Jacob were brothers, twin brothers, although not identical twins but opposites. They did grow up in the same family and had the same father and mother. There was a struggle between them from the very beginning. There was a hatred and a bitterness that was never healed. It was never healed even when they became two great nations.

We find, however, that God had something to say to His people about their relationship to Edom. In Psalm 137:7 we read, "Remember, O LORD, the children of Edom in the day of Jerusalem; who said, Rase it, rase it, even to the foundation thereof." Edom, instead of befriending Israel in the dark hour when the Babylonians destroyed that nation, stood on the sidelines and, in fact, became the cheering section, urging the Babylonians on in their brutalities. But God had said to Israel at the very beginning, when they came into the land, "Thou shalt not abhor an Edomite; for he is thy brother: thou shalt not abhor an Egyptian; because thou wast a stranger in his land" (Deut. 23:7). Israel's tie with the Edomite was greater—he was his brother, a blood brother—and because of that, God said they were not to hate him. However, we will see that Edom manifested a hatred and bitterness toward Israel throughout the entire length of the history of their nation.

There are five specific actions mentioned here which are derived from pride, from their attitude that they could live without God.

The first one is violence—

**For thy violence against thy brother Jacob shame shall cover thee, and thou shalt be cut off for ever [Obad. 10].**

Two things were to happen to them. (1) "Shame shall cover thee." Finally, Babylon was able to capture the city of Petra and take the inhabitants into captivity. There was a period in which they were a captive people. (2) "Thou shalt be cut off for ever." Edom as a nation would be utterly destroyed. It is interesting that in our day we hear a great deal about Israel but nothing whatever about Edom.

Edom was a nation that attempted to live without God, and they were a violent, warlike people. Violence is not God's method. In my own country we have discovered that very little can be settled by war and violence. It does not *finally* settle any matter at all.

The second charge against Edom is that they joined the enemies of Israel—

**In the day that thou stoodest on the other side, in the day that the strangers carried away captive his forces, and foreigners entered into his gates, and cast lots upon Jerusalem, even thou wast as one of them [Obad. 11].**

Instead of attempting to befriend and help the people of Israel, to whom they were related by blood, they went over to the side of the brutal enemy which had invaded the land.

**But thou shouldest not have looked on the day of thy brother in the day that he became a stranger; neither shouldest thou have rejoiced over the children of Judah in the day of their destruction; neither shouldest thou have spoken proudly in the day of distress [Obad. 12].**

They rejoiced over the calamity that had come to Judah. That is always an action of pride. When you hear someone rejoicing over the trouble that another individual is having, you may be sure that you are listening to someone who is very proud. Pride is something that God says He *hates*.

Now the fourth heartless action of the Edomites is looting—

**Thou shouldest not have entered into the gate of my people in the day of their calamity; yea, thou shouldest not have looked on their affliction in the day of their calamity, nor have laid hands on their substance in the day of their calamity [Obad. 13].**

Not only did they join with the enemy against Israel, but they actually moved in to loot and plunder after the enemy had taken Israel away into captivity.

My friend, pride will lead a man to do some terrible things, and one of them is to steal.

Many a man, in order to keep up a front in his business or to keep up with the fellows at the club, will resort to dishonest methods. Also, many a man, in order to win a woman as his wife, will actually resort to dishonest methods. Our contemporary society is honeycombed with dishonesty. What is our problem? Well, the root problem is pride. A proud man, living his life apart from God, will drift into this sort of thing.

The Bible is still the best book on psychology. It will get down to the root of the problem in the human heart. Let's forget all these little psychological courses on how to improve ourselves and, rather, get back to the Word of God. Perhaps you did not realize that in the little Book of Obadiah you would find the root of the thing that is leading our own nation to selfdestruction—*pride*, the attitude of life that declares its ability to live without God.

Now here is the fifth action that springs from pride—

**Neither shouldest thou have stood in the crossway, to cut off those of his that did escape; neither shouldest thou have delivered up those of his that did remain in the day of distress [Obad. 14].**

In my opinion, this is their lowest action—they hit bottom when they did this. In this they revealed their animal philosophy of the survival of the fittest. They betrayed their brothers. You see, when Nebuchadnezzar invaded Jerusalem, the inhabitants scattered and many of them fled to the rugged country of Edom where they could hide. The Edomites, standing at the crossroads, would betray their hiding places. When the Babylonian soldiers were hot on their trail, the Edomites would say, "Yes, we saw a bunch of Israelites come by here. They went that way. You'll find them holed up in that canyon." They betrayed their brothers.

Not long ago a businessman in Los Angeles, California, told me that the business world is "dog-eat-dog." That is what man has come to by living without God. Man wants to make a name for himself. He wants to make money. He wants to be a success. What is in back of it? *Pride*. What is pride? It is an attitude of living life without God. It leads men to betray others. It will cause people to betray fellow workers in order to obtain their jobs. Many men will pretend to be friends when, in fact, they are enemies. There are many men in government today who will betray at the drop of a hat. It is sickening when you take a good look at our society today.

Although I hate to say it, there is also pride in the church. I was a pastor for over forty years and served with many wonderful, faithful men upon whom I could depend. But I learned to my sorrow that, when I had a member on the staff who was a proud young man, he would bear watching. A proud young man, trying to get on in the world, is willing to climb the ladder of success by stepping on the fingers of those who are below him. And every now and then I would add a man to my staff who, for personal advancement, would even be willing to put a knife in my back although I had been helpful to him.

The head of the Church of England was speaking to a bishop many years ago when he made this statement which has a double meaning, "Every bishop has a crook on his staff." Primarily he was referring to the crook on a shepherd's staff which is used to correct the sheep, but he was also saying that every bishop had a crook in his staff of helpers. There would always be at least one who would try to put a knife in the bishop's back.

Do you see now why God hates pride? It leads men to act like animals—in fact, the horrible truth is that when a man attempts to live without God, he is lower than animals. Therefore, the Book of Obadiah is God's devastating answer to the theory of the evolution of the species. What consummate conceit of man, living apart from God, to think that he has evolved from an animal when he is *living* like an animal. He boasts, "I have evolved from the animal world, and look at me today!" In effect, God says, "Do you really know where you have come from? I created you in My own image, and you fell—you fell so low that you are below the animal world." Repeatedly God says that He *hates* pride, and He has never asked me to apologize for Him.

To see the final issue of Edom and Israel, come with me to the time of Christ. I see a man walking by the Sea of Galilee, over the dusty roads of Samaria, and through the narrow streets of Jerusalem. His name is Jesus. He is in the line of Jacob. Also, I see a man on the throne during those years. His name is Herod, and the Scriptures are very careful to identify him—Herod, the Idumaean, the Edomite, in the line of Esau. When a warning came to the Lord Jesus to flee because Herod would kill Him, He said, "Go tell that fox. . . ." Fox? Yes. "Go, and tell that fox, Behold, I cast out demons, and I do cures today and tomorrow, and the third day I shall have finished" (Luke 13:32, *New Scofield Reference Bible*). And when the Lord Jesus was finally brought before him for judgment, He wouldn't even open His mouth before Herod. There they stand, Jesus and Herod, the final issue of Jacob and Esau.

## CATASTROPHE TO EDOM

**For the day of the LORD is near upon all the heathen: as thou hast done, it shall be done unto thee: thy reward shall return upon thine own head [Obad. 15].**

"For the day of the LORD is near." Let me remind you that the phrase, "day of the LORD," is a technical expression which covers a period of time beginning with the Great Tribulation Period. You and I are living in the day of grace or the day of Christ. The emphasis in our day is upon the Holy Spirit who takes the things of Christ and shows them unto us. After the removal of true believers (collectively called the church), the Day of the Lord will begin, and it will begin with the darkness and judgment of the Great Tribulation Period. Following that terrible time, the Sun of Righteousness will arise with healing in His wings, which will be the coming of the Lord Jesus Christ to the earth to establish His kingdom here.

"For the day of the LORD is near upon all the heathen"—that is, all the *nations*. When the Lord Jesus Christ has come to earth to establish His kingdom, there will be a judgment of the nations, described by our Lord Himself in Matthew 25. Now, very frankly, it is not clear whether the ancient nations of the past, which have long since disappeared from view, will be raised for this judgment or if their judgment will be the final judgment at the Great White Throne (see Rev. 20:11–15). I find that the commentators differ on this, but I'll give you my private viewpoint. When I go out on a limb, you better not go with me because the limb may break off, but it is my opinion that when Obadiah says, "The day of the LORD is near upon all the nations," he means that Edom will again become a nation during the end times. If you doubt that this is possible, look at the nation Israel. For twenty-five hundred years Israel was not a nation, but in 1948 she again became a nation. When Obadiah says that the Day of the Lord is near upon *all* nations, I interpret that as meaning *all* the nations, including the ancient nations which will come back into existence and will be judged.

Some expositors believe that Edom will experience the full wrath of God when the Lord Jesus Himself executes the judgment of God upon Edom and her allies (see Isa. 63:1–6).

You see, a nation is responsible to God. The Word of God makes that clear. For example, in Deuteronomy 21:1–3 we read: "If one be found slain in the land which the LORD thy God giveth thee to possess it, lying in the field, and it be not known who hath slain him: Then thy elders and thy judges shall come forth, and they shall measure unto the cities which are round about him that is slain: And it shall be, that the city which is next unto the slain man, even the elders of that city shall take an heifer, which hath not been wrought with, and which hath not drawn in the yoke." In other words, when a man was found slain out on the highway, they were to measure to determine which city was closest to that slain man, and that city was responsible for taking over the case and attempting to find out who killed that man. I think that is a great principle that God put down.

Christians talk about their citizenship being in heaven; and it's true that the Head of the church is in heaven, but the feet of the church are on earth. Christians have a responsibility as citizens of the nation of which they are members to exert an influence for God as much as they can. I don't mean to say that a Christian should jump into politics, but I do believe that God could use many more genuine, Bible-believing Christians on the political scene. Some folk say that politics has become so dirty that no Christian should get involved in them. Well, I am of the opinion that a real Christian, willing to stand on his two feet and be counted, could be used by God in our governmental processes. Our nation is responsible to God, and we are part of it.

This does not mean that God will judge nations on the basis of whether or not they have accepted or rejected Christ, because never yet has any nation accepted Christ wholeheartedly. It is a mistake to speak of any nation as a Christian nation. While it is true that Christians have had a great influence on nations like England and our own country, they never were truly Christian nations, and certainly both are far from God at the present time.

"As thou hast done, it shall be done unto thee: thy reward shall return upon thine own head." Edom was destroyed just as Obadiah had predicted. First it was captured by Babylon some time after Jerusalem was destroyed. That was accomplished by getting spies inside the capital, Petra, the impregnable fortress-city. Later, the Maccabees further subjugated

Edom, and finally, the Romans destroyed Edom when they destroyed Jerusalem in A.D. 70. At that time Edom as a nation disappeared from the world scene and has not been heard of since.

Whether or not Edom will live again as a nation is debatable and makes no real difference to you and me. If Edom is around during the Millennium, I'll be happy; and if it is not, I'll still be happy because I know that God is working out His own plan.

**For as ye have drunk upon my holy mountain, so shall all the heathen drink continually, yea, they shall drink, and they shall swallow down, and they shall be as though they had not been [Obad. 16].**

In other words, God says to Edom, "As you have done, it is going to be done to you. You will be rewarded in the same way." This is what we call today poetic justice. *Lex talionis* is the law of retaliation. The Lord Jesus said, "As you judge, so shall you be judged" (see Matt. 7:1). Or, "Whatsoever a man sows, that shall he also reap" (see Gal. 6:7). Edom will suffer in the same ways that she caused others to suffer. I very frankly shudder when I consider that my nation was the first nation to drop an atom bomb and that we have been a warlike nation. I do not think that God lets any nation get by with that. The history of all nations confirms that, as they have dealt it out, in a similar way it has come back to them. This is something which has worked itself out throughout the history of the world.

In verses 17 through 21 we come to the second and last major division of the Book of Obadiah. It is only a few verses, and it concerns the nation Israel. For Edom it was *destruction*, but for Israel it is to be *restoration*. The little nation of Israel fits into the program of almighty God. Everything fits into the program of almighty God. For every individual, it does not matter who you are, the interesting thing is that had not God thought of you, you wouldn't be around. You were in the mind of God. The great question is: Are you going to be in step with Him? Are you going to move into eternity with Him or against Him? His plan and program *will* be carried out, and you will do well to be on His side.

## CONDITION OF ISRAEL

Although God judged Israel, they were not to be destroyed as a nation—

**But upon mount Zion shall be deliverance, and there shall be holiness;**

**and the house of Jacob shall possess their possessions [Obad. 17].**

"But upon mount Zion shall be deliverance." Salvation is to be offered upon Mount Zion for the world. That is where it is offered to you and me today. The Lord Jesus came and died on Golgotha for you and me. He is coming back to this earth again. Although we are told that at that time His feet shall stand on the Mount of Olives, He will be coming into Jerusalem, and He will, I believe, rule from the top of Mount Zion.

"And there shall be holiness." There is no holiness there today. I have been on Mount Zion half a dozen times, and I have not found any holiness there. They are just as far from God there as they are over in the Arab section of the old city of Jerusalem. There is no holiness there today, but there *shall* be holiness when the Lord Jesus reigns.

"And the house of Jacob shall possess their possessions." I like this expression. They are not possessing their possessions today. They are in the land—that's true. They have a nation—that's true. They've returned to the land, but they have not returned to God, and as a result they do not possess their possessions. There is a great deal of difference between *having* a possession and *possessing* it.

## CONFLAGRATION OF THE HOUSE OF ESAU

**And the house of Jacob shall be a fire, and the house of Joseph a flame, and the house of Esau for stubble, and they shall kindle in them, and devour them; and there shall not be any remaining of the house of Esau, for the LORD hath spoken it [Obad. 18].**

There will be ultimate, final judgment of Esau. I believe that "the house of Esau" is a kingdom that will not enter into the eternal kingdoms of this earth which will become the kingdoms of our Lord and Savior Jesus Christ. What is it that keeps them from being there? Pride of heart—that attitude of a life that declares its ability to live without God. Friend, if it is your decision to live without God, you are going to live without Him not only now but throughout eternity.

## CONSUMMATION OF ALL THINGS

**And they of the south shall possess the mount of Esau; and they of the plain the Philistines: and they shall possess the fields of Ephraim, and the fields of**

**Samaria: and Benjamin shall possess Gilead [Obad. 19].**

The southern section of Judah will expand to possess "the mount of Esau." Those on the west will include the coastland of the Philistines. "The fields of Ephraim, and . . . Samaria"—that is, the northern kingdom—will be restored to the nation, and Benjamin will include Gilead, which is on the east bank of the Jordan River.

**And the captivity of this host of the children of Israel shall possess that of the Canaanites, even unto Zarephath; and the captivity of Jerusalem, which is in Sepharad, shall possess the cities of the south [Obad. 20].**

Zarephath is way up north between Tyre and Sidon in Lebanon. "The cities of the south" refers to Negeb, the southern part, actually, the Sinaitic peninsula. Israel will occupy all the land that God promised to them. He had promised to Abraham a land that contains about three hundred thousand square miles. Even at their zenith, they occupied only about thirty thousand square miles.

**And saviours shall come up on mount Zion to judge the mount of Esau; and the kingdom shall be the Lord's [Obad. 21].**

"Saviours" should be translated "deliverers." "And the kingdom shall be the Lord's." God

is moving forward today undeviatingly, unhesitatingly toward the accomplishment of His purpose; that is, of putting His King on Mount Zion. He says that He will turn and turn and overturn the nations until He comes whose right it is to rule (see Ezek. 21:27).

Nothing can deter or detour or defer God in His plan and in His program. No son of Esau, no animal, can stop Him. No proud man walking this earth can cause God to relinquish or retreat one inch. He is moving today to victory. The kingdom is the Lord's!

There is only One who can lift the heads of men and women walking through life with their heads down like animals (only humans look up as they walk; animals look down). Evolution has not lifted mankind one inch. Look at our world that has been schooled in this godless philosophy. The deadly poison of godless materialism and humanism will bring upon us the judgment of God! God says, "Though you be lifted up, little man, I'll bring you down."

But He also says, through the lips of His Son, our Savior: "And I, if I be lifted up from the earth, will draw all men unto me" (John 12:32). Which way are you going, my friend? Down the way of pride, pessimism, unbelief and rebellion, down, down, down? You who were made in the likeness of God can be restored. You will have to lay aside your pride and come in helplessness to this Savior. He can lift you.

# BIBLIOGRAPHY

(Recommended for Further Study)

Feinberg, Charles L. *The Minor Prophets.* Chicago, Illinois: Moody Press, 1976.

Gaebelein, Arno C. *The Annotated Bible.* 1917. Reprint. Neptune, New Jersey: Loizeaux Brothers, 1971.

Ironside, H. A. *The Minor Prophets.* Neptune, New Jersey: Loizeaux Brothers, n.d.

Jensen, Irving L. *Minor Prophets of Judah.* Chicago, Illinois: Moody Press, 1975. (Obadiah, Joel, Micah, Nahum, Zephaniah, and Habakkuk.)

Tatford, Frederick A. *The Minor Prophets.* Minneapolis, Minnesota: Klock & Klock, n.d.

Unger, Merrill F. *Unger's Commentary on the Old Testament*, Vol. 2. Chicago, Illinois: Moody Press, 1982.

# The Book of
# JONAH
## INTRODUCTION

Jonah is the book of the Bible which perhaps has been criticized more than any other. Unfortunately, many Christians thoughtlessly cast aspersions upon this important book in the canon of Scripture without realizing that they are playing into the hands of the critics and innocently becoming the dupes of the skeptics. You hear even Christians say, when they hear a tall story, "My, that's a Jonah!" What they really mean is that it is something that is hard, or maybe even impossible, to believe.

In warfare the tactic of the enemy is always to feel out the weak spot in the line of the opposition and to center his attack at that vantage point. Judging by this criterion, many critics have evidently come to the conclusion that the Book of Jonah is the vulnerable part of the divine record. This book is the spot where the enemy has leveled his heaviest artillery. As a result, the average Christian today feels that this is the weakest of the sixty-six links in the chain of the Scriptures. If this link gives way, then the chain is broken.

Is the Book of Jonah "the Achilles' heel" of the Bible? It is, if we are to accept the ridiculous explanations of the critics. The translators of the Septuagint were the first to question the reasonableness of this book. They set the pattern for the avalanche of criticism which has come down to the present day. The ancient method of modernism is to allegorize the book and to classify it with *Robinson Crusoe* and *Gulliver's Travels*. Today liberalism uses the same tactics. They make of it an allegory, saying that actually it never took place at all.

Some of the extravagant theories of the critics are so farfetched and fantastic that they are almost ridiculous. It is much easier to believe the Book of Jonah as given than to believe their explanations of it. I would like to pass on to you some of these outlandish explanations of the Book of Jonah:

1. Some critics, without a scrap of evidence to support their claim, say that Jonah was the son of the widow of Zarephath.

2. There are some who have put forth the theory that Jonah had a dream in the ship while he was asleep during the storm and that the Book of Jonah is the account of his dream.

3. Some relate the Book of Jonah to the Phoenician myth of Hercules and the sea monster. There is no similarity at all and, again, they are reaching for an explanation.

4. Another group holds that, although Jonah was a real character and did take a ship to Tarshish, a storm wrecked the ship. Then after the storm and shipwreck, Jonah was picked up by another ship on which there was a fish for its figurehead, and that gives support for the record in the Book of Jonah. I can well understand that if Jonah had been picked up after the storm, he might have been unconscious for awhile. I can also imagine that he might have felt like he was in a fish at that time. But I'm of the opinion that after recovering, on about the second day, Jonah would have come to the conclusion that he was on a ship and not inside a fish!

5. Still others resort to the wild claim that there was a dead fish floating around and that Jonah took refuge in it during the storm. This group has a dead fish and a live Jonah. Before we are through with this book, I am going to turn it around and say that what we have is a live fish and a dead Jonah.

Therefore, liberalism largely takes the position that the Book of Jonah is nothing in the world but an allegory, that it is merely a fairy story to be put in the same category as *Aesop's Fables*. The producers of these speculations claim that the Book of Jonah is unreasonable, and they bring forth these theories to give credence to their story. It would be very interesting indeed to get Jonah's reaction to their "very reasonable" explanations.

We must dismiss all of these speculations as having no basis in fact, no vestige of proof from a historical standpoint, and as having existence only in the imaginations of the critics. It *can* be established that Jonah was an historical person, not a character from mythology. It *can* be ascertained on good authority that the account is accurate. And it can be shown that the message of the book is of utmost significance even for this crucial time in which we live.

Jonah is an historical character and the author of this book. I want to turn to an historical book, 2 Kings, where we read: "In the fifteenth year of Amaziah the son of Joash king of Judah Jeroboam the son of Joash king of Israel began to reign in Samaria, and reigned forty and one years" (2 Kings 14:23). As far as I know, no one has ever questioned that Jeroboam II lived, that he was a king in the northern kingdom of Israel, and that he reigned forty-one years. This is an historical record. We read further: "And he did that which was evil in the sight of the LORD: he departed not from all the sins of Jeroboam the son of Nebat, who made Israel to sin. He restored the coast of Israel from the entering of Hamath unto the sea of the plain, according to the word of the LORD God of Israel, which he spake by the hand of his servant *Jonah, the son of Amittai, the prophet, which was of Gath-hepher*" (2 Kings 14:24–25, italics mine). Jeroboam was a real person, Israel was a real nation, Hamath was a real place, and it is quite unlikely that this man Jonah is just a figment of the imagination. This is an historical record, and it is reasonable to conclude that Jonah is an historical character.

It is begging the point to say that this is *another* Jonah. It is not reasonable to believe that there were two Jonahs whose fathers were named Amittai and who were both prophets. This is especially evident when it is observed that the name of Jonah was not a common name; after all, Jonah is not like our American surname of Jones! The only times that the name occurs in the Bible are in this reference in 2 Kings, in the Book of Jonah itself, and in the New Testament references to that book. There is only one Jonah in the Bible, and he is an historical person.

It is quite interesting in this regard to compare the case of Jonah with another of the prophets, Obadiah. As far as I know, no critic has ever questioned the existence of a man by the name of Obadiah who wrote the Book of Obadiah; yet there is not one historical record in either the Old or New Testament concerning Obadiah. The liberals accept Obadiah, but they reject Jonah. Why? Because they want to deny the miracle that is recorded here.

We have an historical record of Jonah in the Old Testament, and we also have one in the New Testament given by the greatest authority who has ever lived on this earth, the Lord Jesus Christ. He personally gave authenticity to the historical character of Jonah and to his experience in the fish. We read in Luke 11:30, "For as Jonas was a sign unto the Ninevites, so shall also the Son of man be to this generation." Then in Matthew 12:39–41 we read: "But he answered and said unto them, An evil

and adulterous generation seeketh after a sign; and there shall no sign be given to it, but the sign of the prophet Jonas: For as Jonas was three days and three nights in the whale's belly; so shall the Son of man be three days and three nights in the heart of the earth. The men of Nineveh shall rise in judgment with this generation, and shall condemn it: because they repented at the preaching of Jonas; and, behold, a greater than Jonas is here."

The moment you question the historical record of the Book of Jonah, you question the credibility of the Lord Jesus Christ. It is very strange to hear the liberal say, "Jesus was the greatest teacher that ever lived," since one of the marks of a great teacher is that what he teaches is accurate and truthful. If Jesus is a great teacher, my friend, then His authentication of the Book of Jonah has to stand.

I want to conclude this section in which I have attempted to meet the objections of the critics by quoting the late Sir Winston Churchill on the subject of the inspiration of the Scriptures:

> We reject with scorn all those learned and laboured myths that Moses was but a legendary figure upon whom the priesthood and the people hung their essential social, moral and religious ordinances. We believe that the most scientific view, the most up-to-date and rationalistic conception, will find its fullest satisfaction in taking the Bible story literally, and in identifying one of the greatest human beings with the most decisive leap forward ever discernible in the human story. We remain unmoved by the tomes of Professor Gradgrind and Dr. Dryasdust. We may be sure that all these things happened just as they are set out according to Holy Writ.

Jonah was a prophet, but his little book is not a prophecy—that is, there is no prophecy of the future recorded in it. It is, instead, a personal account of a major event in the life of Jonah; as the narrator, he tells us his experience.

This narrative carries two great messages. We have here in miniature a picture of the nation Israel in the Great Tribulation Period, a picture of how God will preserve His people, the 144,000 who are sealed in the Book of Revelation. We also have here a marvelous teaching concerning the resurrection of Jesus Christ. This book is actually prophetic of the Resurrection. The Lord Jesus Himself said that just as Jonah was a sign to the Ninevites, He also would be a sign to His generation in His resurrection from the dead.

The Book of Jonah is not a fish story, and that is something which really disturbs the gainsaying world which makes a great deal of how impossible it is to believe it. This book is a picture of a man who was raised from the dead, and of a throne in the midst of which "stood a Lamb as it had been slain." This Lamb is a resurrected Lamb, and a Christ-rejecting world will some day cry out, ". . . hide us from the face of him that sitteth on the throne, and from the wrath of the Lamb" (Rev. 6:16).

Sometimes the literary excellence of this brief brochure is lost in the din made by the carping critics. It is well to recall the tribute paid by Charles Reade, the English literary critic and author, who wrote, "Jonah is the most beautiful story ever written in so small a compass." It is well to keep in mind that we have before us a literary gem, not a fish story.

Another salient point that I want to make is that the fish is neither the hero of the story nor the villain of the story. This book is not even about a fish, although the fish does become very important. The chief difficulty is in keeping a correct perspective. The fish is merely window dressing and cake trimming. In every play there are certain props and settings. It does not really matter whether *Hamlet* is played against a black, red, blue or white backdrop—that is not the important thing. In the story of Jonah, the fish is among the props and does not occupy the star's dressing room.

In dealing with any book of the Bible, we need to distinguish between what Dr. G. Campbell Morgan calls the essentials and the incidentals. The incidentals in the Book of Jonah are the fish, the gourd, the east wind, the boat, and even the city of Nineveh. The essentials here are Jehovah and Jonah—God and man—that is what the book is all about.

Conservative scholars place the writing of the Book of Jonah before 745 B.C. The incidents took place about that time. Some even place it as early as 860 B.C. In my judgment, it seems best to place it between 800 and 750 B.C. Students of history will recognize this as the period when Nineveh, founded by Nimrod, was in its heyday, when the Assyrian nation was the great world power of the day. That nation was destroyed about 606 B.C. By the time of Herodotus, the Greek historian, the city of Nimrod had ceased to exist. When Xenophon passed the city, it was deserted, but he testified that the walls still stood and

were 150 feet high. Historians now estimate they were 100 feet high and 40 feet thick. Nineveh, as we are going to see, was a great city, and we are told as much here in the record.

The brevity of the Book of Jonah is apt to lead the casual reader to the conclusion that there is nothing of particular significance here except the diatribe about the whale that swallowed Jonah. (The Greek word for whale is *kêtos*, meaning "a great sea monster." Although it could have been a whale, I do not think it was—for the Scripture tells us that a special fish was prepared.) But the Book of Jonah has four very brief chapters, and it is only a little more than twice as long as the Book of Obadiah, which is the shortest book in the Old Testament. Because it is very brief, we are apt to pass over it. However, we should not call any of these books "minor" prophets, for each is like a little atom bomb, just loaded with power and with a program of God.

There are six significant subjects which are suggested and developed in the Book of Jonah which make it very relevant for us today:

1. This is the one book of the Old Testament which sets forth *the resurrection of Jesus Christ*. All of the great doctrines of the Christian faith are set forth in certain books of the Old Testament. For instance, the Book of Exodus sets forth redemption. The deliverance from sin for the sinner who comes to Christ is illustrated in that book. In the Book of Ruth you have the romance of redemption, the love side of redemption. In the Book of Esther, you have the romance of providence. The Book of Job, I believe, teaches repentance. You can go through the Scriptures and find that the great doctrines of our faith are illustrated in various books of the Old Testament. The little Book of Jonah illustrates and teaches the resurrection of the Lord Jesus. If this book does not teach the great doctrine of resurrection, then this most important doctrine of the Christian faith is not illustrated by a book in the Old Testament. For this reason alone, I would say this is a significant book.

2. The Book of Jonah teaches that *salvation is not by works*, but by faith which leads to repentance. This little book is read by orthodox Jews on the great Day of Atonement, Yom Kippur. The way to God is not by works of righteousness which we have done, but by the blood of a substitutionary sacrifice provided by the Lord. The most significant statement in the Book of Jonah is in the second chapter: "Salvation is of the LORD"

(Jonah 2:9). He is the author of salvation; He erected the great building of our salvation; He is the architect.

3. The third great purpose of this book is to show that *God's purpose of grace cannot be frustrated.* Jonah refused to go to Nineveh, but God was still going to get the message to Nineveh. The interesting thing in this particular case is that Jonah was going to be the witness for God in Nineveh—he didn't know he was going there, but he did go.

4. The fourth great truth in this book is that *God will not cast us aside for faithlessness.* He may not use you, but He will not cast you aside. There are a lot of football players sitting on the bench; in fact, more sit on the bench than play in the game. A player is called out to play only when it is believed that he can make a contribution to the game. If you and I are faithless, God may bench us; but we are still wearing our uniform, and He will not cast us aside. Anytime we want to get back in the game of life and do His will, He will permit us to do it.

5. The fifth great truth is that *God is good and gracious.* Read Jonah 4:2 for the most penetrating picture of God in the entire Bible. It is wrong to say that the Old Testament reveals a God of wrath and the New Testament reveals a God of love. He is no vengeful deity in the Book of Jonah.

6. The sixth and last great teaching is that *God is the God of the Gentiles.* When God chose Abraham, in effect He said to the Gentiles, "I'm going to have to leave you for awhile because of the sin that has come into the human family. I'm going to prepare salvation for you through a man and a nation, and I'll bring the Redeemer, the Savior, into the world through them." Now God has a salvation for all mankind. I have written Romans 3:29 over the Book of Jonah in my Bible. Paul writes, "Is he the God of the Jews only? is he not also of the Gentiles? Yes, of the Gentiles also." The Book of Jonah reveals that even in the Old Testament God did not forget the Gentiles. If He was willing to save a woman like Rahab the harlot, and a brutal, cruel nation like the Assyrians, including inhabitants of Nineveh, its capital, then I want to say to you that God is in the business of saving sinners.

# OUTLINE

There are two approaches to the study of the Book of Jonah. The one that is the most popular and is followed by most commentators is to note the striking resemblance between Jonah and Paul. Both Paul and Jonah were missionaries to the Gentiles, both were cast into the sea, both were witnesses to the sailors on board the boat, and both were used to deliver those sailors from death. There are other striking comparisons, which a careful study would reveal. Including his trip to Rome, which I consider to be a missionary journey, there were actually four missionary journeys of the apostle Paul. The four chapters of the Book of Jonah may be divided into four missionary journeys of Jonah. The first journey was into the fish; the second was to the dry land; the third was to Nineveh; and the fourth brought him to the heart of God.

That is a very good and reliable division of this little book, but it never actually satisfied me, and I have attempted to make an outline of the book without making a comparison with Paul. Very frankly, I had more difficulty outlining the little Book of Jonah than I did the Book of Revelation.

I have another approach to outlining Jonah, and I want to tell you how it came about. Many years ago, I was waiting for the train one night in Nashville, Tennessee. I was returning to seminary, and at that time I was working on outlines for each book of the Bible, for I started early in that type of ministry. But I couldn't figure out an outline for Jonah. When I got to the Union Station in Nashville, I discovered that the train was late and that I would have to wait thirty minutes to an hour. I did what I'm sure you do whenever you must wait in an airport or railroad station. I walked around for quite awhile before I sat down. I walked by the popcorn machine; I walked by the cigar stand (today they call them gift shops); I walked by the soda pop vendor; and I walked by the restaurant that was there. I just kept walking around, and I came to the railroad timetable. As I was looking at the timetable, it occurred to me that the Book of Jonah could be outlined according to a timetable.

Three important things are to be found on a timetable. The first is the time and place that the train or plane is leaving. Second, there is the destination of the train or plane. Finally, you need to know the time it will arrive at its destination. I go to many places today on speaking engagements, and if I fly, there are three things that are important to know: the time I leave, my destination, and the time of my arrival.

Therefore, if we look at the Book of Jonah as a timetable, this becomes my outline for the book:

|           | LEAVE | DESTINATION | ARRIVE |
|-----------|-------|-------------|--------|
| Chapter 1 | Israel (Samaria or Gath-hepher) | Nineveh | Fish |
| Chapter 2 | Fish | Nineveh | Dry Land |
| Chapter 3 | Dry Land | Nineveh | Nineveh |
| Chapter 4 | Nineveh | Gourd Vine | Heart of God |

# CHAPTER 1

*THEME: Call and commission of Jonah; Jonah goes west; the great wind; Jonah arrives in the fish*

## CALL AND COMMISSION OF JONAH

**Now the word of the LORD came unto Jonah the son of Amittai, saying [Jonah 1:1].**

Jonah is identified for us as a prophet and as the son of Amittai. See the Introduction for a detailed discussion of the evidence that Jonah was an historical character.

**Arise, go to Nineveh, that great city, and cry against it; for their wickedness is come up before me [Jonah 1:2].**

This is God's call and commission of Jonah to go to Nineveh. The city of Nineveh is called "that great city." It was the capital of the Assyrian Empire and was located on the Tigris River. It was *the* world power in that day. Later on, we will deal with the matter of the size of the city, because it is emphasized two more times in this book. Here the emphasis is actually upon the wickedness of the city. It is a great city but great in wickedness. Its wickedness is so great that it has come up before God, and He has now determined that He will judge the city—that is, if the city does not turn to Him.

## JONAH GOES WEST

**But Jonah rose up to flee unto Tarshish from the presence of the LORD, and went down to Joppa; and he found a ship going to Tarshish: so he paid the fare thereof, and went down into it, to go with them unto Tarshish from the presence of the LORD [Jonah 1:3].**

Jonah leaves his hometown of Gath-hepher in the northern kingdom of Israel and, with this call and commission from God, you would think that he plans to head for the city of Nineveh. Jonah would have had to go *east* from Israel to get to Nineveh. Instead of going in that direction, he does a very strange thing. He goes down to Joppa and buys a ticket on the first boat for Tarshish. Tarshish was a city founded by the Phoenicians on the southern coast of Spain. It was the jumping-off place of the *west*.

What we have before us is a greater problem than the problem of Jonah in the fish. The problem in the Book of Jonah is not the fish—

it's Jonah. God asks him to go to Nineveh, but he buys a ticket for Tarshish. God tells him to go east—Jonah decides not to obey God, and he goes west. The question naturally arises: Why did Jonah do this? There are several reasons:

1. Jonah hated the Ninevites, and he did not want them saved. There was a basis for his hatred. Assyria was one of the most brutal nations of the ancient world. They were feared and dreaded by all the peoples of that day. They used very cruel methods of torture and could extract information from their captives very easily. One of the procedures was to take a man out onto the sands of the desert and bury him up to his neck—nothing but his head would stick out. Then they would put a thong through his tongue and leave him there to die as the hot, penetrating sun would beat down upon his head. It is said that a man would go mad before he died. That was one of the "nice little things" the Assyrians hatched up.

As an army, the Assyrians moved in an unusual manner. One of the reasons the Babylonians were able to overcome them was the slowness of the march of the Assyrian army. They took their families with them and had very little order in the army. They moved as a mob across the countryside. It is very easy to see that their disorder would militate against them. However, when they moved down like a plague of locusts upon a town or village, it is said that they were so feared and dreaded that on some occasions an entire town would commit suicide rather than fall into the hands of the brutal Assyrians. You can see that they were not loved by the peoples round about.

We also know that at this time the Assyrians were making forays into the northern kingdom of Israel. For a long time, it was Syria and the northern kingdom that fought against each other, but they finally came to an alliance because of the threat of Assyria to the north and east of them. However, Assyria eventually took both Syria and Israel into captivity. When the Assyrians were beginning to penetrate into a nation they hoped to conquer, they would make a surprise attack upon a city, take captive the women, and then brutally slay the men and the children. We don't know this for sure, but it is reasonable to conceive that the Assyrians had come down against Jonah's hometown of Gath-hepher at one time. They may have come even to his home, and he may have seen his own father and mother cruelly, brutally slain before his eyes. Or he might have seen his sisters raped by the Assyrians. At least we know that Jonah hated the Assyrians, and he did not want them saved. Therefore, he goes in the opposite direction—he's not going to carry God's message to them.

2. There is a second reason that Jonah went west. Somebody might point out that Jonah's message was not one of salvation. His message was to be one of judgment. Although it is true that it was to be a message of judgment, Jonah knew God, and it was because Jonah knew God that he went in the opposite direction. He knew that if he went to Nineveh with a message of judgment and if the people of the city turned to God in repentance, God would not judge them but would save the city! Jonah didn't want that city saved. It just wasn't something he looked forward to. And so he went in the opposite direction.

3. A third reason that Jonah went in the opposite direction was because he was a disobedient prophet of God—there is no question about that. He was out of the will of God, very much like the prodigal son. The prodigal son ran away from home. He didn't want to live under the will of his father, and so he went to the far country. Jonah was out of the will of God. He was a prophet who is certainly not in step with God. We will find that the entire fourth chapter deals with his rebellion and how God brought him back into step with Himself.

4. Here is a fourth and final reason that Jonah disobeyed God. Have you ever noticed that in the Old Testament God never sent His messengers as missionaries to other countries? The method that God used in the Old Testament was really the opposite of His method today. Israel was to serve and worship God as a nation that was located at the crossroads of the world, where the three continents of Europe, Asia, and Africa meet. The nations of that day, if they were not traveling by water, would take the route through the land of Israel. God took the people of Israel, put them there at the crossroads, and had them build a temple to worship Him in order that they might witness to God by serving Him. Their witness was to a world that was looking in on them. The invitation was, "Come, and let us go up to the house of the Lord and worship Him." Israel witnessed by serving God at the crossroads of the world, and the world came to them.

For example, the Queen of Sheba came from the ends of the earth to Israel. Why did she come? She had heard how they worshiped and, when she got there, she found that there was an altar there for sinners. That was the thing which brought her to a saving knowledge of God. If you read the historical record, you will find that not only did she come but also the kings of the earth came to hear the wisdom of Solomon. During that brief period, Israel did witness to the world; they witnessed not by going out as missionaries but by the world coming in to them.

We are given only the one example of the Queen of Sheba in the Old Testament. In the New Testament we have the examples of one son of Ham, one son of Japheth, and one son of Shem who were converted—the Ethiopian eunuch, Saul of Tarsus, and Cornelius, the Roman centurion. Although we are given only these examples, there were literally thousands and, later, millions who were led to Christ.

However, for the church today the method is the opposite of that in the Old Testament. I think it was rather startling for the twelve disciples, all of whom were Israelites brought up on the Old Testament, when the Lord Jesus said to them, ". . . Go ye into all the world, and preach the gospel . . ." (Mark 16:15). I imagine they looked at each other and said, "My, this is something brand new! We did not know that it was to be done this way." Instead of, "Come up to Jerusalem," the Lord Jesus said, "Beginning at Jerusalem, you are to go now to Judea, Samaria, and on to the ends of the earth" (see Acts 1:8). That is the method today. We often criticize Israel for their failure, but we build a church on the corner and expect the world to come to us, when instead we are supposed to be going out to the world. It took me years to learn that, but that is why the burden of my ministry today is to get the Word of God out to the world via radio. We believe that this is God's method today.

But that wasn't the method in Jonah's day, and Jonah was surprised when God said to him, "Arise, go to Nineveh." I think Jonah was the same kind of man as Simon Peter, and he probably talked back to the Lord. I think he said, "Wait a minute here! You never sent Elijah down to Egypt, and You never sent Elisha over into India. Why are You asking me to do something You've never asked a prophet to do before?" I have great sympathy for Jonah. He didn't understand why God would want to change His method. However, this book reveals that God is the God of the Gentiles. Paul wrote in Romans 3:29, "Is he the God of the Jews only? is he not also of the Gentiles? Yes, of the Gentiles also." Jonah could say amen to that statement but not at this point in time. It wasn't until after the experiences related in this book that he realized that God is the God of the Gentiles also.

"And he found a ship going to Tarshish: so he paid the fare thereof, and went down into it, to go with them unto Tarshish from the presence of the LORD." Jonah's experience may be helpful to you if you are having a difficult time and wonder if you are in the will of God. Although I cannot tell you whether or not you are in God's will, I can say this to you: The fact that you are having a difficult time is *not* a proof that you are out of the will of God. Rather, it may be a proof that you are *in* the will of God. If you are having it too easy today and things are breaking just right for you in every direction, and if that is all you are using to interpret that you are in the will of God, then you are leaning on a poor, broken reed, and it will not hold you up in time of a crisis.

Let's look closely at the illustration of Jonah. Here is a man who hears God's call and heads in the opposite direction. He is definitely out of the will of God. He goes down to Joppa, and when he goes down there, he encounters no problems. He finds a ship. He buys a ticket. He gets on board the ship, and he goes to sleep! Everything is lovely.

I'm of the opinion that Jonah could give a testimony, the kind of which I have often heard. Jonah went down to buy the ticket, perhaps wondering if he were in God's will or not. (He should have known he wasn't. But a lot of us say that we wonder whether we are or not.) He was standing in line to buy a ticket, and the ticket agent said to the man right ahead of Jonah, "I'm sorry, but all space is sold." Jonah was about to turn away when the phone rang and the ticket agent answered it. A Mr. Goldberg was calling to say that he was in the hospital, having suddenly taken sick, and he would not be able to make the trip. So Jonah waited, and the ticket agent turned to him and said, "Brother, are you lucky! I've just had a cancellation." Jonah must have thought, *I sure feel lucky. I feel more than that—maybe this means I'm in God's will.*

How many Christians think like that today? If they are having a difficult time, they say,

"Oh, I am out of the will of God." If things are going easy and everything works out well, they say, "Oh, I must be in the will of God." My friend, I am of the opinion that if you are having problems, it may be that the Devil is getting a little uneasy because you are growing and proving effective for God. I have found this to be true in my own ministry. Just because you are having trouble does not mean you are out of the will of God.

Everything seemed to be propitious for a very pleasant journey for Jonah. Everything had worked out so well. Someone has called this "the fortuitous occurrence of circumstances." But we know that Jonah is going in the wrong direction and that God will have to put him inside a fish in order to turn him around.

God's men down through the centuries, both in the Bible and out of the Bible, have not found the going so easy. It hasn't always been so propitious. Things have been difficult. I have thrilled at the story of David Livingstone, but that man really suffered. If I had been penetrating dark Africa as he did, after a few of the rough experiences that he had, it would have been very easy to say in a very pious voice, "I think it is the will of God for us to turn around and go home." Likewise, John G. Patton, a missionary in the New Hebrides, met disappointment on every hand. He had to overcome handicaps daily, but this is the way God leads.

We read in the Book of Hebrews, "And others had trial of cruel mockings and scourgings, yea, moreover of bonds and imprisonment: They were stoned, they were sawn asunder, were tempted, were slain with the sword: they wandered about in sheepskins and goatskins; being destitute, afflicted, tormented; (Of whom the world was not worthy:) they wandered in deserts, and in mountains, and in dens and caves of the earth" (Heb. 11:36–38). We read also in Hebrews that some *escaped* the edge of the sword by faith, but others by faith were *slain* by the sword. Therefore, you cannot always interpret the good circumstances as being God's will and the unfavorable circumstances as not being God's will.

Jonah is on shipboard now; and, as the ship pulls out, I imagine that Jonah stands on the top deck, smiling as the land fades away in the distance. He may be saying to himself, "My, what a beautiful journey this is going to be!" But we will find that this man is not going to have it quite that easy.

## THE GREAT WIND

**But the LORD sent out a great wind into the sea, and there was a mighty tempest in the sea, so that the ship was like to be broken [Jonah 1:4].**

"**B**ut the LORD sent out a great wind into the sea." God was responsible for this storm. I call your attention to that at the very beginning. This storm is supernatural.

The storm on the Sea of Galilee, during which our Lord was asleep in the boat, was such that those men on board knew that they were going to perish. They were experienced with that sea and knew that it was a storm which they could not weather and that their boat soon would be at the bottom of the sea. It was a supernatural storm also, but Satan was responsible for that one in an attempt to destroy the Lord Jesus. Peter came to Him and said, ". . . carest thou not that we perish?" (Mark 4:38)—for that is what would have happened had He not intervened.

Here in the Book of Jonah, God is using a storm, and He is using it for a good purpose. He is going to save a city with this storm. He is going to turn around a prophet who has been going the wrong way and start him going the right way.

**Then the mariners were afraid, and cried every man unto his god, and cast forth the wares that were in the ship into the sea, to lighten it of them. But Jonah was gone down into the sides of the ship; and he lay, and was fast asleep [Jonah 1:5].**

These "mariners" are sailors accustomed to the Mediterranean, and they detect that this is no *natural* storm.

"But Jonah was gone down into the sides of the ship; and he lay, and was fast asleep." I once entertained the popular viewpoint that if a man gets out of the will of God and into sin, he will be tormented with a bad conscience and will simply be in misery. Is that true of Jonah? Jonah is definitely out of the will of God, going the opposite way, actually running away from the presence of God. He wants to get as far from Nineveh as he possibly can, and he is headed for Tarshish. Yet he is confident that everything is all right. He can sleep in this storm when even the sailors are frightened, and these sailors are a bunch of pagans, worshiping all kinds of gods.

**So the shipmaster came to him, and said unto him, What meanest thou, O sleeper? arise, call upon thy God, if so be that God will think upon us, that we perish not [Jonah 1:6].**

In effect, the shipmaster says, "You sleepy-head, you! Do you mean that you can sleep in a storm like this?" Jonah could. In fact, he is the only one on board who could sleep! The shipmaster goes on, "Arise, call upon thy God, if so be that God will think upon us, that we perish not." So Jonah now comes up on deck, and he sees this great storm they are in which is threatening to send the ship to the bottom.

**And they said every one to his fellow, Come, and let us cast lots, that we may know for whose cause this evil is upon us. So they cast lots, and the lot fell upon Jonah [Jonah 1:7].**

On other occasions when I have taught the Book of Jonah, some folk have misunderstood me at this point and have thought that I approved of gambling. I hope you will follow me very carefully at this time. I think that gambling is an awful curse. I believe that the use of the lottery and of gambling in order to raise revenue for the government will ultimately corrupt our people and our nation. In the end it will be more destructive than it could possibly be helpful.

Other folk are quick to point out that this was a superstitious thing the sailors were doing, casting lots to see why this evil had come upon them. They cast lots, and it fell on Jonah. Apparently God was in this and used this, but that does not mean that God approved of it.

These sailors cast lots. Can God use something like that? I want to share with you an experience that I had in my first pastorate. The very wonderful pastor whom I followed there told me about a certain family in the church. The wife and the little girl, a beautiful, redheaded little girl, were both believers and attended the church, but the pastor had not been able to reach the father, the head of the home. At Christmastime that year, the father came to church. I whispered to several people to be friendly to him, and they all shook hands with him and greeted him. His criticism was that we overdid it. We were too friendly. So at Eastertime when he again came to church, I simply told the folk that he didn't want us to shake hands with him and be friendly. So they didn't, and I just barely shook his hand at the door. His criticism of the church then was that we were too cold. Now there was a fellow you couldn't please at all!

When I went to visit him, he practically ordered me out of the house—he didn't want me to talk to him about the Lord.

About six months later, as I was getting ready for bed one night—in fact, I already had on my pajamas—the doorbell rang. I opened the door, and there stood this man with a very frightened look on his face. I let him in, and we sat down to talk. He told me that he ran a dry cleaning place and had a woman working there for him at the desk as a cashier. One morning she had come to work and told him, "I went to a fortune teller last night, and the fortune teller told me that I'm going to die suddenly." Both he and the woman had laughed about it. Then she went on to say, "The fortune teller also said that the man I am working for is going to die suddenly." They laughed again because they thought it was all preposterous and ridiculous.

But about two days later, as she stepped off the streetcar, that woman was hit by a car and was killed almost instantly. I want to tell you, when he heard it, he really became frightened. It was the very night when he came and knocked on my door. He said to me, "I must be next."

I told him, "Well, I think I can relieve your fear there. The fortune teller had nothing in the world to do with her death—she had no prior knowledge of it. This is just one of those strange circumstances of life which we call a coincidence. This doesn't mean that you will die."

He said, "But I want to be prepared. Would you explain to me the plan of salvation?" I got down on the floor in my pajamas, with some wrapping paper and a piece of crayon, and I outlined the plan of salvation for him. I explained to him how God had sent Christ into the world to die for our sins. That man was ready that night, and he accepted Christ as his Savior.

I have always thought that the Devil had pushed that fellow a little too far, because he was responsible for the man getting saved. Very frankly, God can use things like that. He says that He will make the wrath of man to praise Him, and He can also make the superstition of man to praise Him.

Those sailors on board with Jonah were superstitious fellows. God used their superstition. They cast lots, and the lot fell upon Jonah. Notice what happens—

**Then said they unto him, Tell us, we pray thee, for whose cause this evil is upon us; What is thine occupation? and**

**whence comest thou? what is thy country? and of what people art thou? [Jonah 1:8].**

Jonah apparently has had some time to talk to these sailors, but he hasn't told them much about himself. He certainly is no witness for God. A man out of the will of God can never be an effective witness for God. That is something very important for us to keep in mind.

Notice what Jonah did not tell them. First of all they say to him, "We want to ask you some questions since this evil has fallen on us. What is thine occupation?" Jonah hasn't told anybody he is a prophet; he's kept quiet on that. "And whence comest thou?" Jonah hasn't told them he is from Gath-hepher in the northern kingdom of Israel. He hasn't said anything about his hometown. "What is thy country?" He hasn't said that he is a citizen of Israel. "And of what people art thou?" He hasn't said that he belongs to the Israelite people who have a revelation of the living and true God. He hasn't explained that he is a prophet who represents the living God and who has been called to go to Nineveh to bring a message of hope and salvation. Jonah hasn't said any of that. Why? He is entirely out of the will of God.

**And he said unto them, I am an Hebrew; and I fear the LORD, the God of heaven, which hath made the sea and the dry land [Jonah 1:9].**

"I am an Hebrew"—that meant a lot. The Hebrews were known to be monotheistic; that is, they worshiped *one* God, never an idol. They had no other gods before them but worshiped the God who is the Creator. Jonah says, "I fear the LORD, the God of heaven, which hath made the sea and the dry land." Jonah tells them that he worships the God who made the ocean which they could see right before them being so stirred up by the storm. He made the sea, and He made the dry land also. I think these sailors knew about Israel, but they were pagan and had no knowledge of the living and true God.

**Then were the men exceedingly afraid, and said unto him, Why hast thou done this? For the men knew that he fled from the presence of the LORD, because he had told them [Jonah 1:10].**

Although he could sleep with it very nicely, without question Jonah had a bad conscience. Jonah tells the sailors, "The reason I am taking this trip is for a pleasure trip. Actually, I had business over in Nineveh, but I decided not to go over there. I know that I am getting away from my God in making this trip." But Jonah hasn't divulged too much information to them.

These men say to Jonah, "Why hast thou done this?" May I say to you, that is the good question that the unbeliever sometimes asks of the believer—and can be an embarrassing one.

When I was a pastor of a church in Los Angeles, an unsaved man who had visited the church came to see me. I had met him before in a business in downtown Los Angeles and had invited him to come to church. He said to me, "Is So-and-so a member of your church?" I said, "Yes, and he's an officer in the church." He said, "I've known that man for several years, and I've done business with him. I never would have dreamed that he is a Christian. If I were a Christian, I would not do the things that man does." You know, it's embarrassing when an unbeliever says to a Christian, "Why are you doing this? I thought you were a child of God." I think Jonah must have turned three or four different shades of red at this particular time.

## JONAH ARRIVES IN THE FISH

**Then said they unto him, What shall we do unto thee, that the sea may be calm unto us? for the sea wrought, and was tempestuous [Jonah 1:11].**

These men recognize that they are up against a very hard decision, and they want Jonah to make that decision. They ask him, "What shall we do unto thee, that the sea may be calm unto us?" And Jonah gives them a very straightforward answer—

**And he said unto them, Take me up, and cast me forth into the sea; so shall the sea be calm unto you: for I know that for my sake this great tempest is upon you [Jonah 1:12].**

Jonah recognizes that the hand of God is in all of this and that God is moving in his life at this time. He knows that the only solution to the problem of the storm is to get him off the ship going to Tarshish. God has determined that this man is not going to Tarshish but to the place where He wants him to go.

**Nevertheless the men rowed hard to bring it to the land; but they could not: for the sea wrought, and was tempestuous against them [Jonah 1:13].**

These pagan sailors certainly stand in a good light at this point. Although they are pagan and heathen, they do not want to throw him overboard. They try their best to get the ship out of the storm. They row as hard as they can to bring the ship to land, but they cannot do it. At this particular point in the book, these pagan sailors stand in a better light than Jonah does and prove to be rather outstanding men.

**Wherefore they cried unto the LORD, and said, We beseech thee, O LORD, we beseech thee, let us not perish for this man's life, and lay not upon us innocent blood: for thou, O LORD, hast done as it pleased thee [Jonah 1:14].**

Notice the change that is taking place in these men's lives. They are turning now to the living and true God. Of course, they are turning in their desperation. They call upon God to forgive them for what they are going to do, because they have no other alternative.

**So they took up Jonah, and cast him forth into the sea: and the sea ceased from her raging [Jonah 1:15].**

This reveals very definitely that it was a supernatural storm under God's control.

**Then the men feared the LORD exceedingly, and offered a sacrifice unto the LORD, and made vows [Jonah 1:16].**

The fear of the Lord, we are told in Scripture, is the beginning of wisdom. "Then the men feared the LORD exceedingly." Did they fear their god? No. They feared the one who is the Creator of the sea and of the land.

"And offered a sacrifice unto the LORD." That sacrifice points to Jesus Christ—there is no alternative.

"And made vows." What vows do these men make? They vow to the Lord that they will now serve Him. Through this experience, they now turn to the living and true God. So something good is accomplished by the storm, by Jonah's being on board the ship, and by his being cast overboard.

Notice now what happens to Jonah—

**Now the LORD had prepared a great fish to swallow up Jonah. And Jonah was in the belly of the fish three days and three nights [Jonah 1:17].**

The Greek word translated as "whale" in Matthew 12:40 is *kêtos*, meaning "a huge fish." It is called here "a great fish." I do not think it was a whale, but the thing that is important is the fact that the fish was prepared by the Lord for this special event. I am of the opinion that we have a miracle in this fish in the sense that it was a specially prepared fish to swallow up Jonah.

"And Jonah was in the belly of the fish three days and three nights." Notice that it does not say that Jonah was alive inside the fish.

A review of my timetable for the Book of Jonah shows that in chapter 1 Jonah leaves Israel, his destination is Nineveh, but he arrives in the fish.

# CHAPTER 2

**THEME:** *When did Jonah pray? Jonah's prayer; Jonah arrives on the dry land*

Our timetable for chapter 2 tells us that Jonah is going to leave the fish, his destination is still Nineveh, and he will arrive on the dry land. First, however, we want to examine the experience of this man inside the fish.

## WHEN DID JONAH PRAY?

**Then Jonah prayed unto the LORD his God out of the fish's belly [Jonah 2:1].**

Immediately someone is going to say to me, "You believe that Jonah was dead inside the fish and that God raised him from the dead, but it says here that Jonah prayed unto the Lord God out of the fish's belly—that means he was alive inside the fish." That is true, but my question is: *When* did Jonah pray this prayer? Did he pray this prayer when he first got into the fish? Or, when Jonah found himself inside the fish, did he say to himself, "My, I am really here in a precarious position, and things sure don't look good for me. I want to prepare a prayer to send to God that He'll hear and answer"? Did he decide to write out his prayer, work on it for a couple of days, memorize it, and then on the third day say the prayer to God? If Jonah did that, then my interpretation of this is all wrong—I'm all wet, if you please. But if I know human nature at all, Jonah didn't wait very long to pray this prayer. When he found himself in this condition, you can be sure of one thing: he *immediately* went to prayer before God. In fact, I think he prayed on the way down, and by the time he got into the fish's tummy, it was time to say amen.

Men don't pray a prepared prayer in time of crisis. They get down to business immediately when the crisis comes. I am reminded of a friend of mine in the ministry who lost the

index finger on his right hand below the first joint—there was nothing left but a stub. When anyone would ask him how he was called to the ministry, he would hold up that little stub of a finger and wiggle it, and then he would tell his story.

When he was a boy, an evangelist came to their church to hold meetings. The first night of the meetings, his dad, who was an officer in the church, made him sit on the front row, and the preacher really made that seat hot for him. He knew the preacher was talking right to him, although the preacher himself didn't realize it. His dad made him go to the meeting the second night, and he knew that if he went yet another time, he not only would accept Christ as his Savior but would also give his life to enter the ministry. He had a feeling even at that time that that would be his call. So that night after everybody went to bed, he got an extra shirt and his pajamas and ran off to Mississippi. There he got a job in a sawmill. I don't know if you are acquainted with the old-time sawmill. A man would take a great hook and would roll the logs over onto the carriage which would take the log on down to the big saw. The saw would then rip that log right down through the middle. My friend's job was to roll the logs onto the carriage.

One afternoon after he had worked there for about two weeks, he ran out of logs. So the foreman got some old logs which had not been run through the saw for one reason or another. There was one log among them that had already been ripped about halfway. For some reason they hadn't finished it but had pulled it back out. When my friend rolled that particular log over onto the carriage which carried it into the band saw, the place where the log had previously been ripped opened up, and the index finger on his right hand got caught in it. He felt himself being pulled along the carriage toward that big band saw. He began to yell at the top of his voice, but by that time, the other end of the log had hit the saw and was already going through. If you have ever been around a sawmill, you know that that makes a terrible racket—nobody could hear him. He was yelling at the top of his voice, very frightened as he found himself being pulled against his will right into that saw.

It would take only about forty-five seconds for him to get to the saw. His finger was way out in front of him, and the place where the log had been sawed was clamped down tight on it. His finger hit the saw and was cut off. But that released him, and he rolled to the side and was safe. In that forty-five seconds, he had prayed to the Lord. He accepted Christ as his Savior, promised the Lord he would go into the ministry and do His will, and told Him a lot of other things also! My preacher friend used to say that he told the Lord more in that forty-five seconds than he has ever told Him in an hour's prayer since then.

May I say to you, he prayed that prayer immediately when the crisis came. That's when I pray; that's when you pray. You don't *wait* to pray in a time of emergency. I recall one time on a plane when we got into unusually rough weather—I don't like flying even in good weather, and this rough weather was terrific. The minute the plane began to drop—it seemed to me like it was never going to quit dropping!—I began to pray. I didn't say, "I'm going to wait until we are off the plane, I'm going to wait until we get out of this storm before I pray." I began to pray right there and then. I'm sure that's what you do, and I'm almost sure that's what Jonah did, also.

So Jonah prayed this prayer as he went down from the mouth of the fish and through the esophagus. By the time he went "kerplunk" into the fish's tummy, this man Jonah had already completed his prayer and had said amen. I think he prayed a great deal more than is recorded here—I think we have "the abridged edition" of it.

Some folk put a great deal of emphasis upon the time word *then*—"*Then* Jonah prayed unto the Lord his God out of the fish's belly." They assume that this means that after he had been in the fish three days and three nights, *then* he prayed. This is not what it means at all. It is characteristic of the Hebrew language to give the full account of something

and then to go back and emphasize that which is important. This same technique is used in Genesis concerning the creation. We are given the six days of creation, and then God goes back and gives a detailed account of the creation of man, adding a great deal. To attempt to build an assumption on the little word *then* is very fallacious. It simply means that now Jonah is going to tell us the story in detail; he is going to tell us what really happened inside the fish.

## JONAH'S PRAYER

**And said, I cried by reason of mine affliction unto the Lord, and he heard me; out of the belly of hell cried I, and thou heardest my voice [Jonah 2:2].**

"I cried by reason of mine affliction unto the Lord, and he heard me." Notice first that God heard Jonah's prayer.

"Out of the belly of hell cried I." *The New Scofield Reference Bible* translates this as "out of the belly of *sheol*," and that certainly is accurate for that is the original Hebrew word. *Sheol* is sometimes translated in Scripture by the word "grave" and in other places as "the unseen world," meaning where the dead go. This is a word that, anyway you look at it, has to do with death. It is a word that always goes to the cemetery, and you cannot take it anywhere else. Therefore, my interpretation of what Jonah is saying is that the belly of the fish was his grave, and a grave is a place for the dead—you do not put a live man in a grave. Jonah recognized that he was going to die inside that fish and that God would hear him and raise him from the dead.

Many years ago when I was still a young seminary student, I was asked to preach for a brief period of time at the Westminster Presbyterian Church in Atlanta, Georgia. I made the Sunday evening service an evangelistic service. One night several young people came forward when I gave the invitation. After the service I talked to them, and then I went to the rear of the church. A young fellow was standing there, and he told me, "I'm a student at Georgia Tech, and I would like to accept Christ, but I have a hurdle, a problem that I can't overcome." I asked him what his problem was, and he replied, "I just can't believe that a man could live three days and three nights inside a fish."

I said, "Who told you that?"

"Well," he said, "I thought the Bible said so, and I know I've heard preachers say so.

And I've got a professor at school who spends his time ridiculing that."

"My Bible doesn't say that Jonah was alive inside the fish," I told him. Then I opened my Bible to the second chapter of Jonah and said, "To begin with, this man Jonah makes it very clear that the belly of the fish was his grave. A grave is a place for the dead."

"Do you mean that he *died?* Then that means that God raised him from the dead!" the young man said. I told him he was exactly right—that is exactly what happened. He said, "That's a greater miracle than Jonah's being kept alive in the fish for three days." I agreed with him that it was a greater miracle because, as we shall see, we have records of other men who have lived through such experiences.

The important thing to note here is that Jonah cried unto the Lord out of the fish's belly, out of the belly of hell, out of the belly of *sheol,* out of the belly of the grave—and that is the place for the dead. Jonah felt like he was there to die and that he was in his grave. You must remember that he did not write this account while he was inside the fish but afterward.

I realize there are those who will not accept my viewpoint concerning this. When I wrote my first booklet on it, I felt very much alone. However, when the late Dr. M. R. DeHaan also took this viewpoint, many folk accepted it because of their confidence in him.

If you hold the other viewpoint that Jonah was alive, that's all right. God certainly could have kept Jonah alive. But, my friend, don't hold that viewpoint to the extent that you prevent a lot of young people from defending the Bible. This young man from Georgia Tech went back to college, and when his professor again brought up the subject of Jonah, he said to the professor, "Who told you that Jonah was alive inside the fish?" The professor said, "The Bible says so." This young fellow said to him, "Not my Bible." When they got out a Bible (which they had trouble finding) and looked at the Scripture, they found that it does not say that Jonah was alive inside the fish.

I want to share with you a letter that came to me from Austin, Texas, and which reveals the popular interpretation of the Book of Jonah:

Thank you for responding to my letter concerning Jonah. It is a mark of your dedication that you take time to answer such letters, since I am sure you get many. I believe you are doing a fine work for the Lord, and in listening to you over the years, I think you are not getting older but getting better.

(May I say to you, I'm getting older, but no one's kidding me, I'm not getting better!) The letter continues:

Your story about your fear of flying and how you conquered it brings meaning to a living faith, but as far as Jonah goes, you are, I believe, putting in a private interpretation. You're straining the Word to make it say something it doesn't say. May I go on to say that the fact that Jonah lived three days in the whale's belly doesn't do any damage to the reference in Matthew 12:39–40.

Why don't you take your Bible and read it again? If we forget the chapter designation, it helps. "And Jonah was in the belly of the fish three days and three nights. *Then* Jonah prayed unto the Lord his God out of the fish's belly." I guess that Jonah did a lot of soul-searching during those three days. If you interpret this passage like you do, you must believe the writer didn't have enough sense to put the story down in the sequence it occurred.

. . . You state that it is assumed that Jonah was alive. Well, I don't believe it is, but if you want to say that, I think your assumption [that he was dead] is the greater assumption, and I hope you realize you are only assuming. My question to you is: Why?

I appreciate that letter, and I recognize that the general and popular interpretation is that Jonah was alive for three days and three nights inside the fish, that he apparently had a very comfortable weekend inside a "fish-tel" instead of a motel. I don't think he could have been as comfortable as he would have been in a Holiday Inn, a Ramada Inn, or a Hilton Hotel, but at least it is popularly believed that he spent three days and three nights in there alive. In fact, when I was a boy in Sunday school, I was given a little card on which Jonah was shown inside the fish, sitting at a table! I don't know where that came from, but that was the way he was pictured and, although I was just a little fellow, it rather disturbed me.

If you hold the viewpoint that Jonah was

alive, you are with the majority today, even with the majority of the expositors of the Book of Jonah. You can feel comfortable in being with the majority, but of course, if you want to be *right*, you'll want to go along with me, I'm sure! I say this facetiously, of course.

However, I want to make this point very carefully and very seriously. It is not a question of whether God was *able* to keep Jonah alive inside the fish or not. God *could* keep him alive. The question is: *Did* God keep him alive? Was the miracle one of keeping him alive, or was the miracle in raising him from the dead? Since this book illustrates resurrection, I'm of the opinion that God raised him from the dead.

If, after I have had a little talk with Jonah in heaven, I learn that he was *alive* for three days and three nights inside that fish, then you can come by and say, "I told you so." Then I will have to confess that I was wrong. I am not, however, as the writer of this letter seems to think, taking an assumption and making a dogmatic statement.

I do want to say that I have had the privilege of teaching the Book of Jonah on quite a few college campuses, and I have found that the position I take does give ammunition to young people today. If you want to hold to the opposite viewpoint, don't get enraged and become irritated with my viewpoint, for you must recognize that it has been very helpful to a great many students. It has been the means, as in the case of the Georgia Tech student years ago, of bringing some to a saving knowledge of Christ.

It is also not a question of whether a man *can* live in a fish. Men have been swallowed by a fish or by a whale and have lived to tell the story. There have been recorded some remarkable stories. So that leads me to say that, if you believe Jonah was alive inside the fish, that is not too great a miracle because other men have had the same experience.

Many years ago here in Pasadena, California, there was a very excellent Bible teacher by the name of Miss Grace W. Kellogg. She gave me a copy of her little book, *The Bible Today*. She held the old viewpoint that Jonah was alive inside the fish, and she wanted me to see that Jonah could have been alive. Of course, I agree that he could have been alive, and if that is what Jonah means to have said, then I have really misunderstood him. Nonetheless, I would like to give you a quotation from Miss Kellogg's book which shows that it is possible for a man to be swallowed by a fish and live. There are many examples of it, and I am going to give you a few of those that she gave:

There are at least two known monsters of the deep who could easily have swallowed Jonah. They are the Balaenoptera Musculus or sulphur-bottom whale, and the Rhinodon Typicus or whale shark. Neither of these monsters of the deep have any teeth. They feed in an interesting way by opening their enormous mouths, submerging their lower jaw, and rushing through the water at terrific speed. After straining out the water, they swallow whatever is left. A sulphur-bottom whale, one hundred feet long, was captured off Cape Cod in 1933. His mouth was ten or twelve feet wide—so big he could easily have swallowed a horse. These whales have four to six compartments in their stomachs, in any one of which a colony of men could find free lodging. They might even have a choice of rooms, for in the head of this whale is a wonderful air storage chamber, an enlargement of the nasal sinus, often measuring seven feet high, seven feet wide, by fourteen feet long. If he has an unwelcome guest on board who gives him a headache, the whale swims to the nearest land and gets rid of the offender as he did Jonah.

The *Cleveland Plain Dealer* recently quoted an article by Dr. Ransome Harvey who said that a dog was lost overboard from a ship. It was found in the head of a whale six days later, alive and barking.

Frank Bullen, F.R.G.S., who wrote, "The Cruise of the Cathalot," tells of a shark fifteen feet in length which was found in the stomach of a whale. He says that when dying the whale ejects the contents of its stomach.

The late Dr. Dixon stated that in a museum at Beirut, Lebanon, there is a head of a whale shark big enough to swallow the largest man that history records! He also tells of a white shark of the Mediterranean which swallowed a whole horse; another swallowed a reindeer minus only its horns. In still another Mediterranean white shark was found a whole sea cow, about the size of an ox.

These facts show that Jonah could have been swallowed by either a whale or a shark. But has any other man besides

Jonah been swallowed and lived to tell the tale? We know of two such instances.

The famous French scientist, M. de Parville, writes of James Bartley, who in the region of the Falkland Islands near South America, was supposed to have been drowned at sea. Two days after his disappearance, the sailors made a catch of a whale. When it was cut up, much to their surprise they found their missing friend alive but unconscious inside the whale. He revived and has been enjoying the best of health ever since his adventure.

Dr. Harry Rimmer, President of the Research Science Bureau of Los Angeles, writes of another case. "In the *Literary Digest* we noticed an account of an English sailor who was swallowed by a gigantic Rhinodon in the English Channel. Briefly, the account stated that in the attempt to harpoon one of these monstrous sharks, this sailor fell overboard, and before he could be picked up again, the shark turned and engulfed him. Forty-eight hours after the accident occurred, the fish was sighted and slain. When the shark was opened by the sailors, they were amazed to find the man unconscious but alive! He was rushed to the hospital where he was found to be suffering from shock alone, and a few hours later was discharged as being physically fit. The account concluded by saying that the man was on exhibit in a London Museum at a shilling admittance fee; being advertised as 'The Jonah of the Twentieth Century.' "

In 1926 Dr. Rimmer met this man, and writes that his physical appearance was odd; his body was devoid of hair and patches of yellowish-brown color covered his entire skin.

If two men could exist for two days and nights inside of marine monsters, could not a prophet of God, under His direct care and protection, stand the experience a day and a night longer—so why should we doubt God's Word?

This demonstrates the fact that a man *could* live in a fish, but it also takes away from the unusual character of Jonah's experience; that is, if these men lived and Jonah lived—and I am told there are even other records of such experiences—then what you have in the Book of Jonah is a record of something that is not really a great miracle. You simply have a record of an unusual incident that took place. I personally believe that the greater miracle is the fact that God raised him from the dead.

Again, I remind you that the question before us is not whether God could make a man live for three days and three nights inside a fish; the question is: Did God do that? Is that what the record says?

**For thou hadst cast me into the deep, in the midst of the seas; and the floods compassed me about: all thy billows and thy waves passed over me [Jonah 2:3].**

We cannot treat this lightly. If Jonah lived in the fish, he also lived like a fish, because he was swamped by water. He says, "The floods compassed me about: all thy billows and thy waves passed over me." In other words, Jonah is saying, "I got wet." I think it is all wet to try to say that the man lived three days and three nights. I personally feel that the Devil gets us to argue about that, while we miss the great truth of the resurrection.

**Then I said, I am cast out of thy sight; yet I will look again toward thy holy temple [Jonah 2:4].**

"Then I said, I am cast out of thy sight"—Jonah is speaking of death. "Yet I will look again toward thy holy temple." Jonah believed that he would be raised from the dead. He had been brought up on the Old Testament, and I think that Jonah was one of the many in the northern kingdom who faithfully went down to Jerusalem to worship in the temple. The Israelites knew that Solomon's temple was the place to worship the living and true God. Jonah says, "I'm going to look again toward thy holy temple. God will raise me up again."

Does this sound to you like a man who is alive?—

**The waters compassed me about, even to the soul: the depth closed me round about, the weeds were wrapped about my head [Jonah 2:5].**

"The waters compassed me about, even to the soul." He's saying, "I got drenched. The depth closed me round about, the weeds were wrapped about my head." This sea monster had been eating a bunch of seaweeds. Some seaweeds that I have pulled out along the Pacific Coast are twenty-five feet long—and this monster had his tummy full of them! Jonah says, "I was down there, and I got these things all wrapped around my head." Do you think this man is describing a very pleasant weekend inside a fish? I don't think so—I think he is trying to tell us that he went down to the very depths and that he *died*.

**I went down to the bottoms of the mountains; the earth with her bars was about me for ever: yet hast thou brought up my life from corruption, O Lord my God [Jonah 2:6].**

"I went down to the bottoms of the mountains; the earth with her bars was about me for ever." This is a very interesting translation because it is in Elizabethan English; this is the way that death was spoken of. "The earth with her bars was about me for ever"—Jonah is speaking here of the bars of death, and that is the meaning of this translation.

"Yet hast thou brought up my life from corruption, O Lord my God." "Corruption" is death. The apostle Peter so used this word on the Day of Pentecost when he said that the Lord Jesus did not see corruption (see Acts 2:25–31). The miracle about the Lord Jesus is that when He died He *did not* see corruption—His body did not corrupt. That is the difference between Jonah's experience and our Lord's experience. Jonah *did* see corruption. His body apparently began to decay in those three days and three nights. "Yet hast thou brought up my life from corruption." What we have here, in my judgment, is a definite statement by Jonah that he *died*. The miracle here is resurrection, and that is a much greater miracle than for a man to live for three days inside a fish.

I think it is very important that we have a book in the Old Testament which teaches the resurrection of Jesus Christ. The Resurrection is one of the two pillars of our salvation upon which the ark of the church rests—the death of Christ and the resurrection of Christ. They are both taught in the Old Testament, and this book illustrates His resurrection.

**When my soul fainted within me I remembered the Lord: and my prayer came in unto thee, into thine holy temple [Jonah 2:7].**

I think a normal explanation of this would be that when this man was swallowed by the fish, he was frightened. He began immediately to call out to God to deliver him as he found himself going down the esophagus of that fish.

"My soul fainted within me." It must have been at least five minutes before Jonah lapsed into unconsciousness, but before he did, he said, "I remembered the Lord." *This* is when

he prayed his prayer. Don't try to tell me that he prayed his prayer on the third day, after he'd spent three days in there under conviction and soul-searching! Jonah has said that his soul got wet, and now he says that his soul fainted within him—that means he lost consciousness inside the fish.

"And my prayer came in unto thee, into thine holy temple." Before he lapsed into unconsciousness and before death came to him, this man had already prayed his prayer.

Jonah now makes an observation here, and it is one of the many maxims that you find in the Word of God—

**They that observe lying vanities forsake their own mercy [Jonah 2:8].**

I have tried to arrive at a satisfactory explanation of this verse, and so far I have been unable to do so. However, I will have to give you the explanation I have: This is another of the great principles in Scripture. Vanity is emptiness. Jonah is speaking here of those who observe that which is empty, that which is vain, that which is just a dream and is not going to come to pass. Jonah calls it a *lying* emptiness. He says that they forsake the only mercy they can receive. Jonah says at this time, "I called out to the living and true God. I no longer was playing the pouting prophet, rushing off to Tarshish in the opposite direction because I hated the Ninevites and didn't want them saved. *Now* I am dealing with reality. I'm getting right down to the nitty-gritty." (And, my friend, there was a whole lot of nitty-gritty inside that fish!) This man says, "I'm getting right down to business with God. I appealed to Him, to His mercy, and I found that He was merciful to me."

Jonah cried out to God, and now he shows his gratitude by saying this:

**But I will sacrifice unto thee with the voice of thanksgiving; I will pay that that I have vowed. Salvation is of the Lord [Jonah 2:9].**

"But I will sacrifice unto thee with the voice of thanksgiving." Friend, I don't suppose you and I can possibly conceive of the thanksgiving that was in this man's heart and life when the fish vomited him out onto the dry land. He was a mess at that time, but he lifted his voice in thanksgiving to God for having delivered him and raised him from the dead.

"I will pay that that I have vowed." Do you know what Jonah's vow was? Can't you imagine what it was? I believe that he now says to the Lord, "I'll go to Nineveh." Before he had said, "I won't go to Nineveh." But he's changed his mind—God has changed it for him—and now he makes a vow that he will go to Nineveh.

The Lord has to deal with many of us like that. He has never put me through a fish, but He did give me cancer. Don't misunderstand me, I'm not blaming Him for that—He was judging me. He has also chastised me since then, because I thought that I had learned all the lessons an old man ought to learn, but I found out that I hadn't learned them. I am prepared to say the same thing Jonah said. I am thankful to Him for the trials He has permitted to come to me and for His deliverance from them. I've made vows to God; I've promised Him that I would devote the rest of my life to giving out His Word—that is what He has called me to do. Many people find fault and do not like the way I do it—I'm not entirely satisfied myself; I wish I could do it better—but I've made a vow to God, and I understand the vow this man Jonah made. He said, "I'm going to Nineveh, Lord, and I'm going to do what You want me to do."

"Salvation is of the LORD." In my judgment this is the most important statement that we find in the Book of Jonah. I think it is very, very important. Notice what he says: "I will pay that that I have vowed. Salvation is of the LORD"—he is speaking of deliverance.

There are several things about this that we need to note. Salvation is *God's work for us*. Salvation is *never* man's work for God. God cannot save us by our works, because the only thing that we can present to Him is imperfection, and God simply does not accept imperfection. However, we are unable to present perfection to Him. If it depended on us or our works, if it depended on our *doing* something, we could never be saved. To begin with, we are lost sinners, dead in trespasses and sins. If deliverance is to come, it will have to come to us like it did to Jonah, who was dead and hopeless in that fish. If he is to live, if he is to be used of God (and he *is* going to be used), it will be because "Salvation is of the LORD." And if you ever get saved, it is because salvation is of the Lord.

Salvation is such a wonderful thing that you can put it into three tenses: I *have been* saved—past tense; I *am being* saved—present tense; I *shall be* saved—future tense. So salvation is God's work from beginning to end. Let's look for a moment at what Scripture has to say about this.

1. *I have been saved*—past tense. The Lord Jesus Christ said, "Verily, verily, I say unto you, He that heareth my word, and believeth on him that sent me, hath everlasting life . . ." (John 5:24). The moment you trust Christ you *have* everlasting life. That is something that took place in the past for those who are Christians today. If sometime in the past you trusted Christ, that was all His work—you trusted what He did. "He that believeth on the Son hath everlasting life . . ." (John 3:36). You received life when you trusted Christ. You did nothing, nothing whatsoever—He offered it to you as a gift. ". . . the gift of God is eternal life through Jesus Christ our Lord" (Rom. 6:23). I have been saved. How was I saved? By trusting Christ and *His* work. It was "Not by works of righteousness which we have done, but according to his mercy he saved us, by the washing of regeneration, and renewing of the Holy Ghost" (Titus 3:5).

2. *I am being saved*—present tense. God is not through with us; He intends to continue to work in our lives. We are told ". . . work out your own salvation with fear and trembling. For it is God which worketh in you both to will and to do of his good pleasure" (Phil. 2:12–13). You can't work it out until God has worked it in. Paul could say, "For by grace are ye saved through faith; and that not of yourselves: it is the gift of God: Not of works, lest any man should boast" (Eph. 2:8–9). That's great, but the apostle didn't stop there; he went on to say, "For we are his workmanship . . ." (Eph. 2:10). His workmanship? Yes. "Created in Christ Jesus"—we were given a new life; Paul adds, "Created in Christ Jesus *unto good works*." So that now by the power of the Holy Spirit, the child of God is to produce fruit. The Lord Jesus said that He wanted us to bring forth *much* fruit (see John 15:1–5). Paul writes in Galatians, "But the fruit of the Spirit is love, joy, peace, longsuffering, gentleness, goodness, faith, Meekness, temperance: against such there is no law" (Gal. 5:22–23). All of these marvelous, wonderful graces are His work, and He wants to work them in you today.

You and I ought to be growing in grace and in the knowledge of Christ. I am being saved—I ought to be a better Christian today than I was last year. I get a little discouraged in that connection, because sometimes I feel that I'm like the proverbial cat which climbed up three feet on the pole in the daytime but slipped back five feet at night! I feel like I haven't gotten very far, but nevertheless, there has been some growth. Don't be satisfied with me, because He is not through with me yet. "Salvation is of the LORD."

3. *I will be saved*—future tense. There is coming a day when I will be saved. Paul said to that young preacher, Timothy, "All scripture is given by inspiration of God, and is profitable for doctrine, for reproof, for correction, for instruction in righteousness" (2 Tim. 3:16). As Paul talked to him about the wonderful Word of God, he also said, ". . . from a child thou hast known the holy scriptures, which are able to make thee wise unto salvation . . ." (2 Tim. 3:15). Since Timothy was already saved, what did Paul mean when he said, "which are able to make thee wise unto salvation"? He meant that the Scriptures would enable Timothy to grow and enable him to live for God.

But even when we come to the end of life, we are not complete. Dwight L. Moody, the great evangelist, used to tell about the time when he heard Henry Varley, then an unknown preacher. As Moody sat in the balcony, he heard Varley say, "The world has yet to see what God can do with a man who is fully yielded to Him." Dwight L. Moody, just a young fellow at that time, said to himself, "By the grace of God, I will be that man." But when he was dying, Moody said, "I wanted to be that man, but it is still true that the world has *yet* to see what God can do with a man who is fully yielded to Him." My friend, I am of the opinion that when you and I get to the end of our lives, the same will be true of you and me. It can still be said that the world has yet to see a person completely yielded to God.

So don't be discouraged with me, and I won't be discouraged with you, because, be-

loved, ". . . it doth not yet appear what we shall be: but we know that, when he shall appear, we shall be like him; for we shall see him as he is" (1 John 3:2). We are going to see Him some day, and then we are going to be like Him. Until then, I'll probably be very unlike Him. Maybe you will make it; I don't think I will. But in that day, I will be like Him, and at that time you are going to be delighted with me, and you are really going to love me. That is one thing that will make heaven so wonderful. Not only am I going to love everybody, but everybody is going to love me! When we get to heaven, we are going to be like Him.

"Salvation is of the LORD." This is a wonderful statement, and it is found in the Old Testament in the Book of Jonah. Do you know where this man learned that? He learned that when he was swallowed by a fish and then vomited out—then he was able to make this statement.

## JONAH ARRIVES ON THE DRY LAND

**And the LORD spake unto the fish, and it vomited out Jonah upon the dry land [Jonah 2:10].**

I cannot resist making this corny statement: It just goes to show that you can't keep a good man down! Someone else has put it like this, "Even a fish couldn't digest Jonah, the backsliding prophet." But Jonah is a different man now. He's made some vows to God, and one of them is that he is going to Nineveh. His ticket is now to Nineveh.

# CHAPTER 3

***THEME:** The God of the second chance; Jonah arrives in Nineveh; Nineveh believes God; Nineveh is not destroyed*

Our timetable for the Book of Jonah tells us that all along Jonah's destination has been the city of Nineveh. As we come to chapter 3, his destination is still Nineveh, he leaves the dry land, and he is going to arrive *in Nineveh!* It has taken him three chapters, and he has had to detour through a fish, but he finally makes it. The turning around place for him was that fish—it turned him around and headed him in the right direction.

I would like to write over this third chapter the words of the Lord Jesus in His day: "For as Jonas was a sign unto the Ninevites, so

shall also the Son of man be to this generation" (Luke 11:30).

## THE GOD OF THE SECOND CHANCE

**And the word of the LORD came unto Jonah the second time, saying [Jonah 3:1].**

"The word of the LORD came unto Jonah *the second time*." I was speaking on the Book of Jonah many years ago at a summer conference, and there was a school teacher attending the meetings. She was a lovely person, but after every session, she would come to me with a question. (School teachers always could ask me questions that I couldn't answer!) One day she asked me this question: "Suppose that after Jonah got out of the fish, he went back to Joppa and bought another ticket to go to Tarshish. What would have happened?" I had never been asked that question before, but I told her—and I still believe it—that there would have been a second fish out there waiting for him. But that wasn't necessary because Jonah had already learned his lesson. Now he was going to Nineveh—there's no question about that—he was headed for Nineveh.

I think the same thing could be said of the prodigal son. Suppose that the next year that boy had said, "Dad, stake me again. I'm going to the far country." Do you think the father would have staked him? I think he would have. The interesting thing is that the boy didn't go to the far country. Why? Because he is a son of the father, and he didn't want to get into the pigpen again. God's children may get into sin, but they surely are not going to live in sin. Pigs live in pigpens, and sons live in the father's house. It is just that simple and just that important.

"And the word of the LORD came unto Jonah the second time." Our God is the God of the second chance—what a marvelous, wonderful thing that is! God will give you a second chance, and He will give you more than that. I know that He has given me a dozen different chances. He is long-suffering and patient. He is not willing that any should perish. If you are His child, He is going to hold on to you— you may be sure of that.

Jonah now gets the call from God a second time. I do not believe that the great corporations of our day would give a man a second chance. General Motors or Standard Oil or General Foods—I have a notion that they would not give a man a second chance. Years ago here in California I became acquainted with a man who was the first vice-president of the Bank of America, which is a tremendous banking corporation. He is a very wonderful Christian and a personal friend of mine. I asked him one time, "Suppose that in one of the branches of your bank the manager absconded with all the funds, disappeared down to South America somewhere, and then, after a few years, came back and asked to be forgiven and given another chance. Would you give him a job?" He replied, "No. He's through." Such a man would not be given an-other chance. Isn't it wonderful that God gives us a second chance?

This is not something unusual that God did just in Jonah's case. God is not making an exception with Jonah. Remember the story of Jacob way back in the Book of Genesis? Jacob failed again and again and again and again until he actually became a disgrace to God and a source of embarrassment to Him. But God never let him go. Jacob was a trickster. He was clever. He tried to live by his own ability even when he went down to live with his uncle Laban. Laban was smarter than Jacob and put it over on him, but Jacob did what he could, and he did pretty well. In the end, Jacob had to flee from Laban and get out of the country. He had antagonized both his father-in-law and his brother, Esau, because of his conduct. But he could not keep on like that because he was God's man. He did want to serve God, but what a poor showing he made of it. As far as I'm concerned, I would have gotten rid of him and would have gotten someone else if I had been the Lord, but God didn't do that.

At Peniel, when Jacob came back to the land, God wrestled with him one night. Sometimes it is said that Jacob wrestled with God. Jacob didn't wrestle with God, my friend. With his father-in-law behind him and his brother ahead of him, both of them wishing Jacob dead, you may be sure of one thing: Jacob was not looking for another wrestling match! He had enough problems on his hands, and he was not about to do any wrestling. It was God who wrestled with him at Peniel. That man had to learn something that night. God crippled him before He got him, but when Jacob saw that he was losing, he finally just held on and asked for a blessing.

From that day on, Jacob was a different man. He was changed, as we can see down there in Egypt when he met his grandchildren, Joseph's sons. I'm a grandfather, and I know that a grandpa is inclined to boast just a little; you would like your grandsons to think well of you. But old Jacob didn't tell his grandsons how smart he was or how clever he was, how he put it over on Esau or how he put it over on his father-in-law Laban. This is what he did say: "May the Lord, who kept me from evil, keep the lads" (see Gen. 48:16). What a change had come over him! How humble he was. He was now resting in God, and he was a different man.

Then there is the story of David. Even to-day there are a great many folk who like to criticize David. One evil old man came to me with a leer in his eyes and a sneer in his voice, and he said to me, "Why did God say that David was a man after His own heart?"

I asked him, "Are you trying to say that it was because David committed murder and adultery that God said that about him? Is that what you are trying to say?" "Well, it certainly looks that way," he said.

That man simply hadn't read the record at all. It is true that David committed an awful sin, but God punished him for it. God took him to the woodshed and whipped him within an inch of his life. Finally his heart was broken when his son Absalom was slain. That was the boy he had wanted to be king, but Absalom betrayed him. He led a rebellion against David and was murdered. How David wept! He cried, "Oh, Absalom, my son, Absalom; would to God that I had died in your stead!" (see 2 Sam. 18:33). David feared that Absalom did not know God, and so he was heartbroken the rest of his life. God punished David because of his sin, but God forgave David when he came to Him and said, "Restore unto me the joy of thy salvation . . ." (Ps. 51:12).

I went on to tell that old man who had come to me, "You know, you ought to be very glad that God said David was a man after His own heart because of his relationship with God. If God would save a man like David, He might save you, and He might save me. You ought to be thankful He's that kind of a God. He gave David a second chance, and He will give you a second and a third chance."

Simon Peter also stumbled and fell and got himself dirty. He denied Christ, and when he looked through that judgment hall, he caught the eyes of the Lord. They were not eyes looking at him in anger but in pity and in mercy. Peter went outside and wept. And then when our Lord came back from the dead, He appeared to Simon Peter privately so that Simon Peter could get things straightened out with Him.

My friend, if you are a child of God and get into sin, you can come back to Him, but you'd better mean business, and you'd better be sincere. You can go to Him and tell Him what you can tell no one else. He will accept you and receive you—He is the God of the second chance.

There is another man who failed—John Mark. He wasn't much of a missionary at first. In fact, he was chicken; he turned and went home. I once heard of a man who said that the reason he didn't fly in airplanes was because he had back trouble. When he was asked what kind of back trouble he had, he replied, "I've got a yellow streak up and down my back." John Mark had a yellow streak up and down his back—he turned and left that first missionary journey of the apostle Paul. Good old Barnabas wanted to forgive him and take him on the second missionary journey, but Paul said, "I won't take him again. I'm through with him. I'm not about to take with me anyone who turns and runs home to mama as that boy did." Paul had to change his mind later, because God will receive, and God did receive John Mark. So when Paul wrote his swan song, 2 Timothy, he said, "Take Mark, and bring him with thee: for he is profitable to me for the ministry" (2 Tim. 4:11). John Mark made good. Aren't you glad that God gives us a second chance?

My final illustration is one not from the Bible but is very much up-to-date. Years ago here in Southern California, I was teaching the Book of Jonah on an evening radio broadcast that I had at that time. A day or two after I had enlarged on this first verse of the third chapter, I received a letter from a medical doctor in Beverly Hills, California. He said, "I want you to know that this verse is now the most important verse in the Bible to me. When you said that God is the God of the second chance, I came back to Him." He went on in his letter to tell me his story. He had come from Chicago where he had been a prominent doctor and also an officer in the church. Problems arose in the church which involved the handling of property and funds. He was blamed for the problems, although he was not guilty and had not been involved at all. He became bitter and actually left the Chicago area. He came to California and established an office here, but he never would darken the door of a church. He did, however, listen to me on the radio. When I said that God is a God of the second chance, this man wrote that "it was just like a cool drink of water to a man who was out on the desert, dying of thirst. That meant more to me than anything." I sat down and wrote that man a letter, and I did what any preacher would do—I urged him to get into a church and to get busy again for the Lord. He wrote again and said, "I'm already back in church and busy for the Lord." God is the God of the second chance, my friend; He is wonderful.

Jonah's story is an illustration of how God treats His children when they sin and come back to Him. The prodigal son came home. When he came home, he didn't get a beating; he got a banquet. He didn't get kicked around; he got kisses. Instead of the poor boy being put out of the house and rejected, the father took the boy back. How wonderful this is!

## JONAH ARRIVES IN NINEVEH

Now we are going to see how God is gracious to a sinful city. This is a record of perhaps the greatest revival in the history of the world; that is, what we call a revival—people turning to God. What happened in Nineveh makes the Day of Pentecost look very small. A few thousand turned to God on the Day of Pentecost, but there were several hundred thousand in the city of Nineveh who turned to God. There has never been anything quite like it—an entire city turned to God! No one else has ever seen that happen. The apostle Paul never stayed in a city until everyone was converted; he just preached the Word and moved on to the next town. No one from that day down to the present has seen such a moving of the Spirit of God as took place in Nineveh so long ago.

It is interesting to note that all this happened in Nineveh before the church arrived on the scene, and the greatest revival of all time will take place *after* the church leaves the earth. You see, God is simply not dependent upon the church. If you have the notion that the church or *your* church or *your* group are the only ones God has ever had in mind, I say to you very candidly that it is a false notion. God has something even bigger in mind than the church. Now the church is to be the bride of Christ and will, I think, occupy the very closest place to the Son of God throughout eternity, but God had a purpose in mind before the church got here and even before man appeared on this earth. God was not sitting around, twiddling His thumbs and waiting for man to come along, my friend!

Today His purpose is to call out a people from every tribe, tongue, and nation. We believe that we are coming to the end of the age and that God wants the Word to go out so that everyone might hear. However, the greatest revival, the greatest turning to God, is yet in the future, and the story of Nineveh is just a small adumbration of that.

**Arise, go unto Nineveh, that great city, and preach unto it the preaching that I bid thee [Jonah 3:2].**

We have been told before that this city of Nineveh was a great city (see Jonah 1:2), and the last verse of the Book of Jonah also says, "And should not I spare Nineveh, that great city, wherein are more than sixscore thousand persons that cannot discern between their right hand and their left hand; and also much cattle?" (Jonah 4:11). The unbeliever has criticized the Book of Jonah on many counts, and one of them is the fact that three times in this book it says that Nineveh was a great city, an exceeding great city. The Ninevites were great in sin, to be sure, but they also had a very large city.

However, nothing was known about Nineveh until 1845 when Sir Austen Layard was the first to examine the ruins of this city; he and George Smith excavated the ancient city of Nineveh. Nineveh proper, that is, the tell of Nineveh, was across the Tigris River from the modern city of Mosul. It was built in the shape of a trapezium, which was about two and one-half miles in length and a mile and one-third in breadth. That would make it a pretty good-sized place, but I would say very frankly that that does not meet the demands of the Book of Jonah.

The city of Nineveh lay in a plain which was almost entirely surrounded by rivers. The Tigris River came along to a point at which the Upper Zab River ran into it, forming a V-shaped valley between the two rivers. Then across the top of them, at the north, there was a range of mountains. This entire area, therefore, was protected by the natural fortifications of the rivers and the mountains. There were several prominent cities in this natural enclosure. Nineveh was located up on the Tigris River. Down at the fork where the Upper Zab flowed into the Tigris was Calah, as it is called in Scripture, now known as the Nimrud ruins. Calah was eighteen miles southeast of Nineveh proper. The city of Khorsabad was twelve miles to the northeast of Nineveh on the Upper Zab River.

This statement by Jonah that Nineveh was a great city sounds strange for a day when cities were walled and were by necessity very compact and small. What surprises many folk when they go to Jerusalem is the fact that the walled city is so small. It was even smaller in Christ's day and certainly in David's day than it is today. The walled city of ancient days was very compact. It was really a fortress for the people to come into in time of siege. In Nineveh there were really three walled cities—Nineveh proper, Calah, and Khorsabad. Nineveh became the capital, and the entire area was known by its name. In that fertile valley, then, there lived a great multitude of folk who in time of siege would go into these cities. They tell us that one of the reasons Nineveh fell was not primarily because of the enemy from the outside, but because of a flood that took out one whole section of the wall of the city.

It is quite interesting that when we go back to the Book of Genesis, we read this: "Out of that land went forth Asshur, and builded Nineveh, and the city Rehoboth, and Calah, And Resen between Nineveh and Calah: the same is a great city" (Gen. 10:11–12). All the way through the Word of God, the greatness of this city is emphasized. All of this area was given the name of Nineveh because it was the capital.

One of the ancient writers, Ctesias, describes Nineveh as a city whose circuit is 480 stadia. This would mean that its circumference was over twenty-seven miles.

So we find that Nineveh was "an exceeding great city" with one community after another. Here in Southern California we have a situation very similar to Nineveh's. The Los Angeles area includes at least twenty-five smaller municipalities besides the actual city of Los Angeles. We speak of all of them as being a part of "the greater Los Angeles area," which covers a great deal of ground. In fact, the joke during World War II was that a soldier who got lost up in Alaska and was trying to find his way back finally came to a sign that said, LOS ANGELES CITY LIMITS, and he knew he was no longer lost!

Nineveh was a great city—great in size and great in wickedness. This city was guilty of the same sins, which we read about in the other prophetic books, that brought God's judgment. In the Books of Amos and Hosea, we find that the reason God brought judgment upon the people was because of their luxurious living and sexual immorality, because of their godless music, and because of their drunkenness. The same things could be said of Nineveh. They were given over to idolatry, their cruelty and brutality to their enemies were unspeakable, and there was gross immorality in the city. It was a city of wine and women, of the bottle and the brothel, of sauce and sex. These were the things that identified the great city of Nineveh.

It is into this great city that Jonah is now called to go and to minister.

**So Jonah arose, and went unto Nineveh, according to the word of the LORD. Now Nineveh was an exceeding great city of three days' journey [Jonah 3:3].**

Notice that Jonah is now doing things "according to the word of the LORD." The first time he

had set sail for Tarshish, which was *not* according to the word of the Lord; now he is going into Nineveh according to the word of the Lord.

"Now Nineveh was an exceeding great city of three days' journey." This, of course, is the statement which caused the critics to laugh and to ridicule. The fact of the matter is, as we have explained, it would take several hours to go through just one of these cities, but there were three cities as well as a great area between them in which was a population estimated at several million. It is into this area that Jonah is now coming. It was "an exceeding great city of three days' journey."

**And Jonah began to enter into the city a day's journey, and he cried, and said, Yet forty days, and Nineveh shall be overthrown [Jonah 3:4].**

The point is that it took Jonah quite a while to cover this ground. He didn't have radio, he didn't even have a loud speaker—and I've often wondered how he did it. I think of Nineveh's similarity to the Los Angeles area. I live in a city called Pasadena, about ten miles from downtown Los Angeles. To the south of Pasadena about twenty-five miles is Long Beach, and to the west about twenty miles is Santa Monica. All in between there is just one city after another. Imagine Jonah starting out walking here in Southern California (he didn't have a car, by the way). He would stop at a street corner, a busy intersection, and give his message. Then he would move on down the street to another intersection and, while he was waiting for the traffic signal to change, he would speak to another crowd. In this manner it would take him quite some time to get through a city.

At this point someone is going to ask me, "How did Jonah get a crowd?" Drawing a crowd is always a problem for a preacher. It's natural and normal for us to want as many people as possible to hear the Word of God. How did Jonah do it? He didn't use any of our modern methods or our modern tactics. He didn't rent a great auditorium and put on a great campaign—there's nothing wrong with that; in fact, that's very right to do today— but Jonah didn't do it. He didn't use any gimmicks. He didn't bring in celebrities or some great singer. He didn't entertain the crowd. That was not his method.

Jonah used a method that is a little different from any that we could use today. His method was that he was a man from the dead, and I think he was rather spectacular to see. A man who has spent three days and three nights in a fish simply cannot come out looking like he did when he went in!

If you will recall the illustrations which I gave earlier of the men who had been swallowed by a fish and lived to tell the story, you will remember that the late Dr. Harry Rimmer told about seeing one man who had spent two days inside a fish. The man was put on display in London as "the Jonah of the twentieth century." When Dr. Rimmer interviewed him two years after it had happened, this man didn't have a hair on his body, and his skin was a yellowish-brown color. You see, the gastric juices of the fish had reacted upon the individual as the fish had tried to digest him.

Those chemicals were bound to have an effect upon him, and this is apparently what happened to Jonah also. You can imagine the color of Jonah's skin, and you can imagine how he must have looked. When he stopped at a corner and the crowd gathered, they would say, "Brother, where have you been?" Jonah told them, "I am a man from the dead. A fish swallowed me because God had sent me to Nineveh but I tried to run away to Tarshish." People didn't ridicule Jonah's story. They listened to him.

I am told that in Russia today, out through the rural areas, there is a great company of people who have turned to the Lord. On one of our tours to Bible lands, I went ahead of the group and was fortunate to go through Belgrade, Yugoslavia. There was a mix-up about the time we were to be there, but I understand that there were some five hundred Christians who were going to be there to welcome us had they known our arrival time. This happened because some of our tapes are being translated into Yugoslavian, Romanian, and several other languages and are being used by folk behind the Iron Curtain today. There is a real moving of the spirit of God in places where we would not expect it.

Who would have thought that in the wicked city of Nineveh people would listen to the Word of God and to a man who said, "I'm back from the dead"? By the way, that is the same message we have. We have a message concerning a man who came back from the dead. Paul writes, ". . . if we believe on him that raised up Jesus our Lord from the dead; Who was delivered for our offences, and was raised again for our justification" (Rom. 4:24–25).

Jonah entered the city with a message of judgment: "Yet forty days, and Nineveh shall be overthrown." I think Jonah gave that message with relish—he didn't like Ninevites!

## NINEVEH BELIEVES GOD

**So the people of Nineveh believed God, and proclaimed a fast, and put on sackcloth, from the greatest of them even to the least of them [Jonah 3:5].**

"So the people of Nineveh believed God"—that is a marvelous statement to find in the Old Testament. All God has ever asked any person, any sinner, to do is simply to believe Him. What does He ask you to believe? Believe what He has done for you. Believe that Christ died for you—that He died for *you* and for *your* sins. Believe that He was raised again and is now at God's right hand. The people of Nineveh *believed God*—that is still the important thing today.

I am afraid that we have in our churches many people who are as busy as termites—they take little courses, and they talk a great deal about the Bible—but they do not know God. I was speaking with a man the other day who is that type of an individual; he goes to everything that comes along. I had gotten a little weary of hearing him tell about where he'd been and what he'd seen. He has done very little, but he is always telling about the great meetings he attends. I asked him point-blank, "Do you *believe God?*" He thought for a minute and then said, "Well, I think I do." May I say to you, all of his work is of no value because he does not really believe God.

"So the people of Nineveh believed God, and proclaimed a fast." They *demonstrated* their belief. Faith always leads to works. "And put on sackcloth, from the greatest of them even to the least of them."

**For word came unto the king of Nineveh, and he arose from his throne, and he laid his robe from him, and covered him with sackcloth, and sat in ashes [Jonah 3:6].**

Friend, when people start doing these things they no longer will be committing sin. They are in deep repentance before God and are asking God for mercy. And when you ask God for mercy, you are going to find out that He is merciful.

**And he caused it to be proclaimed and published through Nineveh by the decree of the king and his nobles, saying, Let neither man nor beast, herd nor flock, taste any thing: let them not feed, nor drink water [Jonah 3:7].**

These people, many of whom were alcoholics, are now told not even to drink water.

> **But let man and beast be covered with sackcloth, and cry mightily unto God: yea, let them turn every one from his evil way, and from the violence that is in their hands [Jonah 3:8].**

You, also, must turn from sin, my friend. If you come to Christ, you can come just as you are, but when you come, you will turn from sin. You cannot possibly accept Him and not turn from sin.

"Let them turn every one from his evil way, and from the violence that is in their hands." The Ninevites were a brutal and violent people. They were given to riots. They were given to cruelty and brutality and mob rule. Now the king says, "Turn from all of that and cry to God for mercy."

The strangest thing happened—the whole city turned to God! Now that was remarkable; in fact, it was quite amazing. From the king on the throne to the peasant in the hovel, they all turned to the Lord. They cried mightily to God, and they believed God. What a glorious, wonderful time this was!

We hear today that we are having revival in certain places. I do not think that you can call what is taking place anywhere (certainly not in the United States) a revival. I do think we are seeing a great moving of the spirit of God in certain places. Wherever the Word of God is preached and taught, you will see a moving of the spirit of God; but we are not seeing revival. Instead, we find that the church is quite inactive as far as getting out the Word of God, winning people to Christ, and building them up in the faith.

When I speak of the church, I mean you and me, all of us who are believers, regardless of the group with which we are identified or the local assembly to which we go. Someone sent me this little quote because he had heard me say that there are a great many church members who are *not* real believers. Here it is: "Church members are either pillars or caterpillars. The pillars hold up the church; the caterpillars just crawl in and out." That's accurate, my friend. That is our problem today. We have too many caterpillars and not enough pillars to hold up the church.

## NINEVEH IS NOT DESTROYED

Jonah went to the city of Nineveh, and the entire city turned to God. This was something that had never happened before. Certainly Noah didn't have this kind of ex-

perience!—but Jonah did. What will God do now that the city has turned to Him? The king himself asks the question—

> **Who can tell if God will turn and repent, and turn away from his fierce anger, that we perish not?**

> **And God saw their works, that they turned from their evil way; and God repented of the evil, that he had said that he would do unto them; and he did it not [Jonah 3:9–10].**

We have come to what is probably the strongest statement in Scripture about God repenting. What does it mean when Scripture says that God repented? Does God repent? The word *repentance* as it is used in both the Old and New Testaments primarily means "a change of mind." In the Septuagint (the Greek translation of the Old Testament), the word is *metanoesen*, meaning "to change your mind." The question arises then: *Does* God change His mind?

One of the attributes of God is that He is immutable, which means that He never changes. There is no reason for God to change. He knows the end from the beginning. When the *Los Angeles Times* came out this morning, it didn't tell God a thing. God has not learned anything from the politicians or from our colleges today—they haven't taught Him anything. God knows the end from the beginning, and there is no reason for Him to change His mind. He is carrying on the program that He outlined at the beginning, and He is simply following through on it. Therefore, God does not change.

But Scripture does say that God repents. Follow me carefully here: There are expressions used in the Word of God which are called anthropomorphic terms; that is, there are certain attributes of man which are ascribed to God. In the Bible certain physical and psychological attributes of man are attributed to God.

First of all, let us look at some physical attributes of mankind that are ascribed to God. It says in Scripture that ". . . the *eyes* of the LORD run to and fro throughout the whole earth . . ." (2 Chron. 16:9, italics mine). Does that mean that God has eyes like I have? If He does, are they blue or brown or gray eyes? God is a Spirit, and He does not have eyes like we have. But the one who made the eye can see, and He can see *without* the eye. The Lord knew that Vernon McGee would have a problem understanding that, and so He said, "The eyes of the LORD run to and fro throughout the whole earth." I can understand that now—that means that God sees everything. That is an anthropomorphic term, ascribing to God an attribute that belongs to man in order that we can understand.

The Bible also speaks of the *arm* of the Lord and the *hand* of the Lord. That is very helpful to my understanding, but the one who made my hand and my arm does not have a hand or an arm like I have because God is a Spirit. But the Bible says, "The heavens declare the glory of God; and the firmament sheweth his handiwork" (Ps. 19:1)—that really means *finger* work. John Wesley put it like this: "God created the heavens and the earth, and He didn't even half try." Finger work is like crocheting or knitting; it doesn't require a great deal of muscle. You don't have to do sitting up exercises for six months before you can learn to knit. God created the heavens and the earth—that is His finger work.

However, when Isaiah was speaking of God's salvation and His redemption, he said, "Who hath believed our report? and to whom is the [bared] *arm* of the LORD revealed?" (Isa. 53:1, italics mine). I understand now what I would not have understood before: It cost God more, and it was more difficult for Him to redeem man than it was for Him to create a universe.

These are examples of anthropomorphic terms, of physical attributes of man being attributed to God for the sake of our understanding. The Scriptures also attribute certain psychological attributes of man to God. For example, the *anger* of the Lord. Does God get angry? He surely does. He is angry with the wicked all of the time. God can get angry, but His anger is not like my anger. I get angry when I hear that someone has said something bad about me, but that doesn't bother God at all. His anger is not peevish or petulant but is an anger that is against all wickedness and sin.

Scripture tells us that God *loves*, and that is something I can understand. In fact, in the little Book of Ruth, God takes a very human relationship—the love of a man for a woman—as a picture of His love for us. Also, the church is called the bride of Christ. That tells us something of the love of God. God loves you, and you cannot keep Him from loving you.

Here in Jonah we have another example: God *repents*. To repent means to change your mind; that is what it means when it applies to me. When I repent, I change my mind. I did something wrong, and I now see that it was wrong. I turn from it, and I go to God and ask forgiveness for it—I come over on God's side. To confess your sin is to come over and agree with God about your sin.

But does God repent like that? Does He change His mind? Does He say, "My, I made a mistake there; I shouldn't destroy Nineveh"? No. We need to see that the city of Nineveh had two options when this man Jonah entered it with his message of judgment. They could reject God's message, they could ignore it, they could pay no attention to it, and if they did, they would be destroyed—God never changed that. Or they could accept God's message, they could turn to Him, and God would deliver and save them. God is immutable—He never changes. When His Word is rejected, when people turn from Him, they are lost. But when they turn to Him, He will always save them, regardless of who they are.

Therefore, *who* changed? Did God change? No, but it looked as if He did. Jonah had said, "Yet forty days, and this city is going to be destroyed. God is going to destroy it." But God did not destroy Nineveh. Did God break His Word? No. God is the same yesterday, today, and forever. The city had two options. If they had not accepted His Word, they would have been destroyed. But they *did* accept God's message, they believed God, and they turned from their wickedness. God didn't change; He will always save people when they turn to Him. Although it looked as if God changed, it was really the city of Nineveh that changed, and that makes all the difference in the world.

# CHAPTER 4

**THEME:** *Jonah's displeasure; God's gracious dealing with Jonah*

This fourth chapter is like an addendum to the Book of Jonah, because at the end of chapter 3 the mission is accomplished. As you know, I arranged each chapter of this book according to a timetable. In chapter 1, Jonah left the northern kingdom of Israel, probably from Gath-hepher, his hometown. His destination was Nineveh, and it took him three chapters to get there. But he accomplished his mission, and the entire city turned to God. It would seem that the book ought to end there. But the problem no longer is Nineveh—the problem now is Jonah. Jonah was a problem child. God had more trouble with a backsliding prophet by the name of Jonah than He had with an entire city of brutal, cruel, pagan sinners.

If I had had the privilege of being the one who brought God's message to Nineveh and had seen the result that Jonah saw, I believe that I would have gone down to the Western Union office and sent a telegram back to my hometown. I would want to tell people what had happened and cause them to praise and thank God for what had been accomplished. I would rejoice in it, but that is because of where I am and because I am under altogether different circumstances. If I had been in Jonah's shoes, if I had been in Jonah's fish, I might have had the same feeling that he did. Yet his reaction is something that seems unbelievable. In fact, I have no problem with the fish, but I have a lot of problems with this man Jonah. At the very beginning, he was called to go in one direction, and he headed in the other direction. I don't understand that—until I look closely at my own heart and see that I have headed in the wrong direction several times when it was very clear that God wanted me to go in the opposite direction.

Jonah now has a new destination. He is going to leave Nineveh, and he is glad to get out of town. His destination now is a gourd vine or, as I would like to imagine, a trailer court outside the city. Jonah goes out of the city and finds himself a little spot where he can park his camper for awhile. As he leaves Nineveh, his destination is a little spot outside the city, and he is going to arrive in the heart of God. I do not know of a better place for anybody to arrive than in the heart of God, and that is where this prophet is going to arrive.

God is going to seek to win Jonah over to His viewpoint. This chapter will demonstrate to us the fact that God will never interfere with your free will. He is not going to force you on any issue whatsoever, for you are a free moral agent. God has actually moved heaven and hell and has come by way of a cross to knock at your heart's door. But, my friend, He will not come any farther than that until that door is opened, and it must be opened from the inside. He will never crash the door of your heart; He will never push it in; He will never come in uninvited. God is now going to have to deal with a backsliding prophet who has a pretty strong will and who hates Ninevites. He is going to try to win Jonah over to His viewpoint.

## JONAH'S DISPLEASURE

**But it displeased Jonah exceedingly, and he was very angry [Jonah 4:1].**

It didn't simply displease Jonah a little bit; it displeased him *exceedingly*. He wasn't angry just a little bit; he was *very* angry. What is this man angry about? He's angry because the city of Nineveh turned to God—he didn't like that.

**And he prayed unto the LORD, and said, I pray thee, O LORD, was not this my saying, when I was yet in my country? Therefore I fled before unto Tarshish: for I knew that thou art a gracious God, and merciful, slow to anger, and of great kindness, and repentest thee of the evil [Jonah 4:2].**

"And he prayed unto the LORD"—the last time Jonah prayed he was inside the fish. Here he is outside of Nineveh, with his camper parked up there in a little trailer court, and as he sits in the shade of it, he prays. He's very unhappy; in fact, he's miserable.

You may have felt that I was inaccurate in the Introduction when I said that Jonah had hatred and bitterness in his heart against the Ninevites, that he probably had justification for it, and that it was one of the reasons he did not want to go to Nineveh. But listen to him now: "O LORD, was not this my saying, when I was yet in my country? Therefore I fled before unto Tarshish: for I knew that thou art a gracious God, and merciful, slow to anger, and of great kindness, and repentest thee of the evil."

Years ago I heard a liberal lecturing at Vanderbilt University who said that Jonah's problem was that he did not know God. I don't like to say it like this, but the problem with that lecturer was that he didn't know the Book of Jonah. It is very clear that Jonah *did* know God and that he knew Him very well, probably better than that lecturer knew God. Jonah says to God, "I knew You were gracious, I knew You were merciful, I knew You were slow to anger, and I knew You were of great kindness. And I knew that although You said You would destroy Nineveh in forty days, if Nineveh would turn to You, You would save them because that's what You always do." Jonah knew God and, knowing God, he said, "I hate Ninevites. I don't want them saved. I want God to judge them." So he had headed in the opposite direction from Nineveh. Jonah said, "If those Ninevites would turn to God, God would save them, and you just can't depend on Ninevites—they might put up a good front. They might say that they've turned to God." Jonah should have known that God knew their hearts and knew whether they were genuine or not. But Jonah did know how merciful and good and gracious God is.

Jonah is in great bitterness and anger. Listen to him—

**Therefore now, O Lord, take, I beseech thee, my life from me; for it is better for me to die than to live [Jonah 4:3].**

Two of the great prophets of Scripture said the same thing, that they wanted God to take their lives. In other words, they were actually on the verge of suicide. When the prophet Elijah ran from Jezebel—another man running away, and it was unlike him—he went all the way to Beer-sheba, which was the jumping-off place for the Sinai Peninsula. Elijah left his servant there and kept on going as long as he could. When he was out of breath, he crawled up under a juniper tree and he said, "Oh, Lord, let me die!" When God's man does that, that man is exhausted and drained physically, mentally, psychologically, and spiritually. Every drop is drained out of him. That was true of Elijah. He had been busy, and I mean *busy*, friend! He had withstood the prophets of Baal way up at Mount Carmel. He had been before the public. Although Elijah loved the spectacular and he loved the dramatic, it drained him after awhile. So

when he heard that Jezebel was after him, he simply took out for the far country.

Now I think you'll agree that Jonah has really been through the mill—in fact, he's been through a fish. He had quite an experience. Then he came into the city of Nineveh, he gave out God's Word faithfully, and the city turned to God. This man is now overwrought, overstimulated. He is exhausted, absolutely drained—and he wants to die. Many of us reach this stage sometimes. We get to the place where we feel like saying, "This is it. I give up. I quit. I don't want to go any farther." We're tired; we're exhausted. But to wish that you were dead is just about as foolish a thing as you can possibly do. As far as I know, no one has ever died by wishing. People die of cancer, of heart trouble, and of all kinds of things, but they just don't die of *wishing* to be dead. Jonah is wasting his time.

## GOD'S GRACIOUS DEALING WITH JONAH

Notice how graciously God deals with this man—

**Then said the Lord, Doest thou well to be angry? [Jonah 4:4].**

Dr. G. Douglas Young has given us what I believe is a much better translation here. He has translated it like this: "Is doing good displeasing to you?"—that's what God meant. God says, "Jonah, I have saved Nineveh because I'm in the saving business and I save sinners. I wanted you to bring them the message of judgment to see whether or not they would turn to Me. If they turned to Me, I would save them. They did turn to Me, and I have saved them." My friend, if there is joy in heaven over one sinner turning to God, they must have had a real big time up there when all the folk in Nineveh turned to God. God asks Jonah, "Is this displeasing to you that I have saved these Ninevites?"

Jonah is in a huff, and he's pouting. Notice what he does—

**So Jonah went out of the city, and sat on the east side of the city, and there made him a booth, and sat under it in the shadow, till he might see what would become of the city [Jonah 4:5].**

"So Jonah went out of the city, and sat on the east side of the city." The east side of the city was up in the hill country, up at an elevation. Jonah got himself a good spot where he could look out over the city. Why? Because he didn't trust the Ninevites. He thought they would go right back into their sinning; and if they did, he knew God would destroy them because God never changes. Jonah wanted to be up there if the fire fell. That's the kind of man we are dealing with here—and he's the man who had brought God's message.

"And there made him a booth, and sat under it in the shadow, till he might see what would become of the city." He didn't believe Nineveh would stick by their conversion, their confession of faith. He's up there, and he's waiting for the fire of God's judgment to fall.

God is now going to move in on this man Jonah, and He's going to deal with him personally. We are going to have an answer here to the question that is often asked: Do you have to love people before you can bring the Word of God to them? Do you have to love a people before you can go as a missionary to them? Jonah may be a good example in this particular connection, for one thing is sure: Jonah didn't love the Ninevites.

**And the LORD God prepared a gourd, and made it to come up over Jonah, that it might be a shadow over his head, to deliver him from his grief. So Jonah was exceeding glad of the gourd [Jonah 4:6].**

"And the LORD God prepared a gourd." This gourd was prepared in the same way that God prepared the fish. If you don't believe in the fish, you ought not to believe in the gourd. I believe in the gourd; I believe in the fish.

"And made it to come up over Jonah, that it might be a shadow over his head, to deliver him from his grief. So Jonah was exceeding glad of the gourd." Jonah is made happy at last by this little green gourd growing up. Every day Jonah would go down to the Tigris River, fill a bucket with water, and come up and water this gourd that was growing in that dry country. He trained it to run up over his camper, you know. He sat under the shade of it, and he became very attached to it.

If we understand a little about human nature, we can understand Jonah a little better. It is amazing how people can get attached to living things other than human beings, especially if they are lonely. If they have no person to love, they will have a dog or cat or even a vine to love. Several years ago I visited a friend in Chicago who lived in an apartment. She had several plants, and one of them was a geranium. She took me over to show me the geranium which was just a little old stub sticking up out of the pot. In my yard in Pasadena I have to cut back the geraniums with a hoe in order to keep them from taking over! But this lady said to me, "Dr. McGee, look here at this little geranium. I know you grow them in California, but this one is such a sweet one. It grows up each year and has flowers on it. It dies back in wintertime, although the apartment is warm—I don't know why it does that." I told her, "Well, geraniums have a habit of lunging out in a spurt of growth at times." But hers hadn't done much lunging, you can be sure of that—it was just a little, bitty thing. As we walked away, she *patted* that little geranium and said, "You sweet little thing, you!" I thought, *My gracious, does she talk to the geranium?* I guess she did. She certainly was a very sensible and intelligent woman, but she lived alone and really did not have many friends.

Jonah has no friends, he doesn't like Ninevites, and there's not a person in that city whom he cares about visiting. He's alone, and he's out of fellowship with God at this time. So God lets him get attached to a little old gourd. I have a notion that Jonah would come panting up the hill with a bucket of water every afternoon and would say to the gourd, "Little gourd, I've brought you your drink for today." Can you imagine that? Well, people can get attached to dogs in that way also. One evening when my daughter was just a little thing, I took her for a walk. We came to a corner where there were a lot of vines, and we couldn't see around the corner, but we could hear a woman talking. I have never heard such sweet talk in my life! I thought we were interrupting a romance; so I took my daughter and started to cross the street. But then the woman came around the corner, and she was carrying a little dog. Imagine talking to a dog like that! I do not know if she was married or not, but if she was, I'll bet that her husband wasn't hearing sweet talk like that. We speak of some people leading "a dog's life"—there are some men who wish they could lead a dog's life! Jonah talked that way to this gourd vine—he's attached to it!

Watch how God is going to move in on Jonah—

**But God prepared a worm when the morning rose the next day, and it smote the gourd that it withered [Jonah 4:7].**

"But God prepared a worm"—this worm is just as miraculous as the fish. "And it smote the gourd that it withered." This worm cut the vine down because worms just don't fall in love with gourds—they like to eat them.

**And it came to pass, when the sun did arise, that God prepared a vehement east wind; and the sun beat upon the head of Jonah, that he fainted, and wished in himself to die, and said, It is better for me to die than to live [Jonah 4:8].**

Here he goes again, *wishing*—but it won't do him a bit of good.

**And God said to Jonah, Doest thou well to be angry for the gourd? And he said, I do well to be angry, even unto death [Jonah 4:9].**

Jonah says, "The only thing that I had that was living and that I cared for was this little gourd vine that grew up here and that You gave to me. And now the worm has cut the thing down, and here I am all alone."

**Then said the LORD, Thou hast had pity on the gourd, for the which thou hast not laboured, neither madest it grow; which came up in a night, and perished in a night [Jonah 4:10].**

God says to Jonah, "Jonah, a gourd is nothing." My friend, I hate to say this, but a pussycat is nothing, a little dog is nothing, but a human being has a soul that is either going to heaven or hell. And God didn't ask you to *love* the lost before you go to them. He said, "*I* love the lost, and I want you to go to them." That is what He is saying to Jonah: "Jonah, I love the Ninevites."

**And should not I spare Nineveh, that great city, wherein are more than sixscore thousand persons that cannot discern between their right hand and their left hand; and also much cattle? [Jonah 4:11].**

God says, "I have spared this city." What does He mean by "sixscore thousand [120,000] persons that cannot discern between their right hand and their left hand"? He means little children. God says, "You wouldn't want Me to destroy that city, would you, Jonah? If you can fall in love with a gourd vine, can't you at least fall in love with Ninevite children?"

Now may I make this application? When I was teaching in a Bible institute, I used to say, like all the other teachers were saying, that if you are called to go as a missionary, you ought to love the people to whom you go. I disagree violently with that now, because how can you love people before you know them? I first applied that to myself. I have never accepted a call to a church because I loved the people; I didn't know them to begin with. I went because I felt that God had called me to go there and preach. But I also have never been in a church in which I didn't become involved with the people. I have stood at their bedsides in hospitals, I've been at their gravesides when death came, I've been with them in the marriages that have taken place in their families, and I can truthfully say that I have never yet left a church where there wasn't a great company of people whom I loved—and I really mean that I *love* them in the Lord. But I did not love them when I went there because I did not know them.

God is saying to a great many people today, "I want you to go and take the Word of God to those who are lost." And they say, "But I don't love them." God says, "I never asked you to love them; I asked you to *go*." I cannot find anywhere that God ever asked Jonah to go because he loved the Ninevites. He said, "Jonah, I want you to go because I love them. I love Ninevites. I want to save Ninevites. And I want you to take the message to them."

Again may I say that I am afraid there are a great many people in the church who are caterpillars. Church members are either pillars or caterpillars; the pillars hold up the church, and the caterpillars just crawl in and out. There are a lot of people just crawling in and out of the church, waiting for some great wave of emotion, waiting for some feeling to take hold of them—and they have never done anything yet. God says that we are to get busy for Him.

I remember talking to a missionary who was home from Africa, and he was showing me a picture of some little black boys in the orphans' home there. I could tell by the way he looked at the picture that he loved those little boys. I said to him, "When you first went to Africa, did you love the Africans?" He said, "No, I really wanted to go to my people in Greece, but at that time the door was closed, and I could not go; so I had to go to Africa." As he held that picture, I said to him, "But do you love those little fellows now?" Tears came down from his eyes. He said, "I love them now." God says to you and me, "You go with the Word. I love the lost. You take the Word to them, and when they are saved and you get acquainted with them and know them, you will love them, too."

Since Jonah wrote the book, I think it is reasonable to say that after this experience, Jonah left the dead gourd vine and went down to where the living were walking the streets of Nineveh, and I think that he rejoiced with them that they had come to a saving knowledge of God. My friend, what a message this is! Why don't you get involved in getting the Word of God out to people? Don't wait for some great feeling to sweep over your soul. Don't wait to be moved by a little picture of an orphan. There are so many people waiting to be motivated by things that are emotional. Take the Word of God to them because God loves them; and if you'll do that, I will guarantee that you will learn to love them also.

# BIBLIOGRAPHY

(Recommended for Further Study)

Feinberg, Charles L. *The Minor Prophets.* Chicago, Illinois: Moody Press, 1976.

Gaebelein, Arno C. *The Annotated Bible.* 1917. Reprint. Neptune, New Jersey: Loizeaux Brothers, 1971.

Ironside, H. A. *The Minor Prophets.* Neptune, New Jersey: Loizeaux Brothers, n.d.

Jensen, Irving L. *Minor Prophets of Judah.* Chicago, Illinois: Moody Press, 1975.

Tatford, Frederick A. *The Minor Prophets.* Minneapolis, Minnesota: Klock & Klock, n.d.

Unger, Merrill F. *Unger's Commentary on the Old Testament*, Vol. 2. Chicago, Illinois: Moody Press, 1982.

# The Book of
# MICAH
## INTRODUCTION

It is important to know something about the man Micah as well as his message. His name means "who is like Jehovah?" The word has the same derivation as Michael (the name of the archangel) which means "who is like God?" There are many Micahs mentioned in the Scriptures, but this man is identified as a Morasthite (Mic. 1:1), since he was an inhabitant of Moresheth-gath (Mic. 1:14), a place about twenty miles southwest of Jerusalem, near Lachish. He is not to be confused with any other Micah of Scripture.

Micah prophesied during the reigns of Jotham, Ahaz, and Hezekiah (see Mic. 1:1), who were kings of Judah. However, his prophecy concerns Samaria and Jerusalem. Samaria was the capital of the northern kingdom of Israel, while Jerusalem was the capital of the southern kingdom of Judah. Although he was a man from the southern kingdom, a great deal of his prophecy had to do with the northern kingdom. He spoke to the nation during the time that the northern kingdom was being attacked by Assyria. Although the southern kingdom was attacked also, it was the northern kingdom that actually was carried away into Assyrian captivity.

Micah was a contemporary of three other prophets: Isaiah, Hosea, and Amos. It is possible that he was a friend of Isaiah, and his prophecy has been called that of a miniature Book of Isaiah. There are many striking similarities between the two. For many people, Micah is the favorite of the minor prophets. It is one of the most remarkable books as to style. If you appreciate beautiful language, if you appreciate poetry, and if you appreciate literature, you will appreciate Micah. The writing is pungent and personal. Micah was trenchant, touching, and tender. He was realistic and reportorial—he would have made a good war correspondent. There is an exquisite beauty about this brochure which combines God's infinite tenderness with His judgments. There are several famous passages which are familiar to the average Christian, although he may not recognize them as coming from Micah. Through the gloom of impending judgment, Micah saw clearly the coming glory of the redemption of Israel, which makes this a remarkable book.

Micah pronounced judgment on the cities of Israel and on Jerusalem in Judah. These centers influenced the people of the nation. These were the urban problems that sound very much like our present-day problems. Micah condemned violence, corruption, robbery, covetousness, gross materialism, spiritual bankruptcy, and illicit sex. He well could be labeled "the prophet of the city."

The theme of Micah is very important to understand. Customarily, Micah is considered a prophet of judgment. That seems to be true since in the first three chapters there is a great emphasis on judgment. However, although the first three chapters are denunciatory, the last four chapters are consolatory. His great question is found in one of the loveliest passages of Scripture. "Who is like unto Thee?" that is, unto God. We find that Micah emphasizes that theme as he goes along. In the first three chapters: Who is like unto God in proclaiming—that is, in witnessing? In chapters 4 and 5: Who is like unto God in prophesying, in consoling? In chapter 6: Who is like unto God in pleading? Finally, in chapter 7: Who is like unto God in pardoning? This is what makes Micah a wonderful little book. The main theme of the book is God's judgment and redemption—both are there. The key verse, to me, is Micah 7:18 which says, "Who is a God like unto thee, that pardoneth iniquity, and passeth by the transgression of the remnant of his heritage? he retaineth not his anger for ever, because he delighteth in mercy."

God hates sin, but He loves the souls of sinners, and He wants to save them. Judgment is called God's "strange work." It is strange because He does not like to judge. But since He is a holy God and hates sin, He must deal with any rebellion. He couldn't do otherwise. But He still loves the souls of sinners; He wants to save them, and He will save them if they come to Him in faith.

This little book can be divided in an interesting way. The more natural division of the prophecy is to note that Micah gave three messages, each beginning with the injunction, "Hear" (Mic. 1:2; 3:1; 6:1). The first message is addressed to "all people," and the second message is addressed specifically to the leaders of

Israel. The third message is a personal word of pleading to Israel to repent and return to God.

Now let me refer briefly to the attack upon the unity of this book by the German higher critics of many years ago. They made the same attack which they made upon the prophecy of Isaiah, which has been well answered by conservative scholarship. Therefore we will not waste time by delving into it. I find it interesting that Jeremiah quoted from Micah, which reveals the importance of Micah in his day. "Micah the Morasthite prophesied in the days of Hezekiah king of Judah, and spake to all the people of Judah, saying, Thus saith the LORD of hosts; Zion shall be plowed like a field, and Jerusalem shall become heaps, and the mountain of the house as the high places of a forest" (Jer. 26:18). Of course, the people paid no more attention to Jeremiah than they had to Micah, and what Micah had prophesied did happen to Jerusalem exactly as he said it would.

Many folk, especially young preachers who want to give an exposition, have asked me how to begin. I would say, not only to young preachers but to everyone who wants to study the Bible, first of all, get a grasp of the message of an entire book. What is it all about? What is the author trying to say? What is the main message? To get this information you must outline the book. In Micah we find that the message is, "Who is like God in proclaiming, in prophesying, in pleading, and in pardoning?" That is how the Book of Micah is divided.

# OUTLINE

### "WHO IS A GOD LIKE UNTO THEE?"

**I. Proclaiming Future Judgment for Past Sins, Chapters 1–3**
   A. Prophet's First Message Directed Against Samaria, Reaches to Jerusalem, Chapter 1
   B. Prophet's Second Message Describes Specific Sins, Chapter 2
   C. Prophet's Third Message Denounces Leaders for Sins, Chapter 3

**II. Prophesying Future Glory Because of Past Promises, Chapters 4–5**
   A. Prophecies of Last Days, Chapter 4
   B. Prophecy of First Coming of Christ Before Second Coming and Kingdom, Chapter 5

**III. Pleading Present Repentance Because of Past Redemption, Chapter 6**

**IV. Pardoning All Iniquity Because of Who God Is and What He Does, Chapter 7**

# CHAPTER 1

*THEME: The prophet's first message; directed against Samaria, reaches to Jerusalem*

The first three chapters, as I have indicated in the introduction, are denunciatory.

In every chapter of this remarkable little book there will be a striking statement—sometimes in a single verse, sometimes in many verses as in this first chapter.

**The word of the LORD that came to Micah the Morasthite in the days of Jotham, Ahaz, and Hezekiah, kings of Judah, which he saw concerning Samaria and Jerusalem [Mic. 1:1].**

Let me repeat, Samaria was the capital of the northern kingdom. The city was built originally by Omri, king of Israel, and was the seat of idolatry. It was made famous—or infamous—by Ahab and Jezebel who built there a temple to Baal. The city stood in a very lovely location, but it lies in ruins today. I have pictures of it, which I took while on a trip to Israel. The desolate ruins bear mute testimony to the accuracy of Micah's prophecy concerning Samaria.

"Micah the Morasthite" means that he was a native of Moresheth of Gath, which is southwest of Jerusalem. Although he was in the kingdom of Judah, he prophesied to both kingdoms, but his main message was directed to the northern kingdom. I have often wondered about that. His contemporary, Isaiah, was a prophet to the southern kingdom; and perhaps, since Micah was probably a younger man, he felt that Isaiah could take care of the southern kingdom while God directed him to speak to the northern kingdom. You will never misunderstand Micah, because he makes it very clear to whom he is speaking.

## THE PROPHET'S FIRST MESSAGE

**Hear, all ye people; hearken, O earth, and all that therein is: and let the Lord GOD be witness against you, the Lord from his holy temple [Mic. 1:2].**

"Hear, all ye people" means *all* people. That includes you wherever you are today. Micah has a message for us. As with all the prophets, although speaking into a particular situation which has long since disappeared, his message is relevant for our day because certain principles are laid down. Micah gives a philosophy of human government. He deals with that which is false and that which is true authority in government. This would be a good book for both Republicans and Democrats in Washington to consider. It wouldn't hurt them to look at *God's* philosophy of government because, very candidly, their form of government is not working today. The reason it cannot work properly is because it was originally put together by men who, although some of them were not Christians, had a respect and reverence for the Bible. They felt that the great principles stated in the Bible were worth following, and therefore they wove them into the warp and woof of our government. It will never work in the hands of godless men. Frankly, that is our problem. Actually, the *form* of government is not the important feature, although we think it is. Let me give you an example: when Cromwell was a dictator in England, they had about the best form of government they could possibly have had. Don't misunderstand me, I am not recommending a dictatorship, but it is good if you have the right dictator. When Jesus comes to reign on this earth, my friend, *He* is going to be a dictator and the right kind of dictator. The character of the ruler is of utmost importance. It makes no difference if there is a monarchy, a limited monarchy, an autocracy, a democracy, or a representative form of government; if the right *men* are in charge, it will work. I hope that I am getting it over to you that I am not talking politics, but I am speaking of a philosophy of government and am attempting to pinpoint our current problem. We need men in government who have *character*. The concern of the American people is whether or not their government leaders have TV personalities. We are more interested in charisma than character. Micah deals with this matter in the third chapter: "The heads thereof judge for reward, and the priests thereof teach for hire, and the prophets thereof divine for money: yet will they lean upon the LORD, and say, Is not the LORD among us? none evil can come upon us" (Mic. 3:11). Micah puts his finger on the fact that they had *false* prophets, false religion, and false leaders.

"Hearken, O earth, and all that therein is." Since most of us are on this earth, he means all of us.

"And let the Lord GOD be witness against

you." Micah is calling God as a witness to the thing which he is going to say.

"The Lord from his holy temple." The Lord was in His holy temple, in His heaven, then as now.

The Lord will come down in judgment—

**For, behold, the LORD cometh forth out of his place, and will come down, and tread upon the high places of the earth [Mic. 1:3].**

This language is absolutely beautiful, although it is frightful in many ways.

"Tread upon the high places of the earth." You recall that the high places were the locations of idol worship. Idols were set up in groves upon the hills and mountains. Also in that day the cities were situated on elevated places. Both Samaria and Jerusalem were built on mountains. The Lord Jesus mentioned that a city that is set upon a hill cannot be hid, and the city has a tremendous influence upon the area around it (see Matt. 5:14). When the city is the seat of government, it has a tremendous influence not only upon the immediate area but often upon the entire world. That is the case of many great cities in the past and present. Also cities are centers of great sin. For these reasons God is coming down upon them in judgment—He will "tread upon the high places of the earth."

**And the mountains shall be molten under him, and the valleys shall be cleft, as wax before the fire, and as the waters that are poured down a steep place [Mic. 1:4].**

"The mountains shall be molten [melted] under him, and the valleys shall be cleft." This is definitely a picture of volcanic action and of earthquakes. We find this same language in the Scriptures from Judges through Habakkuk. For example, Psalm 18:7–10: "Then the earth shook and trembled; the foundations also of the hills moved and were shaken, because he was wroth. There went up a smoke out of his nostrils, and fire out of his mouth devoured: coals were kindled by it. He bowed the heavens also, and came down: and darkness was under his feet. And he rode upon a cherub, and did fly: yea, he did fly upon the wings of the wind." Although this language is highly figurative, it is a tremendous, actual, exact picture of what took place.

This raises a question about what or who controls the weather and natural forces. Well, God is the One who controls nature and earthquakes and volcanoes and weather. I believe that God judges nations and that He judges

peoples, and these things are warnings. I have always felt that the Great Depression of the 1930s and the dust storms in the midwest were warnings from God. But America didn't listen to God. Then we entered World War II, and we have not recovered from that yet. God is still moving in the affairs of this world.

I think of Turkey, especially along the west coast, and the ruins of the great cities like Ephesus and Pergamos which at one time were the very lifeblood of the Roman Empire. Now they are lying in ruins. Why is it that there is no great population but only little towns there today? Well, you may say, it is earthquake territory. You are right. It is interesting that man always flocks to earthquake territory. That is true in California where I live. I have seen people come out here by the millions. We are ready for an earthquake, let me tell you. The greatest population of the Roman Empire was in modern Turkey, and look what happened to it. Historians tell us that an earthquake destroyed the cities and caused the people to flee. That was the judgment of God, you see.

God makes it clear here about His judgment—

**For the transgression of Jacob is all this, and for the sins of the house of Israel. What is the transgression of Jacob? is it not Samaria? and what are the high places of Judah? are they not Jerusalem? [Mic. 1:5].**

"For the transgression of Jacob . . . and for the sins of the house of Israel." You see, he is speaking to both kingdoms and their capitals—Samaria of Israel and Jerusalem of Judah (or Jacob).

"What is the transgression of Jacob?" Rather, *who* is responsible for the transgression of Jacob? The answer is: "Is it not Samaria? and what are the high places of Judah? are they not Jerusalem?" The prophet places the blame on the capital cities, Jerusalem and Samaria. Jerusalem was the place where they were to worship God. Were they worshiping Him there? Well, yes, they would go to the temple, but they also were going to the high places where idolatry and the grossest forms of immorality took place. And God says that it is for these things He is going to judge these two great cities because of their tremendous influence over the nations of Israel and Judah.

This has, I believe, an application to my own nation because we have a philosophy of government that is wrong. As we have seen, it is not the *form* of government that is wrong;

it is the *people* who head it up who are wrong. I do not know that there is too much difference between having one godless dictator or having a whole godless Senate and a whole godless House of Representatives. The founders of our nation formed three branches of government because they had had a bad experience with old King George back in England, and they knew they could not trust men. Their theory was that the three branches of government could watch each other. Well, in our day all three need watching. Why? Because it takes the right kind of men for any government to function properly.

The problem in Micah's day was that Samaria and Jerusalem had become corrupt, and God was going to judge them. What about my own country? It is my personal opinion that America has gone over the hill. The United States does not appear in the prophecies of the end times for one of two reasons: either it will have disappeared as a nation or it will no longer be a world power. We had a marvelous opportunity to lead the world following World War II. So what did we give the world? We gave it rock music, hippies, the new morality, a love of pleasure, and a love of affluence. And today the United States of America is on the way down. This is distressing to me because I *love* my country, and I hate to see a godless outfit take over and spoil this nation which I do believe was founded under God for a very definite purpose. It is a government *under God* that Micah is espousing. This is God's philosophy of government, you see.

Now we come to the first striking statement, and it is the longest one. It goes through the remainder of the chapter, from verse 6 to verse 16. It is a miniature of the great destruction that will come in the last days. We will return to the subject of judgment during the last days when we come to the fourth chapter of Micah; but, here in the first chapter of Micah, it is a local judgment in which Assyria will destroy Samaria. I wish I could show you some of my pictures of Samaria. At one time it was a lovely city. It was a city of great influence and culture. It was a city of great promise, but today it lies in dust and ashes.

**Therefore I will make Samaria as an heap of the field, and as plantings of a vineyard: and I will pour down the stones thereof into the valley, and I will discover the foundations thereof [Mic. 1:6].**

"I will make Samaria as an heap of the field, and as plantings of a vineyard." That is what it is today. I saw a little vineyard planted by Arabs growing right in the ruins of one section of Samaria. There are other places where you can find an orchard planted in the ruins and different kinds of trees which were planted here and there.

"I will pour down the stones thereof into the valley." I have stood on the acropolis, the very highest place in Samaria, and have looked down the steep embankment. Do you know what is down there? There are all kinds of pillars and stones that formerly had been hewn out and used in buildings. They have been rolled down, down into the valley. I can't think of anything more literal than this fulfillment of "I will pour down the stones thereof into the valley."

"And I will discover [uncover] the foundations thereof." I would like to show you the pictures I took of the foundations which were there in the time of Ahab and Jezebel. Also I have pictures of the later foundations which were built by the Romans. God has uncovered them all, and they are all there in ruins for you to take a good look at today. The foundations reveal that there had been a tremendous city there, but it has long since gone out of business.

**And all the graven images thereof shall be beaten to pieces, and all the hires thereof shall be burned with the fire, and all the idols thereof will I lay desolate: for she gathered it of the hire of an harlot, and they shall return to the hire of an harlot [Mic. 1:7].**

"And all the graven [carved] images thereof shall be beaten to pieces." When I was there, I asked my guide, "Are there any images around here? Have the archaeologists found any images?" His answer was, "No. There is no evidence of idolatry although we know that there was idolatry here." Let me remind you that the high places which are mentioned were places where idols stood and where the basest kind of worship took place. For example, in the worship of Molech, the idol formed a red-hot oven where children were actually offered? What an awful thing that was! And the grossest forms of immorality were carried on in connection with idol worship. In other words, religion and illicit sex were very much the same thing. It is abroad again today in Satan worship and outgrowths of the occult.

"And all the hires thereof shall be burned

with the fire." The word *hires* is very interesting. It refers to the costly vessels that had been given to the heathen temples. My guide told me that, in the ruins of the palace of Jezebel, archaeologists have found remains of quite a few smaller ivory vessels which were evidently jars to hold perfume and some larger ones to hold wine. There has been a great deal of excavation done there.

"She gathered it of the hire of an harlot, and they shall return to the hire of an harlot." Sex was at the heart of these idolatrous rites. In Corinth, for instance, they know today that in the worship of Aphrodite upon the Acropolis, there were a thousand "vestal virgins," who were nothing in the world but prostitutes. Sex was a part of the religion. A man had to *pay* when he went into one of their places of worship. Whether in temples or out-of-doors, they were brothels. It was all done in the name of religion. This was true among the Phoenicians; it was true among the Philistines; and Israel had adopted their religions.

It is quite interesting that contemporary thought is returning to that viewpoint. The so-called "new morality" is as old as the worship of Molech and of Baal and of other heathen religions of antiquity. This is one reason I insist that religion has not been a blessing to the world. If you want to see what religion has done, go to India. There religion has kept a wonderful people in a pitiful state. The people are absolutely impoverished and *bound* by the fetters of religion. Christianity, of course, is not a religion; Christianity is a Person. The Lord Jesus made that clear when He said, "If the Son therefore shall make you free, ye shall be free indeed" (John 8:36). He can deliver you from things that are sinful, and He can also deliver you from the bondage of religion.

The last part of the verse says, "she gathered it of the hire of an harlot, and they shall return to the hire of an harlot." Micah is saying that the hires will go right back and be used for sin again. Some of these vessels were apparently used again in Roman times. It was Herod who rebuilt that city. He liked the location; it was a delightful place to live, but it also has been destroyed and is in ruins today. Heathen worship was the main sin. It was number one on the sin parade, but Micah is going to mention some other sins, too.

## LAMENTATION OF MICAH

The remainder of the chapter is Micah's lamentation. He is deeply affected by Israel's sins and their consequences. Micah is not just a paid preacher; he is a prophet called of God. He is very much like Jeremiah and Hosea in that he had a tender heart. We tend to think of all the Old Testament prophets as being hard-nosed like Elijah and Ezekiel. You may remember that, when God commissioned Ezekiel, He warned him that He was sending him to an impudent and hardhearted people. But, He said, "I am going to make your head harder than theirs." There was a need for hardheaded prophets, and these men could speak right out; but many of God's prophets were very tenderhearted, and Micah was one of them. Listen to him—

**Therefore I will wail and howl, I will go stripped and naked: I will make a wailing like the dragons, and mourning as the owls [Mic. 1:8].**

"I will go stripped and naked." When a man removed his outer garments, it meant that he was in deep mourning and deep trouble.

"I will make a wailing like the dragons [jackals], and mourning as the owls [ostriches]." If you have ever heard a wolf or a hyena howl at night, you know it is a mournful and terrible sound. Job uses this same expression: "I am a brother to dragons [jackals], and a companion to owls [ostriches]" (Job 30:29). I did not know that ostriches mourn until several years ago when my wife and I were visiting the San Diego Zoo. We were walking around when we heard a mournful sound. It was a very plaintive and pitiful sort of a sound. At first I thought an animal had been trapped or hurt in some way. As we continued our walk, we met a man and I asked him, "Do you know what is making that sound?" He replied, "It's the ostriches." I thought the man was pulling my leg. I didn't even thank him for the information because I thought he was kidding. But soon we walked around a bend in the road, and there were the ostriches. They were all standing there, just looking around. I didn't see any reason for their mourning, but they were making the most mournful sound I have ever heard. Micah said that he would mourn like the ostriches. He would wail like they did.

In other words, the message that this man was giving to the people was affecting him just as the message that Jeremiah gave affected him. This is another example of the type of man God wants to deliver a harsh message. It must be a man with a tender heart if the message is to be harsh. Why? Because before God judges a people, He wants them to know how *He* feels; so He sent the weeping prophet Jeremiah and then this weeping prophet Micah. When the people listen to his message, then to his mourning and wailing, they understand how God feels about their sin. God is not vindictive. Although He takes no delight in judgment, He must judge sin. If you will turn that over in your mind a little, my friend, you will recognize that God cannot permit evil and wrong to be done to one of His creatures without His judging the guilty party. He would not be God if He did not give justice to His creatures. When evil is done and sin is committed, God is going to move in judgment. It takes Him a little while to get around to it; but, when He moves, nothing can stop Him.

**For her wound is incurable; for it is come unto Judah; he is come unto the gate of my people, even to Jerusalem [Mic. 1:9].**

"Her wound is incurable." The nation had passed over an invisible line from which there was no possibility of returning. While I do not know where that line is, I do know it exists. And when an individual or a nation passes over that line, there is no possibility of reclamation. It is not that God is not merciful and gracious, but the individual or the nation is so bent to sin and has turned a deaf ear to God for so long that there is nothing left but judgment. The wound is incurable. They will no longer hear God.

This disturbs me, because I wonder if my own country may have passed over that line. All I know is that they are not hearing the voice of God and do not want to hear it. In spite of the fact that there is a tremendous reception today for the Word of God, I sometimes wonder how deep it is. Are the *hearing* of the Word of God and *obedience* to the Word of God synonymous? I actually know of folk who are living in sin or have lived in sin and have never repented of it, yet speak of *loving* the Word of God! Is it possible that they have stepped over that invisible line and that there is nothing left for them but judgment?

"For her wound is incurable; for it is come unto Judah; he is come unto the gate of my people, even to Jerusalem." The Assyrian army under Sennacherib came down from the north and mowed down the northern kingdom. They got as far south as the walls of Jerusalem, and the king Hezekiah was afraid that they were going to take the city; but God instructed Isaiah to tell the king that Jerusalem would not be invaded but that this was a warning to them. Well, Judah heeded the warning for awhile, but it wore off and they turned back to their idol worship and their sin. The day came when God had to judge Judah as He had judged Israel.

Now we are given a series of names of ten different urban centers that were affected by Samaria and Jerusalem. Not all of these places are on the map, but the list begins in the north with Samaria and moves south toward Jerusalem and beyond Jerusalem. The meanings of the names reveal a play upon words.

**Declare ye it not at Gath, weep ye not at all: in the house of Aphrah roll thyself in the dust [Mic. 1:10].**

"Declare ye it not at Gath." The name *Gath* means "weep-town." God is saying, "Weep not at Weep-town." Gath belonged to the Philistines, the inveterate enemies of Israel, and He is saying, "Don't let them know that judgment is coming upon you."

"In the house of Aphrah roll thyself in the dust." *Aphrah* means "dust-town." To put dust on the head was the sign of the deepest grief. The site of this town is not known, but the thought seems to be that the people were to lament in their own territory.

**Pass ye away, thou inhabitant of Saphir, having thy shame naked: the inhabitant of Zaanan came not forth in the mourning of Beth-ezel; he shall receive of you his standing [Mic. 1:11].**

*Saphir* means "beauty-town." Believe me, the inhabitants passed away and also the town itself so that the site of it is absolutely unknown. Beauty-town would be no longer beautiful—"having thy shame naked."

"The inhabitant of Zaanan came not forth in the mourning." *Zaanan* means "march-town." March-town didn't march. The site of this town is also unknown to us.

**For the inhabitant of Maroth waited carefully for good: but evil came down from the LORD unto the gate of Jerusalem [Mic. 1:12].**

"The inhabitant of Maroth waited carefully [anxiously] for good." The name *Maroth* means "bitterness." They waited for a good report, for good news, but it was a bitter report—"evil came down from the LORD unto the gate of Jerusalem." The Assyrians were marching to the very walls of Jerusalem.

**O thou inhabitant of Lachish, bind the chariot to the swift beast: she is the beginning of the sin to the daughter of**

**Zion: for the transgressions of Israel were found in thee [Mic. 1:13].**

*Lachish* was "Horse-town." There were great stables of horses there. It is a city southwest of Jerusalem, over near the Philistine country, the place where idolatry was first introduced into the southern kingdom of Judah. Apparently Lachish was the link of idolatry between Israel and Judah.

"Bind the chariot to the swift beast" is a reference to the horse, and we now know that this is the place where horses were kept which were used in the worship of the sun. You will recall that even the Greeks had their Apollo driving a chariot across the sky in connection with their worship of the sun. God is condemning Lachish because she introduced this idolatry into Judah, the southern kingdom.

**Therefore shalt thou give presents to Moresheth-gath: the houses of Achzib shall be a lie to the kings of Israel [Mic. 1:14].**

"Moresheth-gath" was, of course, the hometown of Micah; it was in the southern kingdom of Judah.

"The houses of Achzib shall be a lie to the kings of Israel." *Achzib* means "lie-town." Lie-town, as did all these other towns, lived up to its name. The inhabitants were given over to lies. The name *Achzib* is the Hebrew word for a "winter brook" or a "lie." The reason for this is that the brooks in Israel are very much like the brooks in Southern California. In fact, a friend of mine was riding with me one day when we crossed over the Los Angeles River. In the winter, during the wet season, this river can really go on a rampage, but in the dry season there is not much more than a trickle of water in it. As we crossed the river, my friend said, "That's a good place for a river." I replied, "It sure is, and in the winter there *is* a river there." In Israel there are many dry river beds like that. But a flash flood out in the desert can transform them into raging torrents. Now you can see why *achzib* means a "winter brook" or a "lie." And the town of Achzib was Lie-town because they had promised help to the northern kingdom, but they actually gave no help at all. "The houses of Achzib shall be a lie to the kings of Israel."

**Yet will I bring an heir unto thee, O inhabitant of Mareshah: he shall come unto Adullam the glory of Israel [Mic. 1:15].**

Here is a suggestion that help is coming to Israel but not at this time. It is only a faint suggestion that "the glory of Israel" is the heir in the line of David, and the Lord Jesus Christ is the only one who fits this description. One of His names is *Faithful*—He is faithful and true, and He *is* coming to deliver them. He will not come from Lie-town, that's for sure. However, in Micah's day Israel was deceived, greatly deceived, and no help came to them when the Assyrian army came down from the north and overran their land.

Now Micah calls upon Israel to mourn as a nation—

**Make thee bald, and poll thee for thy delicate children; enlarge thy baldness as the eagle; for they are gone into captivity from thee [Mic. 1:16].**

When Assyria invaded Israel the first time, they took the young people into captivity, and the people are called upon to mourn because of that. Making themselves bald was an indication of grief. Although in the Mosaic Law they were told not to trim their beards nor shave their beards, now because of the sin that had come into the nation they are told to express their grief in this manner.

Isaiah, who was a contemporary of Micah, had something to say about this custom. In Isaiah 15:2 we read, "He is gone up to Bajith, and to Dibon, the high places [of idolatry], to weep: Moab shall howl over Nebo, and over Medeba: on all their heads shall be baldness, and every beard cut off." This verse describes deep mourning and wailing. They had lost their children, you see. This is the judgment of God upon them.

# CHAPTER 2

*THEME:* The prophet's second message describes specific sins

## THE PROPHET'S SECOND MESSAGE

In this chapter Micah describes the specific sins of the people. Judgment came upon these people because they had gone into idolatry with all that that implies. Idolatry in that day represented gross immorality, and the wages of the harlots ran the "high places." Prostitution was the source of funds for their religion since sex was associated with idolatry. We find that the same thing is true today in the occult and in Satan worship. I think there is a connection between the occult of today and the idolatry of Micah's day. Sex plays a very prominent part in both of them. They are a revelation of man breaking God's commandment. Sexual sin and idolatry seem to go together. They destroy the home and destroy the sweet and tender relationship between a man and a woman in marriage. When sex is kept within the marriage relationship, it can become the sweetest and most precious thing on earth. When a nation moves sex out of that context and encourages illicit sex in the name of religion or "new morality," it is evidence of the fact that the nation is in decline and is actually on its way out.

The sins which Micah will denounce in this chapter are sins against one another, sins against mankind, while in the first chapter their sins were in their relationship with God. You see, when a man is not right with God, he cannot be right with his fellowman. And when a man is right with God, he can be (although he doesn't always choose to be) right with his fellowman. We have had an illustration of this in the lovey-dovey movement which started several years ago with the "flower children" in the San Francisco area. Because they were far from the Lord, the movement lapsed into gross immorality, and it wrecked the lives of many young people. My friend, when you are not right with God, you will not be right with other people.

Chapter 2 is not going to be pretty. You will not find it to be the most beautiful chapter in the Word of God. But it reveals the sin of a nation, which caused its destruction. It is well for us as God's people and also for our nation to listen to Micah and to wake up.

**Woe to them that devise iniquity, and work evil upon their beds! when the morning is light, they practise it, because it is in the power of their hand [Mic. 2:1].**

Although this may include the practice of illicit sex, it primarily refers to evil of other sorts. When they go to bed at night, they don't go to sleep but lie there and devise and plan iniquity—and chances are they are engaging in it at the same time. I have had some experience with folk like this. A wife complained to me bitterly that when her husband comes home, he doesn't leave his work in the office but brings it with him. And when he goes to bed at night, he lies there conniving what he will do the next day. No wonder the wife was contemplating divorce.

"When the morning is light, they practise it, because it is in the power of their hand." That is, they are able to execute what they have planned. It is also true in our contemporary society that the sinner and the ungodly are successful. The wealth of my own country is not in the hands of the godly today—although it was at one time. Money means power, and the ungodly are able to carry through that which is wrong. This is the chief reason that my nation is in its present predicament. The real problem is not an energy shortage nor the incapability of this or that political party. The root of the problem is that power is in the hands of the ungodly. This is the same sin which brought Israel down. Micah, as we have already noted, presents a philosophy of human government which God follows. If you doubt this, read the history of the fall of great nations. When wealth and power get into the hands of a few ungodly people, God moves in judgment.

Micah is still speaking of those in his day whose lives were characterized by doing evil—twenty-four hours a day. Now he is being specific—

**And they covet fields, and take them by violence; and houses, and take them away: so they oppress a man and his house, even a man and his heritage [Mic. 2:2].**

"They covet fields, and take them by violence." We have an example of this being done by Israel's royalty in the case of Ahab and Jezebel. In 1 Kings 21 we have the record of King Ahab coveting the vineyard of Naboth. Like a spoiled brat, he wanted it, although he didn't make a move to get it. However, his wife Jezebel was a sinner who believed in action. She immediately set about getting the vineyard by eliminating Naboth. So what the heads of government practiced, those down below began to practice. The wealthy began to seize the fields that they coveted because they had the money and the power to do it.

My, how that method is being used in our contemporary society! The little businessman doesn't stand much of a chance for survival in the culture we have produced. The big operators are in control, and they frankly say that they are in for the profits. But sometimes the word *profit* is a synonym for *covetousness*. And this was the great sin of Israel.

I have never understood why any man would want more than one million dollars. I have always thought that if I had that much money I would never want any more. It seems, however, that when a man gets one million dollars, he desires two million dollars. With two million dollars he can't eat any more. He can't sleep any more. He can't indulge himself any more—he can only drink so much, and he can only sin so much. A million dollars will enable a man to do all that he wants, but men want to continue to get richer and richer and richer. The old bromide "The rich get richer and the poor get poorer" is the story of mankind. And Micah is speaking into that situation.

Notice that evil men will covet fields and houses and take them by violence. God not only gave the Land of Promise to the nation Israel and put them in it, but He also gave each tribe a particular portion of the land. Then He gave each individual a particular plot in the tribe to which he belonged, and that plot was his heritage. Then God instituted certain laws so that a man could not lose his land forever. During the Year of Jubilee every mortgage was canceled, and every bit of property was returned to its original owner. However, the Year of Jubilee only came every fifty years. If you lost your land the second year after Jubilee, you would have to wait forty-eight years to reclaim it. You could get very hungry in that length of time! Even though God had made laws to protect the poor, the rich always found ways to get around them, of course. All through the Scriptures we see that God is on the side of the poor. As Abraham Lincoln used to say, "God must love poor people because He made so many of them." And the Lord Jesus Himself experienced the poverty of this earth.

**Therefore thus saith the LORD; Behold, against this family do I devise an evil, from which ye shall not remove your necks; neither shall ye go haughtily: for this time is evil [Mic. 2:3].**

This is a very interesting verse. God has said, "I condemn you because you lie on your beds and plot evil." Now He says, "I am going to plot evil against you." What does He mean by that? Was God actually going to do that which was evil? No, God intended to punish the evildoers, which was right, but from *their* viewpoint it was wrong because they wouldn't like that. They would call it evil.

Today even some Christians condemn God for permitting certain things to take place. In other words, they are saying that God is doing evil. Well, God beat them to it; He said that He would do evil from *their* viewpoint. If they continued sinning, He would stop them with judgment. In fact, He said to Israel, "I devise an evil, from which ye shall not remove your necks." God intended to put around those necks the chains of bondage. And the people of Israel were led captive into Assyria, one of the most brutal nations that has ever been on the topside of this earth. God adds, "Neither shall ye go haughtily: for this time is evil." How haughty and proud they had been!

My own nation is presently in this same position. In many countries that I have visited—South America, Europe, Africa, and Asia—I have found that Americans are not loved, and we haven't been loved for many years. Why? Because we have been haughty and proud. Yet we had the temerity after World War II to tell the world that we were going to lead it to peace! We thought the American dollar would solve the problems of the world. Well, we have gotten this world into a mess, haven't we? And American diplomacy has been nothing to boast about since World War II. Why has our record been so poor? My personal opinion is that the judgment of God is already taking place. I love my country, and it breaks my heart to see it continue to fall into the hands of the godless rich. Let me repeat that it is not the *method* of government but the character of the *men* who govern that makes a nation great.

**In that day shall one take up a parable against you, and lament with a doleful lamentation, and say, We be utterly spoiled: he hath changed the portion of my people: how hath he removed it from me! turning away he hath divided our fields [Mic. 2:4].**

Great confusion was coming and "doleful lamentation"—a very unusual expression in the

Hebrew language. It probably would not be possible to translate into English exactly what Micah was saying. There was no hope at all— "We be utterly spoiled [destroyed]."

**Therefore thou shalt have none that shall cast a cord by lot in the congregation of the Lord [Mic. 2:5].**

There have been various interpretations of this. Perhaps it means that there will be no more worship of God in that place.

**Prophesy ye not, say they to them that prophesy: they shall not prophesy to them, that they shall not take shame.**

**O thou that art named the house of Jacob, is the spirit of the Lord straitened? are these his doings? do not my words do good to him that walketh uprightly? [Mic. 2:6–7].**

This was a time when God cut off the flow of the spirit of prophecy. Why? Because the people wouldn't hear it, and there came a famine of the Word of God.

"Are these his doings?" God has told them that He, too, is plotting evil—that is, what *they* call evil, because it is going to be a judgment against them.

"Do not my words do good to him that walketh uprightly?" Though the message is harsh, God's people will accept it, and they will obey it. This is not a delightful passage like Psalm 23 or John 14, but God gives it just as much prominence. In fact, He put it in the second chapter, rather than in the fourteenth or the twenty-third, so we would not miss it.

**Even of late my people is risen up as an enemy: ye pull off the robe with the garment from them that pass by securely as men averse from war [Mic. 2:8].**

God is saying that, although they are His people, they have become His enemies, and one of the evidences of this is the way they treat the poor. God always insists upon justice for the poor. His charge is: "Ye pull off the robe with the garment from them." A man's robe was what he slept in. In other words, they would take a man's bed out from under him. That was how far they were willing to go to rob the poor.

**The women of my people have ye cast out from their pleasant houses; from their children have ye taken away my glory for ever [Mic. 2:9].**

"The women of my people have ye cast out from their pleasant houses" probably refers to unprotected widows who had inherited homes from their husbands.

"From their children have ye taken away my glory for ever." Even the young children were deprived of what God had given to them. And they would grow up in rebellion. In our day the rebellion of youth is, in my opinion, permitted by God to try to shake us out of our lethargy.

**Arise ye, and depart; for this is not your rest: because it is polluted, it shall destroy you, even with a sore destruction [Mic. 2:10].**

They were attempting to solve their problems and to be at rest without being at peace with God. "Because it is polluted, it shall destroy you, even with a sore [great] destruction." Because of the pollution of their sin and their heartless oppression, the land would cast out its inhabitants.

**If a man walking in the spirit and falsehood do lie, saying, I will prophesy unto thee of wine and of strong drink; he shall even be the prophet of this people [Mic. 2:11].**

This is biting sarcasm. God is saying, "The kind of prophets you want are those who will approve of your sins." My friend, in our day many people do not want the preacher to say that drinking is wrong and that drunkenness is bad. Even in our churches many pastors are approving of social drinking. They insist that we are living in a new day, and, since we are not under the Mosaic Law, we can do these things. While it is true that we are under grace, there is one sure thing: if you love God, you are going to keep His commandments, and He certainly does condemn drunkenness. The false prophets in Micah's day were not condemning the sins of the people. They were popular preachers, saying what the people wanted to hear.

## PROMISE TO THE REMNANT

The message of judgment which Micah has been delivering has been very harsh, but here at the close of the chapter is a very beautiful little prophecy which shines like a ray of sunshine that breaks through the dark clouds on a stormy day.

**I will surely assemble, O Jacob, all of thee; I will surely gather the remnant of Israel; I will put them together as the**

**sheep of Bozrah, as the flock in the midst of their fold: they shall make great noise by reason of the multitude of men [Mic. 2:12].**

You have noticed, I am sure, that when God speaks to them of their sin, He addresses them by the name *Jacob*. So when He uses that term in this verse, the implication is that He is going to show mercy to them, not because of their worthiness or because of some fine character trait, but because of His own grace.

"I will surely assemble, O Jacob, all of thee." This was not fulfilled after the Babylonian captivity, and it has not been fulfilled in their recent return to their land because He says that He will assemble *"all* of thee." At the present time, there are more of the nation Israel in New York City than there are in the whole land of Israel. Also, there is a great company still in Russia and in other countries of the world. So God has not yet assembled all of them according to this prophecy.

"I will surely gather the remnant of Israel." Now for the remnant He uses the name Israel. God has always had a faithful remnant out of the nation, and actually He has never had more than the remnant. There never has been a time when it could be said that 100 percent of the nation had turned to God. And it was always for the sake of the remnant that God was gracious to the nation. In the future day that is coming, even in the Great Tribulation Period when we are told that all Israel shall be saved, who is meant? Well, it is all of Israel which belongs to that company of 144,000. The Book of Revelation makes it clear that they will be sealed (sealed, I believe, by the Holy Spirit of God) and will be able to survive the Great Tribulation. But that will be only a remnant of the nation. After all, there are probably three million Jews in Israel and probably twelve million in other lands, so that 144,000 could be nothing more than a remnant.

"I will put them together as the sheep of Bozrah." Bozrah was a place of many flocks of sheep because of the excellent pasture lands. When God brings His people together like the sheep of Bozrah, the Twenty-third Psalm will be fulfilled: "The LORD is my shepherd; I shall not want. He maketh me to lie down in green pastures . . ." (Ps. 23:1–2).

"They shall make great noise by reason of the multitude of men." The great noise will be due to the fact that a great number will return to the land. When God returns the nation to their land, it does not mean that all of them are going to be saved by any means; but it will be a tremendous event. Since what *we* have seen of the return of Israel to the land has caused such great rejoicing among prophetic teachers, think what it will be in this future day!

**The breaker is come up before them: they have broken up, and have passed through the gate, and are gone out by it: and their king shall pass before them, and the LORD on the head of them [Mic. 2:13].**

"The breaker is come up before them." The "breaker" is the one who clears the way, removes the obstacles, and leads them. I believe this refers to their entering the millennial kingdom when the Lord Jesus Christ will be the one to lead them, as He will have returned to the earth at that time. This verse refers to Him as the Breaker, their King, and the Lord (Jehovah).

# CHAPTER 3

**THEME:** *The prophet's third message denounces leaders for their sins*

## THE PROPHET'S THIRD MESSAGE

Micah denounces the leaders of Israel for their sins—first, the princes; second, the prophets, who were the spiritual leaders; and last, all the leaders of Jerusalem, including the princes, the prophets, and the priests.

## SINS OF THE PRINCES

This section begins with the call to hear, as does every major division of the Book of Micah.

**And I said, Hear, I pray you, O heads of Jacob, and ye princes of the house of Israel; Is it not for you to know judgment? [Mic. 3:1].**

"Hear, I pray you, O heads of Jacob." He is speaking to the leadership of the nation.

"Is it not for you to know judgment?" What does he mean by this? Well, he is addressing the rulers of Israel who were the judges and magistrates. When the people were found guilty of a crime, they were brought before these men for judgment. Now *they* certainly should know what judgment and justice are. The same thought is expressed in the New Testament: "Therefore thou art inexcusable, O man, whosoever thou art that judgest: for wherein thou judgest another, thou condemnest thyself; for thou that judgest doest the same things" (Rom. 2:1). "The same things" does not mean *identical* but *similar* things. An example of this is found in 2 Samuel 12. The prophet Nathan came before King David and told him about a rich man in his kingdom who had great flocks of sheep. However, when he needed meat to serve his guest, instead of taking a lamb from his own flock, he took a poor man's little ewe lamb—the only lamb he owned—and roasted it for his guest. When David heard this, he stood up, hot with anger, and pronounced judgment upon the man who would do such a thing. He could see the injustice of it; yet he himself had done a similar thing. And Nathan said to David, ". . . Thou art the man . . ." (2 Sam. 12:7). David accepted the judgment and confessed his guilt before God. It is amazing, friend, how we can see another man's sin but overlook our own. This is the reason God says to these leaders in Israel, "You have judged others for their misdeeds, but you are doing the same things."

This charge is certainly applicable to our day also. My feeling is that the reason many judges in our land have been so lenient with criminals and have not wanted the death penalty is that they are bothered by a guilt complex themselves. I have a notion that many times when a judge on the bench hears a case of an offender who is brought before him and hands down a light sentence, it is because it salves his own conscience to do so. It is almost a joke when a group of congressmen investigate the wrongdoing of someone in politics. Probably every one of them sitting there judging the other fellow has a skeleton in his own closet. It takes men of character to judge fairly, you see.

This is exactly what Micah is saying to the leadership in his day, "Is it not for you to know judgment?" You are not acting in ignorance; you have had experience in this. You have judged men who were guilty; now *you* are guilty.

**Who hate the good, and love the evil; who pluck off their skin from off them, and their flesh from off their bones [Mic. 3:2].**

"Who hate the good, and love the evil." It is difficult for a judge who had been at a cocktail party the night before and had become a little tipsy himself to sentence a man the next day who has killed somebody because he was driving while drunk. No wonder the judge lets him off easy. I know what I am talking about, my friend, because my mother was killed by a drunken driver right here in Pasadena. I didn't feel that I should press charges, but when I was called in as a witness, I told the court, "All I ask is that *justice* be done." And, believe me, he got off with a light sentence. As I looked at that judge, I had the feeling that he had a pretty bad conscience.

In Micah's day the leadership actually hated the good and loved the evil. Folk like that are not fit to be in positions of leadership then or now. If it is discovered that a man in a high position in government—a congressman, a senator, or a judge—is unfaithful to his wife, is he fit to make laws relative to marriage? I don't think so. The present breakdown in morality goes back to the lawmakers. And God puts the blame on the leadership of the nation Israel in Micah's day. As we have seen before, God is presenting in this little Book of Micah a philosophy of human government, the basis of which is men of good character in positions of leadership.

"Who pluck off their skin from off them, and their flesh from off their bones." He uses a vivid illustration of their barbarous conduct against the poor.

**Who also eat the flesh of my people, and flay their skin from off them; and they break their bones, and chop them in pieces, as for the pot, and as flesh within the caldron [Mic. 3:3].**

In other words, they are like unfeeling human cannibals in their treatment of the poor. They are unprincipled and merciless. May I say that a godless man is the last man I want to sit in judgment upon me in any matter. And, very frankly, I am thankful that I don't have to stand before *you* in judgment, even if you are a Christian. And you ought to be delighted that you will not have to stand before me in judgment. I believe we will fare better in the presence of the Lord Jesus Christ than we would if we were judged by mankind. My case has already been appealed to Him, and I will not have to stand before any man to be judged. It is comforting to know this.

**Then shall they cry unto the LORD, but he will not hear them: he will even hide his face from them at that time, as they have behaved themselves ill in their doings [Mic. 3:4].**

Who is the prophet talking about? He is talking about the leaders in Israel. As long as they had been in their high positions, they had had no regard for the human side, and they had had no real sympathy or love. Now they are in trouble because a power greater than they has come down upon them.

"Then shall they cry unto the LORD, but he will not hear them." These leaders are going to cry out to God. Isn't that interesting? We all cry out to God in times of real trouble. I have been rather amused at times—I shouldn't be, but I can't help it—when I hear of the trouble that is coming upon us today and somebody says, "May God help us!" That is interesting because they bowed Him out of His universe many years ago. God isn't mentioned much today, except in profanity, but every now and then I find people saying, "May God help us." Well, my friend, I don't know whether He will hear you or not, because in Micah's day He said to the people who

had ignored Him and lived godless lives that He would not hear their cry for help. In fact, He said that He would hide His face from them. My friend, we are living in a period of the silence of God. It does not look as if God is doing much to alleviate the present world situation. Yet His grace is still abundant, and He is rich in mercy to those who will bow before Him and accept His Son as Savior.

## SINS OF THE PROPHETS

**Thus saith the LORD concerning the prophets that make my people err, that bite with their teeth, and cry, Peace; and he that putteth not into their mouths, they even prepare war against him [Mic. 3:5].**

The false prophets were like vicious animals or like serpents with forked tongues and fangs that would poison—actually, they were worse than that because they used smooth words to comfort the people, assuring them that peace was coming.

The futile effort of man to achieve peace ought to alert us to the fact that man by his own resources cannot bring peace to the world. Just wanting it and saying often enough that it is coming and voting for it will not bring peace. Again Micah makes it very clear that it is not a surface problem. It is not that folk don't *want* peace. The problem is that the human heart is wicked, and Isaiah, a contemporary of Micah, wrote, "There is no peace, saith my God, to the wicked" (Isa. 57:21). In fact, Isaiah repeats this fact three times in the last part of his prophecy. The great climax to which he came in each of those three times was that the real problem was the *wickedness* of the human heart.

When I make the statement that we cannot have peace in our day, I generally get two or three letters from well-meaning folk. They write lovely letters that chide me for being pessimistic. They insist that we should continue to *try* to bring peace in the world. They are sincere and their argument sounds good, but it is one of the most false teachings abroad that *man* can make peace in *his* way. I want peace as much as anyone, but I want to go at it God's way. First of all, the individual must know what the peace of God is. How are they going to know it? "Therefore being justified by faith, we have peace with God through our Lord Jesus Christ" (Rom. 5:1). It is not possible to have peace with your fellow man until you have peace with God. The human heart cannot be trusted; it is desperately wicked (see Jer. 17:9). You and I do not know how bad we really are. We can sink lower than any other creature on earth. One of the proofs that mankind has not descended from animals is that man can sink lower than animals—animals don't go out and get drunk or beat their mates or abuse their offspring. The human race must have the peace of God in their hearts before they can bring peace to their world.

In Micah's day the false prophets were prophesying peace, while in the north Assyria was getting ready to come down upon them. In our day efforts are being made in certain sections of the world to get people to sit down at a peace table and settle their differences without going to war. Yet for about six thousand years of recorded history, mankind has gone to war and still fights—one nation against another nation, one tribe against another tribe, one family against another family, and one individual against another individual. Why do we do this? We know that it is not to the advantage of either side. But we do it because we are alienated from God and in rebellion against Him. We won't face up to the real problem, but we listen to the smooth words of false prophets who predict peace. Because they do this sort of thing, God pronounces upon them the calamities which are coming—

**Therefore night shall be unto you, that ye shall not have a vision; and it shall be dark unto you, that ye shall not divine; and the sun shall go down over the prophets, and the day shall be dark over them [Mic. 3:6].**

"Therefore night shall be unto you." As we see in the other books of the prophets, darkness always speaks of judgment. It speaks of judgment in two different ways: the direct intervention of God in the punishment of the offender and also in the silence of God in not giving any new revelation to man.

"Ye shall not have a vision"—that is, God will not reveal any new truth to you.

"It shall be dark unto you." The judgment which is coming to them is called darkness; there will not be any light from the Word of God. There will be a cessation of prophesying.

In the New Testament the apostle Paul made reference to this in 1 Corinthians 13:8: "Charity never faileth: but whether there be prophecies, they shall fail. . . ." The English word *fail* is the Greek *ekpiptō*, meaning "to fall off or away." Prophecies will fail in two different ways: (1) they will be fulfilled; and

(2) God will no longer reveal anything new. There was a hiatus of approximately four hundred years between the Old Testament and the New Testament in which God was silent. The sun had gone down. Malachi, the last prophet, prophesied that the sun would come up again—"But unto you that fear my name shall the Sun of righteousness arise with healing in his wings . . ." (Mal. 4:2). Malachi would not have prophesied of the sun arising if the night had not been coming, and it *did* come. The people of Israel entered the long night of four hundred years until the coming of Christ. This is the same picture that Micah presents.

At the present time the United States has moved into the same position as that into which Israel had moved in Micah's day. It is easy for the very sophisticated historians to characterize as narrow-minded and bigoted the men and women who first came to settle in this country. Well, they were imperfect human beings, but even those who were not Christians had a knowledge of and a reverence for the Word of God. Both Harvard and Yale universities were founded to train ministers so that the people in this country would not be in the darkness of ignorance concerning the Word of God. Well, I tell you, their light has gone out, hasn't it? The very places that were supposed to be great educational centers and great lights for this country turned away from God a long time ago. The night is upon us today. At the universities we have had some of the worst riots this nation has ever seen. They have been the very hotbeds of darkness. It is at the university where the worship of Satan originated, and that is where it is being propagated. I have a newspaper clipping telling about a professor who is now involved in the worship of Satan and who indulges in the occult. We are in a period of time, it seems to me, when the sun of revelation has gone down. When I speak of revelation, I am talking about the illumination of the Word of God. The very centers which should be giving light from the Word of God are not doing it anymore. In fact, they are rejecting and turning their backs on God and turning to the occult. This is what Micah is talking about when he says, "Therefore night shall be unto you, that ye shall not have a vision; and it shall be dark unto you, that ye shall not divine; and the sun shall go down over the prophets, and the day shall be dark over them."

**Then shall the seers be ashamed, and the diviners confounded: yea, they shall**

**all cover their lips; for there is no answer of God [Mic. 3:7].**

Micah is saying that there shall be such gross darkness that those who are false prophets will make fools of themselves because of the fact that their prophecies will not come to pass. You will recall that this was the thing Ahab discovered, only he discovered it too late. All of the false prophets told him to go and fight in the war. Only one prophet, God's man, told him that if he went to war he would not come back but would be slain. That true prophet was Micaiah. It was too bad Ahab didn't listen to him, because Ahab went to war and was slain, just as Micaiah said (see 1 Kings 22:1–28).

God's men tell it like it is, and they tell the truth. My friend, there is no use trying to cover up the sins in the church. It has become revolting to hear of the many men who are classed as religious leaders, yet are involved in reprehensible conduct, and who, under the guise of being Christians, are prospering.

We need to read again Hebrews 12:6: "For whom the Lord loveth he chasteneth, and scourgeth every son whom he receiveth." Why does the Lord do that? He does it because He doesn't want us to be illegitimate. He says to us, "I chasten you and I discipline you so that you can know and the world can know that you are My child." Did you know that William the Conqueror actually signed his name William the Bastard because he was illegitimate? I am of the opinion that many church members could sign their names the same way. You might be able to say, "I am a deacon in the church, I am a Sunday school teacher, I am a leader in the church, or I am a preacher," but you would have to write under your name what William the Conqueror wrote under his name when he signed it. You would have to admit, "I am really not a legitimate child of God. I have not really been born again. I do not really know Jesus Christ as my personal Savior. I do not love Him. I do not seek to serve Him. I am not interested in His Word at all."

In Micah's day the false prophet was in that same position. He was speaking smooth words to comfort the people. The people had itching ears, and the prophet would scratch them, you see, by saying what they wanted to hear. Then they in turn would scratch the ears of the prophet by telling him how wonderful he was. "My, what a great preacher you are because you say such nice things. Everything

must be all right." They were living in luxury, but the level of immorality was frightening.

Now notice that Micah is very careful to separate himself from that group.

**But truly I am full of power by the spirit of the Lord, and of judgment, and of might, to declare unto Jacob his transgression, and to Israel his sin [Mic. 3:8].**

It took intestinal fortitude to be an unpopular preacher delivering a message the people hated, but Micah could say, "I know that the Spirit of God is leading me to say what I am saying." It is wonderful to be in that position, my friend.

## SINS OF THE LEADERS OF JERUSALEM

In this final division, Micah turns specifically to Jerusalem. Heretofore he has been speaking to the northern kingdom of Israel; but now he bundles together the prophets, the princes, and the priests of the southern kingdom, and he pronounces judgment upon all of them.

**Hear this, I pray you, ye heads of the house of Jacob, and princes of the house of Israel, that abhor judgment, and pervert all equity [Mic. 3:9].**

He says, "Listen to me, I have something to say to you." Then he details their sins.

**They build up Zion with blood, and Jerusalem with iniquity.**

**The heads thereof judge for reward, and the priests thereof teach for hire, and the prophets thereof divine for money: yet will they lean upon the Lord, and say, Is not the Lord among us? none evil can come upon us [Mic. 3:10–11].**

"The heads thereof judge for reward . . . the priests thereof teach for hire . . . the prophets thereof divine for money." What is the thing that they all have in common? Greed, covetousness. My friend, that was the worst kind of idolatry even in the day of idols! Today we don't have an idol sitting around—at least I hope you don't. While it is true that superstition is gaining ground and multitudes of folk are following the horoscope, we still have not reverted to the base idolatry that existed in Micah's day; yet our covetousness is idolatry. Micah brings into focus Israel's real sin: idolatry, since covetousness is idolatry. The judges were judging for *reward;* the priests were teaching for *hire;* and the prophets were divining for *money.* They were all doing it for what they could get out of it for themselves. They did not take God into consideration, nor did they take the people into consideration. They were willing to walk over them. No wonder the charge was made: "You eat them up like cannibals because of your greed and love of money."

When the leadership of a nation—both civil and religious—is evil, no form of government will work. This is Micah's message to us.

**Therefore shall Zion for your sake be plowed as a field, and Jerusalem shall become heaps, and the mountain of the house as the high places of the forest [Mic. 3:12].**

This is a prediction that for their sins there will be a complete desolation of the city of Jerusalem. Jeremiah quotes Micah as having said this (see Jer. 26:18), which is a confirmation of the prophecy. The destruction did take place when Nebuchadnezzar destroyed Jerusalem. In the first chapters of the Book of Nehemiah, we see the significance of it. When Nehemiah went back to Jerusalem, he found it in a mess. It was nothing but debris, ashes, rubble, and ruin. It seemed like a hopeless task to rebuild the city. The Talmud, which is a Jewish writing, records the fact that at the destruction of Jerusalem by Rome in A.D. 70, an officer of the Roman army (Rufus, by name) actually plowed up the foundations of the temple with a plowshare. Many scholars reject that tradition, although the Jewish historian Jerome also noted it, as did the Jewish philosopher Maimonides. Personally, I think the tradition is accurate. Both Nebuchadnezzar and Titus the Roman were certainly capable of doing a thing like that. Whether or not that particular tradition is accurate, Jerusalem even today bears the scars of the accurate fulfillment of Micah's prophecy.

# CHAPTER 4

*THEME: Prophecies of the last days*

The little prophecy of Micah could be compared to a Jewish day in that it goes from evening to morning. It opens in the darkness of night—the first three chapters pronounce judgment, as we have seen: "Who is a God like unto thee" (Mic. 7:18) in proclaiming future judgment for past sins? But even in the darkness of judgment there was a ray of light which broke through momentarily. Now we have come to a new section, in which Micah prophesies future glory. This we will see in chapters 4 and 5. There will also be a little judgment in this section, but in the main it is glorious light with every now and then a cloud passing across the brightness of the sun.

## PROPHECIES OF THE LAST DAYS

**But in the last days it shall come to pass, that the mountain of the house of the Lord shall be established in the top of the mountains, and it shall be exalted above the hills; and people shall flow unto it [Mic. 4:1].**

This is a remarkable passage of Scripture and may sound familiar to you because it is similar to the second chapter of Isaiah. Micah, you may recall, was a contemporary of Isaiah, and through the years scholars have been trying to determine if Micah copied Isaiah or if Isaiah copied Micah. Candidly, I feel that such debate is a waste of time, because nobody has the answer to it. I would rather look at it this way: Since the Holy Spirit was the author, He was able to say the same things through Isaiah and through Micah; and the reason He said it twice was because of its importance. Therefore, we should look at this section very carefully.

Notice that this fourth chapter opens with the little conjunction "but," which is a connective that contrasts it to the last verse of chapter 3: "Therefore shall Zion for your sake be plowed as a field, and Jerusalem shall become heaps, and the mountain of the house as the high places of the forest."

"But in the last days." Micah is moving now beyond the destruction of Jerusalem by Nebuchadnezzar and the destruction under Titus the Roman, and beyond all other destructions, to the last days. In the Old Testament, "the last days" is a technical term with a very definite meaning. Our Lord Jesus called it "the tribulation, the great one" (see Matt. 24:21) we designate it as the Great Tribulation Period, which begins "the last days." Then after the Tribulation (which will be a brief period of approximately seven years), the Lord Jesus Christ will return to the earth. In fact, His coming will end the Tribulation Period, and He Himself will establish His kingdom upon the earth. So "the last days" embrace the Tribulation, the return of Christ to the earth, and the millennial kingdom of Christ. Therefore, when Micah says "in the last days," he has moved out and beyond all local situations, and he is looking way down into the future. The darker it became in Israel, the brighter the future appeared. And this is true for all of us. I am told that if you go far enough down in a well, you can see the stars. And when Israel hit bottom, God let them see the stars, the light out yonder in the future.

"The mountain of the house of the LORD shall be established in the top of the mountains." The word *mountain* is used both literally and figuratively. Daniel uses it in a figurative way when he says, "Thou sawest till that a stone was cut out without hands, which smote the image upon his feet that were of iron and clay, and brake them to pieces. Then was the iron, the clay, the brass, the silver, and the gold, broken to pieces together, and became like the chaff of the summer threshingfloors; and the wind carried them away, that no place was found for them: and the stone that smote the image became a great mountain, and filled the whole earth" (Dan. 2:34–35). That stone pictures Christ who is coming. "The stone . . . became a great mountain, and filled the whole earth." The mountain Daniel is talking about is Christ's kingdom, which is to be established here upon the earth. That is the spiritual interpretation. We have no right to spiritualize a passage unless there is scriptural authority for doing so, and we do have it for this. However, I would not want to rob it of its literal sense, because the fact is that the city of Jerusalem is located upon a hill. Not only does Scripture make that clear, but all you have to do is to take a look at it. Micah is talking about Jerusalem, as we shall see. And the millennial kingdom will be centered there. Jerusalem will be the capital of the earth.

"And people shall flow unto it." The word *flow* indicates spontaneous movement—from the desire in their hearts. Right now—as I am writing this—the flow is in the opposite direc-

tion. However, the way world conditions are changing, it could be different by the time you read this. But the point is that this prophecy of Micah's is not being fulfilled today and will not be fulfilled until the Messiah comes.

**And many nations shall come, and say, Come, and let us go up to the mountain of the LORD, and to the house of the God of Jacob; and he will teach us of his ways, and we will walk in his paths: for the law shall go forth of Zion, and the word of the LORD from Jerusalem [Mic. 4:2].**

Here is another chapter, among the many chapters in the prophetic books of the Bible, which makes it clear that the present return of the Jews to the land of Israel is not a fulfillment of prophecy. In this day in which we live the nations of the world are not going to Jerusalem to hear from the Lord! Neither is the Word of the Lord going forth from Jerusalem. I could supply you with the names of several Christian missionaries in the city of Jerusalem who themselves are Jewish, but who have been persecuted for presenting Christ and the Word of God. Believe me, the Word of God is not flowing from Jerusalem!

My friend, all the current sensationalism which declares that prophecy is being fulfilled in that land just produces an itch in what I call baby Christians. They want the bottle to be warm and sweet; and, therefore, it is nice to hear that we are seeing a fulfillment of prophecy, which means that the end is just around the corner. Some folk are even setting dates for our Lord's return. Well, nobody *knows*. Although I *think* we are drawing near to the end, I have no inside information from the Lord to confirm it, and certainly there is nothing in His Word to confirm it. I wish these sensational speakers who major in prophecy would read *all* the prophecies throughout the Bible. If they would do that, it would be quite obvious to them that prophecies like Micah gives us here are not now being fulfilled. The Word of God is *not* going out from Jerusalem today. For example, no Bible society is printing Bibles in Jerusalem and sending them out to the ends of the earth! To circulate the New Testament from that place would be utterly impossible. The Word of God is not going forth from Jerusalem as Micah said it would do. The wonderful prophecies in this chapter will be fulfilled during the millennial kingdom when Christ Himself is reigning in Jerusalem. *Then* the heads of the capitals of the world— Peking, Berlin, London, Washington—will be going to Jerusalem to be taught by Christ Himself of His ways!

**And he shall judge among many people, and rebuke strong nations afar off; and they shall beat their swords into plowshares, and their spears into pruninghooks: nation shall not lift up a sword against nation, neither shall they learn war any more [Mic. 4:3].**

"And he shall judge among many people." This again is the Lord Jesus Christ, the Messiah, when He returns to the earth the second time to reign. Imagine the nations of the world bringing their disputes to *Him* for arbitration! The things mentioned in this verse cannot come to pass until He does come.

"They shall beat their swords into plowshares, and their spears into pruninghooks." This verse appears on the building of the United Nations. Believe me, it doesn't belong there! If those boys have beaten their swords into plowshares, it only means that they have a bigger instrument with which to beat each other over the head. And if they are turning their spears into pruninghooks, they are not using them to catch fish but to gouge other nations, especially those that are weaker than they are. This verse certainly is not being fulfilled by the United Nations! They are really knocking each other out there, and there is very little agreement. It will not be fulfilled until Christ comes.

"Nation shall not lift up a sword against nation, neither shall they learn war any more." Obviously, we have not come to this position and will not until the Prince of Peace is ruling. Because He is not ruling in our day, we are not to beat our swords into plowshares; we are to keep our powder dry. This is not the time to disarm. Certainly everyone who wants peace would like to see our armaments cut back and our tax dollars going to something else, but as long as we are living in a big, bad world—not of make-believe but of reality—we need to be armed. The Lord Jesus said, ". . . a strong man armed keepeth his palace . . ." (Luke 11:21). Does he keep it by turning the other cheek? To read about turning the other cheek, you must read the Sermon on the Mount, and remember that it is the King who is speaking and He is referring to the time when He will be reigning upon the earth. When He is reigning, we can get rid of all our protection. We can even take the locks off our doors—but until then I not only have one lock on my door, I have two locks. We are living in that kind of world. These prophecies

that Micah is giving are not for the present hour; they are for the last days. Let's put them in their proper context.

**But they shall sit every man under his vine and under his fig tree; and none shall make them afraid: for the mouth of the LORD of hosts hath spoken it [Mic. 4:4].**

"They shall sit every man under his vine and under his fig tree; and none shall make them afraid." Do you want to tell me that this verse is being fulfilled in Israel today? In our day they are absolutely afraid. Why? Because they are not there according to fulfilled prophecy.

"For the mouth of the LORD of hosts hath spoken it." God Himself has said this. God says that when He puts them in the land, they will live in peace and prosperity.

**For all people will walk every one in the name of his god, and we will walk in the name of the LORD our God for ever and ever [Mic. 4:5].**

The American Standard Version has a much better translation of this verse: "For all the peoples walk every one in the name of his god; and we will walk in the name of Jehovah our God for ever and ever." The thought is that in the past they walked after their own gods, but in the future they are going to walk in the name of Jehovah, our God.

**In that day, saith the LORD, will I assemble her that halteth, and I will gather her that is driven out, and her that I have afflicted [Mic. 4:6].**

"In that day" reminds us that He is still speaking of the millennial kingdom.

"Will I assemble her that halteth." Who is this whom God describes as halting, driven out, and afflicted? It is the nation Israel. Notice that He says, "That I have afflicted." It looks as if God takes the blame for that which has happened to the nation Israel.

I had a conversation with a Jewish man in front of the King David Hotel in Jerusalem several years ago. He was one of the Jews who had come out of Nazi persecution alive, although he had spent time in a concentration camp. He said that he had become an atheist. He asked, "Where was God during the time of our trouble? Why didn't He deliver us?"

I told him, "To tell the truth, I think God was around. Maybe you would like to blame Him for the trouble you had."

He replied, "I certainly do. If there is a God, He would have responded to us."

I said, "No, because you folk had an opportunity to know Him and obey Him way ahead of the rest of us. When your nation had a knowledge of the living and true God, my ancestors were heathens. One tribe was in Germany, and the other tribe was in Scotland. They were dirty, filthy, ignorant pagans, but you had the *light*. Finally some of your people brought the light to my people, and I'm grateful for it. But God has made it very clear in your own writings, your own books, that when you have a knowledge of the true and living God, you cannot turn your back on Him without being punished. If you will read your writings, you will find that not only can you blame Him for your trouble, but He is also not through with you as a nation. He intends to regather you. By that time you will have learned (and obviously you have not learned it yet) that this is God's universe and that you cannot reject the knowledge of Himself that He has given you without suffering His judgment."

My friend, our own nation is coming to this same position and condition, and it alarms me. In this land of ours there is a growing ignorance of the Word of God. Even worse than that, the Word of God is being ridiculed and made light of. A comedian says, "The Devil made me do it." This is simply not true. You don't do evil because the Devil made you do it. You do evil because you have an old nature that is as mean and as alienated and as far from God as it can possibly be. Also I hear it flippantly said, "I'll tell God on you!" Well, of course, you don't have to tell Him about somebody else's sin. He already knows it, and He knows yours as well. My friend, we cannot make light of Him and reject Him without experiencing His judgment. In Micah's day He took the blame for afflicting Israel, and He has not asked me to apologize for Him or to try to explain away that statement. This ought to serve as a warning to us as a nation.

**And I will make her that halted a remnant, and her that was cast far off a strong nation: and the LORD shall reign over them in mount Zion from henceforth, even for ever [Mic. 4:7].**

"I will make her that halted a remnant." Never throughout the long history of Israel did 100 percent of the nation worship God. Always only a remnant was faithful to Him. God always preserved a remnant. Actually, it was a remnant of those which came out of Egypt that entered the land. Practically the entire generation that came out of Egypt died in the wilderness. It was their children who entered the land. God preserved a remnant. Even in Elijah's day God had a faithful remnant. Elijah was very pessimistic. He cried, "Lord, I only am left" (see 1 Kings 19:10). But God told him, "You aren't the only one; I have seven thousand in these mountains who have not bowed the knee to Baal." Because they were hiding from Ahab and Jezebel, Elijah didn't know about them (And I am of the opinion that in our day there are more believers than we think there are. There are many believers like those seven thousand. Although we don't hear about them, they are true believers.) Also, there was a remnant of believers at the coming of Christ; although the leaders of the nation rejected Him and had Him crucified, there was a remnant that received Him. Later, on the Day of Pentecost, a great company turned to Christ; yet it was a remnant. It always has been a remnant. Coming down to our day, there is a remnant even in the church that bears His name. Although I have made the statement that I think there are more believers in our world than we realize, it is also true that in the church there is only a remnant of true believers in Christ.

Many of us would be surprised if we knew how few church members were genuine believers even though they are quite active in Christian circles and in Christian service. Many people in our affluent society have become church members. We are living in a period that has produced a lot of pseudo-saints. They are not genuine by any means. They have not been born again. The Book of Hebrews makes it very clear that ". . . whom the Lord loveth he chasteneth . . ." (Heb. 12:6). And every son whom He receives, He is going to put through the fire. He is going to test him. If you have some metal which you think is gold, you can take it to the assayer's office. He will put the metal under heat so that you will find out whether what you have is gold or something else. And God puts the heat to those who are His own. The day of persecution is going to come to church members, and it will reveal quickly who are the true believers and who are not. God has a remnant in the church today.

Also in our day there is a remnant of believers among the people of Israel—probably more than we realize. In every nation there is a remnant of true believers, although they may not be identified with a local church. Unfortunately, the actions of some church members are shutting the door to a great many believers. Yet God always has His faithful remnant. The word *remnant* in Scripture is very important; don't just rush over it.

In Micah's day God is saying that of the afflicted ones He will make a remnant; He will regather them and make them "a strong nation: and the Lord shall reign over them in mount Zion from henceforth, even for ever."

**And thou, O tower of the flock, the strong hold of the daughter of Zion, unto thee shall it come, even the first dominion; the kingdom shall come to the daughter of Jerusalem [Mic. 4:8].**

"O tower of the flock, the strong hold of the daughter of Zion." God is probably addressing the land itself, informing it that its former dominion under David and Solomon will be restored, the far greater kingdom of the Messiah shall come. This has not happened yet; the kingdom has not come. If the people of Israel are back in their land for anything, they are back there for the Great Tribulation Period. The kingdom is still in the far future.

### THE NEAR FUTURE

At this point a cloud passes over the sun. A great many Bible scholars believe the next two verses refer to the Babylonian captivity.

**Now why dost thou cry out aloud? is there no king in thee? is thy counsellor perished? for pangs have taken thee as a woman in travail.**

**Be in pain, and labour to bring forth, O daughter of Zion, like a woman in travail: for now shalt thou go forth out of the city, and thou shalt dwell in the field, and thou shalt go even to Babylon; there shalt thou be delivered; there the Lord shall redeem thee from the hand of thine enemies [Mic. 4:9–10].**

This is so specific that I feel it could refer to nothing else but the Babylonian captivity which was coming to the southern kingdom. When Micah directs his remarks to the "daughter of Zion," he refers to the southern kingdom of Judah. The word that interests me here is *travail*. Frankly, I can't speak about travail firsthand. One half of the human family does not know what it is to travail in birth. Only the women know about that. The only thing I know about birth pangs is what I saw my own wife go through and what I have been told by others. Birth pains are frightful. They

are something no person could bear for a long period of time. It has to be temporary.

The picture Micah gives us here is that of Nebuchadnezzar taking Jerusalem. He came to that city three times, and the third time he destroyed the temple area, left it in wrack and ruin, leveled the city, and burned it. The suffering of the people of Judah is described as a woman in travail, a woman with birth pangs. This had to be a brief period or the nation would not have continued to exist. That kind of trouble could not go on forever because the people could not have endured it. It would have been too frightful, too terrible. For this same reason the Great Tribulation Period must be brief. The Lord Jesus Christ made that clear: "And except those days should be shortened, there should no flesh be saved: but for the elect's sake those days shall be shortened" (Matt. 24:22).

"Thou shalt go forth out of the city, and thou shalt dwell in the field, and thou shalt go even to Babylon." When Nebuchadnezzar captured the city, the remaining inhabitants fled and tried to live in the fields. Eventually they were taken captive to Babylon.

Let me call your attention to the fact that Micah in these two verses is looking beyond the Assyrian captivity of Israel to the later captivity of Judah by Babylon. However, in the next breath he predicts deliverance: "There shalt thou be delivered; there the Lord shall redeem thee from the hand of thine enemies." Although they shall be captives in Babylon, God will deliver them from there. We know from history that God did deliver them by the hand of Cyrus (see Isa. 44:28; 2 Chron. 36:22–23). The point that Micah is making here is that the travail and suffering of God's people will end in joy.

### THE DISTANT FUTURE

Now in this closing section Micah moves ahead to the far distant future, the time of the Great Tribulation and specifically to the final war, the war (not the battle) of Armageddon.

**Now also many nations are gathered against thee, that say, Let her be defiled, and let our eye look upon Zion [Mic. 4:11].**

"Many nations are gathered against thee"— the mention of *many* nations makes it clear that Micah has moved away from the Babylonian invasion and is speaking of something else here. The many nations gathered against Jerusalem are mentioned by several other prophets. For example: Joel 3; Zechariah 12 and 14; Ezekiel 38 and 39 all refer to the war of Armageddon during the Great Tribulation Period.

**But they know not the thoughts of the Lord, neither understand they his counsel: for he shall gather them as the sheaves into the floor [Mic. 4:12].**

"They know not the thoughts of the Lord, neither understand they his counsel." They do not know what God is going to do. They are coming against Israel blindly, unaware that God is bringing them there for judgment.

**Arise and thresh, O daughter of Zion: for I will make thine horn iron, and I will make thy hoofs brass: and thou shalt beat in pieces many people: and I will consecrate their gain unto the Lord, and their substance unto the Lord of the whole earth [Mic. 4:13].**

"Arise and thresh, O daughter of Zion." The nations of the world are as sheaves for the threshing floor, and Israel will do the threshing. Today Israel is a weak nation and absolutely dependent upon other nations, but in that day they are going to be dependent upon the *Lord.* Psalm 75:6 says, "For promotion cometh neither from the east, nor from the west, nor from the south." Psalm 75:7 goes on to say, "But God is the judge: he putteth down one, and setteth up another." In that day help for Israel will not come from the north (Russia), or from the south (Egypt), or from the west (Europe or the United States), or from the east (China and the Arab countries). Their help will come from the Lord who made heaven and earth.

These final three verses look forward to the war which concludes the Great Tribulation Period, the war of Armageddon.

# CHAPTER 5

*THEME: Prophecy of the first coming of Christ*

This chapter continues the subject begun in chapter 4: prophesying future glory because of past promises. In chapter 4 we saw prophecies regarding the last days; now we shall see prophecies regarding the *first* coming of Christ.

**Now gather thyself in troops, O daughter of troops: he hath laid siege against us: they shall smite the judge of Israel with a rod upon the cheek [Mic. 5:1].**

In the Hebrew Scriptures this verse concludes chapter 4. Frankly, I feel that it belongs there, not here, and that it continues the thought of chapter 4 verse 9 regarding the Babylonian captivity. You will recall that Micah projects the horrors of the Babylonian invasion right on down to the "last days," that is, to the Great Tribulation Period and the war of Armageddon. Now in the verse before us, he again picks up the thought of the Babylonian invasion.

"He hath laid siege against us" refers, I believe, to the siege of the Babylonian army against Jerusalem.

"They shall smite the judge of Israel with a rod upon the cheek." There are those who take the position that the "judge" refers to the Lord Jesus Christ. However, in the gospel record we read that they smote Him with their hands, not with a rod. Neither was Christ smitten in any siege. He was not smitten by a foreign enemy but by His own people. I do not believe that this can refer to the mistreatment of Christ at His first coming.

It seems obvious to me that the "judge of Israel" refers to the last king of the Davidic kingdom, Zedekiah. In 2 Kings 25:7 we read, "And they slew the sons of Zedekiah before his eyes, and put out the eyes of Zedekiah, and bound him with fetters of brass, and carried him to Babylon." I believe that Micah is referring to the shameful treatment which Zedekiah received at that time. It denotes what looks to be the very end of the Davidic line. However, Zedekiah was not in the direct line. You will recall that Jehoiakim rebelled against the king of Babylon. He stood against him at first; then Nebuchadnezzar, king of Babylon, took Jehoiakim into captivity. Then Jehoiachin was put on the throne. Later, he too was taken captive. In 2 Kings 24:15 we read, "And he carried away Jehoiachin to Babylon, and the king's mother, and the king's wives, and his officers, and the mighty of the land, those carried he into captivity from Jerusalem to Babylon." This was the Davidic line which was carried into captivity, and out of this line came both Joseph and Mary, the mother of the Lord Jesus. Then Nebuchadnezzar put Zedekiah (the uncle of Jehoiachin) on the throne at Jerusalem. When *he* rebelled against Babylon, Nebuchadnezzar became tired of fooling with the line of kings at Jerusalem; so he took Zedekiah, slew all of his sons before his eyes, and carried him into captivity.

You might assume from this devastating experience that the Davidic line had come to an end and that the promise God made to David, that one was to come in his line who would reign forever, could never be fulfilled.

This brings us to a remarkable verse that is in contrast to all we have been considering.

## PROPHECY OF THE FIRST COMING OF CHRIST

Now this verse is part of the Christmas story; and, if you are not reading this during December, you may feel that you have chosen an inappropriate time. However, we can be almost sure that Jesus was not born on December 25. That day was chosen to try to identify His birth with the winter solstice. But it is more likely that He was born in the spring, because in December the shepherds would not be out on the hillsides with their sheep. The sheep would be sheltered in the caves which are located all along that area. Around A.D. 532 a calendar was set up, which is a reasonable facsimile of the one we use today. It was set up incorrectly for the number of days in the year, and that is why we have a leap year every now and then. In 1752 the calendar was jumped ahead eleven days. George Washington was not born on February 22; he was actually born on February 11. Therefore, a person could not be sure that Jesus Christ was born on December 25 even if all of the other circumstances fit into it. This raises a question about observing the Sabbath day, too. Which day is the Sabbath day? Actually, it is not important, nor is the exact day of Jesus' birth important. The *time* of the year is immaterial. It is the *place* that is all important. Christ was born in Bethlehem. That is the historical fact. This fact has been authenticated by history.

But thou, Beth-lehem Ephratah, though thou be little among the thousands of Judah, yet out of thee shall he come forth unto me that is to be ruler in Israel; whose goings forth have been from of old, from everlasting [Mic. 5:2].

"But" is a little conjunction that presents the other side of the coin. "But thou, Beth-lehem." In spite of what happened to Zedekiah and the Davidic line—which went into captivity and finally returned to the land of Israel as peasants—the one in David's line *is* coming.

"But thou, Beth-lehem Ephratah"—since there were two Bethlehems, the word *ephratah*, meaning "fruitful", is added to distinguish between them. Micah named the place where Christ was to be born seven hundred years *before* He was born there. After seven hundred years, with so many intervening events, there was little likelihood that one in the line of David could be born in Bethlehem. It was almost entirely out of the question. The odds were against it. No members of the family of David were living in Bethlehem any longer. They were scattered. The Dispersion had driven them from the land. There was one family in the line of David living in Nazareth; yet Bethlehem must be the place where the Son of God was to be born, according to Micah. This prophecy was the sole basis on which the scribes directed the wise men to Bethlehem. The scribes quoted from the prophecy of Micah because they believed that it was the place where He would be born, although they didn't believe it would be fulfilled at that time.

The circumstances which led up to the birth of Jesus in Bethlehem are so familiar to us that we may not realize how remarkable they were. The record in Luke's gospel gives us some of the details: Caesar Augustus signed the tax bill which moved Mary out of Nazareth. If that little donkey on which Mary rode had stumbled and Mary had fallen, Jesus would probably have been born somewhere along the route. But—I say this very carefully—that little donkey could not have stumbled, because seven hundred years earlier Micah had written that Jesus would be born in Bethlehem. The little donkey got her there on schedule; it was timed from eternity. It was more punctual and precise than any jet plane could be in our day.

"Out of thee shall he come forth unto me." The words *unto me* indicate that this One was coming to do the will of the Father and to accomplish His plan.

"Whose goings forth have been from of old, from everlasting." His birth, the Incarnation, has to do with His humanity. He clothed Himself in humanity when He came to Bethlehem. But His existence was before His birth.

Isaiah, a contemporary of Micah, verifies this: ". . . Behold, a virgin shall conceive, and bear a son, and shall call his name Immanuel" (Isa. 7:14). And he has more to say of this coming one: "For unto us a child is born, unto us a son is given . . ." (Isa. 9:6). When Isaiah wrote "unto us," he was not thinking of the United States; it was Israel that he had in mind. "A child is born"—that's His humanity. "A son is given"—not born, because this speaks of His divinity. The "child" was born in Bethlehem, but the "Son" was "from everlasting."

The psalmist mentions this: "Before the mountains were brought forth, or ever thou hadst formed the earth and the world, even from everlasting to everlasting, thou art God" (Ps. 90:2). The Hebrew language expresses this very vividly: "from the vanishing point in the past to the vanishing point in the future, thou art God." Just as far back as you can go in your thinking, He is God. He came out of eternity. He is the eternal Son of God.

In Proverbs 8:23 we find, "I was set up from everlasting, from the beginning, or ever the earth was." "Set up" in this verse means "anointed" and could read, "I was anointed from everlasting, from the beginning, or ever the earth was." The next two verses say, "When there were no depths, I was brought forth; when there were no fountains abounding with water. Before the mountains were settled, before the hills was I brought forth" (Prov. 8:24–25). Before there was any creation, He was God; yet into creation He came, at the appointed time, into a little out-of-the-way town, Bethlehem.

The Lord Jesus said, "I came forth from the Father, and am come into the world: again, I leave the world, and go to the Father" (John 16:28). His goings forth have been of old. He is the everlasting God. He told the Pharisees, ". . . Before Abraham was, I am" (John 8:58). Christ appeared many times in the Old Testament. Go back to the creation. In John 1:3 we read concerning Christ, "All things were made by him; and without him was not any thing made that was made." He was the Creator. In Colossians 1:16 we read this about our Lord, "For by him were all things created, that are in heaven, and that are in earth,

visible and invisible, whether they be thrones, or dominions, or principalities, or powers: all things were created by him, and for him." In the Garden of Eden He was the voice of the Lord God walking in the garden in the cool of the day. He was the articulation of God. He was the Word of God. He was the communication from God to man. We find Him in pursuit of man throughout the Old Testament. He appeared to Moses in the burning bush. He said, "I have come down to deliver you." He was the Redeemer. You see, what Micah is saying here is of tremendous significance. Although He was born in Bethlehem almost two thousand years ago, His goings forth have been from old, from everlasting.

We have been considering His pre-incarnation; now let's look again at His incarnation, His humanity. When God came to Bethlehem, He got something He never had before, and that was the name of *Jesus*. He received a humanity, and Jesus was His human name. He was Jehovah. That is the name of deity. He is Jesus now, and He is a Savior. He came out of Bethlehem to save. Remember, the angels said to the shepherds, "For unto you is born this day in the city of David a Saviour, which is Christ the Lord" (Luke 2:11). Matthew 1:23 says, "Behold, a virgin shall be with child, and shall bring forth a son, and they shall call his name Emmanuel, which being interpreted is, God with us." But His name was to be Jesus. He can't be Jesus unless He is Emmanuel, which means "God with us." He must be a man to take our place, to be our representative, to die a substitutionary death.

In the books of the prophets are many predictions about the coming of the Messiah which are totally unrelated and seem even to contradict each other. How could they all come to pass? Although *Bethlehem* was designated as Christ's birthplace, connected with His birth we are told that there will be weeping in *Ramah*, a place north of Bethlehem. Also, He is to be called out of *Egypt*, and He is to be called a *Nazarene*. It seems utterly impossible for all of these prophecies to be true. How can they all fit into place? Well, Matthew gives the account and, without any strain on the circumstances, all of these things come together normally and naturally—let me change that to *super*naturally. God was overruling.

As you can see, Micah 5:2 is a very remarkable verse, and we have only stayed on the surface of it.

Now we come to an interval which takes

place between the time of Christ's rejection and the time of His return as the King to rule on this earth.

**Therefore will he give them up, until the time that she which travaileth hath brought forth: then the remnant of his brethren shall return unto the children of Israel [Mic. 5:3].**

You may think that this verse still has reference to the birth of Christ. Well, it is true that it speaks of the fact that Mary travailed, but you can't read this passage without realizing that it also refers to the nation of Israel. It speaks not only of their worldwide dispersion—they were scattered by the judgment of God—but of their travail. The Great Tribulation Period is the travail through which the nation must pass. *"Then* the remnant of his brethren shall return unto the children of Israel." The Jews will be regathered from their worldwide dispersion.

**And he shall stand and feed in the strength of the LORD, in the majesty of the name of the LORD his God; and they shall abide: for now shall he be great unto the ends of the earth [Mic. 5:4].**

Here the Lord Jesus is depicted as the Shepherd who feeds His flock. He is the Shepherd to the church, and He is also the Shepherd to the nation Israel. The One who was born in Bethlehem, the One who was rejected, will feed His flock. I can't think of anything that sets Him forth more wonderfully than the figure of the shepherd. It speaks of His care, His protection, and His salvation. He is the *Good* Shepherd who will lay down His life for the sheep (see Ps. 22); He is the *Great* Shepherd who keeps His sheep even today (see Ps. 23); and He is the *Chief* Shepherd who is coming in glory (see Ps. 24). His entire ministry is set forth under the office of a shepherd.

**And this man shall be the peace, when the Assyrian shall come into our land: and when he shall tread in our palaces, then shall we raise against him seven shepherds, and eight principal men [Mic. 5:5].**

"The Assyrian," as we find in the prophecy of Isaiah, sets forth the enemies that shall come up against the nation Israel in the last days. In Micah's day the Assyrian was brutal, and he did take the northern kingdom into captivity.

"Then shall we raise against him seven

shepherds, and eight principal men." The two numbers seem to denote the fact of fullness and that God will make adequate provision for them. These two numbers carry that meaning in other instances (see Prov. 6:16; Eccl. 11:2).

**And they shall waste the land of Assyria with the sword, and the land of Nimrod in the entrances thereof: thus shall he deliver us from the Assyrian, when he cometh into our land, and when he treadeth within our borders [Mic. 5:6].**

"They shall waste the land of Assyria with the sword" continues the prediction of the last days when "the Assyrian" represents the confederacy of nations which will come against Israel at the end of the Tribulation Period. Israel, strengthened by their Shepherd, will not only repulse the attack but will carry the battle into enemy territory.

It is interesting to see how Micah completely sets forth Christ: first, as the One to be born in Bethlehem. When He was born on earth, He came in humility. We need to note that He humbled Himself (see Phil. 2:5–8). We don't humble ourselves; sometimes some other people humble us, but Christ humbled Himself. There was an emptying on the part of Christ. Of what did He empty Himself? Not His deity. That little baby, reclining so helplessly on His mother's bosom, could have spoken this universe out of existence. He is God of very God and man of very man, but He limited Himself. Self-limitation was something that He took willingly. We do not limit ourselves willingly. In fact, we expand ourselves. We are aggressive. We want to win. We want to be on top. Man is self-assertive. He is self-centered. He is selfish. But Jesus Christ is the Shepherd. He was born not in a royal city or in the capital, but in the insignificant town of Bethlehem—and in a *stable.* That is no place for a king to be born! When Christ came to earth, He emptied Himself of His glory. Second, Micah indicates that He is the eternal one "whose goings forth have been from . . . everlasting." Third, Micah depicts Him as the Shepherd who came to die for His sheep and to watch over His own. And finally, when He comes again, He will be the Chief Shepherd, coming in might and power and glory to deliver His people.

**And the remnant of Jacob shall be in the midst of many people as a dew from the LORD, as the showers upon the grass, that tarrieth not for man, nor waiteth for the sons of men [Mic. 5:7].**

The dew and rain refer to the blessing the people of Israel will be among the nations.

**And the remnant of Jacob shall be among the Gentiles in the midst of many people as a lion among the beasts of the forest, as a young lion among the flocks of sheep: who, if he go through, both treadeth down, and teareth in pieces, and none can deliver [Mic. 5:8].**

This certainly does not depict the people of Israel in our day. Israel has been in a precarious position for years. But God promises that in the future, when Israel is obeying the Lord and is in fellowship with Him, He will make them the head and not the tail of the nations (see Deut. 28:13).

**Thine hand shall be lifted up upon thine adversaries, and all thine enemies shall be cut off [Mic. 5:9].**

In that day God is going to give them victory over their enemies.

**And it shall come to pass in that day, saith the Lord, that I will cut off thy horses out of the midst of thee, and I will destroy thy chariots [Mic. 5:10].**

Now, just in case an amillennialist is applying this to some other time, Micah wants to make sure you realize that this will come to pass "in that day," which is still future.

**And I will cut off the cities of thy land, and throw down all thy strong holds [Mic. 5:11].**

This is thought to mean that God will remove all the things on which Israel had leaned for support—horses and chariots and fortified cities. They won't need them anymore, for their Messiah is bringing peace to earth.

**And I will cut off witchcrafts out of thine hand; and thou shalt have no more soothsayers:**

**Thy graven images also will I cut off, and thy standing images out of the midst of thee; and thou shalt no more worship the work of thine hands [Mic. 5:12–13].**

He is going to get rid of idolatry and false religion. They will worship only the living and true God.

**And I will pluck up thy groves out of the midst of thee: so will I destroy thy cities [Mic. 5:14].**

As we have seen, the "groves" were places of idol worship.

**And I will execute vengeance in anger and fury upon the heathen, such as they have not heard [Mic. 5:15].**

"The heathen" are the nations who are persecuting His people. The Messiah will bring blessing and peace to the remnant of Israel and to the remnant of the other nations of the world who turn to Him, but He will "execute vengeance in anger and fury upon the heathen"—this, I believe, refers to the Great Tribulation Period.

# CHAPTER 6

**THEME:** *Pleading present repentance because of past redemption*

Chapter 6 begins Micah's third and final message to the nations of the world and to Israel in particular. Although chapters 6 and 7 are one message, I have taken the privilege of dividing these last two chapters and of making a major division out of each one of them.

## PLEADING PRESENT REPENTANCE BECAUSE OF PAST REDEMPTION

**Hear ye now what the Lord saith; Arise, contend thou before the mountains, and let the hills hear thy voice [Mic. 6:1].**

This section begins as the other major sections of this book have begun: "Hear ye now what the Lord saith." This is a call not only to the northern kingdom, but again I take it that it is also a call to the entire world to "hear." God will now register His complaint against Israel. God has a contention with His people Israel, and from it we can learn great lessons.

"Arise, contend thou before the mountains, and let the hills hear thy voice." This is an expression that we find several times in the writings of the prophets. This is actually a call to nature, a call, it says, to the mountains and to the hills. But I believe that there is also an application here that we see elsewhere in Scripture, too. A mountain represents a great kingdom, and a hill represents a lesser kingdom. I would say, therefore, that this is a call not only to nature but also to the *nations* of the world. In other words, here is a message which is applicable to all the nations of the world.

**Hear ye, O mountains, the LORD'S controversy, and ye strong foundations of the earth: for the LORD hath a controversy with his people, and he will plead with Israel [Mic. 6:2].**

"Hear ye, O mountains, the LORD'S controversy"—the nations of the world are to hear. "And ye strong foundations of the earth"—that is, the great peoples and nations of the world which have been in existence for thousands of years and yet have been far from God. God now gives a message to them.

"For the LORD hath a controversy with his people, and he will plead with Israel." God has a controversy with His people, and He is actually calling them into court.

Then God does a very startling and surprising thing. When He goes into court, instead of immediately lodging a charge against them, He says, "What am I guilty of?" Can you imagine this condescension of Almighty God to little man down here on this earth!

**O my people, what have I done unto thee? and wherein have I wearied thee? testify against me [Mic. 6:3].**

In other words, God is saying to them, "Why have you turned from Me? Why have you rejected Me? What have I done to you?" We find this question again in the prophecy of Malachi, the last book of the Old Testament. After their captivity, the people returned to the land and became very blasé, very sophisticated. They forgot about the Babylonian captivity. The city of Jerusalem had been rebuilt, and they were enjoying prosperity again. When Malachi spoke to them, they said, "Well, to tell the truth, this going through the religious rituals is very boring indeed, and it's wearisome." I would more or less agree with them in that, but the problem was not with God—the problem was with them. Micah is going to be very specific here as to the real problem.

God had asked the people to testify against Him and to tell Him what He has done. Now He is going to tell them what He has done to them. What is it that God has done? Has He been ugly to them? Has He mistreated them? Did He take them down to the land of Egypt and leave them there and forget about them? He could have done that. He didn't have to deliver them out of the land of Egypt, but He did deliver them. Listen to Him—

**For I brought thee up out of the land of Egypt, and redeemed thee out of the house of servants; and I sent before thee Moses, Aaron, and Miriam [Mic. 6:4].**

"For I brought thee up out of the land of Egypt, and redeemed thee out of the house of servants." They had been slaves, and God says, "I redeemed you. I didn't do you wrong. I didn't harm you, but I redeemed you. You were slaves, bending under the yoke of the taskmaster down in the land of Egypt, and there was no one to deliver you. You were not an attractive people; you were a slave people. You had dropped down to the lowest level of humanity, but I loved you and redeemed you out of the house of servants."

"And I sent before thee Moses, Aaron, and Miriam." God says, "I gave you leadership to lead you out of the land—Moses, Aaron, and Miriam." It is interesting that Miriam is mentioned here. I would like to call to the attention of the women's liberation movement the fact that God did not pass them by. Miriam was one of the leaders out of the land of Egypt. She was on a par with Aaron, but she was not on a par with Moses because Moses was the one that God had chosen. Actually, at one time, Miriam wanted to lead a rebellion against her own brother. When the people got out into the wilderness, Moses really took charge, for he was leading under God. But Miriam said, "Who is he to tell me anything? I remember when he was a little, bitty fellow and Mother and I took him down to the river and put him in the bullrushes because he would have been put to death by Pharaoh. I stayed at a distance, and I watched over him. Who does he think he is to tell me what to do?" I guess Miriam was the first women's liberationist that we ever had. But she *was* a leader, and she was chosen of God. I have a notion that she had a real ministry with the women of Israel. Can you imagine the problems that would arise with the women and children on that wilderness march? There would be problems that Moses would not know too much about. So Miriam must have been a great help.

The people of Israel in Micah's day complained that they were weary, tired of worshiping God. They said, "After all, what has He done for us?" So God went back and recited their history. God is pleading from His heart with these people—

**O my people, remember now what Balak king of Moab consulted, and what Balaam the son of Beor answered him from Shittim unto Gilgal; that ye may know the righteousness of the LORD [Mic. 6:5].**

What we have here is the reminder of a very wonderful incident that goes back to the time when the children of Israel were ready to pass into the Promised Land. They had had to go all the way around Edom because Edom would not let them through their land. God led them around Edom, and then they came to Moab. The king of Moab at that time was Balak. Balak wanted to curse the children of Israel, and he hired the prophet Balaam who was a lover of money. Balaam was a hired preacher; yet he was a prophet who seemed to have information from God. God certainly spoke through him, but God finally judged him.

Balaam was called in by Balak to curse the children of Israel. "Balaam the son of Beor answered him from Shittim unto Gilgal." Shittim was the last camping spot before they entered Moab after Balaam began his ministry against them. Gilgal was the first place they camped when they got into the Promised Land. I will not go back over each of the prophecies which Balaam gave but will only say that each time he could not curse Israel— God would not let him curse Israel.

Balak took Balaam up to a mountain, and as he looked down at the camp of Israel, Balaam said, "How shall I curse, whom God hath not cursed? . . ." (Num. 23:8). God was not doing them evil; God was on their side. Now, if you had gone down into the camp, you would have found that they were not perfect—God was dealing with them and with their sin down there—but no enemy on the outside was going to find fault with them. The children of Israel did not know that there was an enemy trying to curse them and that God was protecting and defending them. Even old Balaam had to say, "How shall I curse, whom God hath not cursed? I am not able to do it." God did not permit them to be cursed (see Num. 22–24).

The wonderful thing for the child of God today is that we are told that we have an Advocate with the Father, Jesus Christ, the Righteous One (see 1 John 2:1). God deals with His children personally. I know that He has dealt with me and has done so severely. I am confident that the cancer which I had was a judgment of God upon me. I accept it as that from Him, and I thank Him for hearing prayers for my healing. But I am also very thankful that I have an Advocate, Jesus Christ the Righteous, who defends me. He is on my side; He is my Advocate. He is the one who says that I am His child, that I am in the family of God. He is not going to let anyone on the outside curse me.

May I say to you, this ought to answer the superstitious and wild views that are circulating today that God's children can be demon possessed. However, I do believe that the Devil can oppress the child of God and give him a whole lot of trouble. He can certainly deceive you and make life miserable for you, but no demon is going to possess you if you are truly God's child—because you have an Advocate. It does not matter who you are; if you are a child of God, He's on your side, and He is defending you. When it seemed like the whole world had turned against him at one time, Martin Luther said, "One with God is a majority." I am on the side of the majority. How about you? That is the important question.

God is telling His people here, "I have defended you. I defended you even when Balaam attempted to curse you." Balak got disgusted with Balaam as he took him to the top of four mountains one by one, and Balaam could not curse Israel. But he did give some awful advice to Balak. He said, "Since you can't curse them, and you can't fight them, *join* them." It's the same old story, "If you can't fight 'em, join 'em." Balaam told the king of Moab, "Go down and intermarry with them." And that is exactly what happened— and that introduced the idolatry of Moab among the people of Israel. All of this happened because of the advice of a false prophet.

I want to say something very carefully at this point. Today we are getting a whole lot of so-called marriage counseling from false "prophets." I hear a great deal of it secondhand. My friend, much of it doesn't happen to be scriptural. I know that it is based on pulling out a little verse here and a little verse there, and you can build quite a case that way. But may I say that the only thing which is going to make a marriage work is *love*. If you can look at her and say, "I love you," and she can look back at you and say, "I love you," then, my friend, the Word of God will give you all you need to solve your problems.

God reminds Israel that He is a righteous

God, but He was *defending* them. He was on *their* side. And it is wonderful to have God on our side today.

In each chapter of this book we have found a wonderful, unusual passage, and we are coming now to another in verses 6–8 of this chapter. The liberals delight especially in verse 8, saying, "This is what pure religion is. This is the greatest statement in the Old Testament." I rather agree with the liberals that it is a great statement, but I do not agree with them in the interpretation of it.

God has pleaded with these people to come back to Him, to repent of their gross negligence and sins, and to turn to Him. He has cited His redemption of them in the past, how He redeemed them out of the land of Egypt and brought them through the wilderness. Now the people have four questions that they ask, and they are good questions. The answer to them is all-important.

This is a very important passage of Scripture, because it has been used and abused by the liberals today probably more than any other passage. This is a wonderful section, but we need to be very careful to keep it in the context of what Micah is talking about here, especially as it relates to the Old Testament as a whole.

I am confident that every person who believes in a god wants to ask the question, "How am I going to approach him?" Unless you are an atheist, that has to be a question which would cross your mind. The pagan nations of the past and the heathen of the present have asked that question, and they have answered it. The pagan viewpoint is first of all revealed in their idols—they're horrible looking. Their viewpoint is also revealed in the fact that when trouble comes they think he's angry, and they've got to do something to appease him. Today that is even the viewpoint of the pagan and heathen in my own sophisticated, civilized country. The children of Israel here ask a question, and it is a legitimate question, one that the average man would ask.

**Wherewith shall I come before the Lord, and bow myself before the high God? shall I come before him with burnt offerings, with calves of a year old? [Mic. 6:6].**

The people's first question is: "Wherewith shall I come before the Lord, and bow myself before the high God?" In other words, "What is wrong with God? Why is He displeased with us? We're going through the rituals and the liturgy and the rites of religion. We are going through an outward form, and it is the form which He gave us to go through." But God had also given them a relationship with Himself which they had lost.

Again, the question is: "Wherewith shall I come before the Lord, and bow myself before the high God? What can I bring to God? What can I give Him? He's way up yonder—I'm way down here. How am I going to reach Him? How am I going to communicate with Him? How am I going to make contact with Him? How will I please Him? And—how will I be saved?" The Philippian jailer, who was as pagan as they come, asked, "What must I do to be saved? How can I be right with God?" This is a good question. There is nothing wrong with the question.

The people's second question is: "Shall I come before him with burnt offerings, with calves of a year old?" God had required sacrifices of them. God had given them, in the first part of the Book of Leviticus, five offerings which they were to make, which were to be their approach to Him. So they asked the question, "Will it be adequate simply to go through the form of religion?" Man's reasoning always degenerates down to one thing: "I have to *do* something for God. He wants me to do something." May I say, this probably reveals the proud heart of man more than anything else. We want to do something for God. We feel very warm on the inside when we are generous and make a gift. The unsaved man says, "I go to church; in fact, I'm a church member. I give generously to the church. When they ask me to do something, I do it. I'm a civilized man; I don't go around hitting people on the head. I'm considered a pretty good Joe. I'm a fellow that everybody likes. Now what in the world does God want of me? Shall I do something else? I feel like I should do something."

You see, we have the whole thing backwards. We ask, "What must I *do* to be saved?" The people came to the Lord Jesus and asked, ". . . What shall we do, that we might work the works of God?" And the Lord Jesus said, ". . . This is the work of God, that ye believe on him whom he hath sent" (John 6:28–29). He is saying, ". . . Believe on the Lord Jesus Christ, and thou shalt be saved . . ." (Acts 16:31). That is the only work that God is asking you to do—*believe*. Faith is just about the opposite of works. Saving faith produces works, but it certainly does not originate salvation. Your works have nothing to do with your salvation. This is the second question of the children of Israel, and it is the normal question of man.

The people now ask a third question—

**Will the LORD be pleased with thousands of rams, or with ten thousands of rivers of oil? shall I give my firstborn for my transgression, the fruit of my body for the sin of my soul? [Mic. 6:7].**

"Will the LORD be pleased with thousands of rams, or with ten thousands of rivers of oil?" Now that is really being generous! In other words, they ask, "Is it because we haven't done enough for God? Should we do more for God to try to please Him?" We hear the same question asked today. Years ago I used to play volleyball with a wealthy man who was a member of the YMCA with me in Nashville, Tennessee. It was near Christmastime, and he told me, "I want you to know what my religion is. I believe in being generous. Every Christmas I give my employees a bonus, and I give to this cause and that cause and the other cause. I give to my church, too. Now what else could God ask of me?" In other words, "I go the second mile. I'm a big spender as far as the Lord is concerned. I'm doing all this— what else could He ask me to do?" This is the question: Is it that we need to be very *generous* in what we do? Is that our problem? Many folk express it this way: "Well, maybe I'm not doing enough. I just don't feel like I'm right with God. I don't seem to be doing enough." These are sincere people; but because they are not saved, although they are church members, they feel that they need to do a little bit more than they are doing.

This line of thinking is something that the liberal preacher can work on; he can use a psychological approach. He can say, "Now look here, you folk are not doing enough." And so the fellow digs down a little deeper in his pocket, especially if he is a man of means, and says, "I'll give a little bit more. God will be tickled to death with that. My, He is sure going to be pleased with me." Just like Little Jack Horner, man becomes pleased with himself and with what he does—

Little Jack Horner
Sat in the corner,
Eating of Christmas pie:
He put in his thumb,
And pulled out a plum,
And said, "What a good boy am I!"

There are a lot of church members who are pulling out a plum and saying, "God surely must want to pat me on the head for what I am doing!"

The fourth question the people of Israel ask is going the limit: "Shall I give my firstborn for my transgression, the fruit of my body for the sin of my soul?" This was very meaningful to these people because they were surrounded by pagan peoples who in their worship of Molech and Baal offered human sacrifices. There were instances when even Israel turned in this direction. Two of the most godless kings of the southern kingdom indulged in human sacrifices—old Ahaz and old Manasseh. These two godless men offered their own children as burnt offerings, but is that what God would ask?

I want to make it very clear that God never asked these people to offer a child as a human sacrifice. God did require that they give to Him the firstborn male of everything that was born to them, whether it be a cow, a sheep, an ox, or their son. But God made it very clear to them that He did not require human sacrifice.

There are many passages of Scripture on this, but I will have to confine myself to just a few which I feel are ample to illustrate my point. In the eighteenth chapter of Numbers, God gave to the people certain regulations and told them what He required of them. We read there, "Every thing that openeth the matrix in all flesh, which they bring unto the LORD, whether it be of men or beasts, shall be thine: nevertheless the firstborn of man shalt thou surely redeem, and the firstling of unclean beasts shalt thou redeem" (Num. 18:15). God claimed the firstborn, you see. God required that the firstborn male child belonged to Him, but redemption money, silver, was to be taken and paid for that firstborn. In other words, God would not accept a human sacrifice, and He also would not accept the sacrifice of an unclean animal. I think that is interesting—man is unclean.

We have the practice today of dedicating our children to the Lord, and I think that that is a very fine thing to do. It has been my privilege to dedicate several thousand children in my days as a pastor. Some of them have turned out wonderfully well. One mother brought her son to me at a seminary where I was speaking, and she said, "Dr. McGee, you dedicated him when he was an infant." I thank the Lord that he has turned out well, but I have also dedicated some who have wound up in some of our best jails. It is nice to dedicate your child to the Lord, but that does not guarantee that he will turn out well.

In the Old Testament, God said, "You're to

redeem the child, put up redemption money for him. I will not take him now." Why? He is like that unclean animal; he's unclean. That is the reason that a woman who had brought a child into the world was unclean—she had brought an unclean thing into the world. David said, "Behold, I was shapen in iniquity, and in sin did my mother conceive me" (Ps. 51:5). God doesn't want a child until he is redeemed. We are going to have to wait until our child has received Jesus Christ as his Savior; when he does that, God can take that child and use him. God will not take him and use him until then.

In Exodus we read, "Sanctify unto me all the firstborn, whatsoever openeth the womb among the children of Israel, both of man and of beast: it is mine" (Exod. 13:2). But then in Leviticus we find: "And thou shalt not let any of thy seed pass through the fire to Molech, neither shalt thou profane the name of thy God: I am the Lord" (Lev. 18:21). In other words, God said, "Do not offer a human sacrifice. Do not take your child and offer him as a human sacrifice. You would profane Me if you did that."

People say to me, "I surely hope that your little grandson is going to follow in your footsteps and become a preacher. I am praying that he will do that." I do not mean to be coldhearted, but I do not pray that way about my grandsons. In the best way that I can as a grandfather, I lift them to the Lord, and I have told the Lord that first of all I want them to be saved. Then I pray that the Lord will use them in whatever way He wills. If it is His will for one of them to be a pharmacist and roll pills, that would tickle me to death. If it is the Lord's will for one to dig ditches, I'm going to be for that. You and I cannot take a little child who has our fallen nature and force him into Christian service. It simply won't work; that's not the way it is done, if you please.

**He hath shewed thee, O man, what is good; and what doth the Lord require of thee, but to do justly, and to love mercy, and to walk humbly with thy God? [Mic. 6:8].**

Verse 8 is the joy and delight of liberals because they think that it presents a works religion, that it teaches that man can be saved by his works. What Micah is doing here is answering the questions of many sincere people in the northern kingdom of Israel who were in darkness, who had not been taught the Word of God. They wanted to know how to come before God. They wanted to know

whether they should bring burnt offerings, whether they should bring many offerings, and whether they should offer even their own children as human sacrifices. Micah answers all of these questions: *None* of these things does God require. External religion without an internal experience, without reality on the inside, is absolutely valueless. There must be a rebirth, a new nature given to the individual. Externalities are not important—God never begins there. If you want to know what God takes delight in, what He requires of man, this verse will tell you. I want us to consider this verse carefully and in detail. Mr. Liberal, I insist that you interpret this accurately, and when you do, you will find that you are not saved by your good works because you do not *have* any good works.

"He hath shewed thee, O man, what is good." We notice first of all that this is addressed to *man*. This means not only the man in Israel but also the man in the United States, not only the person of the seventh century B.C. but also the person of the twentieth century A.D. This is for mankind.

These are the three things that God requires: (1) You are "to do justly"—that is, you must have a righteousness to present to God, you must be a righteous person. You are to be just in your dealings with your fellow man; you are to be honest and true. (2) You are "to love mercy." You are not only to love the mercy of God but also to be merciful in your own dealings with others. And (3) you are "to walk humbly with thy God."

How are you going to do these things, brother? Can you do them in your own strength? Do you think that you can do them without God's help? Do you think that you can do them without God's salvation? If you do, (I'm going to say something very strong, but I'm far enough away from you that you cannot hit me), you are a hypocrite! Don't tell me that you live by this moral code without the power of God. You cannot, for the very simple reason that all of these are the fruit of the Holy Spirit. "But the fruit of the Spirit is love, joy, peace, longsuffering, gentleness, goodness, faith, Meekness, temperance: against such there is no law" (Gal. 5:22–23). All three of these things which Micah lists are the work of the Holy Spirit in the life of the believer. None of us has any one of these things in his life today.

Let's turn to the New Testament and see what is said there concerning this. Listen to a man who lived under the Law. In the fifteenth chapter of Acts, when the apostles were deciding whether the Gentiles would have to keep the Law in order to be saved, Simon Peter stood up and said, "But we believe that through the grace of the Lord Jesus Christ we shall be saved, even as they" (Acts 15:11). Why did he say that? Because he had just said in Acts 15:10, "Now therefore why tempt ye God, to put a yoke upon the neck of the disciples, which neither our fathers nor we were able to bear?" Simon Peter said, "I lived under the law" (and I don't think he ever got very far away from it even after he was saved), "yet I did not measure up to it."

God has made this very clear through the words of the apostle Paul also: "For they that are after the flesh do mind the things of the flesh; but they that are after the Spirit the things of the Spirit. For to be carnally minded is death; but to be spiritually minded is life and peace. Because the carnal mind is enmity against God: for it is not subject to the law of God, neither indeed can be. *So then they that are in the flesh cannot please God.* But ye are not in the flesh, but in the Spirit, if so be that the Spirit of God dwell in you . . ." (Rom. 8:5–9, italics mine).

My friend, how does the Spirit of God dwell in you? The Lord Jesus said, ". . . Ye must be born again" (John 3:7). You must be born again by receiving Christ. "But as many as received him, to them gave he power [the right, the authority, the *exousian* power] to become the sons of God, even to them that believe on his name" (John 1:12).

In Romans 3:9–18 the apostle Paul sets before us the condition of man. He brings man before the judgment bar of God and shows that he is guilty. Then Paul takes man into the clinic of God and shows that he is sick, sick nigh unto death—in fact, he is ". . . *dead* in trespasses and sins" (Eph. 2:1, italics mine). No man, therefore, whoever he is, can present these things to God. God requires righteousness, but we cannot meet that standard. Paul says, ". . . There is none righteous, no, not one" (Rom. 3:10). Someone says, "Well, that is in the New Testament." My friend, all that Paul is doing in this section of Romans is quoting the Old Testament. In Psalm 14:1 we find, "The fool hath said in his heart, There is no God. They are corrupt, they have done abominable works, there is none that doeth good." This is what God says about you. But God also says that He requires righteousness. How are you going to be able to present it to Him, my friend?

Paul goes on to say in Romans 3:11: "There is none that understandeth, there is none that seeketh after God." In other words, there is none that acts even on the knowledge that he has. Do you, if you are not a Christian, really live up to your ideals? Have you attained the goal that you have set? Have you come to the plateau in life where you are satisfied with your living? May I say to you, none of us even act on the knowledge which we have—"there is none that seeketh after God." Again, this idea is found in the Old Testament in Psalm 14:2–3: "The LORD looked down from heaven upon the children of men, to see if there were any that did understand, and seek God. They are all gone aside, they are all together become filthy: there is none that doeth good, no, not one."

I could multiply from the Old Testament such statements again and again. Righteousness is what God requires, but the Old Testament makes it very obvious that we cannot present our righteousness to God—because we don't have any. Since God requires righteousness, there must be a change in the life because there is none righteous. We are told that Jesus was ". . . delivered for our offences, and was raised again for our *justification*" (Rom. 4:25, italics mine). The Lord Jesus was raised for our righteousness, that we might have righteousness, that by the Spirit of God we might produce righteousness in our lives.

The "love of mercy"—we do not have that in our human hearts. We are dead in trespasses and sins. Paul says, "They are all gone out of the way, they are together become unprofitable; there is none that doeth good, no, not one" (Rom. 3:12). This is the picture of man; this is the way that man is today. The same point is presented to us by Isaiah: "All we like sheep have gone astray; we have turned every one to his own way; and the LORD hath laid on him the iniquity of us all" (Isa. 53:6). Evidently, "us all" have iniquity, or Isaiah would not have made a statement like that.

Therefore, let's not be hypocritical when we come to this verse in Micah that tells us that we are to walk humbly with our God. *None* seeketh after God; instead, we want to come to Him *our* way.

I want to say this in all kindness, but I trust that it might startle some and awaken them out of their condition today. If you believe that your church membership or your character or your good works are going to get you to God, then may I say that you are bypassing God's way. The Lord Jesus said, ". . . I am the way, the truth, and the life: no man cometh unto the Father, but by me" (John 14:6). If you can get to God by this route presented here—by doing justly, by loving mercy, and by walking humbly with God—and you can do that on your own, when you get to heaven, you can tell God to move over. You can tell Him that you want to share His throne with Him, that you got there by yourself, that you didn't need Him since you are your own god. But, my friend, God says that He does not share His glory with another, and I do not think He will share His throne with you. So why don't you come God's way and not man's way?

Doing justly, loving mercy, and walking humbly with God are things which God requires. Who are you kidding when you claim that you do these things in your natural state? My, how verses like this, when held up to the human family, show us what we really are like! Some commend themselves for being polite and nice folk, especially on Sundays when they seem so genteel and loving—and yet they have never come to God *His* way. How can you continue on and on in a hypocrisy like that? Why not be honest with God? Just come right out with it, go to Him, and tell Him that you are a sinner. He already knows it, but it would be nice if you told Him. Instead of climbing onto a psychiatrist's couch and talking to him, talk to God. Tell Him the thing that is wrong with you. Tell Him about your hangups. Tell Him about the sin in your life. God wants to save you, my friend. God wants to forgive your sins and give you the righteousness of Christ.

Having presented to these people what God requires, Micah is now going to show them how far they have fallen short of it. The reason that God will judge them is because of their willful and continual sinning.

**The LORD's voice crieth unto the city, and the man of wisdom shall see thy name: hear ye the rod, and who hath appointed it [Mic. 6:9].**

"The LORD's voice crieth unto the city." We have seen that Micah has been directing his prophecies largely to the urban areas, to the cities. His writing reveals that he is a very sophisticated writer. He was in the know; he belonged to the upper echelon. He is in contrast to Amos who said, "I'm no prophet. I'm just a gatherer of sycamore fruit. I'm a farmhand, just a country boy who has come to town." But Amos happened to be God's man. Micah is God's man too, but a different type of man from Amos—he is crying to the city.

"And the man of wisdom shall see thy name: hear ye the rod, and who hath appointed it." The rod is for judgment. We read in the second psalm, "Thou shalt break them with a rod of iron; thou shalt dash them in pieces like a potter's vessel" (Ps. 2:9). The rod represents the judgment of God. Judgment is coming upon this nation. The man of wisdom—that is, the man in that day who believed God and who would listen—would recognize that judgment was coming upon the nation and would act accordingly. The voice of God is lifted, and He speaks forth in judgment. The man is a wise man who sees the dealings of God which reveal His righteous character as well as the fact that He is longsuffering, patient, and will pardon iniquity. But God also punishes, and the rod is the badge of His authority as the judge who *will* judge.

There was still sin in the nation, and Micah is now going to reveal these sins specifically; he is going to spell them out.

**Are there yet the treasures of wickedness in the house of the wicked, and the scant measure that is abominable? [Mic. 6:10].**

"Treasures of wickedness" refers to the wealth they had accumulated in their unjust dealings.

**Shall I count them pure with the wicked balances, and with the bag of deceitful weights? [Mic. 6:11].**

Many of these people were coming into the temple, bringing a sacrifice, going through the outward ceremony, and saying that they were doing justly and loving mercy. But what were they doing during the week? God says, "Shall I count them pure with the wicked balances?" I tell you, the butchers in that day were weighing their thumbs—and some butchers had thumbs worth several drachmas! Businessmen were dishonest in their business dealings. He says, "And with the bag of deceitful weights?" They were absolutely crooked. They were avaricious, they were covetous, and they were greedy; yet they tried to pass themselves off as religious folk.

**For the rich men thereof are full of violence, and the inhabitants thereof have spoken lies, and their tongue is deceitful in their mouth [Mic. 6:12].**

The rich were guilty of violence; they were liars. They were deceitful—you could not believe them.

Is this not a picture today of my own nation? Is this not a picture of this wonderful land in which you and I live? We cannot believe the news media today. We cannot believe the politicians, no matter what their party affiliation. It's a day when it is difficult to believe businessmen. It is difficult to believe those in the military leadership. We are living in a nation today where most of us little folk are confused—we don't know whom to believe. This was the situation in Israel in Micah's day, and God did not approve of it. In fact, this is one of the things that brought the nation down and brought the judgment of God upon them.

I want to say this very carefully but clearly because I love my country and I hate to see what is happening to it today. I have taught for years that the United States would have to go down at the end of this age for the very simple reason that we are not mentioned in Bible prophecy. We are a world power today, but will we be tomorrow? It seems that we are going down very fast. At the time that I am writing this, things look very dark in this land. An energy crisis has come upon us. It didn't come suddenly; it has been coming for many years. A few of us have been crying out that America is going to be judged. We are apparently moving into that orbit today. Many warned years ago after World War II that oil should have been brought out of the Middle East at that time and that we should never have used our own reserves. But because of greed (it was called "good business" because it was making money), we went into an age of affluence and plenty, and we really left God out. And He is pretty much left out of our national affairs today. There has been no mention, at the time that I am writing this, that we need to turn to God in this emergency in which we find ourselves.

The northern kingdom of Israel in Micah's day was in the same condition in which we are today, and God brought judgment upon them. Although they were His chosen people as a nation, He brought judgment upon them.

**Therefore also will I make thee sick in smiting thee, in making thee desolate because of thy sins [Mic. 6:13].**

In effect, God says, "First of all, I am going to start taking the oil away from you, but I'm not going to stop there. You're going to find that you will run short on many things before I am through judging you."

**Thou shalt eat, but not be satisfied; and thy casting down shall be in the midst of thee; and thou shalt take hold, but shalt not deliver; and that which thou deliverest will I give up to the sword [Mic. 6:14].**

God says in effect, "You will no longer be able to enjoy all of these things that you have enjoyed, all these little goodies that you have had. Shortages and eventual famine will come. Attempts to remove your wealth to a safe place will be fruitless—the enemy will get it."

**Thou shalt sow, but thou shalt not reap; thou shalt tread the olives, but thou shalt not anoint thee with oil; and sweet wine, but shalt not drink wine [Mic. 6:15].**

The enemy would take them from their land—take them to Assyria as captives.

God intended to cut them down but to cut them down gradually. That, of course, would give them an opportunity to turn to Him. The next chapter will make it clear that God would have pardoned them anytime that they would have turned to Him. But, my friend, you must turn to Him, for God will judge sin.

The people of Israel were going through the externalities of religion, but internally they were far from God. There was dishonesty in their business dealings. There was impurity in their lives. There was violence. There was lying and deceit. Every kind of flagrant sin was committed. And God cannot bless a people or a nation that engages in these things.

**For the statutes of Omri are kept, and all the works of the house of Ahab, and ye walk in their counsels; that I should make thee a desolation, and the inhabitants thereof an hissing: therefore ye shall bear the reproach of my people [Mic. 6:16].**

A question would naturally be asked by a new reader of this: "Who in the world is Omri, and who in the world is Ahab? I have never heard of them before. Why is God saying what He is saying about them?" Such a question demonstrates the need for a different approach to the study of the Old Testament which I have for many years thought would be most helpful. I would suggest that when you study the historical books of the Old Testament, also consider the prophetic book or books that correspond to the same time period as the historical book. For example, that would mean that Micah should be studied along with the historical account of the reigns of Hezekiah in the southern kingdom and of Ahab and Jezebel in the northern kingdom. If the historical books were considered along with the prophetic books, they would give you a complete picture. I had hoped to introduce this approach when I was head of the English Bible department at the Bible Institute of Los Angeles years ago, but I never got around to it.

However, if we will now turn to the historical book of 1 Kings, it will shed some light on this verse here in Micah. Omri was one of the kings in the northern kingdom; in fact, he was one of the meanest. Omri and Zimri, then Tibni, reigned as rival kings until both died, and Omri prevailed to rule over the entire northern kingdom. In 1 Kings 16:24 we read: "And he bought the hill Samaria of Shemer for two talents of silver, and built on the hill, and called the name of the city which he built, after the name of Shemer, owner of the hill, Samaria." That city is called Samaria to this day, and the ruins of the city which Omri built are still there. But Omri is not really the one who developed the city. After the death of Omri, Ahab came to the throne. We read further: "So Omri slept with his fathers, and was buried in Samaria: and Ahab his son reigned in his stead. . . . And Ahab the son of Omri did evil in the sight of the LORD above all that were before him" (1 Kings 16:28,30). Now that was something, let me tell you, but one of the reasons he was able to do that was because he had a great little helper in his wife, Jezebel. "And it came to pass, as if it had been a light thing for him to walk in the sins of Jeroboam the son of Nebat, that he took to wife Jezebel the daughter of Ethbaal king of the Zidonians, and went and served Baal, and worshipped him" (1 Kings 16:31). Ahab and Jezebel made the worship of Baal the religion of Israel!

"The statutes of Omri are kept, and all the works of the house of Ahab." Instead of following the statutes of the Lord, they followed the statutes of Omri and Ahab. They rejected the Word of the Lord and walked in *their* counsels instead. Now in Micah's day, almost two hundred years later, the effect and influence of their evil reigns are apparent.

We see the same effect evident in our own day. The leadership of any nation, if that nation is to prosper under God, must be godly. People like to criticize Queen Victoria and the Victorian Era in England—even the English ridicule it. However, I think it should be said that that happens to have been the greatest period in their history—that is when they had an empire. Victoria was Empress of India; she ruled an empire. Today Great Britain has really been cut down to size, for their leadership since then has not been what it should have been.

When Princess Anne was married, I rejoiced in watching the ceremony. Tears came into our eyes as my wife and I watched it on television, for in the ceremony there was a restoration of the sacredness of marriage. Since that example came from the leadership, I am sure that it had an influence.

My own country has not had a very good example set by either the White House or the Congress in a long, long time. My lifetime pretty much spans this century, and may I say, the example emanating from Washington has not been good. As a result, gross immorality has spread throughout this nation. I do believe, because of this verse here, that God would say that He holds the leaders of our nation during this century responsible for plunging the country into gross immorality through the example which they have set.

Micah presents God's philosophy of government. This is not being taught in any of our universities—that is part of our problem also. As a result, we're not really getting the facts, and our nation continues to decay and deteriorate. We will continue to do so unless a great revival should come to our land, but there is certainly no evidence at the present time that it will come.

# CHAPTER 7

**THEME:** *Pardoning all iniquity because of who God is and what He does; closing prayer; God's answer; paean of praise*

## PARDONING ALL INIQUITY BECAUSE OF WHO GOD IS AND WHAT HE DOES

In the first nine verses of chapter 7, the prophet Micah confesses that God is accurate in His complaint against Israel. The charge and the accuracy of it touch the heart of the prophet. He is not unfeeling. He is moved and motivated by the judgment which is coming upon his people. We have in this first section, therefore, a soliloquy of sorrow, a saga of suffering, a wail of woe, an elegy of eloquent grief.

**Woe is me! for I am as when they have gathered the summer fruits, as the grapegleanings of the vintage: there is no cluster to eat: my soul desired the firstripe fruit [Mic. 7:1].**

Micah begins in a very personal way—he says, "Woe is me!" He is not only very personal, but he is also affected a great deal by God's message which he has relayed, just as Jeremiah was. He is overwhelmed by it. He is grieved by it. He finds no delight in saying these things. There is no fun today in my saying things that are rather pessimistic about the United States. A great many people will not agree with me about them. They will rebuke me for not being patriotic and for not showing a love for my country. My friend, I love my country as much as the normal American loves his country. I find no joy in saying these things. I wish that I could make an announcement to say, "Friends, a great revival is breaking out across this land!" That would be good news, and that would be wonderful, but I just have to say along with Micah, "Woe is me!"

"For I am as when they have gathered the summer fruits, as the grapegleanings of the vintage: there is no cluster to eat: my soul desired the firstripe fruit." Remember that in Scripture the vine is used to picture the nation Israel. Micah's contemporary, Isaiah, is the one who enlarged upon this and set this forth (see Isa. 5). He said very clearly that Israel is the vine and the vine is Israel. Micah looked about at his nation and said, "I've looked for a good cluster of grapes, and there are none on the vine. I desired the firstripe fruit, and there was none. The vine is not producing fruit."

Micah is going to deal now with the specifics—

**The good man is perished out of the earth: and there is none upright among men: they all lie in wait for blood; they hunt every man his brother with a net [Mic. 7:2].**

It is not safe to walk on the streets of our country—today lawlessness abounds. It does seem that the good man is perished; yet there are a lot of wonderful people left in this nation of ours. I am sure there were godly people left in Israel also, but Micah is speaking generally. The good man is not the ideal, and he's not the one in the majority. "The good man is perished out of the earth."

**That they may do evil with both hands earnestly, the prince asketh, and the judge asketh for a reward; and the great man, he uttereth his mischievous desire: so they wrap it up [Mic. 7:3].**

"That they may do evil with both hands earnestly." They are not satisfied to do evil in just a minor way with one hand—they are going at it with both hands. Believe me, doing evil really kept them busy.

"The prince asketh, and the judge asketh for a reward." They were doing evil for a reward. They were not only willing to stoop to do the thing that was wrong, but they did it also because of greed and covetousness on their part. "The prince . . . and the judge"—there was crookedness in government, you see. You would expect the prince and the judge to rule justly and righteously, but that was not the picture.

"And the great man, he uttereth his mischievous desire." The writers of our literature are clever writers today. I watch a great deal of television in order to keep up with what is going on in this world. I find that everything that is presented by our writers has a little hook in it. There's that little hook of liberalism, that little hook of immorality, that little hook of ridicule of the things we have considered sacred in this country. And it is all done in the name of the sacred cow of the freedom of the press and the freedom of speech. But there is very little freedom of religion today, unless it is weird and way out in left field somewhere and not that which is Bible-centered and Bible-anchored. We need a Bibliocentric thrust in this nation of ours today.

**The best of them is as a brier: the most upright is sharper than a thorn hedge: the day of thy watchmen and thy visitation cometh; now shall be their perplexity [Mic. 7:4].**

Even the best people were like a brier—you had to be careful. You can get stuck with a brier, you know, if you're not careful with it. That was the condition of even the best people in Micah's day—you couldn't depend on them. "The best of them is as a brier: the most upright is sharper than a thorn hedge."

Our writers are clever and sophisticated today, but we have no geniuses writing, just clever boys. They write clever plays. They say clever things. They write clever articles. But there are no geniuses. They write nothing of depth, nothing that is actually worthwhile. I believe that God will do with our contemporary culture what He did with Israel in that day and what He did later on with the Greek and Roman cultures. He simply wiped them off the face of the earth. Why preserve it? What is being done today that has eternal value? Oh, my friend, what a parallel there is here, and how accurate Micah is!

"The day of thy watchmen and thy visitation cometh; now shall be their perplexity." The Lord Jesus said, "And there shall be signs in the sun, and in the moon, and in the stars; and upon the earth distress of nations, with perplexity; the sea and the waves roaring" (Luke 21:25). In other words, one thing that would characterize the end of the age is perplexity of nations, confusion of nations. The biggest sign that we are near the end of the age is not found in Israel. Israel is not a sign. We are living in the church age today. We don't need to look for a day, we need to look at a weather report: the sea and the waves roaring, the storms breaking upon the earth, and the nations seething—that is the picture that God's Word presents of the nation in the last days.

Micah has been telling out the difficulty that these people were having, the sin that was in their lives. The lovely statement that was made back in Micah 6:8 was: "He hath shewed thee, O man, what is good; and what doth the LORD require of thee, but to do justly, and to love mercy, and to walk humbly with thy God?" The people just were not doing it, and they found that they *could* not do it. As Peter said, "We were under the yoke of the law. Our forefathers didn't keep it, and we cannot keep it today" (see Acts 15:10). Yet there are a great many people going to church, thinking they are saved by their own good works and are acceptable to God on the basis of what they do. There is no hypocrisy like that kind of hypocrisy! The people living back yonder under the law might be excused for thinking that, but we have an open Bible which makes clear to us that we are saved only by the grace of God.

**Trust ye not in a friend, put ye not confidence in a guide: keep the doors of thy mouth from her that lieth in thy bosom [Mic. 7:5].**

This reveals something of the awful condition that existed in that day, and it has been true pretty much of all the so-called civilizations of this world. It is a big, mean world outside. We need to recognize this, especially if we are to take a stand for God. The Lord Jesus said, "Think not that I am come to send peace on earth: I came not to send peace, but a sword" (Matt. 10:34). As long as there is evil in the world, there will be a conflict and a war between that which is of the flesh and that which is of the Spirit, between light and darkness, between good and evil.

I generally get up very early in the morning because I like to do my studying at home early. I get up while it is still dark, and my study is where I can look out toward the east. It is interesting to watch how the darkness wrestles with the light until finally the sun comes bursting over the horizon and the darkness then vanishes. There is always that period of dawn when it would seem that the darkness is wrestling with the light. The same thing takes place in the evening at dusk when again darkness wants to take over. There is that kind of a *spiritual* struggle going on in the world.

The Lord Jesus went on to say in Matthew, "For I am come to set a man at variance against his father, and the daughter against her mother, and the daughter in law against her mother in law. And a man's foes shall be they of his own household" (Matt. 10:35–36). You will not be able to trust your own family. Micah says, "Trust ye not in a friend, put ye not confidence in a guide: keep the doors of thy mouth from her that lieth in thy bosom." Over the years I have heard of many such instances—and it works both ways, of course—when a wife has not been able to trust her husband, and a husband has not been able to trust his wife.

We live in a day when the word of man seems to carry less value than it ever has before. You cannot believe what you read, and you cannot believe what you hear on radio or on television. The child of God should test everything. I say this very candidly: test every radio program you listen to by the Word of God. Test my Bible-teaching broadcast; test them all. You will be wise if you do this because the human nature is not to be trusted.

**For the son dishonoureth the father, the daughter riseth up against her mother, the daughter in law against her mother in law; a man's enemies are the men of his own house [Mic. 7:6].**

Notice that this is exactly what the Lord Jesus said will come, and it had come in Micah's day also. When this sort of a situation arises, it is a day of decadence, a day of deterioration, a day of decay. It is a day that is very dark, by the way. We live in a day like that. We have gotten to the place where government is having to watch everything. But who is going to watch government? They need watching also. Whom can you trust? In whom can you believe today? We are living at a very sad time in the history of the world. This verse reveals the condition of that day of Micah's grief. This is not something to boast of, not something to rejoice in. It is something to be deplored, something which should grieve your heart and my heart.

**Therefore I will look unto the LORD; I will wait for the God of my salvation: my God will hear me [Mic. 7:7].**

We see here the confidence and the assurance and the faith of Micah. He knows that God is going to hear him, and he knows that God will work this thing out. The Lord Jesus said that there would be distress of nations, the sea and the waves would roar, and the nations of the world would be in great turmoil. But it does not matter how dark it is today and how high the waves are rolling—these things ought not to disturb the child of God, they ought not to detour us. For the Lord Jesus said, "Men's hearts [will be] failing them for fear, and for looking after those things which are coming on the earth: for the powers of heaven shall be shaken. . . . And when these things begin to come to pass, then look up, and lift up your heads; for your redemption draweth nigh" (Luke 21:26, 28). Micah says, "Therefore I will

look unto the LORD; I will wait for the God of my salvation: my God will hear me." These are the days when God's children need to stay very close to God, and we need to stay close to the Word of God.

**Rejoice not against me, O mine enemy: when I fall, I shall arise; when I sit in darkness, the LORD shall be a light unto me [Mic. 7:8].**

This is a great principle that we find running through the Scriptures. Though God's man may fall, God will raise him up. When we sit in darkness, the Lord shall be a light for us. God's people, again may I repeat this, must stay close to the Word of God in dark and difficult days.

Now in verse 9, on behalf of his people, Micah makes a confession to God, or as *The New Scofield Reference Bible* has labeled it, "submission to the LORD." There is sweet submission here and, in spite of the darkness, there is on his lips a praise to God. He has just said to the enemy, "Don't you rejoice against me. God is going to lift me up, and then I will be able to rejoice. Though I sit in darkness, the Lord is going to be a light unto me." Micah had the confidence that God would deliver him and would deliver his people.

**I will bear the indignation of the LORD, because I have sinned against him, until he plead my cause, and execute judgment for me: he will bring me forth to the light, and I shall behold his righteousness [Mic. 7:9].**

Micah is making a public confession of the sin of the people. What confidence this man has! He submits himself to the will of God. That should be the position of every child of God in this dark hour in the history of the world. What is it that we should do? Well, there is one thing that is sure: God has permitted all things to happen, and He is still in control. Therefore we should submit ourselves to God. We should confess our sins and keep our accounts with God right up to date and make sure that we have settled every account with Him. This is the thing that is all-important.

Notice that Micah says, "I will bear the indignation of the LORD." Why? "Because I have sinned against him." My friend, we as a nation have sinned. You have sinned; I have sinned. We have gone along with this affluent society and have accepted its comforts. We have rather smiled at the lack of integrity that there is in public life, and we have shut our eyes to the gross immorality that is around us.

It is time that some of us are confessing our sin.

"Until he plead my cause, and execute judgment for me." God will use the "rod" of Assyria to punish His children for their sins, but afterward He will restore them and bring them "forth to the light." Then they will "behold his righteousness"—they will realize that God was just in punishing them.

**Then she that is mine enemy shall see it, and shame shall cover her which said unto me, Where is the LORD thy God? mine eyes shall behold her: now shall she be trodden down as the mire of the streets [Mic. 7:10].**

God will ultimately triumph, but the thing that is tragic is that, because of the sins of the people, they must be judged. Their enemy asks the question: "You boasted of the fact that you serve God, but where is He? Why doesn't He help you? Why doesn't He deliver you? You have said that He would." Well, the enemy could not see the righteousness of God. He did not see that God was dealing with His people in a righteous way by judging them.

After God restores His people, He will punish the nations that abused them and attempted to annihilate them—then *they* shall "be trodden as the mire of the streets."

Since the Assyrian captivity lay ahead of the people of Israel, the "enemy" is interpreted as the nation of Assyria; yet the following two verses indicate that a later and final enemy is also in view.

Micah has predicted the destruction of Israel's enemies and now turns to Israel's restoration. The nation of Israel is likened to a vineyard in several passages of Scripture. Notice especially Isaiah's song of the vineyard (see Isa. 5:1–7). The walls Micah speaks of are the walls around a vineyard.

**In the day that thy walls are to be built, in that day shall the decree be far removed [Mic. 7:11].**

In the early days of their history, the people of Israel were sent by God down to Egypt to become a nation. Then God hedged them into the land of Palestine, gave them the Law, made them a peculiar people, and kept them from intermarrying with other folk. Then, because of their sin, God sent them into Assyrian and Babylonian captivity. They had a ministry to the world, both at the time of the containment and then again when they were scattered throughout the world.

**In that day also he shall come even to thee from Assyria, and from the fortified cities, and from the fortress even to the river, and from sea to sea, and from mountain to mountain [Mic. 7:12].**

As we have seen in chapter 4, during the millennial kingdom all nations shall come to Zion—even their former enemy, Assyria. "And many nations shall come, and say, Come, and let us go up to the mountain of the LORD, and to the house of the God of Jacob; and he will teach us of his ways, and we will walk in his paths: for the law shall go forth of Zion, and the word of the LORD from Jerusalem" (Mic. 4:2).

However, Micah reminds them that before this time of blessing, punishment lies before them.

**Notwithstanding the land shall be desolate because of them that dwell therein, for the fruit of their doings [Mic. 7:13].**

You see, the land and the people are pretty well tied together. That land was not always desolate as it is today. When the blessing of God comes upon the people, it will also come again upon that land—but it has not yet come upon them.

## CLOSING PRAYER

Now Micah in a very wonderful way commits his people to the Shepherd's care—

**Feed thy people with thy rod, the flock of thine heritage, which dwell solitarily in the wood, in the midst of Carmel: let them feed in Bashan and Gilead, as in the days of old [Mic. 7:14].**

"Feed thy people with thy rod, the flock of thine heritage." In Micah 6:9 the rod was a rod of judgment; here it is a rod of comfort. ". . . thy rod and thy staff they comfort me" (Ps. 23:4). I think it simply refers to the staff of the shepherd which could be used in two ways: it could be used to protect and help the sheep, and it could also be used to discipline the sheep. "Feed thy people with thy rod"—God disciplines us, and He instructs us.

"Which dwell solitarily in the wood, in the midst of Carmel: let them feed in Bashan and Gilead, as in the days of old." These are great grazing lands up in the north and across the Jordan River.

Micah has come to God in beautiful submission and in confession of sin—confession of his sins and of the sins of the people. The prophets always identified themselves with the people in any confession of sin. (We do it a little differently; we like to confess the sin of the other fellow while we try to leave ours out.)

## GOD'S ANSWER

God gives an answer to the prayer of the prophet. There has always been some question as to what this passage makes reference to, but it is the consensus of most expositors that it looks to the future and to the day when the Lord Jesus will come to set up His kingdom.

> According to the days of thy coming out of the land of Egypt will I shew unto him marvellous things [Mic. 7:15].

God led Israel out of Egypt by miracle, but He did not bring them out of Babylon by miracle. No miracles are mentioned in connection with that, although their return to the land was a wonderful thing. It was the deliverance out of Egypt that was miraculous, and God says here that that will be the pattern for the day when He again brings them into the land. We have not seen anything like that in their present-day return to the land. We ought to recognize, therefore, that God has not yet fulfilled this prophecy.

> The nations shall see and be confounded at all their might: they shall lay their hand upon their mouth, their ears shall be deaf [Mic. 7:16].

When God begins again to move them back into the land, the world will stand in amazement, just as the peoples round about them did at the time of their exodus from Egypt. You remember the confession of the harlot, Rahab: "For we have heard how the LORD dried up the water of the Red sea for you, when ye came out of Egypt; and what ye did unto the two kings of the Amorites, that were on the other side Jordan, Sihon and Og, whom ye utterly destroyed. And as soon as we had heard these things, our hearts did melt, neither did there remain any more courage in any man, because of you: for the LORD your God, he is God in heaven above, and in earth beneath" (Josh. 2:10–11). The word has gotten around as to how God had taken care of His people.

> They shall lick the dust like a serpent, they shall move out of their holes like worms of the earth: they shall be afraid of the LORD our God, and shall fear because of thee [Mic. 7:17].

This refers to the godless nations which have attempted to destroy Israel. In that day when He comes to deliver Israel, "they shall be afraid of the LORD our God, and shall fear because of thee."

## PAEAN OF PRAISE

Micah waxes eloquent now, and he asks a question—

> Who is a God like unto thee, that pardoneth iniquity, and passeth by the transgression of the remnant of his heritage? he retaineth not his anger for ever, because he delighteth in mercy [Mic. 7:18].

We will discuss this verse at length in a moment, but Micah goes on here to say that because of who God is, this is what He will do—

> He will turn again, he will have compassion upon us; he will subdue our iniquities; and thou wilt cast all their sins into the depths of the sea.

> Thou wilt perform the truth to Jacob, and the mercy to Abraham, which thou hast sworn unto our fathers from the days of old [Mic. 7:19–20].

Israel's sin put them out of the land temporarily, but God will make good His promises in spite of their sin. Their sin does not cancel out God's promises and God's covenant with these people any more than a child of God loses his salvation when he sins. His sin means that he is going to the woodshed for a good whipping if he doesn't confess it and get it straightened out; but if he will come back to God, God will graciously pardon him. The prodigal son did not get a whipping when he came home to his father; he got his whipping in the far country. And you can be sure of one thing: God's child will never be able to get by with sin. We see that again and again in Scripture.

Now let's come back to this marvelous statement that we have here: "Who is a God like unto thee." I want to make a very startling statement: There is something that God has not seen but which you see every day. Perhaps you didn't know that you could see something that God cannot see—but that is a true statement. It may sound rather impertinent for me to say that; it may sound irrelevant, irreverent, or inappropriate; it may even sound flippant or facetious. It may sound to you like I am making a parody or a pun, a riddle or a rhyme, a trick or a treat, but

I want to assure you that this is a serious and sober subject with a sensible and Scriptural answer. The prophet here asks a profound question: "Who is a God like unto thee?" And it demands a thoughtful answer. The very nature of the question suggests an answer to an enigmatic subject.

This is not the first time in Scripture that this question has been asked, by the way. It was asked in that wonderful song sung by Israel after they crossed the Red Sea. In Exodus 15:11 we read, "Who is like unto thee, O LORD, among the gods? who is like thee, glorious in holiness, fearful in praises, doing wonders?" The people had just come out from Egypt where there were many gods. Egypt was absolutely—if I may use the slang expression—lousy with idols; they had many gods and many lords. The ten plagues in Egypt had been leveled at their various gods—that was God's strategy in it all. And then again at the end of the forty years of the wilderness march, Moses said, "There is none like unto the God of Jeshurun, who rideth upon the heaven in thy help, and in his excellency on the sky. The eternal God is thy refuge, and underneath are the everlasting arms: and he shall thrust out the enemy from before thee; and shall say, Destroy them" (Deut. 33:26–27). This question was again asked by Solomon in 1 Kings 8:23, ". . . LORD God of Israel, there is no God like thee, in heaven above, or on earth beneath, who keepest covenant and mercy with thy servants that walk before thee with all their heart." The psalmist exclaimed: "Who is like unto the LORD our God, who dwelleth on high, Who humbleth himself to behold the things that are in heaven, and in the earth!" (Ps. 113:5–6).

This question is asked in Exodus, Deuteronomy, Kings, Psalms, and in other passages which I have not cited, but now let's answer it. The answer was suggested by my statement at the beginning: God has not seen something which you see every day. What is it that God has not seen? My friend, God has not seen His *equal*. "Who is a God like unto thee?" God has never seen His equal, but you and I see our equals every day.

There are many ways in which God is alone, in which God is unequaled. Only one of them is suggested by our passage here in Micah, but because this is such a profound question and one that is so basic to this book, I want to look at this subject closely: Who is a God like unto our God?

1. *The God of the Bible is the Creator*. The God of the Bible is the Creator, but the gods of the heathen are creatures. The apostle Paul wrote: "Because that, when they knew God, they glorified him not as God, neither were thankful; but became vain in their imaginations, and their foolish heart was darkened. Professing themselves to be wise, they became fools, And changed the glory of the uncorruptible God into an image made like to corruptible man, and to birds, and fourfooted beasts, and creeping things" (Rom. 1:21–23). They worshiped the creature rather than the Creator.

Isaiah, Micah's contemporary, wrote concerning the heathen who make images from trees: "He burneth part thereof in the fire; with part thereof he eateth flesh; he roasteth roast, and is satisfied: yea, he warmeth himself, and saith, Aha, I am warm, I have seen the fire: And the residue thereof he maketh a god, even his graven image: he falleth down unto it, and worshippeth it, and prayeth unto it, and saith, Deliver me; for thou art my god" (Isa. 44:16–17). Isaiah went on to say, "Remember these, O Jacob and Israel; for thou art my servant: I have formed thee; thou art my servant: O Israel, thou shalt not be forgotten of me" (Isa. 44:21). God is the Creator.

You may say, "But we don't have idols today." The Book of Micah has been dealing with a form of idolatry of which Israel was guilty and of which we are guilty also: covetousness is idolatry. Secularism, materialism, that to which you give yourself is your god. That which takes your time and your money is your god. It can be pleasure, it can be sex, it can be money—whatever you are giving yourself to, my friend, is your god. It does not matter what church you might belong to, whatever you are giving yourself to is your god.

With biting irony, God asks the question through the prophet Isaiah: "To whom will ye liken me, and make me equal, and compare me, that we may be like?" (Isa. 46:5). He is the Creator—you cannot make a picture of Him. "They lavish gold out of the bag, and weigh silver in the balance, and hire a goldsmith; and he maketh it a god: they fall down, yea, they worship. They bear him upon the shoulder, they carry him . . ." (Isa. 46:6–7). The supreme question is this: Is your religion carrying you, or are you carrying it? Many people say to me, "Oh, I find Christian work extremely boring. It is hard; it is difficult." If you are finding it that way, then I would suggest that you give up what you are doing—quit teaching your Sunday school class, quit singing in the choir, and do not be an officer in the church. If it is burdensome to you, He does not want you to do it. He doesn't want you carrying Him around—He wants to carry you. He wants to carry all of His children. Somebody said to me the other day, "Why in the world don't you retire? You are in your seventies now, you've been in the pastorate for forty years, and you've given your time to teaching the Bible on radio. Why don't you retire?" Do you want to know something? I would rather teach the Word of God than eat ice cream any day. I'd rather do this than eat a chicken dinner. My friend, God has been carrying me for a long time, even though I think I have been a heavy load for Him.

So God is unique; He is the Creator, and He carries us. "In the beginning God created the heaven and the earth" (Gen. 1:1)—and it is blasphemy to go beyond that. You cannot go beyond Him— ". . . from everlasting to everlasting [from the vanishing point to the vanishing point], thou art God" (Ps. 90:2). He is the Creator.

2. *The God of the Bible is holy and righteous.* This is something that is very important to this little Book of Micah and to all sixty-six books of the Bible. God is a holy and righteous God. The gods of the heathen are little, they're contemptible, they're base, they're ignoble, they're shabby, they're evil, they're mean, and they're ugly—just think about the heathen images which you have seen. The gods of the Greeks on top of Mount Olympus were simply man's projection of himself. They were the enlargement of mankind. What did they do? They acted like overgrown children with overgrown faults and sins; they were spiteful and vengeful. The gods of the heathen are not pretty, my friend.

What a reflection and slur upon God! Have you ever noticed how many times in Scripture we read of "the *beauty* of holiness"? Oh, my friend, our God is beautiful—He is the beautiful one. Remember that He said to His people, ". . . thou thoughtest that I was altogether such an one as thyself . . ." (Ps. 50:21). He says, "I am not like you. You are sinful; you stoop to do low, mean things. I am holy; I am righteous." In Isaiah God says, "For my thoughts are not your thoughts, neither are your ways my ways . . ." (Isa. 55:8).

God is holy, and He says that He hates sin. He is angry with sin. He gets wrought-up over it, my friend. And the wrath of God must be revealed against sin. That is the reason judgment must come. There is no escape from

it; there is no way out. The judgment of God is something that is going to come to pass.

Again the little Book of Micah has real application to my own nation today. This country has really been shaken in the past ten years. Consider this whole century and the things which have actually shaken this world in which you and I live. It is not the same world I was born into. I never dreamed that I would live to see the things which have taken place in my own days. What is back of all this? Well, our God is a holy God, and He reveals His anger against sin—He will judge it. I know that a judgment day is coming in the future for sinners who will not accept Christ, but God is moving today, and I believe that we are experiencing the anger of God.

A godless nation, a nation which rejects God, must bear the consequences. We must also recognize that as individuals you and I are sinners and must come to God. This is what it means to "walk humbly with thy God." You do not come to Him boasting of what you have done. You come to Him confessing. "I'm a sinner, and I need Your salvation." You must accept His salvation, recognizing that you could not go to heaven in your own righteousness. Anselm, one of the great thinkers of the eleventh century, wrote, "I would rather go to hell without sin than go to heaven with sin." That's a great statement. That will shake you, my friend. In this day of "weak tea" theology, we need to hear strong statements like this.

3. *The God of the Bible pardons iniquity and delights in mercy.* Verse 18 says, "Who is a God like unto thee, that pardoneth iniquity, and passeth by the transgression of the remnant of his heritage? he retaineth not his anger for ever, because he delighteth in mercy." Here is where our God is wonderfully and amazingly different. He has no equal here; there is no one even in His neighborhood.

". . . who is like thee, glorious in holiness, fearful in praises, doing wonders?" (Exod. 15:11). What are some of the wonders that God does? Read Exodus 33:18–19: "And he said, I beseech thee, shew me thy glory. And he said, I will make all my goodness pass before thee, and I will proclaim the name of the LORD before thee; and will be gracious to whom I will be gracious, and will shew mercy on whom I will shew mercy." God said, "Moses, I'm going to do this for you, not because you are Moses and the leader of My people, but I'm doing this because I am gracious, because I show mercy, and I do it for everybody." All you have to do is come to Him and claim His mercy, friend; He is just that good, and there is none like Him.

Again in Exodus we read: "And the LORD descended in the cloud, and stood with him there, and proclaimed the name of the LORD. And the LORD passed by before him, and proclaimed, The LORD, The LORD God, merciful and gracious, longsuffering, and abundant in goodness and truth, Keeping mercy for thousands, forgiving iniquity and transgression and sin, and that will by no means clear the guilty . . ." (Exod. 34:5–7). My friend, how wonderful He is! God does not clear the *guilty*. "Wrong is wrong, from the moment it happens till the crack of doom," says the hero of the play, *The Great Divide*. All the angels in heaven working overtime cannot change that by a hair. But God can forgive the sinner and clear him of all charges because His holiness has been satisfied by Christ's vicarious death.

God's forgiveness is set forth in the Scripture by many figures of speech. I would like to mention just a few of them. His forgiveness is like a *debt* which has been paid. In Isaiah He says, "I, even I, am he that blotteth out thy transgressions for mine own sake, and will not remember thy sins" (Isa. 43:25). Peter said, "Repent ye therefore, and be converted, that your sins may be blotted out . . ." (Acts 3:19). On His ledger I am in debt, because there it is written, ". . . the wages of sin is death . . ." (Rom. 6:23), and ". . . in Adam all die . . ." (1 Cor. 15:22). God's forgiveness is set forth in Scripture as the healing of a *disease*. Jeremiah writes, "Return, ye backsliding children, and I will heal your backslidings . . ." (Jer. 3:22). And in Isaiah 61:1 He has promised to ". . . bind up the brokenhearted. . . ." Finally, God's forgiveness is pictured as the cleansing of a *pollution*, a *contamination*. The Scriptures tell us that ". . . according to his mercy he saved us, by the washing of regeneration, and renewing of the Holy Ghost" (Titus 3:5). And we read also, ". . . the blood of Jesus Christ his Son cleanseth us

from all sin" (1 John 1:7). How wonderful our God is!

How does God forgive? God is different for there is none like Him in forgiving. His forgiveness is very different from yours and mine. If you step on my toe in a crowd, you turn to me and say, "Pardon me, will you forgive me?" I say, "Sure," but I'm thinking that, of course, you ought to give me the money to renew the shoeshine you have just ruined! But I say that I forgive you. Another example is a letter that I received some time ago from a man who confessed that he had been talking about me behind my back. Now he had found out that he was wrong, and he asked me to forgive him. I told him, "Don't ask me for forgiveness. Simply get it straightened out with the people you talked to and with the Lord." That's all I asked of him, because I had never known about it before I received his letter. Human forgiveness is pretty easy to come by.

However, God never forgives until the debt is paid. And on the cross Christ paid the debt. He redeemed us. We are sold under sin. We today have offended the holiness of God. We are in debt to Him. We have a disease, and God is not going to take the disease of sin into heaven. But Christ paid our debt, and Christ is the one who will forgive us. He cleanses us, and He makes us acceptable in God's sight so that we might go to heaven someday.

"Who is a God like unto thee, that pardoneth iniquity, and passeth by the transgression of the remnant of his heritage? he retaineth not his anger for ever, because he delighteth in mercy." Isn't He a wonderful God? He is someday going to restore Israel to the land, not because *they* are wonderful, but because *He* is wonderful. And, my friend, I am going to heaven someday, but I am not going there because I am good or righteous—I am not. I'm going to heaven because Jesus died for me. I'm going because the debt has been paid, and there is no God like my God.

# BIBLIOGRAPHY

(Recommended for Further Study)

Feinberg, Charles L. *The Minor Prophets.* Chicago, Illinois: Moody Press, 1976.

Gaebelein, Arno C. *The Annotated Bible.* 1917. Reprint. Neptune, New Jersey: Loizeaux Brothers, 1971.

Ironside, H. A. *The Minor Prophets.* Neptune, New Jersey: Loizeaux Brothers, n.d.

Jensen, Irving L. *Minor Prophets of Judah.* Chicago, Illinois: Moody Press, 1975. (Obadiah, Joel, Micah, Nahum, Zephaniah, and Habakkuk.)

Tatford, Frederick A. *The Minor Prophets.* Minneapolis, Minnesota: Klock & Klock, n.d.

Unger, Merrill F. *Unger's Commentary on the Old Testament*, Vol. 2. Chicago, Illinois: Moody Press, 1982.

# The Book of
# NAHUM
## INTRODUCTION

As I come to each new book and chapter of the Bible, some folk kid me that I always say it is the *greatest* book or chapter. Very candidly, I must say that the little Book of Nahum is not the *greatest* in the Bible, but it is a great book, and it is in the Word of God for a very definite purpose. I dare say that very few people have ever heard a sermon from the little Book of Nahum. This book has received some attention from those who speak "the wild utterances of prophecy mongers," as Sir Robert Anderson calls them. These sensationalists would have us believe that Nahum prophesied of the automobile when in the second chapter he says that "The chariots shall rage in the streets" (Nah. 2:4). That, of course, has no reference at all to the automobile, as we will see when we come to it.

What we do have in the Book of Nahum is a remarkable prophecy, but one which seems very much out of date. To begin with, we know very little about Nahum personally, and he has just one theme, the judgment of Nineveh, the capital of the Assyrian Empire. This is all his prophecy is about, and it has already been fulfilled; so how can this book be meaningful to us today? How can it fit into our common and contemporary culture? Does Nahum have a message for us? The remarkable thing about the Word of God is that no matter where we turn we find a message for us. Some is specifically directed *to* us, but all of it is *for* us—that is, it has a message for us.

The writer is Nahum, and his name means "comforter," but the message that he gives is one of judgment. How in the world can Nahum live up to his name? How can he be a comforter? Well, it is owing to how you look at the judgment. If it is a judgment upon your enemy, one of whom you are afraid, one who dominates you, then judgment can be a comfort to you.

Nahum is identified in the first verse of the book: "The burden of Nineveh. The book of the vision of Nahum the Elkoshite." Who is an Elkoshite? Well, there are several possible identifications of the city of Elkosh. (1) There was a city of Elkosh in Assyria, a few miles north of the ruins of Nineveh. Nahum could well have lived there and prophesied to Nineveh, as Daniel did to Babylon later on. Very candidly, I do not think that is true; I

believe that the content of the book reveals that Nahum did not go to Nineveh. I do not think he was there, nor was he ever called to go there. (2) Another explanation which is offered is that there was a village by the name of Elkosh in Galilee. Jerome recorded that a guide pointed out to him such a village as the birthplace of Nahum. I had that pointed out to me also when I was over there. However, the first time this was ever pointed out was a thousand years after Nahum lived, making such a view largely traditional. Also, Dr. John Davis gives the meaning for Capernaum as "the village of Nahum." If Capernaum is a Hebrew word, then this is the evident origin, and we have no reason to believe otherwise. Nahum was either born there, or he lived there as a boy. (3) Also, down in Judah there was a place called Elkosh. Elkosh seems to have been a common name. We have certain place names in this country of which you will find one in practically every state. You will find a city of the same name in California, in Texas, and then maybe way up in Connecticut. Evidently, Elkosh was a common name like that.

It is the belief of many that what actually happened was that Nahum was born up in the northern kingdom of Israel—which would explain his great attachment to the northern kingdom—but that he later moved down to Elkosh, a place in the south of Judah. He probably went down there as a lad and was raised in the southern kingdom.

The man who wrote this prophecy evidently knew something about Sennacherib's attack upon Jerusalem. It seems to be an eyewitness account that is given in the first chapter. When Sennacherib, king of Assyria, invaded Judah during the reign of Hezekiah, Nahum was probably an eyewitness. This would mean that Nahum was a contemporary of both Isaiah and Micah, and this is the belief of some Bible expositors. I personally have not decided on any definite date at all. There are many dates which have been assigned to this book and this prophet. Dates are suggested anywhere from 720 B.C. to 636 B.C. by conservative scholars. It seems reasonable to locate Nahum about one hundred years after Jonah. He probably lived during the reign of Hezekiah and saw the destruction of the northern kingdom of Israel, and he was greatly moved by that, of course.

Nahum sounds the death knell of Nineveh. He pronounces judgment by the total destruction of Assyria, Nineveh being the capital of that nation. Nahum maintains that God is just in His judgment of this nation.

Actually, I like to study the little Books of Jonah and Nahum together because it was between 100 and 150 years before Nahum appeared on the scene that Jonah went to Nineveh with a message from God. When God told Jonah to go to Nineveh and to bring a message there, a remarkable thing happened—the entire city turned to God—100 percent. Frankly, there has never been anything quite like it in the history of the world. We simply do not seem to have anything else that could compare to an entire city, 100 percent, turning to God. How far-reaching it was in the nation I do not know, but certainly Nineveh as the capital city had a tremendous effect upon the nation, and there was a great turning to God in that day.

The question naturally arises: How did it work out? Did it last? Did this nation become a godly nation? And the answer is no—they didn't. In time the revival wore off. In time they went back to their paganism. In time they became as brutal as they had been before. This nation had had a message from God, but now here comes Nahum with another message. I do not think that Nahum actually went to Nineveh. I believe that this man lived in the southern kingdom of Israel, and I don't think he left there. But if God sent Jonah to Nineveh, why did He not send Nahum? Well, God's methods vary. God certainly is immutable—He never changes—but He does change His methods at times. He sent Jonah to Nineveh because Nineveh was a great, wicked city, but they were totally ignorant of God. When the message was brought, the city turned to God, all the way from the king on the throne to the peasant in the hovel. As a result, God spared the city. Now 100 to 150 years have gone by, and the city has relapsed and returned back to its old way. Why doesn't Nahum go? Because they have already had the light, and they've rejected it.

The Lord Jesus spoke about light that is rejected. He said, ". . . If therefore the light that is in thee be darkness, how great is that darkness!" (Matt. 6:23). How can light be darkness in anyone? Light that is darkness is the rejection of the Word of God. There are more Bibles in this country of ours than any other book; it is the best selling, but least read, book. Assyria was a nation that had had light, but what was the net result? "If therefore the light that is in thee be darkness, how great is that darkness!"

Assyria had had light—God had sent a message to them—and for awhile they turned and served the living and true God. It was a revival in the common sense of the term. It was wonderful, but it didn't last. Isn't that really the history of revivals? At the same time that France had a revolution, England had a revival under the Wesleys and Whitefield. There was a great turning to God, but how did England make out? Well, look at her today. At that time they were a first-rate nation. They were number one among the great nations of the world, but they are not number one today. They aren't number two; they aren't even number three. They are way down on the list today. What happened? They departed from the living and true God.

The first time I visited England, I asked my guide to take me to the cemetery across from Wesley's church where Wesley is buried. The guide had difficulty. He and the driver talked it over, looked at the city map, and finally wound their way through the streets of London until we arrived at the place. The guide said to me, "This is the first time I've ever brought anyone here. I think I will put it on our route and will bring people here when we take tours. I didn't know it was here." England had forgotten John Wesley. They had forgotten the great revival that took place under him. As a result, she has sunk down to a very low level for a nation which has had such a tremendous history. Those of us who had ancestors in the British Isles—whether in England, Wales, Scotland, or Ireland—have to bow our heads today in shame. We feel like weeping when we think of the greatness of that nation and how at one time they listened to the voice of God. How like Nineveh! When Nineveh was no longer listening, Nahum said, "I'm not going over there. I'm not going to waste my time because there is no point in it. They have passed the point of no return."

And has this nation of mine come to that place today? This little book has a message for us, my friend. Quite a few years ago I cut out this little clipping which reads:

A United States Senator has stated that the average life of the great civilizations of the world has been about 200 years. He goes on to say that these civilizations have progressed (if that's the right word) through the following stages:

from bondage to spiritual faith
from spiritual faith to courage
from courage to liberty
from liberty to abundance
from abundance to selfishness
from selfishness to complacency
from complacency to apathy
from apathy back to bondage

The Senator points out the interesting fact that the United States of America will be 200 years old in 12 years. Which of the above stages do you think we're in? How much longer is our civilization going to last?

This nation has now passed its two hundredth anniversary. Think about this for just a moment. Where are we today? Are we a nation of abundance? Yes, but the Lord is beginning to cut us short. "From abundance to selfishness, from selfishness to complacency"—is that a picture of us today? "From complacency to apathy"—there is an apathetic condition in our nation today. The next step, according to the senator, is "from apathy back to bondage."

This is the picture that is given of Nineveh, and this is the message of Nahum. A great world power, Assyria, with Nineveh as its capital, had a message from God. They turned to God and served God for a period of time. I do not know how long they served Him, but after 100 to 150 years had gone by, they were right back where they were before. Now God is going to judge them. The question arises: Is He right in doing it? Nahum will say that He is not only *right* in doing it, but that He is also *good* when He does it. Some folk think the Book of Nahum should be called "Ho hum"! However, Nahum is a thrilling book to study because it reveals the other side of the attributes of God. God is love, but God is also holy and righteous and good. And God still moves in the lives of nations; therefore, this book speaks right into where we are today.

# OUTLINE

I. **Justice and Goodness of God, Chapter 1:1–8**

II. **Justice and Goodness of God Demonstrated in Decision to Destroy Nineveh and to Give the Gospel, Chapter 1:9–15**

III. **Justice and Goodness of God Exhibited in Execution of His Decision to Destroy Nineveh, Chapters 2–3**
   A. Annihilation of Assyria, Chapter 2
   B. Avenging Action of God Justified, Chapter 3

# CHAPTER 1

**THEME:** *Justice and goodness of God*

The little Book of Nahum is a remarkable prophecy. The prophet has just one theme, the judgment of Nineveh, the capital of the Assyrian Empire, but we will find that he also has a meaningful message for us today.

### The burden of Nineveh. The book of the vision of Nahum the Elkoshite [Nah. 1:1].

"The burden of Nineveh"—*burden* means "judgment," as it is also used in the prophecy of Isaiah. Earlier, Jonah had brought a message to Nineveh which revealed the *love* of God, and now the message of the Book of Nahum reveals the *justice* of God—the two go together. Although God will judge a nation, He is still love, and He still loves—you cannot escape that. The thing which makes the judgment of God so frightful is the fact that God does not do it as a petulant person. He doesn't do it in a vindictive manner whatsoever. He does not do it in a spirit of revenge or of trying to get even. He does not judge because He has become angry for a moment in a sudden emotional outburst. God judges because He is just. He still loves, but He is just. Since He is just in His dealings, He must deal with sin even in the lives of those whom He loves.

Nineveh was a city that God loved—He told Jonah that. Jonah wanted the city destroyed, but God said, "And should not I spare Nineveh, that great city, wherein are more than sixscore thousand persons that cannot discern between their right hand and their left hand; and also much cattle?" (Jonah 4:11). God wanted to spare the city and the people who were in it, many of whom were little children. And God *had* spared Nineveh, but now judgment is going to fall upon this great city—this is Nahum's message. Jonah, almost a century and a half before, had brought a message from God, and Nineveh had repented. However, the repentance was transitory. God has patiently given this new generation opportunity to repent (see v. 3), but the day of grace now ends and the moment of doom comes. In Nahum 3:19 we read, "There is no healing of thy bruise; thy wound is grievous: all that hear the bruit [news] of thee shall clap the hands over thee: for upon whom hath not thy wickedness passed continually?" In other words, Nineveh has come to a place where there is no healing for her people.

I believe that for a nation and for an individual it is possible to continue in sin until you cross over a mark. I do not know where that mark is—I don't pretend to be able to say when this takes place—but there is such a place. When you pass over that mark, it is not that the grace of God cannot reach you but that you cannot reach God for the simple reason that you have come to the place where you are hardened and in a state of unbelief which cannot be changed. This can be true of a nation, and it can be true of an individual.

As you consider the things which are happening today, you are apt to be discouraged. I am sure that many of God's people are disturbed today. I believe that this is the reason we have had such an interest in prophecy. The wilder the prophetic teachers are, the more popular they seem to be. They are coming up with all kinds of interpretations. The explanation is that God's people, ignorant of the Word of God, are desperately reaching out because of the things which are happening today. The Lord Himself said, "Men's hearts [will be] failing them for fear, and for looking after those things which are coming on the earth: for the powers of heaven shall be shaken" (Luke 21:26). We are at that state for sure; we've come into that particular orbit today. These things are disturbing to us, but, my friend, let us understand that God is still running the affairs of this world. He is still in charge. It hasn't slipped out from His hands. God is not sitting on the edge of His throne, biting His fingernails. He is not nervous today about what is happening. God is carrying out His plan and purpose, and He is overruling the sin of man. This should be very comforting to the child of God in this day.

Assyria had served God's purpose and is now to be destroyed. The destruction of Nineveh, according to the details given in this written prophecy, is almost breathtaking. This is a message, therefore, of comfort to a people who live in fear of a powerful and godless nation: God will destroy any godless nation. All you need do is to pick up your history book and start reading at the beginning of written history. You will find that every great world power went down, and they went down at a time when they were given over to wine, women, and song. When a nation reaches that place, you can be sure that it is on the skids and will soon pass out into the limbo of the lost. That is where all the former great nations of the world are today.

Where is the United States today? We are on the way down, my friend. It is a nice ride while we are having it. Dr. J. Gresham Machen said years ago, "America today is going downhill with a godly ancestry." America, which has had a godly ancestry, is going downhill on a toboggan. And Dr. Machen added, "God pity America when we reach the bottom of the hill." How close are we to the bottom of the hill? I'm no prophet nor the son of a prophet. I'm just a poor preacher, and all I can say is that it seems to me like we're getting very close to the bottom of the hill. The reason that the Book of Nahum is such a remarkable prophecy is that it speaks right into our own situation today.

"The book of the vision of Nahum the Elkoshite." This is all that is known of the writer of this book, and I have discussed this at some length in the Introduction. Nahum was apparently born in the northern kingdom of Israel, and that was his native country; but he moved to the southern part of Judah sometime when he was very young. He had a great concern for the northern kingdom, and he apparently was alive when it was carried away into captivity by Assyria. His message is of the judgment that is coming upon Nineveh.

> **God is jealous, and the LORD revengeth; the LORD revengeth, and is furious; the LORD will take vengeance on his adversaries, and he reserveth wrath for his enemies [Nah. 1:2].**

*Jealous*, according to Webster's dictionary, means "exacting exclusive devotion." God is a jealous God, and He demands that His people worship Him alone. When any people, no matter who they are, turn to idolatry or turn to sin (all that which is contrary to God), and when they give themselves to it, God is jealous. I hear folk say, "Well, there is just a little bit of difference between the jealousy of God and the jealousy of man." There is not as much difference as you think there is, my friend. In Exodus 20:3–6 we read: "Thou shalt have no other gods before me. Thou shalt not make unto thee any graven image, or any likeness of any thing that is in heaven above, or that is in the earth beneath, or that is in the water under the earth: Thou shalt not bow down thyself to them, nor serve them: for I the LORD thy God am a jealous God, visiting the iniquity of the fathers upon the children unto the third and fourth generation of them

that hate me; And shewing mercy unto thousands of them that love me, and keep my commandments."

God loves you. It does not make any difference who you are, you cannot keep Him from loving you. You can, however, get into a place where you will not experience the love of God. When you put up an umbrella of sin, the sunshine of God's love will not fall on you, but it is still there for you. You can put up the umbrella of indifference. You can put up the umbrella of turning your back upon Him and not doing His will. There are several different umbrellas you can put up that will keep the love of God from shining upon you, but you cannot keep Him from loving you.

Since God loves you, He is actually jealous of you. That means that He wants *you*. Actually, God doesn't want what you possess. We preachers are always asking you for what you have. I wish that I didn't ever have to mention giving—frankly, I don't *like* to. If God's people would just give enough to cover our radio broadcasting expenses, you would never hear me mention it. But God doesn't want what you've got—He wants *you*. And He's jealous when you give yourself, your time, and your substance to other things. When you give yourself to sin, God is jealous.

I once heard a woman say, "I have a very wonderful husband. He's not jealous of me." Well, I don't think that what she said was a compliment at all. We're living in a day when people are supposed to be broad-minded, especially about this matter of sex. They argue that it's all right for a woman to give herself to the first man who comes along. May I say to you, my friend, if you are that type of woman, you will never get a good husband because the good husband is one who is going to love you and want you above everything else. And he won't want to share you with anybody. If you say that you don't have a jealous husband, I feel sorry for you, because you do not have a good relationship.

God very frankly says, "I'm a jealous God. I want you. I don't want to share you with the sin of the world and with the Devil's crowd and with idolatry. I don't want to share you— I want you to belong to Me." There is nothing wrong with God's saying that He is jealous, and Nahum says, "God is jealous." I'm glad that He is.

Any good wife will say, "I don't want to share my husband with anybody else. He is mine. He belongs to me." This is something which is pretty important today but which the world has forgotten. It is no wonder that in

Southern California we have more divorces than marriages. Of course that is what has happened, because people are playing a little game. You used to find the harlots in the brothels; but today it is called "consecutive harlotry," which means that you take one partner at a time, live with him for a little while, and then move on to another. It adds up to the same thing, however. My friend, if you are going to be loved, and if you love, there will be a measure of jealousy in the relationship—there has to be if it is a real love.

"The LORD revengeth; the LORD revengeth, and is furious." The correct translation is not "revengeth," as it is in our Authorized Version—rather, it should be *avengeth*. There is a great difference between the two words. ". . . Vengeance is mine; I will repay, saith the Lord" (Rom. 12:19). God says to you and me, "Don't you indulge in vengeance because, to begin with, you will never exercise it in the right way. Turn it over to Me. I handle it without any heat of anger. I handle it in justice. I will do the right thing. And I know all the issues and side issues—I know everything about it."

The Lord avengeth; and, whether we like it or not, anything God does is right. We need to get that fixed in our minds and, on the other end of the stick, we need to recognize that you and I are just little creatures who really don't know very much—even the smartest ones don't. Frankly, I hate to say this, but I have quit listening to newscasts and talk programs on which they interview some egghead who is supposed to know something. I've discovered that most of these folk, as far as knowing what really is going on in this world, are ignoramuses who are just talking. We ought to recognize that we don't know much and that whatever God does is *right*. If you don't think so, you are wrong. God is not wrong—you are wrong. I wonder if you are willing to take that position. If you're not, my friend, you're in trouble as far as God is concerned because there are many things He is not going to tell you or me about. He is simply going to go ahead and do them. He is running this universe His way. Oh, I know that we get a few power-hungry human beings, but they don't hang around long. Hitler didn't last long and and neither did Mussolini nor Stalin. The others who are on the front page of our newspapers today will be in obituary notices in a few days—it won't be long. May I say to you, God is still on the throne, and He is still running things.

God is "furious." God does not take any delight in the sin of man. God hates sin, and He is furious at it. "The LORD will take vengeance on his adversaries, and he reserveth wrath for his enemies." God is glorified when He judges a nation, as we see especially in Ezekiel 38–39. When Assyria went down, God was glorified in that. They were a brutal, hated, sinful nation, and God brought them down to wrack and ruin and into the debris and dust of the earth. He is glorified when He does things like that. Maybe you don't like it, but the Word of God says that that is the way He moves. I would suggest that you get yourself reconciled to the way God does things, because that is the way they are going to be done.

In verse 3 Nahum puts down a great principle by which God not only judged Assyria (and Nineveh, the capital, in particular), but also the way that God judges the world and will judge the world in the future.

**The LORD is slow to anger, and great in power, and will not at all acquit the wicked: the LORD hath his way in the whirlwind and in the storm, and the clouds are the dust of his feet [Nah. 1:3].**

"The LORD is slow to anger." Nahum makes this very clear. You see, God had sent Jonah to Nineveh to tell them that they were to be destroyed because of their awful sin. They were known as probably the most brutal people in the ancient world, and God said that judgment would come to them. But the entire city of Nineveh repented and turned to God at that time. Obviously, the message of Jonah penetrated the entire empire, and there was a great change. We would say that a great revival rose up. However, it didn't last very long. It has been characteristic of the great waves of revival which have come that they have never lasted permanently. The Wesleyan revival had tremendous impact upon England and this country, as well as side effects upon other nations, but it was of brief duration. There has been some carry-over from it, of course, even down to the present hour. This is true also of the great revivals under Moody in this country, when entire cities moved toward God. Nahum says that God is slow to anger, but this great city of Nineveh has now turned back to its old ways. One hundred years after Jonah, Nahum comes to say, "The clock has struck twelve, and time has run out. There is no longer any delay. Judgment is coming."

"The LORD . . . will not at all acquit the wicked." The justice of God is seen in His judgment because He is slow to anger. It took Him one hundred years to get around to executing judgment against this city, and He is just and righteous in doing it. He is not going to let the wicked off. Never will He let the wicked off unless they turn to Him. Unless they accept Christ as their Savior because He paid the penalty for their sins, they will have to be judged for their sins. God is not going to let them off—He is just and righteous.

You see, the forgiveness of God is different from our forgiveness. When somebody does us wrong, we say, "I forgive you"—and that's it. A penalty has not been paid. Our forgiveness is generally for something that is just a trifle, although it could be a matter of some importance. But when God forgives, the penalty has already been paid. God is the Judge of this earth. He is not only its Creator, He is not only running it, but He is also the *moral* ruler of this universe. And God is not a crooked judge. You cannot slip something under the table to get Him to let you off easy. You cannot tell Him that you belong to a certain family, that your father is very influential and will be able to get you off. Nor can you say you are wealthy and will see that the Judge loses His job, nor that you will pay Him just a little extra to be lenient with you. You cannot deal with God like that.

God must judge the wicked, and we are all told that the heart of man is desperately wicked—not just a little wicked, but desperately wicked (see Jer. 17:9). You and I do not really know the depths of the iniquity that is in our hearts; we do not know what we are capable of. Now God cannot acquit the wicked; therefore, if we are going to be acquitted, someone must pay the penalty. That is the reason He has provided a Redeemer for us. When an individual or a nation turns its back on God's redemption provided now in Christ, then judgment must follow—there is no other alternative.

"The LORD hath his way in the whirlwind and in the storm, and the clouds are the dust of his feet." God today moves even in nature. The storms which come are under His control, and they serve His purpose. So-called Mother Nature doesn't really have anything to do with it. Mother Nature does what *He* tells Mother Nature to do. Our God is the Creator, and He is the Redeemer, and He is also the Judge. He's running things, friend. Just leave it in His hands, and rest in Him today because He is good, He is gracious, and He is the Savior.

**He rebuketh the sea, and maketh it dry, and drieth up all the rivers: Bashan languisheth, and Carmel, and the flower of Lebanon languisheth [Nah. 1:4].**

"He rebuketh the sea, and maketh it dry, and drieth up all the rivers." God had already shown His power to do this—He dried up the Red Sea and the Jordan River.

Bashan, Carmel, and Lebanon are the three fertile areas in that land. Carmel is actually the valley of Esdraelon, and Megiddo was the main city there. This is one of the most fertile spots on the topside of the earth. When you go farther north, along the coast of Lebanon all the way from Beirut down to the ruins of old Tyre, you see beautiful country. In the spring of the year, you can see the fruit trees blooming and in the distance the Anti-Lebanons covered with snow. The fruit trees—apricots, peaches, cherries, bananas, and citrus fruit—everything is grown there, and the land is very fertile.

Nahum says that a drought is to come. I am sure there are many of you who remember the dust storms in this country in the 1930s. I have always felt that those storms were a judgment from God. If there had been any kind of a revival at that time, I am confident we would never have had to fight World War II or to have been involved in all that we have since then. But unfortunately, that judgment from God carried no message for this country at that time.

**The mountains quake at him, and the hills melt, and the earth is burned at his presence, yea, the world, and all that dwell therein [Nah. 1:5].**

He is the Creator, and He's also the Preserver of this universe—He's the One who holds it together.

"The mountains quake at him, and the hills melt" refers, of course, to earthquakes and volcanic eruptions. You can hold Him responsible for anything that takes place, for the floods and the earthquakes that come. But don't hold Him responsible for the people who are killed at that time, because man has been given an intelligence which tells him that he ought not to build too close to a river due to the danger of a flood. Maybe those of us who live here in Southern California ought to listen to Him. We are told that an earthquake is coming, and that is probably true. The San Andreas fault runs very close to where I live, but if an earthquake comes and a loved one of mine is slain by it, I am not going to cry out to God that He is the one who killed him. No— God is not responsible. We would be responsible. We know better. We probably ought to move to another location; but very frankly, my entire family likes Southern California, so we're going to stay right here and take the chance. God does control nature, but you cannot say that He is to blame when these great tragedies take place. Man is responsible for them. He ought not to get too close to a river, and he ought to stay away from where he knows there are going to be earthquakes.

**Who can stand before his indignation? and who can abide in the fierceness of his anger? his fury is poured out like fire, and the rocks are thrown down by him [Nah. 1:6].**

Man has learned that you cannot stand up against nature. Victor Hugo wrote three great novels. He wrote *Les Misérables* to show that society is the enemy of man; he wrote *The Hunchback of Notre Dame* to show that religion is the enemy of man; and he wrote *The Toilers of the Sea* to show that nature is the enemy of man. Well, it is owing to how man approaches each of these. Religion has been an enemy of man. Society is the enemy of man—this civilization today is no friend of grace, I can assure you of that. It is true that nature can be an enemy of man, but it can also be his friend. The issue is that if you are going to try to fight against nature, you're fighting a losing battle. This is what Victor Hugo tried to show in his novel.

"Who can stand before his indignation? and who can abide in the fierceness of his anger?" This question was directed to the people of Nineveh who had rejected the mercy of this all-powerful God. Do *you* have the answer to that question? I'd like to ask that of you if you are unsaved. Maybe you are depending upon your own righteousness and goodness. Do you really believe that you can stand in the presence of a holy God who absolutely hates sin and intends to judge it? Are you able to stand in His holy presence?

The very brilliant Oxford don, C. S. Lewis, wrote a story in which he tells about a bus trip that was run from hell to heaven. It was the sort of tour in which those who were in hell could take a bus trip to heaven. The bus was filled and, when it arrived in heaven, the driver parked the bus in a parking lot (I'm sure there is plenty of parking space up there). The driver told everyone on the bus,

"At four o'clock this afternoon, the bus is going to leave and head for home." Home just happened to be hell. And at four o'clock that afternoon, the bus was filled—everyone was back. The bus driver told them, "If you want to stay, you can stay." Why didn't they stay? It was because they had found out they had no place in heaven. One of the great saints of the past put it this way: "I would rather go to hell without sin than go to heaven with sin."

"Who can stand before his indignation?" If you don't have a Savior, how are you going to stand as a sinner in the presence of a holy God? Do you think that you've got a chance? You don't have a ghost of a chance, my friend. You cannot stand there without a Savior. To be able to stand in His presence is what it means to be accepted into the beloved and to be in Christ. This is a tremendous principle that Nahum is putting down here. God *must* judge sin. There is something radically wrong with God if He doesn't judge sin.

Nahum's description of the power and the anger of God was to reassure the people of Judah of the protection of their all-powerful God when Assyria would invade their land.

**The LORD is good, a strong hold in the day of trouble; and he knoweth them that trust in him [Nah. 1:7].**

"The LORD is good." Let's keep that in mind. Remember that the psalmist said, "O give thanks unto the LORD, for he is good: for his mercy endureth for ever. Let the redeemed of the LORD say so . . ." (Ps. 107:1–2). If the redeemed don't say so, nobody's going to say so. So I am going to say so: *God is good.* God is good, friend—that's wonderful to know. I do not know who you are, where you are, or how you are, but I do know that God loves you and He wants to save you. If you are not saved, it is simply because you will not come to Him, for He *can* save you and He *will* save you. God is good—that is an axiom of Scripture and an axiom of life. "The LORD is good."

"A strong hold in the day of trouble." Are you having any trouble? Do you want to get to a good shelter? The Lord is that shelter which you need.

"And he knoweth them that trust in him." I'm very happy that I'm not going to get lost in the shuffle, that I won't get lost in the multitudes. As I travel from city to city, I sometimes think that everyone has moved to the West Coast. I get on one of our freeways here, and I think, *My, how many people there are!* But then I go back to Dallas, Texas, and I think that everyone has followed me from

California to Texas! The crowds are everywhere. I go to Florida or to New York City, and it seems the people have followed me there. I have never seen such crowds in my life! I went to Europe several years ago and found that the people were there also! The multitudes which are in the Orient almost shock us. And in Egypt, in the Arab countries, and in Turkey there are multitudes of people. It causes me to think, *My, I hope the Lord remembers that my name is Vernon McGee and that I have trusted Him.* I am very happy that the Scripture says, "He knoweth them that trust in him." My friend, He doesn't need a computer to record your name. Actually, He has you written on His heart; He's written your name on the palms of His hands. He knows you—He knows those who have trusted Him.

**But with an overrunning flood he will make an utter end of the place thereof, and darkness shall pursue his enemies [Nah. 1:8].**

The Lord will overwhelm and destroy the Assyrians. "An overrunning flood" pictures a river that is overflowing its banks and causing devastation as it moves. It is believed that this refers to the invading army of the Babylonians which overcame Nineveh. The Greek historian Ctesias of the fifth century B.C. records that the Babylonian army was able to invade Nineveh when the Tigris River suddenly overflowed and washed away the floodgates of the city and the foundations of the palace.

"Darkness shall pursue his enemies" raises a question in my mind regarding the place of permanent punishment. There is more said in Scripture about darkness being the lot of the lost than there is about fire. Darkness is mentioned here—"and darkness shall pursue his enemies." Even the Lord Jesus used the term: "But the children of the kingdom shall be cast out into outer darkness: there shall be weeping and gnashing of teeth" (Matt. 8:12; see also Matt. 22:13). Literal fire could only affect the physical, never the spiritual. But, oh, the fires of a conscience that has been suddenly alerted to the awful thing one did in rejecting Christ and in not doing the things he should have done. Think of the darkness of a lost eternity! Think of not being able to see where you are going at all. Darkness, to me, is a better and more fearful description of hell than fire is. That may be a new thought for you, and I would urge you to pursue it in the Word of God.

## GOD'S DECISION TO DESTROY NINEVEH AND TO GIVE THE GOSPEL

**What do ye imagine against the LORD? he will make an utter end: affliction shall not rise up the second time [Nah. 1:9].**

"What do ye imagine against the LORD?" Nahum puts this question directly to the Assyrian invaders. In effect he is asking, as Dr. Charles Feinberg has stated it, "Can you cope with such a God as Israel has?"

"He will make an utter end"—that is, the Assyrian power will be completely destroyed. It will give you a better understanding of this to read the fulfillment in the historical account in Isaiah 37.

"Affliction shall not rise up the second time." In other words, Nineveh will not be given a second chance. They have had their last chance. They've crossed over that invisible line—I do not know where it is, but it is there somewhere, and you can step over it in your rejection of God. This does not mean that the grace of God could not reach you but that you can no longer reach it after you have come to that particular point.

**For while they be folden together as thorns, and while they are drunken as drunkards, they shall be devoured as stubble fully dry [Nah. 1:10].**

"For while they be folden together as thorns" probably describes the Assyrian army, which presented such a united front that they seemed like entangled thorns—impossible to break through.

"While they are drunken as drunkards, they shall be devoured as stubble fully dry." God would completely destroy them. The fulfillment of this is recorded in Isaiah 37:36–37.

I would say this especially to young people today: Make your decision for Christ while you are young and have a sharp mind. You can keep playing around with intellectualism (which I tried in college and almost got detoured), or you can play around as many are doing with drugs and alcohol, but Nahum says that the day will come when you will stumble around like a drunkard. If you stumble around like a drunkard, you cannot make a decision. A man who had been drinking called me the other night from back East. I refused to talk with him. I told him, "The liquor is speaking and not you. When you are willing to sober up, call me, and I'll be glad to talk with you, but I will not talk to liquor." May I say to you, Nineveh had reached the place where they could make no decision.

Along with the other minor prophets, Nahum makes a contribution to God's philosophy of government and His manner of dealing with individuals and with nations. The point Nahum is going to make is that whether you believe it or not, whether you can understand it or not, God is just and God is good when He judges a nation or an individual. God is still the God of love. He loves the lost. He is, as the apostle John tells us, ". . . the propitiation [the mercy seat] for our sins: and not for ours only, but also for the sins of the whole world" (1 John 2:2).

Men are lost because they are sinners, and they are saved because they accept the overture of salvation that God extends to them. God will get that invitation to any individual on the topside of this earth who will accept it. I have come to believe that we may see a turning to God. I do not mean in great numbers, but I believe there will be a turning to God in response to the invitation given to every people on the topside of this earth. It looks to me right now that radio broadcasting will be the means of bringing that invitation to the unreached.

Nahum is going to be very extreme in what he says. God is going to judge Nineveh, and He is just and righteous in doing it. But God is love also. His judgment is actually an act of His love—that is very difficult for us to comprehend, but it is absolutely true.

**There is one come out of thee, that imagineth evil against the LORD, a wicked counsellor [Nah. 1:11].**

Nahum says now that there had come up against Judah this enemy—the enemy is Assyria with its capital city of Nineveh. I think that there is agreement among all conservative Bible expositors that the invader that is spoken of here as "a wicked counsellor" was Sennacherib, the king of Assyria. This invasion by Sennacherib is recorded three times in Scripture: in 2 Kings 18–19; 2 Chronicles 32; and also in Isaiah 36–37. When God says something three times, we ought to stop, look, and listen. When He says it once, that should be enough. When He says it twice— sometimes He says, "Verily, verily, I say unto you"—it is extra important. But when He repeats something three times, you can just put it down that it is all-important.

Nahum is referring now to this wicked counselor who had come against Jerusalem.

We read in the historical accounts that Sennacherib sent Rabshakeh against Jerusalem with the great army of Assyria. Rabshakeh threatened Hezekiah, the king of Judah, and Hezekiah was almost frightened to death by it all. I think that poor man probably couldn't sleep at night during that period of time. However, Hezekiah went into the temple and called upon God, and then the prophet Isaiah brought the message that Rabshakeh would not even shoot an arrow into the city of Jerusalem. Instead, he had to withdraw because of Assyria's campaign against Egypt in which Sennacherib needed his reinforcements. Then God Himself *destroyed* the army of the Assyrians! Assyria was greatly feared in Judah since during that period they had taken the northern kingdom of Israel into captivity and had dealt with them in a very brutal manner.

**Thus saith the LORD; Though they be quiet, and likewise many, yet thus shall they be cut down, when he shall pass through. Though I have afflicted thee, I will afflict thee no more [Nah. 1:12].**

This is a rather remarkable verse, and we do not want to miss the point that is here. This expression, "Though they be quiet, and likewise many," does not quite make sense to me. What is it that God is saying here?

I know most of the men who worked as editors on *The New Scofield Reference Bible*, and all of them are just as human as you and I are. They are subject to mistakes and not one of them, as far as I know, feels that their notes were inspired. However, every now and then, they have really put in a helpful note. Their note on this verse is an example of how archaeology has confirmed many things in Scripture that we would not have known or understood otherwise, thus revealing the accuracy of the Word of God. *The New Scofield Reference Bible* (pp. 950–951) uses the following note on verse 12:

In the context the expression "quiet, and likewise many," although a literal translation of the Hebrew, does not seem to make much sense. Actually the Hebrew here represents a transliteration of a long-forgotten Assyrian legal formula. Excavation in the ruins of ancient Nineveh, buried since 612 B.C., has brought to light thousands of ancient Assyrian tablets, dozens of which contain this Assyrian legal formula. It proves, on investigation, to indicate joint and several responsibility for carrying out an obligation. Nahum quotes the LORD as using this Assyrian formula in speaking to the Assyrians, saying in effect, "Even though your entire nation joins as one person to resist me, nevertheless I shall overcome you." As the words would have been equally incomprehensible to the later Hebrew copyists, their retention is striking evidence of the care of the scribes in copying exactly what they found in the manuscripts, and testifies to God's providential preservation of the Bible text.

Therefore, you can see that God used an Assyrian legal formula in expressing what He wanted to say. He was talking about Assyria, and He wanted them to understand what He was saying. When we look at this verse in light of what archaeology has discovered today, God was saying something that made sense to the Assyrians although it does not make sense to us today. When the Hebrew scholars later came along, they didn't know what this meant either, but they translated it literally into English because they believed in the plenary, verbal inspiration of the Scriptures. Thank God for that!

This leads me to say that this is one of the reasons I cannot approve of a lot of these so-called modern translations. They are not translations at all because many of them were done by men who do not believe that the Bible is the Word of God. Other men, although they believe it is the Word of God, have wanted to put it into a form that modern man could understand. I rather disagree with that method. I am very happy that *The Living Bible* calls itself "a paraphrased text." I would say concerning *The Living Bible* that it is a bad translation, but in many places it is a marvelous paraphrased text. If you will treat it as a paraphrase, that's fine, but do not believe that you are getting the literal text of Scripture.

This passage here in Nahum reveals that, although you might not understand something in Scripture, God says, "You take it as I have given it to you, and you will find out someday what it means—that is, if you will work and study hard enough." The trouble is that we are trying to make the Word of God like pabulum, and we are trying to spoon-feed a bunch of babies who are too lazy to really study the Word of God. Although I certainly am one who is accused of making the Word of God simple, I do believe that there ought to be a real reverence for the text of Scripture. I'm no Bible worshiper, I'm no bibliophile, by any means, but I do believe that there should be a reverence for the text of Scripture.

I have spent time on this verse because it contains this expression that I did not understand until this archaeological discovery was made. Archaeology has done a great deal of work yonder at the ancient city of Nineveh. The tell of Nineveh, across the Tigris River from the modern city of Mosul, was first excavated in the last century.

**For now will I break his yoke from off thee, and will burst thy bonds in sunder [Nah. 1:13].**

This seemed impossible in the day when Nahum wrote it because the nation of Assyria was to continue for a long time yet. But God said at that time, "I am going to break the yoke of this nation."

He also said:

**And the LORD hath given a commandment concerning thee, that no more of thy name be sown: out of the house of thy gods will I cut off the graven image and the molten image: I will make thy grave; for thou art vile [Nah. 1:14].**

What God says to Nineveh is harsh. He says, "I'm going to bury you." Nikita Khrushchev wasn't the first one who used that expression; he said that to the people of the United States, and it seemed very terrifying to us, naturally. Actually, Khrushchev was using a biblical expression, but he didn't know it. God said to Nineveh, "I'm going to bury you, and when I bury you, you'll go out of business as a nation." When was the last time you saw an Assyrian running around? There are not many, and they have no nation today. God said to them, "I'll bury you," and that is what He did.

He also said, "I'm going to get rid of your gods, that is, your idolatry." It was the Medes and the Babylonians who eventually came and destroyed the city of Nineveh in 612 B.C. The Assyrian idolatry was destroyed by the Medes who were a monotheistic people and did not worship idols. They were really iconoclasts, and they broke up the idolatry of Assyria.

**Behold upon the mountains the feet of him that bringeth good tidings, that publisheth peace! O Judah, keep thy solemn feasts, perform thy vows: for the wicked shall no more pass through thee; he is utterly cut off [Nah. 1:15].**

God is saying through Nahum, "Don't leave Me. Don't withdraw from the Mosaic system. Don't give it up, because I intend to destroy your enemy and to send to you the Messiah, who will bring tidings of great joy."

Nahum says this in reference to Assyria, and you will find that Isaiah actually uses the same expression in Isaiah 52:7, where it is amplified: "How beautiful upon the mountains are the feet of him that bringeth good tidings, that publisheth peace; that bringeth good tidings of good, that publisheth salvation; that saith unto Zion, Thy God reigneth!" Isaiah spoke this in reference to the destruction of Babylon as he wrote to the southern kingdom of Judah. Nahum, writing to the northern kingdom, says the same thing but concerning Assyria. Then notice that Paul quotes this in his Epistle to the Romans: "For whosoever shall call upon the name of the Lord shall be saved. How then shall they call on him in whom they have not believed? and how shall they believe in him of whom they have not heard? and how shall they hear without a preacher? And how shall they preach, except they be sent? as it is written, How beautiful are the feet of them that preach the gospel of peace, and bring glad tidings of good things!" (Rom. 10:13–15).

I think Nahum was the first to say this and then Isaiah. Finally, Paul quotes Isaiah and makes a different application of it in the section of his epistle that refers to Israel, that is, in the dispensational section of Romans. Paul is arguing there that God is not through with the nation Israel and that in the future there will again come to them the good tidings of great joy. But it is also a worldwide message that is applicable to today. Paul writes, "For whosoever shall call upon the name of the Lord shall be saved" (Rom. 10:13).

But how will people hear without somebody bringing the message to them? The messengers must be sent, and I believe that God will do the sending. Isaiah wrote, "How beautiful upon the mountains are the feet of him that bringeth good tidings . . ." (Isa. 52:7). That's not because they have beautiful feet, but because they have come to bring the message of the gospel. They may have traveled by boat, or they may have come by plane, or they may have come by radio, but they have come bringing the message. In our radio ministry we believe that the gospel should begin here at our own Jerusalem, and therefore we are attempting to continue to reach this country with the Word of God as well as we can. But we want also to go right to the ends of the earth via radio. Very frankly, I want my feet to be beautiful, and I want my feet to be ". . . shod with the preparation of the gospel of peace" (Eph. 6:15). I want to walk all over this earth by radio, and I want to reach out to folk with the Good News today.

This is a marvelous way in which the Spirit of God uses Scripture. You get a good course in hermeneutics (the methods of interpretation of Scripture) when you read the little Book of Nahum. Nahum tells you how to interpret the Word of God. He has already shown us that we are to take it literally whether we understand it or not. There is an explanation, and the trouble is not with the Word of God; the trouble is with us when we do not understand it. Then we have also seen that God made direct interpretation of this Scripture to one nation at one time, to another nation at another time, and it now has a worldwide application today.

# CHAPTER 2

***THEME:*** *Execution of God's decision to destroy Nineveh*

In chapters 2–3 we are going to see the justice and goodness of God exhibited in the execution of His decision to destroy Nineveh. God didn't just talk about destroying Nineveh—God did it, and He did it in a very remarkable way.

## ANNIHILATION OF ASSYRIA

In chapter 2 Nahum prophesies a frightful judgment upon Assyria, and history testifies to its literal fulfillment. God has made it very clear in chapter 1 where He says, "I will make thy grave; for thou art vile" (Nah. 1:14); in other words, He says to Assyria, "I'm going to bury you." And, believe me, that is exactly what happened.

**He that dasheth in pieces is come up before thy face: keep the munition, watch the way, make thy loins strong, fortify thy power mightily [Nah. 2:1].**

This refers to the Medo-Babylonian forces that came against Assyria and destroyed it in 612 B.C. under the leadership of Cyaxares and Nabopolassar. It is very interesting that Nahum, with biting sarcasm, tells Assyria, "You sure had better fortify yourself." The Assyrians spared no one, and they thought that their capital was impregnable and that they could withstand any kind of a judgment. But God is saying to this nation, "You are going to be destroyed."

**For the LORD hath turned away the excellency of Jacob, as the excellency of Israel: for the emptiers have emptied them out, and marred their vine branches [Nah. 2:2].**

Nahum is saying that the time has come for Assyria's judgment because God has completed the judgment of His own people and intends to restore them. The mention of both "Jacob" and "Israel" is a reference to both the southern kingdom of Judah and the northern kingdom of Israel. "The emptiers" are the enemies of God's people, especially the nation of Assyria. The "vine branches" is probably a symbol of the nation of Israel (see Ps. 80:8–16).

This chapter is Nahum's detailed prophecy, which today is an accurate, historical record of what took place about one hundred years after Nahum. It speaks of the finality of the judgment of God upon the nation of Assyria; it speaks of the fact that Assyria would never make a comeback. Assyria never did make a comeback, and she never will. According to the Word of God, Babylon will resurge as well as some other nations. But Assyria, one of the great powers in the ancient world, will not make a comeback—God makes that very, very clear.

The capture of Nineveh is described here in rather lurid terms. This passage reveals just how terrible it was, and you could write over this chapter, ". . . whatsoever a man soweth, that shall he also reap" (Gal. 6:7). Assyria had been a very brutal nation, one of the most brutal nations the world has ever seen. For example, one of the things which the Assyrians did to an enemy was to bury him out in the desert sand right up to his chin. Then they would put a thong through his tongue and leave him out in the hot blazing sun, first to go mad, and then to die. That was one of the "nice little things" the Assyrians came up with. They also had several other little surprises for their enemies. It is said that when the Assyrians were on the march, in many places an entire community which lay in the line of their march would commit suicide rather than fall into the hands of brutal Assyrians. They were dreaded and feared in the ancient world. We find here in the Book of Nahum that Assyria is again beginning to move, but now their movement is in retreat. They are no longer the aggressor, but the Medes and the Babylonians are coming up against them.

**The shield of his mighty men is made red, the valiant men are in scarlet: the chariots shall be with flaming torches in the day of his preparation, and the fir trees shall be terribly shaken [Nah. 2:3].**

"The shield of his mighty men is made red." This does not mean that their shields were made red with blood as some have suggested. The Assyrians were especially fond of the color of red, or scarlet. In all of their art, the color red is frequently found, and they evidently were very much interested in it. They made everything red. Some scholars believe that they used copper shields and that the reflection of the sunlight on the copper appeared red. Why did they do this? It is believed that they did this to frighten their enemies. As you well know, in warfare you intend to do as much bluffing as you do fighting. You want to frighten your enemies as much as you possibly can.

In World War II, when the United States issued a warning before the atom bomb was dropped, the Japanese thought that America was bluffing. That was one time when we were not bluffing, but they did not pay any attention to our warning at all. Today there are many who are using the crying towel, who flagellate this nation, declaring that we are guilty of this awful thing. I personally do not feel that our nation should go into sackcloth and ashes because of what we did at that time. It was an awful, horrible thing, but after all, war is a very awful, horrible thing. Our boys were being slain, and we were not winning the war by any means. The dropping of the bomb was what brought the war to an end, and my feeling is that we were justified in it. But I am also very frank to say that we see God's principle working out here in the Book of Nahum, that this enemy who was so brutal reaped exactly what they sowed. I do not think it will be any different with the United States. We happened to be the first ones to drop an atom bomb, and I am not sure that God is going to forget that.

The whole point is that in warfare you do attempt to bluff your enemy, and that is probably the reason the Assyrians used the color red. "The valiant men are in scarlet"—again we have the color red, you see. The Assyrians had uniforms which were red.

"The chariots shall be with flaming torches in the day of his preparation, and the fir trees shall be terribly shaken." This refers to the armor that was on the chariots and the way in which they were built. The Assyrian chariots were not built of wood like the chariots you see in the museum in Cairo, Egypt. The Egyptians used a great deal of wood in building their chariots, but apparently the Assyrians were the ones who got the latest model in chariots. They were sort of the General Motors of chariot building.

**The chariots shall rage in the streets, they shall justle one against another in the broad ways: they shall seem like torches, they shall run like the lightnings [Nah. 2:4].**

Verse 4 will illustrate to us a method of interpretation of Scripture which is entirely wrong. Let me just say that Nahum is talking here about the battle between the chariots of the Assyrians and the chariots of the enemy.

What happened was that when the enemy came against Assyria, they faced the well-defended city of Nineveh. Diodorus Siculus, a Greek historian, tells us that Nineveh had fifteen hundred towers, each of which was two hundred feet high. But at the time of the siege, the Tigris River rose up and flooded, and it took out an entire section of the wall of the city. The river did what the enemy could not do—it breached the walls of Nineveh. Then the enemy was able to come in and penetrate the city itself. They opened the canals used for irrigation and thus flooded the palace. This is the way in which the enemy was able to take the city. The breach in the wall was so great that the chariots of the enemy could get in, and what is described in verse 4 is nothing in the world but the chariot battle which took place at that time.

There is a type of interpretation of prophecy which I deplore, and I regret that at the present hour we see so much of it. For example, there are those who say that this verse is a prophecy of the automobile! That is what Sir Robert Anderson calls "the wild utterances of prophecy mongers." There is a great interest in prophecy today because great world events and world crises are taking place. But we need to recognize that we can become fanatical and go overboard concerning prophecy. I believe it was Winston Churchill who said, "A fanatic is one who cannot change his mind, and he won't change the subject." Some folk today are just dwelling on prophecy (after all, it is a limited subject), and they become fanatical in their interpretations.

My friend, this prophecy has nothing in the world to do with the automobile. I do not think you could even make that kind of application of it for the very simple reason that automobiles don't rage in the streets. To tell the truth, sometimes the drivers rage when they get tied up in traffic, but the automobiles don't rage. Sometimes an automobile manages to stay right where it is and not move at all when it gets a vapor lock! And automobiles do not "justle one against another in the broad ways." Actually, when one jostles against another, it means you have a wreck. One New Year's Eve, as I was out on the freeways of Southern California with a friend, we saw one wreck after another—apparently there were quite a few drunk drivers out that evening. The point is that automobiles don't jostle one against another.

What *is* Nahum talking about when he says, "The chariots shall rage in the streets, they shall justle one against another in the broad ways"? Well, if you have ever been in a museum which had some of the Assyrian relics, you have perhaps seen that on the chariot wheels, that is, on the hub of the wheels, there was a sharp blade. It was like a sword or a sickle, a very dangerous instrument which extended out from the wheel. The one driving the chariot would go up as close as he could get to the enemy, and this very sharp instrument would cut off the wooden wheel of the enemy's chariot. It would put a chariot out of business right away if you could cut off the wheel on one side. That is the jostling together that Nahum mentions here, and it hasn't anything to do with the automobile!

"They shall seem like torches, they shall run like the lightnings." The chariots moved very fast in that day, although in our day it would seem very slow. The Assyrians had developed the art of fighting by chariot to a very fine degree, and the enemy had picked that up so that when they clashed in the broad ways of the city and outside the city, the battle was a frightful, horrible thing. That, my friend, is all that Nahum is talking about here.

I believe that you can make moral and spiritual applications from the Word of God, but I don't think that you can take this prophecy and interpret it in a literal way for our day. Do you see what a remarkable book Nahum is? We have here another great principle for interpreting the Word of God. For example, when you read in Isaiah, ". . . therefore shalt thou plant pleasant plants, and shalt set it with strange slips" (Isa. 17:10), you cannot interpret that to mean the orange trees which today abound in that land. The natural habitat of the orange tree is the land of Israel. In fact, that whole area grew oranges way back even in the days of Solomon. When Solomon speaks in the Song of Solomon of dwelling under the apple tree, the "apple" referred to is actually a *citron* fruit, probably an orange tree (see Song 2:3). My point is that we cannot take Scriptures that have an interpretation for a different people at a different time and try to bring them up to date and interpret them for our own day.

I want to mention again that the little Books of Jonah and Nahum go together. What you have in the Book of Jonah is actually not a prophecy but rather an account of Jonah's missionary activity in the city of Nineveh when the total population turned to God and God spared them from judgment. But time went by, and they departed from the Lord again. One hundred years after Jonah, God raised up Nahum, and his entire message is directed against Nineveh. What we have, therefore, in the Book of Nahum is a very vivid prophecy of the total annihilation of this city. The city was so completely destroyed that it was not until 1850 that the site of Nineveh was located and excavated. A great deal has been learned about the city of Nineveh and the Assyrian civilization through that excavation.

**He shall recount his worthies: they shall stumble in their walk; they shall make haste to the wall thereof, and the defence shall be prepared [Nah. 2:5].**

The destruction of Nineveh came about when the Medes came against the city under Cyaxares. Babylon at that time was not the greatest kingdom, but they did join with the Medes in this battle.

The king of Assyria depended upon his military leaders, but because of their fear, they stumbled and fell in their march. Of course, the defense of the city's wall was of primary importance in the battle.

**The gates of the rivers shall be opened, and the palace shall be dissolved [Nah. 2:6].**

Nahum prophesies here that the Tigris River will be turned into the city. At the time this campaign was carried on, the heavy rains in that area caused the Tigris River to reach flood stage. The floodwaters took out a section of the wall, and the city became like a pool of water. "The gates of the rivers shall be opened, and the palace shall be dissolved." I think that the foundations of the palace were swept out and that the water absolutely brought the palace down. Secular history tells us that part of the city wall was taken out. About two and one-half miles of the wall of Nineveh was right along by the side of the Tigris River. The city was situated well above the normal flow of the river, but with the river at flood stage, it took out a whole section of the wall, and the enemy was able to enter the city. In other words, the overflowing river made the breach that the enemy was attempting to make themselves. It would seem as though the Lord cooperated in the destruction of the city. The floodgates were opened, and even the palace was brought down by the flooding. We are told that the enemy opened the irrigation ditches and the palace was completely inundated with water.

**And Huzzab shall be led away captive, she shall be brought up, and her maids**

shall lead her as with the voice of doves, tabering upon their breasts [Nah. 2:7].

*Huzzab* literally means "it is decreed." This verse should read, "And it is decreed, she shall be led away captive, she shall be brought up, and her maids shall lead her as with the voice of doves, tabering [or, *beating*] upon their breasts." I used to hunt doves in Texas as a young fellow. Late in the afternoon, we would hunt down where a dam had been put up and there was a body of water used for the watering of cattle—we called it a tank in those days. The birds would come there late in the afternoon, and as we would come up over the embankment, we'd be able to get a good shot at the doves. They would all take flight, and the flapping of their wings would be like the sound of beating upon your chest. This is the picture that is given to us here by Nahum. The beating upon their breast was just like the noise made by doves taking flight. The dove's call, by the way, is a mourning noise, and that is the reason it is called the mourning dove. I have been told that that mourning noise is actually the love call of the dove.

**But Nineveh is of old like a pool of water: yet they shall flee away. Stand, stand, shall they cry; but none shall look back [Nah. 2:8].**

"But Nineveh is of old like a pool of water." The flood had entered, and the city became like a lake.

"Stand, stand, shall they cry; but none shall look back." The command was given to them to hold their ground, but when they saw the flood coming in along with the enemy, they decided it was time not to listen to their commanders but to turn and run away as fast as possible.

**Take ye the spoil of silver, take the spoil of gold: for there is none end of the store and glory out of all the pleasant furniture [Nah. 2:9].**

"Take ye the spoil of silver, take the spoil of gold." The enemy is invited to take the spoil of silver and to take the spoil of gold. "For there is none end of the store and glory out of all the pleasant furniture." The city of Nineveh was very wealthy and highly ornate. The palaces were beautiful, and the people lived in luxury because of the success they had had in warfare. You see, the Assyrians had brought in booty from all of the great nations of that day—even the southern kingdom of Judah was paying tribute to them at that time—so that the city had become very wealthy.

**She is empty, and void, and waste: and the heart melteth, and the knees smite together, and much pain is in all loins, and the faces of them all gather blackness [Nah. 2:10].**

"She is empty, and void, and waste." Assyria had brought in booty from everywhere else and had gathered it all in one place, but their enemies came in and took it all out.

"And the heart melteth, and the knees smite together." When your knees smite together, it means that you are afraid, it means there is fear in your heart. This is what happened to the Assyrians.

"And much pain is in all loins, and the faces of them all gather blackness." This was a time of great fear and dread because the Assyrians knew that they were hated by the world of that day. All their neighbors hated them because of their brutality. Now vengeance was being taken out upon them. Instead of the blood being all drawn from their faces, Nahum says that "the faces of them all gather blackness." I take it that this means that they were putting on sackcloth and throwing ashes upon their heads.

**Where is the dwelling of the lions, and the feedingplace of the young lions, where the lion, even the old lion, walked, and the lion's whelp, and none made them afraid? [Nah. 2:11].**

Both Assyria and Babylon used the lion as the symbol of their empires. Nahum could be referring here to the actual lions which the Assyrians had there, or he could be referring to their strong young men because the lion was the symbol of the strength of the kingdom. The whole point is that, whether it is the literal lions or the strength of their army, they are gone—they've left, or they've been killed.

**The lion did tear in pieces enough for his whelps, and strangled for his lionesses, and filled his holes with prey, and his dens with ravin [Nah. 2:12].**

Whether these were the literal lions or the Assyrian army, they had once been well fed, but now all of that is ended. They no longer have anything to eat because all has been taken away by the enemy.

**Behold, I am against thee, saith the LORD of hosts, and I will burn her chariots in the smoke, and the sword shall devour thy young lions: and I will cut off thy prey from the earth, and the voice of thy messengers shall no more be heard [Nah. 2:13].**

"Behold, I am against thee, saith the LORD of hosts." God doesn't say that very often. He says it only here and to Gog and Magog in Ezekiel 38 and 39. Many of us believe that the reference in Ezekiel is directed to modern Russia. That is pretty much established today by conservative scholarship. No one but a liberal who disregards facts and evidence would say that that passage does not refer to modern Russia. God says there to Russia, "I am against you," and He sets down a pattern for us. Russia has had the gospel; actually, they had it before we did. But today communism is opposed to God. It is atheistic; its basic philosophy is that it is opposed to God. But God beat them to the draw. He said to them long before they appeared as a nation, "I am against you."

Here in Nahum He also says, "I am against you," and He is talking to Nineveh. They were a people who had had a personal messenger from God (Jonah), and they had turned to the living God, but now they have turned from Him. When you have had the light and you reject it, the Lord Jesus put it like this: ". . . If therefore the light that is in thee be darkness, how great is that darkness!" (Matt. 6:23). In other words, if the light is shining right into your eyes and you say you cannot see, that means you are blind. This reminds me of the story of a young man who was in a mine explosion together with other men. The rescuers got to them as quickly as they could, taking away all of the wreckage and debris between those on the outside and the trapped miners. When they got through to them, the first thing they did was to turn on a light. But this young man stood there after the light came on and said, "Why don't they turn on the light?" Everybody looked at him in amazement because they knew then that the explosion had blinded him. But, you see, as long as they were in darkness, nobody could tell that he was blind. He couldn't tell it himself because he thought the lights were still out. "If therefore the light that is in thee be darkness, how great is that darkness!"—it means you are blind. This is the picture that Nahum gives to us. The Assyrians had had light, but they rejected it; and when you reject light, your responsibility is greater.

"I will burn her chariots in the smoke, and the sword shall devour thy young lions." Again, this could be literal lions or the young men, but I believe it refers to their young men because the lion was the symbol of the strength of the nation.

"And I will cut off thy prey from the earth, and the voice of thy messengers shall no more be heard." This is a note of finality. One hundred years earlier God had graciously saved Nineveh when they repented and turned to Him; but time has marched on, they have lapsed into an awful apostasy, and God is now going to judge them. He says to them, "I'm against you. I'm going to bring you down. I will annihilate you, and you will never appear again." This ought to be a message today to those who have completely turned their backs upon God: it means total judgment.

# CHAPTER 3

**THEME:** *Avenging action of God justified*

In chapter 3 Nahum gives the cause for and justifies God's destruction of the city of Nineveh. Nineveh's destruction is an example of the fact that ". . . whatsoever a man soweth, that shall he also reap" (Gal. 6:7). This is also true of a nation. You will find that in many ways God deals with individuals and nations in a very similar manner.

Many literary critics have found in this third chapter one of the most vivid descriptions of the destruction of a city that is imaginable. You will not find anything in any language more descriptive than this.

**Woe to the bloody city! it is all full of lies and robbery; the prey departeth not [Nah. 3:1].**

We are given here a picture of the internal condition of the city of Nineveh. "Woe to the bloody city!" Nineveh, as the capital of Assyria, was known in the ancient world to be very brutal, very bloody. They were feared and dreaded by other nations. The army of the Assyrians, although it actually moved rather slowly, was just like a hurricane which devours everything in its pathway. As I mentioned before, at times an entire community would commit suicide rather than suffer the brutal attack of Assyria.

"It is all full of lies." Assyria was a nation which could never be depended upon. She was not faithful to fulfill the promises which she made to other nations to help them and protect them.

What better description could you have even of our own country right now? I feel that we are given very few facts but a great deal of propaganda today. This is true not only of Washington, D.C., and the news media but of all areas of our society. This is true of our government regardless of which party the information comes from. My opinion of our two-party system is that what we have is Tweedledum and Tweedledee—you can pick either one of them. At one point in my life I thought I needed to change from one party to the other, and I did change. But now I need another change, not back to where I came from but to be free of this whole thing in which I am fed nothing in the world but propaganda and never given the truth. The one thing that is needed today is the truth.

One of the reasons God judged the city of Nineveh was that it was "all full of lies and robbery." These things characterized the life of the city. Likewise, our homes today are not safe. I was recently in the home of friends in Louisville, Kentucky. They are lovely folk, and they have a very lovely southern home in which they have some beautiful antiques. Do you know that they have had to put bars on their windows and double and triple locks on their doors! Where do you think we live today? We say that we live in a nation of law and order—but it hasn't been that. What an apt description this verse is of the United States! When I first began to study this, I felt like asking Nahum, "Are you talking about us? You're giving a vivid description of Nineveh, but it is also a picture of my own nation."

The Books of Jonah and Nahum reveal that God deals with gentile nations and that He did so back in the days of the Old Testament. They also show that the government of God moves in the governments of men. God today will overrule the sin of man. He will overrule a nation. As you come down through history, you see great civilizations, one after another, crumbling in the dust and the debris of the ages. Why? Because God judged them, friend—that is the reason why. The United States is no pet of God. We're not something special. We think we are. We can boast of the fact that right now we are the strongest na-

tion in the world, but even that might be questionable today. We live in a security that may be a false security, because God brings great nations down, and He makes that very clear here.

**The noise of a whip, and the noise of the rattling of the wheels, and of the prancing horses, and of the jumping chariots [Nah. 3:2].**

Nahum gives a graphic description of these chariots. They are like armored tanks—they were the tanks of the ancient world. As they came inside the city, you could hear the noise of the whip as the driver whipped up his horse. You could hear the rattling of the wheels and the noise "of the prancing horses, and of the jumping [bounding] chariots." The chariots were leaping over everything, especially dead bodies.

The first two verses of this chapter describe the internal condition of Nineveh. Lies and robbery marked the culture and the climate of the city. This is the reason they acted as they did on the outside toward their enemies—their brutality, their total unconcern for other nations, their lording it over others. The very cause for their methods is that *internally* they were wrong. You see, man does not become a sinner because he sins. He sins because he *is* a sinner. Fundamentally, on the inside, man is a sinner, and that accounts for his actions. I am sure that many people in that day said of the Assyrians, "These people are uncivilized!" Inside the city, it was full of lies and robbery. That which did not characterize our nation years ago (there was a great deal of it, but it wasn't the predominant thing)—lies and robbery—just happens to characterize the internal condition of our nation today. Why? Because we are highly civilized? No. It is because we are sinners. My friend, we are sinners.

**The horseman lifteth up both the bright sword and the glittering spear: and there is a multitude of slain, and a great number of carcases; and there is none end of their corpses; they stumble upon their corpses [Nah. 3:3].**

The number of the dead was unbelievable. I tell you, if a well-placed bomb were dropped somewhere in this country, we would probably see the same sort of thing. There are nations who may pretend to be friendly but who would not hesitate for five seconds to drop that bomb on this country if they thought they could get by with it. And I'm beginning to think that they believe they can get by with it.

We have in verses 3–4 that which characterized the external conditions of Nineveh. They had been a brutal and cruel enemy, and they were now reaping what they had sown.

**Because of the multitude of the whoredoms of the wellfavoured harlot, the mistress of witchcrafts, that selleth nations through her whoredoms, and families through her witchcrafts [Nah. 3:4].**

"Because of the multitude of the whoredoms of the wellfavoured harlot." The city of Nineveh is here likened unto a harlot. She was the one whom all the nations played up to. Note the shame of this city. God likens her to a harlot, a "wellfavoured harlot," suggesting that all the world courted her.

"The mistress of witchcrafts, that selleth nations through her whoredoms, and families through her witchcrafts." Witchcraft is mentioned twice here. This is a reference to the occult. Don't for one moment think that the idolatry of the ancient world was meaningless. The apostle Paul called an idol ". . . nothing in the world . . ." (1 Cor. 8:4), but *back* of the idol is Satan, and back of idolatry is that which is satanic. I do not need to labor this point today. If you are not acquainted with what is happening today in the world of the occult, then you have not been to Southern California. It is not happening just among a bunch of down-and-outers or a bunch of criminals or in the underworld. The occult is active on our college campuses today and in the best sections of our cities. People are given over to witchcraft today. It is amazing how many people will buy their horoscope, which they will then follow. Many folk carry amulets, good luck pieces, charms, little dolls, and all that sort of thing. This is growing by leaps and bounds in a materialistic age and culture, which thought it had graduated from such things, but now we find there has been a return to it. This is exactly what the great city of Nineveh had turned to, and God says that He is justified in judging the city because of its harlotry and witchcraft.

The Book of Revelation tells us that when we come to the end of this age, the organized church will become a harlot, engaging in this type of thing. I am of the opinion that we can see a movement in that direction even now. All of this is very dangerous today. I know a very fine Pentecostal preacher who preaches the Word of God and believes in speaking in tongues and in healing. He expressed to me that there is a real danger in the tongues movement. He said, "Not only does our group speak in tongues, there are those today in the occult who are also doing it. In my own church, we are being very careful about this sort of thing." This man is a spiritually enlightened man, and he is rather reluctant to engage in "tongues" speaking. I would put up a warning to you today, friend: just because a thing seems to have a mark of the supernatural on it does not mean it is scriptural. You had better examine it very carefully to see whether it is scriptural. If it is supernatural and not scriptural, it is not of God. And there is only one other fellow who is in the business of the supernatural other than God, and that is Satan. Satan will ape God and imitate Him in every way that he possibly can.

God is giving to us the reason He judged Nineveh. He is justifying His actions in destroying this city. Now He makes this very remarkable statement—

**Behold, I am against thee, saith the LORD of hosts; and I will discover thy skirts upon thy face, and I will shew the nations thy nakedness, and the kingdoms thy shame [Nah. 3:5].**

"Behold, I am against thee, saith the LORD of hosts." This is the second time that God says this to Nineveh. He also says this to Gog and Magog in Ezekiel 38–39. We believe that definitely refers to Russia. When I graduated from seminary, I would not accept that Ezekiel 38–39 referred to Russia. So I decided to make a study of it on my own, and I now have several reasons why I am confident that it is Russia which is mentioned there. Russia is a nation which wasn't even in existence in Ezekiel's day, but God said to them, "I am against you." Well, we now know why He said that— they are an atheistic nation.

Assyria was a nation to whom God said, "I am against you," not because they were atheistic but because they were polytheistic. Assyria was given over to idolatry—back of the idol was the occult, back of the idol was witchcraft. Witchcraft has become a reality to many today. Men are finding that there is a reality to it. And it is those in the upper echelon who are making this discovery. I have been told on rather good authority, from those who are in our capital of Washington, that it is amazing and alarming to see the number of people there who appeal to fortune-tellers and to horoscopes in an attempt to interpret the future. Men want to know the future. But God said to Nineveh, a city greatly involved in the occult, "I am against thee."

"I will discover thy skirts upon thy face." In other words, "I am going to uncover thy skirts from thy face." We live in a day of a great deal of nudity. With their tongues in their cheeks, men try to call it art to present that which is salacious and sinful and suggestive. There is a great display of the nude by both men and women today. The Assyrian civilization had sunk pretty low but not as low as we have. They did not display the human body—they were not given over to that. It was a *disgrace* for a woman to be displayed nude. God speaks here of the shame that He is going to bring upon Nineveh. He says, "I will uncover thy skirts from thy face. I am going to pull your skirts up over your face. You have been a harlot, and I'm going to reveal you and all of the lurid details." Believe me, that was a real disgrace for them.

"I will shew the nations thy nakedness, and the kingdoms thy shame." That is what God said He would do to this nation. Assyria went down, my friend. A great nation, a great civilization, with all its riches and power, went down into the dust never to rise again. God said that is what He would do to them.

**And I will cast abominable filth upon thee, and make thee vile, and will set thee as a gazingstock [Nah. 3:6].**

God says to Nineveh through Nahum, "I am going to bring you down. I'm opposed to you. I will expose you to the world for what you are." The excavations which have brought to light this great civilization reveal that all of this is quite accurate. And the Book of Nahum just happens to be a vivid prophecy which was given long before this actually took place. This is something quite amazing, is it not?

All of this description which is given here is something I do not want to pass over lightly because it has such a tremendous application for us today and is such an apt picture of the present day. The Book of Nahum reveals God's method in dealing with the nations of the world. I do not think He has changed His method, and if He hasn't, we are in trouble, and I mean deep trouble, my friend. We ought to be praying for our nation.

God calls this city a harlot, saying that He is absolutely going to display all of the shame and filth and vileness of this great civilization and make it a gazingstock, a spectacle, to the world. Such was the end of the great Assyrian Empire.

**And it shall come to pass, that all they that look upon thee shall flee from thee, and say, Nineveh is laid waste: who will bemoan her? whence shall I seek comforters for thee? [Nah. 3:7].**

In other words, God says, "Where in the world will I get people to come and mourn over this city? Nobody will mourn over it. Nobody will weep over it. There will be no mourners there." That is a very sad situation, a very sad one indeed. Several funeral home directors here in Pasadena became my personal friends over the years and would sometimes call me to conduct a funeral. One of the saddest experiences that I ever had was the funeral I conducted for a dear old man. He was a Christian who had come out here from the East with his wife for the sake of her health. She had died, and then he became bedridden, and people forgot about him. When he died, I guess many didn't even recognize his name. When I went down to conduct the funeral, there wasn't anybody there. Nobody came—to me it was the saddest thing. I knew the funeral director pretty well, and I went to him and said, "Get all your office workers and come on in there. We're going to have a funeral service." He rounded up everyone that he could and brought them in. We had about a dozen folk. So I brought a gospel message, a message of hope for the Christian. It was wonderful to be able to say, "Jesus died for our sins, and He rose again for our justification." But it was sad to have a funeral service like that, where no friends attended. God said that there were not going to be any mourners at the funeral of Nineveh. Nahum prophesied that the whole world would rejoice in that day, and they did. When God said this through Nahum, no one would have believed it unless he had believed God and accepted it by faith, but it came to pass just as God said it would.

**Art thou better than populous No, that was situate among the rivers, that had the waters round about it, whose rampart was the sea, and her wall was from the sea? [Nah. 3:8].**

"Art thou better than populous No?"—No-Amon was what we know as Thebes, the great capital of upper Egypt. Dr. Charles Feinberg's books on the minor prophets are very excellent—I know of none better. I would like to quote from his book, *Jonah, Micah and Nahum* (p. 147), in which he describes the city of No-Amon:

It was the capital city of the Pharaohs of the Eighteenth to the Twentieth Dynasties, and boasted such architecture as the Greeks and Romans admired. The Greeks called it Diospolis, because the Egyptian counterpart of Jupiter was worshipped there. It was located on both banks of the river Nile. On the eastern bank were the famous temples at Karnak and Luxor. Homer, the first Greek poet, spoke of it as having 100 gates. Its ruins cover an area of some 27 miles. Amon, the chief god of the Egyptians, was shown on Egyptian relics as a figure with a human body and a ram's head. The judgment of this godless and idolatrous city was foretold by Jeremiah (46:25) and Ezekiel (30:14–16). No-Amon was situated favorably among the canals of the Nile with the Nile itself as a protection. The Nile appears as a sea when it overflows its banks annually. Nineveh can read her fate in that of No-Amon, for she is no better than the mighty Egyptian capital.

God is saying to Nineveh that the city of Thebes should have been an example to the Assyrian Empire. The Assyrians were the ones who had destroyed Thebes, a great city which had seemed impregnable. It seemed that no one could take it, but the Assyrians did take it and destroy it. This should have been an example to the Assyrians. God had judged Thebes, and He is here justifying the fact that He will also judge Nineveh. The government of God moves in the governments of men in this world today.

"Art thou better than populous No, that was situate among the rivers." "Rivers" is used in the plural to mean a great deal of water. When the Nile River would overflow at the flood season, it looked like the ocean. "That had the waters round about it, whose rampart was the sea, and her wall was from the sea?" Thebes was built so that at the flood season it would not be flooded at all. Rather, the water provided a natural protection for the city.

**Ethiopia and Egypt were her strength, and it was infinite; Put and Lubim were thy helpers [Nah. 3:9].**

These were the allies of Thebes which were located around her. The city of Thebes, at one time the capital of the Egyptian Empire, felt that it could never fall because there was a big desert on both sides, the Nile River was a protection, and they had allies to the north and to the south. How could anybody get to them? But the Assyrians did. The Assyrians, in turn, felt that they were impregnable in their day. And today we feel that we have enough atomic weapons and other sophisticated hardware to defend ourselves. My friend, when God's time comes, we will go down. Our best defense today simply does not happen to be in the area of military weapons. Our best defense would be a return to God and to a recognition of Him in our government. I am not impressed by what I see in Washington. They have a little prayer breakfast and then, I'm told, some of them step outside and cuss up a storm! Some men make a profession of being Christians, and yet their language is so vile you cannot even listen to it. What hypocrisy there is today! Is God going to let us off? Are we something special? I think not. Our best defense today would be once again to have men of character in government—even if they were not Christians, if they would at least espouse the great morality set forth in the Word of God. That is the thing that built our nation. I am not greatly impressed with some of our founding fathers. I do not think, for example, that Thomas Jefferson was a Christian, but I will say that he had a respect for the Word of God. He believed in the morality of the Word of God. When we despise and contradict that morality as we do today, God cannot bless us as a nation, and I do not think He will.

**Yet was she carried away, she went into captivity: her young children also were dashed in pieces at the top of all the streets: and they cast lots for her honourable men, and all her great men were bound in chains [Nah. 3:10].**

This is what Assyria had done to Thebes, and now chickens are coming home to roost. "Be not deceived; God is not mocked: for whatsoever a man soweth, that shall he also reap" (Gal. 6:7).

**Thou also shalt be drunken: thou shalt be hid, thou also shalt seek strength because of the enemy [Nah. 3:11].**

The Assyrians will try to fortify their courage by getting drunk, but that is not going to help them a bit.

**All thy strong holds shall be like fig trees with the firstripe figs: if they be shaken, they shall even fall into the mouth of the eater [Nah. 3:12].**

I used to have a fig tree in my yard. When the figs were ripe, all you had to do was just touch a branch, and they all would come tumbling down. This is what Nahum says to Nineveh here: "All your defenses are like that. The minute the enemy comes, he is going to break right through them."

**Behold, thy people in the midst of thee are women: the gates of thy land shall be set wide open unto thine enemies: the fire shall devour thy bars [Nah. 3:13].**

I believe that the thought here is that the men were acting like women. The men were very womanly. Or this could mean that women were actually the ones in the positions of authority. Frankly, I do not think God is for the women's liberation movement which we have today. I still believe that woman's place is in the home. I feel very frankly that the church is at fault in using women in too many offices in the church. A woman's first place is not to teach a Sunday school class. She is to raise her own family—that is her place. Women are being taken away from their homes by church work and every other kind of work. Unless she is forced to work for a living because her husband has passed on or is unable to work, I do not believe a woman's working is justified. I know that I will get reactions for saying this, but I am saying it because I think that this is one mark of the disintegration and downfall of civilization.

**Draw thee waters for the siege, fortify thy strong holds: go into clay, and tread the mortar, make strong the brickkiln [Nah. 3:14].**

At the last minute, the Assyrians would get busy making bricks to fortify themselves. They would heat up water, which they would carry to the top of the city wall. They would then pour a bucket of the scalding water down upon the fellow who was scaling the wall. He was through scaling the wall, I can assure you of that—he would soon find himself back on the ground.

**There shall the fire devour thee; the sword shall cut thee off, it shall eat thee up like the cankerworm: make thyself many as the cankerworm, make thyself many as the locusts [Nah. 3:15].**

Nahum prophesies that they will try to bring in reinforcements but that they will not help.

**Thou hast multiplied thy merchants above the stars of heaven: the canker-worm spoileth, and flieth away [Nah. 3:16].**

Each year their national wealth increased, for they were great merchants, but all of that was going to come to an end.

**Thy crowned are as the locusts, and thy captains as the great grasshoppers, which camp in the hedges in the cold day, but when the sun ariseth they flee away, and their place is not known where they are [Nah. 3:17].**

When the time came, the leaders would manage to escape, that is, for a little while anyway.

**Thy shepherds slumber, O king of Assyria: thy nobles shall dwell in the dust: thy people is scattered upon the mountains, and no man gathereth them [Nah. 3:18].**

The leadership of Assyria disintegrated to the place where they no longer attempted to lead the nation.

I trust that I will not be misunderstood because I am not discussing politics, certainly not from any party viewpoint. (As far as I am concerned, I am disgusted with both of the major political parties in this nation of ours.) I believe that one of the great evidences of our disintegration and deterioration as a nation is the lack of leadership that exists on the national level, the state level, the county level, and even at the city and community levels. There is a lack of real leadership at all levels. It seems that the one with the big mouth and the big talk is the one who is elected. And it seems that the rich man is the one elected. Abraham Lincoln could not run for the office of president today—he wouldn't have enough money. God says that the lack of leadership, along with the other things He has mentioned, is what brought Assyria down.

What God has said in this chapter concerning Assyria fits our nation like a glove. One glove fits Assyria—and that's been fulfilled. The other glove fits the United States. But are we listening to God today? No. No one to speak of is paying any attention. Certainly the leadership of our nation is not. The tragedy of the hour is our retreat from God and our rejection of Jesus Christ, the Prince of Peace, the Savior of the world.

Listen to God's final words to Nineveh. He says this with a note of finality and of dogmatism. This makes your spine tingle. It is frightening indeed—

**There is no healing of thy bruise; thy wound is grievous: all that hear the bruit of thee shall clap the hands over thee: for upon whom hath not thy wickedness passed continually? [Nah. 3:19].**

The Assyrian people had sinned and sinned and sinned—it was a way of life with them. When people want to point a finger and say that God is wrong, that God permits evil and does nothing about evil, God says to them, "I *do* do something about it." My friend, you can look around today at the many injustices in our world, but God *is* doing something about them. God is just and righteous. He was a God of love even when He destroyed Nineveh and wiped it clean like a dish. It disappeared off the face of the map and off the face of the earth—and God took full responsibility for it's judgment.

# BIBLIOGRAPHY

(Recommended for Further Study)

Feinberg, Charles L. *The Minor Prophets*. Chicago, Illinois: Moody Press, 1976.

Freeman, Hobart E. *Nahum, Zephaniah, and Habakkuk*. Chicago, Illinois: Moody Press, 1973.

Gaebelein, Arno C. *The Annotated Bible*. 1917. Reprint. Neptune, New Jersey: Loizeaux Brothers, 1971.

Ironside, H. A. *The Minor Prophets*. Neptune, New Jersey: Loizeaux Brothers, n.d.

Jensen, Irving L. *Minor Prophets of Judah*. Chicago, Illinois: Moody Press, 1975. (Obadiah, Joel, Micah, Nahum, Zephaniah, and Habakkuk.)

Tatford, Frederick A. *The Minor Prophets*. Minneapolis, Minnesota: Klock & Klock, n.d.

Unger, Merrill F. *Unger's Commentary on the Old Testament*, Vol. 2. Chicago, Illinois: Moody Press, 1982.

# The Book of

# HABAKKUK

## INTRODUCTION

Nahum, Habakkuk, and Zephaniah have a great deal in common. Each one gives a different facet of the dealings of God with mankind. They show how the government of God is integrated into the government of men. They also show God's dealings with the individual.

Another similarity is the fact that they come from approximately the same time period. In fact, they all could have been contemporaries, and the possibility is that they were. (It is difficult to nail down the specific dates of the prophets—and of many of the other Old Testament books. The reason, of course, is that the exact dates are not important.) At least we know that all three prophets fit into the period between the reigns of Kings Josiah and Jehoiakim, which would also be the time of the prophet Jeremiah. The northern kingdom had already gone into captivity, and the southern kingdom was right on the verge of captivity. After Josiah, every king in the southern kingdom was a bad king. Nahum, Habakkuk, and Zephaniah all fit into that period of decline.

Although there are similarities, these books also differ from each other. Nahum dealt only with Nineveh, the capital of the Assyrian Empire. Nahum showed that God is just, righteous, and a God of love; yet He was absolutely right in judging that city.

Habakkuk approaches the problem from a little different viewpoint. He is a man with questions. He is disturbed about God's seeming indifference to the iniquity of His own people. Habakkuk asks God, "Why don't You *do* something?" In our day a great many folk feel as Habakkuk did. They are asking, "Why doesn't God *do* something? Why doesn't He move into the affairs of men and stop the violence and injustice and suffering?"

God answered the question for Habakkuk by informing him that He was preparing a nation, Babylon, to punish Judah and to take her into captivity—unless she changed her ways. Well, if you think Habakkuk had a problem before, you can see that he really had a problem then! Habakkuk asked, "Why will You use Babylon—a nation that is definitely more wicked, more pagan, and more given over to idolatry than Your own people—to punish Judah?" God reveals to Habakkuk that He was not through with Babylon but would judge her also. This is God's method.

This book is very important in its relationship to the New Testament. It is generally conceded that the three great doctrinal books of the New Testament are Romans, Galatians, and Hebrews, all of which quote from Habakkuk. In fact, Habakkuk 2:4 is the background of their message: "The just shall live by his faith." So this little book looms upon the horizon of Scripture as being important. Don't let the brevity of it deceive you. Importance is not determined by *how much* you say but by *what* you say.

The name *Habakkuk* means "to embrace." Dr. Charles Feinberg (*Habakkuk, Zephaniah, Haggai*, p. 11) described Martin Luther's striking definition of this name:

> Habakkuk signifies an embracer, or one who embraces another, takes him into his arms. He embraces his people, and takes them to his arms, i.e., he comforts them and holds them up, as one embraces a weeping child, to quiet it with the assurance that, if God wills, it shall soon be better.

Habakkuk told us nothing of his personal life, even of the era in which he lived. I call him the doubting Thomas of the Old Testament because he had a question mark for a brain. His book is really unusual. It is not a prophecy in the strict sense of the term. It is somewhat like the Book of Jonah in that Habakkuk told of his own experience with God—his questions to God and God's answers. We could say that Habakkuk was born in the objective case, in the past pluperfect tense, in the subjunctive mood. We write over him a big question mark until, in the last chapter and especially in the final two or three verses, we can put down an exclamation point. This book is the personal experience of the prophet told in poetry, as Jonah's was told in prose.

Habakkuk was an interesting man, and he has written a lovely book with real literary excellence. The final chapter is actually a song or psalm of praise and adoration to God, a very beautiful piece of literature.

The closing statement in the book, "To the chief singer [musician] on my stringed instruments," reveals that this book is a song. That little note was put there for the director of the orchestra and the choir. The final chapter of the book is a psalm of beauty. In fact, the entire prophecy is a gem. It has been translated into a metric version by A. C. Gaebelein (*The Annotated Bible*, pp. 214–219). Delitzsch wrote, "His language is classical throughout, full of rare and select turns and words." Moorehouse wrote, "It is distinguished for its magnificent poetry."

This little book opens in gloom and closes in glory. It begins with a question mark and closes with an exclamation point. Habakkuk is a big WHY? Why God permits evil is a question that every thoughtful mind has faced. I think that this book is the answer to that question. Will God straighten out the injustice of the world? This book answers that question. Is God doing anything about the wrongs of the world? This book says that He is. In my opinion it is possible to reduce the doubt of Thomas in the New Testament, of Habakkuk in the Old Testament, and of modern man into the one word: *Why?* It is the fundamental question of the human race. When we reduce all questions to the lowest common denominator, we come to the basic question: Why?

You can see that the message of Habakkuk is almost the opposite of the message of Nahum. In the Book of Nahum God was moving in judgment, and the question was: How can God be a God of love and judge as He is doing? Here in Habakkuk it is just the opposite: Why doesn't God do something about the evil in the world?

The theme of Habakkuk is faith. He has been called the prophet of faith. The great statement of Habakkuk 2:4, "the just shall live by his faith," has been quoted three times in the New Testament: Romans 1:17; Galatians 3:11; and Hebrews 10:38.

# OUTLINE

### I. Perplexity of the Prophet, Chapter 1
   A. First Problem of the Prophet, Chapter 1:1–4
      *Why does God permit evil?*
   B. God's Answer, Chapter 1:5–11
      *God was raising up Chaldeans to punish Judah (v. 6).*
   C. Second Problem of the Prophet (greater than first), Chapter 1:12–17
      *Why would God permit His people to be punished by a nation more wicked than they? Why did He not destroy the Chaldeans?*

### II. Perception of the Prophet, Chapter 2
   A. Practice of the Prophet, Chapter 2:1
      *He took the secret problem to the secret place.*
   B. Patience of the Prophet, Chapter 2:2–3
      *He waited for the vision.*
   C. Pageant for the Prophet, Chapter 2:4
      *The great divide in humanity: One group, which is crooked, is flowing toward destruction; the other group, by faith, is moving toward God. This is inevitable.*
   D. Parable to the Prophet, Chapter 2:5–20
      *The application is self-evident from the vision. The Chaldeans, in turn, would be destroyed. God was moving among the nations.*

### III. Pleasure of the Prophet, Chapter 3
   A. Prayer of the Prophet, Chapter 3:1–2
      *The prophet, who thought God was doing nothing about evil, now asks Him to remember to be merciful. Was he afraid that God was doing too much?*
   B. Program of God, Chapter 3:3–17
      *God rides majestically in His own chariot of salvation (v. 8).*
   C. Position of the Prophet, Chapter 3:18–19
      *He will rejoice (v. 18). He has come from pain to pleasure.*

# CHAPTER 1

*THEME: The perplexity of the prophet*

**The burden which Habakkuk the prophet did see [Hab. 1:1].**

"The burden" means the judgment. Actually, this is not Habakkuk's question, but rather it is the Lord's answer. The answer of God is really the prophecy of the Book of Habakkuk. The Lord's answer is judgment which Habakkuk called, as did the other prophets, "the burden."

## FIRST PROBLEM OF THE PROPHET

Habakkuk's first problem is this: Why does God permit evil?

**O Lord, how long shall I cry, and thou wilt not hear! even cry out unto thee of violence, and thou wilt not save! [Hab. 1:2].**

"O Lord, how long shall I cry, and thou wilt not hear!" Habakkuk is telling God that He is refusing to answer his prayers. He cries out in a night of despair as he sees violence among his people. And God is doing nothing and saying nothing. This is the elegy of Habakkuk. As we shall see, the book concludes with a paean of praise and a note of joy.

My friend, if you have a question, my feeling is that you ought to take it to the Lord as Habakkuk did. If you are sincere, you will get an answer from God.

**Why dost thou shew me iniquity, and cause me to behold grievance? for spoiling and violence are before me: and there are that raise up strife and contention.**

**Therefore the law is slacked, and judgment doth never go forth: for the wicked doth compass about the righteous; therefore wrong judgment proceedeth [Hab. 1:3–4].**

Here is his big question: Why does God permit this evil to continue among His own people—the iniquity, the injustice, the strife, and contention?

This is both an old question and a new question. It is one which you could ask today. Let's look at it in detail.

Habakkuk, as I suggested in the Introduction, probably wrote sometime after the time of King Josiah, the last good king of the southern kingdom of Judah. After Josiah there was Jehoahaz, a bad one who didn't last more than three months; then Jehoiakim came along and reigned eleven years, and he was a bad one. It was a time of disintegration, deterioration, and degradation in the kingdom. There was a breaking down of the Mosaic Law, and the people were turning away from God. The question was: Why was God permitting this evil?

While I was in a Bible conference in the East several years ago, I talked with two young professors, one from Vanderbilt University and the other from Missouri. They both were Christians and brilliant young men. They told me that the godless professors would use this method to try to destroy young people's faith in the integrity of the Word of God. They would begin like this: "You do not believe that a God of love would permit evil in the world, do you? Do you think a loving God, kind in heart, would permit suffering in the world?"

The enemy, you will recall, used that same method with Eve, as recorded in Genesis 3. He said something like this: "Do you mean to tell me that God does not want you to eat of *that* tree? Why? That tree has the most delicious fruit of any tree in the garden, and if you eat it, your eyes will be opened, and you will become like God. I can't believe that a good God would forbid your eating of that tree. I just can't understand it!" He was destroying, you see, her confidence in the goodness of God. That is always where the enemy starts.

Habakkuk's question fitted into the local situation of his day. People were getting by with sin, and God was seemingly doing nothing about it. His question was, Why doesn't God judge the wicked? Why does God permit evil men and women to prosper? And isn't that a good question in our day? I'm sure that many of God's people have asked, "Why doesn't God judge the evil in our nation today? Why does He permit the rich to get richer? And why is it that the average person is having to bear the burden of taxation and inflation? Why doesn't God do something about it?" Is this your question?

That was the psalmist's question in Psalm 73:2–3: "But as for me, my feet were almost gone; my steps had well nigh slipped. For I was envious at the foolish, when I saw the prosperity of the wicked." As he looked around, he saw that the ones who were prospering were the *wicked*! It almost robbed him of his faith. Why wasn't God doing something about it?

The people of Judah apparently felt that they were God's little pets and that He would not punish them for their sins. Probably the first time they did something evil they were apprehensive, wondering if God would punish them. When He did nothing, they assumed that He hadn't noticed or didn't care. The writer of Ecclesiastes says in chapter 8 verse 11: "Because sentence against an evil work is not executed speedily, therefore the heart of the sons of men is fully set in them to do evil."

I can remember when I was a boy and swiped my first watermelon. It was in the summertime, and a storm was coming up. By the time I had pulled a watermelon off the vine and had started to the fence with it, there was a flash of lightning and a clap of thunder the like of which you can only have in southern Oklahoma! I thought the Lord was judging me right there and then for what I had done. But the day came when I discovered that it wasn't judgment from God and I could do that sort of thing without fear.

Human nature does not change. The sins which were committed undercover in the backyard are now done openly in the front yard. Does that change the fact that sin is wrong in the sight of God and that He is going to judge every sin? No, God has not changed His standards or His procedures. Even though His execution against an evil work is not performed speedily, His judgment is sure to come eventually.

In our day very few people believe in the judgment of God. They feel like Habakkuk did when he saw his nation getting worse and worse until sin was flagrant and God was doing nothing about it. Don't you feel that way about conditions as they are? Is God doing anything about it today? It doesn't look as if He is. He even let a group of theologians up in New England come up with the idea a few years ago that God was dead. What they actually meant was that there is no God and there has never been a God. What made them arrive at such a conclusion? It is because they don't see Him interfering in the affairs of men today. But isn't He interfering? Isn't God overruling in the affairs of mankind today? He permitted us to go through a period of affluence, and folk became careless—even God's people became careless. Now we are in such a state that we wonder how much longer we are going to survive as a nation.

Habakkuk was a man with a very tender heart, and he hated to see lawlessness abounding and going unpunished. He hated to see the innocent people being threatened and exploited and destroyed. He was asking, "God, why aren't you doing something about it?"

Well, God had an answer for him, and He has an answer for you if this is your question.

## GOD'S ANSWER
**Behold ye among the heathen, and regard, and wonder marvellously: for I will work a work in your days, which ye will not believe, though it be told you [Hab. 1:5].**

"Behold ye among the heathen," or better, "Behold ye among the nations." God is challenging Habakkuk to open his eyes and look about him, to get a world view of what He is doing. One great crisis after another has taken place. The great Assyrian Empire in the north has been conquered, and Nineveh, its capital, has been destroyed. On the banks of the Euphrates River, a kingdom is arising which already has won a victory over Egypt at Carchemish. Nebuchadnezzar is the victor, and he is bringing Babylon to the fore as a world power. God is saying to Habakkuk, "Behold ye among the nations—you think I'm not doing anything? I am not sitting on the fifty-yard line watching this little world. I am very much involved." He is not involved to the extent that He is subject to it and has to make certain plays because they are forced upon Him. God is moving in a sovereign way in the universe. He *is* doing something about sin—"Behold ye among the nations, and regard, and wonder marvellously."

"For I will work a work in your days, which ye will not believe, though it be told you." God is saying, "When I tell you what I am really doing, it is going to be difficult for you to believe it. Instead of doing nothing, I am doing a great deal." In fact, Habakkuk is going to ask God to slow down when he finds out what God is doing.

"For I will work a work in your days, which ye will not believe, though it be told you" is quoted by Paul in the great sermon he gave in Antioch of Pisidia. (I have always felt that this is one of the greatest sermons Paul preached, and yet it is receiving very little attention in our day.) It is recorded in Acts 13. Now notice these words: "Be it known unto you therefore, men and brethren, that through this man [the Lord Jesus Christ] is preached unto you the forgiveness of sins: And by him all that believe are justified from all things, from which ye could not be justified by the law of Moses. Beware therefore, lest that come upon you, which is spoken of in the prophets; Behold, ye despisers, and wonder, and perish: for I work a work in your days, a work which ye shall in no wise believe, though a man declare it unto you" (Acts 13:38–41). As you can see, Paul is quoting from Habakkuk 1:5. It is an amazing application of this verse. Paul is saying that God has provided a salvation, and He didn't do it (as Paul said elsewhere) in a *corner*. At the time of the Crucifixion, Jews from all over the world were in Jerusalem to celebrate the Passover. They carried the word everywhere that Jesus of Nazareth had died on a cross, and it was rumored that He was raised from the dead. Also, Jews from all over the world were back in Jerusalem for the celebration of Pentecost when the Holy Spirit came upon the little group of believers. Multitudes were saved at that time and in succeeding days. When that news went out, the Roman world ignored it at first. Paul is telling them that God has worked a work in their days, "a work which ye shall in no wise believe, though a man declare it unto you."

Today the world asks, "Why doesn't God do something about sin?" My friend, God *has* done something about it! Over nineteen hundred years ago He gave His Son to die. He intruded into the affairs of the world. And He says that He is going to intrude *again* in the affairs of the world—yet today the world goes merrily along picking daisies and having a good time in sin. But God is moving. It is marvelous how Paul used Habakkuk 1:5.

And in Habakkuk's day God was moving. In spite of all the lawlessness, the war, and the sin in all the nations, God was overruling and moving in judgment.

Now God is specific in what He was doing—

**For, lo, I raise up the Chaldeans, that bitter and hasty nation, which shall march through the breadth of the land, to possess the dwellingplaces that are not theirs [Hab. 1:6].**

God is saying to Habakkuk, "Look around you. Down there on the banks of the Euphrates River, a nation is rising which will become the first great world power." (We can check with Daniel on that because Babylon is the head of gold, and it is the lion of Daniel's visions.) Babylon was number one on the parade of the great nations of the world.

"To possess the dwellingplaces that are not theirs." God is telling Habakkuk that the Babylonians are going to take the land of Judah away from them. It was a shock to Habakkuk to hear this.

A "bitter and hasty nation" is a good description of the Babylonian Empire. They were bitter, hateful, and hotheaded, marching for world conquest. They actually took the city of Jerusalem three times, and the third time they burned it to the ground. The Babylonians were a law unto themselves. They considered themselves the superior race, the dominant race, and did not recognize anyone as being equal to them.

**They are terrible and dreadful: their judgment and their dignity shall proceed of themselves [Hab. 1:7].**

"Their dignity shall proceed of themselves"— that is, they rely upon themselves. They have great self-confidence and are great boasters. These qualities are evident in Nebuchadnezzar, the founder of this great empire. In the Book of Daniel we find that Nebuchadnezzar suffered from a form of insanity, egomania, called hysteria by modern psychiatry. It was sort of a manic-depressive psychosis. The time came when he didn't even know who he was. In fact, he went out and ate grass like an animal.

**Their horses also are swifter than the leopards, and are more fierce than the evening wolves: and their horsemen shall spread themselves, and their horsemen shall come from far; they shall fly as the eagle that hasteth to eat [Hab. 1:8].**

What a picture this is! The Babylonians used the cavalry as probably no other nation has used it. The Egyptians used chariots, and the Assyrians had the latest model in chariots. Now the Babylonians have a different method, the cavalry.

"More fierce than the evening wolves." I remember the hungry wolves in west Texas when I was a boy. After the snow had fallen, my dad warned us to be careful when we went outside. If there were a pack of wolves, it would be necessary to shoot one of them. Then when the blood began to flow, the pack would turn on the wounded wolf and devour him so that we could escape.

"They shall fly as the eagle that hasteth to eat." The Babylonian army would come like hungry animals and ferocious birds and seize upon their prey. That was the story of the Chaldeans, the Babylonians.

**They shall come all for violence: their faces shall sup up as the east wind, and**

**they shall gather the captivity as the sand [Hab. 1:9].**

"They shall come all for violence." God's people had been engaging in violence, but they hadn't seen anything yet. Wait until the Babylonians get there. God is going to give them a good dose of violence! You see, chickens do come home to roost—". . . whatsoever a man soweth, that shall he also reap" (Gal. 6:7).

"Their faces shall sup up as the east wind" has also been translated as "the set of their faces is forward." In both translations the thought seems to be that the enemy will be formidable and irresistible in its advance.

"And they shall gather the captivity as the sand." Nebuchadnezzar led his forces against Jerusalem three times. At the final attack, he burned the city and also the temple and took the survivors into captivity. The Babylonians had only one purpose in view, which was to capture as many nations and as many peoples as possible and make slaves of them. This is what happened to the southern kingdom of Judah.

**And they shall scoff at the kings, and the princes shall be a scorn unto them: they shall deride every strong hold; for they shall heap dust, and take it [Hab. 1:10].**

"And they shall scoff at the kings, and the princes shall be a scorn unto them." They were confident in their own strength and in the power of their heathen gods. As the Assyrians before them, they were arrogant as they marched through the earth.

"They shall deride every strong hold; for they shall heap dust, and take it." They had only to cast up bulwarks to capture walled cities; and, when the cities surrendered, they took the inhabitants into captivity.

**Then shall his mind change, and he shall pass over, and offend, imputing this his power unto his god [Hab. 1:11].**

This is exactly what Nebuchadnezzar did. In Daniel 4:30 we read the words of this man: "The king spake, and said, Is not this great Babylon, that I have built for the house of the kingdom by the might of my power, and for the honour of my majesty?" He was lifted up with pride. He was an egomaniac. He trusted completely in himself with no trust in God. And we have a few of those around today—trusting in self rather than in God. In my own nation there is a lack of humility. And, as in

Nebuchadnezzar, it is a form of insanity. Each political party—not one, but all of them—boasts about what it can do or has done. They point the finger of guilt at the other party and at those holding office. Well, I agree they should repent, but my feeling is that everyone who is at the other end of the pointing fingers should also repent. Our big problem in America is that we depend upon our own strength, our own power, and our own ability. I turn off certain television programs because I am tired of listening to individuals boasting of their accomplishments, which are not very much. It reminds me of that scriptural suggestion of a mountain travailing. What did it bring forth? Another mountain? No, it brought forth a mouse! Although the boasting of great men today sounds like a mountain, what they have accomplished is about as big as a mouse.

In these verses God is saying to Habakkuk, "You think I am doing nothing about the sin of My people, but I am preparing a nation down yonder on the banks of the Euphrates River, and if My people do not repent, I'm going to turn the Babylonians loose." My friend, they came, and the record indicates that their destruction of Jerusalem was fierce and terrible. Some of the things they did when they took the people of Judah captive were almost unspeakable.

## SECOND PROBLEM OF THE PROPHET

Now when God says that He is going to use the Babylonians to judge His people, this raises another question in Habakkuk's mind. If you think he had a question before, he *really has a question now.*

**Art thou not from everlasting, O LORD my God, mine Holy One? we shall not die. O LORD, thou hast ordained them for judgment; and, O mighty God, thou hast established them for correction [Hab. 1:12].**

This was Habakkuk's problem: Since the Babylonians were even more wicked than the people of Judah, why would God choose a more wicked nation to punish a nation which was comparatively less wicked? This would not be the first time God had used such a method. In Isaiah 10:5 the Assyrian is called the rod of God's anger. In other words, God used Assyria like a whip in order to chastise the northern kingdom. After God had used Assyria for the chastisement of Israel, He judged Assyria for her own sins.

We find the same thing repeated here. God is going to use a wicked nation, Babylon, to chastise His people. When He is through with that chastisement, He will judge Babylon. God did just that. He moves in the affairs of men.

But the problem remains: How can a holy God use a sinful nation to accomplish His purposes?

This may be a new thought for you. You probably have heard it said—even from some pulpits—that God would never let Russia overcome the United States because we are the fair-haired boys, the good guys, the fine people. We are the ones who send missionaries to godless nations. God would never use Russia to chastise us. My friend, if you believe the Bible, you will see that God's method is to use a sinful nation to judge a people who are less sinful. If we could see what God is doing today behind the scenes, I am sure it would terrify us. I believe He is actually moving against our nation. Why? Because at one time our nation had a knowledge of God, superficial though it may have been. The Bible was once held in reverence. Very few people knew much about it, but it was respected. In our day the Bible is ignored and absolutely rejected by the nation. They may take an oath by placing their hand upon it, but they neither know nor care to know what is between its covers. Will God allow our nation to continue in its godlessness and in its flagrant sins? I don't think so. Will God use a godless nation to chastise us? Well, that was Habakkuk's question. Why would God, who is a holy God, use a pagan, heathen people to chastise His people?

Listen to Habakkuk's eloquent complaint. "Art thou not from everlasting, O Lord my God, mine Holy One?" God has come out of eternity; He is the *eternal* God. "O Lord my God, mine Holy One"—Habakkuk says, in effect, "You are a Holy God. How can you use a nation like Babylon? Word has come to us that there is a great nation rising down there on the banks of the Euphrates River, but I never dreamed that You would use them against *us*! They have been friendly to us." When King Hezekiah was sick, they sent ambassadors to him, and he gave them the red-carpet treatment, showing them all the treasures of the kingdom. Of course, the ambassadors made note of that because they would be coming back one day to get that gold. But Habakkuk didn't realize all that. He never dreamed that God would use Babylon to chastise Judah. He didn't understand why a holy God would use such a method.

Then he says, "We shall not die." He was right about that. This goes back to the promises of God to Abraham, to Isaac, and to Jacob. God made promises to Moses and to Joshua and to David. He gave promises to the prophets who had appeared on the scene before Habakkuk. God had said that He would never let the nation perish. "We shall not die."

That is a good statement, by the way, to drop down upon our amillennial friends who believe that God is through with the nation Israel. God is not through with them; God has an eternal purpose with *them*, just as He has with the church which He is calling out of this world. And, thank God, the child of God today can say, "We shall not die." The Lord Jesus Christ came to this earth to die—He said He did—to die in your stead and in my stead. He said, "I am the resurrection and the life," and He came back from the dead. He ". . . was delivered for our offences, and was raised again for our justification" (Rom. 4:25). The Lord Jesus said to the two weeping sisters of Lazarus, ". . . I am the resurrection, and the life: he that believeth in me, though he were *dead* [think of that!], yet shall he live." When Habakkuk said, "We shall not die," he was right; they wouldn't. "And whosoever liveth and believeth in me shall never die. Believest thou this?" (John 11:25–26, italics mine). This is the message of the gospel. It is something for you and me to believe. Of course, someday you are going to die physically, but are you dead now spiritually? If you are, you will be dead in trespasses and sins for the rest of eternity, and that means eternal separation from God. God is a holy God, and He is not going to take *sin* to heaven. But He has promised that if we will trust His Son, He will give us eternal life. God says, "If you will believe that you are a sinner, that you don't deserve salvation and can't work for it, then I offer it to you as a gift. And by My grace you can be saved. You will receive eternal life. He that hath the Son hath life." My friend, do you have the Son today? If you do, you have life, eternal life, and you will not die.

When Habakkuk said to God, "We shall not die," he was on the right track, but he just couldn't understand (as many of us can't understand) some of the performance of God in this world. God had told Habakkuk earlier that he needed to get a perspective of it. You and I have a tremendous advantage in our day because we have the perspective of history. We can look back to Habakkuk's day and even beyond to the very beginning of the human family. We have a very good perspective of

God's dealing with the nations of this world and of God's dealing with the nation Israel. Also, God is dealing today with His church that is in the world.

God moves in a mysterious way His wonders to perform. He has told us that His ways are not our ways, that His thoughts are not our thoughts. "For my thoughts are not your thoughts, neither are your ways my ways, saith the LORD. For as the heavens are higher than the earth, so are my ways higher than your ways, and my thoughts than your thoughts" (Isa. 55:8–9).

My friend, do not be disturbed if you are not thinking as God thinks. You are not God. Unfortunately, many folk try to take His place. They are trying to work for their salvation, thinking that their character and their good works will merit them salvation. They expect God to pat them on the head someday and say, "You were certainly a nice, sweet little boy down there." Yet, actually, they were corrupt sinners, alienated from the life of God, with no capacity for God whatsoever. If you come to the Father, you will come *His* way, or you are not going to get there. We need to recognize this, my friend. We are a nation of proud people who need to be deflated as a pin deflates a balloon. Instead of blaming everyone else for the problems in our nation, or the problems in our church, or the problems in our home, we should fall on our knees before God and confess our own sins—"not my brother, nor my sister, but it's *me*, oh, Lord, standin' in the need of prayer."

This was the condition of the nation of Judah in the days of Habakkuk. He said to God, "We shall not die."

"O LORD thou hast ordained *them* for judgment." Here is Habakkuk pointing his finger at Babylon. "*They* are the bad guys, and we are the good guys." It is amazing how quickly we can change our point of view. For years I went out to Flagstaff, Arizona, to the Southwest Bible and Missionary Conference. I always enjoyed being out there with the opportunity it offered to have fellowship with the Indians. It was there I learned a good example of man's way of looking at things. One of the young Indian pastors said to me, "You know, Dr. McGee, in the old days when the Indians would raid a village and kill some of the whites, it was called a massacre. But when the whites raided an Indian village and destroyed *all* the Indians, it was called a victory." It is interesting how we always class ourselves with the good guys.

"O mighty God, thou hast established them

for correction." In other words, Habakkuk is saying, "Lord, it really isn't us who are bad after all. They are the mean fellows. They are the ones You should judge and correct." Has he forgotten that he went to the Lord and asked the Lord why He wasn't doing something about the evil among His own people? Habakkuk had pointed out that the people were flaunting the Law and were ignoring God, paying no attention to God's commands. Habakkuk had accused God of not doing anything about the situation. Has he forgotten that?

Now here is Habakkuk's argument—

**Thou art of purer eyes than to behold evil, and canst not look on iniquity: wherefore lookest thou upon them that deal treacherously, and holdest thy tongue when the wicked devoureth the man that is more righteous than he? [Hab. 1:13].**

"Thou art of purer eyes than to behold evil, and canst not look on iniquity." That is a true statement. A holy God cannot look upon evil and iniquity. That is the reason no one can go to heaven with his sin on him. That is why we must all have the forgiveness for our sins. We all need the cleansing power of the blood of the Lamb. We must be given a new nature. We must be born again. Even Nicodemus, a very religious man, needed to be born again and to receive a new nature. Religion will not wash away sin. It is the blood of the Lord Jesus Christ who died and rose again that will wash away sin. God cannot look on iniquity, and He never will look on iniquity. That is why there is no entrance into heaven for you until your sin has been dealt with.

You see, when God forgives you, it is because the penalty for your sin has been paid for by His Son. God is not a sentimental old gentleman who doesn't have the heart to judge little man down here on this earth. God is a holy God who will not look upon iniquity. Your sin will have to be confessed and forgiven before you can be accepted by Him.

"Wherefore lookest thou upon them that deal treacherously." Habakkuk says, "You can't trust those Babylonians. They are sinners and a bunch of crooks!" He was right. They were. But God was going to use them to accomplish His purpose.

This is frightening to me. Don't ever get the idea that God cannot use a godless nation to chasten another nation. I speak now from the point of view of a white man and an American. For years the white man in all the great nations of Europe ruled the world through those great, proud nations. Then America became one of the leading nations of the world. God humiliated us in the war with Vietnam. He is humiliating us in our dealings with the Middle East. All they need to do is turn off the supply of oil, and suddenly we take a nose dive. God deals with the nations of the world in interesting ways. I watch what has been happening in the world with a great deal of interest. I have come to the conclusion that God is still moving among the nations of the world today. You and I may be frightened as we contemplate what lies ahead, but God is not frightened. He is still in charge. Nothing is out of His control. He is still running this universe.

"Wherefore lookest thou upon them that deal treacherously, and holdest thy tongue when the wicked devoureth the man that is more righteous than he?" Habakkuk said the wrong thing here. It is not "the man that is more righteous than he" because *none* are righteous. He should have said, "the man who is a greater sinner than he." But God didn't say that He was going to punish on that basis. God is going to *use* the Babylonians to punish His people.

This brings us to one of the most eloquent sections of the Word of God.

**And makest men as the fishes of the sea, as the creeping things, that have no ruler over them?**

**They take up all of them with the angle, they catch them in their net, and gather them in their drag: therefore they rejoice and are glad.**

**Therefore they sacrifice unto their net, and burn incense unto their drag; because by them their portion is fat, and their meat plenteous [Hab. 1:14–16].**

"And makest men as the fishes of the sea, as the creeping things, that have no ruler over them" refers to the callousness with which the Babylonians handled their enemies, treating them as fish of the sea or as creeping things in the soil which have no defense.

The angle and the net and the drag represent the armies and the weapons used by the Babylonians to carry on their military conquests.

God also uses the catching of fish as a figure of speech, but He catches fish to save them, not to destroy them. You remember that the Lord Jesus said to some of His own disciples who were fishermen, "You have been catching fish and that's fine, but I am going to give you a job of catching *men*" (see Matt. 4:19). My friend, to me the greatest business in the world is to be a fisherman, and that is all I claim to be. We are to fish for men in our day.

"Therefore they sacrifice unto their net, and burn incense unto their drag." The Babylonians were pagans, of course, and gave no credit to the true and living God for their successes.

There are fishermen here in Southern California who think that they get a good catch because their priest has blessed the fishing fleet. That has nothing in the world to do with it, my friend. The reason that you can get plenty to eat is that God is *good*, and that is the only reason. *God* is good, and He is the one who provides.

**Shall they therefore empty their net, and not spare continually to slay the nations? [Hab. 1:17].**

Habakkuk is asking God, "Are You going to permit them to go on into the future, destroying people after people?" God's answer is, "No. I'm going to send Judah into captivity in Babylon as a chastisement, a judgment for her sins, but then I will judge Babylon." My friend, God did exactly that, and in our day Babylon lies under the dust and rubble of the ages. It is a silent but eloquent testimony that God does judge evil.

Now let's translate this interrogation of Habakkuk into the times in which we live. Why does God permit evil? Well, He permits it because He is long-suffering. He is not willing that any should perish, and He has provided a cross, a crucified Savior, so that no one needs to perish. This He did at the first coming of Christ.

Habakkuk's second question is, "Why does not God judge the wicked?" God will answer that at the second coming of Christ, because at that time He will judge sin. All we need is a perspective to see the answers to these two questions. Christ came the first time to wear a crown of thorns and to die upon a cross. The next time He comes, He will wear a crown of glory and will hold the scepter that will rule the earth.

To make a personal application of this, we ask the question, "Why does God permit this trial to happen to me?" I do not know what the answer is for you, but God has an answer.

Several years ago I stayed in a motel in Siloam Springs, Arkansas, at a location where I could throw a rock into the state of Oklahoma. My dad is buried over there. When I was a boy of fourteen, I stood by his grave and wept. He had been killed in an accident at a cotton gin. After the funeral service was over and everyone had gone, I rode back on my bicycle to his grave. I wept and cried, "Why, oh God, did You take him?" Time has gone by, and today I have an answer for that. I know now that it was God's method of dealing with a boy who would never have entered the ministry otherwise.

Actually, what right do we have to question our Maker? What right does little man have to look into the face of heaven and demand, "*Why* do You do this?" Well, to begin with, it is none of our business. It is God's business. This is His universe, and He is running it to please Himself. We are to trust Him.

I can remember when I was a little boy in Oklahoma, we lived in an area that had many tornadoes. In the night my dad would pick me up, and I would begin to cry and ask, "Where are we going?" He would take me down to the storm cellar where it was dark and damp and not very comfortable. He would put me on a pallet, and in the morning I would awaken and be safe and secure. When I was a crying little boy, my dad didn't explain tornadoes to me. He simply protected me from them. All I knew was that I trusted my dad. After my dad died, I learned more and more to trust my Heavenly Father. There are times He has done things to me that He hasn't explained. He took my first child, and I really had a question about that. Do you want to know something? I still have a question mark about it. But I do know this: He has the answer. Someday He will tell me the answer. In the meantime, I'll trust Him.

# CHAPTER 2

**THEME:** *The perception of the prophet*

In chapter 1 we saw the perplexity of the prophet. Now the prophet has learned that God has answers for his questions. He answered his first question, which raised a bigger question, but God has an answer for that also.

My friend, if you have a question, don't smother it in pious phraseology. I often hear people say, "Oh, I'm trusting the Lord," when they are not trusting Him; they are questioning Him every step of the way. There is no sin in questioning the Lord. Just go to Him and tell Him that you don't understand. This is what Habakkuk did.

## PRACTICE OF THE PROPHET

**I will stand upon my watch, and set me upon the tower, and will watch to see what he will say unto me, and what I shall answer when I am reproved [Hab. 2:1].**

Habakkuk says that he is going to the watchtower to wait. (When he says, "watchtower," he doesn't mean that he is going to read a magazine!) Prophets are compared to watchmen in several of the books of prophecy. For instance, in Ezekiel it was, "Son of man, I have made thee a watchman unto the house of Israel: therefore hear the word at my mouth, and give them warning from me" (Ezek. 3:17). The prophets were watchmen who were to prophesy to the nation, and God would hold them responsible for giving out His warning. In a walled city the watchman was the one who watched for enemies during the night; if he was faithful, the city was safe. But if he should betray the city or fail to sound the alarm when an enemy approached, the city was in deep trouble. So Habakkuk, God's prophet, says that he is going to the watchtower to wait for a message from God.

"I . . . will watch to see what he will say unto me." Habakkuk is saying, "I'm going to the watchtower, and I'm going to wait patiently, because I know that God has an answer. I don't know what it will be, but I know He has an answer and He will give that answer in due time."

"And what I shall answer when I am reproved." The word *reprove* here is not the best translation of the original word: Habakkuk did not expect God to rebuke him or, to use the common colloquialism, "bawl him out" because he was questioning God's ways. Habakkuk felt that God would give him the right answer so he would understand God's ways. And he was willing to wait for it.

God often delays. He moves slowly in all

that He does. God intends to give Habakkuk an answer, but it will come in His own time. We are the ones who are in a hurry; God is not. For example, sometimes we hear Christians speak of the "soon coming of Christ." Can you show me in the Bible where that is found? I have never found it. Jesus said, "Behold, I come *quickly* . . ." (Rev. 22:7, italics mine). He didn't say He was coming *soon*. It has now been over nineteen hundred years since He spoke those words, and that could hardly be called soon. He said He would return quickly, because the things that are mentioned in Revelation, which will happen just before he returns to earth, are going to happen quickly. The thing which will introduce the last seven years before Christ comes to establish His kingdom will be the Rapture of the church. When the church leaves the earth, events will move quickly—like a trip-hammer, one blow right after another. Christ will come quickly. He will come right on schedule. We are not to look for the soon coming of Christ but the imminent coming of Christ.

Neither will Christ "delay" His coming, as I hear some pious brothers say. The Lord is coming on His schedule—not mine nor yours. He will not delay. But we must remember that the Lord is long-suffering. He is patient. He is not willing that any should perish. And in Habakkuk's day there was a company of people down yonder in Babylon whom God was going to save. That seventy-year captivity of the children of Israel was going to be a glorious time for God because He was going to reach even the heart of Nebuchadnezzar, king of the Babylonians!

Habakkuk says, "I'm going to retire now to my watchtower. I don't have the answer, but I'm going to wait for an answer from God." And, my friend, you and I are to walk by faith and not by sight. In 2 Corinthians 5 the apostle Paul speaks of the time when our bodies will be put into the grave. The day will come when Christ will call us and raise up our bodies from the grave. In the meantime, when we are absent from the body, we are present with the Lord. When we leave these bodies, we are going to be at home with the Lord. There is an interval of time between the burial of our bodies and the resurrection of our bodies. The Lord moves slowly as judged by the way we look at things. That is why Paul interposes here, "For we walk by faith, not by sight:" (2 Cor. 5:7). Do you have questions which have not been answered? I do. But I have learned, as I did as a little boy when my dad picked me up and carried me to the storm cellar, that my

Heavenly Father also has reasons for the things He does in my life. Although I don't always understand them now, I know that He has the answer, and someday He will give it to me. We need to trust Him.

## PATIENCE OF THE PROPHET

**And the LORD answered me, and said, Write the vision, and make it plain upon tables, that he may run that readeth it [Hab. 2:2].**

God is saying, "Write it so that those folk in the twentieth century—especially that fellow, McGee, who will have some questions [and I think He had you in mind also]—will have an answer from Me during the days when they will be walking by faith."

"That he may run that readeth it." We sometimes get that turned around and make it say, "That he who runs may read it." That is not what God is saying. He says that we need to have a road map with us. We need to know where we are going. We need to know a great deal about the way so that, after we have read it, we may run. That is, the one reading it was to run to tell it forth; he was to be the messenger of God's Word.

My friend, there are many folk today who are trying to preach and trying to teach God's Word without adequate preparation. They need to do more reading before they start running. I remember when I wanted to enter into the ministry, I thought I would skip part of my college training and bypass seminary and go immediately to a Bible school and then start preaching. I thank God for a marvelous, wonderful pastor who told me to get all the training I could get. Learn to read before you start running. Before you begin to witness, be able to give a reason for the hope that is in you.

**For the vision is yet for an appointed time, but at the end it shall speak, and not lie: though it tarry, wait for it; because it will surely come, it will not tarry [Hab. 2:3].**

"For the vision is yet for an appointed time, but at the end it shall speak." There is no better way to explain this than to quote a note on this verse in *The New Scofield Reference Bible* (p. 954):

To the watching prophet comes the response of the vision (vv. 2–20). Three elements are to be distinguished: (1) The moral judgment of the LORD upon the evils practiced by Israel (vv. 5–13, 15–19). (2) The future purpose of God that "the earth shall be filled with the knowledge of the glory of the Lord, as the waters cover the sea" (v. 14). That this revelation awaits the return of the Lord in glory is shown (a) by the parallel passage in Isa. 11:9–12; and (b) by the quotation of v. 3 in Heb. 10:37–38, where the "it" of the vision becomes "he" and refers to the return of the Lord. It is then, after the vision is fulfilled, that "the knowledge of the glory," etc. shall fill the earth. But (3) meantime, "the just shall live by his faith." This great evangelical word is applied to Jews and Gentiles in Rom. 1:17; to the Gentiles in Gal. 3:11–14; and to the Hebrews especially in Heb. 10:38. This opening of life to faith alone, makes possible not only the salvation of the Gentiles, but also makes possible a believing remnant in Israel while the nation, as such, is in blindness and unbelief (see Rom. 11:1 and 5, *notes*), with neither priesthood nor temple, and consequently unable to keep the ordinances of the law. Such is the Lord! In disciplinary government His ancient Israel is cast out of the land and judicially blinded (2 Cor. 3:12–15), but in covenanted mercy the individual Jew may resort to the simple faith of Abraham (Gen. 15:6; Rom. 4:1–5) and be saved. This, however, does not set aside the Palestinian and Davidic Covenants (see Dt. 30:3 and 2 Sam. 7:16, *notes*), for "the earth shall be filled," etc. (v. 14), and the Lord will again be in His Temple (v. 20). Cp. Rom. 11:25–27.

My friend, you can depend on the fact that someday God will give us the answers to all of our questions. That is going to be a great day! I am not interested in heaven's golden streets, but I am very interested in learning the answers to a great many questions that puzzle mankind in our day. In the meantime, we are to walk by faith.

## PAGEANT FOR THE PROPHET

This brings us to one of the most important verses in the Scriptures. It is the key to the little Book of Habakkuk. And, actually, it gives the key to the three great doctrinal epistles in the New Testament that quote this verse: Romans 1:17; Galatians 3:11; and Hebrews 10:38.

**Behold, his soul which is lifted up is not upright in him: but the just shall live by his faith [Hab. 2:4].**

"The just shall live by his faith." There have been many ways of attempting to sidestep the tremendous impact of this verse. Some have attempted to interpret "faith" as faithfulness or right dealing—the just shall live by his faithfulness. However, this verse gives us the two ways which are opened up to mankind.

Notice that the verse mentions two groups of individuals which are in the world: (1) the lifted-up or puffed-up soul; and (2) the just man who is living by his faith. In other words, you could call them the lost and the saved, those who have trusted God and those who have not believed God. Or you can call them the saints and the ain'ts—that makes a sharp division also.

You remember that verse 1 told us that Habakkuk has gone to his watchtower to wait for the answer of God. It will be God's great message which will explain His dealings with individuals and with nations. So here in verse 4 we have a great principle that God has laid down. Actually, it is an axiom of the Bible.

You will remember that when you studied geometry, you accepted certain axioms which were self-evident and you didn't have to prove. For example, a straight line is the shortest distance between two points. And there are certain statements in the Scriptures which are great axioms. This is one of them: "Behold, his soul which is lifted up is not upright in him."

"His soul which is lifted up is not upright in him" describes a group of people who are proud. Either they are attempting to work out their own salvation, or they are just living for today with the philosophy of "eat, drink, and be merry for tomorrow we die." They have no real goal in life. "His soul . . . is not upright in him." He is wrong. He is going down the wrong pathway. "There is a way which seemeth right unto a man, but the end thereof are the ways of death" (Prov. 14:12). You know, I am sure, many folk in this group of humanity. They have a lifted-up or puffed-up soul. They are lifted up with pride. As they meander along their way, picking daisies as they go, they move as on a slow-moving river and will finally arrive at the sea of destruction. That is their end. The Scriptures seldom enlarge upon the fate of the lost, but our Lord Jesus followed them through when He told of the rich man and Lazarus (see Luke 16). When Lazarus died, he was carried to paradise; when the rich man died, he went to hades. He went, as it was said of Judas, to his own place. If you go through life like this, your end will be the same.

"The just shall live by his faith" describes the second group of the human family. They are flowing down the river of life toward the city of God and toward full knowledge—". . . then shall I know even as also I am known" (1 Cor. 13:12, italics mine). Between the moment of salvation and the then, the saved ones will walk by faith. We may not have the answers to our questions now, but God will give them to us when we arrive in His presence.

Now because Habakkuk 2:4 is quoted in the New Testament and is actually the key to the Epistles of Romans, Galatians, and Hebrews, let's look at these quotations more carefully.

In the Epistle to the Romans, the emphasis is upon justification by faith for salvation. "For I am not ashamed of the gospel of Christ: for it is the power of God unto salvation to every one that believeth; to the Jew first, and also to the Greek. For therein is the righteousness of God revealed from faith to faith: as it is written, The just shall live by faith" (Rom. 1:16–17, italics mine). The point here is that "the just," the one who has been justified by faith, shall also live by faith. And that is the great message of the Epistle to the Romans.

In the Epistle to the Galatians, the quotation is this: "But that no man is justified by the law in the sight of God, it is evident: for, The just shall live by faith" (Gal. 3:11, italics mine). The emphasis is a little different here, for we find in Galatians 2:20, "I am crucified with Christ: nevertheless I live; yet not I, but Christ liveth in me: and the life which I now live in the flesh I live by the faith of the Son of God, who loved me, and gave himself for me." While in Romans the emphasis was on justification by faith for salvation, in Galatians the emphasis is not only on faith that saves, but on a faith by which you live throughout life.

In the Epistle to the Hebrews, the quotation from Habakkuk 2:4 is this: "Now the just shall live by faith: but if any man draw back, my soul shall have no pleasure in him" (Heb. 10:38). Here the emphasis is upon the word live—"the just shall live by faith." And in the following chapter, we read of men and women who lived by faith—the emphasis is upon living.

When Habakkuk looked into the future, he asked, "Why, God?" Now from our vantage point, we can look back into history and see the answer to Habakkuk's question. God sent His own people into captivity because it served the purpose of chastisement for their sins. And now we see His greater purpose: it enabled Him to bring the Savior into the world—in the fullness of time.

Again I want to draw your attention to Paul's great sermon at Antioch of Pisidia: "But he, whom God raised again, saw no corruption. Be it known unto you therefore, men and brethren, that through this man is preached unto you the forgiveness of sins: And by him all that believe are justified from all things, from which ye could not be justified by the law of Moses. Beware therefore, lest that come upon you, which is spoken of in the prophets; Behold, ye despisers, and wonder, and perish: for I work a work in your days, a work which ye shall in no wise believe, though a man declare it unto you" (Acts 13:37–41). Therefore, Paul shuts them in to only one way to God—faith. The message is: ". . . Christ died for our sins according to the scriptures; And that he was buried, and that he rose again the third day according to the scriptures" (1 Cor. 15:3–4).

And what are we to do? We are to accept Him as our Savior. We are to trust Him and walk by faith—not by law. I am disturbed when I see so many folk today who are attempting to put believers back under the Ten Commandments or under some little legal system that they have worked out, such as rules and regulations for the family—for the husband and for the wife and for the child. Oh, my friend, if you have been saved by faith in the Lord Jesus Christ, love Him. Loving Him will work out your problems. Loving Him will enable you to walk in the Spirit; and walking in the Spirit, you will be filled with the Spirit, and you will have joy in your heart. You will be a better husband or a better wife or a better child. You will be a better employee or a better employer. Wherever you are, you will be a better person if you walk by faith, and one of these days you will walk right into His presence and be with Him throughout eternity.

Habakkuk was a man of faith. He said, "I'll go to my watchtower and wait for God's answer. I am trusting the One who does have the answer." You see, ". . . without faith it is impossible to please him; for he that cometh to God must believe that he is, and that He is a rewarder of them that diligently seek him" (Heb. 11:6). And the "just shall live by his faith." My friend, today God is asking you to come to Him, and the only way you can come to Him is by faith. The man of faith receives life by faith, he walks by faith, and he moves into eternity by faith—not by his own ability but on the strength and the ability of Another.

Let me repeat that Habakkuk 2:4 gives the two ways which are opened up to mankind. Our Lord Jesus put it like this: "Enter ye in at the strait gate: for wide is the gate, and broad is the way, that leadeth to destruction, and many there be which go in thereat: Because strait is the gate, and narrow is the way, which leadeth unto life, and few there be that find it" (Matt. 7:13–14).

The broad way is actually like a funnel. It is very wide at the place where you enter, but it narrows down so that the follower ends up in only one place—destruction. That is the story of the unbelieving sinner. It is like going down a canyon. I have experienced this when I have been hunting out here in the West. You can start out in the desert in a very wide, open spot. Soon you enter into a canyon; and, as you go deeper and deeper into the canyon, the floor of the canyon gets narrower and narrower. That is the picture here. The entrance is wide, but the end narrows down to destruction.

The strait gate, or the narrow gate, is also an entrance into a funnel. In this case, the gate or entrance is very narrow. Jesus Christ said, ". . . I am the way, the truth, and the life: no man cometh unto the Father, but by me" (John 14:6). That entrance is narrowed down to one person. He is the way. He doesn't just show us the way; He is the way. "He that hath the Son hath life; and he that hath not the Son of God hath not life" (1 John 5:12). You either have Christ, or you don't have Him. You either trust Him, or you don't trust Him. Your salvation has nothing in the world to do with going through a ceremony or making pledges or going forward in a meeting or in joining a church. Your salvation is dependent upon your relationship with Jesus Christ. That is the reason it is a narrow gate. God has given to the world just this one way. The issue is what you will do with Jesus Christ who died on the cross and rose again. That is why Jesus said, ". . . strait is the gate, and narrow is the way, which leadeth unto life, and few there be that find it" (Matt. 7:14).

This gate is also like a funnel. You enter in at the narrow gate—Christ is the way. But as you enter, it doesn't narrow down even more. No, it widens out. Jesus said, ". . . I am come that they might have life, and that they might have it more abundantly" (John 10:10). Oh,

the freedom and liberty He gives to those who are His own!

Let me give an example. Alcohol addiction and drug addiction can look like a broad road of liberty, but they end in the narrow canyon of destruction. My dad used to say, "I can drink, or I can let it alone." He died when I was fourteen. He was a heavy drinker, but he was never an alcoholic. When I was a boy, I would talk to him about his heavy drinking and ask why he didn't give it up. He would say, "Son, I can give it up any time I want to." Do you know what his problem was? He didn't want to. Had he lived longer, I am confident the day would have come when he would have found himself in a very narrow canyon with only one alternative, and that would be to take another drink.

Now the Christian who went in the narrow gate by trusting Christ as his Savior never gets to the place where it narrows down. He really is *living*. If you really want to live, come to Christ.

## PARABLE TO THE PROPHET

Now how about the other crowd—those whose soul "is not upright in him"? The following "woes" are directed to them and refer primarily to the plundering Babylonians who would conquer Judah. These "woes" are just about as systematic and orderly as anything you will find in Scripture. They are presented in five stanzas of three verses each.

**Yea also, because he transgresseth by wine, he is a proud man, neither keepeth at home, who enlargeth his desire as hell, and is as death, and cannot be satisfied, but gathereth unto him all nations, and heapeth unto him all people [Hab. 2:5].**

"Yea also, because he transgresseth by wine." He is talking about the Babylonians. At that moment Babylon was not the great nation that it became later at the time of Daniel.

The first charge is that they transgressed by wine and were proud. "Neither keepeth at home"—they longed to go forth and conquer. "But gathereth unto him all nations, and heapeth unto him all people." They were inflamed with an ambition for conquest. They were never satisfied but kept attacking nation after nation, gathering spoil and captives. Babylon became the first great world power. They wanted to rule the world. That has been the ambition of a great many nations of the world. I am afraid that after World War II the United States got that insane notion also. We stuck our nose into the affairs of other countries when we should have kept our nose at home where it belonged. This has been the fallacy of the nations of the world, and it was the fallacy of Babylon. They were lifted up with pride and felt they were capable of ruling the world.

Notice that God mentions their sin of drunkenness. This issue comes up several times in the writings of the prophets: in Amos, Joel, Nahum, and now Habakkuk. Nahum makes it clear that drunkenness brought down the kingdom of Assyria. Amos tells us that it was drunkenness that caused God to send the northern kingdom into captivity. Now Habakkuk says that it is drunkenness that will cause God to destroy Babylon. In other words, drunkenness works out its own destruction. Drunkenness characterized Babylon. Read Daniel 5, which tells of Belshazzar's great feast. That was the night that Babylon fell. Why? They were drunk! It was a night of revelry and drunkenness. They felt perfectly safe and secure in their fortified city.

Drunkenness brought down Rome also. On our tour to Bible lands, I have taken groups of people to a place many of them had never heard of. It is Ostia, about fifteen miles from Rome, down by the Tiber River on the seacoast. The ruins at Ostia reveal that there the Romans gave themselves over to revelry and drunkenness—those were the things that brought them there. It was the playground of the Romans.

And drunkenness will destroy our own nation. As I travel across this country, I stay in many of the hotels, motels, and inns where conventions are in progress. As I have observed them, they are times of great revelry and drinking. Recently in Dallas, Texas, there were two conventions going on at one time while we were there. On the way to the service in the evening, we would pass two big rooms where cocktail parties were in progress. Now these were the conventions of two reputable companies in this country, but that was the way they carried on their business. How long will a nation last that has millions of alcoholics?

Here in the little Book of Habakkuk, God says that drunkenness has led to pride and has made you like "hell" or sheol—you want to gobble up everything. The Book of Proverbs puts it this way: "The horseleach hath two daughters, crying, Give, give. There are three things that are never satisfied, yea, four things say not, It is enough: The grave. . ."

(Prov. 30:15–16). The grave is sheol, and it is first on the list. Habakkuk uses the same expression, "who enlargeth his desire as hell [sheol]"—continuing to expand their borders, moving out, never, never satisfied.

Now God spells out the five woes upon Babylon.

**Shall not all these take up a parable against him, and a taunting proverb against him, and say, Woe to him that increaseth that which is not his! how long? and to him that ladeth himself with thick clay! [Hab. 2:6].**

The first woe is a taunting proverb against Babylon because they were seizing by force that which was not theirs.

"Shall not all these take up a parable against him." The "all these" probably refers to the nations that have been victims of Babylon's aggression.

"To him that ladeth himself with thick clay!" A better translation is "and maketh himself rich with loans," which makes more sense. It is one thing to buy property and pay for it, but it is another thing to take it by force. God is pronouncing a woe against this nation for wanting more and taking that which does not belong to them.

You see, God has planned that man by the sweat of his brow is going to make his living. And, my friend, if you are not earning your living by the sweat of your brow, somebody else is doing it for you. Babylon wanted somebody else to do the work, and then they by force would take it away. That is the first woe—God is going to judge Babylon for that, and He is just and righteous for doing it.

**Shall they not rise up suddenly that shall bite thee, and awake that shall vex thee, and thou shalt be for booties unto them? [Hab. 2:7].**

"And thou shalt be for booties unto them?" is the principle that whatever a man sows, that shall he also reap. God is saying, "You take it away from somebody, then somebody else will take it away from you." The fact is that when Media-Persia became a great nation, they took Babylon. By night the River Euphrates, which flowed through the city of Babylon, was cut off and the water diverted into other channels, leaving a dry riverbed through the city. And Gobryas, the Median general, marched his army along that riverbed into the city and took it by surprise.

**Because thou hast spoiled many nations, all the remnant of the people**

shall spoil thee; because of men's blood, and for the violence of the land, of the city, and of all that dwell therein [Hab. 2:8].

Man is bloodthirsty, and man is covetous.

The second woe is for their covetousness and their self-aggrandizement—

**Woe to him that coveteth an evil covetousness to his house, that he may set his nest on high, that he may be delivered from the power of evil!**

**Thou hast consulted shame to thy house by cutting off many people, and hast sinned against thy soul.**

**For the stone shall cry out of the wall, and the beam out of the timber shall answer it [Hab. 2:9–11].**

Covetousness was a sin of Babylon along with drunkenness. Their covetousness was an evil kind of coveting. They wanted that which did not belong to them. God tells us we are not to covet our neighbor's property or our neighbor's wife or our neighbor's wealth.

"That he may set his nest on high, that he may be delivered from the power of evil!" This is likening Babylon to an eagle who feels that his nest is absolutely impregnable.

"Thou hast consulted shame to thy house . . . and hast sinned against thy soul." Babylon brought the judgment of God upon itself by its covetousness and bloodshed. Even the stones would cry out against them. Contrast this to the time in the life of the Lord Jesus when the religious rulers tried to silence the crowd who were singing hosannas to Him. He said, ". . . I tell you that, if these should hold their peace, the stones would immediately cry out" (Luke 19:40).

The third woe has to do with murder and pillage, slaughter and violence—

**Woe to him that buildeth a town with blood, and stablisheth a city by iniquity! [Hab. 2:12].**

This was the method of destruction that built Babylon. They became rich by warfare.

My friend, if you stand back and look at the history of mankind, you come to the conclusion that he must be insane the way that he has lived on this earth. And, actually, he is insane—insane with a sinful nature so that he can't even direct his path. He thinks he is right in what he does. People have never waged war without thinking they were doing the right thing. We see here God's condemna-

tion of Babylon, but it can be stretched out and brought up to date and fitted like a glove on any modern nation you choose.

**Behold, is it not of the LORD of hosts that the people shall labour in the very fire, and the people shall weary themselves for very vanity? [Hab. 2:13].**

This verse could be translated: "Behold, is it not of the LORD of hosts that the peoples shall labor only for fire, and the nations shall weary themselves for nothing?" Think of the futile efforts that have been made by the great nations of the past. Instead of building up, they have spent more time in tearing down. Look at Greece, for instance, and their marvelous, wonderful pieces of architecture, the statues, the art, and literature; but actually, the Greeks spent more time in destruction. If you follow the march of Alexander the Great as he crossed over into Asia, you will notice that he did nothing in the world but destroy one city after another, one great civilization after another. That was the thing that marked him out. And that is the thing that marked out Babylon, the nation about which Habakkuk is prophesying.

**For the earth shall be filled with the knowledge of the glory of the LORD, as the waters cover the sea [Hab. 2:14].**

This is the far-off goal toward which God is moving. This will be fulfilled when the Lord Jesus Christ returns to the earth (see Isa. 11:9).

**Woe unto him that giveth his neighbour drink, that puttest thy bottle to him, and makest him drunken also, that thou mayest look on their nakedness! [Hab. 2:15].**

This is actually a little different from the drunkenness mentioned in verse 5. There God says, "He transgresseth by wine." Here He says, "Woe unto him that giveth his neighbour drink, that puttest thy bottle to him, and makest him drunken also, that thou mayest look on their nakedness!" The tragic thing is that liquor is something that leads to gross immorality. It leads to the breaking down of morals. It leads men to commit sins they otherwise probably would not commit— dishonesty and many other sins.

Drunkenness is an alarming problem in many of our large corporations today. I have talked with a man here in Southern California who holds a very responsible position in a large corporation and with another man who is connected with one of the big banks in our state. They both tell me that their corporations have employed certain officials whose business it is to watch for any of their men who are beginning to drink too much. They have many ways of discerning this. They will even talk to his wife and have him followed at night if certain things begin to show in his work—if he is late to work or perhaps doesn't even show up for work. Because some of these men are brilliant men, good men, the company officials will go to them, confront them with their drinking problem, and offer to help them to give it up. But notice how crazy this is: on one hand, these companies have cocktail parties where their men get drunk, and on the other hand, they have a process for drying them out! That is sort of like running a hospital where you bring in healthy people, give them disease germs, and then treat them for the disease they get! Man becomes sort of a guinea pig in this crazy world in which we live today. So many illogical things are being done even by large corporations.

This is the condemnation that is here brought against Babylon. God says to them, "You are making drunkards. Not only are you drinking yourselves, but you are also making drunkards of others."

Again may I refer to an authority, a man and his wife who are working with young people who are caught up in the drug culture. They tell me that many of these young people have come out of homes where cocktails are served. If Mama and Papa are going to have cocktails and live their lives, why can't Junior have his drugs? I would like to have a good answer for that because Junior has asked that question of me. I don't have an answer for him because I think Mama and Papa are responsible for his going into this drug culture. I believe that behind the problem of drugs has been drunkenness. Drunkenness is the thing that has brought this to pass in our nation today.

I know that these things are not being said today, and I know that it does not make me very popular to say them. But I don't think Habakkuk was too popular himself—certainly not down in Babylon when this word percolated down there. But they found out that God condemns drunkenness and that God condemns making drunkards of others.

Notice that drunkenness leads to gross immorality—

**Thou art filled with shame for glory: drink thou also, and let thy foreskin be uncovered: the cup of the LORD's right hand shall be turned unto thee, and shameful spewing shall be on thy glory [Hab. 2:16].**

Drunkenness leads to gross immorality. It leads to divorce. It leads to the breaking up of homes. It leads to a life of sin. I have come to the place in my own life that I have lost respect for men in government. These fellows talk so big about honesty, and they talk so big and brave about helping the poor, while it is a well-known fact that many of them are actually alcoholics who drink like fish. May I ask you, how can we have respect for government when this sort of thing is all out in the open? Yet they ask us to respect them, to look up to them, and to give them our support. It makes me bow my head in shame to see what is happening in this great land of ours. My friend, Habakkuk spelled it out here years ago. God says, "The reason I will bring Babylon down is because of these sins."

**For the violence of Lebanon shall cover thee, and the spoil of beasts, which made them afraid, because of men's blood, and for the violence of the land, of the city, and of all that dwell therein [Hab. 2:17].**

Violence is another of the fruits which comes from drunkenness. You see, all kinds of immoralities spring from drunkenness. The drug culture, the gross immorality, the prevalence of divorce—all of these sins that are abroad in our land today—have come out of drunkenness.

The fifth woe is God's condemnation of the greatest sin of all—

**What profiteth the graven image that the maker thereof hath graven it; the molten image, and a teacher of lies, that the maker of his work trusteth therein, to make dumb idols?**

**Woe unto him that saith to the wood, Awake; to the dumb stone, Arise, it shall teach! Behold, it is laid over with gold and silver, and there is no breath at all in the midst of it [Hab. 2:18–19].**

Actually, drunkenness is not the greatest sin. The greatest sin is idolatry, false religion, turning to an idol instead of turning to God. This is the worst sin of all.

In the Book of Judges a great principle of government is presented, a principle which is also stated very clearly in the prophecy of Isaiah. All of the subsequent prophets simply bear out and apply this principle which has already been stated. The principle is this: There are three steps in the downfall of a nation. First of all, there is *religious apostasy*. The second step is *moral awfulness*. And the third step is *political anarchy*. These are the three steps by which nations pass off the stage of human history. That has always been the way it has moved. You see, the primary problem never was political anarchy. The primary problem never was moral awfulness. As bad as these are, the root problem goes back to religious or spiritual apostasy, a turning away from the living and true God.

This is the thing which has happened to my nation today, and I am not the only one who is saying this, by any means. A prominent professor of history has made the statement that the American dream is vanishing in the midst of terrifying realities and visible signs of decadence in our contemporary society. Clinton Rossiter, at one time a professor of American history at Cornell University, said that in our youth we had a profound sense of national purpose that we lost over the years of our rise to glory. James Reston of the *New York Times* (and I don't think anybody has ever called him a conservative) has said that in public they talk about how optimistic and wonderful the future is, but that the private conversations of thoughtful men in Washington are quite different. It is his opinion that for the first time since World War II, one begins to hear of doubts that mortal man is capable of solving or even controlling the political, social, and economic problems that life has placed before him. This is the picture and this is the story of the downfall of nations, and it alarms me. This great principle, which this man Habakkuk has again restated in the Word of God, was fulfilled in the nation of Babylon.

The downfall of a nation begins in idolatry; it begins in turning away from the living and true God. We would like to think that idolatry has gone out of style, that no one today in this country is bowing down to an idol. That, of course, is not true. Many a man today is worshiping the almighty dollar. Many a man worships sex. Many a man worships pleasure. Many a woman has given her virtue in order to become a famous star or in order to be promoted. May I say to you, anything that you give yourself to, anything that takes all your time or energy, anything that takes all of you is what you worship. That, my friend, is your god, that is your idol, and that is what God condemns. God says that He is a jealous God. God says, "I made you. I created you. I have redeemed you. And I want you." When a man turns his back on God, he is doing the worst thing any man can possibly do.

**But the LORD is in his holy temple: let all the earth keep silence before him [Hab. 2:20].**

Personally, I believe this looks to the future when the Lord Jesus Christ will come to the earth. When He is in His temple down here, the whole earth will be silent before Him. All of the noise, all of the clamor, all of the protest, all of the confusion will disappear at that time. But it is also true that it applies to today. The reason we are having all these difficulties and problems down here is that, although He is yonder in heaven, although the Lord is in His temple, man does not bow before Him and recognize Him. It would be a wonderful thing if we could just have a week of silence. Wouldn't it be wonderful if everyone in Washington, D.C., would keep his mouth shut for a week? Wouldn't it be wonderful if all of us preachers on radio would keep our mouths shut? Wouldn't it be a wonderful thing if everyone who is doing so much talking would just keep quiet and wait before almighty God?

"The LORD is in his holy temple: let all the earth keep silence before him." But the second psalm opens with a question mark—Why? Just like Habakkuk's questions, the psalmist asks, "Why do the heathen rage, and the people imagine a vain thing?" (Ps. 2:1). Why all the clamor? Why all the protest? Because they are far from God. The nations have forgotten that God today is in His heaven. Browning was wrong when he said that God is in His heaven and all's right with the world. God is in His heaven, but all is *wrong* with the world because man is not rightly related to God. Our problem today is a problem of man's relationship to God. My friend, there is only one alternative, there is only one way out: "The just shall live by his faith" (v. 4).

# CHAPTER 3

**THEME:** *The pleasure of the prophet*

As we come to the third chapter of Habakkuk, a tremendous change has taken place in the life of this man Habakkuk. When we get to the end of this chapter, we will see that this man has made a right about-face. The book opened in gloom—Habakkuk has a question mark for a brain, and he has questioned God. But now it closes in glory with a great exclamation point. It closes on a high note of praise, and you will not find any more confident faith than that which is expressed in the last part of this book.

We can divide this chapter into three very definite sections. In the first two verses, we have the prayer of the prophet. We have the program of God in verses 3–17, and then we have the position of the prophet in verses 18–19.

## PRAYER OF THE PROPHET

### A prayer of Habakkuk the prophet upon Shigionoth [Hab. 3:1].

*Shigionoth* is a word having to do with music. Some think it might have been some sort of a musical point used to indicate to the musician the way the piece was to be played. Others think it was a musical instrument. We also find this word in the Book of Psalms (the singular form, *shiggaion*, is used in the title to (Psalm 7). We know it has to do with music, and Habakkuk's prayer is Hebrew poetry. It is a song of high praise.

What a change has taken place in the life of Habakkuk! His glorious experience on the watchtower and his patient waiting for an answer from God have brought him into a place of real faith and have opened his eyes to something he was not conscious of before. Therefore, this chapter is his song. I would call it a folk song; it's a happy song. It is to be played with a stringed instrument, according to the last sentence of this chapter, which says, "To the chief singer on my stringed instruments" (v. 19). I suppose that this is a little notation which Habakkuk put there to indicate how this song was to be sung. Perhaps he is telling the soloist to get with it, that this was something to be sung with a stringed instrument. Aren't most of the folk songs today sung with a stringed instrument? You and I may not like these stringed instruments and what is coming from them, but nevertheless, stringed instruments are used for folk singing.

Apparently, that is what we have here in this chapter, but it was on a much higher plane than the music I hear today.

I do not choose to listen to our modern music, but I often have to hear it. It is amazing that we hear so much about freedom of speech, but what about freedom of hearing? I'd like to have my ears protected today. Just because some vile person insists upon his freedom of speech, my ears are offended because I have to listen to singing that I don't care for. I am forced to hear at least a segment of a dirty song—in my judgment, it is a dirty song—but he's got to have *his* liberty. We today don't consider that we ought to have a little freedom of our ears and not have to listen to a lot of the junk that is being passed around.

**O Lord, I have heard thy speech, and was afraid: O Lord, revive thy work in the midst of the years, in the midst of the years make known; in wrath remember mercy [Hab. 3:2].**

Habakkuk's song is a wonderful song. I do not think this would be offensive to anyone's ears. It is a beautiful prayer. Habakkuk says, "O Lord, I have heard thy speech." In other words, God has answered him. God has said to him, "Now look here, Habakkuk. I want you to stay in your watchtower, and I want you to walk by faith. I want you to trust Me. You think that I am not doing anything about the sins of My people, but I am. I am preparing a nation, the Chaldeans, or the Babylonians, and they are going to be used as I used the Assyrians against the northern kingdom of Israel—they were the 'rod of mine anger.' But when I am through with the Babylonians, I am going to judge them, and I will judge them on a righteous basis." God's judgment of Babylon was spelled out in chapter 2 in the five woes, the great national sins which brought that nation down. God was moving to bring Babylon down.

The very interesting thing is that Habakkuk now reverses himself. He says, "I've heard Your speech, and I am afraid." What is he afraid of? Well, he had thought that God wasn't doing anything. Now he is afraid the Lord is doing too much!

Notice what Habakkuk says: "O Lord, revive thy work in the midst of the years, in the midst of the years make known; in wrath remember mercy." He says, "Lord, I didn't think You were working. I didn't think that You were doing anything, but I see now that You are moving in judgment. And since You are moving in judgment, remember to be merciful even to the Chaldeans, and be merciful to Your people." Before, Habakkuk had been calling down fire from heaven not only upon his own nation who had departed from God but also upon the Chaldeans. Now he is saying, "Lord, don't forget to be merciful." Well, God is merciful, and God is gracious. He is not willing that any should perish.

It does look today as if God is not doing anything, but if you and I could ascend to the watchtower of Habakkuk, if we could learn that the just shall live by his faith, if we could have a living faith in God and see what is moving behind the scenes and see the wheels that are turning, I think that we would be as surprised as this man was. I am not sure but that we, too, would cry out to God for mercy. A great many Christians today have thrown up their hands about the conditions in our own country—they've just given up. We all feel that way at times, don't we? But, may I say to you, God *is* moving today in judgment, and somebody needs to cry out to Him and say, "Oh, Lord, in wrath, as You are moving in judgment, don't forget to be merciful to us. We need Your mercy." This great nation of ours needs the mercy of God today. Since World War II, we have been on an ego trip. We have really had a flight of pride, of being the greatest nation in the world, and now even our little gas buggies have been slowed down. We feel almost helpless today. What would we do in the time of a major crisis? Suppose we were attacked from the outside, how much gasoline would there be? How much of the many other chemicals that are so needed would there be? How long would we really last? It is my belief that God is moving in judgment, and we need to ask Him to be merciful to us. Shakespeare has Portia say in *The Merchant of Venice* (Act IV, Scene i):

The quality of mercy is not strain'd
It droppeth as the gentle rain from heaven
Upon the place beneath: it is twice blest.

We need His mercy. We talk about showers of blessing—what we need today are showers of mercy from Almighty God.

What a reversal has taken place in the thinking of this man Habakkuk. At first he said, "You are not doing anything, Lord. Why don't You do something? Why do You let them get by with their sin?" Now God has let Habakkuk see that He is doing something, and Habakkuk cries out for the mercy of God. If we really knew how much God is moving in judgment, I am of the opinion that it would bring America to her knees before Almighty God.

Let us move on down into this very wonderful prayer. Habakkuk's prayer is actually a recital of what God has done in the past history of the people of Israel. In view of the fact that He has done it in the past, He intends to do it again in the future—that is the thought here. You can depend upon God's continuing to do what He has done in the past. Paul wrote about this to us as believers—in fact, this is my life verse: "Being confident of this very thing, that he which hath begun a good work in you will perform it until the day of Jesus Christ" (Phil. 1:6). My friend, has God begun a good work in you? He has brought you up to this present moment, has He not? He has begun a good work in you, and you can be sure He will perform it until the day of Jesus Christ, until He takes you out of this world and you will be in His likeness. This is our confidence, and this is the great confidence of this psalm of Habakkuk.

## PROGRAM OF GOD

In this section I believe there are three men in the background. However, none of them is mentioned by name, because this is not a psalm about what any man has done; it is a psalm about what God has done through men. Therefore, the men are not mentioned by name. Many scholars see only two men here. But I believe that we have Abraham (vv. 3–6), Moses (vv. 7–10), and Joshua (vv. 11–15). However, there are many who feel that Moses is the only one mentioned in verses 3–10.

**God came from Teman, and the Holy One from mount Paran. Selah. His glory covered the heavens, and the earth was full of his praise [Hab. 3:3].**

Teman is in Edom, and Paran is nearby in the Sinaitic Peninsula. Many think this is a reference to the time when the children of Israel came up out of the land of Egypt. However, you will recall that Abraham went down to Egypt even before that time.

*Selah* is a very interesting word which is also found in the Psalms. Its use here would indicate again that this is a psalm. There is a difference of viewpoint as to what *selah* means. Some believe that it marks a pause in the music, a breathing place. Some think it means that this is where the drums should come in and the music reach a high crescendo. Well, I'm not very musical—in fact, I am not musical at all. To me, I think of it as meaning, "Stop, look, and listen." At all the railroad crossings when I was a boy a cross was put up which said, "Stop, Look, and Listen." That is what I think *selah* means. God is saying, "Now sit up and take notice. Be sure to hear this." The singer is to really let go and the drummer to really pound the drums at this point. *Selah* is to call attention to what has been said. Whether this verse speaks of Abraham or Moses is unimportant because God was present with both of these men.

We have a marvelous, wonderful picture here of the glory of God: "His glory covered the heavens, and the earth was full of his praise." Well, that hasn't taken place quite yet. But certainly, as far as Abraham was concerned, there was praise in his heart. And for the children of Israel when they came out of Egypt, at first, at least, there was praise in their hearts. Of course, they became complainers and whiners during the rest of the journey.

"His glory covered the heavens." We need to be impressed today as believers with the glory of our God. How majestic, how powerful, how wonderful is our God!

**And his brightness was as the light; he had horns coming out of his hand: and there was the hiding of his power [Hab. 3:4].**

"And his brightness was as the light; he had horns coming out of his hand." These "horns" are spokes of light, rays of light. As you know, when the sun comes up, rays of light shoot up from it. This is the picture we are given of His approach. I think that when the Lord Jesus comes back to take His church out of this world, a glory will be present that was not present when He was born in Bethlehem. That will also be true when He comes to the earth to establish His kingdom.

"And there was the hiding of his power." In other words, the glory of God so covered Him that you could not see Him. The very glory of God obscures the glory of God, if you please. Oh, the majesty of His person! This is something which believers need to recognize and respect.

**Before him went the pestilence, and burning coals went forth at his feet [Hab. 3:5].**

This could apply to the time of Moses in Egypt and the ten plagues; but it also could apply to Abraham who went down to Egypt because there was a famine, a pestilence, in the land.

**He stood, and measured the earth: he beheld, and drove asunder the nations; and the everlasting mountains were scattered, the perpetual hills did bow: his ways are everlasting [Hab. 3:6].**

"He stood, and measured the earth." Remember that God said to Abraham, "I am going to give you this land," and He measured it out to him. God has made the statement that He has lined up the nations of the world according to the way He gave that land to Abraham. That is an amazing thing, by the way.

"He beheld, and drove asunder the nations; and the everlasting mountains were scattered, the perpetual hills did bow: his ways are everlasting." Oh, the ways of our God are past finding out! This is a marvelous psalm, my friend.

**I saw the tents of Cushan in affliction: and the curtains of the land of Midian did tremble [Hab. 3:7].**

"I saw the tents of Cushan in affliction"— Cushan is Ethiopia. "And the curtains of the land of Midian did tremble." You will recall that this man Moses went down into the land of Midian for a time. It is believed now by some scholars that Moses, as the son of Pharaoh's daughter, probably led a campaign into Ethiopia. That, of course, is not really a matter of record but rather the belief of some scholars. We do know that he ". . . was mighty in words and in deeds" (Acts 7:22).

**Was the LORD displeased against the rivers? was thine anger against the rivers? was thy wrath against the sea, that thou didst ride upon thine horses and thy chariots of salvation? [Hab. 3:8].**

This is a reference to the children of Israel crossing the Red Sea and crossing the Jordan River. God opened up the waters for them. This is highly figurative, beautiful language, by the way. It is Hebrew poetry, and it speaks of the fact that God was not angry with the rivers because they blocked the way; rather, He merely opened up the Red Sea and let the people cross over, as He did again later with the Jordan River.

**Thy bow was made quite naked, according to the oaths of the tribes, even thy word. Selah. Thou didst cleave the earth with rivers [Hab. 3:9].**

"Thy bow was made quite naked, according to the oaths of the tribes, even thy word. Selah." God was making good His covenant, His promise, to His people. Believe me, "selah" means that you need to pound those drums again, drummer. This should wake them up and cause them to listen to what God has to say.

"Thou didst cleave the earth with rivers." Have you ever stopped to think how God has sliced this earth with rivers? The rivers are like great slices down through the earth. What a highly figurative but accurate picture is given to us here!

**The mountains saw thee, and they trembled: the overflowing of the water passed by: the deep uttered his voice, and lifted up his hands on high [Hab. 3:10].**

When Moses went up to receive the Law on top of Mount Sinai, the mountain trembled, and the children of Israel were so frightened that they actually did not want to come near it. They didn't want God to speak to them at all—they were absolutely frightened.

These verses are a picture of how God through Moses delivered the children of Israel. First, God made a covenant with Abraham, and He made it good. Then God made a covenant with Moses that He would deliver the children of Israel out of the land of Egypt. He made that covenant good also, and He delivered them as He had said He would.

In verse 11 we come to Joshua. I think it is quite clear that Joshua is in the background here but, as I said before, the names of these men are not mentioned because the emphasis is upon the acts of God.

**The sun and moon stood still in their habitation: at the light of thine arrows they went, and at the shining of thy glittering spear [Hab. 3:11].**

"The sun and moon stood still in their habitation"—this immediately identifies this with Joshua.

"At the light of thine arrows they went, and at the shining of thy glittering spear." In other words, the very shining of the sun was like a glittering spear.

**Thou didst march through the land in indignation, thou didst thresh the heathen in anger [Hab. 3:12].**

When God put His people in that land, He put them in there and removed the Amorites because of the sin in their lives. The Amorites who occupied the section in which Jericho was located were eaten up with venereal disease. God moved them out of that land because they would have infected the entire human family. It was almost a plague among them in those days.

**Thou wentest forth for the salvation of thy people, even for salvation with thine anointed; thou woundedst the head out of the house of the wicked, by discovering the foundation unto the neck. Selah [Hab. 3:13].**

There has been a question as to whether "thine anointed" refers to Israel or to the Messiah. Personally, I think it means the Messiah here. "Thou wentest forth for the salvation of thy people, even for salvation with thine anointed"—it is the Lord Jesus who is the Savior as well as the Anointed One, the Messiah.

"Thou woundedst the head out of the house of the wicked, by discovering the foundation unto the neck. Selah." When the "anointed one" is mentioned here, the music is to reach the highest crescendo, what is called fortissimo. Here is where you need a good soprano and a good basso. This is great praise unto God for the salvation which He wrought for these people. He delivered them out of Egypt under Moses, and He brought them into the land through Joshua, but these were all the acts of God.

**Thou didst strike through with his staves the head of his villages: they came out as a whirlwind to scatter me: their rejoicing was as to devour the poor secretly.**

**Thou didst walk through the sea with thine horses, through the heap of great waters [Hab. 3:14–15].**

This was God making good His promises, and this was His salvation to them.

We come now to the reaction of the prophet to all of this. I could only wish that I could do justice to the remainder of this little book and of this chapter. I know that I am totally inadequate to present it as it should be presented to you. This is one of the great passages of the Word of God. I wish that somehow I could convey to your heart something of the grandeur and the glory that is here.

**When I heard, my belly trembled; my lips quivered at the voice: rottenness entered into my bones, and I trembled**

**in myself, that I might rest in the day of trouble: when he cometh up unto the people, he will invade them with his troops [Hab. 3:16].**

At the end of this book, Habakkuk now gives us his own personal experience. He opened the book, as we have seen, with his own personal experience. He tells now about his own physical reaction to all of this. Did you ever have that sinking feeling in the pit of your tummy when some crisis faced you or you came to some place in life where there was a great emergency? This was Habakkuk's experience. He says, "When I heard, my belly trembled; my lips quivered at the voice." Have you ever been so frightened that you could not speak audibly? I am sure that most of us have had an experience like that.

I had that kind of an experience as a young man when I was going to see a certain young lady. The girl who lived next door to her also had a young man who was keeping company with her. After this other young man and I would leave their homes in the evening, there apparently was a Peeping Tom who had found a place on the porch where he could look into both of their bedrooms at the same time. Each of these girls had a sister, so that there were two girls in each home. Apparently, he had been doing this for some time. One evening, the girls next door thought they saw him pass by their window, and so they called to the home where I was. Very foolishly, the girl brought me her father's pistol, and I walked to the alley in the back where there was a high fence. I was walking back to the house, getting ready to tell the girls there was no use being afraid and that there wasn't anybody back there. All of a sudden, a form appeared right above me on that fence. That fellow could have jumped down upon me, but he was so frightened at seeing me that he didn't budge—and neither did I! I tried to raise the gun to shoot, and I thank God I was so frightened that I was not able to do it. I tried to talk, but I couldn't say anything. The girl called her father and said, "He's choking Vernon out there!" He wasn't choking me—I was so scared I just couldn't open my mouth. Instead of being a hero like I intended to be that evening, I turned out to be a very sorry one. That fellow, whoever he was, dropped down on the other side of the fence and started running. I set the gun on the fence because I couldn't hold it steady, and I shot at him twice, but he was perfectly safe. I don't think my shots got in his neighborhood at all! I remember that experience as a time when I felt what Habakkuk describes, but mine was only a chance encounter.

Habakkuk says, "Rottenness entered into my bones." That means he couldn't stand up—he had to hold on to something. "And I trembled in myself, that I might rest in the day of trouble." He saw that God was going to move in judgment, and he knew that it was going to be a hard and difficult time.

**Although the fig tree shall not blossom, neither shall fruit be in the vines; the labour of the olive shall fail, and the fields shall yield no meat; the flock shall be cut off from the fold, and there shall be no herd in the stalls [Hab. 3:17].**

Habakkuk says, "There will be no fruit on the trees, there will be no grapes, the livestock will be gone." All of this will be a part of the judgment of God.

## POSITION OF THE PROPHET

In spite of the impending judgment, Habakkuk is able to say—

**Yet I will rejoice in the LORD, I will joy in the God of my salvation.**

**The LORD God is my strength, and he will make my feet like hinds' feet, and he will make me to walk upon mine high places. To the chief singer on my stringed instruments [Hab. 3:18–19].**

I want you to understand that God is our strength and our joy. God has not promised peace and prosperity in these days in which we live. So much is being promised to us today! I just threw into the wastebasket a magazine which comes from a so-called Christian organization and which told about all the things that you can get through prayer. The magazine promised that God will make you prosperous, that He will give you health, and that He will give you everything. My friend, God is not a glorified Santa Claus! But our God *is* moving in a very definite way. If you want an answer to your problems, Habakkuk gives you the answer here. That answer is simply this: *God* is the answer to your problems.

In the beginning of this book, Habakkuk came to God and said, "Why are You doing these things? Why are You permitting me to see evil? Why don't You move?" God brought Habakkuk to the watchtower and let him see what He was doing, and now Habakkuk says,

"I am going to walk by faith with God." My friend, God is the answer to your problem today. I don't know who you are or what your problem is, but God is the answer. You can have faith and confidence in Him. God has a purpose in your life, and He intends to carry it through. You can trust Christ, and, when you trust Him, you will find that He begins to work in you. He wants to conform you to His image—it is God's intention to make you like Christ.

The apostle Paul writes: "And we know that all things work together for good to them that love God, to them who are the called according to his purpose. For whom he did foreknow, he also did predestinate to be conformed to the image of his Son, that he might be the firstborn among many brethren" (Rom. 8:28–29). Regardless of the big words Paul uses, he simply means that God's eternal purpose with you is to make you like Jesus Christ. Again, he writes in 2 Corinthians: "But we all, with open face beholding as in a glass the glory of the Lord, are changed into the same image from glory to glory, even as by the Spirit of the Lord" (2 Cor. 3:18). My friend, God has a purpose for you. It does not matter who you are. To say that someone else has a greater purpose in life than you have is entirely wrong. You are as important in God's plan and purpose as any individual who has ever lived on this earth or who ever will live on this earth. He wants to make you like Christ. We read in 1 Corinthians 15:47–49: "The first man is of the earth, earthy: the second man is the Lord from heaven. As is the earthy, such are they also that are earthy: and as is the heavenly, such are they also that are heavenly. And as we have borne the image of the earthy, we shall also bear the image of the

heavenly." We are down here in these human bodies which have actually been taken out of the dirt; and God has made us human beings, but that is not His final purpose. We are earthy, but He wants us to be heavenly, and that is His goal for us.

Imagine that you live in the day of Michelangelo. One day you visit his studio, and you see there a rough piece of stone, which is dirty and polluted because it has come out of a dark and damp quarry. It is a hard piece of marble—crude, unyielding, cold, unlovely, and unsightly. But you come back in six months, and what has happened? Why, it has become a statue of David or of the archangel Michael. May I say to you, just as Michelangelo had a purpose for that crude piece of marble, God has a purpose for you and me today. We are earthy, but He has a heavenly purpose for us. You see, the ideal of the artist (who is the Holy Spirit) is to conform us to the image of Christ. The chisel He uses is the discipline of the Lord—"For whom the Lord loveth he chasteneth . . ." (Heb. 12:6). And the hammer is the Word of God. And therefore we can say with the psalmist, ". . . I shall be satisfied, when I awake, with thy likeness" (Ps. 17:15).

My friend, God is the answer to your questions. God is the answer to your problems. Therefore, it does not matter who you are or where you are; you can rejoice in Him, and you can rejoice in His salvation. You can say with Habakkuk, who was such a pessimist in the beginning, "I will joy in the God of my salvation." This book opened in gloom, but it closes in glory. It opened with a question mark, but it closes with a mighty exclamation point. And it ends with his wonderful song. May you and I be encouraged today by the Word of God!

# BIBLIOGRAPHY

(Recommended for Further Study)

Feinberg, Charles L. *The Minor Prophets*. Chicago, Illinois: Moody Press, 1976.

Freeman, Hobart E. *Nahum, Zephaniah, and Habakkuk*. Chicago, Illinois: Moody Press, 1973.

Gaebelein, Arno C. *The Annotated Bible*. 1917. Reprint. Neptune, New Jersey: Loizeaux Brothers, 1971.

Ironside, H. A. *The Minor Prophets*. Neptune, New Jersey: Loizeaux Brothers, n.d.

Jensen, Irving L. *Minor Prophets of Judah*. Chicago, Illinois: Moody Press, 1975. (Obadiah, Joel, Micah, Nahum, Zephaniah, and Habakkuk.)

Tatford, Frederick A. *The Minor Prophets*. Minneapolis, Minnesota: Klock & Klock, n.d.

Unger, Merrill F. *Unger's Commentary on the Old Testament*, Vol. 2. Chicago, Illinois: Moody Press, 1982.

# The Book of
# ZEPHANIAH
## INTRODUCTION

Zephaniah identifies himself better than any of the other minor prophets. Habakkuk concealed himself in silence—we know nothing about his background—but Zephaniah goes to the opposite extreme and tells us more than is ordinary. He traces his lineage back to his great-great-grandfather, Hizkiah (whom we know as Hezekiah), king of Judah. In other words, Zephaniah was of the royal line.

Zephaniah located the time of his writing just as clearly as he did his identification: "in the days of Josiah the son of Amon, king of Judah" (Zeph. 1:1). It was a dark day for the nation. According to the arrangement of the Hebrew Scriptures, Zephaniah was the last of the prophets before the Captivity. He was contemporary with Jeremiah and perhaps with Micah, although I doubt that. His was the swan song of the Davidic kingdom, and he is credited with giving impetus to the revival during the reign of Josiah.

The little Book of Zephaniah will never take the place of John 3:16 and the Gospel of John as number one in Bible popularity. The contents of this book have never been familiar, and I doubt that it has been read very much. I dare say that few have ever heard a sermon on Zephaniah. One Sunday morning several years ago, as I was about to preach on this book, I asked the congregation how many had ever heard a message on Zephaniah before. Out of the 2500–3000 who were present, only two hands were raised! Such neglect is not due to the mediocrity or the inferiority of this little book. If its theme were known, I think it would be very much appreciated because it has the same theme as the Gospel of John. John is called the apostle of love; and as we study this book, we will find that Zephaniah is the prophet of love. That may be difficult for you to believe, but let me give you a verse to demonstrate my point. You are acquainted with John 3:16, but are you acquainted with Zephaniah 3:17?—"The LORD thy God in the midst of thee is mighty; he will save, he will rejoice over thee with joy; he will rest in his love, he will joy over thee with singing." This is lovely, is it not? However, Zephaniah is a little different from the Gospel of John, for this verse is just a small island which is sheltered in the midst of a storm-tossed sea. Much

of this book seems rather harsh and cruel; it seems as if it is fury poured out. Chapter 3 opens in this vein: "Woe to her that is filthy and polluted, to the oppressing city!" (Zeph. 3:1). There is so much judgment in this little book; therefore, how can love be its theme? To find proof that love is the theme of this little book is like looking for the proverbial needle in a haystack, but I will illustrate my point by telling you a mystery story. This may seem to be a very peculiar way to begin a study of Zephaniah, but it is going to help us understand this little book. The title of my story is—

### THE DARK SIDE OF LOVE

It was late at night in a suburban area of one of our great cities in America. A child lay restless in her bed. A man, with a very severe and stern look, stealthily entered her bedroom and softly approached her bed. The moment the little girl saw him, a terrified look came over her face, and she began to scream. Her mother rushed into the room and went over to her. The trembling child threw her arms about her mother.

The man withdrew to the telephone, called someone, who was evidently an accomplice, and in a very soft voice made some sort of an arrangement. Hastily the man reentered the room, tore the child from the mother's arms, and rushed out to a waiting car. The child was sobbing, and he attempted to stifle her cries. He drove madly down street after street until he finally pulled up before a large, sinister, and foreboding-looking building. All was quiet, the building was partially dark, but there was one room upstairs ablaze with light.

The child was hurriedly taken inside, up to the lighted room, and put into the hands of the man with whom the conversation had been held over the telephone in the hallway. In turn, the child was handed over to another accomplice—this time a woman—and these two took her into an inner room. The man who had brought her was left outside in the hallway. Inside the room, the man plunged a gleaming, sharp knife into the vitals of that little child, and she lay as if she were dead.

Your reaction at this point may be, "I certainly hope they will catch the criminal who abducted the little girl and is responsible for such an awful crime!"

However, I have not described to you the depraved and degraded action of a debased mind. I have not taken a chapter out of the life of the man in Cell 2455, Death Row. I have not related to you the sordid and sadistic crime of a psychopathic criminal. On the contrary, I have described to you a tender act of love. In fact, I can think of no more sincere demonstration of love than that which I have described to you. I am sure you are amazed when I say that. Let me fill in some of the details, and then you will understand.

You see, that little girl had awakened in the night with severe abdominal pain. She had been subject to such attacks before, and the doctor had told her parents to watch her very carefully. It was her father who had hurried into the room. When he saw the suffering of his little girl, he went to the telephone, called the family physician, and arranged to meet him at the hospital. He then rushed the little girl down to the hospital and handed her over to the family physician who took her to the operating room and performed emergency surgery.

Through it all, every move and every act of that father was of tender love, anxious care, and wise decision. I have described to you the dark side of love—but *love*, nevertheless. The father loved the child just as much on that dark night when he took her to the hospital and delivered her to the surgeon's knife as he did the next week when he brought her flowers and candy. It was just as much a demonstration of deep affection when he delivered her into the hands of the surgeon as it was the next week when he brought her home and delivered her into the arms of her mother. My friend, love places the eternal security and permanent welfare of the object of love above any transitory or temporary comfort or present pleasure down here upon this earth. Love seeks the best interests of the beloved. That is what this little Book of Zephaniah is all about—the dark side of love.

In our nation we have come through a period when the love of God has been exaggerated out of all proportion to the other attributes of our God. It has been presented in such a way that the love of God is a weakness rather than a strength. It has been presented on the sunny side of the street with nothing of the other side ever mentioned. There is a "love" of God presented that sounds to me like the doting of grandparents rather than the vital and vigorous concern of a parent for the best interests of the child.

The liberal preacher has chanted like a parrot. He has used shopworn clichés and tired adjectives. He has said, "God is love, God is love, God is love" until he has made it saccharine sweet; yet he has not told about the dark side of the love of God. He has watered down love, making it sickening rather than stimulating, causing it to slop over on every side like a sentimental feeling rather than an abiding concern for the object of love.

However, I want you to notice that there is the dark side of the love of God. He deals with us according to our needs, my friend. The Great Physician will put His child on the operating table. He will use the surgeon's knife when He sees a tumor of transgression or a deadly virus sapping our spiritual lives or the cancerous growth of sin. He does not hesitate to deal with us severely. We must learn this fact early: He loves us when He is subjecting us to surgery just as much as when He sends us candy and flowers and brings us into the sunshine.

Sometimes the Great Physician will operate without giving us so much as a sedative. But you can always be sure of one thing. When He does this, He will pour in the balm of Gilead. When He sees that it is best for you and for me to go down through the valley of suffering, that it will be for our eternal welfare, He will not hesitate to let us go down through that dark valley. Someone has expressed it in these lines:

Is there no other way, Oh, God,
   Except through sorrow, pain and loss,
To stamp Christ's likeness on my soul,
   No other way except the cross?

And then a voice stills all my soul,
   As stilled the waves of Galilee.
Can'st thou not bear the furnace,
   If midst the flames I walk with thee?

I bore the cross, I know its weight;
   I drank the cup I hold for thee.
Can'st thou not follow where I lead?
   I'll give thee strength, lean hard on
   Me!

My friend, He loves us most when He is operating on us, "For whom the Lord loveth he chasteneth . . ." (Heb. 12:6)—in other words, He child-trains, He disciplines us.

Under another figure, the Lord Jesus presented it yonder in the Upper Room to those who were His own. He said, in John 15:1–2: "I am the true vine, and my Father is the husbandman. Every branch in me that beareth not fruit he taketh away: and every branch that beareth fruit, he purgeth [prunes] it, that it may bring forth more fruit." We must remember that the Father reaches into your life and mine and prunes out that which is not fruitbearing—and it hurts! But, as a Puritan divine said years ago, "The husbandman is never so close to the branch as when he is trimming it." The Father is never more close to you, my friend, than when He is reaching in and taking out of your heart and life those things that offend.

It was Spurgeon who noticed a weather vane that a farmer had on his barn. It was an unusual weather vane, for on it the farmer had the words, GOD IS LOVE. Mr. Spurgeon asked him, "Do you mean by this that God's love is as changeable as the wind?" The farmer shook his head. "No," he said, "I do not mean that God's love changes like that. I mean that whichever way the wind blows, *God is love*."

Today it may be the soft wind from the south that He brings to blow across your life, for He loves you. But tomorrow He may let the cold blasts from the north blow over your life—and if He does, He still loves you.

It has been expressed in these familiar lines in a way I never could express it myself:

God hath not promised skies always blue,
    Flower-strewn pathways all our lives
        through;
God hath not promised sun without rain,
    Joy without sorrow, peace without
        pain.

God hath not promised we shall not know
    Toil and temptation, trouble and woe;
He hath not told us we shall not bear
    Many a burden, many a care.

But God hath promised strength for the
    day,
    Rest for the laborer, light for the way,
Grace for the trials, help from above,
    Unfailing sympathy, undying love.
          —Annie Johnson Flint

Beloved, if you are a child of God and are in a place of suffering, be assured and know that God loves you. Regardless of how it may appear, He loves you, and you cannot ever change that fact.

Sweetness and light are associated with love on every level and rightly so, but this aspect does not exhaust the full import of love. Love expresses itself always for the good of the one who is loved. This is the reason that it is difficult to associate love with the judgment of God. The popular notion of God is that He is a super Dr. Jekyll and Mr. Hyde. One nature of His is expressed by love, and the other nature is expressed by wrath in judgment. These two appear to be contrary to the extent that there seem to be two Gods. The Book of Zephaniah is filled with the wrath and judgment of God (see Zeph. 1:15; 3:8), but there is the undertone of the love of God (see Zeph. 3:17).

Let me now tell you a true story to illustrate the dark side of love. One Mother's Day, while I was still a pastor in downtown Los Angeles, I looked out over my congregation, and I could tell that there were many mothers present. They were dressed a little special for the day, and many of them were wearing corsages. But I also noticed one mother who did not look as happy as the others. There was a note of sorrow on her face, although she wore a beautiful orchid corsage, the biggest one I had ever seen. I knew that it came from her son in the East. He is a prominent businessman, and high up in government circles as well, but he is not a Christian. He turns a deaf ear to his mother's pleadings. She prays for him constantly and asks others to pray for him. I recall that one Sunday morning she came to me, with tears streaming down her cheeks, and she said, "Oh, Dr. McGee, I pray that God will save my boy. I pray that He will save him even if He has to put him on a sickbed." Then, almost fiercely, she said, "Even if He has to *kill* him, I pray that God will save him before it is too late!" Suppose a detective from the police department had been listening to our conversation. Would he have arrested her for making that statement? No. He could not have arrested her at all. What she said was not a threat but was actually a statement of love. Because she loved that boy, she was actually willing to give him up and to let him go down through the doorway of death if it would mean the salvation of his soul.

The little prophecy of Zephaniah presents the dark side of the love of God. He is a God of love, but He is also a God of judgment. Zephaniah opens with the rumblings of judgment, and you will not find judgment enunciated in any more harsh manner than it is in this book.

Two thoughts stand out in this brief book:

1. "The day of the LORD" occurs seven times in this little prophecy. Obadiah and

Joel, the first of the writing prophets, were the first to use this expression. All of the prophets refer to it; and now Zephaniah, the last of the writing prophets, before the Captivity, brings it to our attention again. He uses it more than any of the other prophets. The actual phrase occurs seven times, but there are other references to it. This expression has particular application to the Great Tribulation Period, which precedes the kingdom; but the Day of the Lord also includes the time of the kingdom. The Great Tribulation Period is ended by the coming of Christ personally to the earth to establish the millennial kingdom—and all of that is included in the Day of the Lord. The emphasis in the Book of Zephaniah is upon judgment. Joel also opens his prophecy with a description of a great locust plague, which he likens to the Day of the Lord that is coming in the future. Joel says that the Day of the Lord is not light; it is darkness. It is on the black background of man's sin that God writes in letters of light the wonderful gospel story for you and me.

2. "Jealousy" occurs twice in this book. God's jealousy is on a little different plane from that of yours and mine. In our jealousy, we seek to do evil. God is jealous of those who are His own. He is jealous of mankind. He created him, and He has purchased a redemption for him, and made it possible for him to be saved. It is not His will that any should perish; He wants them saved—He is jealous for mankind. But when they don't turn to Him, He is going to judge them. The thing which the Book of Zephaniah makes clear is that God is glorified in judging as well as He is glorified in saving. A great many people cannot understand how that is possible. Ezekiel 38–39 speaks of the time in the future when God will judge Russia. We read there, "And thou shalt come up against my people of Israel, as a cloud to cover the land; it shall be in the latter days, and I will bring thee against my land, that the heathen may know me, when I shall be sanctified in thee, O Gog, before their eyes" (Ezek. 38:16). In other words, God is saying, "I intend to judge this godless nation, and when I do, I shall be glorified in that judgment." That is a tremendous statement for God to make, and for a great many people, it is a bitter pill to swallow. But it might be well for us to learn to think God's thoughts after Him, realizing that our thoughts are not His thoughts and our ways are not His ways at all.

# OUTLINE

I. Judgment of Judah and Jerusalem, Chapter 1

II. Judgment of the Earth and of All Nations, Chapters 2:1–3:8

III. All Judgments Removed; Kingdom Established, Chapters 3:9–20

# CHAPTER 1

*THEME: Judgment of Judah and Jerusalem*

**The word of the LORD which came unto Zephaniah the son of Cushi, the son of Gedaliah, the son of Amariah, the son of Hizkiah, in the days of Josiah the son of Amon, king of Judah [Zeph. 1:1].**

Zephaniah identifies himself as being of the royal family. Hezekiah, king of Judah, was his great-great-grandfather. Zephaniah prophesied during the days of the reign of Josiah, which was the period of the last spiritual movement that took place in the southern kingdom of Judah. There was a revival during that time—it wasn't a great one, it didn't last long, but there was a revival. Zephaniah knew something of the reigns of Amon, an evil king, and of Manasseh, also a terrible king. He saw that judgment was coming upon his nation and upon his people, and his message is a very harsh one.

**I will utterly consume all things from off the land, saith the LORD [Zeph. 1:2].**

This is certainly strong language. God says, "I intend to judge, and when I do, I will actually scrape the land. The land will be as if a dirt scraper had been run over it. Just as you wipe clean a dish, that is the way I intend to judge them."

As we move further into this prophecy, we will recognize that this judgment covers more than just the land of Israel. It is a worldwide devastation that is predicted here. The Book of Revelation confirms this and places the time of this judgment as the Great Tribulation Period. During that period, this earth will absolutely be denuded by the judgments that will come upon it. This will occur right before God brings in the millennial kingdom and renews the earth.

**I will consume man and beast; I will consume the fowls of the heaven, and the fishes of the sea, and the stumblingblocks with the wicked; and I will cut off man from off the land, saith the LORD [Zeph. 1:3].**

"I will consume man and beast"—all living creatures are included in this judgment. When I was in the land of Israel, I was told that they have a zoo somewhere up around the Sea of Galilee. They are making an effort to gather together the animals that were in existence in Bible days and to put them in this zoo. Obviously, as the population of Israel increases, the same thing will happen as has happened in the United States. Certain animal species will become extinct and disappear. God says that this is exactly what is going to happen when He judges that land. Many species—in fact, all of them—will become extinct at that time. This is to be a very severe judgment.

**I will also stretch out mine hand upon Judah, and upon all the inhabitants of Jerusalem; and I will cut off the remnant of Baal from this place, and the name of the Chemarims with the priests [Zeph. 1:4].**

"I will also stretch out mine hand upon Judah, and upon all the inhabitants of Jerusalem." God now makes it clear that Judah and Jerusalem are to be singled out for judgment.

"I will cut off the remnant of Baal from this place." The thing that brings the judgment of God upon the land is very specific—it is idolatry. In the prophecy of Habakkuk, God mentions five woes He was going to bring upon the people because of certain sins which they had committed. Idolatry was the last one; it was the fifth woe. But here Zephaniah narrows it down and puts his hand on idolatry—that is, false religion.

The Scriptures, beginning with the Book of Judges, teach a philosophy of human government, which you will find was true of God's people and which has been true of every nation. The first step in a nation's decline is *religious apostasy*, a turning from the living and true God. The second step downward for a nation is *moral awfulness*. The third step downward is *political anarchy*.

A great many people in the United States today think that our problem is in Washington, D.C.—I don't think so. Another group of people feel that if people could be reformed, if we could get people to act nicely, not be violent and not steal, if we could just lift our moral standards, then that would solve our problems. Again, I don't think that is the problem. Very frankly, I believe that the problem in this country is religious apostasy. The problem is out yonder with you and right here with me. The problem is that the church has failed to give God's message. I am not talking about *every* church or *your* church necessarily. There are many Bible-teaching churches across this country which have wonderful pastors who are standing for God—and I thank God for them. But the great denominations, by and large, have now departed from the faith. They have come to the place where they no longer give an effective message to the nation. As a result, from this religious apostasy have flowed moral awfulness and political anarchy.

If you think that this is just the wild raving of a fundamentalist preacher, you are wrong. Let me quote an excerpt from an editorial in a major metropolitan newspaper a number of years ago. Speaking of the failure of the churches to present any spiritual message whatsoever, the editorial concluded:

This betrayal of Christ in the name of Christianity is one reason for the moral and spiritual malaise with which this country is afflicted. The melancholy fact is that the churches no longer influence the development of national character. People go to church mainly because of an impulse to participate in a service of worship, not because of any spiritual guidance they expect from the clergyman.

What a note of condemnation this is! This is true not just of our nation but of every nation.

The historian Gibbon concluded that there were five reasons for the decline and fall of Rome. Gibbon was not a Christian, but here is why he says Rome fell: (1) The undermining of the dignity and sanctity of the home, which is the basis of human society. (2) Higher and higher taxes; the spending of public money for free bread and circuses for the populace. (3) The mad craze for pleasure; sports becoming every year more exciting, more brutal, more immoral. (4) The building of great armaments when the great enemy was within; the decay of individual responsibility. (5) The decay of religion, fading into mere form, losing touch with life, losing power to guide the people.

The message of Zephaniah carries out this scriptural principle of human government, and he puts his finger right down on the sore spot in the southern kingdom of Judah—idolatry. Zephaniah saw what was happening. The people were now on the toboggan; they were on the way down and out, and judgment was coming. Idolatry is where every great nation has gone off the track. When a nation departs from the living and true God or when it gives up great moral principles which were based on religion, when it goes into idolatry,

these factors eventually lead it into gross immorality and into political anarchy.

The interesting thing is that three kinds of idolatry, I believe, are mentioned to us here. "I will cut off the remnant of Baal from this place." The first form of idolatry is the worship of Baal which was introduced into the northern kingdom by Jezebel whose father was the high priest of the worship among the Sidonians. In the southern kingdom, the worship of Baal was popularized and the altars of Baal were rebuilt during the reign of Manasseh. This is an instance which illustrates why it would be wonderful to study at the same time the corresponding portions of the prophetic and historical books of Scripture. At this point it would be helpful to read the background of the reign of Manasseh (see 2 Kings 21; 2 Chron. 33). No king ever departed as far from God as this man did. He reintroduced the worship of Baal, which was a very immoral form of worship. Along with the worship of Baal was worship of Astoreth. When the female principal is introduced in deity, you have gross immorality; and that, of course, came into the life of the nation during this period. Baal worship was a form, therefore, of nature worship and was very crude indeed. When Josiah became king (he was a good king), the first thing he did was to try to remove the worship of Baal.

"And the name of the Chemarims with the priests." *Chemarims* actually means "black priests"—they wore black garments. Have you noticed that those who engage in the worship of Satan today don black garments? It is quite interesting that it is not original with them. It comes all the way down from these idolatrous priests who wore black robes. Zephaniah says that these priests are to be judged.

**And them that worship the host of heaven upon the housetops; and them that worship and that swear by the LORD, and that swear by Malcham [Zeph. 1:5].**

"And them that worship the host of heaven upon the housetops." Zephaniah now mentions the second form of idolatry that became prevalent in that land. It was more subtle and very dangerous indeed. Their housetops were flat—that is true even today in the land of Israel. It is the place where the family gathered in the evening. In fact, God gave a law about putting a banister, a railing, around the roof so that no one would fall off. Zephaniah says that the housetop became a place of worship, and you can see how idolatry was moving into the homes. It meant that actually every home was a little heathen temple where idolatry was practiced; idolatry was really reaching into the homes.

"Them that worship the host of heaven"— the sun, the moon, the stars. It was a worship of the creature rather than the Creator. They worshiped that which had been made rather than worshiping the Creator. This was the second form of idolatry which they adopted.

The worst, the most sophisticated and the most subtle of all the forms of idolatry, is the one that is mentioned next—"and them that worship and that swear by the LORD, and that swear by Malcham." Malcham is the name for Molech, the god of the Ammonites. It was a worship in which they actually sacrificed their children. The subtlety of it was that at the same time they professed to worship the living and true God. They went to the temple. They said that they knew the Lord, that they believed in God. But they also worshiped Molech—they were doing both.

This is the subtle thing that is also taking place today. There are many so-called churches that by the wildest stretch of the imagination could never be called Christian churches. The true church is built around a person, and that person is Jesus Christ. The early church met together to worship and adore *Him*, to come to know Him, and to have fellowship around Him. Everything they did pointed to Jesus Christ. How many churches do you know of where Christ is not even mentioned? If He is mentioned, He is mentioned in a derogatory manner. In other words, His deity is denied. They deny that He is God. They do not worship Him, but they give lip service to Him. They talk about the teachings of Jesus and about what a wonderful man He was. They even call Him a "superstar"! But they deny everything that has been set down in the Scriptures for us as Christians. It is a castrated Christianity that is abroad today.

This is the kind of subtle idolatry that was coming up in the land of Judah in that day. People were still going through the rituals, still going to the temple on the Sabbath. I don't think they came any other time, but they were there then. However, they were actually worshiping Molech. Molech was the god of the flesh. It was a fleshly worship— again, there was gross immorality. Likewise today, there are those who go to church—they have a churchianity but not a Christianity. They deny the great facts of the Christian faith. They practice immorality, or they prac-

tice things that are contrary to the Word of God. This is the picture of Judah in that day, and it is the subtlety of the hour in which we live. A great many people think that if a building has a steeple on it, a bell in that steeple, an organ, a big center aisle for weddings, a pulpit down front, and a choir loft, these make it a church. My friend, it may be one of the worst spots in town! It may be worse than any barroom, any gambling establishment, or any brothel in town. This is the thing that is so deceptive. The thing that undermined the nation of Judah is that they *pretended* that they were serving the living and true God, but they were giving themselves over to Molech idolatry.

**And them that are turned back from the LORD; and those that have not sought the LORD, nor inquired for him [Zeph. 1:6].**

The people have turned completely from God. Two classes are mentioned: backsliders and those who were never saved.

**Hold thy peace at the presence of the Lord GOD: for the day of the LORD is at hand: for the LORD hath prepared a sacrifice, he hath bid his guests [Zeph. 1:7].**

"Hold thy peace at the presence of the Lord GOD." The suggestion is, "Hush, hush. Don't talk out. Don't speak out. No protesting. You are in the presence of the living God." There is a great lack of reverence for God today. This notion that Jesus is sort of a buddy, that God is the man upstairs, and that we can be very flippant when we speak of Him, is all wrong. May I say to you, our God is a holy God. If you and I were to come within a billion miles of Him, we would fall down on our faces before Him because of who He is. He is the great God, the Creator of the universe, and we are merely little creatures.

"Hold thy peace at the presence of the Lord GOD." Why? "For the day of the LORD is at hand." This is the first mention of the Day of the Lord in this book. The Day of the Lord is presented here primarily as the time of judgment. If you want to fit it into God's program, it is the Great Tribulation Period—that is when it begins. Today, you and I are living in the day of Christ, the day of grace. The Day of the Lord will begin when the church leaves this earth. Then God will begin to move in judgment.

Prior to that day, which is still in the future, there have been times which have been likened unto the Day of the Lord. When Nebuchadnezzar finally came and destroyed Jerusalem, burned it to the ground, and plowed it under, he left that land denuded. If you go to that land today, there are very few trees. Oh, I know that Israel has planted millions of trees, but you see barren hills everywhere. At one time those hills were all covered with trees and vineyards. It was a land of milk and honey, but it is not that today. There is still evidence of that which the enemy did. The Babylonians who came under Nebuchadnezzar were followed later by the Media-Persians, then Alexander the Great, and finally the Romans. Enemy after enemy has come into that land. As a result, very few trees are left, and the land is almost completely denuded today. God made it very clear that that was what He was going to do—and He did it. The evidence is still there today. That judgment was for those people "the day of the LORD," but it does not completely satisfy these prophecies. Zephaniah makes it very clear that the Day of the Lord is that day which is yet in the future and which will be consummated when Christ comes and establishes His kingdom here upon this earth.

With almost biting sarcasm, Zephaniah says, "For the LORD hath prepared a sacrifice, he hath bid his guests." The guests are going to be the sacrifice, by the way, and the sacrifice is the judgment that is coming upon this nation.

**And it shall come to pass in the day of the LORD's sacrifice, that I will punish the princes, and the king's children, and all such as are clothed with strange apparel [Zeph. 1:8].**

The thought here is that the rulers had turned away from God. All you have to do is to refer to the time when Zedekiah reigned. He was the last of the kings, and he actually saw his own children killed right before his eyes, and then his own eyes were put out (see 2 Kings 24–25). That was surely harsh judgment, but they had had the warning from God. To these people, this was like the Day of the Lord.

**In the same day also will I punish all those that leap on the threshold, which fill their masters' houses with violence and deceit [Zeph. 1:9].**

Dr. Charles Feinberg (*Habakkuk, Zephaniah, Haggai, and Malachi, p. 48*) writes, "What is referred to is the zeal with which the servants of the rich hastened from their homes to plunder the property of others to enrich their masters." There were those who would take over the land and the homes of the poor. What was happening in that day was that the great middle class disappeared and you had the extreme rich and the extreme poor. The same thing is certainly happening in my own country today. God says to these people that He is going to judge them for this.

**And it shall come to pass in that day, saith the LORD, that there shall be the noise of a cry from the fish gate, and an howling from the second, and a great crashing from the hills [Zeph. 1:10].**

"And it shall come to pass in that day"—this is clearly a reference to the Day of the Lord.

"That there shall be the noise of a cry from the fish gate." The fish gate is what is known today as the Damascus Gate. It was the gate through which they brought the fish from the Sea of Galilee and the Jordan River. It is located on the north side of the city of Jerusalem.

"And an howling from the second, and a great crashing from the hills." The Damascus Gate today is down in a rather low place. If you are acquainted with Jerusalem, you know that the city is surrounded by hills. Zephaniah is saying that in any direction you would want to move, there will be this wailing of the people when the time of judgment has come upon them.

**Howl, ye inhabitants of Maktesh, for all the merchant people are cut down; all they that bear silver are cut off [Zeph. 1:11].**

*Maktesh* means "mortar". There is supposed to have been a depression in the city of Jerusalem where the marketplace was situated. It was perhaps the cheesemakers' valley. It was the valley that went alongside the temple where the Wailing Wall is today—which is a good place for it. "Howl, ye inhabitants of Maktesh, for all the merchant people are cut down; all they that bear silver are cut off."

**And it shall come to pass at that time, that I will search Jerusalem with candles, and punish the men that are settled on their lees: that say in their heart, The LORD will not do good, neither will he do evil [Zeph. 1:12].**

"And it shall come to pass at that time, that I will search Jerusalem with candles." In other words, it is like taking a flashlight and going to look for an individual who is hiding in the dark. God says, "I intend to search out Jerusalem just like that. I will bring to light all the evil and the sin."

"And punish the men that are settled on their lees." This is an idiomatic expression that corresponds, I think, to our idiom today when we say, "Take it easy." These people were taking it easy. They lived in an affluent society, and they were taking it easy. They did not believe they would be judged any more than people today believe that we are to be judged as a nation.

"That say in their heart, The LORD will not do good, neither will he do evil." They are saying, "God's doing nothing. God is not going to do anything about it." Habakkuk's question was, "Why don't you do something about the evil, Lord?" God told him, "I *am* doing something." And when Habakkuk was given a vision and saw what God was really doing, he cried out to God for mercy for the people. A great many people today say, "I'll ignore God. He doesn't do good. He doesn't do evil." They are absolutely neutral about God. This type of thinking, of course, is what led to the abominable theology that God is dead. Only a society like ours could have produced that kind of theology, because people in an affluent society say, "We don't need God at all." As a result, they think that He doesn't do good, He doesn't do evil, He doesn't do anything. But they are greatly mistaken, and Zephaniah is going to make that very clear to us.

**Therefore their goods shall become a booty, and their houses a desolation: they shall also build houses, but not inhabit them; and they shall plant vineyards, but not drink the wine thereof [Zeph. 1:13].**

"Therefore their goods shall become a booty." The goods which they took by plundering and pillaging and robbing are going to be taken away from them in just the same way as they got them.

"And their houses a desolation"—in other words, there would be ghost towns in Israel.

"They shall also build houses, but not inhabit them; and they shall plant vineyards, but not drink the wine thereof." God had given a law to these people that when a man planted a vineyard, he was not to go to war until he had eaten the fruit of that vineyard. Another law said that if a man married, he was to be excused from going to war for a year. Here God is saying that they are going to plant vineyards, but they are not going to drink the wine of them because they have sinned. They won't be able to take time off

from warfare. Neither will they be able to take time off when they get married because the enemy is going to come in like a flood.

**The great day of the LORD is near, it is near, and hasteth greatly, even the voice of the day of the LORD: the mighty man shall cry there bitterly [Zeph. 1:14].**

"The great day of the LORD is near." This great Day of the Lord is the time of the Great Tribulation in the future. In Zephaniah's day, after Josiah ruled, there never arose in the southern kingdom another good king. Every one of them was bad. Jehoahaz, Jehoiakim, Jehoiachin, Zedekiah—every one of them was a corrupt king. Now judgment is going to come upon the nation and upon the people for their departure from God. But they are only going to experience a very small portion of what is in the future in the great Day of the Lord.

Zephaniah says, "It is near, and hasteth greatly, even the voice of the day of the LORD: the mighty man shall cry there bitterly." In other words, the concept of the Wailing Wall would come into existence. And it is going to be there until after the Great Tribulation Period because Israel will never know peace until the Prince of Peace comes and they acknowledge their Messiah.

**That day is a day of wrath, a day of trouble and distress, a day of wasteness and desolation, a day of darkness and gloominess, a day of clouds and thick darkness [Zeph. 1:15].**

Dr. Charles Feinberg is an excellent Hebrew scholar, and he calls our attention to many things that you and I would normally pass over. I would highly recommend to you his work on the minor prophets. There is a play upon words in this verse that Dr. Feinberg brings out which we miss in the English, of course: "The Hebrew words for wasteness and desolation—sho'ah and umesho'ah—are alike in sound to convey the monotony of the destruction." But we do have in the English an alliteration that reveals something of it. It is a day of trouble, then distress, desolation, darkness, and thick darkness, so that there is a play upon words even in the English.

Zephaniah is speaking here of the harshness, the intensity of the judgment that is coming, and the question naturally arises: How can a God of love do a thing like this? We will find before we finish our study of this book that it is like the story I told in the Introduction of the father who took his little child to the surgeon to be operated upon. The picture can be presented in such a way that it looks like he is being cruel and harsh to bring her to the doctor who will plunge his knife into her. But actually, everything the father did was out of love for his little girl. Even the great day of wrath is a judgment of God, but it has in it the love of God. Regardless of what takes place, God is love. It is like the farmer who had on his barn the weather vane which said on it, GOD IS LOVE. The farmer explained it by saying, "Regardless of which way the wind blows, God is love." That is true, my friend.

Even in judgment, God is still a God of love. And He judges because it is essential for Him to judge that which is evil. He does that because He has to be true to Himself, and He could not be good to His creatures unless He did that. If God is going to permit sin throughout eternity, if God does not intend to judge sin, if you and I are going to have to wrestle with disease and with heartbreak and with disappointment and with sorrow throughout eternity, I cannot conceive that He is a God of love. But if you tell me that God is going to judge sin, that He is coming in with a mighty judgment, and that He is going to remove sin from His universe, I'm going to say, "Hallelujah!" And I will believe that He is a God of love even when He does that.

### A day of the trumpet and alarm against the fenced cities, and against the high towers [Zeph. 1:16].

When God gave to the nation Israel the trumpets that they were to blow on the wilderness march, there were several ways in which they were to be used. Having mentioned the different ways the two silver trumpets were to be used, the Lord says in Numbers 10:9, "And if ye go to war in your land against the enemy that oppresseth you, then ye shall blow an alarm with the trumpets; and ye shall be remembered before the LORD your God, and ye shall be saved from your enemies." Zephaniah says here that it is "a day of the trumpet"; they are going to blow the alarm, but God does not intend to deliver them. Why? He intends to judge them. He intends to deliver them over *to* the enemy, not deliver them *from* the enemy. It is to be "A day of the trumpet and alarm against the fenced cities, and against the high towers."

**And I will bring distress upon men, that they shall walk like blind men, because they have sinned against the LORD: and their blood shall be poured out as dust, and their flesh as the dung [Zeph. 1:17].**

This is extreme judgment, I'll grant you. But, you know, surgery today is extreme. After my doctor operated on me the first time for cancer, I was asking him about the operation. He told me, "I cut on you until there was almost a question as to which pile was McGee!" It's a pretty harsh thing to cut on a fellow like that, but my doctor didn't do it because he was angry with me. He didn't do it even in judgment. He did it actually to save my life, and I believe that on the human level he did save my life by that severe method. May I say to you, God will judge, and He does it in an *extreme* way. He does extreme surgery, but He does it for the sake of the body politic.

**Neither their silver nor their gold shall be able to deliver them in the day of the LORD's wrath; but the whole land shall be devoured by the fire of his jealousy: for he shall make even a speedy riddance of all them that dwell in the land [Zeph. 1:18].**

It has been quite interesting that this nation in which I live has spent billions of dollars throughout the world trying to *buy* friends, trying to win friends and influence people. But we are hated throughout the world today—we are not loved. You cannot buy love; you cannot win people over with silver and gold. But in this country we still believe that money solves all the ills of this life, that money is the answer to all the problems. God says that when He begins to judge, "neither their silver nor their gold shall be able to deliver them in the day of the LORD's wrath."

"But the whole land shall be devoured by the fire of his jealousy: for he shall make even a speedy riddance of all them that dwell in the land." God removed them from the land. Why did He do that? He did that because He loved them. If He had not done it, it would have been necessary to exterminate totally succeeding generations. For the sake of the future generations—so not all would have to be slain—God had to move in and cut away the cancer of sin that was destroying the nation.

# CHAPTER 2

**THEME:** *Judgment of the earth and of all nations*

God has not only judged His own people, but God also judges the nations; and that is the subject of this chapter and through verse 8 of chapter 3. But God is gracious, long-suffering, and not willing that any should perish; therefore, He sends out a final call. Although you would think that He had reached the end of His patience, in the first three verses, we find Zephaniah sending out God's last call to the nation of Judah to repent and to come to Him.

**Gather yourselves together, yea, gather together, O nation not desired [Zeph. 2:1].**

"Gather yourselves together." They are to come together as a people, as Dr. Feinberg has stated it, ". . . to a religious assembly to entreat the favor of the Lord in order that by prayer He may turn away His judgment" (*Habakkuk, Zephaniah, Haggai, and Malachi*, p. 53).

"Yea, gather together, O nation not desired." Their sin, of course, has caused God to bring judgment upon them. But it is not that He does not desire them; it is not because He does not love them. Judgment came upon them because of their sin. They were repugnant, they were repulsive; yet they were insensible to the shame of their sinful condition. Their sin had reached a very low stage, and they were dead to shame; they had no sense of decency at all. They were shameless in their conduct. We would say that they had no sensitivity to sin whatsoever. They sinned with impudence. They would sin openly and actually boast of it.

We have come to that same place as a nation today. Someone said to me not long ago, "Dr. McGee, you speak as if America is sinning more and is in a worse condition today than it ever was before." I do not mean to imply that at all. However, I do believe that there was just as much sin when I was growing up as there is today, but the sin was carried on behind the curtain or in the backyard or someplace else where it could not be seen. It was not flaunted before the world. It was not boasted of. In other words, it was not *shameless* sin as it is at the present time. I heard a very beautiful young woman on a talk program on television boast of the fact that she is living with a man to whom she is not married. The others on the program congratulated her

for her "courage" and "broad-mindedness." Nobody called it shameless sin. Sin is right out in the open today. I don't think there is more sin—it is just out in the open where you can see it. They sinned in my day, that's for sure, but it was done under cover. It was done secretly, and there was a sense of sorrow for sin which we seem to have lost today. You and I do not know how repulsive our sin is to God. We spend very little time weeping over our sins.

**Before the decree bring forth, before the day pass as the chaff, before the fierce anger of the LORD come upon you, before the day of the LORD's anger come upon you [Zeph. 2:2].**

God says, "Come together for prayer. Come together for repentance. Come together and turn to Me." There is a note of urgency here. Zephaniah is saying to the people, "Do this before God begins to move in judgment, because when you pass over the line and God begins to move in judgment, you will find out it's too late."

One of the things that is needed today in my country is for someone whose voice is heard to call our nation to prayer and to repentance. My nation has almost reached the end of its rope. This is a great need, and that kind of prayer God will hear and answer.

**Seek ye the LORD, all ye meek of the earth, which have wrought his judgment; seek righteousness, seek meekness: it may be ye shall be hid in the day of the LORD's anger [Zeph. 2:3].**

"Seek ye the LORD, all ye meek of the earth, which have wrought his judgment." There has always been a remnant of those people who are true to God just as there is a remnant in the church today. I doubt that there are many churches—no matter how liberal they may be—who are without some members who are real believers. Now I don't understand why they are there, and I don't propose to sit in judgment on them, but there *is* a remnant within the liberal church today. God has always had a remnant in the world, and apparently He is speaking here to those who are the godly remnant in Judah.

"Seek righteousness." The remnant also should be very careful of the way they live their lives. "Seek meekness." They are not to be lifted up by arrogance and pride and self-sufficiency, for that was one of the great sins of the nation. This is also a danger among believers today. Someone has said that there is "a pride of race, a pride of face, and a pride of grace." Some people are even proud that they have been saved by grace! They feel that that is something for them to boast about. They feel that they are the peculiar and particular pets of almighty God because of their salvation! My friend, we have nothing to glory in. The apostle Paul said that *he* had nothing to glory in, and believe me, if Paul didn't have anything to glory in, I'm sure that none of *us* has. There is a danger of being proud of the fact that we are God's children, but it ought rather to lead to meekness. He says here, "Seek righteousness, seek meekness."

"It may be ye shall be hid in the day of the LORD's anger." It is a glorious, wonderful thing to be hidden in the cleft of the rock and to be covered by His wings. God's children need to recognize that, although they will not go through the Great Tribulation Period, they may experience a great deal of judgment and a great deal of trouble just as these people did. Judah did not go through the Great Tribulation, the great Day of the Lord, but they certainly were going through, as I like to put it, "the *little* tribulation period." All of us are going to have tribulation to a certain extent in this life—we are going to have trouble. I heard the story years ago of a woman who was a maid and was complaining about her troubles. Apparently she had quite a few of them. When the lady of the house rather rebuked her for complaining, the woman replied, "When the good Lord sends me tribulation, I intend to tribulate." I agree with her. I believe we ought to tribulate. Paul says that we groan within these bodies, but that does not mean we are in the Great Tribulation nor that there is a chance of our going through it.

We come now to a section, beginning with verse 4 and going on down to verse 8 of chapter 3, in which we see the judgment of the nations. This passage reveals that God judges *all* the nations of this earth. The God of the Bible is not a local deity. He is not one that you put on a shelf. He is not one that is local or national. It has been the great error of the white race when attempting to "Christianize" a people by bringing them the gospel, also to try to make them live as we live and to adopt our customs and our methods. Well, there are a lot of different people on the topside of this earth, and they are all people for whom Christ died. Our business is to get them to hear the gospel, to get the Word of God to them, and

then let *them* work their Christian life into their own customs and into their own patterns of life. I am told that my ancestors in Europe were pagan, eating raw meat, and living in caves, and when the gospel was brought to them, it did a great deal for them. The early missionaries who came to my ancestors didn't try to make them like they were. Apparently, the missionaries let them develop their own civilization, and we should do the same thing with others.

The God of the Bible is the God of this universe. He is the Creator of the universe and of mankind. And He is the Redeemer of mankind. Notice that He is going to judge these other nations, not just His own people. And He judges other nations for their *sin*. God has put up certain standards that have become worldwide. They have been written into the Ten Commandments, which God gave to Moses. All nations have a sense of right and wrong, although they may vary on what is right and what is wrong. A missionary was telling me about a tribe he had worked with out in the South Seas. They were headhunters; they were cannibals. But he said that they had a high sense of honesty. He told me that you could take your pocketbook with your money in it and put it down in the center of where the tribe dwelt and leave it there for a week, and nobody would touch it. But, of course, they didn't mind eating their mother-in-law for dinner. (You would never know exactly what they meant when they said they had their mother-in-law for dinner—whether she came over to eat with them or whether they ate *her*!) But they did have a high sense of honesty, which is something I don't think we have in my country today. A lady told me that she left her purse on the counter in a department store, and when she returned in less than a minute, the purse was gone with no trace of it anywhere. But, of course, that thief was not going to eat his mother-in-law for dinner that evening. Standards apparently vary, but God has given to the nations of the world certain standards. You find them in all the nations of the earth. No nation could be a civilized nation if it did not recognize some of these. But when a people depart from the living and true God, they go into the deepest kind of paganism and heathenism and reach a place where God gives them up.

God now begins His judgment of the nations—

**For Gaza shall be forsaken, and Ashkelon a desolation: they shall drive out**

**Ashdod at the noon day, and Ekron shall be rooted up [Zeph. 2:4].**

Mentioned here are four of the cities of the Philistines which are going to be judged. Somebody might ask, "Why didn't He mention Gath? It was a prominent place." Well, at this time Gath was pretty much under the control of the southern kingdom of Judah. These four cities are to be judged—Gaza, Ashkelon, Ashdod, and Ekron.

"For Gaza shall be forsaken, and Ashkelon a desolation." It is interesting that Gaza is forsaken today, and Ashkelon is a desolation. There is a place called Ashkelon, but it is not over the ruins of the old city. The old one is right down by the sea. I have been there and have seen the ruins of the temple of Dagon that are there.

"They shall drive out Ashdod at the noon day." Ashdod was driven out, and it was done at noonday. In that land, the people always take time off at noontime; that is, they have what is called south of the border a siesta. In some places in South America, you cannot get into a store from around twelve to two o'clock in the afternoon. You are just wasting your time if you try to go shopping because nothing will be open. You can get into a store at nine o'clock at night, but they take time for a siesta in the heat of the day. At Ashdod it's pretty warm. Although it is by the sea, it gets very warm there in the summer. Zephaniah says that it will be destroyed and that they will be driven out at noonday. In other words, the enemy will take them off guard. Ashdod was completely obliterated. Israel possesses that territory today. They have built apartment building after apartment building, an oil refinery, and also a port there. It is one of the principal ports now. But in that day it was absolutely cleaned off. There are no ruins there at all.

"And Ekron shall be rooted up." Ekron was rooted up; it was completely removed.

**Woe unto the inhabitants of the sea coast, the nation of the Cherethites! the word of the LORD is against you; O Canaan, the land of the Philistines, I will even destroy thee, that there shall be no inhabitant [Zeph. 2:5].**

"Woe unto the inhabitants of the sea coast." All these places are along the seacoast.

"The nation of the Cherethites!" The Cherethites were people who came from the island of Crete, and they evidently were the Philistines. The word *Philistine* comes from the Hebrew word for *migration*. They immigrated to that country. This, by the way, ought to answer the question that some people, especially the liberals, have raised: "What right did Israel have to drive the Philistines out of their native land?" It was *not* their native land. Actually, Israel was there long before the Philistines were there. Abraham, Isaac, and Jacob, and their offspring were in that land, and then they went down to the land of Egypt. In that interval, the Philistines came into that country.

"The word of the LORD is against you; O Canaan, the land of the Philistines, I will even destroy thee, that there shall be no inhabitant." He says that they are to be judged. By the way, when was the last time you saw a Philistine? They have disappeared.

**And the sea coast shall be dwellings and cottages for shepherds, and folds for flocks [Zeph. 2:6].**

This took place, and this condition existed for over a thousand years—in fact, almost nineteen hundred years.

**And the coast shall be for the remnant of the house of Judah; they shall feed thereupon: in the houses of Ashkelon shall they lie down in the evening: for the LORD their God shall visit them, and turn away their captivity [Zeph. 2:7].**

This is God's promise to His people that He will return them from their captivity to inhabit the land of Philistia, which was a part of the territory God had given to Abraham. I have pictures of Israelis lying on the beach at Ashkelon during a holiday. It is a beautiful, sandy beach on the Mediterranean Sea. This prophecy is a picture of a scene that can be demonstrated any day of the year, although it may change tomorrow. However, I do not consider what we see there today as a fulfillment of prophecy, because I believe that Israel will be driven from that land again before their final return under God.

Now He moves over from the west to the east and to the nations which were contiguous to the land of Judah—

**I have heard the reproach of Moab, and the revilings of the children of Ammon, whereby they have reproached my people, and magnified themselves against their border.**

**Therefore as I live, saith the LORD of hosts, the God of Israel, Surely Moab shall be as Sodom, and the children of**

**Ammon as Gomorrah, even the breeding of nettles, and saltpits, and a perpetual desolation: the residue of my people shall spoil them, and the remnant of my people shall possess them [Zeph. 2:8–9].**

I have visited a few countries in my lifetime, and the poorest country that I have ever been in is the modern nation of the Hashimite Kingdom of Jordan. It occupies what was the land of the Moabites and the Ammonites. The modern capital there is Amman. You just do not find any more desolate country than that. All of this prophecy has been fulfilled in the past.

**This shall they have for their pride, because they have reproached and magnified themselves against the people of the Lord of hosts [Zeph. 2:10].**

They are judged for their pride, and as you know, pride is the way the devil sinned at the beginning.

**The Lord will be terrible unto them: for he will famish all the gods of the earth; and men shall worship him, every one from his place, even all the isles of the heathen [Zeph. 2:11].**

God is going to judge the nations of the world because they have ignored Him. They have not recognized Him. ". . . when they knew God, they glorified him not as God, neither were thankful; but became vain in their imaginations, and their foolish heart was darkened. Professing themselves to be wise, they became fools, And changed the glory of the uncorruptible God into an image made like to corruptible man, and to birds, and fourfooted beasts, and creeping things" (Rom. 1:21–23). This is the reason God will judge them.

**Ye Ethiopians also, ye shall be slain by my sword [Zeph. 2:12].**

Ethiopia is in Africa. You see, this is a *worldwide* judgment.

**And he will stretch out his hand against the north, and destroy Assyria; and will make Nineveh a desolation, and dry like a wilderness [Zeph. 2:13].**

"And he will stretch out his hand against the north, and destroy Assyria." Ethiopia is in the south, but now we move to the north and find that Assyria also is to be judged. In Zephaniah's day, Assyria was making quite a splash in the world.

"And will make Nineveh a desolation, and dry like a wilderness." That is the way Nineveh is today. The modern city of Mosul is across the Tigris River from the site of old Nineveh, and it is a miserable place, so I'm told. Nineveh and all of that area is still a desolation.

**And flocks shall lie down in the midst of her, all the beasts of the nations: both the cormorant and the bittern shall lodge in the upper lintels of it; their voice shall sing in the windows; desolation shall be in the thresholds: for he shall uncover the cedar work [Zeph. 2:14].**

In other words, their buildings are to be torn down.

**This is the rejoicing city that dwelt carelessly, that said in her heart, I am, and there is none beside me: how is she become a desolation, a place for beasts to lie down in! every one that passeth by her shall hiss, and wag his hand [Zeph. 2:15].**

"Every one that passeth by her shall hiss." People will hiss at Nineveh in the sense that it will be sort of an explosive expletive that comes from a person who is surprised: "Why, I thought that Assyria was a great nation and that Nineveh was a great city! Just look at it in desolation and ruin!" They hiss, and their breath is just blown out of them, as it were.

"And wag his hand." They will simply shake their hands back and forth, being absolutely stupefied to see what has taken place through God's judgment of the nations.

God has judged nations in the past, and God judges nations today. The Lord Jesus says that He will judge nations in the future. As we see in the Book of Habakkuk, God was moving in that day in a way that the prophet never suspected. And, my friend, God is moving in the nations of the world today. He has judged them in the past. He will judge them in the future.

# CHAPTER 3

*THEME: Judgment of the earth and of all nations; all judgments removed and the kingdom established*

The first eight verses of this chapter conclude this section, which deals with the judgment of the earth and of all nations. By now you may be tired of listening to Zephaniah talk about the harsh, the extreme, the unmitigating judgment of God upon His people. This is probably the strongest language you will find in the Scriptures until you come to the language which the Lord Jesus used in Matthew 23. If you will read that passage in connection with this chapter, you will see that the Lord Jesus topped even Zephaniah in the extreme language of judgment, which He used. It is bloodcurdling, if you please.

We saw in chapter 2 that the judgment of God is worldwide, it is global in its extent, and it includes every nation on the topside of the earth. In verses 1–5 of this chapter, God returns to the judgment that is coming upon His people, and He is very specific. He reveals that the light which a person has will determine the extent of the judgment—in other words, privilege creates responsibility. Your responsibility is measured by the privilege that you have. I like to express it like this: I would rather be a Hottentot in the darkest part of Africa than to be sitting in a Bible-believing church today, hearing the gospel but doing nothing about it. I won't argue about the judgment of the Hottentots in Africa, as that is not what we are talking about here, but I *do* know what God will do with a person of privilege, one who has had the opportunity of hearing the Word of God and has turned his back upon it. This is very extreme language that is used to express the judgment on Jerusalem, a judgment that is in ratio to her privilege—

**Woe to her that is filthy and polluted, to the oppressing city! [Zeph. 3:1].**

Jerusalem was the city in which the temple was located. The priests were there, and the scribes had the Word of God. When wise men came from the east, seeking the King of the Jews, the scribes had no problem in telling them where the Messiah was to be born, but they simply did not manifest any interest in checking to see if the wise men had any valid information about the Messiah. The scribes knew the letter of the Law, but that is all they knew. They did not know the Author of the Book, and they were far from Him. God's condemnation of Jerusalem is on the basis of all the light they had.

"Woe to her that is filthy and polluted." This matter of pollution is not something that is new today, but the pollution spoken of here is not physical pollution. This pollution is not on the outside of man; it is on the *inside* of man. The thing that is causing the pollution on the outside today is that man is polluted and filthy on the inside—that is, before God he is not right.

When a man gets right with God, he is not going to dump his garbage on another man's property, and he is not going to fill a lovely, babbling brook with filth. The ones who are polluting this earth are the godless folk. For example, in one of the beach towns here in Southern California several years ago, there was a meeting of some hippies, a godless crowd. They met in a pasture to hold a protest meeting against pollution. They were decrying the pollution caused by the large factories with their smokestacks which pour out all the dregs and waste materials resulting from industrial production. Very candidly, I agree with them that that's a terrible thing to have taking place. But the interesting thing is that after they held their protest meeting, the city had to spend two thousand dollars to clean up the pasture which those who were protesting pollution had polluted! May I say to you, pollution is on the inside, and when you are godless and wrong with God, you are certainly going to pollute this earth.

Man today is actually wrecking this earth that we are living on, and God's condemnation of Jerusalem is that it is a polluted city, although it was a privileged city, a city that had glorious and wonderful opportunities. This is the picture of that city, but it is also a picture of mankind in general. Notice Paul's verdict in Romans 3:16, "Destruction and misery are in their ways." What a picture of mankind! Man has always left a pile of tin cans and rubbish wherever he has gone on the earth.

Why did God single out the city of Jerusalem? It was a privileged city. This city had the temple of God. It had the Word of God. Therefore, its judgment will be harsher than that of any other city.

God calls Jerusalem not only filthy and polluted, but He also calls it "the oppressing city." It is the oppressing city because of the fact that she did not regard the rights of her people, especially of the poor. She did not consider them; she oppressed the poor.

This is something that I think is so hypocritical in my own government. I am not talking politics now, nor am I speaking of any one party because this is true of the whole structure that we have in Washington, D.C., today. Constantly our congressmen are coming up with programs to help the poor. It is interesting that it is always some rich senator who comes up with such a program. To begin with, he does not know how poor folk feel. He does not know our hardships. Such men have never experienced poverty, and their programs never help the poor; they help some bureaucrats but not the poor. I do not think the poor will ever be helped by any of the plans that men devise. Part of the problem is that the middle-class people are taxed to finance any such program. The middle class are the ones making it possible for the upper class to take our money to help the poor or the lower class. I personally would like to move into one of the other brackets—it would be more comfortable there today. God said that He would judge the city of Jerusalem for their oppression of the poor; so we know how He feels about our oppression.

God is not through with His judgment; He goes on to spell out their sin—

**She obeyed not the voice; she received not correction; she trusted not in the LORD; she drew not near to her God [Zeph. 3:2].**

"She obeyed not the voice." She was disobedient to God. This city had heard the voice of God but had been disobedient to Him.

"She received not correction." God had sent judgment. One hundred eighty-five thousand Assyrians outside the walls of Jerusalem scared the living daylights out of these people—they were frightened beyond measure (see 2 Kings 18–19). They had been partially judged, but God had let the judgment pass over. You would think that they would have learned their lesson and would have turned to God, but they didn't. Likewise, there are many Christians today who suffer but never learn why God permits it. He *never* lets anything happen to His own unless there is a purpose back of it. This city, like many of us, "received not correction." She did not learn the lesson.

"She trusted not in the LORD." The city had no trust in Him at all but looked to something else. When the modern nation of Israel celebrated her twentieth anniversary, they displayed this motto: "Science will bring peace to this land." My friend, the Bible says that the Messiah is the Prince of Peace, and He is the only one who can bring peace. But they don't trust Him—they trust science. After that twentieth anniversary, believe me, Israel got into hot water. Science did *not* bring peace to that land, and my nation has not brought peace to them either.

"She drew not near to her God." Today men are not running to God; they are running from Him as fast as they possibly can. What a picture this is of the city of Jerusalem!

**Her princes within her are roaring lions; her judges are evening wolves; they gnaw not the bones till the morrow [Zeph. 3:3].**

"Her princes within her are roaring lions." God is now talking about the leadership of the nation; and, when you speak of judgment, you must talk about the leadership of any nation or city. In my country, when men are running for office, they are always telling us that they are going to think about us, they are going to help us, and they are going to do something for us. So far, as best I can tell, nobody has ever done anything, either from the city level, the state level, or the national level. Why? Because "her princes within her are *roaring* lions"—they make a big noise.

"Her judges are evening wolves." We have a second meaning for *wolf* today, and I'm not sure but that the Lord included that thought here also. "Her judges are evening wolves"—in other words, they are willing to work day and night—not for the people but for themselves.

"They gnaw not the bones till the morrow." These men are willing to get all they can. Dr. Charles L. Feinberg comments: "The judges of the people were filled with insatiable greed, devouring all at once in their ravenous hunger. They left nothing till the morning" (*Habakkuk, Zephaniah, Haggai, and Malachi,* p. 64). Many of the men who go into office in our country, promising to help us, have not helped us, but they have done well themselves. By the time they retire from office, many of these men have become well-to-do. This is the thing that God judges. Judah was a nation like ours that had the Word of God. That which is said of Jerusalem could apply to us also. If God spoke out of heaven today, He would have to say these same things concerning us.

**Her prophets are light and treacherous persons: her priests have polluted the sanctuary, they have done violence to the law [Zeph. 3:4].**

"Her prophets are light." This does not mean that they give light! It means that they do not really give the Word of God, but they give a little smattering of psychology with a few Scripture verses put over it like a sugarcoated pill. That's the sort of thing that is being dished out today. They do not talk about judgment or the need for sinners to come to Christ.

"Her prophets are . . . treacherous persons." That is, they are racketeers, religious racketeers. Again, let me suggest that you read Matthew 23 to see if God has changed. You will find there the Lord Jesus' denouncement of religious rulers.

"Her priests have polluted the sanctuary." This is a terrible thing. How have they polluted the sanctuary? They have caused the world outside to lose respect for that which was sacred. By their lives, they brought disrespect upon the temple, upon the sanctuary. The same thing took place in Samuel's day when old Eli was priest. Men no longer had respect for religion. And today men decry the fact that the church has lost its influence. I decry it also, but, very frankly, I do not think that the church deserves the respect of the outside world when we cannot and do not present to them a church that is holy and that is living for God.

"They have done violence to the law." In other words, they did not interpret it accurately. In fact, they did violence to it by omitting the teaching of the Word of God. "The law" here means the total Word of God.

**The just LORD is in the midst thereof; he will not do iniquity: every morning doth he bring his judgment to light, he faileth not; but the unjust knoweth no shame [Zeph. 3:5].**

"The just LORD is in the midst thereof; he will not do iniquity." God is not going to do evil. The minute that His people do evil while God does nothing, it looks as if God approves that sort of thing. However, God says that He intends to move in judgment—God will not do iniquity.

"Every morning doth he bring his judgment to light, he faileth not; but the unjust knoweth no shame." The unjust simply continue on in sin with no shame at all that it is public knowledge.

We have now in verses 6–8 the picture of the Great Tribulation Period that is coming in the future, the great Day of the Lord which Zephaniah has talked about. Zephaniah moves from speaking of the city of Jerusalem to talking about the nations of the world in the last days. This is Armageddon, which ends with the return of Christ to earth.

**I have cut off the nations: their towers are desolate; I made their streets waste, that none passeth by: their cities are destroyed, so that there is no man, that there is none inhabitant [Zeph. 3:6].**

It has been my privilege to walk through the ruins of great civilizations of the past. Recently, I walked through the ruins of Ostia, the playground of the Romans. It is just fifteen miles from Rome, but not very well known. It will become well known later, as Rome is developing it, and it will become a tourist attraction. Ostia was where Rome lived it up. It was the Las Vegas of the Roman Empire. As you stand in the ruins of that city and see the stones of the Roman road which were worn by chariot wheels, it is difficult to think that those streets were once crowded and that that city was a great city in its heyday. God says here, "I'm going to make them desolate." It's very difficult to believe that Los Angeles could become that desolate, but it could. It is difficult to believe that New York City could become desolate, but it could.

**I said, Surely thou wilt fear me, thou wilt receive instruction; so their dwelling should not be cut off, howsoever I punished them: but they rose early, and corrupted all their doings [Zeph. 3:7].**

The warnings of judgment and the little judgment that did come had no effect upon them. Eventually that will bring down finally the great Day of the Lord, the final time of judgment, which is coming upon this earth.

**Therefore wait ye upon me, saith the LORD, until the day that I rise up to the prey: for my determination is to gather the nations, that I may assemble the kingdoms, to pour upon them mine indignation, even all my fierce anger: for all the earth shall be devoured with the fire of my jealousy [Zeph. 3:8].**

This earth which you and I are living on is moving toward a judgment. Although folk don't believe it, they are moving to judgment. It is this judgment which will be initiated when the Lord Jesus Christ returns to this earth for His church. It begins then with the Great Tribulation Period and ends when He comes to establish His kingdom on this earth.

## ALL JUDGMENTS REMOVED AND THE KINGDOM ESTABLISHED

We are now going to pass from the darkness to the day and to see the blessings which are in store. The storm is over as far as the little Book of Zephaniah is concerned. The book opens with dark forebodings and with ominous rumblings of judgment. The first part of this chapter, which deals with the judgment of the city of Jerusalem, is almost frightening to read. It *is* frightening when you come to that picture of the Great Tribulation Period when God will judge all nations when they are brought up against Jerusalem in that last day (see Zech. 14:1–3). We have seen two kinds of judgment in the Book of Zephaniah. There is God's judgment of His own people, which is always chastisement. "For whom the Lord loveth he chasteneth . . ." (Heb. 12:6)— in other words, He child-trains, or disciplines, them. Then God must judge the unbelieving world also. This is the picture of judgment that is before us in this little book. The Book of Zephaniah is like a Florida hurricane, a Texas tornado, a Mississippi River flood, a Minnesota snowstorm, and a California earthquake all rolled into one.

As you read this book you might think that God hates His people and that He hates mankind in general; you might think that He is vindictive, cruel, and brutal, that He is unfeeling and unmoved. However, the little story that I told in the Introduction is the story that illustrates the message of Zephaniah. It is the story of the man who took a little child into the darkness of the night and rushed her away from home. It looked as if he were kidnapping the child. It was frightful when he turned her over to another man who plunged a knife into her abdomen. But when you know the whole story, you find that the man was the father of that little girl. His own precious little girl had been having attacks of appendicitis, and that night he picked her up and rushed her to the hospital to put her into the hands of the family physician. Everything was done in tenderness. We find today that our Great Physician takes His own, the ones He loves, and puts them on the operating table. Even in judgment, God is love. When He is judging the unsaved or when He is judging those who are His own, God is love.

Someday the final curtain is coming down on this world in which we live. Man's little day will be over, and judgment will come for lost mankind. But God will restore His children, and we will find out that what we endured down here was actually a blessing in disguise. Let me tell you another little story, one that actually happened. It is the story of a boy who was away from home in school, and things got rough for him there. The lessons were difficult, and he was homesick. He wrote home and said, "Dad, it's hard here. The assignments are too heavy, and the dormitory rules are too strict. I'm homesick and I want to come home." The father wrote back a stern and severe letter in which he said, "You stay on there and study hard. Apply yourself to your work." When the boy got that letter, he thought, *I don't think my dad loves me anymore. My dad couldn't love me, or he wouldn't want me to go through this torture that I'm going through here.* We have a Heavenly Father who tells us, "You stay down there in the college of life. I'm preparing a place for you, and I am also preparing *you* for that place." With this in mind, let us turn to this final passage of Zephaniah.

**For then will I turn to the people a pure language, that they may all call upon the name of the LORD, to serve him with one consent [Zeph. 3:9].**

God has this far-off purpose—it is called the teleological purpose of God. We will find it all through this section because now we are in the light. We are no longer in the darkness of the judgment, no longer in the Day of the Lord which begins at night. The sun has now arisen, and light has broken upon mankind.

"For then will I turn to the people a pure language." He does not mean that everybody is going to speak Hebrew, although a great many people think that that is the meaning. Nor is He going to turn them to some other, perhaps unknown, language which everybody will speak. Nor is the "pure language" English spoken with a Texas accent! Many people find my Texas accent rather distasteful. I thought for awhile that you were going to have to get accustomed to it because it was what everybody would be speaking in heaven—but this doesn't mean that at all. "Pure language" means exactly what it says: the language will be pure. There will be no blasphemy heard. There will be no vileness nor vulgarity. There will be nothing repulsive. The language will be pure.

At one time we had a neighbor who was a very big-hearted woman in many ways, but she was unsaved. She not only had a mean tongue, but she also had the vilest tongue that I have ever heard. It was offensive to people whenever she would lose her temper, for you could hear her throughout the entire neighborhood. It was very distasteful, so much so that some wanted to report her. In heaven, my friend, there will be nobody to report because there is going to be a pure language. Heaven will be pure in thought, word, and deed.

"That they may all call upon the name of the LORD, to serve him with one consent." There will be no rebellion against God in that day. Heaven is going to be a really nice neighborhood to live in. In fact, it is going to be a glorious place, and you are going to have some good neighbors there.

**From beyond the rivers of Ethiopia my suppliants, even the daughter of my dispersed, shall bring mine offering [Zeph. 3:10].**

This verse of Scripture has been variously translated, and all sorts of interpretations have been presented for it. One interpretation is that the ark of the covenant is down in Ethiopia and that it will be brought up to Jerusalem as an offering at this time. I do not think that that is the thing Zephaniah has in mind here at all. Others call attention to a tribe in Ethiopia or Abyssinia known as the *Falashas*, which comes from the same root as the word *Philistine*, meaning migrant. They claim that they can trace their origin back to Israel, that they are Israelites. It is argued that these are the "suppliants" referred to here. Many feel that this verse speaks of those converted from the nations of the world who will bring dispersed Israelites back to their land as an offering to the Lord. My position is that this verse means that Ethiopia will enter the millennial kingdom—that is what is important for us to see. The offering that they will bring is the sacrifice of Christ Himself; in other words, they will come, having accepted His redemption.

**In that day shalt thou not be ashamed for all thy doings, wherein thou hast transgressed against me: for then I will take away out of the midst of thee them that rejoice in thy pride, and thou shalt no more be haughty because of my holy mountain [Zeph. 3:11].**

God is talking to His own here. We have seen that one of the things for which God was judging them was that there was no shame in their vile acts and gross immorality—they were not ashamed of it. But, my friend, God's people will never reach the place where they can be satisfied in sin. If you can live in sin and be happy—you can be sure of one thing—you are not a child of God. The prodigal son was never happy in the pigpen, and since he was the son of the father, he *had* to say, "I'm going home to my father." That revealed that he wasn't a pig. Pigs love pigpens, but sons don't love pigpens. A son wants to go to the father's house because he has the nature of the father. God makes this very clear here: "In that day shalt thou not be ashamed for all thy doings, wherein thou hast trangressed against me."

"For then I will take away out of the midst of thee them that rejoice in thy pride, and thou shalt no more be haughty because of my holy mountain." This speaks of the day when the meek shall inherit the earth. The other crowd has it now, and they are not doing very well with it.

**I will also leave in the midst of thee an afflicted and poor people, and they shall trust in the name of the LORD [Zeph. 3:12].**

When the Babylonians took Judah into captivity, there were three deportations of slaves taken, but they never took all of the people. The poor, the afflicted, and the crippled were not taken to Babylon. You can imagine how they felt. It was terrible to go into Babylonian captivity to become a slave, but it was actually worse to be left behind. God says here, "I intend to take care of the afflicted and the poor." You will notice that all the way through Scripture, the Lord often mentions the fact that He intends someday to see that the poor get an honest deal and that they are treated right. The only one in the world today who has a helpful program for the poor is the Lord Jesus Christ. If you are poor and needy, He is the one to go to. He can help you, and He is the only one who can help.

**The remnant of Israel shall not do iniquity, nor speak lies; neither shall a deceitful tongue be found in their mouth: for they shall feed and lie down, and none shall make them afraid [Zeph. 3:13].**

"The remnant of Israel shall not do iniquity." God has always had a remnant, and there will be this very large remnant in the Millennium.

"Nor speak lies; neither shall a deceitful tongue be found in their mouth." That the day is coming when they will not do these things would seem to indicate that they once did them. Even God's people indulged in sin—but not permanently. They cannot continue to live in sin. They may get their feet dirty, they may get down in the pigpen, but they simply will not stay in the pigpen.

"For they shall feed and lie down, and none shall make them afraid." All of this has reference to the day when God will put His people back in their land and give them the land. Therefore, are you prepared to say that what has happened and is happening in that land today is a fulfillment of prophecy? Is it true that "none shall make them afraid"? My friend, Israel has not had a moment, since they've been in that land, that they have not been frightened.

We come now to a description of the day when the King is going to set up His kingdom on the earth.

**Sing, O daughter of Zion; shout, O Israel; be glad and rejoice with all the heart, O daughter of Jerusalem.**

**The LORD hath taken away thy judgments, he hath cast out thine enemy: the king of Israel, even the LORD, is in the midst of thee: thou shalt not see evil any more [Zeph. 3:14–15].**

The Lord Jesus will come to the earth, evil will be put down, and ". . . the earth shall be full of the knowledge of the LORD, as the waters cover the sea" (Isa. 11:9).

**In that day it shall be said to Jerusalem, Fear thou not: and to Zion, Let not thine hands be slack [Zeph. 3:16].**

"In that day it shall be said to Jerusalem, Fear thou not." Jerusalem has reason to be afraid now, but she will have nothing to fear in that day.

"And to Zion, Let not thine hands be slack." In other words, "Be busy for the Lord."

Verse 17 is a marvelous verse—

**The LORD thy God in the midst of thee is mighty; he will save, he will rejoice over thee with joy; he will rest in his love, he will joy over thee with singing [Zeph. 3:17].**

My friend, God has a purpose. He goes through the night of judgment in order to bring us into the light of a new day. He does all of this that the day might come when He can rest in His love. God loves you and me today. I don't know about you, but I doubt very seriously whether He can rest in His love for Vernon McGee. He could say of me, "He's

not perfected yet. He seems so immature. He is so filled with faults. He is apt to digress, apt to detour, at any moment." God cannot rest in His love today. But the day is coming when we will be in His likeness—after He has put us on the "operating table". Then He is going to bring us to Himself. What a wonderful and glorious picture this is!

**I will gather them that are sorrowful for the solemn assembly, who are of thee, to whom the reproach of it was a burden.**

**Behold, at that time I will undo all that afflict thee: and I will save her that halteth, and gather her that was driven out; and I will get them praise and fame in every land where they have been put to shame.**

**At that time will I bring you again, even in the time that I gather you: for I will make you a name and a praise among all people of the earth, when I turn back your captivity before your eyes, saith the LORD [Zeph. 3:18–20].**

Oh, this is the day of light that will come. It will be glorious for the nation Israel, and it will be glorious for the church also. God is putting many of us through the furnace, and He is putting us through trials. The glorious thing about heaven will not be the golden streets, it will not be the gates of pearl, and it will not be the fact that He is going to wipe away all tears. The glorious thing in heaven will be that we are going to thank Him for every trial we had and for every burden that He put on us in this life.

I conclude with this wonderful little poem, "In the Crucible"—

Out from the mine and the darkness,
    Out from the damp and the mold,
Out from the fiery furnace,
    Cometh each grain of gold.
Crushed into atoms and leveled
    Down to the humblest dust
With never a heart to pity,
    With never a hand to trust.

Molten and hammered and beaten,
    Seemeth it ne'er to be done.
Oh! for such fiery trial,
    What hath the poor gold done?
Oh! 'twere a mercy to leave it
    Down in the damp and the mold.

If this is the glory of living,
  Then better to be dross than gold.

Under the press and the roller,
  Into the jaws of the mint,
Stamped with the emblem of freedom
  With never a flaw or a dint.
Oh! what a joy the refining
  Out of the damp and the mold!

And stamped with the glorious image,
  Oh, beautiful coin of gold!

Someday, when you and I are in the presence of our Savior, we will thank Him for every burden, every trial, every heartache. We will thank Him for dealing with us as a wise father deals with his children, and we will thank Him for the dark side of His love.

# BIBLIOGRAPHY

(Recommended for Further Study)

Feinberg, Charles L. *The Minor Prophets*. Chicago, Illinois: Moody Press, 1976.

Gaebelein, Arno C. *The Annotated Bible*. 1917. Reprint. Neptune, New Jersey: Loizeaux Brothers, 1971.

Ironside, H. A. *The Minor Prophets*. Neptune, New Jersey: Loizeaux Brothers, n.d.

Jensen, Irving L. *Minor Prophets of Judah*. Chicago, Illinois: Moody Press, 1975. (Obadiah, Joel, Micah, Nahum, Zephaniah, and Habakkuk.)

Unger, Merrill F. *Unger's Commentary on the Old Testament*, Vol. 2. Chicago, Illinois: Moody Press, 1982.

# The Book of

# HAGGAI

## INTRODUCTION

The prophets to the returned remnant were Haggai, Zechariah, and Malachi. Haggai, the writer of this short book, is mentioned in Ezra 5:1–2 and 6:14 as one of the two prophets who encouraged the remnant (that returned after the Babylonian captivity) to rebuild the temple in spite of the difficulties that beset them on every hand. From this and the brief references that he made to himself in his prophecy, four things become apparent:

1. Haggai was self-effacing—he exalted the Lord. He took the same position that John the Baptist took: "He must increase, but I must decrease" (John 3:30).

2. He was God's messenger. The expression "Thus saith the Lord" characterizes his message.

3. He not only rebuked the people; he also cheered and encouraged them in a marvelous way.

4. He not only preached; he also practiced.

Haggai begins his book by saying, "In the second year of Darius the king, in the sixth month, in the first day of the month." Hystaspes (the Darius mentioned here) began to reign in 521 B.C., making the second year of his reign about 520 B.C. "The second year of Darius" enables the historian to pinpoint the time of this prophet in profane history. It is interesting to note that the post-Captivity prophets begin to date their prophecies according to the reign of gentile rulers. Those prophets who prophesied before the Captivity always tied the dates of their writings into the reign of either a king of Israel or a king of Judah or both. After the Captivity, since there was no king in either the northern or the southern kingdom, Haggai dates his prophecy according to a gentile king. The Lord Jesus said, ". . . Jerusalem shall be trodden down of the Gentiles, until the times of the Gentiles be fulfilled" (Luke 21:24). In Haggai's day the "times of the Gentiles" had already begun (in fact, it began with the captivity of Judah under Nebuchadnezzar). Since that time Jerusalem has been under gentile domination, and Haggai dates his prophecy accordingly.

The theme of Haggai is the temple. The reconstruction and refurbishing of the temple were the supreme passion of this prophet. He not only rebuked the people for their delay in rebuilding the temple, but he also encouraged them and helped them in this enterprise.

Haggai constantly referred to the "word of the LORD" as the supreme authority. He willingly humbled himself that the Lord might be exalted. His message was practical. It was as simple and factual as $2+2=4$. The prophecy of Haggai and the Epistle of James have much in common. Both put the emphasis upon the daily grind. Action is spiritual. A "do nothing" attitude is wicked. Both place this yardstick down upon life. Work is the measure of life.

Haggai's contemporary, Zechariah, was visionary and had his head in the clouds, but pragmatic Haggai had both feet on the ground. The man of action and the dreamer need to walk together. First Corinthians 15:58 can appropriately be written over this book: "Therefore, my beloved brethren, be ye stedfast, unmoveable, always abounding in the work of the Lord, forasmuch as ye know that your labour is not in vain in the Lord."

There are two key verses in this book: "Go up to the mountain, and bring wood, and build the house; and I will take pleasure in it, and I will be glorified, saith the LORD. . . . And the LORD stirred up the spirit of Zerubbabel the son of Shealtiel, governor of Judah, and the spirit of Joshua the son of Josedech, the high priest, and the spirit of all the remnant of the people; and they came and did work in the house of the LORD of hosts, their God" (Hag. 1:8, 14).

# OUTLINE

The compass of this book is three months and fourteen days, according to the calendar. There are five messages in the book, and each was given on a specific date. The calendar furnishes the clue for the contents.

I. **September 1, 520 B.C., Chapter 1:1–11**
   *A Challenge to the People*
   A. A Charge of Conflict of Interest, Chapter 1:1–4
   B. A Call to Consider Their Ways, Chapter 1:5–7
   C. A Command to Construct the Temple, Chapter 1:8–11

II. **September 24, 520 B.C., Chapter 1:12–15**
   *The Response to the Challenge*
   A. Construction of the Temple; People Obeyed, Chapter 1:12
   B. Confirmation from God, Chapter 1:13–15

III. **October 21, 520 B.C., Chapter 2:1–9**
   *The Discouragement of the People; The Encouragement of the Lord*

IV. **December 24, 520 B.C., Chapter 2:10–19**
   *An Appeal to the Law; The Explanation of the Principle*

V. **December 24, 520 B.C., Chapter 2:20–23**
   *A Revelation of God's Program; An Expectation for the Future*

# CHAPTER 1

*THEME: Challenge to the people; charge of conflict of interest; call to consider their ways; command to construct the temple; construction of the temple—obedience of the people; confirmation from God*

Haggai was a prophet to the restored remnant who returned to Jerusalem after the seventy-year captivity in Babylon. In the study of this prophecy we will note how important it is to consider the historical books along with the prophetic books. There is a little cluster of books that belong together: Ezra, Nehemiah, and Esther for the historical record; and Haggai, Zechariah, and Malachi for the prophetic section—also, the Book of Daniel probably should be studied first. These books belong together and constitute a unit.

## CHALLENGE TO THE PEOPLE

Haggai and Zechariah prophesied during the same period, yet their approach was altogether different. They both challenged and encouraged the returned remnant to rebuild the temple and then to rebuild the walls of Jerusalem. "Then the prophets, Haggai the prophet, and Zechariah the son of Iddo, prophesied unto the Jews that were in Judah and Jerusalem in the name of the God of Israel, even unto them. Then rose up Zerubbabel the son of Shealtiel, and Jeshua the son of Jozadak, and began to build the house of God which is at Jerusalem: and with them were the prophets of God helping them" (Ezra 5:1–2). So, you see, both Haggai and Zechariah are mentioned in this historical Book of Ezra as the two prophets who encouraged the people to rebuild the temple and also aided them in it. Also, in Ezra 6:14 we read: "And the elders of the Jews builded, and they prospered through the prophesying of Haggai the prophet and Zechariah the son of Iddo. And they builded, and finished it, according to the commandment of the God of Israel, and according to the commandment of Cyrus, and Darius, and Artaxerxes king of Persia."

## CHARGE OF CONFLICT OF INTEREST

**In the second year of Darius the king, in the sixth month, in the first day of the month, came the word of the LORD by Haggai the prophet unto Zerubbabel the son of Shealtiel, governor of Judah, and to Joshua the son of Josedech, the high priest, saying [Hag. 1:1].**

"In the second year of Darius the king, in the sixth month, in the first day of the month" gives us the date of this prophecy, which is September 1, 520 B.C., according to the Jewish calendar. This is a book we can date very easily. As we said in the Introduction, the dating is according to the gentile ruler, Darius. The dating is no longer geared to the king of Israel or Judah because Haggai is writing during the "times of the Gentiles," which began with the Babylonian captivity and continues to the present day. The Lord Jesus said, "And they shall fall by the edge of the sword, and shall be led away captive into all nations: and Jerusalem shall be trodden down of the Gentiles, until the times of the Gentiles be fulfilled" (Luke 21:24).

"Came the word of the LORD by Haggai the prophet." We will find all the way through this little book that Haggai repeatedly refers to the Word of the Lord. He is making it clear that he is not speaking his own thoughts but is giving the Word of God to his people.

"Unto Zerubbabel the son of Shealtiel, governor of Judah." The name *Zerubbabel* means "sown in Babylon"; that is, he was born in captivity down in Babylon. It is actually a heathen name, by the way. He was in the line of David, the grandson of Jehoiachin (see 1 Chron. 3:16–19), and was appointed by Cyrus to be governor of Judah.

"And to Joshua the son of Josedech, the high priest." Joshua was the son of Jehozadak who was high priest at the time of the Babylonian invasion (see 1 Chron. 6:15). This man was the religious head. So, you see, God is sending His message first to the leaders, the religious and civil rulers.

When the Israelites returned from Babylonian captivity to their own land, they returned with great anticipation, and their enthusiasm for rebuilding ran high. But they met gigantic obstacles which required herculean effort and hardships. After they had gone through a period like that, they were discouraged when they began to build the temple. The difficulties seemed insurmountable. Therefore they rationalized and decided that it was not the time to build. In other words, this was their pseudoconsolation. They decided to maintain the status quo. They said, "It is so hard, evidently God doesn't intend us to do it." They had laid the foundation of the temple, but the opposition of the Samaritans was so intense that they simply stopped building, and their excuse was, "Well, the time has not come."

**Thus speaketh the Lord of hosts, saying, This people say, The time is not come, the time that the Lord's house should be built [Hag. 1:2].**

If you will read the Book of Nehemiah, you will see that, when they were rebuilding the walls of Jerusalem, the opposition was terrific. Well, they had the same kind of opposition in rebuilding the temple, and the people said, "Well, this is not the Lord's time to build it."

Notice that God says, "This people say"—ordinarily He calls them *My* people, but not here. By this He doesn't mean that He has disowned them; He is just displeased with them. They are not in His will, and they are covering their disobedience with the pious-sounding excuse, "It is just not the right time to build the Lord's house."

What Haggai is going to say will hurt a little. He is going to stick the knife in the trouble spot that, by the way, touches the lives of many Christians. Have you ever heard people say that they had given up trying to do something or that they did not go someplace because it was not the Lord's will? They will sometimes say that the Lord directed them to do something else. Saying that it is the Lord's will to do this or not to do that is a Christian cliché that covers a multitude of sins. It is so easy, when things get hard and rough, to turn in a report to everyone that says, "The Lord wanted me to do something else." Many a preacher, when things got tough in his church, has said, "The Lord needs me somewhere else." My heart goes out to pastors who are really trying to serve God but are having trouble and end up saying, "The Lord is leading me elsewhere." When the Lord's people started building the temple and the going got rough, they said, "It's not the Lord's time to build."

I remember when we attempted to remodel the church in downtown Los Angeles, California, where I served as pastor. The church in its long history had never been remodeled, and the seats, which numbered four thousand, were built to take care of people who lived fifty or sixty years ago. We discovered that people today are about 2½ inches wider than they were fifty years ago! We decided to put in new cushioned seats. Some of the very pious folks said, "We don't feel that money should be spent for cushions. We should give

that money to missions." Now the majority of the people wanted the cushioned seats, and I did too, so I made a proposition to the congregation. I said, "There are so many people enthusiastic about remodeling that they are going to give enough money to cushion their seat and yours too, so those of you who don't want to pay for cushioned seats can give your twenty-five dollars to missions. I hope that we can take an offering today for several hundred twenty-five dollar checks." Well, there were very few twenty-five dollar checks. Why? The truth was that the folk who were objecting to the cushioned seats never intended to give at all, and "missions instead of cushions" was their excuse. But what they *said* was, "It isn't God's will to have cushioned seats. The time hasn't come to remodel the church."

It was my privilege to remodel every church which I served as pastor. I never built a new church, but I remodeled each of them. And I always encountered the same problem. In each church there was a little group—a very small group, thank God for that—which didn't *do* anything, but they were good at criticizing. And the excuse was always the same—"The money shouldn't be spent on us here; it should go to missions." Then they should have given it to missions, but they did not.

The crowd that Haggai is addressing rationalized in the same way. He is pulling the Band-Aid off and exposing the sore. And it isn't an "ouchless" Band-Aid—it *hurts*, you may be sure of that.

Now here is message number one, given on September 1, 520 B.C. Notice that Haggai is giving the *Word* of the Lord.

**Then came the word of the Lord by Haggai the prophet, saying,**

**Is it time for you, O ye, to dwell in your ceiled houses, and this house lie waste? [Hag. 1:3–4].**

These folk who said it was not time to build the Lord's house had all built their *own* houses—it seemed the time to do that! And the Lord pointed out that their houses were "ceiled houses." This means that they were beautifully paneled; they were luxuriously built. And for fifteen years, while they had been building their elaborate homes, the Lord's house had been lying waste.

It is amazing, but I have found it true thoughout my many years in the ministry, that a great many people say, "I feel it is God's will for me to help you in your ministry," and then when the going gets a little rough, say, "It doesn't seem to be the Lord's will for me to help at this time." You see, the minute that things become difficult, that is the time most people decide their resolve is not the *Lord's* will. But when it is something for their own selfish ends, they usually go ahead and do it, don't they? Most people are that way. We make the effort to accomplish that which will always be to our advantage.

In Haggai's day, how in the world were the people able to build their lovely paneled homes? Surely they encountered difficulties, but they were not willing to face the same difficulties to build the Lord's house. Their lame excuse was, "It's just not the Lord's will right now for us to do that."

Oh, I get so weary of hearing people give that excuse for not doing something for God! What do they know about the Lord's will? Just because something is difficult and hard and is going to cost you something, does that mean it is not the Lord's will? May I say to you, that is *not* the way to interpret the Lord's will. Sometimes the Lord's will is very rugged. If we could just listen to the stories of some of God's choice saints of the past, they would tell us that God's will was not always a smooth path.

I wonder what Abraham would say to the people today who say, "It is not God's will for me to do this or that." Abraham lived in Ur of the Chaldees. This man who was to be the father of the Israelites was no doubt a good businessman. He had a nice business in Ur, a highly civilized city in those days and a prosperous one. It was a city of luxury. One day God said to Abraham, "I want you to leave Ur." It would have been easy for Abraham to rationalize, "I must have misunderstood the Lord. He would not ask me to leave this place. The life here is soft and easy. It couldn't be the Lord's will for me to leave this city."

There are literally thousands of missionaries on the mission field today who are making great sacrifices. Why? They do it because they believe it is God's will for them to be on the mission field. I wonder how many of us here at home should be on the mission field. I wonder how many church members there are today who are as busy as termites arranging social events that require no sacrifice or hardship, instead of standing up to the opposition and really getting out the Word of God.

Notice again that Haggai is making it clear that these are not his own words; they are the words of *God*.

I always feel badly when I am in a place like Mexico, and I see all of those ornate cathedrals and the people living in poverty around them. It is easy for us to point a finger and say, "That just isn't right." I agree that it isn't right, but neither is it right for a church to be in a state of disrepair. A church needs to be attractive in order to attract the sinner. One excuse I heard for a church being in such terrible shape was that the congregation gave all of its money to missions. A deacon in that church told me that the reason their church did not have a carpet on the floor or new pews was that all their money had gone to missions. When that deacon took me to his home, he treated me royally. He put me in a guest room that was nicer than any room I had ever been in. His home, I was told, cost over one hundred thousand dollars back in the old days. I have a notion it is worth a great deal more today. It was all I could do to keep quiet. I had to bite my tongue to keep from saying, "You believe in giving to missions, and you don't put a rug on the floor of your church, but look at your home! You could have been a little less lavish and still could have had money for missions *and* your church."

Let me ask you a question, friend, "How much are you spending on yourself, and how much are you doing for God?" That question gets close to us, doesn't it?

May I use another illustration concerning this subject? I went to dinner with a friend of mine who is a fine Christian layman. The dinner was rather expensive, and he left a generous tip for the waitress. Then we went to a church service that evening in order to hear a certain preacher. We heard a good sermon, and when the offering plate was passed, my friend put in one dollar, which was much less than he had given the waitress. I thought, *My, he's not even tipping God!* My friend, this gets right down to where we live.

The Israelites were saying, "It is just not the time for the Lord's house to be built." God says, "Then why is it time for *your* houses to be built?" There is a lot of hypocrisy in the church today. It is sickening to hear people boast about what they do for God when what they do for themselves is a thousand times more than what they are doing for God.

I told you that what Haggai has to say will hurt. He would never win a popularity contest. He is rather like an alarm clock. The alarm clock will never become the most treasured possession of the average American. It is an institution of our contemporary American society but not one that will win a loving cup or a popularity contest. We do not like to be awakened from a sound and restful sleep. The culprit who does it is a criminal, and he should be punished, not rewarded. There are manufacturers today who are making alarm clocks with pleasant sounds, but they are still alarm clocks. Today America is prosperous and powerful and comfortable and satisfied and satiated. We have come to a place where it is woe to anyone who disturbs us, sounds an alarm, blows a whistle, or turns on a siren. In one community a church was restrained from putting up chimes because it would wake up the people in the neighborhood on Sunday morning. If Paul Revere rode again today, he would be arrested for disturbing the peace. John the Baptist would lose his head, not for rebuking a king's sinful life but for being a rabble-rouser and a calamity-howler.

That is the reason God's prophets never won a popularity contest. They were stoned, not starred. And Haggai is an alarm clock. He wakes us up, and he disturbs us. We don't like that. And the people in his day didn't like it. They had just come out of the Babylonian captivity, and they didn't want to hear his message. Haggai occupied a very difficult position. He stood between a rock and a hard place. Yet he attempted to wake up his people to do something for God, and his method was very unusual, though not original by any means. Although his method is not being used in our day, I think it would still be effective in God's work.

## CALL TO CONSIDER THEIR WAYS

Now God calls their attention to something which is very practical. This gets right down to the nitty-gritty of life.

**Now therefore thus saith the LORD of hosts; Consider your ways [Hag. 1:5].**

"Consider your ways" is literally, set your heart upon your ways. Look at what is happening to you. Now He goes into detail—

**Ye have sown much, and bring in little; ye eat, but ye have not enough; ye drink, but ye are not filled with drink; ye clothe you, but there is none warm; and he that earneth wages earneth wages to put it into a bag with holes.**

**Thus saith the LORD of hosts; Consider your ways [Hag. 1:6–7].**

God was judging them concerning their material things, and they were not recognizing it as His judgment. We see in the Book of Hebrews, "If ye endure chastening, God dealeth

with you as with sons; for what son is he whom the father chasteneth not?" (Heb. 12:7). When God disciplines us, there is a reason for it. The child of God needs to consider his ways. He needs to examine his own heart to see why God is putting him through the mill or using sandpaper on him. God wants to smooth the rough edges off our lives; so He does use sandpaper.

For the people of Israel there had been crop failure. There had been famine. There had been little money to buy clothes or food, and they had no savings account. But they never once attributed this to their disobedience. They were trying to explain it in other ways. What about God's children in our day? "Oh," they say, "that's just my luck." It is not *luck* if you are God's child. Difficulties come to you for a purpose. God won't let anything happen to you unless it has a purpose. God is trying to develop something valuable in your heart and life. That is why God said, "Consider your ways." Man's ways always seem right to him. The writer of the Book of Proverbs says, "There is a way which seemeth right unto a man, but the end thereof are the ways of death" (Prov. 14:12). In Isaiah 53:6 we read, "All we like sheep have gone astray; we have turned every one to his *own* way . . ." (italics mine). The problem with mankind today is that we all want to go our *own* way. Again the writer of Psalm 1 says, "For the LORD knoweth the way of the righteous: but the way of the ungodly shall perish" (Ps. 1:6).

Notice how the Word of God enlarges upon the things that reveal man's way as opposed to God's way: "Let the wicked forsake his way, and the unrighteous man his thoughts: and let him return unto the LORD, and he will have mercy upon him; and to our God, for he will abundantly pardon" (Isa. 55:7). And in Proverbs 13:15 He says that ". . . the way of transgressors is hard." It certainly is hard! Again in Isaiah He says, "For as the heavens are higher than the earth, so are my ways higher than your ways, and my thoughts than your thoughts" (Isa. 55:9). And then—"O LORD, I know that the way of man is not in himself: it is not in man that walketh to direct his steps" (Jer. 10:23). Also, "Thus saith the LORD, Stand ye in the ways, and see, and ask for the old paths, where is the good way, and walk therein, and ye shall find rest for your souls. But they said, We will not walk therein" (Jer. 6:16). Man is in rebellion against God. In Jeremiah 10:2 God says, ". . . Learn not the way of the heathen. . . ." And God says, ". . . This is the way, walk ye in it . . ."

(Isa. 30:21). And the Lord Jesus said, "Verily, verily, I say unto you, He that entereth not by the door into the sheepfold, but climbeth up some other way, the same is a thief and a robber. But he that entereth in by the door is the shepherd of the sheep" (John 10:1–2). He goes on to say, "I am the door: by me if any man enter in, he shall be saved, and shall go in and out, and find pasture" (John 10:9). How tremendous this is!

This is what God is saying to His people. He wants them to consider their *ways*. He wants them to set their hearts upon their ways. He asks, "Don't you see what is happening to you?"

Now let me ask you, "What *way* are you on today? What path are you taking? Where is that path leading you? Have you ever considered where drugs are going to lead you? It is a broad way where you start out, and you can do as you please, but that broad way is actually a funnel, and it grows narrower and narrower until there is only one little opening, which leads only to destruction. But God says that the way which leads to life is a narrow way—Christ is that way; He is the *only* way to the Father. When you enter the narrow way, it becomes broader and broader as you go along until you can go in and out and find pasture. You will have life and have it abundantly. My friend, it is time to consider your ways. Set your heart upon your ways. Where are you headed today? How is your marriage working out? If you are a young person in college, do you have a goal in life? If you are a young lady, how about the young man you are dating? Where is he leading you? What is going to happen to you? Why don't you consider your ways?

Folk from all walks of life write to me. Many are headed in the right direction; others very frankly say that they are on the wrong path, and they are suffering broken homes, broken hearts, and wrecked lives. God says, "Consider your ways."

## COMMAND TO CONSTRUCT THE TEMPLE

Now God is going to give them the solution to their problems. It is so simple, so clear that you may wonder why it is necessary to emphasize it. God gives them a command to construct the temple, and He tells them three things that they are to do. You see, the children of Israel had a conflict of interests. They had put their own homes before God's house. They were putting their selfish ends ahead of God's program. The Lord Jesus, in the Sermon on the Mount, said that we are to seek first the kingdom of God and His righteousness (see Matt. 6:33). That "righteousness" is in Christ. When you have Christ, you have everything—you have all those things you are after. Money can be spiritual, depending on what you use it for. Your home can be spiritual if it is a place where God is honored. It can be a place where a testimony for the Lord is given, where friends can come and be refreshed, or where a Bible class can be taught. It can be a place as sacred as your church. The things that people are after today may not be wrong, but it is wrong when they put them *first* in their lives and use them for their own selfish ends.

Now God tells the people in Haggai's day what they are to do:

**Go up to the mountain, and bring wood, and build the house; and I will take pleasure in it, and I will be glorified, saith the LORD [Hag. 1:8].**

The solution is so simple—there are only three things they are to do: (1) "Go up to the mountain, and" (2) "bring wood, and" (3) "build the house." I'll be honest with you, I wonder why some of the children of Israel had not realized this sooner. When people get that big "I" in front of their eyes, it obscures everything else, and they are blind to the things they should see. That which should be very simple becomes a very complex problem. People today say, "Life is so complicated. We need a psychiatrist. We need to get things straightened out." My friend, if you just put God in His rightful place, He will straighten out a great many things for you. But first, you must get the big "I" out of the way.

"Go up to the mountain, and bring wood." If you have visited the land of Israel, you may wonder about God's command to go up to the mountain and bring down trees since that land is almost denuded of trees today. For many years now Israel has been carrying on a project of tree planting. Although they have planted millions of trees, the hills still look bare to me. Very few of them have any sign of green on them. At one time that land was covered with trees, as this verse reveals. God wouldn't tell them to go up to the mountain and get wood if there were not wood up there. Then what happened to the trees? Well, when the enemy invaded Israel in A.D 70, the forces of Rome not only destroyed the cities, they also denuded the land of trees. They cut down practically every tree.

Now notice again God's simple solution to

their problems: (1) "Go up to the mountain, and" (2) "bring wood, and" (3) "build the house." Going up to the mountain, felling the trees, and making them into lumber would take work and a great deal of effort.

My friend, if you are not ready to go to *work* for the Lord, if you are not willing to do what God wants you to do—whatever that might be—Bible study is really not going to help you very much. God believes in *work*, and the message of this little Book of Haggai is the gospel of work.

As we have seen in this marvelous little book, first there was God's challenge to His people. They were kidding themselves that they were doing God's will. But the reason they had not built the temple was that they were just plain lazy. They tried to conceal that fact with the very pious platitude, "The time isn't right. It isn't the will of God to build at this time." God told them to get off their haunches and go to work. He said, "You have been attributing the fact that you have had bad crops and that things are difficult for you to other causes. You have been blaming your circumstances. Why don't you blame Me? I am the One who has sent trouble to you. I'm trying to wake you up." He tells them to consider their ways, to set their hearts on their ways. And now He says to get busy. He charged them with a conflict of interests, then He called them to consider their ways, and now He commands them to start to build the temple. And it is very simple, "Go to the mountain and bring down wood. You can't expect the logs to roll down to you. It is up to you to go to work."

There are so many voices today encouraging Christians to expect a miracle in their lives. They say, "God is going to deal with you by a miracle!" Well, I'm here to tell you that He is not. It would have been very easy for someone to have come along and to have told these Israelites to expect a miracle, but God says, "Go up there and bring down wood. Go to work." My friend, there is no easy shortcut in our service for God.

Very frankly, laziness is the reason Sunday school teachers don't succeed. Laziness is the reason preachers don't succeed. Laziness is the reason people fail in their Christian lives. You have to *work* at it. I do not think that the Holy Spirit will ever bless laziness.

In seminary I remember one of the students complaining to the professor, "Doctor, that book you assigned for us to read is really *dry!*" The professor looked up and smiled, "Well, dampen it with a little sweat from your brow."

That's the way to do it, friend. Don't expect the Christian life to be handed to you on a silver platter. The miracle comes in the work that you do. God told His people in Haggai's day to go to work.

Dr. Frank Morgan has called it (1) the *appeal to the mind*. God told them at the very beginning, "You say it is not time to build God's house? I want you to *think* about that. How is it that *you* are living in fine houses?" That was His appeal to the mind. (2) He *appealed to the heart*. He called them to consider, to set their heart on this. They had not done so, but that was His challenge. (3) God gave them a command, and that command was an *appeal to the will*. "Go up, bring wood, and build"—so simple yet so important.

My friend, roll up your sleeves, and let's go to work for God today. So many people are sitting on the sidelines. This is a day of spectator sports; but frankly, it is a day of spectator Christians also. They like to sit on the sidelines and watch somebody else do it. Many a preacher is being worked to death. He is called upon to visit all the sick folk in his congregation. He does all the administrative work—he is expected to supervise everything. What about you deacons? Why don't you go to work? What about you members of the church? Are you visiting the sick? The pastor is to train you to do the work of the ministry. He is not the one to do it all. The work should be divided and shared. The burden of the ministry should not fall on just a few folk. If you are a member of a local congregation, you should go to work. Work is something which is desperately needed in our churches today.

Let me illustrate what I mean. My first pastorate after I was ordained was my home church, the church in which I had been raised. One morning a deacon made a special trip to the study to talk with me. He said, "Vernon, I can't pray in public. I don't know why, but I can't do it. The fact of the matter is, I can't speak in public either. Don't ever call on me to speak or pray in public. If you do, I will embarrass you, and I will embarrass myself. I simply can't do either one of these things in public, and I can't seem to overcome the weakness." Tears were in his eyes as he spoke. Then he said, "But anytime anything needs to be done in this church, whether it is to replace a light bulb that has burned out or to put a new roof on the church, you can call on me. I will be glad to do it." Do you know what I did after that? If something needed repairing or remodeling around the church, I would call on him. Sometimes in less than an hour, a whole crew of men would be at the church to work, and that deacon would work right along with them. I learned very early that he was one of the most valuable members I ever had in a church. He was a Haggai. He believed in getting down to business and doing the work that needed to be done. Often I heard visiting speakers and others say, "My, this church is certainly kept up; what a lovely place to come and worship!" Do you know why that church looked so nice? A man in my church could not pray in public. Thank God he couldn't pray in public, because most churches have too many men who love to pray in public. We need people who are working people, too. We need people who are willing to roll up their sleeves and go to work.

Actually, the Book of Haggai is too simple to be in God's Word. It should be a little bit more complicated. Haggai gave the people a sermon. He said, "Go up to the mountain." That is the first point. Then he said, "Bring down the wood." That is point number two. Then he said, "Build a house." That is the third point. Those were God's simple instructions. There was nothing more to say, but there was something to do.

Now God explains why the people of Israel had been having such a difficult time—

**Ye looked for much, and, lo, it came to little; and when ye brought it home, I did blow upon it. Why? saith the Lord of hosts. Because of mine house that is waste, and ye run every man unto his own house [Hag. 1:9].**

"And ye run every man unto his own house" indicates the zeal and enthusiasm with which they had been taking care of their own interests and building their own homes.

They had been wondering why all of these difficulties had come upon them, but they were too pious to blame God. They claimed that their bad luck was due to circumstances. It was a bad year. "We had a drought, you know," they would say. But God told them, "I want you to know that I caused the drought. I saw to it that you were not successful in your different schemes, and I will tell you why I did it. It is because My house is lying in waste while every man improves his own home."

Let me repeat that the Lord Jesus stated the great principle in the Book of Haggai, which is applicable for all people of all ages, when He said, "But seek ye first the kingdom of God, and his righteousness; and all these things shall be added unto you" (Matt. 6:33).

When God is put first in our lives, all other things will take care of themselves. What a message this is! Yet it is so simple, I'm afraid we will miss it.

**Therefore the heaven over you is stayed from dew, and the earth is stayed from her fruit [Hag. 1:10].**

Naturally, when there was no rain, there were no crops. The wheat and the barley would not grow, and the vines would not produce. God says, "I turned off the spigot; I didn't give you any water."

In our contemporary society we don't interpret life like that. Because we live in a mechanical society, an electronic age, we blame our problems on someone's failure to push a button or on pushing the wrong button. I wonder if God would like to get through to America and say, "Look, has it ever occurred to you that I may be behind the problems you are having? Did it ever occur to you that I am trying to get your attention off *things* and onto Me?"

Notice that God takes the blame for all of these trials which have come upon Israel—

**And I called for a drought upon the land, and upon the mountains, and upon the corn, and upon the new wine, and upon the oil, and upon that which the ground bringeth forth, and upon men, and upon cattle, and upon all the labour of the hands [Hag. 1:11].**

God is saying to them, "Material blessings have been withheld from you because *I* withheld them. *I* am responsible."

In our day, the tendency is to blame first the police—they should have been on the job. Then we blame the mayor, we blame the legislature, and we blame Washington. Very possibly all of them are guilty. But, my friend, has it occurred to you that *you* yourself are to blame? Although we blame men and machines for the conditions of the world, *God* has brought it all to pass. Do you want to blame Him? Go ahead. He told Israel that He was responsible. But He also told them why. They had neglected Him. You see, the solution to our problems is very simple; yet it is complicated. We think that if we put in a new method or a new machine or a new man, our problems will be solved. My friend, why don't we recognize what our problem really is, who caused it, and how it can be solved?

Now Haggai tells us the response to the challenge which God has given to the people of Israel.

## CONSTRUCTION OF THE TEMPLE— OBEDIENCE OF THE PEOPLE

**Then Zerubbabel the son of Shealtiel, and Joshua the son of Josedech, the high priest, with all the remnant of the people, obeyed the voice of the Lord their God, and the words of Haggai the prophet, as the Lord their God had sent him, and the people did fear before the Lord [Hag. 1:12].**

Zerubbabel is the governor, Joshua is the high priest, and "all the remnant of the people" refers to the people who returned to the land of Israel from Babylonian captivity.

Notice that they did two things: (1) They obeyed God. As Samuel the prophet had said to a disobedient king, ". . . to obey is better than sacrifice, and to hearken than the fat of rams" (1 Sam. 15:22). And the apostle John put it this way, ". . . if we walk in the light, as he is in the light, we have fellowship one with another, and the blood of Jesus Christ his Son cleanseth us from all sin" (1 John 1:7). You see, we must walk in the light of the Word of God, and the Word will humble us and show us our failures. A great many of us don't like to have them called to our attention; but if we will recognize them and deal with them, we will find that the blood of Jesus Christ will just keep on cleansing us from all sin, and we will have fellowship with God. So we see that the people of Israel obeyed God.

Also (2) they feared God. The writer of Proverbs says that "The fear of the Lord is the beginning of wisdom . . ." (Prov. 9:10).

It is significant that the leaders of the people, Zerubbabel and Joshua, are mentioned first in their obedience to God. The need today in our country is for obedient Christians in places of leadership. William Gladstone, the famous British statesman, was asked what was the mark of a great statesman. His reply was that a statesman is a man who knows the direction God is moving for the next fifty years. Well, we don't seem to have men in leadership who know the direction God is moving for the next fifty minutes. Oh, how we need men who really know God and are being led by Him!

### CONFIRMATION FROM GOD

When they obey God and fear Him, they receive this wonderful confirmation from Him.

**Then spake Haggai the Lord's messenger in the Lord's message unto the peo-ple, saying, I am with you, saith the Lord [Hag. 1:13].**

He says, "I am *with* you." How wonderful! You remember that the Lord Jesus said to His own, "Lo, I am with you alway, even unto the end of the age." And notice that the promise of His presence rested upon their obedience: "Go ye therefore, and teach all nations, baptizing them in the name of the Father, and of the Son, and of the Holy Ghost: Teaching them to observe all things whatsoever I have commanded you: and, lo, I am with you alway, even unto the end of the world [the age]. Amen" (Matt. 28:19–20). He didn't say that He will be with you if you sit on your haunches and don't do anything for God. He didn't promise to be with you there. He said that He will be with you when you obey Him. That is the place of blessing and of fellowship. And you can't have anything better than that.

Now notice that the leaders enter enthusiastically into the work.

**And the Lord stirred up the spirit of Zerubbabel the son of Shealtiel, governor of Judah, and the spirit of Joshua the son of Josedech, the high priest, and the spirit of all the remnant of the people; and they came and did work in the house of the Lord of hosts, their God [Hag. 1:14].**

It is pretty important to see the leadership of the nation in action. Zerubbabel was the civil leader, the governor. He was in the kingly line and was the son of Shealtiel, whose name means "asking of God in prayer." And Joshua, the high priest, was the son of Josedech (Jehozadak) who was high priest at the time of the Babylonian invasion. So we see here the civil and religious leaders joining in with the people in doing the work of the Lord.

This second message was given, and Haggai dates it—

**In the four and twentieth day of the sixth month, in the second year of Darius the king [Hag. 1:15].**

This is September 24, 520 B.C. The first message, as we have seen, was given on September 1, 520 B.C.—that was when God challenged them. They had responded to the challenge, had come together, had organized the project, were cutting down trees, were making them into lumber, and had started to build the temple. Now, twenty-four days later, Haggai gives them this second message from God, the assurance of His presence.

Haggai was an orderly man, as his book indicates. He was also an administrator. He was a man who was right down to earth. He helped the people rebuild the temple, and as they worked together he continually encouraged and challenged them in their work. The results would be great. God would be pleased, and God would be glorified.

# CHAPTER 2

**THEME:** *Discouragement of the people; encouragement of the Lord; appeal to the Law; explanation of the principle; revelation of God's program; expectation for the future*

In the second chapter we see the discouragement of the people and the encouragement of the Lord. The obvious inferiority of the second temple to the temple of Solomon became a cause of discouragement, but God responded to it.

## DISCOURAGEMENT OF THE PEOPLE

**In the seventh month, in the one and twentieth day of the month, came the word of the LORD by the prophet Haggai, saying [Hag. 2:1].**

Notice that this took place in the seventh month—the previous time they heard God's message of encouragement was in the sixth month. So now they had been working for a month. They had spent about twenty-four days getting organized, and now the temple is beginning to go up. There is great enthusiasm as they see their progress. And they remember God's encouraging, "I am with you."

Now we come to the second item of discouragement.

**Speak now to Zerubbabel the son of Shealtiel, governor of Judah, and to Joshua the son of Josedech, the high priest, and to the residue of the people, saying [Hag. 2:2].**

This message is directed to the same group of people whom God had encouraged in the previous chapter, the same leaders and the same people.

Now here is the second hurdle which Haggai had to clear as he prophesied to these folk—

**Who is left among you that saw this house in her first glory? and how do ye see it now? is it not in your eyes in comparison of it as nothing? [Hag. 2:3].**

Many of those who had returned from the Babylonian captivity could remember—although they had been very young at the time—the beauty and the richness of Solomon's temple. This little temple which they were putting up looked like a tenant farmer's barn in Georgia in comparison to the richness and glory of Solomon's temple. Although Solomon's temple had not been a large temple, as temples go, they could remember its ornate richness, the jewels, the gold, and the silver which had been put into it. Before inflation the estimated value of the materials that went into Solomon's temple varied between five million and twenty million dollars—that is quite a difference, of course, but in that day either five or twenty million dollars was quite a sum of wealth. That temple had been like a beautiful little jewel box.

Now let me draw your attention again to the dating of this third message from God: "the seventh month, in the one and twentieth day of the month." If you check this date in Leviticus 23, you will find that it was the seventh day of the Feast of Tabernacles, the final feast of ingathering for the Jews. I am of the opinion that the builders had really pushed and speeded up their building in order to get the temple as far along as possible in order to use it for the celebration of the Feast of Tabernacles. So when some of the old-timers came into it and saw the lack of beauty and richness which had characterized Solomon's temple, they were disappointed. As you know, any kind of structure, whether it is a home or a great office building, doesn't look very impressive before it is completed. You have to wait until the building is finished to really appreciate it. But this little temple in Haggai's day, even when it was finished, was no comparison to Solomon's temple. And there was a mixed reaction to it.

The Book of Ezra, chapter 3:8–13, gives us more background as to what went on at this time: "Now in the second year of their coming unto the house of God at Jerusalem, in the second month, began Zerubbabel the son of Shealtiel, and Jeshua the son of Jozadak, and the remnant of their brethren the priests and the Levites, and all they that were come out of the captivity unto Jerusalem; and appointed the Levites, from twenty years old and upward, to set forward the work of the house of the LORD. Then stood Jeshua with his sons and his brethren, Kadmiel and his sons, the sons of Judah, together, to set forward the workmen in the house of God: the sons of Henadad, with their sons and their brethren the Levites. And when the builders laid the foundation of the temple of the LORD, they set the priests in their apparel with trumpets, and the Levites the sons of Asaph with cymbals, to praise the LORD, after the ordinance of David king of Israel. And they sang together by course in praising and giving thanks unto the LORD; because he is good, for his mercy endureth for ever toward Israel. And all the people shouted with a great shout, when they praised the LORD, because the foundation of the house of the LORD was laid."

It may have been just the foundation and a few uprights, but they had to celebrate it. Ezra's record continues—"But many of the priests and Levites and chief of the fathers, who were ancient men, that had seen the first house, when the foundation of this house was laid before their eyes, wept with a loud voice; and many shouted aloud for joy: So that the people could not discern the noise of the shout of joy from the noise of the weeping of the people: for the people shouted with a loud shout, and the noise was heard afar off."

You see, amid all of the shouts of joy there was another sound—a weeping and howling by those who were making a comparison between the two. They were saying, "Look, this little temple that you are putting up here doesn't amount to a hill of beans. In comparison to Solomon's temple, it doesn't amount to anything." This internal criticism was like a wet blanket on the celebration of the construction of the new temple. It dulled the edge of the zeal to rebuild the temple. It poured cold water on the enthusiasm generated by the prodding of Haggai. If you want to dampen a project, all you have to say is, "You think this is great, but you should have seen the original back in the good old days."

When I was a boy, I remember some of the adults talking about the good old days. Well, I don't remember any good old days when I was a boy—those days when I was growing up were hard. I remember the first little church I served in Georgia. It was a little white building sitting on a red clay hill. During my first year there as a student pastor I preached a series of evangelistic messages on the Book of Revelation. I haven't been able to do that again in my ministry, but I did it then, and God blessed. Many young people were saved. On the Sunday night of the final message some of us sat on the steps of the church because it was a warm Georgia evening—most of us were young people—and we were talking about what a wonderful meeting it had been. There was one old man there with whiskers like Methuselah. He said, "You've had some good meetings, young man, but I remember . . . ." When someone starts that, you are headed for the toboggan, and soon you're on the downhill run. He took us for quite a ride down the hill. He told us, "When I was a young man, we really had a meeting here!" As he told us about the meeting, ours seemed pretty small compared to his, although I learned later that he exaggerated a little. Yet what he said was discouraging.

And in Haggai's day the folk, who had been so enthusiastic about the temple they were building, became discouraged.

How is God going to meet this situation? Well, I'll tell you how we in the church would handle it. We would appoint a committee to see what could be done. As someone has said, a committee is a group of people who individually can do nothing and who collectively decide that nothing can be done. Or, as another has said, a committee is a group of incompetents, appointed by the indifferent, to do the unnecessary. Having been a pastor for many years, I am confident that we would use the committee approach to handle this problem. But that is not the way God solved it. He faced the problem squarely and came up with a very simple solution.

**Yet now be strong, O Zerubbabel, saith the LORD; and be strong, O Joshua, son of Josedech, the high priest; and be strong, all ye people of the land, saith the LORD, and work: for I am with you, saith the LORD of hosts [Hag. 2:4].**

God's challenge is twofold here. First, He says, "Be strong," three times. He says *be strong* to the civil ruler. He says *be strong* to the religious ruler. Then when He speaks to the people, does He have something new for them? No, it's the same thing—*be strong*.

Now that is very simple, but it is very important.

My friend, you and I live in a big, bad world today. What is our encouragement? God's work in many places is small and doesn't seem to amount to very much. What is the solution? Well, here is God's answer to us: "Finally, my brethren, be strong in the Lord, and in the power of his might" (Eph. 6:10). We need to recognize that we can't do anything but that God can do a great deal. Be strong in the Lord. How wonderful that is.

Also in Hebrews 11:34 it says that believers "Quenched the violence of fire, escaped the edge of the sword, out of *weakness* were made *strong* . . ." (italics mine). Doesn't God say that He chooses the weak things of the world? God does not choose these big, ornate buildings. He doesn't choose these beautiful mausoleums that have steeples on top of them. Nothing very great is happening in places like that, but things are really jumping in some suburban areas, and many of the smaller churches are packed. I know what I am talking about because I have had the privilege of going across this country several times since I have retired, and this is what I have seen. I have also been abroad several times. I visited one of the great churches in London, England. At one time that church was filled with several thousand people three times a week on a regular basis. When I visited the church on a Sunday night, there were not more than two hundred people in attendance. That great imposing building with its impressive name was not very formidable any more. This same thing is true in my own nation. I have been in some of our great churches, and, my, the amount of lumber I can see in the pews—but nobody is sitting in them. Yet when I go out to some of our small churches, I find that they are packed to the doors and are having two and three morning services.

Today we are to be *strong* in the Lord. This is repeated many times in the Word of God. Paul, writing to a young preacher, said, "Thou therefore, my son, be *strong* in the grace that is in Christ Jesus" (2 Tim. 2:1, italics mine). The Epistle of 2 Timothy is Paul's swan song, and in his final message to this son in the faith, he is saying, "You are a son of God. Be strong now." What a word of encouragement that should be.

Somebody says, "My ministry is so insignificant and my group is so small that I don't think it amounts to very much." My friend, if that is what you are thinking, it is the Devil who is talking to you. Don't listen to him. It is God who is going to put the measuring rod down on it and determine who is great and who is not. There are a whole lot of straw stacks being built today, and they look impressive. I myself have always been fearful that I was building a straw stack. Oh, I know there is some gold in it, but have you ever tried to find a needle in a straw stack? How will you find a little piece of gold that is the same color as the straw? God makes it clear that size is not the important thing.

God is saying to you and me, "Watch ye, stand fast in the faith, quit you like men, be strong" (1 Cor. 16:13). Paul wrote this to a bunch of baby Christians over in Corinth. He was urging them to get out of the crib, get out of their high chairs, and grow up. Be *strong* in the Lord. Oh, how we need that sort of thing in God's work, my friend.

Paul wasn't through with the Corinthians— he wrote a second letter to them in which he said, "(For the weapons of our warfare are not carnal, but *mighty through God* to the pulling down of strong holds;)" (2 Cor. 10:4, italics mine).

It was my privilege to pastor a downtown church in Los Angeles and to have succeeded some great men. Although I may not have approved of everything they had done, I certainly had great respect for them. They were great preachers. Dr. R. A. Torrey had been the founder of that church. I never walked into that pulpit without first looking to God and saying, "Lord, I am unable, I am insufficient for this task. I call upon You today." I say to you that I am thanking God that out of weakness He can make us strong. For the weapons of our warfare are not carnal, but *mighty through God* to the pulling down of strong holds. And I told God many times, "Lord, if anything happens here today, *You* will have to do it because You and I know that this poor boy can't do it at all."

In 2 Corinthians 10:5–6, Paul goes on to say, "Casting down imaginations, and every high thing that exalteth itself against the knowledge of God, and bringing into captivity every thought to the obedience of Christ; And having in a readiness to revenge all disobedience, when your obedience is fulfilled." In other words, make very sure you are being obedient to God. It doesn't make any difference how large or how small the work is. We need to remember, "Be strong." God said to Israel, "Sure, this temple is not as impressive as the other temple was. I know that, but be *strong*.

That is My challenge to you." He said three times, "Be strong!"

God's second word of challenge was "and *work*." Just keep at the job. Let God be the One to determine who is doing the greatest work. When we get to heaven and stand in the presence of Christ, I suspect that we will find out that there were people who were greater than Luther in Luther's day, greater than Wesley in Wesley's day, greater than Billy Sunday in his day, and greater than Billy Graham in his day. I used to tell the pastoral staff at the Church of the Open Door, "Someday when we stand before God, He may call some woman to come forward and say, 'This woman was a member of the Church of the Open Door while Vernon McGee was pastor, and she is the most honored one. I am going to reward her.' I'll nudge you fellows and ask you if you knew her. You all will say, 'No, we never heard of her.' She is one of the unknown members. All she had was only one little boy. Her husband deserted her, and she raised that boy alone. Then she sent him to the mission field and, my, what a work he did! She was faithful. She didn't have the opportunity to speak to thousands, but she had the opportunity of speaking to one, and that is all God asked her to do." My friend, I think we are going to get our eyes opened in that day when we stand in His presence. He says, "Be strong and work." We are to be faithful at the task which God has given us to do.

Now here is God's glorious word of encouragement: "For I am with you, saith the LORD of hosts."

The fact of the matter is that the *shekinah* glory had departed from the temple of Solomon long before the temple was destroyed. I have always taken the position that the *shekinah* glory departed in the days of King Manasseh. He was a ruler who sinned so wickedly that the nation of Israel sank lower than it ever had gone before. If the *shekinah* glory did not leave during his reign, I can't figure out any other time afterward that it would have been more inclined to leave. If I am correct in this, the *shekinah* glory, which was the visible presence of God Himself, had left the temple about one hundred twenty-five years before the temple was destroyed by Babylon. Therefore, in Haggai's day, the old men, the ancients, who had seen Solomon's temple, had seen only its outward glory. The *shekinah* glory had long since gone.

There is no doubt that the outward glory of Solomon's temple was tremendous. As you know, the Mosque of Omar stands on that temple site now, and its dome is gold. I have been told that it is gold leaf. Whether that is true or not, it is really a thing of beauty. I have looked at that dome from the Mount of Olives, and I could have looked at it from Zion. I have looked at it from the tower of a Lutheran church, and I have looked at it from hotel windows—my, how it shines! As I looked at that pagan mosque, I thought of how Solomon's temple must have looked in the bright sunlight of that semidesert air. We know that it was a very ornate, rich temple and that the boards were covered with real gold. How beautiful it must have been! Of course there was no comparison between it and the temple which was then under construction, but God considered Zerubbabel's temple in the different stages of its construction—Solomon's temple, Zerubbabel's temple, and later Herod's temple—as *one* house, not three houses. Therefore it is in the same line as the house (called Herod's temple) into which the Lord Jesus Christ would come. Christ was the *shekinah* glory. He was God manifest in the flesh. The apostle John said, ". . . we beheld his glory . . ." (John 1:14)— but it was veiled in human flesh. And the Lord Jesus walked into that temple not one time but many times.

So God says to these discouraged builders in the days of Haggai, "Yes, this little temple you are building is not much, but *I am with you.*" My friend, that is a great deal better than having a magnificent temple without God being there. This is the same contrast between that contemporary big church with empty pews—cold, indifferent, and dead— and the little church around the corner packed with people and with a faithful pastor teaching the Word of God. We need to get a correct perspective of what is real and what is not real, what God is blessing and what He is not blessing.

**According to the word that I covenanted with you when ye came out of Egypt, so my spirit remaineth among you: fear ye not [Hag. 2:5].**

Though this new building was not impressive, God says, "My spirit remaineth among you." That was a great deal better than a very ornate temple which was devoid of the presence of God.

This reveals the difference between the ministry of the Holy Spirit in Old Testament and New Testament times. In that day He was *among* the people. In our day He is *in* believers. He has certainly changed positions.

This is one of the great benefits we have as believers in Christ.

"Fear ye not." If *they* had no reason to fear, certainly the child of God today should not fear.

**For thus saith the LORD of hosts; Yet once, it is a little while, and I will shake the heavens, and the earth, and the sea, and the dry land;**

**And I will shake all nations, and the desire of all nations shall come: and I will fill this house with glory, saith the LORD of hosts [Hag. 2:6–7].**

First of all, we need to recognize what God is doing here. He is attempting to get their minds and hearts and eyes off that which is local, that which is very limited, and get their eyes fixed upon God's program for the people of Israel. He wants them to see what is out yonder in the future—extending all the way into the Millennium.

My friend, for us today it is so easy to get the wrong perspective of the Christian life. We get our nose pressed right up to the window of the present, and we don't see anything else. As you know, you can put a dime so close to your eye that it blots out the sun. Well, a dime is like the present that blots out God's plan and purpose for our life. Don't be discouraged because present circumstances are not working out for you. Recognize that for the child of God, ". . . all things work together for good to them that love God, to them who are the called according to his purpose" (Rom. 8:28). That is, "the good" is out yonder in the distance.

"I will shake the heavens, and the earth, and the sea, and the dry land." In other words, God intends to move in judgment. We are going to see, before we finish this little Book of Haggai, that God is looking forward and speaking of the Great Tribulation, which is the Day of the Lord, and later of the coming of Christ to the earth and the setting up of the millennial temple, events which are also included in the Day of the Lord.

"I will fill this house with glory." Although it was a series of houses—Solomon's temple, Zerubbabel's temple (which was torn down by Herod), and Herod's temple—God saw it as *one* house. And into that temple came the Lord Jesus Christ. The glory was there, although in human flesh. Then Herod's temple was destroyed (even before it was finished) in A.D. 70 by the forces of Rome under Titus. On that temple site no other temple has been built from that time to this. Actually, the Mosque of Omar stands there today, and the Islamic world would never permit it to be removed because it is either the second or third holiest spot in the world of Islam. However, later there *will* be built the temple which will be designated as the Great Tribulation temple. And after that, the millennial temple will be built on that site. Therefore, seeing it as one house, God says that the day is coming when "this house" will be filled with glory. I believe that the *shekinah* glory will come with Christ when He returns to the earth. In Matthew 24:30 we read, "And then shall appear the sign of the Son of man in heaven: and then shall all the tribes of the earth mourn, and they shall see the Son of man coming in the clouds of heaven with power and great glory." This verse speaks of the sign of the Son of man in heaven, then immediately speaks of the *glory* of the Lord. I believe that His glory, the *shekinah* glory, will be seen in the temple which we designate as the great tribulation temple. But when He comes to occupy it, it won't be a Great Tribulation temple that is in rebellion against Him. There won't be in it the image of Antichrist, but Christ Himself will be present there.

"I will shake all nations." Today it is difficult to believe that there will be more shaking than there has been in the past century. This century was practically ushered in by World War I. That was rather world-shaking. And there have been earthshaking events since then. There was a worldwide depression. There was World War II. Also, oil crises and energy shortages have shaken all nations, but all of these things are nothing compared to the shaking that will come in the future.

"The desire of all nations shall come." The commentators from the very beginning, in fact, the early church fathers, interpreted "the desire of all nations" to be Christ. Frankly, that has disturbed me from the time I was a younger preacher, because I never could believe that Christ was the *desire* of all nations. There are those who interpret the *desire* of all nations to be the *longing* of all nations for the Deliverer, whether or not they realize that the Deliverer is Christ. This may be true, but whom are they going to accept when he comes? They will accept Antichrist. Antichrist is the world's messiah, the world's savior, and they will accept him. I do not think that the nations have any desire for the Lord Jesus Christ.

It is my feeling that the meaning of this

passage becomes clear if we continue reading. Now, let's put verses 7–8 together:

**And I will shake all nations, and the desire of all nations shall come: and I will fill this house with glory, saith the LORD of hosts.**

**The silver is mine, and the gold is mine, saith the LORD of hosts [Hag. 2:7–8].**

What is the desire of all nations? It is silver and gold. In our day many nations have had to go off the gold standard. When they did this, the economic foundation of the entire world was rocked. Why? Because there still is a desire for gold and silver. When Solomon's temple was built, from five to twenty million dollars worth of precious metals and jewels were used in its construction. It was very valuable. As you read the historical record in Kings and Chronicles, it seems as if Solomon had cornered the gold market in his day. When Nebuchadnezzar captured Jerusalem, all that wealth was taken away. You may remember that in 2 Kings 20:12–17 the record tells of ambassadors who came from the king of Babylon to the king of Judah (which was Hezekiah at that time), and the king of Judah showed them all his treasures, all the wealth of Jerusalem. They made note of it, and in due time they captured Jerusalem and moved all that gold to Babylon. Certainly gold was the desire of the nation of Babylon, and it is still the desire of the nations of the world.

"The silver is mine, and the gold is mine." All the silver and gold in the world belong to God, and there will be plenty of it to adorn God's house in the future. The future millennial temple will be, I am confident, a thing of beauty.

**The glory of this latter house shall be greater than of the former, saith the LORD of hosts: and in this place will I give peace, saith the LORD of hosts [Hag. 2:9].**

"The glory of this latter house" is, rather, "the latter glory of this house." Remember that God views the series of temples as one house, and He is saying that the latter glory of this house, which will be that of the millennial temple, will be greater than the former. It will be even greater than Solomon's and certainly greater than the temple they were then building.

"In this place" designates the temple area as the site of the house in all of its stages. "In this place will I give peace, saith the LORD of hosts." I never visit Jerusalem without going to the temple area. Although I have seen it at least a dozen times, I still like to go there. Do you know why? It is because at that spot there will be accomplished what the United Nations and the League of Nations failed to do, which is to bring peace to the earth. When Jesus Christ comes to this earth, His feet will touch down on the Mount of Olives, and when He enters that temple area, *peace* will come to this earth, for He is the Prince of Peace. He will bring world peace at that time. The "peace" to which He refers in the verse before us means finally that.

This peace, however, could also include the peace which He brought at His first coming. At that time He brought peace to men of good will; that is, to men who were rightly related to God. As the apostle Paul put it, "Therefore being justified by faith, we have peace with God through our Lord Jesus Christ (Rom. 5:1). He also brought the peace that passes all understanding, which is for the Christian heart today. He came the first time to bring that kind of peace.

In a day which is yet future He will bring *world peace*, the kind of peace which this world wants and needs.

So the "desire of all nations" is not Christ. I believe that the proper word is *treasure*—the treasure of all nations. He said, "The silver is mine, and the gold is mine," speaking of material treasure. The thought seems to be that the lack of adornment in Zerubbabel's temple would be more than compensated for by the rich treasures which are going to be brought in the day when the millennial temple will be built. Therefore, this passage looks forward to the final days when the millennial kingdom will be established here on earth. God was encouraging the discouraged builders of Haggai's day to see their temple in the perspective of the ultimate purpose of God.

Oh, that you and I might see our present circumstances in that same way! We need to look at them in the light of eternity and to look at them in the light of God's purpose for us. If God be for us, who can be against us? Hallelujah! Let's not be overcome nor overwhelmed by the circumstances of the moment.

I think of that preacher in Scotland who turned in his resignation at the end of the year. When the elders asked him why, he said, "Because we haven't had any conversions this year except wee Bobbie Moffat." Well, my friend, that discouraged preacher couldn't see that "wee Bobbie Moffat" would become Robert Moffat, the great missionary to Africa, who probably did as much if not more than David Livingstone in opening Africa to Christian missions. That year, which the preacher considered a failure, was probably the greatest year of his ministry. All of us need to see things in light of God's plan and purpose for our lives.

## APPEAL TO THE LAW

**In the four and twentieth day of the ninth month, in the second year of Darius, came the word of the Lord by Haggai the prophet, saying [Hag. 2:10].**

This, now, is the fourth message that God gives to Haggai. Notice again how the dating is geared into the reign of Darius, a gentile ruler, because there was no king on the throne of either Israel or Judah. The date is December 24, 520 B.C. The previous message was given in the seventh month; this message was given in the ninth month.

**Thus saith the Lord of hosts; Ask now the priests concerning the law, saying,**

**If one bear holy flesh in the skirt of his garment, and with his skirt do touch bread, or pottage, or wine, or oil, or any meat, shall it be holy? And the priests answered and said, No.**

**Then said Haggai, If one that is unclean by a dead body touch any of these, shall it be unclean? And the priests answered and said, It shall be unclean [Hag. 2:11–13].**

You see, on December 24, 520 B.C., Haggai went to the priests and asked them two questions. Putting it very simply, these are the questions: (1) If that which is holy touches that which is unholy, will it make the unholy holy? The answer is no. (2) If that which is unclean touches that which is clean (holy), will the unclean make it unclean (unholy)? The answer is yes, that is what it will do.

Now these questions are important; so let's get the background before us. There were many facets of everyday life in Israel which were not covered in detail by the Mosaic Law. There were involved situations and there were knotty and thorny problems which arose in their daily lives, and there was nothing specific given in the Law which would adequately cover them. Then how did Israel function under the Law when there was no specific law to govern certain situations? Well, there is a case in point in Numbers 27 regarding the inheritance of Zelophehad's daughters. The Mosaic Law had made no inheritance provision when a man had daughters but no sons. Zelophehad didn't have any sons, but he had a house full of girls. When their father died, the girls went to Moses and said, "Look here, what about our father's property? The Law says that sons are to inherit, but our father had no sons; he had only girls. So we should have the property." Maybe Moses was not too enthusiastic about this women's lib movement; so he took the matter to the Lord. Well, it is quite interesting to see that the Lord was on the side of the girls. He said, "The daughters of Zelophehad speak right; thou shalt surely give them a possession of an inheritance among their father's brethren." So this took care of that particular question.

God made adequate provision for justice under the Law. This is the way it worked: When a matter arose that was not covered by the Law, they were to appeal to the priests. Deuteronomy 17:8–11 says: "If there arise a matter too hard for thee in judgment, between blood and blood, between plea and plea, and between stroke and stroke, being matters of controversy within thy gates: then shalt thou arise, and get thee up into the place which the Lord thy God shall choose; And thou shalt come unto the priests the Levites, and unto the judge that shall be in those days, and inquire; and they shall shew thee the sentence of judgment: And thou shalt do according to the sentence, which they of that place which the Lord shall choose shall shew thee; and thou shalt observe to do according to all that they inform thee: According to the sentence of the law which they shall teach thee, and according to the judgment which they shall tell thee, thou shalt do: thou shalt not decline from the sentence which they shall shew thee, to the right hand, nor to the left." When a certain situation arose that was not covered by the Law, the people were to appeal to the priest; he would make a decision, and his decision became the law for cases which dealt with the same issue. That was God's method, and it seems to me that we follow this same method today. I once took a course in commercial law, and although I don't remember much of what was taught, I do recall the difference between what is known as statute law and what is known as common law. Statute law is that which is passed by the legislature. When a certain bill comes before that body of lawmakers and is passed, it becomes statute law. That law is written down and stands as law. There are so many statute laws that I am sure no one person knows all of them.

There is also that which is known as common law. For example, a matter is brought into court. Let's say it is the case of John Doe versus Mary Roe. The lawyer for each side of the case looks for a similar case in the books, one that has already been tried, because there is nothing on the statute books that covers that specific issue. So finally they find a similar case that was decided years ago by Judge Know-It-All in Washington. Such decisions which were handed down by courts are known as common law. Therefore, we have two kinds of law: statute law and common law.

And this is the provision God made for Israel. Not every specific case was covered by the Mosaic Law, although great principles were laid down. The priests were to *know* the Old Testament, and when a case arose which was not covered specifically by the Law, the people were to bring the matter before the priests for a decision. And the priests would interpret the Mosaic Law for the people according to the great principles found in the Word of God.

## EXPLANATION OF THE PRINCIPLE

Keep in mind that in the Book of Haggai we have come to the post-Captivity period. God's people had already spent seventy years in captivity in Babylon. Only a small remnant had returned to the land, and those people were discouraged. God raised up three prophets to encourage them; and, since Haggai was the very practical prophet, God sent him to the priests to ask the two questions which were not specifically covered by the Mosaic Law.

Remember that when the captives first returned to Jerusalem, they had the enthusiasm to build, but after fifteen years in the debris of Jerusalem and with their enemies outside, they had done nothing about building the temple. They consoled themselves because they had lost their esprit de corps; and sinking into complacency, they were saying, "It's not time to build the Lord's house," and so they did nothing about building it. Haggai spoke into this situation. He encouraged the people; they began to build, and then some of the oldtimers, who had seen the first temple, began to weep and say, "This little temple isn't worth anything." However, for three months the people worked. Then a mercenary spirit entered in, and the people said, "You told us to go to work and build the temple, and if we did, God would bless us. We have obeyed, but God is not blessing us." It was at this juncture that God sent Haggai to the priests with a twofold inquiry. It is actually one question with two facets. Here are the questions and the answers he received: Is holiness communicated by contact? "No," is the answer. The holy cannot make the unholy holy by contact. Holiness is noncommunicable. Is unholiness communicated by contact? "Yes," is the answer. Uncleanness is communicated to the clean by contact. When holy and unholy come in contact, both are unholy. In therapeutics, measles is communicated by contact. In the physical realm, dirty water will discolor clean water—not the opposite. In the moral realm, the evil heart of man cannot perform good deeds. In the religious realm, a ceremony cannot cleanse a sinner.

For God's application of this principle to Israel, we'll have to move ahead to pick up verse 17: "I smote you with blasting and with mildew and with hail in all the labours of your hands; yet ye turned not to me, saith the LORD." God says that when the remnant returned to the land, they didn't turn to Him. They went through the rituals, and they brought sacrifices, and they expected God to bless them, but He did not. Religion, you see, is not a salve you can rub on the outside. Friend, you can *swim* in holy water, and it won't make you holy. You can go through a ritual, you can be baptized in water and be held under until you drown, but that won't make you a child of God. We sometimes put too much emphasis on a rite. Don't misunderstand me, I think baptism is very important, but it does not impart holiness. It will not change a man's heart.

Now let's look at the second inquiry again: "If one that is unclean by a dead body touch any of these, shall it be unclean?" And the priests gave this answer: "It shall be unclean." Perhaps the key passage that deals with this matter is Leviticus 22:4–6. The Word of God is quite specific. Uncleanness is communicable; unholiness is transferable.

An evil heart cannot perform good deeds. A bitter fountain cannot give forth sweet water. Grapes are not gathered from thorns. Figs do not come from thistles.

There is a syllogism in philosophy where you state a major premise, a minor premise, and a conclusion. In the Book of Haggai the major premise is this: holiness is not communicated. The minor premise is this: unholiness is communicated. The conclusion is that when the holy and unholy come into contact, both are unholy. The Lord Jesus Christ asked the question, ". . . Do men gather grapes of thorns, or figs of thistles?" (Matt. 7:16). As a man thinks in his heart, so is he. An act or a ritual cannot change the heart. A good deed is actually tarnished when an evil heart performs it. This is ceremonial law, friend, but it is applicable to every phase of life—just like the law of gravitation, it is universal.

Let's go into a chemistry lab. I fill two large beakers with water. One container I fill with good, clear, clean water, and the other one I fill with the dirtiest water possible. I begin to pour the clean water into the unclean water. How long will I have to pour the clean water into the dirty water before it becomes clear? I will never make the dirty water clean by pouring clean water into it. What happens when I put one drop of the dirty, black water into the clean water? The clean water becomes unclean. So it is in the material world.

In the world of medicine, how do you cure the measles, and how do you get the measles? Do you take a well boy and have him rub up against the sick boy to make him well? Will that cure the boy with the measles? Of course it won't. What happens? The boy who was well will probably have a good case of the measles.

This principle is also true in the moral realm. The liquor industry gives money to charity, and the race track has a day in which they give all their proceeds to charity. Hollywood produces biblical stories, and we are supposed to applaud them—well, you might applaud, but I won't. The liquor industry can never cover up the awful thing it is doing to human lives by giving a few dollars to charity. Why? Because, when a clean thing and an unclean thing come together, the unclean always makes the clean unclean. May I say to you, young man and young woman, you cannot run with the wrong crowd and stay clean. If you are running with an unclean crowd, one of these days you are going to find out it has rubbed off on you. If you are going to play in the mud, you are going to get dirty.

And this great principle certainly holds true in the religious realm. Most of the religions in the world teach that if you go through their prescribed rituals and ceremonies, you are acceptable to God. However, the Word of God is clear on the fact that going through a ceremony—baptism or any other rite—or doing anything externally will not meet the conditions which God has put down for man.

After all, man's condition is a sad one. We read in Jeremiah 17:9, "The heart is deceitful above all things, and desperately wicked: who can know it?" What a picture this is of the human heart! No one but God can know how bad it is. If we could see ourselves as God sees us, we could not *stand* ourselves. We don't realize how bad we really are. The Lord Jesus made this abundantly clear in Matthew 15: 18–20, "But those things which proceed out of the mouth come forth from the heart; and they defile the man. For out of the heart proceed evil thoughts, murders, adulteries, fornications, thefts, false witness, blasphemies: These are the things which defile a man: but to eat with unwashen hands defileth not a man." Just because you wash your hands, have been through a ceremony, or have performed a ritual does not make you right with God, you see.

I often think of a man I played golf with several years ago in Tulsa, Oklahoma. He told me, "I was a church hypocrite for years. I was a member of a big downtown liberal church. I had been through the ceremonies and had served on every committee. To tell the truth, I was not a Christian, and during the week I was practicing things which no Christian should do. I was a typical hypocrite. Then one day I found out that I was a sinner and needed a Savior. That is the thing that transformed my life." You see, the *heart* must be changed. Listen to the Lord Jesus as He talks along this line: "Ye shall know them by their fruits. Do men gather grapes of thorns, or figs of thistles? Even so every good tree bringeth forth good fruit; but a corrupt tree bringeth forth evil fruit [this is the principle at work]. A good tree cannot bring forth evil fruit, neither can a corrupt tree bring forth good fruit. Every tree that bringeth not forth good fruit is hewn down, and cast into the fire. Wherefore by their fruits ye shall know them" (Matt. 7:16–20). Out of the *heart* proceed the issues of life. The heart must be changed.

Shakespeare had it right when he portrayed Lady Macbeth walking in her sleep, rubbing her little hand, and exclaiming, "Out, damned spot! out, I say! . . . . Here's the smell of the blood still: all the perfumes of Arabia will not sweeten this little hand." How true! Neither can all the perfumes of Arabia make the *heart* right with God.

Trying to make yourself acceptable with God through ceremonies and all of that sort of thing is like pouring a gallon of Chanel No. 5 on a pile of fertilizer out in the barnyard in an effort to make it clean and fragrant. My friend, it won't work. The apostle Peter said to Simon the sorcerer, ". . . thy heart is not right in the sight of God" (Acts 8:21). God demands a clean heart. In Ephesians 6:6 God speaks of ". . . doing the will of God from the heart." And in Hebrews 10:22, "Let us draw near with a true heart. . . ." How can a man's heart be made clean when his heart by nature is unclean? Is there something man can do to make his heart clean? No! This is rather like the sign I saw in a dry cleaner's shop in a certain city back East which read: "We clean everything but the reputation." Believe me, that is something you can't get cleaned on earth. The writer of the Book of Proverbs asks the question, "Who can say, I have made my heart clean, I am pure from my sin?" (Prov. 20:9).

Well, God has the prescription: "Come now, and let us reason together, saith the LORD: though your sins be as scarlet, they shall be as white as snow; though they be red like crimson, they shall be as wool" (Isa. 1:18). Peter wrote, "Forasmuch as ye know that ye were not redeemed with corruptible things, as silver and gold, from your vain conversation received by tradition from your fathers; But with the precious blood of Christ, as of a lamb without blemish and without spot" (1 Pet. 1:18–19). One song asks the question, "What can wash away my sin?" That same song answers the question—"Nothing but the blood of Jesus." That is one of the greatest principles ever stated.

God says to the people through the prophet Haggai, "The reason you haven't been blessed is because you have been coming to Me with unclean hands and unclean hearts."

**Then answered Haggai, and said, So is this people, and so is this nation before me, saith the LORD; and so is every work of their hands; and that which they offer there is unclean [Hag. 2:14].**

Their unclean hearts made their service for God unclean. This is the reason that an unsaved person can do *nothing* that is acceptable to God.

Now, you will find a difference of opinion among Bible expositors on verses 15–19. Some hold that the verses review the condition of the returned remnant when they were indifferent to the Lord's house *before* they obeyed the Lord and began to build the temple. Other expositors hold that they refer to the people's discouragement *after* they had built the temple because it had not turned the tide of their misfortunes. Haggai tells them that there has not been time for the change to work, that evil has an infectious power greater than that of holiness and that its effects are more lasting.

However, it is my understanding that God is applying to Israel the great principle of the unclean defiling the clean to illustrate to them that although they had rebuilt the temple, their *hearts* were still far from Him, and He was not able to bless them.

**And now, I pray you, consider from this day and upward, from before a stone was laid upon a stone in the temple of the LORD [Hag. 2:15].**

He is saying that from this day on He is going to bless them because now they have turned to Him.

**Since those days were, when one came to an heap of twenty measures, there were but ten: when one came to the pressfat for to draw out fifty vessels out of the press, there were but twenty.**

**I smote you with blasting and with mildew and with hail in all the labours of your hands; yet ye turned not to me, saith the LORD.**

**Consider now from this day and upward, from the four and twentieth day of the ninth month, even from the day that the foundation of the LORD's temple was laid, consider it.**

**Is the seed yet in the barn? yea, as yet the vine, and the fig tree, and the pomegranate, and the olive tree, hath not brought forth: from this day will I bless you [Hag. 2:16–19].**

God says, "Now that your hearts are right before Me, I'll bless you." You see, they had rebuilt the temple and had been performing the services of the temple, yet that alone was not enough. In fact, when God had sent them into captivity, they had been going through the temple services. The problem was that their hearts were not right.

My friend, one of the ways that *you* can make *your* church a good church—that is, if you have a Bible-teaching preacher—is to go there all prayed up and confessed up and repented up and cleaned up. Then *you* won't block any blessing that might come to the church that day. Remember that when the unclean touches the clean, what happens is that the clean becomes unclean. Your heart has to be right with God before there is blessing. This is a tremendous principle. I know of nothing more practical.

## REVELATION OF GOD'S PROGRAM

**And again the word of the LORD came unto Haggai in the four and twentieth day of the month, saying [Hag. 2:20].**

66**T**he four and twentieth day of the month" is the same day on which the previous message was given—December 24. On one occasion I was asked why Haggai gave two messages on the same day, and I replied that probably it was because Haggai wanted to go home for Christmas—so he gave both messages before he left. Well, some folk took me seriously, and I received a ten-page letter explaining that in Haggai's day they weren't celebrating Christmas yet! Another letter informed me that no one should *ever* celebrate Christmas! Well, the fact is that when I don't have the answer to a question, I generally give some facetious answer. And if you won't let this word get out, I'll confess to you that I don't know why Haggai gave two messages on a particular day—but here they are.

**Speak to Zerubbabel, governor of Judah, saying, I will shake the heavens and the earth [Hag. 2:21].**

"Speak to Zerubbabel, governor of Judah." This message is to the civil ruler, the man in the kingly line of David, and it is God's promise to him.

**And I will overthrow the throne of kingdoms, and I will destroy the strength of the kingdoms of the heathen; and I will overthrow the chariots, and those that ride in them; and the horses and their riders shall come down, every one by the sword of his brother [Hag. 2:22].**

"I will destroy the strength of the kingdoms of the heathen [the nations]." When God says that He will shake the heavens and the earth and will overthrow the ruling governments, He is speaking of the Great Tribulation Period, as He did in verses 6 and 7 of this chapter. He says that He "will overthrow the chariots," because it was that in which the people trusted; in our day it is nuclear weapons. God says, "I am going to remove all of that."

## EXPECTATION FOR THE FUTURE

**In that day, saith the LORD of hosts, will I take thee, O Zerubbabel, my servant, the son of Shealtiel, saith the LORD, and will make thee as a signet: for I have chosen thee, saith the LORD of hosts [Hag. 2:23].**

66**I**n that day"—notice it is not "in *this* day." It looks forward to the end times.

"I . . . will make thee as a signet." The signet was the mark and identification of royalty. A man used it to sign letters and documents. Since it represented him, he guarded it very carefully and usually wore it. It came to represent a most prized possession.

"I have chosen thee, saith the LORD of hosts." As we have seen, Zerubbabel is in the line of David. God's promise is that not only will the Messiah come through David, He will also come through Zerubbabel. Although the name Zerubbabel (Zorobabel) appears in the genealogy of both Matthew and Luke, the one in Matthew is, of course, an entirely different man. God made good His promise to Zerubbabel. The Lord Jesus Christ is just as much the Son of Zerubbabel as He is the Son of David.

The prophecy looks forward to the day when the Lord Jesus will come at the end of the Great Tribulation Period. And God intends to put this line of Zerubbabel, this line of David, in the person of the Lord Jesus Christ, upon the throne of the universe. He is the King of Kings and the Lord of Lords. He will come to the earth to rule. This little Book of Haggai puts Christ in His proper position as the moral ruler, the civil ruler, and the King to rule over this earth in that day, which makes this an important book.

Now it is true that the little temple built in Haggai's day, which became known as Zerubbabel's temple, was not very impressive. But it is very important because it is in the line of temples into which the Messiah Himself will come some day.

Someone has poetically summarized the message of this little Book of Haggai. I regret that I do not know the author, but I shall quote it as we conclude this study—

'Mid blended shouts of joy and grief were laid
    The stones whereon the exile's hopes were based.
    Then foes conspired. The king his course retraced,
His throne against the enterprise arrayed.

And now self-seeking, apathy, invade
    All hearts. The pulse grows faint, the will unbraced.
    They rear their houses, let God's house lie waste.

So heaven from dew and earth from fruit
   are stayed.

There comes swift messenger from
   higher court,
   With rugged message, of divine im-
      port:—
   "Your ways consider; be ye strong and
      build;
   With greater glory shall this house be
      filled."

He touched their conscience, and their
   spirit stirred

To nerve their hands for work, their
   loins regird.
                              —Author unknown

My friend, again let me say this: Who in our
day is going to determine who is doing the great
work and who is doing the small work? *Your*
Sunday school class or other seemingly insignificant ministry may be far more important than an impressive work that is well
known in our day. Only God can know the
importance of it. Let's be found faithful, and
then let's *work*. This is the message of the
little Book of Haggai.

# BIBLIOGRAPHY

(Recommended for Further Study)

Feinberg, Charles L. *The Minor Prophets*.
   Chicago, Illinois: Moody Press, 1976.

Gaebelein, Arno C. *The Annotated Bible*.
   1917. Reprint. Neptune, New Jersey:
   Loizeaux Brothers, 1971.

Ironside, H. A. *The Minor Prophets*. Neptune, New Jersey: Loizeaux Brothers, n.d.

Jensen, Irving L. *Haggai, Zechariah, and
   Malachi*. Chicago, Illinois: Moody Press,
   1976.

Tatford, Frederick A. *The Minor Prophets*.
   Minneapolis, Minnesota: Klock & Klock,
   n.d.

Unger, Merrill F. *Unger's Commentary on the
   Old Testament*, Vol. 2. Chicago, Illinois:
   Moody Press, 1982.

Wolfe, Herbert. *Haggai and Malachi*. Chicago, Illinois: Moody Press, 1976.

# The Book of
# ZECHARIAH
## INTRODUCTION

Zechariah, whose name means "whom Jehovah remembers," is identified as the son of Berechiah, which means "Jehovah blesses," and his father was the son of Iddo, which means "the appointed time." Certainly this cluster of names with such rich meanings is suggestive of the encouragement given to the remnant that had returned to Jerusalem after the Babylonian captivity—God remembers and blesses at the appointed time.

Although the name *Zechariah* was common among the Hebrew people (twenty-eight Zechariahs are mentioned in the Old Testament), there are Bible teachers who identify the Zechariah of this book with the "Zacharias" whom our Lord mentioned in Matthew 23:35 as having been martyred. Many expositors discount this possibility, but it is interesting to note that the Jewish Targum states that Zechariah was slain in the sanctuary and that he was both prophet and priest. In Nehemiah 12:4 Iddo is mentioned as one of the heads of a priestly family. And the historian "Josephus (*Wars*, iv. 5, 34) recounts the murder of a 'Zecharias, the son of Baruch,' i.e., Barachiah, as perpetrated in the Temple by the Zealots just before the destruction of Jerusalem" (*Ellicott's Commentary on the Whole Bible*).

Another interesting observation is that Zechariah's prophecy practically closes the Old Testament—it is next to the final book—and the New Testament opens chronologically with Luke's account of another *Zacharias* (meaning "Jehovah remembers") and his wife Elisabeth (meaning "His oath"). Zacharias was a priest who was serving at the altar of incense when an angel appeared to him with a message from God after four hundred years of silence. So again God remembered His oath.

The prophecy was written in 520 B.C. Zechariah was contemporary with Haggai (see Ezra 5:1; 6:14), although he was probably a younger man (see Zech. 2:4).

This book has the characteristics of an apocalypse. The visions resemble those in the Books of Daniel and Ezekiel and Revelation. Daniel and Ezekiel were born in the land of Israel but wrote their books outside of it. Zechariah was born outside of the land down by the canals of Babylon, but he wrote in the land. It is interesting that Daniel, Ezekiel, and John were all outside Israel when they wrote. Only Zechariah was in that land when he wrote his apocalyptic visions. In the dark day of discouragement which blanketed the remnant, he saw the glory in all of the rapture and vision of hope. He has more messianic prophecies than any of the other minor prophets. This is therefore an important and interesting book.

Zechariah was contemporary with Haggai, but his book is in direct contrast to Haggai. They definitely knew each other and prophesied to the same people at the same period of time. Yet their prophecies are just about as different as any two could be. They are literally ages apart even though they were given to the same people at the same time.

Haggai was down there at the foundation of the temple measuring it. He really had his feet on the ground. Zechariah was a man with his head in the air. Anyone who has ten visions in one night is doing pretty well! He is entirely visionary, whereas Haggai is entirely practical. Yet they were both speaking for God to the same people at the same time concerning the same problem. Also they both speak to us today, but each in his own manner.

We need to recognize that these two types of men are still needed today. They fit together. We need the practical, pragmatic man to go along with the man who is visionary, because there is a danger in the dreamer. Too often the dreamers are not practical. On the other hand, the practical man so often lacks vision. So when you put these two together, you have a happy combination.

# OUTLINE

I. **Apocalyptic Visions (Messianic and Millennial), Chapters 1–6**
   A. Introduction and Message of Warning, Chapter 1:1–6
   B. Ten Visions (All in One Night), Chapters 1:7–6:15
      1. Riders under Myrtle Trees, Chapter 1:7–17
      2. Four Horns, Chapter 1:18–19
      3. Four Smiths, Chapter 1:20–21
      4. Man with Measuring Line, Chapter 2
      5. Joshua and Satan, Chapter 3:1–7
      6. The Branch, Chapter 3:8–10
      7. Lampstand and Two Olive Trees, Chapter 4
      8. Flying Roll, Chapter 5:1–4
      9. Woman in the Ephah, Chapter 5:5–11
      10. Four Chariots, Chapter 6

II. **Historic Interlude, Chapters 7–8**
   A. Question Concerning a Religious Ritual (Fasting), Chapter 7:1–3
   B. Threefold Answer, Chapters, 7:4–8:23
      1. When the Heart Is Right, the Ritual Is Right, Chapter 7:4–7
      2. When the Heart Is Wrong, the Ritual Is Wrong, Chapter 7:8–14
      3. God's Purpose Concerning Jerusalem Unchanged by Any Ritual, Chapter 8

III. **Prophetic Burdens, Chapters 9–14**
   A. First Burden: Prophetic Aspects Connected with First Coming of Christ, Chapters 9–11
   B. Second Burden: Prophetic Aspects Connected with Second Coming of Christ, Chapters 12–14

# CHAPTER 1

*THEME: Apocalyptic visions: of riders under myrtle trees; of four horns; of four smiths*

## APOCALYPTIC VISIONS

The first six chapters are messianic and millennial. In this section is the record of ten visions, and Zechariah was given all of those ten visions in a single night. I would say that this was a good night's work, by the way!

## INTRODUCTION AND MESSAGE OF WARNING

The first verse serves as an introduction to the Book of Zechariah.

**In the eighth month, in the second year of Darius, came the word of the LORD unto Zechariah, the son of Berechiah, the son of Iddo the prophet, saying [Zech. 1:1].**

"In the eighth month, in the second year of Darius" gears this prophetic book into the reign of a gentile king because this is the period of the return of a remnant of Israel back to their land after the seventy-year captivity in Babylon. There is no king in either Israel or Judah now. The line of David is off the throne, and the Times of the Gentiles are in progress. "The second year of Darius" is the same year in which Haggai prophesied. They prophesied to the same people during the same period of time. Haggai began in the sixth month of that year, and Zechariah began two months later. It is the year 520 B.C. Haggai was given a prophecy in September, October, and December, but none in November. So this man Zechariah was given a prophecy in November, the month Haggai missed.

"Came the word of the LORD unto Zechariah." This is the same expression that Haggai used. In other words, Zechariah is speaking by the same authority that Haggai spoke. This same phrase occurs fourteen times in this book. Since the Book of Zechariah has fourteen chapters, it occurs on the average of once every chapter. As you can see, this is another book which places a great emphasis on the *Word* of God.

Now the second verse begins the message of warning which God has given Zechariah. Speaking by the same authority that Haggai did, the Word of the Lord, he is warning the returned remnant not to follow in the footsteps of their pre-Captivity fathers.

**The LORD hath been sore displeased with your fathers [Zech. 1:2].**

Zechariah is telling them that the reason they had been in captivity was that "The LORD hath been sore displeased with your fathers." They had sinned against God, and he is warning them against making the same blunder, the same mistakes.

**Therefore say thou unto them, Thus saith the LORD of hosts; Turn ye unto me, saith the LORD of hosts, and I will turn unto you, saith the LORD of hosts [Zech. 1:3].**

"Thus saith the LORD of hosts." That title for God has become almost a cliché for us; in fact many of the titles of God are almost meaningless to us, although we use them a great deal. What does "the LORD of hosts" really mean? It occurs fifty-two times in this book, which indicates its importance. The word *hosts* is derived from the Hebrew *tsaba* (plural: tsabaoth), meaning "service" or "strength" or even "warfare." The way it is used here "implies the boundless resources at His command for His people's good." That is Dr. Fausset's definition, and I can't improve on it. In the New Testament it says, "He is rich in mercy" (see Eph. 2:4), and "He has all power" (Matt. 28:18). So what do *you* need today, my friend? Do you need a little mercy? Well, he has an abundance of it. He is *rich* in it, and He can extend mercy to you. My, how we all need it! He is the Lord of Hosts—that title occurs three times in this verse and again in the fourth and sixth verses.

"Turn ye unto me, saith the LORD of hosts, and I will turn unto you." You see how He is extending *mercy* to them.

**Be ye not as your fathers, unto whom the former prophets have cried, saying, Thus saith the LORD of hosts; Turn ye now from your evil ways, and from your evil doings: but they did not hear, nor hearken unto me, saith the LORD [Zech. 1:4].**

This is God's very practical warning. He is saying, "Your fathers paid no attention to the prophets whom I sent to them. I sent Hosea. I sent Joel. I sent Amos. I sent to them Isaiah and Jeremiah. I sent all of these prophets, but your fathers did not listen to them nor heed their message. That is the reason they went into captivity."

Now God asks a question—

**Your fathers, where are they? and the prophets, do they live for ever? [Zech. 1:5].**

The voices of the former prophets are no longer sounding. Jeremiah and Isaiah and Hosea and Joel and Amos are gone. They are dead, and their voices are silent. And, by the way, "your fathers, where are they?" Well, they are buried down yonder in Babylon. That is the wrong place for an Israelite to be buried, because he wants to be buried in his own land. Even old Jacob down in the land of Egypt made Joseph take an oath that he would not bury him there in Egypt. He said, "I want to be taken back up yonder and be buried with my fathers." And that is where his body is today—there in Hebron. The hope of the patriarchs and the godly Israelites was to be in their land at the time of the resurrection of the dead. If you have ever been to Jerusalem, you know that before the Eastern Gate, down through the Valley of Kidron and all up the side of the Mount of Olives are graves of Israelites. The Arabs mutilated a great many of them, but they are being restored by Israel. They want to be buried in that location because they expect to see the Messiah come to the earth at that place. And, personally, I believe that they will be raised from the dead when Christ returns to the earth to establish His kingdom. Let me remind you that at the time of the Rapture the Lord Jesus will not come to the earth. Rather, He will call His own out of the earth and will meet them in the air. At that time He will not come to establish His kingdom upon earth. First the world will go through the Great Tribulation Period, and *then* Christ will come to the earth to reign personally here. So you see that there would be no point in raising the Old Testament saints (both Jews and Gentiles) before the Tribulation, because they would just have to stand around and wait until the Tribulation was over so that they could enter the kingdom.

Therefore, you can see that God's question through Zechariah is very pertinent: "Your fathers, where are they?" They are buried down by the canals of Babylon, which is a bad place to be when your hope is in the land of Israel.

**But my words and my statutes, which I commanded my servants the prophets, did they not take hold of your fathers? and they returned and said, Like as the LORD of hosts thought to do unto us, according to our ways, and according to our doings, so hath he dealt with us [Zech. 1:6].**

"Did they not take hold of your fathers?" means "did they not overtake your fathers?" The judgment for their sins overtook them.

"And they returned and said, Like as the LORD of hosts thought to do unto us, according to our ways, and according to our doings, so hath he dealt with us." They were finally willing to admit that the judgment which had come to them was just and righteous on the part of God—because He had warned them but they had not listened to Him.

This concludes the practical section. I don't mean that the next section is impractical; I simply mean that it deals with the visions which Zechariah had.

## TEN VISIONS

While most expositors and commentators say that there are eight visions here, we will make a further division, as you will see.

## VISION OF RIDERS UNDER MYRTLE TREES

The first vision is that of the horses and riders under the myrtle trees.

**Upon the four and twentieth day of the eleventh month, which is the month Sebat, in the second year of Darius, came the word of the LORD unto Zechariah, the son of Berechiah, the son of Iddo the prophet, saying [Zech. 1:7].**

Since the Hebrew months do not begin with January, the eleventh month would be equivalent to our February—February 24, 520 B.C. We will see the significance of this in a few minutes.

Now let's get the background before us. Five months prior to this vision, the Lord had appeared to Haggai and had given him a message of challenge for the remnant to resume the rebuilding of the temple. And the work of building the temple was begun. Then two months before Zechariah's vision, the prophet Haggai had delivered a very sharp message to the priests because they were impure and yet were expecting God to bless them. Also, his message had been directed to the people because of their delay in building and their hesitation in moving forward with it. At this time Haggai also had told them about the coming destruction of gentile world power before God would establish His kingdom here upon the earth. He had told them that the one who would rule would be the Messiah and that He was coming from the line of Zerubbabel, who was the civil ruler of Jerusalem at this time and was in the royal line of King David.

Now it was during this time, while the temple was being rebuilt, that Zechariah was given ten visions.

**I saw by night, and behold a man riding upon a red horse, and he stood among the myrtle trees that were in the bottom; and behind him were there red horses, speckled, and white [Zech. 1:8].**

"I saw by night"—he doesn't say, "I dreamed by night." You may get the impression that because Zechariah had these visions at night that they were dreams, but he makes it clear that they were visions, not dreams. He was wide awake, and I don't think that any tranquilizer or sleeping pill could have put him to sleep on that night!

Many people differ with me in my stand that God does not speak through dreams or by visions in our day. I don't try to correct them when they say to me, "I saw a vision last night," I simply ask them if they saw the vision in a dream. If they did, I know immediately that God has not given them a message but that the dream was caused by something they ate for dinner the evening before, or it came out of some experience they had. In sleep the mind is unlatched or released, and it generally wanders back over some experience that produces the dream. Therefore, I think we can be sure that God does not speak to *us* in dreams.

Notice that Zechariah said, "I *saw*." It is important to understand how God revealed Himself to this prophet at this time.

"Behold"—Zechariah introduces his vision in a dramatic way. Frankly, I think the translator should have put an exclamation mark after that word. *Behold* means "to look." "Look! There's a man riding upon a red horse!"

"A man riding upon a red horse." Who is this man? He is the Lord Jesus Christ before His incarnation. You may ask how I know that. Well, He is identified as the "angel of the Lord" in verses 11 and 12. In the Old Testament *the* angel of the Lord is designated as God. Therefore, *the* angel of the Lord in the Old Testament is the Lord Jesus Christ of the New Testament. He is the angel of the *Presence*; He is Jehovah Himself, the Messiah.

Here in Christ's preincarnation Zechariah sees Him watching over this world. Now, it is true that Satan is called the prince of this world, that is, of this world system—the carnality of this world today is all under Satan's control—but God has not given up this earth to Satan. Even at this very moment, the Lord Jesus Christ is standing in the shadows, keeping watch over His own. Here in Zechariah's vision it is the nation of Israel in particular over which He is watching. What a comfort it is to know that, out of all the galaxies about us which cannot be numbered for multitude, the God of the universe is watching, keeping watch over His own. What a message this vision has for us. Zechariah will give many messages of comfort, and certainly this is one of them.

Notice that the man is riding "upon a red horse." What is the significance of the color red? Well, red speaks of blood and bloodshed; in the Book of Revelation it speaks of bloodshed in war. But for this one who is riding the red horse, it speaks of His own blood that was to be shed. He is watching over this earth because He would die and shed His blood for the human family on this earth. What a picture we have here!

"Behind him were there red horses, speckled, and white." It does not say that there were riders on the horses, but I feel that we can rightly assume that each horse had a rider. Here is an instance where God has not given us complete information, but we assume that the riders are angelic beings under Christ's command whose business it is to watch over this earth and report their findings to Him. I believe that the colors of the horses—red, sorrel (called speckled in the King James version), and white—all have significance.

I haven't seen the word *sorrel* since I was a boy in West Texas and Southern Oklahoma when horses were the means of transportation. I can remember when I saw my first automobile in Springer, Oklahoma. We stood and looked at it for two hours. Can you imagine going to a parking lot today and looking at a car for that long? Well, we did. A doctor owned it, and everyone in that little town in which I lived came out to look at the car. It was fearful to behold and an unusual contraption. Nobody thought it could ever supplant the horse in our day of muddy roads. I remember well the sorrel horses; they were spotted, brownish orange—I always thought of them as a dirty yellow. You might not like that description if a sorrel horse is your pet, but as a boy that is the way they looked to me.

As I said, I believe there is a significance in

the colors of the horses. Red horses would be symbolic of warfare. White horses would probably represent victory, symbolic of the fact that the one riding the horse is marching to victory. The sorrel is a mixture of the other colors.

"He stood among the myrtle trees." The myrtle tree is what we here in California call the laurel tree. We find it down in the desert regions. The Southern Pacific Railroad Company has planted them all along their tracks in the Palm Springs area so that the sand won't cover the tracks. In the land of Israel, which apparently is their native habitat, there were many myrtle-covered valleys. The myrtle is considered sort of a badge of Israel. You see, certain trees and plants represent the nation—the olive tree, the fig tree, the myrtle tree, the grapevine all have their significance. In Isaiah 41:19 (literal translation mine), God says, "I will put in the wilderness the cedar, the acacia, and the myrtle, and the olive, and I will set in the desert the cypress, the plane and the pine together." And in Isaiah 55:13 He says, "Instead of the thorn shall come up the cypress, and instead of the brier shall come up the myrtle: and it shall be to the Lord for a memorial for an everlasting sign which shall not be cut off." In modern Israel the tremendous planting of trees—and most of them are myrtle—could have real significance. It is interesting that myrtle branches together with palm branches were used in the ritual of constructing booths in the celebration of the Feast of Tabernacles. In fact, the name *myrtle* is the Hebrew *hadhas*, from which the name of Esther, *hadhassah*, is derived—so that a girl named Esther and another girl named Myrtle actually have the same name, referring to the myrtle tree.

"The myrtle trees that were in the bottom" —what does he mean by "the bottom"? It means down in a valley. The grove of myrtle trees would be in a valley where there was a water supply. The myrtle trees in the valley may be representative of Israel, for she was certainly down in a valley at this time.

Before we leave this verse, let me say that the rider on the red horse is a picture, I believe, of the Lord Jesus just waiting for the day to come when He will take over this earth. And in the meantime He is patrolling the earth, watching over it. And I assume that the riders on the other horses are created intelligences, supernatural beings, or angels, who are there with Him.

**Then said I, O my lord, what are these? And the angel that talked with me said unto me, I will shew thee what these be [Zech. 1:9].**

"Then said I, O my lord, what are these?" That is the same question *we* have; so let's listen. He says that he will show us what these things are—

**And the man that stood among the myrtle trees answered and said, These are they whom the Lord hath sent to walk to and fro through the earth [Zech. 1:10].**

"To walk to and fro" means that they were patrolling the earth.

**And they answered the angel of the Lord that stood among the myrtle trees, and said, We have walked to and fro through the earth, and, behold, all the earth sitteth still, and is at rest [Zech. 1:11].**

"All the earth sitteth still, and is at rest" means that there was peace on the earth at this time. That sounds good, because during five thousand years of recorded history, there have been only about two hundred years of peace. Man is a fierce, warlike creature— there is war in his heart. So a period of peace sounds wonderful. But what kind of peace was it? Well, it was the kind of peace that does not last very long.

**Then the angel of the Lord answered and said, O Lord of hosts, how long wilt thou not have mercy on Jerusalem and on the cities of Judah, against which thou hast had indignation these threescore and ten years? [Zech. 1:12].**

"Against which thou hast had indignation these threescore and ten years"—that is, for seventy years now Jerusalem has been lying in ruin, debris, and ashes. But the remnant of Israel which has returned to the land is beginning to rebuild. The cry is, "How long will it be before God is going to bring real blessing to us?"

God will make it clear that He is displeased with the nations which are at peace and ignore Jerusalem's plight. God is jealous for Jerusalem, and all the nations of the world are indifferent to it. God returned to Jerusalem with mercies, and the nations have a responsibility also. But the nations are at peace, although they won't be at peace very long.

My friend, this has application to our present world situation. The world can never have permanent peace until the Lord Jesus is reigning in Jerusalem, because He is the Prince of Peace. In the meantime, the peace which He offers is peace with God because of sins forgiven. If we are right with God, we can have peace with our neighbors and even peace among nations. But the so-called civilized— not Christian—nations are the ones that have carried on two world wars in this century. It is interesting that during World War II when some of our United States troops were fighting in the South Pacific, they expected to find on many of the little islands headhunters and cannibals, but instead they found Christian churches and Christians who received them joyfully. The so-called heathen were at peace, and the so-called Christians were at war! The world cannot have peace apart from Christ.

Jerusalem is the key to world peace. In Zechariah's day the world was trying to have peace and ignore Jerusalem. This was during the world domination by Media-Persia. You remember that Babylon had put down both Egypt and Assyria; then Media-Persia had put down the Babylonian Empire and was reigning all the way from the Indus River to the Mediterranean Sea and all the way from the snow of the mountains around the Black Sea and Caspian Sea to the burning sands of the Sahara Desert. Their dominion brought a brief period of peace to the world. But it wouldn't be long until Alexander the Great would come out of the West and upset the apple cart again. Peace could not be permanent because the city of Jerusalem was the key to peace.

**And the LORD answered the angel that talked with me with good words and comfortable words [Zech. 1:13].**

Notice that they were *good* words and *comforting* words, words that were helpful to the remnant. During this time Haggai was pronouncing judgment, but not Zechariah—he was giving God's message of comfort.

**So the angel that communed with me said unto me, Cry thou, saying, Thus saith the LORD of hosts; I am jealous for Jerusalem and for Zion with a great jealousy [Zech. 1:14].**

"I am jealous for Jerusalem." God's jealousy is not a human sort of jealousy that might be just a flare of bad temper. But men's jealousy, which is a burning passion for that which is their own and is dear to them and may be taken away from them, may be similar to the jealousy of God. "I am jealous for Jerusalem

and for Zion with a *great* jealousy." Jerusalem is His city, and the Israelites are His people. He is fully aware of the worldwide woe of oppressed Israel even in our day, and He is exceedingly jealous for His people. I believe that in time God is going to move on their behalf. The world then and now is ready to forsake them.

**And I am very sore displeased with the heathen that are at ease: for I was but a little displeased, and they helped forward the affliction [Zech. 1:15].**

"I was but a little displeased," that is, God's chastisement was intended for a brief period, but the nations of the world wanted her annihilation.

**Therefore thus saith the LORD; I am returned to Jerusalem with mercies: my house shall be built in it, saith the LORD of hosts, and a line shall be stretched forth upon Jerusalem [Zech. 1:16].**

"I am returned to Jerusalem with mercies." God had come back to deal with His people in mercy. The Scriptures tell us that He is *rich* in mercy.

"A line shall be stretched forth upon Jerusalem." There are those who believe that this "line" stretching forth upon Jerusalem means that there would be a great building boom in Jerusalem, that it would expand and become a great city in that day. I think that is probably true. But in the Scriptures, whenever we find a man with a measuring rod or a measuring line, it means that God is getting ready to move *directly* in that particular case. In this case, Israel had just returned from the seventy-year captivity, and God is turning to His people again, turning to those who have returned to Him.

All the nations of the earth are to understand that there will never be peace on earth until there is peace in Jerusalem. That is the key to peace on this earth. Haven't we seen this demonstrated again in these last few years? Haven't the events since Israel became a nation again rather indicated that? That little nation found out how few friends she really had in the world at the beginning of the oil crisis. The nations which they thought were their friends fell away like dead flies because they wanted oil more than they wanted the friendship of Israel. But, of course, modern Israel has not returned to God in spite of the fact that there is a great building boom over there today. They have returned back to the land and have begun rebuilding the cities, and

Zionism is very much a reality, yet they are actually still scattered throughout the world in disbelief. And they are still suffering persecution. The peace of Jerusalem is the key to world peace. You can see this by checking back in the history of the past.

It is certainly true that Jerusalem is crucial in the prophecies of the future: "For the LORD hath chosen Zion; he hath desired it for his habitation. This is my rest for ever: here will I dwell; for I have desired it" (Ps. 132:13–14). Also, "Moreover he refused the tabernacle of Joseph, and chose not the tribe of Ephraim: But chose the tribe of Judah, the mount Zion which he loved" (Ps. 78:67–68). God says that Jerusalem is the spot He loves. I must confess that I do not love Jerusalem as it is today. I must be very frank to say that it is not an attractive place to me. But God is going to make it a wonderful place some day. Although the judgment of God is upon Jerusalem even in this day, God still loves it.

**Cry yet, saying, Thus saith the LORD of hosts; My cities through prosperity shall yet be spread abroad; and the LORD shall yet comfort Zion, and shall yet choose Jerusalem [Zech. 1:17].**

This looks into the future so that these people can recognize that they are working in the plan and program of God which extends into the future.

Allow me to make an application for Christians today. Are you and I working in something that has eternal value? What are you doing today? What value will it be ten years from today? A hundred years from today? A million years from today? Are you and I actually working in the light of eternity? We should keep that in mind.

## VISION OF FOUR HORNS

This is the second vision given to Zechariah.

**Then lifted I up mine eyes, and saw, and behold four horns.**

**And I said unto the angel that talked with me, What be these? And he answered me, These are the horns which have scattered Judah, Israel, and Jerusalem [Zech. 1:18–19].**

I consider the vision of the four horns as one vision, and the vision of the four carpenters as another vision. Most expositors combine them and consider them as a single vision, but I do not interpret them that way.

Zechariah sees four horns, and these four horns are the ones that scattered Jerusalem and Judah and Israel. They have scattered both the northern and the southern kingdoms.

A horn represents a gentile ruler. We find this in Daniel 7:24: "And the ten horns out of this kingdom are ten kings that shall arise. . . ." Again, in Revelation 17:12: "And the ten horns which thou sawest are ten kings, which have received no kingdom as yet; but receive power as kings one hour with the beast." I think you can see from these other references that horns represent gentile world powers. So these four horns which Zechariah saw represent four gentile world powers.

Well, who are they? The four gentile powers that scattered Israel are: Babylon, Media-Persia, Greece, and Rome. The interesting thing is that in the next vision God makes it very clear that these four horns will be dealt with.

## THE VISION OF FOUR SMITHS

In our text they are called carpenters, but they are actually skilled workmen or artisans—or they can be called smiths because a smith is a trained workman.

**And the LORD shewed me four carpenters.**

**Then said I, What come these to do? And he spake, saying, These are the horns which have scattered Judah, so that no man did lift up his head: but these are come to fray them, to cast out the horns of the Gentiles, which lifted up their horn over the land of Judah to scatter it [Zech. 1:20–21].**

"Then said I, What come these to do?" That is, "What are these skilled workmen doing here?"

"And he spake, saying, These are the horns which have scattered Judah, so that no man did lift up his head: but these are come to fray [terrify] them, to cast out the horns of the Gentiles [nations], which lifted up their horn over the land of Judah to scatter it." This is, without doubt, one of the most remarkable prophecies we have in the Scriptures.

Who are the four smiths? There have been many suggestions. Jerome and Cyril and Calvin considered them symbolic of the supernatural means which God uses. Well, I don't quite agree with that. The smiths or artisans are workmen which build up something. I am greatly indebted to Dr. Merrill Unger for his interpretation, which I consider to be the correct one. (By the way, Dr. Unger's book on Zechariah is the finest I have seen.) Since the four horns are symbolic of four successive world empires spanning ". . . the times of the Gentiles . . ." (Luke 21:24), the four smiths must also represent four successive powers used by God to terrify and to cast down the enemies of God's people Israel. Now let me quote Dr. Unger from *Unger's Bible Commentary: Zechariah* (p. 40):

In line with Daniel's great prophecies concerning "the times of the Gentiles" (Dan. 2:31–45; 7:2–13) three of the **horns** in turn and under the punitive hand of God *become* **smiths,** while the fourth and last horn is cast down by the world-wide kingdom set up by the returning Christ, coming to dash to pieces His enemies who are at the same time His peoples' enemies (Ps. 2:1–12). Thus the first horn (Babylon) is cast down by Medo-Persia, the second horn. The second horn (Medo-Persia), accordingly, in turn becomes the first smith. The second horn (Medo-Persia) is cast down by the third horn, and thus becomes the second smith. The third horn (Macedonian Greece), is in turn cast down by the fourth horn (Rome), which thus becomes the third smith. The fourth horn (Rome), the most dreadful of all, *does not* become a smith but in its revived ten-kingdom form of the last days is destroyed by the fourth smith, *the millennial kingdom* set up by the returning "King of kings and Lord of lords" (Rev. 19:16).

The interesting thing is that if you study the history of Rome, you will see that Rome was not destroyed by an outside power. In fact, according to prophecy, the Roman Empire will come back together again. It never did die—it just fell apart because of the internal corruption of the kingdom. There is one who is coming, the Antichrist, who will restore the Roman Empire. He will be a world dictator. Who is going to put him down? Christ will put him down when He returns to the earth. Therefore, Christ is represented by the fourth carpenter or smith. He is the one who will put down the Roman Empire when He comes at the end of the Great Tribulation Period.

My friend, I hope this enables you to see how important it is to study the entire Word of God, because ". . . no prophecy of the scripture is of any private interpretation . . ." (2 Pet. 1:20)—that is, it is not to be interpreted by itself. It must be fitted into God's tremendous program that reaches on into eternity.

It is interesting that, when the Lord Jesus came to earth the first time, He had the title of the carpenter of Nazareth. And He is coming again someday as a carpenter to put down this world dictator and establish His kingdom here upon this earth with Jerusalem as its center. Someone has expressed it in these words:

Then let the world forbear their rage,
The Church renounce her fear;
Israel must live through every age,
And be the Almighty's care.
                              —Author unknown

Before we leave this chapter, I would like to call your attention to the fact that great prominence is given in each of the ten visions to these truths: (1) that God is not through with the nation Israel; and (2) when God says *Israel* and *Judah* and *Jerusalem*, He means exactly those geographic locations. The modern cult which teaches that Great Britain and the United States are the "ten lost tribes" is entirely wrong. I suppose that it helps our national pride to believe that we might be the "chosen people." However, the only way God chooses people today is in Christ. It makes no difference who you are, what your color is, or what your station in life happens to be, if you are *in* Christ, you are chosen and accepted in the Beloved. Unless we are in Christ, it makes no difference to what nation we belong—right now it wouldn't be helpful even to belong to the nation of Israel. We are looking for a ". . . city . . . whose builder and maker is God" (Heb. 11:10), and it is coming from God out of heaven someday. That is our hope.

But God is going to make good His promises to Israel. He will be faithful to them. If you could persuade me that He is going to be unfaithful to the nation Israel, then I do not know on what basis I could believe that He is going to be faithful to the church. But God *is* faithful, both to us and to Israel.

# CHAPTER 2

*THEME: Vision of the man with the measuring line*

The vision of this chapter prophesies the rebuilding of the temple and the city of Jerusalem by the remnant of Israel in the days of Zechariah. However, this in no way concludes the prophecy. Zechariah—and this is true of all the other prophets—looks forward to the very end times and sees the rebuilding of Jerusalem and the temple during the Millennium. During this period the desert will blossom as the rose—and there is a whole lot of desert to blossom over there! And the Lord Himself will dwell in the city of Jerusalem. Although I don't like Jerusalem as it is today, when the Lord moves into it, I think both you and I will like it then. (However, we won't be living there, because the New Jerusalem will be the home of the church.) But the earthly Jerusalem will be inhabited and will become the center of this earth. Keep in mind that the *Lord* will do this—He has already said in chapter 1 verse 17, "My cities through prosperity shall yet be spread abroad; and the LORD shall yet comfort Zion, and shall yet choose Jerusalem." So you see, everything that was to be done in Zechariah's day had eternal significance. God has a purpose with Israel—He is not about to cast her off. Although local circumstances in Zechariah's day were discouraging and it seemed that God has deserted them, He wanted them to know that not only had He not deserted them, but He has an eternal plan and purpose for them. They could say with us, "Being confident of this very thing, that he which hath begun a good work in you will perform it until the day of Jesus Christ" (Phil. 1:6).

## VISION OF THE MAN
## WITH THE MEASURING LINE

**I lifted up mine eyes again, and looked, and behold a man with a measuring line in his hand [Zech. 2:1].**

"I lifted up mine eyes again, and looked." Zechariah sees it with his physical eyes; he is not asleep.

"Behold a man with a measuring line." The appearance of this man reveals that He is the angel of the Lord, the preincarnate Christ, the same one who appeared in the first vision as the rider on the red horse. You may wonder why I say that He is the angel of the Lord when Zechariah simply calls him a man. Well, Zechariah presents Him as a man (*ish* in He-

brew). In chapter 6 verse 12 Zechariah will say, "Thus speaketh the LORD of hosts, saying, Behold the man whose name is The BRANCH." That is the branch of David, the sprout which is coming from Jesse, the Lord Jesus Christ.

To determine the meaning of the "measuring line," I want to call your attention to other verses of Scripture: "Behold, the days come, saith the LORD, that the city shall be built to the LORD from the tower of Hananeel unto the gate of the corner. And the measuring line shall yet go forth over against it upon the hill Gareb, and shall compass about to Goath" (Jer. 31:38–39). When you find God using a measuring line, it simply means that He is getting ready to move again in behalf of that which He is measuring. In the Jeremiah reference He is measuring the city of Jerusalem. The prophet Ezekiel also speaks of measuring: "In the visions of God brought he me into the land of Israel, and set me upon a very high mountain, by which was as the frame of a city on the south. And he brought me thither, and, behold, there was a man, whose appearance was like the appearance of brass, with a line of flax in his hand, and a measuring reed; and he stood in the gate. And the man said unto me, Son of man, behold with thine eyes, and hear with thine ears, and set thine heart upon all that I shall shew thee; for to the intent that I might shew them unto thee art thou brought hither: declare all that thou seest to the house of Israel" (Ezek. 40:2–4). If we read further we would see that this is the vision of the building of the millennial temple in Jerusalem. There is another reference concerning a measuring line: "And there was given me a reed like unto a rod: and the angel stood, saying, Rise, and measure the temple of God, and the altar, and them that worship therein. But the court which is without the temple leave out, and measure it not; for it is given unto the Gentiles: and the holy city shall they tread under foot forty and two months" (Rev. 11:1–2). Without going into detail, let me say that this again is the measuring of the millennial temple that is to be built.

**Then said I, Whither goest thou? And he said unto me, To measure Jerusalem, to see what is the breadth thereof, and what is the length thereof [Zech. 2:2].**

"Whither goest thou?" Zechariah is interested and asks, "Where in the world are you going with that measuring line?"

"To measure Jerusalem, to see what is the breadth . . . and what is the length." He is saying that the city is to be expanded. It did that in Zechariah's day, and it is certainly doing that now. It spilled over the walls long ago. On every hill around the old city of Jerusalem there is construction going on. I don't consider the current building program to be a fulfillment of Zechariah's prophecy because I believe the fulfillment is yet future. The Jews could be driven out of the land of Israel again without disturbing God's promise to eventually and finally bring them back to that land—for that is exactly what He intends to do.

**And, behold, the angel that talked with me went forth, and another angel went out to meet him,**

**And said unto him, Run, speak to this young man, saying, Jerusalem shall be inhabited as towns without walls for the multitude of men and cattle therein [Zech. 2:3–4].**

"Run, speak to this young man." The young man is evidently Zechariah.

"Jerusalem shall be inhabited as towns without walls." In our day the walls of Jerusalem surround only the older city, the small Arab city. Most of the city is outside the walls, scattered on the surrounding hills. This will also be true when this prophecy is fulfilled in the future. It won't be needful to have walls because (1) in modern warfare walls afford no protection, and (2) the city will be at peace, which means that the Prince of Peace will be reigning in Jerusalem.

**For I, saith the LORD, will be unto her a wall of fire round about, and will be the glory in the midst of her [Zech. 2:5].**

This certainly is not true in our day. Their help comes from other nations. But God says that in the future He will be a wall of fire around them. This means that *God* will be their protection. And, my friend, when God protects them, that will be miraculous. Not only will He be their protection, but He Himself will be in their midst. In other words, the *shekinah* glory will then be back in the temple—it did not return to the little temple which the remnant built in the days of Zechariah. But to the harassed little remnant God is promising His protection. He is saying essentially the same thing which He said to

Abraham after he had delivered Lot: ". . . Fear not, Abram: I am thy shield, and thy exceeding great reward" (Gen. 15:1). This means that God will make good all that He had promised them.

Daniel, Ezekiel, Zechariah, and Revelation are the four apocalyptic books in the Bible. They all look to the future when the kingdom is to be established here upon earth. I would like to quote a rather extensive passage from Ezekiel 43 to show the glory that is coming. It describes the coming of the Lord Jesus, the Messiah, coming into His temple. "Afterward he brought me to the gate, even the gate that looketh toward the east: And, behold, the glory of the God of Israel came from the way of the east: and his voice was like a noise of many waters: and the earth shined with his glory."

This is the Lord Jesus, the Messiah, coming into the temple. Notice that He is coming from the east, which is the reason the Eastern Gate in the wall of Jerusalem is so prominent even in our day, although it is sealed up. Facing that gate are graves of thousands of Israelites because they believe they will be resurrected when this prophecy is fulfilled—and they want to be present when the Messiah comes. "And it was according to the appearance of the vision which I saw, even according to the vision that I saw when I came to destroy the city: and the visions were like the vision that I saw by the river Chebar; and I fell upon my face. And the glory of the LORD came into the house by the way of the gate whose prospect is toward the east. So the spirit took me up, and brought me into the inner court; and, behold, the glory of the LORD filled the house. And I heard him speaking unto me out of the house; and the man stood by me. And he said unto me, Son of man, the place of my throne, and the place of the soles of my feet, where I will dwell in the midst of the children of Israel for ever, and my holy name, shall the house of Israel no more defile, neither they, nor their kings, by their whoredom, nor by the carcases of their kings in their high places" (Ezek. 43:1–7).

Notice it says, "I will dwell in the midst of the children of Israel for ever." Forever is a long time, my friend. You see, this is a prophecy that does not find its fulfillment in the days of Ezekiel but looks down through the ages to the Millennium, the time when the Lord Jesus will come and establish His kingdom here on earth.

Now note again what Zechariah has prophesied: "For I, saith the LORD, will be unto her a wall of fire round about, and will be the glory in the midst of her."

**Ho, ho, come forth, and flee from the land of the north, saith the LORD: for I have spread you abroad as the four winds of the heaven, saith the LORD [Zech. 2:6].**

"Ho, ho" is a call to listen. One "ho" would be enough, but when there is a double "ho," it means that He is giving them something very important, and in this case it is a warning.

"Come forth, and flee from the land of the north." In the following verse we shall see that Babylon is referred to as "the land of the north," although it is actually situated in an easterly direction from Palestine. It is called the land of the *north* because invading armies and trading caravans from that land to Jerusalem came around the route called the "fertile crescent" and entered Palestine from the north.

"I have spread you abroad as the four winds of the heaven, saith the LORD." Although historical Babylon did fall two years after this prophecy was given, the final fulfillment will be in the last days, when God will regather them from their worldwide dispersion.

**Deliver thyself, O Zion, that dwellest with the daughter of Babylon [Zech. 2:7].**

This means to get out of Babylon. Why? Because Babylon was going to fall. God was going to bring it down. Let me revert to the two visions about the horns and the carpenters. The first horn is Babylon, and now the carpenter (representing Medo-Persia) is coming, and he is going to tear Babylon down. But Medo-Persia will become a great power, a horn, and then he will persecute God's people. So God will move that nation off the scene by bringing in another carpenter, which will be Greece. And Greece will become a proud nation. And under a ruler, Antiochus Epiphanes, who will come out of the divided empire of Alexander the Great, Israel will be severely persecuted. Then God will raise up another carpenter, Rome, and he will cut down the power of Greece. When the Roman Empire becomes a great power, where is the carpenter who will cut it down? History tells us that the great Roman Empire fell apart, but prophecy tells us that it will come back together again in the last days. Then who will put it down? The Lord Jesus is going to come from heaven. He is the carpenter of Nazareth, and He is also the man with the measuring

rod. He will put down the Antichrist and his kingdom. Then Christ will establish His own kingdom here upon the earth. This is the picture given to us in these visions, which makes them of utmost significance.

**For thus saith the LORD of hosts; After the glory hath he sent me unto the nations which spoiled you: for he that toucheth you toucheth the apple of his eye [Zech. 2:8].**

"Apple of his eye" is an unusual expression, although it occurs elsewhere in Scripture. In this instance it is the Hebrew *babah*, meaning "the pupil" or "the gate" (through which light enters). It is an expression which indicates that which is most precious, most easily injured, and most demanding of protection. This is what Israel is to the Lord God.

**For, behold, I will shake mine hand upon them, and they shall be a spoil to their servants: and ye shall know that the LORD of hosts hath sent me [Zech. 2:9].**

"I will shake mine hand upon them"—that is, all God needs to do is to shake His hand threateningly against the enemies of His people. "And they shall be a spoil to their servants." Those who served them shall become their masters.

Now here is one of the great prophecies of Scripture.

**Sing and rejoice, O daughter of Zion: for, lo, I come, and I will dwell in the midst of thee, saith the LORD [Zech. 2:10].**

"Sing and rejoice, O daughter of Zion." Zion is a hill over in Jerusalem. There are cults that want to appropriate this verse to themselves; so they have moved "Zion" to England or to the United States. Let's be clear on this: When God speaks of Zion, He is not talking about Illinois or Utah or any place other than Palestine. There is a constant danger of taking these prophecies which were given to Israel and relating them to us by way of *interpretation*. Certainly we can make *application* to our own country and to our own lives because great principles are stated here. But when God is talking about geography, He means exactly what He says. "But," somebody says, "this is a *vision*." Granted, but a vision is a vision of reality. A friend of mine disagreed with my interpretation of the Book of Revelation. He said, "It doesn't mean that."

I said, "Then you tell me what it means."

"It is a symbol."

"All right, now you tell me what it is a symbol *of*."

"Oh, it's just a symbol."

"Don't you know that a symbol has to be a symbol *of* something? And it has to make sense. You can't just pull an explanation out of a hat and say, 'This is what it means.' How do you know what it means? It is a symbol of something, and by careful study and comparison with parallel passages, you are to determine what it is. No prophecy is of 'private interpretation'; it must be tested by the whole Word of God."

Therefore, when God uses a geographical term like Zion, He is talking about Zion in Israel. And notice that He is addressing the "daughter of Zion," which is the nation Israel. This is a very familiar figure for Israel, and it cannot mean any other people.

"Lo, I come, and I will dwell in the midst of thee, saith the Lord." God means this literally. He intends to come to that geographical spot on the earth called Zion and to a certain group of people who will be there, Israel the daughter of Zion.

**And many nations shall be joined to the Lord in that day, and shall be my people: and I will dwell in the midst of thee, and thou shalt know that the Lord of hosts hath sent me unto thee.**

**And the Lord shall inherit Judah his portion in the holy land, and shall choose Jerusalem again [Zech. 2:11–12].**

"And many nations shall be joined to the Lord in that day." Notice that it is not only Israel, but *many* nations will be converted to Christ in that day. To be "joined to the Lord" is to be united to Him in faith and spiritual experience.

"And the Lord shall inherit Judah." The conversion of "many nations" does not imply that God will not fulfill His promises to Judah. Zechariah reminds his people again that they are God's inheritance and His portion.

This ought to answer once and for all the anti-Semite who insists that *Judah* refers to Jews and that *Israel* refers to another race. God says that He intends to inherit *Judah*.

"His portion in the holy land." This is the only place in the Bible where the phrase "holy land" is used. It is not the *holy* land today. When I make this statement publicly, it is generally challenged by somebody who says, "But it *is* the holy land. That is the place where Jesus walked!" Well, His footprints are all gone. He is not walking there now. However, someday He will return, and when He does, it will be the holy land again.

"And shall choose Jerusalem again" implies that He is not choosing Jerusalem right now—and I wouldn't either! But when He does choose it, it will become the capital of this earth.

Remember that no prophecy is of any "private interpretation." It must parallel other Scriptures. So let me call your attention to a parallel passage in Isaiah: "And it shall come to pass in the last days, that the mountain of the Lord's house shall be established in the top of the mountains, and shall be exalted above the hills; and all nations shall flow unto it. And many people shall go and say, Come ye, and let us go up to the mountain of the Lord, to the house of the God of Jacob; and he will teach us of his ways, and we will walk in his paths: for out of Zion shall go forth the law, and the word of the Lord from Jerusalem" (Isa. 2:2–3). All of this looks forward to the time of the Millennium.

**Be silent, O all flesh, before the Lord: for he is raised up out of his holy habitation [Zech. 2:13].**

In that day the whole earth will keep silence. Today we hear a lot about freedom of speech, but in that future day there is going to be a marvelous freedom of silence. Why? Because God will be in His holy temple. This looks forward to His visible presence on earth during the Millennium.

This prospect for the future should have been an encouragement to those people in the day of Zechariah. I'm sure it was. And it ought to be an encouragement for us today. God has a plan and purpose for each one of us. He is working in your life and in my life. He works in our hearts both to will and to do of His good pleasure. Oh, to be in step with Him and to be going in the same direction as He is going!

# CHAPTER 3

*THEME: Vision of Joshua and Satan; Vision of the Branch*

As we continue in our study of the ten visions which God gave to Zechariah, keep in mind that we are in a highly figurative section of the Word of God. These ten visions should be considered together as focusing on one particular message. An overall viewpoint will give us a perspective of what each vision is trying to tell us. Also, we need to compare them with other prophetic Scripture passages. As the apostle Peter said, ". . . no prophecy of the scripture is of any private interpretation" (2 Pet. 1:20). That is, we are not to interpret it by itself, but compare it with the whole program of prophecy to get the overall viewpoint which reaches from eternity past to eternity future.

## VISION OF JOSHUA AND SATAN

**And he shewed me Joshua the high priest standing before the angel of the LORD, and Satan standing at his right hand to resist him [Zech. 3:1].**

"He shewed me Joshua the high priest." Keep in mind that this is not the Joshua who led the children of Israel into the Promised Land. This is the Joshua who served as high priest among the remnant of Israel who returned to Jerusalem after the Babylonian captivity. The name *Joshua* means "Jehovah saves," and in the Greek language of the New Testament, the name is translated as "Jesus." You remember that the angel in announcing His approaching birth said, ". . . thou shalt call his name JESUS: for he shall save his people from their sins" (Matt. 1:21). So you can see that the name *Joshua* is especially appropriate for this high priest and prefigures what the nation Israel ought to have been—that is, a holy, high-priestly nation.

"Standing before the angel of the LORD." This angel is the Lord Jesus Christ before His incarnation, as we have seen in the previous chapters.

"And Satan standing at his right hand." It is quite obvious that if Zechariah *saw* Joshua, he also *saw* Satan, which means that Satan is a reality and a person.

In our contemporary culture we see a revival in interest regarding Satan. He pretty much had dropped out of the vocabulary of most people in so-called Christian lands for the past fifty years. They had forgotten about him; or perhaps they felt that by not mentioning him he would go away. But he hasn't gone away. He is very much a reality. The current interest in the supernatural has turned, unfortunately, to Satan and to demons rather than to God and the Lord Jesus Christ. The Bible tells us, and modern thinking demands, that evil be incarnate, that it be represented by a person. Therefore, many folk have gone off into demonology. Logically, if evil must be personified, then good must also be personified. Good is God, and God is good. God in the person of the Lord Jesus Christ will be the final answer to men who are seeking a solution to their own problems and to the ills of the world.

"To resist him." The fact that Satan is standing at Joshua's right hand could mean that he is there to support him or defend him, but, no, he is there to bring charges against him. This is typical in the workings of Satan. Scripture tells us that you and I have an advocate with the Father. Why do we need an advocate with God the Father? Because of the enemy who is accusing us. In Revelation 12:10 he is called ". . . the accuser of our brethren . . . which accused them before our God day and night." I have a notion that this very day he has made a charge against McGee, and I'm sure it is a valid charge. And I am confident that he has been making charges against me from the time I became a child of God. When I was in my teens, working in a Nashville bank, I had tried every form of sin imaginable at that time and was one of a very fast crowd. I was the last person in that crowd that anybody would have imagined would ever go into the ministry and become a teacher of the Word of God. After God had saved me and when I felt God was calling me into the ministry, I made that announcement at the bank and resigned from my position. I wish you could have heard the guffaws that went out. "Imagine McGee!" And I suppose that Satan had a busy day accusing me before the Lord— "You would be very foolish to let him into the ministry. That fellow is the last person in this entire area who ought to go into the ministry." And Satan was standing at the right hand of Joshua to resist him, to accuse him. He was probably saying to God, "How can you put up with this man—he is filthy!" Also Satan was the accuser of the nation Israel. He is really an anti-Semite. If you want to know who is the leader of anti-Semitism, it is the Devil himself.

However, as God's children we have an advocate with the Father. John, writing to believers, says, "My little children, these things write I unto you, that ye sin not. [I wish we didn't, but we do.] And if any man sin, we have an advocate with the Father, Jesus Christ the righteous" (1 John 2:1). And Jesus Christ is the "angel of the LORD" before whom Joshua the high priest is standing in this vision of Zechariah.

**And the LORD said unto Satan, The LORD rebuke thee, O Satan; even the LORD that hath chosen Jerusalem rebuke thee: is not this a brand plucked out of the fire? [Zech. 3:2].**

"The LORD rebuke thee" is very gentle, according to my standards. I could think of a stronger rebuke than that, but God respects this one whom He created. Remember that God created him ". . . Lucifer, son of the morning . . ." (Isa. 14:12), probably the highest creature that He ever created. Then sin was found in him. What kind of sin? Lust or stealing? No. Pride was found in him. He had a free will, and he set that will against the will of God. My friend, that is sin. "All we like sheep have gone astray; we have turned every one to his own way . . ." (Isa. 53:6). Specific sins such as murder, stealing, lying, adultery all come under the heading of "his own way." This is the problem of mankind.

"Even the LORD that hath chosen Jerusalem rebuke thee." This reveals that the rebuke comes not on the account of Joshua the person but on the account of Jerusalem, the capital of the nation.

"Is not this a brand plucked out of the fire?" It looked as if Jerusalem could never be rebuilt after Nebuchadnezzar destroyed it, and it lay in dust and ashes for seventy years. Then out of the ruins the city is rebuilt—a brand plucked out of the burning.

John Wesley called himself a brand plucked out of the burning. I'm of the opinion that many of us today think of ourselves in that way. As I look back, it seems like an accident that I got saved. It just didn't seem that it could possibly have happened to me. But it did happen, and I know now that it was no accident at all. It can be said of any sinner who comes to Christ that he is a brand plucked out of the fire.

**Now Joshua was clothed with filthy garments, and stood before the angel [Zech. 3:3].**

This vision of Joshua the high priest actually goes beyond the man himself. We will learn that this vision gives us the answer to a very difficult question. This is the problem: We have learned so far that God is going to return the nation Israel to the land and that He will dwell in the midst of them. They will be totally restored as His people. That hasn't happened yet, but He says He is going to do that. He will bless them in that land. How can God do that when the people are far from Him? In the day of Zechariah they were far from God and living in sin. Today the same thing is true. How can it ever be a *holy* land when sinners are living in it?

Unger states the problem in this way:

In the preceding visions the marvellous purposes of God's grace toward Israel appear in the judgment of her enemies and the restoration of both the land and of the people. But a crucial question arises: How can an infinitely holy God accomplish such plans with a sinful and besmirched people? How can the wondrous manifestations of divine mercy to them be consistent with God's righteousness? (*Unger's Bible Commentary: Zechariah*, p. 55).

I think the explanation to this problem will become clear as we study the vision. Joshua was to represent the nation. As we read on, we will find him clothed with a filthy garment, very dirty. If you will remember our study of the high priest, you will recall that the high priest had to be dressed spotlessly or else he was not permitted to serve God. Joshua really was the high priest at this time, but in this vision he also represented the entire nation.

Joshua as an individual was not a perfect individual. Even though he was God's high priest, he was described as dirty and filthy. That might have been true of him personally, I do not know. But I do know that the high priest has always represented the nation Israel. For example, on the great Day of Atonement, the high priest went into the Holy of Holies for the entire nation. In just the same way, Jesus Christ is our high priest. He is the representative for the corporate body of believers, the church. He appears before God for us today. To see Joshua in the context of all the ten visions of Zechariah and as a prophetic picture of the nation Israel will deliver us from a very limited interpretation.

Leupold says of the high priest:

He represents and practically impersonates Israel in his holy office. For the nation he prays; for it he enters the Holy Place, he bears the nation's guilt. We must, therefore, not refer the issues and implications of this chapter to Joshua as an individual, nor merely to Joshua, the high priest. We must conclude that *his* condition is *Israel's* condition, *his* acquittal a typical way of expressing *theirs*; the words of comfort and assurance given *him* apply with equal validity to *them* (*Exposition of Zechariah*, p. 64).

That is a very fine statement. Leupold is not always one we can follow in his interpretations, but in this instance he is especially good.

Joshua was a symbol, a type, a representative. God had chosen him, and God had also chosen the nation Israel.

The high priest was to be clothed in fine-twined, white linen undergarments. And over them were to be placed the garments of beauty and glory. Joshua was pictured here as the high priest representing the nation, and his garments, which should have been clean, were unclean. In fact, he "was clothed with filthy garments." That word *filthy* means that there was human excrement on them! Not only was he dirty looking, but he smelled bad. My friend, that is the way the sins of the nation Israel looked to Almighty God. How can this be remedied?

A man with a question called me by telephone from Indianapolis. His question was an old one which has been asked over and over by many people down through the years. It was this: "Have I committed the unpardonable sin?" I told him, "Of course you haven't. Jesus died for *all* your sins. Regardless of who you are or what you have done, you can come to Him right now, confessing your sins and trusting Christ as your Savior. If you do that and mean it, He will forgive you. 'For Christ is the end of the law for righteousness to every one that believeth' (Rom. 10:4). So it doesn't make any difference what you have done, you can come to God through Jesus Christ."

**And he answered and spake unto those that stood before him, saying, Take away the filthy garments from him. And unto him he said, Behold, I have caused thine iniquity to pass from thee, and I will clothe thee with change of raiment [Zech. 3:4].**

This is, without doubt, one of the most beautiful pictures we have in the Old Testament. Joshua could not stand before a righteous, holy God with these dirty garments on. Also his weakness was revealed. You see, being dirty and filthy as he was gave Satan an advantage because the adversary could point his finger at him. Let me give you Dr. Unger's translation of verse 4: "And he answered and spake unto those that stood before him, saying, Take the filthy garments from off him. And unto him he said, Behold, I have caused thine iniquity to pass from thee, and I will clothe thee with rich apparel" (*Unger's Bible Commentary: Zechariah*, p. 60).

Joshua represented not only the nation of Israel, he represents us today. In him we see the sin of the believer. Joshua was a priest before God—God appointed priests in the Old Testament. In our day every believer is a priest before God, but some of us are standing in dirty garments. "Yes," you may say, "but I have been clothed in the righteousness of Christ." If you have been saved, that is true. And that is exactly the picture which is given to us here. You see, the dirty garments, representing sin, must be removed from him, and he must be clothed with clean garments, symbolic of the righteousness of Christ. This pictures your salvation and mine, which makes this such a precious passage of Scripture. Let me refer you to the Epistle to the Romans. In the first three chapters mankind is set before us as a sinner before God. We all stand dirty before Him. And our righteousness—even the best that we can do—is filthy rags in God's sight. We stand in Joshua's condition. What are we going to do about our plight?

Here is God's answer: "But now the righteousness of God without the law is manifested, being witnessed by the law and the prophets; Even the righteousness of God which is by faith of Jesus Christ unto all and upon all them that believe: for there is no difference: For all have sinned, and come short of the glory of God; Being justified freely [without cause] by his grace through the redemption that is in Christ Jesus" (Rom. 3:21–24). Why? Because Christ died, shed His blood, that it might be possible for you and me to come in our filthy rags to Him. He will not accept the filthy rags of our own righteousness. He will take them off and clothe us in the righteousness of Christ. When we stand clothed in Christ's righteousness, nobody, no created thing, can bring any charge against us because we are God's elect. Notice what Paul writes in Romans 8: "What shall we then say to these things? If God be for us, who can be against us? He that spared not his own Son, but delivered him up for us all, how shall he not with him also freely [without a cause] give us all things? Who shall lay any thing to the charge of God's elect? It is God that justifieth. Who is he that condemneth? It is Christ that died, yea rather, that is risen again, who is even at the right hand of God, who also maketh intercession for us" (Rom. 8:31–34). What a Savior we have! When we trust Him as our Savior, He not only takes from us our sins, removes the dirty garment, but He puts on us the robe of His righteousness, and no one can bring any charge against God's elect.

But wait—can God's child get into sin? Yes. Then what is the child of God to do? Well, "If we confess our sins, he is faithful and just to forgive us our sins, and to cleanse us from all unrighteousness" (1 John 1:9). When you and I are out of fellowship with God, we have lost a great deal. We have lost all joy from our lives. We have lost all power from our lives. And it is possible to lose our assurance. I am of the opinion that many folk lack the assurance of their salvation because of sin in their lives. Another thing we lose is our privilege of being of service to God.

You see, if Joshua is to stand before God as His high priest, he must be wearing clean garments. And *God* provides clean garments. How? By mercy. There was a mercy seat in the temple. And we today have a mercy seat—"And he [Christ] is the propitiation [the mercy seat] for our sins . . ." (1 John 2:2). How wonderful this is, and what a glorious picture it gives of God's provision!

Now, you may have an objection to God's choosing the nation Israel. Did He choose them because they were attractive? No. He didn't choose *me* for that reason either. I think of Ruth when she asked Boaz, ". . . Why have I found grace in thine eyes . . . ? (Ruth 2:10). Well, I could say to her, "All you have to do is go home and look in the mirror and you will find out why he fell in love with you and why he extended grace to you. You are beautiful. You are lovely." But, my friend, don't tell *me* to look in the mirror. I have already done it, and what did I see? A sinner, a sinner who needs to be clothed with the righteousness of Christ.

**And I said, Let them set a fair mitre upon his head. So they set a fair mitre upon his head, and clothed him with garments. And the angel of the LORD stood by [Zech. 3:5].**

The adding of this mitre or turban is a little something which is beautiful in its symbolism. The garments of the high priest included a turban, and on that turban were the words: HOLINESS UNTO THE LORD, as in chapter 14 verse 20. This man Joshua didn't have a turban, because in those dirty old garments he certainly was not holy to the Lord. But a turban is given to him now on which is inscribed "Holiness unto the Lord." He will be used of God now just as Israel will be used of the Lord in the future. After the church has been removed in the Rapture, Israel will be the witness for God during the Tribulation, and then during the Millennium the entire nation will be a priesthood down here upon this earth.

**And the angel of the LORD protested unto Joshua, saying,**

**Thus saith the LORD of hosts; If thou wilt walk in my ways, and if thou wilt keep my charge, then thou shalt also judge my house, and shalt also keep my courts, and I will give thee places to walk among these that stand by [Zech. 3:6–7].**

The interpretation of this is quite obvious. Joshua had been dirty, but God had a redemption which enabled Him to extend His grace and mercy to him. Now Joshua is saved, but God says, "If you want to be *used*, you will have to stay clean. You will have to walk in My ways. You will have to be obedient to Me."

Not only is God saying this to Joshua, He is saying it to the nation, and He is saying it to you and me today. Jesus said, "If ye love me, keep my commandments" (John 14:15). Some folk seem to have the idea that if they are saved by grace, they can do as they please. My friend, that is inconsistent. If you do as *you* please, you are not saved by grace— because certainly you are going to love the one who died to save you. If you have really accepted Him and are really trusting Him, you are resting upon Him. And if you are resting in Him, you will want to be obedient to Him and do as He wants you to do. It can't be any other way.

## VISION OF THE BRANCH

**Hear now, O Joshua the high priest, thou, and thy fellows that sit before**

thee: for they are men wondered at: for, behold, I will bring forth my servant the BRANCH [Zech. 3:8].

"**M**y servant the BRANCH" is a marvelous picture of the Lord Jesus Christ. "The Branch" is a familiar figure of the Messiah. Isaiah used that figure to predict His first coming as Savior: "And there shall come forth a rod out of the stem of Jesse, and a Branch shall grow out of his roots" (Isa. 11:1). And Jeremiah uses it to speak of Christ's coming as King to this earth: "Behold, the days come, saith the LORD, that I will raise unto David a righteous Branch, and a King shall reign and prosper, and shall execute judgment and justice in the earth" (Jer. 23:5).

"Hear now, O Joshua the high priest, thou, and thy fellows that sit before thee." God is here addressing Joshua and his fellow priests. Now what is the message He is giving them? Leupold's paraphrase of verse 8 provides the answer: "I shall not let you, Joshua, and your fellow priests be removed from office, nor your office be discontinued, for I have a destiny for you—you are a type of the coming Messiah, who will do My work perfectly ('Servant'), and who will bring the priestly office to undreamed of glory ('Shoot') when He springs forth" (op. cit., in loc.).

> **For behold the stone that I have laid before Joshua; upon one stone shall be seven eyes: behold, I will engrave the graving thereof, saith the LORD of hosts, and I will remove the iniquity of that land in one day [Zech. 3:9].**

The "Branch" is also the stone, the stone which Daniel saw in the vision of the great image: "Thou sawest till that a stone was cut out without hands, which smote the image upon his feet that were of iron and clay, and brake them to pieces. Then was the iron, the clay, the brass, the silver, and the gold, broken to pieces together, and became like the chaff of the summer threshingfloors; and the wind carried them away, that no place was found for them: and the stone that smote the image became a great mountain, and filled the whole earth" (Dan. 2:34–35).

"Upon one stone shall be seven eyes." Seven is not the number of perfection but the number of completeness. The "seven eyes" indicate that Christ has complete knowledge and wisdom. In the New Testament it is said of Christ, "In whom are hid all the treasures of wisdom and knowledge" (Col. 2:3). And the Lord Jesus has been made unto us wisdom because He is all wisdom (see 1 Cor. 1:30).

"I will remove the iniquity of that land in one day." Has that happened in our day? No, it certainly has not happened yet. But it will happen in the future. When the Lord Jesus Christ comes, He will remove the iniquity of Israel in one day.

> **In that day, saith the LORD of hosts, shall ye call every man his neighbour under the vine and under the fig tree [Zech. 3:10].**

"In that day" refers to the Day of the Lord. "Shall ye call every man his neighbour under the vine and under the fig tree" means that they will be dwelling in peace and enjoyment in that day.

# CHAPTER 4

***THEME:*** *Vision of the lampstand and two olive trees*

**W**e have come now to Zechariah's seventh vision. Thinking back over the visions he has had, we can see a story unfolding. He has seen (1) the riders under the myrtle trees, (2) the four horns, (3) the four smiths or carpenters, (4) the man with the measuring line, (5) Joshua and Satan, and then (6) the Branch and the Stone with seven eyes in it. The first four visions symbolize the outward deliverance from the slavery and oppression of Babylon. The visions also look to the end times when Israel again will be scattered throughout the world, as they are today, then returned to their land when the Lord Jesus brings them back.

The fifth and sixth visions symbolized inner salvation. The high priest Joshua, clothed in dirty garments which God replaced with clean garments, tells the story of a people brought back to the land for a purpose, but they can't be used in their sin. They will have to be cleansed; but they cannot cleanse themselves, and their religion won't do it. The cleansing has to come from someone outside themselves. "Come now, and let us reason together, saith the LORD: though your sins be as scarlet, they shall be as white as snow; though they be red like crimson, they shall be as wool" (Isa. 1:18). God Himself provides the redemption ". . . with the precious blood of Christ, as of a lamb without blemish and without spot" (1 Pet. 1:19). The cleansing is actually salvation—"Not by works of righteousness which we have done, but according to his mercy he saved us, by the washing of regeneration, and renewing of the Holy Ghost" (Titus 3:5).

Now that Joshua, the high priest, is cleansed, you may think that he is ready for service. No, he is not quite ready. We come now to the vision of the golden lampstand, which is going to show us *how* Joshua is to fulfill the office of high priest.

## VISION OF THE LAMPSTAND AND TWO OLIVE TREES

**And the angel that talked with me came again, and waked me, as a man that is wakened out of his sleep [Zech. 4:1].**

Let me call your attention again to the fact that Zechariah was awake when he received these visions. At this point he already has had six tremendous visions. He was working the swing shift and the night shift and it was time to have a little rest. So after he had been given the sixth vision, he dozed off. Now the angel has to wake him up because he is not to be given this vision in a dream; he will *see* every bit of it.

**And said unto me, What seest thou? And I said, I have looked, and behold a candlestick all of gold, with a bowl upon the top of it, and his seven lamps thereon, and seven pipes to the seven lamps, which are upon the top thereof [Zech. 4:2].**

The word *candlestick* in the Authorized Version is properly translated "lampstand" because this is the seven-branched lampstand which stood in the Holy Place of the tabernacle and later in the temple, and in our day it is one of the symbols of the nation Israel. There are other symbols of this nation which are used in Scripture, such as the burning bush, the vine, and the olive tree, but here it is the menorah, the lampstand.

In the tabernacle, and later in the temple, the seven-branched lampstand was the most beautiful of the pieces of furniture. It was handwrought of solid gold. Bezaleel, the skilled artisan, was the one who fashioned it originally. There were three branches going out on each side of the main stem, and on top of each were bowls beautifully made like open almond flowers in which the lamps were placed. The high priest had charge of the lampstand. He would light the lamps and keep them filled with oil. Also it was his business to trim the wicks and to see that they burned continually. In the Book of Revelation we have a picture of the Lord Jesus Christ, our Great High Priest, walking in the midst of the lampstands which represented the seven churches in Asia Minor. He warned them that if they didn't repent of their sins He would remove their lampstands. And He did just that. In modern Turkey today not one of those churches is in existence. They all lie in ruins. Christ removed their lampstands. And in our own land our Great High Priest has closed the door of many a church which was not giving out the Word of God. Our Lord has a snuffer, and He just snuffs them out.

And here in Zechariah's vision the picture is of the nation Israel, represented by the menorah, which will in the future become a witness for God in the world.

"With a bowl upon the top of it." This is something new which is added that you don't find in the instructions given to Moses for fashioning the original lampstand. Here there is a "bowl" which acts as a reservoir or oil tank *over* the seven lamps so that the oil flows by gravity into the lamps from the elevated bowl. The oil is the all-important factor in the vision.

The lampstand speaks of Christ; the lamps with the oil in them speak of the Holy Spirit. We have no better picture of the Holy Spirit than the oil of the lampstand. Hengstenberg is correct in saying that "oil is one of the most clearly defined symbols in the Bible," and the symbolism is that of the Holy Spirit. While the oil represents the Holy Spirit, the light which is given out represents Christ because He is the Light of the World. The lampstand probably presents the most complete picture of Christ that the symbolism of the tabernacle gives to us. The measurement of the lampstand was not given because it is impossible to measure deity. It was fashioned in a very wonderful way with open almond blossoms at the top into which the little lamps were placed after they had been filled with oil and their wicks trimmed.

When the Lord Jesus was preparing to leave this earth, He told His disciples that He would send the Holy Spirit, adding, "Howbeit when he, the Spirit of truth, is come, he will guide you into all truth: for he shall not speak of himself; but whatsoever he shall hear, that shall he speak. . . . He shall glorify me: for he shall receive of mine, and shall shew it unto you" (John 16:13–14). With that in mind, look at the lampstand. The lampstand supported the lamps with the light shining from them, and the light, in turn, revealed the beauty and glory of the lampstand. In just such a way, the Holy Spirit does not speak of Himself, but He reveals the glories and the beauties of the Lord Jesus Christ.

**And two olive trees by it, one upon the right side of the bowl, and the other upon the left side thereof [Zech. 4:3].**

The two olive trees were identified in Zechariah's day. Zerubbabel, who was the king in the line of David, is one of the olive trees. The other olive tree was Joshua, the high priest. They would be the two instruments God would use to bring light back into the nation Israel and to make them a light to the world.

The olive oil, as I have already indicated (the word in the Hebrew is beautiful: *golden oil*), represents the Holy Spirit. This prophecy is also destined for a future day, the Great Tribulation Period. This is clearly identified for us in the Book of Revelation: "And I will give power unto my two witnesses, and they shall prophesy a thousand two hundred and threescore days, clothed in sackcloth. These are the two olive trees, and the two candlesticks [lampstands] standing before the God of the earth" (Rev. 11:3–4). Out yonder in the Great Tribulation Period there will be no witness on the earth because the Antichrist, with the power of Satan (since God withdraws His hand for that brief moment), will have stopped the mouth of every witness on the topside of the earth—with the exception of two. God says that always in the mouth of two witnesses a thing is established. Also God says He will never leave Himself without a witness. During that period there will be these two men who will witness for Him. Who they are is speculation. I think Elijah may be one of them, but whether the other is Enoch, whether he is Moses, whether he is John the Baptist, or somebody else, I do not know. But their identity is not the important thing. God will have two witnesses, and they will speak in the power of the Holy Spirit in that day. They will be *God's* witnesses. That is His

promise for the future just as He used Zerubbabel and Joshua in Zechariah's day.

Let me say again that the visions of Zechariah are like stepping-stones which tell out a story. They reveal a very beautiful and complete picture when we put them together. God gave these to the returned remnant for their encouragement. The children of Israel had been in Babylonian captivity and now had returned to the land of Israel. God had made it clear to them that all of this had happened according to His plan and purpose. Now back in the land, they had to be cleansed from their sins and brought into a right relationship with God so that they could render an effective testimony for Him.

Although these visions of Zechariah had a local fulfillment for the past, they also looked forward to the future. The *complete* fulfillment will be during the millennial period when God will return the Jewish people to the land of Israel. And God will cleanse them in that future day. In chapter 13 of Zechariah we will find that a fountain will be opened for the cleansing of David's offspring and for the inhabitants of Jerusalem. After they have been cleansed, they will become a light to the world—which was God's original intention for them. In Deuteronomy 32:8 we read this remarkable verse: "When the Most High divided to the nations their inheritance, when he separated the sons of Adam, he set the bounds of the people according to the number of the children of Israel." Why did He arrange the nations according to the number of the children of Israel? The reason is that God intended them to be His witnesses.

The land of Israel is a very sensitive piece of real estate. God has chosen it and made it that way. He chose it because it was the very center of the three major continents: Africa, Asia, and Europe. It is right on the crossroads of those three continents. There is no place on earth that is more sensitive or that has caused more international problems than that little spot. I think that God intended that it should be that way. And there will be trouble until Israel becomes the center for the proclamation of the Word of God. In Ezekiel 5:5 we read these words: "Thus saith the Lord GOD; This is Jerusalem: I have set it in the midst of the nations and countries that are round about her." Why? So she could be a witness. And in that future day they will be a witness in every corner and crevice of this world.

It is interesting that the popular symbol of Israel today is the menorah. When I have visited in Israel, the fig tree, the vine, and the olive tree symbols have not been in evidence, but I have seen the menorah in many places. I was there during their twenty-fifth anniversary, and I saw the menorah symbol everywhere. Someday the people of Israel will be the witness which God intended them to be.

Israel has failed in the past, but the church is failing in the present. Although Christ has commanded us to go into all the world with the gospel, there are many places in the world that have no witness at all. I am delighted to be penetrating some of those unreached places by means of radio. A letter came to me from South America telling of a young man who had come to know Christ through listening to our Bible teaching by radio, and he immediately became the preacher to his village. Why? Because there wasn't any preacher there, and he was the only witness in the town. He became a flaming evangel, a light for the Lord in that place.

In that future day the Jewish people will be witnesses in every corner of the world, and the Word of God shall go out from Jerusalem. "And it shall come to pass in the last days, that the mountain of the LORD'S house shall be established in the top of the mountains, and shall be exalted above the hills; and all nations shall flow unto it. And many people shall go and say, Come ye, and let us go up to the mountain of the LORD, to the house of the God of Jacob; and he will teach us of his ways, and we will walk in his paths: for out of Zion shall go forth the law, and the word of the LORD from Jerusalem" (Isa. 2:2–3).

**So I answered and spake to the angel that talked with me, saying, What are these, my lord? [Zech. 4:4].**

This young man Zechariah has no inhibitions, so he says, "I see these things, but what is the meaning of them?"

**Then the angel that talked with me answered and said unto me, Knowest thou not what these be? And I said, No, my lord [Zech. 4:5].**

The answer of the angel implies that Zechariah should know what it means. In effect he is saying, "You ought to be able to understand it. You are looking at the golden lampstand, and you ought to know the meaning of that." Well, Zechariah didn't. He said, "No, my lord, I don't understand it at all."

**Then he answered and spake unto me, saying, This is the word of the LORD unto Zerubbabel, saying, Not by might, nor by power, but by my spirit, saith the LORD of hosts [Zech. 4:6].**

Notice that this is God's message to Zerubbabel. Now who is Zerubbabel? He is serving as the civil head of Jerusalem (while Joshua is serving as the religious head). He was the head of the tribe of Judah at the time of their return to Jerusalem after the seventy-year Babylonian captivity. He is the one who led the first group of his people back to their homeland, as described in the Book of Ezra. Zerubbabel's great work was that of rebuilding the temple, but the work was dogged by danger from the outside and discouragement from within. God is giving this vision to strengthen the faith of Zerubbabel. It has real meaning for him, and also it contains a great principle for you and me.

Here is the message: "Not by might, nor by power, but by my spirit, saith the LORD of hosts." The words *might* and *power* are quite interesting. *Might* is a general word for human resources such as physical strength, human ability or efficiency, or wealth. *Power* also denotes mere human strength—physical, material, and mental strength. Therefore, let me give you my translation of this verse: "It is not by brawn nor by brain, but by my spirit, saith the LORD of hosts." You can see that this would be a great encouragement to Zerubbabel, the civil ruler. He and Joshua, the religious ruler, were represented by the two olive trees who were supplying oil to the lampstand. The message is simply this: It will not be by your cleverness, your ability, or your physical strength that the temple will be rebuilt, but by the spirit of God.

My friend, if the spirit of God is not in our enterprises today, they will come to naught, because God is not carrying on His work by our brain or brawn. We speak of clever preachers who deliver very well-composed sermons and all of that, but God's work is not carried on that way. Sometimes a clever preacher is a dangerous man. The fellow who is sharp mentally may be sharp in the wrong direction and cause a great deal of difficulty among God's people. I have had to stand on the sidelines and see a great deal of religious racketeering going on when I couldn't lift my voice against it without being misunderstood. It is quite evident that some clever fellows were good backslappers, good public relations men, good administrators, had nice personalities and a great deal of charisma, and they made an appeal. But God does not carry on His work by the human instrument. It is "not by might nor by power"; it is not by brain nor by brawn, but it is "by my spirit, saith the LORD."

Let me be personal and very frank. Anything that Vernon McGee does in the flesh, that is by his own effort, God hates. He can't use it. It will come to nothing because it is nothing in the world but Vernon McGee building a haystack which ultimately is going to be consumed by fire. God wants to do His work *through* us, by the power of the Holy Spirit. This is important for us to see.

Now looking into the future, this will be especially true during the Millennium. Again, it will not be by brain or by brawn, "but by my spirit, saith the LORD." David Baron has put it like this: "It is in *His* light, and by means of the golden oil of His Spirit, which shall then be shed upon them abundantly, that Israel's candlestick shall yet shine with a sevenfold brilliancy for the illumination of all the nations of the earth." That, my friend, is a great statement.

Back in the days of Zechariah there was a remnant that needed this encouragement because they were overwhelmed by opposition, and they were beset by doubts and by fears. So the vision was given—it is the Word of the Lord unto Zerubbabel—to encourage them.

**Who art thou, O great mountain? before Zerubbabel thou shalt become a plain: and he shall bring forth the headstone thereof with shoutings, crying, Grace, grace unto it [Zech. 4:7].**

"Who art thou, O great mountain?" The mountain represents opposition. This vision encourages them to believe that Zerubbabel will be able to remove the mountain of opposition. The Lord Jesus used "mountain" in that sense. The Lord Jesus said to His disciples, ". . . If ye have faith as a grain of mustard seed, ye shall say unto this mountain, Remove hence to yonder place; and it shall remove; and nothing shall be impossible unto you" (Matt. 17:20). I don't think our Lord was speaking of removing physical mountains—we don't know of any physical mountains being moved in that day—but the faith that removes mountains is the faith that removes obstacles and opposition to the work of God. And that is the picture this vision gives. God's temple will be rebuilt regardless of the seeming impossibilities.

"And he shall bring forth the headstone thereof with shoutings, crying, Grace, grace unto it." The headstone is the finishing or gable stone which marks the completion of a building. He is saying that the temple will be completed with the shoutings and cheers of the people. What an encouragement this was to the disheartened remnant!

**Moreover the word of the LORD came unto me, saying,**

**The hands of Zerubbabel have laid the foundation of this house; his hands shall also finish it; and thou shalt know that the LORD of hosts hath sent me unto you [Zech. 4:8–9].**

This is God's promise that the work won't drag on and finally be completed by someone else, but that Zerubbabel himself is going to finish it. It reminds me of the promise in the New Testament: "Being confident of this very thing, that he which hath begun a good work in you will perform it until the day of Jesus Christ" (Phil. 1:6). God is saying to Zerubbabel, "You have laid the foundation, and I was with you. Well, you are going to put the roof on it, too, and I will be with you."

**For who hath despised the day of small things? for they shall rejoice, and shall see the plummet in the hand of Zerubbabel with those seven; they are the eyes of the LORD, which run to and fro through the whole earth [Zech. 4:10].**

"For who hath despised the day of small things?" I can tell you who has—*we* despise the day of small things. We Americans are impressed with the big and brassy. We like our Christian work to be a success story. And we measure success by the size of the building and the crowds that come to it. Well, I am becoming more and more convinced that the Lord is working in quiet ways and in quiet places today. I am talking to myself when I say that we should quit despising small things.

"For they shall rejoice, and shall see the plummet in the hand of Zerubbabel with those seven." The "plummet" or "plumb" is a weight on the end of a string, and it is used to determine if a building is vertical to the earth. I wish I had thought of using a plummet when I put up a little shed on my place—because it isn't quite straight.

"They are the eyes of the LORD, which run to and fro through the whole earth" indicates that God knows what is going on, and He is still overruling.

**Then answered I, and said unto him, What are these two olive trees upon the**

**right side of the candlestick and upon the left side thereof?**

**And I answered again, and said unto him, What be these two olive branches which through the two golden pipes empty the golden oil out of themselves?**

**And he answered me and said, Knowest thou not what these be? And I said, No, my lord [Zech. 4:11–13].**

Zechariah is asking again for an explanation. And the angel's answer, "Knowest thou not what these be?" implies that he *ought* to know. But he doesn't know.

**Then said he, These are the two anointed ones, that stand by the Lord of the whole earth [Zech. 4:14].**

These are the two Spirit-filled men, Zerubbabel, the civil ruler, and Joshua, the religious ruler. We have already seen that Joshua, representing the nation, has been cleansed and now stands in clean garments. When the remnant of Israel confessed their sin and accepted God's redemption, they were cleansed and now stand in the righteousness of Christ. Therefore, they can be Spirit-filled and can be used of God.

This has a message for you and for me. God wants to fill us with the Holy Spirit. But there are certain conditions to be met. Two of them are negative: (1) ". . . grieve not the holy Spirit of God, whereby ye are sealed unto the day of redemption" (Eph. 4:30). We cannot be filled with the Spirit if there is sin in our lives—we have to be *clean* in God's sight. (2) "Quench not the Spirit" (1 Thess. 5:19). Quenching the Spirit is being out of the will of God. And when we are out of the will of God, God cannot use us. If God wants you in Africa and you are still in your homeland, I don't think that God is going to use you here. But, my friend, if you are in Africa and God wants you to be in your own country, He won't use you there either. The third condition to be met for the filling of the Spirit is positive: (3) ". . . Walk in the Spirit . . ." (Gal. 5:16). Walking in the Spirit is a very practical sort of thing. It is to walk by means of the Spirit, to rest on Him, depending upon Him to do what we cannot do ourselves.

The vision of the lampstands was an encouragement to the remnant in Zechariah's day; it has an application to our day; and it looks forward to the day when God will pour out His Spirit without measure. I see very little of a genuine pouring out of His Spirit in our contemporary society, but during the Millennium He is going to pour out His Spirit upon *all* flesh. That day is yet future, my friend.

# CHAPTER 5

**THEME:** *Vision of the flying roll; vision of a woman in an ephah*

We come now to the two visions which are the most highly symbolic and unusual of this series of visions. The first, the flying roll or scroll, marks a sharp division in the meaning of the visions which Zechariah received. In the first two chapters God makes it clear that He intends to put down all the enemies of Israel and that the nation will become the nation of priests which was God's original intention. God told them that this was His desire for them when He brought them out of Egyptian bondage, but, because of their sin, only one tribe—the tribe of Levi—was chosen for the priesthood. Then in the vision of Joshua and Satan we learned that the nation first had to be cleansed. Then the vision of the branch and the stone with seven eyes looked forward to the kingdom age when God, having cleansed them, would use them, and they would become a light to the world, symbolized by the lampstand being fed oil from the olive trees. The oil, representing the Holy Spirit, signified that they would witness in the power of the Holy Spirit.

That is all well and good, but it does raise a question. Does it mean that every member of this nation, every Israelite, will be chosen—even those who live in continual rebellion and sin? In the visions before us, we will see that the judgment of God will come upon those who do *not* become obedient unto Him. He will ferret out those who are rebellious, and He will judge them.

By the same token, God will do this in the

whole world. Although these visions have in mind the local nation, they also have a world view. There is here a global gospel that looks forward to the establishment of God's kingdom here upon the earth. This makes very clear the thing that God said regarding Israel: ". . . For they are not all Israel, which are of Israel" (Rom. 9:6). It is the national unity, the corporate body—not every member—that will be accepted. Each individual will have to be obedient to God, come God's way for cleansing, as we have seen, and will have to receive the Messiah.

What is said of the nation Israel is also true of the church. Not every church *member* is a genuine Christian—that is, a member of the body of believers which is called the church. There will come a day when there will be a separation of believers and unbelievers. The great division of the church will be at the Rapture, and the division for Israel and for all the nations on the earth will be at the second coming of Christ when He gathers His elect into His kingdom. Then there will be a judgment, and Satan will be bound for one thousand years. All of this is in the picture that is given to us here. You can see that this was for the encouragement of the godly remnant of Israel in Zechariah's day as well as for us today.

## VISION OF THE FLYING ROLL

**Then I turned, and lifted up mine eyes, and looked, and behold a flying roll [Zech. 5:1].**

The first thing that we should establish is that this flying roll is a scroll which represents the Word of God. We get this explanation from the prophet Ezekiel. "And when I looked, behold, an hand was sent unto me; and, lo, a roll of a book was therein; And he spread it before me; and it was written within and without: and there was written therein lamentations, and mourning, and woe. Moreover he said unto me, Son of man, eat that thou findest; eat this roll, and go speak unto the house of Israel. So I opened my mouth, and he caused me to eat that roll. And he said unto me, Son of man, cause thy belly to eat, and fill thy bowels with this roll that I give thee. Then did I eat it; and it was in my mouth as honey for sweetness. And he said unto me, Son of man, go, get thee unto the house of Israel, and speak with my words unto them" (Ezek. 2:9–3:4). Ezekiel was to digest the Word of God and then he was to give it out to the people. This is a tremendous picture for us

who are preachers. We ought to digest the Word of God. It might be bitter in our tummies, but in our mouths it should be as sweet as honey—that is, something that we delight in giving out.

I should add that there is a great difference of opinion and many interpretations regarding the meaning of the flying scroll. But the solid interpretation which has come down through the centuries is that the scroll represents the Word of God in general and the Ten Commandments in particular.

**And he said unto me, What seest thou? And I answered, I see a flying roll; the length thereof is twenty cubits, and the breadth thereof ten cubits [Zech. 5:2].**

The size of the scroll was twenty cubits by ten cubits—that's a very large scroll. The scrolls in the days of Zechariah were made of papyrus or animal skins with a roller at each end so that the ones reading could roll it off one roller and onto the other roller as they read it. Instead of turning pages, as we do when we read a book, they would unroll more of the scroll as they read along. But the scroll of Zechariah's vision was 20x10 cubits (a cubit was the measurement from the end of the middle finger to the elbow and would vary depending upon the size of the individual but was about eighteen inches), which would make the scroll about 15x30 feet, much larger than a bed sheet, even a king-sized sheet. The only way it could be seen would be spread out, and he sees it as a great *flying* scroll, that is, traveling rapidly over the whole land. I imagine that it was completely unrolled as it moved over the earth.

The size of the scroll is probably significant, as it is the same size as the Holy Place of the tabernacle and of the Porch of Solomon in the temple. "And the porch before the temple of the house, twenty cubits was the length thereof, according to the breadth of the house; and ten cubits was the breadth thereof before the house" (1 Kings 6:3). That was the place where the priest could come and worship according to the law. No one could ever go inside the veil unless the blood was put in there. That was done by the high priest only once a year when he went in as a representative of the whole nation. When the high priest went in there, he stood on redeemed ground, having been redeemed by the blood.

You and I today stand on redeemed ground. We have not been redeemed by gold and silver or by any precious stones or precious jewels, but by the precious blood of Christ.

You and I are not standing on a flying carpet. We do not rest on a missile sent from heaven. We have been delivered from the penalty and the power of sin. "And as Moses lifted up the serpent in the wilderness, even so must the Son of man be lifted up: That whosoever believeth in him should not perish, but have eternal life" (John 3:14–15).

**Then said he unto me, This is the curse that goeth forth over the face of the whole earth: for every one that stealeth shall be cut off as on this side according to it; and every one that sweareth shall be cut off as on that side according to it [Zech. 5:3].**

Apparently the Ten Commandments were written on the scroll, and the Ten Commandments are divided into two parts. The first four commandments deal with man's relationship to God, and the last six commandments deal with man's relationship to man. Therefore, the commandment regarding stealing cited here, "for every one that stealeth shall be cut off as on this side according to it," probably represents the section which deals with man's relationship to man. This is clearly identified in Psalm 50: "When thou sawest a thief, then thou consentedst with him [*Thou shalt not steal*], and hast been partaker with adulterers [*Thou shalt not commit adultery*]. Thou givest thy mouth to evil, and thy tongue frameth deceit. Thou sittest and speakest against thy brother; thou slanderest thine own mother's son [*Thou shalt not bear false witness against thy neighbour*]. These things hast thou done, and I kept silence; thou thoughtest that I was altogether such an one as thyself: but I will reprove thee, and set them in order before thine eyes" (Ps. 50:18–21). Now, because men in that day were able to break the Ten Commandments without suffering God's punishment, they came to the conclusion that He was just like they were and would not do anything about their transgressions. But God says that He *is* going to do something about them.

The Mosaic Law was given to the nation of Israel, and it was to be the *Law* of that nation, and they were to obey the law. Well, they disobeyed it, of course, and so God put them out of their land. And in their dispersion among the nations, they scattered the Mosaic Law. The mark of civilization has been the commandments of God which relate especially to man's relationship with man.

I want you to notice here the great principle which is put down concerning the Law and especially the Ten Commandments. The Ten Commandments were given to the nation Israel as they stood in the crossroads of the world, and they took them with them wherever they went. They had a tremendous influence upon Egypt as they became a nation down there. When they went into Assyrian and Babylonian captivity, they had a great influence upon those first great empires. They had an influence upon the Greco-Macedonian Empire and the Roman Empire.

The Ten Commandments produced a civilization. You can say what you please, but the great civilizations of this world have had these laws as a basis: Thou shalt not kill. Thou shalt not steal. Thou shalt not bear false witness. Thou shalt not commit adultery. These have been basic to a nation, building the homes, building a way of life, and establishing a civilization. As long as our nation had them as bedrock, we were blessed of God, and our problems were few compared to what they are today. But our contemporary world society has abandoned them, and we have come to the same place to which the nation Israel had come. God has given Israel as an example. God is saying, "Although I have chosen Israel as a nation, I will judge every individual that breaks My commandments." And so this flying scroll represents for the whole earth the basis upon which God deals with nations. The interesting thing is that it is very difficult to find anything wrong with the Law.

Now God goes ahead and says this—

**I will bring it forth, saith the LORD of hosts, and it shall enter into the house of the thief, and into the house of him that sweareth falsely by my name: and it shall remain in the midst of his house, and shall consume it with the timber thereof and the stones thereof [Zech. 5:4].**

"It shall enter into the house of the thief"— that represents the commandments which have to do with man's relationship to man.

"And into the house of him that sweareth falsely by my name" refers to the first section of the Ten Commandments. Even by the name of God a man would perjure himself!

The Ten Commandments were never given to the Christian as a way of life. We as believers have been called to a much higher plane, and we attain that plane by grace. Actually, man cannot even attain the plane of the Mosaic Law unaided. God gave them the Law, but He gave them no aid to go with it. That is, He did not give them the filling of the Spirit;

the Holy Spirit did not indwell the Old Testament saints. Therefore man in his own strength and ability could never measure up to the Ten Commandments. You and I live in the dispensation of grace, and God has given to us the Holy Spirit whereby we can produce the fruit of the Spirit in our lives (love, joy, peace, longsuffering, etc.), which were never in the Mosaic Law.

## VISION OF A WOMAN IN AN EPHAH

Suppose I told you that last night a missile from outer space landed in my backyard and two little men in green came out of it and talked with me. Would you believe it? Well, if you won't, I won't tell you such a thing. But there are intelligent people today (as well as others) who actually believe in flying saucers. Some have even testified to having seen them. They have even said they saw little people inside. I understand the U.S. Navy has been giving this serious investigation over the years. We hear from two groups. One believes sincerely and vociferously that there are flying saucers. The other group doubts it and denies it equally vociferously.

While I was a pastor in downtown Los Angeles, I had an invitation to go out to Apple Valley to a large rock that is out in that desert area, which was declared to be the landing field where the missiles from outer space came in. I was told they would give me a ride in one of the flying saucers. I didn't go out there for two reasons. One was that I wasn't sure there were flying saucers out there—I'm very much of a skeptic. The other reason was that I was afraid if I did go out there and they put me in one of them, they would take me off and not bring me back—no one assured me of a round-trip ticket. So I didn't go out there. I voiced my skepticism and cynicism about the whole business, but there were some who sincerely believed that missiles from outer space were landing and taking off out in that area. I have driven by that location many times since then, and I don't know why, but I always pick up speed going by that big rock!

Zechariah didn't believe in flying saucers either, but he saw two flying objects in his visions. He saw some strange missiles from outer space. Remember that I said at the beginning that the Book of Zechariah is one of the apocalyptic books of the Bible. It is ethereal, seraphic, spiritual, and highly symbolic. In other words, what he writes is out of this world. We need to avoid fanaticism on one hand and materialism on the other hand.

We're at the launching pad, and we are ready to see another vision. Actually, we are going to see the first astronaut. Believe it or not, we will learn that it is a woman who is in one of those capsules. It is called an ephah or a bushel basket.

**Then the angel that talked with me went forth, and said unto me, Lift up now thine eyes, and see what is this that goeth forth [Zech. 5:5].**

Again he has his eyes wide open—this is no dream. And the interpreting angel says, "Look up, please."

**And I said, What is it? And he said, This is an ephah that goeth forth. He said moreover, This is their resemblance through all the earth [Zech. 5:6].**

"And I said, What is it?" After all, this is the first astronaut Zechariah had ever seen, and he didn't know what it was. Possibly you can remember the great thrill it was when you heard about Alan Shepard making his trip in space. He didn't get very far, but he was the first American in space. Well, here is a woman in space, and Zechariah wants an explanation. "This is an ephah that goeth forth." An ephah is a dry measure equal to a little more than a bushel. It was used to measure such commodities as flour and barley; therefore, this symbolized trade or commerce.

**And, behold, there was lifted up a talent of lead: and this is a woman that sitteth in the midst of the ephah [Zech. 5:7].**

What we have in this vision is a continuation of judgment upon the sin and iniquity of Israel. It looks forward to the Millennium when sin and iniquity will be removed from the land. Also, it looks forward to the judgment of Babylon, which will precede the Millennium. We need to compare it with Revelation 18 where we see the judgment of commercial Babylon. (Revelation 17 pictures the judgment of religious Babylon.) God will judge this matter of covetousness. His command is, "Thou shalt not covet." And God will judge the love of money and the greed that are connected with commercialism. The "talent" was the largest measure of weight, and it was made of lead, the most common heavy metal which was employed in all commercial transactions for weighing out money.

We find that one of the great sins of the Israelites when they returned from Babylon was an insatiable love for money and desire for material things. You may recall that Nehemiah had to deal with them on this issue because they were lending to their brothers at high rates of interest (usury). They had been forbidden by the Mosaic Law to do this, and Nehemiah really straightened them out. The last book of the Old Testament, Malachi, pictures life in that land after the temple had been built. Malachi asks the question, "Will a man rob God? . . ." (Mal. 3:8). Believe me, God answered that question. He said that the whole nation had robbed Him. You see, they were guilty of covetousness; they were bent on accumulating riches for themselves, and they were willing to rob God and hurt their brother in order to do it. That is what they were doing in Zechariah's day, and God is revealing to him that He intends to remove that spirit of covetousness from the land.

"This is a woman that sitteth in the midst of the ephah." Anytime in the Scriptures that we see a woman out of place, there is an evil connotation. For example, the woman in the parable the Lord Jesus gave (see Matt. 13:33) who put leaven in flour. That leaven represents evil, and the leaven of evil is a principle all the way through the Word of God. And when the Scripture pictures a woman in religion, such as the church at Thyatira which had ". . . that woman Jezebel, which calleth herself a prophetess . . ." (Rev. 2:20), and the "great whore" of Revelation 17, she represents evil. In Zechariah's vision, the woman represents the nation of Israel that had gone into commercialism. God wants to bless them, but their awful sin of covetousness must be dealt with first.

**And he said, This is wickedness. And he cast it into the midst of the ephah; and he cast the weight of lead upon the mouth thereof [Zech. 5:8].**

Let me give you Merrill Unger's translation and amplification of this verse (pp. 96–97):

Having announced concerning the woman, This is wickedness, thereupon he [the interpreting angel] cast her [the woman] into the middle of the ephah and cast the lead stone [weight] upon its mouth [opening]. . . . She has been all along sitting or dwelling in the ephah, contentedly, but now that the time has come for commercial Babylon to be removed, to be destroyed, the woman tries to escape from it, because she does not want to be removed with it, and so share its inevitable fate. Therefore, she tries to escape.

**Then lifted I up mine eyes, and looked, and, behold, there came out two women, and the wind was in their wings; for they had wings like the wings of a stork: and they lifted up the ephah between the earth and the heaven [Zech. 5:9].**

Sometime ago a movie was produced called "The Flying Nun"; so I call these two women the two flying nuns. But what do they represent? Well, we may be sure that they represent agents of evil because they are associated with and protective of the woman in the ephah—and the angel had said of her, "This is wickedness."

"They had wings like the wings of a stork"—that is, powerful wings. In Scripture the stork is not a picture of an angel. It is a dirty bird, an unclean bird.

**Then said I to the angel that talked with me, Whither do these bear the ephah?**

**And he said unto me, To build it an house in the land of Shinar: and it shall be established, and set there upon her own base [Zech. 5:10–11].**

God is moving this matter of godless and heartless commercialism out of the land of Palestine.

Now I want you to see something here. The children of Israel were originally a pastoral and agricultural people, and most of the Mosaic Law has to do with that type of life-style. It gives instructions regarding the land itself, the vineyards, the grain, the livestock, and all that sort of thing. And in our day, the Jews who have returned to Palestine have returned, in a large measure, to the soil. However, when they are out of that land, they get into other businesses. I have never heard of a Jewish farmer in America, have you?

When they were in Babylonian captivity they learned commercialism, and they learned it from the Gentiles. They became good businessmen, and they acquired an insatiable love for riches which they saw among the Gentiles in Babylon.

Let me refer you again to the Book of Revelation where, in chapter 18, we find that God is going to judge commercial Babylon at the setting up of His kingdom; in fact, He is going to get rid of it.

My friend, the Bible is a rather revolutionary book, which may be one reason why some people don't like it. It is said that John Calvin got capitalism from the Bible; and I think that he did. But I want to remind you that there is a great deal more in the Bible on the side of the poor people than on the side of the rich. In the Epistle of James, we find this harsh condemnation: "Go to now, ye rich men, weep and howl for your miseries that shall come upon you. Your riches are corrupted, and your garments are motheaten. Your gold and silver is cankered; and the rust of them shall be a witness against you, and shall eat your flesh as it were fire. Ye have heaped treasure together for the last days" (James 5:1–3). He speaks out against the gathering of money just for the sake of gathering it. Then he goes on, "Behold, the hire of the labourers who have reaped down your fields, which is of you kept back by fraud, crieth: and the cries of them which have reaped are entered into the ears of the Lord of sabaoth" (James 5:4).

I wonder what God has to say to some of these great corporations and the great labor unions of our contemporary society. That sort of thing is not going into the kingdom of God upon this earth. God is going to judge it and get rid of it. If there ever was a revolutionary book, it is this Book, the Word of God. It is too hot for a lot of folk to handle!

Now notice that Zechariah asks the interpreting angel, "Whither do these bear the ephah?" And the angel answered, "To build it an house in the land of Shinar." Where is Shinar? It is the land of Babylon. God will return this evil system to the place it came from, and its final destruction was seen by the apostle John: "And after these things I saw another angel come down from heaven, having great power; and the earth was lightened with his glory. And he cried mightily with a strong voice, saying, Babylon the great is fallen, is fallen, and is become the habitation of devils, and the hold of every foul spirit, and a cage of every unclean and hateful bird. For all nations have drunk of the wine of the wrath of her fornication, and the kings of the earth have committed fornication with her, and the merchants of the earth are waxed rich through the abundance of her delicacies. And I heard another voice from heaven, saying, Come out of her, my people, that ye be not partakers of her sins, and that ye receive not of her plagues. For her sins have reached unto heaven, and God hath remembered her iniquities" (Rev. 18:1–5).

My friend, in our contemporary civilization, is God in big business? Is God in the stock market? Is God in the labor unions? Is God in the entertainment business? Anyone with any intelligence recognizes that God is left out of all of them. And God intends to remove them from the earth someday. "And a mighty angel took up a stone like a great millstone, and cast *it* into the sea, saying, Thus with violence shall that great city Babylon be thrown down, and shall be found no more at all. And the voice of harpers, and musicians, and of pipers, and trumpeters, shall be heard no more at all in thee; and no craftsman, of whatsoever craft *he be*, shall be found any more in thee; and the sound of a millstone shall be heard no more at all in thee; And the light of a candle shall shine no more at all in thee; and the voice of the bridegroom and of the bride shall be heard no more at all in thee: for thy merchants were the great men of the earth; for by thy sorceries were all nations deceived. And in her was found the blood of prophets, and of saints, and of all that were slain upon the earth" (Rev. 18:21–24, italics mine).

When this evil system is removed, Palestine will become truly the *holy* land; and when wickedness is destroyed from the whole earth, the kingdom of God will come to the earth. What a glorious prospect this is as you and I live in this present evil age!

# CHAPTER 6

*THEME: Vision of the four chariots; the symbolic crowning of Joshua*

We come now to the final vision of the ten which were given to Zechariah in one night. To get them before us as a background, let me enumerate them again: (1) The riders under the myrtle trees; (2) the four horns; (3) the four smiths; (4) the man with the measuring line; (5) Joshua and Satan; (6) the branch and the stone with seven eyes; (7) the lampstand and the two olive trees; (8) the flying scroll; and (9) the woman in the ephah; and now the tenth, the four chariots. Let me say again that some expositors find only eight visions in this series, but I believe that it is highly consistent to see the visions as ten.

## VISION OF THE FOUR CHARIOTS

**And I turned, and lifted up mine eyes, and looked, and, behold, there came four chariots out from between two mountains; and the mountains were mountains of brass [Zech. 6:1].**

"I . . . lifted up mine eyes, and looked" indicates again that his eyes were wide open; he saw these things—this was not a dream.

"Two mountains; and the mountains were mountains of brass." The majority of the outstanding commentators agree that these two mountains are Mount Zion and the Mount of Olives, which would locate these four chariots down in the Kidron Valley.

"There came four chariots"—we assume that horses were hitched to the chariots and that there were charioteers or drivers for each of them. As we read on, we will find that this is true. These chariots could be interpreted as representing the four great world empires that Daniel saw in his vision. All of them were gentile empires, and all of them have been judged of God. That part of Daniel's vision has been literally fulfilled. These four chariots *could* represent that very easily.

However, I am inclined to identify these four chariots with the vision which John saw in the Apocalypse, speaking of that which is yet future. In fact, Revelation 6 opens with John's vision of the Great Tribulation Period by presenting to us four horsemen, and there is a striking correspondence between them and Zechariah's vision of the four chariots. We have seen in chapter 5 the visions of judgment

primarily with reference to the people of Israel, but here in chapter 6 God's judgment is upon the gentile nations which have oppressed God's people. It reveals not only a past judgment but a future judgment which is to come during the Great Tribulation Period.

"And the mountains were mountains of brass." These mountains were of brass, or literally of bronze. Bronze was known in the earth at a very early period. We can go back in history to the Old Stone Age and the New Stone Age, back to the Neolithic and the Paleolithic periods. We find that bronze appears almost at the beginning of civilization.

Symbolically, bronze is used in the Old Testament to represent judgment. It was one of the metals that was used in the tabernacle in the two articles of furniture which were used in the judgment of sin. The brazen altar was made of bronze as was the laver of brass. These both stood in the outer court of the tabernacle, and both had to do with the judgment of the sin of the people.

Since the mountains in this vision are mountains of brass, it would indicate that these mountains speak of judgment. Judgment is going to come forth from God from the Kidron Valley. There are four judgments that go forth, and they are pictured here as four chariots.

**In the first chariot were red horses; and in the second chariot black horses;**

**And in the third chariot white horses; and in the fourth chariot grisled and bay horses [Zech. 6:2–3].**

The colors of these horses are significant. We have the same colors in the four horsemen of the Apocalypse in Revelation 6. I don't think it is accidental that Zechariah had a vision of four chariots and John of four horsemen. They are probably referring to the same events. The red horse in John's vision represents war. The black horse represents famine, and the pale horse is identified as picturing death. All of these picture judgments from almighty God.

Now what does the first horse, the white horse of the Apocalypse, represent? There are white horses here in Zechariah's vision also, which probably symbolize victory. In John's vision, the white horse is immediately followed by the red horse of war. Therefore, I think that the first horseman represents Antichrist and that he will bring a false peace into the world—because after him rides the red horse of war, and war breaks out upon the earth. My friend, I don't think that we have seen an actual *world* war yet; but in the end times the whole earth will be inflamed by war because man is a warlike creature as long as there is sin in his heart. And when that red horseman rides through the earth—I say it reverently—all hell will break loose. It seems to me that no one today is emphasizing how frightful the Great Tribulation is going to be when it breaks upon this earth. Well, it is symbolized by the riding of that red horse of war.

The "grisled and bay horses" of Zechariah's vision are probably more accurately translated as dappled (lit., as if sprinkled with hail) and would correspond to the pale horse of the Apocalypse.

This tenth vision was given to Zechariah for the encouragement of his people, knowing that God would judge the gentile nations as He would judge His own people.

**Then I answered and said unto the angel that talked with me, What are these, my lord?**

**And the angel answered and said unto me, These are the four spirits of the heavens, which go forth from standing before the Lord of all the earth [Zech. 6:4–5].**

"These are the four spirits of the heavens." The "spirits" are obviously angels so that the four chariots are, as David Baron (*The Visions and Prophecies of Zechariah*, p. 175) puts it,

. . . *angelic beings, or heavenly powers*— those invisible "messengers" of His "who excel in strength, and who ever stand in His presence, hearkening unto the voice of His word," and then go forth in willing obedience, as swift as the "winds," to carry out His behests (Ps. ciii. 20, 21, civ. 4).

In other words, the angels are in charge of the judgments which will be coming upon the gentile nations, as we see also in the Book of Revelation.

Now we get the interpretation—

**The black horses which are therein go forth into the north country; and the white go forth after them; and the grisled go forth toward the south country.**

**And the bay went forth, and sought to go that they might walk to and fro through the earth: and he said, Get you hence, walk to and fro through the earth. So they walked to and fro through the earth [Zech. 6:6–7].**

The black and white horses will go forth into the north country. The "grisled" or dappled and "bay" will go forth into the south country.

**Then cried he upon me, and spake unto me, saying, Behold, these that go toward the north country have quieted my spirit in the north country [Zech. 6:8].**

Notice that none of the horses go to the west—that would put them into the Mediterranean Sea, and none of these are sea horses! Neither do any of the horses go to the east because the great Arabian desert is out there. They go to the north and to the south, which is the way one would go from Israel to any other part of the world. The directions given simply mean that they go out from Israel throughout the whole earth.

It says that the black and the white horses go up into the north country. I personally believe that the judgment of the Great Tribulation Period begins with Russia coming down into the land of Israel, so that judgment will first go to the king of the north, to Gog and Magog in the north. Judgment will also go south toward Egypt. However, the riding of the horses is not the main issue here. In the Book of Revelation we are given the series of events in the Great Tribulation Period, one event after another, one crisis after another. When the white horse rides forth, he will bring a victory that will set up a false peace upon the earth. The world will think that it is entering the Millennium when actually it will be entering the Great Tribulation Period. Immediately after the white horse there will come the red horse of war—war breaks out worldwide—followed by the black horse of famine. Famine generally follows war as do plagues and death, which are symbolized by the fourth, the pale horse. In contrast to this, in the vision of the four chariots which was given to Zechariah, the order is not the important thing. Rather, the emphasis is upon the fact that God intends to judge *all* the nations of the earth, and the four chariots represent those judgments. All of them are to take place during the Tribulation Period. This concludes the ten visions given to Zechariah.

## THE SYMBOLIC CROWNING OF JOSHUA

Now we come to an event which takes place during the days of Zechariah.

**And the word of the LORD came unto me, saying,**

**Take of them of the captivity, even of Heldai, of Tobijah, and of Jedaiah, which are come from Babylon, and come thou the same day, and go into the house of Josiah the son of Zephaniah [Zech. 6:9–10].**

Here we are given the names of three men who came from Babylon. They had not come with either of the two groups of the remnant that returned to the land of Israel, but they came on their own. The name *Heldai* means "robust"; *Tobijah* means "God's goodness"; and *Jedaiah* means "God knows." Linking these names together indicates that God knows that through His goodness He intends to put His King upon the throne, and He will do it in a robust and powerful manner.

What will take place here is a symbolic crowning, but it pictures the coming of Christ to this earth to reign, which is, of course, yet future.

**Then take silver and gold, and make crowns, and set them upon the head of Joshua the son of Josedech, the high priest [Zech. 6:11].**

This seems like a strange thing to do. Why did they place the crown on the head of Joshua the high priest rather than on the head of Zerubbabel who was in the line of David? The reason they were not to crown Zerubbabel is that God was not going to restore the line of David to the throne at that time. The fact of the matter is that the next one who will wear the crown of David will be the Lord Jesus Christ when He comes to this earth to establish His kingdom. But crowning the high priest was very unusual because God kept the offices of king and priest entirely separate.

The explanation is found in the fact that Joshua, the high priest, in this passage is representative of the Lord Jesus Christ who is our Great High Priest today. The Epistle to the Hebrews tells us to *consider* our Great High Priest. Christ, after His resurrection, ascended into heaven, and as our Great High Priest He has passed within the veil. He is

seated now at God's right hand and is waiting for the time when his enemies will be made His footstool. He will come forth and establish His kingdom here upon this earth. The chapter before us pictures His coronation.

Notice the sequence that is followed in this little Book of Zechariah. After the visions that depicted the judgment of God upon His people and upon all the gentile nations of the world, we have this, the coming of Christ and His crowning as the King of Kings and Lord of Lords.

It is interesting to see the threefold ministry of the Lord Jesus Christ in time spans. The first time span is His ministry as God's *Prophet* when he came to this earth over nineteen hundred years ago. He came down here to *speak* for God, and He Himself was the *Word* of God as He revealed *God* in human form. And He revealed the *love* of God by dying upon the cross for your sins and my sins. He was God's Prophet.

In the day in which you and I live He is God's *Priest*. When He ascended into heaven, He passed within the veil, and in the Holy of Holies He presented His own blood for our sins. Today He is there to make intercession for us. He intervenes for us when there is sin in our lives and we confess that sin to Him. He serves there as our High Priest.

One day in the future He will be coming out again. The Book of Revelation makes it very clear that he will come as King of Kings and Lord of Lords. Prophet, Priest, and King is the threefold ministry of Christ.

Now Christ is presented under another figure of speech—

**And speak unto him, saying, Thus speaketh the LORD of hosts, saying, Behold the man whose name is The BRANCH; and he shall grow up out of his place, and he shall build the temple of the LORD [Zech. 6:12].**

"The BRANCH" is not the name of Joshua. It is a prophetic name which is given to the Lord Jesus Christ. He came to this earth over nineteen hundred years ago as the Branch, a root out of dry ground (see Isa. 53:2). The very fact that He came to humanity and came to a people at a time when they were subject to Rome is the most amazing thing in the world. He was called a root out of Jesse, the peasant, because by the time the Lord Jesus was born, the royal line of David had sunk back into poverty. The Lord Jesus was born into poverty and obscurity. He was indeed the root out of a dry ground.

Suppose you were walking in a desert area—like the extremely desolate desert east of here in California. As you walk along you see no growing thing except a few cacti and a rattlesnake or two. Then suddenly you come upon a plant of iceberg lettuce growing there, luscious and green. You would be amazed. You would be unable to account for it. Well, the Lord Jesus was like that—a root out of a dry ground.

Jesus Christ is coming again as the Branch, and this time the Branch is going to rule the world.

"He shall grow up out of his place, and he shall build the temple of the LORD." You see, this is given as an encouragement to the remnant in their struggle to rebuild the temple. As we saw in the Book of Haggai, it looked small and insignificant to many of them, but in God's eyes His temple was *one* house. Although there is a series of temples—the wilderness tabernacle, Solomon's temple, Zerubbabel's temple, Herod's temple, the Great Tribulation temple, the millennial temple—God calls it one house. He didn't view Zerubbabel's temple as a separate house. Although it was considered unimportant by some of the people, God says that He is the one to judge its importance. And it is in His plan and purpose.

Many letters come to me with the lament, "I can't be very much for God." Well, that was also the cry of the discouraged remnant in Zechariah's day. The temple they were building seemed like nothing compared to the grandeur of Solomon's temple. But God was assuring them that the temple they were building was in His will and that He was the one to determine the importance of it.

Again let me say that I believe that some of the greatest pulpits we have in Southern California are not in churches; they happen to be sickbeds where some dear saint of God is confined. Recently I heard of a young man who listens to our Bible-teaching radio program. He is paralyzed from his neck down but is a radiant Christian and sends out Christian literature continually. I'm not sure but what his ministry for God is more important than mine or that of anyone which seems to be doing something great for God. We are to let God decide that. The important thing for you and me is to get into the will of God.

That was the point that Haggai and Zechariah were trying to get over to these people. They were encouraging them. They were saying, "You are doing what God wants you to do. Sure it looks small, but it is in the plan and

purpose of God. That makes it great and big. It is going to eventuate in the coming of the Lord Jesus Christ to this earth to establish His Kingdom."

"Behold the man whose name is The BRANCH." The word of God speaks of the Lord Jesus Christ as "The Branch" in a fourfold way. (1) He is called the Branch of David: "Behold, the days come, saith the LORD, that I will raise unto David a righteous Branch, and a King shall reign and prosper, and shall execute judgment and justice in the earth" (Jer. 23:5). Here Christ is presented as the *King*, the Branch of David. (2) He is spoken of as Jehovah's *Servant*, the Branch; as we have already seen in chapter 3 verse 8: "Here now, O Joshua the high priest, thou, and thy fellows that sit before thee: for they are men wondered at: for, behold, I will bring forth my servant the BRANCH." (3) And here in chapter 6 verse 12 He is called "the *man* whose name is The BRANCH" (italics mine). (4) Finally, He is presented as the Branch of Jehovah: "In that day shall the branch of the LORD [Jehovah] be beautiful and glorious, and the fruit of the earth shall be excellent and comely for them that are escaped of Israel" (Isa. 4:2).

It is interesting that the gospel records in the New Testament present the Lord Jesus in the same fourfold way. In the Gospel of Matthew He is the *King*, the Branch of David; in the Gospel of Mark He is Jehovah's *Servant*, the Branch; in the Gospel of Luke He is presented as the perfect *Man* whose name is the Branch; and in the Gospel of John He is the Branch of Jehovah, *God* the Son. This is a marvelous portrait that we have of Jesus as He was when He walked on this earth as a member of the human family.

**Even he shall build the temple of the LORD; and he shall bear the glory, and shall sit and rule upon his throne; and he shall be a priest upon his throne: and the counsel of peace shall be between them both.**

**And the crowns shall be to Helem, and to Tobijah, and to Jedaiah, and to Hen the son of Zephaniah, for a memorial in the temple of the LORD [Zech. 6:13–14].**

"Even he shall build the temple of the LORD." "Even he" is the sprout, the Branch who grew out of poverty and obscurity. "He shall build the temple of the LORD," refers to the millennial temple.

Christ the Messiah, "shall sit and rule upon

his throne; and he shall be a priest upon his throne." He shall be both King and Priest. The two offices will be combined in one person.

"The crowns shall be . . . for a memorial in the temple of the LORD." Joshua did not wear these crowns. They were placed upon his head only for the symbolic crowning. Then, according to Jewish tradition, they were placed as symbols in the top windows of the temple for a memorial, serving as a reminder that the Messiah would come and that He would be not only the King but He also would be the Priest.

**And they that are far off shall come and build in the temple of the LORD, and ye shall know that the LORD of hosts hath sent me unto you. And this shall come to pass, if ye will diligently obey the voice of the LORD your God [Zech. 6:15].**

"And they that are far off shall come and build in the temple of the LORD." Notice Merrill Unger's comments on this verse (p. 115):

The deputation from far away Babylon bringing an offering of silver and gold for the temple, which was then in the process of construction, was the occasion for Zechariah's prediction of a future glorious temple to be established in Jerusalem as a House of Prayer for all nations, and to which even the Gentile peoples from afar shall flow, bringing their worship and their gifts.

Isaiah also speaks of the coming of gentile nations to the temple in Jerusalem during the Millennium: "And it shall come to pass in the last days, that the mountain of the LORD'S house shall be established in the top of the mountains, and shall be exalted above the hills; and all nations shall flow unto it" (Isa. 2:2).

Let me remind you that back in verses 12 and 13 of this chapter it says that Christ (the Branch) shall build the temple of the Lord. And in the verse before us it says that "they that are far off shall come and build *in* the temple of the LORD." The nations shall build *in* the temple of the Lord in that they will bring their wealth into it. We need to make this distinction because only the Lord Jesus Himself will build the temple. Isaiah also says, "Also the sons of the stranger [Gentile], that join themselves to the LORD, to serve him, and to love the name of the LORD. . . . Even them will I bring to my holy mountain, and make them joyful in my house of prayer: their burnt

offerings and their sacrifices shall be accepted upon mine altar; for mine house shall be called an house of prayer for all people" (Isa. 56:6–7).

"And ye shall know that the LORD of hosts hath sent me unto you." Apparently this means that Christ, the Messiah, will Himself establish the truth of God's Word.

"And this shall come to pass, if ye will diligently obey the voice of the LORD your God." I do not understand this to mean that the *fulfillment* of the prophecy will depend upon their obedience, because the prophecy is in the eternal plan and purpose of God. Rather, their *participation* in it depends upon their faith and obedience.

As we conclude the first major division of the Book of Zechariah, we need to locate it in the stream of history and prophecy. It is possible to lose our way through this section and, by so doing, miss one of the greatest lessons of Scripture and one of the greatest principles that God puts down in His Word. I urge those who attempt to teach prophecy to study this little book very carefully. It will deliver them from making some wild and weird interpretations.

Because the visions of Zechariah are highly symbolic, we are apt to come to the conclusion that they are just haphazard dream-stuff of a prophet of long ago. Folk who consider them totally unrelated to each other feel free to interpret them in any way they choose. There is a danger of lifting out one of the visions from its context and giving it an absurd interpretation. We must remember that one of the great rules of interpreting prophecy is that no prophecy is of any *private* interpretation—that is, it must be fitted into its proper place in the whole body of prophecy.

We need to keep in mind that all of the visions given to Zechariah are connected and related. They have meaning which is local and also they give an outline of history. They picture the whole future of the nation Israel, including the destruction of her enemies and her cleansing and restoration to her high priestly witness. The section finalizes with the coming of Christ to the earth as the great Priest-King to reign on the earth.

All of this was given by God through Zechariah as an encouragement to the discouraged remnant in his day who were struggling to build the temple. Not only was the work moving slowly and with difficulty, but it seemed so small and inconsequential compared to Solomon's temple and to the great heathen temples they had seen in Babylon and later in the Medo-Persian Empire.

However, Israel was in a time of peace, and it was time for them to build.

Now I would like to call your attention to the threefold meaning. There is what is known as (1) the contemporary meaning, (2) the continuing meaning, and (3) the consummation of all things.

The *contemporary* meaning is that Zechariah was speaking into a local situation. He was addressing the people of his day regarding their problems. He was urging his own people not to be discouraged but to know that they are in the eternal plan and purpose of God. The little temple they were building would finally usher in the great millennial temple which the Messiah Himself would build.

The *continuing* meaning is a message for our day. You see, "All scripture is given by inspiration of God, and is profitable . . ." (2 Tim. 3:16). All of it has a message *for* us although not all of it was written *to* us. For instance, God has not asked us to build a temple. A few years ago many Christians tried to get stone out of Indiana and move it over to Israel to help them build the temple. That was a ridiculous idea. Our business is not to get the marble to Israel to help them build the temple; our business is to get to them the message of the one who is the Rock of Ages, the one who is the Stone cut out without hands (see Dan. 2:45), who said of Himself, "And whosoever shall fall on this stone shall be broken: but on whomsoever it shall fall, it will grind him to powder" (Matt. 21:44). If we don't fall upon Him, come in repentance to Him, in this age of grace, the day will come when we will have to bear His judgment. We have seen that God judges nations—the Babylonian, Media-Persian, and Graeco-Macedonian Empires have come and gone. My friend, are you blind to the fact that God is moving today in the history of this world? Do you realize that God is judging our own nation? Vietnam was a place of shame and humiliation. What did we actually accomplish over there? The billions of dollars spent on war costs should have been invested years earlier in Bibles and missionaries.

Current events should certainly teach us how quickly God can raise up a nation and how quickly He can bring it down. America rose to be the strongest nation on the earth, but we stumbled along in our sin and in our arrogance. Fifty years ago absolutely no one would have believed that the United States would yield to the demands of a few desert sheiks who ruled over a few people and some mangy camels. No one would have seen the relationship between the camel and a Cadillac. Yet today we see the wealth of the world going into Arabian oil. They will bankrupt our nation; yet we close our eyes to what is going on. God can raise nations and bring down nations in whatever way He chooses.

If you listen to the news media, you will become discouraged. Besides that, you'll get brainwashed. If you look at Washington, D.C., you will feel like giving up—or throwing up! I don't know about you, but I am tired of hearing panel discussions by politicians, educators, the military, athletes, and the movie colony. I don't think that any of them have a message for us right now. Perhaps you can hear the still small voice of God in the visions of Zechariah. His visions are not weird and wild, and no weird and wild interpretation is satisfactory. They teach us that God's purpose will prevail and that God is moving in history to accomplish *His* purpose.

The final of the threefold meanings is the *consummation* of all things. History is flowing in the channel of prophecy. Again let me repeat verse 12: "Thus speaketh the LORD of hosts, saying, Behold the man whose name is The BRANCH; and he shall grow up out of his place, and he shall build the temple of the LORD." The Branch, as we have seen, is none other than the Lord Jesus Christ, a root out of dry ground, who died on a cross for us. But He is coming again to reign. "In that day shall the branch of the LORD be beautiful and glorious, and the fruit of the earth shall be excellent and comely for them that are escaped of Israel" (Isa. 4:2). He shall be the *priest* upon His *throne*.

Knowing this should help us to keep things in perspective. There may be some little group of believers who meet on a back street, but they are meeting in the name of Christ and they are seeking to honor Him. They are studying His Word, and they really want to do His will. They sing with sincerity,

My Jesus, I love Thee, I know Thou art
    mine,
    For Thee all the follies of sin I resign;
My gracious Redeemer, my Saviour art
    Thou;
    If ever I loved Thee, my Jesus, 'tis
    now.

—William R. Featherstone

That little group may be unknown to the world, but it is more important in the plan and program of God than the meetings held by heads of state in the capitals of the world. This is hard for many folk to believe because the world does not see things from God's point of view.

You see, that little group of believers will join in with a mighty chorus in heaven some day, singing to the Lamb: ". . . Thou art worthy to take the book, and to open the seals thereof: for thou wast slain, and hast redeemed us to God by thy blood out of every kindred, and tongue, and people, and nation; And hast made us unto our God kings and priests: and we shall reign on the earth" (Rev. 5:9–10). That is the goal toward which we are moving. The world may ignore these believers and multitudes simply pass them by; yet they are important in the plan and purpose of God.

This section of Zechariah should help us see things from God's perspective. This tremendous passage of Scripture still has a message for you and me today.

# CHAPTER 7

**THEME:** *Historic interlude; question concerning a religious ritual (fasting); threefold answer; when the heart is right, the ritual is right; when the heart is wrong, the ritual is wrong*

## HISTORIC INTERLUDE

In chapters 7 and 8 we have what I have labeled an historic interlude. It is very similar to what we also have in the little prophecy of Haggai. In the middle of that prophecy, Haggai was sent to the priest to ask concerning a law: When anything that is ceremonially clean touches that which is unclean, will it make it clean? And, of course, the answer is that it will not. And when that which is ceremonially unclean touches that which is clean, will it make it unclean? The answer is yes, it will. In this historic interlude here in Zechariah, we have the same problem approached from a little different angle.

## QUESTION CONCERNING A RITUAL (FASTING)

**And it came to pass in the fourth year of king Darius, that the word of the LORD came unto Zechariah in the fourth day of the ninth month, even in Chisleu [Zech. 7:1].**

The impressive thing here is that again Zechariah is going to have a message for these people, and it is a very important message. He makes it clear that it is not his own message, but it is "the word of the LORD."

"In the fourth year of king Darius . . . in the fourth day of the ninth month, even in Chisleu." If you want me to put this in terms of our calendar, it was December 4, 518 B.C. This is the same period in which Haggai was speaking to the people in a very practical way.

**When they had sent unto the house of God Sherezer and Regemmelech, and their men, to pray before the LORD [Zech. 7:2].**

David Baron's comment (p. 210) will help us better understand this verse: "It will be noticed that, together with the Revised Version, and almost all modern scholars, we discard the rendering given of the first line of the 2nd verse in the Authorized Version, namely, *'When they sent unto the House of God.'* Now, Beth-el does mean literally 'House of God'; but it is never used of the Temple, but only and always of the well-known town of Ephraim, one of the great centers of the Israelitish idolatrous worship set up by Jeroboam the son of Nebat." In other words, what we have here is a delegation of men sent from Beth-el, which means "house of God." It was called the house of God by Jacob at that time in his life when he thought he was running away from God as well as from his father and his brother Esau. He spent the night at this place, and God gave him a vision. Jacob said of Beth-el, ". . . this is none other but the house of God, and this is the gate of heaven" (Gen. 28:17).

Beth-el was located in the northern kingdom of Israel and is the place where Jeroboam put one of the golden calves to be worshiped. This delegation was *not* made up of men of the tribe of Judah. They were probably of the tribe of Ephraim. The fact that this delegation came down from Beth-el indicates that people from the ten so-called "lost-tribes" were not lost at all—some of them were living at Beth-el. If you will read the Book of Ezra very carefully, you will find that many people who returned from the Babylonian captivity returned to towns that were actually north of the Sea of Galilee, an area that belonged to the ten tribes which constituted the northern kingdom of Israel. All twelve tribes were represented in those who returned, although very few actually returned, less than 60,000 all told.

My friend, there are no "ten lost tribes of Israel." Those who returned from the captivity naturally went back to the places from which they had come, and many of them went to the northern part which was the kingdom of Israel. They happened to be folk born in the Babylonian captivity (Sherezer and Regemmelech are Babylonian names) who returned as Jews back to their own tribe. If you feel that Anglo-Saxons or any other gentile race makes up the "ten lost tribes," may I say to you, you are very much lost in the maze of Scripture. You may be lost, but the ten tribes are not lost.

**And to speak unto the priests which were in the house of the LORD of hosts, and to the prophets, saying, Should I weep in the fifth month, separating myself, as I have done these so many years? [Zech. 7:3].**

These men have come down from Beth-el to speak to the priests in the temple at Jerusalem, and they have come with a question. The question has to do with a ritual: Is a ritual right or is a ritual wrong? The people had begun to fast before the Babylonian captivity and had continued to do so during the Captivity. Psalm 137:1–2 says, "By the rivers of Babylon, there we sat down, yea, we wept, when we remembered Zion. We hanged our harps upon the willows in the midst thereof." They just sobbed out their souls there, and that became a religious function. Actually, God had never given them fast days; He gave seven *feast* days. It was their own idea to fast. They had set aside days of fasting and days of weeping and mourning during their captivity, and they continued it after the Captivity, but God was not blessing them. A certain amount of prosperity had come; many of them were building their homes and were getting very comfortable, even affluent. Yet they were weeping and mourning, and they said, "We've been doing this but God hasn't blessed us." The question here is of the right and wrong of a ritual.

This is an important question for us because we are seeing today a recrudescence of ritualistic religion. There is a movement toward formalism, toward adopting a ritual. Formalism is always in evidence when people cease to think. When people get away from the person of Christ, they start either getting up and down or marching around—they have to start doing something. This indicates a time of spiritual decline. There was a time when people fought over the prayer book in Europe, as if that were important—whether you should stand up or sit down or kneel or just how you should pray. There are many people who want a liturgy or an elaborate ritual. There are religions that are called Christian religions that are ritualistic or liturgical. Even we nonconformists who have come out of the Reformation say that a ritual is repugnant, we despise it, we see in it evil continually, but our services have a certain amount of ritual. We open with the doxology, and everyone stands up for that. We close with a benediction, and somewhere in between there is an offering and a sermon.

God gave to the nation Israel a religion—it is the only religion He ever gave—and it was ritualistic. Is a ritual right or is a ritual wrong?—that is the question of these people. They say, "We've been fasting and weeping and wailing, and it looks pretty silly now. It's gotten very boring. After all, it is a religious rite we are going through, and we're not getting any results. God doesn't seem to be blessing us. Should we keep on doing this?"

## THREEFOLD ANSWER

Zechariah will give the people God's answer concerning this question. God doesn't come out and say that it is wrong to fast, nor does He say it is right. He doesn't answer the question directly, and yet He *answers* the question. We will find that there is actually a threefold answer to this question concerning a religious ritual. The first answer is that when the heart is right, the ritual is right (vv. 4–7). The second answer is that when the heart is wrong, the ritual is wrong (vv. 8–14). The third answer is found in chapter 8: God's purpose concerning Jerusalem is unchanged by any ritual. That will answer a great many folk today who are saying, "Let's do this or that to hasten the coming of Christ." My friend, you cannot move it up one second by anything you do. Don't you know that He is running this universe? Anything that you do is not going to interfere with His plan or program. These people thought that a ritual might have something to do with changing

God's plan. In chapter 8 God will let them know that He intends to accomplish His purpose.

## WHEN THE HEART IS RIGHT, THE RITUAL IS RIGHT

**Then came the word of the Lord of hosts unto me, saying,**

**Speak unto all the people of the land, and to the priests, saying, When ye fasted and mourned in the fifth and seventh month, even those seventy years, did ye at all fast unto me, even to me? [Zech. 7:4–5].**

"When ye fasted and mourned in the fifth and seventh month"—that would be the months of August and October. "Even those seventy years"—that is, while Israel was in captivity.

"Did ye at all fast unto me, even to me?" God says to them, "When you went through your ritual, did you do it for Me? Did you do it to honor Me and to praise Me? Or did you do it as a legalistic sort of an exercise that would build up something on the credit side which would make you acceptable to Me and cause Me to bless you?" God does not approve nor does He condemn the ritual. He inquires into their *motive.*

The people say that they have been fasting "these so many years." Oh boy, you can read between the lines there! Worshiping God had really become boring to them. And the Lord is saying to them, "If you really want to know the truth, I was bored with you also. I thought you were very boring." I think there are a lot of so-called Christian services which cause God to yawn. I think that He says, "Ho hum, there they go again, jumping through some little hoop as though they think that it will please Me."

**And when ye did eat, and when ye did drink, did not ye eat for yourselves, and drink for yourselves? [Zech. 7:6].**

God says, "You didn't fast unto Me, and when the fasting was over, you couldn't wait to get to the table. And when you were eating, did you do it unto Me?" Paul wrote to the Corinthians, "But meat commendeth us not to God: for neither, if we eat, are we the better; neither, if we eat not, are we the worse" (1 Cor. 8:8). He went on to say later, "Whether therefore ye eat, or drink, or whatsoever ye do, do all to the glory of God" (1 Cor. 10:31). If you can fast to the glory of God, go ahead and fast, but if you are doing it for

some reason other than that high motive, don't do it. Our Christian faith is not a Sunday affair. The test of the Sunday service is the life that is lived the next day. In the last part of this chapter, God is going to deal with Israel on the very specifics of their business dealings, their social contacts, and their amusements. These were the things that revealed that they did not live their lives unto the Lord at all. There is something more important than the ritual which will determine whether the ritual is right or not.

**Should ye not hear the words which the Lord hath cried by the former prophets, when Jerusalem was inhabited and in prosperity, and the cities thereof round about her, when men inhabited the south and the plain? [Zech. 7:7].**

"The south [the Negeb] and the plain." That section all the way up from Beer-sheba, whether you go to Hebron or over to the coast toward Ekron, looks like a big pasture land. It reminds me of the plains of west Texas where I lived as a boy in the days before they irrigated that land. When a wind would come through, it could really blow up a sandstorm the likes of which you had never seen or heard of before. The plains around Beer-sheba are the same kind of land. God says to the people here, "You went through all these rituals before when you were in the land, and what happened? You went into captivity because you did not obey Me, you did not listen to the voice of My prophets."

## WHEN THE HEART IS WRONG, THE RITUAL IS WRONG

Beginning with verse 8, God is going to show that a ritual is wrong if the heart is wrong. This is not another way of saying the same thing as He has just said. God will put down on the people's lives specific commandments, the commandments that have to do with a man's relationship to man as well as to God, and it will show that their hearts were not right. My friend, it is wrong to think that we can serve Christ and go through a little ritual of doing something while we are not really right with Him. What the Lord Jesus said to Simon Peter following His resurrection is truly beautiful. Do you know what I would have done if I had been in the Lord's place and had come to Simon Peter? I would have bawled him out for denying me. I would have told him what kind of fellow I thought he was. But the Lord Jesus said to him, "Do you love Me?" My friend, it is not the ritual you go through but it is the attitude of your heart that is important to Him.

To some church members, religion is a rite or a ritual or a legalistic and lifeless form, a liturgical system marked by meaningless and wearisome verbiage. There is a lot of religious garbage in our so-called conservative and evangelical churches also. There is a ceaseless quoting of tired adjectives and a jumble of pious platitudes. We so often hear people say, "We want to share our faith." My friend, most people don't have enough faith to share. It's not your faith you share about how wonderful you are or what wonderful things God did for you. You are to witness to Jesus Christ, who He is and what He did for you. In talking about salvation, people say, "Commit your life to Him." If you ask them what they mean, they say, "Yield your life to Him." Do you really think He wants your life? He says that our righteousness and even our so-called good deeds are filthy rags in His sight. God doesn't want your dirty laundry, my friend. I am afraid that we have gotten into the habit of using words that take away the real meaning of the gospel. There is another word that is surely being worn out and whose tread is really becoming thin. Love is a high word of Scripture, but it has been worn out on the freeway of present-day usage. It has been emasculated of its rich, vital, virile, and vigorous Bible meaning. It's been degraded to the level of a bumper sticker which says, "Honk if you love Jesus!" The other day I noticed that the people ahead of me were honking and going around a little car that was being driven very slowly in the fast lane of the freeway. Car after car had to detour around this man. As I came up to him, I thought that I would honk at him also, but then I saw his bumper sticker which said, "Honk if you love Jesus!" As I went around him, I gave him a hard look. If I could have had an opportunity to speak to him, I would have told him that if you love Jesus, you don't run around honking your horn. If you love Jesus you're going to live a life of obedience to Him, and you will be courteous to other people.

My point is that today there is a great deal of "churchianity" that is bland and bloodless, tasteless and colorless. It is devoid of warmth and feeling. There is no personal relationship with Christ that is meaningful and productive. One liberal pastor wrote that it made him sick to hear people talk of a personal relationship with Christ. I would surely make him sick if he would listen to me, because the thing you have to have, my friend, is a personal relationship with Christ. Your ritual and your liturgy are not worth the snap of your fingers unless you have a life that is related to Jesus Christ.

If there is no deep yearning for a life that is well pleasing to Him, if there is no stimulating desire to know Him and His Word, church membership is just like a young man falling in love with a furnished apartment and marrying an electric stove, a refrigerator, a vacuum cleaner, a garbage disposal, and a wet mop! That is just about all it amounts to. A maiden lady was asked why she had never gotten married, and she gave a very interesting answer. "I have a stove that smokes, I have a dog that growls around the house, I have a parrot that cusses, and I have a lazy cat that loafs around all day and then is out half the night—so why do I need a husband?" May I say to you, that is the kind of relationship that a great many folk have to God and to Christ. Let's stop playing church today and start loving Christ and living for Him!

I want to share with you two of the most remarkable letters that I have received in many a day. The first comes from a little town in Tennessee:

I discovered your program out of Memphis only about six months ago, just when I needed it most. Isn't that just like our lovely Lord? I am a born again Christian, only two years old. That is truly something for a 55-year-old grandmother to have to admit. My husband is a retired regular army dentist—a heart patient. We moved 33 times in 26 years before retiring on this little farm here in the boondocks. We played church. I even taught a women's Sunday school class, and my husband was a deacon. I can't speak for him, but all I had was head knowledge and very little heart knowledge. The young minister in the church where we have gone for 14 years is so liberal he thinks the belief in the virgin birth unnecessary and sees no conflict between transcendental meditation and Christianity. We stuck it out for a year and then left the church. I would be less than honest to say I don't miss a church home since I've had church homes like that.

The other letter comes from Southern California:

I am a wife and mother under 30, and I've been a Christian since I was 3½. I have often thought of writing but didn't think I had anything meaningful to say. Well, I've changed my mind. Several years ago I knew a lady quite well who was constantly pushing your program at me. This lady was a terrible housekeeper, had an unhappy husband and marriage and five unruly children. But she listened to her Christian programs from morning till night. Naturally, I associated her fanaticism with you and would not listen. During the past three years, however, I have been listening to you weekdays and sometimes on Sunday before church . . . I love the study of the Word. I get so much from your theology and your knowledge of the Scriptures. I wish that I could find a pastor locally who preached as well. Our time is so short, and I'm glad you're filling each minute with vital news of God. I wish I could have seen past that lady's disorderly life a long time ago. God bless you in your work, thou good and faithful servant.

Here was a woman who listened to all the Christian programs, who was a fanatical Christian, but who had a home and a life that were a disgrace to the cause of Christ. My friend, a ritual is no good to a person like that. Likewise, there's nothing wrong with a ritual if you are right with God and if you love Jesus Christ.

This reminds me of the little girl and the story of the three bears. The little girl's mother was having guests for dinner and she sent the little girl upstairs to go to bed early. She gave her instructions, telling her she knew how to undress, put on her pajamas, and kneel down to have her prayer. The next morning at the breakfast table, the mother asked the little girl how she did. "Just fine" was the reply.

"Did you say your prayers?"

"Well, kind of."

"What do you mean 'kind of'?" the mother asked.

The little girl explained, "Well, I got down on my knees to say that prayer I always say, and I just thought that maybe God got tired of hearing the same thing all the time, so I just crawled into bed, and I told Him the story of the three little bears."

I think God enjoyed that evening when that precious little girl already sensed that there is something wrong with a ritual when the heart is not in it. I think God listened to the story of the three bears. I wish that some church ser-

vices today could be that interesting, and I think it would get God's attention. Why do we have all these problem churches today? Why do we have all these problem Christians today? It is because we are going through a rite, we are going through a ritual, we are performing a liturgy without a heart for God Himself. Even we in fundamental churches open with the doxology, close with a benediction, with something in between, and we feel like we've been to church. Have we really? Have we been drawn to the person of Christ? Do we know Him? Do we love Him? You can go through any ritual you want to, and it will be all right if you are right with the Lord, my friend.

The importance of ritual is still a very moot question for people today. Should I go through this ceremony or should I do this or should I do that? I believe that certain ceremonies, certain rituals are important. I believe there are two sacraments in the church, and I believe they are all-important. One sacrament is baptism, and the other is the Lord's Supper. The important thing is that baptism is believer's baptism. The emphasis should be taken off the mode and put on the heart of the one being baptized: Is he born again? I personally believe in immersion, although I was raised in a church that taught otherwise. I have been both sprinkled and immersed—that way I can't miss, as you can see. My wife was Southern Baptist, she was immersed, and she still thinks that was pretty important. I like to kid her, "It will sure be embarrassing for you if you and I get to heaven and find that immersion was not the right mode. I've had the other, and you haven't." I say that facetiously, and I say it for this reason: As important as the sacraments are, they are no good unless the heart is right. Baptism is no good, my friend, unless you've turned to Jesus Christ and you have a personal relationship with Him and your sins have been forgiven. I am also afraid that the Lord's Supper is absolutely meaningless for many people—it would be better for them if they didn't go through with it. But if your heart is right, the Lord's Supper is absolutely important. It was Lange who made this statement: "God's eye of grace and our eye of faith meet in the sacraments."

Before the Captivity, God judged Jerusalem when the hearts of the people were far from Him, although they were going through the rituals. In verse 7 God said to them, "Should ye not hear the words which the LORD hath cried by the former prophets, when Jerusalem was inhabited and in prosperity, and the cities thereof round about her, when men inhabited the south and the plain?" In effect He said, "You went through the rituals before the Captivity, and I sent you into captivity. Why? The ritual had nothing to do with it. It was because your hearts were wrong, and the heart is the thing that is important."

In the last section of this chapter, God very specifically spells out those things the people were doing which alienated them from Himself. He will be dealing with that part of the Ten Commandments which have to do with man's relationship to man. The previous section of the chapter had to do with a man's relationship to God—when the heart is not rightly related to God, the ritual is wrong. In this section the ritual is wrong if the heart is wrong. By putting these commandments right down upon their lives, God will specifically reveal the things they were doing wrong.

We are not dealing with sin today as we should. If you knew me like I know myself, you would not continue to read what I have to say. But wait a minute, if I knew you like you know yourself, I don't think I'd bother to write to you. May I say to you, we are sinners. When I was a pastor in downtown Los Angeles, I knew a dear little lady who had been a Bible teacher. Whenever I would talk about the fact that we are saved sinners, she always wanted to correct me. She would say, "Dr. McGee, after we are saved, we're not sinners."

"I don't know about you, but I'm still a sinner," I would tell her.

"If your sins have been forgiven, you're not a sinner."

"No, I'm a saved sinner, I'm a forgiven sinner, but I'm still a sinner, and I will be a sinner as long as I live on this earth. 'Beloved, now are we the sons of God, and it doth not yet appear what we shall be: but we know that, when he shall appear, we shall be like him; for we shall see him as he is' (1 John 3:2). In that day when you see Vernon McGee, I won't be a sinner, but until that day, I'm a sinner."

My friend, both you and I are sinners. All of us are sinners before God, and I am delighted to know that this belief is coming back into style. I have a clipping of a prominent doctor of psychology who states that he used to go along with Freudian psychology which teaches that the reason you are such a lousy person is because your mama didn't give you the proper affection that you should have had or that maybe you weren't a breast-fed baby

and that is the reason you have gone in for promiscuous sex. My friend, what nonsense that is! Now this doctor has changed his position, and he writes, "The realities of personal guilt and sin have been glossed over as only symptoms of emotional illness or environmental conditioning for which the individual isn't considered responsible. But there is sin which cannot be subsumed under verbal artifacts such as disease, delinquency, deviancy. There is immorality. There is unethical behavior. There is wrongdoing." In other words, my friend, you and I are sinners. I have been saying that for years. Even when I studied psychology in college, I did not buy behaviorism. I frankly believe that God alone knows about humanity and about our hearts. "The heart is deceitful above all things, and desperately wicked: who can know it?" (Jer. 17:9). Only God knows it, and He alone knows it.

If we could see ourselves as God sees us, we couldn't stand ourselves. Only God could put up with us, and only God does put up with us. Oh, if we would just come to the Word of God and rest in the Word of God! God is going to be specific with them and put these commandments right down upon their lives. This is what we need to do also. I do not mean to step on your toes, but I am trying to tell you what the Word of God says. Let me illustrate my point. If all the church officers in this country would simply read the pastoral epistles (1 and 2 Timothy and Titus) to see what are God's requirements for being an officer in the church, and if they would simply follow those requirements, over one half of the church officers in this country would resign before next Sunday. The church would be better off, and I think a revival would break out in many places. When I teach those epistles, I receive less mail from my listeners than during any other period of time. Why? Because they do not like to hear what the Word of God has to say. Even some of us preachers would have to walk out of the pulpit and never enter it again if we really followed what the Word of God says.

There is little wonder that the church has the problem that it has. There is little wonder that it is filled with a bunch of babies, sucking their thumbs, crying loud and long unless they are given some attention, a rattle to play with, or maybe a yo-yo. They take some little course of instruction and think that that makes them a full-grown child of God in a few weeks. These little courses are not even an all-day sucker for the babe. During the

Second World War when there was a shortage of officers, they instituted a ninety-day course to produce second lieutenants. They were called "the wonder boys." We sure have a lot of "wonder Christians" who know nothing about the Word of God.

Again let me illustrate what I am talking about. Although I have taken as long as five years to teach the entire Bible, I feel like I am a babe as far as the Word of God is concerned. I've missed so much even teaching at that slow pace. I hesitate to teach the Book of Revelation, although I consider it the most mechanical, the most simple book in the Word of God. I approach it with fear and trembling. Yet there are pastors and teachers who have been in a church or with a group for just a short period of time who are already teaching Revelation. My friend, there are sixty-five books that come before Revelation, but prophecy is popular and made to be sensational. Sir Robert Anderson calls this "the wild utterances of prophecy mongers." Many of us are willing to settle for the better things of life when God wants us to have the best things. Oh, that we would put our lives under the spotlight of the Word of God.

**And the word of the LORD came unto Zechariah, saying [Zech. 7:8].**

Zechariah isn't just giving his opinion. He is saying to the people, "This is what God has to say, and this is God's answer to you. The ritual is wrong if the heart is wrong."

Now God is going to put the spotlight down on the people—

**Thus speaketh the LORD of hosts, saying, Execute true judgment, and shew mercy and compassions every man to his brother:**

**And oppress not the widow, nor the fatherless, the stranger, nor the poor; and let none of you imagine evil against his brother in your heart [Zech. 7:9–10].**

It will be helpful for us to take a close look at the last of the Ten Commandments. The first four commandments have to do with a man's relationship to God. The next commandment is a bridge and has to do with man's relationship to his parents. There is a period in his life when that little fellow in the home looks up to his mama and papa; they are actually God to him, and that is the way God intended it to be. The reason children are to obey their parents when they're growing up is so that later on they will be able to obey the Lord Jesus. Now

notice the last five commandments: "Thou shalt not kill. Thou shalt not commit adultery. Thou shalt not steal. Thou shalt not bear false witness against thy neighbour. Thou shalt not covet thy neighbour's house, thou shalt not covet thy neighbour's wife, nor his manservant, nor his maidservant, nor his ox, nor his ass, nor any thing that is thy neighbour's" (Exod. 20:13–17). You are not to covet his Cadillac nor the lovely home that he lives in—you are not to covet these things at all.

Notice how we can put these commandments right down upon our lives. "Thus, speaketh the LORD of hosts, saying, Execute true judgment"—don't bear false witness. "And shew mercy and compassions every man to his brother"—you are not to steal, not to lie, not to covet. "And oppress not the widow, nor the fatherless, the stranger, nor the poor"—oh boy, this is getting right down where we live. "Let none of you imagine evil against his brother in your heart." The Lord Jesus brought all the commandments up to a higher plane, although He only cited two commandments as illustrations. But He said that if you are angry with your brother, you are guilty of murder.

God is saying that although Israel went through the rituals, you ought to have met them on Sunday, Monday, Tuesday, Wednesday, Thursday, and Friday! On Friday night they started through the rituals again, and they would weep and mourn and fast and bring sacrifices. In the Book of Malachi God says to them, "You say that those sacrifices made you sick. You ought to have been in My position—they *nauseated* Me."

**But they refused to hearken, and pulled away the shoulder, and stopped their ears, that they should not hear [Zech. 7:11].**

The people did not want to hear what God wanted them to hear, and there are people today in the same position.

They "pulled away the shoulder"—how vivid this is! When I was a little fellow in southern Oklahoma, the little country school put on a program. I think I was in about the fifth grade, and my class was sitting down front. I was causing some kind of disturbance (I don't know why—I was such a good boy!), and my father, who was sitting in the back, walked down and touched me on the shoulder. I turned and pulled that shoulder away. Oh, what a brat I was to do a thing like that! My dad took me by the hand, led me out the side door, and he said, "Son, I'm going to give you a whipping." That wasn't anything new, but he went on to say, "I'm not going to give it to you because you were making a disturbance. I'm going to give it to you because you pulled away from me when I put my hand on your shoulder. You were disobedient." Then for the next few minutes he impressed upon me that I wasn't to do that sort of thing.

God says of Israel, "I touched them on the shoulder, and they pulled away the shoulder." There are many people in our churches today whom God is touching on the shoulder and saying, "Wait a minute. Don't do that. Don't live that kind of life." They pull away their shoulder, they stop their ears, and they don't want to hear what God has to say.

I was baby-sitting my little grandson out in the yard when he did something he shouldn't have done. He got into my flower bed and was ruining one of my camellias. I told him to get out, but he looked at me and said, "I'm not going to get out." (He takes after his grandmother quite a bit, as you can see!) He started back in, and I put my hand on his shoulder to stop him. He did that same little thing—he pulled away. It reminded me of another little boy about sixty-five years ago. I knew what my dad had done, and since I'm his grandfather, I took him and turned him across my knee, and I gave him quite a little lesson. My daughter applauded me for it and said, "I thought you had him so spoiled that you'd never correct him."

"But they refused to hearken, and pulled away the shoulder, and stopped their ears, that they should not hear." This is what these spoiled brats who had come down from Beth-el had been doing; in fact, the whole nation had been doing it. The reason Israel had gone into captivity was not because they didn't have light. God had put His hand on their shoulder, the prophets had spoken to them, but they "stopped their ears, that they should not hear." In other words, they turned their backs on God. They had broken the commandments which relate to God, and they were guilty before Him.

Going through a religious ritual will not do you a bit of good if your heart is not right, my friend. Until you get your life straightened out, there is no use becoming religious. Actually, that will only make you a member of the crowd the Lord Jesus called hypocrites. Have you ever noticed that He never called a believer a hypocrite? In the Bible, you'll never find a real believer called a hypocrite. It is those who pretend, those who have religion, those who have, as the Lord Jesus said,

washed the outside of the cup while the inside is still putrid, who are called hypocrites (see Matt. 23:25–26). This was the problem with the people of Israel. God simply put down on their lives the Ten Commandments, beginning with the commandments which relate to man. How were they acting in their business and social and home lives? When He did this, it really showed them up, and it showed the reason why God had not heard and answered their prayers.

**Yea, they made their hearts as an adamant stone, lest they should hear the law, and the words which the Lord of hosts hath sent in his spirit by the former prophets: therefore came a great wrath from the Lord of hosts [Zech. 7:12].**

"Therefore came a great wrath from the Lord of hosts." The destruction of Jerusalem by Nebuchadnezzar and the carrying away of these people into Babylon was a sad thing, a tragic thing, an awful thing. They were religious, they were going through a ritual, but their hearts were far from God, and they were a disgrace to Him.

**Therefore it is come to pass, that as he cried, and they would not hear; so they cried, and I would not hear, saith the Lord of hosts [Zech. 7:13].**

God says to these people, "I cried to you, and I pled with you, but you would not listen to Me." Then when they got into trouble, they said, "We don't want to go into captivity. We'll come back to You." And God now says, "I didn't hear you." There are a lot of prayers today that God doesn't hear. I get a little weary of this sentimental rot that is shown on our television screens. In these weepy sob stories, some reprobate—either man or woman—lives any kind of life he wants, but when his little child gets sick, he goes in and kneels by the bed to plead with God for the life of the child! I don't think God hears that prayer, my friend. I'll be honest with you: you've got to get right with God yourself before you are going to get anywhere with Him by praying. God makes it clear that the other is nothing in the world but religious rot, and it will not get you anywhere at all.

**But I scattered them with a whirlwind among all the nations whom they knew not. Thus the land was desolate after them, that no man passed through nor returned: for they laid the pleasant land desolate [Zech. 7:14].**

I want you to note that God says that He made the pleasant land desolate. He not only judged the people but also the land. Many people go to that land today and are greatly disappointed because they've heard that it is the land of milk and honey. It was that at one time; it was like the Garden of Eden. But I think people are trying to kid themselves when they say today, "Oh, isn't this a beautiful land!" My friend, it is rocky, it is dry, it is a most desolate place. If you can find anything pretty on the way down from Jerusalem to Jericho and the Dead Sea, I wish that you would point it out to me. It is as bad as the desert in eastern California and in Arizona. It is really a desolate place, and there are very few beautiful spots in that land. It *was* the pleasant land, but it's the desolate land today.

One of the proofs that prophecy is not being fulfilled today is the fact that the land has not been restored. I know that the Jews have moved back there and have become a nation, but they have been in trouble ever since. At the time I am writing this, I have just heard from a friend who has recently returned from there. He tells me that taxes in Israel are higher than in any place in the world. Are you going to call that "the promised land," and are you going to hold God responsible for that? I don't think He has returned the people back to that land at the present time. My friend also reported to me that a great many of the people who are there now want to leave the land. What is that going to do to these Bible teachers who are trying to date everything in prophecy from the beginning of the modern nation of Israel? My friend, Israel is still a desolate land today, but it's going to become the pleasant land again someday.

# CHAPTER 8

**THEME:** *God's purpose concerning Jerusalem unchanged by any ritual*

Chapter 8 is God's third explanation to the people concerning their question: We have gone through the ritual and the liturgy—why hasn't God blessed us? His first answer was that, when the heart is right, the ritual is all right. His second answer was that, when the heart is wrong, the ritual is wrong. In other words, the ritual doesn't have anything to do with it; it is the heart that is important. Some expositors call chapter 8 the positive answer to this question, with chapter 7 being the negative aspect of the answer. I want to say to you, the answer in chapter 8 is positively positive: God's purpose concerning Jerusalem is unchanged by any ritual. Whether you go through a ritual or you don't go through it, you are not going to change God's plan and purpose. Thank God for that. Thank God that He will carry through His plan and His purpose.

Five words occur in this chapter which are very important. In fact, you can hang the meaning of this chapter on these words.

1. First is the expression, "LORD of hosts." Dr. Merrill Unger gives the interpretation of this expression as "LORD of armies," and that probably is a more literal translation. "The LORD of hosts" or "the LORD of armies" occurs eighteen times in this chapter. Apparently, He is very important in this chapter—"the LORD of hosts."

2. *Jerusalem* occurs six times, and *Zion* occurs twice. Jerusalem is a geographical city located in Israel, over in the Middle East today. It never has changed; it is still the same place. When God says Jerusalem, He means Jerusalem. He does not mean London or Washington, D.C., or Rome or Los Angeles or any other place. When He says Jerusalem, God means Jerusalem.

3. The word *jealous* occurs three times.

4. The word *remnant* occurs twice. Remember that it was only a remnant from all twelve tribes that returned to the land—they did not return from only the two southern tribes. There were very few, even from Judah, who came back. Approximately sixty thousand returned to that land.

5. The final expression, "Thus saith the LORD," occurs ten times. When God keeps repeating that, do you know what it means? It means "thus saith *the* LORD"—not Vernon McGee, not any man, but it is God who is saying this. I do not speak or write in order to

be popular today. I would change my tactics quite a bit if I wanted to do that. I'm attempting to teach the Word of God, and if your toes get stepped on, God is the one who is stepping on them. I'm simply reading what the Word of God has to say. The reason that a book like Zechariah is not being taught today is that people do not like to have their toes stepped on. Yet I am thankful for and amazed at the number of people who are hearing the Word of God. It's a glorious day in which to live, unlike the day in which I began my ministry.

Some commentators feel that chapter 8 puts the Ten Commandments down on the people of Israel even more than chapter 7 did. I do not feel that that is accurate. My feeling is that the last part of chapter 7 put the Ten Commandments down on them, and they were weighed in the balances and were found wanting—they did not measure up to God's standard at all. Then in chapter 8, especially in the first eight verses, we find that God's ultimate purpose is not changed concerning His people—the nation Israel, the land, and Jerusalem. At the present moment, God is not fulfilling any prophecy concerning Israel. He is dealing today with the church; He is calling out a body of believers in the church. And the church and Israel are entirely two separate entities. When God will get through calling out the church, I do not know. It's not geared to any man's calendar at all. It's on God's calendar, but He has never let any of us see it. God's Word doesn't tell us when He will take the church out of this earth, but when He does, He will turn to the people of Israel again. These prophecies here in chapter 8 are simply saying that their return to the land in Zechariah's day was very small but that it is an adumbration, a little miniature picture, of a return to the land that is coming in the future.

**Again the word of the LORD of hosts came to me, saying,**

**Thus saith the LORD of hosts; I was jealous for Zion with great jealousy, and I was jealous for her with great fury [Zech. 8:1–2].**

When God says that He is jealous, it is not the same as man's jealousy, but He does have the same thing in mind. I feel sorry for any woman who makes the statement, "My husband is not jealous of me." If it is true, it means that her husband does not love her. I don't know about you, but I'm jealous of my wife. I married her for myself because I love her. I don't intend to share her with anybody

else, and I will not—that's for sure. I'm jealous of her. God says that concerning Israel, and He says it to the church today. If you think that you can live for the world and the flesh and the Devil and then serve God on Sunday, you are wrong. You won't make it, my friend. If you are His child and try to do that, He will judge you. If you do that and live in that, it means that you're not God's child because He is jealous of those who are His own. He has told us concerning sin in our lives, "For if we would judge ourselves, we should not be judged" (1 Cor. 11:31). And we are also told, "If we confess our sins, he is faithful and just to forgive us our sins, and to cleanse us from all unrighteousness" (1 John 1:9). Sin has to be confessed. You cannot have fellowship with Him and have sin in your life, Christian friend.

**Thus saith the LORD; I am returned unto Zion, and will dwell in the midst of Jerusalem: and Jerusalem shall be called a city of truth; and the mountain of the LORD of hosts the holy mountain [Zech. 8:3].**

This prophecy was not fulfilled then, which was obvious to those people. Rather, this looks to the future. It has not been fulfilled since then, and it's not being fulfilled today. God makes it clear that He will return to Zion, and He makes it clear that He is going to dwell in the midst of Jerusalem.

"And Jerusalem shall be called a city of truth." Today it is a city where there are more religions than you can imagine! Every Christian organization has built something there, and there are all kinds of cults and "isms" there. It is not the city of truth today.

"And the mountain of the LORD of hosts the holy mountain." I have never seen anything there that I thought you could call holy. It's just not holy today, my friend. It will be holy when He gets back there, but He is not back there yet. This prophecy looks to the future.

"Thus saith the LORD; I am returned unto Zion, and will dwell in the midst of Jerusalem: and Jerusalem shall be called a city of truth." Earlier, Isaiah had made it very clear that Jerusalem is to become the capital of the earth. In the second chapter of his prophecy, we read, "The word that Isaiah the son of Amoz saw concerning Judah and Jerusalem. And it shall come to pass in the last days, that the mountain of the LORD'S house shall be established in the top of the mountains, and shall be exalted above the hills; and all nations shall flow unto it" (Isa. 2:1–2). Zechariah is here looking on toward the last days and is encouraging the people. They have returned to the land, and God has blessed them to a certain degree, but this is a miniature of what is going to come in the future. There is a glorious day in the future which does not depend upon a ritual or a liturgy or a ceremony or jumping through some little hoop and thinking that that will please God. God says that it is the heart which will have to be changed, and He says that He is going to change these people's hearts. The Word of God will go forth from Jerusalem, and it will be called a city of truth. Isaiah goes on to say in his prophecy, "And many people shall go and say, Come ye, and let us go up to the mountain of the LORD, to the house of the God of Jacob; and he will teach us of his ways, and we will walk in his paths: for out of Zion shall go forth the law, and the word of the LORD from Jerusalem. And he shall judge among the nations, and shall rebuke many people: and they shall beat their swords into plowshares, and their spears into pruninghooks: nation shall not lift up sword against nation, neither shall they learn war any more" (Isa. 2:3–4). But we have not come to that day yet—we had better keep our atom bombs dry and ready for use. You never know in this mean, big, bad world when you will need things like that. Yet there is coming a day when "Jerusalem shall be called a city of truth; and the mountain [or, kingdom] of the LORD of hosts the holy mountain." In other words, Zechariah is speaking of the establishment of the millennial kingdom which is yet in the future.

**Thus saith the LORD of hosts; There shall yet old men and old women dwell in the streets of Jerusalem, and every man with his staff in his hand for very age [Zech. 8:4].**

Jerusalem will be a place where old people can live. People will not have to go to retirement centers or to senior citizens' cities. I want to say something here that I know is not very popular today. These senior citizens' places of retirement are painted to be very delightful places. I have been to several of them, and I may have to move to one before it is all over, but frankly, I do not think they are very healthful. My wife and I stop at a certain one every now and then to eat lunch because they have good food which is reasonably priced. I tell my wife—and she agrees with me—that it makes me feel very, very downcast to go there and see nothing but old gray heads

around. It will be nice that in Jerusalem they will not have to have a retirement center. In the Millennium they are going to improve on the method which we have today. It will be a place for old people where they will be safe and welcome and where they will enjoy living.

**And the streets of the city shall be full of boys and girls playing in the streets thereof [Zech. 8:5].**

This means they will not have automobiles, and we will get rid of the smog and the pollution. There are not going to be any cars, and the streets of Jerusalem will be playgrounds for the boys and girls. Jerusalem will be a place for old people and for young people, boys and girls. I think it's nice for grandma and grandpa to see the little grandchildren every now and then. They don't want them for too long, though. When the little ones get tired, they become ornery like their grandmother, and that makes it a little difficult for grandfather, and so he likes to send them home after awhile! But it is wonderful when they can mingle. It's good for the little folk to have a grandma and a grandpa to put their arms around them and tell them how much they are loved. Children need all the love they can get in this world. This is a beautiful picture here—a picture of old age and childhood in the Millennium.

At that future time, Jerusalem will be the capital of the earth, Jesus will be reigning there, and the church will be out yonder in space, dwelling in the New Jerusalem. Someone will say, "I thought that the church would be with Christ." Yes, Scripture assures us that the church will be with Him; therefore, I think He is going to commute every day. In the Millennium, there will not be all the tie-up on the freeways that we have today. I do not think it will take Him more than a couple of seconds—maybe not even that long—to commute between the New Jerusalem in space and the city of Jerusalem, the capital of the earth.

**Thus saith the LORD of hosts; If it be marvellous in the eyes of the remnant of this people in these days, should it also be marvellous in mine eyes? saith the LORD of hosts [Zech. 8:6].**

When the delegation came down to Jerusalem from Beth-el, they were greatly impressed. The temple was being rebuilt, many of the people had built their homes, and there was an air of prosperity in Jerusalem. They said, "My, it does look like God is really moving here." And God says, "You don't see what I see in the future. You think that this is something wonderful, but this is nothing compared to what it is going to be like in the future."

Notice again how often the words, "the LORD of hosts" or "the LORD of armies," occur—

**Thus saith the LORD of hosts; Behold, I will save my people from the east country, and from the west country [Zech. 8:7].**

This is quite interesting. "The east country" is the place from which the remnant had returned. A great many come out of Yemen even in our day, and I am told that there are still great numbers of Jews in the Orient. God says, "I will bring My people from the east country and from the west country." Where is "the west country"? My nation is part of it, I think. When I take a plane from Jerusalem, it flies out toward the west and just keeps going west until I finally get back to Los Angeles. The Jews will be leaving this country someday. Just think what New York City will become. It will practically become a ghost town because there are more Jews there than there are in Israel today. God is going to bring His people back to the land of Israel. He is telling the people of Zechariah's day, "If you of the remnant think that what you see is wonderful, think of what I see out yonder in the future."

**And I will bring them, and they shall dwell in the midst of Jerusalem: and they shall be my people, and I will be their God, in truth and in righteousness [Zech. 8:8].**

The Jews are not His people now. Somebody asks me, "Do you believe that the Jews are God's chosen people?" I probably shock them a little when I say, "No, I don't think so." God's chosen people today are the church. Peter writes, ". . . ye are a chosen generation, a royal priesthood, an holy nation, a peculiar people . . ." (1 Pet. 2:9). What is Peter talking about? The church—that is, he is talking about the body of believers in which both Jew and Gentile have been brought together and made one in Christ. The only real brotherhood that there can be in this world today is in the church of Jesus Christ. Someday the church will be removed from the earth, and then God will take His chosen people, the Jews, and return them to their land.

We have already seen in Zechariah's visions that God will cleanse these people. They need cleansing just as we in the church do. The church is a blood-bought, blood-washed people. Why? Because we are sinners. We are saved sinners right now, but we are still sinners. One of these days, I am going to be a real saint. I am a saint now by name, but my life doesn't always look saintly. But one of these days, I am going to be like Christ, and that will be a glorious day. The people of Israel are going to be transformed also. God says, "They shall be my people." When? In that day when they go back to Jerusalem. They are not in the city of Jerusalem today. I have been through the old city of Jerusalem, and it is filled with Arabs. The Arabs are the ones who are living there even at the present time.

"And I will be their God, in truth and in righteousness." They are not back there in truth today. They still deny the Lord Jesus Christ as their Messiah; they do *not* accept Him. I am amazed how little reference there is to God in that land today; in fact, there is practically nil. The leaders of Israel say less about God than anybody else. I heard an Arab leader say, "If Allah wills it." He didn't seem to be ashamed of his concept of God, but Israel doesn't mention her God today. They are not boasting of Him at all. However, in the kingdom age God "will be their God, in truth and in righteousness." And "righteousness" means that things are going to be made right.

In verses 9–19, we see that God expects the delegation newly come from Babylon to hear the prophets, Haggai and Zechariah, in view of the perspective of the glorious future. Also, these people are to keep the commandments. Just because they didn't come back with the remnant does not mean that they are excused from the commandments. They are to listen to Haggai and Zechariah.

**Thus saith the LORD of hosts; Let your hands be strong, ye that hear in these days these words by the mouth of the prophets, which were in the day that the foundation of the house of the LORD of hosts was laid, that the temple might be built [Zech. 8:9].**

"The prophets" are Haggai and Zechariah. They are the ones encouraging the people to build the temple. They are encouraging these newcomers to help with the building of the temple, and they did help, by the way.

**For before these days there was no hire for man, nor any hire for beast; neither was there any peace to him that went out or came in because of the affliction:**

for I set all men every one against his neighbour [Zech. 8:10].

"For before these days there was no hire for man, nor any hire for beast." In other words, unemployment was a real factor in the economics of the country at that time.

"Neither was there any peace to him that went out or came in because of the affliction: for I set all men every one against his neighbour." In my nation today, we have practically forgotten God. There are very few in public life today who make any reference to Him except to ridicule Him. God is pretty well left out; yet we are wondering why we are having all this trouble with the different groups which we call "minority groups." Not only are there the racial divisions, but also there are social divisions, economic divisions, and geographic divisions. There has never been a time when there has been so much talk like: "Let's get together. Let's stand together as a nation. Let's do this as one people." We get a great deal of that kind of talk from our leaders. They encourage us to do this and to do that in order to accommodate this minority group and that minority group. And yet we get farther and farther apart. Do you know why? Because we have left God out. God told Israel, "You're not having peace, and there are divisions among you." Certainly there are all kinds of divisions among us—it is almost warfare that is taking place. There is turmoil and violence on every hand. Every politician who runs for office thinks that he's got the solution to it. The problem is that he *doesn't* have the solution. And I want to say to you, *I* don't have the solution, but the Word of God says, "There is no peace, saith my God, to the wicked" (Isa. 57:21). The answer is that we need to get God back in the picture today. We need to turn to Him.

**But now I will not be unto the residue of this people as in the former days, saith the LORD of hosts [Zech. 8:11].**

God says to them, "I don't intend to bless you as you are now or as you were before I sent you into captivity, but I am going to bless you."

**For the seed shall be prosperous; the vine shall give her fruit, and the ground shall give her increase, and the heavens shall give their dew; and I will cause the remnant of this people to possess all these things [Zech. 8:12].**

God brought prosperity to that nation for a period of time. The great judgment came upon them, of course, when they rejected the Messiah—Titus the Roman destroyed Jerusalem and scattered the people throughout the Roman Empire. They have never returned from that dispersion, according to the Word of God.

**And it shall come to pass, that as ye were a curse among the heathen, O house of Judah, and house of Israel; so will I save you, and ye shall be a blessing: fear not, but let your hands be strong [Zech. 8:13].**

At the time that I am writing this, there are still fingers being pointed at Israel. Practically all of Europe has deserted them because of the oil situation, and they are finding out that they are not worth more than a gallon of gasoline. It is a tragic situation. They have become a curse among the nations. Anti-Semitism is growing again throughout the world. God says, "When I save them and bring them back to that land, they are going to be a blessing to the world." I believe that the nation of Israel will be the priests for the gentile nations of the earth. They will stand between God and the gentile nations during the Millennium.

**For thus saith the LORD of hosts; As I thought to punish you, when your fathers provoked me to wrath, saith the LORD of hosts, and I repented not [Zech. 8:14].**

"For thus saith the LORD of hosts." Notice how often this phrase occurs. "As I thought to punish you, when your fathers provoked me to wrath, saith the LORD of hosts, and I repented not." In other words, God says, "I didn't change my mind about that."

In this section we are looking forward to the time when God is going to make Jerusalem the capital of this earth. God says that nothing can detour or detract Him from His purpose. He intends to do this by His marvelous infinite grace. In writing to the Romans Paul says, "For he saith to Moses, I will have mercy on whom I will have mercy, and I will have compassion on whom I will have compassion. So then it is not of him that willeth, nor of him that runneth, but of God that sheweth mercy" (Rom. 9:15–16). Moses went to God and prayed about whether or not God would destroy the children of Israel. God said in effect, "I'm going to hear you, Moses, but I'm not going to hear you because you are *Moses*. I will show mercy and grace to those whom I will show mercy and grace. Therefore, it is not him that runneth—to him that trots through a ritual or goes to a lot of church services—it is the Lord Jesus Christ who shows mercy." My friend, we can say with the apostle Paul we are what we are by the *grace* of God.

**So again have I thought in these days to do well unto Jerusalem and to the house of Judah: fear ye not [Zech. 8:15].**

God says to these people, "It is not because you have been through the ritual or because you have omitted the ritual. Whether you do or whether you don't, I am showing *mercy* to you." But this is not the end in itself, this time of blessing is a very small thing. God looks down through the centuries and says, "The day is coming when I intend to deal again with you, and in that day I will do a glorious thing upon the earth." He is looking down to the time of the Millennium.

Now since they are going to represent God in the end times, it does not mean that they can do as they please. The grace and mercy of God extended to us does not mean that we can live any kind of life, although some people think that. Listen to what God says now—

**These are the things that ye shall do; Speak ye every man the truth to his neighbour; execute the judgment of truth and peace in your gates [Zech. 8:16].**

"These are the things that ye shall do." Have you trusted Christ as your Savior? Then you have been saved by grace and mercy. But wait a minute, He says, "If ye love me, keep my commandments" (John 14:15). If you love Him, you are going to keep His commandments. You do not keep His commandments in order to get saved, because you *have been* saved by His grace and mercy. The obedience of your life will never add anything to your salvation.

"Speak ye every man the truth to his neighbour." Ours is the day when lying is acceptable in every walk of life. Business cannot be depended upon today to tell the truth. Advertising is very inaccurate. The news media cannot be depended upon to tell the truth. The government cannot be depended upon to tell the truth, and it does not make any difference what party you are talking about. It would seem that you cannot trust men in any walk of life—not the military nor educators nor scientists. In all of these areas today, we are finding that truth has suddenly gone out of style. It is about time that boys and girls were taught in school certain moral standards, and one of them is that if you don't tell the truth, you're a liar—there is no other way around that.

"Execute the judgment of truth and peace in your gates." "The gates" were where the courts of law convened in that day. Many today have confessed that they have lied even to a grand jury, that they have lied when they were under oath!

"Execute the judgment of truth." What He is talking about here is not the *act* of judging. You and I are going to judge. Whether we judge honestly or dishonestly, whether we judge truthfully or untruthfully, we are going to judge. What He has in mind here is the *motive*. The thing that should motivate judging is truth.

**And let none of you imagine evil in your hearts against his neighbour; and love no false oath: for all these are things that I hate, saith the LORD [Zech. 8:17].**

"And let none of you imagine evil in your hearts against his neighbour." That means that you're not to covet anything that is your neighbor's.

"And love no false oath: for all these are things that I hate, saith the LORD." Actually, Zechariah is again referring to the Ten Commandments. The Ten Commandments show us some of the things which God hates. They are not given to save us but to show us the things in our lives that God hates. They are given to show us that we need to turn to Him. We have all these bumper stickers that say that God is love. That is great—God *is* love— but God also hates. You cannot love something without hating something else. If you love the truth, you're going to hate the lie. If you love your child, you'll hate a mad dog that comes into the yard to bite the child. You would kill that mad dog if you love your child. God hates certain things—I'd like to see that put up on billboards today. God hates lying. God hates covetousness. He hates a whole lot of things that the world is doing today.

**And the word of the LORD of hosts came unto me, saying [Zech. 8:18].**

Zechariah says it again—what repetition we have! God wants you to know that *He* said these things.

**Thus saith the LORD of hosts; The fast of the fourth month, and the fast of the fifth, and the fast of the seventh, and the fast of the tenth, shall be to the**

**house of Judah joy and gladness, and cheerful feasts; therefore love the truth and peace [Zech. 8:19].**

God says to them, "I never gave you any fast days. These days that you have set up to fast and to go through a nice little religious ritual, I'm going to turn them into feast days, days of rejoicing, days of love and truth and peace." These are the things that are absent in our contemporary culture and society. I wonder if it has ever occurred to anyone that if we would go back and teach the great biblical and moral values that are stated in the Word of God, it might have a tremendous effect upon our society today. Some of us believe that it would.

In effect God is saying, "I don't want you to come before Me with a long face and that pious look that you have. I want you to come before Me with joy." My friend, a lot of us are not enjoying being Christians as we should. God wants us to have a whole lot of fun. I think that the big fun center for Christians ought to be the local church. Someone says, "Oh, do you mean we ought to have a volleyball court?" No, I mean to come together and study the Word of God—that ought to be fun. And there's something wrong with you, Christian, if studying the Word of God is not fun.

**Thus saith the LORD of hosts; It shall yet come to pass, that there shall come people, and the inhabitants of many cities:**

**And the inhabitants of one city shall go to another, saying, Let us go speedily to pray before the LORD, and to seek the LORD of hosts: I will go also [Zech. 8:20–21].**

This looks to the fact that Jerusalem will become the capital of the earth—not only the political capital but also the religious capital. It looks forward to that time which we call the Millennium. "It shall yet come to pass"—this is something that is for the future.

**Yea, many people and strong nations shall come to seek the LORD of hosts in Jerusalem, and to pray before the LORD [Zech. 8:22].**

"Yea, many people and strong nations shall come to seek the LORD of hosts in Jerusalem." I take it that that does not mean Los Angeles—it means Jerusalem.

"And to pray before the LORD." Very frankly, Jerusalem is not an ideal place to go to pray; it just isn't geared for that today. Actually, you see more religion manifested there and less Christianity than any place that I know of. But it will become the center of God's government during the Millennium.

We referred earlier to the second chapter of Isaiah, and there are many other Scriptures along this line. This illustrates why it is so important to study the Book of Zechariah. A great many teachers in our day have zeroed in on the Book of Daniel. If you go to the average seminary library or to any good library, you will notice that there is volume after volume written on Daniel. Go down the shelves a little farther and see how many books you find that are written on Zechariah—there is a dearth of them. I have a friend who does not believe that there is going to be a Millennium on this earth. He doesn't believe that God will turn to Israel ever again or that He will ever turn again to Jerusalem. He believes that God is through with the people of Israel. He has written a book on Daniel, and he told me, "I have proved my point in Daniel."

I said to him, "Has it ever occurred to you that no prophecy is of any private interpretation? You do not study the Book of Daniel by itself. Why didn't you bring in a little of Zechariah?"

He looked at me rather funny and said, "I didn't need to." So I frankly said to him, "Well, if you hold the theory that God is through with Israel, you can't handle the Book of Zechariah." My friend, Zechariah makes it clear that God is not through with Jerusalem and He's not through with the nation Israel.

**Thus saith the LORD of hosts; In those days it shall come to pass, that ten men shall take hold out of all languages of the nations, even shall take hold of the skirt of him that is a Jew, saying, We will go with you: for we have heard that God is with you [Zech. 8:23].**

"In those days"—what days? This is that expression that we find again and again in Scripture. "In that day," or "in those days"—this is the Millennium that is coming. The Great Tribulation is actually the beginning of it, and it ushers in the coming of Christ and the thousand-year reign of Christ that is called the Millennium. The Millennium, in turn, ushers in Christ's eternal kingdom on this earth.

"In those days it shall come to pass, that ten men shall take hold out of all languages of the nations, even shall take hold of the skirt of him that is a Jew, saying, We will go with you:

for we have heard that God is with you." Is God through with the Jew? In the Millennium, the church will have been removed from the earth. You see, the church could not be here in a period like this. I believe that the number ten here rather suggests a whole number, that it represents the fact that all the gentile nations in that day will find Jerusalem very attractive and they will go there. Why? Because the Lord Jesus will be there, the millennial temple will be there, and it will be the place to worship God.

# CHAPTER 9

**THEME:** *First prophetic burden; The coming of Christ*

We have come to the end of the historic interlude, and we now enter the third and last major division, which I call "Prophetic Burdens." And I have divided this final section into two divisions: The first "burden" deals with the prophetic aspects which are connected with the first coming of Christ (chs. 9–11). The second "burden" deals with the prophetic aspects which are connected with the second coming of Christ (chs. 12–14).

We will see that this new division goes over the same ground that was covered in the ten visions, but it is approached from a different viewpoint. It begins with the people of Israel as they were in the days of Zechariah when they were a small, discouraged remnant attempting to rebuild the temple. God had raised up Haggai and Zechariah to encourage them to rebuild the temple. Zechariah begins with that local, contemporary scene, then moves on down into the immediate future when they would experience for a time the blessing of God. Then he moves on down through the centuries—God had a plan and purpose—to the coming of the Messiah. We shall see the two comings of the Messiah, coming first as the Savior and coming the second time as the Sovereign. His coming the first time had the cross in view; His second coming will have the crown in view.

## FIRST BURDEN—
## JUDGMENT UPON GENTILE NATIONS

In the first eight verses we read of the judgment upon the gentile nations which was accomplished by Alexander the Great—an amazing section.

In the days of Zechariah some folk could have become a little too optimistic. They could have said, "Well, this is going to be the Millennium now that we are back in the land and the temple is rebuilt." So Zechariah is telling them, "No, out in the future there is coming another world ruler." And we will see the contrast between that world ruler and the One whom God will send to the earth for His first coming. The world ruler is Alexander the Great, an arrogant, insolent, highly conceited young man but probably the most brilliant general the world has ever seen. Not only was he a tremendous military leader, but he was a great political leader as well. He had a certain charisma, and multitudes followed him.

**The burden of the word of the LORD in the land of Hadrach, and Damascus shall be the rest thereof: when the eyes of man, as of all the tribes of Israel, shall be toward the LORD [Zech. 9:1].**

"The burden of the word of the LORD." This word *burden* means judgment, a judgment of God. Alexander the Great was unwittingly God's instrument of judgment. His forces subjugated "the land of Hadrach," taking the key towns, Damascus and Hamath. Damascus was the capital of Syria and still is today. Also, it continues to cause Israel a great deal of difficulty.

The cities mentioned in verses 1–7 trace the march of Alexander's great army down into the Promised Land. It is history now; but, when it was written, it was prophecy. Its literal fulfillment makes it one of the most remarkable accounts we find in the Word of God. This is so disturbing to the liberal theologian that he attempts to move the time of the writing of Zechariah up to the time of Alexander the Great!

Alexander left Europe and crossed over into Asia Minor (modern Turkey), and he took city after city. He was a cruel and brutal man. However, we must understand that he had an army of only fifty thousand men, which in that day was rather small. Therefore, he could not leave any of his men behind to control the cities that he conquered. He had to either destroy the cities or so weaken them that they could not attack him from the rear. He obliterated many of these cities mentioned here. It is interesting to note that Alexander, brilliant though he was, died of alcoholism at the age of thirty-two, almost the same age as the Lord Jesus when He died. In the Book of Daniel the Graeco-Macedonian Empire is represented as the third great world power of Daniel 2, the panther of Daniel 7, and the rough goat of Daniel 8 (the goat is the Graeco-Macedonian Empire, and the horn is Alexander the Great himself).

Here Zechariah presents to us the march of Alexander. I am looking at the works of Flavius Josephus in which are recorded the Jewish wars, including details of the march of Alexander as he came with his army into the land of Palestine.

**And Hamath also shall border thereby; Tyrus, and Zidon, though it be very wise [Zech. 9:2].**

"Tyrus, and Zidon" were wealthy commercial cities of that day.

**And Tyrus did build herself a strong hold, and heaped up silver as the dust, and fine gold as the mire of the streets.**

**Behold, the Lord will cast her out, and he will smite her power in the sea; and she shall be devoured with fire [Zech. 9:3–4].**

Everyone felt that Tyre was impregnable as it was situated out on its island fortress. The inhabitants were Phoenicians, a seagoing people who had developed a great commercial nation and had accumulated a great deal of wealth. Alexander besieged it for seven months and finally conquered it by scraping the ruins of the old city into the sea to build a causeway out to the island city. Today we can see all of this, and I have pictures which I have taken that reveal how that prophecy was literally fulfilled.

After taking Tyre, Alexander moved down into the Philistine country.

**Ashkelon shall see it, and fear; Gaza also shall see it, and be very sorrowful, and Ekron; for her expectation shall be ashamed; and the king shall perish from Gaza, and Ashkelon shall not be inhabited [Zech. 9:5].**

I have been in this area and have pictures of ruins of the old temple of Dagon. That area

has been returned to the nation Israel today. At Ashdod they have built an artificial harbor, and they have built apartment after apartment there. Literally thousands have moved into Ashdod. Farther inland as you go down the coast you will find Ashkelon. It is a thriving city today, but it is not in the same location as the old Ashkelon. The original Ashkelon was right on the seacoast, and the ruins are still there today. It is more or less a park now, a beautiful area, but it is not inhabited. It is not a city anymore. It is interesting to see how God's Word was literally fulfilled. Alexander the Great destroyed these cities and broke the power of the Philistines.

**And a bastard shall dwell in Ashdod, and I will cut off the pride of the Philistines [Zech. 9:6].**

"A bastard shall dwell in Ashdod." It does not say that Ashdod will not be inhabited; it just says that there won't be a very high class of people living there. And Ashdod *is* inhabited today.

"I will cut off the pride of the Philistines." Alexander the Great brought the Philistine nation to an end. They never again emerged as a nation.

**And I will take away his blood out of his mouth, and his abominations from between his teeth: but he that remaineth, even he, shall be for our God, and he shall be as a governor in Judah, and Ekron as a Jebusite [Zech. 9:7].**

"And I will take away his blood out of his mouth, and his abominations from between his teeth" refers to the polluted food and idolatrous sacrifices they engaged in. God would take away the idolatry of Philistia. However, when Christ returns they will be converted to the God of Israel—"he shall be for our God," says Zechariah. Philistia will become a part of the people of God and will inherit the blessings of Israel.

This man Alexander the Great destroyed everything that was ahead of him. If he had to wait around a few months to capture a city, like he did at Tyre, he didn't mind doing it, because he would not leave any strong fortress behind him anywhere.

Now he is approaching Jerusalem. What will he do to Jerusalem? Well, we have a very strange statement here—

**And I will encamp about mine house because of the army, because of him that passeth by, and because of him**

that returneth: and no oppressor shall pass through them any more: for now have I seen with mine eyes [Zech. 9:8].

"I will encamp about mine house," refers, I believe, to that little temple they were building. God said that He was going to protect it from Alexander the Great. God said it, and Zechariah had the nerve to record it because he could depend upon the accuracy of God's Word and believed that it would be fulfilled.

Well, was it fulfilled? Let me give you the record of the historian Flavius Josephus. According to him, the high priest in Jerusalem had a vision in which he was instructed to go out and meet the conqueror who was coming, and so he waited for the coming of Alexander the Great.

And when he understood that he was not far from the city, he went out in procession with the priests and the multitude of the citizens. The procession was venerable, and the manner of it different from that of other nations . . . and when the Phoenicians and the Chaldeans that followed him, thought they should have liberty to plunder the city, and torment the high priest to death, which the king's displeasure fairly promised them, the very reverse of it happened; for Alexander, when he saw the multitude at a distance, in white garments, while the priests stood clothed in fine linen, and the high priest in purple and scarlet clothing, with his mitre on his head, having the golden plate whereon the name of God was engraved, he approached by himself, and adored that name, and first saluted the high priest. The Jews also did altogether, with one voice, salute Alexander, and encompass him about; whereupon the kings of Syria and the rest were surprised at what Alexander had done, and supposed him disordered in his mind. However, Parmenio alone went up to him, and asked him how it came to pass that, when all others adored him, he should adore the high priest of the Jews? To whom he replied, "I did not adore him, but that God who hath honoured him with his high-priesthood; for I saw this very person in a dream, in this very habit, when I was at Dios in Macedonia, who, when I was considering with myself, how I might obtain the dominion of Asia, exhorted me to make no delay, but boldly to pass over the sea thither, for that he

would conduct my army, and would give me the dominion over the Persians; whence it is, that having seen no other in that habit, and now seeing this person in it, and remembering that vision, and the exhortation which I had in my dream, I believe that I bring this army under the divine conduct, and shall therewith conquer Darius, and destroy the power of the Persians, and that all things will succeed according to what is in my own mind. (Flavius Josephus, *The Antiquities of the Jews* Book XI, chap. VIII, p. 350).

Then he entered into the city of Jerusalem and worshiped God in the temple. Another tradition says that not only did the high priest approach him arrayed in his priestly garments, but that he also brought along the Book of Daniel and showed Alexander the prophecy concerning him. This so moved him that he went into the city and offered sacrifices and worshiped in the temple. The fact that he did not destroy Jerusalem makes Zechariah's prophecy very remarkable, and it doesn't contradict the fact that Alexander, though the most brilliant general of the day, was still highly cruel, brutal, and arrogant.

## THE COMING KING

The next verse is one of the most remarkable in the Scriptures. Generally we hear a message from it on Palm Sunday because it has to do with the so-called triumphal entry of Christ into Jerusalem.

Rejoice greatly, O daughter of Zion; shout, O daughter of Jerusalem: behold, thy King cometh unto thee: he is just, and having salvation; lowly, and riding upon an ass, and upon a colt the foal of an ass [Zech. 9:9].

I am going to spend quite a bit of time on this verse because it is a key verse. It is the hinge on which the prophecy turns. I hope you will carefully follow this through with me. May I point out first that *salvation* would be better translated as "victory" or "deliverance." He is the King who is bringing victory or who is coming to deliver.

Although all the gospel writers record the so-called triumphal entry of the Lord Jesus, only Matthew quotes from Zechariah. The Gospel of John gives almost a running commentary on the prophecy of Zechariah. For example, instead of saying "Rejoice," he says, "Fear," which is actually a good, sound interpretation. Now notice Matthew's record:

"And when they drew nigh unto Jerusalem, and were come to Bethphage, unto the mount of Olives, then sent Jesus two disciples, Saying unto them, Go into the village over against you, and straightway ye shall find an ass tied, and a colt with her: loose them, and bring them unto me. And if any man say aught unto you, ye shall say, The Lord hath need of them, and straightway he will send them. All this was done, that it might be fulfilled which was spoken by the prophet, saying, Tell ye the daughter of Sion, Behold, thy King cometh unto thee, meek, and sitting upon an ass, and a colt the foal of an ass" (Matt. 21:1–5).

Notice that Matthew says, "Tell ye the daughter of Sion" instead of "Rejoice greatly, O daughter of Zion" as Zechariah has it. Also note that Matthew leaves out "he is just, and having salvation" (a better translation would be "he is just and having *deliverance* or *victory*"). Matthew quoted only a definite portion of verse 9. Why did he leave out certain things and include others? Well, that which Matthew quoted—and also which John interpreted—has to do with the first coming of Christ. The remainder of the verse has to do with the second coming of Christ.

The Lord Jesus came riding on the little animal of peace and came bringing peace at His first coming. He will come riding upon the white horse, the animal of warfare, at His second coming. But He is going to bring peace. How? By putting down all unrighteousness. You see, the world has had over nineteen hundred years to decide what it is going to do with Jesus Christ, and He is pretty much rejected in our day. So God is going to make it very clear that the Son is coming back to *reign*. He came the first time to die for our redemption, but the next time He will come to reign.

This was something that I'm sure puzzled Zechariah (it is still puzzling some folk today), but Simon Peter made it clear that not only Zechariah but the other prophets were puzzled. Peter wrote, "Of which salvation the prophets have inquired and searched diligently, who prophesied of the grace that should come unto you: Searching what, or what manner of time the Spirit of Christ which was in them did signify, when it testified beforehand the sufferings of Christ, and the glory that should follow" (1 Pet. 1:10–11). When the first and second comings of Christ were tied together in one passage, the prophets "inquired and searched diligently," but they were unable to make the distinction. They just had to write it down as the Spirit

gave it to them although they themselves didn't understand it. Simon Peter by the Spirit of God makes the distinction. Christ came one time to suffer, to bring redemption; He will come the next time in glory to reign upon this earth. And Matthew by the Spirit was able to make that separation so that in his quotation of verse 9 he used only that portion of the verse which speaks of the first coming of Christ.

Frankly, I think that the church has misnamed it the *triumphal* entry. I was in San Francisco the night Gen. Douglas MacArthur arrived from Japan a great while after World War II had ended. He was whisked from the airport to the hotel in what they thought would be a private or at least semi-private procession. Well, instead there was a public demonstration that snarled traffic. I was leaving on the train that night to return to Los Angeles. A friend had warned me, "You'd better get down to the train if you intend to catch it, and you ought to leave now." So I took my suitcase down to the train station and checked it. Then I went back into San Francisco to eat dinner. When I came out of the restaurant, I had never seen such a crowd in all my life! No traffic could move. I tried to get back to the railroad station by taxi, but the taxi couldn't move. I finally got out and walked from the civic center to the railroad station. It was the only way I could have gotten there on time. The next day the same thing was repeated when MacArthur arrived in New York. *That* was a triumphal entry.

By comparison, the so-called triumphal entry of Christ into Jerusalem would seem very poor indeed. It was actually a parade of poverty. It was no ticker tape parade but was the coming in of a very poor man with a few very poor followers. If there had been a Roman in Jerusalem that day who had stepped out of a building at that moment, he would have asked someone what was going on. If they had said, "This is the triumphal entry of Jesus," he would have laughed. He would have said, "You think this is a triumphal entry? You should have been in Rome when Caesar came back from Gaul. There was a parade that lasted over three days as he brought back the booty and the captives." To a Roman, this entry of Jesus would have looked mighty poor and beggarly.

Well, Christ did not intend that it be triumphal. When He rode into Jerusalem, it actually marked a crisis in His life, a life that was filled with crises. It marked a change of tactics. Heretofore He had slipped into the city silently. He had entered unobtrusively. He had sought the shadows. There was no publicity. He was always withdrawing from the crowd, not courting attention. It was foretold that He would not cry or strive or cause His voice to be heard in the street (see Isa. 42:2). He entered by the Sheep Gate and would attempt to come in eluding the mob, evading the crowd. Even after He had performed a miracle, He put a hush-hush on it. Now there is an about-face in His approach. It would seem to us that there is an inconsistency here if we did not recognize this as a crisis point. Now He comes out into the open. He enters publicly. He demands attention. He requires a decision. He forces the issue. For one brief moment the nation must consider Him as their King and their Messiah. The Pharisees were accurate when they said, ". . . the world is gone after him" (John 12:19). Jerusalem was stirred when He came in. In spite of His pushing Himself to the front, He was meek. Matthew lifts that out of Zechariah's text which says that He was just and lowly. I disagree with several good Bible commentators who assume that His riding on the little animal, the donkey, denotes His meekness. Far from it. That little donkey was an animal that kings rode upon. You see, the horse was the animal of warfare and is so used in Scripture. The little donkey was the animal that kings rode upon when they were at peace. It was a royal animal. In Judges 10:3–4 we see a judge who had thirty sons, and he got all of them donkeys to ride upon. In this day it would be like buying them each a Jaguar sports car. Riding a donkey did not denote meekness. The thought in Zechariah's prophecy was that in spite of the fact that the coming Messiah would be riding in as the King, He would still be meek and lowly.

In this incident there is another false impression that needs to be corrected. There is the assumption that there was *one* so-called triumphal entry. Bible teachers in Great Britain and Europe have largely recognized that Christ entered Jerusalem on *three* consecutive days. He came the first time on the Sabbath day, which was Saturday. Also He came in on Sunday and again on Monday. He came in the first time on the Sabbath day as the *King*. Notice Mark's record: "And Jesus entered into Jerusalem, and into the temple: and when he had looked round about upon all things, and now the eventide was come, he went out unto Bethany with the twelve" (Mark 11:11). He just looked around. The money changers were not there—it was the Sabbath; He just looked

around and left. His very action was one of rejection. He came in as *King* on Palm Saturday, if you please. Then, when He came in on Sunday, the first day of the week, the money changers were in the temple, and He cleansed the temple at that time. "And Jesus went into the temple of God, and cast out all them that sold and bought in the temple, and overthrew the tables of the moneychangers, and the seats of them that sold doves" (Matt. 21:12). This is quite remarkable. It is the only action that He ever performed as *Priest* when he was here upon this earth. The writer to the Hebrews makes it clear that He was not a priest here on earth: "For if he were on earth, he should not be a priest, seeing that there are priests that offer gifts according to the law" (Heb. 8:4). No priest dared to cleanse the temple, but *He* did when He came back to the temple on Palm Sunday.

Then He came back in on Monday, and on the way He cursed the fig tree, then—". . . when he was come into the temple, the chief priests and the elders of the people came unto him as he was teaching, and said, By what authority doest thou these things? and who gave thee this authority?" (Matt. 21:23). Notice that on this day He was *teaching;* He was speaking for God. He was God's *Prophet.* At that time He met every objection; He silenced the enemy. His was the voice of God. He said, ". . . he that hath seen me hath seen the Father . . ." (John 14:9), and certainly it was equally as true that he that *heard* Him had heard the Father.

So you see that Christ's entry into Jerusalem was not one but three times. His final appearance before the nation was in His threefold office of Prophet, Priest, and King.

We have seen that His entry was not meant to be a triumphal entry, but was it an entry at all? No, actually He was making an exit not an entrance. He was not arranging to take up residence in Jerusalem and reign as King. He sent His disciples ahead to arrange for a room to eat the Passover, but He didn't send them in to rent an apartment. He was not preparing for His reign; He was preparing for His passion, His suffering, His death, and His passing through the portals of death.

His entrance into Jerusalem was not a one-way ticket but a round-trip ticket, and it was part of the program which led to His death, His resurrection, His ascension, His intercession, His coming at the Rapture, and finally His coming as King. The fact of the matter is that the trail of triumph cannot be confined to a ride on a little donkey from Bethany to Jerusalem. That is only a minor segment of a trip which began in eternity past—when He was the Lamb slain before the foundation of the world—and extends into eternity future. My friend, when you see it in those terms, it becomes meaningful. Without that perspective it is meaningless. The one who came out of eternity is the one who came into Jerusalem— ". . . the high and lofty One that inhabiteth eternity, whose name is Holy . . ." (Isa. 57:15). As Moses wrote, ". . . even from everlasting to everlasting, thou art God" (Ps. 90:2). That is, from the vanishing point to the vanishing point, He is God.

The church calls it a triumphal entry, but I think it is a triumphal exit. That crowd who followed Him crying "Hosanna" did not think of Him as the Son of God, the Savior of the world. That same crowd that said "Hosanna" on one day said "Crucify Him" on the next day. One of the most expressive pictures I have ever seen, painted by an artist whose name I do not know, depicts a little donkey in the foreground chewing on a palm frond while in the background there stand three crosses. That tells the story. It wasn't a triumphal entry; it was a triumphal exit. Six months earlier He had steadfastly set His face to go to Jerusalem to die. He moved by a prearranged program, an avowed arrangement, a definite decision. Nothing was accidental. When He rode into Jerusalem, He had come out of eternity, and He was going into eternity. It was an exit rather than an entry. The cross and the empty tomb were not His final destination. Neither was the ascension the end of His story. He could say to the dying thief, ". . . To-day shalt thou be with me in paradise" (Luke 23:43).

When He returns He will come as King. As we look into the future, we can sing,

Crown Him with many crowns,
  The Lamb upon His throne;
Hark! how the heavenly anthem drowns
  All music but its own!
Awake, my soul, and sing
  Of Him who died for thee;
And hail Him as thy matchless King
  Through all eternity.
—Matthew Bridges

As we leave verse 9, I hope you see the importance of it. It is the hinge of the door on which the interpretation of this section of the book swings.

Now we have seen something of the march of Alexander the Great as he crossed what is now modern Turkey and destroyed those great Greek cities. (It was almost a shame to destroy some of those lovely things, but he did it, of course, because he was moving swiftly to world rulership.) Then he made the turn to go down across the land bridge which is the land of Israel. He destroyed the great cities which were in Assyria in the north, then we saw him as he entered into the Promised Land, first the land of the Philistines, then he came to Jerusalem. Everyone expected him to destroy Jerusalem because the high priest there had refused to pay the tribute money to Alexander which he had been paying to Media-Persia. The high priest felt obligated to keep the treaty with Media-Persia. Naturally this infuriated Alexander, and he was intending to destroy Jerusalem. But he did not destroy it because of the vision he had had of the high priest.

Zechariah presents a contrast here. The triumphal entry of Alexander into Jerusalem was something to behold. Then here comes Jesus riding into Jerusalem on a little donkey. And Jesus is not coming to destroy the world; He is coming to *save* the world. He is not coming to form a great kingdom and attract a great following that would minister to Him. "For even the Son of man came not to be ministered unto, but to minister, and to give his life a ransom for many" (Mark 10:45).

As we have said, when Jesus came into Jerusalem as Israel's King, it was not a triumphal entry; it was an exit. He was getting ready to leave. But He will be coming back. The world will have had a long time to decide what they are going to do with Jesus. They have to make a decision concerning Him.

He is coming someday to bring peace to the world. So He says—

**And I will cut off the chariot from Ephraim, and the horse from Jerusalem, and the battle bow shall be cut off: and he shall speak peace unto the heathen: and his dominion shall be from sea even to sea, and from the river even to the ends of the earth [Zech. 9:10].**

"Ephraim" represents the northern kingdom, "Jerusalem" the southern kingdom—one went into Assyrian captivity, the other into Babylonian captivity. However, they are one people and will be reunited under Christ's rule.

"I will cut off the chariot . . . the horse . . . the battle bow." These stand for the whole class of offensive weapons. The Jews won't need their armaments anymore.

"He shall speak peace unto the heathen [nations]." This earth, my friend, will never have peace until Jesus Christ comes and establishes peace. I always shiver when I hear each succeeding president of my nation talk about bringing peace to the world. None of them has been willing to recognize that he is not able to bring peace to the world. *Only* Jesus Christ can bring world peace—it is just as simple as that. For this reason we have armed soldiers throughout the world today, and we have fought two terrible wars since World War II—in Korea and Vietnam. I agree that we should stay prepared, but we are not going to bring peace to the earth by war. Only Jesus Christ can bring peace by putting down unrighteousness, and that will not take place until He comes again to this earth. Instead of trying to make peace throughout the world, we just need to keep prepared to protect ourselves because this is a big, bad world that we live in today. We talk "brotherhood" among nations, which is not scriptural at all. The only brotherhood that can be formed today is in the body of Christ among those who have been redeemed by the blood of Christ.

I know it is not popular to talk like this, but I have discovered that the doctor gives me medication and puts me on the operating table and keeps cutting and cutting on me to get rid of the cancer. It is not fun, but the only way in the world that I can have health is by that route. And the only way the world is going to have peace is through Jesus Christ, whether the world likes it or not. There is no alternative.

**As for thee also, by the blood of thy covenant I have sent forth thy prisoners out of the pit wherein is not water [Zech. 9:11].**

"As for thee" refers to the godly remnant in Israel which was suffering. The best I can do is to make a spiritual interpretation of this verse. The only deliverance for mankind is through the blood of the covenant, and that blood of the covenant is the blood of the New Testament, the blood of Christ. Man talks about his freedom and his liberty. Man in this world today does not recognize that he is actually a prisoner. He is "sold under sin" (Rom. 7:14) He is a slave to sin. In a day in which we hear so much about liberty, I receive hundreds of letters from former drug addicts who have been delivered. How? Only by the blood of Christ, my friend, only by turning to Him for deliverance. He alone can deliver prisoners from "the pit wherein is no water."

**Turn you to the strong hold, ye prisoners of hope: even to day do I declare that I will render double unto thee;**

**When I have bent Judah for me, filled the bow with Ephraim, and raised up thy sons, O Zion, against thy sons, O Greece, and made thee as the sword of a mighty man [Zech. 9:12–13].**

"When I have bent Judah for me." We are looking now toward the Millennium, to the time when Christ will reign. All the nations of the world are going to bow to Him. My friend, when Christ comes again, *that* is going to be a triumphal entry.

**And the LORD shall be seen over them, and his arrow shall go forth as the lightning: and the Lord GOD shall blow the trumpet, and shall go with whirlwinds of the south.**

**The LORD of hosts shall defend them; and they shall devour, and subdue with sling stones; and they shall drink, and make a noise as through wine; and they shall be filled like bowls, and as the corners of the altar [Zech. 9:14–15].**

I would say that this is a picture of how it is going to be *until* Christ comes. Man is not going to bring the Millennium to this earth!

**And the LORD their God shall save them in that day as the flock of his people: for they shall be as the stones of a crown, lifted up as an ensign upon his land [Zech. 9:16].**

"In that day" is an expression which Zechariah will use a great deal in chapter 12. "That day" is the Day of the Lord, which will begin after the church makes its exit from the earth by way of the Rapture. It ushers in the Great Tribulation Period, and it ends, we believe, after the seven years of tribulation when the Lord Jesus Christ will return to establish His kingdom here upon this earth. Then upon this earth will be the thousand-year reign of Christ.

"They shall be as the stones of a crown" or like the glittering jewels of a crown. The prophet Malachi tells us that the Lord is going to make up His jewels in that day: "Then they that feared the LORD spake often one to another: and the LORD hearkened, and heard it, and a book of remembrance was written before him for them that feared the LORD, and that thought upon his name" (Mal. 3:16). This refers to the godly of Israel and of the gentile nations. The church, the ". . . pearl of great price . . ." (Matt. 13:46), is not included, by the way. Christ paid a tremendous price for that pearl.

**For how great is his goodness, and how great is his beauty! corn shall make the young men cheerful, and new wine the maids [Zech. 9:17].**

"How great is his goodness, and how great is his beauty!" This is the goodness of the One who is coming in contrast to Alexander who was not known for his goodness—he was cruel, brutal, and filled with pride. The Lord Jesus was meek and lowly, and He is great in His goodness and in His beauty. There was ". . . no beauty that we should desire Him" (Isa. 53:2) when He came the first time. The cross was a horrible thing. But when He comes again—oh, how beautiful He will be! We speak of beautiful people in our day, but He is the beautiful one, and He puts His beauty on those who are His own.

"Corn shall make the young men cheerful, and new wine the maids." New wine is not intoxicating—it hasn't had a chance to ferment. So what we have here is a reference to abundance of food. There will be no famine or energy shortage during Jesus' reign upon this earth. It will be a joyous time of plenty; that will be one of the characteristics of His kingdom.

# CHAPTER 10

**THEME:** *Judah and Israel to be scattered and regathered*

We have seen in chapter 9 the future deliverance of both the northern and southern kingdoms of Israel and how God is going to use them in the future when they will serve, actually, as priests to the gentile nations of the world. There are those who interpret chapter 10 as a continuation of chapter 9. Some very fine Bible expositors feel, however, that only the first verse belongs to chapter 9, and I accept that view.

The remainder of the chapter is separate, which we will see as we go along.

**Ask ye of the LORD rain in the time of the latter rain; so the LORD shall make bright clouds, and give them showers of rain, to every one grass in the field [Zech. 10:1].**

This first verse, as we have seen, belongs to chapter 9. It continues the description of the prosperous conditions which will prevail during the millennial reign of Christ on the earth.

The rain mentioned in this verse means exactly what it says—literal rain. You see, God has promised Israel, who are an earthly people, *earthly* blessings. (To the church He has not promised earthly blessings but spiritual blessings.) The fall and spring rainfall is a very important part of Israel's temporal blessings and would make that land like the Garden of Eden. In our day it looks almost the opposite because judgment has come upon the land as well as upon the people of Israel. The thing that denotes God's judgment is the withholding of rain. I would say that Israel's greatest problem next to the Arab problem is the water problem—how to get more water. Well, the best and the easiest thing for them would be to turn to God and experience the physical blessings which would come through rain. But they have not returned to God, and the rain has not returned.

I have been told that the latter rains have returned to the land. They are getting more rainfall, that is true; but if you are there in late summer, you will see that the groves they have set out need rain and need it badly. There is not nearly enough water to irrigate the amount of land that needs to be irrigated. The latter rains, the spring rains, come during March and April. Although they do get some rain at that time, it is not nearly the amount of rain indicated in the verse before us. During the Millennium God will send them rain so that there will be plenty of grass for the stock and other animals. There will be plenty of rain for the crops and the trees which they would like to set out. The interpretation of this verse pertains to physical rainfall.

However, rain is also a symbol of spiritual refreshment, and it is used that way in other passages of Scripture. For instance, Joel 2:28

has that connotation. That which physical rain does for the land, the spiritual rain, or the pouring out of the Holy Spirit, does for the spiritual lives of these people. Both the prophecy in Joel and the prophecy here in Zechariah have definite reference to the Millennium of the future. There will be a pouring out of the Spirit of God in that day. Therefore, the rain has a twofold meaning.

## JUDGMENT FOR ISRAEL'S DECEPTION

Now beginning with verse 2 we have a turning back again to the subject of judgment. Although God intends to strengthen them for the last days and intends to bring them into the Millennium, there are certain things which are radically wrong in their midst. He immediately puts his finger down on what was wrong in Israel. The thing which was really causing the trouble in the nation was idolatry.

**For the idols have spoken vanity, and the diviners have seen a lie, and have told false dreams; they comfort in vain: therefore they went their way as a flock, they were troubled, because there was no shepherd [Zech. 10:2].**

"The idols have spoken vanity." The word for "idols" is actually *teraphim*. They were small household oracular divinities, which are spoken of elsewhere in Scripture. Merrill F. Unger, who is quite a Hebrew scholar, has written several books in the area of demonism in our day and also in the past. I am indebted to him for this bit of information which modern archaeology has uncovered regarding the nature of the teraphim. At an ancient site which is right near Nineveh, called Nuzu, excavations were made between 1925 and 1941. They found tablets which illustrate customs which went as far back as the patriarchs. You will recall that Jacob had trouble with his uncle Laban, and he left with his two wives, Leah and Rachel. He was glad to leave, and Rachel actually took the teraphim from the home of Laban and concealed them. Now, with the Nuzu evidence, we know that the possession of those household gods implied leadership of the family. When she stole those gods, she was getting for her husband the right to her father's property, and the theft was a very serious matter. This explains why Laban was so wrought up over it. He certainly didn't want Jacob to get his estate. He felt that Jacob had gotten more than he should have already.

The second medium of deception was used by the diviners, and the verse before us says that "the diviners have seen a lie" or envisioned a falsehood. Divination is an occult, heathen imitation of biblical prophecy. The Devil has always imitated that which was biblical; he never gets far from the Bible. And every one of the cults and "isms" here in Southern California, including Satan worship, uses the Bible. That is the Devil's method of deception.

It is quite interesting that just this morning there have come in the mail box six different communications from cults and "isms", and each of them has some weird interpretation of the Word of God. You see, every one of them uses the Bible.

The Hebrew word for divination means "to cut or divide." It had to do with the taking of a sacrificial animal, cutting it open, and looking at its liver—the form of the liver and the way that it was shaped. This ancient form of divination was called hepatoscopy. (It sounds like a medical term, and it seems to me that the doctors used a word like that in reference to my gall bladder surgery, but I don't think they were looking at my liver for purposes of divination!) The liver was considered to be the seat of the victim's life, and the shape of the liver supposedly told them the shape of things to come. We have reference to this procedure in Ezekiel 21:21: "For the king of Babylon stood at the parting of the way, at the head of the two ways, to use divination: he made his arrows bright, he consulted with images, he looked in the liver." The Babylonians had diviners (Balaam was a diviner), the Philistines had them, and the false prophets of Israel used their methods. Now God, through Zechariah, is saying that "the diviners have seen a lie." It was demonic inspiration; they were not getting their information from God. God had put down a law forbidding His people to use divination; it was entirely satanic. All the prophets warned against this sort of thing.

Many years ago in downtown Los Angeles, I spoke on the subject of demonology in a Sunday evening series, and we averaged about three thousand people in attendance at each service. Some of my preacher friends kidded me about it. One friend with whom I played golf said, "McGee, you will do anything to get a crowd! Now you are speaking on demonology." Well, I spoke on that subject because I felt it was needed in that day.

However, the pendulum of the clock has swung over to the other side, and now there is too much discussion in the church regarding demons and Satan. It is true that there is a manifestation of demonism in our contemporary society, but we need to keep our attention centered upon the Lord Jesus Christ rather than upon Satan.

I am convinced that Satan is out working on the front where the Word of God goes out. And I suspect that the many physical problems that I have had in recent years may be because God has let Satan get through to me. I am sure that Satan would like to stop the teaching of the Word of God today—that would naturally be his priority. No wonder so many of our so-called Bible churches have gone off on an ego trip, playing up some novel program that brings the crowds. My friend, the only thing that God is going to honor permanently is His Word. And during these days I have attempted to keep my eyes centered on the person of Christ. What is the reason for all the froth and even false teaching which is invading our conservative churches today? I think the explanation is that the Devil is out to deceive Christians. And he can destroy the reputation of almost anyone. That is the reason we need the protection of God in this hour as we have never needed His protection before. And we need to keep our eyes upon Jesus Christ. If we stay very close to Him, we will be very far away from the Devil and demons.

Instead of centering our attention on the casting out of demons, we need to think instead of *casting in Christ*. That's the important thing. You will remember that the Lord told a parable about a man who had a demon. The demon went out of the man, and the man got all swept and garnished. Although he was rid of the demon, he had nothing to fill up the empty apartment. Well, when this demon got tired of walking around, he remembered this fellow, and he went back into him because he was an easy mark. Also, he brought some of his demon friends with him so that the last state of the man was worse than the first. So, you see, it is not enough to cast out a demon, the life must then be filled with Christ.

You see, when Israel rejected God's messengers and God's message, they failed in their obedience to God. As a result, they turned to all sorts of satanic deception. God says to them through Zechariah, "The idols have spoken vanity, and the diviners have seen a lie, and have told false dreams; they comfort in vain: therefore they went their way as a flock, they were troubled, because there was no shepherd." Israel no longer had a true shepherd to lead them.

My friend, you and I are living in a day when there is a manifestation again of demonic power. A great many folk are judging individuals and judging organizations by the apparent success they are having. It never occurs to them that we are to *test* the spirits. The apostle John warned: "Beloved, believe not every spirit, but try the spirits whether they are of God: because many false prophets are gone out into the world" (1 John 4:1). The need of the hour is not for more youth programs or more new methods in our churches. What we need today are true shepherds who will feed the sheep the Word of God.

**Mine anger was kindled against the shepherds, and I punished the goats: for the LORD of hosts hath visited his flock the house of Judah, and hath made them as his goodly horse in the battle [Zech. 10:3].**

"Mine anger was kindled against the shepherds." These shepherds were false prophets in Israel who had turned to the occult, had turned to the supernatural which was satanic.

"And I punished the goats." God is calling the leaders of Israel "the goats." When I was a young fellow I worked in an abattoir, a place where they killed cattle, sheep, and pigs for the butcher shop. It was a very bloody business, and during the first two days I worked there, I had to go outside occasionally to recover from it. But the thing that seemed to me more cruel than anything was the use of an old goat with a bell around his neck. He was called a Judas goat because he would lead sheep to the slaughter. Instead of the workmen driving the sheep, they would start this old goat up the ramp, and all the sheep would follow him. Then the goat would step aside while the sheep went to the slaughter. Now when the Lord said, "I punish the goats," He is talking about the leaders in Israel. They should have been leading their people into the Word of God, to the place where they could have peace with God, peace in their own hearts. Instead, they were false prophets, giving them false comfort, and actually leading them away from God. God said that He was angry with them.

"For the LORD of hosts hath visited his flock the house of Judah, and hath made them as his goodly horse in the battle." God, you see, intends to strengthen them against their enemies.

## PROPHECY OF THE MESSIAH

Then He looks on to the future when there *will* come the Messiah, and I believe He is clearly identified in this next verse.

> **Out of him came forth the corner, out of him the nail, out of him the battle bow, out of him every oppressor together [Zech. 10:4].**

"Out of him"—out of whom? Out of the One who *is coming*—the tense is future. It means that from Him shall come forth the corner, the cornerstone. As you know, a cornerstone is placed in a building structure where two walls meet at a ninety-degree angle. The square cornerstone is fitted in there. This is a marvelous picture of Christ as the cornerstone because, you see, there was the wall of Judah and the wall of the ten tribes. The message is that Christ will be the cornerstone to unite them and permanently bring them back together.

However, the cornerstone has a wider meaning than this. It gives us another very wonderful picture. Notice what the prophet Isaiah has written about it: "Therefore thus saith the Lord GOD, Behold, I lay in Zion for a foundation a stone, a tried stone, a precious corner stone, a sure foundation: he that believeth shall not make haste" (Isa. 28:16). Peter quotes this in his epistle and makes it clear that the cornerstone is Christ. "Wherefore also it is contained in the scripture, Behold, I lay in Sion a chief corner stone, elect, precious: and he that believeth on him shall not be confounded" (1 Pet. 2:6). Notice that Peter used the word *confounded*, while Isaiah had used the expression "not make haste," meaning "did not get in a hurry, did not get confused." They both are expressing the same thought. My friend, in these days in which we live, what is the answer to the occult, to the satanic? Well, in the first place, we should have nothing to do with it. We are not to meddle with it. Secondly, we should stay close to the Word of God and close to the person of Christ. Here in Zechariah note that immediately after He has warned against the occult, He introduces the cornerstone.

We need not imagine that we are too intelligent to be deceived by the occult. The Greeks in their day were a very intelligent people; yet they made constant trips to Delphi. The way that the priests interpreted the blowing of the leaves in that cave at Delphi would put the Greek army out to sea or would take a man off his throne. It would change the course of history. If you think they were just following a superstition, I think you are wrong. It is my conviction that the Devil was using it to direct the Greek Empire. He was having a heyday. Frankly, it concerns me to hear of our leaders in Washington consulting fortune-tellers and others who deal in the occult. I am afraid that we are getting our guidance from the wrong source.

What should we do? Turn to the person of Christ. He is the cornerstone. He is the foundation on which we can rest. "Unto you therefore which believe he is precious: but unto them which be disobedient, the stone which the builders disallowed, the same is made the head of the corner, And a stone of stumbling, and a rock of offence, even to them which stumble at the word, being disobedient: whereunto also they were appointed" (1 Pet. 2:7–8). It is my observation that the people who go into the cults have heard the Word of God and have heard the gospel, but they have turned their backs on it. When an individual rejects the truth, God sends them ". . . strong delusion, that they should believe a lie" (2 Thess. 2:11). That principle is still in operation today.

The Lord Jesus made a very startling statement when He called Himself a stone: ". . . whosoever shall fall on this stone shall be broken: but on whomsoever it shall fall, it will grind him to powder" (Matt. 21:44). What happens to you is determined by your relationship to the stone. You can fall on it, or it will fall on you. You can accept and receive Jesus Christ. You can come to Him as a sinner and fall upon Him. You can trust Him, rest upon Him. This means that you are broken in that you no longer trust yourself; you trust Him. But if you reject Him, He will become the stone that will fall on you and grind you to powder. In other words, He is going to be your judge.

Daniel mentioned this in chapter 2 of his prophecy. He was given a vision of the times at the end of the gentile world rule when a stone cut out without hands (representing the Lord Jesus Christ) will smite the earth— every government and everyone in rebellion against God. He is *that* kind of a stone.

Now not only does Zechariah call Him the cornerstone, but also "out of him the *nail*." This is an interesting word. A nail is, of course, a stake or a tent peg used to fasten a tent securely to the ground. In the case of the wilderness tabernacle, the Israelites had tent pins which they used to keep the tabernacle from taking off with the wind. They had to nail it down with pins driven deeply into the desert sand. And here Christ is pictured as the nail or the tent pin. He is the one who holds things down, and we need to allow Him to hold us to the faith. What a picture this is of Him!

Also, that nail or peg was used in another way. A tent pin was used inside a tent to hang things on. Women could hang their jewelry on it and men could hang their valuables on it. This also pictures Christ as the one on whom the Father will hang all His glory—"And the key of the house of David will I lay upon his shoulder; so he shall open, and none shall shut; and he shall shut, and none shall open. And I will fasten him as a nail in a sure place; and he shall be for a glorious throne to his father's house" (Isa. 22:22–23). Although this prophecy was directed to Eliakim, Revelation 3:7 makes it clear that the final fulfillment will be in Christ Himself. He is the one who will become a throne of honor to His Father's house, and only on Him will rest all the glory of His Father's house. To gain Him is to gain that which is more precious than anything in the world.

Notice that Zechariah presents Him not only as the cornerstone and the nail, but he also presents Him as the "battle bow," meaning the warrior and conqueror. He is the one who is going to come to this earth to put down all unrighteousness, and the armies of heaven are going to follow Him. He is going to put down "every oppressor"—the false leaders, both religious and political, whom He has called "goats."

**And they shall be as mighty men, which tread down their enemies in the mire of the streets in the battle: and they shall fight, because the LORD is with them, and the riders on horses shall be confounded [Zech. 10:5].**

This refers to the very dark period of the Great Tribulation. God is going to undertake for His people and enable them to go through it, because at the close of that period Christ will come.

Down through the years when they have rejected Christ, of course there has been no hope for them. When Titus the Roman was outside the gates of Jerusalem in A.D. 70, the walls came down, the city was destroyed, and the people of Israel were scattered throughout the world. It is the current belief of several outstanding expositors that the nation Israel is not now in that land permanently. I'm not sure but what the accurate interpretation of the Word of God is that they will again be put out of the land of Israel and that subsequently *God Himself* will return them to the land. When God brings them back to the land, they won't have any trouble with the Arabs. Their neighbors will not try to exterminate them. Rather, when the Lord regathers them, they will be there permanently and will be a blessing to the world.

**And I will strengthen the house of Judah, and I will save the house of Joseph, and I will bring them again to place them; for I have mercy upon them: and they shall be as though I had not cast them off: for I am the LORD their God, and will hear them [Zech. 10:6].**

"I will strengthen the house of Judah, and I will save the house of Joseph." The "house of Judah" is, of course, the southern kingdom and "the house of Joseph", the northern kingdom. That is, the whole nation will share in the joyful victory and blessing of the coming kingdom.

Even in the time of Zechariah, the small remnant that had returned was made up of all the tribes. We know this because a delegation had come down from Beth-el, and that was one of the capitals of the northern kingdom.

Now why does God protect them during this interval which we call the intertestamental period? Well, His answer is, "For I have mercy upon them." We can ask ourselves the same question: How did you and I get saved? It was "Not by works of righteousness which we have done, but according to his mercy . . ." (Titus 3:5). God is rich in mercy. He had to have a lot of it to save me—maybe He didn't need that much to save you. But He is *rich* in mercy; He has an abundance of it. And it is on the basis of His mercy that He preserved them during that period. After the last book of the Old Testament, Malachi, had been written, God went off the air, and He did not broadcast for about four hundred years. During that silent interval the people of Israel probably suffered more than at any other time (except perhaps during the time of Hitler and the Nazi regime in Germany). Although God was silent during that four-hundred-year period between Malachi in the Old Testament and Matthew in the New Testament, we have a very good record of what transpired because of the prophecies given to Daniel and Zechariah, as we are seeing here.

**And they of Ephraim shall be like a mighty man, and their heart shall re-**

joice as through wine: yea, their children shall see it, and be glad; their heart shall rejoice in the LORD [Zech. 10:7].

Now just in case you think that the ten tribes got lost, "Ephraim" is one of the names which God gave to the ten northern tribes of Israel. If you want to check on that, turn to Hosea. Notice how tenderly God said, "How shall I give thee up, Ephraim? how shall I deliver thee, Israel? . . ." (Hos. 11:8). Well God *didn't* give them up. They are not lost. It is by His grace that they have been preserved as a nation.

"They of Ephraim shall be like a mighty man." The records we have of the intertestamental period give the most thrilling accounts of how the Israelites stood against the Syrian conqueror, Antiochus Epiphanes. His persecution of these people was frightful; yet they were enabled to stand. "They of Ephraim shall be like a mighty man."

"And their heart shall rejoice as through wine." It was a very difficult period, and they were far from God many times, but also there were periods when they rejoiced in the Lord.

I will hiss for them, and gather them; for I have redeemed them: and they shall increase as they have increased [Zech. 10:8].

It is estimated that there must have been around twelve million people in the land of Israel by the time Jerusalem was destroyed by the Romans under Titus in A.D. 70, which is a far greater Jewish population than is there in our day.

God says, "I will hiss for them." The word *hiss* doesn't quite express what He is saying. Have you ever been sitting in an auditorium when you hear somewhere behind you a "Pssst!"? You turn around to see who is trying to get your attention. That is what "hiss" means. Merrill Unger gives a translation with a new twist, and it is a good one. He says that it means, "I will whistle for them." I like that. God says, "I'll whistle for them and gather them."

We know that this has not yet been fulfilled, because in the very next verse it speaks of their being scattered again among the nations. Although there was a great population in Israel at the time of Christ, the Lord Jesus made it very clear that Jerusalem would be destroyed after He had gone. He was crucified somewhere around A.D. 30, and in A.D. 70 Jerusalem was destroyed, and the Jews were scattered throughout the Roman Empire.

And I will sow them among the people: and they shall remember me in far countries; and they shall live with their children, and turn again [Zech. 10:9].

"And turn again." Turn to what? To the land? No, to God. The Jews who have returned to the land in our day have not returned to God. I am in agreement with the Bible expositors who believe that the Jews will be put out of the land of Israel again and will be scattered among the nations. We do know that there is some disillusionment in the land and that many of the Jews want to leave and go back to the countries they came from. I believe the day will come when the Jews will again leave Israel.

I will bring them again also out of the land of Egypt, and gather them out of Assyria; and I will bring them into the land of Gilead and Lebanon; and place shall not be found for them [Zech. 10:10].

"I will bring them again also out of the land of Egypt." There are very few Jews in the land of Egypt in our day. I believe this refers to future dispersion.

"I will bring them into the land of Gilead and Lebanon." If you read the Book of Joshua very carefully and notice where the borders were placed, you will see that Lebanon was part of the Promised Land. Some expositors believe that when the Bible speaks of the land of milk and honey, it has reference to the southern part of the Lebanese coast, which even today is a very rich and fertile area. Well, I don't agree with that because we know that at the time the spies searched out the land, the rainfall was adequate, the hills were wooded, and there was fruit in abundance. Actually, a few years of withholding rainfall can make a desert. But Lebanon was part of the Promised Land. God certainly has not given Lebanon to the Jews in our day, but someday it will be theirs. If you are Lebanese, you won't like that, but don't worry, because it will not happen until the Millennium—and everything will be so wonderful at that time that you won't mind at all.

And he shall pass through the sea with affliction, and shall smite the waves in the sea, and all the deeps of the river shall dry up: and the pride of Assyria shall be brought down, and the sceptre of Egypt shall depart away.

And I will strengthen them in the LORD; and they shall walk up and down in his name, saith the LORD [Zech. 10:11–12].

Notice that the language reflects God's miraculous deliverance of Israel from Egypt the first time He returned them to the Promised Land. But when He regathers them in the future, it will be by even greater miracles—so much so that Jeremiah wrote: "Therefore, behold, the days come, saith the LORD, that they shall no more say, The LORD liveth, which brought up the children of Israel out of the land of Egypt; But, The LORD liveth, which brought up and which led the seed of the house of Israel out of the north country, and from all countries whither I had driven them; and they shall dwell in their own land" (Jer. 23:7–8). In other words, when God regathers them in the future, it will be by a so much greater miracle that they will forget the miraculous deliverance from Egypt.

My friend, I do not think that the wildest interpretation of prophecy in our day would dare say that the present return of Israel to Palestine is a fulfillment of this Scripture. It could not possibly be. It clearly refers to a future regathering.

# CHAPTER 11

*THEME: Jesus rejected as King at His first coming; the Good Shepherd—Christ; the foolish Shepherd—Antichrist*

This chapter concludes the division of "burdens" which hinge on the first coming of Christ. It brings us to the Roman period. This, as the Maccabean period before it, was a very dark period.

We have seen that Zechariah is the prophet of *hope*—many expositors call attention to this. And his name actually means "the Lord remembers." It is quite interesting that his is one of the last voices to speak for God in the Old Testament. And then the New Testament opens with an angel appearing to another man by the name of Zechariah, the husband of Elisabeth who gave birth to John the Baptist, the forerunner of Christ. Again, God remembers His people.

Not only is Zechariah the prophet of hope, he is also the prophet of *truth*. Being a prophet of hope is not enough, because it could be a false hope such as the false prophets were giving the people. Temporarily, there is to be great blessing materially and otherwise, but out of the west are coming other conquerors—first Alexander the Great, then the Roman armies. It will mean great suffering for the people of Israel.

This chapter also presents the Good Shepherd of His people, the Good Shepherd who will give His life for the sheep. Then another shepherd is presented, the foolish shepherd, who will come much later. He pictures the Antichrist, the one who will shear the sheep and kill them for food.

## JUDGMENT RESULTING FROM MESSIAH'S REJECTION

Open thy doors, O Lebanon, that the fire may devour thy cedars [Zech. 11:1].

This doesn't sound very promising. This reveals that there is to be a scattering of the people of Israel even after the time of Zechariah. This was, I think, performed by the Romans.

The Romans used the same method that Alexander the Great used—they came down from the north. If you go to Lebanon today, you will see above Beirut a river which is known as the Dog River. There, right at the entrance by the sea, on the face of the mountain are inscriptions which have been labeled "The Calling Cards of the Nations of the World." Every great general of every great nation who went through there carved his name in the rock. I have looked at it, and the translation was given to me. The only one I could read for myself was the one in Greek—I finally figured out that one. All the great generals came that route because it is the beginning of what is known as the Great Rift, which moves inland and extends into North Africa. The Sea of Galilee, the Jordan River, and the Dead Sea are all part of the Great Rift. So Zechariah is describing here the advance of the conqueror who is coming into Palestine.

"That the fire may devour thy cedars." The

cedars of Lebanon were famous. Much of Solomon's temple was built of the cedars of Lebanon, as was his own palace. The cedar trees have largely disappeared today. There are very few of them left. The nicest one I saw was actually in a park right outside Jerusalem. It was a beautiful tree, well cared for. The one I saw in Beirut was a scrawny sort of tree, but it had grown up very large. The place where they would grow the best is up in the snow country. In fact, *Lebanon* means "white or snowy," taking its name from the snow covered mountains of the area. The Great Rift comes down right beside them. That was a tremendous passageway for the great world conquerors of the past—Egypt, Babylon, Media-Persia, Syria, Greece—and here Zechariah is giving, I think, the description of Rome coming down into Palestine.

**Howl, fir tree; for the cedar is fallen; because the mighty are spoiled: howl, O ye oaks of Bashan; for the forest of the vintage is come down [Zech. 11:2].**

"Howl, O ye oaks of Bashan." Bashan was an area in the northern part of Israel. There were a lot of oaks in that country—I think we call them live oaks.

**There is a voice of the howling of the shepherds; for their glory is spoiled: a voice of the roaring of young lions; for the pride of Jordan is spoiled [Zech. 11:3].**

"There is a voice of the howling of the shepherds." These are the false shepherds who had been giving the people wrong directions and a false security.

"A voice of the roaring of young lions" probably refers to the young princes.

**Thus saith the Lord my God; Feed the flock of the slaughter [Zech. 11:4].**

"Feed the flock of the slaughter." This is almost terrifying! The "flock" refers to those of the remnant who had returned to the land of Israel. But for what had they returned? Although there would be a time of blessing, the conqueror was coming, and untold suffering lay ahead.

**Whose possessors slay them, and hold themselves not guilty: and they that sell them say, Blessed be the Lord; for I am rich: and their own shepherds pity them not [Zech. 11:5].**

How accurate this prophetic picture is of that which did happen to these people when the Romans came down.

**For I will no more pity the inhabitants of the land, saith the Lord: but, lo, I will deliver the men every one into his neighbour's hand, and into the hand of his king: and they shall smite the land, and out of their hand I will not deliver them [Zech. 11:6].**

God says that He will permit this to take place because they had not only turned from Him, but they also rejected the Messiah when He came.

**And I will feed the flock of slaughter, even you, O poor of the flock. And I took unto me two staves; the one I called Beauty, and the other I called Bands; and I fed the flock [Zech. 11:7].**

"And I will feed the flock of slaughter, even you, O poor of the flock." Expositors differ in their interpretations of this. Did Zechariah actually become a shepherd during this time? Was this a parable he was giving, or did he act it out? I personally think that this is a parable in action. Several of the prophets used that method—Ezekiel certainly did. You may recall that Ezekiel locked himself in his house, dug himself out, and came up in the street outside. Here in Pasadena where I live, digging up streets is nothing new. I think that every street in this city has been dug up sometime during the past year—they may have missed one or two, but I doubt it. But in Ezekiel's day it was unusual. In fact, it would be unusual today if someone locked himself in his house and dug himself out! Well, Ezekiel did that, and he had a message when he came up out there in the street. Also he had a crowd. It was a good crowd-getter, and I am of the opinion that Zechariah used the same method.

"And I took unto me two staves." One he called *Beauty*, which means "grace or graciousness." That was the shepherd's crook, the one that he used to keep the little sheep in line. If one started to wander into a place of danger, he reached out with that crook and pulled him right back in line. The other stave he called *Bands*. The English word *Bands* is probably a good translation, because it has to do with the making of a covenant. That speaks of another staff which the shepherd carried. It was a heavy stick, not like the shepherd's crook but a heavy club. He used it to fight off wild animals and even human beings who would try to steal the sheep. So Zechariah speaks of taking two staves: Beauty and Bands, or Grace and Covenants.

"And I fed the flock." I think that Zechariah did this literally.

**Three shepherds also I cut off in one month; and my soul loathed them, and their soul also abhorred me [Zech. 11:8].**

"Three shepherds also I cut off in one month" were probably the false prophets.

**Then said I, I will not feed you: that that dieth, let it die; and that that is to be cut off, let it be cut off; and let the rest eat every one the flesh of another [Zech. 11:9].**

I believe here he is speaking against the false prophets, and he is speaking against the kinds of sacrifices the people were bringing to the Lord. We learn from Malachi that some of the people in that day were stingy; they were skinflints who didn't even like to give a tenth. They didn't like to bring their animals to sacrifice to the Lord. So if a man had an old sick cow, he would tell his boys to rush the animal up to the temple, to the altar, and get the cow killed for a sacrifice before it died a natural death. Then they would pretend they had given the Lord one of their prize cattle. Malachi's prophecy really zeroes in on the people for doing that which was phony and false. God, of course, would not accept such an offering. "That that dieth, let it die." That is, don't slaughter it hurriedly and use it. He is calling them back to honesty and to be clear-cut in their dealings.

**And I took my staff, even Beauty, and cut it asunder, that I might break my covenant which I had made with all the people [Zech. 11:10].**

"I took my staff, even Beauty, and cut it asunder." Remember that *Beauty* means "graciousness," and Zechariah is saying that he is chopping that staff to pieces, signifying that God's grace would be withdrawn. You see, when God put His people in the Promised Land, He promised to bless them and protect them from their enemies. God was dealing with the returned remnant in *grace*. Back in 10:6 God had said, "I will strengthen the house of Judah, and I will save the house of Joseph, and I will bring them again to place them; for I have mercy upon them. . . ." God was going to do this for them—not because they were worthy or because they were obedient. They were disobedient, but God was dealing with them in mercy. However, there would come a time when His mercy would be exhausted, and then He would withdraw His covenant. He would no longer deal with them in mercy; He would no longer be gracious to them.

"That I might break my covenant which I had made with all the people." What does God mean when He says that He will break His covenant? Hasn't He repeatedly told us that He will never break His covenant? Well, we need to understand the difference between a conditional and an unconditional covenant. God *never* breaks an unconditional covenant. But a conditional covenant depends upon a response from the human side. The covenant of the verse before us is conditional. God's promised protection of Israel against their enemies depended upon Israel's obedience to Him. When they disobeyed Him, He followed through by removing His protection. It is in this sense that He broke His covenant.

We have examples of this in the New Testament. For instance, God's promise, "If ye shall ask any thing in my name, I will do it" (John 14:14) is a conditional promise. Dr. Harry Ironside was sitting on a platform with a young pastor during a meeting one night. A young lady entered the meeting, and the pastor told him that she formerly had been an active leader among his members, then began to run with the world, and that this was the first time he had seen her in church in months. Dr. Ironside preached on this passage of Scripture that night. She was greatly incensed and came to see him after the meeting. "How dare you tell these people that if you ask anything in the name of Jesus, He will do it?" she asked him. Dr. Ironside answered, "Why don't you sit down and tell me about it." She told him that her father had been desperately ill some months before, and while the doctor was up in his room, she had knelt in the living room, claimed that promise, and prayed in Jesus' name for his recovery. When the doctor came down from the room, he told her that her father was dead. "Now," she said, "don't tell me that God keeps His promises!" Dr. Ironside said, "Did you read the next verse, 'If ye love me, keep my commandments'?" Then Dr. Ironside asked her what would happen if she found a check made out to someone else and tried to cash it by signing that name. She said "I would be a forger." So he referred her to this verse, "If ye love me, keep my commandments." Then he asked her, "Have you been doing that?" Instead of replying she turned red. Then he explained that what she was trying to do was the same thing as trying to cash a check made out to somebody else. We all need to recognize, friend, that obedience to Him is the evidence of our love for Him, and this promise is given to those who *love* Him.

**And it was broken in that day: and so the poor of the flock that waited upon me knew that it was the word of the LORD [Zech. 11:11].**

"So the poor of the flock that waited upon me" refers to those of the remnant who actually obeyed God and believed the Word of God.

My friend, the fundamental, primary thing for us as believers is to *believe* the Word of God. If you don't believe that the Bible is the Word of God, you are not ready for any growth in the Christian life. Belief in the Word of God has to be settled. And God will establish you in that belief as you study His Word. You may start out a little skeptical and find certain things in the Bible difficult to believe. That is the way I started, but I have now reached the place where I don't just believe the Bible is the Word of God; I *know* it is the Word of God. This is the reason I don't waste my time preaching apologetic sermons. I recognize that most such sermons are needed, and I thank the Lord for young preachers because they generally get into the apologetic field. I spent the first two or three years of my ministry proving that the Bible was true. Now I consider it a waste of time. I like the illustration used by the late Dr. Bob Shuler, who was the great Methodist preacher in downtown Los Angeles years ago. One day he said to me, "If you had a lion in a cage in your backyard, you wouldn't employ a guard to stay at the door of the cage to protect the lion from pussycats in the neighborhood. All you would need to do would be to open the door of the cage, and the lion would take care of himself." That is a great illustration, and I have attempted to follow it in my ministry. I just attempt to open the door of the Word of God and let it prove itself. It can take care of itself. I don't have to try to protect it from the pussycats in the neighborhood. I just give out the Word of God as it is.

Zechariah is saying that "the poor of the flock," the remnant of the remnant, believed it was the Word of the Lord.

## THE GOOD SHEPHERD—CHRIST

There would be coming in their line one who would be their Messiah, and the majority of the nation would reject Him. Only a very small remnant would receive Him at that time. For their rejection, the nation would be judged and scattered throughout the world. Now notice this next verse—

**And I said unto them, If ye think good, give me my price; and if not, forbear. So they weighed for my price thirty pieces of silver [Zech. 11:12].**

This is a very remarkable prophecy that has been literally fulfilled in a most remarkable way. Notice Matthew's record: "Then one of the twelve, called Judas Iscariot, went unto the chief priests, And said unto them, What will ye give me, and I will deliver him unto you? And they covenanted with him for thirty pieces of silver" (Matt. 26:14–15). This is exactly the price that Zechariah mentions. It is quite interesting that the chief priests didn't want to pay very much. I wonder if Judas had a little difficulty agreeing on the price—"So they weighed for my price thirty pieces of silver."

Over in Matthew 27:9–10, we find something else that is quite interesting: "Then was fulfilled that which was spoken by Jeremy the prophet, saying, And they took the thirty pieces of silver, the price of him that was valued, whom they of the children of Israel did value; And gave them for the potter's field, as the Lord appointed me." You will find this prophecy alluded to in Jeremiah 18:1–4 and evidently quoted from Zechariah 11: 12–13. It is credited to Jeremiah simply because in Jesus' day Jeremiah was the first of the books of the prophets, and that section was identified by the name of the first book.

**And the LORD said unto me, Cast it unto the potter: a goodly price that I was prised at of them. And I took the thirty pieces of silver, and cast them to the potter in the house of the LORD [Zech. 11:13].**

"A goodly price" is sometimes translated a "lordly" price. I think an even better word would be a *fancy* price. You have heard the expression, "Well, that's a fancy price for such and such an article."

"That I was prised at of them." Thirty pieces of silver—imagine that! They paid very little for Jesus. They weren't willing to pay a high ransom price of several million dollars to have Him delivered to them. No, they would give only thirty pieces of silver. How *cheap* that was.

What did Judas do with the thirty pieces of silver? "And I took the thirty pieces of silver, and cast them to the potter in the house of the LORD." There has been some disagreement on what was meant by this. Some expositors even think that "cast . . . to the potter" should be translated "cast . . . to the treasury." Well, Judas came into the temple and threw the money down there, but the record says, "And the chief priests took the silver pieces, and said, It is not lawful for to put them into the treasury, because it is the price of blood. And they took counsel, and bought with them the potter's field, to bury strangers in" (Matt. 27:6–7). Zechariah had already said, "And I took the thirty pieces of silver, and cast them to the potter in the house of the LORD." That was no accident. This is one of the most remarkable passages of Scripture that we have.

What is the potter's field? The potter's field was property belonging to the potter. When he had clay on his wheel, attempting to make a pot, a vessel, a vase, but it didn't yield to his fingers or it wouldn't bend where he wanted or a piece came off, he would take it off the wheel and throw it into the field. The clay wasn't the right texture to be molded. It was discarded as useless.

In Jeremiah's prophecy, God likens Himself to the potter. God puts the clay, mankind, on the potter's wheel and attempts to fashion it into the vessel He has in mind. But the clay has to yield to Him. The clay that won't yield to Him is thrown out into the potter's field. He can't use it.

It is interesting that the price of Christ was thirty pieces of silver, and the priests took the coins—they were very pious about not using the price of blood for religious purposes—and bought the potter's field as a burial place for the poor.

My friend, the Lord Jesus has been working in the potter's field for a long, long time. He purchased it. But He didn't purchase it for thirty pieces of silver. He paid the full price— far more than any amount of silver or gold— His own precious blood. He paid the price so that He might buy this old world in which you and I live, a world filled with the broken lives of mankind—broken physically, broken mentally, broken morally, broken spiritually. The great Potter, the Lord Jesus, takes the clay that was thrown away, puts it on the wheel of circumstance, and shapes it into a vessel of honor. We are the clay. He is the Potter. And even in these days of His rejection, He is working in the potter's field.

**Then I cut asunder mine other staff, even Bands, that I might break the brotherhood between Judah and Israel [Zech. 11:14].**

The chopping up of this second staff indicates the complete severance of all relationships between the Shepherd and Israel, His flock. It is as if God is saying, "When you sold Me, when you turned Me over into the hands of the Gentiles to be crucified, I broke my covenant. Titus the Roman will soon be here, and you will be scattered throughout the world." Their Messiah came, the nation rejected Him, and the Jewish people are still scattered throughout the world.

## THE FOOLISH SHEPHERD—ANTICHRIST

**And the LORD said unto me, Take unto thee yet the instruments of a foolish shepherd [Zech. 11:15].**

This, I think, is another parable that Zechariah is to act out. He is to take again the instruments of a shepherd.

**For, lo, I will raise up a shepherd in the land, which shall not visit those that be cut off, neither shall seek the young one, nor heal that that is broken, nor feed that that standeth still: but he shall eat the flesh of the fat, and tear their claws in pieces [Zech. 11:16].**

Zechariah has presented the Good Shepherd, sold for thirty pieces of silver, delivered to His enemies, then crucified on a Roman cross. But that cross became a brazen altar where the Lamb of God was offered to take away the sin of the world. He was the Good Shepherd who gave His life for the sheep.

Now Zechariah presents the foolish shepherd, who will appear much later in history. There is an interval of time between the coming of Christ and the coming of Antichrist that does not concern Zechariah at all. He is prophesying to the remnant of Israel who had returned to Palestine after the Babylonian captivity. If you think he has in mind the church age, you are entirely wrong. The "foolish shepherd" will be coming *after* God completes His purpose with the church and turns again to Israel as a nation.

Notice how Antichrist will deal with the people of Israel: he "shall not visit those that be cut off, neither shall seek the young one, nor heal that that is broken, nor feed that that standeth still: but he shall eat the flesh of the fat, and tear their claws in pieces." He will shear the sheep and kill them for food. What a contrast to the Good Shepherd who gave His life for the sheep!

The Lord Jesus said, "I am come in my

Father's name, and ye receive me not: if another shall come in his own name, him ye will receive" (John 5:43). Frankly, when I began my ministry, I thought we must be very far away from the appearance of the Antichrist because there was not the world climate nor psychological background for the appearance of a man like he will be. However, we have come a long way since I was a young minister. Today, as I look about me, I think that the world is ripe for Antichrist. I don't mean that I think he is coming shortly, because I do not know that; only God has that information. But I am confident that if a man appeared on the scene who had the right credentials (and Antichrist will have them), a man who could bring peace in the world and bring order out of the chaos we are in and bring prosperity, the world would receive him with open arms. Do you think that the world would ask if he came from heaven or hell? I don't think that people would care where he came from. In our day every country seems to be accepting almost any kind of leadership. The world is not blessed with great leaders—certainly our country is not. We are ready for the Antichrist when he comes. His coming may be a long way off, but we have the right climate for it today which we did not have when I first began in the ministry.

**Woe to the idol shepherd that leaveth the flock! the sword shall be upon his arm, and upon his right eye: his arm shall be clean dried up, and his right eye shall be utterly darkened [Zech. 11:17].**

He is called here "the idol shepherd," meaning the *worthless* shepherd. He is no good, he is of no value, he is the great deceiver. Dr. Merrill Unger is quite a Hebrew scholar, and I like his translation of this verse: "Woe! Worthless shepherd, forsaker of the flock! Let the sword be against his arm and against his right eye! His arm shall be completely dried up and his right eye shall be completely blind."

This "foolish" shepherd is of no benefit, but the world will go after him. When Israel rejected the Good Shepherd who was promised, they were scattered worldwide. And the gospel, which the Lord Jesus said would begin at Jerusalem and go to the ends of the earth, is being preached today. It is my personal conviction that through the medium of radio we will be enabled to get the gospel to the ends of the earth. The interval in which the gospel has been going out has already been a long one—over nineteen hundred years. Then this false shepherd will appear. He is worthless, but he is going to promise everything. He will be the supreme politician, promising everything in the book and out of the book.

"Woe to the idol [worthless] shepherd that leaveth the flock!" The word *woe* is the Hebrew *hoy,* and the very sound of it denotes trouble that is coming—"*Hoy, hoy, hoy!*"

"The sword shall be upon his arm, and upon his right eye: his arm shall be clean dried up, and his right eye shall be utterly darkened." What does this mean? Well, he used his eye, not to protect the sheep, but he kept his eye on them to see which was the fattest that he could use. His arm should have been wielding the crook and the club to protect the sheep from harm. But he didn't do that. He exposed them instead of watching over them. God says that judgment will come upon him. His right eye shall be blinded and his arm shriveled or atrophied. In the Book of Revelation we find that God is going to judge the false shepherd, Antichrist—in fact, *he* will make it to the lake of fire even before the Devil gets there!

The false shepherd, the Antichrist, will actually be the one who brings in the Great Tribulation in all its fury. In the first part of the Tribulation Israel will be deceived into thinking that Antichrist is their Good Shepherd, but by the time they discover his real character, he will be the world dictator, and the armies of the world will come against Jerusalem.

# CHAPTER 12

***THEME:*** *Second prophetic burden connected with Christ's second coming*

In chapters 12–14 we come to the prophetic aspects connected with the second coming of Christ. This is the second and final division of this last major section of Zechariah's prophecy. The primary reason that this is such an important section is that it is quite obvious that Zechariah is presenting God's program here. In chapter 11, the prophet first showed us that the true Shepherd, the One who gave His life for the sheep, is rejected. In fact, He was sold for thirty pieces of silver—how cheap! Our redemption was not purchased with silver and gold but with the precious blood of Christ, but what a cheap price He was sold for in that day. The Lord Jesus said when He was on earth, "I am come in my Father's name, and ye receive me not: if another shall come in his own name, him ye will receive" (John 5:43). That one who is coming some day is the one Zechariah calls the idol or worthless shepherd. That shepherd is identified as being the Antichrist. After the church is removed from the earth, after the interval in which the true Shepherd is presented to the world as the One who gave His life for the sheep, we come to the time when the worthless shepherd will present himself. He will be accepted, and he will bring in the Great Tribulation, not the Millennium. As a result, we see here that Jerusalem—which will become the capital of the earth where Jesus will reign some day in the Millennium—is under attack by Antichrist, and we see how it will be delivered.

The second reason that this section of Scripture is so important is that this area of prophecy is rejected today by many Bible expositors, even by so-called conservative expositors. They will not face up to the fact that God presents here a panoramic program of His purposes with this world and with Israel in the future. That is a sad thing to say, but it is true. We also have some men who are called fundamentalists but who border on the sensational and lift out certain statements from this section. I don't think that it is honest to lift certain things out of a passage and try to fit them into the events of today when they have to do with the future. Any interpretation must fit into the entire program that Zechariah is presenting.

Chapter 12 deals with the final siege of Jerusalem and the lifting of that siege. "Jerusalem" is mentioned ten times in this chapter, and "in that day" is mentioned seven times. These two expressions occur again and again. "In that day" is a reference to the Day of the Lord which begins with the Great Tribulation Period and eventuates and goes into the millennial kingdom which the Lord Jesus will usher in when He comes again. The Antichrist brings in the Great Tribulation; the Lord Jesus brings in the Millennium. I want us to note these expressions—"in that day" and "Jerusalem"—for they are the subject of this chapter.

There is so much confusion today as to the meaning of the Day of the Lord. Even as far back as 1951 when I was participating in several summer conferences, I heard two other Bible teachers present a very hazy, indefinite, and uncertain view of the Day of the Lord. It occurred to me that if the man in the pulpit is so fuzzy and foggy on this subject, what about those in the pew? Is there a clearcut understanding of what the Day of the Lord is? What do you think of when you hear the expression, the Day of the Lord? Do you have a definite conception of what it means? Or is it just a nebulous and incoherent expression that is like some sort of umbrella that you can put down over a great many things and it can mean almost anything to you? We hear people use the word *glory*. What does it mean? When people say *amen* to something, what do they mean by that?

I am reminded of the Englishman who went into a restaurant here in the United States after he had been here for just a short time. He asked the waitress, "What kind of soup do you have?" She started out by saying, "Well, we have bean. . . ." He stopped her immediately and said, "I don't care where you have been. I want to know what kind of soup you have." Then there was the preacher in the South years ago who said in the church business meeting, "Now we're going to call on the president to share his report and let us know the status quo of the church." One of the deacons got up and said. "Mr. Preacher, I think you ought to explain to us what the status quo is." The preacher replied. "Well, that's Latin for the mess we're in." My friend, these expressions can mean different things to different people.

The Day of the Lord is an important expression. It occurs eighteen times in the Book of Zechariah alone. We find it in both the Major and the Minor Prophets. The Day of the Lord is actually the theme of Joel's book. Malachi speaks of ". . . the coming of the great and dreadful day of the LORD" (Mal. 4:5). In one sense it is a theme of the Old Testament and one of the most important themes. It would be helpful for us to break down this expression and take a closer look at it.

"The day of the Lord." Let's understand clearly that this does not refer to the Lord's Day. The Day of the Lord and the Lord's Day are two different things. Like a chestnut horse and a horse chestnut or like antifat and fat Auntie—they are simply two different things.

The Day of the Lord is not a twenty-four-hour day. Peter says, "But, beloved, be not ignorant of this one thing, that one day is with the Lord as a thousand years, and a thousand years as one day" (2 Pet. 3:8). The events that the prophets include in the Day of the Lord preclude the possibility of their happening in a 24-hour day. In fact the tremendous things which are going to take place during the Great Tribulation have made some men actually reject it and ridicule that viewpoint. They argue that you just cannot have that many crisis events take place in that brief seven-year period. But things are different since we have gotten into the twentieth century. In one issue of their magazine, *U.S. News and World Report* took the ten-year period from 1960–70 and listed the many crisis events that took place in that brief period of time. There has been a tremendous speeding up of crises in the world today. I do not think that God will have any trouble fulfilling all the prophecies concerning the Great Tribulation Period. The Day of the Lord, therefore, is a period of time. It includes the Great Tribulation Period and the millennial kingdom, which means that it is over a thousand years in length.

Has the Day of the Lord come? Are we living in it? The Old Testament closes with that day still in the future. The Old Testament pointed ahead to it, and the New Testament still anticipated it. The apostle Paul made it very clear that it was still in the future as far as he was concerned: "For yourselves know perfectly that the day of the Lord so cometh as a thief in the night" (1 Thess. 5:2). The Day of the Lord had not come up to Paul's time, and nothing has happened since then that would indicate that it has come.

Concerning the character of the Day of the Lord, it is a good day and it is a bad day. Good news and bad news can come in one message. It is like the pilot on the Italian airplane who came on the air and introduced himself. Then he said, "We welcome you aboard this flight. I have some good news for you, and I have some bad news for you. First of all, I'll give you the bad news. We've lost contact with the ground. Our entire radar system has gone out, and we have no radio contact. In fact, we don't know where we are. That's the bad news. Now for the good news: We're making good time."

May I say to you, the Day of the Lord is good news and bad news. The bad news first: the Great Tribulation. The good news next: the millennial kingdom. Both features will be emphasized beginning here in chapter 12. Zechariah will give you the bad news in verses 2 and 3: "Behold, I will make Jerusalem a cup of trembling unto all the people round about, when they shall be in the siege both against Judah and against Jerusalem. And in that day will I make Jerusalem a burdensome stone for all people: all that burden themselves with it shall be cut in pieces, though all the people of the earth be gathered together against it." That's the bad news. But there is also some good news coming in chapter 14, beginning at verse 8: "And it shall be in that day, that living waters shall go out from Jerusalem." There is bad news and good news, and in chapter 12 we will be dealing with the bad news.

We have, therefore, presented to us the Great Tribulation and Jerusalem under siege. This is the time that Jeremiah called "the time of Jacob's trouble." In Jeremiah 30:5–7 we read: "For thus saith the LORD; We have heard a voice of trembling, of fear, and not of peace. Ask ye now, and see whether a man doth travail with child? wherefore do I see every man with his hands on his loins, as a woman in travail, and all faces are turned into paleness? Alas! for that day is great, so that none is like it: it is even the time of Jacob's trouble; but he shall be saved out of it."

Daniel also wrote concerning this time: "And at that time shall Michael stand up, the great prince which standeth for the children of thy people: and there shall be a time of trouble, such as never was since there was a nation even to that same time: and at that time thy people shall be delivered, every one that shall be found written in the book" (Dan. 12:1).

The Lord Jesus spoke of this time, He identified it, and He Himself labeled it the "great tribulation": "For then shall be great tribulation, such as was not since the beginning of the world to this time, no, nor ever shall be. And except those days should be shortened, there should no flesh be saved: but for the elect's sake those days shall be shortened" (Matt. 24:21–22).

## THE GREAT TRIBULATION

We have in chapter 12 a description of this Great Tribulation Period, and it is presented to us like this—

**The burden of the word of the Lord for Israel, saith the Lord, which stretcheth forth the heavens, and layeth the foundation of the earth, and formeth the spirit of man within him [Zech. 12:1].**

"The burden of the word of the Lord for Israel." The word *burden* here means "a prophecy, a judgment." A judgment is coming to them—it is a burden in that sense. This prophecy had to do with the siege of Jerusalem which precedes the Battle of Armageddon.

"The burden of the word of the Lord for Israel, saith the Lord." In this section of Scripture which is rejected by so many men today, there is a particular emphasis upon the statement of Zechariah again and again that he is not giving you *his* idea but "thus saith the Lord." This prophecy comes directly from God. If you reject this, you are not just a higher critic with a little superficial knowledge who is able to make very intellectual statements about what you do and don't believe—but, my friend, you are making Zechariah a liar. Zechariah says here that this is *the Word of the Lord.* He is either accurate and means what he says or he is a liar—there is no "in-between." When you reject this—no matter who you are—you're making this man a liar. Well, I don't think *he* is a liar, but I think *you* are the liar if you reject him.

There are three great statements in this verse which give to us a sublime description of God as the Creator of this universe and of everything that is in it. This is a tremendous and overwhelming statement that we have here:

1. He is the One "which stretcheth forth the heavens." The psalmist says, "The heavens declare the glory of God; and the firmament sheweth his handiwork" (Ps. 19:1). All of that above us declares His glory, and it shows His handiwork. And it is being stretched out. Quite a few years ago now, Sir James Jeans, an English astronomer, advanced a theory which has been pretty well accepted today among astronomers. I understand that Jeans was a Christian. His proposal suggests that this universe has grown—even since you have started reading this chapter—and is now several million miles bigger. That is really stretching things! You and I are living in a universe in which these tremendous creations of God are moving away from each other, streaking across the universe. He "stretcheth forth the heavens." How great God is!

2. "And layeth the foundation of the earth." God has given particular attention to this little earth that we live on. Man just isn't satisfied that he lives in a universe in which he is the only human being around. So we have been sending missiles out to the other worlds. We aren't electronically bugging them in order to tape anything they might say, but we are sure looking in their front window to see if they might be there. There's been nobody there. God made this earth the habitation for human beings.

3. This is the most remarkable thing: He "formeth the spirit of man within him." Man is a little different creation from anything else that is on this earth. He is above anything that is on this earth, but he is not equal to the created intelligences which we call angels. I think that the universe today is filled with God's created intelligences. I do not mean that there are men from Mars. (They have now found Mars to be the kind of place that if you lived there, you would want to move right away!) Although we live in a universe that looks as if it's not inhabited, I do not think that God has a "Vacancy" sign hanging out anywhere. I believe that if you moved out of our solar system, you would find that God's created intelligences are in this universe. They are spiritual creatures, and our cameras are not apt to pick up any of them, I can assure you. What a glorious picture this verse gives of God as the Creator!

Men years ago who were called deists—none of them were evolutionists—believed that there was a Creator, and they believed that God created the universe but that He went off and left it. He just forgot about it. He wound it up, started it off, and then He walked away. However, this verse reveals that God did not walk off and leave the universe. It reveals that God is immanent in His universe as well as outside of it. This passage portrays the tremendous activity of God out yonder in the heavens as He moves in our great universe. We live in a universe that is filled with energy. It is man who has depleted the energy on this little world on which we live. I think that God put just enough energy down here to last us until He is ready to move in and take it over again. It looks as if the filling station which we live on down here is running out of gas. This is another reason I believe that we are moving on to the end of this age.

We see here that God is working with a very definite and positive action as far as this universe is concerned. He is that One who has formed the spirit of man. He is our omnipotent (all-powerful), omniscient (all-knowing) God. He is wisdom and knowledge. As Dr. Unger expresses it, this "comprises one of the most magnificent eschatological vistas to be found in the Word of God"; yet it is disbelieved by even a great many who call themselves conservative or evangelical.

**Behold, I will make Jerusalem a cup of trembling unto all the people round about, when they shall be in the siege both against Judah and against Jerusalem [Zech. 12:2].**

Jerusalem is mentioned twice here in this one verse. As we have already indicated, it is mentioned ten times in this chapter alone. Here we have Jerusalem becoming the very center of the activity which will take place when Antichrist takes over. Jerusalem becomes the center of attack and of judgment.

"Behold, I will make Jerusalem a cup of trembling unto all the people round about." Better words for "cup" are bowl or goblet or mug.

Let's identify when this will take place: "When they shall be in the siege both against Judah and against Jerusalem." When is that? In the last days, in the time that the Lord Jesus called the Great Tribulation Period. Therefore, the interpretation of this entire section is for a future day. But it *is* going to have a message and a tremendous lesson for us.

In Dr. Unger's words, God will make Jerusalem "a goblet of intoxication," "a goblet of staggering" for those who are concerning themselves with it. In other words, they will be staggering because of it.

**And in that day will I make Jerusalem a burdensome stone for all people: all that burden themselves with it shall be cut in pieces, though all the people of the earth be gathered together against it [Zech. 12:3].**

In effect God says, "You're going to get hurt fooling with Jerusalem." Again, this hasn't anything in the world to do with Rome or Paris or London or Washington, D.C., or Los Angeles or your town. When He says Jerusalem, He means Jerusalem. Although He says it ten times, somehow or another it doesn't get through to us. Some of the commentators don't quite get the message. Jerusalem means Jerusalem, and when He puts Judah with Jerusalem, He is talking about Jerusalem which is in Judah.

"And in that day will I make Jerusalem a burdensome stone for all people." Now that seems strange, doesn't it? Jerusalem is a rather isolated place, an old city, and actually not very attractive today. Despite the fact that it has so many spots which are sacred and meaningful to us, I know a lot of places I like better than I like Jerusalem. I always enjoy staying there because there are so many things to see that are identified with the Bible. But why should this place be so prominent and significant in the last days? How do you explain that? Well, that city even today has become a burdensome stone, but we have not seen the fulfillment of prophecy—it is nonsense to talk like that. This prophecy fits into a program that is yet future, but God just wants you to know that He was not making an exaggerated statement when He said that Jerusalem can become a burdensome stone. I believe that what we have seen is nothing compared with what it will be in that day. It almost broke up the Common Market, it almost wrecked NATO—Jerusalem became a burdensome stone. Consider the list of the nations of the world which have captured that city and have tried to rule it. For example, at the time when General Allenby took Jerusalem and delivered it from the Turks, Great Britain was the number one power, and the sun never set on the British Empire. But, my friend, today the British Empire's sun has set. It went down because they got involved with that city. Frankly, I hope that the United States doesn't get too involved. God says, "Keep your hands off. I am the One running that place."

**In that day, saith the LORD, I will smite every horse with astonishment, and his rider with madness: and I will open mine eyes upon the house of Judah, and will smite every horse of the people with blindness [Zech. 12:4].**

Again God says, "In that day"—this is going to get monotonous before we finish this book.

The horse represents warfare, and when a horse goes blind and the rider is mad, you are certainly going to have confusion. God says here that when the enemy comes against Israel, He is going to make them ineffective.

**And the governors of Judah shall say in their heart, The inhabitants of Jerusalem shall be my strength in the LORD of hosts their God [Zech. 12:5].**

In that day Jerusalem will become a refuge for God's people on the earth.

This siege of Jerusalem in which the enemy comes in from every direction is the result of the activity of Antichrist, but God will intervene on their behalf. When they have rejected Him, why in the world does He intervene on their behalf? We will find the answer in this section of Scripture.

**In that day will I make the governors of Judah like an hearth of fire among the wood, and like a torch of fire in a sheaf; and they shall devour all the people round about, on the right hand and on the left: and Jerusalem shall be inhabited again in her own place, even in Jerusalem [Zech. 12:6].**

Again I remind you that we are talking about Jerusalem—not about Rome or Washington, D.C., or Geneva, Switzerland. We are talking about Jerusalem, the geographical spot located in Judah. He has already identified both Judah and Jerusalem, and He will do that again here—

**The LORD also shall save the tents of Judah first, that the glory of the house of David and the glory of the inhabitants of Jerusalem do not magnify themselves against Judah [Zech. 12:7].**

In other words, Jerusalem would be looking down, as it were, on the rest of the country. People today in one section of our country have a tendency to look down upon people from other sections of the country. I have been very much amused at the reactions which people have to my accent. Many of them very frankly write letters and say, "When I started listening to you, I thought you were just some wild-eyed ignoramus." Well, there are some people who still think that, but the letters go on to say, "But we kept listening and saw beyond that accent." They realized that I had been to school or at least had finished the sixth grade! My point is that this is a tendency we all have. We folk who have been born in Texas have been given the impression that there is nothing beyond the borders of Texas, that the chosen people are in Texas. There are some of my fellow Texans who still believe that, and such is human nature.

Zechariah is saying that if the Lord manifested Himself first to Jerusalem and to the house of David, then they would look down upon the rest of Judah. They would say, "These are country rubes and hillbillies. After all, the Lord didn't manifest Himself to them first." But God says, "I shall save the tents of Judah first." Remember that the Lord Jesus said, "But many that are first shall be last; and the last shall be first" (Matt. 19:30).

We are going to get many shocks when we get to heaven. I think that one of the greatest surprises is that we will find people up there whom we didn't think were going to be there. And there are going to be some missing whom we thought were going to be there. That's the number one shock we will get. Then we are also going to find out who really are the people that God recognizes as those who were His servants and who were doing faithfully that which He wanted done. And they are not going to be the ones we would have chosen. God makes it clear here in Zechariah, "I am going to manifest Myself to Judah first," and that will give Jerusalem and the house of David something to think about.

**In that day shall the LORD defend the inhabitants of Jerusalem; and he that is feeble among them at that day shall be as David; and the house of David shall be as God, as the angel of the LORD before them [Zech. 12:8].**

"In that day shall the LORD defend the inhabitants of Jerusalem; and he that is feeble among them at that day shall be as David." David was quite a soldier. If you don't believe that, read the account concerning his son Absalom, or read how he took that nation which was scattered and divided and brought it together and how he dealt with the Philistines. David was a great administrator, a great soldier, a general of great strategy, a man of tremendous ability. In that day, even the weakest man will be like David.

"And the house of David shall be as God." To me this is one of the most thrilling statements in Scripture: David will be like God. I want you to know that there came One in David's line who is God. David is going to be like God. That One is the Lord Jesus Christ who was born to Mary of the household of David. He was born in the city of Bethlehem.

Mary went down there to be enrolled because she belonged to the house of David. And Joseph also had to be enrolled for he was of the house of David, but he had nothing to do with the birth of the Lord Jesus. They went down to Bethlehem, and Jesus was born into the family of David. Matthew writes. "The book of the generation of Jesus Christ, the son of David, the son of Abraham" (Matt. 1:1)—that is the way the New Testament opens. That He is the Son of David is the first thing that is mentioned. He is also "the son of Abraham," but David is mentioned first.

**And it shall come to pass in that day, that I will seek to destroy all the nations that come against Jerusalem [Zech. 12:9].**

There will be a converging of all the nations against Jerusalem, which we see in a great deal of detail in the Book of Revelation. All of these great prophecies are like trains or planes coming into a train station or airport. All of these great themes of prophecy which originate elsewhere in the Bible converge into the Book of Revelation like a great airport or Union Station.

## ISRAEL'S DELIVERANCE

There is coming against Jerusalem in that day the enemy from the outside. Why is God going to protect them, and why is God going to deliver them? The reason is given here in verse 10—

**And I will pour upon the house of David, and upon the inhabitants of Jerusalem, the spirit of grace and of supplications: and they shall look upon me whom they have pierced, and they shall mourn for him, as one mourneth for his only son, and shall be in bitterness for him, as one that is in bitterness for his firstborn [Zech. 12:10].**

"And I will pour upon the house of David, and upon the inhabitants of Jerusalem, the spirit of grace and of supplications." This is another reason why I do not believe the present return to the land is a fulfillment of any prophecy of Scripture. The Scriptures make it clear, not only here but also in Joel, that God is going to pour out upon them the Spirit of Grace, that is, the Holy Spirit. He will pour out the Holy Spirit upon these people during this period. Because of this effusion of the Holy Spirit that is to come upon them, they

will be His witnesses, and He will protect them during the Great Tribulation Period. Revelation speaks of the angel who seals these people: "And I heard the number of them which were sealed: and there were sealed an hundred and forty and four thousand of all the tribes of the children of Israel" (Rev. 7:4). This 144,000 means the people that we know as Israel who live in that land. It does not refer to any people who arbitrarily claim it for themselves without any basis at all. This has to rest upon facts, and the Book of Revelation makes it very clear that it is 12,000 out of each of the twelve tribes (see Rev. 7:5–8). If you are going to claim to be one of the 144,000, that means that you are unsaved today and that if the Rapture took place, you would not leave the earth but would go into the Great Tribulation Period when they are to be sealed. Therefore, the 144,000 does not mean any group that we have today, but it does mean a certain group among the people of Israel.

There is another large group of people who are to be sealed, but we are not given the number of them. They are Gentiles who are to be sealed during that period. They will go through the Great Tribulation Period, and they will stand for God in that time.

When the church is removed from the earth, the Holy Spirit, as I understand Scripture, does not leave the earth, but He will be on a different mission. He then will return to what He was doing before the Day of Pentecost—that is, He will come upon certain people. Zechariah tells us that there is to be a pouring out of the Spirit upon the remnant that will be back in the land. I do not think that, in what has happened over there since they became a nation in 1948, there has been any time that you could say there has been the pouring out of the Spirit of God.

When that pouring out of the Spirit takes place, they are going to recognize Christ as their Savior. "And they shall look upon me whom they have pierced, and they shall mourn for him, as one mourneth for his only son, and shall be in bitterness for him, as one that is in bitterness for his firstborn." This will be the fulfillment of the great Day of Atonement when they are going to look upon Him. Chapter 13 will develop this a great deal for us. It opens with this: "In that day there shall be a fountain opened to the house of David and to the inhabitants of Jerusalem for sin and for uncleanness" (Zech. 13:1). Then verse 6 in chapter 13 reads, "And one shall say unto him, What are these wounds in thine hands? Then he shall answer, Those with which I was wounded in the house of my friends." In that day they are going to look upon Him whom they pierced, and the question will be asked of Him, "What do these wounds mean? We didn't expect our Messiah, our King, to come with these wounds that You have in Your hands and feet and in Your side." He will say to them, "I got these wounds in the house of My friends. I came before, but you didn't accept Me or receive Me, and now I've come back." They will then mourn because of that.

The explanation is given here as to why God is going to defend Jerusalem. He will pour out the Spirit of grace upon them. My friend, that is the only way today that you and I are indwelt by the Spirit of God. You don't have to seek and groan and grunt and think that you become a super-duper saint in order to have the Holy Spirit. All you must do is to come as a sinner to Jesus Christ and accept and receive Him as your Savior. Then you are indwelt by the Holy Spirit of God. Paul called the Corinthian believers babies, he called them carnal, he called them fleshly; yet he could say to them, "What? know ye not that your body is the temple of the Holy Ghost which is in you, which ye have of God, and ye are not your own?" (1 Cor. 6:19). He is the Spirit of *grace*. He does not indwell me or fill me because I'm super-duper or because I'm a little ahead of somebody else—I'm not, I'm way behind most. It is because of His *grace* that He does these things. And that is the way that He is going to do this for Israel. Since He's been so gracious to me, I'm not going to object to His being gracious to these people.

Israel will know Him when the veil is lifted from their eyes, as Paul put it in 2 Corinthians 3:13-16. That veil doesn't mean that they are not responsible. Any time any one of them will turn his heart to Christ, Paul makes it very clear that the veil will be removed, and he will see Christ as his Savior. My friend, this is true of any sinner today. You are not lost because you haven't heard the gospel; you are not lost because of this, that, or another thing. You're lost today because you have made a definite decision to reject Jesus Christ. This is a false idea today that somehow or another we are not responsible. Although it is by grace, you and I are responsible to respond to the marvelous, infinite, wonderful grace of God. Therefore, God saves us not because of our ability, not even by our faith, but He saves us by the precious blood of Christ. This is a wonderful passage of Scripture.

**In that day shall there be a great mourning in Jerusalem, as the mourning of Hadadrimmon in the valley of Megiddon [Zech. 12:11].**

"In that day"—aren't you getting just a little bit tired of hearing Zechariah talk about "in that day"? Well, you haven't heard anything yet. All the way through the very last chapter and the last verse, he is going to talk about "in that day." By now we ought to know what "in that day" means. It is that period of time known as the Day of the Lord. The Day of the Lord begins when the church leaves at the Rapture and the Great Tribulation Period begins, and then it will continue right on through the millennial kingdom, to the time when all rebellion is put down and the eternal kingdom begins. The eternal kingdom simply continues the thousand-year kingdom, except that it is no longer a time of testing but everything is then fixed for eternity.

"In that day shall there be a great mourning in Jerusalem." This is the real Day of Atonement. The Day of Atonement in the Mosaic system was the only day Israel was to weep. It was the day that atonement was made for their sins. "In that day shall there be a great mourning." May I just pause and say that there is today a great deal of so-called gospel preaching that says, "Come to Jesus. He will make you over. You are going to be a new personality, and you are going to attain your goal." All kinds of attractions are offered to you. But may I say, what do you really think about your sins? Have you ever mourned about them? Has it ever broken your heart that you have been a sinner? This is the one thing that this poor preacher right now can say to you: When I look back on my life and see some of the things that I did in the past, I tell you, it breaks my heart. It is for *that* that my Savior died. There ought to be that mourning, that repentance in the Christian life. The one thing that is missing today is that which used to take place at the Methodist altars in the old days. In those meetings men and women would come *weeping* down to the altar to accept Christ—but I see very little of that today. They come down smiling, thinking they're going to get a new personality. My friend, the truth is that you're an old, rotten, dirty, filthy sinner in His sight, and even your good things are bad to Him. He says that our righteousness is as filthy rags in His sight. And if my *righteousness* is filthy rags, think what my filthy rags are! If you and I could see ourselves as God sees us, we couldn't stand ourselves. We would get rid of our conceit and our self-sufficiency. Oh, how the church needs a real baptism of repentance! This is the thing that is needed today—repentance on the part of believers, a repenting of their sins.

"As the mourning of Hadadrimmon in the valley of Megiddon." This refers to the valley at Megiddon and to the time of Josiah. Josiah was a king greatly loved of the people, and when he died there was great mourning for him. Jeremiah wept over Josiah as he wept over no one else.

**And the land shall mourn, every family apart; the family of the house of David apart, and their wives apart; the family of the house of Nathan apart, and their wives apart [Zech. 12:12].**

They shall mourn "apart." That is, it will be done in a private manner. Such repentance is something that many of us even today need to do privately.

**The family of the house of Levi apart, and their wives apart; the family of Shimei apart, and their wives apart;**

**All the families that remain, every family apart, and their wives apart [Zech. 12:13–14].**

This will be a real mourning. What great sin have they committed? They had rejected their Messiah when He came the first time. Think what it will be like when He comes the second time and there are those who have heard the gospel message but have turned it down. May I say to you, that day is coming on this earth when He will come again. Today if you will hear His voice, harden not your heart. Open up your heart and receive Christ as your Savior.

# CHAPTER 13

***THEME:*** *The cleansing of Israel*

You are seeing, I trust, that this Book of Zechariah is a very important book. I have always appreciated it and felt that it is a neglected book. Each time I go through it I learn something new. In fact, this final section is so tremendous that I do not feel competent to interpret it on the high plane that it belongs. I would love to make it mean as much to you as it means to me. Perhaps my feeling is best expressed in the lovable language of the Pennsylvania Dutch: "We grow too soon old and too late smart." That fits my case.

In the previous chapters we have seen a very definite progress through a program which began with the first coming of Christ to the earth. At that time He had entered Jerusalem, and He had been sold for just a few pieces of silver. Only part of the prophecy of Zechariah was fulfilled at His first coming, which indicates that the other part will be fulfilled at His second coming.

He was rejected as the Good Shepherd who gave His life for the sheep. Another is to come in the future. He hasn't come yet and won't appear until the church is removed from the earth. He will be the false shepherd who will lead the nation of Israel, as well as the world, into the Great Tribulation Period. The only deliverance at that time will be the second coming of Christ to the earth when He comes to establish His kingdom. He alone can bring peace to this earth.

It was back in December, 1959, on a Thursday evening, that a Boeing 707 took off from Andrews Air Force Base in Maryland and headed toward the sunrise. That jet plane bore the insignia of the president of the United States. The president was beginning the longest trip that any president had made previously. He was to visit three continents, confer with a dozen rulers, and be seen by thousands of people. The supreme objective of that trip was *peace*. President Eisenhower at that time expressed it by stating that it was an effort to attain *peace* with *justice*. Certainly that was a laudable and worthy objective, and he traveled 22,370 miles in 19 days in his attempt to achieve it.

Since that time, every other president has traveled farther in his efforts to bring peace to this earth. But at the time President Eisenhower made the trip, the longing and the prayers of over a billion people were with him because the world *wants* peace. The human heart desires peace above all else. It was very interesting that he went in the season of the year when we celebrate the birth of a Baby, when it was said, "Glory to God in the highest and on earth peace, good will toward men" (Luke 2:14). Well, I must confess that back there in 1959 I very sincerely prayed for peace. My good wishes and my prayers went with the president for success and a bon voyage. You know, I am sure, that I did not entertain the delusion that the president or any mere man could bring permanent peace to the earth. Actually I got the impression, as I listened to him on television, that he didn't believe he could achieve peace in the world. I do not think he entertained any grandiose ideas. As a military man, he faced reality. But I think he hoped to relieve the tensions so as to postpone the evil day and to make plain the purpose and intents of this nation by clearing up misunderstanding and misrepresentations.

Well, after all the years which have gone by since then, it is still true that the Baby born over nineteen hundred years ago is the only hope for permanent peace. He alone can and will bring peace to this earth. He holds in perpetuity the title ". . . The Prince of Peace" (Isa. 9:6). He has a program and a plan to bring in permanent peace. He will establish the kingdom of heaven on earth.

The prophets, especially Zechariah, sketch this program in some detail. In this book, as elsewhere, we find out something of the character of that kingdom, which we will note as we go along. We have already seen that the kingdom has a great many physical aspects that appeal to men: the desert will blossom as a rose, the lame will leap, the blind will see, and there are those who like to think of the golden streets in the New Jerusalem. But when we get off on that tangent we forget the spiritual aspects. We have already seen in this little book that the kingdom will be characterized by *truth*: "Thus saith the LORD; I am returned unto Zion, and will dwell in the midst of Jerusalem: and Jerusalem shall be called a city of truth . . ." (Zech. 8:3). It certainly is not that today, but it will be the city of truth when Christ reigns there. I should add that there is *no* capital in the world today which is noted for truth.

Not only will Christ's kingdom be characterized by truth, it will be characterized by *holiness* and *righteousness*, as we will see in verses 1 and 2 of the chapter before us. And in chapter 14 we shall see that even the bells on the horses and the pots and pans in the temple will be holiness to the Lord.

Also, the kingdom will be characterized by *freedom from fear*—we will find that aspect in chapter 14.

Added to this, the kingdom will be characterized by *joy*, as we have seen in chapter 10: "And I will strengthen the house of Judah, and I will save the house of Joseph, and I will bring them again to place them; for I have mercy upon them: and they shall be as though I had not cast them off: for I am the LORD their God, and will hear them. And they of Ephraim shall be like a mighty man, and their heart shall rejoice as through wine: yea, their children shall see it, and be glad; their heart shall rejoice in the LORD" (Zech. 10:6–7). It will be a time of great joy, you see.

All of these are spiritual—not physical—aspects of the kingdom, and the chief one is peace. When Christ comes to reign, He "will speak peace unto the nations."

We have been following in Zechariah's prophecy God's program which will ultimately bring permanent peace to the world. When Christ came the first time, He was rejected and sold and turned over to the Gentiles who crucified Him. Then a period of time lapses which Zechariah does not deal with. It is the church period in which we are living today. When it ends, there will appear the worthless shepherd, the Antichrist. He won't usher in the kingdom; he will bring in the Great Tribulation Period. His world dictatorship can only be ended by the coming of Christ to establish His kingdom upon the earth. This is what we have before us in chapter 13.

All of this should be taken in a literal way. The reason that many folk in our day think that God has no future purpose with Israel is that they don't believe that God means what He says. You couldn't read the section before us and dismiss it unless you spiritualize it away. If you do that, you do not have a very high view of the inspiration of Scripture. The very center of God's plan, as we saw back in chapter 12, is Jerusalem. In the last three chapters of this book, chapters 12–14, the name *Jerusalem* occurs twenty-one times. My friend, God wouldn't have used it that many times unless He had meant literal Jerusalem. He was not talking about London or Paris or Berlin or Moscow or Peking. He was speaking about the actual city of Jerusalem. It is quite interesting that even President Eisenhower, back in his day, bypassed Jerusalem, and heads of state have been bypassing it ever since. You will find that the better conservative expositors take the position that this section should be interpreted literally.

Let me share with you a quotation from Dr. Merrill F. Unger, whom I value very highly as an interpreter of the Book of Zechariah. I feel that his book, *Unger's Bible Commentary: Zechariah*, is the finest I have found. It is scholarly, and you need a little smattering of Hebrew to get through it, but it is a wonderful book. Here on page 221 is his comment:

> Only a literal application of these prophecies to the restoration and conversion of the Jewish nation at the second advent of Christ can satisfy the scope of these prophetic disclosures. Other interpretations ignore the true scope of Zechariah's prophecies as a whole, violate the immediate context, resort to pointless mysticalizing, and end up in a morass of uncertainty and confusion.

I say amen to that. I believe that spiritualizing it is practically a denial of the inspiration of the Word of God.

## THE NATIONAL CLEANSING OF ISRAEL

**In that day there shall be a fountain opened to the house of David and to the inhabitants of Jerusalem for sin and for uncleanness [Zech. 13:1].**

❝**I**n that day." We have already determined that "that day" refers to the Great Tribulation and moves on into the millennial kingdom. Christ will come to this earth at the end of the Great Tribulation, and then He will establish His kingdom.

This verse does not refer to the first coming of Christ. At that time He did not open up a fountain to the house of David and to the inhabitants of Jerusalem "for sin and for uncleanness." Instead, they rejected Him and crucified their Savior. Even Paul writes in Romans 10:3: "For they being ignorant of God's righteousness, and going about to establish their own righteousness, have not submitted themselves unto the righteousness of God."

"A fountain" is God's cleansing power which was opened by Christ's death upon the cross. At His first coming Israel rejected their Messiah-Savior, and this fountain will be opened to them at His second coming to the earth. The chapter before us continues the presentation of God's program, and we saw in chapter 12 that in "that day" God would pour out His Spirit upon the people of Israel. The prophet

Joel spoke of that also. It is at this time that the "fountain" will be opened to them, which will be when they realize the fact that Christ was crucified for them. We have seen that they are going to look upon Him. Remember that this is God's Word, and He puts it very definitely, "They shall look upon *me* whom they have pierced, and they shall mourn for him." It is going to be a real Day of Atonement for these people when Christ comes the second time. They are going to be greatly moved, and the Spirit of God will remove the veil from their eyes. Paul makes it clear that the veil can be taken away even today if they really want to give up their sin.

You see, the problem with man is heart trouble, not head trouble. No man really has an intellectual problem. He hasn't got enough mentality to deal with the Creator of this universe, with an infinite God. His problem is that he does not want to give up his *sin*. That is true of the people of Israel, and it is true of the Gentiles. It is true of all of us—let's face up to it.

**And it shall come to pass in that day, saith the LORD of hosts, that I will cut off the names of the idols out of the land, and they shall no more be remembered: and also I will cause the prophets and the unclean spirit to pass out of the land [Zech. 13:2].**

"And it shall come to pass in that day"—again he dates it as being "in that day."

"I will cut off the names of the idols out of the land." When they were in Babylonian captivity, they took the "gold cure," that is, they gave up idolatry as they had observed it before. The golden calves were never put back at Dan and Beth-el. But they were still using the little household teraphim and other little fetishes. Even today a great many so-called civilized folk think that if they wear a certain object or if they put up a certain little gadget somewhere, it will ward off harm. That was the kind of idolatry that the people of Israel were engaged in. Also they dealt with the zodiac.

"And also I will cause the prophets and the unclean spirit to pass out of the land." The "prophets" are, of course, the false prophets. The "unclean spirit" refers to demons. We live in a world where demons are very active, and attention is being called to them at the present time. It may be that we are seeing an outbreak of demonic activity as we draw near the end of the age, but, candidly, I think there has been a subtle manifestation of them all along. The reason this passage is so important is that it is the only place that speaks of the demons being put out of this earth during the Millennium. The Book of Revelation tells about the false prophet and the Antichrist being put out of the earth: "And the beast was taken, and with him the false prophet that wrought miracles before him, with which he deceived them that had received the mark of the beast, and them that worshipped his image. These both were cast alive into a lake of fire burning with brimstone" (Rev. 19:20). And Satan will be bound during the millennial period (see Rev. 20:1–3). So we know that the false prophet and the Antichrist will be in the lake of fire and the Devil will be bound in the bottomless pit. Nothing is said in the Book of Revelation about the final casting out of demons, but it is logical to believe that it will be done at this time also and that they will be put in one place or the other. At least we know that they will be removed from the earth.

You would think that once a people had been delivered from paganism and heathenism, they would not go back to it. But in our day the world is going back to it because the human family is gradually moving into the darkness again due to a lack of knowledge of the Word of God. And this is the explanation for the demonic dynamic being manifested in our day. Ignorance of God's Word gives energy to the occult—there is no energy shortage in that particular connection.

What a different world this will be when there is a complete extermination of idolatry and demons are removed from the entire earth.

**And it shall come to pass, that when any shall yet prophesy, then his father and his mother that begat him shall say unto him, Thou shalt not live; for thou speakest lies in the name of the LORD: and his father and his mother that begat him shall thrust him through when he prophesieth [Zech. 13:3].**

That seems like strong language, but the day is coming, my friend, when God's children are going to put *Him* first. They betrayed Him the first time He came, and He is being betrayed in our day, but in that future day they are going to be faithful to Him even if the one who prophesies falsely is their own son.

**And it shall come to pass in that day, that the prophets shall be ashamed every one of his vision, when he hath prophesied; neither shall they wear a rough garment to deceive [Zech. 13:4].**

There are two things that interest me here. First, when the Lord comes the false prophets will be ashamed, deeply convicted, of their deceptive "vision." They will be disgraced because the Lord Jesus has come and made liars out of every one of them. The second thing that we note is that "neither shall they wear a rough garment to deceive." The garment worn by prophets was a mantle of rough, untanned sheepskin or goatskin or a cloak of camel's hair. (When Esau was born it is said that he looked like this kind of hairy garment!) The prophet Elijah wore this type of mantle, and it was this mantle that fell upon his successor, Elisha. It was a garment which distinguished a man as a prophet of God, and the false prophets will feel guilty about trying to impersonate a true prophet. You see, Zechariah was not introducing something new but something that was very familiar to the folk of his day.

**But he shall say, I am no prophet, I am an husbandman; for man taught me to keep cattle from my youth [Zech. 13:5].**

The men who were false prophets will go back to the farm.

The next two verses are startling. In fact, the critics have tried to eliminate them from the text because they say that it is shocking to find this prophecy given at this time. And it is! That is the wonder of it. Certainly it is no excuse to reject it; it is there to *alert* us. I should mention that there is a difference of opinion as to who is addressed in this verse. I believe that it is Christ.

**And one shall say unto him, What are these wounds in thine hands? Then he shall answer, Those with which I was wounded in the house of my friends [Zech. 13:6].**

"Wounded in the house of my friends" has been translated by some of the higher critics as "wounded in the house of those who loved me." Well, they didn't *love* Him the first time He came—they hated Him. Scripture says that they hated Him without cause. "He came unto his own, and his own received him not" (John 1:11). But to as many as received Him at that time He gave the authority to become sons of God. Well, when the Spirit is poured out, they (that is, the remnant) are going to receive Him. And they will wonder, saying, "Where did you get those wounds in your hands?" He will answer, "I was wounded here when I came the first time." He came to His own people, the Jewish race (remember that the woman of Samaria recognized Him as a Jew). These were His people, and only a remnant received Him at that time. And, actually, it will be only a remnant who will receive him at His second coming, although I think it will be a much larger remnant. "And *one* shall say unto him" probably refers to the spokesman for the remnant, just as Peter spoke for the other apostles when he said to Jesus, ". . . Thou art the Christ, the Son of the living God" (Matt. 16:16).

There is a song in which Jesus is called "the Stranger of Galilee." I don't know about you, but I don't like that song. He is not the stranger of Galilee to those who *know* Him. When He came the first time He was the stranger of Galilee to His own people, but when He comes the second time He will not be the stranger of Galilee to them. Certainly He is not the stranger of Galilee to Christians in this age in which we live, and I don't think we should sing that song. To *know Him* is life eternal. The apostle Paul at the end of his life wrote, "That I may know him, and the power of his resurrection, and the fellowship of his sufferings, being made conformable unto his death" (Phil. 3:10). But it is true that they did not know Jesus when He came the first time.

This matter of mistaken identity has been the source of plots for writers of both comedy and tragedy down through the years. Shakespeare used it in *The Comedy of Errors*. Dickens used it in *The Tale of Two Cities*. Many dramatic productions are based upon this idea—Alexandre Dumas' *The Count of Monte Cristo*, for example. It becomes even more tragic when it is a *real* life story. I read of a mother who had not seen her daughter for seventeen years, and when she went to meet her in New York, she walked right past her. It took some time to meet again because the mother didn't recognize her own daughter. In Reedley, California, I met a mother who had come from Russia and had not seen her daughter since she was a baby—of course she wouldn't be able to recognize her.

However, I think that the greatest tragedy of the ages is expressed in just eleven words: "He came unto His own, and His own received him not." What a picture! John the Baptist elaborated upon it when he said, ". . . I baptize with water: but there standeth one among you, *whom ye know not*" (John 1:26, italics mine). And the Lord Jesus Himself said that they knew not the time of their visitation—what a tremendous statement! And Paul wrote: "But their minds were blinded: for until this day remaineth [notice that!] the

same veil untaken away in the reading of the old testament; which veil is done away in Christ. But even unto this day, when Moses is read, the veil is upon their heart" (2 Cor. 3:14–15). Notice that the veil is upon their heart—but when the heart is right, they can turn to Him. He is a stranger only to those who do not know Him as Savior. Zechariah speaks of this. In His first coming they didn't know Him.

There is a striking contrast between the first and second comings of Christ. *Redemption* is the high word of His first coming; *revelation* is the high word of His second coming. It was *reconciliation* at His first coming and *recognition* at His second coming. It was the *Incarnation* at His first coming and *identification* at His second coming. It was the *mystery* at His first coming, and it will be *manifestation* at His second coming. At His first coming it was *propitiation;* at His second coming it will be *proclamation*. What a picture this gives of Christ!

## THE SMITTEN SHEPHERD AND THE SCATTERED SHEEP

**Awake, O sword, against my shepherd, and against the man that is my fellow, saith the LORD of hosts: smite the shepherd, and the sheep shall be scattered: and I will turn mine hand upon the little ones [Zech. 13:7].**

This refers to the time that He was smitten. In fact, when Christ was here the first time, He said that this verse applied to Himself, as we shall see. We immediately identify this remarkable passage of Scripture with ". . . they shall look upon me whom they have pierced, and they shall mourn for him . . ." of Zechariah 12:10.

"Awake, O sword, against my shepherd, and against the man that is my fellow, saith the LORD of hosts." The Lord God is the speaker, and Christ, the Messiah, is the person spoken of. The phrase, "the man that is my fellow" would be better translated, "the man my equal" or "the man of my union." This is an unmistakable Old Testament reference to the deity of Christ.

"Smite the shepherd, and the sheep shall be scattered." Who would have thought that this would refer to the Lord Jesus Christ? We know it does because Jesus Himself quotes it. "Then saith Jesus unto them, All ye shall be offended because of me this night: for it is written, I will smite the shepherd, and the sheep of the flock shall be scattered abroad"

(Matt. 26:31). You see that He makes it applicable to *Himself*. If you doubt that God has a future purpose for Israel, you need to note this carefully. In the prophecies that we have here which relate to the first and second comings of Christ, did the Lord Jesus lie? He says that Zechariah was referring to *Him* when he said, "Smite the shepherd, and the sheep shall be scattered." And when He comes the second time, they will ask "What are these wounds, these nail prints, in Your hands?" And His answer will be, "I received these in the house of My friends." And, as we saw in chapter 12, "They shall look upon me whom they have pierced, and they shall mourn for him, as one mourneth for his only son." This will be the great Day of Atonement for the Jewish people, and obviously it is for a future time.

The final two verses of this chapter refer to the Great Tribulation Period.

**And it shall come to pass, that in all the land, saith the Lord, two parts therein shall be cut off and die; but the third shall be left therein [Zech. 13:8].**

"The third shall be left therein" refers to the same remnant that shall ask, "What are these wounds in thine hands?" They will have come through the horrors of the Great Tribulation Period in which two-thirds of their people have perished.

**And I will bring the third part through the fire, and will refine them as silver is refined, and will try them as gold is tried: they shall call on my name, and I will hear them: I will say, It is my people: and they shall say, The Lord is my God [Zech. 13:9].**

Isn't that a wonderful statement? These are the ones who will take a stand for Christ and will be faithful to Him. They will make it through the Great Tribulation because He has sealed them (see Rev. 7:1–8). Then we see them again in Revelation 14: "And I looked, and, lo, a Lamb stood on the mount Sion, and with him an hundred forty and four thousand, having his Father's name written in their foreheads. . . . And they sung as it were a new song before the throne, and before the four beasts, and the elders: and no man could learn that song but the hundred and forty and four thousand, which were redeemed from the earth" (Rev. 14:1, 3).

# CHAPTER 14

**THEME:** *The second coming of Christ, the Messiah*

Chapter 14 concludes the second division of the last section of the Book of Zechariah. This last section, chapters 9–14, deals with prophetic burdens. There was the first burden, dealing with the prophetic aspects connected with the *first* coming of Christ (chs. 9–11). In the second and last division (chs. 12–14), we have the second burden in which we have the prophetic aspects connected with the *second* coming of Christ. This final chapter just gathers together everything and ties up any loose strings there might be.

The very interesting thing is that we have had a very definite program given to us in the Book of Zechariah, and that has been true in all three of its major divisions. We had the ten visions, then the historic interlude, and now this last major division of prophetic burdens. We always start where Israel was at that particular time (and they were in a certain amount of difficulty), and then we move through the national conversion of Israel when the nation will turn to God and there will be a pouring out of the Spirit of God. All of this prepares the scene for the return of Messiah, because at that time they have entered the Great Tribulation Period.

This last chapter is a great climactic chapter, but it also follows the entire program that has been given to us in Zechariah. This is a section that leads up to and into the establishment of the kingdom at the second coming of Christ. In each of these major divisions, Zechariah, encouraging the people of that day, looks on to the future and outlines a prophetic program.

There are certain things which we need to make clear about this chapter. The first is that it is *wholly prophetic*—it is entirely that. The other is that it has no prophecy which is being fulfilled in this present age. In other words, it is speaking of *the end of the age* that ushers in the kingdom. You will find that many commentators, especially of the higher, critical school (and I believe that largely all amillennialists follow this same plan and purpose), teach that this does not actually speak of prophecy, that it is not literal, and that it can be fitted into the present age. Believe me, that leads to some strange interpretations! Lowe and DeWette, who belonged to that camp, both said: "This chapter defies all historical explanation." We can certainly say amen to that, as nothing like this has ever happened in the past. Therefore, this chapter is entirely prophetic; that is, it is prophetic from where we are today, and it looks to the future.

The only interpretation of this chapter which will satisfy is a literal interpretation; that is the only one that will give the meaning. And any interpretation must be in harmony with the context. In interpreting prophecy or interpreting Scripture anywhere, you cannot disregard the context before and after. Also, you must interpret this in keeping with the spirit and the feel of the entire Word of God. You absolutely cannot reach in here and come out with some wild interpretation that has no basis in fact. I believe that this is a very, very important passage of Scripture, because it demonstrates the difference between literal interpretation of Scripture and that which spiritualizes or mysticalizes it, making it mean practically nothing at all. Such interpretation merely makes this passage something that is allegorical or something that is mythical or something that actually can be dissipated into thin air. It is an attempt to explain it away rather than to explain it.

Let me make a suggestion that is really a mean one. If you are wanting to know the position of a pastor whom you're not sure about, if you really want to know what he *believes*, take the fourteenth chapter of Zechariah to him and ask him to explain it to you. You will find out what a man really believes when he deals with this chapter.

Certain of the liberal commentators, actually great scholars of the past, and Hengstenberg specifically, refer chapter 14 "to the whole of the Messianic era." What he really means is that it refers to this church period today. You cannot, by the wildest kind of interpretation, fit that in. That is the reason he does not go into detail. Leupold, another outstanding liberal scholar, says:

Our verses do not, therefore, apply to any one situation. They do not describe a siege, capture, and captivity which actually occurred. By means of a figure they describe a situation which obtains continually through New Testament times. God's people shall continually be antagonized and suffer bitter adversity at the hands of their foes and shall in consequence be brought low; but there shall always be an imperishable remnant, and that not so extremely small.

Would you tell me what he really means by that? He means that he doesn't know what to do with this chapter at all. So the thing he does is spiritualize it—he spreads it out like butter on toast, and it melts just about the same way!

May I say that these verses are not just figurative, they do not apply to New Testament times, and the remnant that is spoken of here—it's been made clear to us in this book— is a *Jewish* remnant. We need to recognize that this chapter is entirely eschatological.

There have been other scholars who identify this chapter with "the error of so-called 'Jewish Chiliasm.' " The fact of the matter is, as Dr. Unger goes on to say, " 'Jewish Chiliasm' was wrong *only* in the fact that it *overlooked the prophesied rejection and death of the Messiah as the indispensable prelude to His manifestation in kingdom glory.*"

With that as a background, let us come to the text itself—

**Behold, the day of the LORD cometh, and thy spoil shall be divided in the midst of thee [Zech. 14:1].**

"Behold, the day of the LORD cometh"—this would make a good headline for the newspaper. Many times, when you get down into an article, it moves behind the headline and gives you the preliminaries that led up to the headline. That is what happens here.

"Behold, the day of the LORD." Here we are again with this very impressive statement. We will find that the thing which is before us in these first three verses is the last siege of Jerusalem. Then in verses 4–7, we have the personal advent of the Messiah. We have seen all of this in other chapters of Zechariah, but now we have it brought in from a little different angle. For instance, regarding the Great Tribulation Period and the siege of Jerusalem, the thing that was important in the other passages was an emphasis on the latter part of the Tribulation and the deliverance that came, and Zechariah was prophesying to the people for their encouragement. But here we see how tragic it is actually going to be during that period of the Day of the Lord. The thing that Joel had said was that the Day of the Lord is not light; it is darkness. It begins in darkness. The hopelessness and the helplessness of these people in that period is difficult for us to understand.

"Behold, the day of the LORD cometh." The Hebrew idiom that is employed here is *yom-ba' leyahweh*. (I pass that on to you just to let you know that I did study Hebrew, although I've forgotten most of it by now.) This is the expression that is headline material here, and it refers to this coming day which is yet in the future (after the church is removed) when Antichrist brings on the Great Tribulation, although the world will believe that he is bringing in the Millennium. We certainly have had quite a few presidents in my day who were going to bring in the Millennium. Not one of them has gotten within four miles of the Millennium, but that does not prevent Americans from believing that the next candidate is going to do it. Well, none of them is going to do it—only Jesus Christ can do that.

Dr. Unger's rendering of this verse is: "Lo, a day is coming—the Lord's—when thy spoil shall be distributed in the midst of thee." The enemy is going to take Jerusalem again, and this will be the last siege.

**For I will gather all nations against Jerusalem to battle; and the city shall be taken, and the houses rifled, and the women ravished; and half of the city shall go forth into captivity, and the residue of the people shall not be cut off from the city [Zech. 14:2].**

This is the last siege of Jerusalem, and it is not a pretty picture that is given to us here. The enemy takes the city, and when Zechariah says "all nations," I am of the opinion that he means that each nation will have representatives there. You might ask how that could be. Well, we have that same thing today with the United Nations. At the time that I am writing this, there are United Nations troops in Israel again. The soldiers come from different nations, and they more or less serve as a buffer between Israel and the enemy. It will be different in that day, but it will be an army that is made up of those who represent all the nations. They will come against Jerusalem, and they're going to take that city.

Again, let me give you Dr. Unger's translation. It is a sad state: "And the city shall be captured and the houses plundered, and the women raped, and half of the city shall go into captivity, but the rest of the people shall not be cut off from the city." Apparently, some will be able to escape. There are those, including myself, who believe that it will probably be the rock-hewn city of Petra to which they will go. Masada would also be a good place. That is where the Jews escaped to at the time of the invasion by Titus in A.D. 70. The only thing is that Masada would sure be a good target for bombers if they went there. I believe that the rock-hewn city of Petra could be the place.

This is a sad thing that is revealed to these people through Zechariah. The city is taken, the houses are plundered, and the women are raped. These are the three things that Zechariah mentions here.

**Then shall the LORD go forth, and fight against those nations, as when he fought in the day of battle [Zech. 14:3].**

This is a picture of the Deliverer who is coming. It is at this time that their help will not come from the north or south or east or west, but their help will come from the Lord, the Maker of heaven and earth. This will be none other than the Lord Jesus Himself coming to the earth to deliver these people.

**And his feet shall stand in that day upon the mount of Olives, which is before Jerusalem on the east, and the mount of Olives shall cleave in the midst thereof toward the east and toward the west, and there shall be a very great valley; and half of the mountain shall remove toward the north, and half of it toward the south [Zech. 14:4].**

"And his feet shall stand in that day upon the mount of Olives." This is a tremendous statement that is made here, and it is quite literal. The Mount of Olives is literal, Jerusalem is literal, these people are literal. When the Lord Jesus comes, His feet will stand upon the Mount of Olives. When Zechariah says His feet, he's talking about His feet, not His hands. Zechariah says that they will touch the Mount of Olives, and apparently he means that that's where the touchdown is going to be. I'm of the opinion that if men can send a missile that goes out to the moon and spends a few days there and comes back, and if they can put a battleship out in the Pacific and have that little capsule come down within two or three miles of the battleship, then God is not going to have any trouble with the Lord Jesus Christ touching down at the Mount of Olives. He is the glorified Christ today. He has nail prints in those feet, but those feet left the

Mount of Olives when He left this earth, and He's coming back to the Mount of Olives when He comes again. This is exactly what was told His disciples. When He ascended, two witnesses came and said, ". . . Ye men of Galilee, why stand ye gazing up into heaven? this same Jesus, which is taken up from you into heaven, shall so come in like manner as ye have seen him go into heaven" (Acts 1:11). This is the fulfillment of it that will take place in the future. When? In the Day of the Lord, in the time when they are in great trouble, when Jerusalem has been besieged and taken for the last time.

"Upon the mount of Olives, which is before Jerusalem on the east." This mention of the east is not a casual statement. You will notice throughout Scripture that help for Israel is coming from the east. This is the reason they pay great attention to that eastern gate which some call the golden gate. I personally believe that the reference to the golden gate is the gate in the temple that shall be built. If you want to call it the golden gate, that's fine—it is the eastern gate. He will probably come in from the east.

Ezekiel also tells us that help is coming to them from the east. I think that it is interesting that we have been on the side of Israel from the very time that it became a nation—but we happen to be a *western* nation, you see. The real help for them is coming from the Lord, and there is no fulfillment of prophecy taking place there today. We can see that clearly when we put this prophecy down on what is going to happen.

"And the mount of Olives shall cleave in the midst thereof toward the east and toward the west, and there shall be a very great valley; and half of the mountain shall remove toward the north, and half of it toward the south." Great physical changes that are going to take place are mentioned to us here. There will be a great earthquake, and the Mount of Olives will be split right down the middle. Half of it will go to the north and half to the south.

"And there shall be a very great valley." Jerusalem today is surrounded by the roughest terrain that I know of anywhere. I frankly have been no place that can compare to it. It is rugged if you go north or if you go east or if you go south or if you go west—any direction that you might go. If you go south to Bethlehem, you would think you were riding one of the toboggan rides at Disneyland. Up and down you go—mountain after mountain—and it is rugged. If you go north, it is rugged. If you go west, it is rugged—big boulders and

rocks. You've never seen such great big rocks. Going east down to Jericho—again, it is a rugged trip. The only thing is that the United States put in a wonderful macadam highway there. It is not a freeway, but it is a good highway, and it makes such an easy trip that the tourist doesn't realize what rough terrain it actually is.

**And ye shall flee to the valley of the mountains; for the valley of the mountains shall reach unto Azal: yea, ye shall flee, like as ye fled from before the earthquake in the days of Uzziah king of Judah: and the LORD my God shall come, and all the saints with thee [Zech. 14:5].**

"And ye shall flee to the valley of the mountains." This is the reason that many commentators believe that they will flee over yonder to the rock-hewn city of Petra in the old country of Edom. However, we cannot be dogmatic because Scripture has not told that.

"And the LORD my God shall come, and all the saints with thee." This is a very interesting passage of Scripture. It is a picture of the Lord Jesus coming back to the earth. We find this also in Revelation 19 where we are told that the armies of heaven will follow Him. Here it says that all the saints will come with Him. Let us look for a moment at Romans 11:25 which says, "For I would not, brethren, that ye should be ignorant of this mystery, lest ye should be wise in your own conceits; that blindness in part is happened to Israel, until the fulness of the Gentiles be come in." This is the time of the fullness of the Gentiles when all the nations come up against Jerusalem. Romans 11:26 reads: "And so all Israel shall be saved: as it is written, There shall come out of Sion the Deliverer, and shall turn away ungodliness from Jacob." That time has definitely not come. The Lord Jesus' first coming doesn't satisfy this, and the Jews' present return to the land does not satisfy any of these Scriptures.

**And it shall come to pass in that day, that the light shall not be clear, nor dark:**

**But it shall be one day which shall be known to the LORD, not day, nor night: but it shall come to pass, that at evening time it shall be light [Zech. 14: 6–7].**

There will be changes in the lighting of the earth. We are moving through that period of dawn to the coming of Christ to establish His kingdom. This is, of course, a definite reference to the Day of the Lord, which is actually not a twenty-four-hour day.

We come now to a new section in which we find the establishment of Israel's kingdom here upon the earth.

**And it shall be in that day, that living waters shall go out from Jerusalem; half of them toward the former sea, and half of them toward the hinder sea: in summer and in winter shall it be [Zech. 14:8].**

"The former sea" is the Dead Sea, and "the hinder sea" is the Mediterranean Sea. In other words, this will be a spring that will gush up water, and I think it means literal water. Apparently, Jerusalem, which has been an inland city, will suddenly become a seagoing city, that is, a port town. If you want to find in this verse a suggestion of the spiritual Water of Life, I think that will be true also because Zechariah also tells us that the Law, the Word of God, will go out from Jerusalem in that day. But this is literal water that Zechariah is talking about here.

**And the LORD shall be king over all the earth: in that day shall there be one LORD, and his name one [Zech. 14:9].**

This is another very marvelous passage of Scripture. It refers to the Day of the Lord and to the fact that the Lord will be King—this is none other than the Lord Jesus Christ, of course. In that day there will be one Lord and one language. I'd like to turn to Zephaniah 3:9 which reads: "For then will I turn to the people a pure language, that they may all call upon the name of the LORD, to serve him with one consent." I do not think that we can be definite about which language this will be. God put up language as a barrier to mankind. No wall could be built any higher than the wall of a language barrier. That was the way in which He was enabled to scatter mankind and then, down through the years, to prepare for the coming of a Savior. Today the gospel is going back into those languages throughout the world. This is another of the great signs which indicate that we are moving toward the end of the age. There will be one language in that day, and I am going to be glad of that. I don't care what language it is, but everybody will speak that same language.

**All the land shall be turned as a plain from Geba to Rimmon south of Jeru-**

**salem: and it shall be lifted up, and inhabited in her place, from Benjamin's gate unto the place of the first gate, unto the corner gate, and from the tower of Hananeel unto the king's winepresses [Zech. 14:10].**

This is very important as we are now looking at what is really the finale—this brings us to the end.

"All the land shall be turned as a plain [the Arabah]." The Arabah is the geographical name of that deep rift that comes down from above the Sea of Galilee, through the Jordan Valley, through the Dead Sea, down into the Gulf of Aqaba, and on into North Africa. It has been called the Great Rift. It begins at the Dog River at the coast north of Beirut in Lebanon. Zechariah is saying that there will be another great valley that resembles the Arabah.

Zechariah says that this great valley will go all the way "from Geba to Rimmon south of Jerusalem." This indicates the hill country of the ancient tribe of Judah to the border of Simeon on the south. It goes all the way from up north where Geba is located in the tribe of Benjamin to Rimmon, which is thirty-three miles southwest of Jerusalem. That will be a tremendous valley. All of that rugged terrain that is around Jerusalem is going to be smoothed out, and, apparently, Jerusalem will be elevated—"and it shall be lifted up."

"And it shall be lifted up, and inhabited in her place, from Benjamin's gate unto the place of the first gate, unto the corner gate, and from the tower of Hananeel unto the king's winepresses." One commentator years ago said that this could not be literal because nobody could find the tower of Hananeel. The interesting thing is that archaeologists have since located it, and this brother is going to have to come up with another interpretation!

**And men shall dwell in it, and there shall be no more utter destruction; but Jerusalem shall be safely inhabited [Zech. 14:11].**

This will be the first time in the history of Jerusalem that it will be a safe place to live. It is not so today, and it never has been. It is a very tender spot. The most sensitive spot in this universe is there. But when the Millennium has come, the Lord Jesus has come, His feet have touched the Mount of Olives, and these tremendous physical changes have taken place, then the people can dwell in Jerusalem safely. In other words, peace will have come to the earth for the first time.

**And this shall be the plague wherewith the LORD will smite all the people that have fought against Jerusalem; Their flesh shall consume away while they stand upon their feet, and their eyes shall consume away in their holes, and their tongue shall consume away in their mouth [Zech. 14:12].**

"Their flesh shall consume away while they stand upon their feet." This is a living death against the enemies of God that will take place. The Book of Revelation tells us that this will take place in the Great Tribulation Period.

"And their eyes shall consume away in their holes [sockets], and their tongue shall consume away in their mouth." May I say, this is a terrible thing.

**And it shall come to pass in that day, that a great tumult from the LORD shall be among them; and they shall lay hold every one on the hand of his neighbour, and his hand shall rise up against the hand of his neighbour [Zech. 14:13].**

That the enemy will be able to take the city will largely be due to this tremendous revolution that apparently will be taking place in the city.

**And Judah also shall fight at Jerusalem; and the wealth of all the heathen round about shall be gathered together, gold, and silver, and apparel, in great abundance.**

**And so shall be the plague of the horse, of the mule, of the camel, and of the ass, and of all the beasts that shall be in these tents, as this plague [Zech. 14: 14–15].**

Jerusalem will become the commercial center of the world. We are told elsewhere in prophecy that, just as they brought great wealth out of Egypt in the days of Moses, they will bring great wealth into the land of Israel when they return—that is, when *God* returns them.

We come now to a description of the kingdom itself in contrast to the setting up of it. In the coming of Christ to the earth, He will put down all unrighteousness, all rebellion.

**And it shall come to pass, that every one that is left of all the nations which came against Jerusalem shall even go up from year to year to worship the King, the LORD of hosts, and to keep the feast of tabernacles [Zech. 14:16].**

This verse means that there will not only be a remnant of Israel saved, but also a remnant out of each nation of the Gentiles. And they will be the ones who enter the kingdom.

"Every one that is left of all the nations which came against Jerusalem shall even go up [that is, face in] from year to year to worship the King." They are going to face in to Jerusalem. There are great changes taking place at this time—not only physically, not only spiritually, not only economically, and in fact, in every area of life, but also the manner of witnessing for God will be different during the Millennium. Today we have been told, beginning at Jerusalem, to go to the ends of the earth (see Acts 1:8). Here we find that people from all nations are to go up to Jerusalem—that is what they did before the Lord Jesus came and died on the cross. But after His death and resurrection He said, "Go to the ends of the earth with this message."

They shall "go up from year to year to worship the King, the LORD of hosts, and to keep the feast of tabernacles." The Feast of Tabernacles is the feast that the Israelites celebrated when they came out of Egypt. In that day, they will celebrate it because they have been brought from the ends of the earth back to Jerusalem.

**And it shall be, that whoso will not come up of all the families of the earth unto Jerusalem to worship the King, the LORD of hosts, even upon them shall be no rain [Zech. 14:17].**

Someone will say, "I thought this was the Millennium!" It is, but the Millennium will be a time of testing those in this great multitude—a remnant, but a large remnant, I believe—who have turned to God. It is like being a church member—not all church members are Christians, by any means. Therefore, this period of the Millennium will be a time of testing.

**And if the family of Egypt go not up, and come not, that have no rain; there shall be the plague, wherewith the LORD will smite the heathen that come not up to keep the feast of tabernacles.**

**This shall be the punishment of Egypt, and the punishment of all nations that come not up to keep the feast of tabernacles [Zech. 14:18–19].**

Egypt is used as an example.

**In that day shall there be upon the bells of the horses, HOLINESS UNTO THE**

**LORD; and the pots in the LORD'S house shall be like the bowls before the altar [Zech. 14:20].**

"In that day"—Zechariah will not let loose of this expression!

"In that day shall there be upon the bells of the horses, HOLINESS UNTO THE LORD." Even a harness on a horse will be holiness unto the Lord. What does that mean? Everything will be for the service of God. The vessels in the tabernacle were called *holy* vessels. Why? They weren't unusual. I have a notion that after forty years in the wilderness they were beaten and battered, and I think they looked like they had really *had* it. But they were *holy* because they were for the service of God. And everything in that day will be for the service of God.

"And the pots in the LORD'S house shall be like the bowls before the altar." Everything will be for the service of God then, but today we are living in a world where practically nothing is used for the service of God.

**Yea, every pot in Jerusalem and in Judah shall be holiness unto the LORD of hosts: and all they that sacrifice shall come and take of them, and seethe therein: and in that day there shall be no more the Canaanite in the house of the LORD of hosts [Zech. 14:21].**

"Yea, every pot in Jerusalem and in Judah shall be holiness unto the LORD of hosts." Just think of that! That skillet that you have, the pot for cooking beans or cabbage—in that day, all will be for the service of God. Everything will be dedicated to Him.

"And all they that sacrifice shall come and take of them." Are they going to offer sacrifices in that day? We read also in Ezekiel that they will. Certainly these sacrifices will look *back* to the death of Christ just as the sacrifices before Christ looked forward to His coming.

"And in that day there shall be no more the Canaanite in the house of the LORD of hosts." This means that all the hypocrites are going to be removed. This means that every unbeliever will be removed, and there will be none in the service of God unless they belong to Him. This will be the Millennium, my friend. What a glorious picture this is! This is a great finale and climax for the prophecy of Zechariah.

# BIBLIOGRAPHY

(Recommended for Further Study)

Baron, David. *The Visions and Prophecies of Zechariah*. London, England: Hebrew Christian Testimony to Israel, 1918.

Feinberg, Charles L. *The Minor Prophets*. Chicago, Illinois: Moody Press, 1976.

Gaebelein, Arno C. *The Annotated Bible*. 1917. Reprint. Neptune, New Jersey: Loizeaux Brothers, 1971.

Ironside, H. A. *The Minor Prophets*. Neptune, New Jersey: Loizeaux Brothers, n.d.

Jensen, Irving L. *Haggai, Zechariah, and Malachi*. Chicago, Illinois: Moody Press, 1976.

Tatford, Frederick A. *The Minor Prophets*. Minneapolis, Minnesota: Klock & Klock, n.d.

Unger, Merrill F. *Unger's Bible Commentary: Zechariah*. Grand Rapids, Michigan: Zondervan Publishing House, 1963.

Unger, Merrill F. *Unger's Commentary on the Old Testament*, Vol. 2. Chicago, Illinois: Moody Press, 1982.

# The Book of
# MALACHI
## INTRODUCTION

Malachi brings down the curtain on the Old Testament. He is the last in a long succession of prophets who foretold the coming of the Messiah. In fact, if we were to go back one thousand years before Malachi and then come down through the centuries, we would find that God was increasing the tempo of telling the people about the coming of the Messiah. And the last voice is that of this man Malachi. I like to think of him as a sort of radio announcer for the Lord. It is as if he were saying, "The next voice you hear will be John the Baptist four hundred years from now." Well, four hundred years is a long time to wait for station identification!

Malachi is a very interesting person although we know nearly nothing about him. We will find that he has a wonderful sense of humor. I do not think you can be a prophet or a preacher without a sense of humor, and if you haven't found humor in the Bible, my friend, you are not reading it aright.

We will also see that this man Malachi in a very definite way was a messenger. The name *Malachi* means "my messenger." The Septuagint gives its meaning as "angel," since *angelos* is the Greek word for "messenger." An angel was a messenger and could be either human or supernatural. In fact, there were a few church fathers who actually thought that Malachi was a *spiritual* angel, that an angel wrote this book—but there are no grounds for this. At the opposite extreme we have the liberal school of higher criticism which claims that the book is actually anonymous. They argue that Malachi means just messenger that it is only a title and not a name at all. Surely our information of Malachi is as limited as it is regarding angels. If the book were anonymous, it would be the only book of prophecy to be so, and I do not think that Malachi would want to be the exception to the rule, especially since he was the last one to write.

There is a reason that we do not know very much about Malachi. He is a messenger, God's messenger with a message, and frankly, we don't need to know about the messenger. When the Western Union boy rings your doorbell at one o'clock in the morning with a very important message for you, you do not question him about his ancestors! He doesn't tell you all about himself and his family. You're not interested in the Western Union boy's ancestors, and you don't care whether or not they came over on *The Mayflower*—especially at one in the morning! The fact of the matter is that you don't even get his name. The important thing is *the message* that he brings. Malachi was just a messenger, and the important thing is the content of his message.

We have this same method used by the Spirit of God in the Gospel of Mark where the Lord Jesus' genealogy is not given at all. The reason is that each of the four Gospels presents Christ in a different way. Matthew presents Him as the King. If He's the King, He will have to be in the line of David, and that is the way the Gospel of Matthew opens: "The book of the generation of Jesus Christ, the son of David . . ." (Matt. 1:1). The important thing is that He is the Son of David because Matthew is presenting Him as the King. But when you come to the Gospel of Mark, which presents Him as the Servant of God, Mark is not concerned about giving His genealogy, and there's none given. The important thing about a servant is whether or not he can get the job done. That is the thing you want to know about anyone who comes into the place of service for you. And Mark shows that the Lord Jesus could get the job done, and He *did* get it done. In the same way, it is *the message*, not the messenger, which is important in the prophecy of Malachi.

There is some difference of opinion about the time at which Malachi wrote. The date that I suggest is 397 B.C., which is probably a late date. It is the belief of conservative scholars today that Malachi prophesied in the last part of the fifth century. That would be near 397 B.C. but somewhat earlier than that. The important thing is that Malachi was the prophet at the time of Nehemiah as Haggai and Zechariah were the prophets at the time of Zerubbabel and Joshua. This man Malachi concluded the prophetic books as Nehemiah concluded the historical books of the Old Testament. He probably prophesied during the time of Nehemiah's governorship or immediately afterwards.

As we have said, Malachi was a messenger, but the thing that is important is his message. He himself uses the term *messenger* three times, and he makes three tremendous and significant references to other messengers.

1. In Malachi 2:7 he refers to Levi as the messenger of the Lord: "For the priest's lips should keep knowledge, and they should seek the law at his mouth: for he is the messenger of the LORD of hosts." This suggests that every messenger, every witness, every teacher of the Word is an angel of the Lord, a messenger of the Lord. In the Book of Revelation where we have the messages addressed to the seven churches, it is expressed in this way: "Unto *the angel* of the church of Ephesus write . . ." (Rev. 2:1, italics mine). I believe that this means the messenger of the church—not a supernatural being, but just the human messenger—in other words, the pastor of the church. I was a pastor for a long time, and I rather like this idea of calling the pastor an angel. I've heard him called everything else, so I don't know why we shouldn't include "angel."

2. Malachi also announced the coming of John the Baptist as "my messenger"—"Behold, I will send my messenger, and he shall prepare the way before me . . ." (Mal. 3:1). John the Baptist was the Malachi of the New Testament and began where Malachi of the Old Testament left off.

3. The third reference to a messenger is to Christ as "the messenger of the covenant." Again in Malachi 3:1 we read, ". . . and the Lord, whom ye seek, shall suddenly come to his temple, even the messenger of the covenant, whom ye delight in: behold, he shall come, saith the LORD of hosts." The angel of the Lord in the Old Testament is definitely the preincarnate Christ.

I want you to see something that makes Malachi one of my favorite books of the Bible (of course, I have sixty-five other favorite books in the Bible), and that is that Malachi has such a wonderful sense of humor. He had to have one in order to deal with the group he had to deal with in that day. He adopted a question-and-answer method. First, he would quote a declaration or an interrogation which God had made to Israel. Then he would give Israel's answer which in every case was supercilious and sophisticated sarcasm. It was arrogant and haughty and presumptuous and even insulting. But, believe me, Malachi has some good answers from the Lord! And since they are the Lord's answers, it is the Lord who has a sense of humor. I hope you enjoy this book because it is a great little book, by the way.

# OUTLINE

# CHAPTER 1

**THEME:** *The love of God for Israel; the priests reproved for profanity*

Malachi is going to deal with those same problems with which Nehemiah dealt, and this reveals that Malachi was speaking into that same day. The first problem is the defilement of the priesthood. The second is their foreign marriages and the divorce of their Israelite wives—believe me, God is going to come down hard on this. Many folk ask me to deal with the subject of divorce. Well, I take whatever comes up in the Word of God, and God will talk about divorce in Malachi. Then the third problem is that the people of Israel were neglecting their giving the tithe and the offering to God. You can be sure that you won't like what God has to say about those who are kidding everybody about their giving to the Lord.

### The burden of the word of the LORD to Israel by Malachi [Mal. 1:1].

*Malachi* means "my messenger." He is the Western Union boy who brings the last message from God to the people of Israel.

"The burden of the word of the LORD to Israel." A "burden" is a judgment, a judgment from God, and it will be a very strong and rigorous rebuke that God will give to them.

Something else that we should note is that Malachi is addressing Israel, that is, all of the twelve tribes. It is obvious that the tribes of Israel didn't really get lost. Although they seem to be "lost" to some people today, they never were lost. This message is "to Israel," to all twelve of the tribes. There had returned to the land just a remnant from each tribe, very few from each one. But God addressed them and, very frankly, I think that Malachi's message went out from here to the others who had not returned. The Book of Nehemiah reveals that there was communication back and forth. There were messengers, travelers, going back and forth between Israel and the place of captivity where they had been in slavery. We are going to see that, apparently, the message went out to all twelve of the tribes.

### I have loved you, saith the LORD. Yet ye say, Wherein hast thou loved us? Was not Esau Jacob's brother? saith the LORD: yet I loved Jacob,

### And I hated Esau, and laid his mountains and his heritage waste for the dragons of the wilderness [Mal. 1:2–3].

Malachi's message starts out in this very marvelous, wonderful way: "I have loved you, saith the LORD." Isn't that a wonderful way to begin!

Now how do you think that these people are going to respond to that? Remember that they have returned to the land, and by the time of Nehemiah, although they are discouraged about the rebuilding of the walls of Jerusalem, there is a show of prosperity, and they are going through the form of worship in the rebuilt temple. They are going through the ritual of it, and on the surface everything looks good. But, oh, are they a sarcastic, supercilious, sophisticated, blasé group! God says to them, "I have loved you, saith the LORD." And listen to them!—"Yet ye say, Wherein hast thou loved us?" Can you believe that these people would have the audacity to speak to God like that? They say, "In what way have You loved us?" I'm not sure but what there are a great many today in the church who would raise that same question and say, "Look at the things that are happening to us today. How can you say that God loves us?" Well, God made it very clear to Israel from the very beginning that He loved them.

It is interesting that you go a long way into the Bible before you find God telling anybody that He loved them. But when you get to Deuteronomy (by that time you've come to Moses), you're out in the wilderness and you've been out there for forty years, and it is going to be pretty hard to make anybody believe that God loves him. But listen to what Moses says in Deuteronomy 10:15: "Only the LORD had a delight in thy fathers to love them . . . ." God simply had not been saying that to anyone. You go through the time of the Flood and afterwards, and God never told anybody that. God didn't tell Abraham that He loved him, but He *did*, of course. The point is that God was in no hurry to let mankind know that He loved them. But He says here, "Only the LORD had a delight in thy fathers to love them, and he chose their seed after them, even you above all people, as it is this day."

Now God is prepared to prove what He has said, and His answer is this: "Was not Esau Jacob's brother? saith the LORD: yet I loved Jacob, And I hated Esau, and laid his mountains and his heritage waste for the dragons of the wilderness." This is a tremendous statement that God makes to them. The people were questioning, they were doubting the love of God, and God reminds them of the origin of their nation. Jacob and Esau were twins. God made a difference between them at the very beginning (see Gen. 25:22–23), but it was about fifteen hundred years before He stated as He does here that He loved Jacob.

This presents a problem: Why should God say that He loved Jacob and hated Esau? A student came to the late Dr. Griffith Thomas with that question. "I have a problem," he said. "Why does God say that He *hated* Esau?"

"Well, I have a problem with that verse, too," Dr. Thomas replied. "But my problem is why God said that He *loved* Jacob. That's the real problem."

My friend, the real problem here is why God would say that He loved this people. But let's understand one thing: God never said this until Jacob and Esau had become two great nations which had long histories. Therefore, God said that He loved Jacob because of the fact that He knew what was in Jacob's heart. He knew that here was a man who had a desire for Him and that Esau did not have a desire for Him at all. But it had to be worked out in fifteen hundred years of history before God was prepared to make the kind of statement He makes here in Malachi. We need to understand that the difference here between loving and hating is simply that the life of the nation that came from Esau, which is Edom, and the life of the nation which came from Jacob, which is Israel, demonstrate that God was right when He said that He loved one and hated the other.

All this reveals something that we need to face up to today. We have majored so much on the love of God. Do you know that if God loves, God also hates—because you cannot love without hating? As someone has said, love and hate are very close together. If God loves the good, He has to hate the evil—it couldn't be otherwise—and that is exactly what we find here. The histories of the nation of Israel and the nation of Edom are altogether different. God says that because of Esau's life, because of the evil which was inherent in this man and which worked itself out into the nation of Edom, He is justified in making this statement.

**Whereas Edom saith, We are impoverished, but we will return and build the desolate places; thus saith the Lord**

**of hosts, They shall build, but I will throw down; and they shall call them, The border of wickedness, and, The people against whom the Lord hath indignation for ever.**

**And your eyes shall see, and ye shall say, The Lord will be magnified from the border of Israel [Mal. 1:4–5].**

What God is saying to them is this: "My action and conduct with these nations which came from Esau and Jacob reveal that I loved Jacob and that I hated Esau." After God judged Edom, they never made a comeback. When was the last time you saw an Edomite? They are just not doing business today. They went out of style years ago. God judged Edom, and this action of His looks like loving and hating. And God says to Israel, "I demonstrated that I loved you." At the beginning, He never made that statement because He had to wait until it worked itself out. This reveals, therefore, that God's choice is neither capricious nor is it an arbitrary choice. God does not make choices like that. There has to be something to back it up. God had a real relationship with His people. He was the Father of the nation; He was their Lord, their God, and also their Judge. And He judged them most severely. In fact, it would seem that later on He judged Israel more severely than He judged Edom—but that was when they rejected the Messiah.

There is a great deal said today about "God is love." It is an abstract statement to say that God is love. God doesn't say to Israel that He is love. He says, "I have loved you and I have demonstrated it." God was a long time telling the human family that He loved them, but He demonstrated it long before He said it. He demonstrated it from the very beginning, in the lives of Adam and Eve, from the time of the call of Abraham, and right down to the present.

**A son honoureth his father, and a servant his master: if then I be a father, where is mine honour? and if I be a master, where is my fear? saith the Lord of hosts unto you, O priests, that despise my name. And ye say, Wherein have we despised thy name? [Mal. 1:6].**

"A son honoureth his father, and a servant his master: if then I be a father, where is mine honour?" Now God was never Father to an *individual* Israelite. Even of both Moses and David, the best that was said was that they were servants of Jehovah—each was a servant of Jehovah. But God called the whole nation His son. Here He reminds them that He has this relationship with the nation.

"And if I be a master [that is, your Lord], where is my fear? saith the LORD of hosts unto you, O priests, that despise my name. And ye say, Wherein have we despised thy name?" They are greatly offended that God would say this about them. They say, "My, we're such nice, wonderful little Sunday school boys and girls. We go to the temple, we go through the rituals, we are very faithful, and we are really the pillars of the whole nation of Israel. And then You dare ask us about despising Your name? How in the world are we despising Your name?"

Of course, you've got to go way back into "uncivilized" times to find children honoring their parents. The modern way and the civilized way is not to honor your parents. But back in that day they did, and so God uses that as the illustration: "A son will honor his father, and a servant his master, but you don't honor Me." This is something that should have gotten to them, but it didn't get to them because they had a hard shell about them. They were a very arrogant and haughty and self-sufficient people. You couldn't tell them anything. I am of the opinion that that is a picture not only of youth today but of all people. We accuse young people of not listening, but the older folk are not listening either—they certainly are not listening to God at all. God said to Israel, "You despise My name." And they act hurt; they act as if they really don't know what He is talking about. Very frankly, had you been in Jerusalem in that day, you would have seen the crowds flocking into the temple. They were bringing their sacrifices. They were going through the ritual. They gave an outward show of being very religious. Their pious performance was very impressive. I am sure that most of us would have said, "This certainly is an alive group, and they're certainly worshiping God." To tell the truth, they were very far from God. Down underneath they actually despised His name.

**Ye offer polluted bread upon mine altar; and ye say, Wherein have we polluted thee? In that ye say, The table of the LORD is contemptible [Mal. 1:7].**

How could they despise His name when they were going to the temple so regularly? God begins to lay it out for them: "Ye offer polluted bread upon mine altar." I think we should make it very clear that the bread refers to the offering that was made on the altar. It would be what we would call a meat offering, that is, it would be an animal sacrifice. God will make it clear in verse 8 that that is really what He is talking about.

God says that their sacrifice was polluted, but they wouldn't acknowledge that. They ask the question, "Wherein have we polluted thee?" My, are they offended that God would dare say this to them because they are such lovely people! To pollute God, by the way, was a serious charge if it were true, but the people dismiss the charge with an indifferent nod of the head and a pretended ignorance. They act as if God doesn't know what He is talking about.

Then God says to them, "In that ye say, The table of the LORD is contemptible." They said that it was contemptible, and they despised it by the way they treated it and by the way they acted.

God is speaking to these people, the Jewish remnant which has returned to the land and has settled upon their lees. They are very happily situated now. They have been back for over one hundred years. The Captivity is now in the background, and things are prosperous in the land. They've become just a little self-sufficient. They have a temple now, and they are going through the ritual of it, but they actually are far from God. They have become insolent as they talk back to God as He says things to them. Maybe you will want to tune me out because what the Lord says now is really going to hurt.

**And if ye offer the blind for sacrifice, is it not evil? and if ye offer the lame and sick, is it not evil? offer it now unto thy governor; will he be pleased with thee, or accept thy person? saith the LORD of hosts [Mal. 1:8].**

"And if ye offer the blind for sacrifice, is it not evil? and if ye offer the lame and sick, is it not evil?" It is clear now that He is talking about *animal* sacrifices. God made it clear to Israel at the very beginning that nothing which was in any way maimed or defiled or any of that sort of thing was to be offered to Him. In other words, when you give secondhand clothing to the rescue mission, don't put that down on your books, thinking you will get credit from God. Don't misunderstand me—the mission can use the secondhand clothes, but you're not giving sacrificially to God when you give that sort of thing. Listen to the instructions God had given to them: "But whatsoever hath a blemish, that shall ye not offer: for it shall not be acceptable for you. And whosoever offereth a sacrifice of peace offerings unto the LORD to accomplish his vow, or a freewill offering in beeves or sheep, it shall be perfect to be accepted; there shall be no blemish therein. Blind, or broken, or maimed, or having a wen, or scurvy, or scabbed, ye shall not offer these unto the LORD, nor make an offering by fire of them upon the altar unto the LORD. Either a bullock or a lamb that hath any thing superfluous or lacking in his parts, that mayest thou offer for a freewill offering; but for a vow it shall not be accepted" (Lev. 22:20–23).

God was telling them that the offering they offered was really a picture of the Lord Jesus Christ who is the perfect Lamb of God who takes away the sin of the world. Any imperfect offering was an insult to the Lord Jesus Christ. In case they missed it in Leviticus, God interprets the law for them in Deuteronomy 15:21: "And if there be any blemish therein, as if it be lame, or blind, or have any ill blemish, thou shalt not sacrifice it unto the LORD thy God."

Now what was happening in Malachi's day was something like this: Imagine there is a man living up in the hill country of Ephraim who has prize cattle. He always gets the blue ribbon at the cattle show. But one day his prize bull becomes sick, and when he calls the veterinarian, the veterinarian says, "I don't think he's going to make it. I think he'll die." So the man says, "Well, let's load him in the truck in a hurry and rush him down to the temple where I'll offer him for a sacrifice." When the man brings the bull to the temple, the priests can see that the old bull is sick, but they go through with it because this is a very prominent fellow who lives up in Ephraim, you see. But when the people see this prize, blue-ribbon bull being offered, they say, "Mr. So-and-so sure is a generous fellow. Look at what he is offering to the Lord!"

What do we do today that corresponds to that which was taking place in Israel in Malachi's day? Remember that the apostle Paul described the men in the last days as "having a form of godliness, but denying the power thereof . . ." (2 Tim. 3:5). Men will be very pious. There is a great deal of pompous piousity that is demonstrated by many so-called Christians today. Paul describes them as "having a form of godliness." You can pour oleomargarine into a butter mold, and it may look like butter, it may even smell like butter, but it is not butter. You probably have heard the story of the very stingy man who gave his wife a mink coat—at least, it was supposed to be a mink coat. No one could understand why this man would be so generous until one day when he and his wife went walking down the street. As they passed a rabbit hound, the coat jumped off his wife and started running! It just happened to be rabbit, you see—not mink.

We should recognize God's rebuke here as a danger signal and as a red light for us. This is a message for folk who go to church—they listen, they are very orthodox, very fundamental, and they say amen. They know the language. They can quote any number of pious platitudes. They are satisfied with a tasteless morality. They go through a form of truth and all the shibboleths, and they are satisfied. But may I say to you, they actually *despise God* when they approach worship like that. It was Dr. G. Campbell Morgan who years ago made the statement, "I am more afraid of the profanity of the sanctuary than I am of the profanity of the street." The profanity of the streets is bad enough, my friend.

You may protest, "But I've never brought a sick cow to God and offered Him that!" Will you notice what God says here in our verse: "Offer it now unto thy governor; will he be pleased with thee, or accept thy person? saith the LORD of hosts." In other words, try paying your taxes with that old sick cow! This is a good question: Do you pay more in taxes than you give to the Lord? I want to say very candidly, shame on you if you are paying more taxes than you are giving to the Lord. I believe that when the offering is taken in the average church, there is actually lots more profanity taking place there than down in the slums of the city where the drunkards are. Why? Because there is a great deal of put-on, of hypocrisy, taking place in the sanctuary today.

I know a very prominent businessman who lives in the East. He's a man that I greatly respect, but I have suspected his generosity for many years. He likes to give, and he'll give generously if you'll put up a building with his name on it. When we obtained our new headquarters facilities some years ago, I had a suggestion or two from folk who would be glad to give if the building were named in their honor. We simply don't do business that way at the "Thru the Bible" radio ministry. When you give to this ministry, you're giving to get out the Word of God. You're not giving to get your name engraved on anything. I realize that our policy causes many prominent, wealthy people to turn from us, but that is perfectly all right. The Lord is speaking to a whole lot of other folk, and I rejoice in that. I happen to know that this particular business-man has buildings named for him on two college campuses. He's a big shot. When he gives, you can be sure it will be with the blowing of the horn, the blare of the trumpet, and the beating of the drum. The Lord Jesus told about the Pharisee who went down to the street corner to give to the poor, and he had somebody down there blowing a horn. Everybody said, "Oh, look at Pharisee So-and-so! Isn't he generous? He's down there on the corner, just giving money away to the poor!" One time this prominent businessman invited me out for an evening meal, and we had good fellowship. He's a likable fellow. He has real charisma. Afterwards, he came with me to the church where I was preaching that night. The pastor of the church invited him up to the platform to lead in prayer. He's a wealthy man, let me tell you, and so he was invited up there to lead in prayer. I saw with my own eyes that this man who had given the waitress a two-dollar tip for our dinner put only a one-dollar bill in the offering plate. I thought, *My, he didn't even tip God generously tonight!*

When the One who was here nineteen hundred years ago sat by the treasury and watched how the people gave, I am sure that some of them thought, "What business has He to see how I give?" He happened to be the Lord Jesus Christ, and I'm not sure but that on Sunday morning He looks over your shoulder as you give. Are you giving what you give for a good meal when you eat out? Are you giving as generously to the Lord's work as you do to other things where it makes a show? My friend, the old sick cow is still being taken to church today. That is the method that Israel used; and, believe me, the Lord didn't let it pass.

This is burning sarcasm—listen to Him: "And if ye offer the blind for sacrifice, is it not evil? and if ye offer the lame and sick, is it not evil? offer it now unto thy governor; will he be pleased with thee, or accept thy person? saith the LORD of hosts." I will say it again, and it is none of my business, but I'm just telling you what the Lord says. He is saying here in a very definite way that you cannot bring Him a sick cow. You don't pay your taxes with a sick cow. Are you giving to the Lord as much or more than you are giving in taxes today? You may argue, "I *have* to pay my taxes." Yes, you sure do, but what about your giving to the Lord? That is supposed to be on the basis of love. The Lord Jesus said. "If ye love me, keep my commandments" (John 14:15). I do not think we are under the tithe today at all. It is interesting to note, however, that in the Mosaic Law there was more than one tithe; we know that there were two tithes, and many think that there were three tithes. That would mean that the people actually gave *thirty percent* of what they made to the Lord.

When the Lord Jesus looked over the treasury, He saw how the rich gave—and they gave large sums—but He didn't commend them for it because they kept so much more for themselves. But He saw that poor widow —and those few little coppers which she dropped in there, compared to the wealth of the temple, very candidly, were nothing. She gave *nothing!* But the Lord Jesus took those copper coins, He kissed them into the gold of heaven, and He said that she gave more than anybody else.

I am amazed at how our Bible-teaching radio ministry is carried on. It is carried on by many widows who send in a dollar bill, and they always say, "It isn't anything." Maybe in comparison to our costs, it isn't much, but when a whole lot of widows get together it sure makes an impression. It is the people who regularly send in the five-dollar and ten-dollar gifts that sustain this radio ministry.

The Israelites in Malachi's day were being very clever. When an old cow got sick or a lamb broke his leg, they would patch it up and rush it off to the temple to offer it as a sacrifice to God. God says that He will not accept such a sacrifice. I wonder how many offerings are really made acceptable to God today? We are told that any offering we make to God is like the priest making an offering back in Old Testament times. Believers today are priests before God, and we are to give by grace, but grace does not mean that we give as little as we possibly can. I am afraid that we are actually seeing a sacrilege committed in the church every Sunday. Someone will say, "But a sacrilege means that somebody steals something in the church." Yes, that is the meaning. The Israelites were guilty of sacrilege because their offerings really cost them nothing. They were valueless, though they may have been large. And, my friend, it is sacrilege to enter the church and put something into the offering plate when there is no blood or sacrifice on the gift.

Frankly, I think that it is sometimes wrong to give. Many people pay ten dollars to see a football or baseball game, and God says to them, "If you pay that kind of money for that and then come into My house and drop a one-dollar bill into the offering and think you have done something for Me, you are wrong. Why, you didn't even give Me the kind of tip that you give to a waitress!" This is pretty strong language here, is it not?

**And now, I pray you, beseech God that he will be gracious unto us: this hath been by your means: will he regard your persons? saith the LORD of hosts [Mal. 1:9].**

Is it possible that these people could continue giving an outward show but not realize that in their hearts they are not right with God? Their hearts are polluted, and their offering, therefore, is polluted.

**Who is there even among you that would shut the doors for nought? neither do ye kindle fire on mine altar for nought. I have no pleasure in you, saith the LORD of hosts, neither will I accept an offering at your hand [Mal. 1:10].**

God says, "All this ritual that you are going through is absolutely meaningless. It is for nothing. It doesn't profit." But they continue on in it.

**For from the rising of the sun even unto the going down of the same my name shall be great among the Gentiles; and in every place incense shall be offered unto my name, and a pure offering: for my name shall be great among the heathen, saith the LORD of hosts [Mal. 1:11].**

Israel was bringing the name of God into disrepute by the way they were serving Him. They were not serving Him as they did in the days of Solomon, for instance, when the Queen of Sheba was greatly impressed with what she saw. At this time, the unsaved were not impressed because it was just a form and a ceremony.

God says that there is a day coming when His name will be great among the Gentiles. If you think that this has been fulfilled today, you're entirely wrong. It will be fulfilled in the Millennium but not today. God's name is not great among the nations today.

"And in every place incense shall be offered unto my name, and a pure offering." "Incense" speaks of prayer. That "pure offering" is Christ.

"For my name shall be great among the heathen, saith the LORD of hosts." God's purpose in choosing Israel was that they might witness to the nations of the world.

**But ye have profaned it, in that ye say, The table of the LORD is polluted; and the fruit thereof, even his meat, is contemptible [Mal. 1:12].**

The Gentiles profaned the name of God because of the lives and actions of God's people whose hearts were polluted and whose ritual was contemptible.

**Ye said also, Behold, what a weariness is it! and ye have snuffed at it, saith the LORD of hosts; and ye brought that which was torn, and the lame, and the sick; thus ye brought an offering: should I accept this of your hand? saith the LORD [Mal. 1:13].**

"Ye said also, Behold, what a weariness is it! and ye have snuffed at it, saith the LORD of hosts." In effect they were saying, "It makes us tired to go to church, to go through all of these things. Oh, what a weariness!" My friend, when the heart is not in the thing, it becomes weariness.

One morning my daughter and I were driving in the morning rush-hour traffic. At the time I was a pastor in downtown Los Angeles. I couldn't wait to get to the church that morning. I had broadcast tapes to make, and I was looking forward to it. I said to her, "Look at the faces of all these people in this big traffic jam. They are bored to tears, dreading to go to work. The worst thing in the world that I can think of is to be doing a job you hate to do. It makes the hours long, and there is no joy in it whatsoever. Going to church is just as boring to a great many people." This is the reason we so often hear it asked, "What can we do to interest our people in the church?" Have you ever heard that discussed? Or, "What can we do to get people to come on Sunday nights?" Somebody will suggest, "Let's serve a dinner. Let's have a banquet. Or let's have a little different service. Instead of all this boring Bible study, let's have some special music, and let's put on an entertaining program. We could have some sort of pageant."

What is wrong, my friend, when people are saying that God is becoming boring to them? Why do you think that men ever adopted a ritual to begin with? Why do they wear robes and chant and burn incense and march around? They are tired of spiritual worship—that's it—and they need something to tickle the flesh. Somebody says, "But I love an orderly service." I do too, but there is danger in loving order, and there is danger in loving a ritual.

I recognize that ritual has its place and that there are many fine folk who were brought up that way. When I was a pastor in downtown Los Angeles, I knew a lovely couple who really loved the Word of God but who were members of a very formal, a very high church. He was actually enraged by the informality of the way in which I began the service. He and his wife would not come until we had completed the brief preliminaries of the service. He very frankly told me, "I just can't stand that informality"—but he loved the Word of God, and so I forgave him for the other.

Way back in the stern days of our fathers, the Puritans, they would sit on log benches and listen to a sermon for two hours. Today there are people who will sit on bleachers for three hours out in the hot sun to watch a baseball game. There are folk who will sit out in the cold to watch a football game. And there are those who will sit for three hours listening to an opera, or for two hours watching a movie, or for four hours to see *Hamlet*. I find it thrilling to sit and listen to a Shakespearean play. When my wife and I were at Stratford-on-Avon and saw *Richard III*, I didn't sit on the edge of my seat, but I sat back, relaxed, and thoroughly enjoyed it for three hours. My friend, why are you weary when your preacher speaks for one hour? I'm a long-winded preacher and always have been. I would speak for an hour, and do you know who complained about it? It wasn't the average person; many people said they didn't think it was too long. It was some of the leaders, the so-called spiritual leaders of the church, who complained. We love the ritual, and we love the form. We go to church, we stand up and sit down, and we sing the doxology loudly, but really where are our hearts? Do we do it because of a love for Him? Do we desire to worship Him? We sing, "Were the whole realm of nature mine, that were a present far too small." Is that a gift far too small? It sure is. Then why did you put just a dollar in the offering plate? If the whole realm of nature isn't big enough for a gift to God, then what about that dollar bill which isn't worth very much today?

It is so easy to get tired and weary in church work. Dwight L. Moody came home one time, and although he was very weary, he was going to another meeting without taking time out to rest. His family begged him to cancel it because he was so weary, but he said this, "I get tired *in* the work, but I never get tired *of* the work."

> **But cursed be the deceiver, which hath in his flock a male, and voweth, and sacrificeth unto the Lord a corrupt thing: for I am a great King, saith the LORD of hosts, and my name is dreadful among the heathen [Mal. 1:14].**

"For I am a great King, saith the LORD of hosts, and my name is dreadful [to be reverenced] among the heathen." His name is going to be reverenced someday, but it's not reverenced even today.

One of the things that has brought God's name into disrepute has been the ministry and those who represent Him here, the believers. I don't question their salvation—and yet I'm afraid I do question the salvation of some. Have you ever noticed that God never called a real believer a hypocrite? But the Lord Jesus really laid it on the line when He was talking about the religious Pharisees of His day. Very frankly, He said *terrible* things about them. He called them "whited sepulchres." Can you imagine that? That is an awful thing to call these people, but that is what He called them. And He likened them to a dish that on the outside is beautiful, but on the inside it hasn't even been washed. It didn't get into the dishwasher, and it is filled with all kinds of garbage. The Lord Jesus said, "That's the hypocrite" (see Matt. 23:25–29). And that's what these people were in Malachi's day—they were merely going through a form of religion.

Let's put it on the line today: Do you have religion, or do you have Christ? Are you real, or are you just going through the form of it? Do you wear your Christianity like a garment that you can take off and put aside at any time, and do you generally put it aside when you are not in church? Perhaps you assume a certain pious attitude and can quote pious platitudes, but how real is Christ to you?

The first thing that Israel did was to bring those old sick cows as sacrifices. Now they are saying, "Oh, this is boring! All these long services. Bible study certainly is boring." I thank God that over a period of twenty-one years, we averaged fifteen hundred people for Bible study in our midweek service in downtown Los Angeles. I have always thanked God for that. But when someone would come and pat me on the back and tell me how wonderful it was, I would remind them of those great office buildings there in downtown Los Angeles. Each afternoon well over two hundred thousand people would empty out of those buildings to go home. Out of that number only about fifteen hundred would return on Thursday nights for Bible study. Our batting average was not really very good, was it? Most of the people who worked in those buildings were church members, and probably they were all out to church on *Easter* Sunday. They could always make it to the ball game at Dodger Stadium on Sunday afternoon, but they would find it *impossible* to get to the Sunday evening service. Today there is a great deal of religion, but very little real Christianity. A great many folk are just playing church. When I was a kid, we played store. I used to fill tin cans with dirt and sell them to the other kids in the neighborhood. My, I ran a store! Playing store never got anywhere, but it was a lot of fun. And there are a lot of adults having fun playing church today.

At the time that I was ordained into the ministry, the man who gave me the charge of entering the ministry said that there are three great sins of the ministry that I should avoid. Maybe I haven't followed through as I should, but I have always remembered those three sins.

The number one sin of the ministry is laziness. Yes, that's right. The reason we don't have more expositors of the Word of God today is because it requires study to be an expositor. It is so easy for a pastor to get busy during the week. Shame on you, if you're taking your preacher's time during the week and not letting him study if he wants to study. Any church that has a man who is an expositor and wants to spend time in study should let him study. He needs that time, and he'll have to have it if he's going to be an expositor. He cannot be lazy and expect to be a real teacher of the Word of God.

One young fellow who was a student of mine at Biola became a pastor in California's San Joaquin Valley. After he had been up there about three years, he came down and said he wanted to talk to me. We went to lunch, and I asked him, "What's your problem?"

"I'm getting ready to get out of the ministry. I've run out of things to preach. I'm beginning simply to repeat myself, and people notice it."

So I said, "How long do you take to prepare a sermon?"

"Well, I've preached all of yours that I have. And I've preached others. Generally, I prepare one in three hours."

I told him, "Although my sermons may not look like it, I spent over twenty-four hours just preparing each sermon. I have never preached a sermon until I was ready to preach."

Laziness is a great sin, and I don't think that God excuses it. I dealt with a young fellow recently who wanted to go into the ministry, and at one time he had high hopes of going to seminary. Now he has the vain notion that he can become a preacher by just going out and letting the Holy Spirit teach him. My friend, the Holy Spirit has never yet taught a *lazy* preacher. He will only teach the one who is willing to go all the way in study.

Spiritual worship became wearisome to the people of Israel because they didn't love the Word of God. You have to love the Word of God. This is one way in which the Bible is different from any other book. Any other book you must read before you love it, and you must understand it before you can love it. But, my friend, you must love the Word of God before you can understand it. The Spirit of God is not teaching lazy folk.

Then the *second* great sin of the ministry is an overweening ambition. This can manifest itself in several different ways. It's a form of covetousness, of desiring fame, of wanting to be a big preacher, of wanting to preach to the crowd. This is a great sin in the ministry today: wanting to speak to crowds. I am convinced that the great preachers today are not in the big churches, and they are not always the ones getting the big crowds. I listened to a man some time ago preach a sermon, and I do not think there were a hundred people present. But it was a great sermon, an expository sermon. It just thrilled my heart to hear that young man preach. I asked him, "How long did you spend preparing that sermon?" He told me that he had been working on it all week. I suppose that boy put in over twenty hours getting up that message, and he's *willing* to be a pastor to a small group of people. However, too many are eager to become great and to minister to a large church.

I heard the story of a preacher somewhere in Texas who came home and told his wife one day, "The next town over has a church which has asked me if I would consider a call to their church. It's a larger town, a larger church, they pay a larger salary, and they are really lots better people over there. I'm going upstairs to pray about it and to see what the Lord wants me to do."

She said, "I'll go up and pray with you."

"Oh, no," he said, "you stay down here and start packing!" I am afraid that there are a great many in the ministry who are just like that.

The *third* great sin of the ministry is to be dull and boring, to be tedious and wearisome. The reason this happens, of course, is that a man does not stay enough in the Book. A man doesn't have to have charisma—many do not—but there is no excuse for being apathetic, very prosaic, colorless, and lackluster.

I mentioned earlier that my wife and I went to see *Richard III*. Shakespeare was a great writer. I don't think he just dashed it off, all of a sudden. We are told that he spent hours writing his plays. I listened to the two young men, one of them playing the part of Richard III and the other playing the one who was supposed to have been his friend but who finally dethroned him and put him in the Tower of London. Of course Shakespeare was a genius, but the thing that impressed me about the play above everything else was the way these young men enunciated, how clearly they spoke, and how they had worked on their lines. I watched purposefully because I had been in Shakespearean plays when I was very young. They didn't miss a cue. There wasn't one slip of the tongue. They went right through it. Do you know why? They had worked and worked and rehearsed and rehearsed and rehearsed. If the actor in the world can spend all that time preparing for a performance, why can't we spend time preparing to give out the Word of God? Any preacher who goes into the pulpit unprepared despises the name of the Lord, and he is causing people to say, "Boy, the Bible is boring! And going to church is tiresome. Next Sunday I'll do something *interesting*." Being a dull preacher is another great sin of the ministry.

Verse 14 says, "But cursed be the deceiver, which hath in his flock a male, and voweth, and sacrificeth unto the Lord a corrupt thing." Here is something else people do: making vows to God and then not following through on them. We find it taught both in Leviticus and Proverbs that God does not want us telling Him something unless we mean it. If you promise to do something for God, you had better go through with it because God means business. He doesn't ask you to make the vow—it is voluntary—but if you make that vow, be sure that you go through with it.

There were people in Israel who were making great protestations, saying, "It looks like we're going to have a bumper crop this year. I am going to give the Lord not only a tenth, but I'm going to give some freewill offerings to Him." But then when the harvest came in in abundance, they decided they would keep it for themselves. They decided they would not turn it over to the Lord after all. Instead, they offered to God the corrupt, the lame, and the sick.

# CHAPTER 2

***THEME:*** *The priests reproved for profanity and the people rebuked for social sins*

In this chapter we come to another section, but it is still dealing with the priests. God is reproving the priests for their profanity. They were profane (*fanus* means "temple"); they were against the temple. Instead of serving God, they were opposed to God, disgracing God in the very service they were performing in the temple.

In the first chapter we saw that the priests were despising God's name, and I mentioned the old sick cows which they presented as an offering to God. The real condemnation of that practice was not because they were giving a valueless thing to God and He was rebuking them because they were not giving as they should. A little later He will come to that and will ask the very pointed question, "Will a man rob God?" But here the emphasis is not upon the *value* of the offering but upon the *character* of the offering that was placed on the altar. In the Book of Leviticus we find that there are five great offerings mentioned, and each of them points to Jesus Christ. Each offering had to represent the One who was coming, and this One was holy, harmless, undefiled, and separate from sinners. He was perfect, and the offering which represented and pointed to Him must be without blemish. The sweet savor and even the nonsweet savor offerings pointed to the Son of God. Now in

the days of Malachi the priests were despising
God's name in that they were bringing to God
an imperfect offering—an old sick cow! It was
blasphemy to bring a diseased or crippled animal to the altar as a representation of the
perfect One who was coming.

The same thing is being done in our day. A
few years ago the very popular rock opera
*Jesus Christ, Superstar* presented the Lord
Jesus as an immoral, confused man. Well, the
world cannot forget Him that's for sure, but
the world is not thinking *rightly* of Him.
Those who misrepresent Him in books and
plays and even in the liberal pulpit are despising the name of God. We hear flippant expressions like "the Devil made me do it."
Well, the Devil didn't make you do it; you did
it because you have that old sinful nature.
Another expression is "God will get you!" No,
He won't! Do you think God is running around
paddling little boys and girls? Oh, my friend,
let's guard against misrepresenting God.

Our God is gracious, and He is to be held in
reverence. He does judge sin and will judge
sin in the future. He is called the awful God,
that is, the awe-inspiring God. He is the rev-
erend God. He is to be respected. He is to be
worshiped. He is to be adored.

The other night I was listening to snatches
of Bach's music and was struck by the fact
that it was nothing in the world but praise to
God. We don't have much of pure praise to
God even today in our so-called fundamental
churches. Our failure to praise God and our
praise of men instead is another way in which
we despise God's name. This is a condemnation of our contemporary church.

Since all true believers are priests in the
age in which we live, this prophecy of
Malachi's which is directed to priests has real
meaning for us.

In chapter 1, verse 6, God addresses the
priests and rebukes them for despising His
name. Now in chapter 2, verse 1, He addresses them again—

**And now, O ye priests, this command-
ment is for you [Mal. 2:1].**

You see, He is still dealing with the priests.

**If ye will not hear, and if ye will not lay
it to heart, to give glory unto my name,
saith the LORD of hosts, I will even send
a curse upon you, and I will curse your
blessings: yea, I have cursed them
already, because ye do not lay it to
heart [Mal. 2:2].**

They were not taking their office seriously.
And God was going to judge them more severely than He would judge the people. Why?
Because of their position of responsibility.
They were permitting this sordid condition to
exist. They were shutting their eyes to the
fact that people were bringing lame and sick
animals for sacrifice. God had given them the
law of truth, and they were to teach it to their
people.

Now I am going to make a very strong
statement. I would rather be the worst sinner
on this earth—even a gangster or a murderer—than to be a minister who goes into the
pulpit with an unbelieving heart and gives
only a few little pious platitudes to the congregation. God is certainly going to hold that
man responsible.

**Behold, I will corrupt your seed, and
spread dung upon your faces, even the
dung of your solemn feasts; and one
shall take you away with it [Mal. 2:3].**

"Behold, I will corrupt your seed." Apparently God had been blessing the people, and
they had been getting abundant harvests at
this time. You will remember that the priests
were to be given the tithe of the crops—
wheat, barley, figs, grapes—a tenth was
given to the Lord to support the priests. Now
God says that He will corrupt the seed out
there so that they wouldn't be getting the
tithe that they had been getting. Their
affluent society was about done with.

"And [I will] spread dung upon your faces."
The interesting thing was that all the maw of
the sacrificial animal was given to the priests,
but the dung in the maw was rejected and
taken away. It could never be left in the sacrificial animal. Therefore, when God says that
He will spread dung upon the faces of the
priests, it is as if He is saying that He is going
to rub their noses in it. And when that happens, they will not be able to serve at His
altar. Why? Because no unclean thing can
come there, and they will certainly be unclean! This is strong language that God is using here.

**And ye shall know that I have sent this
commandment unto you, that my covenant might be with Levi, saith the LORD
of hosts.**

**My covenant was with him of life and
peace; and I gave them to him for the
fear wherewith he feared me, and was
afraid before my name.**

**The law of truth was in his mouth, and iniquity was not found in his lips: he walked with me in peace and equity, and did turn many away from iniquity [Mal. 2:4–6].**

This tells us the reason that God chose the tribe of Levi. If we look at Levi, the son of Jacob, we would never choose him because he had nothing to commend himself to God. And when old Jacob was dying, he called his twelve sons to stand around his bedside, and he gave a prophecy concerning each of them, which we find in Genesis 49. He combined Simeon and Levi into one prophecy: "Simeon and Levi are brethren; instruments of cruelty are in their habitations. O my soul, come not thou into their secret; unto their assembly, mine honour, be not thou united: for in their anger they slew a man, and in their selfwill they digged down a wall." They felt justified in doing it because their sister had been raped, but they were murderers. Jacob's prophecy continues: "Cursed be their anger, for it was fierce; and their wrath, for it was cruel: I will divide them in Jacob, and scatter them in Israel" (Gen. 49:5–7).

How was God going to scatter Levi in Israel? They would become the priestly tribe. They didn't get any territory of the land but were scattered among the tribes. But how could they become the priestly tribe when Levi himself was such a rascal and a murderer? We need to follow along in history to see why God chose the tribe of Levi.

Centuries later, when the children of Israel went into idolatry and made the golden calf to worship, Moses called for the idolaters to be slain. It was the tribe of Levi who did according to the word of Moses. When Moses was about to die, he gathered the tribes around him. The twelve sons of Jacob had become more than a million people who were gathered around Moses. Now Moses gives a prophecy to each of the tribes, and this is his blessing on Levi: ". . . Let thy Thummim and thy Urim be with thy holy one, whom thou didst prove at Massah, and with whom thou didst strive at the waters of Meribah; Who said unto his father and to his mother, I have not seen him; neither did he acknowledge his brethren, nor knew his own children: for they have observed thy word, and kept thy covenant. They shall teach Jacob thy judgments, and Israel thy law: they shall put incense before thee, and whole burnt sacrifice upon thine altar" (Deut. 33:8–10).

Notice that although Levi himself was a brutal murderer, the tribe that came from him observed the Word of God; they kept His covenant. And God made them the priestly tribe to teach the people of Israel the law of God and to offer prayers and sacrifices before Him—those sacrifices pointed to Christ. Therefore, "Bless, LORD, his substance, and accept the work of his hands: smite through the loins of them that rise against him, and of them that hate him, that they rise not again" (Deut. 33:11).

That is the covenant which God made with the tribe of Levi. He was to teach Israel, he was to serve at the place of prayer, the altar of incense, and he was to offer the burnt sacrifices which point to Christ. When we move forward in history to the time of Malachi and the remnant which had returned to the land of Israel after the Babylonian captivity, what is the tribe of Levi like now? Well, we have seen that he is willing to shut his eyes when a sick cow is brought as a sacrifice to God. He is despising the name of God, and he is disobeying God. Therefore, how can he teach God's Word to the people? What a change has taken place! Even after the seventy-year captivity, Levi hasn't learned the lesson. "My covenant was with him of life and peace; and I gave them to him for the fear wherewith he feared me, and was afraid before my name." God is saying through Malachi that Levi previously feared Him, but now the tribe doesn't. "The law of truth was in his mouth." He had taught the truth of God. But these priests are not only failing to teach the truth of God, they also are *breaking* the commandments of God. He continues, "The law of truth was in his mouth, and iniquity was not found in his lips: he walked with me in peace and equity, and did turn many away from iniquity." He had been a good example, you see, to the people. What a change has taken place.

There is a real application in this for us today. No one can serve God without a reverence for His name. That means that Christ must be lifted up before the people. If Christ is lifted up, He will draw men to Himself. He is lifted up by our witness, and that must be by our lives as well as by our words. Our example is just as important as what we say.

**For the priest's lips should keep knowledge, and they should seek the law at his mouth: for he is the messenger of the LORD of hosts [Mal. 2:7].**

The priests are to be messengers of the Lord of hosts. The word *messenger* as I have pointed out before, is also translated "angel," and in the Book of Revelation we find the Lord addressing the "angel" of the church of Ephesus, etc. To whom is He speaking? He is addressing the one who is the leader of the church, the one who is teaching the Word of God in the church.

Now let me sum this up by giving my interpretation of this—and you may not agree with it. I believe that the sole duty of the pastor of a church is to *teach* the Word of God. God have mercy on the church that expects its pastor to be the public relations man, running all over the countryside visiting sick babies and burping them, and expects him to spend his time in the administration of church affairs when he should be studying the Word of God and then teaching it to his people.

Once I had a telephone call from a man back East who was an officer in his church and was dissatisfied with his pastor. He said that his pastor spent his time studying instead of administering the affairs of the church. So I asked him, "Did you tell me that you are a deacon?"

"Yes."

"Have you yourself been visiting the sick?"

"No, sir, I keep pretty busy."

"Do you know that that is your business? *You* are to visit the sick. *You* are to take charge of the administration of the church. His business is to teach the Word of God. If he is not teaching the Word of God when he gets into the pulpit, that is another story. But if he is spending his time in studying and giving out God's Word, then he is doing what God has called him to do."

Remember that a situation like this confronted the apostles in the early church. The Hellenistic Jews were complaining that their widows were being neglected and preference was being given to the native-born widows. The matter was brought before the apostles, and they did a marvelous job of handling it. They told the church to appoint deacons to handle it. They said, ". . . It is not reason that we should leave the word of God, and serve tables" (Acts 6:2).

Having completed my ministry in the church, I stand at a great vantage point today. I thank God that I have reached the place where I no longer have to burp babies and, although I have a little to do with administration, that is not how I spend my time. I am currently spending more time in the study of the Word than ever before, and I thank God for it. If I could relive my days as a pastor, I would spend more time studying the Word— some folk thought I spent too much time as it

was. But I believe that studying the Word and teaching it is the pastor's business.

God says that it was Levi's business, but in Malachi's day the priests were not doing it. Therefore, God says to the priests,

**But ye are departed out of the way; ye have caused many to stumble at the law; ye have corrupted the covenant of Levi, saith the LORD of hosts.**

**Therefore have I also made you contemptible and base before all the people, according as ye have not kept my ways, but have been partial in the law [Mal. 2:8–9].**

There was a time in our own land when ministers were listened to, but that day is past. God said this would happen when the ministry is not giving out His Word.

**Have we not all one father? hath not one God created us? why do we deal treacherously every man against his brother, by profaning the covenant of our fathers? [Mal. 2:10].**

"Have we not all one father?" There are some expositors who say that the "father" refers to Abraham since both Israel and Judah are mentioned in the verse that follows. However, I think that the next question makes it clear that Malachi is speaking about God as the Father: "Hath not one God created us?"

He also makes it clear in what way God is the Father. He is the Father by creation. But man lost that relationship. Adam was called the son of God, but after the Fall, he begat a son in his own likeness—not in the likeness of God, but in the likeness of his own fallen nature. Therefore, when the nation Israel comes into view, we do not find God speaking specifically of any individual Israelite as His son. Rather, He speaks of the corporate body of the nation as a son. Never in the Old Testament does God refer to an individual as His son. Even of two men who were outstanding, Moses and David, it was "Moses my *servant*" and "David my *servant*." Never does God say, "Moses my *son*" or "David my *son*." Individuals become sons of God through faith in Jesus Christ. God is the Father of mankind in the sense that He is the Creator.

This is something that has been greatly emphasized in our contemporary society, and I think properly so. On a telecast I heard a man, who was definitely an unsaved man, play up the fact that we are all human beings and that we ought to show respect and consideration for one another. Well, that is true. As far as he went, he was entirely accurate. You are a human being and I am a human being, and I should accord to you the same rights and privileges and respect that I would like to have for myself. "Have we not all one father? hath not one God created us?" We all are the creation of God.

"Why do we deal treacherously every man against his brother, by profaning the covenant of our fathers?" Now here they were, a chosen people, yet breaking God's covenant and dealing treacherously one with the other. They were not right with God, and so they were not right with each other.

This is certainly true of man in our day. I personally have to say that there are a great many unsaved people that I wouldn't trust. And, unfortunately, having been in the church most of my life, I have to say that there are a lot in the church whom I would not trust either. I have no confidence in them at all. Why? They deal treacherously. There is nothing that hurts the cause of Christ more than a church fight, conflicts in the church, and leaders who are at each other's throats. Regardless of how evangelistic a church may be, its witness is nil when those conditions exist.

### THE SINS OF DIVORCE AND REMARRIAGE

**Judah hath dealt treacherously, and an abomination is committed in Israel and in Jerusalem; for Judah hath profaned the holiness of the LORD which he loved, and hath married the daughter of a strange god [Mal. 2:11].**

He is very specific now: "*Judah* hath dealt treacherously, and an abomination is committed in *Israel* and in Jerusalem." Now we know whom Malachi is talking about: "Judah" is the tribe of Judah, "Israel" includes all the twelve tribes, and "Jerusalem" is the capital.

"An abomination is committed in Israel and in Jerusalem." God is talking about how they profane the covenant of the fathers by dealing treacherously with one another. They are profaning the holiness of the Lord. God is holy, and God loves holiness. God doesn't love sin; He hates sin. Now God will spell it out to them. He specifically tells them what He is talking about (see Gen. 6:1–7).

"And hath married the daughter of a strange [foreign] god." The men saw the beautiful foreign girls who lived around them when they returned from the Captivity. So they were leaving their wives and marrying these foreign girls who served heathen, pagan deities, and brought idolatry into the nation.

We see this same thing all the way through the Word of God. I believe this is the situation in Genesis 6:1–7 where we are told that the sons of God were marrying the daughters of men. I certainly do not hold the view of some expositors that the "sons of God" were angels who were cohabiting with human women and producing some sort of monstrous offspring. Our Lord expressly said that angels do not marry (Matt. 22:30). Rather, this marks the beginning of the breaking down of the godly line of Seth as they intermarried with the ungodly line of Cain.

We see this happening again when the children of Israel were nearing the Promised Land. The king of Moab hired Balaam to curse Israel because the Moabites feared them. When God would not permit Balaam to curse them, he gave the king of Moab some very bad advice—bad for Israel. He said to let the daughters of Moab marry the sons of Israel. They did intermarry, and this brought the idolatry of Moab into Israel.

Again after the kingdom of Israel was divided, the idolatry of Phoenicia was introduced into the northern kingdom by the marriage of Ahab with Jezebel, the daughter of Ethbaal, who was first an idolatrous priest, then king of Tyre and Sidon.

Now this was happening again in Malachi's day. We learn from Nehemiah that there were all kinds of pagan people living around the returned remnant. A young Israelite would see some good-looking foreign girl and decide that he would like to have her for a wife. So he would get rid of his own Israelite wife and marry this pagan girl.

It is the same old story that is being reenacted in our day. I have been sounding a warning here in Southern California since 1940, but the divorce rate keeps climbing. Nobody is paying any attention to me, but I'll keep on saying that a believer and an unbeliever ought not to get married. Any girl or any boy who flies in the face of God's very definite and specific instructions in this connection is just flirting with trouble. Believe me, problems will be coming their way. It cannot be otherwise.

**The LORD will cut off the man that doeth this, the master and the scholar, out of the tabernacles of Jacob, and him that offereth an offering unto the LORD of hosts [Mal. 2:12].**

"The LORD will cut off the man that doeth this, the master and the scholar." It doesn't make any difference who he is, he will suffer the same judgment. "And him that offereth an offering unto the LORD of hosts." Neither will he escape if he goes through the temple ritual but continues to live in sin.

My friend, a true child of God will not continue to live in sin. That is the reason the prodigal son down there in the pigpen finally came to himself and said, "I will arise and go to my father . . ." (Luke 15:18). He was a son and not a pig. He had the nature of his father and could not continue to live as a pig.

I received a startling letter from a church officer here in Southern California who asked for help because he "couldn't give up the awful sin of adultery." If he is a child of God, he will get out of the pigpen. Nothing but pigs love the pigpen and are satisfied to stay down there. A son will get out of it.

**And this have ye done again, covering the altar of the LORD with tears, with weeping, and with crying out, insomuch that he regardeth not the offering any more, or receiveth it with good will at your hand [Mal. 2:13].**

The wives of these men who were divorcing them and marrying foreign girls came to the altar weeping. They shed their tears upon the altar, and God said, "I heard them. Then later you came along very piously and placed your offering upon the same altar on which were the tears of your wives! I want you to know that I paid no attention to your offering."

The church officer who wrote me the letter (to which I referred earlier) may be the treasurer of the church or the head deacon. I can assure him that God is paying no attention to his "good works." In fact, it would be better if he stayed at home and kept out of sight. God makes it very clear that He "regardeth not the offering any more, or receiveth it with good will at your hand." He knows your hypocrisy and will not accept your service.

Now the men in Malachi's day, with feigned innocence and pretended ignorance, ask why—

**Yet ye say, Wherefore? Because the LORD hath been witness between thee and the wife of thy youth, against whom thou hast dealt treacherously: yet is she thy companion, and the wife of thy covenant [Mal. 2:14].**

"Yet ye say, Wherefore?" God is offensive even to suggest that He wouldn't accept their offering. The thought is that they were saying, "Why wouldn't He accept it? I brought a very nice fat lamb to offer." When they ask the question, Malachi spells out the answer for them in neon lights so they cannot misunderstand Him—

"Because the LORD hath been witness between thee and the wife of thy youth, against whom thou hast dealt treacherously." You see, the Israelite married a Hebrew girl when he was a young man. But when he grew older and moved among the pagan and heathen about him, he decided that he wanted to marry a pagan girl with whom he had gotten acquainted.

"Yet is she thy companion, and the wife of thy covenant." His Hebrew wife was the one with whom he stood before the priest and covenanted to be faithful and true to her.

The next verse has always been a difficult passage to interpret, but it is my feeling that Dr. Charles Feinberg is accurate when in his book, *The Minor Prophets*, he says that the natural interpretation is that the prophet is speaking of divorce. And the reference is to the original institution of marriage by God Himself.

**And did not he make one? Yet had he the residue of the spirit. And wherefore one? That he might seek a godly seed. Therefore take heed to your spirit, and let none deal treacherously against the wife of his youth [Mal. 2:15].**

"And did not he make one?" goes back to the original creation of man and woman. Adam was a half and Eve was a half, and together they made one. This is evident when a child is born—he is part of both parents. The two are certainly one in the child.

"Yet had he the residue of the spirit. And wherefore [why] one? That he might seek a godly seed." You see, she is to be like he is—spiritually as well as physically for the sake of the family. A home where there is divorce or where there is polygamy is not a fit place in which to raise children.

My friend, if you are a young lady, you ought not marry that young man unless he believes as you do because, actually, you are supposed to go his way. And you are going to find the going rough if you are a child of God and he is not.

If you are a young man or a young woman, let me say this to you. If you think that you can win your sweetheart to Christ, make sure that you do it *before* your marriage because that is when you have the greatest influence. I tell you, a young fellow in love will do almost anything to please the girl he wants to marry. But after marriage he will not be so anxious to please her. And, of course, that holds true for a young woman in love also. If you don't win your sweetheart to Christ before marriage, you are in trouble, and I mean *deep* trouble.

"Therefore take heed to your spirit, and let none deal treacherously against the wife of his youth." Malachi is warning them to watch what they are doing. God had specifically forbidden His people to intermarry with the heathen.

You may remember that Nehemiah, after he had built the walls of Jerusalem, had returned to his job as the king's cupbearer down in the capital of Media-Persia. But after he had been there for awhile, he got a vacation and came back to Jerusalem. He found that old Tobiah, an Ammonite, an enemy of God, had been moved into an apartment in the temple! The high priest had made this arrangement for him because his son had married the daughter of Tobiah. Do you know what Nehemiah did about it? He went over there and pitched out all of Tobiah's belongings, even the furniture, and told him to take off. You may think that is pretty rough and certainly not very polite. No, it wasn't polite, but it sure did cleanse the temple! As a matter of fact, Nehemiah was pretty rough with his own people whom he found had intermarried with the pagans of Ashdod, of Ammon, and of Moab. Nehemiah himself records his treatment of them: "And I contended with them, and cursed them, and smote certain of them, and plucked off their hair, and made them swear by God, saying, Ye shall not give your daughters unto their sons, nor take their daughters unto your sons, or for yourselves" (Neh. 13:25). And he reminded them of the disaster which had come to their nation through intermarriage with the heathen. Oh, how we need laymen like Nehemiah in our day to stand for the Word of God!

**For the LORD, the God of Israel, saith that he hateth putting away: for one covereth violence with his garment, saith the LORD of hosts: therefore take heed to your spirit, that ye deal not treacherously [Mal. 2:16].**

In the Old Testament, when a man married a girl, he took his garment, his outer garment, and put it over her. This lovely custom was to signify that he was going to protect her.

This was the lovely thing which Boaz did to Ruth. Ruth was a widow and, according to the Mosaic Law, she had to claim Boaz as her kinsman-redeemer before he could act. He could not ask her to marry him; she had to claim him. So Naomi, acting like a regular matchmaker, sent Ruth down to the threshing floor. It was harvest time, and all the families were camped around the threshing floor. At night, to protect the grain, the men slept around it with their heads toward the heap of grain and their feet stuck out like spokes of a wheel. Ruth followed Naomi's instructions and laid at the feet of Boaz. When he realized that someone was there and asked who it was, she replied, ". . . I am Ruth thine handmaid: spread therefore thy skirt over thine handmaid; for thou art a near kinsman" (Ruth 3:9). She was asking him to put his cloak over her, asking for his protection as her kinsman-redeemer—in other words, asking him to marry her. In marriage a man offers a woman his protection and his love. And she offers her devotion and her life to him. This is a beautiful picture of Christ's relationship with believers.

In Malachi's day the men of Israel were dealing treacherously with their wives. They had covered them with their garments in marriage, but now they were covering their garment with violence. In other words, they had divorced their wives.

Notice that God says that He *hates* divorce—"the LORD, the God of Israel, saith that he hateth putting away."

God's ideal for man from the very beginning was that there should be no divorce. We know that, because Jesus said that Moses allowed divorce because of the hardness of men's hearts but that from the beginning it was not so. Then how was it at the beginning? "And Adam gave names to all cattle, and to the fowl of the air, and to every beast of the field; but for Adam there was not found an help meet for him" (Gen. 2:20). To begin with, we learn that among all the creation of God that was beneath man, none could take the place of what God would create for Adam, that is, a wife. God had created all other creatures by twos. Neither could man find a mate from the angels which were created above man. So man was pretty much alone. God let Adam give names to all the animals so that Adam would discover for himself that he was alone and that he needed somebody there with him. Only half of him had really been created at the beginning. He needed somebody like he was and yet different from him. He needed one who was a help "meet" or *fit* for him. He needed someone to be fitted to him. He was just a half, and he needed the other half to be put there so that together they could be one. That was the thing God had in mind. God created Adam first and allowed him time to realize that he needed someone else.

I really get provoked when I hear people talk as if sex is something that is bad. Of course, the sex act outside of marriage is wrong. But after all, who was it that thought of sex? God is the One who thought of it and made it. He is the One who designed man and woman. He had in mind a marvelous arrangement when He created the sexes.

"And the LORD God caused a deep sleep to fall upon Adam, and he slept: and he took one of his ribs, and closed up the flesh instead thereof" (Gen. 2:21). Why did God do that? Why didn't he take her from the ground as He had done with Adam? Because she was to be like Adam and yet different from him. She must come from man because man is not really a whole person. She was made from his side. This is not some foolish story. God wants to impress upon man that woman is part of man, that he is only half a man without a woman.

It has been said that God did not take Eve from Adam's head so that she should be his superior. Neither did He take Eve from his foot to be his servant. He took Eve from Adam's side to be his equal and to be his companion. She came from near his heart so that he would love her. She is to be his helper. Together they become one. One plus one equals one. That is God's arithmetic, and that is accurate.

The Scripture knows nothing about this idea of either women's lib or the other extreme, the inferiority of women. God put woman on a high plane. It is obvious to us already that the people in the days of Malachi had lost that vision. That is why God was reminding them, "When you sin against the wife of your youth, you are sinning against Me." God protects the status of women.

"And the rib, which the LORD God had taken from man, made he a woman, and brought her unto the man" (Gen. 2:22). She must have been a beautiful creation. God brought her and gave her unto the man. Certainly God made *that* marriage. The institution of marriage was made in heaven. God's intention was for marriage to be a blessing. God blessed it, and He intended for it to work for man's benefit.

"And Adam said, This is now bone of my bones, and flesh of my flesh: she shall be called Woman, because she was taken out of Man" (Gen. 2:23). What is woman? Adam was *ish*, and woman is *ishshah*. She is the other side or other half of the male. We call them male and female. She is "bone of my bones and flesh of my flesh." She is called woman because she was taken out of man.

"Therefore shall a man leave his father and his mother, and shall cleave unto his wife: and they shall be one flesh" (Gen. 2:24). This excommunicates mothers-in-law and fathers-in-law. This removes them from the new family. I'm afraid a great many folk today do not get the right instruction about marriage. A marriage establishes a new creation. Papa and mamma are not a part of that new creation. The young couple has left them. And they, the man and wife, shall be one flesh.

"And they were both naked, the man and his wife, and were not ashamed" (Gen. 2:25). This was before sin had entered into the world. Neither one looked with lust upon the other because at that time they were innocent. They looked upon each other with tenderness and with love. There was a mutual respect. Each of them could truly say, "You are the one for me." The creation of Eve made Adam a man, all man. The presence of Adam made Eve a woman, all woman.

Then sin entered into the world. It marred everything, including the relationship in marriage. When we get to the time of Moses and the Law, we find that divorce was permitted. This does not mean that it was God's intention when He instituted marriage, but He permitted it, as Jesus said, because of the hardness of man's heart. The Mosaic Law said this: "When a man hath taken a wife, and married her, and it come to pass that she find no favour in his eyes, because he hath found some uncleanness in her: then let him write her a bill of divorcement, and give it in her hand, and send her out of his house" (Deut. 24:1). "Uncleanness" in the bride infers that her husband found that she was not a virgin; then he could write her a bill of divorcement. She had deceived her husband by not being what she claimed to be. He had been "taken in" by her. Naturally, this would lead to trouble in the home, and lead to fighting later on.

By the time of the New Testament, the interpretation of "uncleanness" had become so broad that if a wife even burned the biscuits, that would be grounds for divorce. When Jesus was asked the question, "Is it lawful for a man to put away his wife for every cause?" the rabbis were teaching that a wife could be divorced upon the slightest whim, which was certainly contrary to the intent of the Mosaic Law.

There were other specifics in this Mosaic

Law: "And when she is departed out of his house, she may go and be another man's wife. And if the latter husband hate her, and write her a bill of divorcement, and giveth it in her hand, and sendeth her out of his house; or if the latter husband die, which took her to be his wife; Her former husband, which sent her away, may not take her again to be his wife, after that she is defiled; for that is abomination before the LORD: and thou shalt not cause the land to sin, which the LORD thy God giveth thee for an inheritance" (Deut. 24:2–4). That would be progressive prostitution, and it would lead to the sort of thing we are seeing in our contemporary society, to people being married and divorced seven or eight times! To do that is absolutely to ridicule the marriage vow.

The problem that was prevalent in Israel at the time of Malachi is prevalent in our contemporary culture today. We have certainly changed our viewpoint on divorce in recent years in this country. I suppose that divorce is one of the most controversial subjects that any Bible teacher has to answer today because there is confusion as to what the Bible really says on that problem, and there is a great difference and wide diversion of interpretation. If I may use the colloquialism of the street—it is a hot potato. You cannot say that there are *no* grounds for divorce, although that was the unanimous decision of the church one hundred years ago—in spite of what the Word of God had to say.

The Lord Jesus made two things very clear on this subject of divorce: (1) Moses had permitted divorce because of the hardness of heart of the people; and (2) there is one clear-cut basis for divorce—that is fornication, unfaithfulness on the part of either the man or the woman. Notice this record in Matthew's gospel: "The Pharisees also came unto him, tempting him, and saying unto him, Is it lawful for a man to put away his wife for every cause? And he answered and said unto them, Have ye not read, that he which made them at the beginning made them male and female, And said, For this cause shall a man leave father and mother, and shall cleave to his wife: and they twain shall be one flesh?" (Matt. 19:3–5).

As I mentioned before, Jesus goes back to the beginning, to the time of creation, when God instituted marriage. "Wherefore they are no more twain, but one flesh. What therefore God hath joined together, let not man put asunder. They say unto him, Why did Moses then command to give a writing of divorce-ment, and to put her away? He saith unto them, Moses because of the hardness of your hearts suffered you to put away your wives: but from the beginning it was not so" (Matt. 19:6–8).

Then He sets down the one reason for which divorce is allowed: "And I say unto you, Whosoever shall put away his wife, except it be for fornication, and shall marry another, committeth adultery: and whoso marrieth her which is put away doth commit adultery" (Matt. 19:9).

It is quite interesting how the disciples followed up that statement with a question: "His disciples say unto him, If the case of the man be so with his wife, it is not good to marry" (Matt. 19:10). In other words, "If it is really that strict, if there is one and only one reason for divorce, then it would be better not to get married at all."

Then our Lord explained the liberty that we have: "But he said unto them, All men cannot receive this saying, save they to whom it is given. For there are some eunuchs, which were so born from their mother's womb: and there are some eunuchs, which were made eunuchs of men: and there be eunuchs, which have made themselves eunuchs for the kingdom of heaven's sake. He that is able to receive it, let him receive it" (Matt. 19:11–12). It is not necessary for everyone to get married. There are some men and some women who do not need to marry. By no means is it a sin to be single. Some folk simply do not need to get married—they are eunuchs from birth. Others are made eunuchs by man, such as Daniel in the court of Nebuchadnezzar. It was forced upon them and served the purpose of making captives more docile toward the king, and it also enabled them to devote more time to their studies. Then there are eunuchs for the kingdom of heaven's sake. There are men who have kept themselves eunuchs in order to serve the cause of Christ and the cause of the church. It is wonderful if a man or a woman feels able to do that. I have known several preachers who have never married. I thought I would do the same in my ministry and decided that I would be an old bachelor all my life. But I soon learned that bachelorhood wasn't for me. This is an area in which God has given us great liberty. But the important thing is this: Christ said that if you do choose to get married, it is a lifelong commitment. The only ground for divorce is fornication by your mate.

In the days of the early church this matter of fornication arose in the Corinthian church.

People of different religious backgrounds were in the church, and there were couples who had married when they were pagans, then one of the spouses became a Christian. What should be their relationship after one of them became converted? Paul addresses himself to this new situation: "And unto the married I command, yet not I, but the Lord, Let not the wife depart from her husband: But and if she depart, let her remain unmarried, or be reconciled to her husband: and let not the husband put away his wife" (1 Cor. 7:10–11). If a couple had been married when they were pagans and now one is converted to Christianity, the Christian is not to walk out on the marriage. If the believer departs, he is to remain unmarried or else be reconciled again.

"But to the rest speak I, not the Lord: If any brother hath a wife that believeth not, and she be pleased to dwell with him, let him not put her away. And the woman which hath an husband that believeth not, and if he be pleased to dwell with her, let her not leave him. For the unbelieving husband is sanctified by the wife, and the unbelieving wife is sanctified by the husband: else were your children unclean; but now are they holy. But if the unbelieving depart, let him depart. A brother or a sister is not under bondage in such cases: but God hath called us to peace" (1 Cor. 7:12–15). Although Jesus said that fornication was the only cause for divorce, the pagan member of a marriage may want to walk out on the marriage. After the partner becomes a believer, the pagan party may say, "I don't like this arrangement. Things are different now from when I married you. I'm going to leave." In such a case Paul says to let the unbeliever go. Whether the unbeliever goes out and gets married again or not, in this situation I assume it would mean that the believing husband or wife would be free to marry again.

When Paul said, "A brother or a sister is not under bondage in such cases," what is the bondage? It is the marriage vows.

When he says, "God hath called us to peace," I believe he is saying that God does not ask any man or woman to live in a hell at home. Never. If they find that they cannot get along together, that they fight like cats and dogs, I think that they ought to separate. On several occasions I have advised couples to separate—but neither of them is to remarry. Their problem is not divorce, it is marriage. They should not have married in the first place. God has called us to peace; therefore the home is not to be a boxing ring. It is not a place for karate; it is a place for love.

A home of love is God's ideal for man. From the beginning God did not intend to have divorce, but, because of man's sin, He permitted it. You may say, "Well, divorce is sinful." Sure it is, and so is murder. But a murderer can be saved. In fact, one was dying on a cross next to Jesus, and he got saved. When Jesus Christ died on the cross, He died for all sins. The thief on the cross was both a thief and a murderer, and his faith in the Lord Jesus Christ and His shed blood saved him. A thief can be saved, and a divorced person can be saved, too. So let's not put divorce in a special category all by itself. If an unsaved person has been a thief and then repents and gets saved by coming to Jesus Christ, he is forgiven for his thievery. We would permit such a man to get married. We would do the same for a murderer. Then let us be fair about divorce. There are people who get divorced before they are saved. When they come to the Lord Jesus Christ, they are forgiven for that sin. I think such a person is free to marry again, and I feel that this is implied in the Scriptures.

Now as an addendum to this important section on marriage and divorce, I would like to look at it from a little different viewpoint by including a message which I have entitled *The Best Love* (which is also available in booklet form).

## THE BEST LOVE

There is an obsession with sex today that is positively frightening and absolutely alarming! You need only consult contemporary literature to recognize this. In a leading British paper some time ago, this statement was made: "Popular morality is now a wasteland, littered with the debris of broken convictions." And it was Judge Barron of the Superior Court of Massachusetts who said, "At too many colleges today, sexual promiscuity among students is a dangerous and growing evil." The Billy Graham paper, *Decision*, had an editorial (I suppose it was way back in 1964) on the church and the moral crisis in which there is this quotation: "So our young people go riding down the highroad to hell in an atmosphere that would make any self-respecting animal sick to its stomach, and no one thinks that matters are as bad as they seem." That is a tremendous statement. An outstanding Christian writer in America says, "But where are the compelling external cries to match the inner voices of the soul which at times murmur darkly and other times shout clamorously that all is not well, that wayward feet are treading the way of wrath, the path of judgment?" Then he goes on to say, "The answer is not simply in passing more laws. It is to be found in regeneration by His Spirit, who alone can set men's souls on fire with a divinely sent thirst for greater purity, both for the individual and for the body politic. Apart from such spiritual burning and purging, men sink beneath the weight and corruption of their own sin." These quotations go back to about 1965. But there are other voices being lifted in alarm.

Yet all about us are the advocates of this erotic cult that falsely claim that all of this emphasis on sex is a signal of a new, broadminded and enlightened era. The facts are that there is nothing new about it. Furthermore, it does not mark the entrance upon abundant living. On the contrary, it has characterized the demise of all decadent and decaying civilizations—Egypt, Babylon, Greece, and Rome to name but a few. The sex symbol marks the decline and fall of many a great and noble people. It is part of the death rattle of a fading nation. The French Revolution marked the departure of the glory of France, and it was during that time that a prostitute was placed on an altar and worshiped.

The excuse for paying this abnormal attention to the subject, given by these purveyors of filth and licentiousness, is that a blue-nosed generation of the past put the lid down on it. The false charge is made that the Bible and the church have frowned upon the subject of sex until it is taboo today and can only be whispered of in secret. They go on to place the blame for present-day marriage failures and the increase in divorce on the gross ignorance of young people. "If only they knew more about this fascinating subject," they counsel, "there would be success in marriage." It is true that the Puritans were blue-nosed, and they probably were a little extreme. I would certainly agree with that, and I would not want to go back to that period. But the tragedy of it is that this present generation hasn't found the solution either. After all, the Bible doesn't go with either crowd. I do not think that the Puritans had a Bible basis for their beliefs in this area. Who was it that thought of sex? This crowd in Hollywood thinks they originated it. *God* is the One who started all of this, my friend, and He wanted it put on a holy basis.

This modern crowd also plays upon the fact that we Americans do not like censorship, and therefore they should be free to say and publish what they choose. Well, these modern Pied Pipers of Hamlin are leading the younger generation into a moral morass of debauchery with dirty sex books and pornographic literature. They give the impression that you must be knowledgeable of this lascivious and salacious propaganda in order to be sophisticated and suave and sharp. The bible of this group is *Playboy* magazine. These filthy dreamers have flooded the marketplace and the schoolroom today with this smut and depravity—so much so that a modern father said, "It is not how much shall I tell my son, but how much does he know that *I* don't know!" In spite of all this new emphasis on sex, the divorce courts continue to grind out their monotonous story of the tragedy of modern marriage in ever increasing numbers.

Now a knowledge of the physical may have its place in preparation for a happy marriage, but it is inadequate *per se* to make a happy home, and it gives a perverted and abnormal emphasis which does not belong there. As Dan Bennett said, "One of the troubles with the world is that people mistake sex for love, money for brains, and transistor radios for civilization." That is the problem of the hour.

The Word of God treats the subject of sex with boldness, frankness, and directness. It is not handled as a dirty subject, and it is not taboo nor theoretical, but it is plain and theological. The Bible is straightforward, and it deals with it in high and lofty language. This is the reason we are spending time on this subject here in Malachi. God lays it on the line to these people that this is part of the reason they went into captivity, and it is part of the reason they have been scattered. I think it is time that God is heard. I feel that the pulpit is long overdue in presenting what God has to say on this subject, but it should be kept on the right plane.

In the very beginning it was *God* who created them male and female. It was *God* who brought the woman to the man. And I would like to add this: He did not need to give Adam a lecture on the birds and bees. God blessed them, and marriage became sacred and holy and pure. And, my friend, it is the only relationship among men and women that God does bless down here—He promises to bless no other. He says that if marriage is made according to *His* plan, He will bless it, and there will be happiness.

God *wants* His children to be happily married. He has a plan and purpose for every one of us if we would only listen to Him. The Lord Jesus says to the church at Ephesus, "Nevertheless I have somewhat against thee, because thou hast left thy first love" (Rev. 2:4). Yet the church in Ephesus is the church at its best. The church has never been on a higher spiritual level since then. It is difficult for us in this cold day of apostasy to conceive of the lofty plane to which the Holy Spirit had brought the early church in its personal relationship to Christ. The believers in the early church were *in love with Christ*. They loved Him! And five million of them sealed that love with their own blood by dying as martyrs for Him.

I would like to make a couple of changes in the translation of Revelation 2:4. The word for "first love" is *protan* in the Greek. It means actually the "best." It is the same word our Lord used in the parable of the prodigal son where the father put on the son the *protan* robe—that is, the "best" robe. And to the Ephesian believers Christ is talking about the *best* love. To this church on its high plane, into which a coolness was creeping, Christ says, "Nevertheless I have against thee that thou art leaving [not *had* left] the best love."

Salvation is a love affair. The question that the Lord asks all of us is, "Do you love Me?" He is not asking, "Are you going to be faithful?" or, "Are you going to the mission field?" He is not asking "How much are you going to give?" or, "How much are you going to do?" He is asking "Do you love Me?" Then He will tell you that you are to obey Him and that there will be something for you to do. The apostle John put it like this: "We love him, because he first loved us" (1 John 4:19). The second book I ever wrote was on the little Book of Ruth. My reason for writing it was to show that redemption is a romance. God took the lives of two ordinary people, a very strong and virile man and a very beautiful and noble woman, and He told their love story. In that story God revealed to man His great love for him. It was a way to get this amazing fact through to us: Salvation is a love affair.

In Christ's last letter to the Ephesian church in the Book of the Revelation, He sounds a warning. We do not quite understand this. But I go back thirty or forty years to His first letter to these believers, written through Paul. We call it the Epistle of Paul to the Ephesians. In this epistle He discussed this matter of marital love and compared it to the love of Christ for the church. This has been one of the most misunderstood passages in the Word of God. Listen: "Wives, submit yourselves unto your own husbands, as unto the Lord" (Eph. 5:22). There has been natural resentment against this on the part of

some, especially very dominant women, for many years. And the women's liberation movement would oppose it. But to resent this is to miss the meaning that is here. Submission is actually for the purpose of headship in the home. It is not a question of one lording it over the other; it is headship for the purpose of bringing order into the home.

But in addition to this it reveals something else that is quite wonderful. He says, "For the husband is the head of the wife, even as Christ is the head of the church: and he is the saviour of the body" (Eph. 5:23). The analogy, you see, is to Christ and the church. Christian marriage down here, if it is made under the Lord, is a miniature of the relationship of Christ and the church. Christian marriage is an adumbration of that wonderful relationship between Christ and the believer. Christian marriage and the relationship of Christ and the church are sacred.

Now will you listen to me very carefully. The physical act of marriage is sacred. It is a religious ritual. It is a sacrament. I do not mean a sacrament made by a church, nor is it made by a man-made ceremony. But it is a sacrament that is made by God Himself, one which He sanctifies, and He says that this relationship is to reveal to you the love of Christ for your soul. Therefore, the woman is to see in a man one to whom she can yield herself in glorious abandonment. She can give herself wholly and completely and find perfect fulfillment and satisfaction in this man, because this is the man for her.

She delights in her husband, in his person, his character, his affection; to her he is not only the chief and foremost of mankind, but in her eyes he is all in all. Her heart's love belongs to him, and to him only. He is her little world, her Paradise, her choice treasure. She is glad to sink her individuality in his. She seeks no renown for herself; his honor is reflected upon her, and she rejoices in it. She will defend his name with her dying breath; safe enough is he where she can speak of him. His smiling gratitude is all the reward she seeks. Even in her dress she thinks of him and considers nothing beautiful which is distasteful to him. He has many objects in life, some of which she does not quite understand; but she believes in them all, and anything she can do to promote them she delights to perform. . . . Such a wife, as a true spouse, realizes the model marriage relation and sets forth what our oneness with the Lord ought to be (Richard Ellsworth Day, *The Shadow of the Broad Brim*, p. 104).

My beloved, that is a marvelous picture of the wife in a real Christian marriage. The man is to see in the woman one he can worship. Someone says, "Do you mean worship?" I mean exactly that. What does worship mean? You will find that worship is respect that is paid to worth. If you go back and read the old marriage ceremonies, you will find that the bridegroom always said, "I with my body worship you." That is, he sees in her everything that is worthwhile. He must love her so much that he is willing to die for her.

Now the Bible is very expressive, and I do not know why we should be so reluctant to speak as plainly. If you turn back to the Song of Solomon, you will see the picture of the bridegroom and what he thinks of his bride: "Thou art all fair, my love; there is no spot in thee. . . . As the lily among thorns, so is my love among the daughters" (Song 4:7, 2:2). That is rather expressive, is it not? That is what the bridegroom says. Now hear the words of the bride: "My beloved is mine, and I am his: he feedeth among the lilies" (Song 2:16). You do not go any higher than that! In that moment of supreme and sweet ecstasy, either the wife will carry him to the skies or plunge him down to the depths of hell. Either the husband will place her on a pedestal and say, "I worship you because I find no spot in you," or else he will treat her with brutality. When the latter happens, he will kill her love, and she will hate him and become cold and frigid. In counseling we find that this is one reason that a great many marriages are breaking up.

Bacteriologist Rene Dubos of the Rockefeller Institute has made this statement, "Aimlessness and lack of fulfillment constitute the most common cause of organic and mental disease in the Western world." This is breaking up many a marriage. A wife becomes dissatisfied and frustrated. She becomes nervous, neurotic, and nagging. And the husband settles down to a life of mediocrity. He becomes lonely and either develops into a henpecked Mr. Milquetoast or a domineering brute. You will find both in our society.

Now let me ask a question, and this is rather personal: Are you the kind of woman that a man would die for? I am going to be very frank. If you are just one of these little beetle-brains who is merely a sex kitten making eyes at every boy that comes along, although you may have a hairdo like a Navy balloon that is ready to make an ascension on the poop deck of a destroyer, you will never be the kind of woman that a man would die for. If you do not have beauty of character, if you do not have nobility of soul, you will be but a flame without heat, a rainbow without color, and a flower without perfume. The Word of God deals with that outward adorning—and do not misunderstand, the Bible does not militate against it. All of us ought to look the best we can—some of us have our problems, but we should do the best we can with what we have. God intends us to enhance the beauty He has given us. There is no reason for any woman not to dress in style. But God puts the emphasis, not on the outward adorning, but on the meek and quiet spirit, the inward adorning, which is with God of great price. "Whose adorning let it not be that outward adorning of plaiting the hair, and of wearing of gold, or of putting on of apparel; But let it be the hidden man of the heart, in that which is not corruptible, even the ornament of a meek and quiet spirit, which is in the sight of God of great price" (1 Pet. 3:3–4).

Now, young man, are you the kind of man that a woman would follow to the ends of the earth? You may look like a model for Hart, Schaffner and Marx but have no purpose, no ambition, no heart for serving God as a Christian, no capacity for great and deep things, no vision at all. If you are that kind, a woman will not follow you very far. She may go with you down to get the marriage license, but she also will be going down to get the divorce later on.

All across our West there are monuments erected to the pioneer wife and mother. I noticed one as I was traveling through Colorado. She is a fine-looking woman, crowned with a sunbonnet, the children about her holding on to her long, flowing dress. You know she did not go to the psychiatrist or the marriage counselor. Do you know why she never had to go to the preacher to talk about her marriage breaking up? Because one day a man came to her and said, "I am going West to build a career and home. Will you follow me?" She said, "I will." And she learned that this man would stand between her and danger; she had many experiences when he protected her from the menacing Indians of that day. She had no problems about whether he loved her or not. And he did not doubt her loyalty. They loved each other. These are the kind of people who built our country. It is the other element that is tearing it to pieces—my lovely country—how I hate to see it happening.

I know that someone is saying right now, "Preacher, I am not that kind of person. I'm no hero." Young man, God never said that every girl would fall in love with you. Ninety-nine women may pass you by and see in you only the boy next door who uses that greasy kid stuff. That's all. But let me say to you very seriously, one of these days there will come by a woman who will see in you the knight in shining armor. It is God who gives that highly charged chemistry between a certain man and a certain woman.

A young woman may be saying, "But I'm not beautiful of face or figure." May I say this to you, God never said that you would attract every male—only animals do that. Ninety-nine men will pass you by and see in you no more than what Kipling described as "a rag, a bone and a hank of hair." But one of these days there will come by a man who will love you if you are the right kind of person. You will become his inspiration. You may inspire him to greatness—to write a book, to compose a masterpiece of poetry or music, to paint a picture, or even to preach a sermon. If you are his inspiration, do not ignore him, do not run from him. God may have sent you together for that very purpose. There *will come* that one.

Perhaps you are thinking, "Preacher, you are in the realm of theory. What you are talking about is idealistic. It sounds good in a storybook, but it does not happen in life." You are wrong. It *does* happen.

I think of the story of Matthew Henry. I'm sitting right now in my office looking at a set of books called *Matthew Henry's Commentary*. If anyone ever wrote a musty commentary, Matthew Henry did. Although a great work, it is to me the most boring thing I have ever read. I never knew that fellow was romantic at any time in his life. But when he came to London as a young man, he met a very wealthy girl of the nobility. He fell in love with her, and she loved him. Finally she went to her father to tell him about it. The father, trying to discourage her, said, "Why, that young man has no background. You do not even know where he came from!" She answered, "You are right. I do not know where he came from, but *I know where he is going*, and I want to go with him." She went.

Nathaniel Hawthorne was merely a clerk that anybody would have passed by, working at the customs in New York City—until he was fired for inefficiency. He came home and sank into a chair, discouraged and defeated. His wife came behind him, placed before him pen and paper, and putting her arm about him, said, "Now, Nathaniel, you can do what you always wanted to do—you can write." He wrote *The House of Seven Gables, The Scarlet Letter*, and other enduring literature—because a wife was his inspiration. Theirs was an eternal love. "In one of her last letters the widow of Nathaniel Hawthorne penned this ineradicable hope, which became an anchor of comfort in her soul's sorrow: 'I have an eternity, thank God, in which to know him more and more, or I should die in despair' " (Walter A. Maier, *For Better Not For Worse*, p. 556).

You say I am talking about theory? I am talking about fact. Let us go back to the very beginning. Consider Adam and Eve. That was a romance! Listen to this: "So ought men to love their wives as their own bodies. He that loveth his wife loveth himself. [She is the other part of you. She's you.] For no man ever yet hated his own flesh; but nourisheth and cherisheth it, even as the Lord the church: For we are members of his body, of his flesh, and of his bones. For this cause shall a man leave his father and mother, and shall be joined unto his wife, and they two shall be one flesh" (Eph. 5:28–31).

Eve was created to be a help meet—a help that fit—for Adam. The language is tremendous. She was taken from his side, not molded from the ground as were the animals, but taken from a part of him so that he actually was incomplete until they were together. God fashioned her the loveliest thing in His creation, and He brought her to Adam. She was a helpmeet; she compensated for what he lacked, for he was not complete in himself. She was made for him, and they became one.

"And Adam said, This is now bone of my bones, and flesh of my flesh: she shall be called Woman, because she was taken out of Man. Therefore shall a man leave his father and his mother, and shall cleave unto his wife: and they shall be one flesh" (Gen. 2:23–24).

Let me move down in history. I want to take a story that always has thrilled me. It is the story of Abelard and Heloise. When John Lord wrote his *Great Women*, he used Heloise as the example of love, marital love. The story concerns a young ecclesiastic by the name of Abelard. He was a brilliant young teacher and preacher in what became the University of Paris. The canon there had a niece by the name of Heloise whom he sent to be under Abelard's instruction. She was a remarkable woman; he was a remarkable man. You know the story—they fell madly in love. But according to the awful practice of that day—and this day as well—the marriage of a priest was deemed a lasting disgrace. When John Lord wrote their story, he gave this introduction, which I would like to share with you. It is almost too beautiful to read in this day. It is like a dew-drenched breeze blowing from a flower-strewn mountain meadow over the slop bucket and pigsty of our contemporary literature. Here is what he wrote:

When Adam and Eve were expelled from Paradise, they yet found one flower, wherever they wandered, blooming in perpetual beauty. This flower represents a great certitude, without which few would be happy,—subtle, mysterious, inexplicable,—a great boon recognized alike by poets and moralists, Pagan and Christian; yea, identified not only with happiness, but human existence, and pertaining to the soul in its highest aspirations. Allied with the transient and the mortal, even with the weak and corrupt, it is yet immortal in its nature and lofty in its aims,—at once a passion, a sentiment, and an inspiration.

To attempt to describe woman without this element of our complex nature, which constitutes her peculiar fascination, is like trying to act the tragedy of Hamlet without Hamlet himself,—an absurdity; a picture without a central figure, a novel without a heroine, a religion without a sacrifice. My subject is not without its difficulties. The passion or sentiment is degrading when perverted, it is exalting when pure. Yet it is not vice I would paint, but virtue; not weakness, but strength; not the transient, but the permanent; not the mortal, but the immortal,—all that is ennobling in the aspiring soul [John Lord, *Beacon Lights of History*, pp. 23–24].

Abelard and Heloise, having fallen in love, were not permitted by the church to marry. Therefore, they were married secretly by a friend of Abelard. He continued to teach. But the secret came out when a servant betrayed them, and she was forced into a nunnery. She was never permitted to visit him, and he was never permitted to visit her. Abelard was probably the boldest thinker whom the Middle Ages produced. At the beginning of the twelfth century, he began to preach and teach that the Word of God was man's authority, not the church. This man, a great man, became bitter and sarcastic in his teaching because of what had been denied him. When he was on his deathbed, for he died a great while before Heloise, being twenty years her senior, he asked that she be permitted to come to see him. The church did the cruelest thing of all—they would not allow her to come. Therefore he penned her a letter. To me it is the most pathetic thing I have ever read. He concludes it with this prayer:

When it pleased Thee O Lord, and as it pleased Thee, Thou didst join us, and Thou didst separate us. Now what Thou hast so mercifully begun, mercifully complete; and after separating us in this world, join us together eternally in heaven.

It is my personal belief that in God's heaven they are together.

This brings us to a tremendous verse. Malachi has concluded the section on social sins which relate to the family and divorce. They were sins which were like a cancer gnawing at the vitals of the nation. And they will destroy any nation—ours will not be an exception, I am sure.

**Ye have wearied the Lord with your words. Yet ye say, Wherein have we wearied him? When ye say, Every one that doeth evil is good in the sight of the Lord, and he delighteth in them; or, Where is the God of judgment? [Mal. 2:17].**

"Ye have wearied the Lord with your words." I can't help but laugh at that. God says, "I'm so tired of those long, pious prayers that you say. And I am so tired of your testimonies. You really make Me weary." You remember that back in the first chapter they had said of their perfunctory service to God, "Behold, what a weariness is it." God says, "You don't know the half of it. *You* bore Me to tears by your hypocritical service."

"Yet ye say, Wherein have we wearied him?" We see again the feigned injured innocence of these people. They are offended that God would *dare* say this of them—they are entirely ignorant of their sins. They ask, "In what way have we wearied Him?"

Note that this is the fifth sarcastic question of the people to God's charge of their phony and pseudo worship. Contemptuously and impudently, they contradict God—"In what way have we wearied Him?"

Well, God has an answer for them. He lays it on the line and tells it to them like it is: "When ye say, Every one that doeth evil is good in the sight of the LORD, and he delighteth in them; or, Where is the God of judgment [justice]?" They are maligning the character of God.

This is a philosophy that arises rather frequently in the history of mankind. Man says, "Look, I see men who are big sinners and yet they are prosperous. They don't seem to have problems or trouble like I have—yet I am trying to serve the Lord. Why does God permit that sort of thing?"

The psalmist expresses this same complaint. He saw folk about him who were getting by with evil and not serving God at all. Yet they were the ones who seemed to prosper the most. He wrote: "But as for me, my feet were almost gone; my steps had well nigh slipped. For I was envious at the foolish, when I saw the prosperity of the wicked" (Ps. 73:2–3). As he looked around, he saw the rascals getting richer and richer while the poor got poorer and poorer. And the poor saints of God were the ones who were not prospering at all.

This was exactly the complaint of the people in Malachi's day. And that attitude produces very quickly a "new morality." When they feel that "every one that doeth evil is *good* in the sight of the LORD," they begin to call evil good and good evil. It pays to do evil.

We have much the same attitude in our day. Most people would say that crime does pay. People get by with as much as they possibly can. This applies to the big corporations as well as to the average man. The government spends our money without any kind of responsibility to the people. The lackadaisical attitude in Washington is one of the real problems in the world today. The politicians try to curry favor with the rich and please the powerful. The little man is stepped on, and nobody cares. Why doesn't God do something about it?

The psalmist got his answer to this problem because he went to God. "Until I went into the sanctuary of God; then understood I their end" (Ps. 73:17). You see, he had been looking at the immediate present. But how about the far-off future? What about their eternal state? From where you and I stand, their little day is ancient history, but way back then they made

their decision for eternity. And for our generation time is slipping through the shuttle fast, let me tell you. So what about the godless today? Well, they can build a "new morality," they can accumulate as much money as they can, but those who do evil today will face the Judge tomorrow. They are going to have to answer to Him. We need to be very careful about sitting in judgment upon the apparent inaction of God in our contemporary society.

This reminds me of an incident when two of us seminary students were traveling together and picked up a hitchhiker who reeked of alcohol. He smelled like a still that had just come out of the Kentucky hills. He apologized for it and said that he knew he shouldn't drink. We witnessed to him of Christ, and my friend said something that was startling to me at that time, but I certainly concur with it now. He said to him, "We're not condemning you for getting drunk. You are a lost man on the way to hell; so you had better squeeze this life like an orange and get all you can of its juice while you're here. You won't have this liquor when you get over there. Go ahead and live it up. But you are moving into eternity. Did you ever stop to think about that?"

Any unsaved person who is familiar with the Word of God knows that he is a sinner and that there is a God of justice. But don't expect God to move in judgment immediately.

When I was a kid in southern Oklahoma, we used to swipe watermelons. I am honest with you when I say that every time I went into the watermelon patch to swipe a watermelon, I thought that there would be lightning out of heaven that would strike me dead. But I was going to steal those watermelons regardless! That is the willfulness of the human heart—even of a little boy.

However, the Lord doesn't operate quite like that, although He *may* do so. Because God does not always judge immediately, man interprets this to mean that God will not judge him at all. "Because sentence against an evil work is not executed speedily, therefore the heart of the sons of men is fully set in them to do evil" (Eccl. 8:11). If a man gets by with it once, he will figure that he can just keep on getting by with it.

The people in Malachi's day asked, "Where is the God of justice?" Well, God will give them His answer in the following chapter.

# CHAPTER 3

*THEME: The prediction of the two messengers; the people rebuked for religious sins*

Chapter 3 opens with God's answer to the question raised by the people of Israel at the end of the previous chapter.

**Behold, I will send my messenger, and he shall prepare the way before me: and the Lord, whom ye seek, shall suddenly come to his temple, even the messenger of the covenant, whom ye delight in: behold, he shall come, saith the LORD of hosts [Mal. 3:1].**

Here in one verse we have two messengers. The first messenger who is to go before and to prepare the way is John the Baptist. The second is "the messenger of the covenant," the Lord Jesus Christ.

The prophecy concerning the first messenger is quoted in all four of the Gospels as applying to John the Baptist; there is no guesswork here. However, the messenger of the covenant is never quoted anywhere in the Gospels, and the reason is obvious. This messenger of the covenant *is* the Lord Jesus, but this passage hasn't anything to do with His first coming. This is His coming not in grace, not as a Redeemer, but as a Judge, as the One who will establish His kingdom and put down the rebellion that is on this earth. You remember that on one occasion He even said to a man, ". . . who made me a judge or a divider over you?" (Luke 12:14). He hasn't come yet to judge. He came the first time to save. He came to bring grace, not government. He came as the One who is the Savior, not the Sovereign.

I would like to turn now to the Gospel passages which quote this verse in reference to John the Baptist. The first one is in Matthew 11:9–10: "But what went ye out for to see? A prophet? yea, I say unto you, and more than a prophet. For this is he, of whom it is written, Behold, I send my messenger before thy face, which shall prepare thy way before thee." Over in Mark's Gospel we find: "As it is written in the prophets, Behold, I send my messenger before thy face, which shall prepare thy way before thee" (Mark 1:2). Then in the Gospel of Luke we read, "This is he, of whom it is written, Behold, I send my messenger before thy face, which shall prepare thy way before thee" (Luke 7:27). Finally, John 1:23 records, "He said, I am the voice of one crying in the wilderness, Make

straight the way of the Lord, as said the prophet Esaias." This is a direct quote from Isaiah, but we can see that Malachi also had this to say about John the Baptist.

Therefore, this is God's answer to the people of Israel: God will send Him first as a Savior because He is gracious and He wants to save. But that doesn't end it all: He is coming again as the messenger of the covenant, that is, to execute justice and judgment on this earth.

If you could convince me that God does not intend to judge sin and that He intends to let sinners get by with their injustice today, then I say very frankly that I would turn my back on Him. But He's made it very clear that *He does intend to judge mankind.* My friend, if you will not have Him as your Savior, you're going to have Him as your Judge whether you like it or not. He said, "For the Father judgeth no man, but hath committed all judgment unto the Son" (John 5:22). And in the Book of Revelation, we see a Great White Throne upon which He is seated. And those who are the lost—both rich and poor, high and low, great and small—are going to stand before it. It does not matter who you are, you are not going to get by with sin, my friend.

When it says "the messenger of the covenant," we need to understand which covenant is meant. A great many have thought that it is the New Covenant in the New Testament. Actually, this has no reference to the first coming of Christ but rather to the covenant which God has made with the people of Israel. This covenant is expressed in several places in the Scriptures. For instance, in Leviticus 26:9–13 we read: "For I will have respect unto you, and make you fruitful, and multiply you, and establish my covenant with you. And ye shall eat old store, and bring forth the old because of the new. And I will set my tabernacle among you: and my soul shall not abhor you. And I will walk among you, and will be your God, and ye shall be my people. I am the LORD your God, which brought you forth out of the land of Egypt, that ye should not be their bondmen; and I have broken the bands of your yoke, and made you go upright."

This is the covenant which God made with the children of Israel. You will find that He confirmed it in Deuteronomy, as the Book of Deuteronomy is a confirmation of the Mosaic

Law and the Israelites' experience with it after forty years. Deuteronomy 4:23 says, "Take heed unto yourselves, lest ye forget the covenant of the LORD your God, which he made with you, and make you a graven image, or the likeness of any thing, which the LORD thy God hath forbidden thee." Of course, Israel had done the very thing which He had forbidden, turning even to the occult.

Therefore, Malachi tells us that the messenger of the covenant is coming someday to make good this covenant. God will dwell in their midst, and this is the reason we will also find in these first verses of Malachi 3 the cleansing and the purifying that will take place. God will not walk among them unless they are obedient unto Him, unless He has cleansed them and purified them. This is true, of course, of any Christian work today as well.

"The Lord, whom ye seek." This will be the Lord Jesus Christ, who is God manifest in the flesh.

"Shall suddenly come to his temple." This does not mean that He will *soon* come to His temple, but that when He comes it will be suddenly. A man once said to me, "You talk about the Rapture in which the Lord will take the church out of the world. Well, when that takes place and He removes the church and I see them leaving, then I'm going to accept Christ." But I said, "It will be too late then because the reason that He's taking the church out is that it is completed. So you would not be able then to be a part of the church. You could accept Christ and go through the Great Tribulation, but I think you're a fool to wait until then."

He is called the Lord, this is His temple, and He's the messenger of the covenant—so we know this is the Lord Jesus Christ. The One whom we know in the New Testament as the Lord Jesus Christ is the angel of the covenant in the Old Testament.

**But who may abide the day of his coming? and who shall stand when he appeareth? for he is like a refiner's fire, and like fullers' soap [Mal. 3:2].**

We know that Malachi refers to the second coming of Christ because it is judgment that is in view here. Note the expression: "But who may abide the day of his coming?" This is the second coming of Christ.

"And who shall stand when he appeareth? for he is like a refiner's fire." In the refining process, the metal is put over red-hot fire, and as it begins to melt, the dross can be drawn off, and the metal is finally made pure.

"And like fullers' soap." He intends to purify, and He intends to clean. Purify and clean—there's not going to be any pollution when He establishes the Millennium on this earth.

**And he shall sit as a refiner and purifier of silver: and he shall purify the sons of Levi, and purge them as gold and silver, that they may offer unto the LORD an offering in righteousness [Mal. 3:3].**

"And he shall sit as a refiner and purifier of silver: and he shall purify the sons of Levi." He is going to cleanse those who enter the Millennium.

"And purge them as gold and silver." There are two processes: cleansing and purifying. Cleansing is the use of soap as it is expressed here. And the fire is used for testing—this is another way which God has of purifying us and testing us.

**Then shall the offering of Judah and Jerusalem be pleasant unto the LORD, as in the days of old, and as in former years [Mal. 3:4].**

"Then shall the offering of Judah and Jerusalem be pleasant unto the LORD." The Lord will take a great delight in their sacrifice because the ones who are offering it are now cleansed and purified. God is not interested in your going through rituals *until* your heart is right, until you have forsaken your sin and turned from it. You can get into sin, but if you stay in it, God is not accepting your religion at all.

"As in the days of old, and as in former years." In the time of Solomon, there was a period in which Israel served God in such a way that they witnessed to the entire world.

**And I will come near to you to judgment; and I will be a swift witness against the sorcerers, and against the adulterers, and against false swearers, and against those that oppress the hireling in his wages, the widow, and the fatherless, and that turn aside the stranger from his right, and fear not me, saith the LORD of hosts [Mal. 3:5].**

"And I will come near to you to judgment; and I will be a swift witness against the sorcerers." Again, through these mixed marriages, through marrying heathen and pagan women who worshiped idols, their sorcery, the occult, and demon worship were brought in.

And in order to fill the great spiritual vacuum that is in our country, multitudes are turning to the occult today. This is the reason the movie *The Exorcist* was so popular. What a reflection this is on the church which certainly has failed to fill that void.

"And against the adulterers." This is a reference to those who had made the mixed marriages by divorcing their wives and marrying these foreign heathen women.

"And against false swearers"—that is, liars.

"And against those that oppress the hireling in his wages, the widow, and the fatherless, and that turn aside the stranger from his right, and fear not me, saith the LORD of hosts." In other words, the people were not witnessing for God. The stranger in that day, to whom they should have witnessed, actually turned from God because of the way he was treated by God's people.

**For I am the LORD, I change not; therefore ye sons of Jacob are not consumed. [Mal. 3:6].**

God is a God of judgment, but He is also gracious. The reason that they had not been absolutely obliterated like the Edomites was because of His grace; it was because God is gracious. And He is still gracious because He never changes. Thank God for that. God today is still a God of judgment—that is a terror to the wicked. But He's also a God who never changes in reference to His grace—and that is a comfort to anyone who will accept the grace of God.

We come now to the sixth of these very smart-alecky retorts which these people give to God. There are eight of them in the book; we've seen five of them, and now we've come to the sixth. These people are, as it were, putting God on a quiz program. God makes a statement, and they ask Him to prove it. God brings eight incriminating accusations against the nation, and they counter by asking eight very impertinent and presumptuous questions. God answers them politely but emphatically. He is attempting to detour them from the destruction to which they are headed.

To interpret these questions it might be well to pause here again to consider the generation who asked them. After the people of Israel had been in captivity for seventy years, a remnant returned to the land. Reluctantly and halfheartedly, they set about restoring the city and rebuilding the temple. They had known the rigors and suffering of slavery. Like their fathers in the brickyards of Egypt, they had certainly been groaning. And even upon returning, they endured hardships, severe persecutions, and dis-

couragements. Believe me, they thought that when they returned everything would be happy and nice and easy for them—but that was not the case. These were God's methods of discipline; it was a form of correction, but it did not have the desired effect. Discipline will either soften or harden you, and these people became hardened and embittered under the yoke which galled them. They became as hard as nails. They were like a prison inmate who has been released but not reformed. They had come out of slavery but apparently had not learned the lesson.

Actually, there is not much more that God could have done for them. Even God exhausted His infinite arsenal of correction. It was out of the soil of this generation that there grew up the poisonous plant of the Pharisees, the Sadducees, and the scribes who were in existence at the time when the Lord Jesus came four hundred years later. What was a pimple of rebellion against God in the time of Malachi, just a scratch on the surface of the nation, became at the time of the Lord Jesus an internal cancer.

God tried to stem the spread of the virus, to cauterize it, and He brought these eight charges against them. Their response reveals their attitude. They pled not guilty to every one of them, and they expressed surprise that God would even suspect them. They affected an injured innocence. They feigned hurt feelings. They assumed ignorance. They played the part of being highly offended, and with a wave of the hand, they dismissed the charges as unworthy of them.

This now is the sixth sarcastic question that the people give to God's penetrating charge. God is now going to call on the people to do something—

**Even from the days of your fathers ye are gone away from mine ordinances, and have not kept them. Return unto me, and I will return unto you, saith the LORD of hosts. But ye said, Wherein shall we return? [Mal. 3:7].**

Oh, what smart alecks they were! They say to God, "You say that we should return to You. We didn't know that we had gone away. We've been going up to the temple to all the services. We tithe to a certain extent. We're doing this, that, and the other thing, but how can we return when we haven't even left You?" They were actually so far gone that they did not realize their true condition.

I would say that this is pretty much the picture of a great many folk in the church today. Ritualism has been substituted for reality. Pageantry has been substituted for power. The aesthetic has been substituted for the spiritual, and form for feeling. Even in the orthodox, conservative, and evangelical circles, they know the vocabulary, but the power of God is gone. They are satisfied with a tasteless morality, they follow a few little shibboleths, and they feel that everything is all right.

But God says, "Return! You've departed from Me." What does He mean by returning to Him? He means to repent. To repent is to return to Him. God has said only to those who are His people, "Repent. Return to Me." You see, the unbeliever can't quite fulfill the song which says, "Lord, I'm coming home." The unbeliever hasn't even been home; he doesn't even have a home. The prodigal son had to *leave* a home before he could come back to his home. He was a son all the time. But he left home, and he had to repent and to change his mind. This is what repentance actually means.

We do not get the full meaning of repentance until we come to the New Testament. *Metanoia*, the Greek word, means "to change your mind." It means to be walking in one direction, you find out you're going the wrong way, and then you turn right around and go the opposite way. The other day Mrs. McGee and I drove over to Glendale, which is a city right next to Pasadena here in Southern California. We asked for directions for getting to a certain place, and a girl gave us the wrong directions. She said, "Turn left," but when we turned left, we ran right up to the side of a mountain. I said to Mrs. McGee, "I think the girl told us wrong." So what did we do? We turned around. We had to return back to where we had turned off, and then we went the other direction and found that the other direction was the right direction. When I turned around, it was because I had found out I was wrong and I wanted to go the right way—that's repentance.

Now God speaks to His own about repentance. The interesting thing is that in the New Testament it is always believers to whom God says, "Repent." It is to those who are supposed to have been His children that He says, "Repent." In the Book of Revelation God had a message for each of the seven churches. To five of those churches God said, "Repent," but to the martyr church of Smyrna He didn't say that. They were dying for Him, and therefore He wouldn't say that. And to the church of Philadelphia, which was holding to the Word of God, He did not say, "Repent." But to all the rest of them, including the church at Laodicea, His message to the churches is to repent.

We have the notion today of telling the unsaved that they are to repent. Well, what are they to repent of? Do they need to change their direction? Yes, but repentance is not the message to be given to the unsaved. It is my feeling that the message of repentance is being given over the heads of believers to unbelievers, and it is falling on deaf ears, naturally. The people to whom it should be given are sitting right down in front. Believers are the ones to whom you should say, "Repent."

Somebody says, "Do you mean that the unsaved person who comes to Christ should not repent?" My friend, all the repentance that he is asked to do is in the word *believe*. Consider Paul's message to the Thessalonians. Paul had a very marvelous ministry there, and he said, "For they themselves shew of us what manner of entering in we had unto you, and how ye turned to God from idols to serve the living and true God" (1 Thess. 1:9). When Paul went into the city of Thessalonica, he did not preach to them against idolatry. It was running riot, but he didn't preach against it. He didn't preach against alcoholism or any of that type of thing. This is the reason that I don't follow the pattern of preaching against certain sins; only when the Word of God touches on these things do I touch on them. Our message to the lost world is what Paul gave to the Philippian jailer: ". . . Believe on the Lord Jesus Christ, and thou shalt be saved . . ." (Acts 16:31). In the word *believe* is all the repentance you need. When Paul went to Thessalonica and preached, did he preach repentance? No. He preached *Christ*. He said, "How ye turned *to* God *from* idols." The Thessalonians were going in one direction, and Paul said, "I want to tell you about Jesus Christ who died for your sins." And the Thessalonians turned to Christ. But when they turned to Him, they turned away from idols, and turning away is repentance—they turned around, you see—but it is in the word *believe*.

You must have something to turn *to*, my friend. You cannot just say to a man, "Repent." When I went down to an altar as a little boy, nobody counseled with me. I just wept—that was all. I wept because the boy next to me wept. His mother was a shoutin' Methodist, and she wept. She started all the weeping. The fellow across from me jumped up and said, "He's prayed through!" I don't know what he meant by that, but whatever it was I didn't do it. Nobody presented Christ to me. I was ready to repent because I wasn't the best boy in the world, although my mother thought so. I could weep for my sins, but I needed Christ. And when you turn to Christ, you'll turn from these things.

However, many of God's children, like the prodigal son, get into a far country, and He says, "Repent. Come home." That's the fellow who should come home. There are a lot of believers who need to come home. God is not talking about the unsaved fellow down the street. He's talking to you, and He says, "Come home." What are you doing in that liberal church? What are you doing committing adultery? God says, "Come on home. Turn around, and come on home." This is a message to believers. To these in Israel who were His children He said, "Return to me, and I will return unto you."

The prodigal son didn't get a whipping when he got home; he had gotten a whipping in the far country. If you think that pigpen was delightful, you are wrong. Any Christian who gets into sin will testify that it is not nearly as much fun as he thought it was going to be—many of us could say that. The important thing is to get out of the pigpen. My friend, there's not but one class of living creatures that like pigpens, and that is pigs. Sons just don't like pigpens, and they are going to get out.

The people of Malachi's day deny that they need to return to God and need to repent. They act as if they haven't been anywhere. They say, "The temple is crowded. We're going through the ritual. What do You mean, 'Repent'? What do You mean, 'Return to You'? We're already here. We haven't gone anywhere!" But God says, "Yes, you have. You may be going through the ritual, but your heart is far from Me."

This is also true even in many conservative churches today. People go through the little ritual that we conservative folk have. We have a certain vocabulary. Folk know when to say, "Praise the Lord" and "Hallelujah," but their hearts are far from Him. He's asking us to repent, but it seems to be the most difficult thing to do, especially for Christians. I don't know why, because it should be easier for us than for any other people in the world.

I heard of a church where one of the officers got up and suggested to the board who was finding fault with everything, including the pastor, that he felt the officers needed to repent. Do you know that they rebuffed that man and insulted him so that it apparently brought on his death? That was the way he was treated for even suggesting to a group of church officers that they needed to repent! Israel said, "Wherein shall we return? How can we repent? We're beautiful people. We don't need to repent. That crowd outside needs to repent." There are a lot of folk in our churches today who think that everybody else needs to repent and that they don't. But we do need it, my friend. We need to return to God today.

When the people respond like this, believe me, God really opens up the wound here—and this will hurt. At this juncture some readers will want to tune me out because this is not going to be pleasant. I don't think that Malachi has been a very pleasant book, but I enjoy it because I think Malachi is talking right to me as well as to you or anybody else, and we *need* to be talked to like this.

My cancer doctor was a very wonderful doctor, but he treated me rougher than any doctor I have had. I tried to get him to give me an encouraging word every now and then. He wouldn't do it. I tried to get him to give me a prescription for easing pain, you know, but he wouldn't do it. He just laid it right on the line. I love the man, and I love him because of the fact that he told it like it was. When you've had cancer and you may still have it in your system, you really want to be told the truth. And in spiritual matters that have to do with my eternal soul, I want somebody to tell me the truth even if it hurts. God doesn't mind telling you the truth at all.

We come now to the seventh sarcastic remark that these people make. Eight times in this book these people will return to God a flippant answer. Eight times they will dismiss His charges like petulant children. Eight times they will evade the fact by affecting ignorance. Eight times they will avoid answering by pretending they are pious.

**Will a man rob God? Yet ye have robbed me. But ye say, Wherein have we robbed thee? In tithes and offerings [Mal. 3:8].**

Instead of pronouncing the benediction in many of our churches, the thing that probably should be said is this: "Stop thieves! You've been robbing God!" The congregation would be apt to say, "You don't mean us! We put a generous offering in the plate." Did you, my friend? Listen to this: "Will a man rob God? Yet ye have robbed me. But ye say, Wherein have we robbed thee?" And God's answer is,

"In tithes and offerings, you have robbed Me."

If you think that God is a Shylock of the sky who was trying to take something away from these people, you are wrong. What God was doing was actually blessing them and saying, "I'm going to let you have nine-tenths, and you return to Me one-tenth."

There are several rather important things that we do need to correct in our understanding at this point. To begin with, the people of Israel did not give just one tithe, as you would discover if you would examine the Scriptures carefully. I am indebted to Dr. Feinberg's excellent book on Malachi (pp. 125–126) in which he lists the tithes given by Israel:

The offerings in Israel were the first-fruits, not less than one-sixtieth of the corn, wine, and oil. (Deuteronomy 18:4). There were several kinds of tithes: (1) the tenth of the remainder after the first-fruits were taken, this amount going to Levites for their livelihood (Leviticus 27:30–33); (2) the tenth paid by Levites to the priests (Numbers 18:26–28); (3) the second tenth paid by the congregation for the needs of the Levites and their own families at the tabernacle (Deuteronomy 12:18); and (4) another tithe every third year for the poor (Deuteronomy 14:28–29).

I would like to look more closely at this last Scripture because this is something that I feel should be observed today. I realize that our government has done much in an effort to help the poor—or maybe it's to help the bureaucrats. There is a real question as to who gets the money which is allocated for the poor. But my feeling is that the church ought to have more of an emphasis on helping the poor. Let's look at God's instructions to Israel: "At the end of three years thou shalt bring forth all the tithe of thine increase the same year, and shalt lay it up within thy gates: And the Levite, (because he hath no part nor inheritance with thee,) and the stranger, and the fatherless, and the widow, which are within thy gates, shall come, and shall eat and be satisfied; that the LORD thy God may bless thee in all the work of thine hand which thou doest" (Deut. 14:28–29).

Therefore, every third year there was this extra tithe that was given for the poor. When you say that God required a tithe of Israel, what do you mean by it? We need to understand that there were several tithes which were given.

The second thing that we need to straighten out in our thinking is that we are living in the day of grace. The giving of believers today is on an altogether different basis than Israel's. We *are* to give but on a different basis. The church is not under the tithe system as a legal system. That does not mean that some people couldn't give a tenth to the Lord—that may be the way the Lord would lead them to give. But let's notice the way the early church gave. When Paul wrote to the Corinthians, he used the Macedonians as an example: "How that in a great trial of affliction the abundance of their joy and their deep poverty abounded unto the riches of their liberality" (2 Cor. 8:2).

Though very poor, the Macedonians gave generously. "For to their power, I bear record, yea, and beyond their power they were willing of themselves" (2 Cor. 8:3).

They gave way beyond any tenth—the tithe didn't even enter into their thinking. They simply gave because of their love of the Lord. And Paul tells us another reason they gave—"Praying us with much entreaty that we would receive the gift, and take upon us the fellowship of the ministering to the saints" (2 Cor. 8:4).

You see, giving is fellowship. It is part of the fellowship and part of the worship of the church. "And this they did, not as we hoped, but first gave their own selves to the Lord, and unto us by the will of God" (2 Cor. 8:5).

This is the reason that from time to time I make it very clear that if you are an unsaved person, if you are not a Christian, we don't want you to give to our Bible-teaching radio ministry. To begin with, giving couldn't be a blessing to you, and I don't think that in the long run it would ever be a blessing to us. God asks *His children* to give. Have you ever noticed that the ark of the covenant was carried on the shoulders of the priests of Israel? The Lord could have called in somebody from the outside to carry it, or He could have had a cart to carry it because a cart carried some of the other things. But the ark of the covenant, which speaks of Christ, was carried on the shoulders of the priests. If we are going to carry forth His message about what He has done for us, it has to be carried upon the shoulders of those who are priests, those who are His. He's not asking you to give if you are not a Christian. "I speak not by commandment, but by occasion of the forwardness of others, and to prove the sincerity of your love" (2 Cor. 8:8).

Your giving proves your love for Christ. He doesn't ask you to give. The song which says, "I gave, I gave My life for thee, What hast thou given for Me?" is as unscriptural as anything can be. He never asks you that question. He says, "If ye *love* me, keep my commandments" (John 14:15, italics mine). "For ye know the grace of our Lord Jesus Christ, that, though he was rich, yet for your sakes he became poor, that ye through his poverty might be rich" (2 Cor. 8:9).

Paul says that you should give hilariously, joyfully. When I was in Israel, I was shown several new government buildings, and one of them was their internal revenue service for the collection of taxes. My Jewish guide very wryly said, "We call that 'the new Wailing Wall.' " Let me tell you, when the offering is taken in our churches, it also is a wailing wall for some. People think, *Oh my, they are going to take an offering!* My friend, the offering ought to be a joyful part of the service. If you can't give joyfully, you ought not to be giving. It won't do you a bit of good, I can assure you of that.

In chapter 8 and on into chapter 9 of 2 Corinthians, Paul continues to discuss the basis upon which Christians are to give. I think that most Christians in this affluent society ought to be giving more than a tenth. Israel gave more than a tenth—there were four tithes.

When I was a pastor in Texas during the Depression, an elder in my church was the only one who was in a business that was really making money. I used to hunt on his ranch and also fish in the river which went right through his property. He and I were in his boat one day fishing, when he said to me, "Preacher, why don't you preach more on the tithe?" I said, "Well, I don't believe in it." He did believe in the tithe and that was the way he gave. Every time he and I would get together he wanted to know why I didn't speak on the tithe. Finally, I went through 2 Corinthians 8 with him. Then I said, "There are a lot of Christians who ought to be giving more than a tenth. For example, I would say that you are probably making more money than any other individual in the church except the doctors." We had five doctors in the church, and they did well financially. But the point was that this man was really making money during the Depression. I told him, "I think that you ought to give more than a tenth." I looked him right straight in the eye when I said that, and he winced a little. He never again asked me to preach on the tithe

because he was glad to give only his tenth. It eased his conscience to feel that that was all he ought to give.

A lot of folk ought to be giving more than a tenth, but when I say "ought to," that's me speaking. Jesus says, "Don't do it unless you are giving it because of love for Me and because you really want to get the Word out."

God says, "Will a man rob God?" What do you think? Again I say, instead of having the benediction at the end of the church service, they ought to let the people start to leave and then have somebody yell out, "Stop thieves!" There sure would be a whole lot of thieves who wouldn't want to be caught and would take off running. Why? Because they have robbed God. How did they rob God? Well, it *all* belongs to Him, but to Israel He said, "You keep nine-tenths, but I want you to give Me the other tenth to recognize Me."

It is amazing how some of the great businessmen of the past were Christians who gave to God and gave to God generously. The founder of the Hershey Chocolate Company was a Christian who was very regular in giving to the Lord. William Wrigley, the founder of the Wrigley Gum Company also gave generously to the Lord. I'm talking about the founders of these companies, not about the present generation. The J.C. Penney stores were started by a preacher's son whose father died when he was a boy. There were no arrangements made to care for his mother, except for people to say, "The Lord bless you." As a little boy, he had to go out and collect the clothes which his mother washed for a living, and he said, "When I grow up, I'm going to make money and see to it that no preacher's widow has to work like this." He made good, and he established villages where retired preachers and their wives can live. God has blessed these men in the past who have recognized Him. I believe that this is still true today, but, my friend, you will have to do it out of love—that is the only way He will accept it.

**Ye are cursed with a curse: for ye have robbed me, even this whole nation [Mal. 3:9].**

Under grace God wants you to give as you are able to give. For some people that would be less than the tithe, and for other people it would be more than the tithe. And I'm of the opinion that a great many in this affluent society ought to be giving more to God.

Here in Southern California there are

headquarters or semi-headquarters of three of the major cults. One of the things that they do is to put their people back under the Mosaic Law and insist that they keep the law, including the tithes—that's part of the system. If you're going to belong to their group, you're going to give a tithe. Those three cults are very wealthy. We think that this little operation that we represent is great—we thank God for it—but we are actually a Mickey Mouse operation if you put us down by the side of these other organizations where millions of dollars are just rolling in. Even on the tithe, the old legal system, look at how much would come in. Doesn't that tell you that God's people who are under grace are surely not giving to the Lord's work as they should?

This is one of the reasons that we do not see the blessing that should attend God's work. Many churches have a minister who is teaching the Word of God, but they don't seem to be going anywhere. God makes it clear that our giving is something that He looks at. If a church or an individual is not giving, God has not promised to bless them at all. I believe that God is going to bless any person who is devoted to Him—but not necessarily with material blessings. Paul tells us in Ephesians that we are blessed with ". . . all spiritual blessings in heavenly places in Christ" (Eph. 1:3). Therefore God, in a very gracious manner, will bless those who are generous with Him. This is a great principle that runs through the entire Word of God. Many churches which were Bible churches have just dried up and died on the vine, and it can all be traced to the fact that the people were not giving as they should unto God. If we open our heart to Him, He'll open His heart to us. Not for *physical* blessings—God promised those to His people Israel; He promises us *spiritual* blessings—"all spiritual blessings in heavenly places in Christ."

God made good His promises to His people. In the time of Hezekiah there was a period of revival. In 2 Chronicles 31:10 we read: "And Azariah the chief priest of the house of Zadok answered him, and said, Since the people began to bring the offerings into the house of the LORD we have had enough to eat, and have left plenty: for the LORD hath blessed his people; and that which is left is this great store."

In other words, the people were giving *more* than enough. At the time that Israel built the tabernacle, Moses asked for offerings, and he had to stop the people from giving because they were bringing too much! That is the only case on record that I have heard of people being stopped from giving—but they did it in that day.

**Bring ye all the tithes into the storehouse, that there may be meat in mine house, and prove me now herewith, saith the LORD of hosts, if I will not open you the windows of heaven, and pour you out a blessing, that there shall not be room enough to receive it [Mal. 3:10].**

Again I would remind you that we are not under the tithe system today. There are many humble believers with very little income for whom a tenth would be too much to give. There are others whom God has blessed in such a wonderful way that they could easily give even as much as the government will allow for deductions. There are those who have an income such that they could give that to the Lord, but we find very few who are giving like that. The tithe is certainly a yardstick by which you could measure yourself, but I don't think that it is legal or binding at all.

"Bring ye all the tithes into the storehouse." There are many churches and some denominations which have said that the storehouse is the local church or the denomination. Frankly, just as the tithe is not for the church today, neither is the storehouse. The storehouse was a part of the temple. There were many buildings around the temple which were storerooms. When people brought their tithe, it was stored away in these storerooms. When Nehemiah came back to Jerusalem (sometime before the time of Malachi), he found Tobiah, the enemy of God, living in one of the storerooms that had been cleaned out. It had been cleaned out because the people were not giving generously, and they had made an apartment out of it for Tobiah! But Nehemiah cleaned up the place. He took Tobiah's things and pitched them out the window and told him to get out of town. Then the people began to bring their offerings to fill up the storeroom again (see Neh. 13:4–9).

There is no such thing today as that which is called "storehouse giving." That's not quite the way we give, because Israel's giving was in the form of produce. In fact, if you will notice the law concerning the offerings, God gave a certain part of the animal to the priests, and He always said that they were to eat it right there. They didn't have any refrigerators, any kind of icebox, in which to freeze the meat. In that warm climate the meat would have gone bad in a hurry, and so

God told them to eat it right there. But the other produce was stored until it was needed.

**And I will rebuke the devourer for your sakes, and he shall not destroy the fruits of your ground; neither shall your vine cast her fruit before the time in the field, saith the LORD of hosts [Mal. 3:11].**

When they were generous with God, He said, "I'll open up the heavens and pour you out a blessing, and I'll rebuke the devourer." "The devourer" evidently means the locust. The locust had a ravenous and insatiable appetite. He was a regular gourmet on green salad—so he just took all the green stuff that was ahead of him. Many of the plagues came to Israel through the locust, but now God says, "I will rebuke the devourer for your sakes."

Even today judgment comes from God upon a nation when they reject Him. I think that this explains the fact that we are having so many shortages—not only an energy shortage but shortages in many areas. For years the shelves of our supermarkets were groaning because they were so full. My supermarket still does pretty well, but there are some things that are absent. You cannot always get the cut of meat that you would like to have. Even if they have it, you can't pay for it unless you mortgage your home! No one seems to be interpreting these things as a judgment or a warning from God. I think it is a warning of that which is to come in the future; in other words, I don't think we've seen anything yet.

"And he shall not destroy the fruits of your ground; neither shall your vine cast her fruit before the time in the field, saith the LORD of hosts." In other words, their vineyards were to produce abundantly.

**And all nations shall call you blessed: for ye shall be a delightsome land, saith the LORD of hosts [Mal. 3:12].**

When Israel was right with God, they became a blessing to the other nations of the world. Honesty with God—and you cannot have holiness without honesty—was the thing that made them a blessing to all nations. In Zechariah 8:13 we read: "And it shall come to pass, that as ye were a curse among the heathen, O house of Judah, and house of Israel; so will I save you, and ye shall be a blessing: fear not, but let your hands be strong."

This looks forward to a future day, but God said at that time that He would make them a blessing to the nations. When Israel is serving God, it becomes a blessing to the other nations.

In verse 13 we come to the eighth and last sarcastic remark which the people of Israel make to God in response to His statements.

**Your words have been stout against me, saith the LORD. Yet ye say, What have we spoken so much against thee? [Mal. 3:13].**

The people respond, "We don't recall that we have said anything against You!" In each of His responses God puts it right on the line—

**Ye have said, It is vain to serve God: and what profit is it that we have kept his ordinance, and that we have walked mournfully before the LORD of hosts? [Mal. 3:14].**

Israel says, "What good is it for us to serve God? It is an *empty* thing." For them it was an empty thing because their hearts were not in it. And since their hearts were not in it, God had not blessed them. So they blamed God for the situation. They said, "It's not worthwhile to serve God." Well, the way they were doing it, it wasn't worthwhile.

I want to make a very strong statement right now. There are some people who attend church who, very frankly, I think would do better if they would just take a drive on Sundays. Their hearts are not in it. They go to church to criticize. As someone has said, "Some people go to eye the clothes and others to close their eyes." Some folk go to church because it's a nice place to get a nap. If your heart is not in it, my friend, if you don't love God, if you don't want to praise Him and serve Him and worship Him, it is of no value.

Today our worship is on a very marvelous, wonderful plane. This is what the Lord Jesus said to the woman at the well: ". . . Woman, believe me, the hour cometh, when ye shall neither in this mountain, nor yet at Jerusalem, worship the Father. Ye worship ye know not what: we know what we worship: for salvation is of the Jews. But the hour cometh, and now is, when the true worshippers shall worship the Father in spirit and in truth: for the Father seeketh such to worship him. God is a Spirit: and they that worship him must worship him in spirit and in truth" (John 4: 21–24).

The Lord Jesus told this woman that the hour is coming when true worshipers will not worship God in that mountain; but believe me, they are still offering bloody sacrifices at that mountain. He said, "Nor yet at Jerusalem"—

Jerusalem is not a place to worship God. Every form of so-called Christianity is found there, and most of it is as far from the message of the Lord Jesus and the early apostles as anything possibly could be. The Lord Jesus went on to say that true worshipers are going to worship God in spirit and in truth. They are going to love the Word of God. They'll want to serve Him. They'll want to obey Him. They'll want to worship and to praise Him.

A man said to me one time, "Well, McGee, I guess you think that I'm going to hell because I play golf on Sunday." I said, "No. You're not going to hell because you play golf on Sunday. You're going to hell because you've rejected the Lord Jesus Christ. Golf hasn't anything to do with it. I know a lot of church members who I wish would go play golf on Sunday to get them out of the church because they are troublemakers. They are not worshiping God in spirit and in truth." My friend, all of this outward religion is not good. The crucial thing is the condition of your heart and your relationship to Jesus Christ.

It was vain and empty for these people in Malachi's day to worship God, but the problem wasn't with Him—the problem was with them. I went to see a man in the hospital many years ago. Outside the door of his room, his wife told me that the doctors said that he was dying. I went in to see him, to have prayer with him, and to say a word, not only of comfort but that his wife might have the assurance of his salvation. He said to me, "Dr. McGee, I'm about to freeze to death. Would you get that blanket over there and put it on me?" And I did. That room was hot—oh, it was warm—but that man thought he was freezing to death. He blamed it on the room and said, "They never keep these rooms warm." But the room was overheated. There are a great many people who say that the church they attend is cold. Are you sure that the church is cold, or is it maybe you who are cold? It might be well to check up, because the problem here was with the people—it was not with God at all.

I would like to look at a good definition of real worship which is given to us in the Scriptures in Isaiah 58: "Wherefore have we fasted, say they, and thou seest not? wherefore have we afflicted our soul, and thou takest no knowledge? Behold, in the day of your fast ye find pleasure, and exact all your labours" (Isa. 58:3).

You see, they had the same problem way back in Isaiah's day that they had in Malachi's day. They fasted and they afflicted their souls, and God didn't do anything about it. "Behold, ye fast for strife and debate, and to smite with the fist of wickedness: ye shall not fast as ye do this day, to make your voice to be heard on high" (Isa. 58:4).

God says, "I don't care about your fasting, your going through all of that ritual, and your wanting to debate religion." They just wanted to have a religious argument. Quite frequently there comes to my desk a very fat letter from someone who wants to enter into a controversy with me or to straighten me out on some doctrinal point. Generally there are fifteen to twenty pages, sometimes closely typewritten or written in such a way that I couldn't even read it if I wanted to. I never read those letters. I'm sorry—maybe I'm missing something—but I just put them into the wastebasket. We won't get anywhere by arguing, my friend. You can differ with my interpretation if you want to. But if you believe that the Bible is the Word of God as I do, why don't you just pray for me if you think my interpretation is wrong. And my interpretation *could* be wrong, by the way—you ought to test it.

Now here is our definition of real worship: "Is not this the fast that I have chosen? to loose the bands of wickedness, to undo the heavy burdens, and to let the oppressed go free, and that ye break every yoke? Is it not to deal thy bread to the hungry, and that thou bring the poor that are cast out to thy house? when thou seest the naked, that thou cover him; and that thou hide not thyself from thine own flesh? Then shall thy light break forth as the morning, and thine health shall spring forth speedily: and thy righteousness shall go before thee; the glory of the LORD shall be thy rereward" (Isa. 58:6–8).

What Isaiah is saying is that when you come in to worship God, make sure you have a life to back it up. This is very important. God wants a life that will back up what you have to say. Here we have an Old Testament definition of real worship. The ritual itself has no value unless the heart is right before God. This is something that we need to remember and keep before us.

**And now we call the proud happy; yea, they that work wickedness are set up; yea, they that tempt God are even delivered [Mal. 3:15].**

It looked as if they could tempt God and get by with it, but as Habakkuk had found out in his day, God was moving in the life of the nation and was going to judge them. I am of the opinion that if we could see behind the scenes today and see the wheels of God that are moving, we would cry out to God to have mercy. He is moving, but we don't seem to recognize it.

**Then they that feared the LORD spake often one to another: and the LORD hearkened, and heard it, and a book of remembrance was written before him for them that feared the LORD, and that thought upon his name [Mal. 3:16].**

"Then they that feared the LORD spake often one to another." In other words, there was a little remnant who loved God and met together, and they feared the Lord. They spoke to one another—they were having fellowship.

"And the LORD hearkened, and heard it, and a book of remembrance was written before him for them that feared the LORD, and that thought upon his name." Running all through the Scripture, there is this idea that God keeps books. I do not think there is a book up there in which He is writing. God never forgets, and He doesn't need that book, and He doesn't even need a computer.

This matter of the book that was written is also mentioned in the Book of Revelation, and in chapter 3 we find the suggestion that He is apt to erase a name: "Thou hast a few names even in Sardis which have not defiled their garments; and they shall walk with me in white: for they are worthy. He that overcometh, the same shall be clothed in white raiment; and I will not blot out his name out of the book of life, but I will confess his name before my Father, and before his angels" (Rev. 3:4–5).

This is about as strong a language as you can get, and it is, very frankly, one of the most difficult passages in the Book of Revelation to understand. I do not think that God has a set of books that He is keeping in heaven. But the only way that you and I can understand this is through this figure of speech that He uses. I can understand it when He says that He puts down in the Book of Life the names of those who are saved. I can understand that He puts down in a book those who will receive a reward or some recognition. This makes it clear to me. But I don't believe that God has a literal book up there—although He may have. We are also told in the last part of the Book of Revelation that when the lost are brought before the Great White Throne, the books will be opened, and there

are several of them. There is also the book of those who are saved (see Rev. 20).

I would like to illustrate it in this way: To me it is more or less like the report card I used to get in school. You get a report card if you are a student; all you have to do to get a report card is to enroll. You get into the Lamb's Book of Life by accepting Christ as your Savior, and that will never be removed. You have a report card; you are in the Lamb's Book of Life; you're enrolled. *Now* you are going to start making grades. *Now* He's going to put down how you are doing with your Bible study. What grade is He giving you on that? Are you making *A*'s these days? Or are you failing the course? How is your life for Him? How is your service for Him? He takes note of all these things, and they are recorded.

Therefore I believe that when He says to the church of Sardis that names are removed from the Book of Life, that names are blotted out; it has to do with service because that is what He is talking about there. It has to do with the *service* that they render. There will be many of us who get a report card, but some are going to be a failure in the Christian life. Paul said in his Epistle to the Corinthians that our works are to be tested by fire (see 1 Cor. 3:11–15). If a man's work is all hay and stubble and it is all consumed by fire, will he be saved? Paul says, "Yes. He'll be saved, but so as by fire." There are going to be a lot of people in heaven who will smell like they were bought at a fire sale—and they were—a brand plucked from the burning, if you please. They did nothing, and nothing was put on the report card.

"A book of remembrance was written before him for them that feared the LORD, and that thought upon his name." God simply doesn't need a book to remember things because He is the One who really has a computer mind—it's all there. The record is of their works, their service, their love for Him— those are the things that are recorded. Salvation is free. It is by faith, never by works. After you have been saved, that is when your works really begin to count, and they become all-important. This book of remembrance is a very beautiful and wonderful thing.

We find God's "book" mentioned elsewhere in the Old Testament. In Psalm 56:8 we read, "Thou tellest my wanderings: put thou my tears into thy bottle: are they not in thy book?" The psalmist says, "Thou tellest my wanderings." The Lord knows exactly where you've been all the time. Maybe your neighbors, your church members, and your pastor don't know—but God knows. The darkness is light to Him. He knows where you've been, and He knows what you've done. "Put thou my tears into thy bottle"—I think that is a very lovely thing. My friend, that godly mother who is weeping because of a wayward child, God has put those tears into a bottle. Can you imagine that? How wonderful it is that He has taken note of them! The man who has served God but has been disappointed by how his brethren have treated him and has wept tears over it—to him God says, "I've put those tears in a bottle." Finally, the psalmist says, "Are they not in thy book?" There is a book that records our lives, my friend. I have always thought that is probably going to be sort of like a movie that He will run through for us. You will see your life from birth to death, and it will all be there. It won't be what the preacher said about you at your funeral, about how wonderful you were and what a great church member you were. God is going to run it just like it was. I don't know about you, but I don't want to see mine. But I guess I'll have to take a look at it someday.

**And they shall be mine, saith the LORD of hosts, in that day when I make up my jewels; and I will spare them, as a man**

**spareth his own son that serveth him [Mal. 3:17].**

Isn't this a lovely way to express it? God is going to make up His jewels, and the church is going to be there. The church is the pearl of great price. Israel never valued pearls very much; Gentiles always have. And so the pearl of great price is His church purchased with His own precious blood. God is going to make up His jewels, and there will be many of them.

"And I will spare them, as a man spareth his own son that serveth him." This speaks of the remnant of believers that there will be during this time.

**Then shall ye return, and discern between the righteous and the wicked, between him that serveth God and him that serveth him not [Mal. 3:18].**

We are living in a day like the day in which Malachi lived and like it will be at the end of the age. You really won't be able to tell the righteous from the unrighteous. However, in the day which God has appointed, the day of His judgment when He comes again, it will be evident who are the true believers and who are the make-believers.

# CHAPTER 4

*THEME: The prediction of the Day of the Lord and of the Sun of Righteousness*

In the Hebrew Bible there is no fourth chapter of the Book of Malachi; it is just the end of the third chapter. However, in the English translations, these six brief verses are made a separate chapter. In chapter 4 we have the prediction of the Day of the Lord and of the Sun of Righteousness who ushers it in. The first verse is a vivid description of the Great Tribulation Period—

**For, behold, the day cometh, that shall burn as an oven; and all the proud, yea, and all that do wickedly, shall be stubble: and the day that cometh shall burn them up, saith the LORD of hosts, that it shall leave them neither root nor branch [Mal. 4:1].**

"For, behold, the day cometh"—this is the Day of the Lord.

"That shall burn as an oven; and all the proud, yea, and all that do wickedly, shall be stubble." In other words, they shall be consumed. In the Book of Revelation we read that at one fell swoop one fourth of the population of the world will be wiped out (see Rev. 6:8).

"And the day that cometh shall burn them up, saith the LORD of hosts, that it shall leave them neither root nor branch." This hasn't anything in the world to do with the doctrine that death ends all for the unsaved, that death for the unsaved is annihilation. The Bible doesn't teach that. The Bible teaches that the body goes into the grave whether a person is lost or saved. Your soul and spirit go into eternity, my friend—either to heaven or to hell. This verse teaches that the unsaved are to be judged in the Great Tribulation Period and removed from the earth's scene.

**But unto you that fear my name shall the Sun of righteousness arise with healing in his wings; and ye shall go forth, and grow up as calves of the stall [Mal. 4:2].**

The Sun of Righteousness in the Old Testament is the same person who is the Bright and Morning Star in the New Testament. However, Christ is never called the Sun of Righteousness in the New Testament, and He's never called the Bright and Morning Star in the Old Testament. We will look at this verse more closely in a moment and see the reason for this.

**And ye shall tread down the wicked; for they shall be ashes under the soles of your feet in the day that I shall do this, saith the LORD of hosts [Mal. 4:3].**

When He comes to this earth to establish His kingdom, the wicked *will be* put down. He will break them into pieces like a potter's vessel. That is the language of Scripture, and it is just too bad if you don't like it.

**Remember ye the law of Moses my servant, which I commanded unto him in Horeb for all Israel, with the statutes and judgments [Mal. 4:4].**

Following this prophecy by Malachi, Israel is going to move into a period in which heaven goes off the air. God will not be broadcasting. There will appear another Zechariah [Zacharias] four hundred years later. He will be serving in the temple when the angel Gabriel will appear to him and announce the birth of John the Baptist (see Luke 1:5–25). The silence of four hundred years will then be broken. In the meantime, Israel is to remember the law of Moses. It will be their life; it will be God's Word for them. They were under the Mosaic system.

**Behold, I will send you Elijah the prophet before the coming of the great and dreadful day of the LORD [Mal. 4:5].**

Revelation speaks of two witnesses who are to appear in the last days (see Rev. 11:3–12). I do not know who the second witness will be, but I am almost sure that one of them will be Elijah. At the Passover Feast, in the orthodox Jew's home, a chair is put at the table in which no one sits. It is for Elijah who shall come. When John the Baptist appeared, the Jews thought he was Elijah, but John the Baptist was not Elijah in any sense of the word. The Scriptures do say that he could have been, but he wasn't—and that's the important thing. If Christ had established His kingdom, then John would have been Elijah. How could that be? I do not know because it didn't happen that way. That's an "iffy" question for which we cannot really have an answer.

"Behold, I will send you Elijah the prophet before the coming of the great and dreadful day of the LORD." John the Baptist was not the fulfillment of this prophecy because he was announcing the Messiah, the Savior of the world. John said, ". . . Behold the Lamb of God, which taketh away the sin of the world" (John 1:29). That is a little different from announcing the great and terrible Day of the Lord that is coming.

**And he shall turn the heart of the fathers to the children, and the heart of the children to their fathers, lest I come and smite the earth with a curse [Mal. 4:6].**

The last word of the Old Testament is *curse*. The curse came when Adam and Eve were in the Garden of Eden and disobeyed God. At that time God said that the ground would be cursed and that the curse would rest upon them. The curse was sin, and it will not be removed until the Lord comes to this earth the second time. It is still in the human family today. All you have to do is to look about you to see that. If you are living in a place where you do not have snails, termites, or some other kind of blight eating away at whatever you are trying to raise—whether it is vegetables or flowers or trees—then you must have moved into the Millennium, my friend. And if you are living in a community where there is no sin, I'd have to say that you've already moved into the Millennium. But I'm of the opinion that, as we look about us today, we can recognize that the curse of sin is upon the human race and upon this earth.

This is a very doleful way to end the Old Testament, but it has been a book of expectations. Therefore, I think that the emphasis should be back on verse 2 of this chapter: "But unto you that fear my name shall the Sun of righteousness arise with healing in his wings; and ye shall go forth, and grow up as calves of the stall." The Old Testament does not close with only a curse. It closes with a great hope that, although the sun has gone down and it is very dark, there is coming a new day. We are living now in the night of sin, and the world is dark. It seems that we are at the darkest moment today. But there is coming a day when the Sun of Righteousness will rise and spiritual light will break upon this little planet.

That Sun of Righteousness is none other than the Lord Jesus Christ. I want to call your attention to something that is very remarkable and very important. In the Old Testament Christ is presented as the Sun of Righteousness. In the New Testament He's presented in a different way altogether. There He is presented to us as the Bright and Morning Star. Listen to Him as He speaks in Revelation 22:16, and this concludes Revelation: "I Jesus have sent mine angel to testify unto you these things in the churches. I am the root and the offspring of David, and the bright and morning star." "The root and the offspring of David" means that He is the King who will reign on this earth, but He is also something else—"the bright and morning star," which is something new, by the way.

It is interesting that man's attention has always been drawn to the heavens. Astronomy is the oldest science known to man, but like many other sciences, it had its origin in the occult and superstition, in the mythological and the mystical. Astronomy as we know it actually had its origin in astrology, that which is filled with superstition. You might say, "That was way back yonder in the Dark Ages when men were very superstitious, but today we've improved." Have we improved? Right now there are probably more people in this country who are interested in the horoscope and the star under which they were born than are interested in the Bible, the Word of God, or anything else, for that matter. To those who are playing with the zodiac and its signs, may I say to you that it is something which borders on the occult. We're seeing today the worship of Satan as we've never seen it before. It is quite interesting that research shows that some years ago only 3 percent of those interviewed believed in a personal devil. More recently the percentage had jumped to 37–48 percent who believe and are convinced that there is a devil. Apparently, some of them are not convinced that there is a God to whom they are responsible, but at least they believe in the Devil.

The heavenly bodies are being observed by men today. At first they were observed with the naked eye because of curiosity about the beauty of the heavens. Then the mechanical eye came into existence, and now scientists are making a greater study of the heavens than they have ever made before.

Scripture does turn man's attention repeatedly to the heavens. Psalm 8 reads: "When I consider thy heavens, the work of thy fingers, the moon and the stars, which thou hast ordained; What is man, that thou art mindful of him? and the son of man, that thou visitest him?" (Ps. 8:3–4).

The answer to that question is that man happens to be the astronomer. He's the one who can view all of this and can give praise and glory to God. "The heavens declare the glory of God; and the firmament sheweth his handiwork" (Ps. 19:1). God said to Abraham, ". . . Look now toward heaven, and tell the stars, if thou be able to number them . . ." (Gen. 15:5).

The Old Testament closes here in Malachi with God directing man to look toward the heavens, and it is well that man looks up. Malachi closes with a thud: "Lest I come and smite the earth with a curse," and the curtain comes down before the human story is over. Darkness closes in on man, but the play is not over. There are the good guys and the bad guys, and the good guys haven't won yet. God says, "Look up at the heavens. Don't miss it." It is important that you see, my friend. He says, "But unto you that fear my name shall the Sun of righteousness arise with healing in his wings; and ye shall go forth, and grow up as calves of the stall." This is a promise of a sunrise. There is a song that says that the world is waiting for a sunrise—and I believe it is—but the church is waiting for something else. Kipling wrote a poem that has been made into a song which says in part, "An' the dawn comes up like thunder outer China 'crost the Bay!" When Christ the Sun of Righteousness comes, that's the way He's going to come: out of the East He'll come up like *thunder* to put down all unrighteousness.

The Old Testament is *expectation*. In one sense it is the most disappointing book in the world if it stands by itself. But it points to the heavens, and it speaks of the Lord Jesus Christ, *the Sun of Righteousness*. This is a fitting figure for Him because He comes to usher in a new day and to end the night of man's sin. The Day of the Lord is coming, and His kingdom will be established upon the earth. God is called a sun throughout the Old Testament. Listen to Psalm 84:11: "For the LORD God is a sun and shield: the LORD will give grace and glory: no good thing will he withhold from them that walk uprightly."

Then in Isaiah 60:19 we read: "The sun shall be no more thy light by day; neither for brightness shall the moon give light unto thee: but the LORD shall be unto thee an everlasting light, and thy God thy glory."

What a picture we have of Him in the Old Testament!

On the other hand, the New Testament is *realization*, and it closes with a little different hope. Let me repeat this marvelous verse: "I Jesus have sent mine angel to testify unto you these things in the churches. I am the root and the offspring of David, and the bright and morning star" (Rev. 22:16).

Not only is He the Sun of Righteousness, but He is also *the Bright and Morning Star*. It is quite interesting that the New Testament does not open with the Sun of Righteousness. The first public announcement was made privately to Zacharias. Then there was a promise of the coming of a forerunner, John the Baptist. The forerunner of whom? Of the Messiah who was coming, who was to be born of Mary. Wise men came to Jerusalem seeking what? They said, ". . . Where is he that is born King of the Jews? for we have seen his *star* in the east, and are come to worship him" (Matt. 2:2, italics mine). By the way, that is not an eastern star. If they had seen an eastern star, they would have ended up in China. The wise men in the East saw the star, the star was in the West, and they came that direction. Isn't it interesting that the sun comes up from the East, but this star was in the West?

How did the wise men associate the coming of Christ with a star? Way back in the Book of Numbers, the heathen prophet Balaam, in the East in Moab, made this prophecy: "I shall see him, but not now: I shall behold him, but not nigh: there shall come a Star out of Jacob, and a Sceptre shall rise out of Israel, and shall smite the corners of Moab, and destroy all the children of Sheth" (Num. 24:17).

Always the star is separated from the sceptre. The star is separated from the sun. The star is the sign of the coming of Christ to take His church out of the world, and the sun is the sign of His second coming to the earth to establish His kingdom. The Jewish apostles were told at the time of His ascension, ". . . this same Jesus, which is taken up from you into heaven, shall so come in like manner as ye have seen him go into heaven" (Acts 1:11), and Zechariah tells us that His feet shall touch the Mount of Olives (see Zech. 14:4). The star, therefore, is the sign of His first coming to take His church out of the world, but He doesn't come to the earth. When He came

before, the entire mission of Christ was wrapped up in a star and not as the Sun of Righteousness. The emphasis is not on His birth but rather on His death. It is interesting that He never asked anybody to remember His birth, but He did say to remember His death. When He established the Lord's Supper, over that Passover Feast, He took the dying embers of a fading feast, and He said, ". . . this do in remembrance of me" (Luke 22:19). The death of Christ as well as His birth is in that star. The star speaks not only of where He was born but also of why He died. The star tells out who He is, why He came. He said, ". . . Lo, I come (in the volume of the book it is written of me,) . . ." (Heb. 10:7). The star points to a manger, but it also points to a cross. It speaks of the fact that He came to bear my sins and yours upon the cross.

A little boy was walking down the street with his father during World War II. He noticed that there were blue stars in many windows, but every now and then there would be a gold star in a window which meant that someone had given a son to die for this country. It was in the early evening, and as they came to a vacant lot, the evening star was just appearing above the horizon. The little fellow said to his dad, "Look, Dad! God gave *His* Son!" Yes, God gave His Son, and the star speaks of that. The little fellow was right, by the way.

Certainly, in two world wars nothing was won—or in any war which we have fought since then. We thought we were going to make the world safe for democracy. Every president, from Woodrow Wilson down to the present time, has thought that he was going to bring peace into the world and make the world unsafe for dictators. Yet today over half the world is under dictators. We won the wars, all right, but we sure lost the victory. In the war against sin the Lord Jesus died to bring men life, to free men from sin, and to bring victory over the grave and death. "O death, where is thy sting? O grave, where is thy victory?" (1 Cor. 15:55).

The future is not in the stars, my friend. In *Julius Caesar* Shakespeare has Cassius say to Brutus:

The fault, dear Brutus, is not in our stars,
But in ourselves, that we are underlings
[act 1, scene 2].

Your future is not in stars out there and neither is your present. If you want help for the present, you need to live victoriously for

Jesus Christ who said, "These things I have spoken unto you, that in me ye might have peace. In the world ye shall have tribulation: but be of good cheer; I have overcome the world" (John 16:33). Are you defeated and discouraged? There's no help in the stars for you, my friend! You're nothing in the world but a pagan and a heathen if you believe that. Look to Jesus. It's not some magic formula; it's not lady luck; it's not chance; it's not fatalism; it's not superstition. If you are defeated by life, if you are overcome by some habit—drink, dishonesty, temper, sex, or materialism—if you are cold and indifferent to spiritual things, may I say to you, He is the answer for you.

> Somewhere beyond the stars
>    Is a Love that is better than Fate,
> And when night unlocks her bars,
>    I shall see Him, and I shall wait.
>                        —Author unknown

If you have no hope for the future, you can look back to the past to an historical event that took place over nineteen hundred years ago when Christ died on the cross for you and for me who were sinners. And you can trust Him as your Savior. Then you can turn your face to the sunrise because the Bright and Morning Star is going to appear one of these days.

Is there hope for the future? Oh, my friend, the bright and morning star appears right before the sun comes up. In my bedroom, I have four windows from which I can look out and see the sun come up. In winter the sun comes up on the extreme right; in the summer it comes up on the extreme left. I watch the sun as it marches back and forth from one window to another. Last March and April I was watching as the bright and morning star appeared nearly an hour before the sun came up. The bright and morning star appears first, then the sun comes up. So we are waiting for the Bright and Morning Star to appear. Christ is the Bright and Morning Star for the church today—that is important to see. Peter speaks of Him in that way: "We have also a more sure word of prophecy; whereunto ye do well that ye take heed, as unto a light that shineth in a dark place, until the day dawn, and the day star arise in your hearts" (2 Pet. 1:19).

That day star speaks of the Rapture of the church when He will take the church out of the world. The Rapture could take place at any moment in time for there are no signs for it at all. John Wesley put it like this: "He will appear as the day-spring from on high, before the morning light. Oh, do not set us a time—expect Him every hour! Now He is nigh, even at the doors!" Job said that ". . . the morning stars sang together, and all the sons of God shouted for joy?" (Job 38:7), but then sin entered God's universe. But the day is coming when that Day Star shall appear, and He shall take the church out. That will be the signal that the sun will be coming up pretty soon. However, the Sun is none other than the Sun of Righteousness, the Lord Jesus Christ.

We leave now the Old Testament where the hope is the coming of Christ to the earth to establish His kingdom. But in the New Testament we ought to be like the wise men who were looking for the star. We are still to be looking for the Day Star to appear when He will take His church out of this world.

# BIBLIOGRAPHY

(Recommended for Further Study)

Feinberg, Charles L. *The Minor Prophets*. Chicago, Illinois: Moody Press, 1976.

Gaebelein, Arno C. *The Annotated Bible*. 1917. Reprint. Neptune, New Jersey: Loizeaux Brothers, 1971.

Ironside, H. A. *The Minor Prophets*. Neptune, New Jersey: Loizeaux Brothers, n.d.

Jensen, Irving L. *Haggai, Zechariah, and Malachi*. Chicago, Illinois: Moody Press, 1976.

Morgan, G. Campbell. *Malachi's Message for Today*. Grand Rapids, Michigan: Baker Book House, n.d.

Tatford, Frederick A. *The Minor Prophets*. Minneapolis, Minnesota: Klock & Klock, n.d.

Unger, Merrill F. *Unger's Commentary on the Old Testament*, Vol. 2. Chicago, Illinois: Moody Press, 1982.

Wolfe, Herbert. *Haggai and Malachi*. Chicago, Illinois: Moody Press, 1976.